Standard Catalog of®

World Paper Money

Edition

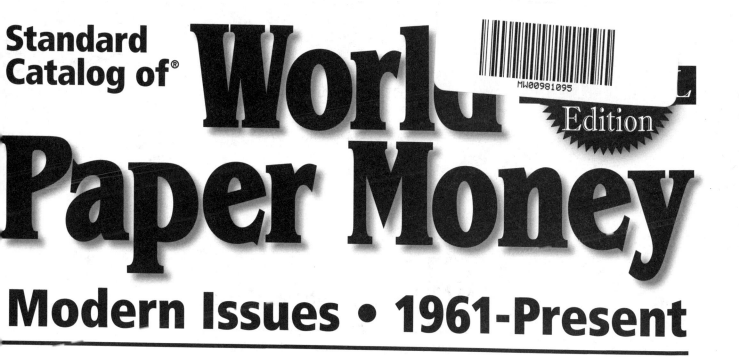

Modern Issues • 1961-Present

Edited by George S. Cuhaj

Book Designer
Sally Olson

Color Section Designer
Sandi Morrison

Special Contributors
Colin R. Bruce II, Flemming Lyngbeck Hansen, Art Matz,
Jon Morowitz, Tony Pisciotta, Neil Shaferr

Published by

krause publications
An Imprint of F+W Publications

700 East State Street • Iola, WI 54990-0001
715-445-2214 • 888-457-2873
www.krausebooks.com

Our toll-free number to place an order or obtain
a free catalog is (800) 258-0929.

ISSN: 1538-2028

ISBN 978-0-89689-502-7

Printed in the United States of America

INTRODUCTION

Welcome to this 13th edition of the Standard Catalog of World Paper Money, Modern Issues.

For those of you already familiar with this volume, you will be glad to see an upgrade in illustration quality. Numerous additions to the text as well as price increases where warrented. Extensive speciman varieties continue to be added throughout

In our constant endeavor to provide as much detail as possible, we have added illustrations and detailed signature information. Extensive price analysis has been performed to provide timely insight to the ever-changing world paper money marketplace. Renumbering has been held to an absolute minimum, except for Fiji which received extensive review in 2006.

For the ease of identification, notes are listed under their historic country identification (British Honduras is no longer hidden within Belize). Please consult the country or bank issuer index. Notes of a particular bank are listed in release date order, and then grouped in ascending denomination order. In the cases of countries where more than one issuing authority is in effect at a single time, follow the bank headings in the listings and it will become apparent if that country's listing is by date or alphabetical by issuing authority. In the cases where a country has changed from a kingdom to a republic all the banknotes of the kingdom's era would be listed before that of the republic.

An Invitation

Users of this catalog may find a helpful adjunct to be the Bank Note Reporter, the only monthly newspaper devoted exclusively to North American and world paper money. Each issue presents up-to-date news, feature articles and valuable information. All purchasers of this catalog are invited to subscribe to the Bank Note Reporter. Requests for a sample copy should be addressed to Bank Note Reporter, 700 East State Street, Iola, WI, 54990-0001.

A review of modern paper money collecting

Paper money collecting is probably as old as paper money itself. However, this segment of the numismatic hobby did not begin to reach a popularity approaching that of coin collecting until the latter half of the 1970's. While coins and paper money are alike in that both served as legal obligations to facilitate commerce, long-time paper money enthusiasts know the similarity ends there.

Coins were historically guaranteed by the intrinsic value of their metallic content - at least until recent years when virtually all circulating coins have become little more than legal tender tokens, containing little or no precious metal - while paper money possesses a value only when it is accepted for debts or converted into bullion or precious metals. With many note issues, this conversion privilege was limited and ultimately negated by the imposition of redemption cutoff dates.

The development of widespread collector interest in paper money of most nations was inhibited by a near total absence of adequate documentation. No more than four decades ago collectors could refer to only a few catalogs and dealer price lists of limited scope, most of which were difficult to acquire, or they could build their own knowledge through personal collecting pursuits and contact with fellow collectors.

The early catalogs authored by Albert Pick chronicled issues of Europe and the Americas and were assembled as stepping-stones to the ultimate objective, which became reality with publication of the first Standard Catalog of World Paper Money in 1975. That work provided collectors with fairly complete listings and up-to-date valuations of all recorded government note issues of the 20th century, incorporating Pick's previously unpublished manuscripts on Africa, Asia and Oceania, plus many earlier issues.

This completely revised and updated 13th Edition of Volume III, Modern Issues, along with the companion 11th Edition Volume II General Issues, presents a substantial extension of the cataloging effort initiated in 1975 and revised in succeeding editions. As the most comprehensive world paper money references ever assembled, they fully document the many and varied legal tender paper currencies issued and circulated by over 380 past and current government issuing authorities of the world from 1300's to present.

George S. Cuhaj
Editor

TABLE OF CONTENTS

ADVERTISER INDEX

COUNTRY INDEX

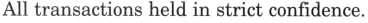

— 13th EDITION —
ACKNOWLEDGMENTS

Over time contributor enhancements to this catalog have been many and varied, and to recognize them all would be a volume in itself. Accordingly, we wish to acknowledge these invaluable collectors, scholars and dealers in the world paper money field, both past and present, for their specific contributions to this work through the submission of notes for illustration, improved descriptive information and market valuations.

Emmanuel K. Aboagye
Dundar Acikalin
Jim Adams
Esko Ahlroth
Jan Alexandersson
Paulo Almeida
Milan Alusic
Carl A. Anderson
Dr. Jorge E. Arbelaez
Donald Arnone
David B. August
Thomas Augustsson
Keith Austin
Cem Barlok
Adriaan C. F. Beck
Dan Bellan
Daniel Bena
Abdullah Beydoun
Milt Blackburn
Ed Bohannon
Joseph E. Boling
Arthur John Boyko
Wilfried A. Bracke
Jean Bricaud
Alejandro Brill
Mahdi Bseiso
Christopher J. Budesa
Weldon D. Burson
Doru Calin
Lance K. Campbell
David Carew
Arthur Chadwick
Arthur D. Cohen
George Conrad
Scott E. Cordry
Guido Crapanzano
Ray Czahor
Thomas Dallmann
Howard A. Daniel III
C. M. Desai
Jacques Desbordes
Adnan Georges Djaroveh
Bruce Donahue
Duane Douglas
Michel Dufour
James A. Downey
Arnoldo Efron
Wilhelm Eglseer
Jos F. M. Eijsermans
Esko Ekman
Wilfred Faroh
Ricardo Faillace
Edward Feltcorn
Mark Fox
W. A. Frick
Brian Giese
Vanjo Grobljar
Edmund Hakimian
Murray Hanewich
Flemming Lyngbeck Hansen
Len Harsel
Mark Hartford
Allan Hauck
William G. Henderson
Robert W. Holbrook
Victor S. Holden
Anton Holt
Armen Hovsepian
Yu Jian Hua
Mikhail Istomin
Jaya Hari Jha
A. J. Jacobs
Edouard Jean-Pierre
Kishore Jhunjhunwalla
Erik Johansen
William M. Judd
Reese Kayhani
Alex Kaglyan
Dimitri Kharitonov
Olaf Kiemer
Josef Klaus
Ladislav Klaus
Michael E. Knabe
Tristan Kolm
Lazare Kouami
David C. Kranz
Chester L. Krause
Michael Kvasnica
Samson K.C. Lai
Michael Lang
Morris Lawing
Akos Ledai
Dr. Edmund Lee
C. K. Leong
Owen Linzmayer
Raymond Lloyd
Claire Lobel
Don Ludwig
Alan Luedeking
Stu Lumsden
Dr. Dennis Lutz
Martin MacDaid
Ma Tak Wo
Ranko Mandic
Claudio Marana
Rolf Marklin
Ian Marshall
John T. Martin
Arthur C. Matz
William McNatt
Ali Mehilba
Marvin E. Mericle
Daniel Meyer
Juozas Minikevicius
Arthur Morowitz
Jon Morowitz
Michael Morris
Rene Muller
Richard Murdoch
Wiliam J. Myers
Quoc Nguyen
Andrew Oberbillig
Fred O'Connell
Geoffrey P. Oldham
Frank Passic
Antonio E. Pedraza
Juan Pena
Tony Pisciotta
Laurence Pope
Savo Popovic
Yahya J. Qureshi
Nazir Rahemtulla
Kavan Ratnatunga
Rudolph Richter
Mircea Raicopol
Bob Reis
Ilan Rinetzky
John Rishel
Alistar Robb
Kerry Rodgers
William Rosenblum
Alan Sadd
Remy Said
Karl Saethre
Robert Sayre
Walter Schmidt
Wolfgang Schuster
Harmut Schoewa
Christian Selvais
Victor C. Seper
Joel Shafer
Neil Shafer
Ladislav Sin
Lee Sing Song
Evzen Sknouril
Gary F. Snover
Mauricio Soto
Jimmie C. Steelman
Herbert Stein
Jeremy Steinberg
Mel Steinberg
Tim Steiner
Georg H. Stocker
Zeljko Stojanovic
Alim A. Sumana
Peter Symes
Imre Szatmari
Steven Tan
Frank Tesson
Reinhardt Tetting
Anthony Tumonis
W. J. van der Drift
Jan Vandersade
Norbert von Euw
Michael Vort-Ronald
Ludek Vostal
Evangelos Vyzas
Wakim Wakim
Pam West
Stewart Westdal
Trevor Wilkin
Peter L. Willems
Dr. Heinz Wirz
Joseph Zaffern
Christof Zellweger

ASSOCIATION & CENTRAL BANKS

American Numismatic Association
International Bank Note Society
American Numismatic Society
L.A.N.S.A.
Smithsonian Institution
East Midland Chapter, I.B.N.S.

Le Change des Monnaies Etrangers
by R. L. Martin. 12, rue Poincaré, F 55800 Revigny, France.
(Illustrated guide of current world bank notes.)

MRI Bankers' Guide to Foreign Currency
by Arnoldo Efron, Monetary Research Institute, P.O. Box 3174, Houston, Texas, U.S.A., 77253-3174.
(Quarterly illustrated guide of current world bank notes and travelers checks.)

Issuer and Bank Index

HOW TO USE THIS CATALOG

Catalog listings consist of all regular and provisional notes attaining wide circulation in their respective countries for the period covered. Notes have been listed under the historical country name. Thus Dahomey is not under Benin, and so on, as had been the case in some past catalogs. Where catalog numbers have changed, and you may find some renumbering in this edition, the old catalog numbers appear in parentheses directly below the new number. The listings continue to be grouped by issue range rather than by denomination, and a slight change in the listing format should make the bank name, issue dates as well as catalog numbers and denominations easier to locate. These changes have been made to make the catalog as easy to use as possible for you.

The editors and publisher make no claim to absolute completeness, just as they acknowledge that some errors and pricing inequities will appear. Correspondence is invited with interested persons who have notes previously unlisted or who have information to enhance the presentation of existing listings in succeeding editions of this catalog.

Catalog Format

Listings proceed generally according to the following sequence: country, geographic or political, chronology, bank name and sometimes alphabetically or by date of first note issue. Release within the bank, most often in date order, but sometimes by printer first.

Catalog number — The basic reference number at the beginning of each listing for each note. For this Modern Issues volume the regular listings require no prefix letters except when 'A' or 'B' appear within the catalog number. (Military and Regional prefixes are explained later in this section.)

Denomination — the value as shown on the note, in western numerals. When denominations are only spelled out, consult the numerics chart.

Date — the actual issue date as printed on the note in day-month-year order. Where more than one date appears on a note, only the latest is used. Where the note has no date, the designation ND is used, followed by a year date in parentheses when it is known. If a note is dated by the law or decree of authorization, the date appears with an L or D and is italicized.

Descriptions of the note are broken up into one or more items as follows:

Color — the main color(s) of the face, and the underprint are given first. If the colors of the back are different, then they follow the face design description

Design — The identification and location of the main design elements if known. Back design elements identified if known.

If design elements and or signatures are the same for an issue group then they are printed only once at the heading of the issue, and apply for the group that follows.

Printer — often a local printer has the name shown in full. Abbreviations are used for the most prolific printers. Refer to the list of printer abbreviations elsewhere in this introduction. In these listings the use of the term "imprint" refers to the logo or the printer's name as usually appearing in the bottom frame or below in the margin of the note.

Valuations — are generally given under the grade headings of Good, Fine and Extremely Fine for early notes; and Very Good, Very Fine and Uncirculated for the later issues. Listings that do not follow these two patterns are clearly indicated. UNC followed by a value is used usually for specimens and proofs when lower grade headings are used for a particular series of issued notes.

Catalog prefix or suffix letters

A catalog number preceded by a capital 'A' indicated the incorporation of an earlier listing as required by type or date; a capital letter following the catalog number usually shows the addition of a later issue. Both may indicate newly discovered lower or higher denominations to a series. Listings of notes for regional circulation are distinguished from regular national issues with the prefix letter 'R'; military issues use a 'M' prefix; foreign exchange certificates are assigned a 'FX' prefix. Varieties, specific date or signature listings are shown with small letters 'a' following a number within their respective entries. Some standard variety letters include: 'p' for proof notes, 'r' for remainder notes, 's' for specimen notes and 'x' for errors.

Denominations

The denomination as indicated on many notes issued by a string of countries stretching from eastern Asia, through western Asia and on across northern Africa, often appears only in unfamiliar non-Western numeral styles. With the listings that follow, denominations are always indicated in Western numerals.

A comprehensive chart keying Western numerals to their non-Western counterparts is included elsewhere in this introduction as an aid to the identification of note types. This compilation features not only the basic numeral systems such as Arabic, Japanese and Indian, but also the more restricted systems such as Burmese, Ethiopian, Siamese, Tibetan, Hebrew, Mongolian and Korean. Additionally, the list includes other localized variations that have been applied to some paper money issues.

In consulting the numeral systems chart to determine the denomination of a note, one should remember that the actual numerals styles employed in any given area, or at a particular time, may vary significantly from these basic representations. Such variations can be deceptive to the untrained eye, just as variations from Western numeral styles can prove deceptive to individuals not acquainted with the particular style employed.

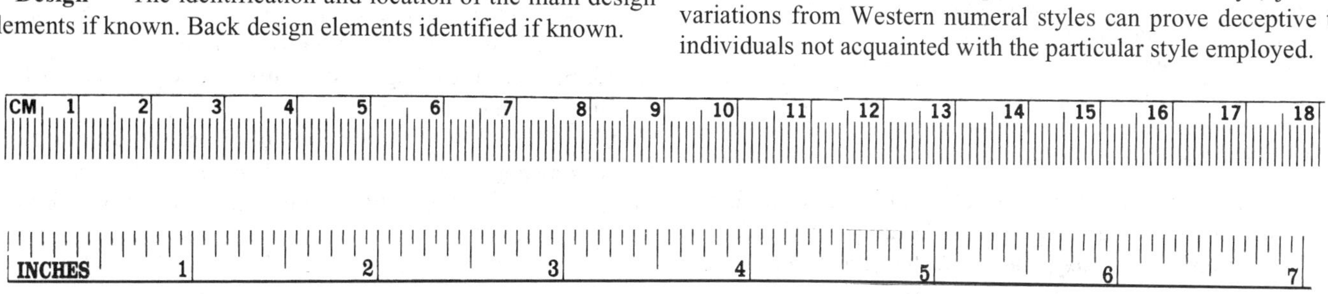

Dates and Date Listing Policy

In previous editions of this work it was the goal to provide a sampling of the many date varieties that were believed to exist. In recent times, as particular dates (and usually signature combinations) were known to be scarcer, that particular series was expanded to include listings of individual dates. At times this idea has been fully incorporated, but with some series it is not practicable, especially when just about every day in a given month could have been an issue date for the notes.

Accordingly, where it seems justifiable that date spans can be realistically filled with individual dates, this has been done. In order to accommodate the many new dates, the idea of providing variety letters to break them up into narrower spans of years has been used. If it appears that there are too many dates for a series, with no major differences in value, then a general inclusive date span is used (beginning and ending) and individual dates within this span are not shown.

For those notes showing only a general date span, the only important dates become those that expand the range of years, months or days earlier or later. But even they would have no impact on the values shown.

Because a specific date is not listed does not necessarily mean it is rare. It may be just that it has not been reported. Those date varieties known to be scarcer are cataloged separately. Newly reported dates in a wide variety of listings are constantly being reported. This indicates that research into the whole area is very active, and a steady flow of new dates is fully expected upon publication of this edition.

Abbreviations

Certain abbreviations have been adopted for words occurring frequently in note descriptions. Following is a list of these:

#	-	number (catalog or serial)
bldg.	-	building
ctr.	-	center
dk.	-	dark
FV	-	face value
Gen.	-	General
govt.	-	government
Kg.	-	king
l.	-	left
lg.	-	large
lt.	-	light
m/c	-	multicolored
ND	-	no date
ovpt.	-	overprint
portr.	-	portrait
Qn.	-	queen
r.	-	right
sign.	-	signature or signatures
sm.	-	small
unpt.	-	underprint (background printing)
wmk.	-	watermark
w/	-	with
w/o	-	without

Valuations

Valuations are given for most notes in three grades. Earlier issues are usually valued in the grade headings of Good, Fine and Extremely Fine; later issues take the grade headings of Very Good, Very Fine and Uncirculated. While it is true that some early notes cannot be valued in Extremely Fine and some later notes have no premium value in Very Good, it is felt that this coverage provides the best uniformity of value data to the collecting community. There are exceptional cases where headings are adjusted for either single notes or a series that really needs special treatment.

Valuations are determined generally from a consensus of individuals submitting prices for evaluation. Some notes have NO values; this does not necessarily mean they are expensive or even rare, but it shows that no pricing information was forthcoming. A number of notes have a 'Rare' designation, and no values. Such notes are generally not available on the market, and when they do appear the price is a matter between buyer and seller. No book can provide guidance in these instances except to indicate rarity.

Valuations used in this book are based on the IBNS grading standards and are stated in U.S. dollars. They serve only as aids in evaluating paper money since actual market conditions throughout the worldwide collector community are constantly changing. In addition, particularly choice examples of many issues listed often bring higher premiums than values listed. Users should remember that a catalog such as this is only a guide to values.

FV (for Face Value) is used as a value designation on new issues as well as older but still redeemable legal tender notes in lower conditions. FV may appear in one or both condition columns before Uncirculated, depending on the relative age and availability of the note in question.

Collection care

The proper preservation of a collection should be of paramount importance to all in the hobby - dealers, collectors and scholars. Only a person who has housed notes in a manner giving pleasure to him or herself and others will keep alive the pleasure of collecting for future generations. The same applies to the way of housing as to the choice of the collecting specialty: it is chiefly a question of what most pleases the individual collector.

Arrangement and sorting of a collection is most certainly a basic requirement. Storing the notes in safe paper envelopes and filing boxes should, perhaps, be considered only when building a new section of a collection, for accommodating varieties or for reasons of saving space when the collection has grown quickly.

Many paper money collections are probably housed in some form of plastic-pocketed album, which are today manufactured in many different sizes and styles to accommodate many types of world paper money. Because the number of bank note collectors has grown continually over the past thirty-five years, some specialty manufacturers of albums have developed a paper money selection. The notes, housed in clear plastic pockets, individually or in groups, can be viewed and exchanged without difficulty. These albums are not cheap, but the notes displayed in this manner do make a lasting impression on the viewer.

A word of concern: certain types of plastic and all vinyl used for housing notes may cause notes to become brittle over time, or cause an irreversible and harmful transfer of oils from the vinyl onto the bank notes.

The high demand for quality that stamp collectors make on their products cannot be transferred to the paper money collecting fraternity. A postage stamp is intended for a single use, then is relegated to a collection. With paper money, it is nearly impossible to acquire uncirculated specimens from a number of countries because of export laws or internal bank procedures. Bends from excessive counting, or even staple holes, are commonplace. Once acquiring a circulated note, the collector must endeavor to maintain its state of preservation.

The fact that there is a classification and value difference between notes with greater use or even damage is a matter of course. It is part of the opinion and personal taste of the individual collector to decide what is considered worthy of collecting and what to pay for such items.

For the purposed of strengthening and mending torn paper money, under no circumstances should one use plain cellophane tape or a similar material. These tapes warp easily, with sealing marks forming at the edges, and the tape frequently discolors. Only with the greatest of difficulty (and often not at all) can these tapes be removed, and damage to the note or the printing is almost unavoidable. The best material for mending tears is an archival tape recommended for the treatment and repair of documents.

There are collectors who, with great skill, remove unsightly spots, repair badly damaged notes, replace missing pieces and otherwise restore or clean a note. There is a question of morality by tampering with a note to improve its condition, either by repairing, starching, ironing, pressing or other methods to possibly deceive a potential future buyer. Such a question must, in the final analysis, be left to the individual collector.

IBNS GRADING STANDARDS FOR WORLD PAPER MONEY

The following introduction and Grading Guide is the result of work prepared under the guidance of the Grading Committee of the International Bank Note Society (IBNS). It has been adopted as the official grading standards of that society.

Introduction

Grading is the most controversial component of paper money collecting today. Small differences in grade can mean significant Vdifferences in value. The process of grading is so subjective and dependent on external influences such as lighting, that even a very experienced individual may well grade the same note differently on separate occasions.

To facilitate communication between sellers and buyers, it is essential that grading terms and their meanings be as standardized and as widely used as possible. This standardization should reflect common usage as much as practicable. One difficulty with grading is that even the actual grades themselves are not used everywhere by everyone. For example, in Europe the grade 'About Uncirculated' (AU) is not in general use, yet in North America it is widespread. The European term 'Good VF' may roughly correspond to what individuals in North America call 'Extremely Fine' (EF).

The grades and definitions as set forth below cannot reconcile all the various systems and grading terminology variants. Rather, the attempt is made here to try and diminish the controversy with some common-sense grades and definitions that aim to give more precise meaning to the grading language of paper money.

How to look at a banknote

In order to ascertain the grade of a note, it is essential to examine it out of a holder and under a good light. Move the note around so that light bounces off of it at different angles. Try holding the note obliquely, so the note is even with your eye as you look up at the light. Hard-to-see folds or slight creases will show up under such examination. Some individuals also lightly feel along the surface of the note to detect creasing.

Cleaning, Washing, Pressing of Banknotes

a) Cleaning, washing or pressing paper money is generally harmful and reduces both the grade and the value of a note. At the very least, a washed or pressed note may lose its original sheen and its surface may become lifeless and dull. The defects a note had, such as folds and creases, may not necessarily be completely eliminated and their telltale marks can be detected under a good light. Carelessly washed notes may also have white streaks where the folds or creases were (or still are).

b) Processing of a note which started out as Extremely Fine will automatically reduce it at least one full grade.

Unnatural Defects

Glue, tape or pencil marks may sometimes be successfuly removed. While such removal will leave a cleaned surface, it will improve the overall appearance of the note without concealing any of its defects. Under such circumstances, the grade of that note may also be improved.

The words "pinholes", "staple holes", "trimmed", "graffiti", "writing on face", "tape marks" etc. should always be added to the description of a note. It is realized that certain countries routinely staple their notes together in groups before issue. In such cases, the description can include a comment such as "usual staple holes" or something similar. After all, not everyone knows that certain notes cannot be found otherwise.

The major point of this section is that one cannot lower the overall grade of a note with defects simply because of the defects. The value will reflect the lowered worth of a defective note, but the description must always include the specific defects.

GRADING

Definitions of Terms

UNCIRCULATED: A perfectly preserved note, never mishandled by the issuing authority, a bank teller, the public or a collector.

Paper is clean and firm, without discoloration. Corners are sharp and square without any evidence of rounding. (Rounded corners are often a tell-tale sign of a cleaned or "doctored" note.)

NOTE: Some note issues are most often available with slight evidence of very light counting folds which do not "break" the paper. Also, French-printed notes usually have a slight ripple in the paper. Many collectors and dealers refer to such notes as AU-UNC.

ABOUT UNCIRCULATED: A virtually perfect note, with some minor handling. May show very slight evidence of bank counting folds at a corner or one light fold through the center, but not both. An AU note canot be creased, a crease being a hard fold which has usually "broken" the surface of the note.

Paper is clean and bright with original sheen. Corners are not rounded.

NOTE: Europeans will refer to an About Uncirculated or AU note as "EF-Unc" or as just "EF". The Extremely Fine note described below will often be referred to as "GVF" or "Good Very Fine".

EXTREMELY FINE: A very attractive note, with light handling. May have a maximum of three light folds or one strong crease.

Paper is clean and firm, without discoloration. Corners are sharp and square without any evidence of rounding. (Rounded corners are often a tell-tale sign of a cleaned or "doctored" note.)

VERY FINE: An attractive note, but with more evidence of handling and wear. May have several folds both vertically and horizontally.

Paper may have minimal dirt, or possible color smudging. Paper itself is still relatively crisp and not floppy.

There are no tears into the border area, although the edges do show slight wear. Corners also show wear but not full rounding.

FINE: A note that shows consideralble circulation, with many folds, creases and wrinkling.

Paper is not excessively dirty but may have some softness.

Edges may show much handling, with minor tears in the border area. Tears may not extend into the design. There will be no center hole because of excessive folding.

Colors are clear but not very bright. A staple hole or two would would not be considered unusual wear in a Fine note. Overall appearance is still on the desirable side.

VERY GOOD: A well used note, abused but still intact.

Corners may have much wear and rounding, tiny nicks, tears may extend into the design, some discoloration may be prsent, staining may have occurred, and a small hole may sometimes be seen at center from excessive folding.

Staple and pinholes are usually present, and the note itself is quite limp but NO pieces of the note can be missing. A note in VG condition may still have an overall not unattractive appearance.

GOOD: A well worn and heavily used note. Normal damage from prolonged circulation will include strong multiple folds and creases, stains, pinholes and/or staple holes, dirt, discoloration, edge tears, center hole, rounded corners and an overall unattractive appearance. No large pieces of the note may be missing. Graffiti is commonly seen on notes in G condition.

FAIR: A totally limp, dirty and very well used note. Larger pieces may be half torn off or missing besides the defects mentioned under the Good category. Tears will be larger, obscured portions of the note will be bigger.

POOR: A "rag" with severe damage because of wear, staining, pieces missing, graffiti, larger holes. May have tape holding pieces of the note together. Trimming may have taken place to remove rough edges. A Poor note is desiralble only as a "filler" or when such a note is the only one known of that particular issue.

> **A word on crimps to otherwise uncirculated notes.** Due to inclusion of wide security foils, crimps appear at the top and bottom edge during production or counting. Thus notes which are uncirculated have a crimp. Examples without these crimps are beginning to command a premium.

STANDARD INTERNATIONAL GRADING TERMINOLOGY AND ABBREVIATIONS

U.S. and ENGLISH SPEAKING LANDS	UNCIRCULATED	EXTREMELY FINE	VERY FINE	FINE	VERY GOOD	GOOD	POOR
Abbreviation	UNC	EF or XF	VF	FF	VG	G	PR
BRAZIL	(1) DW	(3) S	(5) MBC	(7) BC	(8)	(9) R	UTGeG
DENMARK	O	01	1+	1	1÷	2	3
FINLAND	0	01	1+	1	1?	2	3
FRANCE	NEUF	SUP	TTB or TB	TB or TB	B	TBC	BC
GERMANY	KFR	II / VZGL	III / SS	IV / S	V / S.g.E.	VI / G.e.	G.e.s.
ITALY	FdS	SPL	BB	MB	B	M	—
JAPAN	未使用	極美品	美品	並品	—	—	—
NETHERLANDS	FDC	Pr.	Z.F.	Fr.	Z.g.	G	—
NORWAY	0	01	1+	1	1÷	2	3
PORTUGAL	Novo	Soberbo	Muito bo	—	—	—	—
SPAIN	Lujo	SC, IC or EBC	MBC	BC	—	RC	MC
SWEDEN	0	01	1+	1	1?	2	—

FOREIGN EXCHANGE TABLE

The latest foreign exchange rates below apply to trade with banks in the country of origin. The left column shows the number of units per U.S. dollar at the official rate. The right column shows the number of units per dollar at the free market rate.

Country	Official #/$	Market #/$
Afghanistan (New Afghani)	49.6	–
Albania (Lek)	93	–
Algeria (Dinar)	69	–
Andorra uses Euro	.757	–
Angola (Readjust Kwanza)	80	–
Anguilla uses E.C. Dollar	2.7	–
Antigua uses E.C. Dollar	2.7	–
Argentina (Peso)	3.06	–
Armenia (Dram)	365	–
Aruba (Florin)	1.79	–
Australia (Dollar)	1.273	–
Austria (Euro)	.757	–
Azerbaijan (Manat)	4,600	–
Bahamas (Dollar)	1.0	–
Bahrain Is. (Dinar)	.377	–
Bangladesh (Taka)	70	–
Barbados (Dollar)	2.0	–
Belarus (Ruble)	2,140	–
Belgium (Euro)	.757	–
Belize (Dollar)	1.97	–
Benin uses CFA Franc West	490	–
Bermuda (Dollar)	1.0	–
Bhutan (Ngultrum)	45	–
Bolivia (Boliviano)	7.99	–
Bosnia-Herzegovina (Conv. marka)	1.47	–
Botswana (Pula)	6.05	–
British Virgin Islands uses U.S. Dollar	1.00	–
Brazil (Real)	2.14	–
Brunei (Dollar)	1.54	–
Bulgaria (Lev)	1.47	–
Burkina Faso uses CFA Fr.West	490	–
Burma (Kyat)	6.42	1,250
Burundi (Franc)	1,040	–
Cambodia (Riel)	4,050	–
Cameroon uses CFA Franc Central	490	–
Canada (Dollar)	1.149	–
Cape Verde (Escudo)	83.1	–
Cayman Is.(Dollar)	0.82	–
Central African Rep.	490	–
CFA Franc Central	490	–
CFA Franc West	490	–
CFP Franc	90	–
Chad uses CFA Franc Central	490	–
Chile (Peso)	525	–
China, P.R. (Renminbi Yuan)	7.825	–
Colombia (Peso)	2,280	–
Comoros (Franc)	370	–
Congo uses CFA Franc Central	490	–
Congo-Dem.Rep. (Congolese Franc)	490	–
Cook Islands (Dollar)	1.73	–
Costa Rica (Colon)	517	–
Croatia (Kuna)	5.74	–
Cuba (Peso)	1.00	27.00
Cyprus (Pound)	.43	–
Czech Republic (Koruna)	21.1	–
Denmark (Danish Krone)	5.65	–
Djibouti (Franc)	178	–
Dominica uses E.C. Dollar	2.7	–
Dominican Republic (Peso)	32.8	–
East Caribbean (Dollar)	2.7	–
Ecuador uses U.S. Dollar		
Egypt (Pound)	5.72	–
El Salvador (U.S. Dollar)	1.00	–
England (Sterling Pound)	.512	–
Equatorial Guinea uses CFA Franc Central	490	–
Eritrea (Nafka)	15	–
Estonia (Kroon)	11.9	–
Ethiopia (Birr)	8.75	–
Euro	.757	–
Falkland Is. (Pound)	.512	–
Faroe Islands (Krona)	5.65	–
Fiji Islands (Dollar)	1.67	–
Finland (Euro)	.757	–
France (Euro)	.757	–
French Polynesia uses CFP Franc	90	–
Gabon (CFA Franc)	490	–
Gambia (Dalasi)	28	–
Georgia (Lari)	1.73	–
Germany (Euro)	.757	–
Ghana (Cedi)	9,200	–
Gibraltar (Pound)	.512	–
Greece (Euro)	.757	–
Greenland uses Danish Krone	5.65	–
Grenada uses E.C. Dollar	2.7	–
Guatemala (Quetzal)	7.63	–
Guernsey uses Sterling Pound	.512	–
Guinea Bissau (CFA Franc)	490	–
Guinea Conakry (Franc)	5,550	–
Guyana (Dollar)	200	–
Haiti (Gourde)	38.9	–
Honduras (Lempira)	18.9	–
Hong Kong (Dollar)	7.773	–
Hungary (Forint)	195	–
Iceland (Krona)	69.5	–
India (Rupee)	44.7	–
Indonesia (Rupiah)	9,075	–
Iran (Rial)	9,230	–
Iraq (Dinar)	1,425	–
Ireland (Euro)	.757	–
Isle of Man uses Sterling Pound	.512	–
Israel (New Sheqalim)	4.19	–
Italy (Euro)	.757	–
Ivory Coast uses CFA Franc West	490	–
Jamaica (Dollar)	67	–
Japan (Yen)	116.3	–
Jersey uses Sterling Pound	.512	–
Jordan (Dinar)	.71	–
Kazakhstan (Tenge)	130	–
Kenya (Shilling)	70	–
Kiribati uses Australian Dollar	1.273	–
Korea-PDR (Won)	2.2	500
Korea-Rep. (Won)	920	–
Kuwait (Dinar)	.289	–
Kyrgyzstan (Som)	39	–
Laos (Kip)	9720	–
Latvia (Lats)	.53	–
Lebanon (Pound)	1,510	–
Lesotho (Maloti)	7.09	–
Liberia (Dollar)	53.3	–
Libya (Dinar)	1.27	–
Liechtenstein uses Swiss Franc	1.205	–
Lithuania (Litas)	2.62	–
Luxembourg (Euro)	.757	–
Macao (Pataca)	8.0	–
Macedonia (New Denar)	46	–
Madagascar (Franc)	2,040	–
Malawi (Kwacha)	140	–
Malaysia (Ringgit)	3.55	–
Maldives (Rufiya)	12.8	–
Mali uses CFA Franc West	490	–
Malta (Lira)	3.1	–
Marshall Islands uses U.S.Dollar		
Mauritania (Ouguiya)	270	–
Mauritius (Rupee)	32.5	–
Mexico (Peso)	10.82	–
Moldova (Leu)	13.1	–
Monaco uses Euro	.757	–
Mongolia (Tugrik)	1,165	–
Montenegro uses Euro	.757	–
Montserrat uses E.C. Dollar	2.7	–
Morocco (Dirham)	8.44	–
Mozambique (New Metical)	26.3	–
Myanmar (Burma) (Kyat)	6.42	1,250
Namibia (Rand)	7.09	–
Nauru uses Australian Dollar	1.456	–
Nepal (Rupee)	71.6	–
Netherlands (Euro)	.757	–
Netherlands Antilles (Gulden)	1.79	–
New Caledonia uses CFP Franc	90	–
New Zealand (Dollar)	1.493	–
Nicaragua (Cordoba Oro)	17.9	–
Niger uses CFA Franc West	490	–
Nigeria (Naira)	128	–
Northern Ireland uses Sterling Pound	.512	–
Norway (Krone)	6.16	–
Oman (Rial)	.385	–
Pakistan (Rupee)	60.9	–
Palau uses U.S.Dollar		
Panama (Balboa) uses U.S.Dollar		
Papua New Guinea (Kina)	3.02	–
Paraguay (Guarani)	5,400	–
Peru (Nuevo Sol)	3.21	–
Philippines (Peso)	50	–
Poland (Zloty)	2.9	–
Portugal (Euro)	.757	–
Qatar (Riyal)	3.64	–
Romania (New Leu)	2.6	–
Russia (New Ruble)	26.3	–
Rwanda (Franc)	550	–
St. Helena (Pound)	.512	–
St. Kitts uses E.C. Dollar	2.7	–
St. Lucia uses E.C. Dollar	2.7	–
St. Vincent uses E.C. Dollar	2.7	–
San Marino uses Euro	.757	–
Sao Tome e Principe (Dobra)	6,780	–
Saudi Arabia (Riyal)	3.75	–
Scotland uses Sterling Pound	.512	–
Senegal uses CFA Franc West	490	–
Serbia (Dinar)	59.9	–
Seychelles (Rupee)	5.59	6.40
Sierra Leone (Leone)	2,990	–
Singapore (Dollar)	1.55	–
Slovakia (Sk. Koruna)	26.8	–
Slovenia (Tolar)	180	–
Solomon Is.(Dollar)	7.63	–
Somalia (Shilling)	1,370	–
Somaliland (Somali Shilling)	1,800	4,000
South Africa (Rand)	7.09	–
Spain (Euro)	.757	–
Sri Lanka (Rupee)	110	–
Sudan (Dinar)	200	300
Surinam (Dollar)	2.75	–
Swaziland (Lilangeni)	7.09	–
Sweden (Krona)	6.87	–
Switzerland (Franc)	1.205	–
Syria (Pound)	52.2	–
Taiwan (NT Dollar)	32.4	–
Tajikistan (Somoni)	3.40	–
Tanzania (Shilling)	1,280	–
Thailand (Baht)	35.5	–
Togo uses CFA Franc West	490	–
Tonga (Pa'anga)	1.99	–
Transdniestra (Ruble)	6.51	–
Trinidad & Tobago (Dollar)	6.28	–
Tunisia (Dinar)	1.3	–
Turkey (New Lira)	1.43	–
Turkmenistan (Manat)	5,200	–
Turks & Caicos uses U.S. Dollar		
Tuvalu uses Australian Dollar	1.273	–
Uganda (Shilling)	1,800	–
Ukraine (Hryvnia)	5.03	–
United Arab Emirates (Dirham)	3.673	–
Uruguay (Peso Uruguayo)	24.3	–
Uzbekistan (Sum)	1,235	–
Vanuatu (Vatu)	106	–
Vatican City uses Euro	.757	–
Venezuela (Bolivar)	2,150	2,300
Vietnam (Dong)	16,050	–
Western Samoa (Tala)	2.66	–
Yemen (Rial)	198	–
Zambia (Kwacha)	4,050	–
Zimbabwe (revalued Dollar)	250	–

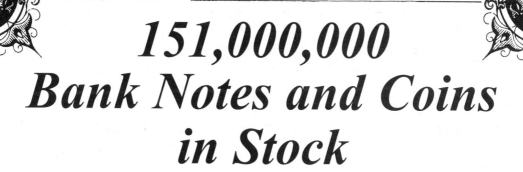

STANDARD INTERNATIONAL NUMERAL SYSTEMS

Prepared especially for the *Standard Catalog of World Coins*© 2007 by Krause Publications

Western	0	½	1	2	3	4	5	6	7	8	9	10	50	100	500	1000
Roman			I	II	III	IV	V	VI	VII	VIII	IX	X	L	C	D	M
Arabic-Turkish	٠	١/٢	١	٢	٣	٤	٥	٦	٧	٨	٩	١٠	٥٠	١٠٠	٥٠٠	١٠٠٠
Malay-Persian	٠	١/٢	١	٢	٣	۴	۵	٦ or ۶	٧	٨	٩	١٠	۵٠	١٠٠	۵٠٠	١٠٠٠
Eastern Arabic	۰	۱/۲	۱	۲	۳	۴	۵	۶	۷	۸	۹	۱۰	۵۰	۱۰۰	۵۰۰	۱۰۰۰
Hyderabad Arabic	۰	١/٢	١	٢	٣	۴	۵	۶	٧	٨	٩	١۰	۵۰	١۰۰	۵۰۰	١۰۰۰
Indian (Sanskrit)	०	१/२	१	२	३	४	५	६	७	८	९	१०	५०	१००	५००	१०००
Assamese	০	১/২	১	২	৩	৪	৫	৬	৭	৮	৯	১০	৫০	১০০	৫০০	১০০০
Bengali	০	১/২	১	২	৩	৪	৫	৬	৭	৮	৯	১০	৫০	১০০	৫০০	১০০০
Gujarati	૦	૧/૨	૧	૨	૩	૪	૫	૬	૭	૮	૯	૧૦	૫૦	૧૦૦	૫૦૦	૧૦૦૦
Kutch	०	१/२	१	२	३	४	५	६	७	८	९	१०	५०	१००	५००	१०००
Devavnagri	०	१/२	१	२	३	४	५	६ or ६	७	८	९ or ९	१०	५०	१००	५००	१०००
Nepalese	०	१/२	१	२	३	४	५	६	७	८	९	१०	५०	१००	५००	१०००
Tibetan	༠	༡/༢	༡	༢	༣	༤	༥	༦	༧	༨	༩	༡༠	༥༠	༡༠༠	༥༠༠	༡༠༠༠
Mongolian	᠐	᠑/᠒	᠑	᠒	᠓	᠔	᠕	᠖	᠗	᠘	᠙	᠑᠐	᠕᠐	᠑᠐᠐	᠕᠐᠐	᠑᠐᠐᠐
Burmese	၀	၁/၂	၁	၂	၃	၄	၅	၆	၇	၈	၉	၁၀	၅၀	၁၀၀	၅၀၀	၁၀၀၀
Thai-Lao	๐	๑/๒	๑	๒	๓	๔	๕	๖	๗	๘	๙	๑๐	๕๐	๑๐๐	๕๐๐	๑๐๐๐
Lao-Laotian	໐		໑	໒	໓	໔	໕	໖	໗	໘	໙	໑໐				
Javanese	꧐		꧑	꧒	꧓	꧔	꧕	꧖	꧗	꧘	꧙	꧑꧐	꧕꧐	꧑꧐꧐	꧕꧐꧐	꧑꧐꧐꧐
Ordinary Chinese Japanese-Korean	零	半	一	二	三	四	五	六	七	八	九	十	十五	百	百五	千
Official Chinese			壹	貳	叁	肆	伍	陸	柒	捌	玖	拾	拾伍	佰	佰伍	仟
Commercial Chinese			〡	〢	〣	〤	〥	〦	〧	〨	〩	十	〥十	〡百	〥百	〡千
Korean		반	일	이	삼	사	오	육	칠	팔	구	십	오십	백	오백	천
Georgian			ა	ბ	გ	დ	ე	ვ	ზ	ჱ	თ	ი	ნ	რ	ფ	ჩ
			11 ია	20 კ	30 ლ	40 მ	60 ჲ	70 ო	80 პ	90 ჟ	200 ს	300 ტ	400 უ	600 ქ	700 ღ	800 ყ
Ethiopian	◆		፩	፪	፫	፬	፭	፮	፯	፰	፱	፲	፶	፻	፭፻	፲፻
				20 ፳	30 ፴	40 ፵	60 ፷	70 ፸	80 ፹	90 ፺						
Hebrew			א	ב	ג	ד	ה	ו	ז	ח	ט	י	נ	ק	תק	
				20 כ	30 ל	40 מ	60 ס	70 ע	80 פ	90 צ	200 ר	300 ש	400 ת	600 תר	700 תש	800 תת
Greek			A	B	Γ	Δ	E	T	Z	H	Θ	I	N	P	Φ	A
				20 K	30 Λ	40 M	60 Ξ	70 O	80 Π		200 Σ	300 T	400 Y	600 X	700 Ψ	800 Ω

COMPANION CATALOGS

Volume 1 - Specialized Issues
Volume 2 - General Issues, 1368-1960

The Companion Catalogs in the Standard Catalog of World Paper Money series include a volume on Specialized Issues of the World - listed are those banknotes which were issued on a limited circulation basis rather than the central monetary authority note issues detailed in this work. The Specialized volume is currently in its 10th edition, and it is updated periodically. The General Issues volume lists notes circulated on a national scope and dated before 1960. It's currently in the 11th edition. Inquiries about the availability of both these volumes are invited to contact Book Department, Krause Publications, 700 East State Street, Iola, WI 54990-0001 or you may call 1-800-258-0929 or www.krausebooks.com.

Dating

Determining the date of issue of a note is a basic consideration of attribution. As the reading of dates is subject not only to the vagaries of numeric styling, but to variations in dating roots caused by the observation of differing religious eras or regal periods from country to country, making this determination can sometimes be quite difficult. Most countries outside the North African and Oriental spheres rely on Western date numerals and the Christian (AD) reckoning, although in a few instances note dating has been tied to the year of a reign or government.

Countries of the Arabic sphere generally date their issues to the Muslim calendar that commenced on July 16, 622 AD when the prophet Mohammed fled from Mecca to Medina. As this calendar is reckoned by the lunar year of 354, its is about three percent (precisely 3.3 percent) shorter than the Christian year. A conversion formula requires you to subtract that percent from the AH date, and then add 621 to gain the AD date.

A degree of confusion arises here because the Muslim calendar is not always based on the lunar year (AH). Afghanistan and Iran (Persia) used a calendar based on a solar year (SH) introduced around 1920. These dates can be converted to AD by simply adding 621. In 1976, Iran implemented a solar calendar based on the founding of the Iranian monarchy in 559 BC. The first year observed on this new system was 2535(MS) which commenced on March 20, 1976.

Several different eras of reckoning, including the Christian (AD) and Muslim (AH), have been used to date paper money of the Indian subcontinent. The two basic systems are the Vikrama Samvat (VS) era that dates from October 18, 58 BC,. and the Saka (SE) era, the origin of which is reckoned from March 3, 78 AD. Dating according to both eras appears on notes of several native states and countries of the area.

Thailand (Siam) has observed three different eras for dating. The most predominant is the Buddhist (BE) era originating in 54 3 BC. Next is the Bangkok or Ratanakosind-sok (RS) era dating from 1781 AD (and consisting of only 3 numerals), followed by the Chula-Sakarat (CS) era dating from 638 AD, with the latter also observed in Burma.

Other calendars include that of the Ethiopian (EE) era that commenced 7 years, 8 months after AD dating, and that of the Hebrew nation beginning on October 7, 3761 BC. Korea claims a dating from 2333 BC which is acknowledged on some note issues.

The following table indicates the years dating from the various eras that correspond to 2007 by Christian (AD) calendar reckoning. It must be remembered that there are overlaps between the eras in some instances:

Christian Era (AD)	—	2008
Mohammedan era (AH)	—	AH1429
Solar year (SH)	—	SH1387
Monarchic Solar era (MS)	—	MS2567
Vikrama Samvat era (VS)	—	SE2065
Saka era (SE)	—	Saka 1930
Buddhist era (BE)	—	BE2551
Bangkok era (RS)	—	RS227
Chula-Sakarat era (CS)	—	CS1370
Ethiopian era (EE)	—	EE2000
Jewish era	—	5768
Korean era	—	4341

Paper money of Oriental origin - principally Japan, Korea, China, Turkestan and Tibet - generally date to the year of the government, dynastic, regnal or cyclical eras, with the dates indicated in Oriental characters usually reading from right to left. In recent years some dating has been according to the Christian calendar and in Western numerals reading from left to right.

More detailed guides to the application of the less prevalent dating systems than those described, and others of strictly local nature, along with the numeral designations employed, are presented in conjunction with the appropriate listings.

Some notes carry dating according to both the locally observed and Christian eras. This is particularly true in the Arabic sphere, where the Muslim date may be indicated in Arabic numerals and the Christian date in Western numerals.

In general the date actually shown on a given paper money issue is indicated in some manner. Notes issued by special Law or Decree will have L or D preceding the date. Dates listed within parentheses may differ from the date appearing on the note; they have been documented by other means. Undated notes are listed with ND, followed by a year only when the year of actual issue is known.

Timing differentials between the 354-day Muslim and the 36 5-day Christian year cause situations whereby notes bearing dates of both eras have two date combinations that may overlap from one or the other calendar system.

China — Republic 9th year, 1st month, 15th day (15.1.1920), read r. to l.

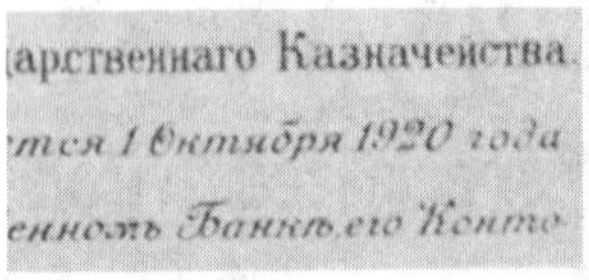

Russia — 1 October 1920

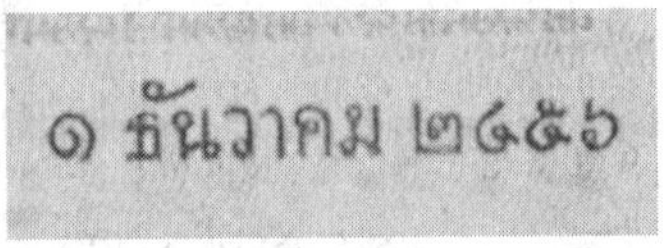

Thailand (Siam) — 1 December 2456

Korea — 4288 (1955)

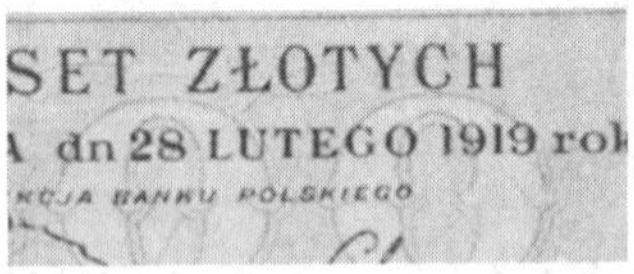

Poland — 28 February 1919

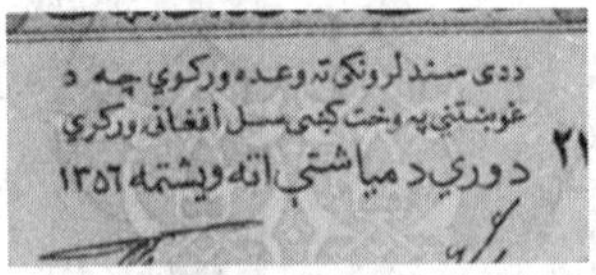

Afghanistan — Solar Year 1356

Israel — 1973, 5733

Indonesia — 1 January 1950

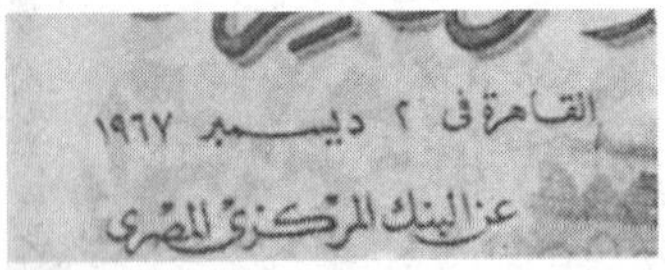

Egypt — 1967 December 2

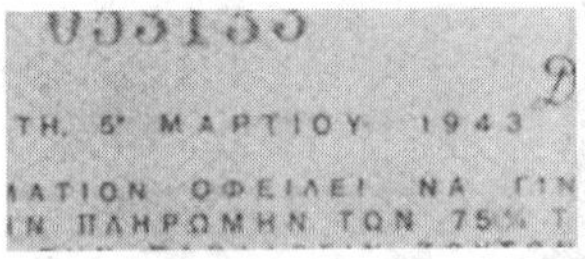

Greece — 5 March 1943

WORLD BANK NOTES WANTED!

Olmstead Currency, *in business for over thirty years and long known as* ***"The Higher Buyer,"*** *is very, very interested in all of your bank notes.*

From **ANGOLA** *to* **ZAIRE, US paper, Canadian paper,** *you name it & we are strong buyers.*

Olmstead Currency *is especially interested in Replacement Notes, Error Notes, & Low Serial Numbers under number 10.*

Olmstead Currency *pays promptly by confidential money order in the currency of your choice.*

If you have notes to sell, contact **Olmstead Currency, The Higher Buyer**, *today.* **Why sell for less?**

Don Olmstead

OLMSTEAD CURRENCY

The Higher Buyer

P.O. Box 487
St. Stephen, NB
Canada E3L 3A6

OR

Fax: 506-466-5726

P.O. Box 135
Calais, ME
04619 USA

www.olmsteadcurrency.com

506-466-2078 • banknote@nbnet.nb.ca

HEJIRA DATE CONVERSION CHART

HEJIRA (Hijira, Hegira), the name of the Muslim era (A.H. = Anno Hegirae) dates back to the Christian year 622 when Mohammed "fled" from Mecca, escaping to Medina to avoid persecution from the Koreish tribemen. Based on a lunar year the Muslim year is 11 days shorter.

*=Leap Year

(Christian Calendar)

AH Hejira	AD Christian Date
1010	1601, July 2
1011	1602, June 21
1012	1603, June 11
1013	1604, May 30
1014	1605, May 19
1015	1606, May 19
1016	1607, May 9
1017	1608, April 28
1018	1609, April 6
1017	1608, April 28
1018	1609, April 6
1019	1610, March 26
1020	1611, March 16
1021	1612, March 4
1022	1613, February 21
1023	1614, February 11
1024	1615, January 31
1025	1616, January 20
1026	1617, January 9
1027	1617, December 29
1028	1618, December 19
1029	1619, December 8
1030	1620, November 26
1031	1621, November 16
1032	1622, November 5
1033	1623, October 25
1034	1624, October 14
1035	1625, October 3
1036	1626, September 22
1037	1627, Septembe 12
1038	1628, August 31
1039	1629, August 21
1040	1630, July 10
1041	1631, July 30
1042	1632, July 19
1043	1633, July 8
1044	1634, June 27
1045	1635, June 17
1046	1636, June 5
1047	1637, May 26
1048	1638, May 15
1049	1639, May 4
1050	1640, April 23
1051	1641, April 12
1052	1642, April 1
1053	1643, March 22
1054	1644, March 10
1055	1645, February 27
1056	1646, February 17
1057	1647, February 6
1058	1648, January 27
1059	1649, January 15
1060	1650, January 4
1061	1650, December 25
1062	1651, December 14
1063	1652, December 2
1064	1653, November 22
1065	1654, November 11
1066	1655, October 31
1067	1656, October 20
1068	1657, October 9
1069	1658, September 29
1070	1659, September 18
1071	1660, September 6
1072	1661, August 27
1073	1662, August 16
1074	1663, August 5
1075	1664, July 25
1076	1665, July 14
1077	1666, July 4
1078	1667, June 23
1079	1668, June 11
1080	1669, June 1
1081	1670, May 21
1082	1671, May 10
1083	1672, April 29
1084	1673, April 18
1085	1674, April 7
1086	1675, March 28
1087	1676, March 16*
1088	1677, March 6
1089	1678, February 23
1090	1679, February 12
1091	1680, February 2*
1092	1681, January 21
1093	1682, January 10
1094	1682, December 31
1095	1683, December 20
1096	1684, December 8*
1097	1685, November 28
1098	1686, November 17
1099	1687, November 7
1100	1688, October 26*
1101	1689, October 15
1102	1690, October 5
1103	1691, September 24
1104	1692, September 12*
1105	1693, September 2
1106	1694, August 22
1107	1695, August 12
1108	1696, July 31*
1109	1697, July 20
1110	1698, July 10
1111	1699, June 29
1112	1700, June 18
1113	1701, June 8
1114	1702, May 28
1115	1703, May 17
1116	1704, May 6*
1117	1705, April 25
1118	1706, April 15
1119	1707, April 4
1120	1708, March 23*
1121	1709, March 13
1122	1710, March 2
1123	1711, February 19
1124	1712, Feburary 9*
1125	1713, January 28
1126	1714, January 17
1127	1715, January 7
1128	1715, December 27
1129	1716, December 16*
1130	1717, December 5
1131	1718, November 24
1132	1719, November 14
1133	1720, November 2*
1134	1721, October 22
1135	1722, October 12
1136	1723, October 1
1137	1724, September 19
1138	1725, September 9
1139	1726, August 29
1140	1727, August 19
1141	1728, August 7*
1142	1729, July 27
1143	1730, July 17
1144	1731, July 6
1145	1732, June 24*
1146	1733, June 14
1147	1734, June 3
1148	1735, May 24
1149	1736, May 12*
1150	1737, May 1
1151	1738, April 21
1152	1739, April 10
1153	1740, March 29*
1154	1741, March 19
1155	1742, March 8
1156	1743, Febuary 25
1157	1744, February 15*
1158	1745, February 3
1159	1746, January 24
1160	1747, January 13
1161	1748, January 2
1162	1748, December 22*
1163	1749, December 11
1164	1750, November 30
1165	1751, November 20
1166	1752, November 8*
1167	1753, October 29
1168	1754, October 18
1169	1755, October 7
1170	1756, September 26*
1171	1757, September 15
1172	1758, September 4
1173	1759, August 25
1174	1760, August 13*
1175	1761, August 2
1176	1762, July 23
1177	1763, July 12
1178	1764, July 1*
1179	1765, June 20
1180	1766, June 9
1181	1767, May 30
1182	1768, May 18*
1183	1769, May 7
1184	1770, April 27
1185	1771, April 16
1186	1772, April 4*
1187	1773, March 25
1188	1774, March 14
1189	1775, March 4
1190	1776, February 21*
1191	1777, February 91
1192	1778, January 30
1193	1779, January 19
1194	1780, January 8*
1195	1780, December 28*
1196	1781, December 17
1197	1782, December 7
1198	1783, November 26
1199	1784, November 14*
1200	1785, November 4
1201	1786, October 24
1202	1787, October 13
1203	1788, October 2*
1204	1789, September 21
1205	1790, September 10
1206	1791, August 31
1207	1792, August 19*
1208	1793, August 9
1209	1794, July 29
1210	1795, July 18
1211	1796, July 7*
1212	1797, June 26
1213	1798, June 15
1214	1799, June 5
1215	1800, May 25
1216	1801, May 14
1217	1802, May 4
1218	1803, April 23
1219	1804, April 12*
1220	1805, April 1
1221	1806, March 21
1222	1807, March 11
1223	1808, February 28*
1224	1809, February 16
1225	1810, Febauary 6
1226	1811, January 26
1227	1812, January 16*
1228	1813, Janaury 26
1229	1813, December 24
1230	1814, December 14
1231	1815, December 3
1232	1816, November 21*
1233	1817, November 11
1234	1818, October 31
1235	1819, October 20
1236	1820, October 9*
1237	1821, September 28
1238	1822, September 18
1239	1823, September 18
1240	1824, August 26*
1241	1825, August 16
1242	1826, August 5
1243	1827, July 25
1244	1828, July 14*
1245	1829, July 3
1246	1830, June 22
1247	1831, June 12
1248	1832, May 31*
1249	1833, May 21
1250	1834, May 10
1251	1835, April 29
1252	1836, April 18*
1253	1837, April 7
1254	1838, March 27
1255	1839, March 17
1256	1840, March 5*
1257	1841, February 23
1258	1842, February 12
1259	1843, February 1
1260	1844, January 22*
1261	1845, January 10
1262	1845, December 30
1263	1846, December 20
1264	1847, December 9
1265	1848, November 27*
1266	1849, November 17
1267	1850, November 6
1268	1851, October 27
1269	1852, October 15*
1270	1853, October 4
1271	1854, September 24
1272	1855, September 13
1273	1856, September 1*
1274	1857, August 22
1275	1858, August 11
1276	1859, July 31
1277	1860, July 20*
1278	1861, July 9
1279	1862, June 29
1280	1863, June 18
1281	1864, June 6*
1282	1865, May 27
1283	1866, May 16
1284	1867, May 5
1285	1868, April 24*
1286	1869, April 13
1287	1870, April 3
1288	1871, March 23
1289	1872, March 11*
1290	1873, March 1
1291	1874, February 18
1292	1875, Febuary 7
1293	1876, January 28*
1294	1877, January 16
1295	1878, January 5
1296	1878, December 26
1297	1879, December 15
1298	1880, December 4*
1299	1881, November 23
1300	1882, November 12
1301	1883, November 2
1302	1884, October 21*
1303	1885, October 10
1304	1886, September 30
1305	1887, September 19
1306	1888, September 7*
1307	1889, August 28
1308	1890, August 17
1309	1891, August 7
1310	1892, July 26*
1311	1893, July 15
1312	1894, July 5
1313	1895, June 24
1314	1896, June 12*
1315	1897, June 2
1316	1898, May 22
1317	1899, May 12
1318	1900, May 1
1319	1901, April 20
1320	1902, april 10
1321	1903, March 30
1322	1904, March 18*
1323	1905, March 8
1324	1906, February 25
1325	1907, February 14
1326	1908, February 4*
1327	1909, January 23
1328	1910, January 13
1329	1911, January 2
1330	1911, December 22
1332	1913, November 30
1333	1914, November 19
1334	1915, November 9
1335	1916, October 28*
1336	1917, October 17
1337	1918, October 7
1338	1919, September 26
1339	1920, September 15*
1340	1921, September 4
1341	1922, August 24
1342	1923, August 14
1343	1924, August 2*
1344	1925, July 22
1345	1926, July 12
1346	1927, July 1
1347	1928, June 20*
1348	1929, June 9
1349	1930, May 29
1350	1931, May 19
1351	1932, May 7*
1352	1933, April 26
1353	1934, April 16
1354	1935, April 5
1355	1936, March 24*
1356	1937, March 14
1357	1938, March 3
1358	1939, February 21
1359	1940, February 10*
1360	1941, January 29
1361	1942, January 19
1362	1943, January 8
1363	1943, December 28
1364	1944, December 17*
1365	1945, December 6
1366	1946, November 25
1367	1947, November 15
1368	1948, November 3*
1369	1949, October 24
1370	1950, October 13
1371	1951, October 2
1372	1952, September 21*
1373	1953, September 10
1374	1954, August 30
1375	1955, August 20
1376	1956, August 8*
1377	1957, July 29
1378	1958, July 18
1379	1959, July 7
1380	1960, June 25*
1381	1961, June 14
1382	1962, June 4
1383	1963, May 25
1384	1964, May 13*
1385	1965, May 2
1386	1966, April 22
1387	1967, April 11
1388	1968, March 31*
1389	1969, march 20
1390	1970, March 9
1391	1971, February 27
1392	1972, February 16*
1393	1973, February 4
1394	1974, January 25
1395	1975, January 14
1396	1976, January 3*
1397	1976, December 23*
1398	1977, December 12
1399	1978, December 2
1400	1979, November 21
1401	1980, November 9*
1402	1981, October 30
1403	1982, October 19
1404	1984, October 8
1405	1984, September 27*
1406	1985, September 16
1407	1986, September 6
1409	1987, August 26
1409	1988, August 14*
1410	1989, August 3
1411	1990, July 24
1412	1991, July 13
1413	1992, July 2*
1414	1993, June 21
1415	1994, June 10
1416	1995, May 31
1417	1996, May 19*
1418	1997, May 9
1419	1998, April 28
1420	1999, April 17
1421	2000, April 6*
1422	2001, March 26
1423	2002, March 15
1424	2003, March 5
1425	2004, February 22*
1426	2005, February 10
1427	2006, January 31
1428	2007, January 20
1429	2008, January 10*
1430	2008, December 29
1431	2009, December 18
1432	2010, December 8
1433	2011, November 27*
1434	2012, November 15
1435	2013, November 5
1436	2014, October 25
1437	2015, October 15*
1438	2016, October 3
1439	2017, September 22
1440	2018, September 12
1441	2019, September 11*
1442	2020, August 20
1443	2021, August 10
1444	2022, July 30
1445	2023, July 19*
1446	2024, July 8
1447	2025, June 27
1448	2026, June 17
1449	2027, June 6*
1450	2028, May 25

The Islamic Republic of Afghanistan, which occupies a mountainous region of Southwest Asia, has an area of 251,773 sq. mi. (652,090 sq. km.) and a population of 25.59 million. Presently about a fifth of the total population reside mostly in Pakistan in exile as refugees. Capital: Kabul. It is bordered by Iran, Pakistan, Tajikistan, Turkmenistan, Uzbekistan and Peoples Republic of China's Sinkiang Province. Agriculture and herding are the principal industries; textile mills and cement factories are recent additions to the industrial sector. Cotton, wool, fruits, nuts, sheepskin coats and hand-woven carpets are exported but foreign trade has been sporadic since 1979.

Because of its strategic position astride the ancient land route to India, Afghanistan - formerly known as Aryana and Khorasan - was conquered by Darius I, Alexander the Great, various Scythian tribes, the Arabs, the Turks, Genghis Khan, Tamerlane, the Mughals, the Persians, and in more recent times by Great Britain.

It was a powerful empire under the Kushans, Hephthalites, Ghaznavids and Ghorids. The name Afghanistan, *Land of the Afghans,* came into use in the eighteenth and nineteenth centuries to describe the realm of the Afghan kings. Previously this mountainous region was the easternmost frontier of the Iranian world, with strong cultural influences from the Turks and Mongols to the north and India to the south.

The first Afghan king, Ahmad Shah Abdali, founder of the Durrani dynasty, established his rule at Qandahar in 1747. He conquered large territories in India and eastern Iran, which were lost by his grandson Zaman Shah. A new family, the Barakzays, drove the Durrani king out of Kabul in 1819, but the Durranis were not eliminated completely until 1858. Further conflicts among the Barakzays prevented full unity until the reign of 'Abd al-Rahman in 1880. In 1929 a commoner, Baccha-i-Saqao, *Son of the Water-Carrier,* drove King Amanullah from the throne and ruled as Habibullah Ghazi for less than a year before he was defeated by Muhammad Nadir Shah. The last king, Muhammad Zahir Shah, became a constitutional, though still autocratic, monarch in 1964. In 1973 a *coup d'etat* displaced him and created the Republic of Afghanistan. A subsequent military *coup* established the pro-Soviet Khalq Democratic Republic of Afghanistan under Nur Muhammad Taraqi in 1978. Mounting resistance and violence led to the Soviet invasion of late 1979 and the installation of Babrak Kamal as prime minister. A brutal civil war ensued, even after Soviet forces withdrew in 1989 and Kamal's government was defeated in 1992. An unstable coalition of former *Mujahideen* (Freedom Fighters) factions attempted to govern for several years but were gradually overcome by the Taliban, a Muslim fundamentalist force supported from Pakistan. On Sept. 26, 1996 Taliban forces captured Kabul and set up a government under Mohammed Rabbani. Afghanistan was declared a complete Islamic state under Sharia law.

In the Fall of 2001 the continuing revolution came to a head and by December the Taliban government was overthrown with the assistance of the U.S. military and a grand council endorsed the Transitional Authority, which continues to govern the country and is preparing for elections to take place in late 2004.

RULERS:

Muhammad Zahir Shah, SH1312-1352/1933-1973AD

MONETARY SYSTEM:

1 Rupees = 10 Afghani, 1925-
1 Afghani = 100 Pul
1 Amani = 20 Afghani

KINGDOM

BANK OF AFGHANISTAN

1961-63 ISSUES

#37-42 Kg. Muhammad Zahir (third portrait) at l. and as wmk. Printer: TDLR.

		VG	VF	UNC
37	**10 Afghanis** SH1340 (1961). Brown on multicolor underprint. Mosque of Khwajeh Mohammad Abu-Nasr Parsa in Balkh at center on back.			
	a. Issued note.	.25	1.00	5.00
	s. Specimen.	—	—	—

		VG	VF	UNC
38	**20 Afghanis** SH1340 (1961). Blue on multicolor underprint. Independence monument in Kabul at center on back.	.25	1.00	7.00

		VG	VF	UNC
39	**50 Afghanis** SH1340 (1961). Green on multicolor underprint. Mausoleum of King Nadir Shah in Kabul at center on back.			
	a. Issued note.	.50	1.50	12.50
	s. Specimen.	—	—	—

		VG	VF	UNC
40	**100 Afghanis** SH1340 (1961). Red on multicolor underprint.	1.25	7.50	32.50

		VG	VF	UNC
40A	**500 Afghanis** SH1340 (1961). Orange on multicolor underprint.			
	a. Issued note.	5.00	25.00	100.
	s. Specimen.	—	—	—

41 500 Afghanis

SH1340 (1961); SH1342 (1963). Olive-brown on multicolor underprint.

	VG	VF	UNC
a. 8 digit serial #. SH1340.	5.00	25.00	100.
b. Serial # with prefix. SH1342.	3.50	15.00	75.00
s. Specimen.	—	—	—

42 1000 Afghanis

SH1340 (1961); SH1342 (1963). Blue-gray on multicolor underprint. Arch of Qila'-e Bost in Lashkargah at right on back.

	VG	VF	UNC
a. 8 digit serial #. SH1340.	4.00	32.50	175.
b. Prefix serial #. SH1342.	4.00	25.00	150.

1967 Issue

#43-46 Kg. Muhammad Zahir at l. and as wmk. W/o imprint.

43 50 Afghanis

SH1346 (1967). Green on multicolor underprint. Arg-e Shahi, King's palace at center right on back.

	VG	VF	UNC
a. Issued note.	.50	1.50	6.00
s. Specimen.	—	—	—

44 100 Afghanis

SH1346 (1967). Lilac on multicolor underprint. Mosque in Kabul at center right on back.

	VG	VF	UNC
a. Issued note.	.75	2.50	9.00
s. Specimen.	—	—	—

45 500 Afghanis

SH1346 (1967). Black and dark blue on multicolor underprint. Qandahar Airport at right on back.

	VG	VF	UNC
a. Issued note.	1.50	17.50	50.00
s. Specimen.	—	—	—

46 1000 Afghanis

SH1346 (1967). Brown on multicolor underprint.

	VG	VF	UNC
a. Issued note.	3.50	15.00	75.00
s. Specimen.	—	—	—

Republic

SH1352-1358/1973-1979 AD

Bank of Afghanistan

1973-78 Issue

#47-53 Pres. Muhammad Daud at l. and as wmk.

Note: It is possible that all notes #47-53 dated SH1354 are replacements.

47 10 Afghanis

SH1352 (1973); SH1354 (1975); SH1356 (1977). Green on multicolor underprint. Arch of Qila'-e Bost in Lashkargah at center right on back.

	VG	VF	UNC
a. Issued note.	.10	.50	2.25
s. Specimen.	—	—	—

48 20 Afghanis

SH1352 (1973); SH1354 (1975); SH1356 (1977). Purple on multicolor underprint. Canal at right on back.

	VG	VF	UNC
a. Issued note.	.10	.50	3.00
s. Specimen.	—	—	—

49 50 Afghanis

SH1352 (1973); SH1354 (1975); SH1356 (1977). Green on multicolor underprint. Men riding yaks at center on back.

	VG	VF	UNC
a. Issued note.	.20	1.00	4.50
s. Specimen.	—	—	—

50 100 Afghanis

SH1352 (1973); SH1354 (1975); SH1356 (1977). Brown-lilac on multicolor underprint. Friday Mosque in Herât at center right on back.

	VG	VF	UNC
a. Issued note.	.25	2.00	10.00
s. Specimen.	—	—	—

51 500 Afghanis

SH1352 (1973); SH1354 (1975). Blue on multicolor underprint. Fortified tribal village at center right on back.

	VG	VF	UNC
a. Issued note.	.50	3.00	20.00
s. Specimen.	—	—	—

52 500 Afghanis

SH1356 (1977). Brown on multicolor underprint. Like #51.

	VG	VF	UNC
a. Issued note.	1.00	5.00	25.00
s. Specimen.	—	—	—

53 1000 Afghanis

	VG	VF	UNC
SH1352 (1973); SH1354 (1975); SH1356 (1977). Brown on multicolor underprint. Mosque of Mazâr-e Sharîf, the Noble Shrine at center right on back.	.75	3.50	20.00

have filtered into the market via Pakistan recently.

KHALQ DEMOCRATIC REPUBLIC

SH1357-1370/1978-1992 AD

DA AFGHANISTAN BANK

1978 ISSUE

#53A and 54 w/Khalq Government emblem from flag at top l. or r. ctr.

53A 20 Afghanis

	VG	VF	Unc
AH1357 (1978). Purple on multicolor underprint. Fortress at center on back. Specimen, punched hole cancelled.			

54 50 Afghanis

	VG	VF	UNC
SH1357 (1978). Blue-green on multicolor underprint. Dar-al-Aman Palace in Kabul on back.	.50	3.00	20.00

DEMOCRATIC REPUBLIC

DA AFGHANISTAN BANK

1979 ISSUE

#55-61 bank arms w/horseman at top ctr. or ctr. r. on face.

		VG	VF	UNC
55	**10 Afghanis** SH1358 (1979). Green and blue on multicolor underprint. Mountain road scene at center on back.			
	a. Issued note.	.10	.20	.60
	s. Specimen. Punch hole cancelled, ovpt: *SPECIMEN.*	—	Unc	8.00

		VG	VF	UNC
56	**20 Afghanis** SH1358 (1979). Purple on multicolor underprint. Building and mountains at center on back. Signature varieties.			
	a. Issued note.	.10	.25	1.00
	s. Specimen. Punch hole cancelled, ovpt *SPECIMEN.*	—	Unc	20.00

		VG	VF	UNC
57	**50 Afghanis** SH1358-70 (1979-91). Greenish black with black text on multicolor underprint. Similar to #54.			
	a. SH1358 (1979). 2 signature varieties.	.10	.20	.75
	b. SH1370 (1991).	.10	.25	1.00
	s. Specimen. As a. Punch hole cancelled. Ovpt: *SPECIMEN.*	—	Unc	40.00

		VG	VF	UNC
58	**100 Afghanis** SH1358-70 1979-91). Deep red-violet on multicolor underprint. Farm worker in wheat field at right. Hydroelectric dam in mountains at center on back.			
	a. SH1358 (1979). 2 signature varieties.	.10	.50	2.00
	b. SH1369 (1990).	.10	.50	2.50
	c. SH1370 (1991).	.10	.25	1.00

		VG	VF	UNC
59	**500 Afghanis** SH1358 (1979). Violet and dark blue on multicolor underprint. Horsemen competing in Buzkashi at right. Fortress at Kabul at left center on back.	.50	2.00	12.50

		VG	VF	UNC
60	**500 Afghanis** SH1358-70 (1979-91). Reddish-brown, deep green and deep brown on multicolor underprint. Like #59. Back deep green on multicolor underprint.			
	a. SH1358 (1979).	.20	.75	2.50
	b. SH1369 (1990).	.25	1.00	4.00
	c. SH1370 (1991).	.10	.25	1.50

		VG	VF	UNC
61	**1000 Afghanis** SH1358-70 (1979-91). Dark brown and deep red-violet on multicolor underprint. Mosque at Mazar-e-Sharif at right. Victory Arch near Kabul at left center on back.			
	a. SH1358 (1979).	.50	2.50	7.50
	b. SH1369 (1990).	.10	.50	2.50
	c. SH1370 (1991).	.10	.25	1.50

1993 ISSUE

#62-64 bank arms w/horseman at top l. ctr. Wmk: Bank arms.

		VG	VF	UNC
62	**5000 Afghanis** SH1372 (1993). Violet and blue-black on multicolor underprint. Mosque with minaret at right. Tomb of King Habibullah, Jalalabad at center on back.	.20	.50	2.00

		VG	VF	UNC
63	**10,000 Afghanis** SH1372 (1993). Black, deep olive-green and deep blue-green on multicolor underprint. Gateway between minarets at right. Arched gateway at Bost in center on back.			
	a. Without small space between *Da* and *Afghanistan* on back.	.20	.75	3.00
	b. With small space between *Da* and *Afghanistan* on back.	.15	.50	2.00

REPUBLIC (2001)

DA AFGHANISTAN BANK

2002 ISSUE

1000 'old' afghani = 1 'new' afghani.

		VG	VF	UNC
64	**1 Afghani** SH 1381 (2002). Purple on multicolor underprint. Bank name around ancient coin, cornucopia pair below. Mosque at Mazar-i Sharif at center on back.	FV	FV	.50

		VG	VF	UNC
65	**2 Afghanis** SH 1381 (2002). Slate blue on multicolor underprint. Bank name around ancient coin, cornucopia pair below. Victory Arch near Kabul on back.	FV	FV	.50

		VG	VF	UNC
66	**5 Afghanis** SH 1381 (2002). Olive on multicolor underprint. Bank name around ancient coin, cornucopia pair below. Fortress at Kabul at center on back.	FV	FV	.75

		VG	VF	UNC
67	**10 Afghanis** SH 1381 (2002). Green and brown on multicolor underprint. Mosque at right. Victory Arch near Kabul at center on back. Segmented security thread.	FV	FV	1.25

		VG	VF	UNC
68	**20 Afghanis** SH 1381 (2002). Green and purple on multicolor underprint. Tomb at right. Arg-e Shahi, King's Palace at center on back.	FV	FV	1.50

		VG	VF	UNC
69	**50 Afghanis** SH 1381 (2002). Green and brown on multicolor underprint. Salang Pass at center on back.	FV	FV	3.00

		VG	VF	UNC
70	**100 Afghanis** SH 1381 (2002). Arch at Qila'-e Bost on back.	FV	FV	6.00

		VG	VF	UNC
71	**500 Afghanis** SH 1381 (2002). Violet and blue on multicolor underprint. Airport tower on back.	FV	FV	25.00

		VG	VF	UNC
72	**1000 Afghanis** SH 1381 (2002). Orange and brown on yellow and multicolor underprint. Tomb on back.	FV	FV	50.00

The Republic of Albania, a Balkan republic bounded by the rump Yugoslav state of Montenegro and Serbia, Macedonia, Greece and the Adriatic Sea, has an area of 11,100 sq. mi. (28,748 sq. km.) and a population of 3.5 million. Capital: Tirana. The country is mostly agricultural, although recent progress has been made in the manufacturing and mining sectors. Petroleum, chrome, iron, copper, cotton textiles, tobacco and wood products are exported.

Since it had been part of the Greek and Roman Empires, little is known of the early history of Albania. After the disintegration of the Roman Empire, Albania was overrun by Goths, Byzantines, Venetians and Turks. Skanderbeg, the national hero, resisted the Turks and established an independent Albania in 1443, but in 1468 the country again fell to the Turks and remained part of the Ottoman Empire for more than 400 years.

Independence was re-established by revolt in 1912, and the present borders established in 1913 by a conference of European powers which, in 1914, placed Prince William of Wied on the throne; popular discontent forced his abdication within months. In 1920, following World War I occupancy by several nations, a republic was set up. Ahmet Zogu seized the presidency in 1925, and in 1928 proclaimed himself king with the title of Zog I. King Zog fled when Italy occupied Albania in 1939 and enthroned King Victor Emanuel of Italy. Upon the surrender of Italy to the Allies in 1943, German troops occupied the country. They withdrew in 1944, and communist partisans seized power, naming Gen. Enver Hoxha provisional president. In 1946, following a victory by the communist front in the 1945 elections, a new constitution modeled on that of the USSR was adopted. In accordance with the constitution of Dec. 28, 1976, the official name of Albania was changed from the People's Republic of Albania to the People's Socialist Republic of Albania. A general strike by trade unions in 1991 forced the communist government to resign. A new government was elected in March 1992. In 1997 Albania had a major financial crisis which caused civil disturbances and the fall of the administration.

PEOPLES REPUBLIC

BANKA E SHTETIT SHQIPTAR

1964 ISSUE

#33-39 arms at upper r. on back. Wmk: Curved *BSHSH* repeated.

		VG	VF	UNC
33	**1 Lek** 1964. Green and deep blue on multicolor underprint. Peasant couple at center. Shkoder fortress at left center on back.			
	a. Issued note.	.15	.50	1.50
	s. Specimen ovpt: *MODEL* or *SPECIMEN*.	—	—	3.00

		VG	VF	UNC
34	**3 Lekë** 1964. Brown and lilac on multicolor underprint. Woman with basket of grapes at left. Saranda view at left center on back.			
	a. Issued note.	.20	.65	2.25
	s. Specimen ovpt: *MODEL* or *SPECIMEN*.	—	—	4.00

		VG	VF	UNC
35	**5 Lekë** 1964. Purple and dark blue on multicolor underprint. Truck and steam passenger train crossing viaduct at left center. Ship at left on back.			
	a. Issued note.	.25	.90	3.00
	s. Specimen ovpt: *MODEL* or *SPECIMEN*.	—	—	5.00

		VG	VF	UNC
36	**10 Lekë** 1964. Dark green on multicolor underprint. Woman working with cotton spinning frame. People at left center, male portrait at upper right on back.			
	a. Issued note.	.35	1.20	4.00
	s. Specimen ovpt: *MODEL* or *SPECIMEN*.	—	—	6.00

		VG	VF	UNC
37	**25 Lekë** 1964. Blue-black on multicolor underprint. Peasant woman with sheaf at left. Combine and truck at center. Farm tractor at left center on back.			
	a. Issued note.	.60	2.00	7.00
	s. Specimen ovpt: *MODEL* or *SPECIMEN*.	—	—	7.50

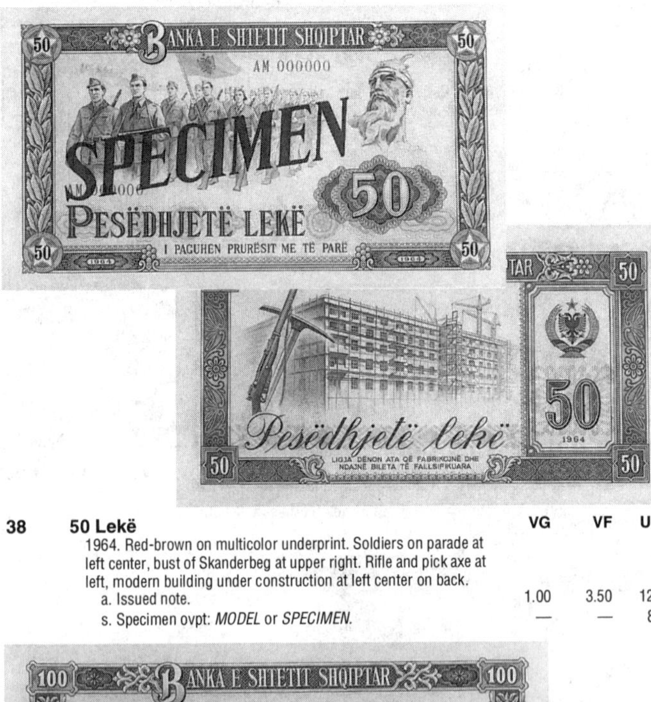

		VG	VF	UNC
38	**50 Lekë** 1964. Red-brown on multicolor underprint. Soldiers on parade at left center, bust of Skanderbeg at upper right. Rifle and pick axe at left, modern building under construction at left center on back.			
	a. Issued note.	1.00	3.50	12.00
	s. Specimen ovpt: *MODEL* or *SPECIMEN*.	—	—	8.50

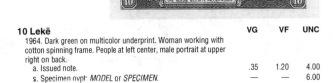

39	100 Lekë	VG	VF	UNC
	1964. Brown-lilac. Worker and boy at coffer dam at left center. Steel worker and well rigger at center on back.			
	a. Issued note.	2.25	7.50	25.00
	s. Specimen ovpt: *MODEL* or *SPECIMEN*.	—	—	10.00

PEOPLES SOCIALIST REPUBLIC

BANKA E SHTETIT SHQIPTAR

1976 ISSUE

#40-46 like #33-39. Arms at upper r. on back. Wmk: Bank name around radiant star, repeated.

40	1 Lek	VG	VF	UNC
	1976. Green and deep blue on multicolor underprint.			
	a. Issued note.	.05	.15	.50
	s1. Red ovpt: *SPECIMEN* with all zeros serial #.	—	—	3.50
	s2. Red ovpt: *SPECIMEN* with normal serial #.	—	—	.50
	s3. Large blue ovpt: *SPECIMEN* on face. Black ovpt: *E PRANUESHME* on back.	—	—	—

Note: #40 w/lg. blue ovpt: *SPECIMEN* on face and black rectangular ovpt. for bank 25th anniversary on back is a private issue.

41	3 Lekë	VG	VF	UNC
	1976. Brown and lilac on multicolor underprint.			
	a. Issued note.	.10	.25	.75
	s1. Red ovpt: *SPECIMEN* with all zeros serial #.	—	—	4.00
	s2. Red ovpt: *SPECIMEN* with normal serial #.	—	—	.75

42	5 Lekë	VG	VF	UNC
	1976. Lilac and blue on multicolor underprint.			
	a. Issued note.	.10	.35	1.25
	s1. Red ovpt: *SPECIMEN* with all zeros serial #.	—	—	4.50
	s2. Red ovpt: *SPECIMEN* with normal serial #.	—	—	1.00
	s3. Large blue ovpt: *SPECIMEN* on face. Black ovpt: *E PRANUESHME* on back.	—	—	—

Note: #42 w/lg. blue ovpt: *SPECIMEN* on face and black rectangular ovpt. for bank 25th anniversary on back is a private issue.

43	10 Lekë	VG	VF	UNC
	1976. Dark green on multicolor underprint.			
	a. Issued note.	.10	.40	1.50
	s1. Red ovpt: *SPECIMEN* with all zeros serial #.	—	—	5.50
	s2. Red ovpt: *SPECIMEN* with normal serial #.	—	—	1.25

44	25 Lekë	VG	VF	UNC
	1976. Blue-black on multicolor underprint.			
	a. Issued note.	.15	.50	3.50
	s1. Red ovpt: *SPECIMEN* with all zeros serial #.	—	—	6.50
	s2. Red ovpt: *SPECIMEN* with normal serial #.	—	—	1.75

45	50 Lekë	VG	VF	UNC
	1976. Red-brown on multicolor underprint.			
	a. Serial # prefix without serifs. Chinese printing.	.30	1.00	6.00
	b. Serial # prefix with serifs. Crossbar of 4 is thicker than bottom serif. (1st European printing).	.45	1.25	8.00
	c. Serial # prefix with serifs. Crossbar of 4 is same thickness as bottom serif. (2nd European printing).	.25	.75	5.00
	s1. Red ovpt: *SPECIMEN* with all zeros serial #.	—	—	7.50
	s2. Red ovpt: *SPECIMEN* with normal serial #.	—	—	2.50
	s3. Large blue ovpt: *SPECIMEN* on face. Black ovpt: *E PRANUESNHME* on back.	—	—	—

Note: #45 w/lg. blue ovpt: *SPECIMEN* on face and black rectangular ovpt. for bank 25th anniversary on back is a private issue.

46	100 Lekë	VG	VF	UNC
	1976. Brown-lilac on multicolor underprint.			
	a. Issued note.	.30	1.50	10.00
	s1. Red ovpt: *SPECIMEN* with all zeros serial #.	—	—	8.50
	s2. Red ovpt: *SPECIMEN* with normal serial #.	—	—	3.00

ND Issue

46A	100 Lekë	VG	VF	UNC
	ND. Steel workers at left, steel mill at center. Oil well derricks at left center, arms at upper right on back. Specimen only.			
	a. Blue and dull red on light green and light yellow underprint.	—	—	200.
	b. Brown and dull red on light green and light yellow underprint.	—	—	200.

1991 Issue

#47 and 48 arms at upper r. on back. Wmk: Bank name around radiant star, repeated.

47	100 Lekë	VG	VF	UNC
	1991. Deep brown and deep purple on pale orange and multicolor underprint. Steel workers at left, steel mill at right. Refinery at left center on back.			
	a. Issued note.	.50	2.00	6.00
	s. Specimen.	—	—	5.00

48	500 Lekë	VG	VF	UNC
	1991; 1996. Purple, red and blue-green on light blue and light orange underprint. Peasant woman by sunflowers at left center. Evergreen trees, mountains at left center on back.			
	a. 1991.	FV	FV	14.00
	b. Enhanced UV printing. 1996.	FV	FV	10.00

1992 ND Issue

#48A-50 steelworker at ctr. Electrical transmission towers at l., arms at upper ctr., hydroelectric generator at r. on back. Wmk: *B.SH.SH.* below star, repeated.

48A	1 Lek Valutë (= 50 Lekë)	VG	VF	UNC
	ND (1992). Purple and gray-green on multicolor underprint. (Not issued).	—	—	35.00

49	10 Lek Valutë (= 500 Lekë)	VG	VF	UNC
	ND (1992). Deep green and purple on multicolor underprint.			
	a. With serial #.	2.00	5.00	15.00
	b. Without serial #.	2.00	5.00	15.00
	s. Specimen.	—	—	—

Note: Many examples of #49 have mismatched serial #'s. No additional premium is given for such.

50	50 Lek Valutë (= 2500 Lekë)	VG	VF	UNC
	ND (1992). Deep brown-violet and gray-green on multicolor underprint.			
	a. With serial #.	8.00	18.00	60.00
	b. Without serial #.	2.00	6.00	15.00
	s. Specimen.	—	—	25.00

#51 not assigned.

Republic

Banka e Shqiperise

1992 Issue

#52-54 wmk: Repeated ring of letters *B.SH.SH.*

		VG	VF	UNC
52	**200 Lekë**			
	1992. Deep reddish-brown on multicolor underprint. Ismail Qemali at left. Citizens portrayed in double-headed eagle outline on back.			
	a. Issued note.	FV	FV	6.00
	s. Specimen.	—	—	—

		VG	VF	UNC
53	**500 Lekë**			
	1992. Deep blue on blue and multicolor underprint. Naim Frasheri at left. Rural mountains at left, candle at center on back.			
	a. Issued note.	FV	FV	14.00
	s. Specimen.	—	—	—

		VG	VF	UNC
54	**1000 Lekë**			
	1992. Deep green and green on multicolor underprint. Skanderbeg at left. Kruja Castle at left, crowned arms at center on back.			
	a. Issued note.	FV	FV	25.00
	s. Specimen.	—	—	12.00

1993-94 Issue

		VG	VF	UNC
55	**100 Lekë**			
	1993-96. Purple on multicolor underprint. L. Kombetar at left. Mountain peaks at left center. Lanner Falcon at center on back.			
	a. 1993.	FV	FV	6.00
	b. 1994.	FV	FV	4.00
	c. Enhanced U-V printing. 1996.	FV	FV	3.00
	s. Specimen.	—	—	2.50

		VG	VF	UNC
56	**200 Lekë**			
	1994. Deep reddish brown on multicolor underprint. Like #52.			
	a. Issued note.	FV	FV	4.50
	s. Specimen.	—	—	4.00

		VG	VF	UNC
57	**500 Lekë**			
	1994. Deep blue on blue and multicolor underprint. Like #53.			
	a. Issued note.	FV	FV	10.00
	s. Specimen.	—	—	6.50
58	**1000 Lekë**			
	1994. Deep green on green and multicolor underprint. Like #54.			
	a. Issued note.	FV	FV	20.00
	s. Specimen.	—	—	12.50

1995-96 Issue

#59-61 like #56-58 but w/segmented foil over security thread.

		VG	VF	UNC
59	**200 Lekë**			
	1996. Deep reddish brown on multicolor underprint. Like #56.	FV	FV	5.00
60	**500 Lekë**			
	1996. Deep blue on blue and multicolor underprint. Like #57.	FV	FV	10.00

61	1000 Lekë	VG	VF	UNC
	1995-96. Deep green and green on multicolor underprint.			
	a. 1995. Olive-green signature	FV	FV	25.00
	b. 1995. Black signature	FV	FV	20.00
	c. 1996. Black signature	FV	FV	20.00

1996 ISSUE

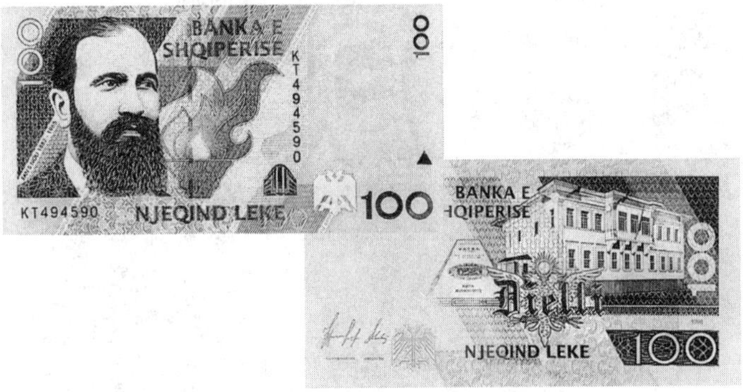

		VG	VF	UNC
62	**100 Lekë** 1996 (1997). Purple, dark brown and orange on multicolor underprint. Fan S. Noli at left and as watermark. First Albanian parliament building at upper right on back.	FV	FV	2.50
63	**200 Lekë** 1996 (1997). Brown and brown-orange on multicolor underprint. Niam Frasheri at left and as watermark. Frasheri's birthplace at upper right on back.	FV	FV	4.50
64	**500 Lekë** 1996 (1997). Dark blue, purple and brown on multicolor underprint. Ismail Qemali at left and as watermark. Conference table and movie projector at center. Independence house in Vlora at upper right on back.	FV	FV	8.50
65	**1000 Lekë** 1996 (1997); 1999. Green and dark green on multicolor. Pjeter Bogdani at left and as watermark. Church of Vau i Dejes at upper right on back.	FV	FV	17.50
66	**5000 Lekë** 1996 (1999). Olive green and multicolor. Skanderbeg at left and as watermark. Kruja castle, equestrian statue, crown on back.	FV	FV	110.

2001 ISSUE

#68-70 like #63-65 but with new sign. and enhanced security features.

67	200 Lekë	VG	VF	UNC
	2001. Brown and brown-orange on multicolor underprint. N. Frasheri at left and as watermark. Frasheri's birthplace at upper right on back.	FV	FV	3.50

68	500 Lekë	VG	VF	UNC
	2001. Dark blue, purple and brown on multicolor underprint. I. Qemali at left and as watermark. Independence House at upper right, conference table and movie projector at center on back.	FV	FV	7.50

69	1000 Lekë	VG	VF	UNC
	2001. Green and dark green on multicolor underprint. P. Bogadani at left and as watermark. Sun at center, Church of Vau i Dejes at upper right on back.	FV	FV	15.00

70	5000 Lekë	VG	VF	UNC
	2001 (2004). Olive green and multicolor. Skanderbeg at left and as watermark. Kruja castle, equestrian statue, crown on back.	FV	FV	95.00

FOREIGN EXCHANGE CERTIFICATES

BANKA E SHTETIT SHQIPTAR

1965 ISSUE

#FX21-FX27 arms at r. Bank arms at ctr. on back.

FX21	.05 Lek	VG	VF	UNC
	1965. Deep blue-green on pink and pale yellow-orange underprint.	—	—	40.00

FX22 .10 Lek VG — VF — UNC 40.00
1965. Deep olive-brown on pink and pale blue underprint.

FX23 1/2 Lek VG — VF — UNC 40.00
1965. Deep purple on pink and lilac underprint.

FX24 1 Lek VG — VF — UNC 40.00
1965. Blackish green on pale yellow and pale yellow-orange underprint.

FX25 5 Lek VG — VF — UNC 110.
1965. Blue-black on pale yellow-green underprint.

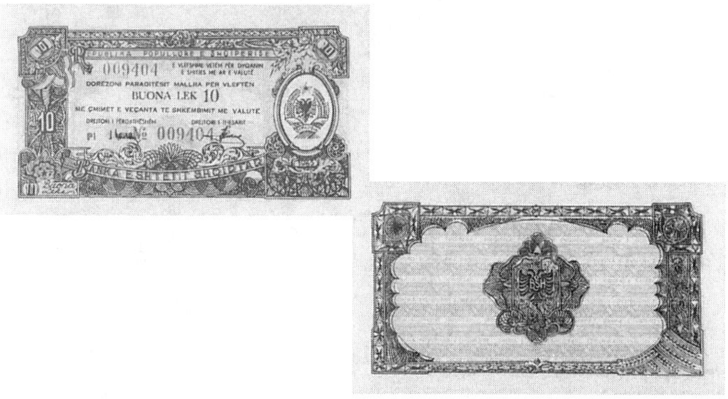

FX26 10 Lek VG — VF — UNC 110.
1965. Blue-green on pale yellow and pale grayish green underprint.

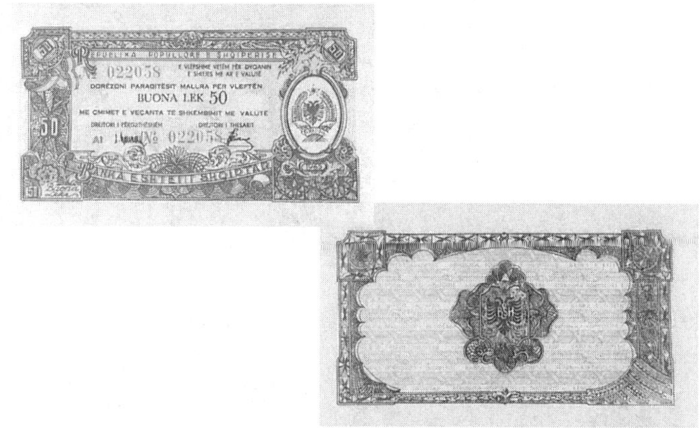

FX27 50 Lek VG — VF — UNC 110.
1965. Deep red-brown on pink and pale yellow underprint.

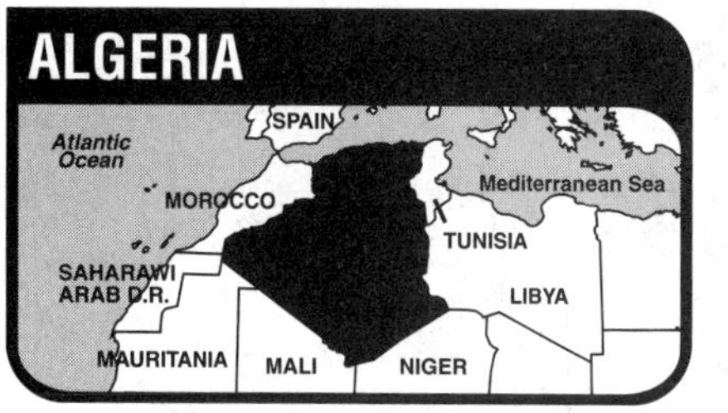

The Democratic and Popular Republic of Algeria, a North African country fronting on the Mediterranean Sea between Tunisia and Morocco, has an area of 919,595 sq. mi. (2,381,741 sq. km.) and a population of 28.6 million. Capital: Algiers (Alger). Most of the country's working population is engaged in agriculture although a recent industrial diversification, financed by oil revenues, is making steady progress. Wines, fruits, iron and zinc ores, phosphates, tobacco products, liquified natural gas, and petroleum are exported.

Algiers, the capital and chief seaport of Algeria, was the site of Phoenician and Roman settlements before the present Moslem city was founded about 950. Nominally part of the sultanate of Tlemcen, Algiers had a large measure of independence under the amirs of its own. In 1492 the Jews and Moors who had been expelled from Spain settled in Algiers and enjoyed an increasing influence until the imposition of Turkish control in 1518. For the following three centuries Algiers was the headquarters of the notorious Barbary pirates. The French took Algiers in 1830, and after a long and wearisome war completed the conquest of Algeria and annexed it to France, 1848. Following the armistice signed by France and Nazi Germany on June 22, 1940, Algeria fell under Vichy Government control until liberated by the Allied invasion forces under the command of Gen. Dwight D. Eisenhower on Nov. 8, 1942. The inability to obtain equal rights with Frenchmen led to an organized revolt which began on Nov. 1, 1954 and lasted until a ceasefire was signed on July 1, 1962. Independence was proclaimed on July 5, 1962, following a self-determination referendum.

RULERS:

French to 1962

MONETARY SYSTEM:

1 Franc = 100 Centimes to 1960
1 Nouveau Franc = 100 Old Francs, 1959-64
1 Dinar = 100 Centimes, 1964-

FRENCH ADMINISTRATION

BANQUE DE L'ALGÉRIE

1959 ISSUE

		VG	VF	UNC
118	**5 Nouveaux Francs**			
	1959. Green and multicolor. Ram at bottom center, Bacchus at right. Like #106.			
	a. 31.7.1959; 18.12.1959.	12.50	75.00	300.
	s. Specimen. 31.7.1959.	—	—	160.

		VG	VF	UNC
119	**10 Nouveaux Francs**			
	1959-61. Brown and yellow. Isis at right. Like #104.			
	a. 31.7.1959-2.6.1961.	12.50	85.00	325.
	s. Specimen. 31.7.1959.	—	—	165.

		VG	VF	UNC
120	**50 Nouveaux Francs**			
	1959. Multicolor. Pythian Apollo at left. Like #109.			
	a. 31.7.1959; 18.12.1959.	32.50	165.	500.
	s. Specimen. 31.7.1959.	—	—	375.

		VG	VF	UNC
121	**100 Nouveaux Francs**			
	1959-61. Blue and multicolor. Seagulls with city of Algiers in background. Like #110.			
	a. 31.7.1959; 18.12.1959.	60.00	200.	550.
	b. 3.6.1960; 25.11.1960; 10.2.1961; 29.9.1961.	20.00	100.	375.
	s. Specimen. 31.7.1959.	—	—	175.

> **NOTICE**
>
> Readers with unlisted dates, signature varieties, etc. are invited to submit photocopies of their notes to: Standard Catalog of World Paper Money, 700 East State St. Iola, WI 54990-0001, E-Mail: george.cuhaj@fwpubs.com.

REPUBLIC

BANQUE CENTRALE D'ALGÉRIE

1964 ISSUE

#122-125 wmk: Amir Abd el-Kader.

		VG	VF	UNC
122	**5 Dinars**			
	1.1.1964. Purple and lilac. Griffon vulture, tawny eagle perched on rocks at left center. Native objects on back. 2 styles of numerals in date and serial #.			
	a. Issued note.	5.00	40.00	200.
	s. Specimen.	—	—	—

		VG	VF	UNC
123	**10 Dinars**			
	1.1.1964. Lilac and multicolor. Pair of storks and minaret. Native craft on back. 2 styles of numerals in date and serial #.			
	a. Issued note.	2.50	20.00	65.00
	s. Specimen.	—	—	—

124	50 Dinars	VG	VF	UNC
	1.1.1964. Light brown and multicolor. 2 mountain sheep. Camel caravan on back.			
	a. Issued note.	4.00	25.00	85.00
	s. Specimen.	—	—	—

125	100 Dinars	VG	VF	UNC
	1.1.1964. Multicolor. Harbor scene. Modern building complex at left center on back. 2 styles of numerals in date and serial #.			
	a. Issued note.	3.00	15.00	60.00
	s. Specimen.	—	—	—

1970 Issue

#126 and 127 wmk: Amir Abd el-Kader.

126	5 Dinars	VG	VF	UNC
	1.11.1970. Blue and multicolor. Warrior with shield and sword at center right. Ruppel's sand fox at left center, village in background at center right on back. Signature varieties.			
	a. Issued note.	.50	6.00	20.00
	s. Specimen.	—	—	30.00

127	10 Dinars	VG	VF	UNC
	1.11.1970. Red-brown and multicolor. Sheep at left, peacock at right. Seated elderly man at left, ornate building at right on back. Minor plate varieties in French text on back.			
	a. Issued note.	1.50	6.00	25.00
	s. Specimen.	—	—	30.00

128	100 Dinars	VG	VF	UNC
	1.11.1970. Brown, brown-orange, blue-gray and pale yellow-orange. Two men at at left, airport at center, wheat ears at right. Scenery with edmi gazelle at right on back.			
	a. Deep brown.	2.50	12.50	55.00
	b. light brown.	2.50	10.00	45.00
	s. Specimen.	—	—	50.00

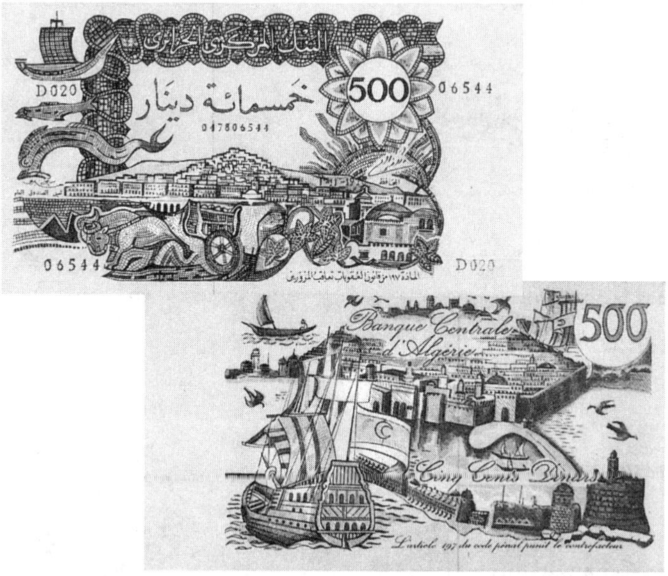

129	500 Dinars	VG	VF	UNC
	1.11.1970. Purple. View of city. Galleon, fortress on back.			
	a. Issued note.	4.00	25.00	75.00
	s. Specimen.	—	—	50.00

1977; 1981 ISSUE

#130 and 131 wmk: Amir Abd el-Kader.

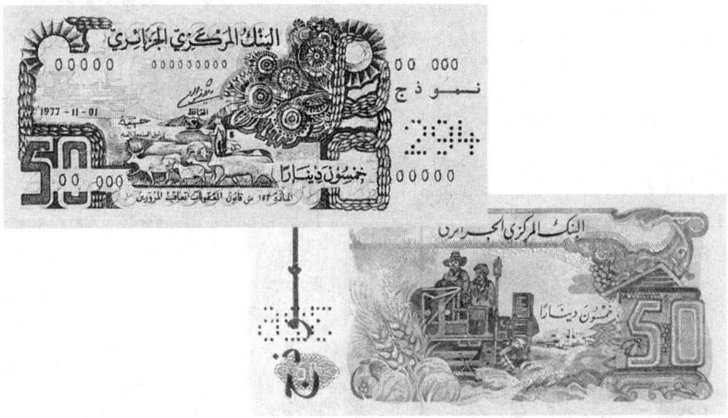

		VG	VF	UNC
130	**50 Dinars** 1.11.1977. Dark green on multicolor underprint. Shepherd with flock at lower left center. Farm tractor on back. Signature varieties.			
	a. Issued note.	1.00	2.00	7.50
	s. Specimen.	—	—	—

		VG	VF	UNC
131	**100 Dinars** 1.11.1981. Dark blue and aqua on light blue underprint. Village with minarets at left. Man working with plants at center on back.			
	a. Issued note.	1.50	4.00	12.50
	s. Specimen.	—	—	—

1982-83 ISSUE

#132-135 wmk: Amir Abd el-Kader.

		VG	VF	UNC
132	**10 Dinars** 2.12.1983. Black on brown and blue-green underprint. Diesel passenger train at center. Back blue, blue-green and brown; mountain village at center.			
	a. Issued note.	FV	.40	2.50
	s. Specimen.	—	—	—

		VG	VF	UNC
133	**20 Dinars** 2.1.1983. Red-brown on ochre underprint. Vase at left center, handcrafts at right. Tower at center on back.			
	a. Issued note.	FV	.50	3.50
	s. Specimen.	—	—	—

		VG	VF	UNC
134	**100 Dinars** 8.6.1982. Pale blue and gray. Similar to #131 but without bird at upper right on face.			
	a. Issued note.	FV	17.50	50.00
	s. Specimen.	—	—	—

		VG	VF	UNC
135	**200 Dinars** 23.3.1983. Brown and dark green on multicolor underprint. Monument to the Algerian martyrs at left, bridge over canyon at center, amphora at right on back.			
	a. Issued note.	FV	4.00	15.00
	s. Specimen.	—	—	—

#136 not assigned.

BANQUE D'ALGÉRIE

1992 DATED (1995; 1996) ISSUE

		VG	VF	UNC
137	**100 Dinars** 21.5.1992 (1996). Dark blue with black text on pale blue and multicolor underprint. Army charging at right. Seal with horsemen charging at left, ancient galley at center on back. Watermark: Horse's head.	FV	FV	6.00

138 200 Dinars — VG | VF | UNC

21.5.1992 (1996). Dark brown and red-brown on multicolor underprint. Koranic school at center right, building at center on back. Watermark: Horse's head. — FV | FV | 12.50

139 500 Dinars — VG | VF | UNC

21.5.1992 (1996). Deep purple, violet and red-violet on multicolor underprint. Hannibal's troops and elephants engaging the Romans at center right. Waterfalls at left, tomb ruins of Numid King Massinissa at left center, elephant mounted troops at center right on back. Watermark: Elephant heads. — FV | FV | 25.00

140 1000 Dinars — VG | VF | UNC

21.5.1992 (1995). Red-brown and orange on multicolor underprint. Tassili cave carvings of animals at lower center, water buffalo's head at right and as watermark Hoggar cave painting of antelope at left, ruins at center on back. — FV | FV | 35.00

1998 Dated (2000) Issue

Similar to #139-140 but with holographic band at l.

141 500 Dinars — VG | VF | UNC

10.6.1998. Deep purple, violet and red-violet on multicolor underprint. Similar to #139. Holographic band at left center. — FV | FV | 20.00

142 1000 Dinars — VG | VF | UNC

21.5.1992; 10.6.1998. Red-brown and orange on multicolor underprint. Similar to #140. Holographic band at left center.

	VG	VF	UNC
a. 21.5.1992.	FV	FV	35.00
b. 6.10.1998.	FV	FV	25.00

2005 Commemorative Issue

143 1000 Dinars — VG | VF | UNC

22.3.2005. Red-brown and orange on multicolor underprint. Arab League's 60th Anniversary seal and holographic band added. — — | — | 27.50

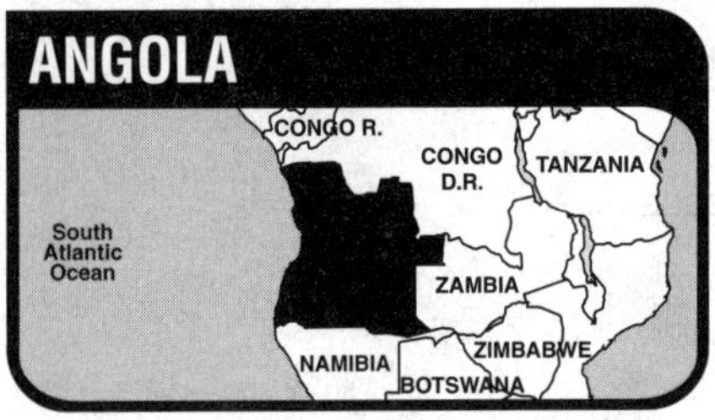

The Peoples Republic of Angola, a country on the west coast of southern Africa bounded by Zaïre, Zambia and Namibia (South-West Africa), has an area of 481,354 sq. mi. (1,246,700 sq. km.) and a population of 12.78 million, predominantly Bantu in origin. Capital: Luanda. Most of the people are engaged in subsistence agriculture. However, important oil and mineral deposits make Angola potentially one of the richest countries in Africa. Iron and diamonds are exported.

Angola was discovered by Portuguese navigator Diogo Cao in 1482. Portuguese settlers arrived in 1491, and established Angola as a major slaving center which sent about 3 million slaves to the New World.

A revolt against Portuguese rule, characterized by guerrilla warfare, began in 1961 and continued until 1974, when a new regime in Portugal offered independence. The independence movement was actively supported by three groups, the National Front, d in Zaïre, the Soviet-backed Popular Movement, and the moderate National Union. Independence was proclaimed on Nov. 11, 1975.

RULERS:

Portuguese to 1975

MONETARY SYSTEM:

1 Milreis = 1000 Reis = 20 Macutas to 1911
100 Centavos - 1 Escudo, 1911
1 Escudo = 1 Milreis
1 Escudo = 100 Centavos, 1954-77
1 Kwanza = 100 Lwei, 1977-95
1 Kwanza Reajustado = 1,000 "old" Kwanzas, 1995-

SIGNATURE VARIETIES

1	Governor	Administrator
2	Governor	Administrator
3	Governor	Administrator
4		Vice-Governor
5	Governor	Vice-Governor
6	Governor	Vice-Governor
7	Governor	Administrator
8	Governor	Administrator
9	Governor	Administrator
10	Governor	Administrator
11	Governor	Vice-Governor

SIGNATURE VARIETIES

12	Governor	Administrator
13	Governor	Administrator
14	Governor	Vice-Governor
15	Governor	Vice-Governor
16	Governor	Vice-Governor
17	Governor	Vice-Governor
18	Governor	Vice-Governor
19	Governor	Vice-Governor
20	Governor	Administrator

PORTUGUESE ADMINISTRATION

BANCO DE ANGOLA

1962 ISSUE

Escudo System

#92-96 portr. Americo Tomas. at l. or r. Printer: TDLR.

		VG	VF	UNC
92	**20 Escudos** 10.6.1962. Black on multicolor underprint. Dock at left. Gazelles running on back. Signature 1.	1.25	6.50	32.50

		VG	VF	UNC
93	**50 Escudos** 10.6.1962. Light blue on multicolor underprint. Airport at left. Various animals at water hole on back. Signature 2.	2.50	12.50	50.00
94	**100 Escudos** 10.6.1962. Lilac on multicolor underprint. Salazar bridge at left. Elephants at watering hole on back. Signature 3.	4.00	30.00	125.
95	**500 Escudos** 10.6.1962. Red on multicolor underprint. Port of Luanda at center 2 black rhinoceros on back. Signature 4.	9.50	50.00	325.
96	**1000 Escudos** 10.6.1962. Blue on multicolor underprint. Dam at center. Herd on back. Signature 4.	8.00	45.00	260.

1970 ISSUE

#97-98 portr. Americo Tomas at l. or r. Printer: TDLR.

		VG	VF	UNC
97	**500 Escudos** 10.6.1970. Red on multicolor underprint. Like #95. Signature 5.	10.00	40.00	215.
98	**1000 Escudos** 10.6.1970. Blue on multicolor underprint. Like #96. Signature 5.	12.50	45.00	225.

1972 ISSUE

#99-103 Arms at l., M. Carmona at ctr. r. and as wmk. Printer: TDLR.

		VG	VF	UNC
99	**20 Escudos** 24.11.1972. Red and brown on multicolor underprint. Flowers on back. Signature 7.	.30	1.25	6.50

		VG	VF	UNC
100	**50 Escudos** 24.11.1972. Green and brown on multicolor underprint. Plants on back. Signature 8.	.30	1.25	6.50

		VG	VF	UNC
101	**100 Escudos** 24.11.1972. Light and dark brown on multicolor underprint. Tree and plants on back. Signature 7.	.50	1.50	6.50

		VG	VF	UNC
102	**500 Escudos** 24.11.1972. Blue on multicolor underprint. Rock formation at Pungo Andongo at center right on back. Signature 6.	1.00	5.00	20.00

		VG	VF	UNC
103	**1000 Escudos** 24.11.1972. Purple on multicolor underprint. Waterfall on back. Signature 5.	1.75	6.00	37.50

1973 ISSUE

#104-108 Luiz de Camoes at r. and as wmk.

		VG	VF	UNC
104	**20 Escudos** 10.6.1973. Blue, purple and green on multicolor underprint. Cotton plant on back. Signature 10.			
	a. Issued note.	1.00	5.00	22.50
	s. Specimen.	—	—	—
	ct. Color trial.	—	—	225.

105 50 Escudos

10.6.1973. Blue and brown on multicolor underprint. Plant on back. Signature 9.

	VG	VF	UNC
a. Issued note.	.25	1.00	3.75
s. Specimen.	—	—	—
ct. Color trial. Blue, purple and green on multicolor underprint.	—	—	225.

106 100 Escudos

10.6.1973. Brown, black and maroon on multicolor underprint. Back dark green and maroon on multicolor underprint. Tree at left. Signature 10.

VG	VF	UNC
.50	1.50	5.00

107 500 Escudos

10.6.1973. Dark brown, violet and purple on multicolor underprint. High rock formation on back. Signature 11.

VG	VF	UNC
1.50	4.50	20.00

108 1000 Escudos

10.6.1973. Olive and blue on multicolor underprint. Waterfall on back. Signature 11.

VG	VF	UNC
2.00	9.00	37.50

PEOPLES REPUBLIC

BANCO NACIONAL DE ANGOLA

1976 ISSUE

Kwanza System

#109-113 Antonio Agostinho Neto at r. Arms at lower l. on back.

109 20 Kwanzas

11.11.1976. Brown, green and orange. Soldiers in field on back. Signature 12.

	VG	VF	UNC
a. Issued note.	.50	3.50	12.75
s. Specimen.	—	—	—

110 50 Kwanzas

11.11.1976. Purple, brown and black. Field workers on back. Signature 12.

	VG	VF	UNC
a. Issued note.	.50	2.00	9.50
s. Specimen.	—	—	—

111 100 Kwanzas

11.11.1976. Green on multicolor underprint. Textile factory workers on back. Signature 12.

	VG	VF	UNC
a. Issued note.	.50	1.50	6.25
s. Specimen.	—	—	—

NOTICE

Readers with unlisted dates, signature varieties, etc. are invited to submit photocopies of their notes to: Standard Catalog of World Paper Money, 700 East State St. Iola, WI 54990-0001, E-Mail: george.cuhaj@fwpubs.com.

112	500 Kwanzas	VG	VF	UNC
	11.11.1976. Blue on multicolor underprint. Cargo ships dockside on back. Signature 12.			
	a. Issued note.	2.00	6.00	25.00
	s. Specimen.	—	—	—

113	1000 Kwanzas	VG	VF	UNC
	11.11.1976. Red on multicolor underprint. School class on back. Signature 12.			
	a. Issued note.	2.00	9.50	40.00
	s. Specimen.	—	—	—

1979 ISSUE

#114-117 w/2 serial #. Sign. titles, date of independence added under bank name on face. Arms at lower l. on back.

114	50 Kwanzas	VG	VF	UNC
	14.8.1979. Purple, brown and black. Like #110. Signature 13.	.40	2.50	10.00

115	100 Kwanzas	VG	VF	UNC
	14.8.1979. Green on multicolor underprint. Like #111. Signature 13.	.30	1.75	7.50
116	**500 Kwanzas**			
	14.8.1979. Blue on multicolor underprint. Like #112. Signature 13.	2.75	17.50	75.00

117	1000 Kwanzas	VG	VF	UNC
	14.8.1979. Red on multicolor underprint. Like #113. Signature 13.			
	a. Issued note.	2.50	10.00	47.50
	s. Specimen.	—	—	—

1984-87 ISSUE

#118-125 conjoined busts of José Eduardo dos Santos and Antonio Agostinho Neto at r. Arms at lower l. on back. Wmk: bird (weak).

Replacement notes: Serial # prefixes *ZA, ZB, ZC*, etc.

118	50 Kwanzas	VG	VF	UNC
	7.1.1984. Deep brown and green on light green and tan underprint. Classroom and teacher on back. Signature 14.	.25	1.25	5.00

Note: #118 dated 11.11.1987 may exist (see #122).

119	100 Kwanzas	VG	VF	UNC
	7.1.1984; 11.11.1987. Deep blue, violet and brown on light blue and multicolor underprint. Picking cotton on back. Signature 14.	2.00	10.00	25.00

Note: #119 dated 1987 was issued only w/ovpt. (see #125).

120	500 Kwanzas	VG	VF	UNC
	1984; 1987. Brown, red-brown and red on lilac and multicolor underprint. Offshore oil platform at left, worker at right on back.			
	a. Signature 14. 7.1.1984.	2.50	11.00	50.00
	b. Signature 15. 11.11.1987.	2.25	10.00	45.00

121	1000 Kwanzas	VG	VF	UNC
	1984; 1987. Purple, blue-black and blue on light blue and multicolor underprint. Soldiers embarking dockside at left center and soldier at right on back.			
	a. Signature 14. 7.1.1984.	2.75	12.50	65.00
	b. Signature 15. 11.11.1987.	2.50	11.00	57.50

1991 Provisional Issue

#121-125 portr. conjoined bust of José Eduardo dos Santos and Antonio Agostinho Neto at r. and as wmk. Arms at lower l. on back.

122	50 Novo Kwanza on 50 Kwanzas	VG	VF	UNC
	ND (-old date 11.11.1987). Ovpt: *NOVO KWANZA* on unissued date of #118. Signature 15.	—	—	—

123	500 Novo Kwanza on 500 Kwanzas	VG	VF	UNC
	ND (-old date 11.11.1987). Ovpt: *NOVO KWANZA* in light green on #120b.	2.50	13.00	65.00

124	1000 Novo Kwanza on 1000 Kwanzas	VG	VF	UNC
	ND (-old date 11.11.1987). Ovpt: *NOVO KWANZA* in red on #121b.	3.00	13.00	65.00

125	5000 Novo Kwanza on 100 Kwanzas	VG	VF	UNC
	ND (-old date 11.11.1987). Ovpt: *NOVO KWANZA 5000* in brown on unissued date of #119. Signature 15.	25.00	100.	285.

1991 Issue

#126-134 portr. conjoined busts of Jose Eduardo dos Santos and Antonio Agostinho Neto at r. and as wmk. Arms at lower l. on back.

#126-131 replacement notes: Serial # prefixes *AZ, BZ, CZ, DZ, EZ.*

126	100 Kwanzas	VG	VF	UNC
	4.2.1991. Purple, green and brown. Rock formation at Pungo Andongo at left center. Tribal mask at right on back. Signature 16.	.30	1.25	5.75
127	**500 Kwanzas**			
	4.2.1991. Blue and violet. Back blue, violet, green and brown. Like #126. Specimen.	—	—	—

128	500 Kwanzas	VG	VF	UNC
	4.2.1991. Purple and deep blue-green on multicolor underprint. Serra da Leba at left center, native pot at right on back.			
	a. Signature 16.	.75	5.00	25.00
	b. Signature 17.	.50	2.50	10.00
	c. Signature 18.	.60	3.25	12.50

129	1000 Kwanzas	VG	VF	UNC
	4.2.1991. Brown, orange, purple and red-violet on multicolor underprint. Banco Nacional at left center, native doll at right on back.			
	a. Signature 16.	1.25	7.50	37.50
	b. Signature 17.	.40	2.75	12.75
	c. Signature 18.	.75	5.00	16.00

130	5000 Kwanzas	VG	VF	UNC
	4.2.1991. Dark green, blue-green and dark brown on multicolor underprint. Waterfall and stylized statue of "The Thinker" on back.			
	a. Signature 16.	2.25	15.00	50.00
	b. Signature 17.	1.00	5.00	20.00
	c. Signature 18.	1.50	7.50	22.50

		VG	VF	UNC
131	**10,000 Kwanzas**			
	4.2.1991. Red, olive-green and purple on multicolor underprint. Sable antelope herd and shell on back.			
	a. Signature 17.	2.00	15.00	80.00
	b. Signature 18.	.60	3.25	12.50

		VG	VF	UNC
132	**50,000 Kwanzas**			
	4.2.1991. Bright green, yellow-green and dark brown on multicolor underprint. Like #130. Signature 18.	.50	2.50	9.50

		VG	VF	UNC
133	**100,000 Kwanzas**			
	4.2.1991 (1993). Orange and aqua on emerald green and multicolor underprint. Like #131 except for value. Signature 18.			
	a. Microprint around watermark area reads: *100000 BNA*, latent print: *100000 CEM MIL*. watermark: *100000*.	1.00	5.00	9.50
	x. Microprint around watermark. area reads: *10000 BNA*, latent print: *10000 DEZ MIL*. watermark: *10,000*. (error).	2.00	15.00	57.50

		VG	VF	UNC
134	**500,000 Kwanzas**			
	4.2.1991 (1994). Red, brown and violet on multicolor underprint. Rhinoceros at left. on back. Signature 19.	.50	2.00	6.50
134A	**1,000,000 Kwanzas**			
	4.2.1991. Reported not confirmed.	—	—	—

1995 ISSUE

Kwanza Reajustado System

#135-142 portr. conjoined busts of José Eduardo dos Santos and Antonio Agostinho Neto at r. Arms at lower l., mask at upper r. on back. Wmk: Sculpture.

		VG	VF	UNC
135	**1000 Kwanzas Reajustados**			
	1.5.1995. Black and blue on multicolor underprint. Sable antelope at left on back. Signature 20.	.50	1.50	3.75

		VG	VF	UNC
136	**5000 Kwanzas Reajustados**			
	1.5.1995. Green and brown on multicolor underprint. Banco Nacional at left on back. Signature 20.	.50	2.25	9.00

		VG	VF	UNC
137	**10,000 Kwanzas Reajustados**			
	1.5.1995. Red and purple on multicolor underprint. Off shore oil platform at left on back. Signature 20.	.50	2.25	9.50
138	**50,000 Kwanzas Reajustados**			
	1.5.1995. Orange and green on multicolor underprint. Telecommunications station in Luanda at left center on back. Signature 20.	.50	2.50	9.00

		VG	VF	UNC
139	**100,000 Kwanzas Reajustados**			
	1.5.1995. Dark blue and brown-violet on multicolor underprint. Mask and pottery at left center on back. Signature 20.	.50	2.75	6.50

		VG	VF	UNC
140	**500,000 Kwanzas Reajustados** 1.5.1995. Dark brown and red-brown on multicolor underprint. Matala dam at left center on back. Signature 20.	1.00	3.00	7.50

		VG	VF	UNC
141	**1,000,000 Kwanzas Reajustados** 1.5.1995. Bright blue and red-brown on multicolor underprint. School girl at left center on back. Signature 20.	1.00	3.50	9.50

		VG	VF	UNC
142	**5,000,000 Kwanzas Reajustados** 1.5.1995. Violet and red-brown on multicolor underprint. Serra da Leba at left center on back. Signature 20.	1.50	7.50	50.00

1999; 2003 ISSUE

1 Kwanza = 1,000,000 reajustados Kwanzas.

#143-146 portr. conjoined busts of Jose Eduardo dos Santos and Antonio Agostinho Neto at r. Arms at lower l., mask at at upper r. on back. Wmk: Sculpture. Printer: FCO.

		VG	VF	UNC
143	**1 Kwanza** 10.1999. Dark brown, pink and light blue on multicolor underprint. Women picking cotton on back. Signature 21	FV	FV	1.00
144	**5 Kwanzas** 10.1999. Purple, light-blue and dark blue on multicolor underprint. Mountain pass on back. Signature 21.	FV	FV	1.75
145	**10 Kwanzas** 10.1999. Brown, orange and purple on multicolor underprint. Two antelope on back. Signature 21.	FV	FV	3.00

		VG	VF	UNC
146	**50 Kwanzas** 10.1999. Off-shore oil rig on back.	FV	FV	6.00
147	**100 Kwanzas** 10.1999. Olive and multicolor underprint. Banco Nacional building on back.	FV	FV	10.00

		VG	VF	UNC
148	**200 Kwanzas** 11.2003. Mauve, aqua, pink and orange on multicolor underprint. Aerial view of Luanda's coastline boulevard on back. Signature 22.	FV	FV	15.00

		VG	VF	UNC
149	**500 Kwanzas** 11.2003. Mauve, yellow and green on multicolor underprint. Cotton harvesting scene on back. Signature 22.	FV	FV	26.00

		VG	VF	UNC
150	**1000 Kwanzas** 11.2003. Red, oragne, blue and purple on multicolor underprint. Coffee plantation on back. Signature 22.	FV	FV	50.00

		VG	VF	UNC
151	**2000 Kwanzas** 11.2003. Light and dark green on multicolor underprint.	FV	FV	75.00

The Argentine Republic, located in South America, has an area of 1,068,301 sq. mi. (2,766,889 sq. km.) and a population of 37.03 million. Capital: Buenos Aires. Its varied topography ranges from the subtropical lowlands of the north to the towering Andean Mountains in the west and the windswept Patagonian steppe in the south. The rolling, fertile pampas of central Argentina are ideal for agriculture and grazing, and support most of the republic's population. Meat packing, flour milling, textiles, sugar refining and dairy products are the principal industries. Oil is found in Patagonia, but most of the mineral requirements must be imported.

Argentina was discovered in 1516 by the Spanish navigator Juan de Solis. A permanent Spanish colony was established at Buenos Aires in 1580, but the colony developed slowly. When Napoleon conquered Spain, the Argentines set up their own government in the name of the Spanish king on May 25, 1810. Independence was formally declared on July 9, 1816.

MONETARY SYSTEM:

1 Peso (m/n) = 100 Centavos to 1970
1 'New' Peso (Ley 18.188) = 100 'Old' Pesos (m/n), 1970-83
1 Peso Argentino = 10,000 Pesos, (Ley 18.188) 1983-85
1 Austral = 100 Centavos = 1000 Pesos Argentinos, 1985-92
1 Peso = 10,000 Australes, 1992-
1 Peso = 8 Reales = 100 Centavos

REPLACEMENT NOTES:

#260d onward: *R* prefix before serial #. Note: The listings encompassing issues circulated by various bank and regional authorities are contained in Volume 1.

REPUBLIC

BANCO CENTRAL

1960-69 ND ISSUE

W/o Ley- Moneda Nacional

#275-277, 279-280 Portr. Gen. José de San Martín in uniform at r. Sign. varieties.

Notes begin with *SERIE A* unless noted.

		VG	VF	UNC
275	**5 Pesos** ND (1960-62). Brown on yellow underprint. People gathering before building on back. Printer: CMN. 3 signature varieties. Serie A.			
	a. Signature titles: D.	.30	1.50	6.00
	b. Signature titles: C.	.75	3.00	12.50
	c. Signature titles: E.	.40	1.75	5.50

		VG	VF	UNC
276	**50 Pesos** ND (1968-69). Green. Army in mountains on back. *SERIE D.* Signature titles: C.	.35	1.25	5.00

277 100 Pesos

ND (1967-69). Red-brown. Spanish and Indians on back. *SERIE E, F, G.* 2 signature varieties. Signature titles: C.

	VG	VF	UNC
277	.25	1.25	4.00

278 500 Pesos

ND (1964-69). Blue on blue and gold underprint. Portrait elderly Gen. J. de San Martín not in uniform at right. Grand Bourg House in France on back. 4 signature varieties. Serie A.

	VG	VF	UNC
a. Signature titles: E.	3.00	10.00	17.50
b. Signature titles: C.	1.50	4.00	10.00

279 1000 Pesos

ND (1966-69). Purple. Portrait young Gen J. de San Martín in uniform at right. Sailing ship on back. Serie C, D. 3 signature varieties.

	VG	VF	UNC
a. Signature titles: E.	1.00	3.75	15.00
b. Signature titles: C.	.75	3.25	10.00

280 5000 Pesos

ND (1962-69). Brown on yellow green underprint. Portrait young Gen. J. de San Martín in uniform. Capitol on back. 6 signature varieties. Serie A.

	VG	VF	UNC
a. Signature titles: E.	4.50	15.00	50.00
b. Signature titles: C.	3.50	12.50	37.50
s. As a. Specimen.	—	—	200.

281 10,000 Pesos

ND (1961-69). Deep red on blue and yellow underprint. Portrait elderly Gen J. de San Martín not in uniform at right. Armies in the field on back. Serie A, B. 5 signature varieties.

	VG	VF	UNC
a. Signature titles: E. Serie A, B.	4.50	15.00	50.00
b. Signature titles: C. Serie B.	2.50	12.50	35.00
s. As a. Specimen.	—	—	200.

1969 ND Provisional Issue

Ley 18.188.

#282-286 Overprint in wmk. area on face. Sign. titles: C.

282 1 Peso on 100 Pesos

ND (1969-71). Red-brown. Ovpt: New denomination on #277. Serie G.

	VG	VF	UNC
282	.50	3.00	10.00

Albania, 500 Leke, #57

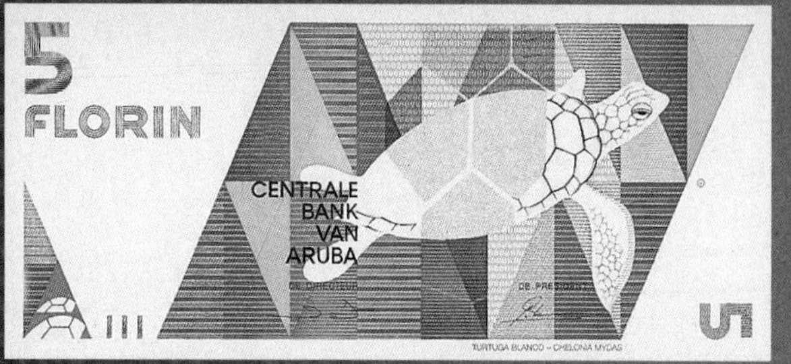

Aruba, 5 Florin, #6

Austria, 20 Schilling, #148

Australia, 10 Dollar, #49

Bahrain, 20 Dinars, #22

Belarus, 1000 Rublei, #28

Belgium, 1000 Francs, #144

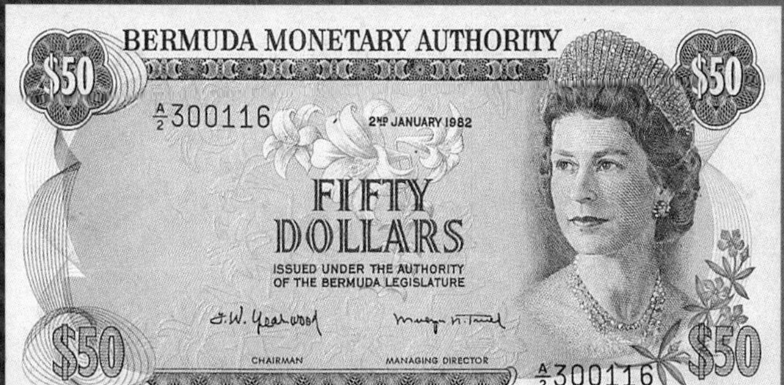

Bermuda, 50 Dollars, #32

Bhutan, 500 Ngultrum, #21

Brunei, 10 Ringgit, #24

Cape Verde, 200 Escudos, #63

Chad, 5000 Francs, #8

Central African Republic, Congo
2000 Francs, #103c

Chile, 2000 Pesos, #158

China, 5 Yuan, #886

Cook Islands, 50 Dollars, #10

Comoros, 5000 Francs, #9

Congo, 20 Centimes, #83

Cuba, 1 Peso, #114

Cyprus, 10 Lira, #59

Denmark, 200 Kroner, #57

Dominican Republic, 5 Pesos Oro, #152

Egypt, 5 Pounds, #59

European Community, 500 Euro, #7

Faeroe Islands, 10 Kronor, #16

France, 50 Francs, #52

Gambia, 25 Dalasis, #14

Georgia, 10 Lari, #56

Germany - Federal Republic, 1000 Mark, #24

Germany - Democratic Republic , 500 Mark, Fx7

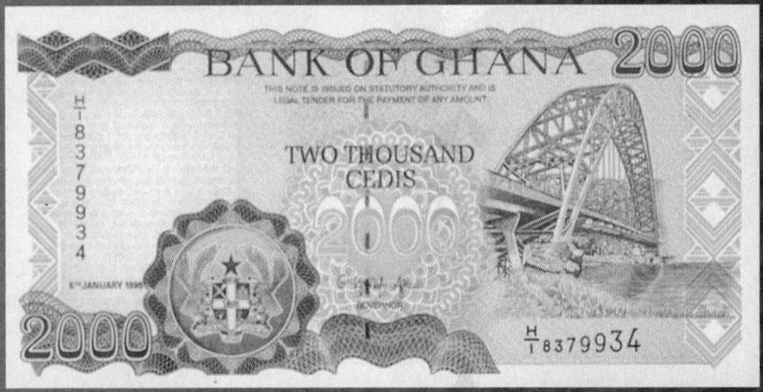

Ghana, 2000 Cedis, #33

Great Britain, 1 Pound, #37

Guatemala, 50 Centavos, #72

Equatorial Guinea, 5000 Francs, #22

Hong Kong, 20 Dollars, #285

Hungary, 50 Forint, #170

India, 50 Rupees, #90

Israel, 50 New Sheqalim, #55

Italy, 5000 Lire, #11

Japan, 5000 Yen. #101

Kenya, 200 Shillings, #38

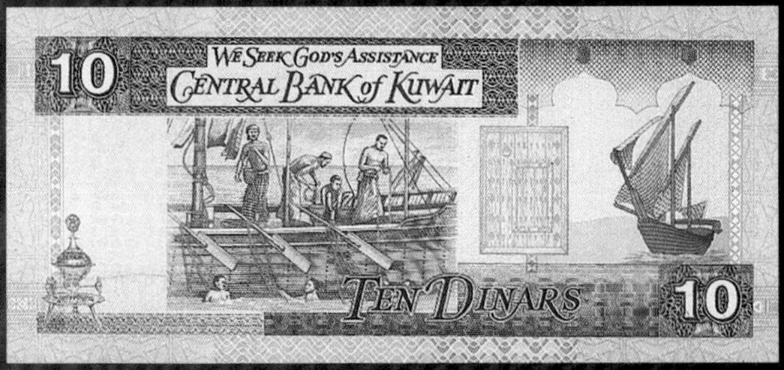

Kuwait, 10 Dinars, #26

Lebanon, 100 Livres, #60

Maldives, 10 Rufiyaa, #19

Netherlands, 100 Gulden, #101

North Korea, 10 Won, Part CS2

Norway, 1000 Kroner, #35

Oman, 20 Rials, #20

Pakistan, 10 Rupees, #R4

Papua New Guinea, 20 Kina, #23

Poland, 20 Zlotych, #174

Peru, 100,000 Intis, #144a

South Africa, 20 Rand, #108

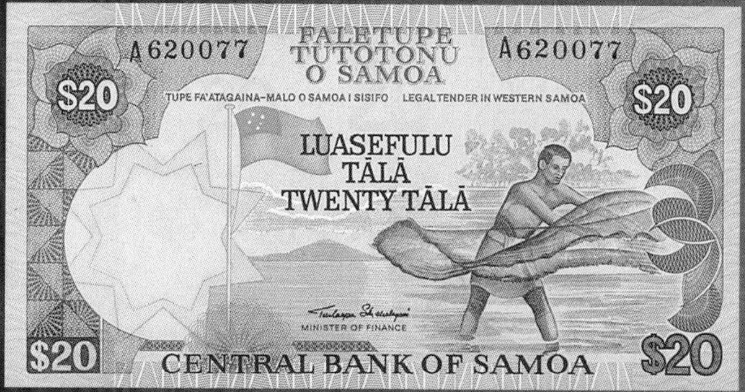

Samoa, 20 Tala, #28

South Korea, 10,000 Won, #49

Slovakia, 500 Korun, #38

Uruguay, 1000 New Pesos, #62

St. Thomas & Prince, 50,000 Dobras, #68

Switzerland, 1000 Francs, #52

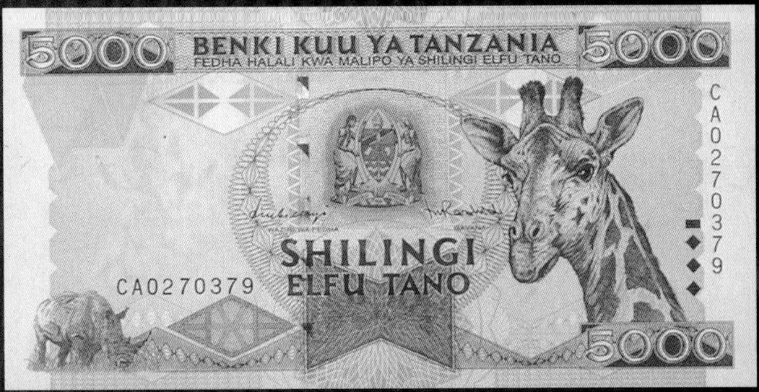

Tanzania, 5000 Shilling, #32

Tonga, 5 Pa'anga, #33

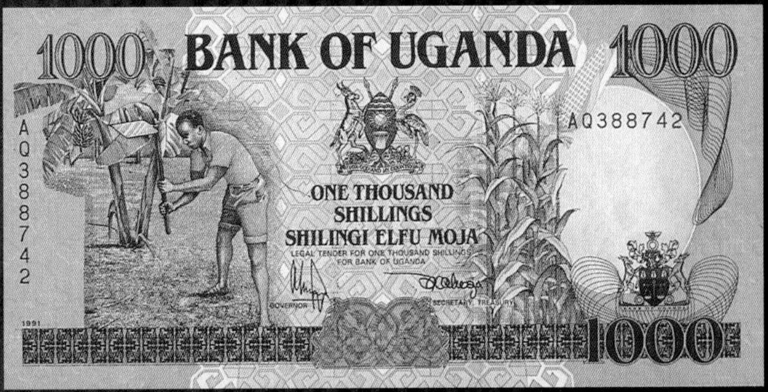

Uganda, 1000 Shilling, #39

Uzbekistan, 10 Som, #76

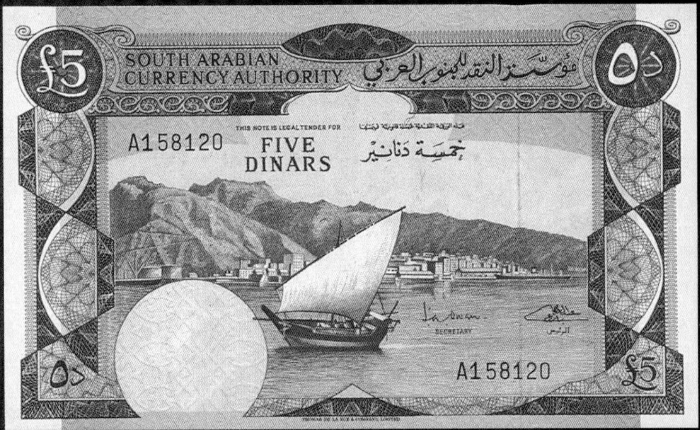

Yemen, 5 Dinars, #4

283 5 Pesos on 500 Pesos

ND (1969-71). Blue on blue and gold underprint. Ovpt: New denomination on #278. 2 signature varieties. *Serie A.*

VG	VF	UNC
1.50	7.50	22.50

284 10 Pesos on 1000 Pesos

ND (1969-71). Purple. Ovpt: New denomination on #279. *SERIE D, E.*

VG	VF	UNC
1.50	7.50	22.50

285 50 Pesos on 5000 Pesos

ND (1969-71). Brown on yellow green underprint. Ovpt: New denomination on #280. *SERIE A.*

VG	VF	UNC
2.25	12.50	37.50

286 100 Pesos on 10,000 Pesos

ND (1969-71). Deep red on blue and yellow underprint. Ovpt: New denomination on #281. *SERIE B.* 2 signature varieties.

VG	VF	UNC
10.00	22.50	75.00

LEY 18.188; 1970-73 ND ISSUE

#287-289 Gen. Manuel Belgrano at r. Printer: CMN. Many sign. varieties. W/o colored threads in white or grayish tint paper. Wmk. varieties.

#287-292 replacement notes: Serial # prefix *R*.

287 1 Peso

ND (1970-73). Orange on multicolor underprint. Scene of Bariloche-Llao-Llao at center on back. *SERIE A-E.* 5 signature varieties.

VG	VF	UNC
.15	.40	1.50

288 5 Pesos

ND (1971-73). Blue on multicolor underprint. Monument to the Flag at Rosario at center on back. 2 signature varieties.

VG	VF	UNC
.25	1.00	4.50

289	10 Pesos	VG	VF	UNC
	ND (1970-73). Purple on multicolor underprint. Waterfalls at Iguazu at center on back. *SERIE A, B.* 6 signature varieties.	.10	.30	2.00

#290-292 Gen. José de San Martín at r. Colored threads in paper. Wmk: Arms.

290	50 Pesos	VG	VF	UNC
	ND (1972-73). Black and brown on multicolor underprint. Hot springs at Jujuy at center on back. 3 signature varieties.	.50	3.00	15.00

291	100 Pesos	VG	VF	UNC
	ND (1971-73). Red on multicolor underprint. Coastline at Ushuaia at center on back. *SERIE A, B.* 4 signature varieties.	1.00	5.00	20.00

292	500 Pesos	VG	VF	UNC
	ND (1972-73). Green on multicolor underprint. Army monument at Mendoza at center on back. 2 signature varieties.	1.50	10.00	30.00

DECRETO-LEY 18.188/69; 1973-76 ND ISSUE

#293-295 Gen. Manuel Belgrano at r. Sign. varieties. W/o colored threads in paper (varieties). Wmk: Arms. Wmk. varieties.

#293-299 replacement notes: Serial # prefix *R*.

293	1 Peso	VG	VF	UNC
	ND (1974). Orange on multicolor underprint. Like #287. Scene of Bariloche-Llao-Llao at center on back. *SERIE E, F.*	.15	.50	1.50

294	5 Pesos	VG	VF	UNC
	ND (1974-76). Blue on multicolor underprint. Like #288. Monument to the Flag at Rosario at center on back. *SERIE A, B.* 2 signature varieties.	.10	.40	1.25

295	10 Pesos	VG	VF	UNC
	ND (1973-76). Purple on multicolor underprint. Like # 289. Waterfall at Iguazu at center on back. *SERIE C, D.* 4 signature varieties.	.15	.50	2.50

NOTICE

Readers with unlisted dates, signature varieties, etc. are invited to submit photocopies of their notes to: Standard Catalog of World Paper Money, 700 East State St. Iola, WI 54990-0001, E-Mail: george.cuhaj@fwpubs.com.

#296-299 Gen. José de San Martín at r. Sign. varieties. Colored threads in paper. Wmk: Arms.

296	50 Pesos	VG	VF	UNC
	ND (1974-75). Black and brown on multicolor underprint. Like #290. Hot springs at Jujuy at center on back. *SERIE A, B.* 2 signature varieties.	.15	.50	1.50

297	100 Pesos	VG	VF	UNC
	ND (1973-76). Red on multicolor underprint. Like #291. Usukaja Harbor scene at center on back. *SERIE B, C.* 3 signature varieties.	.25	1.00	3.50

298	500 Pesos	VG	VF	UNC
	ND (1974-75). Green on multicolor underprint. Like #292. Army monument at Mendoza at center on back. 2 signature varieties.			
	a. Signature titles: C.	1.00	3.00	10.00
	b. Signature titles: F.	.50	2.00	7.50
	c. Signature titles :I.	1.00	3.00	10.00

299	1000 Pesos	VG	VF	UNC
	ND (1973-76). Brown on multicolor underprint. *Plaza de Mayo* in Buenos Aires at center on back. *SERIE A-C.* 3 signature varieties.	1.25	5.00	12.50

1976-83 ND Issue

W/o Decreto or Ley

#301-310 Replacement notes: Serial # prefix *R*.

#300-302 wmk: Arms.

300	10 Pesos	VG	VF	UNC
	ND (1976). Purple on multicolor underprint. Like #289. Gen. M. Belgrano at right. Waterfall at Iguazu at center on back. *SERIE D, E.*	.10	.20	1.00

#301-310 Gen José de San Martín at r. Sign. and wmk. varieties.

301	50 Pesos	VG	VF	UNC
	ND (1976-78). Black on multicolor underprint. Like #290. Hot springs at Jujuy at center on back. *SERIE B, C.* 2 signature varieties. Engraved or lithographed back.			
	a. Without colored threads in paper.	1.25	5.00	10.00
	b. Colored threads in paper.	.10	.20	.75

302	100 Pesos	VG	VF	UNC
	ND (1976-78). Red on multicolor underprint. Like #291. Coastline at Ushuaia at center on back. *SERIE C-E.*			
	a. Without colored threads in paper. 2 signature varieties.	.15	.50	2.50
	b. Colored threads in paper. 2 signature varieties.	.10	.30	1.00

303	500 Pesos	VG	VF	UNC
	ND (1977-82). Green on multicolor underprint. Like #292. Army monument at Mendoza at center on back. *SERIE A-D.* 4 signature varieties.			
	a. Watermark: Arms. without colored threads in paper.	.10	.20	1.50
	b. Watermark: Arms. Colored threads in paper.	.15	.50	2.50
	c. Watermark: Multiple sunbursts. Colored threads. Back lithographed. *SERIE C, D.*	.05	.20	.75

#304-305 Color varieties in underprint: yellow or green, maroon or ochre.

304	1000 Pesos	VG	VF	UNC
	ND (1976-83). Brown on multicolor underprint. Like #299. *Plaza de Mayo* in Buenos Aires at center on back. *SERIE C-I.* 5 signature varieties.			
	a. Watermark: Arms. without colored threads in paper.	.10	.30	2.00
	b. Watermark: Arms. Colored threads in paper. 2 signature varieties.	.05	.20	1.50
	c. Watermark: Multiple sunbursts. Back engraved.	.05	.20	1.00
	d. Watermark: Multiple sunbursts. Back lithographed. *SERIE I.*	.05	.15	.75

#305-310 w/colored threads.

305	5000 Pesos	VG	VF	UNC
	ND (1977-83). Blue and olive-green on multicolor underprint. Coastline of Mar del Plata on back.			
	a. Watermark: Arms. 2 signature varieties. *SERIE A, B.*	.20	.40	2.00
	b. Watermark: Multiple sunbursts. 2 signature varieties. *SERIE B.*	.10	.20	1.00

306	10,000 Pesos	VG	VF	UNC
	ND (1976-83). Orange and red on multicolor underprint. National park on back. 4 signature varieties.			
	a. Watermark: Arms. 3 signature varieties. *SERIE A-G.*	.25	.75	3.00
	b. Watermark: Multiple sunbursts. *SERIE G.*	.20	.50	1.50

307	50,000 Pesos	VG	VF	UNC
	ND (1979-83). Brown on multicolor underprint. Banco Central building at left center on back. Watermark: Arms. 2 signature varieties.	.25	1.00	3.00

308	100,000 Pesos	VG	VF	UNC
	ND (1979-83). Gray and red on multicolor underprint. Mint building at left center on back.			
	a. Watermark: Arms. *SERIE A, B.*	.25	2.00	10.00
	b. Watermark: Multiple sunbursts. *SERIE B.*	.25	1.00	3.00

309	500,000 Pesos	VG	VF	UNC
	ND (1980-83). Green, brown and blue on multicolor underprint. Founding of Buenos Aires at left center on back. Watermark: Multiple sunbursts. 2 signature varieties.	.25	1.00	5.00

310	1,000,000 Pesos	VG	VF	UNC
	ND (1981-83). Blue and pink on multicolor underprint. Independence Declaration with *25 de Mayo* at left center on back. Watermark: Multiple sunbursts. *SERIE A, B*. 3 signature varieties.	1.50	7.50	17.50

1983-85 ND Issue

Peso Argentino System

#311-319 w/colored threads. Watermark varieties. Replacement notes: Serial # prefix *R*.

#311-317 face design w/San Martín at r.

#311-316 wmk: Multiple sunbursts. Printer: CdM.

311	1 Peso Argentino	VG	VF	UNC
	ND (1983-84). Red-orange and purple on blue and multicolor underprint. Like #287. Scene of Bariloche-Llao-Llao at center on back. *SERIE A, B*. 2 signature varieties.			
	a. Issued note.	.05	.15	.75
	s. Specimen.	—	—	25.00

312	5 Pesos Argentinos	VG	VF	UNC
	ND (1983-84). Brown-violet and black on multicolor underprint. Like #288. Monument to the Flag at Rosario at center on back. 2 signature varieties. White or grayish tint paper.			
	a. Issued note.	.05	.15	.75
	s. Specimen.	—	—	25.00

313	10 Pesos Argentinos	VG	VF	UNC
	ND (1983-84). Black and red on green and multicolor underprint. Like #289. Waterfall at Iguazu at center on back. *SERIE A, B*. 2 signature varieties. White or grayish tint paper.			
	a. Issued note.	.05	.15	.75
	s. Specimen.	—	—	25.00

314	50 Pesos Argentinos	VG	VF	UNC
	ND (1983-85). Brown on green and multicolor underprint. Like #290. Hot springs at Jujuy at center on back. 2 signature varieties.			
	a. Issued note.	.05	.15	.75
	s. Specimen.	—	—	25.00

315	100 Pesos Argentinos	VG	VF	UNC
	ND (1983-85). Blue on multicolor underprint. Like #291. Coastline at Ushuaia at center on back. *SERIE A, B*. 2 signature varieties.			
	a. Issued note.	.15	.50	1.50
	s. Specimen.	—	—	25.00

316	500 Pesos Argentinos	VG	VF	UNC
	ND (1984). Purple on multicolor underprint. Town meeting of May 22, 1810 on back. White or grayish tint paper.			
	a. Issued note.	.15	.50	1.50
	s. Specimen.	—	—	25.00

317	1000 Pesos Argentinos	VG	VF	UNC
	ND (1983-85). Blue-green and brown on multicolor underprint. *El Paso de los Andes* battle scene on back.			
	a. *SERIE A, B.* 2 signature varieties.	.25	1.50	7.00
	b. Watermark: Multiple sunbursts (1984). *SERIE C, D.*	.15	.50	1.50
	s1. As a. Specimen. Ovpt: *MUESTRA.*	—	—	25.00
	s2. As b. Specimen. Ovpt.: *MUESTRA.*	—	—	25.00

318	5000 Pesos Argentinos	VG	VF	UNC
	ND (1984-85). Red-brown on multicolor underprint. J. B. Alberdi at right. Constitutional meeting of 1853 on back. Watermark: Young San Martín. *SERIE A, B.*			
	a. Issued note.	.50	2.00	10.00
	s. Specimen.	—	—	25.00

319	10,000 Pesos Argentinos	VG	VF	UNC
	ND (1985). Blue-violet on multicolor underprint. M. Belgrano at right. Creation of Argentine flag on back. Watermark: Young San Martín.			
	a. Issued note.	.75	3.50	15.00
	s. Specimen.	—	—	25.00

1985 ND Provisional Issue

Austral System

#320-322 ovpt. on Peso Argentino notes. Rectangle on wmk. area on face.

320	1 Austral	VG	VF	UNC
	ND (1985). New denomination overprint in numeral and wording in box, green on face and blue on back of #317b. Series D. Watermark: sunburst.	.15	.50	2.50

321	5 Australes	VG	VF	UNC
	ND (1985). New denomination overprint as #320, purple on face and brown on back of #318, Series B. Watermark: San Martín.	.50	2.00	5.00

322	10 Australes	VG	VF	UNC
	ND (1985). New denomination overprint as #320 on #319.			
	a. Blue overprint on face and back. watermark: San Martín. Series A; B.	.50	4.00	9.00
	b. Like a. but watermark: Multiple sunbursts. Series A-C.	.25	1.75	6.00
	c. Blue ovpt on face, light olive-green overprint on back. Series B; C.	.25	1.75	5.00
	d. Series B without overprint	7.50	30.00	60.00
	s. As b. Specimen.	—	—	25.00

NOTICE

Readers with unlisted dates, signature varieties, etc. are invited to submit photocopies of their notes to: Standard Catalog of World Paper Money, 700 East State St. Iola, WI 54990-0001, E-Mail: george.cuhaj@fwpubs.com.

1985-91 ND ISSUE

#323-330 latent image "BCRA" on face. Liberty (Progreso) w/torch and shield seated at l. ctr. on back. Printer: CdM. Sign. varieties.

Replacement notes: Serial # prefix *R*.

323	1 Austral	VG	VF	UNC
	ND (1985-89). Blue-green and purple on multicolor underprint. B. Rivadavia at center. Watermark: Multiple sunbursts.			
	a. Signature titles E. Series A.	.10	.75	3.00
	b. Signature titles C. Series B; C. 2 Signature varieties.	.05	.15	.40
	s. Signature titles C. Series A. Specimen.	—	—	25.00

324	5 Australes	VG	VF	UNC
	ND (1986-89). Brown and deep olive-green on multicolor underprint. J. J. de Urquiza at center. Watermark: Multiple sunbursts.			
	a. Signature titles E. Series A.	.10	.25	2.00
	b. Signature titles C. Series A.	.05	.15	.40

325	10 Australes	VG	VF	UNC
	ND (1985-89). Dark blue and purple on multicolor underprint. S. Derqui at center. Watermark: Multiple sunbursts.			
	a. Coarse portrait in heavy horizontal wavy lines. signature titles E. Series A.	.25	.75	3.50
	b. Modified portrait in finer horizontal wavy lines. signature titles C. Series A; B; C.	.05	.15	.40

326	50 Australes	VG	VF	UNC
	ND (1986-89). Purple and deep brown on multicolor underprint. B. Mitre at center. Watermark: Multiple sunbursts.			
	a. Signature titles E. Series A.	.50	6.00	20.00
	b. Signature titles C. Series A. 3 Signature varieties.	.10	.15	.50
	s. As b. Specimen.	—	—	25.00

327	100 Australes	VG	VF	UNC
	ND (1985-90). Dark red and purple on multicolor underprint. D. F. Sarmiento at center. Watermark: Multiple sunbursts.			
	a. Signature titles E. Series A.	.50	4.00	15.00
	b. Signature titles C. Engraved back. Series A; B. 3 Signature varieties.	.10	.20	.75
	c. Signature titles C. Back pink and lithographed; without purple and blue. Series C; D.	.05	.15	.50
	s. As b. Specimen.	—	—	25.00

328	500 Australes	VG	VF	UNC
	ND (1988-90). Pale olive-green on multicolor underprint. N. Avellaneda at center. Signature titles: C. 2 signature varieties.			
	a. Metallic green guilloche by *500*. Back olive-green, black and multicolor. watermark: Liberty. Series A. (1988).	.10	.50	2.00
	b. dark olive-green guilloche by *500*. Back pale olive-green and multicolor; lithographed (without black). watermark: Multiple sunbursts. Series A. (1990).	.05	.20	.75
	s. As a. Specimen.	—	—	25.00

		VG	VF	UNC
329	**1000 Australes** ND (1988-90). Violet-brown and purple on multicolor underprint. J. A. Roca at center. Signature titles: *GERENTE GENERAL* and *PRESIDENTE*.			
	a. Vertical green guilloche near *1000*. watermark: Liberty. Series A.	.05	.20	.75
	b. Vertical brown-violet guilloche near *1000*. watermark: Liberty. Series B.	.05	.25	1.00
	c. Like b. but watermark: Multiple sunbursts.	.05	.25	1.00
	d. Like c. but signature titles: F. Series C.	.10	.50	2.00
	s. As a. Specimen.	—	—	25.00

		VG	VF	UNC
330	**5000 Australes** ND (1989-91). Dark brown and red-brown on multicolor underprint. M. Juarez at center.			
	a. Green shield design at upper center r. Sign titles: E. watermark: Liberty. Series A.	.50	3.00	12.50
	b. Green shield design at upper center r. Sign titles: C. watermark: Liberty. Series A.	.75	5.00	17.50
	c. dark brown shield design at upper center r. signature titles: E. watermark: Liberty. Series B.	.50	2.50	8.00
	d. dark brown shield designature signature titles: C. watermark: Liberty. Series B.	.50	2.00	7.00
	e. dark brown shield designature signature titles: F. Lithographed back. watermark: Multiple sunbursts. Series C.	.20	1.00	4.00
	f. Series D (1991).	20.00	60.00	125.

1989; 1991 ND Provisional Issue

#331-333 use modified face plates from earlier issue. Wmk: Multiple sunbursts. Series M. Printer: CdM-A. Replacement notes: Serial # prefix *R*.

		VG	VF	UNC
331	**10,000 Australes** ND (1989). Black-blue, deep blue-green and brown on multicolor underprint. Face similar to #306. Overprint value in olive-green in box at left. Word "PESOS" at center blocked out. Denomination repeated in lines of text and overprint value at right on back. Signature titles: C.	2.00	7.50	25.00

		VG	VF	UNC
332	**50,000 Australes** ND (1989). Deep olive-green and blue on multicolor underprint. Face similar to #307. Overprint value in violet in box at left. Word "PESOS" at center blocked out. Back similar to #331. Value in light brown at right. Signature titles: E.	2.00	8.00	27.50
333	**500,000 Australes** ND (1990). Black, purple and red on multicolor underprint. Face similar to #309. Overprint value in box at left. Word "PESOS" at bottom right blocked out. Back similar to #331. Value at right. Signature titles: F.	7.50	30.00	75.00

1989-91 ND Issue

#334-338 Liberty (Progreso) w/torch and shield seated at l. ctr. on back. Wmk: Liberty head. Printer: CdM-A. Replacement notes: Serial # prefix *R*.

		VG	VF	UNC
334	**10,000 Australes** ND (1989-91). Black on deep blue, brown and multicolor underprint with brown diamond design at upper center right. C. Pellegrini at center.			
	a. Signature titles: C. Series A; B.	.25	1.25	3.50
	b. Signature titles: F. Series C. watermark: sunbursts.	.50	1.50	6.00

		VG	VF	UNC
335	**50,000 Australes** ND (1989-91). Black on ochre, olive-green and multicolor underprint with black flower design at upper center right. Saenz Peña at center signature titles: C. Series A; B.	1.00	6.00	25.00

NOTICE

Readers with unlisted dates, signature varieties, etc. are invited to submit photocopies of their notes to: Standard Catalog of World Paper Money, 700 East State St. Iola, WI 54990-0001, E-Mail: george.cuhaj@fwpubs.com.

336 100,000 Australes

ND (1990-91). Dark brown and reddish brown on pale brown and multicolor underprint. Coarsely engraved portrait of J. Evaristo Uriburu at center. Black signature titles: F. Series A; B.

VG	VF	UNC
2.00	10.00	45.00

337 100,000 Australes

ND (1991). Dark brown and reddish brown on brown and multicolor underprint. Finely engraved portrait of J. Evaristo Uriburu at center. Brown signature titles. Series B.

VG	VF	UNC
1.50	8.00	50.00

338 500,000 Australes

ND (1991). Black-violet, red and blue on multicolor underprint. M. Quintana at center. Series A, B. 2 signature varieties.

VG	VF	UNC
4.00	25.00	75.00

1991-92 ND Issue

Peso System

#339-341 wmk: Multiple sunbursts. Printer: CdM-A.

#339-345 replacement notes: Serial # prefix *R*.

339 1 Peso

ND (1992-94). Dark blue and violet-brown on multicolor underprint. C. Pelligrini at right. Back gray on multicolor underprint; National Congress building at left center.

	VG	VF	UNC
a. Signature titles: F. (1992). Series A, B.	FV	FV	3.00
b. Signature titles: G. (1993). Series B, C, D.	FV	FV	2.50
c. Signature titles as a. Serial # prefix L. (1994).	FV	FV	5.00

340 2 Pesos

ND (1992-97). Deep blue and red-violet on multicolor underprint. B. Mitre at right. Back light blue on multicolort underprint; Mitre Museum at left center.

	VG	VF	UNC
a. Signature titles: F. (1992). Series A.	FV	FV	5.00
b. Signature titles: H. (1993). Series A-C.	FV	FV	4.00

341 5 Pesos

ND (1992-97). Deep olive-green and red-orange on multicolor underprint. Gen. J. de San Martín at right. Back light olive-gray on multicolor underprint; monument to the Glory of Mendoza at left center.

	VG	VF	UNC
a. Signature titles: F. (1992). Series A.	FV	FV	8.00
b. Signature titles: G. (1993). Series A-C.	FV	FV	9.00
c. Signature titles as a. Serial # prefix L. (1994).	FV	FV	10.00

#342-343 wmk: Liberty head. Printer: CdM-A.

342 10 Pesos

ND (1992-97). Deep brown and dark green on multicolor underprint. M. Belgrano at right. Monument to the Flag at Rosario with city in background at left center on back.

	VG	VF	UNC
a. Signature titles: F. (1992). Series A-B.	FV	FV	20.00
b. Signature titles: H. (1993). Series C-E.	FV	FV	17.50

343 20 Pesos

	VG	VF	UNC
ND (1992-97). Carmine and deep blue on multicolor underprint. J. Manuel de Rosas at right. *Vuelta de Obligado* battle scene at left center on back.			
a. Signature titles: F. (1992). Series A.	FV	FV	35.00
b. Signature titles: G. (1993). Series A-B.	FV	FV	30.00

344 50 Pesos

	VG	VF	UNC
ND (1992-97). Black and red on multicolor underprint. D. Faustino Sarmiento at right and as watermark. Plaza de Mayo in Buenos Aires at left center on back.			
a. Signature titles: F. (1992). Series A.	FV	FV	75.00
b. Signature titles: H. (1993). Series A-B.	FV	FV	70.00

345 100 Pesos

	VG	VF	UNC
ND (1992-97). Violet, lilac and green on multicolor underprint. J. A. Roca at right and as watermark. Back violet and m/c; *La Conquista del Desierto* scene at left center.			
a. Signature titles: F. (1992). Series A.	FV	FV	125.
b. Signature titles: G. (1993). Series A-D.	FV	FV	110.

1997-2000 ND Issue

#346-351 ascending size serial # at upper r. Printer: CdM-A. Replacement notes: Serial # prefix *R*.

346 2 Pesos

	VG	VF	UNC
ND (1997-2002). Deep blue and brown-violet on multicolor underprint. B. Mitre at right and as watermark. Ornate gate at center. Mitre Museum at left center on back. Signature titles: H. 2 signature varieties. Series A-D.	FV	FV	3.00

347 5 Pesos

	VG	VF	UNC
ND (1998-2003). Deep olive-green and purple on multicolor underprint. Gen. J. de. San Martín at right and as watermark, Gen. San Martín on horseback with troops at center. Monument to the Glory at Mendoza at left center on back. Signature titles: G. 4 signature varieties. Series A-C.	FV	FV	7.00

348 10 Pesos

	VG	VF	UNC
ND (1998-2003). Deep brown and dark green on multicolor underprint. M. Belgrano at right and as watermark, Liberty with flag at center. Monument to the Flag at Rosario with city in background at left center on back. Signature titles: H. 3 signature varieties. Series A-E.	FV	FV	15.00

349 20 Pesos

	VG	VF	UNC
ND (1999-2003). Red-brown and purple on multicolor underprint. J. Manuel de Rosas at right and as watermark. *Vuelta de Obligado* battle scene at left center on back. Signature titles: G. 4 signature varieties. Series A, B.	FV	FV	30.00

350 50 Pesos

	VG	VF	UNC
ND (1999-2003). Multicolor. D. Faustino Sarmiento at right and as watermark. Government office with monuments, palm trees in foreground at left center on back. Signature titles: H. 3 signature varieties. Series A.	FV	FV	65.00

351 100 Pesos — VG FV | VF FV | UNC 120.
ND (1999-2002). Multicolor. J. A. Roca at right and as watermark *La Conquista del Desierto* scene at left center on back. Signature titles: G. 4 signature varieties. Series A, B.

2002-03 ND Issue

#352-357 similar to #346-351 but no clause: *CONVERTIBLES DE CURSO LEGAL.*

		VG	VF	UNC
352	**2 Pesos** ND (2002). Similar to #346. Series D-G. 4 signature varieties.	FV	FV	3.00

		VG	VF	UNC
353	**5 Pesos** ND (2003). Similar to #347. Series C-D. 2 signature varieties.	FV	FV	7.00

		VG	VF	UNC
354	**10 Pesos** ND (2003). Similar to #348. Series E-H. 3 signature varieties.	FV	FV	15.00

		VG	VF	UNC
355	**20 Pesos** ND (2003). Similar to #349. Series B-C. 3 signature varieties.	FV	FV	30.00
356	**50 Pesos** ND (2003). Similar to #350. Series A-C. 3 signature varieties.	FV	FV	65.00
357	**100 Pesos** ND (2003). Similar to #351. Series B-G. 2 signature varieties.	FV	FV	120.

The Republic of Armenia (formerly the Armenian S.S.R.) is bounded to the north by Georgia, to the east by Azerbaijan and to the south and west by Turkey and Iran. It has an area of 11,490 sq. mi. (29,800 sq. km) and a population of 3.7 million. Capital: Yerevan. Agriculture including cotton, vineyards and orchards, hydroelectricity, chemicals - primarily synthetic rubber and fertilizers, and vast mineral deposits of copper, zinc and aluminum and production of steel and paper are major industries.

The earliest history of Armenia records continuous struggles with Babylonia and later Assyria. In the sixth century B.C. it was called Armina. Later under under the Persian empire it was a vassal state. Conquered by Macedonia, it later defeated the Seleucids and thus Greater Armenia was founded under the Artaxis dynasty. Christianity was established in 303 A.D. which led to religious wars with the Persians and Romans who then divided it into two zones of influence. The Arabs succeeded the Sassanids. In 862 A.D. Ashot V was recognized as the "prince of princes" and established a throne recognized by Baghdad and Constantinople in 886 A.D. The Seljuks overran the whole country and united with Kurdistan whic eventually ran the new government. From 1240 A.D. onward the Mongols occupied almost all of western Asia until their downfall in 1375 A.D. when various Kurdish, Armenian and Turkoman independent principalities arose. After the defeat of the Persians in 1516 A.D. the Ottoman Turks gradually took control with Kurdish tribes settling within Armenian lands. In 1605 A.D, the Persians relocated thousands of Armenians as far as India to develop colonies. Persia and the Ottoman Turks were again at war, with the Ottomans once again prevailing. The Ottomans later gave absolute civil authority to a Christian bishop allowing the Armenians free enjoyment of their religion and traditions.

Russia occupied Armenia in 1801 until the Russo-Turkish war of 1878. British intervention excluded either side from remaining although the Armenian remained more loyal to the Ottoman Turks. In 1894 the Ottoman Turks sent in an expeditionary force of Kurds fearing a revolutionary movement. Large massacres were followed by retaliations, an amnesty was proclaimed which continued to 1916, when Armenia was occupied by Russian forces. From 1917-1918 the Georgians, Armenians and Azerbaijanis formed the short-lived Transcaucasian Federal Republic which split into three independent republics on May 26, 1918. Communism developed and in Sept. 1920 the Turks attacked the Armenian Republic; the Russians soon followed suit, routing the Turks. On Nov. 29, 1920 Armenia was proclaimed a Soviet Socialist Republic. On March 12, 1922, Armenia, Georgia and Azerbaijan were combined to form the Transcaucasian Soviet Federated Socialist republic, which on Dec. 30, 1922, became a part of U.S.S.R. On Dec. 5, 1936, the Transcaucasian federation was dissolved and Armenia became a constituent republic of the U.S.S.R.

A new constitution was adopted in April 1978. Elections took place on May 20, 1990. The Supreme Soviet adopted a declaration of sovereignty in Aug. 1991, voting to unite Armenia with Nagorno-Karabakh. This newly constituted Republic of Armenia became independent by popular vote in Sept. 1991. It joined the CIS in Dec.1991.

Fighting between Christians in Armenia and Muslim forces of Azerbaijan escalated in 1992 and continued through early 1994. Each country claimed the Nagorno-Karabakh, an Armenian ethnic enclave in Azerbaijan. A temporary cease-fire was announced in May 1994.

MONETARY SYSTEM:

1 Ruble = 100 Kopeks
1 Dram = 100 Lumma

Note: For later issues of the Armenian Socialist Soviet Republic refer to Volume 1, Russia-Transcaucasia, and for current issues of the new Republic refer to Volume 3.

Republic

Armenian Republic Bank

1993-95 Issue

#33-38 wmk: Crude outlined coat, or refined coat. Printer: G&D (w/o imprint).

		VG	VF	UNC
33	**10 Dram** 1993. Dark brown, light blue and pale orange on multicolor underprint. Statue of David from Sasoun at upper center right, main railway station in Yerevan at upper left center. Mt. Ararat at upper center right on back.	.05	.25	1.00

		VG	VF	UNC
34	**25 Dram** 1993. Brown and light red on multicolor underprint. Frieze with lion from Erebuni Castle at center right, cuneiform tablet at upper left center. Arched ornament at upper center right on back.	.10	.25	1.25

		VG	VF	UNC
35	**50 Dram** 1993. Dark blue on pink and multicolor underprint. State Museum of History and National Gallery at upper left center. Parliament building at upper center right on back.	.10	.25	1.25

		VG	VF	UNC
36	**100 Dram** 1993. Purple, light blue and light red on multicolor underprint. Mt. Ararat at upper left center, Church of Zvarnots at center right. Opera and ballet theater in Yerevan at upper center right on back.			
	a. Watermark: Crude outline arms.	.10	.25	1.75
	b. Watermark: Refined arms.	.10	.25	1.50

		VG	VF	UNC
37	**200 Dram** 1993. Brown, green and red on multicolor underprint. Church of St. Hripsime in Echmiadzin at center right. Circular design at upper center right on back.			
	a. Watermark: Crude outline arms.	.10	.50	3.00
	b. Watermark: Refined arms.	.10	.50	3.00

		VG	VF	UNC
38	**500 Dram** 1993. Dark green and red-brown on multicolor underprint. Tetradrachm of King Tigran II the Great at center right, Mt. Ararat at upper left. Center Open book and quill pen at upper center right on back.			
	a. Watermark: Crude outline arms.	.10	.50	3.00
	b. Watermark: Refined arms.	.10	.50	3.00

		VG	VF	UNC
39	**1000 Dram** 1994. Dark brown and brown on multicolor underprint. Statue of Mesrop Mashtotz at left. Matenadaran facade at right on back. Watermark: Arms.	.25	1.00	5.00

		VG	VF	UNC
40	**5000 Dram** 1995. Brown-violet on multicolor underprint. Temple of Garni at center. Goddess Anahit on back.	.50	1.00	8.00

CENTRAL BANK OF THE REPUBLIC OF ARMENIA

1998-99 ISSUE

#41-45, 48 printer: (T)DLR (w/o imprint.) Wmk. is portr. #41, 42, 44 replacement notes serial # first digit is 9.

		VG	VF	UNC
42	**100 Dram** 1998. Light and dark blue on multicolor underprint. Victor Hambartsumyan at left, solar system map at right. Byurakan Observatory on Mt. Arakadz on back.	.15	.50	1.50

#43 Not assigned.

42	50 Dram	VG	VF	UNC
	1998. Brownish pink and slate blue on multicolor underprint. Aram Khachaturian at left, opera house at right. Scene from *Gayaneh* Ballet and Mt. Ararat on back.	.15	.50	1.25

44	500 Dram	VG	VF	UNC
	1999 (2000). Black on red and multicolor underprint. Alexander Tamanyan and city plan. House of the Government in Yerevan at left center on back.	.15	.75	4.00

45	1000 Dram	VG	VF	UNC
	1999. Aqua and green on multicolor underprint. Yeghishe Charents at left, lines of poetry at right. Old Yerevan city scene on back.	.75	2.50	8.00

46	5000 Dram	VG	VF	UNC
	1999 (2000).Dk and light brown on green, gold and multicolor underprint. H. Tumanyan at left. Saryan's picture of Lory mountains on back. Printer: JEZ.	1.00	4.00	17.50

47	20,000 Dram	VG	VF	UNC
	1999. Brown and yellow on multicolor underprint. Martiros Saryan, painter at left, abstract painting in center. Hologram at right. Saryan painting *Armenia* on back.	2.00	7.50	30.00

2001 COMMEMORATIVE ISSUE

#48, 1700 years of Christianity in Armenia

48	50,000 Dram	VG	VF	UNC
	2001. Brown and multicolor. Cathedral of Holy Echmiatzin at center, holographic strip at left with commemorative text vertically. St Gregory and King Tiridat holding church on back.	25.00	75.00	200.

#49 Not assigned.

2001; 2003 ISSUE

50	1000 Dram	VG	VF	UNC
	2001 (2002). Aqua and green on multicolor underprint. Like #45 but with additional security features.	1.00	3.00	10.00

51	5000 Dram	VG	VF	UNC
	2003. H. Tumanyuan at left. Saryan's picture of Lory Mountains on back.	13.00	15.00	35.00

52 **10,000 Dram**
2003. Avetik Isahakyan Gyumri at left.

	VG	VF	UNC
	25.00	35.00	50.00

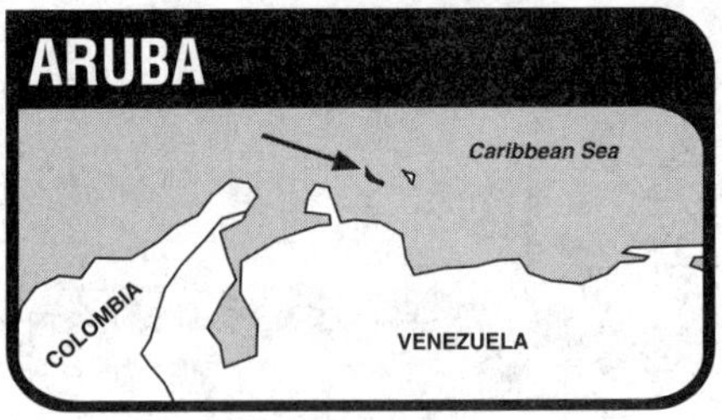

Aruba, formerly a part of the Netherlands Antilles, achieved on Jan. 1, 1986 a special status "status aparte" as the third state under the Dutch crown, together with the Netherlands and the remaining five islands of the Netherlands Antilles. On Dec. 15, 1954 the Netherlands Antilles were given complete domestic autonomy and granted equality within the Kingdom of the Netherlands.

Aruba was the second-largest island of the Netherlands Antilles and is situated near the Venezuelan coast. The island has an area of 74-1/2 sq. mi. (193 sq. km.) and a population of 68,000. Capital: Oranjestad, named after the Dutch royal family. Chief industry is tourism. For earlier issues see Curaçao and the Netherlands Antilles. During Jan. 1986 the banknotes of the Netherlands Antilles were redeemed at a ratio of 1 to 1.

MONETARY SYSTEM:

1 Florin = 100 Cents

DUTCH ADMINISTRATION

BANCO CENTRAL DI ARUBA

1986 ISSUE

#1-5 flag at l., coastal hotels at ctr. Arms of Aruba at ctr. on back. Printer: JEZ.

1 **5 Florin**
1.1.1986. Green.

	VG	VF	UNC
	FV	FV	17.50

2 **10 Florin**
1.1.1986. Green.

	VG	VF	UNC
	FV	FV	27.50

3 **25 Florin**
1.1.1986. Green.

	VG	VF	UNC
	FV	FV	45.00

		VG	VF	UNC
4	**50 Florin** 1.1.1986. Green.	FV	FV	65.00
5	**100 Florin** 1.1.1986. Green.	FV	FV	130.

Centrale Bank van Aruba

1990 Issue

#6-10 geometric forms with pre-Columbian Aruban art on back. Wmk: Stylized tree. Printer: JEZ.

		VG	VF	UNC
6	**5 Florin** 1.1.1990. Purple and multicolor. Tortuga Blanco (sea turtle) at center right.	FV	FV	17.50

		VG	VF	UNC
7	**10 Florin** 1.1.1990. Blue and multicolor. Calco Indian conch at center right.	FV	FV	17.50

		VG	VF	UNC
8	**25 Florin** 1.1.1990. Brown and multicolor. Rattlesnake at right.	FV	FV	35.00

		VG	VF	UNC
9	**50 Florin** 1.1.1990. Red-brown and multicolor. Burrowing owl at center right.	FV	FV	62.50
10	**100 Florin** 1.1.1990. Olive-green and multicolor. Frog at center right.	FV	FV	200.

1993 Issue

#11-15 like #7-10 but w/text: *Wettig Betaalmiddel* (legal tender). Wmk: Stylized tree. Printer: JEZ.

		VG	VF	UNC
11	**10 Florin** 16.7.1993 (1996). Blue and multicolor. Like #7.	FV	FV	16.50

		VG	VF	UNC
12	**25 Florin** 16.7.1993 (1996). Brown and multicolor. Like #8.	FV	FV	32.50

		VG	VF	UNC
13	**50 Florin** 16.7.1993 (1996). Red-brown and multicolor. Like #9.	FV	FV	60.00

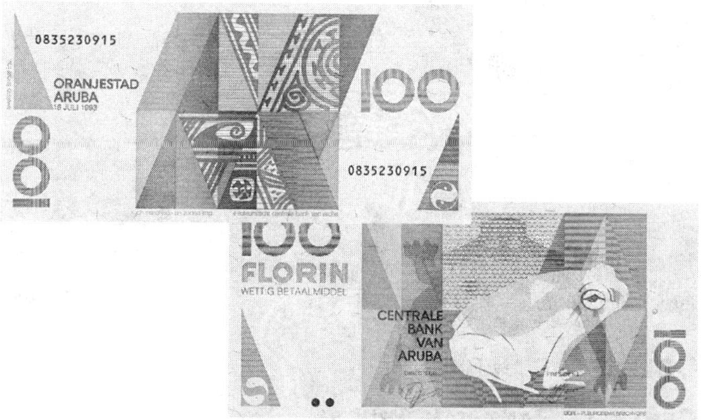

		VG	VF	UNC
14	**100 Florin** 16.7.1993 (1996). Olive-green and multicolor. Like #10.	FV	FV	115.
15	**500 Florin** 16.7.1993. Blue and multicolor. Grouper fish at center right.	FV	FV	460.

2003 Issue

#16-20 like #11-15 but w/additional security features and different signatures. Printer:JEZ.

		VG	VF	UNC
16	**10 Florin** 1.12.2003. Blue and multicolor. Like #11.	FV	FV	12.50

		VG	VF	UNC
17	**25 Florin** 1.12.2003. Brown and multicolor. Like #12.	FV	FV	27.50

		VG	VF	UNC
18	**50 Florin** 1.12.2003. Red-brown and multicolor. Like #13.	FV	FV	52.50

		VG	VF	UNC
19	**100 Florin** 1.12.2003. Olive-green and multicolor. Like #14.	FV	FV	105.
20	**500 Florin** 1.12.2003. Blue and multicolor. Like #15.	FV	FV	400.

Collector Series

Centrale Bank van Aruba

1990 Issue

		IP	MV
CS1	**1990 5-100 Florin** #6-10 with low matched serial # in six page special presentation folder. 200 sets produced.	—	450.

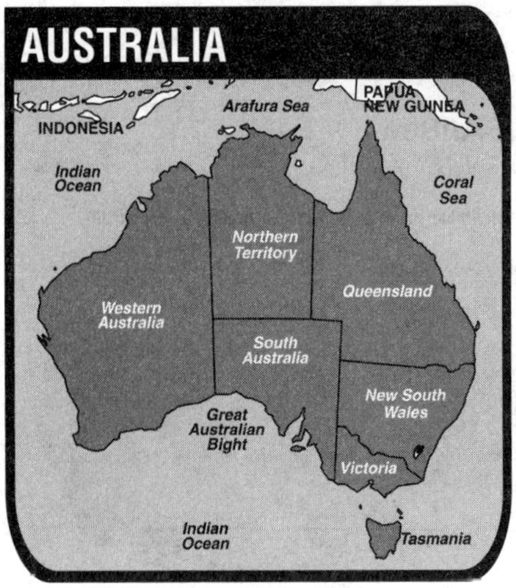

The Commonwealth of Australia, the smallest continent and largest island in the world, is located south of Indonesia between the Indian and Pacific oceans. It has an area of 2,967,909 sq. mi. (7,686,849 sq. km.) and a population of 18.84 million. Capital: Canberra. Due to its early and sustained isolation, Australia is the habitat of such curious and unique fauna as the kangaroo, koala, platypus, wombat and barking lizard. The continent possesses extensive mineral deposits, the most important of which are gold, coal, silver, nickel, uranium, lead and zinc. Livestock raising, mining and manufacturing are the principal industries. Chief exports are wool, meat, wheat, iron ore, coal and nonferrous metals.

The first caucasians to see Australia probably were Portuguese and Spanish navigators of the late 16th century. In 1770, Captain James Cook explored the east coast and annexed it for Great Britain. The Colony of New South Wales was founded by Captain Arthur Phillip on Jan. 26, 1788, a date now celebrated as Australia Day. Dates of creation of six colonies that now comprise the states of the Australian Commonwealth are: New South Wales, 1823; Tasmania, 1825; Western Australia, 1838; South Australia, 1842; Victoria, 1851; Queensland, 1859. A constitution providing for federation of the colonies was approved by the British Parliament in 1900; the Commonwealth of Australia came into being in 1901. Australia passed the Statute of Westminster Adoption Act on Oct. 9, 1942, which officially established Australia's complete autonomy in external and internal affairs, thereby formalizing a situation that had existed for years.

During WWII Australia was the primary supply and staging area for Allied forces in the South Pacific Theatre.

Australia is a member of the Commonwealth of Nations. Elizabeth II is Head of State as Queen of Australia.

RULERS:

British

MONETARY SYSTEM:

1 Shilling = 12 Pence
1 Pound = 20 Shillings = 2 Dollars
1 Pound = 20 Shillings; to 1966
1 Dollar = 100 Cents, 1966-

Commonwealth of Australia

Reserve Bank

1960-61 ND Issue

#33-36 like #29-32. Sign. H. C. Coombs w/title: *GOVERNOR/RESERVE BANK of AUSTRALIA* below lower l. sign. R. Wilson. Wmk: Capt. James Cook. Replacement notes: Serial # suffix *.

		VG	VF	UNC
33	**10 Shillings** ND (1961-65). Dark brown on orange and green underprint. Arms at lower left, portrait Matthew Flinders at right. Old Parliament House in Canberra on back. Like #29.			
	a. Issued note.	20.00	70.00	250.
	r. Serial # suffix *, replacement.	300.	1100.	15,000.
	s. Specimen.	2500.	15,000.	50,000.

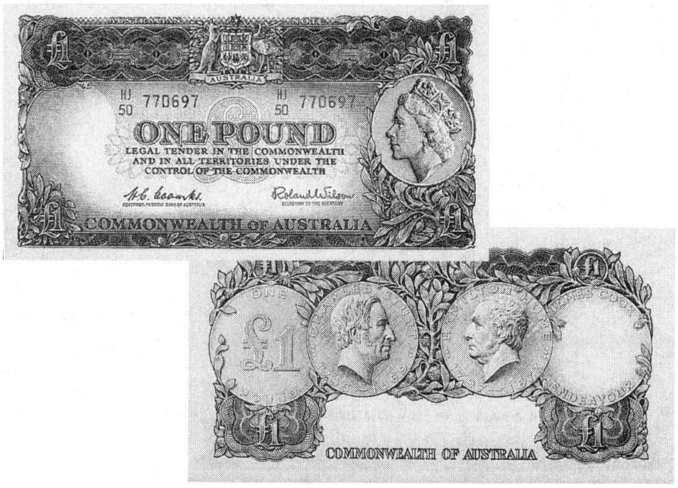

34 1 Pound

ND (1961-65). Black on green and yellow underprint. Arms at upper center, cameo portrait Queen Elizabeth II at right. Back green; facing portrait Charles Sturt and Hamilton Hume. Like #30.

	VG	VF	UNC
a. Issued note.	10.00	40.00	150.
r. Serial # suffix *, replacement.	275.	1200.	16,000.
s. Specimen.	2500.	15,000.	50,000.

35 5 Pounds

ND (1960-65). Black on blue underprint. Arms at upper left, portrait Sir John Franklin at right. Back blue; cattle, sheep and agricultural products across center Like #31.

	VG	VF	UNC
a. Issued note.	20.00	45.00	400.
r. Serial # suffix *, replacement.	750.	7500.	30,000.
s. Specimen.	1250.	8500.	35,000.

36 10 Pounds

ND (1960-65). Black on red underprint. Arms at top center, portrait Gov. Arthur Philip at left. Symbols of science and industry on back. Like #32.

	VG	VF	UNC
a. Issued note.	40.00	100.	1200.
s. Specimen.	1500.	9000.	38,000.

1966-67 ND Issue

#37-41 w/text: *COMMONWEALTH OF* in heading. Wmk: Capt. James Cook. Replacement notes: Serial # prefixes *ZAA-ZXA* w/suffix *.

37 1 Dollar

ND (1966-72). Dark brown on orange and multicolor underprint. Arms at center, Queen Elizabeth II at right. Stylized aboriginal figures and animals on back.

	VG	VF	UNC
a. Signature H. C. Coombs and R. Wilson. (1966).	5.00	15.00	60.00
b. Signature H. C. Coombs and R. J. Randall. (1968).	25.00	150.	600.
c. Signature J. G. Phillips and R. J. Randall. (1969).	3.00	10.00	45.00
d. Signature J. G. Phillips and F. H. Wheeler. (1972).	3.00	10.00	45.00
s1. Specimen in oval on each side.	—	3500.	9500.
s2. Specimen eight times each side.	—	5000.	17,500.
s3. Specimen twice diagonally each side.	—	3000.	12,000.
ar. As a, serial # suffix *, replacement.	75.00	550.	2850.
br. As b, serial # suffix *, replacement.	250.	3000.	8500.
cr. As c, serial # suffix *, replacement.	75.00	575.	2900.

38 2 Dollars

ND (1966-72). Black on green, blue and yellow multicolor underprint. John MacArthur at right, sheep at center William Farrer at left, wheat at center on back.

	VG	VF	UNC
a. Signature H. C. Coombs and R. Wilson. (1966).	8.00	20.00	55.00
b. Signature H. C. Coombs and R. J. Randall. (1967).	15.00	45.00	140.
c. Signature J. G. Phillips and R. J. Randall. (1968).	7.00	18.00	55.00
d. Signature J. G. Phillips and F. H. Wheeler. (1972).	6.00	17.00	55.00
ar. As a, serial # suffix *, replacement.	70.00	500.	2750.
as. As a. Specimen.	—	3500.	9500.
br. As b, serial # suffix *, replacement.	550.	2500.	6500.
cr. As c, serial # suffix *, replacement.	70.00	550.	2750.

39 5 Dollars VG VF UNC

ND (1967-72). Deep purple on multicolor underprint. Sir Joseph Banks at right, plants at center. Caroline Chisholm, ship, buildings, and women on back.

		VG	VF	UNC
39	**5 Dollars**			
	a. Signature J. G. Phillips and R. J. Randall. (1969).	20.00	55.00	200.
	b. Signature H. C. Coombs and R. J. Randall. (1967).	18.00	50.00	170.
	c. Signature J. G. Phillips and F. H. Wheeler. (1972).	16.00	48.00	165.
	s1. As a. Specimen in oval each side.	—	3500.	9500.
	s2. As b. Specimen eight time each side.	—	5750.	18,000.
	s3. As c. Specimen twice diagonally each side.	—	3500.	13,000.
	ar. As a, serial # suffix *, replacement.	500.	2000.	5000.
	br. As b, serial # suffix *, replacement.	1100.	4000.	15,000.

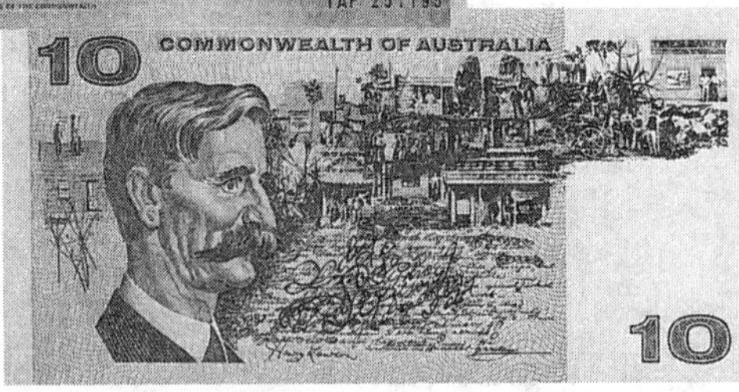

		VG	VF	UNC
40	**10 Dollars**			
	ND (1966-72). Black on blue, orange and multicolor underprint. Francis Greenway at right, village scene at center. Henry Lawson and buildings on back.			
	a. Signature H. C. Coombs and R. Wilson. (1966).	20.00	35.00	70.00
	b. Signature H. G. Coombs and R. J. Randall. (1967).	40.00	150.	450.
	c. Signature J. G. Phillips and R. J. Randall. (1968).	20.00	30.00	75.00
	d. Signature J. G, Phillips and F. H. Wheeler. (1972).	20.00	30.00	70.00
	s1. As a. Specimen in oval each side.	—	3500.	9500.
	s2. As b. Specimen eight time each side.	—	5500.	17,000.
	s3. As c Specimen twice diagonally each side.	—	4500.	13,000.
	ar. As a, serial # suffix *, replacement.	150.	1750.	3700.
	br. As b, serial # suffix *, replacement.	575.	1850.	10,000.
	cr. As c, serial # suffix *, replacement.	350.	2500.	6000.

		VG	VF	UNC
41	**20 Dollars**			
	ND (1966-72). Black on red, yellow and multicolor underprint. Sir Charles Kingsford-Smith at right. Lawrence Hargrave at left, aeronautical devices on back.			
	a. Signature H. C. Coombs and R. Wilson. (1966).	30.00	40.00	70.00
	b. Signature H. G. Coombs and R. J. Randall. (1968).	100.	1000.	3300.
	c. Signature J. G. Phillips and R. J. Randall. (1968).	35.00	75.00	240.
	d. Signature J. G. Phillips and F. H. Wheeler. (1972).	40.00	85.00	300.
	s1. As a. Specimen in oval each side.	—	1850.	10,000.
	s2. As b. Specimen eight times each side.	—	6000.	18,000.
	s3. As c. Specimen twice diagonally each side.	—	4500.	13,000.
	cr. As c, serial # suffix *, replacement.	900.	4000.	14,000.

AUSTRALIA, RESERVE BANK

1973; 1984 ND ISSUE

#42-48 w/o text: *COMMONWEALTH OF* in heading.

#42-46 like #37-41. Wmk: Capt. James Cook.

		VG	VF	UNC
42	**1 Dollar**			
	ND (1974-83). Dark brown on orange and multicolor underprint. Like #37.			
	a. Signature J. G. Phillips and F. H. Wheeler. (1974).	5.00	15.00	45.00
	b1. Signature H. M. Knight and F. H. Wheeler. (1976). Center security thread.	3.00	10.00	28.00
	b2. As b1. Side security thread.	2.00	5.00	18.00
	b3. KW test note DBP.	20.00	45.00	125.
	c. Signature H. M. Knight and J. Stone. (1979).	2.00	3.00	8.00
	d. Signature R. A. Johnston and J. Stone. (1983).	1.00	2.00	4.00
	s1. As a. Specimen twice diagonally each side.	—	6000.	18,000.
	s2. As b1. Specimen twice diagonally each side.	—	7500.	19,500.

		VG	VF	UNC
43	**2 Dollars**			
	ND (1974-85). Black on green, blue and yellow underprint. Like #38.			
	a. Signature J. G. Phillips and F. H. Wheeler. (1974).	6.00	18.00	55.00
	b1. Signature H. M. Knight and F. H. Wheeler. (1976). Gothic serial #.	22.00	50.00	135.
	b2. Signature H. M. Knight and F. H. Wheeler. (1976). Ocrb serial #. Center thread.	8.00	25.00	80.00
	b3. Signature H. M. Knight and F. H. Wheeler. (1976). Ocrb serial #. Side thread.	3.00	10.00	30.00
	c. Signature H. M. Knight and J. Stone. (1979).	3.00	5.00	12.00
	d. Signature R. A. Johnston and J. Stone. (1983).	2.00	4.00	11.00
	e. Signature R. A. Johnston and B. W. Fraser. (1985).	2.00	3.00	6.00
	s1. As a. Specimen twice diagonally each side.	—	6000.	18,000.
	s2. As b. Specimen twice diagonally each side.	—	6500.	19,500.

		VG	VF	UNC
44	**5 Dollars**			
	ND (1974-91). Deep purple on multicolor underprint. Like #39.			
	a. Signature J. G. Phillips and F. H. Wheeler. (1974).	25.00	55.00	145.
	b1. H.M. Knight and F.H. Wheeler. Centre metal thread.	6.00	18.00	55.00
	b2. H.M. Knight and F.H. Wheeler. Side metal thread.	5.00	15.00	50.00
	b3. H.M. Knight and F.H. Wheeler. Ocrb (last type) serials.	5.00	12.00	45.00
	c. Signature H. M. Knight and J. Stone. (1979).	5.00	10.00	30.00
	d. Signature R. A. Johnston and J. Stone. (1983).	5.00	8.00	25.00
	e. Signature R. A. Johnston and B. W. Fraser. (1985). 2 serial # varieties.	5.00	8.00	26.00
	f. Signature B. W. Fraser and C. I. Higgins. (1990).	5.00	8.00	26.00
	g. Signature B. W. Fraser and A. S. Cole. (1991).	5.00	7.00	16.00
	s1. As a. Specimen twice diagonally each side.	—	6000.	18,000.
	s2. As b1. Specimen twice diagonally each side.	—	7500.	19,500.
	as. As a. Specimen.	—	—	—

45	10 Dollars	VG	VF	UNC
	ND (1974-91). Black on blue and orange underprint. Like #40.			
	a. Signature J. G. Phillips and F. H. Wheeler. (1974).	35.00	60.00	185.
	b. Signature H. M. Knight and F. H. Wheeler. (1976).	30.00	50.00	155.
	c. Signature H. M. Knight and J. Stone. (1979). 2 serial # varieties.	15.00	30.00	90.00
	d. Signature R. A. Johnston and J. Stone. (1983).	10.00	25.00	65.00
	e. Signature R. A. Johnston and B. W. Fraser. (1985).	10.00	15.00	35.00
	f. Signature B. W. Fraser and C. I. Higgins. (1990).	10.00	15.00	35.00
	g. Signature B. W. Fraser and A. S. Cole. (1991).	10.00	15.00	32.00
	as. As a. Specimen.	—	6000.	18,000.

46	20 Dollars	VG	VF	UNC
	ND (1974-94). Black on red, yellow and multicolor underprint. Like #41.			
	a. Signature J. G. Phillips and F. H. Wheeler. (1974).	50.00	125.	280.
	b. Signature H. M. Knight and F. H. Wheeler. (1975).	40.00	85.00	200.
	c. Signature H. M. Knight and J. Stone. (1979). 2 serial # varieties.	35.00	50.00	115.
	d. Signature R. A. Johnston and J. Stone. (1983).	35.00	50.00	120.
	e. Signature R. A. Johnston and B. W. Fraser. (1985) 2 serial # varieties.	20.00	30.00	70.00
	f. Signature M. J. Phillips and B. W. Fraser. (1989).	20.00	35.00	75.00
	g. Signature B. W. Fraser and C. I. Higgins. (1989).	20.00	35.00	80.00
	h. Signature B. W. Fraser and A. S. Cole. (1991).	20.00	35.00	70.00
	i. Signature B. W. Fraser and E. A. Evans. (1994).	20.00	30.00	65.00
	as. As a. Specimen.	—	8500.	19,000.

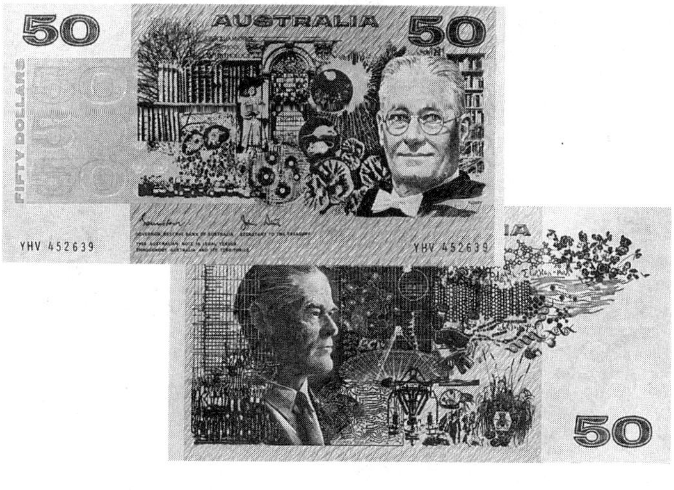

47	50 Dollars	VG	VF	UNC
	ND (1973-94). Dark brown and black on multicolor underprint. Teaching implements at center, Lord Howard Walker Florey at right. Ian Clunies-Ross at left, space research at center on back.			
	a. Signature J. G. Phillips and F. H. Wheeler. (1973).	75.00	125.	300.
	b. Signature H. M. Knight and F. H. Wheeler. (1975).	65.00	85.00	200.
	c. Signature H. M. Knight and J. Stone. (1979).	65.00	85.00	200.
	d. Signature R. A. Johnston and J. Stone. (1983).	65.00	80.00	195.
	e. Signature R. A. Johnston and B. W. Fraser. (1985). 2 serial # varieties.	65.00	85.00	200.
	f. Signature M. J. Phillips and B. W. Fraser. (1989).	60.00	80.00	150.
	g. Signature B. W. Fraser and C. I. Higgins. (1989).	65.00	85.00	210.
	h. Signature B. W. Fraser and A. S. Cole. (1991).	55.00	70.00	120.
	i. Signature B. W. Fraser and E. A. Evans. (1994).	50.00	65.00	115.

48	100 Dollars	VG	VF	UNC
	ND (1984-92). Blue and gray on multicolor underprint. Sir Douglas Mawson at center J. Tebbutt at left center on back.			
	a. Signature R. A. Johnston and J. Stone. (1984).	110.	150.	235.
	b. Signature R. A. Johnston and B. W. Fraser. (1985).	110.	145.	230.
	c. Signature B. W. Fraser and C. I. Higgins. (1990).	110.	140.	225.
	d. Signature B. W. Fraser and A. S. Cole. (1992).	105.	135.	220.

Note: See also "Collector Series" following note listings.

1988 ND Commemorative Issue

#49, Bicentennial of British Settlement

Polymer plastic. Printer: NPA.

49	10 Dollars	VG	VF	UNC
	1988; ND. Brown and green on multicolor underprint. Capt. Cook OVD at upper left, colonists across background; Cook's ship *Supply* at lower right shoreline. Aboriginal youth, rock painting and ceremonial *Morning Star* pole at center on back. Signature right. A. Johnston and B. W. Fraser. Polymer plastic.			
	a. Serial # prefix AA. 26.1.1988. Issued in folder.	—	—	25.00
	b. Issued note. Serial # prefix AB. ND.	FV	15.00	25.00

NOTICE

Readers with unlisted dates, signature varieties, etc. are invited to submit photocopies of their notes to: Standard Catalog of World Paper Money, 700 East State St. Iola, WI 54990-0001, E-Mail: george.cuhaj@fwpubs.com.

1992-2001 Issues

#50-56 Dates are indicated by the first two digits of the serial #. Printer: NPA.

#	Denomination / Description	VG	VF	UNC
50	**5 Dollars**			
	ND (1992); (19)93. Black, red and blue on multicolor underprint. Branch at left, Queen Elizabeth II at center right. Back black on lilac and multicolor underprint, the old and the new Parliament Houses in Canberra at center, gum flower OVD at lower right.			
	a. Signature B. W. Fraser and A. S. Cole. (1992).	FV	15.00	40.00
	b. Signature B. W. Fraser and E. A. Evans. (1993).	FV	10.00	20.00

#	Denomination / Description	VG	VF	UNC
51	**5 Dollars**			
	(19)95-(20)01. Black, red and bright purple. Like #50 but with orientation bands in upper and lower margins, gum flower OVD at lower right. Back with darker underprint. colors.			
	a. With 4 diagonal white lines in orientation band at lower left signature B. W. Fraser and E. A. Evans. (1995-96).	FV	10.00	20.00
	b. As a, but with 11 diagonal white lines in orientation band at lower left Plate error. (1995).	FV	10.00	20.00
	c. Signature I. Macfarlane and E. A. Evans. (1996-98) 2002-03.	FV	9.00	15.00

#	Denomination / Description	VG	VF	UNC
52	**10 Dollars**			
	(19)93-(20)01. Dark blue and purple on multicolor underprint. Man on horseback at left, A. B. "Banjo" Paterson at center, windmill OVD in transparent window at lower right. Dame Mary Gilmore at center right on back.			
	a. Signature B. W. Fraser and E. A. Evans. (1993-94).	FV	18.00	40.00
	b. Signature I. Macfarlane and E. A. Evans. (1996-98).	FV	15.00	35.00

#	Denomination / Description	VG	VF	UNC
53	**20 Dollars**			
	(19)94-(20)01. Black and red on orange and pale green underprint. Mary Reiby at center, sailing ship at left. Compass OVD in transparent window at lower right. Biplane at left, Rev. John Flynn at center right, camel at right on back.			
	a. Signature B. W. Fraser and E. A. Evans. (1994-96).	FV	35.00	60.00
	b. Signature I. Macfarlane and E. A. Evans. (1997-98).	FV	30.00	50.00

#	Denomination / Description	VG	VF	UNC
54	**50 Dollars**			
	(19)95-(20)01. Black and deep purple on yellow-brown, green and multicolor underprint. David Unaipon at left. center, Mission Church at Point McLeay at lower left, patent drawings at upper center right, Southern Cross constellation OVD in transparent window at lower right. Edith Cowan, foster mother with children at center, W. Australia's Parliament House at upper left, Cowan at lectern at right on back.			
	a. Signature B. W. Fraser and E. A. Evans. (1995-96).	FV	80.00	110.
	b. Signature I. Macfarlane and E. A.	FV	70.00	90.00

#	Denomination / Description	VG	VF	UNC
55	**100 Dollars**			
	(19)96-(20)01. Black and green on orange and multicolor underprint. Opera stage at left, Dame Nellie Melba at center, stylized peacock OVD in transparent window at lower right. Sir John Monash and WWI battle scenes and insignia on back.			
	a. Signature B. W. Fraser and E. A. Evans. (1996).	FV	150.	200.
	b. Signature I. Macfarlane and E. A. Evans. (1998-99).	FV	120.	160.

2001 Commemorative Issue

#56, Centennial of the Commonwealth

#	Denomination / Description	VG	VF	UNC
56	**5 Dollars**			
	1.1.2001. Black, violet and blue on multicolor underprint. Sir Henry Parkes at center. Catherine Helen Spence at center on back.	FV	9.00	16.00

2002-03 Issue

#57-61 as previous issue but w/names added below portrait.

#	Denomination / Description	VG	VF	UNC
57	**5 Dollars**			
	(20)04. Expected new issue.	—	—	—
58	**10 Dollars**			
	(20)02. Dark blue and purple on multicolor underprint. Like #52.	FV	FV	10.00

#	Denomination / Description	VG	VF	UNC
59	**20 Dollars**			
	(20)02. Black and red on orange and pale green underprint. Like #53.	FV	FV	17.50
60	**50 Dollars**			
	(20)03. Expected new issue.	—	—	—
61	**100 Dollar**			
	(20)04. Expected new issue.	—	—	—

COLLECTOR SERIES

AUSTRALIA, RESERVE BANK

Many varieties of products have been produced for collectors in the form of uncut sheets, special serial # prefixes, various coin fair ovpts., souvenir folders including coin and bank note sets too numerous to list. These are documented occasionally in *Australian Coin Review* by Michael Vort-Ronald.

The Republic of Austria (Oesterreich), a parliamentary democracy located in mountainous central Europe, has an area of 32,374 sq. mi. (83,849 sq. km.) and a population of 8.1 million. Capital: Vienna. Austria is primarily an industrial country. Machinery, iron and steel, textiles, yarns and timber are exported.

The territories later to be known as Austria were overrun in pre-Roman times by various tribes, including the Celts. Upon the fall of the Roman Empire, the country became a margravate of Charlemagne's Empire. Premysl 2 Otakar, King of Bohemia, gained possession in 1252, only to lose the territory to Rudolf of Habsburg in 1276. Thereafter, until World War I, the story of Austria was that of the ruling Habsburgs, Holy Roman emperors from 1438-1806. From 1815-1867 it was a member of the *Deutsche Bund* (German Union).

During World War I, the Austro-Hungarian Empire was one of the Central Powers with Germany, Bulgaria and Turkey. At the end of the war, the empire was dissolved and Austria established as an independent republic. In March 1938, Austria was incorporated into Germany's Third Reich. Allied forces of both East and West liberated Austria in April 1945, and subsequently divided it into four zones of military occupation. On May 15, 1955, the four powers formally recognized Austria as a sovereign independent democratic state.

MONETARY SYSTEM:

1 Schilling = 100 Groschen, 1924-1938, 1945-2002
1 Euro = 100 Cents, 2002-

REPUBLIC

OESTERREICHISCHE NATIONALBANK

AUSTRIAN NATIONAL BANK

1956-65 ISSUES

		VG	VF	UNC
136	**20 Schilling** 2.7.1956. Brown on red-brown and multicolor underprint. Carl Auer Freiherr von Welsbach at right, arms at left. Village Maria Rain, church and Karawanken mountains on back.			
	a. Issued note.	.75	7.50	15.00
	s. Specimen.	—	—	50.00

		VG	VF	UNC
137	**50 Schilling** 2.7.1962 (1963). Purple on multicolor underprint. Richard Wettstein at right, arms at bottom center. Mauterndorf castle in Salzburg on back.			
	a. Issued note.	1.50	9.00	20.00
	s. Specimen.	—	—	50.00

138	100 Schilling	VG	VF	UNC
	1.7.1960 (1961). Dark green on multicolor underprint. Violin and music at lower left, Johann Strauss at right, arms at left. Schönbrunn Castle on back.			
	a. Issued note.	3.00	10.00	40.00
	s. Specimen.	—	—	50.00

139	500 Schilling	VG	VF	UNC
	1.7.1965 (1966). Red-brown on multicolor underprint. Josef Ressel at right. Steam powered screw propeller ship *Civetta* at left, arms at lower right on back.	20.00	50.00	120.
140	**1000 Schilling**			
	2.1.1961 (1962). Dark blue on multicolor underprint. Viktor Kaplan at right. Dam and Persenburg Castle, arms at right on back. 148 x 75mm.			
	a. Issued note. Rare.	—	—	—
	s. Specimen.	—	400.	800.

Note: #140 was in use for only 11 weeks.

141	1000 Schilling	VG	VF	UNC
	2.1.1961 (1962). Dark blue on multicolor underprint. Like #140 but with blue lined underprint. up to margin. 158 x 85mm.			
	a. Issued note.	35.00	90.00	185.
	s. Specimen. Overprint and perforated: *Muster.*	—	Unc	1500.

1966-70 Issues

142	20 Schilling	VG	VF	UNC
	2.7.1967 (1968). Brown on olive and lilac underprint. Carl Ritter von Ghega at right, arms at lower center. Semmering Railway bridge over the Semmering Pass (986 meters) on back.	1.00	2.50	4.50

143	50 Schilling	VG	VF	UNC
	2.1.1970 (1972). Purple on multicolor underprint. Ferdinand Raimund at right, arms at left. Burg Theater in Vienna at left center on back.			
	a. Issued note.	3.00	6.00	12.00
	s. Specimen. Overprint: *Muster.*	—	—	500.

144	50 Schilling	VG	VF	UNC
	2.1.1970 (1983). Like #143 but with ovpt. *2. AUFLAGE* (2nd issue) at lower left center.	3.00	6.00	12.00

145	100 Schilling	VG	VF	UNC
	2.1.1969 (1970). Dark green on multicolor underprint. Angelika Kauffmann at right. Large house on back.			
	a. Issued note.	FV	10.00	22.50
	s. Specimen. Overprint: *Muster.*	—	—	750.

146 **100 Schilling**

2.1.1969 (1981). Like #145 but with ovpt: *2 AUFLAGE* (2nd issue) at upper left.

	VG	VF	UNC
	FV	12.00	22.50

147 **1000 Schilling**

1.7.1966 (1970). Blue-violet on multicolor underprint. Bertha von Suttner at center right, arms at right. Leopoldskron Castle and Hohensalzburg Fortress on back.

	VG	VF	UNC
a. Issued note.	FV	90.00	150.
s. Specimen. Overprint: *Muster*.	—	—	1250.

1983-88 Issue

#148-153 Federal arms at upper l. Wmk: Federal arms and parallel vertical lines.

148 **20 Schilling**

1.10.1986 (1988). Dark brown and brown on multicolor underprint. Moritz Daffinger at right. Vienna's Albertina Museum at left center on back.

VG	VF	UNC
FV	FV	3.25

149 **50 Schilling**

2.1.1986 (1987). Purple and violet on multicolor underprint. Sigmund Freud at right. Vienna's *Josephinum* Medical School at left center on back.

VG	VF	UNC
FV	FV	7.00

150 **100 Schilling**

2.1.1984 (1985). Dark green, gray and dark brown on multicolor underprint. Eugen Böhm v. Bawerk at right. Wissenschaften Academy in Vienna at left center on back. 3 serial # varieties.

VG	VF	UNC
FV	FV	15.00

151 **500 Schilling**

1.7.1985 (1986). Dark brown, deep violet and orange-brown on multicolor underprint. Architect Otto Wagner at right. Post Office Savings Bank in Vienna at left center on back.

VG	VF	UNC
FV	FV	65.00

152 **1000 Schilling**

3.1.1983. Dark blue and purple on multicolor underprint. Erwin Schrödinger at right. Vienna University at left center on back.

VG	VF	UNC
FV	FV	135.

153 **5000 Schilling**

4.1.1988 (1989). Light brown and purple on multicolor underprint. Woflgang Amadeus Mozart at right, kinegram of Mozart's head at lower left. Vienna Opera House at center on back.

VG	VF	UNC
FV	FV	575.

NOTICE

Readers with unlisted dates, signature varieties, etc. are invited to submit photocopies of their notes to: Standard Catalog of World Paper Money, 700 East State St. Iola, WI 54990-0001, E-Mail: george.cuhaj@fwpubs.com.

1997 Issue

154	500 Schilling	VG	VF	UNC
	1.1.1997. Brown on multicolor underprint. Rosa Mayreder at left. Rosa and Karl Mayreder with group at right on back.	FV	FV	60.00

155	1000 Schilling	VG	VF	UNC
	1.1.1997. Blue on multicolor underprint. Karl Landsteiner at left. Landsteiner working in his laboratory in Licenter at right on back.	FV	FV	125.

Note: For later issues used in Austria, see European Union listings.

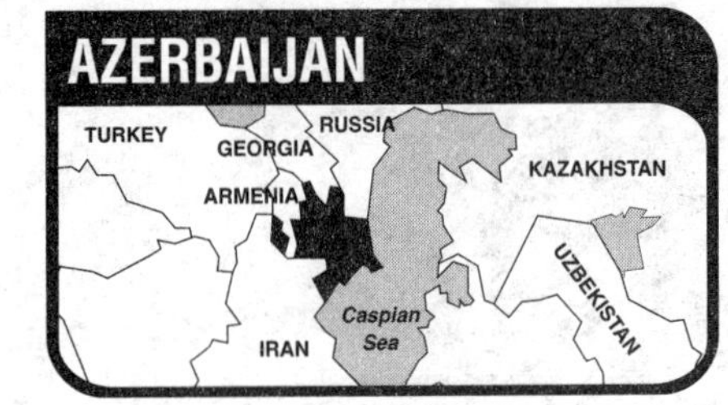

The Republic of Azerbaijan includes the Nakhichevan Autonomous Republic and Nagorno-Karabakh Autonomous Region (which was abolished in 1991). Situated in the eastern area of Transcaucasia, it is bordered in the west by Armenia, in the north by Georgia and the Russian Federation of Dagestan, to the east by the Caspian Sea and to the south by Iran. It has an area of 33,430 sq. mi. (86,600 sq. km.) and a population of 7.83 million. Capital: Baku. The area is rich in mineral deposits of aluminum, copper, iron, lead, salt and zinc, with oil as its leading industry. Agriculture and livestock follow in importance.

In ancient times home of Scythian tribes and known under the Romans as Albania and to the Arabs as Arran, the country of Azerbaijan formed at the time of its invasion by Seljuk Turks a prosperous state under Persian suzerainty. From the 16th century the country was a theatre of fighting and political rivalry between Turkey, Persia and later Russia. Baku was first annexed to Russia by Czar Peter I in 1723. After the Russian retreat in 1735, the whole of Azerbaijan north of the Aras River became a khanate under Persian control until 1813 when annexed by Czar Alexander I into the Russian empire.

Until the Russian Revolution of 1905 there was no political life in Azerbaijan. A Mussavat (Equality) party was formed in 1911. After the Russian Revolution of March 1917, the party started a campaign for independence, but Baku, the capital, with its mixed population, constituted an alien enclave in the country. While a national Azerbaijani government was established at Gandzha (Elizavetpol), a Communist-controlled council assumed power at Baku. The Gandzha government joined first, on Sept. 20, 1917, a Transcaucasian federal republic, but on May 28, 1918, proclaimed the independence of Azerbaijan. On June 4, 1918, at Batum, a peace treaty was signed with Turkey and a Turko-Azerbaijani force started an offensive against Baku, but it was occupied on Aug. 17, 1918 by 1,400 British troops coming by sea from Anzali, Persia. On Sept. 14 the British evacuated Baku, returning to Anzali, and three days later the Azerbaijan government, headed by Fath Ali Khan Khoysky, established itself at Baku.

After the collapse of the Ottoman empire the British returned to Baku, at first ignoring the Azerbaijan government. A general election with universal suffrage for the Azerbaijan constituent assembly took place on Dec. 7, 1918 and out of 120 members there were 84 Mussavat supporters; Ali Marden Topchibashev was elected speaker, and Nasib Usubekov formed a new government. On Jan. 15, 1920, the Allied powers recognized Azerbaijan de facto but on April 27 of the same year the Red army invaded the country and a Soviet Republic of Azerbaijan was proclaimed the next day.

The Azerbaijan Communist party held its first congress at Baku in Feb. 1920. From 1921 to 1925 its first secretary was a Russian, S.M. Kirov, who directed a mass deportation to Siberia of about 120,000 Azerbaijani "nationalist deviationists," among them the country's first two premiers. Later it became a member of the Transcaucasian Federation joining the U.S.S.R. on Dec. 30, 1922. It became a self-constituent republic in 1936.

In 1990 it adopted a declaration of republican sovereignty, and in Aug. 1991 declared itself formally independent; this was approved by a vote of referendum in Jan. 1992.

The Armed forces of Azerbaijan and the Armenian separatists of the Armenian ethnic enclave of Nagurno-Karabakh supported in all spheres by Armenia fought over the control of the enclave in 1992-94. A cease-fire was declared in May 1994 with Azerbaijan actually losing control over the territory. A Treaty of Friendship and Cooperation w/Russia was signed on 3 July 1997.

Republic

Azerbaycan Milli Banki

1992 ND Issue

In 1993, due to a cash crisis, bonds of the State Loan of Azerbaijan Republic were officially used as currency; however, they were not freely accepted in the local bazaars. The acceptance term of these bonds in the branches of the State Savings Bank was until 1 June 2000.

11	1 Manat	VG	VF	UNC
	ND (1992). Deep olive-green on multicolor underprint.	.10	.25	3.00

12	10 Manat	VG	VF	UNC
	ND (1992). Deep brown-violet on multicolor underprint.	.20	.50	7.50

		VG	VF	UNC
13	**250 Manat** ND (1992). Deep blue-gray on multicolor underprint.			
	a. Original issue with fraction prefix.	1.50	10.00	50.00
	b. Reissue with 2 prefix letters.	.25	.75	2.50

AZERBAYCAN REPUBLIC STATE LOAN BONDS

1993 ISSUE

#13A-13C printer: Goznak.

		VG	VF	UNC
13A	**250 Manat** 1993. Olive-green on multicolor underprint.	—	—	—
13B	**500 Manat** 1993. Pinkish-red on multicolor underprint.	—	—	—
13C	**1000 Manat** 1993. Steel-blue on multicolor underprint.	—	—	—

AZERBAYCAN MILLI BANKI (RESUMED)

1993 ND; 1994-95 ISSUE

#14-20 ornate "value" backs. Wmk: 3 flames.

#14-18 different view Maiden Tower ruins at ctr.

#13b, 17b, 18b, 19b, 20b replacement notes: Serial # prefix *BZ*.

		VG	VF	UNC
14	**1 Manat** ND (1993). Deep blue on tan, dull orange and green underprint.	FV	FV	3.00

		VG	VF	UNC
15	**5 Manat** ND (1993). Deep brown on lilac and multicolor underprint.	FV	FV	5.00

		VG	VF	UNC
16	**10 Manat** ND (1993). Deep grayish blue-green on pale blue and multicolor underprint.	FV	FV	7.00

		VG	VF	UNC
17	**50 Manat** ND (1993). Red on ochre and multicolor underprint.			
	a. Original issue with fraction prefix.	FV	FV	10.00
	b. Reissue with 2 prefix letters.	FV	FV	1.00

		VG	VF	UNC
18	**100 Manat** ND (1993). Red-violet on pale blue and multicolor underprint.			
	a. Original issue with fraction prefix.	FV	FV	12.50
	b. Reissue with 2 prefix letters.	FV	FV	1.75

		VG	VF	UNC
19	**500 Manat** ND (1993). Deep brown on pale blue, pink and multicolor underprint. Portrait N. Gencevi at right.			
	a. Original issue with fraction prefix.	FV	FV	15.00
	b. Reissue with 2 prefix letters.	FV	FV	3.00

		VG	VF	UNC
20	**1000 Manat** ND (1993). Dark brown and blue on pink and multicolor underprint. M. E. Resulzado at right.			
	a. Original issue with fraction prefix.	FV	FV	9.00
	b. Reissue with 2 prefix letters.	FV	FV	3.00

		VG	VF	UNC
21	**10,000 Manat**			
	1994. Dull dark brown and pale violet on multicolor underprint. Shirvansha's Palace at center right. Watermark: AMB repeated.			
	a. Security thread.	5.00	20.00	60.00
	b. Segmented foil over security thread.	FV	FV	10.00

		VG	VF	UNC
22	**50,000 Manat**	FV	FV	40.00
	1995. Blue-green and light brown on multicolor underprint. Mausoleum in Nachziban at center right. Carpet design at left on back. Segmented foil over security thread.			

2001 Issue

		VG	VF	UNC
23	**1000 Manat**	FV	FV	4.00
	2001. Slate blue on light blue and multicolor underprint. Oil rigs and pumps at center right. Value on back.			

BAHAMAS

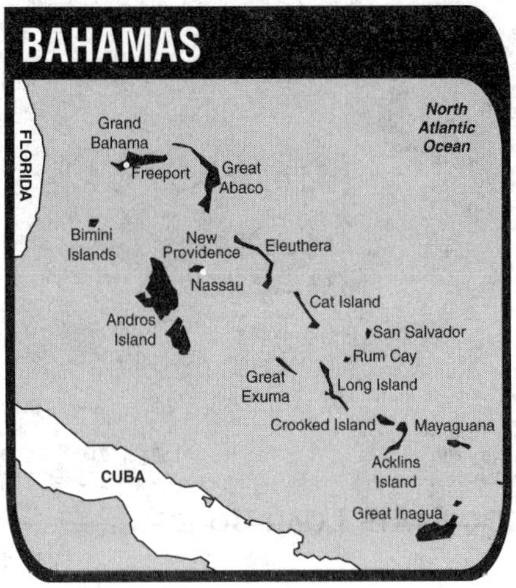

The Commonwealth of The Bahamas is an archipelago of about 3,000 islands, cays and rocks located in the Atlantic Ocean east of Florida and north of Cuba. The total land area of the 800-mile (1.287 km.) long chain of islands is 5,380 sq. mi. (13,935 sq. km.). They have a population of 302,000. Capital: Nassau. The Bahamas imports most of their food and manufactured products and exports cement, refined oil, pulpwood and lobsters. Tourism is the principal industry.

The Bahamas were discovered by Columbus in October, 1492, but Spain made no attempt to settle them. British influence began in 1626 when Charles I granted them to the lord proprietors of Carolina. They continued under British proprietors until 1717, when the civil and military governments were surrendered to the King and the islands designated a British Crown Colony. The Bahamas obtained complete internal self-government under the constitution of Jan. 7, 1964. Full independence was achieved on July 10, 1973. The Bahamas is a member of the Commonwealth of Nations. Elizabeth II is Head of State, as Queen of Bahamas.

RULERS:
British

MONETARY SYSTEM:
1 Shilling = 12 Pence
1 Pound = 20 Shillings to 1966
1 Dollar = 100 Cents 1966-

Commonwealth

Government of the Bahamas

1965 Currency Note Act

#17-25 Qn. Elizabeth II at l. Sign. varieties. Arms at r. on back. Wmk: Shellfish. Printer: TDLR. Replacement notes: Serial # prefix *Z*.

		VG	VF	UNC
17	**1/2 Dollar**	2.00	5.00	17.50
	L.1965. Purple on multicolor underprint. Straw market on back.			

		VG	VF	UNC
18	**1 Dollar**			
	L.1965. Green on multicolor underprint. Sea garden on back.			
	a. 2 signature	3.25	6.50	55.00
	b. 3 signature	3.25	9.00	70.00
	s. As b. Specimen.	—	—	—
19	**3 Dollars**	VG	VF	UNC
	L.1965. Red on multicolor underprint. Paradise Beach on back.			
	a. Signature Sands and Higgs.	4.00	7.50	47.50
	b. Signature Francis and Higgs. Specimen.	—	—	300.

		VG	VF	UNC
20	**5 Dollars**			
	L.1965. Green on multicolor underprint. Government House on back.			
	a. Issued note.	12.00	30.00	125.
	s. Specimen.	—	—	—
21	**5 Dollars**			
	L.1965. Orange on multicolor underprint. Like #20.			
	a. 2 signature	15.00	45.00	365.
	b. 3 signature	30.00	275.	825.

		VG	VF	UNC
22	**10 Dollars**			
	L.1965. Dk. blue on multicolor underprint. Flamingos on back.			
	a. 2 signature	20.00	75.00	700.
	b. 3 signature	40.00	375.	1275.
23	**20 Dollars**			
	L.1965. Dk. brown on multicolor underprint. Surrey on back.			
	a. 2 signature	60.00	250.	1000.
	b. 3 signature	200.	400.	1750.
	s. Specimen. 3 signature	—	—	100.
24	**50 Dollars**			
	L.1965. Brown on multicolor underprint. Produce market on back.			
	a. Issued note.	100.	300.	1650.
	s. Specimen. 3 signature	—	—	200.
25	**100 Dollars**			
	L.1965. Blue on multicolor underprint. Deep sea fishing on back.			
	a. 2 signature	175.	600.	2750.
	b. 3 signature	450.	—	—
	s. Specimen. 3 signature	—	—	300.

BAHAMAS MONETARY AUTHORITY

1968 MONETARY AUTHORITY ACT

#26-33 Qn. Elizabeth II at l. Back designs like #17-25. Wmk: Shellfish. Printer: TDLR. Replacement notes: Serial # prefix *Z*.

		VG	VF	UNC
26	**1/2 Dollar**			
	L.1968. Purple on multicolor underprint. Back like #17.			
	a. Issued note.	.65	1.50	12.50
	s. Specimen.	—	—	40.00

		VG	VF	UNC
27	**1 Dollar**			
	L.1968. Green on multicolor underprint. Back like #18.			
	a. Issued note.	1.25	2.25	30.00
	s. Specimen.	—	—	40.00

		VG	VF	UNC
28	**3 Dollars**			
	L.1968. Red on multicolor underprint. Back like #19.			
	a. Issued note.	3.50	7.50	45.00
	s. Specimen.	—	—	40.00

		VG	VF	UNC
29	**5 Dollars**			
	L.1968. Orange on multicolor underprint. Back like #20.			
	a. Issued note.	7.00	50.00	200.
	s. Specimen.	—	—	70.00
30	**10 Dollars**			
	L.1968. Dk. blue on multicolor underprint. Back like #22.			
	a. Issued note.	25.00	150.	750.
	s. Specimen.	—	—	80.00
31	**20 Dollars**			
	L.1968. Dk. brown on multicolor underprint. Back like #23.			
	a. Issued note.	60.00	300.	1350.
	s. Specimen.	—	—	140.
32	**50 Dollars**			
	L.1968. Brown on multicolor underprint. Back like #24.			
	a. Issued note.	150.	450.	2000.
	s. Specimen.	—	—	250.
33	**100 Dollars**			
	L.1968. Blue on multicolor underprint. Back like #25.			
	a. Issued note.	300.	700.	3250.
	s. Specimen.	—	—	375.

#34 not assigned.

NOTICE

Readers with unlisted dates, signature varieties, etc. are invited to submit photocopies of their notes to: Standard Catalog of World Paper Money, 700 East State St. Iola, WI 54990-0001, E-Mail: george.cuhaj@fwpubs.com.

CENTRAL BANK OF THE BAHAMAS

1974 CENTRAL BANK ACT

#35-41 Qn. Elizabeth II at l. Back designs like #18-25 and #27-33. Wmk: Shellfish. Printer: TDLR. Replacement notes: Serial # prefix *Z*.

		VG	VF	UNC
35	**1 Dollar**			
	L.1974. Dk. blue-green on multicolor underprint. Back like #18.			
	a. Signature T. B. Donaldson.	1.25	2.00	17.50
	b. Signature W. C. Allen.	1.50	7.50	30.00

#36 not assigned.

		VG	VF	UNC
37	**5 Dollars**			
	L.1974. Orange on multicolor underprint. Back like #20.			
	a. Signature T. B. Donaldson.	6.50	18.50	90.00
	b. Signature W. C. Allen.	10.00	50.00	225.

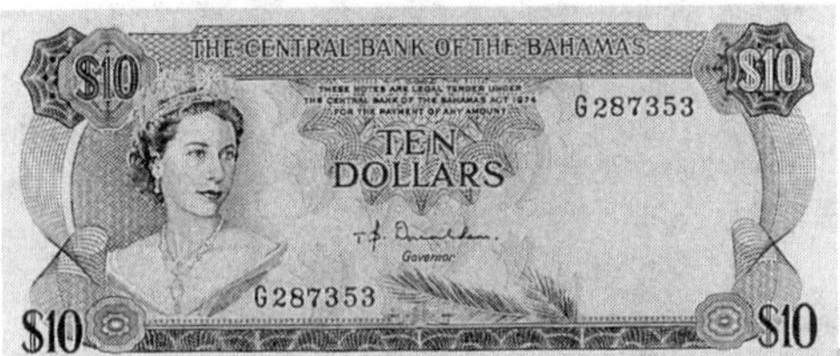

		VG	VF	UNC
38	**10 Dollars**			
	L.1974. Dk. blue on multicolor underprint. Back like #22.			
	a. Signature T. B. Donaldson.	11.00	40.00	350.
	b. Signature W. C. Allen.	20.00	150.	550.

		VG	VF	UNC
39	**20 Dollars**			
	L.1974. Dk. brown on multicolor underprint. Back like #23.			
	a. Signature T. B. Donaldson.	27.50	85.00	450.
	b. Signature W. C. Allen.	42.50	185.	750.
40	**50 Dollars**			
	L.1974. Brown on multicolor underprint. Back like #24.			
	a. Signature T. B. Donaldson.	75.00	250.	1200.
	b. Signature W. C. Allen.	85.00	350.	1750.
41	**100 Dollars**			
	L.1974. Blue on multicolor underprint. Back like #25.			
	a. Signature T. B. Donaldson.	135.	400.	2000.
	b. Signature W. C. Allen.	200.	600.	3000.

1974 CENTRAL BANK ACT; 1984 ND ISSUE

#42-49 map at l., mature portr. Qn. Elizabeth II at ctr. r. Arms at r. on back. Wmk: Sailing ship. Printer: TDLR. Replacement notes: Serial # prefix *Z*.

		VG	VF	UNC
42	**1/2 Dollar**			
	L.1974 (1984). Green on multicolor underprint. Baskets at left. Sister Sarah in Nassau market on back. Signature W. C. Allen.			
	a. Issued note.	FV	FV	4.50
	s. Specimen.	—	—	—

		VG	VF	UNC
43	**1 Dollar**			
	L.1974 (1984). Deep green on multicolor underprint. Fish at left. Royal Bahamas Police band at center on back.			
	a. Signature W. C. Allen.	FV	FV	8.00
	b. Signature F. H. Smith. 2 horizontal serial #.	FV	FV	9.00
44	**3 Dollars**			
	L.1974 (1984). Red-violet on multicolor underprint. Paradise Beach at left. Family Island sailing regatta on back. Signature W. C. Allen.	FV	FV	15.00

45	5 Dollars	VG	VF	UNC
	L.1974 (1984). Orange on multicolor underprint. Statue at left. Local dancers Junkanoo at center.			
	a. Signature W. C. Allen.	FV	9.50	75.00
	b. Signature F. H. Smith. 2 horizontal serial #.	FV	9.00	60.00

46	10 Dollars	VG	VF	UNC
	L.1974 (1984). Pale blue on multicolor underprint. Two flamingos at left. Lighthouse and Abaco Settlement on back.			
	a. Signature W. C. Allen.	FV	15.00	115.
	b. Signature F. H. Smith. 2 horizontal serial #.	FV	40.00	180.

47	20 Dollars	VG	VF	UNC
	L.1974 (1984). Red and black on multicolor underprint. Horse and carriage at left. Nassau harbor on back.			
	a. Signature W. C. Allen.	FV	30.00	190.
	b. Signature F. H. Smith. 2 horizontal serial #.	FV	22.50	100.

48	50 Dollars	VG	VF	UNC
	L.1974 (1984). Purple, orange and green on multicolor underprint. Lighthouse at left. Central Bank on back.			
	a. Signature W. C. Allen.	65.00	150.	515.
	b. Signature F. H. Smith. 2 horizontal serial #.	100.	300.	1325.

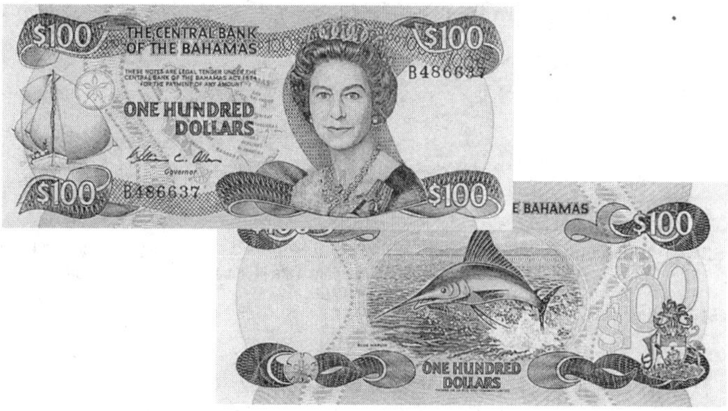

49	100 Dollars	VG	VF	UNC
	L.1974 (1984). Purple, deep blue and red-violet on multicolor underprint. Sailboat at left. Blue marlin on back. Signature W. C. Allen.	FV	200.	800.

1992 Commemorative Issue

#50, Quincentennial of First Landfall by Christopher Columbus

50	1 Dollar	VG	VF	UNC
	ND (1992). Dark blue and deep violet on multicolor underprint. Commercial seal at left, bust of Christopher Columbus right with compass face behind. Flamingos, rose-throated parrots, lizard, islands, ships across back with arms at lower right. Printer: CBNC.			
	a. Issued note.	FV	FV	7.50
	s. Specimen.	—	—	—

1974 Central Bank Act; 1992-95 ND Issue

#51-56 arms at r. on back. Wmk: Caravel sailing ship. Sign. F.H. Smith.

51	1 Dollar	VG	VF	UNC
	L.1974 (1992). Deep green on multicolor underprint. Like #43b but with serial # vertical and horizontal. Printer: BABN.	FV	FV	6.50

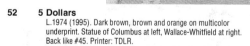

52	5 Dollars	VG	VF	UNC
	L.1974 (1995). Dark brown, brown and orange on multicolor underprint. Statue of Columbus at left, Wallace-Whitfield at right. Back like #45. Printer: TDLR.	FV	FV	25.00

		VG	VF	UNC
53	**10 Dollars**			
	L.1974 (1992). Pale blue on multicolor underprint. Like #46b but with serial # vertical and horizontal. Printer: BABN.	FV	20.00	100.

#54-56 printer: TDLR.

		VG	VF	UNC
54	**20 Dollars**			
	L.1974 (1993). Black and red on multicolor underprint. Sir Milo B. Butler at right, horse drawn surrey at left. Aerial view of ships in Nassau's harbor at center.	FV	25.00	80.00

		VG	VF	UNC
55	**50 Dollars**			
	L.1974 (1992). Brown, blue-green and orange on multicolor underprint. Like #48b but with serial # vertical and horizontal.	FV	70.00	230.
56	**100 Dollars**			
	L.1974 (1992). Purple, deep blue and red-violet on multicolor underprint. Like #49 but with serial # vertical and horizontal.	FV	125.	430.

1974 Central Bank Act; 1996 Series

#57, 59, 61, and 62 mature bust of Qn. Elizabeth II. Ascending size serial # at lower l. Arms at r. on back. Sign. F. H. Smith.

		VG	VF	UNC
57	**1 Dollar**			
	1996. Deep green on multicolor underprint. Like #51. Printer: BABN.	FV	FV	6.00

#58 *Deleted*. See #63.

		VG	VF	UNC
59	**10 Dollars**			
	1996. Deep blue-green, green and violet on multicolor underprint. Like #53. Printer: TDLR.	FV	FV	42.50

#60 not assigned.

		VG	VF	UNC
61	**50 Dollars**			
	1996. Red-brown and deep green on multicolor underprint. Like #55. Printer: TDLR.	FV	FV	160.

Note: The following notes were stolen and are not redeemable. Serial # G101,001-103,000; G104,001-G105,000; G108,001-G109,000.

		VG	VF	UNC
62	**100 Dollars**			
	1996. Purple, deep blue and violet on multicolor underprint. Like #56. Printer: BABN.	FV	FV	245.

Note: The following notes were stolen and are not redeemable. Serial # G541,001-G548,000.

1974 Central Bank Act; 1997; 2000; 2001 Series

Serial #'s vertical and ascending size horizontal.

		VG	VF	UNC
63	**5 Dollars**			
	1997. Dark brown, brown and orange on multicolor underprint. Like #52. Printer: TDLR. 2 signature varieties.			
	a. 1997. *GOVERNOR* title in orange.	FV	FV	22.50
	b. 2001. *GOVERNOR* in black.	FV	FV	17.50

		VG	VF	UNC
64	**10 Dollars** 2000. Deep blue-green, green and violet on multicolor underprint. Sir Stafford Sands and OVD at right, pair of flamingos at left.	FV	FV	35.00
65	**20 Dollars** 1997; Multicolor. Sir Milo B. Butler at right. Aerial view of ships in Nassau's Harbor at center on back. 1997. 2 signature varieties.	FV	FV	65.00
65A	**20 Dollars** 2000; Multicolor. As 42 but with modified security features.			
	a. Issued note.	FV	FV	57.50
	r. Replacement	FV	FV	160.

		VG	VF	UNC
66	**50 Dollars** 2000. Sir Roland Symonette and OVD at right, lighthouse at left.	FV	FV	120.

		VG	VF	UNC
67	**100 Dollars** 2000. Multicolor. Queen Elizabeth II, OVD at right.	FV	FV	210.

2000 Central Bank Act; 2001 Series

		VG	VF	UNC
68	**1/2 Dollar** 2001. Slate blue and green on tan and multicolor underprint. Queen Elizabeth II at right, baskets at left. Sister Sarah in Nassau market on back.	FV	FV	3.00

		VG	VF	UNC
69	**1 Dollar** 2001. Green, brown and multicolor. Sir. Lynden O. Pindling at right. Police band on back. Printer: TDLR.	FV	FV	5.00

2000 Central Bank Act; 2002 Series

		VG	VF	UNC
70	**1 Dollar** 2002. Deep green on multicolor underprint. Like #43. Segemnted foil security strip added. Printer TDLR.			
71	**3 Dollars** 2002. Multicolor.	FV	FV	10.00

2000 Central Bank Act; 2006 Series

#72-75 is the new CRISP Series.

		VG	VF	UNC
72	**5 Dollars** 2006. Multicolor. Wallace-Whitfield at r.	FV	FV	15.00
73	**10 Dollars** 2005. Multicolor. Sit. Stafford Sands at r. Printer: TDLR	FV	FV	32.50
74	**20 Dollars** 2006. Multicolor. Sir Milo B. Butler at r. Printer: FC-O.	FV	FV	50.00
75	**50 Dollars** 2006. Multicolor. Sir Roland T. Symonette at r. Printer: FC-O.	FV	FV	110.

Collector Series

Bahamas Government

1965 Issue

		Issue	Mkt.	Value
CS1	**1/2-100 Dollars** L.1965. #17-26 ovpt: SPECIMEN. (100 sets).		—	2500.—

Bahamas Monetary Authority

1968 Issues

		Issue	Mkt.	Value
CS2	**1/2-100 Dollars** L.1968. #26-33 ovpt: SPECIMEN.	—	—	975.—
CS3	**1/2-100 Dollars** L.1968. #26-33 ovpt: SPECIMEN, punched hole cancelled.	—	—	450.—

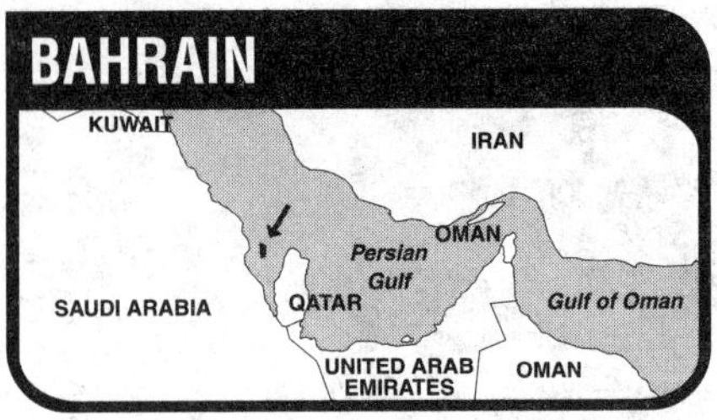

The State of Bahrain, a group of islands in the Persian Gulf off Saudi Arabia, has an area of 258 sq. mi. (622 sq. km.) and a population of 618,000. Capital: Manama. Prior to the depression of the 1930s, the economy was d on pearl fishing. Petroleum and aluminum industries and transit trade are the vital factors in the economy today.

The Portuguese occupied the islands in 1507 but were driven out in 1602 by Arab subjects of Persia. They in turn were ejected by Arabs of the Ataiba tribe from the Arabian mainland who have maintained possession up to the present time. The ruling sheikh of Bahrain entered into relations with Great Britain in 1805 and concluded a binding treaty of protection in 1861. In 1968 Great Britain decided to terminate treaty relations with the Persian Gulf sheikhdoms. Unable to agree on terms of union with the other sheikhdoms, Bahrain decided to seek independence as a separate entity and became fully independent on August 15, 1971.

A new constitution establishing Bahrain as a kingdom was published on December 14, 2002.

RULERS:

Isa Bin Sulman al-Khalifa, 1961-

MONETARY SYSTEM:

1 Dinar = 1000 Fils

KINGDOM

BAHRAIN CURRENCY BOARD

AUTHORIZATION 6/1964

#1-6 dhow at l., arms at r. Wmk: Falcon's head. For specimen notes with a maltese cross serial # prefix, see CS1 at the end of the country listing.

		VG	VF	UNC
1	**100 Fils** L.1964. Ochre on multicolor underprint. Back green and orange; palm trees at center.			
	a. Issued note.	FV	2.00	10.00
	s. Specimen.	—	—	35.00

		VG	VF	UNC
2	**1/4 Dinar** L.1964. Brown on multicolor underprint. Oil derricks on back.			
	a. Issued note.	FV	3.00	12.00
	s. Specimen.	—	—	35.00

		VG	VF	UNC
3	**1/2 Dinar** L.1964. Purple on multicolor underprint. Ships at the Mina Sulman Jetty on back.			
	a. Issued note.	FV	4.00	15.00
	s. Specimen.	—	—	40.00

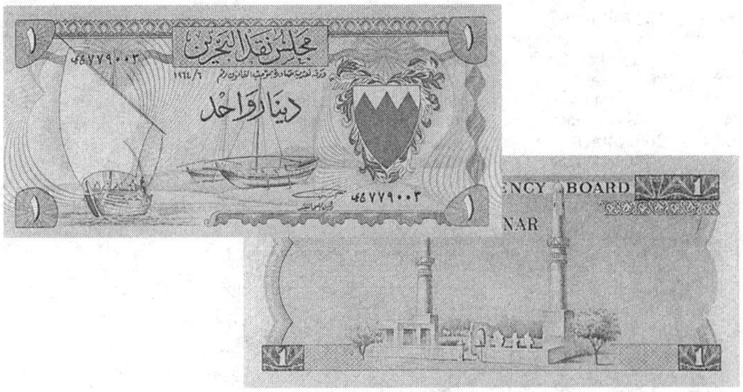

		VG	VF	UNC
4	**1 Dinar** L.1964. Brownish red on multicolor underprint. Ruins of the Suq al-Khamis mosque, dominated by two minarets, on back.			
	a. Issued note.	FV	6.00	18.00
	s. Specimen.	—	—	40.00

		VG	VF	UNC
5	**5 Dinars** L.1964. Blue-black on multicolor underprint. Two pearling dhows on back.			
	a. Issued note.	FV	75.00	300.
	s. Specimen.	—	—	200.

		VG	VF	UNC
6	**10 Dinars** L.1964. Green on multicolor underprint. Aerial view of the town of Isa on back.			
	a. Issued note.	FV	60.00	150.
	s. Specimen.	—	—	150.

BAHRAIN MONETARY AGENCY

AUTHORIZATION 23/1973

#7-11 map at l., dhow at ctr., arms at r. Wmk: Falcon's head.

7 **1/2 Dinar**

L.1973. Brown on multicolor underprint. Cast copper head of bull at lower left. Smelting works of Aluminium Bahrain at left on back.

VG	VF	UNC
FV	4.00	7.00

8 **1 Dinar**

L.1973. Red on multicolor underprint. Minaret of the Manama Mosque at left. Headquarters of Bahrain Monetary Agency at left on back.

VG	VF	UNC
FV	4.00	8.00

8A **5 Dinars**

L.1973. Dark blue on multicolor underprint. Minaret of the Suq al-Khamis mosque at left. Pearling dhows at left on back.

VG	VF	UNC
FV	14.00	45.00

9 **10 Dinars**

L.1973. Green on multicolor underprint. Wind tower at left. Dry dock at left on back.

	VG	VF	UNC
a. 2 horizontal serial #.	FV	35.00	65.00
b. Serial # vertical and horizontal.	FV	40.00	65.00

10 **20 Dinars**

L.1973. Reddish-brown on multicolor underprint. Minaret of the al-Fadhel mosque at left. Government House at left on back.

	VG	VF	UNC
a. Issued note.	FV	75.00	175.
s. Specimen.	—	—	—

11 **20 Dinars**

L.1973. Face like #10, but with symbol changed at right of map. Silvering added at lower left denomination. Back has open frame and symbol around watermark area. Also various color differences.

	VG	VF	UNC
a. 2 horizontal serial #.	FV	60.00	110.
b. Serial # vertical and horizontal.	FV	65.00	125.

AUTHORIZATION 23/1973; 1993 ND ISSUE

#12-16 arms at ctr., outline map at l. Wmk: Antelope's head.

12 **1/2 Dinar**

L.1973 (1986). Dark brown and violet on violet on multicolor underprint. Red shield at center Man weaving at right. Back brown and violet on multicolor underprint. "Aluminum Bahrain" facility at left center.

VG	VF	UNC
FV	1.50	4.00

13 **1 Dinar**

L.1973 (1993). Violet and red-orange on multicolor underprint. Ancient Dilmun seal at right. Bahrain Monetary Agency building at left center on back. Narrow security thread.

VG	VF	UNC
FV	4.00	9.00

		VG	VF	UNC
14	**5 Dinars** L.1973 (1993). Dark blue and deep blue-green on multicolor underprint. Riffa Fortress at right. Bahrain International Airport at left center on back.	FV	14.00	55.00

		VG	VF	UNC
15	**10 Dinars** L.1973 (1993). Deep olive-green and green on multicolor underprint. Dhow at right. Aerial view of King Fahad Causeway at left center on back.	FV	45.00	80.00

		VG	VF	UNC
16	**20 Dinars** L.1973 (1993). Purple and violet multicolor underprint. Bab al-Bahrain gate at right. Ahmed al-Fateh Islamic Center at left center on back.	VF	65.00	150.

Note: A second printing was ordered using a false authorization. These are easily distinguished by a space between the 2 Arabic letters in the serial # prefix and are not redeemable. Collector value is approximately $10.00.

Authorization 23/1973; 1996 ND Issue

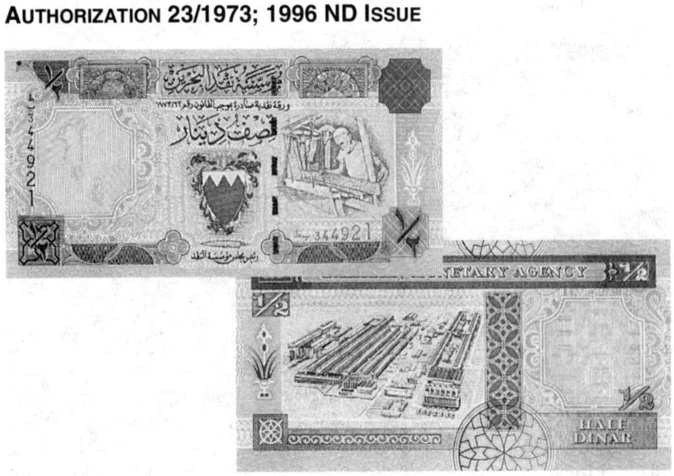

		VG	VF	UNC
17	**1/2 Dinar** L.1973 (1996). Deep brown, violet and brown with deep brown shield at center Like #12. Narrow security thread.	FV	FV	5.00

Authorization 23/1973; 1998 ND Issue

#18-20 arms at lower ctr., wide security thread.

#20-23 with hologram at lower l.

		VG	VF	UNC
18	**1/2 Dinar** L.1973 (1998). Similar to #17.			
	a. With microprinting.	FV	FV	5.00
	b. Without microprinting.	FV	FV	3.50
19	**1 Dinar** L.1973 1998. Similar to #13.			
	a. With *BMA* microprinting on security thread.	FV	FV	9.00
	b. Without microprinting on security thread.	FV	FV	6.00

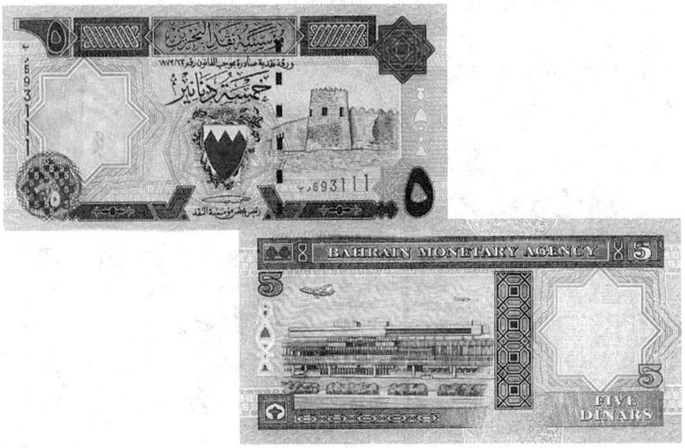

		VG	VF	UNC
20	**5 Dinars** L.1973 (1998). Blue on multicolor underprint. Like #14.			
	a. With *BMA* microprinting on security thread.	FV	40.00	60.00
	b. Without microprinting on security thread.	FV	FV	35.00

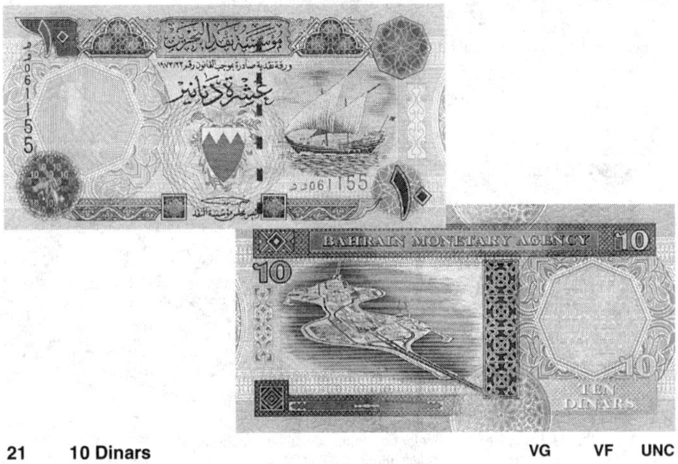

		VG	VF	UNC
21	**10 Dinars** L.1973 (1998). Green on multicolor underprint. Like #15.			
	a. With *BMA* microprinting on security thread.	FV	60.00	125.
	b. Without microprinting on security thread.	FV	FV	50.00

		VG	VF	UNC
22	**20 Dinars** L.1973 (1998). Purple on multicolor underprint. Like #16 but with hologram and wide micro-printed security thread.	50.00	200.	400.
23	**20 Dinars** L. 1973 (1998). Orange and black on multicolor underprint. Like #16.	FV	75.00	150.

AUTHORIZATION 23/1973; 2001 ND ISSUE

		VG	VF	UNC
24	**20 Dinars** ND (2001). Orange on multicolor underprint. Shaikh Hamad bin Issa al Khalifa, King of Bahrain at right.	FV	FV	100.

2001 ND SECOND ISSUE

		VG	VF	UNC
25	**5 Dinars** ND (2002). Blue on multicolor underprint. Hologram added to #20.	FV	FV	30.00

COLLECTOR SERIES

BAHRAIN MONETARY AGENCY

AUTHORIZATION 23/1973

#7-11 map at l., dhow at ctr., arms at r. Wmk: Falcon's head.

		Issue	Mkt.	Value
CS1	**100 Fils - 20 Dinars** ND (1978). #1-6 and 10 with ovpt: *SPECIMEN* and Maltese cross serial # prefix.	—	—	80.00

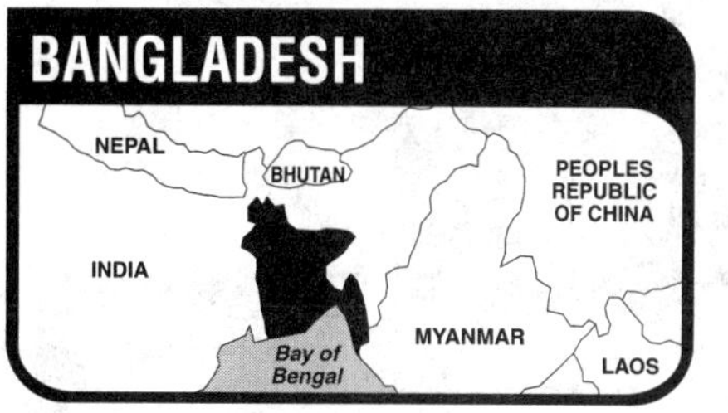

The Peoples Republic of Bangladesh (formerly East Pakistan), a parliamentary democracy located on the Bay of Bengal bordered by India and Burma, has an area of 55,598 sq. mi. (143,998 sq. km.) and a population of 128.31 million. Capital: Dhaka (Dacca). The economy is predominantly agricultural. Jute products and tea are exported.

British rule over the vast Indian sub-continent ended in 1947 when British India attained independence and was partitioned into the two successor states of India and Pakistan. Pakistan consisted of East and West Pakistan, two areas united by the Moslem religion but separated by culture and 1,000 miles of Indian territory. Restive under the de facto rule of the militant but fewer West Pakistanis, the East Pakistanis unsuccessfully demanded greater economic benefits and political reforms. The inability of the leaders of East and West Pakistan to resolve a political breakdown occasioned by the East Pakistan success in the general elections of 1970 precipitated massive civil disobedience in East Pakistan which West Pakistan sought to suppress militarily. East Pakistan seceded from Pakistan, March 26, 1971, and with the support of India declared an independent Peoples Republic of Bangladesh led by Mujibur Rahman who was later assassinated on Aug. 15, 1975. Bangladesh is a member of the Commonwealth of Nations. The president is the Head of State and of Government.

MONETARY SYSTEM:

1 Rupee = 100 Paise to 1972
1 Taka = 100 Paisas 1972-

REPUBLIC

PEOPLES REPUBLIC OF BANGLADESH

1971 ND PROVISIONAL ISSUE

#1-3 w/*BANGLADESH* ovpt. in English or Bengali on Pakistan notes. The Bangladesh Bank never officially issued any Pakistan notes w/ovpt. These are considered locally issued by some authorities.

		VG	VF	UNC
1	**1 Rupee** ND (1971). Blue. Purple overprint *BANGLADESH* on Pakistan #9. Four different overprints are documented.	7.50	30.00	90.00

		VG	VF	UNC
1A	**1 Rupee** ND (1971). Blue. Purple Bengali overprint on Pakistan #9. Two different overprints are documented.	7.50	30.00	90.00

		VG	VF	UNC
2	**5 Rupees** ND (1971). Brown-violet. Purple Bengali overprint on Pakistan #15.	10.00	32.50	100.
2A	**5 Rupees** ND (1971). English overprint on Pakistan #15.	10.00	32.50	100.

		VG	VF	UNC
3	**10 Rupees** ND (1971). Brown. Purple Bengali overprint on Pakistan #13.	10.00	35.00	120.
3A	**5 Rupees** ND (1971). English overprint on Pakistan #18.	20.00	75.00	175.

		VG	VF	UNC
3B	**10 Rupees** ND (1971). English overprint on Pakistan #19.	25.00	125.	225.

1972-89 ND Issues

		VG	VF	UNC
4	**1 Taka** ND (1972). Brown on orange and blue underprint. Map of Bangladesh at left.	.20	.75	6.00

		VG	VF	UNC
5	**1 Taka** ND (1973). Purple and ochre. Hand holding rice plants at left. Arms at right on back.			
	a. With watermark: Tiger's head.	.20	.75	5.00
	b. Without watermark. (2 signature varieties).	.20	.75	5.00

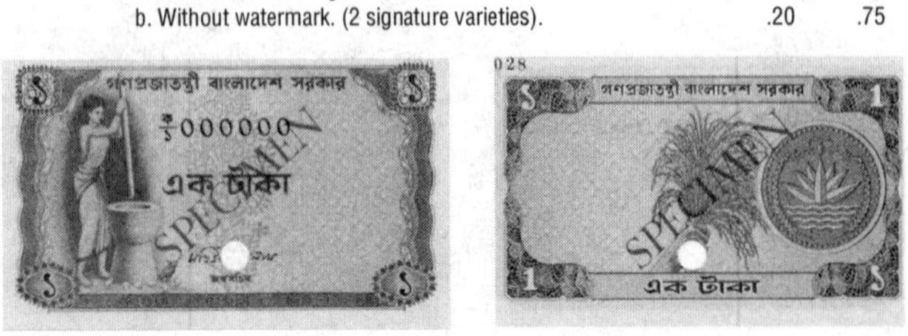

		VG	VF	UNC
6	**1 Taka** ND (1973). Purple on ochre and blue underprint. Woman preparing grain at left. Hand holding rice plants at center, arms at right on back. Watermark: Tiger's head.			
	a. Issued note.	.20	.60	7.00
	s. Specimen.	—	—	100.

		VG	VF	UNC
6A	**1 Taka** ND (1979). Purple on multicolor underprint. Arms at right. Deer at left center on back. Watermark: Tiger's head.	.10	.50	2.00

		VG	VF	UNC
6B	**1 Taka** ND (1982). Purple on multicolor underprint. Similar to #6A but no printing on watermark area at left. Modified tiger watermark.			
	a. Signature title in Bengali: *FINANCE SECRETARY*. Solid security thread. Six Signature varieties.	.05	.10	.75
	b. Signature title in Bengali: *PRINCIPAL FINANCE SECRETARY*. Solid security thread. 1 Signature variety.	.05	.10	.50
	c. Signature title in Bengali: *FINANCE SECRETARY*. Micro-printed security thread. One Signature variety.	.05	.10	.50

		VG	VF	UNC
6C	**2 Taka** ND (1988). Gray-green on orange and green underprint. Monument at right. Dhyal or Magpie-robin at left on back. 6 signature varieties. Watermark: Tiger's head.			
	a. Solid security thread. Four signature varieties.	FV	FV	.75
	b. Security thread reads: *BANGLADESH BANK* in Bengali.	FV	FV	.50
	c. Security thread reads: *GOVERNMENT OF BANGLADESH* in Bengali. One signature	FV	FV	.50
	d. As c, but smaller watermark.	FV	FV	.50
	e. Dated 2002 on back.	FV	FV	.50
	f. Dated 2003 on back.	FV	FV	.50
	g. Dates 2004 on back.	FV	FV	.50

Bangladesh Bank

1972 ND Issue

#7-9 map of Bangladesh at l., portr. Mujibur Rahman at r.

		VG	VF	UNC
7	**5 Taka** ND (1972). Purple on multicolor underprint.	.50	3.00	17.50

		VG	VF	UNC
8	**10 Taka** ND (1972). Blue on multicolor underprint.	1.00	5.00	27.50

		VG	VF	UNC
9	**100 Taka** ND (1972). Green on multicolor underprint.	2.00	8.00	75.00

1973 ND Issue

#10-12 Mujibur Rahman at l. Wmk: Tiger's head.

		VG	VF	UNC
10	**5 Taka** ND (1972). Red on multicolor underprint. Lotus plants at center right on back.			
	a. Issued note.	.25	1.50	10.00
	s. Specimen.	—	—	—

		VG	VF	UNC
11	**10 Taka** ND (1972). Green on multicolor underprint. River scene on back.			
	a. Serial # in Western numerals.	.50	4.00	17.50
	b. Serial # in Bengali numerals.	2.00	7.50	25.00
	s. Specimen.	—	—	—

		VG	VF	UNC
12	**100 Taka** ND (1972). Brown on multicolor underprint. River scene on back.			
	a. Serial # in western numerals.	.75	3.00	17.50
	b. Serial # in Bengali numerals.	25.00	50.00	100.

1974 ND Issue

#13-14 Mujibur Rahman at r. Wmk: Tiger's head.

		VG	VF	UNC
13	**5 Taka** ND (1973). Red on multicolor underprint. Aerial view of factory on back. 2 signature varieties.			
	a. Issued note.	.25	1.50	12.50
	s. Specimen.	—	—	110.

		VG	VF	UNC
14	**10 Taka** ND (1973). Green on multicolor underprint. Rice harvesting scene at left center on back. 2 signature varieties.			
	a. Issued note.	.25	1.00	10.00
	s. Specimen.	—	—	110.

1976; 1977 ND Issue

#15-17, 19 Star mosque in Dhaka at r. Wmk: Tiger's head.

		VG	VF	UNC
15	**5 Taka** ND (1977). Light brown on multicolor underprint. Back like #13.			
	a. Issued note.	.10	.25	5.00
	s. Specimen.	—	—	100.

		VG	VF	UNC
16	**10 Taka** ND (1977). Violet on multicolor underprint. Back like #14.			
	a. Issued note.	.25	.75	7.50
	s. Specimen.	—	—	110.

17	50 Taka	VG	VF	UNC
	ND (1976). Orange on multicolor underprint. Harvesting scene on back.			
	a. Issued note.	.25	1.00	15.00
	s. Specimen.	—	—	100.

18	100 Taka	VG	VF	UNC
	ND (1976). Blue-violet on multicolor underprint. Back like #12. Watermark: Tiger's head.	1.00	7.50	50.00

19	500 Taka	VG	VF	UNC
	ND (1976). Blue and lilac on multicolor underprint. High Court in Dhaka on back.	25.00	90.00	250.

Note: For similar 500 Taka but w/o printing on wmk. area, see #30.

1978-82 ND Issue

#20-24 wmk: Tiger's head.

20	5 Taka	VG	VF	UNC
	ND (1978). Brown on multicolor underprint. Mihrab in *Kushumba* mosque at right. Back like #13.			
	a. Issued note.	.20	.50	4.00
	s. Specimen.	—	—	100.

21	10 Taka	VG	VF	UNC
	ND (1978). Violet on multicolor underprint. *Atiya Jam-e* mosque in Tangali at right. Back like #14.			
	a. Issued note.	.25	.50	6.00
	s. Specimen.	—	—	110.

22	20 Taka	VG	VF	UNC
	ND (1979). Dark blue-green on multicolor underprint. *Chote Sona* mosque at right. Harvesting scene on back. Underprint over watermark area at left. Micro-printed security thread.	.25	.75	6.00

23	50 Taka	VG	VF	UNC
	ND (1979). Orange on multicolor underprint. Sat Gamnbuj Mosque in Dhaka at right. Women harvesting tea on back.	.25	1.00	8.00

24	100 Taka	VG	VF	UNC
	ND (1977). Blue-violet, deep brown and orange on multicolor underprint. Star mosque in Dhaka at right. Underprint throughout watermark area at left. Ruins of Lalbagh Fort at left center on back.	.50	3.00	20.00

1982-88 ND Issue

#25-32 wmk: Modified tiger's head. Sign. varieties.

		VG	VF	UNC
25	**5 Taka** ND (1981). Similar to #20 but without printing on watermark area at left on face.			
	a. Solid security thread. Black signature Large serial #. 1 signature variety.	.10	.25	1.50
	b. Micro-printed security thread. Black signature Sm. serial #. 2 signature varieties.	FV	.15	1.00
	c. Micro-printed security thread. Brown signature Sm. serial #. 3 signature varieties.	FV	FV	.75
	s. Specimen.	—	—	—

		VG	VF	UNC
26	**10 Taka** ND (1982). Violet and red-violet on multicolor underprint. *Atiya Jam-e* mosque in Tangali at right. Hydroelectric dam at left center on back.			
	a. With curved line of text above and below mosque. Solid security thread.	.10	.25	2.50

		VG	VF	UNC
	b. Without curved line of text above mosque. Solid security thread. 2 signature varieties.	FV	.40	1.25
	c. Micro-printed security thread. 3 signature varieties.	FV	FV	1.25

		VG	VF	UNC
27	**20 Taka** ND (1988); 2002. Blue-green on multicolor underprint. Similar to #22 but without printing on watermark area. 3 signature varieties.			
	a. Black signature Large serial #. 2 signature varieties.	FV	FV	4.00
	b. Green signature Sm. serial #. 2 signature varieties.	FV	FV	3.50
	c. Foil security thread. Green signature small serial #.	FV	FV	3.50

		VG	VF	UNC
28	**50 Taka** ND (1987). Black, red and deep green on multicolor underprint. National Monument at Savar at center National Assembly building at center on back. 3 signature varieties.			
	a. 7-digit serial #.	FV	FV	5.00
	b. 8-digit serial #.	FV	FV	5.00
	c. Different tiger in watermark. Clouds on back have been re-engraved. Underprint colors changed.	FV	FV	5.00

		VG	VF	UNC
29	**100 Taka** ND (1981). Blue-violet, deep brown and orange on multicolor underprint. Similar to #24, but without printing on watermark area at left.	FV	FV	10.00

		VG	VF	UNC
30	**500 Taka** ND (1982). Gray, blue and violet on multicolor underprint. Similar to #19 but without printing on watermark area at left on face.			
	a. Without segmented foil. 2 signature varieties.	FV	FV	55.00
	b. With segmented foil over security thread. 2 signature varieties.	FV	FV	30.00
	c. Eight numerals in serial #.	FV	FV	30.00

		VG	VF	UNC
31	**100 Taka** ND (1983). Like #29 but with circular toothed border added around watermark area on face and back.			

		VG	VF	UNC
31	**100 Taka**			
	a. Solid security thread. 2 signature varieties.	FV	FV	6.50
	b. Micro-printed security thread. 2 signature varieties.	FV	FV	6.00
	c. Segmented foil security thread. 2 signature varieties.	FV	FV	6.00
	d. Segmented foil thread with micro-printing. 1 signature variety.	FV	FV	6.00
	e. Solid foil thread with micro-printing.	FV	FV	6.00

1996 ND Commemorative Issue

#35, Victory Day. Ovpt: *VICTORY DAY SILVER JUBILEE '96* in lower l. wmk. area.

		VG	VF	UNC
33	**10 Taka** ND (1996). Violet on multicolor underprint. Commemorative overprint on #26b at lower left in watermark area.	FV	FV	3.00

1997 ND Issue

		VG	VF	UNC
32	**10 Taka** ND (1997). Dark brown and deep blue-green on multicolor underprint. M. Rahman at right and as watermark. Arms at left, Lalbagh Fort mosque at left center on back. 2 signature varieties.	FV	FV	2.50

1998 ND Issue

		VG	VF	UNC
34	**500 Taka** ND (1998). Brown, blue, purple and red on multicolor underprint. National Monument in Savar at center right. Black slate blue; High Court building in Dhaka.	FV	FV	30.00

2000-01 Issue

		VG	VF	UNC
35	**10 Taka** 2000. Brown, red and multicolor. Mujibur Rahman at left. National Assembly building on back. Polymer plastic.	FV	FV	2.00

		VG	VF	UNC
36	**50 Taka** ND (2000). Brown and blue on multicolor underprint. National Assembly building at left. Bagha Mosque of Rajshahi at right on back.	FV	FV	3.00

		VG	VF	UNC
37	**100 Taka** 2001. Dark blue on light red-brown underprint. Mujibur Rahman at left, Sixty Dome Mosque at right. Bangabandhu Bridge on back.	FV	FV	5.00

		VG	VF	UNC
38	**500 Taka** 2000. Brownish purple on multicolor underprint. Mujibur Rahman at right, Sat Gambuj Mosque in center. High Court building in Dhaka on back.	FV	FV	22.50

2002 Issue

		VG	VF	UNC
39	**10 Taka** 2002; 2003; 2004; 2005. Brown, red and multicolor. National emblem at left; building at lower right. National Assembly building on back.	FV	FV	2.00

		VG	VF	UNC
40	**20 Taka** 2002; 2003; 2004. Blue-green on multicolor underprint. Similar to #27 but reduced size. Enhanced security features.	FV	FV	3.50

		VG	VF	UNC
41	**50 Taka** 2003; 2004; 2005. Brown and blue on multicolor underprint. Similar to #36 but reduced size. Iridescent security thread, sight impaired features.	FV	FV	4.00

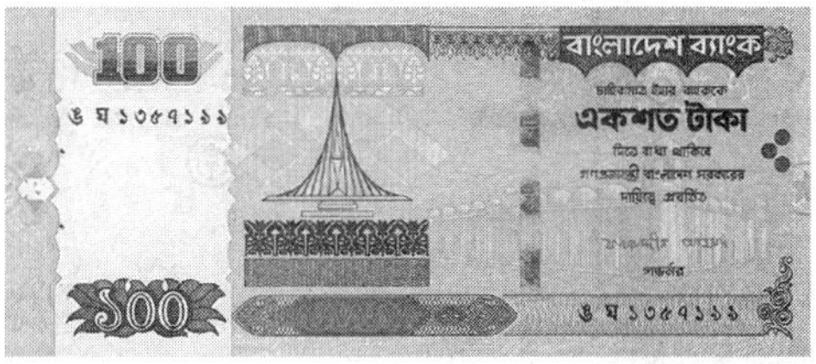

		VG	VF	UNC
42	**100 Taka** 2002; 2003; 2004. Dark blue on light red-brown underprint. National monument at Savar at center. Bangabandhu Bridge on back.	FV	FV	5.00
43	**500 Taka** 2002; 2003. Brownish purple on multicolor underprint. National Monument at Savar at right, Sat Gambuj Mosque in center. High Court building in Dhaka on back.	FV	FV	22.50

2004-05 Issue

		VG	VF	UNC
44	**100 Taka** 2005. Multicolor like #42. But value in upper left is a solid color.	FV	FV	5.00

		VG	VF	UNC
45	**500 Taka** 2003; 2004. Like # 43. Value at upper left is in solid color. Value in text is in color shifting ink.	FV	FV	22.50

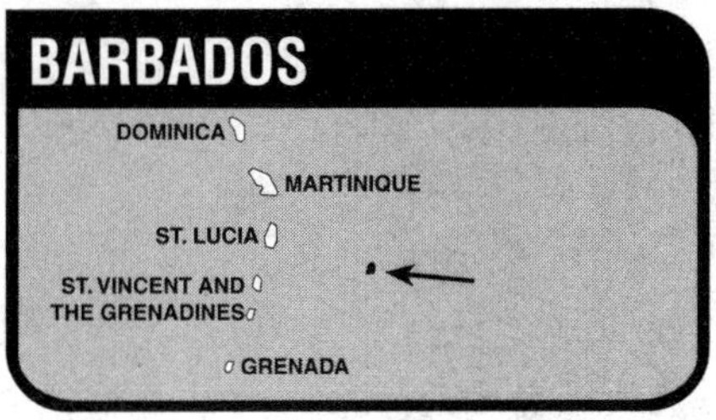

Barbados, an independent state within the British Commonwealth, is located in the Windward Islands of the West Indies east of St. Vincent. The coral island has an area of 166 sq. mi. (431 sq. km) and a population of 269,000. Capital: Bridgetown. The economy is d on sugar and tourism. Sugar, petroleum products, molasses and rum are exported.

Barbados was named by the Portuguese who achieved the first landing on the island in 1563. British sailors landed at the site of present-day Holetown in 1624. Barbados was under uninterrupted British control from the time of the first British settlement in 1627 until it obtained independence on Nov. 30, 1966. It is a member of the Commonwealth of Nations. Elizabeth II is Head of State, as Queen of Barbados.

Barbados was included in the issues of the British Caribbean Territories - Eastern Group and later the East Caribbean Currency Authority until 1973.

RULERS:

British to 1966

MONETARY SYSTEM:

1 Dollar = 100 Cents, 1950-

STATE

CENTRAL BANK OF BARBADOS

1973 ND ISSUE

#29-35 arms at l. ctr. Trafalgar Square in Bridgetown on back. Sign. C. Blackman. Wmk: Map of Barbados. Printer: (T)DLR. Replacement notes: serial # prefix *Z1*.

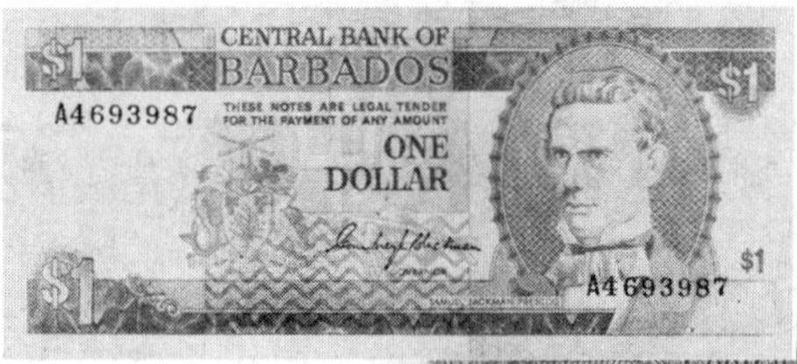

			VG	VF	UNC
29	**1 Dollar**				
	ND (1973). Red on multicolor underprint. Portrait S. J. Prescod at right.				
		a. Issued note.	FV	1.00	10.00
		s. Specimen.	—	—	50.00

		VG	VF	UNC
30	**2 Dollars**			
	ND (1980). Blue on multicolor underprint. Portrait J. R. Bovell at right.	FV	3.00	16.00

			VG	VF	UNC
31	**5 Dollars**				
	ND (1973). Green on multicolor underprint. Portrait S. J. Prescod at right.				
		a. Issued note.	FV	8.00	30.00
		s. As a. Specimen.	—	—	50.00

		VG	VF	UNC
32	**5 Dollars**			
	ND (1975). Dark green on multicolor underprint. Portrait Sir. F. Worrell at right.	FV	8.00	25.00

		VG	VF	UNC
33	**10 Dollars**			
	ND (1973). Dark brown on multicolor underprint. Portrait C. D. O'Neal at right.	FV	10.00	37.50

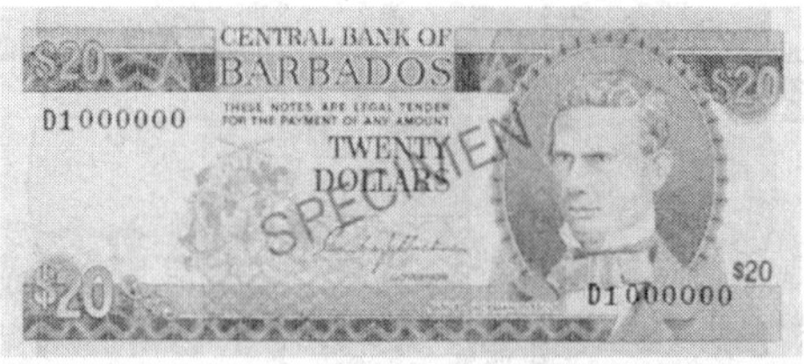

		VG	VF	UNC
34	**20 Dollars**			
	ND (1973). Purple on multicolor underprint. Portrait S. J. Prescod at right.	FV	17.50	52.50

		VG	VF	UNC
35	**100 Dollars** ND (1973). Gray and blue on multicolor underprint. Portrait Sir. G. H. Adama at right. Treetops are grayish blue on back. Serial # to E3200000.	FV	80.00	190.

1986 ND ISSUE

		VG	VF	UNC
35A	**10 Dollars** ND. Dark Brown and green on multicolor underprint. Like #38 but without seahorse at left. Signature K. King.	FV	15.00	40.00

		VG	VF	UNC
35B	**100 Dollars** ND. Brown, purple and gray-blue on multicolor underprint. Like #41, but signature C. Blackman	FV	75.00	185.

1986-89 ND ISSUE

#36-41 sign. K. King. Printer: (T)DLR. Replacement notes: serial # prefix *Z1*.

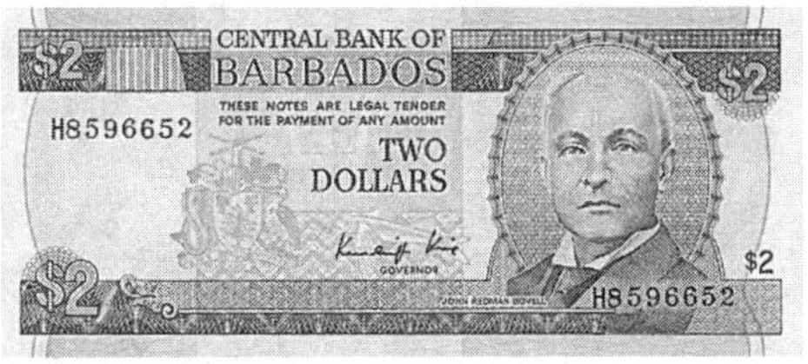

		VG	VF	UNC
36	**2 Dollars** ND (1986). Blue on multicolor underprint. Portrait J. R. Bovell at right.	VF	3.00	15.00

		VG	VF	UNC
37	**5 Dollars** ND (1986). Dark green on multicolor underprint. Portrait Sir. F. Worrell at right.	FV	6.00	22.50

		VG	VF	UNC
38	**10 Dollars** ND (1986). Dark Brown and green on multicolor underprint. Like #33 but seahorse in rectangle at left on face and at right on back.	FV	7.00	27.50
39	**20 Dollars** ND (1988). Purple on multicolor underprint. Like #34 but bird emblem in rectangle at left on face and at right on back.	FV	15.00	45.00

		VG	VF	UNC
40	**50 Dollars** ND (1989). Orange, blue and gray on multicolor underprint. Portrait Prime Minister E. W. Barrow at right. Trident emblem at left on face and right on back.	FV	40.00	105.

		VG	VF	UNC
41	**100 Dollars** ND (1986). Brown, purple and gray-blue on multicolor underprint. Like #35 but seahorse emblem at right on face and left on back. Treetops are green. Serial # above E3200000.	FV	65.00	155.

1993-94 ND Issue

#42-45 arms at l. ctr. Trafalgar Square in Bridgetown on back. Sign. C. M. Springer. Wmk: Map of Barbados. Printer: (T)DLR. Replacement notes: serial # prefix *Z1*.

		VG	VF	UNC
42	**2 Dollars** ND (1993). Blue on multicolor underprint. Portrait J. R. Bovell at right.	FV	FV	12.50
43	**5 Dollars** ND (1993). Dark green on multicolor underprint. Portrait Sir. F. Worrell at right.	FV	FV	17.50
44	**20 Dollars** ND (1993). Purple on multicolor underprint. Portrait S. J. Prescod at right.	FV	FV	40.00

		VG	VF	UNC
45	**100 Dollars** ND (1994). Brown, purple and gray-blue multicolor underprint. Portrait Sir. G. H. Adams at left.	FV	FV	145.

1995-96 ND Issue

#46-49 ascending size serial # at upper l. Enhanced security features. Printer (T)DLR. Replacement notes: serial # prefix *Z1*.

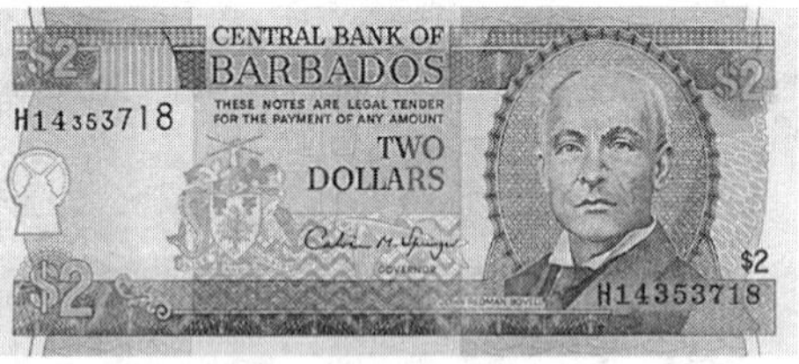

		VG	VF	UNC
46	**2 Dollars** ND (1995). Blue on multicolor underprint. Similar to #42.	FV	FV	11.00

		VG	VF	UNC
47	**5 Dollars** ND (1996). Dark green on multicolor underprint. Similar to #43.	FV	FV	15.00

		VG	VF	UNC
48	**10 Dollars** ND (1995). Dark brown and green on multicolor underprint. Similar to #38.	FV	FV	22.50

		VG	VF	UNC
49	**20 Dollars** ND (1996). Red-violet and purple on multicolor underprint. Similar to #39.	FV	FV	37.50

1996-97 ND Issue

#50-52 w/enlarged denomination numerals at upper l. Sign. C. M. Springer. Printer: (T)DLR. Replacement notes: serial # prefix *Z1*.

		VG	VF	UNC
50	**20 Dollars** ND (1997). Red-violet and purple on multicolor underprint. Similar to #49.	FV	FV	35.00

		VG	VF	UNC
51	**50 Dollars** ND (1997). Orange, blue and gray on multicolor underprint. Similar to #40.	FV	FV	80.00
52	**100 Dollars** ND (1996). Brown, purple and blue-gray on multicolor underprint. Similar to #45.	FV	FV	130.

1997 ND Commemorative Issue

#53, 25th Anniversary Central Bank

53	100 Dollars	VG	VF	UNC
	ND (1997). Brown, purple and blue-gray on multicolor underprint. Commemorative overprint on #52 at left.			
	a. Issued note.	FV	FV	135.
	r. Replacement note.	FV	FV	190.
	s. Specimen.	—	—	—

1998 ND Issue

#54-59 enhanced security features. Sign. W. Cox. Printer: (T)DLR. Replacement notes: serial # prefix *Z1*.

54	2 Dollars	VG	VF	UNC
	ND (1998). Blue on multicolor underprint. Similar to #46.			
	a. ND (1998). Face-to-back register device of windmill with blades dark.	FV	FV	8.50
	b. ND (1999). Face-to-back register device of windmill with two quarters filled in.	FV	FV	7.50

55	5 Dollars	VG	VF	UNC
	ND (1999). Dark green on multicolor underprint. Similar to #47.	FV	FV	12.50

56	10 Dollars	VG	VF	UNC
	ND (1999). Dark brown and green on multicolor underprint. Similar to #48.	FV	FV	17.50
57	**20 Dollars**			
	ND (1999). Red-violet and purple on multicolor underprint. Similar to #50.	FV	FV	27.50

58	50 Dollars	VG	VF	UNC
	ND (1999). Orange, blue and gray on multicolor underprint. Similar to #51.	FV	FV	75.00

59	100 Dollars	VG	VF	UNC
	ND (1999). Brown, purple and blue-gray on multicolor underprint. Similar to #52.	FV	FV	125.

2000 ND Issue

#60-65 similar to #54-59 but with enhanced security features. Sign. M. Williams. Printer: (T)DLR. Replacement notes: Serial # prefix *Z1*.

60	2 Dollars	VG	VF	UNC
	ND (2000). Blue on multicolor underprint. Similar to #54.	FV	FV	6.50

61	5 Dollars	VG	VF	UNC
	ND (2000). Dark green on multicolor underprint. Similar to #55.	FV	FV	10.00

62	10 Dollars	VG	VF	UNC
	ND (2000). Dark brown and green on multicolor underprint. Similar to #56.	FV	FV	15.00

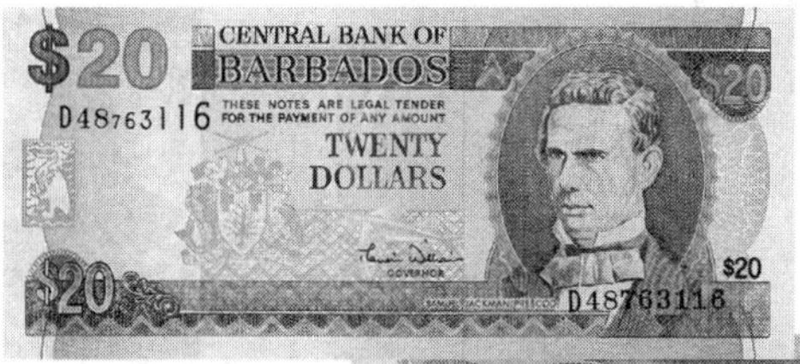

63	20 Dollars	VG	VF	UNC
	ND (2000). Red-violet and purple on multicolor underprint. Similar to #57.	FV	FV	25.00

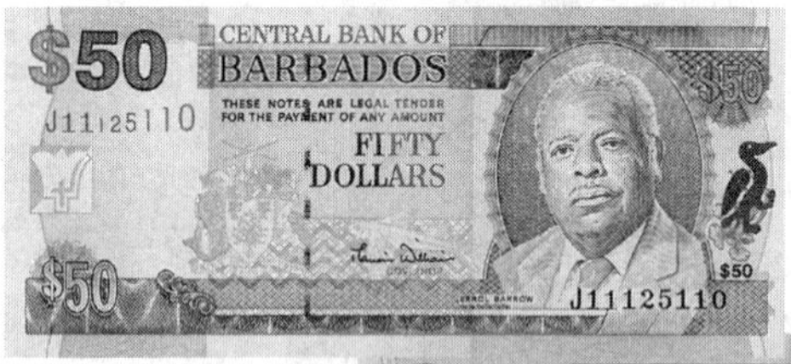

64	50 Dollars	VG	VF	UNC
	ND (2000). Orange, blue and gray on multicolor underprint. Similar to #58.	FV	FV	62.50

65	100 Dollars	VG	VF	UNC
	ND (2000). Brown, purple and blue-gray on multicolor underprint. Similar to #59.	FV	FV	110.

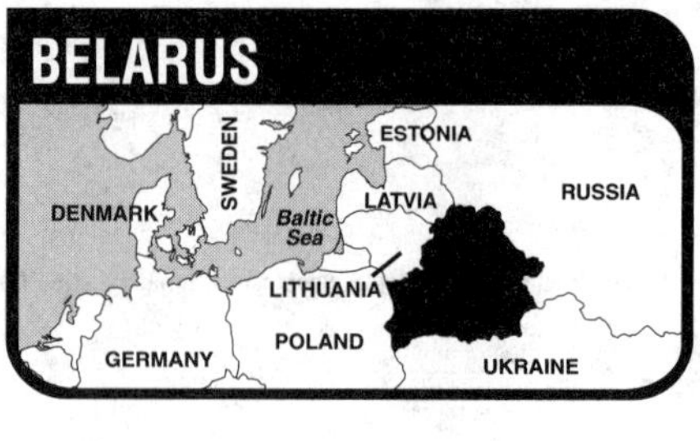

Belarus (Byelorussia, Belorussia, or White Russia) is bounded in the west by Poland, to the north by Latvia and Lithuania, to the east by Russia and the south by the Ukraine. It has an area of 80,134 sq. mi. (207,600 sq. km.) and a population of 10.3 million. Capital: Minsk. Peat, salt, agriculture including flax, fodder and grasses for cattle breeding and dairy products, along with general manufacturing industries comprise the economy.

An independent state of Byelorussia never existed. When Kiev was the center of Rus, there were a few feudal principalities in the Byelorussian lands, those of Polotsk, Smolensk and Turov being the most important. The principalities, protected by the Pripet marshes, escaped invasion until, in the first half of the 13th century, the Tatars destroyed the Kievan Rus. The area was soon incorporated into the Grand Duchy of Lithuania. They respected the Christianity of the conquered and gradually Byelorussian became the official language of the grand duchy. When Lithuania was absorbed by Poland in the 16th century, Polish replaced Byelorussian as the official language of the country. Until the partitions of Poland at the end of the 18th century, the history of Byelorussia is identical with that of Lithuania.

When Russia incorporated the whole of Byelorussia into its territories in 1795, it claimed to be recovering old Russian lands and denied that the Byelorussians were a separate nation. The country was named Northwestern territory and in 1839 Byelorussian Roman Catholics of the Uniate rite were forced to accept Orthodoxy. A minority remained faithful to the Latin rite. The German occupation of western Byelorussia in 1915 created an opportunity for Byelorussian leaders to formulate, in December 1917 their desire for an independent Byelorussia. On February 25, 1918, Minsk was occupied by the Germans, and in the Brest-Litovsk peace treaty of March 3rd between the Central Powers and Soviet Russia the existence of Byelorussia was ignored. Nevertheless, on March 25, the National council proclaimed an independent republic. After the collapse of Germany, the Soviet government repudiated the Brest treaties and on January 1, 1919, proclaimed a Byelorussian S.S.R. The Red army occupied the lands evacuated by the Germans, and by February all Byelorussia was in Communist hands. The Polish army started an eastward offensive, however, and on August 8th entered Minsk. The peace treaty between Poland and the U.S.S.R. in March 1921, partitioned Byelorussia. In its eastern and larger part a Soviet republic was formed, which in 1922 became a founder member of the U.S.S.R. The eastern frontier was identical with the corresponding section of the Polish-Russian frontier before 1772. The first premier of the Byelorussian S.S.R., The Moscow treaty of August 16, 1945, fixed the Polish-Soviet frontier, and left Bialystok to Poland. From January 1, 1955, the republic was divided into seven oblasti or provinces: Minsk, Brest, Grodno, Molodechno, Mohylev (Mogilev), Homel (Gomel) and Vitebsk. On August 25, 1991, following an unsuccessful coup, the Supreme Soviet adopted a declaration of independence, and the "Republic of Belarus" was proclaimed in September. In December it became a founding member of the Commonweath of Independent States.

MONETARY SYSTEM:

1 Ruble = 100 Kapeek

REPUBLIC

КУПОН РЭСПУБЛІКА БЕЛАРУСЬ

BELARUS REPUBLIC

1991 FIRST RUBLE CONTROL COUPON ISSUE

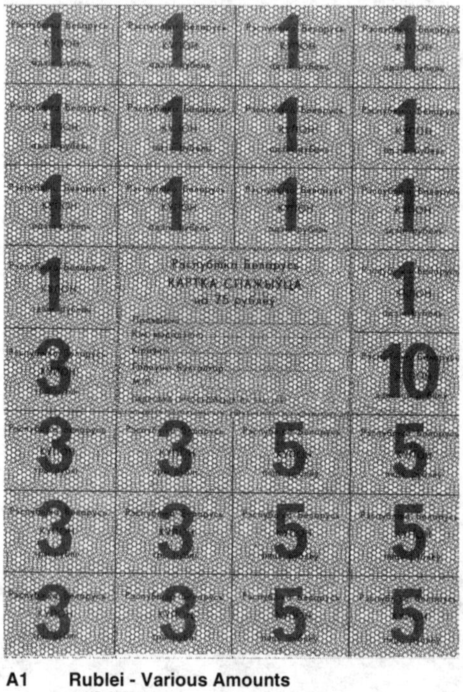

A1	Rublei - Various Amounts	VG	VF	UNC
	ND (1991).	.25	1.50	6.00

Note: The 50, 75, and 100 Rublei denominations were issued in various colors on a sheet of 28 coupons. Uniface.

		VG	VF	UNC
AA1	**20 Rublei** ND (1991).	.25	1.50	6.00

Note: The 20 Rublei denomination was issued on a sheet of 14 coupons. Uniface.

1991 Second Ruble Control Coupon Issue

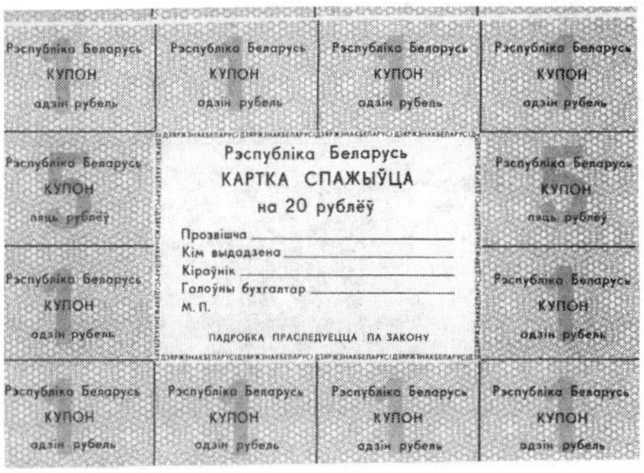

		VG	VF	UNC
A3	**20 Rublei** ND (1991).	.50	.75	2.50

Note: The 20 Rublei denomination was issued on a sheet of 12 coupons. Uniface.

		VG	VF	UNC
A4	**Rublei - Various Amounts** ND (1991).	.50	1.50	5.00

Note: The 50, 75, 100, 200, 300, and 500 Rublei denominations were issued in various colors on a sheet of 28 coupons. Uniface.

НАЦЫЯНАЛЬНАГА БАНКА БЕЛАРУСІ

Belarus National Bank

1992-96 РАЗЛІКОВЫ БІЛЕТ - Exchange Note Issue

#1-10 "Pagonya," a defending warrior wielding sword on horseback at ctr. Wmk. paper.

		VG	VF	UNC
1	**50 Kapeek** 1992. Red and brown-orange on pink underprint. Squirrel at center right on back.	.05	.10	.50

		VG	VF	UNC
2	**1 Ruble** 1992. Blue-green and blue. Back brown on multicolor underprint. Rabbit at center right on back.	.05	.50	4.00

		VG	VF	UNC
3	**3 Rublei** 1992. Green, red-orange and pale olive-green on multicolor underprint. Two beavers at center right on back.	.05	.50	4.00

		VG	VF	UNC
4	**5 Rublei** 1992. Deep blue on light blue, lilac, violet and multicolor underprint. Two wolves at center right on back.	.05	.25	2.00

		VG	VF	UNC
5	**10 Rublei** 1992. Deep green on light green, orange and multicolor underprint. Lynx with kitten at center right on back.	.05	.10	.50

		VG	VF	UNC
6	**25 Rublei** 1992. Violet on red, green and multicolor underprint. Moose at center right on back.	.05	.10	.50

		VG	VF	UNC
7	**50 Rublei** 1992. Deep purple on red and green underprint. Bear at center right on back.	.05	.10	.50

		VG	VF	UNC
8	**100 Rublei** 1992. Brown, gray and tan on multicolor underprint. Wisent (European Bison) at center on back.	.05	.10	.50

		VG	VF	UNC
9	**200 Rublei** 1992. Deep brown-violet, orange, green and ochre on multicolor underprint. City view at center right on back.	.10	.35	3.00

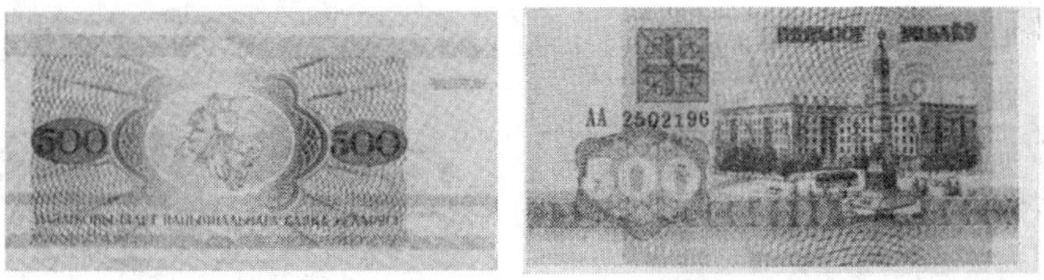

		VG	VF	UNC
10	**500 Rublei** 1992. Violet, tan, light blue and orange on multicolor underprint. Victory Plaza in Minsk at center right on back.	.10	1.50	8.00

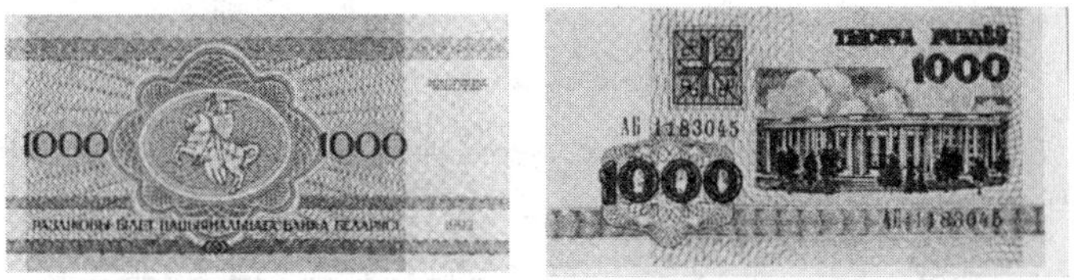

		VG	VF	UNC
11	**1000 Rublei** 1992 (1993). Light blue, pale olive-green and pink. Back dark bluc and dark green on multicolor underprint.; Academy of Sciences building at center right on back.	.10	.50	1.50

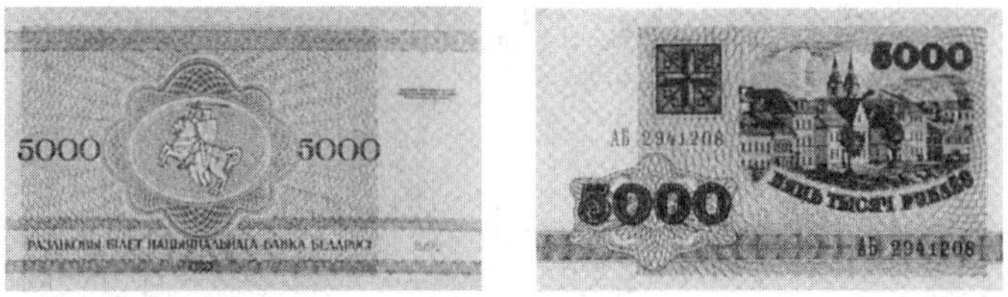

		VG	VF	UNC
12	**5000 Rublei** 1992 (1993). Purple and red-violet on multicolor underprint. Back brown-violet and olive-green on multicolor underprint. Buildings in Minsk lower city at center right.	.10	.50	2.50

1994-96 Issue

		VG	VF	UNC
13	**20,000 Rublei** 1994. Dark brown on multicolor underprint. National Bank building at left center, *Pagonya* (National emblem) on back. Watermark: Tower and tree.	.50	1.00	5.00

		VG	VF	UNC
14	**50,000 Rublei** 1995. Dark brown on multicolor underprint. Yellow paper. Brest's tower, Holmsky Gate at left, tapestry at center right. Star shaped war memorial gateway at center right on back.	.75	2.50	8.00

		VG	VF	UNC
15	**100,000 Rublei** 1996. Deep blue and violet on multicolor underprint. Bolshoi Opera and Ballet Theatre at center, tapestry at left. Scene from Glebov's ballet *Vibrannitsa* at center on back.	1.00	3.00	12.50

1998 Issue

		VG	VF	UNC
16	**1000 Rublei** 1998. Light blue, pale olive-green and pink. Similar to #11 but single value moved to oval replacing *Pagonya*, warrior on horseback at left center. Watermarked paper.	.05	.10	.50

1998-99 Issue

		VG	VF	UNC
17	**5000 Rublei** 1998. Multicolor. Back like #12.	.05	.10	.60

		VG	VF	UNC
18	**500,000 Rublei** 1998. Light red and green on yellow underprint. Palace of Culture building at center façade fragment on back.	1.00	3.00	10.00

19	1,000,000 Rublei	VG	VF	UNC
	1999. Green on multicolor underprint. National Museum of Art at center Artwork: *Wife's Portrait with Flowers and Fruits* on back.	1.00	3.50	10.00

20	5,000,000 Rublei	VG	VF	UNC
	1999. Purple and green on multicolor underprint. Minsk sports complex at center. Winter sports complex on back.	2.00	4.50	15.00

2000 ISSUE

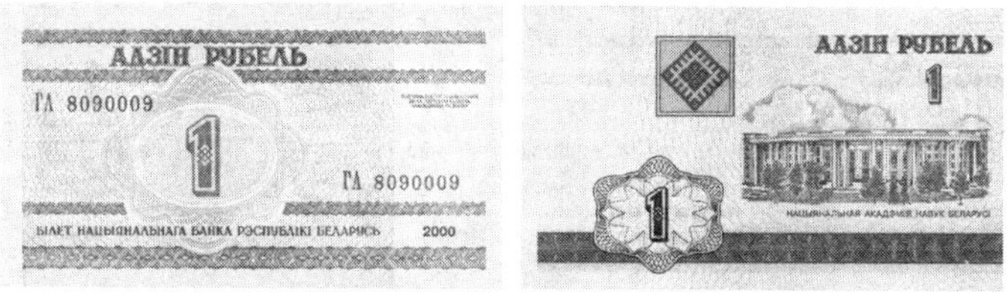

21	1 Ruble	VG	VF	UNC
	2000. Green on multicolor underprint. Back similar to #11.	—	.25	1.00

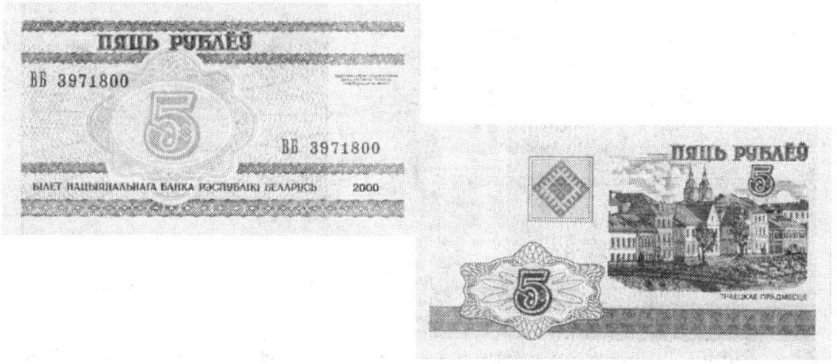

22	5 Rublei	VG	VF	UNC
	2000. Pale red and violet on multicolor underprint. Back similar to #17.	—	.25	1.00

23	10 Rublei	VG	VF	UNC
	2000. Lilac on multicolor underprint. National Library at right on back.	—	.25	1.00

24	20 Rublei	VG	VF	UNC
	2000. Brown on multicolor underprint. National Bank building at left center. Interior view on back.	—	.25	1.00

25	50 Rublei	VG	VF	UNC
	2000. Red-borwn on multicolor underprint. Similar to #14. Holmsky Gate at left center. War memorial gateway on back.	—	.25	1.50

26	100 Rublei	VG	VF	UNC
	2000. Green on multicolor underprint. Similar to #15. Bolshoi Opera and Ballet Theater. Scene from ballet *Vibrannitsa* on back. Watermark: Ballerina.	—	.25	3.00

27	500 Rublei	VG	VF	UNC
	2000. Brown and green on tan underprint. Palace of Culture. Façade fragment on back.	.20	1.50	6.00

28 **1000 Rublei**
2000. Blue on yellow underprint. National Museum of Art at left center. Flowers and fruits still life on back.

VG	VF	UNC
.50	2.50	8.00

29 **5000 Rublei**
2000. Purple and slate gray on multicolor underprint. Minsk Sports complex at center. Winter sports complex (three ski jump hills) on back.

VG	VF	UNC
1.00	3.00	12.50

30 **10,000 Rublei**
2000 (2001). Orange and blue on multicolor underprint. Vitebsk city view. Amphitheater on back.

VG	VF	UNC
1.00	3.00	17.50

31 **20,000 Rublei**
2000 (2001). Olive on multicolor underprint. Palaces in Gomel at center. Mountaintop palace on back.

VG	VF	UNC
1.00	4.50	25.00

32 **50,000 Rublei**
2000 (2002). Blue, gray, lilac on multicolor underprint. Mirski Zanak castle at left center. Details of Mirski Zanak on back. Printer: Goznak.

VG	VF	UNC
2.00	6.00	50.00

2001 Commemorative Issue

#33, 10th Anniversary National Bank of Belarus

33 **20 Rublei**
2001. Brown on multicolor underprint. #24 with OVD denomination at upper center right and gold-stamped dates *1991-2001* with bank initials at right. Issued in a special folder.

VG	VF	UNC
.75	1.50	6.00

2005 Issue

34 **100,000 Rublei**
ND (2005). Brown on rose and multicolor underprint. Building at center. Castle on back.

VG	VF	UNC
FV	FV	80.00

Collector Series

Belarus National Bank

2000 Commemorative

CS1 **Rublei - Various Amounts**
10-piece set of notes in blue folder. Set consists of #21-30 dated 2000 and with matching serial #. The 20 Rublei and higher include an overprint: *MILLENNIUM* at the lower left on the back.

Issue Prince	Mkt.	Value
—	—	25.00

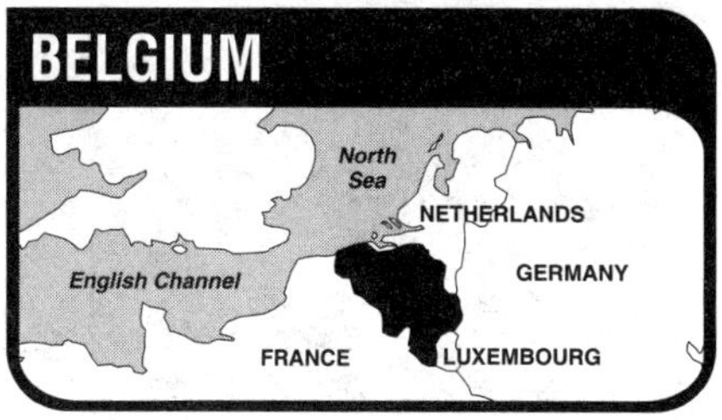

The Kingdom of Belgium, a constitutional monarchy in northwest Europe, has an area of 11,779 sq. mi. (30,513 sq. km.) and a population of 10.26 million, chiefly Dutch-speaking Flemish and French-speaking Walloons. Capital: Brussels. Agriculture, dairy farming, and the processing of raw materials for re-export are the principal industries. "Beurs voor Diamant" in Antwerp is the world's largest diamond trading center. Iron and steel, machinery, motor vehicles, chemicals, textile yarns and fabrics comprise the principal exports.

The Celtic tribe called "Belgae," from which Belgium derived its name, was described by Caesar as the most courageous of all the tribes of Gaul. The Belgae eventually capitulated to Rome and the area remained for centuries as a part of the Roman Empire known as Belgica.

As Rome began its decline, Frankish tribes migrated westward and established the Merovingian, and subsequently, the Carolingian empires. At the death of Charlemagne, Europe was divided among his three sons Karl, Lothar and Ludwig. The eastern part of today's Belgium lay in the Duchy of Lower Lorraine while much of the western parts eventually became the County of Flanders. After further divisions, the area was absorbed into the Duchy of Burgundy from whence it passed into Hapsburg control when Marie of Burgundy married Maximilian of Austria. Phillip I (the Fair), son of Maximilian and Marie, then added Spain to the Hapsburg empire by marrying Johanna, daughter of Ferdinand and Isabella. Charles and Ferdinand, sons of Phillip and Johanna, began the separate Spanish and Austrian lines of the Hapsburg family. The Burgundian lands, along with the northern provinces which make up present day Netherlands, became the Spanish Netherlands. The northern provinces successfully rebelled and broke away from Hapsburg rule in the late 16th century and early 17th century. The southern provinces along with the Duchy of Luxembourg remained under the influence of Spain until the year 1700 when Charles II, last of the Spanish Hapsburg line, died without leaving an heir and the Spanish crown went to the Bourbon family of France. The Spanish Netherlands then reverted to the control of the Austrian line of Hapsburgs and became the Austrian Netherlands. The Austrian Netherlands along with the Bishopric of Liege fell to the French Republic in 1794.

At the Congress of Vienna in 1815 the area was united with the Netherlands but in 1830 independence was gained and the constitutional monarchy of Belgium was established. A large part of the Duchy of Luxembourg was incorporated into Belgium and the first king was Leopold I of Saxe-Coburg-Gotha. It was invaded by the German army in Aug. 1914 and the German forces carried on a devastating occupation of most of the territory until the Armistice. Belgium joined the League of Nations. On May 10, 1940 it was invaded again by Nazi German armies. The Belgian and Allied forces were quickly overwhelmed and were evacuated through Dunkirk. Allied troops reached Belgium again in Sept. 1944. Prince Charles, Count of Flanders assumed King Leopold's responsibilities until his liberation by the U.S. army in Austria on May 8, 1945. From 1920-1940 and since 1944 Eupen-Malmedy went from Germany to Belgium.

RULERS:

Baudouin I, 1952-93
Albert II, 1993-

MONETARY SYSTEM:

1 Franc = 100 Centimes to 2001
1 Belga = 5 Francs
1 Euro = 100 Cents, 2002-

KINGDOM

BANQUE NATIONALE DE BELGIQUE

NATIONALE BANK VAN BELGIE

1961-71 ISSUE

#134-137 wmk: Kg. Baudouin I.

		VG	VF	UNC
134	**100 Francs** 1.2.1962-2.6.1977. Violet on multicolor underprint. Lambert Lombard at left. Allegorical figure at center on back. 4 signature varieties.			
	a. Serial # 00001 A 001 to 10000 Z 999. Sign (1 and 7), (1 and 8).	4.00	6.00	10.00
	b. Serial # 1001 A 0001 to 2350 Z 999. signature (1 and 8), (2 and 8) and (3 and 8).	4.00	6.00	10.00
	c. Series 3000. Coated with plastic. signature (2 and 8).	15.00	25.00	50.00

#135-137 replacement notes: Serial # prefix *Z/1*.

		VG	VF	UNC
135	**500 Francs** 2.5.1961-28.4.1975. Blue-gray and multicolor. Bernard Van Orley at center. Margaret of Austria and Malines Palace façade at right. 4 signature varieties.			
	a. Serial # 0001 A 001 to 2500 Z 999. signature (1 and 7) and (1 and 8).	20.00	30.00	60.00
	b. Serial # 251 A 0001 to 556 Z 9999. signature (1 and 8), (2 and 8) and (3 and 8).	20.00	30.00	60.00

		VG	VF	UNC
136	**1000 Francs** 2.1.1961-8.12.1975. Brown and blue. Gérard Kremer (called Mercator) at left. Atlas holding globe on back. 4 signature varieties.			
	a. Serial # 0001 A 001 to 10400 Z 999. signature (1 and 7).	35.00	50.00	80.00
	b. Serial # 1041 A 0001 to 1877 Z 999. signature (1 and 8), (2 and 8) and (3 and 8).	35.00	50.00	80.00

		VG	VF	UNC
137	**5000 Francs** 6.1.1971-15.9.1977. Green. André Vesalius at center. Escapelus statue and temple of Epidaure on back. Signature (1 and 8), (2 and 8), (3 and 8) and (3 and 9).	225.	275.	400.

ROYAUME DE BELGIQUE - KONINKRIJK BELGIE

TRÉSORERIE - THESAURIE (TREASURY NOTES)

1964-66 ISSUE

#138 and 139 replacement notes: Serial # prefix *Z/1*.

		VG	VF	UNC
138	**20 Francs** 15.6.1964. Black on blue, orange and multicolor underprint. King Baudouin I at left and as watermark, arms at lower right. Atomium complex in Brussels at right on back. Signature 18, 19, 20.	.25	.50	2.00

139 50 Francs

16.5.1966. Brown-violet and orange-brown on multicolor underprint. Arms at lower left center, King Baudouin I and Queen Fabiola at right. Parliament building in Brussels on back. Watermark: Baudouin I. Signature 18, 19, 20, 21.

VG	VF	UNC
1.00	2.00	4.00

BANQUE NATIONALE DE BELGIQUE

1978; 1980 ND ISSUE

#140-142 wmk: Kg. Baudouin I. Sign. only on face side.

140 100 Francs

ND (1978-81). Maroon, blue and olive-green on multicolor underprint. Hendrik Beyaert at center right. Architectural view and plan at left. Geometric design on back. Signature (3 and 9), (3 and 10).

VG	VF	UNC
15.00	20.00	30.00

141 500 Francs

ND (1980-81). Deep blue-violet and deep green on blue and multicolor underprint. Constantin Meunier at left center underprint of two coal miners and mine conveyor tower at center right. Five circular designs on back. Signature (3 and 8).

VG	VF	UNC
35.00	50.00	75.00

1981-82 ND ISSUE

#142-145 wmk: K. Baudouin I.

142 100 Francs

ND (1982-94). Like #140 but with signature on face and back. Signature (3 and 10), (4 and 10), (4 and 11), (4 and 12), (4 and 13), (5 and 14), (5 and 15).

VG	VF	UNC
4.00	6.00	10.00

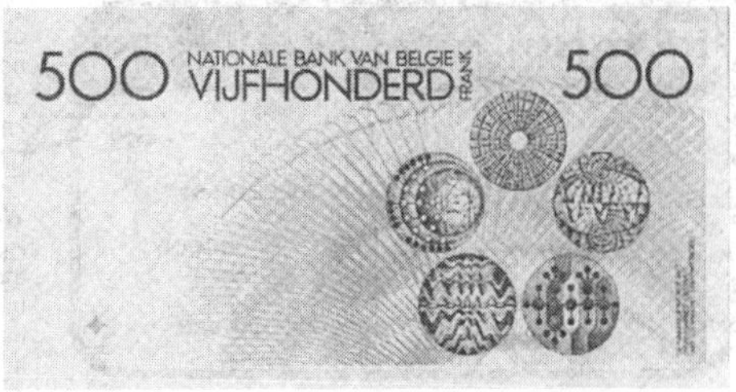

143 500 Francs

ND (1982-98). Like #141 but with signature on face and back. Signature (3 and 10), (4 and 10), (4 and 11), (4 and 12), (4 and 13), (5 and 14), (5 and 15).

VG	VF	UNC
20.00	25.00	50.00

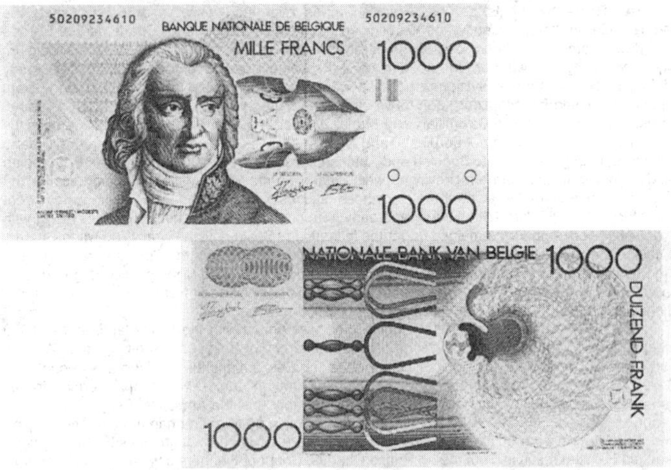

144 1000 Francs

ND (1980-96). Brown and green on multicolor underprint. André Gretry at left center, bass violin center right in background. Tuning forks and view of inner ear on back. Signature (3 and 10), (4 and 10), (4 and 11), (4 and 12), (4 and 13), (5 and 14), (5 and 15).

	VG	VF	UNC
a. Name as: *ANDRÉ ERNEST MODESTE GRETRY. 1741-1813.*	40.00	60.00	90.00
x1. Name as: *• ERNEST • MODESTE.*	50.00	120.	300.
x2. Name as: *ANDRÉ ERNEST MODESTE TRY.*	60.00	75.00	120.

145 5000 Francs

ND (1982-92). Green on multicolor underprint. Guido Gezelle at left center. Tree and stained glass window behind. Back green, red and brown; dragonfly and leaf at center signature (4 and 10), (4 and 11), (4 and 12), (4 and 13), (5 and 14).

VG	VF	UNC
175.	225.	350.

1992 ND ISSUE

146 10,000 Francs

ND (1992-97). Grayish purple on multicolor underprint. King Baudouin I and Queen Fabiola at left and as watermark, aerial map as underprint. Flora and greenhouses at Laeken (royal residence) at center on back. Signature (5 and 15).

VG	VF	UNC
350.	475.	600.

1994-97 ND Issue

147 100 Francs

ND (1995-2001). Red-violet and black on multicolor underprint. James Ensor at left and as watermark, masks at lower center and at right. Beach scene at left on back. Signature (5 and 15), (6 and 16).

VG	VF	UNC
3.00	5.00	7.50

148 200 Francs

ND (1995). Black and brown on yellow and orange underprint. Adolphe Sax at left and as watermark, saxophone at right. Saxophone players outlined at left, church, houses in Dinant outlined at lower right on back. Signature (5 and 15).

VG	VF	UNC
6.00	10.00	15.00

149 500 Francs

ND (1998). Blue-black, purple and blue-green on multicolor underprint. René Magritte at left and as watermark, birds in plants at lower center, tree at right. Six men, chair at left, men at center right on back. Signature (5 and 15).

VG	VF	UNC
15.00	25.00	35.00

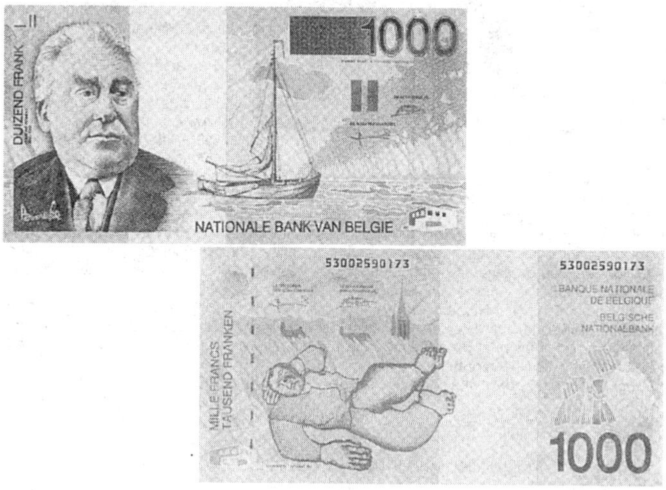

150 1000 Francs

ND (1997). Dark brown on multicolor underprint. Constant Permeke at left and as watermark, sailboat at center *Sleeping Farmer* painting at left on back. Signature (5 and 15).

VG	VF	UNC
30.00	40.00	60.00

151 2000 Francs

ND (1994-2001). Purple and blue-green on multicolor underprint. Baron Victor Horta at left and as watermark. Flora and *Art Nouveau* design at left on back. Signature (5 and 15).

VG	VF	UNC
60.00	80.00	100.

152 10,000 Francs

ND (1997). Deep purple on multicolor underprint. King Albert II and Queen Paola at left, aerial view of Parliamentary chamber at right. Greenhouses at Laeken (royal residence) on back. Watermark: King Albert II. Signature (5 and 15).

VG	VF	UNC
325.	375.	450.

Note: For later issues used in Belgium, see European Union listings.

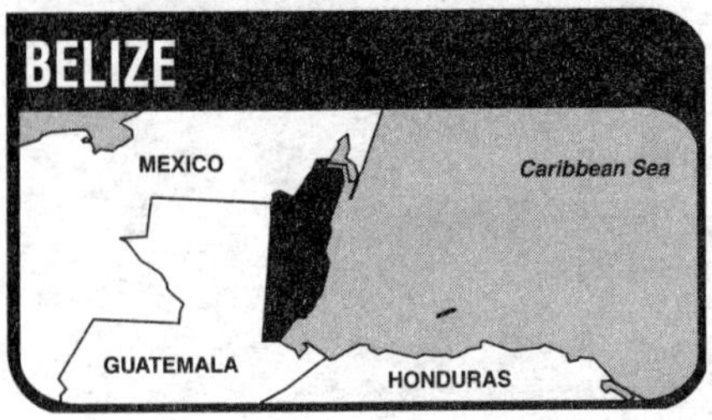

Belize (formerly British Honduras) is situated in Central America south of Mexico and east and north of Guatemala. It has an area of 8,867 sq. mi. (22,965 sq. km.) and a population of 242,000. Capital: Belmopan. Sugar, citrus fruits, chicle and hard woods are exported.

The area, site of the ancient Mayan civilization, was sighted by Columbus in 1502, and settled by shipwrecked English seamen in 1638. British buccaneers settled the former capital of Belize in the 17th Century. Britian claimed administrative right over the area after the emancipation of Central America from Spain, and declared it a dependency of the Colony of Jamaica in 1862. It was established as the separate Crown Colony of British Honduras in 1884. The anti-British People's United Party, which attained power in 1954, won a constitution, effective in 1964 which established self-government under a British appointed Governor. British Honduras became Belize on June 1, 1973, following the passage of a surprise bill by the People's United Party, but the consititutional relationship with Britain remained unchanged.

In Dec. 1975, the U.N. General Assembly adopted a resolution supporting the right of the people of Belize to self-determination, and asked Britian and Guatemala to renew their negotiations on the future of Belize. They obtained independence on Sept. 21, 1981. Elizabeth II is Head of State, as Queen of Belize.

For earlier bank notes, see British Honduras.

MONETARY SYSTEM:

1 Dollar = 100 Cents

BELIZE

GOVERNMENT OF BELIZE

1974-75 ISSUE

#33-37 arms at l., portr. Qn. Elizabeth II at r.

33	1 Dollar	VG	VF	UNC
	1974-76. Green on multicolor underprint.			
	a. 1.1.1974.	1.50	10.00	70.00
	b. 1.6.1975.	1.00	6.00	55.00
	c. 1.1.1976.	1.00	5.00	50.00
	s. Specimen.	—	—	100.
	ct. Color trial. Blue, green and pale orange.	—	—	300.

34	2 Dollars	VG	VF	UNC
	1974-76. Violet on lilac and multicolor underprint.			
	a. 1.1.1974.	4.00	20.00	95.00
	b. 1.6.1975.	3.00	10.00	75.00
	c. 1.1.1976.	2.50	9.00	70.00
	s. Specimen.	—	—	125.
	ct. Color trial. Brown, orange and red.	—	—	225.

35	5 Dollars	VG	VF	UNC
	1975; 1976. Red on multicolor underprint.			
	a. 1.6.1975.	7.50	30.00	175.
	b. 1.1.1976.	5.00	25.00	150.
	s. Specimen.	—	—	150.
	ct. Color trial. Red on multicolor underprint.	—	—	200.

36	10 Dollars	VG	VF	UNC
	1974-76. Black on multicolor underprint.			
	a. 1.1.1974.	20.00	75.00	650.
	b. 1.6.1975.	17.50	60.00	450.
	c. 1.1.1976.	15.00	50.00	375.
	s. Specimen.	—	—	375.
	ct. Color trial. Green and orange.	—	—	725.

37	20 Dollars	VG	VF	UNC
	1974-76. Brown on multicolor underprint.			
	a. 1.1.1974.	50.00	250.	1250.
	b. 1.6.1975.	25.00	125.	700.
	c. 1.1.1976.	25.00	100.	625.
	s. Specimen.	—	—	650.
	ct. Color trial. Blue, green and pale yellow.	—	—	1200.

MONETARY AUTHORITY OF BELIZE

ORDINANCE NO. 9 OF 1976; 1980 ISSUE

#38-42 linear border on arms in upper l. corner, Qn. Elizabeth II at ctr. r. 3/4 looking l., underwater scene w/reef and fish in ctr. background. House of Representatives at ctr. Jabiu stork at r. on back. Wmk: Carved head of the "sleeping giant." Replacement notes: Serial # prefix *Z/1; Z/2; Z/3; Z/4; Z/5*.

38	1 Dollar	VG	VF	UNC
	1.6.1980. Green on multicolor underprint.			
	a. Issued note.	2.00	10.00	40.00
	s. Specimen.	—	—	—

39	**5 Dollars**	VG	VF	UNC
	1.6.1980. Red on multicolor underprint.			
	a. Issued note.	5.00	25.00	100.
	s. Specimen.	—	—	—

40	**10 Dollars**	VG	VF	UNC
	1.6.1980. Violet on multicolor underprint.			
	a. Issued note.	9.00	45.00	190.
	s. Specimen.	—	—	—

41	**20 Dollars**	VG	VF	UNC
	1.6.1980. Brown on multicolor underprint.	30.00	95.00	400.

42	**100 Dollars**	VG	VF	UNC
	1.6.1980. Blue on multicolor underprint.	125.	375.	1500.

CENTRAL BANK OF BELIZE

ACT 1982; 1983 ISSUE

#43-45 similar to #38, 40 and 41. Wreath border on arms at upper l. Replacement notes: Serial # prefix *Z/1; Z/3; Z/4.*

43	**1 Dollar**	VG	VF	UNC
	1.7.1983. Green on multicolor underprint. Like #38.	1.50	6.50	30.00

44	**10 Dollars**	VG	VF	UNC
	1.7.1983. Black on red and multicolor underprint. Like #40.			
	a. Issued note.	7.50	35.00	120.
	s. Specimen.	—	—	—

45	**20 Dollars**	VG	VF	UNC
	1.7.1983. Brown on multicolor underprint. Like #41.	32.50	100.	425.

ACT 1982; 1983-87 ISSUE

#46-50 like #38-42. Lg. tree behind arms at upper l. Sign. varieties. Replacement notes: Serial # prefix *Z/1; Z/2; Z/3; Z/4; Z/5.*

46	**1 Dollar**	VG	VF	UNC
	1983-87. Green on multicolor underprint. Like #38.			
	a. 1.11.1983.	FV	5.00	25.00
	b. 1.1.1986.	FV	4.50	22.50
	c. 1.1.1987.	FV	4.00	18.00
	s. Specimen.	—	—	—

47	**5 Dollars**	VG	VF	UNC
	1987; 1989. Red on multicolor underprint. Like #39.			
	a. 1.1.1987.	15.00	65.00	250.
	b. 1.1.1989.	FV	15.00	60.00

		VG	VF	UNC
48	**10 Dollars**			
	1987; 1989. Black on red and multicolor underprint. Like #40.			
	a. 1.1.1987.	7.50	27.50	120.
	b. 1.1.1989.	27.50	90.00	400.

		VG	VF	UNC
49	**20 Dollars**			
	1986; 1987. Brown on multicolor underprint. Like #41.			
	a. 1.1.1986.	FV	60.00	225.
	b. 1.1.1987.	FV	15.00	75.00

		VG	VF	UNC
50	**100 Dollars**			
	1983; 1989. Blue on multicolor underprint. Like #42.			
	a. 1.11.1983.	65.00	150.	750.
	b. 1.1.1989.	60.00	175.	850.

ACT 1982; 1990 ISSUE

#51-57 older facing portr. of Qn. Elizabeth II at r. Wmk: Carved head of the "sleeping giant." Printer: TDLR.

		VG	VF	UNC
51	**1 Dollar**	FV	1.25	9.00
	1.5.1990. Green on light brown, blue and multicolor underprint. Lobster at left. Back green and red; marine life of Belize across center.			

		VG	VF	UNC
52	**2 Dollars**			
	1990; 1991. Purple on light green, blue and multicolor underprint. Carved stone pillar at left. Mayan ruins of Belize on back.			
	a. 1.5.1990.	FV	1.50	15.00
	b. 1.6.1991.	FV	1.50	15.00

		VG	VF	UNC
53	**5 Dollars**			
	1990; 1991. Red-orange, orange and violet on multicolor underprint. C. Columbus medallion at left, silver tiger fish below. St. George's Caye, coffin, outline map and building on back.			
	a. 1.5.1990.	FV	3.50	30.00
	b. 1.6.1991.	FV	3.50	25.00

		VG	VF	UNC
54	**10 Dollars**			
	1990; 1991. Black, olive-brown and deep blue-green on multicolor underprint. Court House clock tower at left. Government House, Court House and St. John's Cathedral on back.			
	a. 1.5.1990.	FV	7.50	45.00
	b. 1.6.1991.	FV	7.50	35.00

		VG	VF	UNC
55	**20 Dollars**	FV	17.50	55.00
	1.5.1990. Dark brown on multicolor underprint. Upper left dog-like bat; lower left Kinkajou; upper center Black Howler Monkey; lower center left Collared Peccary; upper center right Northern Tamandua; lower center right Red Brocket; upper right Ringtail; lower right Jaguar. Fauna of Belize on back.			

		VG	VF	UNC
56	**50 Dollars**			
	1990; 1991. Purple, brown and red on multicolor underprint. Boats at left. Bridges of Belize on back.			
	a. 1.5.1990.	FV	35.00	120.
	b. 1.6.1991.	FV	30.00	100.

57 **100 Dollars**

1990-94. Blue-violet, orange and red on multicolor underprint. Keel-billed toucan at left. Birds of Belize - jabiru stork, brown pelican, red-footed booby, magnificent frigate bird, yellow-headed parrot and king vulture on back.

	VG	VF	UNC
a. 1.5.1990.	FV	75.00	275.
b. 1.6.1991.	FV	75.00	300.
c. 1.5.1994.	FV	70.00	225.

ACT 1982; 1996 ISSUE

#58-59 like #53-54 but w/segmented foil over security strip and ascending size serial # at upper r. Printer: TDLR.

		VG	VF	UNC
58	**5 Dollars** 1.3.1996. Red-orange, orange and violet on multicolor underprint. Like #53.	FV	3.50	22.50
59	**10 Dollars** 1.3.1996. Black, olive brown and deep blue-green on multicolor underprint. Like #54.	FV	6.00	32.50

1997-2002 ISSUES

#60-65 reduced size.

60 **2 Dollars**

1999; 2002. Purple on light green, blue and multicolor underprint. Like #52.

	VG	VF	UNC
a. 1.1.1999.	FV	FV	9.00
b. 1.1.2002.	FV	FV	7.50

61 **5 Dollars**

1999; 2002. Red-orange, orange and violet on multicolor underprint. Like #53.

	VG	VF	UNC
a. 1.1.1999.	FV	FV	15.00
b. 1.1.2002.	FV	FV	10.00

62 **10 Dollars**

1997; 2001. Black, olive-brown and deep blue-green on multicolor underprint. Like #59.

	VG	VF	UNC
a. 1.6.1997.	FV	FV	30.00
b. 1.2001. (no day)	FV	FV	25.00

63 **20 Dollars**

1997; 2000. Dark Brown on multicolor underprint. Like #55.

	VG	VF	UNC
a. 1.6.1997.	FV	FV	45.00
b. 1.10.2000.	FV	FV	37.50

64 **50 Dollars**

1997; 2000. Purple, brown and red on multicolor underprint. Like #56.

	VG	VF	UNC
a. 1.6.1997.	FV	FV	90.00
b. 1.9.2000.	FV	FV	85.00

		VG	VF	UNC
65	**100 Dollars** 1.6.1997. Blue-violet, orange and red on multicolor underprint. Like #57.	FV	FV	165.

2003 ISSUE

#66-71 like #60-65 but additional security features. Printer: TDLR.

		VG	VF	UNC
66	**2 Dollars** 1.6.2003.	FV	FV	5.00

67	**5 Dollars** 2003-05.			
	a. 1.6.2003.	—	Unc	7.50
	b. 1.1.2005.	—	Unc	6.00
	r. 1.1.2005. Replacement.	—	Unc	75.00

		VG	VF	UNC
68	**10 Dollars** 2003-5.			
	a. 1.3.2003.	FV	FV	12.50
	b. 1.1.2005.	FV	FV	10.00

		VG	VF	UNC
69	**20 Dollars** 2003-05.			
	a. 1.1.2003.	FV	FV	22.50
	b. 1.1.2005.	FV	FV	20.00

		VG	VF	UNC
70	**50 Dollars** 1.3.2003.	FV	FV	50.00

		VG	VF	UNC
71	**100 Dollars** 1.1.2003.	FV	FV	100.

COLLECTOR SERIES

CENTRAL BANK OF BELIZE

1984 ND ISSUE

Note: The Central Bank of Belize will no longer exchange these notes for regular currency. (It is illegal to export the currency afterwards). Value is thus speculative.

		Issue Price	Mkt.	Value
CS1	**ND (1984) Collection** Stamped from paper bonded within gold foil. Denominations: $1 (1 pc.), $2 (2 pcs.) $5 (3 pcs.), $10 (4 pcs.), $20 (2 pcs.), $25 (6 pcs.), $50 (7 pcs.), $75 (5 pcs.), $100 (6 pcs.). Total 36 pcs. All have Queen Elizabeth II and building on face, different animals, ships, fish, birds etc. on backs.		—	325.

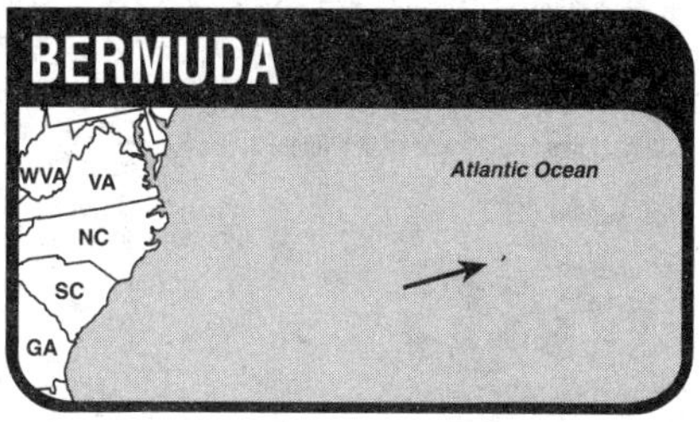

The Parliamentary British Colony of Bermuda, situated in the western Atlantic Ocean 660 miles (1,062 km.) east of North Carolina, has an area of 20.6 sq. mi. (53 sq. km.) and a population of 60,100. Capital: Hamilton. Concentrated essences, beauty preparations, and cut flowers are exported. Most Bermudians derive their livelihood from tourism.

Bermuda was discovered by Juan de Bermudez, a Spanish navigator, in 1503. British influence dates from 1609 when a group of Virginia-bound British colonists under the command of Sir George Somers was shipwrecked on the islands for 10 months. The islands were settled in 1612 by 60 British colonists from the Virginia Colony and became a crown colony in 1684. Internal autonomy was obtained by the constitution of June 8, 1968.

In February, 1970, Bermuda converted from its former currency, the British pound, to a decimal currency, termed a dollar, On July 31, 1972, Bermuda severed its monetary link with the British pound and pegged its dollar to be the same value as the U.S. dollar.

RULERS:

British

MONETARY SYSTEM:

1 Shilling = 12 Pence
1 Pound = 20 Shillings, to 1970
1 Dollar = 100 Cents, 1970-

BRITISH ADMINISTRATION

BERMUDA GOVERNMENT

1952 ISSUE

Royal crest on back. Printer: BWC.

		VG	VF	UNC
18	**5 Shillings** 1952; 1957. Brown on multicolor underprint. Portrait Queen Elizabeth II at upper center Hamilton Harbor in frame at bottom center.			
	a. 20.10.1952.	10.00	35.00	135.
	b. 1.5.1957.	8.00	30.00	100.
	s. As b. Specimen.	—	—	—

1952-66 ISSUE

#18-22 arms at ctr. on back. Printer: BWC.

		VG	VF	UNC
19	**10 Shillings** 1952-66. Red on multicolor underprint. Portrait Queen Elizabeth II at upper center Gate's Fort in St. George in frame at bottom center.			
	a. 20.10.1952.	25.00	70.00	350.
	b. 1.5.1957.	15.00	40.00	175.
	c. 1.10.1966.	18.00	60.00	250.
	s. As b. Specimen.	—	—	—

		VG	VF	UNC
20	**1 Pound** 1952-66. Blue on multicolor underprint. Queen Elizabeth II at right. Bridge at left.			
	a. 20.10.1952.	30.00	90.00	450.
	b. 1.5.1957. without security strip.	25.00	70.00	375.
	c. 1.5.1957. with security strip.	22.50	70.00	350.
	d. 1.10.1966.	20.00	60.00	275.
	s. As d. Specimen.	—	—	—

		VG	VF	UNC
21	**5 Pounds** 1952-66. Orange on multicolor underprint. Portrait Queen Elizabeth II at right, Large value at left. ship entering Hamilton Harbor at left. Back orange and green.			
	a. 20.10.1952.	100.	300.	1400.
	b. 1.5.1957. without security strip.	110.	325.	1600.
	c. 1.5.1957. with security strip.	65.00	200.	1250.
	d. 1.10.1966.	60.00	200.	950.
22	**10 Pounds** 28.7.1964. Purple on multicolor underprint. Portrait Queen Elizabeth II at right.	150.	500.	2000.

1970 ISSUE

#23-27 Qn. Elizabeth II at r. looking 3/4 to l., arms at l. ctr. Wmk: Tuna fish.

		VG	VF	UNC
23	**1 Dollar** 6.2.1970. Dark blue on tan and aqua underprint. Bermuda petrel or cahow at center. Sailboats at left center, buildings at upper right on back.			
	a. Issued note.	1.50	4.00	27.50
	s. Specimen.	—	—	25.00

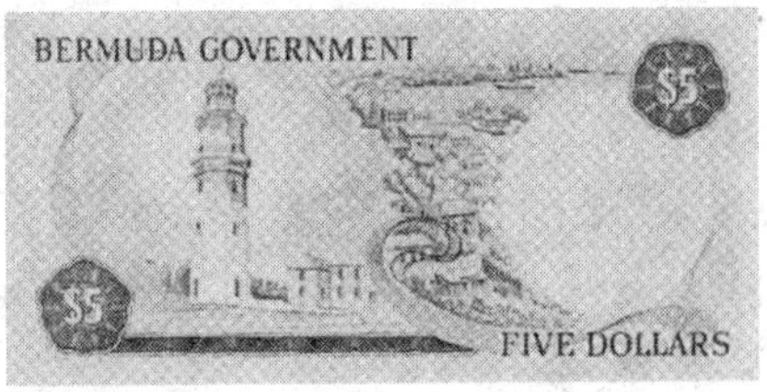

24	5 Dollars	VG	VF	UNC
	6.2.1970. Red-violet on aqua and multicolor underprint. Lighthouse at left, buildings at center right on back.			
	a. Issued note.	6.50	10.00	45.00
	s. Specimen.	—	—	25.00

25	10 Dollars	VG	VF	UNC
	6.2.1970. Purple on brown and multicolor underprint. Bermuda petrel and seashell at center, beach at left on back.			
	a. Issued note.	FV	15.00	95.00
	s. Specimen.	—	—	25.00

26	20 Dollars	VG	VF	UNC
	6.2.1970. Green on multicolor underprint. Building, sailboat and bridge at left center on back.			
	a. Issued note.	FV	30.00	150.
	s. Specimen.	—	—	35.00

27	50 Dollars	VG	VF	UNC
	6.2.1970. Brown on multicolor underprint. Lighthouse at left, map at upper right on back.			
	a. Issued note.	FV	80.00	300.
	s. Specimen.	—	—	60.00

Bermuda Monetary Authority

1974-82 Issue

#28-33 Qn. Elizabeth II at r. looking 3/4 to l. Wmk: Tuna fish. Replacement notes: Serial # prefix *Z/1*.

#28-32 like #23-27.

28	1 Dollar	VG	VF	UNC
	1975-88. Dark blue on tan and aqua underprint. Like #23.			
	a. Signature titles: *CHAIRMAN* and *MANAGING DIRECTOR.* 1.7.1975; 1.12.1976.	1.00	5.00	35.00
	b. 1.4.1978; 1.9.1979; 2.1.1982; 1.5.1984.	1.00	3.00	17.50
	c. Signature titles: *CHAIRMAN* and *GENERAL MANAGER.* 1.1.1986.	1.00	3.50	17.50
	d. Signature titles: *CHAIRMAN* and *DIRECTOR.* 1.1.1988.	1.00	3.00	17.50
	s. Specimen, punch hole cancelled.	—	—	—

29	5 Dollars	VG	VF	UNC
	1978-88. Red-violet on aqua and multicolor underprint. Like #24.			
	a. Signature titles: *CHAIRMAN* and *MANAGING DIRECTOR.* 1.4.1978.	FV	8.00	40.00
	b. 2.1.1981.	FV	7.50	35.00
	c. Signature titles: *CHAIRMAN* and *GENERAL MANAGER.* 1.1.1986.	FV	7.50	35.00
	d. Signature titles: *CHAIRMAN* and *DIRECTOR.* 1.1.1988.	FV	7.50	32.50
	s. Specimen, punch hole cancelled.	—	—	—

30	10 Dollars	VG	VF	UNC
	1978; 1982. Purple on brown and multicolor underprint. Like #25.			
	a. 1.4.1978.	FV	40.00	150.
	b. 2.1.1982.	FV	40.00	120.
	s. Specimen, punch hole cancelled.	—	—	—

31	20 Dollars	VG	VF	UNC
	1974-86. Green on multicolor underprint. Like #26.			
	a. 1.4.1974.	25.00	125.	500.
	b. 1.3.1976.	FV	45.00	185.
	c. 2.1.1981; 1.5.1984.	FV	25.00	90.00
	d. Signature title: *GENERAL MANAGER* at right. 1.1.1986.	FV	25.00	95.00
	s. Specimen, punch hole cancelled.	—	—	—

32	50 Dollars	VG	VF	UNC
	1974-82. Brown on multicolor underprint. Like #27.			
	a. 1.5.1974.	85.00	350.	1700.
	b. 1.4.1978; 2.1.1982.	FV	100.	450.
	s. Specimen, punch hole cancelled.	—	—	—

33	100 Dollars	VG	VF	UNC
	1982-86. Orange and brown on multicolor underprint. House of Assembly at left, Camden building at upper center right on back.			
	a. 2.1.1982.	FV	FV	385.
	b. Signature title: *GENERAL MANAGER* overprint at right. 14.11.1984.	FV	FV	375.
	c. Signature title: *GENERAL MANAGER* at right. 1.1.1986.	FV	FV	350.
	s. Specimen, punch hole cancelled.	—	—	—

NOTICE

Readers with unlisted dates, signature varieties, etc. are invited to submit photocopies of their notes to: Standard Catalog of World Paper Money, 700 East State St. Iola, WI 54990-0001, E-Mail: george.cuhaj@fwpubs.com.

1988-89 Issue

#34-39 mature bust of Qn. Elizabeth II at r. Back similar to #29-33 but w/stylistic changes; arms added at upper l. Sign. titles: *CHAIRMAN* and *DIRECTOR*. Wmk.: Tuna fish. Replacement notes: Serial # prefix *Z/1, Z/2*.

34	2 Dollars	VG	VF	UNC
	1988; 1989. Blue-green on green and multicolor underprint. Dockyards clock tower building at upper left, map at center, arms at center right on back.			
	a. Serial # prefix: *B/1*. 1.10.1988.	FV	FV	10.00
	b. Serial # prefix: *B/2*. 1.8.1989.	FV	FV	9.50

35	5 Dollars	VG	VF	UNC
	20.2.1989. Red-violet and purple on multicolor underprint. Similar to #29.			
	a. Signature title: *DIRECTOR* on silver background at bottom center Serial # prefix: *B/1*.	FV	7.00	25.00
	b. Signature title: *DIRECTOR* without silver background. Serial # prefix: *B/1, B/2*.	FV	FV	12.50

36	10 Dollars	VG	VF	UNC
	20.2.1989. Purple, blue and ochre on multicolor underprint. Similar to #30.	FV	FV	25.00

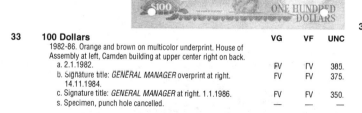

37	20 Dollars	VG	VF	UNC
	20.2.1989. Green and red on multicolor underprint. Similar to #31.			
	a. Serial # prefix: *B/1*.	FV	FV	42.50
	b. Serial # prefix: *B/2*.	FV	FV	40.00

38	50 Dollars	VG	VF	UNC
	20.2.1989. Brown and olive on multicolor underprint. Similar to #32.	FV	FV	100.

39	100 Dollars	VG	VF	UNC
	20.2.1989. Orange, brown and violet on multicolor underprint. Similar to $33.	FV	FV	185.

1992 Commemorative Issue; Act 1969

#40, Quincentenary of Christopher Columbus

40	50 Dollars	VG	VF	UNC
	12.10.1992. Dark blue, brown and red on multicolor underprint. Face like #38 but with commemorative details. Maltese cross as serial # prefix at upper left, c/c fractional prefix at right, and overprint: *Christopher Columbus / Quincentenary / 1492-1992* at left. Scuba divers, shipwreck at left, island outline at upper center right above arms.	FV	FV	120.

Act 1969; 1992-96 Issue

#40A-45 issued under Bermuda Monetary Authority Act 1969. Like #34-39 but w/Authorization text in 3 lines at ctr. Wmk: Tuna fish.

40A	2 Dollars	VG	VF	UNC
	1996-97. Blue and green on multicolor underprint. Like #34 but with 3-line text at center.			
	a. 29.2.1996.	FV	FV	9.00
	b. 6.6.1997.	FV	FV	5.00

41	5 Dollars	VG	VF	UNC
	1992-97. Red-violet and purple on multicolor underprint. Like #35 but with 3-line text at center.			
	a. 12.11.1992.	FV	FV	12.50
	b. 25.3.1995.	FV	FV	11.00
	c. 20.2.1996.	FV	FV	10.00
	d. 10.6.1997.	FV	FV	10.00

42	10 Dollars	VG	VF	UNC
	1993-99. Purple, deep blue and orange on multicolor underprint. Like #36 but with 3-line text at center.			
	a. 4.1.1993.	FV	FV	22.50
	b. 15.3.1996.	FV	FV	20.00
	c. 17.6.1997.	FV	FV	20.00
	d. 31.5.1999. with security strip.	FV	FV	20.00

43	20 Dollars	VG	VF	UNC
	1996; 1999. Green and red on multicolor underprint. Like #37 but with 3-line text at center.			
	a. 27.2.1996.	FV	FV	40.00
	b. 13.5.1999. with security strip.	FV	FV	37.50

44 **50 Dollars**
1992-96. Dark blue, brown and red on multicolor underprint. Similar to #40 but without commemorative details.

	VG	VF	UNC
a. 12.10.1992.	FV	FV	100.
b. 25.3.1995.	FV	FV	90.00
c. 23.2.1996.	FV	FV	85.00

45 **100 Dollars**
14.2.1996. Orange, brown and violet on multicolor underprint. Like #39 but with 3-line text at center.

VG	VF	UNC
FV	FV	175.

1994 Commemorative Issue

#46, 25th Anniversary Bermuda Monetary Authority

46 **100 Dollars**
20.2.1994. Orange, brown and violet on multicolor underprint. Like #45 but with overprint: *25th Anniversary....*

VG	VF	UNC
FV	FV	170.

1997 Commemorative Issue

#47, Opening of Burnaby House

47 **20 Dollars**
17.1.1997. Green and red on multicolor underprint. Overprint on #43. *To commemorate the opening of Burnaby House...* in watermark area at left.

VG	VF	UNC
FV	FV	37.50

1997 Regular Issue

48 **50 Dollars**
6.6.1997. Dark blue, brown and red on multicolor underprint. Like #44 but with segmented foil over security thread.

VG	VF	UNC
FV	FV	87.50

49 **100 Dollars**
30.6.1997. Orange and brown on multicolor underprint. Like #45 but with segmented foil over security thread.

VG	VF	UNC
FV	FV	165.

2000 Issue

Mature portr. Qn. Elizabeth II at r. Backs like #40A-45. Replacement notes: Serial # prefix *Z/I*.

50 **2 Dollars**
24.5.2000. Blue and green on multicolor underprint. Sea horse at center. Boats and building at left, island map at center on back.

	VG	VF	UNC
a. Issued note.	FV	FV	4.00
s. Specimen, punch hole cancelled.	—	—	—

51 **5 Dollars**
24.5.2000. Purple and burgundy on multicolor underprint. Shell and fish at center Lighthouse at left, bay view at center on back.

	VG	VF	UNC
a. Issued note.	FV	FV	8.50
s. Specimen.	—	—	—

NOTICE

Readers with unlisted dates, signature varieties, etc. are invited to submit photocopies of their notes to: Standard Catalog of World Paper Money, 700 East State St. Iola, WI 54990-0001, E-Mail: george.cuhaj@fwpubs.com.

52	10 Dollars	VG	VF	UNC
	24.5.2000. Dark blue and mauve on multicolor underprint. Flower and Bermuda Petrel at center. Bay scene, Bermuda Petrel and shell on back.			
	a. Issued note.	FV	FV	17.00
	s. Specimen.	—	—	—

53	20 Dollars	VG	VF	UNC
	24.5.2000. Green and red on multicolor underprint. Building at center. Bridge and harbor scene on back.			
	a. Issued note.	FV	FV	37.50
	s. Specimen.	—	—	—

54	50 Dollars	VG	VF	UNC
	24.5.2000. Bluish black, red and brown on multicolor underprint. Building at center Scuba divers and wreck at left, map at upper center on back.			
	a. Issued note.	FV	FV	85.00
	s. Specimen.	—	—	—

55	100 Dollars	VG	VF	UNC
	24.5.2000. Red-orange and brown on multicolor underprint. Flowers and shell at center. House of Assembly at left on back.			
	a. Issued note.	FV	FV	165.
	s. Specimen.	—	—	—

2003 Commemorative Issue

56	50 Dollars	VG	VF	UNC
	2.6.2003. Similar to #54 but with golden crown at right with overprint: *TO COMMEMORATE THE CORONATION OF QUEEN ELIZABETH II 1953-2003.* "	FV	FV	95.00

Collector Series

Bermuda Monetary Authority

1978-84 Dated Issue (1985)

CS1	1978-84 1-100 Dollars	Issue Price	Mkt.	Value
	#22-33 with normal serial #, punched hole cancelled, overprint: *SPECIMEN* (1985).		—	65.00

1981-82 Issue (1985)

CS2	1981-82 1-100 Dollars	Issue Price	Mkt.	Value
	#28-33 with all zero serial #, punched hole cancelled in all 4 corners, overprint: *SPECIMEN* (1985).		—	65.00

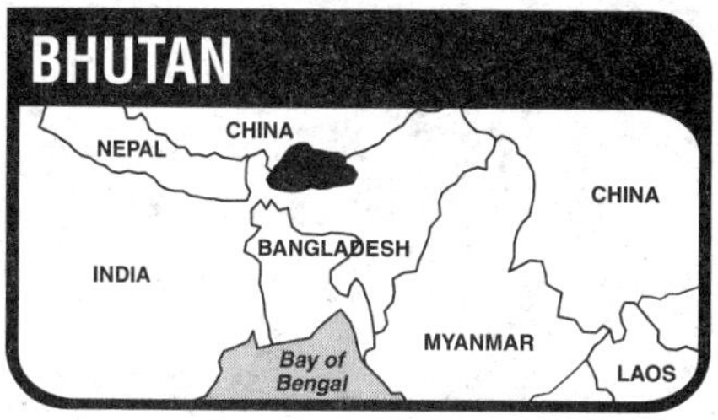

The Kingdom of Bhutan, a landlocked Himalayan country bordered by Tibet, India, and Sikkim, has an area of 18,147 sq. mi. (47,000 sq. km.) and a population of 2.03 million. Capital: Thimphu; Paro is the administrative capital. Virtually the entire population is engaged in agricultural and pastoral activities. Rice, wheat, barley, and yak butter are produced in sufficient quantity to make the country self-sufficient in food. The economy of Bhutan is primitive and many transactions are conducted on a barter basis.

Bhutan's early history is obscure, but is thought to have resembled that of rural medieval Europe. The country was conquered by Tibet, which still claims sovereignty over Bhutan, in the 9th century, and subjected to a dual temporal and spiritual rule until the mid-19th century, when the southern part of the country was occupied by the British and annexed to British India. Bhutan was established as a hereditary monarchy in 1907, and in 1910 agreed to British control of its external affairs. In 1949, India and Bhutan concluded a treaty whereby India assumed Britain's role in subsidizing Bhutan and conducting its foreign affairs.

RULERS:

Jigme Singye Wangchuk, 1972-

MONETARY SYSTEM:

1 Ngultrum (= 1 Indian Rupee) = 100 Chetrums, 1974-

SIGNATURE CHART	
Chairman Ashi Sonam Wangchuck	Bank of Bhutan Yeshe Dorji
Chairman Dorji Tsering	

KINGDOM

ROYAL GOVERNMENT OF BHUTAN

1974-78 ND ISSUE

#1-4 wmk: 4-petaled symbol, called a *dorje*, the Buddhist version of a thunderbolt, symbol of a "flash" of enlightenment.

		VG	VF	UNC
1	**1 Ngultrum** ND (1974). Blue on multicolor underprint. Dragon design at left and right.	.50	2.50	6.00

		VG	VF	UNC
2	**5 Ngultrum** ND (1974). Red-brown on multicolor underprint. Portrait J. Singye Wangchuk at center. Simtokha Dzong palace center right on back.	1.50	15.00	50.00

		VG	VF	UNC
3	**10 Ngultrum** ND (1974). Blue-violet on multicolor underprint. Portrait J. Dorji Wangchuk at top center. Paro Dzong palace center right on back.	3.50	30.00	200.

		VG	VF	UNC
4	**100 Ngultrum** ND (1978). Green and brown on multicolor underprint. Portrait J. Singye Wangchuk at center, circle with 8 good luck symbols at right. Tashichho Dzong palace at left center on back.	300.	1000.	—

1981 ND ISSUE

#5-11 serial # at upper l. and r.

		VG	VF	UNC
5	**1 Ngultrum** ND (1981). Blue on multicolor underprint. Royal emblem between facing dragons at center. Simtokha Dzong palace at center on back.	.10	.25	3.00

		VG	VF	UNC
6	**2 Ngultrum** ND (1981). Brown and green on multicolor underprint. Like #5. Royal emblem between facing dragons at center. Simtokha Dzong palace at center on back.	.15	.50	4.50

		VG	VF	UNC
7	**5 Ngultrum** ND (1981). Brown on multicolor underprint. Royal emblem between facing birds at center. Paro Dzong palace at center on back.	.50	2.50	10.00

#8-11 royal emblem at l.

		VG	VF	UNC
8	**10 Ngultrum** ND (1981). Purple on multicolor underprint. Royal emblem at left, portrait J. Singye Wangchuk at right. Paro Dzong palace at center on back.	.75	5.00	17.50

		VG	VF	UNC
9	**20 Ngultrum** ND (1981). Olive on multicolor underprint. Facing portrait Jigme Dorji Wangchuk at right. Punakha Dzong palace at center on back.	1.25	7.50	30.00

		VG	VF	UNC
10	**50 Ngultrum** ND (1981). Purple, violet and brown on multicolor underprint. Face like #9. Tongsa Dzong palace at center on back.	3.00	15.00	75.00

		VG	VF	UNC
11	**100 Ngultrum** ND (1981). Dark green, olive-green and brown-violet on multicolor underprint. Bird at center, portrait J. Singye Wangchuk at right. Tashichho Dzong palace at center on back.	5.00	27.50	150.

ROYAL MONETARY AUTHORITY OF BHUTAN

1985-92 ND ISSUE

#12-18 similar to #5-11. Serial # at lower l. and upper r.

#12-15 reduced size.

		VG	VF	UNC
12	**1 Ngultrum** ND (1986). Blue on multicolor underprint. 2 signature varieties. Similar to #5.	FV	FV	.50

		VG	VF	UNC
13	**2 Ngultrum** ND (1986). Brown and green on multicolor underprint. Similar to #6.	FV	FV	.75
14	**5 Ngultrum** ND (1985). Brown on multicolor underprint. Similar to #7.	FV	FV	1.50

15 10 Ngultrum

ND (1986; 1992). Purple on multicolor underprint. Similar to #8.

	VG	VF	UNC
a. Serial # prefix fractional style. (1986).	FV	FV	1.75
b. Serial # prefix 2 Large letters (printed in China.) (1992).	FV	FV	2.00

16 20 Ngultrum

ND (1986; 1992). Olive on multicolor underprint. Similar to #9.

	VG	VF	UNC
a. Serial # prefix fractional style. (1986).	FV	FV	4.00
b. Serial # prefix 2 Large letters (printed in China.) (1992).	FV	FV	3.50

17 50 Ngultrum

ND (1985; 1992). Violet and brown on multicolor underprint. Similar to #10.

	VG	VF	UNC
a. Serial # prefix fractional style. (1986)	FV	3.00	15.00
b. Serial # prefix letters 2 Large letters (printed in China.) (1992).	FV	2.00	6.50

18 100 Ngultrum

ND (1986; 1992). Green and brown on multicolor underprint. Similar to #11.

	VG	VF	UNC
a. Serial # prefix fractional style. (1986).	FV	5.00	25.00
b. Serial # prefix 2 Large letters (printed in China.) (1992).	FV	4.00	17.50

1994 ND ISSUE

#19 and 20 similar to #17 and 18 but with modified unpt. including floral diamond shaped registry design at upper ctr. Wmk: Wavy *ROYAL MONETARY AUTHORITY* repeated.

19 50 Ngultrum

	VG	VF	UNC
ND (1994). Purple, violet and brown on multicolor underprint. Similar to #17.	FV	FV	6.00

20 100 Ngultrum

	VG	VF	UNC
ND (1994). Green and brown on multicolor underprint. Similar to #18.	FV	FV	9.00

1994 ND COMMEMORATIVE ISSUE

#21, National Day

21 500 Ngultrum

	VG	VF	UNC
ND (1994). Red-orange on multicolor underprint. Portrait King Jigme Singye Wangchuk in headdress at right. Punakha Dzong palace on back. Both serial #s ascending size. Watermark: 4-petaled symbol.	FV	FV	40.00

NOTICE

Readers with unlisted dates, signature varieties, etc. are invited to submit photocopies of their notes to: Standard Catalog of World Paper Money, 700 East State St. Iola, WI 54990-0001, E-Mail: george.cuhaj@fwpubs.com.

2000-01 ND Issue

		VG	VF	UNC
22	**10 Ngultrum** ND (2000). Purple and blue on multicolor underprint. Royal emblem at left, portrait King Jigme Singye Wangchuk at right. Back like #15.	FV	FV	1.75
23	**20 Ngultrum** ND (2000). Olive on multicolor underprint. Like #16 but with signature 3.	FV	FV	4.00

		VG	VF	UNC
24	**50 Ngultrum** ND (2000). Violet and brown on multicolor underprint. Like #19.	FV	FV	6.50

		VG	VF	UNC
25	**100 Ngultrum** ND (2000). Green and brown on multicolor underprint. Portrait King Jigme Singye Wangchuk at right, vertical serial # at right, both ascending size. Back similar to #18. Watermark: 4-petaled symbol.	FV	FV	17.50

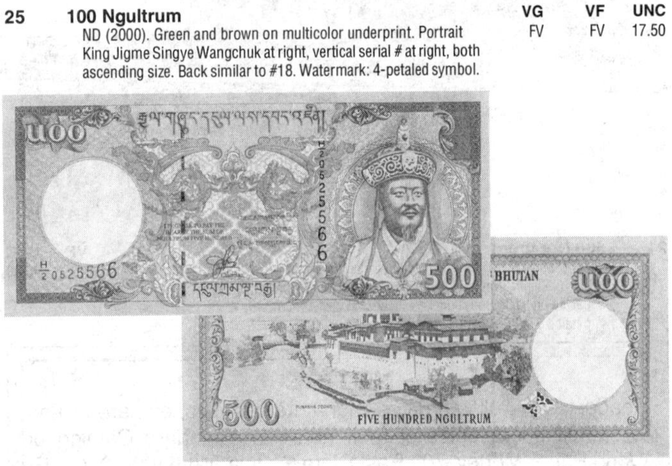

		VG	VF	UNC
26	**500 Ngultrum** ND (2000). Red-orange on multicolor underprint. Portrait King Jigme Singye Wangchuk in headdress at right. Punakha Dzong palace on back.	FV	FV	32.50

BIAFRA

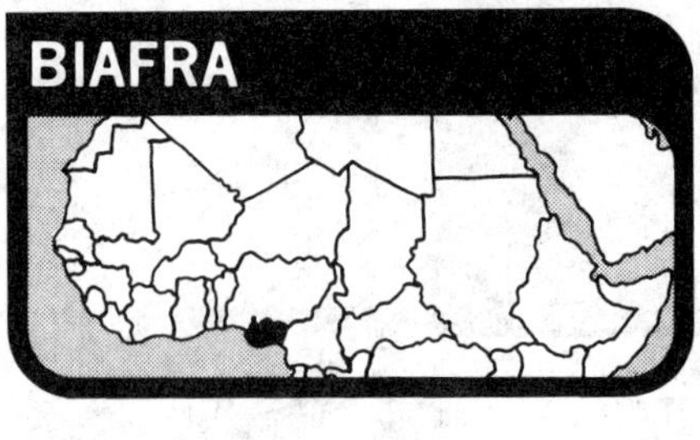

On May 27, 1967, Gen. Yakubu Gowon, head of the Federal Military Government of Nigeria, created three states from the Eastern Region of the country. Separation of the region, undertaken to achieve better regional and ethnic balance, caused Lt. Col. E. O. Ojukwu, Military Governor of the Eastern Region, to proclaim on May 30, 1967, the independence of the Eastern Region as the "Republic of Biafra." Fighting broke out between the Federal Military Government and the forces of Lt. Col. Ojukwu and continued until Biafra surrendered on Jan. 15, 1970. Biafra was then reintegrated into the Republic of Nigeria as three states: East-Central, Rivers, and South-Eastern.

For additional history, see Nigeria.

MONETARY SYSTEM:

1 Shilling = 12 Pence
1 Pound = 20 Shillings

Republic

Bank of Biafra

1967 ND Issue

#1-2 palm tree, lg. rising sun at l.

		VG	VF	UNC
1	**5 Shillings** ND (1967). Blue on lilac underprint. (Color varies from orange to yellow for rising sun.) Back brown on light blue underprint; four girls at right.	.50	3.00	12.50

		VG	VF	UNC
2	**1 Pound** ND (1967). Blue and orange. Back brown on light blue underprint., arms at right.	1.00	25.00	100.

1968 ND Issue

#3-7 palm tree and small rising sun at l. to ctr.

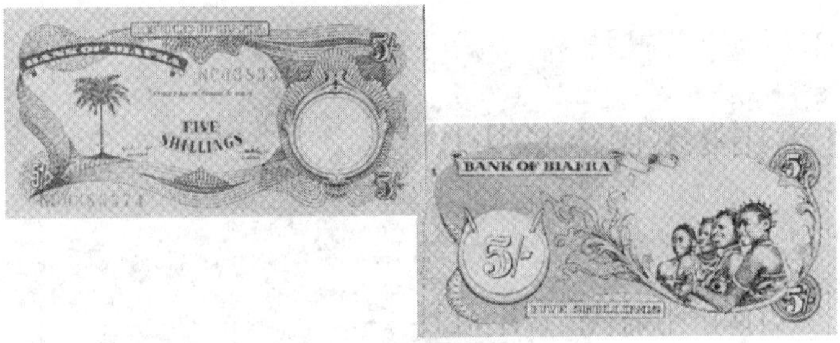

		VG	VF	UNC
3	**5 Shillings** ND (1968-69). Blue on green and orange underprint. Back similar to #1.			
	a. Issued note.	.50	5.00	15.00
	b. Without serial #.	1.00	12.50	35.00

4 **10 Shillings**

	VG	VF	UNC
ND (1968-69). Dark green on blue and and orange underprint. Buildings at right on back.	.25	1.50	4.50

5 **1 Pound**

	VG	VF	UNC
ND (1968-69). Dark brown on green, brown and orange underprint. Back similar to #2.			
a. Issued note.	.10	.25	1.00
b. Without serial #.	.50	5.00	20.00

6 **5 Pounds**

	VG	VF	UNC
ND (1968-69). Purple on green and orange underprint. Arms at left, weaving at left center on back.			
a. Issued note.	4.00	17.50	65.00
b. Without serial #.	2.00	6.00	27.50

7 **10 Pounds**

	VG	VF	UNC
ND (1968-69). Black on blue, brown and orange underprint. Arms at left, carver at left center on back.			
a. Issued note.	4.00	15.00	75.00
b. Without serial #.	2.50	7.50	35.00

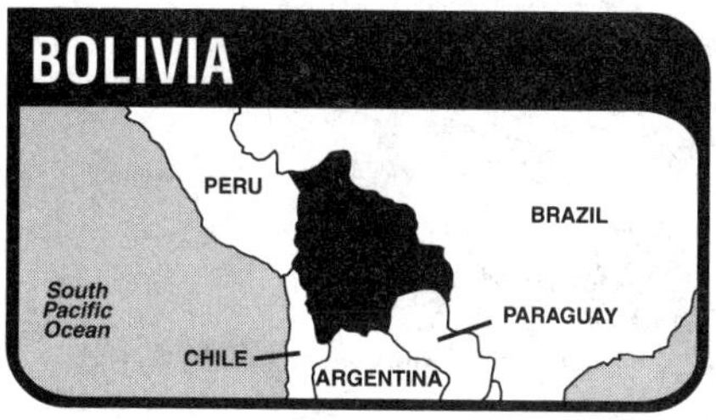

The Republic of Bolivia, a landlocked country in west central South America, has an area of 424,165 sq. mi. (1,098,581 sq. km.) and a population of 8.33 million. Capitals: La Paz (administrative); Sucre (constitutional). Mining is the principal industry and tin the most important metal. Minerals, petroleum, natural gas, cotton and coffee are exported.

The Incas, who ruled one of the world's greatest dynasties, incorporated the area that is now western Bolivia into their empire about 1200AD. Their control was maintained until the Spaniards arrived in 1535 and reduced the predominantly Indian population to slavery. When Napoleon occupied Madrid in 1808 and placed his brother Joseph on the Spanish throne, a fervor of revolutionary activity quickened in Bolivia, culminating with the 1809 proclamation of independence. Sixteen years of struggle ensued before the republic, named for the famed liberator General Simón Bolívar, was established on August 6, 1825. Since then, Bolivia has had more than 60 revolutions, 70 presidents and 11 constitutions.

MONETARY SYSTEMS:

1 Boliviano = 100 (Centavos) to 1965
1 Bolivar = 100 Centavos, 1945-1962
1 Peso Boliviano = 100 Centavos, 1962-1987
1 Boliviano = 100 Centavos, 1987-

SPECIMEN NOTES:

All *SPECIMEN, MUESTRA, MUESTRA SIN VALOR* and *ESPECIMEN* notes always have serial #'s of zero.

REPUBLIC

BANCO CENTRAL DE BOLIVIA

LEY DE 13 DE JULIO DE 1962 - FIRST ISSUE

Peso Boliviano System

#152-157 old and new denomination on back at bottom. Arms at l. Sign. varieties. Printer: TDLR.

152 **1 Peso Boliviano**

	VG	VF	UNC
L.1962. Black on multicolor underprint. Portrait Campesino at right. Agricultural scene at center right on back. Series A-E.			
a. Issued note.	2.00	7.50	20.00
s. Specimen with red ovpt: *SPECIMEN.* Series A.	—	—	20.00

153 **5 Pesos Bolivianos**

	VG	VF	UNC
L.1962. Blue on multicolor underprint. Portrait Mayor Gualberto Villarroel Lopez at right. Petroleum refinery on back. Series A-B1. 11 signature varieties.			
a. Issued note.	1.00	3.00	12.00
b. Uncut sheet of 4 signed notes.	—	—	100.
s. Specimen with red ovpt: *SPECIMEN.* Series A; T; Z.	—	—	40.00

154 10 Pesos Bolivianos

L.1962. Olive-green on multicolor underprint. Portrait Colonel Germán Busch Becerra at right. Mountain of Potosí on back. Series A-U3. 18 signature varieties.	VG	VF	UNC
a. Issued note.	.05	.20	.75
b. Uncut sheet of 4 signed notes. Series U2.	—	—	30.00
s1. Specimen with red ovpt: *SPECIMEN.* Series A.	—	—	—
s2. As s1 but with punched hole cancellation and TDLR oval stamp. Series A.	—	—	—
s3. Specimen ovpt: *SPECIMEN.* Series A.	—	—	8.00
s4. Uncut sheet of 4 specimen notes. Series U2.	—	—	25.00

155 20 Pesos Bolivianos

L.1962. Purple on multicolor underprint. Portrait Pedro Domingo Murillo at right. La Paz mountain on back. Series A.	VG	VF	UNC
a. Issued note.	1.00	15.00	50.00
s. Specimen with red ovpt: *SPECIMEN.* Series A.	—	—	20.00

156 50 Pesos Bolivianos

L.1962. Orange on multicolor underprint. Portrait Antonio Jose de Sucre at right. Puerta del Sol on back. Series A.	VG	VF	UNC
a. Issued note.	30.00	85.00	225.
s. Specimen with red ovpt: *SPECIMEN.* Series A.	—	—	20.00

157 100 Pesos Bolivianos

L.1962. Red on multicolor underprint with green at left, blue at right. Portrait Simón Bolívar at right. Red serial #, and security thread at left center. Back darker red; engraved, scene of the declaration of the Bolivian Republic. Series A.	VG	VF	UNC
a. Issued note. Large, wide, dark signatures.	30.00	85.00	225.
b. Issued note. Small, thin, light signatures.	30.00	75.00	185.
s. Specimen with red ovpt: *SPECIMEN.* Series A.	—	—	20.00

Ley de 13 de Julio de 1962 - Second Issue

#158, 161-164A only new denomination on back. Sign. varieties. Printer: TDLR.

158 1 Peso Boliviano

L.1962. Like #152. Series F-F1. 7 signature varieties.	VG	VF	UNC
a. Issued note.	.25	.75	8.00
s. Specimen with red ovpt: *SPECIMEN.* Series Y.	—	—	—

#159, 160 not assigned.

161 20 Pesos Bolivianos

L.1962. Like #155. Series B-H. 4 signature varieties.	VG	VF	UNC
a. Issued note.	.25	1.00	10.00
s. Specimen with red ovpt: *SPECIMEN.* Series E.	—	—	—

#162-164 replacement notes: Serial # prefixes: *ZX; ZY; ZZ.*

162 50 Pesos Bolivianos

L.1962. Like #156. Series A-W7. 22 signature varieties.	VG	VF	UNC
a. Issued note.	.10	.25	1.00
b. Uncut sheet of 4 signed notes. Series L2, Y2.	—	—	10.00
r. Uncut sheet of 4 unsigned notes. Series AZ.	—	—	20.00
s1. Specimen with red ovpt: *SPECIMEN.* Series F; X; D1.	—	—	—
s2. As s1 but with punched hole cancellation (in l. signature area) and TDLR oval stamp. Series C.	—	—	125.
bx. Uncut sheet of 4 notes with signature at top of notes. Series L2; Y2. (error).	—	—	10.00

163 100 Pesos Bolivianos

L.1962. Red on multicolor underprint. Like #157. Brighter red back, engraved. Lower # prefixes (from B to T9). 19 signature varieties.

	VG	VF	UNC
a. Issued note. Prefix Z2.	.10	.25	1.00
b. Uncut sheet of 4 signed notes. Series X4; D5; U5.	—	—	12.50
r. Uncut sheet of 4 unsigned notes. Series AZ.	—	—	—
s. Specimen with red ovpt: *SPECIMEN.* Series G.	—	—	—

164 100 Pesos Bolivianos

L.1962 (1983). Red on multicolor underprint. Like #163.

	VG	VF	UNC
a. Back dull red, lithographed with poor detail. Black serial #. without security thread. Prefixes #10E-13D. 2 signature varieties.	.25	.75	4.00
b. As a. but with solid black security thread.	.25	.75	5.00
c. As a. but with segmented security thread.	.50	2.00	8.00
r. Unsigned remainder. Prefix #12H.	—	—	17.50
s. Specimen with red ovpt: *SPECIMEN.* Prefix #10E.	—	—	—

164A 100 Pesos Bolivianos

	VG	VF	UNC
L.1962. Red on multicolor underprint. Like #163 including engraved back, security thread and red serial #. Higher # prefixes (13E-19T) than for 164a. 2 signature varieties.	.10	.25	2.00

1981-84 Various Decrees ND Issue

#165-171 replacement notes: Serial # prefixes: *Z; ZY; ZZ.*

165 500 Pesos Bolivianos

D. 1.6.1981. Deep blue, blue-green and black on multicolor underprint. Arms at center, portrait Eduardo Avaroa at right and as watermark at left. Back blue on multicolor underprint. View of Puerto de Antofagasta, ca. 1879 at center Series A. Printer: ABNC.

	VG	VF	UNC
a. Issued note. 2 signature varieties.	.10	.25	2.00
r. Remainder without series, decreto or signature printing.	20.00	45.00	75.00
s. Specimen with red ovpt: *MUESTRA.*	—	—	—

NOTICE

Readers with unlisted dates, signature varieties, etc. are invited to submit photocopies of their notes to: Standard Catalog of World Paper Money, 700 East State St. Iola, WI 54990-0001, E-Mail: george.cuhaj@fwpubs.com.

166 500 Pesos Bolivianos

D. 1.6.1981. Like #165 but Series B; C. Printer: TDLR.

	VG	VF	UNC
a. Issued note.	.25	.30	1.25
b. Specimen with red ovpt: *SPECIMEN.* Series B.	—	—	50.00

167 1000 Pesos Bolivianos

D. 25.6.1982. Black on multicolor underprint. Arms at center, portrait Juana Azurday de Padilla at right and as watermark at left. House of Liberty on back. Series A1-Z9; (6 digits) A-L; (8 digits) each only to 49,999,999). Printer: TDLR. 3 signature varieties.

	VG	VF	UNC
a. Issued note.	.25	.30	1.00
s. Specimen with red ovpt: *SPECIMEN.* Series A1.	—	—	—

168 5000 Pesos Bolivianos

D. 10.2.1984. Deep brown on multicolor underprint. Arms at center, Marshal J. Ballivian y Segurola at right and as watermark at left. Stylized condor and leopard on back. Printer: BDDK. Series A.

	VG	VF	UNC
a. Issued note. signature varieties.	.50	1.00	2.00
s1. Specimen with red ovpt: *MUESTRA SIN VALOR.* Series A.	—	—	—
s2. Specimen pin-holed cancelled: *SPECIMEN.*	—		

169	10,000 Pesos Bolivianos	VG	VF	UNC
	D. 10.2.1984. Blackish purple and purple with dk. green arms on multicolor underprint. Arms at center portrait Marshal Andres de Santa Cruz at right and as watermark at left. Back brown, bluish purple and green; Legislative palace at center Printer: BDDK. Series A.			
	a. Issued note.	.05	.20	.75
	s. Specimen with red ovpt: *MUESTRA SIN VALOR*. Series A.	—	—	—

170	50,000 Pesos Bolivianos	VG	VF	UNC
	D. 5.6.1984. Deep green on multicolor underprint. Arms at left, portrait Gualberto Villarroel Lopez at center Petroleum refinery on back. Printer: TDLR. Series A; B.			
	a. Issued note. 2 signature varieties.	.05	.25	1.00
	s. Specimen with red ovpt: *MUESTRA SIN VALOR*. Series A.	—	—	—

171	100,000 Pesos Bolivianos	VG	VF	UNC
	D. 5.6.1984. Brown-violet on multicolor underprint. Arms at left, portrait Campesino at right. Agricultural scene at center right on back. Printer: TDLR. Series A; B.			
	a. Issued note. 2 signature varieties.	.15	.50	2.00
	s. Specimen with red ovpt: *MUESTRA SIN VALOR*. Series A.	—	—	—

1982-86 Monetary Emergency

Banco Central de Bolivia

W/o Branch

Decreto Supremo No. 19078, 28 Julio 1982

Cheque de Gerencia Issue

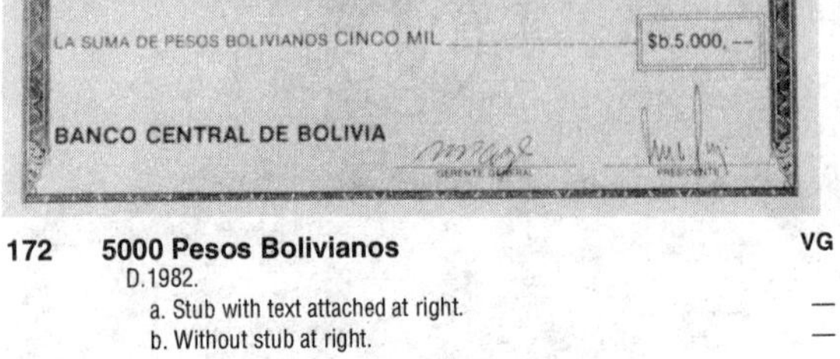

172	5000 Pesos Bolivianos	VG	VF	UNC
	D.1982.			
	a. Stub with text attached at right.	—	—	8.00
	b. Without stub at right.	—	—	7.00

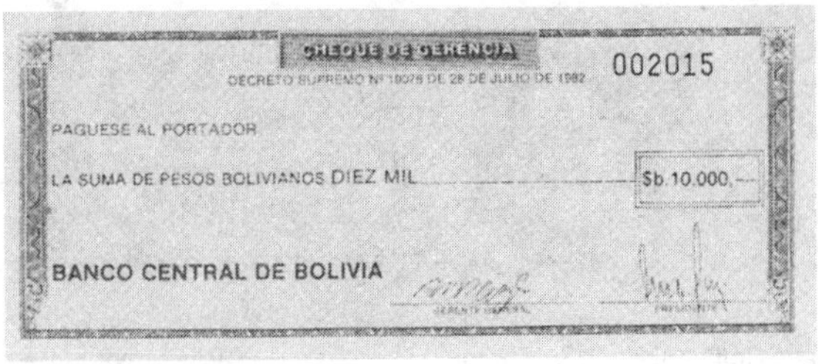

173	10,000 Pesos Bolivianos	VG	VF	UNC
	D.1982.			
	a. Stub with text attached at right.	—	—	10.00
	b. Without stub at right.	—	—	9.00

#174 and 175 not assigned.

Santa Cruz

1984 Cheque de Gerencia Issue

#176; 178 black, Mercury in green circular unpt. at ctr.

176	50,000 Pesos Bolivianos	Good	Fine	XF
	4.6.1984; 7.6.1984.			
	a. Issued note.	—	—	—
	b. Ovpt: *ANULADO* (cancelled) across face.	40.00	90.00	200.

#177 not assigned.

178	1,000,000 Pesos Bolivianos	Good	Fine	XF
	4.6.1984; 7.6.1984.			
	a. Issued note.	—	—	—
	b. Ovpt: *ANULADO* across face.	60.00	100.	250.

#179 not assigned.

La Paz

1984 Cheque de Gerencia Issue

#180-182 like #176-178.

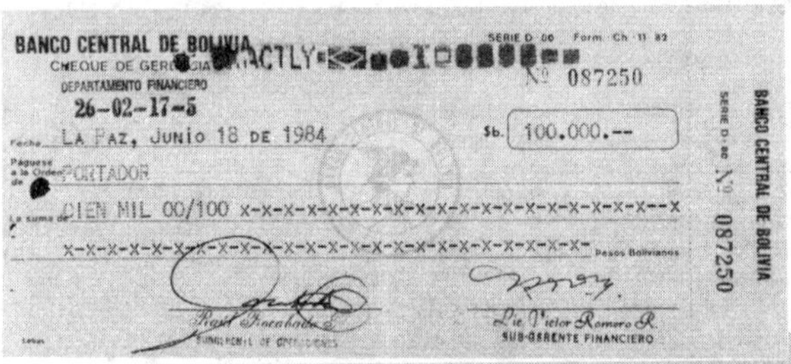

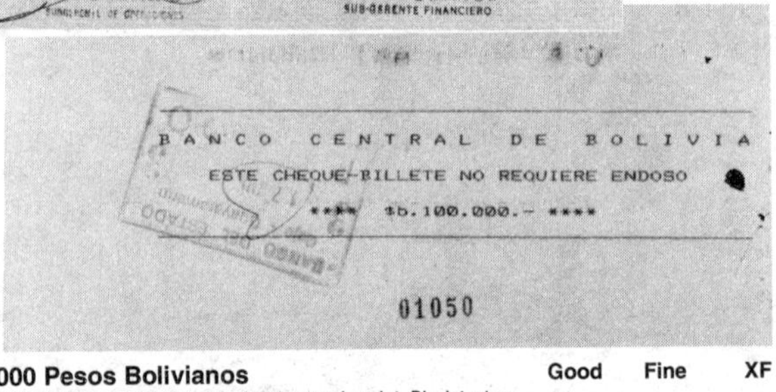

180	100,000 Pesos Bolivianos	Good	Fine	XF
	18.6.1984. Olive-green text on pale green underprint. Black text on back.			
	a. Issued note.	—	—	—
	b. Ovpt: *ANULADO* across face.	50.00	100.	210.
	c. Paid. Punched hole cancelled.	70.00	150.	275.

181	500,000 Pesos Bolivianos	Good	Fine	XF
	4.6.1984; 18.6.1984.			
	a. Issued note.	—	—	—
	b. Ovpt: *ANULADO* across face.	60.00	110.	225.
	c. Paid. Punched hole cancelled.	60.00	175.	300.

182	1,000,000 Pesos Bolivianos	Good	Fine	XF
	18.6.1984.			
	a. Issued note.	—	—	—
	b. Ovpt: *ANULADO* across face.	70.00	120.	240.
	c. Paid. Punched hole cancelled.	100.	210.	425.

Decreto Supremo No. 20272, 5 Junio 1984, First Issue

#183-185 brown on pink unpt. Mercury at upper l. Series A. Printer: JBNC. Usable for 90 days after date of issue (Spanish text at lower r. on back).

Note: Unpt. of "B.C.B." and denom. boxes easily fade from pink to lt. tan to pale yellow.

183	10,000 Pesos Bolivianos	VG	VF	UNC
	D.1984.	3.00	7.00	20.00

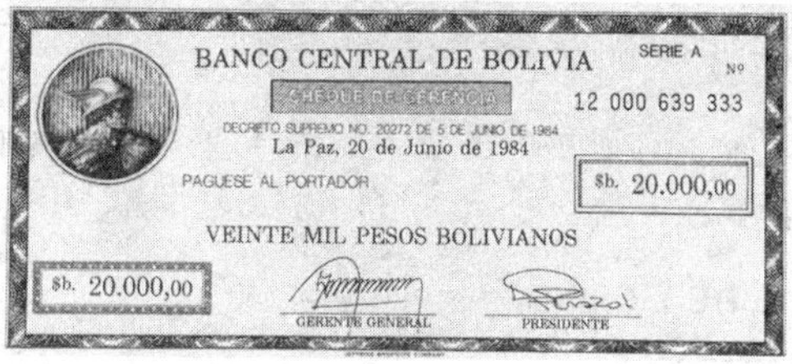

184	20,000 Pesos Bolivianos	VG	VF	UNC
	D.1984.	15.00	50.00	125.

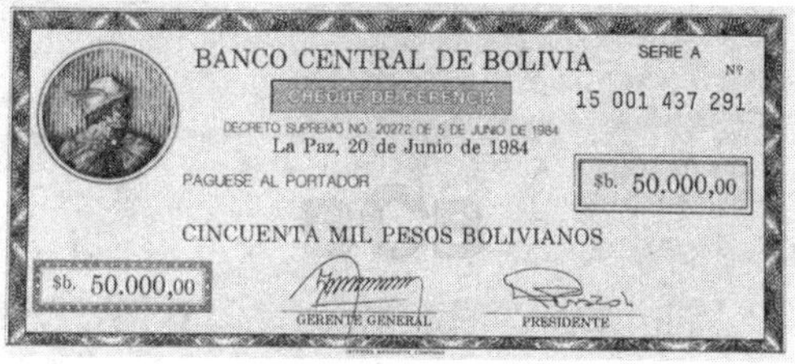

185	50,000 Pesos Bolivianos	VG	VF	UNC
	D.1984.	1.00	5.00	17.50

DECRETO SUPREMO NO. 20272, 5 JUNIO 1984, SECOND ISSUE

#186-187 like #183-184 but w/o 90 day use restriction text on back.

186	10,000 Pesos Bolivianos	VG	VF	UNC
	D.1984. light blue on pink underprint. Series A.	1.00	2.50	8.00
187	20,000 Pesos Bolivianos	VG	VF	UNC
	D.1984. Green on pink underprint. Series A.	1.00	2.50	8.50

#188 has 90-day use restriction clause similar to #183-185.

188	100,000 Pesos Bolivianos	VG	VF	UNC
	21.12.1984. Reddish brown on light blue and light reddish brown underprint. 90 day usage clause at lower right on back. Series A. Imprint and watermark: CdMB.	.20	.75	3.00

DECRETO SUPREMO NO. 20272, DE 5 DE JUNIO DE 1984

189	500,000 Pesos Bolivianos	VG	VF	UNC
	D.1984. Deep green on green and peach underprint. No 90-day clause on back. Printer: CdMB without imprint.	.20	.75	3.50

DECRETO SUPREMO NO. 20732, 8 MARZO 1985; FIRST ISSUE

190	1 Million Pesos Bolivianos	VG	VF	UNC
	D.1985. Blue on yellow and pale blue underprint. Similar to previous issue. No 90-day restriction clause at lower right on back. Series A. Printer: CdMB without imprint.			
	a. Issued note.	.25	1.00	5.50
	s. Specimen perforated: *SPECIMEN.*	—	—	—

#191 and 192 Series A. Printer: G&D.

191	5 Million Pesos Bolivianos	VG	VF	UNC
	D.1985. Brown-orange and red-brown on multicolor underprint. Similar to previous issues but higher quality printing and appearance. Multicolor back; bank initials in ornate guilloche at center. No 90-day restriction clause. Series A.			
	a. Issued note.	.30	1.50	8.00
	s. Specimen ovpt: *SPECIMEN.*	—	—	—

192	10 Million Pesos Bolivianos	VG	VF	UNC
	D.1985. Rose, violet and purple on multicolor underprint. Similar to #191. Series A.			
	a. Issued note.	2.00	8.00	20.00
	s. Specimen ovpt: *SPECIMEN.*	—	—	35.00

DECRETO SUPREMO NO. 20732, 8 MARZO 1985; SECOND ISSUE

#192A and 192B similar to #191 and 192. Printer: CdM-Brazil.

192A	5 Million Pesos Bolivianos	VG	VF	UNC
	D.1985. Similar to #191. Series B.	.50	2.00	7.50

192B	10 Million Pesos Bolivianos	VG	VF	UNC
	D.1985. Rose, violet and purple on multicolor underprint. Similar to #192. Series B.	.75	3.50	10.00

Decreto Supremo No. 20732, 8 Marzo 1985; Third Issue

#192C-194 printer: CdM-Argentina.

192C	1 Million Pesos Bolivianos	VG	VF	UNC
	D.1985. Blue and multicolor. Large guilloche at left, Mercury head in underprint at right. Series left.			
	a. Issued note.	.20	.75	3.25
	s. Specimen with black ovpt: *MUESTRA.*	—	—	15.00

193	5 Million Pesos Bolivianos	VG	VF	UNC
	D.1985. Brown with reddish brown text on multicolor underprint. Similar to #192C. Series N.			
	a. Issued note.	.75	3.25	7.50
	s. Specimen with black ovpt: *MUESTRA.*	—	—	30.00

194	10 Million Pesos Bolivianos	VG	VF	UNC
	D.1985. Violet with lilac text on multicolor underprint. Similar to #192C. Series M.			
	a. Issued note.	1.00	4.00	20.00
	s. Specimen with black ovpt: *MUESTRA.*	—	—	40.00

Republic, 1986-

Banco Central de Bolivia

1987 ND Provisional Issue

195	1 Centavo on 10,000 Pesos Bolivianos	VG	VF	UNC
	ND (1987). Overprint at right on back of #169.	.10	.25	1.00

196	Bolivianos5 Centavos on 50,000 Pesos	VG	VF	UNC
	ND (1987). Overprint at right on back of #170.	.15	.50	2.25
196A	Bolivianos10 Centavos on 100,000 Pesos			
	ND (1987). Overprint at right on back of #171.	.50	1.50	7.00

197	10 Centavos on 100,000 Pesos Bolivianos	VG	VF	UNC
	ND (1987). Overprint at right on back of #188.	.15	.50	3.00

NOTICE

Readers with unlisted dates, signature varieties, etc. are invited to submit photocopies of their notes to: Standard Catalog of World Paper Money, 700 East State St. Iola, WI 54990-0001, E-Mail: george.cuhaj@fwpubs.com.

198 **olivianos50 Centavos on 500,000 Pesos B**

ND (1987). Overprint at right on back of #189.

VG	VF	UNC
.20	.75	3.25

199 **1 Boliviano on 1,000,000 Pesos Bolivianos**

ND (1987). Overprint at right on back of #192C.

VG	VF	UNC
.25	.50	2.50

200 **5 Bolivianos on 5,000,000 Pesos Bolivi-anos**

ND (1987). Overprint at left on back of #192A.

	VG	VF	UNC
a. Issued note.	.30	1.25	6.00
x1. Error. Inverted overprint on left end.	1.00	6.00	15.00
x2. Error. overprint on r. end.	—	—	—

Note: Several varieties of "errors" have been reported and all should be looked upon as suspect.

201 **10 Bolivianos on 10,000,000 Pesos Bolivi-anos**

ND (1987). Overprint at left on back of #192B.

VG	VF	UNC
1.00	4.00	20.00

LEY 901 DE 28.11.1986;1987-2001 ND ISSUES

#202-208 arms at lower l., ctr. or r. Wmk: S. Bolívar, unless otherwise noted. Printer: F-CO.

Series A sign. titles: *PRESIDENTE BCB* and *MINISTRO DE FINANZAS*. Serial # suffix *A*.

Series B sign. titles: *PRESIDENTE DEL B.C.B.* and *GERENTE GENERAL B.C.B.* Serial # suffix *B*.

Series E sign. titles: *PRESIDENTE BCB* and *GERENTE GENERAL BCB*. Serial # suffix *E*.

202 **2 Bolivianos**

L.1986. (1987; 1990). Black on multicolor underprint. Antonio Vaca Diez at right, arms at lower center. Trees and buildings at center on back.

	VG	VF	UNC
a. Series A (1987). with control #.	FV	FV	3.50
b. Series B. (1990). with control #.	FV	FV	4.00
s. As a. Specimen with red ovpt: *ESPECIMEN*.	—	—	—

203 **5 Bolivianos**

L.1986. (1987; 1990; 1998). Olive-green on multicolor underprint. Adela Zamudio at right, arms at lower left. Religious shrine at left center on back.

	VG	VF	UNC
a. Series A (1987). with control #.	FV	FV	6.00
b. Series B (1990). with control #.	FV	FV	6.50
c. Series E (1998). without control #.	FV	FV	4.00
s. As a. Specimen with red ovpt: *ESPECIMEN*.	—	—	—

204 **10 Bolivianos**

L.1986. (1987-97). Blue-black on multicolor underprint. Cecilio Guzman de Rojas at right, arms at lower left. Figures overlooking city view on back.

	VG	VF	UNC
a. Series A (1987). with control #.	FV	FV	9.50
b. Series B (1990). with control #.	FV	FV	12.50
c. Series E (1997). without control #.	FV	FV	5.00
s. As a. Specimen with red ovpt: *ESPECIMEN*.	—	—	—

205 20 Bolivianos

	VG	VF	UNC
L.1986. (1987; 1990). Orange on multicolor underprint. Pantaleon Dalence at right, arms at lower center. Building at center on back.			
a. Series A (1987). with control #.	FV	FV	20.00
b. Series B (1990). with control #.	FV	FV	25.00
c. Series E (1997). without control #.	FV	FV	8.50
s. As a. Specimen with red ovpt: *ESPECIMEN.*	—	—	—

206 50 Bolivianos

	VG	VF	UNC
L.1986 (1987; 1997). Purple on multicolor underprint. Melchor Perez de Holguin at right, arms at lower center Tall building at center on back.			
a. Series A (1987). with control #.	FV	FV	50.00
b. Series E (1997). without control #.	FV	FV	17.50
s. As a. Specimen with red ovpt: *ESPECIMEN.*	—	—	—

207 100 Bolivianos

	VG	VF	UNC
L.1986 (1987; 1997). Red-violet and orange on multicolor underprint. Gabriel Rene Moreno at right, arms at lower right. University building at center on back.			
a. Watermark: Simon Bolívar.	FV	FV	110.
b. Series E (1997). without control #. watermark: Gabriel Rene Moreno.	FV	FV	35.00
s. As a. Specimen with red ovpt: *ESPECIMEN.*	—	—	—

208 200 Bolivianos

	VG	VF	UNC
L.1986 (1987; 1997). Brown and dark brown on multicolor underprint. Franz Tamayo at right, arms at lower center Ancient statuary on back.			
a. Series A (1987). with control #.	FV	FV	225.
b. Series E (1997). without control #. watermark: F. Tamayo.	FV	FV	60.00
s. As a. Specimen with red ovpt: *ESPECIMEN.*	—	—	—

LEY 901 DE 28.11.1986; 1993 ND ISSUE

#209-214 similar to #203-208 but many stylistic differences. Sign. titles: *PRESIDENTE BCB* and *GERENTE GENERAL BCB.* Serial # suffix *C.* Printer: FNMT.

#209-212 wmk: S. Bolívar.

209 5 Bolivianos

	VG	VF	UNC
L.1986 (1993). Olive-green on multicolor underprint. Series C. Similar to #203.	FV	FV	17.50

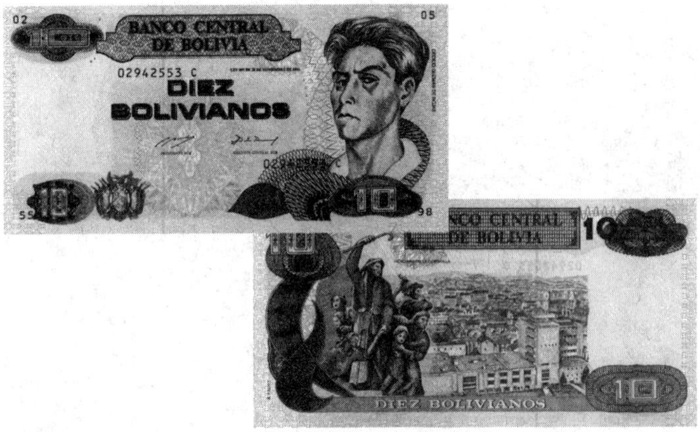

210 10 Bolivianos

	VG	VF	UNC
L.1986 (1993). Blue-black on multicolor underprint. Series C. Similar to #204.	FV	FV	6.50

211 20 Bolivianos

	VG	VF	UNC
L.1986 (1993). Orange on multicolor underprint. Series C. Similar to #205.	FV	FV	10.00

212 **50 Bolivianos**
L.1986 (1993). Purple on multicolor underprint. Series C. Similar to #206.

VG	VF	UNC
FV	FV	22.50

213 **100 Bolivianos**
L.1986 (1993). Red and orange on multicolor underprint. Series C. Similar to #207.

VG	VF	UNC
FV	FV	45.00

214 **200 Bolivianos**
L.1986 (1993). Brown and dark brown on multicolor underprint. Series C. Similar to #208.

VG	VF	UNC
FV	FV	90.00

LEY 901 DE 28.11.1986; 1995 ND INTERIM ISSUE

#215 and 216 like #209 and 210 but w/many stylistic differences including sign. titles. Wmk: S. Bolívar. Printer: TDLR.

215 **5 Bolivianos**
L.1986 (1995). Olive-green on multicolor underprint. Series C. Like #209.

	VG	VF	UNC
a. Issued note.	FV	FV	6.00
s. Specimen with red ovpt: *MUESTRA SIN VALOR.*	—	—	—

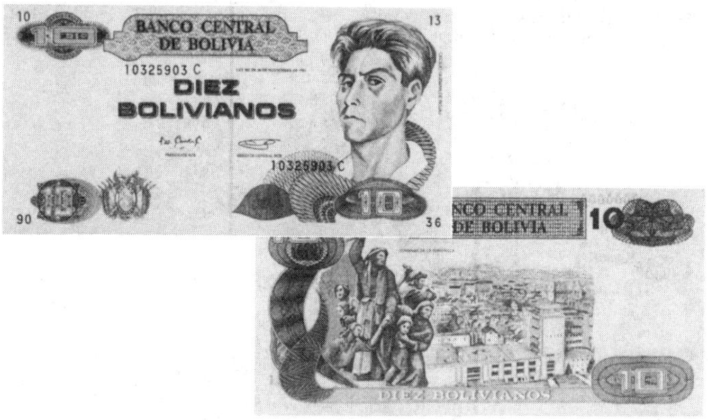

216 **10 Bolivianos**
L.1986 (1995). Blue-black on multicolor underprint. Series C. Like #210.

	VG	VF	UNC
a. Issued note.	FV	FV	12.00
s. Specimen with red ovpt: *MUESTRA SIN VALOR.*	—	—	—

LEY 901 DE 28.11.1986; 1995-96 ND ISSUE

#217-222 like #209-214 but w/many stylistic differences and sign. titles: *PRESIDENTE BCB* and *GERENTE GENERAL BCB*. W/o 4 control #'s. Printer: TDLR.

#217-220 wmk: S. Bolívar.

217 **5 Bolivianos**
L.1986 (1995). Olive-green on multicolor underprint. Series D. Like #209.

VG	VF	UNC
FV	FV	3.50

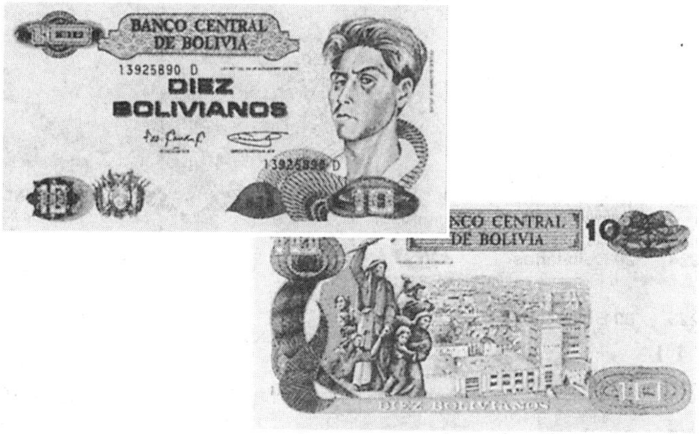

218 **10 Bolivianos**
L.1986 (1995). Blue-black on multicolor underprint. Series D. Like #210.

VG	VF	UNC
FV	FV	5.00

		VG	VF	UNC
219	**20 Bolivianos** L.1986 (1995). Orange on multicolor underprint. Series D. Like #211.	FV	FV	9.00

		VG	VF	UNC
220	**50 Bolivianos** L.1986 (1995). Purple on multicolor underprint. Series D. Like #212.			
	a. Issued note.	FV	FV	20.00
	s. Specimen with red ovpt: *MUESTRA SIN VALOR.*	—	—	—
221	**100 Bolivianos** L.1986 (1996). Red and orange on multicolor underprint. Watermark: Gabriel Rene Moreno. Series D. Like #213.	FV	FV	35.00
222	**200 Bolivianos** L.1986 (1996). Brown and dark brown on multicolor underprint. Watermark: F. Tamayo. Series D. Like #214.	FV	FV	65.00

Note: For Series E, see #203a-208a.

LEY 901 DE 28.11.1986; 2001 ND ISSUE

#223-227, like #207b, 208b, 210-212 but w/ addition of raised marks for the blind and narrow clear text security thread. Printer: F-CO. Sign. titles: PRESIDENTE BCB and GERENTE GENERAL BCB. W/o 4 control #'s. Wmk. Simon Bolívar or as noted.

		VG	VF	UNC
223	**10 Bolivianos** L. 1986 (2001). Blue-black on multicolor underprint. Series F. Like #210.	FV	FV	4.00
224	**20 Bolivianos** L.1986 (2001). Orange and brown-orange on multicolor underprint. Series F. Like #211.	FV	FV	7.00
225	**50 Bolivianos** L.1986 (2001). Purple on multicolor underprint. Series F. Like #212.	FV	FV	15.00
226	**100 Bolivianos** L.1986 (2001). Red-violet and orange on multicolor underprint. Series F. Like #207b.	FV	FV	30.00
227	**200 Bolivianos** L.1986 (2001). Brown and dark brown on multicolor underprint. Series F. Like #208b.	FV	FV	60.00

LEY 901 DE 28.11.1986; 2005 ND ISSUE

#228-232 like #223-227. Wide clear text security thread. Printer: F-CO. Sign. titles: *PRESIDENTE BCB* and *GENENTE GENERAL BCB*. W/o 4 control #s. Wmk: as portr., with value in numerals vertically.

		VG	VF	UNC
228	**10 Bolivianos** L.1986 (2005). Blue-black on multicolor underprint. Like #223. Without security thread. Series G.	FV	FV	4.00
229	**20 Bolivianos** L.1986 (2005). Orange and brown-orange on multicolor underprint. Like #224. Narrow security thread. Series G.	FV	FV	7.00
230	**50 Bolivianos** L.1986. (2005). Purple on multicolor underprint. Like #225. Wide security thread. Series G.	FV	FV	15.00
231	**100 Bolivianos** L.1986 (2005). Red-violet and orange on multicolor underprint. Like #226. Wide security thread. Series G.	FV	FV	30.00
232	**200 Bolivianos** L.1986. (2005). Brown and dark brown on multicolor underprint. Like #227. Wide security thread. Series G.	FV	FV	60.00

BOSNIA AND HERZEGOVINA

The Republic of Bosnia-Herzegovina borders Croatia to the north and west, Serbia to the east and Montenegro in the southeast with only 12.4 miles of coastline. The total land area is 19,735 sq. mi. (51,129 sq. km.). It has a population of 4.34 million. Capital: Sarajevo. Electricity, mining and agriculture are leading industries.

Bosnia's first ruler of importance was the Ban Kulin, 1180-1204. Stephen Kotromanió was invested with Bosnia, held loyalty to Hungary and extended his rule to the principality of Hum or Zahumlje, the future Herzegovina. His daughter Elisabeth married Louis the Great and he died in the same year. His nephew Tvrtko succeeded and during the weakening of Serbian power he assumed the title *Stephen Tvrtko, in Christ God King of the Serbs and Bosnia and the Coastland.* Later he assumed the title of *King of Dalmatia and Croatia,* but died before he could consolidate power. Successors also asserted their right to the Serbian throne.

In 1459 the Turks invaded Serbia. Bosnia was invaded in 1463 and Herzegovina in 1483. During Turkish rule Islam was accepted rather than Catholicism. During the 16th and 17th centuries Bosnia was an important Turkish outpost in continuing warfare with the Habsburgs and Venice. When Hungary was freed of the Turkish yoke, the imperialists penetrated Bosnia, and in 1697 Prince Eugene captured Sarajevo. Later, by the Treaty of Karlowitz in 1699, the northern boundary of Bosnia became the northernmost limit of the Turkish empire while the eastern area was ceded to Austria, but later restored to Turkey in 1739 lasting until 1870 following revolts of 1821, 1828, 1831 and 1862. On June 30, 1871 Serbia and Montenegro declared war on Turkey and were quickly defeated. The Turkish war with Russia led to the occupation by Austria-Hungary. Insurgents attempted armed resistance and Austria-Hungary invaded, quelling the uprising in 1878. The Austrian occupation provided a period of prosperity while at the same time prevented relations with Serbia and Croatia. Strengthening political and religious movements from within forced the annexation by Austria on Oct. 7, 1908. Hungary's establishment of a dictatorship in Croatia following the victories of Serbian forces in the Balkan War roused the whole Yugoslav population of Austria-Hungary to feverish excitement. The Bosnian group, mainly students, devoted its efforts to revolutionary ideas. After Austria's Balkan front collapsed in Oct. 1918 the union with Yugoslavia developed and on Dec. 1, 1918 the former Kingdom of the Serbs, Croats and Slovenes was proclaimed (later to become the Kingdom of Yugoslavia on Oct. 3, 1929).

After the defeat of Germany in WWII during which Bosnia was under the control of Pavelic of Croatia, a new Socialist Republic was formed under Marshal Tito having six constituent republics all subservient, quite similar to the constitution of the U.S.S.R. Military and civil loyalty was with Tito. In Jan. 1990 the Yugoslav government announced a rewriting of the constitution, abolishing the Communist Party's monopoly of power. Opposition parties were legalized in July 1990. On Oct. 15, 1991 the National Assembly adopted a Memorandum on Sovereignty that envisaged Bosnian autonomy within a Yugoslav Federation. In March 1992 an agreement was reached under EC auspices by Moslems, Serbs and Croats to set up 3 autonomous ethnic communities under a central Bosnian authority. Independence was declared on April 5, 1992. The 2 Serbian members of government resigned and fighting broke out between all 3 ethnic communities. The Dayton (Ohio, USA) Peace Accord was signed in 1995 which recognized the Federation of Bosnia-Herzegovina and the Srpska (Serbian) Republic. Both governments maintain separate military forces, schools, etc., providing humanitarian aid while a treaty allowed NATO "Peace Keeping" forces be deployed in Dec. 1995 replacing the United Nations troops previously acting in a similar role.

RULERS:

Ottoman, until 1878
Austrian, 1878-1918
Yugoslavian, 1918-1941

MONETARY SYSTEM:

1 Dinar = 100 Para 1992-1998
1 Convertible Marka = 1 Deutschemark
1 Convertible Marka = 100 Convertible Pfeniga, 1998-

REPUBLIKA BOSNA I HERCEGOVINA

MOSLEM REPUBLIC

НАРОДНА БАНКА БОСНЕ И ХЕРЦЕГОВИНЕ

NARODNA BANKA BOSNE I HERCEGOVINE

1992 FIRST PROVISIONAL ISSUE

#1-2 violet handstamp: *NARODNA BANKA BOSNE I HERCEGOVINE,* also in Cyrillic around Yugoslav arms, on Yugoslav regular issues. Handstamp varieties exist.

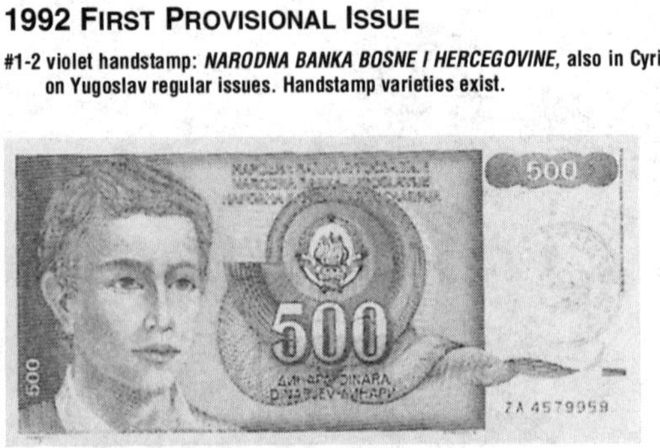

		Good	Fine	XF
1	**500 Dinara** ND (1992). 27mm or 31mm handstamp on Yugoslavia #109.			
	a. Handstamp without numeral.	10.00	30.00	100.
	b. Handstamp with numeral: *1.*	10.00	30.00	100.
	c. Handstamp with numeral: *2.*	10.00	30.00	100.

2	1000 Dinara	Good	Fine	XF
	ND (1992). 48mm handstamp on Yugoslavia #110.			
	a. Handstamp without numeral.	8.00	25.00	125.
	b. Handstamp with numeral 1.	8.00	25.00	125.
	c. Handstamp with numeral 2.	8.00	25.00	125.

#3 and 4 not assigned.

1992 Second Provisional Novcani Bon Issue

#6-9 issued in various Central Bosnian cities. Peace dove at upper l. ctr. Example w/o indication of city of issue are remainders.

6	100 Dinara	Good	Fine	XF
	1992. Deep pink on gray and yellow underprint.			
	a. Handstamped: *BREZA* on back.	7.50	25.00	100.
	b. Circular red handstamp: *FOJNICA* on back.	3.00	10.00	50.00
	c. Rectangular purple handstamp on face, circular purple handstamp: *KRESEVO* on back.	6.50	20.00	80.00
	d. Handstamped: *TESANJ* on back.	5.50	20.00	80.00
	e. Handstamped: *VARES* on back.	10.00	35.00	110.
	f1. Handstamped: *VISOKO* 31mm on back.	2.00	6.00	30.00
	f2. Handstamped: *VISOKO* 20mm on back.	3.00	10.00	55.00
	g. Circular red ovpt: *ZENICA*, 11.5.1992. on back r. with printed signature at either side.	1.00	3.00	9.00
	r. Remainder, without handstamp or overprint	1.00	3.00	10.00

7	500 Dinara	Good	Fine	XF
	1992. Pale greenish-gray on gray and yellow underprint.			
	a. Handstamped: *BREZA* on back.	5.00	17.50	70.00
	b. Circular red handstamp: *FOJNICA* on back.	5.00	17.50	70.00
	c. Handstamped: *KRESEVO* on back.	12.50	45.00	120.
	d. Handstamped: *TESANJ* on back.	2.00	7.50	35.00
	e. Handstamped: *VARES* on back.	5.00	17.50	70.00
	f. Circular red handstamp: *VISOKO* on back.	3.00	12.50	40.00
	g. Circular red handstamp on back, details as #6g: *ZENICA* (small or large), 11.5.1992.	.50	2.00	7.00

8	1000 Dinara	Good	Fine	XF
	1992. Blue on gray underprint.			
	a. Handstamped: *BREZA* on back.	5.00	15.00	65.00
	b. Handstamped: *FOJNICA* on back.	5.00	15.00	65.00
	c. Handstamped: *KRESEVO* on back.	8.00	30.00	90.00
	d. Handstamped: *TESANJ* on back.	6.50	20.00	75.00
	e. Handstamped: *VARES* on back.	6.50	20.00	75.00
	f1. Handstamped: *VISOKO* 31mm on back.	2.00	9.00	35.00
	f2. Handstamped: *VISOKO* 20mm on back.	9.00	30.00	100.
	g. Handstamped: *ZENICA* on face, no date on stamping.	8.00	25.00	75.00
	h. Circular red overprint on back, details as 6g: *ZENICA*, 11.5.1992.	.50	2.00	10.00

9	5000 Dinara	Good	Fine	XF
	1992. Dull brown on gray and yellow underprint.			
	a. Handstamped: *BREZA* on back.	3.00	10.00	35.00
	b. Circular red handstamp: *FOJNICA* on back.	2.00	8.00	30.00
	c. Handstamped: *KRESEVO* on back.	12.50	50.00	125.
	d. Handstamped: *TESANJ* on back.	25.00	85.00	350.
	e. Handstamped: *VARES* on back.	7.00	20.00	75.00
	f1. Handstamped: *VISOKO* on back.	2.00	6.00	18.00
	f2. Handstamped: *VISOKO* 32mm on back.	7.50	30.00	90.00
	f3. Handstamped: *VISOKO* 20mm on back.	3.00	10.00	35.00
	g. Handstamped: *ZENICA* on face, without date in stamping.	7.00	22.50	65.00
	h. Circular violet overprint on back, details as 6g: *ZENICA*, 11.5.1992.	.50	2.00	7.50
	r. Remainder, without handstamp or overprint	1.00	5.00	20.00

1992-93 Issues

#10-15 guilloche at l. ctr. 145x73mm. Wmk: Repeated diamonds. Printer: Cetis (Celje, Slovenia).

#10-18 serial # varieties.

10	10 Dinara	VG	VF	UNC
	1.7.1992. Purple on pink underprint. Mostar stone arch bridge at right on back.			
	a. Issued note.	.10	.25	1.00
	s. Specimen.	—	—	30.00

11	25 Dinara	VG	VF	UNC
	1.7.1992. Blue-black on light blue underprint. Crowned arms at center right on back.			
	a. Issued note.	.10	.20	1.25
	s. Specimen.	—	—	30.00

12 50 Dinara

1.7.1992. Blue-black on red-violet underprint. Mostar stone arch bridge at right on back.

	VG	VF	UNC
a. Issued note.	.10	.50	1.50
s. Specimen.	—	—	30.00

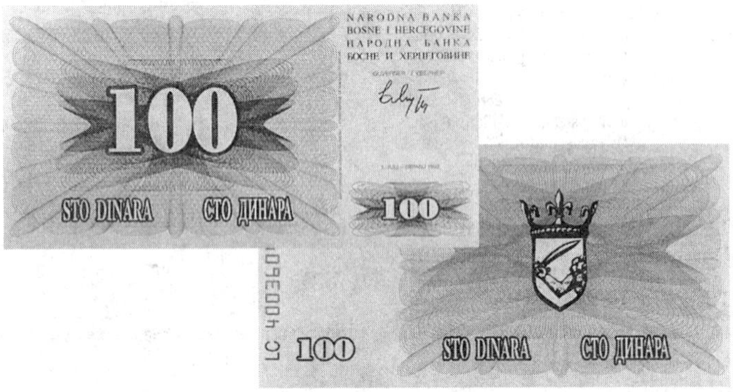

13 100 Dinara

1.7.1992. Dull black on olive-green underprint. Crowned arms at center right on back.

	VG	VF	UNC
a. Issued note.	.10	.50	1.75
s. Specimen.	—	—	30.00

14 500 Dinara

1.7.1992. Dull violet-brown on pink and ochre underprint. Crowned arms at center right on back.

	VG	VF	UNC
a. Issued note.	.20	.75	3.50
s. Specimen.	—	—	30.00

15 1000 Dinara

1.7.1992. Deep purple on light green and lilac underprint. Mostar stone arch bridge at right on back.

	VG	VF	UNC
a. Issued note.	.25	1.00	4.50
s. Specimen.	—	—	30.00

#16 and 17 grayish blue shield w/fleur-de-lis replaces crowned shield w/raised scimitar on back. Reduced size notes. Printed in Zenica.

16 5000 Dinara

25.1.1993. Pale olive-green on yellow-orange underprint. Arms at center right on back.

	VG	VF	UNC
a. Issued note.	1.00	3.00	7.50
b. With overprint: *SDK..ZENICA* on back With handstamp or machine printing.	1.75	5.00	15.00

17 10,000 Dinara

25.1.1993. Brown on pink underprint. Arms at center right on back.

	VG	VF	UNC
a. Issued note.	1.25	3.50	8.50
b. With overprint: *SDK..ZENICA* on back With handstamp or machine printing.	1.75	5.00	15.00

1992-94 Bon Issue

#21-33 shield at l. on back. Issued during the seige of Sarajevo. Grayish green or yellow unpt. on back.

21 10 Dinara

1.8.1992. Violet.

	VG	VF	UNC
a. Issued note.	2.00	6.00	35.00
s. Specimen.	—	—	30.00

22 20 Dinara

1.8.1992. Blue-violet.

	VG	VF	UNC
a. Issued note.	1.50	5.00	30.00
s. Specimen.	—	—	30.00

23 50 Dinara

1.8.1992. Pink.

	VG	VF	UNC
a. Issued note.	2.00	6.00	35.00
s. Specimen.	—	—	30.00

24 **100 Dinara**

1.8.1992. Green.

	VG	VF	UNC
a. Issued note.	5.00	25.00	125.
s. Specimen.	—	—	30.00

25 **500 Dinara**

1.8.1992. Orange. Back red-orange on pale purple and grayish green underprint.

	VG	VF	UNC
a. Issued note.	3.00	8.00	40.00
s. Specimen.	—	—	30.00

26 **1000 Dinara**

1.8.1992. Brown.

	VG	VF	UNC
a. Issued note.	1.50	6.00	35.00
s. Specimen.	—	—	30.00

27 **5000 Dinara**

1.8.1992. Violet.

	VG	VF	UNC
a. Issued note.	1.50	6.00	35.00
s. Specimen.	—	—	30.00

28 **10,000 Dinara**

6.4.1993. Light Blue.

VG	VF	UNC
1.50	6.00	35.00

29 **50,000 Dinara**

1.5.1993. Pink.

VG	VF	UNC
2.50	10.00	40.00

30 **100,000 Dinara**

1.8.1993. Green on multicolor underprint. Back green on gray underprint.

VG	VF	UNC
1.50	5.00	30.00

31 **100,000 Dinara**

1.8.1993. Green. Back green on yellow underprint.

VG	VF	UNC
1.50	5.00	30.00

32 **500,000 Dinara**

1.1.1994. Brown. Back brown on pale yellow-green underprint.

VG	VF	UNC
1.50	5.00	25.00

33 **1,000,000 Dinara**

1.1.1994. Red.

VG	VF	UNC
1.50	5.00	25.00

1993 NOVCANI BON EMERGENCY ISSUE

34	100,000 Dinara	VG	VF	UNC
	1993 (-old date 1.7.1992). Rectangular crenalated framed ovpt: *NOVCANI BON 100,000*...on face and back of #10.			
	a. Purple overprint 1.9.1993.	2.00	7.50	17.50
	b. Blue overprint and signature overprint 10.11.1993.	2.00	7.50	17.50

35	1,000,000 Dinara	VG	VF	UNC
	10.11.1993 (old date-1.7.1992). Blue-violet overprint on #11. (Not issued)			
	a. Purple overprint 1.9.1993.	.50	8.00	20.00
	b. Blue overprint and signature overprint 10.11.1993.	.50	3.50	9.00

36	10,000,000 Dinara	VG	VF	UNC
	10.11.1993 (old date-1.7.1992). Blue-violet overprint on #12. (Not issued)	—	4.00	12.50

37	100,000,000 Dinara	VG	VF	UNC
	10.11.1993 (old date-1.7.1992). Blue-violet overprint on #13. (Not issued)	—	4.00	12.50

1994 ISSUE

Currency Reform, 1994

1 New Dinar = 10,000 Old Dinara

#39-46 alternate with shield or Mostar stone bridge at ctr. r. on back. Wmk: block design. Printer: DD "Dom Stampe" Zenica.

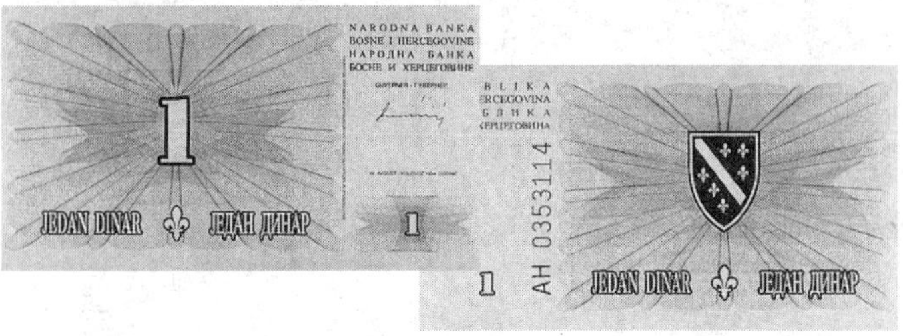

39	1 Dinar	VG	VF	UNC
	15.8.1994. Purplish gray on red-violet and pale green underprint.			
	a. Issued note.	.05	.15	.75
	s. Specimen.	—	—	—

40	5 Dinara	VG	VF	UNC
	15.8.1994. Purplish gray on lilac, red and orange underprint.			
	a. Issued note.	.05	.15	.75
	s. Specimen.	—	—	—

41	10 Dinara	VG	VF	UNC
	15.8.1994. Purple on red, orange and red-violet underprint.			
	a. Issued note.	.10	.25	1.00
	s. Specimen.	—	—	—

42	20 Dinara	VG	VF	UNC
	15.8.1994. Brown on violet, red and yellow underprint.			
	a. Issued note.	.15	.50	1.50
	s. Specimen.	—	—	—

43	50 Dinara	VG	VF	UNC
	15.8.1994. Purplish gray on red-violet and pale purple underprint.			
	a. Issued note.	.15	.50	2.00
	s. Specimen.	—	—	—

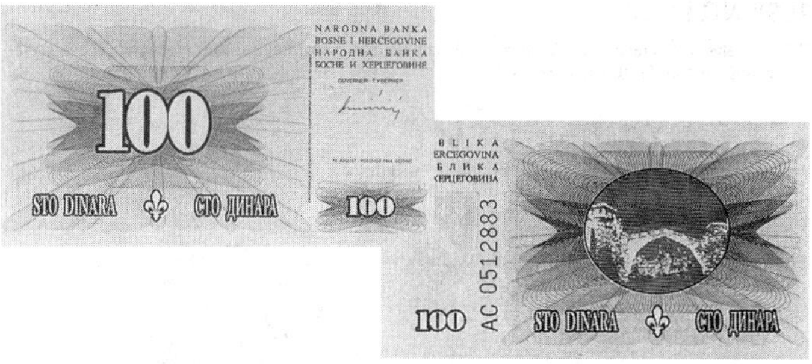

		VG	VF	UNC
44	**100 Dinara** 15.8.1994. Dull black on aqua, yellow and olive-green underprint.			
	a. Issued note.	.15	.50	2.25
	s. Specimen.	—	—	—
45	**500 Dinara** 15.8.1994. Dull brown on lilac and yellow underprint.			
	a. Large #'s.	.25	1.50	6.00
	b. Small #'s.	.25	1.50	6.00
	s. Specimen.	—	—	—

		VG	VF	UNC
46	**1000 Dinara** 15.8.1994. Blue-gray on gray-green, red-violet and light green underprint.			
	a. Large #'s.	1.00	4.50	12.50
	b. Small #'s.	1.00	4.50	12.50
	s. Specimen.	—	—	—

1995 ND ISSUE

#47-47C Printed in London but unable to be delivered.

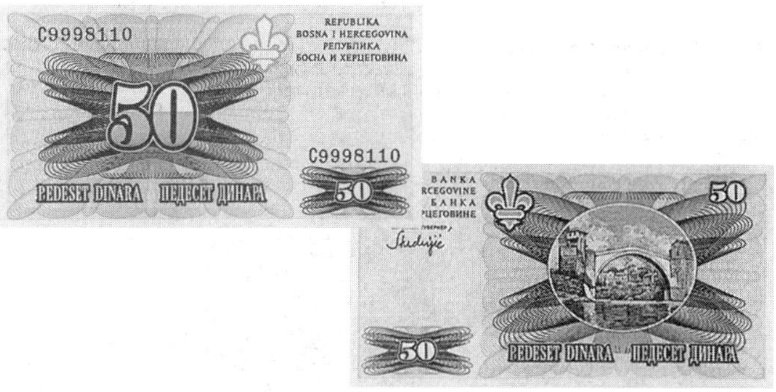

		VG	VF	UNC
47	**50 Dinara** ND (1995). Purple on pink and ochre underprint. Bridge at right. Watermark: Lis.	1.00	6.00	20.00
47A	**100 Dinara** ND (1995). Design as #47. (Not issued).	—	—	—
47B	**500 Dinara** ND (1995). Design as #47. (Not issued).	—	—	—

		VG	VF	UNC
47C	**1000 Dinara** ND (1995). Design as #47. (Not issued).	—	—	—

TRAVNIK, NOVI TRAVNIK AND VITEZ

1992 ND NOVCANI BON ISSUE

#48-52 plain design w/value at ctr. w/Travnik, Novi Travnik or Vitez Branch handstamps.

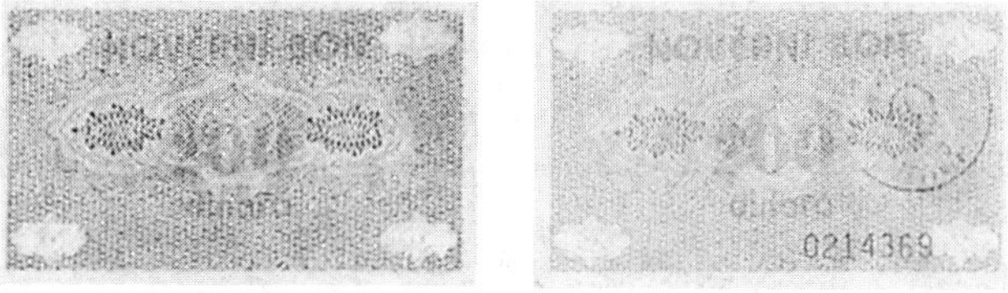

		VG	VF	UNC
48	**200 Dinara** ND (1992). Orange.			
	a. Handstamped: *TRAVNIK.*	2.50	10.00	40.00
	b. Handstamped: *NOVI TRAVNIK.*	5.00	20.00	80.00
	c. Handstamped: *VITEZ.*	7.50	35.00	110.

		VG	VF	UNC
49	**500 Dinara** ND (1992). Brown.			
	a. Handstamped: *TRAVNIK.*	2.50	15.00	55.00
	b. Handstamped: *NOVI TRAVNIK.*	7.50	30.00	95.00
	c. Handstamped: *VITEZ.*	10.00	45.00	120.

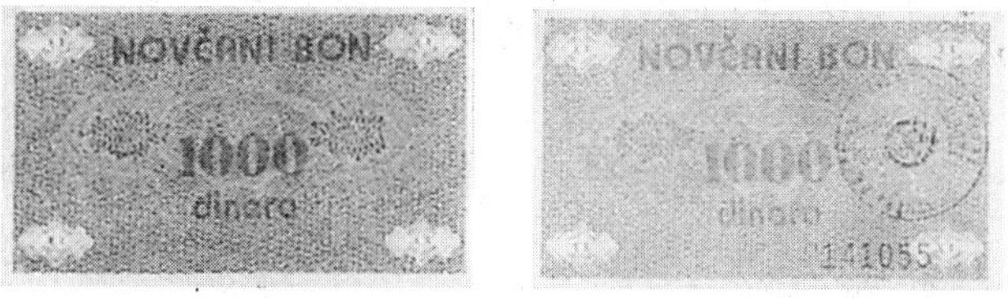

		VG	VF	UNC
50	**1000 Dinara** ND (1992). Lilac.			
	a. Handstamped: *TRAVNIK.*	2.50	8.00	30.00
	b. Handstamped: *NOVI TRAVNIK.*	4.00	18.00	70.00
	c. Handstamped: *VITEZ.*	5.00	25.00	95.00

		VG	VF	UNC
51	**5000 Dinara** ND (1992). Light blue.			
	a. Handstamped: *TRAVNIK.*	10.00	70.00	500.
	b. Handstamped: *NOVI TRAVNIK.* Rare.	—	—	—
	c. Handstamped: *VITEZ.* Rare.	—	—	—

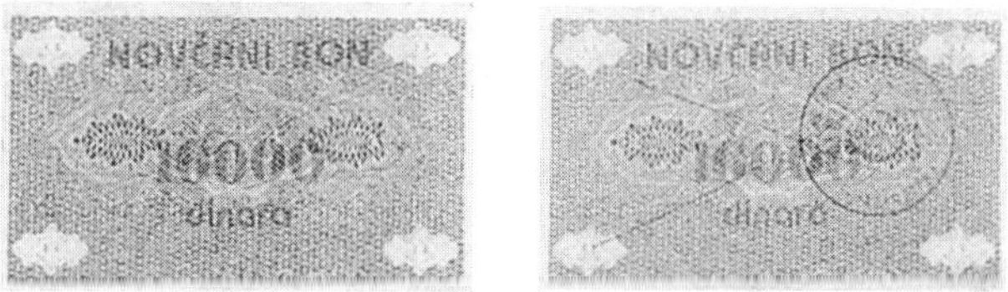

		VG	VF	UNC
52	**10,000 Dinara** ND (1992). Red on blue underprint.			
	a. Handstamped: *TRAVNIK.*	2.50	15.00	45.00
	b. Handstamped: *NOVI TRAVNIK.*	5.00	25.00	95.00
	c. Handstamped: *VITEZ.*	7.50	35.00	110.

1993 Emergency Issue

#53-56 like #10-13 w/additional 3 solid zeroes printed after large value on face w/Travnik Branch dated handstamp.

53	10,000 Dinara	VG	VF	UNC
	1993. Red on yellow underprint.			
	a. 15.10.1993. Short green zeroes.	1.00	2.50	7.50
	b. 15.10.1993. Short red zeroes.	1.00	2.50	7.50
	c. 24.12.1993. Tall green zeroes.	1.00	2.50	7.50
	d. 24.12.1993. Tall red zeroes.	1.00	2.50	7.50

54	25,000 Dinara	VG	VF	UNC
	1993. Green on blue underprint.			
	a. 15.10.1993. Short green zeroes.	1.00	2.50	7.50
	b. 15.10.1993. Short red zeroes.	1.00	2.50	7.50
	c. 24.12.1993. Tall green zeroes.	1.00	2.50	7.50
	d. 24.12.1993. Tall red zeroes.	1.00	2.50	7.50

55	50,000 Dinara	VG	VF	UNC
	1993. Red.			
	a. 15.10.1993. Short green zeroes.	1.00	2.50	7.50
	b. 15.10.1993. Short red zeroes.	1.00	2.50	7.50
	c. 24.12.1993. Tall green zeroes.	1.00	2.50	7.50
	d. 24.12.1993. Tall red zeroes.	1.00	2.50	7.50

56	100,000 Dinara	VG	VF	UNC
	1993. Green.			
	a. 15.10.1993. Short green zeroes.	1.00	2.50	7.50
	b. 15.10.1993. Short red zeroes.	1.00	2.50	7.50
	c. 24.12.1993. Tall green zeroes.	1.00	2.50	7.50
	d. 24.12.1993. Tall red zeroes.	1.00	2.50	7.50

1998 ND Issue

#57-70 w/alternating texts of bank name and denominations. Wmk: Central bank monogram repeated vertically. Printer: F-CO (w/o imprint).

57	50 Convertible Pfeniga	VG	VF	UNC
	ND (1998). Dark blue on blue and lilac underprint. Portrait S. Kulenovic at right. *Stecak Zgosca* fragment at left center on back.			
	a. Issued note.	FV	FV	.75
	s. Specimen.	—	—	—

58	50 Convertible Pfeniga	VG	VF	UNC
	ND (1998). Dark blue on blue and lilac underprint. Portrait B. Copic at right. Open book, cabin at left center on back.			
	a. Issued note.	FV	FV	.75
	s. Specimen.	—	—	—

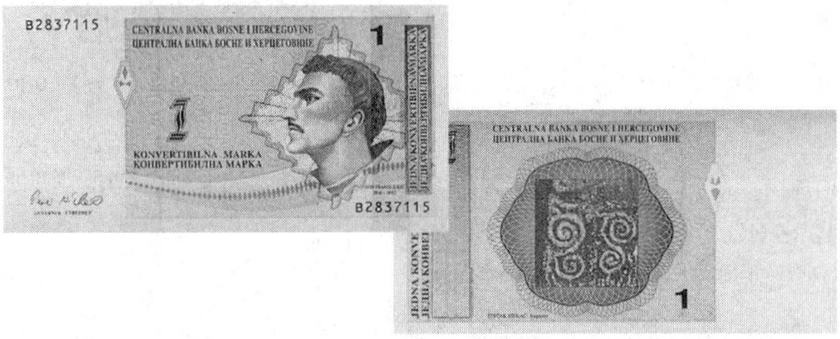

59	1 Convertible Marka	VG	VF	UNC
	ND (1998). Dark green on green and yellow-green underprint. I. F. Jukic at right. *Stecak Stolac* fragment at left center on back.			
	a. Issued note.	FV	FV	1.50
	s. Specimen.	—	—	—

60	1 Convertible Marka	VG	VF	UNC
	ND (1998). Dark green on green and yellow-green underprint. I. Andric at right. Bridge at left center on back. (Not issued).	—	—	—

Note: Some examples of #60 were stolen and have been offered on the market at about $80.00-100.00.

61	5 Convertible Maraka	VG	VF	UNC
	ND (1998). Violet on multicolor underprint. M. Selimovic at right. Trees at left center on back. English letters in bank name as top line.			
	a. Issued note.	FV	FV	7.50
	s. Specimen.	—	—	—

62	5 Convertible Maraka	VG	VF	UNC
	ND (1998). Violet on multicolor underprint. Like #61 but Cyrillic bank name and denomination as top line.			
	a. Issued note.	FV	FV	7.50
	s. Specimen.	—	—	—

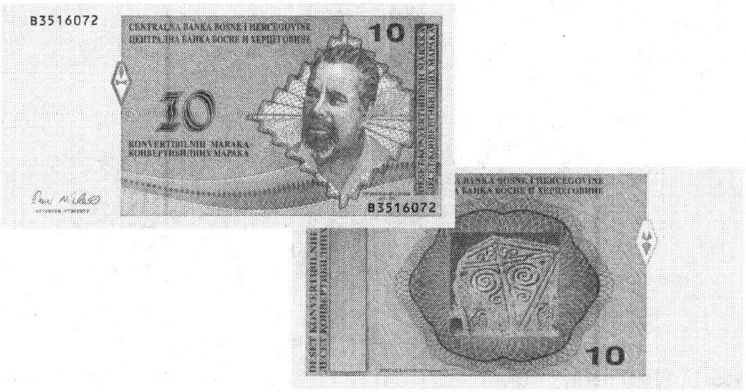

63	10 Convertible Maraka	VG	VF	UNC
	ND (1998). Orange-brown on dull purple and orange-brown underprint. M. M. Dizdar at right. *Stecak Radimlja* fragment at left center on back.			
	a. Issued note.	FV	FV	12.50
	s. Specimen.	—	—	—

64	10 Convertible Maraka	VG	VF	UNC
	ND (1998). Orange-brown on dull purple and orange-brown underprint. A. Santic at right. Loaf of bread at left center on back.			
	a. Issued note.	FV	FV	12.50
	s. Specimen.	—	—	—

#65-70 variable optical device at upper l. ctr.

65	20 Convertible Maraka	VG	VF	UNC
	ND (1998). Dark brown on multicolor underprint. A. B. Simic at right. *Stecak Radimilja* fragment at left center on back.			
	a. Issued note.	FV	FV	20.00
	s. Specimen.	—	—	—

66	20 Convertible Maraka	VG	VF	UNC
	ND (1998). Dark brown on multicolor underprint. F. Visjic at right. "Gusle" musical instrument at left center on back.			
	a. Issued note.	FV	FV	20.00
	s. Specimen.	—	—	—

67	50 Convertible Maraka	VG	VF	UNC
	ND (1998). Purple on lilac and multicolor underprint. M. C. Catic at right. Stone relief at left center on back.			
	a. Issued note.	FV	FV	55.00
	s. Specimen.	—	—	—

68	50 Convertible Maraka	VG	VF	UNC
	ND (1998); 2002. Purple on lilac and multicolor underprint. I. Ducic at right. Pen, glasses and book at left center on back.			
	a. Issued note.	FV	FV	55.00
	s. Specimen.	—	—	—

69	100 Convertible Maraka	VG	VF	UNC
	ND (1998). Dark brown on yellow and multicolor underprint. N. Sop at right. "Stecak Sgosca" fragment at left center on back.			
	a. Issued note.	FV	FV	100.
	s. Specimen.	—	—	—

70	100 Convertible Maraka	VG	VF	UNC
	ND (1998). Dark brown on yellow and multicolor underprint. P. Kocic at right. Pen, glasses and book at left center on back.			
	a. ND.	FV	FV	100.
	b. 2002.	FV	FV	85.00
	s. Specimen.	—	—	—

71	200 Convertible Maraka	VG	VF	UNC
	ND (2002). Blue.	FV	FV	165.

SRPSKA (SERBIAN) REPUBLIC

НАРОДНА БАНКА СРПСКЕРЕПУБЛИКЕ

БОСНЕ И ХЕРЦЕГОВИНЕ

NARODNA BANKA SRPSKE REPUBLIKE

BOSNE I HERCEGOVINE

NATIONAL BANK OF THE SERBIAN REPUBLIC OF BOSNIA-HERZEGOVINA

1992-93 BANJA LUKA ISSUE

#133-139 arms at l., numerals in heart-shaped design below guilloche at ctr. r. Curved artistic design at l. ctr., arms at r. on back.

#133-135 wmk: Portr. of a young girl.

133	10 Dinara	VG	VF	UNC
	1992. Deep brown or orange and silver underprint. Back with ochre underprint.			
	a. Issued note.	.10	.50	1.50
	s. Specimen.	—	—	5.00

134	50 Dinara	VG	VF	UNC
	1992. Deep olive-gray on ochre and multicolor underprint.			
	a. Issued note.	.15	.50	1.50
	s. Specimen.	—	—	5.00

135	100 Dinara	VG	VF	UNC
	1992. Dark blue on lilac and silver underprint.			
	a. Issued note.	.25	1.00	3.00
	s. Specimen.	—	—	5.00

#136-140 wmk: Portr. of a young boy.

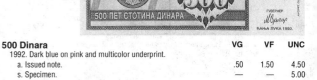

136	500 Dinara	VG	VF	UNC
	1992. Dark blue on pink and multicolor underprint.			
	a. Issued note.	.50	1.50	4.50
	s. Specimen.	—	—	5.00

137	1000 Dinara	VG	VF	UNC
	1992. Slate gray on peach and tan underprint. Back with orange underprint.			
	a. Issued note.	.50	1.25	3.75
	s. Specimen.	—	—	5.00

		VG	VF	UNC
138	**5000 Dinara**			
	1992. Violet on lilac and light blueunderprint.			
	a. Issued note.	.50	2.50	10.00
	s. Specimen.	—	—	5.00
139	**10,000 Dinara**			
	1992. Gray on tan and light blue underprint.			
	a. Issued note.	.50	2.50	10.00
	s. Specimen.	—	—	5.00
140	**50,000 Dinara**			
	1993. Brown on olive-green and multicolor underprint.			
	a. Issued note.	2.00	8.00	30.00
	s. Specimen.	—	—	7.50

Note: For similar notes to #136-140 but differing only in text at top, sign., and Knin as place of issue, see Croatia-Regional.

		VG	VF	UNC
141	**100,000 Dinara**			
	1993. Purple on brown and multicolor underprint. Watermark: portrait of young woman with head covering.			
	a. Issued note.	.50	1.50	4.00
	s. Specimen.	—	—	7.50

#142-144 wmk: Portr. of a young girl.

		VG	VF	UNC
142	**1 Million Dinara**			
	1993. Deep purple on pink, yellow and multicolor underprint.			
	a. Issued note.	2.00	8.00	40.00
	s. Specimen.	—	—	7.50
143	**5 Million Dinara**			
	1993. Dark brown on light blue and yellow-orange underprint.			
	a. Issued note.	.25	1.00	3.00
	s. Specimen.	—	—	7.50

		VG	VF	UNC
144	**10 Million Dinara**			
	1993. Dark blue-violet on olive-green and yellow-orange underprint.			
	a. Issued note.	.50	1.50	4.50
	s. Specimen.	—	—	7.50

SRPSKA (SERBIAN) REPUBLIC

НАРОДНА БАНКА РЕПУБЛИКЕСРПСКЕ

NARODNA BANKA REPUBLIKE SRPSKE

NATIONAL BANK OF THE SERBIAN REPUBLIC

1993 BANJA LUKA FIRST ISSUE

		VG	VF	UNC
145	**50 Million Dinara**			
	1993. Dark brown on pink and gray underprint.			
	a. Issued note.	.75	2.50	7.50
	s. Specimen.	—	—	5.00

		VG	VF	UNC
146	**100 Million Dinara**			
	1993. Pale blue-gray on light blue and gray underprint.			
	a. Issued note.	.50	1.50	4.00
	s. Specimen.	—	—	5.00

		VG	VF	UNC
147	**1 Milliard Dinara**			
	1993. Orange on pale blue and light orange underprint.			
	a. Issued note.	.50	1.50	5.00
	s. Specimen.	—	—	5.00

		VG	VF	UNC
148	**10 Milliard Dinara**			
	1993. Black on pink and pale orange underprint.			
	a. Issued note.	.50	1.50	5.00
	s. Specimen.	—	—	5.00

1993 Banja Luka Second Issue

#149-155 P. Kocic at l. Serbian arms at ctr. r. on back. Wmk: Greek design repeated.

		VG	VF	UNC
149	**5000 Dinara**			
	1993. Red-violet and purple on pale blue-gray underprint.			
	a. Issued note.	.25	1.00	3.00
	s. Specimen.	—	—	7.50

		VG	VF	UNC
150	**50,000 Dinara**			
	1993. Brown and dull red on ochre underprint.			
	a. Issued note.	.25	1.00	3.00
	s. Specimen.	—	—	7.50

		VG	VF	UNC
151	**100,000 Dinara**			
	1993. Violet and blue-gray on pink underprint.			
	a. Issued note.	.25	1.00	3.00
	s. Specimen.	—	—	7.50

		VG	VF	UNC
152	**1,000,000 Dinara**			
	1993. Black and blue-gray on pale purple underprint.			
	a. Issued note.	.50	1.50	5.00
	s. Specimen.	—	—	7.50

		VG	VF	UNC
153	**5,000,000 Dinara**			
	1993. Orange and gray-blue on pale orange underprint.			
	a. Issued note.	.50	1.50	5.00
	s. Specimen.	—	—	7.50

		VG	VF	UNC
154	**100,000,000 Dinara**			
	1993. Dull grayish green and pale olive-brown on light blue underprint.			
	a. Issued note.	.50	1.50	5.00
	s. Specimen.	—	—	7.50

		VG	VF	UNC
155	**500,000,000 Dinara**			
	1993. Brown-violet and grayish green on pale olive-brown underprint.			
	a. Issued note.	.50	1.50	5.00
	s. Specimen.	—	—	7.50

		VG	VF	UNC
156	**10,000,000,000 Dinara**			
	1993. Blue and red. (Not issued.)	—	—	150.

		VG	VF	UNC
157	**50,000,000,000 Dinara**			
	1993. Brown. (Not issued.)	—	—	150.

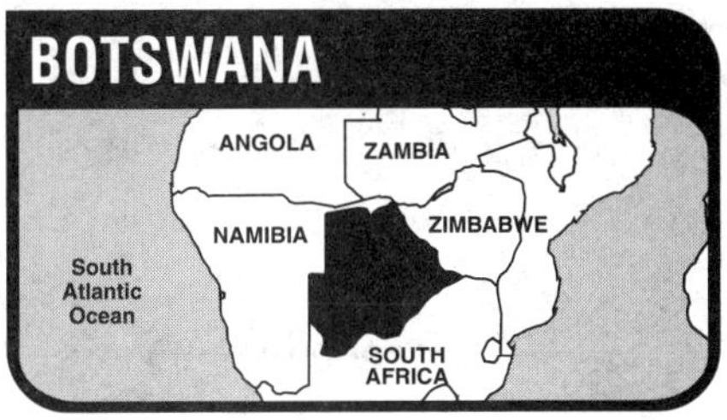

The Republic of Botswana (formerly Bechuanaland), located in south central Africa between Southwest Africa, (Namibia) and Zimbabwe has an area of 231,805 sq. km.) and a population of 1.62 million. Capital: Gaborone. Botswana is a member of a Customs Union with South Africa, Lesotho, and Swaziland. The economy is primarily pastoral with a rapidly developing mining industry, of which diamonds, copper and nickel are the chief elements. Meat products and diamonds comprise 85 percent of the exports.

Little is known of the origin of the peoples of Botswana. The early inhabitants, the Bushmen, did not develop a recorded history and are now dying out. The ancesters of the present Botswana probably arrived about 1600 AD in Bantu migrations from the north and east. Bechuanaland was first united early in the 19th century under Chief Khama III to more effectively resist incursions by the Boer trekkers from Transvaal and by the neighboring Matabeles. As the Boer threat intensified, appeals for protection were made to the British Government, which proclaimed the whole of Bechuanaland a British protectorate in 1885. In 1895, the southern part of the protectorate was annexed to Cape Province. The northern part, known as the Bechuanaland Protectorate, remained under British administration until it became the independent Republic of Botswana on Sept. 30, 1966. Botswana is a member of the Commonwealth of Nations. The president is Chief of State and Head of Government.

MONETARY SYSTEM:

1 Pula (Rand) = 100 Thebe (Cents)

	MINISTER OF FINANCE	GOVERNOR
1	Sir Q.K.J. Masire	Q. Hermans
2	Sir Q.K.J. Masire	B.C. Leavitt
3	P.S. Mmusi	F.G. Mogae
4	P.S. Mmusi	C. Kilonyogo
5	P.S. Mmusi	Q. Hermans
6a	F.G. Mogae	Q. Hermans
6b	F.G. Mogae	Q. Hermans
7a	P.H.K. Kedikilwe	B. Gaolatlhe
7b	P.H.K. Kedikilwe	B. Gaolatlhe
8a	B. Gaolatlhe	Mrs. L.K. Mohohlo
8b	B. Gaolatlhe	Mrs. L.K. Mohohlo

REPUBLIC

BANK OF BOTSWANA

1976-79 ND ISSUE

#1-5 Pres. Sir Seretse Khama at l., arms at upper r. Wmk: Rearing zebra. Printer: TDLR. Replacement notes: Serial # prefixes *Z/1, X/1, Y/1* for 1, 10, and 20 respectively. For specimen notes with a maltese cross serial # prefix see the CS1 listing at the end of the country.

		VG	VF	UNC
1	**1 Pula** ND (1976). Brown on multicolor underprint. Bird at center Farmer milking cow at center right on back.			
	a. Issued note.	.60	1.75	6.00
	s. Specimen. Serial # prefix: *A/1.*	—	—	95.00

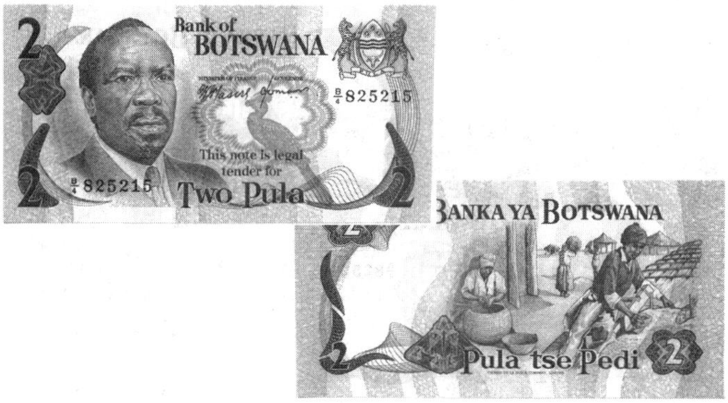

		VG	VF	UNC
2	**2 Pula** ND (1976). Blue on multicolor underprint. Bird at center. Various workers at center right on back.			
	a. Issued note.	FV	3.00	14.00
	s. Specimen. Serial # prefix: *B/1.*	—	—	95.00

		VG	VF	UNC
3	**5 Pula** ND (1976). Purple on multicolor underprint. Bird at center. Gemsbok antelope at center right on back.			
	a. Issued note.	FV	6.00	35.00
	s. Specimen. Serial # prefix: *C/1.*	—	—	90.00

		VG	VF	UNC
4	**10 Pula** ND (1976). Green on multicolor underprint. Bird at center. Large building at center right on back.			
	a. Signature 1.	7.50	30.00	150.
	b. Signature 2.	12.50	45.00	300.
	s1. As a. Specimen. Serial # prefix: *D/1.*	—	—	95.00
	s2. As b. Specimen. Serial # prefix: *D/4.*	—	—	95.00

5	20 Pula	VG	VF	UNC
	ND (1979). Red, purple and brown on multicolor underprint. Bird at center. Mining conveyors at center right on back.			
	a. Signature 1.	15.00	50.00	300.
	b. Signature 2.	17.50	55.00	400.
	s1. As a. Specimen. Serial # prefix: *E/1*.	—	—	95.00
	s2. As b. Specimen. Serial # prefix: *E/2*.	—	—	95.00

1982-83 ND ISSUE

#6-10 Pres. Q.K.J. Masire at l. wearing coarser pin-stripe suit. Printer: TDLR. Replacement notes: Serial # prefix *Z/1*, *X/1*, *Y/1* for 1, 10 and 20 respectively.

6	1 Pula	VG	VF	UNC
	ND (1983). Dark brown. Cattle, arms and plants on back. Signature 4.			
	a. Issued note.	FV	.75	4.00
	s. Specimen. Serial # prefix: *A/1*.	—	—	70.00

#7-10 Pres. Q.K.J. Masire at l., arms at upper r. Wmk: Rearing zebra.

7	2 Pula	VG	VF	UNC
	ND (1982). Blue on multicolor underprint. Grey lourie at center. Various workers at center right on back.			
	a. Signature 3.	1.00	2.50	16.00
	b. Signature 4.	FV	1.00	8.50
	c. Signature 5.	FV	1.50	13.00
	d. Signature 6a.	—	1.00	7.00
	s1. As a. Specimen. Serial # prefix *B/6*.	—	—	70.00
	s2. As b. Specimen. Serial # prefix *B/7*.	—	—	70.00
	s3. As c. Specimen. Serial # prefix *B/16*.	—	—	70.00
	s4. As d. Specimen. Serial # prefix *B/21*.	—	—	70.00

8	5 Pula	VG	VF	UNC
	ND (1982). Deep violet on multicolor underprint. Helmeted guinea fowl at center. Gemsbok antelope at center right on back.			
	a. Signature 3.	1.50	5.00	35.00
	b. Signature 4.	FV	2.00	19.00
	c. Signature 5.	FV	1.50	15.00
	s1. As a. Specimen. Serial # prefix *C/5*.	—	—	70.00
	s2. As b. Specimen. Serial # prefix *C/6*.	—	—	70.00
	s3. As c. Specimen. Serial # prefix *C/10*.	—	—	70.00

9	10 Pula	VG	VF	UNC
	ND (1982). Green on multicolor underprint. Crowned hornbill at center. Large building at center right on back.			
	a. Signature 3.	2.50	10.00	50.00
	b. Signature 4.	FV	3.50	28.50
	c. Signature 5.	FV	4.00	35.00
	d. Signature 6a.	FV	3.00	22.50
	s1. As a. Specimen. Serial # prefix: *D/7*.	—	—	70.00
	s2. As b. Specimen. Serial # prefix: *D/12*.	—	—	70.00
	s3. As c. Specimen. Serial # prefix: *D/21*.	—	—	70.00
	s4. As d. Specimen. Serial #	—	—	70.00

10	20 Pula	VG	VF	UNC
	ND (1982). Red, purple and brown on multicolor underprint. Ostrich at center. Mining conveyors at center right on back.			
	a. Signature 3.	6.00	17.50	70.00
	b. Signature 4.	FV	7.50	58.00
	c. Signature 5.	FV	8.50	60.00
	d. Signature 6a.	FV	5.00	37.50
	s1. As a. Specimen. Serial # prefix: *E/2*.	—	—	70.00
	s2. As b. Specimen. Serial # prefix: *E/5*.	—	—	70.00
	s3. As c. Specimen. Serial # prefix: *E/9*.	—	—	70.00
	s4. As d. Specimen. Serial # prefix: *E/13*.	—	—	70.00

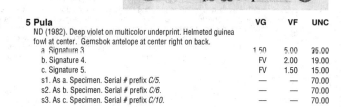

1992-95 ND ISSUE

#11-15 Pres. Q.K.J. Masire at l., arms at upper r. Wmk: Rearing zebra.

#11-13 printer: Harrison.

		VG	VF	UNC
11	**5 Pula**			
	ND (1992). Deep violet on multicolor underprint. Similar to #8; small stylistic differences. Signature 6a.			
	a. Issued note.	FV	1.50	6.00
	s. *C/18, C/19, C/27.*	—	—	125.

		VG	VF	UNC
12	**10 Pula**			
	ND (1992). Green on multicolor underprint. Similar to #9; small stylistic differences. Signature 6a.			
	a. Issued note.	FV	2.50	10.00
	s. Specimen. Serial # prefix: *D/45, D/46.*	—	—	135.

		VG	VF	UNC
13	**20 Pula**			
	ND (1993). Red, purple and brown on multicolor underprint. Similar to #10; small stylistic differences. Signature 6a.			
	a. Issued note.	FV	6.00	20.00
	s. Specimen. Serial # prefix: *E/21, E/29.*	—	—	150.

NOTICE

Readers with unlisted dates, signature varieties, etc. are invited to submit photocopies of their notes to: Standard Catalog of World Paper Money, 700 East State St. Iola, WI 54990-0001, E-Mail: george.cuhaj@fwpubs.com.

		VG	VF	UNC
14	**50 Pula**			
	ND (ca. 1992). Dark brown and dark green on multicolor underprint. Malachite kingfisher at center. Man in canoe and African fish eagle at center right on back. Signature 6b. Printer: Fidelity Printers (Zimbabwe - Harare). Without imprint.			
	a. Issued note.	FV	15.00	65.00
	s1. Specimen. Serial # *F000000A.*	—	—	60.00
	s2. Specimen. Serial # *F000000A.* Punch-hole cancelled.	—	—	60.00
15	**50 Pula**			
	ND(1995). Similar to #14. Printer: TDLR.			
	a. Issued note.	FV	12.50	52.50
	s. Specimen. Serial # prefix: *F...C.* (suffix)	—	—	60.00

		VG	VF	UNC
16	**100 Pula**			
	ND (1993). Blue-violet and ochre on multicolor underprint. Diamond and fish eagle at center. Worker sorting rough diamonds at center right on back. Signature 6. Printer: TDLR.			
	a. Issued note.	FV	FV	75.00
	b. Specimen. Serial # prefix: *G/1, G/6.*	—	—	60.00

1997 ND ISSUE

#17-19 President Q.K.J. Masire at l. wearing finer stripped pin suit, arms at upper r. Wmk: Rearing zebra. Printer as: *...RUE, LIMITED.*

		VG	VF	UNC
17	**10 Pula**			
	ND(1997). Similar to #12.			
	a. Issued note. signature 6a.	FV	3.00	17.50
	s. Specimen. Serial # prefix: *D/54.*	—	—	60.00
18	**20 Pula**			
	ND(1997). Similar to #13.			
	a. Issued note. signature 6a.	FV	5.00	22.50
	s. Specimen. Serial # prefix: *E/33.*	—	—	60.00
19	**50 Pula**			
	ND(1997). Similar to #14.			
	a. Issued note. signature 6b.	FV	12.50	42.50
	s. Specimen. Serial # prefix: *F/13.*	—	—	60.00

1999-2000 ND ISSUE

#20-23 Wmk: Rearing zebra.

20 **10 Pula**

ND(1999). Green on multicolor underprint. Pres. F. Mogae at left, arms at upper right, Hornbill at center. Parliament on back. Printer: F-CO.

	VG	VF	UNC
a. Signature 7a.	FV	FV	11.00
b. Sign 8a.	FV	FV	6.50
s1. As a. Specimen. Serial # prefix *D/62*.	—	—	60.00
s2. As b. Specimen. Serial # prefix *D/72*.	—	—	60.00

21 **20 Pula**

ND (1999). Red, purple and brown on multicolor underprint. K. Motsete at left, arms at upper right. Ostrich center. Mining conveyors at center right on back. Printer: SABN.

	VG	VF	UNC
a. Sign 7b.	FV	FV	16.00
s1. As a. Specimen. Serial # prefix *E/42*.	—	—	60.00

22 **50 Pula**

ND (2000). Dark brown and dark green on multicolor underprint. Sir Seretse Khama at left, malachite kingfisher at center, Arms on right. Optical variable ink star at right. Man in canoe and fish eagle at center right on back. Printer: F-CO.

	VG	VF	UNC
a. Signature 8a.	FV	FV	22.50
s. As a. Specimen. Serial # prefix *F/18*.	—	—	60.00

23 **100 Pula**

ND (2000). Blue-violet and ochre on multicolor underprint. Three chiefs: Sebeli I, Bathoen I and Khama III at left, fisheagle at center, arms and optical variable ink diamond at right. Worker sorting rough diamonds at center on back. Printer: F-CO.

	VG	VF	UNC
a. Signature 8a.	FV	FV	52.50
s. As a. Specimen. Serial # prefix *G/11*.	—	—	60.00

2002 ND Issue

#24-25 wide security thread added.

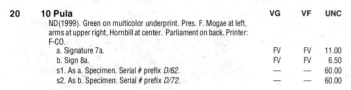

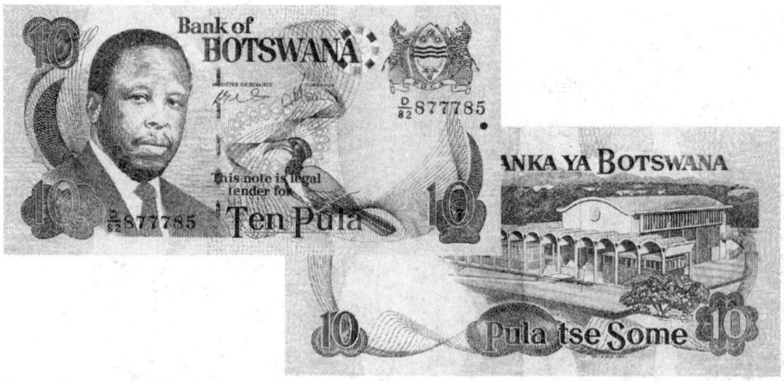

24 **10 Pula**

2002. Green on multicolor underprint. Printer: DLR.

	VG	VF	UNC
a. Signature 8b.	FV	FV	6.50
s. As a. Specimen. Serial # prefix D/82.	—	—	60.00

25 **20 Pula**

2002. Red, purple and brown on multicolor underprint. Printer: DLR.

	VG	VF	UNC
a. Sign 8b.	FV	FV	9.50
s. As a. Specimen. Serial # prefix E/52.	—	—	60.00

2005 ND Issue

26 **100 Pula**

ND. Like #23a but with circular Kinegram added at lower right.

	VG	VF	UNC
	FV	FV	52.50

COLLECTOR SERIES

BANK OF BOTSWANA

1979 ND ISSUE

		Issue Price	Mkt.	Value
CS1	**ND (1979) 1-20 Pula** #1-3, 4a, 5a. Ovpt: *SPECIMEN* and Maltese cross serial # prefix.	—	—	40.00

The Federative Republic of Brazil, which comprises half the continent of South America, is the only Latin American country deriving its culture and language from Portugal. It has an area of 3,286,470 sq. mi. (8,511,965 sq. km.) and a population of 169.2 million. Capital: Brasília. The economy of Brazil is as varied and complex as any in the developing world. Agriculture is a mainstay of the economy, although but 4 percent of the area is under cultivation. Known mineral resources are almost unlimited in variety and size of reserves. A large, relatively sophisticated industry ranges from basic steel and chemical production to finished consumer goods. Coffee, cotton, iron ore and cocoa are the chief exports.

Brazil was discovered and claimed for Portugal by Admiral Pedro Alvares Cabral in 1500. Portugal established a settlement in 1532 and proclaimed the area a royal colony in 1549. During the Napoleonic Wars, Dom João VI established the seat of Portuguese government in Rio de Janeiro. When he returned to Portugal, his son Dom Pedro I declared Brazil's independence on Sept. 7, 1822, and became emperor of Brazil. The Empire of Brazil was maintained until 1889 when a republic was established. The Federative Republic was established in 1946 by terms of a constitution drawn up by a constituent assembly. Following a coup in 1964, the armed forces retained overall control under dictatorship until a civilian government was restored on March 15, 1985. The current constitution was adopted in 1988.

RULERS:

Pedro II, 1831-1889

MONETARY SYSTEM:

1 Cruzeiro = 100 Centavos, 1942-1967
1 Cruzeiro Novo = 1000 Old Cruzeiros, 1967-1985
1 Cruzado = 1000 Cruzeiros Novos, 1986-1989
1 Cruzado Novo = 1000 Cruzados, 1989-1990
1 Cruzeiro = 1 Cruzado Novo, 1990-1993
1 Cruzeiro Real (pl. Reals) = 1000 Cruzeiros, 1993-

SIGNATURE VARIETIES

8	Sebastião P. Almeida	
9	Clemente Mariani	Carlos A. Carrílho
10	Walter M. Salles	Reginaldo F. Nunes
11	Reginaldo F. Nunes, 1962	Walter M. Salles
12	Reginaldo F. Nunes, 1963	Miguel Calmon
13	Reginaldo F. Nunes, 1964	Otávio Gouvex Bulhões
14	Sérgio A. Ribeiro, 1964-66	Otávio Gouvex Bulhões
15	Dénio Nogueira, 1966-67	Otávio Gouvex Bulhões

SIGNATURE VARIETIES

16	Ruy Leme, 1967	Antônio Delfim Netto
17	Ername Galveas, 1967-72	Antônio Delfim Netto
18	Mário Henrique Simonsen, 1974-79	Paulo H.P. Lira
19	Karlos Rischbieter. 1979-80	Ernane Galvêas
20	Ernane Galvêas, 1980-81	Carlos P. Langoni
21	Ernane Galvêas, 1983-85	Alfonso C. Pastore
22	Francisco Dornélles, 1985	Antonio Lengruber
23	Dilson Funaro, 1985-86	Fernao C.B. Bracher
24	Dilson Funaro, 1987	Francisco Gross
25	Luiz Carlos Bresser Pereira, 1987	Fernando M. Oliveira
26	Maílson Ferreira Da Nóbrega, 1988-89	Elmo Camões
27	Maílson Ferreira Da Nóbrega, 1989-90	Wadico Bucchi
28	Zélia Cardoso De Mello, 1990	Ibrahim Éris
29	Marcílio M. Moreira, 1991-92	Francisco Gross
30	Paulo R. Haddad, 1993	Gustavo Loyola
31	Elizeu Resende, 1993	Paulo Ximenes
32	Fernando H. Cardoso, 1993	Paulo Ximenes

SIGNATURE VARIETIES

33	Fernando H. Cardoso, 1993-94	Pedro Malan
34	Rubens Ricúpero, 1994	Pedro Malan
35	Ciro Gomes, 1994	Pedro Malan
36	Pedro Malan, 1995	Pérsio Arida
37	Pedro Malan, 1995-97	Gustavo Loyola
38	Pedro Malan, 1998	Gustavo Franco
39	Pedro Malan, 1999-	Arminia Fraganeto
40	Antonio Palocci Filho, 2003-	Henrique De Campos Meirelles

TESOURO NACIONAL, VALOR RECEBIDO

ESTAMPA 3; 1961 ND ISSUE

		VG	VF	UNC
166	**5 Cruzeiros** ND (1961-62). Dark brown and brown. Raft with sail at left, male Indian at right. Flower on back. Printer: CdM-B.			
	a. Signature 8. Series #1-75.	.10	.50	2.00
	b. Signature 10. Series #76-111.	.10	.25	1.25

NOTICE

Readers with unlisted dates, signature varieties, etc. are invited to submit photocopies of their notes to: Standard Catalog of World Paper Money, 700 East State St. Iola, WI 54990-0001, E-Mail: george.cuhaj@fwpubs.com.

TESOURO NACIONAL, VALOR LEGAL

ESTAMPA 1A; 1961 ND ISSUE

#167-173 dk. blue on m/c unpt. 2 printed sign. Printer: ABNC.

167	10 Cruzeiros	VG	VF	UNC
	ND (1961-63). Portrait G. Vargas at center. Back green; allegory of "Industry" at center.			
	a. Signature 9. Series #331-630. (1961).	.15	.50	2.00
	b. Signature 12. Series #631-930. (1963).	.15	.50	1.75
	s. As a or b. Specimen.	—	—	110.

168	20 Cruzeiros	VG	VF	UNC
	ND (1961-63). Portrait D. da Fonseca at center. Back red; allegory of "the Republic" at center.			
	a. Signature 9. Series #461-960. (1961).	.15	.50	2.25
	b. Signature 12. Series #961-1260. (1963).	.15	.50	2.00
	s. As a or b. Specimen.	—	—	115.

169	50 Cruzeiros	VG	VF	UNC
	ND (1961). Portrait Princess Isabel at center. Back purple; allegory of "Law" at center. Signature 9. Series #721-1220.			
	a. Issued note.	.15	1.50	7.50
	s. Specimen.	—	—	115.

170	100 Cruzeiros	VG	VF	UNC
	ND (1961-64). Portrait D. Pedro at center. Back red-brown; allegory of "National Culture" at center.			
	a. Signature 9. Series #761-1160. (1961).	.25	2.25	9.00
	b. Signature 13. Series #1161-1360. (1964).	.25	1.00	4.50
	c. Signature 14. Series #1361-1560. (1964).	.25	2.00	8.00
	s. As a, b or c. Specimen.	—	—	125.

171	200 Cruzeiros	VG	VF	UNC
	ND (1961-64). Portrait D. Pedro at center. Back olive-green; battle scene at center.			
	a. Signature 9. Series #671-1070. (1961).	.50	3.50	15.00
	b. Signature 13. Series #1071-1370. (1964).	.50	3.00	12.00
	c. Signature 14. Series #1371-1570. (1964).	.50	3.00	12.00
	s. As a, b or c. Specimen.	—	—	125.

172	500 Cruzeiros	VG	VF	UNC
	ND (1961-62). Portrait D. Joao VI at center. Back blue-black; allegory of "Maritime Industry" at center.			
	a. Signature 9. Series #261-660. (1961).	1.00	5.00	25.00
	b. Signature 11. Series #661-1460. (1962).	.75	4.00	20.00
	s. As a, b. Specimen.	—	—	125.

173	1000 Cruzeiros			
	ND (1961-63). Portrait P. Alvares Cabral at center. Back orange; scene of the "First Mass" at center.			
	a. Signature 9. Series #1331-1730. (1961).	.75	8.00	50.00
	b. Signature 11. Series #1731-3030. (1962).	.75	6.00	40.00
	c. Signature 12. Series #3031-3830. (1963).	1.00	7.00	45.00
	s. As a, b or c. Specimen.	—	—	135.

174	5000 Cruzeiros	VG	VF	UNC
	ND (1963-64). Blue-gray on multicolor underprint. Portrait Tiradentes at right. Back red; Tiradentes in historical scene at center. Printer: ABNC.			

174	5000 Cruzeiros	VG	VF	UNC
	a. Signature 12. Series #1-400. (1963).	1.00	5.00	35.00
	b. Signature 13. Series #401-1400. (1964).	1.00	4.50	30.00
	c. Signature 14. Series #1401-1650. (1965).	1.75	8.00	50.00
	s. As a, b or c. Specimen.	—	—	150.

ESTAMPA 2A; 1962-63 ND ISSUE

#175 *Deleted*, see #182B.

#176-182 2 printed sign. Printer: TDLR.

176	5 Cruzeiros	VG	VF	UNC
	ND (1962-64). Brown on multicolor underprint. Portrait Barao do Rio Branco at center.			
	a. Signature 11. Series #2301-3500. (1962).	.10	.25	1.00
	b. Signature 12. Series #3501-3700. (1963).	.10	.25	2.50
	c. Signature 13. Series #3701-3748; 4149-4180; 4201-4232. (1964).	.10	.25	5.00
	d. Signature 14. Series #3749-4148; 4181-4200; 4233-4700. (1964).	.10	.25	.75
177	**10 Cruzeiros**			
	ND (1962). Green on multicolor underprint. Like #167.			
	a. Signature 10. Series #2365-3055.	.10	.25	1.50
	b. Signature 11. Series 2394A.	.10	.25	1.50

178	20 Cruzeiros	VG	VF	UNC
	ND (1962). Red-brown on multicolor underprint. Like #168. Signature 11. Series #1576-2275.	.15	.50	2.25

179	50 Cruzeiros	VG	VF	UNC
	ND (1963.) Purple on multicolor underprint. Like #169. Signature 12. Series #586-785.	.25	1.00	4.00
180	**100 Cruzeiros**			
	ND (1963). Red on multicolor underprint. Like #170. Signature 12. Series #216-415.	.25	2.00	9.00

NOTICE

Readers with unlisted dates, signature varieties, etc. are invited to submit photocopies of their notes to: Standard Catalog of World Paper Money, 700 East State St. Iola, WI 54990-0001, E-Mail: george.cuhaj@fwpubs.com.

181	1000 Cruzeiros	VG	VF	UNC
	ND (1963). Orange on multicolor underprint. Like #173. Signature 12. Series #791-1590.	.50	3.00	15.00

182	5000 Cruzeiros	VG	VF	UNC
	ND (1963-64). Red on multicolor underprint. Like #174. Signature at left with *Director Caixa de Amortizacao*.			
	a. Signature 12. Series #1-400. (1963).	1.00	4.50	30.00
	b. Signature 13. Series #401-1400. (1964).	.75	4.00	25.00
	c. Signature 14. Series #1401-1700. (1964).	1.50	6.00	40.00

BANCO CENTRAL DO BRASIL

1965; 1966 ND ISSUE

182A	5000 Cruzeiros	VG	VF	UNC
	ND (1965). Red on multicolor underprint. Like #174. Signature D. Nogueira with title: *Presidente do Banco Central* and O. Gouvea de Bulhões. Sign 15. Series #1701-2200.	1.00	5.00	35.00

182B	10,000 Cruzeiros	VG	VF	UNC
	ND (1966). Gray on multicolor underprint. Portrait S. Dumont at right. Back blue; early airplane at right. Signature 15. Printer: ABNC.			
	a. Series #1-493.	4.00	17.50	70.00
	b. Series #561-590.	45.00	175.	350.
	s. As a. Specimen.	—	—	175.

1966; 1967 ND PROVISIONAL ISSUE

Feb. 1967 Monetary Reform: 1 Cruzeiro Novo = 1,000 Cruzeiros

#183-190 black circular ovpt: *BANCO CENTRAL* and new currency unit in black circle on Tesouro Nacional notes.

183	1 Centavo on 10 Cruzeiros	VG	VF	UNC
	ND (1966-67). Green on multicolor underprint. Overprint on #177. Signature 15.			

183 1 Centavo on 10 Cruzeiros

	VG	VF	UNC
a. Error: *Minstro* below r. signature (2 types of 1 in ovpt.) (1966). Series #3056-3151.	.10	.20	1.00
b. *Ministro* below r. signature (1967). Series # 3152-4055.	.10	.20	1.00
s. As b. Specimen ovpt: *MODELO.*	—	—	—

184 5 Centavos on 50 Cruzeiros

ND (1966-67). Purple on multicolor underprint. Overprint on #179. Signature 15.

	VG	VF	UNC
a. Type of #183a. Series #786-1313.	.10	.25	1.50
b. Type of #183b. Series #1314-1885.	.10	.25	1.50

185 10 Centavos on 100 Cruzeiros

ND (1966-67). Red on multicolor underprint. Overprint on #180. Signature 15.

	VG	VF	UNC
a. Type of #183a. Series #416-911.	.10	.25	2.00
b. Type of #183b. Series #912-1515.	.10	.25	1.75

186 50 Centavos on 500 Cruzeiros

ND (1967). Blue on multicolor underprint. Overprint on #172. Signature 15. Series #1461-2360.

	VG	VF	UNC
a. Issued note.	.75	2.00	4.50
s. Specimen.	—	—	100.

187 1 Cruzeiro Novo on 1000 Cruzeiros

ND (1966-67). Blue on multicolor underprint. Overprint on #173.

	VG	VF	UNC
a. Signature 14. Series #3831-3930.	2.00	7.50	22.50
b. Signature 15. Series #3931-4830.	1.50	2.50	7.50
s. As b. Specimen.	—	—	115.

188 eiros5 Cruzeiros Novos on 5000 Cruz

ND (1966-67). Blue-green on multicolor underprint. Overprint on #174.

	VG	VF	UNC
a. Signature 14. Series #1651-1700.	10.00	30.00	60.00
b. Signature 15. Series #1701-2900.	2.00	8.00	22.50
s. As b. Specimen.	—	—	115.

189 10 Cruzeiros Novos on 10,000 Cruzeiros

ND (1966-67). Gray on multicolor underprint. Bold or semi-bold overprint on #182B. Printer: ABNC.

	VG	VF	UNC
a. Signature 15. Series #494-560 and 591-700. (1966).	2.50	25.00	85.00
b. Signature 16. Series #701-1700. (1967).	1.00	6.00	25.00
c. Signature 17. Series #1701-2700. (1967).	1.00	5.00	20.00
s. As b. Specimen.	—	Unc	150.

190 10 Cruzeiros Novos on 10,000 Cruzeiros

ND (1967). Brown on pink and multicolor underprint. Like #182B. Printer: TDLR.

	VG	VF	UNC
a. Signature 16. Series #1-1000.	1.00	3.50	15.00
b. Signature 17. Series #1001-2100.	.75	2.25	10.00

1970 ND Issues

#191-195 portr. as wmk. Sign. varieties. 5 digit series # above serial #.

#191-194, 195A printer: CdM-B.

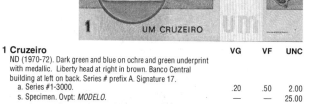

191 1 Cruzeiro

ND (1970-72). Dark green and blue on ochre and green underprint with medallic. Liberty head at right in brown. Banco Central building at left on back. Series # prefix A. Signature 17.

	VG	VF	UNC
a. Series #1-3000.	.20	.50	2.00
s. Specimen. Ovpt: *MODELO.*	—	—	25.00

191A 1 Cruzeiro

ND (1972-80). Dark green and blue with medallic. Liberty head in green. Series # prefix B.

	VG	VF	UNC
a. Signature 17. Series #1-3781 (1972).	.10	.25	1.00
b. Signature 18. Series #3782-13194 (1975).	.05	.15	.75
c. Signature 20. Series #13195-18094 (1980).	.05	.10	.50
s. As a. Specimen overprint and perforated: *MODELO.*	—	—	25.00

192 5 Cruzeiros

ND (1970-80). Blue on orange and green underprint. Portrait D. Pedro I at right. Back maroon; parade square at left.

	VG	VF	UNC
a. Back darkly printed. signature 17. Series # prefix A. Series #1-107 (1970-71).	.25	5.00	20.00
b. Back lightly printed. signature 17. Series # prefix B. Series #1-2467 (1973).	.10	.25	1.25
c. Signature 18. Series #2468-6050 (1974).	.10	.25	1.50
d. Signature 19. Series #6051-6841 (1979).	.10	.25	2.00
s. As a. Specimen ovpt: *SEM VALOR*, perforated: *MODELO.*	—	—	25.00

193 10 Cruzeiros

ND (1970-80). Grayish purple and dark brown on orange-brown blue-green and multicolor underprint. Portrait D. Pedro II at right. Back green, violet and brown; statue of the Prophet Daniel.

	VG	VF	UNC
a. Back darkly printed. signature 17. Series # prefix A. Series #1-1429 (1970).	.50	2.50	15.00
b. As a. signature 18. Series #1430-7745 (1974).	.15	.50	1.75
c. Back lightly printed. signature 18. Series # prefix B. Series #1-2394 (1979).	.25	1.00	5.00
d. As c. signature 19. Series #2395-2870 (1980).	.15	.50	2.50
e. As d. signature 20. Series #2871-5131 (1980).	.10	.50	2.00
s. Specimen.	—	—	25.00

194 50 Cruzeiros

ND (1970-81). Black, purple, blue-black and violet on lilac and multicolor underprint. Portrait D. da Fonseca at right. Back brown, lilac and blue; coffee loading at left.

	VG	VF	UNC
a. Signature 17. Series #1-1250 (1970).	1.00	3.00	20.00
b. Signature 18. Series #1251-3841 (1974).	.20	.50	3.00
c. Signature 20. Series #3842-5233 (1980).	.15	.50	2.50
s. Specimen.	—	—	25.00

195 100 Cruzeiros

ND (1970-81). Purple and violet on pink and multicolor underprint. Portrait Marshal F. Peixoto at right. Back blue, brown and violet; National Congress at left. Printer: TDLR. Signature 17 (with imprint CdM-B). Series #1-01358.

	VG	VF	UNC
a. Issued note.	1.50	6.00	35.00
s. Specimen.	—	—	—

195A 100 Cruzeiros

ND (1974-81). Purple and violet on pink and multicolor underprint. Like #195. Printer: CdM-B.

	VG	VF	UNC
a. Signature 18. Series #01359-10455 (1974).	.25	.75	6.00
b. Signature 20. Series #10456-12681 (1981).	.25	.75	6.00
s. Specimen.	—	—	25.00

Note: The difference between #195 and 195A is in the wmk.

1972 Commemorative Issue

#196, 196A, 150th Anniversary of Brazilian Independence

196 500 Cruzeiros

1972 (1972-74). Dark olive-green and brown on violet and multicolor underprint. Portrait of five men of differing racial groups. Watermark: Dates *1822 1972* in clear area at left. 5 different historical maps of Brazil on back. Printer: CdM-B.

	VG	VF	UNC
a. Signature 17. Series # prefix A. #1-90 (1972).	35.00	100.	300.
b. As a. signature 18. Series #91-2636 (1974).	1.00	5.00	35.00
s1. Specimen. signature 17. Ovpt: *MODELO.*	—	—	70.00
s2. Specimen. signature 18. Ovpt: *MODELO.*	—	—	50.00

196A	500 Cruzeiros	VG	VF	UNC
	1972 (1979-80). Like #196 but watermark area has vertical lines printed on face and back.			
	a. Signature 18. Series # prefix B. #1-1401 (1979).	1.00	4.00	25.00
	b. As a. signature 19. Series #1402-1959 (1979).	1.00	4.00	25.00
	c. As a. signature 20. Series #1960-2763 (1980).	1.00	4.00	25.00
	s. Specimen.	—	—	50.00

1978 ND Issue

#197, the first 4 digits of the serial # represent the series #.

197	1000 Cruzeiros	VG	VF	UNC
	ND (1978-80). Green and brown. Double portrait B. do Rio Branco and as watermark *BANCO CENTRAL DO BRASIL* in two lines. Double view of machinery on back. Also, small plate modification on back.			
	a. Signature 18. Series #1-665 (1978).	1.50	8.00	50.00
	b. Signature 19. Series #666-2072 (1979).	1.75	6.00	32.50
	c. Signature 20. Series #2073-3297 (1980).	.75	6.00	35.00

1981-85 ND Issue

#198-205 portr. as wmk. Sign. varieties. Printer: CdM-B. The first 4 digits of the serial # represent the series #.

#198-202 double portr. and vignettes.

198	100 Cruzeiros	VG	VF	UNC
	ND (1981-84). Red and purple on multicolor underprint. D. de Caxias at center. Back gray-blue and red; battle scene and sword at center.			
	a. Signature 20. Series #1-4081 (1981).	.05	.15	.50
	b. Signature 21. Series #4082-8176 (1984).	.05	.15	.50

199	200 Cruzeiros	VG	VF	UNC
	ND (1981-84). Green and violet on multicolor underprint. Princess Isabel at center. Back brown and green; two women cooking outdoors.			
	a. Signature 20. Series #1-2996 (1981).	.05	.15	.50
	b. Signature 21. Series #2997-4960 (1984).	.05	.15	.50

200	500 Cruzeiros	VG	VF	UNC
	ND (1981-85). Blue and brown on multicolor underprint. D. da Fonseca at center. Back pink, brown and purple; group of legislators.			
	a. Signature 20. Series #1-3510 (1981).	.05	.20	1.00
	b. Signature 21. Series #3511-4238 (1985).	.05	.15	.75

201	1000 Cruzeiros	VG	VF	UNC
	ND (1981-86). Brown and dark olive on multicolor underprint. Similar to #197, but bank name in one line. Back tan and blue.			
	a. Signature 20. Series # prefix A, #1-5733 (1981).	.10	.50	2.50
	b. As a. signature 21. Series #5734-7019 (1984).	.05	.15	.75
	c. As b. signature 22. Series #7020-9999 (1985).	.05	.15	.75
	d. Signature 22. Series # prefix B, #1-788 (1986).	.05	.15	.75

202 5000 Cruzeiros

ND (1981-85). Purple and brown on multicolor underprint. C. Branco at center. Back brown, purple and blue; antennas.

	VG	VF	UNC
a. Signature 20. Series # prefix A, #1-9205 (1981).	.15	.75	6.50
b. As a. signature 21. Series #9206-9999 (1983).	.10	.25	1.50
c. Signature 21. Series # prefix B, #1-2118 (1984).	.10	.25	1.00
d. As c. signature 22. Series #2119-2342 (1985).	.25	.50	2.00

203 10,000 Cruzeiros

ND (1984-85). Brown on multicolor underprint. Desk top at center, Rui Barbosa at center right. Conference scene on back.

	VG	VF	UNC
a. Signature 21. Series #1-3619 (1984).	.25	1.25	4.50
b. Signature 22. Series #3620-3696 (1985).	.75	4.00	22.50

204 50,000 Cruzeiros

ND (1984-86). Purple on multicolor underprint. Microscope at center, O. Cruz at right. Cruz Institute at center on back.

	VG	VF	UNC
a. Signature 21. Series #1-1673 (1984).	.50	3.75	20.00
b. Signature 22 (reversed). Series #1674-2170 (1985).	1.00	5.00	15.00
c. Signature 22 (corrected). Series #2171-3248 (1985).	.25	1.75	7.00
d. Signature 23. Series #3249-3290 (1986).	.50	2.00	12.50

		VG	VF	UNC
205	**100,000 Cruzeiros** ND (1985). Black on blue, gold and multicolor underprint. Electric power station at center, Pres. J. Kubitschek at right. Old and modern buildings at center on back. Signature 23. Series #1-4347.	.50	2.50	5.50

1986 ND Provisional Issue

Feb. 1986 Monetary Reform: 1 Cruzado = 1,000 Cruzeiros

#206-208 black circular ovpt: *Banco Central Do Brasil* and new currency unit on #203-205.

		VG	VF	UNC
206	**s10 Cruzados on 10,000 Cruzeiro** ND (1986). Overprint on #203. Signature 23. Series #3697-5124.	.10	.20	1.50

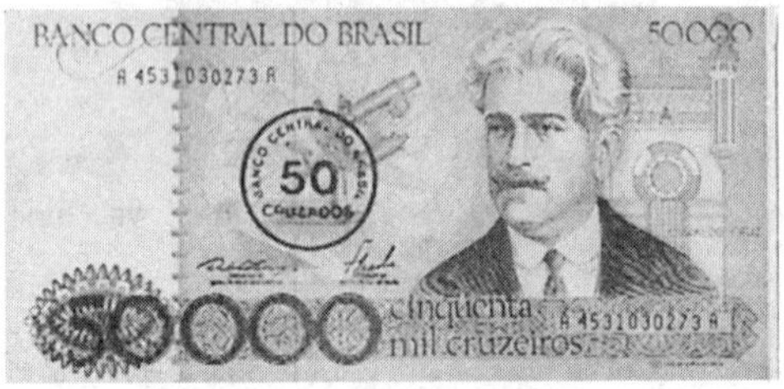

		VG	VF	UNC
207	**50 Cruzados on 50,000 Cruzeiros** ND (1986). Overprint on #204. Signature 23. Series #3291-4592.	.20	.75	2.50

		VG	VF	UNC
208	**ros100 Cruzados on 100,000 Cruzei** ND (1986). Overprint on #205. Signature 23. Series #4348-6209.	.20	.75	5.00

1986 ND Issue

#209-211 printer: CdM-B.

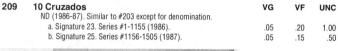

209 10 Cruzados

ND (1986-87). Similar to #203 except for denomination.

	VG	VF	UNC
a. Signature 23. Series #1-1155 (1986).	.05	.20	1.00
b. Signature 25. Series #1156-1505 (1987).	.05	.15	.50

210 50 Cruzados

ND (1986-88). Similar to #204 except for denomination.

	VG	VF	UNC
a. Signature 23. Series #1-1617 (1986).	.05	.20	.75
b. Signature 25. Series #1618-2044 (1987).	.05	.20	.75
c. Signature 26. Series #2045-2051 (1988).	2.50	15.00	100.

211 100 Cruzados

ND (1986-88). Similar to #205 except for denomination.

	VG	VF	UNC
a. Signature 23. Series #1-1176 (1986).	.10	.40	2.00
b. Signature 24. Series #1177-1582 (1987).	.10	.40	2.00
c. Signature 25. Series #1583-3045 (1987).	.05	.15	.50
d. Signature 26. Series #3046-3059 (1988).	.50	3.00	17.50

1986 ND Commemorative Issue

#212, Birth Centennial of H. Villa-Lobos

212 500 Cruzados

ND (1986). Blue-green on green and multicolor underprint. H. Villa-Lobos at center right and as watermark. Villa-Lobos conducting at left center on back. Printer: CdM-B.

	VG	VF	UNC
a. Signature 23. Series #1-2352 (1986).	.10	.50	3.00
b. Signature 24. Series #2353-2842 (1987).	.10	.50	2.50
c. Signature 25. Series #2843-7504 (1987).	.05	.15	.50
d. Signature 26. Series #7505-8309 (1988).	.05	.20	1.00

1987 ND Regular Issue

#213-215 portr. as wmk. Printer: CdM-B. Series # are first 4 digits of serial #.

213 1000 Cruzados

ND (1987-88). Purple and brown-violet on multicolor underprint. J. Machado at right. Street scene from old Rio de Janeiro on back.

	VG	VF	UNC
a. Signature 25. Series #1-2744 (1987).	.20	1.00	6.00
b. Signature 26. Series #2745-9919 (1988)	.05	.15	.75

214 5000 Cruzados

ND (1988). Blue on multicolor underprint. Portion of mural at left center, C. Portinari at right. C. Portinari painting at center on back. Signature 26. Series #1-1757.

VG	VF	UNC
.25	1.00	4.00

215 10,000 Cruzados

ND (1989). Red and brown on multicolor underprint. C. Chagas at right. Chagas with lab instruments on back. Signature 26. Series #1-1841.

VG	VF	UNC
.25	1.00	7.00

1989 ND Provisional Issue

Jan. 1989 Monetary Reform: 1 Cruzado Novo = 1,000 Cruzados

#216-218 black triangular ovpt. of new currency unit on #213-215.

		VG	VF	UNC
216	**1 Cruzado Novo on 1000 Cruzados** ND (1989). Purple and brown-violet on multicolor underprint. Overprint on #213.			
	a. Signature 26. Series # prefix A, #9920-9999 (1989).	.10	.50	2.00
	b. Signature 26. Series # prefix B, #1-1617 (1989).	.10	.15	.50
	c. As b. Signature 27. Series #1618-1792 (1989).	.10	.25	1.25

		VG	VF	UNC
217	**dos5 Cruzados Novos on 5000 Cruza** ND (1989). Blue on multicolor underprint. Overprint on #214.			
	a. Signature 26. Series #1758-3531 (1989).	.10	.50	1.75
	b. Signature 27. Series #3532-3818 (1989).	.10	.50	1.75

		VG	VF	UNC
218	**10 Cruzados Novos on 10,000 Cruzados** ND (1989-90). Red and brown on multicolor underprint. Overprint on #215.			
	a. Signature 26. Series #1842-4171 (1989).	.10	.25	1.50
	b. Signature 27. Series #4172-4502 (1990).	.10	.50	2.50

1989 ND Issue

#219 and 220 printer: CdM-B. Wmk: Liberty head.

		VG	VF	UNC
219	**50 Cruzados Novos** ND (1989-90). Brown and black on multicolor underprint. C. Drummond de Andrade at right. Back black, red-brown and blue; de Andrade writing poetry.			
	a. Signature 26. Series #1-3340 (1989).	.10	.25	1.50
	b. Signature 27. Series #3341-3358 (1990).	.25	2.00	15.00

		VG	VF	UNC
220	**100 Cruzados Novos** ND (1989). Orange, purple and green on multicolor underprint. C. Meireles at right. Back brown, black and multicolor; child reading and people dancing.			
	a. Signature 26. Series #1-6772.	.15	.75	1.50
	b. Signature 27. Series #6773-8794.	.20	1.00	5.00

1989 ND Commemorative Issue

#221, Centenary of the Republic

		VG	VF	UNC
221	**200 Cruzados Novos** ND (1989). Blue and black on multicolor underprint. Political leaders at center, sculpture of the Republic at center right, arms at right. Oil painting "Patria" by P. Bruno with flag being embroidered by a family on back. Watermark: Liberty head. Printer: CdM-B. Signature 27. Series #1-1964.	.20	1.00	5.00

1990 ND Issue

		VG	VF	UNC
222	**500 Cruzados Novos** ND (1990). Green and purple on multicolor underprint. Orchids at center, A. Ruschi at right. Back light orange, purple and blue; swalow-tailed hummingbird, orchids and A. Ruschi at center watermark: Liberty head. Signature 27. Series #1-3700.	.75	2.00	7.50

NOTICE

Readers with unlisted dates, signature varieties, etc. are invited to submit photocopies of their notes to: Standard Catalog of World Paper Money, 700 East State St. Iola, WI 54990-0001, E-Mail: george.cuhaj@fwpubs.com.

1990 ND Provisional Issue

March 1990 Monetary Reform: 1 Cruzeiro = 1 Cruzado Novo

#223-226 black rectangular ovpt. of new currency unit on #219-222. Sign. 27.

		VG	VF	UNC
223	**50 Cruzeiros on 50 Cruzados Novos** ND (1990). Brown and black on multicolor underprint. Overprint on #219. Series #3359-5338.	.10	.15	.50

		VG	VF	UNC
224	**100 Cruzeiros on 100 Cruzados Novos** ND (1990). Orange, purple and green on multicolor underprint. Overprint on #220.			
	a. Series #8601.	10.00	50.00	140.
	b. Series #8795-9447.	.10	.40	1.50

		VG	VF	UNC
225	**200 Cruzeiros on 200 Cruzados Novos** ND (1990). Blue and black on multicolor underprint. Overprint on #221.			
	a. Series #1725.	20.00	75.00	175.
	b. Series #1965-2668.	.10	.50	1.00

		VG	VF	UNC
226	**500 Cruzeiros on 500 Cruzados Novos** ND (1990). Green and purple on multicolor underprint. Overprint on #222.			
	a. Series #3111.	10.00	35.00	100.
	b. Series #3701-7700.	.10	.25	.75

1992 ND Emergency Issue

		VG	VF	UNC
227	**5000 Cruzeiros** ND (1990). Deep olive-green and deep brown on multicolor underprint. Liberty head in green at right and as watermark Arms at left on back. Printer: CdM-B. Provisional type. Signature 28. Series #1-1520.	.20	.75	2.00

1990-93 ND Regular Issue

#228-236 printer: CdM-B.

#228-231 similar to #220-223 but w/new currency unit and new sign. titles.

		VG	VF	UNC
228	**100 Cruzeiros** ND (1990). Like #220. Signature 28. Series #1-1045.	.10	.20	.50

		VG	VF	UNC
229	**200 Cruzeiros** ND (1990). Like #221. Signature 28. Series #1-1646.	.05	.15	.50

		VG	VF	UNC
230	**500 Cruzeiros** ND (1990). Like #222. Signature 28. Series #1-0210.	.30	.75	3.00

231 1000 Cruzeiros

ND (1990-91). Dark brown, brown, violet and black on multicolor underprint. C. Rondon at right, native hut at center, map of Brazil in background. Two Indian children and local food from Amazonia on back. Watermark: Liberty head.

	VG	VF	UNC
a. Signature 28. Upper Signature title: *MINISTRO DA ECONOMIA,...* Series #1-4268 (1990).	.10	.40	2.50
b. Upper signature title: *MINISTRA DA ECONOMIA,...* Series #4269-6796 (1990).	.10	.30	2.00
c. Signature 29. Series #6797-8453 (1991).	.05	.15	.50

232 5000 Cruzeiros

ND (1990-93). Blue-black, black, and deep brown on light blue and multicolor underprint. C. Gomes at center right, Brazilian youths at center. Statue of Gomes seated, grand piano in background at center on back.

	VG	VF	UNC
a. Signature 28. Series #1-4489 (1990).	.10	.50	2.00
b. Signature 29. Series #4490-5501 (1992).	.10	.25	1.50
c. Signature 30. Series #5502-6041 (1993).	.10	.20	1.00

233 10,000 Cruzeiros

ND (1991-93). Black and brown-violet on multicolor underprint. V. Brazil at right and as watermark. Extracting poisonous venom at center. One snake swallowing another at center on back.

	VG	VF	UNC
a. Signature 28. Series #1-3136 (1991).	.10	.50	3.00
b. Signature 29. Series #3137-6937 (1992).	.10	.25	1.25
c. Signature 30. Series #6938-7365 (1993).	.05	.15	1.00

234 50,000 Cruzeiros

	VG	VF	UNC
ND (1992). Dark brown and red-orange on multicolor underprint. C. Cascudo at center right and as watermark. Two men on raft in background at left center. Folklore dancers at left center on back. Signature 29. Series #1-6289.	.10	.25	1.25

#235 and 236 wmk: Sculptured head of *Brasilia*.

235 100,000 Cruzeiros

ND (1992-93). Brown, green and purple on multicolor underprint. Hummingbird feeding nestlings at center, butterfly at right. Butterfly at left, Iguacú cataract at center on back.

	VG	VF	UNC
a. Signature 29. Series #1-6052 (1992).	.15	.50	6.00
b. Signature 30. Series #6053-6226 (1993).	.15	.50	5.00
c. Signature 31. Series #6227-6290 (1993).	.15	.50	5.00
d. Signature 32. Series #6291-6733 (1993).	.10	.25	1.25

236 500,000 Cruzeiros

ND (1993). Red-violet, brown and deep purple on multicolor underprint. M. de Andrade at right, native Indian art in underprint. Building; de Andrade teaching children at center on back.

	VG	VF	UNC
a. Signature 30. Series #1-3410 (1993).	.50	2.50	12.00
b. Signature 31. Series #3411-4404 (1993).	.50	2.00	10.00
c. Signature 32. Series #4405-8291 (1993).	.20	.50	4.00

1993 ND Provisional Issue

August 1993 Monetary Reform: 1 Cruzeiro Real = 1,000 Cruzeiros

#237-239 black circular ovpt. of new value on #234-236. Sign. 32.

237 50 Cruzeiros Reais on 50,000 Cruzeiros

	VG	VF	UNC
ND (1993). Dark brown and red-orange on multicolor underprint. Overprint on #234. Series #6290-6591.	.05	.20	1.00

238 100 Cruzeiros Reais on 100,000 Cruzeiros

	VG	VF	UNC
ND (1993). Brown, green and purple on multicolor underprint. Overprint on #235d. Series #6734-7144.	.10	.20	1.00

		VG	VF	UNC
239	**500 Cruzeiros Reais on 500,000 Cruzeiros** ND (1993). Red-violet, brown and deep purple on multicolor underprint. Overprint on #236c.			
	a. Series prefix A, #8292-9999.	.10	.50	3.00
	b. Series prefix B, #1-717.	.10	.25	2.25

1993-94 ND Issue

#240-242 wmk: Sculptured head of *"Brasilia."* Printer: CdM-B. Sign. 33.

		VG	VF	UNC
240	**1000 Cruzeiros Reais** ND (1993). Black, dark blue and brown on multicolor underprint. A. Teixeira at center right. "Parque" school at left center. Children and workers on back. Series #1-2515.	.10	.50	2.00

		VG	VF	UNC
241	**5000 Cruzeiros Reais** ND (1993). Black, red-brown and dark olive-green on multicolor underprint. Gaucho at center right, ruins of São Miguel das Missões at left center. Back vertical format; gaucho on horseback roping steer at center. Series #1-9999.	.50	2.50	12.50

		VG	VF	UNC
242	**50,000 Cruzeiros Reais** ND (1994). Deep purple and brown-violet on multicolor underprint. Dancer at left center, Baiana at center right. Back vertical format; Baiana do Acarajé preparing food at center Series #1-1200.	5.00	25.00	50.00

1994 ND Issue

July 1994 Monetary Reform: 1 Real = 2750 Cruzeiros Reals

#243-247 sculpture of the Republic at ctr. r. Back vertical format. Printer: CdM-B or w/additional imprint of secondary printer. Series # is first 4 digits of serial #. Sign. varieties.

		VG	VF	UNC
243	**1 Real** ND (1994-97). Black, olive-green and blue-green on aqua and pale green underprint. White-necked jacobin hummingbirds at center on back.			
	a. Signature 33. without text *DEUS SEJA LOUVADO,* Series #1-2409 (1994). Serial #A-A.	.50	1.00	6.00
	b. Signature 34. Series 2410-3833 (1994).	.50	1.00	6.00
	c. Signature 34. with text: *DEUS SEJA LOUVADO* at lower left Series #3834-6568.	.50	1.00	6.00
	d. Signature 35. Series 6569-7019.	.50	1.00	9.00
	e. Signature 37. Series 7020-9999.	.50	1.00	5.00
	f. Signature 37. Series 0001-0072, serial #A-B.	.50	2.00	17.50
243A	**1 Real** ND (1997-). Black, olive-green and blue-green on aqua and pale green underprint. Similar to #243 but watermark: Flag. Serial #A-B, B-B or C-B.			
	a. Signature 37. Series #0001-3247.	.50	1.00	4.00
	b. Signature 38. Series #3248-7561.	.50	1.00	4.00
	c. Signature 39. Series #7562-8948.	.50	1.00	6.00
	d. Signature 39. Series #8949-9999.	.50	1.00	4.00
	e. Signature 39. Series #0001-9999, series B-B.	FV	FV	3.00
	f. Signature 39. Serial C-B. Series #0001-3382.	FV	FV	2.00
	g. Signature 40. Series 3383-.	FV	FV	2.00

		VG	VF	UNC
244	**5 Reais** ND (1994-97). Violet, dark brown and blue on lilac underprint. Great egret at center on back. Serial #A-A. Watermark: Republic.			
	a. Signature 33. without text: *DEUS SEJA LOUVADO.* Series #0001-1411.	2.00	5.00	22.50
	b. Signature 33. without text. Printer: G & D. Series A-B,#1-1000.	5.00	20.00	55.00
	c. Signature 34. without text. Series A-A: #1412-1609.	10.00	50.00	130.
	d. Signature 34. with text: *DEUS SEJA LOUVADO. Series #1610-4093.*	2.00	5.00	17.50
	e. Signature 35. with text. Series 4094-5378.	2.00	5.00	17.50
	f. Signature 36. with text. Series 5379-5798.	2.00	5.00	22.50
	g. Signature 37. with text. Series #5799-8232.	2.00	5.00	17.50
244A	**5 Reais** ND (1997-). Violet, dark brown and blue on lilac underprint. Similar to #244 but watermark: Flag and series A-C.			
	a. Signature 37. Series #0001-1504.	2.00	5.00	17.50
	b. Signature 38. Series #1505-3034.	2.00	5.00	17.50

244A 5 Reais

	VG	VF	UNC
c. Signature 39. Series #3035-3196.	2.00	7.50	22.50
d. Signature 39. Series #3197-8817.	FV	2.00	6.00
e. Signature 40. Series #8818-.	FV	FV	5.00

245 10 Reais

ND (1994). Dark brown, brown-violet and brown-orange on lilac and pale orange underprint. Macaw at center on back. Watermark: Republic.

	VG	VF	UNC
a. Signature 33. without text: *DEUS SEJA LOUVADO*. Series A-A: #1-0713.	5.00	10.00	45.00
b. Signature 33. Printer: TDLR. Series #A-B: #0001-1200.	5.00	15.00	55.00
c. Signature 34. without text: *DEUS SEJA LOUVADO* at lower left Series #0714-1817.	5.00	10.00	30.00
d. Signature 34. with text at lower left Series #1818-3403.	5.00	10.00	30.00
e. Signature 35. Series #3404-6102.	5.00	10.00	30.00
f. Signature 36. Series #6103-6714.	5.00	15.00	55.00
g. Signature 37. Series #6715-9999.	5.00	10.00	30.00
h. Signature 37. Series #0001-4844. Serial A-B.	5.00	15.00	55.00

245A 10 Reais

ND (1997-). Dark brown, brown-violet and brown-orange on lilac and pale orange underprint. Similar to #245. Watermark: flag.

	VG	VF	UNC
a. Signature 37. Series #0001-4571. Serial A-C.	4.00	7.00	22.50
b. Signature 38. Series #4572-9179.	4.00	7.00	22.50
c. Signature 39. Series #9180-9999.	4.00	7.00	22.50
d. Signature 39. Series #0001-0075. Serial B-C.	4.00	10.00	27.50
e. Signature 39. Series #0076-9999.	4.00	5.00	12.50
f. Signature 39. Serial C-C. Series #0001-1136.	FV	FV	8.00
g. Signature 40. Series #1136-.	FV	FV	8.00

246 50 Reais

ND (1994-). Dark brown and red-brown on multicolor underprint. Jaguar on back.

	VG	VF	UNC
a. Signature 33. without text: *DEUS SEJA LOUVADO*. Series A-A: #0001-1249.	25.00	50.00	115.
b. Sing. 33. without text. Printer: F-CO. Series A-B: #0001-0400.	25.00	50.00	165.
c. Sing. 34. without text. Series #1250-1338.	20.00	40.00	135.
d. Signature 34. with text. Series #1339-1438.	25.00	50.00	165.
e. Signature 36. Series #1439-1636.	50.00	100.	550.
f. Signature 37. Series #1637-8405.	25.00	50.00	120.
g. Signature 38. Series #8406-9999.	20.00	40.00	135.
h. Signature 38. Series #0001-1004. Serial #B-A.	20.00	40.00	135.
i. Signature 39. Series #1005-1483. Serial #B-A.	20.00	40.00	135.
j. Signature 39. Series #1484-9057.	20.00	25.00	60.00
k. Signature 40. Series #9058-.	FV	FV	30.00

247 100 Reais

ND (1994-). Blue-green and purple on multicolor underprint. Garoupa fish on back.

	VG	VF	UNC
a. Signature 33. without text: *DEIS SEJA LOUVADO. Series #0001-1198.*	50.00	100.	175.
b. Signature 34. Series #1199-1201.	60.00	150.	325.
c. With text: *DEUS SEJA LOUVADO* at lower left signature 34. Series #1202-1300.	50.00	125.	225.

2000 Commemorative Issue

#248, 500th Anniversary of the Discovery of Brazil

248 10 Reais

ND (2000). Dark Blue, blue and orange. Pedro Alvares Cabral at center compass to left. Map and many portraits on back. Polymer plastic.

	VG	VF	UNC
a. Name as: *PEDRO A. CABRAL*. Series #0001-0586.	FV	FV	15.00
b. Name as: *PEDRO ALVARES CABRAL*. Series #0587-2536.	FV	FV	10.00

#248 Series #0001 was also available in a special folder, value $20.00.

2001-02 Issue

249 2 Reais

ND (2001-). Blue-green and black on multicolor underprint. Tartaruga Marinha turtles on back.

	VG	VF	UNC
a. Signature 39. Series #0001-2798.	FV	FV	2.50
b. Signature 40. Series #2799-.	FV	FV	2.50

250	20 Reais	VG	VF	UNC
	ND (2002-). Yellow and rose on multicolor underprint. Lion monkey on back.			
	a. Signature 39. Series #0001-2125.	FV	FV	12.50
	b. Signature 40. Series #2126-.	FV	FV	10.00

REPUBLICA FEDERATIVA DO BRAZIL

BANCO CENTRAL DO BRAZIL

2003 ISSUE

		VG	VF	UNC
251	1 Real			
	ND (2003-). Serial #A-C. Similar to #243A.			
	a. Signature 40. Series 0001-.	FV	FV	2.00
252	5 Reais			
	ND (2005). Violet. Expected new issue.	—	—	—
253	10 Reais			
	ND (2005). Dark brown. Expected new issue.	—	—	—
254	20 Reais			
	ND (2005). Expected new issue.	—	—	—
255	50 Reais			
	ND (2005). Dark brown. Expected new issue.	—	—	—

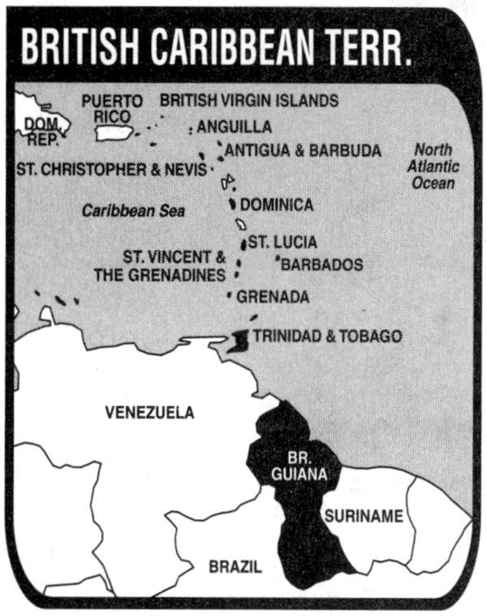

The British Caribbean Territories (Eastern Group), a currency board formed in 1950, comprised the British West Indies territories of Trinidad and Tobago; Barbados; the Leeward Islands of Anguilla, Saba, St. Christopher, Nevis and Antigua; the Windward Islands of St. Lucia, Dominica, St. Vincent and Grenada; British Guiana and the British Virgin Islands.

As time progressed, the members of this Eastern Group varied.

For later issues see East Caribbean States listings in Volume 3, Modern issues.

RULERS:
British

MONETARY SYSTEM:
1 Dollar = 100 Cents

BRITISH ADMINISTRATION

BRITISH CARIBBEAN TERRITORIES, EASTERN GROUP

1953 ISSUE

#7-12 map at lower l., portr. Qn. Elizabeth II at r. Arms in all 4 corners on back. Printer: BWC.

7	1 Dollar	VG	VF	UNC
	1953-64. Red on multicolor underprint.			
	a. Watermark: Sailing ship. 5.1.1953.	15.00	75.00	325.
	b. Watermark: Queen Elizabeth II. 1.3.1954-2.1.1957.	8.00	30.00	225.
	c. 2.1.1958-2.1.1964.	7.00	25.00	185.

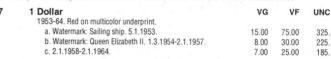

8	2 Dollars	VG	VF	UNC
	1953-64. Blue on multicolor underprint.			
	a. Watermark: Sailing ship. 5.1.1953.	30.00	225.	850.
	b. Watermark: Queen Elizabeth II. 1.3.1954-1.7.1960.	20.00	85.00	650.
	c. 2.1.1961-2.1.1964.	18.00	75.00	550.

		VG	VF	UNC
9	**5 Dollars**			
	1953-64. Green on multicolor underprint.			
	a. Watermark: Sailing ship. 5.1.1953.	35.00	275.	1100.
	b. Watermark: Queen Elizabeth II. 3.1.1955-2.1.1959.	25.00	100.	925.
	c. 2.1.1961-2.1.1964.	22.50	90.00	850.

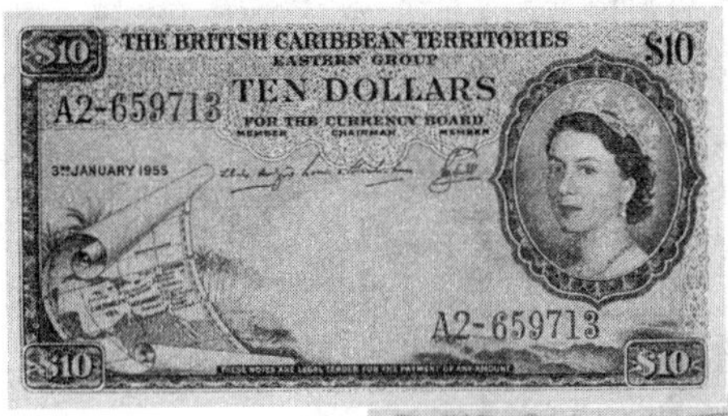

		VG	VF	UNC
10	**10 Dollars**			
	1953-64. Brown on multicolor underprint.			
	a. Watermark: Sailing ship. 5.1.1953.	60.00	400.	—
	b. Watermark: Queen Elizabeth II. 3.1.1955-2.1.1959.	40.00	250.	1750.
	c. 2.1.1961; 2.1.1962; 2.1.1964.	37.50	200.	1500.

		VG	VF	UNC
11	**20 Dollars**			
	1953-64. Purple on multicolor underprint.			
	a. Watermark: Sailing ship. 5.1.1953.	90.00	600.	—
	b. Watermark: Queen Elizabeth II. 2.1.1957-2.1.1964.	45.00	300.	—
12	**100 Dollars**			
	1953-63. Black on multicolor underprint.			
	a. Watermark: Sailing ship. 5.1.1953.	500.	2000.	—
	b. Watermark: Queen Elizabeth II. 1.3.1954; 2.1.1957; 2.1.1963.	300.	1350.	—
	s. As b. Specimen.	—	—	2500.

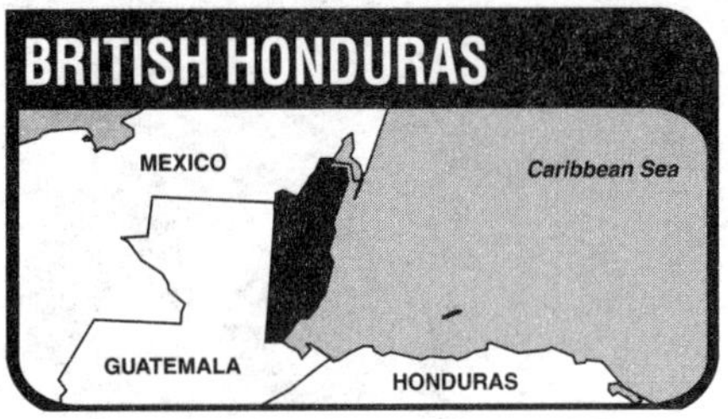

The former British colony of British Honduras is now Belize, a self-governing dependency of the United Kingdom situated in Central America south of Mexico and east and north of Guatemala, has an area of 8,867 sq. mi. (22,965 sq. km.) and a population of 209,000. Capital: Belmopan. Sugar, citrus fruits, chicle and hard woods are exported.

The area, site of the ancient Mayan civilization, was sighted by Columbus in 1502, and settled by shipwrecked English seamen in 1638. British buccaneers settled the former capital of Belize in the 17th century. Britain claimed administrative right over the area after the emancipation of Central America from Spain, and declared it a colony subordinate to Jamaica in 1862. It established as the separate Crown Colony of British Honduras in 1884. The anti-British People's United Party, which attained power in 1954, won a constitution, effective in 1964 which established self-government under a British appointed governor. British Honduras became Belize on June 1, 1973, following the passage of a surprise bill by the Peoples United Party, but the constitutional relationship with Britain remained unchanged.

In Dec. 1975, the U.N. General Assembly adopted a resolution supporting the right of the people of Belize to self-determination, and asking Britain and Guatemala to renew their negotiations on the future of Belize. Belize obtained independence on Sept. 21, 1981.

RULERS:
British

MONETARY SYSTEM:
1 Dollar = 100 Cents

BRITISH HONDURAS

GOVERNMENT OF BRITISH HONDURAS

1952-53 ISSUE

#28-32 arms at l., portr. Qn. Elizabeth II at r.

		VG	VF	UNC
28	**1 Dollar**			
	1953-73. Green on multicolor underprint.			
	a. 15.4.1953-1.10.1958.	6.00	30.00	225.
	b. 1.1.1961-1.5.1969.	5.00	15.00	100.
	c. 1.6.1970-1.1.1973.	5.00	10.00	90.00
	s. As a, b, c. Specimen.	—	—	75.00

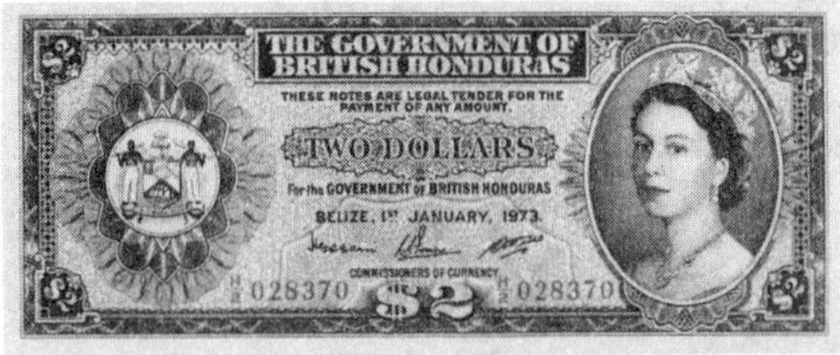

		VG	VF	UNC
29	**2 Dollars**			
	1953-73. Purple on multicolor underprint.			
	a. 15.4.1953-1.10.1958.	10.00	65.00	550.
	b. 1.10.1960-1.5.1965.	7.50	30.00	225.
	c. 1.1.1971-1.1.1973.	5.00	20.00	175.
	s. As a, b, c. Specimen.	—	—	50.00

30	5 Dollars	VG	VF	UNC
	1953-73. Red on multicolor underprint.			
	a. 15.4.1953-1.10.1958.	15.00	85.00	700.
	b. 1.3.1960-1.5.1965.	10.00	45.00	450.
	c. 1.1.1970-1.1.1973.	10.00	35.00	275.
	s. As a, c. Specimen.	—	—	75.00

31	10 Dollars	VG	VF	UNC
	1958-73. Black on multicolor underprint.			
	a. 1.10.1958-1.11.1961.	35.00	200.	—
	b. 1.4.1964-1.5.1969.	20.00	100.	900.
	c. 1.1.1971-1.1.1973.	15.00	75.00	700.
	s. As a, c. Specimen.	—	—	150.

32	20 Dollars	VG	VF	UNC
	1952-73. Brown on multicolor underprint.			
	a. 1.12.1952-1.10.1958.	50.00	285.	—
	b. 1.3.1960-1.5.1969.	37.50	200.	1650.
	c. 1.1.1970-1.1.1973.	30.00	175.	1500.
	s. As a, c. Specimen.	—	—	200.

Note: For similar notes but w/BELIZE heading, see Belize listings.

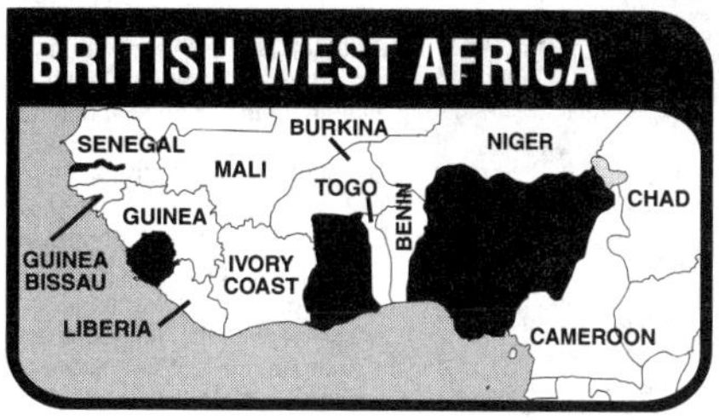

British West Africa was an administrative grouping of the four former British West Africa colonies of Gambia, Sierra Leone, Nigeria and Gold Coast (now Ghana). All are now independent republics and members of the British Commonwealth of Nations. These four colonies were supplied with a common currency by the West African Currency Board from 1907 through 1962.

Also see Gambia, Ghana, Nigeria and Sierra Leone for related currency and for individual statistics and history.

RULERS:

British to 1952

MONETARY SYSTEM:

1 Shilling = 12 Pence
1 Pound = 20 Shillings

BRITISH ADMINISTRATION

WEST AFRICAN CURRENCY BOARD

1962 ISSUE

12	20 Shillings	VG	VF	UNC
	17.4.1962. Black and red. River scene with palm trees at left. Harvesting on back. Printer: TDLR.	12.50	35.00	225.

BRUNEI

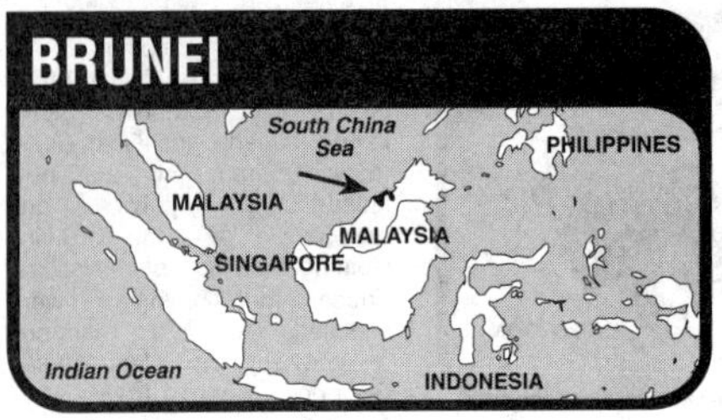

Negara Brunei Darussalam (The State of Brunei), a member of the British Commonwealth is located on the northwest coast of the island of Borneo, has an area of 2,226 sq. mi. (5,765 sq. km.) and a population of 326,000. Capital: Bandar Seri Begawan. Crude oil and rubber are exported.

Magellan was the first European to visit Brunei in 1521. It was a powerful state, ruling over Northern Borneo and adjacent islands from the 16th to the 19th century. Brunei became a British protectorate in 1888 and a British dependency in 1905. The Constitution of 1959 restored control over internal affairs to the sultan, while delegating responsibility for defense and foreign affairs to Britain.

On Jan. 1, 1984, Brunei became a fully independent member of the Commonwealth.

RULERS:

Sultan Sir Omar Ali Saifuddin III, 1950-1967
Sultan Hassanal Bolkiah I, 1967-

MONETARY SYSTEM:

1 Dollar = 100 Sen to 1967
1 Ringgit (Dollar) = 100 Sen, 1967-

STATE

KERAJAAN BRUNEI

GOVERNMENT OF BRUNEI

1967 ISSUE

#1-5 Sultan Omar Ali Saifuddin III w/military cap at r. and as wmk. Mosque on back. Printer: BWC.

		VG	VF	UNC
1	**1 Ringgit** 1967. Dark blue on multicolor underprint. Back gray and lavender on pink underprint.			
	a. Issued note.	7.00	25.00	50.00
	s. Specimen.	—	—	—

		VG	VF	UNC
2	**5 Ringgit** 1967. Dark green on multicolor underprint. Back green on pink underprint.			
	a. Issued note.	15.00	40.00	125.
	s. Specimen.	—	—	—

		VG	VF	UNC
3	**10 Ringgit** 1967. Red on multicolor underprint. Back red.			
	a. Issued note.	40.00	80.00	175.
	s. Specimen.	—	—	—

> **NOTICE**
> Readers with unlisted dates, signature varieties, etc. are invited to submit photocopies of their notes to: Standard Catalog of World Paper Money, 700 East State St. Iola, WI 54990-0001, E-Mail: george.cuhaj@fwpubs.com.

		VG	VF	UNC
4	**50 Ringgit** 1967. Dark brown on multicolor underprint. Back olive.	75.00	150.	300.

		VG	VF	UNC
5	**100 Ringgit** 1967. Blue on multicolor underprint. Back purple.	175.	300.	550.

1972-79 ISSUE

#6-10 Sultan Hassanal Bolkiah I in military uniform at r. and as wmk. Mosque on back. Printer: BWC.

		VG	VF	UNC
6	**1 Ringgit** 1972-88. Blue on multicolor underprint.			
	a. 1972; 1976; 1978.	2.00	5.00	12.50
	b. 1980; 1982.	2.00	4.00	10.00
	c. 1983-1986.	2.00	3.00	8.00
	d. 1988.	2.00	3.00	8.00
	s. Specimen.	—	—	130.

		VG	VF	UNC
7	**5 Ringgit** 1979-86. Green on multicolor underprint.			
	a. 1979; 1981.	5.00	15.00	40.00
	b. 1983; 1984; 1986.	4.00	12.50	35.00
	s. Specimen.	—	—	150.

8	10 Ringgit	VG	VF	UNC
	1976-86. Red on multicolor underprint.			
	a. 1976; 1981.	11.00	30.00	80.00
	b. 1983; 1986.	10.00	27.50	70.00
	s. Issued note.	—	—	175.

9	50 Ringgit	VG	VF	UNC
	1973-86. Dark brown on multicolor underprint.			
	a. 1973.	FV	100.	150.
	b. 1977; 1982.	FV	90.00	125.
	c. 1981.	FV	110.	100.
	d. 1986.	FV	70.00	200.
	s. Specimen.	—	—	250.

10	100 Ringgit	VG	VF	UNC
	1972-88. Blue on multicolor underprint.			
	a. 1972; 1976.	FV	100.	300.
	b. 1978; 1980.	FV	90.00	225.
	c. 1982; 1983; 1988.	FV	80.00	225.
	s. Specimen.	—	—	400.

1979; 1987 ISSUE

#11 and 12 Sultan Hassanal Bolkiah I in royal uniform at r. and as wmk. Printer: BWC.

11	500 Ringgit	VG	VF	UNC
	1979; 1987. Orange on multicolor underprint. Mosque at center on back.			
	a. 1979.	FV	450.	1000.
	b. 1987.	FV	425.	900.
	s. Specimen.	—	—	1100.

12	1000 Ringgit	VG	VF	UNC
	1979; 1986; 1987. Gray, brown and greenish blue. Brunei Museum on back.			
	a. 1979.	FV	900.	1500.
	b. 1986-87.	FV	850.	1350.
	s. Specimen.	—	—	1750.

NEGARA BRUNEI DARUSSALAM

1989 ISSUE

#13-20 Sultan Hassanal Bolkiah I at r. and as wmk.

13	1 Ringgit	VG	VF	UNC
	1989-95. Purple on multicolor underprint. Aerial view on back.			
	a. 1989; 1991.	FV	2.00	4.00
	b. 1994-95.	FV	FV	3.50

14	5 Ringgit	VG	VF	UNC
	1989-91; 1993; 1995. Blue-gray and deep green on multicolor underprint. Houses and boats on back.	FV	FV	12.50

15	10 Ringgit	VG	VF	UNC
	1989-92; 1995. Purple and red-orange on multicolor underprint. Waterfront village with mosque on back.	FV	FV	18.00

16	50 Ringgit	VG	VF	UNC
	1989-91; 1994; 1995. Brown, olive-green, and orange on multicolor underprint. People in power launch on back.	FV	FV	75.00

17	100 Ringgit	VG	VF	UNC
	1989-92; 1994. Blue and violet on multicolor underprint. River scene on back.	FV	FV	150.

18	500 Ringgit	VG	VF	UNC
	1989-92. Red-orange, purple, olive and black on multicolor underprint. Houses at left center. Padian woman paddling her boat in Kampong Ayer on back.	FV	FV	650.

19	1000 Ringgit	VG	VF	UNC
	1989-91. Red-violet, purple, olive and blue-green on multicolor underprint. Waterfront village of Kampong Ayer and Istana Nurul Iman on back.	FV	FV	1000.

		VG	VF	UNC
20	**10,000 Ringgit** 1989. Dark brown and dark green on multicolor underprint. Aerial view of Bandar Seri Begawan harbor on back.			
	a. Issued note.	FV	FV	8500.
	s. Specimen. Ovpt: *CONTOH SPECIMEN* in two lines.	—	—	4500.

1992 Commemorative Issue

#21, 25th Anniversary of Accession

		VG	VF	UNC
21	**25 Ringgit** 1992. Brown, lilac, green and multicolor. Royal procession at center, Sultan at right and as watermark at left. Crown at left, coronation at center on back. Dates *1967* and *1992* with text at top.	FV	FV	40.00

1996 Issue

#22-27 Sultan Jam'Asr Hassan Bolkiah I at r.

#22-24 arms at upper l. Polymer plastic. Printer: NPA (w/o imprint).

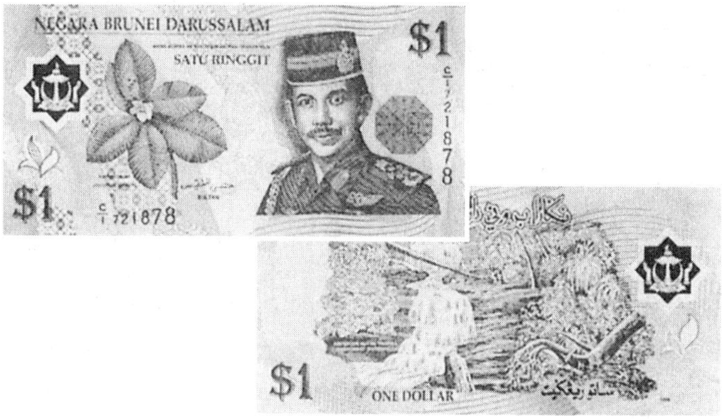

		VG	VF	UNC
22	**1 Ringgit** 1996. Blue-black and deep green on multicolor underprint. Riverside simpur plant at left center. Back blue and multicolored; rain forest waterfall at left center.	FV	FV	2.50

		VG	VF	UNC
23	**5 Ringgit** 1996; 2002. Black on green and multicolor underprint. Pitcher plant at left center. Rain forest floor on back.	FV	FV	8.00

		VG	VF	UNC
24	**10 Ringgit** 1996; 1998. Dark brown and brown on red and multicolor underprint. Purple-leafed forest yam at left center. Rain forest canopy on back.	FV	FV	14.00

#25-27 are paper issues.

		VG	VF	UNC
25	**50 Ringgit** 1996. Brown, blue and purple on multicolor underprint. Offshore oil rig on back.	FV	FV	55.00

		VG	VF	UNC
26	**100 Ringgit** 1996. Brown and orange on multicolor underprint. Brunei International Airport on back.	FV	FV	90.00

		VG	VF	UNC
27	**500 Ringgit** 2000. Deep orange and brown on multicolor underprint. Bolkiah Mosque on back.	FV	FV	500.

NOTICE

Readers with unlisted dates, signature varieties, etc. are invited to submit photocopies of their notes to: Standard Catalog of World Paper Money, 700 East State St. Iola, WI 54990-0001, E-Mail: george.cuhaj@fwpubs.com.

2004 Commemorative Issue

		VG	VF	UNC
28	**50 Ringgit** 15.7.2004. Brown, green and blue on multicolor underprint. Kantan medicinal flower at center. Polymer plastic.	FV	FV	50.00

		VG	VF	UNC
29	**100 Ringgit** 15.7.2004. Brown, orange and yellow on multicolor underprint. Kjojk medicinial flower at center. Polymer plastic.	FV	FV	90.00

BULGARIA

The Republic of Bulgaria (formerly the Peoples Republic of Bulgaria), a Balkan country on the Black Sea in southeastern Europe, has an area of 42,855 sq. mi. (110,993 sq. km.) and a population of 8.31 million. Capital: Sofia. Agriculture remains a key component of the economy but industrialization, particularly he- avy industry, has been emphasized since the late 1940's. Machinery, tobacco and cigarettes, wines and spirits, clothing and metals are the chief exports.

The area now occupied by Bulgaria was conquered by the Bulgars, an Asiatic tribe, in the 7th century. Bulgarian kingdoms continued to exist on the peninsula until it came under Turkish rule in 1395. In 1878, after nearly 500 years of Turkish rule, Bulgaria was made a principality under Turkish suzerainty. Union seven years later with Eastern Rumelia created a Balkan state with borders approximating those of present-day Bulgaria. A Bulgarian kingdom fully independent of Turkey was proclaimed Sept. 22, 1908.

During WWI Bulgaria had been aligned with Germany. After the Armistice certain land concessions were granted to Greece and Romania. In 1934 King Boris III suspended all political parties and established a dictatorial monarchy. In 1938 the military began rearming through the aid of the Anglo-French loan. As WWII developed Bulgaria again supported the Germans but Boris protected its Jewish community. Boris died mysteriously in 1943 and Simeon II became king at the age of six. The country was then ruled by a pro-Nazi regency until it was invaded by Soviet forces in 1944. The monarchy was abolished and Simeon was ousted by plebiscite in 1946, and Bulgaria became a People's Republic in the Soviet pattern. Following demonstrations and a general strike, the communist government resigned in Nov. 1990. A new government was elected in Oct. 1991.

Thrace, a name applied at various periods to areas of different extent, is a territory divided at present between Greece, Turkey and Bulgaria. Bulgaria's claim came as a result of the end of the first Balkan War of 1912, at which time it took control of most of Thrace.

The second Balkan War altered this status but the whole area remained in turmoil until after the end of World War I. At that point, Greece had taken most of Thrace, but the Allies believed Bulgaria needed an economic outlet to the Aegean Sea. Article 48 of the Treaty of Neuilly declared that Bulgaria had the right of transit over its former Thracian territory to the various ports assigned to Greece. Nothing worked out as planned, and the area was again reapportioned in 1923.

TITLES:

Bulgarian People's Republic:
НАРОДНА РЕПУБЛИКА БЪЛГАРИЯ
Bulgarian National Bank:
БЪЛГАРСКА НАРОДНА БАНКА

MONETARY SYSTEM:

1 Lev ЛВ = 100 Stotinki STOTINKI until 1999
1 Lev = 1,000 "Old" Lev, 1999
Silver Lev = Lev Srebro
Gold Lev = Lev Zlato

Peoples Republic

БЪЛГАРСКА НАРОДНА БАНКА

Bulgarian National Bank

1962 Issue

#88-92 arms at l.

		VG	VF	UNC
88	**1 Lev** 1962. Brown-lilac on multicolor underprint. Monument for the Battle of Shipka Pass (1877) at left center on back.			
	a. Issued note.	.10	.25	1.75
	s. Specimen.	—	—	17.50

		VG	VF	UNC
89	**2 Leva** 1962. Black and blue on green underprint. Woman picking grapes in vineyard at right on back.			
	a. Issued note.	.20	.40	2.50
	s. Specimen.	—	—	17.50

90	5 Leva	VG	VF	UNC
	1962. Red on blue and multicolor underprint. Coastline village.			
	a. Issued note.	.25	.50	4.50
	s. Specimen.	—	—	20.00

91	10 Leva	VG	VF	UNC
	1962. Black on blue and multicolor underprint. G. Dimitrov at left on back.			
	a. Issued note.	.25	.50	7.50
	s. Specimen.	—	—	22.50

92	20 Leva	VG	VF	UNC
	1962. Brown-lilac on multicolor underprint. Factory. G. Dimitrov at left on back.			
	a. Issued note.	.25	.50	12.50
	s. Specimen.	—	—	25.00

1974 ISSUE

#93-97 modified arms w/dates *681-1944* at l.

#93-95 wmk: Decorative design.

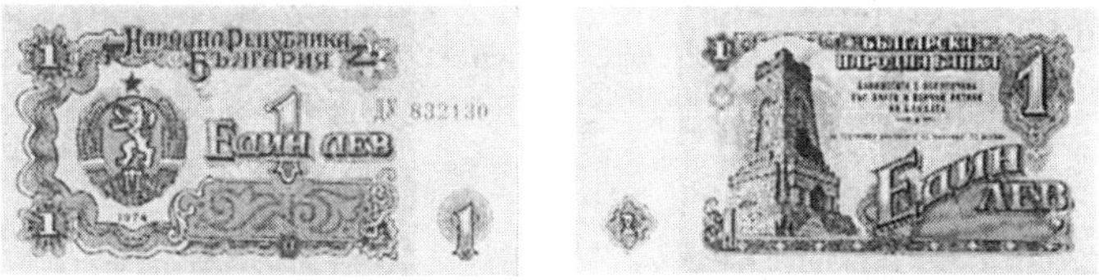

93	1 Lev	VG	VF	UNC
	1974. Brown on multicolor underprint. Like #88.			
	a. Issued note.	.10	.20	1.00
	s. Specimen.	—	—	15.00

94	2 Leva	VG	VF	UNC
	1974. Black and blue on green underprint. Like #89.			
	a. Issued note.	.10	.25	1.75
	s. Specimen.	—	—	15.00

95	5 Leva	VG	VF	UNC
	1974. Red on blue and multicolor underprint. Like #90.			
	a. Issued note.	.15	.50	1.75
	s. Specimen.	—	—	17.50

#96 and 97 wmk: Hands holding hammer and sickle.

96	10 Leva	VG	VF	UNC
	1974. Black on blue and multicolor underprint. Like #91.			
	a. Issued note.	.15	.50	4.50
	s. Specimen.	—	—	20.00

97	20 Leva	VG	VF	UNC
	1974. Brown-lilac on multicolor underprint. Like #92.			
	a. Issued note.	.50	1.00	8.50
	s. Specimen.	—	—	22.50

1989; 1990 ISSUES

98	50 Leva	VG	VF	UNC
	1990. Brown and dark blue on multicolor underprint. Arms at left center. Back brown and dark green; castle ruins at center right on back. Watermark: Hands holding hammer and sickle.			
	a. Issued note.	.50	1.00	6.00
	s. Specimen.	—	—	120.

#98 was withdrawn from circulation shortly after its release.

		VG	VF	UNC
99	**100 Leva** 1989. Purple on lilac underprint. Arms at left center. Horseman with two dogs at center right on back. Watermark: Rampant lion. (Not issued).	—	—	150.

#99 carries the name of the Bulgarian Peoples Republic, probably the reason it was not released. An estimated 500-600 pieces were "liberated" from the recycling process.

REPUBLIC

БЪЛГАРСКА НАРОДНА БАНКА

BULGARIAN NATIONAL BANK

1991-94 ISSUE

#100-103 wmk: Arms (lion).

		VG	VF	UNC
100	**20 Leva** 1991. Blue-black and blue-green on multicolor underprint. Dutchess Sevastokrat Oritza Desislava at left center. Boyana Church at right on back.	FV	FV	.25

		VG	VF	UNC
101	**50 Leva** 1992. Purple and violet on multicolor underprint. Khristo G. Danov at left. Platen printing press at right on back.	FV	FV	.40

		VG	VF	UNC
102	**100 Leva** 1991; 1993. Dark brown and maroon on multicolor underprint. Zhary Zograf (artist) at left center. Wheel of Life at right on back.			
	a. 1991.	FV	FV	1.25
	b. 1993.	FV	FV	.40

		VG	VF	UNC
103	**200 Leva** 1992. Deep violet and brown-orange on multicolor underprint. Ivan Vazov at left, village in underprint. Lyre with laurel wreath at right on back.	FV	FV	.60

		VG	VF	UNC
104	**500 Leva** 1993. Dark green and black on multicolor underprint. D. Christov at left and as watermark. Opera house in Varna at center right, herring gulls at lower right on back.	FV	FV	1.00

		VG	VF	UNC
105	**1000 Leva** 1994; 1997. Dark green and olive-brown on multicolor underprint. V. Levski at left and as watermark., Liberty with flag, sword and lion at upper center right. Monument and writings of Levski at center right on back.	FV	FV	1.50

1994-96 Issue

#106-109 w/wide hologram foil strip at l.

106	1000 Leva	VG	VF	UNC
	1996. Dark green and olive-brown on multicolor underprint. Like #105 but with wide hologram foil strip at left.	FV	FV	1.50

107	2000 Leva	VG	VF	UNC
	1994; 1996. Black and dark blue on multicolor underprint. N. Ficev at left and as watermark, building outlines at center, wide hologram foil strip at left. Steeple, building plans at center right on back.	FV	1.00	3.50

108	5000 Leva	VG	VF	UNC
	1996. Violet on multicolor underprint. Z. Stoyanov at left and as watermark, quill pen at center right. Monument (two views) at center, and *1885 Proclamation to the Bulgarian People* at right on back.	FV	4.00	9.00

109	10,000 Leva	VG	VF	UNC
	1996. Brown and purple on multicolor underprint. V. Dimitrov at left and as watermark, palette, brushes, Academy of the Arts at center. Sketches at center, "Bulgarian Madonna" at right on back.	FV	6.00	17.50

#110 Deleted, see #105.

1997 Issue

111	5000 Leva	VG	VF	UNC
	1997. Violet on multicolor underprint. Like #108. without wide holographic foil strip at left.	FV	4.00	9.00

#112 and 113 w/wide hologram foil strip at l. Reduced size.

112	10,000 Leva	VG	VF	UNC
	1997. Multicolor. Dr. P. Beron at left. Telescope at right on back.	FV	6.00	18.00

113	50,000 Leva	VG	VF	UNC
	1997. Purple on multicolor underprint. St. Cyril at left, St. Methodius at center right. Architectural monuments of the ancient Bulgarian capitals of Pliska and Preslav on back.	FV	25.00	50.00

1999-2003 Issue

Monetary Reform: 1 Lev = 1000 "Old" Leva.

#114-119 w/holographic strip at l.

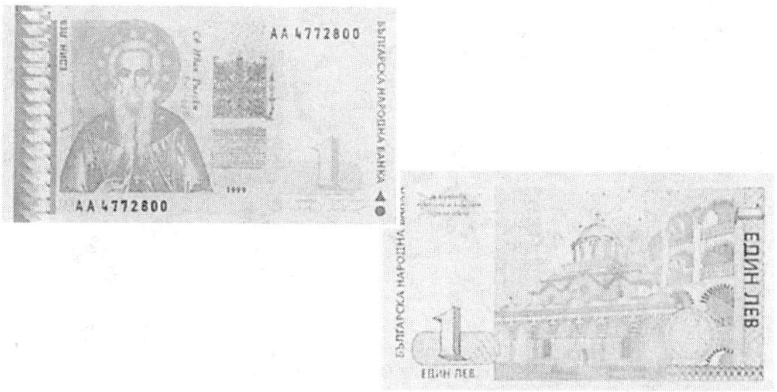

114	1 Lev	VG	VF	UNC
	1999. Red and blue on yellow underprint. Icon of St. John of Rila at left. Rila Monastery on back.	FV	FV	.85

115	2 Leva	VG	VF	UNC
	1999. Violet and pink on light blue underprint. Paisii Hilendarski at left. Heraldic lion on back.	FV	FV	1.75

116 **5 Leva**

1999. Red, brown and green on multicolor underprint. Ivan Milev at left. Parts of paintings on back.

VG	VF	UNC
FV	FV	4.50

117 **10 Leva**

1999. Dark green on ochre underprint. Dr. Peter Beron at left. Astronomy sketches and telescope on back.

VG	VF	UNC
FV	FV	9.00

118 **20 Leva**

1999. Blue on multicolor underprint. S. Stambolov at left. National Assembly building and Eagles' and Lions' Bridges in Sofia on back.

VG	VF	UNC
FV	FV	17.50

119 **50 Leva**

1999. Brown and yellow on multicolor underprint. Pencho Slaveykov at left. Illustrations from his poetry works on back.

VG	VF	UNC
FV	FV	45.00

120 **100 Leva**

2003. Green on multicolor underprint. Aleka Konstantinov at right. His character "Uncle Ganyo" on back.

VG	VF	UNC
FV	FV	85.00

FOREIGN EXCHANGE CERTIFICATES

CORECOM

1966 ND ISSUE

			VG	VF	UNC
FX1	1 Lev	ND (1966). Light brown on yellow underprint.	3.00	10.00	15.00
FX2	2 Leva	ND (1966). Light brown on yellow underprint.	5.00	12.50	20.00
FX3	5 Leva	ND (1966). Light brown on yellow underprint.	10.00	20.00	30.00
FX4	10 Leva	ND (1966). Light brown on yellow underprint.	12.50	25.00	40.00
FX5	20 Leva	ND (1966). Light brown on yellow underprint.	20.00	40.00	60.00
FX6	50 Leva	ND (1966). Light brown on yellow underprint.	22.50	60.00	100.
FX7	100 Leva	ND (1966). Light brown on yellow underprint.	40.00	75.00	150.

1968 ND ISSUE

			VG	VF	UNC
FX8	1 Lev	ND (1968). Brown on light green underprint.	3.00	10.00	15.00
FX9	2 Leva	ND (1968). Brown on light green underprint.	5.00	12.50	20.00

			VG	VF	UNC
FX10	5 Leva	ND (1968). Brown on light green underprint.	7.50	15.00	25.00
FX11	10 Leva	ND (1968). Brown on light green underprint.	10.00	20.00	30.00
FX12	20 Leva	ND (1968). Brown on light green underprint.	15.00	30.00	40.00
FX13	50 Leva	ND (1968). Brown on light green underprint.	22.50	50.00	80.00
FX14	100 Leva	ND (1968). Brown on light green underprint.	30.00	60.00	100.

1975 ND ISSUE

			VG	VF	UNC
FX14A	.05 Lev	ND (1975).	2.00	5.00	9.00

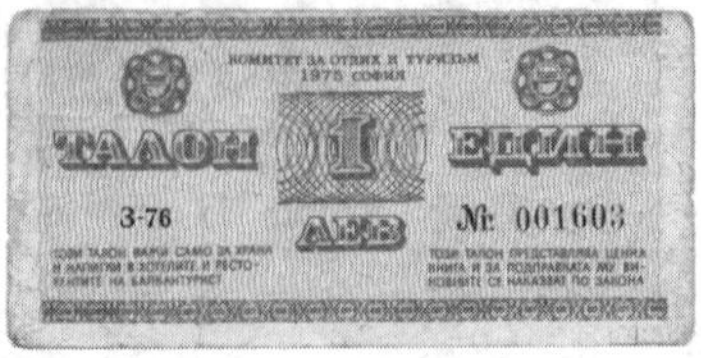

			VG	VF	UNC
FX15	1 Lev	ND (1975). Brown on light pink underprint.	3.00	6.00	10.00

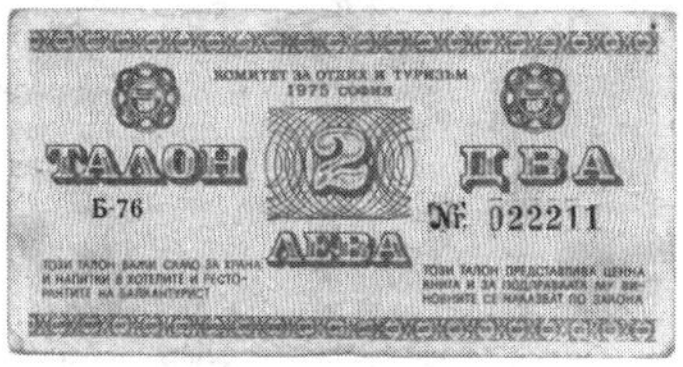

		VG	VF	UNC
FX16	**2 Leva** ND (1975).	5.00	10.00	15.00

		VG	VF	UNC
FX17	**5 Leva** ND (1975).	7.50	12.50	20.00
FX18	**10 Leva** ND (1975).	10.00	20.00	30.00
FX19	**20 Leva** ND (1975).	15.00	30.00	40.00
FX20	**50 Leva** ND (1975).	20.00	40.00	60.00
FX21	**100 Leva** ND (1975).	22.50	50.00	80.00

1978 ND Issue

#FX22-28 Wmk: Wavy lines.

		VG	VF	UNC
FX22	**1 Lev** ND (1978). Red on light blue underprint.	1.00	3.00	5.00
FX23	**2 Leva** ND (1978).	2.00	5.00	10.00
FX24	**5 Leva** ND (1978).	3.00	7.50	15.00
FX25	**10 Leva** ND (1978).	7.50	12.50	20.00
FX26	**20 Leva** ND (1978).	15.00	30.00	40.00
FX27	**50 Leva** ND (1978).	30.00	40.00	50.00
FX28	**100 Leva** ND (1978).	35.00	50.00	60.00

Bulgarian National Bank

1981 Issue

#FX29-35 Wmk: BNB in oval, repeated. Specimens exist.

		VG	VF	UNC
FX29	**1 Lev** 1981. Light brown on pale red underprint. a. Issued note.	1.00	3.00	5.00
	s. Specimen.	—	—	—

		VG	VF	UNC
FX30	**2 Leva** 1981. a. Issued note.	2.00	5.00	10.00
	s. Specimen.	—	—	—

		VG	VF	UNC
FX31	**5 Leva** 1981. Green-blue on yellow underprint. a. Issued note.	3.00	8.00	15.00
	s. Specimen.	—	—	—

		VG	VF	UNC
FX32	**10 Leva** 1981. a. Issued note.	5.00	12.50	20.00
	s. Specimen.	—	—	—
FX33	**20 Leva** 1981.	15.00	30.00	40.00
FX34	**50 Leva** 1981.	25.00	50.00	80.00
FX35	**100 Leva** 1981.	30.00	100.	125.

1986 Issue

#FX36-FX42 specimens exist.

		VG	VF	UNC
FX36	**1 Lev** (19)86. Red on ochre underprint. a. Issued note.	1.00	3.00	5.00
	s. Specimen.	—	—	—

		VG	VF	UNC
FX37	**2 Leva** (19)86. Blue on grey underprint. a. Issued note.	2.00	6.00	10.00
	s. Specimen.	—	—	—

		VG	VF	UNC
FX38	**5 Leva** (19)86. s. Specimen.	—	—	—

		VG	VF	UNC
FX39	**10 Leva**			
	(19)86.			
	a. Issued note.	5.00	12.50	20.00
	s. Specimen.	—	—	—

		VG	VF	UNC
FX40	**20 Leva**			
	(19)86.			
	a. Issued note.	10.00	20.00	30.00
	s. Specimen.	—	—	—
FX41	**50 Leva**			
	(19)86.	20.00	35.00	50.00
FX42	**100 Leva**			
	(19)86. Olive on light brown underprint.	30.00	50.00	100.

Note: A 1988 dated issue is not confirmed.

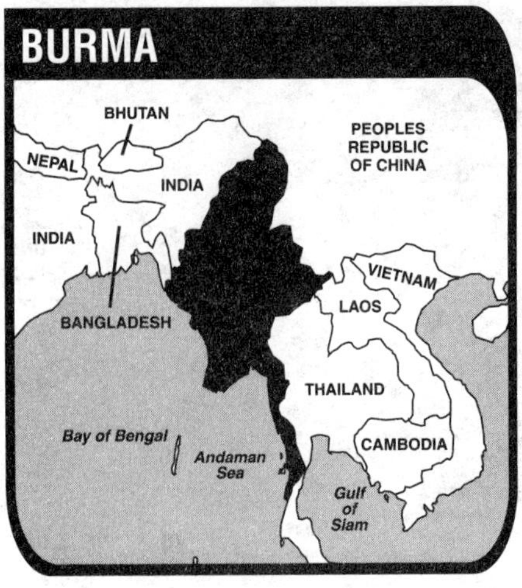

The Socialist Republic of the Union of Burma (now called Myanmar), a country of Southeast Asia fronting on the Bay of Bengal and the Andaman Sea, has an area of 261,228 sq. mi. (676,577 sq. km.) and a population of 49.34 million. Capital: Rangoon. Myanmar is an agricultural country heavily dependent on its leading product (rice) which embodies two-thirds of the cultivated area and accounts for 40 percent of the value of exports. Petroleum, lead, tin, silver, zinc, nickel, cobalt and precious stones are exported.

The first European to reach Burma, about 1435, was Nicolo Di Conti, a merchant of Venice. During the beginning of the reign of Bodawpaya (1782-1819AD) the kingdom comprised most of the same area as it does today including Arakan which was taken over in 1784-85. The British East India Company, while unsuccessful in its 1612 effort to establish posts along the Bay of Bengal, was enabled by the Anglo-Burmese Wars of 1824-86 to expand to the whole of Burma and to secure its annexation to British India. In 1937, Burma was separated from India, becoming a separate British colony with limited self-government. The Japanese occupied Burma in 1942, and on Aug. 1, 1943 Burma became an "independent and sovereign state" under Dr. Ba Maw who was appointed the Adipadi (head of state). This puppet state later collapsed with the surrender of Japanese forces. Burma became an independent nation outside the British Commonwealth on Jan. 4, 1948, the constitution of 1948 providing for a parliamentary democracy and the nationalization of certain industries. However, political and economic problems persisted, and on March 2, 1962, Gen. Ne Win took over the government, suspended the constitution, installed himself as chief of state, and pursued a socialistic program with nationalization of nearly all industry and trade. On Jan. 4, 1974, a new constitution adopted by referendum established Burma as a "socialist republic" under one-party rule. The country name was changed formally to the Union of Myanmar in 1989.

For later issues refer to Myanmar.

RULERS:

British to 1948
Japanese, 1942-45

MONETARY SYSTEM:

1 Rupee (Kyat) = 10 Mu = 16 Annas (Pe) to 1942, 1945-52
1 Rupee = 100 Cents, 1942-43
1 Kyat = 100 Pya, 1943-45, 1952-89

REPUBLIC

PEOPLES BANK OF BURMA

1965 ND ISSUE

#52-55 portr. Gen. Aung San at ctr. Arms at upper l. on back. Wmk: pattern throughout paper. Printed in East Berlin. Replacement notes have special Burmese characters w/serial #.

		VG	VF	UNC
52	**1 Kyat**			
	ND (1965). Purple and blue-gray on multicolor underprint. Fisherman at center on back. Serial # varieties.	.15	.30	1.00

		VG	VF	UNC
53	**5 Kyats**			
	ND (1965). Green and light blue. Back green; man with ox at center.	.25	1.00	2.50

54 **10 Kyats**

	VG	VF	UNC
ND (1965). Red-brown and violet. Back red-brown, woman picking cotton at right.	.50	1.50	5.00

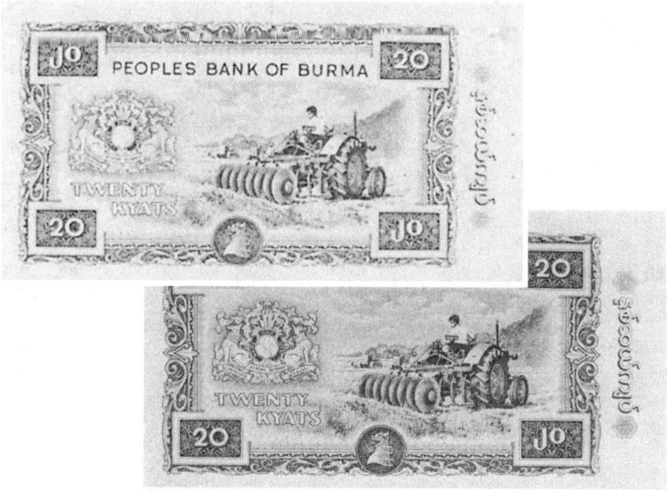

55 **20 Kyats**

	VG	VF	UNC
ND (1965). Brown and tan. Farmer on tractor at center right on back.	.75	2.50	8.00

UNION OF BURMA BANK

1972-79 ND ISSUE

#56-61 various military portrs. of Gen. Aung San at l. and as wmk.

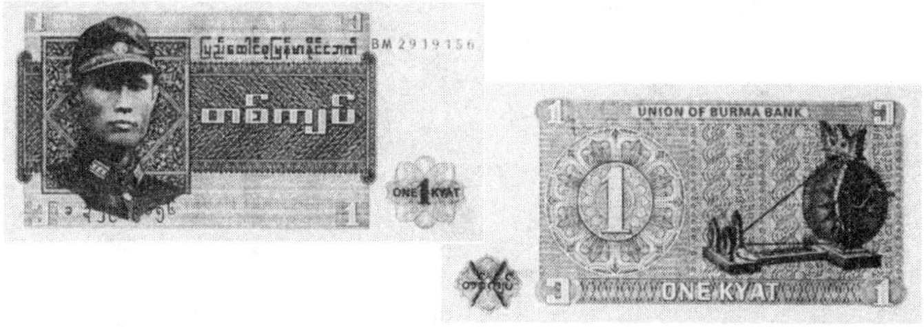

56 **1 Kyat**

	VG	VF	UNC
ND (1972). Green and blue on multicolor underprint. Ornate native wheel assembly at right on back.	.10	.15	.40

57 **5 Kyats**

	VG	VF	UNC
ND (1973). Blue and purple on multicolor underprint. Palm tree at left center on back.	.15	.25	1.00

58 **10 Kyats**

	VG	VF	UNC
ND (1973). Red and violet on multicolor underprint. Native ornaments at left center on back.	.15	.50	1.00

59 **25 Kyats**

	VG	VF	UNC
ND (1972). Brown and tan on multicolor underprint. Mythical winged creature at center on back.	.25	.75	1.50

60 **50 Kyats**

	VG	VF	UNC
ND (1979). Brown and violet on multicolor underprint. Mythical dancer at left center on back.	3.00	10.00	25.00

61 **100 Kyats**

	VG	VF	UNC
ND (1976). Blue and green on multicolor underprint. Native wheel and musical string instrument at left center on back.	1.50	4.00	15.00

NOTICE

Readers with unlisted dates, signature varieties, etc. are invited to submit photocopies of their notes to: Standard Catalog of World Paper Money, 700 East State St. Iola, WI 54990-0001, E-Mail: george.cuhaj@fwpubs.com.

1985-87 ND ISSUE

#62-66 reduced size notes. Various portrs. Gen. Aung San as wmk.

		VG	VF	UNC
62	**15 Kyats** ND (1986). Blue-gray and green on multicolor underprint. Gen. Aung San at left center. Mythical dancer at left on back.	FV	FV	2.00

		VG	VF	UNC
63	**35 Kyats** ND (1986). Brown-violet and purple on multicolor underprint. Gen. Aung San in military hat at left center. Mythical dancer at left on back.	.20	.50	1.50

		VG	VF	UNC
64	**45 Kyats** ND (1987). Blue-gray and blue on multicolor underprint. Po Hla Gyi at right. Two workers with rope and bucket at left center, oil field at center on back.	FV	FV	4.00

		VG	VF	UNC
65	**75 Kyats** ND (1985). Brown on multicolor underprint. Gen. Aung San at left center. Dancer at left on back.	.20	.75	2.75

		VG	VF	UNC
66	**90 Kyats** ND (1987). Brown, green and blue on multicolor underprint. Seya San at right. Farmer plowing with oxen at left center, rice planting at upper right on back.	FV	FV	6.00

Note: For later issues see Myanmar.

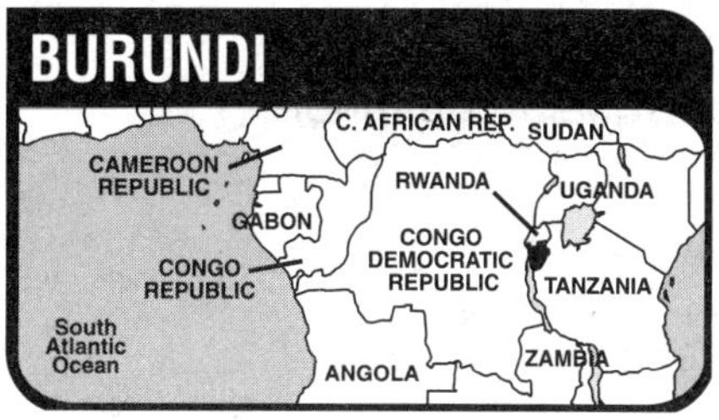

The Republic of Burundi, a landlocked country in central Africa, east of Lake Taganyila has an area of 10,759 sq. mi. (27,834 sq. km.) and a population of 6.97 million. Capital: Bujumbura. Burundi has a predominantly agricultural economy. Coffee, tea and cotton are exported.

The original inhabitants of Burundi are believed to be the Twa (pygmy); they were there when the Hutu (Bantu) arrived in the 14th century, imposing their language and customs. The development of the state structure began in the 15th centruy when migrating Tutsi, imposed themselves as feudal rulers over the Hutu. Burundi had a caste system and was ruled by a monarch, so-called the *Mwami;* however, the political and social structures were not rigid, the marriages between the two communites were common, and the Hutu enjoyed greater economic independence.

Since 1820, the caravans of Zanzibar traversed the country, but the Islamic infulence was minimal. In 1858 the first British travelers arrived in the country, and in 1871 the explorer Livingstone and journalist Stanley. As a result of Bismark's continuing interest in Africa, Burundi (then called Urundi) was occupied in the 1880s and the German Protectorate established in 1890. The country was incorporated with Rwanda (called Ruanda), into German East Africa.

During World War I, Belgium occupied Ruanda-Urundi and later the League of Nations gave the mandate area as part of Belgian Congo. After World War II, it was made a UN trust territory administrated by Belgium. The indigenous social structures were maintained in Urundi, including the presence of a local monarch, King Mwambutsa IV Bangiricenge The UN supervised election of 1961 established limited self-governoment. Burundi became a constitutional monarchy on July 1, 1962 and was admitted to the UN. Political rivalry between the Hutu and Tutsi intensified. The monarchy was overthrown in a military *coup* in 1966, A 1972 Hutu uprising lead to widespread massacres. Additional *coups* occured in 1976, 1987 and 1992. Since elections of 1993, there has been continual civil unrest.

RULERS:

Mwambutsa IV, 1962-1966
Ntare V, 1966

MONETARY SYSTEM:

1 Franc = 100 Centimes

KINGDOM

BANQUE DU ROYAUME DU BURUNDI

1964 ND PROVISIONAL ISSUE

#1-7 lg. *BURUNDI* ovpt. on face only of Banque d'Emission du Rwanda et du Burundi notes.

			Good	Fine	XF
1	**5 Francs**	ND (1964 - old dates 15.5.1961; 15.4.1963). Light brown. Black overprint on Rwanda-Burundi #1.	10.00	45.00	200.

			Good	Fine	XF
2	**10 Francs**	ND (1964 - old date 5.10.1960). Gray. Red overprint on Rwanda-Burundi #2.	15.00	75.00	250.

			Good	Fine	XF
3	**20 Francs**	ND (1964 - old date 5.10.1960). Green. Black overprint on Rwanda-Burundi #3.	20.00	75.00	250.

			Good	Fine	XF
4	**50 Francs**	ND (1964 - old dates 15.9.1960-1.10.1960). Red. Black overprint on Rwanda-Burundi #4.	20.00	75.00	250.

			Good	Fine	XF
5	**100 Francs**	ND (1964 - old dates 1.10.1960; 31.7.1962). Blue. Red overprint on Rwanda-Burundi #5.	15.00	65.00	235.
6	**500 Francs**	ND (1964 - old dates 15.9.1960-15.5.1961). Lilac brown. Black overprint on Rwanda-Burundi #6.	150.	650.	1150.
7	**1000 Francs**	ND (1964 - old date 31.7.1962). Green. Black overprint on Rwanda-Burundi #7.	100.	400.	1250.

KINGDOM

BANQUE DU ROYAUME DU BURUNDI

1964; 1965 REGULAR ISSUE

#8-14 arms at ctr. on back.

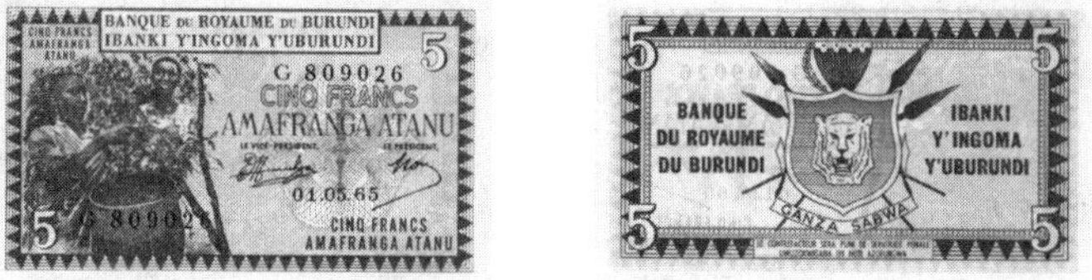

			VG	VF	UNC
8	**5 Francs**	1.10.1964; 1.12.1964; 1.5.1965. Light brown on gray-green underprint. Two young men picking coffee beans at left.	2.00	10.00	30.00
9	**10 Francs**	20.11.1964; 25.2.1965; 20.3.1965; 31.12.1965. Dark brown on lilac-brown underprint. Cattle at center.	2.00	10.00	35.00
10	**20 Francs**	20.11.1964; 25.2.1965; 20.3.1965. Blue-green. Dancer at center.	7.50	35.00	125.

			VG	VF	UNC
11	**50 Francs**	1964-66. Red-orange. View of Bujumbura.			

		VG	VF	UNC
11	**50 Francs**			
	a. Signature titles: *LE VICE-PRESIDENT* and *LE PRESIDENT.* 1.10.1964-31.12.1965.	15.00	65.00	200.
	b. Signature titles: *L'ADMINISTRATEUR* and *LE PRESIDENT.* 1.7.1966.	—	—	—

Note: #11b was prepared but apparently not released w/o ovpt. See #16b.

		VG	VF	UNC
12	**100 Francs**			
	1964-66. Bluish purple. Prince Rwagasore at center.			
	a. Signature titles: *LE VICE-PRESIDENT* and *LE PRESIDENT.* 1.10.1964; 1.12.1964; 1.5.1965.	6.00	65.00	200.
	b. Signature titles: *L'ADMINISTRATEUR* and *LE PRESIDENT.* 1.7.1966.	—	—	—
13	**500 Francs**			
	5.12.1964; 1.8.1966. Brown on yellow underprint. Bank at right.	45.00	175.	—
14	**1000 Francs**			
	1.2.1965. Green on multicolor underprint. King Mwami Mwambutsa IV at right.	150.	625.	—

REPUBLIC

BANQUE DE LA RÉPUBLIQUE DU BURUNDI

1966 ND PROVISIONAL ISSUE

#15-19 black ovpt: *DE LA REPUBLIQUE* and *YA REPUBLIKA* on face only of Banque du Royaume du Burundi notes.

		VG	VF	UNC
15	**20 Francs**			
	ND (1966 - old date 20.3.1965). Overprint on #10.	15.00	55.00	200.
16	**50 Francs**			
	ND (1966 - old dates 1.5.1965; 31.12.1965; 1.7.1966).			
	a. overprint on #11a.	17.50	75.00	250.
	b. overprint on #11b.	22.50	85.00	275.

Note: Ovpt. on #16 has letters either 3.2 or 2.6mm high.

		VG	VF	UNC
17	**100 Francs**			
	ND (1966).			
	a. overprint on #12a. (- old date 1.5.1965).	10.00	55.00	200.
	b. overprint on #12b. (- old date 1.7.1966).	10.00	55.00	200.

Note: Ovpt. on #17 has letters either 3.2 or 2.6mm high.

		VG	VF	UNC
18	**500 Francs**			
	ND (1966 - old dates 5.12.1964; 1.8.1966). Overprint on #13.	85.00	250.	—
19	**1000 Francs**			
	ND (1966 - old date 1.2.1965). Overprint on #14.	225.	725.	—

REPUBLIC

BANQUE DE LA RÉPUBLIQUE DU BURUNDI

1968-75 ISSUES

Sign. varieties.

		VG	VF	UNC
20	**10 Francs**			
	1968; 1970. Red on green and blue underprint. "Place De La Revolution" monument at right. Signature titles: *L'ADMINISTRATEUR* and *LE PRESIDENT.*			
	a. 1.11.1968.	1.00	4.00	12.50
	b. 1.4.1970.	.50	1.25	4.00
21	**20 Francs**			
	1968-73. Blue on green and violet underprint. Dancer at center. Text on back.			
	a. Signature titles: *LE PRESIDENT* and *LE VICE-PRESIDENT.* 1.11.1968.	3.00	10.00	40.00
	b. Signature titles: *LE PRESIDENT* and *L'ADMINISTRATEUR.* 1.4.1970; 1.11.1971; 1.7.1973.	2.00	7.00	30.00
22	**50 Francs**			
	1968-73. Pale red on multicolor underprint. Drummer at left center.			
	a. Signature titles: *LE VICE-PRESIDENT* and *LE PRESIDENT.* 15.5.1968; 1.10.1968.	3.50	25.00	100.
	b. Signature titles: *ADMINISTRATEUR* and *PRESIDENT.* 1.2.1970; 1.8.1971; 1.7.1973.	2.50	15.00	40.00
	s. Specimen.	—	—	200.

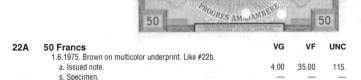

		VG	VF	UNC
22A	**50 Francs**			
	1.6.1975. Brown on multicolor underprint. Like #22b.			
	a. Issued note.	4.00	35.00	115.
	s. Specimen.	—	—	—

		VG	VF	UNC
23	**100 Francs**			
	1968-75. Brown on pale orange, lilac and blue underprint. Prince Rwagasore at right.			
	a. Signature titles: *LE VICE-PRESIDENT* and *LE PRESIDENT.* 15.5.1968; 1.10.1968.	4.00	50.00	150.
	b. Signature titles: *ADMINISTRATEUR* and *LE PRESIDENT.* 1.2.1970; 1.8.1971; 1.7.1973; 1.6. 1975.	3.00	30.00	100.
	s. Specimen.	—	—	200.
24	**500 Francs**			
	1968-75. Brown. Bank building at right.			
	a. Signature titles: *LE PRESIDENT* and *LE VICE-PRESIDENT.* 1.8.1968.	75.00	250.	900.
	b. Signature titles: *LE PRESIDENT* and *L'ADMINISTRATEUR.* 1.4.1970; 1.8.1971.	75.00	200.	750.
	c. Signature titles: *LE PRESIDENT* and *LE VICE-PRESIDENT.* 1.7.1973; 1.6.1975.	75.00	200.	750.

25	1000 Francs	VG	VF	UNC
	1968-75. Blue and multicolor. Paradise whydah and flowers. Back blue and light brown; cattle at center.			
	a. Signature titles: *L'ADMINISTRATEUR* and *LE PRESIDENT.* 1.4.1968; 1.5.1971; 1.2.1973.	45.00	175.	550.
	b. Signature title: *LE VICE-PRESIDENT* 1.6.1975; 1.9.1976.	35.00	150.	500.
	s. Specimen.	—	—	850.

26	5000 Francs			
	1968; 1971; 1973. Blue. Pres. Micombero in military uniform at right. Loading at dockside on back.			
	a. Signature titles: *LE VICE-PRESIDENT* and *LE PRESIDENT.* 1.4.1968; 1.7.1973.	200.	500.	1500.
	b. Signature title: *L'ADMINISTRATEUR.* 1.5.1971.	200.	500.	1750.

1975-78 Issue

#27-31 face like #20-26. Arms at ctr. on back.

27	20 Francs	VG	VF	UNC
	1977-2005. Red on multicolor underprint. Face design like #21. Signature titles: *LE GOUVERNEUR* and *L'ADMINISTRATEUR.*			
	a. 1.7.1977; 1.6.1979; 1.12.1981.	FV	.50	2.00
	b. 1.12.1983; 1.12.1986; 1.5.1988; 1.10.1989.	FV	.40	1.25
	c. 1.10.1991; 25.5.1995.	FV	FV	.75
	d. Signature titles: *LE GOUVERNEUR* and *LE 2e VICE-GOUVERNEUR.* 5.2.1997; 1.8.2001; 1.7.2003; 5.2.2005.	FV	FV	.75
	s. Specimen.	—	—	100.

28	50 Francs	VG	VF	UNC
	1977-93. Brown on multicolor underprint. Face like #22.			
	a. 1.7.1977; 1.5.1979.	.15	.75	3.00
	b. 1.12.1981; 1.12.1983.	FV	.50	2.00
	c. 1.5.1988; 1.10.1989; 1.10.1991; 1.5.1993.	FV	FV	1.25
	s. Specimen.	—	—	100.

29	100 Francs	VG	VF	UNC
	1977-93. Purple on multicolor underprint. Face design like #23. Signature titles: *L'ADMINISTRATEUR* and *LE GOUVERNEUR.*			
	a. 1.7.1977; 1.5.1979.	FV	1.00	3.50
	b. 1.1.1981; 1.7.1982; 1.11.1984; 1.11.1986.	FV	.75	3.00
	c. 1.5.1988; 1.7.1990; 1.5.1993.	FV	FV	2.00
	s. Specimen.	—	—	100.

30	500 Francs	VG	VF	UNC
	1977-88. Dark blue on multicolor underprint. Face design like #24. Numeral and date style varieties. Signature titles: *LE GOUVERNEUR* and *LE VICE-GOUVERNEUR.*			
	a. 1.7.1977; 1.9.1981.	FV	10.00	40.00
	b. 1.7.1985; 1.9.1986.	FV	7.00	20.00
	c. 1.5.1988.	FV	5.00	12.50
	s. Specimen. 1.1.1980; 1.7.1985.	—	—	175.

31	1000 Francs	VG	VF	UNC
	1977-91. Dark green on multicolor underprint. Like #25.			
	a. Signature titles: *LE VICE-GOUVERNEUR* and *LE GOUVERNEUR.* 1.7.1977; 1.1.1978; 1.5.1979; 1.1.1980.	FV	15.00	50.00
	b. 1.1.1981; 1.5.1982; 1.1.1984; 1.12.1986.	FV	12.50	35.00
	c. Signature titles: *L'ADMINISTRATEUR* and *LE VICE-GOUVERNEUR.* 1.6.1987.	FV	20.00	65.00
	d. Signature titles: *LE VICE-GOUVERNEUR* and *LE GOUVERNEUR.* 1.5.1988; 1.10.1989; 1.10.1991.	FV	7.50	12.50
	s. Specimen.	—	—	175.

32	5000 Francs	VG	VF	UNC
	1978-95. Dark brown and grayish purple on multicolor underprint. Arms at upper center; building at lower right. Ship dockside on back.			
	a. 1.7.1978; 1.10.1981.	30.00	60.00	200.
	b. 1.1.1984; 1.9.1986.	FV	30.00	100.
	c. 1.10.1989; 1.10.1991.	FV	20.00	80.00
	d. Sign titles: *LE 1ER VICE-GOUVERNEUR* and *LE GOUVERNEUR*. 19.5.1994; 25.5.1995.	FV	FV	62.50

1979-81 Issues

#33 and 34 replacement notes: Serial # prefix *Z*.

33	10 Francs	VG	VF	UNC
	1981-2005. Blue-green on tan underprint. Map of Burundi with arms superimposed at center. Text on back.			
	a. Signature titles: *LE GOUVERNEUR* and *ADMINISTRATEUR*. 1.6.1981; 1.12.1983.	FV	FV	1.00
	b. 1.12.1986; 1.5.1988; 1.10.1989; 1.10.1991.	FV	FV	.75
	c. 25.5.1995.	FV	FV	.50
	d. Signature titles: *LE GOUVERNEUR* and *LE 2E GOUVERNEUR*. 5.2.1997; 1.8.2001; 1.7.2003; 5.2.2005.	FV	FV	.50
	e. Signature titles: *LE GOUVERNEUR* and *LE 2E VICE GOUVERNEUR*. 5.2.2005.	FV	FV	.50

34	500 Francs	VG	VF	UNC
	1.6.1979; 1.1.1980; Tan, blue-black, purple and green on multicolor underprint. Back purple on multicolor underprint. Similar to #30. Signature titles: *LE GOUVERNEUR* and *LE VICE-GOUVERNEUR*.	5.00	12.50	50.00

1993-97 Issue

#35 not assigned.

36	50 Francs	VG	VF	UNC
	19.5.1994; 5.2.1999; 1.8.2001; 1.7.2003; 5.2.2005. Dull brown-violet on multicolor underprint. Man in dugoout canoe at left, arms at lower center. Four men with canoe at center, hippopotamus at lower right on back.	FV	FV	2.00

37	100 Francs	VG	VF	UNC
	1.10.1993; 1.12.1997; 1.8.2001; 1.5.2004; 1.5.2006. Dull purple on multicolor underprint. Archway at left center, Prince Rwagasore at right. Arms lower left, home construction at center on back. Signature titles: *LE 2eme VICE-GOUVERNEUR* and *LE GOUVERNEUR*.			
	a. Issued note.	FV	FV	3.00
	s. Specimen.	—	—	125.

38	500 Francs	VG	VF	UNC
	1995-2003. Gray and violet on multicolor underprint. Native painting at left. Back blue on multicolor underprint; bank building at center, arms at right. Watermark: Ox.			
	a. 5.2.1995	FV	FV	7.50
	b. 1.5.1997.	FV	FV	7.50
	c. 5.2.1999.	FV	FV	6.00
	d. 1.7.2003.	FV	FV	6.00
39	**1000 Francs**			
	1994; 1997; 2000. Greenish black and brown-violet on multicolor underprint. Cattle at left, arms at lower center Monument at center on back. Signature titles: *LE GOUVERNEUR* and *LE 1ER VICE-GOUVERNEUR*. Watermark: Pres. Micombero.			
	a. 19.5.1994.	FV	FV	17.50
	b. 1.12.1997.	FV	FV	9.00
	c. 1.7.2000.	FV	FV	9.00
40	**5000 Francs**			
	5.2.1997. Olive-green and dark green on multicolor underprint. Like #32 but with date moved to left and segmented foil over security thread.	FV	FV	55.00

NOTICE

Readers with unlisted dates, signature varieties, etc. are invited to submit photocopies of their notes to: Standard Catalog of World Paper Money, 700 East State St. Iola, WI 54990-0001, E-Mail: george.cuhaj@fwpubs.com.

1999-2001 ISSUE

		VG	VF	UNC
41	**2000 Francs** 25.6.2001. Blue and green on multicolor underprint. Harvest scene at right. Lake and dam on back.	FV	FV	15.00

		VG	VF	UNC
42	**5000 Francs** Green, olive and 1999; 2003. Light red on multicolor underprint. Like #40, but printed bull's head with OVD ink at lower left center on face.			
	a. 5.2.1999.	FV	FV	40.00
	b. 1.7.2003.	FV	FV	25.00
	c. 5.2.2005.	FV	FV	25.00

		VG	VF	UNC
43	**10,000 Francs** 25.10.2004; 1.5.2006. Multicolor. Two men at lower left. Three students at center on back.	FV	FV	60.00

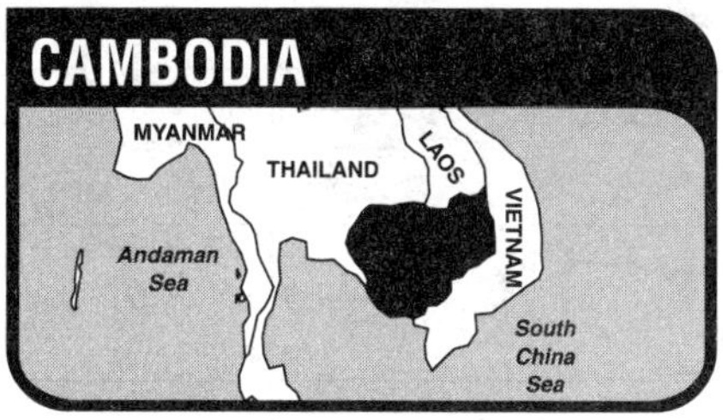

Cambodia, formerly known as Democratic Kampuchea and the Khmer Republic, a land of paddy fields and forest-clad hills located on the Indo-Chinese peninsula fronting on the Gulf of Thailand, has an area of 69,898 sq. mi. (181,035 sq. km.) and a population of 9.86 million. Capital: Phnom Penh. Agriculture is the basis of the economy, with rice the chief crop. Native industries include cattle breeding, weaving and rice milling. Rubber, cattle, corn, and timber are exported.

The region was the nucleus of the Khmer empire which flourished from the 5th to the 12th century and attained an excellence in art and architecture still evident in the magnificent ruins at Angkor. The Khmer empire once ruled over much of Southeast Asia, but began to decline in the 13th century as the Thai and Vietnamese invaded the region and attached its territories. At the request of the Cambodian king, a French protectorate attached to Cochin-China was established over the country in 1863, saving it from dissolution, and in 1885, Cambodia was included in the French Union of Indo-China. France established a constitutional monarchy for Cambodia within the French Union in 1949. The 1954 Geneva Convention resulted in full independence for the Kingdom of Cambodia. King Sihanouk abdicated to his father and won the office of Prime Minister.

Prince Sihanouk was toppled by a bloodless coup led by Lon Nol in March of 1970. Sihanouk moved to Peking to head a government-in-exile. On Oct. 9, 1970, Cambodia became the Khmer Republic, and Lon Nol its President. The government of Lon Nol was in turn toppled, April 17, 1975, by the Khmer Rouge insurgents who took control of the government and renamed the country Democratic Kampuchea.

The Khmer Rouge completely eliminated the economy and created a state without money, exchange or barter. Everyone worked for the state and was taken care of by the state. The Vietnamese supported People's Republic of Kampuchea was installed in accordance with the constitution of January 5, 1976. The name of the country was changed from Democratic Cambodia to Democratic Kampuchea, afterwards reverting to Cambodia.

In the early 1990's the UN supervised a ceasefire and in 1992 Norodom Sihanouk returned as Chief of State. He was crowned king in 1993, and in 2004 abdicated in favor of one of his sons.

RULERS:

Norodom Suramarit, 1955-1960
Norodom Sihanouk (as Chief of State), 1960-1970
Lon Nol, 1970-1975
Pol Pot, 1975-1979
Heng Samrin, 1979-1985
Hun Sen, 1985-1991
Norodom Sihanouk (as Chairman, Supreme National Council), 1991-1993
Norodom Sihanouk (as King), 1993-2002
Boromneath Norodom Sihamoni, 2004-

MONETARY SYSTEM:

1 Riel = 100 Sen

SIGNATURE CHART

	Governor	Chief Inspector	Advisor	Date
1				28.10.1955
2				1956
3				1956
4				Late 1961
5				Mid 1962
6				1963
7				1965
8				1968
9				1968

SIGNATURE CHART				
10				1969
11				1970
12				1972
13				1972
14				1974
15				March, 1975 (printed 1974)
16	Le Gouverneur Thor Peng Leath (08-07-93/23-03-98)		Le Caissier General Tieng Seng, 1995-	
17	Le Gouverneur Chea Chanto 23-03-98-		Le Caissier General Tieng Seng, 1995-	

CAMBODIA - KINGDOM

BANQUE NATIONALE DU CAMBODGE

1956; 1958 ND SECOND ISSUE

		VG	VF	UNC
4	**1 Riel** ND (1956-75). Grayish green on multicolor underprint. Boats dockside in port of Phnom-Penh. Royal palace throne room. Printer: BWC (without imprint).			
	a. Signature 1; 2.	.50	3.00	15.00
	b. Signature 6; 7; 8; 10; 11.	.15	.25	3.00
	c. Signature 12.	.10	.15	1.00
	s. Specimen. Signature 1. Perforated and printed: *SPECIMEN.*	—	—	150.

		VG	VF	UNC
5	**20 Riels** ND (1956-75). Brown on multicolor underprint. Combine harvester at right. Phnom Penh pagoda. Watermark: Buddha. Printer: BWC (without imprint).			
	a. Signature 3.	.25	1.00	10.00
	b. Signature 6.	.25	.75	4.00
	c. Signature 7; 8; 10.	.20	.50	2.00
	d. Signature 12.	.10	.25	1.00

#6 not assigned.

		VG	VF	UNC
7	**50 Riels** ND (1956-75). Blue and orange. Fishermen fishing from boats with Large nets in Lake Tonle Sap at left and right. Blue and brown. Angkor Wat. Watermark: Buddha. Printer: TDLR (without imprint).			
	a. Western numeral in plate block designator. Signature 3.	.50	3.00	20.00
	b. Cambodian numeral in plate block designator. 5-digit serial #. Signature 7; 10.	.25	1.00	3.00
	c. As b. Signature 12.	.25	.50	1.00
	d. Cambodian serial # 6-digits. Signature 12.	.10	.20	1.00
	s. As c. Specimen.	—	—	100.
	s2. As a. Specimen.	—	—	100.

		VG	VF	UNC
8	**100 Riels** ND (1957-75). Brown and green on multicolor underprint. Statue of Lokecvara at left. Long boat. Watermark: Buddha.			
	a. Imprint: *Giesecke & Devrient AG, Munchen.* Signature 3.	.50	3.00	20.00
	b. As a. Signature 7; 8; 11.	.50	1.00	4.00
	c. Imprint: *Giesecke & Devrient-Munchen.* Signature 12; 13.	.20	.50	2.00
	s. Specimen. As a. Signature 3. Perforated *Specimen. Uniface printings.*	—	—	200.

		VG	VF	UNC
9	**500 Riels** ND (1958-70). Green and brown on multicolor underprint. Sculpture of two royal women dancers - *Devatas* at left. Two royal dancers in ceremonial costumes. Watermark: Buddha. Printer: G&D.			

9	500 Riels	VG	VF	UNC
	a. Signature 3.	3.00	20.00	75.00
	b. Signature 6.	2.00	17.50	55.00
	c. Signature 9.	1.00	3.00	12.50
	s. Specimen. Signature 3.			

Note: This banknote was withdrawn in March 1970 because of counterfeiting.

1962-63 ND Third Issue

10	5 Riels	VG	VF	UNC
	ND (1962-75). Red on multicolor underprint. Bayon stone 4 faces of Avalokitesvara at left. Royal Palace Entrance - Chanchhaya at right. Watermark: Buddha. Printer: BWC (without imprint).			
	a. Signature 4; 6.	.50	3.00	20.00
	b. Signature 7; 8; 11.	.20	.50	4.00
	c. Signature 12.	.10	.25	1.00
	s. Specimen. Signature 4, 8. Perforated *SPECIMEN.*	—	—	200.
11	**10 Riels**			
	ND (1962-75). Red-brown on multicolor underprint. Temple of Banteay Srei at right. Central Market building at Phnom-Penh at left. Watermark: Buddha. Printer: TDLR (without imprint).			
	a. Signature 5; 6.	.50	3.00	20.00
	b. Signature 7; 8; 11.	.20	.50	3.00
	c. Signature 12. 5 digit serial #.	.10	.25	1.00
	d. As c. 6 digit serial #.	.20	.50	2.00
	s. Specimen. Signature 6, 8.	—	—	125.
	s2. TDLR Specimen. Signature 6.	—	—	125.

12	100 Riels	VG	VF	UNC
	ND (1963-72). Blue-black, dark green and dark brown on multicolor underprint. Sun rising behind Temple of Preah Vihear at left. Blue, green and brown. Aerial view of the Temple of Preah Vihear. Watermark: Buddha. Printer: G&D.			
	a. Signature 6.	.50	3.00	20.00
	b. Signature 13. (Not issued).	.10	.20	1.00
	s. Specimen. Signature 6.	—	—	200.

13 100 Riels
ND (1956-1972). Blue on light blue underprint. Two oxen at right. Three ceremonial women.

13	100 Riels	VG	VF	UNC
	a. Printer: ABNC with imprint on lower margins, face and back. Signature 3.	3.00	20.00	100.
	b. Without imprint on either side. Signature 12.	.10	.25	2.00
	p. Uniface proofs.	FV	FV	75.00
	s. As a. Specimen. Signature 3.	—	—	200.

14	500 Riels	VG	VF	UNC
	ND (1958-1970). Multicolor. Farmer plowing with two water buffalo. Pagoda at right, doorway of Preah Vihear at left. Watermark: Buddha. Printer: BdF (without imprint).			
	a. Signature 3.	.50	4.00	30.00
	b. Signature 5; 7.	.50	2.00	10.00
	c. Signature 9.	.50	1.50	9.00
	d. Signature 12.	.15	1.00	5.00
	x1. Lithograph counterfeit; watermark. barely visible. Signature 3; 5.	20.00	50.00	100.
	x2. As x1. Signature 7; 9.	15.00	45.00	80.00
	x3. As x1. Signature 12.	7.50	22.50	55.00

Khmer Republic

Banque Nationale du Cambodge

1973 ND Issue

#15 and 16 replacement notes: Series #90.

15	100 Riels	VG	VF	UNC
	ND. Purple and violet on multicolor underprint. Carpet weaving. Angkor Wat on back. Watermark: Man's head. Printer: TDLR (without imprint). (Not issued).			
	a. Signature 13.	.10	.35	2.00
	b. Signature 14.	.25	1.25	7.50

NOTICE

Readers with unlisted dates, signature varieties, etc. are invited to submit photocopies of their notes to: Standard Catalog of World Paper Money, 700 East State St. Iola, WI 54990-0001, E-Mail: george.cuhaj@fwpubs.com.

16	500 Riels	VG	VF	UNC
	ND(1973-75). Green and black on multicolor underprint. Girl with vessel on head at left. Rice paddy scene on back. Watermark: Man's head. Printer: TDLR (without imprint).			
	a. Signature 13; 14.	.25	2.00	10.00
	b. Signature 15.	.10	.20	1.00
	s. As a. Specimen.	—	—	—

17	1000 Riels	VG	VF	UNC
	ND. Green on multicolor underprint. School children. Head of Lokecvara at Ta Som on back. Watermark: School girl. Signature 13. Printer: BWC. (Not issued).	.10	.20	1.00
17A	5000 Riels			
	ND (1974). Brown, tan, yellow and green. Male bust at right. Building on back. Unissued. Only released starting in 2005.	—	—	25.00

KAMPUCHEA

BANK OF KAMPUCHEA

1975 ISSUE

#18-24 prepared by the Khmer Rouge but not issued. New regime under Pol Pot instituted an "agrarian moneyless society." All notes dated 1975.

#20-24 wmk: Angkor Wat.

18	0.1 Riel (1 Kak)	VG	VF	UNC
	1975. Purple and green on orange and multicolor underprint. Mortar crew left. Threshing rice on back.			
	a. Issued note.	.20	.50	3.00
	s. Specimen.	—	—	200.

19	0.5 Riel (5 Kak)	VG	VF	UNC
	1975. Red on light green and multicolor underprint. Troops marching at left center. Bayon sculpture at left, machine and worker at right on back.			
	a. Issued note.	.20	.50	3.00
	s. Specimen.	—	—	200.

20	1 Riel	VG	VF	UNC
	1975. Red-violet and red on multicolor underprint. Women farm workers at left center. Woman operating machine on back.			
	a. Issued note.	.20	.50	3.00
	s. Specimen.	—	—	200.

21	5 Riels	VG	VF	UNC
	1975. Deep green on multicolor underprint. Ancient temples of Angkor Wat at center right. Landscaping crew on back.			
	a. Issued note.	.20	.40	3.50
	s. Specimen.	—	—	200.

22	10 Riels	VG	VF	UNC
	1975. Brown and red on multicolor underprint. Soldiers (Machine gun crew) at center right. Rice harvesting on back.			
	a. Issued note.	.20	.75	6.00
	s. Specimen.	—	—	200.

23	50 Riels	VG	VF	UNC
	1975. Purple on multicolor underprint. Planting rice at left, Bayon sculpture at right. Woman's militia at center right on back.			
	a. Issued note.	.50	2.00	12.00
	s. Specimen.	—	—	200.

24	100 Riels	VG	VF	UNC
	1975. Deep green on multicolor underprint. Factory workers at left. center. Back black; harvesting rice.			
	a. Issued note.	.75	4.00	17.50
	s. Specimen.	—	—	200.

STATE BANK OF DEMOCRATIC KAMPUCHEA

1979 ISSUE

#25-32 issued 20.3.1980 by the Vietnamese-backed regime of Heng Samrin which overthrew Pol Pot in 1979.

25	0.1 Riel (1 Kak)	VG	VF	UNC
	1979. Olive-green on light blue underprint. Arms at center. Water buffalos on back.			
	a. Issued note.	.05	.15	.50
	s. Specimen.	—	—	15.00

26	0.2 Riel (2 Kak)	VG	VF	UNC
	1979. Grayish green on tan underprint. Arms at center. Rice workers on back.			
	a. Issued note.	.10	.20	.50
	s. Specimen.	—	—	15.00

27	0.5 Riel (5 Kak)	VG	VF	UNC
	1979. Red-orange on tan and gray underprint. Arms at left, modern passenger train at right. Men fishing from boats with nets on back.			
	a. Issued note.	.10	.20	1.00
	s. Specimen.	—	—	15.00

28	1 Riel	VG	VF	UNC
	1979. Brown on yellow and multicolor underprint. Arms at center. Women harvesting rice on back.			
	a. Issued note.	.10	.20	.50
	s. Specimen. 2 serial # var.	—	—	15.00

29	5 Riels	VG	VF	UNC
	1979. Dark brown on light green and multicolor underprint. Four people at left, arms at right. Independence from France (now Victory) monument on back.			
	a. Issued note.	.10	.30	2.00
	s. Specimen.	—	—	15.00
	x. Counterfeit (contemporary).	—	1.00	3.00

30	10 Riels	VG	VF	UNC
	1979. Dark gray on lilac and multicolor underprint. Arms at left, harvesting fruit trees at right. School on back.			
	a. Issued note.	.20	.50	4.00
	s. Specimen.	—	—	15.00

31	20 Riels	VG	VF	UNC
	1979. Purple on pink and multicolor underprint. Arms at left. Water buffalos hauling logs on back. Watermark: Arms.			
	a. Issued note.	.10	.35	5.00
	s. Specimen.	—	—	20.00
	x. Counterfeit (contemporary).	1.00	2.00	4.00

		VG	VF	UNC
32	**50 Riels**			
	1979. Deep red on yellow-green and multicolor underprint. Arms at left, Bayon stone head at center. Angkor Wat on back. Watermark: Arms.			
	a. Issued note.	.10	.35	7.50
	s. Specimen.	—	—	20.00

1987 Issue

		VG	VF	UNC
33	**5 Riels**			
	1987. Like #29 but red and brown on light yellow and light green underprint. Back red on pale yellow underprint.	.10	.35	2.00

		VG	VF	UNC
34	**10 Riels**			
	1987. Like #30 but green on light blue and multicolor underprint. Back deep green and lilac on light blue underprint.	.10	.35	2.00

Cambodia

Peoples National Bank of Cambodia

1990-92 Issue

#35-37 wmk: Stylized lotus flowers.

		VG	VF	UNC
35	**50 Riels**			
	1992. Dull brown on multicolor underprint. Arms at center, male portrait at right. Ships dockside on back. Printer: NBC (without imprint).			
	a. Issued note.	.10	.25	2.00
	s. Specimen.	—	—	35.00

		VG	VF	UNC
36	**100 Riels**			
	1990. Dark green and brown on light blue and lilac underprint. Independence from France (now Victory) monument at left center, male portrait at right. Rubber trees on back.			
	a. Issued note.	.10	.50	3.00
	s. Specimen.	—	—	50.00

		VG	VF	UNC
37	**200 Riels**			
	1992. Dull olive-green and tan on multicolor underprint. Floodgates at right. Bayon sculpture in Angkor Wat center on back. Printer: NBC.			
	a. Issued note.	.15	.50	2.00
	s. Specimen. 1993.	—	—	125.

		VG	VF	UNC
38	**500 Riels**			
	1991. Red, purple and brown-violet on multicolor underprint. Arms above Angkor Wat at center. Animal statue at left, cultivating with tractors at center on back. Watermark: Sculptured heads.			
	a. Issued note.	.25	.50	3.00
	s. Specimen. (two different serial # varieties.)	—	—	50.00

		VG	VF	UNC
39	**1000 Riels**			
	1992. Dark green, brown and black on multicolor underprint. Bayon Temple ruins in Angkor Wat. Fishermen fishing in boats with large nets in Lake Tonle Sap on back. Watermark: Chinze. (Not released).	—	—	10.00

NOTICE

Readers with unlisted dates, signature varieties, etc. are invited to submit photocopies of their notes to: Standard Catalog of World Paper Money, 700 East State St. Iola, WI 54990-0001, E-Mail: george.cuhaj@fwpubs.com.

		VG	VF	UNC
40	**2000 Riels** 1992. Black, deep blue and violet-brown on multicolor underprint. King N. Sihanouk at left and as watermark, Temple portal at Preah Vihear at right. (Not released).	—	—	10.00

NATIONAL BANK OF CAMBODIA

1995 ISSUE

SIGNATURE VARIETIES		
16	Le Gouverneur Thor Peng Leath,	Le Caissier Général Tieng Seng, 1999-
17	Chea Chanto, 1999-	Tieng Seng, 1999-

#41-43 arms at upper l. Wmk: Stylized lotus flowers. Printer: NBC. Sign. 16 or 17.

		VG	VF	UNC
41	**100 Riels** 1995; 1998. Grayish green and brown on multicolor underprint. Chinze, Independence from France (Now Victory) monument at right. Tapping rubber trees on back.			
	a. 1995. signature 16.	.10	.20	1.00
	b. 1998. signature 16; 17.	.10	.20	.50
	s. Specimen. 1995.	—	—	35.00

		VG	VF	UNC
42	**200 Riels** 1995; 1998. Dark olive-green and brown on multicolor underprint. Similar to #37 but smaller size. Signature 16.			
	a. 1995.	FV	FV	2.00
	b. 1998.	FV	FV	.35
	s. Specimen. 1995.	—	—	25.00

		VG	VF	UNC
43	**500 Riels** 1996, 1998. Red and purple on multicolor underprint. Angkor Wot at right. Mythical animal at left, rice fields at center on back.			
	a. 1996. signature 16.	FV	FV	1.00
	b. 1998. signature 16; 17.	FV	FV	1.00
	s. Specimen. 1996.	—	—	25.00

#44-50 Replacement notes have an *0* at the end of the serial # prefix, eg. *A0*. Printer: F-CO. #44 and 45 wmk: Cube design.

		VG	VF	UNC
44	**1000 Riels** ND (1995). Blue-green on gold and multicolor underprint. Bayon stone four faces of Avalokitesvara at left. Prasat Chan Chaya at right on back.			
	a. ND (1995).	FV	FV	2.00
	s. Specimen.	—	—	30.00

		VG	VF	UNC
45	**2000 Riels** ND (1995). Reddish brown on multicolor underprint. Fishermen fishing from boats with nets in Lake Tonie Sap at left and right. Temple ruins at Angkor Wat on back.			
	a. Issued note.	FV	FV	3.50
	s. Specimen.	—	—	30.00

#46-49 Kg. N. Sihanouk at r. and as wmk.

		VG	VF	UNC
46	**5000 Riels** ND (1995); 1998. Deep purple and blue-black with black text on multicolor underprint. Temple of Banteai Srei at lower left center. Central market in Phnom-Penh on back.			
	a. ND (1995). signature 16.	FV	FV	10.00
	b. 1998. signature 16, 17.	FV	FV	6.50
	s. Specimen. ND (1995); 1998.	—	—	30.00

47 10,000 Riels

ND (1995); 1998. Blue-black, black and dark green on multicolor underprint. Statue of Lokecvara at lower left center. People rowing long boat during the water festival at lower center on back.

	VG	VF	UNC
a. ND (1995). signature 16.	FV	FV	12.50
b. 1998. signature 16, 17.	FV	FV	12.00
s. Specimen. ND(1995); 1998.	—	—	30.00

48 20,000 Riels

ND (1995). Violet and red on multicolor underprint. Boats dockside in Port of Phnom-Penh at center. Throne Room in National Palace on back. Signature 16.

	VG	VF	UNC
a. Issued note.	FV	FV	20.00
s. Specimen.	—	—	30.00

49 50,000 Riels

ND (1995); 1998. Dark brown, brown and deep olive-green on multicolor underprint. Preah Vihear Temple at center. Road to Preah Vihear Temple on back.

	VG	VF	UNC
a. ND (1995). signature 16.	FV	FV	52.50
b. 1998. signature 16, 17.	FV	FV	50.00
s. Specimen. ND (1995); 1998.	—	—	35.00

50 100,000 Riels

ND (1995). Green, blue-green and black on multicolor underprint. Chief and First Lady at right and as watermark. Chief and First Lady receiving homage of people at center right on back. Signature 16.

	VG	VF	UNC
a. Issued note.	FV	FV	95.00
s. Specimen. Ovpt: *SPECIMEN.*	—	—	40.00

1999 Issue

51 1000 Riels

1999. Dark brown and dark olive-green on multicolor underprint. Temples at center right. Back brown and slate blue; construction site at center signature 17.

	VG	VF	UNC
a. Issued note.	FV	FV	1.25
s. Specimen.	—	—	30.00

2001-02 Issue

#52-54 naga heads sculpture at lower l. ctr. Wmk: Bayon sculpture in Angkor Wat.

52 50 Riels

2002. Dark brown and tan on multicolor underprint. Preah Vihear temple at center. Dam at center on back. Signature 17.

	VG	VF	UNC
a. Issued note.	FV	FV	.35
s. Specimen.	—	—	25.00

53 100 Riels

2001. Purple, brown and green. Independence Monument at right center. Students and school on back. Watermark: multiple lines of text. Signature 17.

	VG	VF	UNC
a. Issued note.	FV	FV	.50
s. Specimen.	—	—	15.00

#53-56 Kg. Norodom Sihanouk at r.

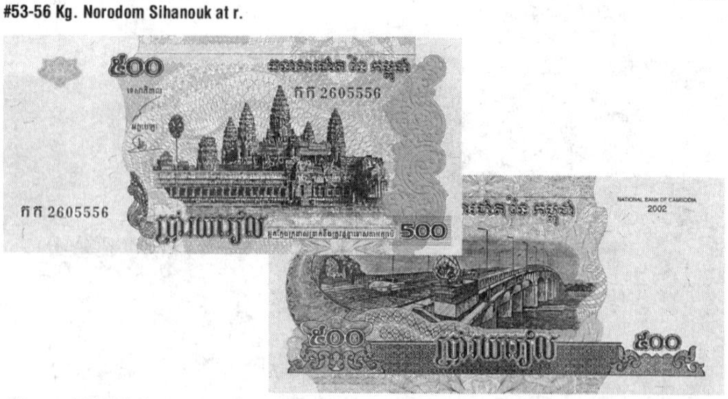

54 500 Riels

2002; 2004. Red and purple on multicolor underprint. Angkor Wat temple at center. Bridge spanning Mekong river at Kampong Cham at center on back. Signature 17.

	VG	VF	UNC
a. 2002.	FV	FV	1.50
b. 2004.	FV	FV	1.00
s. Specimen.	FV	FV	15.00

		VG	VF	UNC
55	**5000 Riels** 2001; 2004. Green and gray. Bridge of Kampong Kdei in Siemreap Province on back. Signature 17.			
	a. 2001.	FV	FV	6.00
	b. 2004.	FV	FV	5.00
	s. Specimen.	—	—	15.00

		VG	VF	UNC
56	**10,000 Riels** 2001. Violet, brown and blue. Water festival before Royal Palace on back. Signature 17.			
	a. Issued note.	FV	FV	8.00
	s. Specimen.	—	—	15.00

		VG	VF	UNC
57	**50,000 Riels** 2001. Violet, brown and blue. Angkor Wat temple on back. Signature 17.			
	a. Issued note.	FV	FV	40.00
	s. Specimen.	—	—	30.00

2005 ISSUE

		VG	VF	UNC
58	**1000 Riels** 2005. Brown and lilac on multicolor underprint. Temple at center. Cargo ships on back.	FV	FV	2.25

NOTICE

Readers with unlisted dates, signature varieties, etc. are invited to submit photocopies of their notes to: Standard Catalog of World Paper Money, 700 East State St. Iola, WI 54990-0001, E-Mail: george.cuhaj@fwpubs.com.

REGIONAL

KHMER ROUGE INFLUENCE

1993 ND ISSUE

#R1-R5 w/sign. of Pres. Khieu Samphan.

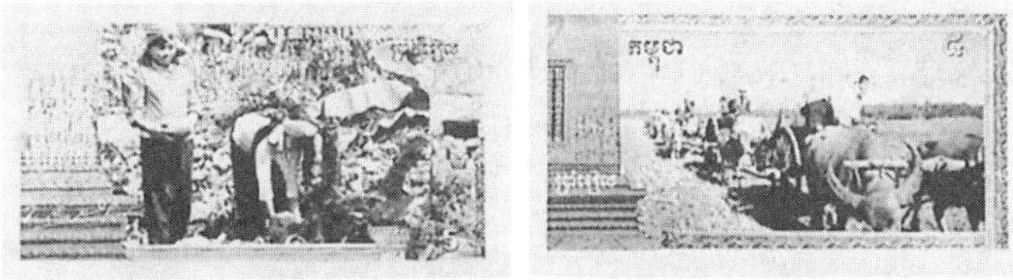

		VG	VF	UNC
R1	**5 Riels** ND (1993-99). Multicolor. Children harvesting vegetables at center, temple carvings at left and right. Caravan of ox carts at center, temple carvings at left on back.	.50	3.00	10.00

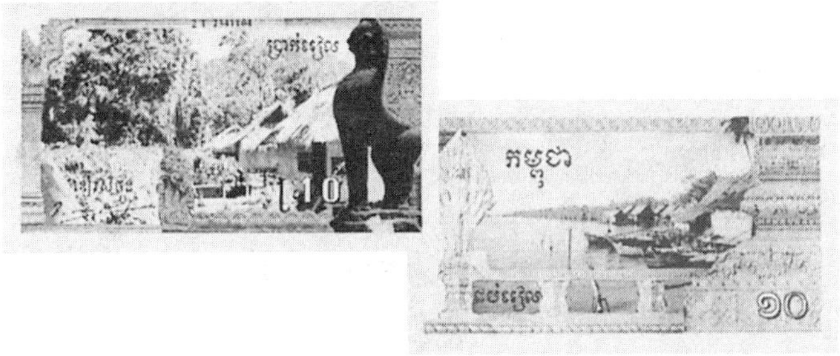

		VG	VF	UNC
R2	**10 Riels** ND (1993-99). Multicolor. Village at center right, temple carvings at left and right. Fishing village, boats at center, temple carvings at left and right on back.	.50	3.00	10.00

		VG	VF	UNC
R3	**20 Riels** ND (1993-99). Multicolor. Villagers leading cattle along road at center, temple carvings at left and right. Street scene at center, temple carvings at left and right on back.	1.00	4.00	15.00
R4	**50 Riels** ND (1993-99). Multicolor. Planting rice at center Ox-drawn carts at left center. Temple carvings at left and right on back.	1.00	4.00	15.00

		VG	VF	UNC
R5	**100 Riels** ND (1993-99). Multicolor. Field workers at center, temple carvings at left. Temples of Angkor Wat at center, temple carvings at left and right on back.	2.00	10.00	55.00

FOREIGN EXCHANGE CERTIFICATES

MINISTERE DU TOURISME DU CAMBODGE

1960'S BON TOURISTIQUE ISSUE

#FX1-FX5 black text. Shoreline at l. ctr., royal dancer at r. Black text on back. Perforated along l. edge.

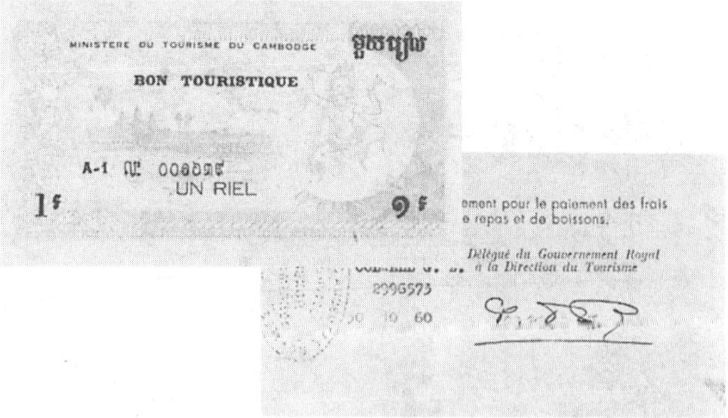

		VG	VF	UNC
FX1	**1 Riel** ca. 1960's. Pink and tan.	25.00	60.00	125.

		VG	VF	UNC
FX2	**2 Riels** 1961. Light green and violet.	25.00	60.00	125.

		VG	VF	UNC
FX3	**5 Riels** ca. 1960's. Dark purple and orange.	25.00	60.00	125.
FX4	**10 Riels** ca. 1960's. Yellow and light green.	25.00	60.00	125.
FX5	**20 Riels** ca. 1960's. Brown and pale green.	25.00	60.00	125.

COLLECTOR SERIES

NATIONAL BANK OF CAMBODIA

1995 ND ISSUE

		Issue Price	Mkt. Value
CS1	**1000 - 100,000 Riels** ND (1995). #44-50. Specimen.	—	250.

Note: Issued in a special folder w/notes laminated in plastic including 50, 100, 200 and 500 Riels coins dated BE2538 (1994).

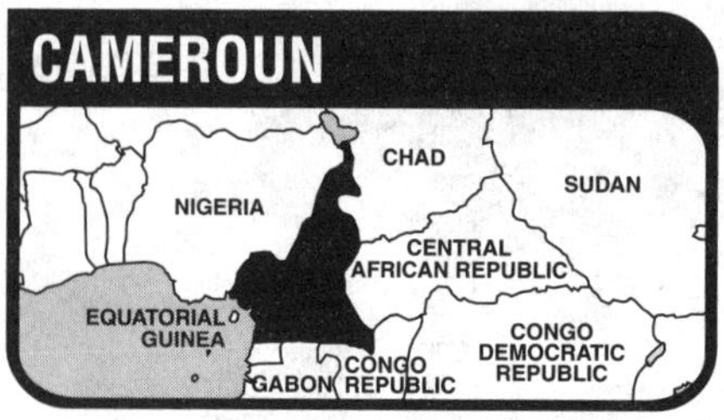

The United Republic of Cameroun, located in west-central Africa on the Gulf of Guinea, has an area of 185,568 sq. mi. (475,440 sq. km.) and a population of 15.13 million. Capital: Yaounde. About 90 percent of the labor force is employed on the land; cash crops account for 80 percent of the country's export revenue. Cocoa, coffee, aluminum, cotton, rubber and timber are exported.

European contact with what is now the United Republic of Cameroun began in the 16th century with the voyage of Portuguese navigator Fernando Po. The following three centuries saw continuous activity by Spanish, Dutch and British traders and missionaries. The land was spared colonial rule until 1884, when treaties with tribal chiefs brought German domination. After Germany's defeat in WWI, the League of Nations in 1919 divided the Cameroons between Great Britain and France, with the larger eastern area going to France. The French and British mandates were converted into United Nations trusteeships in 1946. French Cameroon became the independent Cameroun Republic on Jan. 1, 1960. The federation of East (French) and West (British) Cameroun was established in 1961 when the southern part of British Cameroun voted for reunification with the Cameroun Republic, and the northern part for union with Nigeria. On Nov. 1, 1995 the Republic of Cameroun joined the Commonwealth. Issues continue under Central African States.

MONETARY SYSTEM:

1 Franc = 100 Centimes

SIGNATURE VARIETIES:

Refer to introduction of Central African States.

RÉPUBLIQUE DU CAMEROUN

BANQUE CENTRALE

1961 ND ISSUE

#7-9 denominations in French only, or French and English.

		Good	Fine	XF
7	**1000 Francs** ND (1961). Multicolor. Man with basket harvesting cocoa. Signature 1A.	175.	750.	1850.
8	**5000 Francs** ND (1961). Multicolor. Pres. A. Ahidjo at right. Signature 1A.	75.00	300.	1500.

		Good	Fine	XF
9	**5000 Francs** ND. Like #8 but denomination also in English words at lower left center. Signature 1A.	150.	600.	1900.

NOTICE

Readers with unlisted dates, signature varieties, etc. are invited to submit photocopies of their notes to: Standard Catalog of World Paper Money, 700 East State St. Iola, WI 54990-0001, E-Mail: george.cuhaj@fwpubs.com.

RÉPUBLIQUE FÉDÉRALE DU CAMEROUN

BANQUE CENTRALE

1962 ND ISSUE

#10-13 denominations in French and English.

		VG	VF	UNC
10	**100 Francs** ND (1962). Multicolor. President of the Republic at left. Ships on back. Signature 1A. Watermark: Antelope's head.	5.00	30.00	125.

		VG	VF	UNC
11	**500 Francs** ND (1962). Multicolor. Man with 2 oxen. Man with bananas at left, truck on road at center right, two ships in background at upper right on back. Signature 1A.	15.00	125.	450.

Note: Engraved (intaglio) and lithographic varieties.

		VG	VF	UNC
12	**1000 Francs** ND (1962). Multicolor. Like #7 but with title: *RÉPUBLIQUE FÉDÉRALE* . . . on back. Signature 1A.	30.00	150.	650.

Note: Engraved (intaglio) and lithographic varieties.

		VG	VF	UNC
13	**5000 Francs** ND (1962). Multicolor. Like #9 but with title: *RÉPUBLIQUE FÉDÉRALE* . . . on back. Signature 1A.	150.	500.	1500.

1972 ND ISSUE

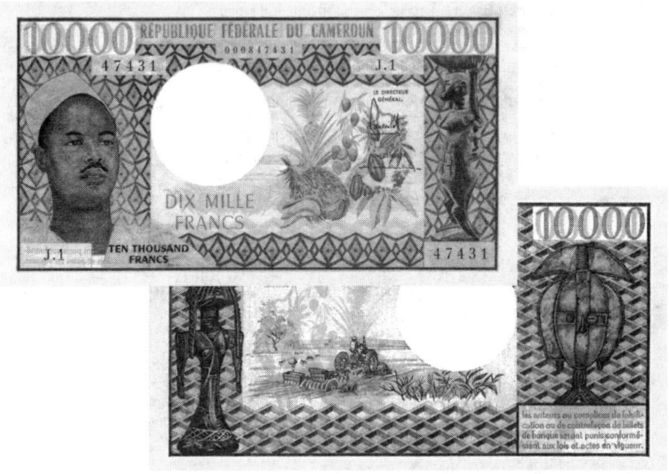

		VG	VF	UNC
14	**10,000 Francs** ND (1972). Multicolor. Pres. A. Ahidjo at left, fruit at center, wood carving at right. Statue at left and right, tractor plowing at center on back. Signature 2.	40.00	125.	375.

RÉPUBLIQUE UNIE DU CAMEROUN

BANQUE DES ÉTATS DE L'AFRIQUE CENTRALE

1974 ND ISSUE

		VG	VF	UNC
15	**500 Francs** ND (1974; 1984); 1978-83. Red-brown and multicolor. Woman wearing hat at left, aerial view of modern buildings at center. Mask at left, students and chemical testing at center, statue at right on back.			
	a. Signature titles: *LE DIRECTEUR GÉNÉRAL* and *UN CENSEUR*. Engraved. watermark: Antelope in half profile. Signature 3. ND (1974).	20.00	75.00	250.
	b. As a. signature 5.	1.50	8.00	35.00
	c. Signature titles: *LE GOUVERNEUR* and *UN CENSEUR*. watermark: Antelope in profile. Signature 10. 1.4.1978.	1.00	6.00	30.00
	d. Signature 12. 1.6.1981; 1.1.1983.	1.00	4.00	15.00
	e. Signature 12. 1.1.1982.	5.00	25.00	75.00

		VG	VF	UNC
16	**1000 Francs**			
	ND (1974); 1978-83. Blue and multicolor. Hut at center, girl with plaits at right. Mask at left, trains, planes and bridge at center, statue at right on back.			
	a. Signature titles: *LE DIRECTEUR GÉNÉRAL* and *UN CENSEUR.* Engraved. watermark: Antelope in half profile. Signature 5. ND (1974).	1.50	10.00	40.00
	b. Signature titles like a. Lithographed. watermark. like c. Signature 8. ND (1978).	20.00	55.00	175.
	c. Signature titles: *LE GOUVERNEUR* and *UN CENSEUR.* Lithographed. watermark: Antelope in profile. Signature 10. 1.4.1978, 1.7.1980.	1.00	7.50	30.00
	d. Signature 12. 1.6.1981; 1.1.1982; 2; 1.1.1983.	1.00	4.50	25.00
	s. As a. Specimen.	—	—	—

		VG	VF	UNC
17	**5000 Francs**			
	ND (1974). Brown and multicolor. Pres. A. Ahidjo at left, railway loading equipment at right. Mask at left, industrial college at center, statue at right on back.			
	a. Signature titles: *LE DIRECTEUR GÉNÉRAL* and *UN CENSEUR.* Engraved. Signature 3. ND (1974).	50.00	175.	550.
	b. Like a. signature 5.	30.00	100.	350.
	c. Signature titles: *LE GOUVERNEUR* and *UN CENSEUR.* Signature 11; 12.	15.00	80.00	150.

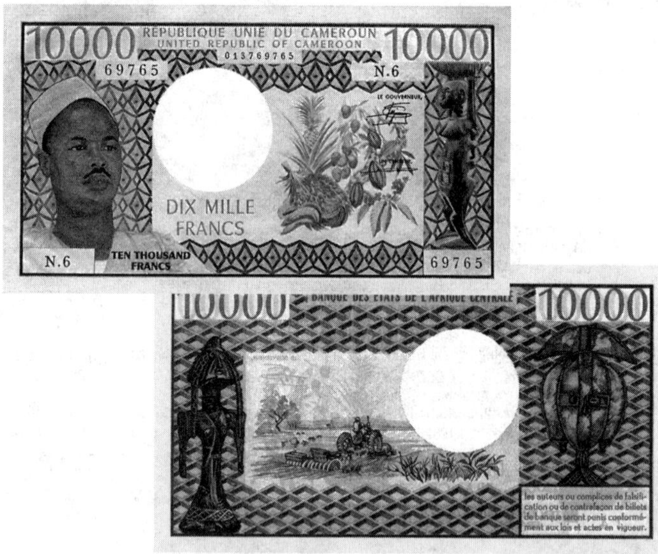

		VG	VF	UNC
18	**10,000 Francs**			
	ND (1974; 1978; 1981). Multicolor. Pres. A. Ahidjo at left. Similar to #14 except for new bank name on back.			
	a. Signature titles: *LE DIRECTEUR GÉNÉRAL* and *UN CENSEUR.* Signature 5. ND (1974).	25.00	75.00	350.
	b. Signature titles: *LE GOUVERNEUR* and *UN CENSEUR.* Signature 11; 12. ND (1978; 1981).	20.00	60.00	225.

NOTICE

Readers with unlisted dates, signature varieties, etc. are invited to submit photocopies of their notes to: Standard Catalog of World Paper Money, 700 East State St. Iola, WI 54990-0001, E-Mail: george.cuhaj@fwpubs.com.

1981 ND Issue

		VG	VF	UNC
19	**5000 Francs**			
	ND (1981). Brown and multicolor. Mask at left, woman carrying bundle of fronds at right. Plowing and mine ore conveyor on back. Signature 12.	5.00	20.00	85.00

		VG	VF	UNC
20	**10,000 Francs**			
	ND (1981). Brown, green and multicolor. Stylized antelope heads at left, woman at right. Loading of fruit onto truck at left on back. Signature 12.	10.00	35.00	150.

République du Cameroun

Banque des États de l'Afrique Centrale

1984 ND Issue

		VG	VF	UNC
21	**1000 Francs**			
	1.6.1984. Blue and multicolor. Like #16 except for new country name. Signature 12.	2.00	7.50	30.00
22	**5000 Francs**			
	ND (1984; 1990; 1992). Brown and multicolor. Like #19 except for new country name. Signature 12; 13; 15.	5.00	20.00	75.00
23	**10,000 Francs**			
	ND (1984; 1990). Brown, green and multicolor. Like #20 except for new country name. Signature 12; 13.	10.00	40.00	130.

1985-86 Issue

#24-26 wmk: Carving (as on notes).

24	500 Francs	VG	VF	UNC
	1985-90. Brown on multicolor underprint. Carving and jug at center. Man carving mask at left center on back.			
	a. Signature 12. 1.1.1985-1.1.1988.	.50	2.50	8.00
	b. Signature 13. 1.1.1990.	.50	1.50	7.00

25	1000 Francs	VG	VF	UNC
	1.1.1985. Dark blue on multicolor underprint. Carving at left, small figurines at center, man at right. Incomplete map of Chad at top. Elephant at left, carving at right on back.	1.50	5.00	30.00

26	1000 Francs	VG	VF	UNC
	1986-92. Like #25 but with completed outline map of Chad at top center.			
	a. Signature 12. 1.1.1986-1.1.1989.	1.00	6.50	15.00
	b. Signature 13. 1.1.1990.	1.00	4.50	15.00
	c. Signature 15.1.1.1992.	1.00	4.50	15.00

CANADA

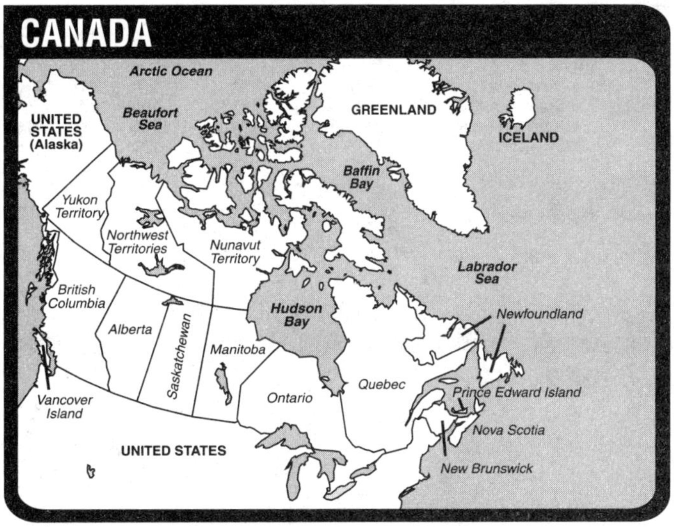

Canada is located to the north of the United States, and spans the full breadth of the northern portion of North America from Atlantic to Pacific oceans, except for the State of Alaska. It has a total area of 3,850,000 sq. mi. (9,970,610 sq. km.) and a population of 30.68 million. Capital: Ottawa.

Jacques Cartier, a French explorer, took possession of Canada for France in 1534, and for more than a century the history of Canada was that of a French colony. Samuel de Champlain helped to establish the first permanent colony in North America, in 1604 at Port Royal, Acadia - now Annapolis Royal, Nova Scotia. Four years later he founded the settlement of Quebec.

The British settled along the coast to the south while the French, motivated by a grand design, pushed into the interior. France's plan for a great American empire was to occupy the Mississippi heartland of the country, and from there to press in upon the narrow strip of English coastal settlements from the rear. Inevitably, armed conflict erupted between the French and the British; consequently, Britain acquired Hudson Bay, Newfoundland and Nova Scotia from the French in 1713. British control of the rest of New France was secured in 1763, largely because of James Wolfe's great victory over Montcalm near Quebec in 1759.

During the American Revolution, Canada became a refuge for great numbers of American Royalists, most of whom settled in Ontario, thereby creating an English majority west of the Ottawa River. The ethnic imbalance contravened the effectiveness of the prevailing French type of government, and in 1791 the Constitutional act was passed by the British parliament, dividing Canada at the Ottawa River into two parts, each with its own government: Upper Canada, chiefly English and consisting of the southern section of what is now Ontario; and Lower Canada, chiefly French and consisting principally of the southern section of Quebec. Subsequent revolt by dissidents in both sections caused the British government to pass the Union act, July 23, 1840, which united Lower and Upper Canada (as Canada East and Canada West) to form the Province of Canada, with one council and one assembly in which the two sections had equal numbers.

The union of the two provinces did not encourage political stability; the equal strength of the French and British made the task of government all but impossible. A further change was made with the passage of the British North American act, which took effect on July 1, 1867, and established Canada as the first federal union in the British Empire. Four provinces entered the union at first: Upper Canada as Ontario, Lower Canada as Quebec, Nova Scotia and New Brunswick. The Hudson's Bay Company's territories were acquired in 1869 out of which were formed the provinces of Manitoba, Saskatchewan and Alberta. British Columbia joined in 1871 and Prince Edward Island in 1873. Canada took over the Arctic Archipelago in 1895. In 1949 Newfoundland came into the confederation. Canada is a member of the Commonwealth. Elizabeth II is Head of State as Queen of Canada.

RULERS:

French 1534-1763
British 1763-

MONETARY SYSTEM:

100 Cents = 1 Dollar

DOMINION

BANQUE DU CANADA / BANK OF CANADA

1954 MODIFIED HAIR STYLE ISSUE

74	1 Dollar	VG	VF	UNC
	1954 (1955-72). Black on green underprint. Like #66 but Queen's hair in modified style. Green. Western prairie scene. Printer: CBNC.			
	a. Signature Beattie-Coyne. (1955-61).	1.00	2.50	15.00
	b. Signature Beattie-Rasminsky. (1961-72).	1.00	2.00	12.50

75 1 Dollar

1954 (1955-74). Black on green underprint. Queen's hair in modified style. Like #74. Green. Western prairie scene. Printer: BABNC.

	VG	VF	UNC
a. Signature Beattie-Coyne. (1955-61).	1.00	2.50	20.00
b. Signature Beattie-Rasminsky. (1961-72).	1.00	1.50	7.50
c. Signature Bouey-Rasminsky. (1972-73).	1.00	1.50	8.50
d. Signature Lawson-Bouey. (1973-74).	1.00	1.50	7.50

76 2 Dollars

1954 (1955-75). Black on red-brown underprint. Like #67 but Queen's hair in modified style. Red-brown. Quebec scenery. Printer: BABNC.

	VG	VF	UNC
a. Signature Beattie-Coyne. (1955-61).	1.75	4.00	30.00
b. Signature Beattie-Rasminsky. (1961-72).	1.75	3.00	20.00
c. Signature Bouey-Rasminsky. (1972-73).	1.75	3.00	15.00
d. Signature Lawson-Bouey. (1973-75).	1.75	3.00	15.00

77 5 Dollars

1954 (1955-72). Black on blue underprint. Like #68 but Queen's hair in modified style. Blue. River in the north country. Printer: CBNC.

	VG	VF	UNC
a. Signature Beattie-Coyne. (1955-61).	5.00	10.00	65.00
b. Signature Beattie-Rasminsky. (1961-72).	4.50	7.50	35.00
c. Signature Bouey-Rasminsky. (1972).	4.50	7.50	30.00

78 5 Dollars

	VG	VF	UNC
1954 (1955-61). Black on blue underprint. Queen's hair in modified style. Like #77. Signature Beattie-Coyne. Blue. River in the north country. Printer: BABNC.	4.50	10.00	65.00

79 10 Dollars

1954 (1955-71). Black on purple underprint. Like #69 but Queen's hair in modified style. Purple. Rocky Mountain scene. Printer: BABNC.

	VG	VF	UNC
a. Signature Beattie-Coyne. (1955-61).	9.00	12.50	55.00
b. Signature Beattie-Rasminsky. (1961-71).	9.00	12.50	45.00

80 20 Dollars

1954 (1955-70) Black on olive olive-green underprint. Like #70 but Queen's hair in modified style. Olive-green. Laurentian hills in winter. Printer: CBNC.

	VG	VF	UNC
a. Signature Beattie-Coyne. (1955-61).	17.50	25.00	100.
b. Signature Beattie-Rasminsky. (1961-70).	FV	20.00	65.00

81 50 Dollars

1954 (1955-75). Black on orange underprint. Like #71 but Queen's hair in modified style. Orange. Atlantic coastline. Printer: CBNC.

	VG	VF	UNC
a. Signature Beattie-Coyne. (1955-61).	FV	50.00	175.
b. Signature Beattie-Rasminsky. (1961-72).	FV	50.00	150.
c. Signature Lawson-Bouey. (1973-75).	FV	65.00	200.

82 100 Dollars

1954 (1955-76). Black on brown underprint. Queen's hair in modified style. Brown. Mountain lake. Printer: CBNC.

	VG	VF	UNC
a. Signature Beattie-Coyne. (1955-61).	FV	100.	275.
b. Signature Beattie-Rasminsky. (1961-72).	FV	100.	225.
c. Signature Lawson-Bouey. (1973-76).	FV	100.	250.

83 1000 Dollars

1954 (1955-87). Black on rose underprint. Like #73 but Queen's hair in modified style. Rose. Central Canadian landscape.

	VG	VF	UNC
a. Signature Beattie-Coyne. (1955-61).	800.	1250.	2500.
b. Signature Beattie-Rasminsky. (1961-72).	FV	950.	1750.
c. Signature Bouey-Rasminsky. (1972).	FV	950.	1700.
d. Signature Lawson-Bouey. (1973-84).	FV	FV	1250.
e. Signature Thiessen-Crow. (1987).	FV	1000.	1500.

NOTICE

Readers with unlisted dates, signature varieties, etc. are invited to submit photocopies of their notes to: Standard Catalog of World Paper Money, 700 East State St. Iola, WI 54990-0001, E-Mail: george.cuhaj@fwpubs.com.

1967 COMMEMORATIVE ISSUE

#84, Centennial of Canadian Confederation

84 1 Dollar

1967. Black on green underprint. Queen Elizabeth II at right. Signature Beattie-Rasminsky. Green. First Parliament Building.

	VG	VF	UNC
a. Centennial dates: *1867-1967* replaces serial #.	1.00	1.50	3.50
b. Regular serial #'s.	1.00	1.50	5.00

1969-75 ISSUE

#85-91 arms at l.

85 1 Dollar

1973. Black on light green and multicolor underprint. Queen Elizabeth II at right. Parliament Building as seen from across the Ottawa River on back.

	VG	VF	UNC
a. Engraved back. signature Lawson-Bouey.	FV	1.00	5.00
b. Lithographed back. signature as a. Serial # prefix: *AFF-*.	FV	1.00	5.50
c. Signature Crow-Bouey.	FV	1.00	3.50

Note: Two formats of uncut 40-note sheets of #85b were sold to collectors in 1988 (BABN) and again in 1989 (CBNC). BABN format: 5x8 notes regular serial # prefixes *BFD, BFK, BFL* and replacement prefix *BAX*. CBNC format: 4x10 notes regular serial # prefixes *ECP, ECR, ECV, ECW* and replacement prefix *EAX*.

86 2 Dollars

1974. Red-brown on multicolor underprint. Queen Elizabeth II at right. Inuits preparing for hunt on back.

	VG	VF	UNC
a. Signature Lawson-Bouey.	FV	2.25	12.50
b. Signature Crow-Bouey.	FV	2.25	10.00

Note: Two formats of uncut 40-note sheets of #86b were sold to collectors in 1995-96. BABN format: 5x8 notes. CBNC format: 4x10 notes.

87 5 Dollars

1972. Blue on multicolor underprint. Sir Wilfred Laurier at right. Serial # on face. Salmon fishing boat at Vancouver Island on back.

	VG	VF	UNC
a. Signature Bouey-Rasminsky.	FV	6.00	37.50
b. Signature Lawson-Bouey.	FV	6.00	35.00

88 10 Dollars

1971. Purple on multicolor underprint. Sir John A. MacDonald at right. Oil refinery at Sarnia, Ontario, on back.

	VG	VF	UNC
a. Signature Beattie-Rasminsky.	FV	12.50	60.00
b. Signature Bouey-Rasminsky.	FV	15.00	75.00
c. Signature Lawson-Bouey.	FV	FV	45.00
d. Signature Crow-Bouey.	FV	FV	40.00
e. Signature Thiessen-Crow.	FV	FV	42.50

89 20 Dollars

1969. Green on multicolor underprint. Arms at left. Queen Elizabeth II at right. Serial # on face. Alberta's Lake Moraine and Rocky Mountains on back.

	VG	VF	UNC
a. Signature Beattie-Rasminsky.	FV	25.00	95.00
b. Signature Lawson-Bouey.	FV	22.50	90.00

90 **50 Dollars**

1975. Red on multicolor underprint. William Lyon MacKenzie King at right. Mounted Police in *Dome* formation (from their Musical Ride program) on back.

	VG	VF	UNC
a. Signature Lawson-Bouey.	FV	65.00	220.
b. Signature Crow-Bouey.	FV	55.00	185.

91 **100 Dollars**

1975. Brown on multicolor underprint. Sir Robert Borden at right. Lunenburg, Nova Scotia harbor scene on back.

	VG	VF	UNC
a. Signature Lawson-Bouey.	FV	105.	250.
b. Signature Crow-Bouey.	FV	100.	225.

1979 Issue

#92 and 93 arms at l.

92 **5 Dollars**

1979. Blue on multicolor underprint. Similar to #87, but different design element at upper center. Serial # on back.

	VG	VF	UNC
a. Signature Lawson-Bouey.	FV	FV	30.00
b. Signature Crow-Bouey.	FV	FV	35.00

93 **20 Dollars**

1979. Deep olive-green on multicolor underprint. Similar to #89, but different guilloches on face. Serial # on back.

	VG	VF	UNC
a. Signature Lawson-Bouey.	FV	FV	75.00
b. Signature Crow-Bouey.	FV	FV	70.00
c. Signature Thiessen-Crow.	FV	FV	55.00

1986-91 Issue

#94-100 arms at upper l. ctr. Replacement notes: Third letter of serial # prefix is *X*.

94 **2 Dollars**

1986. Brown on multicolor underprint. Queen Elizabeth II, Parliament building at right. Pair of robins on back.

	VG	VF	UNC
a. Signature Crow-Bouey.	FV	FV	8.50
b. Signature Thiessen-Crow.	FV	FV	3.50
c. Signature Bonin-Thiessen.	FV	FV	3.50

95 **5 Dollars**

1986. Blue-gray on multicolor underprint. Sir Wilfrid Laurier, Parliament buildings at right. Kingfisher on back.

	VG	VF	UNC
a1. Signature Crow-Bouey. with yellow plate # on back.	FV	5.50	30.00
a2. Signature Crow-Bouey. with blue plate # on back.	FV	FV	25.00
b. Signature Thiessen-Crow.	FV	FV	12.00
c. Signature Bonin-Thiessen.	FV	FV	10.00
d. Signature Knight-Thiessen.	FV	FV	9.00
e. Signature Knight-Dodge.	FV	FV	8.50

96 **10 Dollars**

1989. Purple on multicolor underprint. Sir John A. Macdonald, Parliament buildings at right. Osprey in flight on back.

	VG	VF	UNC
a. Signature Thiessen-Crow.	FV	FV	17.00
b. Signature Bonin-Thiessen.	FV	FV	16.00
c. Signature Knight-Thiessen.	FV	FV	15.00

97 **20 Dollars**

1991. Deep olive-green and olive-green on multicolor underprint. Green foil optical device with denomination at upper left. Queen Elizabeth II, Parliament library at right. Common loon on back.

	VG	VF	UNC
a. Signature Thiessen-Crow.	FV	FV	35.00
b. Signature Bonin-Thiessen.	FV	FV	32.50
c. Signature Knight-Thiessen.	FV	FV	30.00
d. Signature Knight-Dodge.	FV	FV	30.00

Note: The letter "I" in prefix exists serif and sans-serif.

98	50 Dollars	VG	VF	UNC
	1988. Red on multicolor underprint. William Lyon MacKenzie King, Parliament building at right, gold optical device with denomination at upper left. Snowy owl on back.			
	a. Signature Thiessen-Crow.	FV	FV	95.00
	b. Signature Bonin-Thiessen.	FV	FV	90.00
	c. Signature Knight-Thiessen.	FV	FV	85.00
	d. Signature Knight-Dodge.	FV	FV	75.00

99	100 Dollars	VG	VF	UNC
	1988. Dark brown on multicolor underprint. Sir Robert Bordon, Parliament building at right, green optical device with denomination at upper left. Canadian geese on back.			
	a. Signature Thiessen-Crow.	FV	FV	175.
	b. Signature Bonin-Thiessen.	FV	FV	200.
	c. Signature Knight-Thiessen.	FV	FV	150.
	d. Signature Knight-Dodge.	FV	FV	135.

100	1000 Dollars	VG	VF	UNC
	1988. Pink on multicolor underprint. Queen Elizabeth II, Parliament library at right. Optical device with denomination at upper left. Pine grosbeak pair on branch at right on back.			
	a. Signature Thiessen-Crow.	FV	FV	1500.
	b. Signature Bonin-Thiessen.	FV	FV	1350.

NOTICE

Readers with unlisted dates, signature varieties, etc. are invited to submit photocopies of their notes to: Standard Catalog of World Paper Money, 700 East State St. Iola, WI 54990-0001, E-Mail: george.cuhaj@fwpubs.com.

2001-03 Issue

#101-105 redesigned portraits, new back designs. The "Canadian Journey" series.

101	5 Dollars	VG	VF	UNC
	2002. Blue and tan-yellow. Sir Wilfrid Laurier at left, west block of Parliament at center. Winter sports - children skating, tobogganing, and playing hockey on back. Signature Knight-Dodge.	FV	FV	8.50
101A	5 Dollars			
	2006. Blue and tan-yellow. Sir Wilfrid Lauier at left, west block of Parliament at center. Winter sports - children skating, tobogganing, and playing hocket on back. Holographic strip at left. Sign. Jenkens-Dodge.	FV	FV	7.50

102	10 Dollars	VG	VF	UNC
	2001. Purple and tan on multicolor. Sir John A. Macdonald at left, Parliament Library at center. Veteran and children at memorial at right, peacekeeper with binoculars at center, poppies, doves and and the first verse of *In Flanders Fields* at right on back.			
	a. Signature Knight-Thiessen.	FV	FV	13.50
	b. Signature Knight-Dodge.	FV	FV	12.50
102A	10 Dollars			
	2005. Purple and tan on multicolor underprint. As #102 but with holographic strip at left. Signature Jenkins-Dodge.	FV	FV	12.00

103	20 Dollars	VG	VF	UNC
	2004. Green and tan on multicolor underprint. Queen Elizabeth II at left. Bill Reid sculpture, westcoast native art theme on back. Signature Jenkins-Dodge.	FV	FV	25.00
104	50 Dollars			
	2004. Red-orange and tan on multicolor underprint. William Lyon MacKenzie King at left. Accomplishments of the Famous Five and Thérèse Casgrain on back. Signature Jenkins-Dodge.	FV	FV	65.00

		VG	VF	UNC
105	**100 Dollars** 2004. Brown and green on multicolor underprint. Sir Robert Borden at right. Historic and satellite maps of Canada on back. Signature Jenkins-Dodge.	FV	FV	120.

CAPE VERDE

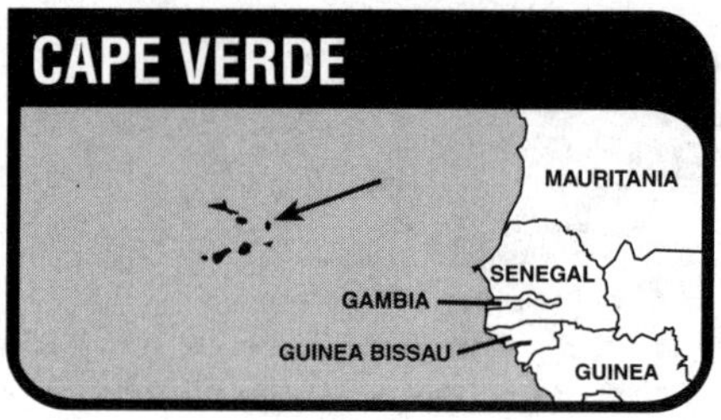

The Republic of Cape Verde, is located in the Atlantic Ocean, about 370 miles (595 km.) west of Dakar, Senegal off the coast of Africa. The 14-island republic has an area of 1,557 sq. mi. (4,033 sq. km.) and a population of 437,000. Capital: Praia. The refueling of ships and aircraft is the chief economic function of the country. Fishing is important and agriculture is widely practiced, but the Cape Verdes are not self-sufficient in food. Fish products, salt, bananas, coffee, peanuts and shellfish are exported.

The date of discovery of the islands is uncertain. Possibly they were visited by Venetian Captain Alvise Cadamosto in 1456. Portuguese navigator Diogo Gomes claimed them for Portugal in May of 1460. Settlement began two years later. The early importance and wealth of the islands, which caused them to be attacked by Sir Francis Drake and the Dutch, resulted from the monopoly of the Guinea slave trade granted the inhabitants in 1466. Poverty and famine occasioned by frequent periods of severe drought have marked the history of the country since abolition of the slave trade in 1876.

After 500 years of Portuguese rule, the Cape Verdes became independent on July 5, 1975.

RULERS:

Portuguese to 1975

MONETARY SYSTEM:

1 Mil Reis = 1000 Reis
1 Escudo = 100 Centavos, 1911-

PORTUGUESE ADMINISTRATION

BANCO NACIONAL ULTRAMARINO

CABO VERDE

1971; 1972 ISSUE

Decreto Lei 39221 and 44891

#52 and 53 portr. S. Pinto at r., bank seal at l., arms at lower ctr. Allegorical woman w/ships on back. W/security thread. Sign. titles: *ADMINISTRADOR* and *VICE-GOVERNADOR*.

		VG	VF	UNC
52	**20 Escudos** 4.4.1972. Green on multicolor underprint. Two signature varieties.			
	a. Issued note.	12.00	45.00	125.
	s. Specimen.	—	—	150.

		VG	VF	UNC
53	**50 Escudos** 4.4.1972. Blue on multicolor underprint.			
	a. Issued note.	20.00	75.00	200.
	s. Specimen.	—	—	225.

53A	500 Escudos	VG	VF	UNC
	16.6.1971; 29.6.1971. Olive-green on multicolor underprint. Infante D. Henrique at right.			
	a. Issued note.	35.00	135.	350.
	s. Specimen.	—	—	375.
	ct. Color trial. Blue on multicolor underprint.	—	—	450.

REPUBLIC

BANCO DE CABO VERDE

1977 ISSUE

#54-56 A. Cabral w/native hat at r. and as wmk. Printer: BWC.

54	100 Escudos	VG	VF	UNC
	20.1.1977. Red and multicolor. Bow and musical instruments at left. Mountain at left center on back.			
	a. Issued note.	1.25	2.50	15.00
	s. Specimen.	—	—	75.00

55	500 Escudos	VG	VF	UNC
	20.1.1977. Blue and multicolor. Shark at left. Harbor at Praia on back.			
	a. Issued note.	6.00	12.50	25.00
	s. Specimen.	—	—	100.

56	1000 Escudos	VG	VF	UNC
	20.1.1977. Brown and multicolor. Electrical appliance at left. Workers at quarry at left center, banana stalk at right on back.			
	a. Issued note.	12.50	25.00	50.00
	s. Specimen.	—	—	135.

1989 ISSUE

#57-61 A. Cabral at r. and as wmk. Serial # black at l., red at r. Printer: TDLR.

57	100 Escudos	VG	VF	UNC
	20.1.1989. Red and dark purple on multicolor underprint. Festival at left center on back.			
	a. Issued note.	FV	FV	5.00
	s. Specimen.	—	—	30.00

58	200 Escudos	VG	VF	UNC
	20.1.1989. Green and black on multicolor underprint. Modern airport collage in vertical format on back.			
	a. Issued note.	FV	FV	8.00
	s. Specimen.	—	—	35.00

		VG	VF	UNC
59	**500 Escudos** 20.1.1989. Blue on multicolor underprint. Shipyard on back.			
	a. Issued note.	FV	FV	17.50
	s. Specimen.	—	—	40.00

		VG	VF	UNC
60	**1000 Escudos** 20.1.1989. Brown and red-brown on multicolor underprint. Insects at left center on back.			
	a. Issued note.	FV	FV	35.00
	s. Specimen.	—	—	50.00

		VG	VF	UNC
61	**2500 Escudos** 20.1.1989. Violet on multicolor underprint. Palace of National Assembly on back.			
	a. Issued note.	FV	FV	67.50
	s. Specimen.	—	—	75.00

1992 ISSUE

#63-64 wmk: A. Cabral. Printer: TDLR.

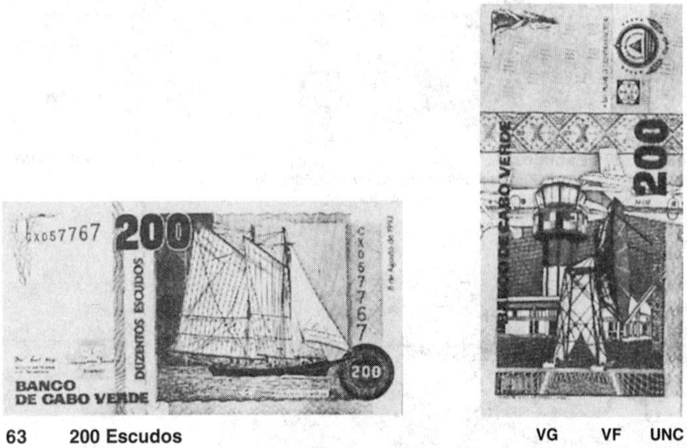

		VG	VF	UNC
63	**200 Escudos** 8.8.1992. Black and blue-green on multicolor underprint. Sailing ship *Ernestina* at center right. Back like #58.	FV	FV	6.00

		VG	VF	UNC
64	**500 Escudos** 23.4.1992. Purple, blue and dark brown on multicolor underprint. Dr. B. Lopes da Silva at center right. Back like #59.	FV	FV	12.50

		VG	VF	UNC
65	**1000 Escudos** 5.6.1992. Dark brown, red-orange and purple on multicolor underprint. Cape Verde warbler at center right. Insects at left center on back.	FV	FV	22.50

1999-2000 ISSUE

		VG	VF	UNC
66	**2000 Escudos** 1.7.1999. Brown, green, red and multicolor. Eugenio Tavares at bottom. Cardeal flower and stanza from poem *Morna de Aguada* on back.	FV	FV	30.00

		VG	VF	UNC
67	**5000 Escudos** 5.7.2000. Orange, red and multicolor. Woman carrying stones. Fortress details on back.	FV	FV	65.00

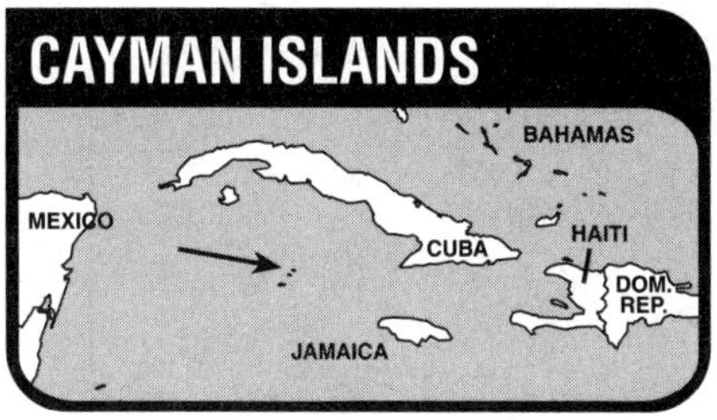

The Cayman Islands, a British Crown Colony situated about 180 miles (290 km.) northwest of Jamaica, consists of three islands: Grand Cayman, Little Cayman and Cayman Brac. The islands have an area of 102 sq. mi. (259 sq. km.) and a population of 41,000. Capital: Georgetown. Seafaring, commerce, banking and tourism are the principal industries. Rope, turtle shells and shark skins are exported.

The islands were discovered by Columbus in 1503, and were named by him, Tortugas (Spanish for "turtles") because of the great number of turtles in the nearby waters. The Cayman Islands were colonized from Jamaica by the British and remained dependencies of Jamaica until 1959, when they became a unit territory within the West Indies Federation. They became a separate colony when the Federation was dissolved in 1962.

RULERS:

British

MONETARY SYSTEM:

1 Dollar = 100 Cents

BRITISH ADMINISTRATION

CAYMAN ISLANDS CURRENCY BOARD

1971 CURRENCY LAW

#1-4 arms at upper ctr., Qn. Elizabeth II at r. Wmk: Tortoise. Printer: TDLR. Replacement notes: Serial # prefix *Z/1*.

1	**1 Dollar**	VG	VF	UNC
	L.1971 (1972). Blue on multicolor underprint. Fish, coral at center on back.			
	a. Issued note.	2.00	3.50	20.00
	r. Replacement. Serial # Prefix *Z/1*.	—	—	75.00
	s. Specimen.	—	—	—

2	**5 Dollars**	VG	VF	UNC
	L.1971 (1972). Green on multicolor underprint. Sailboat at center on back.			
	a. Issued note.	9.00	11.00	65.00
	r. Replacement. Serial # prefix *Z/l*.	—	—	150.
	s. Specimen.	—	—	—

3	**10 Dollars**	VG	VF	UNC
	L.1971 (1972). Red on multicolor underprint. Beach scene at center on back.	15.00	30.00	220.

4	**25 Dollars**	VG	VF	UNC
	L.1971 (1972). Brown on multicolor underprint. Compass and map at center on back.	40.00	125.	675.

1974 CURRENCY LAW

#5-11 arms at upper ctr., Qn. Elizabeth II at r. Wmk: Tortoise. Printer: TDLR. Replacement notes: Serial # prefix *Z/1*.

5	**1 Dollar**	VG	VF	UNC
	L.1974 (1985). Blue on multicolor underprint. Like #1.			
	a. Signature as #1 illustration.	2.00	3.00	17.50
	b. Signature Jefferson.	1.50	2.00	13.00
	r1. Replacement. As a. Serial # prefix *Z/1*.	—	—	70.00
	r2. Replacement. As b. Serial # prefix *Z/1*.	—	—	65.00
	s. Specimen.	—	—	—

6	**5 Dollars**	VG	VF	UNC
	L.1974. Green on multicolor underprint. Like #2.			
	a. Issued note.	9.00	12.00	40.00
	r. Replacement. Serial # prefix *Z/1*.	—	—	50.00
	s. Specimen.	—	—	—

7	**10 Dollars**	VG	VF	UNC
	L.1974. Red on multicolor underprint. Like #3.			
	a. Issued note.	FV	50.00	165.
	r. Replacement. Serial # prefix *Z/1*.	—	—	350.
	s. Specimen.	—	—	—

8	**25 Dollars**	VG	VF	UNC
	L.1974. Brown on multicolor underprint. Like #4.			
	a. Issued note.	FV	35.00	100.
	r. Replacement. Serial # prefix *Z/1*.	—	—	150.
	s. Specimen.	—	—	—

9 **40 Dollars**

L.1974 (1981). Purple on multicolor underprint. Pirates Week Festival (crowd on beach) at center on back.

	VG	VF	UNC
a. Issued note.	FV	60.00	125.
r. Replacement. Serial # prefix *Z/1.*	FV	65.00	150.

10 **50 Dollars**

L.1974 (1987). Blue on multicolor underprint. Government house at center on back.

	VG	VF	UNC
a. Issued note.	FV	110.	195.
r. Replacement. Serial # prefix *Z/1.*	100.	250.	650.

11 **100 Dollars**	VG	VF	UNC
L.1974 (1982). Deep orange on multicolor underprint. Seacoast view of George Town at center on back.	125.	175.	320.

1991 Issue

#12-15 arms at upper ctr., Qn. Elizabeth II at r., treasure chest at lower l. ctr. Red coral at l. on back. Wmk: Tortoise. Printer: TDLR. Replacement notes: Serial # prefix *Z/1.*

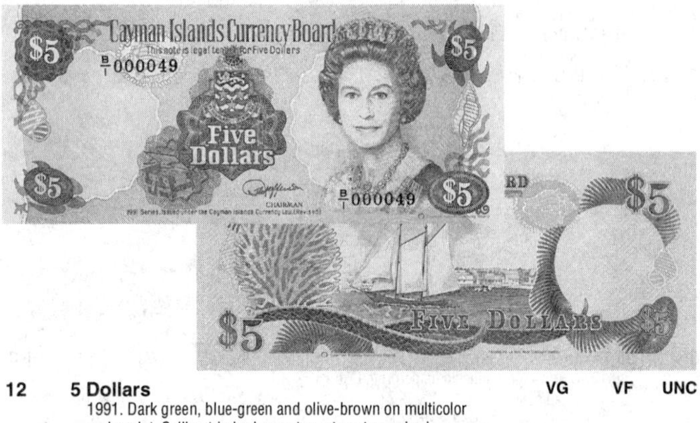

12 **5 Dollars**

1991. Dark green, blue-green and olive-brown on multicolor underprint. Sailboat in harbor waters at center on back.

	VG	VF	UNC
a. Issued note.	6.00	10.00	35.00
r. Replacement. Serial # prefix *Z/1.*	20.00	35.00	70.00

13 **10 Dollars**	VG	VF	UNC
1991. Red and purple on multicolor underprint. Open chest, palm tree along coastline at center on back. (2 varieties in color of conch shell at upper center on back.)	FV	FV	100.

14 **25 Dollars**	VG	VF	UNC
1991. Deep brown, tan and orange on multicolor underprint. Island outlines and compass at center on back.	FV	FV	75.00

15 **100 Dollars**	VG	VF	UNC
1991. Orange and dark brown on multicolor underprint. Harbor view at center on back.	FV	FV	250.

1996 Issue

#16-20 Qn. Elizabeth at r. Wmk: Tortoise. Printer: TDLR.

16 **1 Dollar**	VG	VF	UNC
1996. Purple, orange and deep blue on multicolor underprint. Back similar to #1.	FV	3.00	12.00

17 **5 Dollars**

1996. Dark green, blue-green and olive-brown on multicolor underprint. Back similar to #12.

	VG	VF	UNC
	FV	FV	30.00

18 **10 Dollars**

1996. Red and purple on multicolor underprint. Back similar to #13.

	VG	VF	UNC
a. Serial # prefix *B/I.*	FV	FV	35.00
b. Serial # prefix *X/I.* Experimental paper. (100,000 pieces issued).	150.	750.	—

19 **25 Dollars**

1996. Deep brown, tan and orange on multicolor underprint. Back similar to #14.

	VG	VF	UNC
	FV	FV	75.00

20 **100 Dollars**

1996. Orange and brown on multicolor underprint. Back similar to #15.

	VG	VF	UNC
	FV	150.	225.

CAYMAN ISLANDS MONETARY AUTHORITY

1998 ISSUE; 1996 LAW

#21-25 Qn. Elizabeth at r. Segmented foil over security thread. Wmk: Tortoise. Printer: (T)DLR.

21 **1 Dollar**

1998. Purple, orange and deep blue on multicolor underprint. Like #16.

	VG	VF	UNC
a. Issued note.	FV	3.50	9.50
r. Replacement. Serial # prefix *Z/1.*	7.50	15.00	60.00

22 **5 Dollars**

1998. Olive-green and blue-green on multicolor underprint. Like #17.

	VG	VF	UNC
a. Issued note.	FV	12.00	22.50
r. Replacement. Serial # prefix *Z/I*	12.50	25.00	75.00

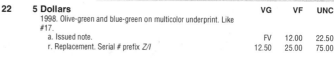

23 **10 Dollars**

1998. Red and purple on multicolor underprint. Like #18.

	VG	VF	UNC
	FV	22.50	40.00

24 **25 Dollars**

1998. Deep brown, tan and orange on multicolor underprint. Like #19.

	VG	VF	UNC
	FV	FV	75.00

25	100 Dollars	VG	VF	UNC
	1998. Orange and brown on multicolor underprint. Like #20.	FV	FV	210.

2001 Issue; 2001 Law Revision

#26-29 Qn. Elizabeth at r. Segmented full over security thread. Wmk: Tortoise and CIMA. Printer: (T)DLR.

26	1 Dollar	VG	VF	UNC
	2001. Multicolor. Like #21.			
	a. Issued note.	FV	FV	7.50
	r. Replacement. Serial # prefix *Z/1*.	FV	7.50	55.00
	s. Specimen.	—	—	—

27	5 Dollars	VG	VF	UNC
	2001. Multicolor. Like #22.			
	a. Issued note.	FV	FV	17.50
	s. Specimen.	—	—	—

28	10 Dollars	VG	VF	UNC
	2001. Multicolor. Like #23.			
	a. Issued note.	FV	FV	30.00
	s. Specimen.	—	—	—

29	50 Dollars	VG	VF	UNC
	2001. Multicolor.			
	a. Issued note.	FV	FV	125.
	r. Replacement. Serial # prefix *Z/1*.	FV	100.	295.
	s. Specimen.	—	—	—

2003 Commemorative Issue; 2002 Law Revision

500th Anniversary of discovery.

30	1 Dollar	VG	VF	UNC
	2003. Multicolor.			
	a. Issued note.	FV	FV	7.50
	b. Issued note in presentation folder (4000 made).	—	—	50.00
	s. Specimen.	—	—	—

2003 Issue; 2002 Law Revision

31	25 Dollars	VG	VF	UNC
	2003. Multicolor.			
	a. Issued note.	FV	FV	60.00
	s. Specimen.	—	—	—

		VG	VF	UNC
32	**50 Dollars**			
	2003. Multicolor.			
	a. 2003. Serial # prefix *C1.*	FV	FV	120.
	b. 2003 (2007). Serial # prefix *C2.*	FV	FV	110.
	s. Specimen.	—	—	—

2005-2006 Issue; 2004 Law Revision

#33-37 Sign. titles: Financial Secretary and Managing Director. Wmk. in each corner.

		VG	VF	UNC
33	**1 Dollar**			
	2006. Multicolor.			
	a. Issued note.	FV	FV	4.00
	s. Specimen.	—	—	—
34	**5 Dollars**			
	2006. Multicolor.			
	a. Issued note.	FV	FV	12.50
	s. Specimen.	—	—	—
35	**10 Dollars**			
	2005. Multicolor.			
	a. Issued note.	FV	FV	25.00
	r. Replacement note. Serial # prefix *Z/1.*	FV	50.00	125.
	s. Specimen.	—	—	—

		VG	VF	UNC
36	**25 Dollars**			
	2006. Multicolor.			
	a. Issued note.	FV	FV	55.00
	s. Specimen.	—	—	—

NOTICE

Readers with unlisted dates, signature varieties, etc. are invited to submit photocopies of their notes to: Standard Catalog of World Paper Money, 700 East State St. Iola, WI 54990-0001, E-Mail: george.cuhaj@fwpubs.com.

		VG	VF	UNC
37	**100 Dollars**			
	2006. Multicolor.			
	a. Issued note.	FV	FV	180.
	s. Specimen.	—	—	—

Collector Series

Cayman Islands Currency Board

1974 Currency Law Issue

		Issue Price	Mkt. Value
CS1	***L.1974.* 1-100 Dollars**		
	#5-11 ovpt: *SPECIMEN.* (300 sets.)	—	750.

1991 Issue

		Issue Price	Mkt. Value
CS2	**1991 5-100 Dollars**		
	#12-15 ovpt: *SPECIMEN.* (300 sets.)	—	400.

1996 Issue

		Issue Price	Mkt. Value
CS3	**1996 1-100 Dollars**		
	#16-20 ovpt: *SPECIMEN.* (300 sets.)	—	375.

1998 Issue

		Issue Price	Mkt. Value
CS4	**1998 1-100 Dollars**		
	#21-25 ovpt: *SPECIMEN.* (Only 100 complete sets exist.)	—	675.

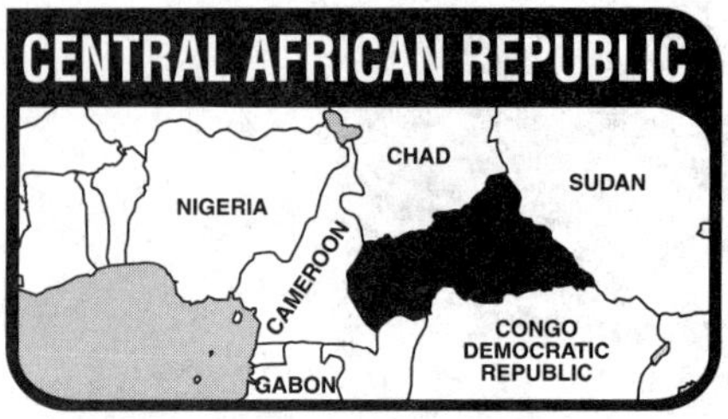

The Central African Republic, a landlocked country in Central Africa, bounded by Chad on the north, Cameroon on the west, Democratice Republic of the Congo and the Republic of the Congo on the south, and The Sudan on the east, has an area of 240,535 sq. mi. (622,984 sq. km.) and a population of 3.64 million. Capital: Bangui. Deposits of uranium, iron ore, manganese and copper remain to be developed. Diamonds, cotton, timber and coffee are exported.

The area that is now the Central African Republic was constituted as the French territory of Ubangi-Shari in 1894. It was united with Chad in 1905 and joined with Middle Congo and Gabon in 1910, becoming one of the four territories of French Equatorial Africa. Upon dissolution of the federation on Dec. 1, 1958, the constituent territories became full autonomous members of the French Community. Ubangi-Shari proclaimed its complete independence as the Central African Republic on Aug. 13, 1960.

On Jan. 1, 1966, Col. Jean-Bedel Bokassa, Chief of Staff of the Armed Forces, overthrew the government of President David Dacko and assumed power as president of the republic. President Bokassa abolished the constitution of 1959 and dissolved the National Assembly. In 1972 the Congress of the sole political party appointed Bokassa president for life. The republic became a constitutional monarchy on Dec. 4, 1976; President Bokassa was named Emperor Bokassa I. Bokassa was ousted as Central African emperor in a bloodless takeover of the government led by former president David Dacko on Sept. 20, 1979, and the African nation was proclaimed once again a republic. In 1996-97 a mutiny of army personnel created great tensions. It is a member of the "Union Monetaire des Etats de l'Afrique Centrale."

See also Central African States, Equatorial African States, and French African States.

RULERS:

Emperor J. B. Bokassa I, 1976-79

MONETARY SYSTEM:

1 Franc = 100 Centimes

SIGNATURE VARIETIES:

Refer to introduction to Central African States.

RÉPUBLIQUE CENTRAFRICAINE

BANQUE DES ÉTATS DE L'AFRIQUE CENTRALE

1974-76 ND ISSUE

#1-4 Pres. J. B. Bokassa at r. Wmk: Antelope's head.

		VG	VF	UNC
1	**500 Francs** ND (1974). Lilac-brown and multicolor. Landscape at center. Mask at left, students and chemical testing at center, statue at right on back. Signature 6.	10.00	40.00	175.

		VG	VF	UNC
2	**1000 Francs** ND (1974). Blue and multicolor. Rhinoceros at left, water buffalo at center. Mask at left, trains, planes and bridge at center, statue at right on back. Signature 6.	20.00	60.00	250.

		VG	VF	UNC
3	**5000 Francs** ND (1974). Brown and multicolor. Field workers hoeing at left, combine at center. Mask at left, buildings at center, statue at right on back.			
	a. Signature 4.	35.00	150.	600.
	b. Signature 6.	30.00	125.	550.

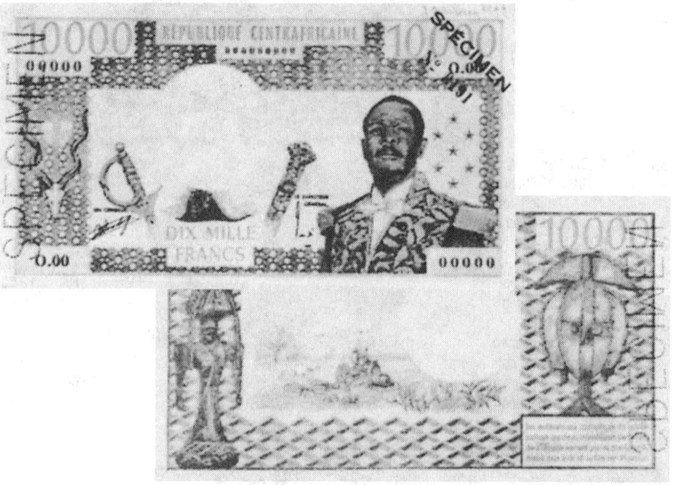

		VG	VF	UNC
4	**10,000 Francs** ND (1976). Multicolor. Sword hilts at left and center. Mask at left, tractor cultivating at center, statue at right on back. Signature 6.	75.00	300.	900.

EMPIRE CENTRAFRICAIN

BANQUE DES ÉTATS DE L'AFRIQUE CENTRALE

1978-79 ISSUE

#5-8 Emp. J. B. Bokassa I at r. Wmk: Antelope's head.

		VG	VF	UNC
5	**500 Francs** 1.4.1978. Similar to #1. Specimen.	—	—	2000.

		VG	VF	UNC
6	**1000 Francs** 1.4.1978. Similar to #2. Signature 9.	50.00	200.	800.

		VG	VF	UNC
7	**5000 Francs** ND (1979). Similar to #3. Signature 9.	50.00	225.	900.

		VG	VF	UNC
8	**10,000 Francs** ND (1978). Similar to #4. Signature 6.	50.00	200.	800.

RÉPUBLIQUE CENTRAFRICAINE

BANQUE DES ÉTATS DE L'AFRIQUE CENTRALE

1980 ISSUE

		VG	VF	UNC
9	**500 Francs** 1.1.1980; 1.7.1980; 1.6.1981. Red and multicolor. Woman weaving basket at right. Back like #1. Lithographed. Signature 9.	1.50	4.00	15.00

		VG	VF	UNC
10	**1000 Francs** 1.1.1980; 1.7.1980; 1.6.1981; 1.1.1982; 1.6.1984. Blue and multicolor. Butterfly at left, waterfall at center, water buffalo at right. Back like #2. Lithographed. Signature 9.	4.50	8.00	25.00

		VG	VF	UNC
11	**5000 Francs** 1.1.1980. Brown and multicolor. Girl at left, village scene at center. Carving at left, airplane, train crossing bridge and tractor hauling logs at center, man smoking a pipe at right on back. Similar to Equatorial African States #6. Signature 9.	12.50	50.00	250.

1983-84 ND ISSUE

		VG	VF	UNC
12	**5000 Francs** ND (1984). Brown and multicolor. Mask at left, woman with bundle of fronds at right. Plowing and mine ore conveyor on back.			
	a. Signature 9.	12.50	22.50	80.00
	b. Signature 14.	10.00	20.00	70.00

		VG	VF	UNC
13	**10,000 Francs** ND (1983). Brown, green and multicolor. Stylized antelope heads at left, woman at right. Loading fruit onto truck at left on back. Signature 9.	22.50	35.00	100.

1985 ISSUE

#14-16 wmk: Carving (as printed on notes). Sign. 9.

		VG	VF	UNC
14	**500 Francs** 1985-91. Brown on orange and multicolor underprint. Carving and jug at center Man carving mark at left center on back.			
	a. 1.1.1985.	2.00	4.00	12.50
	b. 1.1.1986.	1.75	3.50	8.00
	c. 1.1.1987.	1.75	3.25	7.00
	d. 1.1.1989; 1.1.1991.	1.75	3.25	7.00

		VG	VF	UNC
15	**1000 Francs** 1.1.1985. Dull blue-violet on multicolor underprint. Carving at left, map at center, Gen. Kolingba at right. Incomplete map of Chad at top center. Elephant at left, animals at center, carving at right on back.	3.50	7.50	20.00

1986 ISSUE

		VG	VF	UNC
16	**1000 Francs** 1.1.1986-1.1.1990. Dull blue-violet on multicolor underprint. Like #15 but complete outline map of Chad at top center. Watermark: Carving. Signature 9.	2.75	5.00	12.50

CENTRAL AFRICAN STATES

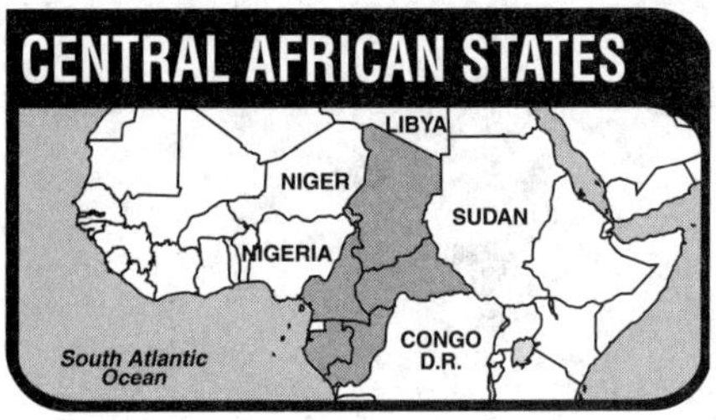

The Bank of the Central African States (BEAC) is a regional central bank for the monetary and customs union formed by Cameroun, Central African Republic, Chad, Congo (Brazzaville), Gabon, and (since 1985) Equatorial Guinea. It succeeded the Equatorial African States Bank in 1972-73 when the latter was reorganized and renamed to provide greater African control over its operations. The seat of the BEAC was transferred from Paris to Yaounde in 1977 and an African governor assumed responsibility for direction of the bank in 1978. The BEAC is a member of the franc zone with its currency denominated in CFA francs and pegged to the French franc at a rate of 50-1.

BEAC notes carry country names on the face and the central bank name on the back. The 1974-84 series had common back designs but were face-different. A new series begun in 1983-85 uses common designs also on the face except for some 1000 franc notes. The notes carry the signatures of *LE GOUVERNEUR (LE DIRECTEUR GENERAL* prior to 1-4-78) and *UN CENSEUR* (since 1972). Cameroun, Gabon, and France each appoint one censeur and one alternate. Cameroon and Congo notes carry the Cameroun censeur signature. Central African Republic, Equatorial Guinea, and Gabon notes carry the Gabon censeur signature. Chad notes have been divided between the two.

Prior to 1978, all BEAC notes were printed by the Bank of France. Since 1978, the 500 and 1000 franc notes have been printed by the private French firm F. C. Oberthur. The Bank of France notes are engraved and usually undated. The F. C. Oberthur notes are lithographed and most carry dates.

See individual member countries for additional note listings. Also see Equatorial African States and French Equatorial Africa.

CONTROL LETTER or CODE

Country	1993 Onward
Cameroun	E
Central African Republic	F
Chad	P
Congo	C
Equatorial Guinea	N
Gabon	L

SIGNATURE VARIETIES

1	Le Directeur-Genera Panouillot	Le President Gautier	
1a	Le Directeur-Genera Panouillot	Un Censeur Duouedi	
2	Le Directeur-Genera Panouillot	Un Censeur Koulla	1955-72
3	Le Directeur-Genera Joudiou	Un Censeur Koulla	1961-72
4	Le Directeur-Genera Joudiou	Un Censeur Renombo	1972-73
5	Le Directeur-Genera Joudiou	Un Censeur Ntang	1974-77
6	Le Directeur-Genera Joudiou	Un Censeur Ntoutoume	1974-78

SIGNATURE VARIETIES			
7	Le Directeur-Genera Joudiou	Un Censeur Beke Bihege	1977
8	Le Directeur-Genera Joudiou	Un Censeur Kamgu	1978
9	Le Gouvemeur Oye Mba	Un Censeur Ntoutoume	1979-90
10	Le Gouvemeur Oye Mba	Un Censeur Kamgueu	1978-86
11	Le Gouvemeur Oye Mba	Un Censeur Kamgueu	1978-80
12	Le Gouvemeur Oye Mba	Un Censeur Tchepannou	1981-89
13	Le Gouvemeur Oye Mba	Un Censeur Dang	1990
14	Le Gouvemeur Mamalepot	Un Censeur Ntoutoume	1991
15	Le Gouvemeur Mamalepot	Un Censeur Mebara	1991-93
16	Le Gouvemeur Mamalepot	Un Censeur Ognagna	1994-2000
17	Le Gouvemeur Mamalepot	Un Censeur Kaltjob	1994-98
18	Le Gouvemeur Mamalepot		1998-99
19	Le Gouvemeur Mamalepot		2000-2002
20	Le Gouvemeur Mamalepot		2000-2002

CENTRAL AFRICAN STATES

BANQUE DES ÉTATS DE L'AFRIQUE CENTRALE(1993-2001)

C FOR CONGO

1993; 1994 ISSUE

#101C-103C map of Central African States at lower l. ctr. First 2 digits of serial # are year of issue.

		VG	VF	UNC
101C	**500 Francs** (19)93-(20)00. Dark brown and gray on multicolor underprint. Shepherd at right and as watermark, zebus at center Baobab, antelopes and Kota mask on back.			
	a. Signature 15. (19)93.	FV	FV	5.00
	b. Signature 16. (19)94.	FV	FV	4.50
	c. Signature 16. (19)95.	FV	FV	4.50
	d. Signature 16. (19)97.	FV	FV	4.00
	e. Signature 16. (19)98.	FV	FV	4.00
	f. Signature 16. (19)99.	FV	FV	4.00
	g. Signature 19. (20)00.	FV	FV	4.00
	h. Signature 19. (20)02.	FV	FV	4.00
102C	**1000 Francs** (19)93-(20)00. Dark brown and red with black text on multicolor underprint. Young man at right and as watermark, harvesting coffee beans at center Forest harvesting, Okoume raft and Bakele wood mask on back.			
	a. Signature 15. (19)93.	FV	FV	9.00
	b. Signature 16. (19)94.	FV	FV	8.00
	c. Signature 16. (19)95.	FV	FV	8.00
	d. Signature 16. (19)97.	FV	FV	7.50
	e. Signature 16. (19)98.	FV	FV	7.50
	f. Signature 16. (19)99.	FV	FV	7.50
	g. Signature 19. (20)00.	FV	FV	7.00
	h. Signature 19. (20)02.	FV	FV	7.50
103C	**2000 Francs** (19)93-(19)99. Dark brown and green with black text on orange and multicolor underprint. Woman's head at right and as watermark surrounded by tropical fruit. Exchange of passengers and produce with ship at left center on back.			
	a. Signature 15. (19)93.	FV	FV	14.00
	b. Signature 16. (19)94.	FV	FV	12.50
	c. Signature 16. (19)95.	FV	FV	12.00
	d. Signature 16. (19)97.	FV	FV	12.00
	e. Signature 16. (19)98.	FV	FV	12.00
	f. Signature 16. (19)99.	FV	FV	12.00
	g. Signature 19. (20)00.	FV	FV	9.00
	h. Signature 19. (20)02.	FV	FV	10.00
104C	**5000 Francs** (19)94-(20)00. Dark brown, brown and blue with violet text on multicolor underprint. Laborer wearing hard hat at center right, riggers with well drill at right. Woman with head basket at lower left, gathering cotton at center on back.			
	a. Signature 16. (19)94.	FV	FV	27.50
	b. Signature 16. (19)95.	FV	FV	27.50
	c. Signature 16. (19)97.	FV	FV	25.00
	d. Signature 16. (19)98.	FV	FV	25.00
	e. Signature 16. (19)99.	FV	FV	25.00
	f. Signature 16. (20)00.	FV	FV	25.00
105C	**10,000 Francs** (19)94-(20)00. Dark brown and blue with blue-black text on multicolor underprint. Modern building at center, young woman at right. Fisherman, boats and villagers along shoreline at left center on back.			
	a. Signature 16. (19)94.	FV	FV	47.50
	b. Signature 16. (19)95.	FV	FV	45.00
	c. Signature 16. (19)97.	FV	FV	42.50
	d. Signature 16. (19)98.	FV	FV	45.00
	e. Signature 16. (19)99.	FV	FV	45.00
	f. Signature 19. (20)00.	FV	FV	45.00
	g. Signature 19. (20)02.	FV	FV	45.00

T FOR CONGO

2002 ISSUE

		VG	VF	UNC
106T	**500 Francs** 2002. Signature 19.	FV	FV	4.00
107T	**1000 Francs** 2002. Signature 19.	FV	FV	7.00
108T	**2000 Francs** 2002. Signature 19.	FV	FV	10.00

		VG	VF	UNC
109T	**5000 Francs** 2002. Signature 19.	FV	FV	25.00
110T	**10,000 Francs** 2002. Signature 19.	FV	FV	45.00

E FOR CAMEROUN

1993; 1994 ISSUE

201E 500 Francs
(19)93-(20)02. Dark brown and gray on multicolor underprint. Like #101C.

	VG	VF	UNC
a. Signature 15. (19)93.	FV	FV	5.00
b. Signature 17. (19)94.	FV	FV	4.50
c. Signature 17. (19)95.	FV	FV	4.50
d. Signature 17. (19)97.	FV	FV	4.50
e. Signature 18. (19)98.	FV	FV	4.50
f. Signature 18. (19)99.	FV	FV	4.50
g. Signature 20. (20)00.	FV	FV	4.00
h. Signature 20. (20)02.	FV	FV	4.00

202E 1000 Francs
(19)93-(20)02. Dark brown and red with black text on green and multicolor underprint. Like #102C.

	VG	VF	UNC
a. Signature 15. (19)93.	FV	FV	9.00
b. Signature 17. (19)94.	FV	FV	8.00
c. Signature 17. (19)95.	FV	FV	8.00
d. Signature 17. (19)97.	FV	FV	8.00
f. Signature 18. (19)99.	FV	FV	7.00
g. Signature 20. (20)00.	FV	FV	6.50
h. Signature 20. (20)02.	FV	FV	6.50

203E 2000 Francs
(19)93-(20)02). Dark brown and green with black text on orange and multicolor underprint. Like #103C.

	VG	VF	UNC
a. Signature 15. (19)93.	FV	FV	15.00
b. Signature 17. (19)94.	FV	FV	12.50
c. Signature 17. (19)95.	FV	FV	12.50
d. Signature 17. (19)97.	FV	FV	12.00
e. Signature 18. (19)98.	FV	FV	11.00
f. Signature 18. (19)99.	FV	FV	12.00
g. Signature 20. (20)00.	FV	FV	12.00
h. Signature 20. (20)02.	FV	FV	12.00

204E 5000 Francs
(19)94-(20)02). Dark brown, brown and blue with violet text on multicolor underprint. Like #104C.

	VG	VF	UNC
a. Signature 17. (19)94.	FV	FV	27.50
b. Signature 17. (19)95.	FV	FV	27.50
c. Signature 17. (19)97.	FV	FV	25.00
d. Signature 18. (19)98.	FV	FV	25.00
e. Signature 18. (19)99.	FV	FV	25.00
f. Signature 20. (20)00.	FV	FV	22.00
g. Signature 20. (20)02.	FV	FV	22.00

205E 10,000 Francs
(19)94-(20)00. Dark brown and blue with blue-black text on multicolor underprint. Like #105C.

	VG	VF	UNC
a. Signature 17. (19)94.	FV	FV	45.00
b. Signature 17. (19)95.	FV	FV	45.00
c. Signature 17. (19)97.	FV	FV	45.00
d. Signature 18. (19)98.	FV	FV	45.00
e. Signature 18. (19)99.	FV	FV	45.00
f. Signature 20. (20)00.	FV	FV	45.00
h. Signature 20. (20)02.	FV	FV	45.00

BANQUE DES ÉTATS DE L'AFRIQUE CENTRALE (2003-)

U FOR CAMEROUN

2002 ISSUE

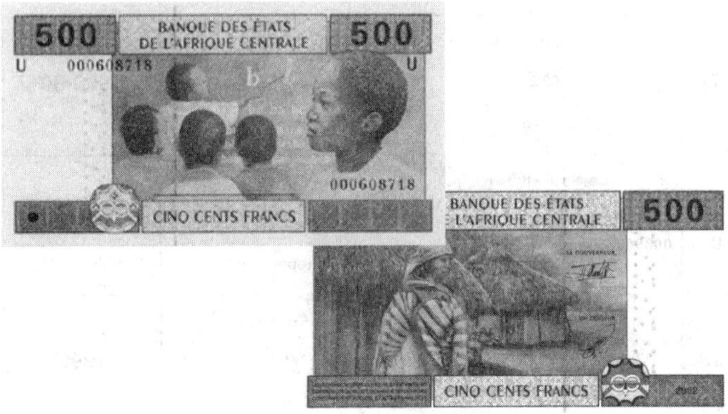

		VG	VF	UNC
206U	**500 Francs** 2002. Signature 20.	FV	FV	4.00

		VG	VF	UNC
207U	**1000 Francs** 2002. Signature 20.	FV	FV	7.00

		VG	VF	UNC
208U	**2000 Francs** 2002. Signature 20.	FV	FV	10.00

		VG	VF	UNC
209U	**5000 Francs**			
	2002. Signature 20.	FV	FV	25.00

		VG	VF	UNC
210U	**10,000 Francs**			
	2002. Signature 20.	FV	FV	45.00

F FOR CENTRAL AFRICAN REPUBLIC

1993; 1994 ISSUE

		VG	VF	UNC
301F	**500 Francs**			
	(19)93-(19)99. Dark brown and gray on multicolor underprint. Like #101C.			
	a. Signature 15. (19)93.	FV	FV	6.00
	b. Signature 16. (19)94.	FV	FV	5.00
	c. Signature 16. (19)95.	FV	FV	5.00
301F	**500 Francs**			
	d. Signature 16. (19)97.	FV	FV	4.00
	e. Signature 16. (19)98.	FV	FV	4.00
	f. Signature 16. (19)99.	FV	FV	4.00
	g. Signature 19. (20)00.	FV	FV	4.00
302F	**1000 Francs**			
	(19)93-(19)99. Dark brown and red with black text on green and multicolor underprint. Like #102C.			
	a. Signature 15. (19)93.	FV	FV	9.00
	b. Signature 16. (19)94.	FV	FV	8.50
	c. Signature 16. (19)95.	FV	FV	8.00
	d. Signature 16. (19)97.	FV	FV	7.50
	e. Signature 16. (19)98.	FV	FV	7.00
	f. Signature 16. (19)99.	FV	FV	7.00
303F	**2000 Francs**			
	(19)93-(19)99. Dark brown and green with black text on orange and multicolor underprint. Like #103C.			
	a. Signature 15. (19)93.	FV	FV	17.50
	b. Signature 16. (19)94.	FV	FV	15.00
	c. Signature 16. (19)95.	FV	FV	13.00
	d. Signature 16. (19)97.	FV	FV	13.00
	e. Signature 16. (19)98.	FV	FV	13.00
	f. Signature 16. (19)99.	FV	FV	12.00
304F	**5000 Francs**			
	(19)94-(19)99. Dark brown, brown and blue with violet text on multicolor underprint. Like #104C.			
	a. Signature 16. (19)94.	FV	FV	32.50
	b. Signature 16. (19)95.	FV	FV	30.00
	c. Signature 16. (19)97.	FV	FV	25.00
	d. Signature 16. (19)98.	FV	FV	25.00
	e. Signature 16. (19)99.	FV	FV	25.00
305F	**10,000 Francs**			
	(19)94-(19)99. Dark brown and blue with blue-black text on multicolor underprint. Like #105C.			

		VG	VF	UNC
305F	**10,000 Francs**			
	a. Signature 16. (19)94.	FV	FV	55.00
	b. Signature 16. (19)95.	FV	FV	50.00
	c. Signature 16. (19)97.	FV	FV	45.00
	d. Signature 16. (19)98.	FV	FV	45.00
	e. Signature 16. (19)99.	FV	FV	45.00
	f. Signature 19. (20)00.	FV	FV	45.00

M FOR CENTRAL AFRICAN REPUBLIC

2002 ISSUE

		VG	VF	UNC
306M	**500 Francs**			
	2002. Signature 19.	FV	FV	4.00
307M	**1000 Francs**			
	2002. Signature 19.	FV	FV	7.00
308M	**2000 Francs**			
	2002. Signature 19.	FV	FV	10.00
309M	**5000 Francs**			
	2002. Signature 19.	FV	FV	25.00
310M	**10,000 Francs**			
	2002. Signature 19.	FV	FV	45.00

L FOR GABON

1993; 1994 ISSUE

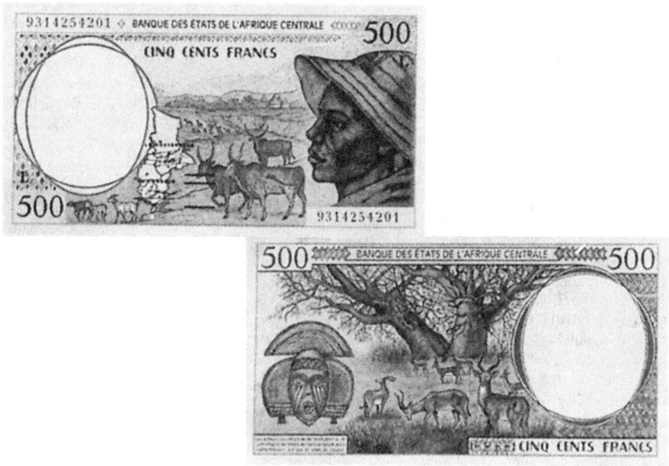

		VG	VF	UNC
401L	**500 Francs**			
	(19)93-(20)00. Dark brown and gray on multicolor underprint. Like #101C.			
	a. Signature 15. (19)93.	FV	FV	5.00
	b. Signature 16. (19)94.	FV	FV	4.50
	c. Signature 16. (19)95.	FV	FV	4.50
	g. Signature 16. (20)00.	FV	FV	4.50

		VG	VF	UNC
402L	**1000 Francs**			
	(19)93-(20)00. Dark brown and red with black text on green and multicolor underprint. Like #102C.			
	a. Signature 15. (19)93.	FV	FV	8.50
	b. Signature 16. (19)94.	FV	FV	8.00
	c. Signature 16. (19)95.	FV	FV	7.50
	d. Signature 16. (19)97.	FV	FV	7.50
	e. Signature 16. (19)98.	FV	FV	7.50
	f. Signature 16. (19)99.	FV	FV	7.50
	g. Signature 19. (20)00.	FV	FV	7.50
	h. Signature 19. (20)02.	FV	FV	7.50

No.	Denomination	VG	VF	UNC
403L	**2000 Francs** (19)93-(20)00. Dark brown and green with black text on orange and multicolor underprint. Like #103C.			
	a. Signature 15. (19)93.	FV	FV	15.00
	b. Signature 16. (19)94.	FV	FV	15.00
	c. Signature 16. (19)95.	FV	FV	15.00
	d. Signature 16. (19)97.	FV	FV	12.50
	e. Signature 16. (19)98.	FV	FV	12.50
	f. Signature 16. (19)99.	FV	FV	12.50
	g. Signature 19. (20)00.	FV	FV	12.50
	h. Signature 19. (20)02.	FV	FV	7.50
404L	**5000 Francs** (19)94-(20)00. Dark brown, brown and blue with violet text on multicolor underprint. Like #104C.			
	a. Signature 16. (19)94.	FV	FV	25.00
	b. Signature 16. (19)95.	FV	FV	25.00
	c. Signature 16. (19)97.	FV	FV	25.00
	d. Signature 16. (19)98.	FV	FV	25.00
	e. Signature 16. (19)99.	FV	FV	25.00
	f. Signature 16. (20)00.	FV	FV	25.00
405L	**10,000 Francs** (19)94-(20)00. Dark brown and blue with blue-black text on multicolor underprint. Like #105C.			
	a. Signature 16. (19)94.	FV	FV	52.50
	b. Signature 16. (19)95.	FV	FV	47.50
	c. Signature 16. (19)97.	FV	FV	45.00
	d. Signature 16. (19)98.	FV	FV	45.00
	e. Signature 16. (19)99.	FV	FV	45.00
	f. Signature 19. (20)00.	FV	FV	45.00
	g. Signature 19 (20)02.	FV	FV	45.00

A FOR GABON

2002 ISSUE

No.	Denomination	VG	VF	UNC
406A	**500 Francs** 2002. Signature 19.	FV	FV	4.00
407A	**1000 Francs** 2002. Signature 19.	FV	FV	7.00
408A	**2000 Francs** 2002. Signature 19.	FV	FV	10.00
409A	**5000 Francs** 2002. Signature 19.	FV	FV	25.00
410A	**10,000 Francs** 2002. Signature 19.	FV	FV	45.00

N FOR EQUATORIAL GUINEA

1993; 1994 ISSUE

No.	Denomination	VG	VF	UNC
501N	**500 Francs** (19)93-(20)00. Dark brown and gray on multicolor underprint. Like #101C.			
	a. Signature 15. (19)93.	FV	FV	6.00
	b. Signature 16. (19)94.	FV	FV	6.00
	c. Signature 16. (19)95.	FV	FV	6.00
	d. Signature 16. (19)97.	FV	FV	4.50
	f. Signature 16. (19)99.	FV	FV	4.50
	g. Signature 19. (20)00.	FV	FV	4.50
502N	**1000 Francs** (19)93-(20)00. Dark brown and red with black text on multicolor underprint. Like #102C.			
	a. Signature 15. (19)93.	FV	FV	9.00
	b. Signature 16. (19)94.	FV	FV	8.00
	c. Signature 16. (19)95.	FV	FV	7.50
	d. Signature 16. (19)97.	FV	FV	7.50
	e. Signature 16. (19)98.	FV	FV	7.50
	f. Signature 16. (19)99.	FV	FV	7.50
	g. Signature 16. (20)00.	FV	FV	7.00
	h. Signature 19. (20)00.	FV	FV	7.50

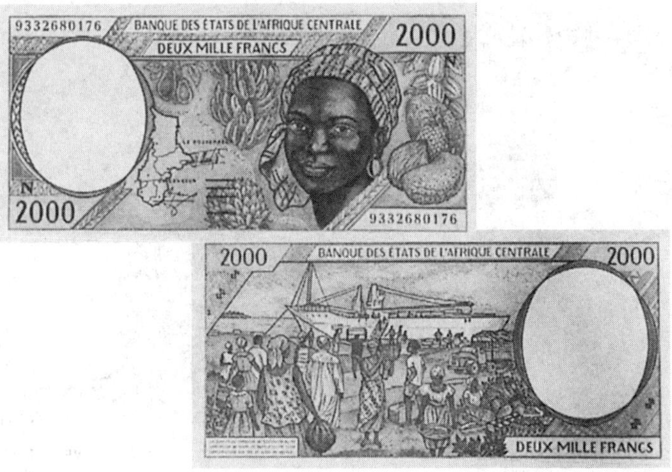

No.	Denomination	VG	VF	UNC
503N	**2000 Francs** (19)93-(20)00. Dark brown and green with black text on multicolor underprint. Like #103C.			
	a. Signature 15. (19)93.	FV	FV	15.00
	b. Signature 16. (19)94.	FV	FV	15.00
	c. Signature 16. (19)95.	FV	FV	15.00
	d. Signature 16. (19)97.	FV	FV	12.50
	g. Signature 19. (20)00.	FV	FV	12.50
504N	**5000 Francs** (19)94-(20)00. Dark brown, brown and blue with violet text on multicolor underprint. Like 104C.			
	a. Signature 16. (19)94.	FV	FV	25.00
	b. Signature 16. (19)95.	FV	FV	25.00
	d. Signature 16. (19)98.	FV	FV	25.00
	e. Signature 16. (19)99.	FV	FV	25.00
	f. Signature 19. (20)00.	FV	FV	25.00
505N	**10,000 Francs** (19)94-(20)00. Dark brown and blue with blue-black text on multicolor underprint. Like #105C.			
	a. Signature 16. (19)94.	FV	FV	47.50
	b. Signature 16. (19)95.	FV	FV	47.50
	c. Signature 16. (19)97.	FV	FV	45.00
	d. Signature 16. (19)98.	FV	FV	47.50
	e. Signature 16. (19)99.	FV	FV	45.00
	f. Signature 19. (20)00.	FV	FV	45.00

F FOR EQUATORIAL GUINEA

2002 ISSUE

No.	Denomination	VG	VF	UNC
506F	**500 Francs** 2002. Signature 19.	FV	FV	4.00
507F	**1000 Francs** 2002. Signature 19.	FV	FV	7.00
508F	**2000 Francs** 2002. Signature 19.	FV	FV	10.00
509F	**5000 Francs** 2002. Signature 19.	FV	FV	25.00
510F	**10,000 Francs** 2002. Signature 19.	FV	FV	45.00

P FOR CHAD

1993; 1994 ISSUE

No.	Denomination	VG	VF	UNC
601P	**500 Francs** (19)93-(20)00. Dark brown and gray on multicolor underprint. Like #101C.			
	a. Signature 15. (19)93.	FV	FV	6.00
	b. Signature 16. (19)94.	FV	FV	5.00
	c. Signature 16. (19)95.	FV	FV	5.00
	d. Signature 16. (19)97.	FV	FV	5.00
	e. Signature 16. (19)98.	FV	FV	4.50
	f. Signature 16. (19)99.	FV	FV	4.50
	g. Signature 19. (20)00.	FV	FV	4.50

602P 1000 Francs	VG	VF	UNC
(19)93-(20)00. Dark brown and red with black text on green and multicolor underprint. Like #102C.			
a. Signature 15. (19)93.	FV	FV	8.50
b. Signature 16. (19)94.	FV	FV	7.50
c. Signature 16. (19)95.	FV	FV	7.00
d. Signature 16. (19)97.	FV	FV	7.00
e. Signature 16. (19)98.	FV	FV	7.50
f. Signature 16. (19)99.	FV	FV	7.50
g. Signature 19. (20)00.	FV	FV	7.50

603P 2000 Francs	VG	VF	UNC
(19)93-(20)00. Dark brown and green with black text on orange and multicolor underprint. Like #103C.			
a. Signature 15. (19)93.	FV	FV	15.00
b. Signature 16. (19)94.	FV	FV	15.00
c. Signature 16. (19)95.	FV	FV	12.50
d. Signature 16. (19)97.	FV	FV	12.50
e. Signature 16. (19)98.	FV	FV	12.50
f. Signature 16. (19)99.	FV	FV	12.50

604P 5000 Francs	VG	VF	UNC
(19)94-(20)00. Dark brown, brown and blue with violet text on multicolor underprint. Like #104C.			
a. Signature 16. (19)94.	FV	FV	30.00
b. Signature 16. (19)95.	FV	FV	27.50
c. Signature 16. (19)97.	FV	FV	27.50
d. Signature 16. (19)98.	FV	FV	25.00
e. Signature 16. (19)99.	FV	FV	25.00
f. Signature 19. (20)00.	FV	FV	25.00

605P 10,000 Francs	VG	VF	UNC
(19)94-(20)00. Dark brown and blue with blue-black text on multicolor underprint. Like #105C.			
a. Signature 16. (19)94.	FV	FV	50.00
b. Signature 16. (19)95.	FV	FV	50.00
c. Signature 16. (19)97.	FV	FV	47.50
d. Signature 16. (19)98.	FV	FV	45.00
e. Signature 16. (19)99.	FV	FV	45.00
f. Signature 19. (20)00.	FV	FV	45.00

C FOR CHAD

2002 ISSUE

	VG	VF	UNC
606C 500 Francs 2002. Signature 19.	FV	FV	4.00
607C 1000 Francs 2002. Signature 19.	FV	FV	7.00
608C 2000 Francs 2002. Signature 19.	FV	FV	10.00
609C 5000 Francs 2002. Signature 19.	FV	FV	25.00
610C 10,000 Francs 2002. Signature 19.	FV	FV	45.00

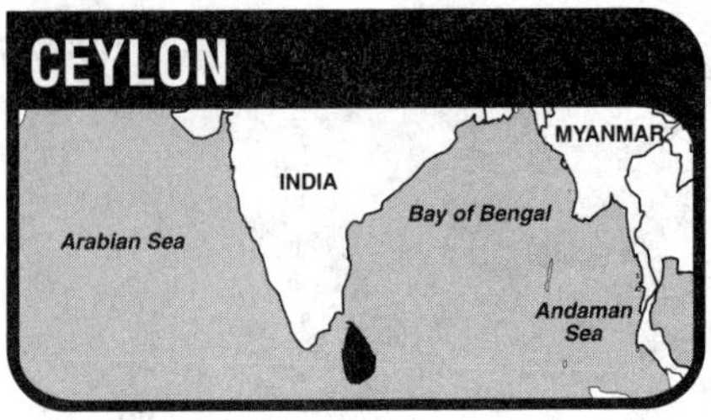

Ceylon (later to become the Democratic Socialist Republic of Sri Lanka), situated in the Indian Ocean 18 miles (29 km.) southeast of India, has an area of 25,332 sq. mi. (65,610 sq. km.) and a population of 18.82 million. Capital: Colombo. The economy is chiefly agricultural. Tea, coconut products and rubber are exported.

The earliest known inhabitants of Ceylon, the Veddahs, were subjugated by the Sinhalese from northern India in the 6th century BC. Sinhalese rule was maintained until 1498, after which the island was controlled by China for 30 years. The Portuguese came to Ceylon in 1505 and maintained control of the coastal area for 150 years. They were supplanted by the Dutch in 1658, who were in turn supplanted by the British who seized the Dutch colonies in 1796, and made them a Crown Colony in 1802. In 1815, the British conquered the independent Kingdom of Kandy in the central part of the island. Constitutional changes in 1931 and 1946 granted the Ceylonese a measure of autonomy and a parliamentary form of government. Ceylon became a self-governing dominion of the British Commonwealth on February 4, 1948. On May 22, 1972, the Ceylonese adopted a new constitution which declared Ceylon to be the Republic of Sri Lanka - "Resplendent Island." Sri Lanka is a member of the Commonwealth of Nations. The president is Chief of State. The prime minister is Head of Government.

For later issues, see Sri Lanka.

RULERS:

Dutch to 1796
British, 1796-1972

MONETARY SYSTEM:

1 Rix Dollar = 48 Stivers
1 Rupee = 100 Cents

Note: Certain listings encompassing issues circulated by various bank and regional authorities are contained in Volume 1.

STATE

CENTRAL BANK OF CEYLON

1956 ISSUE

#56-61 arms of Ceylon at l. W/o bank name in English. Various date and sign. varieties. Wmk: Chinze. Printer: BWC.

		VG	VF	UNC
56	**1 Rupee** 1956-63. Blue on orange, green and brown underprint. Arms of Ceylon at left. Without bank name in English. Ornate stairway. Watermark: Chinze. Printer: BWC.			
	a. Without security strip. 30.7.1956.	1.00	5.00	25.00
	b. Without security strip. 31.5.1957; 9.4.1958; 7.11.1958; 11.9.1959.	.75	2.00	10.00
	c. With security strip. 18.8.1960; 29.1.1962; 5.6.1963.	.50	1.50	7.50

		VG	VF	UNC
57	**2 Rupees** 1956-62. Brown and lilac on blue and green underprint. Arms of Ceylon at left. Without bank name in English. Pavilion. Watermark: Chinze. Printer: BWC.			
	a. Without security strip. 30.7.1956-11.9.1959.	2.00	6.00	30.00
	b. Security strip. 18.8.1960; 29.1.1962.	2.00	6.00	22.50

		VG	VF	UNC
58	**5 Rupees** 1956-62. Orange on aqua, green and brown underprint. Arms of Ceylon at left. Without bank name in English. Standing figure. Watermark: Chinze. Printer: BWC.			
	a. Without security strip. 30.7.1956; 31.5.1957; 10.6.1958; 1.7.1959.	3.00	9.00	70.00
	b. Security strip. 18.8.1960; 29.1.1962.	2.50	6.00	45.00

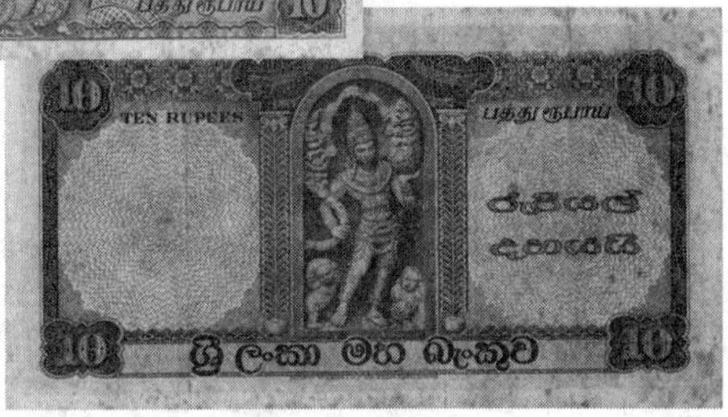

		VG	VF	UNC
59	**10 Rupees** 1956-63. Green on violet, brown and blue underprint. Arms of Ceylon at left. Without bank name in English. Ceremonial figures. Watermark: Chinze. Printer: BWC.			
	a. Without security strip. 30.7.1956; 7.11.1958; 11.9.1959.	3.00	8.00	50.00
	b. Security strip. 18.8.1960; 7.4.1961; 5.6.1963.	2.00	7.00	45.00

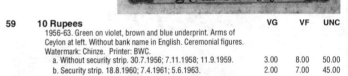

		VG	VF	UNC
60	**50 Rupees** 30.7.1956; 7.11.1958; 11.9.1959. Blue and violet on multicolor underprint. Arms of Ceylon at left. Without bank name in English. Ornate stairway. Watermark: Chinze. Printer: BWC.	22.50	60.00	250.
61	**100 Rupees** 24.10.1956. Brown on multicolor underprint. Arms of Ceylon at left. Without bank name in English. Two women in national dress. Watermark: Chinze. Printer: BWC.	25.00	100.	450.

Note: For later issues see Ceylon and Sri Lanka listings in Volume 3, Modern Issues.

1962-64 ISSUE

#62-66 S. Bandaranaike at r. Wmk: Chinze. Printer: BWC.

No.	Description	VG	VF	UNC
62	**2 Rupees** 1962-65. Light brown on lilac, green and blue underprint. Pavilion at left center on back.			
	a. Signature P. B. G. Kaluga and D. W. Rajapatirana. 8.11.1962.	2.50	6.00	15.00
	b. Signature T. B. Illangaratue and D. W. Rajapatirana. 11.4.1964; 12.6.1964.	2.50	5.00	12.50
	c. Signature U. B. Wanninayake and D. W. Rajapatirana. 6.4.1965.	2.00	5.00	10.00

No.	Description	VG	VF	UNC
63	**5 Rupees** 1962; 1964. Orange and brown on multicolor underprint. Back green and orange; standing figure at center on back.			
	a. Signature P. B. G. Kalugalla and D. W. Rajapatirana. 8.11.1962.	2.50	7.50	20.00
	b. Signature N. M. Perera and D. W. Rajapatirana. 12.6.1964.	2.00	7.00	15.00

No.	Description	VG	VF	UNC
64	**10 Rupees** 12.6.1964; 28.8.1964; 19.9.1964. Green and purple on orange and blue underprint. Ceremonial figures on back.	2.50	8.00	30.00

No.	Description	VG	VF	UNC
65	**50 Rupees** 1961-65. Blue and purple on multicolor underprint. Back blue; ornate stairway.			
	a. Signature F. R. D. Bandaranaike and D. W. Rajapatirana. 2.11.1961.	5.00	20.00	100.
	b. Signature T. B. Illangaratne and D. W. Rajapatirana. 5.6.1963.	4.50	17.50	80.00
	c. Signature U. B. Wanninayake and D. W. Rajapatirana. 6.4.1965.	3.75	15.00	70.00

Note: An issue was prepared dated 12.6.1964 which was later destroyed.

No.	Description	VG	VF	UNC
66	**100 Rupees** 5.6.1963. Brown and blue on multicolor underprint. Two women in national dress on back.	12.50	30.00	100.

1965-68 ISSUE

#67-71 statue of Kg. Parakkrama at r. W/o bank name in English. Back designs like #57-61. Various date and sign. varieties. Wmk.: Chinze. Printer: BWC.

No.	Description	VG	VF	UNC
67	**2 Rupees** 1965-68. Light brown on lilac, light green and blue underprint.			
	a. Signature U. B. Wanninayake and D. W. Rajapatirana. 9.9.1965; 15.7.1967.	1.00	2.50	7.00
	b. Signature U. B. Wanninayake and W. Tennekoon. 10.1.1968.	1.00	2.50	6.00
68	**5 Rupees** 1965-68. Orange and brown on multicolor underprint. Back green and orange.			
	a. Signature U. B. Wanninayake and D. W. Rajapatirana. 9.9.1965; 15.7.1967.	1.00	3.00	12.00
	b. Signature U. B. Wanninayake and W. Tennekoon. 1.9.1967; 10.1.1968.	1.00	2.00	10.00
69	**10 Rupees** 10.1.1968. Green and purple on orange and blue underprint.	1.50	4.00	20.00
70	**50 Rupees** 1967; 1968. Blue and purple on multicolor underprint.			
	a. Signature U. W. Wanninayake and D. W. Rajapatirana. 7.3.1967.	10.00	40.00	125.
	b. Signature U. B. Wanninayake and W. Tennekoon. 10.1.1968.	10.00	35.00	110.
71	**100 Rupees** 1966-68. Brown and blue on multicolor underprint.			
	a. Signature U. W. Wanninayake and D. W. Rajapatirana. 28.5.1966; 22.11.1966.	7.50	40.00	200.
	b. Signature U. B. Wanninayake and W. Tennekoon. 10.1.1968.	5.00	35.00	175.

1968-69 ISSUE

#72-76 w/bank name in English on both sides. Various date and sign. varieties. Wmk.: Chinze. Printer: BWC.

No.	Description	VG	VF	UNC
72	**2 Rupees** 1969-77. Light brown on lilac, light green and blue underprint. Like #67.			
	a. Signature U. B. Wanninayake and W. Tennekoon. 10.5.1969.	.50	1.50	6.00
	b. Signature N. M. Perera and W. Tennekoon. 1.6.1970; 1.2.1971; 7.6.1971; 12.5.1972; 21.8.1973; 27.8.1974.	.25	1.25	5.00
	c. Signature R. J. G. de Mel and H. E. Tennekoon. 26.8.1977.	.25	1.00	4.00

No.	Description	VG	VF	UNC
73	**5 Rupees** 1969-77. Orange and brown on multicolor underprint. Back green and orange. Like #68.			
	a. Signature U. B. Wanninayake and W. Tennekoon. 10.5.1969.	.50	2.00	8.00
	b. Signature N. M. Perera and W. Tennekoon. 1.6.1970; 1.2.1971; 21.8.1973; 16.7.1974; 27.8.1974.	1.00	3.50	7.00
	c. Signature F. R. D. Bandaranaike and H. E. Tennekoon. 26.8.1977.	.40	1.50	6.00
	ct. Color trial.	—	—	150.

		VG	VF	UNC
74	**10 Rupees**			
	1969-77. Green and purple on orange and blue underprint. Like #69.			
	a. Signature U. B. Wanninayake and W. Tennekoon. 20.10.1969.	2.00	7.00	20.00
	b. Signature N. M. Perera and W. Tennekoon. 1.6.1970; 1.2.1971; 7.6.1971; 21.8.1973; 16.7.1974.	.50	2.50	10.00
	c. Signature F. R. D. Bandaranaike and H. E. Tennekoon. 6.10.1975.	.50	2.25	9.00
	d. Signature R. J. G. de Mel and H. E. Tennekoon. 26.8.1977.	.50	2.00	8.00
	ct. Color trial.	—	—	175.
75	**50 Rupees**			
	20.10.1969. Blue and purple on multicolor underprint. Like #70.	10.00	40.00	125.

		VG	VF	UNC
76	**100 Rupees**			
	10.5.1969. Brown and blue on multicolor underprint. Like #71.	7.50	30.00	95.00

1970 Issue

#58 and 59 Smiling Pres. Bandaranaike w/raised hand. Wmk.: Chinze. Printer: TDLR. Replacement notes serial # prefix *W/1* and *V/1*.

		VG	VF	UNC
77	**50 Rupees**			
	26.10.1970; 29.12.1970. Blue on lilac, yellow and brown underprint. Monument on back.	3.00	15.00	75.00

		VG	VF	UNC
78	**100 Rupees**			
	26.10.1970; 9.12.1970. Red-violet on multicolor underprint. Female dancers on back.	5.00	25.00	100.

1971-72 Issue

#79 and 80 smiling Pres. Bandaranaike w/o hand raised. Wmk.: Chinze. Printer: BWC.

		VG	VF	UNC
79	**50 Rupees**			
	28.12.1972; 27.8.1974. Purple and multicolor. Landscape on back.			
	a. Issued note.	3.00	12.50	60.00
	s. Specimen.	—	—	175.

		VG	VF	UNC
80	**100 Rupees**			
	1971-75. Brown and purple on multicolor underprint. Ornate stairway on back.			
	a. Signature N. M. Perera and H. E. Tennekoon. 18.12.1971; 16.7.1974; 27.8.1974.	4.00	17.50	85.00
	b. Signature F. R. D. Bandaranaike and H. E. Tennekoon. 6.10.1975.	3.75	15.00	75.00

Note: For later issues see Sri Lanka.

CHAD

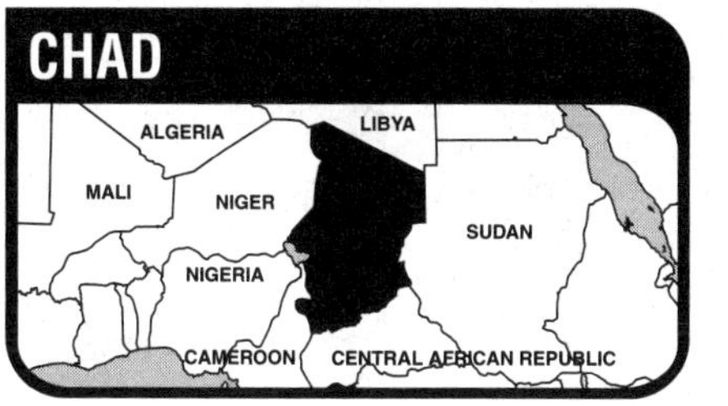

The Republic of Chad, a landlocked country of central Africa, is the largest country of former French Equatorial Africa. It has an area of 495,755 sq. mi. (1,284,000 sq. km.) and a population of 7.27 million. Capital. N'Djaména. An expanding livestock industry produces camels, cattle and sheep. Cotton (the chief product), ivory and palm oil are important exports.

Although supposedly known to Ptolemy, the Chad area was first visited by europeans in 1823. Exaggerated estimates of its economic importance led to a race for its possession (1890-93) which resulted in territory being divided by treaty between Great Britain, France and Germany. As a consequence of World War I, the German area was mandated to France in 1919. Chad was absorbed into the colony of French Equatorial Africa, as a part of Ubangi-Shari, in 1910 and became a separate colony in 1920. Upon dissolution of French Equatorial Africa in 1959, the component states became autonomous members of the French Union. Chad became an independent republic on Aug. 11, 1960.

Conflicts between the government and secessionists began in 1965 and developed into civil war. A ceasefire in 1987 was followed by an attempted coup. In 1990, Idress Déby declared himself president.

For later issues, see Central African States.

MONETARY SYSTEM:

1 Franc = 100 Centimes

SIGNATURE VARIETIES:

Refer to introduction to Central African States.

RÉPUBLIQUE DU TCHAD

BANQUE CENTRALE

1971 ISSUE

		VG	VF	UNC
1	**10,000 Francs**			
	ND (1971). Multicolor. Pres. Tombalbaye at left, cattle watering at center right. Mask at left, tractor plowing at center, statue at right on back. Signature 1.	150.	750.	2250.

BANQUE DES ÉTATS DE L'AFRIQUE CENTRALE

1974-78; ND ISSUE

		VG	VF	UNC
2	**500 Francs**			
	ND (1974); 1978. Brown and red on multicolor underprint. Woman at left; flamingos, crowned cranes, abdim's stork at center and at right. Mask at left, students and chemical testing at center, statue at right on back.			
	a. Signature titles and watermark. like #3a. Signature 6. (1974).	2.50	12.50	40.00
	b. Signature titles, watermark. and date like #3c. Signature 10. 1.4.1978.	20.00	75.00	200.

		VG	VF	UNC
3	**1000 Francs**			
	ND; 1.4.1978. Blue and brown on multicolor underprint. Woman at right. Mask at left, trains, planes and bridge at center, statue at right on back.			
	a. Signature titles: *LE DIRECTEUR GÉNÉRAL* and *UN CENSEUR*. Engraved. watermark: Antelope. in half profile. Signature 5; 7.	4.00	15.00	90.00
	b. Signature titles: *LE DIRECTEUR GÉNÉRAL* and *UN CENSEUR*. Lithographed. watermark: Antelope in profile. Signature 8.	3.00	12.50	50.00
	c. Signature titles: *LE GOUVERNEUR* and *UN CENSEUR*. Signature 10. 1.4.1978.	2.00	8.00	35.00

		VG	VF	UNC
4	**5000 Francs**			
	ND (1974). Brown-orange on multicolor underprint. President Tombalbaye at left. Mask at left, industrial collage at center, statue at right on back. Signature 4.	100.	250.	650.

		VG	VF	UNC
5	**5000 Francs**			
	ND. Brown on multicolor underprint. Woman at left. Like #4 on back.			
	a. Signature 6. (1976).	25.00	75.00	275.
	b. Signature 9. (1978).	20.00	50.00	200.

NOTICE

Readers with unlisted dates, signature varieties, etc. are invited to submit photocopies of their notes to: Standard Catalog of World Paper Money, 700 East State St. Iola, WI 54990-0001, E-Mail: george.cuhaj@fwpubs.com.

1980 Issue

		VG	VF	UNC
6	**500 Francs** 1.6.1980; 1.6.1984. Red and brown on multicolor underprint. Woman weaving basket at right. Like #2 on back. Signature 10.	1.50	4.00	25.00

		VG	VF	UNC
7	**1000 Francs** 1.6.1980; 1.6.1984. Blue and dull purple on multicolor underprint. Water buffalo at right. Back like #3. Signature 9; 10.	3.00	10.00	40.00

		VG	VF	UNC
8	**5000 Francs** 1.1.1980. Brown and multicolor. Girl at lower left, village scene at center. Back with carving, airplane, train, tractor and man smoking pipe. Similar to Central African Republic #11 and others. Signature 9.	15.00	40.00	200.

1984-85; ND Issue

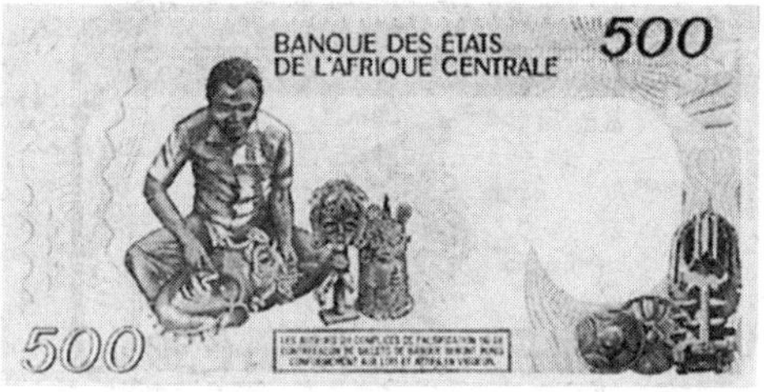

		VG	VF	UNC
9	**500 Francs** 1985-92. Brown on multicolor underprint. Carved statue and jug at center. Man carving mask at left center on back. Watermark: Carving.			
	a. Signature 10. 1.1.1985; 1.1.1986.	.50	1.50	10.00
	b. Signature 12. 1.1.1987.	.50	1.50	8.50
	c. Signature 13. 1.1.1990.	.50	1.50	8.50
	d. Signature 15. 1.1.1991.	.50	1.50	7.50
	e. Signature 15. 1.1.1992.	.50	1.50	7.50

		VG	VF	UNC
10	**1000 Francs** 1.1.1985. Dull blue-violet on multicolor underprint. Animal carving at lower left, map at center, starburst at lower right. Incomplete outline map of Chad at top center. Elephants at left, statue at right on back. Watermark: Animal carving. Signature 9.	15.00	40.00	100.

#10 was withdrawn shortly after issue because of the incompleteness of the map at top.

		VG	VF	UNC
10A	**1000 Francs** 1985-92. Like #10 but complete outline map of Chad at top center.			
	a. Signature 9. 1.1.1985; 1.1.1988; 1.1.1989; 1.1.1990.	2.00	7.50	25.00
	b. Signature 15. 1.1.1991.	3.50	15.00	35.00
	c. Signature 15. 1.1.1992.	2.00	7.50	25.00

		VG	VF	UNC
11	**5000 Francs** ND (1984-91). Brown on multicolor underprint. Mask at left, woman with bundle of fronds at right. Plowing and mine ore conveyor on back. Signature 9; 15.	5.00	20.00	85.00

		VG	VF	UNC
12	**10,000 Francs** ND (1984-91). Black, brown and dark green on multicolor underprint. Stylized antelope heads at left, woman at right and as watermark. Loading fruit onto truck at left on back.			
	a. Signature 9.	10.00	35.00	150.
	b. Signature 15.	10.00	30.00	130.

Note: For notes with similar back designs see Cameroun Republic, Central African Republic, Congo (Brazzaville) and Gabon.

The Republic of Chile, a ribbonlike country on the Pacific coast of southern South America, has an area of 292,258 sq. mi. (756,945 sq. km.) and a population of 15.21 million. Capital: Santiago. Historically, the economic of Chile has been the rich mineral deposits of its northern provinces. Copper, of which Chile has about 25 percent of the world's reserves, has accounted for more than 75 per cent of Chile's export earnings in recent years. Other important exports are iron ore, iodine, fruit and nitrate of soda.

Diego de Almargo was the first Spaniard to attempt to wrest Chile from the Incas and Araucanian tribes, 1536. He failed, and was followed by Pedro de Valdivia, a favorite of Pizarro, who founded Santiago in 1541. When the Napoleonic Wars involved Spain, leaving the constituent parts of the Spanish Empire to their own devices, Chilean patriots formed a national government and proclaimed the country's independence, Sept. 18, 1810. Independence, however, was not secured until Feb. 12, 1818, after a bitter struggle led by Generals Bernardo O'Higgins and José de San Martín.

In 1925, the constitution was ratified to strengthen the Executive branch at the expense of the Legislature.

MONETARY SYSTEM:

1 Condor = 10 Pesos to 1960
1 Escudo = 100 Centesimos, 1960-75
1 Peso = 100 "old" Escudos, 1975-

REPLACEMENT NOTES:

#140, 143, 145-148 w/*R* next to serial #.
#149-158 w/*R* near to plate position #.

REPUBLIC

BANCO CENTRAL DE CHILE

1960 ND PROVISIONAL ISSUE

1 Escudo = 1000 Pesos (= 100 Centesimos)

#124-133 Escudo denominations in red as part of new plates overprinted in wmk. area on back. Wmk: D. Diego Portales. Sign. titles: *PRESIDENTE* and *GERENTE GENERAL*. Sign. varieties. Printer: CdM-Chile.

		VG	VF	UNC
124	**1/2 Centesimo on 5 Pesos** ND (1960-61). Blue. Portrait Bernard O'Higgins at left. Signature titles: PRESIDENTE and GERENTE GENERAL. Watermark: D. Diego Portales. Printer: CdM-Chile. Rare.	—	—	—

		VG	VF	UNC
125	**1 Centesimo on 10 Pesos** ND (1960-61). Red-brown. Portrait Manuel Bulnes at left. Series F. Signature titles: PRESIDENTE and GERENTE GENERAL. Watermark: D. Diego Portales. Printer: CdM-Chile.	1.00	2.50	12.50

126 5 Centesimos on 50 Pesos
ND (1960-61). Green. Portrait Anibal Pinto at left. Series C. 3 signature varieties. Signature titles: PRESIDENTE and GERENTE GENERAL. Watermark: D. Diego Portales. Printer: CdM-Chile.

	VG	VF	UNC
a. Imprint on face 25mm wide.	.25	1.00	2.50
b. Imprint on face 22mm wide.	.10	.20	2.00
s. Specimen.	—	—	12.50

127 10 Centesimos on 100 Pesos
ND (1960-61). Red. Portrait Arturo Prat at left. 3 signature varieties. Series C-K. Signature titles: PRESIDENTE and GERENTE GENERAL. Light and dark varietes. Watermark: D. Diego Portales. Printer: CdM-Chile.

	VG	VF	UNC
a. Issued note.	.25	1.00	2.50
s. Specimen.	—	—	12.50

	VG	VF	UNC
128 50 Centesimos on 500 Pesos ND (1960-61). Blue. Portrait Manuel Montt at right. Series A. Signature titles: PRESIDENTE and GERENTE GENERAL. Watermark: D. Diego Portales. Printer: CdM-Chile.	.50	2.50	15.00

	VG	VF	UNC
129 1 Escudo on 1000 Pesos ND (1960-61). Dark brown. Portrait Manuel Blanco Encalada at left. Series A. Signature titles: PRESIDENTE and GERENTE GENERAL. Watermark: D. Diego Portales. Printer: CdM-Chile.	.50	2.00	12.50
130 5 Escudos on 5000 Pesos ND (1960-61). Brown-violet. Portrait Manuel Antonio Tocornal at left. 2 signature varieties. Series J. Signature titles: PRESIDENTE and GERENTE GENERAL. Watermark: D. Diego Portales. Printer: CdM-Chile.	1.00	5.00	25.00
131 10 Escudos on 10,000 Pesos ND (1960-61). Purple on light blue underprint. Portrait Jose Manuel Balmaceda at left. Series F. Signature titles: PRESIDENTE and GERENTE GENERAL. Watermark: D. Diego Portales at left, words *DIEZ MIL* at right. Printer: CdM-Chile.	2.00	10.00	40.00
132 10 Escudos on 10,000 Pesos ND (1960-61). Red-brown. Portrait Jose Manuel Balmaceda at left. Similar to #131. Series F. Signature titles: PRESIDENTE and GERENTE GENERAL. Watermark: D. Diego Portales. Printer: CdM-Chile.	2.00	15.00	55.00
133 50 Escudos on 50,000 Pesos ND (1960-61). Blue-green and brown on multicolor underprint. Portrait Arturo Alessandri at left. Series A. Signature titles: PRESIDENTE and GERENTE GENERAL. Watermark: D. Diego Portales. Printer: CdM-Chile.	4.50	25.00	75.00

1962-75 ND Issue

#134-141 sign. varieties. Wmk: D. Diego Portales P. at l. Printer: CdM-Chile.

134 1/2 Escudo
ND. Dark blue on pale orange and light blue underprint. Portrait Gen. Bernardo O'Higgins at center. Explorer on horseback at left center on back. Red serial #.

	VG	VF	UNC
a. Paper of #122. Series A. 3 signature varieties.	.15	.50	3.00
b. Paper of #121. Series B. 2 signature varieties.	.15	.50	3.00
s. Specimen.	—	—	15.00

134A 1/2 Escudo
ND. Like #134, but tan underprint. Black serial #.

	VG	VF	UNC
a. Paper of #121. Series B-G.	.10	.25	1.50
s. Specimen.	—	—	17.50

135 1 Escudo
ND. Brown-violet with lilac guilloche on tan underprint. Portrait Arturo Prat at center. Red-brown arms with founding of Santiago on back. Engraved. Watermark: Balmaceda.

	VG	VF	UNC
a. Large and sm. brown serial #. watermark: *1000* at right. Series A.	.50	3.00	10.00
b. Large and sm. black serial #. watermark: *500* at right. Series A.	1.00	5.00	20.00
c. Without watermark. at right. Series A; B.	.50	1.50	5.00
d. Sm. black serial #. without watermark. at right. Arms in red-brown at left. on back.	.20	.50	2.00
s. As c. Specimen.	—	—	17.50

135A 1 Escudo

ND. Like #135c but with arms in olive at left on back. 2 signature varieties.

	VG	VF	UNC
a. Series G-I. without watermark. at right.	.10	.20	1.00
b. With *V* under portrait Paper of #121. Series J-N.	.10	.20	1.00

136 1 Escudo

	VG	VF	UNC
ND (1964). Dull violet on tan underprint. Portrait Arturo Prat. Like #135 but arms on back in light olive. Lithographed. 3 signature varieties. 6 or 7 digit serial #. Series N; P; Q.	.10	.25	.75

137 5 Escudos

ND. Reddish brown on multicolor underprint. Portrait Manuel Bulnes at center. Battle of Rancagua at center, yellow-orange arms at left on back.

	VG	VF	UNC
a. Series A.	.75	2.00	12.50
s. Specimen.	—	—	17.50

138 5 Escudos

	VG	VF	UNC
ND (1964). Red and brown-violet on multicolor underprint. Like #137. Red-brown arms at left. on back. 4 signature varieties. 6 or 7 digit serial #. Series A-E.	.10	.25	2.00

139 10 Escudos

ND. Violet, blue-gray and dull purple on multicolor underprint. Portrait Jose Manuel Balmaceda at center. Dark or light brown arms at left, soldiers meeting at center on back. 3 signature varieties.

	VG	VF	UNC
a. Series A-G.	.25	.75	5.00
s. Specimen.	—	—	25.00

140 50 Escudos

ND. Dark green and olive-brown on multicolor underprint. Porr. Arturo Alessandri at center. Back brown and green; Banco Central building 5 signature varieties.

	VG	VF	UNC
a. Series A-D.	1.00	1.75	8.00
b. Series E-F.	.10	.25	2.00
s. Specimen.	—	—	25.00

141	100 Escudos	VG	VF	UNC
	ND. Blue-gray and violet-brown on tan underprint. Portrait Manuel Regifo at right. Sailing ships at center arms at left on back. 2 signature varieties.			
	a. Series A-G.	.25	.75	4.00
	s. Specimen.	—	—	25.00

1967-76 ND Issues

#142-148 sign. varieties. Wmk: D. Diego Portales P. at l. Printer: CdM-Chile. Replacement notes: Serial # suffix *R* or *R* in area of sheet position #.

142	10 Escudos	VG	VF	UNC
	ND (1970). Gray-green, violet-brown and blue-gray on multicolor underprint. Portrait Jose Manuel Balmaceda at right. Red-brown lower margin on back. Engraved. Series A. 2 signature varieties.	.20	.50	2.00

142A	10 Escudos	VG	VF	UNC
	ND. Like #142 but with green lower margin on back. Lithographed.			
	a. Series B.	.20	.50	2.00
	s. Specimen.	—	—	20.00

143	10 Escudos	VG	VF	UNC
	ND. Grayish brown on tan underprint. Like #142. Lithographed. 3 signature varieties. Series A.	.10	.25	1.50
144	500 Escudos			
	1971. Red-brown on multicolor underprint. Copper worker at left. Strip mining at center right on back. Without 3-line text: *NO DEBEMOS CONSENTIR...* at bottom. Rare.	—	—	—

145	500 Escudos	VG	VF	UNC
	1971. Like #144 but with 3-line text: *NO DEBEMOS CONSENTIR...*at bottom on back. 2 signature varieties. Series A; B.	.15	.50	2.50

Note: #144 and 145 commemorate the nationalization of iron and copper mines.

146	1000 Escudos	VG	VF	UNC
	ND. Purple and violet on multicolor underprint. Jose Miguel Carrera at left. Back like #147. 2 signature varieties. Series A; B.	.15	.50	3.00

147	5000 Escudos	VG	VF	UNC
	ND. Dark green and brown on multicolor underprint. Jose Miguel Carrera at left. Carrera House at center right on back.			
	a. Back with deep green vignette. Lithographed. Series A.	.50	1.50	5.00
	b. Back with dark olive-green vignette. Partially engraved. Series B. 2 signature varieties.	.25	.75	3.00

148	10,000 Escudos	VG	VF	UNC
	ND. Orange-brown on multicolor underprint. Gen. Bernardo O'Higgins at left. Blue serial #. Battle of Rancagua on back. Series A. 2 signature varieties.	1.00	3.50	6.00

1975-89 ISSUES

#149-152 wmk: D. Diego Portales P. Sign. varieties. Replacement notes: *R* serial # suffix. #149-156 printer: CdM-Chile.

149	5 Pesos	VG	VF	UNC
	1975-76. Green on olive underprint. Jose Miguel Carrera at right. Back similar to #147.			
	a. 1975.	.50	1.50	5.00
	b. 1976.	10.00	25.00	55.00
	s. As a. Specimen.	—	—	25.00

150	10 Pesos	VG	VF	UNC
	1975-76. Red on multicolor underprint. Gen. Bernardo O'Higgins at right and as watermark. Back similar to #148.			
	a. *B. O'HIGGINS* under portrait 1975.	.75	1.75	8.00
	b. *LIBERTADOR B. O'HIGGINS* under portrait 1975; 1976.	.50	1.00	6.00
	s. As a. Specimen.	—	—	25.00

151	50 Pesos	VG	VF	UNC
	1975-81. Dark blue and aqua on green and light blue underprint. Portrait Captain Arturo Prat at right. Sailing ships at center on back. 3 signature varieties.			
	a. 1975; 1976; 1977; 1978.	.20	.50	3.00
	b. 1980; 1981 (2 signature varieties.)	.15	.25	2.00
	s. Specimen. 1975.	—	—	25.00

152	100 Pesos	VG	VF	UNC
	1976-84. Purple and red-violet on multicolor underprint. Diego Portales at right. 1837 meeting at left center on back. 6 signature varieties.			
	a. Normal serial # without prefix letter. Series A. 1976.	1.50	4.00	10.00
	b. Electronic sorting serial # with prefix letter. 1976-77, 1979-84. 6 signature varieties (2 for 1981).	.30	.50	3.00
	s. Specimen. 1976.	—	—	25.00

153	500 Pesos	VG	VF	UNC
	1977-2000. Dark brown and brown-violet with black text on multicolor underprint. Pedro de Valdivia at right. Watermark: Carrera. Founding of Santiago at center on back. 11 signature varieties.			
	a. 1977; 1978.	FV	1.50	7.50
	b. 1980-82; 1985-90.	FV	FV	4.50
	c. Signature titles: *PRESIDENTE* and *GERENTE GENERAL INTERINO.* 1991.	FV	2.00	7.50
	d. 1991-93.	FV	FV	4.00
	e. 1994-2000. (1999 without imprint).	FV	FV	3.00
	s. Specimen. 1977.	—	—	25.00

154	1000 Pesos	VG	VF	UNC
	1978-. Deep blue-green, dark olive-brown on multicolor underprint. Ignacio Carrera Pinto at right and as watermark, military arms at center Monument to Chilean heroes on back. 12 signature varieties.			
	a. Signature titles: *PRESIDENTE* and *GERENTE GENERAL*. 1978-80.	FV	4.00	25.00
	b. 1982.	FV	FV	10.00
	c. 1984-90.	FV	FV	9.50
	d. Signature titles: *PRESIDENTE* and *GERENTE GENERAL INTERINO.* 1990.	FV	FV	9.00
	e. Signature titles as a. 1991-94. (2 Signature varieties in 1994).	FV	FV	7.50
	f. Designer's names omitted from lower left and right. 1995-2005. (without imprint 1999; 2001-2002, 2004-2005).	FV	FV	5.00
	s. Specimen. 1978. Overprint: *Especimen.*	—	—	50.00

155	5000 Pesos	VG	VF	UNC
	1981. Brown and red-violet on multicolor underprint. Allegorical woman with musical instrument, seated male at center. Statue of woman with children at left center, Gabriela Mistral at right on back and as watermark. 9 signature varieties.			
	a. Signature titles: *PRESIDENTE* and *GERENTE GENERAL*. 1981. Plain security thread.	FV	FV	70.00
	b. 1986-90.	FV	FV	50.00
	c. Signature titles: *PRESIDENTE* and *GERENTE GENERAL INTERINO*. 1991.	FV	FV	35.00
	d. Signature titles: *PRESIDENTE* and *GERENTE GENERAL*. 1991-94.	FV	FV	27.50
	e. As d but with segmented foil security thread. 1994-2005. (without imprint, 2002-2005).	FV	FV	20.00
	s. Specimen. 1981; 1993.	—	—	100.

156	10,000 Pesos	VG	VF	UNC
	1989-95. Dark blue and dark olive-green on multicolor underprint. Captain Arturo Prat at right and as watermark. Statue of Liberty at left, Hacienda San Agustin de Punual Cuna at left center on back. 5 signature varieties.			
	a. Plain security thread. 1989-93.	FV	FV	60.00
	b. As a. 1994.	FV	FV	50.00
	c. With imprint. Segmented foil over security thread. 1994-95.	FV	FV	45.00
	s. Specimen. 1994.	—	—	100.

1994 Issue

157	10,000 Pesos	VG	VF	UNC
	1994-99; 2001-05. Dark blue and deep olive-green on multicolor underprint. Like #156c. Printer: TDLR (without imprint). 2 signature varieties.	FV	FV	35.00

1997 Issue

158	2000 Pesos	VG	VF	UNC
	1997; 1999 (with imprint); 2001-03 (without imprint). Purple and dark brown on multicolor underprint. Manuel Rodríguez E. at right and as watermark, statue of Manuel Rodríguez on horseback at center Iglesia de los Dominicos (church) at center on back. Printer: CdM-C.	FV	FV	9.00

1998 Issue

159	20,000 Pesos	VG	VF	UNC
	1998-2001. Lilac brown, green and multicolor. Don Andres Bello at right. University building on back. Printer: CdM-C.	FV	FV	60.00

2004 Polymer Issue

160	2000 Pesos	VG	VF	UNC
	2004. Lilac and brown on multicolor underprint. Manuel Rodríguez E. at right and as statue on horseback. Polymer plastic. Similar to #158.	FV	FV	7.50

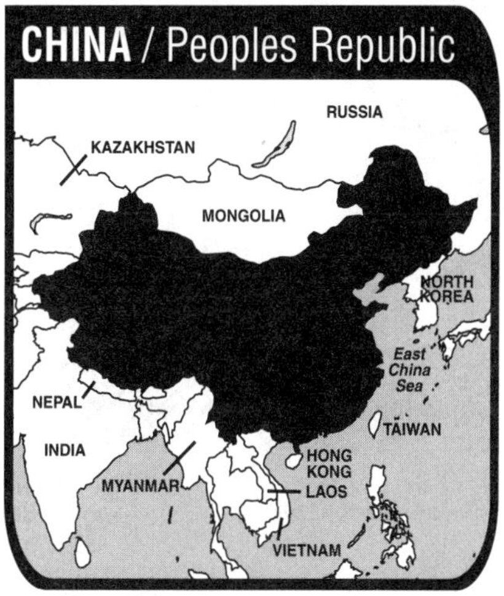

The Peoples Republic of China, located in eastern Asia, has an area of 3,696,100 sq. mi. (9,572,900 sq. km.), including Manchuria and Tibet, and a population of 1.276 billion. Capital: Beijing. The economy is based on agriculture, mining and manufacturing. Textiles, clothing, metal ores, tea and rice are exported.

In the fall of 1911, the middle business class of China and Chinese students educated in Western universities started a general uprising against the Manchu dynasty which forced the abdication on Feb. 12, 1912, of the boy emperor Hsuan T'ung (Pu-yi), thus bringing to an end the dynasty that had ruled China since 1644. Five days later, China formally became a republic with physician and revolutionist Sun Yat-sen as first provisional president.

Dr. Sun and his supporters founded a new party called the Kuomintang, and planned a Chinese republic based upon the Three Principles of Nationalism, Democracy and People's Livelihood. They failed, however, to win control over all of China, and Dr. Sun resigned the presidency in favor of Yuan Shih Kai, the most powerful of the Chinese Army generals. Yuan ignored the constitution of the new republic and tried to make himself emperor.

After the death of Yuan in 1917, Sun Yat-sen and the Kuomintang established a republic in Canton. It failed to achieve the unification of China, and in 1923 Dr. Sun entered into an agreement with the Soviet Union known as the Canton-Moscow Entente. The Kuomintang agreed to admit Chinese communists to the party. The Soviet Union agreed to furnish military advisers to train the army of the Canton Republic. Dr. Sun died in 1925 and was succeeded by one of his supporters, General Chiang Kai-shek.

Chiang Kai-shek launched a vigorous campaign to educate the Chinese and modernize their industries and agriculture. Under his command, the armies of the Kuomintang captured Nanking (1927) and Peking (1928). In 1928, Chiang was made president of the Chinese Republic. His government was recognized by most of the great powers, but he soon began to exercise dictatorial powers. Prodded by the conservative members of the Kuomintang, he initiated a break between these members and the Chinese Communists which, once again, prevented the unification of China.

Persuaded that China would fare better under the leadership of its businessmen in alliance with the capitalist countries than under the guidance of the Chinese Communists in alliance with the Soviet Union, Chiang expelled all Communists from the Kuomintang, sent the Russian advisers home, and hired German generals to train his army.

The Communists responded by setting up a government and raising an army that during the period of 1930-34 acquired control over large parts of Kiangsi, Fukien, Hunan, Hupeh and other provinces.

When his army was sufficiently trained and equipped, Chiang Kai-shek led several military expeditions against the Communist Chinese which, while unable to subdue them, dislodged them south of the Yangtze, forcing them to undertake in 1935 a celebrated "Long March" of 6,000 miles (9,654 km.) from Hunan northwest to a refuge in Shensi province just south of Inner Mongolia from which Chiang was unable to displace them.

The Japanese had now assumed warlike proportions. Chiang rejected a Japanese offer of cooperation against the Communists, but agreed to suppress the movement himself. His generals, however, persuaded him to negotiate a truce with the Communists to permit united action against the greater of Japanese aggression. Under the terms of the truce, Communists were again admitted to the Kuomintang. They, in turn, promised to dissolve the Soviet Republic of China and to cease issuing their own currency.

The war with Japan all but extinguished the appeal of the Kuomintang, appreciably increased the power of the Communists, and divided China into three parts. The east coast and its principal cities - Peking, Tientsin, Nanking, Shanghai and Canton - were in Japanese-controlled, puppet-ruled states. The Communists controlled the countryside in the north where they were the de facto rulers of 100 million peasants. Chiang and the Kuomintang were driven toward the west, from where they returned with their prestige seriously damaged by their wartime performance.

At the end of World War II, the United States tried to bring the Chinese factions together in a coalition government. American mediation failed, and within weeks the civil war resumed.

By the fall of 1947, most of northeast China was under Communist control. During the following year, the war turned wholly in favor of the Communists. The Kuomintang armies in the northeast surrendered, two provincial capitals in the north were captured, a large Kuomintang army in the Huai river basin surrendered. Four Communist armies converged upon the demoralized Kuomintang forces. The Communists crossed the Yangtse in April 1949. Nanking, the Nationalist capital, fell. The civil war on the mainland was virtually over.

Chiang Kai-shek relinquished the presidency to Li Tsung-jen, his deputy, and after moving to Canton, to Chungking and Chengtu, retreated from the mainland to Taiwan (Formosa) where he resumed the presidency.

The Communist Peoples Republic of China was proclaimed on September 21, 1949. Thereafter relations between the Peoples Republic and the Soviet Union steadily deteriorated. China emerged as an independent center of Communist power in 1958.

MONETARY SYSTEM:

1 Yüan = 10 Chiao
1 Chiao = 10 Fen

MONETARY UNITS

Yuan	圓 or 圜
Pan Yuan	圓 半
5 Jiao	角伍
1 Jiao	角壹
1 Fen	分壹

NUMERICAL CHARACTERS

No.	CONVENTIONAL			FORMAL	
1	一	正	元	壹	弌
2	二			弍	貳
3	三			弎	叁
4	四			肆	
5	五			伍	
6	六			陸	
7	七			柒	
8	八			捌	
9	九			玖	
10	十			拾	什
20	十 二	廿		拾貳	念
25	五 十 二	五廿		伍拾貳	
30	十 三	卅		拾叁	
100	百 一			佰壹	
1,000	千 一			仟壹	
10,000	萬 一			萬壹	
100,000	萬 十	億 一		萬拾	億壹
1,000,000	萬百一			萬佰壹	

PEOPLES BANK OF CHINA

行銀民人國中
Chung Kuo Jen Min Yin Hang

中國人民銀行
Zhong Guo Ren Min Yin Hang

1953 SECOND ISSUE

#860-870 arms at ctr. on back.

		VG	VF	UNC
860	**1 Fen** 1953. Brown on yellow-orange underprint. Produce truck at right.			
	a. Roman control numerals and serial #.	.25	1.00	3.00
	b. 3 Roman control numerals only.	—	—	.50
	c. 2 Roman control numerals.	—	—	.20
861	**2 Fen** 1953. Dark blue on light blue underprint. Airplane at right.			
	a. Roman control numerals and serial #.	.25	1.25	4.00
	b. Roman control numerals only.	FV	.20	.50
862	**5 Fen** 1953. Dark green on green underprint. Cargo ship at right.			
	a. Roman control numerals and serial #.	1.50	7.00	18.00
	b. Roman control numerals only.	—	.20	.50

1962; 1965 ISSUE

#877-879 arms at r. on back.

		VG	VF	UNC
877	**1 Jiao** 1962. Brown on multicolor underprint. Workers at left.			
	a. Back brown on green and light orange underprint. without watermark.	5.00	20.00	90.00
	b. As a. watermark: stars.	30.00	90.00	270.
	c. Serial # prefix: 3 blue Roman numerals. Back brown. without watermark.	FV	.20	1.00
	d. Like c, serial # prefix: 2 blue Roman numerals.	FV	.30	1.50
	e. Like b, partially engraved. Serial # prefix: 2 red Roman numerals. watermark: Stars.	FV	.20	.80
	f. Like c but lithographed, serial # prefix: 2 red Roman numerals. without watermark.	FV	.15	.50
878	**2 Jiao** 1962. Green. Bridge over Yangtze River at left.			
	a. Engraved face. Serial # prefix: 3 Roman numerals.	FV	.25	2.00
	b. Lithographed face. Serial # prefix: 3 Roman numerals.	FV	.20	.50
	c. As b. Serial # prefix: 2 Roman numerals.	FV	.15	.50
	x. As b. Red back. Post production chemical alteration.	FV	1.00	3.50

		VG	VF	UNC
879	**10 Yüan** 1965. Black on multicolor underprint. Representatives of the National Assembly at center. Palace gate at left on back. Watermark: Great Hall with rays.			
	a. Serial # prefix: 3 Roman numerals.	FV	2.00	15.00
	b. Serial # prefix: 2 Roman numerals.	FV	1.50	10.00

1972 ISSUE

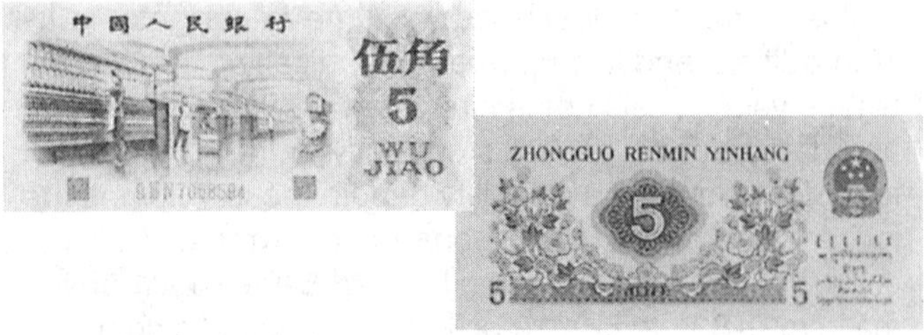

		VG	VF	UNC
880	**5 Jiao** 1972. Purple and multicolor. Women working in textile factory. Arms at right on back.			
	a. Engraved bank title and denomination. Serial # prefix: 3 Roman numerals. watermark: Stars.	FV	.40	1.50
	b. As a. but lithographed face. with watermark.	FV	.50	2.00
	c. Lithographed face. without watermark.	FV	.20	.75

1980 ISSUE

#881-888 illustrate 14 persons of various minorities.
#881-883 arms at ctr. on back.

		VG	VF	UNC
881	**1 Jiao** 1980. Brown and dark brown on multicolor underprint. Two Taiwanese men at left.	FV	FV	.50

		VG	VF	UNC
882	**2 Jiao** 1980. Grayish olive-green on multicolor underprint. Native *Pu Yi* and Korean youth at left.	FV	FV	.50

		VG	VF	UNC
883	**5 Jiao** 1980. Purple and red-violet on multicolor underprint. *Miao* and *Zhuang* children at left. Back: brown-violet on multicolor underprint.	FV	FV	.75

#884-889 arms at upper l., stylized birds in unpt. at ctr., dot patterns for poor of sight at lower l. or r.

		VG	VF	UNC
884	**1 Yüan** 1980; 1990; 1996. Brown-violet on multicolor underprint. *Dong* and *Yao* youths at right. Great Wall at center on back.			
	a. Engraved. dark blue serial #. watermark: Ancient *Pu* (pants) coin repeated. 1980.	FV	FV	1.50
	b. Partially engraved. watermark. as a. Black serial #. 1990.	FV	FV	.75
	c. Litho. watermark: Stars. Black serial #. 1996.	FV	FV	.50

885 2 Yüan | VG | VF | UNC

1980; 1990. Dark olive-green on multicolor underprint. *Hyger* and *Ye Yien* youths at right. Rocky shoreline of South Sea on back. Watermark: Ancient *Pu* (pants) coin repeated.

	VG	VF	UNC
a. Engraved back. 1980.	FV	FV	4.00
b. Litho. back. 1990.	FV	FV	.75

886 5 Yüan | VG | VF | UNC

	VG	VF	UNC
1980. Dark brown on multicolor underprint. Old Tibetan man and young Islamic woman at right. Yangtze Gorges on back. Watermark: Ancient *Pu* (pants) coin repeated.	FV	FV	2.50

887 10 Yüan | VG | VF | UNC

	VG	VF	UNC
1980. Black on blue and multicolor underprint. Elder Han and youthful Mongolian man at right. Mountains on back. Watermark: Young Mongolian man.	FV	FV	4.00

888 50 Yüan | VG | VF | UNC

1980; 1990. Black on light green and multicolor underprint. Intellectual, farm girl and industrial male worker at center. Waterfall of Yellow River on back. Watermark: Industrial male worker.

	VG	VF	UNC
a. 1980.	FV	FV	22.00
b. Security thread at right. 1990.	FV	FV	12.50

889 100 Yüan | VG | VF | UNC

1980; 1990. Black on multicolor underprint. Four great leaders at center. Mountains at Ding Gang Sha (starting point of the "Long March") on back. Watermark: Bust of Mao Tse-tung.

	VG	VF	UNC
a. 1980.	FV	FV	30.00
b. Security thread at right. 1990.	FV	FV	20.00

890 500 Yüan

	VG	VF	UNC
1990. Black on multicolor underprint.	—	—	—

Note: #890 was used for inter-bank transfers only.

1999 COMMEMORATIVE ISSUE

891, 50th Anniversary of Revolution

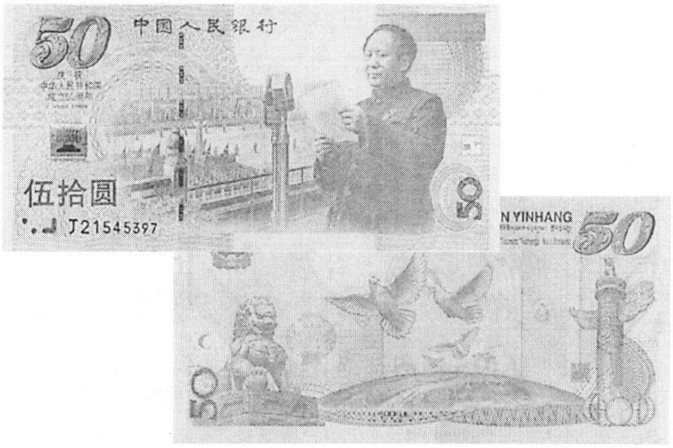

891 50 Yüan | VG | VF | UNC

	VG	VF	UNC
1999. Red on multicolor underprint. Mao Tse-tung delivering speech. Five pigeons in flight, carvings to left and right on back.	FV	FV	15.00

#892-894 held in reserve.

1999 REGULAR ISSUE

#892-901 Mao Tse-tung at r., flora at lower ctr. and as wmk.

895 1 Yüan

	VG	VF	UNC
1999.	FV	FV	.50

#896 held in reserve.

		VG	VF	UNC
897	**5 Yüan** 1999 (2002). Purple on multicolor underprint. Mountain valley veiw on back.	FV	FV	1.00

		VG	VF	UNC
898	**10 Yüan** 1999 (2000). Slate blue and multicolor. Three gorges of Yangtze river on back.	FV	FV	2.50

		VG	VF	UNC
899	**20 Yüan** 1999. Brown on multicolor underprint. River scene on back.	FV	FV	4.50

		VG	VF	UNC
900	**50 Yüan** 1999 (2001). Green and multicolor. Potala of Tibet on back.	FV	FV	10.00
901	**100 Yüan** 1999. Red and multicolor. Hall of the People on back.	FV	FV	20.00

2000 COMMEMORATIVE ISSUE

#902, Year 2000 commemorative

		VG	VF	UNC
902	**100 Yüan** 2000. Orange, red and green. Polymer plastic. Dragon at center, clear window with image at lower left, OVD at upper right. Scientific building on back.	FV	FV	32.50

FOREIGN EXCHANGE CERTIFICATES

BANK OF CHINA

This series has been discontinued and is no longer redeemable.

中國銀行

Chung Kuo Yin Hang

1979 ISSUE

#FX1-FX7 only uncirculated examples command a premium.

		VG	VF	UNC
FX1	**10 Fen** 1979. Brown on multicolor underprint. Waterfall at center.			
	a. Watermark: 1 Large and 4 sm. stars.	—	—	.50
	b. Watermark: Star and torch.	—	—	1.00

#FX2-FX4 wmk: Star and Torch.

		VG	VF	UNC
FX2	**50 Fen** 1979. Purple on multicolor underprint. Temple of Heaven at left center.	—	—	1.50
FX3	**1 Yüan** 1979. Deep green on multicolor underprint. Pleasure boats in lake with mountains behind at center.	—	—	1.00
FX4	**5 Yüan** 1979. Deep brown on multicolor underprint. Mountain scenery at center.	—	—	2.00

		VG	VF	UNC
FX5	**10 Yüan** 1979. Deep blue on m/c/ underprint. Yangtze Gorges at center.	—	—	2.50

#FX6-FX9 wmk: National badge.

		VG	VF	UNC
FX6	**50 Yüan** 1979. Purple and red on multicolor underprint. Mountain lake at Kweilin at center.	—	—	20.00
FX7	**100 Yüan** 1979. Black and blue on multicolor underprint. Great Wall at center.	—	—	25.00

1988 ISSUE

#FX8-FX9 only uncirculated examples command a premium.

		VG	VF	UNC
FX8	**50 Yüan** 1988. Black, orange-brown and green on multicolor underprint. Shoreline rock formations at center.	—	Unc	15.00
FX9	**100 Yüan** 1988. Olive-green on multicolor underprint. Great Wall at center.	—	—	20.00

PEOPLES REPUBLIC - MILITARY

MILITARY PAYMENT CERTIFICATES

軍用代金券

Chün Yung Tai Chin Ch'üan

1965 ISSUE

		VG	VF	UNC
M41	**1 Fen** 1965. Greenish brown. Airplane at left center.	5.00	15.00	60.00
M42	**5 Fen** 1965. Red. Airplane at center.	6.00	30.00	90.00
M43	**1 Chiao** 1965. Purple. Steam passenger train at center right.	15.00	60.00	175.

#M44 Held in reserve.

		VG	VF	UNC
M45	**1 Yüan** 1965. Green. Truck convoy at left.	15.00	75.00	300.
M46	**5 Yüan** 1965. Truck convoy at left.	25.00	125.	500.

CHINESE ADMINISTRATION OF TAIWAN

The Republic of China, comprising Taiwan (an island located 90 miles off the southeastern coast of mainland China), the islands of Quemoy and Matsu and nearby islets of the Pescadores chain, has an area of 14,000 sq. mi. (35,981 sq. km.). and a population of 20.2 million. Capital: Taipei. In recent years, manufacturing has replaced agriculture in importance. Fruits, vegetables, plywood, textile yarns, fabrics and clothing are exported.

Chinese migration to Taiwan began as early as the sixth century. The Dutch established a base on the island in 1624 and held it until 1661, when they were driven out by supporters of the Ming dynasty who used it as a stage for their unsuccessful attempt to displace the ruling Manchu dynasty on the mainland. Manchu forces occupied the island in 1683 and remained under the suzerainty of China until its cession to Japan in 1895. Following World War II Taiwan was returned to China, and on December 8, 1949 it became the last remnant of Dr. Sun Yat-sen's Republic of China when Chiang Kai-shek moved his army and government from the mainland to the islands following his defeat by the Communist forces of Mao Tse-tung.

BANK OF TAIWAN

臺灣銀行

T'ai Wan Yin Hang

CIRIULATING BANK CASHIER'S CHECKS

PORTRAIT ABBREVIATIONS

SYS = Dr. Sun Yat-sen, 1867-1925
President of Canton Government, 1917-25
Taiwan, 1949-1975

CKS = Chiang Kai-shek, 1886-1975
President in Nanking, 1927-31
Head of Formosa Government,

Note: Because of the frequency of the above appearing in the following listings, their initials are used only in reference to their portraits.

PRINTERS

CPF:
(Central Printing Factory) 中央印製廠

CPFT:
(Central Printing Factory, Taipei) 中央印製廠台北廠

FPFT:
(First Printing Factory) 第一印刷廠

PFBT:
(Printing Factory of Taiwan Bank) 臺灣銀行印刷所

1961 ISSUE

#1971-1975 portr. SYS at l. Printer: CPF.

		VG	VF	UNC
1971	**1 Yüan** 1961. Dark blue-green and purple on multicolor underprint. Steep coastline at right. Printer: PFBT.			
	a. Engraved.	.20	.75	5.00
	b. Lithographed. (1972).	.10	1.50	3.00

NOTICE
Readers with unlisted dates, signature varieties, etc. are invited to submit photocopies of their notes to: Standard Catalog of World Paper Money, 700 East State St. Iola, WI 54990-0001, E-Mail: george.cuhaj@fwpubs.com.

		VG	VF	UNC
1972	**5 Yüan** 1961. Red on multicolor underprint. House with tower at right.	.20	.75	4.00

		VG	VF	UNC
1973	**5 Yüan** 1961. Brown on multicolor underprint. Similar to #972.	.25	1.50	10.00
1974	**50 Yüan** 1961. Purple on multicolor underprint.	FV	3.00	20.00
1975	**100 Yüan** 1961. Green on multicolor underprint. SYS at left.	FV	3.25	22.00

1964 ISSUE

#1976 and 1977 portr. SYS at l. Printer: CPF.

		VG	VF	UNC
1976	**50 Yüan** 1964. Purple on multicolor underprint. Similar to #1974.	FV	2.00	15.00

		VG	VF	UNC
1977	**100 Yüan** 1964. Green on multicolor underprint. Similar to #1975.	FV	3.00	20.00

REPUBLIC OF CHINA-TAIWAN BANK

中華民國 臺灣銀行

Chung Hua Min Kuo-T'ai Wan Yin Hang

1969 ISSUE

#1978 and 1979 portr. SYS at l. Printer: CPF.

		VG	VF	UNC
1978	**5 Yüan** 1969. Blue on multicolor underprint.			
	a. Issued note.	.15	.40	3.00
	s. Specimen. Uniface impression of each side.	—	—	150.

		VG	VF	UNC
1979	**10 Yüan**			
	1969. Red on multicolor underprint. Similar to #1978.			
	a. Without plate letter.	.20	.50	3.00
	b. Plate letter A at lower right. on face.	.15	.35	2.50
	s. As a. Specimen. Uniface printing of each side.	—	—	150.

1970 ISSUE

#1980-1983 SYS at l. Printer: CPF.

		VG	VF	UNC
1980	**50 Yüan**			
	1970. Purple on multicolor underprint.	FV	2.25	10.00
1981	**100 Yüan**			
	1970. Green on multicolor underprint.	FV	4.50	15.00

1972 ISSUE

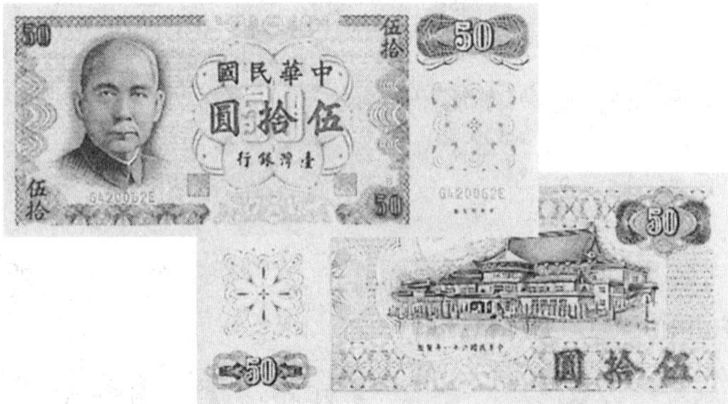

		VG	VF	UNC
1982	**50 Yüan**			
	1972. Purple and light blue on multicolor underprint. Chungshan building on back. Wide margin with guilloche at right.			
	a. Issued note.	FV	2.00	6.00
	s. Specimen. Uniface printing of each side.	—	—	150.

		VG	VF	UNC
1983	**100 Yüan**			
	1972. Dark green, light green and orange on multicolor underprint. Palace on back.			
	a. Issued note.	FV	3.50	8.00
	s. Specimen. Uniface printing of each side.	—	—	150.

1976 ISSUE

#1984-1986 printer: CPF.

		VG	VF	UNC
1984	**10 Yüan**			
	1976. Red on multicolor underprint. SYS at left. Bank on back.	FV	.50	2.00
1985	**500 Yüan**			
	1976. Olive, purple and multicolor. CKS at left. Chungshan building on back. Without watermark at right.	FV	20.00	45.00

		VG	VF	UNC
1986	**1000 Yüan**			
	1976. Blue-black, olive-brown and violet on multicolor underprint. CKS at left. Presidential Office building on back. Without watermark at right.	FV	40.00	120.

1981 ISSUE

#1987 and 1988 CKS at l. Printer: CPF.

		VG	VF	UNC
1987	**500 Yüan**			
	1981. Brown and red-brown on multicolor underprint. Similar to #1985 but watermark of CKS at right.	FV	FV	40.00

#	Denomination	VG	VF	UNC
1988	**1000 Yüan** 1981. Blue-black on multicolor underprint. Similar to #1986 but watermark: CKS at right.	FV	FV	80.00

1987 Issue

#	Denomination	VG	VF	UNC
1989	**100 Yüan** 1987 (1988). Red, red-brown and brown-violet on multicolor underprint. SYS at left and as watermark. Chungshan building on back.	FV	FV	7.00

1999 Commemorative Issue

#1990, 50th Anniversary of Taiwan

#	Denomination	VG	VF	UNC
1990	**50 Yüan** Red on multicolor underprint. Currency and high-speed train at left. Bank building on back. Polymer plastic.	FV	FV	4.00

1999; 2001 Issue

#	Denomination	VG	VF	UNC
1991	**100 Yüan** 2001. Multicolor.	FV	FV	7.50

#	Denomination	VG	VF	UNC
1992	**200 Yüan** 2001. Green.	FV	FV	8.50
1993	**500 Yüan** 1999; 2001. Brown and rose on multicolor underprint. Boy's baseball team at center, Professional Pitcher at right. Formosan Sika Deer family on back.	FV	FV	25.00

#	Denomination	VG	VF	UNC
1994	**1000 Yüan** 1999. Light and dark blue on light green underprint. School children studying globe at center. Two Mikado Pheasant and mountian vista on back.	FV	FV	40.00

#	Denomination	VG	VF	UNC
1995	**2000 Yüan** 2002. Purple and lilac on multicolor underprint. Satellite Dishes and rocket. Two salmon and Mt. Nanhu on back.	FV	FV	80.00

2005 Issue

#	Denomination	VG	VF	UNC
1996	**500 Yüan** 2005. As #1993 but with wide security foil at right.	FV	FV	25.00
1997	**1000 Yüan** 2005. Like #1994 but with wide security foil at right.	FV	FV	40.00

NOTICE

Readers with unlisted dates, signature varieties, etc. are invited to submit photocopies of their notes to: Standard Catalog of World Paper Money, 700 East State St. Iola, WI 54990-0001, E-Mail: george.cuhaj@fwpubs.com.

OFF-SHORE ISLAND CURRENCY

BANK OF TAIWAN

行銀灣臺

T'ai Wan Yin Hang

Notes of the Bank of Taiwan and later notes of the Republic of China/Bank of Taiwan w/ovpt: 門金

KINMEN (QUEMOY) BRANCH

1949-51 (1963; 1967) ISSUE

#R101-R109 portr. SYS at upper ctr. Vertical format.

#R101, R106 and R107 portr. SYS at upper ctr. Vertical format.

用通門金限

Hsien Chin Men T'ung Yung

		VG	VF	UNC
R101	**1 Yüan** 1949 (1963). Green on multicolor underprint. Printer: CPF.	.25	2.00	10.00

1950-51 ISSUES

		VG	VF	UNC
R106	**10 Yüan** 1950 (1963). Blue. Printer: CPF.	.50	1.50	10.00
R107	**50 Yüan** 1951 (1967). Green. Printer: FPFT.	3.00	20.00	120.

1955-72 ISSUES

		VG	VF	UNC
R109	**5 Yüan** 1966. Violet-brown. Printer: CPF.	.75	3.00	20.00
R110	**10 Yüan** 1969 (1975). Red on multicolor underprint. Red overprint on #1979a.	1.00	2.00	10.00

		VG	VF	UNC
R111	**50 Yüan** 1969 (1970). Dark blue on multicolor underprint. SYS at right.	2.00	3.50	25.00

		VG	VF	UNC
R112	**100 Yüan** 1972 (1975). Green overprint on #1983.	4.00	7.50	40.00

1976; 1981 ISSUE

		VG	VF	UNC
R112A	**10 Yüan** 1976. Overprint on #1984.	.25	.75	10.00
R112B	**100 Yüan** 1981. Overprint on #1988.	5.00	8.00	30.00
R112C	**1000 Yüan** 1981. Overprint on #1988.	35.00	50.00	200.

MATSU BRANCH

1950-51 DATED (1964; 1967) ISSUE

#R113-R115 horizontal format.

#R117 and 118 portr. SYS at upper ctr. Vertical format.

		VG	VF	UNC
R117	**10 Yüan** 1950 (1964). Blue on multicolor underprint. Printer: CPF.	1.00	3.00	25.00

		VG	VF	UNC
R118	**50 Yüan** 1951 (1967). Green on multicolor underprint. Printer: FPDT.	3.00	8.00	80.00

1969; 1972 ISSUE

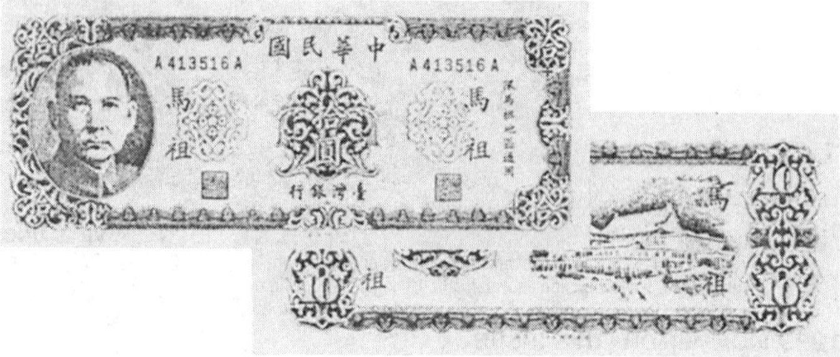

		VG	VF	UNC
R122	**10 Yüan** 1969 (1975). Red on multicolor underprint. Overprint on #1979a. Printer: CPF.	.50	1.00	10.00

		VG	VF	UNC
R123	**50 Yüan** 1969 (1970). Violet on multicolor underprint. Printer: CPF.	2.00	4.00	30.00
R124	**100 Yüan** 1972 (1975). Dark green, light green and orange on multicolor underprint. Green overprint on #1983. Printer: CPF.	4.00	10.00	80.00

1976; 1981 ISSUE

		VG	VF	UNC
R125	**10 Yüan** 1976. Red on multicolor underprint. Overprint on #1984.	.40	1.00	8.00
R126	**500 Yüan** 1981. Brown and red-brown on multicolor underprint. Overprint on #1987.	FV	20.00	80.00
R127	**1000 Yüan** 1981. Blue-black on multicolor underprint. Overprint on #1988.	FV	37.50	200.

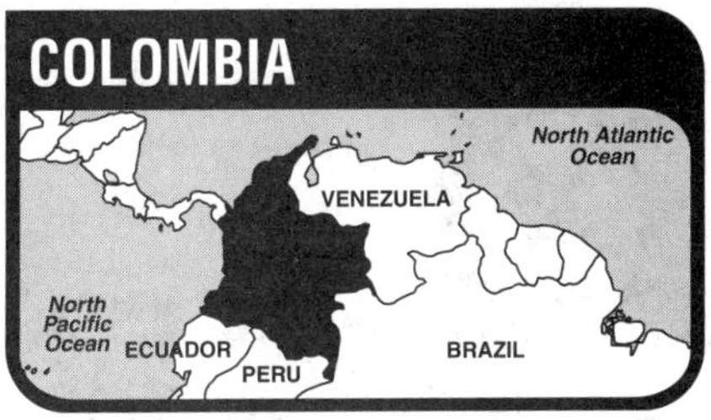

The Republic of Colombia, located in the northwestern corner of South America, has an area of 439,737 sq. mi. (1,138,914 sq. km.) and a population of 42.3 million. Capital: Bogotá. The economy is primarily agricultural with a mild, rich coffee the chief crop. Colombia has the world's largest platinum deposits and important reserves of coal, iron ore, petroleum and limestone; precious metals and emeralds are also mined. Coffee, crude oil, bananas, sugar, coal and flowers are exported.

The northern coast of present Colombia was one of the first parts of the American continent to be visited by Spanish navigators, and the site, at Darien in Panama, of the first permanent European settlement on the American mainland in 1510. New Granada, as Colombia was known until 1861, stemmed from the settlement of Santa Maria in 1525. New Granada was established as a Spanish Colony in 1549. Independence was declared in 1810, and secured in 1824. In 1819, Simón Bolívar united Colombia, Venezuela, Panama and Ecuador as the Republic of Greater Colombia. Venezuela withdrew from the Republic in 1829; Ecuador in 1830; and Panama in 1903.

MONETARY SYSTEM:

1 Peso = 100 Centavos 1993
1 Peso Oro = 100 Centavos to 1993

REPLACEMENT NOTES:

Earlier issues, small *R* just below and between signatures. Larger *R* used later. Some TDLR printings have *R* preceding serial number. Later Colombian-printed notes use circled asterisk usually close to sign. or a star at r. of upper serial #. Known replacements: #389-407, 409, 413-15, 417-19, 421-22, 425-29, 431-433, 436-41, 443, 445-48.

REPUBLIC

BANCO DE LA REPÚBLICA

1943 PESOS ORO ISSUE

		VG	VF	UNC
392	**20 Pesos Oro** 1943-63. Purple and multicolor. Bust of Francisco José de Caldas at left, bust of Simon Bolívar at right. Liberty at center. Printer: ABNC.			
	a. Series U in red. 20.7.1943.	20.00	200.	500.
	b. Series U in purple. 20.7.1944; 1.1.1945.	10.00	60.00	200.
	c. Series U. Prefix A. 7.8.1947.	3.00	15.00	80.00
	d. Series DD. 1.1.1950; 1.1.1951.	1.50	7.50	50.00
	e. Series DD. 2.1.1963.	1.50	7.50	50.00
	s. Specimen.	—	—	65.00

1953 PESOS ORO ISSUE

#400-401 printer: TDLR.

		VG	VF	UNC
400	**10 Pesos Oro** 1953-61. Blue on multicolor underprint. Similar to #377, but palm trees at right instead of watermark. Portrait General Antonio Nariño with Mercury alongside at left. Bank building at Cali. Series N. Printer: TDLR.			
400	**10 Pesos Oro**			
	a. 1.1.1953.	1.00	7.50	35.00
	b. 1.1.1958; 1.1.1960.	1.00	7.50	35.00
	c. 2.1.1961.	1.00	7.50	35.00
	s. Specimen. With red TDLR and *SPECIMEN* overprint. Punched hole cancelled.	—	—	100.

		VG	VF	UNC
401	**20 Pesos Oro** 1953-65. Red-brown on multicolor underprint. Similar to #378, but Liberty in circle at right instead of watermark. Portrait Francisco José de Caldas and allegory at left. Series O. Newer bank building at Barranquilla on back. Printer: TDLR.			
	a. 1.1.1953.	1.00	7.50	35.00
	b. 1.1.1960.	1.00	7.50	35.00
	c. 2.1.1961; 2.1.1965.	1.00	6.00	30.00
	s1. Specimen. With red TDLR overprint and *SPECIMEN*. Punched hole cancelled.	—	—	100.
	s2. Specimen. Red overprint: *SPECIMEN*. Punched hole cancelled.	—	—	65.00

1958 PESOS ORO ISSUE

#402-403 printer: ABNC.

		VG	VF	UNC
402	**50 Pesos Oro** 1958-67. Light brown on multicolor underprint. Portrait Antonio José de Sucre at lower left. Series Z. Olive-green. Liberty at center. Printer: ABNC. 1958-67.			
	a. 20.7.1958; 7.8.1960.	1.00	10.00	60.00
	b. 1.1.1964; 12.10.1967.	1.00	8.00	50.00
	s1. Specimen.	—	—	135.
	s2. Specimen. Red overprint: *SPECIMEN*. Punched hole cancelled.	—	—	135.

		VG	VF	UNC
403	**100 Pesos Oro** 1958-67. Gray on multicolor underprint. Portrait General Francisco de Paula Santander at right. Series Y. Green. Like #402. Printer: ABNC.			
	a. 7.8.1958.	1.00	8.00	60.00
	b. 1.1.1960; 1.1.1964.	1.00	6.00	40.00
	c. 20.7.1965; 20.7.1967.	1.00	6.00	40.00
	p1. Face proof. Without date, signatures, series or serial #. Punched hole cancelled.	—	—	150.
	s. Specimen.	—	—	75.00

1959-60 PESOS ORO ISSUE

Printer: Imprenta de Billets - Bogota.

404 1 Peso Oro

1959-77. Blue on multicolor underprint. Portrait Simón Bolívar at left, portrait General Francisco de Paula Santander at right. Liberty head and condor with waterfall and mountain at center. Printer: Imprenta de Billets-Bogota.

	VG	VF	UNC
a. Security thread. 12.10.1959.	.25	2.50	10.00
b. Security thread. 2.1.1961; 7.8.1962; 2.1.1963; 12.10.1963; 2.1.1964; 12.10.1964.	.20	2.00	7.50
c. As b. 20.7.1966.	1.25	10.00	40.00
d. Without security thread. 20.7.1966; 20.7.1967; 1.2.1968; 2.1.1969.	.15	1.25	5.00
e. Without security thread. 1.5.1970; 12.10.1970; 7.8.1971; 20.7.1972; 7.8.1970; 7.0.1974.	.10	.50	3.00
f. As e. 1.1.1977.	.75	5.00	30.00
s1. Specimen.	—	—	50.00
s2. Specimen. Red overprint: *ESPECIMEN.*	—	—	50.00

1961-64 ISSUE

#406-407 replacement notes: Serial # prefix *R* or *.

406 5 Pesos Oro

1961-81. Deep greenish black and deep brown on multicolor underprint. Condor at left, José María Córdoba at right. Fortress at Cartagena at center on back.

	VG	VF	UNC
a. Security thread. 2.1.1961; 1.5.1963; 2.1.1964.	1.00	6.00	30.00
b. Security thread. 11.11.1965; 12.10.1967; 20.7.1968.	.50	3.00	15.00
c. Security thread. 20.7.1971.	.25	2.50	10.00
d. As c. 1.1.1973.	10.00	50.00	200.
e. Without security thread. 1.1.1973; 20.7.1974; 20.7.1975; 20.7.1976; 20.7.1977.	.15	1.00	4.00
f. Without security thread. 1.10.1978; 1.4.1979; 1.1.1980; 1.1.1981.	.10	.75	2.50
s. Specimen.	—	—	40.00

407 10 Pesos Oro

1963-80. Lilac and slate blue on green and multicolor underprint. General Antonio Nariño at left, condor at right. Back red-brown and slate blue; archaeological site with monoliths.

	VG	VF	UNC
a. Security thread. 20.7.1963.	1.50	10.00	40.00
b. As a. 20.7.1964.	.75	4.00	25.00
c. 20.7.1965; 20.7.1967; 2.1.1969.	.50	4.00	17.50
d. As c. with segmented security thread. 12.10.1970; 1.1.1973.	.50	2.00	10.00
e. As d. 20.7.1974.	15.00	75.00	300.
f. Without security thread. 20.7.1974; 1.1.1975; 20.7.1976; 1.1.1978.	.25	.75	5.00
g. As f. 7.8.1979; 7.8.1980.	.05	.35	3.00
h. Like f., but *SERIE AZ* at left center and upper right. on face. 7.8.1980. *Serie AZ.*	.10	.50	4.00
s. Specimen.	—	—	40.00

408 500 Pesos Oro

20.7.1964. Olive-green on multicolor underprint. Portrait Simon Bolívar at right. Back has no open space under Liberty head. Printer: ABNC. Series *AA*. 6 or 7 digit serial #.

	VG	VF	UNC
a. Issued note.	10.00	50.00	150.
s. Specimen. overprint *MUESTRA* and punched hole cancelled.	—	—	150.

1966-68 ISSUE

#409 replacement note: Serial # prefix *R* or *.

409 20 Pesos Oro

1966-83. Brown, gray and green on multicolor underprint. Francisco José de Caldas with globe at right. Back brown and green on multicolor underprint; *Balsa Muisca* from the Gold Museum.

	VG	VF	UNC
a. Security thread. 12.10.1966; 2.1.1969; 1.5.1972; 1.5.1973.	.75	4.00	25.00
b. As a. 20.7.1974.	25.00	150.	400.
c. Without security thread. 20.7.1974; 20.7.1975; 20.7.1977.	.50	2.00	10.00
d. As c. 1.4.1979; 1.1.1981; 1.1.1982; 1.1.1983.	.25	.75	5.00
s. Specimen.	—	—	40.00

410 100 Pesos Oro

1968-71. Blue on multicolor underprint. General Francisco de Paula Santander at right. Capitol at Bogotá on back. Watermark: Simon Bolívar. Series Y. Printer: TDLR.

	VG	VF	UNC
a. 1.1.1968.	1.25	10.00	45.00
b. 2.1.1969.	1.50	6.00	35.00
c. 1.5.1970; 20.7.1971.	1.25	4.00	22.50
s. Specimen.	—	—	50.00

NOTICE

Readers with unlisted dates, signature varieties, etc. are invited to submit photocopies of their notes to: Standard Catalog of World Paper Money, 700 East State St. Iola, WI 54990-0001, E-Mail: george.cuhaj@fwpubs.com.

411	500 Pesos Oro	VG	VF	UNC
	1968; 1971. Green on multicolor underprint. Simón Bolívar at right. Zipaquirá subterranean salt cathedral. Watermark: Liberty head. Series A. Printer: ABNC.			
	a. 1.1.1968.	7.50	30.00	100.
	b. 12.10.1971.	12.50	40.00	100.
	s. Specimen.	—	—	125.

1969 Issue

412	50 Pesos Oro	VG	VF	UNC
	1969-70. Purple on pale blue, lilac and pink underprint. Blue design without border at left, Camilo Torres at right and as watermark. Arms and flowers on back. Printer: TDLR.			
	a. 2.1.1969.	1.00	6.00	35.00
	b. 12.10.1970.	.75	4.00	25.00
	s. Specimen. Punched hole cancelled.	—	—	100.

1972-73 Issue

#413-415 replacement notes: Serial # prefix *R* or *.

413	2 Pesos Oro	VG	VF	UNC
	1972-77. Purple on multicolor underprint. Policarpa Salavarietta at left. Back brown; *El Dorado* from the Gold Museum.			
	a. Large size serial #, and # at right. near upper border. 1.1.1972; 20.7.1972; 1.1.1973.	.25	1.00	5.00
	b. Small size serial #, and # at right. far from upper border. 20.7.1976; 1.1.1977; 20.7.1977.	.25	1.00	4.00
	s. Specimen.	—	—	50.00

414	50 Pesos Oro	VG	VF	UNC
	20.7.1973; 20.7.1974. Purple on pale blue, lilac and pink underprint. Similar to #412, but curved dark border added at left and right, also at right on back. Printer: TDLR.	.75	3.00	17.50

415	100 Pesos Oro	VG	VF	UNC
	20.7.1973; 20.7.1974. Similar to #410 but curved dark border added at left and right, also at right on back. Series Y. Printer: TDLR.	1.00	4.00	25.00

416	500 Pesos Oro	VG	VF	UNC
	7.8.1973. Red on multicolor underprint. Like #411. Series A. Printer: ABNC.			
	a. Issued note.	12.50	40.00	80.00
	s. Specimen.	—	—	100.

1974 Issue

#417 replacement note: Serial # prefix *R*.

417	200 Pesos Oro	VG	VF	UNC
	1974; 1975. Green on multicolor underprint. Simón Bolívar at center right and as watermark, church at right. *BOGOTÁ COLOMBIA* at lower left center. Man picking coffee beans on back. Printer: TDLR.			

417	200 Pesos Oro	VG	VF	UNC
	a. 20.7.1974.	2.50	12.50	45.00
	b. 7.8.1975.	1.00	5.00	20.00

1977-79 ISSUE

#418-420 replacement notes: Serial # prefix *R* or *.

418	100 Pesos Oro	VG	VF	UNC
	1977-80. Purple and black on multicolor underprint. General Francisco de Paula Santander at center right. Capitol at Bogotá on back. Watermark: Liberty head. Printer: TDLR.			
	a. 1.1.1977.	.25	1.50	8.00
	b. 1.1.1980.	.25	1.25	6.00
	c. Serial # prefix *A-C*. 1.1.1980.	.25	1.25	6.00
	s1. Specimen.	—	—	75.00
	s2. Specimen. Red ovpt: *SPECIMEN*. Punch hole cancelled.	—	—	50.00

Note: Numerals at upper ctr. and upper r. are darker on 1980 dated notes, also the word *CIEN*.

419	200 Pesos Oro	VG	VF	UNC
	20.7.1978; 1.1.1979; 1.1.1980. Like #417 but with only *COLOMBIA* at lower left center. Printer: TDLR.	.50	1.50	8.00

420	500 Pesos Oro	VG	VF	UNC
	1977-79. Olive and multicolor. General Francisco de Paula Santander at left and in profile as watermark. Back gray; subterranean church and Liberty head. Printer: ABNC.			
	a. 20.7.1977.	1.50	6.00	30.00
	b. 1.4.1979.	1.00	4.50	20.00
	s. Specimen.	—	—	100.

421	1000 Pesos Oro	VG	VF	UNC
	1.4.1979. Black and multicolor. José Antonio Galan at right and as watermark. Nariño Palace on back. Printer: ABNC.			
	a. Issued note.	1.00	7.50	30.00
	s. Specimen.	—	—	150.

1980-82 ISSUES

#422 replacement note: Serial # prefix *.

422	50 Pesos Oro	VG	VF	UNC
	1980-83. Purple on pale blue, lilac and pink underprint. *COLOMBIA* added near border at upper left center. Printer: TDLR (without imprint).			
	a. 1.1.1980; 7.8.1981.	FV	1.00	4.00
	b. 1.1.1983.	FV	.50	2.00
	s. Specimen.	—	—	50.00

423	500 Pesos Oro	VG	VF	UNC
	1981-86. Brown, dark green and red-brown on multicolor underprint. General Francisco de Paula Santander at left and in profile as watermark, Bogotá on back; screw coinage press at lower right. Printer: TDLR.			
	a. 20.7.1981.	FV	4.00	20.00
	b. 20.7.1984; 20.7.1985.	FV	2.00	10.00
	c. 12.10.1985; 20.7.1986.	FV	1.00	6.00
	s. Specimen.	—	—	50.00

424	1000 Pesos Oro	VG	VF	UNC
	1982-87. Deep blue and olive-brown on multicolor underprint. Simón Bolívar at left and as watermark. Scene honoring 1819 battle heroes on back. Printer: TDLR.			
	a. 1.1.1982.	FV	5.00	20.00
	b. 7.8.1984.	FV	3.00	10.00
	c. 1.1.1986; 1.1.1987.	FV	2.00	7.00
	s. Specimen.	—	—	75.00

1982-84 Issues

#425-430 replacement notes: Serial # prefix circled-*.

425	50 Pesos Oro	VG	VF	UNC
	1984-86. Purple on pale blue, lilac and pink underprint. Similar to #414. Without watermark. Printer: IBB.			
	a. 12.10.1984; 1.1.1985.	FV	1.00	3.00
	b. 1.1.1986.	FV	FV	2.00
	s. Specimen. Overprint *MUESTRA SIN VALOR.*	—	—	50.00

426	100 Pesos Oro	VG	VF	UNC
	1983-91. Violet, brown, orange and dark red on multicolor underprint. General Antonio Nariño at left and as watermark Villa de Leyva on back; flat bed printing press at lower right. Printer: IBB.			
	a. 1.1.1983; 12.10.1984.	FV	FV	3.00
	b. 12.10.1985; 1.1.1986; 12.10.1986.	FV	FV	2.50
	c. Larger stylized serial #. 12.10.1986; 1.1.1987; 12.10.1988.	FV	FV	2.50
	d. Back colors slightly off shade from earlier issues. 7.8.1989.	FV	FV	2.25
	e. Signature titles: *GERENTE* and *SECRETARIO.* 1.1.1990; 1.1.1991.	FV	FV	1.50
	s. Specimen. Overprint *MUESTRA SIN VALOR.*	—	—	50.00
426A	100 Pesos Oro			
	7.8.1991. Like #426 but red omitted from back. Printer: IBSFB.	FV	FV	1.00

427	200 Pesos Oro	VG	VF	UNC
	1.1.1982. Like #419 but printer: IBB.	FV	FV	5.00

428	200 Pesos Oro	VG	VF	UNC
	1.4.1983. Deep green and black on multicolor underprint. Church and Fr. José Celestino Mutis at left and as watermark, arms at upper right. Bogota Observatory *Observatorio Astronomico Nacional* at right on back. Printer: TDLR.			
	a. Issued note.	FV	1.50	10.00
	s. Specimen.	—	—	50.00

429	200 Pesos Oro	VG	VF	UNC
	1983-91. Deep green and black on multicolor underprint. Like #428.			
	a. Printer: IBB. 1.4.1983; 20.7.1984.	FV	5.00	25.00
	b. 20.7.1984; 1.11.1984; 1.4.1985.	FV	FV	10.00
	c. 1.11.1985.	FV	FV	7.00
	d. Larger stylized and bold serial #. 1.4.1987; 1.4.1988; 1.11.1988; 1.4.1989; 1.11.1989; 1.4.1991.	FV	FV	4.00
	s. Specimen. Red ovpt: *MUESTRA SIN VALOR.* Punch hole cancelled.	—	—	50.00
429A	200 Pesos Oro			
	10.8.1992. Like #439. Printer: IBSFB.	FV	FV	1.25

430	2000 Pesos Oro	VG	VF	UNC
	1983-86. Dark brown and brown-orange on multicolor underprint. Simón Bolívar at left and as watermark. Scene at *Paso del Paramo de Pisba* at center right on back. Printer: TDLR.			
	a. 24.7.1983.	FV	5.00	35.00
	b. 24.7.1984.	FV	4.00	20.00
	c. 17.12.1985.	FV	3.00	15.00
	d. 17.12.1986.	FV	3.00	10.00
	s. Specimen. Some punched hole cancelled.	—	—	50.00

1986-87 ISSUE

#431-433 replacement notes: Serial # prefix *.

		VG	VF	UNC
431	**500 Pesos Oro** 20.7.1986; 12.10.1987; 20.7.1989; 12.10.1990. Like #423. Printer: IBB.	FV	FV	3.00

		VG	VF	UNC
431A	**500 Pesos Oro** 2.3.1992; 4.1.1993. Like #431, but green omitted from back. Printer: IBSFB.	FV	FV	2.50

		VG	VF	UNC
432	**1000 Pesos Oro** 1.1.1987; 1.1.1990; 1.1.1991. Black, blue-green and deep olive-brown on multicolor underprint. Like #424. Printer: IBB.	FV	FV	7.50

		VG	VF	UNC
432A	**1000 Pesos Oro** 31.1.1992; 1.4.1992; 4.1.1993. Like #432. Printer: IBSFB.	FV	FV	4.50

		VG	VF	UNC
433	**2000 Pesos Oro** 17.12.1986; 17.12.1988; 17.12.1990. Dark brown and brown-orange on multicolor underprint. Like #430 but with redesigned *2's* in denomination. Printer: IDD.	FV	FV	9.00

		VG	VF	UNC
433A	**2000 Pesos Oro** 1992. Like #433. Printer: IBSFB.			
	a. 2.3.1992; 1.4.1992.	FV	FV	5.00
	b. 3.8.1992.	5.00	10.00	50.00

1986 COMMEMORATIVE ISSUE

#434, Centennial of the Constitution

		VG	VF	UNC
434	**5000 Pesos Oro** 5.8.1986. Deep violet and red-violet on multicolor underprint. Rafael Nuñez at left and as watermark Statue of Miguel Antonio Caro at center right on back. Printer: BDDK.			
	a. Issued note.	FV	FV	50.00
	s. Specimen with red serial # at upper right.	—	—	75.00

1987 ISSUE

		VG	VF	UNC
435	**5000 Pesos Oro** 5.8.1987; 5.8.1988. Deep violet and red-violet on multicolor underprint. Similar to #434 but printer: IPS-Roma.	FV	FV	35.00

1990 ISSUE

#436 replacement note: Serial # prefix *.

		VG	VF	UNC
436	**5000 Pesos Oro** 1.1.1990. Deep violet and red-violet on multicolor underprint. Like #435. Printer: IBB.	FV	FV	25.00

		VG	VF	UNC
436A	**5000 Pesos Oro** 31.1.1992. 4.1.1993. Like #436. Printer: IBSFB.	FV	FV	25.00

1992 COMMEMORATIVE ISSUE

#437, Quincentennial of Columbus' Voyage, 12.10.1492

		VG	VF	UNC
437	**10,000 Pesos Oro** 1992. Light and dark brown on multicolor underprint. Early sailing ships at center, youthful woman *Mujer Embera* at center right and as watermark, native gold statue at right. Native birds around antique world map at left center, Santa Maria sailing ship at lower right on back. The birds are left to right: greater flamingo, andean condor, green honeycreeper, andean cock of the rock, blue and yellow macaw, hotzin, scarlet ibis, yellow-hooded blackbird, metallic green tanager, white pelican, magnificent frigatebird, keel-billed toucan, baltimore oriole, scarlet macaw, yellow crowned parrot, red-capped cardinal. Printer: BDM.			
	a. Issued note.	FV	FV	60.00
	s. Specimen.	—	—	100.

1993 ISSUE

		VG	VF	UNC
437A	**10,000 Pesos Oro** 1993; 1994. Deep brown and black on multicolor underprint. Like #437. Printer: IBSFB.	FV	FV	40.00

Note: 1,000,000 pieces of #437A dated 1993 were stolen in 1994.

1993-95 ISSUES

Peso System

#437A-441 printer: IBSFB.

		VG	VF	UNC
438	**1000 Pesos** 3.1.1994; 1.11.1994; 1.7.1995; 2.8.1995; 2.10.1995. Like #432 but *EL* omitted from title and *ORO* omitted from value. Black omitted on back.	FV	FV	5.00

#439-443 portr. as wmk.

		VG	VF	UNC
439	**2000 Pesos** 1993-94. Dark brown and brown-orange on multicolor underprint. Like #433 but *EL* deleted from title, *ORO* deleted from value.			
	a. 1.7.1993.	FV	FV	10.00
	b. Orange omitted from back. 1.7.1994; 1.11.1994; 17.12.1994.	FV	FV	8.00

Note: 1,700,000 pieces of #439a were stolen.

		VG	VF	UNC
440	**5000 Pesos** 3.1.1994; 4.7.1994; 2.1.1995. Deep violet and red-violet on multicolor underprint. Like #434-436 but *EL* deleted from the title, *ORO* deleted from the value.	FV	FV	20.00

Note: 2,200,000 pieces of #440 dated 3.1.1994 were stolen in 1994.

441	5000 Pesos	VG	VF	UNC
	1.3.1995; 1.3.1996. Dark brown, brown and deep blue-green on multicolor underprint. José Asunción Silva and bug at upper right, trees at left and center. Watermark: Asunción Silva. Woman, trees and monument at center on back. Printer: IBSFB.			
	a. Issued note.	FV	FV	20.00
	s. Specimen.	—	—	75.00

442	5000 Pesos	VG	VF	UNC
	1.7.1995. Dark brown, brown and deep blue-green on multicolor underprint. Like #441. Printer: TDLR.			
	a. Issued note.	FV	FV	25.00
	s. Specimen.	—	—	75.00
443	10,000 Pesos			
	1.3.1995; 1.8.1996; 23.7.1997; 6.1.1998; 23.7.1998; 23.7.1999; 17.12.1999; 1.6.2001. Deep brown and black on multicolor underprint. Like #437A, but *EL* omitted from title, *ORO* omitted from value, different signature and titles. Printer: IBSFB.			
	a. Issued note.	FV	FV	20.00
	s. Specimen.	—	—	75.00

1995 COMMEMORATIVE ISSUE

#444, 200th Anniversary of Policarpa Salavarrieta *"La Pola"*

Replacement note: Serial # prefix *.

444	10,000 Pesos	VG	VF	UNC
	1.7.1995; 1.8.1995. Red-brown and green on multicolor underprint. Policarpa Salavarrieta at right, Village of Guaduas (ca. 1846) at left center on back. Printer: TDLR.			
	a. Issued note.	FV	FV	30.00
	s. Specimen.	—	—	75.00

1996-97, 2000 ISSUE

#445-449 printer: IBSFB. New arms used afer 1999.

445	2000 Pesos	VG	VF	UNC
	2.4.1996; 6.5.1997; 6.1.1998; 7.8.1998; 9.4.1999; 12.10.1999. Dark olive-green, red-brown and dark brown on multicolor underprint. General Francisco de Paula Santander at right and as watermark. Casa de Moneda building, entrance at left center on back.			
	a. Issued note.	FV	FV	4.00
	s. Specimen.	—	—	50.00

446	5000 Pesos	VG	VF	UNC
	2.1.1997. Dark brown and deep blue-green on multicolor underprint. Like #442.			
	a. Issued note.	FV	FV	10.00
	s. Specimen.	—	—	75.00

447	5000 Pesos	VG	VF	UNC
	12.10.1997; 2.4.1998; 23.7.1999; 12.10.1999. Deep violet and red-violet on multicolor underprint. Like #442 but with bank seal at center.			
	a. Issued note.	FV	FV	8.00
	s. Specimen.	—	—	75.00

448 20,000 Pesos

	VG	VF	UNC
23.7.1996; 6.1.1998; 7.8.1998; 6.5.1999, 1.5.2000; 12.10.2000. Black, deep green and dark blue on multicolor underprint. Julio Garavito Armero at right and as watermark. View of the moon at center. Satellite view of earth at center right, moon's surface along bottom, geometric forms in underprint. on back.			
a. Issued note.	FV	FV	22.50
s. Specimen.	—	—	60.00

449 50,000 Pesos

	VG	VF	UNC
7.8.2000. Purple, green and light orange on multicolor underprint. Jorge Isaacs at lower center. Maria, character from book, at center *Hacienda el Paraiso* on back. Vertical format.			
a. Issued note.	FV	FV	45.00
s. Specimen.	—	—	100.

2001 Issue

#450-455 printer: IBBR.

450 1000 Pesos

	VG	VF	UNC
7.8.2001; 27.9.2001; 17.12.2001; 7.5.2002; 30.5.2003; 16.2.2004; 17.2.2004; 2.3.2005; 3.3.2005. Brown and orange on multicolor underprint. Crowd at center, Jorge Eliécer Gaitán at right and as watermark. Gaitán with right arm raised, crowd behind at center on back.			
a. Issued note.	FV	FV	1.00
s. Specimen.	—	—	50.00

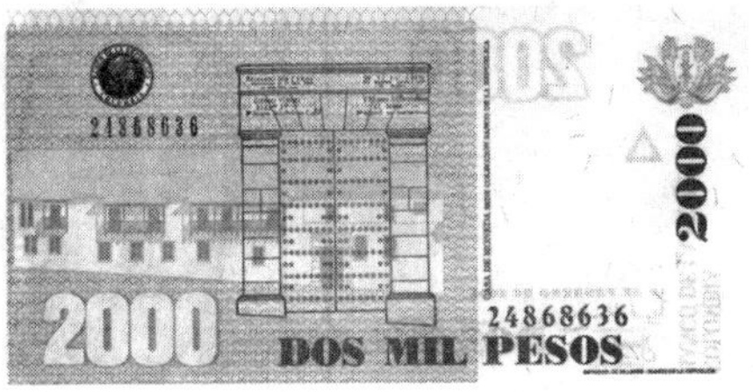

451 2000 Pesos

	VG	VF	UNC
2000-2005. Dark olive-green, red-brown and dark brown on multicolor underprint. Like #445.			
a. 12.10.2000; 23.7.2001; 12.10.2001; 11.11.2001; 8.5.2002; 13.5.2002; 2.6.2003; 18.2.2004.	FV	FV	2.00
b. 19.2.2004; 4.3.2005. Triangles added at left front for visually impaired.	FV	FV	2.00
s. Specimen.	—	—	50.00

452 5000 Pesos

	VG	VF	UNC
11.11.2001; 17.12.2001; 9.5.2002; 6.6.2003. Deep violet and red-violet on multicolor underprint. Like #447.			
a. Issued note.	FV	FV	6.00
s. Specimen.	—	—	50.00

453 10,000 Pesos

	VG	VF	UNC
20.7.2001; 10.5.2002; 20.11.2002; 25.11.2002; 9.6.2003. Deep brown and black on multicolor underprint. Like #443.			
a. Issued note.	FV	FV	11.00
s. Specimen.	—	—	75.00

454 20,000 Pesos

	VG	VF	UNC
1.6.2001; 23.7.2001; 7.8.2001; 14.5.2002; 20.11.2002; 13.6.2003; 16.6.2003; 21.9.2004; 22.9.2004. Black, deep green and dark blue on multicolor underprint. Like #448.			
a. Issued note.	FV	FV	20.00
s. Specimen.	—	Unc	75.00

455	50,000 Pesos	VG	VF	UNC
	1.5.2001; 23.7.2001; 15.5.2002; 20.6.2003; 9.3.2005. Purple, green and light orange on multicolor underprint. Like #449.			
	a. Issued note.	FV	FV	45.00
	s. Specimen.	—	—	100.

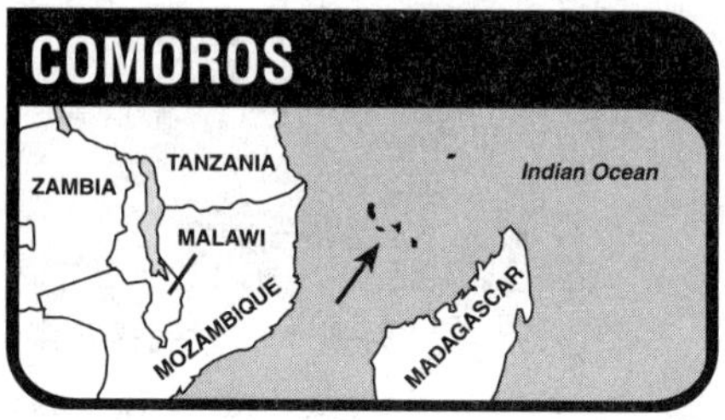

The Federal Islamic Republic of the Comoros, a volcanic archipelago located in the Mozambique Channel of the Indian Ocean 300 miles (483 km.) northwest of Madagascar, has an area of 838 sq. mi. (1,797 sq. km.) and a population of 714,000. Capital: Moroni. The economy of the islands is d on agriculture. There are practically no mineral resources. Vanilla, essence for perfumes, copra and sisal are exported.

Ancient Phoenician traders were probably the first visitors to the Comoros Islands, but the first detailed knowledge of the area was gathered by Arab sailors. Arab dominion and culture were firmly established when the Portuguese, Dutch and French arrived in the 16th century. In 1843 a Malagasy ruler ceded the island of Mayotte to France; the other three principal islands of the archipelago - Anjouan, Moheli and Grand Comore - came under French protection in 1886. The islands were joined administratively with Madagascar in 1912. The Comoros became partially autonomous, with the status of a French overseas territory in 1946 and achieved complete internal autonomy in 1961. On Dec. 31, 1975, after 133 years of French association, the Comoros Islands became the independent Republic of the Comoros.

Mayotte retained the option of determining its future ties and in 1976 voted to remain French. Its present status is that of a French Territorial Collectivity. Euro coinage and currency circulates there.

RULERS:

French to 1975

MONETARY SYSTEM:

1 Franc = 100 Centimes

REPUBLIC

BANQUE DE MADAGASCAR ET DES COMORES

1960 ND PROVISIONAL ISSUE

#2-6 additional red ovpt: *COMORES*.

2	50 Francs	VG	VF	UNC
	ND (1960-63). Brown and multicolor. Woman with hat at right. Man. Overprint on Madagascar #45.			
	a. Signature titles: *LE CONTROLEUR GAL.* and *LE DIRECTEUR GAL.* ND (1960).	—	—	—
	b. Signature titles: *LE DIRECTEUR GAL. ADJOINT* and *LE PRESIDENT DIRECTEUR GAL.* ND (1963). 2 sign varieties.	5.00	25.00	100.
	s. Specimen.	—	—	—

3	100 Francs	VG	VF	UNC
	ND (1960-63). Multicolor. Woman at right, palace of the Queen of Tananariva in background. Woman, boats and animals. Overprint on Madagascar #46.			
	a. Signature titles: *LE CONTROLEUR GAL.* and *LE DIRECTEUR GAL.* ND (1960).	8.00	45.00	150.
	b. Signature titles: *LE DIRECTEUR GAL. ADJOINT* and *LE PRESIDENT DIRECTEUR GAL.* ND (1963).	3.00	15.00	55.00
	s. Specimen.	—	—	—

#4-6 dated through 1952 have titles "a", those dated 1955 or ND have titles "b".

	VG	VF	UNC
4 500 Francs			
ND (1960-63). Multicolor. Man with fruit at center. Overprint on Madagascar #47.			
a. Signature titles: *LE CONTROLEUR GAL* and *LE DIRECTEUR GAL.* - old date 30.6.1950; 9.10.1952 (1960).	25.00	150.	450.
b. Signature titles: *LE DIRECTEUR GAL. ADJOINT* and *LE PRESIDENT DIRECTEUR GAL.* ND (1963).	12.50	100.	350.
5 1000 Francs			
ND (1960-63). Multicolor. Woman and man at left center. Center Ox cart. Overprint on Madagascar #48.			
a. Signature titles: *LE CONTROLEUR GAL.* and *LE DIRECTEUR GAL.* - old date 1950-52; 9.10.1952 (1960).	35.00	200.	550.
b. Signature titles: *LE DIRECTEUR GAL. ADJOINT* and *LE PRESIDENT DIRECTEUR GAL.* ND (1963).	20.00	125.	400.

	VG	VF	UNC
6 5000 Francs			
ND (1960-63). Multicolor. Portrait Gallieni at upper left, young woman at right. Huts at left, woman with baby at right. Overprint on Madagascar #49.			
a. Signature titles: *LE CONTROLEUR GAL.* and *LE DIRECTEUR GAL.* - old date 30.6.1950 (1960).	150.	425.	925.
b. Signature titles: *LE DIRECTEUR GAL. ADJOINT* and *LE PRESIDENT DIRECTEUR GAL.* ND (1963).	100.	325.	800.
c. Signature titles: *LE DIRECTEUR GÉNÉRAL* and *LE PRÉSIDENT DIRECTEUR GAL.*	125.	350.	800.

INSTITUT D'ÉMISSION DES COMORES

1976 ND ISSUE

#7-9 wmk: Crescent on Maltese cross.

	VG	VF	UNC
7 500 Francs			
ND (1976). Blue-gray, brown and red on multicolor underprint. Building at center, young woman wearing a hood at right. Two women at left, boat at right on back. Two signature varieties.			
a. Issued note.	1.00	4.00	15.00
s. Specimen.	—	—	50.00

	VG	VF	UNC
8 1000 Francs			
ND (1976). Blue-gray, brown and green on multicolor underprint. Woman at right, palm trees at water's edge in background. Women on back.			
a. Issued note.	2.00	8.00	25.00
s. Specimen.	—	—	50.00

	VG	VF	UNC
9 5000 Francs			
ND (1976). Green on multicolor underprint. Man and woman at center, boats and building in left background. President Djohr at center on back.			
a. Issued note.	FV	35.00	100.
s. Specimen.	—	—	100.

BANQUE CENTRALE DES COMORES

1984-86 ND ISSUE

#10-12 like to #7-9 but w/new bank name. Wmk: Maltese cross w/crescent.

		VG	VF	UNC
10	**500 Francs** ND (1986-). Blue-gray, brown and red on multicolor underprint. Like #7.			
	a. Partially engraved. signature titles: *LE DIRECTEUR GÉNÉRAL* and *LE PRÉSIDENT DU CONSEIL D'ADMINISTRATION* (1986).	1.00	2.25	10.00
	b. Offset. signature titles: *LE GOUVERNEUR* and *PRÉSIDENT DU...* (1994). (2 signature varieties.)	1.00	2.00	7.00

		VG	VF	UNC
11	**1000 Francs** ND (1984-). Blue-gray, brown and green on multicolor underprint. Like #8.			
	a. Partially engraved. signature titles: *LE DIRECTEUR GÉNÉRAL* and *LE PRÉSIDENT DU CONSEIL D'ADMINISTRATION.* (1986).	1.50	5.00	20.00
	b. Offset. signature titles: *LE GOUVERNEUR* and *PRÉSIDENT DU....* (1994). (2 signature varieties.)	1.50	4.00	15.00

		VG	VF	UNC
12	**5000 Francs** ND (1984-). Green on multicolor underprint. Like #9. Engraved.			
	a. Signature titles: *LE DIRECTEUR GÉNÉRAL* and *LE PRÉSIDENT DU CONSEIL D'ADMINISTRATION.*	5.00	20.00	65.00
	b. Signature titles: *LE GOVERNEUR* and *LE PRESIDENT...*	5.00	20.00	55.00

1997 ND ISSUE

#13 and 14 wmk: 4 stars below crescent (arms).

		VG	VF	UNC
13	**2500 Francs** ND (1997). Purple and blue on multicolor underprint. Woman wearing colorful scarf at left. Sea turtle at lower left center on back.	3.00	10.00	35.00

		VG	VF	UNC
14	**10,000 Francs** ND (1997). Yellow, brown and blue on multicolor underprint. Two seated women weaving baskets at center. Al-Habib Seyyid O. Bin Sumeit at left, mosque at center on back.	10.00	25.00	100.

2006 ISSUE

		VG	VF	UNC
15	**500 Francs** 2006. Pink, blue, green and multicolor. Lemur at upper center. Flowers on back.	FV	FV	5.00
17	**2500 Francs** 1.1.2005. Green and multicolor. Market scene and mosque. Village on back.	FV	FV	25.00
18	**5000 Francs** Expected new issue.	—	—	—
19	**10,000 Francs** 2006. Yellow, cream and multicolor. Friday mosque in Moroni at left, al-Habib Seyyid O. bin Sumeit at center. Cananga tree ylang-ylang flowers and turle on back. Watermark: Four stars and half-moon.	FV	FV	65.00

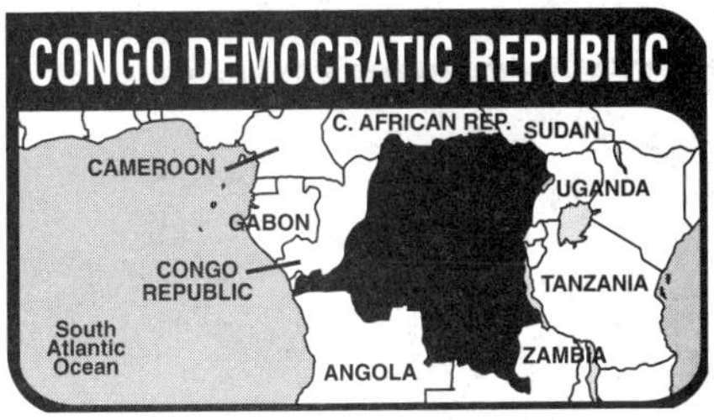

The Congo Democratic Republic (formerly Zaïre), located in the south-central part of Africa, has an area of 905,568 sq. mi. (2,345,409 sq. km.) and a population of 51.75 million. Capital: Kinshasa. The mineral-rich country produces copper, tin, diamonds, gold, zinc, cobalt and uranium.

In ancient times the territory comprising Zaïre was occupied by Negrito peoples (Pygmies) pushed into the mountains by Bantu and Nilotic invaders. The interior was first explored by the American correspondent Henry Stanley, who was subsequently commissioned by King Leopold II of Belgium to conclude development treaties with the local chiefs. The Berlin conference of 1885 awarded the area to Leopold, who administered and exploited it as his private property until it was annexed to Belgium in 1908. Following the eruption of bloody independence riots in 1959, Belgium granted the Belgian Congo independence as the Republic of the Congo on June 30, 1960. The Belgian Congo attained independence with the distinction of being the most ill-prepared country to ever undertake self-government. Without a single doctor, lawyer or engineer, with no organized unit capable of maintaining law and order, independence disintegrated into an orgy of anarchy. Provinces seceded. Intertribal warfare erupted. Belgian troops intervened to protect Belgian citizens from retributive massacre. By 1961, four groups were fighting for political dominance. The most serious threat to the viability of the country was posed by the secession of mineral-rich Katanga province on July 11, 1960.

After two and one-half years of sporadic warfare with a U.N. military force, Katanga's leaders capitulated, Jan. 14, 1963 and the rebellious province was partitioned into three provinces. The nation officially changed its name to Zaïre on Oct. 27, 1971. In May 1997, the dictator was overthrown after a three year rebellion. The country changed its name to the Democratic Republic of the Congo. A change to a Francs-Congolese currency has been considered, but meanwhile "hard" currency such as U.S.A. dollars circulate freely.

See also Rwanda, Rwanda-Burundi, and Zaïre.

MONETARY SYSTEM:

1 Franc = 100 Centimes to 1967
1 Zaïre = 100 Makuta, 1967-71
1 Franc = 100 Centimes, 1997-

CONGO (KINSHASA)

RÉPUBLIQUE DU CONGO
CONSEIL MONÉTAIRE DE LA RÉPUBLIQUE DU CONGO

1962-63 ISSUE

#1-3 various date and sign varieties.

		VG	VF	UNC
1	**100 Francs** 1.6.1963-8.7.1963. Green and multicolor. Dam at left. Dredging at right on back.			
	a. Issued note.	5.00	40.00	100.
	s. Specimen.	—	85.00	145.
	ct. Color trial. Blue on multicolor underprint.	—	—	175.

		VG	VF	UNC
2	**1000 Francs** 15.2.1962. Purple on multicolor underprint. Portrait African man at left. Text: *EMISSION DU CONSEIL MONÉTAIRE DE LA REPUBLIQUE DU CONGO* in place of watermark. Back deep violet on pink underprint.; waterbuck drinking in stream.			
	a. Issued note.	25.00	100.	525.
	s. Specimen.	—	—	385.

		VG	VF	UNC
3	**5000 Francs** 1.12.1963. Gray-green. Portrait African woman at left. Oarsmen on back.			
	a. Issued note.	500.	1750.	—
	s. Specimen.	—	—	4000.
	ct. Color trial. Blue on multicolor underprint.	—	—	4500.

BANQUE NATIONALE DU CONGO

1961 ISSUE

#4-8 sign. 1.

		VG	VF	UNC
4	**20 Francs** 15.11.1961-15.9.1962. Green, blue and brown. Girl seated at right and as watermark. Stylized tree at center on back. Printer: JEZ.			
	a. Issued note.	3.50	15.00	60.00
	s. Specimen.	—	—	75.00

#5-8 long bldg. at bottom on back.

		VG	VF	UNC
5	**50 Francs**			
	1.9.1961-1.7.1962. Green. Lion at left, bridge and lake at center right in background.			
	a. Issued note.	6.00	30.00	145.
	s. Specimen.	—	—	85.00
	ct. Color trial. Brown on multicolor underprint.	—	—	150.

		VG	VF	UNC
6	**100 Francs**			
	1.9.1961-1.8.1964. Dark brown on multicolor underprint. J. Kasavubu at left, two crowned cranes at right. Printer: TDLR.			
	a. Issued note.	5.00	25.00	120.
	s. Specimen.	—	—	95.00

		VG	VF	UNC
7	**500 Francs**			
	15.10.1961; 1.12.1961; 1.1.1962; 1.8.1964. Lilac. Mask at left. Watermark: Bird.			
	a. Issued note.	15.00	55.00	265.
	s. Specimen.	—	—	145.

		VG	VF	UNC
8	**1000 Francs**			
	15.10.1961; 15.12.1961; 1.8.1964. Dark blue on multicolor underprint. J. Kasavubu at left, carving at right. Watermark: Antelope's head. Printer: TDLR.			
	a. Issued note.	12.00	50.00	200.
	s. Specimen.	—	—	120.

1967 ISSUE

#9-13 various date and sign. varieties. Printer: TDLR. Replacement notes: Serial # prefix ZZ.

		VG	VF	UNC
9	**10 Makuta**			
	2.1.1967; 1.9.1968; 14.1.1970; 21.1.1970. Blue on olive-green and multicolor underprint. Stadium at left, Mobutu at right. Long building on back. Signature 1.			
	a. Issued note.	3.00	12.50	60.00
	s. Specimen.	—	—	35.00
10	**20 Makuta**			
	1967-70. Black on green, blue and multicolor underprint. Man with flag at center, P. Lumumba at right. People in long boat at left center on back. Watermark: Antelope's head.			
	a. Signature 1. 24.11.1967; 21.1.1970.	6.00	32.50	130.
	b. Signature 2. 1.10.1970.	5.50	30.00	120.
	s. Specimen. 21.1.1970.	—	—	100.
11	**50 Makuta**			
	1967-70. Red on olive-green and multicolor underprint. Stadium at center left, Mobutu at right. Gathering coconuts on back.			
	a. Signature 1. 2.1.1967; 1.9.1968; 21.1.1970.	6.50	35.00	145.
	b. Signature 2. 1.10.1970.	6.50	35.00	145.
	s. Specimen. 1.9.1968.	—	—	125.

		VG	VF	UNC
12	**1 Zaïre = 100 Makuta**			
	1967-70. Brown and green on multicolor underprint. Stadium at left, Mobutu at right. Mobutu's "time to work" to gathering of people at left center on back. Watermark: Antelope's head.			
	a. Signature 1. 2.1.1967; 24.11.1967; 1.9.1968.	5.50	30.00	120.
	b. Signature 2. 21.1.1970; 1.10.1970.	5.50	30.00	120.
	s1. Specimen. 24.11.1967.	—	—	125.
	s2. Specimen. 1.10.1970.	—	—	125.

		VG	VF	UNC
13	**5 Zaïres = 500 Makuta**			
	1967-70. Green and multicolor. Mobutu at right. Long building at left center on back. Watermark: Antelope's head.			
	a. Signature 1 above title: *LE GOUVERNEUR*. Green date. 2.1.1967; 24.6.1967.	20.00	95.00	385.
	b. Signature 2 below title: *LE GOUVERNEUR*. Black date. 2.1.1967; 24.11.1967; 1.9.1968; 21.1.1970.	15.00	75.00	285.
	s1. Specimen. 2.1.1967.	—	—	275.
	s2. Specimen. 21.1.1970.	—	225.	275.

1971 ISSUE

#14 and 15 portr. Mobutu at l. and as wmk., leopard at lower r. facing r. Sign. 2. Printer: G&D. Replacement notes: Serial # suffix Z.

14	5 Zaïres	VG	VF	UNC
	24.11.1971. Green, black and multicolor. Carving at left center, hydroelectric dam at center right on back.			
	a. Issued note.	20.00	80.00	325.
	s. Specimen.	—	—	250.

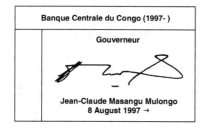

15	10 Zaïres	VG	VF	UNC
	30.6.1971. Blue, brown and multicolor. Arms on back with yellow star.			
	a. Issued note.	20.00	90.00	355.
	s. Specimen.	—	—	250.

DEMOCRATIC REPUBLIC

BANQUE CENTRALE DU CONGO

Banque Centrale du Congo (1997-)	
	Gouverneur  Jean-Claude Masangu Mulongo 8 August 1997 →

1997 ISSUE

#80-90 bank monogram at ctr. Wmk: Single Okapi head or multiple heads repeated vertically.

#80-84 printer imprint is very light.

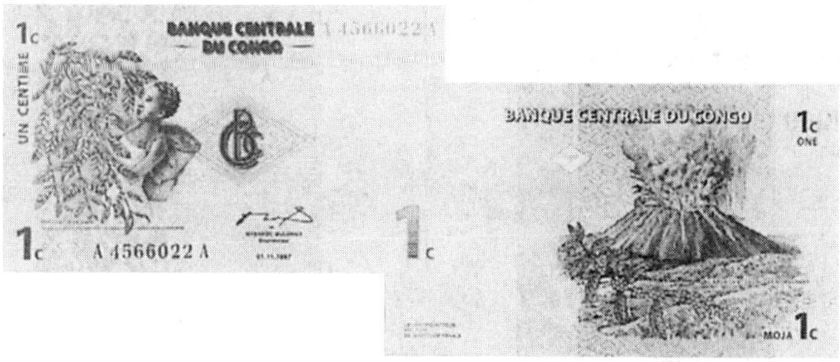

80	1 Centime	VG	VF	UNC
	1.11.1997. Deep olive-green, violet and dark brown on multicolor underprint. Woman harvesting coffee beans at left. Nyiragongo volcano erupting at right on back. Printer: ATB.			
	a. Issued note.	FV	FV	1.00
	s. Specimen.	—	—	3.00

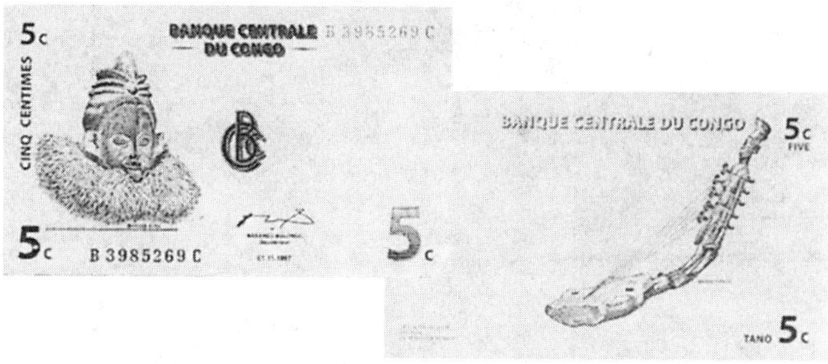

81	5 Centimes	VG	VF	UNC
	1.11.1997. Purple on multicolor underprint. Suku mask at left. Zande Harp at center right on back. Printer: G&D.			
	a. Issued note.	FV	FV	1.00
	s. Specimen.	—	—	10.00

82	10 Centimes	VG	VF	UNC
	1.11.1997. Red-violet and dark brown on multicolor underprint. Pende mask at left. Pende dancers at center right on back. Printer: ATB.			
	a. Issued note.	FV	FV	1.25
	s. Specimen.	—	—	3.00

83	20 Centimes	VG	VF	UNC
	1.11.1997. Blue-green and black on multicolor underprint. Waterbuck at left. Waterbuck herd by large tree at center right on back. Printer: ATB.			
	a. Issued note.	FV	FV	1.25
	s. Specimen.	—	—	4.00

84	50 Centimes	VG	VF	UNC
	1.11.1997. Dark brown and brown on multicolor underprint. Okapi's head at left. Family of Okapis at left center on back. Printer: G&D.			
	a. Issued note.	FV	FV	1.75
	s. Specimen.	—	—	5.00
84A	50 Centimes			
	1.11.1997. As #84. Printer: ATB. Serial # prefix: E; suffix: A-E, T.	FV	FV	1.75

85	1 Franc	VG	VF	UNC
	1.11.1997 (1998). Deep purple and blue-violet on multicolor underprint. Large mining complex at left. Prisoners Lumumba and two companions at center right on back. Printer: G&D.			
	a. Issued note.	FV	FV	4.00
	s. Specimen.	—	—	6.00

86	5 Francs	VG	VF	UNC
	1.11.1997 (1998). Purple and black on multicolor underprint. White rhinoceros at left. Kamwanga Falls at center right on back. Printer: NBBPW.			
	a. Issued note.	FV	FV	5.00
	s. Specimen.	—	—	12.50
86A	5 Francs			
	1.11.1997 (1998). As #86. Printer: HdM.	FV	FV	5.00

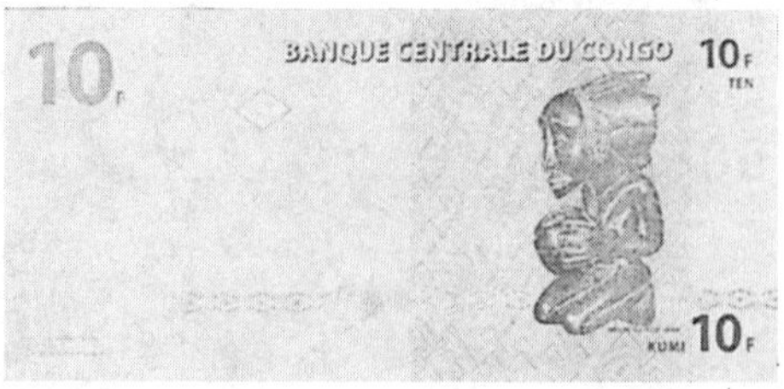

87	10 Francs	VG	VF	UNC
	1.11.1997 (1998). Olive-brown, olive-green and deep blue-green on multicolor underprint. "Apui-tete Chef Luba" carving of a couple at left. "Coupe en Bois Luba" carving at right on back. Printer: NBBPW. Serial # prefix: *H*; suffix: *A*.			
	a. Issued note.	FV	4.00	15.00
	s. Specimen.	—	—	15.00
87A	10 Francs	VG	VF	UNC
	1.11.1997. As 87 but printer G&D. Serial # prefix: H; suffix: B-E.	FV	5.00	17.50
87B	10 Francs	VG	VF	UNC
	1.11.1997. As #87. Printer: HdM.	FV	FV	15.00

88	20 Francs	VG	VF	UNC
	1.11.1997 (1998). Brown-orange and red-orange on multicolor underprint. Male lion's head at left. Lioness lying with two cubs at center right on back. Printer: NBBPW.			
	a. Issued note.	FV	5.00	20.00
	s. Specimen.	—	—	17.50
88A	20 Francs	VG	VF	UNC
	1.11.1997 (1998). As #88. Printer: HdM.	FV	4.00	15.00

89	50 Francs	VG	VF	UNC
	1.11.1997 (1998). Olive-green. Head at left. Village scene on back. Printer: NBBPW.			
	a. Issued note.	FV	10.00	45.00
	s. Specimen.	—	—	25.00

90	100 Francs	VG	VF	UNC
	1.11.1997 (1998). Brown. Elephant at left. Dam on back. Printer: NBBPW.			
	a. Issued note.	FV	17.50	75.00
	s. Specimen.	—	—	30.00
90A	100 Francs			
	1.11.1997. As #90 but printer: HDM.	FV	FV	75.00

2000 ISSUE

		VG	VF	UNC
91	**50 Francs** 4.1.2000. Lilac brown. Like #89. Printer: G&D.	FV	FV	45.00
91A	**50 Francs** 4.1.2000. Like #91 but printer: HDM.	FV	FV	40.00

		VG	VF	UNC
92	**100 Francs** 4.1.2000. Slate blue. Like #90. Printer: G&D.	FV	FV	75.00
92A	**100 Francs** 4.1.2000. Like #92 but printer HdMZ.	FV	FV	75.00

2003 Issue

		VG	VF	UNC
93	**10 Francs** 30.6.2003. Brown and red on orange and blue multicolor underprint. Like #87. Printer G&D.	FV	FV	.25

		VG	VF	UNC
94	**20 Francs** 30.6.2003. Blue-green on green multicolor underprint. Male lion's head at left. Lioness lying with two cubs at center right on back. Printer: HdM-B.O.C.	FV	FV	.50
94A	**20 Francs** 30.6.2003. Like #94 but printer G&D.	FV	FV	.50

		VG	VF	UNC
95	**200 Francs** 30.6.2000 (2003). Lilac and olive green on multicolor underprint. Two farmers at left. Four men working on logs.	FV	FV	.75

		VG	VF	UNC
96	**500 Francs** 4.1.2002 (2004). Blue on multicolor underprint. Miners and diamond at left.	FV	FV	3.25

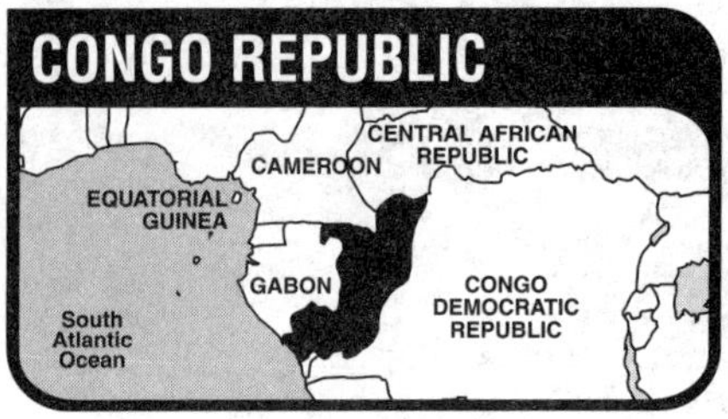

The Republic of the Congo (formerly the Peoples Republic of the Congo), located on the equator in west-central Africa, has an area of 132,047 sq. mi. (342,000 sq. km.) and a population of 2.98 million. Capital: Brazzaville. Agriculture forestry, mining, and food processing are the principal industries. Timber, industrial diamonds, potash, peanuts, and cocoa beans are exported.

The Portuguese were the first Europeans to explore the Congo (Brazzaville) area, 14th century. They conducted a slave trade with the tribal kingdoms of Teke, Loango, and Kongo without attempting developmental colonization. French influence was established in 1883 when the King of Teke signed a treaty with Savorgnan de Brazza, thereby placing his kingdom under the protection of France. While a French protectorate, the area was known as Middle Congo. In 1910 Middle Congo became a part of French Equatorial Africa, which also included Gabon, Ubangi-Shari (now the Central African Republic), and Chad. Following World War II, during which it was an important center of Free French activities, the Middle Congo was given a large measure of internal autonomy, and its inhabitants were made French citizens. Upon approval of the constitution of the Fifth French Republic, 1958, it became a member of the new French Community. On Aug. 15, 1960, Middle Congo became the independent Republic of the Congo-Brazzaville. In Jan. 1970 the country's name was changed to Peoples Republic of the Congo. A new constitution which asserts the government's advocacy of socialism was adopted in 1973. In June and July of 1992, a new 125-member National Assembly was elected. Later that year a new president, Pascal Lissouba, was elected. In November, President Lissouba dismissed the previous government and dissolved the National Assembly. A new 23-member government, including members of the opposition, was formed in December 1992 and the name was changed to République du Congo.

Violence erupted in 1997 nearly emptying the capitol.

RULERS:

French to 1960

MONETARY SYSTEM:

1 Franc = 100 Centimes

SIGNATURE VARIETIES:

Refer to introduction of Central African States.

RÉPUBLIQUE POPULAIRE DU CONGO

BANQUE CENTRALE

1971 ISSUE

		VG	VF	UNC
1	**10,000 Francs** ND (1971). Multicolor. Young Congolese woman at left, people marching with sign at center. Statue at left and right, tractor plowing at center on back. Signature 1.	150.	800.	2250.

BANQUE DES ÉTATS DE L'AFRIQUE CENTRALE

1974 ND ISSUE

		VG	VF	UNC
2	**500 Francs** ND (1974)-1983. Lilac-brown and multicolor. Woman at left, river scene at center. Mask at left, students and chemical testing at center, statue at right on back.			
	a. Signature titles: *LE DIRECTEUR GENERAL* and *UN CENSEUR*. Engraved. Signature 5. ND (1974).	2.50	15.00	50.00
	b. Signature titles: *LE GOUVERNEUR* and *UN CENSEUR*. Lithographed. Signature 10. 1.4.1978.	5.00	25.00	90.00
	c. Titles as b. signature 10; 1.7.1980.	1.50	7.50	25.00
	d. Titles as b. signature 12. 1.6.1981; 1.1.1982; 1.1.1983; 1.6.1984.	1.50	4.00	20.00

		VG	VF	UNC
3	**1000 Francs** ND (1974)-1984. Blue and multicolor. Industrial plant at center, man at right. Mask at left, trains, planes and bridge at center, statue at right on back.			
	a. Signature titles: *LE DIRECTEUR GENERAL* and *UN CENSEUR*. Engraved. watermark: Antelope head in half profile. Signature 3. ND (1974).	10.00	40.00	200.
	b. Like a. signature 5.	4.00	12.50	75.00
	c. Signature titles: *LE DIRECTEUR GENERAL* and *UN CENSEUR*. Lithographed. watermark: Antelope head in profile. Signature 8. ND (1978).	3.00	8.50	35.00
	d. Signature titles: *LE GOUVERNEUR* and *UN CENSEUR*. Lithographed. watermark: like b. Signature 10. 1.4.1978.	2.75	7.50	30.00
	e. Titles as d. signature 12; 1.6.1981; 1.1.1982; 1.1.1983; 1.6.1984.	2.25	6.50	22.50

		VG	VF	UNC
4	**5000 Francs** ND (1974; 1978). Brown. Man at left. Mask at left, buildings at center, statue at right on back.			
	a. Signature titles: *LE DIRECTEUR GENERAL* and *UN CENSEUR*. Signature 3. ND (1974).	35.00	100.	450.
	b. Like a. signature 5.	15.00	75.00	250.
	c. Signature titles: *LE GOUVERNEUR* and *UN CENSEUR*. Signature 11; 12. ND (1978).	13.50	35.00	200.

NOTICE

Readers with unlisted dates, signature varieties, etc. are invited to submit photocopies of their notes to: Standard Catalog of World Paper Money, 700 East State St. Iola, WI 54990-0001, E-Mail: george.cuhaj@fwpubs.com.

5	10,000 Francs	VG	VF	UNC
	ND (1974-81). Multicolor. Like #1 except for new bank name on back.			
	a. Signature titles: *LE DIRECTEUR GENERAL* and *UN CENSEUR*. Signature 5; 7. ND (1974; 1977).	30.00	65.00	275.
	b. Signature titles: *LE GOUVERNEUR* and *UN CENSEUR*. Signature 11; 12. ND (1978; 1981).	25.00	75.00	225.

1983-84 ND ISSUE

6	5000 Francs	VG	VF	UNC
	ND (1984; 1991). Brown and multicolor. Mask at left, woman with bundle of fronds at right. Plowing and mine ore conveyor on back.			
	a. Signature 12. (1984).	15.00	35.00	125.
	b. Signature 15. (1991).	15.00	30.00	100.

7	10,000 Francs	VG	VF	UNC
	ND (1983). Brown, green and multicolor. Stylized antelope heads at left, woman at right. Loading fruit onto truck at left on back. Signature 12.	25.00	40.00	150.

1985-87 ISSUES

Note: For issues w/similar back designs see Cameroun Republic, Central African Republic, Chad and Gabon.

#8-10 sign. titles: *LE GOUVERNEUR* and *UN CENSEUR*.

8	500 Francs	VG	VF	UNC
	1985-91. Brown on multicolor underprint. Statue at left. Center and as watermark, jug at center. Man carving mask at left center on back.			
	a. Signature 12. 1.1.1985; 1.1.1987; 1.1.1989.	FV	1.00	7.00
	b. Signature 12. 1.1.1988.	50.00	—	—
	c. Signature 13. 1.1.1990.	FV	1.00	6.00
	d. Signature 15. 1.1.1991.	FV	1.00	6.00

9	1000 Francs	VG	VF	UNC
	1.1.1985. Dull blue-violet on multicolor underprint. Animal carving at lower left, map of 6 member states at center. Unfinished map of Chad at upper center. Elephant at left, animals at center, carving at right on back. Watermark: Animal carving. Signature 12.	1.25	7.50	20.00

10	1000 Francs	VG	VF	UNC
	1987-91. Dull blue-violet on multicolor underprint. Like #9 but completed map of Chad at top on face.			
	a. Signature 12. 1.1.1987; 1.1.1988; 1.1.1989.	1.00	4.50	15.00
	b. Signature 13. 1.1.1990.	.75	4.00	12.00
	c. Signature 15. 1.1.1991.	.75	3.50	10.00

RÉPUBLIQUE DU CONGO

BANQUE DES ÉTATS DE L'AFRIQUE CENTRALE

1992 ISSUE

		VG	VF	UNC
11	**1000 Francs** 1.1.1992. Dull blue-violet on multicolor underprint. Like #10, but with new country name. Signature 15.	FV	FV	11.00

1992 ND ISSUE

		VG	VF	UNC
12	**5000 Francs** ND (1992). Black text and brown on pale yellow and multicolor underprint. African mask at left and as watermark, woman carrying bundle of cane at right. African string instrument at far left, farm tractor plowing at left center, mineshaft cable ore bucket lift at right on back. Signature 15.	5.00	15.00	45.00

		VG	VF	UNC
13	**10,000 Francs** ND (1992). Greenish-black text, brown on pale green and multicolor underprint. Artistic antelope masks at left, woman's head at right and as watermark. Loading produce truck with bananas at left on back. Signature 15.	5.00	15.00	75.00

Note: For later issues see Central African States.

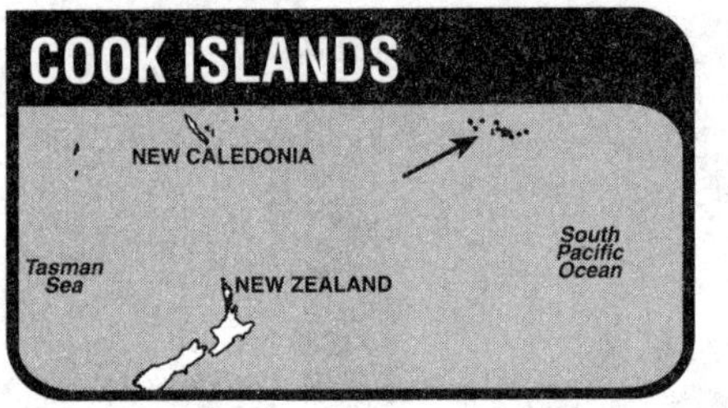

Cook Islands, a political dependency of New Zealand consisting of 15 islands located in the South Pacific Ocean about 2,000 miles (3,218 km.) northeast of New Zealand, has an area of 93 sq. mi. (234 sq. km.) and a population of 20,000. Capital: Avarua. The United States claims the islands of Danger, Manahiki, Penrhyn and Rakahanga atolls. Citrus, canned fruits and juices, copra, clothing, jewelry and mother-of-pearl shell are exported.

The islands were first sighted by Spanish navigator Alvaro de Mendada in 1595. Portuguese navigator Pedro Fernandes de Quieros landed on Rakahanga in 1606. English navigator Capt. James Cook sailed to the islands on three occasions: 1773, 1774 and 1777. He named them Hervey Islands, in honor of Augustus John Hervey, a lord of the Admiralty. The islands were declared a British protectorate in 1888, and were annexed to New Zealand in 1901. They were granted internal self-government in 1965. New Zealand provides an annual subsidy and retains responsibility for defense and foreign affairs.

As a territory of New Zealand, the Cook Islands are considered to be within the Commonwealth of Nations.

Note: In June 1995 the Government of the Cook Islands began redeeming all 10, 20 and 50 dollar notes in exchange for New Zealand currency while most coins originally intended for circulation along with their 3 dollar notes will remain in use.

RULERS:

New Zealand, 1901-

MONETARY SYSTEM:

1 Shilling = 12 Pence
1 Pound = 20 Shillings, to 1967
1 Dollar = 100 Cents, 1967-

NEW ZEALAND ADMINISTRATION

GOVERNMENT OF THE COOK ISLANDS

1987 ND ISSUE

#3-5 Ina and the shark at l.

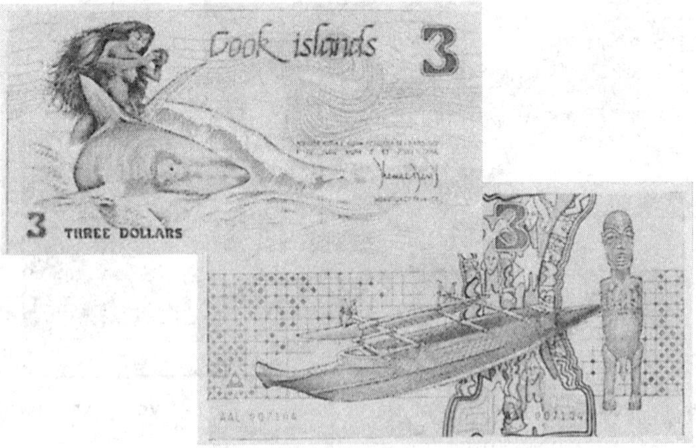

		VG	VF	UNC
3	**3 Dollars** ND (1987). Deep green, blue and black on multicolor underprint. Fishing canoe and statue of the god of Te-Rongo on back.			
	a. Issued note.	FV	3.00	6.50
	s. Specimen.	—	—	25.00

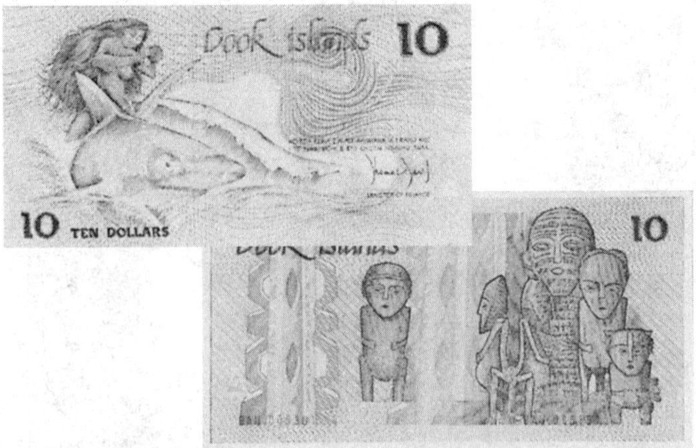

		VG	VF	UNC
4	**10 Dollars** ND (1987). Violet-brown, blue and black on multicolor underprint. Pantheon of gods on back.			
	a. Issued note.	FV	8.50	17.50
	s. Specimen.	—	—	17.50

5	20 Dollars	VG	VF	UNC
	ND (1987). Blue, black and purple on multicolor underprint. Conch shell, turtle shell and drum on back.			
	a. Signature T. Davis.	FV	17.50	37.50
	b. Signature M. J. Fleming.	FV	17.50	35.00
	s. Specimen.	—	—	20.00

1992 Commemorative Issue

#6, 6th Festival of Pacific Arts, Rarotonga, Oct. 16-27, 1992

6	3 Dollars	VG	VF	UNC
	Oct. 1992. Black commemorative text overprint at left on back of #3.	FV	3.00	6.00

1992 ND Issue

#7-10 worshippers at church w/cemetery at ctr. Wmk: Sea turtle.

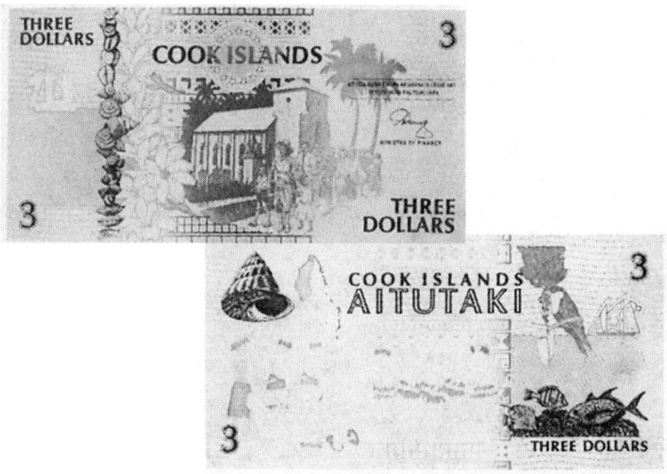

7	3 Dollars	VG	VF	UNC
	ND (1992). Lilac and green on multicolor underprint. Back purple, orange and multicolor. *AITUTAKI* at upper center, local drummers at left, dancers at center, blue lorikeet and fish at right.			
	a. Issued note.	FV	FV	6.00
	s. Specimen.	—	—	20.00

8	10 Dollars	VG	VF	UNC
	ND (1992). Green and olive on multicolor underprint. Cook Islands Fruit Dove. *RAROTONGA* above hillside gathering on back.			
	a. Issued note.	FV	FV	12.50
	s. Specimen.	—	—	25.00

9	20 Dollars	VG	VF	UNC
	ND (1992). Brown-orange and olive on multicolor underprint. *NGAPUTORU & MANGAIA* above two islanders with canoe at center. Mangaia kingfisher at right on back.			
	a. Issued note.	FV	FV	22.50
	s. Specimen.	—	—	20.00

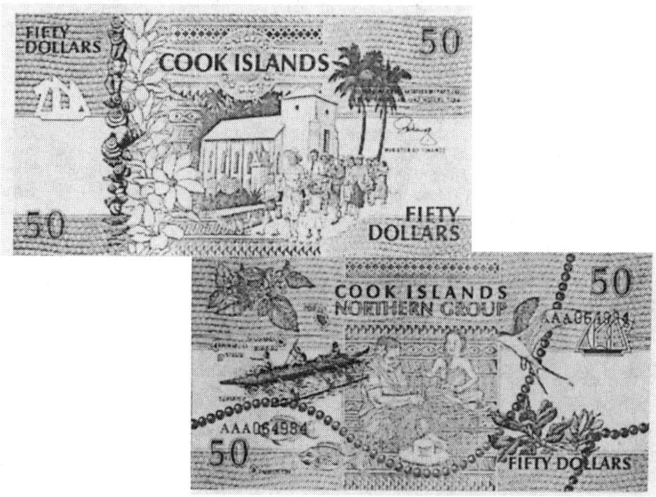

10	50 Dollars	VG	VF	UNC
	ND (1992). Blue and green on multicolor underprint. 3 islanders in canoe at left, *NORTHERN GROUP* above two seated women weaving at center, sooty tern at right on back.			
	a. Issued note.	FV	FV	55.00
	s. Specimen.	—	—	25.00

Collector Series

Government of the Cook Islands

1987 ND Issue

CS1	ND (1987) 3-20 Dollars	Issue Price	Mkt. Value
	#3-5 with matched serial # in special pack.	—	60.00

The Republic of Costa Rica, located in southern Central America between Nicaragua and Panama, has an area of 19,575 sq. mi. (50,700 sq. km.) and a population of 3.8 million. Capital: San Jose. Agriculture predominates; coffee, bananas, beef and sugar contribute heavily to the country's export earnings.

Costa Rica was discovered by Christopher Columbus in 1502, during his last voyage to the new world, and was a colony of Spain from 1522 until independence in 1821. Columbus named the territory Nueva Cartago; the name Costa Rica wasn't generally employed until 1540. Bartholomew Columbus attempted to found the first settlement but was driven off by Indian attacks and the country wasn't pacified until 1530. Costa Rica was absorbed for two years (1821-23) into the Mexican Empire of Agustin de Iturbide. From 1823 to 1848 it was a constituent state of the Central American Republic (q.v.). It was established as a republic in 1848.

Constitution revisions followed in 1871 and 1948. In the early 1990's, Costa Rica was beset with economic problems.

MONETARY SYSTEM:

1 Peso = 100 Centavos to 1090
1 Colon = 100 Centimos

REPUBLIC

BANCO CENTRAL DE COSTA RICA

1951; 1952 ISSUE - SERIES A

		VG	VF	UNC
220	**5 Colones**			
	1951-58. Green on multicolor underprint. Portrait B. Carillo at right. Green. Coffee worker. Printer: ABNC.			
	a. *POR* (for) added to left of signature title at right. 20.11.1952.	3.00	15.00	50.00
	b. Without signature title changes. 2.7.1952-6.8.1958.	3.00	15.00	50.00
	c. Signature title: *SUB-GERENTE* overprint at right. 11.7.1956.	3.00	15.00	50.00
	d. *POR* added to left of signature title at left. 12.9.1951; 26.5.1954.	3.00	15.00	50.00
	s. Specimen.	—	—	—

#221-223 printer: W&S.

		VG	VF	UNC
221	**10 Colones**			
	1951-62. Blue on multicolor underprint. Portrait A. Echeverria at center. Blue. Ox-cart at center. Printer: W & S.			
	a. *POR* added to left of sign title at left. 24.10.1951; 8.11.1951; 19.11.1951; 5.12.1951; 29.10.1952.	6.00	25.00	100.
	b. *POR* added to both signature titles. 28.11.1951.	6.00	25.00	100.
	c. Without *POR* title changes. 2.7.1952; 28.10.1953-27.6.1962.	6.00	25.00	100.
	d. *POR* added to left of signature title at right. 20.11.1952.	6.00	25.00	100.

		VG	VF	UNC
222	**20 Colones**			
	1952-64. Red on multicolor underprint. Portrait C. Picado at center. Red. University building at center. Printer: W & S.			
	a. Date at left center, without signature title changes. 26.2.1952; 11.6.1952; 11.8.1954; 14.10.1955; 13.2.1957; 10.12.62.	15.00	50.00	185.
	b. Signature title: *SUB-GERENTE* overprint at right. 20.4.1955.	15.00	50.00	175.
	c. Date at lower left 7.11.1957-9.9.1964.	15.00	50.00	175.
	d. *POR* added at left of signature title at left. 25.3.1953; 25.2.1954.	15.00	50.00	175.

		VG	VF	UNC
223	**50 Colones**			
	1952-64. Olive on multicolor underprint. Portrait right. F. Guardia at center. Olive. National Library at center. Printer: W & S.			
	a. 10.6.1952-25.11.1959.	15.00	50.00	225.
	b. 14.9.1960-9.9.1964.	15.00	45.00	200.
224	**100 Colones**			
	1952-60. Black on multicolor underprint. Portrait J. R. Mora at center. Black. Statue of J. Santamaría at center.			
	a. Without signature title changes: 11.6.1952-29.4.1960.	15.00	35.00	200.
	b. Signature title: *SUB-GERENTE* overprint at right. 27.3.1957.	15.00	35.00	200.

#225-226 printer: ABNC.

		VG	VF	UNC
225	**500 Colones**			
	1951-77. Purple on multicolor underprint. Portrait M. M. Gutiérrez at right. Purple. National Theater at center. Printer: ABNC.			
	a. 10.10.1951-6.5.1969.	60.00	300.	850.
	b. 7.4.1970-26.4.1977.	50.00	250.	650.
	s. Specimen.	—	—	650.

226	1000 Colones	VG	VF	UNC
	1952-74. Red on multicolor underprint. Portrait J. Pena at left. Red. Central and National Bank at center. Printer: ABNC.			
	a. 11.6.1952-6.10.1959.	125.	500.	1350.
	b. 25.4.1962-6.5.1969.	100.	350.	850.
	c. 7.4.1970-12.6.1974.	60.00	150.	400.
	s. Specimen.	—	—	550.

1958 ISSUE

227	5 Colones	VG	VF	UNC
	29.10.1958-8.11.1962. Green on multicolor underprint. Portrait B. Carrillo at center. Series B. Green. Coffee worker at center. Printer: W & S.	3.50	15.00	50.00

1963-70 ISSUES

#228 and 229 printer: TDLR.

228	5 Colones	VG	VF	UNC
	3.10.1963-29.5.1967. Green on multicolor underprint. Portrait B. Carrillo at center. Back green; coffee worker at center Series C.			
	a. Issued note.	2.50	10.00	45.00
	s. Specimen.	—	—	—

229	10 Colones	VG	VF	UNC
	19.9.1962-9.10.1967. Blue on multicolor underprint. Portrait Echeverría at center. Back blue; ox-cart at center Series B.	5.00	20.00	80.00

230	10 Colones	VG	VF	UNC
	1969-70; ND. Blue on multicolor underprint. Portrait right. Facio Brenes at right. Back blue; Banco Central building at center Series C. Printer: ABNC.			
	a. 4.3.1969; 17.6.1969.	1.50	8.50	35.00
	b. 30.6.1970.	1.00	6.00	25.00
	s. Specimen. overprint *MUESTRA*. Punch hole cancelled.	—	—	—
	x. Without date or signature	—	—	—

Note: It is reported that 10,000 pieces of #230x mistakenly reached circulation. #231-234 printer: TDLR.

231	20 Colones	VG	VF	UNC
	11.11.1964-30.6.1970. Brown on multicolor underprint. Portrait Picado at center. Back brown; University building at center. Series B.			
	a. Issued note.	4.00	15.00	60.00
	s. Specimen.	—	—	—

232	50 Colones	VG	VF	UNC
	9.6.1965-30.6.1970. Greenish-brown on multicolor underprint. Portrait Guardia at center. Back greenish brown; National Library at center. Series B.	7.50	30.00	125.

233	100 Colones	VG	VF	UNC
	1961-66. Black on multicolor underprint. Portrait J. R. Mora at center. Statue of J. Santamaría at center on back. Series B.			
	a. Brown underprint. 18.10.1961-3.12.1964.	10.00	40.00	150.
	b. Olive underprint. and with security thread. 9.6.1965; 14.12.1965; 27.4.1966.	7.50	30.00	150.

234	100 Colones	VG	VF	UNC
	29.8.1966-27.8.1968. Black on multicolor underprint. Portrait Mora at center, without *C* in corners or at right. Back black; statue of J. Santamaría at center. Series C.			
	a. Issued note.	7.50	30.00	135.
	s. Specimen. Ovpt: *MUESTRA*.	—	125.	500.

1967 Provisional Issue

#235 ovpt: *BANCO CENTRAL DE COSTA RICA/SERIE PROVISIONAL* on Banco Nacional notes.

235	2 Colones	VG	VF	UNC
	5.12.1967. Black overprint on #203 (Vol. 2). Series F.	3.00	12.50	45.00

1968-72 Issues

236	5 Colones	VG	VF	UNC
	1968-92. Deep green and lilac on multicolor underprint. Rafael Yglesias Castro at left, flowers at right. Back green on multicolor underprint; National Theater scene. Series D. Printer: TDLR.			
	a. Date at center watermark: *BCCR CINCO*. Security thread. Error name *T. VILLA* on back. 20.8.1968; 11.12.1968.	1.50	5.00	20.00
	b. Date at center r. with watermark. and security thread. Error name *T. VILLA* on back. 1.4.1969; 30.6.1970; 24.5.1971; 8.5.1972.	.50	1.25	9.00
	c. Date at center r. watermark. and security thread. Corrected name *J. VILLA* on back. 4.5.1973-4.5.1976.	FV	.75	6.00
	d. Without watermark. or security thread. Changed signature titles. 28.6.1977-4.10.1989.	FV	FV	3.00
	e. As d. 24.1.1990-15.1.1992.	FV	FV	2.00
	s. As d. Specimen. Ovpt: *MUESTRA*.	—	—	50.00
	x. As d. but with error date: 7.4.1933 (instead of 1983).	5.00	10.00	30.00

237	10 Colones	VG	VF	UNC
	1972-87. Dark blue on multicolor underprint. University building at left, Rodrigo Facio Brenes at right. Central Bank on back. Watermark: *BCCR 10*. Printer: ABNC (without imprint). Series D.			
	a. Security thread. 6.9.1972-1977.	.75	3.00	10.00
	b. Without security thread. 26.4.1977-18.2.1987.	.50	1.00	6.50
	s. As a. Specimen. Ovpt: *MUESTRA*.	—	—	60.00

238	20 Colones	VG	VF	UNC
	1972-83. Dark brown on multicolor underprint. President Cleto González Viquez at left, buildings and trees at right. Allegorical scene of Justice on back. Printer: ABNC (without imprint). Series C.			
	a. Watermark: *BCCR 20*. (error). *BARBA* - etc. text under bldgs. at center signature titles: *EL PRESIDENTE DE LA JUNTA DIRECTIVA* and *EL GERENTE DEL BANCO*. Date at upper right, with security strip. 10.7.1972; 6.9.1972.	1.50	5.00	22.50
	b. Watermark. as a. Text and signature as a., date position at upper center, with security strip. 13.11.1972-26.4.1977.	1.00	2.00	10.00
	c. Without watermark. light brown. signature titles: *PRESIDENTE EJECUTIVO* and *GERENTE*. Without security thread. (corrected). *BARVA*... etc. text under bldgs. at center Date at upper center r. or upper center 1.6.1978-7.4.1983.	.50	1.00	8.50
	s1. Specimen. Ovpt: *MUESTRA*. 1.6.1978.	—	—	80.00
	s2. Specimen. ND.	—	—	80.00

Note: For 20 Colones dated 28.6.1983 Series Z, printed on Tyvek, see #252.

239	50 Colones	VG	VF	UNC
	6.9.1972-26.4.1977. Olive-green multicolor underprint. Meeting scene at left, M. M. de Peralta y Alfaro at right. Casa *Amarilla* (Yellow House) on back. Printer: TDLR (without imprint). Series C.	2.00	7.50	30.00

240	100 Colones	VG	VF	UNC
	26.8.1969-26.4.1977. Black on multicolor underprint. Ricardo Jimenez O. at left, cows and mountains at center. Supreme Court at left center, figures at right on back. Printer: TDLR. Series D.			
	a. Issued note.	3.50	12.50	45.00
	s. Specimen. Ovpt: *MUESTRA*.	—	—	—

1971 Commemorative Issue

#241-246 circular ovpt: 150 *AÑOS DE INDEPENDENCIA* 1821-1971

241	5 Colones	VG	VF	UNC
	24.5.1971. Overprint on #236b. Series D.	2.00	8.50	35.00

242	10 Colones	VG	VF	UNC
	24.5.1971. Overprint on #230. Series C.	5.00	25.00	100.

243	50 Colones	VG	VF	UNC
	24.5.1971. Overprint on #232. Series B.	20.00	75.00	300.

244	100 Colones	VG	VF	UNC
	24.5.1971; 13.12.1971. Overprint on #240. Series D.	30.00	100.	500.

245	500 Colones	VG	VF	UNC
	24.5.1971. Overprint on #225. Series A.	125.	500.	1000.

246	1000 Colones	VG	VF	UNC
	24.5.1971. Overprint on #226. Series A.	200.	650.	1500.

1975 Commemorative Issue

#247, circular ovpt: *XXV ANIVERSARIO BANCO CENTRAL DE COSTA RICA*

247	5 Colones	VG	VF	UNC
	20.3.1975. Overprint on #236. Series D.	1.50	12.50	40.00

1975-79 Issue

248	100 Colones	VG	VF	UNC
	1977-88. Black on multicolor underprint. Ricardo Jimenez O. at left. Series E. Printer: TDLR.			
	a. 26.4.1977-24.12.1981.	1.00	4.00	20.00
	b. 18.5.1982-9.11.1988.	.75	3.00	15.00

NOTICE

Readers with unlisted dates, signature varieties, etc. are invited to submit photocopies of their notes to: Standard Catalog of World Paper Money, 700 East State St. Iola, WI 54990-0001, E-Mail: george.cuhaj@fwpubs.com.

249 500 Colones | VG | VF | UNC
1979-85. Purple on multicolor underprint. M. M. Gutierrez at right. National Theatre at center right on back. Series B. Printer: TDLR.

	VG	VF	UNC
a. Red serial #. 4.6.1979-12.3.1981.	3.50	15.00	75.00
b. Black serial #. 17.9.1981; 24.12.1981; 18.5.1982; 7.8.1984; 20.3.1985.	2.50	12.50	40.00

250 **1000 Colones**	VG	VF	UNC
9.6.1975; 13.11.1978; 24.12.1981; 8.7.1982; 4.11.1982; 7.4.1983; 2.10.1984; 20.3.1985. Red on multicolor underprint. T. Soley Guell at left. National Insurance Institute at center right on back. Series B. Printer: ABNC.	FV	10.00	50.00

1978 COMMEMORATIVE ISSUE

#251, Centennial - Bank of Costa Rica 1877-1977

251 50 Colones
1978-86. Olive-green and multicolor. Obverse of 1866-dated 50 Centimos coin at left, Gaspar Ortunoy Ors at right. Old bank, reverse of 50 Centimos coin and commemorative text: *1877-CENTENARIO...* on back. Series D. Printer: TDLR.

	VG	VF	UNC
a. 30.10.1978; 30.4.1979; 18.3.1980; 2.4.1981.	1.50	6.00	22.50
b. 18.5.1982; 28.8.1984; 22.11.1984; 20.3.1985; 2.4.1986.	1.00	4.00	20.00

1983-88 ISSUE

252 **20 Colones**	VG	VF	UNC
28.6.1983. Design like #238c, but Series Z. Printed on Tyvek.	1.00	5.00	20.00

253 **50 Colones**	VG	VF	UNC
15.7.1987; 26.4.1988. Olive-green on multicolor underprint. Similar to 251 but text: *ANTIGUO EDIFICIO...* on back. Watermark: *BCCR 50* with security thread. Series E. Printer: CdM-Brazil.	FV	2.00	10.00

1986, 1987 ISSUE

254 **100 Colones**	VG	VF	UNC
30.11.1988; 4.10.1989; 5.10.1990. Black on multicolor underprint. Similar to #248. Series F. Printer: ABNC.	.50	2.50	15.00

255 **500 Colones**	VG	VF	UNC
21.1.1987; 14.6.1989. Brown-orange, brown and olive-brown on multicolor underprint. Similar to #249, but clear watermark area at left. Series C. Printer: TDLR.	FV	4.00	20.00

256 1000 Colones

19.11.1986; 17.6.1987; 6.1.1988; 17.1.1989. Red on multicolor underprint. Similar to #250. Series C. Printer: ABNC.

	VG	VF	UNC
a. Issued note.	FV	7.50	40.00
s. Specimen.	—	—	100.

1990-92 ISSUE

257 50 Colones

19.6.1991; 28.8.1991; 29.7.1992; 2.6.1993; 7.7.1993. Olive-green on multicolor underprint. Similar to #253. Series E. Without security thread. Printer: TDLR.

	VG	VF	UNC
a. Issued note.	FV	.50	6.00
s. Specimen. Ovpt: *MUESTRA*.	—	—	120.

258 100 Colones

17.6.1992. Black on multicolor underprint. Like #254. Series G. Printer: CdM-Brazil.

	VG	VF	UNC
	FV	1.00	9.00

259 1000 Colones

1990-94. Red on multicolor underprint. Similar to #250 and #256. Series C. Printer: USBN.

	VG	VF	UNC
a. 24.4.1990; 3.10.1990; 23.10.1991.	FV	4.00	20.00
b. 2.2.1994; 20.4.1994; 15.6.1994; 10.10.1994.	FV	FV	15.00

260 5000 Colones

1991-95. Dark blue, blue and dark brown on multicolor underprint. Local sculpture at left. Center Toucan, leopard, local carving, foliage and sphere on back. Series A. Printer: TDLR.

	VG	VF	UNC
a. 28.8.1991;11.3.1992; 29.7.1992.	FV	20.00	70.00
b. 4.5.1994; 18.1.1995.	FV	FV	55.00

1993-97 ISSUE

261 100 Colones

28.9.1993. Black on multicolor underprint. Like #258. Watermark: *BCCR-100* (repeated). Series H. Printer: ABNC.

	VG	VF	UNC
a. Issued note.	FV	.75	5.00
s. Specimen. Ovpt: *MUESTRA*. 28.9.1993.	—	—	125.

262 500 Colones

6.7.1994. Brown-orange, brown and olive-brown on multicolor underprint. Similar to #255 but with printing in watermark area at left. Ascending size serial # at lower left. Series D. Printer: TDLR.

	VG	VF	UNC
a. Issued note.	FV	FV	12.50
s. Specimen. Ovpt: *MUESTRA*. 6.7.1994.	—	—	150.

#263 *Deleted*. See #259. #264-267 printer: F-CO.

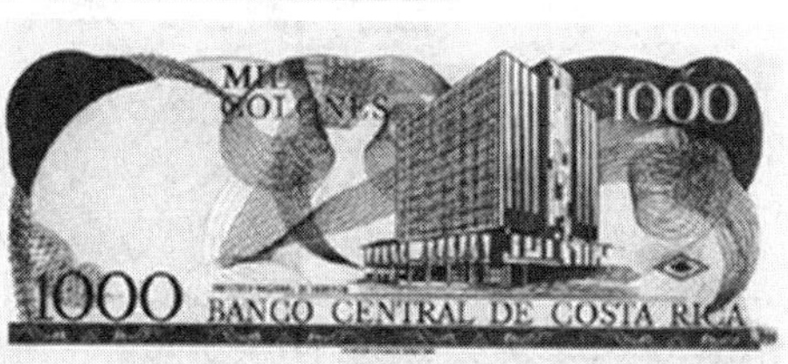

264 1000 Colones

23.7.1997; 23.9.1998; 9.4.2003. Red on multicolor underprint. Like #263 but with ascending size serial # at upper right. Series D.

	VG	VF	UNC
a. Issued note.	FV	FV	15.00
s. Specimen. Ovpt: *MUESTRA*. 23.7.1997.	—	—	200.

265	2000 Colones	VG	VF	UNC
	30.7.1997 (1998). Brown-orange and dark brown on multicolor underprint. C. Picado T. at center right and as watermark, Coco Island in underprint at center. Hammerhead shark at left, dolphin at lower center on back. Series A.			
	a. Issued note.	FV	FV	25.00
	s. Specimen. Ovpt: *MUESTRA* or *MUESTRA SIN VALOR.*	—	—	250.

266	5000 Colones	VG	VF	UNC
	27.3.1996 (1997). Dark blue and dark brown on multicolor underprint. Like #260 but with ascending size serial #. Series B. Printer: TDLR.			
	a. Issued note.	FV	FV	45.00
	s. Specimen. Ovpt: *MUESTRA* or *MUESTRA SIN VALOR.*	—	—	300.

267	10,000 Colones	VG	VF	UNC
	30.7.1997 (1998). Dark blue and deep blue-green on multicolor underprint. E. Gamboa A. at center right and as watermark, volcanoes in underprint at center. Puma at upper center on back. Series A.			
	a. Issued note.	FV	FV	85.00
	s. Specimen. Ovpt: *MUESTRA.* 30.7.1997.	—	—	500.

1999 ISSUE

267A	1000 Colones	VG	VF	UNC
	1999. Multicolor.	FV	FV	10.00

268	5000 Colones	VG	VF	UNC
	24.2.1999. Dark blue and dark brown on multicolor underprint. Like #266 but with microprinting and security thread added. Series C.			
	a. Issued note.	FV	FV	35.00
	s. Specimen. Ovpt: *MUESTRA* or *MUESTRA SIN VALOR.*	—	—	400.

2000 COMMEMORATIVE ISSUE

50th Anniversary Banco Central

#269-273 as #262-267 but w/commemorative ovpt. *50 BCCR ANIVERSARIO* added at lower r. 10,000 notes of each denomination were overprinted, but not all on uncirculated notes. All of #269-271 were sold as collectors' items; however, approximately 1/3 of #272-73 were put into general circulation.

269	500 Colones	VG	VF	UNC
	6.7.1994. Brown-orange, brown on multicolor underprint. As #262 but with commemorative overprint.	FV	FV	10.00

270	1000 Colones	VG	VF	UNC
	23.9.1998. Red on multicolor underprint. As #264 but with commemorative overprint.	FV	FV	15.00

271	2000 Colones	VG	VF	UNC
	30.7.1997. Brown-orange and dark brown on multicolor underprint. As #265 but with commemorative overprint.	FV	FV	30.00

		VG	VF	UNC
272	**5000 Colones** 24.2.1999. Dark blue and dark brown on multicolor underprint. As #266 but with commemorative overprint.	FV	FV	70.00

		VG	VF	UNC
273	**10,000 Colones** 30.7.1997. Dark blue and deep blue-green on multicolor underprint. As #267 but with commmemorative overprint.			
	a. Issued note.	FV	FV	150.
	s. Specimen.	—	—	—

The Republic of Croatia (Hrvatska), formerly a federal republic of the Socialist Federal Republic of Yugoslavia, has an area of 21,829 sq. mi. (56,538 sq. km.) and a population of 4.48 million. Capital: Zagreb.

Countless archeological sites witness the rich history of the area dating from Greek and Roman times, continuing uninterruptedly through the Middle Ages until today. An Independent state under the first Count Borna (about 800 AD), Croatia was proclaimed a kingdom under Tomislav in 925. In 1102 the country joined the personal union with Hungary, and by 1527 all Croatian lands were included in the Habsburg kingdom, staying in the union until 1918, when Croatia became part of the Yugoslav kingdom together with Slovenia and Serbia. In the past, Croats played a leading role in the wars against the Turks, the Antemuralis Christianitatis, and were renown soldiers in the Napoleonic army. From 1941 to 1945 Croatia was an independent military puppet state; from 1945 to 1991 it was part of the Socialist state of Yugoslavia. Croatia proclaimed its independence from Yugoslavia on Oct. 8, 1991.

Local Serbian forces supported by the Yugoslav Federal Army had developed a military stronghold and proclaimed an independent "SRPSKE KRAJINA" state in the area around Knin, located in southern Croatia. In August 1995 Croat forces overran this political-military enclave.

RULERS:

Austrian, 1527-1918
Yugoslavian, 1918-1941

MONETARY SYSTEM:

1 Dinar = 100 Para

Note: Certain listings encompassing issues circulated by various bank and regional authorities are contained in Volume 1.

REPUBLIC

REPUBLIKA HRVATSKA

REPUBLIC OF CROATIA

1991-93 ISSUE

#16-27 R. Boskovic at ctr., geometric calculations at upper r. (Printed in Sweden).

#16-22 vertical back with Zagreb cathedral and artistic rendition of city buildings behind.

		VG	VF	UNC
16	**1 Dinar** 8.10.1991. Dull orange-brown on multicolor underprint. 4.5mm serial #. Watermark: Lozenges.			
	a. Issued note.	.05	.25	.50
	s. Specimen.	—	—	15.00

		VG	VF	UNC
17	**5 Dinara** 8.10.1991. Pale purple on multicolor underprint. 4mm serial #. Watermark: Lozenges.			
	a. Issued note.	.05	.25	.50
	s. Specimen.	—	—	15.00

		VG	VF	UNC
18	**10 Dinara** 8.10.1991. Pale red-brown on multicolor underprint. 4.5mm serial #. Watermark: Lozenges.			
	a. Issued note.	.25	.50	1.00
	s. Specimen.	—	—	20.00

19	25 Dinara	VG	VF	UNC
	8.10.1991. Dull purple on multicolor underprint. Buff paper with 2.8mm serial #. Watermark: 5's in crossed wavy lines.			
	a. Issued note.	.50	1.00	1.50
	b. Inverted watermark.	1.00	10.00	30.00
	s. Specimen.	—	—	20.00

Note: The wmk. paper actually used in the production for #19 was originally prepared for printing Sweden 5 Kroner, #51.

20	100 Dinara	VG	VF	UNC
	8.10.1991. Pale green on multicolor underprint. Without watermark.			
	a. Issued note.	.50	1.50	2.50
	s. Specimen.	—	—	35.00

#21-26 wmk: Baptismal font.

21	500 Dinara	VG	VF	UNC
	8.10.1991. Lilac on multicolor underprint.			
	a. Issued note.	1.00	2.50	10.00
	s. Specimen.	—	—	30.00

22	1000 Dinara	VG	VF	UNC
	8.10.1991. Pale blue-violet on multicolor underprint.			
	a. Issued note.	1.50	3.00	12.00
	s. Specimen.	—	—	30.00

#23-26 statue of seated Glagolica *Mother Croatia* at ctr. on back.

23	2000 Dinara	VG	VF	UNC
	15.1.1992. Deep brown on multicolor underprint.			
	a. Issued note.	.50	2.00	7.00
	s. Specimen.	—	—	30.00

24	5000 Dinara	VG	VF	UNC
	15.1.1992. Dark gray on multicolor underprint.			
	a. Issued note.	.50	2.50	9.00
	s. Specimen.	—	—	30.00

25	10,000 Dinara	VG	VF	UNC
	15.1.1992. Olive-green on multicolor underprint.			
	a. Issued note.	1.00	3.00	12.00
	s. Specimen.	—	—	30.00

26	50,000 Dinara	VG	VF	UNC
	30.5.1993. Deep red on multicolor underprint.			
	a. Issued note.	.25	.50	2.50
	s. Specimen.	—	—	25.00

27	100,000 Dinara	VG	VF	UNC
	30.5.1993. Dark blue-green on multicolor underprint.			
	a. Issued note.	.50	1.00	5.00
	s. Specimen.	—	—	25.00

NARODNA BANKA HRVATSKE

1993 ISSUE

#28-35 shield at upper l. ctr. Printer: G&D.

28	5 Kuna	VG	VF	UNC
	31.10.1993 (1994). Dark green and green on multicolor underprint. F. K. Frankopan and P. Zrinski at right and as watermark. Fortress in Varazdin at left center on back.			

28 5 Kuna

	VG	VF	UNC
a. Issued note.	1.00	2.00	3.00
s. Specimen.	—	—	20.00
x. Error without date or signature	12.00	30.00	60.00

29 10 Kuna

31.10.1993 (1994). Purple and violet on multicolor underprint. J. Dobrila at right and as watermark Pula arena at left center on back.

	VG	VF	UNC
a. Issued note.	2.00	4.00	7.00
s. Specimen.	—	—	20.00

30 20 Kuna

31.10.1993 (1994). Brown, red and violet on multicolor underprint. J. Jelacic at right and as watermark. Pottery dove and castle of Count Eltz in Vukovar at left center on back.

	VG	VF	UNC
a. Issued note.	3.00	5.00	10.00
s. Specimen.	—	—	25.00

31 50 Kuna

31.10.1993 (1994). Dark blue and blue-green on multicolor underprint. I. Gundulic at right and as watermark. Aerial view of old Dubrovnik at left center on back.

	VG	VF	UNC
a. Issued note.	5.00	8.00	20.00
s. Specimen.	—	—	26.00

32 100 Kuna

31.10.1993 (1994). Red-brown and brown-orange on multicolor underprint. I. Mazuranic at right and as watermark. Plan of and church of St. Vitus in Rijeka at left center on back.

	VG	VF	UNC
a. Issued note.	8.00	15.00	35.00
s. Specimen.	—	—	30.00
x. Error without serial #.	12.00	30.00	60.00

33 200 Kuna

31.10.1993 (1994). Dark brown and brown on multicolor underprint. S. Radic at right and as watermark. Town command in Osijek at left center on back.

	VG	VF	UNC
a. Issued note.	15.00	25.00	45.00
s. Specimen.	—	—	30.00

34 500 Kuna

31.10.1993 (1994). Dark brown and olive-brown on multicolor underprint. M. Marulic at right and as watermark. Palace of Diocletian in Spit at left center on back.

	VG	VF	UNC
a. Issued note.	25.00	45.00	95.00
s. Specimen.	—	—	35.00

35 1000 Kuna

31.10.1993 (1994). Dark brown and purple on multicolor underprint. A. Star cevic at right and as watermark. Equestrian statue of King Tomislav at left center, Zagreb Cathedral at center right on back.

	VG	VF	UNC
a. Issued note.	45.00	75.00	185.
s. Specimen.	—	—	40.00

1995 Issue

36	10 Kuna	VG	VF	UNC
	15.1.1995. Black and brown on green and multicolor underprint. Like #29. Printer: G&D.			
	a. Issued note.	FV	FV	4.00
	s. Specimen.	—	—	40.00

Hrvatska Narodna Banka

2001 Issue

#37-39 new bank name arrangement. Wmk. as portrait. Perfect registration devices and microprinting on each. Printer: G&D.

37	5 Kuna	VG	VF	UNC
	7.3.2001. Multicolor. Similar to #28.	FV	FV	2.50

38	10 Kuna	VG	VF	UNC
	7.3.2001. Multicolor. Similar to #29.	FV	FV	4.00

39	20 Kuna	VG	VF	UNC
	7.3.2001. Multicolor. Similar to #30.	FV	FV	9.00

40	50 Kuna	VG	VF	UNC
	7.3.2002. Multicolor. Similar to #31.	FV	FV	18.00

41	100 Kuna	VG	VF	UNC
	2001. Multicolor. Similar to #32.	FV	FV	35.00

42	200 Kuna	VG	VF	UNC
	2001. Multicolor. Similar to #33.	FV	FV	60.00
43	500 Kuna			
	2001. Multicolor. Similar to #34. Expected new issue.	—	—	—
44	1000 Kuna			
	2001. Multicolor. Similar to #35. Expected new issue.	—	—	—

2004 Commemorative Issue

#45, 10th Anniversary of the National Bank of Croatia.

45	10 Kuna	VG	VF	UNC
	2004. Like #38 but large 10 added in watermark area.	FV	FV	4.00

COLLECTOR SERIES

REPUBLIC OF CROATIA

1998 ISSUE

		Issue Price	Mkt. Value
CS1	**1991-93 1-100,000 Dinara** #16-27 with matched serial #. (50,000).	—	—
CS2	**1993 5-1000 Kuna** #28-36 with matched serial #. (50,000).	—	—

Note: #CS1 and CS2 are sold by the Croatian National Bank.

REGIONAL

РЕПУБЛИКА СРПСКА КРАЈИНА

REPUBLIKA SRPSKA KRAJINA

1991 ВРИЈЕДНОСНИ БОН ISSUE

#RA1-RA3 Serbian arms at upper l. Uniface.

		VG	VF	UNC
RA1	**10,000 Dinara** 1991.	—	120.	450.

		VG	VF	UNC
RA2	**20,000 Dinara** 1991.	—	60.00	350.

		VG	VF	UNC
RA3	**50,000 Dinara** 1991.	—	80.00	450.

1992 ISSUE

#R1-R6 arms at l., numerals in heartshaped design below guilloche at ctr. r. Curved artistic design at l. ctr., arms at r. on back. Headings in Serbo-Croatian and Cyrillic.

#R1-R3 wmk: Young girl.

Replacement notes: #R1-R34, ZA prefix letters.

Note: For notes identical in color and design to #R1-R19 but differing only in text at top, sign. and place of issue Banja Luka, see Bosnia-Herzegovina #133-147.

		VG	VF	UNC
R1	**10 Dinara** 1992. Deep brown on orange and silver underprint. Back with ochre underprint.			
	a. Issued note.	.25	1.00	2.00
	b. Specimen.	—	—	10.00

		VG	VF	UNC
R2	**50 Dinara** 1992. Gray on tan and yellow underprint.			
	a. Issued note.	.25	1.00	2.00
	s. Specimen.	—	—	10.00

		VG	VF	UNC
R3	**100 Dinara** 1992. Blue-gray on lilac and silver underprint.			
	a. Issued note.	.50	1.50	3.50
	s. Specimen.	—	—	10.00

		VG	VF	UNC
R4	**500 Dinara** 1992. Blue-gray on pink and multicolor underprint. Watermark: Young boy.			
	a. Issued note.	1.00	4.00	15.00
	s. Specimen.	—	—	15.00

		VG	VF	UNC
R5	**1000 Dinara** 1992. Deep gray on pink and tan underprint.			
	a. Issued note.	1.00	5.00	20.00
	s. Specimen.	—	—	15.00

		VG	VF	UNC
R6	**5000 Dinara**			
	1992. Violet on light blue, pink and lilac underprint.			
	a. Issued note.	1.00	4.00	15.00
	s. Specimen.	—	—	15.00

НАРОДНА БАНКА РЕПУБЛИКЕ СРПСКЕ КРАЈИНЕ

NARODNA BANKA REPUBLIKE SRPSKE KRAJINE

NATIONAL BANK OF THE SERBIAN REPUBLIC - KRAJINA

1992-93 ISSUE

#R7-R12 replacement notes: Serial # prefix *ZA*.

#R7-R16 like #R1-R6.

		VG	VF	UNC
R7	**10,000 Dinara**			
	1992. Deep gray-green on light blue and tan underprint..			
	a. Issued note.	.50	3.00	15.00
	s. Specimen.	—	—	15.00

		VG	VF	UNC
R8	**50,000 Dinara**			
	1992. Brown on pale orange and pale olive-green underprint. Watermark: Young boy.			
	a. Issued note.	1.00	4.50	20.00
	s. Specimen.	—	—	15.00

		VG	VF	UNC
R9	**100,000 Dinara**			
	1993. Dull purple and brown on multicolor underprint. Watermark: Young women.			
	a. Issued note.	1.00	5.00	25.00
	s. Specimen.	—	—	15.00

#R10-R12 wmk: Young girl.

		VG	VF	UNC
R10	**1 Million Dinara**			
	1993. Deep purple on multicolor underprint.			
	a. Issued note.	2.00	8.00	30.00
	s. Specimen.	—	—	20.00

		VG	VF	UNC
R11	**5 Million Dinara**			
	1993. Dark brown on orange and blue-gray underprint.			
	a. Issued note.	.50	2.00	7.00
	s. Specimen.	—	—	10.00

		VG	VF	UNC
R12	**10 Million Dinara**			
	1993. Deep blue on pale olive-green and multicolor underprint.			
	a. Issued note.	.50	2.00	7.00
	s. Specimen.	—	—	10.00

#R13-R19 wmk: Greek design repeated. Replacement notes: Serial # prefix *Z*.

R13	20 Million Dinara	VG	VF	UNC
	1993. Olive-gray on orange and tan underprint.			
	a. Issued note.	1.00	3.00	12.00
	s. Specimen.	—	—	10.00

R14	50 Million Dinara	VG	VF	UNC
	1993. Brown-violet on pink and light gray underprint.			
	a. Issued note.	1.00	3.00	10.00
	s. Specimen.	—	—	10.00

R15	100 Million Dinara	VG	VF	UNC
	1993. Blue-black on light blue and gray underprint.			
	a. Issued note.	.50	1.50	6.00
	s. Specimen.	—	—	10.00

R16	500 Million Dinara	VG	VF	UNC
	1993. Orange on lilac and yellow underprint.			
	a. Issued note.	.50	2.00	8.00
	s. Specimen.	—	—	10.00

R17	1 Milliard Dinara	VG	VF	UNC
	1993. Dull brownish orange on pale blue and light orange underprint.			
	a. Issued note.	.50	2.00	8.00
	s. Specimen.	—	—	10.00

R18	5 Milliard Dinara	VG	VF	UNC
	1993. Purple on lilac and gray underprint.			
	a. Issued note.	1.00	3.50	12.00
	s. Specimen.	—	—	15.00

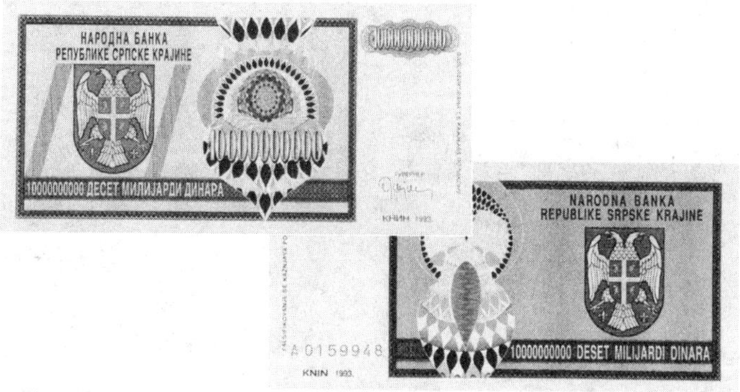

R19	10 Milliard Dinara	VG	VF	UNC
	1993. Black on orange and pink underprint.			
	a. Issued note.	1.50	4.50	15.00
	s. Specimen.	—	—	15.00

1993 ISSUE

#R20-R27 Knin fortress on hill at l. ctr. Serbian arms at ctr. r. on back. Wmk: Greek design repeated. Replacement notes: Serial # prefix *Z*.

R20	5000 Dinara	VG	VF	UNC
	1993. Red-violet and violet on blue-gray underprint.			
	a. Issued note.	.25	1.00	3.00
	s. Specimen.	—	—	10.00

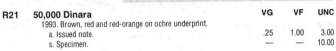

R21 50,000 Dinara

1993. Brown, red and red-orange on ochre underprint.

	VG	VF	UNC
a. Issued note.	.25	1.00	3.00
s. Specimen.	—	—	10.00

R22 100,000 Dinara

1993. Violet and blue-gray on pink underprint.

	VG	VF	UNC
a. Issued note.	.25	1.00	3.00
s. Specimen.	—	—	10.00

R23 500,000 Dinara

1993. Brown and gray-green on pale green underprint.

	VG	VF	UNC
a. Issued note.	.25	1.00	3.00
s. Specimen.	—	—	10.00

R24 5 Million Dinara

1993. Orange and gray-green on pale orange underprint.

	VG	VF	UNC
a. Issued note.	.50	1.00	3.50
s. Specimen.	—	—	10.00

R25 100 Million Dinara

1993. Olive-brown and grayish green on light blue underprint.

	VG	VF	UNC
a. Issued note.	.50	1.00	1.00
s. Specimen.	—	—	10.00

R26 500 Million Dinara

1993. Chocolate brown and gray-green on pale olive-green underprint.

	VG	VF	UNC
a. Issued note.	.50	1.50	4.00
s. Specimen.	—	—	10.00

R27 5 Milliard Dinara

1993. Brown-orange and aqua on gray underprint.

	VG	VF	UNC
a. Issued note.	1.00	2.00	6.00
s. Specimen.	—	—	10.00

R28 10 Milliard Dinara

1993. Purple and red on aqua underprint.

	VG	VF	UNC
a. Issued note.	1.00	2.00	7.00
s. Specimen.	—	—	15.00

R29 **50 Milliard Dinara**

1993. Brown and olive-green on reddish brown underprint.

	VG	VF	UNC
a. Issued note.	1.00	2.00	6.00
s. Specimen.	—	—	15.00

1994 ISSUE

#R30-R34 like #R2-R29.

Replacement notes: Serial # prefix *ZA*.

R30 **1000 Dinara**

1994. Dark brown and slate-gray on yellow-orange underprint.

	VG	VF	UNC
a. Issued note.	.25	.50	2.00
s. Specimen.	—	—	10.00

R31 **10,000 Dinara**

1994. Red-brown and dull purple on ochre underprint.

	VG	VF	UNC
a. Issued note.	.25	.50	2.00
s. Specimen.	—	—	10.00

R32 **500,000 Dinara**

1994. Dark brown and blue-gray on grayish green underprint.

	VG	VF	UNC
a. Issued note.	.50	1.00	3.00
s. Specimen.	—	—	10.00

R33 **1 Million Dinara**

1994. Purple and aqua on lilac underprint.

	VG	VF	UNC
a. Issued note.	.50	1.00	3.00
s. Specimen.	—	—	10.00

R34 **10 Million Dinara**

1994. Gray and red-brown on pink underprint.

	VG	VF	UNC
a. Issued note.	.50	1.50	5.00
s. Specimen.	—	—	10.00

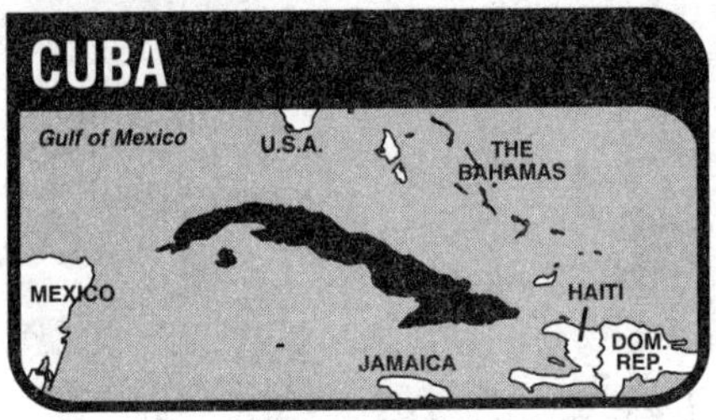

The Republic of Cuba, situated at the northern edge of the Caribbean Sea about 90 miles (145 km.) south of Florida, has an area of 44,218 sq. mi. (114,524 sq. km.) and a population of 11.2 million. Capital: Havana. The Cuban economy is d on the cultivation and refining of sugar, which provides 80 percent of export earnings.

Discovered by Columbus in 1492 and settled by Diego Velasquez in the early 1500s, Cuba remained a Spanish possession until 1898, except for a brief British occupancy in 1762-63. Cuban attempts to gain freedom were crushed, even while Spain was granting independence to its other American possessions. Ten years of warfare, 1868-78, between Spanish troops and Cuban rebels exacted guarantees of right which were never implemented. The final revolt, begun in 1895, evoked American sympathy, and with the aid of U.S. troops independence was proclaimed on May 20, 1902. Fulgencio Batista seized the government in 1952 and established a dictatorship. Opposition to Batista, led by Fidel Castro, drove him into exile on Jan. 1, 1959. A communist-type, 25-member collective leadership headed by Castro was inaugurated in March 1962.

RULERS:

Spanish to 1898

MONETARY SYSTEM:

1 Peso = 100 Centavos
1 Peso Convertible = 1 U.S.A. Dollar, 1995-

REPUBLIC

BANCO NACIONAL DE CUBA

NATIONAL BANK OF CUBA

1961 ISSUE

#94-99 denomination at l. and r. Sign. titles: *PRESIDENTE DEL BANCO* at l., *MINISTRO DE HACIENDA* at r. Printer: STC-P (w/o imprint).

94	1 Peso	VG	VF	UNC
	1961-65. Olive-green on ochre underprint. Portrait J. Martí at center. F. Castro with rebel soldiers entering Havana in 1959 on back.			
	a. 1961.	1.00	3.00	17.00
	b. 1964.	.50	2.50	10.00
	c. 1965.	.40	1.75	8.00
	s. As a. Specimen.	—	—	6.00

95	5 Pesos	VG	VF	UNC
	1961-65. Dull deep green on pink underprint. Portrait A. Maceo at center. Invasion of 1958 on back.			
	a. 1961.	1.00	3.75	19.00
	b. 1964.	.75	3.00	12.50
	c. 1965.	.50	2.50	10.00
	s. As a. Specimen.	—	—	6.00

96	10 Pesos	VG	VF	UNC
	1961-65. Brown on tan and yellow underprint. Portrait M. Gómez at center. Castro addressing crowd in 1960 on back.			
	a. 1961.	1.25	5.00	23.00
	b. 1964.	1.00	4.50	17.50
	c. 1965.	1.00	4.00	15.00
	s. As a. Specimen.	—	—	6.00

97	20 Pesos	VG	VF	UNC
	1961-65. Blue on pink underprint. Portrait C. Cienfuegos at center. Soldiers on the beach in 1956 on back.			
	a. 1961.	2.50	12.50	60.00
	b. 1964.	2.00	8.00	35.00
	c. 1965.	1.75	7.50	30.00
	s. As a. Specimen.	—	—	8.00
	x. U.S.A. counterfeit. Series F69; F70, 1961.	3.50	20.00	100.

Note: Each member of the "Bay of Pigs" invasion force was reportedly issued one hundred each of #97x. They are found w/ or w/o added serial #.

98	50 Pesos	VG	VF	UNC
	1961. Purple on green underprint. Portrait C. García Iñiguez at center. Nationalization of international industries on back.			
	a. Issued note.	10.00	35.00	150.
	s. Specimen.	—	—	10.00

99 **100 Pesos**

1961. Light red on orange underprint. Portrait C. M. de Céspedes at center. Attack on Moncada in 1953 on back.

	VG	VF	UNC
a. Issued note.	25.00	60.00	210.
s. Specimen.	—	—	10.00

Note: #98 and 99 were recalled shortly after release. A small hoard recently appeared in the marketplace.

1966 Issue

#100 and 101 denomination at l. and r. Sign titles: *PRESIDENTE DEL BANCO* at l. and r. Printer: STC-P (w/o imprint).

100 **1 Peso**

1966. Olive-green on ochre underprint. Like #94.

	VG	VF	UNC
a. Issued note.	.25	1.25	5.00
s. Specimen.	—	—	6.00

101 **10 Pesos**

1966. Brown on tan and yellow underprint. Like #96.

	VG	VF	UNC
a. Issued note.	2.00	7.50	20.00
s. Specimen.	—	—	6.00

1967; 1971 Issue

#102-105 denomination at l. Sign. title: *PRESIDENTE DEL BANCO* at lower r. Printer: STC-P (w/o imprint).

102 **1 Peso**

1967-88. Olive-green on ochre underprint. Similar to #94.

	VG	VF	UNC
a. 1967-70; 1972.	.25	1.00	5.00
b. 1978-85.	.25	.50	3.50
c. 1986.	.25	.50	3.00
d. 1988.	.25	.50	2.50
s. Specimen.	—	—	6.00

103 **5 Pesos**

1967-90. Dull deep green on pink underprint. Similar to #95.

	VG	VF	UNC
a. 1967-68.	.25	1.00	15.00
b. 1970; 1972.	.25	.75	12.50
c. 1984-87.	.25	.75	10.00
d. 1988; 1990.	.25	.50	4.00
s. Specimen.	—	—	6.00

104 **10 Pesos**

1967-89. Brown on tan and yellow underprint. Similar to #96.

	VG	VF	UNC
a. 1967-71.	.50	1.00	15.00
b. 1978.	.50	1.00	15.00
c. 1983-84; 1986-87.	.50	1.00	10.00
d. 1988-89.	.50	1.00	10.00
s. Specimen.	—	—	—

105 **20 Pesos**

1971-90. Blue on pink underprint. Similar to #97.

	VG	VF	UNC
a. 1971.	1.00	3.50	20.00
b. 1978.	1.00	3.50	20.00
c. 1983.	1.00	3.50	15.00
d. 1987-90.	1.00	3.50	10.00
s. Specimen.	—	—	6.00

1975 Commemorative Issue

#106, 15th Anniversary Nationalization of Banking

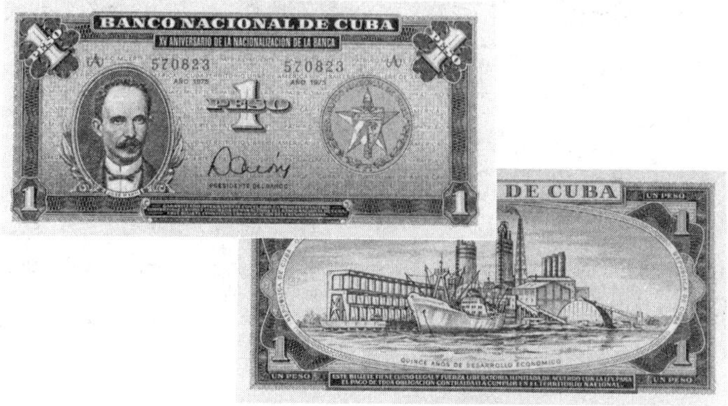

106 **1 Peso**

1975. Olive on violet underprint. Portrait J. Martí at left, arms at right. Ship dockside on back.

	VG	VF	UNC
a. Issued note.	.50	1.25	5.00
s. Specimen.	—	—	5.00

1983 Issue

107	3 Pesos	VG	VF	UNC
	1983-89. Red on multicolor underprint. Portrait E. "Che" Guevara at center. Back red on orange underprint; "Che" cutting sugar cane at center.			
	a. 1983-86.	.50	1.00	5.00
	b. 1988-89.	.50	1.00	2.00
	s. Specimen.	—	—	5.00

1990; 1991 Issue

Replacement notes: #108-112: *EX, DX, CX, BX, AX* series #, by denomination.

108	5 Pesos	VG	VF	UNC
	1991. Deep green and blue on multicolor underprint. A. Maceo at right. Conference between A. Maceo and Spanish General A. Martínez Campos at Mangos de Baraguá in 1878 at left center on back. Watermark: J. Marti.			
	a. Issued note.	.25	.50	1.25
	s. Specimen.	—	—	5.00

109	10 Pesos	VG	VF	UNC
	1991. Deep brown and olive-green on multicolor underprint. M. Gómez at right. "Guerra de todo el Pueblo" at left center on back. Watermark: J. Marti.			
	a. Issued note.	FV	FV	2.50
	s. Specimen.	—	—	5.00

110	20 Pesos	VG	VF	UNC
	1991. Blue-black and purple on multicolor underprint. C. Cienfuegos at right. Agricultural scenes at left center on back. Watermark: Celia Sánchez Manduley.			
	a. Issued note.	FV	FV	5.00
	s. Specimen.	—	—	5.00

111	50 Pesos	VG	VF	UNC
	1990. Deep violet and dark green on multicolor underprint. Arms at center. C. García Iñiguez at right center of Genetic Engineering and Biotechnology at left center on back. Watermark: Celia Sánchez Manduley.			
	a. Issued note.	FV	FV	6.00
	s. Specimen.	—	—	5.00

1995 Issue

#112 and 113 arms at upper ctr. r.

112	1 Peso	VG	VF	UNC
	1995. Dull olive-green and orange on light blue and multicolor underprint. J. Martí at left, arms at upper center right. F. Castro with rebel soldiers entering Havana in 1959 on back.	FV	FV	.75

113	3 Pesos	VG	VF	UNC
	1995. Red-brown, purple and green on multicolor underprint. E. *Che* Guevara at left. Guevara cutting sugar cane on back.	FV	FV	1.50

1995 Dual Commemorative Issue

#114, 45th anniversary of central banking in Cuba and 100th of death of José Martí

114 **1 Peso**

	VG	VF	UNC
1995. Black and olive-green on green and brown underprint. J. Martí at left, arms and commemorative text at center right. Horseback riders at center, commemorative text and dates at left on back. Specimen.	—	—	200.

Note: It is reported that only 1300 examples of #114 were printed, only as specimens. The value is speculative.

BANCO CENTRAL DE CUBA

1997-98 ISSUE

116 **5 Pesos**

	VG	VF	UNC
1997; 1998; 2000; 2001. Green on multicolor underprint. A. Maceo at right. Back similar to #108.	FV	FV	1.25

117 **10 Pesos**

	VG	VF	UNC
1997; 1998; 2001. Brown on multicolor underprint. M. Gómez at right. Back similar to #109.	FV	FV	2.50

118 **20 Pesos**

	VG	VF	UNC
1998; 2000; 2001. Blue-black and light blue on violet and blue underprint. C. Cienfuegos at right. Back similar to #110.	FV	FV	5.00

119 **50 Pesos**

	VG	VF	UNC
1998; 1999; 2001. Light purple on green underprint. C. Garcia Iñiguez at right center. Back similar to #111.	FV	FV	6.00

2000 COMMEMORATIVE ISSUE

#120, 50th anniversary of central banking in Cuba

120 **100 Pesos**

	VG	VF	UNC
2000. Reddish brown on yellow underprint. Carlos Manuel de Cespedes at right, commemorative symbol and text at left. Martí and scene of Havana on back. Watermark: National heroine.	FV	FV	8.00

2001-02 ISSUE

121 **1 Peso**

	VG	VF	UNC
2002. Black and olive green. J. Martí at right. Fidel Castro and victory parade scene on back.	FV	FV	1.25

121A **50 Pesos**

	VG	VF	UNC
2002.	FV	FV	7.50

		VG	VF	UNC
121B	**100 Pesos** 2001. As #120 but without commemorative overprint.	FV	FV	15.00

2003 First Commemorative Issue

150th Anniversary birth of Jose Martí.

		VG	VF	UNC
122	**1 Peso** 2003. José Martí at right. Martí's birthplace on back.	FV	FV	1.50

2004 Commemorative Issue

		VG	VF	UNC
123	**3 Pesos** 2004. Brown on tan underprint. E. "Che" Guevara at right. View of Guevara in sugar cane fields on back.	FV	FV	2.00

2004 Issue

		VG	VF	UNC
124	**1 Peso** 2004. Multicolor. Like #122.	FV	FV	1.50
125	**100 Pesos** 2004. Multicolor. Like #121B.	FV	FV	100.

Foreign Exchange Certificates

The Banco Nacional de Cuba issued four types of peso certificates in series A, B, C and D. The C and D series was issued in two designs and originally required hand issue date and sign. at redemption. Resembling traveler's checks.

Banco Nacional de Cuba

Series A

#FX1-FX5 red-violet. Arms at l. Various Spanish colonial fortresses on back.

		VG	VF	UNC
FX1	**1 Peso** ND (1985). Orange and olive-green underprint. Castillo San Salvador de la Punta on back.	.25	1.50	3.50
FX2	**3 Pesos** ND (1985). Orange and pink underprint. Castillo San Pedro de la Roca on back.	.50	3.50	7.00
FX3	**5 Pesos** ND (1985). Orange and blue-green underprint. Castillo de los Tres Reyes del Morro on back.	1.00	5.00	10.00
FX4	**10 Pesos** ND (1985). Orange and brown underprint. Castillo Nuestra Señora de Los Angeles de Jagua on back.	2.00	9.00	17.50

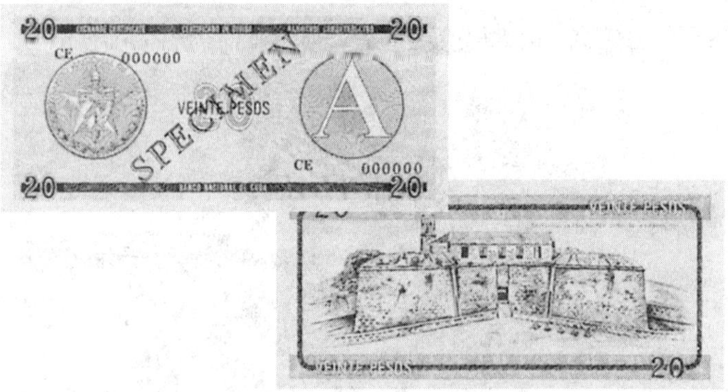

		VG	VF	UNC
FX5	**20 Pesos** ND (1985). Orange and blue underprint. Castillo de la Real Fuerza on back.	4.00	20.00	40.00

Series B

#FX6-FX10 dk. green. Arms at l. Various Spanish colonial fortresses on back.

		VG	VF	UNC
FX6	**1 Peso** ND (1985). Light green and olive-brown underprint. Back like #FX1.	.25	1.00	2.50
FX7	**5 Pesos** ND (1985). Light green and blue-green underprint. Back like #FX3.	1.00	5.00	20.00
FX8	**10 Pesos** ND (1985). Light green and brown underprint. Back like #FX4.	2.00	10.00	30.00
FX9	**20 Pesos** ND (1985). Light green and blue underprint. Back like #FX5.	4.00	20.00	40.00

		VG	VF	UNC
FX10	**50 Pesos** ND (1985). Light green and dull violet underprint. Castillo de la Chorrera on back.	7.50	20.00	70.00

SERIES C FIRST ISSUE

Note: Large quantities were sold into the numismatic market.

#FX11-18 pale blue. Arms at l.

		VG	VF	UNC
FX11	**1 Peso** ND. Light blue and light red-brown underprint.	.10	.25	1.50

		VG	VF	UNC
FX12	**3 Pesos** ND. Light blue and violet underprint.	.10	.30	1.75
FX13	**5 Pesos** ND. Light blue and light olive underprint.	.10	.50	2.50
FX14	**10 Pesos** ND. Light blue and lilac underprint.	.10	.40	2.25
FX15	**20 Pesos** ND. Light blue and tan underprint.	.15	.50	3.00
FX16	**50 Pesos** ND. Light blue and rose underprint.	.20	.60	3.50
FX17	**100 Pesos** ND. Light blue and ochre underprint.	.20	.75	4.00
FX18	**500 Pesos** ND. Light blue and tan underprint.	.20	5.00	20.00

SERIES C SECOND ISSUE

#FX19-FX26 blue-violet. Similar to #FX11-FX18.

		VG	VF	UNC
FX19	**1 Peso** ND.	.15	.50	1.25
FX20	**3 Pesos** ND. Light blue and red underprint.	.15	.50	1.25
FX21	**5 Pesos** ND. Light blue and pale olive-green underprint.	.25	1.00	2.00

		VG	VF	UNC
FX22	**10 Pesos** ND. Light blue and brown underprint.	.50	1.50	3.00
FX23	**20 Pesos** ND. Light blue and orange-brown underprint.	.50	2.50	5.00

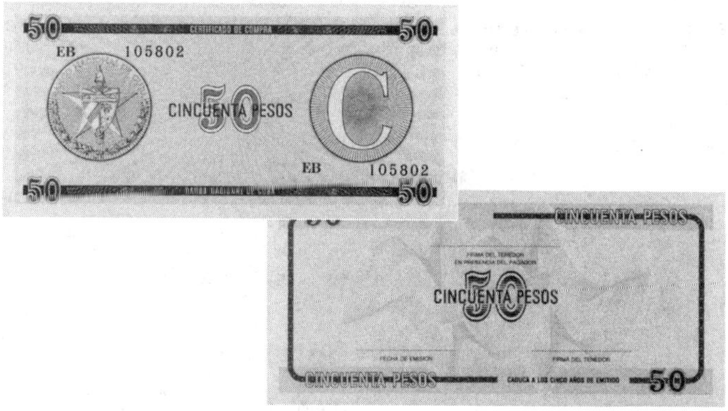

		VG	VF	UNC
FX24	**50 Pesos** ND. Light blue and violet underprint.	.50	1.50	5.00
FX25	**100 Pesos** ND. Light blue and gray underprint.	.50	1.50	5.00
FX26	**500 Pesos** ND.	2.00	5.00	25.00

SERIES D FIRST ISSUE

#FX27-31 pale red-brown. Arms at l.

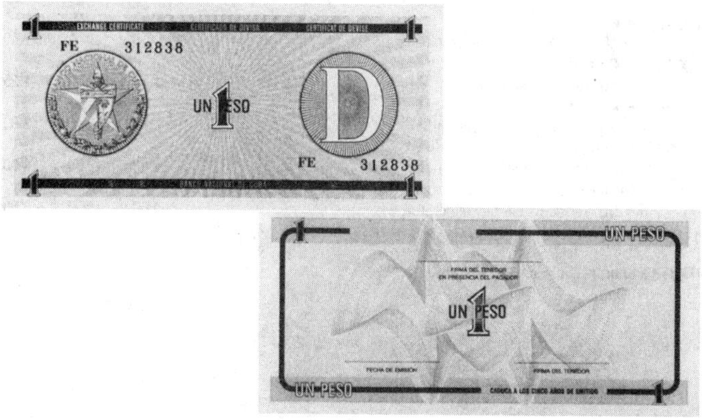

		VG	VF	UNC
FX27	**1 Peso** ND. Light orange and orange-brown underprint.	.25	1.50	3.50
FX28	**3 Pesos** ND. Light orange and pale blue underprint.	.50	3.00	7.00

		VG	VF	UNC
FX29	**5 Pesos** ND. Light orange and light green underprint.	1.00	5.00	10.00

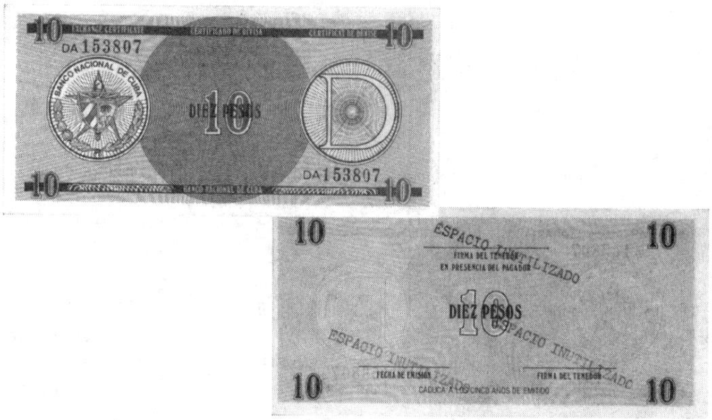

		VG	VF	UNC
FX30	**10 Pesos** ND. Light orange and lilac underprint.	2.00	10.00	17.50

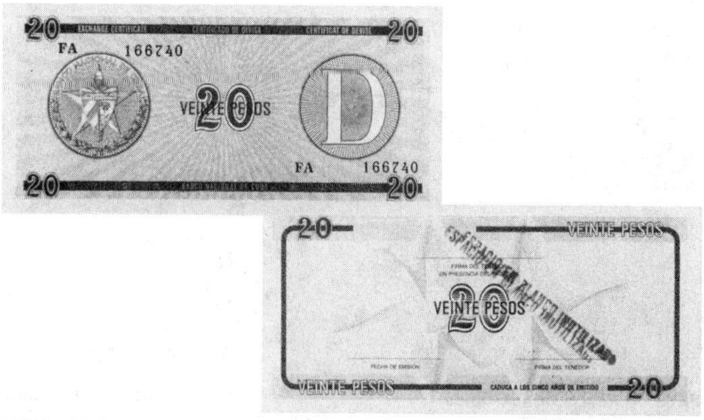

		VG	VF	UNC
FX31	**20 Pesos** ND. Light orange and ochre underprint.	4.00	20.00	32.50

SERIES D SECOND ISSUE

#FX32-FX36 dk. brown. Similar to #FX19-FX23. W/ or w/o various handstamps *ESPACIO EN BLANCO INUTILIZADO* or *ESPACIO INUTILIZADO* on back.

		VG	VF	UNC
FX32	**1 Peso** ND. Tan and pale olive-green underprint.	.10	.30	.60
FX33	**3 Pesos** ND. Tan and red underprint.	.15	.60	1.25
FX34	**5 Pesos** ND. Tan and green underprint.	.25	1.00	2.00
FX35	**10 Pesos** ND. Tan and orange underprint.	.50	2.00	4.00
FX36	**20 Pesos** ND. Tan and blue-gray underprint.	1.00	4.00	8.00

1994 PESOS CONVERTIBLES ISSUE

#FX37-FX43 arms at ctr. on back. Wmk: J. Martí.

		VG	VF	UNC
FX37	**1 Peso Convertible** 1994. Orange, brown and olive-green on multicolor underprint. J. Martí monument at right. Watermark: J. Marti.	FV	FV	2.50

		VG	VF	UNC
FX38	**3 Pesos Convertibles** 1994. Dull red, deep blue-green and brown on multicolor underprint. E. "Che" Guevara monument at right.	FV	FV	7.00

		VG	VF	UNC
FX39	**5 Pesos Convertibles** 1994. Dark green, orange and blue-black on multicolor underprint. A. Maceo monument at right.	FV	FV	10.00

		VG	VF	UNC
FX40	**10 Pesos Convertibles** 1994. Brown, yellow-green and purple on multicolor underprint. M. Gómez monument at right.	FV	FV	17.50

		VG	VF	UNC
FX41	**20 Pesos Convertibles** 1994. Blue, red and tan on multicolor underprint. C. Cienfuegos monument at right.	FV	FV	35.00

		VG	VF	UNC
FX42	**50 Pesos Convertibles** 1994. Purple, brown and orange on multicolor underprint. C. García monument at right.	FV	FV	70.00

		VG	VF	UNC
FX43	**100 Pesos Convertibles** 1994. Red-violet, brown-orange and purple on multicolor underprint. C. Manuel de Céspedes monument at right.	FV	FV	150.

BANCO CENTRAL DE CUBA

2004 PESOS CONVERTIBLES ISSUE

		VG	VF	UNC
FX44	**5 Pesos Convertibles** 2004.	FV	FV	10.00

		VG	VF	UNC
FX45	**10 Pesos Convertibles** 2004.	FV	FV	17.50

2006 PESOS CONVERTIBLES

		VG	VF	UNC
FX46	**1 Peso** 2006. Multicolor.	FV	FV	2.50
FX47	**3 Pesos** 2006. Multicolor.	FV	FV	5.00
FX48	**5 Pesos** 2006. Multicolor.	FV	FV	10.00
FX49	**10 Pesos** 2006. Multicolor.	FV	FV	17.50
FX50	**20 Pesos** 2006. Multicolor.	FV	FV	35.00
FX51	**50 Pesos** 2006. Multicolor.	FV	FV	70.00
FX52	**100 Pesos** 2006. Multicolor.	FV	FV	150.

COLLECTOR SERIES

BANCO NACIONAL DE CUBA

1961-1995 ISSUES

The Banco Nacional de Cuba had been selling specimen notes regularly of the 1961-1989 issues. Specimen notes dated 1961-66 have normal block # and serial # while notes from 1967 to date all have normal block # and all zero serial #.

		Issue Price	Mkt. Value
CS1	**1961 1-100 Pesos** Overprint: *SPECIMEN* on #94a-97a, 98, 99.	—	110.
CS2	**1964 1-20 Pesos** Overprint: *SPECIMEN* on #94b-97b.	—	20.00
CS3	**1965 1-20 Pesos** Overprint: *SPECIMEN* on #94c-97c.	—	14.00
CS4	**1966 1, 10 Pesos** Overprint: *SPECIMEN* on #100, 101.	—	7.00
CS5	**1967 1-10 Pesos** Overprint: *SPECIMEN* on #102a-104a.	—	10.00
CS6	**1968 1-10 Pesos** Overprint: *SPECIMEN* on #102a-104a.	—	10.00
CS7	**1969 1, 10 Pesos** Overprint: *SPECIMEN* on #102a, 104a.	—	7.00
CS8	**1970 1-10 Pesos** Overprint: *SPECIMEN* on #102a, 103b, 104a.	—	7.00
CS9	**1971 10, 20 Pesos** Overprint: *SPECIMEN* on #104a, 105a.	—	8.00
CS10	**1972 1, 5 Pesos** Overprint: *SPECIMEN* on #102a, 103b.	—	7.00
CS11	**1975 1 Peso** Overprint: *SPECIMEN* on #106.	—	10.00
CS12	**1978 1, 10, 20 Pesos** Overprint: *ESPECIMEN* on #102b, 104b, 105b.	—	11.00
CS13	**1979 1 Peso** Overprint: *ESPECIMEN* on #102b.	—	3.00
CS14	**1980 1 Peso** Overprint: *ESPECIMEN* on #102b.	—	3.00
CS15	**1981 1 Peso** Overprint: *ESPECIMEN* on #102b.	—	3.00
CS16	**1982 1 Peso** Overprint: *MUESTRA* on #102b.	—	3.00
CS17	**1983 3, 10, 20 Pesos** Overprint: *MUESTRA* on #104c, 105c, 107a.	—	12.00
CS18	**1984 3, 5, 10 Pesos** Overprint: *MUESTRA* on #103c, 104c, 107a.	—	12.00
CS19	**1985 1, 3, 5 Pesos** Overprint: Ovpt: *MUESTRA* on #102b, 103c, 107a.	—	12.00
CS20	**1986 1-10 Pesos** Overprint: *MUESTRA* on #102b, 103c, 104c, 107a.	—	12.50
CS21	**1987 5, 10, 20 Pesos** Overprint: *MUESTRA* on #103c-105c.	—	12.00
CS22	**1988 1-20 Pesos** Overprint: *MUESTRA* on #102c, 103d-105d, 107b.	—	12.50
CS23	**1989 3, 20 Pesos** Overprint: *MUESTRA* on #105d, 107b.	—	7.00
CS24	**1990 5, 20, 50 Pesos** Overprint: *SPECIMEN* on #103d, 105d, 111.	—	10.00
CS25	**1991 5, 10, 20 Pesos** Overprint: *SPECIMEN* on #108-110.	—	10.00
CS26	**1994 1-100 Peso Convertibles** Overprint: *MUESTRA* on FX37-FX43.	—	60.00
CS27	**1995 1, 3 Pesos** Overprint: *MUESTRA* on #112 and 113.	—	5.00

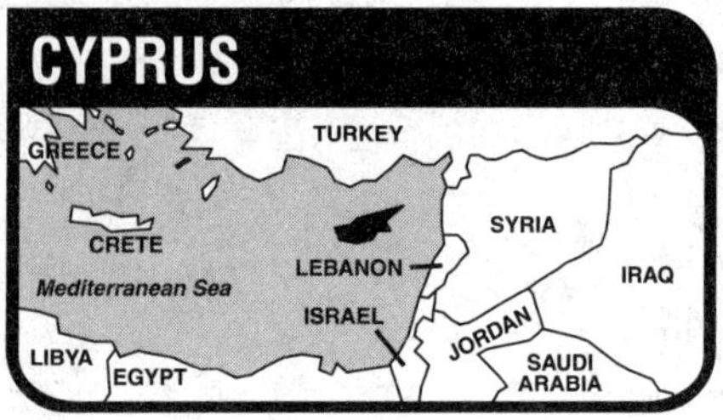

The Republic of Cyprus, a member of the European Commonwealth and Council, lies in the eastern Mediterranean Sea 44 miles (71 km.) south of Turkey and 60 miles (97 km.) west of Syria. It is the third largest island in the Mediterranean Sea, having an area if 3,572 sq. mi. (9,251 sq. km.) and a population of 757,000. Capital: Nicosia. Agriculture and mining are the chief industries. Asbestos, copper, citrus fruit, iron pyrites and potatoes are exported.

The importance of Cyprus dates from the Bronze Age when it was desired as a principal souce of copper (from which the island derived its name) and as a strategic trading center. Its role as an international marketplace made it a prime disseminator of the then prevalent cultures, a role that still influences the civilization of Western man. Because of its fortuitous position and influential role, Cyprus was conquered by a succession of empires; the Assyrian, Egyptian, Persian, Macedonian, Ptolemaic, Roman and Byzantine. It was taken from Isaac Comnenus by Richard the Lion-Hearted in 1191, sold to the Knights Templars, conquered by Venice and Turkey, and made a crown colony of Britain in 1925. Finally on Aug. 16, 1960, it became an independent republic.

In 1964, the ethnic Turks, who favor partition of Cyprus into separate Greek and Turkish states, withdrew from active participation in the government. Turkish forces invaded Cyprus in 1974 and gained control of 40 percent of the island. In 1975, Turkish Cypriots proclaimed their own Federated state in northern Cyprus. The UN held numerous discussions from 1985-92, without any results towards unification.

The president is Chief of State and Head of Government.

RULERS:

British to 1960

MONETARY SYSTEM:

1 Shilling = 9 Piastres
1 Pound = 20 Shillings to 1963
1 Shilling = 50 Mils
1 Pound = 1000 Mils, 1963-83
1 Pound = 100 Cents, 1983-

DEMOCRATIC REPUBLIC

ΚΥΠΡΙΑΚΗ ΔΗΜΟΚΡΑΤΙΑ

KIBRIS CUMHURIYETI

REPUBLIC OF CYPRUS

1961 ISSUE

#37-40 arms at r., map at lower r. Wmk: Eagle's head. Printer: BWC (w/o imprint).

		VG	VF	UNC
37	**250 Mils**			
	1.12.1961. Blue on multicolor underprint. Fruit at left. Mine on back.			
	a. Issued note.	3.00	15.00	115.
	s. Specimen.	—	—	90.00
38	**500 Mils**			
	1.12.1961. Green on multicolor underprint. Mountain road lined with trees on back.			
	a. Issued note.	5.00	40.00	260.
	s. Specimen.	—	—	90.00

		VG	VF	UNC
39	**1 Pound**			
	1.12.1961. Brown on multicolor underprint. Viaduct and pillars on back.			
	a. Issued note.	10.00	30.00	140.
	s. Specimen.	—	—	90.00
40	**5 Pounds**			
	1.12.1961. Dark green on multicolor underprint. Embroidery and floral design on back.			
	a. Issued note.	15.00	55.00	300.
	s. Specimen.	—	—	90.00

ΚΕΝΤΡΙΚΗ ΤΡΑΠΕΖΑ ΤΗΣ ΚΥΠΡΟΥ

KIBRIS MERKEZ BANKASI

CENTRAL BANK OF CYPRUS

1964-66 ISSUE

#41-44 like #37-40. Various date and sign. varieties.

		VG	VF	UNC
41	**250 Mils**			
	1964-82. Like #37.			
	a. 1.12.1964-1.12.1969; 1.9.1971.	2.00	8.00	70.00
	b. 1.3.1971; 1.6.1972; 1.5.1973; 1.6.1974.	2.00	7.50	57.50
	c. 1.7.1975-1.6.1982.	2.00	6.00	47.50
	s. Specimen.	—	—	140.
	ct. Color trial. Brown on multicolor underprint.	—	—	250.

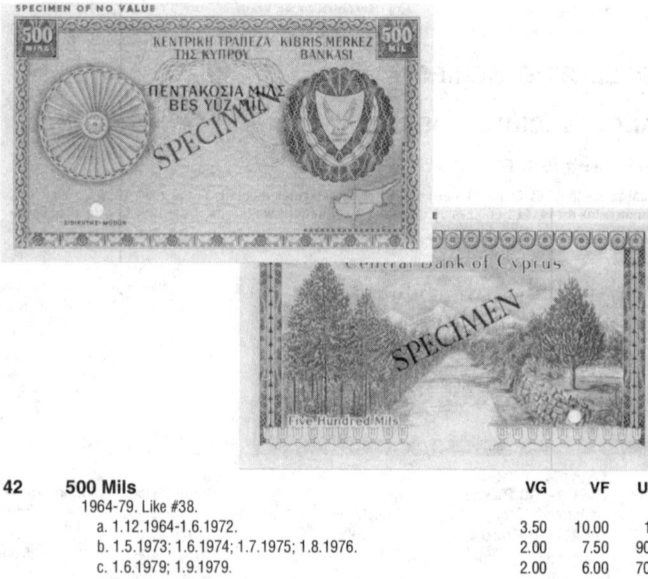

		VG	VF	UNC
42	**500 Mils**			
	1964-79. Like #38.			
	a. 1.12.1964-1.6.1972.	3.50	10.00	110.
	b. 1.5.1973; 1.6.1974; 1.7.1975; 1.8.1976.	2.00	7.50	90.00
	c. 1.6.1979; 1.9.1979.	2.00	6.00	70.00
	s. Specimen.	—	—	140.

43 **1 Pound**

1966-78. Like #39.

	VG	VF	UNC
a. 1.8.1966-1.6.1972.	3.50	12.50	105.
b. 1.11.1972; 1.5.1973; 1.6.1974; 1.7.1975.	3.50	8.00	85.00
c. 1.8.1976; 1.5.1978.	3.50	7.50	80.00
s. Specimen.	—	—	—

44 **5 Pounds**

1966-76. Blue on multicolor underprint. Like #40.

	VG	VF	UNC
a. 1.8.1966; 1.9.1967; 1.12.1969.	17.50	35.00	190.
b. 1.6.1972; 1.11.1972; 1.5.1973.	12.50	30.00	130.
c. 1.6.1974; 1.7.1975; 1.8.1976.	12.50	30.00	120.

1977-82 ISSUE

#45-48 wmk: Moufflon (ram's) head.

45 **500 Mils**

1.6.1982. Light brown on green and multicolor underprint. Woman seated at right, arms at top left center. Yermasoyia Dam on back. Printer: BWC (without imprint).

	VG	VF	UNC
a. Issued note.	1.00	7.50	60.00
s. Specimen.	—	—	130.

46 **1 Pound**

	VG	VF	UNC
1.6.1979. Dark brown and brown on multicolor underprint. Mosaic of nymph Acme at right, arms at top left center. Bellapais Abbey on back. Printer: TDLR (without imprint).	2.00	7.50	32.50

47 **5 Pounds**

	VG	VF	UNC
1.6.1979. Violet on multicolor underprint. Limestone head from Hellenistic period at left, arms at upper center right. Ancient Theater at Salamis on back. Printer: TDLR (without imprint).	10.00	17.50	80.00

48 **10 Pounds**

1977-85. Dark green and blue-black on multicolor underprint. Archaic bust at left, arms at right. Two Cyprus warblers on back. Printer: BWC (without imprint).

	VG	VF	UNC
a. 1.4.1977; 1.5.1978; 1.6.1979.	20.00	35.00	170.
b. 1.7.1980; 1.10.1981; 1.6.1982; 1.9.1983; 1.6.1985.	20.00	25.00	140.
s. As a. Specimen.	—	—	—

1982-87 ISSUE

#49-51 wmk: Moufflon (ram's) head.

49	50 Cents	VG	VF	UNC
	1.10.1983; 1.12.1984. Brown and multicolor. Similar to #45. Printer: BWC (without imprint).			
	a. Issued note.	1.00	4.00	20.00
	s. Specimen.	—	—	130.

50	1 Pound	VG	VF	UNC
	1.2.1982; 1.11.1982; 1.3.1984; 1.11.1985. Dark brown and multicolor. Like #46 but bank name in outlined (white) letters by dark underprint. Printer: TDLR (without imprint).	1.00	5.00	27.50

51	10 Pounds	VG	VF	UNC
	1.4.1987; 1.10.1988. Dark green and blue-black on multicolor underprint. Similar to #48 but with date above at left. of modified arms on right. Printer: TDLR (without imprint).	FV	25.00	130.

1987-92 ISSUE

#53-56 enhanced designs w/micro-printing. Wmk: Moufflon (ram's) head.

52	50 Cents	VG	VF	UNC
	1.4.1987; 1.10.1988; 1.11.1989. Like #49 but with bank name in micro-printing alternately in Greek and Turkish just below upper frame. Printer: BABN (without imprint).	FV	2.50	13.00

53	1 Pound	VG	VF	UNC
	1987-96. Like #50 but with bank name in unbroken line of micro-printing with Greek at left and Turkish at right just below upper frame.			
	a. Without light beige underprint. color on back. Micro-print line under dark bar at top. Printer: TDLR (Without imprint). 1.4.1987; 1.10.1988; 1.11.1989.	FV	FV	27.50
	b. light beige color added to center underprint. on back for security. Printer: F-CO (without imprint). 1.11.1989; 1.2.1992.	FV	FV	16.00
	c. Dot added near upper left. corner. 1.3.1993; 1.3.1994.	FV	FV	14.00
	d. 1.9.1995.	FV	FV	13.00
	e. 1.10.1996.	FV	3.00	21.00

54	5 Pounds	VG	VF	UNC
	1990; 1995. Violet on multicolor underprint. Like #47 but with line of micro-printing added within bank titles. Printer: TDLR (without imprint).			
	a. 1.10.1990.	FV	FV	67.50
	b. 1.9.1995.	FV	FV	62.50

55	10 Pounds	VG	VF	UNC
	1989-95. Dark green and blue-black on multicolor underprint. Similar to #51 but with enhanced security features. Printer: TDLR (without imprint).			
	a. 1.11.1989; 1.10.1990.	FV	FV	115.
	b. 1.2.1992.	FV	FV	110.
	c. 1.6.1994.	FV	FV	105.
	d. 1.9.1995.	FV	FV	90.00

56	20 Pounds	VG	VF	UNC
	1992; 1993. Deep blue on multicolor underprint. Bust of Aphrodite at left, arms at upper center, ancient bird (pottery art) at right. Kyrenia boat at center, ancient pottery jugs at lower right on back. Printer: TDLR (without imprint).			
	a. Error: No dot over 'i' in *YIRMI LIRA*. 1.2.1992.	FV	FV	200.
	b. Corrected: *YiRMi LiRA*. 1.3.1993.	FV	35.00	150.

1997 FIRST ISSUE

#57-60 arms at upper ctr. Wmk: Bust of Aphrodite. Thin security thread. Printer: F-CO (w/o imprint).

57	1 Pound	VG	VF	UNC
	1.2.1997. Brown on pink and multicolor underprint. Cypriot girl at left. Handcrafts and Kato Drys village scene in background on back.	FV	FV	13.00

58	5 Pounds	VG	VF	UNC
	1.2.1997. Purple and violet on multicolor underprint. Archaic limestone head of young man at left. Peristerona church and Turkish mosque on back.	FV	FV	35.00

59	10 Pounds	VG	VF	UNC
	1.2.1997. Olive-green and blue-green on multicolor underprint. Marble head of Artemis at left. Ruppell's warbler green turtle, butterfly, moufflon, tulip and cyclamen plants on back.	FV	FV	67.50

1997-2001 ISSUE

#60-63 arms at upper ctr. Wmk: Bust of Aphrodite. Wide security foil.

60	1 Pound	VG	VF	UNC
	1.10.1997; 1.12.1998; 1.2.2001; 1.4.2004. Brown on light tan and multicolor underprint. Like #57 but with slightly modified colors. Printer: F-CO (without imprint).			
	a. 1.10.1997.	FV	FV	13.00
	b. 1.12.1998.	FV	FV	10.00
	c. 1.2.2001.	FV	FV	9.00
	d. 1.4.2004. Signature Chr. Christodoulou.	FV	FV	9.00

61	5 Pounds	VG	VF	UNC
	1.2.2001; 1.9.2003. Purple and violet on multicolor underprint. Like #58.			
	a. 1.2.2001. Printer: F-CO (without imprint).	FV	FV	32.50
	b. 1.9.2003. Printer: TDLR (without imprint). Signature Chr. Christodoulou.	FV	FV	32.50

62	10 Pounds	VG	VF	UNC
	1.10.1997; 1.12.1998; 1.2.2001; 1.9.2003. Olive-green and blue-green on multicolor underprint. Like #59.			
	a. 1.10.1997. Printer: F-CO (without imprint).	FV	FV	67.50
	b. 1.12.1998. Printer: F-CO (without imprint).	FV	FV	65.00
	c. 1.2.2001. Printer: F-CO (without imprint).	FV	FV	65.00
	d. 1.9.2003. Printer: TDLR (without imprint). Signature Chr. Christodoulou.	FV	FV	62.50
	e. 1.4.2005.	FV	FV	62.50

63	20 Pounds	VG	VF	UNC
	1.10.1997; 1.10.2001; 1.4.2004. Deep blue on multicolor underprint. Similar to #56b. Printer: TDLR (without imprint).			
	a. 1.10.1997.	FV	FV	115.
	b. 1.10.2001.	FV	FV	110.
	c. 1.4.2004. Signature Chr. Christodoulou.	FV	FV	110.

CZECHOSLOVAKIA

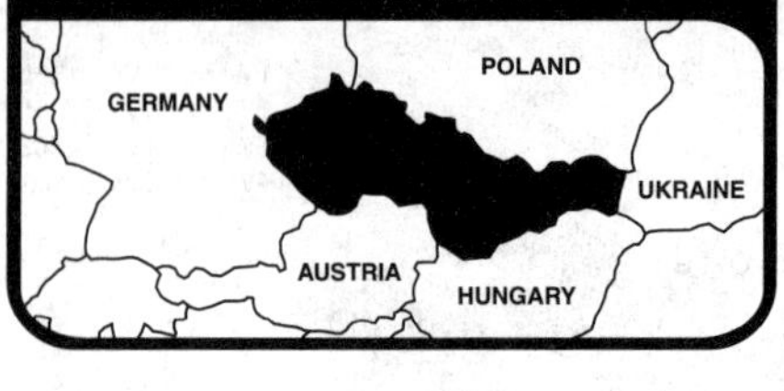

The Republic of Czechoslovakia, located in central Europe, had an area of 49,365 sq. mi. (127,859 sq. km.). Capital: Prague (Praha). Industrial production in the cities and agriculture and livestock in the rural areas were the chief occupations.

The Czech lands to the west were united with the Slovak to form the Czechoslovak Republic on October 28, 1918 upon the dissolution of the Austrian-Hungarian Empire. Tomas G. Masaryk was the first president. In the 1930s Hitlet provoked Czechoslovakia's German minority in the Sudetenland to agitate for autonomy. The territory was broken up for the benefit of Germany, Poland and Hungary by the Munich agreement signed by the United Kingdom, France, Germany and Italy on September 29, 1938. On March 15, 1939, Germany invaded Czechoslovakia and incorporated the Czech lands into the Third Reich as the "Protectorate of Bohemia and Moravia." eastern Slovakia, was constituted as a republic under Nazi infulence. A government-in-exile was set up in London in 1940. The Soviet and American forces liberated the area by May 1945. After World War II the physical integrity and independence of Czechoslovakia was re-established, while bringing it within the Russian sphere of influence. On February 23-25, 1948, the Communists seized control of the government in a *coup d'etat,* and adopted a constitution making the country a "people's republic." A new constitution adopted June 11, 1960, converted the country into a "socialist republic." Communist infulence increased steadily while pressure for liberalization culminated in the overthrow of the Stalinist leader Antonçin Novotny and his associates in January, 1968. The Communist Party then introduced far reaching reforms which received warnings from Moscow, followed by occupation of Warsaw Pact forces on August 21, 1968 resulting in stationing of Soviet troops. Student demonstrations for reform began in Prague on November 17, 1989. The Federal Assembly abolished the Communist Party's sole right to govern. In December, 1989, communism was overthrown. In January, 1990 the Czech and Slovak Federal Republic (CSFR) was formed. The movement for a democratic Slovakia was apparent in the June 1992 elections with the Slovak National Council adopting a declaration of sovereignty. The CSFR was disolved on December 31, 1992, and both new republics came into being on January 1, 1993.

See the Czech Republic and Slovakia sections for additional listings.

MONETARY SYSTEM:

1 Koruna = 100 Haleru

SPECIMEN NOTES:

Large quantities of specimens were made available to collectors. Notes issued after 1945 are distinguished by a perforation consisting of three small holes or a letter S (for Solvakia). Since the difference in value between issued notes and specimen notes is frequently very great, both types of notes are valued. Earlier issues recalled from circulation were perforated: *SPECIMEN* or *NEPLATNE* or with a letter *S* for collectors. Caution should be exercised while examining notes as examples of perforated notes having the holes filled in are known.

NOTE AVAILABILITY:

The Czech National Bank in 1997 made available to collectors uncirculated examples of #78-98, as a full set or in issue groups. As the notes were demonetized they had no cancellation holes nor were overprinted. They have regular serial #'s.

SOCIALIST REPUBLIC

ČESKOSLOVENSKÁ SOCIALISTICKÁ REPUBLIKA

CZECHOSLOVAK SOCIALIST REPUBLIC

1961 ISSUE

#81 and 82 wmk: Star in circle, repeated. Printer: STC-P.

81	3 Koruny	VG	VF	UNC
	1961. Blue on blue-green underprint. Large 3 at center and upper corners. Socialist arms at center on back.			
	a. Issued note. Serial # prefix 2.5mm in height.	.20	.50	2.00
	b. Issued note. Serial # prefix 3mm in height.	.20	.50	2.00
	s. Perforated with 3 holes or *SPECIMEN.*	—	.50	2.00

82	5 Korun	VG	VF	UNC
	1961. Dull black on pale green underprint. Text in frame. Socialist arms at center on back.			

		VG	VF	UNC
82	**5 Korun**			
	a. Issued note. Serial # prefix 2.5mm in height.	.20	.50	2.00
	b. Issued note. Serial # prefix 3mm in height.	.20	.50	2.00
	s. Perforated with 3 holes or *SPECIMEN.*	—	.50	2.00

STÁTNÍ BANKA CESKOSLOVENSKÁ

CZECHOSLOVAK STATE BANK

1960-64 ISSUE

#88-98 printer: STC-Prague.

#88-91 Printed by wet photogravure or dry photogravure (wet printing has smaller image).

		VG	VF	UNC
88	**10 Korun**			
	1960. Brown on multicolor underprint. 2 girls with flowers at right. Orava Dam. Printer: STC-Prague. Printed by wet photogravure or dry photogravure. (Wet printing has smaller image.)			
	a. Series prefix: H; F (wet printing).	2.00	8.00	15.00
	b. Series prefixes: E, J, L, M, S, X (dry printing)	.10	.75	3.00
	s. Specimen.	—	—	—

		VG	VF	UNC
89	**25 Korun**			
	1961 (1962). Blue-black on light blue underprint. Similar to #87 but different arms.			
	a. Series prefix: E. (wet printing).	5.00	15.00	40.00
	b. Series prefix: Q. (dry printing)	.75	1.75	7.50
	s. Perforated: *SPECIMEN.*	—	—	2.00

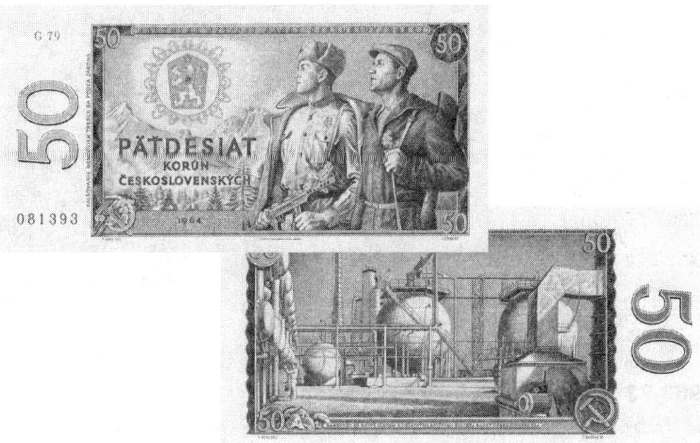

		VG	VF	UNC
90	**50 Korun**			
	1964 (1965). Red-brown. Arms at left, Russian soldier and partisan at right. Slovnaft refinery in Bratislava on back.			
	a. Series prefix: K. (wet printing).	5.00	15.00	80.00
	b. Series prefix: A; N; G; J (dry printing).	1.00	2.50	7.50

		VG	VF	UNC
91	**100 Korun**			
	1961. Deep green on multicolor underprint. Factory at lower left, farm couple at right. Charles Bridge and Hradcany in Prague on back.			
	a. Watermark: Star within linden leaf, repeated. Series prefix: B01-40; C; D (wet printing).	6.00	15.00	40.00
	b. As a. Series prefix: B41-99; P; R; T; Z; X01-24 (dry printing).	1.00	3.00	10.00
	c. Reissue watermark: Multiple stars and linden leaves. Series prefix: X25-96; G; M. (1990-92).	.50	1.00	7.50

Note: #91b or #91c w/added *C-100* adhesive stamp, see Czech Republic. With *SLOVENSKÁ REPUBLIKA* adhesive stamp, see Slovakia.

1970; 1973 ISSUE

		VG	VF	UNC
92	**20 Korun**			
	1970 (1971). Blue on light blue and multicolor underprint. Arms at center, Jan Zizka at right. Husite soldiers on back. Series prefix: F, H, L, M.	.25	1.00	2.50

		VG	VF	UNC
93	**500 Korun**			
	1973. Deep brown-violet and multicolor. Soldiers at right. Medieval shield at lower center, mountain fortress ruins at Devin at right on back. Series prefix: U, W, Z.	2.00	10.00	30.00

Note: For #93 w/additional "D-500" adhesive stamp, see Czech Republic. *SLOVENSKÁ REPUBLIKA* adhesive stamp, see Slovakia.

NOTICE

Readers with unlisted dates, signature varieties, etc. are invited to submit photocopies of their notes to: Standard Catalog of World Paper Money, 700 East State St. Iola, WI 54990-0001, E-Mail: george.cuhaj@fwpubs.com.

1985-89 Issue

		VG	VF	UNC
94	**10 Korun** 1986. Deep brown on blue and multicolor underprint. Pavol Orszag-Hviezdoslav at right. Bird at lower left, view of Orava mountains on back. Series prefix: J, P, V.	.20	.50	2.00

		VG	VF	UNC
95	**20 Korun** 1988. Blue and multicolor. Jan Ámos Komensky at right, circular design with open book at left. Alphabet at left, Tree of life growing from book at center, young couple at right on back. Series prefix: E, H.	.25	.75	2.50

Note: For #95 w/additional *SLOVENSKÁ REPUBLIKA* adhesive stamp, see Slovakia.

		VG	VF	UNC
96	**50 Korun** 1987. Brown-violet and blue on red and orange underprint. Ludovit Stúr at right, shield and spotted eagle at right. Bratislava castle and town view on back.			
	a. Series prefix: *F.*	.50	1.50	3.00
	b. Series prefix: *I.*	1.00	2.50	6.00

Note: For #96 w/additional *SLOVENSKÁ REPUBLIKA* adhesive stamp, see Slovakia.

		VG	VF	UNC
97	**100 Korun** 1989. Dark green on green and red underprint. Klement Gottwald at right. Hradcany in Prague on back. Series prefix: A.	.75	2.25	10.00

Note: #97 was in circulation only from 1.10.1989 to 31.12.1990.

		VG	VF	UNC
98	**1000 Korun** 1985. Blue-black, blue and purple on multicolor underprint. Bedrich Smetana at right. Vysehrad Castle at left on back. Series prefix: C, U.	5.00	20.00	45.00

Note: For #98 w/additional "M-1000" adhesive stamp or printed, see Czech Republic. With *SLOVENSKÁ REPUBLIKA* adhesive stamp, see Slovakia.

Foreign Exchange Certificates

Podniku Zahranicniho Obchodu Tuzex

1961 Issue

		VG	VF	UNC
FX25	**0.50 Koruna** 1961.	5.00	12.50	65.00
FX26	**1 Koruna** 1961.	5.00	15.00	80.00
FX27	**5 Korun** 1961.	10.00	35.00	120.
FX28	**10 Korun** 1961. Rare.	—	—	—
FX29	**20 Korun** 1961. Rare.	—	—	—
FX30	**50 Korun** 1961. Rare.	—	—	—
FX31	**71.5 Korun** 1961. Rare.	—	—	—
FX32	**100 Korun** 1962. Rare.	—	—	—

1962-69 Issues

Printed date of 1966-69 on FX33-FX39, others w/handstamped date.

		VG	VF	UNC
FX33	**0.50 Koruna** 1962-69.			
	a. Regular issue.	2.00	5.00	10.00
	b. Z (zahranicni) Foreign issue.	2.00	5.00	10.00

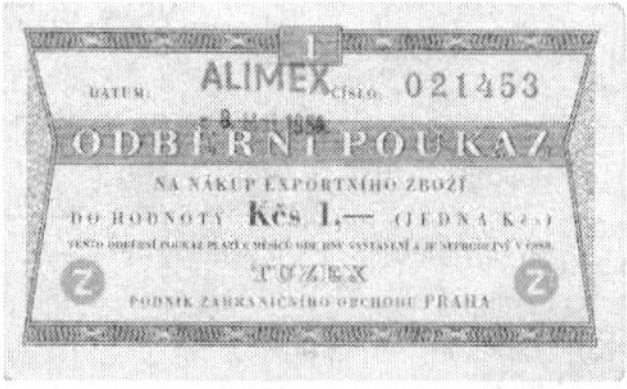

		VG	VF	UNC
FX34	**1 Koruna** 1962-69.			
	a. Regular issue.	2.00	4.00	10.00
	b. Z (zahranicini) Foreign issue.	2.00	4.00	10.00
FX35	**5 Korun** 1962-69.	5.00	15.00	50.00
FX36	**10 Korun** ND (1962).	10.00	35.00	100.
FX37	**20 Korun** ND (1962).	15.00	50.00	150.
FX38	**50 Korun** ND (1962).	20.00	75.00	200.
FX39	**100 Korun** ND (1962).	25.00	100.	250.

1969-73 Issues

Printed date on FX40-FX42, all others w/handstamped date.

		VG	VF	UNC
FX40	**0.50 Koruna** 1969-73.			
	a. Regular issue.	1.25	2.00	5.00
	b. Z (zahranicni) Foreign issue.	3.00	7.50	15.00

		VG	VF	UNC
FX41	**1 Koruna**			
	1969-73.			
	a. Regular issue.	1.25	2.00	5.00
	b. Z (zahranicini) Foreign issue.	3.00	7.50	15.00
FX42	**5 Korun**			
	1969-73.			
	a. Regular issue.	2.00	4.00	10.00
	b. Z (zahranicni) Foreign issue.	5.00	12.50	25.00
FX43	**10 Korun**			
	1969-73.	5.00	15.00	60.00
FX44	**20 Korun**			
	1969-73.	10.00	35.00	100.

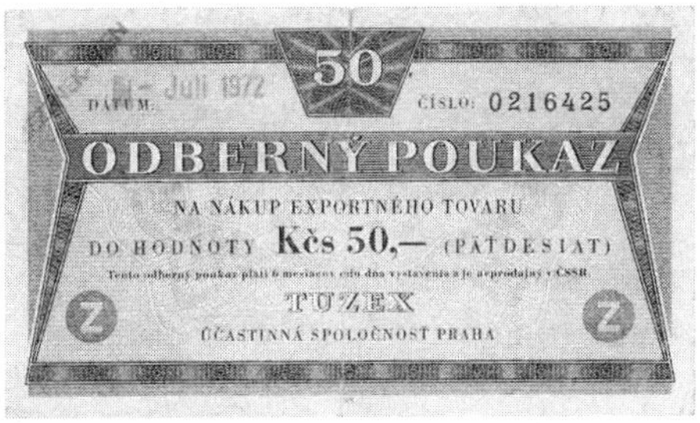

		VG	VF	UNC
FX45	**50 Korun**			
	1969-73.			
	a. Issued note.	15.00	75.00	150.
	b. "Z" imprint.	—	—	—
FX46	**100 Korun**			
	1969-73.	20.00	100.	200.

1973-80 Issues

Printed date on FX47-49, all others w/handstamped date.

		VG	VF	UNC
FX47	**0.50 Koruna**			
	1973-79.			
	a. Regular issue. 1973-79.	.20	.50	1.00
	b. Z (Zahranicni) foreign issue. 1974-78.	.50	1.50	3.00
FX48	**1 Koruna**			
	1973-79.			
	a. Regular issue. 1973-79.	.20	.50	1.00
	b. Z (Zahranicni) foreign issue. 1974-78.	.50	1.50	3.00
FX49	**5 Korun**			
	1973-80.			
	a. Regular issue. 1973-80.	.50	1.50	3.00
	b. Z (Zahranicni) foreign issue. 1974-78.	3.00	7.50	15.00
FX50	**10 Korun**			
	ND (1973).	4.00	8.00	15.00
FX51	**20 Korun**			
	ND (1973).	5.00	15.00	30.00
FX52	**50 Korun**			
	ND (1973).	7.50	25.00	75.00
FX53	**100 Korun**			
	ND (1974).	15.00	90.00	150.
FX54	**500 Korun**			
	ND (1979).	25.00	150.	350.

1980-88 Issue

#FX55-FX62 white outer edge. *TUZEX* once in text. Date printed for FX55-FX57, others w/handstamped date. Printer: STC-P.

		VG	VF	UNC
FX55	**0.50 Koruna**			
	1980-87. Violet and green.	.25	.50	1.00

		VG	VF	UNC
FX56	**1 Koruna**			
	1980-87. Green on ochre underprint.	.25	.50	1.00

		VG	VF	UNC
FX57	**5 Korun**			
	1980-87. Violet on blue and ochre underprint.			
	a. 1980.	2.00	4.00	10.00
	b. 1980-87.	.50	1.50	3.00

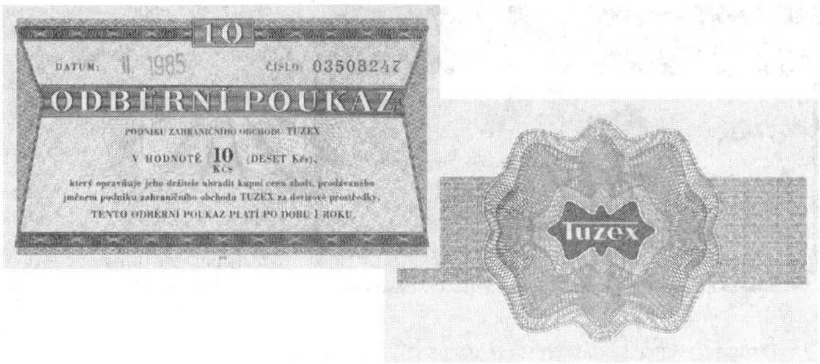

		VG	VF	UNC
FX58	**10 Korun**			
	ND (1980). Dark green on green underprint.	.75	2.00	5.00
FX59	**20 Korun**			
	ND (1980). Brown on orange and green underprint.	2.00	5.00	10.00
FX60	**50 Korun**			
	ND (1980). Brown on pink and orange underprint.	4.00	10.00	20.00
FX61	**100 Korun**			
	ND (1980). Violet on green and violet underprint.	5.00	15.00	30.00
FX62	**500 Korun**			
	ND (1980). Gray on brown underprint.	15.00	75.00	150.

1989-90 Issue

#FX63-FX70 lg. globe w/*TUZEX* at l. and r. Colors as previous issue but outer edge w/solid color. Date printed for FX63-65, others w/handstamped date. Printer: STC-P.

		VG	VF	UNC
FX63	**0.50 Koruna**			
	1989; 1990. Violet edge.	.25	.50	1.00

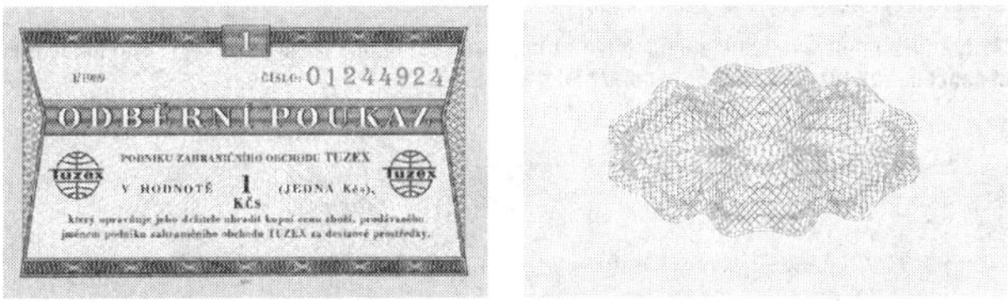

		VG	VF	UNC
FX64	**1 Koruna**			
	1989; 1990. Yellow-brown edge.	.25	.50	1.00
FX65	**5 Korun**			
	1989; 1990. Blue and ochre edge.	.50	1.50	3.00

Note: #FX22-FX26 were redeemable 1 year from issue date.

		VG	VF	UNC
FX66	**10 Korun**			
	ND (1989). Light and dark green edge.	1.25	2.50	5.00
FX67	**20 Korun**			
	ND (1989). Yellow-brown and green edge.	2.00	5.00	10.00
FX68	**50 Korun**			
	ND (1989). Pink and orange edge.	4.00	10.00	20.00
FX69	**100 Korun**			
	ND (1989). Violet and green edge.	5.00	15.00	30.00
FX70	**500 Korun**			
	ND (1989). Brown edge.	10.00	65.00	100.

1990-92 Issue

#FX71-FX78 globe w/TUZEX. Date printed for FX63-FX65, others w/handstamped date. Printer: VEB Leipzig, Germany.

		VG	VF	UNC
FX71	**0.50 Koruna**			
	1990-92.	.25	.50	1.00

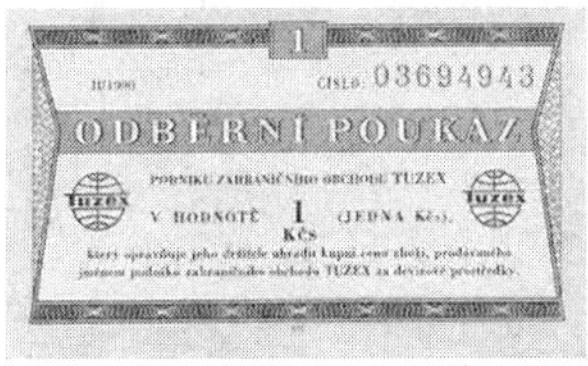

		VG	VF	UNC
FX72	**1 Koruna**			
	1990-92.	.25	.50	1.00
FX73	**5 Korun**			
	1990-92.	.50	1.50	3.00
FX74	**10 Korun**			
	ND (1990).	1.00	2.50	5.00
FX75	**20 Korun**			
	ND (1990).	2.00	5.00	10.00
FX76	**50 Korun**			
	ND (1990).	5.00	12.50	20.00
FX77	**100 Korun**			
	ND (1990).	5.00	15.00	30.00
FX78	**500 Korun**			
	ND (1990).	10.00	50.00	100.

The Czech Republic is bordered to the west by Germany, to the north by Poland, to the east by Slovakia and to the south by Austria. It consists of 3 major regions: Bohemia, Moravia and Silesia. It has an area of 30,431 sq. mi. (78,864 sq. km.) and a population of 10.19 million. Capital: Prague (Praha). Industrial production in cities and agriculture and livestock in the rural areas are chief occupations while coal deposits are the main mineral resources.

The Czech Republic was formed on January 1, 1993 upon the peaceful split of the Czech and Slovak Federal Republic. See the Czechslovakia introduction for earlier history.

MONETARY SYSTEM:

1 Czechoslovak Koruna (Kcs) = 100 Haleru Jan. - Feb. 1993
1 Czech Koruna (Kc) = 100 Haleru since Feb. 1993

REPUBLIC

CESKÁ NÁRODNÍ BANKA

CZECH NATIONAL BANK

1993 ND PROVISIONAL ISSUE

#1-3 were released 8.2.1993 having adhesive revalidation stamps affixed (later a printed *1000* was also circulated). Valid until 31.8.1993 but could be exchanged in deposits until 31.5.1994. Old Czechoslovak notes of 100 Korun and higher denominations became obsolete on 7.2.1993. Smaller denominations remained in circulation until 30.11.1993.

Note: In 1997 the CNB made available uncirculated examples of #1-3a and 3b to collectors. The notes are without cancellation marks and have regular serial #.

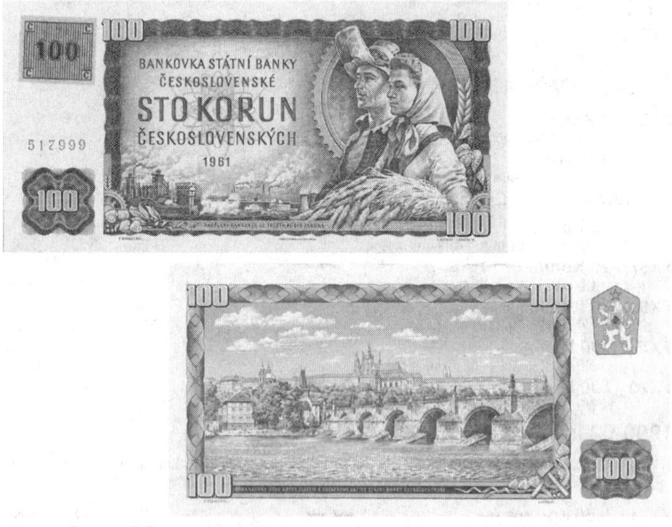

		VG	VF	UNC
1	**100 Korun** ND (1993-old date 1961). Dark green *C-100* adhesive stamp affixed to Czechoslovakia #91a or 91b.			
	a. Stamp on Czechoslovakia #91a.	7.50	12.50	25.00
	b. Stamp on Czechslovakia #91b.	4.00	7.50	15.00
	c. Stamp on Czechslovakia #91c.	2.50	5.00	10.00

		VG	VF	UNC
2	**500 Korun** ND (1993-old date 1973). Dark green *D-500* adhesive stamp affixed to Czechoslovakia #93. Series prefixes: U, W, Z.	7.50	12.50	30.00

		VG	VF	UNC
3	**1000 Korun** ND (1993-old date 1985). Deep green *M-1000* revalidation stamp on Czechoslovakia #98.			
	a. Adhesive stamp affixed. Series prefixes: C, U.	7.50	12.50	50.00
	b. Stamp image printed. Series prefix: U.	7.50	12.50	50.00

1993 REGULAR ISSUE

#4-9 arms at ctr. r.; only value in wmk. area on back.

#4-7 replacement notes: Serial # prefix *Z*.

		VG	VF	UNC
4	**50 Korun** 1993. Violet and black on pink and gray underprint. St. Agnes of Bohemia at right and with crown as watermark. Large A within gothic window frame at left center on back. Printer: TDLR. Serial # prefix *A*.			
	a. Issued note.	2.00	3.00	8.00
	r. Serial # prefix *Z*, replacement.	10.00	20.00	50.00

		VG	VF	UNC
5	**100 Korun** 1993. Blue-green, green and blue-black on lilac and multicolor underprint. King Karel IV at right and as watermark. Large seal of Charles University at left center on back. Printer: TDLR. Serial # prefix *A*.			
	a. Issued note.	4.00	6.00	12.50
	r. Serial # prefix *Z*, replacement.	8.00	17.50	35.00

6 **200 Korun**

1993. Deep brown on light orange and light green underprint. Jan Ámos Komensky at right and as watermark. Hands outreached at left center on back. Printer: STC-P. Serial # prefix *A*.

	VG	VF	UNC
a. Security filament with *200 KCS.*	FV	FV	25.00
b. Security filament with *200 KC.*	FV	FV	15.00
x. Error. Security filament reads: *REPUBLIQUE DU ZAÏRE.*	100.	600.	—

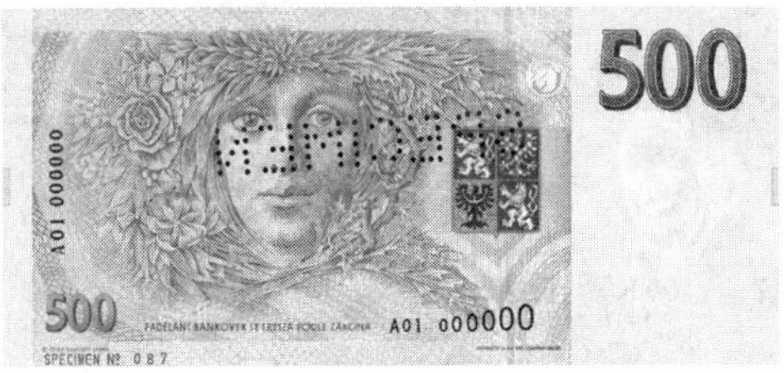

7 **500 Korun**

1993. Dark brown, brown & brown-violet on pink and tan underprint. Rose in underprint at upper center, Bozena Nemcová at right and as watermark. Laureate young woman's head at left center on back. Printer: TDLR. Serial # prefix *A*.

	VG	VF	UNC
a. Issued note.	FV	30.00	60.00
r. Serial # prefix *Z*, replacement.	20.00	50.00	90.00
s. Specimen.	—	—	—

8 **1000 Korun**

1993. Purple and lilac on multicolor underprint. Frantisek Palacky and as watermark. Eagle and Kromeriz Castle on back. Printer: STC-P. Serial # prefix *A*; *B*.

	VG	VF	UNC
a. Issued ntoe.	FV	FV	100.
s. Specimen.	—	—	—

9 **5000 Korun**

	VG	VF	UNC
1993. Black, blue-gray and violet on pink and light gray underprint. President Tomas Garrigue Masaryk at right. Montage of Prague Gothic and Baroque buildings on back. Printer: STC-P. Serial # prefix *A*.	FV	FV	350.

1994-96 ISSUE

#10-16 value and stylized design in wmk. area on back. Printer: STC-P.

10 **20 Korun**

1994. Blue-black and gray on light blue underprint, King Premysl Otakar I at right and as watermark. Crown with seal above at center, stylized crown at lower right on back.

	VG	VF	UNC
a. Serial # prefix *A*; *B*. Security filament at center (74mm from left edge). (1994).	FV	FV	3.00
b. Serial # prefix *B*. Security filament at left. center (50mm from left edge). (1995).	FV	FV	3.00

11 **50 Korun**

	VG	VF	UNC
1994. Violet and black on multicolor underprint. Like #4 but without gray in underprint. Stylized heart at lower right on back. Serial # prefix *B*.	FV	FV	4.00

12 **100 Korun** | VG FV | VF FV | UNC 10.00

1995. Blue-green, green and blue-black on lilac and multicolor underprint. Like #5, but with stylized *K* in circle at lower right on back. Serial # prefix *B*.

13 **200 Korun** | VG FV | VF FV | UNC 15.00

1996. Deep brown on pale orange and light green underprint. Like #6 but with stylized open book at lower right on back. Serial # prefix *B*.

14 **500 Korun** | VG FV | VF FV | UNC 35.00

1995. Dark brown, brown and brown-violet on pink and tan underprint. Like #7 but with stylized rose at lower right on back. Serial # prefix *B*.

15 **1000 Korun** | VG FV | VF FV | UNC 60.00

1996. Purple and lilac on multicolor underprint. Like #8 but with metallic linden leaf at upper center on face, and with stylized *P* and tree at lower right on back. Serial # prefix *C, D, E*.

16 **2000 Korun** | VG FV | VF FV | UNC 110.

1996. Dark olive-green, gray and violet on tan underprint. Ema Destinová at right, lyre at at upper left. in spray. Muse of music and lyric poetry Euterpe at left center, violin and cello and a large *D.*, stylized lyre at lower right on back. Serial # prefix *A*.

1997-99 ISSUE

#17-23 printer: STC-P. CR used in front-to-back perfect register.

17 **50 Korun** | VG FV | VF FV | UNC 3.00

1997. Violet and purple on multicolor underprint. Like #11. Serial # prefix *C, D, E*.

18 **100 Korun** | VG FV | VF FV | UNC 6.00

1997. Dark green, dark olive-green and black on multicolor underprint. Like #12. Serial # prefix *C, D, E*.

19 **200 Korun** | VG FV | VF FV | UNC 12.00

1998. Similar to #13, but fibers added in the paper. Serial # prefix *C, D*.

20	500 Korun	VG	VF	UNC
	1997. Dark brown, brown and brown-violet on pink and tan underprint. Like #14 but fibers added in the paper. Serial # prefix *C*.	FV	FV	28.00

#21 held in reserve.

22	2000 Korun	VG	VF	UNC
	1999. Similar to #16. Three metallic vertical bars in lyre at top center on face. Lyre in watermark area on back. Fibers added in the paper. Serial # prefix *B*.	FV	FV	100.

23	5000 Korun	VG	VF	UNC
	1999. Similar to #9. Metallic hexagon emblem at top center on face. Linden leaf in watermark area on back. Fibers added in the paper. Serial # prefix *B*.	FV	FV	250.

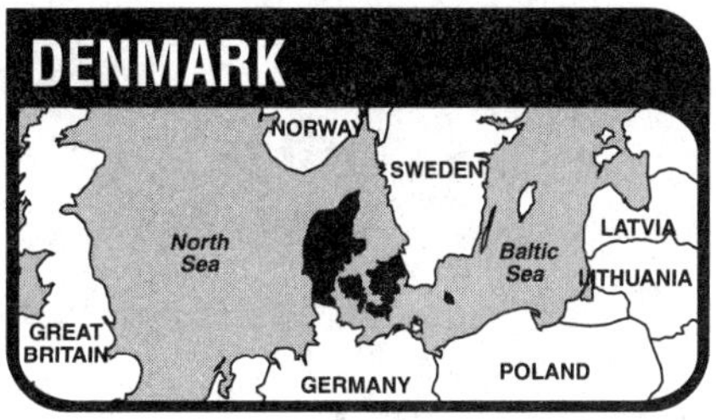

The Kingdom of Denmark, a constitutional monarchy located at the mouth of the Baltic Sea, has an area of 16,639 sq. mi. (43,070 sq. km.) and a population of 5.2 million. Capital: Copenhagen. Most of the country is arable. Agriculture, which used to employ the majority of the people, is now conducted by large farms served by cooperatives. The largest industries are food processing, iron and metal, and shipping. Machinery, meats (chiefly bacon), dairy products and chemicals are exported.

Denmark, a great power during the Viking period of the 9th-11th centuries, conducted raids on western Europe and England, and in the 11th century united England, Denmark and Norway under the rule of King Canute. Despite a struggle between the crown and the nobility (13th-14th centuries) which forced the king to grant a written constitution, Queen Margrethe (1353-1412) succeeded in uniting Denmark, Norway, Sweden, Finland and Greenland under the Danish crown, placing all Nordic countries under the rule of Denmark. Sweden and Finland were lost in 1523, and an unwise alliance with Napoleon caused the loss of Norway to Sweden in 1814. In the following years a liberal movement was fostered, which succeeded in making Denmark a constitutional monarchy in 1849.

The present decimal system of currency was introduced in 1874. As a result of a referendum held Sept. 28, 2000, the currency of the European Monetary Union, the Euro, will not be introduced in Denmark in the forseeable future.

RULERS:

Frederik IX, 1947-1972
Margrethe II, 1972-

MONETARY SYSTEM:

1 Krone = 100 Øre

REPLACEMENT NOTES:

#42-45 although dated (19)50, they were issued from 1952 onwards. #42-47, suffix OJ (for whole sheets) or OK (for single notes). Revalued Notes: For early Danish notes with additional printing and signatures on back refer to Danish West Indies, Faeroe Islands and Iceland.

KINGDOM

DANMARKS NATIONALBANK

1944-46 ISSUE

#35-41 first sign. Svendsen for #35, 36, 37a, 38, 39 - 1944-45. Halberg for #35, 37a, 37b, 38, 40, 1945-49. Riim for #35, 37b, 38, 40, 41 - 1948-62.

41	500 Kroner	VG	VF	UNC
	1944-62. Orange. Farmer with horses at center. Arms.			
	a. 1944. Prefix D. Left signature: Svendsen.	120.	225.	950.
	b. 1945. Prefix D. Left signature: Halberg.	120.	225.	850.
	c. 1948. Prefix D. Left signature: Halberg.	110.	200.	650.
	d. 1948. Prefix D. Left signature: Riim.	110.	200.	675.
	e. 1951. Prefix D. Left signature: Riim.	110.	225.	725.
	f. 1953. Prefix D.	120.	225.	725.
	g. 1954. Prefix D.	110.	200.	675.
	h. 1956. Prefix D.	110.	200.	675.
	i. 1959. Prefix D.	110.	200.	675.
	j. 1961. Prefix D.	110.	200.	725.
	k. 1962. Prefix D.	120.	200.	725.

1950 (1952)-63 ISSUE

Law of 7.4.1936

#42-47 first sign. changes. Usually there are 3 sign. combinations per prefix A0, A1, A2 etc. Second sign. Riim, (19)51-68 for #42, 43, 44a-f, (19)51-68 for #42, 43, 44a-f, 45a-b, 46a-b, 47. Valeur for (19)69 for #44g-h, 45c and 46b. The prefixes mentioned in the listings refer to the first two characters of the left serial #. The middle two digits indicate the date, and the last two characters indicate the sheet position of the note. Replacement Notes: #42-47, Serial # suffix: *OJ* (for whole sheet replacements) or *OK* (for single note replacements).

42 5 Kroner

(19)50; (19)52; (19)54-60. Blue-green. Portrait Bertil Thorvaldsen at left, 3 Graces at right. Kalundborg city view with 5 spire church at center. Watermark: *5* repeated.

	VG	VF	UNC
a. 5 in the watermark. 11mm high. Without dot after *7* in law date. (19)52. Prefix A0; A1.	9.00	45.00	150.
b. As a. (19)52. Prefix A2.	10.00	55.00	155.
c. As a., but with dot after 7 in law date. (19)52. Prefix A2.	7.00	35.00	110.
d. As c. (19)52. Prefix A3.	11.00	60.00	160.
e. As c. (19)54-55. Prefix A3-A9.	5.00	20.00	70.00
f. 5 in the watermark. 13mm high.	4.25	16.00	35.00
g. As f. (19)55. Prefix B1.	6.00	25.00	80.00
h. As f. (19)56. Prefix B1-B3.	4.00	15.00	32.50
i. As f. (19)56. Prefix B4.	6.00	25.00	80.00
j. As f. (19)57. Prefix B4-B6.	3.75	12.50	30.00
k. As f. (19)58-59. Prefix B7-B9, C0-C1.	3.50	8.00	25.00
l. As f. (19)59. Prefix C3.	30.00	100.	250.
m. As f. (19)60. Prefix C3-C4.	3.00	7.50	22.50
r1. As a. Replacement note. (19)50. Suffix OK.	50.00	200.	350.
r2. As e. Replacement note. (19)50. Suffix OJ.	7.50	30.00	90.00
r3. As e. Replacement note. (19)50. Suffix OK.	35.00	140.	260.
r4. As f, h, j. Replacement note. (19)50. Suffix OJ.	6.50	22.50	60.00
r5. As g, i, l. Replacement note. (19)50. Suffix OJ.	8.00	30.00	90.00
r6. As k. Replacement note. (19)50. Suffix OJ.	5.50	18.00	40.00
r7. As m. Replacement note. (19)60. Suffix OJ.	5.50	15.00	30.00
s. Specimen.	—	—	275.

43 10 Kroner

(19)50-52. Black and olive-brown. Portrait Hans Christian Andersen at left, white storks in nest at right. Green landscape of Egeskov Mølle Fyn at center. Watermark: *5* repeated. 125 x 65mm.

	VG	VF	UNC
a. (19)51. Prefix A0; A3; A4.	22.50	55.00	160.
b. (19)52. Prefix A1; A2; A5-A-8.	17.50	45.00	120.
c. (19)52. Prefix A9.	100.	200.	—
d. (19)52. Prefix B0.	17.50	45.00	120.
e. (19)52. Prefix B1.	35.00	80.00	225.
r1. As a. (19)50. Replacement note. Suffix OK.	120.	400.	—
r2. As b or d. Replacement note. Suffix OK.	90.00	300.	—

44 10 Kroner

(19)50; (19)54-74. Black and brown. Similar to #43, but text line added in upper and lower frame. Portrait Hans Christian Andersen at left. Black landscape at center. 125 x 71mm.

	VG	VF	UNC
a. Top and bottom line in frame begins with *10*. watermark: *10* repeated, 11mm high. (19)54. Prefix C0-C1.	9.00	35.00	110.
b. Like a but watermark. 13mm high. (19)54-55. Prefix C1-D5.	6.00	17.50	60.00
c. As b. (19)55. Prefix D6.	9.00	35.00	140.
d. As b. (19)56. Prefix D6.	6.00	17.50	60.00
e. As a. (19)56. Prefix D6-D8.	9.00	30.00	110.

44 10 Kroner

	VG	VF	UNC
f. As b. (19)56-57. Prefix D8-E4.	5.50	15.00	45.00
g. Top and bottom line in frame begins with *Tl*. (19)57. Prefix E4.	40.00	100.	300.
h. As g. (19)57. Prefix E5-E6.	5.50	14.00	35.00
i. As g. (19)57. Prefix E7.	9.00	32.50	120.
j. As g. (19)58. Prefix E7-F3.	5.25	12.50	30.00
k. As g. (19)58-59. Prefix F4.	6.00	15.00	30.00
l. As g. (19)59-60. Prefix F5-G3.	5.00	12.50	22.50
m. As g. (19)61-63. Prefix G4-H6.	4.50	10.00	18.00
n. As g. (19)64-67. Prefix H7-K9.	4.00	6.50	12.00
o. As g. (19)68. Prefix A0-A3.	3.75	5.50	10.00
p. As g. (19)68. Second signature Riim. Prefix A4.	4.50	9.00	17.00
q. As g. (19)69. Second signature Valeur. Prefix A4.	4.50	9.00	17.00
r. As q. (19)69. Prefix A5-A8.	3.25	5.50	10.00
r1. As c or e. Replacement note. (19)50. Suffix OJ.	10.00	40.00	120.
r2. As b, d or f. Replacement note. (19)50. Suffix OJ.	7.50	25.00	80.00
r3. As k or l.Replacement note. (19)50; (19)60. Suffix OJ.	6.00	20.00	60.00
r4. As m-r, t. Replacement note. (19)61-74. Suffix OJ.	4.50	10.00	25.00
r5. As u. Replacement note. (19)71. Suffix OJ.	12.00	50.00	160.
r6. As v or x. Replacement note. (19)72-74. Suffix OJ.	3.00	4.75	8.00
r7. As y. Replacement note. (19)74. Suffix OJ.	3.50	5.00	9.00
r8. As b. (19)50. Replacement note. Suffix OK.	100.	200.	—
r9. As n. Replacement note. (19)62-67. Suffix OK.	12.00	50.00	
r10. As t. Replacement note. (19)70-71. Suffix OK.	8.00	35.00	100.
r11. As t or v. Replacement note. (19)71-73. Suffix OK.	6.00	20.00	50.00
r12. As u. Replacement note. (19)71-73. Suffix OK.	12.00	50.00	160.
r13. As x. Replacement note. (19)74. Suffix OK.	8.00	35.00	100.
s. As q. (19)69. Prefix A9.	10.00	50.00	140.
s1. Specimen.	—	—	250.
t. As q. (19)70-71. Prefix A9-B9.	3.50	5.00	10.00
u. As q. (19)71. Prefix C0.	10.00	50.00	150.
v. As q. (19)72-73. Prefix C0-C9.	3.00	4.50	9.00
w. As q. (19)74. prefix C9.	10.00	50.00	150.
x. As q. (19)74. Prefix D0-D5.	3.00	4.50	8.00
y. As q. (19)74. Prefix D6.	3.50	5.00	10.00

45 50 Kroner

(19)50; (19)56-70. Blue on green underprint. Portrait Ole Rømer at left, Round Tower in Copenhagen at right. Blue. Stone Age burial site Dolmen of Stenvad, Djursland at center.

	VG	VF	UNC
a. Handmade paper. Watermark: Crowns and *50* (19)56-57, Prefix A1.	22.50	65.00	225.
b. As a. (19)57. Prefix A2.	28.00	90.00	260.
c. As a. (19)58. Prefix A2.	20.00	60.00	200.
d. As a. (19)58. prefix B0.	60.00	175.	600.
e. Machine made paper. Watermark: Rhombuses and 50. (19)61/1962. Prefix A4.	25.00	50.00	100.
f. As e. (19)62-63. Prefix A4-A5.	22.50	45.00	80.00
g. As e. (19)66. Prefix A6-A8.	18.00	30.00	65.00
h. As e. (19)70. Prefix A8-A9.	14.00	22.50	50.00
r1. As a. Replacement note. (19)50. Suffix OJ.	20.00	50.00	180.
r2. As a. Replacement note. (19)50. Suffix OJ. Prefix A2, A3.	60.00	175.	600.
r3. As a-d. Replacement note. (19)60/1960. Suffix OJ.	18.00	55.00	180.
r4. As b. Replacement note. (19)50. Suffix OJ.	25.00	65.00	210.
r5. As c. Replacement note. (19)50. Suffix OJ.	20.00	60.00	200.
r6. As e. Replacement note. (19)61/1962. Suffix OK.	18.00	45.00	120.
r7. As f. Replacement note. (19)62-63. Suffix OJ.	17.00	40.00	80.00
r8. As g. Replacement note. (19)66. Suffix OJ.	16.00	30.00	65.00
r9. As g, h. Replacement note. (19)66, (19)70. Suffix OK.	35.00	90.00	300.
r10. As h. Replacement note. (19)70. Suffix OJ.	14.00	22.50	50.00

46	100 Kroner	VG	VF	UNC
	(19)61-70. Red-brown on red-yellow underprint. Portrait Hans Christian Ørsted at left, compass card at right. Brown. Kronborg castle in Elsinore.			
	a. Handmade paper. Watermark: Close wavy lines and compass. (19)61. Prefix A0.	60.00	120.	350.
	b. Machine made paper. Watermark: *100.* (19)61. Prefix A2- A3.	22.50	45.00	130.
	c. (19)62. Prefix A4-A5.	22.50	40.00	120.
	d. (19)65. Prefix A6-B1.	22.50	35.00	90.00
	e. (19)65. Prefix B2.	60.00	120.	250.
	f. (19)70. Prefix B2-B4.	20.00	30.00	65.00
	r1. As a. Replacement note. Suffix OJ.	25.00	45.00	180.
	r2. As a. Replacement note. Suffix OK.	60.00	120.	350.
	r3. As b. Replacement note. Suffix OJ.	20.00	40.00	100.
	r4. As c, d. Replacement note. Suffix OJ.	20.00	35.00	100.
	r5. As e. Replacement note. Suffix OJ.	30.00	70.00	160.
	r6. As f. Replacement note. Suffix OJ.	20.00	30.00	65.00
	r7. As f. Replacement note. Suffix OK.	45.00	100.	200.

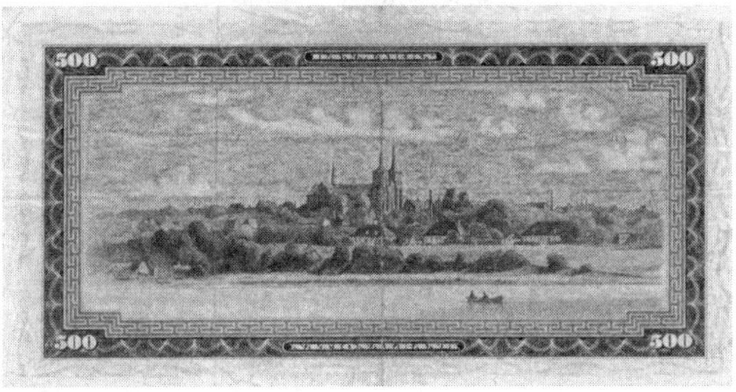

47	500 Kroner	VG	VF	UNC
	1963-67. Green. Portrait C. D. F. Reventlow at left, farmer plowing at right. Roskilde city view.			
	a. 1963. Prefix A0.	100.	175.	500.
	b. 1965. Prefiox A0.	100.	200.	600.
	c. 1967. Prefix A0-A1.	90.00	150.	400.
	r1. As a. Replacement note. Suffix OJ.	100.	200.	550.
	r2. As b. Replacement note. Suffix OJ.	120.	225.	650.
	r3. As c. Replacement note. Suffix OJ.	75.00	150.	425.
	s. Specimen.	—	—	900.

1972; 1979 Issue

Issued under *L. 1936*. The year of issue is shown by the 2 middle numerals within the series code at lower l. or r. Sign. varieties.

#48-52 portr. at r. on all notes painted by Danish artist Jens Juel (1745-1802).

#48-53 printer: Nationalbanken, Copenhagen (w/o imprint). All w/ *SERIE 1972* at lower r. on back.

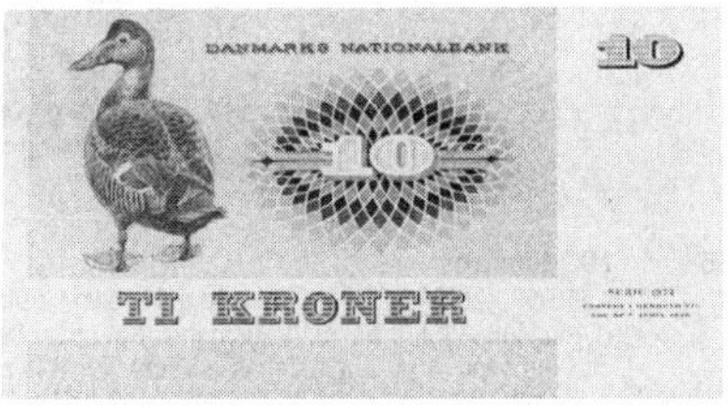

48	10 Kroner	VG	VF	UNC
	(19)72-78. Black on olive and multicolor underprint. Portrait Catherine Sophie Kirchhoff at right. Eider duck at left on back.			
	a. (19)72; (19)75. Prefix A0-A6.	FV	3.00	8.00
	b. (19)76. Prefix A8-B0.	FV	2.50	6.00
	c. (19)77-78. Prefix B1-B8.	FV	FV	5.00

49	20 Kroner	VG	VF	UNC
	(19)79-88. Dark blue on brown and multicolor underprint. Portrait Pauline Tutein at right. Male and female House Sparrow at left center on back. Watermark: Painter's palette, brushes and *20.*			
	a. (19)79. Prefix A0-A4.	FV	4.00	12.00
	b. (19)80. Prefix A5.	FV	4.50	14.00
	c. (19)81. Prefix A6, C0-C1.	FV	4.00	12.00
	d. (19)83. Prefix C2.	FV	FV	12.00
	d. (19)84. Prefix C3-C4.	FV	FV	12.00
	e. (19)85. Prefix C5.	FV	FV	12.00
	f. (19)87. Prefix C6.	FV	FV	11.00
	g. (19)88. Prefix C7-C8.	FV	FV	10.00

50	50 Kroner	VG	VF	UNC
	(19)72-98. Dark gray on pale blue, dull purple and pale green underprint. Portrait Mrs. Ryberg at right. *Carassius-Carassius* fish at left on back.			
	a. (19)72. Prefix A0-A1.	11.00	17.50	70.00
	b. (19)76; (19)78-79. Prefix A2-A6.	FV	12.00	45.00
	c. (19)82; (19)84-85; (19)89-90. Prefix C0-C6.	FV	FV	30.00
	d. (19)92-94. Prefix C7-C9, D0.	FV	FV	20.00
	e. (19)95. Prefix D1.	FV	12.50	50.00
	f. (19)96-98. Prefix D2-D5.	FV	FV	17.50
	s. Specimen.	—	—	400.

51	100 Kroner	VG	VF	UNC
	(19)72-93. Black and red on multicolor underprint. Jens Juel's self-portrait (ca.1773-74) at right. Danish Red Order Ribbon moth at left. on back.			
	a. (19)72. Prefix A0-A2.	FV	25.00	100.
	b. (19)75. Prefix A3-A5.	FV	FV	90.00
	c. (19)76-77. Prefix A6-A7.	FV	16.00	65.00

51	100 Kroner	VG	VF	UNC
	d. (19)78-79; (19)81-85. Prefix A8-A9, B0-B4, C0-C9.	FV	FV	50.00
	e. (19)85; Prefix H0.	17.50	40.00	110.
	f. (19)86-91. Prefix D0-D9, E0-E1.	FV	FV	35.00
	g. (19)86; Prefix R1.	17.50	30.00	90.00
	h. (19)91; Prefix E2.	FV	15.00	40.00
	i. (19)93. Prefix E3-E4.	FV	FV	35.00
	s. Specimen.	—	—	500.

52	500 Kroner	VG	VF	UNC
	(19)72-88. Black on green and multicolor underprint. *Unknown Lady* portrait, possibly von Qualen at right. Lizard on back. Watermark: Jens Juel and *500* repeated.			
	a. (19)72. Prefix A0-A1.	FV	65.00	210.
	b. (19)76. Prefix A2.	FV	FV	180.
	c. (19)80. Prefix A3-A5.	FV	FV	150.
	d. (19)88. Prefix C0-C1.	FV	FV	140.

53	1000 Kroner	VG	VF	UNC
	(19)72-92. Black on gray and multicolor underprint. Portrait Thomasine Heiberg at right. European or Red squirrel on back. Watermark: Double portrait Jens Juel and his wife and *1000*.			
	a. (19)72. Prefix A0.	FV	225.	450.
	b. (19)72. Prefix A1; (19)77. Prefix A2.	FV	200.	375.
	c. (19)80-81. Prefix A3, C0-C1.	FV	FV	300.
	d. (19)86. Prefix C2-C3.	FV	FV	300.
	e. (19)92. Ptrefix C4-C5.	FV	FV	300.

1972A Issue

54	100 Kroner	VG	VF	UNC
	(19)94-98. Black and orange on multicolor underprint. Like #51 but with additional security devices. Watermark: Jens Juul. *Series 1972A* at lower right on back.			
	a. (19)94. Prefix F0.	FV	FV	35.00
	b. (19)95. Prefix F1-F2.	FV	FV	32.50
	c. (19)95. Prefix F3.	FV	FV	35.00
	d. (19)95. Prefix F4-F5.	FV	FV	28.00
	e. (19)96. Prefix F6.	FV	FV	30.00
	f. (19)97. Prefix F7	FV	FV	28.00
	g. (19)97. Prefix F8.	FV	FV	40.00
	h. (19)98. Prefix F9-G0.	FV	FV	28.00

1997-2001 Issue

55	50 Kroner	VG	VF	UNC
	(19)99; (20)00; (20)01; (20)02. Black and deep purple on multicolor underprint. Karen Blixen at right and as watermark. Centaur stone relief from Landet Church, Tåsinge at left center on back.			
	a. (19)99. Prefix A0-A1.	FV	FV	15.00
	b. (20)00. Prefix A2-A3.	FV	FV	14.00
	c. (20)01. Prefix A4-A6.	FV	FV	12.50
	d. (20)01. Prefix A7.	FV	FV	20.00
	e. (20)02. A8-A9.	FV	FV	12.50

56	100 Kroner	VG	VF	UNC
	(19)99; (20)00; (20)01. Black and red-brown on orange and multicolor underprint. Blue latent image at upper left, Carl Nielsen at right and as watermark. Basilisk stone relief from Tømmerby Church in Thy at left center on back.			
	a. (19)99. Prefix A0-A2.	FV	FV	27.50
	b. (20)00. Prefix A3-A4.	FV	FV	27.50
	c. (20)00. Prefix A5.	FV	FV	35.00
	d. (20)01. Prefix A6-A7.	FV	FV	27.50
	e. (20)01. Prefix A8.	FV	FV	40.00

		VG	VF	UNC
57	**200 Kroner** (19)97; (20)00. Black and dark blue on turquoise green and multicolor underprint. Pale red-violet latent image at upper left, J. L. Heiberg at right. Stone lion relief from Viborg Cathedral at left center on back.			
	a. (19)97. Prefix A0-A1.	FV	FV	50.00
	b. (20)00. Prefix A2.	FV	FV	50.00

		VG	VF	UNC
58	**500 Kroner** (19)97; (19)99; (20)00; (20)03. Black on blue, orange and multicolor underprint. N. Bohr at right. Knight and dragon relief from Lihme Church at left center on back.			
	a. (19)97. prefix A0.	FV	FV	130.
	b. (19)97. Prefix A1.	FV	FV	150.
	c. (19)99. Prefix A2.	FV	FV	150.
	d. (20)00. Prefix A3.	FV	FV	125.
	e. (20)00. Prefix A4.	FV	FV	135.
	f. (20)03. Prefix A5.	FV	FV	135.

		VG	VF	UNC
59	**1000 Kroner** (19)98. Violet, purple and green. Purple iridescent metallic strip. A. and M. Ancher at right. Back purple, turquoise, and orange on multicolor underprint. Tournament scene relief from Bislev Church at left center on back. Serial # prefix A0-A1.	FV	FV	240.

2002 Issue

#60-64 similar to #55-59 but with increased security features. Hologram added at upper left.

		VG	VF	UNC
60	**50 Kroner** (20)04; (20)05. Black and deep purple on multicolor underprint. Serial # prefix B. Similar to #55.	FV	FV	12.50

		VG	VF	UNC
61	**100 Kroner** (20)02; (20)04; (20)06. Black and red-brown on orange and multicolor underprint. Similar to #56. Serial # prefix B, C.	FV	FV	22.50

		VG	VF	UNC
62	**200 Kroner** (20)03; (20)05. Black and dark blue on turquoise green and multicolor underprint. Similar to #57. Serial # prefix B.	FV	FV	45.00

		VG	VF	UNC
63	**500 Kroner** (20)03; (20)06. Black on blue, orange and multicolor underprint. Similar to #58. Serial # prefix B.	FV	FV	110.
64	**1000 Kroner** (20)04; (20)06. Violet, purple and green. Similar to #59. Serial # prefix B.	FV	FV	220.

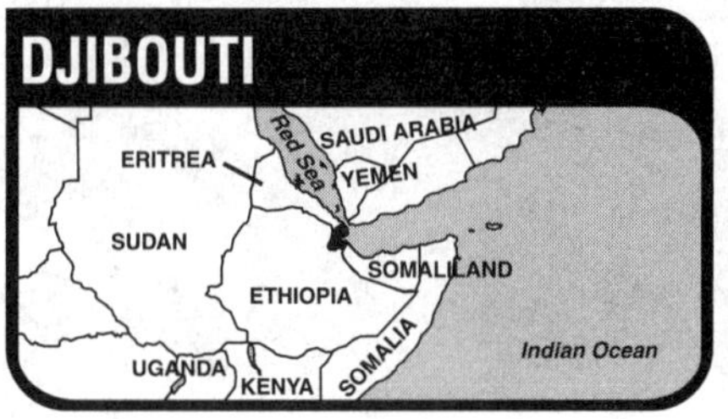

The Republic of Djibouti (formerly French Somaliland or the French Overseas Territory of Afars and Issas), located in northeast Africa at the Bab el Mandeb Strait connecting the Suez Canal and the Red Sea with the Gulf of Aden and the Indian Ocean, has an area of 8,494 sq. mi. (22,000 sq. km.) and a population of 687,000. Capital: Djibouti. The tiny nation has less than one sq. mi. of arable land, and few natural resources of salt, sand and camels. The commercial activities of the trans-shipment port of Djibouti and the Addis Ababa-Djibouti railroad are the basis of the economy also French (and now American) military activity. Salt, fish and hides are exported.

French interest in former French Somaliland began in 1839 with concessions obtained by a French naval lieutenant from the provincial sultans. French Somaliland was made a protectorate in 1884 and its boundaries were delimited by the Franco-British and Ethiopian accords of 1887 and 1897. It became a colony in 1896 and a territory within the French Union in 1946. In 1958, it voted to join the new French Community as an overseas territory, and reaffirmed that choice by a referendum in March 1967. Its name was changed from French Somaliland to the French Territory of Afars and Issas on July 5, 1967.

In 1977 Afars and Issas became independent under the name of the Republic of Djibouti.

Note: For earlier issues see French Afars and Issas.

MONETARY SYSTEM:

1 Franc = 100 Centimes

REPUBLIC OF DJIBOUTI

BANQUE NATIONALE DE DJIBOUTI

1979; 1984 ND ISSUE

		VG	VF	UNC
36	**500 Francs**			
	ND (1979; 1988). Multicolor. Man at left, rocks in sea, storks at right. Stern of ship at right on back.			
	a. Blue underprint. without signature (1979).	FV	7.00	18.00
	b. Pale blue underprint. Sign title: *LE GOUVERNEUR* added. (1988).	FV	6.00	16.00

		VG	VF	UNC
37	**1000 Francs**			
	ND (1979; 1988). Brown and multicolor. Woman at left, people by diesel passenger trains at center Trader with camels at center on back.			
	a. Long Arabic text on back. without signature Engraved. (1979).	FV	12.00	35.00
	b. Signature title: *LE GOUVERNEUR* added above *MILLE*. Short Arabic text at top on back. Lithographed. (1988).	FV	10.00	30.00
	c. Long Arabic text on back. (1991).	FV	10.00	25.00
	d. As c but with security thread. 2 signature varieties.	FV	FV	20.00
	e. as d. but bluish microprint frame on both sides.	FV	FV	20.00

		VG	VF	UNC
38	**5000 Francs**			
	ND (1979). Multicolor. Man at right, forest scene at center. Aerial view at center on back.			
	a. Without signature	FV	40.00	90.00
	b. With signature	FV	40.00	80.00
	c. As b but with security thread.	FV	FV	70.00
	d. as c. but fluorescent security stripe.	FV	FV	70.00

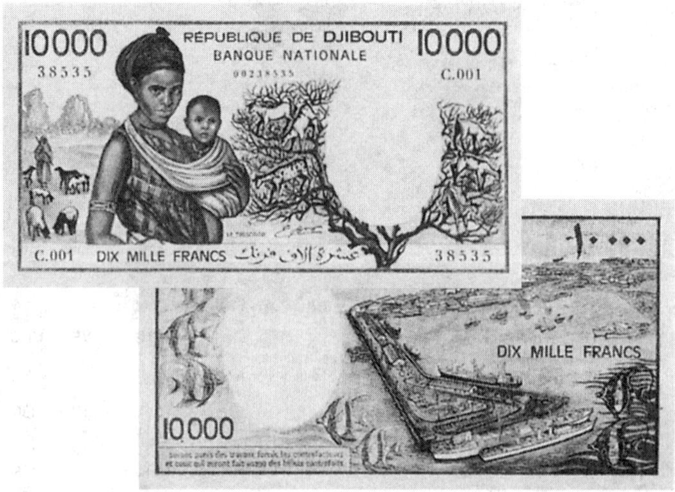

		VG	VF	UNC
39	**10,000 Francs**			
	ND (1984). Brown and red on yellow and green. Woman holding baby at left, goats in tree at right. Fish and harbor scene on back.			
	a. Signature title: *TRÉSORIER*.	FV	80.00	160.
	b. Signature title: *GOUVERNEUR* . with security thread.	FV	FV	130.

1997; 1999 ND ISSUE

		VG	VF	UNC
40	**2000 Francs**			
	ND (1997). Dark blue, blue-black and black on yellow and multicolor underprint. Young girl at right, camel caravan at center. Statue with spear and shield at lower left, government building at center on back.	FV	FV	30.00

Note: #40 reportedly commemorates the 20th anniversary of independence.

NOTICE

Readers with unlisted dates, signature varieties, etc. are invited to submit photocopies of their notes to: Standard Catalog of World Paper Money, 700 East State St. Iola, WI 54990-0001, E-Mail: george.cuhaj@fwpubs.com.

41 **10,000 Francs** | VG | VF | UNC
ND (1999). Blue and multicolor. President Hassan Gouled Aptidon at right, undersea life at center. Building at center on back. | FV | FV | 125.

BANQUE CENTRALE DE DJIBOUTI

2002 ND ISSUE

		VG	VF	UNC
42	**1000 Francs**			
	ND (2005). Reddish brown and multicolor.			
	a. Issued note.	FV	FV	16.00
	r. Replacement note. *Z* prefix.	FV	FV	25.00

		VG	VF	UNC
43	**5000 Francs**			
	ND (2002). Purple and multicolor. Central bank building and M. Harbi. Three females dancing with swords, rock landscape on back.	FV	FV	55.00

The Dominican Republic, occupying the eastern two-thirds of the island of Hispañiola, has an area of 18,816 sq. mi. (48,734 sq. km.) and a population of 8.49 million. Capital: Santo Domingo. The agricultural economy produces sugar, coffee, tobacco and cocoa.

Columbus discovered Hispaniola in 1492, and named it *La Isla Espanola* - "the Spanish Island." Santo Domingo, the oldest white settlement in the Western Hemisphere, was the from which Spain conducted its exploration of the New World. Later, French buccaneers settled the western third of Hispaniola, which in 1697 was ceded to France by Spain, and in 1804 became the Republic of Haiti - "mountainous country." At this time, the Spanish called their part of Hispaniola Santo Domingo, and the French called their part Saint-Domingue. In 1822, the Haitians conquered the entire island and held it until 1844, when Juan Pablo Duarte, the national hero of the Dominican Republic, drove them out of eastern Hispaniola and established an independent Dominican Republic. The republic returned voluntarily to Spanish dominion - after being rejected by France, Britain and the United States - from 1861 to 1865, when independence was restored.

Dictatorships and democratic rule was intersperced and from 1916 to 1924 it was occupied by the U.S. from 1930 to 1961, Rafael Trujillo was dictator. In the 1994 elections, a reform government gained power.

MONETARY SYSTEM:

1 Peso Oro = 100 Centavos Oro

SPECIMEN NOTES:

In 1998 the Banco Central once again began selling various specimens over the counter to the public. Current market valuations are being reflected, subject to change.

REPLACEMENT NOTES:

#53-61: Z prefix and suffix (TDLR printings).
#117-124: Z prefix and suffix (TDLR printings).

REPUBLIC

BANCO CENTRAL DE LA REPÚBLICA DOMINICANA

1961 ND ISSUES

		VG	VF	UNC
85	**10 Centavos Oro**			
	ND (1961). Blue and black. Banco de Reservas in round frame at center. Back blue. Printer: ABNC.			
	a. Issued note.	1.00	3.50	15.00
	s. Specimen.	—	—	20.00

		VG	VF	UNC
86	**10 Centavos Oro**			
	ND (1961). Black on light blue-green safety paper. Banco de Reservas in oval frame at center. Back green. Printer: Banco Central.			
	a. Issued note.	2.00	6.00	30.00
	s. Specimen.	—	—	20.00

		VG	VF	UNC
87	**25 Centavos Oro**			
	ND (1961). Red and black. Entrance to the Banco Central in rectangular frame at center. Back red. Printer: ABNC.			
	a. Issued note.	1.00	4.00	12.50
	s. Specimen.	—	—	20.00

88	25 Centavos Oro	VG	VF	UNC
	ND (1961). Black. Entrance to the Banco Central in oval frame at center. Back green. Printer: Banco Central.			
	a. Pink safety paper.	1.75	5.00	30.00
	b. Plain cream paper.	2.50	7.50	35.00
	s. Specimen.	—	—	20.00

89	50 Centavos Oro	VG	VF	UNC
	ND (1961). Purple and black. Palacio Nacional in circular frame at center. Back purple. Printer: ABNC.			
	a. Issued note.	1.75	4.00	15.00
	s. Specimen.	—	—	20.00

90	50 Centavos Oro	VG	VF	UNC
	ND (1961). Black on yellow safety paper. Palacio Nacional in oval frame at center. Back green. Printer: Banco Central.			
	a. Issued note.	5.50	25.00	80.00
	s. Specimen.	—	—	20.00

1962 ND Issue

#91-98 w/text over seal: *SANTO DOMINGO/DISTRITO NACIONAL/REPÚBLICA DOMINICANA*. Medallic portr. Liberty head at l., arms at r. on back. Printer: ABNC.

91	1 Peso Oro	VG	VF	UNC
	ND (1962-63). Red. Portrait J. P. Duarte at center.			
	a. Issued note.	4.00	20.00	65.00
	s. Specimen.	—	—	125.

92	5 Pesos Oro	VG	VF	UNC
	ND (1962). Red. Portrait J. Sánchez atnright center. Back purple.			
	a. Issued note.	6.00	25.00	80.00
	s. Specimen.	—	—	150.

93	10 Pesos Oro	VG	VF	UNC
	ND (1962). Red. Portrait Mella at center. Back brown.			
	a. Issued note.	12.50	50.00	175.
	s. Specimen.	—	—	240.

94	20 Pesos Oro	VG	VF	UNC
	ND (1962). Red. *Puerta del Conde* at center. Back olive.			
	a. Issued note.	25.00	125.	350.
	s. Specimen.	—	—	400.

95	50 Pesos Oro	VG	VF	UNC
	ND (1962). Red. Tomb of Columbus at center. Back blue-gray.			
	a. Issued note.	50.00	200.	500.
	s. Specimen.	—	—	40.00

96	100 Pesos Oro	VG	VF	UNC
	ND (1962). Red. Woman with coffee pot and cup at center. Back blue-gray.			
	a. Issued note.	75.00	225.	550.
	s. Specimen.	—	—	60.00

97	500 Pesos Oro	VG	VF	UNC
	ND (1962). "Obelisco de Ciudad Trujillo" at center.			
	a. Issued note.	—	—	—
	s. Specimen.	—	—	100.

98	1000 Pesos Oro	VG	VF	UNC
	ND (1962). Minor Basilica of Santa Maria at center.			
	a. Issued note. Unique.	—	—	—
	s. Specimen.	—	—	150.

1964 ND Issue

#99-106 orange bank seal at r. Medallic portr. Liberty head at l., arms at r. on back. Sign. varieties. Printer: TDLR.

99	1 Peso Oro	VG	VF	UNC
	ND (1964-73). Black on multicolor underprint. Portrait J. P. Duarte at center with eyes looking left, white bow tie.			
	a. Issued note.	.50	2.50	12.50
	s. Specimen with black ovpt: *MUESTRA*.	—	—	15.00

100	5 Pesos Oro	VG	VF	UNC
	ND (1964-74). Brown on multicolor underprint. Portrait J. Sánchez at right center.			
	a. Issued note.	3.00	10.00	40.00
	s. Specimen with black ovpt: *MUESTRA*.	—	—	17.50

101	10 Pesos Oro	VG	VF	UNC
	ND (1964-74). Deep green on multicolor underprint. Portrait Mella at center.			
	a. Issued note.	5.00	17.50	55.00
	s. Specimen with black ovpt: *MUESTRA*.	—	—	20.00

102	20 Pesos Oro	VG	VF	UNC
	ND (1964-74). Dark brown on multicolor underprint. *Altar de la Patria* at center.			
	a. Issued note.	8.00	30.00	125.
	s. Specimen with black ovpt: *MUESTRA*.	—	—	20.00

103	50 Pesos Oro	VG	VF	UNC
	ND (1964-74). Purple on multicolor underprint. Ox cart at center.			
	a. Issued note.	20.00	75.00	175.
	s. Specimen with black ovpt: *MUESTRA*.	—	—	22.50

104	100 Pesos Oro	VG	VF	UNC
	ND (1964-74). Orange-brown on multicolor underprint. Banco Central at center.			
	a. Issued note.	40.00	125.	300.
	s. Specimen.	—	—	40.00

		VG	VF	UNC
105	**500 Pesos Oro** ND (1964-74). Dark blue on multicolor underprint. Columbus tomb and cathedral at center.			
	a. Issued note.	100.	400.	850.
	s. Specimen with black ovpt: *MUESTRA*.	—	—	60.00
106	**1000 Pesos Oro** ND (1964-74). Red and multicolor underprint. National Palace at center. Medallic portrait Liberty at left center, arms at right center on back.			
	a. Issued note.	200.	750.	1750.
	s. Specimen.	—	—	125.

1973 ND Issue

		VG	VF	UNC
107	**1 Peso Oro** ND (1973-74). Black on light green and pinkish tan underprint. Like #99 but portrait J. P. Duarte with eyes looking front, black bow tie.			
	a. Issued note.	.50	2.00	10.00
	s. Specimen.	—	—	12.50

1975 Issue

#108-115 dates at ctr. in upper margin on back. Printer: TDLR.

		VG	VF	UNC
108	**1 Peso Oro** 1975-78. Black on light green and pinkish tan underprint. Like #107.			
	a. Issued note.	.25	1.50	7.50
	s. Specimen.	—	—	12.50

		VG	VF	UNC
109	**5 Pesos Oro** 1975-76. Brown on light green and lilac underprint. Like #100.			
	a. Issued note.	.50	5.00	20.00
	s. Specimen.	—	—	—
110	**10 Pesos Oro** 1975-76. Green on light green and lilac underprint. Like #101.			
	a. Issued note.	1.50	10.00	35.00
	s. Specimen.	—	—	—
111	**20 Pesos Oro** 1975-76. Brown on light green and blue underprint. Like #102.			
	a. Issued note.	2.50	15.00	55.00
	s. Specimen.	—	—	20.00

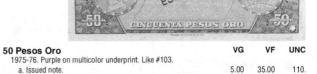

		VG	VF	UNC
112	**50 Pesos Oro** 1975-76. Purple on multicolor underprint. Like #103.			
	a. Issued note.	5.00	35.00	110.
	s. Specimen.	—	—	—

		VG	VF	UNC
113	**100 Pesos Oro** 1975-76. Orange-brown on multicolor underprint. Like #104.			
	a. Issued note.	10.00	60.00	190.
	s. Specimen with black overprint:*ESPECIMEN*. 1976.	—	—	40.00
114	**500 Pesos Oro** 1975. Dark blue on multicolor underprint. Like #105.			
	a. Issued note.	50.00	250.	750.
	s. Specimen.	—	—	60.00

115 1000 Pesos Oro

1975-76. Red on multicolor underprint. Like #106.

	VG	VF	UNC
a. Issued note.	95.00	500.	1500.
s. Specimen with black ovpt: *ESPECIMEN.* 1975.	—	—	125.

1977-80 ISSUES

#116-124 dates in upper margin on back. Replacement notes: Serial # prefix and suffix *Z*.

116 1 Peso Oro

1978-79. Black, dark green and dark brown on multicolor underprint. J. P. Duarte at right, orange seal at left. Sugar refinery on back. Printer: ABNC.

	VG	VF	UNC
a. Issued note.	.20	1.00	5.00
s. Specimen with red ovpt: *MUESTRA - SIN VALOR.* 1978.	—	—	12.50

#117-124 orange bank seal at l. Printer: TDLR.

117 1 Peso Oro

1980-82. Black, dark green and dark brown on multicolor underprint. Like #116. Dates very lightly printed.

	VG	VF	UNC
a. Issued note.	.75	1.00	4.50
s. Specimen with black ovpt: *ESPECIMEN.* 1980; 1981.	—	—	12.50

118 5 Pesos Oro

1978-88. Deep brown, red-brown and red on multicolor underprint. J. Sánchez at right, arms at center. Hydroelectric dam on back.

	VG	VF	UNC
a. 1978.	.50	2.50	8.50
b. 1980-82.	FV	2.00	7.00
c. 1984; 1985; 1987; 1988.	FV	1.50	5.50
s1. Specimen with black ovpt: *ESPECIMEN.* 1978; 1980; 1981.	—	—	15.00
s2. Specimen with red ovpt: *MUESTRA SIN VALOR* and TDLR oval seals. 1985; 1987.	—	—	15.00
s3. Specimen with black ovpt: *MUESTRA SIN VALOR* and red ovpt: TDLR oval seals. 1988.	—	—	15.00

119 10 Pesos Oro

1978-88. Black and green on multicolor underprint. Mella at right, medallic Liberty head at center. Quarry mining scene on back.

	VG	VF	UNC
a. 1978.	1.25	5.00	20.00
b. 1980-82.	FV	3.50	15.00
c. 1985; 1987; 1988.	FV	3.00	10.00
s1. Specimen with black ovpt: *ESPECIMEN.* 1978; 1980; 1981.	—	—	17.50
s2. Specimen with red ovpt: *MUESTRA SIN VALOR* and TDLR oval seals. 1985; 1987.	—	—	20.00
s3. Specimen with black ovpt: *MUESTRA SIN VALOR* and red ovpt: TDLR oval seals. 1988.	—	—	20.00

120 20 Pesos Oro

1978-88. Black, dark brown and olive-brown on multicolor underprint. *Altar de la Patria* at center *Puerta del Conde* on back.

	VG	VF	UNC
a. 1978.	2.00	7.00	25.00
b. 1980-82.	FV	5.50	20.00
c. 1985; 1987; 1988.	FV	5.00	17.50
s1. Specimen with black ovpt: *ESPECIMEN.* 1978; 1980; 1981.	—	—	20.00
s2. Specimen with red ovpt: *MUESTRA SIN VALOR* and TDLR oval seals. 1985; 1987.	—	—	22.50
s3. Specimen with black ovpt: *MUESTRA SIN VALOR* and red ovpt: TDLR oval seals. 1988.	—	—	22.50

121 50 Pesos Oro

1978-87. Black and purple on multicolor underprint. Basilica at center. First cathedral in America at center right on back.

	VG	VF	UNC
a. Watermark: Indian head. 1978; 1980; 1981.	5.00	22.50	50.00
b. Watermark: J. P. Duarte. 1985; 1987.	6.00	25.00	55.00

		VG	VF	UNC
121	**50 Pesos Oro**			
	s1. As a. Specimen with black ovpt: *ESPECIMEN*. 1978; 1980; 1981.	—	—	22.50
	s2. As b. Specimen with perforated *MUESTRA SIN VALOR* and red ovpt: TDLR oval seals. 1985; 1987.	—	—	25.00

		VG	VF	UNC
122	**100 Pesos Oro** 1977-87. Violet, brown-orange and yellow-orange on multicolor underprint. Entrance to 16th century mint at center. Banco Central at center right on back.			
	a. Watermark: Indian head. 1977; 1978; 1980; 1981.	10.00	42.50	125.
	b. Watermark: J.P. Duarte. 1984; 1985; 1987.	FV	50.00	150.
	s1. As a. Specimen with black ovpt: *ESPECIMEN*.1978; 1980; 1981.	—	—	30.00
	s2. As b. Specimen with perforated: *MUESTRA SIN VALOR* and red ovpt: TDLR oval seals. 1985; 1987.	—	—	25.00

		VG	VF	UNC
123	**500 Pesos Oro** 1978-87. Deep blue, blue and brown on multicolor underprint. National Theater at center Fort San Felipe at center right on back.			
	a. Watermark: Indian head. 1978; 1980; 1981.	55.00	225.	450.
	b. Watermark: J. P. Duarte. 1985; 1987.	50.00	200.	400.
	s1. As a. Specimen with black ovpt: *ESPECIMEN*. 1978; 1980; 1981.	—	—	40.00
	s2. As b. Specimen with perforated: *MUESTRA SIN VALOR* and red ovpt: TDLR oval seals. 1985; 1987.	—	—	40.00

		VG	VF	UNC
124	**1000 Pesos Oro** 1978-87. Red, purple and violet on multicolor underprint. National Palace at center Columbus' fortress at center right on back.			
	a. Watermark: Indian head. 1978; 1980.	100.	275.	550.
	b. Watermark: J. P. Duarte. 1984; 1987.	90.00	225.	450.
	s1. As a. Specimen with black ovpt: *ESPECIMEN*. 1978; 1980; 1981.	—	—	50.00
	s2. As b. Specimen with perforated: *MUESTRA SIN VALOR* and red ovpt: TDLR oval seals. 1985; 1987.	—	—	50.00
	s3. As b. Specimen with red ovpt: *MUESTRA SIN VALOR*.	—	—	50.00

1978 Commemorative Issue

#125, Inauguration of new Banco Central bldg.

		VG	VF	UNC
125	**100 Pesos Oro** 15.8.1978 (- old date 1977). Special commemorative text overprint in black script at left on back of #122a. Specimen in red folder.	—	—	200.

1982 Commemorative Issue

#125A, 35th Anniversary Banco Central, 1947-1982

		VG	VF	UNC
125A	**100 Pesos Oro** 22.10.1982 (old dates 1978, 1981). Special commemorative text overprint in black below bank at right on back of #122a.			
	s1. Old date 1978. Face without adhesive stamp or handstamp. Specimen.	—	—	135.
	s2. Old date 1981. Banco Central commemorative adhesive stamp affixed at left, handstamp with date 22.10.1982 at center l. Specimen.	—	—	150.

1984 Issue

		VG	VF	UNC
126	**1 Peso Oro** 1984; 1987; 1988. Black and brown on multicolor underprint. New portrait J. P. Duarte at right, otherwise like #117. Printer: TDLR.			
	a. Issued note.	FV	FV	2.00
	s1. Specimen with red ovpt: *MUESTRA SIN VALOR* and TDLR oval seals. 1987.	—	—	10.00
	s2. Specimen with black ovpt: *MUESTRA SIN VALOR* and red ovpt: TDLR oval seals. 1988.	—	—	10.00

1988 Issue

#127-130 orange bank seal at l. Wmk: Duarte (profile). Printer: USBNC.

		VG	VF	UNC
127	**50 Pesos Oro** 1988. Black and purple on multicolor underprint. Similar to #121.			
	a. Issued note.	FV	FV	17.50
	s. Specimen with red ovpt: *ESPECIMEN MUESTRA SIN VALOR*.	—	—	20.00

		VG	VF	UNC
128	**100 Pesos Oro** 1988. Violet, brown-orange and brown on multicolor underprint. Similar to #122.			
	a. Issued note.	FV	FV	25.00
	s. Specimen with red ovpt: *ESPECIMEN MUESTRA SIN VALOR*.	—	—	22.50

		VG	VF	UNC
129	**500 Pesos Oro**			
	1988. Deep blue, blue, and brown on multicolor underprint. Similar to #123.			
	a. Issued note.	FV	FV	75.00
	s. Specimen with red ovpt: *ESPECIMEN MUESTRA SIN VALOR.*	—	—	35.00

		VG	VF	UNC
130	**1000 Pesos Oro**			
	1988; 1990. Purple, red-violet and violet on multicolor underprint. Similar to #124.			
	a. Issued note.	FV	FV	135.
	s. Specimen with red ovpt: *ESPECIMEN MUESTRA SIN VALOR.* 1988.	—	—	45.00

1990 Issue

#131-134 w/silver leaf-like underlays at l. and r. on face. Printer: H&S.

		VG	VF	UNC
131	**5 Pesos Oro**			
	1990. Deep brown, red-brown and red on multicolor underprint. Similar to #118.	FV	FV	2.50

		VG	VF	UNC
132	**10 Pesos Oro**			
	1990. Deep green and black on multicolor underprint. Similar to #119.	FV	FV	4.00
133	**20 Pesos Oro**			
	1990. Deep brown and brown on multicolor underprint. Similar to #120.	FV	FV	7.00
134	**500 Pesos Oro**			
	1990. Deep blue-green, black and brown on multicolor underprint. Similar to #123.	FV	FV	70.00

1991 Issue

#135-138 orange seal at l. Printer: TDLR.

		VG	VF	UNC
135	**50 Pesos Oro**			
	1991; 1994. Black and purple on multicolor underprint. Like #127 but watermark: Columbus.			
	a. Issued note.	FV	FV	10.00
	s. Specimen with black ovpt: *MUESTRA SIN VALOR* and red ovpt: TDLR oval seals. 1991; 1994.	—	—	20.00

		VG	VF	UNC
136	**100 Pesos Oro**			
	1991; 1994. Orange and violet on multicolor underprint. Like #128.			
	a. Issued note.	FV	FV	20.00
	s. Specimen with black ovpt: *MUESTRA SIN VALOR* and red ovpt: TDLR oval seals. 1994.	FV	FV	35.00

		VG	VF	UNC
137	**500 Pesos Oro**			
	1991; 1994. Deep blue, blue and dark brown on multicolor underprint. Like #134.			
	a. Issued note.	FV	FV	65.00
	s. Specimen with black ovpt: *MUESTRA SIN VALOR* and red ovpt: TDLR oval seals. 1991; 1994.	—	—	35.00

		VG	VF	UNC
138	**1000 Pesos Oro**			
	1991; 1992; 1994. Purple, red-violet and violet on multicolor underprint. Like #130.			
	a. Issued note.	FV	FV	125.
	s. Specimen with black ovpt: *MUESTRA SIN VALOR* and red ovpt: TDLR oval seals. 1991; 1994.	—	—	50.00

1992 Commemorative Issue

#139-142, Quincentennial of First Landfall by Christopher Columbus, 1992

		VG	VF	UNC
139	**20 Pesos Oro**			
	1992. Deep brown and brown on multicolor underprint. Like #133 but with brown commemorative text: *1492-1992 V Centenario...* at left over orange seal. Printer: BABNC.			
	a. Issued note.	FV	FV	5.00
	s. Specimen with red overprintt: *ESPECIMEN* and black ovpt: *ESPECIMEN SIN VALOR.*	—	—	20.00

#140-142 wmk: C. Columbus.

		VG	VF	UNC
140	**500 Pesos Oro** 1992. Brown and blue-black on multicolor underprint. Sailing ships at center, C. Columbus at center right. Arms at left, Columbus Lighthouse, placement of Cross of Christianity and map outline at center on back. Printer: CBNC.			
	a. Issued note.	FV	FV	85.00
	s. Specimen with black ovpt: *MUESTRA SIN VALOR* and red ovpt: TDLR oval seals.	—	—	110.

		VG	VF	UNC
141	**500 Pesos Oro** 1992. Deep blue, blue and dark brown on multicolor underprint. Black commemorative text overprint at right on #137. Printer: TDLR.			
	a. Issued note.	FV	FV	85.00
	s. Specimen with black ovpt: *MUESTRA SIN VALOR* and red ovpt: TDLR oval seals.	—	—	35.00

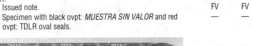

		VG	VF	UNC
142	**1000 Pesos Oro** 1992. Purple, red-violet and violet on multicolor underprint. Black commemorative text overprint at right on #138. Printer: TDLR.			
	a. Issued note.	FV	FV	125.
	s. Specimen with black ovpt: *MUESTRA SIN VALOR* and red ovpt: TDLR oval seals.	—	—	40.00

1993 Regular Issue

		VG	VF	UNC
143	**5 Pesos Oro** 1993. Deep brown, red-brown and red on multicolor underprint. Similar to #131. Printer: USBNC.	FV	FV	2.00
144	**100 Pesos Oro** 1993. Orange and violet on multicolor underprint. Similar to #136. Printer: FNMT.	FV	FV	17.50
145	**1000 Pesos Oro** 1993. Red, purple and violet on multicolor underprint. Similar to #138. Printer: FNMT.	FV	FV	120.

1994 Issue

		VG	VF	UNC
146	**5 Pesos Oro** 1994. Deep brown, red-brown and red on multicolor underprint. Similar to #143. Printer: TDLR.	FV	FV	1.75

1995 Issue

#147-151 orange bank seal at l. Printer: F-CO.

		VG	VF	UNC
147	**5 Pesos Oro** 1995. Deep brown, red-brown and red on multicolor underprint. Similar to #146 but with brighter colored arms at center.			
	a. Issued note.	FV	FV	1.25
	s. Specimen with black ovpt: *ESPECIMEN MUESTRA SIN VALOR.*	—	—	15.00

		VG	VF	UNC
148	**10 Pesos Oro** 1995. Deep green and black on multicolor underprint. Like #132.			
	a. Issued note.	FV	FV	3.00
	s. Specimen with black ovpt: *ESPECIMEN MUESTRA SIN VALOR.*	—	—	20.00

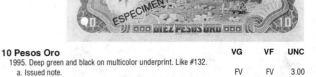

		VG	VF	UNC
149	**50 Pesos Oro** 1995. Purple and black on multicolor underprint. Like #135.			
	a. Issued note.	FV	FV	7.00
	s. Specimen with black ovpt: *ESPECIMEN MUESTRA SIN VALOR.*	—	—	20.00

#150 and 151 w/luminescent strip of cross design w/*BCRD* in angles repeated at r. on back.

150 100 Pesos Oro	VG	VF	UNC
1995. Orange, violet and brown on multicolor underprint. Like #136 but with silver overlays at left and right, purple design with *RD* also at right.			
a. Issued note.	FV	FV	12.50
s. Specimen with black ovpt: *ESPECIMEN MUESTRA SIN VALOR.*	—	—	30.00

151 500 Pesos Oro	VG	VF	UNC
1995. Deep blue, blue and brown on multicolor underprint. Like #137 but with silver overlays at left and right, gold design with *RD* also at right.			
a. Issued note.	FV	FV	70.00
s. Specimen with black ovpt: *ESPECIMEN MUESTRA SIN VALOR.*	—	—	60.00

1996-97 Issue

#152-158 date under bank seal at l. on face. Similar to #147-151 but printer: F-CO.

152 5 Pesos Oro	VG	VF	UNC
1996; 1997. Deep brown, red-brown and red on multicolor underprint. Similar to #147.			
a. Issued note.	FV	FV	2.00
s. Specimen.	—	—	7.50

153 10 Pesos Oro	VG	VF	UNC
1996; 1997; 1998. Deep green and black on multicolor underprint. Similar to #148.			
a. Issued note.	FV	FV	3.00
s. Specimen with black ovpt: *ESPECIMEN SIN VALOR.*	—	—	7.50

154 20 Pesos Oro	VG	VF	UNC
1997; 1998. Deep brown and brown on multicolor underprint. Similar to #133.			
a. Issued note.	FV	FV	5.00
s. Specimen with black ovpt: *ESPECIMEN SIN VALOR.*	—	—	10.00

#155-158 wmk: Duarte.

155 50 Pesos Oro	VG	VF	UNC
1997; 1998. Purple and black on multicolor underprint. Similar to #149.			
a. Issued note.	FV	FV	10.00
s. Specimen.	—	—	15.00

156 100 Pesos Oro	VG	VF	UNC
1997; 1998. Orange and violet on multicolor underprint. Similar to #150.			
a. Issued note.	FV	FV	17.50
s. Specimen.	—	—	20.00

157 500 Pesos Oro	VG	VF	UNC
1996; 1997; 1998. Deep blue, blue and brown on multicolor underprint. Similar to #151.			
a. Issued note.	FV	FV	55.00
s. Specimen.	—	—	25.00

158 1000 Pesos Oro	VG	VF	UNC
1996; 1997; 1998. Red, purple, violet on multicolor underprint. Similar to #145.			
a. Issued note.	FV	FV	120.
s. Specimen.	—	—	40.00

2000 Issue

#159-163 printer F-CO.

All Specimen notes w/black ovpt: *ESPECIMEN MUESTRA SIN VALOR* on both sides.

159 10 Pesos Oro	VG	VF	UNC
2000. Dark green on multicolor underprint. Matías Ramón Mella at right. *Altar de la Patria* on back.			
a. Issued note.	FV	FV	3.00
s. Specimen.	—	—	7.50

160 **20 Pesos Oro**
2000. Brown on multicolor underprint. Gregorio Luperon at right. *Panteón Nacional* at left on back.

	VG	VF	UNC
a. Issued note.	FV	FV	4.00
s. Specimen.	—	—	10.00

#161-163 wmk: Duarte.

161 **50 Pesos Oro**
2000. Purple and dark brown on multicolor underprint. Santa Maria la Menor Cathedral at right. Basilica de Nuestra Señora de la Altagracia at left on back.

	VG	VF	UNC
a. Issued note.	FV	FV	9.00
s. Specimen.	—	—	12.50

162 **500 Pesos Oro**
2000. Dark brown and aqua on multicolor underprint. Salome Ureña de Henriquez and Pedro Henriquez Ureña at right. Banco Central building at left on back.

	VG	VF	UNC
a. Issued note.	FV	FV	45.00
s. Specimen.	—	—	—

163 **1000 Pesos Oro**
2000. Red and deep lilac on multicolor underprint. *Palacio Nacional* at right. Alcazar de Don Diego Colon at left on back.

	VG	VF	UNC
a. Issued note.	FV	FV	125.
s. Specimen.	—	—	—

164 **2000 Pesos Oro**
2000. Black and blue on multicolor underprint. Emillo Prud-Homme and José Reyes at right. *Teatro Nacional* on back.

	VG	VF	UNC
a. Issued note.	FV	FV	220.
s. Specimen.	—	—	—

Note: #166 has a special rendition of the date and a millennium commemorative text.

2000-01 ISSUE

#166, 167 printer: BABN. Wmk: Duarte.

165 **10 Pesos Oro**
2000; 2001. Like #159.

	VG	VF	UNC
a. Issued note.	FV	FV	3.00
s. Specimen.	—	—	7.50

166 **20 Pesos Oro**
2000; 2001. Like #160.

	VG	VF	UNC
a. Issued note.	FV	FV	4.00
s. Specimen.	—	—	10.00

167 **100 Pesos Oro**
2000; 2001. Dark brown and orange on multicolor underprint. F. R. Sanches, J. P. Duarte and M. R. Mella at right. *Puerta del Conde* at left on back.

	VG	VF	UNC
a. Issued note.	FV	FV	20.00
s. Specimen.	—	—	20.00

2001-02 ISSUE

#168-174 like previous issues but for wider border printing at upper ctr. r. on face. Some color shade differences. Printer: (T)DLR.

168 **10 Pesos Oro**
2001; 2002; 2003. Dark green on multicolor underprint. Similar to #159.

	VG	VF	UNC
a. Issued note.	FV	FV	2.00
s. Specimen.	—	—	7.50

		VG	VF	UNC
169	**20 Pesos Oro** 2001; 2002; 2003. Brown on multicolor underprint. Similar to #160.			
	a. Issued note.	FV	FV	3.00
	s. Specimen.	—	—	10.00

#170-174 wmk: Duarte.

		VG	VF	UNC
170	**50 Pesos Oro** 2001; 2002; 2003; 2004. Purple and dark brown on multicolor underprint. Similar to #161.			
	a. Issued note.	FV	FV	8.00
	s. Specimen.	—	—	12.50

		VG	VF	UNC
171	**100 Pesos Oro** 2001; 2002; 2003; 2004. Dark brown and orange on multicolor underprint. Similar to #167.			
	a. Issued note.	FV	FV	17.50
	s. Specimen.	—	—	15.00
172	**500 Pesos Oro** 2002; 2003. Dark brown and aqua on multicolor underprint. Similar to #162.			
	a. Issued note.	FV	FV	40.00
	s. Specimen.	—	—	20.00

		VG	VF	UNC
173	**1000 Pesos Oro** 2002; 2003. Red and deep lilac on multicolor underprint. Similar to #163.			
	a. Issued note.	FV	FV	105.
	s. Specimen.	—	—	30.00

		VG	VF	UNC
174	**2000 Pesos Oro** 2002. Dlack and blue on multicolor underprint. Similar to #164.			
	a. Issued note.	FV	FV	200.
	s. Specimen.	—	—	40.00

2002 COMMEMORATIVE ISSUE

#175, 55th Anniversary of the Central Bank.

		VG	VF	UNC
175	**100 Pesos Oro** 2002. Dark Brown and orange on multicolor underprint. Commemorative overprint on back #171.	FV	FV	17.50

COLLECTOR SERIES

BANCO CENTRAL DE LA REPÚBLICA DOMINICANA

1974 ISSUES

		Issue Price	Mkt. Value
CS1	**1-1000 Pesos Oro** ND(1974). #99-106. Ovpt: *MUESTRA* twice on face.	—	450.
CS2	**1-1000 Pesos Oro** ND(1974). #99-106. Ovpt: *MUESTRA* on face and back.	—	450.

1978 ISSUES

		Issue Price	Mkt. Value
CS3	**Pesos Oro** 1978. #116, 118-124. Ovpt: *MUESTRA/SIN VALOR* on face, *ESPECIMEN* on back.	—	235.

CS4	Pesos Oro	Issue Price	Mkt.	Value
	1978. #116, 118a-120a, 121, 122a, 123, 124a. Overprint: *SPECIMEN* with serial # prefix Maltese cross. #122a is dated 1977.	—	—	60.00—

EAST AFRICA

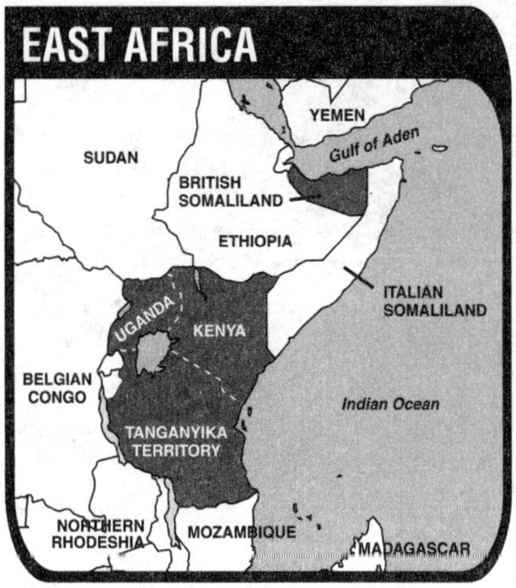

East Africa was an administrative grouping of several neighboring British territories: Kenya, Tanganyika, Uganda and Zanzibar.

The common interest of Kenya, Tanzania and Uganda invited cooperation in economic matters and consideration of political union. The territorial governors, organized as the East Africa High Commission, met periodically to administer such common activities as taxation, industrial development and education. The authority of the Commission did not infringe upon the constitution and internal autonomy of the individual colonies. The common monetary system circulated for the territories by the East African Currency Board and was also used in British Somaliland and the Aden Protectorate subsequent to the independence of India (1947) whose currency had previously circulated in these two territories.

Also see British Somaliland, Zanzibar, Kenya, Uganda and Tanzania. Also see Somaliland Republic, Kenya, Uganda and Tanzania.

RULERS:
British

MONETARY SYSTEM:
1 Shilling = 100 Cents

BRITISH ADMINISTRATION

EAST AFRICAN CURRENCY BOARD, NAIROBI

1961 ND ISSUE

#41-44 portr. Qn. Elizabeth II at upper l. w/3 sign. at l. and 4 at r. Printer: TDLR.

		VG	VF	UNC
41	**5 Shillings** ND (1961-63). Various. Brown on light red underprint. Portrait Queen Elizabeth II at upper left. 3 signatures at left and 4 at right. Printer: TDLR.			
	a. Top left signature: E. B. David. (1961).	5.00	20.00	250.
	b. Top left sign: A. L. Adu. (1962-63).	3.50	15.00	200.
42	**10 Shillings** ND (1961-63). Various. Green on multicolor underprint. Portrait Queen Elizabeth II at upper left. 3 signatures at left and 4 at right. Printer: TDLR.			
	a. Top left signature: E. B. David. (1961).	9.00	25.00	350.
	b. Top left signature: A. L. Adu. (1962-63).	6.00	20.00	300.
43	**20 Shillings** ND (1961-63). Various. Blue on light pink underprint. Portrait Queen Elizabeth II at upper left. 3 signatures at left and 4 at right. Printer: TDLR.			
	a. Top left signature: E. B. David. (1961).	10.00	75.00	500.
	b. Top left signature: A. L. Adu. (1962-63).	7.00	45.00	325.

		VG	VF	UNC
44	**100 Shillings** ND 91961-63). Various. Red on multicolor underprint. Portrait Queen Elizabeth II at upper left. 3 signatures at left and 4 at right. Printer: TDLR.			
	a. Top left signature: E. B. David. (1961).	25.00	125.	950.
	b. Top left signature: A. L. Adu. (1962-63).	20.00	90.00	700.

1964 ND ISSUE

#45-48 wmk: Rhinoceros, wmk. area at l., sailboat at l. ctr. Various plants on back.

45	5 Shillings	VG	VF	UNC
	ND (1964). Brown on multicolor underprint. Watermark area at left, sailboat at left center. Various plants. Watermark: Rhinoceros.	3.00	12.50	90.00

46	10 Shillings	VG	VF	UNC
	ND (1964). Green on multicolor underprint.			
	a. Issued note.	5.00	20.00	120.
	s. Specimen, punch hole cancelled.	—	—	—

47	20 Shillings	VG	VF	UNC
	ND (1964). Blue on multicolor underprint.			
	a. Issued note.	7.50	30.00	300.
	s. Specimen. Punched hole cancelled.	—	—	—

48	100 Shillings	VG	VF	UNC
	ND (1964). Deep red on multicolor underprint.			
	a. Issued note.	9.00	45.00	225.
	s. Specimen. Punched hole cancelled.	—	—	—

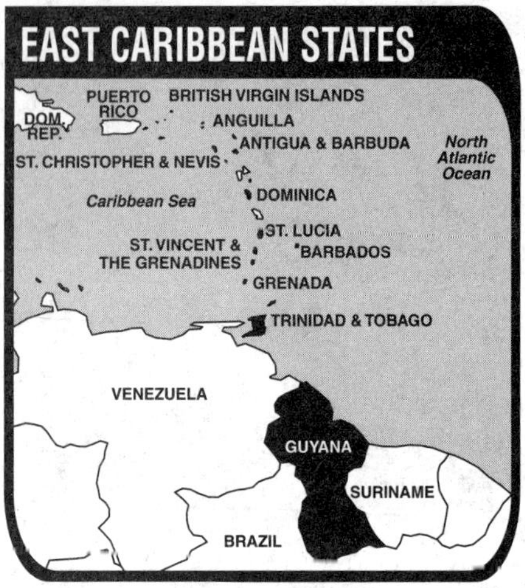

The East Caribbean States, formerly the British Caribbean Territories (Eastern Group), a currency board formed in 1950, comprised the British West Indies territories of Trinidad and Tobago, Barbados, the Leeward Islands of Anguilla, St. Christopher, Nevis and Antigua; the Windward Islands of St. Lucia, Dominica, St. Vincent and Grenada; British Guiana and the British Virgin Islands.

As time progressed, the member countries varied and is reflected on the backs of #13-16. The first issue includes Barbados but not Grenada, while the second issue includes both Barbados and Grenada and the third issue retains Grenada while Barbados is removed. Barbados attained self-government in 1961 and independence on Nov. 30, 1966. On May 26, 1966 British Guiana became independent as Guyana which later became a cooperative Republic on Feb. 23, 1970.

The British Virgin Islands became a largely self-governing dependent territory of the United Kingdom in 1967. United States currency is the official medium of exchange.

St. Christopher and Nevis became fully independent on Sept. 19, 1983.

Trinidad & Tobago became an independent member state of the Commonwealth on August 31, 1962.

RULERS:

British

MONETARY SYSTEM:

1 Dollar = 100 Cents

The variety letters for numbers 19-46 have changed to match the serial # suffix letter of the respective country of issue.

EAST CARIBBEAN CURRENCY AUTHORITY

SIGNATURE VARIETIES

1	Director	Chairman Director	Director	2	Director	Chairman Director	Director
3	Director	Chairman Director	Director	4	Director	Chairman Director	Director
5	Director	Chairman Director	Director	6	Director	Chairman Director	Director
7	Director	Chairman Director	Director	8	Director	Chairman Director	Director
9	Director	Chairman Director	Director	10	Director	Chairman Director	Director

ISLAND PARTICIPATION

Variety I

Variety II

Variety III

VARIETY I: Listing of islands on back includes Barbados but not Grenada.
VARIETY II: Listing includes Barbados and Grenada.
VARIETY III: Listing retains Grenada while Barbados is deleted.

1965 ND ISSUE

#13-16 map at l., Qn. Elizabeth II at r. and as wmk. Coastline w/rocks and trees at l. ctr. on back. Sign. varieties. Printer: TDLR. Replacement notes: Serial # prefix *Z1*.

Beginning in 1983, #13-16 were ovpt. with circled letters at l. indicating their particular areas of issue within the Eastern Group. Letters and their respective areas are as follows:

A, Antigua	L, St. Lucia
D, Dominica	M, Montserrat
G, Grenada	U, Anguilla
K, St. Kitts	V, St. Vincent

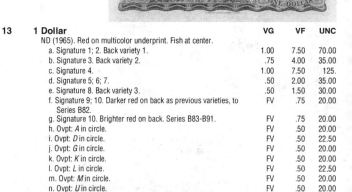

		VG	VF	UNC
13	**1 Dollar**	VG	VF	UNC
	ND (1965). Red on multicolor underprint. Fish at center.			
	a. Signature 1; 2. Back variety 1.	1.00	7.50	70.00
	b. Signature 3. Back variety 2.	.75	4.00	35.00
	c. Signature 4.	1.00	7.50	125.
	d. Signature 5; 6; 7.	.50	2.00	35.00
	e. Signature 8. Back variety 3.	.50	1.50	30.00
	f. Signature 9; 10. Darker red on back as previous varieties, to Series B82.	FV	.75	20.00
	g. Signature 10. Brighter red on back. Series B83-B91.	FV	.75	20.00
	h. Ovpt: *A* in circle.	FV	.50	20.00
	i. Ovpt: *D* in circle.	FV	.50	22.50
	j. Ovpt: *G* in circle.	FV	.50	20.00
	k. Ovpt: *K* in circle.	FV	.50	20.00
	l. Ovpt: *L* in circle.	FV	.50	22.50
	m. Ovpt: *M* in circle.	FV	.50	20.00
	n. Ovpt: *U* in circle.	FV	.50	20.00
	o. Ovpt: *V* in circle.	FV	.50	20.00
	s. As a, j-n. Specimen.	—	—	125.

		VG	VF	UNC
14	**5 Dollars**	VG	VF	UNC
	ND (1965). Green on multicolor underprint. Flying fish at center.			
	a. Signature 1. Back variety 1.	6.00	25.00	180.
	b. Signature 2.	6.00	25.00	180.
	c. Signature 3. Back variety 2. Reported not confirmed.	—	—	—
	d. Signature 4.	4.00	10.00	150.
	e. Signature 5; 6.	3.50	7.50	85.00
	f. Signature 7.	4.00	10.00	85.00
	g. Signature 8. Back variety 3.	2.00	5.00	50.00
	h. Signature 9; 10.	FV	3.00	35.00
	i. Ovpt: *A* in circle.	FV	2.50	35.00
	j. Ovpt: *D* in circle.	FV	2.50	40.00
	k. Ovpt: *G* in circle.	FV	2.50	35.00
	l. Ovpt: *K* in circle.	FV	2.50	35.00
	m. Ovpt: *L* in circle.	FV	7.50	125.
	n. Ovpt: *M* in circle.	FV	2.50	40.00
	o. Ovpt: *U* in circle.	FV	2.50	35.00
	p. Ovpt: *V* in circle.	FV	2.50	35.00
	s. As a, b. Specimen.	—	—	275.

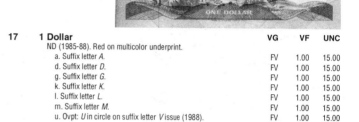

15	20 Dollars	VG	VF	UNC
	ND (1965). Purple on multicolor underprint. Turtles at center.			
	a. Signature 1. Back variety 1.	17.50	65.00	700.
	b. Signature 2.	20.00	75.00	800.
	c. Signature 3. Back variety 2. Reported not confirmed.	—	—	—
	d. Signature 4.	12.50	50.00	425.
	e. Signature 5; 6; 7.	10.00	40.00	315.
	f. Signature 8. Back variety 3.	10.00	12.50	95.00
	g. Signature 9; 10.	FV	10.00	80.00
	h. Ovpt: *A* in circle.	FV	10.00	75.00
	i. Ovpt: *D* in circle.	FV	10.00	90.00
	j. Ovpt: *G* in circle.	FV	10.00	75.00
	k. Ovpt: *K* in circle.	FV	20.00	145.
	l. Ovpt: *L* in circle.	FV	10.00	75.00
	m. Ovpt: *M* in circle.	FV	10.00	75.00
	n. Ovpt: *U* in circle.	FV	10.00	75.00
	o. Ovpt: *V* in circle.	FV	10.00	75.00
	s. As a. Specimen.	—	—	525.

16	100 Dollars	VG	VF	UNC
	ND (1965). Black on multicolor underprint. Sea horses at center.			
	a. Signature 1. Back variety 1.	100.	300.	1750.
	b. Signature 2. Reported not confirmed.	—	—	—
	c. Signature 5. Back variety 2.	110.	325.	1850.
	d. Signature 3; 4; 6; 7. Reported not confirmed.	—	—	—
	e. Signature 8. Back variety 3. Reported not confirmed.	—	—	—
	f. Signature 9; 10.	FV	85.00	500.
	g. Ovpt: *A* in circle.	FV	85.00	500.
	h. Ovpt: *D* in circle.	60.00	140.	900.
	i. Ovpt: *G* in circle.	50.00	120.	600.
	j. Ovpt: *K* in circle.	50.00	125.	825.
	k. Ovpt: *L* in circle.	FV	85.00	500.
	l. Ovpt: *M* in circle.	FV	85.00	500.
	m. Ovpt: *U* in circle.	FV	85.00	500.
	n. Ovpt: *V* in circle.	FV	85.00	500.
	s. As a. Specimen.	—	—	1000.

EASTERN CARIBBEAN CENTRAL BANK

SIGNATURE VARIETIES			
	Governor		Governor
1		2	

1985-87 ND ISSUE

#17-25 windsurfer at l., Qn. Elizabeth II at ctr. r., map at r. Back similar to #13-16. Wmk: QEII. Printer: TDLR. Replacement notes: Serial # prefix *Z1*.

Notes w/suffix letter of serial # indicating particular areas of issue (as with ovpt. letters on previous issue).

#17-20 do not have name Anguilla at island near top of map at r. Palm tree, swordfish at ctr. r., shoreline in background on back. No $10 without Anguilla was issued.

17	1 Dollar	VG	VF	UNC
	ND (1985-88). Red on multicolor underprint.			
	a. Suffix letter *A*.	FV	1.00	15.00
	d. Suffix letter *D*.	FV	1.00	15.00
	g. Suffix letter *G*.	FV	1.00	15.00
	k. Suffix letter *K*.	FV	1.00	15.00
	l. Suffix letter *L*.	FV	1.00	15.00
	m. Suffix letter *M*.	FV	1.00	15.00
	u. Ovpt: *U* in circle on suffix letter *V* issue (1988).	FV	1.00	15.00
	v. Suffix letter *V*.	FV	1.00	15.00

18	5 Dollars	VG	VF	UNC
	ND (1986-88). Deep green on multicolor underprint.			
	a. Suffix letter *A*.	FV	FV	27.50
	d. Suffix letter *D*.	FV	FV	27.50
	g. Suffix letter *G*.	FV	FV	27.50
	k. Suffix letter *K*.	FV	FV	27.50
	l. Suffix letter *L*.	FV	FV	27.50
	m. Suffix letter *M*.	FV	FV	27.50
	u. Ovpt: *U* in circle on suffix letter *V* issue (1988).	FV	FV	27.50
	v. Suffix letter *V*.	FV	FV	27.50
	ur. Replacement note. Z/1 serial # prefix.	5.00	10.00	65.00

19	20 Dollars	VG	VF	UNC
	ND (1987-88). Purple and brown on multicolor underprint.			
	a. Suffix letter *A*.	FV	FV	70.00
	d. Suffix letter *D*.	FV	FV	70.00
	g. Suffix letter *G*.	FV	FV	70.00
	k. Suffix letter *K*.	FV	FV	70.00
	l. Suffix letter *L*.	FV	FV	70.00
	m. Suffix letter *M*.	FV	12.50	80.00
	u. Ovpt: *U* in circle.	FV	FV	70.00
	v. Suffix letter *V*.	FV	FV	70.00

20 100 Dollars
ND (1986-88). Black and orange on multicolor underprint.

	VG	VF	UNC
a. Suffix letter *A*.	FV	50.00	275.
d. Suffix letter *D*.	FV	50.00	275.
g. Suffix letter *G*.	FV	50.00	275.
k. Suffix letter *K*.	FV	50.00	275.
l. Suffix letter *L*.	FV	50.00	275.
m. Suffix letter *M*.	FV	50.00	275.
u. Ovpt: *U* in circle on suffix letter *V* issue (1988).	FV	50.00	275.
v. Suffix letter *V*.	FV	50.00	275.

1985-88 ND Issue

#21-25 with *ANGUILLA* island named near top of map at r

#21, 22, 24 and 25 harbor at St. Lucia on back.

21 1 Dollar
ND (1988-89). Red on multicolor underprint. Like #17 but Anguilla named. Signature 1.

	VG	VF	UNC
d. Suffix letter *D*.	FV	1.00	17.50
k. Suffix letter *K*.	FV	1.00	17.50
l. Suffix letter *L*.	FV	1.00	17.50
m. Suffix letter *M*.	FV	5.00	30.00
u. Suffix letter *U*.	FV	1.00	17.50
ur. As u. Replacement note. Serial # prefix *Z*.	FV	10.00	50.00

22 5 Dollars
ND (1988-93). Deep green on multicolor underprint. Like #18 but Anguilla named.

	VG	VF	UNC
a1. Suffix letter *A*. signature 1.	FV	FV	22.50
a2. Like a1. signature 2.	FV	FV	22.50
d. Suffix letter *D*. signature 1.	FV	FV	22.50
g. Suffix letter *G*. signature 2.	FV	FV	22.50
k1. Suffix letter *K*. signature 1.	FV	FV	22.50
k2. Like k1. signature 2.	FV	FV	22.50
l1. Suffix letter *L*. signature 1.	FV	FV	22.50
l2. Like l1. signature 2.	FV	FV	22.50
m. Suffix letter *M*. signature 1.	FV	FV	22.50
u. Suffix letter *U*. signature 1.	FV	FV	22.50
v. Suffix letter *V*. signature 2.	FV	FV	22.50

23 10 Dollars
ND (1985-93). Blue on multicolor underprint. Harbor at Grenada, sailboats at left and center on back.

	VG	VF	UNC
a1. Suffix letter *A*. signature 1.	FV	FV	35.00
a2. Like a1. signature 2.	FV	FV	35.00
d1. Suffix letter *D*. signature 1.	FV	FV	35.00
d2. Like d1. signature 2.	FV	FV	35.00
g. Suffix letter *G*. signature 1.	FV	FV	35.00
k1. Suffix letter *K*. signature 1.	FV	FV	35.00
k2. Like k1. signature 2.	FV	FV	35.00
l1. Suffix letter *L*. signature 1.	FV	FV	35.00
l2. Like l1. signature 2.	FV	FV	35.00
m. Suffix letter *M*. signature 1.	FV	FV	35.00
u. Suffix letter *U*. signature 1.	FV	FV	35.00
v1. Suffix letter *V*. signature 1.	FV	FV	35.00
v2. Like v1. signature 2.	FV	FV	35.00
ar. As a2. Replacement note. Serial # prefix: *Z*.	FV	25.00	75.00

24 20 Dollars
ND (1988-93). Purple and brown on multicolor underprint. Like #19 but Anguilla named.

	VG	VF	UNC
a1. Suffix letter *A*. signature 1.	FV	FV	60.00
a2. Like a1. signature 2.	FV	FV	60.00
d1. Suffix letter *D*. signature 1.	FV	FV	60.00
d2. Like d1. signature 2.	FV	FV	60.00
g. Suffix letter *G*. signature 1.	FV	FV	60.00
k1. Suffix letter *K*. signature 1.	FV	FV	60.00
k2. Like k1. signature 2.	FV	FV	60.00
l1. Suffix letter *L*. signature 1.	FV	FV	60.00
l2. Like l1. signature 2.	FV	FV	60.00
m1. Suffix letter *M*. signature 1.	FV	FV	60.00
m2. Like m1. signature 2.	FV	FV	60.00
u. Suffix letter *U*. signature 1.	FV	FV	60.00
v. Suffix letter *V*. signature 1.	FV	FV	60.00

25 100 Dollars
ND (1988-93). Black and orange on multicolor underprint. Like #20 but Anguilla named.

	VG	VF	UNC
a1. Suffix letter *A*. signature 1.	FV	FV	250.
a2. Like a1. signature 2.	FV	FV	250.
d1. Suffix letter *D*. signature 1.	FV	FV	250.
d2. Like d1. signature 2.	FV	FV	250.

25	100 Dollars	VG	VF	UNC
	g. Suffix letter *G*. signature 1.	FV	FV	250.
	k1. Suffix letter *K*. signature 1.	FV	FV	250.
	k2. Like k1. signature 2.	FV	FV	250.
	l1. Suffix letter *L*. signature 1.	FV	FV	250.
	l2. Like l1. signature 2.	FV	FV	250.
	m1. Suffix letter *M*. signature 1.	FV	FV	250.
	m2. Like m1. signature 2.	FV	FV	250.
	u. Suffix letter *U*. signature 1.	FV	FV	250.
	v. Suffix letter *V*. signature 1.	FV	FV	250.

1993 ND Issue

Antigua (A)	St. Lucia (L)
Dominica (D)	Montserrat (M)
Grenada (G)	Anguilla (U)
St. Kitts (K)	St. Vincent (V)

#26-30 Qn. Elizabeth II at ctr. r. and as wmk. (profile), turtle at lower ctr., green-throated carib at top l. Island map at ctr. on back. Sign. 2. Printer: TDLR.

26	5 Dollars	VG	VF	UNC
	ND (1993). Dark green, black and violet on multicolor underprint. Admiral's House in Antigua and Barbuda at left, Trafalgar Falls in Dominica at right on back.			
	a. Suffix letter *A*.	FV	FV	20.00
	d. Suffix letter *D*.	FV	FV	20.00
	g. Suffix letter *G*.	FV	FV	20.00
	k. Suffix letter *K*.	FV	FV	20.00
	l. Suffix letter *L*.	FV	FV	20.00
	m. Suffix letter *M*.	FV	FV	30.00
	u. Suffix letter *U*.	FV	FV	20.00
	v. Suffix letter *V*.	FV	FV	20.00

27	10 Dollars	VG	VF	UNC
	ND (1993). Dark blue, black and red on multicolor underprint. Admiralty Bay in St. Vincent and Grenadines at left, sailing ship *Warspite* and brown pelican at right center on back.			
	a. Suffix letter *A*.	FV	FV	30.00
	d. Suffix letter *D*.	FV	FV	30.00
	g. Suffix letter *G*.	FV	FV	30.00
	k. Suffix letter *K*.	FV	FV	30.00
	l. Suffix letter *L*.	FV	FV	30.00
	m. Suffix letter *M*.	FV	FV	50.00
	u. Suffix letter *U*.	FV	FV	30.00
	v. Suffix letter *V*.	FV	FV	30.00

28	20 Dollars	VG	VF	UNC
	ND (1993). Brown-violet, blue-gray and orange on multicolor underprint. Government House in Montserrat at left, nutmeg in Grenada at right on back.			
	a. Suffix letter *A*.	FV	FV	47.50
	d. Suffix letter *D*.	FV	FV	47.50
	g. Suffix letter *G*.	FV	FV	47.50
	k. Suffix letter *K*.	FV	FV	47.50
	l. Suffix letter *L*.	FV	FV	47.50
	m. Suffix letter *M*.	FV	FV	75.00
	u. Suffix letter *U*.	FV	FV	47.50
	v. Suffix letter *V*.	FV	FV	47.50

29	50 Dollars	VG	VF	UNC
	ND (1993). Purple and olive-green on multicolor underprint. Brimstone Hill in St. Kitts at left, Les Pitons mountains in St. Lucia and sooty tern at right on back.			
	a. Suffix letter *A*.	FV	FV	115.
	d. Suffix letter *D*.	FV	FV	115.
	g. Suffix letter *G*.	FV	FV	115.
	k. Suffix letter *K*.	FV	FV	115.
	l. Suffix letter *L*.	FV	FV	115.
	m. Suffix letter *M*.	FV	35.00	180.
	u. Suffix letter *U*.	FV	FV	115.
	v. Suffix letter *V*.	FV	FV	115.

30	100 Dollars	VG	VF	UNC
	ND (1993). Dark brown, dark olive-green and tan on multicolor underprint. Sir Arthur Lewis at left, E.C.C.B. Central Bank building and Lesser Antillean Swift at right on back.			
	a. Suffix letter *A*.	FV	45.00	215.
	d. Suffix letter *D*.	FV	45.00	215.
	g. Suffix letter *G*.	FV	45.00	215.
	k. Suffix letter *K*.	FV	45.00	215.

30	100 Dollars	VG	VF	UNC
	l. Suffix letter *L*.	FV	45.00	215.
	m. Suffix letter *M*.	FV	55.00	280.
	u. Suffix letter *U*.	FV	45.00	215.
	v. Suffix letter *V*.	FV	45.00	215.

1994 ND Issue

#31-35 like #26-30 but w/clear bold values at upper l. and lower r. Thin security thread. Sign. 2. Replacement notes: Serial # prefix *Z* are scarce and command a premium.

31	5 Dollars	VG	VF	UNC
	ND (1994). Dark green, black and violet on multicolor underprint. Like #26.			
	a. Suffix letter *A*.	FV	FV	17.50
	d. Suffix letter *D*.	FV	FV	17.50
	g. Suffix letter *G*.	FV	FV	17.50
	k. Suffix letter *K*.	FV	FV	17.50
	l. Suffix letter *L*.	FV	FV	17.50
	m. Suffix letter *M*.	FV	5.00	32.50
	u. Suffix letter *U*.	FV	FV	17.50
	v. Suffix letter *V*.	FV	FV	17.50

32	10 Dollars	VG	VF	UNC
	ND (1994). Dark blue, black and red on multicolor underprint. Like #27.			
	a. Suffix letter *A*.	FV	FV	27.50
	d. Suffix letter *D*.	FV	FV	27.50
	g. Suffix letter *G*.	FV	FV	27.50
	k. Suffix letter *K*.	FV	FV	27.50
	l. Suffix letter *L*.	FV	FV	27.50
	m. Suffix letter *M*.	FV	FV	45.00
	u. Suffix letter *U*.	FV	FV	27.50
	v. Suffix letter *V*.	FV	FV	27.50

33	20 Dollars	VG	VF	UNC
	ND (1994). Brown-violet, blue-gray and orange on multicolor underprint. Like #28.			
	a. Suffix letter *A*.	FV	FV	40.00
	d. Suffix letter *D*.	FV	FV	40.00
	g. Suffix letter *G*.	FV	FV	40.00
	k. Suffix letter *K*.	FV	FV	40.00
	l. Suffix letter *L*.	FV	FV	40.00
	m. Suffix letter *M*.	FV	FV	75.00
	u. Suffix letter *U*.	FV	FV	40.00
	v. Suffix letter *V*.	FV	FV	40.00

34	50 Dollars	VG	VF	UNC
	ND (1994). Tan, red-orange and green on multicolor underprint. Like #29.			
	a. Suffix letter *A*.	FV	FV	110.
	d. Suffix letter *D*.	FV	FV	110.
	g. Suffix letter *G*.	FV	FV	110.
	k. Suffix letter *K*.	FV	FV	110.
	l. Suffix letter *L*.	FV	FV	110.
	m. Suffix letter *M*.	50.00	95.00	270.
	u. Suffix letter *U*.	FV	FV	110.
	v. Suffix letter *V*.	FV	FV	110.

35	100 Dollars	VG	VF	UNC
	ND (1994). Dark brown and dark green on multicolor underprint. Like #30.			
	a. Suffix letter *A*.	FV	FV	190.
	d. Suffix letter *D*.	FV	FV	190.
	g. Suffix letter *G*.	FV	FV	190.
	k. Suffix letter *K*.	FV	FV	190.
	l. Suffix letter *L*.	FV	FV	190.
	m. Suffix letter *M*.	FV	FV	320.
	u. Suffix letter *U*.	FV	FV	190.
	v. Suffix letter *V*.	FV	FV	190.

1998 ND Issue

#36 Building rendering is long, partially covering signature. Printer: (T)DLR.

36	100 Dollars	VG	VF	UNC
	ND (1998). Dark brown and dark green on multicolor underprint. Like #35 but with gold foil flower enhanced colors and segmented foil over security thread.			

		VG	VF	UNC
36	**100 Dollars**			
	a. Suffix letter *A.*	FV	FV	145.
	d. Suffix letter *D.*	FV	FV	145.
	g. Suffix letter *G.*	FV	FV	145.
	k. Suffix letter *K.*	FV	FV	145.
	l. Suffix letter *L.*	FV	FV	145.
	m. Suffix letter *M.*	FV	FV	210.
	u. Suffix letter *U.*	FV	FV	145.
	v. Suffix letter *V.*	FV	FV	145.

2000 ND ISSUE

#37-41. Modified security features. Segmented security thread. Gold foil devices in upper r. of face. Shorter building rendering above signature.

		VG	VF	UNC
37	**5 Dollars**			
	ND (2000). Green, dark green, slate blue on multicolor underprint. Like #31 but with gold foil fish at right.			
	a. Suffix letter *A.*	FV	FV	12.00
	d. Suffix letter *D.*	FV	FV	12.00
	g. Suffix letter *G.*	FV	FV	12.00
	k. Suffix letter *K.*	FV	FV	12.00
	l. Suffix letter *L.*	FV	FV	12.00
	m. Suffix letter *M.*	FV	FV	17.50
	u. Suffix letter *U.*	FV	FV	12.00
	v. Suffix letter *V.*	FV	FV	12.00

		VG	VF	UNC
38	**10 Dollars**			
	ND (2000). Blue and black on multicolor underprint. Like #32 but with gold foil fish at right.			
	a. Suffix letter *A.*	FV	FV	22.50
	d. Suffix letter *D.*	FV	FV	22.50
	g. Suffix letter *G.*	FV	FV	22.50
	k. Suffix letter *K.*	FV	FV	22.50
	l. Suffix letter *L.*	FV	FV	22.50
	m. Suffix letter *M.*	FV	FV	30.00
	u. Suffix letter *U.*	FV	FV	22.50
	v. Suffix letter *V.*	FV	FV	22.50

		VG	VF	UNC
39	**20 Dollars**			
	ND (2000). Purple and slate blue on multicolor underprint. Like #33 but with gold foil butterfly at right.			
	a. Suffix letter *A.*	FV	FV	32.50
	d. Suffix letter *D.*	FV	FV	32.50
	g. Suffix letter *G.*	FV	FV	32.50
	k. Suffix letter *K.*	FV	FV	32.50
	l. Suffix letter *L.*	FV	FV	32.50
	m. Suffix letter *M.*	FV	FV	45.00
	u. Suffix letter *U.*	FV	FV	32.50
	v. Suffix letter *V.*	FV	FV	32.50

		VG	VF	UNC
40	**50 Dollars**			
	ND (2000). Bronze and orange on multicolor underprint. Like #34 but with gold foil flower at right.			
	a. Suffix letter *A.*	FV	FV	85.00
	d. Suffix letter *D.*	FV	FV	85.00
	g. Suffix letter *G.*	FV	FV	85.00
	k. Suffix letter *K.*	FV	FV	85.00
	l. Suffix letter *L.*	FV	FV	85.00
	m. Suffix letter *M.*	FV	FV	160.
	u. Suffix letter *U.*	FV	FV	85.00
	v. Suffix letter *V.*	FV	FV	85.00

		VG	VF	UNC
41	**100 Dollars**			
	ND (2000). Dark brown and dark green on multicolor underprint. Like #36.			
	a. Suffix letter *A.*	FV	FV	120.
	d. Suffix letter *D.*	FV	FV	120.
	g. Suffix letter *G.*	FV	FV	140.
	k. Suffix letter *K.*	FV	FV	140.
	l. Suffix letter *L.*	FV	FV	140.
	m. Suffix letter *M.*	FV	FV	160.
	u. Suffix letter *U.*	FV	FV	140.
	v. Suffix letter *V.*	FV	FV	140.

2003 ND ISSUE

#42-46 like #37-41 but with modified security features which include silver foil devices in the upper r. of the face and a wider security thread. Printer: (T)DLR.

		VG	VF	UNC
42	**5 Dollars**			
	ND (2003). Green, dark green, slate blue on multicolor underprint.			

42	5 Dollars	VG	VF	UNC
	a. Suffix letter *A.*	FV	FV	7.50
	d. Suffix letter *D.*	FV	FV	8.50
	g. Suffix letter *G.*	FV	FV	8.50
	k. Suffix letter *K.*	FV	FV	8.50
	l. Suffix letter *L.*	FV	FV	8.50
	m. Suffix letter *M.*	FV	FV	13.00
	u. Suffix letter *U.*	FV	FV	8.50
	v. Suffix letter *V.*	FV	FV	8.50

43	10 Dollars	VG	VF	UNC
	ND (2003). Blue and black on multicolor underprint.			
	a. Suffix letter *A.*	FV	FV	12.00
	d. Suffix letter *D.*	FV	FV	13.00
	g. Suffix letter *G.*	FV	FV	13.00
	k. Suffix letter *K.*	FV	FV	13.00
	l. Suffix letter *L.*	FV	FV	13.00
	m. Suffix letter *M.*	FV	FV	17.00
	u. Suffix letter *U.*	FV	FV	13.00
	v. Suffix letter *V.*	FV	FV	13.00

44	20 Dollars	VG	VF	UNC
	ND (2003). Purple and slate blue on multicolor underprint.			
	a. Suffix letter *A.*	FV	FV	20.00
	d. Suffix letter *D.*	FV	FV	22.00
	g. Suffix letter *G.*	FV	FV	22.00
	k. Suffix letter *K.*	FV	FV	22.00
	l. Suffix letter *L.*	FV	FV	22.00
	m. Suffix letter *M.*	FV	FV	27.50
	u. Suffix letter *U.*	FV	FV	22.00
	v. Suffix letter *V.*	FV	FV	22.00

45	50 Dollars	VG	VF	UNC
	ND (2003). Bronze and orange on multicolor underprint.			
	a. Suffix letter *A.*	FV	FV	55.00
	d. Suffix letter *D.*	FV	FV	60.00
	g. Suffix letter *G.*	FV	FV	60.00
	k. Suffix letter *K.*	FV	FV	60.00

45	50 Dollars	VG	VF	UNC
	l. Suffix letter *L.*	FV	FV	60.00
	m. Suffix Letter *M.*	FV	FV	80.00
	u. Suffix letter *U.*	FV	FV	60.00
	v. Suffix letter *V.*	FV	FV	60.00

46	100 Dollars	VG	VF	UNC
	ND (2003). Black Brown and dark green on multicolor underprint.			
	a. Suffix letter *A.*	FV	FV	105.
	d. Suffix letter *D.*	FV	FV	115.
	g. Suffix letter *G.*	FV	FV	115.
	k. Suffix letter *K.*	FV	FV	115.
	l. Suffix letter *L.*	FV	FV	115.
	m. Suffix letter *M.*	FV	FV	150.
	u. Suffix letter *U.*	FV	FV	115.
	v. Suffix letter *V.*	FV	FV	115.

COLLECTOR SERIES

GOVERNMENT OF ANTIGUA AND BARBUDA

1983 ND ISSUE

This set is made with thin gold and silver foil bonded to paper.

CS1	30 Dollars	Issue Price	Mkt. Value
	ND (1983). 12 different notes showing various flowers and animals.	—	350.

1985 ND ISSUE

CS2	30 Dollars	Issue Price	Mkt. Value
	ND (1984). 12 different notes showing various animals and plants.	—	350.
CS3	30 Dollars		
	ND (1985) 10 different notes showing various animals and plants.	—	250.

EAST CARIBBEAN CENTRAL BANK

1988 ND ISSUE

This set is made with gold and silver foil bonded to paper.

CS4	100 Dollars	Issue Price	Mkt. Value
	ND (1988). 30 different notes showing various pirate and treasure sailing ships. (20,000 sets).	—	1100.

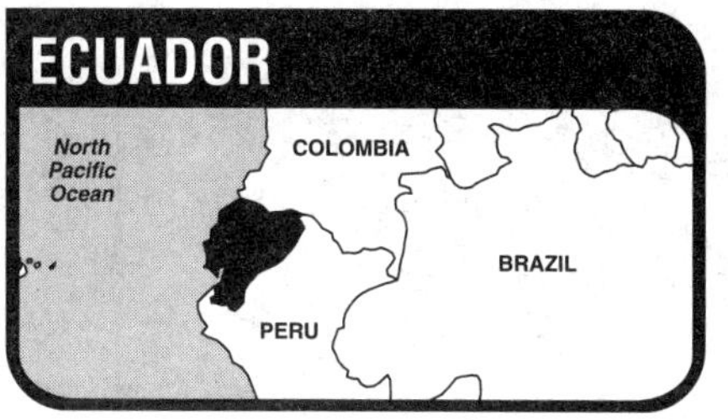

The Republic of Ecuador, located astride the equator on the Pacific coast of South America, has an area of 109,484 sq. mi. (283,561 sq. km.) and a population of 12.65 million. Capital: Quito. Agriculture is the mainstay of the economy but there are appreciable deposits of minerals and petroleum. It is the world's largest exporter of bananas and balsa wood. Coffee, cacao and shrimp are also valuable exports.

Ecuador was first sighted, 1526, by Bartolome Ruiz. Conquest was undertaken by Sebastian de Benalcazar who founded Quito in 1534. Ecuador was part of the province, later Vice-royalty, of Peru until 1739 when it became part of the Vice-royalty of New Granada. After two failed attempts to attain independence in 1810 and 1812, it successfully declared its independence in October 1820, and won final victory over Spanish forces May 24, 1822. Incorporated into the Gran Colombia confederacy, it loosened its ties in 1830 and regained full independence in 1835.

MONETARY SYSTEM:

1 USA Dollar = 25,000 Sucres (March 2001)

REPUBLIC

BANCO CENTRAL DEL ECUADOR

1944-67 ISSUE

#96 and 97 black on m/c unpt. Printer: ABNC.

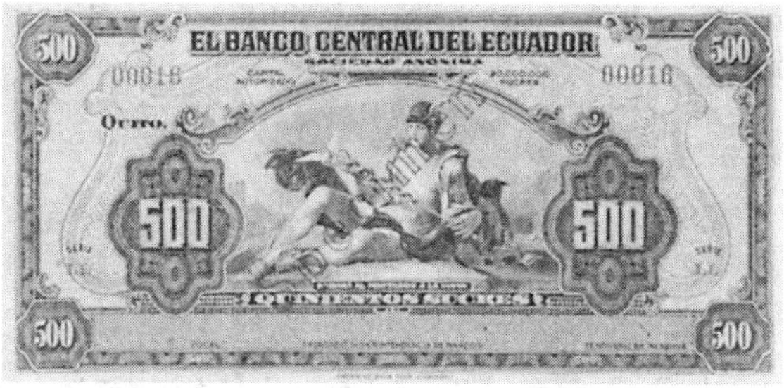

		VG	VF	UNC
96	**500 Sucres** 1944-66. Black on multicolor underprint. Mercury seated at center. With text: *CAPITAL AUTORIZADO 20,000,000 SUCRES.* 3 signature. Deep orange. Printer: ABNC.			
	a. Signature title overprint: *PRESIDENTE* at left. 12.5.1944; 27.6.1944.	175.	400.	—
	b. Signature title overprint: *GERENTE GENERAL* at left, *VOCAL* at right. 31.7.1944; 7.9.1944.	150.	375.	—
	c. Signature title overprint: *GERENTE GENERAL* at right. 12.1.1945-12.7.1947.	125.	300.	—
	d. As c. 21.4.1961-17.11.1966.	125.	300.	—
	s. Specimen. ND.	—	—	400.

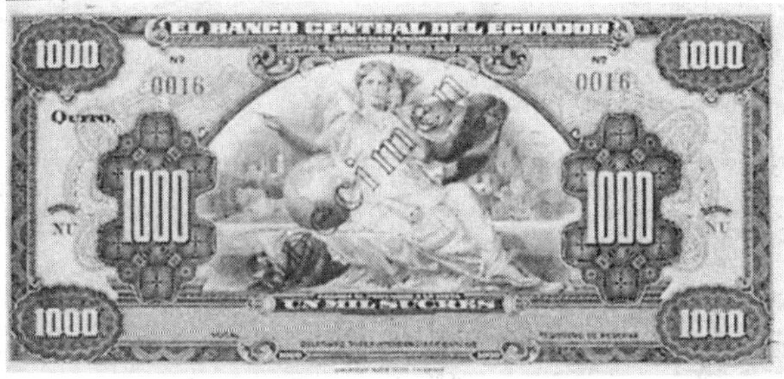

		VG	VF	UNC
97	**1000 Sucres** 1944-67. Woman reclining (Telephone Service") at center. With text: *CAPITAL AUTORIZADO 20,000,000 SUCRES.* 3 signature. Greenish-gray. Printer: ABNC.			
	a. Signature title overprint: *PRESIDENTE* at left. 12.5.1944; 27.6.1944.	300.	650.	—
	b. Signature title overprint: *GERENTE GENERAL* at left, *VOCAL* at right. 31.7.1944; 7.9.1944.	275.	550.	—
	c. Signature title overprint: *PRESIDENTE* at left, *GERENTE GENERAL* at right. 12.1.1945.	250.	500.	—
	d. Signature title overprint: *GERENTE GENERAL* at right. 16.10.1945; 12.7.1947.	225.	450.	—
	e. As d. 21.4.1961; 27.2.1962; 4.3.1964; 23.7.1964; 17.11.1966; 6.4.1967.	150.	350.	—
	s. Specimen. ND.	—	—	400.

Note: The following reduced size notes are listed by printer.

1950 Issue (1950-59) #98-99 printer: W&S.
1950-71 Issue (1950-74) #100-107 printer: ABNC.
1975-80 Issue (1975-83) #108-112 printer: ABNC.
1957-71 Issue (1957-82) #113-118 printer: TDLR.

1950 ISSUE - REDUCED SIZE NOTES

#98-99 arms at ctr. on back. Printer: W&S.

		VG	VF	UNC
98	**5 Sucres** 1950-55. Black on green underprint. Portrait Antonio Jose de Sucre at center. Date at left or right. Back red. Red. Arms at center. Printer: W&S.			
	a. 11.5.1950-13.7.1953.	2.25	15.00	75.00
	b. Signature title overprint: *SUBGERENTE GENERAL* at left. 21.9.1953.	4.50	20.00	85.00
	c. 31.5.1954-28.11.1955.	2.00	12.50	55.00
99	**50 Sucres** 1950-59. Black on green underprint. National monument at center with buildings in background. Green. Arms at center. Printer: W&S.			
	a. 11.5.1950; 26.7.1950; 13.10.1950; 3.4.1951; 26.9.1951.	7.50	50.00	150.
	b. Signature title overprint: *SUBGERENTE GENERAL* at left. 3.9.1952; 8.10.1954; 24.9.1957.	7.50	50.00	150.
	c. 10.12.1953; 19.6.1956; 25.11.1957; 25.11.1958; 8.4.1959.	6.00	40.00	125.
	s1. Specimen. Black overprint: *ESPÉCIMEN* on both sides. ND, with 0000 serial #, unsigned.	—	—	175.
	s2. Specimen. Red overprint: *MUESTRA* twice on both sides. ND, without serial # or signs. Punched hole cancelled.	—	—	175.

1950-71 ISSUE

#100-107 black on m/c unpt. Several date varieties, sign. title ovpts. and serial # styles. Arms on back 31mm. wide, w/o flagpole stems below. Printer: ABNC.

		VG	VF	UNC
100	**5 Sucres** 1956-73. Portrait Antonio Jose de Sucre at center. Red. Arms 31mm. wide, without flagpole stems below. Printer: ABNC. Several date varieties, signature title overprints and serial # styles.			
	a. 19.6.1956; 28.8.1956; 2.4.1957; 19.6.1957; 19.6.1957.	1.00	5.00	40.00
	b. Signature title overprint: *SUBGERENTE GENERAL.* 24.9.1957; 2.1.1958.	.75	5.00	40.00
	c. 2.2.1958; 1.1.1966.	.50	2.50	20.00
	d. 27.2.1970; 3.9.1973. Serial # varieties.	.25	1.50	3.50
101	**10 Sucres** 1950-1955. Portrait Sebastian de Benalcazar at center. Plain background Blue. Arms 31mm. wide without flagpole stems below. Printer: ABNC. Several date varieties, signature title overprints and serial # styles.			
	a. 14.1.1950-28.11.1955.	2.00	8.00	45.00
	b. 21.9.1953; 16.3.1954; 3.10.1955. Overprint: *SUB GERENTE GENERAL.*	2.00	10.00	50.00
	s. Specimen.	—	—	100.

		VG	VF	UNC
101A	**10 Sucres** 1956-74. Portrait Sebastian de Benalcazar at center. Like #101 but different guilloches and ornate background. Arms 31 mm. wide, without flagpole stems below. Printer: ABNC. Several date varieties, signature title overprints and serial # styles.			

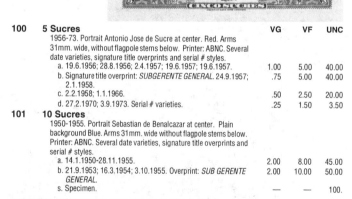

No.	Description	VG	VF	UNC
101A	**10 Sucres**			
	a. 15.6.1956-27.4.1966.	1.00	7.50	35.00
	b. 24.5.1968-2.1.1974.	.50	3.00	15.00
	s. Specimen.	—	—	100.

Note: #101A with date of 24.12.1957 has ovpt: *SUB GERENTE GENERAL*.

No.	Description	VG	VF	UNC
102	**20 Sucres** 28.2.1950-28.7.1960. Church facade at center. Brown. Arms 31 mm. wide, without flagpole stems below. Printer: ABNC. Several date varieties, signature title overprints and serial # styles.	2.50	15.00	50.00
103	**20 Sucres** 1962-73. Like #102. Church facade at center, different guilloches and darker underprint on face. Arms 31 mm. wide, without flagpole stems below. Printer: ABNC. Several date varieties, signature title overprints, and serial # styles.			
	a. 12.12.1962-4.10.1967.	2.00	5.00	25.00
	b. 24.5.1968-3.9.1973.	1.00	3.00	15.00
	s. Specimen. ND.	—	—	125.

No.	Description	VG	VF	UNC
104	**50 Sucres** 1968-71. National monument at center. Like # 99. Green. Arms 31 mm. wide, without flagpole stems below. Printer: ABNC. Several date varieties, signature title overprints, and serial # styles.			
	a. 24.5.1968; 5.11.1969.	2.00	5.00	30.00
	b. 20.5.1971.	1.00	4.00	20.00
	s. Specimen. ND.	—	—	50.00
104A	**100 Sucres** 1952-57. Portrair Simon Bolivar at center. Purple. Arms 31 mm. wide, without flagpole stems below. Printer: ABNC. Several date varieties, signature title overprints, and serial # styles.			
	a. 3.9.1952-19.6.1957.	15.00	75.00	220.
	b. Signature title: *SUBGERENTE*. 3.9.1952; 10.12.1953.	15.00	75.00	220.
105	**100 Sucres** 27.4.1966-7.7.1970. Portrait Simon Bolivar at center, like #104A but different guilloches. Purple. Arms 31 mm. wide, without flagpole stems below. Printer: ABNC. Several date varieties, signature title overprints, and serial # styles.	5.00	10.00	50.00
106	**500 Sucres** ND (ca.1971). Similar to #96. Mercury seated at center with different guilloches and other changes. Back red. Archive example.	—	Unc	1000.

No.	Description	VG	VF	UNC
107	**1000 Sucres** 30.5.1969-20.9.1973. Banco Central building at center. Olive-gray. Arms 31 mm. wide, without flagpole stems below. Printer: ABNC. Several date varieties, signature title overprints, and serial # styles.			
	a. Issued note.	20.00	85.00	250.
	s. Specimen. ND.	—	—	75.00

1957-71 ISSUE

#113-118 black on m/c unpt. Similar to previous issues. Several sign. title ovpt. varieties. Security thread intermittent through 1969. Printer: TDLR.

No.	Description	VG	VF	UNC
113	**5 Sucres** 1958-88. Black on multicolor underprint. Portrait Antonio Jose de Sucre at center, like #108. Red. Red with new rendition of arms. Printer: TDLR.			
	a. 2.1.1958-7.11.1962.	.75	4.00	15.00
	b. 23.5.1963-27.2.1970.	.50	1.00	10.00
	c. 25.7.1979-24.5.1980.	.25	.50	5.00
	d. 22.11.1988.	.10	.25	2.00
	s. Specimen. ND; 24.5.1968; 24.5.1980.	—	—	50.00
114	**10 Sucres** 1968-83. Similar to #109. Back blue.			
	a. 24.5.1968; 20.5.1971.	.50	3.00	20.00
	b. 24.5.1980; 30.9.1982; 20.4.1983.	.25	1.00	10.00
	s1. Specimen. 24.5.1968.	—	—	75.00
	s2. Specimen. 20.5.1971. Series KY.	—	—	50.00
	s3. Specimen. 30.9.1982. Series LI.	—	—	50.00

No.	Description	VG	VF	UNC
115	**20 Sucres** 1961-83. Similar to #110. Back brown.			
	a. 7.6.1961; 29.8.1961; 27.2.1962; 6.7.1962; 7.11.1962; 12.12.1962.	1.50	5.00	35.00
	b. 1.5.1978; 24.5.1980; 20.4.1983.	1.00	2.50	15.00
	s1. Specimen. ND.	—	—	50.00
	s2. Specimen. Series LE. 24.5.1980.	—	—	50.00
116	**50 Sucres** 1957-82. Printer: TDLR. Similar to #111.			
	a. 2.4.1957; 7.7.1959.	2.50	15.00	60.00
	b. 7.11.1962; 29.10.1963; 29.1.1965; 6.8.1965.	1.00	8.00	35.00
	c. 1.1.1966; 27.4.1966; 17.11.1966.	1.00	4.00	25.00
	d. 4.10.1967; 30.5.1969; 17.7.1974.	.75	2.00	15.00
	e. 24.5.1980; 20.8.1982.	.50	1.25	10.00
	s. Specimen. ND; 1.1.1966.	—	—	20.00

No.	Description	VG	VF	UNC
117	**100 Sucres** 29.8.1961-6.8.1965.. Similar to #112 but crude portrait with light clouds behind. Back purple.			
	a. Issued note.	3.50	20.00	50.00
	s. Specimen. without signature Series TW.	—	—	75.00

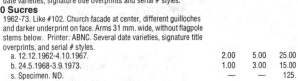

118	100 Sucres	VG	VF	UNC
	1971-77. Like #117 but finer portrait with dark clouds behind. Back purple.			
	a. 20.5.1971; 17.7.1974.	3.00	8.00	40.00
	b. 10.8.1976; 10.8.1977.	2.00	5.00	25.00
	s. Specimen. 20.5.1971.	—	—	50.00

1975-80 ISSUE

#108-112 black on m/c unpt. Face designs like previous issue. New rendition of arms 29mm. wide w/flagpole stems below on back. Printer: ABNC.

108	5 Sucres	VG	VF	UNC
	1975-83. Like #100. Portrait Antonio Jose de Sucre at center. Red with new rendition of arms. Printer: TDLR.			
	a. 14.3.1975; 29.4.1977.	.25	1.50	7.50
	b. 20.8.1982; 20.4.1983.	.25	1.00	4.00

109	10 Sucres	VG	VF	UNC
	14.3.1975; 10.8.1976; 29.4.1977; 24.5.1978. Like #101A. Portrait Sebastian de Benalcazar at center. Blue with new rendition of arms. Printer: TDLR.	.25	2.00	10.00

110	20 Sucres	VG	VF	UNC
	10.8.1976. Like #103. Church façade at center. Brown. Brown with new rendition of arms. Printer: TDLR.	.25	2.50	15.00

111	50 Sucres	VG	VF	UNC
	10.8.1976. Like #104. National monument at center. Back green with new rendition of arms.			
	a. Issued note.	1.00	4.00	22.50
	s. Specimen.	—	—	100.

112	100 Sucres	VG	VF	UNC
	24.5.1980. Like #105. Portrait S. Bolivar at center. Back purple with new rendition of arms.	.25	1.50	12.50

1976 ISSUE

#119 and 120 printer: TDLR.

119	500 Sucres	VG	VF	UNC
	1976-82. Black, violet brown and dark olive on multicolor underprint. Dr. Eugenio de Santa Cruz y Espejo at left. Back blue on multicolor underprint; arms at center and as watermark.			
	a. 24.5.1976; 10.8.1977; 9.10.1978; 25.7.1979.	2.50	12.50	50.00
	b. 20.7.1982.	2.00	7.50	30.00
	s1. Specimen. ND.	—	—	40.00
	s2. As b. Specimen.	—	—	25.00

120	1000 Sucres	VG	VF	UNC
	1976-82. Dark green and red-brown on multicolor underprint. Ruminahui at right. Back dark green on multicolor underprint; arms at center and as watermark.			
	a. 24.5.1976-25.7.1979.	2.50	7.50	50.00
	b. 24.5.1980; 20.7.1982.	1.25	5.00	25.00
	s1. Specimen. ND.	—	—	50.00
	s2. Specimen. Series HP. 24.5.1980.	—	—	25.00

1984-88 ISSUES

#120A-125 w/o text: *SOCIEDAD ANONIMA* below bank title. W/o imprint.

120A	5 Sucres	VG	VF	UNC
	22.11.1988. Black on multicolor underprint. Portrait A. J. de Sucré at center. Arms on back 26mm wide. Back red-violet. Printer: TDLR.	.05	.50	4.00

121	10 Sucres	VG	VF	UNC
	29.4.1986; 22.11.1988. Black on multicolor underprint. Like #114 Back blue.	.10	.75	3.50

121A	20 Sucres	VG	VF	UNC
	1986-88. Black on multicolor underprint. Like #115. Back brown.			
	a. 29.4.1986; 22.11.1988.	.10	.75	5.00
	s. Specimen. 29.4.1986. Series LM.	—	—	20.00

122	50 Sucres	VG	VF	UNC
	5.9.1984; 22.11.1988. Black on multicolor underprint. Similar to #116. Back green.			
	a. Issued note.	.25	1.00	7.50
	s. Specimen. 5.9.1984.	—	—	40.00

123	100 Sucres	VG	VF	UNC
	29.4.1986; 20.4.1990. Black on multicolor underprint. Like #118. Back purple. Black, dark blue or light blue serial #.	.50	2.00	15.00

123A	100 Sucres	VG	VF	UNC
	1988-97. Black on multicolor underprint. Like #123 but with plate differences on face and back. Serial # style varieties. Back purple.			
	a. Blue serial #. 8.6.1988; 21.6.1991; 11.10.1991.	.25	.50	5.00
	b. 9.3.1992; 4.12.1992; 20.8.1993.	.25	.50	5.00
	c. Black serial #. 21.2.1994.	.25	.50	5.00
	d. As c. 3.4.1997.	.25	.50	5.00
	s1. As a. Specimen. 8.6.1988. Punched hole cancelled.	—	—	35.00
	s2. As b. Specimen. 21.6.1991; Series WF. 20.8.1993.	—	—	25.00

#124 and 125 wmk: Arms. W/o imprint. Sign. varieties.

124	500 Sucres	VG	VF	UNC
	5.9.1984. Black, violet-brown and dark olive on multicolor underprint. Like #119.			
	a. Issued note.	.50	2.00	15.00
	s. Specimen.	—	—	40.00

124A	500 Sucres	VG	VF	UNC
	8.6.1988. Black, violet-brown and dark olive on multicolor underprint. Similar to #124 but many minor plate differences.	.25	1.25	10.00

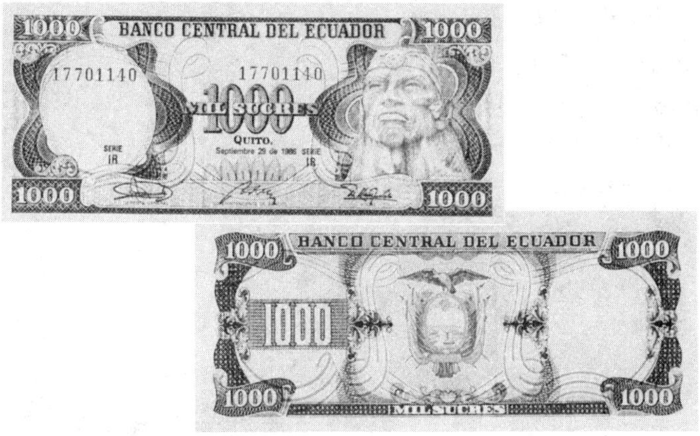

125	1000 Sucres	VG	VF	UNC
	1984-88. Dark green and red-brown on multicolor underprint. Like #120 but without *EL* in bank title. Serial # style varieties.			
	a. 5.9.1984; 29.9.1986.	.25	2.00	15.00
	b. 8.6.1988.	.25	1.50	10.00

Note: Later dates of #123A-#125 were made by different printers (w/o imprint) and vary slightly.

126	5000 Sucres	VG	VF	UNC
	1.12.1987. Purple and brown on multicolor underprint. Juan Montalvo at left and as watermark, arms at center. Flightless cormoran, Galapagos penguin and Galapagos tortoise on back. Printer: BCdE.			
	a. Issued note.	.25	2.00	25.00
	s. Specimen.	—	—	50.00

Note: #126 designed in Mexico.

127	10,000 Sucres	VG	VF	UNC
	1988-98. Dark brown and reddish brown on multicolor underprint. Vicente Rocafuerte at left and as watermark. Arms upper left center, Independence monument in Quito at center right on back. Printer: BCdE. Serial # varieties exist.			
	a. Signature title by itself at l.: *VOCAL*. 30.7.1988; 21.2.1994; 13.10.1994.	.25	2.00	15.00
	b. Signature title at l.: *PRESIDENTE JUNTA MONETARIA*. 6.2.1995; 8.3.1995; 8.8.1995; 4.1.1996; 23.9.1996.	.25	2.00	15.00
	c. Signature title at l.: *PRESIDENTE DEL DIRECTORIO*. 14.12.1998.	.25	.75	10.00
	s1. As a. Specimen. Series AB.	—	—	150.
	s2. As a. Specimen. 13.10.1994 Series AH.	—	—	150.
	s3. As b. Specimen. 8.3.1995. Series AL.	—	—	125.

1991-95 Issue

128	5000 Sucres	VG	VF	UNC
	1991-99. Purple and brown on multicolor underprint. Like #126 but with repositioned signature and both serial # horizontal. Printer: BCdE.			
	a. Signature title by itself at l.: *VOCAL*. 21.6.1991; 17.3.1992; 22.6.1992; 20.8.1993.	.25	1.25	10.00
	b. Signature title at l.: *PRESIDENTE JUNTA MONETARIA*. 31.1.1995; 8.8.1995; 13.1.1996; 31.10.1996.	.25	1.25	7.50
	c. Signature title at l.: *PRESIDENTE DEL DIRECTORIO*. 26.3.1996; 26.3.1999.	.25	1.25	7.50
	s1. Specimen. 21.6.1991. Series AG.	—	—	35.00
	s2. As a. Specimen. 17.3.1992. Series AJ.	—	—	35.00
	s3. As b. Specimen. 31.1.1995.	—	—	25.00

129	20,000 Sucres	VG	VF	UNC
	1995-99. Brown, black and deep blue on multicolor underprint. Dr. Gabriel Garcia Moreno at right and as watermark Arms at center on back.			
	a. Signature title at r.: *PRESIDENTE JUNTA MONETARIA*. 31.1.1995; 20.11.1995.	.75	2.00	20.00
	b. Signature title at r.: *PRESIDENTE JUNTA MONETARIA*. 2.6.1997.	.75	1.50	15.00
	c. Two security threads. signature title at r.: *PRESIDENTE DEL DIRECTORIO*. 10.5.1998; 26.3.1999.	.75	1.50	10.00
	d. Without security thread. signature title at r.: *PRESIDENTE DEL DIRECTORIO*. 10.3.1999.	.75	1.50	7.50
	s1. As a. Specimen, punched hole cancelled. 31.1.1995.	—	—	35.00
	s2. As b. Specimen. 2.6.1997. Series AD.	—	—	25.00
	s3. As c. 10.3.1999.	—	—	25.00

130	50,000 Sucres	VG	VF	UNC
	1995-99. Gray and red-brown on multicolor underprint. Eloy Alfaro at right and as watermark Arms on back. Segmented foil over security thread.			
	a. Two security threads. signature title at l.: *PRESIDENTE JUNTA MONETARIA*. 31.1.1995; 2.6.1997; 20.4.1998; 6.3.1999; 26.3.1999.	1.00	2.50	15.00
	b. 2 security threads. 6.3.1999.	1.00	2.50	10.00
	c. Decreased security features. withoutne security thread. signature title at l.: *GERENTE GENERAL*. 10.3.1999; 26.3.1999.	1.00	2.50	10.00
	s. As a. Specimen. 31.1.1995; 2.6.1997. Series AB.	—	—	25.00

Note: Since September 7, 2000, the U.S. Dollar became legal tender, and the sucre was redeemable until March 30, 2001 at the rate of 25,000 Sucres per U.S. Dollar.

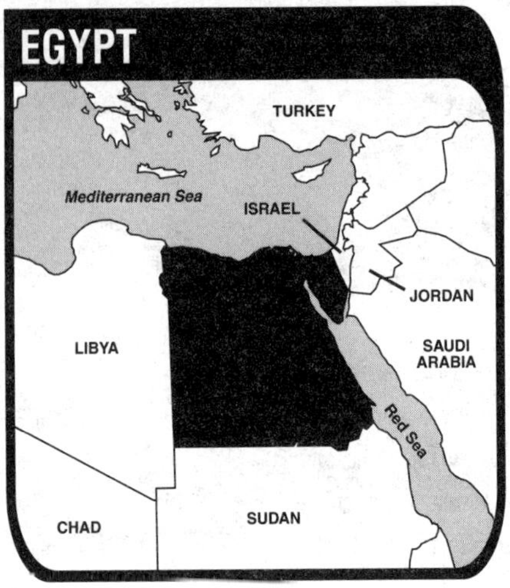

The Arab Republic of Egypt, located on the northeastern corner of Africa, has an area of 386,650 sq. mi. (1,000,000 sq. km.) and a population of 68.12 million. Capital: Cairo. Although Egypt is an almost rainless expanse of desert, its economy is predominantly agricultural. Cotton, rice and petroleum are exported.

Egyptian history dates back to about 4000 B.C. when the empire was established by uniting the upper and lower kingdoms. Following its "Golden Age" (16th to 13th centuries B.C.), Egypt was conquered by Persia (525 B.C.) and Alexander the Great (332 B.C.). The Ptolemies ruled until the suicide of Cleopatra (30 B.C.) when Egypt became a Roman colony. Arab caliphs ruled Egypt from 641 to 1517, when the Turks took it for their Ottoman Empire. Turkish rule, interrupted by the occupation of Napoleon (1798-1801), became increasingly casual, permitting Great Britain to inject its influence by purchasing shares in the Suez Canal. British troops occupied Egypt in 1882, becoming the de facto rulers. On Dec. 14, 1914, Egypt was made a protectorate of Britain. British occupation ended on Feb. 28, 1922, when Egypt became a sovereign, independent kingdom. The monarchy was abolished and a republic proclaimed on June 18, 1952.

On Feb. 1, 1958, Egypt and Syria formed the United Arab Republic. Yemen joined on March 8 in an association known as the United Arab States. Syria withdrew from the United Arab Republic on Sept. 29, 1961, and on Dec. 26 Egypt dissolved its ties with Yemen in the United Arab States. On Sept. 2, 1971, Egypt shed the name United Arab Republic in favor of the Arab Republic of Egypt.

MONETARY SYSTEM:

1 Pound = 100 Piastres

REPLACEMENT NOTES:

Starting in 1969, 2 types exist. Earlier system uses a single Arabic letter as series prefix instead of normal number/letter prefix. Known notes: #42. Later system has the equivalent of English "200", "300" or "400" in front of a single Arabic series letter.

SIGNATURE VARIETIES

11	A. El-Refay, 1961-63	12	A. Zendo, 1962-66
13	A. Nazmy A. A El Hamed, 1967-70	14	A. Zendo, 1972-75
15	M. Ibrahim, 1976-81	16	M. S. A. Shalaby, 1981-84
17	A. Negm, 1985	18	S. Hamed, 1986
19	I. H. Mohamed	20	M. Abou El-Oyoun
21	Farouk Abdel Baky El Okda 1st kind	22	Farouk Abdel Baky El Okda II 2nd kind

NOTICE

Readers with unlisted dates, signature varieties, etc. are invited to submit photocopies of their notes to: Standard Catalog of World Paper Money, 700 East State St. Iola, WI 54990-0001, E-Mail: george.cuhaj@fwpubs.com.

REPUBLIC

CENTRAL BANK OF EGYPT

1961-64 ISSUES

#35-41 sign. and date varieties.

			VG	VF	UNC
35	**25 Piastres** 1.11.1961-18.8.1966. Blue on multicolor underprint. U. A. R. arms at right. Signature 11; 12.				
		a. Issued note.	.75	2.00	6.00
		s. Specimen.	—	—	—

			VG	VF	UNC
36	**50 Piastres** 1.11.1961-14.8.1966. Blackish green multicolor underprint. U. A. R. arms at right, also in watermark signature 11; 12.				
		a. Issued note.	.75	3.00	15.00
		s. Specimen.	—	—	—

			VG	VF	UNC
37	**1 Pound** 1.11.1961-23.2.1967. Blue-green on lilac and multicolor underprint. Tutankhamen's mask at right. Back green. Watermark: Arms. Signature 11; 12; 13.				
		a. Issued note.	1.00	2.50	6.00
		s. Specimen.	—	—	—

		VG	VF	UNC
38	**5 Pounds** 1.11.1961-12.11.1961. Green and brown on multicolor underprint. Circular guilloche at left, Tutankhamen's mask at right. Watermark: Flower. Signature 11.	7.50	25.00	100.

		VG	VF	UNC
39	**5 Pounds** 13.11.1961-16.6.1964. Green and brown on multicolor underprint. Similar to #38, but circular area at left is blank. Guilloche at bottom center on face and back. Watermark: Arms. Signature 11; 12.			
	a. Issued note.	3.00	7.50	25.00
	s. Specimen.	—	—	—

		VG	VF	UNC
40	**5 Pounds** 17.6.1964-13.2.1965. Lilac and brown on multicolor underprint. Like #39. Signature 12.	2.00	5.00	22.50

		VG	VF	UNC
41	**10 Pounds** 1.11.1961-13.2.1965. Dark green and dark brown on multicolor underprint. Tutankhamen's mask at right. Back brown. Watermark: Arms. Signature 11; 12.	3.50	7.50	30.00

1967-69 ISSUE

#42-46 wmk: Archaic Egyptian scribe. Replacement notes: Serial # prefix single Arabic letter.

		VG	VF	UNC
42	**25 Piastres** 6.2.1967-4.1.1975. Blue, green and brown on multicolor underprint. Sphinx with statue at left center U.A.R. arms at center on back. Signature 13; 14.	.15	.50	3.00

		VG	VF	UNC
43	**50 Piastres** 2.12.1967-28.1.1978. Red-brown and brown on multicolor underprint. Al Azhar mosque at right, University of Cairo at left center. Ramses II at center right on back. Signature 13; 14; 15.			
	a. Issued note.	.25	1.00	3.50
	s. Specimen.	—	—	—

44 1 Pound

12.5.1967-19.4.1978. Brown and black on multicolor underprint. Sultan Quayet Bey mosque at left center. Archaic statues on back. Signature 13; 14; 15.

	VG	VF	UNC
a. Issued note.	.50	1.00	4.00
s. Specimen.	—	—	—

45 5 Pounds

1.1.1969-78. Black on blue and multicolor underprint. Ahmad ibn Tulun mosque at Cairo at center right. Ruins at left, frieze at center right on back. Signature 13; 14; 15.

	VG	VF	UNC
a. Issued note.	2.00	3.50	20.00
s. Specimen.	—	—	—

46 10 Pounds

1.9.1969-78. Red-brown and brown on multicolor underprint. Sultan Hassan Mosque at Cairo at left center. Pharaoh and pyramids on back. Signature 13; 14; 15.

VG	VF	UNC
3.00	6.00	25.00

1976 ISSUE

#47 and 48 replacement notes: Serial # prefix single Arabic letter.

47 25 Piastres

12.4.1976-28.8.1978. Blue, green and grayish brown on blue and orange underprint. Face and watermark like #42. A. R. E. arms on back. Signature 15.

	VG	VF	UNC
a. Issued note.	.30	.75	3.50
s. Specimen.	—	—	—

48 20 Pounds

5.7.1976; 1978. Green and black on multicolor underprint. Mohammed Ali mosque at left, Arabic legends at right. Archaic war chariot at left center, frieze at center right on back. Watermark: Egyptian scribe. Signature 15.

VG	VF	UNC
6.00	10.00	35.00

1978-79 ISSUE

#49-62 no longer have conventional dates with Arabic day, month and year. In place of this are six Arabic numerals, the first and last making up the year, the second and third the day, the fourth and fifth the month of issue; YDDMMY; i.e. 825029 will be 25 Feb. 1989. Wmk: Tutankhamen's mask.

Replacement notes: Serial # prefix. Arabic *200* or *300* before single Arabic letter.

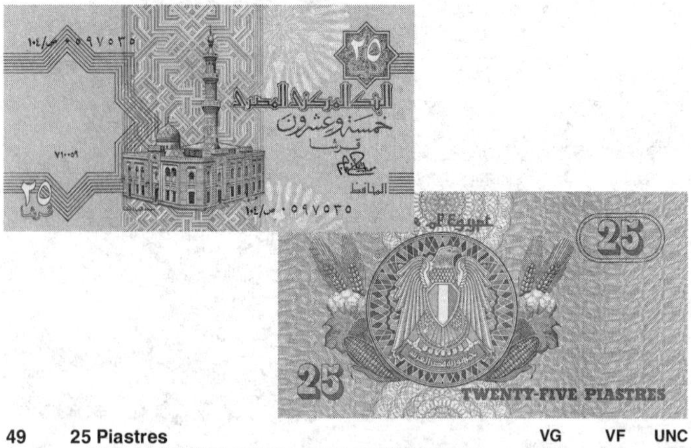

49 25 Piastres

2.1.-11.5.(19)79. Black and brown on gray, pale blue and orange underprint. Al-Sayida Aisha mosque at center. Stylized A. R. E. arms, cotton, wheat and corn plants at center on back. Signature 15.

VG	VF	UNC
FV	.50	2.00

50 **1 Pound** — VG | VF | UNC

29.5.(19)78-. Brown, purple and deep olive-green on multicolor underprint. Sultan Qait Bey mosque at left center. Statues from the Abu Simbel Temple on back.

	VG	VF	UNC
a. Back deep brown. Solid security thread. 29.5.(19)78-10.4.(19)87. signature 15; 16; 17; 18.	FV	FV	1.50
b. Back pale brown. Solid security thread. 19.11.(19)86-9.8.(19)89. signature 18; 19.	FV	FV	1.50
c. Back pale brown. Segmented security thread with bank name repeated. 10.5.(19)89-(20)01. signature 18, 19.	FV	FV	1.50
d. (20)01-(20)03. signature 20.	FV	FV	1.50

51 **10 Pounds** — VG | VF | UNC

24.6.(19)78-27.9.(20)00. Red-brown and brown-violet on multicolor underprint. Al-Rifai mosque at center. Pharaoh on back. Signature 15; 16; 17; 18; 19. — FV | FV | 10.00

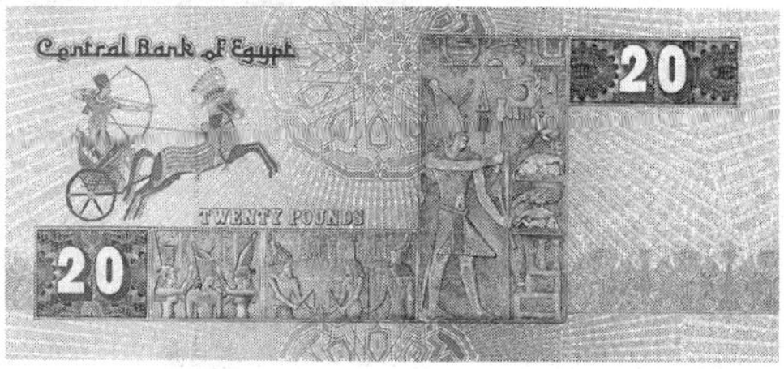

52 **20 Pounds** — VG | VF | UNC

6.9.(19)78-92. Black, gray-violet and deep green on multicolor underprint. Muhammed Ali mosque at center Archaic sculptures from Chapel of Sesostris I and archaic war chariot on back.

	VG	VF	UNC
a. Date below watermark. Solid security thread. 6.9.(19)78-22.4.(19)82. signature 15; 16.	FV	FV	30.00
b. Date at lower right of watermark. Solid security thread. 9.12.(19)86; 3.3.(19)87; 4.10.(19)87. signature 18.	FV	FV	20.00
c. Segmented security thread with bank name repeated. (19)88-(19)92. signature 19.	FV	FV	17.50

53 **100 Pounds** — VG | VF | UNC

(19)78; (19)92. Blue and green on multicolor underprint. Al-Sayida Zainab mosque at center. Pharaoh's mask above frieze at center of vertical format on back.

	VG	VF	UNC
a. Series 1-6.(19)78. signature 15.	FV	30.00	100.
b. (19)92. signature 18.	FV	FV	90.00

1980-81 ISSUE

Replacement notes: Serial # prefix Arabic *200* or *300* before single Arabic series letter.

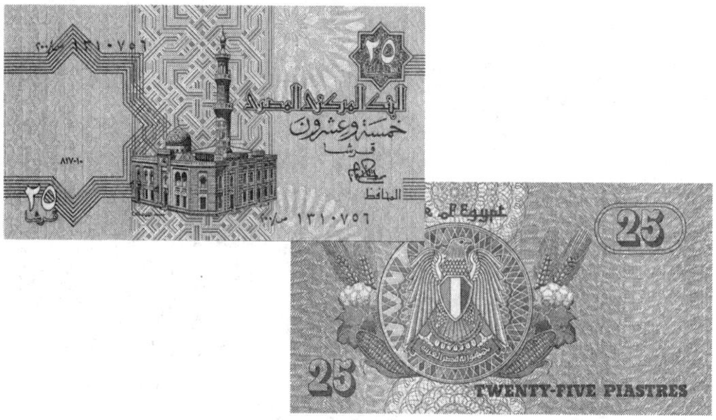

54 **25 Piastres** — VG | VF | UNC

17.1.(19)80-10.1(19)84. Dark green on light green, orange and blue underprint. Like #49. Signature 15; 16. — FV | .30 | 1.50

55 **50 Piastres** — VG | VF | UNC

1.1.(19)81-10.6.(19)83. Green and brown on multicolor underprint. Al Azhar mosque at center. Sculptured wall design at left, Ramses II at center, archaic seal at right on back. Signature 15; 16. — FV | .50 | 2.00

NOTICE

Readers with unlisted dates, signature varieties, etc. are invited to submit photocopies of their notes to: Standard Catalog of World Paper Money, 700 East State St. Iola, WI 54990-0001, E-Mail: george.cuhaj@fwpubs.com.

56	5 Pounds	VG	VF	UNC
	(19)81, (19)86; (19)87. Olive-black and blue-black on multicolor underprint. Ibn Toulon mosque at center. Design symbolizing bounty of the Nile River at center on back.			
	a. 1.2.(19)81. signature 15.	FV	5.00	25.00
	b. (19)86; 6.1.(19)87. signature 16; 17; 18.	FV	3.00	15.00

1985 Issue

Replacement notes: Serial # prefix Arabic *200* or *300* before single Arabic series letter.

57	25 Piastres	VG	VF	UNC
	(19)85-99. Purple and pale blue on pale lilac and multicolor underprint. Face and watermark like #49 and #54. Standard A. R. E. arms at left center on back.			
	a. Solid security thread. 12.1.(19)85-30.1.(19)89. signature 17; 18.	FV	FV	1.00
	b. Segmented security thread with bank name repeated. 5.12.(19)90-(19)99. signature 18; 19.	FV	FV	.75
	c. 8.1.2001. signature 19.	FV	FV	.75
	d. Solid security thread. 22.1.(20)02. signature 20.			—

58	50 Piastres	VG	VF	UNC
	(19)85-94. Black on pale orange, pink and multicolor underprint. Al Azhar mosque at center right. Back like #55.			
	a. No text line at lower left on face. Solid security thead. 2.7.(19)85- . signature 17; 18.	FV	.25	2.00
	b. Text line added at lower left on face. 1.2.(19)87-17.8.(19)89. signature 18; 19.	FV	FV	1.25
	c. Segmented security thread with bank name repeated. 5.1.(19)90-11.8.(19)94.	FV	FV	1.00

1989-94 Issue

Replacement notes: Serial # prefix Arabic *200* or *300* before single Arabic series letter.

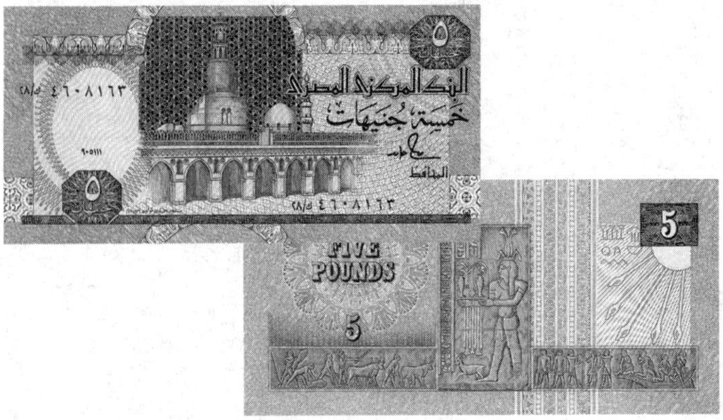

59	5 Pounds	VG	VF	UNC
	2.4.(19)89-. Black and blue-black on multicolor underprint. Like #56 but multicolor scrollwork added in underprint and into watermark area. Archaic design over watermark area at right on back. Signature 18; 19; 20.	FV	FV	5.00

60	50 Pounds	VG	VF	UNC
	9.2.(19)93- . Brown, violet and multicolor. Abu Hariba Mosque at right. Isis above archaic boat, interior view of Edfu temple at left center on back. Signature 18; 19.	FV	FV	30.00

61	100 Pounds	VG	VF	UNC
	14.9.(19)94; (19)97. Dark brown and brown-violet on multicolor underprint. Sultan Hassan Mosque at lower left center. Sphinx at center on back. Signature 19.	FV	FV	60.00

1995 Issue

		VG	VF	UNC
62	**50 Piastres** 6.7.(19)95-17.7.2002. Dull olive-gray on multicolor underprint. Like #58. Signature 19; 20	FV	FV	.75

2000-03 Issue

#63-64 w/wide segmented silver security strip and added rosette printed in optical variable ink.

		VG	VF	UNC
63	**5 Pounds** 21.2.2002. Multicolor.	FV	FV	5.00

		VG	VF	UNC
64	**10 Pounds** 12.8.2003; 31.8.2003. Multicolor.	FV	FV	8.00

		VG	VF	UNC
65	**20 Pounds** 3.10.2001-10.12.2003. Black, gray-violet and deep green on multicolor underprint. Similar to #52. Signature 19, 20, 21.	FV	FV	15.00

		VG	VF	UNC
66	**50 Pounds** 25.11.2001. Multicolor.	FV	FV	27.50

		VG	VF	UNC
67	**100 Pounds** 2000; 29.12.2003. Dark brown and brown-violet on multicolor underprint. Like #61.	FV	FV	50.00

Currency Notes

United Arab Republic

Law 50 of 1940

Face 4: Main heading unchanged from

Face 3 but *EGYPTIAN REGION* (small line of Arabic text) is deleted.

Back 2: *UNITED ARAB REPUBLIC* in English. Various sign. Imprint: Survey Dept.

1961 ND Issue

		VG	VF	UNC
180	**5 Piastres** L.1940. Lilac. Queen Nefertiti at right. Watermark: U A R.			
	a. Signature Baghdady with titles: *VICE-PRESIDENT AND MINISTER OF TREASURY*. Series 15; 16.	1.25	6.00	25.00
	b. Signature Kaissouni with titles: *MINISTER OF TREASURY AND PLANNING*. Series 16-18.	.25	3.00	10.00
	c. Signature Daif with titles: *MINISTER OF TREASURY*. Color lilac to blue. watermark. 3mm tall. Series 18-22.	.20	2.00	10.00
	d. Signature and titles as c. watermark. 5mm tall. Series 22-26.	.20	2.00	8.00
	e. Signature Hegazy with titles as d. Series 26-33.	.20	1.00	8.00
180A	**5 Piastres**	VG	VF	UNC
	L.1940. Face like #180. Back with signature Kaissouni with title: MINISTER OF TREASURY (error). Series 16.	15.00	50.00	150.

181 10 Piastres	VG	VF	UNC
L.1940. Black. Group of militants with flag having only two stars.			
a. Signature Baghdady with titles: *VICE-PRESIDENT AND MINISTER OF TREASURY*. Series 16.	2.00	10.00	30.00
b. Signature Kaissouni with titles: *MINISTER OF TREASURY AND PLANNING*. Series 16-18.	.50	3.00	10.00
c. Signature Kaissouni with titles: *MINISTER OF TREASURY*. Series 16.	15.00	50.00	175.
d. Signature Daif with title as c. Series 18-24.	.25	3.00	10.00
e. Signature Hegazy with title as c. Series 24-29.	.25	3.00	10.00

ARAB REPUBLIC OF EGYPT

Law 50 of 1940

Face 5: *ARAB REPUBLIC OF EGYPT* in Arabic.

Back 3: *THE ARAB REPUBLIC OF EGYPT* in English. Various sign. Printer: Survey Authority or Postal Printing House.

1971 ND ISSUE

182 5 Piastres	VG	VF	UNC
L.1940. Lilac. Similar to #180. Imprint: Survey of Egypt.			
a. Signature Hegazy with title: *MINISTER OF TREASURY*. watermark: *U A R*. Series 33; 34.	1.00	5.00	20.00
b. Signature Hegazy with title: *MINISTER OF TREASURY*. watermark: *A R E*. Series 34-36.	.75	4.00	15.00
c. Signature Ibrahim with title: *MINISTER OF FINANCE*. watermark: *A R E*. Series 36; 37.	.25	1.50	6.00
d. Signature El Nashar with title as c. Series 37.	.75	2.50	10.00
e. Signature Ismail. with title as c. Series 37-40.	.20	.75	3.00
f. Signature M. S. Hamed. Series 40-42.	.25	1.00	4.00
g. Signature Loutfy. Series 42-47.	.20	.75	3.00
h. Signature Meguid. Series 47-50.	.15	.60	3.00
i. Signature Hamed. Series. 50.	2.00	6.00	25.00
j. Like c. Printer: Postal Printing House. signature Hamed. Series 50-72.	.10	.50	2.50
k. Signature El Razaz. Series 72.	.25	1.00	5.00

183 10 Piastres	VG	VF	UNC
L.1940. Black. Simlar to #181. Printer: Survey Authority.			
a. Signature Hegazy with title: *MINISTER OF TREASURY*. watermark: *U A R*. Series 29; 30.	2.00	8.00	35.00
b. Signature Hegazy with title: *MINISTER OF TREASURY*. watermark: *A R E*. Series 30; 31.	1.00	5.00	20.00
c. Signature Ibrahim with title: *MINISTER OF FINANCE*. watermark: *A R E*. Series 31; 32.	.50	2.00	9.00
d. Signature El Nashar with titles as c. Series 32-33.	1.00	4.00	15.00
e. Signature Ismail with titles as c. Series 33-35.	.25	1.00	4.00
f. Signature M. S. Hamed with titles as c. Series 35-38.	.50	1.75	7.00
g. Signature Loutfy with titles as c. Series 38-43.	.25	1.00	4.00
h. Signature Meguid with titles as c. Series 43-46.	.20	.75	3.00
i. Signature Hamed with titles as c. Series 46.	3.00	8.00	30.00

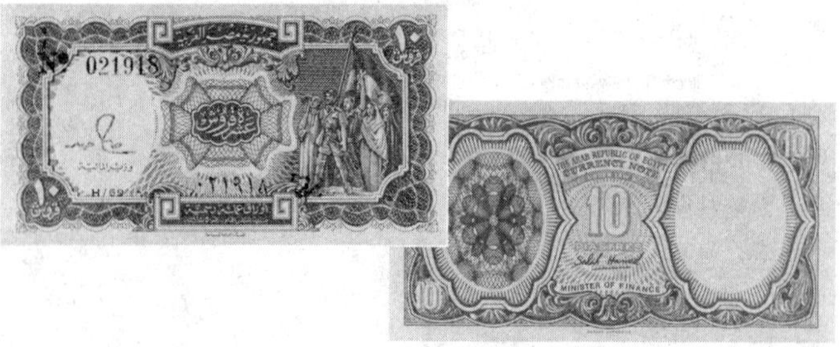

184 10 Piastres	VG	VF	UNC
L.1940. Black. Similar to #183 but new flag with eagle instead of two stars. Signature title: MINISTER OF FINANCE.			
a. Signature Hamed. Series 46-69.	.15	.50	2.50
b. Signature El Razaz. Series 69-75.	.20	.75	3.00

Note: Transitional series numbers from one signature to the next are generally much scarcer and command a premium. As of July, 1991 all Egyptian currency notes had been demonetized and withdrawn from circulation. A new series was released recently because of a coinage shortage.

1997; 1998 ND ISSUE

Law 50 of 1940.

185 5 Piastres	VG	VF	UNC
L.1940. Green and orange. Similar to #182. El-Ghareeb with title: MINISTER OF FINANCE. Arabic Series 1-2. Printer: Postal Printing House. Watermark: King Tut's mask.	.10	.25	1.25

186 5 Piastres	VG	VF	UNC
L.1940. Like #185 but mule issue with signature Salah Hamad with title: MINISTER OF FINANCE on back.	1.00	3.00	12.50

187 10 Piastres	VG	VF	UNC
L.1940. Black and orange. Sphinx, pyramids at right. Mosque of Mohamed Ali at Citadel at left on back. Signature El Ghareeb with title: MINISTER OF FINANCE. Arabic Series 1-2. Watermark: King Tut's mask.	.10	.50	1.50

Note: Because of the error note the production of #185-187 ceased.

1998; 1999 ND ISSUE

Law 50 of 1940

#188 and 189 sign. M. Elghareeb w/title: *MINISTER OF FINANCE*.

188 5 Piastres	VG	VF	UNC
L.1940. Blue-gray on blue and lilac underprint. Similar to #185.	.10	.25	1.25

189 10 Piastres	VG	VF	UNC
L.1940. Dull purple and blue on multicolor underprint. Similar to #187.	.10	.25	1.00

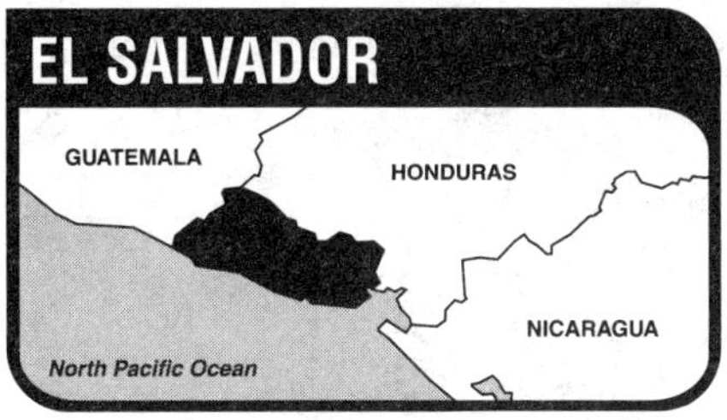

The Republic of El Salvador, a Central American country bordered by Guatemala, Honduras and the Pacific Ocean, has an area of 8,260 sq. mi. (21,041 sq. km.) and a population of 6.32 million. Capital: San Salvador. This most intensely cultivated country of Latin America produces coffee (the major crop), sugar and balsam for export. Gold, silver and other metals are largely unexploited.

The first Spanish attempt to subjugate the area was undertaken in 1523 by Pedro de Alvarado, Cortes' lieutenant. He was forced to retreat by superior Indian forces, but returned in 1525 and succeeded in bringing the region under control of the captaincy general of Guatemala, where it remained until 1821. In 1821, El Salvador and the other Central American provinces declared their independence from Spain. In 1823, the Federal Republic of Central America was formed by the five Central American States. When this federation was dissolved in 1829, El Salvador became an independent republic.

A twelve-year civil war was ended in 1992 with the signing of a UN sponsored Peace Accord. Free elections, with full participation of all political parties, were held in 1994 and 1997. Armando Calderón-Sol was elected as president in 1994 for a 5-year term.

On January 1, 2001, a monetary reform established the U.S. dollar as the accounting unit for all financial transactions, and fixed the exchange rate as 8.75 colones per dollar. In addition, the Central Reserve Bank has indicated that it will cease issuing coins and notes.

MONETARY SYSTEM:

1 Colón = 100 Centavos 1919-

SUPERINTENDENCIA DE BANCOS Y OTRAS INSTITUCIONES FINANCIERAS:

Juan S. Quinteros	1962-1975	Marco T. Guandique	1977-Feb. 1981
Jose A. Mendoza	1968-1975	Rafael T. Carbonell	1981
Jorge A. Dowson	1975-1977	Raul Nolasco	1981-

DATING SYSTEM:

Dates listed for notes are those found on the face, regardless of the ovpt. issue dates on back which were applied practically on a daily basis as notes were needed for circulation.

Republic

Banco Central de Reserva de El Salvador

1962; 1963 Issue

#100-146 w/various date and sign. ovpts. on back w/different shields and seals.

#100-130, 132-142, 144 and 145 portr. C. Columbus at ctr. l. on back, and later as wmk.

#100-104 printer: TDLR.

100	1 Colón	VG	VF	UNC
	12.3.1963; 25.1.1966; 23.8.1966. Black on multicolor underprint. Central Bank at center. Back orange.			
	a. Issued note.	1.00	8.50	30.00
	s. Specimen. 12.3.1963.	—	—	—

101	2 Colones	VG	VF	UNC
	15.2.1962; 9.6.1964. Black on multicolor underprint. Coffee bush at left, workers at left center. Back red-brown.			
	a. Issued note.	3.00	12.50	65.00
	s. Specimen. 15.2.1962.	—	—	—

102	5 Colones	VG	VF	UNC
	15.2.1962; 12.3.1963. Black on multicolor underprint. Woman with basket of fruit on her head at left. Back green.			
	a. Issued note.	3.00	10.00	50.00
	s. Specimen. 15.2.1962.	—	—	—

103	10 Colones	VG	VF	UNC
	15.2.1962; 9.6.1964; 27.12.1966. Black on multicolor underprint. Portrait Manuel José Arce at center, serial # at lower left and upper right. Back brown.			
	a. Issued note.	3.50	17.50	80.00
	s. Specimen. 15.2.1962.	—	—	150.

104	25 Colones	VG	VF	UNC
	1963; 1966. Black on multicolor underprint. 5th of November Dam at center. Back dark blue.			
	a. 12.3.1963.	7.50	25.00	125.
	b. 27.12.1966.	750.	25.00	100.
	s1. As a. Specimen.	—	—	80.00
	s2. As b. Specimen.	—	—	75.00

1964; 1965 Issue

#105-107 printer: ABNC.

105	1 Colón	VG	VF	UNC
	8.9.1964. Black on pink and green underprint. Farmer plowing at center, *SAN SALVADOR* at upper left. Black serial # and series letters. Back orange.			

		VG	VF	UNC
105	**1 Colón**			
	a. Issued note.	2.00	7.50	30.00
	s. Specimen.	—	—	—

		VG	VF	UNC
106	**5 Colones**			
	8.9.1964. Black on green and multicolor underprint. José Matías Delgado addressing crowd at center, *SAN SALVADOR* at upper left. Black serial # at lower left and upper right. Back deep olive-green.			
	a. Issued note.	2.50	10.00	40.00
	s. Specimen.	—	—	—

		VG	VF	UNC
107	**100 Colones**			
	12.1.1965. Brown and green underprint. Independence monument at center but *SAN SALVADOR* at upper left. Serial # at lower left and upper right. Back olive-green.			
	a. Issued note.	20.00	75.00	250.
	s. Specimen. Punched hole cancelled.	—	—	150.

1967 COMMEMORATIVE ISSUE

#108-109 printer: TDLR. These notes are reportedly commemoratives for the Bicentennial of the Birth of José Cañas.

		VG	VF	UNC
108	**1 Colón**			
	20.6.1967. Black on multicolor underprint. Juan José Cañas at right, *UN COLON* at center *SAN SALVADOR* and date at right. Back orange.			
	a. Issued note.	1.00	4.00	25.00
	s. Specimen. Punched hole cancelled.	—	—	40.00

NOTICE

Readers with unlisted dates, signature varieties, etc. are invited to submit photocopies of their notes to: Standard Catalog of World Paper Money, 700 East State St. Iola, WI 54990-0001, E-Mail: george.cuhaj@fwpubs.com.

		VG	VF	UNC
109	**5 Colones**			
	20.6.1967. Black on pink and green underprint. Scene of Juan José Cañas freeing the slaves, *31.12.1823* at center. Back green.			
	a. Issued note.	20.00	125.	325.
	s. Specimen.	—	—	100.

1968-70 ISSUE

#110-114 printer: USBNC.

		VG	VF	UNC
110	**1 Colón**			
	1968; 1970. Black on light orange and pale blue underprint. Juan José Cañas at right, *1 COLON* at center. Back orange.			
	a. Signature title: *CAJERO* at right. 13.8.1968.	.75	3.50	20.00
	b. Signature title: *GERENTE* at right. 12.5.1970.	.75	3.50	20.00
	s1. As a. Specimen.	—	—	35.00
	s2. As b. Specimen.	—	—	35.00

		VG	VF	UNC
111	**5 Colones**			
	1968-70. Black on green and ochre underprint. José Matías Delgado addressing crowd at center, *5 COLONES* at right. Back dark green.			
	a. Signature title: *CAJERO* at right. 13.8.1968; 4.2.1969.	1.25	6.00	30.00
	b. Signature title: *GERENTE* at right. 12.5.1970.	1.25	6.00	30.00
	s1. As a. Specimen. 13.8.1968; 4.2.1969.	—	—	35.00
	s2. As b. Specimen.	—	—	35.00

		VG	VF	UNC
112	**10 Colones**			
	13.8.1968. Black on tan and pale blue underprint. Manuel José Arce at right, *10 COLONES* at center. Back black.			
	a. Issued note.	3.00	12.50	50.00
	s. Specimen.	—	—	40.00

113	25 Colones	VG	VF	UNC
	12.5.1970. Black on light orange and pale blue underprint. 5th of November Dam at right. Back dark blue.			
	a. Issued note.	7.00	20.00	80.00
	s. Specimen.	—	—	50.00

114	100 Colones	VG	VF	UNC
	12.5.1970. Black on pink and pale olive-green underprint. Independence monument at center. Back olive-green.			
	a. Issued note.	20.00	75.00	250.
	s. Specimen.	—	—	200.

1971; 1972 ISSUE

#115-119 Printer: TDLR.

115	1 Colón	VG	VF	UNC
	31.8.1971; 24.10.1972. Black on multicolor underprint. *SAN SALVADOR* and date at left, *UN COLON* at center, Juan José Cañas at right. Back red.			
	a. Issued note.	.25	1.50	8.00
	s. Specimen. 31.8.1971; 24.10.1972.	—	—	30.00

116	2 Colones	VG	VF	UNC
	1972; 1974. Black on multicolor underprint. Colonial church of Panchimalco at center, *DOS COLONES* at right. Back red-brown.			
	a. 24.10.1972.	.25	2.00	10.00
	b. 15.10.1974.	.25	1.75	10.00
	s. As a, b. Specimen.	—	—	30.00

Note: #116 w/o wmk. is reported, not confirmed.

117	5 Colones	VG	VF	UNC
	31.8.1971-24.6.1976. Black on pale blue and multicolor underprint. Face like #111 without *5 COLONES* at left, José Matías Delgado addressing crowd at center. Back green.			
	a. Issued note.	FV	2.50	17.50
	s. Specimen. 31.8.1971; 24.10.1972; 15.10.1974.	—	—	30.00

118	10 Colones	VG	VF	UNC
	31.8.1971-23.12.1976. Black on multicolor underprint. *DIEZ COLONES* at center, Manuel José Arce at right. Back dull black.			
	a. Issued note.	2.50	6.00	30.00
	s. Specimen. 31.8.1971; 24.10.1972; 15.10.1974.	—	—	35.00

119	25 Colones	VG	VF	UNC
	31.8.1971. Black on multicolor underprint. 5th of November Dam at center. Back blue.			
	a. Issued note.	7.50	15.00	55.00
	s. Specimen.	—	—	32.50

1974 ISSUE

#120-122 black on m/c unpt. Printer: TDLR.

120	1 Colón	VG	VF	UNC
	15.10.1974. Cerron Grande Dam at center, without *UN COLON* at left. Back red; like #115.	.25	2.00	9.00

121	25 Colones	VG	VF	UNC
	15.10.1974; 24.6.1976; 23.12.1976. Aerial view of Acajutla port. Back blue.			
	a. Issued note.	5.00	12.50	45.00
	s. Specimen. 15.10.1974.	—	—	—

122	100 Colones	VG	VF	UNC
	1974-79. Indian pyramid at Tazumal at center, arms at lower right. Back olive-green on multicolor underprint.			
	a. Regular serial #. 15.10.1974-11.5.1978.	15.00	20.00	95.00
	b. Electronic sorting serial #. 3.5.1979.	15.00	17.50	75.00
	s. As a. Specimen. 15.10.1974.	—	—	60.00

1976 ISSUE

#123 and 124 black on m/c unpt. Printer: TDLR.

123	1 Colón	VG	VF	UNC
	28.10.1976. Similar to #120 but *UN COLON* at left. Back like #125. without watermark.			
	a. Issued note.	.25	1.00	8.50
	s. Specimen.	—	—	30.00

124	2 Colones	VG	VF	UNC
	24.6.1976. Black on multicolor underprint. Like #116 but with *DOS COLONES* at left and right. Denomination added to face at left. Back brown-violet; without watermark.			
	a. Issued note.	.25	1.75	10.00
	s. Specimen.	—	—	30.00

1977-79 ISSUES

#125-126, 129-130 black on m/c unpt. w/unpt. in margins on face.

125	1 Colón	VG	VF	UNC
	1977-80. Like #123. Printer: TDLR.			
	a. Regular style serial #. 7.7.1977; 11.5.1978.	FV	1.50	8.50
	b. Electronic sorting serial #. 3.5.1979; 19.6.1980.	FV	1.00	7.50
	s. As b. Specimen.	—	—	—

126	5 Colones	VG	VF	UNC
	6.10.1977. Like #117, but *5 COLONES* at left and right. Without watermark. Printer: TDLR.			
	a. Issued note.	FV	2.00	12.00
	s. Specimen.	—	Unc	30.00

Note: For similar 5 Colones dated 19.6.1980, see #132A.

127	10 Colones	VG	VF	UNC
	7.7.1977. Black on multicolor underprint. *DIEZ COLONES* at center, Manuel José Arce at center right. Back black. Printer: ABNC.	FV	4.00	15.00

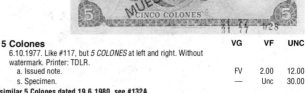

128	10 Colones	VG	VF	UNC
	13.10.1977. Like #127 but blue arms added to face and back.Without watermark. Printer: ABNC.	FV	4.00	15.00

129 **10 Colones**

		VG	VF	UNC
	1978-80. Manuel José Arce at right. Back black. Printer: TDLR.			
	a. Regular serial #. 11.5.1978.	FV	2.25	10.00
	b. Electronic sorting serial #. 3.5.1979; 21.7.1980.	FV	1.50	8.00
	s. As b. Specimen. 3.5.1979.	—	—	30.00

130 **25 Colones**

		VG	VF	UNC
	1978-80. Like #121. Printer: TDLR.			
	a. Regular serial #. 11.5.1978.	FV	5.00	30.00
	b. Electronic sorting serial #. 3.5.1979; 19.6.1980.	FV	3.00	15.00
	s. As b. Specimen. 19.6.1980.	—	—	30.00

131 **50 Colones**

		VG	VF	UNC
	1979; 1980. Purple on multicolor underprint. Large building and statue at left, Captain General Gerardo Barrios at right. Ships at left, Christopher Columbus at center on back. Printer: TDLR.			
	a. 3.5.1979.	FV	8.00	42.50
	b. 19.6.1980.	FV	5.00	20.00
	s. As a. Specimen.	—	—	30.00

132 **100 Colones**

		VG	VF	UNC
	7.7.1977. Deep olive-green on multicolor underprint. Independence monument at right. Printer: ABNC.	FV	20.00	75.00

1980 ISSUE

132A **5 Colones**

		VG	VF	UNC
	19.6.1980 (1992). Like #134. Printer: ABNC.	FV	FV	5.00

133 **100 Colones**

		VG	VF	UNC
	17.7.1980. Black on multicolor underprint. Like #122 but with flag below date at upper left. Printer: TDLR.	FV	17.50	42.50

1982; 1983 ISSUE

#133A-137 w/o sign. title *GERENTE* at r.

#133A-136 black on m/c unpt. W/o unpt. in margins.

133A **1 Colón**

		VG	VF	UNC
	3.6.1982. Black on multicolor underprint. Like #125. Back red. Printer: TDLR.			
	a. Issued note.	FV	FV	7.00
	s. Specimen.	—	—	30.00

#134-137 printer: ABNC.

134 **5 Colones**

		VG	VF	UNC
	1983; 1988. Black on multicolor underprint. Back green. Like #132A.			
	a. 25.8.1983.	FV	FV	5.00
	b. 17.3.1988.	FV	FV	4.00
	s1. As a. Specimen.	—	—	55.00
	s2. As b. Specimen.	—	—	30.00

NOTICE

Readers with unlisted dates, signature varieties, etc. are invited to submit photocopies of their notes to: Standard Catalog of World Paper Money, 700 East State St. Iola, WI 54990-0001, E-Mail: george.cuhaj@fwpubs.com.

135	10 Colones	VG	VF	UNC
	1983; 1988. Black on multicolor underprint. Like #127.			
	a. 25.8.1983.	FV	FV	8.00
	b. 17.3.1988.	FV	FV	7.00
	s1. As a. Specimen.	—	—	55.00
	s2. As b. Specimen.	—	—	30.00

136	25 Colones	VG	VF	UNC
	29.9.1983. Black on multicolor underprint. Bridge and reservoir at center. Back blue.			
	a. Issued note.	FV	FV	15.00
	s. Specimen.	—	—	30.00

137	100 Colones	VG	VF	UNC
	1983; 1988. Deep olive-green on multicolor underprint. Like #132.			
	a. 29.9.1983.	FV	FV	37.50
	b. 17.3.1988.	FV	FV	30.00
	s1. As a. Specimen.	—	—	30.00
	s2. As b. Specimen.	—	—	27.50

1990-93 Issues

#138 and 140 unpt. in margins on face.

138	5 Colones	VG	VF	UNC
	16.5.1990. Black on multicolor underprint. Like #126 but without signature, title: *GERENTE* at right, with electronic sorting serial #. Back olive-green and dark gray. Printer: TDLR.			
	a. Issued note.	FV	FV	5.00
	s. Specimen.	—	—	25.00

#139 *Deleted.* See #132A.

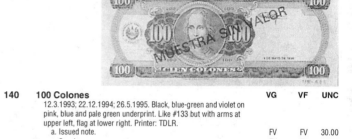

140	100 Colones	VG	VF	UNC
	12.3.1993; 22.12.1994; 26.5.1995. Black, blue-green and violet on pink, blue and pale green underprint. Like #133 but with arms at upper left, flag at lower right. Printer: TDLR.			
	a. Issued note.	FV	FV	30.00
	s. Specimen.	FV	FV	40.00

1995 Issue

#141-143 w/ascending size serial # at upper r. Wmk: Columbus wearing cap. Printer: TDLR.

141	10 Colones	VG	VF	UNC
	26.5.1995. Like #129.			
	a. Issued note.	FV	FV	6.00
	s. Specimen.	—	—	40.00

142	25 Colones	VG	VF	UNC
	26.5.1995; 9.2.1996. Similar to #130 but without signature, title: *GERENTE* at right.			
	a. Issued note.	FV	FV	12.50
	s. Specimen.	—	—	40.00

143	50 Colones	VG	VF	UNC
	26.5.1995. Purple on multicolor underprint. Like #131 but without signature, title: *GERENTE* at right.			
	a. Issued note.	FV	FV	17.50
	s. Specimen.	—	—	40.00

1996 Issue

#144-146 wmk: C. Columbus wearing cap. Printer: CBNC.

144	10 Colones	VG	VF	UNC
	9.2.1996. Black on multicolor underprint. Similar to #141.			
	a. Issued note.	FV	FV	5.00
	s. Specimen.	—	—	40.00

#145 and 146 w/segmented foil over security thread.

145 50 Colones VG VF UNC

9.2.1996. Purple on multicolor underprint. Like #143.

	VG	VF	UNC
a. Issued note.	FV	FV	17.50
s. Specimen.	—	—	40.00

146 100 Colones VG VF UNC

9.2.1996. Black, blue-green and violet on pink, blue and pale green underprint. Like #140.

	VG	VF	UNC
a. Issued note.	FV	FV	25.00
s. Specimen.	—	—	50.00

1997 ISSUE

#147-152 w/special marks for poor of sight above arms at l. ctr. C. Columbus wearing hat at l. on back and as wmk., continents over his 3 ships at ctr. Sign. titles *PRESIDENTE* and *DIRECTOR*.

147 5 Colones VG VF UNC

18.4.1997; 2.3.1998. Black, dark green and brown on multicolor underprint. National Palace at center right.

	VG	VF	UNC
a. Issued note. Series D, E, K.	FV	FV	3.50
s. Specimen. Series A.	—	—	22.50

148 10 Colones VG VF UNC

18.4.1997; 2.3.1998. Dark blue-violet, brown and deep blue-green on multicolor underprint. Izalco volcano at center right.

	VG	VF	UNC
a. Issued note. Series A; C.	FV	FV	5.50
s. Specimen. Series A.	—	—	22.50

149 25 Colones VG VF UNC

1997; 1998. Black, brown and blue-black on multicolor underprint. San Andres pyramid at center right.

	VG	VF	UNC
a. Issued note. Series A-D. 18.4.1997.	FV	FV	12.00
b. Issued note. Series F. 2.3.1998.	FV	FV	9.00
s. Specimen. Series A.	—	—	22.50

150 50 Colones VG VF UNC

18.4.1997. Purple, brown and blue-black on multicolor underprint. Lake Coatepeque at center right.

	VG	VF	UNC
a. Issued note. Series A.	FV	FV	17.50
s. Specimen. Series A.	—	—	50.00

151 100 Colones VG VF UNC

18.4.1997; 4.5.1998. Deep olive-green and dark brown on multicolor underprint. Tazumal pyramid at center right.

	VG	VF	UNC
a. Issued note. Series A.	FV	FV	22.50
s. Specimen. Series A.	—	—	27.50

152	200 Colones	VG	VF	UNC
	1997-98. Brown, red-violet and purple on multicolor underprint. *EL SALVADOR DEL MUNDO* monument at center right.			
	a. 1997; 1998. Series B.	FV	FV	40.00
	s. Specimen. Series A.	—	—	35.00

1999 ISSUE

#153-158 like #147-152 except for added security features.

153	5 Colones	VG	VF	UNC
	19.4.1999. Green and olive on multicolor underprint. National Palace. Like #147.	FV	FV	2.50

154	10 Colones	VG	VF	UNC
	19.4.1999. Purple and green on multicolor underprint. Izalco Volcano. Like #148.	FV	FV	5.00

155	25 Colones	VG	VF	UNC
	19.4.1999. Brown and green on multicolor. San Andres Pyramid. Like #149.	FV	FV	9.50

156	50 Colones	VG	VF	UNC
	19.4.1999. Violet and orange on multicolor underprint. Coatepeque Lake. Like #150.	FV	FV	20.00

157	100 Colones	VG	VF	UNC
	19.4.1999. Dark green and light green on multicolor underprint. Tazumal Pyramid. Like #151.	FV	FV	30.00

158	200 Colones	VG	VF	UNC
	19.4.1999. Brown, red and multicolor. Like #152.	FV	FV	50.00

Note: U.S. Dollars have replaced Salvadorian Colones.

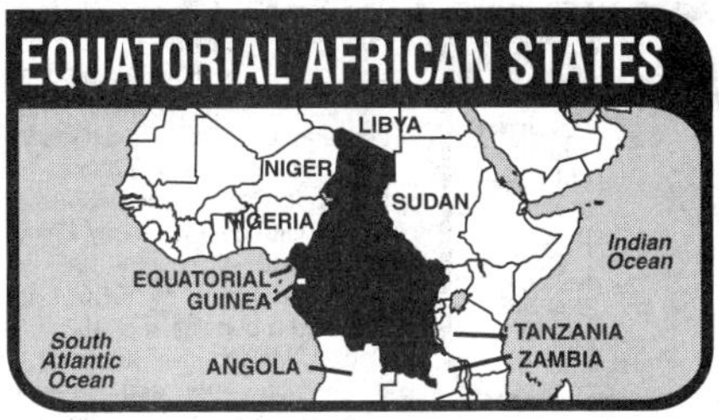

Equatorial African States (Central African States), a monetary union comprising the former French possessions and now independent states of the Republic of Congo (Brazzaville), Gabon, Central African Republic, Chad and Cameroon, issues a common currency for the member states from a common central bank. The monetary unit, the African Financial Community Franc, is tied to and supported by the French franc.

In 1960, an abortive attempt was made to form a union of the newly independent republics of Chad, Congo, Central Africa and Gabon. The proposal was discarded when Chad refused to become a constituent member. The four countries then linked into an Equatorial Customs Unit, to which Cameroon became an associate member in 1961. A more extensive cooperation of the five republics, identified as the Central African Customs and Economic Union, was entered into force at the beginning of 1966.

In 1974 the Central Bank of the Equatorial African States, which had issued coins and paper currency in its own name and with the names of the constituent member nations, changed its name to the Bank of the Central African States.

MONETARY SYSTEM:

1 Franc (C.F.A.) = 100 Centimes

CONTROL LETTER or SYMBOL CODE

Country	1961-72
Cameroun	*
Central African Republic	B
Chad	A
Congo	C
Equatorial Guinea	
Gabon	D

EQUATORIAL AFRICAN STATES

BANQUE CENTRALE DES ÉTATS DE L'AFRIQUE ÉQUATORIALE ET DU CAMEROUN

1961 ND ISSUES

		VG	VF	UNC
1	**100 Francs** ND (1961-62). Blue and multicolor. Portrait Gov. Felix Eboue at center, woman with jug at left, people in canoe at right. Cargo ships at center, man at right on back.			
	a. Code letter *A*.	20.00	125.	450.
	b. Code letter *B*.	20.00	150.	500.
	c. Code letter *C*.	20.00	125.	450.
	d. Code letter *D*.	20.00	125.	450.
	e. * for Cameroun.	50.00	200.	750.
	f. Without code letter.	15.00	40.00	300.
	s. Specimen. Prefix letter O, serial #0s	—	—	500.
2	**100 Francs** ND (1961-62). Multicolor. Like #1 but denomination also in English. with * for Cameroun.	50.00	150.	500.

Note: For similar 100 Francs w/FRANÇAISE in the title see French Equatorial Africa #32. (Vol. II).

BANQUE CENTRALE ÉTATS DE L'AFRIQUE ÉQUATORIALE

1963 ND ISSUE

		VG	VF	UNC
3	**100 Francs** ND (1963). Brown and multicolor. Musical instrument at left, hut at left center, man at right. Elephant at left, tools at right on back.			
	a. Code letter *A*.	10.00	40.00	125.
	b. Code letter *B*.	15.00	50.00	150.
	c. Code letter *C*.	10.00	40.00	125.
	d. Code letter *D*.	10.00	40.00	125.

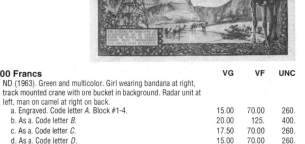

		VG	VF	UNC
4	**500 Francs** ND (1963). Green and multicolor. Girl wearing bandana at right, track mounted crane with ore bucket in background. Radar unit at left, man on camel at right on back.			
	a. Engraved. Code letter *A*. Block #1-4.	15.00	70.00	260.
	b. As a. Code letter *B*.	20.00	125.	400.
	c. As a. Code letter *C*.	17.50	70.00	260.
	d. As a. Code letter *D*.	15.00	70.00	260.
	e. Lithographed. Code letter *A*. Block #5-.	10.00	55.00	240.
	f. As e. Code letter *B*.	10.00	65.00	260.
	g. As e. Code letter *C*.	12.00	55.00	240.
	h. As e. Code letter *D*.	10.00	55.00	240.

		VG	VF	UNC
5	**1000 Francs** ND (1963). Multicolor. People gathering cotton. Young men logging on back.			
	a. Engraved. Code letter *A*. Block #1-5.	15.00	125.	400.
	b. As a. Code letter *B*.	20.00	150.	450.
	c. As a. Code letter *C*.	15.00	125.	400.
	d. As a. Code letter *D*.	15.00	125.	400.
	e. Lithographed. Code letter *A*. Block #7-.	10.00	100.	350.
	f. As e. Code letter *B*.	15.00	125.	400.
	g. As e. Code letter *C*.	10.00	100.	350.
	h. As e. Code letter *D*.	10.00	100.	350.

		VG	VF	UNC
6	**5000 Francs** ND (1963). Multicolor. Girl at left, village scene at center. Carving at left, airplane, train crossing bridge and tractor hauling logs at center, man smoking a pipe at right on back.			

6	**5000 Francs**	VG	VF	UNC
	a. Code letter *A*.	150.	375.	1150.
	b. Code letter *B*.	150.	375.	1150.
	c. Code letter *C*.	150.	375.	1150.
	d. Code letter *D*.	150.	375.	1150.

7	**10,000 Francs**	VG	VF	UNC
	ND (1968). Multicolor. President Bokassa at right, Rock Hotel, Bangui, C.A.R. in background, arms of Central African Republic at lower left.	275.	650.	2150.

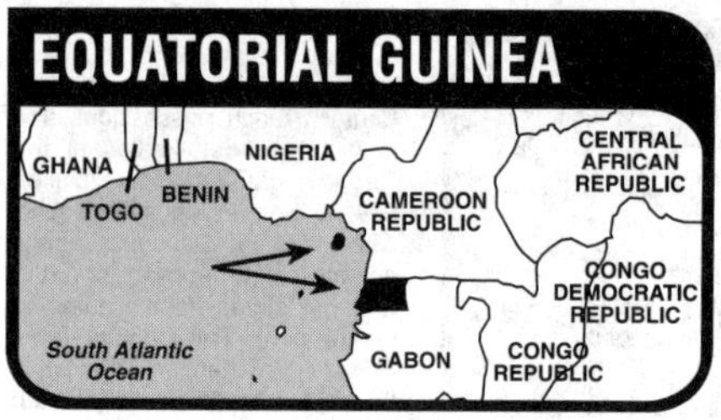

The Republic of Equatorial Guinea (formerly Spanish Guinea) consists of Rio Muni, located on the coast of west-central Africa between Cameroon and Gabon, and the offshore islands of Fernando Po, Annobon, Corisco, Elobey Grande and Elobey Chico. The equatorial country has an area of 10,831 sq. mi. (28,051 sq. km.) and a population of 452,000. Capital: Malabo. The economy is d on agriculture and forestry. Cacao, wood and coffee are exported.

Fernando Po was discovered between 1474 and 1496 by Portuguese navigators charting a route to the spice islands of the Far East. Portugal retained control of it and the adjacent islands until 1778 when they, together with trading rights to the African coast between the Ogooue and Niger rivers, were ceded to Spain. Fernando Po was administered, with Spanish consent, by the British from 1827 to 1844 when it was reclaimed by Spain. Mainland Rio Muni was granted to Spain by the Berlin Conference of 1885. The name of the colony was changed from Spanish Guinea to Equatorial Guinea in Dec. of 1963. Independence was attained on Oct. 12, 1968.

Additional listings can be found under Central African States.

MONETARY SYSTEM:

1 Peseta Guineana = 100 Centimos to 1975
1 Ekuele = 100 Centimos, 1975 80
1 Epkwele (pl. Bipkwele) = 100 Centimos, 1980-85
1 Franc (C.F.A.) = 100 Centimes, 1985-
1 Franco (C.F.A.) = 4 Bipkwele

REPUBLIC

BANCO CENTRAL

1969 ISSUE

#1-3 printer: FNMT.

1	**100 Pesetas Guineanas**	VG	VF	UNC
	12.10.1969. Red-brown on light tan underprint. Banana tree at left. Shoreline and man with boat on back. Watermark: Woman's head.	1.00	5.00	20.00

2	**500 Pesetas Guineanas**	VG	VF	UNC
	12.10.1969. Green on multicolor underprint. Derrick loading logs at left, shoreline at center. Woman with bundle on head at right on back. Watermark: Man's head.	2.00	7.50	30.00

		VG	VF	UNC
3	**1000 Pesetas Guineanas** 12.10.1969. Blue on multicolor underprint. President M. Nguema Biyogo at center. Tree at left, arms at center on back. Watermark: King and queen.	2.75	10.00	45.00

BANCO POPULAR

1975 FIRST DATED ISSUE

#4-8 w/portr. Pres. M. N. Biyogo at r. and as wmk. Name under portrait: *MACIAS NGUEMA BIYOGO*. Printer: TDLR. Replacement notes: Serial # prefix *Z1*.

		VG	VF	UNC
4	**25 Ekuele** 7.7.1975. Purple on light orange and green underprint. Trees at center. Arms at left, bridge at center on back. Name underneath: *PUENTE MACIAS NGUEMA BIYOGO.*	.50	2.00	7.00

		VG	VF	UNC
5	**50 Ekuele** 7.7.1975. Brown on green and pink underprint. Plants at center. Arms at left, logging at center on back.	.50	2.00	7.00

#6-8 arms at ctr.

		VG	VF	UNC
6	**100 Ekuele** 7.7.1975. Green on pink and multicolor underprint. Bridge and boats on back.	.75	2.00	7.00

		VG	VF	UNC
7	**500 Ekuele** 7.7.1975. Blue on multicolor underprint. National Palace on back.	1.25	4.00	15.00

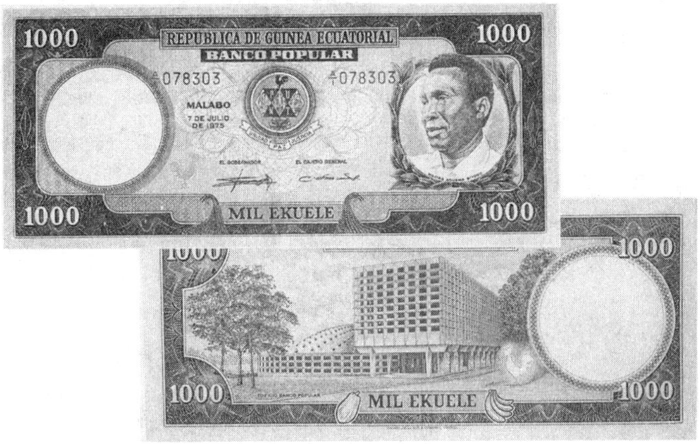

		VG	VF	UNC
8	**1000 Ekuele** 7.7.1975. Red on multicolor underprint. Bank on back.	2.00	5.00	20.00

1975 SECOND DATED ISSUE

#9-13 like #4-8 but name under portrait: *MASIE NGUEMA BIYOGO NEGUE NDONG*. Different sign. at l. Replacement notes: Serial # prefix *Z1*.

		VG	VF	UNC
9	**25 Ekuele** 7.7.1975. Like #4 except for name change on both sides.	1.00	2.00	7.50

		VG	VF	UNC
10	**50 Ekuele** 7.7.1975. Like #5 except for name change.	1.00	2.00	7.50

		VG	VF	UNC
11	**100 Ekuele** 7.7.1975. Like #6 except for name change on both sides.	1.00	2.50	7.50

		VG	VF	UNC
12	**500 Ekuele** 7.7.1975. Like #7 except for name change.	1.50	4.00	15.00
13	**1000 Ekuele** 7.7.1975. Like #8 except for name change.	1.50	4.00	15.00

BANCO DE GUINEA ECUATORIAL

1979 ISSUE

#14-17 wmk: T.E. Nkogo. Printer: FNMT.

		VG	VF	UNC
14	**100 Bipkwele** 3.8.1979. Dark olive-green and multicolor. Arms at center, T. E. Nkogo at right. Boats along pier of Puerto de Bata on back.	1.75	4.00	12.50

		VG	VF	UNC
15	**500 Bipkwele** 3.8.1979. Black on green and pink underprint. Arms at center, right. Uganda at right. Back brown and black; sailboat, shoreline and trees at left center.	4.00	15.00	45.00

		VG	VF	UNC
16	**1000 Bipkwele** 3.8.1979. Brown, black and multicolor. Arms at center, right. Bioko at right. Back maroon and brown; men cutting food plants at left center.	3.50	12.50	35.00

		VG	VF	UNC
17	**5000 Bipkwele** 3.8.1979. Blue-gray on multicolor underprint. Arms at center, E. N. Okenve at right. Back blue-gray and blue; logging scene at center.	3.00	10.00	35.00

1980 PROVISIONAL ISSUE

		VG	VF	UNC
18	**1000 Bipkwele on 100 Pesetas** 21.10.1980 (-old date 12.10.1969). Black overprint of new denomination and date on #1. (Not issued).	—	3.50	15.00

		VG	VF	UNC
19	**5000 Bipkwele on 500 Pesetas** 21.10.1980 (-old date 12.10.1969). Similar red overprint on #2. (Not issued).	—	6.00	25.00

Note: #18 and 19 were prepared for issue but not released to circulation. Shortly afterwards, Equatorial Guinea began the use of CFA franc currency. #3 was not ovpt. because it carries the portrait of former Pres. Biyogo.

BANQUE DES ÉTATS DE L'AFRIQUE CENTRALE

1985 ISSUE

#20-22 wmk: Carving (as printed on notes). Sign. 9. For sign. see Central African States listings.

		VG	VF	UNC
20	**500 Francos** 1.1.1985. Brown on multicolor underprint. Carving and jug at center. Man carving mask at left center on back.	1.00	3.00	10.00

		VG	VF	UNC
21	**1000 Francos** 1.1.1985. Dark blue on multicolor underprint. Animal carving at lower left, map at center, starburst at lower right. Incomplete map of Chad at upper center Elephant at left, statue at right on back.	2.00	5.00	15.00

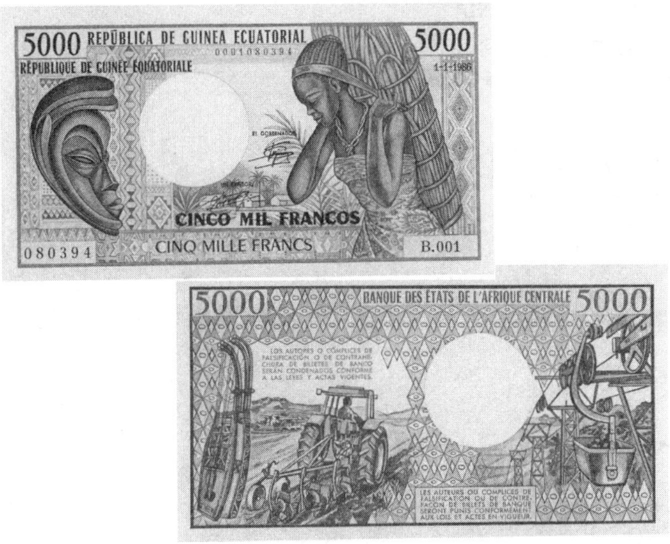

		VG	VF	UNC
22	**5000 Francos** 1.1.1985; 1.1.1986. Brown, yellow and multicolor. Carved mask at left, woman carrying bundle at right. Farmer plowing with tractor at left, ore lift at right on back.			
	a. 1.1.1985.	10.00	20.00	75.00
	b. 1.1.1986.	10.00	17.50	65.00

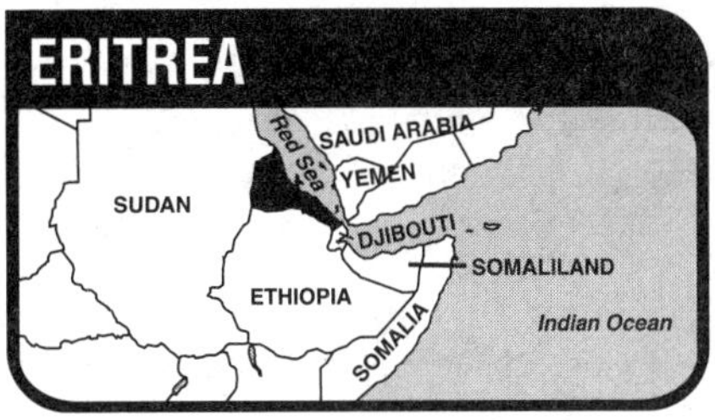

The State of Eritrea, a former Ethiopian province fronting on the Red Sea, has an area of 45,300 sq. mi. (117,600 sq. km.) and a population of 3.53 million. It was an Italian colony from 1889 until its incorporation into Italian East Africa in 1936. It was under the British Military Administration from 1941 to 1952, when the United Nations designated it an autonomous unit within the federation of Ethiopia and Eritrea. On Nov. 14, 1962, it was annexed with Ethiopia. In 1991 the Eritrean Peoples Liberation Front extended its control over the entire territory of Eritrea. Following 2 years of provisional government, Eritrea held a referendum on independence in May 1993. Overwhelming popular approval led to the proclamation of an independent Republic of Eritrea on May 24.

MONETARY SYSTEM:

1 Nakfa = 100 Cents

REPUBLIC

BANK OF ERITREA

1997 ISSUE

#1-6 flag raising at l. Wmk: Camel's head.

Design by Clarence Holbert of the USBEP. Printer: G&D (w/o imprint).

		VG	VF	UNC
1	**1 Nakfa** 24.5.1997. Dark brown and black on multicolor underprint. Three girls at center. Back dark green; children in bush school at center right.	FV	FV	1.00

#2-6 Kinnegram vertical foil strip at l. w/camels repeated.

		VG	VF	UNC
2	**5 Nakfa** 24.5.1997. Dark brown and black on multicolor underprint. Young boy, young and old man at center. Back dark green; cattle grazing under huge Jacaranda tree at center right.	FV	FV	3.50

		VG	VF	UNC
3	**10 Nakfa** 24.5.1997. Dark brown and black on multicolor underprint. Three young women at center. Back dark green; truck on rails hauling box cars across viaduct over the Dogali River at center right.	FV	FV	7.50

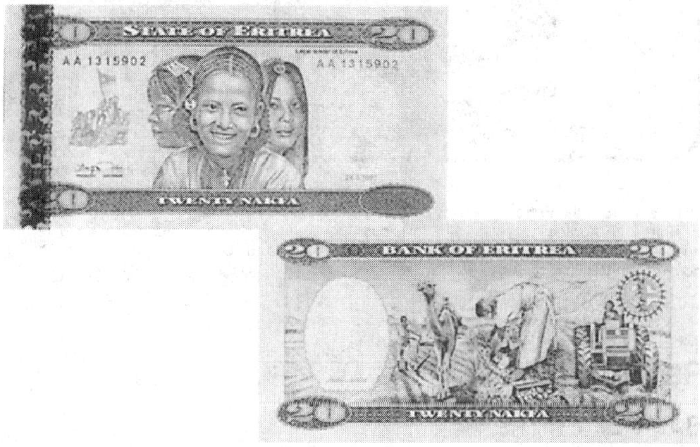

		VG	VF	UNC
4	**20 Nakfa** 24.5.1997. Dark brown and black on multicolor underprint. Three young girls at center. Back dark green; farmer plowing with camel, woman harvesting, woman on farm tractor at center right.	FV	FV	12.50

		VG	VF	UNC
5	**50 Nakfa** 24.5.1997. Dark brown and black on multicolor underprint. Three young women at center. Back dark green; ships in Port of Masawa at center right.	FV	FV	20.00

		VG	VF	UNC
6	**100 Nakfa** 24.5.1997. Dark brown and black on multicolor underprint. Three young girls at center. Back dark green; farmers plowing with oxen at center right.	FV	FV	37.50

2004 Issue

		VG	VF	UNC
7	**50 Nakfa** 24.5.2004. Multicolor.	—	Unc	20.00
8	**100 Nakfa** 24.5.2004. Multicolor.	—	Unc	37.50

The Republic of Estonia (formerly the Estonian Soviet Socialist Republic of the U.S.S.R.) is the northernmost of the three Baltic states in eastern Europe. It has an area of 17,413 sq. mi. (45,100 sq. km.) and a population of 1.42 million. Capital: Tallinn. Agriculture and dairy farming are the principal industries. Butter, eggs, bacon, timber are exported.

This small and ancient Baltic state has enjoyed but two decades of independence since the 13th century. After having been conquered by the Danes, the Livonian Knights, the Teutonic Knights of Germany, the Swedes, the Poles and the Russians. Estonia declared itself an independent republic on Nov. 15, 1917, The peace treaty was signed Feb. 2, 1920. Shortly after the start of World War II, it was again occupied by Russia and incorporated as the 16th state of the U.S.S.R. Germany occupied Estonia from 1941 to 1944, after which it was retaken by Russia.

On August 20, 1991, the Parliament of the Estonian S.S.R. voted to reassert the republic's independence.

MONETARY SYSTEM

1 Kroon = 100 Senti

Republic

Eesti Pank

Bank of Estonia

1991-92 Issue

#69-71 replacement notes: Serial # prefix *.

#69 and 70 wmk: Fortress.

		VG	VF	UNC
69	**1 Kroon** 1992. Brownish black on yellow-orange and dull violet-brown underprint. K. Raud at left. Toampea castle with Tall Hermann (national landmarks) on back.			
	a. Issued note.	FV	FV	1.50
	s. Specimen.	—	—	45.00

		VG	VF	UNC
70	**2 Krooni** 1992. Black on light blue-violet and grayish green underprint. K. E. von Baer at left. Tartu University building at center on back.			
	a. Issued note.	FV	FV	1.50
	s. Specimen.	—	—	45.00

NOTICE

Readers with unlisted dates, signature varieties, etc. are invited to submit photocopies of their notes to: Standard Catalog of World Paper Money, 700 East State St. Iola, WI 54990-0001, E-Mail: george.cuhaj@fwpubs.com.

#71-75 wmk: Arms (3 lions).

71	**5 Krooni**	VG	VF	UNC
	1991 (92); 1992 (94). Black and tan on multicolor underprint. P. Keres at center, chessboard and arms at upper right. Teutonic fortress along Narva River, church on back.			
	a. 1991.	FV	FV	2.00
	b. 1992.	FV	FV	2.00
	s. Specimen.	—	—	60.00

72	**10 Krooni**	VG	VF	UNC
	1991 (92); 1992 (94). Purple and red on multicolor underprint. J. Hurt at left center. Tamme-lauri oak tree at Urvaste at right on back.			
	a. 1991.	FV	FV	4.00
	b. 1992.	FV	FV	2.50
	s. Specimen.	—	—	60.00

73	**25 Krooni**	VG	VF	UNC
	1991 (92); 1992 (94). Deep olive-green on multicolor underprint. A. Hansen-Tammsaare at left center, wilderness in background at right. Early rural log construction farm; view of Vargamäe on back.			
	a. 1991.	FV	FV	10.00
	b. 1992.	FV	FV	4.50
	s. Specimen.	—	—	70.00

74	**100 Krooni**	VG	VF	UNC
	1991 (92); 1992 (94). Black and deep blue on light blue and multicolor underprint. L. Koidula at left center, cuckoo bird at lower right. Waves breaking against rocky cliffs of north coast at center to right on back.			
	a. 1991.	FV	FV	15.00
	b. 1992.	FV	FV	15.00
	s. Specimen.	—	—	85.00

75	**500 Krooni**	VG	VF	UNC
	1991 (92). Blue-black and purple on multicolor underprint. C. R. Jakobson at left center, harvest between two farmers with Sakala above at right. Barn swallow in flight over rural pond at right, value at upper right on back.			
	a. Issued note.	FV	FV	75.00
	s. Specimen.	—	—	200.

1994 Issue

#76-80 ascending size serial # at r.

76	**5 Krooni**	VG	VF	UNC
	1994 (97). Black and tan on multicolor underprint. Like #71 but with modified design at lower right on face and lower left on back.			
	a. Issued note.	FV	FV	1.00
	s. Specimen.	—	—	60.00

77	**10 Krooni**	VG	VF	UNC
	1994 (97). Purple and red on multicolor underprint. Like #72 but with modified design at lower right on face and lower left on back.			
	a. Issued note.	FV	FV	1.50
	s. Specimen.	—	—	60.00

78 **50 Krooni**

1994. Green and black on multicolor underprint. R. Tobias at left center, gates at lower center right. Opera house in Tallinn at center right on back.

	VG	VF	UNC
a. Issued note.	FV	FV	10.00
s. Specimen.	—	—	60.00

79 **100 Krooni**

1994. Black and dark blue on multicolor underprint. Like #74 but with gray seal at upper right on face. Different rosette at lower left on back.

	VG	VF	UNC
a. Issued note.	FV	FV	17.50
s. Specimen.	—	—	75.00

80 **500 Krooni**

1994 (95). Blue-black and purple on multicolor underprint. Like #75 but with dark gray bank seal at upper right. Different rosette at lower left on back.

	VG	VF	UNC
a. Issued note.	FV	FV	80.00
s. Specimen.	—	—	200.

1996 Issue

81 **500 Krooni**

1996 (97). Blue, black and purple on multicolor underprint. Like #80 but with hologram at upper left. Value at lower right on back.

	VG	VF	UNC
a. Issued note.	FV	FV	75.00
s. Specimen.	—	—	200.

1999-2000 Issue

82 **100 Krooni**

1999. Blue on light blue and multicolor underprint. Holographic strip at left. Similar to #79, but many differences. L. Koidula at left center; cuckoo bird at lower center. Back blue on light red underprint. Waves breaking against rocky cliffs of north coast at center to right.

	VG	VF	UNC
a. Issued note.	FV	FV	15.00
s. Specimen withoutvpt: *PROOV.*	—	—	35.00

83 **500 Krooni**

	VG	VF	UNC
2000. Dark blue and blue on multicolor underprint. Similar to #81, but with some differences. C. R. Jakobson at left and as watermark. Barn swallow on back.	FV	FV	75.00

2002 Issue

84 **25 Krooni**

	VG	VF	UNC
2002. Green, black and lilac on multicolor underprint. Anton Hansen-Tammsaare at left, arms at upper right. Estonian farm view Vargamae on back. Wide holographic band at left.	FV	FV	8.00

Collector Series

Eesti Pank

Bank of Estonia

1999 Collector's Set

80th Anniversary of Bank

		Issue Price	Mkt. Value
CS1	**100 Krooni** 1999. Set includes: 100 Krooni specimen note (#82), 5 Krooni coin, and 4 stamps. 3,000 pcs.	—	35.00

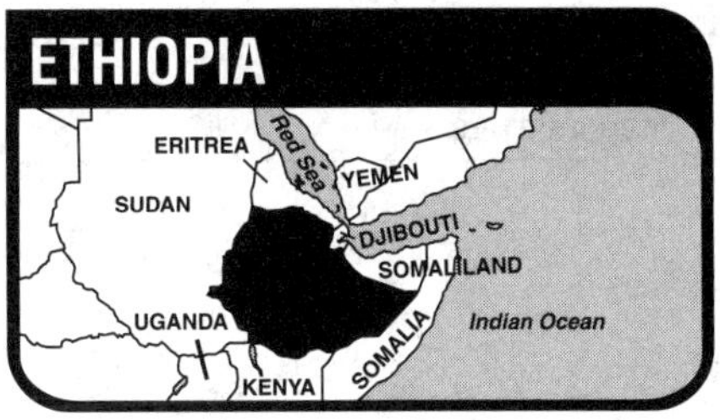

The Federal Republic of Ethiopia (formerly the Peoples Democratic Republic and the Empire of Ethiopia) is located in east-central Africa. The country has an area of 424,214 sq. mi. (1.099,900 sq. km.) and a population of 66.18 million people who are divided among 40 tribes that speak some 270 languages and dialects. Capital: Addis Ababa. The economy is predominantly agricultural and pastoral. Gold and platinum are mined and petroleum fields are being developed. Coffee, oilseeds, hides and cereals are exported.

Legend claims that Menelik I, the son born to Solomon, King of Israel, by the Queen of Sheba, settled in Axum in northern Ethiopia to establish the dynasty which then reigned - with only brief interruptions - until 1974. Modern Ethiopian history began with the reign of Emperor Menelik II (1889-1913) under whose guidance the country emerged from medieval isolation. Ethiopia was invaded by fascist Italy in 1935, and together with Italian Somaliland and Eritrea became part of Italian East Africa until liberated by British and Ethiopian troops in 1941. Haile Selassie I, 225th consecutive Solomonic ruler, was deposed by a military committee on Sept. 12, 1974. In July 1976, Ethiopia's military provisional government referred to the country as Socialist Ethiopia. After establishing a new regime in 1991, Ethiopia became a federated state.

Eritrea, a former Ethiopian province fronting on the Red Sea, was an Italian colony from 1890 until its incorporation into Italian East Africa in 1936. It was under British military administration from 1941 to Sept. 15, 1952, when the United Nations designated it an autonomous unit within the federation of Ethiopia and Eritrea. On Nov. 14, 1962, it was fully integrated with Ethiopia. On May 24, 1993, Eritrea became an independent nation.

RULERS:

Haile Selassie I, 1930-1936, 1941-1974

MONETARY SYSTEM:

1 Birr (Dollar) = 100 Santeems (Cents), since 1944

EMPIRE

STATE BANK OF ETHIOPIA

1961 ND ISSUE

Dollar System

#18-24 Emperor Haile Selassie at r. Arms at ctr. on back. Printer: BWC.

		VG	VF	UNC
18	**1 Dollar** ND (1961). Green on lilac and light orange underprint. Coffee bushes at left.			
	a. Issued note.	4.00	15.00	50.00
	s. Specimen. Punched hole cancelled.	—	—	25.00

		VG	VF	UNC
19	**5 Dollars** ND (1961). Orange on green and multicolor underprint. Addis Ababa University (old palace) at left.			
	a. Issued note.	4.00	25.00	80.00
	s. Specimen. Punched hole cancelled.	—	—	50.00

		VG	VF	UNC
20	**10 Dollars** ND (1961). Red on multicolor underprint. Harbor at Massawa at left.			
	a. Issued note.	10.00	40.00	125.
	s. Specimen. Punched hole cancelled.	—	Unc	110.

		VG	VF	UNC
21	**20 Dollars** ND (1961). Brown on multicolor underprint. Ancient stone monument (Axum) at left.			
	a. Issued note.	25.00	80.00	250.
	s. Specimen. Punched hole cancelled.	—	—	125.
22	**50 Dollars** ND (1961). Blue on multicolor underprint. Bridge over Blue Nile at left.	VG	VF	UNC
	a. Issued note.	50.00	100.	300.
	s. Specimen. Punched hole cancelled.	—	—	175.

		VG	VF	UNC
23	**100 Dollars** ND (1961). Purple on multicolor underprint. Trinity Church at Addis Ababa at left.			
	a. Signature title: *GOVERNOR.*	80.00	150.	400.
	b. Signature title: *ACTING GOVERNOR.*	65.00	125.	350.
	s. Specimen.	—	—	200.
24	**500 Dollars** ND (1961). Dark green on multicolor underprint. Fasilides castle at Gondar at left.			
	a. Issued note.	250.	600.	1500.
	s. Specimen. Punched hole cancelled.	—	—	300.

NATIONAL BANK OF ETHIOPIA

1966 ND ISSUE

#25-29 Emperor Haile Selassie at r. Arms at ctr. on back. Printer: TDLR.

		VG	VF	UNC
25	**1 Dollar** ND (1966). Dark green on multicolor underprint. Aerial view of Massawa harbor, city at left.			
	a. Issued note.	1.50	6.00	20.00
	s. Specimen.	—	—	30.00

26	5 Dollars	VG	VF	UNC
	ND (1966). Brown on multicolor underprint. Bole Airport, Addis Ababa at left. Back orange.			
	a. Issued note.	3.00	17.50	80.00
	r. Replacement note. Serial # prefix *X*.	6.00	30.00	140.
	s. Specimen.	—	—	35.00

27	10 Dollars	VG	VF	UNC
	ND (1966). Dark red on multicolor underprint. National Bank at Addis Ababa at left.			
	a. Issued note.	4.00	20.00	75.00
	s. Specimen.	—	—	50.00

28	50 Dollars	VG	VF	UNC
	ND (1966). Blue on multicolor underprint. Koka High Dam on the Awash River on back.			
	a. Issued note.	15.00	75.00	190.
	s. Specimen.	—	—	165.

29	100 Dollars	VG	VF	UNC
	ND (1966). Purple on green and multicolor underprint. Rock church "Bet Giorgis" in Lalibela at left.			
	a. Issued note.	5.00	20.00	125.
	s. Specimen.	—	—	125.

PEOPLES DEMOCRATIC REPUBLIC

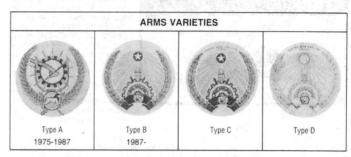

ARMS VARIETIES			
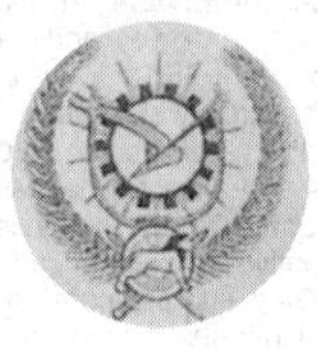	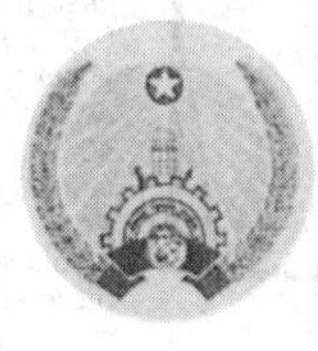		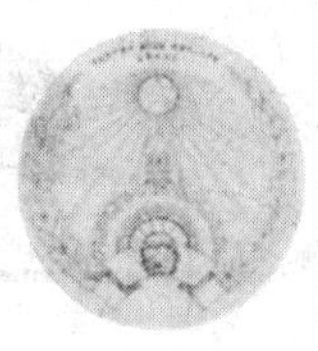
Type A 1975-1987	Type B 1987-	Type C	Type D

SIGNATURE VARIETIES			
1	Teferra Deguefe, 1974-76 CHAIRMAN OF THE BOARD	2	Tadesse G. Kidan, 1978-87 ADMINISTRATOR
3	Bekele Tamirat, 1987-91 ADMINISTRATOR	4	Leikun Berhanu, 1991-97 GOVERNOR
5	Thbale Tala, 1997-98 GOVERNOR	6	Teklewold Atnafu, 1998- GOVERNOR

NATIONAL BANK OF ETHIOPIA

1976 ND ISSUE

Birr System

law EE Masharam 1969 (Sept. 1976 AD) #30-34 have map at l., lion's head in unpt. at l. ctr. Arms Type A at r. on back. Replacement notes: Serial # prefix *ZZ*.

30	1 Birr	VG	VF	UNC
	L.EE1969 (1976). Black and dark green on light brown and green underprint. Young man at center right, longhorns at right. Back black on multicolor underprint; whited-throated bee-eaters and Tisisat waterfalls of Blue Nile on back.			
	a. Signature 1.	.25	2.00	5.00
	b. Signature 2.	.25	1.50	2.50

31	5 Birr	VG	VF	UNC
	L.EE1969 (1976). Black and brown-orange on multicolor underprint. Man picking coffee beans at center right, plant at right. Kudu, caracal and Semien Mountains on back.			
	a. Signature 1.	.75	3.25	9.00
	b. Signature 2.	.75	2.75	7.00

		VG	VF	UNC
32	**10 Birr** L.EE1969 (1976). Brown-violet and red on multicolor underprint. Woman weaving basket at center right, wicker work dining table with lid at right. Plowing with tractor on back.			
	a. Signature 1.	2.00	6.00	15.00
	b. Signature 2.	2.00	4.00	12.00

		VG	VF	UNC
33	**50 Birr** L.EE1969 (1976). Blue-black and dark brown on lilac and multicolor underprint. Science students at center right, musical instrument at right. Fasilides Castle at Gondar on back.			
	a. Signature 1.	10.00	25.00	60.00
	b. Signature 2.	10.00	20.00	50.00

		VG	VF	UNC
34	**100 Birr** L.EE1969 (1976). Purple, violet and dark brown on multicolor underprint. Warrior standing at center right, flowers at right. Young man with microscope on back.			
	a. Signature 1.	20.00	40.00	100.
	b. Signature 2.	20.00	32.50	85.00

1987 ND Issue

Law EE Masharam 1969 (Sept. 1976 AD).

#36-40 similar to #30-34 but w/ornate tan design at l. and r. edges on back. Sign. 3. Arms Type A at r. on back. Replacement notes: Serial # prefix *ZZ*.

		VG	VF	UNC
36	**1 Birr** L.EE1969 (1987). Black and green on light brown and green underprint. Like #30.	.25	1.00	2.50
37	**5 Birr** L.EE1969 (1987). Black and brown-orange on multicolor underprint. Like #31.	.75	2.50	6.00
38	**10 Birr** L.EE1969 (1987). Brown-violet and red on multicolor underprint. Like #32.	1.00	3.50	10.00
39	**50 Birr** L.EE1969 (1987). Blue-black and dark brown on lilac and multicolor underprint. Like #33.	7.50	17.50	40.00
40	**100 Birr** L.EE1969 (1976). Purple, violet and dark brown on multicolor underprint. Like #34 but with flowers and dark silvered shield at right.	15.00	35.00	70.00

Federal Democratic Republic

National Bank of Ethiopia

1991 ND Issue

Law EE Masharam 1969 (Sept. 1976 AD).

#41-45 like #36-40 but w/new arms Type B, C or D at r. on back.

		VG	VF	UNC
41	**1 Birr** L.EE1969 (1991). Dark green on light brown and green underprint. Like #36. Arms Type D.			
	a. Signature 3 with title in Amharic script. Serial # prefix larger sans-serif letters.	.25	.75	1.50
	b. Signature 4 with title: *GOVERNOR* and also in Amharic script.	.20	.75	1.50
	c. As b. but with serial # prefix smaller serif letters.	.25	.75	2.00

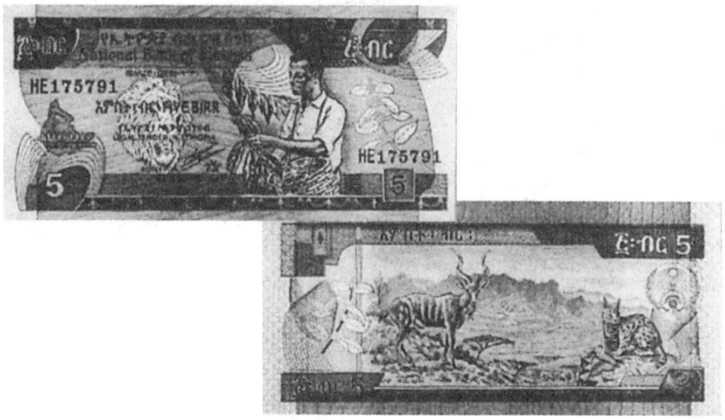

		VG	VF	UNC
42	**5 Birr** L.EE1969 (1991). Black and brown-orange on multicolor underprint. Like #37.			
	a. Sign 3 with title in Amharic script. Arms Type B.	.50	2.00	4.50
	b. Signature 4 with title *GOVERNOR* and also in Amharic script. Arms Type C.	.50	2.00	4.00
	c. As b. Arms Type D. Reported not confirmed.	—	—	—

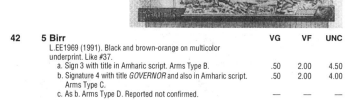

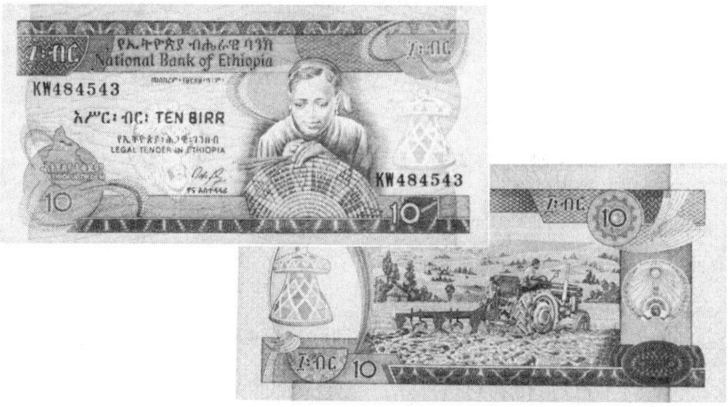

		VG	VF	UNC
43	**10 Birr** L.EE1969 (1991). Brown-violet and red on multicolor underprint. Like #38. Arms Type D.			
	a. Signature 3 with title in Amharic script.	.75	3.75	7.50
	b. Signature 4 with title: *GOVERNOR* and also in Amharic script.	.75	3.00	6.00

		VG	VF	UNC
44	**50 Birr** L.EE1969 (1991). Blue-black and dark brown on lilac and multicolor underprint. Like #39.			
	a. Signature 3 with title in Amharic script. Arms Type B.	5.00	20.00	40.00
	b. Signature 4 with title: *GOVERNOR* and also in Amharic script. Arms Type C.	5.00	17.50	35.00
	c. As b. Arms Type D.	4.00	15.00	30.00

45 **100 Birr** | VG | VF | UNC

L.EE1969 (1991). Purple, violet and dark brown on multicolor underprint. Like #40. Arms Type D.

	VG	VF	UNC
a. Signature 3 with title in Amharic script.	8.00	25.00	50.00
b. Signature 4 with title: *GOVERNOR* and also in Amharic script.	7.00	22.50	45.00

1997/EE1989 Issue

#46-48 similar to #41-43 but w/latent image (map of Ethiopia) w/value at l. W/o arms on back. Sign. 5; 6.

46 **1 Birr**

1997/EE1989; 2000/EE1992. Black on multicolor underprint. Similar to #41.

	VG	VF	UNC
a. 1997/EE 1989. signature 5.	FV	FV	.75
b. 2000/EE 1992. signature 6.	FV	FV	.75
c. 2003/EE 1995. signature 6.	FV	FV	.75

#47-50 w/segmented foil over security thread.

47 **5 Birr**

1997/EE1989; 2000/EE1992. Dark blue on multicolor underprint. Similar to #42.

	VG	VF	UNC
a. 1997/EE1989. signature 5.	FV	FV	3.00
b. 2000/EE1992. signature 6.	FV	FV	2.50
c. 2003/EE 1995. signature 6.	FV	FV	2.50

48 **10 Birr**

1997/EE1989; 2000/EE1992. Deep brown, red and green on multicolor underprint. Similar to #43.

	VG	VF	UNC
a. 1997/EE1989. signature5.	FV	FV	4.00
b. 2000/EE1992. signature 6.	FV	FV	3.00
c. 2003/EE 1995. signature 6.	FV	FV	3.00

49 **50 Birr**

1997/EE1989; 2000/EE1992. Tan and orange-brown on multicolor underprint. Farmer plowing with oxen at center. Back similar to #33.

	VG	VF	UNC
a. 1997/EE1989. signature 5.	FV	FV	15.00
b. 2000/EE1992. signature 6.	FV	FV	12.50
c. 2003/EE1995. signature 6.	FV	FV	10.00

50 **100 Birr**

1997/EE1989; 2000/EE1992. Deep blue-green, olive-green and dark green on multicolor underprint. Face like #49. Back similar to #34.

	VG	VF	UNC
a. 1997/EE1989. signature 5.	FV	FV	30.00
b. 2000/EE1992. signature 6.	FV	FV	27.50

2003/EE1997; 2004/EE1999 Issue

#51-52 increased security features.

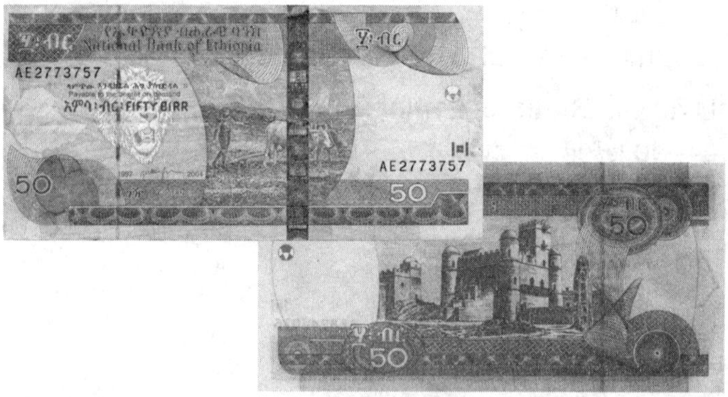

51 **50 Birr**

2004/EE 1997. Tan and orange-brown on multicolor underprint. Farmer plowing with oxen at center.

	VG	VF	UNC
	FV	FV	10.00

52 **100 Birr**

	VG	VF	UNC
2003/EE1995; 2004/EE1997. Deep blue-green, olive-green and dark green on multicolor underprint.	FV	FV	22.50

EUROPEAN UNION

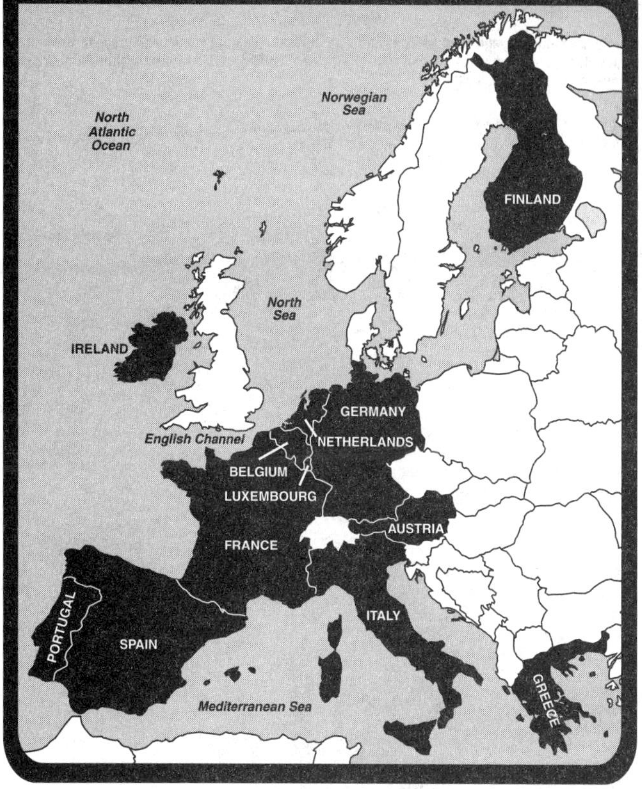

The Treaty of Rome (1958) declared a common European market as a European objective with the aim of increasing economic prosperity and contributing to an ever closer union among the peoples of Europe.

The Single European Act (1986) and the Treaty on European Union (1992) have built on this, introducing the Economic and Monetary Union and laying the foundations for the single currency.

In January 1999 the exchange rate was irrevocably set for the original participating countries. These were: Austria, Belgium, Finland, France, Germany, Ireland, Italy, Luxembourg, Netherlands, Portugal and Spain. Greece became a participating member in January 2001.

Denmark, Sweden and the United Kingdom, although members of the European Union, decided not to participate in the single currency at its inception. The currency was introduced on January 1, 2002.

The French overseas departments: French Guiana, Guadeloupe, Martinique; these dependencies: Saint Martin, Saint Barthélemy; and territories: Saint Pierre et Miquelon and Mayotte all use the Euro Currency, and are depicted on the map section on the notes along with Réunion and the Canary Islands.

MONETARY SYSTEM:

1 Euro = 100 Cent

Central Bank	Serial # Prefix	Printer Code Letters (on face)	Printer
Sweden	K (reserved)	A	Bank of England Printing Works
Finland	L	C	AB Tumba Bruk, Sweden
Portugal	M	D	Setec Oy, Finland
Austria	N	E	F.C. Oberthur, France
Netherlands	P	F	Oesterreichische Nationalbank
Luxembourg	R (reserved)	G	John. Enschede Security Printing
Italy	S	H	Thomas De La Rue, Great Britian
Ireland	T	J	Banca d'Italia
France	U	K	Central Bank of Ireland
Spain	V	L	Banque de France
Denmark	W (reserved)	M	Fabrica Nacional de Moneda y Timbre
Germany	X	N	Bank of Greece
Greece	Y	P	Gieseck & Devrient, Germany
Belgium	Z	R	Bundesdruckerei, Germany
		S	Danmarks Nationalbank
		T	Banque Nationale de Belgique

NOTICE

Readers with unlisted dates, signature varieties, etc. are invited to submit photocopies of their notes to: Standard Catalog of World Paper Money, 700 East State St. Iola, WI 54990-0001, E-Mail: george.cuhaj@fwpubs.com.

EUROPEAN UNION

EUROPEAN CENTRAL BANK

2002 ISSUE

#1-7 various windows, arches and gateways on face. Bridges, map of Europe and European Union flag on back. The theme of the issue is "the ages and styles of Europe," and a differnt architectural era is portraied on each note. 2 Sign. var.

1	5 Euro	VG	VF	UNC
	2002. Gray and multicolor. Classical architecture.			
	l. Serial # prefix *L.*	FV	FV	14.00
	m. Serial # prefix *M.*	FV	FV	11.00
	n. Serial # prefix *N.*	FV	FV	10.00
	p. Serial # prefix *P.*	FV	FV	10.00
	s. Serial # prefix *S.*	FV	FV	10.00
	t. Serial # prefix *T.*	FV	FV	11.00
	u. Serial # prefix *U.*	FV	FV	10.00
	v. Serial # prefix *V.*	FV	FV	11.00
	x. Serial # prefix *X.*	FV	FV	10.00
	y. Serial # prefix *Y.*	FV	FV	10.00
	z. Serial # prefix *Z.*	FV	FV	11.00

2	10 Euro	VG	VF	UNC
	2002. Red and multicolor. Romanesque architecture.			
	l. Serial # prefix *L.*	FV	FV	25.00
	m. Serial # prefix *M.*	FV	FV	22.50
	n. Serial # prefix *N.*	FV	FV	20.00
	p. Serial # prefix *P.*	FV	FV	21.50
	s. Serial # prefix *S.*	FV	FV	20.00
	t. Serial # prefix *T.*	FV	FV	20.00
	u. Serial # prefix *U.*	FV	FV	20.00
	v. Serial # prefix *V.*	FV	FV	21.50
	x. Serial # prefix *X.*	FV	FV	20.00
	y. Serial # prefix *Y.*	FV	FV	20.00
	z. Serial # prefix *Z.*	FV	FV	20.00

3	20 Euro	VG	VF	UNC
	2002. Blue and multicolor. Gothic architecture.			
	l. Serial # prefix *L.*	FV	FV	45.00
	m. Serial # prefix *M.*	FV	FV	42.50
	n. Serial # prefix *N.*	FV	FV	37.50
	p. Serial # prefix *P.*	FV	FV	37.50
	s. Serial # prefix *S.*	FV	FV	37.50

3	20 Euro	VG	VF	UNC
	t. Serial # prefix *T.*	FV	FV	37.50
	u. Serial # prefix *U.*	FV	FV	42.50
	v. Serial # prefix *V.*	FV	FV	37.50
	x. Serial # prefix *X.*	FV	FV	37.50
	y. Serial # prefix *Y.*	FV	FV	37.50
	z. Serial # prefix *Z.*	FV	FV	37.50

4	50 Euro	VG	VF	UNC
	2002. Orange and multicolor. Renaissance architecture.			
	l. Serial # prefix *L.*	FV	FV	100.
	m. Serial # prefix *M.*	FV	FV	95.00
	n. Serial # prefix *N.*	FV	FV	90.00
	p. Serial # prefix *P.*	FV	FV	90.00
	s. Serial # prefix *S.*	FV	FV	90.00
	t. Serial # prefix *T.*	FV	FV	90.00
	u. Serial # prefix *U.*	FV	FV	90.00
	v. Serial # prefix *V.*	FV	FV	100.
	x. Serial # prefix *X.*	FV	FV	90.00
	y. Serial # prefix *Y.*	FV	FV	90.00
	z. Serial # prefix *Z.*	FV	FV	90.00

5	100 Euro	VG	VF	UNC
	2002. Green and multicolor. Baroque and Rococo architecture.			
	l. Serial # prefix *L.*	FV	FV	185.
	m. Serial # prefix *M.*	FV	FV	180.
	n. Serial # prefix *N.*	FV	FV	175.
	p. Serial # prefix *P.*	FV	FV	175.
	s. Serial # prefix *S.*	FV	FV	175.
	t. Serial # prefix *T.*	FV	FV	175.
	u. Serial # prefix *U.*	FV	FV	175.
	v. Serial # prefix *V.*	FV	FV	180.
	x. Serial # prefix *X.*	FV	FV	175.
	y. Serial # prefix *Y.*	FV	FV	175.
	z. Serial # prefix *Z.*	FV	FV	175.

6	200 Euro	VG	VF	UNC
	2002. Yellow-brown and multicolor. Iron and glass architecture.			
	l. Serial # prefix *L*.	FV	FV	360.
	n. Serial # prefix *N*.	FV	FV	350.
	p. Serial # prefix *P*.	FV	FV	335.
	s. Serial # prefix *S*.	FV	FV	335.
	t. Serial # prefix *T*.	FV	FV	335.
	u. Serial # prefix *U*.	FV	FV	335.
	v. Serial # prefix *V*.	FV	FV	350.
	x. Serial # prefix *X*.	FV	FV	335.
	y. Serial # prefix *Y*.	FV	FV	335.
	z. Serial # prefix *Z*.	FV	FV	335.

7	500 Euro	VG	VF	UNC
	2002. Purple and multicolor. Modern 20th century architecture.			
	l. Serial # prefix *L*.	FV	FV	900.
	n. Serial # prefix *N*.	FV	FV	875.
	p. Serial # prefix *P*.	FV	FV	850.
	s. Serial # prefix *S*.	FV	FV	850.
	t. Serial # prefix *T*.	FV	FV	850.
	u. Serial # prefix *U*.	FV	FV	850.
	v. Serial # prefix *V*.	FV	FV	875.
	x. Serial # prefix *X*.	FV	FV	850.
	y. Serial # prefix *Y*.	FV	FV	850.
	z. Serial # prefix *Z*.	FV	FV	850.

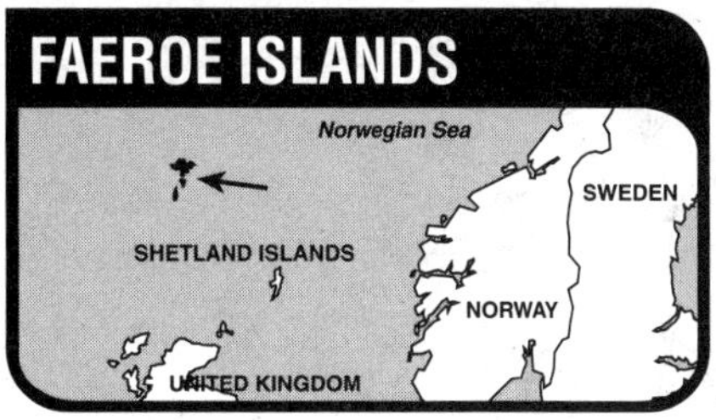

The Faroes, a self-governing community within the kingdom of Denmark, are situated in the North Atlantic between Iceland and the Shetland Islands. The 17 inhabited islets and reefs have an area of 540 sq. mi. (1,399 sq. km.) and a population of 43,678. Capital: Thorshavn. The principal industries are fishing and grazing. Fish and fish products are exported.

While it is thought that Irish hermits lived on the islands in the 7th and 8th centuries, the present inhabitants are descended from the 6th century Norse settlers. The Faroes became a Norwegian fief in 1035 and became Danish in 1380 when Norway and Denmark were united. They have ever since remained in Danish possession and were granted self-government (except for an appointed governor-general) with their own legislature, executive and flag in 1948.

The islands were occupied by British troops during World War II, while the Germans occupied Denmark.

RULERS:

Danish

MONETARY SYSTEM:

1 Króne = 100 Øre

DANISH ADMINISTRATION

FØROYAR

1964-74 ISSUE

#16-18 have coded year dates in the l. series # (the 2 middle digits). Wmk: Anchor chain. Replacement notes: Serial # suffix *OJ; OK*.

16	10 Krónur	VG	VF	UNC
	L.1949 (19)74. Green. Shield with ram at left. Rural scene at center on back. Signature L. Groth and A. P. Dam.			
	a. Issued note.	FV	FV	8.00
	s. Specimen.	—	—	—

17	50 Krónur	VG	VF	UNC
	L.1949 (19)67. Black on light blue and blue-green underprint. Portrait Nölsoyar Pall at left. Back blue on green underprint. Drawing of homes and church across center. Signature M. Wahl and P. M. Dam.	12.50	25.00	65.00

18	100 Krónur	VG	VF	UNC
	L.1949 (19)64; 69; 72; 75. Black on pink and gold underprint. Portrait V. U. Hammershaimb at left. Back blue on tan underprint. Drawing of house and mountains.			
	a. (19)75. signature L. Groth and A.P. Dam.	20.00	30.00	80.00
	r1. (19)64. signature M. Wahl and H. Djurhuus. Suffix OJ.	27.50	75.00	150.
	r2. (19)64. As r1 but suffix OK.	50.00	175.	—
	r3. (19)69. signature M. Wahl and H. Djurhuus. Suffix OJ.	25.00	50.00	130.
	r4. (19)72. signature as r3. Suffix OJ.	22.50	45.00	125.
	r5. (19)75. signature L. Groth and A.P. Dam. Suffix OJ.	20.00	30.00	80.00
	s. Specimen. As a.	—	—	—

1978-86 ISSUE

#19-23 have coded year dates in the l. series # (the 2 middle digits). Wmk: Anchor chain. Replacement notes: Serial # suffix *OJ; OK.*

19	20 Krónur	VG	VF	UNC
	L.1949 (19)86; 88. Deep purple on pink and aqua underprint. Man with ice tool at right. Back red and black; drawing of animals at center.			
	a. Signature N. Bentsen and A. P. Dam. (19)86.	FV	FV	12.00
	b. Signature B. Klinte and A. P. Dam. (19)88.	FV	FV	16.00

20	50 Krónur	VG	VF	UNC
	L.1949 (19)78-94. Black on light blue and gray underprint. Similar to #17 but reduced size. 140 x 72mm. Back black on gray underprint. Watermark: Chain links.			
	a. Signature L. Groth and A. P. Dam. (19)78.	FV	FV	50.00
	b. Signature as a. (19)87.	FV	25.00	90.00
	c. Signature N. Bentsen and A. P. Dam. (19)87.	FV	FV	25.00
	d. Signature B. Klinte and E. Joensen (19)94.	FV	FV	20.00
	s. Specimen. As a.	—	—	—

21	100 Krónur	VG	VF	UNC
	L.1949 (19)78-94. Black on tan underprint. Similar to #18 but reduced size. Back black and green on ochre underprint. Watermark: Chain links.			
	a. Signature L. Groth and A. P. Dam. (19)78.	FV	FV	80.00
	b. Signature N. Bentsen and P. Ellefsen. (19)83.	FV	FV	75.00
	c. Signature N. Bentsen and A. P. Dam. (19)87.	FV	FV	75.00
	d. Signature B. Klinte and A. P. Dam. (19)88.	FV	FV	65.00
	e. Signature B. Klinte and J. Sun Stein. (19)90.	FV	FV	50.00
	f. Signature B. Klinte and E. Joensen. (19)94.	FV	FV	40.00
	s. Specimen. As a.	—	—	—

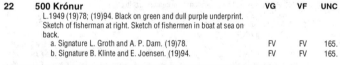

22	500 Krónur	VG	VF	UNC
	L.1949 (19)78; (19)94. Black on green and dull purple underprint. Sketch of fisherman at right. Sketch of fishermen in boat at sea on back.			
	a. Signature L. Groth and A. P. Dam. (19)78.	FV	FV	165.
	b. Signature B. Klinte and E. Joensen. (19)94.	FV	FV	165.

23	1000 Krónur	VG	VF	UNC
	L.1949 (19)78; 83; 87; 89; 94. Blue-green, black and green. J. H. O. Djurhuus at left. Street scene sketch on back.			

		VG	VF	UNC
23	**1000 Krónur**			
	a. Signature L. Groth and A. P. Dam. (19)78.	FV	FV	400.
	b. Signature N. Bentsen and P. Ellefsen. (19)83.	FV	FV	350.
	c. Signature N. Bentsen and A. P. Dam. (19)87.	FV	FV	350.
	d. Signature B. Klinte and A. P. Dam. (19)89.	FV	FV	325.
	e. Signature B. Klinte and M. Petersen. (19)94.	FV	FV	300.

2001-2005 ISSUE

		VG	VF	UNC
24	**50 Krónur** (20)01. Black on gray underprint. Ram's horn at right. Hillside in Sumba on back. Lilac segmented security strip at right.	FV	FV	14.00

		VG	VF	UNC
25	**100 Krónur** (20)02. Dull yellow. Fish tail at right. View from Klaksvík at back.	FV	FV	20.00

		VG	VF	UNC
26	**200 Krónur** (20)03. Dull purple. Moth at right. View from Vágum on back.	FV	FV	60.00

		VG	VF	UNC
27	**500 Krónur** (20)04. Dull green. Crab's claw at right. View from Hvannasundi on back.	FV	FV	125.
28	**1000 Krónur** (20)05. Dull red. Bird's wing at right. View from Sandoy on back.	FV	FV	225.

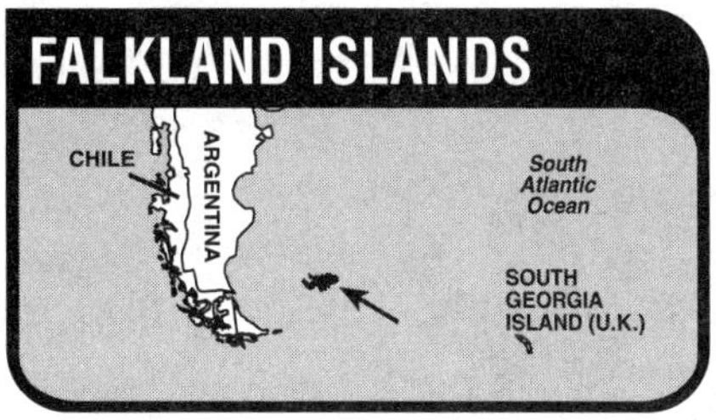

The Colony of the Falkland Islands and Dependencies, a British colony located in the South Atlantic about 500 miles northeast of Cape Horn, has an area of 4,700 sq. mi. (12,173 sq. km.) and a population of 2,564. East Falkland, West Falkland, South Georgia, and South Sandwich are the largest of the 200 islands. Capital: Port Stanley. Fishing and sheep are the industry. Wool, whale oil, and seal oil are exported.

The Falklands were discovered by British navigator John Davis (Davys) in 1592, and named by Capt. John Strong - for Viscount Falkland, treasurer of the British navy - in 1690. French navigator Louis De Bougainville established the first settlement, at Port Louis, in 1764. The following year Capt. John Byron claimed the islands for Britain and left a small party at Saunders Island. Spain later forced the French and British to abandon their settlements but did not implement its claim to the islands. In 1829 the Republic of Buenos Aires, which claimed to have inherited the Spanish rights, sent Louis Vernet to develop a colony on the islands. In 1831 he seized three American sailing vessels, whereupon the men of the corvette *U.S.S. Lexington,* destroyed his settlement and proclaimed the Falklands to be "free of all governance." Britain, which had never renounced its claim, re-established its settlement in 1833.

The Islands were important in the days of sail and steam shipping as a location to re-stock fresh food and fuel, and make repairs after trips around Cape Horn. Argentine forces In 1990 the Argentine congrees declared the Falklands and other islands in the region part of the province of Tierra del Fuego. occupied the islands in April 1982, and after a short military campaign Britain regained control in June.

RULERS:

British

MONETARY SYSTEM:

1 Shilling = 12 Pence
1 Pound = 20 Shillings to 1966
1 Pound = 100 Pence, 1966-

BRITISH ADMINISTRATION

GOVERNMENT

1960-67 ISSUE

#7-9 portr. Qn. Elizabeth II at r. Printer: TDLR.

		VG	VF	UNC
7	**10 Shillings** 10.4.1960. Brown on gray underprint. Queen Elizabeth II at right. Printer: TDLR.			
	a. Issued note.	35.00	150.	500.
	s. Specimen.	—	—	—

		VG	VF	UNC
8	**1 Pound** 1967-82. Blue on gray-green and lilac underprint.			
	a. 2.1.1967.	6.00	25.00	100.
	b. 20.2.1974.	5.00	18.00	70.00
	c. 1.12.1977.	7.50	30.00	125.
	d. 1.1.1982.	5.00	20.00	75.00
	e. 15.6.1982.	5.00	20.00	75.00
	s. Specimen. As a-e.	—	—	—

		VG	VF	UNC
9	**5 Pounds** 1960; 1975. Red on green underprint. Queen Elizabeth II at right. Printer: TDLR.			
	a. Sign: L. Gleadell: 10.4.1960.	25.00	100.	450.
	b. Sign: H. T. Rowlands: 30.1.1975.	20.00	85.00	375.
	s. Specimen. As a-b.	—	—	—

1969; 1975 Issue

#10 and 11 portr. Qn. Elizabeth II at r. Printer: TDLR.

		VG	VF	UNC
10	**50 Pence**			
	1969; 1974. Brown on gray underprint. Like #7.			
	a. Sign: L. Gleadell. 25.9.1969.	4.00	15.00	60.00
	b. Sign: H. T. Rowlands. 20.2.1974.	3.50	12.50	50.00
	s. Specimen. As a-b.	—	—	—

		VG	VF	UNC
11	**10 Pounds**			
	1975-82. Green on light orange and yellow-green underprint. Signature H. T. Rowlands.			
	a. 5.6.1975.	30.00	110.	475.
	b. 1.1.1982.	37.50	135.	575.
	c. 15.6.1982.	27.50	100.	450.
	s. Specimen. As a.	—	—	—

1983 Commemorative Issue

#12, 150th Anniversary of English rule, 1833-1983

		VG	VF	UNC
12	**5 Pounds**			
	14.6.1983. Red on multicolor underprint. Like #13. Commemorative legend at lower center.			
	a. Issued note.	FV	FV	37.50
	s. Specimen.	—	—	—

1984-90 Regular Issue

#13-16 Qn. Elizabeth II at r. King penguins and shield at l., seals at r. Governor's home and church on back.

		VG	VF	UNC
13	**1 Pound**			
	1.10.1984. Blue on brown and yellow underprint. Like #12	FV	12.00	45.00

		VG	VF	UNC
14	**10 Pounds**			
	1.9.1986. Green on blue and multicolor underprint. Like #12.			
	a. Issued note.	FV	FV	60.00
	s. Specimen.	—	—	—

		VG	VF	UNC
15	**20 Pounds**			
	1.10.1984. Brown on multicolor underprint. Like #12.			
	a. Issued note.	FV	55.00	110.
	s. Specimen.	—	—	—

		VG	VF	UNC
16	**50 Pounds**			
	1.7.1990. Blue on multicolor underprint. Like #12.			
	a. Issued note.	FV	FV	205.
	s. Specimen.	—	—	—

2005 Issue

		VG	VF	UNC
17	**5 Pounds**			
	14.6.2005. Red on multicolor underprint. Seals at right, island map at center, Queen Elizabelth II at lright center, king penguins at left. Three signatures. Government House and Christ Church Cathedral in Stanley on back.	FV	FV	32.50

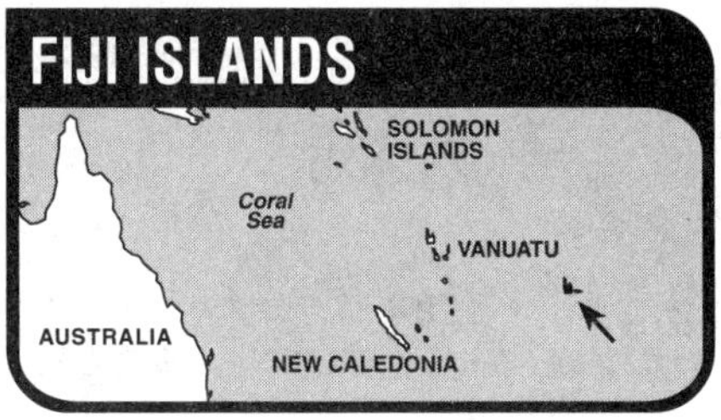

The republic of Fiji is an independent member of the British Commonwealth. It consists of about 320 islands located in the southwestern Pacific 1,100 miles (1,770 km.) north of New Zealand. The islands have a combined area of 7,056 sq. mi. (18,274 sq. km.) and a population of 848,000. Capital: Suva, on the island of Viti Levu. Fiji's economy is based on agriculture and mining. Sugar, coconut products, manganese and gold are exported.

The first European to sign Fiji was the Dutch navigator Abel Tasman in 1643. The island was visited by British naval captain James Cook in 1774. The first complete survey of the island was conducted by the United States in 1840. Settlement by missionaries from Tonga and traders attracted by the sandalwood trade began in 1835. Following a lengthy period of intertribal warfare, the islands were unconditionally and voluntarily ceded to Great Britain in 1874 by King Cakobau. The trading center was Levuka on the island of Ovalau which was also the capital under the British from 1874-82. Fiji became an independent nation on Oct 10, 1970, the 96th anniversary of the cession of the islands to Queen Victoria.

RULERS:

British, 1874-

MONETARY SYSTEM:

1 Shilling = 12 Pence
1 Pound = 20 Shillings to 1969
1 Dollar = 100 Cents, 1969-

REPLACEMENT NOTES:

#37-72: Z/1 prefix.

BRITISH ADMINISTRATION

GOVERNMENT

1954-57 ISSUE

#51-57 arms at upper ctr., portr. Qn. Elizabeth II at r. Wmk: Fijian youth's bust. Printer: BWC.

51 5 Shillings

1957-65. Green and blue on lilac and green underprint. Arms at upper center. Portrait Queen Elizabeth II at right. Watermark: Fijian youth's bust. Printer: BWC.

	VG	VF	UNC
a. 1.6.1957. Signature Davidson, Griffiths, Marais.	10.00	75.00	350.
b. 28.4.1961. Signature Bevington, Griffiths, Cruickshank.	10.00	75.00	350.
c. 1.12.1962. Signature Ritchie, Griffiths, Cruickshank.	8.00	60.00	325.
d. 1.9.1964. Signature Ritchie, Griffiths, Cruickshank.	7.50	50.00	275.
e. 1.10.1965. Signature Ritchie, Griffiths, Cruickshank.	7.50	40.00	225.
s. Specimen. Various dates.	—	—	450.
cs. Commercial (false color) specimen.	—	—	350.

52 10 Shillings

1957-65. Brown on lilac and green underprint. Arms at upper center. Portrait Queen Elizabeth II at right. Watermark: Fijian youth's bust. Printer: BWC.

	VG	VF	UNC
a. 1.6.1957. Signature Davidson, Griffiths, Marais.	17.50	100.	500.
b. 28.4.1961. Signature Bevington, Griffiths, Cruickshank.	17.50	120.	550.
c. 1.12.1962. Signature Ritchie, Griffiths, Cruickshank.	10.00	80.00	450.
d. 1.9.1964. Signature Ritchie, Griffiths, Cruickshank.	12.50	125.	600.
e. 1.10.1965. Signature Ritchie, Griffiths, Cruickshank.	10.00	95.00	600.
s. Specimen. Various dates.	—	—	650.
cs. Commercial (false color) specimen.	—	—	500.

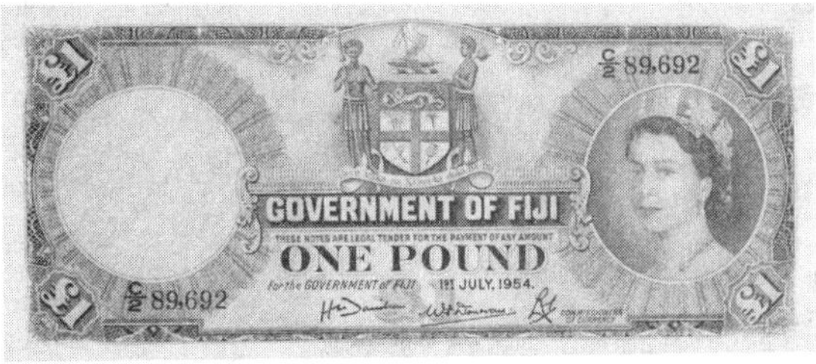

53 1 Pound

1954-67. Green on yellow and blue underprint. Arms at upper center. Portrait Queen Elizabeth II at right. Watermark: Fijian youth's bust. Printer: BWC.

	VG	VF	UNC
a. 1.7.1954. Signature Davidson, Donovan, Davis.	20.00	130.	625.
b. 1.6.1957. Signature Davidson, Griffiths, Marais.	25.00	145.	725.
c. 1.9.1959. Signature Ritchie, Griffiths, Cruickshank.	20.00	130.	625.
d. 1.12.1961. Signature ritchie, Griffiths, Cruickshank.	27.50	145.	725.
e. 1.12.1962. Signature Ritchie, Griffiths, Cruickshank.	25.00	145.	700.
f. 20.1.1964. Signature Ritchie, Griffiths, Cruickshank.	22.50	140.	625.
g. 1.5.1965. Signature Ritchie, Griffiths, Cruickshank.	20.00	130.	600.
h. 1.12.1965. Signature Ritchie, Griffiths, Cruickshank.	25.00	135.	575.
i. 1.1.1967. Signature Ritchie, Griffiths, Cruickshank.	17.50	125.	575.
s. Specimen. Various dates.	—	—	850.
cs. Commercial (false color) specimen.	—	—	700.

54 5 Pounds

1954-67. Purple on light orange and green underprint. Arms at upper center. Portrait Queen Elizabeth II at right. Watermark: Fijian youth's bust. Printer: BWC.

	VG	VF	UNC
a. 1.7.1954. Signature Davidson, Donovan, Davis.	125.	750.	1500.
b. 1.9.1959. Signature Bevington, Griffiths, Marais.	125.	750.	1500.
c. 1.10.1960. Signature Bevington, Griffiths, Cruickshank.	95.00	750.	1500.
d. 1.12.1962. Signature Ritchie, Griffiths, Cruickshank.	85.00	725.	1250.
e. 20.1.1964. Signature Ritchie, Griffiths, Cruickshank.	85.00	700.	1100.
f. 1.1.1967. Signature Ritchie, Griffiths, Cruickshank.	80.00	700.	1100.
s. Specimen. Various dates.	—	—	1000.
cs. Commercial (false color) specimen.	—	—	850.

55 10 Pounds VG VF UNC

1954-64. Blue on blue, orange and green underprint. Arms at upper center. Portrait Queen Elizabeth II at right. Watermark: Fijian youth's bust. Printer: BWC.

		VG	VF	UNC
55	**10 Pounds**			
	a. 1.7.1954. Signature Davidson, Donovan, Davis.	250.	1250.	2000.
	b. 1.9.1959. Signature Bevington, Griffiths, Marais.	250.	1250.	2000.
	c. 1.10.1960. Signature Bevington, Griffiths, Cruickshank.	180.	1100.	2000.
	d. 20.1.1964. Signature Ritchie, Griffiths, Cruickshank.	170.	1000.	1850.
	e. 11.6.1964. Signature Ritchie, Griffiths, Cruickshank.	160.	900.	1750.
	f. 1.5.1965. Not released. Signature Ritchie, Griffiths, Cruickshank.	—	—	—
	s. Specimen. Various dates.	—	—	1100.
	cs. Commercial (false color) specimen.	—	—	950.
56	**20 Pounds**			
	1.1.1953. Black and purple on purple underprint. Arms at upper center. Portrait Queen Elizabeth II at right. Watermark: Fijian youth's bust. Printer: BWC.			
	a. 1.1.1953. Signature Davidson, Donovan, Smith.	950.	1250.	4000.
	s. Specimen.	—	—	3500.
	cs. Commercial (false color) specimen.	—	—	1200.

		VG	VF	UNC
57	**20 Pounds**			
	1.7.1954; 1.11.1958. Red on red and green underprint. Arms at upper center. Portrait Queen Elizabeth II at right. Watermark: Fijian youth's bust. Printer: BWC.			
	a. 1.7.1954. Signature Davidson, Donovan, Davis.	750.	1250.	3000.
	b. 1.11.1958. Signature Bevington, Griffiths, Marais.	600.	1000.	2500.
	s. Specimen.	—	—	2000.
	cs. Commercial (false color) specimen.	—	—	1000.

1969 Currency Board Issue

#58-63 Qn. Elizabeth at r. Arms and heading: *GOVERNMENT OF FIJI* at upper ctr. Sign. Ritchie and Barnes. Wmk: Profile Fijian head. Printer: TDLR.

		VG	VF	UNC
58	**50 Cents**			
	ND (1968). Blue-green on multicolor underprint. Thatched bure (house) and coconut palms on back.			
	a. Issued note.	1.00	5.00	30.00
	s. Specimen.	—	—	200.

		VG	VF	UNC
59	**1 Dollar**			
	ND (1968). Brown on brown, green and pink underprint. Yanuca beach scene in Yasewas on back.			
	a. Issued note.	2.00	10.00	85.00
	s. Specimen.	—	—	250.

#52-55 w/o pictorial scenes on back.

		VG	VF	UNC
60	**2 Dollars**			
	ND (1968). Green on brown and and light blue underprint. Geometric lathe pattern on back.			
	a. Issued note.	4.00	25.00	150.
	s. Specimen.	—	—	300.

		VG	VF	UNC
61	**5 Dollars**			
	ND (1968). Orange on purple and gray underprint. Geometric lathe pattern on back.			
	a. Issued note.	7.00	40.00	350.
	s. Specimen.	—	—	400.

		VG	VF	UNC
62	**10 Dollars**			
	ND (1968). Purple on orange and purple underprint. Geometric lathe pattern on back.			
	a. Issued note.	12.50	85.00	750.
	s. Specimen.	—	—	700.

63	20 Dollars	VG	VF	UNC
	ND (1968). Blue on light green, orange and blue underprint. Geometric lathe pattern on back.			
	a. Issued note.	25.00	125.	1000.
	s. Specimen.	—	—	1000.

1971-73 AD-INTERIM CURRENCY

#64-69 like #68-63 but w/only 1 sign. Wmk: Profile Fijian head. Printer: TDLR.

64	50 Cents	VG	VF	UNC
	ND (1971). Green on multicolor underprint. Like #58.			
	a. Signature Wesley Barrett.	1.00	5.00	35.00
	b. Signature C. A. Stinson.	1.00	3.00	30.00
	s. Specimen.	—	—	150.
	ar. As a. Replacement *Z/1* prefix.	5.00	35.00	150.
	br. As b. Replacement *Z/I* prefix.	7.50	25.00	125.

65	1 Dollar	VG	VF	UNC
	ND (1971). Brown on lilac and light green underprint. Like #59.			
	a. Signature Wesley Barrett.	1.50	20.00	100.
	b. Signature C. A. Stinson.	2.00	25.00	125.
	s. Specimen.	—	—	200.
	ar. As a. Replacement. *Z/I* prefix.	25.00	150.	550.
	br. As b. Replacement. *Z/I* prefix.	10.00	50.00	250.

66	2 Dollars	VG	VF	UNC
	ND (1971). Green on yellow and light blue underprint. Like #60.			
	a. Signature Wesley Barrett.	4.00	15.00	185.
	b. Signature C. A. Stinson. Not issued.	—	—	—
	s. Specimen.	—	—	350.
	ar. As a. Replacement. *Z/I* prefix.	15.00	100.	400.
	br. As b. Replacement. *Z/I* prefix. Not issued.	—	—	—

67	5 Dollars	VG	VF	UNC
	ND (1971). Like #61.			
	a. Signature Wesley Barrett.	6.00	40.00	400.
	b. Signature C. A. Stinson.	7.00	50.00	500.
	s. Specimen.	—	—	500.
	ar. As a. Replacement. *Z/I* prefix.	20.00	200.	850.
	br. As b. Replacement. *Z/I* prefix.	40.00	350.	1000.

68	10 Dollars	VG	VF	UNC
	ND (1971). Like #62.			
	a. Signature Wesley Barrett.	10.00	150.	550.
	b. Signature C. A. Stinson.	12.50	200.	750.
	s. Specimen.	—	—	700.
	ar. As a. Replacement. *Z/I* prefix.	60.00	325.	1000.
	br. As b. Replacement. *Z/I* prefix.	85.00	400.	1250.

69	20 Dollars	VG	VF	UNC
	ND (1971). Like #63.			
	a. Signature Wesley Barrett.		—	
	b. Signature C. A. Stinson.	30.00	125.	925.
	s. Specimen.	25.00	85.00	700.
	ar. As a. Replacement. *Z/I* prefix.	150.	300.	1500.
	br. As b. Replacement. *Z/I* prefix.		—	

CENTRAL MONETARY AUTHORITY

1974 ND ISSUE

#70-75 like #58-63 but w/heading: *FIJI* at top ctr., and issuing authority name across lower ctr. 2 sign. Wmk: Profile Fijian head. Printer: TDLR.

70	50 Cents	VG	VF	UNC
	ND (1974). Like #58. Signature D. J. Barnes and right. J. A. Earland. (Not issued.)			
	s. Specimen.	—	—	—

71	1 Dollar	VG	VF	UNC
	ND (1974). Like #59.			
	a. Signature D. J. Barnes and R. J. Earland.	1.00	5.00	17.50
	b. Signature D. J. Barnes and H. J. Tomkins.	1.00	4.00	17.50
	s. As a, b. Specimen.	—	—	100.
	ar. As a. Replacement. *Z/I* prefix.	2.50	9.00	30.00
	br. As b. Replacement. *Z/I* prefix.	2.00	7.50	25.00

72	2 Dollars	VG	VF	UNC
	ND (1974). Like #60.			
	a. Signature D. J. Barnes and I. A. Craik.	12.50	50.00	200.
	b. Signature D. J. Barnes and R. J. Earland.	2.00	8.50	40.00
	c. Signature D. J. Barnes and H. J. Tomkins.	2.00	10.00	60.00
	s. Specimen.	—	—	175.
	ar. As a. Replacement. *Z/I* prefix.	35.00	200.	550.
	br. As b. Replacement. *Z/I* prefix.	3.00	25.00	135.
	cr. As c. Replacement. *Z/I* prefix.	2.50	15.00	95.00

73	5 Dollars	VG	VF	UNC
	ND (1974). Like #61.			
	a. Signature D. J. Barnes and I. A. Craik.	20.00	100.	550.
	b. Signature D. J. Barnes and R. J. Earland.	5.00	45.00	190.
	c. Signature D. J. Barnes and H. J. Tomkins.	6.00	85.00	250.
	s. Specimen.	—	—	500.
	ar. As a. Replacement. Z/I prefix.	85.00	350.	1000.
	br. As b. Replacement. Z/I prefix.	12.50	225.	750.
	cr. As c. Replacement. Z/I prefix.	15.00	95.00	350.

74	10 Dollars	VG	VF	UNC
	ND (1974). Like #62.			
	a. Signature D. J. Barnes and I. A. Craik.	20.00	100.	750.
	b. Signature D. J. Barnes and R. J. Earland.	8.50	35.00	300.
	c. Signature D. J. Barnes and H. J. Tomkins.	7.50	25.00	225.
	s. As a. Specimen.	—	—	—

75	20 Dollars	VG	VF	UNC
	ND (1974). Like #63.			
	a. Signature D. J. Barnes and I. A. Craik.	125.	425.	1850.
	b. Signature D. J. Barnes and R. J. Earland.	20.00	65.00	450.
	c. Signature D. J. Barnes and H. J. Tomkins.	20.00	85.00	500.
	s. Specimen.	—	—	650.
	ar. As a. Replacement. Z/I prefix.	375.	850.	2500.
	br. As b. Replacement. Z/I prefix.	65.00	225.	900.
	cr. As c. Replacement. Z/I prefix.	95.00	325.	1000.

1980 ND Issue

#76-80 Qn. Elizabeth II at r. ctr., arms at ctr., artifact at r. Denomination figures 8mm high. Wmk: Profile Fijian head. Sign. D. J. Barnes and H. J. Tomkins. Printer: TDLR.

76	1 Dollar	VG	VF	UNC
	ND (1980). Brown on multicolor underprint. Open air Suva markets at center on back.			
	a. Issued note.	FV	4.00	15.00
	r. As a. Replacement. Z/I prefix.	6.00	12.50	60.00
	s. Specimen.	—	—	350.

77	2 Dollars	VG	VF	UNC
	ND (1980). Green on multicolor underprint. Back khaki, sugar cane harvest at center on back.			
	a. Issued note.	FV	8.00	20.00
	r. As a. Replacement. Z/I prefix.	7.50	18.50	90.00
	s. Specimen.	—	—	400.

78	5 Dollars	VG	VF	UNC
	ND (1980). Orange on multicolor underprint. Circle of fishermen with net at center on back.			
	a. Issued note.	FV	15.00	37.50
	r. As a. Replacement. Z/I prefix.	10.00	35.00	150.
	s. Specimen.	—	—	450.

79	10 Dollars	VG	VF	UNC
	ND (1980). Purple on multicolor underprint. Ceremonial tribal dance scene at center on back.			
	a. Issued note.	FV	22.50	125.
	r. As a. Replacement. Z/I prefix.	12.50	75.00	225.
	s. Specimen.	—	—	550.

80	20 Dollars	VG	VF	UNC
	ND (1980). Blue on multicolor underprint. Fijian bure (house) at center on back.			
	a. Issued note.	20.00	40.00	250.
	r. As a. Replacement. Z/I prefix.	15.00	100.	500.
	s. Specimen.	—	—	650.

1983-86 ND ISSUE

#81-85 like #76-80. Backs retouched and lithographed. Denomination figures 9.5mm high. Wmk: Profile Fijian head. Sign. D. J. Barnes and S. Siwatibau. Printer: TDLR .

81	1 Dollar	VG	VF	UNC
	ND (1983). Dark gray on multicolor underprint. Like #76.			
	a. Issued note.	FV	3.00	9.00
	r. As a. Replacement. Z/I prefix.	4.00	10.00	45.00
	s1. Specimen. Signatures punched out.	—	—	225.
	s2. Specimen. Corners punched out.	—	—	150.

82	2 Dollars	VG	VF	UNC
	ND (1983). Green on multicolor underprint. Like #77 but back green.			
	a. Issued note.	FV	7.00	15.00
	r. As a. Replacement. Z/I prefix.	5.00	18.50	85.00
	s1. Specimen. Signatures punched out.	—	—	275.
	s2. Specimen. Corners punched out.	—	—	175.

83	5 Dollars	VG	VF	UNC
	ND (1986). Brown-orange and purple on multicolor underprint. Like #78.			
	a. Issued note.	FV	10.00	35.00
	r. As a. Replacement.	8.50	30.00	125.
	s1. Specimen. Signatures punched out.	—	—	325.
	s2. Specimen. Corners punched out.	—	—	225.

84	10 Dollars	VG	VF	UNC
	ND (1986). Purple and brown on multicolor underprint. Like #79.			
	a. Issued note.	FV	15.00	50.00
	r. As a. Replacement. Z/I prefix.	12.50	50.00	185.
	s1. Specimen. Signatures punched out.	—	—	400.
	s2. Specimen. Corners punched out.	—	—	285.

85	20 Dollars	VG	VF	UNC
	ND (1986). Blue on multicolor underprint. Like #80.			
	a. Issued note.	FV	17.50	75.00
	r. As a. Replacement.	17.50	85.00	250.
	s1. Specimen.	—	—	450.
	s2. Specimen. Corners punched out.	—	—	350.

RESERVE BANK OF FIJI

1987-88 ND ISSUE

#86-88 modified portr. of Qn. Elizabeth II at r., and new banking authority. Similar to #81-2, 85. Sign. S. Siwatibau. Wmk: Profile Fijian head. No replacement notes. Printer: BWC.

86	1 Dollar	VG	VF	UNC
	ND (1987). Dark gray on multicolor underprint. Similar to #81.			
	a. Issued note.	FV	FV	4.50
	s. Specimen.	—	—	25.00

87	2 Dollars	VG	VF	UNC
	ND (1988). Green on multicolor underprint. Similar to #82.			
	a. Issued note.	FV	FV	7.00
	s. Specimen.	—	—	35.00

		VG	VF	UNC
88	**20 Dollars**			
	ND (1988). Dark blue, blue-green and black on multicolor underprint. Similar to #85.			
	a. Issued note.	FV	35.00	60.00
	s. Specimen.	—	—	95.00

1991 ND Issue

#89-92 modified portr. Qn. Elizabeth II at r. Like #81-84. Wmk: Profile Fijian head. Sign. J. Kuabuabola. Printer: TDLR. No replacement notes.

		VG	VF	UNC
89	**1 Dollar**			
	ND (1993). Dark gray on multicolor underprint. Similar to #78. Without segmented security thread.			
	a. Issued note.	FV	FV	3.50
	s. Specimen.	—	—	25.00

		VG	VF	UNC
90	**2 Dollars**			
	ND (1995). Deep green on multicolor underprint. Similar to #79.			
	a. Issued note.	FV	FV	7.00
	s. Specimen.	—	—	35.00

		VG	VF	UNC
91	**5 Dollars**			
	ND (ca.1991). Brown-orange and purple on multicolor underprint. Similar to #75.			
	a. Issued note.	FV	17.50	32.50
	s. Specimen.	—	—	55.00

		VG	VF	UNC
92	**10 Dollars**			
	ND (1989). Purple and brown on multicolor underprint. Similar to #76.			
	a. Issued note.	FV	27.50	50.00
	s. Specimen.	—	—	75.00

1992 ND Issue

#93-95 like #86-92 but vertical and horizontal serial #. single letter serial # prefix, segmented security thread. Wmk: Profile Fijian head. Sign. J. Kubuabola. Printer: TDLR.

		VG	VF	UNC
93	**5 Dollars**			
	ND (1992). Brown-orange and purple on multicolor underprint. Similar to #80.			
	a. Issued note.	FV	8.00	15.00
	s. Specimen.	—	—	50.00

		VG	VF	UNC
94	**10 Dollars**			
	ND (1992). Purple and brown on multicolor underprint. Similar to #81.			
	a. Issued note.	FV	12.50	27.50
	s. Specimen.	—	—	75.00

		VG	VF	UNC
95	**20 Dollars**			
	ND (1992). Dark blue, blue-green and black on multicolor underprint. Similar to #82.			
	a. Issued note.	FV	25.00	45.00
	s. Specimen.	—	—	100.

1992-95 ND Issue

#96-100 mature bust of Qn. Elizabeth II at r., arms at upper r. Segmented foil security thread. Wmk: Profile Fijian head. Printer: TDLR. Replacement notes: Serial # prefix *Z*.

		VG	VF	UNC
96	**2 Dollars**			
	ND (1996). Dark green, blue and olive-brown on multicolor underprint. Kaka bird (Masked Shining Parrot) at lower left. Fijian family of 5 at left. Center on back.			
	a. Single letter prefix.	FV	FV	7.50
	b. Double letter prefix. Amended security thread.	FV	FV	5.00
	r. Replacement. *Z* prefix.	FV	5.00	10.00
	s. Specimen.	—	—	30.00

97 5 Dollars	VG	VF	UNC
ND (1995). Brown-orange on violet and multicolor underprint. Bunedamu bird (White-throated Pigeon) at lower left. Aerial view Nadi International Airport at left center, ferry boat at lower center right on back.			
a. Issued note.	FV	FV	15.00
r. Replacement. *Z* prefix.	5.00	15.00	50.00
s. Specimen.	—	—	50.00

98 10 Dollars	VG	VF	UNC
ND (1996). Purple, violet and brown on multicolor underprint. Kikau bird at lower left. Children swimming at left in background, family in boat constructed of reeds with thatched roof shelter at left center on back.			
a. Single letter prefix.	FV	FV	35.00
b. Double letter prefix.	FV	FV	25.00
r. Replacement. *Z* prefix.	10.00	25.00	75.00
s. Specimen.	—	—	75.00

99 20 Dollars	VG	VF	UNC
ND (1996) Blue, purple and dark blue on multicolor underprint. Manusa bird at lower left. Parliament House at left, Reserve Bank building at center right on back.			
a. Single letter prefix. Novel numbering on l. serial # only.	FV	FV	65.00
b. Double letter prefix.	FV	FV	35.00
r. Replacement. *Z* prefix.	FV	60.00	100.
s. Specimen.	—	—	150.

NOTICE

Readers with unlisted dates, signature varieties, etc. are invited to submit photocopies of their notes to: Standard Catalog of World Paper Money, 700 East State St. Iola, WI 54990-0001, E-Mail: george.cuhaj@fwpubs.com.

100 50 Dollars	VG	VF	UNC
ND (1996). Black, red, orange and violet on multicolor underprint. Kaka bird at lower left. Ascending size vertical serial # at left. Flag raising ceremony at left, signing of Deed of Cession over Cession Stone at center on back.			
a. Novel numbering on l. serial only.	FV	FV	75.00
r. Replacement. *Z* prefix.	FV	60.00	200.
s. Specimen.	—	—	150.

1998 ND Issue

101 5 Dollars	VG	VF	UNC
ND (1998). Brown and orange on multicolor underprint. Like #97.			
a. Signature Kubuabola.	FV	FV	12.50
b. Signature Narube.	FV	FV	15.00
s1. As a. Specimen.	—	—	50.00
s2. As b. Specimen.	—	—	65.00
ar. As a. Replacement. *Z* prefix.	FV	10.00	20.00
br. As b. Replacement. *Z* prefix.	FV	10.00	20.00

2000 Commemorative Issue

#102-103 arms at upper r. *Y2K* at ctr. Segmented foil security thread. Wmk: Profile Fijian head.

102 2 Dollars	VG	VF	UNC
2000. Green and blue on multicolor underprint. Kaka bird at left, Sir Penaia Ganilau at right. Group portrait of islanders and turtle on back.			
a. Issued note.	FV	FV	4.00
b. Uncut pair.	FV	FV	7.50
c. Uncut sheet of 20.	FV	FV	75.00
s. Specimen.	—	—	20.00

103 2000 Dollars
2000. Multicolor. Sir Kamisese Mara at right. Earth, rising sun; island map on back.

	VG	VF	UNC
a. Isused note.	FV	FV	1500.
s. Specimen, individually numbered.	—	—	450.

2002 ND Issue

#104-108 similar to #104-106 but with additional security features. Ascending size serial #. Sign. Savenaca Narube.

104 2 Dollars
ND (2002). Dark green, blue and olive-brown on multicolor underprint. Similar to #96.

	VG	VF	UNC
a. Double letter prefix.	FV	FV	3.00
r. Replacement. *Z* prefix.	3.00	6.00	10.00
s. Specimen.	—	—	20.00

105 5 Dollars
ND (2002). Brown-orange on violet and multicolor underprint. Similar to #97.

	VG	VF	UNC
a. Single letter prefix.	FV	FV	8.00
b. Double letter prefix.	FV	FV	8.00
r. Replacement. *Z* prefix.	FV	7.00	15.00
s. Specimen.	—	—	45.00

106 10 Dollars
ND (2002). Purple, violet and brown on multicolor underprint. Similar to #98.

	VG	VF	UNC
a. Double letter prefix.	FV	FV	13.00
r. Replacement. *Z* prefix.	FV	10.00	20.00
s. Specimen.	—	—	65.00

107 20 Dollars
ND (2002). Blue, purple and dark blue on multicolor underprint. Similar to #99.

	VG	VF	UNC
a. Double letter prefix.	FV	FV	25.00
r. Replacement. *Z* prefix.	FV	15.00	30.00
s. Specimen.	—	—	85.00

108 50 Dollars
ND (2002). Black, red, orange and violet on multicolor underprint. Similar to #100.

	VG	VF	UNC
a. Single letter prefix.	FV	FV	55.00
r. Replacement. *Z* prefix.	FV	30.00	70.00
s. Specimen.	—	—	120.

FINLAND

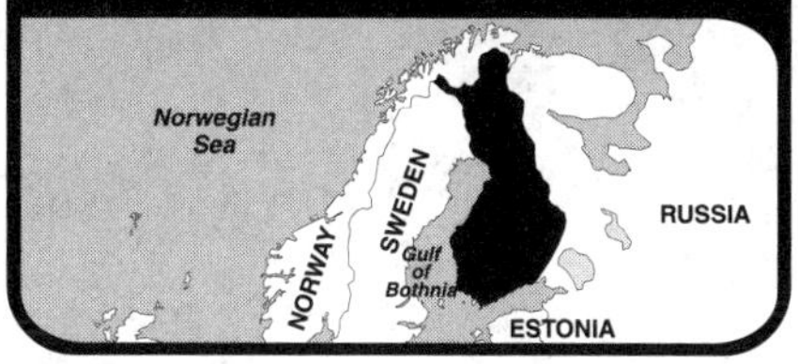

The Republic of Finland, the second most northerly state of the European continent, has an area of 130,120 sq. mi. (337,009 sq. km.) and a population of 5.21 million. Capital: Helsinki. Electrical/optical equipment, shipbuilding, metal and woodworking are the leading industries. Paper, wood pulp, plywood and telecommunication equipment are exported.

The Finns, who probably originated in the Volga region of Russia, took Finland from the Lapps late in the 7th century. They were conquered in the 12th century by Eric IX of Sweden, and brought into contact with Western Christendom. In 1809, Sweden was invaded by Alexander I of Russia, and the peace terms gave Finland to Russia. It became a grand duchy within the Russian Empire until Dec. 6, 1917, when, shortly after the Bolshevik revolution, it declared its independence. After a brief but bitter civil war between the Russian sympathizers and Finnish nationalists in which the Whites (nationalists) were victorious, a new constitution was adopted, and on Dec. 6, 1917 Finland was established as a republic. In 1939 Soviet troops invaded Finland over disputed territorial concessions which were later granted in the peace treaty of 1940. When the Germans invaded Russia, Finland also became involved and in the Armistice of 1944 lost the Petsamo area also to the USSR.

MONETARY SYSTEM:

1 Markka = 100 Penniä, 1860-1963
1 Markka = 100 "Old" Markkaa, 1963-2001
1 Markka = 100 Penniä, 1963-2001
1 Euro = 100 Cents, 2002

REPLACEMENT NOTES:

Replacement notes were introduced in 1955. Until 1980, replacement notes have an asterisk after the serial number. Series 1986 show 2nd and 3rd digits of serial # as 99.

Note: Certain listings encompassing issues by various commercial banks and regional authorities are contained in Volume 1.

REPUBLIC

SUOMEN PANKKI - FINLANDS BANK

1963 DATED ISSUE

#98-102 arms at ctr. or ctr. r. on back. W/o *Litt.* designation.

98	1 Markka	VG	VF	UNC
	1963. Lilac-brown on olive underprint. Wheat ears.			
	a. Issued note.	.30	.50	2.00
	r. Replacement note. Serial # suffix *.	1.00	8.00	25.00
	s. Specimen.	—	—	100.

99	5 Markkaa	VG	VF	UNC
	1963. Blue and blue-green. Conifer branch.			
	a. Issued note.	1.00	3.00	12.50
	r. Replacement note. Serial # suffix *.	10.00	20.00	40.00
	s. Specimen.	—	—	125.

100	10 Markkaa	VG	VF	UNC
	1963. Dark green and blue. Juho Kusti Paasikivi at left. (Watermark. direction varies.)			
	a. Issued note.	3.00	10.00	25.00
	r. Replacement note. Serial # suffix *.	100.	250.	500.
	s. Specimen.	—	—	150.

101	50 Markkaa	VG	VF	UNC
	1963. Brown. Kaarlo Juho Ståhlberg at left.			
	a. Issued note.	10.00	20.00	40.00
	r. Replacement note. Serial # suffix *.	300.	500.	750.
	s. Specimen.	—	—	175.

102	100 Markkaa	VG	VF	UNC
	1963. Violet. Juhana Vilhelm Snellman at left.			
	a. Issued note.	20.00	25.00	50.00
	r. Replacement note. Serial # suffix *.	150.	350.	700.
	s. Specimen.	—	—	200.

1963 DATED ISSUE, LITT. A

103	5 Markkaa	VG	VF	UNC
	1963. Blue and blue-green. Similar to #99 but border and date designs are more detailed.			
	a. Issued note.	1.00	2.50	7.00
	r. Replacement note. Serial # suffix *.	1.00	5.00	30.00

104	10 Markkaa	VG	VF	UNC
	1963. Dark green and blue. Like #100. (Watermark: position varies.)			
	a. Issued note.	2.00	3.00	9.00
	r. Replacement note. Serial # suffix *.	2.00	5.00	10.00

105	50 Markkaa	VG	VF	UNC
	1963. Brown. Like #101.			
	a. Issued note.	10.00	20.00	35.00
	r. Replacement note. Serial # suffix *.	100.	200.	300.

106	100 Markkaa	VG	VF	UNC
	1963. Violet. Like #102.			
	a. Issued note.	20.00	25.00	40.00
	r. Replacement note. Serial # suffix *.	20.00	40.00	75.00

1963 Dated Issue, Litt. B

106A	5 Markkaa	VG	VF	UNC
	1963. Blue and blue-green. Like #99.			
	a. Issued note.	1.00	1.50	4.00
	r. Replacement note. Serial # suffix *.	2.00	5.00	8.00
107	50 Markkaa			
	1963. Brown. Like #101 and #105. (Watermark direction varies.)			
	a. Issued note.	10.00	15.00	35.00
	r. Replacement note. Serial # suffix *.	15.00	30.00	60.00

1975-77 Issue

108	50 Markkaa	VG	VF	UNC
	1977. Brown and multicolor. Kaarlo Juho Ståhlberg at left and as watermark (Watermark position and direction varies.)			
	a. Issued note.	10.00	12.50	20.00
	r. Replacement note. Serial # suffix *.	10.00	20.00	40.00
	s. Specimen.	—	—	200.

109	100 Markkaa	VG	VF	UNC
	1976. Violet. Juhana Vilhelm Snellman at left and as watermark (Watermark position and direction varies.)			
	a. Issued note.	20.00	25.00	35.00
	r. Replacement note. Serial # suffix *.	20.00	25.00	40.00

110	500 Markkaa	VG	VF	UNC
	1975. Blue and violet. Urho Kaleva Kekkonen at left and as watermark. Arms and 9 small shields on back. (Watermark position varies.)			
	a. Thin metallic security thread.	100.	150.	200.
	b. Broad yellow plastic security thread.	100.	100.	150.
	r1. As a. Replacement note. Serial # suffix *.	150.	300.	600.
	r2. As b. Replacement note. Serial # suffix *.	125.	200.	300.
	s. Specimen.	—	—	350.

1980 Issue

111	10 Markkaa	VG	VF	UNC
	1980. Green and brown on orange and multicolor underprint. Like #100 except for color and addition of four raised discs at right center for denomination identification by the blind. Back green and purple. Watermark: Paasikivi.			
	a. Issued note.	2.00	3.00	7.00
	r. Replacement note. Serial # suffix *.	2.50	5.00	14.00

1980 Issue; Litt. A

112	10 Markkaa	VG	VF	UNC
	1980. Similar to #111 but date under portrait, and five small circles at bottom. *Litt. A.*			
	a. Issued note.	2.00	3.00	6.00
	r. Replacement note. *99* as 2nd and 3rd numerial in serial #.	2.50	5.00	10.00

1986 Issue

#113-117 portr. as wmk. Circles above lower r. serial #.
#113-115, and 117 replacement notes: w/*99* as 2nd and 3rd digits in serial # and command a premium.

113	10 Markkaa	VG	VF	UNC
	1986. Deep blue on blue and green underprint. Paavo Nurmi at left and as watermark. Helsinki Olympic Stadium on back.			
	a. Issued note.	2.00	2.50	6.00
	r. Replacement note.	2.25	4.00	12.50

114	50 Markkaa	VG	VF	UNC
	1986. Black on red-brown and multicolor underprint. Alvar Aalto at left and as watermark. Four raised circles at lower right for the blind. Finlandia Hall on back.			
	a. Issued note.	10.00	12.50	25.00
	r. Replacement note.	15.00	30.00	50.00

115	100 Markkaa	VG	VF	UNC
	1986. Black on green and multicolor underprint. Jean Sibelius at left and as watermark. Three raised circles at lower right for the blind. Whooper Swans on back.			
	a. Issued note.	20.00	25.00	40.00
	r. Replacement note.	25.00	40.00	60.00

116	500 Markkaa	VG	VF	UNC
	1986. Black on red, brown and yellow underprint. Elias Lönnrot at left and as watermark. Punkaharju on back.			
	a. Issued note.	100.	125.	175.
	r. Replacement note.	125.	150.	200.

117	1000 Markkaa	VG	VF	UNC
	1986. Blue and purple on multicolor underprint. Anders Chydenius at left and as watermark. King's gate, sea fortress of Suomenlinna in Helsinki harbor, seagulls on back.			
	a. Issued note.	FV	200.	300.
	r. Replacement note.	200.	250.	325.

1986 Dated (1991) Issue, Litt. A

#118-122 like #114-117 with w/*Litt. A* above denomination added to lower l. and optical variable device (OVD) added at upper r. to higher denominations. Circles above bank name. Portr. as wmk.

118	50 Markkaa	VG	VF	UNC
	1986 (1991). Similar to #114. Latent image at upper right.	FV	10.00	20.00
119	**100 Markkaa**			
	1986 (1991). Similar to #115. Latent image at upper right.	FV	17.50	27.50

120	500 Markkaa	VG	VF	UNC
	1986 (1991). Similar to #116.	FV	100.	125.

121	1000 Markkaa	VG	VF	UNC
	1986 (1991). Similar to #117.	FV	100.	225.

1993 ISSUE

122	20 Markkaa	VG	VF	UNC
	1993. Black on blue and gold underprint. Väinö Linna at left and as watermark. Latent image at upper right. Tampere street scene on back.	4.00	7.50	12.50

1993 DATED (1997) ISSUE; LITT. A.

123	20 Markkaa	VG	VF	UNC
	1993 (1997). Black on blue and green underprint. Like #122 but with optical variable device at upper right. *Litt. A.* at lower left.	4.00	5.00	8.00

Note: For later issues made for use in Finland see European Union listings.

The French Republic, largest of the West European nations, has an area of 220,668 sq. mi. (547,026 sq. km.) and a population of 60 million. Capital: Paris. Agriculture, manufacturing and tourism are the most important elements of France's diversified economy. Textiles and clothing, iron and steel products, machinery and transportation equipment, agricultural products and wine are exported.

Charles de Gaulle was unanimously elected president of the Fourth Republic, but resigned in January 1946 when leftists withdrew their support. In actual operation, the Fourth Republic was remarkably like the Third, with the National Assembly the focus of power. The later years of the Fourth Republic were marked by a burst of industrial expansion unmatched in modern French history. The growth rate, however, was marred by a nagging inflationary trend that weakened the franc and undermined the competitive posture of France's export trade. This and the Algerian conflict led to the recall of de Gaulle to power, the adoption of a new constitution vesting strong powers in the executive, and establishment in 1958 of the current Fifth Republic.

Note: Certain listings encompassing issues of various banks and regional authorities are contained in Volume 1, Specialized Issues.

MONETARY SYSTEM:

1 Nouveau Franc = 100 "old" Francs, 1960-1962
1 Franc = 100 Centimes, 1962-2002
1 Euro = 100 Cents, 2002-

REPUBLIC

BANQUE DE FRANCE

1959 ISSUE

#141-145 denomination: *NOUVEAUX FRANCS* (NF).

141	5 Nouveaux Francs	VG	VF	UNC
	5.3.1959-5.11.1965. Blue, orange and multicolor. Panthéon in Paris at left, Victor Hugo at right. Village at right, Victor Hugo at left.			
	a. Issued note.	5.00	20.00	200.
	s. Specimen.	—	—	—

		VG	VF	UNC
142	**10 Nouveaux Francs** 5.3.1959-4.1.1963. Multicolor. Palais Cardinal across, Armand du Plessis, Cardinal Richelieu at right. Town gate (of Richelieu, in Indre et Loire) at right.	5.00	15.00	125.
143	**50 Nouveaux Francs** 5.3.1959-6.7.1961. Multicolor. Henry IV at center, Paris' Pont Neuf bridge in background. Henry IV at center, Château de Pau at left.	30.00	100.	1000.
144	**100 Nouveaux Francs** 5.3.1959-2.4.1964. Multicolor. Arc de Triomphe at left, Napoléon Bonaparte at right. Church of the Invalides in Paris at right, Bonaparte at left.	20.00	40.00	700.

145 500 Nouveaux Francs

1959-66. Multicolor. Jean Baptiste Poquelin called Molière at center Paris' Palais Royal in background. Theater in Versailles.

	VG	VF	UNC
a. Signature G. Gouin D'Ambrières, R. Tondu and P. Gargam. 2.7.1959-8.1.1965.	FV	200.	1000.
b. Signature H. Morant, R. Tondu and P. Gargam. 6.1.1966; 1.9.1966.	FV	200.	1000.
s. Specimen. As b.	—	—	—

Note: #145b dated 1.9.1966 was not released for circulation, but examples with pin-hole cancelations are known.

1962-66 Issue

146 5 Francs

1966-70. Brown, purple and multicolor. Louis Pasteur at left, Pasteur Institute in Paris at right. Laboratory implements, man fighting a rabid dog, Pasteur at right on back.

	VG	VF	UNC
a. Signature R. Tondu, P. Gargam and H. Morant. 5.5.1966-4.11.1966.	10.00	60.00	200.
b. Signature R. Tondu, H. Morant and G. Bouchet. 5.5.1967-8.1.1970.	10.00	60.00	200.
s. Specimen. As a. Overprint and perforated *SPECIMEN.*	—	—	500.

147 10 Francs

1963-73. Red and multicolor. Paris' Palais des Tuileries at center, Voltaire at right and as watermark. Château de Cirey at right, Voltaire at left on back.

	VG	VF	UNC
a. Signature G. Gouin D'Ambrières, P. Gargam and R. Tondu. 4.1.1963-2.12.1965.	FV	30.00	100.
b. Signature H. Morant, P. Gargam and R. Tondu. 6.1.1966-6.4.1967.	FV	8.00	60.00
c. Signature G. Bouchet, H. Morant and R. Tondu. 6.7.1967-4.2.1971.	FV	6.00	40.00
d. Signature G. Bouchet, H. Morant and P. Vergnes. 3.6.1971-6.12.1973.	FV	7.50	20.00
s. Specimen. As a-c. overprint and perforated *SPECIMEN.*	—	—	500.

148 50 Francs

1962-76. Multicolor. Port Royal des Champs Abbey at center, Jean Racine at right. Jean Racine at left, View of La Ferté-Milon on back.

	VG	VF	UNC
a. Signature G. Gouin d'Ambrieres, R. Tondu and P. Gargam. 7.6.1962-4.3.1965.	6.00	50.00	150.
b. Signature H. Morant, R. Tondu and P. Gargam. 2.2.1967.	10.00	70.00	180.
c. Signature H. Morant, R. Tondu and G. Bouchet. 7.12.1967-5.11.1970.	6.00	15.00	100.
d. Signature G. Bouchet, P. Vergnes and H. Morant. 3.6.1971-3.5.1973.	6.00	15.00	100.
e. Signature G. Bouchet, J. J. Tronche and H. Morant. 4.10.1973-2.10.1975.	6.00	15.00	100.
f. Signature P. A. Strohl, G. Bouchet and J. J. Tronche. 2.1.1976-3.6.1976.	6.00	15.00	100.
s. Specimen. overprint and perforated *SPECIMEN.*	—	—	600.

149 100 Francs

1964-79. Multicolor. Pierre Corneille at center, Theater in Versailles around. His bust in cartouche at center, View of Rouen on back.

	VG	VF	UNC
a. Signature R. Tondu. G. Gouin D'Ambrières and P. Gargam. 2.4.1964-2.12.1965.	10.00	35.00	150.
b. Signature R. Tondu, H. Morant and P. Gargam. 3.2.1966-6.4.1967.	10.00	25.00	120.
c. Signature R. Tondu, G. Bouchet and H. Morant. 5.10.1967-1.4.1971.	10.00	25.00	100.
d. Signature P. Vergnes, G. Bouchet and H. Morant. 1.7.1971-3.10.1974.	10.00	25.00	100.
e. Signature J. J. Tronche, G. Bouchet and H. Morant. 6.2.1975-6.11.1975.	10.00	25.00	100.
f. Signature P. A. Strohl, G. Bouchet and J. J. Tronche. 2.1.1976-1.2.1979.	10.00	25.00	70.00
s. Specimen. overprint and perforated *SPECIMEN.*	—	—	600.

1968-81 Issue

150 10 Francs

1972-78. Red, brown and olive. Hector Berlioz at right. conducting in the Chapelle des Invalides, Berlioz at left, musical instrument at right and Rome's Villa Medici on back.

	VG	VF	UNC
a. Signature H. Morant, G. Bouchet and P. Vergnes. 23.11.1972-3.10.1974.	FV	6.00	45.00
b. Signature H. Morant, G. Bouchet and J. J. Tronche. 6.2.1975-4.12.1975.	FV	5.00	20.00
c. Signature P. A. Strohl, G. Bouchet and J. J. Tronche. 2.1.1976-6.7.1978.	FV	4.00	15.00
s. Specimen. As b. overprint and perforated *SPECIMEN.*	—	—	500.

151 20 Francs

1980-97. Dull violet, brown and multicolor. Claude Debussy at right and as watermark, sea scene in background *(La Mer)*. Back similar but with lake scene.

	VG	VF	UNC
a. Signature P. A. Strohl, J. J. Tronche and B. Dentaud. 1980-86.	FV	5.00	40.00
b. Signature P. A. Strohl, D. Ferman and B. Dentaud. 1987.	FV	4.00	25.00
c. Without security thread. signature D. Ferman, B. Dentaud and A. Charriau. 1988; 1989.	FV	3.00	25.00
d. With security thread. signature as c. 1990.	FV	FV	20.00
e. Signature D. Bruneel, B. Dentaud and A. Charriau. 1991.	FV	FV	15.00
f. Signature D. Bruneel, J. Bonnardin and A. Charriau. 1992; 1993.	FV	FV	15.00
g. Signature D. Bruneel, J. Bonnardin and C. Vigier. 1993.	FV	FV	15.00
h. Signature as g. New Ley (law) on back. 1995.	FV	FV	10.00
i. Signature D. Bruneel, J. Bonnardin and Y. Barroux. 1997.	FV	FV	10.00
s. Specimen. Overprint and perforated *SPECIMEN.*	—	—	400.

152 50 Francs

1976-92. Deep blue-black on multicolor underprint. Maurice Quentin de la Tour at center right and as watermark, and Palace of Versailles at left center in background. Q. de la Tour and St. Quentin City Hall at center right in background on back.

	VG	VF	UNC
a. Signature P. A. Strohl, G. Bouchet and J. J. Tronche. 1976-79.	FV	FV	45.00
b. Signature P. A. Strohl, J. J. Tronche and B. Dentaud. 1979-86.	FV	FV	40.00
c. Signature P. A. Strohl, D. Ferman and B. Dentaud. 1987.	FV	FV	35.00
d. Signature D. Ferman, B. Dentaud and A. Charriau. 1988; 1989.	FV	FV	30.00
e. Signature D. Bruneel, B. Dentaud and A. Charriau. 1990; 1991.	FV	FV	20.00
f. Signature D. Bruneel, J. Bonnardin and A. Charriau. 1992.	FV	FV	20.00
s. Specimen. Overprint and perforated *SPECIMEN.*	—	—	450.

153 100 Francs

	VG	VF	UNC
1978. Brown. Eugène Delacroix at left center and as watermark, Marianne holding tricolor, part of Delacroix's painting *La Liberté Guidant le Peuple* at right. Signature P. A. Strohl, G. Bouchet and J. J. Tronche.	FV	50.00	200.

154 100 Francs

1978-95. Brown. Like #153 but *100 CENT FRANCS* retouched with heavier diagonal lines at upper left.

	VG	VF	UNC
a. Signature P. A. Strohl, G. Bouchet and J. J. Tronche. 1978-79.	FV	30.00	150.
b. Signature P. A. Strohl, J. J. Tronche and B. Dentaud. 1979-86.	FV	FV	60.00
c. Signature P. A. Strohl, D. Ferman and B. Dentaud. 1987.	FV	FV	50.00
d. Signature D. Ferman, B. Dentaud and A. Charriau. 1988-90.	FV	FV	50.00
e. Signature D. Bruneel, B. Dentaud and A. Charriau. 1990-91.	FV	FV	100.
f. Signature D. Bruneel, J. Bonnardin and A. Charriau. 1991.	FV	FV	100.
g. Signature D. Bruneel, J. Bonnardin and C. Vigier. 1993.	FV	FV	35.00
h. Signature as g. New Ley (law) on back. 1994; 1995.	FV	FV	30.00
s. Specimen. Overprint and perforated *SPECIMEN.*	—	—	500.

155 200 Francs VG VF UNC

1981-94. Blue-green, yellow and multicolor. Figure with staff at at left, Charles Baron de Montesquieu at right and as watermark. Similar but with Castle of Labrède on back (Montesquieu's birthplace).

155	200 Francs	VG	VF	UNC
	a. Signature P. A. Strohl, J. J. Tronche and B. Dentaud. 1981-86.	FV	FV	120.
	b. Signature P. A. Strohl, D. Ferman and B. Dentaud. 1987.	FV	FV	120.
	c. Signature D. Ferman, B. Dentaud and A. Charriau. 1988; 1989.	FV	FV	95.00
	d. Signature D. Bruneel, B. Dentaud and A. Charriau. 1990; 1991.	FV	FV	90.00
	e. Signature D. Bruneel, J. Bonnardin and A. Charriau. 1992.	FV	FV	70.00
	f. Signature D. Bruneel, J. Bonnardin and C. Vigier. New Ley (law) on back. 1994.	FV	FV	100.
	s. Specimen. Overprint and perforated *SPECIMEN*.	—	—	500.

156	500 Francs	VG	VF	UNC
	1968-93. Yellow-brown and dark brown. Tower of St. Jacques in Paris at left, Blaise Pascal at center Blaise Pascal at left, abbey of Port Royal on back.			
	a. Signature G. Bouchet, R. Tondu and H. Morant. 4.1.1968-8.1.1970.	FV	115.	250.
	b. Signature G. Bouchet, P. Vergnes and H. Morant. 5.8.1971-5.9.1974.	FV	120.	300.
	c. Signature G. Bouchet, J. J. Tronche and H. Morant. 5.12.1974-6.11.1975.	FV	80.00	250.
	d. Signature P. A. Strohl, G. Bouchet and J. J. Tronche. 1.4.1976-7.6.1979.	FV	70.00	150.
	e. Signature P. A. Strohl, J. J. Tronche and B. Dentaud. 7.6.1979-6.2.1986.	FV	FV	130.
	f. Signature P. A. Strohl, D. Ferman and B. Dentaud. 8.1.1987; 22.1.1987; 5.11.1987.	FV	FV	125.
	g. Signature of D. Ferman, B. Dentaud and A. Charriau. 3.3.1988-1.2.1990.	FV	FV	125.
	h. Signature D. Bruneel, B. Dentaud and A. Charriau. 5.7.1990-2.5.1991.	FV	FV	125.
	i. Signature D. Bruneel, J. Bonnardin and A. Charriau. 3.10.1991-7.1.1993.	FV	FV	125.
	j. Signature D. Bruneel, J. Bonnardin and C. Vigier. 2.9.1993.	FV	FV	250.
	s. Specimen. overprint and perforated *SPECIMEN*.	—	—	600.

1993-97 Issue

#157-160 Many technical anti-counterfeiting devices added

157	50 Francs	VG	VF	UNC
	1992-93. Purple and dark blue on blue, green and multicolor underprint. Drawing of *le Petit Prince* at left. Old airplane at top left, topographical map of Africa at center, Antoine de Saint-Exupéry at right and as watermark Breguet XIV biplane on back. Name as Éxupéry, old law clause on back.			
	a. Signature D. Bruneel, J. Bonnardin and A. Charriau. 1992.	—	Unc	30.00
	b. Signature D. Bruneel, J. Bonnardin and C. Vigier. 1993.	—	Unc	25.00

157A	50 Francs	VG	VF	UNC
	1994-99. As 157 but name corrected to Exupéry, new law clause on back.			
	a. Signature D. Bruneel, J. Bonnardin and C. Vigier. 1994. 8 cardinal points in compass solid. Underline *al.* in Signature titles.	FV	FV	12.50
	b. Signature D. Bruneel, J. Bonnardin and C. Vigier. 1994. 8 cardinal points in compass striped. without underlined *al.* in Signature title.	FV	FV	12.50
	c. Signature D. Bruneel, J. Bonnardin and Y. Barroux. 1996.	FV	FV	25.00
	d. Signature as c. 1997, 1998.	FV	FV	15.00

158	100 Francs	VG	VF	UNC
	1997; 1998. Deep brown on orange, pink and light green underprint. Paul Cézanne at right and as watermark. Painting of fruit at left on back. Signature as #157Ac.	FV	FV	25.00

159	200 Francs	VG	VF	UNC
	1995-99. Brown and pink on multicolor underprint. Gustave Eiffel at right and as watermark, observatory at upper left center, Eiffel tower truss at center. View through tower base across exhibition grounds at left0 center on back.			
	a. Signature D. Bruneel, J. Bonnardin and C. Vigier. 1995; 1996.	FV	FV	50.00
	b. Signature D. Bruneel, J. Bonnardin and Y. Barroux. 1996; 1997.	FV	FV	45.00
	c. Signature D. Bruneel, J. Bonnardin and Y. Barroux. 1999.	FV	FV	40.00

160	500 Francs	VG	VF	UNC
	1994-2000. Dark green and black on multicolor underprint. Marie and Pierre Curie at center right. Segmented foil strip at left. Laboratory utensils at left center on back. Watermark: M. Curie.			
	a. 1994-95. signature as #159a.	FV	FV	130.
	b. 1996. signature as #159a.	FV	120.	200.
	c. 1998. signature as #159c.	FV	FV	120.
	d. 2000. signature Y. Barroux, J. Bonnardin, A. Vienney.	FV	FV	140.

Note: For later issues made for use in France see European Union listings.

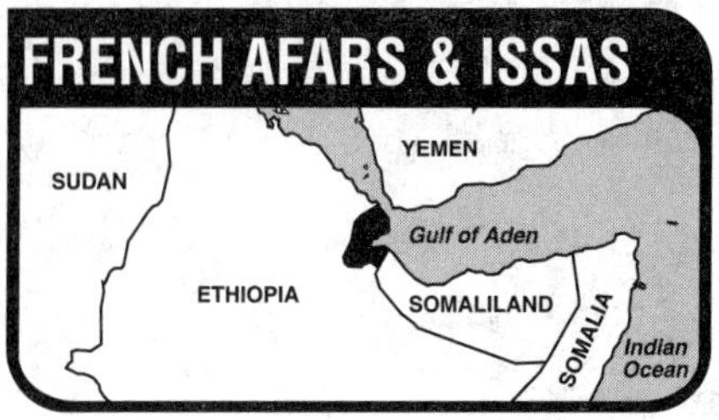

The French Overseas Territory of Afars and Iassas (formerly French Somaliland, later to be independent as Djibouti) is located in northeast Africa at the Bab el Mandeb Strait connecting the Suez Canal and the Red Sea with the Gulf of Aden and the Indian Ocean, has an area of 8,494 sq. mi. (22,000 sq. km.) and a population of 542,000. Capital: Djibouti. The tiny nation has less than one sq. mi. of arable land, and no natural resources except salt, sand and camels. The commercial activities of the trans-shipment port of Djibouti and the Addis Ababa-Djibouti railroad are the basis of the economy. Salt, fish and hides are exported.

French interest in former French Somaliland began in 1839 with concessions obtained by a French naval lieutenant from the provincial sultans. French Somaliland was made a protectorate in 1884 and its boundaries were delimited by the Franco-British and Ethiopian accords of 1887 and 1897. It became a colony in 1896 and a territory within the French Union in 1946. In 1958, it voted to join the new French Community as an overseas territory, and reaffirmed that choice by a referendum in March 1967. Its name was changed from French Somaliland to the French Territory of Afars and Issas on July 5, 1967.

The French Tricolor, which had flown over the strategically important territory for 115 years, was lowered for the last time on June 27, 1977, when French Afars and Issas became Djibouti.

Note: For later issues see Djibouti.

RULERS:

French to 1977

MONETARY SYSTEM:

1 Franc = 100 Centimes

FRENCH ADMINISTRATION

TRÉSOR PUBLIC, TERRITOIRE FRANÇAIS DES AFARS ET DES ISSAS

1969 ND ISSUE

		VG	VF	UNC
30	**5000 Francs** ND (1969). Multicolor. Aerial view of Djibouti harbor at center. Ruins at center on back.	75.00	275.	750.

1973; 1974 ND ISSUE

		VG	VF	UNC
31	**500 Francs** ND (1973). Multicolor. Ships at left center. Rearing antelope at center on back.	12.00	50.00	185.

		VG	VF	UNC
32	**1000 Francs** ND (1974). Multicolor. Woman holding jug at left center on face. Reversed image as face on back.	20.00	80.00	325.

1975 ND ISSUE

		VG	VF	UNC
33	**500 Francs** ND (1975). Multicolor. Man at left, rocks in sea, storks at right. Stern of ship at right on back.	7.00	20.00	80.00

		VG	VF	UNC
34	**1000 Francs** ND (1975). Multicolor. Woman at left, people by diesel passenger trains at center. Trader with camels on back.	10.00	35.00	150.

		VG	VF	UNC
35	**5000 Francs** ND (1975). Multicolor. Man at right, forest scene at center. Aeriel view at center on back.	45.00	85.00	350.

Three French overseas departments, Guiana, Guadeloupe and Martinique which issued a common currency from 1961-1975. Since 1975 Bank of France notes have circulated.

RULERS:

French

MONETARY SYSTEM:

1 Nouveau Franc = 100 "old" Francs
1 Franc = 100 Centimes

SIGNATURE VARIETIES		
	Le Directeur Général	Le Président du Conseil de Surveillance
1	André POSTEL-VINAY	Pierre CALVET 1059-1965
2	André POSTEL-VINAY	Bemard CLAPPIER 1966-1972

FRENCH ADMINISTRATION

INSTITUT D'EMISSION DES DÉPARTEMENTS D'OUTRE-MER

1961 ND PROVISIONAL ISSUE

Nouveau Franc System

#1-3 ovpt: *GUADELOUPE, GUYANE, MARTINIQUE*. Sign. 1.

		VG	VF	UNC
1	**1 Nouveau Franc on 100 Francs** ND (1961). Multicolor. La Bourdonnais at left. Woman at right on back.	15.00	75.00	425.

		VG	VF	UNC
2	**10 Nouveaux Francs on 1000 Francs** ND (1961). Multicolor. Fishermen from the Antilles.	75.00	500.	2000.

		VG	VF	UNC
3	**50 Nouveaux Francs on 5000 Francs** ND (1961). Multicolor. Woman with fruit bowl at center right.	150.	750.	2500.

SECOND 1961 ND PROVISIONAL ISSUE

#4, ovpt: *DÉPARTEMENT DE LA GUADELOUPE - DÉPARTEMENT DE LA GUYANE - DÉPARTEMENT DE LA MARTINIQUE*. Sign. 1.

		VG	VF	UNC
4	**5 Nouveaux Francs on 500 Francs** ND (1961). Brown on multicolor underprint. Sailboat at left, two women at right. Men with carts containing plants and wood on back.	75.00	350.	1500.

INSTITUT D'EMISSION DES DÉPARTEMENTS D'OUTRE-MER RÉPUBLIQUE FRANCAISE

1963 ND ISSUE

#5-10 ovpt: ***DÉPARTEMENT DE LA GUADELOUPE - DÉPARTEMENT DE LA GUYANE - DÉPARTEMENT DE LA MARTINIQUE.*** **Sign. 1.**

5	**10 Nouveaux Francs**	VG	VF	UNC
	ND (1963). Brown and green on multicolor underprint. Girl at right, coastal scenery in background. People cutting sugar cane on back.			
	a. Issued note.	30.00	110.	350.
	s. Specimen.	—	—	250.

6	**50 Nouveaux Francs**	VG	VF	UNC
	ND (1963). Green on multicolor underprint. Banana harvest. Shoreline with houses at left, man and woman at right on back.			
	a. Issued note.	40.00	175.	550.
	s. Specimen.	—	—	350.

1964 ND ISSUE

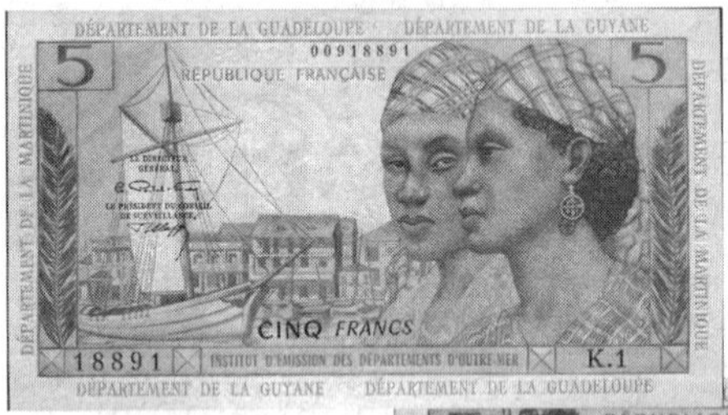

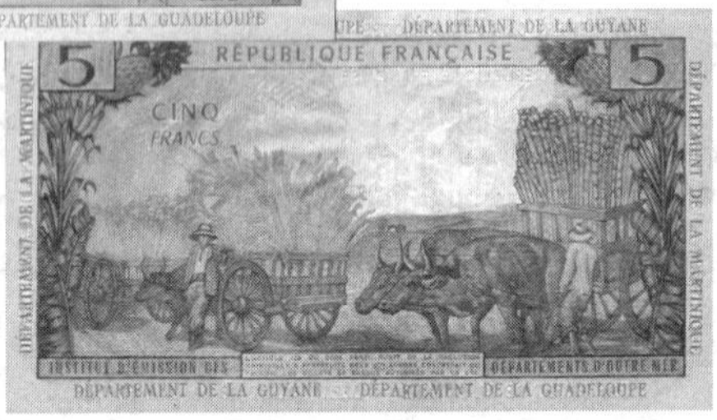

7	**5 Francs**	VG	VF	UNC
	ND (1964). Like #4, but smaller size.			
	a. Signature 1.	50.00	210.	650.
	b. Signature 2.	40.00	175.	550.
	s. As b. Specimen.	—	—	—

8	**10 Francs**	VG	VF	UNC
	ND (1964). Like #5.			
	a. Signature 1.	25.00	100.	325.
	b. Signature 2.	20.00	85.00	275.

9	**50 Francs**	VG	VF	UNC
	ND (1964). Like #6.			
	a. Signature 1.	40.00	175.	550.
	b. Signature 2.	35.00	150.	500.

10	**100 Francs**	VG	VF	UNC
	ND (1964). Brown and multicolor. General Schoelcher at center right. Schoelcher at left center, various arms and galleon around on back.			
	a. Signature 1.	80.00	300.	1100.
	b. Signature 2.	60.00	250.	950.

FRENCH GUIANA

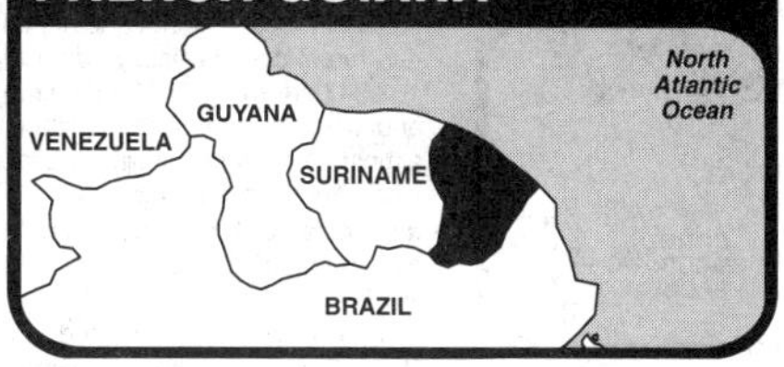

The French Overseas Department of French Guiana, located on the northeast coast of South America, bordered by Surinam and Brazil, has an area of 32,252 sq. mi. (91,000 sq. km.) and a population of 173,000. Capital: Cayenne. Placer gold mining and shrimp processing are the chief industries. Shrimp, lumber, gold, cocoa and bananas are exported.

The coast of Guiana was sighted by Columbus in 1498 and explored by Amerigo Vespucci in 1499. The French established the first successful trading stations and settlements, and placed the area under direct control of the French Crown in 1674. Portuguese and British forces occupied French Guiana for five years during the Napoleonic Wars. Devil's Island, the notorious penal colony in French Guiana where Capt. Alfred Dreyfus was imprisoned, was established in 1852 - and finally closed in 1947. When France adopted a new constitution in 1946, French Guiana voted to remain within the French Union as an overseas department.

RULERS:

French

MONETARY SYSTEM:

1 Franc = 10 Decimes = 100 Centimes to 1960
1 Nouveau (new) Franc = 100 "old" Francs, 1961-

FRENCH ADMINISTRATION

CAISSE CENTRALE DE LA FRANCE D'OUTRE-MER

1961 ND PROVISIONAL ISSUE

#29-33 ovpt: *GUYANE* and nouveau franc denominations on earlier issue. (Vol. 2.)

		VG	VF	UNC
29	**1 Nouveau Franc on 100 Francs** ND (1961). Multicolor. Overprint on #23. B. d'Esnambuc at left, sailing ship at right.	15.00	45.00	325.
30	**5 Nouveaux Francs on 500 Francs** ND (1961). Multicolor. Overprint on #24. Sailboat at left, two women at right.	50.00	165.	675.
31	**10 Nouveaux Francs on 1000 Francs** ND (1961). Multicolor. Overprint on #27. Fishermen.	125.	500.	1300.
32	**10 Nouveaux Francs on 1000 Francs** ND. Multicolor. Overprint on #25. Woman at right.	110.	350.	900.
33	**50 Nouveaux Francs on 5000 Francs** ND. Overprint on #28. Woman with fruit bowl.	375.	800.	1800.

Note: For later issues see French Antilles.

FRENCH PACIFIC TERRITORIES

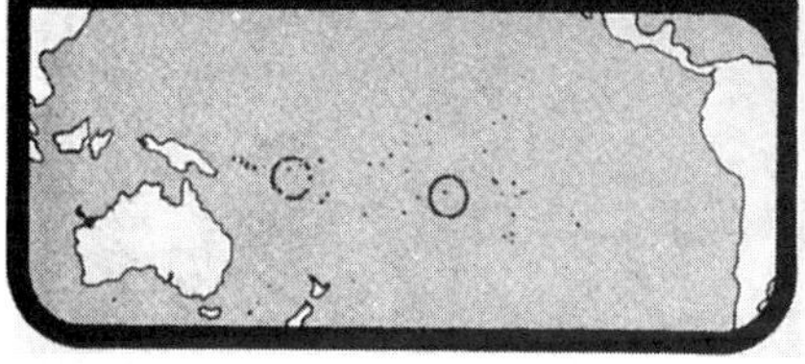

The French Pacific Territories include French Polynesia, New Caledonia and formerly the New Hebrides Condominium. For earlier issues also refer to French Oceania and Tahiti.

FRENCH ADMINISTRATION

INSTITUT D'EMISSION D'OUTRE-MER

1985-96 ND ISSUE

Notes w/o *NOUMEA* or *PAPEETE*.

		VG	VF	UNC
1	**500 Francs** ND (1992). Multicolor. Sailboat at center, fisherman at right. Man at left, objects at right on back.			
	a. 2 signature without security thread. signature 2.	FV	FV	25.00
	b. 3 signature with security thread. signature 3.	FV	FV	20.00

		VG	VF	UNC
2	**1000 Francs** ND (1996). Multicolor. Hut in palm trees at left, girl at right.			
	a. Signature 3.	FV	FV	32.50
	b. Signature 4.	FV	FV	30.00

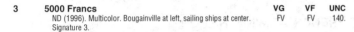

		VG	VF	UNC
3	**5000 Francs** ND (1996). Multicolor. Bougainville at left, sailing ships at center. Signature 3.	FV	FV	140.

		VG	VF	UNC
4	**10,000 Francs** ND (1985). Multicolor. Tahitian girl with floral headdress at upper left topuristic bungalows at center. Fish at center, Melanesian girl wearing flower at right on back. Watermark: 2 ethnic heads.			
	a. 2 signature without security thread. signature 1.	FV	FV	250.
	b. 3 signature with security thread. (New Ley on back.) signature 5.	FV	FV	225.

Note: Above notes in CFP francs (change franc Pacifique). Common currency of French Polynesia, New Caledonia, and Wallis & Futuna Islands. Design types of #1-3 like issues for New Caledonia and New Hebrides but w/o *NOUMEA* or *PAPEETE*. Sign. varieties correspond to those used for New Caledonia and New Hebrides issues.

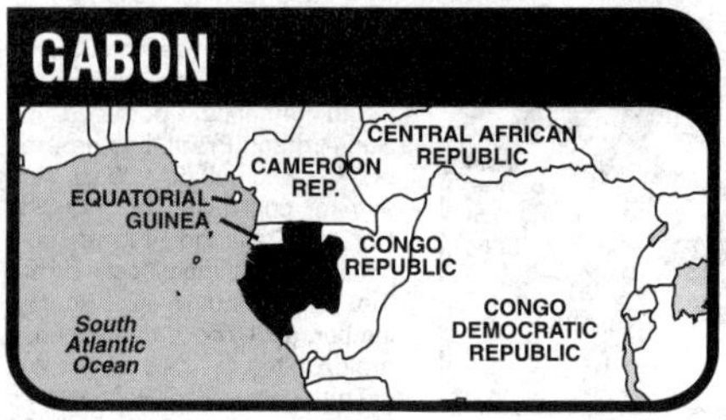

The Gabonese Republic, a member of the French Community, straddles the equator on the west coast of Africa. The hot and humid rain forest country has an area of 103,347 sq. mi. (267,667 sq. km.) and a population of 1.23 million, almost all of Bantu origin. Capital: Libreville. Extravagantly rich in resources, Gabon exports crude oil, manganese ore, gold and timbers.

Gabon was first visited by Portuguese navigator Diego Cam in the 15th century. Dutch, French and British traders, lured by the rich stands of hard woods and oil palms, quickly followed. The French founded their first settlement on the left bank of the Gabon River in 1839 and established their presence by signing treaties with the tribal chiefs. After gradually extending their influence into the interior during the last half of the 19th century, France occupied Gabon in 1885 and, in 1910, organized it as one of the four territories of French Equatorial Africa. It became an autonomous republic within the French Union in 1946, and on Aug. 17, 1960, became a completely independent republic within the new French Community.

Note: For related currency, see the Equatorial African States.

RULERS:

French to 1960

MONETARY SYSTEM.

1 Franc = 100 Centimes

SIGNATURE VARIETIES:

Refer to introduction to Central African States.

RÉPUBLIQUE GABONAISE

BANQUE CENTRALE

1971 ND ISSUE

		VG	VF	UNC
1	**10,000 Francs** ND (1971). Multicolor. President O. Bongo at right, mask at left, mine elevator at center. Statue at left and right, tractor plowing at center on back. Signature 1.	40.00	125.	375.

BANQUE DES ÉTATS DE L'AFRIQUE CENTRALE

1974 ND ISSUE

2	500 Francs	VG	VF	UNC
	ND (1974); 1978. Lilac-brown on multicolor underprint. Woman wearing kerchief at left, logging at center Mask at left, students and chemical testing at center, statue at right on back.			
	a. Engraved. signature 6. ND (1974).	1.75	4.50	22.50
	b. Lithographed. signature 9. 1.4.1978.	1.00	3.00	15.00

3	1000 Francs	VG	VF	UNC
	ND (1974; 1978); 1978-84. Red and blue on multicolor underprint. Ship and oil refinery at center, President O. Bongo at right. Mask at left, trains, planes and bridge at center, statue at right on back.			
	a. Signature 4 with titles: *LE DIRECTEUR GÉNÉRAL* and *UN CENSEUR*. Engraved. watermark: Antelope head in half profile. ND (1974).	45.00	150.	350.
	b. Like a. signature 6.	4.00	15.00	55.00
	c. Signature 6 with titles: *LE DIRECTEUR GÉNÉRAL* and *UN CENSEUR*. Lithographed. watermark. Antelope head in profile. ND (1978).	3.50	10.00	40.00
	d. Signature 9 with titles: *LE GOUVERNEUR* and *UN CENSEUR*. Lithographed. watermark. like b. 1.4.1978; 1.1.1983; 1.6.1984.	3.25	8.00	20.00

4	5000 Francs	VG	VF	UNC
	ND (1974; 1978). Brown. Oil refinery at left, open pit mining and President O. Bongo at right. Mask at left, buildings at center, statue at right on back.			
	a. Signature 4 with titles: *LE DIRECTEUR GENERAL* and *UN CENSEUR*. ND (1974).	35.00	100.	400.
	b. Like a. signature 6.	17.50	50.00	200.
	c. Signature 9 with titles: *LE GOUVERNEUR* and *UN CENSEUR*. ND (1978)	10.00	25.00	150.
	x1. Error. As a. without signature	25.00	60.00	180.
	x2. Error. As c. without signature	20.00	50.00	155.

5	10,000 Francs	VG	VF	UNC
	ND (1974; 1978). Multicolor. Like #1 except for new bank name on back.			
	a. Signature 6 with titles: *LE DIRECTEUR GÉNÉRAL* and *UN CENSEUR*. ND (1974).	27.50	75.00	200.
	b. Signature 9 with titles: *LE GOUVERNEUR* and *UN CENSEUR*. ND (1978).	20.00	50.00	175.

1983; 1984 ND Issue

6	5000 Francs	VG	VF	UNC
	ND (1984-91). Brown on multicolor underprint. Mask at left, woman with fronds at right. Plowing and mine ore conveyor on back.			
	a. Signature 9. (1984).	5.00	15.00	50.00
	b. Signature 14. (1991).	5.00	12.50	40.00

7	10,000 Francs	VG	VF	UNC
	ND (1983-91). Brown and green on multicolor underprint. Stylized antelope heads at left, woman at right. Loading fruit onto truck at left on back.			
	a. Signature 9. (1984).	7.50	27.50	90.00
	b. Signature 14. (1991).	7.50	25.00	75.00

1985 ISSUE

#8-10 wmk: Carving (same as printed on notes).

		VG	VF	UNC
8	**500 Francs** 1.1.1985. Brown on orange and multicolor underprint. Carving and jug at center. Man carving mask at left center on back. Signature 9.	1.25	2.25	7.00

		VG	VF	UNC
9	**1000 Francs** 1.1.1985. Deep blue on multicolor underprint. Carving at left, map at center, President O. Bongo at right. Incomplete outline map of Chad at top center. Elephant at left, animals at center, man carving at right on back. Signature 9.	FV	9.50	20.00

1986 ISSUE

		VG	VF	UNC
10	**1000 Francs** 1986-91. Deep blue on multicolor underprint. Like #9 but with outline map of Chad at top completed.			
	a. Signature 9. 1.1.1986; 1.1.1987; 1.1.1990.	FV	7.50	20.00
	b. Signature 14. 1.1.1991.	FV	7.00	15.00

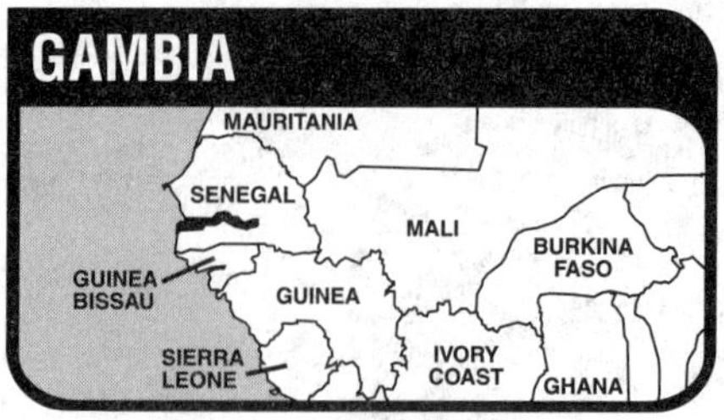

The Republic of The Gambia, an independent member of the British Commonwealth, occupies a strip of land 7 miles (11 km.) to 20 miles (32 km.) wide and 200 miles (322 km.) long encompassing both sides of West Africa's Gambia River, and completely surrounded by Senegal. The republic, one of Africa's smallest countries, has an area of 4,361 sq. mi. (11,295 sq. km.) and a population of 1.24 million. Capital: Banjul. Agriculture and tourism are the principal industries. Peanuts constitute 95 per cent of export earnings.

The Gambia was once part of the great empires of Ghana and Songhay. When Portuguese gold seekers and slave traders visited The Gambia in the 15th century, it was part of the Kingdom of Mali. In 1588 the territory became, through purchase, the first British colony in Africa. English slavers established Fort James, the first settlement, on a small island a dozen miles up the Gambia River in 1664. After alternate periods of union with Sierra Leone and existence as a separate colony, The Gambia became a British colony in 1888. On Feb. 18, 1965, The Gambia achieved independence as a constitutional monarchy within the Commonwealth of Nations, with Elizabeth II as Head of State as Queen of The Gambia. It became a republic on April 24, 1970, remaining a member of the Commonwealth, but with the president as Chief of State and Head of Government.

RULERS:

British to 1970

MONETARY SYSTEM:

1 Shilling = 12 Pence
1 Pound = 20 Shillings to 1970
1 Dalasi = 100 Bututs 1970-

SIGNATURE VARIETIES					
1	CHAIRMAN	DIRECTOR	8		
2	GENERAL MANAGER	GOVERNOR	9	GENERAL MANAGER	GOVERNOR
3			10	GENERAL MANAGER	GOVERNOR
4			11		
5			12		
6			13		
7			14		

REPLACEMENT NOTES:

#13-16, Z prefix.

BRITISH ADMINISTRATION

THE GAMBIA CURRENCY BOARD

1965 ND ISSUE

Pound System

#1-3 sailboat at l. Wmk. Crocodile's head. Sign. 1.

		VG	VF	UNC
1	**10 Shillings**			
	ND (1965-70). Green and brown on multicolor underprint. Workers in field on back.			
	a. Issued note.	5.00	15.00	45.00
	s. Specimen.	—	—	175.
	ct. Color trial. Blue and green on multicolor underprint.	—	—	250.

		VG	VF	UNC
2	**1 Pound**			
	ND (1965-70). Red and brown on multicolor underprint. Loading sacks at dockside on back.			
	a. Issued note.	6.00	22.50	70.00
	s. Specimen.	—	—	175.
	ct. Color trial. Brown and gray on multicolor underprint.	—	—	250.

		VG	VF	UNC
3	**5 Pounds**			
	ND (1965-70). Blue and green on multicolor underprint. Back blue; man and woman operating agricultural machine at center right.			
	a. Issued note.	15.00	40.00	125.
	s. Specimen.	—	—	175.
	ct. Color trial. Gray-brown and green on multicolor underprint.	—	—	250.

REPUBLIC

CENTRAL BANK OF THE GAMBIA

1971; 1972 ND ISSUE

Dalasi System

#4-8 sailboat at l., Pres. D. Kairaba Jawara at r. Sign. varieties. Wmk: Crocodile's head.

		VG	VF	UNC
4	**1 Dalasi**			
	ND (1971-87). Purple on multicolor underprint. Back similar to #1.			
	a. Signature 2.	4.00	15.00	50.00
	b. Signature 3.	4.50	15.00	65.00
	c. Signature 4.	2.50	9.00	20.00
	d. Signature 5.	1.50	5.00	10.00
	e. Signature 6.	.75	2.50	5.00
	f. Signature 7.	.50	2.00	4.00
	g. Signature 8.	1.00	4.00	7.00
	p. Proof.	—	—	250.
	s. Specimen.	—	—	65.00

		VG	VF	UNC
5	**5 Dalasis**			
	ND (1972-86). Red on multicolor underprint. Back similar to #2.			
	a. Signature 2.	17.50	35.00	140.
	b. Signature 4.	3.00	7.00	25.00
	c. Signature 6.	2.00	5.00	15.00
	d. Signature 7.		3.00	8.00
	s. Specimen.	—	—	100.

		VG	VF	UNC
6	**10 Dalasis**			
	ND (1972-86). Green on multicolor underprint. Fishermen in boat with net on back.			
	a. Signature 3.	5.00	15.00	40.00
	b. Signature 4. Reported not confirmed.	—	—	—
	c. Signature 6.	3.25	6.00	14.00
	d. Signature 7.	1.50	4.00	10.00
	s. Specimen.	—	—	100.
	ct. Color trial. Purple-brown on multicolor underprint.	—	—	200.

		VG	VF	UNC
7	**25 Dalasis**			
	ND (1972-83). Blue on multicolor underprint. Back similar to #3 but design is at left center.			
	a. Signature 2.	30.00	65.00	240.
	b. Signature 6.	9.00	17.50	40.00
	s. As a, b. Specimen.	—	—	100.
	ct. Color trial. Slate on multicolor underprint.	—	—	400.

1978 ND COMMEMORATIVE ISSUE

#8, Opening of Central Bank on 18.2.1978

		VG	VF	UNC
8	**1 Dalasi** ND (1978). Purple on multicolor underprint. Central bank building on back; commemorative legend beneath. Signature 5.	6.00	12.50	55.00

1987 ND ISSUE

#9-11 w/line of microprinting under text: *PROMISE TO PAY....* Wmk: Crocodile's head.

		VG	VF	UNC
9	**5 Dalasis** ND (1987-90). Red and orange on multicolor underprint. Like #5.			
	a. Signature 8.	1.00	2.25	9.00
	b. Signature 10.	1.00	2.00	8.00

		VG	VF	UNC
10	**10 Dalasis** ND (1987-90). Green on multicolor underprint. Like #6 but back green and light olive.			
	a. Signature 8 with title: *GOVERNOR* at right.	1.50	3.75	12.00
	b. Signature 9 with title: *ACTING GOVERNOR* at right.	1.50	4.00	12.00

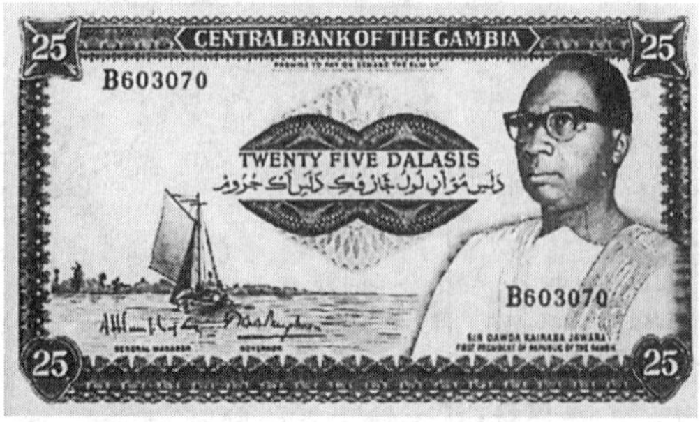

		VG	VF	UNC
11	**25 Dalasis** ND (1987-90).Blue on multicolor underprint. Like #7 but back blue, black and aqua.			
	a. Signature 8 with title: *GOVERNOR* at right.	5.00	12.00	45.00
	b. Signature 9 with title: *ACTING GOVERNOR* at right.	4.00	9.00	35.00
	c. Signature 10.	3.75	7.50	32.50
	s. Specimen.	—	—	100.

1989-91 ND ISSUE

#12-15 Pres. Jawara at r. Microprinting of bank name above and below title. Wmk: Crocodile's head. Replacement notes: serial # prefix *Z/1*.

		VG	VF	UNC
12	**5 Dalasis** ND (1991-95). Red and orange on multicolor underprint. Giant Kingfisher at center. Herding cattle on back.			
	a. Signature 10.	FV	2.00	3.75
	b. Signature 11.	FV	2.00	3.50
	s. Specimen.	—	—	40.00

		VG	VF	UNC
13	**10 Dalasis** ND (1991-95). Dark green, green and olive-green on multicolor underprint. Sacred Ibis at center. Abuko Earth satellite station at left center on back.			
	a. Signature 10.	FV	3.50	5.00
	b. Signature 11.	FV	2.50	4.00
	s. Specimen.	—	—	40.00

		VG	VF	UNC
14	**25 Dalasis** ND (1991-95). Dark blue-violet, black and blue on multicolor underprint. Carmine Bee Eater at center government house at left center on back. Signature 10.			
	a. Issued note.	FV	FV	10.00
	s. Specimen.	—	—	40.00

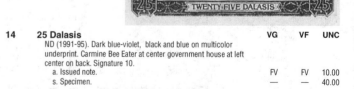

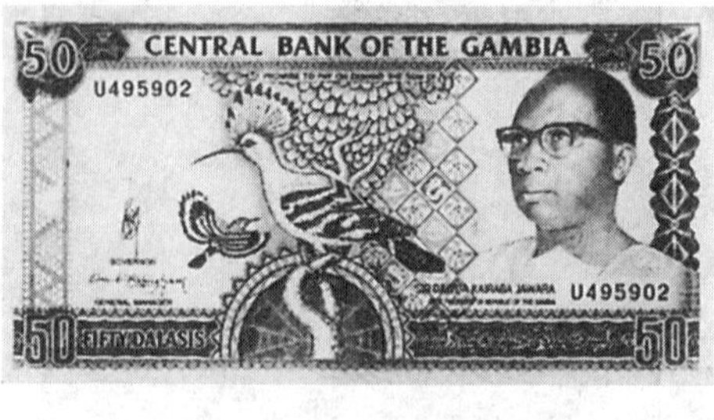

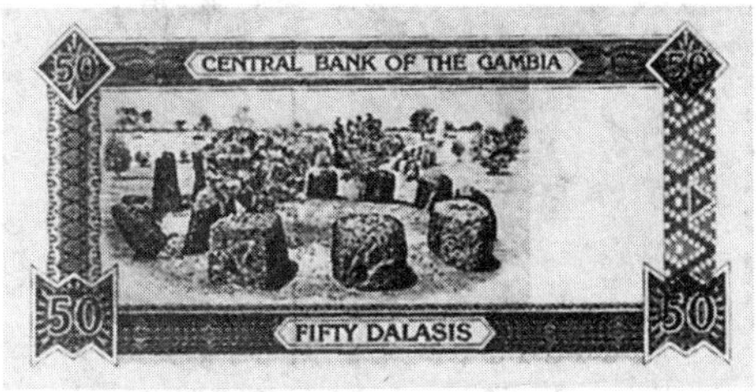

15	50 Dalasis	VG	VF	UNC
	ND (1989-95). Purple and violet on multicolor underprint. Hoopoe birds at center. Stone circles at Wassu on back. Signature 10.			
	a. Issued note.	FV	FV	20.00
	s. Specimen.	—	—	40.00

1996 ND Issue

#16-19 backs similar to #12-15. Wmk: Crocodile's head. W/o imprint. Sign. 12. Replacement notes: Serial # prefix *Z*.

16	5 Dalasis	VG	VF	UNC
	ND (1996). Red, orange and dark brown on multicolor underprint. Giant Kingfisher at center, young girl at right. Back like #12.			
	a. Issued note.	FV	FV	2.50
	s. Specimen.	—	—	35.00

17	10 Dalasis	VG	VF	UNC
	ND (1996). Dark green, bright green and olive-green on multicolor underprint. Sacred Ibis at center, young boy at right. Back like #13.			
	a. Issued note.	FV	FV	4.00
	s. Specimen.	—	—	35.00

18	25 Dalasis	VG	VF	UNC
	ND (1996). Deep blue-violet, black and blue on multicolor underprint. Carmine Bee Eater at center, man at right. Back like #14.			
	a. Issued note.	FV	6.00	10.00
	s. Specimen.	—	—	40.00

19	50 Dalasis	VG	VF	UNC
	ND (1996). Purple and violet on multicolor underprint. Hoopoe birds at center, woman at right. Back like #15.			
	a. Issued note.	FV	FV	15.00
	s. Specimen.	—	—	40.00

2001 ND Issue

#20-24 like #16-19 except that vertical serial # is in ascending size.

20	5 Dalasis	VG	VF	UNC
	ND (2001). Multicolor. Like #16 but with ascending size vertical serial #.			
	a. Signature 13.	FV	FV	2.00
	b. Signature 14.	FV	FV	2.00
	c. Signature 15.	FV	FV	2.00

21	10 Dalasis	VG	VF	UNC
	ND (2001). Multicolor. Like #17 but with ascending size vertical serial #.			
	a. Signature 13.	FV	FV	3.50
	b. Signature 14.	FV	FV	3.50
	c. Signature 15.	FV	FV	3.50

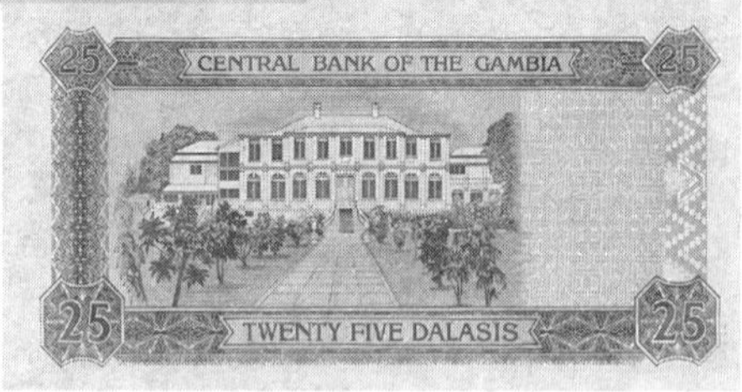

		VG	VF	UNC
22	**25 Dalasis** ND (2001). Multicolor. Like #18 but with ascending size vertical serial #.			
	a. Signature 13.	FV	FV	6.00
	b. Signature 14.	FV	FV	4.00
	c. Signatrure 15.	FV	FV	4.00

23	**50 Dalasis** ND (2001). Multicolor. Like #19 but with ascending size vertical serial #.			
	a. Signature 13.	—	Unc	10.00
	b. Signature 14.	—	Unc	10.00
	c. Signature 15.	FV	FV	10.00

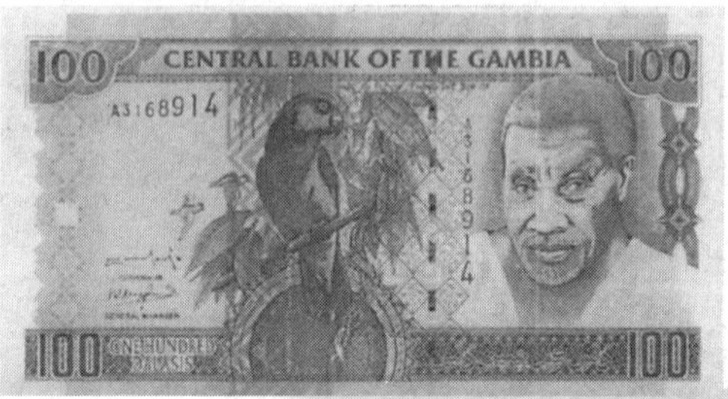

		VG	VF	UNC
24	**100 Dalasis** ND (2001). Multicolor. Senegal Parrot at center, male bust facing at right.			
	a. Signature 13.	FV	FV	20.00
	b. Signature 14.	FV	FV	20.00
	c. Signature 15.	FV	FV	20.00

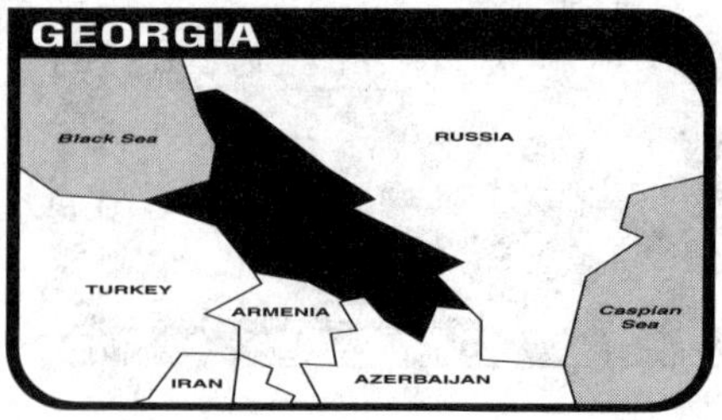

Georgia is bounded by the Black Sea to the west and by Turkey, Armenia and Azerbaijan. It occupies the western part of Transcaucasia covering an area of 26,900 sq. mi. (69,700 sq. km.), and a population of 5.42 million. Capital: Tbilisi. Hydro-electricity, minerals, forestry and agriculture are the chief industries.

The Georgian dynasty first emerged after the Macedonian victory over the Achaemenid Persian empire in the 4th century B.C. Roman "friendship" was imposed in 65 B.C. after Pompey's victory over Mithradates. The Georgians embraced Christianity in the 4th century A.D. During the next three centuries Georgia was involved in the ongoing conflicts between the Byzantine and Persian empires. The latter developed control until Georgia regained its independence in 450-503 A.D. but then it reverted to a Persian province in 533 A.D., then restored as a kingdom by the Byzantines in 562 A.D. It was established as an Arab emirate in the 8th century. Over the following centuries Turkish and Persian rivalries along with civil strife, divided the area under the two influences.

Russian interests increased and a treaty of alliance was signed on July 24, 1773 whereby Russia guaranteed Georgian independence while it acknowledged Russian suzerainty. Persia invaded again in 1795. Russia slowly took over annexing piece by piece and soon developed total domination. After the Russian Revolution, the Georgians, Armenians and Azerbaijanis formed the short- lived Transcaucasian Federal Republic on Sept. 20, 1917, which broke up into three independent republics on May 26, 1918. A Germano-Georgian treaty was signed on May 28, 1918, followed by a Turko-Georgian peace treaty on June 4. The end of WW I and the collapse of the central powers allowed free elections.

On May 20, 1920, Soviet Russia concluded a peace treaty recognizing its independence, but later invaded on Feb. 11, 1921 and a soviet republic was proclaimed. On March 12, 1922 Stalin included Georgia in a newly formed Transcaucasian Soviet Federated Socialist Republic. On Dec. 5, 1936, the T.S.F.S.R. was dissolved and Georgia became a direct member of the U.S.S.R. The collapse of the U.S.S.R. allowed full transition to independence and on April 9, 1991, the republic, as an independent state, d on its original treaty of independence of May 1918 was declared.

Independent from May 26, 1918 to March 18, 1921. Commonly refered to in Russian as 'Gruzia' it was the last area in Transcaucasia to fall under Bolshevik control.

MONETARY SYSTEM:

1 Lari = 1,000,000 'old' Laris, 1995-
1 Lari = 100 Thetri to 1995

REPUBLIC OF GEORGIA

GEORGIAN NATIONAL BANK

FIRST 1993 *KUPONI* ND ISSUE

#25-32, view of Tbilisi at ctr. r. w/equestrian statue of Kg. V. Gorgosal in foreground, Mt. Tatzminda in background. Cave dwellings at l. ctr. on back. Fractional serial # prefix w/1 as denominator. Wmk: Hexagonal design repeated.

#25-28 w/o ornate triangular design at l. and r. of lg. value in box at l. ctr. on face, or at sides of value at r. on back.

#23 and 24 not used.

		VG	VF	UNC
25	**5 (Laris)** ND (1993). Dull brown on lilac underprint with rosettes at sides of value on face and back.	.05	.25	2.50

		VG	VF	UNC
26	**10 (Laris)** ND (1993). Yellow-brown on lilac underprint.	.05	.30	3.00

		VG	VF	UNC
27	**50 (Laris)** ND (1993). Light blue on lilac underprint.	.10	.50	4.00
28	**100 (Laris)** ND (1993). Greenish gray and light brown on lilac underprint.	.15	.75	5.00

29	500 (Laris)	VG	VF	UNC
	ND (1993). Purple on lilac underprint.	.20	.75	5.00

30	1000 (Laris)	VG	VF	UNC
	ND (1993). Blue-gray and brown on lilac underprint.	.30	1.50	10.00

31	5000 (Laris)	VG	VF	UNC
	ND (1993). Green and brown on lilac underprint. Back green on pale brown-orange.	.20	1.00	5.00

32	10,000 (Laris)	VG	VF	UNC
	ND (1993). Violet on lilac and brown underprint.	.50	3.00	15.00

SECOND 1993 *KUPONI* ND ISSUE

#33-38 like #25-28 but w/ornate triangular design at l. and r. of lg. value in box at l. ctr. on face, and at sides of value at r. on back. Fractional serial # prefix w/2 as denominator. Wmk: Hexagonal design repeated.

33	1 (Laris)	VG	VF	UNC
	ND (1993). Red-orange and light brown on lilac underprint. Similar to #25.	.05	.15	1.00

34	3 (Laris)	VG	VF	UNC
	ND (1993). Purple and light brown on lilac underprint. Similar to #25.	.05	.15	1.00

35	5 (Laris)	VG	VF	UNC
	ND (1993). Like #25.	.05	.15	.75

36	10 (Laris)	VG	VF	UNC
	ND (1993). Like #26.	.05	.15	1.00

37	50 (Laris)	VG	VF	UNC
	ND (1993). Like #27.	.05	.20	2.00

38	100 (Laris)	VG	VF	UNC
	ND (1993). Like #28.	.10	.50	3.00

THIRD 1993 DATED ISSUE

#39-42 similar to first 1993 issue but fractional serial # prefix w/3 as denominator.

39	10,000 (Laris)	VG	VF	UNC
	1993. Violet on lilac and brown underprint.	.15	.50	4.00

40	25,000 (Laris)	VG	VF	UNC
	1993. Orange and dull brown on lilac underprint.	.20	1.00	6.00

41	50,000 (Laris)	VG	VF	UNC
	1993. Pale red-brown and tan on lilac underprint. Back dull red-brown on pale brown-orange underprint.	.20	1.00	4.00

42	100,000 (Laris)	VG	VF	UNC
	1993. Olive-green and brown on lilac underprint. Back pale olive-green on dull brown-orange underprint.	.20	1.00	5.00

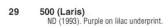

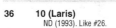

FOURTH 1993 DATED ISSUE

#43-46 griffin at l. and r. of ornate round design at ctr. on face. 2 bunches of grapes w/vine above and below value on vertical format back. Wmk: Isometric rectangular design.

		VG	VF	UNC
43	**250 (Laris)**			
	1993. Dark blue on green, lilac and light blue underprint.			
	a. With security thread.	.05	.15	1.25
	b. Without security thread.	—	—	—

		VG	VF	UNC
44	**2000 (Laris)**			
	1993. Green and blue on gold and green underprint.	.10	.50	2.00

		VG	VF	UNC
45	**3000 (Laris)**			
	1993. Brown and yellow on light brown underprint.	.10	.50	2.00

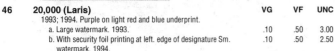

		VG	VF	UNC
46	**20,000 (Laris)**			
	1993; 1994. Purple on light red and blue underprint.			
	a. Large watermark. 1993.	.10	.50	3.00
	b. With security foil printing at left. edge of designature Sm. watermark. 1994.	.10	.50	2.50

NOTICE

Readers with unlisted dates, signature varieties, etc. are invited to submit photocopies of their notes to: Standard Catalog of World Paper Money, 700 East State St. Iola, WI 54990-0001, E-Mail: george.cuhaj@fwpubs.com.

1994 ISSUE

#47-52 similar to #43-46 but w/security foil printing at l. edge of design. Wmk: Isometric rectangular design repeated.

		VG	VF	UNC
47	**30,000 (Laris)**			
	1994. Dull red-brown on pale orange and light gray underprint.	.10	1.00	5.00

		VG	VF	UNC
48	**50,000 (Laris)**			
	1994. Dark olive-green and dull black on pale olive-green and tan underprint.	.15	1.00	5.00

		VG	VF	UNC
48A	**100,000 (Laris)**			
	1994. Dark gray on light blue and light gray underprint.			
	a. With security thread. Large watermark.	.20	.75	5.00
	b. Without security thread. Sm. watermark.	.20	.75	5.00

		VG	VF	UNC
49	**150,000 (Laris)**			
	1994. Dark blue-green on pale blue, light gray and lilac underprint.	.20	1.00	6.00

		VG	VF	UNC
50	**250,000 (Laris)**			
	1994. Brown-orange on pale orange and light green underprint.	.20	.75	4.50

51 **500,000 (Laris)**

	VG	VF	UNC
1994. Deep violet on pale purple and pink underprint.	.20	.75	3.00

52 **1 Million (Laris)**

	VG	VF	UNC
1994. Red on pink and pale yellow-brown underprint.	.25	1.00	7.00

1994 Privatization Check Voucher Issue

52A **Various Denominations**

	VG	VF	UNC
1994. Orange, black and Multicolor.	3.50	7.50	25.00

1995 Issue

#57-59 wmk: Griffin.

#53-59 arms at l. to ctr.

53 **1 Lari**

	VG	VF	UNC
1995. Dull purple on multicolor underprint. N. Pirosmani between branches at center. View of Tbilisi, painting of deer at center right on back.	.50	1.00	3.00

54 **2 Lari**

	VG	VF	UNC
1995. Deep olive-green on multicolor underprint. Bars of music at left, Z. Paliashvili at center right. Opera House in Tbilisi at center right on back.	.75	1.50	6.00

55 **5 Lari**

	VG	VF	UNC
1995. Brown on multicolor underprint. I. Javakhishvili at center. Map above ornate lion statue at left center, Tbilisi State University above open book at right.	.75	1.50	10.00

56 **10 Lari**

	VG	VF	UNC
1995. Blue-black on multicolor underprint. Flowers at left, A. Tseriteli and barn swallow at center right. Woman seated on stump while spinning yarn with a crop spindle between ornamental branches at center right on back. Watermark: Arms repeated vertically.	.75	5.00	12.50

57 **20 Lari**

	VG	VF	UNC
1995. Dark brown on multicolor underprint. Open book and newspaper at upper left, I. Chavchavadze at center. Statue of King V. Gorgosal between views of Tbilisi at center right on back.	5.00	10.00	35.00

58 **50 Lari**

	VG	VF	UNC
1995. Dark brown and deep blue-green on multicolor underprint. Griffin at left, Princess Tamara at center right. Mythical figure at center right on back.	5.00	25.00	50.00

59 **100 Lari**

	VG	VF	UNC
1995. Dark brown, purple and black on multicolor underprint. Carved bust of S. Rustaveli at center right. Frieze at upper center right on back.	5.00	45.00	75.00

		VG	VF	UNC
60	**500 Lari** 1995. Deep purple on multicolor underprint. King David "The Builder" with buildingg at center Early Georgian inscriptions, cross on back. (Not issued).	—	—	500.

1999 Issue

#61-67 similar to #53-59 but for country name change in English to *GEORGIA*.

		VG	VF	UNC
61	**1 Lari** 1999. Deep purple on multicolor underprint. Similar to #53.	.50	.75	1.50
62	**2 Lari** 1999. Deep olive-green on multicolor underprint. Similar to #54.	.50	.75	3.00
63	**5 Lari** 1999. Brown on multicolor underprint. Similar to #55.	.50	2.00	4.50
64	**10 Lari** 1999. Blue-black on multicolor underprint. Similar to #56.	5.00	7.50	17.50
65	**20 Lari** 1999. Dark brown on multicolor underprint. Similar to #57.	8.00	10.00	20.00

		VG	VF	UNC
66	**50 Lari** 1999. Dark brown and deep blue-green on multicolor underprint. Similar to #58.	15.00	20.00	30.00

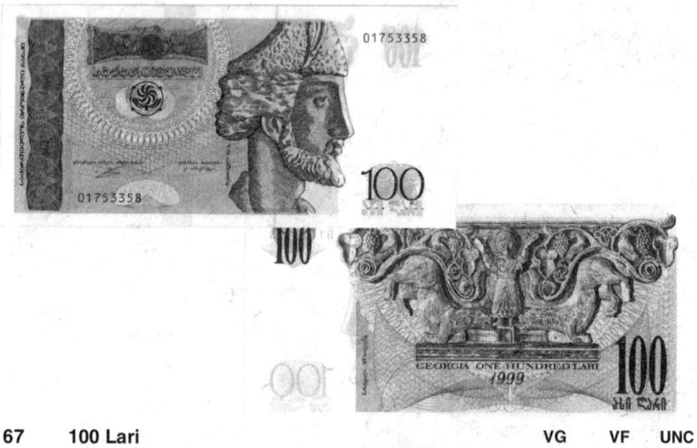

		VG	VF	UNC
67	**100 Lari** 1999. Dark brown, purple and black on multicolor underprint. Similar to #59.	25.00	30.00	55.00

2002; 2004 Issue

		VG	VF	UNC
68	**1 Lari** 2002. Deep purple on multicolor underprint.	.50	.75	1.50

		VG	VF	UNC
69	**2 Lari** 2002. Deep olive-green on multicolor underprint.	.75	1.00	3.50

		VG	VF	UNC
70	**5 Lari** 2002. Brown on multicolor underprint.	1.25	1.50	4.50

		VG	VF	UNC
71	**10 Lari** 2002. Blue-black on multicolor underprint.	2.50	3.00	17.50

		VG	VF	UNC
72	**20 Lari** 2002. Dark brwn on multicolor underprint.	5.00	6.00	20.00

		VG	VF	UNC
73	**50 Lari** 2004.	20.00	25.00	50.00

74	100 Lari	VG	VF	UNC
	2004.	55.00	70.00	110.
75	200 Lari			
	2004.	130.	150.	175.

Note: The 1991-1992 ND Provisional Issues, R1-R6, and the 1993 Georgia Military Issues, M1-M8 have been determined to be spurious in nature and have been eliminated from the listings.

The Federal Republic of Germany (formerly West Germany), located in north-central Europe, since 1990 with the unification of East Germany, has an area of 137,782 sq. mi. (356,854 sq. km.) and a population of 82.69 million. Capital: Berlin. The economy centers about one of the world's foremost industrial establishments. Machinery, motor vehicles, iron, steel, chemicals, yarns and fabrics are exported.

During the post-Normandy phase of World War II, Allied troops occupied the western German provinces of Schleswig-Holstein, Hamburg, Lower Saxony, Bremen, North Rhine-Westphalia, Hesse, Rhineland-Palatinate, Baden-Wurttemberg, Bavaria and Saarland. The conquered provinces were divided into American, British and French occupation zones. Five eastern German provinces were occupied and administered by the forces of the Soviet Union.

The western occupation forces restored the civil status of their zones on Sept. 21, 1949, and resumed diplomatic relations with the provinces on July 2, 1951. On May 5, 1955, nine of the ten western provinces, organized as the Federal Republic of Germany, became fully independent. The tenth province, Saarland, was restored to the republic on Jan. 1, 1957.

The post-WW II division of Germany ended on Oct. 3, 1990, when the German Democratic Republic (East Germany) ceased to exist and its five constituent provinces were formally admitted to the Federal Republic of Germany. An election Dec. 2, 1990, chose representatives to the united federal parliament (Bundestag), which then conducted its opening session in Berlin in the old Reichstag building.

MONETARY SYSTEM:

1 Deutsche Mark (DM) = 100 Pfennig, 1948-2001
1 Euro = 100 Cents, 2002-

FEDERAL REPUBLIC

DEUTSCHE BUNDESBANK

1960 ISSUE

#18-24 portr. as wmk. Replacement notes: Serial # prefix *Y, Z*.
#18-22 w/ or w/o ultraviolet sensitive features.

18	5 Deutsche Mark	VG	VF	UNC
	2.1.1960. Green on multicolor underprint. Young Venetian woman by Albrecht Dürer (1505) at right. Oak sprig at left center.			
	a. Issued note.	FV	FV	14.00
	s. Specimen.	—	—	100.

19	10 Deutsche Mark	VG	VF	UNC
	2.1.1960. Blue on multicolor underprint. Young man by Albrecht Dürer at right. Sail training ship *Gorch Fock*			
	a. Issued note.	FV	12.00	50.00
	s. Specimen.	—	—	100.

20	20 Deutsche Mark	VG	VF	UNC
	2.1.1960. Black and green on multicolor underprint. Elsbeth Tucher by Albrecht Dürer (1499) at right. Violin, bow and clarinet.			
	a. Issued note.	FV	20.00	65.00
	s. Specimen.	—	—	100.

21	50 Deutsche Mark	VG	VF	UNC
	2.1.1960. Brown and olive-green on multicolor underprint. Portrait of Hand Urmiller by Barthel Beham (about 1525) at right. Holsten-Tor gate in Lübeck.			
	a. Issued note.	FV	20.00	80.00
	s. Specimen.	—	—	100.

22	100 Deutsche Mark	VG	VF	UNC
	2.1.1960. Blue on multicolor underprint. *Master Sebastian Münster* by Christoph Amberger (1552) at right. Eagle.			
	a. Issued note.	FV	75.00	190.
	s. Specimen.	—	—	150.

23	500 Deutsche Mark	VG	VF	UNC
	2.1.1960. Brown-lilac on multicolor underprint. Male portrait by Hans Maler zu Schwaz. Eltz Castle.			
	a. Issued note.	FV	375.	750.
	s. Specimen.	—	—	400.

24	1000 Deutsche Mark	VG	VF	UNC
	2.1.1960. Dark brown on multicolor underprint. Astronomer Johann Schöner by Lucas Cranach the Elder at right. Cathedral of Limburg on the Lahn.			
	a. Issued note.	FV	700.	1100.
	s. Specimen.	—	—	600.

BUNDESKASSENSCHEIN

1967 ND ISSUE

#25-29A small change notes. Printed for use in a coin shortage which never developed. Not issued. Replacement notes: Serial # prefix 4 petals (+). Printer: BDDK (w/o imprint).

25	5 Pfennig	VG	VF	UNC
	ND. Black and dark green on lilac underprint. (Not issued).	—	—	—

26	10 Pfennig	VG	VF	UNC
	ND. Dark brown on tan underprint. (Not issued).	—	—	15.00
27	50 Pfennig			
	ND. (Not issued).	—	—	—

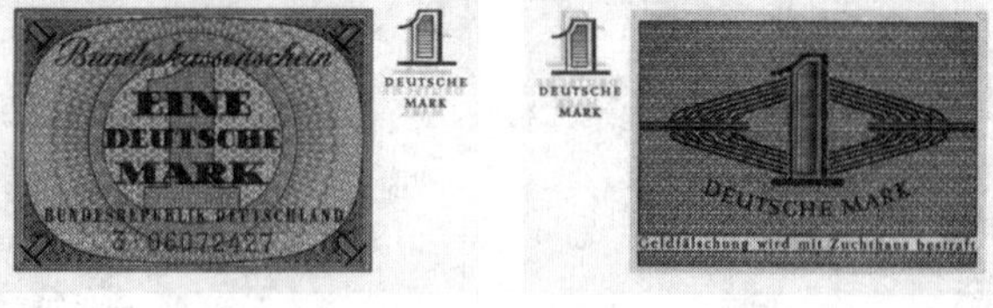

28	1 Deutsche Mark	VG	VF	UNC
	ND. Brown and blue on multicolor underprint. (Not issued).	—	—	75.00

		VG	VF	UNC
29	**2 Deutsche Mark** ND. Purple and tan on multicolor underprint. (Not issued).	—	—	20.00
29A	**5 Deutsche Mark** 1.7.1963. Brown. Young Venetian woman by Albrecht Dürer. Like #18.	—	—	—

DEUTSCHE BUNDESBANK (CONT.)

1970-80 ISSUE

#30-36 portr. as wmk. Replacement notes: Serial # prefix *Y, Z, YA-, ZA-*. Values are significantly higher.

30	**5 Deutsche Mark**	VG	VF	UNC
	1970; 1980. Green on multicolor underprint. Like #18.			
	a. 2.1.1970.	FV	25.00	60.00
	b. With © *DEUTSCHE BUNDESBANK 1963* on back. 2.1.1980.	FV	6.00	9.00
	s. Specimen. As a.	—	—	100.

#31a-34a letters of serial # either 2.8 or 3.3mm in height.

31	**10 Deutsche Mark**	VG	VF	UNC
	1970-80. Blue on multicolor underprint. Like #19.			
	a. 2.1.1970.	FV	10.00	32.50
	b. 1.6.1977.	FV	10.00	25.00
	c. Without © notice. 2.1.1980.	FV	10.00	25.00
	d. With © *DEUTSCHE BUNDESBANK 1963* on back. 2.1.1980.	FV	7.50	12.50
	s. Specimen.	—	—	100.

32	**20 Deutsche Mark**	VG	VF	UNC
	1970-80. Black and green on multicolor underprint. Like #20.			
	a. 2.1.1970.	FV	20.00	60.00
	b. 1.6.1977.	FV	20.00	60.00
	c. Without © notice. 2.1.1980.	FV	20.00	60.00
	d. With © *DEUTSCHE BUNDESBANK 1961* on back. 2.1.1980.	FV	7.50	35.00
	s. Specimen.	—	—	100.

33	**50 Deutsche Mark**	VG	VF	UNC
	1970-80. Brown and olive-green on multicolor underprint. Like #21.			
	a. 2.1.1970.	FV	35.00	85.00
	b. 1.6.1977.	FV	30.00	75.00
	c. Without © notice. 2.1.1980.	FV	30.00	75.00
	d. With © *DEUTSCHE BUNDESBANK 1962* on back. 2.1.1980.	FV	30.00	70.00
	s. Specimen.	—	—	100.

34	**100 Deutsche Mark**	VG	VF	UNC
	1970-80. Blue on multicolor underprint. Like #22.			
	a. 2.1.1970.	FV	70.00	140.
	b. 1.6.1977.	FV	70.00	140.
	c. Without © notice. 2.1.1980.	FV	70.00	140.
	d. With © *DEUTSCHE BUNDESBANK 1962* on back. 2.1.1980.	FV	65.00	125.
	s. Specimen.	—	—	100.
35	**500 Deutsche Mark**			
	1970-80. Brown-lilac on multicolor underprint. Like #23.			
	a. 2.1.1970.	FV	335.	625.
	b. 1.6.1977.	FV	300.	500.
	c. 2.1.1980.	FV	300.	550.
	s. Specimen.	—	—	400.

36 1000 Deutsche Mark
1977-80. Dark brown on multicolor underprint. Astronomer Johannes Schöner by Lucas Cranach "the elder" at right and as watermark Cathedral of Limburg on the Lahn on back.

		VG	VF	UNC
36	**1000 Deutsche Mark**			
	a. 1.6.1977.	FV	675.	1100.
	b. 2.1.1980.	FV	625.	950.
	s. Specimen.	—	—	600.

1989-91 ISSUE

#37-44 replacement notes: Serial # prefix *ZA; YA.*

		VG	VF	UNC
37	**5 Deutsche Mark**			
	1.8.1991. Green and olive-green on multicolor underprint. Bettina von Arnim (1785-1859) at right. Bank seal and Brandenburg Gate in Berlin at left center, script on open envelope at lower right in watermark area on back. Signature Schlesinger-Tietmeyer.	FV	FV	7.50

		VG	VF	UNC
38	**10 Deutsche Mark**			
	1989-99. Purple, violet and blue on multicolor underprint. Carl Friedrich Gauss (1777-1855) at right. Sextant at left center, mapping at lower right in watermark area on back.			
	a. Signature Pöhl-Schlesinger. 2.1.1989.	FV	FV	20.00
	b. Signature Schlesinger-Tietmeyer. 1.8.1991.	FV	FV	15.00
	c. Signature Tietmeyer-Gaddum. 1.10.1993.	FV	FV	10.00
	d. Signature Welteke-Stark. 1.9.1999.	FV	FV	12.50
	e. Uncut sheet of 54 notes, signature as c or d.	—	—	400.

		VG	VF	UNC
39	**20 Deutsche Mark**			
	1991; 1993. Green and red-violet on multicolor underprint. Annette von Droste-Hülshoff (1797-1848) at right. Quill pen and beech-tree at left center, open book at lower right in watermark area on back.			
	a. Signature Schlesinger-Tietmeyer. 1.8.1991.	FV	FV	30.00
	b. Signature Tietmeyer-Gaddum. 1.10.1993.	FV	FV	30.00

		VG	VF	UNC
40	**50 Deutsche Mark**			
	1989-93. Dark brown and red-brown on multicolor underprint. Balthasar Neuman (1687-1753) at right. Architectural drawing of Bishop's residence in Würzburg at left center, building blueprint at lower right in watermark area on back.			
	a. Signature Pöhl-Schlesinger. 2.1.1989.	FV	FV	75.00
	b. Signature Schlesinger-Tietmeyer. 1.8.1991.	FV	FV	70.00
	c. Signature Tietmeyer-Gaddum. 1.10.1993.	FV	FV	70.00

		VG	VF	UNC
41	**100 Deutsche Mark**			
	1989-93. Deep blue and violet on multicolor underprint. Clara Schumann (1819-1896) at center right. Building at left in background, grand piano at center, multiple tuning forks at lower right in watermark area on back.			
	a. Signature Pöhl-Schlesinger. 2.1.1989.	FV	FV	140.
	b. Signature Schlesinger-Tietmeyer. 1.8.1991.	FV	FV	130.
	c. Signature Tietmeyer-Gaddum. 1.10.1993.	FV	FV	135.

		VG	VF	UNC
42	**200 Deutsche Mark**			
	2.1.1989. Red-orange and blue on multicolor underprint. Paul Ehrlich (1854-1915) at right. Microscope at left center, medical science symbol at lower right in watermark area on back. Signature Pöhl-Schlesinger.	FV	FV	225.

43	500 Deutsche Mark	VG	VF	UNC
	1991; 1993. Red-violet and blue on multicolor underprint. Maria Sibylla Merian (1647-1717) at right. Dandelion with butterfly and caterpillar at center, flower at lower right in watermark area on back.			
	a. Signature Schlesinger-Tietmeyer. 1.8.1991.	FV	FV	425.
	b. Signature Tietmeyer-Gaddum. 1.10.1993.	FV	FV	400.

44	1000 Deutsche Mark	VG	VF	UNC
	1.8.1991; 1.10.1993. Deep brown-violet and blue-green on multicolor underprint. City drawing at center, Wilhelm and Jakob Grimm (1786-1859 and 1785-1863) at center right. Bank seal at left, book frontispiece of *Deutches Wörterbuch* over entry for freedom at left center, child collecting falling stars (illustrating fairy tale *Sterntaler*) at lower right in watermark area on back.			
	a. Signature Schlesinger-Tietmeyer. 1.8.1991.	FV	FV	775.
	b. Signature Tietmeyer-Gaddum. 1.10.1993.	FV	FV	800.

1996 ISSUE

#45-47 like #40-42 but w/Kinegram foil added at l. ctr. Sign. Tietmeyer-Gaddum.

45	50 Deutsche Mark	VG	VF	UNC
	2.1.1996. Dark brown and violet on multicolor underprint. Square-shaped Kinegram foil.	FV	FV	65.00

> **NOTICE**
>
> Readers with unlisted dates, signature varieties, etc. are invited to submit photocopies of their notes to: Standard Catalog of World Paper Money, 700 East State St. Iola, WI 54990-0001, E-Mail: george.cuhaj@fwpubs.com.

46	100 Deutsche Mark	VG	VF	UNC
	2.1.1996. Deep blue and violet on multicolor underprint. Lyre-shaped Kinegram foil.	FV	FV	130.

47	200 Deutsche Mark	VG	VF	UNC
	2.1.1996. Red-orange and blue on multicolor underprint. Double hexagon-shaped Kinegram foil.	FV	FV	225.

Note: For later issues made for use in Germany see European Union listings.

The German Democratic Republic (East Germany), located on the great north European plain, ceased to exist in 1990. During the closing days of World War II in Europe, Soviet troops advancing into Germany from the east occupied the German provinces of Mecklenburg, Brandenburg, Saxony-Anhalt, Saxony and Thuringia. These five provinces comprised the occupation zone administered by the Soviet Union after the cessation of hostilities. The other three zones were administered by the United States, Great Britain and France. Under the Potsdam agreement, questions affecting Germany as a whole were to be settled by the commanders in chief of the occupation zones acting jointly and by unanimous decision. When Soviet intransigence rendered the quadripartite commission inoperable, the three western zones were united to form the Federal Republic of Germany, May 23, 1949. Thereupon the Soviet Union dissolved its occupation zone and established it as the Democratic Republic of Germany, Oct. 7, 1949. East and West Germany became reunited as one country on Oct. 3, 1990.

MONETARY SYSTEM:

1 Mark = 100 Pfennig

DEMOCRATIC REPUBLIC

DEUTSCHE NOTENBANK

1964 ISSUE

#22-26 replacement notes: Serial # prefix *YA-YZ; ZA-ZZ*.

#22 and 25 arms at l. on back.

#23, 24 and 26 arms at upper ctr. r. on back.

22	5 Mark	VG	VF	UNC
	1964. Brown on multicolor underprint. Alexander von Humboldt at right. Humboldt University in Berlin at left center on back. Watermark: Hammer and compass.			
	a. Issued note.	1.25	3.00	8.00
	s. Specimen.	—	—	25.00

23	10 Mark	VG	VF	UNC
	1964. Green on multicolor underprint. Friedrich von Schiller at right. Zeiss factory in Jena at left center on back. Watermark: Hammer and compass.			
	a. Issued note.	3.00	6.00	12.50
	s. Specimen.	—	—	25.00

24	20 Mark	VG	VF	UNC
	1964. Red-brown on multicolor underprint. Johann Wolfgang von Goethe at right and as watermark. National Theater in Weimar at left center on back.			
	a. Issued note.	2.00	7.50	15.00
	s. Specimen.	—	—	25.00

25	50 Mark	VG	VF	UNC
	1964. Deep green on multicolor underprint. Friedrich Engels at right and as watermark. Wheat threshing at left center on back.			
	a. Issued note.	5.00	10.00	30.00
	r. Replacement note. Serial # prefix ZA-ZE.	5.00	12.50	35.00
	s. Specimen.	—	—	25.00

26	100 Mark	VG	VF	UNC
	1964. Blue on multicolor underprint. Karl Marx at right and as watermark. Brandenburg Gate in Berlin at left center on back.			
	a. Issued note.	4.00	12.50	45.00
	r. Replacement note. Serial # prefix ZA, ZB.	4.00	15.00	50.00
	s. Specimen.	—	—	25.00

STAATSBANK DER DDR

1971-85 ISSUE

#27-31 arms at upper l. on face. Arms at l. on back. Portr. as wmk. Replacement notes: Serial # prefix *YA-YI, YZ, ZA-ZQ*.

27 **5 Mark**

1975. Purple on multicolor underprint. Thomas Müntzer at right. Harvesting on back.

		VG	VF	UNC
27	**5 Mark**			
	a. 6 digit wide serial #.	.40	1.00	2.50
	b. 6 digit narrow serial #. (1987).	.50	1.25	3.00
	s. As b. Specimen.	—	—	25.00

Note: A large quanity of #27 are known with mis-matched serial numbers. Value $100.00 in EF.

		VG	VF	UNC
28	**10 Mark**			
	1971. Brown on multicolor underprint. Clara Zetkin at right. Woman at radio station on back.			
	a. 6 digit wide serial #.	.75	1.75	4.50
	b. 7 digit narrow serial #. (1985).	.40	1.00	3.50
	s. As a. Specimen.	—	—	25.00

		VG	VF	UNC
29	**20 Mark**			
	1975. Green on multicolor underprint. Johann Wolfgang von Goethe at right. Children leaving school on back.			
	a. 6 digit wide serial #.	.75	2.00	5.00
	b. 7 digit narrow serial #. (1986).	1.25	3.00	7.50
	s. As b. Specimen.	—	—	25.00

		VG	VF	UNC
30	**50 Mark**			
	1971. Dark red on multicolor underprint. Friedrich Engels at right. Oil refinery on back.			
	a. 7 digit wide serial #.	1.35	4.50	15.00
	b. 7 digit narrow serial #. (1986).	1.25	3.50	10.00
	s. Specimen.	—	—	25.00

		VG	VF	UNC
31	**100 Mark**			
	1975. Blue on multicolor underprint. Karl Marx at right. Street scene in East Berlin on back.			
	a. 7 digit wide serial #.	1.75	4.50	20.00
	b. 7 digit narrow serial #. (1986).	1.75	4.50	12.00
	s. Specimen.	—	—	25.00

		VG	VF	UNC
32	**200 Mark**			
	1985. Dark olive-green and dark brown on multicolor underprint. Family at right. Teacher dancing with children in front of modern school building at center on back. Watermark: Dove. (Not issued.)	—	—	40.00

		VG	VF	UNC
33	**500 Mark**			
	1985. Dark brown on multicolor underprint. Arms at right and as watermark. Government Building Staatsrat (in Berlin) at center on back. (Not issued.)	—	—	40.00

FOREIGN EXCHANGE CERTIFICATES

FORUM-AUSSENHANDELSGESELLSCHAFT M.B.H.

1979 ISSUE

Certificates issued by state-owned export-import company. These were in the form of checks for specified amounts for purchase of special (mostly imported) goods.

1 Mark = 1 DM (West German Mark)

#FX1-FX7 replacement notes: Serial # prefix *ZA, ZB*.

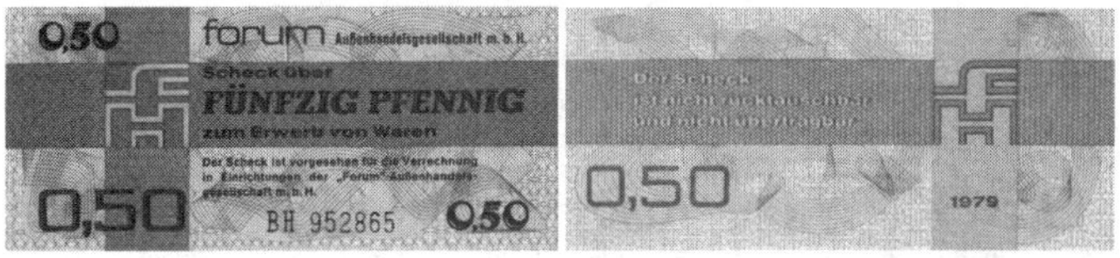

		VG	VF	UNC
FX1	**50 Pfennig**			
	1979. Violet on multicolor underprint. Back violet and orange.	.25	.75	2.00

		VG	VF	UNC
FX2	**1 Mark**			
	1979. Brown and rose.	.25	.75	3.00

		VG	VF	UNC
FX3	**5 Mark**			
	1979. Green and peach.	.50	1.50	5.00

		VG	VF	UNC
FX4	**10 Mark** 1979. Blue and light green.	.50	1.50	5.00

		VG	VF	UNC
FX5	**50 Mark** 1979. Light red and orange.	.50	1.50	5.00

		VG	VF	UNC
FX6	**100 Mark** 1979. Olive and green. Back olive and yellow.	1.00	3.00	7.50

		VG	VF	UNC
FX7	**500 Mark** 1979. Gray-brown and purple. Back gray-brown and blue.	2.50	5.00	10.00

A set of specimens of FX1-FX7 are available in two varieties: w/ovpt: *MUSTER* and w/o serial #s, or perforation *SPECIMEN* and serial # AA000000. Value at $700.

COLLECTOR SERIES

STAATSBANK DER DDR

1989 COMMEMORATIVE ISSUE

#CS1, Opening of Brandenburg Gate, 1989. Not legal tender.

		Issue Price	Market Value
CS1	**20 Mark 22.12.1989** Black and purple on multicolor underprint. Brandenburg Gate in Berlin at center.	—	300.

Note: As stated on this item, #CS1 was never intended to be legal tender.

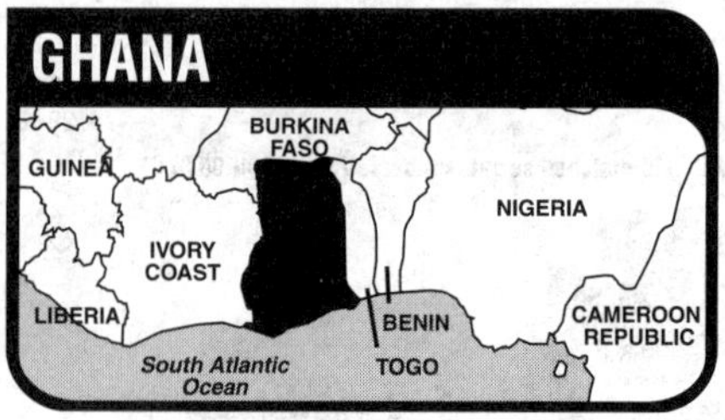

The Republic of Ghana, a member of the British Commonwealth situated on the West Coast of Africa between the Ivory Coast and Togo, has an area of 92,098 sq. mi. (238,537 sq. km.) and a population of 19.93 million, almost entirely African. Capital: Accra. Traditional exports include cocoa, coffee, timber, gold, industrial diamonds, maganese and bauxite. Additional exports include pineapples, bananas, yams, tuna, cola and salt.

Ghana was first visited by Portuguese traders in 1470, and through the 17th century was used by various European powers - England, Denmark, Holland, Germany - as a center for their slave trade. Britain achieved control of the Gold Coast in 1821, and established the colony of Gold Coast in 1874. In 1901, Britain annexed the neighboring Ashanti Kingdom; the same year a northern region known as the Northern Territories became a British protectorate. Part of the former German colony of Togoland was mandated to Britain by the League of Nations and administered as part of the Gold Coast. The state of Ghana, comprising the Gold Coast and British Togoland, obtained independence on March 6, 1957, becoming the first black African colony to do so. On July 1, 1960, Ghana adopted a republican constitution, changing from a ministerial to a presidential form of government. The government was overthrown, the constitution suspended and the National Assembly dissolved by the Ghanaian Army and police on Feb. 24, 1966. The government was returned to civilian authority in Oct. 1969, but was again seized by military officers in a bloodless coup on Jan. 13, 1972. The country was again returned to civilian rule on Sept. 24, 1979. The junior military officers once again seized power on Dec. 31, 1981 and ruled the country until Jan. 7, 1993 when power was handed over to a civilian government. Ghana remains a member of the Commonwealth of Nations, with executive authority vested in the Supreme Military Council.

Ghana's monetary denomination of "cedi" is derived from the word "sedie" meaning cowrie, a shell money commonly employed by coastal tribes.

MONETARY SYSTEM:

1 Shilling = 12 Pence
1 Pound = 20 Shillings to 1965
1 Cedi = 100 Pesewas, 1965-

REPUBLIC

BANK OF GHANA

1958-63 ISSUE

#1-3 wmk: *GHANA* in star.

		VG	VF	UNC
1	**10 Shillings** 1958-63. Green and brown on multicolor underprint. Bank of Ghana building in Accra at center right. Star. Watermark: *GHANA* in star.			
	a. 2 signature. Printer: TDLR. 1.7.1958.	4.00	20.00	55.00
	b. Without imprint. 1.7.1961.	2.50	12.50	35.00
	c. Without imprint. 1.7.1962.	4.25	20.00	57.50
	d. 1 signature 1.7.1963.	1.25	7.00	27.50
	s. As a. Specimen.	—	—	75.00

2 1 Pound

1958-62. Red-brown and blue on multicolor underprint. Bank of Ghana building in Accra at center. Cocoa pods in two heaps. Watermark: *GHANA* in star.

	VG	VF	UNC
a. Printer: TDLR. 1.7.1958; 1.4.1959.	3.25	10.00	30.00
b. Without imprint. 1.7.1961; 1.7.1962.	3.00	9.00	25.00
s. As a. Specimen.	—	—	75.00

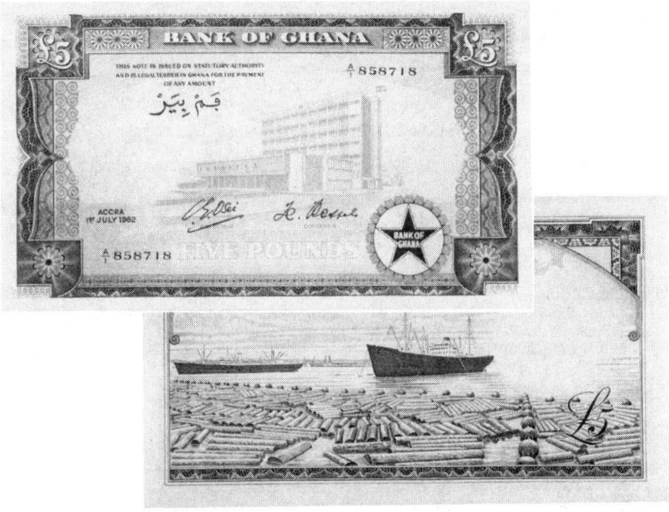

3 5 Pounds

1.7.1958-1.7.1962. Purple and orange on multicolor underprint. Bank of Ghana building in Accra at center Cargo ships, logs in water. Watermark: *GHANA* in star.

	VG	VF	UNC
a. Issued note.	10.00	25.00	80.00
s1. Specimen. 1.7.1958.	—	—	100.
s2. Specimen. Perforated: *CANCELLED*.	—	—	200.

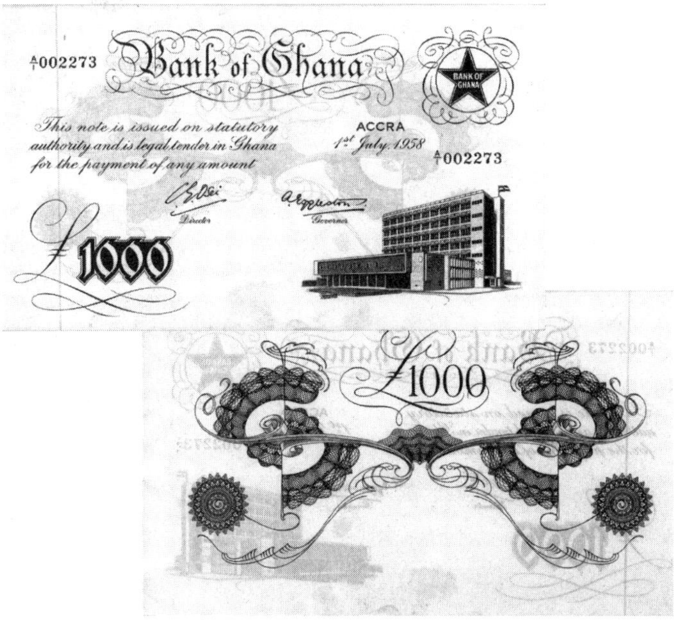

4 1000 Pounds

1.7.1958. Blackish brown. Bank of Ghana building in Accra at lower right. Ornate design. Watermark: *GHANA* in star.

	VG	VF	UNC
	10.00	100.	300.

Note: #4 was used in interbank transactions.

1965 Issue

#5-9 wmk: Kwame Nkrumah.

5 1 Cedi

ND (1965). Blue on multicolor underprint. Portrait K. Nkrumah at upper right. Bank on back.

	VG	VF	UNC
a. Issued note.	2.50	5.50	10.00
s. Specimen, punch hole cancelled.	—	—	35.00
ct. Color trial. Red multicolor underprint.	—	—	200.

6 5 Cedis

ND (1965). Dark brown on multicolor underprint. Portrait K. Nkrumah at upper right. Parliament House at left center on back. Signature 3.

	VG	VF	UNC
a. Issued note.	2.50	6.00	14.00
s. Specimen, punch hole cancelled.	—	—	35.00
ct. Color trial. Green multicolor underprint.	—	—	200.

7 10 Cedis

ND (1965). Green on multicolor underprint. Portrait K. Nkrumah at upper left. Independence Square at center on back. Signature 3.

	VG	VF	UNC
a. Issued note.	4.00	9.00	25.00
s. Specimen, punch hole cancelled.	—	—	35.00
ct. Color trial. dark blue multicolor underprint.	—	—	200.

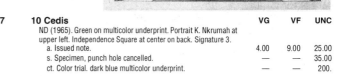

8 50 Cedis

ND (1965). Red on multicolor underprint. Portrait K. Nkrumah at upper left. Island and coconut trees on back. Signature 3.

	VG	VF	UNC
a. Issued note.	8.00	25.00	60.00
s. Specimen, punch hole cancelled.	—	—	35.00
ct. Color trial. light blue on multicolor underprint.	—	—	250.

9 **100 Cedis**
ND (1965). Purple on multicolor underprint. Portrait K. Nkrumah at upper right. Hospital on back. Signature 3.

	VG	VF	UNC
a. Issued note.	15.00	35.00	80.00
s. Specimen.	—	—	55.00
ct. Color trial. Brown multicolor underprint.	—	—	300.

9A **1000 Cedis**
ND(1965). Black. Large star at upper left. Bank of Ghana building in Accra at right on back. Signature 3.

	VG	VF	UNC
a. Issued note.	—	175.	450.
s. Specimen.	—	—	—
ct. Color trial. Purple.	—	—	700.

1967 Issue

Various date and sign. varieties.
#10-16 wmk: Arms - Eagle's head above star. Replacement notes: Serial # prefix *Z/99*.

10 **1 Cedi**
23.2.1967; 8.1.1969; 1.10.1970; 1.10.1971. Blue on multicolor underprint. Cacao tree with pods at right. Shield and ceremonial sword on back. Signature 4, 5.

	VG	VF	UNC
a. 23.2.1967.	1.50	4.00	7.00
b. 8.1.1969.	2.00	5.00	10.00
c. 1.10.1970.	1.25	4.00	7.00
d. 1.10.1971.	1.00	3.50	6.50
s. Specimen.	—	—	45.00

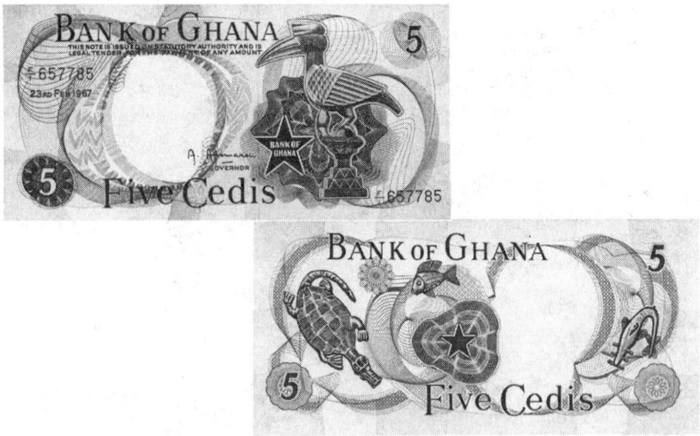

11 **5 Cedis**
23.2.1967; 8.1.1969. Dark brown on multicolor underprint. Wood carving of a bird at right. Animal carvings on back. Signature 4, 5.

	VG	VF	UNC
a. 23.2.1967.	3.00	9.00	35.00
b. 8.1.1969.	3.00	8.50	32.50
s. Specimen.	—	—	45.00

12 **10 Cedis**
23.2.1967; 8.1.1969; 1.10.1970. Red on multicolor underprint. Art products at right. Small statuettes on back. Signature 4, 5.

	VG	VF	UNC
a. 23.2.1967.	2.50	7.00	30.00
b. 8.1.1969.	2.50	8.00	35.00
c. 1.10.1970.	2.50	6.50	27.50
s. Specimen.	—	—	45.00

1972-73 Issue

#13-16 wmk: Arms - Eagle's head above star.

13 **1 Cedi**
1973-76. Dark blue, deep green, and purple on multicolor underprint. Young boy with slingshot at right. Man cutting Cacao pods from tree at left center on back. Signature 5, 6, 7.

	VG	VF	UNC
a. 2.1.1973.	1.25	3.00	7.50
b. 2.1.1975.	.50	2.50	6.00
c. 2.1.1976.	.50	2.00	5.00
d. 2.1.1978.	.30	.75	4.00
s. As a. Specimen.	—	—	45.00

Note: Date 2.1.1976 has two minor varieties in length of *"2nd"* as part of date.

14	2 Cedis	VG	VF	UNC
	1972-78. Green on multicolor underprint. Young man with hoe at right. Workers in field at left center on back. Signature 5, 6, 7.			
	a. 21.6.1972. signature J. J. Ansah.	2.00	4.00	13.00
	b. 21.6.1972. signature G. Nikoi.	2.00	3.50	9.00
	c. 2.1.1977; 2.1.1978.	.50	1.25	4.00
	s. As a. Specimen.	—	—	45.00

15	5 Cedis	VG	VF	UNC
	1973-78. Brown on multicolor underprint. Woman wearing large hat at right. Huts on back. Signature 5, 6, 7.			
	a. 2.1.1973; 2.1.1975; 2.1.1976.	.75	1.50	6.00
	b. 2.1.1977; 4.7.1977; 2.1.1978.	.50	1.00	3.50
	s. As a. Specimen.	—	—	45.00

16	10 Cedis	VG	VF	UNC
	1973-78. Red, violet and dark brown on multicolor underprint. Elderly man smoking a pipe at right. Dam on back. Signature 5, 6, 7.			
	a. 2.1.1973. Serial # prefix *A/1.*	2.00	5.00	8.00
	b. 2.1.1973. Serial # prefix *B/1-.*	1.50	5.00	8.00
	c. 2.1.1975.	2.00	6.00	10.00
	d. 2.1.1976.	.75	2.00	3.75
	e. 2.1.1977.	.75	2.00	3.50
	f. 2.1.1978.	.50	1.50	3.25
	s. As a. Specimen.	—	—	45.00

1979 Issue

#17-22 wmk: Arms - Eagle's head above star. Replacement notes: Serial # prefix *XX; ZZ.*
#17-21, 2 serial # varieties.

17	1 Cedi	VG	VF	UNC
	7.2.1979; 6.3.1982. Green and multicolor. Young man at right. Man weaving at center right on back. Signature 7.			
	a. 7.2.1979.	1.00	1.75	5.00
	b. 6.3.1982.	.50	1.00	3.25
	s. Specimen.	—	—	50.00

18	2 Cedis	VG	VF	UNC
	7.2.1979; 2.1.1980; 2.7.1980; 6.3.1982. Blue and multicolor. School girl at right. Workers tending plants in field at center right on back. Signature 7.			
	a. 7.2.1979.	.75	1.25	4.00
	b. 2.1.1980.	1.00	1.50	5.50
	c. 2.7.1980.	.50	.75	3.00
	d. 6.3.1982.	.75	1.25	3.75
	s. Specimen.	—	—	50.00

19	5 Cedis	VG	VF	UNC
	7.2.1979; 2.1.1980; 6.3.1982. Red and multicolor. Elderly man at right. Men cutting log at left center on back. Signature 7.			
	a. 7.2.1979.	.50	1.75	5.00
	b. 2.1.1980.	.50	1.75	5.00
	c. 6.3.1982.	.50	1.50	4.50
	s. Specimen.	—	—	60.00

20 10 Cedis
7.2.1979; 2.1.1980; 2.7.1980; 6.3.1982. Purple, green and multicolor. Young woman at right. Fishermen with long net at left center on back. Signature 7.

	VG	VF	UNC
a. 7.2.1979.	1.25	6.00	18.00
b. 2.1.1980.	1.25	5.00	11.00
c. 2.7.1980.	1.25	5.00	13.00
d. 6.3.1982.	1.25	5.75	16.00
s. Specimen.	—	—	75.00

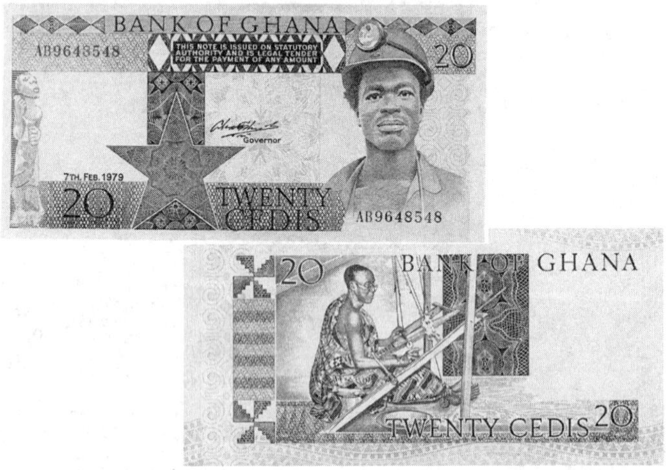

21 20 Cedis
7.2.1979; 2.7.1980; 6.3.1982. Green and multicolor. Miner at right. Man weaving at center right on back. Signature 7.

	VG	VF	UNC
a. 7.2.1979.	1.50	5.50	22.00
b. 2.7.1980.	1.25	5.00	18.00
c. 6.3.1982.	1.25	5.00	17.00
s. Specimen.	—	—	75.00

22 50 Cedis
7.2.1979; 2.7.1980. Brown and multicolor. Old man at right. Men splitting cacao pods on back. Signature 7.

	VG	VF	UNC
a. 7.2.1979.	.75	3.00	10.00
b. 2.7.1980.	.75	2.50	7.50
s. Specimen.	—	—	90.00

1983-91 Issue

#23-31 Replacement notes: Serial # prefix *Z/1*.

#23-27 arms at top ctr. r.

23 10 Cedis
15.5.1984. Purple and multicolor. W. Larbi, F. Otoo, E. Nukpor at left. People going to rural bank at center on back. Without security thread. Signature 8.

	VG	VF	UNC
a. Issued note.	.50	1.25	4.00
s. Specimen.	—	—	—

#24-28 wmk: Arms - Eagle's head above star.

24 20 Cedis
15.5.1984; 15.7.1986. Shades of green and aqua. Queen Mother Yaa Asantewa at left. Workers and flag procession on back. Signature 8.

VG	VF	UNC
.75	1.25	6.00

25 50 Cedis
1.4.1983; 15.5.1984; 15.7.1986. Brown, violet and multicolor. Boy with hat at left center. Drying grain at center on back. Signature 8.

VG	VF	UNC
.75	1.25	6.00

26	100 Cedis	VG	VF	UNC
	1983-91. Purple, blue and multicolor. Woman at left center. Loading produce onto truck at center on back. Signature 8, 9.			
	a. Signature J. S. Addo. 1.4.1983; 15.5.1984; 15.7.1986.	.75	1.50	7.00
	b. Signature G. K. Agama. 19.7.1990; 19.9.1991.	.75	1.50	6.00

27	200 Cedis	VG	VF	UNC
	1983-93. Light brown, orange and multicolor. Old man at left center. Children in classroom at center on back. Signature 8,9.			
	a. Signature J. S. Addo. 1.4.1983; 15.5.1984; 15.7.1986.	.50	1.75	6.00
	b. Signature G. K. Agama. 20.4.1989; 19.7.1990; 19.9.1991; 14.10.1992; 10.8.1993.	.40	1.50	5.00
	s. Specimen. 1.4.1983.	—	—	75.00

28	500 Cedis	VG	VF	UNC
	1986-94. Purple and blue-green on multicolor underprint. Arms at right. Cacao trees with cacao pods and miner at center on back. Signature 8, 9.			
	a. Signature J. S. Addo. 31.12.1986.	FV	2.00	15.00
	b. Signature G. K. Agama. 20.4.1989; 19.7.1990.	FV	FV	7.00
	c. Signature G. K. Agama. 19.9.1991; 14.10.1992; 10.8.1993; 10.6.1994.	FV	FV	5.50
	s. Specimen.	—	—	75.00

#29-31 arms at lower l. and as wmk. Sign. G. K. Agama.

29	1000 Cedis	VG	VF	UNC
	1991-96. Dark brown, dark blue and dark green on multicolor underprint. Jewels at right. Harvesting, splitting cacao pods at left center on back. Signature 9.			

29	1000 Cedis	VG	VF	UNC
	a. 22.2.1991.	FV	1.00	9.00
	b. Segmented foil security thread. 22.7.1993; 6.1.1995; 23.2.1996.	FV	1.00	6.00

30	2000 Cedis	VG	VF	UNC
	15.6.1994; 6.1.1995. 23.2.1996. Red-brown, green and multicolor. Suspension bridge at right. Fisherman loading nets into boat at left center on back. Signature 9.	FV	3.50	14.00

31	5000 Cedis	VG	VF	UNC
	29.6.1994; 6.1.1995; 23.2.1996. Green and red-orange on multicolor underprint. Large stars in underprint at center, supported shield of arms at upper right. Map at left center, freighter in harbor at center, log flow in foreground on back. Signature 9.			
	a. 26.6.1994.	FV	7.00	35.00
	b. 6.1.1995.	FV	6.00	28.00
	c. 23.2.1996.	FV	6.00	25.00

1996 ISSUE

#32-34 like #29-31 but reduced size.

32	1000 Cedis	VG	VF	UNC
	1996-2003. Dark brown, dark blue and dark green on multicolor underprint. Like #29. Signature 9, 10, 11.			
	a. 5.12.1996.	FV	FV	5.50
	b. 1.12.1997; 2.5.1998; 1.7.1999; 1.7.2000.	FV	FV	4.00
	c. 3.9.2001.	FV	FV	10.00
	d. 22.10.2001; 2.9.2002; 4.8.2003.	FV	FV	3.00
	s. Specimen. 1.7.2000.	—	—	35.00

33	2000 Cedis	VG	VF	UNC
	5.12.1996; 1.12.1997; 2.5.1998; 1.7.1999; 1.7.2000; 3.9.2001; 22.10.2001; 2.9.2002; 4.8.2003. Red-brown, green and multicolor. Like #30. Signature 9, 10, 11.			
	a. Issued note.	FV	FV	5.00
	s. Specimen. 2.5.1998.	—	—	35.00

34	5000 Cedis	VG	VF	UNC
	5.12.1996; 1.12.1997; 2.5.1998; 1.7.1999; 1.7.2000; 22.10.2001; 2.9.2002; 4.8.2003. Green and red-orange on multicolor underprint. Like #31. Signature 9, 10, 11.	FV	FV	8.00

2002 Issue

35	10,000 Cedis	VG	VF	UNC
	2.9.2002; 4.8.2003. Purple and red-yellow on multicolor underprint. Kwame Nkrumah and five other leaders at right. Signature 11.			
	a. 2.9.2002.	FV	FV	13.00
	b. 4.8.2003.	FV	FV	10.00

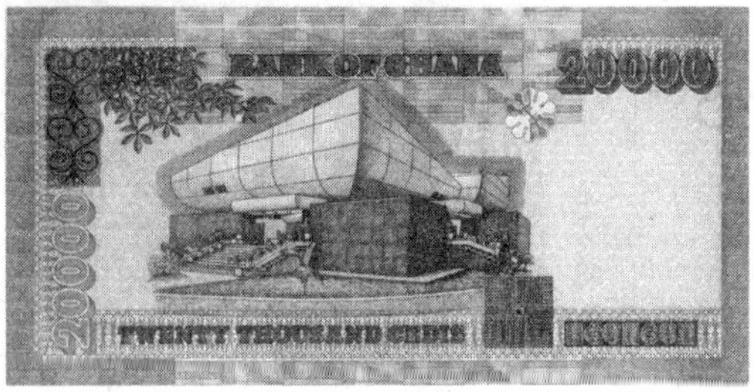

36	20,000 Cedis	VG	VF	UNC
	2.9.2002; 4.8.2003; 4.8.2006. Red-orange and pink-yellow on multicolor underprint. Ephraim Amu, musician, at right. Signature 11.			
	a. 2.9.2002.	FV	FV	20.00
	b. 4.8.2003.	FV	FV	17.50
	c. 4.8.2006.	FV	FV	12.50

Collector Series

Bank of Ghana

1977 Issue

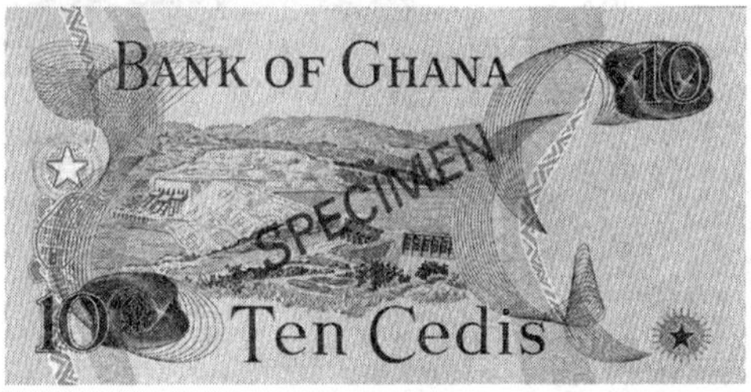

CS1	1977 1-10 Cedis	Issue Price	Mkt. Value
	#13b, 14c, 15b, 16d. with overprint: *SPECIMEN* and Maltese cross prefix serial #.	—	40.00

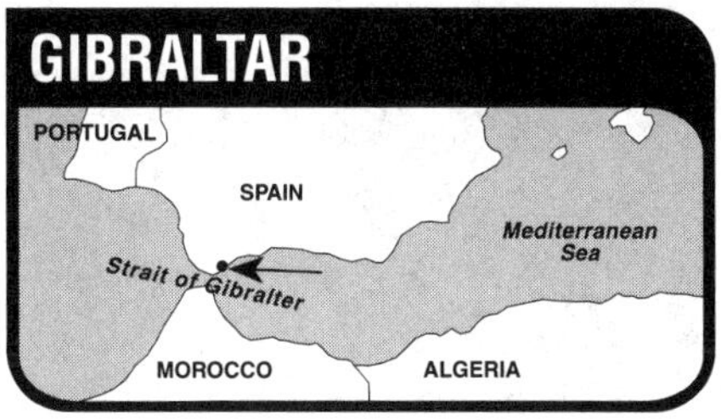

The British Colony of Gibraltar, located at the southernmost point of the Iberian Peninsula, has an area of 2.25 sq. mi. (5.8 sq. km.) and a population of 29,000. Capital (and only town): Gibraltar. Aside from its strategic importance as guardian of the western entrance to the Mediterranean Sea, Gibraltar is also a free port and a British naval .

Gibraltar, rooted in Greek mythology as one of the Pillars of Hercules, has long been a coveted stronghold. Moslems took it from Spain and fortified it in 711. Spain retook it in 1309, lost it again to the Moors in 1333, and retook it in 1462. After Barbarossa sacked Gibraltar in 1540, Spain strengthened its defenses and held it until the War of the Spanish Succession when it was captured by a combined British and Dutch force, 1704. Britain held it against the Franco-Spanish attacks of 1704-05 and through the historic "Great Siege" of 1779-83. Recently Spain has attempted to discourage British occupancy by harassment and economic devices. In 1967, Gibraltar's inhabitants voted to remain under British rule.

RULERS:

British

MONETARY SYSTEM:

1 Shilling = 12 Pence
1 Pound = 20 Shillings to 1971
1 Pound = 100 New Pence, 1971-

BRITISH ADMINISTRATION

GOVERNMENT OF GIBRALTAR

1934 ORDINANCE; 1958 ISSUE

#17-19 arms at ctr. on back. Printer: TDLR.

		VG	VF	UNC
17	**10 Shillings** 3.10.1958; 1.5.1965. Blue on yellow-brown underprint. Rock of Gilbraltar at left. Arms at center. Printer: TDLR.	10.00	60.00	250.

		VG	VF	UNC
18	**1 Pound** 1958-75. Green on yellow-brown underprint. Rock of Gibraltar at bottom center. Arms at center. Printer: TDLR.			
	a. Signature title: *FINANCIAL SECRETARY.* 3.10.1958; 1.5.1965.	4.00	15.00	90.00
	b. Signature title: *FINANCIAL AND DEVELOPMENT SECRETARY.* 20.11.1971.	3.00	10.00	50.00
	c. 20.11.1975.	7.50	30.00	175.
	s. Specimen. As a-c.	—	—	—

		VG	VF	UNC
19	**5 Pounds** 1958-75. Brown. Rock of Gibraltar at bottom center. Arms at center. Printer: TDLR.			
	a. Signature title: *FINANCIAL SECRETARY.* 3.10.1958; 1.5.1965.	25.00	100.	575.
	b. Signature title: *FINANCIAL AND DEVELOPMENT SECRETARY.* 1.5.1965; 20.11.1971; 20.11.1975.	17.50	80.00	400.
	s. Specimen. As a-b.	—	—	—

ORDINANCE CAP 39; 1975; 1986 ISSUE

#20-24 Qn. Elizabeth II at ctr. r. and as wmk. Sign. varieties. Printer: TDLR.

		VG	VF	UNC
20	**1 Pound** 1975-88. Brown and red on multicolor underprint. The Covenant of Gibraltar at left center on back. Three signature varieties.			
	a. 20.11.1975 (1978).	FV	5.00	45.00
	b. 15.9.1979.	FV	4.00	42.50
	c. 10.11.1983.	FV	4.00	40.00
	d. 21.10.1986.	FV	2.50	35.00
	e. 4.8.1988.	FV	FV	12.50
	s. Specimen. As a; b; d.	—	—	—

		VG	VF	UNC
21	**5 Pounds** 1975; 1988. Green on multicolor underprint. Back like #20.			
	a. 20.11.1975.	FV	17.50	80.00
	b. 4.8.1988.	FV	FV	40.00

		VG	VF	UNC
22	**10 Pounds** 1975; 1986. Deep violet, dark brown and deep blue-green on multicolor underprint. Governor's house on back.			
	a. 20.11.1975 (1977).	FV	25.00	95.00
	b. 21.10.1986.	FV	FV	65.00

		VG	VF	UNC
23	**20 Pounds** 1975-86. Light brown on multicolor underprint. Back similar to #22.			
	a. 20.11.1975 (1978).	FV	60.00	325.
	b. 15.9.1979.	FV	60.00	375.
	c. 1.7.1986.	FV	60.00	150.

		VG	VF	UNC
24	**50 Pounds** 27.11.1986. Purple on multicolor underprint. Rock of Gibraltar on back.	FV	FV	220.

1995 ISSUE

#25-28 mature image of Qn. Elizabeth at r. and as wmk., shield of arms at l.

		VG	VF	UNC
25	**5 Pounds** 1.7.1995. Green and purple on multicolor underprint. Urn above gateway at left center. Tavik ibn Zeyad with sword at right, Moorish castle at upper left on back.			
	a. Issued note.	FV	FV	35.00
	s. Specimen.	—	—	—

		VG	VF	UNC
26	**10 Pounds** 1.7.1995. Orange-brown and violet on multicolor underprint. Lighthouse above cannon at left center. Portrait Gen. Eliott at right, scene of "The Great Siege, 1779-85" at upper left center on back.			
	a. Issued note.	FV	FV	60.00
	s. Specimen.	—	—	—

NOTICE

Readers with unlisted dates, signature varieties, etc. are invited to submit photocopies of their notes to: Standard Catalog of World Paper Money, 700 East State St. Iola, WI 54990-0001, E-Mail: george.cuhaj@fwpubs.com.

27	20 Pounds	VG	VF	UNC
	1.7.1995. Purple and violet on multicolor underprint. Bird above cannon at left center. Portrait Admiral Nelson at right, H.M.S. Victory at upper left center on back.			
	a. Issued note.	FV	FV	110.
	s. Specimen.	—	—	—

28	50 Pounds	VG	VF	UNC
	1.7.1995. Red and violet on multicolor underprint. Gibraltar monkey above horse and carriage at left center. Portrait W. Churchill at upper right, Spitfire airplanes at the North Front, 1942 at upper left center on back.			
	a. Issued note.	FV	FV	200.
	s. Specimen.	—	—	—

Note: #28 also honored the 30th anniversary of the death of Churchill.

2000 Issue

#29, Millennium Commemorative

29	5 Pounds	VG	VF	UNC
	2000. Green on multicolor underprint. Face similar to #25, but with enhanced security devices. Gibraltar monkey at left, city & harbor view at center, gondola on right on back.	FV	FV	35.00

30	10 Pounds	VG	VF	UNC
	10.9.2002. Orange-brown and violet on multicolor underprint. Large square with butterflies and grouse within on back.	FV	FV	57.50

2004 Commemorative Issue

31	20 Pounds	VG	VF	UNC
	4.8.2004. Mauve, tan and black on multicolor underprint. Back blue, tan and brown; John Mackintosh Square at center, 19th century townfolk at right edge.			
	a. Issued note.	FV	FV	110.
	s. Specimen.	—	—	—

COLLECTOR SERIES

GOVERNMENT OF GIBRALTAR

1975 ISSUE

		Issue Price	Mkt. Value
CS1	**1975 1-20 Pounds** #20a, 21a, 22, 23a. with overprint: *SPECIMEN* and serial # prefix: Maltese cross.	—	125.

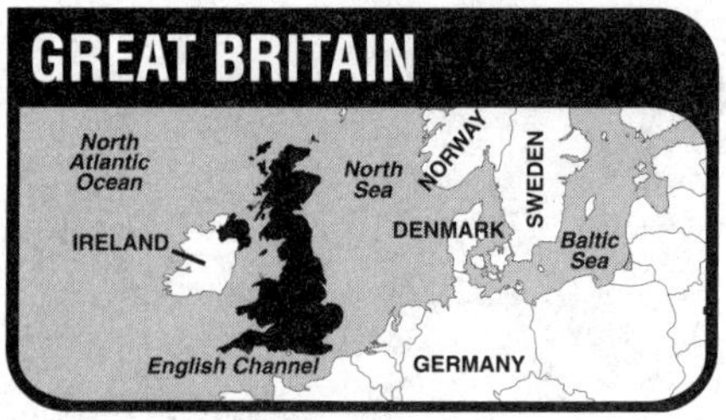

The United Kingdom of Great Britain and Northern Ireland, (including England, Scotland, Wales and Norhtern Ireland) is located off the northwest coast of the European continent, has an area of 94,227 sq. mi. (244,046 sq. km.), and a population of 59.45 million. Capital: London.

The economy is d on industrial activity, trading and financial services. Machinery, motor vehicles, chemicals and textile yarns and fabrics are exported.

After the departure of the Romans, who brought Britain into an active relationship with Europe, Britain fell prey to invaders from Scandinavia and the Low Countries who drove the original Britons into Scotland and Wales, and established a profusion of kingdoms that finally united in the 11th century under the Danish King Canute. Norman rule, following the conquest of 1066, stimulated the development of those institutions which have since distinguished British life. Henry VIII (1509-47) turned Britain from continental adventuring and faced it to the sea - a decision that made Britain a world power during the reign of Elizabeth I (1558-1603). Strengthened by the Industrial Revolution and the defeat of Napoleon, 19th century Britain turned to the remote parts of the world and established a colonial empire of such extent and prosperity that the world has never seen its like. World Wars I and II sealed the fate of the Empire and relegated Britain to a lesser role in world affairs by draining her resources and inaugurating a worldwide movement toward national self-determination in her former colonies.

By the mid-20th century, most of the former British Empire had gained independence and had evolved into the Commonwealth of Nations. This association of equal and and autonomous states, set out to agree views and special relationships with one another (appointing High Commissioners rather than Ambassadors) for mutual benefit, trade interests, etc. The Commonwealth is presently (1999) composed of 54 member nations, including the United Kingdom. All recognize the monarch as Head of the Commonwealth; 16 continue to recognize Queen Elizabeth II as Head of State. In addition to the United Kingdom, they are: Antigua & Barbuda, Australia, The Bahamas, Barbados Belize, Canada, Grenada, Paupa New Guinea, St. Christopher & Nevis, St. Lucia, St. Vincent & the Grenadines, Solomon Islands.

RULERS:

Elizabeth II, 1952-

MONETARY SYSTEM:

1 Shilling = 12 Pence
1 Pound = 20 Shillings to 1971
1 Pound = 100 (New) Pence, 1971-

KINGDOM

BANK OF ENGLAND

1957-61 ND ISSUE

		VG	VF	UNC
371	**5 Pounds** ND (1957-67). Blue and multicolor. Signature L.K. O'Brien. Helmeted Britannia head at left, St. George and dragon at lower center, denomination *£5* in blue print on back.	15.00	50.00	135.
372	**5 Pounds** ND (1961-63). Blue and multicolor. Signature K. O'Brien at left. Helmeted Britannia head at left, St. George and dragon at lower center, denomination *£5* recessed in white on back.	15.00	50.00	135.

1960-64 ND ISSUE

#373-376 portr. Qn. Elizabeth II at r.

#373-375 wmk: Laureate heads in continuous vertical row at l.

373	10 Shillings	VG	VF	UNC
	ND (1960-70). Brown on multicolor underprint. Portrait Queen Elizabeth II at right. Watermark: Laureate heads in continuous vertical row at left. Britannia seated with shield in circle at center right.			
	a. Signature L. K. O'Brien. (1960-61).	1.50	4.00	15.00
	b. Signature J. Q. Hollom. (1962-66).	1.00	3.00	12.50
	c. Signature J. S. Fforde. (1966-70).	1.00	2.50	10.00
	s. Specimen. As a; c.	—	—	—

374	1 Pound	VG	VF	UNC
	ND (1960-77). Deep green on multicolor underprint. Portrait Queen Elizabeth II at right. Watermark: Laureate heads in continuous vertical row at left. Britannia seated with shield in circle at center right.			
	a. Signature L. K. O'Brien. (1960-61).	2.00	4.00	12.00
	b. Signature as a. Small letter *R* (for Research) at lower left center on back. (Notes printed on web press.) Serial # prefixes A01N; A05N; A06N.	125.	375.	1150.
	c. Signature J. Q. Hollom. (1962-66).	FV	4.00	10.00
	d. Signature as c. Letter *G* at lower left center on back. (Printed on experimental German Goebel Press.)	4.00	12.50	25.00
	e. Signature J. S. Fforde. (1966-70).	FV	4.00	9.00
	f. Signature as e. Letter *G* at lower center on back.	4.00	12.50	30.00
	g. Signature J. B. Page. (1970-77).	FV	4.00	9.00
	s. Specimen. As a-c.	—	—	—

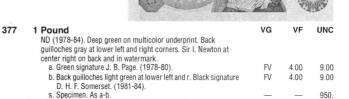

375	5 Pounds	VG	VF	UNC
	ND (1963-71). Deep blue on multicolor underprint. Britannia seated with shield in 8-petalled pattern at center on back.			
	a. Signature J. Q. Hollom. (1963-66).	FV	22.50	75.00
	b. Signature J. S. Fforde. (1966-70).	FV	20.00	65.00
	c. Signature J. B. Page. (1970-71).	FV	22.50	75.00
	s. Specimen. As a.	—	—	950.

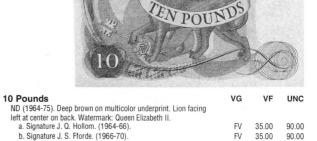

376	10 Pounds	VG	VF	UNC
	ND (1964-75). Deep brown on multicolor underprint. Lion facing left at center on back. Watermark: Queen Elizabeth II.			
	a. Signature J. Q. Hollom. (1964-66).	FV	35.00	90.00
	b. Signature J. S. Fforde. (1966-70).	FV	35.00	90.00
	c. Signature J. B. Page. (1970-75).	FV	35.00	85.00
	r. As c. Replacement note. Serial # prefix *M*.	20.00	45.00	115.
	s. Specimen. As a.	—	—	1100.

1971-82 ND Issue

#377-381 Qn. Elizabeth II in court robes at r.

377	1 Pound	VG	VF	UNC
	ND (1978-84). Deep green on multicolor underprint. Back guilloches gray at lower left and right corners. Sir I. Newton at center right on back and in watermark.			
	a. Green signature J. B. Page. (1978-80).	FV	4.00	9.00
	b. Back guilloches light green at lower left and r. Black signature D. H. F. Somerset. (1981-84).	FV	4.00	9.00
	s. Specimen. As a-b.	—	—	950.

378	5 Pounds	VG	VF	UNC
	ND (1971-91). Blue-black and blue on multicolor underprint. Duke of Wellington at center right, battle scene in Spain at left center on back and in watermark.			

378	5 Pounds	VG	VF	UNC
	a. Blue-gray signature J. B. Page. (1971-72).	FV	17.50	50.00
	b. Black signature J. B. Page. Litho back with small *L* at lower left (1973-80).	FV	15.00	45.00
	c. Black signature D. H. F. Somerset. (1980-87). Thin security thread.	FV	12.00	35.00
	d. As c. without signature	50.00	110.	325.
	e. Signature D. H. F. Somerset. Thick security thread. (1987-88).	FV	18.00	55.00
	f. Signature G. M. Gill (1988-91).	FV	12.50	37.50
	s. Specimen. As a.	—	—	950.

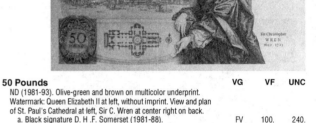

379	10 Pounds	VG	VF	UNC
	ND (1978-92). Deep brown on multicolor underprint. Florence Nightingale at center right, hospital scene with Florence Nightingale as the "Lady with lamp" at left center on back and as watermark.			
	a. J. B. Page. (1975-80).	FV	30.00	75.00
	b. D. H. F. Somerset (1980-84).	FV	40.00	95.00
	c. Signature D. H. F. Somerset. Litho printing with *L* at lower back. (1984-86).	FV	20.00	65.00
	d. D. H. F. Somerset. with segmented security thread. (1987-88).	FV	20.00	75.00
	e. Signature G. M. Gill (1988-91).	FV	20.00	65.00
	f. Signature G. E. A. Kentfield (1991-92).	FV	35.00	100.
	r. As a. Replacement note. Serial # prefix *M*.	45.00	100.	285.

380	20 Pounds	VG	VF	UNC
	ND (1970-91). Purple on multicolor underprint. Shakespeare statue at center right on back.			
	a. Watermark: Queen Elizabeth II. signature J. S. Fforde. (1970).	60.00	175.	450.
	b. Watermark. as a. signature J. B. Page. (1970-80).	FV	55.00	150.
	c. Watermark. as a. signature D. H. F. Somerset. (1981-84).	FV	65.00	190.
	d. Watermark: Shakespeare. Modified background colors. Segmented security thread. D. H. F. Somerset. (1984-88).	FV	55.00	150.
	e. Signature G. M. Gill (1988-91).	FV	50.00	140.
	s. Specimen. As c.	—	—	1100.

381	50 Pounds	VG	VF	UNC
	ND (1981-93). Olive-green and brown on multicolor underprint. Watermark: Queen Elizabeth II at left, without imprint. View and plan of St. Paul's Cathedral at left, Sir C. Wren at center right on back.			
	a. Black signature D. H .F. Somerset (1981-88).	FV	100.	240.
	b. Modified background and guilloche colors. Segmented foil on security thread on surface. signature G. M. Gill (1988-91).	FV	110.	265.
	c. Signature G. E. A. Kentfield (1991-93).	FV	100.	250.

1990-92 ISSUE

#382-384 Qn. Elizabeth II at r. and as wmk. Crown at upper r. corner on face.

382	5 Pounds	VG	VF	UNC
	©1990 (1990-92). Dark brown and deep blue-green on multicolor underprint. Britannia seated at upper left. Rocket locomotive at left, George Stephenson at right on back.			
	a. Signature G. M. Gill (1990-91).	FV	FV	35.00
	b. Signature G. E. A. Kentfield (1991-92).	FV	FV	30.00

383	10 Pounds	VG	VF	UNC
	©1992 (1992-93). Black, brown and red on multicolor underprint. Britannia at left. Cricket match at left, Charles Dickens at right on back. Signature G. E. A. Kentfield (1992).	FV	FV	52.50

384	20 Pounds	VG	VF	UNC
	©1991 (1991-93). Black, teal-violet and purple on multicolor underprint. Britannia at left. Broken vertical foil strip and purple optical device at left center. M. Faraday with students at left, portrait at right on back. Serial # olive-green to maroon at upper left and dark blue at right.			
	a. Signature G. M. Gill (1990-91).	FV	FV	105.
	b. Signature G. E. A. Kentfield (1991-93).	FV	FV	115.

1993 MODIFIED ISSUE

#385-388 Qn. Elizabeth II at r. and as wmk. Value at upper r. corner on face.

385	5 Pounds	VG	VF	UNC
	©1990 (1993-2002). Like #382 but with dark value symbol at upper left corner, also darker shading on back.			
	a. Signature G. E. A. Kentfield (1993-98).	FV	FV	27.50
	b. Signature M. Lowther (1999-2002).	FV	FV	22.50

Note: For #385 with HK serial # prefix, see CS4.

386	10 Pounds	VG	VF	UNC
	©1993 (1993-2000). Like #383 but with enhanced symbols for value and substitution of value £10 for crown at upper right on face. Additional value symbol at top right on back.			
	a. Signature G. E. A. Kentfield (1993-98).	FV	FV	47.50
	b. Signature M. Lowther (1999-2000).	FV	FV	47.50

387	20 Pounds	VG	VF	UNC
	©1993 (1993-99). Like #384 but with dark value symbol at upper left corner and substitution of value symbol for crown at upper right corner on face. Additional value symbol at top right on back.			
	a. Signature G. E. A. Kentfield (1993-98).	FV	FV	85.00
	b. Signature M. Lowther (1999).	FV	FV	140.

388	50 Pounds	VG	VF	UNC
	©1994 (1993-). Brownish-black, red and violet on multicolor underprint. Allegory in oval in underprint at left. Bank gatekeeper at lower left, his house at left and Sir J. Houblon at right on back.			
	a. Signature G. E. A. Kentfield (1993-98).	FV	FV	180.
	b. Signature M. Lowther (1999-).	FV	FV	170.

Note: #388 also honors the 300th anniversary of the Bank of England.

1999-2000 ISSUE

389	10 Pounds	VG	VF	UNC
	2000. Brown, orange and multicolor. Brown and multicolor. Charles Darwin at right on back. Hummingbird magnifying glass and flora to left.			
	a. Copyright notice reads: *THE GOVERNOR AND THE COMPANY...* signature M. Lowther (2000).	FV	FV	42.50
	b. Copyright notice reads: *THE GOVERNOR AND COMPANY...* signature M. Lowther (2000-2003).	FV	FV	35.00
	c. Signature A. Bailey (2004-).	FV	FV	32.50

390	20 Pounds	VG	VF	UNC
	© 1999. Brown and purple on red and green underprint. 20 and Britannia in OVD, modified top left and right value numerals. Worchester Cathedral at left, Sir Edward Elgar at right on back.			
	a. Signature M. Lowther (1999-2003).	FV	FV	65.00
	b. Signature A. Bailey (2004-).	FV	FV	60.00

2002 Issue

		VG	VF	UNC
391	**5 Pounds** 2002. Brown and green on multicolor underprint. Back light blue and Multicolor; Elizabeth Fry at right, scene of women and children in workhouse at left.			
	a. Serial # on varnished paper, easily rubbed off. Withdrawn. From serial # prefix: HA 01. signature M. Lowther (2002).	FV	FV	25.00
	b. Serial # prefix on paper, varnished. From serial # prefix: HC 01. signature M. Lowther (2002-03).	FV	FV	17.50
	c. Signature A. Bailey (2004).	FV	FV	16.00

Military

British Armed Forces, Special Vouchers

1962 ND Fourth Series

#M30-M36 w/o imprint. (Not issued).

		VG	VF	UNC
M30	**3 Pence** ND (1962). Slate on violet and light green underprint. Specimen. Rare.	—	—	—

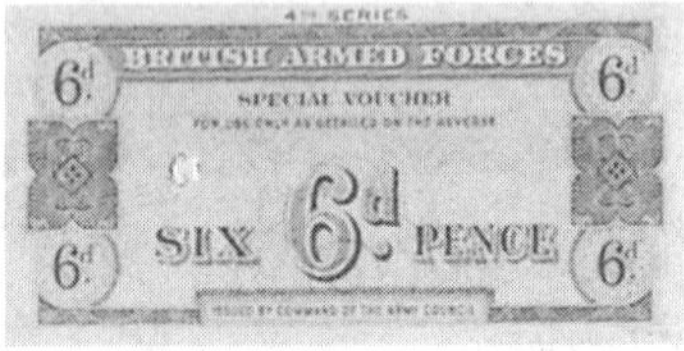

		VG	VF	UNC
M31	**6 Pence** ND (1962). Blue on violet and light green underprint. Specimen. Rare.	—	—	—
M32	**1 Shilling** ND. Dark brown on olive and orange underprint.			
	a. Normal serial #, but without punch cancellations.	6.00	25.00	100.
	b. Cancelled remainder with 2 punched holes.	—	—	3.50
	c. Specimen with 1 punched hole. Rare.	—	—	—
M33	**2 Shillings - 6 Pence** ND (1962). Red-orange on violet and light green underprint. Specimen. Rare.	—	—	—

		VG	VF	UNC
M34	**5 Shillings** ND. Green on light brown underprint. Specimen only. Rare.	—	—	—

		VG	VF	UNC
M35	**10 Shillings** ND. Violet on blue and green underprint.			
	a. Normal serial # but without punch cancellations.	5.00	25.00	125.
	b. Cancelled remainder with normal serial # and 2 punched holes.	—	—	5.00
	c. Specimen with special serial # and 1 punched hole. Rare.	—	—	—

		VG	VF	UNC
M36	**1 Pound** ND. Violet on pale green and lilac underprint.			
	a. Normal serial #, without punch cancellations.	—	—	1.00
	b. Specimen with special serial # and 1 punched hole. Rare.	—	—	—

1960s Fifth Series

#M37-M43 known in specimen form and a few as proofs.

		VG	VF	UNC
M37	**3 Pence** ND. Red-brown, purple and green. Specimen. Rare.	—	—	—
M38	**6 Pence** ND. Green, turquoise and light brown. Specimen. Rare.	—	—	—
M39	**1 Shilling** ND. Lilac and green. Specimen. Rare.	—	—	—
M40	**2 Shillings - 6 Pence** ND. Purple, turquoise and light brown. Specimen. Rare.	—	—	—
M41	**5 Shillings** ND. Blue, red and turquoise. Specimen. Rare.	—	—	—
M42	**10 Shillings** ND. Orange, green and slate. Specimen. Rare.	—	—	—
M43	**1 Pound** ND. Olive and red-brown. Specimen. Rare.	—	—	—

1972 Sixth Series

#M44-M46 printer: TDLR.

		VG	VF	UNC
M44	**5 New Pence** ND (1972). Orange-brown and green.			
	a. Issued note.	—	—	2.00
	s. Specimen.	—	—	5.00

		VG	VF	UNC
M45	**10 New Pence** ND (1972). Violet, green and olive.			
	a. Issued note.	—	—	3.00
	s. Specimen.	—	—	5.00

		VG	VF	UNC
M46	**50 New Pence**			
	ND (1972). Green on pink underprint.			
	a. Issued note.	—	—	4.00
	s. Specimen.	—	—	5.00

1972 Sixth Series Second Issue

#M47-M49 printer: BWC.

		VG	VF	UNC
M47	**5 New Pence** ND (1972). Like #M44.	—	—	.50
M48	**10 New Pence** ND (1972). Like #M45.	—	—	.50
M49	**50 New Pence** ND (1972). Like #M46.	—	—	.75

Collector Series

Bank of England

1995 Issue

#CS1 and CS2, 200th Anniversary of the First 5 Pound Note

		Issue Price	Mkt. Value
CS1	**5 Pounds** Uncut sheet of three notes #385 in folder. Serial #AB16-AB18. Last sheet printing.	—	100.
CS2	**5 Pounds** Uncut sheet of three notes #385 in folder. Serial #AC01-AC03. First web printing.	—	100.
CS3	**10 Pounds** As #386 with serial #HM70. 70th Birthday of Queen Elizabeth II. Issued in a case with £5 Proof coin. 2,000 sets.	—	—
CS4	**20 Pounds** Uncut pair of #384b. Kentfield first issue. 1000 pair in folder.	—	—

1996 Issue

		Issue Price	Mkt. Value
CS5	**5 Pounds** As #386 with serial # prefix *HM70* for the 70th Birthday of Queen Elizabeth II. Limited to 5000.	—	—
CS6	**5 Pounds** Uncut sheet of 8 of #383c. Limited to 5000 sheets.	—	—

1997 Issue

		Issue Price	Mkt. Value
CS7	**5 Pounds** As #385a with serial # prefix HK issued commemorating the Return of Hong Kong to the People's Republic of China.		
	a. Single note in a special card.	—	25.00
	b. Uncut sheet of 12.	—	—
	c. Uncut sheet of 35.	—	—
CS8	**5, 10, 20 Pounds** As #385b, 386b, 387b with serial # prefix BE98 with matching numbers. Limited to 1888.	—	100.

1999 Issue

		Issue Price	Mkt. Value
CS9	**5, 10, 20, 50 Pounds** New Lowther issue. In folder: #385b, 386b, 387b and 388b.	—	—

2000 Issue

		Issue Price	Mkt. Value
CS10	**5 Pounds** As 385b but with serial # prefix *YR20*. Millenium. Limited to 1500.	—	—
CS11	**10 Pounds** As #386b with serial # prefix *YR20*.Millenium. Limited to 1500.	—	—
CS12	**5 Pounds** As #385b with serial # prefix *QM10*. Queen Mother's 100th birthday. Limited to 10,000.	—	—
CS13	**5 Pounds** As #CS12 with CN crown in folder. Limited to 1000.	—	—

The Hellenic Republic of Greece is situated in southeastern Europe on the southern tip of the Balkan Peninsula. The republic includes many islands, the most important of which are Crete and the Ionian Islands. Greece (including islands) has an area of 50,949 sq. mi. (131,957 sq. km.) and a population of 10.6 million. Capital: Athens. Greece is still largely agricultural. Tobacco, cotton, fruit and wool are exported.

Greece, the Mother of Western civilization, attained the peak of its culture in the 5th century BC, when it contributed more to government, drama, art and architecture than any other people to this time. Greece fell under Roman domination in the 2nd and 1st centuries BC, becoming part of the Byzantine Empire until Constantinople fell to the Crusaders in 1202. With the fall of Constantinople to the Turks in 1453, Greece became part of the Ottoman Empire. Independence from Turkey was won with the revolution of 1821-27. In 1833, Greece was established as a monarchy, with sovereignty guaranteed by Britain, France and Russia. After a lengthy power struggle between the monarchist forces and democratic factions, Greece was proclaimed a republic in 1925. The monarchy was restored in 1935 and reconfirmed by a plebiscite in 1946. The Italians invaded Greece via Albania on Oct. 28, 1940 but were driven back well within the Albanian border. Germany began its invasion on April 6, 1941 and quickly overran the entire country, driving off a British Expeditionary force by the end of April. King George II and his new government went into exile. The German - Italian occupation of Greece lasted until Oct. 1944. On April 21, 1967, a military junta took control of the government and suspended the constitution. King Constantine II made an unsuccessful attempt against the junta in the fall of 1968 and consequently fled to Italy. The monarchy was formally abolished by plebiscite, Dec. 8, 1974, and Greece established as the "Hellenic Republic," the third republic in Greek history.

RULERS:

Paul I, 1947-1964
Constantine II, 1964-1973

MONETARY SYSTEM:

1 Drachma = 100 Lepta, 1841-2001
1 Euro = 100 Cents, 2002-

GREEK ALPHABET											
Α	α	Alpha	(ā)	Ι	ι	Iota	(ē)	Ρ	ρ	Rho	(r)
Β	β	Beta	(b)	Κ	κ	Kappa	(k)	Σ	σ	Sigma	(s)6
Γ	γ	Gamma	(g)	Λ	λ	Lambda	(l)	Τ	τ	Tau	(t)
Δ	δ	Delta	(d)	Μ	μ	Mu	(m)	Υ	υ	Upsilon	(o͞o)
Ε	ε	Epsilon	(e)	Ν	ν	Nu	(n)	Φ	φ	Phi	(f)
Ζ	ζ	Zeta	(z)	Ξ	ξ	Xi	(ks)	Χ	χ	Chi	(H)
Η	η	Eta	(ā)	Ο	ο	Omicron	(o)	Ψ	ψ	Psi	(ps)
Θ	θ	Theta	(th)	Π	π	Pi	(p)	Ω	ω	Omega	(ō)

Kingdom

ΤΡΑΠΕΖΑ ΤΗΣ ΕΛΛΑΔΟΣ

Bank of Greece

1964-70 Issue

#195-197 wmk: Head of Ephebus.

		VG	VF	UNC
195	**50 Drachmai** 1.10.1964. Blue on multicolor underprint. Arethusa at left, galley at bottom right. Shipyard on back.			
	a. Issued note.	.50	1.00	2.50
	s. Specimen.	—	—	150.

196	100 Drachmai	VG	VF	UNC
	1966-67. Red-brown on multicolor underprint. Demokritos at left, building and atomic symbol at right. University at center on back.			
	a. Signature Zolotas as Bank President. 1.7.1966.	8.00	15.00	45.00
	b. Signature Galanis as Bank President. 1.10.1967.	.75	1.00	3.00
	s. Specimen. As b.	—	—	150.

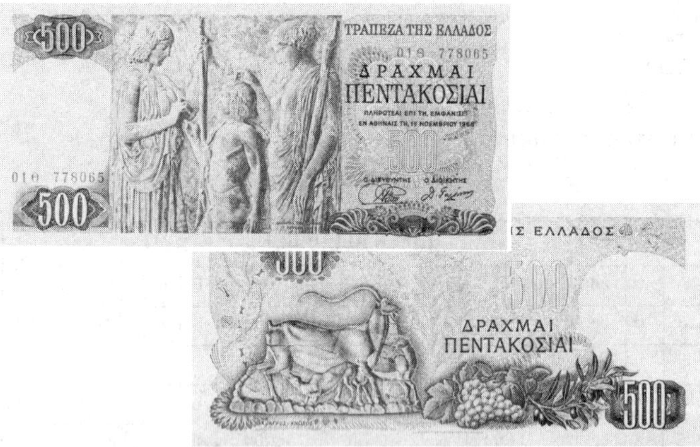

197	500 Drachmai	VG	VF	UNC
	1.11.1968. Olive on multicolor underprint. Relief of Elusis at center. Relief of animals at bottom left, fruit at bottom center on back.			
	a. Issued note.	2.50	6.00	25.00
	s. Specimen.	—	—	150.

198	1000 Drachmai	VG	VF	UNC
	1.11.1970. Brown on multicolor underprint. Zeus at left, stadium at bottom center. Back brown and green; woman at left and view of city Hydra on the Isle of Hydra.			
	a. Watermark: Head of Aphrodite of Knidus (hair in knot at top of head) profile (1970).	20.00	40.00	120.
	b. Watermark: Head of Ephebus of Anticythera in 3/4 profile (1972).	1.00	2.00	10.00
	s. As b. Specimen.	—	—	150.

NOTICE

Readers with unlisted dates, signature varieties, etc. are invited to submit photocopies of their notes to: Standard Catalog of World Paper Money, 700 East State St. Iola, WI 54990-0001, E-Mail: george.cuhaj@fwpubs.com.

REPUBLIC

ΤΡΑΠΕΖΑ ΤΗΣ ΕΛΛΑΔΟΣ

BANK OF GREECE

1978 ISSUE

#199 and 200 wmk: Head of Charioteer Polyzalos of Delphi.

199	50 Drachmai	VG	VF	UNC
	8.12.1978. Blue on multicolor underprint. Poseidon at left. Sailing ship at left center, man and woman at right on back.			
	a. Issued note.	FV	FV	2.50
	r. Replacement note. Series 00A.	FV	FV	45.00
	s. Specimen.	—	—	150.

200	100 Drachmai	VG	VF	UNC
	8.12.1978. Brown and violet on multicolor underprint. Athena Peiraios at left. Back maroon, green and orange; A. Koraes at left, Church of Arkadi Monastery in Crete at bottom right.			
	a. Original issue. without "L" at lower left on back.	FV	FV	2.50
	b. Second issue. with "L" at lower left on back.	FV	FV	2.00
	r. As b. Replacement note. Series 00A.	FV	FV	35.00
	s. Specimen.	—	—	150.

1983-87 ISSUE

#201-203 wmk: Head of Charioteer Polyzalos of Delphi.

201	500 Drachmaes	VG	VF	UNC
	1.2.1983. Deep green on multicolor underprint. I. Capodistrias at left center, his birthplace at lower right. Fortress overlooking Corfu on back.			
	a. Issued note.	FV	FV	4.50
	r. Replacement note. Series 00A.	FV	FV	150.
	s. Specimen.	—	—	150.

202 1000 Drachmaes

1.7.1987. Brown on multicolor underprint. Apollo at center right, ancient coin at bottom left center. Discus thrower and Hera Temple ruins at Olympia on back.

	VG	VF	UNC
a. Issued note.	FV	FV	6.00
r. Replacement note. Series 00A.	FV	FV	100.
s. Specimen.	—	—	150.

203 5000 Drachmaes

23.3.1984. Deep blue on multicolor underprint. T. Kolokotronis at left, Church of the Holy Apostles at Calamata at bottom center right. Landscape and view of town of Karytaina at center right on back.

	VG	VF	UNC
a. Issued note.	FV	FV	45.00
r. Replacement note. Series 00A.	FV	FV	100.
s. Specimen.	—	—	150.

1995-98 Issue

#204 and 205 wmk: Bust of Philip of Macedonia.

204 200 Drachmaes

2.9.1996. Deep orange on multicolor underprint. R. Velestinlis-Feraios at left. Velestinlis-Feraios singing his patriotic song at lower right. Secret school run by Greek priests (during the Ottoman occupation) at center right on back.

	VG	VF	UNC
a. Issued note.	FV	FV	3.75
s. Specimen.	—	—	150.

205 5000 Drachmaes

1.6.1997. Purple and yellow-green on multicolor underprint. Similar to #203 but reduced size.

	VG	VF	UNC
a. Issued note.	FV	FV	35.00
r. Replacement note. Series 00A.	FV	FV	150.
s. Specimen.	—	—	150.

206 10,000 Drachmaes

16.1.1995. Deep purple on multicolor underprint. Dr. Georgios Papanikolaou at left center, microscope at lower center right. Medical care frieze at bottom center, statue of Asklepios at center right on back.

	VG	VF	UNC
a. Issued note.	FV	FV	65.00
r. Replacement note. Series 00A.	FV	FV	200.
s. Specimen.	—	—	200.

Note: For later issues made for use in Greece see European Union listings.

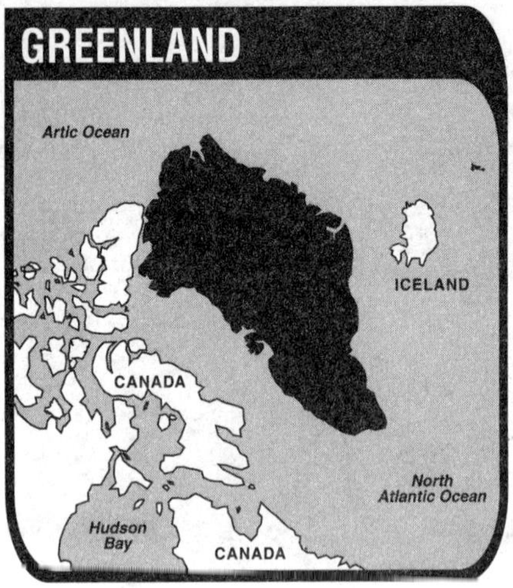

Greenland, an integral part of the Danish realm, is a huge island situated between the North Atlantic Ocean and the Polar Sea, almost entirely within the Artic Circle. It has an area of 840,000 sq. mi. (2,175,600 sq. km.) and a population of 56,087. Capital: Godthab. Greenland is the world's only source of natural cryolite, a fluoride of sodium and aluminum important in making aluminum. Fish products and minerals are exported.

Eric the Red discovered Greenland in 982 and established the first settlement in 986. Greenland was a republic until 1261, when the sovereignty of Norway was extended to the island. The original colony was abandoned about 1400 when increasing cold interfered with the breeding of cattle. Successful recolonization was undertaken by Denmark in 1721. In 1921 Denmark extended its claim to include the entire island, and made it a colony of the crown in 1924. The island's colonial status was abolished by amendment to the Danish constitution on June 5, 1953, and Greenland became an integral part of the Kingdom of Denmark. It has been an autonomous state since May 1, 1979.

RULERS:

Danish

MONETARY SYSTEM:

1 Krone = 100 Óre, 1874-

Danish Administration

Den Kongelige Grønlandske Handel

1953 Issue

#18-20 w/text: *DEN KONGELIGE GRÓNLANDSKE HANDEL* at l. and r. margin, across bottom, and around map at ctr. on back.

18	**5 Kroner**	VG	VF	UNC
	Green. Polar bear on ice at center. Text: DEN KONGELIGE GRONLANDSKE HANDEL at left and right margin, across bottom, and around map			
	a. Issued note.	15.00	40.00	125.
	s. Specimen.	—	—	—

19	**10 Kroner**	VG	VF	UNC
	ND (1953-67). Brown. Hump-back whale at center. Text: DEN KONGELIGE GRONLANDSKE HANDEL at left and right margin, across bottom, and around map			
	a. Issued note.	15.00	60.00	250.
	s. Specimen.	—	—	—

20	**50 Kroner**	VG	VF	UNC
	ND (1953-67). Lilac. Clipper ship at center. Text: DEN KONGELIGE GRONLANDSKE HANDEL at left and right margin, across bottom, and around map			
	a. Issued note.	75.00	300.	800.
	s. Specimen.	—	—	—

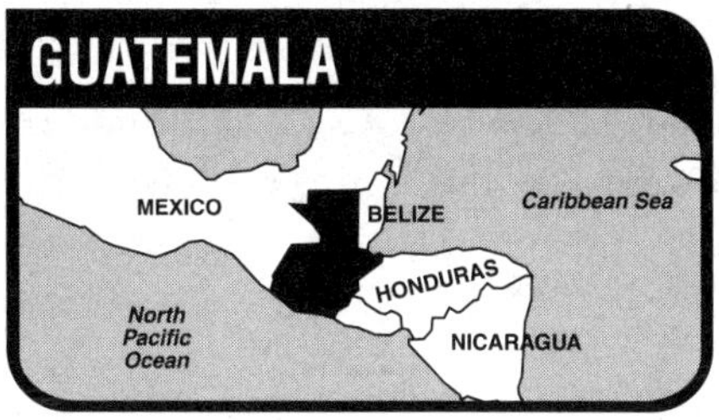

The Republic of Guatemala, the northernmost of the five Central American republics, has an area of 42,042 sq. mi. (108,889 sq. km.) and a population of 12.22 million. Capital: Guatemala City. The economy of Guatemala is heavily dependent on resources which are being developed. Coffee, cotton and bananas are exported.

Guatemala, once the site of the ancient Mayan civilization, was conquered by Pedro de Alvarado, the lieutenant of Cortes who undertook the conquest from Mexico. Skilled in strategy and cruelty, he progressed rapidly along the Pacific coastal lowlands to the highland plain of Quezaltenango where the decisive battle for Guatemala was fought. After routing the Mayan forces, he established the first capital of Guatemala in 1524.

Guatemala of the colonial period included all of Central America but Panama. Guatemala declared its independence of Spain in 1821 and was absorbed into the short-lived Mexican empire of Augustin Iturbide, 1822-23. From 1823 to 1839 Guatemala was a constituent state of the Central American Republic. Upon dissolution of the federation, Guatemala became an independent republic.

MONETARY SYSTEM:

1 Quetzal = 100 Centavos, 1924-

REPUBLIC

BANCO DE GUATEMALA

1957-63 ISSUE

#35-50 sign. title: *JEFE DE...* at r.
#35-39 Printer: ABNC.

No.	Description	VG	VF	UNC
35	**1/2 Quetzal** 22.1.1958. Brown on multicolor underprint. Hermitage of Cerro del Carmen at left. Signature title:*JEFE DE...* Two Guatemalans. Printer: ABNC.	3.00	15.00	75.00
36	**1 Quetzal** 16.1.1957; 22.1.1958. Green on multicolor underprint. Palace of the Captains General at left. Signature title:*JEFE DE...* Lake Atitlan. Printer: ABNC.	3.00	10.00	50.00
37	**5 Quetzales** 22.1.1958. Purple. Vase *Vasija de Uaxactum* at left. Signature title:*JEFE DE...* Mayan-Spanish battle scene. Printer: ABNC.	8.00	35.00	125.
38	**10 Quetzales** 22.1.1958; 12.1.1962; 9.1.1963; 8.1.1964. Red. Round stone carving *Ara de Tikal* at left. Signature title:*JEFE DE...* Founding of old Guatemala. Printer: ABNC.	12.50	65.00	200.
39	**20 Quetzales** 9.1.1963; 8.1.1964; 15.1.1965. Blue. Landivar at left. Signature title:*JEFE DE...* Meeting of Independence. Printer: ABNC.	20.00	75.00	250.

1959-60 ISSUES

#40-50 sign. varieties. Printer: W&S.

No.	Description	VG	VF	UNC
40	**1/2 Quetzal** 18.2.1959. Signature title:*JEFE DE...* at right. Lighter brown shadings around value guilloche at left. 6-digit serial #. Printer: W&S. Printed area 2mm smaller than #41.	2.00	10.00	60.00
41	**1/2 Quetzal** 18.2.1959; 13.1.1960; 18.1.1961. Signature title:*JEFE DE...* at right. Darker brown shadings around value guilloche at left. 7-digit serial #. Printer: W&S.			
	a. Issued note.	2.00	7.50	40.00
	s. Specimen.	—	—	30.00
42	**1 Quetzal** 18.2.1959. Signature title:*JEFE DE...* at right. Building at center right. Green palace. 6-digit serial #. Dull green. Printer: W&S.			
	a. Issued note.	2.00	10.00	60.00
	s. Specimen.	—	—	—
43	**1 Quetzal** 18.2.1959; 13.1.1960; 18.1.1961; 12.1.1962; 9.1.1963; 8.1.1964. Signature title:*JEFE DE...* at right. Black palace. 7-digit serial #. Bright green. Printer: W&S.			
	a. Issued note.	2.00	7.50	40.00
	s. Specimen.	—	—	—
44	**5 Quetzales** 18.2.1959. Value at left center. Vase in purple. Signature title:*JEFE DE...* at right. Printer: W&S.	8.00	30.00	110.

No.	Description	VG	VF	UNC
45	**5 Quetzales** 18.2.1959-8.1.1964. Redesigned guilloche. Value at center. Vase in brown. Signature title:*JEFE DE...* at right. Printer: W&S.			
	a. Issued note.	5.00	25.00	100.
	s. Specimen.	—	—	—
46	**10 Quetzales** 18.2.1959. Signature title:*JEFE DE...* at right. Round red stone at right. Printer: W&S.	15.00	50.00	200.

No.	Description	VG	VF	UNC
47	**10 Quetzales** 18.2.1959; 13.1.1960; 18.1.1961. Similar to #46 but redesigned guilloche. Round stone in brown. Signature title:*JEFE DE...* at right. Printer: W&S.			
	a. Issued note.	15.00	35.00	150.
	s. Specimen.	—	—	—
48	**20 Quetzales** 13.1.1960-15.1.1965. Blue. Signature title:*JEFE DE...* at right. Portrait at right Landivar at right.			
	a. Issued note.	20.00	65.00	200.
	s. Specimen.	—	—	—
49	**100 Quetzales** 18.2.1959. Dark blue. Signature title:*JEFE DE...* at right. *Indio de Nahuala* in blue at center. Printer: W&S.	115.	250.	550.
50	**100 Quetzales** 13.1.1960-15.1.1965. Dark blue. Signature title:*JEFE DE...* at right. Portrait *Indio de Nahuala* in brown at right. Printer: W&S.			
	a. Issued note.	115.	250.	500.
	s. Specimen.	—	—	—

1964-67 ISSUE

#51-57 sign. varieties. Printer: TDLR.

No.	Description	VG	VF	UNC
51	**1/2 Quetzal** 8.1.1964-5.1.1972. Brown on multicolor underprint. Like #41. Hermitage of Cerro del Carmen at left. Two Guatemalans at center on back.	1.50	7.50	35.00

No.	Description	VG	VF	UNC
52	**1 Quetzal** 8.1.1964; 15.1.1965; 21.1.1966; 13.1.1967; 3.1.1968; 3.1.1969; 7.1.1970; 6.1.1971; 5.1.1972. Black and green on multicolor underprint. Palace of the Captains General at center right. Lake Atitlan Printer: TDLR.	1.50	7.50	35.00

#53-57 two wmk. varieties.

No.	Description	VG	VF	UNC
53	**5 Quetzales** 8.1.1964; 15.1.1965; 21.1.1966; 13.1.1967; 3.1.1968; 3.1.1969; 7.1.1970; 6.1.1971. Purple on multicolor underprint. Vase *Vasija de Uaxactum* at right. Watermark: 2 varieties. Printer: TDLR.	3.00	10.00	60.00
54	**10 Quetzales** 15.1.1965-7.1.1970. Red on multicolor underprint. Round carved stone *Arade Tikal* at right. Mayan-Spanish battle scene. Watermark: 2 varieties. Printer: TDLR.	8.00	25.00	100.
55	**20 Quetzales** 15.1.1965-6.1.1971. Blue on multicolor underprint. R. Landivar at right. Founding of Guatemala. Watermark: 2 varieties. Printer: TDLR.	17.50	45.00	200.

		VG	VF	UNC
56	**50 Quetzales** 13.1.1967-5.1.1973. Orange and blue on multicolor underprint. Gen. J. M. Orellana at right. Orange. Bank at center. Watermark: 2 varieties. Printer: TDLR.	50.00	175.	450.

		VG	VF	UNC
57	**100 Quetzales** 21.1.1966; 13.1.1967; 3.1.1968; 3.1.1969; 7.1.1970. Blue-black and brown on pale green and multicolor underprint. Face like #50. *Indio de Nahuala* at right. City and mountain in valley Antihua on back.	60.00	150.	400.

1969-75 Issue

#58-64 Quetzal bird at upper ctr. Various date and sign. varieties. Printer: TDLR. #60-64 wmk: Tecun Uman.

		VG	VF	UNC
58	**1/2 Quetzal** 1972-83. Brown on multicolor underprint. Tecun Uman (national hero) at right. Tikal temple on back.			
	a. Without security (flourescent) imprint. 5.1.1972; 5.1.1973.	.25	1.75	12.00
	b. Security (flourescent) imprint on back. 2.1.1974; 3.1.1975; 7.1.1976; 20.4.1977.	.25	1.25	9.00
	c. 4.1.1978; 3.1.1979; 2.1.1980; 7.1.1981; 6.1.1982; 6.1.1983.	.25	1.50	9.00
	s. Specimen. As c.	—	—	10.00

		VG	VF	UNC
59	**1 Quetzal** 1972-83. Green on multicolor underprint. Gen. J. M. Orellana at right. Banco de Guatemala building on back.			
	a. Security (flourescent) imprint on face. Date at lower right. 5.1.1972; 5.1.1973.	.50	2.50	14.00
	b. Security imprint as a. on face and back. 2.1.1974; 3.1.1975; 7.1.1976.	.40	2.00	10.00
	c. Date at center r. 5.1.1977; 20.4.1977; 4.1.1978; 3.1.1979; 2.1.1980; 7.1.1981; 6.1.1982; 6.1.1983; 30.12.1983.	.25	1.00	7.50
	s. Specimen. As c.	—	—	10.00

		VG	VF	UNC
60	**5 Quetzales** 1969-83. Purple on multicolor underprint. Gen. (later Pres.) J. R. Barrios at right. Classroom scene on back.			
	a. 3.1.1969; 6.1.1971; 5.1.1972; 5.1.1973.	1.25	5.00	27.50
	b. 2.1.1974; 3.1.1975; 7.1.1976; 5.1.1977; 20.4.1977.	1.00	4.00	22.50
	c. 4.1.1978; 3.1.1979; 2.1.1980; 7.1.1981; 6.1.1982; 6.1.1983.	1.00	3.00	17.50
	s. Specimen. As c. ND.	—	—	10.00

		VG	VF	UNC
61	**10 Quetzales** 1971-83. Red on multicolor underprint. Gen. M. G. Granados at right. National Assembly session of 1872 on back.			
	a. 6.1.1971; 5.1.1972; 3.1.1973.	2.50	10.00	45.00
	b. 2.1.1974; 3.1.1975; 7.1.1976; 5.1.1977; 20.4.1977.	2.25	7.50	35.00
	c. 4.1.1978; 3.1.1979; 2.1.1980; 7.1.1981; 6.1.1982; 6.1.1983.	2.00	5.00	22.50
	s. Specimen. As c. ND.	—	—	10.00

		VG	VF	UNC
62	**20 Quetzales** 1972-83; 1988. Blue on multicolor underprint. Dr. M. Galvez at right. Granting of Independence to Central America on back.			
	a. 5.1.1972; 5.1.1973.	4.00	10.00	65.00
	b. 2.1.1974; 3.1.1975; 7.1.1976; 5.1.1977; 20.4.1977.	3.75	8.50	45.00
	c. 4.1.1978; 2.1.1979; 2.1.1980; 7.1.1981; 6.1.1982; 6.1.1983.	3.50	8.50	35.00
	d. 6.1.1988.	FV	6.00	30.00

63	50 Quetzales	VG	VF	UNC
	1974; 1981-83. Orange on multicolor underprint. C. O. Zachrisson at right. Crop workers on back.			
	a. 2.1.1974.	10.00	45.00	175.
	b. 7.1.1981; 6.1.1982; 6.1.1983.	10.00	35.00	125.

64	100 Quetzales	VG	VF	UNC
	1972-83. Brown on multicolor underprint. F. Marroquin at right. University of San Carlos de Borromeo on back.			
	a. 5.1.1972.	22.50	75.00	250.
	b. 3.1.1975; 7.1.1976; 3.1.1979.	20.00	60.00	175.
	c. 6.1.1982; 6.1.1983.	17.50	45.00	140.

1983 Issue

#65-71 similar to #58-64. Wmk: Tecun Uman. Printer: G&D.

65	1/2 Quetzal	VG	VF	UNC
	6.1.1983-4.1.1989. Brown on multicolor underprint. Tecun Uman at right. Tikal temple on back. Similar to #58.	FV	FV	5.00

66	1 Quetzal	VG	VF	UNC
	30.12.1983-4.1.1989. Blue-green and green on multicolor underprint. Gen. J. Orellana at right. Banco de Guatemala building on back. Similar to #59.	FV	FV	5.00

67	5 Quetzales	VG	VF	UNC
	6.1.1983-6.1.1988. Purple on multicolor underprint. J. R. Barrios at right. Classroom scene on back. Similar to #60.	FV	2.50	12.50

68	10 Quetzales	VG	VF	UNC
	30.12.1983-6.1.1988. Red and red-brown on multicolor underprint. Gen. M. G. Granados at right. National Assembly session of 1872 on back. Similar to #61.	FV	5.00	25.00

69	20 Quetzales	VG	VF	UNC
	6.1.1983-7.1.1987. Blue on multicolor underprint. Dr. M. Galvez at right. Similar to #62.	FV	7.50	40.00

70	50 Quetzales	VG	VF	UNC
	30.12.1983-7.1.1987. Orange and yellow-orange on multicolor underprint. C. O. Zachrisson at right. Crop workers on back. Similar to #63.	FV	20.00	65.00

71	100 Quetzales	VG	VF	UNC
	30.12.1983-7.1.1987. Brown on multicolor underprint. F. Marroquin at right. Similar to #64.	FV	30.00	90.00

1989; 1990 ISSUE

#72-74 printer: CBN. Sign. varieties.

		VG	VF	UNC
72	**1/2 Quetzal** 4.1.1989; 14.2.1992. Brown on multicolor underprint. Similar to #65. Without watermark.	FV	FV	5.00

		VG	VF	UNC
73	**1 Quetzal** 3.1.1990; 6.3.1991; 22.1.1992; 14.2.1992. Blue-green on multicolor underprint. Similar to #66. Without watermark.	FV	FV	4.00

		VG	VF	UNC
74	**5 Quetzales** 3.1.1990; 6.3.1991; 22.1.1992. Purple on multicolor underprint. Similar to #67.	FV	FV	7.50

#75-78 similar to #68-71. Vertical serial # at l. Wmk: Tecun Uman. Printer: TDLR. Sign. varieties.

		VG	VF	UNC
75	**10 Quetzales** 4.1.1989; 3.1.1990; 22.1.1992. Brown-violet and red on multicolor underprint. Similar to #68.	FV	FV	12.50

		VG	VF	UNC
76	**20 Quetzales** 4.1.1989; 3.1.1990; 22.1.1992. Blue-black, purple and blue on multicolor underprint. Similar to #69.	FV	FV	17.50

		VG	VF	UNC
77	**50 Quetzales** 4.1.1989; 3.1.1990. Orange and green on multicolor underprint. Similar to #70.	FV	7.50	30.00

		VG	VF	UNC
78	**100 Quetzales** 4.1.1989; 3.1.1990; 22.1.1992. Brown and red-brown on multicolor underprint. Similar to #71. Back lilac and multicolor.	FV	20.00	50.00

1992 ISSUE

#79-82 similar to #65-68 but more colorful backs. Printer: F-CO.

		VG	VF	UNC
79	**1/2 Quetzal** 16.7.1992. Brown on multicolor underprint. Similar to #65.	FV	FV	2.50
80	**1 Quetzal** 16.7.1992. Blue-green on multicolor underprint. Similar to #66.	FV	FV	3.50

		VG	VF	UNC
81	**5 Quetzales** 16.7.1992. Purple on multicolor underprint. Similar to #67.	FV	FV	7.00

#82-85 wmk: Tecun Uman.

		VG	VF	UNC
82	**10 Quetzales** 16.7.1992. Brown-violet and red on multicolor underprint. Similar to #68.	FV	FV	10.00

#83-85 similar to #69-71 but more colorful backs. Printer: BABN.

		VG	VF	UNC
83	**20 Quetzales** 12.8.1992. Blue-black, purple and blue on multicolor underprint. Similar to #69.	FV	FV	15.00
84	**50 Quetzales** 12.8.1992. Orange and green on multicolor underprint. Similar to #70.	FV	FV	30.00

		VG	VF	UNC
85	**100 Quetzales** 27.5.1992. Brown on multicolor underprint. Date at lower left, gold colored device at right. Back light brown and multicolor. Similar to #71.	FV	FV	40.00

1993; 1995 Issue

#86-89 printer: CBNC.

		VG	VF	UNC
86	**1/2 Quetzal** 27.10.1993; 27.9.1994; 6.9.1995. Brown on multicolor underprint. Similar to #79 but with colorful back.	FV	FV	2.00

		VG	VF	UNC
87	**1 Quetzal** 27.10.1993; 6.9.1994; 6.9.1995. Dark green on green and multicolor underprint. Similar to #80 but with colorful back.	FV	FV	3.00

		VG	VF	UNC
88	**5 Quetzales** 1993; 1995. Purple on multicolor underprint. Similar to #81 but with colorful back.			
	a. 27.10.1993; 16.6.1995.	FV	FV	5.50
	b. Without imprint. 16.6.1995.	FV	FV	4.50

		VG	VF	UNC
89	**10 Quetzales** 16.6.1995. Brown-violet and red on multicolor underprint. Similar to #82 but with colorful back. Large and small printer imprint on back.	FV	FV	7.50

1994 Issue

#90 and 91 printer: F-CO.

		VG	VF	UNC
90	**1 Quetzal** 27.9.1994. Dark green on green and multicolor underprint. Similar to #73 but with colorful back.	FV	FV	2.50
91	**10 Quetzales** 29.6.1994. Brown-violet and red on multicolor underprint. Similar to #75 but with colorful back.	FV	FV	7.50

Note: Formerly listed #90A has been determined to be #92.

1994; 1995 Issue

#92-94 Printer: TDLR.

		VG	VF	UNC
92	**5 Quetzales** 29.6.1994. Purple on multicolor underprint. Similar to #74 but with colorful back.	FV	FV	3.50

		VG	VF	UNC
93	**50 Quetzales** 16.6.1995. Orange and green on multicolor underprint. Similar to #77 but with colorful back.	FV	FV	20.00

		VG	VF	UNC
94	**100 Quetzales** 29.6.1994; 16.6.1995. Brown on multicolor underprint. Similar to #78 but with colorful back.	FV	FV	35.00

1995 Issue

		VG	VF	UNC
95	**20 Quetzales** 16.6.1995. Blue-black, purple and blue on multicolor underprint. Similar to #69 but with colorful back. Printer: G&D.	FV	FV	10.00

1996 Issue

#96 and 97 printer: H&S.

		VG	VF	UNC
96	**1/2 Quetzal** 28.8.1996. Brown on multicolor underprint. Similar to #86.			
	a. Issued note.	FV	FV	1.00
	s. Specimen.	—	—	75.00

		VG	VF	UNC
97	**1 Quetzal** 28.8.1996. Dark green on green and multicolor underprint. Similar to #87.			
	a. Issued note.	FV	FV	1.50
	s. Specimen.	—	—	75.00

1998 Issue

#98 and 99 printer: (T)DLR.

		VG	VF	UNC
98	**1/2 Quetzal** 9.1.1998. Brown on multicolor underprint. Similar to #96.	FV	FV	.75
99	**1 Quetzal** 9.1.1998. Dark green and green on multicolor underprint. Similar to #90.	FV	FV	1.00

		VG	VF	UNC
100	**5 Quetzales** 29.7.1998. Purple on multicolor underprint. Similar to #92.	FV	FV	2.50

1998-99 Issue

#100-103 printer: BABN.

		VG	VF	UNC
101	**10 Quetzales** 29.7.1998. Brown-violet and red on multicolor underprint. Similar to #91.	FV	FV	5.00

		VG	VF	UNC
102	**20 Quetzales** 17.6.1999. Similar to #83.	FV	FV	10.00

2001 Issue

		VG	VF	UNC
103	**100 Quetzales** 29.7.1998. Multicolor.	FV	FV	35.00

		VG	VF	UNC
104	**100 Quetzales** 8.4.2001. Multicolor. Printer: G&D.	FV	FV	30.00

2001 Second Issue

		VG	VF	UNC
105	**50 Quetzales** 9.4.2001. Orange and green on multicolor underprint. Printer: G&D.	FV	FV	20.00

2003 Issue

106	5 Quetzales	VG	VF	UNC
	12.2.2003. Purple on multicolor underprint. Printer: F-CO.	FV	FV	2.50

107	10 Quetzales	VG	VF	UNC
	12.2.2003. Brown-violet and red on multicolor underprint. Printer: F-CO.	FV	FV	5.00

108	20 Quetzales	VG	VF	UNC
	12.2.2003. Blue-black, purple and blue on multicolor underprint. Printer: G&D.	FV	FV	8.00

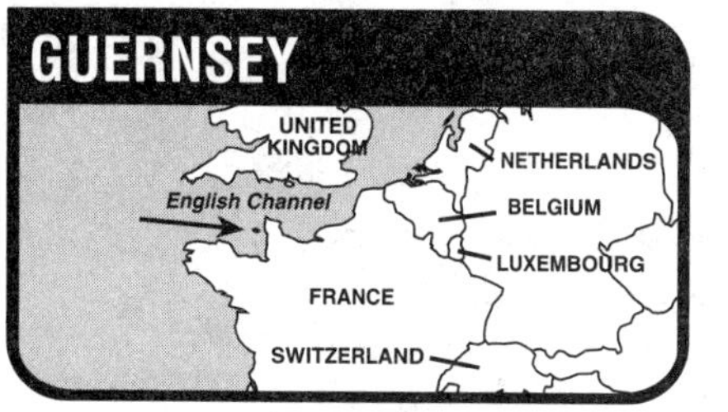

The Bailiwick of Guernsey, a British crown dependency located in the English Channel 30 miles (48 km.) west of Normandy, France, has an area of 30 sq. mi. (78 sq. km.), including the Isles of Alderney, Jethou, Herm, Brechou and Sark, and a population of 58,681. Capital: St. Peter Port. Agriculture and cattle breeding are the main occupations.

Militant monks from the Duchy of Normandy established the first permanent settlements on Guernsey prior to the Norman invasion of England, but the prevalence of prehistoric monuments suggests an earlier occupancy. The island, the only part of the Duchy of Normandy belonging to the British crown, has been a possession of Britain since the Norman Conquest of 1066. During the Anglo-French Wars, the harbors of Guernsey were employed in the building and outfitting of ships for the English privateers preying on French shipping. Guernsey is administered by its own laws and customs. Acts passed by the British Parliament are not applicable to Guernsey unless the island is specifically mentioned. During World War II, German troops occupied the island from 1940 to 1944.

United Kingdom bank notes and coinage circulate concurrently with Guernsey money as legal tender.

RULERS:

British to 1940, 1944-

MONETARY SYSTEM:

1 Penny = 8 Doubles
1 Shilling = 12 Pence
1 Pound = 20 Shillings to 1971
1 Pound = 100 New Pence 1971-

BRITISH ADMINISTRATION

STATES OF GUERNSEY

1945; 1956 ISSUE

#42-44 printer: PBC.

42	10 Shillings	VG	VF	UNC
	1945-66. Lilac on light green underprint. Purple. Printer: PBC.			
	a. 1.8.1945-1.9.1957.	50.00	200.	550.
	b. 1.7.1958-1.3.1965.	20.00	90.00	275.
	c. 1.7.1966.	8.00	45.00	120.
	s. As c. Specimen.	—	—	—

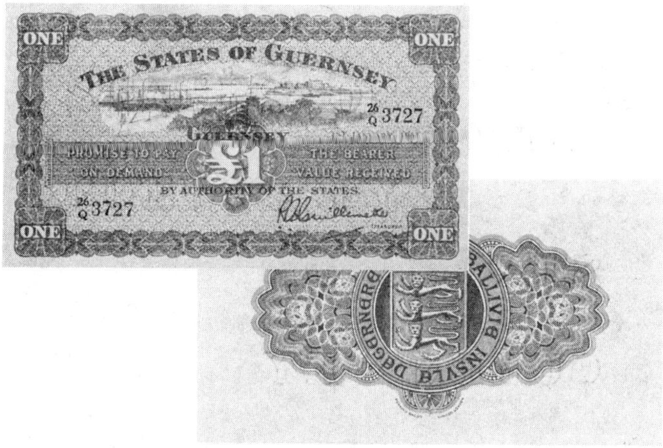

43	1 Pound	VG	VF	UNC
	1945-66. Purple on green underprint. Harbor entrance across center. Green. Printer: PBC.			

		VG	VF	UNC
43	**1 Pound**			
	a. 1.8.1945-1.3.1957.	60.00	275.	650.
	b. 1.9.1957-1.3.1962; 1.6.1963; 1.3.1965.	25.00	120.	375.
	c. 1.7.1966.	15.00	70.00	240.
	s. As c. Specimen.	—	—	—

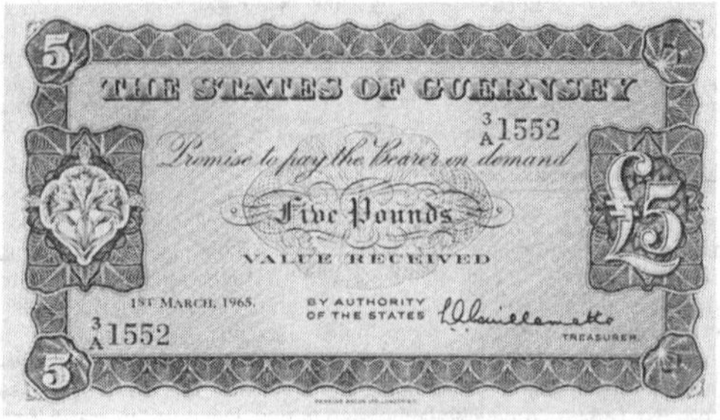

		VG	VF	UNC
44	**5 Pounds** 1.12.1956; 1.3.1965; 1.7.1966. Green and blue. Flowers at left. Printer: PBC.	150.	650.	1500.

1969; 1975 ND Issue

#45-47 printer: BWC. Replacement notes: Serial # prefix *Z*.

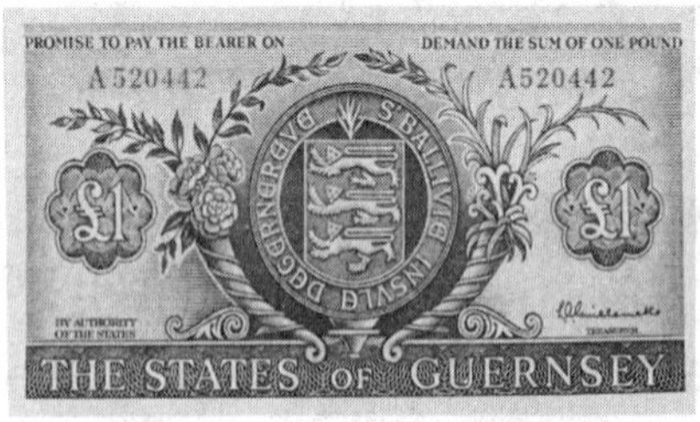

		VG	VF	UNC
45	**1 Pound** ND (1969-75). Olive on pink and yellow underprint. Arms at center. Castle Cornet on back.			
	a. Signature Guillemette.	5.00	20.00	85.00
	b. Signature Hodder.	FV	6.00	35.50
	c. Signature Bull.	FV	6.00	35.00

		VG	VF	UNC
46	**5 Pounds** ND (1969-75). Purple on light brown underprint. Arms at right. City view and harbor wall on back.			
	a. Signature Guillemette.	15.00	75.00	300.
	b. Signature Hodder.	FV	40.00	170.
	c. Signature Bull.	FV	25.00	100.
	s. Specimen.	—	—	—

		VG	VF	UNC
47	**10 Pounds** ND (1975-80). Blue, green and multicolor. Britannia with lion and shield at left. Sir I. Brock and Battle of Queenston Heights on blue back. Signature Hodder.	30.00	125.	525.

1980 ND Issue

#48-51 Guernsey States seal at lower l. on face and as wmk. Printer: TDLR. Replacement notes: Serial # prefix *Z*.

		VG	VF	UNC
48	**1 Pound** ND (1980-89). Dark green and black on multicolor underprint. Market square scene of 1822 at lower center in underprint. D. De Lisle Brock and Royal Court of St. Peter Port on back. 135 x 67mm.			
	a. Signature W. C. Bull.	FV	FV	20.00
	b. Black signature M. J. Brown.	FV	FV	14.00

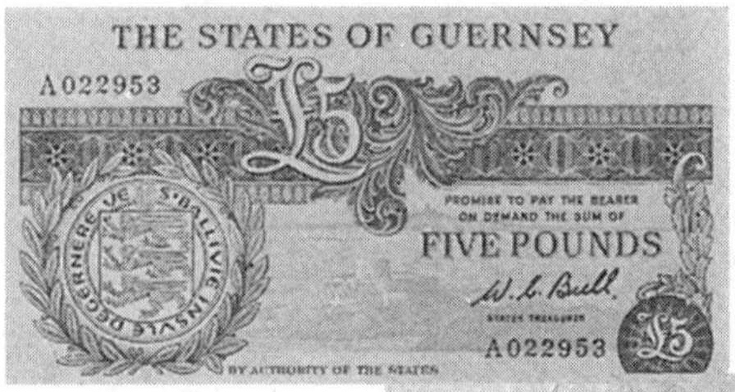

		VG	VF	UNC
49	**5 Pounds** ND (1980-89). Purple, dark brown and olive-brown on multicolor underprint. Fort Grey at lower center in underprint. T. De La Rue and Fountain Street at center, workers at envelope making machine at lower right on back. Signature W. C. Bull. 146 x 78mm.	FV	15.00	55.00

50 10 Pounds | VG | VF | UNC

ND (1980-89). Purple, blue and blue-black on multicolor underprint. Castle Cornet at lower center. Maj. Sir Isaac Brock and battle of Queenston Heights on back. 151 x 85mm.

	VG	VF	UNC
a. Signature W. C. Bull.	FV	30.00	110.
b. Black signature M. J. Brown.	FV	27.50	95.00

51 20 Pounds | VG | VF | UNC

ND (1980-89). Red, red-violet, brown and orange on multicolor underprint. 1815 scene of Saumarez Park at lower center in underprint. Adm. Lord de Saumarez and ships on back. 161 x 90mm.

	VG	VF	UNC
a. Signature W. C. Bull.	FV	65.00	190.
b. Black signature M. J. Brown.	FV	55.00	150.

1990; 1991 ND Issue

#52-55 similar to #48-51 but reduced size. Wmk: Guernsey States seal. Printer: (T)DLR. Replacement notes: Serial # prefix *Z*.

52 1 Pound | VG | VF | UNC

ND (ca.1991-). Dark green and black on multicolor underprint. Similar to #48. 128 x 65mm.

	VG	VF	UNC
a. Green signature M. J. Brown.	FV	FV	9.00
b. Signature D. P. Trestain.	FV	FV	8.00
c. Signature D. M. Clark.	FV	FV	7.00

53 5 Pounds | VG | VF | UNC

ND (1990-95). Purple, dark brown and olive-brown on multicolor underprint. Similar to #49. 136 x 70mm.

	VG	VF	UNC
a. Brown signature M. J. Brown.	FV	12.00	40.00
b. Signature D. P. Trestain.	FV	10.00	35.00

54 10 Pounds

ND (ca.1991-95). Purple, blue and blue-black on multicolor underprint. Similar to #50. 142 x 75mm.

	VG	VF	UNC
a. Blue signature M. J. Brown.	FV	FV	55.00
b. Signature D. P. Trestain.	FV	FV	50.00

55 20 Pounds | VG | VF | UNC

ND (ca.1991-95). Red, red-violet, brown and orange on multicolor underprint. Similar to #51. 149 x 80mm.

	VG	VF	UNC
a. Red-orange signature M. J. Brown.	FV	FV	100.
b. Signature D. P. Trestain.	FV	FV	90.00

1994-96 ND Issue

#56-59 Qn. Elizabeth II at r. and as wmk., Guernsey States seal at bottom ctr. r. Printer: TDLR.

56 5 Pounds | VG | VF | UNC

ND (1996). Dark brown and purple on multicolor underprint. St. Peter Port Town Church at lower left, brown seal at lower center. Fort Grey at upper left center, Hanois Lighthouse at center right on back.

	VG	VF	UNC
a. Signature D. P. Trestain.	FV	FV	30.00
b. Signature D. M. Clark.	FV	FV	25.00

57	10 Pounds	VG	VF	UNC
	ND (1995). Violet, blue and dark blue on multicolor underprint. Elizabeth College at lower left. Saumarez Park above Le Niaux Watermill and Le Trepid Dolmen at left center on back.			
	a. Signature D. P. Trestain.	FV	FV	45.00
	b. Signature D. M. Clark.	FV	FV	40.00

58	20 Pounds	VG	VF	UNC
	ND (1996). Pink, dark brown and orange on multicolor underprint. St. James Concert Hall at lower left. Flowers at lower left, St. Sampson's Church at left center, sailboats below Vale Castle at center right, ship at upper right on back.			
	a. Signature D. P. Trestain.	FV	FV	80.00
	b. Signature D. M. Clark.	FV	FV	75.00

59	50 Pounds	VG	VF	UNC
	ND (1994). Dark brown, dark green and blue-black on multicolor underprint. Royal Court House at lower left. Stone carving, letter of Marque at lower left, St. Andrew's Church at center right on back.	FV	FV	210.

2000 Issue

#60, Millennium Commemorative

60	5 Pounds	VG	VF	UNC
	2000. Dark brown and purple on multicolor underprint. Similar to #56 but with added commemorative text at left on face. Blue seal at lower center Printer: (T)DLR.	FV	FV	20.00

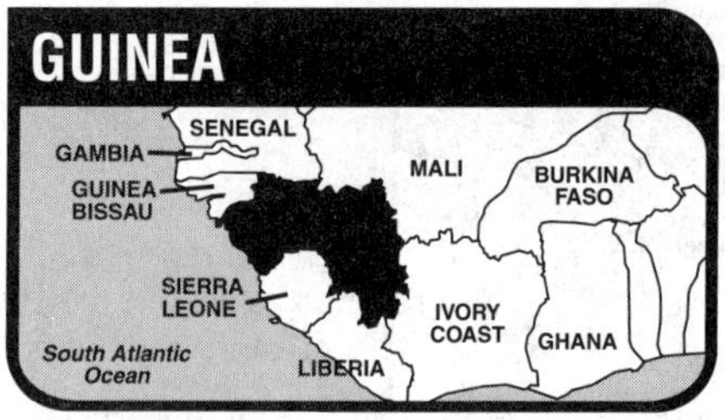

The Republic of Guinea (formerly French Guinea), situated on the Atlantic coast of Africa between Sierra Leone and Guinea-Bissau, has an area of 94,964 sq. mi. (245,957 sq. km.) and a population of 7.86 million. Capital: Conakry. Although Guinea contains one-third of the world's reserves of bauxite and significant deposits of iron ore, gold and diamonds, the economy is still dependent on agriculture. Aluminum, bananas, copra and coffee are exported.

The coast of Guinea was known to Portuguese navigators of the 15th century but was seldom visited by European traders of the 16th-18th centuries because of its dangerous coastal waters. French penetration of the area began in the mid-19th century with the entering into of protectorate treaties with several of the coastal chiefs. After a long struggle with Guinea's native leader Samory Toure, France secured the area and until 1890 administered it as a part of Senegal. In 1895 the colony (Guinee Francaise) became an autonomous part of the federation of French West Africa. The inhabitants were extended French citizenship in 1946 when the colony became an overseas territory of the French Union. Guinea became an independent republic on Oct. 2, 1958, when it declined to enter the new French Community.

MONETARY SYSTEM:

1 Franc = 100 Centimes to 1971
1 Syli = 10 Francs, 1971-1980
Franc System, 1985-

Republic

Banque Centrale de la République de Guinée

1960 Issue

#12-15A Pres. Sekou Toure at l. Wmk: Dove.

12	50 Francs	VG	VF	UNC
	1.3.1960. Brown on multicolor underprint. Heavy machinery on back.			
	a. Issued note.	1.00	4.00	20.00
	s. Specimen.	—	—	25.00

13	100 Francs	VG	VF	UNC
	1.3.1960. Dark brown on pale olive-green, pale orange, pink and lilac underprint. Back dark brown on orange and pink underprint., pineapple field workers.			
	a. Issued note.	2.00	6.00	35.00
	s. As a. Specimen.	—	—	25.00
	x. (Error). dark brown and pale olive-green, light blue and pale yellow-orange underprint. Back dark brown on yellow underprint.	—	—	—

14	500 Francs	VG	VF	UNC
	1.3.1960. Blue on multicolor underprint. Men pulling long boats ashore on back.			
	a. Issued note.	3.00	20.00	150.
	s. Specimen.	—	—	35.00

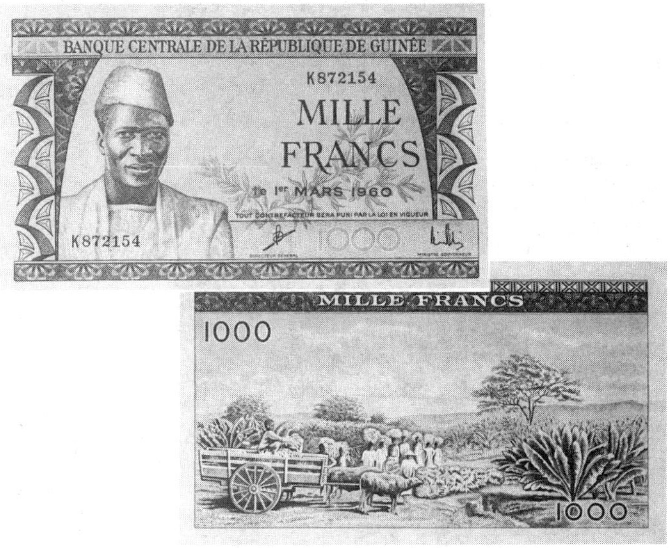

15	1000 Francs	VG	VF	UNC
	1.3.1960. Green on multicolor underprint. Banana harvesting on back.			
	a. Issued note.	3.00	15.00	75.00
	s. Specimen.	—	—	35.00
15A	5000 Francs			
	1.3.1960. Purple on green and multicolor underprint. Pres. Sekou Toure at left. Woman in headdress at left, huts at right. Watermark: Dove. (Not issued). Specimen.	—	—	400.

1971 Issue

#16-19 issued under Law of 1960.

16	10 Sylis	VG	VF	UNC
	1971. Brown on multicolor underprint. Patrice Lumumba at right. People with bananas on back.	.20	.50	1.75

17	25 Sylis	VG	VF	UNC
	1971. Dark brown on multicolor underprint. Man smoking a pipe at right. Man and cows on back.	.25	.75	3.00

18	50 Sylis	VG	VF	UNC
	1971. Green on multicolor underprint. Bearded man at left. Landscape with large dam and reservoir on back.	.50	2.00	10.00

19	100 Sylis	VG	VF	UNC
	1971. Purple on multicolor underprint. A. S. Toure at left. Steam shovel and two dump trucks on back.	.50	2.00	9.00

1980; 1981 Issue

#20-27 issued under Law of 1960.

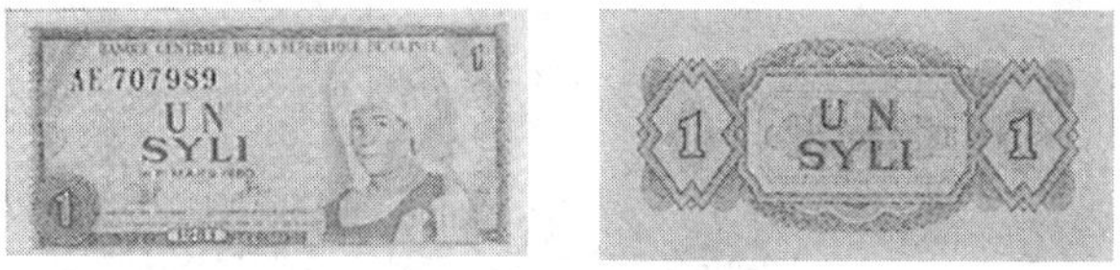

20	1 Syli	VG	VF	UNC
	1981. Olive on green underprint. Mafori Bangoura at right.			
	a. Issued note.	.05	.15	.50
	s. Specimen.	—	—	6.00

21	2 Sylis	VG	VF	UNC
	1981. Black and brown on orange underprint. Green guilloche at center, King Mohammed V of Morocco at left.			
	a. Issued note.	.05	.25	.75
	s. Specimen.	—	—	7.00

22	5 Sylis	VG	VF	UNC
	1980. Blue on pink underprint. Kwame Nkrumah at right. Back like #16.			
	a. Issued note.	.20	.50	2.00
	s. Specimen.	—	—	8.00

23	10 Sylis	VG	VF	UNC
	1980. Red and red-orange on multicolor underprint. Like #16.			
	a. Issued note.	.25	.50	2.50
	s. Specimen.	—	—	9.00

24	25 Sylis	VG	VF	UNC
	1980. Dark green on multicolor underprint. Like #17.			
	a. Issued note.	.25	.50	4.00
	s. Specimen.	—	—	10.00

25	50 Sylis	VG	VF	UNC
	1980. Dark red and brown on multicolor underprint. Like #18.			
	a. Issued note.	.50	1.50	7.00
	s. Specimen.	—	—	10.00

26	100 Sylis	VG	VF	UNC
	1980. Blue on multicolor underprint. Like #19.			
	a. Issued note.	1.00	4.00	17.50
	s. Specimen.	—	—	15.00

27	500 Sylis	VG	VF	UNC
	1980. Dark brown on multicolor underprint. J. Broz Tito at left. Modern building on back.			
	a. Issued note.	.50	2.00	12.50
	s. Specimen.	—	—	20.00

Note: #27 is purported to commemorate Marshal Tito's visit to Guinea.

1985 ISSUE

#28-33 arms at ctr. on face. Issued under Law of 1960.

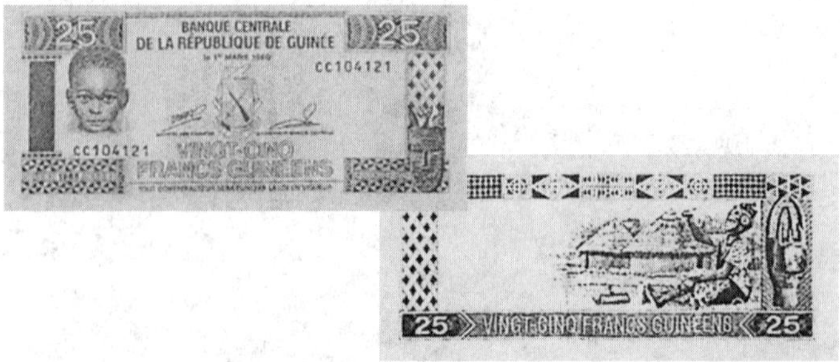

28	25 Francs	VG	VF	UNC
	1985. Blue on multicolor underprint. Young boy at left. Girl by huts at center right on back.			
	a. Issued note.	.05	.20	1.25
	s. Specimen.	—	—	3.00

29	50 Francs	VG	VF	UNC
	1985. Red-violet on multicolor underprint. Bearded man at left. Plowing with water buffalo at center on back.			
	a. Issued note.	.10	.25	1.50
	s. Specimen.	—	—	50.00

30	100 Francs	VG	VF	UNC
	1985. Purple on multicolor underprint. Young woman at left. Harvesting bananas at center on back.			
	a. Issued note.	.10	.25	1.75
	s. Specimen.	—	—	50.00

31	500 Francs	VG	VF	UNC
	1985. Green on multicolor underprint. Woman at left. Minehead at center on back.			
	a. Issued note.	.25	1.00	4.50
	s. Specimen.	—	—	65.00

32	1000 Francs	VG	VF	UNC
	1985. Brown and blue on multicolor underprint. Girl at left. Shovel loading ore into open end dump trucks at center, mask at right on back.			
	a. Issued note.	FV	1.50	6.50
	s. Specimen.	—	—	65.00

33	5000 Francs	VG	VF	UNC
	1985. Blue and brown on multicolor underprint. Woman at left. Dam at center, mask at right on back.			
	a. Issued note.	FV	4.50	20.00
	s. Specimen.	—	—	100.

#34 not assigned.

1998 Issue

35	100 Francs	VG	VF	UNC
	1998. Multicolor. Young woman at left. Harvesting bananas at center on back. Similar to #30.	FV	FV	1.50

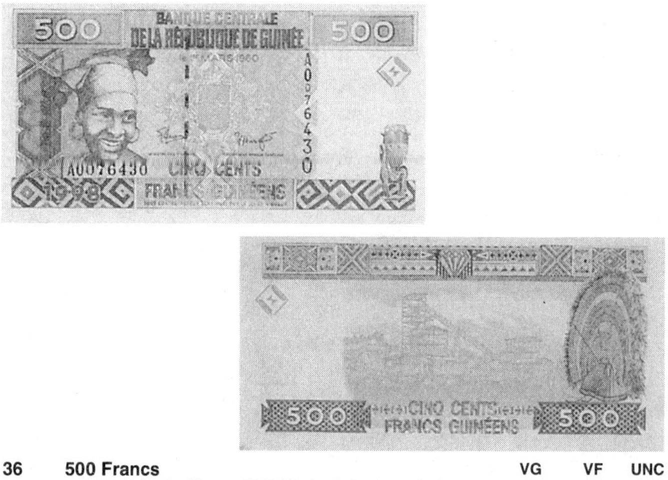

36	500 Francs	VG	VF	UNC
	1998. Multicolor. Woman at left. Minehead at center on back. Similar to #31.	FV	FV	3.50

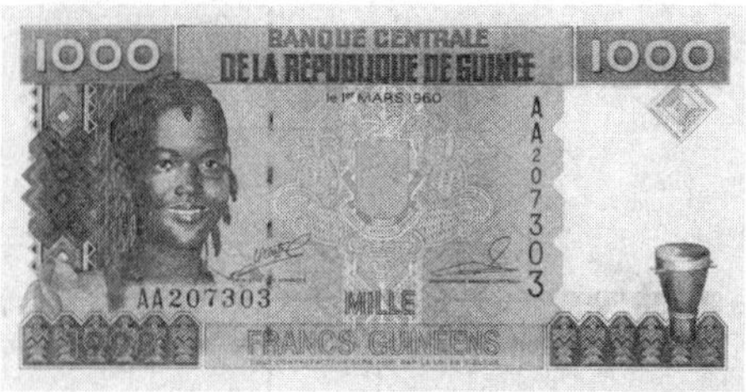

		VG	VF	UNC
37	**1000 Francs** 1998. Brown and red-brown on multicolor underprint. Female head at left. Mining scene on back. Similar to #32.	FV	FV	5.00

		VG	VF	UNC
38	**5000 Francs** 1998. Multicolor. Woman at left. Dam at center, mask at right on back. Similar to #33 but with thick security thread.	FV	FV	17.50

GUINEA-BISSAU

The Republic of Guinea-Bissau, a former Portuguese overseas province on the west coast of Africa between Senegal and Guinea, has an area of 13,948 sq. mi. (36,125 sq. km.) and a population of 1.18 million. Capital: Bissau. The country has undeveloped deposits of oil and bauxite. Peanuts, oil-palm kernels and hides are exported.

The African Party for the Independence of Guinea-Bissau was founded in 1956, and several years later began a guerrilla warfare that grew in effectiveness until 1974, when the rebels controlled most of the colony. Portugal's costly overseas wars in her African territories resulted in a military coup in Portugal in April 1974, that appreciably brightened the prospects for freedom for Guinea-Bissau. In August 1974, the Lisbon government signed an agreement granting independence to Portuguese Guinea effective Sept. 10, 1974. The new republic took the name of Guinea-Bissau.

On Jan. 1, 1997, Guinea-Bissau became a member of the West African States, and has issued CFA currency notes with the code letter `S'. Refer to West African States listings.

RULERS:

Portuguese until 1974

MONETARY SYSTEM:

1 Peso = 100 Centavos, 1975-1997
1 Franc = 65 Pesos, 1997-

REPUBLIC

BANCO NACIONAL DA GUINÉ-BISSAU

1975 ISSUE

#1-3 wmk: A. Cabral. Printed in Algeria.

		VG	VF	UNC
1	**50 Pesos** 24.9.1975. Blue and brown on multicolor underprint. P. Nalsna at left, group at center. Field workers at center, woman at right on back.	2.00	5.00	30.00

		VG	VF	UNC
2	**100 Pesos** 24.9.1975. Brown (shades) on multicolor underprint. D. Ramos at left, group in open hut at lower left center. Objects and woman on back.	1.50	5.00	27.50

		VG	VF	UNC
3	**500 Pesos** 24.9.1975. Green, black and brown on multicolor underprint. Pres. A. Cabral at left, arms at center, soldier at right. Carving and two youths on back.	8.00	30.00	120.

#4 *Deleted.* See #8.

1978-84 Issue

#5-9 arms at lower r. on face. Wmk: A. Cabral. Replacement notes: Serial # prefix *Z*.

		VG	VF	UNC
5	**50 Pesos** 28.2.1983. Orange on blue and multicolor underprint. Artifact at left center, P. Nalsna at right. Local scene on back. Printer: BWC.	.50	2.50	9.00

		VG	VF	UNC
6	**100 Pesos** 28.2.1983. Red on multicolor underprint. Carving at left, D. Ramos at right. Building at left center on back. Without imprint.	.25	1.25	4.50

		VG	VF	UNC
7	**500 Pesos** 28.2.1983. Deep blue on multicolor underprint. Carving at left, F. Mendes at right. Slave trade scene on back. Without imprint.	.50	2.00	6.00

		VG	VF	UNC
8	**1000 Pesos** 24.9.1978. Green on brown and multicolor underprint. Weaver and loom at lower left center, Pres. A. Cabral at right. Allegory with title: *Apoteose ao Triunfo* on back. Printer: BWC.			
	a. Signature titles: *COMISSARIO PRINCIPAL, COMISSARIO DE ESTADO DAS FINANCAS* and *GOVERNADOR.*	7.50	20.00	85.00
	b. Signature titles: *PRIMEIRO MINISTRO, MINISTRO DE ECONOMIA E FINANCAS* and *GOVERNADOR.*	.75	3.00	7.00
	s. As a. Specimen.	—	—	185.

		VG	VF	UNC
9	**5000 Pesos** 12.9.1984. Brown and black on multicolor underprint. Map at left center, Pres. A. Cabral at right. Harvesting grain at center on back. Without imprint.	1.00	4.00	12.00

Note: Date on #9 is the 60th birthday of Cabral.

1990 Issue

#10-15 sign. titles: *MINISTRO-GOVERNADOR* and *VICE-GOVERNADOR*. Printer: TDLR. Replacement notes: Serial # prefixes *AZ; BZ; CZ; DZ; ZA* or *ZZ*.

#10-12 wmk: *BCG*.

		VG	VF	UNC
10	**50 Pesos** 1.3.1990. Pale red on multicolor underprint. Similar to #5 but reduced size. Without watermark area.	.05	.25	1.00

		VG	VF	UNC
11	**100 Pesos** 1.3.1990. Olive-gray on multicolor underprint. Similar to #6 but reduced size. Without watermark area.	.05	.20	.75

		VG	VF	UNC
12	**500 Pesos** 1.3.1990. Deep blue on multicolor underprint. Similar to #7 but reduced size. Without watermark area.	.15	.50	2.50

#13-15 wmk: Portr. A. Cabral.

		VG	VF	UNC
13	**1000 Pesos** 1990; 1993. Dark brown, brown-violet and orange on multicolor underprint. Similar to #8.			
	a. Signature titles: *MINISTRO-GOVERNADOR* and *VICE-GOVERNADOR.* 1.3.1990.	.10	.50	3.50
	b. Signature titles: *GOVERNADOR* and *VICE-GOVERNADOR.* 1.3.1993.	.10	.50	2.50

		VG	VF	UNC
14	**5000 Pesos** 1990; 1993. Purple, violet and brown on multicolor underprint. Similar to #9.			
	a. Signature titles: *MINISTRO-GOVERNADOR* and *VICE-GOVERNADOR.*	.20	1.00	6.00
	b. Signature titles: *GOVERNADOR* and *VICE-GOVERNADOR.* 1.3.1993.	.20	1.00	4.00

		VG	VF	UNC
15	**10,000 Pesos** 1990; 1993. Green, olive-brown and blue on multicolor underprint. Statue at lower left center, outline map at center, A. Cabral at right. Local people fishing with nets in river at center on back.			
	a. Sign titles: *MINISTRO-GOVERNADOR* and *VICE-GOVERNADOR.* 1.3.1990.	.30	2.00	12.50
	b. Signature titles: *GOVERNADOR* and *VICE-GOVERNADOR.* 1.3.1993.	.30	1.00	10.00

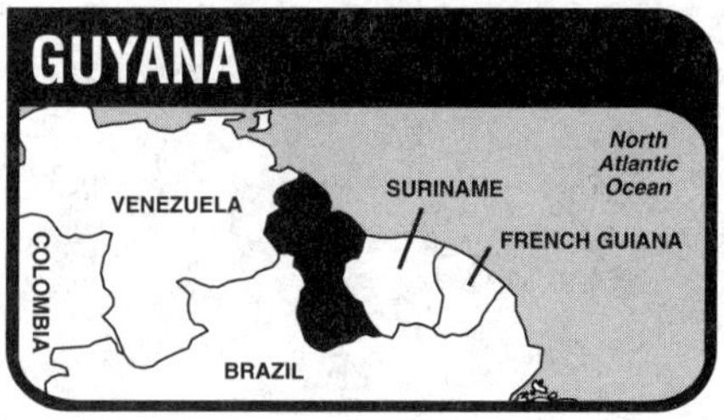

The Cooperative Republic of Guyana, (formerly British Guiana) an independent member of the British Commonwealth situated on the northeast coast of South America, has an area of 83,000 sq. mi. (214,969 sq. km.) and a population of 874,000. Capital: Georgetown. The economy is basically agrarian. Sugar, rice and bauxite are exported.

The original area of Guyana, which included present-day Surinam, French Guiana, and parts of Brazil and Venezuela, was sighted by Columbus in 1498. The first European settlement was made late in the 16th century by the Dutch. For the next 150 years, possession alternated between the Dutch and the British, with a short interval of French control. The British exercised de facto control after 1796, although the area, which included the Dutch colonies of Essequebo, Demerary and Berbice, wasn't ceded to them by the Dutch until 1814. From 1803 to 1831, Essequebo and Demerary were administered separately from Berbice. The three colonies were united in the British Crown Colony of British Guiana in 1831. British Guiana won internal self-government in 1952 and full independence, under the traditional name of Guyana, on May 26, 1966.

Notes of the British Caribbean Currency Board circulated from 1950-1965.

RULERS:

British to 1900

MONETARY SYSTEM:

1 Dollar = 4 Shillings 2 Pence, 1837-1965
1 Dollar = 100 Cents, 1966-

SIGNATURE VARIETIES

1	GOVERNOR / MINISTER OF FINANCE	2	GOVERNOR / MINISTER OF FINANCE
3	GOVERNOR / MINISTER OF FINANCE	4	GOVERNOR / MINISTER OF FINANCE
4A	GOVERNOR / MINISTER OF FINANCE	5	GOVERNOR / MINISTER OF FINANCE
6	GOVERNOR / VICE PRESIDENT ECONOMIC MINISTER OF FINANCE	7	GOVERNOR / MINISTER OF FINANCE
8	GOVERNOR / MINISTER OF FINANCE	9	GOVERNOR / MINISTER OF FINANCE
10	GOVERNOR / MINISTER OF FINANCE	11	GOVERNOR / MINISTER OF FINANCE
12	GOVERNOR / MINISTER OF FINANCE		

REPUBLIC

BANK OF GUYANA

1966 ND ISSUE

#21-29 wmk: Macaw's (parrot) head. Printer: TDLR.

#21-27 arms at ctr., Kaieteur Falls at r. Color shading variations.

21	1 Dollar	VG	VF	UNC
	ND (1966-92). Red on multicolor underprint. Black bush polder at left, rice harvesting at right on back.			
	a. Signature 1; 2.	.75	3.00	15.00
	b. Signature 3; 4.	1.25	6.00	30.00
	c. Signature 4A.	.05	.25	1.50
	d. Signature 5.	.20	1.00	4.00
	e. Signature 6 (1983).	.05	.25	1.50
	f. Serial # prefix *B/1* or higher. signature 7 (1989).	FV	FV	1.00
	g. Signature 8 (1992); 9. Back darker red.	FV	FV	.75
	s. As a. Specimen.	—	—	25.00

22	5 Dollars	VG	VF	UNC
	ND (1966-92). Dark green on multicolor underprint. Cane sugar harvesting at left, conveyor at right on back.			
	a. Signature 1; 2.	1.50	8.00	40.00
	b. Signature 3.	2.00	10.00	50.00
	c. Signature 5.	.20	1.00	5.00
	d. Signature 6 (1983).	.15	.50	3.00
	e. Serial # prefix *A/27* or higher. signature 7 (1989).	FV	FV	1.00
	f. Signature 8 (1992); 9.	FV	FV	.75
	s. As a. Specimen.	—	—	25.00

23	10 Dollars	VG	VF	UNC
	ND (1966-92). Dark brown on multicolor underprint. Bauxite mining at left, aluminum plant at right on back.			
	a. Signature 1; 2; 3.	2.00	10.00	50.00
	b. Signature 4; 5.	.50	2.50	12.50
	c. Signature 6 (1983).	.25	1.25	6.00
	d. Serial # prefix *A/16* or higher. signature 7 (1989).	FV	FV	1.00
	e. Signature 8 (1992).	FV	FV	1.50
	f. Signature 9.	FV	FV	1.00
	s. As a. Specimen.	—	—	25.00

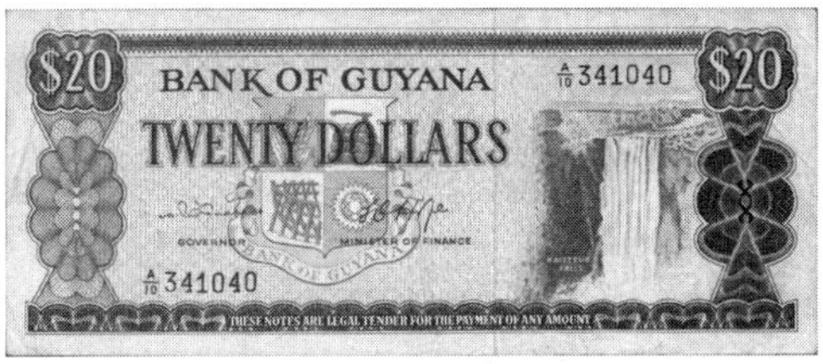

24	20 Dollars	VG	VF	UNC
	ND (1966-89). Brown and purple on multicolor underprint. Shipbuilding at left, ferry *Malali* at right on back.			
	a. Signature 1; 2; 4; 4A.	2.00	10.00	50.00
	b. Signature 5.	FV	3.00	15.00
	c. Signature 6 (1983).	FV	2.50	12.50
	d. Serial # prefix *A/42* or higher. signature 7 (1989).	FV	FV	1.50
	s. As a. Specimen.	—	—	25.00

#25 and 26 not used.

1989; 1992 ND ISSUE

#27-29 printer: TDLR.

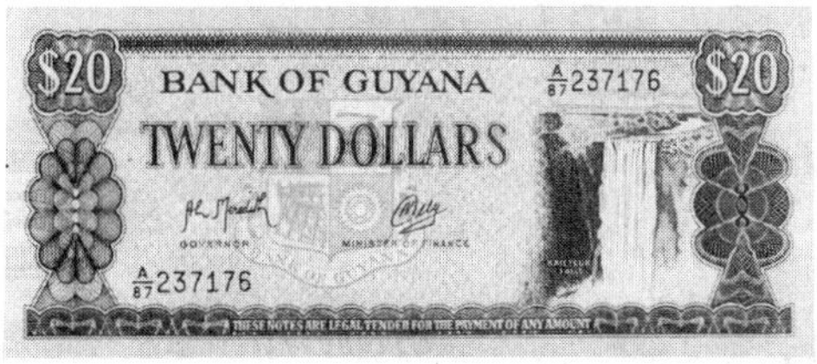

27	20 Dollars	VG	VF	UNC
	ND (1989). Brown and purple on multicolor underprint. Similar to #24, but design element in colored border at left and right. Signature 7; 9.	FV	FV	2.50

#28 and 29 map of Guyana at r., bank arms at ctr.

28	100 Dollars	VG	VF	UNC
	ND (1989). Blue on multicolor underprint. Cathedral at center on back. Signature 7; 8.	FV	FV	6.00

29	500 Dollars	VG	VF	UNC
	ND (ca. 1992). Lilac-brown and purple on multicolor underprint. Public buildings in Georgetown on back.			
	a. Signature 8.	FV	FV	35.00
	b. Signature 9.	FV	FV	10.00
	c. Signature 10.	FV	FV	10.00

1996; 1999 ND ISSUE

#30-33 map of Guyana at r., bank arms at ctr. Ascending size serial # at upper r. Wmk: Macaw's (parrot) head.

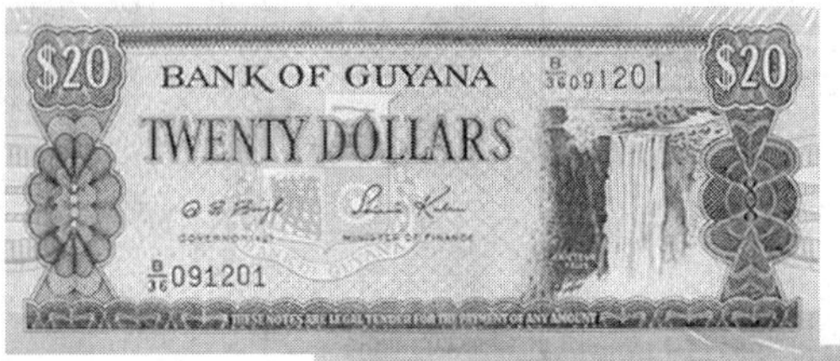

		VG	VF	UNC
30	**20 Dollars** ND (1996). Brown and purple on multicolor underprint. Like #27. Signature 10; 11; 12.	FV	FV	1.00

		VG	VF	UNC
31	**100 Dollars** ND (1999). Like #28. Signature 10; 11; 12.	FV	FV	4.00

		VG	VF	UNC
32	**500 Dollars** ND (1996). Lilac-brown and purple on multicolor underprint. Silver OVD map at right. Segmented foil over security thread. Like #29. Signature 10; 11.	FV	FV	8.50

		VG	VF	UNC
33	**1000 Dollars** ND (1996). Dark green, deep red and brown on multicolor underprint. Gold OVD map at right. Segmented foil over security thread. Bank building at center on back. Signature 10.	FV	FV	15.00

2000 ND ISSUE

		VG	VF	UNC
34	**500 Dollars** ND (2002). Lilac-brown and purple on multicolor underprint. OVD in watermark area at right. Similar to #32.	FV	FV	8.50

		VG	VF	UNC
35	**1000 Dollars** ND (2000). Similar to #33 but with gold OVD shield at right. Various small design and color adjustments also. Signature 11, 12.	FV	FV	15.00

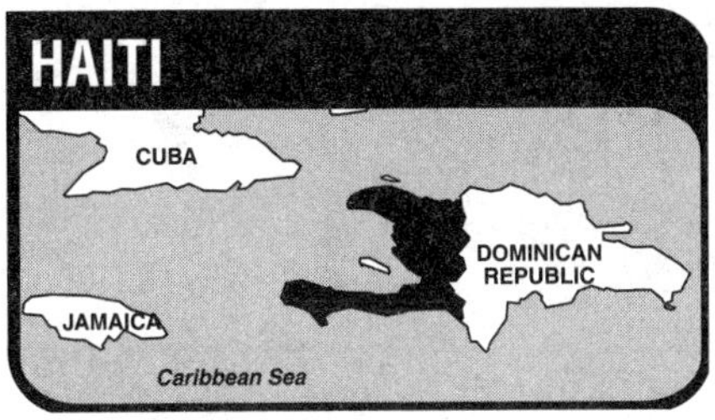

The Republic of Haiti, occupying the western one third of the island of Hispañola in the Caribbean Sea between Puerto Rico and Cuba, has an area of 10,714 sq. mi. (27,750 sq. km.) and a population of 7.82 million. Capital: Port-au-Prince. The economy is based on agriculture, light manufacturing and tourism which is becoming increasingly important. Coffee, bauxite, sugar, essential oils and handicrafts are exported.

Columbus discovered Hispañola in 1492. Spain colonized the island, making Santo Domingo the for exploration of the Western Hemisphere. Later French buccaneers settled the western third of Hispañola which was ceded to France by Spain in 1697. Slaves brought over from Africa to work the coffee and sugar cane plantations made it one of the richest colonies of the French Empire. The Republic of Haiti was established in 1804 after the slave revolts of the 1790's.

As a republic from 1915-1934 it was occupied by the U.S. Francois Duvalier was president 1957-1981, and his son 1981-1986, when a quick succession of governments continued with U.N. and U.S. intervention through the 1990's.

MONETARY SYSTEM:

1 Gourde = 100 Centimes
1 Piastre = 300 Gourdes, 1873
5 Gourdes = 1 U.S. Dollar, 1919-89

REPUBLIC

BANQUE NATIONALE DE LA RÉPUBLIQUE D'HAITI

CONVENTION DU 12 AVRIL 1919
SIXTH ISSUE (CA.1951-64)

#178-184 arms at ctr. on back. First sign. title: *Le President*. Printer: ABNC.

	VG	VF	UNC
178 1 Gourde			
L.1919. dark brown on light blue and multicolor underprint. Closeup view of Citadel Rampart at center Prefix letters AS-BM. 5 signature varieties.			
a. Issued note.	.75	2.00	17.50
s. Specimen.	—	—	35.00

	VG	VF	UNC
179 2 Gourdes			
L.1919. Blue and multicolor. Light green in underprint. Citadel rampart at center Prefix letters Y-AF. 6 signature varieties.			
a. Issued note.	1.00	4.00	25.00
s. Specimen.	—	—	60.00
180 5 Gourdes			
L.1919. Orange and multicolor. Green in underprint. Woman harvesting coffee at left. Prefix letters G-M. 3 signature varieties.			
a. Issued note.	1.25	6.00	35.00
s. Specimen, punch hole cancelled.	—	—	50.00

	VG	VF	UNC
181 10 Gourdes			
L.1919. Green on multicolor underprint. Coffee plant at center Prefix letters B-D. 2 signature varieties.			
a. Issued note.	3.00	12.50	55.00
s. Specimen, punch hole cancelled.	—	—	70.00

#182 not assigned.

	VG	VF	UNC
183 50 Gourdes			
L.1919. Olive-green on multicolor underprint. Cotton bolls at center Specimen.	—	—	225.

	VG	VF	UNC
184 100 Gourdes			
L.1919. Purple on multicolor underprint. Field workers at left. Prefix letter A.			
a. Issued note.	30.00	125.	350.
s. Specimen, punched hole cancelled.	—	—	175.

CONVENTION DU 12 AVRIL 1919
SEVENTH ISSUE (CA.1964)

#185-189 like #178-180 but new guilloche patterns, w/o green in unpt. Arms at ctr. on back. Printer: ABNC.

	VG	VF	UNC
185 1 Gourde			
L.1919. dark brown on light blue and multicolor underprint. Citadel rampart at center Like #178. Prefix letters BK-BT.			
a. Issued note.	.50	1.50	7.50
s. Specimen.	—	—	25.00
186 2 Gourdes			
L.1919. Blue on light blue and multicolor underprint. Citadel rampart at center Like #179. Prefix letters AE-AJ.			
a. Issued note.	.50	1.50	7.50
s. Specimen.	—	—	25.00

		VG	VF	UNC
187	**5 Gourdes**			
	L.1919. Orange on light blue and multicolor underprint. Woman harvesting coffee beans at left. Like #180. Prefix letter N.			
	a. Issued note.	.50	1.00	7.00
	s. Specimen.	—	—	25.00

Note: It is reported that the entire shipment of #187 was stolen and never officially released.

188	**50 Gourdes**			
	L.1919. Olive-green on blue and magenta underprint. Like #183. Cotton bolls at center (Not issued.) Archive example.	—	—	—
189	**100 Gourdes**			
	L.1919. Purple on multicolor underprint. Like #184. Field workers at left. (Not issued.) Archive example.	—	—	—

Convention du 12 Avril 1919
Eighth Issue (ca.1967)

#190-195 arms at ctr. on back. Printer: TDLR.
#190-193, 195 second sign. title: *LE DIRECTEUR*.

		VG	VF	UNC
190	**1 Gourde**			
	L.1919. Brown on multicolor underprint. Similar to #185. Prefix letters DA-DL.			
	a. Issued note.	.25	1.00	7.50
	s. Specimen.	—	—	27.50

		VG	VF	UNC
191	**2 Gourdes**			
	L.1919. Grayish blue on multicolor underprint. Similar to #186. Prefix letters DA-DF.			
	a. Issued note.	.50	1.50	10.00
	s. Specimen.	—	—	27.50

		VG	VF	UNC
192	**5 Gourdes**			
	L.1919. Orange on light blue and multicolor underprint. Similar to #187. Prefix letters DA-DK.			
	a. Issued note.	1.00	4.00	12.50
	s. Specimen.	—	—	27.50

		VG	VF	UNC
193	**10 Gourdes**			
	L.1919. Green on multicolor underprint. Coffee plant at center. Similar to #181. Prefix letters DA.			
	a. Issued note.	3.00	8.00	30.00
	s. Specimen.	—	—	35.00

		VG	VF	UNC
194	**50 Gourdes**			
	L.1919. Olive-green on multicolor underprint. Cotton bolls at center. Similar to #188. Prefix letters DA. Second signature title: UN DIRECTEUR.			
	a. Issued note.	10.00	17.50	80.00
	s. Specimen.	—	—	170.

		VG	VF	UNC
195	**100 Gourdes**			
	L.1919. Purple on multicolor underprint. Field workers at left. Similar to #189. Prefix letters DA.			
	a. Issued note.	20.00	35.00	150.
	s. Specimen.	—	—	—

Convention du 12 Avril 1919
Ninth Issue

#196-198 Pres. Dr. François Duvalier at ctr. or l. Arms at ctr. on back. Printer: TDLR.

		VG	VF	UNC
196	**1 Gourde**			
	L.1919. Dark brown on multicolor underprint. Prefix letters DK-DT.			
	a. Issued note.	.25	.75	3.50
	s. Specimen.	—	—	20.00

		VG	VF	UNC
197	**2 Gourdes**			
	L.1919. Grayish blue on multicolor underprint. Like #196. Prefix letters DG-DK.			
	a. Issued note.	.50	1.25	4.50
	s. Specimen.	—	—	25.00

198	5 Gourdes	VG	VF	UNC
	L.1919. Orange on multicolor underprint. Portrait Pres. Dr. F. Duvalier at left. Prefix letters DG-DK.			
	a. Issued note.	1.00	2.50	7.50
	s. Specimen.	—	—	25.00

CONVENTION DU 12 AVRIL 1919

TENTH ISSUE

#200-203 arms at ctr. on back. Printer: ABNC.

200	1 Gourde	VG	VF	UNC
	L.1919. Dark brown on multicolor underprint. Portrait Pres. Dr. F. Duvalier at center. Prefix letters A-Z; AA-CR. Three signature varieties.			
	a. Issued note.	.25	.75	3.00
	s. Specimen.	—	—	20.00

#201-207 w/4 lines of text on back (like previous issues).

201	2 Gourdes	VG	VF	UNC
	L.1919. Blue on multicolor underprint. Like #200. First issued without prefix, then letters A-Q.	.50	1.25	3.50

202	5 Gourdes	VG	VF	UNC
	L.1919. Orange on multicolor underprint. Portrait Pres. Dr. F. Duvalier at left. First issued without prefix, then letters A-Z; AA-AP. Three signature varieties.			
	a. Issued note.	1.00	2.00	6.50
	s. Specimen.	—	—	25.00
203	10 Gourdes			
	L.1919. Dark green on multicolor underprint. Portrait Pres. Dr. F. Duvalier at center. First issued without prefix, then letter A.			
	a. Issued note.	2.50	5.00	12.50
	s. Specimen.	—	—	30.00

204	50 Gourdes	VG	VF	UNC
	L.1919. Dark gray on multicolor underprint. Portrait Pres. Lysius Félicité Salomon Jeune at center. First issued without prefix, then letters A-C. Two signature varieties.			
	a. Issued note.	10.00	17.50	30.00
	s. Specimen.	—	—	27.50

205	100 Gourdes	VG	VF	UNC
	L.1919. Purple on multicolor underprint. Portrait Henri Christophe (Pres., later King) at left. Without prefix letter. Two signature varieties.	20.00	40.00	75.00

206	250 Gourdes	VG	VF	UNC
	L.1919. Dark yellow-green on multicolor underprint. Jean-Jacques Dessalines at right. Without prefix letter.			
	a. Issued note.	55.00	110.	225.
	s. Specimen.	—	—	225.

207	500 Gourdes	VG	VF	UNC
	L.1919. Red on multicolor underprint. Similar to #203. Without prefix letter.			
	a. Issued note.	80.00	165.	350.
	s. Specimen.	—	—	350.

#208 and 209 not assigned.

ELEVENTH ISSUE (CA.1973)

Lois des 21 Mai 1935 et 15 Mai 1953 et au Décret du 22 Novembre 1973 (issued 1979)
#210-214 arms at ctr. on back. Printer: ABNC.

210	1 Gourde	VG	VF	UNC
	L.1973, etc. Dark brown on multicolor underprint. Like #200. Prefix letters A-Z; AA-AC.	.30	.60	3.00

#211-214 w/3 lines of text on back.

211	2 Gourdes	VG	VF	UNC
	L.1973, etc. Blue on multicolor underprint. Like #201. Prefix letters A-J.	.60	1.25	4.50

212 5 Gourdes — VG | VF | UNC
L.1973, etc. Orange on multicolor underprint. Like #202. Prefix letters A-AA. — 1.00 | 2.00 | 7.50

213 50 Gourdes — VG | VF | UNC
L.1973, etc. Dark gray on multicolor underprint. Like #204. Prefix letter A. — 10.00 | 17.50 | 35.00

214 100 Gourdes
L.1973, etc. Purple on multicolor underprint. Like #205. Without prefix letter. Two serial # varieties. — 20.00 | 35.00 | 70.00

#215-217 not assigned.

Twelfth Issue

Lois des 21 Mai 1935 et 15 Mai 1953 et au Décret du 22 Novembre 1973

218 25 Gourdes — VG | VF | UNC
L.1973, etc. Dark blue and brown-violet on multicolor underprint. Pres. Jean-Claude Duvalier at left, antenna at right. Prefix letters DA-DD. National Palace on back. Printer: TDLR.
a. Issued note. — 3.00 | 7.50 | 17.50
s. Specimen. — — | — | 30.00

#219-229 not assigned.

> **NOTICE**
> Readers with unlisted dates, signature varieties, etc. are invited to submit photocopies of their notes to: Standard Catalog of World Paper Money, 700 East State St. Iola, WI 54990-0001, E-Mail: george.cuhaj@fwpubs.com.

Banque de la République d'Haiti

Loi du 17 Aout 1979 (1980-82)

#230-232, 235-238 sign. titles: *LE GOUVERNEUR, LE GOUVERNEUR ADJOINT* and *LE DIRECTEUR.* Arms at ctr. on back. Printer: ABNC.

230 1 Gourde — VG | VF | UNC
L.1979. Dark brown on multicolor underprint. Like #210. With or without prefix letter. Printed on paper with planchettes. Small size numerals in serial #. — FV | .50 | 1.75

230A 1 Gourde
L.1979. Like #230. Printed on Tyvek. Larger size numerals in serial #.
a. Issued note. — FV | .50 | 3.00
s. Specimen. — — | — | 25.00

231 2 Gourdes — VG | VF | UNC
L.1979. Blue on multicolor underprint. Like #230. Without or with prefix letter. Printed on paper with planchettes. Smaller size numerals in serial #. — FV | .50 | 3.00

231A 2 Gourdes
L.1979. Like #231. Printed on Tyvek. Larger size numerals in serial #. — FV | 1.00 | 5.00

232 5 Gourdes
L.1979. Orange on multicolor underprint. Like #212. Prefix letters A-T, AA-. — FV | 1.25 | 7.50

#233 and 234 held in reserve.

235 50 Gourdes
L.1979. Dark brown on green and multicolor underprint. Like #213. Printed on dull white paper with planchettes. Without prefix letter or with A, B, G.
a. Issued note. — FV | 12.50 | 30.00
s. Specimen. — — | — | 35.00

235A 50 Gourdes
L.1979. Like #235. Printed on Tyvek.
a. Prefix letter C. watermark: American bald eagle symbol of ABNC. — FV | 12.50 | 35.00
b. Without watermark. Prefix letter D, F. — FV | 12.50 | 32.50
s. Specimen. — — | — | 40.00

236 100 Gourdes — VG | VF | UNC
L.1979. Purple on multicolor underprint. Like #205. Printed on paper with planchettes. Prefix letters A; B.
a. Issued note. — FV | 20.00 | 55.00
s. Specimen. — — | — | 35.00

236A 100 Gourdes
L.1979. Like #236. Printed on Tyvek. Prefix letter C, D, E. — FV | 20.00 | 55.00

237 250 Gourdes
L.1979. Dark yellow-green on multicolor underprint. Similar to #206. Printed on Tyvek.
a. Issued note. — FV | 45.00 | 125.
s. Specimen. — — | — | 100.

238 500 Gourdes
L.1979. Red on multicolor underprint. Similar to #207. Printed on Tyvek.

	VG	VF	UNC
a. Issued note.	FV	90.00	250.
s. Specimen.	—	—	300.

1984; 1985 ND Issue

#239-240 arms at ctr. on back. Printer: TDLR. Replacement notes: Serial # prefix *ZZ*.

239 1 Gourde
L.1979 (1984). Dark brown on multicolor underprint. Like #196. Double prefix letters. Signature titles like #230.

VG	VF	UNC
FV	.25	1.50

240 2 Gourdes
L.1979 (1985). Grayish blue on multicolor underprint. Similar to #191.

VG	VF	UNC
FV	.50	2.50

#241-243 sign. title at r: *LE DIRECTEUR GENERAL*. Arms at ctr. on back.

241 5 Gourdes
L.1979 (1985). Orange on multicolor underprint. Portrait Pres. Jean-Claude Duvalier at left and as watermark. Printer: G&D.

	VG	VF	UNC
a. Issued note.	FV	1.00	4.00
s. Specimen.	—	—	35.00

242 10 Gourdes
L.1979 (1984). Green on multicolor underprint. Similar to #203, but portrait Jean-Claude Duvalier at center. Printer: ABNC.

	VG	VF	UNC
a. Issued note.	FV	2.00	7.50
s. Specimen.	—	—	27.50

243 25 Gourdes
L.1979 (1985). Blue on pink and multicolor underprint. Like #241. Printer: G&D.

	VG	VF	UNC
a. Issued note.	FV	4.50	15.00
s. Specimen.	—	—	30.00

#244 *Deleted*. See #240.

1986-88 Issue

#245-252 sign. title at r: *LE DIRECTEUR GENERAL*. Arms at ctr. on back.

245 1 Gourde
1987. Dark brown and brown-black on multicolor underprint. Toussaint L'Ouverture with long hair at center. Printer: G&D.

	VG	VF	UNC
a. Issued note.	FV	FV	1.00
s. Specimen.	—	—	22.50

245A 2 Gourdes
L.1979. Grayish blue on multicolor underprint. Like #240.

VG	VF	UNC
FV	.25	2.00

246 5 Gourdes
1987. Orange and brown on multicolor underprint. Statue of Combat de Vertiéres at upper center. Watermark: Palm tree. Printer: G&D.

	VG	VF	UNC
a. Issued note.	FV	FV	4.00
s. Specimen.	—	—	25.00

247 **10 Gourdes** | VG | VF | UNC
1988. Green, red and blue on multicolor underprint. Catherine Flon Arcahaie seated sewing the first flag of the Republic at right. Back green. Printer: ABNC.

	VG	VF	UNC
a. Issued note.	FV	FV	6.00
s. Specimen.	—	—	27.50

248 **25 Gourdes** | VG | VF | UNC
1988. Dark blue and purple on multicolor underprint. Palace of Justice at center. Watermark: Palm tree. Printer: G&D.

	VG	VF	UNC
a. Issued note.	FV	FV	12.50
s. Specimen.	—	—	28.50

249 **50 Gourdes** | VG | VF | UNC
1986. Dark brown on green and multicolor underprint. Design and signature titles like #235. Printer: ABNC.

	VG	VF	UNC
a. Issued note.	FV	FV	30.00
s. Specimen.	—	—	25.00

250 **100 Gourdes**
1986. Purple on multicolor underprint. Similar to #236 (but more colorful). Printer: TDLR.

	VG	VF	UNC
a. Issued note.	FV	FV	45.00
s. Specimen.	—	—	35.00

251 **250 Gourdes**
1988. Tan on multicolor underprint. Similar to #237. Printer: ABNC.

	VG	VF	UNC
a. Issued note.	FV	FV	80.00
s. Specimen.	—	—	70.00

252 **500 Gourdes**
1988. Red on multicolor underprint. Pres. Alexandre Pétion at right. Printer: ABNC.

	VG	VF	UNC
a. Issued note.	FV	FV	150.
s. Specimen.	—	—	85.00

1989-91 ISSUE

#253-255 arms at ctr. on back. Printer: USBC.

253 **1 Gourde** | VG | VF | UNC
1989. Dark brown and brown-black on multicolor underprint. Toussaint L'Ouverture with short hair at center. Legal clause includes reference to the United States.

	VG	VF	UNC
a. Issued note.	FV	FV	1.00
s. Specimen.	—	—	22.50

254 **2 Gourdes** | VG | VF | UNC
1990. Blue-black on multicolor underprint. Citadel rampart at center. Legal clause without reference to the United States.

	VG	VF	UNC
a. Issued note.	FV	.50	3.00
s. Specimen.	—	—	25.00

255 **5 Gourdes** | VG | VF | UNC
1989. Orange and brown on multicolor underprint. Like #246. Legal clause includes reference to the United States.

	VG	VF	UNC
a. Issued note.	FV	FV	2.00
s. Specimen.	—	—	25.00

#256-258 legal clause on face and back w/o reference to the United States. Arms at ctr. on back. Wmk: Palm tree. Printer: G&D.

256 **10 Gourdes** | VG | VF | UNC
1991; 1998; 1999. Dark green, red and blue on multicolor underprint. Similar to #247, but with C. F. Arcahaie at center.

	VG	VF	UNC
a. Issued note.	FV	FV	4.00
s. Specimen.	—	—	25.00

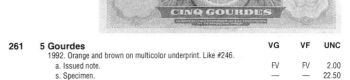

257 50 Gourdes
1991; 1999. Dark olive-green on multicolor underprint. Portrait Pres. L. F. Salomon Jeune at center.

	VG	VF	UNC
a. Issued note.	FV	FV	10.00
s. Specimen.	—	—	50.00

258 100 Gourdes
1991. Purple on multicolor underprint. Portrait H. Christophe at left.

	VG	VF	UNC
a. Issued note.	FV	FV	20.00
s. Specimen.	—	—	25.00

1992-94 ISSUE

#259-264 w/o laws. Shortened clause on face and back: *CE BILLET EST EMIS CONFORMEMENT...* Arms at ctr. on back.
#259-261 printer: TDLR. Replacement notes: Serial # prefix *ZZ*.

259 1 Gourde
1992; 1993. Dark brown and brown-black on multicolor underprint. Like #245.

	VG	VF	UNC
a. Issued note.	FV	FV	.75
s. Specimen.	FV	FV	25.00

260 2 Gourdes
1992. Blue-black on multicolor underprint. Like #254.

	VG	VF	UNC
a. Issued note.	FV	FV	1.25
s. Specimen.	—	—	25.00

261 5 Gourdes
1992. Orange and brown on multicolor underprint. Like #246.

	VG	VF	UNC
a. Issued note.	FV	FV	2.00
s. Specimen.	—	—	22.50

262 25 Gourdes
1993. Dark blue and purple on multicolor underprint. Like #248. Printer: G&D.

	VG	VF	UNC
a. Issued note.	FV	FV	4.50
s. Specimen.	—	—	25.00

263 250 Gourdes
1994. Olive-brown and dark brown on multicolor underprint. Portrait J. J. Dessalines at left. Printer: G&D.

	VG	VF	UNC
a. Issued note.	FV	FV	35.00
s. Specimen.	—	—	100.

264 500 Gourdes
1993. Red-violet on multicolor underprint. Portrait Pres. A. Pétion at left. Printer: G&D.

	VG	VF	UNC
a. Issued note.	FV	FV	60.00
s. Specimen.	—	—	200.

NOTICE

Readers with unlisted dates, signature varieties, etc. are invited to submit photocopies of their notes to: Standard Catalog of World Paper Money, 700 East State St. Iola, WI 54990-0001, E-Mail: george.cuhaj@fwpubs.com.

2000 Issue

#265-270 more colorful, especially on borders. Ascending size serial #. Letters BRH at r. in various color combinations on face.

#265, 267, 269 and 270 printer: (T)DLR. #266 and 268 printer: G&D.

		VG	VF	UNC
265	**10 Gourdes** 2000; 2004. Dark green and multicolor. Similar to #256.	FV	FV	2.50

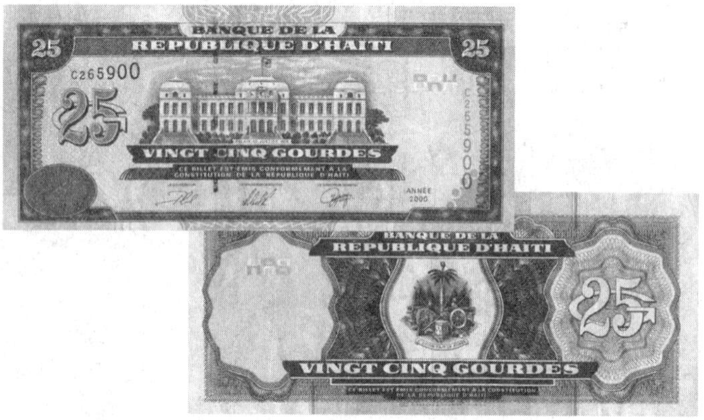

		VG	VF	UNC
266	**25 Gourdes** 2000; 2004. Dark blue and black on multicolor underprint. Similar to #262.	FV	FV	3.00

		VG	VF	UNC
267	**50 Gourdes** 2000; 2003. Dark olive-green and black on multicolor underprint. Similar to #257.	FV	FV	8.00
268	**100 Gourdes** 2000. Purple on multicolor underprint. Similar to #258.	FV	FV	18.00

		VG	VF	UNC
269	**250 Gourdes** 2000; 2003; 2005. Olive-brown and dark brown on multicolor underprint. Similar to #263.	FV	FV	30.00

		VG	VF	UNC
270	**500 Gourdes** 2000; 2003; 2005. Red and violet on multicolor underprint. Similar to #264.	FV	FV	45.00

2001 Commemorative Issue

Bicentennial of the Constitution, 1801-2001

		VG	VF	UNC
271	**20 Gourdes** 2001. Brown, orange and yellow. Bust at left. Foil impressions flank center wreath. Open Constitution book on back.	FV	FV	4.00

2004 Commemorative Issue

#272-277 Bicentennial of Haiti. Signature titles in France French and Haitian Creole.

		VG	VF	UNC
272	**10 Gourdes** 2004. Blue. Sanite Belair at left. Fort Cap-Rouge (Jacmel) on back.			
	a. Issued note.	FV	FV	2.50
	s. Specimen.	—	—	—

273 20 Gourdes — VG | VF | UNC

2004. Purple on tan and green underprint. Nicolas Gieffrard at left. Fortress des Plantons (Dussio) on back.

	VG	VF	UNC
a. Issued note.	FV	FV	3.00
s. Specimen.	—	—	—

274 50 Gourdes

2004. Purple. Francois Cappiox at left. Fort Jalousiere (Marmelade) on back.

	VG	VF	UNC
a. Issued note.	FV	FV	8.00
s. Specimen.	—	—	—

275 100 Gourdes

2004. Blue and gray. Henry Christophé at left. Citadelle Henry (Milot) on back.

	VG	VF	UNC
a. Issued note.	FV	FV	18.00
s. Specimen.	—	—	—

276 250 Gourdes

2004. Blue on tan and brown underprint. Jean-Jacques Dessalines at left. Fort Decidé (Marchand) on back.

	VG	VF	UNC
a. Issued note.	FV	FV	30.00
s. Specimen.		—	

277 500 Gourdes

2004. Purple on tan underprint. Alexandre Petion at left. Fort Jacques (Fermathe) on back.

	VG	VF	UNC
a. Issued note.	FV	FV	45.00
s. Specimen.		—	

2000 Dated 2004 Issue

278 1000 Gourdes

1999 (2006). Purple.

	VG	VF	UNC
a. Issued note.	—	—	—
s. Specimen.	—	—	—

Certificat de Liberation Economique

Loi du 17 Septembre 1962

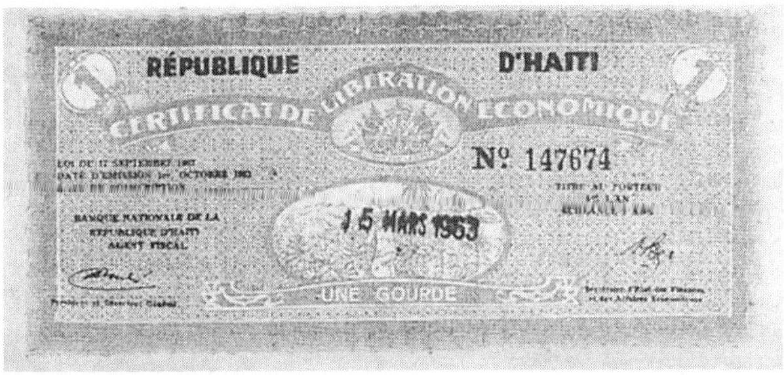

501 1 Gourde

	VG	VF	UNC
1.10.1962. Green with black text.	5.00	25.00	65.00

NOTICE

Readers with unlisted dates, signature varieties, etc. are invited to submit photocopies of their notes to: Standard Catalog of World Paper Money, 700 East State St. Iola, WI 54990-0001, E-Mail: george.cuhaj@fwpubs.com.

		VG	VF	UNC
502	**5 Gourdes**			
	1.10.1962. Red with black text.			
	a. Series A.	5.00	25.00	65.00
	b. Series B.	5.00	25.00	65.00
	c. Series C.	5.00	25.00	65.00
503	**25 Gourdes**			
	1.10.1962. Yellow-orange with black text.	10.00	30.00	80.00

		VG	VF	UNC
504	**100 Gourdes**			
	1.10.1962. Blue with black text.	30.00	100.	250.

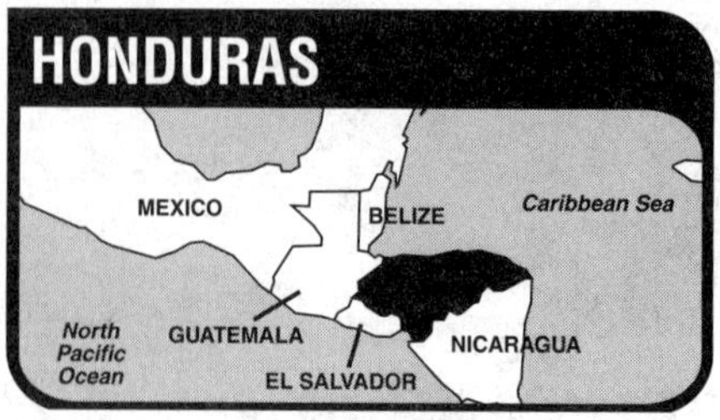

The Republic of Honduras, situated in Central America between El Salvador, Nicaragua and Guatemala, has an area of 43,277 sq. mi. (112,088 sq. km.) and a population of 6.48 million. Capital: Tegucigalpa. Tourism, agriculture, mining (gold and silver), and logging are the chief industries. Bananas, timber and coffee are exported.

Honduras, a site of the ancient Mayan Empire, was claimed for Spain by Columbus in 1502, during his last voyage to the Americas. The first settlement was made by Cristobal de Olid under orders of Hernan Cortes, then in Mexico. The area, regarded as one of the most promising sources of gold and silver in the New World, was a part of the Captaincy General of Guatemala throughout the colonial period. After declaring its independence from Spain in 1821, Honduras fell briefly to the Mexican Empire of Agustin de Iturbide, and then joined the Central American Federation (1823-39). Upon dissolution of the federation, Honduras became an independent republic.

MONETARY SYSTEM:

I Peso = 100 Centavos, 1871-1926
1 Lempira = 100 Centavos, 1926-

REVOLUTION

Banco Territorial de Honduras#S161-S161A

REPUBLIC

Billete Aduanero (Customs Notes)#S162-S171

Note: Certain listings encompassing issues circulated by provincial, state and commercial banking authorities are contained in Volume 1.

REPÚBLICA DE HONDURAS

BANCO CENTRAL DE HONDURAS

1950-51 ISSUE

		VG	VF	UNC
49	**100 Lempiras**			
	1951-73. Yellow on multicolor underprint. Valle at left, arms at right. Village and bridge on back.			
	a. Without security thread, lilac-pink underprint. Printer: W&S. 16.3.1951; 8.3.1957.	70.00	300.	1000.
	b. Without security thread, With fibers at right center, light green and light orange underprint. Printer: W&S. 5.2.1964; 5.11.1965; 22.3.1968; 10.12.1969.	100.	300.	1250.
	c. With security thread, yellow underprint. 13.10.1972. Reported not confirmed.	—	—	—
	d. As c. but without security thread. 13.10.1972; 23.3.1973.	45.00	175.	375.
	s. Specimen, punched hole cancelled.	—	—	250.

#50 not assigned.

1953-56 ISSUE

		VG	VF	UNC
51	**5 Lempiras**			
	1953-68. Gray on multicolor underprint. Morazán at left, arms at right. Serial # at upper left and upper right. Battle of Trinidad on back. Printer: ABNC.			
	a. Date horizontal. 17.3.1953; 19.3.1954; 7.5.1954.	6.00	35.00	175.
	b. As a. 22.11.1957-7.1.1966.	4.00	25.00	125.
	c. Date vertical. 15.4.1966; 29.9.1967; 22.3.1968.	3.50	17.50	70.00

52	10 Lempiras	VG	VF	UNC
	1954-69. Brown on multicolor underprint. Cabañas at left, arms at right. Old bank on back. Date and signature style varieties. Printer: TDLR.			
	a. R. signature title: *MINISTRO DE HACIENDA*... 19.11.1954.	15.00	75.00	300.
	b. R. signature title: *MINISTRO DE ECONOMIA*... 19.2.1960-10.1.1969.	10.00	35.00	250.

53	20 Lempiras	VG	VF	UNC
	1954-72. Green. D. de Herrera at left, arms at right. Waterfalls on back. Printer: TDLR.			
	a. 4.6.1954; 26.11.1954; 5.4.1957; 6.3.1959; 8.5.1959.	22.50	75.00	325.
	b. 19.2.1960; 27.4.1962; 19.4.1963; 6.3.1964.	17.50	50.00	275.
	c. 7.1.1966-18.2.1972.	15.00	45.00	250.

1961 Issue

54A	1 Lempira	VG	VF	UNC
	10.2.1961; 30.7.1965. Red on multicolor underprint. Lempira at left, modified design of #45 with black serial #. Dios del Maiz/Idolo Maya and Mayan artifacts on back. Two signature varieties. Printer: TDLR.			
	a. Issued note.	.75	4.00	25.00
	s. Specimen. Punched hole cancelled. 10.2.1961.	—	—	50.00

1968; 1970 Issue

55	1 Lempira	VG	VF	UNC
	1968; 1972. Red-orange on green and pink underprint. Lempira at left, design different from #45 and 54A. *Ruinas de Copan Juego de Pelota* on back. Printer: TDLR.			
	a. R. signature title: *MINISTRO DE ECONOMIA*... 25.10.1968.	.50	3.00	17.50
	b. R. signature title: *MINISTRO DE HACIENDA*... 21.1.1972.	.25	1.00	12.50

56	5 Lempiras	VG	VF	UNC
	1968-74. Black on multicolor underprint. Morazan at left, arms at right. Similar to #51. Serial # at lower left and upper right. Battle scene of Trinidad at center on back. Printer: ABNC.			
	a. Date horizontal. 29.11.1968; 11.4.1969; 10.3.1970.	3.00	30.00	65.00
	b. Date vertical. 20.11.1970-24.8.1974.	2.00	10.00	60.00

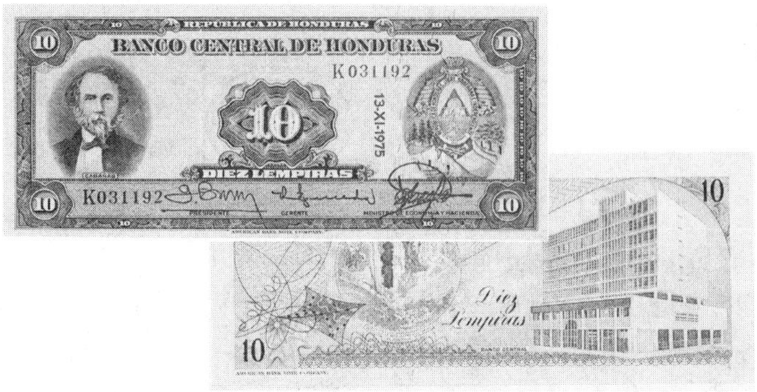

57	10 Lempiras	VG	VF	UNC
	27.8.1970-13.11.1975. Brown on multicolor underprint. Cabañas at left, arms at right. Ruins and new bank on back. Printer: ABNC.	3.50	15.00	65.00

1973; 1974 Issue

58	1 Lempira	VG	VF	UNC
	11.3.1974. Red on green and lilac underprint. Lempira without feather at left, arms at right. Different view of Ruinas de Copan on back. Printer: TDLR.	.25	1.00	8.00

59	5 Lempiras	VG	VF	UNC
	1974-78. Black on multicolor underprint. Morazán at left, arms at right. Battle of Trinidad at left on back. Printer: ABNC.			
	a. Date vertical. 24.10.1974.	2.50	8.00	40.00
	b. Date horizontal. 12.12.1975; 26.2.1976; 16.9.1976; 9.12.1976; 13.1.1977; 3.6.1977; 25.11.1977; 13.2.1978.	2.00	4.00	25.00

60	20 Lempiras	VG	VF	UNC
	2.3.1973; 13.8.1973; 30.11.1973; 1.3.1974; 22.4.1974; 5.6.1975; 15.1.1976; 18.3.1976; 13.1.1977; 3.6.1977. Green on multicolor underprint. D. de Herrera at left, arms at right. Presidential residence on back. Date placement varieties. Printer: (T)DLR.	12.50	40.00	150.

1976 Commemorative Issue

#61, Centennial of the Marco Aurelio Soto Government

61	2 Lempiras	VG	VF	UNC
	23.9.1976. Purple on multicolor underprint. Arms at left, M. A. Soto at right. Island and Port of Amapala on back. Printer: TDLR.	FV	.75	5.00

1975-78 Regular Issue

#62-63 printer: TDLR.

62	1 Lempira	VG	VF	UNC
	30.6.1978. Red. Like #58 but Indian symbols added below bank name on back.	FV	.75	5.00

63	5 Lempiras	VG	VF	UNC
	1978-94. Black, dark blue, and deep olive-green on multicolor underprint. Arms at left, Morazán at right. Battle of Trinidad scene (Nov. 11, 1827) on back.			
	a. 4.10.1978; 8.5.1980.	FV	2.00	10.00
	b. 8.12.1985; 30.3.1989.	FV	1.50	7.50
	c. Red serial # at upper left. in ascending size. 14.1.1993; 25.2.1993.	FV	FV	4.00
	d. Brown serial # as c. 12.5.1994.	FV	FV	4.00
	s. As d. Specimen. *MUESTRA SIN VALOR.*	—	—	—

#64-66 printer: ABNC.

64	10 Lempiras	VG	VF	UNC
	1976-89. Brown on multicolor underprint. Cabañas at left. City University on back.			
	a. 18.3.1976-10.5.1979.	FV	5.00	25.00
	b. 23.6.1982-5.10.1989.	FV	3.00	17.50
65	**20 Lempiras**			
	1978-93. Green on multicolor underprint. D. de Herrera at right and as watermark. Port of Puerto Cortes on back. Date placement varieties.			
	a. 2.11.1978; 10.9.1979.	FV	8.00	30.00
	b. Vertical date at right. 8.1.1981-10.2.1989.	FV	4.00	20.00
	c. Horizontal date at upper left. 22.6.1989-2.10.1992.	FV	3.50	12.50
	d. 10.12.1992; 18.3.1993; 1.7.1993.	FV	FV	7.50

66	50 Lempiras	VG	VF	UNC
	1976-93. Deep blue on multicolor underprint. J. M. Galvez D. at left. National Agricultural Development Bank on back. Watermark: tree.			

			VG	VF	UNC
66	50 Lempiras				
		a. Vertical date at right. 29.1.1976-10.9.1979.	FV	15.00	55.00
		b. 5.1.1984; 3.7.1986; 24.9.1987; 10.2.1989.	FV	8.00	35.00
		c. Horizontal date at upper left. 1.3.1990; 13.12.1990; 29.8.1991.	FV	7.00	25.00
		d. 18.3.1993; 1.7.1993.	FV	FV	17.50

		VG	VF	UNC
67	100 Lempiras 16.1.1975; 29.1.1976; 18.3.1976; 13.1.1977; 12.1.1978; 10.9.1979. Brown-orange on multicolor underprint. Valle at left. Signatepeque school of forestry on back. Printer: TDLR.	FV	25.00	150.

1980-81 Issue

#68-69 printer: TDLR.

			VG	VF	UNC
68	1 Lempira 1980; 1984; 1989. Red on multicolor underprint. Arms at left, Lempira at right. Ruins of Copan on back.				
		a. Without security thread. 29.5.1980; 18.10.1984.	FV	.50	4.00
		b. With security thread. 30.3.1989.	FV	FV	3.00

			VG	VF	UNC
69	100 Lempiras 1981-94. Brown-orange, dark olive-green, and deep purple on multicolor underprint. J. C. del Valle at right and as watermark. Forestry school on back.				
		a. Regular serial #. 8.1.1981; 23.6.1982; 8.9.1983.	FV	15.00	75.00
		b. 5.1.1984-13.12.1989.	FV	12.50	50.00
		c. 21.12.1989-1.7.1993.	FV	FV	35.00

1989 Issue

			VG	VF	UNC
70	10 Lempiras 21.9.1989. Dark brown and red on multicolor underprint. (of vertical stripes). Arms at left, Cabañas at right. City University on back. Printer: TDLR.				
		a. Issued note.	FV	2.50	10.00
		s. Specimen. *MUESTRA SIN VALOR.*	—	—	—

1992-93 Issue

		VG	VF	UNC
71	1 Lempira 10.9.1992. Dark red on multicolor underprint. Similar to #68 but back in paler colors. Printer: CBNC.	FV	FV	2.00

#72-75 printer: TDLR. 1993 dates have red serial #. 1994 and later dates have brown serial #.

			VG	VF	UNC
72	2 Lempiras 14.1.1993; 26.2.1993; 12.5.1994. Purple on multicolor underprint. Like #61 but with light blue underprint at left. Ascending size serial # at upper left.				
		a. Issued note.	FV	FV	3.00
		s. Specimen. *MUESTRA SIN VALOR.*	—	—	—

		VG	VF	UNC
73	**20 Lempiras** 14.1.1993; 25.2.1993; 12.5.1994; 12.12.1996; 18.9.1997. Deep green and dark brown on multicolor underprint. D. de Herrera at right and as watermark. Back vertical; Presidential House at center.			
	a. Issued note.	FV	FV	6.00
	s. Specimen. *MUESTRA SIN VALOR.* 12.5.1994.	—	—	—
73A	**20 Lempiras** 3.9.1998. As #73 but Printer: FC-O.	FV	FV	6.00

		VG	VF	UNC
74	**50 Lempiras** 14.1.1993; 25.2.1993; 12.5.1994; 12.12.1996; 18.9.1997; 3.9.1998. Blue-black and dark brown on multicolor underprint. J. M. Galvez D. at right and as watermark. Back vertical; Central Bank Annex at center.			
	a. Issued note.	FV	FV	14.00
	s. Specimen. *MUESTRA SIN VALOR.* 12.5.1994.	—	—	—

		VG	VF	UNC
75	**100 Lempiras** 14.1.1993; 25.2.1993; 12.5.1994. Brown-orange, dark olive-green and dark brown on multicolor underprint. Like #69 but with engraved date. Serial # at upper left in ascending size. Enhanced underprint in watermark area on back. Black signature. Red serial #. Printer: DLR.			
	a. Issued note.	FV	FV	27.50
	s. Specimen. *MUESTRA SIN VALOR.* 12.5.1994.	—	—	—

1994; 1995 Issue

		VG	VF	UNC
76	**1 Lempira** 12.5.1994. Red on multicolor underprint. Similar to #71 but with brown ascending size serial # at upper left. Printer: TDLR.			
	a. Issued note.	FV	FV	1.50
	s. Specimen. *MUESTRA SIN VALOR.*	—	—	—

		VG	VF	UNC
77	**100 Lempiras** 1994-2003. Brown-orange, black and olive-green on multicolor underprint. J. C. del Valle at center right and as watermark, bridge over the Choluteca River at right. Valle's house at left on back. Brown serial #. Printer: TDLR (without imprint).			
	a. Signature titles: *MINISTRO DE HACIENDA Y CREDITO PUBLICO.* 12.5.1994.	FV	FV	17.50
	b. Signature titles: *SECRETARIO DE FINANZAS.* 18.9.1997; 3.9.1998; 14.12.2000; 30.8.2001; 23.1.2003; 26.8.2004.	FV	FV	20.00

		VG	VF	UNC
78	**500 Lempiras** 1995-2003. Violet and purple on multicolor underprint. Dr. R. Rosa at right and as watermark, National Gallery of Art in background. View of Rosario de San Juancito at left center on back.			
	a. Signature titles: *MINISTRO DE HACIENDA Y CREDITO PUBLICO.* 16.11.1995.	FV	FV	95.00
	b. Signature titles: *SECRETARIO DE FINANZAS.* 3.9.1998; 14.12.2000; 30.8.2001; 23.1.2003.	FV	FV	90.00

NOTICE

Readers with unlisted dates, signature varieties, etc. are invited to submit photocopies of their notes to: Standard Catalog of World Paper Money, 700 East State St. Iola, WI 54990-0001, E-Mail: george.cuhaj@fwpubs.com.

1996-98 ISSUE

#79-81 brown serial # w/ascending size serial # at upper l.

			VG	VF	UNC
79	**1 Lempira**	12.12.1996; 3.9.1998. Dark red on multicolor underprint. Like #71. Printer: F-CO.	FV	FV	1.00
79A	**1 Lempira**	18.9.1997. Dark red on multicolor underprint. Like #79 but printer: TDLR (without imprint).	FV	FV	1.00
80	**2 Lempiras**	18.9.1997 Purple on multicolor underprint. Similar to #72. Printer: TDLR.	FV	FV	1.50
80A	**2 Lempiras**	3.9.1998; 14.12.2000; 30.8.2001; 23.1.2003; 26.8.2004. Purple on multicolor underprint. Like #80 but printer: F-CO.	FV	FV	1.50

			VG	VF	UNC
81	**5 Lempiras**	12.12.1996; 18.9.1997; 3.9.1998. Black, dark blue and deep olive-green on multicolor underprint. Like #63. Printer: TDLR.	FV	FV	2.00

			VG	VF	UNC
82	**10 Lempiras**	12.12.1996; 18.9.1997; 3.9.1998; 14.12.2000. Dark brown and red on multicolor underprint. Like #70. Printer: TDLR.	FV	FV	3.50

2000 COMMEMORATIVE ISSUE

#83, 50th Anniversary of the Central Bank and Year 2000

			VG	VF	UNC
83	**20 Lempiras**	30.3.2000. Dark green and brown on multicolor underprint. D. Herrera and Government House at right. Work, effort and unity sculpture on back.	FV	FV	5.00

2000 ISSUE

			VG	VF	UNC
84	**1 Lempira**	14.12.2000; 30.8.2001; 23.1.2003; 26.8.2004. Dark red on multicolor underprint. Similar to #79. Printer: CBNC.	FV	FV	1.00

			VG	VF	UNC
85	**5 Lempiras**	14.12.2000; 30.8.2001; 23.1.2003; 26.8.2004. Multicolor. Similar to #81. Printer: CBNC.	FV	FV	1.75

			VG	VF	UNC
86	**10 Lempiras**	30.8.2001; 23.1.2003. Multicolor. Similar to #82. Printer: FC-O.	FV	FV	2.75

			VG	VF	UNC
87	**20 Lempiras**	30.8.2001; 23.1.2003; 26.8.2004. Green and violet on multicolor underprint. Printer: G&D.	FV	FV	4.50

88	**50 Lempiras**	VG	VF	UNC
	30.8.2001; 23.1.2003. Multicolor. Similar to #74, but vertical serial # at left. Printer: TDLR.	FV	FV	9.50

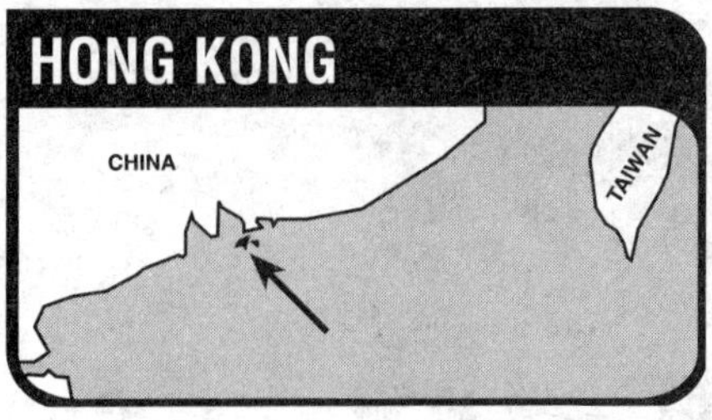

Hong Kong S.A.R., a former British Colony, is situated at the mouth of the Canton or Pearl River 90 miles (145 km.) southeast of Canton, has an area of 409 sq. mi. (1,091 sq. km.) and an estimated population of nearly 7 million. Capital: Central (formerly Victoria). The port of Hong Kong had developed as the commercial center of the Far East, a transshipment point for goods destined for China and the countries of the Pacific rim. Light manufacturing and tourism are important components of the economy.

Long a haven for fishermen-pirates and opium smugglers, the island of Hong Kong was ceded to Britain at the conclusion of the first Opium War (1839-1842). At the time, the acquisition of "a barren rock" was ridiculed by both London and English merchants operating in the Far East. The Kowloon Peninsula and Stonecutter's Island were ceded in 1860 and the so-called New Territories, comprising most of the mainland of the colony, were leased to Britain for 99 years in 1898.

When the Japanese opened hostilities in World War II, on Dec. 7, 1941, they immediately attacked Hong Kong which fell, after some bitter fighting, on Christmas Day. The colony was liberated by British troops on Aug. 30, 1945, when it was found that the population was no more than 600,000, of whom 80 percent were suffering from malnutrition. Hong Kong's economic life was dead. A brief period of military administration was followed by the formal re-establishment of civil government in May 1946. Hong Kong made a dramatic recovery and at the close of 1947 the population had reached 1,800,000. With the disintegration of the Nationalist Chinese forces and the establishment of the Central Peoples government, from 1948 to April 1950, an unprecedented influx of refugees took place, raising the population to about 2,360,000. It is currently near 7 million.

Hong Kong was returned to the Peoples Republic of China on July 1, 1997 and was made a Special Administrative Region, enjoying a high degree of autonomy and vested with executive, legislative and independent judicial power.

RULERS:

British (1842-1997)

MONETARY SYSTEM:

1 Dollar = 100 Cents

NOTE ON VALUATIONS:

Most valuations are for issued notes. At times specimen or proof notes are listed w/valuations, but these are only cases where a regularly issued example is not known to exist.

BRITISH ADMINISTRATION

CHARTERED BANK

行銀打渣

Cha Ta Yin Hang

1961; 1967 ND ISSUES

#68-72 wmk: Helmeted warrior's head. Printer: TDLR.

68	**5 Dollars**	VG	VF	UNC
	1961-62; ND. Black and green on multicolor underprint. Arms at lower left. Chinese junk and sampan at center on back.			
	a. 1.7.1961.	25.00	80.00	250.
	b. 3.3.1962.	35.00	110.	375.
	c. ND (1962-70).	12.00	40.00	120.
	s. Specimen. As a.	—	—	—

69	**5 Dollars**	VG	VF	UNC
	ND (1967). Black and yellow-brown on multicolor underprint. Like #68.	7.00	30.00	120.

70	10 Dollars	VG	VF	UNC
	1961-62; ND. Black and red-violet on red underprint. Arms at left. Chartered Bank building at center on back.			
	a. 1.7.1961.	35.00	110.	350.
	b. 3.3.1962.	20.00	60.00	250.
	c. ND (1962-70).	10.00	25.00	60.00
	s. Specimen. As c.	—	—	—

71	100 Dollars	VG	VF	UNC
	1961; ND. Dark green and brown on multicolor underprint. Arms at center. Harbor view on back.			
	a. 1.7.1961.	225.	750.	1400.
	b. ND (1961-70).	150.	425.	750.

72	500 Dollars	VG	VF	UNC
	1961-77. Black and dark brown on multicolor underprint. Male portrait at left. Ship, harbor view at center on back.			
	a. Signature titles: *ACCOUNTANT* and *MANAGER*. 1.7.1961.	450.	1500.	2250.
	b. Signature titles as a. ND (1962-?).	225.	650.	1500.
	c. Signature titles: *ACCOUNTANT* and *CHIEF MANAGER IN HONG KONG*. ND (?-1975).	225.	600.	1300.
	d. Signature titles as c. 1.1.1977.	125.	300.	750.
	s. Specimen. As d.	—	—	450.

1970 ND; 1975-77 Issue

#73-76 bank bldg. at l., bank crest at ctr. Wmk: Helmeted warrior's head. Printer: TDLR.

73	5 Dollars	VG	VF	UNC
	ND (1970-75); 1975. Dark brown on multicolor underprint. City Hall at center right on back.			
	a. Signature titles: *ACCOUNTANT* and *MANAGER*. ND (1970-75).	.75	4.00	15.00
	b. Signature titles: *ACCOUNTANT* and *CHIEF MANAGER IN HONG KONG* at right. ND; 1.6.1975.	5.00	15.00	45.00
	s. Specimen. As b.	—	—	—

74	10 Dollars	VG	VF	UNC
	ND; 1975; 1977. Dark green on multicolor underprint. Ocean terminal at center right.			
	a. Signature titles: *ACCOUNTANT* and *MANAGER*. ND (1970-75).	3.00	10.00	45.00
	b. Signature titles: *ACCOUNTANT* and *CHIEF MANAGER IN HONG KONG*. ND; 1.6.1975.	5.00	20.00	60.00
	c. Signature titles as b. 1.1.1977.	1.50	6.00	22.50
	s. Specimen. As b.	—	—	250.

75	50 Dollars	VG	VF	UNC
	ND (1970-75). Blue on multicolor underprint. City Hall at center right on back.			
	a. Issued note.	50.00	150.	400.
	s. Specimen.	—	—	400.

76	100 Dollars	VG	VF	UNC
	ND; 1977. Red on multicolor underprint.			
	a. ND (1970-75).	40.00	125.	360.
	b. 1.1.1977.	30.00	60.00	160.
	s. Specimen. As a.	—	—	350.

1979; 1980 Issue

#77-81 bank bldg. at l., arms at ctr. on back. Wmk: Helmeted warrior's head. Printer: TDLR (w/o imprint).

		VG	VF	UNC
77	**10 Dollars** 1.1.1980; 1.1.1981. Green on multicolor underprint. Stylistic carp at right.	FV	4.00	8.00

		VG	VF	UNC
78	**50 Dollars** 1979-82. Blue on multicolor underprint. Chinze at right.			
	a. 1.1.1979.	FV	20.00	75.00
	b. 1.1.1981; 1.1.1982.	FV	FV	50.00
	s. Specimen.	—	—	160.

		VG	VF	UNC
79	**100 Dollars** 1979-82. Red on multicolor underprint. Mythical horse *Qilin* at right.			
	a. 1.1.1979.	FV	40.00	140.
	b. 1.1.1980.	FV	35.00	90.00
	c. 1.1.1982.	FV	30.00	75.00
	s. Specimen.	—	—	175.

		VG	VF	UNC
80	**500 Dollars** 1979; 1982. Brown on multicolor underprint. Mythical phoenix at right.			
	a. 1.1.1979.	FV	FV	300.
	b. 1.1.1982.	FV	FV	250.
	s. Specimen.	—	—	400.

		VG	VF	UNC
81	**1000 Dollars** 1979; 1982. Yellow-orange on multicolor underprint. Dragon at right.			
	a. 1.1.1979.	FV	150.	500.
	b. 1.1.1982.	FV	120.	400.
	s. Specimen.	—	—	500.

HONG KONG & SHANGHAI BANKING CORPORATION

行銀理滙海上港香

Hsiang K'ang Shang Hai Hui Li Yin Hang

HONG KONG

1932-35 ISSUE

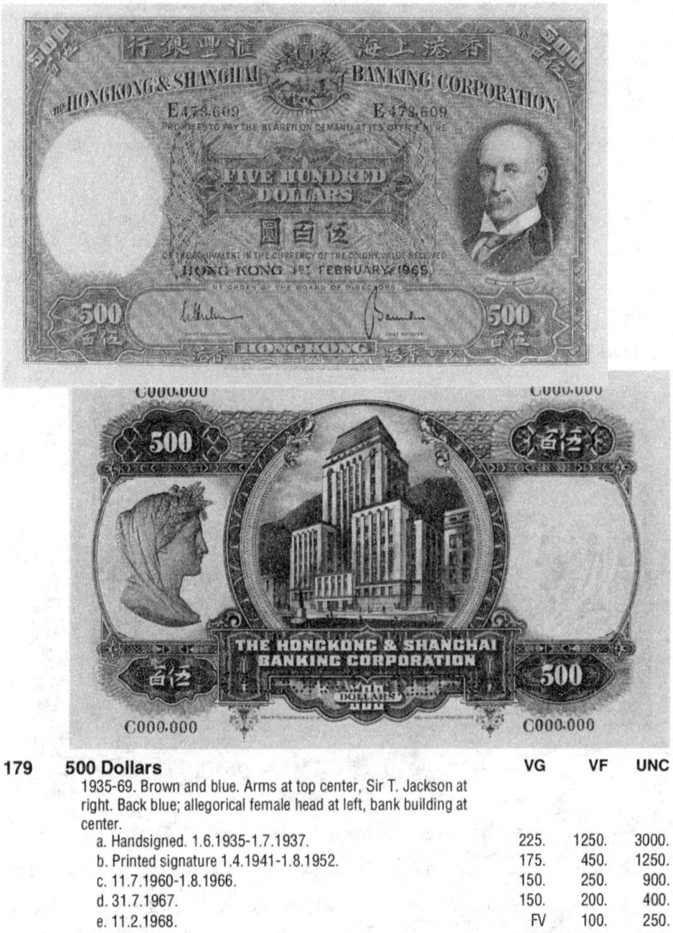

		VG	VF	UNC
179	**500 Dollars** 1935-69. Brown and blue. Arms at top center, Sir T. Jackson at right. Back blue; allegorical female head at left, bank building at center.			
	a. Handsigned. 1.6.1935-1.7.1937.	225.	1250.	3000.
	b. Printed signature 1.4.1941-1.8.1952.	175.	450.	1250.
	c. 11.7.1960-1.8.1966.	150.	250.	900.
	d. 31.7.1967.	150.	200.	400.
	e. 11.2.1968.	FV	100.	250.
	f. 27.3.1969.	FV	100.	300.

1959 ISSUE

#181-183 wmk: Helmeted warrior's head. Printer: BWC.

		VG	VF	UNC
181	**5 Dollars**			
	1959-75. Brown on multicolor underprint. Woman seated at right. New bank building at center on back.			
	a. Signature titles: *CHIEF ACCOUNTANT* and *CHIEF MANAGER.* 2.5.1959-29.6.1960.	3.00	15.00	45.00
	b. 1.5.1963.	50.00	175.	750.
	c. 1.5.1964-27.3.1969.	1.50	4.00	15.00
	d. Signature titles: *CHIEF ACCOUNTANT* and *GENERAL MANAGER.* 1.4.1970-18.3.1971.	1.00	3.50	12.50
	e. 13.3.1972; 31.10.1972.	.75	2.00	9.00
	f. Sm. serial #. 31.10.1973; 31.3.1975.	.75	1.25	7.00
	s. Specimen.	—	—	—

		VG	VF	UNC
182	**10 Dollars**			
	1959-83. Dark green on multicolor underprint. Portrait woman with sheaf of grain at upper left, arms below. Back similar to #184.			
	a. Signature titles: *CHIEF ACCOUNTANT* and *CHIEF MANAGER.* 21.5.1959-1.9.1962.	5.00	15.00	45.00
	b. 1.5.1963; 1.9.1963.	6.00	20.00	60.00
	c. 1.5.1964; 1.9.1964.	5.00	15.00	55.00
	d. 1.10.1964.	40.00	200.	800.
	e. 1.2.1965; 1.8.1966; 31.7.1967.	2.00	6.00	20.00
	f. 20.3.1968; 23.11.1968; 27.3.1969.	2.00	6.00	18.00
	g. Signature titles: *CHIEF ACCOUNTANT* and *GENERAL MANAGER.* 1.4.1970-31.3.1976.	1.50	3.75	10.00
	h. Signature titles: *CHIEF ACCOUNTANT* and *EXECUTIVE DIRECTOR.* 31.3.1977; 31.3.1978; 31.3.1979.	1.50	3.00	12.00
	i. Signature titles: *CHIEF ACCOUNTANT* and *GENERAL MANAGER.* 31.3.1980; 31.3.1981.	1.50	2.00	9.00
	j. Signature titles: *MANAGER* and *GENERAL MANAGER.* 31.3.1982; 31.3.1983.	1.50	2.00	9.00
	s. Specimen.	—	—	—

		VG	VF	UNC
183	**100 Dollars**			
	1959-72. Red on multicolor underprint. Woman seated at left. with open book, arms at upper center watermark: Helmeted warrior's head and denomination.			
	a. Signature titles: *CHIEF ACCOUNTANT* and *CHIEF MANAGER.* 12.8.1959-1.10.1964.	20.00	50.00	175.
	b. 1.2.1965-27.3.1969.	20.00	35.00	125.
	c. Signature titles: *CHIEF ACCOUNTANT* and *GENERAL MANAGER.* 1.4.1970; 18.3.1971; 13.3.1972.	15.00	30.00	90.00

1968-73 ISSUE

#184-186 printer: BWC.

		VG	VF	UNC
184	**50 Dollars**			
	1968-83. Dark blue on light blue and multicolor underprint. Arms at right. New bank building at left center on back. Watermark: Helmeted warrior's head and denomination.			
	a. Signature titles: *CHIEF ACCOUNTANT* and *CHIEF MANAGER.* 31.5.1968; 27.3.1969.	12.00	45.00	120.
	b. Signature titles: *CHIEF ACCOUNTANT* and *GENERAL MANAGER.* 31.10.1973; 31.3.1975; 31.3.1978.	12.00	35.00	90.00
	c. Signature titles as b. 31.3.1977.	12.00	35.00	90.00
	d. Signature titles: *CHIEF ACCOUNTANT* and *EXECUTIVE DIRECTOR.* 31.3.1977.	12.00	35.00	90.00
	e. 31.3.1979.	50.00	150.	350.
	f. Signature titles: *CHIEF ACCOUNTANT* and *GENERAL MANAGER.* 31.3.1980.	FV	12.50	55.00
	g. 31.3.1981.	FV	12.00	50.00
	h. Signature titles: *MANAGER* and *GENERAL MANAGER.* 31.3.1982; 31.3.1983.	FV	10.00	45.00
	s. Specimen.	—	—	—

185	100 Dollars	VG	VF	UNC
	1972-76. Red on multicolor underprint. Arms at left. Facing lions at lower left and right, bank building at center, dragon in medallion at right on back.			
	a. With 4 Large serial # on back. 13.3.1972; 31.10.1972.	15.00	40.00	100.
	b. Smaller electronic sorting serial # on face. without serial # on back. 31.10.1972.	20.00	60.00	160.
	c. 31.10.1973.	15.00	35.00	100.
	d. 31.3.1975; 31.3.1976.	15.00	35.00	80.00

186	500 Dollars	VG	VF	UNC
	1973-76. Brown on multicolor underprint. Arms at left. Bank building at left, lion's head at right on back.			
	a. 31.10.1973.	FV	200.	375.
	b. 31.3.1975.	FV	225.	450.
	c. 31.3.1976.	FV	175.	375.

1977; 1978 Issue

#187, 189 and 190 wmk: Lion's head. Printer: BWC.

187	100 Dollars	VG	VF	UNC
	1977-83. Red on lighter multicolor underprint. Similar to #185.			
	a. Signature titles: *CHIEF ACCOUNTANT* and *EXECUTIVE DIRECTOR*. 31.3.1977; 31.3.1978.	FV	25.00	65.00
	b. Signature titles as a. 31.3.1979.	12.50	25.00	125.
	c. 31.3.1980; 31.3.1981.	FV	FV	50.00
	d. Signature titles: *MANAGER* and *GENERAL MANAGER*. 31.3.1982; 31.3.1983.	FV	FV	40.00

#188 *Deleted*. See #186.

189	500 Dollars	VG	VF	UNC
	1978-83. Brown and black on multicolor underprint. Similar to #186 but with modified frame designs.			
	a. 31.3.1978; 31.3.1980; 31.3.198 1981.	FV	FV	250.
	b. 31.3.1983.	FV	FV	200.

190	1000 Dollars	VG	VF	UNC
	1977-83. Gold and black on multicolor underprint. Arms at right. Lion at left, bank building at center right on back.			
	a. 31.3.1977.	FV	FV	525.
	b. 31.3.1979; 31.3.1980; 31.3.1981; 31.3.1983.	FV	FV	450.

1985-87 Issue

#191-196 arms at l. Facing lions at lower l. and r. w/new bank bldg. at ctr. on back. Sign. varieties. Wmk: Lion's head. Printer: TDLR. Replacement notes: Serial # prefix *ZZ*.

191	10 Dollars	VG	VF	UNC
	1985-92. Deep green on multicolor underprint. Sampan and ship at right on back.			
	a. Signature title: *GENERAL MANAGER*. 1.1.1985; 1.1.1986; 1.1.1987.	FV	FV	4.50
	b. Signature title: *EXECUTIVE DIRECTOR*. 1.1.1988.	FV	FV	4.00
	c. Signature title: *GENERAL MANAGER*. 1.1.1989; 1.1.1990; 1.1.1991; 1.1.1992.	FV	FV	3.50
	s. Specimen. As a.	—	—	250.

192	20 Dollars	VG	VF	UNC
	1986-89. Deep gray-green and brown on purple and multicolor underprint. Clock tower, ferry in harbor view at right on back.			
	a. Signature title: *GENERAL MANAGER.* 1.1.1986; 1.1.1987.	FV	FV	10.00
	b. Signature title: *EXECUTIVE DIRECTOR.* 1.1.1988.	FV	FV	7.50
	c. Signature title: *GENERAL MANAGER.* 1.1.1989.	FV	FV	6.50
	s. Specimen. As a.	—	—	300.

193	50 Dollars	VG	VF	UNC
	1985-92. Purple on multicolor underprint. Men in boats at right on back.			
	a. Signature title: *GENERAL MANAGER.* 1.1.1985; 1.1.1986; 1.1.1987.	FV	FV	25.00
	b. Signature title: *EXECUTIVE DIRECTOR.* 1.1.1988.	FV	FV	20.00
	c. Signature title: *GENERAL MANAGER.* 1.1.1989; 1.1.1990; 1.1.1991; 1.1.1992.	FV	FV	15.00
	s. Specimen.	—	—	400.

194	100 Dollars	VG	VF	UNC
	1985-88. Red on multicolor underprint. Tiger Balm Garden pagoda at right on back.			
	a. Signature title: *GENERAL MANAGER.* 1.1.1985; 1.1.1986; 1.1.1987.	FV	FV	30.00
	b. Signature title: *EXECUTIVE DIRECTOR.* 1.1.1988.	FV	FV	25.00
	s. Specimen.	—	—	450.

195	500 Dollars	VG	VF	UNC
	1987-92. Brown on multicolor underprint. Old tower at right on back.			
	a. Signature title: *GENERAL MANAGER.* 1.1.1987.	FV	FV	120.
	b. Signature title: *EXECUTIVE DIRECTOR.* 1.1.1988.	FV	FV	110.
	c. Signature title: *GENERAL MANAGER.* 1.1.1989; 1.1.1990; 1.1.1991; 1.1.1992.	FV	FV	110.

196	1000 Dollars	VG	VF	UNC
	1.1.1985; 1.1.1986; 1.1.1987. Red, brown and orange on multicolor underprint. Old Supreme Court building at right on back.	FV	FV	180.

1988-90 ISSUE

#197-199 printer: TDLR. Replacement notes: Serial # prefix *ZZ*.

197	20 Dollars	VG	VF	UNC
	1.1.1990; 1.1.1991; 1.1.1992. Like #192 but gray and black on orange, pink and multicolor underprint. Signature title: *GENERAL MANAGER.*	FV	FV	6.00

198	100 Dollars	VG	VF	UNC
	1.1.1989; 1.1.1990; 1.1.1991; 1.1.1992. Similar to #194. Signature title: *GENERAL MANAGER.* Back red and black on multicolor underprint.	FV	FV	25.00

199	1000 Dollars	VG	VF	UNC
	1988-91. Similar to #196. Back orange, brown and olive-brown on multicolor underprint.			
	a. Signature title: *EXECUTIVE DIRECTOR.* 1.1.1988.	FV	FV	210.
	b. Sign. title: *GENERAL MANAGER.* 1.1.1989; 1.1.1990; 1.1.1991.	FV	FV	190.

HONG KONG & SHANGHAI BANKING CORPORATION LIMITED

1993; 1995 ISSUE

#201-205 lion's head at l. and as wmk., city view in unpt. at ctr. Latent image of value in box at lower r. New bank bldg. at ctr. between facing lions on back. Printer: TDLR. Notes dated 1.1.1996 and after w/o imprint. Replacement notes: Serial # prefix *ZZ*.

#200 not assigned.

201	20 Dollars	VG	VF	UNC
	1993-99. Gray and brown on multicolor underprint.			
	a. Signature title: *EXECUTIVE DIRECTOR.* 1.1.1993; 1.1.1994.	FV	FV	10.00
	b. Signature titles as a. Copyright clause on both sides. 1.1.1995; 1.1.1996.	FV	FV	7.50
	c. Signature title: *GENERAL MANAGER.* 1.1.1997; 1.7.1997.	FV	FV	6.00
	d. Signature title as c. 1.1.1998; 1.1.1999; 1.1.2000; 1.1.2001; 1.1.2002.	FV	FV	6.00

202	50 Dollars	VG	VF	UNC
	1993-99. Purple, violet and black on multicolor underprint.			
	a. Signature title: *EXECUTIVE DIRECTOR.* 1.1.1993; 1.1.1994.	FV	FV	19.00
	b. Signature title as a. Copyright clause on both sides. 1.1.1995; 1.1.1996.	FV	FV	15.00
	c. Signature title: *GENERAL MANAGER.* 1.1.1997; 1.7.1997.	FV	FV	12.00
	d. Signature title as a. 1.1.1998; 1.1.2000; 1.1.2001.	FV	FV	12.00
	e. Signature title as c. 1.1.2002.	FV	FV	12.00

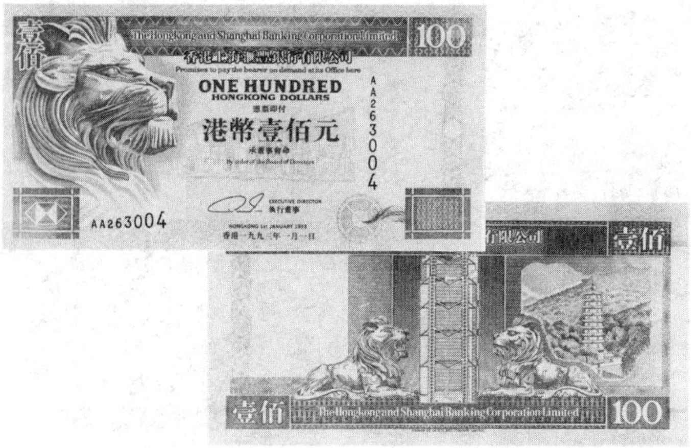

203	100 Dollars	VG	VF	UNC
	1993-99. Red, orange and black on multicolor underprint. Ten Thousand Buddha Pagoda at Chatin at right on back.			
	a. Signature title: *EXECUTIVE DIRECTOR.* 1.1.1993; 1.1.1994; 1.1.1996.	FV	FV	30.00
	b. Signature title: *GENERAL MANAGER.* 1.1.1997; 1.7.1997; 1.1.1998.	FV	FV	30.00
	c. Signature title as a. 1.1.1999; 1.1.2000.	FV	FV	25.00
	d. Signature title as b. 1.1.2001.	FV	FV	25.00
	e. Signature titles as a.	FV	FV	25.00

204	500 Dollars	VG	VF	UNC
	1993-99. Brown and red-orange on multicolor underprint. Government house at upper right on back.			
	a. Signature title: *EXECUTIVE DIRECTOR.* 1.1.1993; 1.1.1994.	FV	FV	140.
	b. Signature title as a. Copyright clause on both sides. 1.1.1995; 1.1.1996.	FV	FV	130.
	c. Signature title: *GENERAL MANAGER.* 1.1.1997; 1.7.1997.	FV	FV	125.
	d. Signature title as a. 1.1.1998; 1.1.1999.	FV	FV	125.
	e. Signature title as c. 1.1.2002.	FV	FV	125.

205	1000 Dollars	VG	VF	UNC
	1993-99. Orange, red-brown and olive-green on pink and multicolor underprint. Legislative Council building at right on back.			
	a. Signature title: *EXECUTIVE DIRECTOR.* 1.1.1993; 1.1.1994.	FV	FV	250.
	b. Signature title: *GENERAL MANAGER.* 1.1.1997; 1.7.1997.	FV	FV	220.
	c. Signature titles as a. 1.1.1998; 1.1.1999.	FV	FV	220.

2000 ISSUE

Wide security thread added.

206	1000 Dollars	VG	VF	UNC
	1.9.2000; 1.1.2002. Orange, red-brown and olive-green on pink and multicolor underprint. Signature title: *GENERAL MANAGER*.	FV	FV	215.

2003 ISSUE

207	20 Dollars	VG	VF	UNC
	1.7.2003; 1.1.2005. Dark blue on light blue and multicolor underprint. The Peak Tram on back. Signature title: *GENERAL MANAGER*.	FV	FV	6.00

208	50 Dollars	VG	VF	UNC
	1.7.2003; 1.1.2005. Green on multicolor underprint. Po Lin Temple on back.	FV	FV	15.00

209	100 Dollars	VG	VF	UNC
	1.7.2003. Red on multicolor underprint. Tsing-Ma Bridge on back.	FV	FV	25.00

210	500 Dollars	VG	VF	UNC
	1.7.2003. Brown on multicolor underprint. Hong Kong Airport on back.	FV	FV	125.

211	1000 Dollars	VG	VF	UNC
	1.7.2003. Orange, red-brown and olive-green on multicolor underprint. Hong Kong Convention and Exhibition Center on back.	FV	FV	215.

MERCANTILE BANK LIMITED

行銀利有 港香

Hsiang K'ang Yu Li Yin Hang

1964 ISSUE

244	100 Dollars	VG	VF	UNC
	1964-73. Red-brown on multicolor underprint. Aerial view of coastline. Woman standing with pennant and shield at center on back. Watermark: Dragon. Printer: TDLR.			
	a. 28.7.1964.	300.	900.	2600.
	b. 5.10.1965.	200.	600.	1350.
	c. 27.7.1968.	250.	750.	1750.
	d. 16.4.1970.	125.	400.	1100.
	e. 1.11.1973.	100.	350.	950.

1974 ISSUE

245	100 Dollars	VG	VF	UNC
	4.11.1974. Red, purple and brown on multicolor underprint. Woman standing with pennant and shield at left. Back red on multicolor underprin., city view at center. Watermark: Dragon. Printer: TDLR.	17.00	65.00	220.

STANDARD CHARTERED BANK

Hong Kong Cha Ta Yin Hang

1985-89 ISSUES

#278 -283 bank bldg. at l., bank arms at ctr. on back. Wmk: Helmeted warrior's head.

278	10 Dollars	VG	VF	UNC
	1985-91. Dark green on yellow-green and multicolor underprint. Mythological carp at right.			
	a. Signature titles: *FINANCIAL CONTROLLER* and *AREA GENERAL MANAGER*. 1.1.1985.	FV	FV	10.00
	b. Signature titles: *AREA FINANCIAL CONTROLLER* and *AREA GENERAL MANAGER*. 1.1.1986; 1.1.1987; 1.1.1988; 1.1.1989.	FV	FV	7.00
	c. Signature titles: *AREA FINANCIAL CONTROLLER* and *GENERAL MANAGER*. 1.1.1990.	FV	FV	6.00
	d. Signature titles: *CHIEF FINANCIAL OFFICER* and *GENERAL MANAGER*. 1.1.1991.	FV	FV	6.00

279	20 Dollars	VG	VF	UNC
	1985; 1992. Dark gray, orange and brown on multicolor underprint. Mythological tortoise at right.			
	a. Signature titles: *FINANCIAL CONTROLLER* and *AREA GENERAL MANAGER*. 1.1.1985.	FV	FV	10.00
	b. Signature titles: *CHIEF FINANCIAL OFFICER* and *AREA GENERAL MANAGER*. 1.1.1992.	FV	FV	7.00

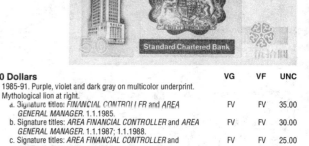

280	50 Dollars	VG	VF	UNC
	1985-91. Purple, violet and dark gray on multicolor underprint. Mythological lion at right.			
	a. Signature titles: *FINANCIAL CONTROLLER* and *AREA GENERAL MANAGER*. 1.1.1985.	FV	FV	35.00
	b. Signature titles: *AREA FINANCIAL CONTROLLER* and *AREA GENERAL MANAGER*. 1.1.1987; 1.1.1988.	FV	FV	30.00
	c. Signature titles: *AREA FINANCIAL CONTROLLER* and *GENERAL MANAGER*. 1.1.1990.	FV	FV	25.00
	d. Signature titles: *CHIEF FINANCIAL OFFICER* and *GENERAL MANAGER*. 1.1.1991.	FV	FV	25.00

281	100 Dollars	VG	VF	UNC
	1985-92. Red on multicolor underprint. Mythological horse (unicorn) at right.			
	a. Signature titles: *FINANCIAL CONTROLLER* and *AREA GENERAL MANAGER*. 1.1.1985.	FV	FV	48.00
	b. Signature titles: *AREA FINANCIAL CONTROLLER* and *AREA GENERAL MANAGER*. 1.1.1986-1.1.1989.	FV	FV	37.50
	c. Signature titles: *FINANCIAL CONTROLLER* and *AREA GENERAL MANAGER*. 1.1.1990.	FV	FV	35.00
	d. Signature titles: *FINANCIAL CONTROLLER* and *AREA GENERAL MANAGER*. 1.1.1991; 1.1.1992.	FV	FV	30.00

282	500 Dollars			
	1988-92. Maroon, gray and green on multicolor underprint. Mythological phoenix at right.			
	a. Signature titles: *FINANCIAL CONTROLLER* and *AREA GENERAL MANAGER*. 1.1.1988; 1.1.1989; 1.10.1989.	FV	FV	150.
	b. Signature titles: *FINANCIAL CONTROLLER* and *AREA GENERAL MANAGER*. 1.1.1990.	FV	FV	140.
	c. Signature titles: *FINANCIAL CONTROLLER* and *AREA GENERAL MANAGER*. 1.1.1991; 1.1.1992.	FV	FV	130.

283	1000 Dollars	VG	VF	UNC
	1985-92. Yellow-orange on multicolor underprint. Mythological dragon at right.			
	a. Signature titles: *FINANCIAL CONTROLLER* and *AREA GENERAL MANAGER*. 1.1.1985.	FV	FV	280.
	b. Signature titles: *AREA FINANCIAL CONTROLLER* and *AREA GENERAL MANAGER*. 1.1.1987.	FV	FV	300.
	c. Signature titles as b. 1.1.1988.	FV	FV	250.
	d. Signature titles: *FINANCIAL CONTROLLER* and *AREA GENERAL MANAGER*. 1.1.1992.	FV	FV	230.

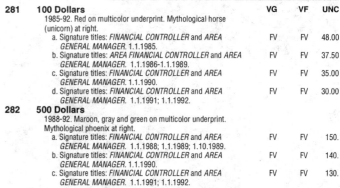

1993 ISSUE

#284-289 Bauhinia flower blossom replaces bank arms at ctr. on back. Wmk: *SCB* above helmeted warrior's head.

284	10 Dollars	VG	VF	UNC
	1993-95. Dark green on yellow-green underprint. Face like #278.			
	a. Signature titles: *CHIEF FINANCIAL OFFICER* and *AREA GENERAL MANAGER*. 1.1.1993.	FV	FV	6.00
	b. Signature titles: *HEAD OF FINANCE* and *GENERAL MANAGER*. 1.1.1994; 1.1.1995.	FV	FV	5.00

285	20 Dollars	VG	VF	UNC
	1993-2002. Dark gray, orange and brown on multicolor underprint. Face like #279.			
	a. Signature titles: *CHIEF FINANCIAL OFFICER* and *AREA GENERAL MANAGER*. 1.1.1993.	FV	FV	10.00
	b. Signature titles: *HEAD OF FINANCE* and *GENERAL MANAGER*. 1.1.1994; 1.1.1995; 1.1.1996; 1.1.1997; 1.7.1997.	FV	FV	7.50
	c. Signature titles: *HEAD OF FINANCE* and *CHIEF EXECUTIVE*. 1.1.1998; 1.1.1999; 1.1.2000; 1.1.2001.	FV	FV	6.00
	d. Signature titles: *CHIEF FINANCIAL OFFICER* and CHIEF EXECUTIVE & GENERAL MANAGER. 1.1.2002.	FV	FV	5.00

286	50 Dollars	VG	VF	UNC
	1993-2002. Purple, violet and dark gray on multicolor underprint. Face like #280.			
	a. Signature titles: *CHIEF FINANCIAL OFFICER* and *AREA GENERAL MANAGER*. 1.1.1993.	FV	FV	17.50
	b. Signature titles: *HEAD OF FINANCE* and *GENERAL MANAGER*. 1.1.1994; 1.1.1995; 1.1.1996; 1.1.1997; 1.7.1997.	FV	FV	15.00
	c. Signature titles: *HEAD OF FINANCE* and *CHIEF EXECUTIVE*. 1.1.1998; 1.1.1999; 1.1.2000; 1.1.2001; 1.1.2002.	FV	FV	15.00

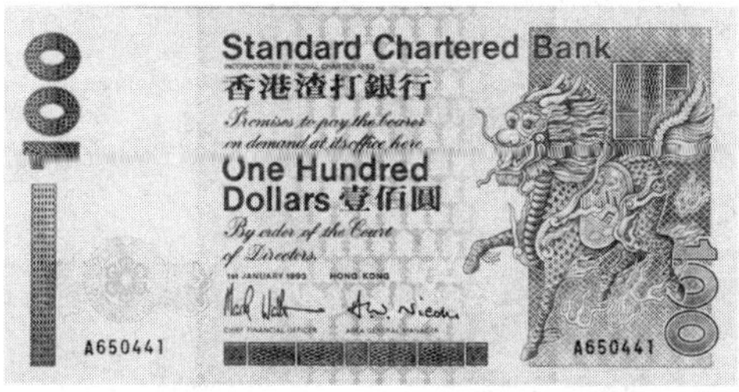

287	100 Dollars	VG	VF	UNC
	1993-2002. Red and purple on multicolor underprint. Face like #281.			
	a. Signature titles: *CHIEF FINANCIAL OFFICER* and *AREA GENERAL MANAGER*. 1.1.1993.	FV	FV	33.00
	b. Signature titles: *HEAD OF FINANCE* and *GENERAL MANAGER*. 1.1.1994; 1.1.1995; 1.1.1996; 1.1.1997; 1.7.1997.	FV	FV	27.50
	c. Signature titles: *HEAD OF FINANCE* and *CHIEF EXECUTIVE*. 1.1.1998; 1.1.1999; 1.1.2000; 1.1.2001.	FV	FV	27.50
	d. Signature titles: *CHIEF FINANCIAL OFFICER* and *CHIEF EXECUTIVE & GENERAL MANAGER*. 1.1.2001; 1.1.2002.	FV	FV	25.00

288	500 Dollars	VG	VF	UNC
	1993-2002. Brown and blue-green on multicolor underprint. Face like #282.			
	a. Signature titles: *CHIEF FINANCIAL OFFICER* and *AREA GENERAL MANAGER*. 1.1.1993.	FV	FV	150.
	b. Signature titles: *HEAD OF FINANCE* and *GENERAL MANAGER*. 1.1.1994; 1.1.1995; 1.1.1996; 1.1.1997; 1.7.1997; 1.1.1998; 1.1.1999; 1.1.2000.	FV	FV	135.
	c. Signature titles: *CHIEF FINANCIAL OFFICER* and CHIEF EXECUTIVE & GENERAL MANAGER. 1.1.2001; 1.1.2002.	FV	FV	130.

289	1000 Dollars			
	1993-2002. Yellow-orange on multicolor underprint. Face like #283.			
	a. Signature titles: *CHIEF FINANCIAL OFFICER* and *AREA GENERAL MANAGER*. 1.1.1993.	FV	FV	250.
	b. Signature titles: *HEAD OF FINANCE* and *GENERAL MANAGER*. 1.1.1994; 1.1.1995; 1.1.1997; 1.7.1997; 1.1.1998.	FV	FV	225.
	c. Signature titles: *HEAD OF FINANCE and CHIEF EXECUTIVE. 1.1.1999; 1.1.2000.*	FV	FV	200.
	d. Signature titles: *CHIEF FINANCIAL OFFICER and CHIEF EXECUTIVE & GENERAL MANAGER. 1.1.2001; 1.1.2002.*	FV	FV	200.

2002 ISSUE

290	1000 Dollars	VG	VF	UNC
	1.1.2002. Yellow-orange and blue-green on multicolor underprint. Like #289 but with enhanced security features. Signature title: *CHIEF FINANCIAL OFFICER* and CHIEF EXECUTIVE & GENERAL MANAGER.	FV	FV	215.

2003 ISSUE

291	20 Dollars	VG	VF	UNC
	1.7.2003. Dark Blue on multicolor underprint. Victoria Harview view ca. 1850 on back. Signature titles: *CHIEF FINANCIAL OFFICER* and *DIRECTOR*.	FV	FV	6.00

292	50 Dollars	VG	VF	UNC
	1.7.2003. Dark green and brown on multicolor underprint. Victoria Harbor view ca. 1890 on back.	FV	FV	15.00

		VG	VF	UNC
293	**100 Dollars** 1.7.2003. Red and brown on multicolor underprint. Victoria Harbor view ca. 1930 on back.	FV	FV	25.00

		VG	VF	UNC
294	**500 Dollars** 1.7.2003. Dark brown and dark blue on multicolor underprint. Victoria Harbor view ca. 1970 on back.	FV	FV	135.

		VG	VF	UNC
295	**1000 Dollars** 1.7.2003. Red-brown, orange and olive on multicolor underprint. Victoria Harbor view ca. 2003 on back.	FV	FV	215.

GOVERNMENT OF HONG KONG

府政港香

Hsiang K'ang Cheng Fu

SIGNATURE VARIETIES			
1	J.J. Cowperthwaite, 1961-71	4	Sir Piers Jacobs, 1986-92
2	C.P. Haddon-Cave, 1971-81	5	Sir Hamish Macleod, 1992-95
3	Sir J.H. Bremridge, 1981-86		

1961 ND ISSUE

#325-327 portr. Qn. Elizabeth II at r. Uniface.

		VG	VF	UNC
325	**1 Cent** ND (1961-95). Brown on light blue underprint.			
	a. Signature 1. (1961-71).	.05	.10	.25
	b. Signature 2. (1971-81).	.05	.25	.50
	c. Signature 3. (1981-86).	.05	.75	2.00
	d. Signature 4. (1986-92).	.05	.10	.25
	e. Signature 5. (1992-95).	.05	.25	.50

		VG	VF	UNC
326	**5 Cents** ND (1961-65). Green on lilac underprint.	.25	1.75	8.00

		VG	VF	UNC
327	**10 Cents** ND (1961-65). Red on grayish underprint.	.25	1.00	5.00

HONG KONG SPECIAL ADMINISTRATION REGION

BANK OF CHINA (HONG KONG) LIMITED

中國銀行

Chung Kuo Yin Hang

1994 ISSUE

#329-#333 Bank of China Tower at l. Wmk: Chinze. Printer: TDLR (HK) Ltd. (W/o imprint).

		VG	VF	UNC
329	**20 Dollars** 1.5.1994; 1.1.1996; 1.7.1997; 1.1.1998; 1.1.1999; 1.1.2000. Blue-black, blue and purple on multicolor underprint. Narcissus flowers at lower center right. Aerial view of Wanchai and Central Hong Kong at center right on back.	FV	FV	6.00

330 **50 Dollars** | VG FV | VF FV | UNC 16.00
1.5.1994; 1.1.1996; 1.7.1997; 1.1.1998; 1.1.1999; 1.1.2000. Purple and blue on violet and multicolor underprint. Chrysanthemum flowers at lower center right. Aerial view of cross-harbor tunnel at center right on back.

331 **100 Dollars** | VG FV | VF FV | UNC 30.00
1.5.1994; 1.1.1996; 1.7.1997; 1.1.1998; 1.1.1999; 1.1.2000. Red-violet, orange and red on multicolor underprint. Lotus flowers at lower center right. Aerial view of Tsimshatsui, Kowloon Peninsula at center right on back.

332 **500 Dollars** | VG FV | VF FV | UNC 150.
1.5.1994; 1.1.1995; 1.1.1996; 1.7.1997; 1.1.1998; 1.1.1999; 1.1.2000. Dark brown and blue on multicolor underprint. Peony flowers at lower center right. Hong Kong Container Terminal in Kwai Chung at center right on back.

333 **1000 Dollars** | VG FV | VF FV | UNC 250.
1.5.1994; 1.1.1995; 1.1.1996; 1.7.1997; 1.1.1998; 1.1.1999; 1.1.2000. Reddish brown, orange and pale olive-green on multicolor underprint. Bauhinia flowers at lower center right. Aerial view overlooking the Central district at center right on back.

2001 ISSUE

334 **1000 Dollars** | VG FV | VF FV | UNC 250.
1.1.2001. Reddish brown, orange and pale olive-green on multicolor underprint. Like #333 but enhanced security features.

2003 ISSUE

335 **20 Dollars** | VG FV | VF FV | UNC 6.00
1.7.2003. Dark blue on multicolor underprint. The Peak on back. Signature title: *CHIEF EXECUTIVE.*

336 **50 Dollars** | VG FV | VF FV | UNC 15.00
1.7.2003. Dark green on multicolor underprint. Aerial view of Tsimshatsui, Kowloon Peninsula on back.

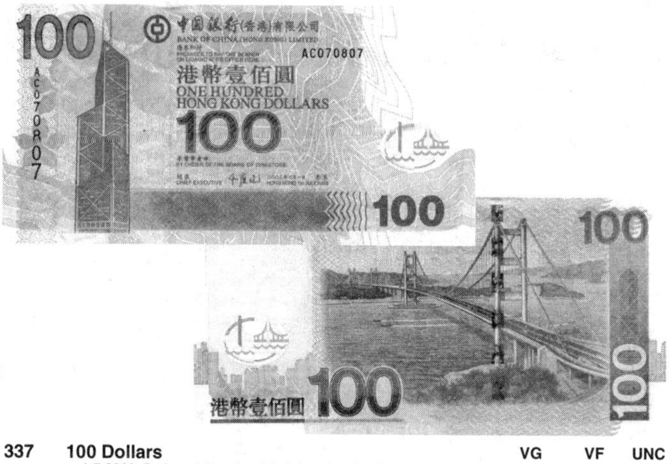

337 **100 Dollars** | VG FV | VF FV | UNC 25.00
1.7.2003. Red on pink and multicolor underprint. Tsing-Ma Bridge on back.

		VG	VF	UNC
338	**500 Dollars** 1.7.2003. Dark brown on multicolor underprint. Hong Kong Airport on back.	FV	FV	135.

		VG	VF	UNC
339	**1000 Dollars** 1.7.2003. Reddish-brown, orange and olive-green on multicolor underprint. Hong Kong Convention and Exhibition Center on back.	FV	FV	220.

GOVERNMENT OF HONG KONG

2002 ISSUE

		VG	VF	UNC
400	**10 Dollars** 1.7.2002; 1.1.2003; 1.1.2005 Purple, blue and multicolor. Geometric patterns.	FV	FV	3.00

The Hungarian Republic, located in central Europe, has an area of 35,919 sq. mi. (93,030 sq. km.) and a population of 9.81 million. Capital: Budapest. The economy is d on agriculture and a rapidly expanding industrial sector. Machinery, chemicals, iron and steel, and fruits and vegetables are exported.

The ancient kingdom of Hungary, founded by the Magyars in the 9th century, expanded its greatest power and authority in the mid-14th century. After suffering repeated Turkish invasions, Hungary accepted Habsburg rule to escape Turkish occupation, regaining independence in 1867 with the Emperor of Austria as king of a dual Austro-Hungarian Empire.

Sharing the defeat of the Central Powers in World War I, Hungary lost the greater part of its territory and population and underwent a period of drastic political revision. The short-lived republic of 1918 was followed by a chaotic interval of communist rule during 1919, and the restoration of the kingdom in 1920 with Admiral Horthy as regent of a kingdom without a king. Although a German ally in World War II, Hungary was occupied by German troops who imposed a pro-Nazi dictatorship in 1944. Soviet armies drove out the Germans in 1945 and assisted the communist minority in seizing power. A revised constitution published on Aug. 20, 1949, had established Hungary as a "People's Republic" of the Soviet type, but it is once again a republic as of Oct. 23, 1989. Entered the European Union in 2004.

RULERS:
Austrian to 1918

MONETARY SYSTEM:
1 Forint = 100 Fillér 1946-

PEOPLES REPUBLIC

MAGYAR NEMZETI BANK

HUNGARIAN NATIONAL BANK

1957-83 ISSUE

#168-171 The variety in the serial # occurs in 1975 when the letter and numbers are narrower and larger.
#170, 172 and 173 arms of 3-bar shield w/star in grain spray.

		VG	VF	UNC
168	**10 Forint** 1957-75. Green and slate black on orange and lilac underprint. Like #164 but new arms and signature Value at left, port. Sándar Petőfi at right. Trees and river, *Birth of the Song* by János Jankó at center on back.			
	a. 23.5.1957.	.30	2.00	10.00
	b. 24.8.1960.	.25	.50	9.50
	c. 12.10.1962.	.10	.50	5.00
	d. 30.6.1969. Blue-green center on back.	.10	.40	5.00
	e. Serial # varieties. 28.10.1975.	.10	.25	7.50
	s1. As a, b, c. Specimen with red overprint and perforated: *MINTA.*	—	—	45.00
	s2. As d, e. Specimen.	—	—	27.50

169	20 Forint	VG	VF	UNC
	1957-80. Blue and green on light green and pink underprint. Like #165 but new arms and signature Value at left, portrait György Dózsa at right. Penthathlete Csaba Hegedüs with hammer and wheat at center on back.			
	a. 23.5.1957.	.25	3.00	12.50
	b. 24.8.1960.	2.00	7.50	45.00
	c. 12.10.1962.	.20	1.50	12.50
	d. 3.9.1965.	.20	1.00	12.50
	e. 30.6.1969.	.20	.75	9.00
	f. Serial # varieties. 28.10.1975.	.15	.50	12.50
	g. 30.9.1980.	.15	.40	12.50
	s1. As a; c; d. Specimen with red overprint and perforated: *MINTA*.	—	—	27.50
	s2. As b. Specimen.	—	—	35.00
	s3. As e; f; g. Specimen.	—	—	25.00

170	50 Forint	VG	VF	UNC
	1965-89. Brown on blue and orange underprint. Value at left, Like #167 but new arms and signature Portrait Prince Ferencz Rákóczi II at right. Battle of the Hungarian insurrectionists (Kuruc) against pro-Austrian soldiers (Labanc) scene at center on back.			
	a. 3.9.1965.	.25	1.50	25.00
	b. 30.6.1969.	.25	1.50	20.00
	c. Serial # varieties. 28.10.1975.	1.00	2.00	12.50
	d. Serial # prefix D. 30.9.1980.	.20	.75	12.50
	e. Serial # prefix H. 30.9.1980.	1.00	2.50	15.00
	f. 10.11.1983.	.10	.50	9.00
	g. 4.11.1986.	.10	.50	27.50
	h. 10.1.1989.	.10	.50	17.50
	s1. As a. Specimen. Ovpt *MINTA*.	—	—	50.00
	s2. As b-h. Specimen.	—	—	25.00

171	100 Forint	VG	VF	UNC
	1957-89. Red-violet on blue and orange underprint. Like #166 but new arms and signature Value at left, portrait Lajos Kossuth at right. Horse-drawn wagon from *Took Refuge from the Storm* by Károly Lotz at center on back.			
	a. 23.5.1957.	1.00	3.00	15.00
	b. 24.8.1960.	2.00	4.00	15.00
	c. 12.10.1962.	1.00	3.00	12.50
	d. 24.10.1968.		FV	12.50
	e. 28.10.1975. Serial # varieties.	FV	2.00	10.00
	f. 30.9.1980.	FV	FV	10.00
	g. 30.10.1984.	FV	FV	10.00
	h. 10.1.1989.	FV	FV	9.00
	s1. As a. Specimen with red overprint and perforted: *MINTA*.	—	—	65.00
	s2. As b; c. Specimen.	—	—	—
	s3. As d; e. Specimen.	—	—	35.00
	s4. As f; g. Specimen.	—	—	30.00
	s5. As h. Specimen.	—	—	30.00

172	500 Forint	VG	VF	UNC
	1969-80. Purple on multicolor underprint. Portrait Endre Ady at right. Aerial view of Budapest and Danube river on back.			
	a. 30.6.1969.	FV	FV	12.50
	b. Serial # varieties. 28.10.1975.	FV	FV	12.50
	c. 30.9.1980.	FV	FV	10.00
	s. As a-c. Specimen.	—	—	30.00

173	1000 Forint	VG	VF	UNC
	1983. Deep green and olive-green on multicolor underprint. Béla Bartók at right. Back green on multicolor underprint; *Anya* sculpture, mother nursing child by F. Medgyessy at center.			
	a. Serial # prefix: *A*; *B*. 25.3.1983.	FV	FV	17.50
	b. Serial # prefix: *B*; *C*; *D*;. 10.11.1983.	FV	FV	17.50
	s. As a, b. Specimen with red overprint and perforated: *MINTA*.	—	—	45.00

REPUBLIC

MAGYAR NEMZETI BANK

HUNGARIAN NATIONAL BANK

1990; 1992 ISSUE

#174-177 St. Stephan's Crown over Hungarian Arms replaces 3-bar shield.

#174-177 numerous photocopy counterfeits began appearing in mid-1999.

174	100 Forint	VG	VF	UNC
	1992-95. Red-violet on multicolor underprint. Like #171 but with new arms.			
	a. 15.1.1992.	FV	FV	3.00
	b. 16.12.1993.	FV	FV	3.00
	c. 20.12.1995.	FV	FV	12.50
	s1. As a, b. Specimen with red. overprint and perforated *MINTA*.	—	—	25.00
	s2. As c. Specimen.	—	—	65.00

NOTICE

Readers with unlisted dates, signature varieties, etc. are invited to submit photocopies of their notes to: Standard Catalog of World Paper Money, 700 East State St. Iola, WI 54990-0001, E-Mail: george.cuhaj@fwpubs.com.

175	500 Forint	VG	VF	UNC
	31.7.1990. Purple on multicolor underprint. Like #172 but with new arms.			
	a. Issued note.	FV	FV	10.00
	s. Specimen.	—	—	30.00
176	1000 Forint			
	1992-96. Deep green and olive-green on multicolor underprint. Like #173 but with new arms.			
	a. Serial # prefix: *D.* 30.10.1992.	FV	FV	17.50
	b. Serial # prefix: *D; E.* 16.12.1993.	FV	FV	17.50
	c. Serial # prefix: *E; F.* 15.1.1996.	FV	FV	17.50
	s. Specimen. Serial # prefix: *A-F.*	—	—	30.00

177	5000 Forint	VG	VF	UNC
	1990-95. Deep brown and brown on orange and multicolor underprint. Portrait Count Istvan Széchenyi at right. Academy of Science at center on back.			
	a. Serial # prefix: *H; J.* 31.7.1990.	2.50	7.50	60.00
	b. Serial # prefix: *J.* 30.10.1992.	2.50	7.50	60.00
	c. Serial # prefix: *J.* 16.12.1993.	2.50	7.50	60.00
	d. Serial # prefix: *J; K.* 31.8.1995.	2.50	7.50	60.00
	s. As a-d. Specimen with red overprint and perforated: *MINTA.*	—	—	50.00

1997-99 ISSUE

#178-183 crowned arms at l. ctr. Latent image in cartouche at upper l.

178	200 Forint	VG	VF	UNC
	1998. Dark green and grayish purple on multicolor underprint. King Robert Károly at right and as watermark. Diósgyóri Castle ruins at left on back. Serial # prefix: *FA-FH.*			
	a. Issued note.	FV	FV	5.00
	s. Specimen.	—	—	25.00

179	500 Forint	VG	VF	UNC
	1998. Brown-violet and brown on multicolor underprint. Ferenc Rákóczi II at right and as watermark. Sárospatak Castle on back. Serial # prefix *EA-EF.*			
	a. Issued note.	FV	FV	10.00
	s. Specimen.	—	—	30.00

180	1000 Forint	VG	VF	UNC
	1998; 1999. Blue and blue-green on multicolor underprint. King Mátyás at right and as watermark. Fountain in the palace at Visegrád on back.			
	a. 1998. Serial # prefix: *DA-DJ.*	FV	FV	17.50
	b. 1999. Serial # prefix: *DA-DD.*	FV	FV	17.50
	s. As a, b. Specimen.	—	—	30.00

#181-183 w/hologram.

181	2000 Forint	VG	VF	UNC
	1998. Dark brown and brown on multicolor underprint. Prince Gabor Bethlen at right and as watermark. Prince G. Bethlen amongst scientists at left center on back. Serial # prefix: *CA-CG.*			
	a. Issued note.	FV	FV	30.00
	s. Specimen.	—	—	50.00

182	5000 Forint	VG	VF	UNC
	1999. Deep violet and purple on multicolor underprint. István Széchenyi at right and as watermark. Széchenyi's home at Nagycenk on back. Serial # prefixes: *BA-BJ*.			
	a. Issued note.	FV	FV	60.00
	s. Specimen.	—	—	75.00

183	10,000 Forint	VG	VF	UNC
	1997-1999. Violet, dull purple and blue-black on multicolor underprint. King St. Stephan at right and as watermark. View of Esztergom at left center on back.			
	a. Serial # prefixes: *AA-AK*. 1997.	FV	FV	120.
	b. Serial # prefixes: *AA-AC* with additional security devices. 1998.	FV	FV	120.
	c. Serial # prefix: *AA-AE*. 1999.	FV	FV	120.
	s. As a-c. Specimen.	—	—	120.

184	20,000 Forint	VG	VF	UNC
	1999. Slate gray on red and multicolor underprint. Ferenc Deák at right and as watermark. Plaza on back. Serial # prefix: *GA-GE*.			
	a. Issued note.	FV	FV	200.
	s. Specimen.	—	—	225.

NOTICE

Readers with unlisted dates, signature varieties, etc. are invited to submit photocopies of their notes to: Standard Catalog of World Paper Money, 700 East State St. Iola, WI 54990-0001, E-Mail: george.cuhaj@fwpubs.com.

2000 Commemorative Issues

#185, Millennium Celebration

185	1000 Forint	VG	VF	UNC
	2000. Blue, light yellow brown on multicolor underprint. Similar to #180 but with MNB in seal at upper left and *MILLENNIUM* at lower left. Serial # prefix: *DA-DE*.			
	a. Issued note.	FV	FV	17.50
	s. Specimen.	—	—	30.00

#186, 1000 Years of the Hungarian State

186	2000 Forint	VG	VF	UNC
	20.8.2000. Brown on tan and multicolor underprint. Crown of St. Stephan at right. St. Stephan as bishop baptizing on back. Serial # prefix: *MM*.			
	a. Issued note.	FV	FV	45.00
	s. Specimen.	—	—	50.00

2001-02 Issue

#187-192 enhanced security features added.

187	200 Forint	VG	VF	UNC
	2001-05. Green and multicolor. Like #178.			
	a. 2001. Serial # prefix: *FA-FE*.	FV	FV	5.00
	b. 2002. Serial # prefix: *FA-FC*.	FV	FV	5.00
	c. 2003. Serial # prefix: *FA-FC*.	FV	FV	9.00
	d. 2004. Serial # prefix: *FA-FC*.	FV	FV	9.00
	e. 2005. Serial # prefix: *FA-FC*.	FV	FV	9.00
	s. Specimen.	—	—	25.00

188 500 Forint

2001-03. Brown-violet and brown on multicolor underprint. Like #179.

	VG	VF	UNC
a. 2001. Serial # prefix: *EA-EC.*	FV	FV	10.00
b. 2002. Serial # prefix: *EA-EB.*	FV	FV	10.00
c. 2003. Serial # prefix: *EA-EC.*	FV	FV	10.00
d. 2005. Serial # prefix: *EA-EC.*	FV	FV	10.00
e. 2006. Serial # prefix: *EA-.*	FV	FV	10.00
s. Specimen.	—	—	30.00

189 1000 Forint

2002-06. Blue and light yellow brown on multicolor underprint. Like #180.

	VG	VF	UNC
a. 2002. Serial # prefix: *DA, DB.*	FV	FV	17.50
b. 2003. Serial # prefix: *DA-DC.*	FV	FV	17.50
c. 2004. Serial # prefix: *DA-DC.*	FV	FV	15.00
d. 2005. Serial # prefix: *DA.*	FV	FV	15.00
e. 2006. Serial # prefix: *DA-DI.*	FV	FV	15.00
s. Specimen.	—	—	30.00

190 2000 Forint

2002-05. Dark brown and brown on multicolor underprint. Like #181.

	VG	VF	UNC
a. 2002. Serial # prefix: *CA, CB.*	FV	FV	25.00
b. 2003. Serial # prefix: *CA.*	FV	FV	25.00
c. 2004. Serial # prefix: *CA-CC.*	FV	FV	25.00
d. 2005. Serial # prefix: *CA-CB.*	FV	FV	25.00
s. Specimen.	—	—	50.00

191 5000 Forint

2005-6. Multicolor.

	VG	VF	UNC
a. 2005. Serial # prefix: *BA-BC.*	FV	FV	60.00
b. 2006. Serial # prefix: *BA-BB.*	FV	FV	60.00
s. Specimen.	—	—	75.00

192 10,000 Forint

2001-06. Multicolor.

	VG	VF	UNC
a. 2001. Serial # prefix: *AA-AC.*	FV	FV	120.
b. 2003. Serial # prefix: *AA-AC.*	FV	FV	120.
c. 2004. Serial # prefix: *AA-AD.*	FV	FV	120.
d. 2005. Serial # prefix: *AA-AC.*	FV	FV	120.
e. 2006. Serial # prefix: *AA-AC.*			
s. Specimen.	—	—	120.

193 20,000 Forint

2004; 2005. Multicolor.

	VG	VF	UNC
a. 2004. Serial # prefix: *GA-GB.*	FV	FV	200.
b. 2005. Serial # prefix: *GA-GC.*	FV	FV	200.
s. Specimen.	—	—	225.

2006 ISSUE

194 500 Forint

23.10.1956. Brown-violet and brown on multicolor underprint. Ferenc Rákóczi at right. Parliament building and tri-color national flag, with a hole thru it on back. Serial # prefix EA-EC.

	VG	VF	UNC
	FV	FV	10.00

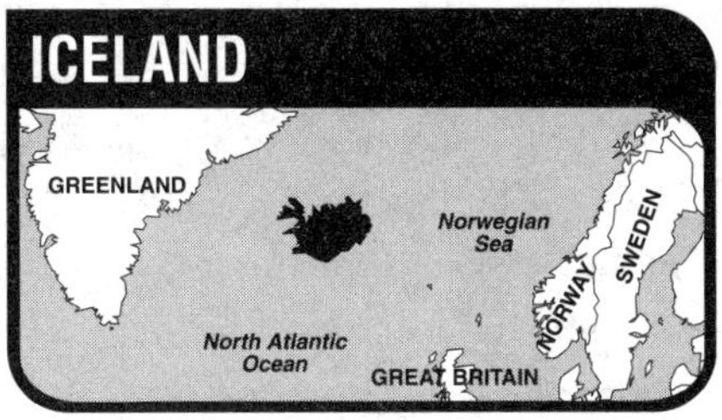

The Republic of Iceland, an island of recent volcanic origin in the North Atlantic east of Greenland and immediately south of the Arctic Circle, has an area of 39,768 sq. mi. (103,000 sq. km.) and a population of 283,000. Capital: Reykjavík. Fishing is the chief industry and accounts for more than 60 percent of the exports.

Iceland was settled by Norwegians in the 9th century and established as an independent republic in 930. The Icelandic assembly called the "Althing," also established in 930, is the oldest parliament in the world. Iceland came under Norwegian sovereignty in 1262, and passed to Denmark when Norway and Denmark were united under the Danish crown in 1384. In 1918, it was established as a virtually independent kingdom in union with Denmark. On June 17, 1944, while Denmark was still under occupation by troops of the Third Reich, Iceland was established by plebiscite as an independent republic.

MONETARY SYSTEM:

1 Krona = 100 Aurar, 1874-

SIGNATURE VARIETIES

31	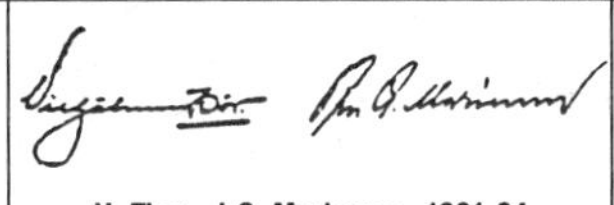 V. Thor - J.G. Mariasson, 1961-64	32	 J. Nordal - V. Thor, 1961-64
33	 J.G. Mariasson - J. Nordal, 1961-67	34	 J. Nordal - J.G. Mariasson, 1961-67
35	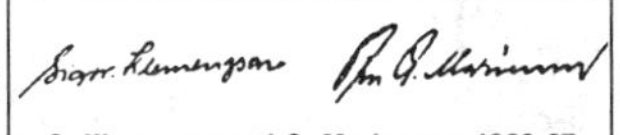 S. Klemenzson - J.G. Mariasson, 1966-67	36	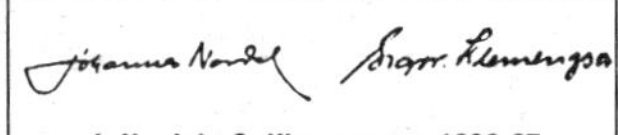 J. Nordal - S. Klemenzson, 1966-67
37	 J. Nordal - D. Olafsson, 1967-86	38	 D. Olafsson - J. Nordal, 1967-86
39	 S. Klemenzson - D. Olafsson, 1967-71	40	 S. Frimannsson - D. Olafsson, 1971-73
41	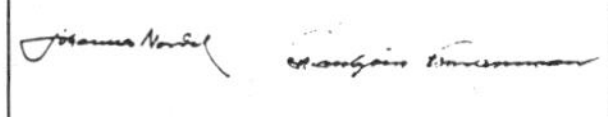 J. Nordal - S. Frimannsson, 1971-73	42	 G. Hjartarson - D. Olafsson, 1974-84
43	 J. Nordal - G. Hjartarson, 1974-84	44	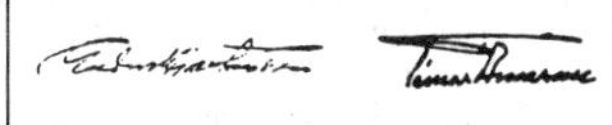 G. Hjartarson - T. Arnason, 1984
45	 T. Arnason - J. Nordal, 1984-93	46	 T. Arnason - D. Olafsson, 1984-93
47	 J. Nordal - T. Arnason, 1984-93	48	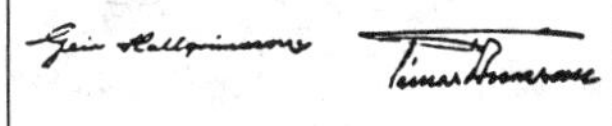 G. Hallgrimsson - T. Arnason, 1986-90
49	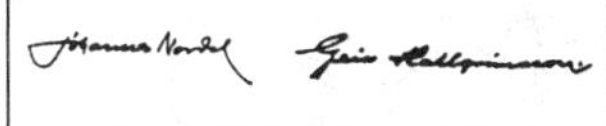 J. Nordal - G. Hallgrimsson, 1986-90	50	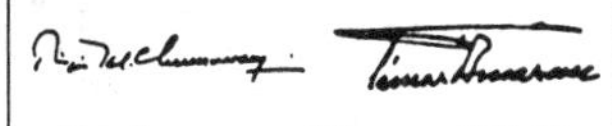 B. I. Gunnarsson - T. Arnason, 1991-93
51	 J. Nordal - B. I. Gunnarsson, 1991-93	52	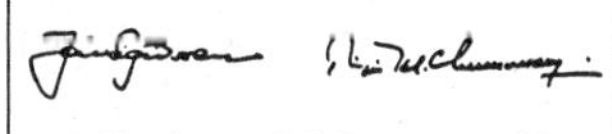 J. Sigurthsson - B. I. Gunnarsson, 1994
53	 B. I. Gunnarsson - J. Sigurthsson, 1994	54	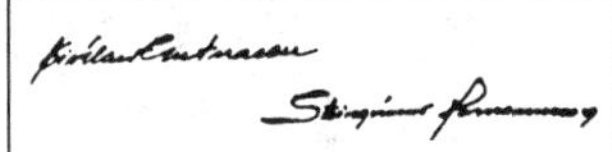 E. Guthnason - S. Hermansson, 1994
55	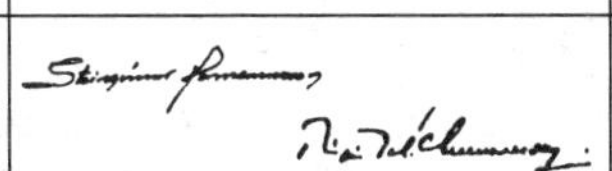 S. Hermansson - E. Guthnason, 1994	56	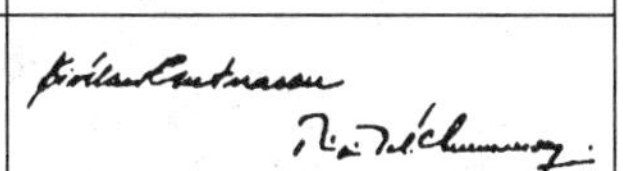 E. Guthnason - S. Hermansson, 1994

REPUBLIC

SEDLABANKI ÍSLANDS

CENTRAL BANK OF ICELAND

LAW OF 29.3.1961

#42-47 printer: BWC (w/o imprint).

#43-47 wmk: S. Bjornsson.

		VG	VF	UNC
42	**10 Krónur** L.1961. Brown-violet on green and orange underprint. Jón Eriksson at left, ships in Port of Reykjavík at lower center. Back green; ships moored at pier. Signature 33; 34.	1.50	3.00	6.25

		VG	VF	UNC
43	**25 Krónur** L.1961. Purple on multicolor underprint. Magnús Stephensen at left, Fjord at center. Fishing boats near Westmen Islands on back. Signature 34.	1.00	2.00	5.25

		VG	VF	UNC
44	**100 Krónur** L.1961. dark blue-green on multicolor underprint. Tryggvi Gunnarsson at left. Sheepherders on horseback, sheep in foreground, Mt. Mekla in background on back. Signature 31-36; 38-44.			
	a. Issued note.	.50	1.50	3.25
	s. Specimen.	—	—	—

45	500 Krónur	VG	VF	UNC
	L.1961. Green on lilac and multicolor underprint. Hannes Hafstein at left. Sailors on back. Signature 36; 38-43.			
	a. Issued note.	1.00	2.50	7.25
	s. Specimen.	—	—	—

46	1000 Krónur	VG	VF	UNC
	L.1961. Blue on multicolor underprint. Jón Sigurthsson at right, building at lower center. Rock formations on back. Signature 31-34; 36; 38-43.			
	a. Issued note.	2.50	6.00	16.25
	s. Specimen.	—	—	—

47	5000 Krónur	VG	VF	UNC
	L.1961. Brown on multicolor underprint. Similar to #41. Einer Benediktsson at left, dam at lower center. Man overlooking waterfall on back. Signature 36; 38-43.			
	a. Issued note.	5.00	16.50	37.50
	s. Specimen.	—	—	—

LAW 29 MARCH 1961 (1981-86) ISSUE

#48-52 Printer: BWC (w/o imprint), then later by TDLR (w/o imprint). These made after takeover of BWC by TDLR.

#48-53 wmk: J. Sigurthsson.

48	10 Krónur	VG	VF	UNC
	L.1961 (1981). Blue on multicolor underprint. Arngrimúr Jónsson at right. Old Icelandic household scene on back. Signature 37; 38; 42; 43.			
	a. Issued note.	FV	FV	1.00
	s. Specimen.	—	—	60.00

49	50 Krónur	VG	VF	UNC
	L.1961 (1981). Brown on multicolor underprint. Bishop Guthbranthur Thorláksson at left. Two printers on back. Signature 37; 38; 42; 43.			
	a. Issued note.	FV	FV	2.00
	s. Specimen.	—	—	60.00

50	100 Krónur	VG	VF	UNC
	L.1961 (1981). Dark green on multicolor underprint. Prof. Arni Magnússon at right. Monk with illuminated manuscript on back. Signature 37; 38; 42; 43; 45-53.			
	a. Issued note.	FV	FV	4.00
	s. Specimen.	—	—	60.00

51	500 Krónur	VG	VF	UNC
	L.1961 (1981). Red on multicolor underprint. Jón Sigurthsson at left center. Sigurthsson working at his desk on back. Signature 37; 38; 42; 43; 45; 48-53.			
	a. Issued note.	FV	FV	17.75
	s. Specimen.	—	—	75.00

		VG	VF	UNC
52	**1000 Krónur**			
	L.1961 (1984-91). Purple on multicolor underprint. Bishop Byrnijólfur Sveinsson with book at right. Church at center on back. Signature 38; 42; 43; 45; 48-51.			
	a. Issued note.	FV	FV	28.50
	s. Specimen.	—	—	80.00

		VG	VF	UNC
53	**5000 Krónur**			
	L.1961 (1986-95). Blue on multicolor underprint. Ragnheithur Jónsdóttir at center. Bishop G. Thorláksson with two previous wives at right. Jónsdóttir teaching two girls embroidery on back.			
	a. Signature 38; 46; 47.	FV	FV	170.
	b. Signature 54-56. (1995).	FV	FV	120.

Law 5 Mai 1986 (1994-00) Issue

#54-56 like #50-52 but w/new sign. and law date.

		VG	VF	UNC
54	**100 Krónur**			
	L.1986 (1994). Signature 52; 53.	FV	FV	3.00

		VG	VF	UNC
55	**500 Krónur**			
	L.1986 (1994). Signature 45; 50-53.	FV	FV	13.00

		VG	VF	UNC
56	**1000 Krónur**			
	L.1986 (1994). Signature 45; 50; 51; 54-56.	FV	FV	21.00

		VG	VF	UNC
57	**2000 Krónur**			
	L.1986 (1995). Brown and blue-violet on multicolor underprint. Painting Inside, Outside at center, Johannes S. Kjarval at right. Painting Yearning for Flight (Leda and the Swan) and Woman with Flower on back. Signature 54-56.	FV	FV	41.50

		VG	VF	UNC
58	**5000 Krónur**			
	22.5.2001. Blue on multicolor underprint. Similar to #53, enhanced security decives.	FV	FV	87.50

Law 5 Mai 1986 (2001) Issue

		VG	VF	UNC
59	**500 Krónur**			
	L. 1986. (2004). As #55 but with designs to edge of paper.	FV	FV	10.00
60	**1000 Krónur**			
	L. 1986. (2005). As #55 but with designs to edge.	FV	FV	16.00

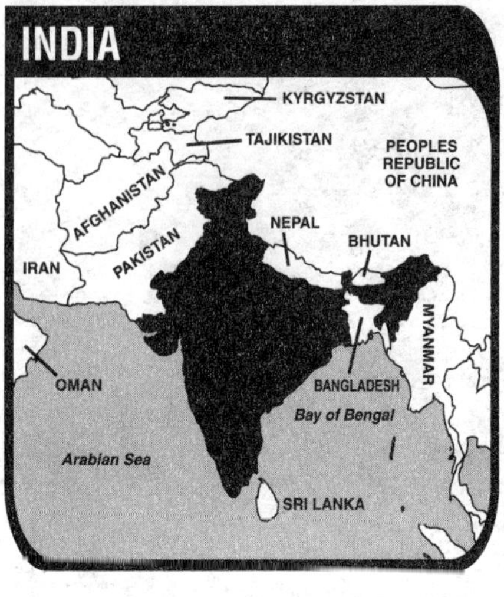

The Republic of India, a subcontinent jutting southward from the mainland of Asia, has an area of 1,266,595 sq. mi. (3,287,590 sq. km.) and a population of 1,006.8 million, second only to that of the Peoples Republic of China. Capital: New Delhi. India's economy is d on agriculture and industrial activity. Engineering goods, cotton apparel and fabrics, handicrafts, tea, iron and steel are exported.

The people of India have had a continuous civilization since about 2500 BC, when an urban culture d on commerce and trade, and to a lesser extent, agriculture, was developed by the inhabitants of the Indus River Valley. The origins of this civilization are uncertain, but it declined about 1500 B.C., when the region was conquered by the Aryans. Over the following 2,000 years, the Aryans developed a Brahmanic civilization and introduced the caste system. Several successive empires flourished in India over the following centuries, notably those of the Mauryans, Guptas and Mughals. In the 7th and 8th centuries AD, the Arabs expanded into western India, bringing with them the Islamic faith. A Muslim dynasty (the Mughal Empire) controlled virtually the entire subcontinent during the period preceding the arrival of the Europeans; an Indo-Islamic style of art and architecture evolved, of which the Taj Mahal is a splendid example.

The Portuguese were the first to arrive, off Calicut in May 1498. It was not until 1612, after Portuguese and Spanish power began to wane, that the English East India Company established its initial settlement at Surat. By the end of the century, English traders were firmly established in Bombay, Madras and Calcutta, as well as in some parts of the interior, and Britain was implementing a policy to create the civil and military institutions that would insure British dominion over the country. By 1757, following the successful conclusion of a war of colonial rivalry with France, the British were firmly established in India not only as traders, but as conquerors. During the next 60 years, the English East India Company acquired dominion over most of India by bribery and force, and ruled directly or through puppet princelings.

The Indian Mutiny (also called Sepoy Mutiny) of 1857-59, begun by Indian troops in the service of the British East India Company, revealed the intensity of the growing resentment against British domination. The widespread rebellion against British rule was unsuccessful, but resulted in the transfer of government from the company to the British crown.

Following World War I, in which India sent six million troops to fight at the side of the Allies, Indian nationalism intensified under the banner of the Indian National Congress and the leadership of Mohandas Gandhi, who called the non-violent revolt against British authority. The Government of India Act of 1935 proposed a federal status linking the British India provinces with the many princely states; in addition, provincial legislatures were to be created. The federal status was never implemented, but the legislatures were created after the election of 1937, with the National Congress winning majorities in most of the provinces.

When Britain declared war on Germany in Sept., 1939, the viceroy declared India also to be at war with a common enemy. The Congress, however, demanded independence as a condition for cooperation. Britain refused. But as the Japanese advanced into Asia, Britain offered to transfer to Indians power over all but military affairs during the war, and set forth a plan for postwar independence. Congress was willing to accept the wartime transfer of power, but both Congress and the Muslim League rejected Britain's plan for independence; Congress because it did not sufficiently safeguard Indian unity, the Muslims (who wanted a separate Muslim state) because of fears of what would happen to Muslims within a united India.

Early in 1947, Prime Minister Clement Attlee announced that Britain would leave India "by a date not later than June 1948," even though the Hindus and Muslims could not agree among themselves on a plan for self-government. The National Congress, aware that the Muslim League would revolt rather than accept an all-India government, reluctantly agreed to the formation of a separate Muslim state. The Muslim-populated provinces of the northwest frontier, Sindh and West Punjab in the west, and East Bengal in the east were separated from India to form the Muslim state of Pakistan, which became independent on August 14, 1947. India became independent on the following day. Initially, Pakistan consisted of East and West Pakistan, two areas separated by 1,000 miles of Indian territory. East Pakistan seceded from Pakistan on March 26, 1971, and with the support of India established itself as the independent Peoples Republic of Bangladesh.

The Republic of India is a member of the Commonwealth of Nations. The president is the Chief of State. The prime minister is the Head of Government.

MONETARY SYSTEM:

1 Rupee = 100 Naye Paise, 1957-1964
1 Rupee = 100 Paise, 1964-

Note: Staple holes and condition:

Perfect uncirculated notes are rarely encountered without having at least two tiny holes made by staples, stick pins or stitching having been done during age old accounting practices before and after a note is released to circulation. Staples were officially discontinued in 1998.

COLONIAL OFFICES

	Allahabad	K	Karachi
B	Bombay	L	Lahore
C	Calcutta	M	Madras
	Calicut	R	Rangoon, refer to Myanmar listings
A	Cawnpore		

DENOMINATION LANGUAGE PANELS

 Bengali	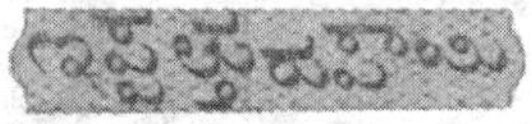 Marathi
 Burmese	 Tamil
 Gujarati	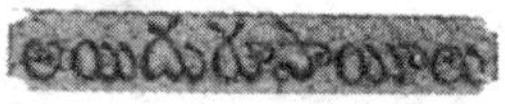 Telugu
 Gujarati (var.)	 Persian (Farsi)
 Hindi	 Urdu
 Kannada	

SIGNATURE VARIETIES

GOVERNORS OF THE RESERVE BANK OF INDIA

71	 Sir C.D. Deshmukh February 1943-June 1949	72	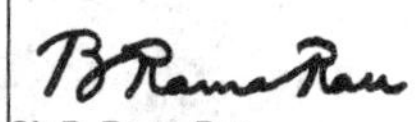 Sir B. Rama Rue July 1949-1957
73	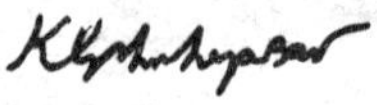 K. G. Ambegoankar January 1957-February 1957	74	 H. V. R. Iengar March 1957-February 1962
75	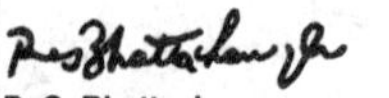 P. C. Bhattacharyya March 1962-June 1967	76	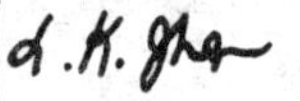 L. K. Jha MJuly 1967-May 1970
77	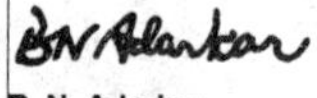 B. N. Adarkar May 1970-June1970	78	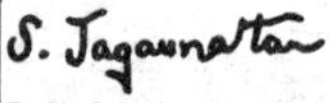 B. N. Adarkar May 1970-June1970
79	 N. C. Sengupta May 1975-August 1975	80	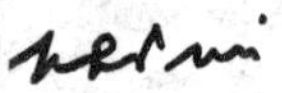 K. R. Puri August 1975-May 1975
81	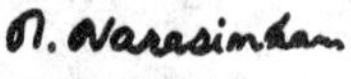 M. Narasimham May 1977-November 1977	82	 I. G. Patel December 1977-September 1982
83	 Manmohan Singh September 198 January 1984-February 1985	84	 Abhitam Ghosh January 1985-February 1985
85	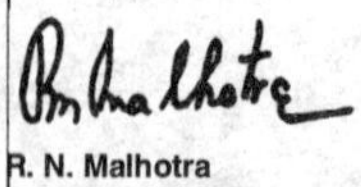 R. N. Malhotra February 1985-December 1990	86	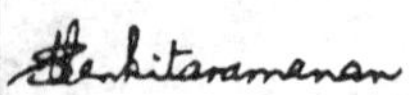 S. Venkitaramanan November 1997-
87	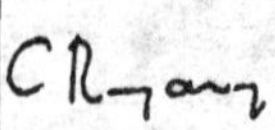 C. Rangarajan December 1992-97 November 1987-88	88	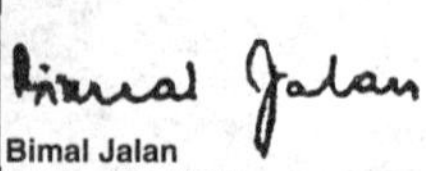 Bimal Jalan November 1997-

Republic of India

Reserve Bank of India

First Series

#27-47 Asoka column at r. Lg. letters in unpt. beneath serial #. Wmk: Asoka column.

रुपया — Error singular Hindi = *RUPAYA*

रुपये — Corrected plural Hindi = *RUPAYE*

VARIETIES: #27-28, 33, 38, 42, 46, 48 and 50 have large headings in Hindi expressing value incorrectly in the singular form Rupaya.

Note: For similar notes but in different colors, please see Haj Pilgrim and Persian Gulf listings at the end of this country listing.

#	Denomination / Description	VG	VF	UNC
27	**2 Rupees** ND. Red-brown on violet and green underprint. Tiger head at left. on back. Value in English and error Hindi on face and back. Hindi numeral *2* at upper right. 8 value text lines on back. Signature 72.	1.50	6.00	20.00
28	**2 Rupees** ND. Similar to #27 but English *2* at upper left and right. Redesigned panels on face. 7 value text lines on back; third line 18mm long. Sign 72.	.50	2.00	5.00

#	Denomination / Description	VG	VF	UNC
29	**2 Rupees** ND. Red-brown on violet and green underprint. Like #28 but value in English and corrected Hindi on both sides. Tiger hea d at left. looking to left, third value text line on back 24mm long.			
	a. Signature 72.	1.00	6.00	10.00
	b. Signature 74.	.75	2.00	5.00

#	Denomination / Description	VG	VF	UNC
30	**2 Rupees** ND. Red-brown on green underprint. Face like #29. Tiger head at left. looking to right, with 13 value text lines at center on back. Signature 75.	.75	4.00	10.00

#	Denomination / Description	VG	VF	UNC
31	**2 Rupees** ND. Olive on tan underprint. Like #30. Signature 75.	.50	2.50	12.50
32	**5 Rupees** ND. Green on brown underprint. English value only on face, serial # at center *Rs. 5* and antelope on back. Signature 72 .	1.00	8.00	40.00

#	Denomination / Description	VG	VF	UNC
33	**5 Rupees** ND. Like #32 but value in English and error Hindi on face, serial # at right. 8 value lines on back, fourth line 21mm long. Signature 72.	.50	2.00	5.00
34	**5 Rupees** ND. Like #33 but Hindi corrected. Fourth value text line on back 26mm long. Signature 72.	1.00	8.00	50.00

#	Denomination / Description	VG	VF	UNC
35	**5 Rupees** ND. Green on brown underprint. Like #34 but redesigned panels at left and right.			
	a. Without letter. signature 74.	.75	4.00	15.00
	b. Letter A. signature 74.	.50	3.50	10.00
	c. Letter A. signature 75.	.75	5.00	15.00
	d. Letter B. signature 75.	.75	5.00	15.00

Note: For similar note but in orange, see #R2 (Persian Gulf listings).

#	Denomination / Description	VG	VF	UNC
36	**5 Rupees** ND (1962-67). Green on brown underprint. Like #35 but signature title: *GOVERNOR* centered. Thirteen value text lines on back.			
	a. Letter A. signature 75.	.50	2.00	10.00
	b. Letter B. signature 75.	.50	3.00	15.00
37	**10 Rupees** ND. Purple on multicolor underprint. English value only on face. *Rs. 10* at lower center, 1 serial #. English in both lower corners, dhow at center on back.			
	a. Signature 71.	4.00	17.50	100.
	b. Signature 72.	3.00	10.00	25.00

#	Denomination / Description	VG	VF	UNC
38	**10 Rupees** ND. Like #37 but value in English and error Hindi on face and back. 2 serial #. Third value text line on back 24mm long. Signature 72.	.75	2.00	5.00
39	**10 Rupees** ND. Purple on multicolor underprint. Like #38 but Hindi corrected. Third value text line on back 29mm long.			
	a. Without letter. signature 72.	1.00	5.00	15.00
	b. Without letter. signature 74.	1.00	5.00	15.00
	c. Letter A. signature 74.	.75	2.00	5.00

Note: For similar note but in red, see #R3 (Persian Gulf listings); in blue, see #R5 (Haj Pilgrim listings).

#	Denomination / Description	VG	VF	UNC
40	**10 Rupees** ND. Like #39 but title: *GOVERNOR* centered. Green on brown underprint. Thirteen value text lines on back.			
	a. Letter A. signature 75.	.75	3.00	12.50
	b. Letter B. signature 75.	.75	3.00	5.00

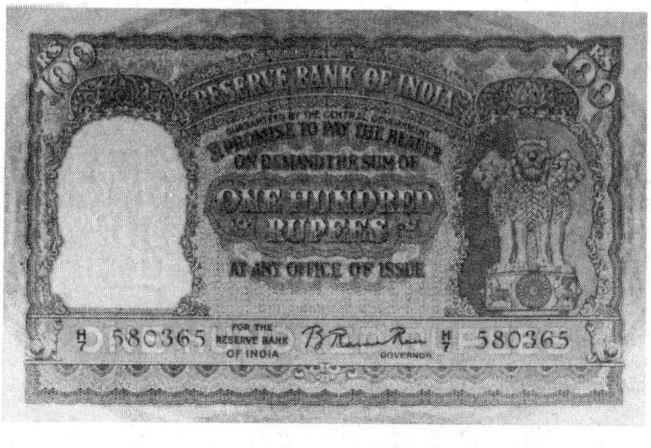

		VG	VF	UNC
41	**100 Rupees**			
	ND. Blue on multicolor underprint. English value only on face. Two elephants at center 8 value text lines below and bank emblem at left. on back.			
	a. dark blue. signature 72.	25.00	60.00	140.
	b. light blue. signature 72.	25.00	60.00	140.
42	**100 Rupees**			
	ND. Purplish-blue on multicolor underprint. Like #41 but value in English and error Hindi on face and back. 7 value text lines on back; third 27mm long.			
	a. Black serial #. signature 72.	15.00	45.00	120.
	b. Red serial #. signature 72.	15.00	45.00	120.

		VG	VF	UNC
43	**100 Rupees**			
	ND. Purplish blue on multicolor underprint. Like #42 but Hindi corrected. Third value text line 40mm long.			
	a. Without letter, thin paper. signature 72.	15.00	45.00	120.
	b. Without letter, thin paper. signature 74.	12.50	40.00	100.

Note: For similar note but in green, see #R4 (Persian Gulf listings); in red, see #R6 (Haj Pilgrim listings).

44	**100 Rupees**			
	ND. Purple and multicolor. Heading in rectangle at top, serial # at upper left and lower right. Title: *GOVERNOR* at center right. Dam at center with 13 value text lines at left. on back. Signature 74.	12.50	30.00	60.00
45	**100 Rupees**			
	ND. Violet and multicolor. Like #44 but signature title: *GOVERNOR* centered. Signature 75.	12.50	30.00	60.00
		Good	**Fine**	**XF**
47	**1000 Rupees**			
	ND. Brown on green and blue underprint. Like #46 but Hindi corrected. Tanjore Temple at center. Thirteen value text lines on back.			
	a. *BOMBAY.* signature 72.	200.	400.	—
	b. *CALCUTTA.* signature 72.	200.	400.	—
	c. *BOMBAY.* signature 74.	400.	800.	—
	d. *BOMBAY.* signature 75.	100.	200.	—
		VG	**VF**	**UNC**
48	**5000 Rupees**			
	ND. Green, violet and brown. Asoka column at left. Value in English and error Hindi on face and back. Gateway of India on back.			
	a. *BOMBAY.* signature 72. Rare.	—	—	—
	b. *CALCUTTA.* signature 72. Rare.	—	—	—
	c. *DELHI.* signature 72. Rare.	—	—	—
49	**5000 Rupees**			
	ND. Green, violet and brown. Like #48 but Hindi corrected.			
	a. *BOMBAY.* signature 74.	200.	375.	800.
	b. *MADRAS.* signature 74.	200.	375.	800.

		Good	Fine	XF
50	**10,000 Rupees**			
	ND. Blue, violet and brown. Asoka column at center Value in English and error Hindi on face and back.			
	a. *BOMBAY.* signature 72.	300.	700.	1500.
	b. *CALCUTTA.* signature 72.	300.	700.	1500.
	s. As B. Specimen. signature 72.			
50A	**10,000 Rupees**			
	ND. Like #50 but Hindi corrected.			
	a. *BOMBAY.* signature 74.	300.	700.	1500.
	b. *MADRAS.* signature 74.	400.	800.	1750.
	c. *NEW DELHI.* signature 74.	400.	800.	1750.
	d. *BOMBAY.* signature 76.	400.	800.	1750.

SECOND SERIES

Most notes of reduced size. Large letters found in unpt. beneath serial #.

#51-65 Asoka column at r.

Urdu Incorrect

Corrected Urdu (actually Farsi)

		VG	VF	UNC
51	**2 Rupees**			
	ND. Brown and multicolor. Numeral *2* at center 7mm high. Incorrect Urdu inscription at bottom left, tiger at center on back.			
	a. Signature 75 with title: *GOVERNOR* centered at bottom.	.25	1.00	5.00
	b. Signature 76 with title: *GOVERNOR* at center r.	.25	1.00	5.00

		VG	VF	UNC
52	**2 Rupees**			
	ND. Deep pink and multicolor. Numeral *2* at center 15mm high. Back like #51, tiger at center. Signature 78.	.20	1.00	4.00
53	**2 Rupees**			
	ND. Deep pink and multicolor. English text at left on face. Like #52 but corrected Urdu at bottom left on back.			
	a. Without letter. signature 78.	.20	1.00	3.00
	b. Without letter. signature 80.	.25	1.00	4.00
	c. Letter A. signature 80.	.20	1.00	3.00
	d. Letter A. signature 82.	.20	.75	2.50
	e. Letter B. signature 82.	.20	.75	2.50
	f. Letter C. signature 82.	.20	.75	2.50
	g. Letter C. signature 83.	.15	.75	2.50

53A **2 Rupees**

ND. Deep pink and multicolor. English text at right on face. Otherwise like #53. Smaller size serial #.

53A	2 Rupees	VG	VF	UNC
	a. Without letter. signature 83.	.15	.50	2.00
	b. Without letter. signature 84.	.75	2.00	6.00
	c. Letter A. signature 85.	.15	.50	2.00
	d. Letter B. signature 85.	.15	.50	2.00
	e. Letter B. signature 86.	.15	.50	2.00

54	5 Rupees	VG	VF	UNC
	ND. Green and multicolor. Numeral *5* at center 11mm high. Incorrect Urdu inscription at bottom left, antelope at center on back.			
	a. Signature 75 with title: *GOVERNOR* centered at bottom.	.25	2.00	7.00
	b. Signature 76 with title: *GOVERNOR* at center r.	.25	2.00	7.00

55	5 Rupees	VG	VF	UNC
	ND. Dark green on multicolor underprint. Numeral *5* at center 17mm high. Back like #54, antelope at center. Signature 78.	.50	2.00	6.00

56	5 Rupees	VG	VF	UNC
	ND. Dark green on multicolor underprint. Like #55 but antelope at center, corrected Urdu at bottom left on back.			
	a. Without letter. signature 78.	.50	2.00	6.00
	b. Letter A. signature 78.	.50	2.00	6.00

#57-58 incorrect Urdu at bottom l. on back.

57	10 Rupees	VG	VF	UNC
	ND. Purple and multicolor. Numeral *10* at center 30mm broad. Dhow at center on back.			
	a. Signature 75 with title: *GOVERNOR* centered at bottom.	1.00	2.50	10.00
	b. Signature 76 with title: *GOVERNOR* at center r.	1.00	2.50	10.00
58	**10 Rupees**			
	ND. Black on brown and pale green underprint. Numeral *10* at center 18mm broad. Heading in English and Hindi on back. Signature 76.	2.00	6.00	17.50

59	10 Rupees	VG	VF	UNC
	ND. Dark brown on multicolor underprint. Like #58. Heading only in Hindi on back.			
	a. Without letter. signature 78.	.75	1.50	4.00
	b. Letter A. signature 78.	.75	1.50	4.00

60	10 Rupees	VG	VF	UNC
	ND. Dark brown on multicolor underprint. Like #59 but corrected Urdu at bottom left on back.			
	a. Letter A. signature 78.	1.00	2.50	9.00
	b. Letter B. signature 78.	1.00	7.50	40.00
	c. Letter B. signature 80.	1.00	2.50	9.00
	d. Letter B. signature 81.	1.00	10.00	50.00
	e. Letter C. signature 81.	.75	1.50	4.00
	f. Letter C. signature 82.	.75	1.50	4.00
	g. Letter D. signature 82.	.75	1.50	4.00
	h. Letter D. signature 83.	.75	1.50	4.00
	i. Letter E. signature 83.	.75	1.50	4.00
	j. Letter E. signature 84.	.75	1.50	4.00
	k. Letter F. signature 85.	.75	1.50	4.00
	l. Letter G. signature 85.	.75	1.50	4.00

60A	10 Rupees	VG	VF	UNC
	ND. Dark brown on multicolor underprint. With Hindi title above *RESERVE BANK OF INDIA* and Hindi text at left of *10* and *I PROMISE...* at right. Sanskrit title added under Asoka column at right.			
	a. Signature 85.	.50	1.50	4.00
	b. Signature 86. Large serial #.	.75	1.50	4.00
	c. Signature 86. Sm. serial #.	.50	1.50	4.00

Incorrect Kashmiri

Corrected Kashmiri (actually Farsi)

61	20 Rupees	VG	VF	UNC
	ND. Orange and multicolor. Parliament House at center on back. Signature 78.			
	a. dark colors under signature, error in Kashmiri in fifth line on back.	2.00	6.00	20.00
	b. light colors under signature, error in Kashmiri in fifth line on back.	1.50	4.00	10.00

61A	20 Rupees	VG	VF	UNC
	ND. Orange and multicolor. Like #61b but corrected Kashmiri in fifth line on back.	1.50	4.00	10.00

62	100 Rupees	VG	VF	UNC
	ND. Blue and multicolor. Numeral *100* at center 43mm broad. Dam at center with only English heading on back.			
	a. Signature 75.	6.00	15.00	50.00
	b. Signature 76.	6.00	15.00	50.00
63	100 Rupees			
	ND. Blue and multicolor. Numeral *100* at center 28mm broad. Dam at center with only Hindi heading on back. Signature 78.	5.00	12.50	35.00

64	100 Rupees	VG	VF	UNC
	ND. Like #63 but corrected Urdu value line on back.			
	a. Without letter. signature 78.	5.00	12.50	35.00
	b. Without letter. signature 80.	5.00	12.50	35.00
	c. Without letter. signature 81.	5.00	12.50	35.00
	d. Letter A. signature 82.	5.00	12.50	35.00

NOTICE

Readers with unlisted dates, signature varieties, etc. are invited to submit photocopies of their notes to: Standard Catalog of World Paper Money, 700 East State St. Iola, WI 54990-0001, E-Mail: george.cuhaj@fwpubs.com.

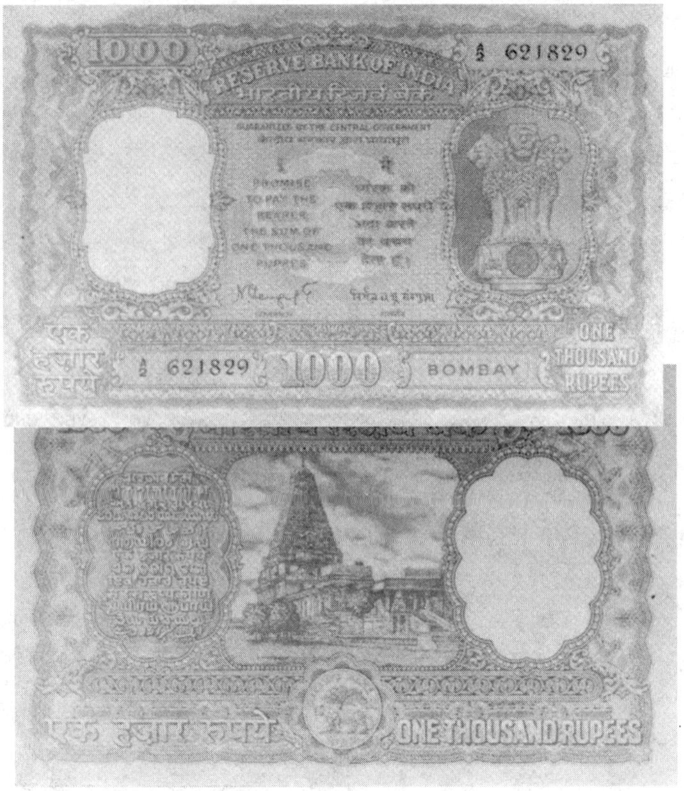

65	1000 Rupees	VG	VF	UNC
	ND. Brown on multicolor underprint. Text in English and Hindi on face. Temple at center on back. *BOMBAY.*			
	a. Signature 79.	40.00	100.	200.
	b. Signature 80.	40.00	100.	200.

Government of India

1969 ND Commemorative Issue

#66, Centennial - Birth of M. K. Gandhi

66	1 Rupee	VG	VF	UNC
	ND (1969-70). Violet and multicolor. Coin with Gandhi and *1869-1948* at right. Reverse of Gandhi coin on back at left. Signature 82.	.75	2.00	6.00

Reserve Bank of India

1969 ND Commemorative Issue

#67-70, Centennial - Birth of M. K. Gandhi

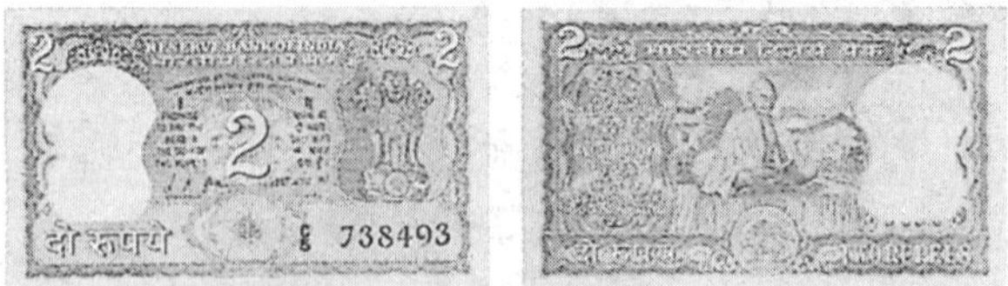

67	2 Rupees	VG	VF	UNC
	ND (1969-70). Red-violet and multicolor. Face like #52. Gandhi seated at center on back.			
	a. Signature 76.	.50	3.00	8.50
	b. Signature 77.	.50	3.00	8.50

		VG	VF	UNC
68	**5 Rupees** ND (1969-70). Dark green on multicolor underprint. Face like #55. Back like #67.			
	a. Signature 76.	.50	3.00	9.00
	b. Signature 77.	.50	4.00	12.50

		VG	VF	UNC
69	**10 Rupees** ND (1969-70). Brown and multicolor. Face like #59. Back like #68.			
	a. Signature 76.	.50	3.50	10.00
	b. Signature 77.	1.00	4.00	12.50
	s. Specimen.	—	—	—

		VG	VF	UNC
70	**100 Rupees** ND (1969-70). Blue and multicolor. Face like #63. Back like #68.			
	a. Signature 76.	5.00	30.00	80.00
	b. Signature 77.	5.00	30.00	80.00
	s. Specimen.	—	—	—

GOVERNMENT OF INDIA

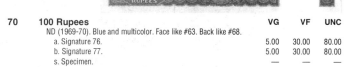

SIGNATURE VARIETIES	
SECRETARIES, MINISTRY OF FINANCE (1 Rupee notes only)	
K. R. K. Menon, 1944	A. K. Roy, 1957
K. G. Ambegaonkar, 1949-1951	L. K. Jha, 1957-1963
H. M. Patel, 1951-1957	

1957; 1963 ISSUE

		VG	VF	UNC
75	**1 Rupee** 1957. Violet on multicolor underprint. Redesigned coin with Asoka column at right. Coin dated 1957 and *100 Naye Paise* in Hindi, 7 value text lines on back. Watermark: Asoka column.			
	a. Letter A. signature H. M. Patel with signature title: *SECRETARY...* (1957).	.50	3.00	10.00
	b. Letter A. signature H. M. Patel with signature title: *PRINCIPAL SECRETARY...* 1957.	.25	2.00	8.00
	c. Letter B. signature A. K. Roy. 1957.	.50	4.00	12.50
	d. Letter B. signature L. K. Jha. 1957.	.75	6.00	40.00
	e. Letter C. signature L. K. Jha. 1957.	.25	1.25	5.00
	f. Letter D. signature L. K. Jha. 1957.	.25	1.25	5.00

Note: For similar note but in red, see #R1 (Persian Gulf listings).

		VG	VF	UNC
76	**1 Rupee** 1963-65. Violet on multicolor underprint. Redesigned note. Coin with various dates and *1 Rupee* in Hindi, thirteen value text lines on back.			
	a. Letter A. signature 35. 1963.	.25	1.25	5.00
	b. Letter B. signature 36. 1964.	1.50	10.00	60.00
	c. Letter B. signature 36. 1965.	.25	1.25	5.00

		VG	VF	UNC
77	**1 Rupee** 1966-80. Violet on multicolor underprint. Redesigned note, serial # at left. Coin with various dates on back.			
	a. Without letter. signature 36. 1966.	.20	.75	3.00
	b. Letter A. signature 37. 1967.	.25	1.25	5.00
	c. Letter A. signature 37. 1968.	.25	1.00	4.00
	d. Letter B. signature 38 with signature title: *SPECIAL SECRETARY...* 1968.	.20	.75	3.00
	e. Letter B. signature 38 with signature title: *SPECIAL SECRETARY...* 1969.	.20	.75	3.00
	f. Letter C. signature 38 with title: *SPECIAL SECRETARY...* 1969.	.20	.75	3.00
	g. Letter C. signature 38. 1970.	.20	.75	3.00
	h. Letter C. signature 38. 1971.	.20	.75	3.00
	i. Letter D. signature 38. 1971.	.20	.75	3.00
	j. Letter D. signature 38. 1972.	.20	.75	3.00
	k. Letter E. signature 38. 1972.	.20	.75	3.00
	l. Letter E. signature 39. 1973.	.20	.75	3.00
	m. Letter F. signature 39. 1973.	.20	.75	3.00
	n. Letter F. signature 39. 1974.	.20	.75	3.00
	o. Letter G. signature 39. 1974.	.20	.75	3.00
	p. Letter G. signature 39. 1975.	.20	.75	3.00
	q. Letter H. signature 39. 1975.	.25	1.00	4.00
	r. Letter H. signature 39. 1976.	.20	.75	3.00
	s. Letter I. signature 39. 1976.	.25	1.25	5.00
	t. Without letter. Sm. serial #. signature 40. 1976.	.20	.75	3.00
	u. Sm. serial #. signature 40. 1977.	.20	.75	3.00
	v. Letter A. signature 40. 1978.	.20	.75	3.00
	w. Letter A. signature 40. 1979.	.20	.75	3.00
	x. Letter A. signature 40. 1980.	.20	.75	3.00
	y. Letter A. signature 41. 1980.	.20	.75	3.00
	z. Letter B. signature 41. 1980.	.20	.75	3.00

		VG	VF	UNC
78	**1 Rupee** 1981. Purple and violet on light blue, brown and multicolor underprint. Coin with Asoka column at upper right. Offshore oil drilling platform and reverse of coin with date on back.			
	a. Signature 41. 1981.	.10	.25	1.00
	b. Signature 42. 1981.	.10	.50	2.00

78A	1 Rupee	VG	VF	UNC
	1983-1994. Similar to #78 but with new coin design.			
	a. Signature 43 with title: *SECRETARY...* 1983-85.	.10	.20	1.00
	b. Signature 44 with title: *FINANCE SECRETARY...* 1985.	.10	.20	1.00
	c. Letter A. signature 44. 1986-89.	.10	.20	1.00
	d. Letter B. signature 45. 1989.	.10	.50	2.00
	e. Letter B. signature 46. 1990.	.10	.50	2.00
	f. Letter B. signature 47. 1991.	.10	.75	2.50
	g. Letter B. signature 48 with title: *SECRETARY...* 1991.	.10	.75	2.50
	h. Letter B. signature 48. 1992.	.10	.75	2.50
	i. Letter B. signature 48 with title: *FINANCE SECRETARY...* 1993.	.10	.75	2.50
	j. Letter B. signature 48. 1994.	.20	1.00	3.00

RESERVE BANK OF INDIA

THIRD SERIES

Lg. letters in unpt. beneath serial #.

#79-88 Asoka column at r. and as wmk.

79	2 Rupees	VG	VF	UNC
	ND(1976). Orange on multicolor underprint. Space craft at center on back.			
	a. Signature 80.	.20	.75	2.00
	b. Signature 81.	.20	.75	2.00
	c. Without letter. Without watermark. signature 82.	.25	.75	2.00
	d. Without letter. With watermark: 6 wheels surrounding Asoka column. signature 82.	.15	.60	2.00
	e. Letter A. signature 82.	.15	.60	2.00
	f. Letter A. signature 83.	.20	.75	2.00
	g. Letter A. signature 84.	.20	.75	2.00
	h. Letter A. signature 85.	.15	.60	2.00
	i. Letter B. signature 85.	.15	.60	2.00
	j. Without letter. signature 85 With *Satyameva Jayate* added below the Ashoka Pillar.	.15	.60	2.00
	k. Letter A. signature 85 with *Satyameva Jayate* added below the Ashoka Pillar.	.15	.60	2.00
	l. Letter B. signature 86.	.10	.50	2.00
	m. Letter B. signature 87.	.10	.50	2.00

80	5 Rupees	VG	VF	UNC
	ND(1975). Grayish green on light blue and orange underprint. Farmer plowing with tractor at center on back.			
	a. Without letter. signature 78.	.50	1.00	2.00
	b. Without letter. signature 80.	.50	1.00	2.00
	c. Letter A. signature 80.	.50	1.00	2.00
	d. Letter A. signature 81.	.50	1.00	2.00
	e. Letter A. signature 82.	.50	1.00	2.00
	f. Letter B. signature 82.	.50	1.00	2.00
	g. Letter C. signature 82.	.50	1.00	2.00
	h. Letter C. signature 83.	.25	.75	2.00
	i. Letter D. signature 83.	.25	.75	2.00
	j. Letter D. signature 84.	.50	1.00	2.00
	k. Letter D. signature 85.	.25	.75	2.00
	l. Letter E. signature 85.	.25	.75	2.00
	m. Letter F. signature 85.	.25	.75	2.00
	n. Letter G. signature 85.	.25	.75	2.00
	o. Without letter. New Seal in Hindi & English. signature 85.	.25	.75	2.00
	p. Letter A. New Seal - do - signature 85.	.25	.75	2.00
	q. Letter B. signature 86.	.15	.50	2.00
	r. Letter B. signature 87.	.15	.50	2.00
	s. Without letter. signature 88.	.15	.50	2.00

81	10 Rupees	VG	VF	UNC
	ND. Brown on multicolor underprint. Tree with peacocks at center on back.			
	a. Without letter. signature 78.	.50	2.00	7.00
	b. Without letter. signature 80.	.50	2.00	7.00
	c. Without letter. signature 81.	.50	2.50	10.00
	d. Letter A. signature 82.	.50	1.50	3.00
	e. Without letter. signature 82.	.50	1.50	3.00
	f. Letter A. signature 83.	.50	1.50	3.00
	g. Letter B. signature 85.	.50	1.50	3.00
	h. Letter C. signature 85.	.50	1.50	3.00

82	20 Rupees	VG	VF	UNC
	ND. Red and purple on multicolor underprint. Back orange on multicolor underprint; Hindu Wheel of Time at lower center.			
	a. Signature 78.	.50	3.50	12.50
	b. Signature 80.	.50	2.50	5.00
	c. Signature 81.	.50	7.50	25.00
	d. Without letter. signature 82.	.50	3.00	9.00
	e. Letter A. signature 82.	.50	2.50	5.00
	f. Letter A. signature 83.	.50	2.00	6.00
	g. Letter A. signature 85.	.50	2.00	6.00
	h. Letter B. signature 85.	.50	2.00	6.00
	i. Letter B. signature 87.	.50	1.50	4.00
	j. Letter C. signature 87.	.50	1.50	4.00
	k. Letter C. signature 88.	.50	1.50	4.00
	l. Letter C. signature 89.	.50	1.50	4.00

83	50 Rupees	VG	VF	UNC
	ND(1975). Black and purple on lilac and multicolor underprint. Parliament House at center without flag at top of flagpole on back.			
	a. Signature 78.	.75	5.00	15.00
	b. Signature 80.	.75	4.00	12.50
	c. Signature 81.	.75	7.50	30.00
	d. Signature 82.	.75	3.50	10.00

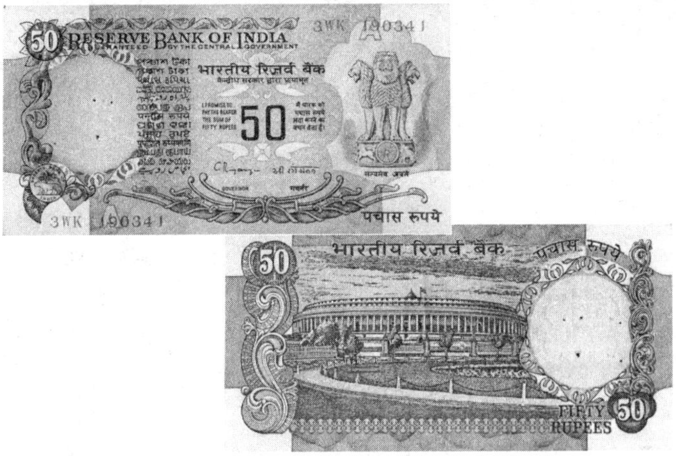

84 50 Rupees

ND(1978). Black and purple on orange, lilac and multicolor underprint. Similar to #83 but with flag at top of flagpole on back.

	VG	VF	UNC
a. Signature 82.	.75	3.00	9.00
b. Signature 83.	.75	3.00	9.00
c. Signature 85.	.75	2.50	9.00
d. Letter A. signature 85.	.75	3.00	9.00
e. Letter B. signature 85.	.75	3.00	9.00
f. Letter A. signature 86.	.75	2.50	7.00
g. Letter B. signature 86.	.75	2.50	7.00
h. Letter A. signature 87.	.75	2.00	5.00
i. Letter B. signature 87.	.75	2.00	5.00
j. Letter C. signature 87.	.75	2.00	5.00
k. Without letter. signature 87. Reported not confirmed.	—	—	—
l. Letter B. signature 88.	1.00	2.00	5.00

85 100 Rupees

ND(1975). Black and blue-violet on brown and multicolor underprint (tan at center.). Dam, agricultural work at center on back. Denomination above bar at lower right. Black signature.

	VG	VF	UNC
a. Signature 78.	3.00	15.00	100.
b. Signature 80.	2.00	6.00	20.00
c. Signature 81.	3.00	12.50	35.00
d. Signature 82.	2.00	6.00	15.00

85A 100 Rupees

	VG	VF	UNC
ND. Like #85 but without bar under denomination at lower right. Signature 85.	2.00	6.00	15.00

86 100 Rupees

ND(1979). Black, deep red and purple on multicolor underprint. (pink at ctr.). Like #85A. Deep red signature.

	VG	VF	UNC
a. Signature 82.	1.50	5.00	15.00
b. Signature 83.	1.50	5.00	15.00
c. Signature 85.	1.50	4.00	12.50
d. Signature 86.	1.50	4.00	8.50
e. Letter A. signature 86.	1.50	4.00	8.50
f. Without letter. signature 87.	1.50	4.00	8.50
g. Letter A. signature 87.	1.50	4.00	8.50
h. Letter B. signature 87.	1.50	4.00	8.50

87 500 Rupees

ND (1987). Brown, deep blue-green and deep blue on multicolor underprint. M. K. Gandhi at center right. Electronic sorting marks at lower left. Gandhi leading followers across back.

	VG	VF	UNC
a. Signature 85.	FV	20.00	40.00
b. Signature 86.	FV	FV	37.50
c. Signature 87.	FV	FV	35.00

1992 Issue

88 10 Rupees

ND (1992). Dull brown-violet on orange, green and multicolor underprint. Back red-violet; rural temple at left center.

	VG	VF	UNC
a. Signature 86.	.50	1.25	3.00
b. Letter A. signature 86.	.50	1.25	3.00
c. Letter A. signature 87.	.50	1.25	3.00
d. Letter B. signature 87.	.50	1.25	3.00
e. Letter C. signature 87.	.50	1.25	3.00
f. Letter D. signature 87.	.25	1.25	2.50
g. Letter E. signature 87.	.25	1.25	2.50

1996-2002 ND Issue

#89-93 M. K. Gandhi at r. and as wmk. Reserve Bank seal at lower r. In 1999 the name was spelled out as Mahatma Gandhi.

88A 5 Rupees
ND(2002). Green-orange on multicolor underprint. Mahatma Gandhi at right and as watermark. Farmer plowing with tractor at center on back.

	VG	VF	UNC
a. Without letter. signature 88.	FV	FV	1.00
b. Letter L; R. signature 88.	FV	FV	1.00
c. Without letter. signature 89.	FV	FV	1.00
d. Letter L, R. signature 89.	FV	FV	1.00

89 10 Rupees
ND (1996). Pale brown-violet on multicolor underprint. Ornamented rhinoceros and elephant heads behind tiger at left center on back.

	VG	VF	UNC
a. Without letter. signature 87.	FV	FV	1.00
b. Letter L; M; R. signature 87.	FV	FV	1.00
c. Letter R; N; A; P; Q; S; T; L; B; M. signature 88.	FV	FV	1.00
d. Without letter. signature 89.	FV	FV	1.00
e. Letter A, R. signature 89.	FV	FV	1.00

89A 20 Rupees
ND(2002). Red-orange on multicolor underprint. Mahatma Gandhi at right and as watermark. Coconut trees on back.

	VG	VF	UNC
a. Without letter. signature 88.	FV	FV	2.00
b. Letter A; R. signature 88.	FV	FV	2.00
c. Without letter. signature 89.	FV	FV	2.00
d. Letter A; R. signature 89.	FV	FV	2.00

90 50 Rupees
ND (1997). Black and purple on multicolor underprint. Parliament house at left center on back.

	VG	VF	UNC
a. Without letter. signature 87.	FV	FV	4.00
b. Without letter. signature 88.	FV	FV	3.50
c. Letter A. signature 88.	FV	FV	3.50
d. Letter R. signature 88.	FV	FV	3.50
e. Letter A. signature 88.	FV	FV	3.50
f. Letter E. signature 88.	FV	FV	3.50
g. Letter L. signature 88.	FV	FV	3.50
h. Without letter. signature 89.	FV	FV	3.50
i. Letter A. signature 89.	FV	FV	3.50
j. Letter E. signature 89.	FV	FV	3.50
k. Letter R. signature 89.	FV	FV	3.50

91 100 Rupees
ND (1996). Black, purple and dark olive-green on pale blue-green and multicolor underprint. Himalaya mountains at left center on back. Segmented foil over security thread.

	VG	VF	UNC
a. Without letter. signature 87.	FV	2.50	9.00
b. Letter E. signature 87.	FV	2.50	9.00
c. Letter L. signature 87.	FV	2.50	9.00
d. Letter A. signature 87.	FV	FV	7.00
e. Letter L. signature 88.	FV	FV	7.00
f. Letter E. signature 88.	FV	FV	7.00
g. Without letter. signature 88.	FV	FV	7.00
h. Letter R. signature 88.	FV	FV	7.00
i. Letter F. signature 88.	FV	FV	7.00
j. Letter B. signature 88.	FV	FV	7.00
k. Without letter. signature 89.	FV	FV	7.00
l. Letter L. signature 89.	FV	FV	7.00
m. Letter R. signature 89.	FV	FV	

92 500 Rupees
ND (1997). Dark brown, olive-green and purple on multicolor underprint. Similar to #87. Segmented foil over security thread.

	VG	VF	UNC
a. Without letter. signature 87.	FV	FV	40.00
b. Without letter. signature 88.	FV	FV	40.00
c. Letter A. signature 88.	FV	FV	40.00
d. Letter C. signature 88.	FV	FV	40.00

2000-02 ND Issue

93 500 Rupees
ND (2000-02). Pale yellow, mauve and brown. Like #92 but different colors. Value at center in optical variable ink.

	VG	VF	UNC
a. Without letter. signature 88.	FV	FV	37.50
b. Letter A. signature 88.	FV	FV	37.50
c. Letter B. signature 88.	FV	FV	37.50
d. Letter C. signature 88.	FV	FV	37.50
e. Without letter. signature 89.	FV	FV	33.50
f. Letter A. signature 89.	FV	FV	33.50
g. Letter B. signature 89.	FV	FV	33.50
h. Letter C. signature 89.	FV	FV	33.50

		VG	VF	UNC
94	**1000 Rupees** ND (2000). Pink and gray. M. K. Gandhi at right. Back brown, red and black; allegory of Indian economy.			
	a. Without letter. signature 88.	FV	FV	65.00
	b. Letter A. signature 88.	FV	FV	65.00
	c. Without letter. signature 89.	FV	FV	65.00
	d. Letter A. signature 89.	FV	FV	65.00

PERSIAN GULF

Intended for circulation in areas of Oman, Bahrain, Qatar and Trucial States during 1950's and early 1960's.
"Z" prefix in serial # Known as "Gulf Rupees".

RESERVE BANK OF INDIA

ND ISSUE

		VG	VF	UNC
R2	**5 Rupees** ND. Orange. Like #35a. Signature H. V. R. Iengar.	100.	200.	500.

		VG	VF	UNC
R3	**10 Rupees** ND. Red. Like #39c. Letter A. Signature H. V. R. Iengar.	25.00	125.	350.

		VG	VF	UNC
R4	**100 Rupees** ND. Green. Like #43b. Signature H. V. R. Iengar.	65.00	350.	1350.

GOVERNMENT OF INDIA

ND ISSUE

		VG	VF	UNC
R1	**1 Rupee** ND. Red. Like #75c. signature A. K. Roy; left. K. Jha or H. V. R. Iengar.	25.00	50.00	200.

NOTICE

Readers with unlisted dates, signature varieties, etc. are invited to submit photocopies of their notes to: Standard Catalog of World Paper Money, 700 East State St. Iola, WI 54990-0001, E-Mail: george.cuhaj@fwpubs.com.

HAJ PILGRIM

Intended for use by Moslem pilgrims in Mecca, Saudi Arabia.

RESERVE BANK OF INDIA

(ND) ISSUE

#R5 and R6 Asoka column at r. Letters *HA* near serial #, and *HAJ* at l. and r. of bank title at top.

		VG	VF	UNC
R5	**10 Rupees** ND. Blue. Like #39c. Signature H. V. R. Iengar.	250.	500.	1000.
R6	**100 Rupees** ND. Red. Like #43b. Signature H. V. R. Iengar.	500.	1000.	—

The Republic of Indonesia, the world's largest archipelago, extends for more than 3,000 miles (4,827 km.) along the equator from the mainland of southeast Asia to Australia. The 13,667 islands comprising the archipelago have a combined area of 735,268 sq. mi. (2,042,005 sq. km.) and a population of 202 million, including East Timor. Capital: Jakarta. Petroleum, timber, rubber and coffee are exported.

Had Columbus succeeded in reaching the fabled Spice Islands, he would have found advanced civilizations a millennium old, and temples still ranked among the finest examples of ancient art. During the opening centuries of the Christian era, the islands were influenced by Hindu priests and traders who spread their culture and religion. Moslem invasions began in the 13th century, fragmenting the island kingdoms into small states which were unable to resist Western colonial infiltration. Portuguese traders established posts in the 16th century, but they were soon outnumbered by the Dutch who arrived in 1602 and gradually asserted control over the islands comprising present-day Indonesia. Dutch dominance, interrupted by British incursions during the Napoleonic Wars, established the Netherlands East Indies as one of the richest colonial possessions in the world.

The Indonesian independence movement, which began between the two world wars, was encouraged by the Japanese during their 3-year occupation during World War II. Indonesia proclaimed its independence on Aug. 17, 1945, three days after the surrender of Japan, and was established on Dec. 28, 1949, after four years of Dutch military efforts to reassert control. West Irian, formerly Netherlands New Guinea, came under the administration of Indonesia on May 1, 1963.

MONETARY SYSTEM:

1 Rupiah = 100 Sen, 1945-

REPUBLIC

REPUBLIK INDONESIA

1961 ISSUE

		VG	VF	UNC
78	**1 Rupiah** 1961. Dark green on orange underprint. Like #76.	.10	.25	.75

		VG	VF	UNC
79	**2 1/2 Rupiah** 1961. Black, dark blue and brown on blue-green underprint. Like #77.	.10	.25	.75

1961 BORNEO ISSUE

#79A and 79B portr. Pres. Sukarno at l. Javanese dancer at r. on back.

		VG	VF	UNC
79A	**1 Rupiah** 1961. Green on orange underprint.	1.00	4.00	10.00

		VG	VF	UNC
79B	**2 1/2 Rupiah** 1961. Blue on gray-brown underprint.	1.00	4.00	10.00

1964 ISSUE (1960 DATED)

#80 and 81 portr. Pres. Sukarno at l. Wmk: Arms at ctr.

		VG	VF	UNC
80	**1 Rupiah** 1964. Black, red and brown.			
	a. Imprint: *Pertjetakan Kebajoran* at bottom center on face.	.25	1.00	3.00
	b. Without imprint.	.50	2.00	6.00
81	**2 1/2 Rupiah** 1964. Black, blue and brown.			
	a. Imprint like #80a.	.75	2.50	7.50
	b. Without imprint.	.85	3.00	8.00

#82-88 Pres. Sukarno at l. Javanese dancers on most backs.

		VG	VF	UNC
82	**5 Rupiah** 1960. Lilac. Female dancer at right on back.			
	a. Watermark: Sukarno.	.25	1.50	5.00
	b. Watermark: Water buffalo.	.30	.60	6.00

BANK INDONESIA

1960 DATED (1964) ISSUE

#82-88 Pres. Sukarno at l. Dancers on back.

		VG	VF	UNC
83	**10 Rupiah** 1960. Green. 2 female dancers. Watermark: Sukarno.	.50	2.00	6.00

		VG	VF	UNC
84	**25 Rupiah** 1960. Green on yellow. Female dancer on back.			
	a. Printer: TDLR. watermark: Sukarno.	1.00	4.00	10.00
	b. Printer: Pertjetakan. watermark: Water buffalo.	1.00	4.00	10.00

		VG	VF	UNC
85	**50 Rupiah** 1960. Dark blue. Female dancer and 2 men on back.			
	a. Printer: TDLR. watermark: Sukarno.	2.00	8.00	20.00
	b. Printer: Pertjetakan. watermark: Water buffalo.	1.50	4.50	12.50

86	100 Rupiah	VG	VF	UNC
	1960. Red-brown. Man and woman dancer on back.			
	a. Printer: Pertjetakan. watermark: Sukarno.	2.50	10.00	22.50
	b. Watermark: Water buffalo. Reported not confirmed.	—	—	—

87	500 Rupiah	VG	VF	UNC
	1960. Black. Two dancers on back.			
	a. Printer: TDLR. watermark: Sukarno.	7.50	15.00	75.00
	b. Printer: Pertjetakan. watermark: Sukarno.	7.50	15.00	75.00
	c. Printer like b. watermark: Water buffalo.	7.50	15.00	75.00
	d. Printer like b. watermark: Arms.	10.00	20.00	80.00

88	1000 Rupiah	VG	VF	UNC
	1960. Dark green. 2 dancers on back.			
	a. Printer: TDLR. watermark: Sukarno.	25.00	60.00	150.
	b. Printer: Pertjetakan. watermark: Water buffalo.	15.00	40.00	110.

1963 Issue

89	10 Rupiah	VG	VF	UNC
	1963. Pale blue and brown on multicolor underprint. Balinese wood carver at left. Balinese houses at center, mythical figure at right on back. Watermark: Water buffalo.	.15	.50	1.50

1964 Issue

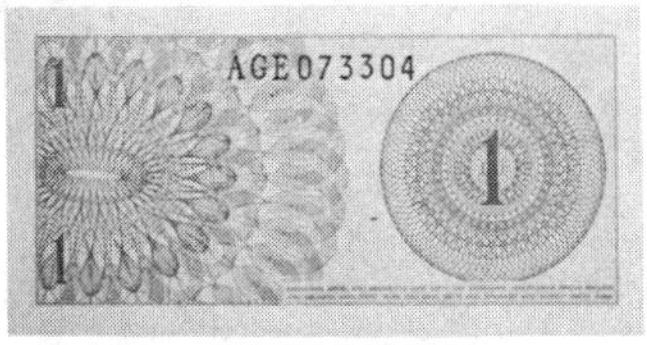

90	1 Sen	VG	VF	UNC
	1964. Green-blue and brown. Peasant with straw hat at right.			
	a. Issued note.	—	.05	.10
	s. Specimen.	—	—	15.00

91	5 Sen	VG	VF	UNC
	1964. Lilac-brown. Female volunteer in uniform at right.			
	a. Issued note.	—	.05	.10
	s. Specimen.	—	—	15.00

92	10 Sen	VG	VF	UNC
	1964. Dark blue on yellow-green underprint. Like #91.			
	a. Issued note.	—	.05	.10
	s. Specimen.	—	—	15.00

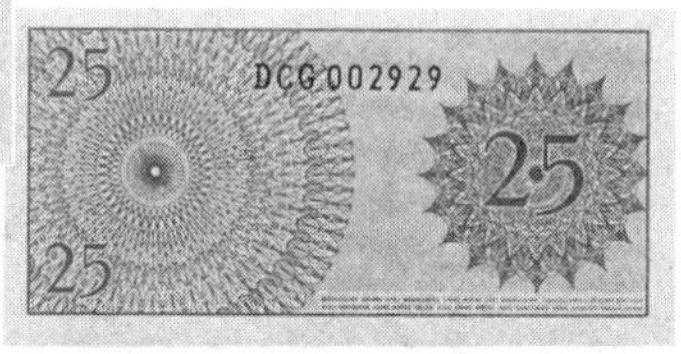

93	25 Sen	VG	VF	UNC
	1964. Red on yellow-green underprint. A volunteer in uniform at right.			
	a. Issued note.	—	.05	.15
	s. Specimen.	—	—	15.00

94	50 Sen	VG	VF	UNC
	1964. Purple and red. Like #93.			
	a. Issued note.	—	.10	.25
	s. Specimen.	—	—	15.00
95	**25 Rupiah**			
	1964. Green on light brown underprint. Batak woman weaver at left, printed arms in brown at right. Batak house at center on back.	.20	.50	2.00

96 50 Rupiah VG VF UNC

1964. Black and green on aqua underprint. Timor woman spinner at left, printed arms in pale green at right. Rice barns at center on back. .15 .50 1.50

97 100 Rupiah VG VF UNC

1964. Brown and red on light tan underprint. Rubber tapper at left. Kalimantan house at center on back. Watermark: Water buffalo.

a. Printer's name: *P. T. Pertjetakan Kebajoran Imp.* 16mm. long at right on back. .50 2.00 6.00

b. Printer's name: *PN Pertjetakan Kebajoran Imp.* 22mm. long at right on back. .25 1.25 4.00

98 100 Rupiah VG VF UNC

1964. Blue on light tan underprint. Like #97b. Printed arms in brown at left. .50 1.50 5.00

99 10,000 Rupiah

1964. Red and dark brown on multicolor underprint. Two fishermen at left. Floating houses at center on back. Watermark: Water buffalo. 1.50 4.00 20.00

100 10,000 Rupiah

1964. Green. Like #99. .75 2.00 6.00

101 10,000 Rupiah VG VF UNC

1964. Green. Like #100, but watermark with printed arms in pale green at right.

a. Watermark. in paper at center. 1.25 5.00 22.50

b. Watermark. in paper at left and r. 1.25 5.00 22.50

1968 ISSUE

#102-112 Gen. Sudirman at l.

#102 and 103 wmk: Arms at ctr.

102 1 Rupiah VG VF UNC

1968. Light red on light blue and purple underprint. Arms at right. Woman collecting copra at left on back.

a. Issued note. .25 .75 2.25

s. Specimen. — — 15.00

103 2 1/2 Rupiah VG VF UNC

1968. Dark blue on red and blue underprint. Arms at right. Woman gathering paddy rice stalks at left on back.

a. Issued note. .25 .75 2.25

s. Specimen. — — 15.00

#104-110 wmk: Arms at r. upper ctr.

104 5 Rupiah VG VF UNC

1968. Pale purple on multicolor underprint. Jatiluhur Dam construction on back.

a. Issued note. .50 1.50 4.50

s. Specimen. — — 15.00

105	10 Rupiah	VG	VF	UNC
	1968. Brown on green and multicolor underprint. Oil refinery on back.			
	a. Issued note.	.25	1.00	3.00
	s. Specimen.	—	—	15.00
106	25 Rupiah			
	1968. Green on light brown and multicolor underprint. Back brown; Ampera lift bridge over Musi River at center right.			
	a. Issued note.	.50	1.50	4.50
	s. Specimen.	—	—	15.00

107	50 Rupiah	VG	VF	UNC
	1968. Purple and dark blue on multicolor underprint. Airplanes in repair hangar at center right on back.			
	a. Issued note.	.75	2.50	7.50
	s. Specimen.	—	—	15.00

108	100 Rupiah	VG	VF	UNC
	1968. Deep red on multicolor underprint. Facility at the port of Tanjung Priok at center right on back.			
	a. Issued note.	.50	1.50	5.00
	s. Specimen.	—	—	15.00

NOTICE

Readers with unlisted dates, signature varieties, etc. are invited to submit photocopies of their notes to: Standard Catalog of World Paper Money, 700 East State St. Iola, WI 54990-0001, E-Mail: george.cuhaj@fwpubs.com.

109	500 Rupiah	VG	VF	UNC
	1968. Black and dark green on multicolor underprint. Yarn spinning in cotton mill on back.			
	a. Issued note.	.75	2.50	7.50
	s. Specimen.	—	—	15.00

110	1000 Rupiah	VG	VF	UNC
	1968. Orange and black on multicolor underprint. P.T. Pusri fertilizer plant at center right on back.			
	a. Issued note.	1.00	3.00	12.00
	s. Specimen.	—	—	15.00

Note: Deceptive forgeries of #110 exist. #111 and 112 wmk: Prince Diponegoro. Two serial # varieties.

111	5000 Rupiah	VG	VF	UNC
	1968. Blue-green on multicolor underprint. Tonasa cememt plant at center right on back.			
	a. Issued note.	5.00	22.50	70.00
	s. Specimen.	—	—	15.00
112	10,000 Rupiah			
	1968. Red-brown and dark brown on multicolor underprint. Back purple; tin mininig facility in Bangla at center right.			
	a. Issued note.	5.00	20.00	60.00
	s. Specimen.	—	—	15.00

1975; ND Issue

#112 A, B, C, 113A, 114A wmk: Prince Diponegoro.

		VG	VF	UNC
112A	**100 Rupiah** ND. Red on multicolor underprint. Prince Diponegoro at left. Mountain scenery at left center on back. (Not issued.)			
	a. Normal serial #.	—	—	—
	s. Specimen.	—	—	—

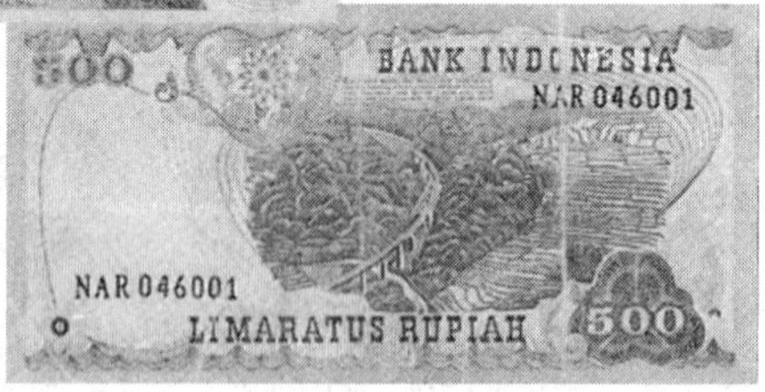

		VG	VF	UNC
112B	**500 Rupiah** ND. Green on multicolor underprint. Prince Diponegoro at left. Terraced rice fields in Sianok Gorge on back. (Not issued.)			
	a. Normal serial #.	—	—	—
	s. Specimen.	—	—	—

		VG	VF	UNC
113	**1000 Rupiah** ND; 1975. Blue-green and blue on multicolor underprint. Prince Diponegoro at left. Farmer plowing in terraced rice fields on back.			
	a. 1975. watermark: Majapahit statue.	.50	2.00	7.50
	s. ND. Specimen. (Not issued.)	—	—	—

		VG	VF	UNC
113A	**5000 Rupiah** ND. Brown on multicolor underprint. Prince Diponegoro at right. Three sailing ships on back. (Not issued.)			
	a. Normal serial #.	—	—	—
	s. Specimen.	—	—	—

		VG	VF	UNC
114	**5000 Rupiah** 1975. Brown and red-brown on multicolor underprint. Fisherman with net at right. Back like #113A. Watermark: Tjut Njak Din.	2.50	7.50	25.00

		VG	VF	UNC
114A	**10,000 Rupiah** ND. Green and red on multicolor underprint. Face like #113A. Peasants at center on back. (Not issued.)			
	a. Normal serial #.	—	—	—
	s. Specimen.	—	—	—

		VG	VF	UNC
115	**10,000 Rupiah** 1975. Brown, red and multicolor. Stone relief at Borobudur Temple. Large mask from Bali at left on back. Watermark: Surkano.	7.50	25.00	75.00

NOTICE

Readers with unlisted dates, signature varieties, etc. are invited to submit photocopies of their notes to: Standard Catalog of World Paper Money, 700 East State St. Iola, WI 54990-0001, E-Mail: george.cuhaj@fwpubs.com.

1977 Issue

		VG	VF	UNC
116	**100 Rupiah** 1977. Red on multicolor underprint. Java Rhinoceros at left. Java Rhinoceros in jungle scene at center on back. Watermark: Arms.	.25	.50	2.00

		VG	VF	UNC
117	**500 Rupiah** 1977. Green on pink and multicolor underprint. Woman with orchids at left. Bank of Indonesia at center on back and as watermark.	.25	1.00	4.00

1979 Issue

		VG	VF	UNC
118	**10,000 Rupiah** 1979. Purple on multicolor underprint. Javanese Gamelan Orchestra at center. Prambanan Temple on back. Watermark: Dr. Soetomo.	3.00	9.00	25.00

NOTICE

Readers with unlisted dates, signature varieties, etc. are invited to submit photocopies of their notes to: Standard Catalog of World Paper Money, 700 East State St. Iola, WI 54990-0001, E-Mail: george.cuhaj@fwpubs.com.

1980 Issue

		VG	VF	UNC
119	**1000 Rupiah** 1980. Blue on multicolor underprint. Dr. Soetomo at center right. Mountain scene in Sianok Valley on back. Watermark: Sultan Hasanudin.	.25	1.00	3.50

		VG	VF	UNC
120	**5000 Rupiah** 1980. Brown on multicolor underprint. Diamond cutter at center. Back brown, green and multicolor. Three Torajan houses from Celebes at center.			
	a. Watermark: D. Sartika.	2.00	6.00	20.00
	p. Proof. watermark: Prince Diponegoro.	—	—	—

1982 Issue

		VG	VF	UNC
121	**500 Rupiah** 1982. Dark green on multicolor underprint. Man standing by Amorphophallus Titanum giant flower at left. Bank of Indonesia on back. Watermark: Gen. A. Yani.	.25	.75	2.50

1984-88 Issue

122	100 Rupiah	VG	VF	UNC
	1984. Red on multicolor underprint. Victoria crowned pigeon at left. Asahan Dam on back. Watermark: Arms.			
	a. Engraved.	.10	.30	1.25
	b. Litho.	.05	.25	.75
	s. As a. Specimen.	—	—	15.00

123	500 Rupiah	VG	VF	UNC
	1988. Brown and dark green on multicolor underprint. Rusa Deer at left. Bank of Indonesia Cirebon branch at right on back. Watermark: Gen. A. Yani.			
	a. Issued note.	.20	.50	1.50
	s. Specimen.	—	—	15.00

124	1000 Rupiah	VG	VF	UNC
	1987. Blue-black on multicolor underprint. Raja Sisingamangaraja XII at center, arms at left. Yogyakarta Court at center on back. Watermark: Sultan Hasanuddin.			
	a. Issued note.	.25	1.00	2.00
	s. Specimen.	—	—	15.00

125	5000 Rupiah	VG	VF	UNC
	1986. Dark brown on multicolor underprint. Teuku Umar at center. Minaret of Kudus mosque at right on back. Watermark: C. Martha Tijahahu.			
	a. Issued note.	1.50	3.50	10.00
	s. Specimen.	—	—	15.00

126	10,000 Rupiah	VG	VF	UNC
	1985. Purple on multicolor underprint. R. A. Kartini at left. Prambanan Temple at center. Female graduate at center right on back. Watermark: Dr. T. Mangoenkoesoemo.			
	a. Issued note.	2.00	6.00	15.00
	s. Specimen.	—	—	15.00

1992 ISSUE

#127-132 arms at upper r. area. Printer: Perum Percetakan Uang.

#127-129 second date appears after imprint.

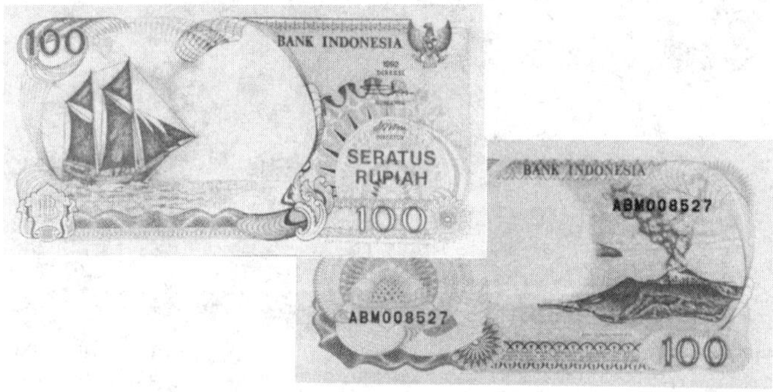

127	100 Rupiah	VG	VF	UNC
	1992-2000. Pale red on orange and multicolor underprint. Sailboat *Pinisi* at left. Volcano *Anak Krakatau* at right on back. Watermark: Ki Hajar Dewantara.			
	a. 1992.	FV	FV	.75
	b. 1992/1993.	FV	FV	.50
	c. 1992/1994.	FV	FV	.50
	d. 1992/1995.	FV	FV	.45
	e. 1992/1996.	FV	FV	.25
	f. 1992/1997.	FV	FV	.25
	g. 1992/1999.	FV	FV	.25
	h. 1992/2000.	FV	FV	.20

128	500 Rupiah	VG	VF	UNC
	1992-99. Brown and green on multicolor underprint. Orangutan resting on limb at left. Native huts at E. Kalimantan at right on back. Watermark: H. O. S. Cokroaminoto.			
	a. 1992.	FV	FV	1.25
	b. 1992/1993.	FV	FV	1.00
	c. 1992/1994.	FV	FV	1.00
	d. 1992/1995.	FV	FV	1.00
	e. 1992/1996.	FV	FV	.50
	f. 1992/1997.	FV	FV	.40
	g. 1992/1998.	FV	FV	.30
	h. 1992/1999.	FV	FV	.20

129	1000 Rupiah	VG	VF	UNC
	1992-2000. Deep blue on light blue and multicolor underprint. Aerial view of Lake Toba at left center. Stone jumping attraction on Nias Island at center on back. Watermark: Cut Nyak Meutia.			
	a. 1992.	FV	FV	2.00
	b. 1992/1993.	FV	FV	1.75
	c. 1992/1994.	FV	FV	1.75
	d. 1992/1995.	FV	FV	1.50
	e. 1992/1996.	FV	FV	1.00
	f. 1992/1997.	FV	FV	.75
	g. 1992/1998.	FV	FV	.75
	h. 1992/1999.	FV	FV	.50
	i. 1992/2000.	FV	FV	.50

130	5000 Rupiah	VG	VF	UNC
	1992-2001. Black, brown and dark brown on multicolor underprint. Sasando musical instrument and Rote Island tapestry at center. Volcano with three-color Lake Kelimutu at center on back. Watermark: Tjut Njak Din.			
	a. 1992.	FV	FV	7.50
	b. 1992/1993.	FV	FV	7.00
	c. 1992/1994.	FV	FV	7.00
	d. 1992/1995.	FV	FV	6.50
	e. 1992/1996.	FV	FV	3.50
	f. 1992/1997.	FV	FV	2.50
	g. 1992/1998.	FV	FV	1.50
	h. 1992/1999.	FV	FV	1.25
	i. 1992/2000.	FV	FV	1.25
	j. 1999/2001.	FV	FV	1.25
	s. Specimen.	—	—	—

131	10,000 Rupiah	VG	VF	UNC
	1992-98. Purple and red on multicolor underprint. Sri Sultan Hamengku Buwono IX at left, girl scouts at center right. Borobudur Temple on hillside on back. Watermark: W. R. Soepratman.			
	a. 1992.	2.00	6.00	12.50
	b. 1992/1993.	2.00	6.00	12.00
	c. 1992/1994.	2.00	5.00	12.00
	d. 1992/1995.	2.00	5.00	10.00
	e. 1992/1996.	1.50	3.00	6.00
	f. 1992/1997.	1.00	2.00	4.00
	g. 1992/1998 & letter prefix.	2.00	7.50	15.00
	s. Specimen.	—	—	—

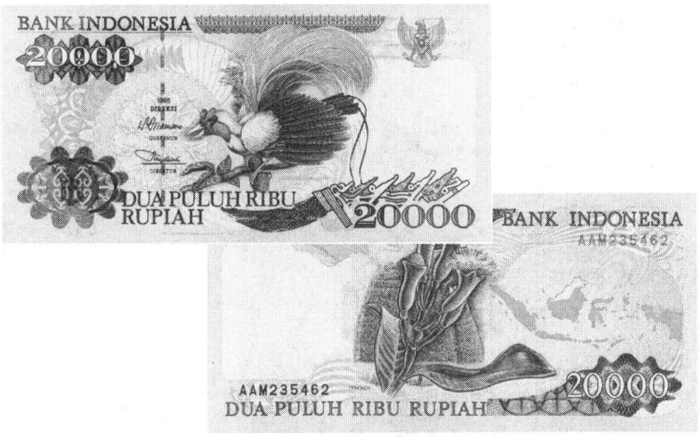

132	20,000 Rupiah	VG	VF	UNC
	1992-95. Black, dark grayish green and red on multicolor underprint. Red bird of paradise at center. Cloves flower at center, map of Indonesian Archipelago at right on back. Watermark: K. H. Dewantara.			
	a. 1992.	3.00	10.00	22.50
	b. 1992/1993.	3.00	10.00	20.00
	c. 1992/1994.	—	8.00	17.50
	d. 1992/1995.	4.00	12.50	25.00
	s. Specimen.	—	—	—

1993 Commemorative Issues

#133 and 134, 25 Years of Development

133	50,000 Rupiah	VG	VF	UNC
	1993-94. Greenish blue, tan and gray on multicolor underprint. Pres. Soeharto at left center, surrounded by various scenes of development activities. Anti-counterfeiting design at right. Jet plane over Soekarno-Hatta International Airport at center on back. Watermark: W. R. Soepratman.			
	a. 1993.	8.00	20.00	40.00
	b. 1993/1994.	8.00	17.50	35.00

		VG	VF	UNC
134	**50,000 Rupiah** 1993. Design like #133, but pale gray. Plastic. Pres. Soeharto in OVD at right.			
	a. Note alone.	8.00	20.00	40.00
	b. Included in souvenir folder.	—	—	50.00

1995 Issue

		VG	VF	UNC
135	**20,000 Rupiah** 1995-98. Black, dark grayish green and red on multicolor underprint. Like #132 but with new engraved date, new signature and segmented foil over security thread.			
	a. 1995.	FV	5.00	15.00
	b. 1995/1996.	FV	4.00	9.00
	c. 1995/1997.	FV	3.00	5.00
	d. 1995/1998.	FV	3.00	5.00
136	**50,000 Rupiah** 1995-98. Greenish blue, tan and gray on multicolor underprint. Like #133 but with new engraved date, new signature and segmented foil over security thread.			
	a. 1995.	FV	7.00	42.50
	b. 1995/1996.	FV	5.00	25.00
	c. 1995/1997.	FV	5.00	15.00
	d. 1995/1998.	FV	5.00	15.00

1998-99 Issue

#137 and 138 printer: Perum Peruri.

		VG	VF	UNC
137	**10,000 Rupiah** 1998-. Deep brownish purple and black on multicolor underprint. Tjut Njak Dhien at right, arms at upper right, bank monogram at lower right. Segara Anak Volcanic Lake at center right on back. Wmk.: W. R. Soepratman.			
	a. 1998.	FV	FV	3.25
	b. 1998/1999.	FV	FV	3.25
	c. 1998/2000.	FV	FV	3.25
	d. 1998/2001.	FV	FV	3.25
	e. 1998/2002.	FV	FV	3.25
	f. 1998/2003.	FV	FV	3.25
	g. 1998/2004.	FV	FV	3.25

		VG	VF	UNC
138	**20,000 Rupiah** 1998-. Deep green and dark brown on multicolor underprint. Ki Hadjar Dewantara at center and as watermark, arms at upper left, Ganesha at left, bank monogram at right. Classroom at center right on back.			
	a. 1998.	FV	FV	6.00
	b. 1998/1999.	FV	FV	5.00
	c. 1998/2000.	FV	FV	5.00
	d. 1998/2001.	FV	FV	5.00
	e. 1998/2002.	FV	FV	5.00
	f. 1998/2003.	FV	FV	5.00
	g. 1998/2004.	FV	FV	5.00

		VG	VF	UNC
139	**50,000 Rupiah** 1999-. Grayish brown on multicolor underprint. W. R. Soepratman at center. Military personnel hoisting flag on Independence Day on back.			
	a. 1999.	FV	FV	22.50
	b. 1999/2000.	FV	FV	20.00
	c. 1999/2001.	FV	FV	20.00
	d. 1999/2002.	FV	FV	20.00
	e. 1999/2003.	FV	FV	20.00
	f. 1999/2004.	FV	FV	20.00
140	**100,000 Rupiah** 1999. Lilac brown, green and orange. Soekarno and Hatta at center. Parliament building on back. Polymer plastic.	FV	FV	30.00

2000 Issue

		VG	VF	UNC
141	**1000 Rupiah** 2000-. Purple on red, blue and multicolor underprint. Kapitan Pattimura at center. Fishing boat and volcano on back.			
	a. 2000.	FV	FV	.50
	b. 2000/2001.	FV	FV	.50
	c. 2000/2002.	FV	FV	.50
	d. 2000/2003.	FV	FV	.50
	e. 2000/2004.	FV	FV	.50
	f. 2000/2005.	FV	FV	.50

2001 Issue

		VG	VF	UNC
142	**5000 Rupiah** 2001-. Brown and green on multicolor underprint. Tuanku Imam Bondjol at center. Purple and green on multicolor underprint; female at hand loom at center.			
	a. 2001.	FV	FV	2.50
	b. 2001/2002.	FV	FV	2.50
	c. 2001/2003.	FV	FV	2.50
	d. 2001/2004.	FV	FV	2.50

143	20,000 Rupiah	VG	VF	UNC
	2004. Blue on multicolor underprint. Otto Iskandar Dinata at center.	FV	FV	5.50

144	100,000 Rupiah	VG	VF	UNC
	2004. Red-brown on multicolor underprint. Similar to #140 but paper.	FV	FV	30.00

REGIONAL - IRIAN BARAT

REPUBLIK INDONESIA

1963 ND PROVISIONAL ISSUE

#R1 and R2 Pres. Sukarno at l. w/ovpt: *IRIAN BARAT* at lower r. on Republik Indonesia issue.

R1	1 Rupiah	VG	VF	UNC
	ND (1963 - old date 1961). Orange.	4.00	10.00	30.00

R2	2 1/2 Rupiah	VG	VF	UNC
	ND (1963 - old date 1961). Violet.	5.00	12.00	35.00

BANK INDONESIA

1963 ND PROVISIONAL ISSUE

#R3-R5 Pres. Sukarno at l. w/ovpt: *IRIAN BARAT* on Bank Indonesia issue.

R3	5 Rupiah	VG	VF	UNC
	ND (1963 - old date 1960). Gray-olive.	7.50	20.00	60.00

R4	10 Rupiah	VG	VF	UNC
	ND (1963 - old date 1960). Red.	6.00	17.50	50.00

R5	100 Rupiah	VG	VF	UNC
	ND (1963 - old date 1960). Green.	20.00	45.00	110.

REGIONAL - RIAU

REPUBLIK INDONESIA

1963 ND PROVISIONAL ISSUE

#R6 and R7 Pres. Sukarno at l. w/ovpt: *RIAU* at lower r. on Republik Indonesia issue.

R6	1 Rupiah	VG	VF	UNC
	ND (1963 - old date 1961). Orange.	7.50	20.00	50.00

R7 **2 1/2 Rupiah** | VG | VF | UNC
ND (1963 - old date 1961). Blue. | 7.50 | 20.00 | 60.00

Note: Contemporary counterfeits on fragile paper w/artificial blue fibers exist.

BANK INDONESIA

1963 ND PROVISIONAL ISSUE

#R8-R10 Pres. Sukarno at l. w/ovpt: *RIAU* on Bank Indonesia issue.

R8 **5 Rupiah** | VG | VF | UNC
ND (1963 - old date 1960). Violet. Overprint on #82b, with prefix *X* in serial #. | 7.50 | 22.50 | 55.00

Note: Modern counterfeits on #82a but w/o prefix X on serial # exist.

R9 **10 Rupiah** | VG | VF | UNC
ND (1963 - old date 1960). Red. | 6.00 | 17.50 | 45.00

R10 **100 Rupiah** | VG | VF | UNC
ND (1963 - old date 1960). Green. | 25.00 | 100. | 400.

IRAN

The Islamic Republic of Iran, located between the Caspian Sea and the Persian Gulf in southwestern Asia, has an area of 636,296 sq. mi. (1,648,000 sq. km.) and a population of 76.43 million. Capital: Tehran. Although predominantly an agricultural state, Iran depends heavily on oil for foreign exchange. Crude oil, carpets and agricultural products are exported.

Iran (historically known as Persia) is one of the world's most ancient and resilient nations. Strategically astride the lower land gate to Asia, it has been conqueror and conquered, sovereign nation and vassal state, ever emerging from its periods of glory or travail with its culture and political individuality intact. Iran (Persia) was a powerful empire under Cyrus the Great (600-529 B.C.), its borders extending from the Indus to the Nile. It has also been conquered by the predatory empires of antique and recent times - Assyrian, Medean, Macedonian, Seljuq, Turk, Mongol - and more recently been coveted by Russia, Germany and Great Britain. Revolts against the absolute power of the Shahs resulted in the establishment of a constitutional monarchy in 1906. In 1931 the Kingdom of Persia became known as the Kingdom of Iran. In 1979, the Pahlavi monarchy was toppled and an Islamic Republic proclaimed.

RULERS: QAJAR DYNASTY

Mohammad Reza Pahlavi, SH1320-58/1941-79AD

PRESIDENTS:

Islamic Republic of Iran
Abolhassan Bani Sadr, SH1358-60 (AD1979-Jun 81)
Mohammad Ali Rajai, SH1360 (AD-1981 Jun-Oct)
Hojjatoleslam Ali Khamene'i, SH1360-(AD1981-)

MONETARY SYSTEM:

1 Rial 100 Dinars = 20 Shahis
1 Toman = 10 Rials SH1310- (1932-)

SIGNATURE AND TITLE VARIETIES

Kingdom: Mohammad Reza Pahlavi

	GENERAL DIRECTOR	MINISTER OF FINANCE
7	Ebrahim Kashani	Abholbagi Shoaii
8	Dr. Ali Asghar Pouhomayoun	Abdul Hossein Behnia
9	Mehdi Samii	Abdul Hossein Behnia
10	Mehdi Samii	Amir Abbas Hoveyda
11	Mehdi Samii	Dr. Jamshid Amouzegar
12	Khodadad Famanfarmaian	Dr. Jamshid Amouzegar
13	Abdul Ali Jahanshahi	Dr. Jamshid Amouzegar
14	Mohammad Yeganeh	Dr. Jamshid Amouzegar
	GENERAL DIRECTOR	MINISTER OF ECONOMIC AND FINANCIAL AFFAIR
15	Mohammad Yeganeh	Hushang Ansary

SIGNATURE AND TITLE VARIETIES

Kingdom: Mohammad Reza Pahlavi

	GENERAL DIRECTOR	MINISTER OF FINANCE
16	Hassan Ali Mehran	Hushang Ansary
17	Hassan Ali Mehran	Mohammad Yeganeh

Note: Some signers used more than one signature (Jamshid Amouzegar), some held more than one term of office (Mehdi Samii) and others held the office of both General Director and Minister of Finance (Mohammad Yeganeh) at different times.

Shah Mohammad Reza Pahlavi, SH1323-58/1944-79 AD

Type V. Imperial Iranian Army (IIA) uniform. Full face. SH1337-40.

Type VI. Imperial Iranian Air Force (IIAF) uniform. Three quarter face. SH1341-44.

Type VII. Imperial Iranian Army (IIA) uniform. Full face. SH1347-48.

Type VIII. Commander in Chief of Iran's Armed Forces. Three quarter face. Large portrait. MS2535 to SH1358.

Type IX. Shah Pahlavi in CinC uniform and his father Shah Reza in Imperial Iranian Army (IIA) uniform. MS2535.

KINGDOM OF IRAN

BANK MARKAZI IRAN

1961; 1962 ISSUE

#71 and 72 Type V portr. of Shah Pahlavi in army uniform at r. Wmk: Young Shah Pahlavi. Yellow security security thread runs vertically. Sign. 7. Printer: Harrison (w/o imprint).

#73-75 Type VI portr. of Shah Pahlavi in air force uniform. Wmk: Young Shah Pahlavi. Yellow security thread runs vertically. Sign. 8. Printer: Harrison (w/o imprint).

		VG	VF	UNC
71	**10 Rials** SH1340 (1961). Blue on green and orange underprint. Geometric design at center. Amir Kabir Dam near Karaj on back.	2.00	4.00	10.00

		VG	VF	UNC
72	**20 Rials** SH1340 (1961). Dark brown on green and pink underprint. Geometric design at center. Statue of Shah and Ramsar Hotel on back.	2.00	6.00	14.00

		VG	VF	UNC
73	**50 Rials** SH1341 (1962). Green on orange and blue underprint. Shah Pahlavi at right. Koohrang Dam and tunnel on back.			
	a. Sm. date 2.5mm high.	2.00	6.00	14.00
	b. Large date 4.0mm high.	3.00	8.00	16.00

		VG	VF	UNC
74	**500 Rials** SH1341 (1962). Black on pink and multicolor underprint. Shah Pahlavi at center. Winged horses on back.	40.00	100.	250.

75	1000 Rials	VG	VF	UNC
	SH1341 (1962). Brown on red and blue underprint. Shah Pahlavi at center. Tomb of Hafez in Shiraz on back.	40.00	125.	350.

1963; 1964 Issue

#76 and 77 Type VI portr. of Shah Pahlavi in armed forces uniform at r. Wmk: Young Shah Pahlavi. Yellow security thread. Printer: Harrison (w/o imprint).

76	50 Rials	VG	VF	UNC
	SH1343 (1964). Dark green on orange and blue underprint. Like #73. Ornate design at center. Koohrang Dam and tunnel on back. Signature 9.	3.00	10.00	20.00

77	100 Rials	VG	VF	UNC
	SH1342 (1963). Maroon on light green and multicolor underprint. Ornate design at center. Oil refinery at Abadan on back. Signature 9.	3.00	10.00	20.00

1965 ND Issue

#78-83 Type VI portr. of Shah Pahlavi in armed forces uniform at r. Wmk: Young Shah Pahlavi. Yellow security thread. Printer: Harrison (w/o imprint).

78	20 Rials	VG	VF	UNC
	ND (1965). Dark brown on pink and green underprint. Ornate design at center. Oriental hunters on horseback on back.			
	a. Signature 9.	1.00	3.00	7.00
	b. Signature 10.	1.00	3.00	7.00

79	50 Rials	VG	VF	UNC
	ND (1965). Dark green on orange and blue underprint. Like #73. Ornate design at center. Koohrang Dam and tunnel on back.			
	a. Signature 9.	3.00	8.00	20.00
	b. Signature 10.	3.00	8.00	20.00

80	100 Rials	VG	VF	UNC
	ND (1965). Maroon on olive-green and multicolor underprint. Like #77. Ornate design at center. Oil refinery at Abadan on back. Signature 10.	3.00	8.00	20.00

81	200 Rials	VG	VF	UNC
	ND (1965). Dark blue on orange and lavender underprint. Multicolor ornate design at center. Railroad bridge on back. Signature 9.	6.00	20.00	50.00

		VG	VF	UNC
82	**500 Rials** ND (1965). Black on pink and purple underprint. Like #74. Shah at center. Winged horses on back. Signature 9.	40.00	100.	250.

		VG	VF	UNC
83	**1000 Rials** ND (1965). Brown on red and blue underprint. Like #75. Shah at center. Tomb of Hafez at Shiraz on back. Signature 9.	50.00	125.	350.

1969 ND Issue

#84-87 Type VII portr. of Shah Pahlavi in army uniform at r. Wmk: Young Shah Pahlavi. Yellow security thread runs vertically. Sign. 11 or 12. Printer: Harrison (w/o imprint).

#84-89A are called *Dark Panel* notes. The bank name is located on a contrasting dk. ornamental panel at the top ctr.

		VG	VF	UNC
84	**20 Rials** ND (1969). Dark brown on pink and green underprint. Ornate design at center. Oriental hunters on horseback on back. Signature 11.	2.00	4.00	10.00

		VG	VF	UNC
85	**50 Rials** ND (1969-71). Green on orange and blue underprint. Ornate design at center. Koohrang Dam and tunnel on back.			
	a. Signature 11.	2.00	5.00	10.00
	b. Signature 12.	2.00	5.00	10.00
86	**100 Rials** ND (1969-71). Maroon on light green and multicolor underprint. Ornate design at center. Oil refinery at Abadan on back.			
	a. Signature 11.	2.00	6.00	12.00
	b. Signature 12.	2.00	6.00	12.00
87	**200 Rials** ND (1969-71). Dark blue on orange and purple underprint. Multicolor ornate design. Railroad bridge on back.			
	a. Signature 11.	5.00	15.00	35.00
	b. Signature 12.	7.00	20.00	50.00

#88-89A Type VII portr. of Shah Pahlavi in army uniform at ctr. Sign. 11.

		VG	VF	UNC
88	**500 Rials** ND (1969). Black on pink and purple underprint. Ornate frame at center. Winged horses on back.	6.00	25.00	80.00

		VG	VF	UNC
89	**1000 Rials** ND (1969). Brown on red and blue underprint. Ornate frame at center. Tomb of Hafez at Shiraz on back.	10.00	40.00	150.
89A	**5000 Rials** ND (1969). Purple on red and multicolor underprint. Ornate frame at center. Golestan Palace in Tehran on back. Printed in Pakistan.	350.	1000.	2000.

1971 ND Issue

#90-96 are called *Light Panel* notes. The bank name is located on a contrasting lt. ornamental background panel at the top ctr.

#90-92 Type VII portr. of Shah Pahlavi in army uniform at r. Wmk: Young Shah Pahlavi. Yellow security thread runs vertically. Printer: Harrison (w/o imprint).

		VG	VF	UNC
90	**50 Rials** ND (1971). Dark green on orange and blue underprint. Like #85 but with light panel. Signature 13.	2.00	4.00	10.00

		VG	VF	UNC
91	**100 Rials** ND (1971-73). Maroon on olive-green and multicolor underprint. Like #86 but with light panel.			
	a. Signature 11.	2.00	5.00	15.00
	b. Signature 12.	2.00	8.00	18.00
	c. Signature 13.	2.00	5.00	15.00

		VG	VF	UNC
92	**200 Rials** ND (1971-73). Dark blue on orange and lavender underprint. Like #87 but with light panel.			
	a. Signature 11.	4.00	16.00	50.00
	b. Signature 12.	6.00	20.00	60.00
	c. Signature 13.	3.00	8.00	20.00

NOTICE

Readers with unlisted dates, signature varieties, etc. are invited to submit photocopies of their notes to: Standard Catalog of World Paper Money, 700 East State St. Iola, WI 54990-0001, E-Mail: george.cuhaj@fwpubs.com.

#93-96 Type VII portr. of Shah Pahlavi in army uniform at ctr. Wmk: Young Shah Pahlavi.

		VG	VF	UNC
93	**500 Rials**			
	ND (1971-73). Black on orange, green and multicolor underprint. Like #88 but with light panel.			
	a. Signature 11.	8.00	20.00	50.00
	b. Signature 12.	15.00	40.00	150.
	c. Signature 13.	12.00	30.00	100.

		VG	VF	UNC
94	**1000 Rials**			
	ND (1971-73). Brown on red, blue and multicolor underprint. Like #89 but with light panel.			
	a. Signature 11.	20.00	60.00	200.
	b. Signature 12.	15.00	50.00	150.
	c. Signature 13.	12.00	40.00	125.

		VG	VF	UNC
95	**5000 Rials**			
	ND (1971-72). Purple on red and multicolor underprint. Ornate frame at center. Golestan Palace in Tehran on back.			
	a. Signature 12.	100.	300.	900.
	b. Signature 13.	70.00	200.	600.

		VG	VF	UNC
96	**10,000 Rials**			
	ND (1972-73). Dark green and brown. Ornate frame at center. National Council of Ministries in Tehran on back.			
	a. Signature 11.	300.	600.	2000.
	b. Signature 13.	200.	400.	1250.

1971 ND COMMEMORATIVE ISSUE

#97 and 98, 2,500th Anniversary of the Persian Empire

#97 and 98 Type VIII portr. of Shah Pahlavi in the "Commander in Chief" of Iranian armed forces uniform at r. Wmk: Young Shah Pahlavi. Yellow security thread runs vertically. Printer: TDLR.

		VG	VF	UNC
97	**50 Rials**			
	SH1350 (1971). Green on blue, brown and multicolor underprint. Floral design at center. Shah Pahlavi giving land deeds to villager on back.			
	a. Signature 11.	2.00	6.00	12.00
	b. Signature 13.	2.50	8.00	16.00

		VG	VF	UNC
98	**100 Rials**			
	SH1350 (1971). Maroon on orange and multicolor underprint. Multicolor geometric and floral design. Three vignettes labeled: *HEALTH, AGRICULTURE* and *EDUCATION* on back. Signature 11.	3.00	8.00	20.00

#99 *Deleted.* See #101a.

1974 ND Issue

#100-107 Type VIII portr. of Shah Pahlavi at r. Wmk: Young Shah Pahlavi. Yellow security thread runs vertically. Printer: TDLR. Replacement notes: For sign. 14, 15, 16 where the prefix for regular notes is a whole number such as 1, 2, 3 or 4, the replacemnt is 01, 02, 03 or 04. For sign. 17 and 18 where the prefix for regular notes is a fraction, the replacemnt is 99/9, 98/9 or 97/9.

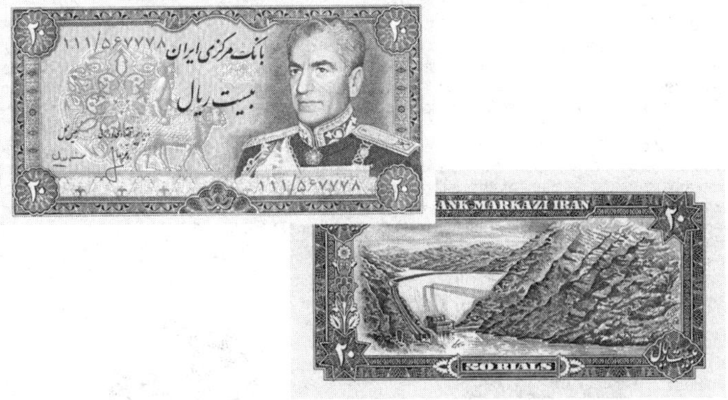

100	20 Rials	VG	VF	UNC
	ND (1974-79). Brown on orange, lilac and multicolor underprint. Persian carpet design, shepherd and ram. Amir Kabir Dam near Karaj on back.			
	a1. Signature 16. Farsi denomination short.	1.00	2.00	6.00
	a2. Signature 16. Farsi denomination long.	1.00	2.00	6.00
	b. Signature 17.	2.00	4.00	8.00
	c. Signature 18.	2.50	5.00	10.00

101	50 Rials	VG	VF	UNC
	ND (1974-79). Green on brown, blue and multicolor underprint. Persian carpet design. Tomb of Cyrus the Great at Pasargarde at left center on back.			
	a. Yellow security thread. signature 14.	2.50	5.00	10.00
	b. Yellow security thread. signature 15.	2.00	4.00	8.00
	c. Yellow security thread. signature 16.	2.00	4.00	8.00
	d. Black security thread. Sign: 17.	2.00	4.00	8.00
	e. Black security thread. signature 18.	2.50	5.00	10.00

102	100 Rials	VG	VF	UNC
	ND (1974-79). Maroon on orange, green and multicolor underprint. Persian carpet design. Pahlavi Museum at left center on back.			
	a. Yellow security thread. signature 15.	2.50	5.00	12.50
	b. Yellow security thread. signature 16.	3.00	6.00	15.00
	c. Black security thread. signature 17.	3.00	7.00	18.00
	d. Black security thread. signature 18.	3.00	6.00	15.00

103	200 Rials	VG	VF	UNC
	ND (1974-79). Blue on green and multicolor underprint. Persian carpet design. Shahyad Square in Tehran on back.			
	a. 6 point star in design on back. Yellow security thread. Monument name as Maidane Shahyad at lower left on back. signature 15.	6.00	20.00	50.00
	b. 12 point star in design on back. Yellow security thread. Monument name as Maidane Shahyad. signature 16.	3.00	10.00	30.00
	d. 12 point star in design on back. Black security thread and Shahyad Aryamer monument. signature 17.	2.00	8.00	25.00
	e. 12 point star in design on back. Black security thread and Shahyad Aryamer monument. signature 18.	2.00	8.00	25.00
	h. 12 point star in design on back. Yellow security thread. Monument name changed to Shahyad Aryamer. signature 16.	2.00	8.00	25.00

104	500 Rials	VG	VF	UNC
	ND (1974-79). Black, dark brown and green on orange and multicolor underprint. Persian carpet design. Winged horses on back.			
	a. 6 point star in design below Shah Pahlavi. Yellow security thread. signature 15.	5.00	15.00	40.00
	b. 6 point star in design below Shah Pahlavi. Yellow security thread. signature 16.	4.00	10.00	25.00
	c. Diamond design below Shah Pahlavi. Black security thread. signature 17.	5.00	15.00	35.00
	d. Diamond design below Shah Pahlavi. Black security thread. signature 18.	4.00	10.00	25.00

105	1000 Rials	VG	VF	UNC
	ND (1974-79). Brown on green, red, yellow and multicolor underprint. Persian carpet design. Tomb of Hafez in Shiraz on back.			
	a. Yellow security thread. signature 15.	10.00	30.00	100.
	b. Yellow security thread. signature 16.	5.00	10.00	30.00
	c. Black security thread. signature 17.	5.00	10.00	30.00
	d. Black security thread. signature 18.	5.00	10.00	30.00

		VG	VF	UNC
106	**5000 Rials**			
	ND (1974-79). Purple on pink, green and multicolor underprint. Persian carpet design. Golestan Palace in Tehran on back.			
	a. Yellow security thread. signature 15.	50.00	100.	300.
	b. Yellow security thread. signature 16.	3.00	10.00	50.00
	c. Black security thread. signature 17.	25.00	75.00	200.
	d. Black security thread. signature 18.	50.00	100.	250.

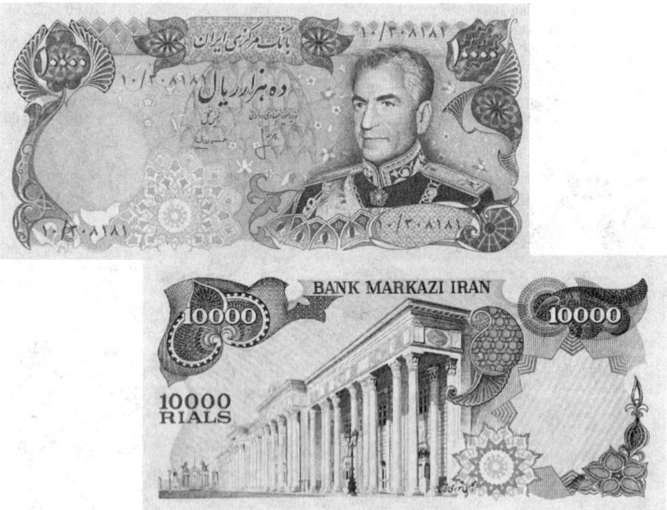

		VG	VF	UNC
107	**10,000 Rials**			
	ND (1974-79). Dark brown and green on multicolor underprint. Persian carpet design. National Council of Ministries in Tehran on back.			
	a. Yellow security thread. signature 15.	75.00	200.	550.
	b. Yellow security thread. signature 16.	10.00	30.00	100.
	c. Black security thread. signature 17.	25.00	100.	300.
	d. Black security thread. signature 18.	35.00	125.	350.

1976 ND Commemorative Issue

#108, 50th Anniversary of the Founding of the Pahlavi Dynasty

#108 Type IX portr. of Shah Pahlavi w/Shah Reza at r. Wmk: Young Shah Pahlavi. Yellow security thread runs vertically. Sign. 16. Printer: TDLR.

		VG	VF	UNC
108	**100 Rials**			
	ND (1976). Maroon on orange, green and multicolor underprint. Persian carpet design with old Bank Melli at bottom center. 50th anniversary design in purple and lavender consisting of fifty suns surrounding Pahlavi Crown on back.	4.00	10.00	25.00

Islamic Republic

REVOLUTIONARY OVERPRINTS

After the Islamic Revolution of 1978-79, the Iranian government used numerous overprints on existing stocks of unissued paper money to obliterate Shah Pahlavi's portrait. There were many unauthorized and illegal crude stampings such as a large "X" and hand obliterations used by zealous citizens which circulated freely, but only three major types types of official overprints were used by the government.

PROVISIONAL ISSUES

All provisional government ovpt. were placed on existing notes of Shah Pahlavi already printed. Overprinting was an interim action meant to discredit and disgrace the deposed Shah as well as to publicize and give credence to the new Islamic Republic. The overprints themselves gave way to more appropriate seals and emblems, changes of watermarks and finally to a complete redesigning of all denominations of notes.

In all cases the Shah's portr. was covered by an arabesque design. Eight different styles and varieties of this ovpt. were used. Watermark ovpt., when used, are either the former Iranian national emblem of Lion and Sun or the calligraphic Persian text of *JUMHURI-YE-ISLAMI-YE-IRAN* (Islamic Republic of Iran) taken from the obverse of the country's new emblem. All ovpt. colors are very dark and require careful scrutiny to distinguish colors other than black.

PORTRAIT OVERPRINT

Overprint A

Overprint B

Overprint C

Overprint D

Overprint E

Overprint F

Overprint G

Overprint H

Obverse 1

Reverse 1

Obverse 2

Obverse 3

GOVERNMENT

TYPE 1 ND PROVISIONAL ISSUE

#110-116 Type I ovpt: Arabesque design over Shah at r. Wmk. area at l. w/o ovpt. Replacement notes: Refer to #100-107.

		VG	VF	UNC
110	**20 Rials**			
	ND.			
	a. Black type A overprint on #100a1 (short Farsi).	2.00	8.00	15.00
	b. Black type A overprint on #100a2 (long Farsi).	3.00	8.00	30.00
	c. Black type C overprint on #100a2.	250.	400.	800.
	d. Black type C overprint on 100b.	300.	500.	1000.
	e. Black type C. overprint on #100c.	600.	1000.	2000.

		VG	VF	UNC
111	**50 Rials**			
	ND. Overprint on #101b.			
	a. Black type B overprint	2.00	5.00	12.00
	b. Green type B overprint	3.00	6.00	20.00

		VG	VF	UNC
112	**100 Rials**			
	ND. Overprint on #102c.			
	a. Black type C overprint	2.50	10.00	25.00
	b. Maroon type C overprint	2.50	10.00	25.00
	c. Black type G. overprint	75.00	150.	300.

		VG	VF	UNC
113	**200 Rials**			
	ND. Overprint on #103.			
	a. Black type E overprint on #103a.	200.	400.	1200.
	b. Black type E overprint on #103b.	250.	500.	1400.
	c. Black type E ovpt on #103d.	3.00	12.00	30.00
	d. Black type G ovpt on #103d.	75.00	150.	300.

		VG	VF	UNC
114	**500 Rials**			
	ND. Overprint on #104.			
	a. Black type F overprint on #104b.	5.00	15.00	50.00
	b. Black type F overprint on #104c.	200.	400.	900.
	c. Black type F overprint on #104d.	5.00	16.00	60.00

		VG	VF	UNC
115	**1000 Rials**			
	ND. Overprint on #105.			
	a. Black type G overprint on #105b.	5.00	15.00	50.00
	b. Black type G overprint on #105d.	7.00	20.00	65.00
	c. Brown type G overprint on #105d.	7.00	20.00	100.

116	5000 Rials	VG	VF	UNC
	ND. Black type H overprint on #106d.	500.	1000.	2000.

TYPE 2 ND PROVISIONAL ISSUE

#117-122 Type II ovpt: Arabesque design over Shah at r. and lion and sun national emblem over wmk. area at l.

117	50 Rials	VG	VF	UNC
	ND. Overprint on #101.			
	a. Black type B overprint on #101c.	5.00	12.00	30.00
	b. Black type B overprint on #101d.	200.	400.	1000.
	c. Black type B overprint on #101e.	100.	200.	600.

118	100 Rials	VG	VF	UNC
	ND. Overprint on #102.			
	a. Black type C overprint on #102c.	70.00	150.	400.
	b. Black type D overprint on #102d.	2.00	4.00	10.00

119	200 Rials	VG	VF	UNC
	ND. Overprint on #103.			
	a. Black Type E overprint on #103d.	8.00	25.00	60.00

120	500 Rials	VG	VF	UNC
	ND. Overprint on #104.			
	a. Black type F overprint on #104b.	350.	700.	2000.
	b. Black type F overprint on #104d.	10.00	30.00	80.00

121	1000 Rials	VG	VF	UNC
	ND. Overprint on #105.			
	a. Black type G overprint on #105b.	400.	800.	3000.
	b. Brown type G overprint on #105b.	8.00	20.00	75.00
	c. Black type G overprint on #105d.	8.00	20.00	75.00

122	5000 Rials	VG	VF	UNC
	ND. Overprint on #106.			
	a. Black type H overprint on #106b.	500.	1000.	2750.
	b. Black type H overprint on #106c.	700.	1500.	3000.
	c. Black type H overprint on #106d.	350.	800.	1750.

TYPE 3 ND PROVISIONAL ISSUE

#123-126 Type III ovpt: Arabesque design over Shah at r. and calligraphic Persian text *JUMHURI-YE ISL-AMI-YE-IRAN* (Islamic Republic of Iran) over wmk. area at l.

123	50 Rials	VG	VF	UNC
	ND. Overprint on #101.			
	a. Black type B ovpt., dark green script on #101c.	2.00	6.00	20.00
	b. Black type D ovpt., black script on #101e.	1.50	4.00	10.00

124	500 Rials	VG	VF	UNC
	ND. Overprint on #104.			
	a. Black type F ovpt., black script on #104b.	5.00	15.00	50.00
	b. Black type D ovpt., black script on #104d.	3.00	10.00	30.00

125	1000 Rials	VG	VF	UNC
	ND. Overprint on #105.			
	a. Black type G ovpt., black script on #105b.	5.00	15.00	50.00
	b. Black type G ovpt., black script on #105d.	5.00	15.00	50.00
	c. Brown type G ovpt., violet script on #105b.	7.50	20.00	75.00
	d. Brown type G ovpt., brown script on #105b.	7.50	20.00	75.00

126	5000 Rials	VG	VF	UNC
	ND. Overprint on #106.			
	a. Purple type H ovpt., purple script on #106b.	500.	1000.	2500.
	b. Black type H ovpt., purple script on #106d.	75.00	150.	350.

Note: Some notes w/Shah portr. are found w/unofficial ovpts., i.e. large purple or black stamped *X* on portr. and wmk. area.

1980 EMERGENCY CIRCULATING CHECK ISSUE

The emergency checks were issed by Bank Melli, the National Bank and not Bank Markazi, the Central Bank, which is only authorized to issue currency. The checks were valid in the country only, not abroad. No English text on the checks.

126A	10,000 Rials	VG	VF	UNC
	ND (1980). Dark blue with black text on green underprint. Bank Melli building at left and center. Two watermark varieties: Bank name repeated. Uniface.	100.	250.	6000.

Note: These Emergency Checks were issued by Bank Melli the National Bank, and not Bank Markazi, the Central Bank which is only authorized to issue currency. The checks were valid in Iran and not abroad. No English text on the check.

BANK MARKAZI IRAN

Notes of the Islamic Republic of Iran		
18	Yousef Khoshkish (on ovpt.)	Mohammad Yeganeh (on ovpt.)
19	Mohammad Ali Mowiavi	Ali Ardalan
20	Ali Reza Nobari	Abol Hassan Bani-Sadr
21	Dr. Mohsen Nourbakhsh	Hossein Nemazi
22	Dr. Mohsen Nourbakhsh	Iravani
23	Ghasemi	Iravani
24	Ghasemi	Dr. Mohsen Nourbakhsh
25	Mohammad Hosein Adeli	Dr. Mohsen Nourbakhsh
26	Mohammad Hosein Adeli	Mohammad Khan
27	Dr. Mohsen Nourbakhsh	Mohammad Khan
28	Dr. Mohsen Nourbakhsh	Hossein Nemazi

1981 ND First Issue

#127-131 calligraphic Persian (Farsi) text from circular republic seal at l., Imam Reza mosque at r. W/o wmk. Yellow security thread w/*BANK MARKAZI IRAN* in black runs through vertically. Back has circular shield w/stars and points at r. Sign. 19. Printer: TDLR (w/o imprint).

#127 and #130 have calligraphic seal printed in the same color as the note (blue and lavender, respectively) and with no variation. #128, 129 and 131 had the calligraphic seal applied locally after notes were printed. Numerous color varieties, misplacement or total omission can be seen on face or back, or both.

		VG	VF	UNC
127	**200 Rials**			
	ND (1981). Blue and green on multicolor underprint. Tomb of Ibn-E-Sina in Hamadan at left on back. Overprint: Dark blue calligraphic seal at right.			
	a. overprint on watermark: Shah profile.	.75	2.00	6.00
	b. overprint on watermark: Lion & Sun.	1.50	4.00	10.00

		VG	VF	UNC
127A	**200 Rials**			
	ND (1981). Blue, blue-violet and deep green on multicolor underprint. Face like #127 with overprint: lion and sun. Victory Monument renamed *Banaye Azadi* at left on back. Signature 19.	2500.	5000.	12,000.

		VG	VF	UNC
128	**500 Rials**			
	ND (1981). Dark brown on orange, green and multicolor underprint. Winged horses on back.	2.00	5.00	12.00

		VG	VF	UNC
129	**1000 Rials**			
	ND (1981). Rust and brown on green and multicolor underprint. Tomb of Hafez in Shiraz on back.	2.50	8.00	22.50

		VG	VF	UNC
130	**5000 Rials**			
	ND (1981). Lavender on green and multicolor underprint. Oil refinery at Tehran on back.			
	a. Security thread.	10.00	30.00	80.00
	b. Without security thread.	15.00	50.00	100.

		VG	VF	UNC
131	**10,000 Rials**			
	ND (1981). Deep green, olive-brown and dark brown on multicolor underprint. National Council of Ministries in Tehran on back.			
	a. dark brown circular seal at left. dark brown circular shield seal at right on back.	20.00	50.00	200.

Note: #131 first ovpt. w/circular gray-yellow lion and sun on both sides, then additional ovpt. regular black calligraphic seal on top of first ovpt. Notes w/o black seal, or misplaced seal, are errors.

1981 ND Second Issue

#132-134 Islamic motifs. White security thread w/*BANK MARKAZI IRAN* in black Persian script runs vertically. Sign. 20 unless otherwise noted. Printer: TDLR (w/o imprint). Replacement notes: Serial # prefix *99/99; 98/99; 97/99;* etc.

		VG	VF	UNC
132	**100 Rials** ND (1981). Maroon and light brown on multicolor underprint. Imam Reza shrine at Mashad at right. Madressa Chahr-Bagh in Isfahan on back. Watermark: Republic seal. Signature 20; 21.	1.00	2.00	5.00

		VG	VF	UNC
133	**5000 Rials** ND (1981). Violet, red-orange and brown on multicolor underprint. Mullahs leading marchers carrying posters of Ayatollah Khomeini at center. Hazrat Masoumeh shrine at left center on back. Watermark: Arms.	7.00	25.00	80.00

		VG	VF	UNC
134	**10,000 Rials** ND (1981). Dark blue and green on yellow and multicolor underprint. Face like #133. Imam Reza shrine in Mashad at center on back.			
	a. Signature 20. watermark: Republic seal.	10.00	30.00	125.
	b. Signature 21. watermark: Arms.	10.00	30.00	125.
	c. Signature 22. watermark: Arms.	10.00	30.00	125.

1982; 1983 ND Issue

#135-139 Islamic motifs. White security thread w/black *BANK MARKAZI IRAN* in Persian letters repeatedly runs vertically. Printer: TDLR (w/o imprint).

		VG	VF	UNC
135	**100 Rials** ND (1982). Maroon on light brown and multicolor underprint. Like #132 except for watermark. Signature 21.	1.00	2.00	4.00

		VG	VF	UNC
136	**200 Rials** ND (1982-). Aqua and blue-black on multicolor underprint. Mosque at center. Farmers and farm tractor at left center on back.			
	a. Signature 21. watermark: Arms.	1.00	3.00	6.00
	b. Signature 23.	FV	FV	4.00
	c. Signature 28. watermark: Khomeini.	FV	FV	3.00
	d. Sign 31. watermark: Khomeini.	FV	FV	3.00

		VG	VF	UNC
137	**500 Rials** ND (1982-2002). Gray and olive. Feyzieh Madressa Seminary at lower left, large prayer gathering at center. Tehran University on back.			
	a. Signature 21. watermark: Arms.	FV	FV	12.00
	b. Signature 22.	5.00	15.00	40.00
	c. Signature 23.	FV	FV	10.00
	d. Signature 23. watermark: Mohd. H. Fahmideh (youth).	FV	FV	8.00
	e. Signature 24.	FV	FV	6.00
	f. Signature 25.	FV	FV	4.00
	g. Signature 26.	FV	FV	4.00
	h. Signature 27. watermark: Arms.	FV	FV	3.00
	i. Signature 27. watermark: Mohd. H. Fahmideh (youth).	FV	FV	3.00
	j. Signature 28. watermark: Khomeini.	FV	FV	3.00
	k. Signature 28. watermark: Mohd. H. Fahmideh (youth).	FV	FV	3.00
	l. Signature 28. watermark: Arms.	FV	FV	3.00

		VG	VF	UNC
137A	**500 Rials**			
	ND (2003-). Gray and olive. Feyzieh Madressa Seminary at lower left, prayer gathering at center. Tehran University on back. Architectural image at lower left in different position than #137.			
	a. Signature 30. watermark: Khomeini.	FV	FV	3.00
	b. Signature 31.	FV	FV	3.00

		VG	VF	UNC
138	**1000 Rials**			
	ND (1982-2002). Dark olive-green, red-brown and brown on multicolor underprint. Feyzieh Madressa Seminary at center. Mosque of Omar (Dome of the Rock) in Jerusalem on back.			
	a. Signature 21. Additional short line of text under mosque on back. watermark: Arms.	FV	FV	20.00
	b. Signature like a. No line of text under building on back.	FV	FV	50.00
	c. Signature 22.	FV	FV	25.00
	d. Signature 23.	FV	FV	15.00
	e. Signature 23. watermark: Mohd. H. Fahmideh (youth).	FV	FV	7.00
	f. Signature 25.	FV	FV	4.00
	g. Signature 26.	FV	FV	4.00
	h. Signature 27.	FV	FV	4.00
	i. Signature 28. watermark: Mohd. H. Fahmideh (youth).	FV	FV	4.00
	j. Signature 28. watermark: Arms.	FV	FV	4.00
138A	**1000 Rials**			
	ND (2003-). Dark olive-green, red-brown and brown on multicolor underprint. Feyzieh Madressa Seminary at center. Mosque of Omar (Dome of the rock) in Jerusalem on back. Architectural element at lower left in different position than on #138.			
	a. Signature 30.	FV	FV	4.00

		VG	VF	UNC
139	**5000 Rials**			
	ND (1983-). Violet, red-orange and brown on multicolor underprint. Similar to #133; reduced crowd. Radiant sun removed from upper left on face. Two small placards of Khomeini added to crowd. Watermark: Arms.			
	a. Signature 21.	FV	FV	75.00
	b. Signature 22.	FV	FV	75.00

Note: #139 exists w/2diff. sign. 21 style of Nemazi.

Central Bank of the Islamic Republic of Iran

1985; 1986 ND Issue

		VG	VF	UNC
140	**100 Rials**			
	ND (1985-). Purple on multicolor underprint. Ayatollah Moddaress at right. Parliament at left on back. Printer: TDLR (without imprint).			
	a. Signature 21. watermark: Arms.	FV	FV	3.00
	b. Signature 22.	FV	FV	2.50
	c. Signature 23.	FV	FV	1.50
	d. Signature 25.	FV	FV	1.25
	e. Signature 26.	FV	FV	1.25
	f. Signature 28. watermark: Khomeini.	FV	FV	1.25
	g. Signature 31.	FV	FV	1.25

		VG	VF	UNC
141	**2000 Rials**			
	ND(1986-). Purple, olive-green and dark brown on multicolor underprint. Revolutionists before mosque at center right. Kaabain Mecca on back.			
	a. Signature 21. watermark: Arms.	FV	FV	10.00
	b. Signature 22.	FV	FV	10.00
	c. Signature 23.	FV	FV	10.00
	d. Signature23. watermark: Mohd. H. Fahmideh (youth).	FV	FV	6.00
	e. Signature 24.	FV	FV	4.00
	f. Signature 25.	FV	FV	4.00
	g. Signature 25. watermark: Arms.	10.00	25.00	125.
	h. Signature 26.	FV	FV	3.00
	i. Signature 27. watermark: Arms.	FV	FV	3.00
	j. Signature 27. watermark: Mohd. H. Fahmideh (youth).	FV	FV	3.00
	k. Signature 28. watermark: Khomeini.	FV	FV	3.00
	l. Signature 28. watermark: Mohd. H. Fahmideh (youth).	FV	FV	3.00

1992; 1993 ND Issue

#142 not assigned.

#143-146 Khomeini at r. Sign. 25.

		VG	VF	UNC
143	**1000 Rials**			
	ND (1992-). Brown and dark green on multicolor underprint. Mosque of Omar (Dome of the Rock) in Jerusalem at center on back.			
	a. Fahmideh (youth).	FV	FV	12.50
	b. Signature 27.	FV	FV	5.00
	c. Signature 28. watermark: Khomeini.	FV	FV	3.00
	d. Signature 31. watermark: Khomeini.	FV	FV	3.00
144	**2000 Rials**			
	ND (2005).	FV	FV	4.50

#145 and 146 wmk: Khomeini.

		VG	VF	UNC
145	**5000 Rials**			
	ND (1993-). Dark brown, brown and olive-green on multicolor underprint. Back red-violet and pale olive-green on multicolor underprint; flowers and birds at center right.			
	a. Signature 25.	FV	FV	10.00
	b. Signature 27.	FV	FV	9.00
	c. Signature 28 (same as 21).	FV	FV	6.00
	d. Signature 29.	FV	FV	6.00
	e. Signature 30.	FV	FV	6.00

		VG	VF	UNC
146	**10,000 Rials**			
	ND (1992-). Deep blue-green, blue and olive-green on multicolor underprint. Mount Damavand at center right on back.			
	a. Signature 25.	FV	FV	20.00
	b. Signature 26.	FV	FV	20.00
	c. Signature 27.	FV	FV	12.50
	d. Signature 28 (same as 21).	FV	FV	12.50
	e. Signature 29.	FV	FV	9.00
	f. Signature 30	FV	FV	9.00
	g. Signature 31.	FV	FV	8.00

Note: Dr. Nourbaksh & Nemazi (sign. 21) were re-appointed to the positions they held several years ago and therefore sign. 28 is the same as sign. 21.

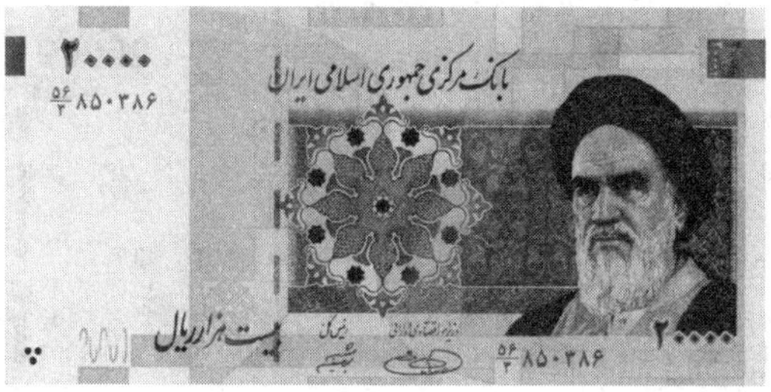

		VG	VF	UNC
147	**20,000 Rials**			
	ND (2004-5). Blue and green on multicolor underprint. Large Imam Khomeini bust at right. Khomeini square in Isfahan on back.			
	a. Signature 30.	FV	FV	18.00

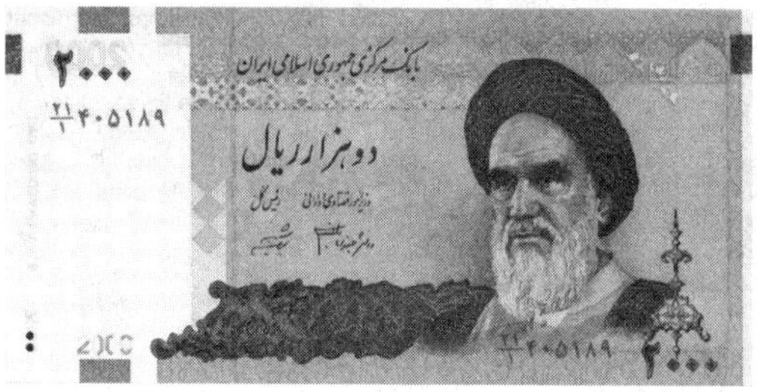

		VG	VF	UNC
148	**20,000 Rials**			
	2005. Blue and green on multicolor underprint. Smaller Iman Khomeini bust at right. Khomeini square in Isfahan on back. Signature 31.	FV	FV	15.00

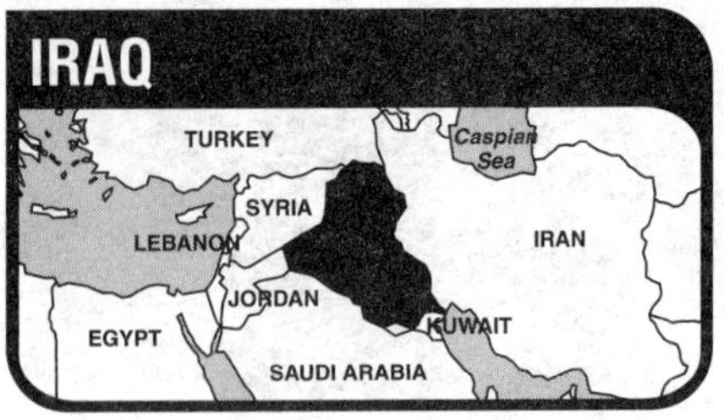

The Republic of Iraq, historically known as Mesopotamia, is located in the Near East and is bordered by Kuwait, Iran, Turkey, Syria, Jordan and Saudi Arabia. It has an area of 167,925 sq. mi. (434,924 sq. km.) and a population of 23.11 million. Capital: Baghdad. The economy of Iraq is based on agriculture and petroleum. Crude oil accounts for 94 percent of the exports before the war with Iran began in 1980.

Iraq was the site of a number of flourishing civilizations of antiquity - Sumerian, Assyrian, Babylonian, Parthian, Persian - and of the Biblical cities of Ur, Nineveh and Babylon. Desired because of its favored location which embraced the fertile alluvial plains of the Tigris and Euphrates Rivers, Mesopotamia - "land between the rivers" - was conquered by Cyrus the Great of Persia, Alexander of Macedonia and by Arabs who made the legendary city of Baghdad the capital of the ruling caliphate. Suleiman the Great conquered Mesopotamia for Turkey in 1534, and it formed part of the Ottoman Empire until 1623, and from 1638 to 1917. Great Britain, given a League of Nations mandate over the territory in 1920, recognized Iraq as a kingdom in 1922. Iraq became an independent constitutional monarchy presided over by the Hashemite family, direct descendants of the prophet Mohammed, in 1932. In 1958, the army-led revolution of July 14 overthrew the monarchy and proclaimed a republic. After several military coups, Saddam Hussein became president in 1979. In 2003 he was overthrown by a coalition of foreign forces lead by the United States.

MONETARY SYSTEM:

1 Dinar = 1000 Fils

REPUBLIC

CENTRAL BANK OF IRAQ

1959 ISSUE

#51-55 new Republic arms w/1958 at r. and as wmk. Sign. 10, 11, 12.

		VG	VF	UNC
51	**1/4 Dinar** ND (1959). Green on multicolor underprint. Palm trees at center on back.			
	a. Without security thread. 1 signature varieties.	1.00	5.00	15.00
	b. With security thread. 2 signature varieties.	1.00	5.00	5.00
	s. Specimen. Punched hole cancelled.	—	—	30.00

		VG	VF	UNC
52	**1/2 Dinar** ND (1959). Brown on multicolor underprint. Ruins of the mosque and spiral minaret at Samarra on back.			
	a. Without security thread. 1 signature variety.	2.00	7.50	30.00
	b. With security thread. 2 signature varieties.	2.00	7.50	30.00
	s. Specimen. Punched hole cancelled.	—	—	30.00

		VG	VF	UNC
53	**1 Dinar** ND (1959). Blue on multicolor underprint. The *Harp of Ur* at center on back.			
	a. Without security thread. 1 signature variety.	1.50	5.00	20.00
	b. With security thread. Blue lines over watermark. area. 2 signature varieties.	1.50	5.00	20.00
	s. Specimen. Punched hole cancelled.	—	—	30.00

		VG	VF	UNC
54	**5 Dinars** ND (1959). Light purple on multicolor underprint. Ancient carving of Hammurabi receiving the laws on back.			
	a. Without security thread. 1 signature variety.	2.50	12.50	35.00
	b. With security thread.	2.50	12.50	35.00
	s. Specimen. Punched hole cancelled.	—	—	30.00

		VG	VF	UNC
55	**10 Dinars** ND (1959). Purple on multicolor underprint. Carvings of a winged Assyrian ox and an Assyrian priest on back.			
	a. Without security thread. 1 signature variety.	3.00	10.00	50.00
	b. With security thread. 2 signature varieties.	3.00	10.00	50.00
	s. Specimen. Punched hole cancelled.	—	—	30.00

Note: Various hoards of #51-55 have appeared on the market during the past several years. Values shown are speculative for all these pieces.

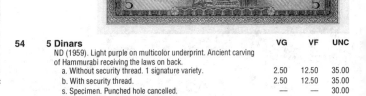

1971 ND Issue

#56-60 wmk: Falcon's head. Sign. #13, 14.

56	1/4 Dinar	VG	VF	UNC
	ND (1971). Green and brown on multicolor underprint. Harbor at center. *1/4 Dinar* at left, palm trees at center on back.	1.00	3.00	9.00

57	1/2 Dinar	VG	VF	UNC
	ND (1971). Brown and blue on multicolor underprint. Cement factory at center. *1/2 Dinar* at left, spiral minaret and ruins of mosque at Samarra at center on back.	2.50	7.50	25.00

58	1 Dinar	VG	VF	UNC
	ND (1971). Blue and brown on multicolor underprint. Oil refinery at center. Entry to the al-Mustansiriyah School at center, *1 Dinar* at left on back. Two signature varieties.	2.00	6.00	17.50

59	5 Dinars	VG	VF	UNC
	ND (1971). Lilac on brown and multicolor underprint. Parliament building across face. Hammurabi (left) in conversation with sun god Shamash at center *5 Dinars* at left on back. Two signature varieties.	5.00	15.00	45.00

60	10 Dinars	VG	VF	UNC
	ND (1971). Purple, blue and brown on multicolor underprint. Dockdan dam at center. Winged statues from the palace complex of Sargon II at Khorsabad at center on back. *10 Dinars* at left on back.	5.00	15.00	45.00

1973 ND; 1978 Issue

#61-66 wmk: Falcon's head. Sign. #14, 15.

61	1/4 Dinar	VG	VF	UNC
	ND (1973). Green and black on multicolor underprint. Similar to #56. *Quarter Dinar* at bottom right on back. Two signature varieties.	.50	1.50	5.00

62	1/2 Dinar	VG	VF	UNC
	ND (1973). Brown on multicolor underprint. Face design similar to #57. *Half Dinar* below Minaret of the Great Mosque at Samarra at center on back. Two signature varieties.	1.25	4.00	12.50

63 **1 Dinar**

ND (1973). Dark blue and aqua on multicolor underprint. Similar to #58. *One Dinar* at bottom right on back.

	VG	VF	UNC
a. 1 line of Arabic caption (factory name) below.	1.00	4.50	32.50
b. Without Arabic caption below factory.	1.00	3.00	10.00

64 **5 Dinars**

	VG	VF	UNC
ND (1973). Deep lilac on multicolor underprint. Similar to #59. *Five Dinars* at bottom on back. Two signature varieties.	.75	2.50	7.50

65 **10 Dinars**

	VG	VF	UNC
ND (1973). Purple and red-brown on blue and multicolor underprint. Dockdan dam at right. Back similar to #60, but *Ten Dinars* at bottom. Two signature varieties.	1.50	4.50	12.50

66 **25 Dinars**

1978; 1980. Green and brown on multicolor underprint. Three Arabian horses at center, date below signature at lower right. Abbasid Palace on back. 182 x 88mm. Two signature varieties.

	VG	VF	UNC
a. 1978/AH1398.	5.00	10.00	30.00
b. 1980/AH1400.	2.50	7.50	22.50
s. Specimen.	—	—	—

1979-86 Issue

#67-72 wmk: Arabian horse's head. Sign. varieties.

67 **1/4 Dinar**

1979/AH1399. Green and multicolor. Palm trees at center. Building on back.

	VG	VF	UNC
a. Issued note.	.15	.30	1.00
s. Specimen.	—	—	—

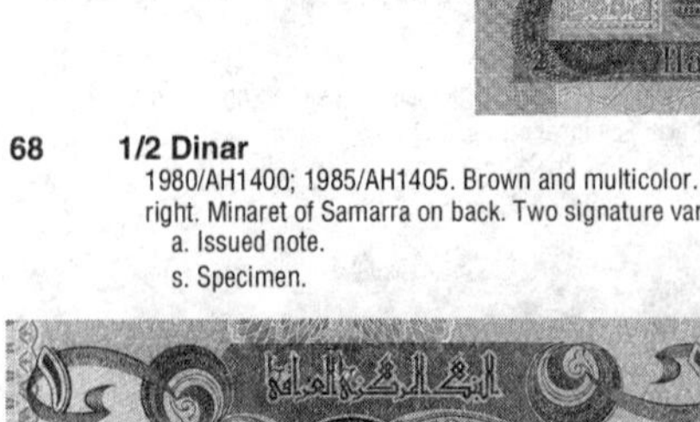

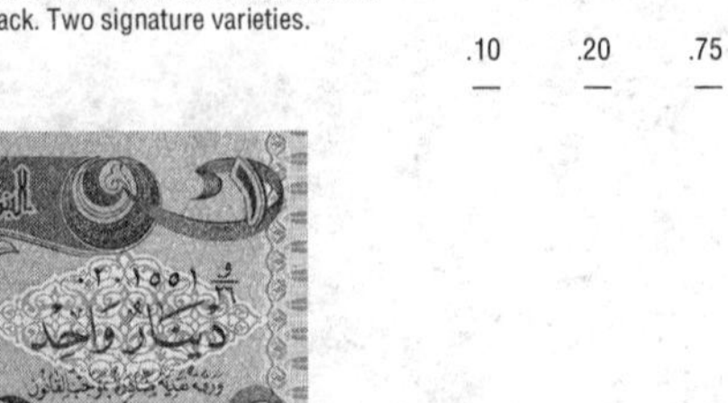

68 **1/2 Dinar**

1980/AH1400; 1985/AH1405. Brown and multicolor. Astrolabe at right. Minaret of Samarra on back. Two signature varieties.

	VG	VF	UNC
a. Issued note.	.10	.20	.75
s. Specimen.	—	—	—

			VG	VF	UNC
69	**1 Dinar**	1979/AH1399; 1980/AH1400; 1984/AH1405. Olive-green and deep blue on multicolor underprint. Coin design at center. Mustansiriyah School in Baghdad on back. Three signature varieties.			
		a. Issued note.	.10	.20	.75
		s. Specimen.	—	—	—

			VG	VF	UNC
70	**5 Dinars**	1980/AH1400; 1981/AH1401; 1982/AH1402. Brown-violet and deep blue on multicolor underprint. Gali-Ali Beg waterfall at center. Al-Ukhether castle at center on back.			
		a. Issued note.	.25	1.00	3.00
		s. Specimen.	—	—	—

			VG	VF	UNC
71	**10 Dinars**	1980/AH1400; 1981/AH1401; 1982/AH1402. Purple on blue, violet and multicolor underprint. Al-Hassan ibn al-Haitham (scientist) at right. Hadba minaret in Mosul on back.	.25	1.00	3.00

			VG	VF	UNC
72	**25 Dinars**	1981/AH1401; 1982/AH1402. Green and brown. Similar to #66 but date below horses. Reduced size, 175 x 80mm.	.25	.75	1.25

			VG	VF	UNC
73	**25 Dinars**	1986. Brown, green and black on blue and multicolor underprint. Charging horsemen at center, Saddam Hussein at right and as watermark. City gate at left, Martyr's monument at center on back.	.25	.75	2.50

Note: In a sudden economic move during summer of 1993, it was announced that all previous 25 Dinar notes issued before #74 had become worthless.

1990 Emergency Gulf War Issue

#74-76 Iraq printing. Many color shade varieties exist because of poor printing quality.

			VG	VF	UNC
74	**25 Dinars**	1990/AH1411. Similar to #72 but green and gray. Lithograph, without watermark.			
		a. Green underprint. with pink highlights and brown ink.	—	.10	.50
		b. Green underprint. without pink highlights and black ink.	—	.10	.50
		c. Green and pink underprint. with pink highlights and brown ink.	—	.10	.50

			VG	VF	UNC
75	**50 Dinars**	1991/AH1411. Brown and blue-green on peach and multicolor underprint. Saddam Hussein at right. Minaret of the Great Mosque at Samarra at center right on back. Lithograph.	—	—	.75

		VG	VF	UNC
76	**100 Dinars** 1991/AH1411. Dark blue-green on lilac and multicolor underprint. Saddam Hussein at right. Victory Arch Monument of crossed swords at center on back.	5.00	15.00	40.00

1992-93 Emergency Issue

#77-79 dull lithograph printing. W/faint indelible ink wmk. Printed in China.

		VG	VF	UNC
77	**1/4 Dinar** 1993/AH1413. Green on multicolor underprint. Like #67.	—	—	.40

		VG	VF	UNC
78	**1/2 Dinar** 1993/AH1413. Brown on multicolor underprint. Like #68.			
	a. dark brown underprint.	—	—	.40
	b. light lilac underprint.	—	—	.40

		VG	VF	UNC
79	**1 Dinar** 1992/AH1412. Green and blue-black on multicolor underprint. Like #69.	—	—	.40

#80 and 81 Saddam Hussein at r. Printed in China.

		VG	VF	UNC
80	**5 Dinars** 1992/AH1412. Dull red-brown on pale orange, lilac and multicolor underprint. Temple at center. Hammurabi in conversation with the sun god Shamash at left. Tomb of the unknown soldier in center on back. Color shade varieties.			
	a. With border around embossed text at center.	—	—	3.00
	b. Without border around embossed text at center.	—	—	3.00
	c. As b. without embossed text at center.	—	—	.60

		VG	VF	UNC
81	**10 Dinars** 1992/AH1412. Purplish black, blue-green and multicolor. Statue of winged beast from the palace complex of Sargon II at Khorsabad at left on back.	—	—	1.50

#82 held in reserve.

1994-95 Issue

#83-85 Saddam Hussein at r.

		VG	VF	UNC
83	**50 Dinars** 1994/AH1414. Brown and pale green on multicolor underprint. Ancient statuette, monument at left center. "Aljahad Project" double deck Saddam bridge at center on back.	—	—	1.50

		VG	VF	UNC
84	**100 Dinars** 1994/AH1414. Dark blue on light blue and pale ochre underprint. Al-Ukhether castle at center. Baghdad clock at center on back. Printed watermark: Falcon's head.			
	a1. First diacritical mark in the text of the denomination is above the first letter (from the right). Printed on white paper which fluoresces.	—	—	1.00
	a2. As a. but printed on dark paper which does not fluoresce under UV light.	—	—	1.00
	b. First diacritical mark in the text of the denomination is below the second letter (from the right).	—	—	1.00

Note: Shade varieties exist.

		VG	VF	UNC
85	**250 Dinars** 1995/AH1415. Lavender on blue and multicolor underprint. Hydroelectric dam at left center. Friese from the Liberty Monument across back.			
	a1. First word of the text for the denomination has its second letters as a long 'a.' Printed on white paper which fluoresces.	—	—	1.25
	a2. As a. but printed on dark paper which does not fluoresce under UV light.	—	—	1.25
	b. First word of the text for the denomination has its second last letters as a long 'i', also with different diacritical marks.	—	—	1.25

2001-02 Issue

#86-88 Saddam Hussein at r.

		VG	VF	UNC
86	**25 Dinars** 2001/AH1422. Brown on light green underprint.	—	—	.75

		VG	VF	UNC
87	**100 Dinars** 2002/AH1422. Blue on blue and yellow underprint. Shenashils of old Baghdad on back.	—	—	1.50

		VG	VF	UNC
88	**250 Dinars** 2002/AH1422. Purple on rose and blue underprint. Dome Rock on back.	—	—	1.50

		VG	VF	UNC
89	**10,000 Dinars** 2002/AH1423. Tomb of unknown soldier in center, Saddam Hussein at right. Al-Mustansiriyah University in Baghdad and Arabic astrolobe on back.	—	—	7.00

Democratic Republic

Central Bank of Iraq

2003-04 Issue

#90-96 printer: TDLR.

		VG	VF	UNC
90	**50 Dinars** 2003/AH1424. Purple on multicolor underprint. Grain silo at Basrah. Date palms on back.	FV	FV	.50

91 **250 Dinars** | VG | VF | UNC
2003/AH1424. Light and dark blue on multicolor underprint. Astrolobe. Spiral Minaret in Samarra on back. | FV | FV | 1.00

92 **500 Dinars** | VG | VF | UNC
2004/AH1425. Green and blue on multicolor underprint. Ducan Dam at center. Winged bull statue on back. | FV | FV | 1.75

93 **1000 Dinars** | VG | VF | UNC
2003/AH1424. Light and dark brown. Medieval dinar coin. Al-Mustansiriyah University in Baghdad on back. | FV | FV | 2.50

94 **5000 Dinars** | VG | VF | UNC
2003/AH1424. Dark blue on multicolor underprint. Gali Ali Beg and waterfall. Al-Ukhether fortress on back. | FV | FV | 10.00

95 **10,000 Dinars** | VG | VF | UNC
2003/AH1424, 2004/AH1425. Green on multicolor underprint. Abu Ali Hasan Ibn al-Haitham (known as Alhazen), physicist and mathematician. Hadba Minaret at the Great Nurid Mosque in Mosul on back. Two signature varieties. | FV | FV | 15.00

96 **25,000 Dinars** | VG | VF | UNC
2003/AH1424; 2004;AH1425. Red, purple and tan on multicolor underprint. Kurdish farmer holding sheaf of wheat, tractor in background. Ancient Babylonian King Hammurabi on back. Two signature varieties. | FV | FV | 27.50

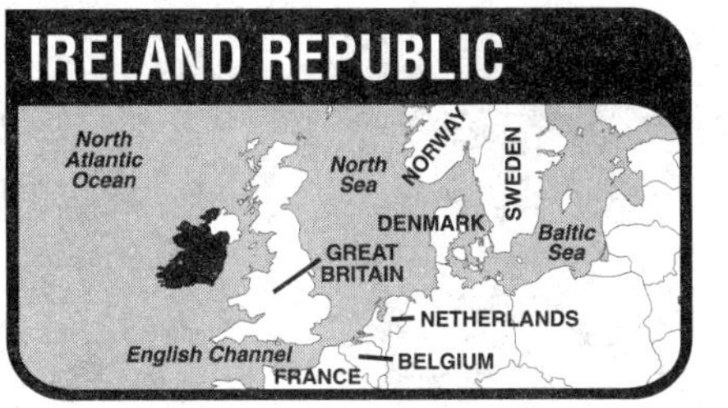

The Republic of Ireland, occupying five-sixths of the island of Ireland located in the Atlantic Ocean west of Great Britain, has an area of 27,136 sq. mi. (70,283 sq. km.) and a population of 3.71 million. Capital: Dublin.

The Fenian Brotherhood was organized in 1858 and consisted of Irish emigrants embittered by British attitude and policy towards Ireland. The leader of the group was John O'Mahoney. The Brotherhood sought Irish independence through pressure and embarassment tactics, perpetrating a number of raids in Canada mostly during the 1860s and 1870s. Though such activities proved largely unsuccessful, the movement continued until World War I when it became part of a newer group with similar aims, the Sinn Fein.

Agriculture and dairy farming are the principal industries. Meat, livestock, dairy products and textiles are exported.

The Irish Free State was established as a dominion on Dec. 6, 1921. Ireland withdrew from the Commonwealth and proclaimed itself a republic on April 18, 1949.

RULERS:

British to 1921

MONETARY SYSTEM:

1 Shilling = 12 Pence
1 Pound = 20 Shillings to 1971
1 Pound = 100 Pence, 1971-2001
1 Euro = 100 Cent, 2002-
1 Dollar = 100 Cents

REPUBLIC

BANC CEANNAIS NA HÉIREANN

CENTRAL BANK OF IRELAND

1961-63 ISSUE

#63-69 representation of river gods at ctr. on back. Replacement notes: From 1974-1976 single letter prefix plus 6-digit serial number for £1-£20. For £1 and £5 dated 1975 a "00" was used in front of a prefix letter.

#63-65 portr. Lady Hazel Lavery at l., denomination at bottom ctr.

63	10 Shillings	VG	VF	UNC
	3.1.1962-6.6.1968. Orange on light green and lilac underprint. Signature M. O'Muimhneacháin and T. K. Whitaker.			
	a. Issued note.	FV	10.00	45.00
	s. Specimen.	—	—	—

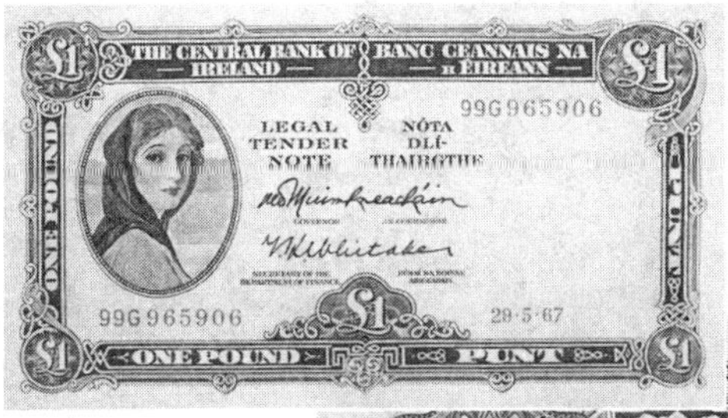

64	1 Pound	VG	VF	UNC
	1962-76. Green on pale gold underprint.			
	a. Signature M. O'Muimhneacháin and T. K. Whitaker. 16.3.1962-8.10.1968.	FV	12.00	60.00
	b. Signature T. K. Whitaker and C. H. Murray. 1.3.1969-17.9.1970.	FV	10.00	40.00
	c. Signature like b, but metallic security thread at left. of center 8.7.1971-21.4.1975.	FV	6.00	27.50
	d. Signature C. H. Murray and M. O'Murchu. 30.9.1976.	FV	5.00	25.00
	r. Replacement note. Serial # prefix *S*.	5.00	15.00	55.00
	s. Specimen.	—	—	—

Note: Replacement notes: Serial # prefix *S* or *00A*.

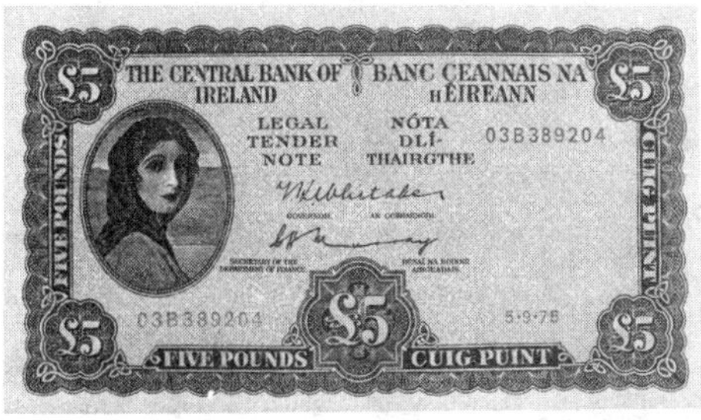

65	5 Pounds	VG	VF	UNC
	1961-75. Dark brown on light gold and orange underprint.			
	a. Signature M. O'Muimhneachain and T. K. Whitaker. 15.8.1961-12.8.1968.	FV	35.00	175.
	b. Signature T. K. Whitaker and C. H. Murray. 12.5.1969; 27.2.1970.	FV	27.50	140.
	c. Signature like b., but metallic security thread at left. of center 18.1.1971-5.9.1975.	FV	25.00	125.

Note: Replacement notes: Serial # prefix *R* or *00K*. #66-69 Lady Hazel Lavery in Irish national costume w/chin resting on her hand and leaning on an Irish harp.

66	10 Pounds	VG	VF	UNC
	1962-76. Blue on multicolor underprint.			
	a. Signature M. O'Muimhneachain and T. K. Whitaker. 2.5.1962-16.7.1968.	FV	60.00	190.
	b. Signature T. K. Whitaker and C. H. Murray. 5.5.1969; 9.3.1970.	FV	50.00	170.
	c. Signature like b, but metallic security thread at left. of center 19.5.1971-10.2.1975.	FV	45.00	150.
	d. Signature C. H. Murray and M. O'Murchu. 2.12.1976.	FV	40.00	140.

Note: Replacement notes: Serial # prefix *T*.

67	20 Pounds	VG	VF	UNC
	1961-76. Red on multicolor underprint.			
	a. Signature M. O'Muimhneachain and T. K. Whitaker. 1.6.1961-15.6.1965.	FV	110.	375.
	b. Signature T. K. Whitaker and C. H. Murray. 3.3.1969-6.1.1975.	FV	80.00	275.
	c. Signature C. H. Murray and M. O'Murchu. 24.3.1976.	FV	65.00	200.

Note: Replacement notes: Serial # prefix *V*.

68	50 Pounds	VG	VF	UNC
	1962-77. Purple on multicolor underprint.			
	a. Signature M. O'Muimhneachain and T. K. Whitaker. 1.2.1962-6.9.1968.	FV	385.	1150.
	b. Signature T. K. Whitaker and C. H. Murray. 4.11.1970-16.4.1975.	FV	365.	1050.
	c. Signature C. H. Murray and M. O'Murchu. 4.4.1977.	FV	350.	1000.

69	100 Pounds	VG	VF	UNC
	1963-77. Green on multicolor underprint.			
	a. Signature M. O'Muimhneachain and T. K. Whitaker. 16.1.1963-9.9.1968.	FV	475.	1350.
	b. Signature T. K. Whitaker and C. H. Murray. 26.10.1970; 3.3.1972; 20.2.1970; 10.4.1076.	FV	425.	1200.
	c. Signature C. H. Murray and M. O'Murchu. 4.4.1977.	FV	400.	1150.

1976-82 ISSUE

#70-74 replacement notes: Serial # prefixes *AAA; BBB;* etc.

70	1 Pound	VG	VF	UNC
	1977-89. Dark olive-green and green on multicolor underprint. Queen Medb at right. Old writing on back. Watermark: Lady Lavery.			
	a. Signature C. H. Murray and M. O'Murchu. 10.6.1977-29.11.1977.	2.00	5.00	15.00
	b. Signature C. H. Murray and T. F. O'Cofaigh. 30.8.1978-30.10.1981.	FV	5.00	14.00
	c. Signature T. F. O'Cofaigh and M. F. Doyle. 30.6.1982-24.4.1987.	FV	5.00	14.00
	d. Signature M. F. Doyle and S. P. Cromien. 23.3.1988-17.7.1989.	FV	4.00	12.50
	s. Specimen. As a, c.	—	—	—

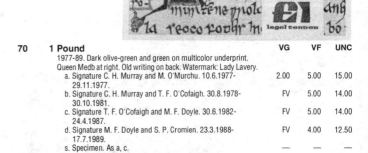

71	5 Pounds	VG	VF	UNC
	1976-93. Brown and red-violet on multicolor underprint. John Scotus Eriugena at right. Old writing on back.			
	a. Signature T. K. Whitaker and C. H. Murray. 26.2.1976.	FV	30.00	60.00
	b. Signature C. H. Murray and M. O'Murchu. 18.5.1976-17.10.1977.	FV	25.00	55.00
	c. Signature C. H. Murray and T. F. O'Cofaigh. 25.4.1979-29.10.1981.	FV	17.50	40.00
	d. Signature T. F. O'Cofaigh and M. F. Doyle. 1982; 17.10.1983-22.4.1987.	FV	17.50	40.00
	e. Signature M. F. Doyle and S. P. Cromien. 12.8.1988-7.5.1993.	FV	15.00	35.00
	s. Specimen. As b, d.	—	—	—

72	10 Pounds	VG	VF	UNC
	1978-92. Violet and purple on multicolor underprint. Jonathan Swift at right. Old street map and canal on back.			
	a. Signature C. H. Murray and T. F. O'Cofaigh. 1.6.1978-28.10.1981.	FV	35.00	85.00
	b. Signature T. F. O'Cofaigh and M. F. Doyle. 1982; 25.2.1983-9.2.1987.	FV	30.00	70.00
	c. Signature M. F. Doyle and S. P. Cromien. 22.12.1987-15.4.1992.	FV	27.50	65.00
	s. Specimen. As a, b.	—	—	—

73	20 Pounds	VG	VF	UNC
	1980-92. Blue on multicolor underprint. William Butler Yeats at right, Abbey Theatre symbol at center. Map on back.			
	a. Signature C. H. Murray and T. F. O'Cofaigh. 7.1.1980-28.10.1981.	FV	55.00	140.
	b. Signature T. F. O'Cofaigh and M. F. Doyle. 11.7.1983-28.8.1986.	FV	50.00	125.
	c. Signature M. F. Doyle and S. P. Cromien. 12.8.1987-14.2.1992.	FV	45.00	100.
	s. Specimen. As b.	—	—	—

74	50 Pounds	VG	VF	UNC
	1982; 1991. Red and brown on multicolor underprint. Turlough O'Carolan playing harp in front of group. Musical instruments on back.			
	a. Signature T. F. O'Cofaigh and M. F. Doyle. 1.11.1982.	FV	120.	325.
	b. Signature M. F. Doyle and S. P. Cromien. 5.11.1991.	FV	100.	275.

1992-96 ISSUE

#75-78 wmk: Lady Lavery and value. Replacement notes: Serial # prefixes *BBB; CCC,* etc.

75	5 Pounds	VG	VF	UNC
	1994-99. Dark brown, reddish brown, and grayish purple on multicolor underprint. Mater Misericordiae Hospital at bottom left center, Sister Catherine McAuley at right. School children at center on back.			
	a. Signature M. F. Doyle and S. P. Cromien. 15.3.1994-28.4.1994.	FV	FV	27.50
	b. Signature M. O'Conaill and P. H. Mullarkey. 21.12.1994-15.10.1999.	FV	FV	20.00

76	10 Pounds	VG	VF	UNC
	1993-99. Dark green and brown on multicolor underprint. Aerial view of Dublin at center, James Joyce at right. Sculpted head representing Liffey River at left, map in underprint on back.			
	a. Signature M. F. Doyle and S. P. Cromien. 14.7.1993-27.4.1994.	FV	FV	37.50
	b. Signature M. O'Conaill and P. H. Mullarkey. 13.3.1995-2.7.1999.	FV	FV	30.00

		VG	VF	UNC
77	**20 Pounds**	VG	VF	UNC
	1992-99. Violet, brown and dark grayish blue on multicolor underprint. Derrynane Abbey at left center, Daniel O'Connell at right. Writings and Four Courts building, Dublin, on back.			
	a. Signature M. F. Doyle and S. P. Cromien. 10.9.1992-29.4.1994.	FV	FV	70.00
	b. Signature M. O'Conaill and P. H. Mullarkey. 14.6.1995-9.12.1999.	FV	FV	65.00

		VG	VF	UNC
78	**50 Pounds**	VG	VF	UNC
	1995-2001. Dark blue and violet on multicolor underprint. Douglas Hyde at right, Áras an Uachtaráin building in background at center. Back dark gray and deep olive-green on multicolor underprint; Uilinn Piper at left, crest of Conradh na Gaeilge at upper center right.			
	a. Signature M. O'Conaill and P. H. Mullarkey. 6.10.1995; 14.2.1996; 19.3.1999.	FV	FV	180.
	b. Signature M. O'Conaill and J. A. Hurley. 8.3.2001.	FV	FV	150.

		VG	VF	UNC
79	**100 Pounds**	VG	VF	UNC
	22.8.1996. Lilac brown, light orange-brown and slate. Charles Stewart Parnell at right, Avondale House and gardens in Rathdrum at lower left center, Irish Wolfhound at lower left. Parts of the Parnell monument in Dublin on back. Signature M. O'Conaill and P. H. Mullarkey.	FV	FV	325.

Note: For later issues made for use in the Republic of Ireland, see European Union listings.

IRELAND - NORTHERN

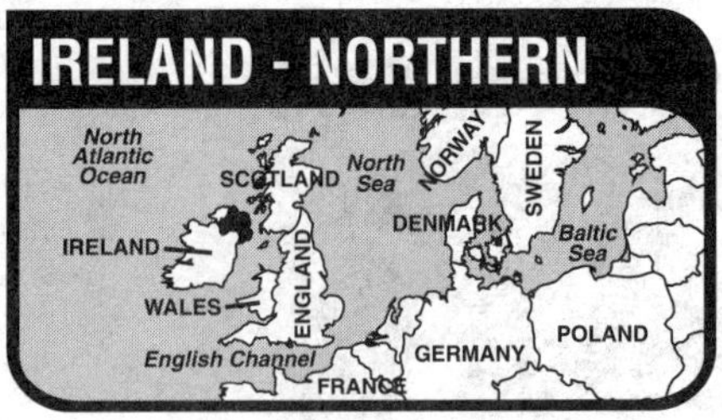

From 1800 to 1921 Ireland was an integral part of the United Kingdom. The Anglo-Irish treaty of 1921 established the Irish Free State of 26 counties within the Commonwealth of Nations and recognized the partition of Ireland. The six predominantly Protestant counties of northeast Ulster chose to remain a part of the United Kingdom with a limited self-government.

Up to 1928 banknotes issued by six of the nine joint stock commercial banks were circulating in the whole of Ireland. After the establishment of the Irish Free State, the commercial notes were issued for circulation only in Northern Ireland, with the Consolidated Banknotes being issued by the eight commercial banks operating in the Irish Free State.

RULERS:

British

MONETARY SYSTEM:

1 Shilling = 12 Pence
1 Pound = 20 Shillings to 1971
1 Pound = 100 New Pence, 1971-

BRITISH ADMINISTRATION

ALLIED IRISH BANKS LTD.

1982 ISSUE

#1-5 designs similar to Provincial Bank of Ireland Ltd. (#247-251) except for bank title and sign. Printer: TDLR.

		VG	VF	UNC
1	**1 Pound** 1.1.1982; 1.7.1983; 1.12.1984. Green on multicolor underprint. Young girl at right. Sailing ship *Girona* at center on back.	3.00	12.00	40.00

		VG	VF	UNC
2	**5 Pounds** 1.1.1982; 1.7.1983. Blue and purple on multicolor underprint. Young woman at right. Dunluce Castle at center on back.	13.00	32.50	85.00

		VG	VF	UNC
3	**10 Pounds** 1.1.1982; 1.12.1984. Brown and gray-green on multicolor underprint. Young man at right. Wreck of the *Girona* at center on back.	25.00	45.00	140.

		VG	VF	UNC
4	**20 Pounds** 1.1.1982; 1.7.1983; 1.12.1984. Purple and green. Elderly woman at right. Chimney at Lacada Point at center on back.	45.00	75.00	325.
5	**100 Pounds** 1.1.1982. Black, olive and green. Elderly man at right. The *Armada* at center on back.	250.	400.	850.

Allied Irish Banks Public Limited Company

1987-88 Issue

#6-9 like #2-5 except for bank title and sign. Printer: TDLR.

		VG	VF	UNC
6	**5 Pounds** 1.1.1987; 1.1.1990. Similar to #2.	15.00	30.00	75.00

		VG	VF	UNC
7	**10 Pounds** 1.6.1988; 1.1.1990; 18.5.1993. Similar to #3.			
	a. 1.6.1988; 1.1.1990.	27.50	45.00	110.
	b. 18.5.1993.	25.00	40.00	90.00

		VG	VF	UNC
8	**20 Pounds** 1.1.1987; 1.4.1987; 1.1.1990. Similar to #4.			
	a. 1.1.1987.	42.50	70.00	180.
	b. 1.4.1987; 1.1.1990.	40.00	65.00	140.

		VG	VF	UNC
9	**100 Pounds** 1.12.1988. Similar to #5.	200.	350.	700.

Bank of Ireland

Belfast

1967 ND Issue

#56-64 Mercury at l., woman w/harp at r. Airplane, bank bldg. and boat on back. Sign. title as Agent.

		VG	VF	UNC
56	**1 Pound** ND (1967). Black on green and lilac underprint. 151 x 72mm. Signature W. E. Guthrie.	5.00	20.00	70.00
57	**5 Pounds** ND (1967-68). Brown-violet.			
	a. Signature W. E. Guthrie. (1967).	22.50	80.00	300.
	b. Signature H. H. M. Chestnutt. (1968).	18.00	70.00	250.
58	**10 Pounds** ND (1967). Brown and yellow. Signature W. E. Guthrie.	60.00	250.	700.

#59 and 60 *Deleted.*

1971-74 ND Issues

W/o word *Sterling* after Pound.

#61-63 replacement notes: Serial # prefix *Z*.

		VG	VF	UNC
61	**1 Pound** ND (1972-77). Black on light green and lilac underprint. Like #56 but smaller size. 134 x 66mm.			
	a. Signature H. H. M. Chestnutt. (1972).	7.00	30.00	60.00
	b. Signature A. S. J. O'Neill. (1977).	5.00	25.00	45.00
62	**5 Pounds** ND (1971-77). Blue on light green and lilac underprint. 146 x 78mm.			
	a. Signature H. H. M. Chestnutt. (1971).	25.00	100.	180.
	b. Signature A. S. J. O'Neill. (1977).	22.50	75.00	150.
63	**10 Pounds** ND (1971-77). Brown on light green and pale orange underprint.			
	a. Signature H. H. M. Chestnutt. (1971).	50.00	300.	600.
	b. Signature A. S. J. O'Neill. (1977).	40.00	200.	375.
64	**100 Pounds** ND (1974-78). Red on multicolor underprint.			
	a. Signature H. H. M. Chestnutt. (1974).	300.	950.	1400.
	b. Signature A. S. J. O'Neill. (1978).	275.	600.	950.

1980s ND Issue

Word *Sterling* added after Pound.

		VG	VF	UNC
65	**1 Pound** ND. Black on light green and lilac underprint. Like #61 but with *STERLING* added below value. Watermark: Bank name repeated. Signature A. S. J. O'Neill.	3.50	12.50	20.00
66	**5 Pounds** ND. Blue on light green and lilac underprint. Like #62 but with £ signs added in corners.			
	a. Signature A. S. J. O'Neill.	17.50	65.00	120.
	b. Signature D. F. Harrison.	14.00	45.00	80.00

		VG	VF	UNC
67	**10 Pounds** ND (1984). Dark brown on light green and pale orange underprint. Like #63.			
	a. Signature A. S. J. O'Neill.	30.00	120.	190.
	b. Signature D. F. Harrison.	25.00	100.	140.
67A	**20 Pounds** ND. Dark olive-green on multicolor underprint.			
	a. Signature A. S. J. O'Neill.	60.00	180.	275.
	b. Signature D. F. Harrison.	60.00	170.	225.
68	**100 Pounds** ND. Red on multicolor underprint. Similar to #64 but with £ sign at upper right and lower left corners on face and back. *Sterling* added at lower center on face.			
	a. Signature A. S. J. O'Neill.	250.	525.	750.
	b. Signature D. F. Harrison.	225.	400.	650.

1983 Commemorative Issue

#69, Bank of Ireland Bicentenary, 1783-1983

		VG	VF	UNC
69	**20 Pounds** 1983. Dark olive-green on multicolor underprint. Like #67A but commemorative text below bank title. Signature A. S. J. O'Neill.	175.	600.	1200.

1990-95 Issue

#70-74 bank seal (Hibernia seated) at l., six county shields at upper ctr. Queen's University in Belfast on back. Sign. D. F. Harrison. Wmk: Medusa head.

		VG	VF	UNC
70	**5 Pounds** 28.8.1990; 16.1.1992. Blue and purple on multicolor underprint.			
	a. Issued note	12.50	22.50	40.00
	s. Specimen.	—	—	100.

		VG	VF	UNC
71	**10 Pounds** 14.5.1991. Purple and maroon on multicolor underprint.			
	a. Issued note.	20.00	35.00	65.00
	s. Specimen.	—	—	120.

		VG	VF	UNC
72	**20 Pounds** 9.5.1991. Green and brown on multicolor underprint.			
	a. Issued note.	42.50	80.00	130.
	s. Specimen.	—	—	200.
73	**100 Pounds** 28.8.1992. Red on multicolor underprint.			
	a. Issued note.	225.	275.	400.
	s. Specimen.	—	—	400.

Note: Specimens and 3-subject sheets were sold to collectors. Low numbers were also available to special folders.

NOTICE

Readers with unlisted dates, signature varieties, etc. are invited to submit photocopies of their notes to: Standard Catalog of World Paper Money, 700 East State St. Iola, WI 54990-0001, E-Mail: george.cuhaj@fwpubs.com.

1995; 1998 ISSUE

#74-76, 78 like #70-73 except for somewhat different color arrangements.
#74-78 w/ascending size serial # at lower r.

		VG	VF	UNC
74	**5 Pounds** 4.8.1998; 5.9.2000. Blue and purple on multicolor underprint. Like #74.	FV	15.00	30.00

		VG	VF	UNC
75	**10 Pounds** 1.7.1995; 1.7.1998; 5.9.2000. Purple and maroon on multicolor underprint. Like #75.	FV	27.50	45.00

		VG	VF	UNC
76	**20 Pounds** 1995; 1.1.1999. Green and brown on multicolor underprint. Like #76.	FV	55.00	85.00

		VG	VF	UNC
77	**50 Pounds** 1.7.1995; 1.9.1999. Brown, olive and multicolor. Seated woman at left. The Queen's University in Belfast on back.	100.	140.	190.

		VG	VF	UNC
78	**100 Pounds** 1.7.1995. Red on multicolor underprint. Like #73.	FV	225.	350.

2003 ISSUE

		VG	VF	UNC
79	**5 Pounds** 1.3.2003. Blue and violet on multicolor underprint. Queen's University, Belfast on back. Signature Sowden.	FV	FV	15.00
82	**100 Pounds** 1.3.2005. Multicolor. Signature McGovern.	FV	FV	275.

BELFAST BANKING COMPANY LIMITED

1922-23 ISSUE

#126-131 arms at top or upper ctr. w/payable text: . . . *at our Head Office, Belfast.*

#127-131 arms at top or upper ctr. w/payable text: . . . *at our Head Office, Belfast.*

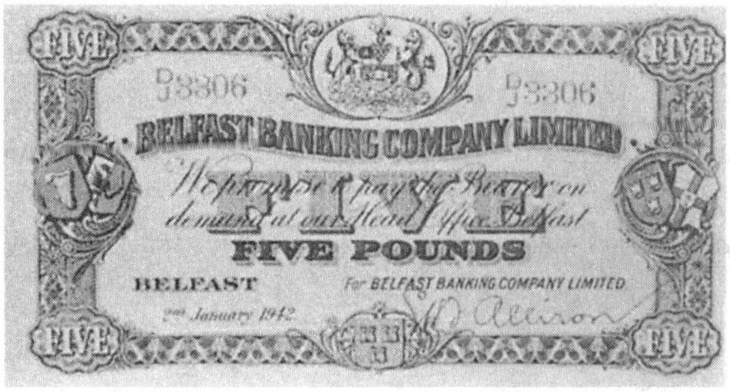

		VG	VF	UNC
127	**5 Pounds** 1923-66. Black on red underprint.			
	a. Black serial #. 3.1.1923; 3.5.1923; 7.9.1927.	200.	300.	700.
	b. Red serial #. 8.3.1928-2.10.1942.	200.	450.	550.
	c. Red serial #. 6.1.1966.	100.	200.	300.

128	10 Pounds	VG	VF	UNC
	1923-65. Black on green underprint.			
	a. Black serial #. 3.1.1923.	300.	500.	850.
	b. Green serial #. 9.1.1929-1.1.1943.	200.	300.	600.
	c. Green serial #. 3.12.1963; 5.6.1965.	65.00	160.	300.
129	20 Pounds			
	1923-65. Black on purple underprint.			
	a. Black serial #. 3.1.1923.	800.	1600.	—
	b. Mauve serial #. 9.11.1939; 10.8.1940.	650.	1200.	—
	c. Black serial #. 3.2.1943.	400.	900.	1500.
	d. Black serial #. 5.6.1965.	200.	350.	550.

130	50 Pounds	VG	VF	UNC
	1923-63. Black on orange underprint.			
	a. Black serial #. 3.1.1923; 3.5.1923.	1000.	2000.	—
	b. Yellow serial #. 9.11.1939; 10.8.1940.	800.	1250.	2000.
	c. Black serial #. 3.2.1943.	650.	900.	1800.
	d. Black serial #. 3.12.1963.	450.	750.	1200.

131	100 Pounds	VG	VF	UNC
	1923-68. Black on red underprint.			
	a. 3.1.1923; 3.5.1923.	750.	1300.	2000.
	b. 9.11.1939; 3.2.1943.	500.	900.	1600.
	c. 3.12.1963.	450.	750.	1400.
	d. 8.5.1968.	450.	700.	1200.

FIRST TRUST BANK

1994 ISSUE

#132-135 five shields at bottom ctr. Printer: TDLR. Sign. title: *GROUP MANAGING DIRECTOR*. Wmk: Young woman.

132	10 Pounds	VG	VF	UNC
	10.1.1994; 1.3.1996. Dark brown and purple. Face similar to #3. Sailing ship Girona at center on back.			
	a. 10.1.1994.	27.50	50.00	80.00
	b. 1.3.1996.	27.50	60.00	110.

133	20 Pounds	VG	VF	UNC
	10.1.1994. Violet, dark brown and red-brown on multicolor underprint. Face similar to #4. Chimney at Lacada Point at center on back.			
	a. 10.1.1994.	45.00	75.00	120.
	b. 1996.	50.00	85.00	140.

134	50 Pounds	VG	VF	UNC
	10.1.1994. Black, dark olive-green and blue on multicolor underprint. Face similar to #5. Cherubs holding Armada medallion at center on back.	110.	160.	250.

135	100 Pounds	VG	VF	UNC
	10.1.1994; 1.3.1996. Black and olive-brown on multicolor underprint. Elderly couple at right. The *Armada* at center on back.			
	a. 10.1.1994.	200.	275.	400.
	b. 1.3.1996.	200.	275.	500.

1998 ISSUE

#136-139 like #132-135 but w/added security features.

		VG	VF	UNC
136	**10 Pounds**			
	1998. Dark brown and purple. Like #132 but with scalloped gold seal over value at upper right.			
	a. Issued note.	FV	25.00	45.00
	s. Specimen.	—	Unc	300.
137	**20 Pounds**			
	1998. Violet, dark brown and red-brown on multicolor underprint. Like #133 but with windowed security thread and gold seal at upper right.			
	a. Issued note.	FV	55.00	90.00
	s. Specimen.	—	—	350.
138	**50 Pounds**			
	1998. Black, dark olive-green and blue on multicolor underprint. Like #134 but with windowed security thread and silver seal at upper right.			
	a. Issued note.	FV	110.	175.
	s. Specimen.	—	—	400.
139	**100 Pounds**			
	1998. Black and olive-brown on multicolor underprint. Like #135 but with windowed security thread and gold seal at upper right.			
	a. Issued note.	FV	250.	350.
	s. Specimen.	—	—	475.

NORTHERN BANK LIMITED

1929 REGULAR ISSUE

#178; 181 sailing ship, plow and man at grindstone at upper ctr.

		VG	VF	UNC
178	**1 Pound**			
	1929-68. Black. Blue guilloche.			
	a. Red serial #. 6.5.1929; 1.7.1929; 1.8.1929.	35.00	110.	200.
	b. Black prefix letters and serial #. 1.1.1940.	25.00	90.00	150.
	c. 1.10.1968.	12.50	40.00	85.00

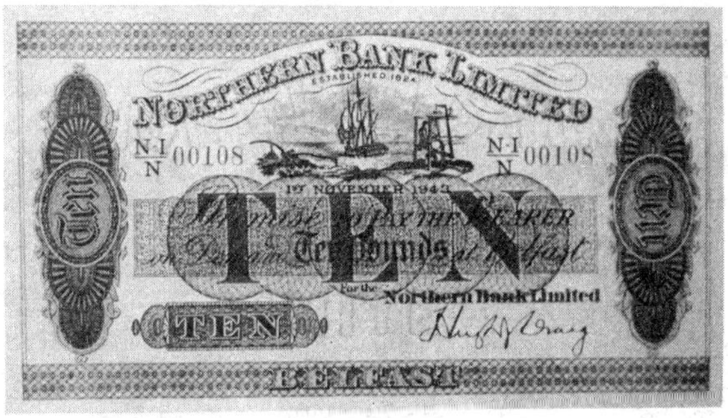

		VG	VF	UNC
181	**10 Pounds**			
	1930-68. Black on red underprint.			
	a. Red serial #. 1.1.1930-1.1.1940.	140.	275.	575.
	b. Black serial #. 1.8.1940; 1.9.1940.	120.	225.	450.
	c. Red serial #. 1.1.1942-1.11.1943.	90.00	200.	350.
	d. Imprint on back below central designature 1.10.1968.	25.00	50.00	200.

1968 ISSUE

		VG	VF	UNC
184	**5 Pounds**			
	1.10.1968. Black on green underprint.	20.00	70.00	130.
185	**50 Pounds**			
	1.10.1968. Black on dark blue underprint. *NBLD* monogram on back.	250.	500.	900.
186	**100 Pounds**			
	1.10.1968. Black on dark blue underprint. *NBLD* monogram on back.	400.	900.	1400.

1970 ISSUE

#187-192 cows at l., shipyard at bottom ctr., loom at r. Stylized arms at ctr. on back. Sign. varieties.

		VG	VF	UNC
187	**1 Pound**			
	1970-82. Green on pink underprint. Printer: BWC.			
	a. Signature Wilson.	8.00	27.50	50.00
	b. Signature Gabbey.	8.00	25.00	50.00
	c. Signatrue Ervin.	6.00	22.50	40.00
188	**5 Pounds**			
	1.7.1970-1.4.1982. Light blue.			
	a. Signature Wilson.	35.00	90.00	170.
	b. Signature Gabbey.	32.50	90.00	160.
	c. Signature Newland.	27.50	60.00	100.
	d. Signature Ervin.	25.00	50.00	80.00
	e. Signature Roberts.	25.00	60.00	100.
189	**10 Pounds**			
	1970-88. Brown.			
	a. Signature Wilson.	32.50	90.00	200.
	b. Signature Gabbey.	90.00	200.	375.
	c. Signature Newland.	80.00	150.	275.
	d. Signature Ervin.	60.00	120.	225.
	e. Signature Roberts.	60.00	100.	190.
	f. Signature Torrens.	45.00	90.00	150.
190	**20 Pounds**			
	1.7.1970; 1.3.1981; 2.3.1987; 15.6.1988. Purple.			
	a. Signature Wilson.	175.	300.	600.
	b. Signature Ervin.	100.	225.	400.
	c. Signature Roberts.	80.00	200.	375.
	d. Signature Torrens.	55.00	130.	200.

		VG	VF	UNC
191	**50 Pounds**			
	1.7.1970; 1.3.1981. Orange.			
	a. Signature Wilson.	250.	450.	700.
	b. Signature Newland.	175.	450.	700.
	c. Signature Ervin.	150.	275.	425.
192	**100 Pounds**			
	1.7.1970; 1.10.1971; 1.1.1975; 1.7.1976; 1.1.1980. Red.			
	a. Signature Wilson.	325.	500.	900.
	b. Signature Gabbey.	300.	450.	850.
	c. Signature Newland.	275.	375.	750.
	d. Signature Ervin.	250.	375.	700.

1988-90 ISSUE

#193-197 dish antenna at l., stylized *N* at ctr. and computer on back. Printer: TDLR.

		VG	VF	UNC
193	**5 Pounds**			
	24.8.1988; 24.8.1989; 24.8.1990. Blue and multicolor. Station above trolley car at center, W. A. Traill at right.			
	a. 24.8.1988; 24.8.1989.	FV	22.50	50.00
	b. 24.8.1990.	FV	20.00	40.00

194 **10 Pounds**
24.8.1988; 14.5.1991; 24.8.1993. Red and brown on multicolor underprint. Early automobile above bicyclist at center, J. B. Dunlop at right.

	VG	VF	UNC
a. 24.8.1988; 24.8.1990.	40.00	100.	160.
b. 14.5.1991; 24.8.1993.	30.00	80.00	140.
c. 30.8.1996.	FV	60.00	100.

195 **20 Pounds**
24.8.1988; 24.8.1989; 24.8.1990; 9.5.1991; 30.3.1992; 8.24.1993. Purple-brown, red and multicolor. Airplane at center, H. G. Ferguson at right, tractor at bottom right.

	VG	VF	UNC
a. 24.8.1988.	75.00	140.	225.
b. 24.8.1989; 24.8.1990; 9.5.1991; 30.3.1992; 8.24.1993.	60.00	100.	175.
c. 30.8.1996.	50.00	90.00	150.

196 **50 Pounds**
1.11.1990. Bluish green, black and multicolor. Tea dryer, centrifugal machine at center, Sir S. Davidson at right.

VG	VF	UNC
110.	180.	275.

197 **100 Pounds**
1.11.1990. Lilac, black, blue and multicolor. Airplanes and ejection seat at center, Sir J. Martin at right.

VG	VF	UNC
250.	375.	500.

1997; 1999 ISSUE

#198-201 city hall in Belfast at ctr., bldgs. and architectural drawings in unpt. on back.

		VG	VF	UNC
198	**10 Pounds** 24.2.1997. Dark brown and violet on multicolor underprint. J. B. Dunlop at right and as watermark, bicycle at lower left.			
	a. 24.2.1997. Signature Savage.	FV	32.50	50.00
	b. 8.10.1999. Signature Price.	FV	27.50	40.00
199	**20 Pounds** 24.2.1997; 8.10.1999. Purple and dark brown on multicolor underprint. H. Ferguson at right and as watermark, farm tractor at lower left.			
	a. 24.2.1997. Signature Savage.	FV	50.00	70.00
	b. 8.10.1999. Signature Price.	FV	55.00	75.00
200	**50 Pounds** 8.10.1999. Olive brown on multicolor underprint. Sir Samuel Davidson at right.	100.	160.	225.
201	**100 Pounds** 8.10.1999. Brown olive on multicolor underprint. Sir James Martin at right. Martin Baker ejection seat at left.	200.	250.	325.

1999 COMMEMORATIVE ISSUE

#202, 175 Years of Banking, 1824-1999

202 **20 Pounds**
1.9.1999 Purple and dark brown on multicolor underprint. Like #199 but with commemorative text and gold rectangle at upper left center on face.

VG	VF	UNC
42.50	65.00	100.

2000 COMMEMORATIVE ISSUE

#203, Millennium and Y2K Commemoratives

203 **5 Pounds**
1999; 2000. Blue, red and multicolor. Ovals, globe pattern. Space shuttle, electronics on back. Polymer plastic.

	VG	VF	UNC
a. 8.10.1999. Serial # prefix MM.	FV	12.50	20.00
b. 1.1.2000. Serial # prefix Y2K.	FV	17.50	32.50

2004 ISSUE

		VG	VF	UNC
204	**5 Pounds** 2004. Multicolor.	FV	FV	15.00
205	**10 Pounds** 29.4.2004. Multicolor.	FV	37.50	80.00

2005 ISSUE

		VG	VF	UNC
206	**10 Pounds** 19.1.2005. Multicolor.	FV	FV	30.00
207	**20 Pounds** 19.1.2005. Multicolor.	FV	FV	65.00
208	**50 Pounds** 19.1.2005. Multicolor.	FV	FV	160.
209	**100 Pounds** 19.1.2005. Multicolor.	FV	FV	275.

PROVINCIAL BANK OF IRELAND LIMITED

BELFAST

1948; 1951 ISSUE

		VG	VF	UNC
240	**10 Pounds** 10.1.1948. Green on red underprint. and green and pink mesh.			
	a. Signature H. Robertson.	25.00	60.00	125.
	b. Signature F. S. Forde.	22.00	55.00	110.
	c. Signature G. A. Kennedy.	20.00	50.00	100.

1954 ISSUE

		VG	VF	UNC
241	**1 Pound** 1.10.1954. Green. 148 x 84mm.	20.00	70.00	140.
242	**5 Pounds** 5.10.1954-5.7.1961. Brown.	30.00	90.00	200.

1965 ISSUE

#243 and 244 cameo portr. archaic woman at upper ctr. Bank bldg. at ctr. on back.
#243-246 printer: TDLR.

		VG	VF	UNC
243	**1 Pound** 1.12.1965. Green.	80.00	300.	500.
244	**5 Pounds** 6.12.1965. Brown.	75.00	200.	300.

1968 ISSUE

		VG	VF	UNC
245	**1 Pound** 1.1.1968-1.1.1972. Green. Like #243. 150 x 71mm.	25.00	60.00	110.
246	**5 Pounds** 5.1.1968; 5.1.1970; 5.1.1972. Brown. Like #244. 139 x 84mm.	25.00	50.00	90.00

1977; 1981 ISSUE

		VG	VF	UNC
247	**1 Pound** 1977; 1979. Green on multicolor underprint. Like #1. Young girl at right. Sailing ship *Girona* at center on back.			
	a. Signature J. G. McClay. 1.1.1977.	5.00	25.00	45.00
	b. Signature F. H. Hollway. 1.1.1979.	5.00	25.00	37.50

		VG	VF	UNC
248	**5 Pounds** 1977; 1979. Blue and purple on multicolor underprint. Like #2. Young woman at right. Dunluce Castle at center on back.			
	a. Signature J. G. McClay. 1.1.1977.	22.50	52.50	125.
	b. Signature F. H. Hollway. 1.1.1979.	18.00	42.50	100.
249	**10 Pounds** 1977; 1979. Brown and gray-green on multicolor underprint. Like #3. Young man at right. Wreck of the *Girona* at center on back.			
	a. Signature J. G. McClay. 1.1.1977.	35.00	100.	175.
	b. Signature F. H. Hollway. 1.1.1979.	32.50	90.00	150.
250	**20 Pounds** 1.3.1981. Purple and green. Like #4. Elderly woman at right. Chimney at Lacada Point at center on back.	60.00	150.	300.
251	**100 Pounds** 1.3.1981. Black, olive and green. Like #5. Elderly man at right. The *Armada* at center on back.	250.	450.	950.

ULSTER BANK LIMITED

1966-70 ISSUE

#321-324 rural and urban views of Belfast at lower l. and r., port w/bridge at lower ctr. below sign., date to r. Arms at ctr. on back. Sign. Jno. J. A. Leitch. Printer: BWC.

		VG	VF	UNC
321	**1 Pound** 4.10.1966. Blue-black on multicolor underprint. 151 x 72mm.			
	a. Issued note.	10.00	35.00	65.00
	s. Specimen.	—	—	90.00

322	5 Pounds	VG	VF	UNC
	4.10.1900. Drown on multicolor underprint. 140 x 85mm.			
	a. Issued note.	25.00	00.00	250
	s. Specimen, punch hole cancelled.	—	—	200.

323	10 Pounds	VG	VF	UNC
	4.10.1966. Green on multicolor underprint. 151 x 93mm.			
	a. Issued note.	50.00	120.	400.
	s. Specimen, punch hole cancelled.	—	—	275.

324	20 Pounds	VG	VF	UNC
	1.7.1970. Lilac on multicolor underprint. 161 x 90mm. Specimen, punch hole cancelled.	—	—	500.

NOTICE

Readers with unlisted dates, signature varieties, etc. are invited to submit photocopies of their notes to: Standard Catalog of World Paper Money, 700 East State St. Iola, WI 54990-0001, E-Mail: george.cuhaj@fwpubs.com.

1971-82 ISSUE

#325-330 printer: BWC.
#325-328 similar to #321-324 but date at l., sign. at ctr. r.

325	1 Pound	VG	VF	UNC
	1971-76. Blue-black on multicolor underprint. Watermark: Bank name repeated. 135 x 67mm.			
	a. Signature H. E. O'B. Traill. 15.2.1971.	7.00	22.50	60.00
	b. Signature R. W. Hamilton. 1.3.1973; 1.3.1976.	5.00	12.50	30.00
	s. As a. Cpooimon.	—	—	100.
326	**5 Pounds**			
	1971-86. Brown on multicolor underprint. 146 x 78mm.			
	a. Signature H. E. O'B. Traill. 15.2.1971.	30.00	125.	300.
	b. Sign R. W. Hamilton. 1.3.1973; 1.3.1976.	17.50	45.00	130.
	c. Signature V. Chambers. 1.10.1982; 1.10.1983; 1.9.1986.	15.00	30.00	65.00

327	10 Pounds	VG	VF	UNC
	1971-89. Green on multicolor underprint. 151 x 86mm.			
	a. Signature H. E. O'B. Traill. 15.2.1971.	45.00	200.	350.
	b. Signature R. W. Hamilton. 1.3.1973; 1.3.1976; 2.6.1980.	35.00	80.00	160.
	c. Signature V. Chambers. 1.10.1982; 1.10.1983; 1.2.1988.	27.50	75.00	140.
	d. Signature J. Wead. 1.12.1989.	27.50	60.00	120.
328	**20 Pounds**			
	1976-83. Violet on multicolor underprint.			
	a. Signature Brian. 15.2.1971.	700.	1300.	2000.
	b. Signature R. W. Hamilton. 1.3.1976.	70.00	150.	250.
	c. Signature V. Chambers. 1.10.1982; 1.10.1983; 1.2.1988.	70.00	140.	200.
329	**50 Pounds**			
	1.10.1982. Brown on multicolor underprint. Signature V. Chambers.			
	a. Issued note.	130.	275.	450.
	s. Specimen.	—	—	550.
330	**100 Pounds**			
	1.3.1973. Red on multicolor underprint. Signature R. W. Hamilton.			
	a. 1.3.1973. Signature Hamilton.	200.	400.	700.
	b. 1.10.1982. Signature Chambers.	200.	400.	700.
	s. Specimen.	—	—	650.

1989-90 ISSUE

#331-334 similar to previous issue but smaller size notes. Sign. J. Wead. Printer: TDLR.
Note: The Bank of Ireland sold to collectors matched serial # sets of £5-10-20 notes as well as 100 sets of replacement serial # prefix *Z*.

331	5 Pounds	VG	VF	UNC
	1.12.1989; 1.1.1992; 4.1.1993. Brown on multicolor underprint. Similar to #326.			
	a. 1.12.1989	FV	22.50	50.00
	b. 1.1.1992; 4.1.1993.	FV	20.00	40.00
	s. Specimen. 4.1.1993	—	—	300.

		VG	VF	UNC
332	**10 Pounds** 1.12.1990. Green on multicolor underprint. Similar to #327.			
	a. Issued note.	22.50	35.00	75.00
	s. Specimen.	—	—	375.
333	**20 Pounds** 1.11.1990. Violet on multicolor underprint. Similar to #328.			
	a. Issued note.	FV	75.00	200.
	s. Specimen.	—	—	450.
334	**100 Pounds** 1.12.1990. Red on multicolor underprint. Similar to #330.			
	a. Issued note.	225.	400.	700.
	s. Specimen.	—	—	650.

1996; 1998 Issue

#335-338 similar to #329, 331-333 but w/ascending size serial # at l. and r.

		VG	VF	UNC
335	**5 Pounds** 2.1.1998; 1.7.1998; 1.1.2001. Similar to #331.			
	a. 1.7.1998. Signature Wilson.	FV	12.50	27.50
	b. 1.1.2001. Signature Wilson.	FV	10.00	17.50

		VG	VF	UNC
336	**10 Pounds** 1.1.1997. Blue and green on multicolor underprint. Similar to #332.			
	a. 1.1.1997. Signature Kells.	FV	22.50	40.00
	b. 1.7.1999. Signature Wilson.	FV	20.00	32.50

		VG	VF	UNC
337	**20 Pounds** 1.1.1996; 1.7.1999. Purple and violet on multicolor underprint. Similar to #333 but with hologram at upper center right.			
	a. 1.1.1996. Signature Kells.	45.00	75.00	150.
	b. 1.7.1999. Signature Wilson.	FV	47.50	80.00
	c. 1.7.2002. Signature Wilson.	FV	42.50	70.00
	d. 6.1.2004. Signature McCarthy.	FV	FV	60.00

		VG	VF	UNC
338	**50 Pounds** 1.1.1997. Brown on multicolor underprint. Similar to #329 but with hologram at upper center right.	FV	120.	220.

Collector Series

Bank of Ireland

1978 ND Issue

		Issue Price	Mkt. Value
CS1	**ND (1978). 1, 5, 10, 100 Pounds** #61b-64b overprint: *SPECIMEN* and Maltese cross prefix serial #.	—	85.00

Provincial Bank of Ireland Limited

1978 Issue

		Issue Price	Mkt. Value
CS2	**1978 1, 5, 10 Pounds** #247a-249a dated 1.1.1977. Overprint: *SPECIMEN* and Maltese cross prefix serial #.	—	60.00

Bank of Ireland

1995 ND Issue

		Issue Price	Mkt. Value
CS3	**ND (1995). 5, 10, 100 Pounds** #62b-64b overprint: *SPECIMEN.*	—	400.

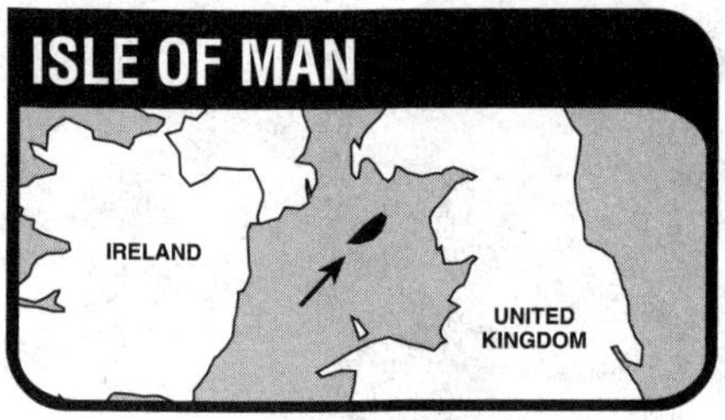

The Isle of Man, a dependency of the British Crown located in the Irish Sea equidistant from Ireland, Scotland and England, has an area of 227 sq. mi. (588 sq. km.) and a population of 71,714. Capital: Douglas. Agriculture, dairy farming, fishing and tourism are the chief industries.

The prevalence of prehistoric artifacts and monuments on the island gives evidence that its mild, almost sub-tropical climate was enjoyed by mankind before the dawn of history. Vikings came to the Isle of Man during the 9th century and remained until ejected by Scotland in 1266. The island came under the protection of the English Crown in 1288, and in 1406 was granted, in perpetuity, to the Earls of Derby. In 1736 it was inherited by the Duke of Atholl. Rights and title were purchased from the Duke of Atholl in 1765 by the British Crown; the remaining privileges of the Atholl family were transferred to the crown in 1829. The Sovereign of the United Kingdom (currently Queen Elizabeth II) holds the title Lord of Man. The Isle of Man is ruled by its own legislative council and the House of Keys, one of the oldest legislative assemblies in the world. Acts of Parliament passed in London do not affect the island unless it is specifically mentioned.

United Kingdom bank notes and coinage circulate concurrently with Isle of Man money as legal tender.

RULERS:
British

MONETARY SYSTEM:
1 Pound = 20 Shillings to 1971
1 Pound = 100 New Pence, 1971-
1 Guinea = 1 Pound 1 Shilling

BRITISH ADMINISTRATION

LLOYDS BANK LIMITED

1955 ISSUE

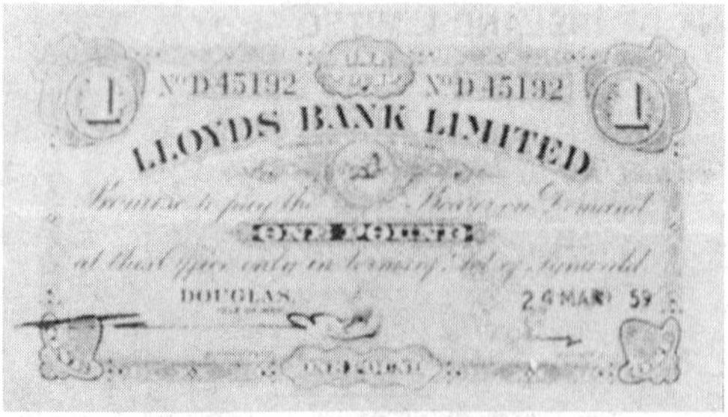

13	1 Pound	Good	Fine	XF
	21.1.1955-14.3.1961. Black on green underprint. Bank arms at upper center Like #12 but bank title enlarged on back.			
	a. Issued note.	180.	350.	750.
	r. Unsigned remainder. ND.	—	—	200.

WESTMINSTER BANK LIMITED

1955 ISSUE

#23A, various date and sign. varieties.

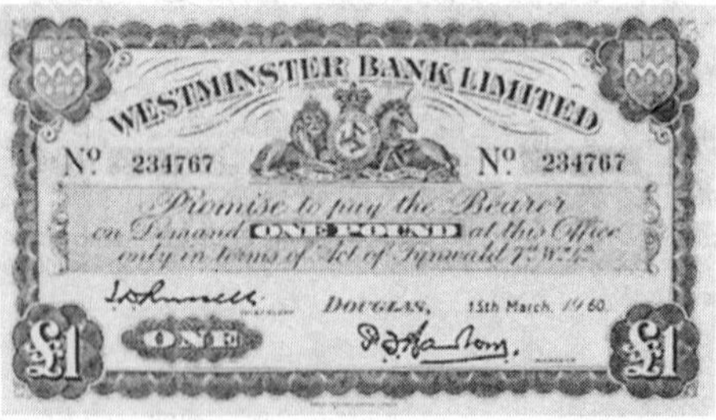

23A	1 Pound	Good	Fine	XF
	1955-61. Black on light yellow underprint. Like #23 but with text: *INCORPORATED IN ENGLAND* added below bank name. Printer: W&S.			
	a. 23.11.1955.	100.	200.	500.
	b. 4.4.1956-10.3.1961.	40.00	100.	225.

GOVERNMENT

1961 ND ISSUE

#24-27 TRISKELE ARMS AT LOWER CTR. AND AS WMK., YOUNG PORTR. QN. ELIZABETH II AT R. PRINTER: BWC.

SIGNATURE VARIETIES			
1	Garvey	2	Stallard
3	Paul (26mm)	4	Paul (20mm)
5	Dawaon	6	Cashen

24	10 Shillings	VG	VF	UNC
	ND (1961). Red on multicolor underprint. Old sailing boat on back.			
	a. Signature 1.	5.00	25.00	75.00
	b. Signature 2.	5.00	20.00	60.00
	s1. Signature 1. Specimen. 00000 serial #. (150 issued).	—	—	190.
	s2. Signature 2. Specimen.	—	—	—

25	1 Pound	VG	VF	UNC
	ND (1961). Purple on multicolor underprint. Tynwald Hill on back.			
	a. Signature 1.	7.50	40.00	140.
	b. Signature 2.	5.00	30.00	120.
	s1. Signature 1. Specimen. 00000 serial #. (150 issued).	—	—	200.
	s2. Signature 2. Specimen.	—	—	200.

26	5 Pounds	VG	VF	UNC
	ND (1961). Green and blue on multicolor underprint. Castle Rushen on back.			
	a. Signature 1.	40.00	200.	1100.
	b. Signature 2.	35.00	165.	1000.
	s1. Specimen with normal serial #.	—	—	500.
	s2. Signature 1. Specimen with normal serial # blocked out, punch hole cancelled. (50 issued).	—	—	350.
	s3. Signature 1. Specimen. 000000 serial #. (150 issued).	—	—	350.

1969 ND ISSUE

27	50 New Pence	VG	VF	UNC
	ND (1969). Blue on multicolor underprint. Back like #24. 139 x 66mm. Signature 2.	2.00	9.00	35.00

1972 ND ISSUE

#28-31 Triskele arms at ctr. and as wmk., older portr. Qn. Elizabeth II at r. Sign. title: *LIEUTENANT GOVERNOR*. Printer: BWC.

28	50 New Pence	VG	VF	UNC
	ND (1972). Blue on multicolor underprint. Back like #24. 126 x 62mm.			
	a. Signature 2.	4.00	20.00	60.00
	b. Signature 3.	2.00	12.50	30.00
	c. Signature 4.	2.00	12.50	30.00
	s1. As a. Specimen. Punched hole cancelled.	—	—	200.
	s2. As b, c. Specimen.	—	—	200.
29	1 Pound			
	ND (1972). Purple on multicolor underprint. Back similar to #25.			
	a. Signature 2.	5.00	25.00	110.
	b. Signature 3. Series D.	50.00	150.	550.
	c. Signature 3. Series E.	5.00	25.00	80.00
	d. Signature 4.	2.50	7.50	45.00
	s1. As a. Specimen. Punched hole cancelled.	—	—	200.
	s2. As b, c. Specimen.	—	—	200.

30	5 Pounds	VG	VF	UNC
	ND (1972). Blue-black and violet on multicolor underprint. Back gray-green; similar to #26.			
	a. Signature 2.	25.00	75.00	525.
	b. Signature 3.	15.00	40.00	275.
	s. As a, b. Specimen. Punched hole cancelled.	—	—	325.

31	10 Pounds	VG	VF	UNC
	ND (1972). Brown and dark green on multicolor underprint. Back brown and orange; Peel Castle ca.1830 at center.			
	a. Signature 2.	175.	500.	1500.
	b. Signature 3.	60.00	150.	600.
	s. As a, b. Specimen, punched hole cancelled.	—	—	700.

1979 COMMEMORATIVE ISSUE

#32, Millennium Year 1979

32	20 Pounds	VG	VF	UNC
	1979. Red-orange, orange and dark brown on multicolor underprint. Triskele at center. Queen Elizabeth II at right. Island outline at upper right. Commemorative text at lower right of triskele. Laxey wheel ca. 1854, crowd of people with hills in background on back. Printer: BWC.	50.00	150.	375.

1979 ND ISSUE

#33-37 Qn. Elizabeth II at r., arms at ctr. Sign. title: *TREASURER OF THE ISLE OF MAN*. Wmk: Triskele arms. Printer: BWC.

#33s-38s were mounted on a board for bank display.

33	50 New Pence	VG	VF	UNC
	ND. Blue on multicolor underprint. Like #28. Signature 5.			
	a. Issued note.	FV	FV	12.00
	s. Specimen. Normal serial #, punched hole cancelled.	—	—	175.
34	1 Pound			
	ND. Purple on multicolor underprint. Like #29. Signature 5.			
	a. Issued note.	FV	FV	20.00
	s. Specimen. Normal serial #, punched hole cancelled.	—	—	175.

		VG	VF	UNC
35	**5 Pounds**			
	ND. Blue-black and violet on multicolor underprint. Like #30.			
	a. Signature 5. Series B-C.	12.50	50.00	175.
	b. Signature 5. Series D. Large 'D' with serifs.	20.00	75.00	300.
35A	**5 Pounds**			
	ND. Blue-black and violet on multicolor underprint. Like #35 but with modified guilloche. Series D. Narrow 'D' without serifs.			
	a. Issued note.	12.50	50.00	175.
	s. Specimen. Normal serial #, punched hole cancelled.	—	—	275.

		VG	VF	UNC
36	**10 Pounds**			
	ND. Brown and dark green on multicolor underprint. Like #31. Signature 5.			
	a. Without prefix.	25.00	90.00	375.
	b. Prefix A.	25.00	100.	375.
	c. Prefix B. (10,000 printed).	300.	600.	1600.
	s. Specimen. Prefix A, normal serial #, punched hole cancelled.	—	—	400.

		VG	VF	UNC
37	**20 Pounds**			
	ND (1979). Red-orange, orange and dark brown on multicolor underprint. Like #32 but without commemorative text.			
	a. Issued note.	40.00	125.	400.
	s. Specimen. Normal serial #, punched hole cancelled.	—	—	450.

1983 ND Issue

		VG	VF	UNC
38	**1 Pound**			
	ND (1983). Green on multicolor underprint. Like #25 but printed on Bradvek, a plastic.	2.00	5.00	25.00

		VG	VF	UNC
39	**50 Pounds**			
	ND (1983). Blue gray, deep green and olive-green on multicolor underprint. Douglas Bay on back.			
	a. Issued note.	FV	100.	175.
	s. Specimen. Normal serial #, punched hole cancelled.	—	—	550.

1983 ND Reduced Size Issue

#40-44 smaller format. Qn. Elizabeth II at r., arms at ctr. Wmk: Triskele. Printer: TDLR. Replacement notes: Serial # prefix *Z*.

		VG	VF	UNC
40	**1 Pound**			
	ND. Purple on multicolor underprint. Back like #25.			
	a. Signature 5.	FV	4.00	12.00
	b. Signature 6.	FV	FV	5.00

		VG	VF	UNC
41	**5 Pounds**			
	ND. Greenish blue and lilac-brown on multicolor underprint. Back like #30.			
	a. Signature 5.	FV	20.00	60.00
	b. Signature 6.	FV	FV	20.00

		VG	VF	UNC
42	**10 Pounds**			
	ND. Brown and green on multicolor underprint. Like #31. Back brown, orange and multicolor.	FV	FV	90.00

		VG	VF	UNC
43	**20 Pounds** ND. Brown and red-orange on multicolor underprint. Back like #32.			
	a. Signature 5.	40.00	100.	375.
	b. Signature 6.	FV	FV	90.00

1998; 2000 ND Issue

#44-45 like #42-43 but w/*LIMITED* deleted from payment clause.

		VG	VF	UNC
44	**10 Pounds** ND (1998). Brown and green on multicolor underprint. Like #42.	FV	FV	37.50
45	**20 Pounds** ND (2000). Brown and red-orange on multicolor underprint. Like #43b.			
	a. Issued note.	FV	FV	60.00
	s. Specimen. Serial # *D000000*. Punch hole cancelled.	—	—	200.

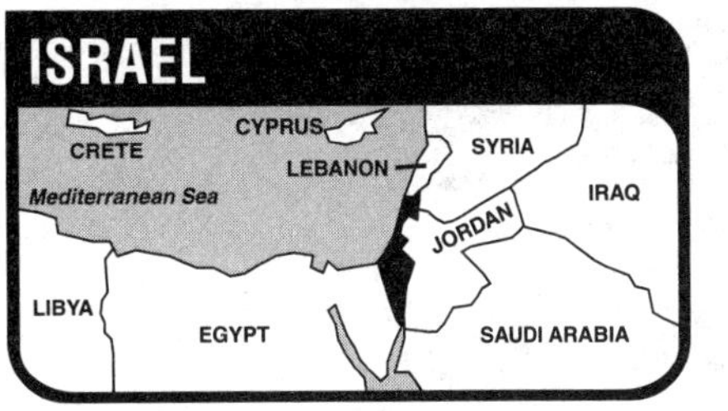

The State of Israel, at the eastern end of the Mediterranean Sea, bounded by Lebanon on the north, Syria on the northeast, Jordan on the east, and Egypt on the southwest, has an area of 7,847 sq. mi. (23,309 sq. km.) and a population of 6.08 million. Capital: Jerusalem. Diamonds, chemicals, citrus, textiles, and minerals are exported, local tourism to religious sites.

Palestine, which corresponds to Canaan of the Bible, was settled by the Philistines about the 12th century B.C. and shortly thereafter was invaded by the Jews who established the kingdoms of Israel and Judah. Because of its position as part of the land bridge connecting Asia and Africa, Palestine was invaded and conquered by nearly all of the historic empires of ancient Europe and Asia. In the 16th century it became a Turkish satrap. After falling to the British in World War I, it, together with Transjordan, was mandated to Great Britain by the League of Nations in 1922.

For more than half a century prior to the termination of the British mandate over Palestine in 1948, Zionist leaders had sought to create a Jewish homeland for Jews dispersed throughout the world. Israel was the logical location choice as it had long been the Jewish religious and cultural homeland. Also, for almost as long, Jews fleeing persecution had immigrated to Palestine. The Nazi persecutions of the 1930s and 1940s increased the Jewish relocation to Palestine and generated international support for the creation of a Jewish state, first promulgated by the Balfour Declaration of 1917 which asserted British support for the endeavor. The dream of a Jewish homeland was realized on May 14, 1948 when Palestine was proclaimed the State of Israel.

MONETARY SYSTEM:

1 Palestine Pound = 1000 Mils to 1948
1 Lira = 1000 Prutot, 1948-1960
1 Lira = 100 Agorot, 1958-1980
1 New Sheqel = 1000 "old" Sheqalim, 1985-
1 New Sheqel = 100 Agorot, 1985-

State of Israel

Bank of Israel

1958-60 / 5718-20 Issue

Lira system

#29-33 wmk. as portrait.

#29, 30 and 33 printer: JEZ (w/o imprint).

		VG	VF	UNC
29	**1/2 Lira** 1958/5718. Green on green and peach underprint. Woman soldier with basket full of oranges at left. Tombs of the Sanhedrin at right on back.			
	a. Issued note.	.50	1.50	5.00
	s. Specimen.	—	—	295.

		VG	VF	UNC
30	**1 Lira** 1958/5718. Blue on light blue and peach underprint. Fisherman with net and anchor at left. Synagogue mosaic at right on back.			
	a. Paper with security thread at left. Black serial #.	.50	1.25	4.00
	b. Red serial #.	.50	1.25	4.00
	c. Paper with security thread and morse tape, brown serial #.	.50	1.00	3.00
	s. Specimen.	—	—	295.

#31 and 32 printer: TDLR (w/o imprint).

		VG	VF	UNC
31	**5 Lirot** 1958/5718. Brown on multicolor underprint. Worker with hammer in front of factory at left. Seal of Shema at right on back.			
	a. Issued note.	.50	2.00	5.00
	s. Specimen.	—	—	295.

		VG	VF	UNC
32	**10 Lirot** 1958/5718. Lilac and purple on multicolor underprint. Scientist with microscope and test tube at left. Dead Sea scroll and vases at right on back.			
	a. Paper with security thread. Black serial #.	.50	2.00	10.00
	b. Paper with security thread and morse tape. Red serial #.	.50	2.00	18.00
	c. Paper with security thread and morse tape. Blue serial #.	.50	2.00	18.00
	d. Paper with security thread and morse tape. Brown serial #.	.50	1.50	7.50
	s. Specimen.	—	—	295.

		VG	VF	UNC
33	**50 Lirot** 1960/5720. Brown and multicolor. Boy and girl at left. Mosaic of menorah at right on back.			
	a. Paper with security thread. Black serial #.	2.00	10.00	45.00
	b. Paper with security thread. Red serial #.	2.00	10.00	45.00
	c. Paper with security thread and morse tape. Blue serial #.	1.50	6.00	45.00
	d. Paper with security thread and morse tape. Green serial #.	1.50	6.00	30.00
	e. Paper with security thread and morse tape. Brown serial #.	1.50	5.00	30.00
	s. Specimen.	—	—	400.

1968 / 5728 Issue

#34-37 printer: JEZ (w/o imprint).

		VG	VF	UNC
34	**5 Lirot** 1968/5728. Gray-green and blue on multicolor underprint. Albert Einstein at right and as watermark. Atomic reactor at Nahal Sorek on back.			
	a. Black serial #.	.75	3.00	9.00
	b. Red serial #.	.75	3.00	9.00
	s. Specimen.	—	—	225.

		VG	VF	UNC
35	**10 Lirot** 1968/5728. Brown, purple and multicolor. Chaim Nahman Bialik at right and as watermark. Bialik's house in Tel Aviv on back.			
	a. Black serial #.	.25	1.00	5.00
	b. Green serial #.	.25	1.00	5.00
	c. Blue serial #.	.25	1.00	5.00
	s. Specimen.	—	—	225.

		VG	VF	UNC
36	**50 Lirot** 1968/5728. Light and dark brown and green on multicolor underprint. Pres. Chaim Weizmann at right and as watermark. Knesset building in Jerusalem on back.			
	a. Black serial #.	.50	2.00	7.00
	b. Blue serial #.	.50	2.00	7.00
	s. Specimen.	—	—	225.

37	100 Lirot	VG	VF	UNC
	1968/5728. Blue and light green on multicolor underprint. Dr. Theodor Herzl at right and as watermark. Menorah and symbols of the twelve tribes of Israel at left center on back.			
	a. Watermark: Profile. Black serial #. 3.5mm.	2.50	10.00	35.00
	b. Watermark: 3/4 profile r. Red serial #.	2.50	10.00	45.00
	c. Watermark: Profile. Black serial #. 2.8mm. without series letter.	2.50	10.00	25.00
	d. Watermark: Profile. Brown serial #.	2.50	10.00	35.00
	s. Specimen.	—	—	225.

1973-75 / 5733-35 ISSUE

#38-51 printer: JEZ (w/o imprint).

All the following notes except #41 and 45 have marks for the blind on the face. #38-46 have barely discernible bar code strips at lower l. and upper r. on back. All have portr. as wmk. Various gates in Jerusalem on backs.

38	5 Lirot	VG	VF	UNC
	1973/5733. Light and dark brown. Henrietta Szold at right. Lion's Gate on back.	.15	.50	1.50

39	10 Lirot	VG	VF	UNC
	1973/5733. Purple on lilac underprint. Sir Moses Montefiore at right. Jaffa Gate on back.			
	a. Issued note.	.15	.50	1.50
	s. Specimen.	—	—	—

40	50 Lirot	VG	VF	UNC
	1973/5733. Green on olive-green underprint. Chaim Weizmann at right. Sichem Gate on back.	.25	1.00	6.00

41	100 Lirot	VG	VF	UNC
	1973/5733. Blue on blue and brown underprint. Dr. Theodor Herzl at right. Zion Gate on back.	.50	1.50	5.00

42	500 Lirot	VG	VF	UNC
	1975/5735. Black on tan and brown underprint. David Ben-Gurion at right. Golden Gate on back.	2.50	10.00	45.00

1978-84 / 5738-44 ISSUE

Sheqel system

43	1 Sheqel	VG	VF	UNC
	1978/5738 (1980). Purple on lilac underprint. Like #39.			
	a. Issued note.	.15	.50	2.00
	s. Specimen.	—	—	—

44	5 Sheqalim	VG	VF	UNC
	1978/5738 (1980). Green on olive-green underprint. Like #40.	.25	.75	3.00

45	10 Sheqalim	VG	VF	UNC
	1978/5738 (1980). Blue on blue and brown underprint. Like #41.	.50	1.50	5.00

46	50 Sheqalim	VG	VF	UNC
	1978/5738 (1980). Black on tan and brown underprint. Like #42.			
	a. Without small bars below serial # or barely discernible bar code strips on back.	.15	.50	2.00
	b. Without small bars below serial #, but With bar code strips on back.	1.00	4.00	25.00
	c. 2 green bars below serial # on back.	20.00	45.00	225.
	d. 4 black bars below serial # on back.	15.00	35.00	175.
	e. As a. 12-subject sheet.	—	—	20.00

Note: Colored bars were used to identify various surface-coated papers, used experimentally.

47	100 Sheqalim	VG	VF	UNC
	1979/5739. Red-brown on light tan underprint. Ze'ev Jabotinsky at right. Herod's Gate on back.			
	a. Without bars below serial # on back.	.50	1.50	8.00
	b. 2 bars below serial # on back.	6.00	30.00	100.
48	**500 Sheqalim**			
	1982/5742. Red on multicolor underprint. Farm workers at center, Baron Edmond de Rothschild at right. Vine leaves on back.	.50	1.50	9.00

49	1000 Sheqalim	VG	VF	UNC
	1983/5743. Green on multicolor underprint. Rabbi Moses Maimonides at right. View of Tiberias at left on back.			
	a. Error in first letter *he* of second word at right. in vertical text (right to left), partly completed letter resembling 7.	1.50	7.50	30.00
	b. Corrected letter resembling *17.*	1.00	5.00	20.00
	c. As a. Uncut sheet of 3 (3,610 sheets).	—	—	45.00
	d. As b. Uncut sheet of 3 (3.365 sheets).	—	—	35.00

50	5000 Sheqalim	VG	VF	UNC
	1984/5744. Blue on multicolor underprint. City view at center, Levi Eshkol at right. Water pipe and modern design on back.			
	a. Issued note.	1.50	7.50	45.00
	b. Uncut sheet of 3 (2,755 sheets).	—	—	55.00

51	10,000 Sheqalim	VG	VF	UNC
	1984/5744. Brown, black, orange and dark green on multicolor underprint. Stylized tree at center, Golda Meir at right and as watermark. Gathering in front of Moscow synagogue on back.			
	a. Issued note.	2.00	10.00	30.00
	b. Uncut sheet of 3 (2,720 sheets).	—	—	75.00

1985-92 / 5745-52 ISSUE

#51A-56 portr. as wmk. Printer: JEZ (w/o imprint). All with marks for the blind.

SIGNATURE VARIETIES			
5	 Mandelbaum, 1986	6	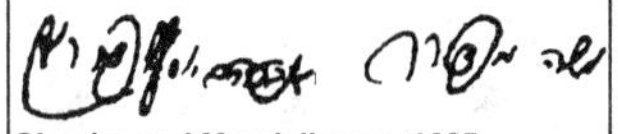 Shapira and Mandelbaum, 1985
7	 Lorincz and Bruno, 1987-91	8	 Lorincz and Frankel, 1992
9			

51A	1 New Sheqel	VG	VF	UNC
	1986/5746. Like #49 except for denomination. Signature 5.			
	a. Issued note.	.25	.50	2.00
	b. Uncut sheet of 3 (2,017 sheets).	—	—	7.00
	c. Uncut sheet of 12 (1,416 sheets).	—	—	35.00
	d. Uncut sheet of 18 (1.503 sheets).	—	—	50.00

52	5 New Sheqalim	VG	VF	UNC
	1985/5745; 1987/5747. Like #50 except for denomination.			
	a. Signature 6. 1985/5745.	.75	3.00	15.00
	b. Signature 7. 1987/5747.	.50	2.50	18.00
	c. As a. Uncut sheet of 3 (1,630 sheets).	—	—	40.00

53	10 New Sheqalim	VG	VF	UNC
	1985/5745; 1987/5747; 1992/5752. Like #51 except for denomination.			
	a. Signature 6. 1985/5745.	1.00	6.00	32.50
	b. Signature 7. 1987/5747.	.75	4.00	20.00
	c. Signature 8. 1992/5752.	.50	2.00	12.50
	d. As a. Uncut sheet of 3 (1,571 sheets).	—	—	50.00

54	20 New Sheqalim	VG	VF	UNC
	1987/5747; 1993/5753. Dark gray on multicolor underprint. Moshe Sharett standing holding flag at center, his bust at right and as watermark. Herzlya High School at center on back.			
	a. Without sm. double circle With dot in watermark. area face and back. signature 7. 1987/5747.	FV	FV	40.00
	b. With sm. double circle With dot in watermark. area face and back. signature 7. 1987/5747.	FV	FV	40.00
	c. Signature 8. 1993/5753.	FV	FV	18.00

55	50 New Sheqalim	VG	VF	UNC
	1985/5745-1992/5752. Purple on multicolor underprint. Shmuel Yosef Agnon at right and as watermark. Various buildings and book titles on back.			
	a. Signature 6. 1985/5745.	FV	FV	90.00
	b. Signature 7. Slight color variations. 1988/5748.	FV	FV	90.00
	c. Signature 8. 1992/5752.	FV	FV	50.00

56	100 New Sheqalim	VG	VF	UNC
	1986/5746; 1989/5749; 1995/5755. Brown on multicolor underprint. Itzhak Ben-Zvi at right and as watermark. Stylized village of Peki'in and carob tree on back.			
	a. Signature 5. Plain security thread and plain white paper. 1986/5746.	FV	FV	90.00
	b. Signature 6. with security thread inscribed: *Bank Israel,* paper with colored threads. 1989/5749.	FV	FV	90.00
	c. Signature 8. 1995/5755.	FV	FV	85.00

NOTICE

Readers with unlisted dates, signature varieties, etc. are invited to submit photocopies of their notes to: Standard Catalog of World Paper Money, 700 East State St. Iola, WI 54990-0001, E-Mail: george.cuhaj@fwpubs.com.

		VG	VF	UNC
57	**200 New Sheqalim** 1991/5751; 1994/5754. Deep red, purple and blue-green on multicolor underprint. Zalman Shazar at right and as watermark. School girl writing at center on back.			
	a. Signature 7. 1991/5751.	FV	FV	135.
	b. Signature 8. 1994/5754.	FV	FV	120.

1998 Commemorative Issue

#58, 50th Anniversary - State of Israel

		VG	VF	UNC
58	**50 New Sheqalim** 1998/5758. Purple on multicolor underprint. Like #55 but with OVI *50* at upper left, 5-digit serial # below. Signature 8.	FV	FV	45.00

Note: #58 was issued in sheets of three in a special folder (10,001) sets. Value $100.

1998 Dated 1999 Issue

#59-62 vertical format.

		VG	VF	UNC
59	**20 New Sheqalim** 1998; 2001. Dark green on multicolor underprint. Moshe Sharett at bottom, flags in background. Scenes of his life and work on back.			
	a. 1998 (1999).	FV	FV	18.00
	b. 2001 (2003).	FV	FV	15.00

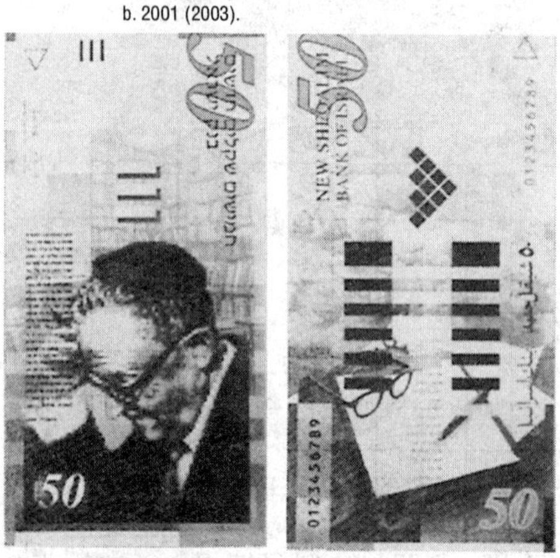

		VG	VF	UNC
60	**50 New Sheqalim** 1998; 2001. Purple on multicolor underprint. Shmuel Yosef Agnon at bottom, library shelves in background. Scenes of his life and work on back.			
	a. 1998.	FV	FV	40.00
	b. 2001 (2003).	FV	FV	28.00

		VG	VF	UNC
61	**100 New Sheqalim** 1998; 2002. Dark brown on multicolor underprint. Itzhak Ben-Zvi at bottom. Scenes of his life and work on back.			
	a. 1998.	FV	FV	50.00
	b. 2002 (2003).	FV	FV	50.00

		VG	VF	UNC
62	**200 New Sheqalim** 1999, 2002. Red and red-orange on multicolor underprint. Zalman Shazar at bottom, classroom in background. Scenes of his life and work on back.			
	a. 1999.	FV	FV	100.
	b. 2002 (2003).	FV	FV	90.00

Collector Series

Bank of Israel

1990 Issue

		Issue Price	Mkt. Value
CS1	**(1990). 1-50 New Sheqalim** 1985-87. #51Aa-55a with matching serial #. Issued in special packaging. (2,000).	—	95.00

1991 Issue

		Issue Price	Mkt. Value
CS2	**(1991). 100, 200 New Sheqalim** 1985-86. #56a and 57a with matching serial # issued in special packaging. (2,000).	—	150.

The Italian Republic, a 700-mile-long peninsula extending into the heart of the Mediterranean Sea, has an area of 116,304 sq. mi. (301,308 sq. km.) and a population of 57.46 million. Captal: Rome. The economy centers about agriculture, manufacturing, forestry and fishing. Machinery, textiles, clothing and motor vehicles are exported.

From the fall of Rome until modern times, "Italy" was little more than a geographical expression. Although nominally included in the Empire of Charlemagne and the Holy Roman Empire, it was in reality divided into a number of independent states and kingdoms presided over by wealthy families, soldiers of fortune or hereditary rulers. The 19th century unification movement fostered by Mazzini, Garibaldi and Cavor attained fruition in 1860-1870 with the creation of the Kingdom of Italy and the installation of Victor Emanuele, King of Italy. Benito Mussolini came to power during the post-World War I period of economic and political unrest, installed a Fascist dictatorship with a figurehead king as titular Head of State.

Mussolini entered Italy into the German-Japanese anti-Comintern pact (Tri-Partite Pact) and withdrew from the League of Nations. The war did not go well for Italy and Germany was forced to assist Italy in its failed invasion of Greece. The Allied invasion of Sicily on July 10, 1943 and bombing Rome brought the Fascist council to a no vote of confidence on July 24, 1943. Mussolini was arrested but soon escaped and set up a government in Salò. Rome fell to the Allied forces in June 1944 and the country was allowed the status of co-belligerent against Germany. The Germans held northern Italy for another year. Mussolini was eventually captured and executed by partisans. Following the defeat of the Axis powers the Italian monarchy was dissolved by plebiscite, and the Italian Republic proclaimed on June 10, 1946.

RULERS:

Umberto I, 1878-1900
Vittorio Emanuele III, 1900-1946

MONETARY SYSTEM:

1 Lira = 100 Centesimi, to 2001
1 Euro = 100 Cents, 2001-

REPLACEMENT NOTES:

#M10-M23, asterisk in front of serial number.

FACE SEAL VARIETIES:

Type B
Facing head of Medusa

Type C
Winged lion of St. Mark of Venice above 3 shields of Genoa, Pisa and Amalfi

REPUBLIC

REPUBBLICA ITALIANA - BIGLIETTO DI STATO

DECRETO MINISTERIALE 5.6.1976

		VG	VF	UNC
95	**500 Lire** 20.12.1976. Like #94.	.50	1.50	3.50

1966 ISSUE

		VG	VF	UNC
93	**500 Lire** 1966-75. Dark gray on blue and multicolor underprint. Eagle with snake at left, Arethusa at right. Three signature varieties.			
	a. 20.6.1966; 20.10.1967; 23.2.1970.	1.00	2.00	25.00
	b. 23.4.1975.	25.00	100.	450.

DECRETO MINISTERIALE 14.2.1974

		VG	VF	UNC
94	**500 Lire** 14.2.1974; 2.4.1979. Grayish purple on blue and multicolor underprint. Mercury at right. Watermark: star in wreath. Three signature varieties.	.50	1.00	2.00

BANCA D'ITALIA

BANK OF ITALY

1962 ISSUE

Decreto Ministeriale 12.4. 1962; Decreto Ministeriale 28.6.1962.

		VG	VF	UNC
96	**1000 Lire** 1962-68. Blue on red and light brown underprint. G. Verdi at right. Watermark: Laureate head. Seal: Type B.			
	a. Signature Carli and Ripa. 14.7.1962; 14.1.1964.	FV	8.00	80.00
	b. Signature Carli and Ripa. 5.7.1963; 25.7.1964.	FV	15.00	150.
	c. Signature Carli and Febbraio. 10.8.1965; 20.5.1966.	FV	9.00	80.00
	d. Signature Carli and Pacini. 4.1.1968.	FV	9.00	300.

		VG	VF	UNC
97	**10,000 Lire** 1962-73. Brown, purple, orange and red-brown with dk. brown text on multicolor underprint. Michaelangelo at right. Piazza del Campidoglio in Rome. Watermark: Roman head. Seal: Type B.			
	a. Signature Carli and Ripa. 3.7.1962; 14.1.1964; 27.7.1964.	FV	10.00	60.00
	b. Signature Carli and Febbraio. 20.5.1966.	FV	10.00	60.00
	c. Signature Carli and Pacini. 4.1.1968.	FV	10.00	90.00
	d. Signature Carli and Lombardo. 8.6.1970.	FV	10.00	60.00
	e. Signature Carli and Barbarito. 15.2.1973; 27.11.1973.	FV	FV	60.00

1967 ISSUE

Decreto Ministeriale 27.6.1967.

		VG	VF	UNC
99	**50,000 Lire** 1967-74. Brownish black, dark brown and reddish brown with black text on multicolor underprint. Leonardo da Vinci at right. City view at center on back. Watermark: bust of Madonna. Seal: Type B.			
	a. Signature Carli and Febbraio. 4.12.1967.	FV	200.	1200.
	b. Signature Carli and Lombardo. 19.7.1970.	FV	150.	800.
	c. Signature Carli and Barbarito. 16.5.1972; 4.2.1974.	FV	100.	600.

		VG	VF	UNC
100	**100,000 Lire** 1967-74. Brownish black, brown and deep olive-green on multicolor underprint. A. Manzoni at right. Mountain lake scene at center on back. Watermark: Archaic female bust. Seal: Type B.			
	a. Signature Carli and Febbraio. 3.7.1967.	80.00	400.	1750.
	b. Signature Carli and Lombardo. 19.7.1970.	80.00	200.	850.
	c. Signature Carli and Barbarito. 6.2.1974.	80.00	225.	950.

1964 Issue

Decreto Ministeriale 20.8.1964.

		VG	VF	UNC
98	**5000 Lire** 1964-70. Green on pink underprint. Columbus at right. Ship at left center on back. Seal: Type B.			
	a. Signature Carli and Ripa. 3.9.1964.	12.00	50.00	260.
	b. Signature Carli and Pacini. 4.1.1968.	12.00	50.00	260.
	c. Signature Carli and Lombardo. 20.1.1970.	12.00	50.00	260.

1969; 1971 Issue

Decreto Ministeriale 26.2.1969; Decreto Ministeriale 15.5.1971.

		VG	VF	UNC
101	**1000 Lire** 1969-81. Black and brown on light blue and lilac underprint. Harp at left center, G. Verdi at right. Paper with security thread. Milan's La Scala opera house at left center on back. Watermark: Vertical row of laureate heads. Seal: Type B.			
	a. Signature Carli and Lombardo. 25.3.1969; 11.3.1971.	FV	1.00	9.00
	b. Signature Carli and Barbarito. 15.2.1973.	FV	1.50	10.00
	c. Signature Carli and Barbarito. 5.8.1975.	FV	1.00	8.00
	d. Signature Baffi and Stevani. 10.1.1977; 10.5.1979.	FV	2.00	15.00
	e. Signature Ciampi and Stevani. 20.2.1980; 6.9.1980; 30.5.1981.	FV	1.00	8.00

		VG	VF	UNC
102	**5000 Lire** 1971-77. Olive, blue and brown on light olive underprint. Mythical seahorse at center, Columbus at right. Three sailing ships of Columbus' at left center on back. Seal: Type C.			
	a. Signature Carli and Lombardo. 20.5.1971.	FV	20.00	100.
	b. Signature Carli and Barbarito. 11.4.1973.	FV	20.00	100.
	c. Signature Baffi and Stevani. 10.11.1977.	FV	25.00	150.

1973; 1974 Issue

Decreto Ministeriale 10.9.1973; Decreto Ministeriale 20.12.1974.

		VG	VF	UNC
103	**2000 Lire** 1973; 1976; 1983. Brown and green on light tan and olive underprint. Galileo at center, ornate arms at left, buildings and leaning tower of Pisa at right. Signs of the Zodiac on back. Watermark: Man's head. Seal: Type C.			
	a. Signature Carli and Barbarito. 8.10.1973.	FV	3.00	30.00
	b. Signature Baffi and Stevani. 20.10.1976.	FV	2.00	15.00
	c. Signature Ciampi and Stevani. 24.10.1983.	FV	FV	5.00

		VG	VF	UNC
104	**20,000 Lire** 21.2.1975. Brownish black and dark brown on red-brown and pale olive-green underprint. Titian at center. Titian's painting *Amor Sacro e Amor Profano* at left center on back. Watermark: Woman's head. Seal: Type C. Signature Carli and Barbarito.	30.00	60.00	340.

1976-79 Issue

Decreto Ministeriale 2.3.1979; Decreto Ministeriale 25.8.1976; Decreto Ministeriale 20.6.1977; Decreto Ministeriale 16.6.1978.

105	5000 Lire	VG	VF	UNC
	1979-83. Brown and green. Man at left. Building and statuary at center right on back. Watermark: Man with cap. Seal: Type C.			
	a. Signature Baffi and Stevani. 9.3.1979.	FV	5.00	20.00
	b. Signature Ciampi and Stevani. 1.7.1980; 3.11.1982; 19.10.1983.	FV	5.00	20.00

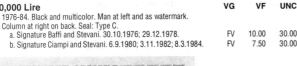

106	10,000 Lire	VG	VF	UNC
	1976-84. Black and multicolor. Man at left and as watermark. Column at right on back. Seal: Type C.			
	a. Signature Baffi and Stevani. 30.10.1976; 29.12.1978.	FV	10.00	30.00
	b. Signature Ciampi and Stevani. 6.9.1980; 3.11.1982; 8.3.1984.	FV	7.50	30.00

107	50,000 Lire	VG	VF	UNC
	1977-82. Blue, red and green. Young women and lion of St. Mark at left. Modern design of arches on back. Seal: Type C.			
	a. Signature Baffi and Stevani. 20.6.1977; 12.6.1978; 23.10.1978.	FV	40.00	100.
	b. Signature Ciampi and Stevani. 11.4.1980.	FV	40.00	100.
	c. Signature Ciampi and Stevani. 2.11.1982.	FV	50.00	250.

108	100,000 Lire	VG	VF	UNC
	D.1978. Red-violet and black on multicolor underprint. Woman's bust at left and as watermark. Modern building design at right on back. Seal: Type C.			
	a. Signature Baffi and Stevani. 20.6.1978.	FV	65.00	180.
	b. Signature Ciampi and Stevani. 1.7.1980-10.5.1982.	FV	65.00	220.

1982; 1983 Issue

Decreto Ministeriale 6.1.1982; Decreto Ministeriale 1.9.1983.

109	1000 Lire	VG	VF	UNC
	D.1982. Dark green and tan. Marco Polo at right and as watermark. Facade of Doge Palace in Venice at bottom of vertical format on back. Printer: ODBI. Seal: Type C.			
	a. Signature Ciampi and Stevani. 6.1.1982.	FV	FV	3.00
	b. Signature Ciampi and Speziali. 6.1.1982.	FV	FV	3.00

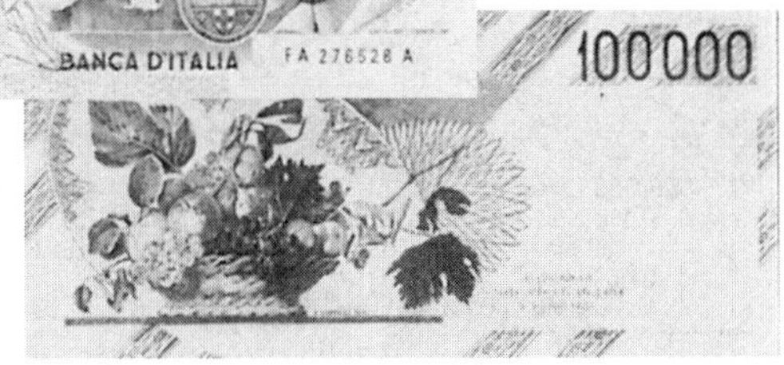

110	100,000 Lire	VG	VF	UNC
	D.1983. Dark brown and brown on green and olive-green underprint. Couple at center, Caravaggio at right and as watermark. Fruit basket at left, castle at upper center on back. Seal: Type C.			
	a. Signature Ciampi and Stevani. 1.9.1983.	FV	FV	150.
	b. Signature Ciampi and Speziali. 1.9.1983.	FV	FV	120.

1984; 1985 Issue

Decreto Ministeriale 4.1.1985; Decreto Ministeriale 3.9.1984; Decreto Ministeriale 6.2.1984.

111	5000 Lire	VG	VF	UNC
	D.1985. Olive-green and blue on multicolor underprint. Coliseum at center, V. Bellini at right and as watermark. Scene from opera Norma at left center on back. Seal: Type C.			
	a. Signature Ciampi and Stevani. 4.1.1985.	FV	FV	30.00
	b. Signature Ciampi and Speziali. 4.1.1985.	FV	FV	10.00
	c. Signature Fazio and Amici.	FV	FV	7.50

112	10,000 Lire	VG	VF	UNC
	D.1984. Dark blue on multicolor underprint. Lab instrument at center, A. Volta at right and as watermark. Mausoleum at left center on back. Seal: Type C.			
	a. Signature Ciampi and Stevani. 3.9.1984.	FV	FV	30.00
	b. Signature Ciampi and Speziali. 3.9.1984.	FV	FV	14.00
	c. Signature Fazio and Speziali. 3.9.1984.	FV	FV	12.50
	d. Signature Fazio and Amici. 3.9.1984.	FV	FV	12.50

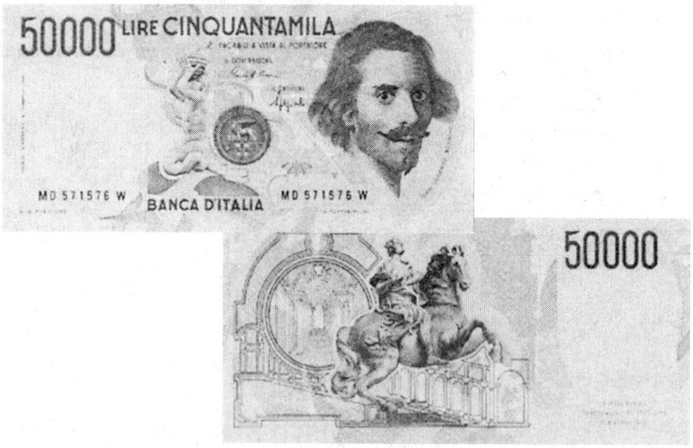

113	50,000 Lire	VG	VF	UNC
	D.1984. Red-violet and multicolor. Figurine at center, G.L. Bernini at right and as watermark. Equestrian statue at left center on back. Seal: Type C.			
	a. Signature Ciampi and Stevani. 6.2.1984; 5.12.1984; 28.10.1985; 1.12.1986.	FV	FV	80.00
	b. Signature Ciampi and Speziali. 25.1.1990.	FV	FV	60.00

1990-94 Issue

Decreto Ministeriale 3.10.1990; Decreto Ministeriale 27.5.1992; Decreto Ministeriale 6.5.1994.

114	1000 Lire	VG	VF	UNC
	D.1990. Red-violet and multicolor. M. Montessori at right and as watermark. Teacher and student at left center on back. Seal: Type C.			
	a. Signature Ciampi and Speziali.	FV	FV	3.00
	b. Signature Fazio and Speziali.	FV	FV	3.00
	c. Signature Fazio and Amici.	FV	FV	3.00

115	2000 Lire	VG	VF	UNC
	D.1990. Dark brown on multicolor underprint. Arms at left center, G. Marconi at right and as watermark. Marconi's yacht Elettra at upper left center, radio towers at left, early radio set at center on back. Seal: Type C. Signature Ciampi and Speziali.	FV	FV	4.50

116	50,000 Lire	VG	VF	UNC
	D.1992. Violet and dull green on multicolor underprint. Similar to #113. Seal: Type C.			
	a. Signature Ciampi and Speziali.	FV	FV	70.00
	b. Signature Fazio and Speziaii.	FV	FV	60.00
	c. Signature Fazio and Amici.	FV	FV	60.00

117	100,000 Lire	VG	VF	UNC
	D.1994. Dark brown, reddish brown and pale green on multicolor underprint. Similar to #110. Seal: Type C.			
	a. Signature Fazio and Speziali. 6.5.1994.	FV	FV	125.
	b. Signature Fazio and Amici.	FV	FV	120.

1997 Issue

Decreto Ministeriale 6.5.1997.

118	500,000 Lire	VG	VF	UNC
	D.1997. Deep purple, dark blue and bright green on multicolor underprint. Raphaël at right, painting of Triumph of Galatée at center. The School of Athens at left center on back. Seal: Type C. Signature Fazio and Amici.	FV	FV	400.

Note: For later issues made for use in Italy, see European Union listings.

Jamaica, a member of the British Commonwealth situated in the Caribbean Sea 90 miles south of Cuba, has an area of 4,232 sq. mi. (10,991 sq. km.) and a population of 2.59 million. Capital: Kingston. The economy is founded chiefly on mining, tourism and agriculture. Alumina, bauxite, sugar, rum and molasses are exported.

Jamaica was discovered by Columbus on May 3, 1494, and settled by Spain in 1509. The island was captured in 1655 by a British naval force under the command of Admiral William Penn, and ceded to Britain by the Treaty of Madrid in 1670. For more than 150 years, the Jamaican economy of sugar, slaves and piracy was one of the most prosperous in the New World. Dissension between the property-oriented island legislature and the home government prompted Parliament to establish a crown colony government for Jamaica in 1866. From 1958 to 1961 Jamaica was a member of the West Indies Federation, withdrawing when Jamaican voters rejected the association. The colony attained independence on Aug. 6, 1962.

Jamaica is a member of the Commonwealth of Nations. Elizabeth II is the Head of State, as Queen of Jamaica.

A decimal standard currency system was adopted on Sept. 8, 1969.

RULERS:
British

MONETARY SYSTEM:
1 Shilling = 12 Pence
1 Pound = 20 Shillings to 1969
1 Dollar = 100 Cents, 1969-

Note: Certain listings encompassing issues circulated by various bank and regional authorities are contained in Volume 1.

BRITISH ADMINISTRATION

BANK OF JAMAICA

SIGNATURE VARIETIES

1	Stanley W. Payton, 1960-64	2	Richard T. P. Hall Acting Governor, 1964-66
3	Richard T. P. Hall Governor, 1966-67	4	G. Arthur Brown, 1967-77
5	Herbert Samuel Walker, 1977-81	6	Dr. Owen C. Jefferson, Acting Governor, 1981-83
7	Horace G. Barber, 1983-86	8	Headley A. Brown, 1986-89
9	Dr. Owen C. Jefferson Acting Governor, 1989-90	10	G. A. Brown, 1990-93
11	R. Rainsford, 1993	12	J. Bussieres, 1994-
13			

LAW 1960

1961 ND ISSUE

Pound System

#49-51 Qn. Elizabeth II at l. Latin motto below arms. Sign. 1. Printer: TDLR.

		VG	VF	UNC
49	**5 Shillings** L.1960. (1961). Red on multicolor underprint. River rapids on back.	5.00	25.00	125.
50	**10 Shillings** L.1960. (1961). Purple on multicolor underprint. Men with bananas on back.	7.50	50.00	350.

		VG	VF	UNC
51	**1 Pound** L.1960. (1961). Green on multicolor underprint. Harvesting on back.	7.50	40.00	300.

1964 ND ISSUE

#51A-51C like #49-51, but English motto below arms. Printer: TDLR.

		VG	VF	UNC
51A	**5 Shillings** L.1960. (1964). Red on multicolor underprint. Like #49.			
	a. Signature 1. Gothic serial #.	3.00	15.00	85.00
	b. Signature 1. Roman numeral serial #.	3.50	25.00	120.
	c. Signature 2.	2.50	15.00	100.
	d. Signature 4.	2.00	7.50	75.00
	e. Specimen. As b.	—	—	—

		VG	VF	UNC
51B	**10 Shillings** L.1960. (1964). Purple on multicolor underprint. Like #50.			
	a. Signature 1. Gothic serial #.	3.50	10.00	160.
	b. Signature 1. Roman numeral serial #.	3.50	15.00	170.
	c. Signature 2.	3.50	12.50	185.
	d. Signature 3.	5.00	17.50	225.
	e. Signature 4.	3.00	8.50	140.

		VG	VF	UNC
51C	**1 Pound** L.1960. (1964). Green on multicolor underprint. Like #51.			
	a. Signature 1. Gothic serial #.	5.00	20.00	285.
	b. Signature 1. Roman numeral serial #.	7.50	35.00	325.
	c. Signature 2.	5.00	20.00	250.
	d. Signature 3.	7.50	35.00	300.
	e. Signature 4.	4.00	25.00	250.
	s. Specimen. As c.	—	—	—

		VG	VF	UNC
52	**5 Pounds** L.1960. Blue on multicolor underprint. Storage plant at center, woman with fruit basket at right on back.			
	a. Signature 1. Gothic serial #.	40.00	450.	1700.
	b. Signature 1. Roman numeral serial #.	50.00	500.	2000.
	c. Signature 3.	45.00	475.	1850.
	d. Signature 4.	40.00	400.	1500.

Law 1960

1970 ND Issue

Dollar System

#53-58 wmk: Pineapple. Sign. 4. Printer: TDLR. Replacement notes: Serial # prefix *ZZ*.

		VG	VF	UNC
53	**50 Cents** L.1960 (1970). Red on multicolor underprint. Marcus Garvey at left, arms in underprint at center. National shrine at right on back.			
	a. Issued note.	.50	2.00	8.00
	s. Specimen.	—	—	—
54	**1 Dollar** L.1960 (1970). Purple on multicolor underprint. Sir Alexander Bustamante at left, arms at bottom center right. Tropical harbor at right on back.	.50	2.00	8.00

		VG	VF	UNC
55	**2 Dollars** L.1960 (1970). Dark green and red-brown on multicolor underprint. Paul Bogle, arms at left, Red-billed streamer trail at center. Group of people on back.			
	a. Issued note.	1.00	4.00	12.50
	s. Specimen.	—	—	—

Note: For #54 and 55 w/red serial # see #CS1-CS3.

		VG	VF	UNC
56	**5 Dollars** L.1960 (1970). Dark brown, green and blue-gray on multicolor underprint. Norman Manley at left, arms at bottom center. Old Parliament at center right on back.	2.50	10.00	55.00

		VG	VF	UNC
57	**10 Dollars** L.1960 (1970). Blue-black, brown and black on multicolor underprint. George William Gordon at left, arms in underprint at center. Bauxite mining scene at center right on back.	5.00	30.00	175.

1973 FAO Commemorative Issue

#58, 25th Anniversary Declaration of Human Rights 1948-73

		VG	VF	UNC
58	**2 Dollars** 1973. Like #55 but *Universal Declaration of Human Rights/1948 - 10 December - 1973. Toward Food Education Employment for All/Articles 23-26* added on back. Serial # double prefix FA-0. Signature 4.	1.00	3.00	15.00

1976; 1977 ND Issue

#59-63 new guilloches in corners and some larger denomination numerals on face and back. Wmk: Pineapple. Printer: TDLR. Replacement notes: Serial # prefix *ZY* or *ZZ*.

		VG	VF	UNC
59	**1 Dollar**			
	L.1960 (1976). Purple on multicolor underprint. Like #54 but with corner design modifications.			
	a. Signature 4.	.25	1.50	7.50
	b. Signature 5.	.25	1.00	6.50
60	**2 Dollars**			
	L.1960 (1976). Dark green on multicolor underprint. Like #55 but with corner design modifications.			
	a. Signature 4.	.50	2.00	12.50
	b. Signature 5.	.50	1.50	10.00

		VG	VF	UNC
61	**5 Dollars**			
	L.1960 (1976). Dark brown, green and blue-green on multicolor underprint. Like #56 but with corner design modifications.			
	a. Signature 4.	1.00	5.00	32.50
	b. Signature 5.	.75	3.50	20.00
62	**10 Dollars**			
	L.1960 (1976). Blue-black and black on multicolor underprint. Like #57 but with corner design modifications. Signature 4.	3.00	20.00	175.

		VG	VF	UNC
63	**20 Dollars**			
	L.1960 (1977). Maroon on multicolor underprint. Noel Nethersole at left, flag in underprint at center, arms below. Bank of Jamaica building on back. Signature 4.	5.00	35.00	200.

1978-84 Issue

Bank of Jamaica Act

#64-68 wmk: Pineapple. Printer: TDLR. Replacement notes: Serial # prefix *ZY* or *ZZ*.

		VG	VF	UNC
64	**1 Dollar**			
	ND (1982-86). Purple on multicolor underprint. Like #59.			
	a. Signature 6.	.15	.50	2.50
	b. Signature 7.	.10	.25	1.50
65	**2 Dollars**			
	ND (1982-86). Dark green and red-brown on multicolor underprint. Like #60.			
	a. Signature 6.	.25	1.50	7.50
	b. Signature 7.	.20	1.00	6.00
66	**5 Dollars**			
	ND (1984). Dark brown, green and blue-gray on multicolor underprint. Similar to #61. Signature 7.	.15	2.00	10.00

		VG	VF	UNC
67	**10 Dollars**			
	1978-81. Bluish purple on multicolor underprint. Like #62.			
	a. Signature 5. 1.10.1978; 1.10.1979.	.50	2.50	25.00
	b. Signature 9. 1.12.1981.	.25	1.00	7.50

		VG	VF	UNC
68	**20 Dollars**			
	1978-83. Red and purple on multicolor underprint. Like #63.			
	a. Signature 5. 1.10.1978; 1.10.1979; 1.10.1981.	1.00	5.00	40.00
	b. Signature 6. 1.12.1981.	.75	3.00	30.00
	c. Signature 7. 1.12.1983.	.75	2.50	25.00

1985 Reduced Size Issue

#68A-72 note size: 144 x 68mm. Wmk: Pineapple. Printer: TDLR. Replacement notes: Serial # prefix *ZY* or *ZZ*.

		VG	VF	UNC
68A	**1 Dollar**			
	1985-90. Purple on multicolor underprint. Similar to #64; lower corner guilloches modified.			
	a. Signature 7. 1.1.1985.	FV	FV	4.00
	b. Signature 8. 1.3.1986; 1.2.1987; 1.9.1987.	FV	FV	2.25
	c. Signature 9. 1.7.1989.	FV	FV	2.00
	d. Signature 10. 1.1.1990.	FV	FV	1.00

69 2 Dollars

1985-93. Dark green and red-brown on multicolor underprint. Similar to #65 but corner numerals modified. Horizontal sorting bar at right.

	VG	VF	UNC
a. Signature 7. 1.1.1985.	FV	FV	3.00
b. Signature 8. 1.3.1986; 1.2.1987; 1.9.1987.	FV	FV	2.25
c. Signature 9. 1.7.1989.	FV	FV	2.00
d. Signature 10. 1.1.1990; 29.5.1992.	FV	FV	1.25
e. Signature 11. 1.2.1993.	FV	FV	1.25

#70-72 arms at bottom ctr.

70 5 Dollars

1985-92. Dark brown, green and blue-gray on multicolor underprint. Similar to #66 but with two horizontal blue-green sorting bars at left and right.

	VG	VF	UNC
a. Signature 7. 1.1.1985.	FV	FV	5.00
b. Signature 8. 1.9.1987.	FV	FV	3.50
c. Signature 9. 1.5.1989.	FV	FV	3.00
d. Signature 10. 1.7.1991; 1.8.1992.	FV	FV	1.75

71 10 Dollars

1985-94. Bluish purple on multicolor underprint. Similar to #67 but three horizontal sorting bars at left and right.

	VG	VF	UNC
a. Signature 7. 1.1.1985.	FV	FV	7.50
b. Signature 8. 1.9.1987.	FV	FV	6.00
c. Signature 9. 1.8.1989.	FV	FV	3.00
d. Signature 10. 1.5.1991; 1.8.1992.	FV	FV	1.50
e. Signature 12. 1.3.1994.	FV	FV	1.50

72 20 Dollars

1985-99. Red-orange, purple and black on multicolor underprint. Similar to #68 but circular electronic sorting mark at left.

	VG	VF	UNC
a. Signature 7. 1.1.1985.	FV	FV	10.00
b. Signature 8. 1.3.1986; 1.2.1987; 1.9.1987.	FV	FV	8.00
c. Signature 9. 1.9.1989.	FV	FV	7.00
d. Signature 10. 1.10.1991.	FV	FV	4.50
e. Signature 12. 1.2.1995.	FV	FV	3.50
f. Signature 13. 24.5.1996;	FV	FV	3.00

1986-91 ISSUE

#73-75 wmk: Pineapple. Printer: TDLR. Replacement notes: Serial # prefix *ZZ; ZY*.

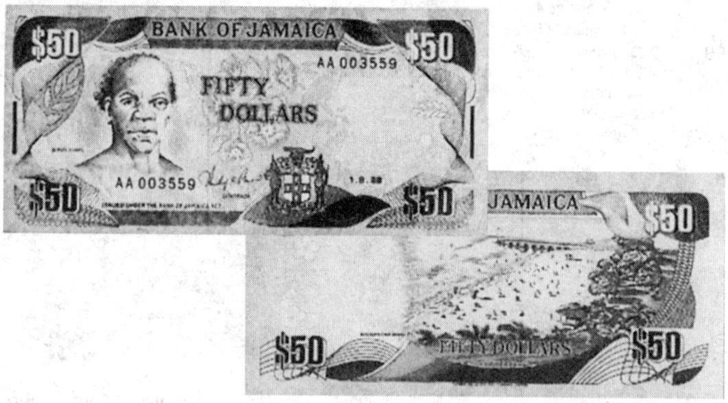

73 50 Dollars

1988. Brown, purple and red-violet on multicolor underprint. Sam Sharpe at left. Doctor's Cave Beach, Mointego Bay, on back.

	VG	VF	UNC
a. Signature 8. 1.8.1988.	FV	FV	12.00
b. Signature 11. 1.2.1993.	FV	FV	7.50
c. Signature 12. 1.2.1995.	FV	FV	5.00
d. Signature 13. 24.5.1996; 12.1.1998.	FV	FV	4.50

74 100 Dollars

1.12.1986; 1.9.1987. Black and purple on multicolor underprint. Sir Donald Sangster at left. Dunn's River Falls, St. Ann, at right on back. Signature 8.

	VG	VF	UNC
	FV	7.00	35.00

75 100 Dollars

1991-93. Black and purple on lilac underprint. Like #74. Two circles at right, each with vertical orange bar. More silver waves added to both *$100* and across bottom on back.

	VG	VF	UNC
a. Signature 10. 1.7.1991.	FV	FV	12.50
b. 1.6.1992.	FV	FV	10.00
c. Signature 11. 1.2.1993.	FV	FV	10.00

1994 ISSUE

#76-78 printer: TDLR. Replacement notes: Serial # prefix *ZY* or *ZZ*.

		VG	VF	UNC
76	**100 Dollars** 1994-2000. Black and purple on lilac underprint. Like #75 but with ascending size serial # and segmented foil over security thread.			
	a. Signature 12. 1.3.1994.	FV	FV	8.50
	b. Signature 13. 24.5.1996; 12.1.1998; 15.2.1999.	FV	FV	7.50
	c. 15.3.2000. watermark: swallow-tailed hummingbird. Improved security thread.	FV	FV	7.00

		VG	VF	UNC
77	**500 Dollars** 1994-99. Purple, violet and brown on multicolor underprint. Nanny of the Maroons at left. Historical map of the islands above Port Royal architecture at center right on back. Watermark: Pineapple.			
	a. Signature 12. 1.5.1994.	FV	FV	25.00
	b. Signature 13. 24.5.1996; 12.2.1998; 15.2.1999.	FV	FV	25.00

2000 Issue

		VG	VF	UNC
78	**1000 Dollars** 15.2.2000; 15.10.2000; 15.1.2001. Dark blue, green and purple on multicolor underprint. Michael Manley at left. Jamaica House on back. Signature 13. Printer: TDLR. (without imprint).	FV	FV	45.00

2001; 2002 Issue

		VG	VF	UNC
79	**50 Dollars** 15.3.2000; 15.1.2001; 15.1.2002; 15.1.2003; 15.1.2004. Multicolor. Like #73. Watermark: Swallow-tailed Hummingbird. Signature 13.	FV	FV	4.00

		VG	VF	UNC
80	**100 Dollars** 15.1.2001; 15.1.2002; 15.1.2004. Black and purple on lilac underprint.	FV	FV	7.00
81	**500 Dollars** 15.1.2002; 15.1.2003; 15.1.2004. Like #77. Watermark: Swallow-Tailed Hummingbird.	FV	FV	22.50
82	**1000 Dollars** 15.1.2002; 15.1.2003; 15.1.2004. Like #78. Signature 13. Printer: (T)DLR.	FV	FV	40.00

Collector Series

Bank of Jamaica

1976 Issue

		Issue Price	Mkt. Value
CS1	**1976 1-10 Dollars** #54-57 with matching red star prefix serial # and *SERIES 1976.* (5000 sets issued).	—	20.00

1977 Issue

		Issue Price	Mkt. Value
CS2	**1977 1-10 Dollars** #59a-61a, 62 with matching red star prefix serial # and *SERIES 1977.* (7500 sets issued).		15.00

1978 Issue

		Issue Price	Mkt. Value
CS3	**1978 1-10 Dollars** #54-57 in double set. One is like #CS1-2 with *SERIES 1978* and the other with additional overprint: *Twenty-fifth Anniversary of the Coronation June 2, 1953* and *SERIES 1978* at right. All with matching red star prefix serial #. (6250 sets issued).		30.00

Japan, a constitutional monarchy situated off the east coast of Asia, has an area of 145,856 sq. mi. (377,819 sq. km.) and a population of 127.13 million. Capital: Tokyo. Japan, one of the three major industrial nations of the free world, exports machinery, motor vehicles, textiles and chemicals.

Founded (so legend holds) in 660 BC by a direct descendant of the Sun Goddess, the country was first brought into contact with the west by a storm-blown Portuguese ship in 1542. European traders and missionaries proceeded to enlarge the contact until the Shogunate, sensing a military threat in the foreign presence, expelled all foreigners and severed relations with the outside world in the 17th century. (Except for one Dutch outpost in Nagasaki.) After contact was reestablished by Commodore Perry of the U.S. Navy in 1854, Japan rapidly industrialized, abolished the Shogunate and established a parliamentary form of government, and by the end of the 19th century achieved the status of a modern economic and military power. A series of wars with China and Russia, and participation with the Allies in World War I, enlarged Japan territorially but brought its interests into conflict with the Far Eastern interests of the United States and Britain, causing it to align with the Axis powers for the pursuit of World War II. After its defeat in World War II, Japan renounced military aggression as a political instrument, established democratic self-government, and quickly reasserted its position as an economic world power.

See also Burma, China (Japanese military issues, Central Reserve Bank, Federal Reserve Bank, Hua Hsing Commercial Bank, Mengchiang Bank, Chanan Bank, Chi Tung Bank and Manchukuo), Hong Kong, Indochina, Malaya, Netherlands Indies, Oceania, the Philippines, Korea and Taiwan.

RULERS:

Yoshihito (Taisho), 1912-1926
Hirohito (Showa), 1926-1989
Akihito (Heisei), 1989-

MONETARY SYSTEM:

1 Sen = 10 Rin
1 Yen = 100 Sen

CONSTITUTIONAL MONARCHY

BANK OF JAPAN

日 本 銀 行 券

Nip-pon Gin-ko Ken

1963-69 ND ISSUE

95	500 Yen	VG	VF	UNC
	ND (1969). Blue on multicolor underprint. Tomomi Iwakura at right. Back steel blue; Mt. Fuji at left center. Watermark: 5-petaled flowers.			
	a. Single letter serial # prefix.	FV	10.00	25.00
	b. Double letter serial # prefix.	FV	6.00	10.00
	s. As b. Specimen.	—	—	—

96	1000 Yen	VG	VF	UNC
	ND (1963). Dark green and brown on multicolor underprint. Hirobumi Ito at right and as watermark. Back brown; Bank of Japan at center.			
	a. Single letter serial # prefix. Black serial #.	FV	20.00	60.00
	b. As a., but with double letter serial # prefix.	FV	10.00	20.00
	c. Single letter serial # prefix. Blue serial #.	FV	10.00	35.00
	d. As c., but with double letter serial # prefix.	FV	FV	16.00
	s. As b. Specimen.	—	—	—

1984 ND ISSUE

#97-99 wmk. same as portr.

#97s-99s were released in a special booklet by Printing Bureau, Ministry of Finance.

97	1000 Yen	VG	VF	UNC
	ND (1984-93). Blue on multicolor underprint. Soseki Natsume at right and as watermark. Two Manchurian cranes on back.			
	a. Single letter serial # prefix. Black serial #	FV	10.00	20.00
	b. As a., but with double letter serial # prefix.	FV	FV	15.00
	c. Single letter serial # prefix. Blue serial #.	FV	10.00	20.00
	d. As c., but with double letter serial # prefix.	FV	FV	15.00
	s. As b. Specimen. Perforated *mihon.*	—	—	1500.

98	5000 Yen	VG	VF	UNC
	ND (1984-93). Purple on multicolor underprint. Inazo Nitobe at right and as watermark. Lake and Mt. Fuji at center on back.			
	a. Single letter serial # prefix. Black serial #.	FV	55.00	75.00
	b. As a., but with double letter serial # prefix.	FV	FV	65.00
	s. As b. Specimen. Perforated *mihon.*	—	—	1500.

		VG	VF	UNC
99	**10,000 Yen**			
	ND (1984-93). Light brown on multicolor underprint. Yukichi Fukuzawa at right and as watermark. Pheasant at left and right on back.			
	a. Single letter serial # prefix.	FV	110.	150.
	b. As a., but with double letter serial # prefix.	FV	FV	120.
	s. As b. Specimen. Perforated *mihon*.	—	—	1500.

1993 ND Issue

#100-102 microprinting added to upper or lower r. corner.

Due to a government reorganization, the Okurasho (Finance Ministry) was renamed Zaimusho (Ministry of Finance). The imprint on the notes (made at the Finance Ministry Pinting Bureau) was changed accordingly in 2001. In 2003 the imprint was changed again, to National Printing Bureau.

Printer a. 8 characters starting *O*.

Printer b. 8 characters starting *Zai*.

Printer c. 7 characters.

		VG	VF	UNC
100	**1000 Yen**			
	ND (1993-). Blue on multicolor underprint. Soseki Natsume at right. Like #97.			
	a. Single letter serial # prefix. Brown serial #. Printer A. (1993).	FV	10.00	18.00
	b. As a. Double letter serial # prefix.	FV	FV	12.50
	c. Single letter serial # prefix. Green serial #.	FV	FV	18.00
	d. As c. Double letter serial # prefix.	FV	FV	12.50
	e. As c. Double letter serial #. Printer B.	FV	FV	13.00
	f. As d, printer C. (2003).	FV	FV	13.00
101	**5000 Yen**			
	ND (1993-). Violet on multicolor underprint. Inazo Nitobe at right. Like #98.			
	a. Single letter serial # prefix. Brown serial # Printer a. (1993).	FV	70.00	80.00
	b. As a., but with double letter serial # prefix.	FV	FV	70.00
	c. As b. Printer b. (2001).	FV	FV	70.00
	d. As c. Printer c. (2003).	FV	FV	65.00
102	**10,000 Yen**			
	ND (1993-). Light brown on multicolor underprint. Yukichi Fukuzawa at right. Like #99.			
	a. Single letter serial # prefix. Brown serial # (1993).	FV	110.	150.
	b. As a., but with double letter serial # prefix.	FV	FV	125.
	c. As b. printer b. (2001).	FV	FV	125.
	d. As b. Printer c. (2003).	FV	FV	125.

2000 Commemorative Issue

#103, G-8 Economic Summit in Okinawa

		VG	VF	UNC
103	**2000 Yen**			
	ND (2000). Slate, green and brown on multicolor underprint. Shureimon Gate in Naha, Okinawa at right and as watermark. Scene from *Genji Monogatari* (Tale of Genji) on back.	FV	FV	25.00

2004 ND Issue

#104-106 include enhanced security features and bar wmk. (in addition to portr. wmk.) Iridescent ink feature is observed by holding the note at a shallow angle to incident light. The iridescent ink glistens like pink mother of pearl from the surface of the ends of the face of the note; it is otherwise virtually invisible and impossible to copy using available copying technologies.

		VG	VF	UNC
104	**1000 Yen**			
	ND (2004). Blue on multicolor underprint. Hideo Noguchi (bacteriologist) at right and as watermark. Mt. Fuji on back.	FV	FV	13.00
105	**5000 Yen**			
	ND (2004). Violet on multicolor underprint. Ichiyo Higuchi (novelist) at right and as watermark. Irises (painting by Korin Ogata) on back.	FV	FV	65.00
106	**10,000 Yen**			
	ND (2004). Brown on multicolor underprint. Yukichi Fukuzawa (educator, futurist) at right and as watermark. Phoenix from Boydo-in Temple on back.	FV	FV	125.

JERSEY

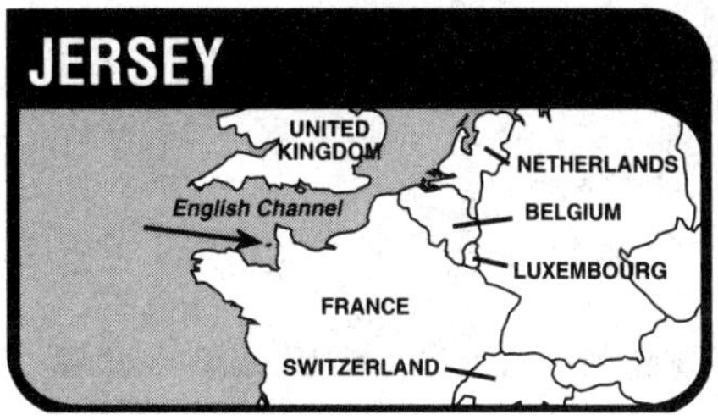

The Bailiwick of Jersey, a British Crown dependency located in the English Channel 12 miles (19 km.) west of Normandy, France, has an area of 45 sq. mi. (117 sq. km.) and a population of 90,000. Capital: St. Helier. The economy is d on agriculture and cattle breeding - the importation of cattle is prohibited to protect the purity of the island's world-famous strain of milk cows.

Jersey was occupied by Neanderthal man 100,000 years B.C., and by Iberians of 2000 B.C. who left their chamber tombs in the island's granite cliffs. Roman legions almost certainly visited the island although they left no evidence of settlement. The country folk of Jersey still speak an archaic form of Norman-French, lingering evidence of the Norman annexation of the island in 933 B.C. Jersey was annexed to England in 1206, 140 years after the Norman Conquest. The dependency is administered by its own laws and customs; laws enacted by the British Parliament do not apply to Jersey unless it is specifically mentioned. During World War II, German troops occupied the island from 1940 until 1944.

United Kingdom bank notes and coinage circulate concurrently with Jersey money as legal tender.

RULERS:

British

MONETARY SYSTEM:

1 Shilling = 12 Pence
1 Pound = 20 Shillings to 1971
1 Pound = 100 New Pence, 1971-

SIGNATURE VARIETIES			
1	F. N. Padgham, 1963-72	2	J. Clennett, 1972-83
3	Leslie May, 1983-93	4	Baird, 1993-

British Administration

States of Jersey, Treasury

1963 ND Issue

#7-10 Qn. Elizabeth II at r. looking l., wearing cape. Wmk: Jersey cow's head. Sign. 3. Printer: TDLR. Replacement notes: Serial # prefix *Z*.

		VG	VF	UNC
7	**10 Shillings**			
	ND (1963). Brown on multicolor underprint. St. Ouen's Manor on back.			
	a. Issued note.	3.00	10.00	35.00
	s. Specimen.	—	—	200.

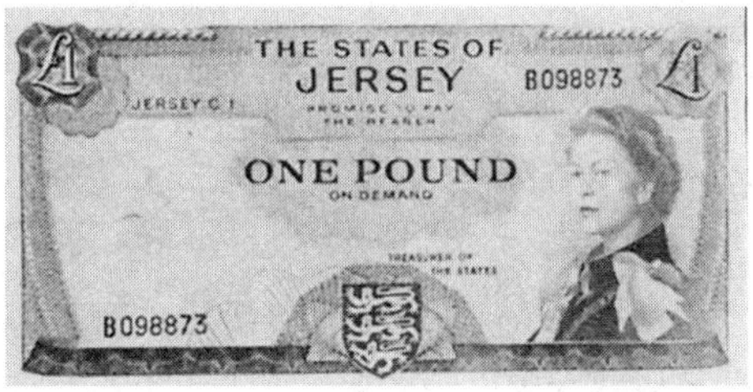

8	1 Pound	VG	VF	UNC
	ND (1963). Green on multicolor underprint. Mont Orgueil Castle on back. Two signature varieties.			
	a. Signature 1.	7.50	35.00	90.00
	b. Signature 2.	5.00	20.00	50.00
	c. Without signature	30.00	85.00	300.
	s. As a. Specimen. Black or red overprint Serial # prefix A-G.	—	—	75.00

9	5 Pounds	VG	VF	UNC
	ND (1963). Dark red on multicolor underprint. St. Aubin's Fort on back.			
	a. Signature 1.	40.00	100.	400.
	b. Signature 2.	10.00	30.00	90.00
	s1. As a. Specimen. Black or red overprint	—	—	100.
	s2. As b. Specimen. Red overprint.	—	—	100.

10	10 Pounds	VG	VF	UNC
	ND (1972). Purple on multicolor underprint. Back similar to #7.			
	a. Signature 2.	20.00	40.00	100.
	s. Specimen. Red overprint.	—	—	135.

1976 ND Issue

#11-14 Qn. Elizabeth at ctr. r. looking l., wearing a tiara. Wmk: Jersey cow's head. Printer: TDLR. Replacement notes: Serial # prefixes *ZB; ZC*.

11	1 Pound	VG	VF	UNC
	ND (1976-88). Blue on multicolor underprint. Battle of Jersey scene on back.			
	a. Signature 2.	FV	5.00	12.00
	b. Signature 3.	FV	4.00	9.00
	s. As a. Specimen.	—	—	17.50

12	5 Pounds	VG	VF	UNC
	ND (1976-88). Brown on multicolor underprint. Elizabeth Castle, sailing ships in foreground on back.			
	a. Signature 2.	FV	20.00	50.00
	b. Signature 3.	FV	20.00	45.00
	s. Specimen.	—	—	27.50

13	10 Pounds	VG	VF	UNC
	ND (1976-88). Green on multicolor underprint. Victoria College on back.			
	a. Signature 2.	FV	35.00	85.00
	b. Signature 3.	FV	30.00	75.00
	s. Specimen.	—	—	45.00

14	20 Pounds	VG	VF	UNC
	ND (1976-88). Red-brown on multicolor underprint. Sailing ship, Gorey Castle on back.			
	a. Signature 2.	FV	60.00	140.
	b. Signature 3.	FV	60.00	150.
	s. Specimen.	—	—	80.00

1989 ND ISSUE

#15-19 Birds at l. corner, arms at ctr., older Qn. Elizabeth II at r. facing, wearing cape. Wmk: Jersey cow's head. Sign. 3. Replacement notes: Serial # prefix *CZ*.

		VG	VF	UNC
15	**1 Pound** ND (1989). Dark green and violet on multicolor underprint. Treecreepers at lower left. Church at left center on back.			
	a. Issued note.	FV	FV	8.00
	s. Specimen.	—	—	6.00

		VG	VF	UNC
16	**5 Pounds** ND (1989). Rose on multicolor underprint. Whitethroat at lower left. La Corbiere lighthouse on back.			
	a. Issued note.	FV	FV	25.00
	s. Specimen.	—	—	17.50

		VG	VF	UNC
17	**10 Pounds** ND (1989). Orange-brown on multicolor underprint. Oyster catchers at lower left. Battle of Jersey on back.			
	a. Issued note.	FV	FV	45.00
	s. Specimen.	—	—	25.00

		VG	VF	UNC
18	**20 Pounds** ND (1989). Blue on multicolor underprint. Brent goose at lower left. St. Ouen's Manor on back.			
	a. Issued note.	FV	FV	85.00
	s. Specimen.	—	—	35.00

		VG	VF	UNC
19	**50 Pounds** ND (1989). Dark gray on multicolor underprint. Fulmers at lower left. Government House on back.			
	a. Issued note.	FV	FV	165.
	s. Specimen.	—	—	75.00

1993 ND ISSUE

#20-24 like #15-19 but w/solid color denomination at upper r. Wmk: Jersey cow's head.

		VG	VF	UNC
20	**1 Pound** ND (1993). Dark green on multicolor underprint. Like #15.			
	a. Signature 4.	FV	FV	6.00
	s. Specimen.	—	—	6.00

		VG	VF	UNC
21	**5 Pounds** ND (1993). Rose on multicolor underprint. Like #16.			
	a. Signature 4.	FV	FV	20.00
	s. Specimen.	—	—	15.00
22	**10 Pounds** ND (1993). Orange-brown on multicolor underprint. Like #17.			
	a. Signature 4.	FV	FV	40.00
	s. Specimen.	—	—	22.50

		VG	VF	UNC
23	**20 Pounds** ND (1993). Blue on multicolor underprint. Like #18.			
	a. Signature 4.	FV	FV	70.00
	s. Specimen.	—	—	30.00

		VG	VF	UNC
24	**50 Pounds**			
	ND (1993). Dark gray on multicolor underprint. Like #19.			
	a. Signature 4	FV	FV	150.
	s. Specimen.	—	—	85.00

1995 Commemorative Issue

#25, 50th Anniversary Liberation of Jersey

		VG	VF	UNC
25	**1 Pound**			
	9.5.1995. Dark green and purple on multicolor underprint. Face like #20 with island outline at upper right, with text: *50th Anniversary...* at left in watermark area. Serial # prefix: *LJ.* Face and back of German occupation 1 Pound #6 on back. Watermark: Cow's head. Signature 4. Printer: TDLR.			
	a. Issued note.	FV	FV	8.00
	s. Specimen.	—	—	25.00

Note: #25 also issued in a special wallet w/commemorative £2 coin. (6000 pcs.). Current market value: $20.00.

2000 ND Issue

#26-30 like #20-24 but sign. Ian Black.

		VG	VF	UNC
26	**1 Pound**			
	ND (2000). Dark green on multicolor underprint. Like #20.	FV	FV	5.00
27	**5 Pounds**			
	ND (2000). Rose on multicolor underprint. Like #21.	FV	FV	17.50

		VG	VF	UNC
28	**10 Pounds**			
	ND (2000). Orange-brown on multicolor underprint. Like #17.	FV	FV	35.00
29	**20 Pounds**			
	ND (2000). Blue on multicolor underprint. Like #23.	FV	FV	65.00
30	**50 Pounds**			
	ND (2000). Dark gray on multicolor underprint. Like #24.	FV	FV	140.

2004 Commemorative Issue

800th Anniversary of the special relationship between Jersey and the British Crown.

		VG	VF	UNC
31	**1 Pound**			
	2004. Dark green and purple on multicolor underprint. Mount Orgueil Castle on back.			
	a. Issued note.	FV	FV	7.50
	s. Specimen.	—	—	12.50

Collector Series

States of Jersey, Treasury

1978 Issue

		Issue Price	Mkt. Value
CS1	**ND (1978) 1-20 Pounds**		
	#11a-14a with overprint: *SPECIMEN* and Maltese cross prefix serial #.	—	75.00

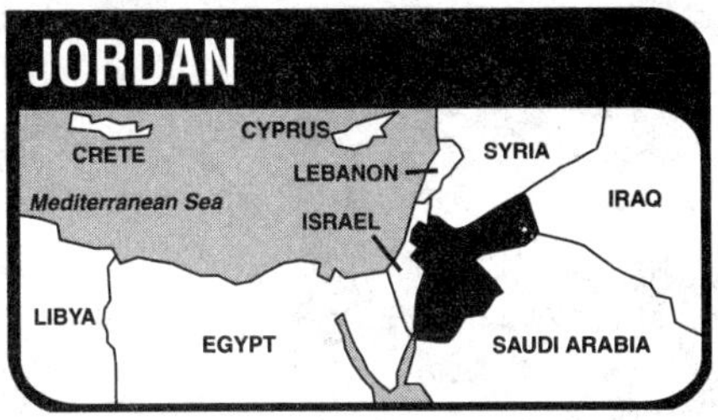

The Hashemite Kingdom of Jordan, a constitutional monarchy in southwest Asia, has an area of 37,738 sq. mi. (97,740 sq. km.) and a population of 5.46 million. Capital: Amman. Agriculture and tourism comprise Jordan's economic . Chief exports are phosphates, tomatoes and oranges.

Jordan is the Edom and Moab of the time of Moses. It became part of the Roman province of Arabia in 106 AD, was conquered by the Arabs in 633-36, and was part of the Ottoman Empire from the 16th century until World War I. At that time, the regions presently known as Jordan and Israel were mandated to Great Britain by the League of Nations as Transjordan and Palestine. In 1922 Transjordan was established as the semi-autonomous Emirate of Transjordan, ruled by the Hashemite Prince Abdullah but still nominally a part of the British mandate. The mandate over Transjordan was terminated in 1946, the country becoming the independent Hashemite Kingdom of Transjordan. The kingdom was renamed The Hashemite Kingdom of The Jordan in 1950.

RULERS:

Hussein I, 1952-1999
Abdullah II, 1999-

MONETARY SYSTEM:

1 Dinar = 10 Dirhams
1 Dirham = 10 Piastres = 10 Qirsh
1 Piastre = 1 Qirsh = 10 Fils

REPLACEMENT NOTES:

#9-27, jj prefix (YY).

KINGDOM

CENTRAL BANK OF JORDAN

SIGNATURE VARIETIES

9			10		
11			12A		
12			13		
14			15		
16			17		
18			19		
20			21		
22			23		
24			25		

FIRST ISSUE - LAW 1959

#9-12 Kg. Hussein at l. w/law date 1959 (in Arabic *1909*).

		VG	VF	UNC
9	**500 Fils**			
	L.1959. Brown on multicolor underprint. Jerash Forum on back. FIVE HUNDRED FILS at bottom margin on back. Signature 10.			
	a. Issued note.	10.00	50.00	100.
	s. Specimen.	—	—	100.

		VG	VF	UNC
10	**1 Dinar**			
	L.1959. Green on multicolor underprint. Al-Aqsa Mosque "Dome of the Rock" at center with columns at right on back. Signature 10.			
	a. Issued note.	4.00	20.00	65.00
	s. Specimen.	—	—	100.

		VG	VF	UNC
11	**5 Dinars**			
	L.1959. Red-brown on multicolor underprint. Al-Hazne, Treasury of Pharaoh at Petra at center right on back.			
	a. Signature 10; 11; 12.	10.00	35.00	125.
	s. Specimen. signature 10.	—	—	125.

12	10 Dinars	VG	VF	UNC
	L.1959. Blue-gray on multicolor underprint. Baptismal site on River Jordan on back.			
	a. Signature 10; 11, 12.	25.00	65.00	235.
	s. Specimen. signature 10.	—	—	125.

SECOND ISSUE - LAW 1959

#13-16 like #9-12. Kg. Hussein I at l., but w/o law date *1959* (in Arabic *1909*). Wmk: Kg. Hussein wearing turban.

13	1/2 Dinar	VG	VF	UNC
	ND. Like #9, but *HALF DINAR* at bottom margin on back.			
	a. Signature 12.	2.00	8.00	30.00
	b. Signature 12A.	2.00	8.00	30.00
	c. Signature 14.	1.00	3.00	12.00

14	1 Dinar	VG	VF	UNC
	ND. Like #10.			
	a. Signature 13.	FV	10.00	40.00
	b. Signature 14.	FV	6.00	25.00

15	5 Dinars	VG	VF	UNC
	ND. Like #11.			
	a. Signature 12.	FV	15.00	60.00
	b. Signature 15.	FV	12.00	35.00
	s. Specimen. signature 10.	—	—	100.

16	10 Dinars	VG	VF	UNC
	ND. Like #12.			
	a. Signature 12; 12A.	FV	45.00	150.
	b. Signature 13; 14.	FV	55.00	175.
	c. Signature 15.	FV	FV	85.00

THIRD ISSUE

#17-21 Kg. Hussein at l. Wmk: Kg. Hussein wearing turban.

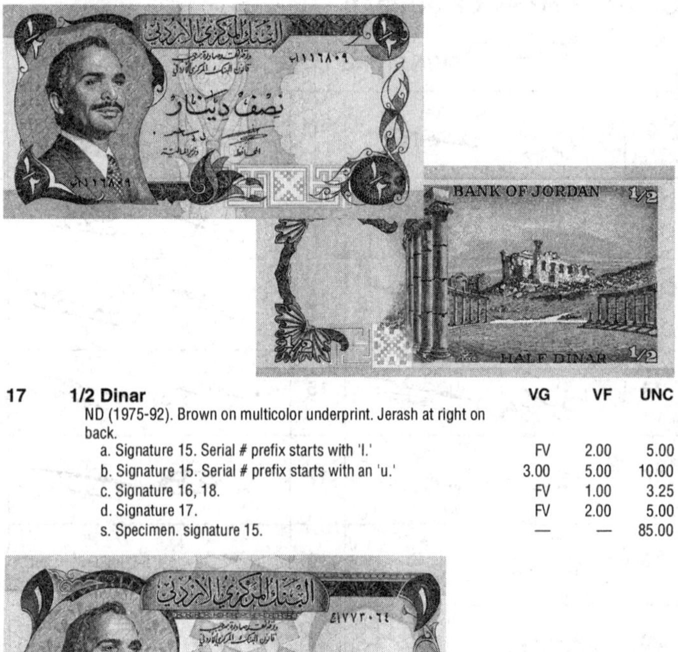

17	1/2 Dinar	VG	VF	UNC
	ND (1975-92). Brown on multicolor underprint. Jerash at right on back.			
	a. Signature 15. Serial # prefix starts with 'I.'	FV	2.00	5.00
	b. Signature 15. Serial # prefix starts with an 'u.'	3.00	5.00	10.00
	c. Signature 16, 18.	FV	1.00	3.25
	d. Signature 17.	FV	2.00	5.00
	s. Specimen. signature 15.	—	—	85.00

18	1 Dinar	VG	VF	UNC
	ND (1975-92). Dark green on multicolor underprint. Al-Aqsa Mosque "Dome of the Rock" in Jerusalem, behind columns at right on back.			
	a. Text above doorway on back. signature 15.	FV	FV	15.00
	b. Without text above doorway on back. signature 15.	FV	FV	12.50
	c. Text above doorway on back. signature 16.	FV	FV	10.00
	d. Signature 17.	FV	FV	8.00
	e. Signature 18.	FV	FV	8.00
	f. Signature 19.	FV	FV	5.00
	s. Specimen. As b. signature 15.	—	—	200.

19 5 Dinars
ND (1975-92). Red on multicolor underprint. Al-Hazne, Treasury of the Pharaoh at Petra at right on back.

	VG	VF	UNC
a. Signature 15.	FV	FV	30.00
b. Signature 16.	FV	FV	27.50
c. Signature 18.	FV	FV	22.50
d. Signature 19.	FV	FV	27.50
s. Specimen. As a.	—	—	250.

20 10 Dinars
ND (1975-92). Blue on multicolor underprint. Cultural palace above and Roman amphitheater at center right on back.

	VG	VF	UNC
a. Signature 15.	FV	FV	85.00
b. Signature 16.	FV	FV	65.00
c. Signature 18.	FV	FV	45.00
d. Signature 19.	FV	FV	35.00
s. Specimen. As a.	—	—	—

21 20 Dinars
1977-1988. Deep brown on multicolor underprint. Electric power station of Zerga on back. Signature 16-18.

	VG	VF	UNC
a. Signature 16. 1977; 1981.	FV	FV	80.00
b. Signature 17. 1985.	FV	FV	75.00
c. Signature 18. 1987; 1988.	FV	FV	70.00
s. Specimen. signature 15. 1977.	FV	FV	300.

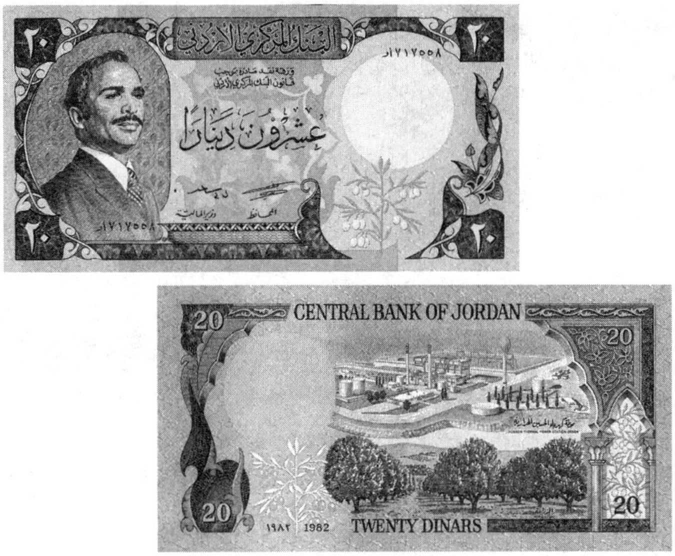

22 20 Dinars
1977-85. Blue on multicolor underprint. Like #21.

	VG	VF	UNC
a. Signature 16. 1977 (1991).	FV	45.00	100.
b. Signature 15. 1982 (1991).	FV	45.00	95.00
c. Signature 17. 1985 (1992).	FV	45.00	85.00

FOURTH ISSUE (1992-93)

#23-27 Kg. Hussein wearing kuffiyeh at ctr. r. and as wmk. Sign. 19.

23 1/2 Dinar
AH1412/1992-AH1413/1993. Lilac-brown and dark brown on multicolor underprint. Qusayr Amra fortress at right on back.

	VG	VF	UNC
a. AH1412/1992.	FV	FV	4.00
b. AH1413/1993.	FV	FV	3.50
s1. As a. Specimen.	—	—	40.00
s2. As b. Specimen.	—	—	25.00

24 1 Dinar
AH1412/1992-AH1413/1993. Green on olive and multicolor underprint. Ruins of Jerash at center right on back.

	VG	VF	UNC
a. AH1412/1992.	FV	FV	6.50
b. AH1413/1993.	FV	FV	5.00
s1. As a. Specimen.	—	—	45.00
s2. As b. Specimen.	—	—	30.00

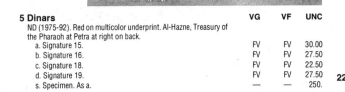

25	5 Dinars	VG	VF	UNC
	AH1412/1992-AH1413/1993. Red and violet-brown on multicolor underprint. Treasury of Petra on back.			
	a. AH1412/1992.	FV	FV	30.00
	b. AH1413/1993.	FV	FV	25.00
	s1. As a. Specimen.	—	—	60.00
	s2. As b. Specimen.	—	—	35.00

26	10 Dinars	VG	VF	UNC
	AH1412/1992. Blue, gray-violet and green on multicolor underprint. Al-Rabadh Castle ruins on back.			
	a. Issued note.	FV	FV	45.00
	s. Specimen.	—	—	75.00

27	20 Dinars	VG	VF	UNC
	AH1412/1992. Dark brown, green and red-brown on multicolor underprint. Al-Aqsa Mosque "Dome of the Rock" at left center on back.			
	a. Issued note.	FV	FV	95.00
	s. Specimen.	—	—	105.

Note: Kg. Hussein financed the restoration of the Al-Aqsa Mosque, as well as the gold-leaf treatment on the dome.

FIFTH ISSUE (1995-2002)

#28-32 w/title: *THE HASHEMITE KINGDOM OF JORDAN* added on back.

28	1/2 Dinar	VG	VF	UNC
	AH1415/1995-. Lilac-brown and dark brown on multicolor underprint. Like #23.			
	a. AH1415/1995. signature 19.	FV	FV	3.50
	b. AH1417/1997. signature 21.	FV	FV	3.00
	s. Specimen.	—	—	25.00

29	1 Dinar	VG	VF	UNC
	AH1415/1995-. Green and olive on multicolor underprint. Like #24.			
	a. AH1415/1995. signature 19.	FV	FV	6.00
	b. AH1416/1996. signature 21.	FV	FV	5.00
	c. AH1417/1997. signature 21.	FV	FV	5.00
	d. AH1422/2001. signature 24.	FV	FV	4.00
	e. AH1423/2001. signature 24.	FV	FV	3.50
	f. AH1423/2002. signature 24.	FV	FV	3.50
	s. As a, b. Specimen.	—	—	35.00

30	5 Dinars	VG	VF	UNC
	AH1415/1995-. Red-violet, purple and orange on multicolor underprint. Similar to #25.			
	a. AH1415/1995. signature 19.	FV	FV	17.50
	b. AH1417/1997. signature 22.	FV	FV	15.00
	c. AH1423/2001. signature 24.	FV	FV	17.50
	s. As a, b. Specimen.	—	—	50.00

31	10 Dinars	VG	VF	UNC
	AH1416/1996; AH1422/2001. Purple, dark blue and black on multicolor underprint. Like #26 but castle ruins renamed *AJLOUN CASTLE.*			
	a. AH1416/1996. signature 20.	FV	FV	35.00
	b. AH1422/2001. signature 24.	FV	FV	27.50
	s. As a. Specimen.	—	—	85.00

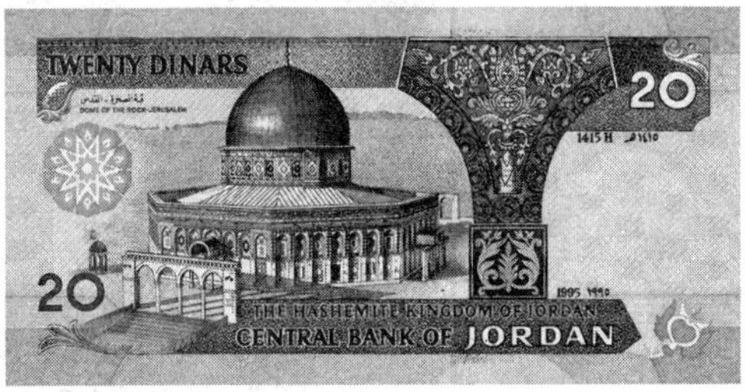

32	20 Dinars	VG	VF	UNC
	AH1415/1995; AH1422/2001. Dark brown, green and red-brown on multicolor underprint. Like #27.			
	a. AH1415/1995. signature 19.	FV	FV	65.00
	b. AH1422/2001. signature 24.	FV	FV	45.00
	s. Specimen.	—	—	100.

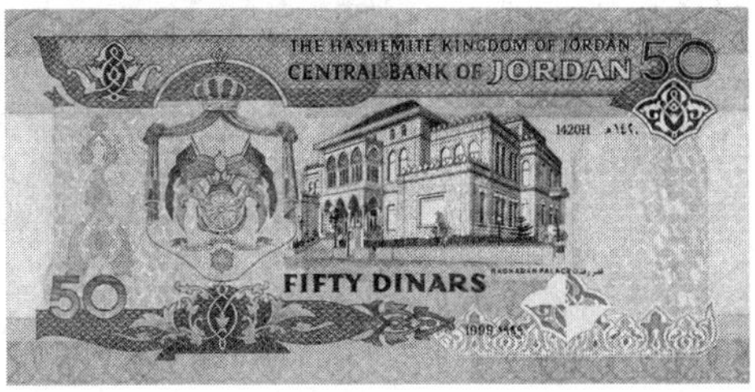

33	50 Dinars	VG	VF	UNC
	AH1420/1999. Light green, blue, red and brown on multicolor underprint. King Abdullah II at right wearing business suit. Raghadan Palace at right center. Coat of Arms at left on back. Signature 23.	FV	FV	125.

SIXTH ISSUE (2002-)

Wmk: same as the portr. Printer: (T)DLR.

34	1 Dinar	VG	VF	UNC
	AH1423/2002. Green, gold and brown on multicolor underprint. Sherif Hussein ibn Ali at right. Silver coins, Great Arab Revolt scene on back. Signature 24.	FV	FV	3.00

35	5 Dinars	VG	VF	UNC
	AH1423/2002. Orange, brown and gold on multicolor underprint. King Abdullah I at right, calvary at center. Ma'an Palace on back. Signature 24.			
	a. Issued note.	FV	FV	12.50
	s. Specimen.	—	—	—

36	10 Dinars	VG	VF	UNC
	AH1423/2002. Blue, green and red on multicolor underprint. King Talal ibn Abdullah at right. First Parliament at center. Camels at Petra on back.			
	a. Signature 24. Foil on vertical serial #.	FV	FV	30.00
	b. Signature 25. Foil to left of vertical serial #.	FV	FV	25.00
	s. Specimen.	—	—	—

		VG	VF	UNC
37	**20 Dinars** AH1423/2002. Blue-green and grey on multicolor underprint. King Hussein at right. Al-Aqsa Mosque "Dome of the Rock" in Jerusalem, on back. Signature 24.	FV	FV	50.00

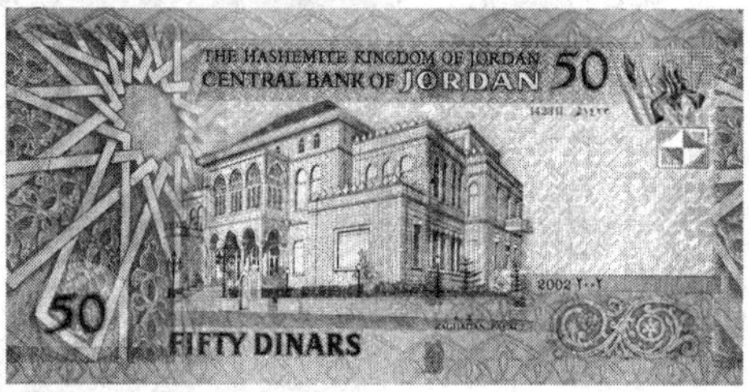

		VG	VF	UNC
38	**50 Dinars** AH1423/2002; AH1425/2004. Light green, blue, red and brown on multicolor underprint. King Abdullah II at right. Raghadan Palace on back. Signature 24; 25.	FV	FV	110.

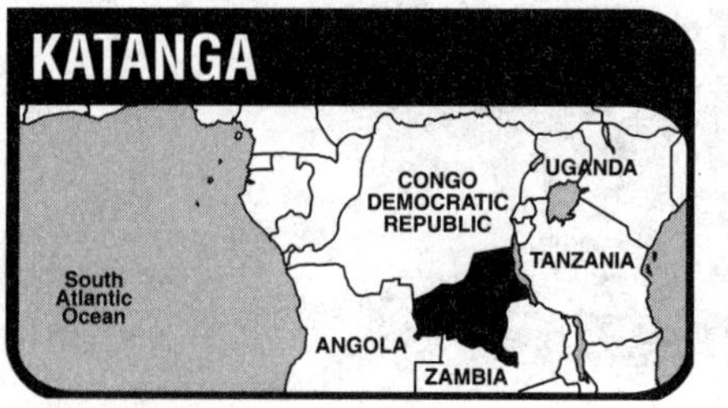

Katanga, the southern province of the former Zaïre extends northeast to Lake Tanganyika, east and south to Zambia, and west to Angola. It was inhabited by Luba and Bantu peoples, and was one of Africa's richest mining areas.

In 1960, Katanga, under the leadership of provincial president Moise Tshombe and supported by foreign mining interests, seceded from newly independent Republic of the Congo. A period of political confusion and bloody fighting involving Congolese, Belgian and United Nations forces ensued. At the end of the rebellion in 1962, Katanga was reintegrated into the republic, and is known as the Shaba region.

For additional history, see Zaïre.

MONETARY SYSTEM:

1 Franc = 100 Centimes

INDEPENDENT

GOVERNMENT

1961 ND PROVISIONAL ISSUE

#1-4 w/red ovpt: *GOUVERNEMENT KATANGA* on face and back of Banque D'Emission du Rwanda et du Burundi notes.

		Good	Fine	XF
1	**5 Francs** ND (1961 - old date 15.5.1961). Overprint on Rwanda & Burundi #1.	—	—	—
2	**10 Francs** ND (1961 - old date 15.9.1960; 5.10.1960). Overprint on Rwanda & Burundi #2. Rare.	—	—	—

		Good	Fine	XF
3	**20 Francs** ND (1961 - old date/15.9.1960; 5.10.1960). Overprint on Rwanda & Burundi #3. Rare.	—	—	—

		Good	Fine	XF
4	**50 Francs** ND (1961 - old date 1.10.1960). Overprint on Rwanda & Burundi #4. Rare.	—	—	—

BANQUE NATIONALE DU KATANGA

1960 ISSUE

#5-10 Moise Tshombe at r. Bldg. at l. on back. Sign. 1.

#5A and 6A Moise Tshombe at l., flag at r. Printer: W&S. (Not issued).

5	10 Francs	VG	VF	UNC
	1.12.1960; 15.12.1960. Lilac and yellow.			
	a. Issued note.	20.00	60.00	125.
	r. Remainder, without serial #.	—	—	80.00
	s. Specimen.	—	75.00	100.

5A	10 Francs	VG	VF	UNC
	1.12.1960. Green, brown and red. Reservoir at center. Foundry at center on back.			
	r. Remainder without date or serial #.	—	—	500.
	s. Specimen.	—	—	150.

6	20 Francs	VG	VF	UNC
	1960. Blue-green and brown.			
	a. 21.11.1960.	30.00	75.00	150.
	b. 1.12.1960.	75.00	150.	300.
	r. Remainder, without serial #.	—	—	125.
	s. Specimen.	—	80.00	150.

6A	20 Francs	Good	Fine	XF
	1.12.1960. Multicolor. Aerial view at center. Miners at center on back. Specimen. Rare.	—	—	—

7	50 Francs	VG	VF	UNC
	10.11.1960. Red-brown and blue.			
	a. Issued note.	40.00	90.00	200.
	r. Remainder, without serial #.	—	—	125.
	s. Specimen.	—	100.	150.

8	100 Francs	VG	VF	UNC
	31.10.1960. Brown, green and yellow.			
	a. Issued note.	40.00	100.	250.
	r. Remainder, without serial #.	—	—	175.
	s. Specimen.	—	150.	200.

9	500 Francs	VG	VF	UNC
	31.10.1960. Green, violet and olive.			
	a. Issued note.	200.	400.	750.
	r. Remainder, without serial #.	—	—	450.
	s. Specimen.	—	200.	300.

10	1000 Francs	VG	VF	UNC
	31.10.1960. Blue and brown.			
	a. Issued note.	150.	450.	900.
	r. Remainder, without serial #.	—	—	450.
	s. Specimen.	—	275.	325.

#11 Not assigned.

1962 Issue

#12-14 wheel of masks and spears on back. Wmk: Elephant. Sign. 2, 3.

		VG	VF	UNC
12	**100 Francs** 18.5.1962; 15.8.1962; 15.9.1962. Dark green and brown on multicolor underprint. Woman carrying ears of corn at right.			
	a. Issued note.	30.00	75.00	180.
	b. 15.1.1963.	50.00	125.	250.
	s. Specimen.	—	—	125.

		VG	VF	UNC
13	**500 Francs** 17.4.1962. Purple and multicolor. Man with fire at right.			
	a. Issued note.	125.	350.	600.
	s. Specimen.	—	—	450.

		VG	VF	UNC
14	**1000 Francs** 26.2.1962. Dark blue, red and brown on multicolor underprint. Woman carrying child on back while picking cotton at right. Ornate wheel at left.			
	a. Issued note.	75.00	180.	350.
	s. Specimen.	—	—	300.

The Republic of Kazakhstan is bordered to the west by the Caspian Sea and Russia, to the north by Russia, in the east by the Peoples Republic of China and in the south by Uzbekistan and Kyrgyzstan. It has an area of 1,049,155 sq. mi. (2,717,300 sq. km.) and a population of 16.93 million. Capital: Astana. The country is rich in mineral resources including coal, tungsten, copper, lead, zinc and manganese with huge oil and natural gas reserves. Agriculture is important also non-ferrous metallurgy, heavy engineering and chemical industries are leaders in its economy.

The Kazakhs are a branch of the Turkic peoples which led the nomadic life of herdsman until WW I. In the 13th century they come under Genghis Khan's eldest son Juji and later became a part of the Golden Horde, a western Mongol empire. Around the beginning of the 16th century they were divided into 3 confederacies, known as zhuz or hordes, in the steppes of Turkistan. At the end of the 17th century an incursion by the Kalmucks, a remnant of the Oirat Mongol confederacy, facilitated Russian penetration. Resistance to Russian settlements varied throughout the 1800's, but by 1900 over 100 million acres was declared Czarist state property and used for a planned peasant colonization. In 1916 the Czarist government ordered mobilization of all males, between 19 and 43 for auxiliary service. The Kazakhs rose in defiance which led the governor general of Turkestan to send troops against the rebels. Shortly after the Russian revolution, Kazakh nationalists asked for full autonomy. The Communist coup d'état of Nov. 1917 led to civil war. In 1919-20 the Red army defeated the "White" Russian forces and occuped Kazakhstan and fought against the Nationalist government formed by Ali Khan Bukey Khan. The Kazakh Autonomous Soviet Socialist Republic was proclaimed on Aug. 26, 1920 within the R.S.F.S.R. Russian and Ukrainian colonization continued. On Dec. 5, 1936, Kazakhstan qualified for full status as an S.S.R. and held its first congress in 1937. Independence was declared on Dec. 16, 1991 and the new Republic joined the C.I.S.

MONETARY SYSTEM:

1 Tengé = 100 Tyin = 500 Rubles (Russian), 1993 -

Republic

КАЗАКСТАН УЛТТЫК БАНКI

Kazakhstan National Bank

1993-98 Issue

#1-6 ornate denomination in circle at r. Circular arms at l. on back. Serial # at l. or lower l. Wmk. paper.

		VG	VF	UNC
1	**1 Tyin** 1993. Red, blue and purple on yellow and multicolor underprint. Two watermark varieties.			
	a. Watermark: large diamond lattice pattern.	.10	.15	.50
	b. Watermark: small snowflake pattern.	.10	.15	.50

		VG	VF	UNC
2	**2 Tyin** 1993. Blue-violet on light blue and multicolor underprint.			
	a. Watermark: large diamond pattern.	.10	.15	.50
	b. Watermark: small snowflake pattern.	.10	.15	.50
	c. Without watermark.	.10	.15	.45

		VG	VF	UNC
3	**5 Tyin** 1993. Violet on light blue and multicolor underprint.	.10	.15	.60

		VG	VF	UNC
4	**10 Tyin** 1993. Deep red on pink and multicolor underprint.	.10	.15	.75

		VG	VF	UNC
5	**20 Tyin** 1993. Black and blue-gray on yellow and multicolor underprint.	.10	.15	.75

		VG	VF	UNC
6	**50 Tyin** 1993. Dark brown and black on multicolor underprint.	.10	.15	1.50

#7-15 arms at upper ctr. r. on back. #7-9 wmk: symmetrical design repeated.

		VG	VF	UNC
7	**1 Tengé** 1993. Dark blue on multicolor underprint. Al-Farabi at center right. Back light blue on multicolor underprint; architectural drawings of mosque at left center, arms at upper right.			
	a. Issued note.	.10	.15	1.50
	s. Specimen.	—	—	100.

		VG	VF	UNC
8	**3 Tengé** 1993. Dark green on multicolor underprint. Suinbai at center right. Mountains, forest, and river at left center on back.			
	a. Issued note.	.10	.15	2.50
	s. Specimen.	—	—	100.

		VG	VF	UNC
9	**5 Tengé** 1993. Dark brown-violet on multicolor underprint. Kurmangazy at center right. Cemetery at left center on back.			
	a. Issued note.	.25	.45	2.50
	s. Specimen.	—	—	100.

		VG	VF	UNC
10	**10 Tengé** 1993. Dark green on multicolor underprint. Shoqan Valikhanov at center right and as watermark. Mountains, forest, and lake at left center on back.			
	a. Issued note.	.25	.50	3.00
	s. Specimen.	—	—	100.

		VG	VF	UNC
11	**20 Tengé** 1993. Brown on multicolor underprint. Abai Kunanbrev at center right and as watermark. Equestrian hunter at left center on back.			
	a. Issued note.	.25	.50	5.00
	s. Specimen.	—	—	100.

		VG	VF	UNC
12	**50 Tengé** 1993. Red-brown and deep violet on multicolor underprint. Abilkhair Khan at center right and as watermark. Native artwork at left center on back.			
	a. Issued note.	.30	1.25	7.00
	s. Specimen.	—	—	125.

13	100 Tengé	VG	VF	UNC
	1993; 2004. Purple and dark blue on multicolor underprint. Gold OVD ink at top left. Abylai Khan at center right and as watermark. Domed building at left center on back.			
	a. 1993.	.60	1.20	7.50
	b. 2004.	.50	1.00	7.50
	s. Specimen.	—	—	125.

#14-17 al-Farabi at r. and as wmk.

14	200 Tengé	VG	VF	UNC
	1993. Red and brown on multicolor underprint. Back blue on multicolor underprint; domes of building at left on back.			
	a. Issued note.	FV	FV	12.00
	s. Specimen.	—	—	135.

15	500 Tengé	VG	VF	UNC
	1994. Blue-black and violet on multicolor underprint. Ancient building on back.			
	a. Issued note.	FV	FV	17.50
	s. Specimen.	—	—	150.

16	1000 Tengé	VG	VF	UNC
	1994. Deep green, red and orange on multicolor underprint. Ancient building on back.			
	a. Issued note.	FV	FV	32.50
	s. Specimen.	—	—	150.

17	2000 Tengé	VG	VF	UNC
	1996. Dark brown and green on multicolor underprint. Gate on back.	12.50	25.00	60.00

18	5000 Tengé	VG	VF	UNC
	1998. Light brown on multicolor underprint. Al Farabi at center. Mausoleum on back.	30.00	35.00	75.00

19 *Not assigned.*

1999-2001 ISSUE

20	200 Tengé	VG	VF	UNC
	1999. Brown and tan on multicolor underprint. Similar to #14.			
	a. Security device at lower right. with white linear design.	1.00	2.00	5.00
	b. Security device at lower right. solid.	1.00	2.00	5.00

NOTICE

Readers with unlisted dates, signature varieties, etc. are invited to submit photocopies of their notes to: Standard Catalog of World Paper Money, 700 East State St. Iola, WI 54990-0001, E-Mail: george.cuhaj@fwpubs.com.

		VG	VF	UNC
21	**500 Tengé** 1999. Dark blue and violet on multicolor underprint. Similar to #15.			
	a. Security device at lower right. with white linear designature	2.00	5.00	7.50
	b. Security device at lower right. solid.	3.00	5.00	7.50

		VG	VF	UNC
22	**1000 Tengé** 2000. Dark green, red and slate blue on multicolor underprint. Similar to #16.	6.00	12.50	27.50

		VG	VF	UNC
23	**2000 Tengé** 2000. Green, brown and purple on multicolor underprint. Similar to #17. Mausoleum of Khodka Akhemd Yassavi on back.	FV	FV	35.00

		VG	VF	UNC
24	**5000 Tengé** 2001. Light brown and red on multicolor underprint. Similar to #18.	FV	FV	65.00

		VG	VF	UNC
25	**10,000 Tengé** 2003. Blue and dark brown on multicolor underprint. Snow leopard with mountains in background on back.	FV	FV	125.

2001 COMMEMORATIVE ISSUE

		VG	VF	UNC
26	**5000 Tengé** 2001. Light brown and red on multicolor underprint. Blue overprint at top of watermark area on face of #18.	FV	FV	65.00

2004 ISSUE

		VG	VF	UNC
27	**500 Tengé** 1999 (2004). Dark blue and blue on violet and multicolor underprint. Al-Farabi at right. Mausoleum of Khodka Akhmed Yassavi on back. Like #21 but additional security features at right.	FV	FV	7.50

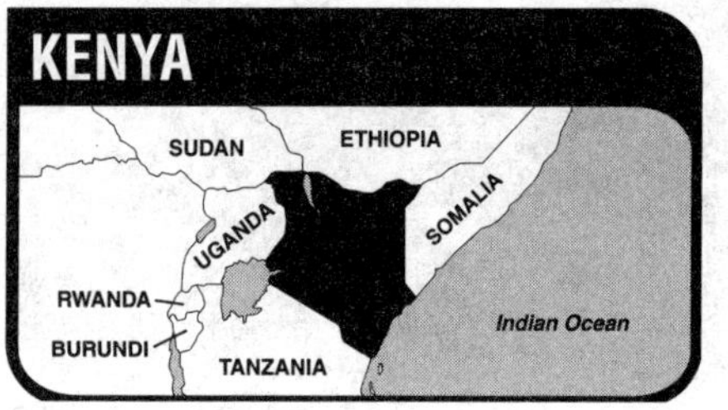

The Republic of Kenya, located on the east coast of Central Africa, has an area of 224,961 sq. mi. (582,646 sq. km.) and a population of 30.34 million. Capital: Nairobi. The predominantly agricultural country exports coffee, tea and petroleum products.

The Arabs came to the coast of Kenya in the 8th century and established posts to conduct an ivory and slave trade. The Portuguese, the inveterate wanderers of the Age of Exploration, followed in the 16th century. After a lengthy and bitter struggle with the sultans of Zanzibar who controlled much of the southeastern coast of Africa, the Portuguese were driven away (late 17th century) and for many years Kenya was simply a port of call on the route to India. German and British interests in the 19th century produced agreements defining their respective spheres of influence. The British sphere was administered by the Imperial East Africa Co. until 1895, when the British government purchased the company's rights in the East Africa Protectorate which in 1920 was designated as Kenya Colony and protectorate - the latter being a 10-mile wide coastal strip together with Mombasa, Lamu and other small islands nominally retained by the Sultan of Zanzibar. Kenya achieved self-government in June of 1963 as a consequence of the 1952-60 Mau Mau terrorist campaign to secure land reforms and political rights for Africans. Independence was attained on Dec. 12, 1963. Kenya became a republic in 1964. It is a member of the Commonwealth of Nations. The president is Chief of State and Head of Government.

Notes of the East African Currency Board were in use during the first years.

RULERS:

British to 1964

MONETARY SYSTEM:

1 Shilling (Shilingi) = 100 Cents

REPUBLIC

CENTRAL BANK OF KENYA

1966 ISSUE

#1-5 Mzee Jomo Kenyatta at l., arms at ctr. in unpt. Values also in Arabic numerals and letters. Wmk: Lion's head.

		VG	VF	UNC
1	**5 Shillings**			
	1966-68. Brown on multicolor underprint. Woman picking coffee beans at right on back.			
	a. 1.7.1966.	4.00	20.00	95.00
	b. 1.7.1967.	3.00	17.50	90.00
	c. 1.7.1968.	3.50	17.50	85.00
	s. As a. Specimen, punched hole cancelled.	—	—	—

		VG	VF	UNC
2	**10 Shillings**			
	1966-68. Green on multicolor underprint. Tea pickers in field on back.			
	a. 1.7.1966.	5.00	25.00	95.00
	b. 1.7.1967.	5.00	27.50	140.
	c. 1.7.1968.	4.00	20.00	120.
	s. As a. Specimen, punched hole cancelled.	—	—	—

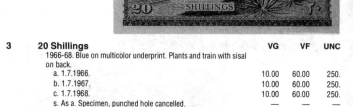

		VG	VF	UNC
3	**20 Shillings**			
	1966-68. Blue on multicolor underprint. Plants and train with sisal on back.			
	a. 1.7.1966.	10.00	60.00	250.
	b. 1.7.1967.	10.00	60.00	250.
	c. 1.7.1968.	10.00	60.00	250.
	s. As a. Specimen, punched hole cancelled.	—	—	—

		VG	VF	UNC
4	**50 Shillings**			
	1966-68. Dark brown on multicolor underprint. Cotton picking below Mt. Kenya on back.			
	a. 1.7.1966.	55.00	300.	950.
	b. 1.7.1967.	65.00	400.	1500.
	c. 1.7.1968.	50.00	350.	1350.
	s. As a. Specimen, punched hole cancelled.	—	—	—

		VG	VF	UNC
5	**100 Shillings**			
	1966; 1968. Purple on multicolor underprint. Workers at pineapple plantation on back.			
	a. 1.7.1966.	12.50	55.00	475.
	b. 1.7.1968.	15.00	60.00	500.
	s. As a. Specimen, punched hole cancelled.	—	—	—

1969 ISSUE

#6-10 Mzee Jomo Kenyatta at l., values w/o Arabic numerals and letters. Different text at lower ctr. Wmk: Lion's head.

		VG	VF	UNC
6	**5 Shillings**			
	1969-73. Brown on multicolor underprint. Similar to #1.			
	a. Signature 2. 1.7.1969.	1.00	5.00	25.00
	b. Signature 3. 1.7.1971.	1.50	6.00	30.00
	c. Signature 3. 1.7.1972.	.75	2.00	25.00
	d. Signature 3. 1.7.1973.	.75	4.00	22.50

		VG	VF	UNC
7	**10 Shillings**			
	1969-74. Green on multicolor underprint. Similar to #2.			
	a. Signature 2. 1.7.1969.	2.50	8.00	60.00
	b. Signature 3. 1.7.1971.	2.00	6.00	50.00
	c. Signature 3. 1.7.1972.	1.50	7.00	55.00
	d. Signature 3. 1.7.1973.	1.50	7.00	55.00
	e. Signature 3. 1.7.1974.	1.50	7.00	57.50

		VG	VF	UNC
8	**20 Shillings**			
	1969-73. Blue on multicolor underprint. Similar to #3.			
	a. Signature 2. 1.7.1969.	3.00	20.00	160.
	b. Signature 3. 1.7.1971.	7.00	40.00	275.
	c. Signature 3. 1.7.1972.	4.00	25.00	180.
	d. Signature 3. 1.7.1973.	5.00	30.00	200.
9	**50 Shillings**			
	1969; 1971. Dark brown on multicolor underprint. Similar to #4.			
	a. Signature 2. 1.7.1969.	50.00	175.	600.
	b. Signature 3. 1.7.1971.	15.00	65.00	200.

		VG	VF	UNC
10	**100 Shillings**			
	1969-73. Purple on multicolor underprint. Similar to #5.			
	a. Signature 2. 1.7.1969.	25.00	125.	500.
	b. Signature 3. 1.7.1971.	10.00	40.00	275.
	c. Signature 3. 1.7.1972.	10.00	40.00	275.
	d. Signature 3. 1.7.1973.	20.00	100.	350.

1974 ISSUE

#11-14 Mzee Jomo Kenyatta at l., values in latent images at bottom l. Wmk: Lion's head.

		VG	VF	UNC
11	**5 Shillings**			
	1974-77. Brown-orange on multicolor underprint. Woman picking coffee beans at right on back.			
	a. Signature 3. 12.12.1974.	.50	2.00	15.00
	b. Signature 4. 1.1.1975.	1.00	4.00	30.00
	c. Signature 4. 1.7.1976.	.25	1.50	10.00
	d. Signature 5. 1.7.1977.	.50	2.00	15.00

		VG	VF	UNC
12	**10 Shillings**			
	1.1.1975; 1.7.1976; 1.7.1977. Dark green and dark brown on multicolor underprint. Back green; cattle at center right on back.			
	a. Signature 4. 1.1.1975.	1.00	3.00	15.00
	b. Signature 4. 1.7.1976.	1.50	6.00	25.00
	c. Signature 5. 1.7.1977.	1.25	4.00	17.50

13 20 Shillings

1974-77. Dark blue on multicolor underprint. Lions on back.

	VG	VF	UNC
a. Signature 3. 12.12.1974.	3.00	15.00	60.00
b. Signature 4. 1.1.1975.	2.00	7.50	35.00
c. Signature 4. 1.7.1976.	4.00	12.50	65.00
d. Signature 5. 1.7.1977.	3.00	9.00	45.00

14 100 Shillings

1974-77. Purple on light green and multicolor underprint. Kenyatta statue and tower on back. 153 x 79mm.

	VG	VF	UNC
a. Signature 3. 12.12.1974.	10.00	35.00	150.
b. Signature 4. 1.1.1975.	5.00	17.50	125.
c. Signature 4. 1.7.1976.	7.50	25.00	140.
d. Signature 5. 1.7.1977.	7.50	30.00	220.

1978 Issue

#15-18 Mzee Jomo Kenyatta at l., w/English value only in 3rd line on face. Wmk: Lion's head.

Note: #15-18 were withdrawn soon after Kenyatta's death. A shortage of currency resulted in a limited reissue during Dec. 1993 - Jan. 1994 of mostly circulated notes.

15 5 Shillings

	VG	VF	UNC
1.7.1978. Brown-orange on multicolor underprint. Similar to #11. with English value only in third line on face. Signature 5.	.50	1.50	3.00

16 10 Shillings

	VG	VF	UNC
1.7.1978. Dark green and dark brown on multicolor underprint. Similar to #12. Signature 5.	.50	1.00	5.00

17 20 Shillings

	VG	VF	UNC
1.7.1978. Blue-black and blue on multicolor underprint. Similar to #13. Signature 5.	1.25	2.75	7.50

18 100 Shillings

	VG	VF	UNC
1.7.1978. Purple, dark brown and dark blue on multicolor underprint. Similar to #14 but with different colors in guilloches. 157 x 81mm. Signature 5.	2.50	7.50	20.00

1980-81 Issue

#19-23 arms at ctr., Pres. Daniel Toroitich Arap Moi at r. Wmk: Lion's head.

19 5 Shillings

1981-84. Orange-brown on multicolor underprint. Three rams with giraffes and mountain in background on back.

	VG	VF	UNC
a. Signature 6. 1.1.1981.	FV	.50	5.00
b. Signature 6. 1.1.1982.	FV	3.00	4.00
c. Signature 7. 1.7.1984.	FV	6.00	7.00

20 10 Shillings

1981-88. Green, blue and brown on multicolor underprint. Two cows at left, two school children drinking milk at center on back.

	VG	VF	UNC
a. Signature 6. 1.1.1981.	FV	1.50	8.00
b. Signature 6. 1.1.1982.	FV	1.25	7.00
c. Signature 7. 1.7.1984.	FV	1.75	9.00
d. Signature 7. 1.7.1985.	FV	2.00	10.00
e. Signature 7. 14.9.1986.	FV	1.50	8.00
f. Signature 8. 1.7.1987.	FV	1.25	8.00
g. Signature 9a. 1.7.1988.	FV	1.25	7.00

21 20 Shillings

1981-87. Blue on multicolor underprint. Four women reading newspaper at center on back.

	VG	VF	UNC
a. Signature 6. 1.1.1981.	FV	1.75	14.00
b. Signature 6. 1.1.1982.	FV	1.50	10.00
c. Signature 7. 1.7.1984.	FV	1.50	10.00
d. Signature 7. 1.7.1985.	FV	2.00	16.00
e. Signature 7. 14.9.1986.	FV	2.25	17.50
f. Signature 8. 1.7.1987.	FV	1.75	14.00

22 50 Shillings

1980-88. Dark red and multicolor. Back olive; jet aircraft flying over Jomo Kenyatta airport.

	VG	VF	UNC
a. Signature 4. 1.6.1980.	FV	3.00	12.50
b. Signature 7. 1.7.1985.	FV	3.50	17.50
c. Signature 7. 14.9.1986.	FV	3.50	18.00
d. Signature 8. 1.7.1987.	FV	5.00	20.00
e. Signature 9a. 1.7.1988.	FV	5.00	20.00

23 100 Shillings

1980-88. Purple and multicolor. Kenyatta statue, tower and mountains on back.

	VG	VF	UNC
a. Signature 4. 1.6.1980.	FV	5.00	25.00
b. Signature 6. 1.6.1981.	FV	6.00	35.00
c. Signature 7. 1.7.1984.	FV	5.00	30.00
d. Signature 7. 14.9.1986.	FV	6.50	40.00
e. Signature 8. 1.7.1987.	FV	7.00	50.00
f. Signature 9a. 1.7.1988.	FV	4.00	22.00

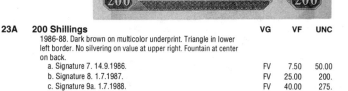

23A 200 Shillings

1986-88. Dark brown on multicolor underprint. Triangle in lower left border. No silvering on value at upper right. Fountain at center on back.

	VG	VF	UNC
a. Signature 7. 14.9.1986.	FV	7.50	50.00
b. Signature 8. 1.7.1987.	FV	25.00	200.
c. Signature 9a. 1.7.1988.	FV	40.00	275.

1986-90 Issue

#24-30 Pres. Daniel Toroitich Arap Moi at r. ctr., arms at l. ctr. Vertical serial # at l. Wmk: Lion's head. Replacement notes: Serial # prefix ZZ.

Note: H&S printed the small date of 2.1.1992.

24	10 Shillings	VG	VF	UNC
	1989-94. Dark green, dark blue and brown on multicolor underprint. University at left center on back.			
	a. Signature 9a. 14.10.1989	FV	FV	3.00
	b. Signature 9a. 1.7.1990.	FV	FV	2.50
	c. Signature 9a. 1.7.1991.	FV	FV	1.75
	d. Signature 10a. 2.1.1992. Small date font.	FV	1.00	4.50
	e. Signature 10a. 1.7.1993. Large date font.	FV	1.00	4.50
	f. Signature 11. 1.1.1994.	FV	1.50	6.00

25	20 Shillings	VG	VF	UNC
	1988-92. Dark blue and multicolor. Moi International Sports Complex on back.			
	a. Signature 9b. 12.12.1988.	1.25	4.00	15.00
	b. Signature 9b. 1.7.1989.	FV	1.00	5.00
	c. Signature 9b. 1.7.1990.	FV	FV	3.50
	d. Signature 9b. 1.7.1991.	FV	2.00	6.00
	e. Signature 10a. 2.1.1992. Large date font.	FV	2.00	6.00

Note: #25 dated 12.12.1988 is believed to be a commemorative for the 25th Anniversary of Independence.

26	50 Shillings	VG	VF	UNC
	1990; 1992. Red-brown on multicolor underprint. Back green; modern buildings at left, flag at right.			
	a. Signature 9b. 10.10.1990.	FV	4.00	16.00
	b. Signature 10b. 1.7.1992.	FV	3.00	14.00

27	100 Shillings	VG	VF	UNC
	1989-95. Purple, dark green and red on multicolor underprint. Monument to 25th Anniversary of Independence with Mt. Kenya on back.			
	a. Signature 9a. 14.10.1989.	FV	3.00	12.50
	b. Signature 9a. 1.7.1990.	FV	3.00	12.50
	c. Signature 9a. 1.7.1991.	FV	2.00	10.00
	d. Signature 10a. 2.1.1992. Small date font.	FV	3.00	12.50
	e. Signature 10a. 1.7.1992. Large date font.	FV	4.00	15.00
	f. Signature 11. 1.1.1994.	FV	3.00	15.00
	g. Signature 12. 1.1.1995.	FV	4.00	17.50

#28 *Deleted.* See #23A.

29	200 Shillings	VG	VF	UNC
	1989-94. Similar to #23A but rose replaces colored triangle to right of *200* at lower left. Additional silver diamond design under 200 at upper right. Vertical serial # at left.			
	a. Signature 9a. 14.10.1989.	FV	4.50	27.50
	b. Signature 9a. 1.7.1990.	FV	4.50	25.00
	c. Signature 10a. 2.1.1992. Small date font.	FV	5.00	37.50
	d. Signature 10a. 1.7.1992. Large date font.	FV	4.00	25.00
	e. Signature 11. 14.9.1993.	FV	3.50	22.50
	f. Signature 11. 1.1.1994.	FV	4.00	25.00

30	500 Shillings	VG	VF	UNC
	1988-95. Black, deep green and red on multicolor underprint. Roses at left. Parliament building, Mt. Kenya on back.			
	a. Signature 9b. 14.10.1988.	10.00	50.00	250.
	b. Signature 9b. 1.7.1989.	FV	25.00	100.
	c. Signature 9b. 1.7.1990.	FV	15.00	55.00
	d. Signature 10a. 2.1.1992. Small date font.	FV	20.00	75.00
	e. Signature 10a. 1.7.1992. Large date font.	FV	15.00	55.00
	f. Signature 11. 14.9.1993.	FV	17.50	65.00
	g. Signature 12. 1.1.1995.	FV	17.50	70.00

1993 Issue

#31 Pres. Daniel Toroitich Arap Moi at ctr. r.

31 20 Shillings | VG | VF | UNC

1993-94. Similar to #25 but with roses added to left border, vertical red serial #. Male runner and other artistic enhancements added on back.

	VG	VF	UNC
a. Signature 11. 14.9.1993.	FV	2.00	5.00
b. Signature 11. 1.1.1994.	FV	2.00	6.00

1994-95 ISSUE

#32-34 Pres. Daniel Toroitich Arap Moi at l. ctr., arms at upper ctr. r. Ascending size serial #. W/o segmented foil over security thread. Wmk: Lion head facing.

32 20 Shillings

	VG	VF	UNC
1.7.1995. Dark blue, brown and blue-green on multicolor underprint. Baton at left, Moi Int'l Sports Complex at left center, runner at center right on back. Signature 13.	FV	FV	2.50

33 500 Shillings

	VG	VF	UNC
1.7.1995. Black, green and red on multicolor underprint. Parliament building at left center on back.	FV	FV	22.50

34 1000 Shillings

	VG	VF	UNC
12.12.1994; 1.7.1995. Brown on multicolor underprint. Water buffalo, elephants and egret on back.	FV	FV	50.00

1996-97 ISSUE

#35-40 like previous issue but w/segmented foil over security thread.

35 20 Shillings

1996-2001. Dark blue on multicolor underprint. Like #32. with security thread.

	VG	VF	UNC
a. 1.1.1996.	FV	FV	3.00
b. 1.7.1997.	FV	FV	5.00
c. 1.7.1998.	FV	FV	7.00

36 50 Shillings

1996-2002 Brown-violet and blue-black on multicolor underprint. Dromedary caravan on back.

	VG	VF	UNC
a. 1.1.1996.	FV	FV	5.00
b. 1.7.1997.	FV	FV	7.00
c. 1.7.1998.	FV	FV	4.00
d. 1.7.1999.	FV	FV	5.00
e. 1.7.2000.	FV	FV	3.00
f. 1.7.2001.	FV	FV	15.00
g. 1.7.2002.	FV	FV	2.50

37 100 Shillings

1996-2002. Purple, red and deep green on multicolor underprint. People by Monument to 25th Anniversary of Independence at center, branch of fruit at left on back.

	VG	VF	UNC
a. 1.7.1996.	FV	FV	6.00
b. 1.7.1997.	FV	FV	12.00
c. 1.7.1998.	FV	FV	5.00
d. 1.7.1999.	FV	FV	7.50
e. 1.7.2000.	FV	FV	4.00
f. 1.7.2001.	FV	FV	8.00
g. 1.7.2002.	FV	FV	4.00
h. 1.9.2002.	FV	FV	5.00

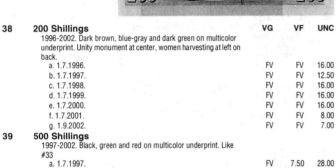

		VG	VF	UNC
38	**200 Shillings**			
	1996-2002. Dark brown, blue-gray and dark green on multicolor underprint. Unity monument at center, women harvesting at left on back.			
	a. 1.7.1996.	FV	FV	16.00
	b. 1.7.1997.	FV	FV	12.50
	c. 1.7.1998.	FV	FV	16.00
	d. 1.7.1999.	FV	FV	16.00
	e. 1.7.2000.	FV	FV	16.00
	f. 1.7.2001.	FV	FV	8.00
	g. 1.9.2002.	FV	FV	7.00
39	**500 Shillings**			
	1997-2002. Black, green and red on multicolor underprint. Like #33			
	a. 1.7.1997.	FV	7.50	28.00
	b. 1.7.1999.	FV	FV	26.00
	c. 1.7.2000.	FV	FV	24.00
	d. 1.7.2001.	FV	FV	18.00

		VG	VF	UNC
40	**1000 Shillings**			
	1997-2002. Brown-violet and olive-green on multicolor underprint. Like #34.			
	a. 1.7.1997.	FV	FV	60.00
	b. 1.7.1999.	FV	FV	45.00
	c. 1.7.2000.	FV	FV	35.00
	d. 1.7.2001.	FV	FV	40.00
	e. 1.7.2002.	FV	FV	35.00

2003-04 Issue

#41-45 like previous issue but w/enhanced security features. 2003 dates ahve thin security thread, 2004 onwards have a thick thread.

		VG	VF	UNC
41	**50 Shillings**			
	1.4.2003; 2.2.2004; 2.8.2004; 1.6.2005; 1.4.2006. Brown-violet and blue-black on multicolor underprint. Dromedary caravan on back.			
	a. Issued note.	FV	FV	2.50
	s. Specimen.	—	—	—

		VG	VF	UNC
42	**100 Shillings**			
	2.2.2004; 2.8.2004; 1.6.2005; 1.4.2006. Purple, orange and green on multicolor underprint. Nyayo monument on back.	FV	FV	3.50
43	**200 Shillings**			
	2.2.2004; 2.8.2004; 1.6.2005. Brown, blue and light green on multicolor underprint. Jomo Kenyatta at left center. Cotton pickers on back. Like #45 but without commemorative text.	FV	FV	6.50

		VG	VF	UNC
44	**500 Shillings**			
	1.4.2003; 2.2.2004; 2.8.2004; 1.6.2005. Black and green on multicolor underprint. National Assembly building.	FV	FV	16.00

		VG	VF	UNC
45	**1000 Shillings**			
	1.4.2003; 2.2.2004; 2.8.2004; 1.6.2005. Brown, lilac and light olive on multicolor underprint. Elephants and other animals on back.	FV	FV	32.50

2003 COMMEMORATIVE ISSUE

40th Anniversary of Independence.

46	200 Shillings	VG	VF	UNC
	12.12.2003. Brown, blue and light green on multicolor underprint. Jomo Kenyatta at left center, commemorative text in watermark area at left. Cotton pickers on back.	FV	FV	6.50

The Democratic Peoples Republic of Korea, situated in in northeastern Asia on the northern half of the Korean peninsula between the Peoples Republic of China and the Republic of Korea, has an area of 46,540 sq. mi. (120,538 sq. km.) and a population of 23.26 million. Capital: Pyongyang. The economy is d on heavy d on heavy industry and agriculture. Metals, minerals and farm produce are exported.

Japan replaced China as the predominant foreign influence in Korea in 1895 and annexed the peninsular country in 1910. Defeat in World War II brought an end to Japanese rule. U.S. troops entered Korea from the south and Soviet forces entered from the north. The Cairo conference (1943) had established that Korea should be "free and independent." The Potsdam conference (1945) set the 38th parallel as the line dividing the occupation forces of the United States and Russia. When Russia refused to permit a U.N. commission designated to supervise reunification elections to enter North Korea, an election was held in South Korea which established the Republic of Korea on Aug. 15, 1948. North Korea held an unsupervised election on Aug. 25, 1948, and on the following day proclaimed the establishment of the Democratic Peoples Republic of Korea.

MONETARY SYSTEM:

1 Won = 100 Chon

DEMOCRATIC PEOPLES REPUBLIC

KOREAN CENTRAL BANK

1959 ISSUE

#12-17 arms at l. or upper l. Wmk. paper.

12	50 Chon	VG	VF	UNC
	1959. Blue on multicolor underprint. Arms at upper left.	.80	2.50	8.00

13	1 Won	VG	VF	UNC
	1959. Red-brown on multicolor underprint. Fishing boat at center.	.60	1.75	6.00

14	5 Won	VG	VF	UNC
	1959. Green on multicolor underprint. Large Building at center.	.75	2.00	7.00

15 **10 Won**

	VG	VF	UNC
1959. Red on multicolor underprint. Fortress gateway at center right. Woman picking fruit on back.	.80	2.25	8.00

16 **50 Won**

	VG	VF	UNC
1959. Purple on multicolor underprint. Bridge and city at center Woman with wheat on back.	1.00	3.50	10.00

17 **100 Won**

	VG	VF	UNC
1959. Green on multicolor underprint. Steam freight train in factory area at center River with cliffs on back.	1.50	4.50	15.00

1978 ISSUE

#18-22 arms at upper l.

Note: Circulation of varieties #18-21:

a. For general circulation.

b. For Socialist visitors.

c. For non-Socialist visitors.

d. Replaced a for general circulation.

e. Use not known.

18 **1 Won**

1978. Olive-green on multicolor underprint. Two adults and two children at center. Back purple and multicolor; soldier at left, woman with flowers at center, woman at right.

	VG	VF	UNC
a. Red and black serial #. No seal on back.	.50	1.25	5.00
b. Black serial #. Green seal at left. on back.	.20	.50	2.50
c. Red serial #. Red seal at left. on back.	.20	.50	2.50
d. Red serial #. Large numeral *1* in red guilloche on back.	.20	.50	2.50
e. Black serial #. Large numeral *1* in blue guilloche on back.	.20	.50	2.50
s. Specimen.	—	—	—

19 **5 Won**

1978. Blue-gray on multicolor underprint. Worker with book and gear, and woman with wheat at center. Mt. Gumgang on back.

	VG	VF	UNC
a. Red and black serial #. No seal on back.	.25	.75	3.00
b. Black serial #. Green seal at left. on back.	.25	.75	3.50
c. Red serial #. Red seal at left. on back.	.25	.75	3.50
d. Red serial #. Large numeral *5* in red guilloche on back.	.25	.75	3.50
e. Black serial #. Large numeral *5* in blue guilloche on back.	.25	.75	3.50
s. Specimen.	—	—	—

20 **10 Won**

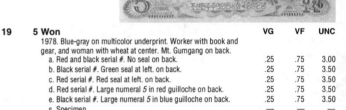

1978. Brown on multicolor underprint. Winged equestrian statue "Chonllima" at center. Waterfront factory on back.

		VG	VF	UNC
20	**10 Won**			
	a. Red and black serial #. No seal on back.	.30	1.00	7.50
	b. Black serial #. Green seal at upper right on back.	.30	1.00	4.00
	c. Red serial #. Red seal at upper right on back.	.30	1.00	4.00
	d. Red serial #. Large numeral *10* in red guilloche on back.	.30	1.00	4.00
	e. Black serial #. Large numeral *10* in blue guilloche on back.	.30	1.00	4.00
	s. Specimen.	—	—	—

		VG	VF	UNC
21	**50 Won**			
	1978. Olive-green on multicolor underprint. Soldier with man holding torch, woman with wheat, man with book at center. Lake scene on back.			
	a. Red and black serial #. No seal on back.	.35	1.25	6.00
	b. Black serial #. Green seal at lower right on back.	.35	1.25	4.50
	c. Red serial #. Red seal at lower right on back.	.35	1.25	4.50
	d. Red serial #. Large numeral *50* in red guilloche on back.	.50	1.25	4.50
	e. Black serial #. Large numeral *50* in blue guilloche on back.	.35	1.25	4.50
	s. Specimen.	—	—	—

		VG	VF	UNC
22	**100 Won**			
	1978. Brown on lilac and multicolor underprint. Kim Il Sung at center right. House with trees on back. Red and black serial #. No seal on back.			
	a. Issued note.	.75	2.50	10.00
	s. Specimen. overprint in red on face.	—	—	200.

1988 "CAPITALIST VISITOR" ISSUE

#23-26 arms at upper l. on face; red serial #. "Value" backs.

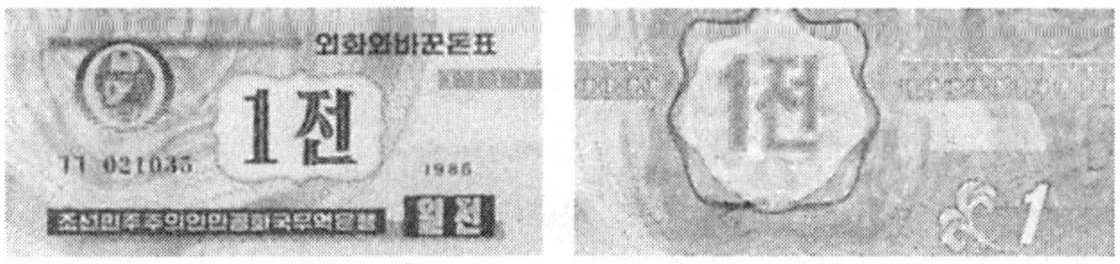

		VG	VF	UNC
23	**1 Chon**			
	1988. Blue on purple underprint.	.10	.20	.40

		VG	VF	UNC
24	**5 Chon**			
	1988. Blue on pink underprint.	.25	.75	1.00

		VG	VF	UNC
25	**10 Chon**			
	1988. Blue and black on green-yellow underprint.	.20	.40	1.00

		VG	VF	UNC
26	**50 Chon**			
	1988. Blue on yellow underprint.	.25	.50	1.00

#27-30 dk. green on blue and pink unpt. w/winged equestrian statue "Chonllima" at ctr., arms at upper r. Red serial #.

		VG	VF	UNC
27	**1 Won**			
	1988.	.25	.75	2.50
28	**5 Won**			
	1988.	.25	1.50	7.50

		VG	VF	UNC
29	**10 Won**			
	1988.	.75	3.00	12.50

		VG	VF	UNC
30	**50 Won**			
	1988.	1.50	8.00	40.00

1988 "SOCIALIST VISITOR" ISSUE

#31-38 arms at upper r. Denomination on back. Black serial #.

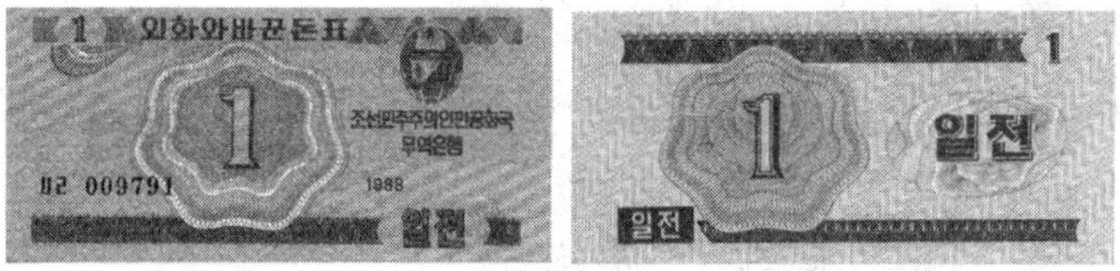

		VG	VF	UNC
31	**1 Chon**			
	1988. Red-brown on pink and blue underprint.	FV	FV	1.25

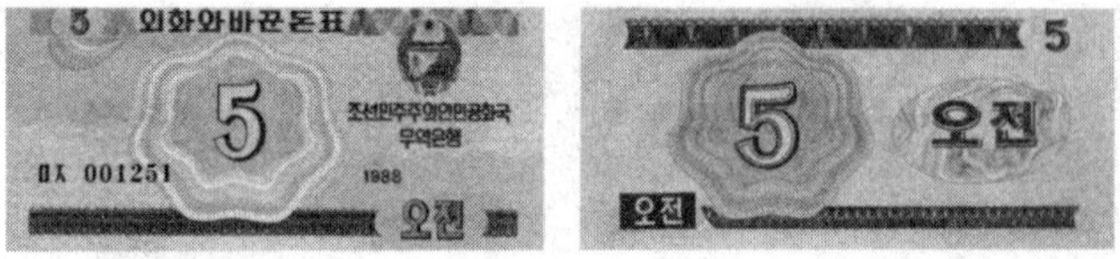

		VG	VF	UNC
32	**5 Chon** 1988. Purple on pink and blue underprint.	FV	FV	1.75

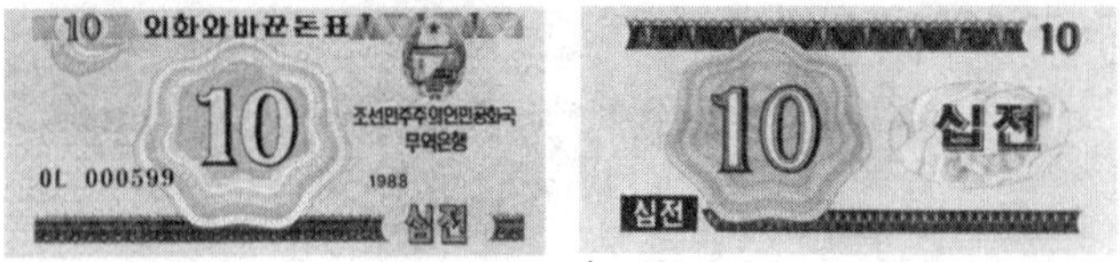

		VG	VF	UNC
33	**10 Chon** 1988. Olive-green on pink and blue underprint.	FV	FV	2.50

		VG	VF	UNC
34	**50 Chon** 1988. Brown-violet on pink and blue underprint.	FV	FV	3.00

#35-38 red on blue and ochre unpt. Temple at ctr., olive sprig on globe at r. Olive sprig on globe on back.

		VG	VF	UNC
35	**1 Won** 1988.	FV	FV	3.50

		VG	VF	UNC
36	**5 Won** 1988.	FV	FV	12.50

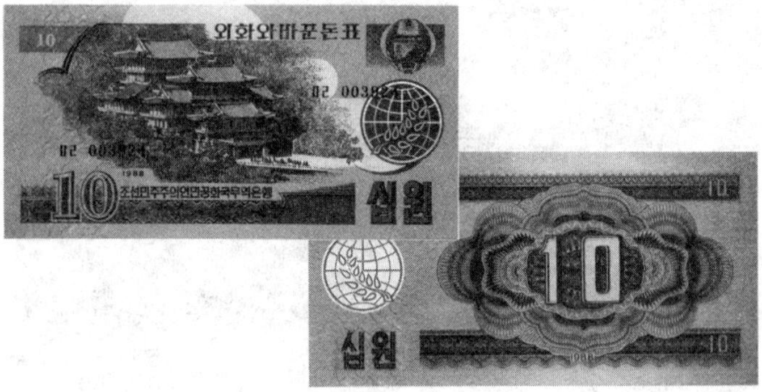

		VG	VF	UNC
37	**10 Won** 1988.	1.50	3.50	15.00

		VG	VF	UNC
38	**50 Won** 1988.	6.00	15.00	60.00

1992; 1998 Issue

#39-42 arms at upper l. Wmk: Winged equestrian statue "Chonllima".

		VG	VF	UNC
39	**1 Won** 1992; 1998. Grayish olive-green and olive-brown on multicolor underprint. Young woman with flower basket at center right. Mt. Gumgang on back.			
	a. Issued note.	.20	.75	2.00
	s. Specimen. 1992.		—	15.00
40	**5 Won** 1992; 1998. Blue-black and deep purple on multicolor underprint. Students at center right with modern building and factory in background. Palace on back.	.80	2.00	8.00
41	**10 Won** 1992; 1998. Deep brown and red-brown on multicolor underprint. Factory worker, winged equestrian statue "Chonllima" at center, factories in background at right. Flood gates on back.			
	a. Issued note.	.40	1.50	3.00
	s. Specimen. 1992.		—	25.00
42	**50 Won** 1992; 1998. Deep brown and deep olive-brown on multicolor underprint. Monument to five year plan at left and as watermark, young professionals at center right, arms at upper right. Landscape of pine trees and mountains on back.	1.00	3.00	10.00
43	**100 Won** 1992; 1998. Deep brown and brown-violet on multicolor underprint. Arms at lower left center, Kim Il Sung at right. Rural home at center on back. Watermark: Arched gateway.	1.50	4.00	12.00
44	**500 Won** 1998. Slate gray on light blue and purple underprint. Assembly Hall. Back red and black. Suspension bridge.	3.00	6.00	30.00

2002 Issue

		VG	VF	UNC
45	**1000 Won** 2002. Dark green on multicolor underprint. Back slate blue on multicolor underprint. Rural home at center. Like #43.	2.00	5.00	20.00

		VG	VF	UNC
46	**5000 Won** 2002. Purple on multicolor underprint. Rural home at center on back. Like #43.	FV	10.00	50.00

COLLECTOR SERIES

KOREAN CENTRAL BANK

1978 ISSUE

		Issue Price	Mkt. Value
CS1	**1978 1-100 Won.** Red overprint Korean characters for specimen on #18a-21a, 22 (with all zero serial #).	—	60.00

1992 ISSUE

		Issue Price	Mkt. Value
CS2	**1992 1-100 Won.** Red, rectangular overprint Korean characters for specimen on #39-43. (39, 42 and 43 with all zero serial #, 40-41 with normal serial #).	—	50.00

2000 ISSUE

#CS3-CS8 ovpt. in Korean or English: ***The 55th Anniversary of Foundation of the Workers' Party of Korea 10th.10.Juche 89 (2000).***

		Issue Price	Mkt. Value
CS3	**1 Won** Black overprint in English on face of #18e.	—	3.00
CS4	**5 Won** Red overprint in Korean on face of #19d.	—	3.00
CS5	**10 Won** Black overprint in English on face of #20e.	—	3.00
CS6	**50 Won** Red overprint in Korean on face of #21b.	—	3.00
CS7	**50 Won** Red overprint in English on face of #21b.	—	3.00
CS8	**50 Won** Black overprint in English on face of #21b.	—	3.00

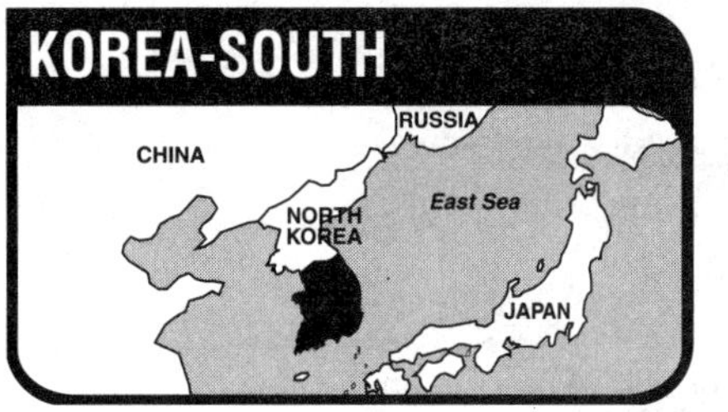

The Republic of Korea, situated in northeastern Asia on the southern half of the Korean peninsula between North Korea and the Korean Strait, has an area of 38,025 sq. mi. (98,484 sq. km.) and a population of 44.61 million. Capital: Seoul. The economy is d on agriculture and textiles. Clothing, plywood and textile products are exported.

Japan replaced China as the predominant foreign influence in Korea in 1895 and annexed the peninsular country in 1910. Defeat in World War II brought an end to Japanese rule. U.S. troops entered Korea from the south and Soviet forces entered from the north. The Cairo Conference (1943) had established that Korea should be "free and independent." The Potsdam Conference (1945) set the 38th parallel as the line dividing the occupation forces of the United States and Russia. When Russia refused to permit a U.N. commission designated to supervise reunification elections to enter North Korea, an election was held in South Korea on May 10, 1948. By its determination, the Republic of Korea was inaugurated on Aug. 15, 1948.

Note: For Bank of Chosen notes issued in South Korea under the Allied occupation during the post WWII period 1945 to 1948 refer to Korea listings.

MONETARY SYSTEM:

1 Won (Hwan) = 100 Chon
1 new Won = 10 old Hwan, 1962-

REPLACEMENT NOTES:

#30-32, 34, 36-37, sm. crosslet design in front of serial #. #35, 38, 38A, 39, 43-49: notes w/first digit 9 in serial number.

DATING:

The modern notes of Korea are dated according to the founding of the first Korean dynasty, that of the house of Tangun, in 2333 BC.

REPUBLIC

BANK OF KOREA

1958-60 ISSUE

		VG	VF	UNC
23	**50 Hwan** 4291 (1958). Green-blue on olive-green underprint. Archway at left. Back green; statue at center, medieval tortoise warship at right.	20.00	60.00	350.
24	**500 Hwan** 4291 (1958); 4292 (1959). Dark green. Portrait Syngman Rhee at right. Back brownish purple.	7.50	40.00	350.

		VG	VF	UNC
25	**1000 Hwan** 4293 (1960); 4294 (1961); 1962. Black on olive underprint. King Sejong the Great at right. Back blue-green and light brown; flaming torch at center.			
	a. 4293 (1960).	2.50	10.00	100.
	b. 4294 (1961).	1.50	6.00	60.00
	c. 1962.	1.75	7.00	65.00

1961-62 ISSUE

Hwan System.

26	100 Hwan	VG	VF	UNC
	1962. Green on orange and multicolor underprint. Woman reading to child at right. Archway at left, date at bottom right margin on back.	15.00	60.00	325.

27	500 Hwan	VG	VF	UNC
	4294 (1961). Blue-green on multicolor underprint. King Sejong the Great at right. Back green; building at right. Eight-character imprint.	17.50	80.00	475.

1962 ND ISSUES

Won System

28	10 Jeon	VG	VF	UNC
	1962. Deep blue on pale blue and pink underprint.	.05	.10	.40

29	50 Jeon	VG	VF	UNC
	1962. Black on pale green and ochre underprint. Back brown.	.05	.10	.50

30	1 Won	VG	VF	UNC
	ND (1962). Violet on brown underprint.			
	a. Issued note.	.05	.10	1.00
	s. Specimen.	—	—	—

31	5 Won	VG	VF	UNC
	ND (1962). Black on gray-green underprint.			
	a. Issued note.	.10	.25	2.00
	s. Specimen.	—	—	—

32	10 Won	VG	VF	UNC
	ND (1962). Brown on green underprint.			
	a. Issued note.	.50	2.00	10.00
	s. Specimen.	—	—	—

33	10 Won	VG	VF	UNC
	1962-65; ND. Brown on lilac and green underprint. Tower at left. Medieval tortoise warship at center, date at lower left on back.			
	a. 1962.	2.50	8.00	50.00
	b. 1963.	2.75	8.50	52.50
	c. 1964.	1.50	4.50	27.50
	d. 1965.	1.00	3.00	20.00
	e. ND.	.15	.50	3.00

34	50 Won	VG	VF	UNC
	ND (1962). Red-brown on blue and lilac underprint. Rock in the sea at left. Torch at center on back.			
	a. Issued note.	4.00	15.00	95.00
	s. Specimen.	—	—	—

35	100 Won	VG	VF	UNC
	1962-69. Green on olive underprint. Archway at left. Underprint: *100 Won* at center. Pagoda and date on back.			
	a. 1962.	5.00	17.50	110.
	b. 1963.	4.00	12.50	80.00
	c. 1964.	4.00	12.50	75.00
	d. 1965.	4.00	12.50	75.00
	e. 1969.	5.00	15.00	90.00

		VG	VF	UNC
36	**100 Won**			
	ND (1962). Green on blue and gold underprint. Archway similar to #35 at left. Five-petaled blossom at center in underprint. Back similar to #34.			
	a. Issued note.	2.00	12.50	80.00
	s. Specimen.	—	—	—

		VG	VF	UNC
37	**500 Won**			
	ND (1962). Blue on lilac and green underprint. Pagoda portal at left. Back similar to #34.			
	a. Issued note.	5.00	22.50	135.
	s. Specimen.	—	—	—

1965; 1966 ND Issue

		VG	VF	UNC
38	**100 Won**			
	ND (1965). Dark green and blue on multicolor underprint. Bank name and denomination in red. King Sejong the Great at right. Building on back.			
	a. Issued note.	.75	1.75	5.50
	s. Specimen.	—	—	—

		VG	VF	UNC
38A	**100 Won**			
	ND (1965). Dark blue-green. Bank name and denomination in brown. Like #38.	.75	2.25	10.00

		VG	VF	UNC
39	**500 Won**			
	ND (1966). Black on multicolor underprint. City gate at left. Medieval turtle warships on back.			
	a. Issued note.	.75	1.50	9.00
	s. Specimen.	—	—	—

1969-73 ND Issue

		VG	VF	UNC
40	**50 Won**			
	ND (1969). Black on green and brown underprint. Pavilion at left. Back blue; torch at center.			
	a. Issued note.	.25	1.00	4.00
	s. Specimen.	—	—	—
41	**5000 Won**			
	ND (1972). Brown on green and multicolor underprint. Yi I at right and as watermark. Large building on back.	7.50	12.50	40.00
42	**10,000 Won**			
	ND (1973). Dark brown on multicolor underprint. King Sejong the Great at left center. Buildings and pavilion on back. Watermark: Woman with headdress.	15.00	25.00	60.00

1973-79 ND Issue

		VG	VF	UNC
43	**500 Won**			
	ND (1973). Blue and green on multicolor underprint. Adm. Yi Sun-shin at left, medieval turtle warship at center. Building with steps on back.	FV	1.00	3.50

NOTICE

Readers with unlisted dates, signature varieties, etc. are invited to submit photocopies of their notes to: Standard Catalog of World Paper Money, 700 East State St. Iola, WI 54990-0001, E-Mail: george.cuhaj@fwpubs.com.

44 1000 Won VG VF UNC
ND (1975). Purple on multicolor underprint. Yi Hwang at right. Do-San Academy in black on back. Watermark: Flowers. FV 2.00 5.00

45 5000 Won VG VF UNC
ND (1977). Brown on multicolor underprint. Yi I at right and as watermark. Small building with steps on back. FV 8.50 20.00

46 10,000 Won VG VF UNC
ND (1979). Black and dark green on multicolor underprint. Water clock at left, King Sejong at right and as watermark. Pavilion at center on back. FV 20.00 40.00

1983 ND ISSUE

47 1000 Won VG VF UNC
ND (1983). Purple on multicolor underprint. Yi Hwang at right and as watermark. One raised colored dot for visually impaired at lower left. Buildings of Tosansowon Academy on back. FV FV 4.00

48 5000 Won VG VF UNC
ND (1983). Brown on multicolor underprint. Yi I at right and as watermark. Two raised colored dots for visually impaired at lower left. Ojukon, birthplace of Yi I on back. FV FV 12.00

49 10,000 Won VG VF UNC
ND (1983). Dark green on multicolor underprint. Water clock at left, King Sejong at right and as watermark in clear area. Three raised colored dots in green for visually impaired at lower left. Kyonghoeru Pavilion at center on back. FV FV 22.50

50 10,000 Won
ND (1994). Dark green on multicolor underprint. Like #49, but with circular dark green lines over watermark area at left, microprinting added under water tower, segmented silver security thread at left center. FV FV 20.00

2000-2002 ISSUE

51 5000 Won VG VF UNC
2002. Brown and orange on multicolor underprint. Scholar Yi I. Ojukon on back. FV FV 9.00

		VG	VF	UNC
52	**10,000 Won** 2000. Dark green on multicolor underprint. Like #50, but watermark area clear. Three raised colored dots in variable ink (brown to green). Copyright 2000 notice in Korean at lower left on face, in English at lower right on back.	FV	FV	20.00

2004 BANK CHECK ISSUE

		VG	VF	UNC
53	**1,000,000 Won** 6.2004.	FV	FV	125.
54	**5000 Won** 2005. Multicolor.	FV	FV	9.00

AUXILIARY MILITARY PAYMENT CERTIFICATE COUPONS

SERIES I

#M1-M8 were issued on Dec. 29, 1969, and were valid only until June or Oct. 7, 1970. Anchor on glove crest. Validation stamp on back. Uniface.

		VG	VF	UNC
M1	**5 Cents** ND (1969). Maroon, red-brown and yellow center. Flowering branch at left, large *5* at right.	—	—	—
M2	**10 Cents** ND (1969). Dark blue with light blue-green center. Flowers at left, large *10* at right.	—	—	—
M3	**25 Cents** ND (1969). Brown and yellow center. Flower at left, large *25* at right.	—	—	—
M4	**50 Cents** ND (1969). Green and yellow center. Flower at left, large *50* at right.	—	—	—
M5	**1 Dollar** ND (1969). Brown and yellow center. Korean flag at left, large *1* at right.	—	—	—
M6	**5 Dollars** ND (1969). Blue and turquoise center. Flowers at left, large *5* at right.	—	—	—
M7	**10 Dollars** ND (1969). Brown and yellow center. Flowers at left.	—	—	—
M8	**20 Dollars** ND (1969). Green and yellow center. Flowers at left.	—	—	—

SERIES II

#M9-M16 were issued June (or Oct.) 1970. Anchor symbol ctr., 702 at l., lg. denomination numerals r. Face and back similar.

		VG	VF	UNC
M9	**5 Cents** ND (1970). Maroon and violet on ochre underprint. Space capsule at left.	20.00	65.00	200.

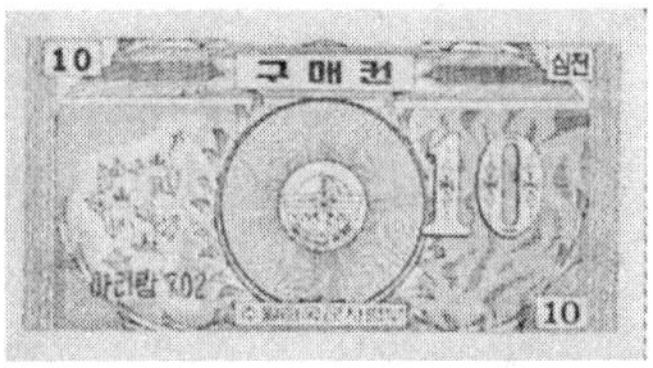

		VG	VF	UNC
M10	**10 Cents** ND (1970). Red and yellow on green paper. Flowers at left. Back red.	30.00	90.00	275.

		VG	VF	UNC
M11	**25 Cents** ND (1970). Green and blue. Crown at left.	90.00	225.	—

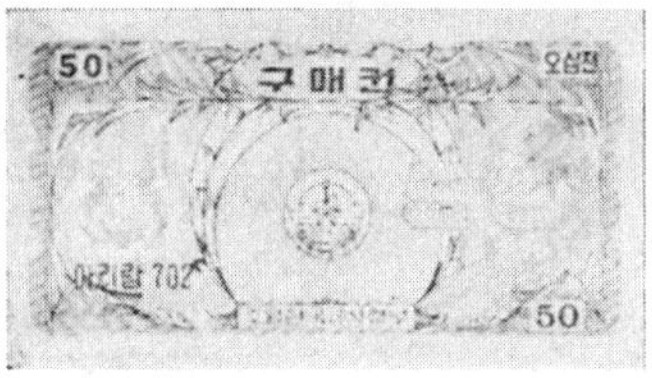

		VG	VF	UNC
M12	**50 Cents** ND (1970). Blue and green. Pottery with legs at left.	90.00	225.	—
M13	**1 Dollar** ND (1970). Maroon and red on light green paper. Torch at left.	—	—	—
M14	**5 Dollars** ND (1970). Red, ochre and yellow on light blue paper. Holed coin at left.	—	—	—
M15	**10 Dollars** ND (1970). Blue on yellow paper. Pagoda at left.	—	—	—
M16	**20 Dollars** ND (1970). Green on pink paper. Vignette at left.	—	—	—

SERIES III

#M17-M24, military symbol in circle at ctr. on face.

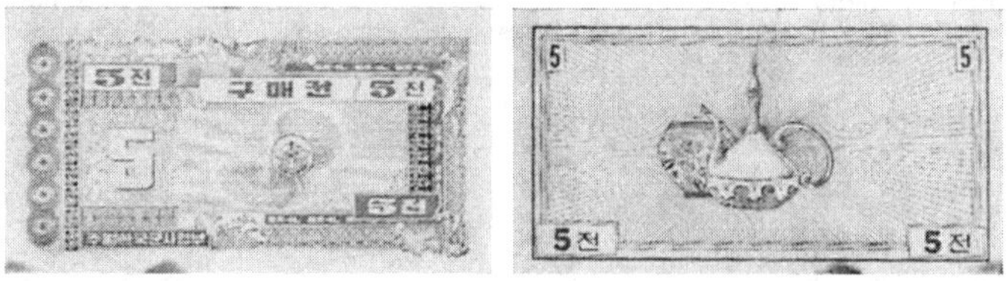

		VG	VF	UNC
M17	**5 Cents** ND. Brown and maroon on yellow paper. "5" at left, clam shell and pearl at center. Kettle on back.	20.00	65.00	200.
M18	**10 Cents** ND. Blue with green tint. "10" at left, snail at center. Candle holder on back.	30.00	75.00	275.

		VG	VF	UNC
M19	**25 Cents** ND. Red, lilac and ochre. "25" at left, crest seal on turtle at right. Back pink; archway at center.	90.00	225.	—
M20	**50 Cents** ND. Green and blue. "50" at left, tiger at center. Balancing rock on back.		225.	—

		VG	VF	UNC
M21	**1 Dollar** ND. Brown and maroon. Flowers at left. Shrine on back.	—	—	—

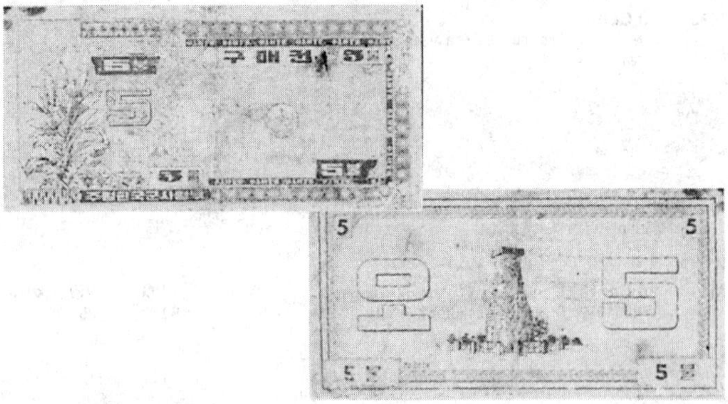

		VG	VF	UNC
M22	**5 Dollars** ND. Blue and light blue on yellow paper. Bush at left, crest seal on rayed cloud at right. Tower at center on back.	—	—	—
M23	**10 Dollars** ND. Yellow and maroon. Pagoda on face. Turtle boat on back.	—	—	—
M24	**20 Dollars** ND. Two dragons at center. Korean house on back.	—	—	—

SERIES IV

#M25-M32, Korean warrior at ctr. on face.

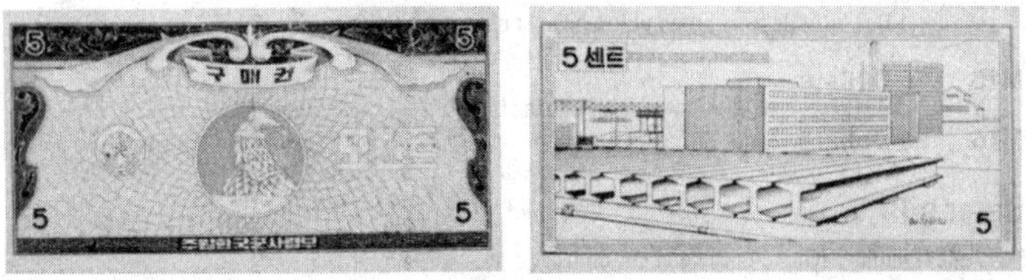

		VG	VF	UNC
M25	**5 Cents** ND. Pink, deep green and light blue. Beams and steel mill at center on back.	20.00	40.00	185.

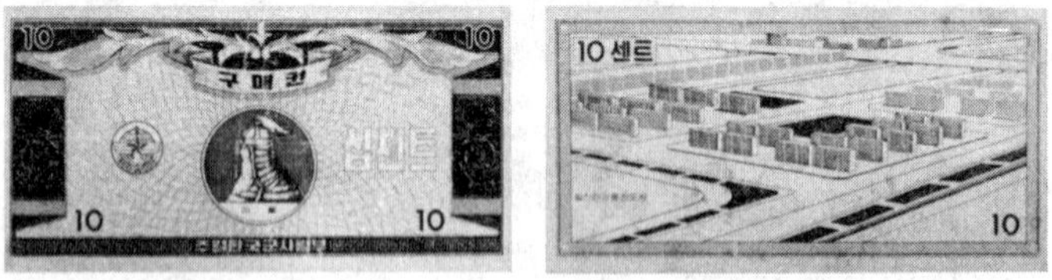

		VG	VF	UNC
M26	**10 Cents** ND. Deep green on yellow-green. Modern city complex on back. Thick or thin paper.	20.00	40.00	185.
M27	**25 Cents** ND. Yellow and maroon. Two bridges on back.	60.00	200.	—
M28	**50 Cents** ND. Blue-green and maroon. Back blue-green and red; dam.	90.00	225.	—

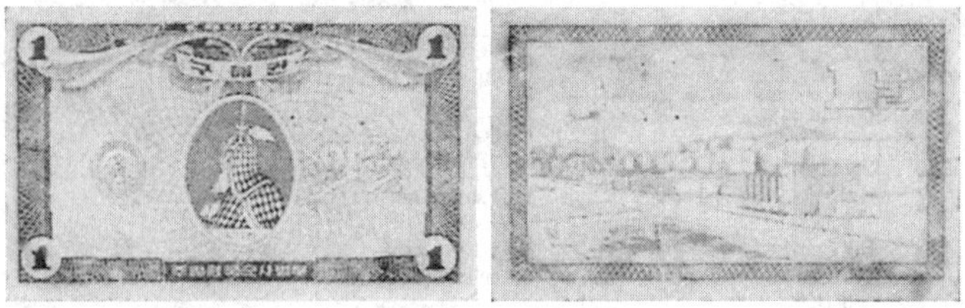

		VG	VF	UNC
M29	**1 Dollar** ND. Green on light green underprint. Oil refinery on back.	35.00	100.	250.

		VG	VF	UNC
M30	**5 Dollars** ND. Brown on gold underprint. Back red-orange; natural gas tank.	350.	700.	—

		VG	VF	UNC
M31	**10 Dollars** ND. Pink and green. Back pink and blue; loading area at docks.	60.00	200.	—
M32	**20 Dollars** ND. Blue and purple. Back green; four-lane superhighway.	—	—	—

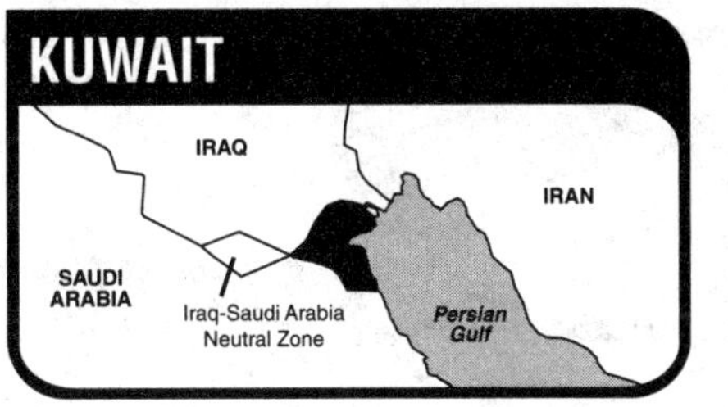

The State of Kuwait, a constitutional monarchy located on the Arabian Peninsula at the northwestern corner of the Persian Gulf, has an area of 6,880 sq. mi. (17,818 sq. km.) and a population of 1.97 million. Capital: Kuwait. Petroleum, the basis of the economy, provides 95 per cent of the exports.

The modern history of Kuwait began with the founding of the men who wandered northward from the region of the Qatar Peninsula of eastern Arabia. Fearing that the Turks would take over the sheikhdom, Shaikh Mubarak entered into an agreement with Great Britain, 1899, placing Kuwait under the protection of Britain and empowering Britain to conduct its foreign affairs. Britain terminated the protectorate on June 19, 1961, giving Kuwait its independence (by a simple exchange of notes) but agreeing to furnish military aid on request.

The Kuwait dinar, one of the world's strongest currencies, is backed 100 percent by gold and foreign exchange holdings.

On Aug. 2, 1990 Iraqi forces invaded and rapidly overran Kuwaiti forces. Annexation by Iraq was declared on Aug. 8. The Kuwaiti government established itself in exile in Saudi Arabia. The United Nations forces attacked on Feb. 24, 1991 and Kuwait City was liberated on Feb. 26. Iraq quickly withdrew remaining forces.

RULERS:

British to 1961
Abdullah, 1961-1965
Sabah Ibn Salim Al Sabah, 1965-1977
Jabir Ibn Ahmad Al Sabah, 1977-2006
Sabah Al Ahmad Al Sabah, 2006-

MONETARY SYSTEM:

1 Dinar = 1000 Fils

SIGNATURE VARIETIES

1	Amir Sheikh Jaber al-Ahmed				
	BANK GOVERNOR	FINANCE MINISTER		BANK GOVERNOR	FINANCE MINISTER
2	Hamza Abbas	A. R. al-Atiquel	3	Hamza Abbas	A. L. al-Hamad
4	A. al-Tammar	A. K. al-Sabah	5	A. al-Tammar	J. M. al-Kharafi
6	S. A. al-Sabah	N. A. al-Rodhan	7	S. A. al-Sabah	A. K. al-Sabah
8	S. A. al-Sabah	N. A. al-Rodhan	9	S. A. al-Sabah	A. S. al-Sabah
10	S. A. al-Sabah	A. A. al-Sabah	11	S. A. al-Sabah	Y. H. Al-Ibrahim

STATE

KUWAIT CURRENCY BOARD

LAW OF 1960, 1961 ND ISSUE

#1-5 Amir Shaikh Abdullah at r. and as wmk. Sign. 1.

		VG	VF	UNC
1	**1/4 Dinar** L.1960 (1961). Brown on multicolor underprint. Aerial view, Port of Kuwait at center on back.	4.00	15.00	45.00

		VG	VF	UNC
2	**1/2 Dinar** L.1960 (1961). Purple on multicolor underprint. School at center on back.	5.00	25.00	90.00

		VG	VF	UNC
3	**1 Dinar** L.1960 (1961). Red-brown on multicolor underprint. Cement plant at center on back.	7.50	40.00	125.

		VG	VF	UNC
4	**5 Dinars** L.1960 (1961). Blue on multicolor underprint. Street scene on back.	30.00	150.	500.

		VG	VF	UNC
5	**10 Dinars** L.1960 (1961). Green on multicolor underprint. Dhow on back.	30.00	150.	475.

CENTRAL BANK OF KUWAIT

LAW #32 OF 1968, FIRST ND ISSUE

#6-10 Amir Shaikh Sabah at r. and as wmk. Sign. #2.

		VG	VF	UNC
6	**1/4 Dinar** L.1968. Brown on multicolor underprint. Back similar to #1.			
	a. Black signature	1.25	6.00	22.50
	b. Brown signature	1.25	6.00	22.50
	s. As a. Specimen.	—	—	250.

		VG	VF	UNC
7	**1/2 Dinar** L.1968. Purple on multicolor underprint. Back similar to #2.			
	a. Black signature	2.00	7.50	30.00
	b. Purple signature	2.00	7.50	30.00
	s. As a. Specimen.	—	—	250.

		VG	VF	UNC
8	**1 Dinar** L.1968. Red-brown and blue on multicolor underprint. Oil refinery on back.			
	a. Issued note.	4.00	8.00	40.00
	s. Specimen.	—	—	350.

		VG	VF	UNC
9	**5 Dinars** L.1968. Blue and aqua on multicolor underprint. View of Kuwait on back.			
	a. Issued note.	15.00	45.00	120.
	s. Specimen.	—	—	350.

		VG	VF	UNC
10	**10 Dinars** L.1968. Green and brown on multicolor underprint. Back similar to #5.			
	a. Issued note.	22.50	60.00	150.
	s. Specimen.	—	—	475.

LAW #32 OF 1968, SECOND ND ISSUE

#11-16 arms at r. Black serial #. #11-15 wmk.: Dhow.

		VG	VF	UNC
11	**1/4 Dinar** L.1968 (1980-91). Brown and purple on multicolor underprint. Oil rig at left. Oil refinery on back.			
	a. Overall ornate underprint. signature 2-4.	1.00	3.00	8.00
	b. Clear margins at top and bottom. signature 6.	.75	1.50	6.00

Note: Contraband stolen by invading Iraqi forces included prefix denominators #54-68.

12	1/2 Dinar	VG	VF	UNC
	L.1968 (1980). Purple on multicolor underprint. Kuwait Towers at left. Harbor scene on back.			
	a. Overall ornate underprint. signature 2-4.	1.25	4.00	10.00
	b. Clear margins at top and at bottom. signature 6.	1.00	3.00	7.00

Note: Contraband stolen by invading Iraqi forces include prefix denominators #30-37.

13	1 Dinar	VG	VF	UNC
	L.1968 (1980-91). Red-violet and purple on multicolor underprint. Telecommunications Center in Kuwait City at left. Old fortress on back.			
	a. Overall ornate underprint. signature 2.	2.00	7.00	20.00
	b. As a. signature 3.	1.50	4.00	10.00
	c. As a. signature 4.	1.50	3.50	8.00
	d. Plain colored underprint. at top and bottom. signature 6.	1.00	3.00	7.00
	s. As a. Specimen.	—	—	100.

Note: Contraband stolen by invading Iraqi forces include prefix denominators #47-53.

14	5 Dinars	VG	VF	UNC
	L.1968 (1980-91). Deep blue and black on multicolor underprint. Minaret at left. The Seif Palace (the Amir's Administration HQ) on back.			
	a. Overall ornate underprint. signature 2, 4.	5.00	12.00	50.00
	b. Clear margins at top and at bottom. signature 6.	3.00	7.50	22.50
	s. Specimen.	—	—	—

Note: Contraband stolen by invading Iraqi forces include prefix denominators #18-20.

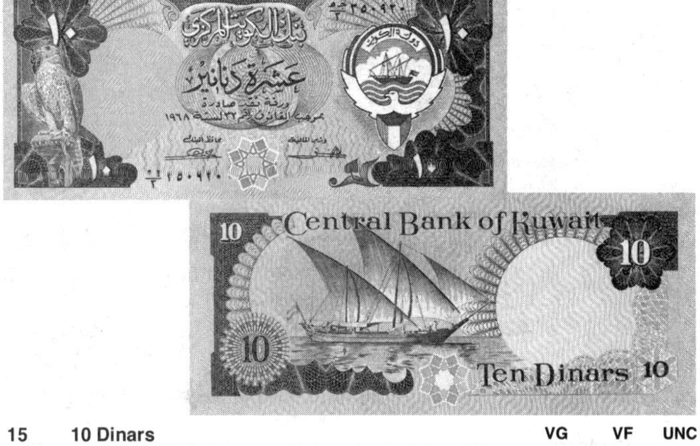

15	10 Dinars	VG	VF	UNC
	L.1968 (1980-91). Green on multicolor underprint. Falcon at left. Sailing boat on back.			
	a. Overall ornate underprint. signature 2-4.	6.00	15.00	60.00
	b. Clear margins at top and at bottom. signature 6.	3.00	7.50	32.50

Note: Contraband stolen by invading Iraqi forces include prefix denominators #70-87.

16	20 Dinars	VG	VF	UNC
	L.1968 (1986-91). Brown and olive-green on multicolor underprint. Façade of Kuwait Stock Exchange at left. The Justice Center of Kuwait at left center on back. Watermark: Eagle's head.			
	a. Signature 5.	25.00	65.00	160.
	b. Signature 6.	3.00	8.00	32.50

Note: Contraband stolen by invading Iraqi forces include prefix denominators #9-13.

LAW #32 OF 1968, 1992 ND POST LIBERATION ISSUE

Note: After the 1991 Gulf War, Kuwait declared all previous note issues worthless.

#17-22 like previous issue. Red serial # at top r. Wmk: Dhow. Sign. 7.

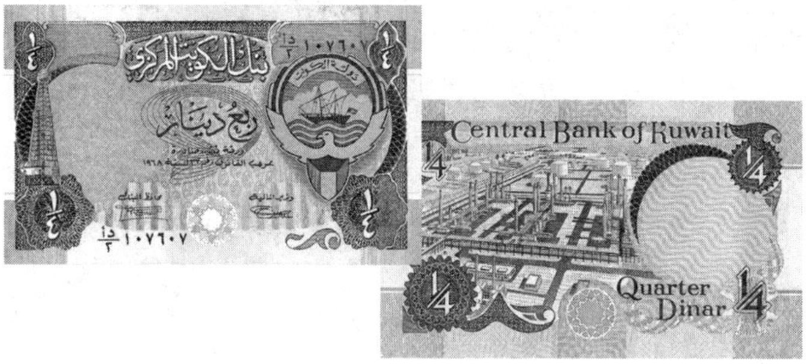

17	1/4 Dinar	VG	VF	UNC
	L.1968 (1992). Violet and black on silver and multicolor underprint. Back brown on multicolor underprint. Like #11.	FV	FV	4.00

18	1/2 Dinar	VG	VF	UNC
	L.1968 (1992). Deep blue, blue-green and deep violet on silver and multicolor underprint. Like #12.	FV	FV	7.00

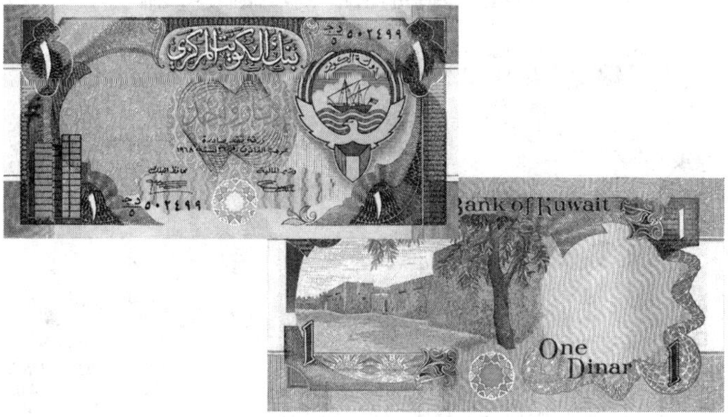

19	1 Dinar	VG	VF	UNC
	L.1968 (1992). Deep olive-green, green and deep blue on silver and multicolor underprint. Like #13.	FV	FV	9.00

20 **5 Dinars** | VG FV | VF FV | UNC 45.00
L.1968 (1992). Olive-brown, green and pink on multicolor underprint. Like #14.

21 **10 Dinars** | VG FV | VF FV | UNC 75.00
L.1968 (1992). Orange-red, olive-brown on multicolor underprint. Like #15. Signature 7, 8.

22 **20 Dinars** | VG FV | VF FV | UNC 125.
L.1968 (1992). Violet-brown on multicolor underprint. Like #16. Signature 7, 8.

LAW #32 OF 1968, 1994 ND ISSUE

#23-28 arms at l., segmented silver vertical thread at ctr. r. Wmk: Falcon's head. Sign. 8-12.

23 **1/4 Dinar** | VG FV | VF FV | UNC 4.00
L.1968 (1994). Brown, grayish purple and deep orange on multicolor underprint. Ship at bottom center right. Outline of falcon's head at lower right near value. Girls playing game on back. Signature 8, 10, 11, 12.

#24-28 outline of falcon's head at upper l. near value.

24 **1/2 Dinar** | VG FV | VF FV | UNC 7.00
L.1968 (1994). Brown and dark grayish green on multicolor underprint. Souk shops at lower right. Boys playing game on back. Signature 8, 10, 11, 12.

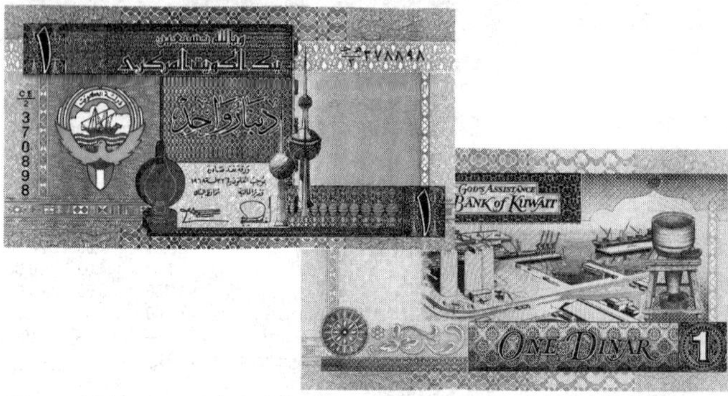

25 **1 Dinar** | VG FV | VF FV | UNC 11.00
L.1968 (1994). Deep brown, purple and dark gray on blue and multicolor underprint. Pinnacles at center right. Aerial view of harbor docks on back. Signature 8, 10, 11, 12.

#26-28 silver foiling of falcon's head at l. ctr.

26 **5 Dinars** | VG FV | VF FV | UNC 42.00
L.1968 (1994). Dark red and grayish green on multicolor underprint. Pinnacle at right. Oil refinery at center on back. Signature 8, 9, 11, 12.

27 **10 Dinars** | VG FV | VF FV | UNC 80.00
L.1968 (1994). Purple, dark blue and dark brown on multicolor underprint. Mosque at lower right. Pearl fisherman at left center, dhow at right on back. Signature 8, 12.

Note: #23-27 were withdrawn in early 1995 because the word *Allah* being present.

		VG	VF	UNC
28	**20 Dinars** L.1968 (1994). Dark olive-green, orange and olive-brown on multicolor underprint. Fortress at lower right. Central Bank at bottom left center, old fortress gate, pinnacle at right on back. Signature 8, 9, 10, 11, 12.	FV	FV	120.

Collector Series

Central Bank of Kuwait

1993 Issue

#CS1 Issued in a special folder for "Second Anniversary of Liberation of Kuwait."

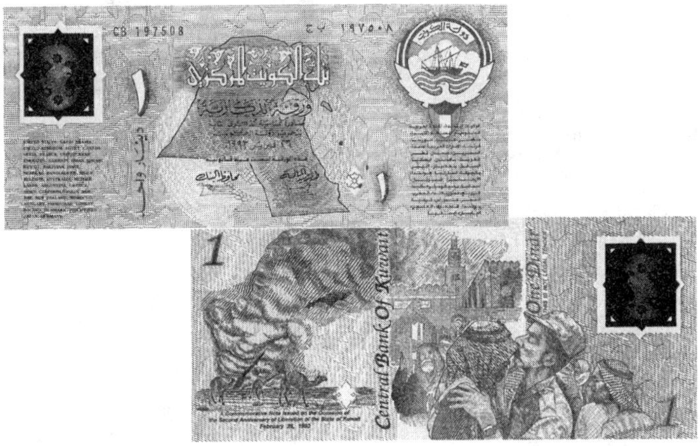

		Issue Price	Mkt. Value
CS1	**1 Dinar** 26.2.1993. Orange-red, violet-blue and blue. Polymer plastic with silver foil window. Text on back includes: *THIS IS NOT LEGAL TENDER.*	—	20.00

Note: Replacement notes for #CS1 have serial # CK000091 and a market value of $175.

2001 Issue

#CS2 issued in a special folder for "10th Anniversary of the Liberation of the State of Kuwait."

		Issue Price	Mkt. Value
CS2	**1 Dinar** 26.2.2001. Light blue and lilac. Arms at right. Military man holding flag, town view on back. Polymer plastic with silver foil window. Text on back includes: *NOT A LEGAL TENDER...* at lower left.	—	17.50

The Republic of Kyrgyzstan, an independent state since Aug. 31, 1991, is a member of the UN and of the C.I.S. It was the last state of the Union Republics to declare its sovereignty. Capital: Bishkek (formerly Frunze). Population of 4.54 million.

Originally part of the Autonomous Turkestan S.S.R. founded on May 1, 1918, the Kyrgyz ethnic area was established on October 14, 1924 as the Kara-Kirghiz Autonomous Region within the R.S.F.S.R. Then on May 25, 1925 the name Kara (black) was dropped. It became an A.S.S.R. on Feb. 1, 1926 and a Union Republic of the U.S.S.R. in 1936. On Dec. 12, 1990, the name was then changed to the Republic of Kyrgyzstan.

MONETARY SYSTEM:
1 SOM = 100 Tyiyn

Republic

КЫРГЫЗ РЕСПУБЛИКАСЫ

Kyrgyz Republic

1993 ND Issue

#1-3 bald eagle at ctr. Ornate design at ctr. on back. Wmk: Eagle in repeating pattern.

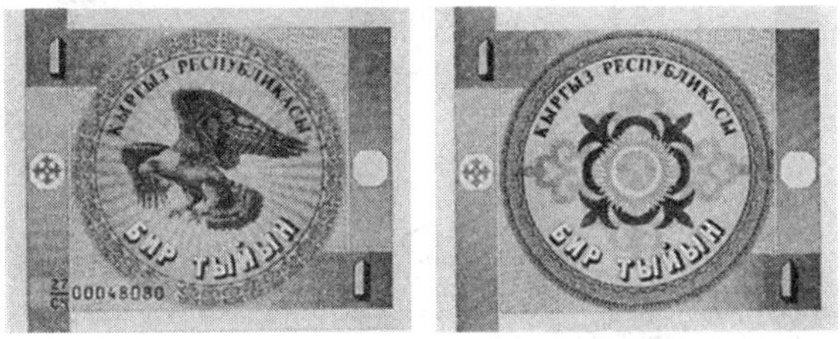

		VG	VF	UNC
1	**1 Tyiyn** ND (1993). Dark brown on pink and brown-orange underprint.	.05	.10	.75

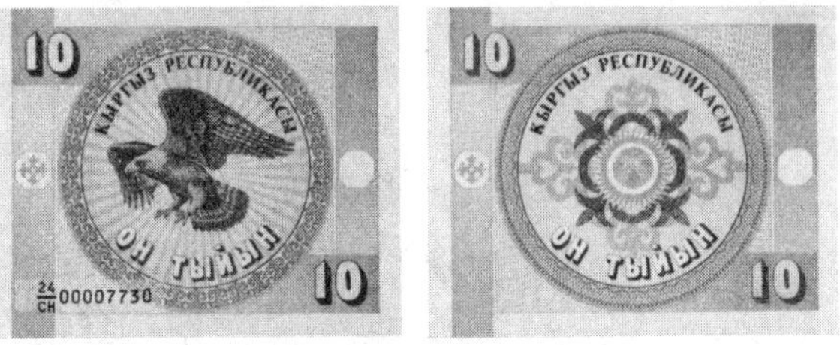

		VG	VF	UNC
2	**10 Tyiyn** ND (1993). Brown on pale green and brown-orange underprint.	.10	.25	.75

		VG	VF	UNC
3	**50 Tyiyn** ND (1993). Gray on blue and brown-orange underprint.	.15	.35	1.00

КЫРГЫЗСТАН БАНКЫ

Kyrgyzstan Bank

1993; 1994 ND Issue

#4-6 Equestrian statue of Manas the Noble at ctr. r. Manas Mausoleum at l. ctr. on back. Wmk: Eagle in repeating pattern.

		VG	VF	UNC
4	**1 Som** ND (1993). Red on multicolor underprint.	.20	.50	1.75

		VG	VF	UNC
5	**5 Som** ND (1993). Deep grayish green on multicolor underprint.	.10	1.50	5.00

		VG	VF	UNC
6	**20 Som** ND (1993). Purple on multicolor underprint.	.25	3.00	20.00

КЫРГЫЗ БАНКЫ

KYRGYZ BANK

1994 ND ISSUE

Replacement notes: Serial # prefix *ZZ*.

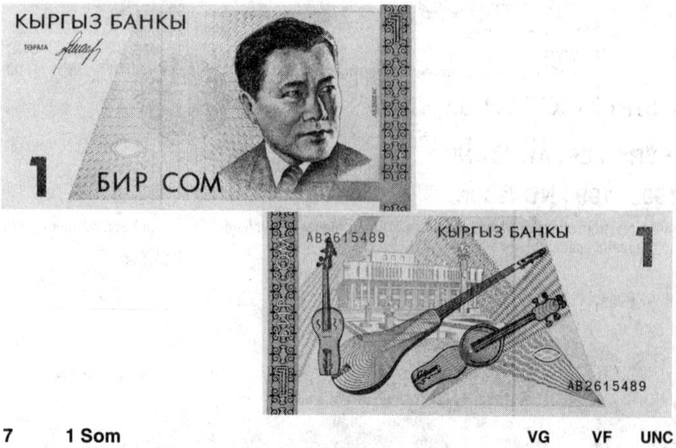

		VG	VF	UNC
7	**1 Som** ND (1994). Brown on yellow and multicolor underprint. A. Maldybayev at right and as watermark. String musical instruments, Bishkek's Philharmonic Society and Manas Architectural Ensemble at left center on back.	.10	.50	2.00

		VG	VF	UNC
8	**5 Som** ND (1994). Dark blue on yellow and multicolor underprint. B. Beishenaliyeva at right and as watermark. National Opera Theatre at left center on back.	.25	1.00	4.50

		VG	VF	UNC
9	**10 Som** ND (1994). Green and brown on multicolor underprint. Kassim at right and as watermark. Mountains on back.	.50	1.50	6.00

		VG	VF	UNC
10	**20 Som** ND (1994). Red-orange on multicolor underprint. T. Moldo at right and as watermark. Manas Mausoleum on back.	1.00	1.50	6.00

		VG	VF	UNC
11	**50 Som** ND (1994). Reddish brown on multicolor underprint. Czarina Kurmanjan Datka at right and as watermark. Uzgen Architectural Ensemble, mausoleum and minaret on back.	1.00	1.50	12.50

		VG	VF	UNC
12	**100 Som** ND (1994). Dark brown on multicolor underprint. Toktogul at right and as watermark. Hydroelectric dam at left center on back.	2.00	5.00	25.00

1997 ISSUE

Replacement notes: Serial # prefix *BZ*.

13	5 Som	VG	VF	UNC
	1997. Dark blue and violet on multicolor underprint. Similar to #8.	.15	.75	2.00

14	10 Som	VG	VF	UNC
	1997. Dark green, purple and red on multicolor underprint. Similar to #9.	.15	.75	3.25

2000 ND ISSUE

15	1 Som	VG	VF	UNC
	1999. Brown and tan on multicolor underprint. Abdilas Maldibayeff at left. Musical instruments on back.	.05	.25	1.25

16	200 Som	VG	VF	UNC
	2000. Brown and tan on multicolor underprint. Alikul Osmonov at right. Poetry verse and lake scene on back.	1.00	3.00	7.50

17	500 Som	VG	VF	UNC
	2000. Rose, brown and olive on multicolor underprint. Sayakbai Karalaiev at right. Karalaiev seated, in background horseman chasing an eagle on back.	1.00	3.50	15.00

18	1000 Som	VG	VF	UNC
	2000. Olive, slate, brown and multicolor. Jusul Balasagbin at right. Gate, tree and mountains on back.	1.00	4.00	25.00

2002 ND ISSUE

#19-20 wmk. as portr.

19	20 Som	VG	VF	UNC
	ND (2002). Dark brown and orange on multicolor underprint. Togolok Moldo at right. Manas Mausoleum on back.	.25	1.00	5.00

20	50 Som	VG	VF	UNC
	ND (2002). Brown and blue on multicolor underprint. Czarina Krumanjan-Datka at right. Uzgen Architectural ensemble: mausoleum and minaret on back.	.50	1.00	7.50

21	100 Som	VG	VF	UNC
	ND (2002). Green, pink and blue on multicolor underprint. Toktogul at right. Khan Tenyiri Mountains at left center on back.	.50	1.00	12.50

		VG	VF	UNC
22	**200 Som** ND (2004). Brown and tan on multicolor underprint. Alikul Osmonov at right. Poetry verse and lake scene on back.	FV	4.00	8.00

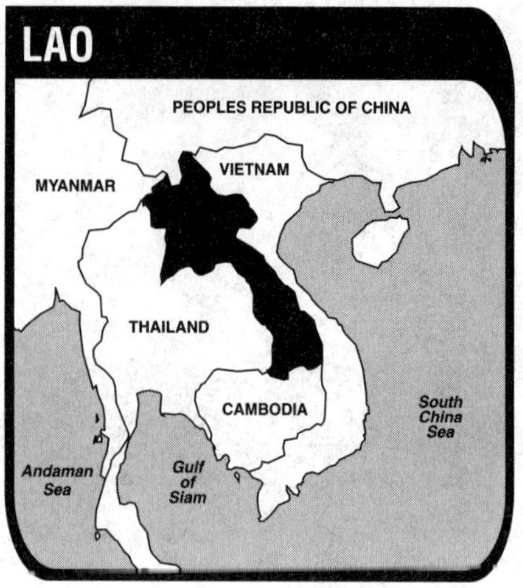

The Lao People's Democratic Republic, located on the Indo-Chinese Peninsula between the Socialist Republic of Vietnam and the Kingdom of Thailand, has an area of 91,429 sq. mi. (236,800 sq. km.) and a population of 5.69 million. Captial: Vientiane. Agriculture employs 95 percent of the people. Tin, lumber and coffee are exported.

The first United Kingdom of Laos was established in the mid-14th century by King Fa Ngum who ruled an area including present Laos, northeastern Thailand, and the southern part of China's Yunnan province from his capital at Luang Prabang. Thailand and Vietnam obtained control over much of the present Lao territory in the 18th century and remained dominant until France established a protectorate over the area in 1893 and incorporated it into the Union of Indo-China. The Independence of Laos was proclaimed in March of 1945, during the last days of the Japanese occupation of World War II. France reoccupied Laos in 1946, and established it as a constitutional monarchy within the French Union in 1949. In 1953, war erupted between the government and the Pathet Lao, a Communist movement supported by the Vietnamese Communist forces. Peace was declared in 1954 with Laos becoming fully independent in 1955 and the Pathet Lao being permitted to occupy two northern provinces. Civil war broke out again in 1960 with the United States supporting the government of the Kingdom of Laos and the North Vietnamese helping the Communist Pathet Lao, and continued, with intervals of truce and political compromise, until the formation of the Lao People's Democratic Republic on Dec. 2, 1975.

RULERS:

Sisavang Vong, 1949-1959
Savang Vatthana, 1959-1975

MONETARY SYSTEM:

1 Kip = 100 At, 1955-1978
1 new Kip = 100 old Kip, 1979-

BANQUE NATIONALE DU LAOS

SIGNATURE VARIETIES		
	ຜູ້ອຳນວຍການ LE GOUVERNEUR	(ຜູ້ກວດກາຜູ້ນຶ່ງ) UN CENSEUR
1		
2		
3		
4		
5		
6		

1962-63 ISSUE

		VG	VF	UNC
8	**1 Kip** ND (1962). Brown on pink and bue underprint. Stylized figure at left. Tricephalic elephant arms at center on back.			
	a. Signature 3; 4.	.10	.20	.50
	s. Signature 3. Specimen.	—	—	40.00

9 5 Kip

ND (1962). Green on multicolor underprint. S. Vong at right. Temple at left, man on elephant at center on back. Watermark: Tricephalic elephant arms.

	VG	VF	UNC
a. Signature 2.	4.50	17.50	50.00
b. Signature 5.	.15	.50	1.25
s. As a. Specimen.	—	—	50.00

10 10 Kip

ND (1962). Blue on yellow and green underprint. Woman at left. (like back of Fr. Indochina #102). Stylized sunburst on back (like face of #102). Watermark: Elephant's head.

	VG	VF	UNC
a. Signature 1.	25.00	60.00	125.
b. Signature 5.	.15	.50	1.75
s1. As a. Specimen. Ovpt: *SPECIMEN.*	—	—	100.
s2. As b. Specimen. TDLR oval overprint	—	—	100.

#11-14, Kf. Savang Vatthana at l. Wmk: Tricephalic elephant arms. Replacement notes: Serial # prefix *S9* (=Z9 in English).

11 20 Kip

ND (1963). Brown on tan and blue underprint. Temple or pagoda at center. Pagoda at center right on back.

	VG	VF	UNC
a. Sign 5.	.10	.40	2.00
b. Sign 6.	.10	.30	1.50
s1. As a. Specimen. Ovpt: *SAN VALEUR.*	—	—	40.00
s2. As a. Specimen. Ovpt: TDLR oval.	—	—	40.00

12 50 Kip

ND (1963). Purple on brown and blue underprint. Pagoda at center. Back purple; building at right.

	VG	VF	UNC
a. Signature 5; 6.	.10	.25	2.00
s1. Signature 5. Specimen. Ovpt: *SAN VALEUR.*	—	—	40.00
s2. Signature 5. Specimen. Ovpt: TDLR oval.	—	—	40.00

13 200 Kip

ND (1963). Blue on green and gold underprint. Temple of That Luang at center. Waterfalls on back.

	VG	VF	UNC
a. Signature 4.	.20	1.00	6.00
b. Signature 6.	.20	.50	3.00
s1. As a. Specimen. Ovpt: *SAN VALEUR.*	—	—	50.00
s2. As a. Specimen. Ovpt: TDLR oval.	—	—	60.00

14 1000 Kip

ND (1963). Brown on blue and gold underprint. Temple at center. Three long canoes on back.

	VG	VF	UNC
a. Signature 5.	.25	1.00	6.00
b. Signature 6.	.25	.75	4.00
s1. As a. Specimen. Ovpt: *SAN VALEUR.*	—	—	60.00
s2. As a. Specimen. Ovpt: TDLR oval.	—	—	60.00

1974; 1975 ND ISSUE

		VG	VF	UNC
15	**10 Kip** ND (1974). Blue on multicolor underprint. King Savang Vatthana at center right. Back blue and brown; ox cart. Signature 6.			
	a. Normal serial #. (Not issued).	—	—	10.00
	s. Specimen. Ovpt: *SAN VALEUR.*	—	—	375.

#16-19 Kg. Savang Vatthana at l. Wml: Tricephalic elephant arms. Sign. 6.

		VG	VF	UNC
16	**100 Kip** ND (1974). Brown on blue, green and pink underprint. Pagoda at center. Ox cart on back.			
	a. Issued note.	.15	.50	3.00
	s. Specimen. Ovpt: *SAN VALEUR.*	—	—	50.00

		VG	VF	UNC
17	**500 Kip** ND (1974). Red on multicolor underprint. Pagoda at center. Hydroelectric dam on back.			
	a. Issued note.	.20	.75	4.00
	s. Specimen. Ovpt: *SAN VALEUR.*	—	—	75.00

		VG	VF	UNC
18	**1000 Kip** ND. Black on multicolor underprint. Elephant on back.			
	a. Normal serial #. (Not issued.)	—	—	15.00
	s. Specimen. Ovpt: *SAN VALEUR.*	—	—	600.

		VG	VF	UNC
19	**5000 Kip** ND (1975). Blue-gray on multicolor underprint. Pagoda at center. Musicians with instruments on back.			
	a. Issued note.	.75	2.25	9.00
	s. Specimen. Ovpt: *SAN VALEUR.*	—	—	75.00

STATE OF LAO

PATHET LAO GOVERNMENT

ND ISSUE

#19A-24 printed in Peoples Republic of China and circulated in areas under control of Pathet Lao insurgents. Later these same notes became the accepted legal tender for the entire country.

		VG	VF	UNC
19A	**1 Kip** ND. Green and blue on yellow and pink underprint. Threshing grain at center. Medical clinic scene on back.			
	a. Issued note.	—	—	10.00
	s. Specimen.	—	—	150.
20	**10 Kip** ND. Red on light blue and gold underprint. Medical examination scene. Fighters in the brush on back.			
	a. Watermark: Temples.	.05	.15	2.00
	b. Watermark: 5-pointed stars.	.05	.15	1.00
	s. As b. Specimen. overprint in Lao.	—	—	50.00

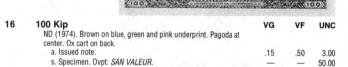

21	20 Kip	VG	VF	UNC
	ND. Brown on light pink and olive-brown underprint. Rice distribution. Forge workers on back.			
	a. Watermark: Temples.	.10	.20	3.00
	b. Watermark: 5-pointed stars.	.10	.20	2.00
	s. As b. Specimen. overprint in Lao.	—	—	50.00

22	50 Kip	VG	VF	UNC
	ND. Purple on multicolor underprint. Factory workers. Plowing ox on back.			
	a. Watermark: Temples.	.10	.25	3.00
	b. Watermark: 5-pointed stars.	.10	.25	2.00
	s. As b. Specimen. overprint in Lao.	—	—	50.00

23	100 Kip	VG	VF	UNC
	ND. Blue on multicolor underprint. Long boats on lake. Scene in textile store on back. Watermark: Temples.			
	a. Issued note.	1.00	3.00	6.00
	s. Specimen. overprint in Lao.	—	—	50.00

23A	200 Kip	VG	VF	UNC
	ND. Green on multicolor underprint. Road and trail convoys. Factory scene on back. Watermark: Temples.			
	a. Issued note.	2.00	4.00	12.00
	s. Specimen. overprint in Lao.	—	—	50.00
	x. Lithograph counterfeit (1974) on plain paper, without serial #. Ho Chi Minh at right on back.	125.	250.	500.

24	500 Kip	VG	VF	UNC
	ND. Brown on multicolor underprint. Armed field workers in farm scene. Soldiers shooting down planes on back. Watermark: Temples.			
	a. Issued note.	2.00	5.00	15.00
	s. Specimen. overprint in Lao.	—	—	50.00

Lao Peoples Democratic Republic

Government

1979 Provisional Issue

24A	50 Kip on 500 Kip	VG	VF	UNC
	ND. New legends and denomination overprint on #24. (Not issued).	100.	300.	700.

Bank of the Lao PDR

1979 ND; 1988 Issue

#25-32 wmk: Stars, hammer and sickles.

#25-29 replacement notes: Serial # prefixes *ZA; ZB; ZC*.

25	1 Kip	VG	VF	UNC
	ND (1979). Blue-gray on multicolor underprint. Militia unit at left, arms at upper right. Schoolroom scene at left on back.			
	a. Issued note.	.05	.15	1.00
	s. Specimen. overprint in Lao.	—	—	15.00

26	5 Kip	VG	VF	UNC
	ND (1979). Green on multicolor underprint. Shoppers at a store, arms at upper right. Logging elephants at left on back.			
	a. Issued note.	.05	.15	1.00
	s. Specimen. overprint in Lao.	—	—	15.00

27	10 Kip	VG	VF	UNC
	ND (1979). Dark brown on multicolor underprint. Lumber mill at left, arms at upper right. Medical scenes at left on back.			
	a. Issued note.	.05	.15	1.00
	s. Specimen. overprint in Lao.	—	—	15.00

28	20 Kip	VG	VF	UNC
	ND (1979). Brown and red-brown on underprint. Arms at left, tank with troop column at center. Back brown and maroon; textile mill at center.			
	a. Issued note.	.10	.20	1.00
	s. Specimen. overprint in Lao.	—	—	15.00

29	50 Kip	VG	VF	UNC
	ND (1979). Violet on multicolor underprint. Rice planting at left center, arms at upper right. Back red and brown; hydroelectric dam at center.			
	a. Issued note.	.10	.20	1.00
	s. Specimen. overprint in Lao.	—	—	15.00

#30-32 replacement notes: Serial # prefixes *AM; ZL; ZK.*

30	100 Kip	VG	VF	UNC
	ND (1979). Deep blue-green and deep blue on multicolor underprint. Grain harvesting at left, arms at upper right. Bridge, storage tanks, and soldier on back.			
	a. Issued note.	FV	FV	2.00
	s. Specimen. overprint in Lao.	—	—	17.50

31	500 Kip	VG	VF	UNC
	1988. Dark brown, purple and deep blue on multicolor underprint. Modern irrigation systems at center, arms above. Harvesting fruit at center on back.			
	a. Issued note.	FV	FV	3.00
	s. Specimen. Overprint in Lao.	—	—	20.00

1998-2003 Issue

32	1000 Kip	VG	VF	UNC
	1992-2003. Dark green, deep purple and green on multicolor underprint. Three women at left, temple at center right, arms at upper right. Cattle at center on back. Watermark: star.			
	a. Without security thread. 1992. Red serial #.	FV	FV	6.00
	b. With security thread. 1994.	FV	FV	3.50
	c. As b. 1995.	FV	FV	3.50
	d. As b. 1996.	FV	FV	3.50
	e. Red and green serial #. 1998.	FV	FV	3.00
	f. 2003.	FV	FV	3.00
	s. As a (overprint in Lao); b (overprint in English). Specimen.	—	—	20.00

#33 and 34 Kaysone Phomvihane at l., arms at upper r.

33	2000 Kip	VG	VF	UNC
	1997; 2003. Blue-black and purple on multicolor underprint. Temple in underprint at center right. Hydroelectric complex at center on back.			
	a. 1997.	FV	FV	2.00
	b. 2003.	FV	FV	2.00
	s. Specimen. Ovpt: *SPECIMEN* on both sides. 1997.	—	—	20.00

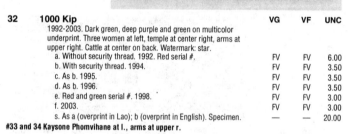

34 **5000 Kip**

1997; 2003. Dark brown and purple on multicolor underprint. Temple in underprint at center right. Cememt factory at center on back. Watermark: Temple.

	VG	VF	UNC
a. 1997.	FV	FV	3.00
b. 2003.	FV	FV	3.00
s. Specimen. Ovpt: *SPECIMEN* on both sides. 1997.	—	—	20.00

35 **10,000 Kip**

2002-03. Slate blue and brown on multicolor underprint. Kaysone Phomuihane at left, temple at center. Bridge over Mekong river at center on back. Brown and green serial #. Blue and green, road at center on back.

	VG	VF	UNC
a. 2002.	FV	FV	5.00
b. 2003.	FV	FV	5.00
s. Specimen.	—	—	—

36 **20,000 Kip**

2002-03. Red-brown on multicolor underprint. Brown and green serial #. Hydroelectric complex at center on back.

	VG	VF	UNC
a. 2002.	FV	FV	9.00
b. 2003.	FV	FV	9.00
s. Specimen.	—	—	—

37 **20,000 Kip**

	VG	VF	UNC
2004. Brown and orange and rose on multicolor underprint.	FV	FV	25.00

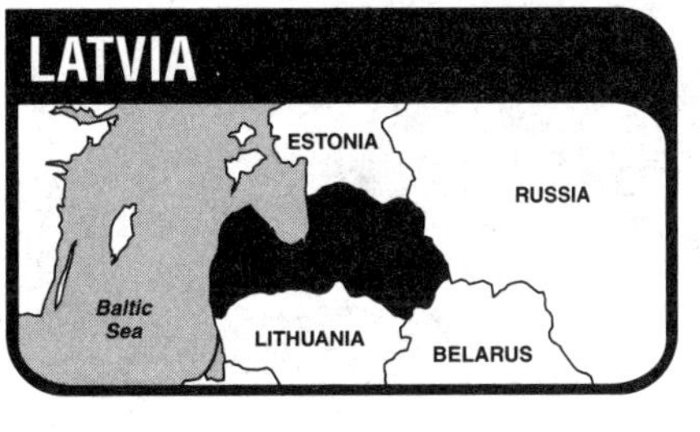

The Republic of Latvia, the central Baltic state in east Europe, has an area of 24,595 sq. mi. (43,601 sq. km.) and a population of 2.4 million. Capital: Riga. Livestock raising and manufacturing are the chief industries. Butter, bacon, fertilizers and telephone equipment are exported.

The Latvians, of Aryan descent, were nomadic tribesmen who settled along the Baltic prior to the 13th century. Lacking a central government, they were easily conquered by the German Teutonic knights, Russia, Sweden and Poland. Following the third partition of Poland by Austria, Prussia and Russia in 1795, Latvia came under Russian domination and did not experience autonomy until the Russian Revolution of 1917 provided an opportunity for freedom. The Latvian republic was established on Nov. 18, 1918. It was occupied by Soviet troops in 1939 and annexed to the Soviet Union in 1940. Following the German occupation of 1941-44, it was retaken by Russia and reestablished as a member S.S. Republic of the Soviet Union. Western countries, including the United States, did not recognize Latvia's incorporation into the Soviet Union. Latvia declared its independence from the former U.S.S.R. on Aug. 22, 1991.

MONETARY SYSTEM:

1 Lats = 100 Santimu, 1923-40; 1992
1 Lats = 200 Rublu, 1993
1 Rublis = 1 Russian Ruble, 1992

REPUBLIC

GOVERNMENT

1992 ISSUE

#35-40 wmk: Symmetrical design.

35 **1 Rublis**

	VG	VF	UNC
1992. Violet on yellow and ochre underprint. Back violet-brown on light green and yellow underprint.	—	.10	.30

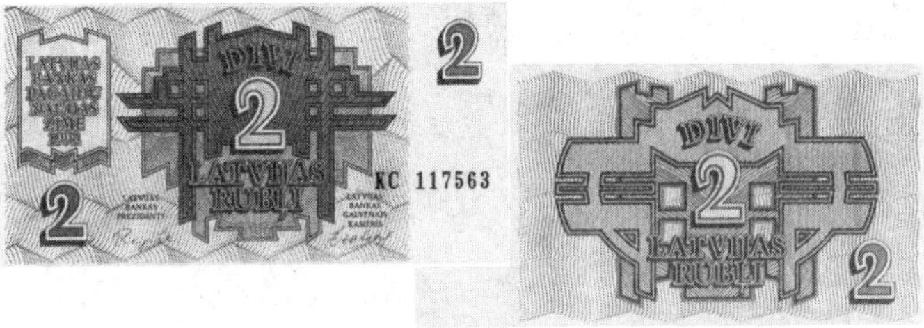

36 **2 Rubli**

	VG	VF	UNC
1992. Purple on brown-orange and yellow underprint.	—	.10	.50

37 **5 Rubli**

	VG	VF	UNC
1992. Deep blue on light blue and light yellow-orange underprint. Back blue-black on blue and light blue underprint.	.20	.75	2.75

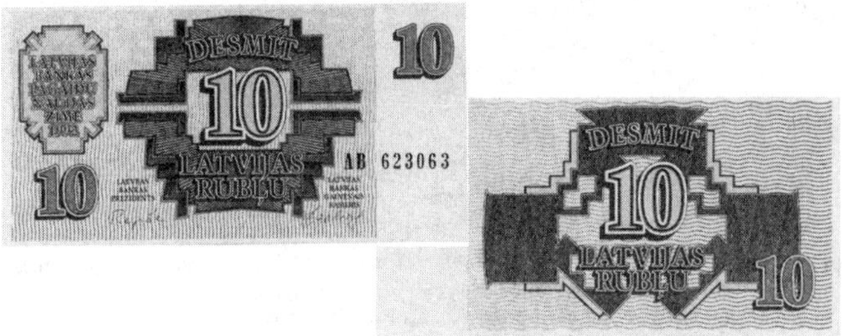

38 **10 Rublu**

	VG	VF	UNC
1992. Purple on red-orange and pale orange underprint.	.10	.25	2.00

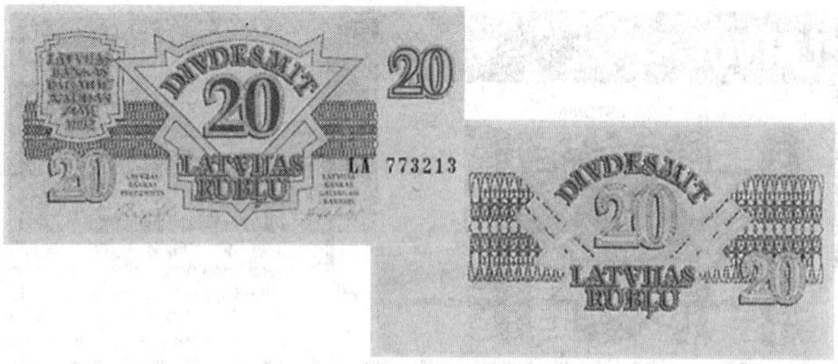

		VG	VF	UNC
39	**20 Rublu** 1992. Violet on lilac and pink underprint.	.15	.50	3.00

		VG	VF	UNC
40	**50 Rublu** 1992. Gray-green on light blue and pink underprint.	.20	.75	4.00

		VG	VF	UNC
41	**200 Rublu** 1992. Greenish black on yellow and blue-green underprint. Back greenish black on light blue and pink underprint.	1.00	3.50	10.00

		VG	VF	UNC
42	**500 Rublu** 1992. Violet-brown on gray and dull orange underprint.	1.50	5.00	18.00

LATVIJAS BANKAS NAUDAS ZIME

1992 DATED 1993-1998 ISSUE

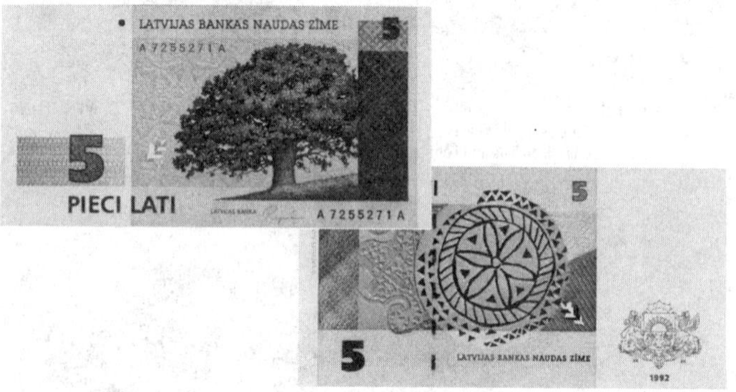

		VG	VF	UNC
43	**5 Lati** 1992 (1993); 1996; 2001. Varied shades of green on tan and pale green underprint. Oak tree at center right. Local art at center on back.			
	a. Small foil strip. 1992.	FV	FV	15.00
	b. Broad foil strip. 1996.	FV	FV	10.00

		VG	VF	UNC
44	**10 Latu** 1992 (1993). Violet and purple on multicolor underprint. Panoramic view of Daugava River at center. Traditional bow broach at center on back.	FV	FV	30.00

		VG	VF	UNC
45	**20 Latu** 1992 (1993). Brown and dark brown on multicolor underprint. Rural homestead at right. Traditional ornamented woven linen at left center on back.	FV	FV	60.00

		VG	VF	UNC
46	**50 Latu** 1992 (1994). Deep blue on multicolor underprint. Sailing ship at right. Two crossed keys and a cross on back (Historical seal of Riga) superimposed on medieval fortifications of Riga.	FV	FV	120.

		VG	VF	UNC
47	**100 Latu** 1992 (1994). Red and dark brown on multicolor underprint. Krisjanis Barons at right. Lielvarde belt ornaments on back.	FV	FV	150.

		VG	VF	UNC
48	**500 Latu** 1992 (1998). Purple on multicolor underprint. Young woman in national costume at right. Small ornamental brass crowns on back.	FV	FV	625.

2000-01 ISSUE

		VG	VF	UNC
49	**5 Lati** 2001. Similar to #43.	FV	FV	10.00
50	**10 Latu** 2000. Violet and purple on multicolor underprint. Similar to # 44 but for some engraving and color modifications.	FV	FV	17.50
51	**20 Latu** 2004.	FV	FV	32.50

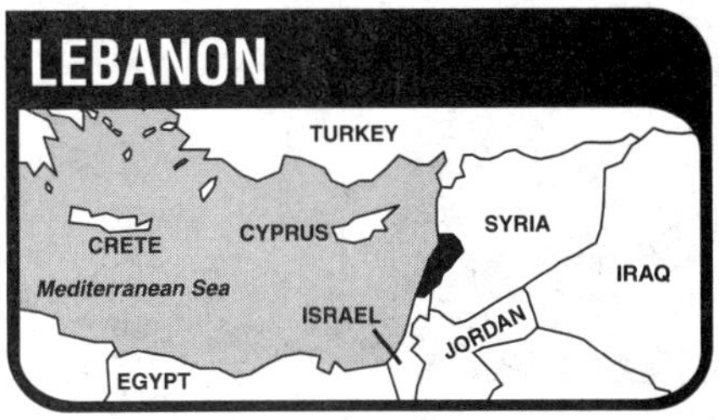

The Republic of Lebanon, situated on the eastern shore of the Mediterranean Sea between Syria and Israel, has an area of 4,015 sq. mi. (10,400 sq. km.) and a population of 3.29 million. Capital: Beirut. The economy is d on agriculture, trade and tourism. Fruit, other foodstuffs and textiles are exported.

Almost at the beginning of recorded history, Lebanon appeared as the well-wooded hinterland of the Phoenicians who exploited its famous forests of cedar. The mountains were a Christian refuge and a Crusader stronghold. Lebanon, the history of which is essentially the same as that of Syria, came under control of the Ottoman Turks early in the 16th century. Following the collapse of the Ottoman Empire after World War I, Lebanon, along with Syria, became a French mandate. The French drew a border around the predominantly Christian Lebanon Sanjak or administrative subdivision and on Sept. 1, 1920 proclaimed the area the State of Grand Lebanon (Etat du Grand Liban), a republic under French control. France announced the independence of Lebanon during WWII after Vichy control was deposed on Nov. 26, 1941. It became fully independent on Jan. 1, 1944, but the last British and French troops did not leave until the end of Aug. 1946.

Since the late 1950's the independent Palestinian movement caused government friction. By 1976 large-scale fighting broke out, which continued thru 1990. In April 1996, Israel staged a 17 day bombardment of the southern areas.

RULERS

French to 1943

MONETARY SYSTEM

1 Livre (Pound) = 100 Piastres

RÉPUBLIQUE LIBANAISE

BANQUE DE SYRIE ET DU LIBAN

1952; 1956 ISSUE

#55-60 all dated 1st of January. Sign. varieties. Printer: TDLR.

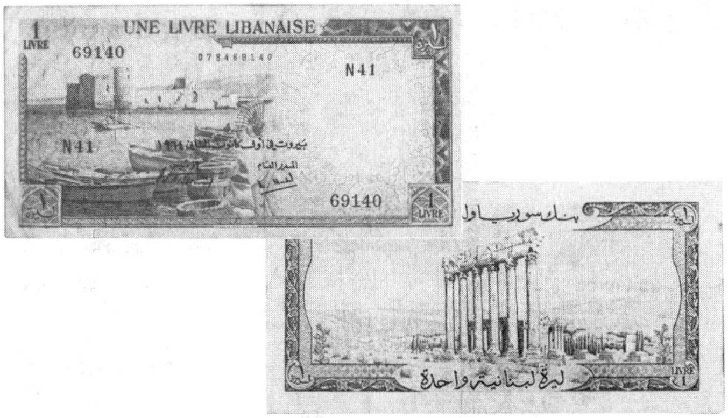

		VG	VF	UNC
55	**1 Livre** 1.1.1952-64. Brown on multicolor underprint. Crusader Castle at Saida (Sidon) at left. Columns of Baalbek on back. with or without security strip.			
	a. Issued note.	1.00	8.00	40.00
	s. Specimen. Oval TDLR stamp, punch hole cancelled.	—	—	30.00

		VG	VF	UNC
56	**5 Livres** 1.1.1952-64. Blue on multicolor underprint. Courtyard of the Palais de Beit-ed-Din. Snowy mountains with trees on back. with or without security strip.			
	a. Issued note.	3.00	35.00	140.
	s. Specimen. Oval TDLR stamp, punch hole cancelled.	—	—	40.00

		VG	VF	UNC
57	**10 Livres** 1.1.1956; 1.1.1961; 1.1.1963. Green on multicolor underprint. Ruins of Temple of Bacchus temple at Baalbek. Shoreline with city in hills on back.			
	a. Issued note.	6.00	45.00	200.
	s. Specimen. Oval TDLR stamp, punch hole cancelled.	—	—	—

		VG	VF	UNC
58	**25 Livres** 1.1.1952; 1.1.1953. Blue-gray on multicolor underprint. Harbor town. Stone arch bridge at center right on back. Watermark: Lion's head.			
	a. Issued note.	50.00	175.	750.
	s. Specimen. Oval TDLR stamp, punch hole cancelled.	—	—	120.

		VG	VF	UNC
59	**50 Livres** 1.1.1952; 1.1.1953; 1.1.1964. Deep brown on multicolor underprint. Coast landscape. Large rock formations in water on back. Watermark: Lion's head.			
	a. Issued note.	45.00	165.	725.
	s. Specimen. Oval TDLR stamp, punch hole cancelled.	—	—	125.

60	100 Livres	VG	VF	UNC
	1.1.1952; 1.1.1953; 1.1.1958; 1.1.1963. Blue on multicolor underprint. View of Beirut and harbor. Cedar tree at center on back and as watermark.			
	a. Issued note.	12.50	35.00	150.
	s. Specimen. Oval TDLR stamp, punch hole cancelled.	—	—	120.

REPUBLIC

BANQUE DU LIBAN

1964; 1978 ISSUE

#61-67 printer: TDLR.

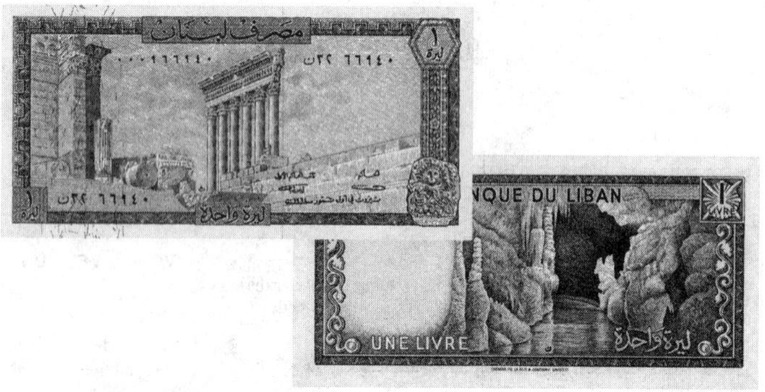

61	1 Livre	VG	VF	UNC
	1964-80. Brown on light blue underprint. Columns of Baalbek. Jeita Cavern on back. Watermark: Two eagles.			
	a. 1964; 1968.	1.00	3.00	15.00
	b. 1971; 1972; 1973; 1974.	1.00	2.00	10.00
	c. 1978; 1980.	.50	1.50	3.50

62	5 Livres	VG	VF	UNC
	1964-86. Green on blue and light yellow underprint. Buildings. Bridge over Kalb at center right on back. Watermark: Ancient galley.			
	a. 1964.	1.50	5.00	15.00
	b. 1967; 1968.	1.00	3.00	12.50
	c. 1972; 1974; 1.2.1978; 1.4.1978.	.50	1.25	4.00
	d. 1986.	.20	.40	1.25

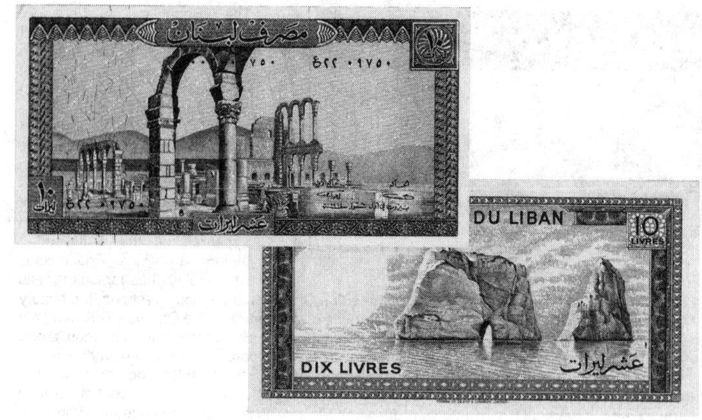

63	10 Livres	VG	VF	UNC
	1964-86. Purple on multicolor underprint. Ruins of Anjar. Large rocks in water near Beirut on back. Watermark: Man's head.			
	a. 1964.	2.00	7.50	20.00
	b. 1967; 1968.	1.50	5.00	15.00
	c. 1971; 1972; 1973; 1974.	1.00	2.75	10.00
	d. 1.2.1978.	2.00	7.50	20.00
	e. 1.4.1978.	1.00	2.75	10.00
	f. 1986.	.20	.40	1.25

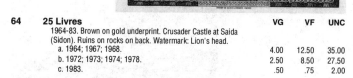

64	25 Livres	VG	VF	UNC
	1964-83. Brown on gold underprint. Crusader Castle at Saida (Sidon). Ruins on rocks on back. Watermark: Lion's head.			
	a. 1964; 1967; 1968.	4.00	12.50	35.00
	b. 1972; 1973; 1974; 1978.	2.50	8.50	27.50
	c. 1983.	.50	.75	2.00

65	50 Livres	VG	VF	UNC
	1964-88. Dark gray, purple and dark olive-green on multicolor underprint. Ruins of Temple of Bacchus at Baalbek. Building on back. Watermark: Cedar tree.			
	a. 1964; 1967; 1968.	4.50	15.00	45.00
	b. 1972; 1973; 1974; 1978.	3.50	10.00	30.00
	c. Guilloche added above temple ruins with 10-petaled rosette at left. in underprint. Clear watermark. area on back. 1983; 1985.	.50	1.00	3.00
	d. Without control # above ruins on face. 1988.	FV	FV	2.50

66	100 Livres	VG	VF	UNC
	1964-88. Blue on light pink and light blue underprint. Palais Beit-ed-din with inner courtyard. Snowy cedars on Lebanon mountains on back. Watermark: bearded male elder.			
	a. 1964; 1967; 1968.	5.00	12.50	40.00
	b. 1972; 1973; 1974; 1977; 1978; 1980.	4.00	8.50	25.00
	c. Guilloche added under bank name on face and back. Clearer watermark. area on back. 1983; 1985.	.25	1.50	4.00
	d. Without control # at upper center 1988.	.25	.75	2.50

67	250 Livres	VG	VF	UNC
	1978-88. Deep gray-green and blue-black on multicolor underprint. Ruins at Tyras on face and back. Watermark: Ancient circular sculpture with head at center from the Grand Temple Podium.			
	a. 1978.	3.00	17.50	50.00
	b. 1983. Control # at top center.	1.25	5.00	15.00
	c. 1985.	.20	1.00	5.00
	d. 1986.	.15	1.00	4.50
	e. Without control # above signature at archway on face. 1986; 1987; 1988.	FV	.50	4.00

1988; 1993 Issue

Law of 1988

#68 and 69 printer: TDLR.

68	500 Livres	VG	VF	UNC
	1988. Brown and olive-green on multicolor underprint. Beirut city view at center. Back brown on multicolor underprint; ruins at left center Watermark: Lion's head.	1.00	1.50	3.50

69	1000 Livres	VG	VF	UNC
	1988; 1990-92. Dark blue, blue-black and green on multicolor underprint. Map at right. Ruins at center, modern building at center right back. Watermark: Cedar tree.			
	a. 1988.	.75	1.50	4.00
	b. 1990; 1991.	.75	1.00	3.50
	c. 1992.	FV	FV	3.00

70	10,000 Livres	VG	VF	UNC
	1993 Purple and olive-brown on multicolor underprint. Ancient ruins at Tyros at center. City ruins with five archaic statues on back. Watermark: Ancient circular sculpture with head at center from the Grand Temple Podium.	FV	10.00	25.00

1994 Issue

#71-74 ornate block designs as unpt. Arabic serial # and matching bar code, #. Wmk: Cedar tree. Printer: BABN.

71	5000 Livres	VG	VF	UNC
	1994; 1995. Dark purple and red on pink and multicolor underprint. Geometric designs on back.			
	a. 1994.	FV	7.00	12.00
	b. 1995.	FV	6.00	12.00

72 **20,000 Livres** — VG: FV | VF: 17.50 | UNC: 40.00

1994; 1995. Red-brown and orange on yellow and multicolor underprint. Geometric designs with large *LIBAN* left center on back.

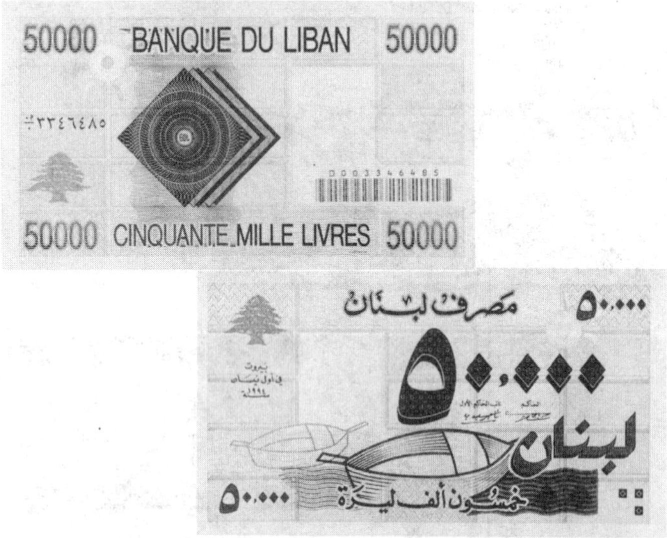

73 **50,000 Livres** — VG: FV | VF: 40.00 | UNC: 90.00

1994; 1995. Blue-black and brown-violet on multicolor underprint. Cedar tree at upper left, artistic boats at lower left center. Large diamond with BDL at left center, cedar tree at lower left on back.

74 **100,000 Livres** — VG: FV | VF: FV | UNC: 120.

1994; 1995. Dark blue-green and dark green on multicolor underprint. Cedar tree at lower right. Artistic bunch of grapes and grain stalks at left center on back.

1998-99 Issue

75 **5000 Livres** — VG: FV | VF: FV | UNC: 10.00

1999. Dark purple and red on multicolor underprint. Like #71 but smaller size and new signature.

76 **10,000 Livres** — VG: FV | VF: FV | UNC: 20.00

1998. Orange and green on yellow and multicolor underprint. Patriotic Monument, stylized landscape on back. Embedded iridescent planchets in paper.

Note: #76 issued on Martyr's Day 1998.

77 **50,000 Livres** — VG: FV | VF: FV | UNC: 70.00

1999. Blue-black and brown-violet on multicolor underprint. Similar to #73 but with enhanced security features and holographic foil strip at left.

		VG	VF	UNC
78	**100,000 Livres** 1999. Dark blue-green and dark green on multicolor underprint. Similar to #74 but with enhanced security features.	FV	FV	100.

2001 Issue

#79-82 wide security thread. Printer: BABN.

		VG	VF	UNC
79	**5000 Livres** 2001. Dark purple and red on multicolor underprint.	FV	FV	6.00

80 *Not assigned.*

		VG	VF	UNC
81	**20,000 Livres** 2001. Red-brown and orange on multicolor underprint.	FV	FV	40.00

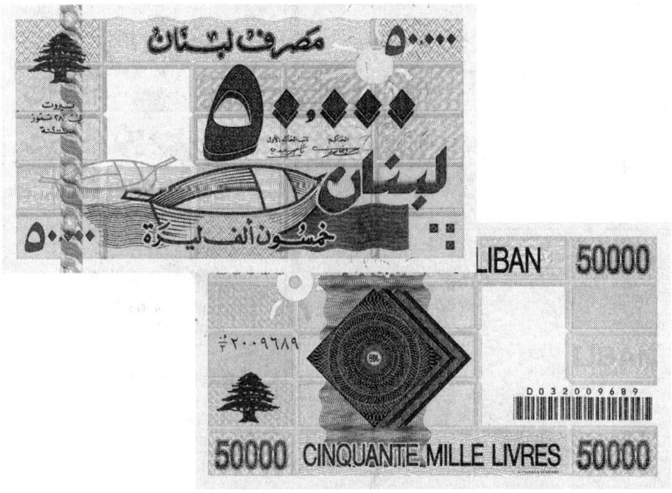

		VG	VF	UNC
82	**50,000 Livres** 2001.	FV	FV	75.00

		VG	VF	UNC
83	**100,000 Livres** 2001. Dark blue-green and dark green on multicolor underprint.	FV	FV	110.

2004 Issue

		VG	VF	UNC
84	**1000 Livres** 2004. Multicolor.	FV	FV	2.00
85	**5000 Livres** 2004. Multicolor.	FV	FV	7.50
86	**10,000 Livres** 2005. Multicolor.	FV	FV	16.00
87	**20,000 Livres** 2005. Multicolor.	FV	FV	35.00

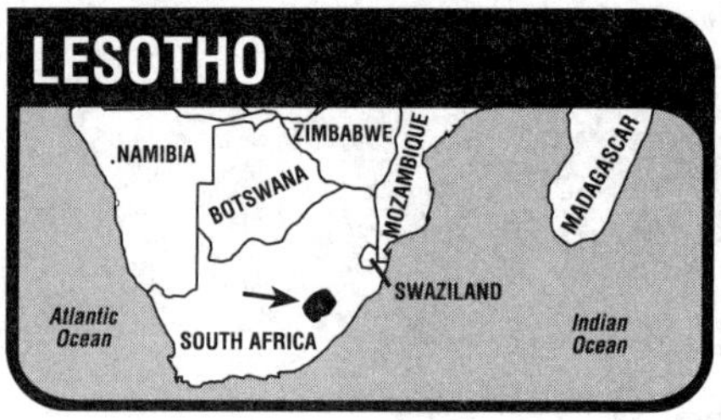

The Kingdom of Lesotho, a constitutional monarchy located within the east-central part of the Republic of South Africa, has an area of 11,716 sq. mi. (30,355 sq. km.) and a population of 2.29 million. Capital: Maseru. The economy is d on subsistence agriculture and livestock raising. Wool, mohair, water through Katse Dam, and cattle are exported. Lesotho (formerly Basutoland) was sparsely populated until the end of the 16th century. Between the 16th and 19th centuries an influx of refugees from tribal wars led to the development of a distinct Basotho group. During the reign of tribal chief Moshoeshoe I (1823-70), a series of wars with the Orange Free State resulted in the loss of large areas of territory to South Africa. Moshoeshoe II appealed to the British for help, and Basutoland was constituted a native state under British protection. In 1871 it was annexed to Cape Colony, but was restored to direct control by the Crown in 1884. From 1884 to 1959 legislative and executive authority was vested in a British High Commissioner. The constitution of 1959 recognized the expressed wish of the people for independence, which was attained on Oct. 4, 1966, when Lesotho became a monarchy under King Moshoeshoe II. Following his death in an automobile accident in Jan. 1996 his eldest son Prince Bereng Seeiso became King Letsie III on Oct. 17, 1997. Lesotho is a member of the Commonwealth of Nations. The king of Lesotho is Chief of State.

RULERS:

King Motlotlehi Moshoeshoe II, 1966-1996
King Letsi III, 1997-

MONETARY SYSTEM:

1 Loti = 100 Lisente

KINGDOM

LESOTHO MONETARY AUTHORITY

1979 ISSUE

#1-3A arms at ctr., military bust of Kg. Moshoeshoe II at r. Wmk: Basotho hat. Sign. 1.

Dating: Partial date given in the 2 numbers of the serial # prefix for #1-8.

		VG	VF	UNC
1	**2 Maloti** (19)79. Dark brown on multicolor underprint. Building and Lesotho flag at left on back.			
	a. Blue and brown underprint. at right. of King	2.00	4.50	24.00
	s. Specimen. Serial # prefix R/79.	—	—	135.

		VG	VF	UNC
2	**5 Maloti** (19)79. Deep blue on multicolor underprint. Craftsmen weaving at left center on back.			
	a. Issued note.	4.00	12.50	37.00
	s. Specimen. Serial # prefix J/79.	—	—	135.

		VG	VF	UNC
3	**10 Maloti** (19)79. Red and purple on multicolor underprint. Basotho horseman in maize field at center on back.			
	a. Issued note.	8.00	30.00	145.
	s. Specimen. Serial # prefix C/79.	—	—	135.

		VG	VF	UNC
3A	**20 Maloti** (19)79. Herdsmen with cattle at left center on back. Specimen (Not issued.)	—	—	—

CENTRAL BANK OF LESOTHO

SIGNATURE VARIETIES

	MINISTER OF FINANCE	GOVERNOR
1	E. R. Sekhonyana	E. K. Molemohi
2A	K. Rakhetla	S. Schoenbeg 08.11.1982-08.11.1985
2B	K. Rakhetla	S. Schoenbeg 08.11.1982-08.11.1985
2C	K. Rakhetla	S. Schoenbeg 08.11.1982-08.11.1985
1985-1988	K. Rakhetla	Mr. E. L. Karlsson 09.11.1985-30.6.1988
3	E. R. Sekhonyana	Dr. A. M. Maruping 01.07.1988-15.05.1998
4	E. L. Thoahlane	Dr. A. M. Maruping 01.07.1988-15.05.1998
5	Dr. L. V. Ketso	Dr. A. M. Maruping 01.07.1988-15.05.1998
6	Dr. L. V. Ketso	S. M. Swaray 9.91998

1981; 1984 Issue

#4-8 arms at ctr., military bust of Kg. Moshoeshoe II at r. Partial year date given as the denominator of the serial # prefix. Wmk: Basotho hat.

4	2 Maloti	VG	VF	UNC
	(19)81; 84. Like #1.			
	a. Signature 1 (19)81.	1.50	4.00	15.00
	b. Signature 2A (19)84.	1.00	3.00	12.50
	s1. Specimen. Serial # prefix A/81.	—	—	135.
	s2. Specimen. Serial # prefix D/84.	—	—	135.

5	5 Maloti	VG	VF	UNC
	(19)81. Face like #2. Waterfalls at center on back. Signature 1.			
	a. Issued note.	1.50	5.00	22.00
	s. Specimen. Serial # prefix A/81.	—	—	135.

6	10 Maloti	VG	VF	UNC
	(19)81. Like #3.			
	a. Signature 1 (19)81.	5.00	15.00	55.00
	b. Signature 2A (19)81 (1984).	1.50	5.00	22.50
	s1. Specimen. Serial # prefix A/81.	—	—	135.
	s2. Specimen. Serial # prefix C/81.	—	—	135.

7	20 Maloti	VG	VF	UNC
	(19)81; 84. Dark green and olive-green on multicolor underprint. Mosotho herdsboy with cattle at left center on back.			
	a. Signature 1 (19)81.	10.00	30.00	110.
	b. Signature 2A (19)84.	7.50	12.50	50.00
	s1. Specimen. Serial # prefix A/81.	—	—	135.
	s2. Specimen. Serial # prefix A/84.	—	—	135.

8	50 Maloti	VG	VF	UNC
	(19)81. Purple and deep blue on multicolor underprint. "Qiloane" mountain at left on back. Signature 1.			
	a. Issued note.	20.00	80.00	375.
	s. Specimen. Serial # prefix A/81.	—	—	175.

1989 Issue

#9-13 arms at ctr., civilian bust of Kg. Moshoeshoe II in new portr. at r. Designs similar to #4-8 but w/Kg. also as wmk. Sign. 3.

9	2 Maloti	VG	VF	UNC
	1989. Similar to #4.			
	a. Issued note.	FV	1.25	2.75
	s. Specimen. Serial # prefix G.	—	—	115.

10	5 Maloti	VG	VF	UNC
	1989. Similar to #5.			
	a. Issued note.	FV	2.00	7.50
	s. Specimen. Serial # prefix C.	—	—	115.

		VG	VF	UNC
11	**10 Maloti** 1990. Similar to #6.			
	a. Issued note.	FV	3.50	12.50
	s. Specimen. Serial # prefix R.	—	—	115.

		VG	VF	UNC
12	**20 Maloti** 1990. Dark green and blue-black on multicolor underprint. Similar to #7.			
	a. 1990.	FV	10.00	40.00
	b. 1993.	20.00	100.	400.
	s1. As a. Specimen. Serial # prefix F.	—	—	115.
	s2. As b. Specimen. Serial # prefix J.	—	—	160.
13	**50 Maloti** 1989. Purple and deep blue on multicolor underprint. Similar to #18.			
	a. Issued note.	12.00	30.00	135.
	s. Specimen. Serial # prefix A.	—	—	115.

1992 ISSUE

		VG	VF	UNC
14	**50 Maloti** 1992. Purple, dark olive-green and dark blue on multicolor underprint. Seated King Moshoeshoe I at right. "Qiloane" mountain at left center on back. Signature 4.			
	a. Issued note.	10.00	20.00	90.00
	s1. As a. 1992. Specimen. Serial # prefix A.	—	—	110.
	s2. As a. 1993. Specimen. Serial # prefix B.	—	—	160.

NOTICE

Readers with unlisted dates, signature varieties, etc. are invited to submit photocopies of their notes to: Standard Catalog of World Paper Money, 700 East State St. Iola, WI 54990-0001, E-Mail: george.cuhaj@fwpubs.com.

1994-2000 ISSUE

#15-20 seated Kg. Moshoeshoe I at l., arms at ctr. and as wmk.

		VG	VF	UNC
15	**10 Maloti** 2000; 2003. Red and purple on multicolor underprint. Traditionally dressed Masotho on horseback, maize crops and mountain on back. Printer: TDLR.			
	a. Signature 6. 2000.	FV	FV	4.50
	b. Signature 7. 2003.	FV	FV	3.50
	s. Specimen. Serial # prefix A.	—	—	100.

		VG	VF	UNC
16	**20 Maloti** 1994; 1999; 2001. Deep olive-green and blue-black on multicolor underprint. Mosotho herdsboy with cattle near huts at center right on back. Printer: TDLR.			
	a. Signature 5. 1994.	FV	6.00	20.00
	b. Signature 6. 1999.	FV	FV	9.00
	c. Signature 6. 2001.	FV	FV	6.50
	s1. As a. Specimen. Serial # prefix A.	—	—	100.
	s2. As b. Specimen. Serial # prefix F.	—	—	100.

		VG	VF	UNC
17	**50 Maloti** 1994; 1997; 1999; 2001. Purple, olive-green and dark blue on multicolor underprint. Herdsman on horseback with pack mule at center, *Qiloane* mountain at right on back. Printer: TDLR.			
	a. Signature 5. 1994.	FV	12.50	50.00
	b. Signature 5. 1997.	FV	—	30.00
	c. Signature 6. 1999.	FV	FV	20.00
	d. Signature 6. 2001.	FV	FV	17.00
	s1. As a. Specimen. Serial # prefix A.	—	—	100.
	s2. As b. Specimen. Serial # prefix C.	—	—	100.
	s3. As c. Specimen. Serial # prefix F.	—	—	100.
18	**100 Maloti** 1994. Dark olive-green, orange and brown on multicolor underprint. Sheep by shed and home at center right on back. Printer: BABN.			
	a. Signature 5.	FV	20.00	65.00
	s. Specimen. Serial # prefix AA.	—	—	100.

		VG	VF	UNC
19	**100 Maloti**			
	1999; 2001. Similar to #18. Printer: TDLR.			
	a. Sign 6.	FV	15.00	55.00
	b. Signature 6. 2001.	FV	FV	45.00
	s. As a. Specimen. Serial # prefix A.	—	—	100.

		VG	VF	UNC
20	**200 Maloti**			
	1994; 2001. Dark brown, brown and orange on multicolor underprint. Herdsman with sheep on back. Kinogram strip vertically at right. Printer: TDLR.			
	a. Signature 5. 1994.	FV	FV	80.00
	b. Signature 6. 2001.	FV	FV	100.
	s. As a. Specimen. Serial # prefix A.	—	—	100.

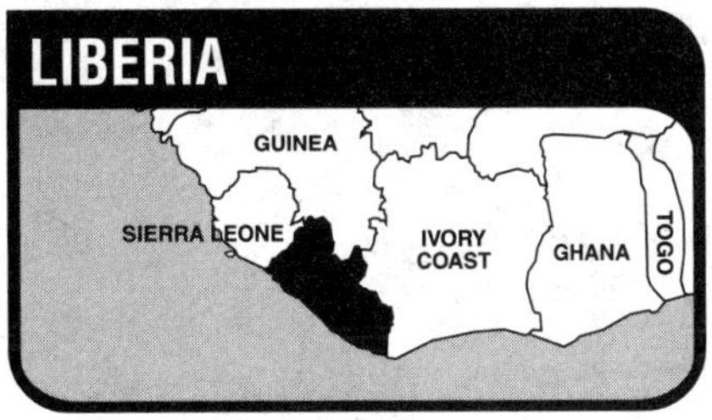

The Republic of Liberia, located on the southern side of the west African bulge between Sierra Leone and the Ivory Coast, has an area of 38,250 sq. mi. (111,369 sq. km.) and a population of 3.26 million. Capital: Monrovia. The major industries are agriculture, mining and lumbering. Iron ore, diamonds, rubber, coffee and cocoa are exported.

The Liberian coast was explored and chartered by Portuguese navigator Pedro de Cintra in 1461. For the following three centuries Portuguese traders visited the area regularly to trade for gold, slaves and pepper. The modern country of Liberia, Africa's first republic, was settled in 1822 by the American Colonization Society as a homeland for American freed slaves, with the U.S. government furnishing funds and assisting in negotiations for procurement of land from the indigenous chiefs. The various settlements united in 1839 to form the Commonwealth of Liberia, and in 1847 established the country as a republic with a constitution modeled after that of the United States.

Notes were issued from 1857 through 1880; thereafter the introduction of dollar notes of the United States took place. U.S. money was declared legal tender in Liberia in 1943, replacing British West African currencies. Not until 1989 was a distinctive Liberian currency again issued.

MONETARY SYSTEM:

1 Dollar = 100 Cents

REPLACEMENT NOTES:

#19, 20: ZZ prefix.

REPUBLIC

NATIONAL BANK OF LIBERIA

1989 ISSUE

#19 replacement note: Serial # prefix *ZZ*.

		VG	VF	UNC
19	**5 Dollars**	1.00	2.50	7.00
	12.4.1989. Black and deep green on multicolor underprint. Latent image star at left, portrait J. J. Roberts at center, tapping trees at right. Back deep green on multicolor underprint; National Bank building at center Printer: TDLR.			

1991 ISSUE

#20 replacement note: Serial # prefix *ZZ*.

		VG	VF	UNC
20	**5 Dollars**	1.00	2.00	6.00
	6.4.1991. Similar to #19 but with arms at center. Printer: TDLR.			

CENTRAL BANK OF LIBERIA

1999 ISSUE

#21-23 arms at l. *REPUBLIC OF LIBERIA* on back.

		VG	VF	UNC
21	**5 Dollars** 1999. Red and brown on yellow underprint. Edward J. Roye at center. Female farmer harvesting rice on back. Date for establishment of Central Bank shown as 1974.	FV	FV	2.50

		VG	VF	UNC
22	**10 Dollars** 1999. Purple and black on multicolor underprint. Joseph Jenkins Roberts at center. Worker tapping rubber on back.	FV	FV	3.50

		VG	VF	UNC
23	**20 Dollars** 1999. Brown, black and olive on multicolor underprint. William V. S. Tubman, Sr. at center. Market on back.	FV	FV	5.00

#24-25 wmk: Arms.

		VG	VF	UNC
24	**50 Dollars** 1999. Purple; red and blue on multicolor underprint. Samuel Kayon Doe at center. Palm nut harvesting on back.	FV	FV	7.50

		VG	VF	UNC
25	**100 Dollars** 1999. Green, brown and black on multicolor underprint. William R. Tolbert, Jr. at center. Market woman and child on back.	FV	FV	15.00

2003 ISSUE

#26-30, *CENTRAL BANK OF LIBERIA* at trop on back. 2 sign. varieties.

		VG	VF	UNC
26	**5 Dollars** 2003. Red and brown on yellow underprint.	FV	FV	2.50

		VG	VF	UNC
27	**10 Dollars** 2003. Purple and black on multicolor underprint.	FV	FV ·	3.50

28	**20 Dollars** 2003; 2004. Brown, black and olive on multicolor underprint.	FV	FV	5.00

		VG	VF	UNC
30	**100 Dollars** 2003. Green, brown and black on multicolor underprint.	FV	FV	15.00

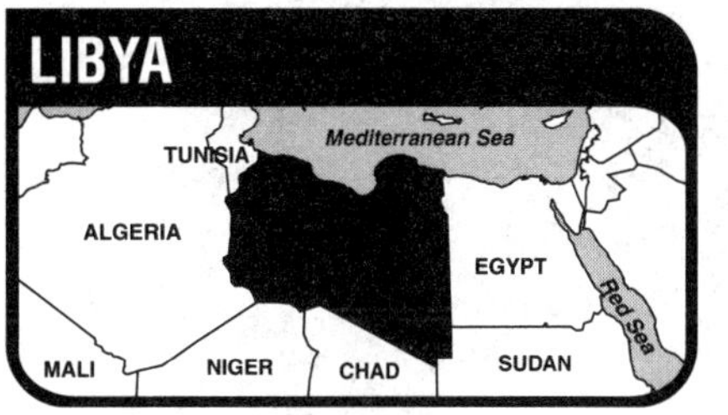

The Socialist People's Libyan Arab Jamahiriya, located on the north central coast of Africa between Tunisia and Egypt, has an area of 679,359 sq. mi. (1,759,540 sq. km.) and a population of 6.39 million. Capital: Tripoli. Crude oil, which accounts for 90 percent of the export earnings, is the mainstay of the economy.

Libya has been subjected to foreign rule throughout most of its history, various parts of it having been ruled by the Phoenicians. Carthaginians, Vandals, Byzantines, Greeks, Romans, Egyptians, and in the following centuries the Arab's language, culture and religion were adopted by the indigenous population. Libya was conquered by the Ottoman Turks in 1553, and remained under Turkish domination, becoming a Turkish vilayet in 1835, until it was conquered by Italy and made into a colony in 1911. The name "Libya", the ancient Greek name for North Africa exclusive of Egypt, was given to the colony by Italy in 1934. Libya came under Allied administration after the fall of Tripoli on Jan. 23, 1943 and was divided into zones of British and French control. On Dec. 24, 1951, in accordance with a United Nations resolution, Libya proclaimed its independence as a constitutional monarchy, thereby becoming the first country to achieve independence through the United Nations. The monarchy was overthrown by a coup d'etat on Sept. 1, 1969, and Libya was established as a republic.

RULERS:

Idris I, 1951-1969

MONETARY SYSTEM:

1 Piastre = 10 Milliemes
1 Pound = 100 Piastres = 1000 Milliemes, 1951-1971
1 Dinar = 1000 Dirhams, 1971-

CONSTITUTIONAL MONARCHY

BANK OF LIBYA

LAW OF 5.2.1963 - FIRST ISSUE

Pound System

#23-27 crowned arms at l. Wmk: Arms.

		VG	VF	UNC
23	**1/4 Pound** L.1963/AH1382. Red on multicolor underprint.			
	a. Issued note.	3.50	15.00	125.
	s. Specimen.	—	—	—
24	**1/2 Pound** L.1963/AH1382. Purple on multicolor underprint.	5.00	30.00	185.
25	**1 Pound** L.1963/AH1382. Blue on multicolor underprint.	8.00	45.00	350.

26	**5 Pounds**	VG	VF	UNC
	L.1963/AH1382. Green on multicolor underprint.	20.00	150.	—
27	**10 Pounds**			
	L.1963/AH1382. Brown on multicolor underprint.	27.50	250.	—

LAW OF 5.2.1963 - SECOND ISSUE

#28-32 crowned arms at l. Reduced size notes. Wmk: Arms.

28	**1/4 Pound**	VG	VF	UNC
	L.1963/AH1382. Red on multicolor underprint.	4.00	20.00	150.
29	**1/2 Pound**			
	L.1963/AH1832. Purple on multicolor underprint.	5.00	32.50	250.
30	**1 Pound**			
	L.1963/AH1382. Blue on multicolor underprint.	10.00	50.00	350.

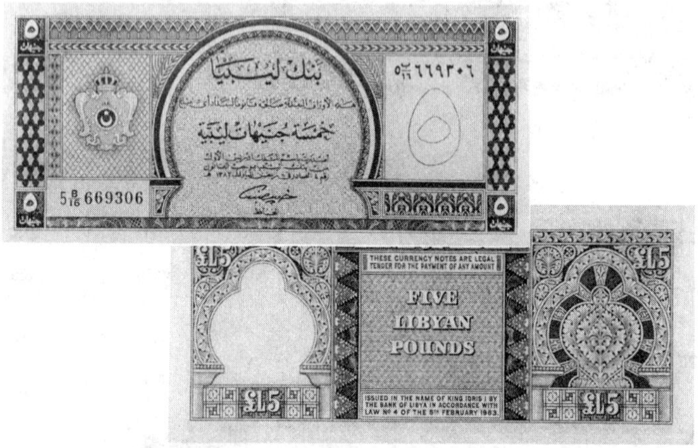

31	**5 Pounds**	VG	VF	UNC
	L.1963/AH1382. Green on multicolor underprint.	20.00	150.	700.

32	**10 Pounds**	VG	VF	UNC
	L.1963/AH1382. Brown on multicolor underprint.	30.00	225.	1500.

SOCIALIST PEOPLES REPUBLIC

CENTRAL BANK OF LIBYA

SIGNATURE VARIETIES			
1		3	
2		4	
5		6	

1971 ISSUE - SERIES 1

Dinar System

#33-37 w/ or w/o Arabic inscription at bottom of wmk. area at lower r. on face. Wmk: Arms (Heraldic eagle).

33	**1/4 Dinar**	VG	VF	UNC
	ND. Orange-brown on multicolor underprint. Arms at left. Doorway on back.			
	a. Without inscription (1971).	5.00	20.00	150.
	b. With inscription (1972).	1.00	3.50	25.00

34	**1/2 Dinar**	VG	VF	UNC
	ND. Purple on multicolor underprint. Arms at left. Oil refinery on back.			
	a. Without inscription (1971).	7.50	35.00	225.
	b. With inscription (1972).	2.00	5.00	35.00

35 1 Dinar

ND. Blue on multicolor underprint. Gate and minaret at left. Hilltop fortress on back.

	VG	VF	UNC
a. Without inscription (1971).	10.00	45.00	425.
b. With inscription (1972).	3.00	7.50	55.00

36 5 Dinars

ND. Olive on multicolor underprint. Arms at left. Fortress at center on back.

	VG	VF	UNC
a. Without inscription (1971).	20.00	75.00	500.
b. With inscription (1972).	5.00	15.00	125.

37 10 Dinars

ND. Blue-gray on multicolor underprint. Omar El Mukhtar at left. Three horsemen at center on back.

	VG	VF	UNC
a. Without inscription (1971).	35.00	100.	650.
b. With inscription (1972).	4.00	12.50	55.00

#38-42 *Deleted.* See #33b-37b.

1980-81 Issue - Series 2

#42A-46 wmk: Heraldic falcon.

42A 1/4 Dinar

ND (1981). Green on multicolor underprint. Ruins at left. Fortress and palms at center right on back.

	VG	VF	UNC
a. Signature 1.	.45	1.75	6.00
b. Signature 2.	.40	1.50	4.50

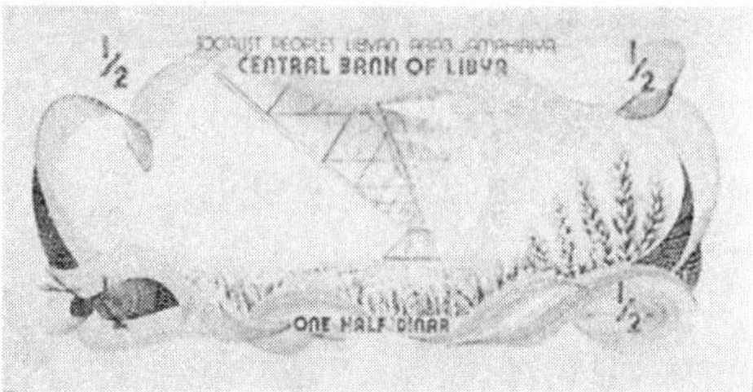

43 1/2 Dinar

ND (1981). Green on multicolor underprint. Petroleum refinery at left. Irrigation system above wheat field on back.

	VG	VF	UNC
a. Signature 1.	.75	3.00	7.50
b. Signature 2.	.50	2.25	6.00

44 1 Dinar

ND (1981). Green on multicolor underprint. Mosque at left. Interior of mosque at center right on back.

	VG	VF	UNC
a. Signature 1.	2.00	4.00	11.50
b. Signature 2.	1.65	3.00	10.00

45 **5 Dinars**

		VG	VF	UNC
	ND (1980). Green on multicolor underprint. Camels at left. Crowd around monument at center right on back.			
	a. Signature 1.	2.00	10.00	37.50
	b. Signature 2.	2.00	9.00	25.00

46 **10 Dinars**

		VG	VF	UNC
	ND (1980). Green on multicolor underprint. Omar El Mukhtar at left. Large crowd below hilltop fortress at center on back.			
	a. Signature 1.	4.00	22.00	85.00
	b. Signature 2.	4.00	20.00	50.00

1984 Issue - Series 3

#47-51 designs generally similar to previous issue. Sign. 2.

47 **1/4 Dinar** — VG .50 — VF 1.50 — UNC 4.00

ND (1984). Green and brown on multicolor underprint. Similar to #42A.

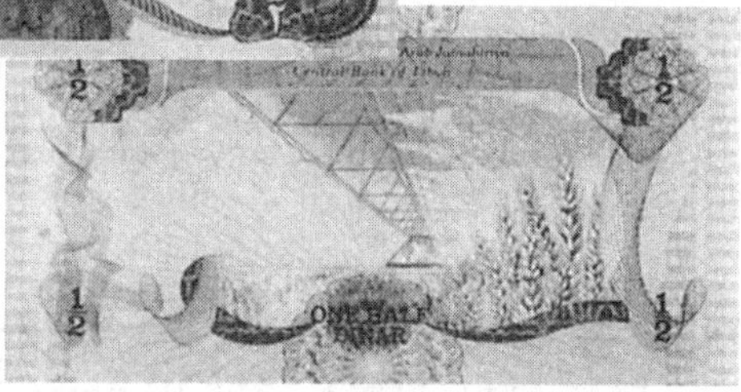

48 **1/2 Dinar** — VG .50 — VF 2.00 — UNC 4.00

ND (1984). Green and purple on multicolor underprint. Similar to #43.

49 **1 Dinar** — VG 1.00 — VF 4.00 — UNC 12.50

ND (1984). Green and dark blue on multicolor underprint. Similar to #44.

50 **5 Dinars** — VG 2.00 — VF 8.50 — UNC 35.00

ND (1984). Dark olive-green and light green on multicolor underprint. Similar to #45.

NOTICE

Readers with unlisted dates, signature varieties, etc. are invited to submit photocopies of their notes to: Standard Catalog of World Paper Money, 700 East State St. Iola, WI 54990-0001, E-Mail: george.cuhaj@fwpubs.com.

			VG	VF	UNC
51	**10 Dinars**	ND (1984). Dark green and blue-green on multicolor underprint. Similar to #46.	3.50	15.00	45.00

1988-90 Issue - Series 4

#52-58 wmk: Heraldic falcon. Sign. 3.

			VG	VF	UNC
52	**1/4 Dinar**	ND (ca.1990). Green, blue and black on multicolor underprint. Ruins at center. Back brown; English text at top, fortress with palm trees at left center. Design features similar to #47.	FV	1.00	2.00

			VG	VF	UNC
53	**1/2 Dinar**	ND (ca.1990). Deep purple and aqua on multicolor underprint. Oil refinery at left center. Back purple; English text at top, irrigation system at left center. Similar to #48.	FV	1.75	3.00

			VG	VF	UNC
54	**1 Dinar**	ND (1988). Blue and green on multicolor underprint. M. Kadaffy at left center. Temple at lower center right on back.	FV	2.00	7.50
55	**5 Dinars**	ND (ca.1991). Brown and violet on multicolor underprint. Camel at center. Crowd and monument on back. English text at top.	FV	7.50	25.00
56	**10 Dinars**	ND (1989). Green on multicolor underprint. Omar el-Mukhtar at left. Arabic text; Large crowd before hilltop fortress at center. Octagonal frame without underprint at upper right on back.	FV	14.00	40.00

1991-93 Issue - Series 4

			VG	VF	UNC
57	**1/4 Dinar**	ND (ca.1991). Green, blue and black on multicolor underprint. Like #52, but with all Arabic text on back. More pink in underprint on face.			
		a. Signature 3.	FV	FV	4.00
		b. Signature 4.	FV	FV	3.00
		c. Signature 5.	FV	FV	2.50

			VG	VF	UNC
58	**1/2 Dinar**	ND (ca. 1991). Deep purple and blue on multicolor underprint. Like #53, but with all Arabic text on back. More color in underprint at upper corners.			
		a. Signature 3.	FV	FV	4.00
		b. Signature 4.	FV	FV	4.00
		c. Signature 5.	FV	FV	4.00

NOTICE

Readers with unlisted dates, signature varieties, etc. are invited to submit photocopies of their notes to: Standard Catalog of World Paper Money, 700 East State St. Iola, WI 54990-0001, E-Mail: george.cuhaj@fwpubs.com.

59	1 Dinar	VG	VF	UNC
	ND (1993). Blue and green on multicolor underprint. Like #54, but with modified green and pink underprint.			
	a. Signature 4.	FV	FV	6.00
	b. Signature 5.	FV	FV	5.00

60	5 Dinars	VG	VF	UNC
	ND (ca. 1991). Brown and violet on multicolor underprint. Like #55, but with all Arabic text on back.			
	a. Signature 3.	FV	FV	20.00
	b. Signature 4.	FV	FV	17.50
	c. Signature 5.	FV	FV	15.00

61	10 Dinars	VG	VF	UNC
	ND (1991). Green on multicolor underprint. Like #56, but with underprint in octagonal frame at upper right on back. Signature 4; 5.	FV	FV	37.50

2002 Issue - Series 5

62	1/4 Dinar	VG	VF	UNC
	ND (2002). Ochre on multicolor underprint. Ruins at center. Walled compound on back. Signature 4.	FV	FV	2.00

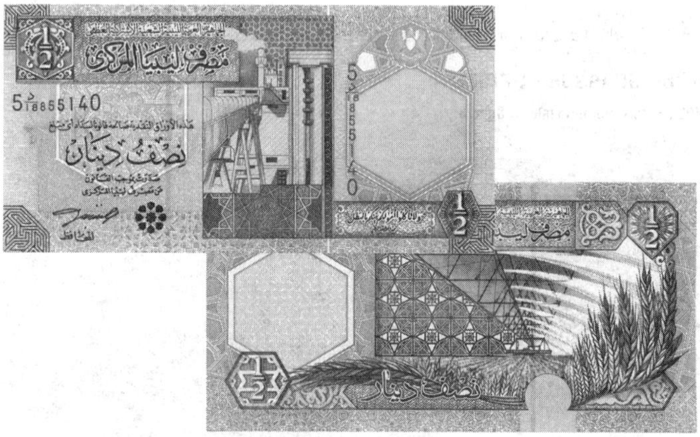

63	1/2 Dinar	VG	VF	UNC
	ND (2002). Dark blue on blue and multicolor underprint. Oil refinery at center. Irrigation system on back. Signature 4.	FV	FV	3.00

64	1 Dinar	VG	VF	UNC
	ND (2002). Blue and green on multicolor underprint. Muammar Qadhafy at center. Mosque on back. Signature 4; 5.	FV	FV	6.00

65	5 Dinars	VG	VF	UNC
	ND (2002). Green and yellow on multicolor underprint. Camels at center. Monument and crowd on back. Signature 4; 5.	FV	FV	15.00

		VG	VF	UNC
66	**10 Dinars** ND (2002). Green and dark green on multicolor underprint. Omar el-Mukhtar at center left. Fortress and crowd on back. Signature 4.	FV	FV	27.50

		VG	VF	UNC
67	**20 Dinars** ND (2002). Green, blue and brown on multicolor underprint. Map with water tunnels at center. Mohmar Kadaffy with OAU members at center, map of Africa at right. 9.9.1999 meeting date on back. Signature 6. Series 1.	FV	FV	40.00

2004 Issue - Series 6

#68-70 like #64-66 but reduced in size.

		VG	VF	UNC
68	**1 Dinar** ND (2004). Multicolor. Muammar Qadhafy at center. Mosque on back.	FV	FV	7.50
69	**5 Dinars** ND (2004). Multicolor. Camels at center. Monument and crowd on back.	FV	FV	12.50
70	**10 Dinars** ND (2004). Multicolor. Omar el-Mukhtar at center. Fortress and crowd on back.	FV	FV	22.50

The Republic of Lithuania southernmost of the Baltic states in east Europe, has an area of 26,173 sq. mi. (65,301 sq. km.) and a population of 3.69 million. Capital: Vilnius. The economy is d on livestock raising and manufacturing. Hogs, cattle, hides and electric motors are exported.

Lithuania emerged as a grand duchy joined to Poland through the Lublin Union in 1569. In the 15th century it was a major power of central Europe, stretching from the Baltic to the Black Sea. Following the 1795 partition of Poland by Austria, Prussia and Russia, Lithuania came under Russian domination and did not regain its independence until shortly before the end of World War I when it declared itself a sovereign republic. The republic was occupied by Soviet troops in June of 1940 and annexed to the U.S.S.R. Following the German occupation of 1941-44, it was retaken by Russia and reestablished as a member republic of the Soviet Union. Western countries, including the United States, did not recognize Lithuania's incorporation into the Soviet Union.

Lithuania declared its independence March 11, 1990. Lithuania was seated in the UN General Assembly on Sept. 17, 1991; and joined the European Union on May 1, 2004.

MONETARY SYSTEM:

1 Litas = 100 Centu

Republic

Lietuvos Bankas

Bank of Lithuania

1991 Issue

Talonas System

#29-31 plants on face, arms at ctr. in gray on back. W/ and w/o counterfeiting clause at bottom. Wmk. paper.

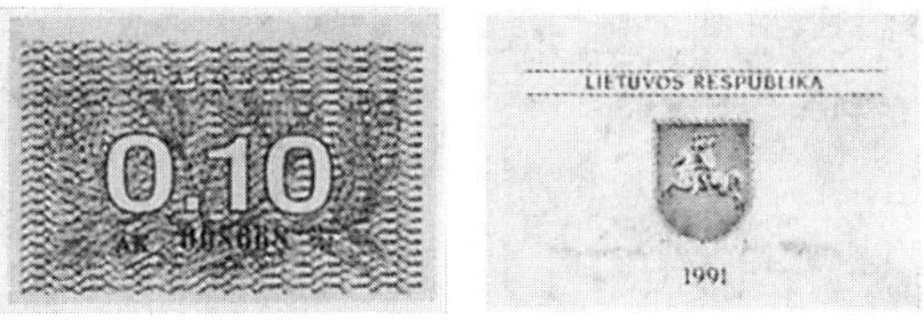

		VG	VF	UNC
29	**0.10 Talonas** 1991. Brown on green and gold underprint.			
	a. Without 3 lines of black text at center.	.10	.25	1.00
	b. With 3 lines of black text at center.	.10	.25	.25
	x. Error. As b. but with text: *PAGAL ISTATYMA* repeated.	.50	.75	3.00

		VG	VF	UNC
30	**0.20 Talonas** 1991. Lilac on green and gold underprint. Three lines of black text at center.	.10	.25	.50

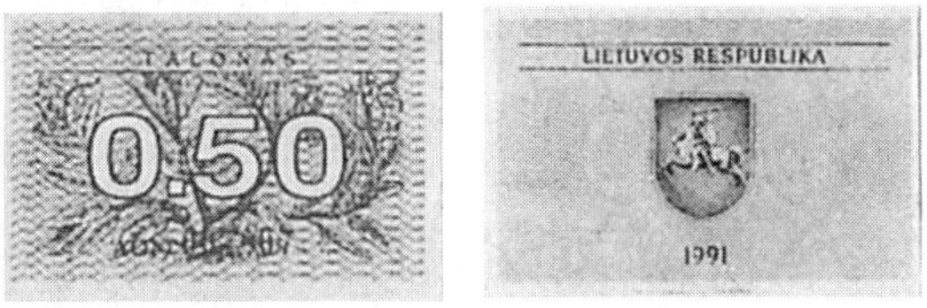

		VG	VF	UNC
31	**0.50 Talonas** 1991. Blue-green on green and gold underprint.			
	a. Without 3 lines of black text at center.	.10	.25	2.00
	b. With 3 lines of black text at center.	.10	.25	.50
	x1. As b. but first word of text: *VALSTYBINIS.* (error).	.50	.75	3.00
	x2. As x1 but with inverted text. (contemporary counterfeit).	—	—	—

#32-38 value w/plants at ctr., arms in gray at r. Animals or birds on back. Wmk: Lg. squarish diamond w/symbol of the republic throughout paper. W/ and w/o counterfeiting clause at bottom of face.

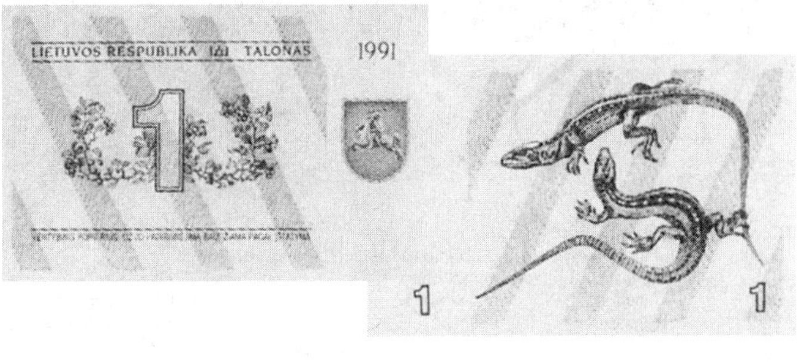

		VG	VF	UNC
32	**1 (Talonas)** 1991. Brown on yellow-gold underprint. Numeral with cranberry branch at center. Two lizards on back.			
	a. Without text.	.10	.25	2.00
	b. With text.	.10	.25	2.00

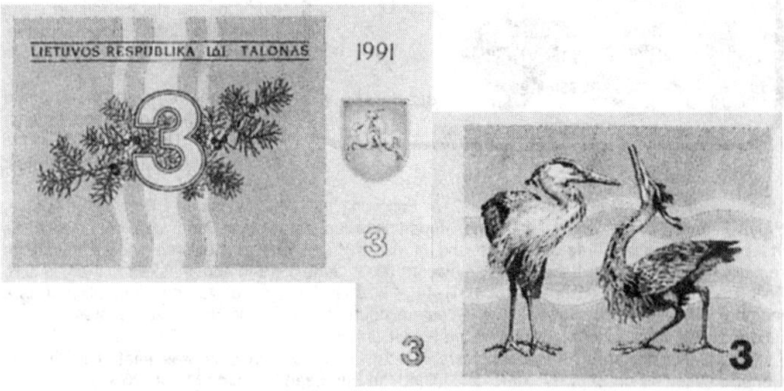

		VG	VF	UNC
33	**3 (Talonas)** 1991. Dark green and gray on blue-green, ochre and brown underprint. Numeral with juniper branch at center. Two Grey Herons on back.			
	a. Without text.	.10	.25	3.00
	b. With text.	.10	.25	3.00

		VG	VF	UNC
34	**5 (Talonas)** 1991. Dark purple and gray on blue and gray underprint. Numeral with oak tree branch at center. Osprey at center on back.			
	a. Without text.	.75	1.00	4.00
	b. With text.	.50	.75	3.00

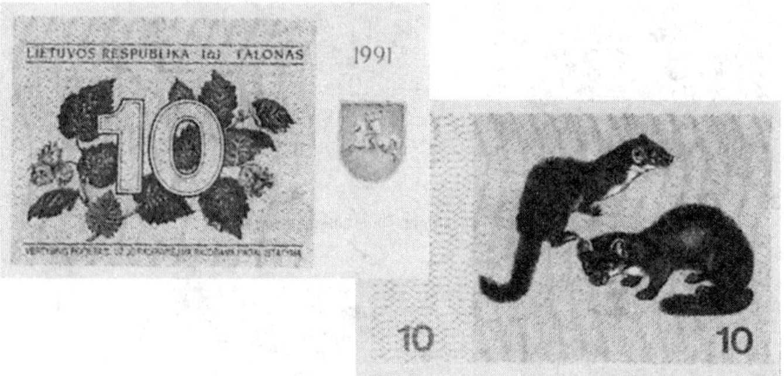

		VG	VF	UNC
35	**10 (Talonas)** 1991. Brown on pinkish underprint. Numerals with walnut tree branch at center. Two martens on back.			
	a. Without text.	.50	1.50	10.00
	b. With text.	.50	1.00	4.00

		VG	VF	UNC
36	**25 (Talonas)** 1991. Purplish gray on blue and orange underprint. Numerals with pine tree branch at center. Lynx on back.			
	a. Without text.	1.00	2.50	15.00
	b. With text.	.50	1.00	5.00

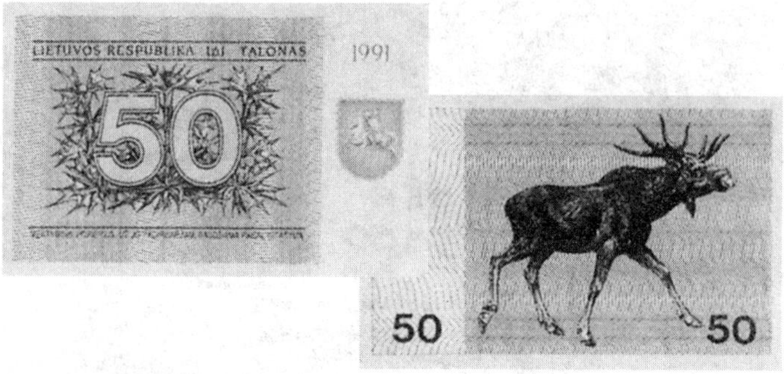

		VG	VF	UNC
37	**50 (Talonas)** 1991. Green and orange on orange underprint. Numerals with seashore plant at center. Moose on back.			
	a. Without text.	1.00	2.00	10.00
	b. With text.	.50	1.00	4.00

		VG	VF	UNC
38	**100 (Talonas)** 1991. Green and brown on brown underprint. Numerals and dandelions at center. European bison on back.			
	a. Without text.	1.50	3.00	15.00
	b. With text.	.50	2.00	5.00

1992 Issue

#39-44 value on plant at ctr., shield of arms at r. on face. Wmk. as #32-38. Smaller size than #32-38.

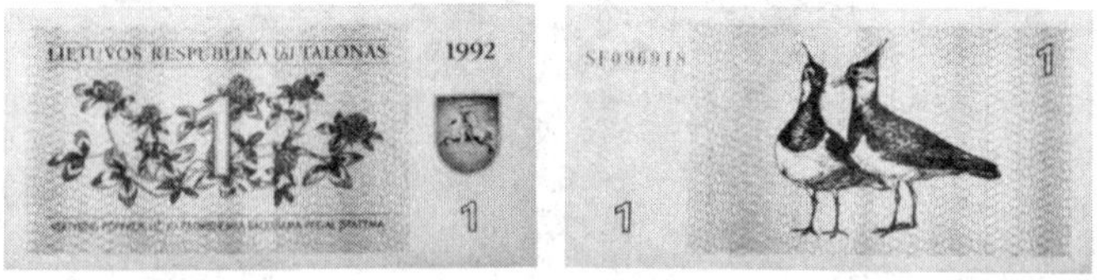

		VG	VF	UNC
39	**1 (Talonas)** 1992. Brown on orange and ochre underprint, dark brown shield. Two Eurasian lapwings on back.	.10	.25	1.00

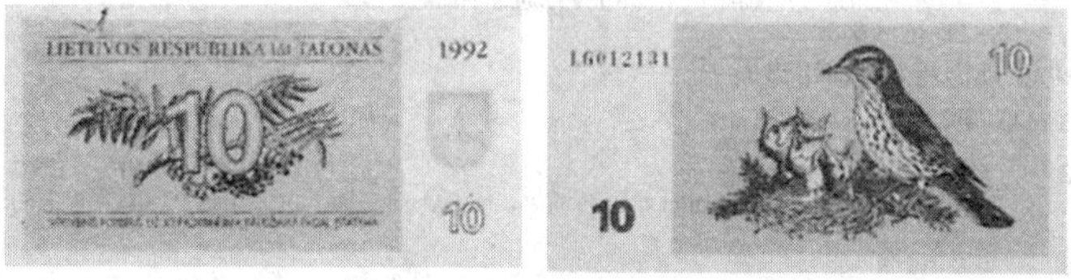

		VG	VF	UNC
40	**10 (Talonas)** 1992. Brown on tan and ochre underprint, gray shield. Nest of mistle thrush on back.	.10	1.00	10.00

		VG	VF	UNC
41	**50 (Talonas)** 1992. Dark grayish green on light green and gray underprint, dark gray-green shield. Two black grouse on back.	1.00	4.00	20.00

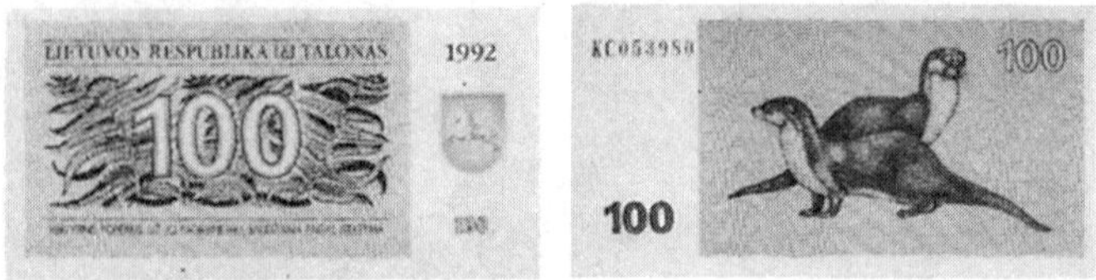

		VG	VF	UNC
42	**100 (Talonas)** 1992. Grayish purple on blue and red-orange underprint, gray shield. Two otters on back.	.25	.75	6.00

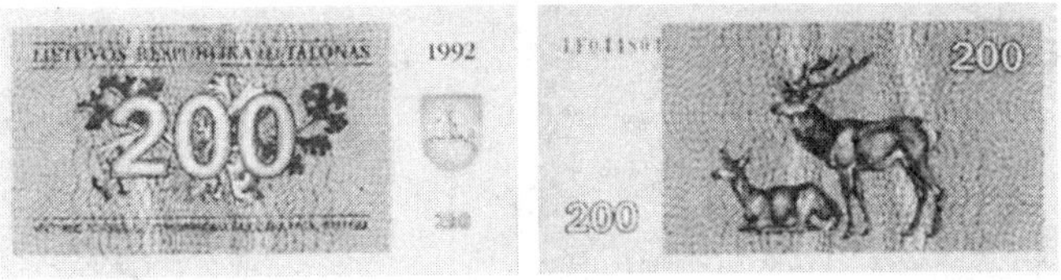

43 200 (Talonas) — VG / VF / UNC

1992. Dark brown on red and brown underprint, gray shield. Two Red Deer on back.

	VG	VF	UNC
a. Issued note.	.40	1.50	6.00
x. Error. without gray shield at right.	—	—	—

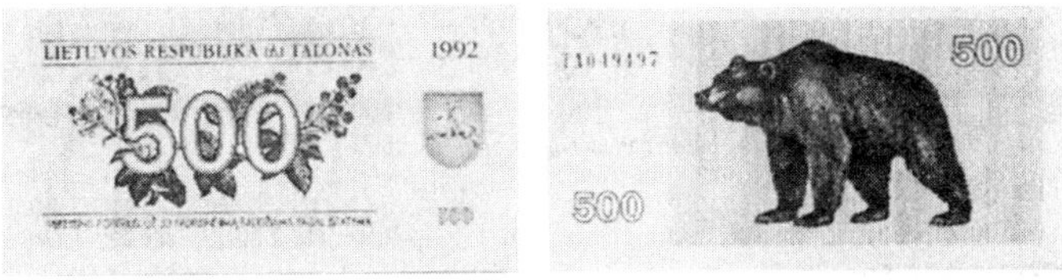

44 500 (Talonas)

	VG	VF	UNC
1992. Brown-violet on blue underprint, brown shield. Brown Bear on back.	1.00	2.25	5.00

1993 Issue

#45 and 46 arms in brown at l., value w/branches at ctr. Animals on back. Wmk: Pattern repeated, circle w/design inside.

45 200 Talonu

	VG	VF	UNC
1993. Brown and red on blue underprint. Two Red Deer on back.	.50	1.25	3.00

46 500 Talonu

	VG	VF	UNC
1993. Brown on blue and brown underprint. Two wolves on back.	.20	.75	2.50

Note: #46 was withdrawn after 6 weeks.

1991 Dated Issue (1993)

Litu System

#47-49 arms "Vytis" at upper r. on back and as wmk. Printer: USBNC (w/o imprint).

47 10 Litu

1991 (1993). Brownish black and brown on tan underprint. Aviators Steponas Darius and Stasys Girénas at center. Monoplane "Lituanica" at upper center on back.

	VG	VF	UNC
a. *GIRENAS* name without accent dot on E (error).	FV	4.00	15.00
b. *GIRÉNAS* name with accent dot on E.	FV	5.00	20.00
x. Quadrupled engraved face printing. Error.	—	—	250.

48 20 Litu

	VG	VF	UNC
1991 (1993). Dark brown and green on violet and tan underprint. Jonas Maironis at right. Liberty at left, Museum of History in Kaunas at center on back.	FV	7.00	30.00

49 50 Litu

1991 (1993). Yellowish black and brown on ochre and tan underprint. Jonas Basanavicius at right. Cathedral at Vilnius at left on back.

	VG	VF	UNC
a. VALDYBOS with regular L.	10.00	20.00	45.00
b. VALDYBOS with heel on L (error).	—	30.00	50.00

50 100 Litu

1991 (1993); 1994. Deep green, blue and brown on multicolor underprint. Arms "Vytis" at center, Simonas Daukantas at right. Back brown and green; aerial view of University of Vilnius at left center.

	VG	VF	UNC
a. 1991. One signature	FV	40.00	110.
b. 1994. Two signature (Not issued.)	—	—	—

51 500 Litu

	VG	VF	UNC
1991. Arms "Vytis" at center, Vincas Kudirka at right. Liberty bell on back. (Not issued).	—	—	—

52 1000 Litu

	VG	VF	UNC
1991. Arms "Vytis" at center, Mykolas Ciurlionis at right. Two kings on back. (Not issued).	—	—	—

1993; 1994 Issue

#53-58 wmk: Arms "Vytis." Shield w/"Vytis" at ctr. r. on back. Printer: TDLR (w/o imprint).

53 1 Litas

1994. Black and dark brown on orange and multicolor underprint. Julija Zemaite at right. Old church at left on back.

	VG	VF	UNC
a. Issued note.	.50	.75	3.00
b. Uncut sheet of 40.	—	—	120.
r. Replacement note, ZZ serial # prefix.	.75	1.00	7.50

54	**2 Litai**	VG	VF	UNC
	1993. Black and dark green on pale green and multicolor underprint. Samogitian Bishop Motiejus Valancius at center right. Trakai castle at left on back.			
	a. Issued note.	.50	1.00	6.00
	b. Uncut sheet of 40.	—	—	200.
	r. Replacement note, ZZ serial # prefix.	1.00	2.00	7.50

55	**5 Litai**	VG	VF	UNC
	1993. Purple, violet and dark blue-green on multicolor underprint. Jonas Jablonskis at center right. Mother and daughter at spinning wheel at left center on back.			
	a. Issued note.	1.50	2.50	10.00
	b. Uncut sheet of 40.	—	—	350.
	r. Replacement note, ZZ serial # prefix.	1.00	4.00	12.50

56	**10 Litu**	VG	VF	UNC
	1993. Dark blue, dark green, and brown-violet on multicolor underprint. Similar to #47 but pilots at right.			
	a. Issued note.	FV	FV	15.00
	r. Replacement note, * serial # prefix.	3.00	7.50	20.00

57	**20 Litu**	VG	VF	UNC
	1993. Dark brown, purple and deep blue-green on multicolor underprint. Similar to #48.			
	a. Issued note.	FV	FV	20.00
	r. Replacement note, * serial # prefix.	4.00	8.00	17.50

58	**50 Litu**	VG	VF	UNC
	1993. Dark brown, red-brown and blue-black on multicolor underprint. Similar to #49.			
	a. Issued note.	FV	FV	40.00
	r. Replacement note, * serial # prefix.	12.50	16.00	50.00

1997-2000 Issue

#59-61 printer: G&D (w/o imprint).

59	**10 Litu**	VG	VF	UNC
	1997. Dark blue, dark green and brown-violet on multicolor underprint. Like #56 but with one signature. Watermark: Arms "Vytis".	FV	FV	15.00

60	**20 Litu**	VG	VF	UNC
	1997. Dark brown, purple and deep green on multicolor underprint. Like #57 but with one signature. Watermark: Jonas Maironis.	FV	FV	20.00

61	**50 Litu**	VG	VF	UNC
	1998. Brown and green on ochre and multicolor underprint. Jonas Basanavicius at right. Vilnius Cathedral, belfry and Gediminas hill on back.	FV	FV	40.00

		VG	VF	UNC
62	**100 Litu** 2000. Dark green and green on multicolor underprint. Simonas Daukantas at right. View of Vilnius's Old Town section on back. Printer: OFZ.	FV	FV	80.00

		VG	VF	UNC
63	**200 Litu** 1997. Dark blue on blue and multicolor underprint. Vilius Vydúnas at right, "Vytis" at lower left center. Klaipeda Lighthouse at left on back. Printer: G&D.	FV	FV	100.

		VG	VF	UNC
64	**500 Litu** 2000. Brown and rose on multicolor underprint. Vincas Kudirka at right. Bell of Freedom of Lithuania against landscape view on back. Printer: G&D.	FV	FV	200.

2001-03 Issue

#65-67 printer: OFZ. Replacement notes *AZ* serial # prefix.

		VG	VF	UNC
65	**10 Litu** 2001. Violet and blue on multicolor underprint. Like #59 but with additional security features and airplane hologram at lower left. Watermark: "Vytis."	FV	FV	9.00

		VG	VF	UNC
66	**20 Litu** 2001. Dark brown on multicolor underprint. Similar to #60 but with additional security features. Book and quill hologram at lower left. Watermark: Jonas Maironis.	FV	FV	12.50

		VG	VF	UNC
67	**50 Litu** 2003. Brown and green on ochre and multicolor underprint. Jonas Basanavicius at right and as watermark. Vilnius Cathedral, belfry and Gediminas hill on back. Like #61 but with addtional security features.	FV	FV	30.00

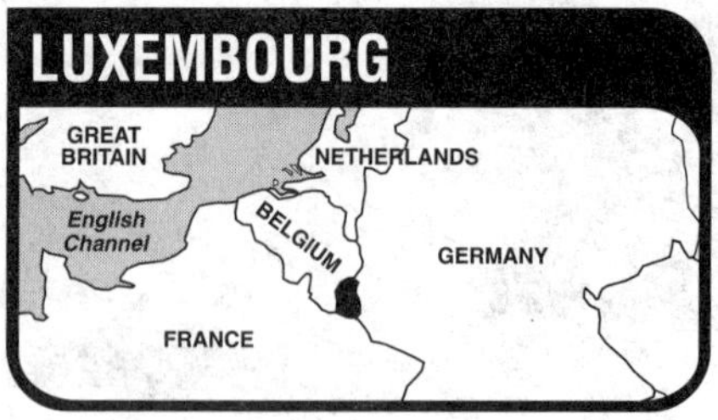

The Grand Duchy of Luxembourg is located in western Europe between Belgium, Germany and France. It has an area of 998 sq. mi. (2,586 sq. km.) and a population of 430,000. Capital: Luxembourg. The economy is d on steel - Luxembourg's per capita production of 16 tons is the highest in the world.

Founded about 963, Luxembourg was a prominent country of the Holy Roman Empire; one of its sovereigns became Holy Roman Emperor as Henry VII, 1308. After being made a duchy by Emperor Charles IV, 1534, Luxembourg passed under the domination of Burgundy, Spain, Austria and France in 1443-1815. It regained autonomy under the Treaty of Vienna, 1815, as a grand duchy in union with the Netherlands, though ostensibly a member of the German Confederation. When Belgium seceded from the Kingdom of the Netherlands, in 1830, Luxembourg was forced to cede its greater western section to Belgium. The tiny duchy left the German Confederation in 1867 when the Treaty of London recognized it as an independent state and guaranteed its perpetual neutrality. Luxembourg was occupied by Germany and liberated by American forces in both world wars.

RULERS:

Charlotte, 1919-64
Jean, 1964-

MONETARY SYSTEM:

1 Franc = 100 Centimes, to 2001
1 Euro = 100 Cents, 2001-

BANQUE INTERNATIONALE A LUXEMBOURG

INTERNATIONAL BANK IN LUXEMBOURG

1968 ISSUE

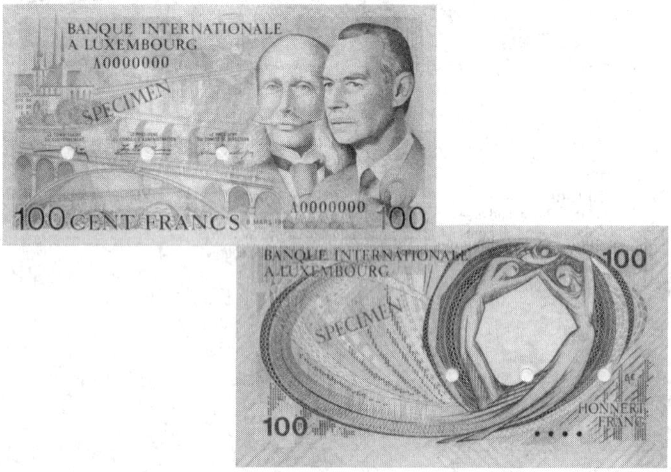

		VG	VF	UNC
14	**100 Francs** 1.5.1968. Green-blue and blue on multicolor underprint. Tower at left, portrait Grand Duke Jean at right. Steelworks and dam on back. Watermark: *BIL*. Printer: F-CO.			
	a. Issued note.	1.25	4.00	15.00
	s. Specimen.	—	—	65.00

1981 ISSUE

		VG	VF	UNC
14A	**100 Francs** 8.3.1981. Brown and tan on multicolor underprint. Bridge to Luxembourg City at left, Grand Duke Jean at right, Prince Henry of the Netherlands in the background. Back purple on multicolor underprint; two stylized female figures swirling around watermark area. Watermark: *BIL*.	1.00	3.50	12.50

GRAND DUCHÉ DE LUXEMBOURG

1961; 1963 ISSUE

#51-52B Portr. Grand Duchess Charlotte at r. and as wmk.

		VG	VF	UNC
51	**50 Francs** 6.2.1961. Brown on multicolor underprint. Landscape with combine harvester on back.			
	a. Issued note.	2.00	4.00	10.00
	s. Specimen, punched hole cancelled.	—	—	45.00
52	**100 Francs** 18.9.1963. Dark red on multicolor underprint. Hydroelectric dam on back.			
	a. Issued note.	5.00	10.00	30.00
	s. Specimen, punched hole cancelled.	—	—	65.00

		VG	VF	UNC
52A	**500 Francs** ND. Ducal Palace on back. Specimen only.	—	—	2400.

		VG	VF	UNC
52B	**1000 Francs** ND. Crowned and mantled arms at center on back. Specimen only.	—	—	3000.

1966-72 ISSUE

#53-56 Grand Duke Jean at l. ctr.

53	**10 Francs**	VG	VF	UNC
	20.3.1967. Green on multicolor underprint. Grand Duchess Charlotte Bridge in city on back.			
	a. Issued note.	.75	2.25	5.00
	s. Specimen, punched hole cancelled.	—	—	75.00

54	**20 Francs**	VG	VF	UNC
	7.3.1966. Blue on multicolor underprint. Moselle River with dam and lock on back.			
	a. Issued note.	1.00	2.25	5.00
	s. Specimen, punched hole cancelled.	—	—	250.

55	**50 Francs**	VG	VF	UNC
	25.8.1972. Dark brown on multicolor underprint. Guilloche underprint at left. Factory on back.			
	a. Signature title: *LE MINISTRE DES FINANCES.*	2.00	4.00	8.50
	b. Signature title: *LE MINISTRE D'ÉTAT.*	2.00	3.50	7.00
	s. As a. Specimen, punched hole cancelled.	—	—	175.

56	**100 Francs**	VG	VF	UNC
	15.7.1970. Red on multicolor underprint. View of Adolphe Bridge on back.			
	a. Issued note.	FV	4.00	12.50
	s. Specimen, punched hole cancelled.	—	—	50.00

1980 ISSUE

57	**100 Francs**	VG	VF	UNC
	14.8.1980. Brownish red on multicolor underprint. Grand Duke Jean at center right, building at left. Back gold and red; city of Luxembourg scene. Signature varieties.			
	a. Issued note.	FV	4.50	7.50
	s. Specimen.	—	—	140.

INSTITUT MONETAIRE LUXEMBOURGEOIS

SIGNATURE VARIETIES MINISTRE DU TRESOR			
1	J. Poos	2	J. Santer

1985-93 ND ISSUE

#58-60 Grand Duke Jean at ctr. r. and as wmk.

58	**100 Francs**	VG	VF	UNC
	ND (1986). Red on multicolor underprint. Like #57, but with new issuer's name.			
	a. Without © symbol. signature 1. Series A-K.	FV	FV	6.50
	b. With © symbol. signature 2. Series L-.	FV	FV	4.50

59	1000 Francs	VG	VF	UNC
	ND (1985). Brown on multicolor underprint. Castle of Vianden at left, Grand Duke Jean at center. Building sketches at center right on back.			
	a. Issued note.	FV	FV	45.00
	s. Specimen.	—	—	275.
60	**5000 Francs**			
	ND(1993); 1996. Green, orange and olive-green on brown and multicolor underprint. Chateau de Clevaux at left. 17th century map, European Center at Luxembourg-Kirchberg at center right on back. Two signature varieties.			
	a. Serial # prefix A. ND.	FV	200.	300.
	b. Serial # Prefix B. 10.1996.	FV	FV	225.

Note: For later issues used in Luxembourg see European Union listings.

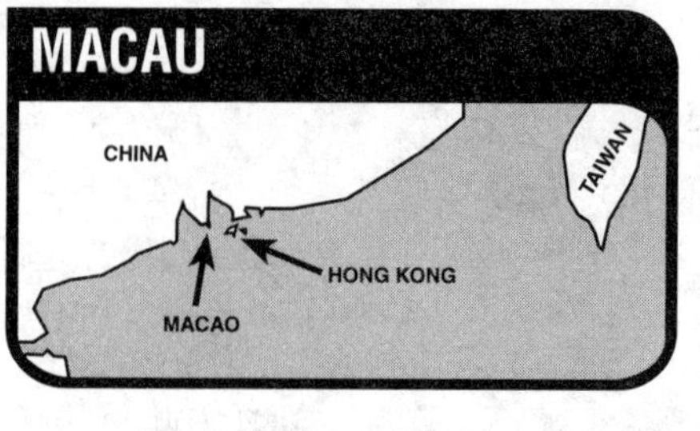

The Macau R.A.E.M., a former Portuguese overseas province located in the South China Sea 35 miles (56 km.) southwest of Hong Kong, consists of the peninsula and the islands of Taipa and Coloane. It has an area of 14 sq. mi. (21.45 sq. km.) and a population of 415,850. Capital: Macau. The economy is d on tourism, gambling, commerce and gold trading - Macau is one of the few entirely free markets for gold in the world. Cement, textiles, vegetable oils and metal products are exported.

Established by the Portuguese in 1557, Macau is the oldest European settlement in the Far East. The Chinese, while agreeing to Portuguese settlement, did not recognize Portuguese sovereign rights and the Portuguese remained largely under control of the Chinese until 1849, when the Portuguese abolished the Chinese custom house and declared the independence of the port. The Manchu government formally recognized the Portuguese right to *perpetual occupation* of Macau in 1887. In March 1940 the Japanese army demanded recognition of the nearby "puppet" government at Changshan. In Sept. 1943 they demanded installation of their "advisors" in lieu of a military occupation.

Macao became a special administrative area known as Macau R.A.E.M. under The Peoples Republic of China on December 20, 1999.

RULERS:

Portuguese from 1849-1999

MONETARY SYSTEM:

1 Pataca = 100 Avos

PORTUGUESE ADMINISTRATION

BANCO NACIONAL ULTRAMARINO

行銀理滙外海國洋西大

Ta Hsi Yang Kuo Hai Wai Hui Li Yin Hang

1963-68 ISSUE

#49, 50, and 52 portr. Bishop D. Belchior Carneiro at lower r. and as wmk. Bank seal w/sailing ship at l. Woman and sailing ships at ctr. on back. Printer: BWC.

49	5 Patacas	VG	VF	UNC
	21.3.1968. Brown on multicolor underprint. Signature varieties.			
	a. Issued note.	10.00	40.00	90.00
	s. Specimen.	—	—	110.

50	10 Patacas	VG	VF	UNC
	8.4.1963. Deep blue-violet on multicolor underprint. Signature varieties.			
	a. Issued note.	7.50	20.00	65.00
	s. Specimen.	—	—	125.

51 **100 Patacas** | VG | VF | UNC

1.8.1966. Brown on multicolor underprint. Portrait M. de Arriaga Brum da Silveira at right. Arms at left, flag atop archway at center on back. Printer: TDLR.

	VG	VF	UNC
a. Issued note.	100.	300.	900.
s. Specimen.	—	—	650.

52 **500 Patacas**

8.4.1963. Green on multicolor underprint.

	VG	VF	UNC
a. Issued note.	150.	300.	800.
s. Specimen.	—	—	600.

1973 Issue

53 **100 Patacas**

13.12.1973. Deep blue-violet on multicolor underprint. Ruins of S. Paulo Cathedral at right and as watermark. Junk at left, bank seal with sailing ship at center on back. Signature titles: *GOVERNADOR and ADMINISTRADOR* above signs.

	VG	VF	UNC
a. Issued note.	100.	225.	600.
s. Specimen.	—	—	450.

1976-79 Issue

#54-57 w/text: *CONSELHO DE GESTAO* at ctr.

54 **5 Patacas**

18.11.1976. Brown on multicolor underprint. Like #49. Signature varieties.

	VG	VF	UNC
a. Issued note.	5.00	25.00	55.00
s. Specimen.	—	—	150.

55 **10 Patacas**

7.12.1977. Deep blue-violet on multicolor underprint. Like #50.

	VG	VF	UNC
a. Issued note.	5.00	15.00	65.00
s. Specimen.	—	—	130.

56 **50 Patacas**

1.9.1976. Greenish-gray on multicolor underprint. Portrait L. de Camoes at right. Bank seal with sailing ship at left, woman and sailing ships at center on back.

	VG	VF	UNC
a. Issued note.	50.00	175.	500.
s. Specimen.	—	—	250.

57	100 Patacas	VG	VF	UNC
	8.6.1979. Blue on multicolor underprint. Like #53. Signature title: *PRESIDENTE* at left signature.			
	a. Issued note.	75.00	175.	450.
	s. Specimen.	—	—	375.

57A	500 Patacas	VG	VF	UNC
	24.4.1979. Green on multicolor underprint. Like #52.			
	a. Issued note.	125.	300.	600.
	s. Specimen. 2 different signature varieties r.h. side.	—	—	400.

1981; 1988 Issue

#58-62 bank seal w/sailing ship at l., 19th century harbor scene on back.

58	5 Patacas	VG	VF	UNC
	8.8.1981. Green on multicolor underprint. Temple at right.			
	a. With signature title: *PRESIDENTE* at left.	4.00	10.00	30.00
	b. With signature title: *VICE-PRESIDENTE* at left.	4.00	10.00	30.00
	c. Without signature title: *PRESIDENTE* at left.	4.00	10.00	30.00
	s. As b. Specimen.	—	—	120.

59	10 Patacas	VG	VF	UNC
	1981; 1984. Brown on multicolor underprint. Lighthouse with flag at right.			
	a. With signature title: *PRESIDENTE* at left. 2 decrees at upper left. 8.8.1981.	5.00	20.00	45.00
	b. As a. without signature title at left. 8.8.1981.	5.00	17.50	45.00
	c. Signature title as a. 3 decrees at upper left. 12.5.1984.	5.00	17.50	40.00
	d. With signature title: *VICE-PRESIDENTE* at left. 12.5.1984.	4.00	15.00	40.00
	e. Without signature title under signature at left. 3 signature varieties. 12.5.1984.	4.00	12.50	35.00
	s1. As a. Specimen.	—	—	100.
	s2. As d. Specimen.	—	—	100.

60	50 Patacas	VG	VF	UNC
	8.8.1981. Purple on multicolor underprint. Portrait L. de Camoes at right and as watermark.			
	a. With signature title: *PRESIDENTE* at left.	10.00	17.50	80.00
	b. Without signature title: *PRESIDENTE* at left.	10.00	17.50	80.00
	s1. As a. Specimen.	—	—	125.
	s2. As b. Specimen.	—	—	125.

61	100 Patacas	VG	VF	UNC
	1981; 1984. Blue and purple on multicolor underprint. Portrait C. Pessanha at right. Watermark: Man's head.			
	a. With signature title: *PRESIDENTE* at left. 8.8.1981; 12.5.1984.	12.50	20.00	100.
	b. Without signature title: *PRESIDENTE* at left. 8.8.1981; 12.5.1984.	12.50	20.00	90.00
	s1. As a. Specimen. 8.8.1981; 12.5.1984.	—	—	160.
	s2. As b. Specimen. 2 signature varieties. 8.8.1981.	—	—	160.

62	500 Patacas	VG	VF	UNC
	1981; 1984. Olive-green on multicolor underprint. Portrait V. de Morais at right. Peninsula on back.			
	a. 8.8.1981; 12.5.1984. signature title: *PRESIDENTE* at left.	65.00	90.00	350.
	b. 8.8.1981; 12.5.1984. signature title: *ADMINISTRADOR* at left.	65.00	90.00	325.
	s1. As a. Specimen.	—	—	300.
	s2. As b. Specimen.	—	—	300.
	s3. Specimen. 12.5.1984. signature title: *VICE-PRESIDENTE* at left.	—	—	600.

63 1000 Patacas

1988. Brown and yellow-orange on multicolor underprint. Stylized dragon at right. Modern view of bridge to Macao on back.

	VG	VF	UNC
a. Issued note.	130.	175.	400.
b. Specimen.	—	—	500.

1988 COMMEMORATIVE ISSUE

#64, 35th Anniversary Grand Prix

64 10 Patacas

	VG	VF	UNC
11.26-27.1988 (- old date 1984). Black overprint at left on face, at center on back of #59a. Issued in a small folder.	3.00	10.00	40.00

1990-96 ISSUE

#65-70 bank seal w/sailing ship at l., bridge and city view on back. Wmk: Junk.

65 10 Patacas

8.7.1991. Brown and olive-green on multicolor underprint. Building at right.

	VG	VF	UNC
a. Issued note.	3.00	6.00	15.00
s. Specimen.	—	—	150.

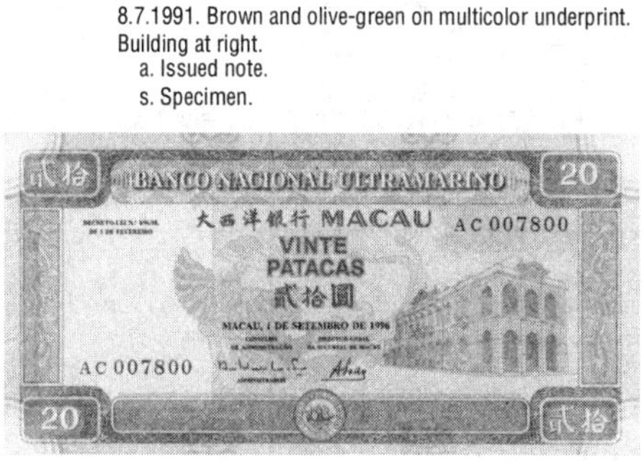

66 20 Patacas

1.9.1996. Lilac and purple on light green and multicolor underprint. B.N.U. building at right, facing dragons in border at left and right.

	VG	VF	UNC
a. Issued note.	4.00	10.00	25.00
s. As a. Specimen.	—	—	250.

67 50 Patacas

13.7.1992. Olive-brown on multicolor underprint. Holiday marcher with dragon costume at center right, man at right.

	VG	VF	UNC
a. Issued note.	12.00	20.00	40.00
s. As a. Specimen.	—	—	300.

68 100 Patacas

13.7.1992. Black on multicolor underprint. Early painting of Settlement at center, junk at right.

	VG	VF	UNC
a. Issued note.	25.00	30.00	75.00
s. As a. Specimen.	—	—	400.

69 500 Patacas

3.9.1990. Olive-green on multicolor underprint. Building at right. Two signature varieties.

	VG	VF	UNC
a. Issued note.	75.00	125.	300.
s1. Specimen. signature as a. Serial # AA00000.	—	—	600.
s2. Specimen. signature different. Serial # AW00000.	—	—	565.

70 1000 Patacas VG VF UNC

8.7.1991. Brown and yellow-orange on multicolor underprint. Like #63. Two signature varieties.

		VG	VF	UNC
70	**1000 Patacas**			
	a. 8.7.1991. signature title at left: *ADMINISTRATOR.* Serial # prefix AP.	175.	200.	450.
	b. 8.7.1991. signature title at left: *PRESIDENTE.* Serial # prefix AQ.	175.	200.	425.
	s. As b. Specimen but different signature Serial # AF00000.	—	—	600.

1999 Issue

All notes issued since 20 December 1999 are issued under Macao as a Special Administrative Region in China.

		VG	VF	UNC
71	**20 Patacas**			
	20.12.1999. Similar to #66.			
	a. Issued note.	FV	FV	12.50
	b. Uncut sheet of 12. Serial # prefix *JJ* or *KK*.	—	—	200.
	s. As a. Specimen.	—	—	100.

		VG	VF	UNC
72	**50 Patacas**			
	20.12.1999. Similar to #67.			
	a. Issued note.	FV	FV	27.50
	b. Uncut sheet of 12. Serial # prefix: *CC*.	—	—	375.
	s. As a. Specimen.	—	—	125.

		VG	VF	UNC
73	**100 Patacas**			
	20.12.1999. Similar to #68.			
	a. Issued note.	FV	FV	45.00
	s. Specimen.	—	—	150.

		VG	VF	UNC
74	**500 Patacas**			
	20.12.1999. Similar to #69.			
	a. Issued note.	FV	FV	195.
	s. Specimen.	—	—	300.

		VG	VF	UNC
75	**1000 Patacas**			
	20.12.1999. Similar to #70.			
	a. Signature title: *PRESIDENTE.*	FV	FV	375.
	b. Signature title: *ADMINISTRADOR.*	FV	FV	325.
	s. Specimen. As a.	FV	FV	400.

2001 Issue

		VG	VF	UNC
76	**10 Patacas**			
	8.1.2001. Dark red and orange with multicolor underprint. Like #65.			
	a. Signature title: *PRESIDENTE.*	FV	FV	9.50
	b. Signature title: *ADMINISTRATOR*	FV	FV	8.50
	c. Uncut sheet of 4. Archive use only.	—	—	—
	d. Uncut sheet of 40.	—	—	285.
	s. As a. Specimen.	—	—	125.

2003 Issue

77	10 Patacas	VG	VF	UNC
	8.6.2003. Dark red and orange on multicolor underprint. Like #76.	FV	FV	8.50

78	100 Patacas	VG	VF	UNC
	8.6.2003. Black on multicolor underprint. Similar to #68.	FV	FV	40.00

79	500 Patacas	VG	VF	UNC
	8.6.2003. Olive-green on multicolor underprint. Similar to #74.	FV	FV	185.

2005 Issue

Begining with the 2005 Issue, the 50 Pataca note was no longer issued.

80	10 Patacas	VG	VF	UNC
	8.8.2005 (2006).	FV	FV	7.50

81	20 Patacas	VG	VF	UNC
	8.8.2005 (2006).	FV	FV	12.50

82	100 Patacas	VG	VF	UNC
	8.8.2005 (2006).	FV	FV	40.00

83	500 Patacas	VG	VF	UNC
	8.8.2005 (2006).	FV	FV	165.

		VG	VF	UNC
04	**1000 Patacas** 8.8.2005 (2006).	FV	FV	300.

BANCO DA CHINA

Chung Kuo Yin Hang

1995; 1996 ISSUE

#90-95 Bank of China - Macau bldg. at l., lotus blossom at lower ctr. on back. Wmk: Lotus blossom(s).

		VG	VF	UNC
90	**10 Patacas** 16.10.1995. Dark brown and deep green on multicolor underprint. Farel de Guia lighthouse at right.	FV	FV	15.00

		VG	VF	UNC
91	**20 Patacas** 1.9.1996. Purple and violet on multicolor underprint. Ama Temple at right.	FV	FV	25.00

		VG	VF	UNC
92	**50 Patacas** 1995; 1997. Black, dark brown and brown on multicolor underprint. University of Macao at right.			
	a. 16.10.1995.	FV	FV	50.00
	b. 1.11.1997.	FV	FV	40.00

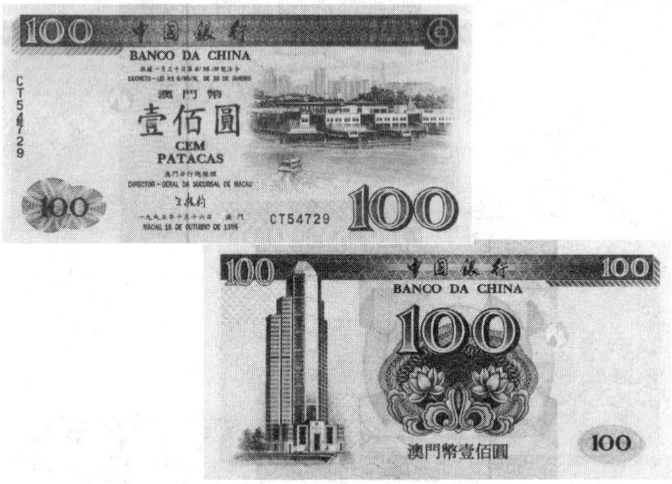

		VG	VF	UNC
93	**100 Patacas** 16.10.1995. Black, brown and purple on multicolor underprint. New terminal of Port Exterior at right.	FV	FV	75.00

		VG	VF	UNC
94	**500 Patacas** 16.10.1995. Dark green and dark blue on multicolor underprint. Ponte de Amizade bridge at right.	FV	FV	300.
95	**1000 Patacas** 16.10.1995. Brown, orange and red on multicolor underprint. Aerial view of Praia Oeste at right.	FV	FV	600.

1999 ISSUE

All notes issued since 20 December 1999 are issued under Macau as a Special Administrative Region in China.

96 **20 Patacas**

	VG	VF	UNC
20.12.1999. Purple and violet on multicolor underprint. Similar to #91.	FV	FV	12.50

97 **50 Patacas**

	VG	VF	UNC
20.12.1999. Black, dark brown and brown on multicolor underprint. Similar to #92.	FV	FV	27.50

98 **100 Patacas**

	VG	VF	UNC
1999; 2002. Black, brown and purple on multicolor underprint. Similar to #93.			
a. 20.12.1999.	FV	FV	42.50
b. 2.2.2002.	FV	FV	40.00

99 **500 Patacas**

	VG	VF	UNC
1999; 2002. Dark green and dark blue on multicolor underprint. Similar to #94.			
a. 20.12.1999.	FV	FV	200.
b. 2.2.2002.	FV	FV	185.

100 **1000 Patacas**

	VG	VF	UNC
20.12.1999. Brown, orange and red on multicolor underprint. Similar to #95.	FV	FV	325.

2001 Issue

101 **10 Patacas**

	VG	VF	UNC
2001; 2002. Red and orange on multicolor underprint. Like #90.			
a. 8.1.2001.	FV	FV	8.50
b. 2.2.2002.	FV	FV	8.00
c. Uncut sheet of 30. 8.1.2001.	—	—	235.

2003 Issue

#102-106 similar to previous issue but include increased security features, two metallic threads, champagne bubbles in the design and graduated serial #s.

Begining with the 2003 issue the 50 Pataca note was no longer issued.

102 **10 Patacas**

	VG	VF	UNC
8.12.2003 (2004). Red and orange on multicolor underprint.	FV	FV	7.50

103 **20 Patacas**

	VG	VF	UNC
8.12.2003 (2005).	FV	FV	13.50

104 **100 Patacas**

	VG	VF	UNC
8.12.2003 (2005).	FV	FV	42.50

		VG	VF	UNC
105	**500 Patacas** 8.12.2003 (2005).	FV	FV	185.
106	**1000 Patacas** 8.12.2003 (2005).	FV	FV	325.

COLLECTOR SERIES

BANCO NACIONAL ULTRAMARINO

1999 ISSUE

		Issue Price	Mkt. Value
CS1	**20-1000 Patacas** One each of #71-74 in a special folder. Matching serial #.	—	675.

BANCO DA CHINA AND BANCO NACIONAL ULTRAMARINO

2001 ISSUE

		Issue Price	Mkt. Value
CS2	**10 Pataca Sheetlets of 4** One mini-sheet from each bank in a special folder.	—	150.

The Republic of Macedonia is land-locked, and is bordered in the north by Yugoslavia, to the east by Bulgaria, in the south by Greece and to the west by Albania. It has an area of 9,923 sq. mi. (25,713 sq. km.) and its population at the 1991 census was 2.23 million. of which the predominating ethnic groups were Macedonians. The capital is Skopje.

The Slavs, settled in Macedonia since the 6th century, who had been Christianized by Byzantium, were conquered by the non-Slav Bulgars in the 7th century and in the 9th century formed a Macedo-Bulgarian empire, the western part of which survived until Byzantine conquest in 1014. In the 14th century it fell to Serbia, and in 1355 to the Ottomans. After the Balkan Wars of 1912-13 Turkey was ousted, and Serbia received the greater part of the territory, the balance going to Bulgaria and Greece. In 1918, Yugoslav Macedonia was incorporated into Serbia as "South Serbia," becoming a republic in the S.F.R. of Yugoslavia. Claims to the historical Macedonian territory have long been a source of contention between Bulgaria and Greece.

On Nov. 20, 1991 parliament promulgated a new constitution, and declared its independence on Nov. 20, 1992 and was admitted to the UN on April 8, 1993.

MONETARY SYSTEM:

1 DHNAR **(Denar) = 100** DHNI **(Deni)**

REPUBLIC

НАРОДНА БАНКА НА МАКЕДОНИЈА

NATIONAL BANK OF MACEDONIA

1992 ISSUE

#1-8 wmk. paper.

#1-6 farmers harvesting at l. Ilenden monument in Krushevo at l. on back.

		VG	VF	UNC
1	**10 (Denar)** 1992. Pale blue on lilac underprint.			
	a. Issued note.	.10	.20	.75
	s. Specimen. Red overprint ПРИМЕРОК.	—	—	—

		VG	VF	UNC
2	**25 (Denar)** 1992. Red on lilac underprint.			
	a. Issued note.	.10	.20	1.00
	s. Specimen.	—	—	—

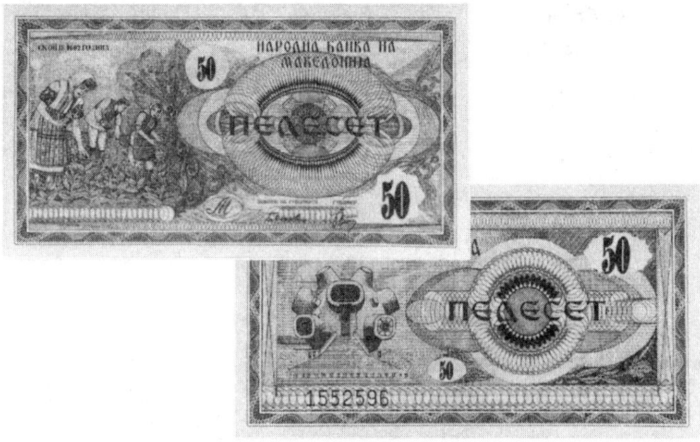

3 **50 (Denar)**
1992. Brown on ochre underprint.

	VG	VF	UNC
a. Issued note.	.10	.20	1.00
s. Specimen.	—	—	—

4 **100 (Denar)**
1992. Blue-gray on light blue underprint.

	VG	VF	UNC
a. Issued note.	—	.20	1.00
s. Specimen.	—	—	—

5 **500 (Denar)**
1992. Bright green on ochre underprint.

	VG	VF	UNC
a. Issued note.	.15	.20	1.25
s. Specimen.	—	—	—

6 **1000 (Denar)**
1992. Dull blue-violet on pink underprint.

	VG	VF	UNC
a. Issued note.	.25	.75	1.75
s. Specimen.	—	—	—

7 **5000 (Denar)**
1992. Deep brown and dull red on multicolor underprint. Woman at desk top computer at center. Ilenden monument at left on back.

	VG	VF	UNC
a. Issued note.	.25	1.50	6.00
s. Specimen.	—	—	—

8 **10,000 (Denar)**
1992. Blue-black on pink and gray underprint. Buildings at center right. Musicians at left of Ilenden monument at center right on back.

	VG	VF	UNC
a. Issued note.	.50	2.50	8.50
s. Specimen.	—	—	—

НАРОДНА БАНКА НА РЕПУБЛИКА МАКЕДОНИЈА

NATIONAL BANK OF THE REPUBLIC OF MACEDONIA

1993 ISSUE

Currency Reform

1 "New" Denar = 100 "Old" Denars

#9-12 wmk: Ilenden monument in Krushevo.

9	10 Denari	VG	VF	UNC
	1993. Light blue on multicolor underprint. Houses on mountainside in Krushevo at center right. Ilenden monument at left center on back.			
	a. Issued note.	FV	FV	1.50
	s. Specimen.	—	—	15.00

10	20 Denari	VG	VF	UNC
	1993. Wine-red on multicolor underprint. 16th century clock Tower in Skopje in vertical format on face. Turkish bath in Skopje at left center on back.			
	a. Issued note.	FV	FV	2.50
	s. Specimen.	—	—	15.00

11	50 Denari	VG	VF	UNC
	1993. Light red on multicolor underprint. National Bank building in Skopje at right. 12th century Orthodox Church of St. Pantileimon at left on back.			
	a. Issued note.	FV	FV	4.00
	s. Specimen.	—	—	15.00

12	100 Denari	VG	VF	UNC
	1993. Brown on multicolor underprint. Bovev Palace, National Museum in Ohrid at right. 11th century Monestery of St. Sophia in Ohrid at left on back.			
	a. Issued note.	FV	FV	8.00
	s. Specimen.	—	—	15.00

13	500 Denari	VG	VF	UNC
	1993. Greenish gray on multicolor underprint. Ohrid castle ruins at upper center. 12th century Orthodox church of St. John in Ohrid at left and as watermark on back.			
	a. Issued note.	FV	FV	35.00
	s. Specimen.	—	—	15.00

1996 ISSUE

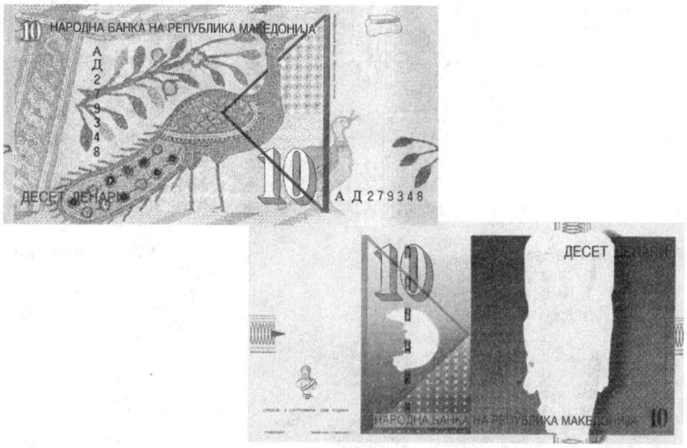

14	10 Denari	VG	VF	UNC
	8.9.1996; 8.1997; 1.2001; 1.2003. Deep olive-green with black text on multicolor underprint. Statue torso of Goddess Isida at center right and as watermark. Back blue-green, deep olive-green with black text on multicolor underprint. Mosaic of branch over peacock and duck.			
	a. Issued note.	FV	FV	1.50
	s. Specimen.	—	—	20.00

15	50 Denari	VG	VF	UNC
	8.9.1996; 8.1997; 1.2001. Brown with black text on multicolor underprint. Byzantine copper follis of Anastasia at center right and as watermark. Archangel Gabriel at left center on back.			
	a. Issued note.	FV	FV	3.00
	s. Specimen.	—	—	20.00

		VG	VF	UNC
16	**100 Denari** 8.9.1996; 8.1997; 1.2000; 1.2002; 5.2004. Brown with purple text on multicolor underprint. Large baroque wooden ceiling rosette in Debar town house at center right and as watermark. J. Harevin's engraving of Skopje "seen" through town house window frame at left center.			
	a. Issued note.	FV	FV	5.00
	s. Specimen.	—	—	25.00

		VG	VF	UNC
17	**500 Denari** 8.9.1996. Black and violet on multicolor underprint. 6th century golden death mask, Trebenista, Ohrid at right and as watermark. Violet poppy flower and plant at left center on back.			
	a. Issued note.	FV	FV	22.50
	s. Specimen.	—	—	25.00

		VG	VF	UNC
18	**1000 Denari** 8.9.1996. Brown and orange on multicolor underprint. 14th century icon of Madonna Episkepsis and Christ Child, church of St. Vrach-Mali, Ohrid at center right. Partial view of the St. Sophia church in Ohrid at left center. Watermark: Madonna.			
	a. Issued note.	FV	FV	40.00
	s. Specimen.	—	—	30.00

NOTICE

Readers with unlisted dates, signature varieties, etc. are invited to submit photocopies of their notes to: Standard Catalog of World Paper Money, 700 East State St. Iola, WI 54990-0001, E-Mail: george.cuhaj@fwpubs.com.

		VG	VF	UNC
19	**5000 Denari** 8.9.1996. Black and violet on olive-green and multicolor underprint. 6th century bronze figurine of Tetovo Maenad VI (horizontally) at center right and as watermark. 6th century mosaic of Cerberus the Dog tied to a fig tree, representing the watcher of Heaven (horizontally) at left center on back.			
	a. Issued note.	FV	FV	175.
	s. Specimen.	—	—	60.00

2000 Commemorative Issue

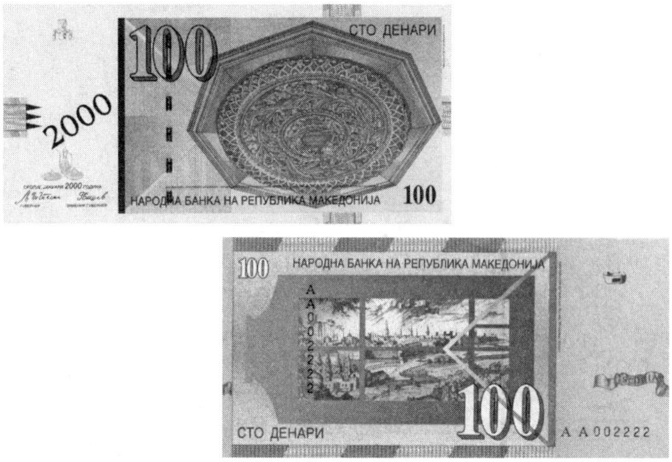

		VG	VF	UNC
20	**100 Denari** 1.2000. Brown with purple text on multicolor underprint. As #16 but with *2000* added at left.	—	35.00	80.00

2003 Issue

		VG	VF	UNC
21	**500 Denari** 1.2003. Black and violet on multicolor underprint. Gold foil at center. Similar to #17.			
	a. Issued note.	FV	FV	22.50
	s. Specimen.	FV	FV	25.00

		VG	VF	UNC
22	**1000 Denari** 1.2003. Brown and orange on multicolor underprint. As #18 but with hologram added on center top.			
	a. Issued note.	FV	FV	40.00
	s. Specimen.	—	—	25.00

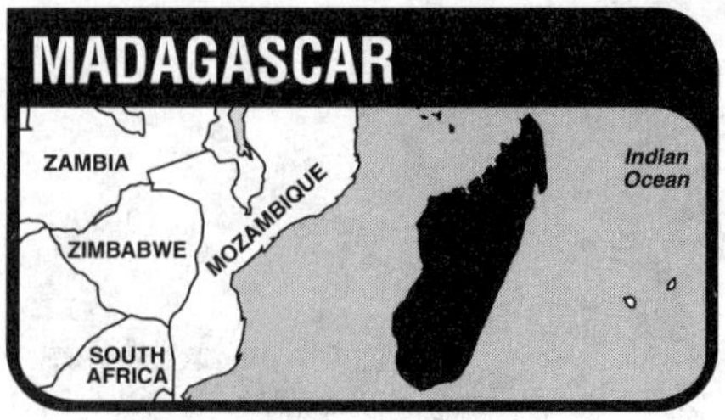

The Democratic Republic of Madagascar, an independent member of the French Community located in the Indian Ocean 250 miles (402 km.) off the southeast coast of Africa, has an area of 226,658 sq. mi. (587,041 sq. km.) and a population of 17.39 million. Capital: Antananarivo. The economy is primarily agricultural; large bauxite deposits are presently being developed. Coffee, vanilla, graphite and rice are exported.

Diago Diaz, a Portuguese navigator, sighted the island of Madagascar on Aug. 10, 1500, when his ship became separated from an India-bound fleet. Attempts at settlement by the British during the reign of Charles I and by the French during the 17th and 18th centuries were of no avail, and the island became a refuge and supply for Indian Ocean pirates. Despite considerable influence on the island, the British accepted the imposition of a French protectorate in 1886 in return for French recognition of Britain's sphere of influence in Zanzibar. Madagascar was made a French colony in 1896 after absolute control had been established by military force. Britain occupied the island after the fall of France in 1942, to prevent its seizure by the Japanese, and gave it to the Free French in 1943. On Oct. 14, 1958, following a decade of intermittent but bitter warfare, Madagascar, as the Malagasy Republic, became an autonomous state within the French Community. On June 27, 1960, it became a sovereign independent nation, though remaining nominally within the French Community. The Malagasy Republic was renamed the Democratic Republic of Madagascar in 1976.

MONETARY SYSTEM:

1 CFA Franc = 0.02 French Franc, 1959-1961
5 Malagasy Francs (F.M.G.) = 1 Ariary, 1961-2003
1 Ariary = 5 Francs, 2003-

MALAGASY

INSTITUT D'EMISSION MALGACHE

1961 ND PROVISIONAL ISSUE

#51-55 new bank name and new Ariary denominations ovpt. on previous issue of Banque de Madagascar et des Comores. Wmk: Woman's head.

		VG	VF	UNC
51	**50 Francs = 10 Ariary** ND (1961). Multicolor. Woman with hat at center right. Man at center on back. Overprint on #45.			
	a. Signature title: *LE CONTROLEUR GENERAL.*	2.00	17.50	70.00
	b. Signature title: *LE DIRECTEUR GENERAL ADJOINT.*	2.50	20.00	75.00
52	**100 Francs = 20 Ariary** ND (1961). Multicolor. Woman at center right, palace of the Queen of Tananariva in background. Woman, boats and animals on back. Overprint on #46b.	3.00	30.00	110.
53	**500 Francs = 100 Ariary** ND (1961 - old date 9.10.1952). Multicolor. Man with fruit at center overprint on #47.	15.00	90.00	400.
54	**1000 Francs = 200 Ariary** ND (1961 - old date 9.10.1952). Multicolor. Man and woman at left. Center Ox cart at center right on back. Overprint on #48.	20.00	175.	500.
55	**5000 Francs = 1000 Ariary** ND (1961). Multicolor. Gallieni at upper left, woman at right. Woman and baby on back. Overprint on #49.	50.00	325.	800.

Note: #53-55 some notes also have old dates of intended or original issue (1952-55).

1963 ND REGULAR ISSUE

56	1000 Francs = 200 Ariary	VG	VF	UNC
	ND (1963). Multicolor. Portrait Pres. P. Tsiranana, people in canoes at left. Ox cart at center right on back. Watermark: Woman's head.			
	a. Without signature and title.	50.00	375.	800.
	b. With signature and title.	40.00	250.	700.

1966 ND Issue

#57-60 wmk: Woman's head.

57	100 Francs = 20 Ariary	VG	VF	UNC
	ND (1966). Multicolor. Three women spinning. Trees on back. Two signature varieties.			
	a. Issued note.	2.50	10.00	30.00
	s. Specimen.	—	—	25.00

58	500 Francs = 100 Ariary	VG	VF	UNC
	ND (1966). Multicolor. Woman at left, landscape in background. River scene on back. Two signature varieties.			
	a. Issued note.	5.00	45.00	185.
	s. Specimen.	—	—	35.00

59	1000 Francs = 200 Ariary	VG	VF	UNC
	ND (1966). Multicolor. Woman and man at left. Similar to #48 and #54 but size 150 x 80mm.			
	a. Issued note.	7.50	65.00	250.
	s. Specimen.	—	—	35.00

60	5000 Francs = 1000 Ariary	VG	VF	UNC
	ND (1966). Multicolor. Portrait Pres. P. Tsiranana at left, workers in rice field at right. Woman and boy on back.			
	a. Issued note.	10.00	45.00	200.
	s. Specimen.	—	—	45.00

1969 ND Issue

61	50 Francs = 10 Ariary	VG	VF	UNC
	ND (1969). Multicolor. Like #51. Different signature title.	2.25	7.50	25.00

Madagascar Democratic Republic

Banky Foiben'ny Repoblika Malagasy

Banque Centrale de la République Malgache

1974 ND Issue

#62-66 replacement notes: Serial # prefix *Z/*.

#64-66 wmk: Zebu's head.

62	50 Francs = 10 Ariary	VG	VF	UNC
	ND (1974-75). Purple on multicolor underprint. Young man at center right. Fruit stand under umbrella at left center on back.			
	a. Issued note.	.50	4.00	12.50
	s. Specimen.	—	—	25.00
63	100 Francs = 20 Ariary			
	ND. Brown on multicolor underprint. Old man at right. Rice planting on back.			
	a. Issued note.	.50	3.00	10.00
	s. Specimen.	—	—	25.00

64	500 Francs = 100 Ariary	VG	VF	UNC
	ND. Green on multicolor underprint. Butterfly at left, young woman at center right holding ornate bag on head. Dancers at center on back.			
	a. Issued note.	1.00	6.00	30.00
	s. Specimen.	—	—	25.00

65	1000 Francs = 200 Ariary	VG	VF	UNC
	ND. Blue on multicolor underprint. Ring-tailed Lemurs at left, man in straw hat at right. Trees and designs on back.			
	a. Issued note.	2.00	8.00	45.00
	s. Specimen.	—	—	25.00

66	5000 Francs = 1000 Ariary	VG	VF	UNC
	ND. Red and violet on multicolor underprint. Oxen at left, young woman at center right. Back violet and orange; tropical plants and African carving at center.			
	a. Issued note.	7.00	30.00	80.00
	s. Specimen.	—	—	25.00

BANKY FOIBEN'I MADAGASIKARA

1988 ND ISSUE

#71-74 vertical serial # at r. Sign. varieties. Wmk: Zebu's head. Replacement notes: Serial # prefix *ZZ*.

71	500 Francs = 100 Ariary	VG	VF	UNC
	ND (1988-93). Similar to #67, but modified underprint.	.25	1.50	5.00

72	1000 Francs = 200 Ariary	VG	VF	UNC
	ND (1988-93). Similar to #68, but modified underprint.	.25	2.00	7.50
72A	2500 Francs = 500 Ariary			
	ND (1993). Red, green, blue and black on multicolor underprint. Older woman at center. Grey heron, tortoise, Verreaux's Sifaka and butterfly in foliage on vertical format back.	.20	.75	2.50

73	5000 Francs = 1000 Ariary	VG	VF	UNC
	ND (1988-94). Similar to #69, but modified underprint.	1.25	4.00	15.00

74	10,000 Francs = 2000 Ariary	VG	VF	UNC
	ND (1988-94). Similar to #70, but modified underprint.	2.00	10.00	30.00

NOTICE

Readers with unlisted dates, signature varieties, etc. are invited to submit photocopies of their notes to: Standard Catalog of World Paper Money, 700 East State St. Iola, WI 54990-0001, E-Mail: george.cuhaj@fwpubs.com.

74A 25,000 Francs = 5000 Ariary
ND (1993) Olive-green and green on multicolor underprint. Old man at center, island outline at left. Scene of traditional bullfighting at right on back.

VG	VF	UNC
1.00	5.00	17.50

1983 ND ISSUE

#67-70 wmk: Zebu's head. Sign. varieties. Replacement notes: Serial # prefix Z/.

67 500 Francs = 100 Ariary
ND (1983-87). Brown and red on multicolor underprint. Boy with fish in net at center. Aerial view of port at right on back.

VG	VF	UNC
.25	1.50	5.00

68 1000 Francs = 200 Ariary
ND (1983-87). Violet and brown on multicolor underprint. Man with hat playing flute at center. Fruits and vegetables at right on back.

VG	VF	UNC
.25	2.00	7.50

69 5000 Francs = 1000 Ariary
ND (1983-87). Blue on multicolor underprint. Woman and child at center. Book at upper center, school at center right, monument at lower right on back.

VG	VF	UNC
1.50	10.00	35.00

70 10,000 Francs = 2000 Ariary
ND (1983-87). Green on multicolor underprint. Young girl with sheaf at center. Harvesting rice at center right on back.

VG	VF	UNC
2.50	20.00	65.00

1994-95 ND ISSUE

#75-80 wmk: Zebu's head.

75 500 Francs = 100 Ariary
ND (1994). Dark brown and dark green on multicolor underprint. Girl at center right, village in underprint at upper center. Herdsmen with Zebus, village in upper background at left center on back.

VG	VF	UNC
.10	.50	1.75

76 1000 Francs = 200 Ariary
ND (1994). Dark brown and dark blue on multicolor underprint. Young man at center right, boats in background. Young woman with basket of shellfish at center, fisherman with net at left center on back.

VG	VF	UNC
.20	.50	1.50

#77 renumbered to 72A.

78	5000 Francs = 1000 Ariary	VG	VF	UNC
	ND (1995). Dark brown and purple on lilac and multicolor underprint. Young male head at right, ox cart, cane cutters at center. Ringtailed Lemur, Diademed Sifaka, Red-ruffed Lemur and birds - Madagascar pigmy kingfisher, Madagascar fody and helmet vanga, plus seashells on back.	.75	1.25	6.00

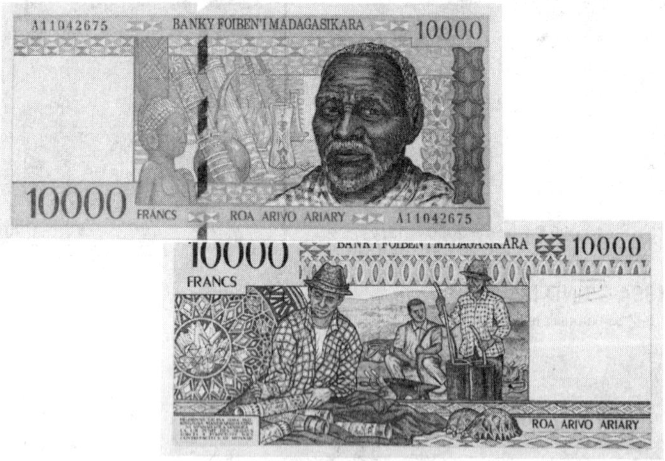

79	10,000 Francs = 2000 Ariary	VG	VF	UNC
	ND (1995). Dark brown on tan and multicolor underprint. Old man at right, statuette, local artifacts at center. Artisans at work on back.	1.00	2.50	10.00

#80 renumbered to #74A.

1998 ND Issue

81	2500 Francs = 500 Ariary	VG	VF	UNC
	ND (1998). Multicolor. Woman at right, village in background. Woman weaving at left center on back.	.25	.75	3.50

> **NOTICE**
> Readers with unlisted dates, signature varieties, etc. are invited to submit photocopies of their notes to: Standard Catalog of World Paper Money, 700 East State St. Iola, WI 54990-0001, E-Mail: george.cuhaj@fwpubs.com.

82	25,000 Francs = 5000 Ariary	VG	VF	UNC
	ND (1998). Multicolor. Mother with child at center right, fruit trees in background. Woman harvesting at center on back.	1.00	3.00	25.00

2003 Issue

83	2000 Ariary	VG	VF	UNC
	ND (2003). Multicolor.	FV	FV	10.00

84	5000 Ariary	VG	VF	UNC
	ND (2003). Multicolor.	FV	FV	20.00

85 **10,000 Ariary** | VG | VF | UNC
ND (2003). Multicolor. | FV | FV | 35.00

2004 Issue

86 **100 Ariary** | VG | VF | UNC
2004. Blue and tan on multicolor underprint. | FV | FV | .75

87 **200 Ariary** | VG | VF | UNC
2004. Green and tan on multicolor underprint. | FV | FV | 1.00

88 **500 Ariary** | VG | VF | UNC
2004. Tan on blue underprint. Man weaving basket at left. Cattle on back. | FV | FV | 2.50

89 **1000 Ariary** | VG | VF | UNC
2004. Purple on multicolor underprint. Lemur on tree branch at left. Plants on back. | FV | FV | 3.50

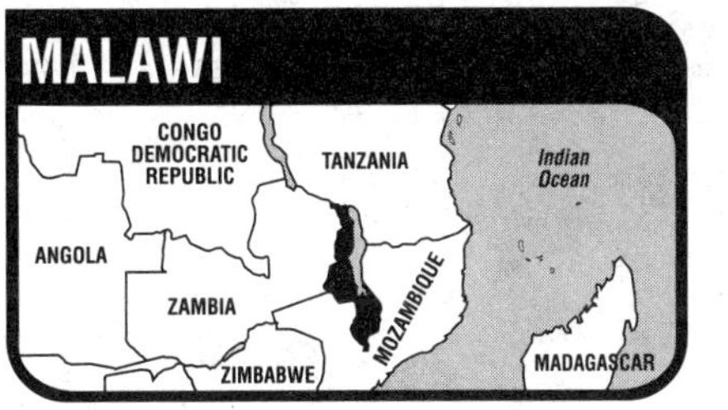

The Republic of Malawi (formerly Nyasaland), located in southeastern Africa to the west of Lake Malawi (Nyasa), has an area of 45,747 sq. mi. (118,484 sq. km.) and a population of 10.98 million. Capital: Lilongwe. The economy is predominantly agricultural. Tobacco, tea, peanuts and cotton are exported.

Although the Portuguese, heirs to the restless spirit of Prince Henry, were the first Europeans to reach the Malawi area, the first meaningful contact was made by missionary-explorer Dr. David Livingstone who arrived at Lake Malawi on Sept. 16, 1859, and remained to make extensive explorations in the 1860s. Subsequent clashes between settlements of Scottish missionaries and Arab slave traders, and the procurement of development rights by Cecil Rhodes, 1884, stimulated British interest and brought about the establishment of the Nyasaland protectorate in 1891. In 1953, Nyasaland reluctantly joined the Federation of Rhodesia and Nyasaland and, after prolonged protest, was granted self-government within the federation. Nyasaland became the independent nation of Malawi on July 6, 1964, and became a republic two years later. As a one party dictatorship lasting 30 years until 1994 when elections returned Malawi to a multi-party democracy. Malawi is a member of the Commonwealth of Nations. The president is the Chief of State and Head of Government.

Also see Rhodesia, Rhodesia and Nyasaland.

RULERS:

British to 1964

MONETARY SYSTEM:

1 Pound = 20 Shillings to 1971
1 Kwacha = 100 Tambala 1971-

REPLACEMENT NOTES:

#13-17, ZZ prefix. #18-22, V/1, W/1, X/1, Y/1, Z/1 prefix by denomination. #23-27, ZZ prefix.

Republic

Reserve Bank of Malawi

1964 Reserve Bank Act; First Issue

Pound System

#1-4 portr. Dr. Hastings Kamuzu Banda at l., fishermen in boat on Lake Malawi at ctr. Sign. title: *GOVERNOR* only. Wmk: Rooster.

1 **5 Shillings** | VG | VF | UNC
L.1964. Blue-gray on multicolor underprint. Arms with bird on back. | 5.00 | 17.50 | 95.00

2 **10 Shillings** | VG | VF | UNC
L.1964. Brown on multicolor underprint. Workers in tobacco field on back. | 7.50 | 75.00 | 250.

3 **1 Pound**
L.1964. Green on multicolor underprint. Workers picking cotton at center right on back. | 10.00 | 85.00 | 350.

4 **5 Pounds** | VG | VF | UNC
L.1964. Blue and brown on multicolor underprint. Tea pickers below Mt. Mulanje on back. | 40.00 | 300. | 1200.

NOTICE

Readers with unlisted dates, signature varieties, etc. are invited to submit photocopies of their notes to: Standard Catalog of World Paper Money, 700 East State St. Iola, WI 54990-0001, E-Mail: george.cuhaj@fwpubs.com.

1964 Reserve Bank Act; Second Issue

#1A-3A portr. Dr. Hastings Kamusu Banda at l., fishermen at ctr. Sign. titles: *GOVERNOR* and *GENERAL MANAGER.*

		VG	VF	UNC
1A	**5 Shillings**			
	L.1964. Blue-gray on multicolor underprint. Like #1.			
	a. Issued note.	3.50	10.00	70.00
	s. Specimen.	—	—	—

		VG	VF	UNC
2A	**10 Shillings**			
	L.1964. Brown on multicolor underprint. Like #2.			
	a. Issued note.	5.00	17.50	100.
	s. Specimen.	—	—	—

		VG	VF	UNC
3A	**1 Pound**			
	L.1964. Green on multicolor underprint. Like #3.			
	a. Issued note.	5.00	40.00	200.
	s. Specimen.	—	—	—

1964 Reserve Bank Act; 1971 Issue

Kwacha System

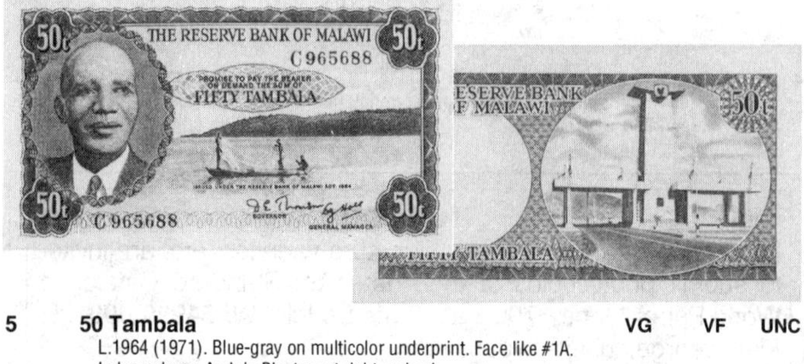

		VG	VF	UNC
5	**50 Tambala**			
	L.1964 (1971). Blue-gray on multicolor underprint. Face like #1A. Independence Arch in Blantyre at right on back.			
	a. Issued note.	10.00	50.00	325.
	s. Specimen.	—	—	—
6	**1 Kwacha**			
	L.1964 (1971). Brown on multicolor underprint. Like #2A.			
	a. Issued note.	12.50	50.00	325.
	s. Specimen.	—	—	—

		VG	VF	UNC
7	**2 Kwacha**			
	L.1964 (1971). Green on multicolor underprint. Like #3A.			
	a. Issued note.	15.00	50.00	300.
	s. Specimen.	—	—	—

		VG	VF	UNC
8	**10 Kwacha**			
	L.1964 (1971). Blue and brown on multicolor underprint. Like #4 but two signs.			
	a. Issued note.	30.00	175.	900.
	s. Specimen.	—	—	—

1973-74 Issue

#9-12 portr. Dr. Hastings Kamuzu Banda as Prime Minister at r., fishermen in boat on Lake Malawi and palm tree at ctr. W/ or w/o dates. Wmk: Rooster.

		VG	VF	UNC
9	**50 Tambala**			
	L.1964 (ND); 1974-75. Blue-gray on multicolor underprint. Sugar cane harvesting on back.			
	a. ND (1973).	5.00	30.00	200.
	b. 30.6.1974.	3.00	15.00	100.
	c. 31.1.1975.	2.00	5.00	40.00
	s. As a. Specimen.	—	—	—
	ct. Color trial. Purple on multicolor underprint.	—	—	275.

10	1 Kwacha	VG	VF	UNC
	L.1964 (ND); 1974-75. Red-brown on multicolor underprint. Plantation worker, hill in background on back.			
	a. ND (1973).	5.00	20.00	135.
	b. 30.6.1974.	4.00	15.00	85.00
	c. 31.1.1975.	3.00	7.00	75.00
	ct. Color trial. Orange on multicolor underprint.	—	—	250.

11	5 Kwacha	VG	VF	UNC
	L.1964 (ND); 1974-75. Red-orange on multicolor underprint. Worker with basket at center, K5 at upper left on back.			
	a. ND (1973).	10.00	55.00	350.
	b. 31.1.1975.	7.50	30.00	225.
	ct. Color trial. Green on multicolor underprint.	—	—	550.
12	**10 Kwacha**			
	L.1964 (ND); 1974-75. Blue and brown on multicolor underprint. Plantation workers with mountains in background on back.			
	a. ND (1973).	15.00	65.00	400.
	b. 30.6.1974.	12.50	75.00	450.
	c. 31.1.1975.	9.00	45.00	325.

1976; 1983 ISSUE

#13-17 portr. Dr. Hastings Kamuzu Banda as President at r. Wmk: Rooster. Sign. varieties.

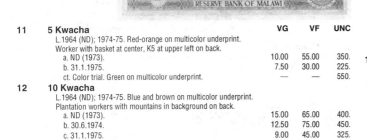

13	50 Tambala	VG	VF	UNC
	1976-84. Blue-gray on multicolor underprint. Cotton harvest on back.			
	a. 31.1.1976.	.50	3.00	25.00
	b. 1.7.1978.	.50	4.50	30.00
	c. 1.1.1981.	.50	5.00	40.00
	d. 1.5.1982.	.50	2.50	12.50
	e. 1.1.1983.	.50	5.00	35.00
	f. 1.11.1984.	1.00	7.50	60.00
	s. As. a. Specimen.	—	—	35.00

14	1 Kwacha	VG	VF	UNC
	1976-84. Red-brown on multicolor underprint. Workers harvesting, mountains in background on back.			
	a. 31.1.1976.	.50	3.00	22.50
	b. 1.7.1978.	.50	3.00	25.00
	c. 30.6.1979.	2.00	15.00	100.
	d. 1.1.1981.	.50	2.00	20.00
	e. 1.5.1982.	.25	1.50	12.50
	f. 1.1.1983.	.50	3.00	25.00
	g. 1.4.1984.	.25	1.50	12.50
	h. 1.11.1984.	.50	2.00	15.00
	s. Specimen. 31.1.1976.	—	—	40.00

15	5 Kwacha	VG	VF	UNC
	1976-84. Red on multicolor underprint. Field workers, *K5* at upper right on back.			
	a. 31.1.1976.	2.00	20.00	175.
	b. 1.7.1978.	2.00	20.00	175.
	c. 30.6.1979.	3.00	30.00	275.
	d. 1.1.1981.	1.50	7.50	60.00
	e. 1.1.1983.	1.00	5.00	50.00
	f. 1.11.1984.	2.00	15.00	175.
	s. Specimen. 31.1.1976.	—	—	50.00

16	10 Kwacha	VG	VF	UNC
	1976-85. Deep blue and brown on multicolor underprint. Capital building at Lilongwe on back.			
	a. 31.1.1976.	7.50	30.00	400.
	b. 1.7.1978.	7.50	25.00	385.
	c. 30.6.1979.	8.50	40.00	500.

		VG	VF	UNC
16	**10 Kwacha**			
	d. 1.1.1981.	7.50	25.00	350.
	e. 1.1.1983.	7.50	22.50	300.
	f. 1.4.1984.	7.50	22.50	300.
	g. 1.11.1984.	8.00	27.50	400.
	h. 1.8.1985.	7.50	27.50	375.
	s. Specimen. 31.1.1976.	—	—	45.00

		VG	VF	UNC
17	**20 Kwacha**			
	1983; 1984. Green, brown-violet on multicolor underprint. Back green; Reserve Bank in Lilongwe at center.			
	a. 1.7.1983.	4.50	15.00	125.
	b. 1.11.1984.	10.00	35.00	300.
	s. Specimen.	—	—	240.

1986 ISSUE

#18-22 portr. Pres. Dr. Hastings Kamuzu Banda at r. Wmk; Rooster.

		VG	VF	UNC
18	**50 Tambala**			
	1.3.1986. Black and dark brown on multicolor underprint. Picking corn on back.	.25	1.00	9.00

		VG	VF	UNC
19	**1 Kwacha**			
	1986; 1988. Red-brown on multicolor underprint. Cultivating tobacco on back.			
	a. 1.3.1986.	.50	1.75	10.00
	b. 1.4.1988.	.25	.75	6.50

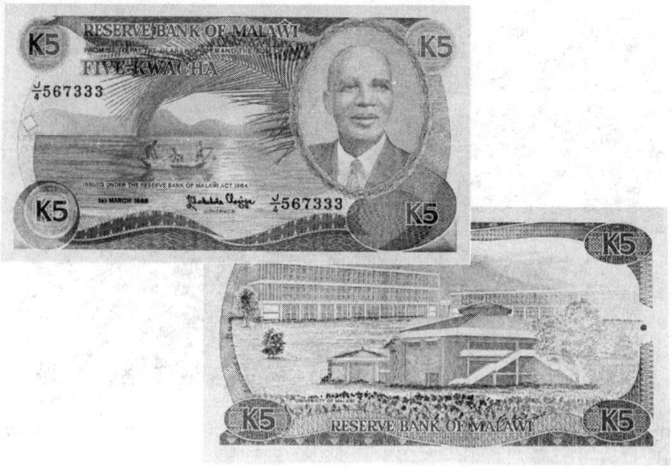

		VG	VF	UNC
20	**5 Kwacha**			
	1986; 1988. Red-orange on multicolor underprint. University of Malawi at Zomba on back.			
	a. 1.3.1986.	1.75	7.00	40.00
	b. 1.4.1988.	1.00	5.00	30.00

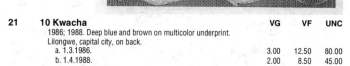

		VG	VF	UNC
21	**10 Kwacha**			
	1986; 1988. Deep blue and brown on multicolor underprint. Lilongwe, capital city, on back.			
	a. 1.3.1986.	3.00	12.50	80.00
	b. 1.4.1988.	2.00	8.50	45.00

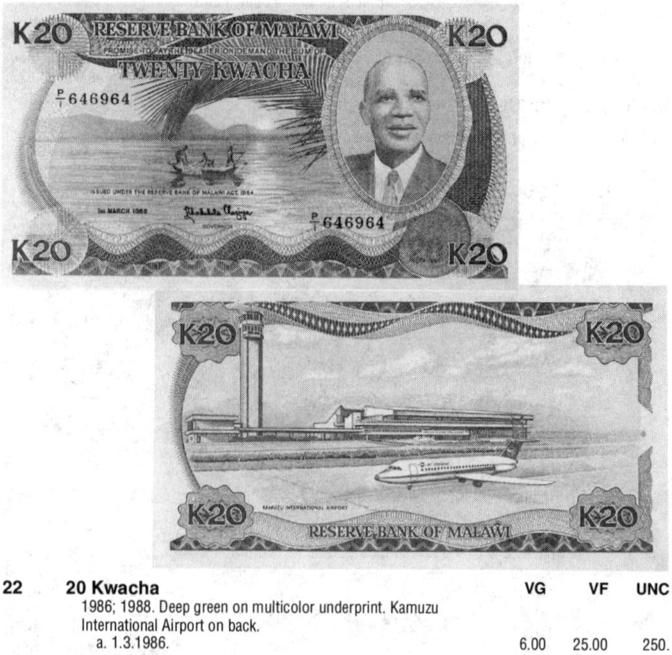

		VG	VF	UNC
22	**20 Kwacha**			
	1986; 1988. Deep green on multicolor underprint. Kamuzu International Airport on back.			
	a. 1.3.1986.	6.00	25.00	250.
	b. 1.4.1988.	3.00	15.00	135.

1989 ACT; 1990; 1993 ISSUE

#23-28 palm tree, man in dugout canoe, and rayed silver circle at ctr., portr. Dr. Hastings Kamuzu Banda as President at r. Ascending size vertical serial # at l. and lower r. Wmk: Rooster.

23	1 Kwacha	VG	VF	UNC
	1990; 1992. Red-brown on multicolor underprint. Back similar to #19.			
	a. 1.12.1990.	FV	FV	5.00
	b. 1.5.1992.	FV	FV	2.00

24	5 Kwacha	VG	VF	UNC
	1990; 1994. Red-orange and olive-green on multicolor underprint. University of Malawi at left center on back.			
	a. 1.12.1990.	FV	FV	6.50
	b. 1.1.1994.	FV	FV	4.50

25	10 Kwacha	VG	VF	UNC
	1990-94. Blue-gray, blue-violet and dark brown on multicolor underprint. Lilongwe City municipal building at left center on back.			
	a. 1.12.1990.	FV	FV	12.50
	b. 1.9.1992.	FV	FV	6.00
	c. Smaller signature as b. 1.1.1994.	FV	FV	4.00
	s. As b. Specimen.	—	—	135.
26	20 Kwacha			
	1.9.1990. Green, orange and blue on multicolor underprint. Kamuzu International Airport at left center on back.	FV	FV	50.00

27	20 Kwacha	VG	VF	UNC
	1.7.1993. Like #26 but with larger airplane on back.	FV	FV	10.00

28	50 Kwacha	VG	VF	UNC
	1990; 1994. Pale purple, violet and blue on multicolor underprint. Independence Arch at Blantyre at center on back.			
	a. 1.6.1990.	FV	12.50	55.00
	b. 1.1.1994.	FV	FV	30.00

29	100 Kwacha	VG	VF	UNC
	1993; 1994. Blue, green and dark brown on multicolor underprint. Trucks hauling maize to storage facility at center on back.			
	a. 1.4.1993.	FV	30.00	65.00
	b. 1.1.1994.	FV	FV	40.00

1995 ISSUE

#30-35 Pres. Muluzi at r., bird at upper l., sunrise above fisherman in boat on Lake Malawi at ctr., bird over silver segmented sunburst at l. Wmk: Fish.

		VG	VF	UNC
30	**5 Kwacha** 1.6.1995. Red and orange-brown on multicolor underprint. Spoonbill at top left. Zebras at left on back.	FV	FV	1.75

		VG	VF	UNC
31	**10 Kwacha** 1.6.1995. Black, dark blue and dark brown on multicolor underprint. Crowned crane at top left. Capital Hill, Lilongwe at left center on back.	FV	FV	4.00

		VG	VF	UNC
32	**20 Kwacha** 1.6.1995. Deep green and dark brown on multicolor underprint. Lesser striped swallow at top left. Harvesting tea leaves at left center on back.	FV	FV	7.50

		VG	VF	UNC
33	**50 Kwacha** 1.6.1995. Purple and violet on multicolor underprint. Pink-backed pelican at top left. Independence Arch in Blantyre at left center on back.	FV	FV	12.00

		VG	VF	UNC
34	**100 Kwacha** 1.6.1995. Purple and deep ultramarine on multicolor underprint. Sacred ibis at top left. Trucks hauling maize to storage facility at left center on back.	FV	FV	25.00

		VG	VF	UNC
35	**200 Kwacha** 1.6.1995. Brown-violet and blue-green and silver on multicolor underprint. African fish eagle at top left. Elephants on back.	FV	FV	40.00

1989 ACT; 1997 ISSUE

#36-41 J. Chilembwe at r. and as wmk., sunrise, fishermen at ctr., bank stylized logo at lower l.

#36-39 bank seal at top ctr. r. on back.

		VG	VF	UNC
36	**5 Kwacha** 1.7.1997; 1.3.2004; 1.12.2005. Deep olive-green, green and olive-brown on multicolor underprint. Villagers mashing grain at left on back.			
	a. 1.7.1997.	FV	FV	1.25
	b. 1.3.2004; 1.12.2005.	FV	FV	.50

37	10 Kwacha	VG	VF	UNC
	1.7.1997. Dark brown and brown-violet on multicolor underprint. Children in "bush" school at left center on back.	FV	FV	1.50

38	20 Kwacha	VG	VF	UNC
	1.7.1997. Blackish purple, purple and violet on multicolor underprint. Workers harvesting tea leaves, mountains in background at left on back.			
	a. Even height serial #s.	FV	FV	3.50
	b. Ascending size serial #.	FV	FV	3.25

39	50 Kwacha	VG	VF	UNC
	1.7.1997. Dark green, deep blue and aqua on multicolor underprint. Independence arch in Blantyre at left center on back.	FV	FV	5.00

40	100 Kwacha	VG	VF	UNC
	1.7.1997. Purple, red and violet on multicolor underprint. Circular kinegram bank seal at right. Capital Hill Lilongwe at left center on back.	FV	FV	12.50

41	200 Kwacha	VG	VF	UNC
	1.7.1997. Dark gray, dull blue and deep blue-green on multicolor underprint. Oval kinegram bank seal at right. Reserve Bank building in Lilongwe at left center on back.	FV	FV	17.50

#42 has been merged into #48.

2001-03 Issue

#43-48 with ascending size serial #.

43	10 Kwacha	VG	VF	UNC
	1.1.2003; 1.10.2003; 1.6.2004. Dark brown and brown-violet on multicolor underprint. Children in "bush" school at left center on back.			
	a. 1.1.2003.	FV	FV	1.50
	b. 1.10.2003.	FV	FV	1.50
	c. 1.6.2004.	—	—	1.50

44	20 Kwacha	VG	VF	UNC
	1.10.2001; 1.4.2004; 1.6.2004. Black and purple on multicolor underprint.			
	a. 1.10.2001.	FV	FV	3.00
	b. 1.4.2004.	FV	FV	2.00
	c. 1.6.2004.	FV	FV	2.00

45	50 Kwacha	VG	VF	UNC
	1.10.2001; 1.1.2003; 31.10.2005. Dark green, deep blue and aqua on multicolor underprint.			
	a. 1.10.2001.	FV	FV	4.00
	b. 1.1.2003.	FV	FV	2.75
	c. 31.10.2005.	FV	FV	2.00

		VG	VF	UNC
46	**100 Kwacha** 1.10.2001; 1.1.2003. Dark purple and red on red and multicolor underprint.			
	a. 1.10.2001.	FV	FV	10.00
	b. 1.1.2003.	FV	FV	5.00
47	**200 Kwacha** 1.7.2001; 1.10.2003; 1.6.2004. Multicolor. As #41 but with holographic band at right.			
	a. 1.7.2001.	FV	FV	15.00
	b. 1.10.2003.	FV	FV	9.00
	c. 1.6.2004.	FV	FV	7.00

		VG	VF	UNC
48	**500 Kwacha** 1.12.2001; 1.6.2003; 1.11.2005. Multicolor.			
	a. 1.12.2001. Holographic square at left.	FV	FV	30.00

		VG	VF	UNC
48A	**500 Kwacha**			
	b. 1.6.2003. Holographic strip at right.	FV	FV	17.50
	c. 1.11.2005.	FV	FV	15.00

2004 Commemorative Issue

#49, 40th Anniversary of Independence.

		VG	VF	UNC
49	**50 Kwacha** 6.7.2004. Blue on yellow-orange underprint. Modern buildings on back.	FV	FV	5.00

MALAYA & BRITISH BORNEO

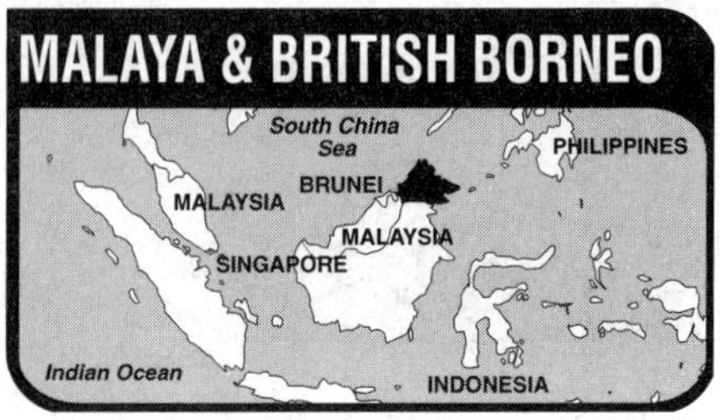

Malaya and British Borneo, a Currency Commission named the Board of Commissioners of Currency, Malaya and British North Borneo, was initiated on Jan. 1, 1952, for the purpose of providing a common currency for use in Johore, Kelantan, Kedah, Perlis, Trengganu, Negri Sembilan, Pahang, Perak, Salangor, Penang, Malacca, Singapore, North Borneo, Sarawak and Brunei.

For later issues see Brunei, Malaysia and Singapore.

RULERS:
British

MONETARY SYSTEM:
1 Dollar = 100 Cents

British Administration

Board of Commissioners of Currency

1959-61 Issue

#8-9 wmk: Tiger's head.

		VG	VF	UNC
8	**1 Dollar** 1.3.1959. Blue on multicolor underprint. Sailing boat at left. Men with boat and arms of 5 states on back. Printer: W&S.			
	a. Issued note.	6.00	25.00	150.
	s. Specimen.	—	—	—
8A	**1 Dollar** 1.3.1959. Blue on multicolor underprint. Like #8. Printer: TDLR.	4.00	40.00	75.00

		VG	VF	UNC
9	**10 Dollars** 1.3.1961. Red and dark brown on multicolor underprint. Farmer plowing with ox at right. Printer: TDLR.			
	a. Sm. serial #. Series A.	50.00	125.	450.
	b. Large serial #. Series A.	120.	225.	800.
	c. Large serial #. Series B.	150.	400.	1200.
	s. As a. Specimen.	—	—	—

MALAYSIA

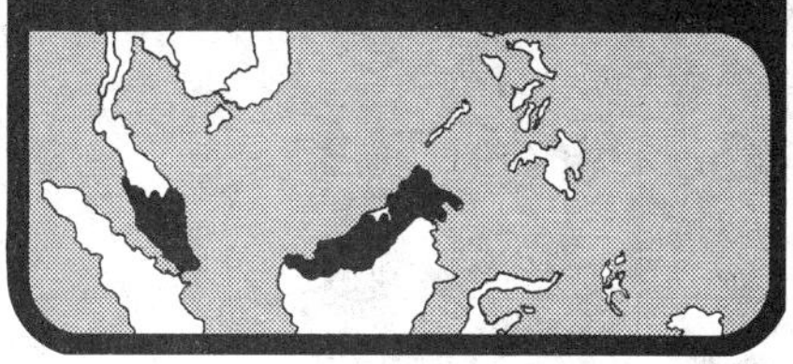

Malaysia, an independent federation of southeast Asia consisting of 11 states of West Malaysia on the Malay Peninsula and two states of East Malaysia on the island of Borneo, has an area of 127,316 sq. mi. (329,747 sq. km.) and a population of 22.3 million. Capital: Kuala Lumpur. The federation came into being on Sept. 16, 1963. Rubber, timber, tin, iron ore and bauxite are exported.

The constituent states of Malaysia are Johore, Kedah, Kelantan, Malacca, Negri Sembilan, Pahang, Penang, Perak, Perlis, Selangor and Trengganu of West Malaysia; and Sabah and Sarawak of East Malaysia. Singapore joined the federation in 1963, but broke away on Aug. 9, 1965, to become an independent republic. Malaysia is a member of the Commonwealth of Nations. The "Paramount Ruler" is Chief of State. The prime minister is Head of Government.

MONETARY SYSTEM:

1 Ringgit (Dollar) = 100 Sen

DEMONETIZED NOTES:

All 500 and 1000 Ringgitt notes ceased to be legal tender on July 1, 1999.

FEDERATION

BANK NEGARA MALAYSIA

1967 ND ISSUE

#1-6 old spelling of *DI-PERLAKUKAN*. Arms on back. Wmk: Tiger's head. Sign. of Ismail Md. Ali w/title: *GABENOR*.

#1, 2, and 6 printer: BWC.

		VG	VF	UNC
1	**1 Ringgit** ND (1967-72). Blue on multicolor underprint.			
	a. Solid security thread.	FV	3.00	10.00
	b. Segmented security thread.	FV	5.00	12.00

		VG	VF	UNC
2	**5 Ringgit** ND (1967-72). Green on multicolor underprint.			
	a. Solid security thread.	FV	8.00	42.50
	b. Segmented security thread.	FV	8.00	47.50

#3-5 printer: TDLR. Replacement notes: Serial # prefix *Z/*.

		VG	VF	UNC
3	**10 Ringgit** ND (1967-72). Red-orange on multicolor underprint. *(SA-PULOH)*.			
	a. Solid security thread.	FV	15.00	55.00
	b. Segmented security thread.	FV	15.00	60.00
4	**50 Ringgit** ND (1967-72). Blue and greenish gray on multicolor underprint. *(LIMA PULOH)*.			
	a. Solid security thread.	FV	60.00	220.
	b. Segmented security thread.	FV	70.00	230.

NOTICE

Readers with unlisted dates, signature varieties, etc. are invited to submit photocopies of their notes to: Standard Catalog of World Paper Money, 700 East State St. Iola, WI 54990-0001, E-Mail: george.cuhaj@fwpubs.com.

		VG	VF	UNC
5	**100 Ringgit** ND (1967-72). Purple and brown on multicolor underprint. *(SA-RATUS)*.			
	a. Solid security thread.	FV	250.	575.
	b. Broken security thread.	FV	250.	575.
6	**1000 Ringgit** ND (1967-72). Brown-violet on multicolor underprint. *(SA-RIBU)*. Printer: BWC.	450.	1250.	2500.

1972; 1976 ND ISSUE

#7-12 new spelling *DIPERLAKUKAN*. Arms on back. Wmk: Tiger's head. Sign. of Ismail Md. Ali w/title: *GABENUR*.

#7, 8, 11 and 12 printer: BWC.

		VG	VF	UNC
7	**1 Ringgit** ND (1972-76). Blue on multicolor underprint. Like #1.	FV	2.00	6.00

		VG	VF	UNC
8	**5 Ringgit** ND (1976). Green on multicolor underprint. Like #2.			
	a. Issued note.	FV	6.00	20.00
	s. Specimen.	—	—	—

#9 and 10 printer: TDLR.

		VG	VF	UNC
9	**10 Ringgit** ND (1972-76). Red-orange and brown on multicolor underprint. *(SEPULUH)*. Like #3.			
	a. Solid security thread.	FV	10.00	40.00
	b. Broken security thread.	FV	6.00	40.00
	s. Specimen.	—	—	—

		VG	VF	UNC
10	**50 Ringgit**			
	ND (1972-76). Blue and greenish gray on multicolor underprint. *(LIMA PULUH)*. Like #4.			
	a. Solid security thread.	FV	90.00	230.
	b. Broken security thread.	FV	110.	250.
11	**100 Ringgit**			
	ND (1972-76). Purple and brown on multicolor underprint. *(SERATUS)*. Like #5.	FV	160.	375.
12	**1000 Ringgit**			
	ND (1972-76). Brown-violet on multicolor underprint. *(SERIBU)*. Like #6.	500.	900.	2300.

1976; 1981 ND Issues

#13-18 arms on back. Wmk: Tiger's head.

#13-16 different guilloche w/latent image numeral at lower l.

#13-15 printer: BWC.

		VG	VF	UNC
13	**1 Ringgit**			
	ND (1976-81). Blue on multicolor underprint. Like #7.			
	a. Signature Ismail Md. Ali. (1976).	FV	1.00	5.00
	b. Signature Abdul Aziz Taha. (1981).	FV	1.00	6.00
	s. Specimen.	—	—	—
14	**5 Ringgit**			
	ND (1976-81). Green on multicolor underprint. Like #8.			
	a. Signature Ismail Md. Ali. (1976).	FV	5.00	20.00
	b. Signature Abdul Aziz Taha. (1981).	FV	5.00	18.00
	s. Specimen.	—	—	—
15	**10 Ringgit**			
	ND (1976-81). Red-orange and brown on multicolor underprint. Like #9. Signature Ismail Md. Ali. (1976).	FV	15.00	30.00

#15A, 16A and 17b replacement notes: Serial # prefix *X/*.

		VG	VF	UNC
15A	**10 Ringgit**			
	ND (1976-81). Like #15 but printer: TDLR. Signature Abdul Aziz Taha.			
	a. Issued note.	FV	15.00	30.00
	s. Specimen.	—	—	—

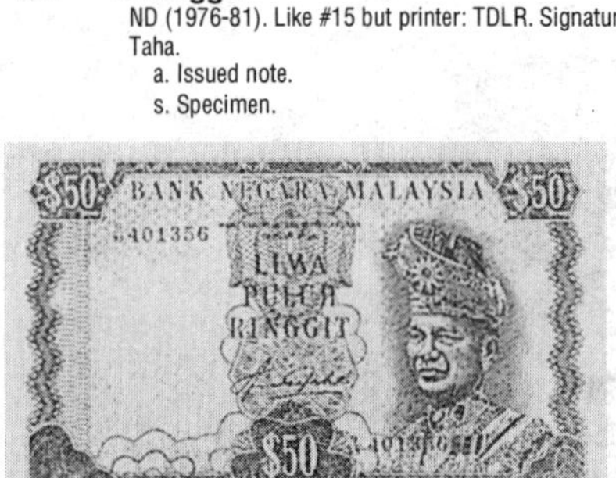

		VG	VF	UNC
16	**50 Ringgit**			
	ND (1976-81). Blue and greenish gray on multicolor underprint. Like #10. Signature Ismail Md. Ali (1976). Printer: BWC.	FV	80.00	180.
16A	**50 Ringgit**			
	ND (1981-83). Blue and greenish gray on multicolor underprint. Like #16 but printer: TDLR. Signature Abdul Aziz Taha (1981).	FV	70.00	160.
17	**100 Ringgit**			
	ND (1976-81). Purple and brown on multicolor underprint. Like #11. Printer: TDLR.			
	a. Signature Ismail Md. Ali. (1976).	FV	90.00	250.
	b. Signature Abdul Aziz Taha. (1981).	FV	250.	550.

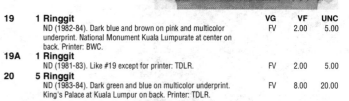

		VG	VF	UNC
18	**1000 Ringgit**			
	ND (1976-81). Purple and green on multicolor underprint. Face like #12. Parliament building in Kuala Lumpur on back. Signature Ismail Md. Ali. Printer: BWC.	—	600.	1500.

1981-83 ND Issues

#19-26 new design w/marks for the blind. Sign. of Abdul Aziz Taha. T. A. Rahman at r. and as wmk. Replacement notes: Serial # prefixes *BA; WA; UZ; ZZ*.

		VG	VF	UNC
19	**1 Ringgit**			
	ND (1982-84). Dark blue and brown on pink and multicolor underprint. National Monument Kuala Lumpurate at center on back. Printer: BWC.	FV	2.00	5.00
19A	**1 Ringgit**			
	ND (1981-83). Like #19 except for printer: TDLR.	FV	2.00	5.00
20	**5 Ringgit**			
	ND (1983-84). Dark green and blue on multicolor underprint. King's Palace at Kuala Lumpur on back. Printer: TDLR.	FV	8.00	20.00

		VG	VF	UNC
21	**10 Ringgit**			
	ND (1983-84). Red and brown on multicolor underprint. Railway station at Kuala Lumpur on back. Printer: TDLR.	FV	15.00	30.00

22 **20 Ringgit**

	VG	VF	UNC
ND (1982-84). Deep brown and dark blue on multicolor underprint. Bank Negara Malaysia building in Kuala Lumpur on back. Printer: BWC.	FV	15.00	30.00

23 **50 Ringgit**

	VG	VF	UNC
ND (1983-84). Black and blue-gray on multicolor underprint. National Museum at Kuala Lumpur on back. Printer: TDLR.	FV	60.00	100.

24 **100 Ringgit**

	VG	VF	UNC
ND (1983-84). Red-brown and violet on multicolor underprint. National Mosque in Kuala Lumpur on back. Printer: TDLR.	FV	80.00	150.

25 **500 Ringgit**

	VG	VF	UNC
ND (1982-84). Dark red and purple on multicolor underprint. High Court building in Kuala Lumpur on back. Printer: BWC.	FV	300.	500.

26 **1000 Ringgit**

	VG	VF	UNC
ND (1983-84). Gray-green on multicolor underprint. Parliament building in Kuala Lumpur on back. Printer: TDLR.	500.	700.	1100.

1986-95 ND ISSUES

#27-34 similar to #19-26 but no mark for the blind, white space for wmk. (both sides), and vertical serial #. Sign. Datuk Jaafar Hussein. Wmk: T. A. Rahman.

#27-31, 32, 33 and 34 printer: TDLR. Replacement notes: Serial # prefixes *BA; WA; UZ or ZZ*.

27 **1 Ringgit**

	VG	VF	UNC
ND (1986; 1989). Dark blue and purple on multicolor underprint. Similar to #19.			
a. Usual security thread (1986).	FV	FV	2.50
b. Segmented foil over security thread (1989).	FV	FV	2.50

28 **5 Ringgit**

	VG	VF	UNC
ND (1986-91). Dark green and green on multicolor underprint. Similar to #20.			
a. Usual security thread (1986).	FV	FV	10.00
b. Segmented foil over security thread (1989).	FV	FV	8.00
c. Flagpole without crossbar at top of back (1991).	FV	FV	6.00

		VG	VF	UNC
29	**10 Ringgit** ND (1989). Red-orange and brown on multicolor underprint. Segmented foil over security thread. Similar to #21.	FV	FV	12.50
29A	**10 Ringgit** ND (1989). Brown, red-orange and violet on multicolor underprint. Like #29 but printer: BABN.	FV	FV	10.00

		VG	VF	UNC
30	**20 Ringgit** ND (1989). Deep brown and olive on multicolor underprint. Similar to #22.	FV	FV	15.00

		VG	VF	UNC
31	**50 Ringgit** ND (1987). Blue and black on multicolor underprint. Segmented foil over security thread. Signature Jafar Hussein. Similar to #23.	FV	FV	40.00
31A	**50 Ringgit** ND (1991-92). Like #31, but printer: BABN. Signature Jafar Hussein.	FV	FV	50.00
31B	**50 Ringgit** ND (1995). Like #31, but printer: F-CO. Signature Ahmad M. Don.	FV	FV	40.00
31C	**50 Ringgit** ND (1995). Like #31, but printer: TDLR. Signature Ahmad M. Don.	FV	FV	40.00
31D	**50 Ringgit** ND (1997). Like #31 but printer: BABN. Signature Ahmad M. Don.	FV	FV	40.00

		VG	VF	UNC
32	**100 Ringgit** ND (1989). Purple on multicolor underprint. Segmented foil over security thread. Similar to #24. Printer: TDLR.	FV	FV	80.00
32A	**100 Ringgit** ND (1992). Like #32, but printer: USBNC. Signature Jafar Hussein.	FV	FV	150.
32B	**100 Ringgit** ND (1995). Like #32, but printer: TDLR. Signature Ahmad M. Don.	FV	FV	70.00
32C	**100 Ringgit** ND (1998). Like #32, but printer: H&S. Signature Ahmad M. Don.	FV	FV	65.00
33	**500 Ringgit** ND (1989). Red and brown on yellow and multicolor underprint. Segmented foil over security thread. Similar to #25. Printer: TDLR.	FV	300.	440.
33A	**500 Ringgit** ND (1989). Red and brown on yellow and multicolor underprint. As #33 but printer: H&S.	FV	300.	440.

		VG	VF	UNC
34	**1000 Ringgit** ND (1987). Blue, green and purple on multicolor underprint. Segmented foil over security thread. Printer: TDLR. Similar to #26. Signature Jafar Hussein.	FV	550.	750.
34A	**1000 Ringgit** ND (1995). Blue, green and purple on multicolor underprint. As #34 but printer: G&D. Signature Ahmad M. Don.	FV	500.	750.

1995 ND ISSUES

#35-38 sign. Ahmed Mohd. Don. Wmk: T.A. Rahman.

		VG	VF	UNC
35	**5 Ringgit** ND (1995). Dark blue on multicolor underprint. Like #28. Printer: TDLR.	FV	FV	3.50
35A	**5 Ringgit** ND (1998). Dark green. Like #35. Segmented security thread. Printer: CBN.	FV	FV	3.50

		VG	VF	UNC
36	**10 Ringgit** ND (1995). Dark brown, red-orange and violet on multicolor underprint. Like #29. Printer: F-CO.	FV	FV	6.50

37	10 Ringgit	VG	VF	UNC
	ND (1995). Dark brown, red-orange and violet on multicolor underprint. Like #29. Printer: BABN.	FV	FV	10.00

38	10 Ringgit	VG	VF	UNC
	ND (1995). Dark brown, red-orange and violet on multicolor underprint. Like #29. Printer: G&D.	FV	FV	6.50

1996-2000 ND Issue

#39-44 T. A. Rahman at r. and as wmk. Ascending size serial #. 3 sign. varieties.

39	1 Ringgit	VG	VF	UNC
	ND (2000). Blue and multicolor. Flora and mountain landscape with lake on back.	FV	FV	.75

40	2 Ringgit	VG	VF	UNC
	ND (1996-99). Purple and red-violet on multicolor underprint. Modern tower at left, communications satellite at upper center on back. Printer: NBM (without imprint).			
	a. Signature Ahmad M. Don vertical at left.	FV	FV	1.50
	b. Signature Ali Abu Hassan vertical at left.	FV	FV	1.50
	c. Signature Ali Abu Hassan horizontal at lower center.	FV	FV	1.50

41	5 Ringgit	VG	VF	UNC
	ND (1999; 2001). Green on multicolor underprint. Modern buildings on back. Printer: CBNC.			
	a. ND (1999). Signature Ali Abu Hassan.	FV	FV	2.00
	b. ND (2001). Signature Zeti Akhtar Aziz.	FV	FV	2.00

42	10 Ringgit	VG	VF	UNC
	ND (1997-). Red on multicolor underprint. Modern passenger train at left, passenger jet airplane, freighter ship at center on back.			
	a. ND (1997). Signature Ahmad M. Don vertical at left.	FV	FV	5.00
	b. ND (1999). Signature Ali Abu Hassan vertical at left.	FV	FV	5.00
	c. ND (1999). Signature Ali Abu Hassan at center.	FV	FV	5.00
	d. ND (2001). Signature Zeti Akhtar Aziz.	FV	FV	5.00

43	50 Ringgit	VG	VF	UNC
	ND (1998-). Dark green and green on multicolor underprint. Offshore oil platform at left on back.			
	a. ND (1998). Signature Ahmad M. Don vertical at left.	FV	FV	20.00
	b. ND (1999). Signature Ali Abu Hassan vertical at left.	FV	FV	25.00
	c. ND (1999). Signature Ali Abu Hassan at center.	FV	FV	20.00
	d. ND (2001). Signature Zeti Akhtar Aziz.	FV	FV	20.00

		VG	VF	UNC
44	**100 Ringgit** ND (1998-). Purple and brown on multicolor underprint. Automobile production themes on back.			
	a. ND (1998). Signature Ahmad M. Don vertical at left.	FV	FV	40.00
	b. ND (1999). Signature Ali Abu Hassan vertical at left.	FV	FV	50.00
	c. ND (1999). Signature Ali Abu Hassasn at center.	FV	FV	40.00
	d. ND (2001). Signature Zeti Akhtar Aziz.	FV	FV	40.00

1998 Commemorative Issue

#45, XVI Commonwealth Games, Kuala Lumpur, 1998. Polymer plastic.

		VG	VF	UNC
45	**50 Ringgit** (19)98. Black and purple on multicolor underprint. T. A. Rahman at right, Petronas Towers at center, multimedia corridor in underprint at right. Utama Bukit Jalil Stadium at center, games logo at left on back. Serial # prefix: *KL/98.*	FV	FV	40.00

2004 ND First Issue

		VG	VF	UNC
46	**10 Ringgit** ND (2004). Red and orange on multicolor underprint. Wide holographic strip at right.	FV	FV	20.00

2004 ND Polymer Issue

		VG	VF	UNC
47	**5 Ringgit** ND (2004). Green. Polymer plastic.	FV	FV	2.00
48	**10 Ringgit** ND (2004). Red. Polymer plastic.	FV	FV	20.00

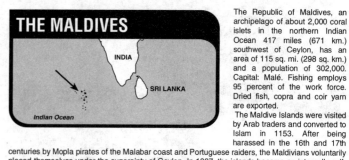

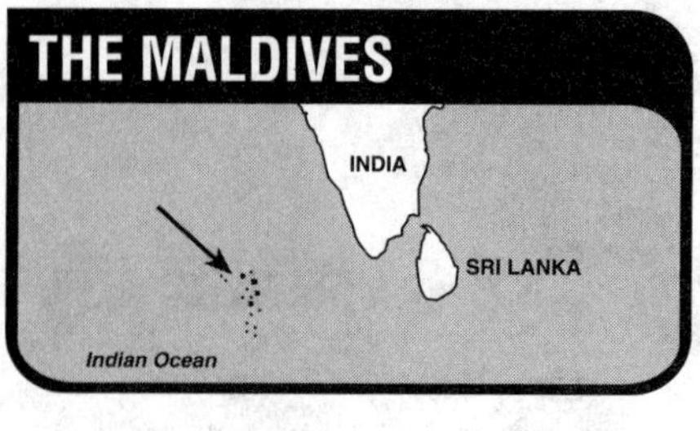

The Republic of Maldives, an archipelago of about 2,000 coral islets in the northern Indian Ocean 417 miles (671 km.) southwest of Ceylon, has an area of 115 sq. mi. (298 sq. km.) and a population of 302,000. Capital: Malé. Fishing employs 95 percent of the work force. Dried fish, copra and coir yarn are exported.

The Maldive Islands were visited by Arab traders and converted to Islam in 1153. After being harassed in the 16th and 17th centuries by Mopla pirates of the Malabar coast and Portuguese raiders, the Maldivians voluntarily placed themselves under the suzerainty of Ceylon. In 1887, the islands became an internally self-governing British protectorate and a nominal dependency of Ceylon. Traditionally a sultanate, the Maldives became a republic in 1953 but restored the sultanate in 1954. The Sultanate of the Maldive Islands attained complete internal and external autonomy within the Commonwealth on July 26, 1965, and on Nov. 11, 1968 again became a republic.

RULERS:

British to 1965

MONETARY SYSTEM:

1 Rufiyaa (Rupee) = 100 Lari

Republic

Maldivian State, Government Treasurer

1951; 1960; 1980 Issue

		VG	VF	UNC
6	**50 Rupees** 1951-80. Blue on multicolor underprint. Royal Embarkation Gate at Male at center on back			
	a. 1951/AH1371.	35.00	150.	400.
	b. 4.6.1960/AH1379.	4.00	20.00	60.00
	c. Litho. 1.8.1980/AH17.7.1400.	5.00	25.00	85.00
	s. As c. Specimen.	—	—	175.

		VG	VF	UNC
7	**100 Rupees**			
	1951; 1960. Green on multicolor underprint. Back brown, violet and m/c; park and building complex at center.			
	a. 1951/AH1371.	45.00	175.	500.
	b. 4.6.1960/AH1379.	7.50	30.00	100.

#8 not assigned.

MALDIVES MONETARY AUTHORITY

1983 ISSUE

#9-14 dhow at r. Wmk: Arms. Printer: BWC.

		VG	VF	UNC
9	**2 Rufiyaa**			
	7.10.1983/AH1404. Dark olive-green on multicolor underprint. Shoreline village on back.			
	a. Issued note.	FV	FV	4.00
	s. Specimen.	—	—	30.00

		VG	VF	UNC
10	**5 Rufiyaa**			
	7.10.1983/AH1404. Deep purple on green and multicolor underprint. Fishing boats at center on back.			
	a. Issued note.	FV	FV	4.00
	s. Specimen.	—	—	30.00

		VG	VF	UNC
11	**10 Rufiyaa**			
	7.10.1983/AH1404. Brown on green and multicolor underprint. Villagers working at center on back.			
	a. Issued note.	FV	FV	4.00
	s. Specimen.	—	—	30.00

		VG	VF	UNC
12	**20 Rufiyaa**			
	1983; 1987. Red-violet on multicolor underprint. Fishing boats at dockside in Malé Harbour on back.			
	a. 7.10.1983/AH1404. Imprint at bottom center on back.	FV	FV	7.00
	b. 25.8.1987/AH1408. Without imprint at bottom center on back.	FV	FV	5.50
	s. Specimen. As a.	—	—	30.00

		VG	VF	UNC
13	**50 Rufiyaa**			
	1983; 1987. Blue-violet on multicolor underprint. Village market in Malé at center on back.			
	a. 7.10.1983/AH1404. Imprint at bottom center on back.	FV	FV	25.00
	b. 25.8.1987/AH1408. Without imprint at bottom center on back.	FV	FV	17.50
	s. Specimen.	—	—	30.00

		VG	VF	UNC
14	**100 Rufiyaa**			
	1983; 1987. Dark green and brown on multicolor underprint. Tomb of Medhuziyaaraiy at center on back.			
	a. 7.10.1983/AH1404. Imprint at bottom center on back.	FV	FV	35.00
	b. 25.8.1987/AH1408. Without imprint at bottom center on back.	FV	FV	27.50
	s. Specimen.	—	—	30.00

1990 ISSUE

#15-17 wmk: Arms. Printer: TDLR.

15 **2 Rufiyaa** | VG FV | VF FV | UNC 2.50
26.7.1990/AH1411. Dark olive-green on multicolor underprint. Like #9, but darker dhow and trees, also slightly different underprint colors and less clouds.

16 **5 Rufiyaa** | FV | FV | 3.00
26.7.1990/AH1411. Deep purple on multicolor underprint. Like #10, but brown underprint at center, also darker boats on back.

17 **500 Rufiyaa** | VG FV | VF FV | UNC 120.
26.7.1990/AH1411. Orange and green on multicolor underprint. Grand Friday Mosque and Islamic Center on back.

1995-98 ISSUE

#18-21 w/design into borders. Ascending size serial # at l. and lower r. Wmk: Arms. Printer: TDLR.

18 **5 Rufiyaa** | VG FV | VF FV | UNC 2.00
27.4.1998/AH1419; 2000/AH1421. Deep purple, dark blue and violet on multicolor underprint. Like #16.

19 **10 Rufiyaa** | VG FV | VF FV | UNC 3.00
25.10.1998/AH1419. Dark brown, green and orange on multicolor underprint. Like #11.

20 **20 Rufiyaa** | VG FV | VF FV | UNC 5.50
2000/AH1421. Red-violet and green on multicolor underprint. Like #12.

21 **50 Rufiyaa** | VG FV | VF FV | UNC 12.50
2000/AH1421. Blue-violet and light green on multicolor underprint. Like #13.

22 **100 Rufiyaa**
1995; 2000; 2002. Dark green and brown on multicolor underprint. Like #14 but light blue underprint at left.

	VG	VF	UNC
a. 29.7.1995/AH1416.	FV	FV	25.00
b. 2000/AH1421. Enhanced UV features.	FV	FV	22.50
c. 2002/AH1423. Expected new issue.	—	—	—

23 **500 Rufiyaa** | VG FV | VF FV | UNC 90.00
1.5.1996/AH1416; 2000/AH1421. Orange and green on multicolor underprint. Like #17 but ship and other design elements in dark color.

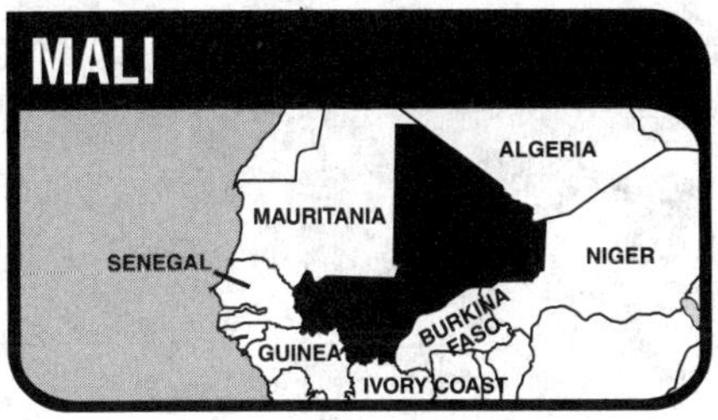

The Republic of Mali, a landlocked country in the interior of West Africa southwest of Algeria, has an area of 478,764 sq. mi. (1,240,000 sq. km.) and a population of 12.56 million. Capital: Bamako. Livestock, fish, cotton and peanuts are exported.

Malians are descendants of the ancient Malinke Kingdom of Mali that controlled the middle Niger from the 11th to the 17th centuries. The French penetrated the Sudan (now Mali) about 1880, and established their rule in 1898 after subduing fierce native resistance. In 1904 the area became the colony of Upper Senegal-Niger (changed to French Sudan in 1920), and became part of the French Union in 1946. In 1958 French Sudan became the Sudanese Republic with complete internal autonomy. Senegal joined with the Sudanese Republic in 1959 to form the Mali Federation which, in 1960, became a fully independent member of the French Community. Upon Senegal's subsequent withdrawal from the Federation, the Sudanese, on Sept. 22, 1960, proclaimed their nation the fully independent Republic of Mali and severed all ties with France.

Mali seceded from the African Financial Community in 1962, then rejoined in 1984. Issues specially marked with letter *D* for Mali were made by the Banque des Etats de l'Afrique de l'Ouest. See also French West Africa, and West African States.

MONETARY SYSTEM:

1 Franc = 100 Centimes

SIGNATURE VARIETIES			
1	Ministre Des Finances		Gouverneur de La Banque
2	Ministre d'Etat	Ministre Des Finances	Gouverneur de La Banque
3	Le Président du Council d' Administration		Le Directeur Genéral
4	Le Président du Council d' Administration		Le Directeur Genéral
5	Le Président du Council d' Administration		Le Directeur Genéral
6	Le Président du Council d' Administration		Le Directeur Genéral
7	Le Président du Council d' Administration		Le Directeur Genéral
8	Le Président du Council d' Administration		Le Directeur Genéral
9	Le Président du Council d' Administration		Le Directeur Genéral

BANQUE DE LA RÉPUBLIQUE DU MALI

FIRST 1960 (1962) ISSUE

Note: Post-dated on Day of Independence.

#1-5 Pres. Modibo Keita at l. Sign. 1.

			VG	VF	UNC
1	**50 Francs** 22.9.1960. Purple on multicolor underprint. Village on back.		10.00	35.00	125.

		VG	VF	UNC
2	**100 Francs** 22.9.1960. Brown on yellow underprint. Cattle on back.	10.00	50.00	165.
3	**500 Francs** 22.9.1960. Red on light blue and orange underprint. Woman and tent on back.	60.00	400.	1000.

		VG	VF	UNC
4	**1000 Francs** 22.9.1960. Blue on light green and orange underprint. Farmers with oxen at lower right. Back blue; man and huts.	25.00	100.	500.
5	**5000 Francs** 22.9.1960. Green on multicolor underprint. 2 farmers plowing with oxen at right. Market scene and building on back.	85.00	285.	—

SECOND 1960 (1967) ISSUE

Note: Post-dated on Day of Independence.

#6-10 Modibo Keita at r. Sign 2. Printer: TDLR.

		VG	VF	UNC
6	**50 Francs** 22.9.1960 (1967). Purple on blue and light green underprint. Dam at lower left. Back purple; woman and village.	17.50	50.00	220.

		VG	VF	UNC
7	**100 Francs** 22.9.1960 (1967). Brown on green and lilac underprint. Tractors at lower left. Back brown; old man at right, canoes at center, city view behind.	15.00	50.00	215.

		VG	VF	UNC
8	**500 Francs** 22.9.1960 (1967). Green on yellow, blue and red underprint. Building at lower left. Longhorn cattle on back.	30.00	125.	550.

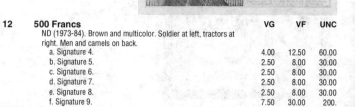

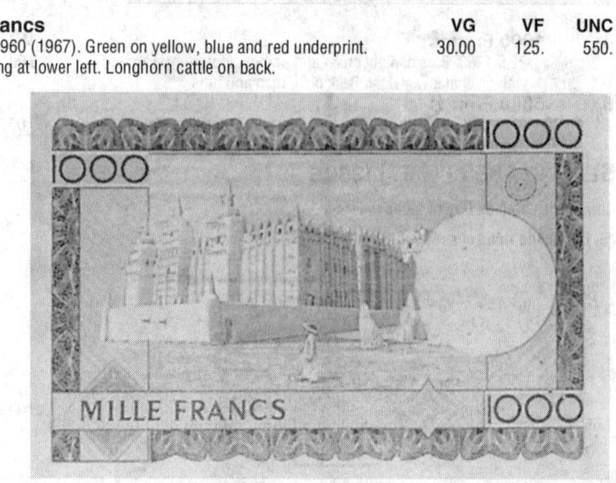

		VG	VF	UNC
9	**1000 Francs** 22.9.1960 (1967). Blue on lilac and brown underprint. Bank at lower left. Back blue; people and Djenne mosque.	60.00	300.	950.

		VG	VF	UNC
10	**5000 Francs** 22.9.1960 (1967). Dark red on green underprint. Farmers at center. Market scene and buildings on back.	65.00	300.	1000.

BANQUE CENTRALE DU MALI

1970-73 ND ISSUES

#12-15 wmk: Man's head. Sign. varieties.

		VG	VF	UNC
11	**100 Francs** ND (1972-73). Brown and multicolor. Woman at left, hotel at right. Woman at left, boats docking at center on back. Signature 4.	6.00	25.00	100.

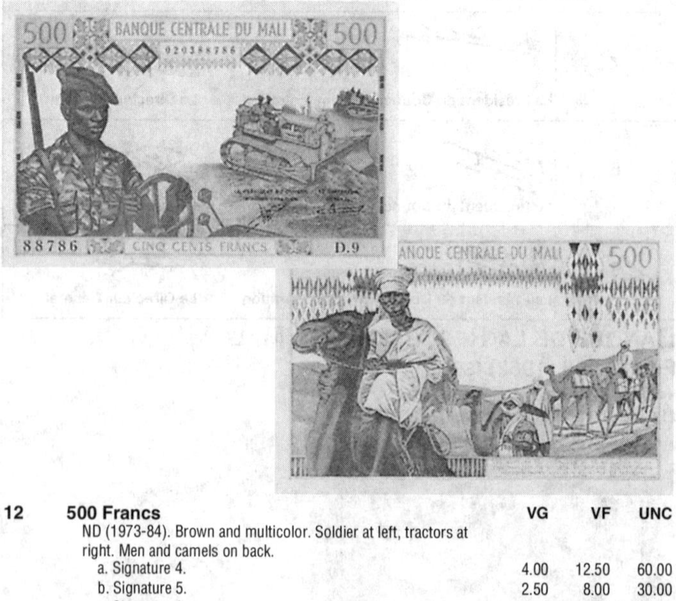

		VG	VF	UNC
12	**500 Francs** ND (1973-84). Brown and multicolor. Soldier at left, tractors at right. Men and camels on back.			
	a. Signature 4.	4.00	12.50	60.00
	b. Signature 5.	2.50	8.00	30.00
	c. Signature 6.	2.50	8.00	30.00
	d. Signature 7.	2.50	8.00	30.00
	e. Signature 8.	2.50	8.00	30.00
	f. Signature 9.	7.50	30.00	200.

13 **1000 Francs**

ND (1970-84). Brownish black, purple and multicolor. Building at left, older man at right. Carvings at left, mountain village at center on back.

	VG	VF	UNC
a. Signature 4.	3.50	12.50	35.00
b. Signature 5.	3.50	12.50	35.00
c. Signature 6.	3.50	10.00	30.00
d. Signature 7.	3.50	10.00	30.00
e. Signature 8.	3.50	10.00	30.00

14 **5000 Francs**

ND (1972-84). Blue, brown and multicolor. Cattle at lower left, man with turban at right. Woman and flowers at left center, woman at textile machinery at right on back.

	VG	VF	UNC
a. Signature 4.	12.50	35.00	225.
b. Signature 5.	12.50	30.00	200.
c. Signature 6.	12.50	30.00	200.
d. Signature 7.	12.50	30.00	200.
e. Signature 8.	12.50	30.00	175.

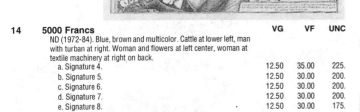

15 **10,000 Francs**

ND (1970-84). Multicolor. Man with fez at left, factory at lower right. Weaver at left, young woman with coin headband at right on back.

	VG	VF	UNC
a. Signature 3.	20.00	65.00	300.
b. Signature 4.	20.00	60.00	250.
c. Signature 5.	20.00	60.00	275.
d. Signature 6.	25.00	75.00	250.
e. Signature 7.	20.00	60.00	250.
f. Signature 8.	20.00	60.00	250.
g. Signature 9.	20.00	65.00	275.

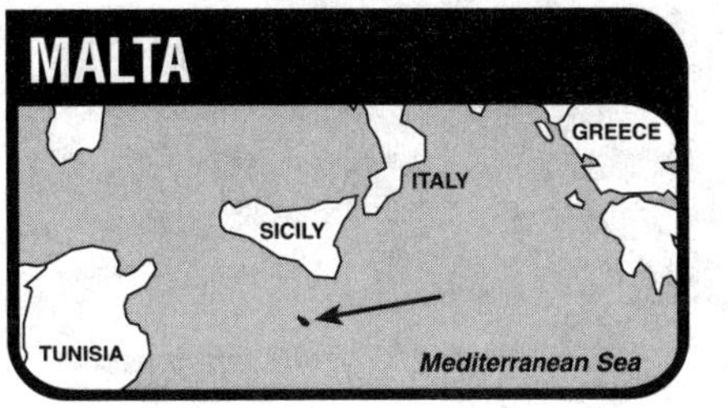

The Republic of Malta, an independent parliamentary democracy within the British Commonwealth, is situated in the Mediterranean Sea between Sicily and North Africa. With the islands of Gozo and Comino, Malta has an area of 122 sq. mi. (316 sq. km.) and a population of 379,000. Capital: Valletta. With the islands of Gozo (Ghawdex), Comino, Cominetto and Filfla, Malta has no proven mineral resources, an agriculture insufficient to its needs and a small but expanding, manufacturing facility. Clothing, textile yarns and fabrics, and knitted wear are exported.

For more than 3,500 years Malta was ruled, in succession, by Phoenicians, Carthaginians, Romans, Arabs, Normans, the Knights of Malta, France and Britain. Napoleon seized Malta by treachery in 1798. The French were ousted by a Maltese insurrection assisted by Britain, and in 1814, Malta, of its own free will, became part of the British Empire. The island was awarded the George Cross for conspicuous corrage during World War II. Malta obtained full independence in September 1964, electing to remain within the Commonwealth with Elizabeth II as Head of State as Queen of Malta.

RULERS:

British to 1974

MONETARY SYSTEM:

1 Shilling = 12 Pence
1 Pound = 20 Shillings to 1971

REPUBLIC

GOVERNMENT

1949 ORDINANCE; 1963 ND ISSUE

#25-27 Qn. Elizabeth II at r. Printer: BWC.

25 **10 Shillings**

L.1949 (1963). Green and blue on multicolor underprint. Cross at center. Mgarr Harbor, Gozo on back.

	VG	VF	UNC
a. Issued note.	9.00	50.00	225.
s. Specimen.	—	—	—

26 **1 Pound**

L.1949 (1963). Brown and violet on multicolor underprint. Cross at center. Industrial Estate, Marsa on back.

	VG	VF	UNC
a. Issued note.	10.00	50.00	225.
s. Specimen.	—	—	—

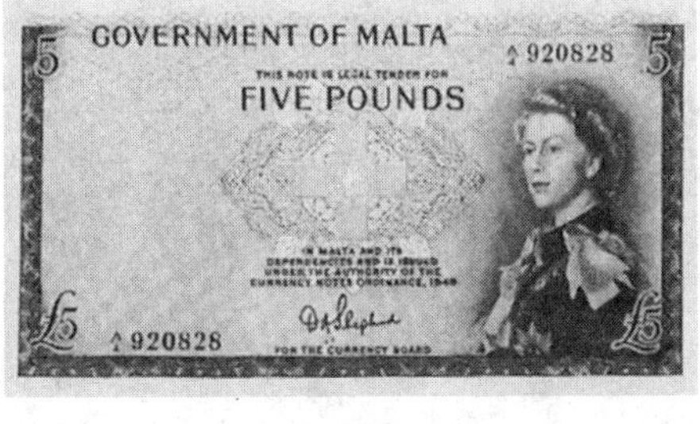

27	5 Pounds	VG	VF	UNC
	L.1949 (1961). Blue on multicolor underprint. Cross at center. Grand Harbor on back.			
	a. Signature D. A. Shepherd (1961).	35.00	200.	1100.
	b. Signature R. Soler (1963).	40.00	225.	1250.
	s. As a. Specimen, punch hole cancelled.	—	—	450.

Central Bank of Malta

1967 Central Bank Act; 1968-69 ND Issue

#28-30 designs similar to #25-27. Printer: BWC.

28	10 Shillings	VG	VF	UNC
	L.1967 (1968). Red on multicolor underprint. Similar to #25.			
	a. Issued note.	4.00	15.00	80.00
	ct. Color trial. Dark olive on multicolor underprint.	—	Unc	250.

29	1 Pound	VG	VF	UNC
	L.1967 (1969). Olive-green on multicolor underprint. Similar to #26.			
	a. Issued note.	7.50	25.00	125.
	s. Specimen.	—	Unc	100.
	ct. Color trial. Blue on multicolor underprint.	—	Unc	275.

30	5 Pounds	VG	VF	UNC
	L.1967 (1968). Brown and violet on multicolor underprint. Similar to #27.	20.00	50.00	225.

Bank Centrali ta' Malta

1967 Central Bank Act; 1973 ND Issue

#31-33 arms at r., map at ctr. Wmk: Allegorical head of Malta. Printer: TDLR. Replacement notes: Serial # prefix *X/1, Y/1 or Z/1* (by denomintation).

31	1 Lira	VG	VF	UNC
	L.1967 (1973). Green on multicolor underprint. War Memorial at left. Prehistoric Temple in Tarxien at left, old capital city of Medina at center on back.			
	a. Signature J. Sammut and A. Camilleri.	1.00	7.50	35.00
	b. Signature H. de Gabriele and J. Laspina.	1.00	7.50	35.00
	c. Signature H. de Gabriele and A. Camilleri.	1.00	7.50	35.00
	d. Signature J. Laspina and J. Sammut.	1.00	7.50	35.00
	e. Signature A. Camilleri and J. Laspina.	1.00	7.50	35.00
	f. Signature J. Sammut and H. de Gabriele.	1.00	7.50	35.00

32	5 Liri	VG	VF	UNC
	L.1967 (1973). Blue on multicolor underprint. Neptune at left. Marina at left, boats at center right on back.			
	a. Signature H. de Gabriele and J. Laspina.	3.00	15.00	80.00
	b. Signature H. de Gabriele and A. Camilleri.	3.00	15.00	80.00
	c. Signature J. Laspina and J. Sammut.	3.00	15.00	80.00
	d. Signature A. Camilleri and J. Laspina.	3.00	10.00	70.00
	e. Signature J. Sammut and H. de Gabriele.	3.00	10.00	70.00
	f. Signature J. Sammut and A. Camilleri.	3.00	10.00	70.00

33 10 Liri VG VF UNC

L.1967 (1973). Brown on multicolor underprint. Like #32. View of Grand Harbour and boats on back.

	VG	VF	UNC
a. Signature H. de Gabriele and A. Camilleri.	4.50	35.00	180.
b. Signature J. Laspina and J. Sammut.	4.50	35.00	220.
c. Signature A. Camilleri and J. Laspina.	4.50	35.00	220.
d. Signature J. Sammut and H. de Gabriele.	4.50	35.00	220.
e. Signature L. Spiteri with title: *DEPUTAT GOVERNATUR.*	4.50	35.00	150.

1979 ND Issue

Central Bank Act, 1967

#34-36 map at upper l., arms at upper r. Wmk: Allegorical head of Malta. Printer: TDLR. Replacement notes: Serial prefix *X/2*, *Y/2* or *Z/2* (by denomination).

34 1 Lira VG VF UNC

L.1967 (1979). Brown on multicolor underprint. Watch tower "Gardjola" at center. New University at left center on back.

	VG	VF	UNC
a. Without dot.	FV	5.00	14.00
b. With 1 dot added for blind at upper right.	FV	5.00	12.50

35 5 Liri VG VF UNC

L.1967 (1979). Purple and violet on multicolor underprint. Statue of "Culture" at center. Aerial view of Marsa Industrial Estate at left center on back.

	VG	VF	UNC
a. Without 2 dots.	FV	20.00	50.00
b. With 2 dots added for blind at upper right.	FV	17.50	42.50

36 10 Liri VG VF UNC

L.1967 (1979). Gray and pink on multicolor underprint. Statue of "Justice" at center. Aerial view of Malta drydocks at left center on back.

	VG	VF	UNC
a. Without 3 dots.	FV	35.00	80.00
b. With 3 dots added for blind at upper right.	FV	35.00	90.00

1986 ND Issue

#37-40 sailing craft and map of Malta at ctr., A. Barbara at r. Wmk: Allegorical head of Malta. Printer: TDLR. Replacement notes: Serial # prefix *W/2*, *X/2*, *Y/2* or *Z/2* (by denomination).

37 2 Liri VG VF UNC

L.1967 (1986). Red-orange on multicolor underprint. Dockside crane at left, aerial harbor view at right on back. FV FV 25.00

38 5 Liri VG VF UNC

L.1967 (1986). Gray-green and blue on multicolor underprint, with two black horizontal accounting bars at lower right. Sailboats in harbor and repairing of fishing nets on back. FV FV 50.00

39 10 Liri VG VF UNC

L.1967 (1986). Olive and dark green on multicolor underprint, with three dark green horizontal accounting bars at lower right. Shipbuilding on back. FV FV 85.00

40 20 Lira VG VF UNC

L.1967 (1986). Brown and red-brown on multicolor underprint, With four brown horizontal accounting bars at lower right. Statue and government building at center on back. FV FV 165.

1989 ND Issue

#41-44 doves at l., Malta standing w/rudder at ctr. r. Wmk: Turreted head of Malta. Printer: TDLR. Replacement notes: Serial # prefix *W/2*, *X/2*, *Y/2* or *Z/2* (by denomination).

		VG	VF	UNC
41	**2 Liri** L.1967 (1989). Purple on multicolor underprint. Buildings in Malta and Gozo on back.	FV	FV	17.50
42	**5 Liri** L.1967 (1989). Blue on multicolor underprint. Historical tower on back.	FV	FV	35.00
43	**10 Liri** L.1967 (1989). Green on multicolor underprint. Wounded people being brought into National Assembly on back.	FV	FV	60.00
44	**20 Lira** L.1967 (1989). Brown on multicolor underprint. Prime Minister Dr. G. B. Olivier on back.	FV	FV	120.

1994 ND Issue

#45-48 like #41-44 but w/enhanced colors, segmented foil over security threads and ascending size serial # at upper l.

		VG	VF	UNC
45	**2 Liri**			
	L.1967 (1994). Purple on multicolor underprint. Like #41.			
	a. Signature Anthony P. Galdes.	FV	FV	15.00
	b. Signature Francis J. Vasallo.	FV	FV	12.00
	c. Signature Emanuel Ellul.	FV	FV	10.00

		VG	VF	UNC
46	**5 Liri**			
	L.1967 (1994). Blue on multicolor underprint. Like #42.			
	a. Signature Anthony P. Galdes.	FV	FV	35.00
	b. Signature Francis J. Vassallo.	FV	FV	27.50
	c. Signature Emanuel Ellul.	FV	FV	22.50

		VG	VF	UNC
47	**10 Liri**			
	L.1967 (1994). Green on multicolor underprint. Like #43.			
	a. Signature Anthony P. Galdes.	FV	FV	65.00
	b. Signature Emanuel Ellul.	FV	FV	52.50
	c. Signature Michael P. Bonello.	FV	FV	45.00

		VG	VF	UNC
48	**20 Lira**			
	L.1967 (1994). Brown on multicolor underprint. Signature Anthony P. Galdes. Like #44.	FV	FV	90.00

2000 Issue

#49-51 Millennium Commemorative issue.

#49-51 like #45-47 but w/map and clock hologram on wmk. area.

		VG	VF	UNC
49	**2 Liri**			
	2000. *(L. 1967.)* Purple on multicolor underprint. Like #45.	FV	FV	24.50

		VG	VF	UNC
50	**5 Liri**			
	2000. *(L.1967.)* Blue on multicolor underprint. Like #46.	FV	FV	35.00

		VG	VF	UNC
51	**10 Liri**			
	2000. *(L. 1967.)* Green on multicolor underprint. Like #47.	FV	FV	50.00

Collector Series

Bank Centrali ta' Malta

1979 Issue

		Issue Price	Mkt. Value
CS1	**ND (1979) 1-10 Liri**		
	#34a-36a with overprint: *SPECIMEN* and Maltese cross prefix serial #.	—	50.00

2000 Issue

		Issue Price	Mkt. Value
CS2	**ND (2000) 2-5-10 Liri**		
	#49-51 in individual folders titled: *Special Millennium Issue.* Hologram on watermark area: *1999 Towards a New Millennium 2000.* 25,000 sets issued.	—	100.

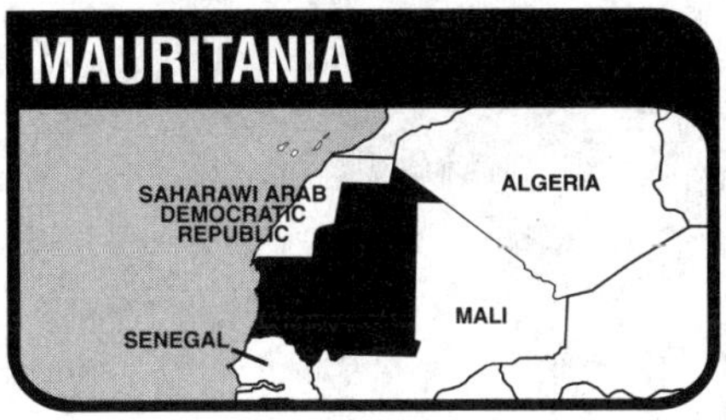

The Islamic Republic of Mauritania, located in northwest Africa bounded by Spanish Sahara, Mali, Algeria, Senegal and the Atlantic Ocean, has an area of 397,955 sq. mi. (1,030,700 sq. km.) and a population of 2.58 million. Capital: Nouakchott. The economy centers on herding, agriculture, fishing and mining. Iron ore, copper concentrates and fish products are exported.

The indigenous Negroid inhabitants were driven out of Mauritania by Berber invaders of the Islamic faith in the 11th century. The Berbers in turn were conquered by Arab invaders, the Beni Hassan, in the 16th century. Arab traders carried on a gainful trade in gum arabic, gold and slaves with Portuguese, Dutch, English and French traders until late in the 19th century when France took control of the area, and in 1920 made it a part of French West Africa. Mauritania became a part of the French Union in 1946 and was made an autonomous republic within the new French Community in 1958, when the Islamic Republic of Mauritania was proclaimed. The republic became independent on November 28, 1960, and withdrew from the French Community in 1966.

On June 28, 1973, in a move designed to emphasize its non-alignment with France, Mauritania converted its currency from the old French-supported CFA franc unit to a new unit called the Ouguiya.

MONETARY SYSTEM:

1 Ouguiya = 5 Khoum
100 Ouguiya = 500 CFA Francs, 1973-

Note: Issues specially marked with letter *E* for Mauritania were issued by the Banque Centrale des Etats de l'Afrique de l'Ouest. These issues were used before Mauritania seceded from the French Community of the West African States in 1973. For those listings see West African States.

REPUBLIC

BANQUE CENTRALE DE MAURITANIE

1973 ISSUE

#1-3 printed in Algeria.

		VG	VF	UNC
1	**100 Ouguiya**			
	20.6.1973. Blue on multicolor underprint. Mauritanian girl at center. Men loading boat on back.			
	a. Issued note.	10.00	20.00	75.00
	s. Specimen.	—	—	35.00

		VG	VF	UNC
2	**200 Ouguiya**			
	20.6.1973. Brown on multicolor underprint. Bedouin woman at left, tents in background. Camels and huts on back.			
	a. Issued note.	12.50	25.00	90.00
	s. Specimen.	—	—	40.00

NOTICE

Readers with unlisted dates, signature varieties, etc. are invited to submit photocopies of their notes to: Standard Catalog of World Paper Money, 700 East State St. Iola, WI 54990-0001, E-Mail: george.cuhaj@fwpubs.com.

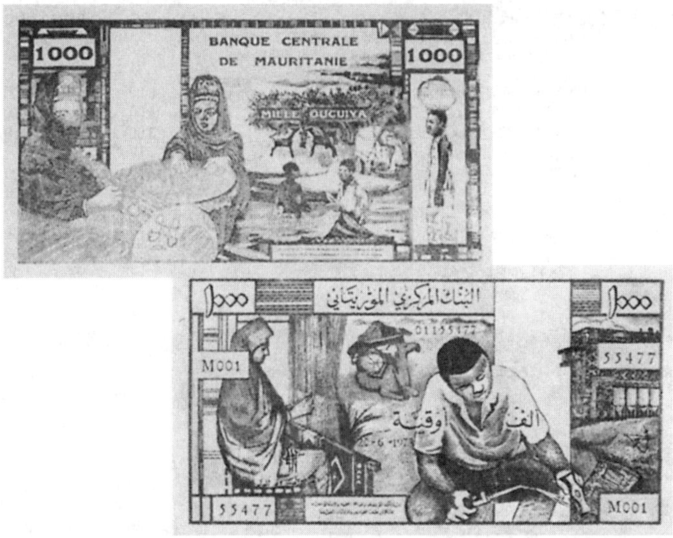

		VG	VF	UNC
3	**1000 Ouguiya**			
	20.6.1973. Green and multicolor. Woman weaving on loom at left, metal worker at right center. Local musicians and scenes on back.			
	a. Issued note.	15.00	40.00	175.
	s. Specimen.	—	—	75.00

1974; 1979 ISSUE

#4-7 wmk: Old man w/beard. Sign. varieties. Printer: G&D (w/o imprint).

		VG	VF	UNC
4	**100 Ouguiya**			
	1974-. Purple, violet and brown on multicolor underprint. Musical instruments at left, cow and tower at right on back.			
	a. 28.11.1974. Narrow black security thread.	3.00	10.00	25.00
	b. 28.11.1983.	6.00	15.00	35.00
	c. 28.11.1985.	2.00	7.50	15.00
	d. 28.11.1989. Wide green security thread.	1.50	5.00	12.50
	e. 28.11.1992.	FV	4.00	10.00
	f. 28.11.1993.	FV	3.00	9.00
	g. 28.11.1995.	FV	2.50	6.00
	h. 28.11.1996.	FV	2.00	5.00
	i. 28.11.1999.	FV	2.00	5.00
	j. 28.11.2001.	FV	2.00	5.00
	k. 28.11.2002	FV	2.00	5.00
	s. As a. Specimen.	—	—	25.00

5	200 Ouguiya	VG	VF	UNC
	1974-. Brown, dark olive-green and brown-orange on multicolor underprint. Bowl and rod at left, dugout canoe and palm tree at right on back.			
	a. 28.11.1974. Thin security thread.	6.00	15.00	30.00
	b. 28.11.1985.	4.00	10.00	25.00
	c. 28.11.1989. Thick security thread.	3.00	6.00	22.50
	d. 28.11.1992.	FV	5.00	20.00
	e. 28.11.1993.	FV	5.00	15.00
	f. 28.11.1995.	FV	5.00	10.00
	g. 28.11.1996.	FV	5.00	9.00
	h. 28.11.1999.	FV	5.00	8.50
	i. 28.11.2001.	FV	5.00	8.00
	j. 28.11.2002.	FV	FV	8.00
	s. As a. Specimen.	—	—	35.00

6	500 Ouguiya	VG	VF	UNC
	1979-. Green, brown and dark green on multicolor underprint. Back brown, green and black; field workers at left, mine entrance complex at right.			
	a. 28.11.1979. Thin security thread.	15.00	40.00	90.00
	b. 28.11.1983.	12.50	35.00	90.00
	c. 28.11.1985.	7.50	15.00	35.00
	d. 28.11.1989. Thick security thread.	5.00	12.00	36.00
	e. 28.11.1991.	FV	10.00	30.00
	f. 28.11.1992.	FV	8.00	25.00
	g. 28.11.1993.	FV	8.00	22.50
	h. 28.11.1995.	FV	8.00	20.00
	i. 28.11.1996.	FV	8.00	20.00
	s. As a. Specimen.	—	—	50.00

7	1000 Ouguiya	VG	VF	UNC
	1974-. Blue, violet and blue-black on multicolor underprint. Bowl of fish at left, camel, hut and tower at right back.			
	a. 28.11.1974. Thin security thread.	17.50	40.00	85.00
	b. 28.11.1985.	10.00	30.00	55.00
	c. 28.11.1989. Thick security thread.	8.00	25.00	45.00
	d. 28.10.1991.	FV	20.00	40.00
	e. 28.11.1992.	FV	15.00	40.00
	f. 28.11.1993.	FV	15.00	35.00
	g. 28.11.1995.	FV	15.00	27.50
	h. 28.11.1996.	FV	12.50	25.00
	s. As a. Specimen.	—	—	75.00

1999 ISSUE

8	500 Ouguiya	VG	VF	UNC
	28.11.1999; 28.11.2001; 28.11.2002. Green, brown and dark green on multicolor underprint. Similar to #6 but hologram image added to right center.	FV	FV	17.50

9	1000 Ouguiya	VG	VF	UNC
	28.11.1999; 28.11.2001; 28.11.2002. Blue on tan underprint. Similar to #7 but with hologram value added at right center.	FV	FV	22.50

2004 ISSUE

#10-14 Printer: G&D (w/o imprint) Replacement notes: Second letter of serial # prefix: *Z*.

10	100 Ouguiya	VG	VF	UNC
	28.11.2004. Green and purple on multicolor underprint. Geometric design at right. Musical instruments at left, cow feeding before tower at center on back.	FV	FV	3.00

NOTICE

Readers with unlisted dates, signature varieties, etc. are invited to submit photocopies of their notes to: Standard Catalog of World Paper Money, 700 East State St. Iola, WI 54990-0001, E-Mail: george.cuhaj@fwpubs.com.

11 **200 Ouguiya** — VG: FV | VF: FV | UNC: 5.00
28.11.2004. Brown and blue on multicolor underprint. Geometric pattern at right. Bowl at left, canoe at center on back.

12 **500 Ouguiya** — VG: FV | VF: FV | UNC: 10.00
28.11.2004. Green and brown on multicolor underprint. Geometric pattern at right. Men harvesting at left, factory at center on back.

13 **1000 Ouguiya** — VG: FV | VF: FV | UNC: 15.00
28.11.2004. Multicolor.

14 **2000 Ouguiya** — VG: FV | VF: FV | UNC: 25.00
28.11.2004. Multicolor.

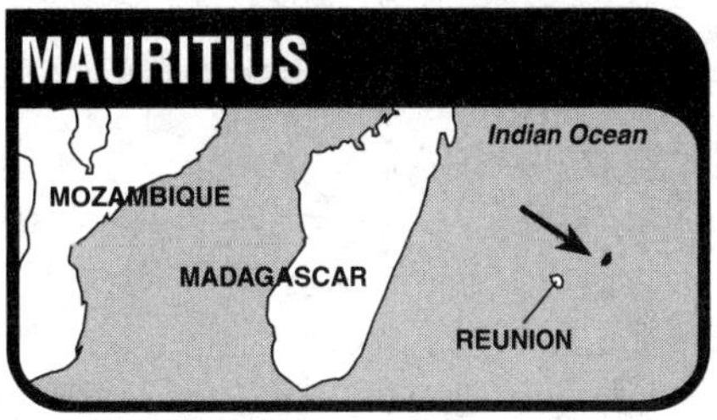

The island of Mauritius, a member of the British Commonwealth located in the Indian Ocean 500 miles (805 km.) east of Madagascar, has an area of 790 sq. mi. (2,045 sq. km.) and a population of 1.18 million. Capital: Port Louis. Sugar provides 90 percent of the export revenue.

Cartographic evidence indicates that Arabs and Malays arrived at Mauritius during the Middle Ages. Domingo Fernandez, a Portuguese navigator, visited the island in the early 16th century, but Portugal made no attempt at settlement. The Dutch took possession, and named the island, in 1598. Their colony failed to prosper and was abandoned in 1710. France claimed Mauritius in 1715 and developed a strong and prosperous colony that endured until the island was captured by the British in 1810, during the Napoleonic Wars. British possession was confirmed by the Treaty of Paris, 1814. Mauritius became independent on March 12, 1968, with Elizabeth II as Head of State as Queen of Mauritius. Mauritius became a Republic on March 12, 1992, with a President as Head of State.

RULERS:
British

MONETARY SYSTEM:
1 Rupee = 100 Cents, 1848-

BRITISH ADMINISTRATION

BANK OF MAURITIUS

SIGNATURE VARIETIES

	GOVERNOR	MANAGING DIRECTOR
1	 Mr. A. Beejadhur 1.7.1967-31.12.1972	 Mr. D. G. H. Cook 1.7.1967-27.7.1968
2	 Mr. A. Beejadhur 1.7.1967-31.12.1972	 Mr. D. C. Keys 28.7.1968-27.21920
3	 Mr. A. Beejadhur 1.7.1967-31.12.1972	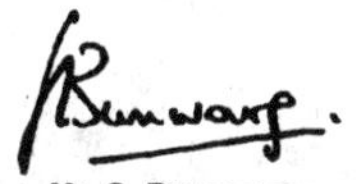 Mr. G. Bunwaree 28.2.1970-31.12.1972
4	 Mr. G. Bunwaree 1.1.1973-9.6.1982	 Sir I. Ramphul 1.1.1973-9.6.1982
5	 Sir I. Ramphul 10.6.1982-31.3.1996	 Mr. R. Tacouri 10.6.1982-28.2.1997
6	 Mr. D. Maraye 1.4.1996-30.11.1998	 Mr. B. Gujadhur 1.3.1997-1.12.1998
7	 Mr. R. Basant Roi 1.12.1998-	 Mr. B. R. Gujadhur 17.12.1998-

NOTICE

Readers with unlisted dates, signature varieties, etc. are invited to submit photocopies of their notes to: Standard Catalog of World Paper Money, 700 East State St. Iola, WI 54990-0001, E-Mail: george.cuhaj@fwpubs.com.

1967 ND Issue

#30-33 Qn. Elizabeth II at r. Wmk: Dodo bird. Printer: TDLR. Replacement notes: Serial # prefix Z/#.

30	5 Rupees	VG	VF	UNC
	ND (1967). Blue on multicolor underprint. Sailboat on back.			
	a. Signature 1.	1.00	5.00	35.00
	b. Signature 3.	1.50	7.50	50.00
	c. Signature 4.	.75	2.50	10.00
	s. As a. Specimen.	—	—	—

31	10 Rupees	VG	VF	UNC
	ND (1967). Red on multicolor underprint. Government building on back.			
	a. Signature 1.	1.50	7.50	50.00
	b. Signature 2.	2.50	10.00	75.00
	c. Signature 4.	.75	4.00	15.00

32	25 Rupees	VG	VF	UNC
	ND (1967). Green on multicolor underprint. Ox cart on back.			
	a. Signature 1.	2.50	12.50	75.00
	b. Signature 4.	2.25	10.00	65.00

33	50 Rupees	VG	VF	UNC
	ND (1967). Purple on multicolor underprint. Ships docked at Port Louis harbor on back.			
	a. Signature 1.	10.00	40.00	185.
	b. Signature 2.	12.50	50.00	225.
	c. Signature 4.	5.00	20.00	85.00

1985-91 ND Issue

#34-41 replacement notes: Serial # prefix Z/#.

#34-36 outline of Mauritius map on back. Wmk: Dodo bird. Printer: TDLR. Sign. 5.

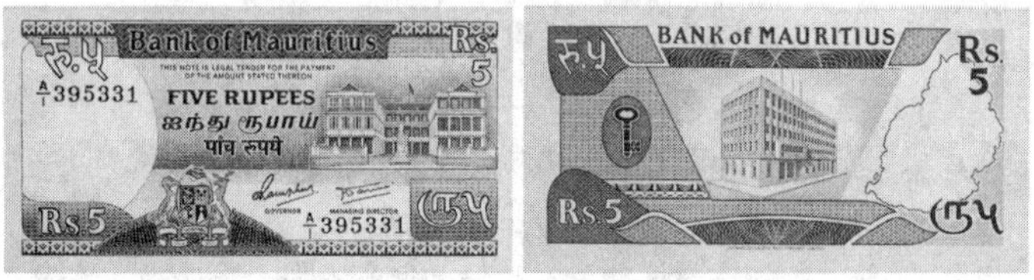

34	5 Rupees	VG	VF	UNC
	ND (1985). Dark brown. Arms at lower left center, building with flag at right. Bank on back.	FV	FV	3.00

35	10 Rupees	VG	VF	UNC
	ND (1985). Green on multicolor underprint. Arms at lower left center, building with flag at center right. Bridge on back.			
	a. Orange UV latent printing. dark green printing.	FV	.75	4.00
	b. Dark green printing. Green UV latent printing.	FV	FV	3.00

Note: the light green variety formerly listed is the result of fading.

36	20 Rupees	VG	VF	UNC
	ND. Bluish purple, blue-green, blue and orange on multicolor underprint. Lady Jugnauth at left, arms at center, building with flag at lower right. Satellite dishes at center on back.	FV	FV	7.00

#37 and 38 arms at lower l. to lower ctr., bldg. w/flag at r. Wmk: Dodo bird. Printer: BWC (w/o imprint).

37 **50 Rupees**

ND (1986). Dark blue on multicolor underprint. Two deer, butterfly and Mauritius Kestrel on back.

	VG	VF	UNC
a. Printer's name on back.	FV	2.50	15.00
b. Without printer's name on back.	FV	FV	10.00

38 **100 Rupees**

	VG	VF	UNC
ND (1986). Red on multicolor underprint. Landscape on back.	FV	FV	20.00

39 **200 Rupees**

ND (1985). Blue on multicolor underprint. Sir Seewoodsagur Ramgoolam at left. Large home (Le Réduit) on back. Printer: TDLR.

	VG	VF	UNC
a. Orange UV latent printing.	FV	7.50	45.00
b. Green UV latent printing.	FV	FV	35.00

40 **500 Rupees**

ND (1988). Brown and orange on multicolor underprint. Building with flag at center, arms below, Sir A. Jugnaurh (Prime Minister) at right. Sugar cane field workers loading wagon with mountains in background on back. Watermark: Dodo bird. Printer: TDLR (without imprint).

	VG	VF	UNC
a. Orange UV latent printing.	FV	20.00	100.
b. Green UV latent printing.	FV	FV	90.00

41 **1000 Rupees**

	VG	VF	UNC
ND (1991). Blue and red on multicolor underprint. Sir V. Ringadoo at left, palm trees and building with flag at center. Port Louis harbor on back. Watermark: Dodo bird. Printer: TDLR.	FV	FV	160.

1998 Issue

#42-48 arms at lower l., bldg. facades at ctr., standing Justice w/scales at lower r. in unpt. Wmk: Dodo bird's head. Ascending size serial #.

#42-48 raised much public controversy being printed w/the values in English/ Sanskrit/ Tamil instead of the normal order of English/ Tamil/ Sanskrit. They have been withdrawn and replaced with #49-55.

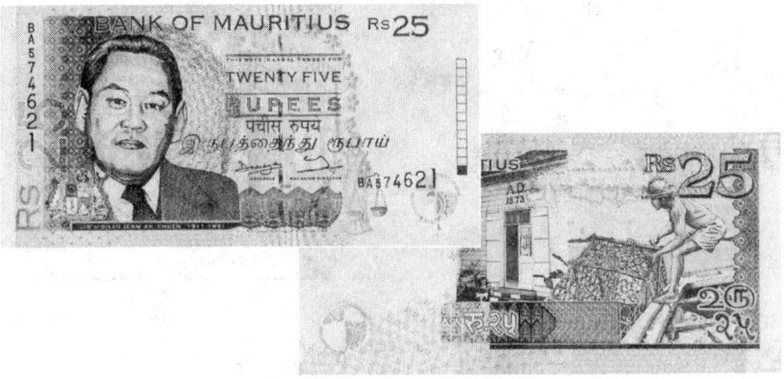

42 **25 Rupees**

	VG	VF	UNC
1998. Black, violet and brown on multicolor underprint. Sir M. J. Ah-chuen at left. Building facade at center, worker at right on back.	FV	FV	6.00

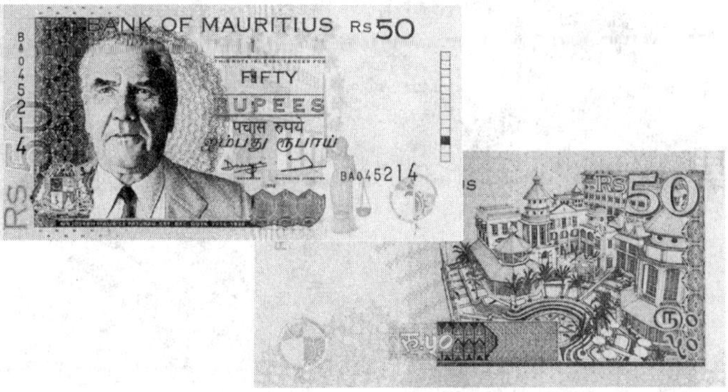

43 **50 Rupees**

	VG	VF	UNC
1998. Black, purple and deep blue on multicolor underprint. J. M. Paturau at left. Building complex at center right on back.	FV	FV	10.00

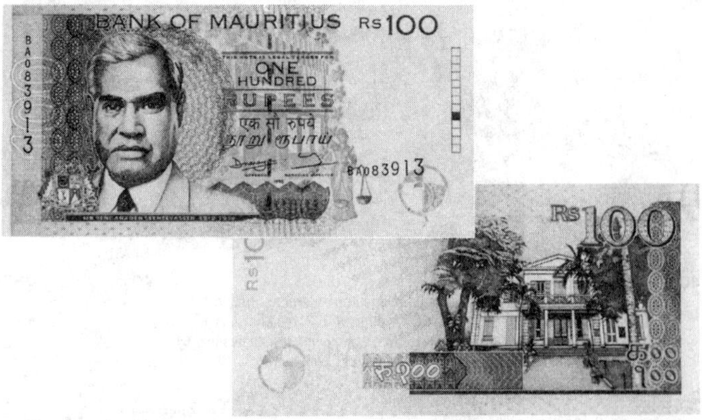

44	100 Rupees	VG	VF	UNC
	1998. Black, blue and deep blue-green on multicolor underprint. R. Seeneevassen at left. Building at left on back.	FV	FV	17.50

45	200 Rupees	VG	VF	UNC
	1998. Black, deep green and violet on multicolor underprint. Sir A. R. Mohamed at left. Market street scene at right on back.	FV	FV	30.00

46	500 Rupees	VG	VF	UNC
	1998. Black, brown and orange on multicolor underprint. S. Bissoondoyal at left. University of Mauritius at center right on back.	FV	FV	55.00

47	1000 Rupees	VG	VF	UNC
	1998. Black and blue on multicolor underprint. Sir Charles G. Duval at left. Women dancing at center right on back.	FV	FV	100.

48	2000 Rupees	VG	VF	UNC
	1998. Rose, orange, black, yellow-brown on multicolor underprint. Seewoosagur Ramgoolam at left. Ox cart on back.	FV	FV	185.

1999 Issue

#49-55 as 42-48 but language text correctly ordered as: English/ Tamil/ Sanskrit. Sign. 7.

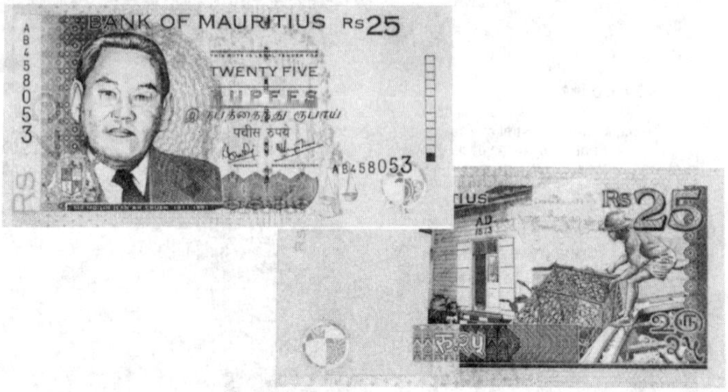

49	25 Rupees	VG	VF	UNC
	1999; 2003. Similar to #42.	FV	FV	2.50

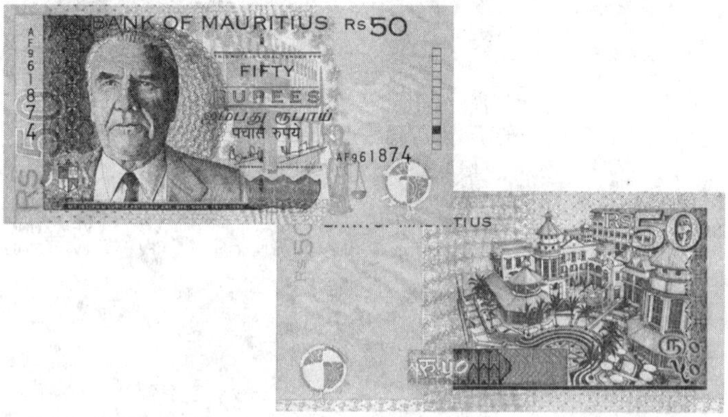

50	50 Rupees	VG	VF	UNC
	1999; 2001; 2003. Similar to #43.			
	a. 1999.	FV	FV	6.00
	b. 2001.	FV	FV	5.50
	c. 2003.	FV	FV	5.00

51	100 Rupees	VG	VF	UNC
	1999; 2001. Similar to #44.			
	a. 1999.	FV	FV	10.00
	b. 2001.	FV	FV	8.50

		VG	VF	UNC
52	**200 Rupees**			
	1999; 2001. Similar to #45.			
	a. 1999.	FV	FV	17.50
	b. 2001.	FV	FV	15.00

		VG	VF	UNC
53	**500 Rupees**			
	1999. Similar to #46.			
	a. 1999.	FV	FV	35.00

		VG	VF	UNC
54	**1000 Rupees**			
	1999. Slate black, light blue and red underprint. Sir Charles Duval at left. Back light blue and red. Building at center.			
	a. 1999.	FV	FV	65.00

		VG	VF	UNC
55	**2000 Rupees**			
	1999. Similar to #48.	FV	FV	125.

2001 Issue

		VG	VF	UNC
56	**100 Rupees**			
	2001. Similar to #51 but iridescent strip added.	FV	FV	6.00
57	**200 Rupees**			
	2001. Similar to #52 but iridescent strip added.	FV	FV	12.50
58	**500 Dollars**			
	2003.	FV	FV	30.00

		VG	VF	UNC
59	**1000 Dollars**			
	2003.	FV	FV	55.00
60	**2000 Rupees**			
	2003.	FV	FV	105.

Collector Series

Bank of Mauritius

1978 ND Issue

		Issue Price	Mkt. Value
CS1	**ND (1978) 5-50 Rupees**		
	#30c, 31c, 32b, 33c with overprint.: *SPECIMEN* and Maltese cross prefix serial #.	—	80.00

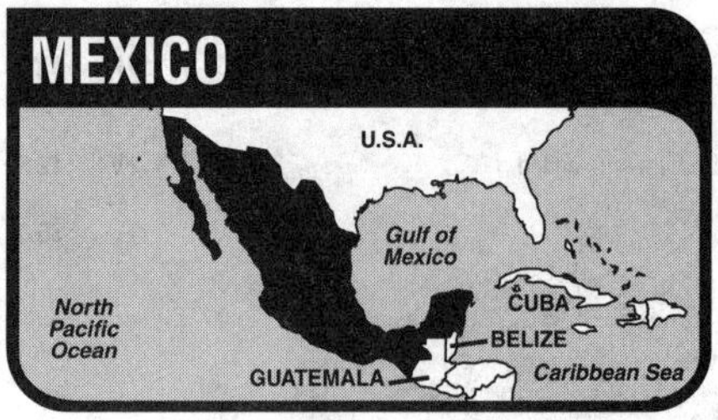

The United States of Mexico, located immediately south of the United States, has an area of 1,222,612 sq. mi. (1,967,183 sq. km.) and a population of 98.88 million. Capital: Mexico City. The economy is based on agriculture, manufacturing and mining. Cotton, sugar, coffee and shrimp are exported.

Mexico was the site of highly advanced Indian civilizations 1,500 years before conquistador Hernando Cortes conquered the wealthy Aztec empire of Montezuma, 1519-1521, and founded a Spanish colony which lasted for nearly 300 years. During the Spanish period, Mexico, then called New Spain, stretched from Guatemala to the present states of Wyoming and California, its present northern boundary having been established by the secession of Texas (1836) and the war of 1846-1848 with the United States.

Independence from Spain was declared by Father Miguel Hidalgo on Sept. 16, 1810, Mexican Independence Day, and was achieved by General Agustin de Iturbide in 1821. Iturbide became emperor in 1822 but was deposed when a republic was established a year later. For more than half a century following the birth of the republic, the political scene of Mexico was characterized by turmoil which saw two emperors (including the unfortunate Maximilian), several dictators and an average of one new government every nine months passing swiftly from obscurity to oblivion. The land, social, economic and labor reforms promulgated by the Reform Constitution of Feb. 5, 1917 established the basis for a sustained economic development and participative democracy that have made Mexico one of the most politically stable countries of modern Latin America.

MONETARY SYSTEM:

1 Peso = 100 Centavos, 1863-
1 Nuevo Peso = 1000 "old" Pesos, 1992-1996
1 Peso = 1 Nuevo Peso, 1996-

ESTADOS UNIDOS MÉXICANOS

UNITED STATES OF MEXICO

BANCO DE MÉXICO

1945-51 ISSUE

#49-53 sign. varieties. Printer: ABNC.

49 50 Pesos

1948-72. Blue on multicolor underprint.Like #41 but middle signature title: *INTERVENTOR DE LA COM. NAC. BANCARIA.* Engraved dates. Back blue; Independence Monument at center.

	VG	VF	UNC
a. 22.12.1948. Black series letters. Series: BA-BD.	3.00	6.00	15.00
b. 23.11.1949. Series: BU-BX.	3.00	6.00	15.00
c. 26.7.1950. Series: BY-CF.	3.00	5.00	15.00
d. 27.12.1950. Series: CS-DH.	3.00	5.00	15.00
e. 19.1.1953. Series: DK-DV.	2.00	4.00	15.00
f. 10.2.1954. Series: DW-EE.	2.00	4.00	15.00
g. 8.9.1954. Series: EF-FF.	2.00	4.00	15.00
h. 11.1.1956. Series: FK-FV.	2.00	4.00	15.00
i. 19.6.1957. Series: FW-GP.	2.00	4.00	15.00
j. 20.8.1958. Series: HC-HR.	2.00	4.00	15.00
k. 18.3.1959. 2 red series letters. Series: HS-IP.	2.00	4.00	15.00
l. 20.5.1959. Series: IQ-JN.	2.00	4.00	15.00
m. 25.1.1961. Series: JO-LB.	1.00	3.00	8.00
n. 8.11.1961. Series: LC-AID.	1.00	3.00	8.00
o. 24.4.1963. Series: AIE-BAP.	1.00	3.00	6.00
p. 17.2.1965. Series: BAQ-BCD.	1.00	2.50	6.00
q. 10.5.1967. Series: BCY-BEN.	1.00	2.50	6.00
r. 19.11.1969. Series: BGK-BIC.	1.00	2.50	4.00
s. 22.7.1970. Series: BIG-BKN.	1.00	2.50	4.00
t. 27.6.1972. Series: BLI-BMG.	1.00	2.50	3.00
u. 29.12.1972. Series: BMO-BRB.	1.00	2.00	3.00
v. Specimen, punched hole cancelled.	—	—	135.

50 100 Pesos

17.1.1945. Brown on multicolor underprint. Portrait M. Hidalgo at left, series letters above serial #. Middle signature title: *INTERVENTOR DEL GOBIERNO.* Printed date. Back olive-green. Coin with national coat-of-arms at center Series: S-Z.

	VG	VF	UNC
a. Issued note.	5.00	15.00	70.00
s. Specimen, punched hole cancelled.	—	—	200.

NOTICE

Readers with unlisted dates, signature varieties, etc. are invited to submit photocopies of their notes to: Standard Catalog of World Paper Money, 700 East State St. Iola, WI 54990-0001, E-Mail: george.cuhaj@fwpubs.com.

51 500 Pesos

1948-78. Black on multicolor underprint. Like #43 but without *No.* above serial #. Middle signature title: *INTERVENTOR DE LA COM. NAC. BANCARIA.* Back green; Palace of Mining at center.

	VG	VF	UNC
a. 22.12.1948. Series: BA.	10.00	40.00	125.
b. 27.12.1950. Series: CS; CT.	4.00	12.00	30.00
c. 3.12.1951. Series: DI; DJ.	4.00	12.00	30.00
d. 19.1.1953. Series: DK-DN.	4.00	12.00	30.00
e. 31.8.1955. Series: FG-FJ.	4.00	12.00	30.00
f. 11.1.1956. Series: FK-FL.	4.00	12.00	30.00
g. 19.6.1957. Series: FW-GB.	4.00	12.00	30.00
h. 20.8.1958. Series: HC-HH.	4.00	12.00	30.00
i. 18.3.1959. Series: HS-HX.	4.00	12.00	30.00
j. 20.5.1959. Series: IQ-IV.	4.00	12.00	30.00
k. 25.1.1961. Series: JO-JT.	3.00	8.00	25.00
l. 8.11.1961. Series: LC-MP.	2.00	7.00	20.00
m. 17.2.1965. Series: BAQ-BCN.	4.00	12.00	25.00
n. 24.3.1971. Series: BKO-BKT.	2.50	5.00	12.50
o. 27.6.1972. Series: BLI-Blight	2.50	5.00	12.50
p. 29.12.1972. Series: BNG-BNP.	2.50	5.00	12.50
q. 18.7.1973. Series: BUY-BWB.	1.50	5.00	12.50
r. 2.8.1974. Series: BXV-BZI.	1.50	3.50	10.00
s. 18.2.1977. Series: BZJ-CCK.	1.00	3.50	10.00
t. 18.1.1978. Series: CCL-CDY.	1.00	3.50	8.50

52 1000 Pesos

1948-77. Black on multicolor underprint. Like #44 but middle signature title: *IN-TERVENTOR DE LA COM. NAC. BANCARIA.* Back brown; Chichen Itza pyramid at center.

	VG	VF	UNC
a. 22.12.1948. Series: BA.	5.00	15.00	60.00
b. 23.11.1949. Series: BU.	5.00	15.00	60.00
c. 27.12.1950. Series: CS.	5.00	15.00	60.00
d. 3.12.1951. Series: DI; DJ.	5.00	15.00	60.00
e. 19.1.1953. Series: DK; DL.	5.00	15.00	60.00
f. 31.8.1955. Series: FG; FH.	5.00	15.00	60.00
g. 11.1.1956. Series: FK; FL.	5.00	15.00	60.00
h. 19.6.1957. Series: FW-FZ.	5.00	15.00	60.00
i. 20.8.1958. Series: HC-HE.	5.00	15.00	60.00
j. 18.3.1959. Series: HS-HU.	5.00	15.00	60.00
k. 20.5.1959. Series: IQ-IS.	5.00	15.00	60.00
l. 25.1.1961. Series: JO-JQ.	5.00	15.00	60.00
m. 8.11.1961. Series: LC-LV.	3.00	10.00	20.00
n. 17.2.1965. Series: BAQ-BCN.	2.00	8.00	15.00
o. 24.3.1971. Series: BKO-BKT.	2.00	6.00	10.00
p. 27.6.1972. Series: BLI-BLM.	2.00	6.00	10.00
q. 29.12.1972. Series: BNG-BNK.	1.00	3.00	5.00
r. 18.7.1973. Series: BUY-BWB.	2.00	6.00	10.00
s. 2.8.1974. Series: BXV-BYY.	1.00	5.00	8.00
t. 18.2.1977. Series: BZJ-CBQ.	1.00	5.00	8.00
x. Error: *EERIE HD* rather than SERIE at left.	25.00	45.00	85.00

1950; 1951 ISSUE

#53-55 sign. varieties. Printer: ABNC.

		VG	VF	UNC
53	**10 Pesos** 1951; 1953. Black on multicolor underprint. Like #47 but without *No.* above serial #.			
	a. 3.12.1951. Series: DI, DJ.	.25	2.00	5.00
	b. 19.1.1953. Series: DK-DL.	.25	2.00	5.00

1950 ISSUE

#54 and 55 sign. varieties. Printer: ABNC.

		VG	VF	UNC
54	**20 Pesos** 1950-70. Black on multicolor underprint. Like #48 but without *No.* above serial #. Back olive-green; Federal Palace courtyard at center.			
	a. 27.12.1950. Black series letters. Series: CS; CT.	1.00	3.00	15.00
	b. 19.1.1953. Series: dark	1.00	3.00	15.00
	c. 10.2.1954. Red series letters. Series: DW.	1.00	2.00	10.00
	d. 11.1.1956. Series: FK.	1.00	2.00	10.00
	e. 10.6.1957. Series: FW.	1.00	2.00	10.00
	f. 20.8.1958. Series: HC, HD.	1.00	2.00	10.00
	g. 18.3.1959. Series: HS, HT.	1.00	2.00	10.00
	h. 20.5.1959. Series: IQ, IR.	1.00	2.00	10.00
	i. 25.1.1961. Series: JO, JP.	.50	1.50	10.00
	j. 8.11.1961. Series: LC-Large	.50	1.50	10.00
	k. 24.4.1963. Series: AIE-AIH.	.50	1.50	5.00
	l. 17.2.1965. Series: BAQ-BAV.	.50	1.50	5.00
	m. 10.5.1967. Series: BCY-BDB.	.50	1.50	5.00
	n. 27.8.1969. Series: BGA; BGB.	.50	1.50	5.00
	o. 18.3.1970. Series: BID-BIF.	.50	1.50	5.00
	p. 22.7.1970. Series: BIG-BIK.	.50	1.50	5.00
	s. Specimen, punched hole cancelled.	—	Unc	135.
55	**100 Pesos** 1950-61. Brown on multicolor underprint. Like #50 but middle signature title: *INTERVENTOR DE LA COM. NAC. BANCARIA.* Engraved dates. Back olive-green; coin with national seal at center.			
	a. 27.12.1950. Black series letters. Series: CS-CZ.	4.00	8.00	30.00
	b. 19.1.1953. Series: DK-DP.	2.00	7.00	25.00
	c. 10.2.1954. Series: DW-DZ.	2.00	7.00	25.00
	d. 8.9.1954. Series: EI-ET.	2.00	7.00	25.00
	e. 11.1.1956. Series: FK-FV.	2.00	7.00	25.00
	f. 19.6.1957. Series: FW-GH.	2.00	7.00	25.00
	g. 20.8.1958. Series: HC-HR.	2.00	7.00	25.00
	h. 18.3.1959. Series: HS-IH.	2.00	7.00	25.00
	i. 20.5.1959. Series: IQ-JF.	2.00	7.00	25.00
	j. 25.1.1961. Series: JO-KL.	2.00	7.00	25.00

1954 ISSUE

		VG	VF	UNC
58	**10 Pesos** 1954-67. Black on multicolor underprint. Portrait E. Ruiz de Velazquez at right. Like #53 but with text: *MEXICO D.F.* above series letters. Back brown; road to Guanajuato at center Printer: ABNC.			
	a. 10.2.1954. Series: DW, DX.	.50	1.50	5.00
	b. 8.9.1954. Series: EI-EN.	.50	1.50	5.00

		VG	VF	UNC
58	**10 Pesos**			
	c. 19.6.1957. Series: FW, FX.	.50	1.50	5.00
	d. 24.7.1957. Series: GQ.	.50	1.50	5.00
	e. 20.8.1958. Series: HC-HF.	.25	1.50	6.00
	f. 18.3.1959. Series: HS-HU.	.25	1.00	5.00
	g. 20.5.1959. Series: IQ-IS.	.25	1.00	4.00
	h. 25.1.1961. Series: JO-JT.	.25	1.00	4.00
	i. 8.11.1961. Series: LC-LV.	.25	1.00	4.00
	j. 24.4.1963. Series: AIE-AIT.	.25	1.00	3.00
	k. 17.2.1965. Series: BAQ-BAX.	.25	1.00	3.00
	l. 10.5.1967. Series: BCY-BDA.	.25	1.00	3.00
	s. Specimen, punched hole cancelled.	—	Unc	150.

1957; 1961 ISSUE

#59-61 printer: ABNC.

		VG	VF	UNC
59	**1 Peso** 1957-70. Black on multicolor underprint. Aztec calendar stone at center Like #56 but with text: *MEXICO D.F.* added above date at lower left. Back red, Independence monument at center.			
	a. 19.6.1957. Series: FW-GF.	.10	1.00	4.50
	b. Deleted.	—	—	—
	c. 4.12.1957. Series: GS-HB.	.10	1.00	4.50
	d. 20.8.1958. Series: HC-HL.	.10	.75	2.50
	e. 18.3.1959. Series: HS-IB.	.10	.50	2.50
	f. 20.5.1959. Series: IQ-IZ.	.10	.50	2.50
	g. 25.1.1961. Series: JO-KC.	.10	.25	2.00
	h. 8.11.1961. Series: LC; LD.	.10	.50	2.00
	i. 9.6.1965. Series: BCO-BCX.	.10	.25	2.00
	j. 10.5.1967. Series: BCY-BEB.	.10	.25	1.00
	k. 27.8.1969. Series: BGA-BGJ.	.10	.25	1.00
	l. 22.7.1970. Series: BIG-BIP.	.10	.20	1.00
	s. Specimen.	—	—	—

		VG	VF	UNC
60	**5 Pesos** 1957-70. Black on multicolor underprint. Portrait gypsy at center Like #57 but with Text: *MEXICO D.F.* before date. Back gray; Independence Monument at center.			
	a. 19.6.1957. Series: FW, FX.	.25	2.00	7.00
	b. 24.7.1957. Series: GQ, GR.	.25	2.00	7.00
	c. 20.8.1958. Series: HC-HJ.	.25	1.50	6.00
	d. 18.3.1959. Series: HS-HV.	.25	1.50	6.00
	e. 20.5.1959. Series: IQ-IT.	.25	1.50	6.00
	f. 25.1.1961. Series: JO-JV.	.15	.50	4.00
	g. 8.11.1961. Series: LC-MP.	.15	.50	3.00
	h. 24.4.1963. Series: AIE-AJJ.	.15	.50	2.50
	i. 27.8.1969. Series BGJ.	.15	.50	2.50
	j. 19.11.1969. Series: BGK-BGT.	.15	.50	2.50
	k. 22.7.1970. Series: BIG-BII.	.15	.50	2.50

61 100 Pesos

1961-73. Brown on multicolor underprint. Like #55 but series letters below serial #.

	VG	VF	UNC
a. 8.11.1961. Red series letters. Series: LE-ZZ; AAA-AEQ.	2.00	5.00	12.50
b. 24.4.1963. Series: AIK-AUG.	2.00	5.00	12.50
c. 17.2.1965. Series: BAQ-BCD.	1.00	3.00	8.00
d. 10.5.1967. Series: BCY-BFZ.	1.00	3.00	8.00
e. 22.7.1970. Series: BIO-BJK.	1.00	3.00	8.00
f. 24.3.1971. Series: BKP-BLH.	1.00	3.00	8.00
g. 27.6.1972. Series: BLI-BNF.	1.00	3.00	8.00
h. 29.12.1972. Series: BNG-BUX.	.50	1.50	5.00
i. 18.7.1973. Series: BUY-BXU.	.50	1.50	5.00

1969-74 Issue

#62-66 bank title w/*S.A.* 3 sign. and sign. varieties. Printer: BdM.

62 5 Pesos

1969-72. Black on multicolor underprint. J. Ortiz de Dominguez at right. Yucca plant, aqueduct, village of Queretaro and national arms on back.

	VG	VF	UNC
a. 3.12.1969.	.15	.50	3.00
b. 27.10.1971.	.15	.25	2.00
c. 27.6.1972.	.15	.25	1.50

63 10 Pesos

1969-77. Dark green on multicolor underprint. Bell at left, M. Hidalgo y Castilla at right. National arms and Dolores Cathedral on back.

	VG	VF	UNC
a. 16.9.1969.	.25	.50	5.00
b. 3.12.1969.	.15	.25	1.50
c. 22.7.1970.	.15	.25	1.50
d. 3.2.1971.	.15	.25	1.25
e. 29.12.1972.	.15	.25	1.25
f. 18.7.1973.	.10	.20	1.25
g. 16.10.1974.	.10	.20	1.00
h. 15.5.1975.	.10	.20	.75
i. 18.2.1977.	.10	.20	.75
s. Specimen.	—	—	—

Note: #63a bears the date of Mexican Independence Day.

64 20 Pesos

1972-77. Red and black on multicolor underprint. J. Morelos y Pavon at right with building in background. Pyramid of Quetzalcoatl on back.

	VG	VF	UNC
a. 29.12.1972.	.25	.50	3.00
b. 18.7.1973.	.10	.30	2.25
c. 8.7.1976.	.10	.20	2.00
d. 8.7.1977.	.10	.20	1.50

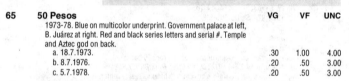

65 50 Pesos

1973-78. Blue on multicolor underprint. Government palace at left, B. Juárez at right. Red and black series letters and serial #. Temple and Aztec god on back.

	VG	VF	UNC
a. 18.7.1973.	.30	1.00	4.00
b. 8.7.1976.	.20	.50	3.00
c. 5.7.1978.	.20	.50	3.00

66 100 Pesos

1974; 1978. Purple on multicolor underprint. V. Carranza at left, "La Trinchera" painting at center. Red and black series letters and serial #. Stone figure on back.

	VG	VF	UNC
a. 30.5.1974.	.30	1.00	3.00
b. 5.7.1978.	.30	1.00	3.00
s. Specimen.	—	—	—

1978-80 Issue

#67-71 bank title w/*S.A.* W/3 sign. Printer: BdM.

		VG	VF	UNC
67	**50 Pesos**			
	1978; 1979. Blue on multicolor underprint. Like #65 but only red series letters and a black serial #.			
	a. 5.7.1978.	.30	.75	2.00
	b. 17.5.1979.	.20	.40	1.50
68	**100 Pesos**			
	1978-79. Purple on multicolor underprint. Like #66 but only red series letters and a black serial #.			
	a. 5.7.1978.	.20	.40	1.50
	b. 17.5.1979. Engraved. Litho back. Series before LL.	.20	.40	1.00
	c. 17.5.1979. Litho back. Series LS and later.	.20	.40	1.00

		VG	VF	UNC
69	**500 Pesos**			
	29.6.1979. Black on dark olive-green on multicolor underprint. F. I. Madero at left and as watermark. Aztec calendar stone on back. Pink paper.	1.00	3.00	11.00

		VG	VF	UNC
70	**1000 Pesos**			
	1978-79. Dark brown and brown on multicolor underprint. J. de Asbaje at right and as watermark. Santo Domingo plaza at left center on back. Light tan paper.			
	a. 5.7.1978.	2.00	4.50	20.00
	b. 17.5.1979.	1.00	4.00	12.50
	c. 29.6.1979.	1.00	3.00	10.00

		VG	VF	UNC
71	**5000 Pesos**			
	25.3.1980. Red on multicolor underprint. Cadets at left center, one of them as watermark. Chapultepec castle on back. Light blue paper.	5.00	15.00	45.00
72	**10,000 Pesos**			
	18.1.1978. Purple on multicolor underprint. Portrait M. Romero at left. Back green; National Palace at center. Printer: ABNC. Series CCL-CES.	5.00	20.00	75.00

1981 ISSUE

#73-78 bank title w/*S.A.* W/4 sign. and sign. varieties. Printer: BdM.

		VG	VF	UNC
73	**50 Pesos**			
	27.1.1981. Blue on multicolor underprint. Like #67 but four signatures.	.10	.25	1.00

		VG	VF	UNC
74	**100 Pesos**			
	1981-82. Purple on multicolor underprint. Like #68 but four signatures.			
	a. 27.1.1981.	.10	.30	1.50
	b. 3.9.1981.	.10	.30	1.50
	c. 25.3.1982.	.10	.20	.75

		VG	VF	UNC
75	**500 Pesos**			
	1981-82. Green on multicolor underprint. Like #69 but four signatures and narrow serial # style.			
	a. 27.1.1981.	.25	1.25	4.50
	b. 25.3.1982.	.25	1.25	4.50

		VG	VF	UNC
76	**1000 Pesos**			
	1981-82. Dark brown and brown on multicolor underprint. Like #70 but four signatures and narrow serial # style.			
	a. Engraved buildings on back. 27.1.1981. Black or red serial #.	.50	2.00	10.00
	b. Litho. buildings on back. 27.1.1981.	.50	2.00	10.00
	c. 3.9.1981.	.50	2.00	9.00
	d. 25.3.1982.	.50	1.50	7.00

77	5000 Pesos	VG	VF	UNC
	1981; 1982. Red and black on multicolor underprint., light blue paper. Like #71 but four signatures and narrower serial #.			
	a. 27.1.1981.	1.00	6.00	30.00
	b. 25.3.1982.	1.00	6.00	30.00

78	10,000 Pesos	VG	VF	UNC
	1981-82. Blue-black, brown and deep blue-green on multicolor underprint. Power plant at center, Gen. Lazaro Cardenas at right and as watermark. Back dark green, red and blue; Coyolxauhqui stone carving at center. Light green paper.			
	a. 8.12.1981.	10.00	25.00	55.00
	b. 25.3.1982.	2.00	15.00	50.00
	c. Red and blue serial #. 30.9.1982.	2.00	15.00	50.00
	d. Green and red serial #. 30.9.1982.	2.00	15.00	50.00

1983-84 Issues

#79-84 *S.A.* removed from bank title. W/4 sign. Printer: BdM.

79	500 Pesos	VG	VF	UNC
	1983; 1984. Green on multicolor underprint. Similar to #75 but with silk threads and without watermark. Design continued over watermark area on both sides. White paper.			
	a. 14.3.1983.	.25	1.00	4.00
	b. 7.8.1984.	.20	.75	2.50

80	1000 Pesos	VG	VF	UNC
	1983; 1984. Dark brown and brown on multicolor underprint. Like #76 but *S.A.* removed from title.			
	a. 13.5.1983.	.50	2.00	5.00
	b. 7.8.1984.	.50	2.00	5.00
81	1000 Pesos			
	30.10.1984. Dark brown and brown on multicolor underprint. Similar to #80 but radiant quill pen printed over watermark area at left.	.25	.75	3.00

82	2000 Pesos	VG	VF	UNC
	1983-84. Black, dark green and brown on multicolor underprint. J. Sierra at left center. University building at right. 19th century courtyard on back.			
	a. 26.7.1983.	1.00	3.00	10.00
	b. 7.8.1984.	.75	1.25	5.00
	c. 30.10.1984.	.75	1.25	5.00

83	5000 Pesos	VG	VF	UNC
	1983. Red and black on multicolor underprint. Like #77 but *S.A.* removed from title.			
	a. 13.5.1983.	1.25	3.50	12.50
	b. 26.7.1983.	1.00	3.00	9.00
	c. 5.12.1983.	1.00	3.00	9.50
84	10,000 Pesos			
	1983. Blue-black, brown and deep blue-green on multicolor underprint. Similar to #78 but *S.A.* removed from bank title.			
	a. 13.5.1983.	2.00	4.50	15.00
	b. Red and dark blue serial #. 26.7.1983.	2.00	4.50	15.00
	c. Green and blue serial #. 26.7.1983.	2.00	4.50	15.00
	d. Purple and blue serial #. 26.7.1983.	2.00	4.50	17.50
	e. 5.12.1983.	2.00	5.00	20.00

1985 Issues

#85-94 w/3 sign. *S.A.* removed from bank title. Printer: BdM.

85	1000 Pesos	VG	VF	UNC
	19.7.1985. Dark brown and brown on multicolor underprint. Like #81 but only three signatures.	.35	.75	2.50

86 **2000 Pesos**

1985-89. Black, dark green and brown on multicolor underprint. Like #82 but only three signatures.

	VG	VF	UNC
a. With *SANTANA* at lower left 2 date positions. 19.7.1985.	.60	1.25	4.00
b. As a. 24.2.1987.	.60	1.25	3.00
c. Without *SANTANA*. 28.3.1989.	.60	1.00	2.25

87 **5000 Pesos**

	VG	VF	UNC
19.7.1985. Red on multicolor underprint. Blue tint paper. Like #83 but only three signatures.	1.75	2.25	7.50

88 **5000 Pesos**

1985-89. Purple and brown-orange on multicolor underprint. Similar to #87 but design continued over watermark area. Without watermark. Light tan paper.

	VG	VF	UNC
a. With *SANTANA* vertically at lower left 19.7.1985.	.60	2.00	6.00
b. As a. 24.2.1987.	.60	1.75	5.00
c. Without *SANTANA*. 28.3.1989.	.50	1.50	3.00

89 **10,000 Pesos**

1985; 1987. Blue-black, brown and deep blue-green on multicolor underprint. Like #84 but only three signatures.

89 **10,000 Pesos**

	VG	VF	UNC
a. Purple and blue serial #. 19.7.1985.	2.00	5.00	12.50
b. Green and blue serial #. 19.7.1985.	2.00	5.00	12.50
c. Red and blue serial #. 24.2.1987.	2.00	5.00	12.50
d. Green and blue serial #. 24.7.1987.	2.00	5.00	12.50

90 **10,000 Pesos**

1987-91. Deep blue-black on brown and blue-green underprint. Similar to #89 but watermark area filled in. Light tan paper.

	VG	VF	UNC
a. With *SANTANA*. at lower left under refinery designature 24.2.1987.	1.50	3.00	10.00
b. Without *SANTANA*. 1.2.1988.	1.50	2.50	7.00
c. 28.3.1989.	1.50	2.50	6.00
d. 16.5.1991.	1.25	2.00	6.00

91 **20,000 Pesos**

1985-87. Deep blue on blue and multicolor underprint. Fortress above coastal cliffs at center, Don A. Quintana Roo at right and as watermark. Artwork on back.

	VG	VF	UNC
a. 19.7.1985.	4.00	7.00	22.50
b. 24.2.1987.	3.50	6.50	17.50
c. 27.8.1987.	3.50	6.50	17.50

92 **20,000 Pesos**

1988; 1989. Blue-black on blue and pink underprint. Similar to #91 but design continued over watermark area.

	VG	VF	UNC
a. 1.2.1988.	3.50	5.00	15.00
b. 28.3.1989.	3.50	5.00	12.50

93 **50,000 Pesos**

1986-90. Purple on multicolor underprint. Aztec symbols at center, Cuauhtémoc at right and as watermark. Aztec and Spaniard fighting at left center on back. Pink paper.

	VG	VF	UNC
a. 12.5.1986; 24.2.1987; 27.8.1987; 1.2.1988.	7.50	17.50	60.00
b. 28.3.1989; 10.1.1990; 20.12.1990.	6.50	15.00	45.00

		VG	VF	UNC
94	**100,000 Pesos** 1988; 1991. Blue-black and maroon on multicolor underprint. P. E. Calles at left and as watermark, Banco de Mexico at center. Desert Mule Deer, cactus, lake and mountain at center right on back.			
	a. 4.1.1988.	12.50	27.50	85.00
	b. 2.9.1991.	12.50	27.50	85.00

1992 First Issue

Nuevos Pesos System

1000 "old" Pesos = 1 Nuevo Peso

#95-98 similar to #90-94. 3 sign. and sign. varieties. Printer: BdM.

		VG	VF	UNC
95	**10 Nuevos Pesos** 31.7.1992. Blue-black, brown and deep blue-green on multicolor underprint. Similar to #90. Series A-Y.	FV	FV	7.50

		VG	VF	UNC
96	**20 Nuevos Pesos** 31.7.1992. Deep blue on blue and multicolor underprint. Similar to #92. Series A-Q.	FV	FV	12.50

		VG	VF	UNC
97	**50 Nuevos Pesos** 31.7.1992. Purple on multicolor underprint. Similar to #93. Series A-P.	FV	FV	27.50

		VG	VF	UNC
98	**100 Nuevos Pesos** 31.7.1992. Blue-black and maroon on multicolor underprint. Similar to #94. Series A-Q.	FV	FV	40.00

1992 (1994) Second Issue

#99-104 printer: BdM.

		VG	VF	UNC
99	**10 Nuevos Pesos** 10.12.1992 (1994). Deep blue-green and gold on multicolor underprint. E. Zapata at right, hands holding corn at center. Machinery at lower left, statue of Zapata on horseback near peasant at center right, building in background. Series A-T.	FV	FV	4.00

		VG	VF	UNC
100	**20 Nuevos Pesos** 10.12.1992 (1994). Purple and dark blue on multicolor underprint. B. Juárez at right, eagle on cactus with snake (arms) at center. Monument, statues "Hemiciclo a Juárez" on back. Series A-T.	FV	FV	6.50

		VG	VF	UNC
101	**50 Nuevos Pesos** 10.12.1992 (1994). Red-violet and black on multicolor underprint. J. M. Morelos at right, crossed cannons on outlined bow and arrow below his flag at left center. Butterflies at left, boat fishermen at center on back. Series A-AF.	FV	FV	15.00

102	100 Nuevos Pesos	VG	VF	UNC
	10.12.1992 (1994). Red and brown on multicolor underprint. Nezahualcóyotl at right and as watermark; Aztec figure at center. Xochipilli statue on back. Series A-V.	FV	FV	25.00

103	200 Nuevos Pesos	VG	VF	UNC
	10.12.1992 (1994). Dark olive-green, dark brown and olive-brown on multicolor underprint. J. de Asbaje at right and as watermark, open book and quill pen at center. Temple de San Jerónimo on back. Series A-E.	FV	FV	45.00

104	500 Nuevos Pesos	VG	VF	UNC
	10.12.1992 (1994). Red-brown, deep purple and dark brown-violet on multicolor underprint. I. Zaragoza at center right and as watermark, Battle of Puebla at left center. Cathedral at Puebla at center on back. Series A-G	FV	FV	110.

1994; 1995 (1996) ISSUE

#105-116 similar to #99-104 but *EL* omitted from bank title, *NUEVOS* and *PAGARÁ A LA VISTA AL PORTADOR* are omitted. 2 sign. Printer: BdM.

105	10 Pesos	VG	VF	UNC
	1994 (1996); 1996. Deep blue-green and gold on multicolor underprint. Similar to #99. Series A-.			
	a. 6.5.1994.	FV	FV	3.00
	b. 10.5.1996.	FV	FV	3.00

106	20 Pesos	VG	VF	UNC
	1994 (1996); 1996. Purple and dark blue on multicolor underprint. Similar to #100. Series A-.			
	a. 6.5.1994.	FV	FV	6.00
	b. 10.5.1996.	FV	FV	5.50
	c. 3.17.1998.	FV	FV	5.50
	d. 23.4.1999.	FV	FV	5.50

107	50 Pesos	VG	VF	UNC
	1994-98 (1996). Red-violet and black on multicolor underprint. Similar to #101. Series A-.			
	a. 6.5.1994.	FV	FV	15.00
	b. 10.5.1996.	FV	FV	10.00
	c. 17.3.1998.	FV	FV	10.00
	d. 23.4.1999.	FV	FV	10.00

108	100 Pesos	VG	VF	UNC
	1994 (1996); 1996. Red and brown-orange on multicolor underprint. Similar to #102. Series A-.			
	a. 6.5.1994.	FV	FV	22.50
	b. 10.5.1996.	FV	FV	22.50
	c. 23.4.1999.	FV	FV	22.50

NOTICE

Readers with unlisted dates, signature varieties, etc. are invited to submit photocopies of their notes to: Standard Catalog of World Paper Money, 700 East State St. Iola, WI 54990-0001, E-Mail: george.cuhaj@fwpubs.com.

109	200 Pesos	VG	VF	UNC
	1995-98 (1996). Dark olive-green, dark brown and olive-brown on multicolor underprint. Similar to #103. Series A-.			
	a. 7.2.1995.	FV	FV	45.00
	b. 10.5.1996.	FV	FV	37.50
	c. 17.3.1998.	FV	FV	37.50
	d. 23.4.1999.	FV	FV	37.50

110	500 Pesos	VG	VF	UNC
	1995 (1996); 1996. Red-brown, deep purple and dark brown-violet on multicolor underprint. Similar to #104. Series A-.			
	a. 7.2.1995.	FV	FV	95.00
	b. 10.5.1996.	FV	FV	95.00
	c. 17.3.1998.	FV	FV	95.00
	d. 23.4.1999.	FV	FV	95.00

2000 Commemorative Issue

#111-115, 75th Anniversary Banco de Mexico. Commemorative text immediately below bank name.

111	20 Pesos	VG	VF	UNC
	25.8.2000. Purple and dark blue on multicolor underprint. Like #106.	FV	3.50	9.50

112	50 Pesos	VG	VF	UNC
	25.8.2000. Red-violet and black on multicolor underprint. Like #107.	FV	9.00	17.50
113	**100 Pesos**			
	25.8.2000. Red and brown-orange on multicolor underprint. Like #108.	FV	15.00	35.00

114	200 Pesos	VG	VF	UNC
	25.8.2000. Dark olive-green, dark brown and olive-brown on multicolor underprint. Like #109.	FV	30.00	70.00

115	500 Pesos	VG	VF	UNC
	25.8.2000. Red-brown, deep purple and dark brown-violet on multicolor underprint. Like #110.	FV	65.00	150.

2000-01 Issue

116	20 Pesos	VG	VF	UNC
	2001; 2002; 2003. Blue and multicolor underprint. Similar to #106. Polymer plastic. Printer: NPA and BdM.			
	a. 17.5.2001. Series A-F. Two electronic sorting bars at upper left.	FV	FV	5.50
	b. 17.5.2001. Series G-T. Three electronic sorting bars at upper left.	FV	FV	4.50
	c. 26.3.2002. Two electronic sorting bars. Series U.	FV	FV	4.50
	d. 23.5.2003. Two electronic sorting bars. Series V-.	FV	FV	4.50

#117-120 w/vertical iridescent strip at l. Additional enhanced security features.

		VG	VF	UNC
117	**50 Pesos** 18.10.2000 (2001); 26.3.2002; 23.5.2003. Similar to #107.	FV	FV	10.00

		VG	VF	UNC
118	**100 Pesos** 18.10.2000 (2001); 26.3.2002; 23.5.2003; 21.11.2003. Similar to #108.	FV	FV	18.00
119	**200 Pesos** 18.10.2000 (2001); 23.3.2002. Similar to #109.	FV	FV	32.50
120	**500 Pesos** 18.10.2000 (2001). Similar to #110.	FV	FV	80.00

		VG	VF	UNC
121	**1000 Pesos** 26.3.2002. Multicolor. Similar to #111.	FV	FV	150.

The area of Moldova is bordered in the north, east, and south by the Ukraine and on the west by Romania.

The historical Romanian principality of Moldova was established in the 14th century. It fell under Turkish suzerainty in the 16th century. From 1812 to 1918, Russians occupied the eastern portion of Moldova which they named Bessarabia. In March 1918, the Bessarabian legislature voted in favor of reunification with Romania.

At the Paris Peace Conference of 1920, the union was officially recognized by several nations, but the new Soviet government did not accept the union. In 1924, to pressure Romania, a Moldovan Autonomous Soviet Socialist Republic (A.S.S.R.) was established within the USSR on the border, consisting of a strip extending east of the Dniester River. Today it is Transnistria (see country listing).

Soviet forces reoccupied the region in June 1940, and the Moldovan S.S.R. was proclaimed. Transniestria was transferred to the new republic. Ukrainian S.S.R. obtained possession of the southern part of Bessarabia. The region was liberated by the Romanian army in 1941. The Soviets reconquered the territory in 1944. A declaration of independence was adopted in June 1990 and the area was renamed Moldova. It became an independent republic in August 1991. In December 1991, Moldova became a member of the Commonwealth of Independent States.

MONETARY SYSTEM:

100 Rubles = 1000 Cupon, 1992
1 Leu = 1000 Cupon, 1993-

REPUBLIC

MINISTER OF FINANCE

RUBLE CONTROL COUPONS

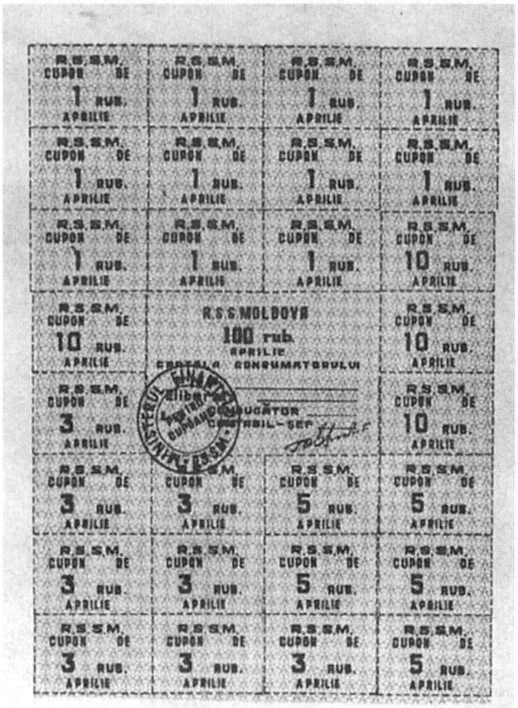

		VG	VF	UNC
A11	**Various amounts** 1992.			
	a. Full sheet.	—	.50	1.00
	b. Coupon.	—	—	.10

BANCA NATIONALA A MOLDOVEI

1992; 1993 "CUPON" ISSUE

#1-4 arms at l. Castle at r. on back. Wmk. paper (varies).

1 **50 Cupon**

	VG	VF	UNC
1992. Gray-green on gray underprint.	.10	.40	2.25

2 **200 Cupon**

	VG	VF	UNC
1992. Purple on gray underprint. Back purple on lilac underprint.	.10	.40	2.25

3 **1000 Cupon**

	VG	VF	UNC
1993. Brown on pale blue-green and ochre underprint. Bank monogram at upper left.	.15	.75	3.00

4 **5000 Cupon**

	VG	VF	UNC
1993. Pale brown-violet on orange and pale olive-green underprint. Bank monogram at upper left. Back pale brown-violet on pale brown-orange underprint.	.50	1.50	5.00

1992 (1993) ISSUE

#5-7 Kg. Stefan at l., arms at upper ctr. r. Soroca Fortress at ctr. r. on back. Sign. L. Talmaci. Printed in Romania on watermarked paper.

5 **1 Leu**

	VG	VF	UNC
1992 (1993). Brown and dark olive-green on ochre underprint.	.10	.50	2.00

6 **5 Lei**

	VG	VF	UNC
1992 (1993). Purple on light blue and ochre underprint.	.25	1.00	5.00

7 **10 Lei**

	VG	VF	UNC
1992 (1993). Red brown and olive-green on pale orange underprint.	.50	1.50	7.50

1992; 1994 ISSUE

#8-16 Kg. Stefan at l. and as wmk., arms at upper ctr. r.
#8-14 bank monogram at upper r. corner.

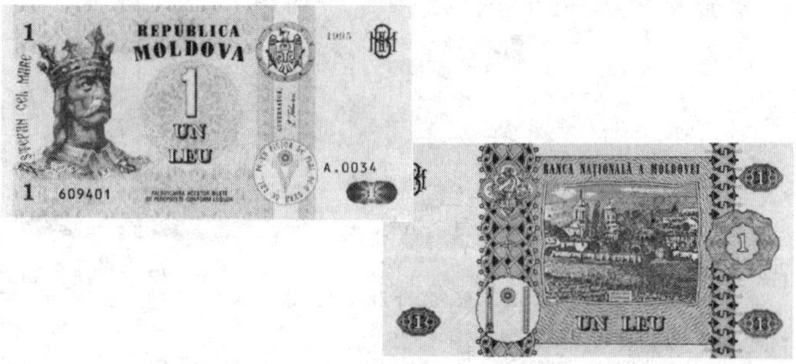

8 **1 Leu**

	VG	VF	UNC
1994; 1995; 1997; 1998; 1999; 2002; 2005; 2006. Brown on ochre, pale yellow-green and multicolor underprint. Monastery at Capriana at center right on back.	.10	.50	1.50

9 **5 Lei**

	VG	VF	UNC
1994; 1995; 1999. Blue-green on lilac and pale aqua underprint. Basilica of St. Dumitru in Orhei at center right on back.	.25	1.00	2.75

10 **10 Lei**

	VG	VF	UNC
1994; 1995; 1998; 2005; 2006. Red-brown on pale blue and gold underprint. Monastery at Hîrjauca at center right on back.	.75	1.25	4.00

#11 and 12 held in reserve.

13 **20 Lei**

	VG	VF	UNC
1992 (1994); 1995; 1997; 1999; 2002; 2005. Blue-green on light green, aqua and ochre underprint. Soroca Fortress at center right on back.	1.50	3.00	8.00

14 **50 Lei**

	VG	VF	UNC
1992 (1994); 2002; 2005. Red-violet on lilac and multicolor underprint. Monastery at Hîrbovet at center right on back.	2.00	5.00	15.00

1992 (1995) ISSUE

15 **100 Lei**

	VG	VF	UNC
1992 (1995). Brown on multicolor underprint. Thighina Fortress on back.	5.00	7.50	25.00

16 **200 Lei**

	VG	VF	UNC
1992 (1995). Purple on multicolor underprint. Chisinau City Hall on back.	12.50	17.50	45.00

1992 (1999) ISSUE

17 **500 Lei**

	VG	VF	UNC
1992 (1999). Slate black, orange and green on multicolor underprint. Chisinau Cathedral on back.	35.00	60.00	100.

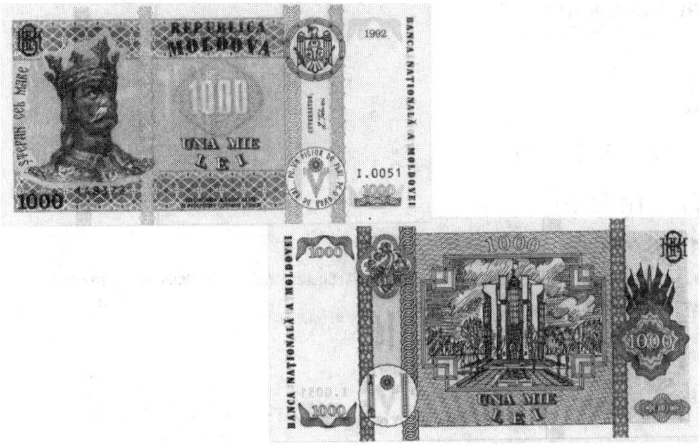

18 **1000 Lei**

	VG	VF	UNC
1992 (2003). Blue and purple on multicolor underprint. King Stefan at left.	FV	100.	150.

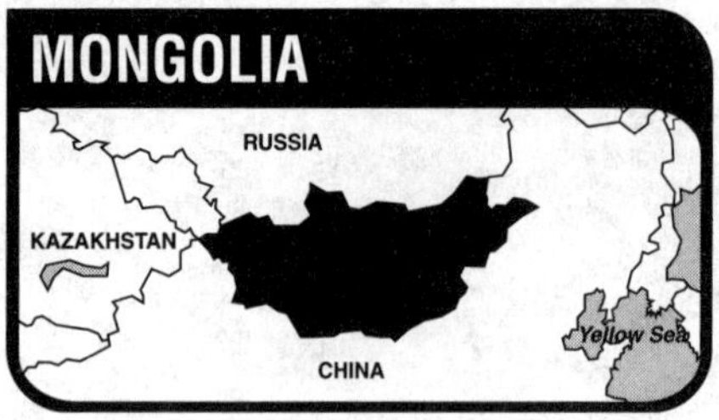

The State of Mongolia, a landlocked country in central Asia between Russia and the Peoples Republic of China, has an area of 604,247 sq. mi. (1,565,000 sq. km.) and a population of 2.74 million. Capital: Ulan Bator. Animal herds and flocks are the chief economic asset. Wool, cattle, butter, meat and hides are exported.

Mongolia (often referred to as Outer Mongolia), one of the world's oldest countries, attained its greatest power in the 13th century when Genghis Khan and his successors conquered all of China and extended their influence westward as far as Hungary and Poland. The empire dissolved in later centuries and in 1691 was brought under suzerainty of the Manchus, who had conquered China in 1644. Mongolia, with the support of Russia, proclaimed its independence from China on March 13, 1921, when the Provisional Peoples Government was established. Later, on November 26, 1924, the government proclaimed the Mongolian Peoples Republic. Opposition to the communist party developed in late 1989 and on March 12, 1990 and the new State of Mongolia was organized.

RULERS:

Chinese to 1921

MONETARY SYSTEM:

1 Tugrik (Tukhrik) = 100 Mongo

REPLACEMENT NOTES:

#28-41, 3A, 3B, or WA **prefix.**
#42-48, WA, WV **prefix.**

STATE

УЛСЫН БАНК

STATE BANK

1966 ISSUE

#35-41 Socialist arms at upper l. Backs are m/c. Wmk: Circles forming a 6-petaled flower-like pattern.

#36-41 portr. Sukhe-Bataar at r.

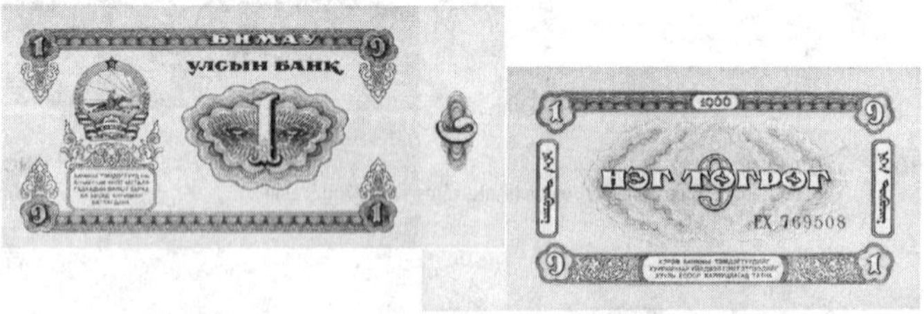

		VG	VF	UNC
35	**1 Tugrik** 1966. Brown on pale green and yellow underprint.			
	a. Issued note.	.20	.40	.75
	s. Specimen.	—	—	15.00
36	**3 Tugrik** 1966. Dark green on light green and pink underprint.			
	a. Issued note.	.25	.50	1.00
	s. Specimen.	—	—	15.00
37	**5 Tugrik** 1966. Dark blue on light blue and pale green underprint.			
	a. Issued note.	.25	.50	1.00
	s. Specimen.	—	—	15.00
38	**10 Tugrik** 1966. Red on pale red and blue underprint.			
	a. Issued note.	.25	.75	1.25
	s. Specimen.	—	—	15.00
39	**25 Tugrik** 1966. Brown-violet on pale green underprint.			
	a. Issued note.	.50	1.00	1.50
	s. Specimen.	—	—	15.00
40	**50 Tugrik** 1966. Dark green on light green and gold underprint. Government Building at Ulan-Bator on back.			
	a. Issued note.	1.00	2.50	3.00
	s. Specimen.	—	—	15.00

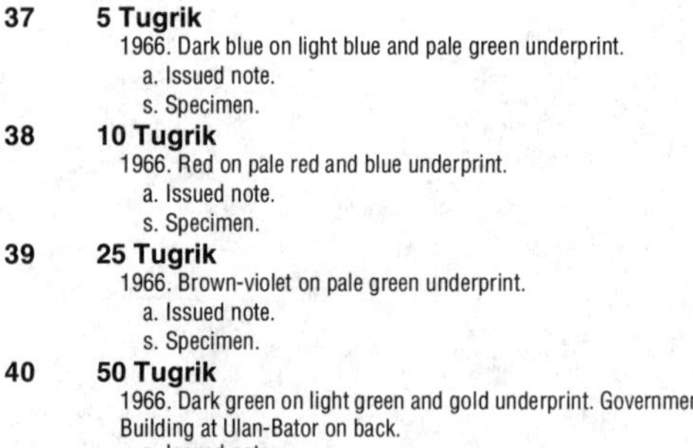

		VG	VF	UNC
41	**100 Tugrik** 1966. Dark brown on ochre and blue-green underprint. Back like #40.			
	a. Issued note.	2.00	4.00	7.50
	s. Specimen.	—	—	15.00

1981-83 ISSUE

#42-45 and 47-48 like #36-41. Replacement notes: Serial # prefix ЯА.

		VG	VF	UNC
42	**1 Tugrik** 1983. Brown on pale green and yellow underprint. Like #35.	.05	.25	1.00

		VG	VF	UNC
43	**3 Tugrik** 1983. Dark green on light green and pink underprint. Like #36.	.10	.25	1.25

		VG	VF	UNC
44	**5 Tugrik** 1981. Blue on light blue and pale green underprint. Like #37.	.10	.25	1.75

		VG	VF	UNC
45	**10 Tugrik** 1981. Red on pale red and blue underprint. Like #38.	.10	.25	2.00

		VG	VF	UNC
46	**20 Tugrik** 1981. Yellow-green on light green and brown underprint. Sukhe-Bataar at center, arms at left. Power station at Ulan-Bator at center right on back.	.10	.35	2.25

47 **50 Tugrik** — VG .10 | VF 1.00 | UNC 5.00
1981. Dark green on light green and gold underprint. Like #40.

48 **100 Tugrik** — VG | VF .10 | UNC 9.00
1981. Dark brown on ochre and blue-green underprint. Like #41.

МОНГОЛ БАНК

MONGOL BANK

1993 ND; 1994-95 ISSUE

#49-51 "Soemba" arms at upper ctr. Replacement notes: Serial # prefix *ZZ*.

#49#50#51

49 **10 Mongo** — VG — | VF .10 | UNC .75
ND (1993). Red-violet on pale red-orange underprint. Two archers at lower center on face and back.

50 **20 Mongo** — VG — | VF .15 | UNC .75
ND (1993). Brown on ochre and yellow-brown underprint. Two athletes at lower center on face and back.

51 **50 Mongo** — VG — | VF .50 | UNC .75
ND (1993). Greenish-black on blue and pale green underprint. Two horsemen at lower center on face and back.

#52-60 wmk: Genghis Khan.

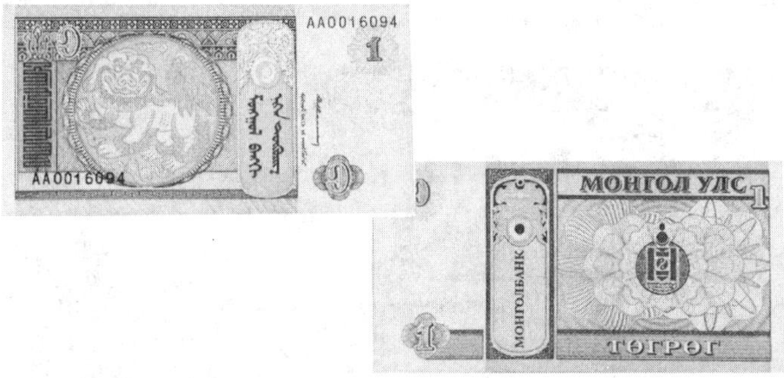

52 **1 Tugrik** — VG .05 | VF .15 | UNC 1.00
ND (1993). Dull olive-green and brown-orange on ochre underprint. Chinze at left. "Soemba" arms at center right on back.

#53-57 youthful portr. Sukhe-Bataar at l., "Soemba" arms at ctr. Horses grazing in mountainous landscape at ctr. r. on back.

53 **5 Tugrik** — VG .05 | VF .25 | UNC 1.25
ND (1993). Deep orange, ochre and brown on multicolor underprint.

54 **10 Tugrik** — VG .05 | VF .25 | UNC 1.25
ND (1993). Green, blue and light green on multicolor underprint.

55 **20 Tugrik** — VG .05 | VF .25 | UNC 1.25
ND (1993). Violet, orange and red on multicolor underprint.

56 **50 Tugrik** — VG .05 — VF .25 — UNC 1.50
ND (1993). Dark brown on multicolor underprint.

57 **100 Tugrik** — VG .05 — VF .50 — UNC 2.00
ND (1993); 1994. Purple, brown and dark blue on multicolor underprint.

#58-61 Genghis Khan at l. and as wmk., "Soemba" arms at ctr. Ox drawn yurte, village at ctr. r. on back.

58 **500 Tugrik** — VG .25 — VF 1.00 — UNC 5.00
ND (1993); 1997. Dark green, brown and yellow-green on multicolor underprint.

59 **1000 Tugrik** — VG 1.00 — VF 5.00 — UNC 10.00
ND (1993); 1997. Blue-gray, brown and blue on multicolor underprint.

60 **5000 Tugrik** — VG 4.00 — VF 7.50 — UNC 17.50
1994. Purple, violet and red on multicolor underprint. Building complex, tree, people on back.

61 **10,000 Tugrik** — VG 8.50 — VF 16.00 — UNC 35.00
1995. Black, dark olive-green and orange on multicolor underprint. Building complex, tree, people on back.

2000; 2003 Issue

62 **10 Tugrik** — VG FV — VF FV — UNC .50
2000; 2002; 2005. Dark green and multicolor.

63 **20 Tugrik** — VG FV — VF FV — UNC .75
2000; 2002. Multicolor.

64 **50 Tugrik** — VG FV — VF FV — UNC 1.25
2000. Brown-gold. Sukhe-Bataar at left. Segmented security thread. Microprinting, UV ink and embossed *50* below arms.

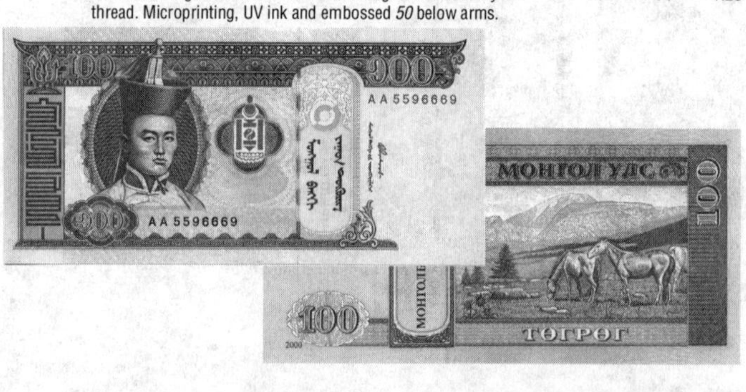

		VG	VF	UNC
65	**100 Tugrik** 2000. Multicolor.	FV	FV	2.00
65A	**500 Tugrik** 2000. Multicolor.	FV	FV	5.00

		VG	VF	UNC
66	**500 Tugrik** 2003. Blue and brown on multicolor underprint. Wide security thread added to #65A.	FV	FV	5.00

		VG	VF	UNC
67	**1000 Tugrik** 2003. Blue and brown on multicolor underprint.	FV	FV	10.00

		VG	VF	UNC
68	**5000 Tugrik** 2003. Purple and orange on multicolor underprint.	FV	FV	17.50

		VG	VF	UNC
69	**10,000 Tugrik** 2003. Dark green and orange on multicolor underprint.	FV	FV	35.00

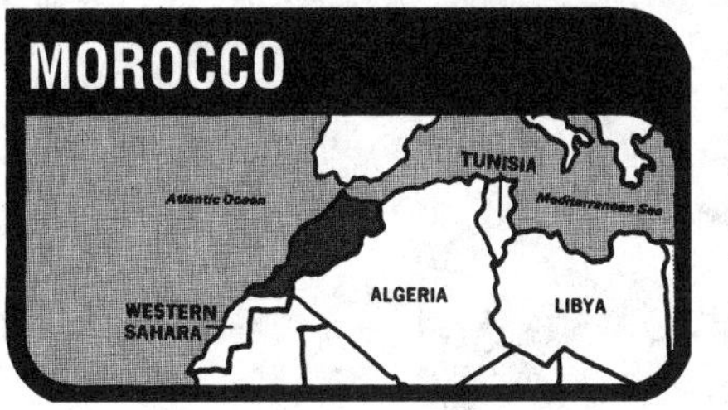

The Kingdom of Morocco, situated on the northwest corner of Africa south of Spain, has an area of 172,413 sq. mi. (712,550 sq. km.) and a population of 28.98 million. Capital: Rabat. The economy is essentially agricultural. Phosphates, fresh and preserved vegetables, canned fish and raw material are exported.

Morocco's strategic position at the gateway to western Europe has been the principal determinant of its violent, frequently unfortunate history. Time and again the fertile plain between the rugged Atlas Mountains and the sea has echoed the battle's trumpet as Phoenicians, Romans, Vandals, Visigoths, Byzantine Greeks and Islamic Arabs successively conquered and occupied the land. Modern Morocco is a remnant of an early empire formed by the Arabs at the close of the 7th century which encompassed all of northwest Africa and most of the Iberian Peninsula. During the 17th and 18th centuries, while under the control of native dynasties, it was the headquarters of the famous Sale pirates. Morocco's strategic position involved it in the competition of 19th century European powers for political influence in Africa, and resulted in the division of Morocco into French and Spanish spheres of interest which were established as protectorates in 1912. Morocco became independent on March 2, 1956, after France agreed to end its protectorate. Spain signed similar agreements on April 7 of the same year.

RULERS:

Muhammad V, AH1346-1380/1927-1961AD
Hassan II, AH1380-1420 /1961-1999AD
Muhammad VI, AH1420- /1999- AD

MONETARY SYSTEM:

1 Dirham = 100 Francs, 1921-1974
1 Dirham = 100 Centimes = 100 Santimat, 1974-

SIGNATURE VARIETIES

	GOVERNMENT COMISSONER	GOVERNOR
1	Mohamed Tahiri, 1960	M'hamed Zeghari
2	Ahmed Ben Nani, 1963-65	M'Hamed Zeghari
3		Driss Slaovi
4	Mohamed Lemniai, 1966	Driss Slaovi
5	Abdelaziz El Alami, 1967	Driss Slaovi
6	Abdelkrim Lazrek, 1968	M'hamed Zeghari
7	Abdelkrim Lazrek, 1969	Prince Moulay Hassan Ben Mehdi El Alaovi
8	Mohamed El Mdaghri, 1970	Prince Moulay Hassan Ben Mehdi El Alaovi
9	Hassan Lukash, 1985-89	Ahmed Ben Nani
10	Hassan Lukash	Mohamed Es Sakat
11	Abdul el Fatah ben Mansour	Mohamed Es Sakat
12	Noureddin Omary	Mohamed Es Sakat

Kingdom

Banque du Maroc

1960 (ND); 1965 Issue

#53-55 wmk: Lion's head. French printing.

53	5 Dirhams	VG	VF	UNC
	ND (1960); 1965-69. Brown and multicolor. King Muhammad V wearing a fez at right. Harvesting at left, man holding sheaf at right on back.			
	a. Signature 1. ND (1960).	2.00	8.50	40.00
	b. Signature 2. ND (1963).	1.75	7.50	35.00
	c. Signature 3. 1965/AH1384.	1.50	6.00	35.00
	d. Signature 4. 1966/AH1386.	1.25	5.00	35.00
	e. Signature 6. 1968/AH1387.	1.25	5.00	35.00
	f. Signature 7. 1969/AH1389.	1.25	5.00	35.00

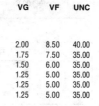

54	10 Dirhams	VG	VF	UNC
	ND (1960); 1965-69. Brown and multicolor. King Muhammad V wearing fez at left, Hassan Tower in Rabat at center. Orange picking on back.			
	a. Signature 1. ND (1960).	2.75	12.50	50.00
	b. Signature 2. ND (1963).	2.50	10.00	45.00
	c. Signature 3. 1965/AH1384.	2.00	8.00	40.00
	d. Signature 6. 1968/AH1387.	2.00	8.00	40.00
	e. Signature 7. 1969/AH1389.	2.00	8.00	40.00

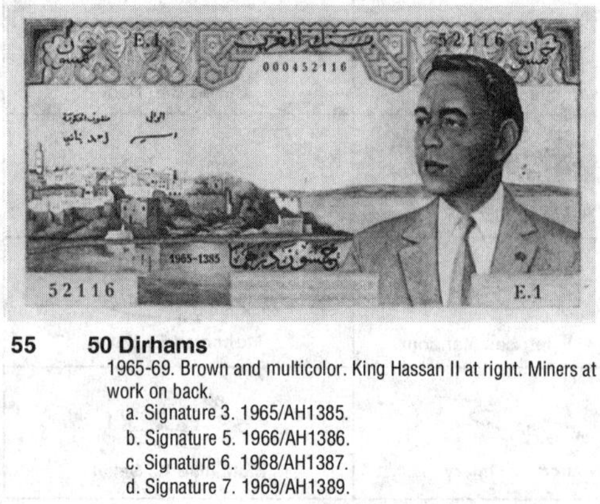

55	50 Dirhams	VG	VF	UNC
	1965-69. Brown and multicolor. King Hassan II at right. Miners at work on back.			
	a. Signature 3. 1965/AH1385.	15.00	60.00	375.
	b. Signature 5. 1966/AH1386.	12.50	55.00	350.
	c. Signature 6. 1968/AH1387.	10.00	45.00	300.
	d. Signature 7. 1969/AH1389.	10.00	42.50	285.

1970 Issue

#56-59 Kg. Hassan II at l. and as wmk. Printer: TDLR.

56	5 Dirhams	VG	VF	UNC
	1970/AH1390. Purple on light blue and multicolor underprint. Castle at center. Industrial processing on back. Signature 8. Replacement notes: Serial # prefix *Z*.			
	a. Issued note.	.50	1.50	4.50
	s. Specimen.	—	—	32.50

57	10 Dirhams	VG	VF	UNC
	1970; 1985. Brown on light green and multicolor underprint. Villa at center. Processing oranges on back. Replacement notes: Serial # prefix *Y*.			
	a. Signature 8. 1970/AH1390.	.75	2.00	6.50
	b. Signature 9. 1985/AH1405.	.75	1.50	5.50
	s. As a. Specimen.	—	—	35.00

58	50 Dirhams	VG	VF	UNC
	1970; 1985. Green and brown on multicolor underprint. City at center. Dam on back. Replacement notes: Serial # prefix *X*.			
	a. Signature 8. 1970/AH1390.	3.00	10.00	22.50
	b. Signature 9. 1985/AH1405.	3.00	8.00	20.00
	s. As b. Specimen.	—	—	50.00

59	100 Dirhams	VG	VF	UNC
	1970; 1985. Brown and blue on light green and multicolor underprint. Building at center. Oil refinery on back. Replacement notes: Serial # prefix *W*.			
	a. Signature 8. 1970/AH1390.	5.00	15.00	37.50
	b. Signature 9. 1985/AH1405.	5.00	12.50	35.00
	s. As b. Specimen.	—	—	70.00

BANK AL-MAGHRIB

1987 ISSUE

#60-62 Kg. Hassan II facing at r. and as wmk. 2 sign. varieties.

60	10 Dirhams	VG	VF	UNC
	1987/AH1407. Red-brown and red on multicolor underprint. Musical instrument and pillar at left center on back.			
	a. Signature 9.	FV	3.00	10.00
	b. Signature 10.	FV	2.50	8.00

61	50 Dirhams	VG	VF	UNC
	1987/AH1407. Green on multicolor underprint. Mounted militia charging, flowers at center on back.			
	a. Signature 9.	FV	FV	25.00
	b. Signature 10.	FV	FV	20.00
62	100 Dirhams			
	1987/AH1407. Brown on multicolor underprint. Demonstration on back.			
	a. Signature 9.	FV	FV	30.00
	b. Signature 10.	FV	FV	30.00

1987 (1991) ISSUE

#63-66 older bust of Kg. Hassan II at r. facing half l. Wmk: Kg. facing.

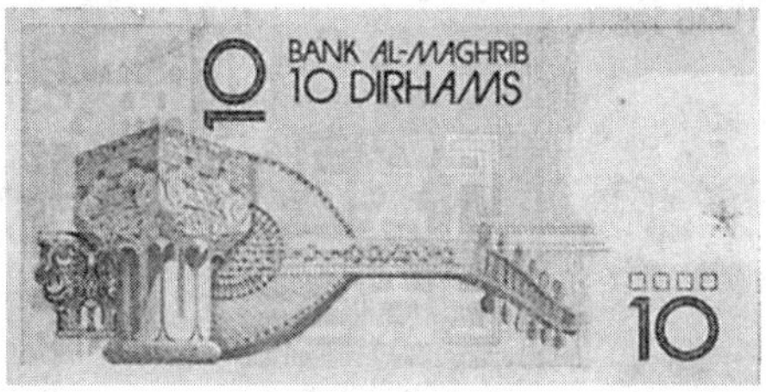

63	10 Dirhams	VG	VF	UNC
	1987/AH407 (ca.1991). Brown-violet and purple on multicolor underprint. Back like #60, but different colors of underprint.			
	a. Signature 10.	FV	FV	6.00
	b. Signature 11.	FV	FV	3.50

64	50 Dirhams	VG	VF	UNC
	1987/AH1407 (ca.1991). Green on multicolor underprint. Back like #61.			
	a. Signature 10.	FV	FV	20.00
	b. Signature 11.	FV	FV	15.00
	c. Signature 12.	FV	FV	12.50
	d. Signature 13.	FV	FV	12.50

65	100 Dirhams	VG	VF	UNC
	1987/AH1407 (ca.1991). Brown and blue on multicolor underprint. Back like #62.			
	a. Signature 10.	FV	FV	30.00
	b. Signature 11.	FV	FV	25.00
	c. Signature 12.	FV	FV	20.00
	d. Signature 13.	FV	FV	20.00

66	200 Dirhams	VG	VF	UNC
	1987/AH1407 (ca.1991). Blue-violet and blue on multicolor underprint. Mausoleum of King Muhammad V at center. Sailboat, shell and coral on back.			
	a. Signature 10.	FV	FV	50.00
	b. Signature 11.	FV	FV	47.50
	c. Signature 12.	FV	FV	45.00
	d. Signature 13.	FV	FV	40.00
	e. Signature 16.	FV	FV	37.50

1996 ISSUE

		VG	VF	UNC
67	**20 Dirhams** 1996. Multicolor. King Hassan II at left, Great Mosque of Casablanca at center. Fountain on back.			
	a. Signature 12.	FV	FV	5.00
	b. Signature 13.	FV	FV	4.50
	c. Signature 14.	FV	FV	4.50
	d. Signature 15.	FV	FV	4.50
	e. Signature 16.	FV	FV	4.50

2002 (2004-) ISSUE

		VG	VF	UNC
68	**20 Dirhams** 2004/AH1425. Mohammed VI.	FV	FV	4.50
69	**50 Dirhams** 2002/AH1423. Mohammed VI.	FV	FV	12.50

		VG	VF	UNC
70	**100 Dirhams** 2002/AH1423. Brown on multicolor underprint. Mohammed VI, Hassan II and Mohammed V at right. People with flags marching on back.	FV	FV	20.00

		VG	VF	UNC
71	**200 Dirhams** 2002/AH1423. Mohammed VI and Hassan II.	FV	FV	35.00

MOZAMBIQUE

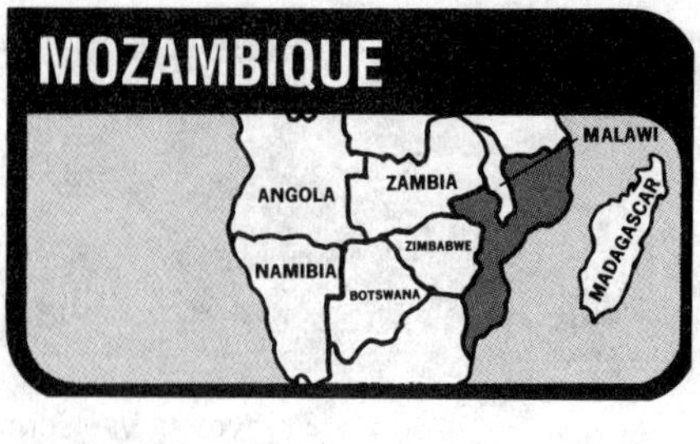

The People's Republic of Mozambique, a former overseas province of Portugal stretching for 1,430 miles (2,301 km.) along the southeast coast of Africa, has an area of 309,494 sq. mi. (783,030 sq. km.) and a population of 19.56 million. Capital: Maputo. Agriculture is the chief industry. Cashew nuts, cotton, sugar, copra and tea are exported.

Vasco da Gama explored all the coast of Mozambique in 1498 and found Arab trading posts already along the coast. Portuguese settlement dates from the establishment of the trading post of Mozambique in 1505. Within five years Portugal absorbed all the former Arab sultanates along the east African coast. The area was organized as a colony in 1907 and became an overseas province in 1952. In Sept. of 1974, after more than a decade of guerrilla warfare with the forces of the Mozambique Liberation Front, Portugal agreed to the independence of Mozambique, effective June 25, 1975. Mozambique became a member of the Commonwealth of Nations in November 1995. The President is Head of State; the Prime Minister is Head of Government.

RULERS:

Portuguese to 1975

MONETARY SYSTEM:

1 Escudo = 100 Centavos, 1911-1975
1 Escudo = 1 Metica = 100 Centimos, 1975-

REPLACEMENT NOTES:

#116, 117, 119: Z prefix.
#125-133, ZA, ZB, ZC prefix.
#134-137, AW, BW, CY, DZ prefix by denomination.

BANCO NACIONAL ULTRAMARINO

MOÇAMBIQUE BRANCH

1961; 1967 ISSUE

#109 and 110 printer: BWC.

		VG	VF	UNC
109	**100 Escudos** 27.3.1961. Green on multicolor underprint. Portrait A. de Ornelas at right, arms at upper center. Bank steamship seal at left on back. Printer: BWC without imprint.			
	a. Watermark: Arms.	1.50	4.00	17.50
	b. Without watermark.	1.00	3.00	10.00
	s. As a. Specimen.	—	—	140.

		VG	VF	UNC
110	**500 Escudos** 22.3.1967. Purple on multicolor underprint. Portrait C. Xavier at right, arms at upper center. Printer: BWC without imprint.			
	a. Issued note.	4.00	20.00	75.00
	s. Specimen.	—	—	150.

1970 ISSUE

Sign. varieties.

		VG	VF	UNC
111	**50 Escudos** 27.10.1970. Black on multicolor underprint. J. de Azevedo Coutinho at left center, arms at upper center right. Back green; bank steamship seal at left. Watermark: Arms.	1.00	3.00	15.00

FIRST 1972 ISSUE

		VG	VF	UNC
112	**1000 Escudos** 16.5.1972. Black-blue on multicolor underprint. King Afonso V at right and as watermark, arms at upper center. Allegorical woman with ships at left on back, bank steamship seal at upper center. Three signature varieties.	10.00	22.50	125.

Note: #112 has 2 1/2mm. serial # w/o prefix or 3mm. serial # and 3-letter prefix.

SECOND 1972 ISSUE

		VG	VF	UNC
113	**100 Escudos** 23.5.1972. Blue on multicolor underprint. G. Coutinho and S. Cabral at left center. Surveyor at center on back. Watermark: Coutinho.	2.00	7.50	50.00

		VG	VF	UNC
114	**500 Escudos** 23.5.1972. Purple on multicolor underprint. G. Coutinho at left center and as watermark. Cabral and airplane on back.	4.00	15.00	85.00

		VG	VF	UNC
115	**1000 Escudos** 23.5.1972. Green on multicolor underprint. Face similar to #114. Two men in cockpit of airplane at left center on back.	5.00	25.00	120.

PEOPLES REPUBLIC

BANCO DE MOÇAMBIQUE

1976 ND PROVISIONAL ISSUE

#116-119 black ovpt. of new bank name.

		VG	VF	UNC
116	**50 Escudos** ND (1976 - old date 27.10.1970). Black on multicolor underprint. Overprint on #111.	.10	.25	1.00

		VG	VF	UNC
117	**100 Escudos** ND (1976 - old date 27.3.1961). Green on multicolor underprint. Overprint on #109.			
	a. Issued note.	.10	.25	1.50
	s. Specimen.	—	—	100.

118	500 Escudos	VG	VF	UNC
	ND (1976 - old date 22.3.1967). Purple on multicolor underprint. Overprint on #110.			
	a. Issued note.	.25	.50	2.50
	s. Specimen.	—	—	115.

119	1000 Escudos	VG	VF	UNC
	ND (1976 - old date 23.5.1972). Green on multicolor underprint. Overprint on #115.	.25	.75	3.00

1976 Issue

#120-124 Pres. S. Machel at l. ctr. Printer: TDLR. These appear to be unadopted designs.

120	5 Meticas	VG	VF	UNC
	25.6.1976. Brown and multicolor. Kudu on back. Specimen, punched hole cancelled.	—	—	—

121	10 Meticas	VG	VF	UNC
	25.6.1976. Blue on multicolor. Lions on back. Specimen, punched hole cancelled.	—	—	—

122	20 Meticas	VG	VF	UNC
	25.6.1976. Red and multicolor. Giraffes on back. Specimen, punched hole cancelled.	—	—	—
123	50 Meticas			
	25.6.1976. Purple and multicolor. Cape buffalo on back. Specimen, punched hole cancelled.	—	—	—

124	100 Meticas	VG	VF	UNC
	25.6.1976. Green and multicolor. Elephants on back. Specimen, punched hole cancelled.	—	—	—

República Popular de Moçambique

1980 Issue

#125-128 arms at ctr. Large size serial #.

125	50 Meticais	VG	VF	UNC
	16.6.1980. Dark brown and brown on multicolor underprint. Soldiers at left, flag ceremony at right. Soldiers in training on back.	.15	.50	2.00

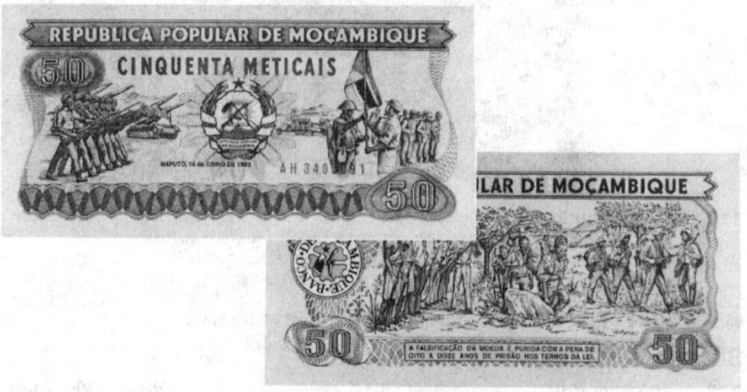

126	100 Meticais	VG	VF	UNC
	16.6.1980; 16.6.1983. Green on multicolor underprint. Soldiers at flagpole at left, E. Mondlane at right. Public ceremony on back.	.20	.75	3.00

127	500 Meticais	VG	VF	UNC
	16.6.1980. Deep blue-violet and dark blue-green on multicolor underprint. Government assembly at left, chanting crowd at right. Chemists and school scene on back.	.25	.50	4.50

		VG	VF	UNC
128	**1000 Meticais** 16.6.1980. Deep red on multicolor underprint. Pres. S. Machel with three young boys at right, revolutionary monument at left. Mining and harvesting scenes on back.	.75	1.75	8.50

1983-88 ISSUE

#129-132 modified arms at ctr. Smaller size serial #.

		VG	VF	UNC
129	**50 Meticais** 16.6.1983; 16.6.1986. Similar to #125 except for arms.	.10	.25	1.50

		VG	VF	UNC
130	**100 Meticais** 16.6.1983; 16.6.1986; 16.6.1989. Similar to #126 except for arms.	.15	.50	2.00

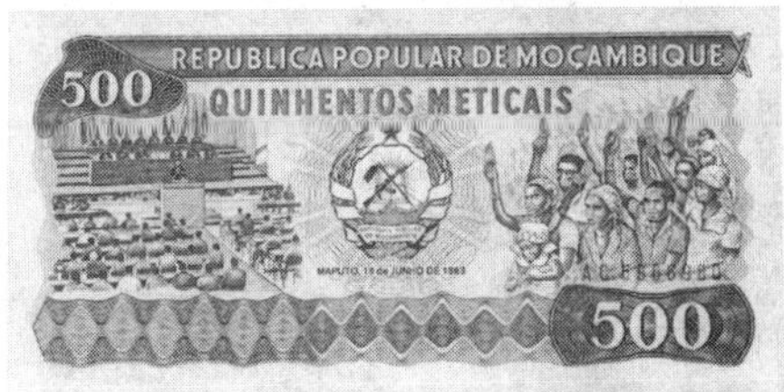

		VG	VF	UNC
131	**500 Meticais** 16.6.1983; 16.6.1986; 16.6.1989. Similar to #127 except for arms.	.25	.50	2.50

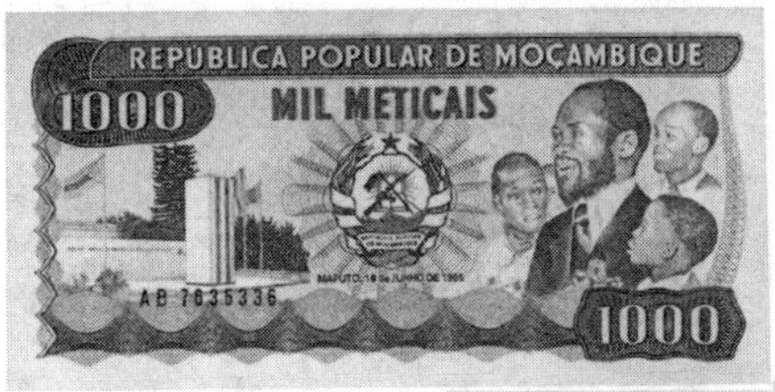

		VG	VF	UNC
132	**1000 Meticais** 16.6.1983; 16.6.1986; 16.6.1989. Similar to #128 except for arms.			
	a. 16.6.1983.	.50	1.50	6.00
	b. 16.6.1986.	.50	2.00	7.50
	c. 16.6.1989.	.50	.50	3.00

		VG	VF	UNC
133	**5000 Meticais** 3.2.1988; 3.2.1989. Purple, brown and violet on multicolor underprint. Carved statues at left, painting at right. Dancers and musicians on back.	.75	1.75	5.00

1991-93 ISSUE

#134-137 arms at upper ctr. r. printed on silver or gold underlay. Bank seal at lower l. on back. Wmk: J. Chissano. Printer: TDLR.

		VG	VF	UNC
134	**500 Meticais** 16.6.1991. Brown and blue on multicolor underprint. Native carving of couple in grief at left center, native art at right. Dancing warriors at center on back.	FV	FV	1.00

135 **1000 Meticais**

	VG	VF	UNC
16.6.1991. Brown and red on multicolor underprint. E. Mondlane at left center, military flag raising ceremony at right. Monument at left center on back.	FV	FV	2.00

136 **5000 Meticais**

	VG	VF	UNC
16.6.1991. Purple, violet and orange-brown on multicolor underprint. S. Machel at left center, monument to the Socialist vanguard at right. Foundry workers at center on back.	FV	FV	1.50

137 **10,000 Meticais**

	VG	VF	UNC
16.6.1991. Blue-green, brown and orange on multicolor underprint. J. Chissano at left center, high tension electrical towers at right, with farm tractor in field and high-rise city view in background at right. Plowing with oxen at center on back.	FV	FV	1.50

#138 and 139 Bank of Mozambique bldg. at l. ctr., arms at upper r. Cabora Bassa hydroelectric dam on back. Wmk: Bank monogram.

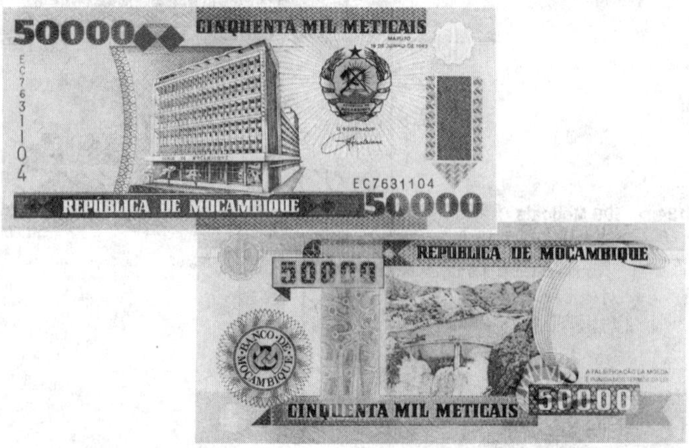

138 **50,000 Meticais**

	VG	VF	UNC
16.6.1993 (1994). Dark brown, red-brown on multicolor underprint.	FV	FV	6.50

139 **100,000 Meticais**

	VG	VF	UNC
16.6.1993 (1994). Red, brown-orange and olive-brown on multicolor underprint.	FV	FV	12.50

1999 ISSUE

140 **20,000 Meticais**

	VG	VF	UNC
16.6.1999. Green on multicolor underprint. Young woman seated writing at center. Maputo city hall on back.	FV	FV	2.50

2004 ISSUE

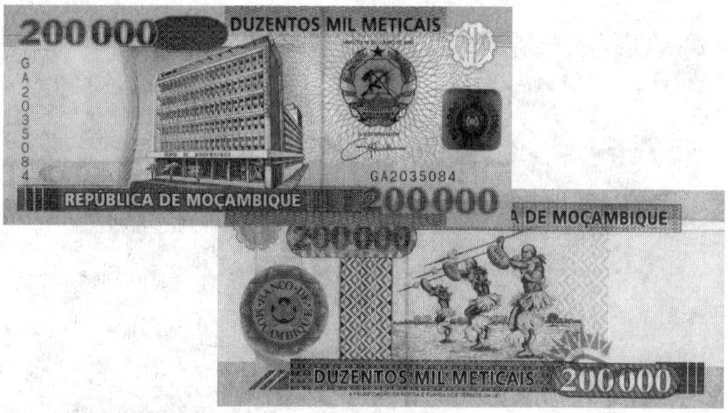

141 **200,000 Meticais**

	VG	VF	UNC
16.6.2003 (2004). Dark blue and aqua on multicolor underprint. Dancing warriors on back.	FV	FV	25.00

142 **500,000 Meticais**

	VG	VF	UNC
16.6.2003 (2004). Purple, tan and multicolor. Holographic seal at right. Serial #s in green and black.	FV	FV	55.00

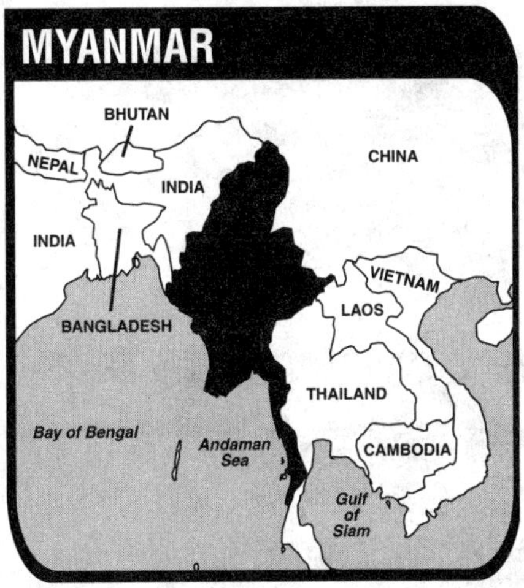

The Socialist Republic of the Union of Myanmar (formally called Burma), a country of Southeast Asia fronting on the Bay of Bengal and the Andaman Sea, has an area of 261,789 sq. mi. (676,552 sq. km.) and a population of 49.34 million. Capital: Rangoon. Myanmar is an agricultural country heavily dependent on its leading product (rice) which embodies two-thirds of the cultivated area and accounts for 40 percent of the value of exports. Petroleum, lead, tin, silver, zinc, nickel, cobalt and precious stones are exported.

The first European to reach Burma, about 1435, was Nicolo Di Conti, a merchant of Venice. During the beginning of the reign of Bodawpaya (1782-1819AD) the kingdom comprised most of the same area as it does today including Arakan which was taken over in 1784-85. The British East India Company, while unsuccessful in its 1612 effort to establish posts along the Bay of Bengal, was enabled by the Anglo-Burmese Wars of 1824-86 to expand to the whole of Burma and to secure its annexation to British India. In 1937, Burma was separated from India, becoming a separate British colony with limited self-government. The Japanese occupied Burma in 1942, and on Aug. 1, 1943 Burma became an "independent and sovereign state" under Dr. Ba Maw who was appointed the Adipadi (head of state) which collpased with the surrender of Japanese forces. Burma became an independent nation outside the British Commonwealth on Jan. 4, 1948, the constitution of 1948 providing for a parliamentary democracy and the nationalization of certain industries. However, political and economic problems persisted, and on March 2, 1962, Gen. Ne Win took over the government, suspended the constitution, installed himself as chief of state, and pursued a socialistic program with nationalization of nearly all industry and trade. On Jan. 4, 1974, a new constitution adopted by referendum established Burma as a "socialist republic" under one-party rule. The country name in English was changed to Union of Myanmar in 1989.

MONETARY SYSTEM:

1 Kyat = 100 Pyas, 1943-1945, 1952-

REPUBLIC

CENTRAL BANK OF MYANMAR

1990 ND ISSUE

			VG	VF	UNC
67	**1 Kyat**	ND (1990). Pale brown and orange on multicolor underprint. Gen. Aung San at left and as watermark. Dragon carving at left on back.	FV	FV	.30

1991-98 ND ISSUE

			VG	VF	UNC
68	**50 Pyas**	ND (1994). Dull purple and dull brown on gray and tan underprint. Musical string instrument at center. Watermark: B/CM.	FV	FV	.30

			VG	VF	UNC
69	**1 Kyat**	ND (1996). Gray, blue and purple on multicolor underprint. Chinze at right. Watermark: B/CM.	FV	FV	.30

			VG	VF	UNC
70	**5 Kyats**	ND (1996). Dark brown and blue-green on multicolor underprint. Chinze at left center. Ball game scene on back.			
		a. Watermark: Chinze. (1996).	FV	FV	.75
		b. Watermark: Chinze bust over value. (1997).	FV	FV	.50

			VG	VF	UNC
71	**10 Kyats**	ND (1996). Deep purple and violet on multicolor underprint. Chinze at right center. Elaborate barge on back.			
		a. Watermark: Chinze. (1996).	FV	FV	1.00
		b. Watermark: Chinze bust over value. (1997).	FV	FV	.50

			VG	VF	UNC
72	**20 Kyats**	ND (1994). Deep olive-green, brown and blue-green on multicolor underprint. Chinze at left. Fountain of elephants in park at center right on back. Watermark: Chinze bust over value.	FV	FV	1.00

			VG	VF	UNC
73	**50 Kyats**	ND (1994-). Red-brown, tan and dark brown on multicolor underprint. Chinze at right and as watermark. Coppersmith at left center on back.			
		a. Watermark: Chinze. (1994).	FV	FV	3.00
		b. Watermark: Chinze bust over value. (1997).	FV	FV	2.00

74 **100 Kyats**

ND (1994). Blue-violet, blue-green and dark brown on multicolor underprint. Chinze at left. Workers restoring temple and grounds at center right on back.

	VG	VF	UNC
a. Security thread in negative script. watermark: Chinze.	FV	FV	4.00
b. Security thread in positive script. watermark: Chinze above value.	FV	FV	3.00

75 **200 Kyats**

ND (ca.1991; 1998). Dark blue and green on multicolor underprint. Chinze at right, his head as watermark. Elephant pulling log at center right on back.

	VG	VF	UNC
a. Security thread in negative script. watermark: Chinze.	FV	FV	8.00
b. Security thread in positive script. watermark: Chinze above value.	FV	FV	6.00

76 **500 Kyats**

ND (1994). Brown, purple and brown-orange on multicolor underprint. Chinze at left. Workers restoring medieval statue, craftsman and water hauler at center right on back.

	VG	VF	UNC
a. Security thread in negative script. watermark: Chinze.	FV	FV	14.00
b. Security thread in positive script. watermark: Chinze above value.	FV	FV	10.00

77 **1000 Kyats**

ND (1998). Deep green and purple on multicolor underprint. Chinze at right. Central Bank building at left center on back.

	VG	VF	UNC
a. Security thread in negative script. watermark: Chinze.	FV	FV	15.00
b. Security thread in positive script. watermark: Chinze above value.	FV	FV	15.00

2004 ND Reduced Size Issue

		VG	VF	UNC
78	**200 Kyats** ND (2004).	FV	FV	6.00
79	**500 Kyats** ND (2004).	FV	FV	10.00

		VG	VF	UNC
80	**1000 Kyats** ND (2004).	FV	FV	15.00

Foreign Exchange Certificates

Central Bank

1993 ND Issue

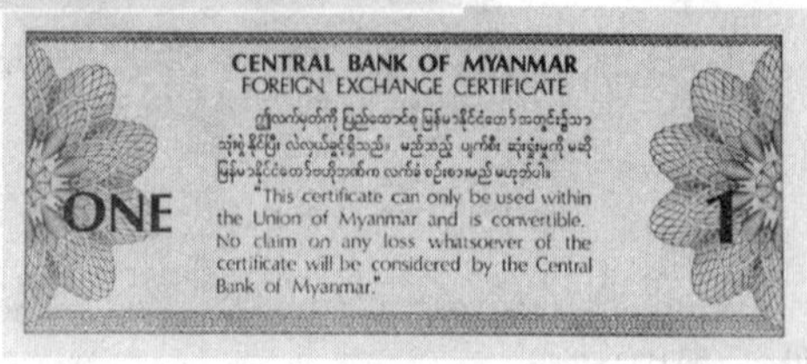

		VG	VF	UNC
FX1	**1 Dollar (USA)** ND (1993). Blue, brown, yellow and green.	—	—	4.00

		VG	VF	UNC
FX2	**5 Dollars (USA)** ND (1993). Maroon, yellow and blue.	—	—	12.50

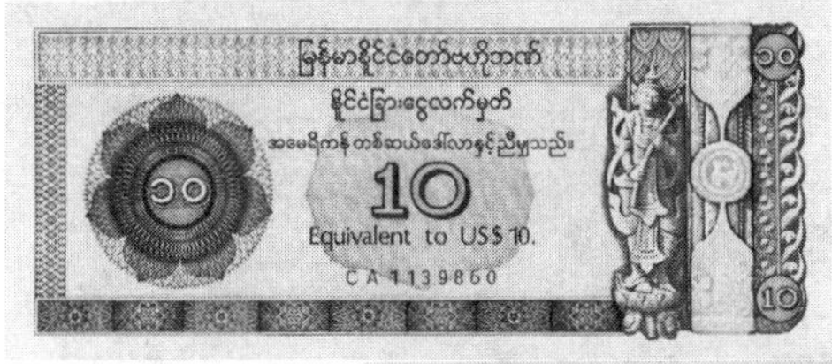

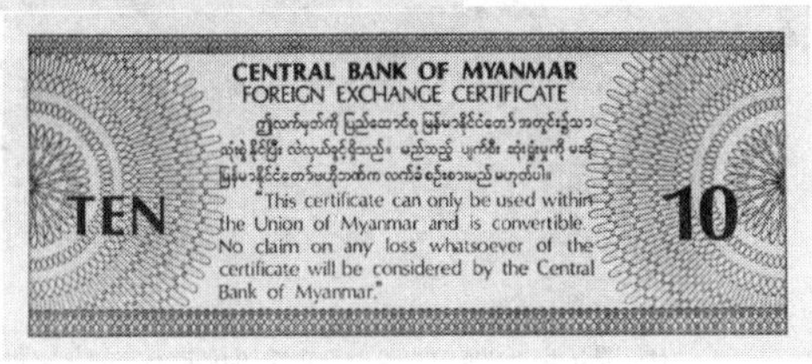

		VG	VF	UNC
FX3	**10 Dollars (USA)** ND (1993). Blue, green and gray.	—	—	27.50
FX4	**20 Dollars (USA)** ND (1997). Maroon, yellow and brown.	—	—	35.00

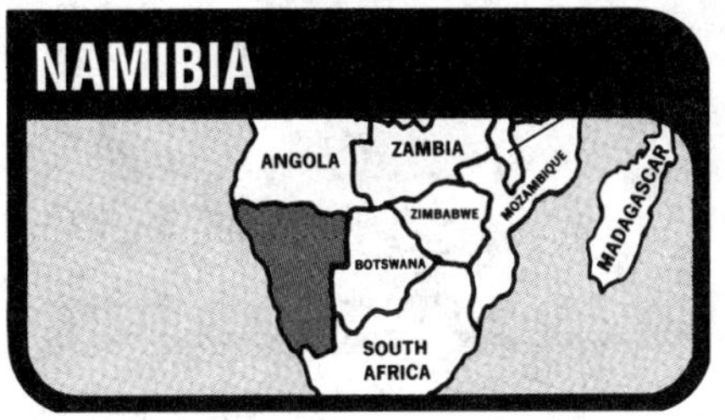

The Republic of Namibia, once the German colonial territory of German South West Africa, is situated on the Atlantic coast of southern Africa, bounded on the north by Angola, on the east by Botswana, and on the south by South Africa. It has an area of 318,261 sq. mi. (824,290 sq. km.) and a population of 1.73 million. Capital: Windhoek. Diamonds, copper, lead, zinc and cattle are exported.

South Africa undertook the administration of South West Africa under the terms of a League of Nations mandate on Dec. 17, 1920. When the League of Nations was dissolved in 1946, its supervisory authority for South West Africa was inherited by the United Nations. In 1946 the UN denied South Africa's request to annex South West Africa. South Africa responded by refusing to place the territory under a UN trusteeship. In 1950 the International Court of Justice ruled that South Africa could not unilaterally modify the international status of South West Africa. A 1966 UN resolution declaring the mandate terminated was rejected by South Africa, and the status of the area remained in dispute. In June 1968 the UN General Assembly voted to rename the territory Namibia. In 1971 the International Court of Justice ruled that South Africa's presence in Namibia was illegal. In Dec. 1973 the UN appointed a UN Commissioner, and a multi-racial Advisory Council was also appointed. An interim government was formed in 1977 and independence was to be declared by Dec. 31, 1978. This resolution was rejected by major UN powers. In April 1978 South Africa accepted a plan for UN-supervised elections which led to political abstention by the South West Africa People's Organization (SWAPO) party. The result was the dissolution of the Minister's Council and National Assembly in Jan. 1983. A Multi-Party Conference (MPC) was formed in May 1984 which held talks with SWAPO. The MPC petitioned South Africa for Namibian self-government and on June 17, 1984 the Transitional Government of National Unity was installed. Negotiations were held in 1988 between Angola, Cuba and South Africa reaching a peaceful settlement on Aug. 5, 1988. By April 1, 1989, Cuban troops were to withdraw from Angola and South African troops from Namibia. The Transitional Government resigned on Feb. 28, 1988 for the upcoming elections of the constituent assembly in Nov. 1989. Independence was finally achieved on March 21, 1990, within the Commonwealth of Nations. The President is Head of State; the Prime Minister is Head of Government.

MONETARY SYSTEM:

1 Namibia Dollar = 100 Cents

Note: For notes of the 3 commercial banks circulating until 1963, see Southwest Africa listings in Vol. II.

SIGNATURE VARIETIES	
	Dr. W. L. Benard **16 July 1990-31 August 1991**
1	**Mr. Erik L. Karlsson** **Acting: 1 Semtember 1991-24 November 1992** **25 November 1992-31 December 1993**
2	**Dr. Jaafar B. Ahmad** **1 January 1994-31 December 1996**
3	**Mr. Tom K. Alweendo** **1 January 1997-**

REPUBLIC

NAMIBIA RESERVE BANK

1990 ISSUE

#A1-E1 printer: BWC. Unadopted designs.

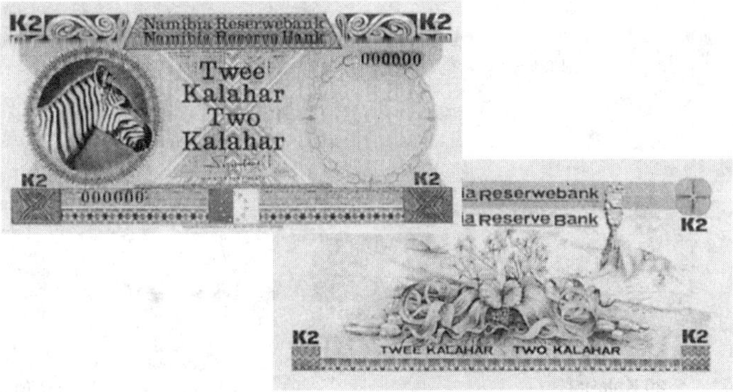

		VG	VF	UNC
A1	**2 Kalahar** ND. Red on multicolor underprint. Zebra head at left. Plant at center, rock formation at right. Unissued specimen.	—	—	—

B1	5 Kalahar	VG	VF	UNC
	ND. Red and purple on multicolor underprint. Oryx head at left. Back blue; road graders at center. Unissued specimen.	—	—	—

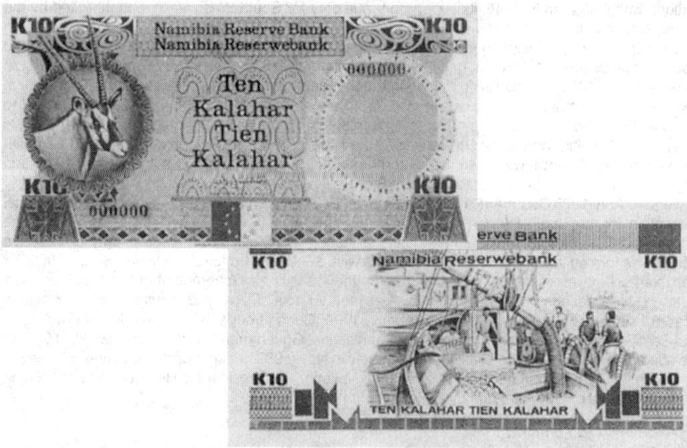

C1	10 Kalahar	VG	VF	UNC
	ND. Red and purple on multicolor underprint. Oryx head at left. Commercial fishing boat at center on back. Unissued specimen.	—	—	—

D1	20 Kalahar	VG	VF	UNC
	ND. Purple on multicolor underprint. Lion head in round frame at left, watermark circle at right. Sheep herd on back, herdsman on horseback. Unissued specimen.	—	—	—

E1	20 Kalahar	VG	VF	UNC
	ND. Purple on multicolor underprint. Lion head at left, flag at center. Sheep herd on back, walking herdsman. Unissued specimen.	—	—	—

BANK OF NAMIBIA

1993 ND ISSUE

#1-3 Capt. H. Wittbooi at l. ctr. and as wmk. Printer: Tumba Bruk A.B. (Sweden - w/o imprint). Sign. 1. Replacement notes: Serial # prefix *X; Y; Z* for #1, 2 and 3 respectively.

1	10 Namibia Dollars	VG	VF	UNC
	ND (1993). Blue-black on multicolor underprint. Arms at upper left. Springbok at right on back.			
	a. Signature 1.	FV	2.00	8.25
	s. Specimen. Serial # prefix *S*.	—	—	150.

2	50 Namibia Dollars	VG	VF	UNC
	ND (1993). Blue-green and dark brown on multicolor underprint. Arms at upper center. Kudu at right on back.			
	a. Signature 1.	FV	11.00	38.50
	s. Specimen. Serial # prefix *S*.	—	—	150.

3	100 Namibia Dollars	VG	VF	UNC
	ND (1993). Red, brown and red-brown on multicolor underprint. Arms at upper center right. Oryx at right on back.			
	a. Signature 1.	FV	20.00	70.00
	s. Specimen. Serial # prefix *S*.	—	—	150.

#4 not assigned.

1996-2001 ND ISSUE

#4-8 Capt. H. Wittbooi at l. ctr. and as wmk. Segmented foil over security thread and ascending size serial #. Replacement notes: Serial # prefix *X; V; Y; Z; W* respectively for #4-8.

4	10 Namibia Dollars	VG	VF	UNC
	ND (2001). Blue on multicolor underprint. Arms at upper left. Springbok on back. Signature 3. Like #1. Printer: F-CO.			
	a. Issue note.	FV	FV	3.75
	s. Specimen. Serial # prefix *A*.	—	—	120.

		VG	VF	UNC
5	**20 Namibia Dollars** ND (1996). Orange and violet on multicolor underprint. Arms at upper left. Red hartebeest at center right on back. Printer: TDLR. 7-digit serial #.			
	a. Signature 2.	FV	FV	15.00
	s. Specimen. Serial # prefix *H*.	—	—	140.
6	**20 Namibia Dollars** ND (2002). Similar to #5. Printer: SABN.			
	a. Signature 3. 8-digit serial #.	FV	FV	6.75
	s. Specimen. Serial # prefix *J*.	—	—	120.

		VG	VF	UNC
7	**50 Namibia Dollars** ND (1999). Blue-green and dark brown on multicolor underprint. Arms at upper center. Kudu at right on back. Like #2. Printer: TDLR.			
	a. Signature 3. 7-digit serial #.	FV	FV	23.00
	s. Specimen. Serial # prefix *P*.	—	—	130.
8	**50 Namibia Dollars** ND (1999). Similar to #7. Printer: SABN.			
	a. Signature 3. 8-digit serial #.	FV	FV	17.00
	s. Specimen. Serial # prefix *N*.	—	—	120.

		VG	VF	UNC
9	**100 Namibia Dollars** ND (1999). Red, brown and red-brown on multicolor underprint. Arms at center right. Oryx at right on back. Like #3. Printer: TDLR.			
	a. Signature 3. Seven digit serial #.	FV	FV	47.50
	b. Signature 3. Eight digit serial #.	FV	FV	35.00
	c. Signature 3. 7-digit serial #. Prefix TT.	FV	30.00	100.
	s. Specimen. Serial # prefix *T*.	—	—	130.

		VG	VF	UNC
10	**200 Namibia Dollars** ND (1996). Purple and violet on multicolor underprint. Arms at upper center. Roan antelope at center right on back. Printer: TDLR.			
	a. Signature 2.	FV	FV	80.00
	s. Specimen. Serial # prefix *U*.	—	—	130.

2003 ISSUE

#11-12 8-digit serial #. Printer:SABN.

		VG	VF	UNC
11	**50 Namibia Dollars** ND (2003). Blue-green and dark brown on multicolor underprint.	FV	FV	22.50
12	**100 Namibia Dollars** ND (2003). Red, brown and red-brown on multicolor underprint.	FV	FV	30.00

COLLECTOR SERIES

BANK OF NAMIBIA

1993 ND ISSUE

		Issue Price	Mkt. Value
CS1	**10, 50, 100 Dollars** ND (1993). #1-3 with matched serial # mounted in a special plexiglass frame.	—	225.

1996; 1999 ND ISSUE

		Issue Price	Mkt. Value
CS2	**20, 50, 100, 200 Dollars** ND (1996; 1999). #5, 7, 9, 10 with matched serial #.	—	330.

Note: Issued only to current owners of #CS1 to complete matched serial sets.

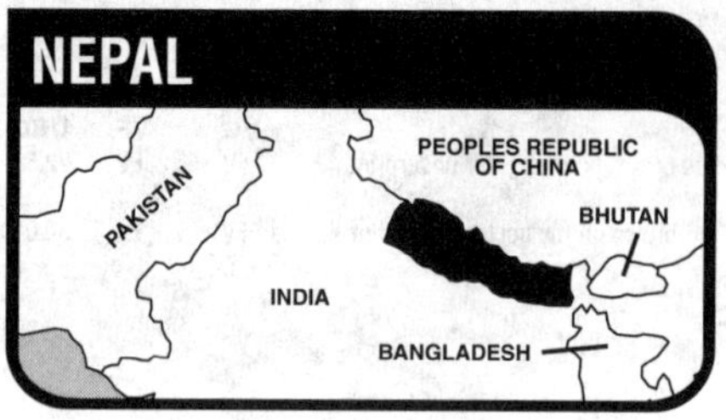

The Kingdom of Nepal, the world's only Hindu kingdom, is a landlocked country located in central Asia along the southern slopes of the Himalayan Mountains. It has an area of 56,136 sq. mi. (140,797 sq. km.) and a population of 24.35 million. Capital: Káthmandu. Nepal has substantial deposits of coal, copper, iron and cobalt but they are largely unexploited. Agriculture is the principal economic activity. Livestock, rice, timber and jute are exported.

Prithvi Narayan Shah, ruler of the principality of Gurkha, formed Nepal from a number of independent mountain states in the latter half of the 18th century. After his death a period of political instability ensued which lasted until the 1840's when the Rana family reduced the monarch to a figurehead and established itself as hereditary Prime Ministers. A popular revolution (1950-51) toppled the Rana family and reconstituted the power in the throne. In 1959 King Mahendra declared Nepal a constitutional monarchy. A new constitution promulgated in 1962 instituted a system of panchayat (village council) democracy from the village to the national levels. In 1990, following political unrest, the king's powers were reduced, and the country adopted a system of parliamentary democracy.

RULERS:

Mahendra Vira Vikrama Shahi Deva, 1955-1972
Birendra Bir Bikram Shahi Deva, 1972-2001
Ginendra, 2001-

MONETARY SYSTEM:

1 Rupee = 100 Paisa, 1961-

SIGNATURE VARIETIES

1	Janak Raj	2	Bharat Raj
3	Narendra Raj	4	Himalaya Shamsher (J.B. Rama)
5	Lekshmi Nath Gautam	6	Pradhumna Lai (Rajbhandari)
7	Bekh Bahadur Thapa	8	Yadav Prasad Pant
9	Kul Shekhar Sharma	10	Kalyan Dikram Adhikary
11	Ganesh Bahadur Thapa	12	Harishankar Trfipathi
13	Satyendra Pyara Shrestha	14	Dipendra Purush Dhakal
15	Dr. Tilak Rawal	16	

KINGDOM

CENTRAL BANK OF NEPAL

1961; 1965 ND ISSUE

#12-15 denominations in Nepalese language changed from "Mohru" on previous issue to "Rupees" on both face and back. Wmk: Plumed crown.

			VG	VF	UNC
12	**1 Rupee** ND (1965). Lilac and olive-green. Like #8. Coin at left, temple at center. Back lilac and green; arms at center, coin at right. Signature 8.		.25	.75	3.50

#13-15 portr. Kg. Mahendra Vira Vikrama at upper l.

			VG	VF	UNC
13	**5 Rupees** ND (1961). Purple and aqua. Like #9. Stupa at center. Himalayas on back. Signature 5; 7; 8.		.50	1.50	4.00

			VG	VF	UNC
14	**10 Rupees** ND (1961). Dark brown and red. Like # 10. Temple at center. Arms at center on back. Signature 5; 6; 7; 8.		1.00	3.00	8.00

			VG	VF	UNC
15	**100 Rupees** ND (1961). Green and brown. Like #11. Temple at Lalitpor at center. Indian rhinoceros at center on back. Signature 5; 6; 7; 8.		3.00	10.00	35.00

1972 ND ISSUE

#16-21 Kg. Mahendra Vira Vikrama wearing military uniform w/white cap at l. Wmk: Plumed crown. Sign. 8.

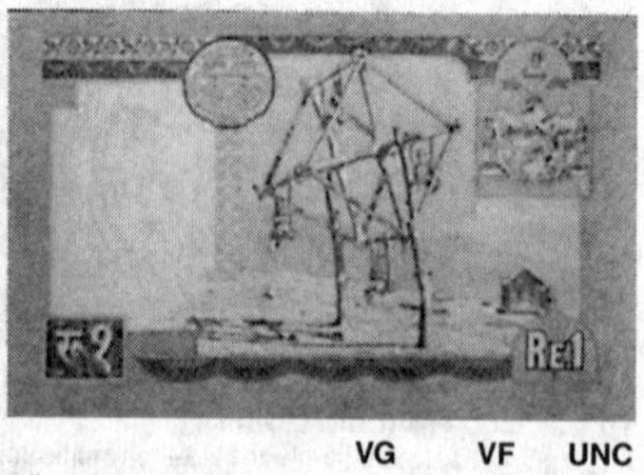

			VG	VF	UNC
16	**1 Rupee** ND (1972). Light brown on blue underprint. Back brown and purple; four-chair rotary swing at center right, arms at upper right on back.		.20	.75	1.75

		VG	VF	UNC
17	**5 Rupees** ND (1972). Light green on lilac underprint. Back green and blue; terraced hillside with Himalayas in background.	.25	1.00	2.50

		VG	VF	UNC
18	**10 Rupees** ND (1972). Light brown on dull olive-green and light blue underprint. Back green and brown; Singha Dunbar at Kathmandu at center.	.25	1.00	2.50

		VG	VF	UNC
19	**100 Rupees** ND (1972). Green on lilac underprint. Himalayas at center. Ornate building, temple and arms at right on back.	3.00	7.00	17.50
20	**500 Rupees** ND (1972). Brown and violet. Two tigers on back.	25.00	75.00	200.

		VG	VF	UNC
21	**1000 Rupees** ND (1972). Blue and multicolor. Great Stupa at Bodhnath. House and mountains on back.	25.00	60.00	175.

NOTICE

Readers with unlisted dates, signature varieties, etc. are invited to submit photocopies of their notes to: Standard Catalog of World Paper Money, 700 East State St. Iola, WI 54990-0001, E-Mail: george.cuhaj@fwpubs.com.

1974 ND Issue

#22-28 Kg. Birendra Bir Bikram in military uniform w/dk. cap at l. Wmk: Plumed crown.

		VG	VF	UNC
22	**1 Rupee** ND (1974). Blue on purple and gold underprint. Temple at center. Back blue and brown; two musk deer at center, arms at upper right. Signature 9; 10; 11; 12.	.05	.25	1.00

		VG	VF	UNC
23	**5 Rupees** ND (1974). Red, brown and green. Temple at center. Back red and brown; Two yaks at center right. Signature 9; 10; 11.			
	a. Issued note.	.15	.50	3.25
	s. Specimen.	—	—	100.
	ct. Color trial. Green and purple face, back blue.	—	—	165.

		VG	VF	UNC
24	**10 Rupees** ND (1974). Dark and light brown on multicolor underprint. Vishnu on Garnda at center. Back brown and green; Two Black Buck Antelope at center, arms at right. Signature 9; 10; 11.			
	a. Issued note.	.25	.75	3.25
	s. Specimen.	—	—	100.
	ct. Color trial. Green and purple on multicolor underprint.	—	—	165.

		VG	VF	UNC
25	**50 Rupees** ND (1974). Purple on green and multicolor underprint. Building at center. Back blue and brown; Himalayan Tahr standing facing right at center, arms at right. Signature 9.			
	a. Issued note.	1.50	3.50	10.00
	s. Specimen.	—	—	135.

		VG	VF	UNC
26	**100 Rupees** ND (1974). Green and purple on multicolor underprint. Mountains at center, temple at right. Back green; Indian Rhinoceros walking left, "eye" at upper left corner, arms at upper right. Signature 9.	3.00	7.00	20.00

		VG	VF	UNC
27	**500 Rupees** ND (1974). Brown on multicolor underprint. Monastery at center. Back brown and gold; Two tigers at center right, arms at upper right. Signature 9; 10.	25.00	75.00	200.

		VG	VF	UNC
28	**1000 Rupees** ND (1974). Blue on multicolor underprint. Temple and Great Stupa at center. Elephant at center, arms at upper right on back. Signature 9.			
	a. Issued note.	25.00	80.00	225.
	s. Specimen.	—	—	—

1981-87 ND Issue

#29-36 Kg. Birendra Bir Bikram wearing plumed crown at l. Wmk: Plumed crown.

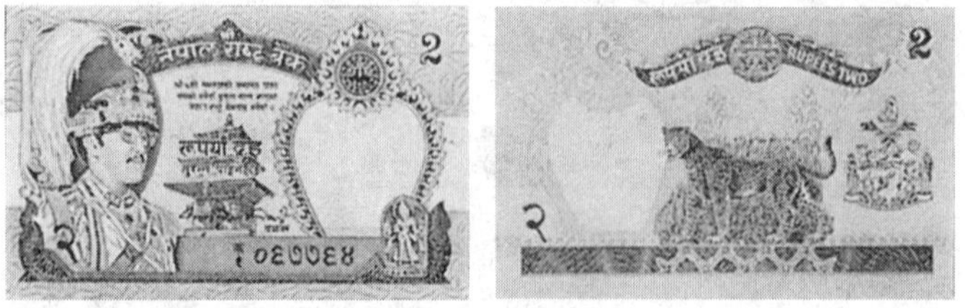

		VG	VF	UNC
29	**2 Rupees** ND (1981-). Green on light blue and lilac underprint. Temple at center. Back multicolored; leopard at center.			
	a. Line from king's lower lip extending downward. Serial # 24mm long. signature 10.	FV	FV	2.00
	b. No line from king's lower lip. signature 10; 11; 13.	FV	FV	.50
	c. As b. Serial # 20mm long. signature 12.	FV	FV	.75

		VG	VF	UNC
30	**5 Rupees** ND (1987-). Brown on red and multicolor underprint. Temple at center. Back similar to #23.			
	a. Serial # 24mm long. signature 11; 12; 13.	FV	FV	1.25
	b. Serial # 20mm long. signature 12.	FV	FV	1.25

		VG	VF	UNC
31	**10 Rupees** ND (1985-87). Dark brown and orange on lilac and multicolor underprint. Vishnu on Garnda at center. Antelopes at center, arms at right on back.			
	a. Serial # 24mm long. signature 11; 12.	FV	FV	2.00
	b. Segmented foil over security thread. signature 13, 14.	FV	FV	1.75

		VG	VF	UNC
32	**20 Rupees** ND (1982-87). Orange on multicolor underprint. Janakpur Temple at center. Back orange and multicolor; Sambar Deer at center, arms at right. Serial # 24mm long. Signature 10; 11.			
	a. Issued note.	FV	FV	5.00
	s. Specimen.	—	—	135.

		VG	VF	UNC
33	**50 Rupees** ND (1983-). Blue on multicolor underprint. Palace at center. Himalayan Tahr at center, arms at right on back.			

		VG	VF	UNC
33	**50 Rupees**			
	a. With title at right. Serial # 24mm long. signature 10. (1983).	FV	FV	5.50
	b. With title at center Serial # 20mm long. signature 11; 12.	FV	FV	3.50
	c. Segmented foil over security thread. signature 13.	—	—	3.00

		VG	VF	UNC
34	**100 Rupees**			
	ND (1981-). Green on pale lilac and multicolor underprint. Temple at right. Rhinoceros walking left, arms at upper right on back. Similar to #26, but without "eye" at upper left.			
	a. Line from king's lower lip extending downward. with security thread. Serial # 24mm long. signature 10.	FV	FV	6.50
	b. No line from king's lower lip. Serial # at lower left signature 10.	FV	FV	6.00
	c. Serial # 20mm long. signature 11.	FV	FV	5.50
	d. As b. Segmented foil over security thread. signature 12.	FV	FV	5.00
	e. Serial # 20mm long. signature 13.	FV	FV	4.50
	f. Serial # 24mm long. signature 13.	FV	FV	4.50

		VG	VF	UNC
35	**500 Rupees**			
	ND (1981-). Brown and blue-violet on multicolor underprint. Temple at center. Back brown and gold on blue underprint; Two tigers at center right, arms at upper right.			
	a. Line from King's lip extending downwards. Serial # 24mm long. signature 10.	FV	FV	45.00
	b. Serial # 20mm long. signature 11.	FV	FV	20.00
	c. Segmented foil over security thread. signature 12.	FV	FV	17.50
	d. Signature 13. (1996).	FV	FV	17.50

		VG	VF	UNC
36	**1000 Rupees**			
	ND (1981-). Red-brown and gray on multicolor underprint. Stupa and temple on face. Elephant at center, arms at upper right on back.			
	a. Line from King's lip extending downwards. Serial # 24mm long. signature 10.	FV	FV	85.00
	b. Serial # 20mm long. signature 11.	FV	FV	37.50
	c. Segmented foil over security thread. signature 12.	FV	FV	37.50
	d. Signature 13. (1996).	FV	FV	35.00

1988-96 ND ISSUE

#37 and 38 Kg. Birendra Bir Bikram wearing plumed crown at l. Wmk: Crown.

		VG	VF	UNC
37	**1 Rupee**			
	ND (1991-) Purple and dull blue on multicolor underprint. Back like #22. Signature 12; 13.	FV	FV	.40

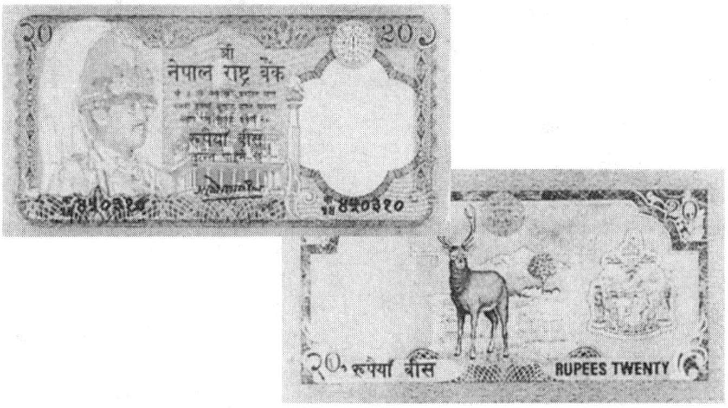

		VG	VF	UNC
38	**20 Rupees**			
	ND (1988-). Orange on multicolor underprint. Like #32, but multicolor border on face and back.			
	a. Serial # 24mm long. signature 11; 12.	FV	FV	2.25
	b. Segmented foil over security thread. Serial # 20mm long. signature 13.	FV	FV	2.00
	s. As a. Specimen.	—	—	115.

Note: #39 and 40 have been renumbered 35d and 36d respectively.

1997 ND COMMEMORATIVE ISSUE

#41 and 42, Silver Jubilee of Accession, 1972-1997

#41 and 42 portr. Kg. Birenda Bir Bikram wearing plumed crown at l. Wmk: Plumed crown.

		VG	VF	UNC
41	**25 Rupees**			
	ND (1997). Black and dark brown on multicolor underprint. Royal palace at center right. Back dull green and orange; pillars with chinze at left, steer at center, arms at right.	FV	FV	2.25

		VG	VF	UNC
42	**250 Rupees**			
	ND (1997). Dark gray and blue-gray on multicolor underprint. House of Representatives in underprint at center, royal palace at center right. Back blue and orange on green underprint; pillars with chinze at left, steer at center, arms at right.	FV	FV	17.50

#42 was also issued in a special folder.

2000 ND ISSUE

		VG	VF	UNC
43	**500 Rupees**			
	ND (2000). Brown, blue-violet and silver on multicolor underprint. Similar to #35 but larger portrait.	FV	FV	17.50

44 **1000 Rupees** | VG FV | VF FV | UNC 35.00

ND (2000). Blue, brown and silver on multicolor underprint. Similar to #36 but larger portrait.

2002 ND Commemorative Issue

Accession to the throne of Kg. Gyanendra Bir Bikram

45 **10 Rupees** | VG FV | VF FV | UNC 1.50

ND (30.9.2002). Multicolor. Commemorative text in horse-shoe shaped window: *This is issued on the occasion of King Gyanendra Bir Bikram Shah Dev's accession to the throne in BS 2058. Printer: NPA.*

2002 ND Issue

#46-51 portr. Kg. Gyanendra Bir Bikram at r. Sign. Tilak Rawal.

46 **5 Rupees** | VG FV | VF FV | UNC 2.50

ND (2002). Red and brown on multicolor underprint. Portrait is darkly engraved.

47 **20 Rupees** | VG FV | VF FV | UNC 2.25

ND (2002). Deer at center.

48 **50 Rupees** | VG FV | VF FV | UNC 4.00

ND (2002). Black and blue on multicolor underprint. Building at center. Himalayan Tahr at center on back.

49 **100 Rupees** | VG FV | VF FV | UNC 6.00

ND (2002). Rhinocerous walking left at center on back.

50 **500 Rupees** | VG FV | VF FV | UNC 17.50

ND (2002). Black and orange on multicolor underprint. Building at center. Two tigers at center on back.

51 **1000 Rupees** | VG FV | VF FV | UNC 35.00

ND (2002). Black and red on multicolor underprint. Temple at center. Elephant at center on back.

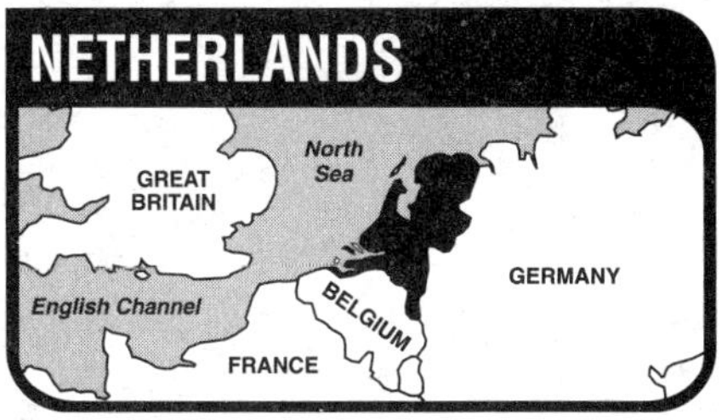

The Kingdom of the Netherlands, a country of western Europe fronting on the North Sea and bordered by Belgium and Germany, has an area of 15,770 sq. mi. (40,844 sq. km.) and a population of 15.87 million. Capital: Amsterdam, but the seat of government is at The Hague. The economy is d on dairy farming and a variety of industrial activities. Chemicals, yarns and fabrics, and meat products are exported.

After being a part of Charlemagne's empire in the 8th and 9th centuries, the Netherlands came under the control of Burgundy and the Austrian Hapsburgs, and finally were subjected to Spanish domination in the 16th century. Led by William of Orange, the Dutch revolted against Spain in 1568. The seven northern provinces formed the Union of Utrecht and declared their independence in 1581, becoming the Republic of the United Netherlands. In the following century, the "Golden Age" of Dutch history, the Netherlands became a great sea and colonial power, a patron of the arts and a refuge for the persecuted. In 1814, all the provinces of Holland and Belgium were merged into the Kingdom of the United Netherlands under William I. The Belgians withdrew in 1830 to form their own kingdom, the last substantial change in the configuration of European Netherlands. German forces invaded in 1940 and the royal family fled to England where a government in exile was formed. German High Commissioner Arthur Seyss-Inquart was placed in command until 1945 when the arrival of Allied military forces ended the occupation. Reigning since 1948, Queen Juliana abdicated in 1981. Her daughter, Beatrix, is now Queen.

RULERS:

Juliana, 1948-1981
Beatrix, 1981-

MONETARY SYSTEM:

1 Gulden = 100 Cents, to 2001
1 Euro = 100 Cents, 2002-

KONINKRIJK - KINGDOM

DE NEDERLANDSCHE BANK

NETHERLANDS BANK

1966-72 ISSUE

		VG	VF	UNC
90	**5 Gulden**			
	26.4.1966. Green on multicolor underprint. Joost van den Vondel at right. Modern design of Amsterdam Play-house on back. Watermark: Inkwell, quill pen and scroll.			
	a. Serial # at upper left and lower right. Gray paper with clear watermark.	FV	FV	10.00
	b. Serial # at upper left and lower right. White paper with vague watermark. Series XA/XM.	FV	FV	12.50
	c. Serial # at upper left and center r. in smaller type. (Experimental issue; circulated initally in the province of Utrecht.) Series 6AA.	50.00	125.	625.

		VG	VF	UNC
91	**10 Gulden**			
	25.4.1968. Dark blue on violet and multicolor underprint. Stylized self-portrait of Frans Hals at right. Modern design on back. Watermark: Cornucopia.			
	a. *0* in "bullseye" at upper left. on back.	FV	6.00	12.00
	b. Plain "bullseye" at upper left. on back.	FV	FV	10.00

		VG	VF	UNC
92	**25 Gulden**			
	10.2.1971. Red on orange and pink underprint. Jan Pietersz Sweelinck at right. Modern design on back. Watermark: Rectangular wave design.			
	a. Issued note.	FV	FV	35.00
	s. Specimen.	—	—	950.

		VG	VF	UNC
93	**100 Gulden**			
	14.5.1970. Dark brown on multicolor underprint. Michiel Adriaensz de Ruyter at right. Compass-card or rhumbcard design at center on back.			
	a. Issued note.	FV	FV	165.
	s. Specimen.	—	—	1100.

		VG	VF	UNC
94	**1000 Gulden**			
	30.3.1972. Black and dark green on multicolor underprint. Baruch d' Espinoza at right. Watermark: Pyramid in bowl on slab.			
	a. Issued note.	FV	FV	750.
	s. Specimen.	—	—	1400.

1973 ISSUE

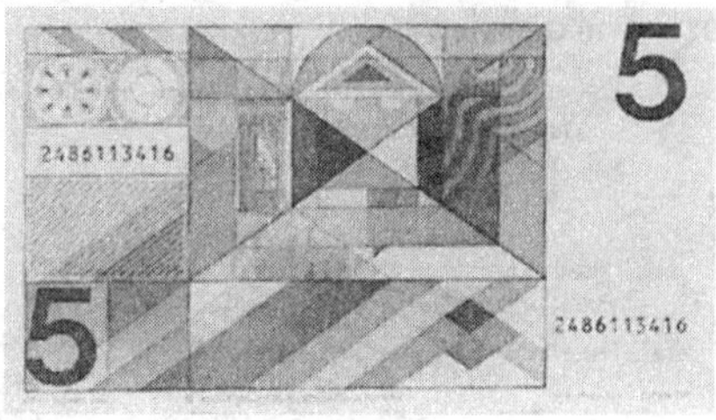

95 **5 Gulden** | VG | VF | UNC
28.3.1973. Dark green on green and multicolor underprint. Joost van den Vondel at right. Watermark like #90.

	VG	VF	UNC
a. Issued note.	FV	FV	7.50
s. Specimen.	—	—	1300.

1977-85 Issue

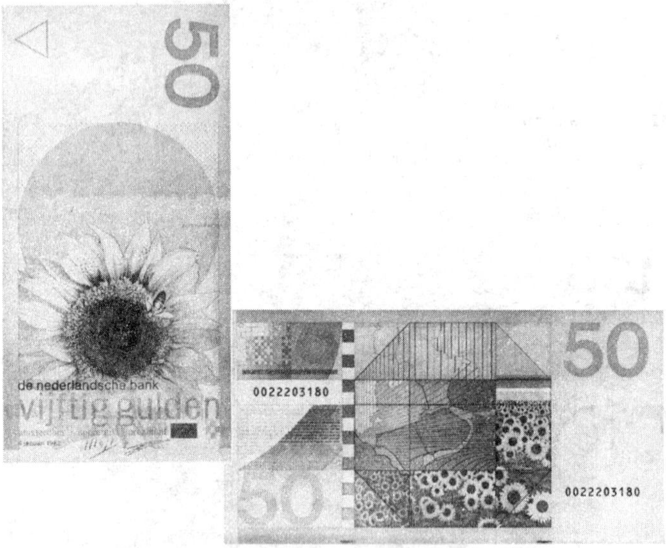

96 **50 Gulden**

VG	VF	UNC
FV	FV	35.00

4.1.1982. Orange and yellow on multicolor underprint. Sunflower with bee at lower center. Vertical format. Map and flowers on back. Watermark: Bee.

97 **100 Gulden**
28.7.1977 (1981). Dark brown on multicolor underprint. Snipe at right. Head of great snipe on back and as watermark.

	VG	VF	UNC
a. Issued note.	FV	FV	140.
s. Specimen.	—	—	1200.

NOTICE

Readers with unlisted dates, signature varieties, etc. are invited to submit photocopies of their notes to: Standard Catalog of World Paper Money, 700 East State St. Iola, WI 54990-0001, E-Mail: george.cuhaj@fwpubs.com.

98 **250 Gulden**
25.7.1985 (1986). Violet on multicolor underprint. Lighthouse. Vertical format. Lighthouse and map on back. Watermark: Rabbit and *VHP*.

	VG	VF	UNC
a. Issued note.	FV	FV	150.
s. Specimen.	—	—	1700.

1989-97 Issue

99 **10 Gulden**

VG	VF	UNC
FV	FV	7.50

1.7.1997. Purple and blue-violet on multicolor underprint. Value and geometric designs on face and back. Watermark: Bird.

100 **25 Gulden**

VG	VF	UNC
FV	FV	17.50

5.4.1989. Red on multicolor underprint. Value and geometric designs on face and back. Watermark: Robin.

101	100 Gulden	VG	VF	UNC
	9.1.1992 (7.9.1993). Dark and light brown, gray and gold on multicolor underprint. Value and geometric designs on face and back. Watermark: Little owl.	FV	FV	75.00

102	1000 Gulden	VG	VF	UNC
	2.6.1994 (1996). Dark gray and green. Geometric designs on face and back. Watermark: Lapwing's head.	FV	FV	600.

Note: For later issues used in the Netherlands see European Union listings.

The Netherlands Antilles, part of the Netherlands realm, comprise two groups of islands in the West Indies: Bonaire and Curacao near the Venezuelan coast; St. Eustatius, Saba, and the southern part of St. Martin (St. Maarten) southeast of Puerto Rico. The island group has an area of 385 sq. mi. (961 sq. km.) and a population of 210,000. Capital: Willemstad. Chief industries are the refining of crude oil, and tourism. Petroleum products and phosphates are exported.

On Dec. 15, 1954, the Netherlands Antilles were given complete domestic autonomy and granted equality within the Kingdom with Surinam and the Netherlands. The island of Aruba gained independence in 1986.

RULERS:
Dutch

MONETARY SYSTEM:
1 Gulden = 100 Cents

DUTCH ADMINISTRATION

NEDERLANDSE ANTILLEN

1955 MUNTBILJET NOTE ISSUE

A1	2 1/2 Gulden	VG	VF	UNC
	1955; 1964. Blue. Ship in dry dock at center Crowned supported arms at center on back. Printer: ABNC.			
	a. 1955.	7.50	35.00	215.
	b. 1964.	5.00	25.00	190.
	s. As a or b. Specimen.	—	—	240.

1962 ISSUE

#1-7 woman seated w/scroll and flag in oval at l. Crowned arms at ctr. r. on back. Wmk: *NA* monogram. Printer: JEZ.

1	5 Gulden	VG	VF	UNC
	2.1.1962. Blue on multicolor underprint. View of Curaçao at center.			
	a. Issued note.	4.00	15.00	75.00
	s. Specimen.	—	—	35.00

2	10 Gulden	VG	VF	UNC
	2.1.1962. Green on multicolor underprint. High-rise building (Aruba) at center.			
	a. Issued note.	7.50	25.00	110.
	s. Specimen.	—	—	45.00

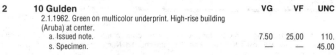

3	25 Gulden	VG	VF	UNC
	2.1.1962. Black-gray on multicolor underprint. View of Bonaire at center.			
	a. Issued note.	FV	25.00	145.
	s. Specimen.	—	—	60.00

4	50 Gulden	VG	VF	UNC
	2.1.1962. Brown on multicolor underprint. City by the seaside (St. Maarten) at center.			
	a. Issued note.	35.00	100.	300.
	s. Specimen.	—	—	75.00

5	100 Gulden	VG	VF	UNC
	2.1.1962. Violet on multicolor underprint. Monument (St. Eustatius) at center.			
	a. Issued note.	60.00	175.	450.
	s. Specimen.	—	—	100.

6	250 Gulden	VG	VF	UNC
	2.1.1962. Olive-green on multicolor underprint. Boats on the beach (Saba) at center.			
	a. Issued note.	125.	375.	—
	s. Specimen.	—	—	135.

7	500 Gulden	VG	VF	UNC
	2.1.1962. Red on multicolor underprint. Oil refinery (Curacao) at center.			
	a. Issued note.	250.	450.	—
	s. Specimen.	—	—	185.

1967 ISSUE

#8-13 monument *Steunend op eigen Kracht...* at l. Crowned arms at ctr. on back. Wmk: *NA* monogram. Printer: JEZ.

8	5 Gulden	VG	VF	UNC
	1967; 1972. Dark blue and green on multicolor underprint. View of Curaçao at center.			
	a. 28.8.1967.	3.50	7.50	45.00
	b. 1.6.1972.	3.50	5.00	35.00
	s. As a. Specimen.	—	—	30.00

9	10 Gulden	VG	VF	UNC
	1967; 1972. Green on multicolor underprint. View of Aruba at center.			
	a. 28.8.1967.	FV	10.00	55.00
	b. 1.6.1972.	FV	7.50	47.50
	s. As a. Specimen.	—	—	—

		VG	VF	UNC
10	**25 Gulden** 1967; 1972. Black-gray on multicolor underprint. View of Bonaire at center.			
	a. 28.8.1967.	FV	27.50	125.
	b. 1.6.1972.	FV	20.00	95.00
	s. As a. Specimen.	—	—	—

		VG	VF	UNC
11	**50 Gulden** 1967; 1972. Brown on multicolor underprint. Beach (St. Maarten) at center.			
	a. 28.8.1967.	FV	65.00	225.
	b. 1.6.1972.	FV	45.00	175.
	s. As a. Specimen.	—	—	—

		VG	VF	UNC
12	**100 Gulden** 1967; 1972. Violet on multicolor underprint. Boats and fishermen on the beach (St. Eustatius) at center.			
	a. 28.8.1967.	FV	125.	365.
	b. 1.6.1972.	FV	85.00	275.
	s. As a. Specimen.	—	—	150.

		VG	VF	UNC
13	**250 Gulden** 28.8.1967. Olive-green on multicolor underprint. Mountains (Saba) at center.			
	a. Issued note.	125.	250.	525.
	s. Specimen.	—	—	350.

#14 *Deleted.* See #A1.

1979; 1980 ISSUE

#15-19 like #8-13. Printer: JEZ.

		VG	VF	UNC
15	**5 Gulden** 1980; 1984. Purplish blue on multicolor underprint. Like #8.			
	a. 23.12.1980.	FV	7.50	35.00
	b. 1.6.1984.	FV	6.00	32.50

		VG	VF	UNC
16	**10 Gulden** 1979; 1984. Green and blue-green on multicolor underprint. Like #9.			
	a. 14.7.1979.	FV	10.00	50.00
	b. 1.6.1984.	FV	7.50	45.00
17	**25 Gulden** 14.7.1979. Blue and blue-green on multicolor underprint. Like #10.	FV	50.00	200.

		VG	VF	UNC
18	**50 Gulden** 23.12.1980. Red on multicolor underprint. Like #11.	FV	65.00	325.
19	**100 Gulden** 14.7.1979. Red-brown and violet on multicolor underprint. Like #12.			
	a. 14.7.1979.	FV	90.00	450.
	b. 9.12.1981.	FV	100.	500.

1970 MUNTBILJET ISSUE

#20 and 21 crowned arms at r. on back. Printer: JEZ.

		VG	VF	UNC
20	**1 Gulden** 8.9.1970. Red on orange underprint. Aerial view of harbor at left center.			
	a. Issued note.	FV	2.00	10.00
	s. Specimen.	—	—	110.

21	2 1/2 Gulden	VG	VF	UNC
	8.9.1970. Blue on light blue underprint. Jetliner at left center.			
	a. Issued note.	FV	3.00	20.00
	s. Specimen.	—	—	120.

1986 BANK ISSUE

#22-27 back and wmk: Shield-like bank logo. Sign. and sign. title varieties. Printer: JEZ.

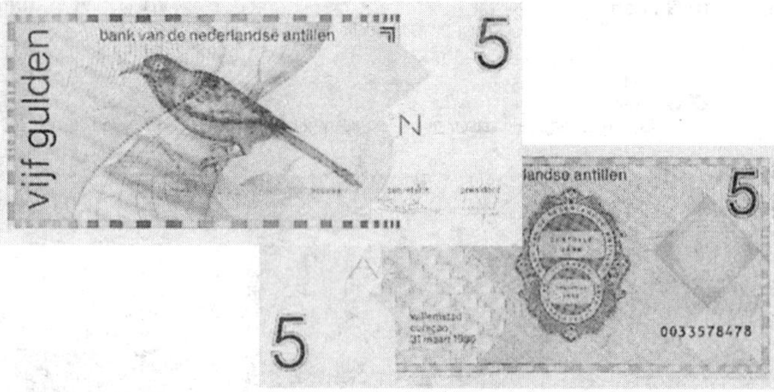

22	5 Gulden	VG	VF	UNC
	1986; 1990; 1994. Dark blue on multicolor underprint. Troupial at center.			
	a. Signature titles: *SEKRETARIS; PRESIDENT.* 31.3.1986.	FV	FV	35.00
	b. Signature titles: *DIRECTEUR SEKRETARIS; PRESIDENT.* 1.1.1990.	FV	FV	32.50
	c. 1.5.1994.	FV	FV	32.50
	s. As a. Specimen.	—	—	—

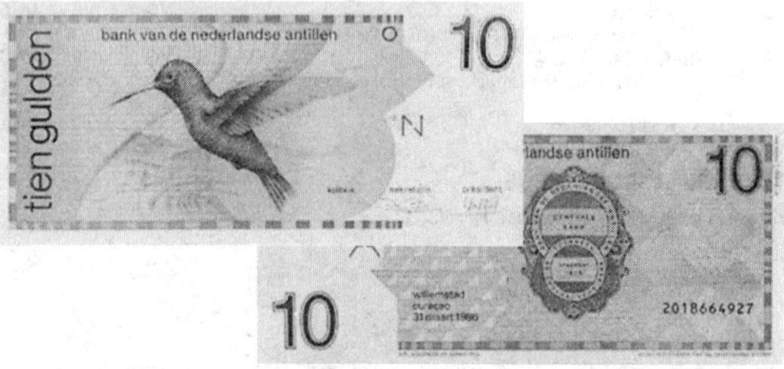

23	10 Gulden	VG	VF	UNC
	1986; 1990; 1994. Dark green on multicolor underprint. Purple-throated carib at left center.			
	a. 31.3.1986. signature titles as 22a.	FV	FV	50.00
	b. 1.1.1990. signature titles as 22b.	FV	FV	45.00
	c. 1.5.1994.	FV	FV	40.00
	s. As a. Specimen.	—	—	—

24	25 Gulden	VG	VF	UNC
	1986; 1990; 1994. Red on multicolor underprint. Flamingo at left center.			
	a. 31.3.1986. signature titles as 22a.	FV	FV	105.
	b. 1.1.1990. signature titles as 22b.	FV	FV	100.
	c. 1.5.1994.	FV	FV	95.00
	s. As a. Specimen.	—	—	—

25	50 Gulden	VG	VF	UNC
	1986; 1990; 1994. Brown and orange on multicolor underprint. Rufous-collared sparrow at left center.			
	a. 31.3.1986. signature titles as 22a.	FV	FV	170.
	b. 1.1.1990. signature titles as 22b.	FV	FV	150.
	c. 1.5.1994.	FV	FV	140.
	s. As a. Specimen.	—	—	—

26	100 Gulden	VG	VF	UNC
	1986; 1990; 1994. Brown on multicolor underprint. Bananaquit at left center.			
	a. 31.3.1986.	FV	FV	265.
	b. 1.1.1990.	FV	FV	250.
	c. 1.5.1994.	FV	FV	225.
	s. As a. Specimen.	—	—	—

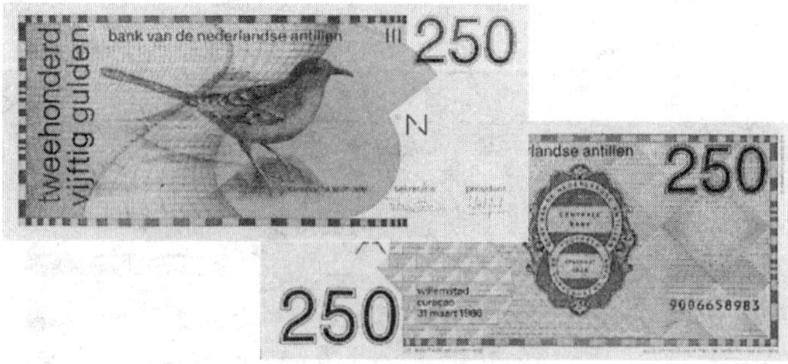

27	250 Gulden	VG	VF	UNC
	31.3.1986. Purple and red-violet on multicolor underprint. Caribbean mockingbird at left center.			
	a. Issued note.	FV	FV	500.
	s. Specimen.	—	—	—

1998; 2001; 2003 ISSUE

#28-31 similar to #23-26 but w/gold foil at lower r. Additional enhanced security devices include surface overlays on face and small sparkling dots at top and bottom on back. 2 sign. varieties.

28	10 Gulden	VG	VF	UNC
	1998; 2001; 2003. Dark and light green on multicolor underprint. Similar to #23.			
	a. 1.1.1998.	FV	FV	37.50
	b. 1.12.2001.	FV	FV	35.00
	c. 1.12.2003.	FV	FV	27.50

29	25 Gulden	VG	VF	UNC
	1998; 2001; 2003. Red on multicolor underprint. Similar to #24.			
	a. 1.1.1998.	FV	FV	85.00
	b. 1.12.2001.	FV	FV	65.00
	c. 1.12.2003.	FV	FV	50.00

30	50 Gulden	VG	VF	UNC
	1998; 2001; 2003. Brown-orange on multicolor underprint. Similar to #25.			
	a. 1.1.1998.	FV	FV	125.
	b. 1.12.2001.	FV	FV	105.
	c. 1.12.2003.	FV	FV	90.00

31	100 Gulden	VG	VF	UNC
	1998; 2001; 2003. Brown on multicolor underprint. Similar to #26.			
	a. 1.1.1998.	FV	FV	200.
	b. 1.12.2001.	FV	FV	175.
	c. 1.12.2003.	FV	FV	155.

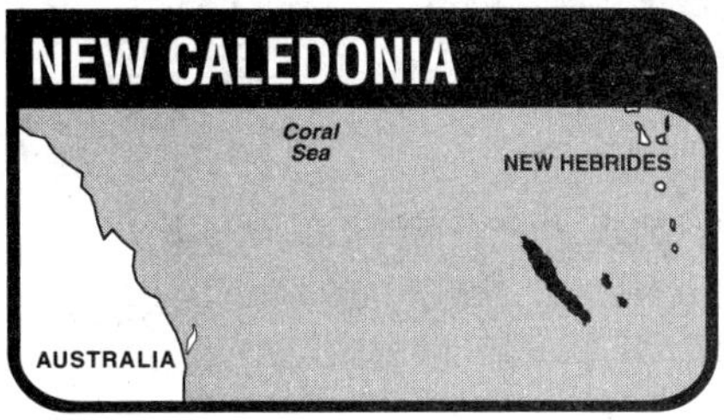

The French Overseas Territory of New Caledonia, a group of about 25 islands in the South Pacific, is situated about 750 miles (1,207 km.) east of Australia. The territory, which includes the dependencies of Ile des Pins, Loyalty Islands, Ile Huon, Isles Belep, Isles Chesterfield, and Ile Walpole, has a total land area of 6,530 sq. mi. (19,058 sq. km.) and a population of 152,000. Capital: Noumea. The islands are rich in minerals; New Caledonia has the world's largest known deposit of nickel. Nickel, nickel castings, coffee and copra are exported.

British navigator Capt. James Cook discovered New Caledonia in 1774. The French took possession in 1853, and established a penal colony on the island in 1854. The European population of the colony remained disproportionately convict until 1894. New Caledonia became an overseas territory within the French Community in 1946, and in 1958 and 1972 chose to remain affiliated with France.

RULERS:

French

MONETARY SYSTEM:

1 Franc = 100 Centimes

SIGNATURE VARIETIES

	DIRECTEUR GÉNÉRAL	PRÉSIDENT DU CONSEIL DE SURVEILLANCE
1	André Postel-Vinay, 1967-1972	Bernard Clappier, 1966-1972
2	Claude Panouillot, 1972-1973	André De Lattre, 1973
3	Claude Panouillot, 1974-1978	Marcel Theron, 1974-1979
4	Yves Roland-Billecart, 1979-1984	Gabriel Lefort, 1980-1984
5	Yves Roland-Billecart, 1985-1973	Jacques Waitzenegger, 1985-

INSTITUT D'EMISSION D'OUTRE-MER

NOUMÉA

1969 ND ISSUE

59	100 Francs	VG	VF	UNC
	ND (1969). Brown on multicolor underprint. Girl wearing wreath and playing guitar at right. Without overprint: *REPUBLIQUE FRANÇAISE* at lower center. Girl at left, harbor scene at center on back. Intaglio. Signature 1.	10.00	40.00	135.

60 500 Francs

ND (1969-92). Blue, brown and multicolor. Dugout canoe with sail at center, fisherman at right. Man at left, rock formation at left center, native art at right on back.

		VG	VF	UNC
60	**500 Francs**			
	a. Signature 1.	9.00	25.00	70.00
	b. Signature 2.	9.00	22.50	65.00
	c. Signature 3.	8.00	22.50	60.00
	d. Signature 4.	8.00	20.00	60.00
61	**1000 Francs**			
	ND (1969). Orange, brown and multicolor. Hut under palm tree at left, girl at right. Without overprint: *RÉPUBLIQUE FRANÇAISE* at lower left. Building, Kagu bird at left, deer near hut at right on back. Signature 1.	17.50	50.00	225.

#62 *Deleted.* See #65.

1971 ND Issue

		VG	VF	UNC
63	**100 Francs**			
	ND (1971; 1973). Brown on multicolor underprint. Like #59 but with overprint: *RÉPUBLIQUE FRANÇAISE* at lower center.			
	a. Intaglio. signature 1 (1971).	7.50	27.50	85.00
	b. Lithographed. Series beginning #H2, from #51,000. signature 1 (1973).	7.50	25.00	75.00
	c. As. b. signature 2 (1975).	5.00	17.50	50.00
	d. As b. signature 3 (1977).	4.00	12.50	40.00
	s. As a. Specimen.	—	—	—
64	**1000 Francs**			
	ND (1971; 1983). Orange, brown and multicolor. Like #61 but with overprint: *RÉPUBLIQUE FRANÇAISE* at lower left.			
	a. Signature 1 (1971).	15.00	35.00	125.
	b. Signature 4 (1983).	12.50	30.00	100.

		VG	VF	UNC
65	**5000 Francs**			
	ND (1971-84). Multicolor. Bougainville at left, sailing ships at center. Overprint: *RÉPUBLIQUE FRANÇAISE.* Admiral Febvrier-Despointes at right, sailboat at center right on back.			
	a. Signature 1 (1971).	65.00	125.	350.
	b. Signature 2 (1975).	60.00	120.	325.
	c. Signature 4 (1982-84).	60.00	110.	300.
	s. As a. Specimen.	—	—	400.

Note: For current 500 and 10,000 Francs see French Pacific Territories.

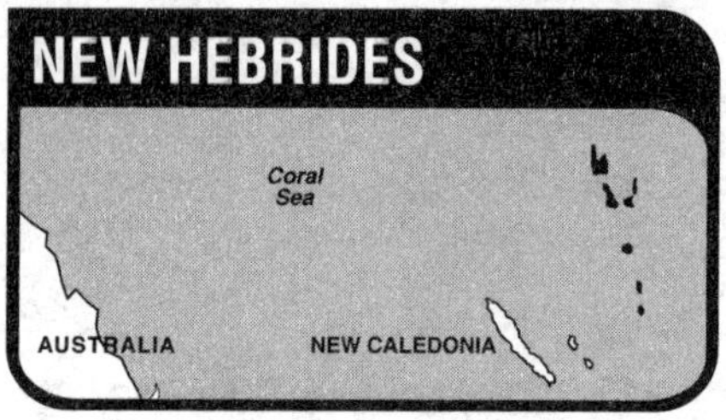

New Hebrides Condominium, a group of islands located in the South Pacific 500 miles (800 km.) west of Fiji, were under the joint sovereignty of Great Britain and France. The islands have an area of 5,700 sq. mi. (14,763 sq. km.) and a population of mainly Melanesians of mixed blood. Capital: Port-Vila. The volcanic and coral islands, while malarial and subject to frequent earthquakes, are extremely fertile, and produce copra, coffee, tropical fruits and timber for export.

The New Hebrides were discovered by Portuguese navigator Pedro de Quiros in 1606, visited by French explorer Bougainville in 1768, and named by British navigator Capt. James Cook in 1774. Ships of all nations converged on the islands to trade for sandalwood, prompting France and Britain to relinquish their individual claims and declare the islands a neutral zone in 1878. The New Hebrides were placed under the control of a mixed Anglo-French commission of naval officers during the native uprisings of 1887, and established as a condominium under the joint sovereignty of France and Great Britain in 1906.

RULERS:

British and French to 1980

MONETARY SYSTEM:

1 Franc = 100 Centimes

SIGNATURE VARIETIES		
	DIRECTEUR GÉNÉRAL	PRÉSIDENT DU CONSEIL DE SURVEILLANCE
1	André Postel-Vinay, 1967-1972	Bernard Clappier, 1966-1972
2	Claude Panouillot, 1972-1973	André De Lattre, 1973
3	Claude Panouillot, 1974-1978	Marcel Theron, 1974-1979
4	Yves Roland-Billecart, 1979-1984	Gabriel Lefort, 1980-1984
5	Yves Roland-Billecart, 1985-1973	Jacques Waitzenegger, 1985-

British and French Administration

Institut d'Emission d'Outre-Mer, Nouvelles Hébrides

1965; 1967 ND Issue

		VG	VF	UNC
16	**100 Francs**			
	ND (1965-71). Brown and multicolor. Girl with guitar at right. Girl at left, harbor scene at center with overprint: *NOUVELLES-HÉBRIDES* in capital letters on back. Signature 1.	15.00	70.00	250.

		VG	VF	UNC
17	**1000 Francs** ND (1967-71). Red. Hut under palm tree at left, girl at right. Building, Kagu bird at left, deer near hut at right. With overprint: *NOUVELLES HÉBRIDES* in capital letters at upper center on back. Signature 1.	25.00	120.	400.

1970 ND ISSUE

		VG	VF	UNC
18	**100 Francs** ND (1970; 1972; 1977). Multicolor. Like #16, but red and blue underprint. *Nouvelles Hébrides* in script on face and back.			
	a. Intaglio plates. signature 1. (1970).	7.50	25.00	75.00
	b. Lithographed series beginning E1, from no. 51,000. signature 1. (1972).	7.00	22.50	65.00
	c. As b. signature 2. (1975).	7.00	22.50	65.00
	d. As b. signature 3. (1977).	6.00	20.00	50.00

		VG	VF	UNC
19	**500 Francs** ND (1970-80). Blue, brown and multicolor. Dugout canoe with sail at center, fisherman at right. Man at left, rock formation at left center, native art at right on back.			
	a. Signature 1. (1970).	15.00	40.00	150.
	b. Signature 3. (1979).	12.50	32.50	120.
	c. Signature 4. (1980).	10.00	27.50	100.

		VG	VF	UNC
20	**1000 Francs** ND (1970-80). Orange, brown and multicolor. Like #17. *Nouvelles Hébrides* in script on face and back.			
	a. Signature 1. (1970).	20.00	55.00	200.
	b. Signature 2. (1975).	15.00	40.00	150.
	c. Signature 3. (1980).	15.00	35.00	135.

Note: For later issues see Vanuatu.

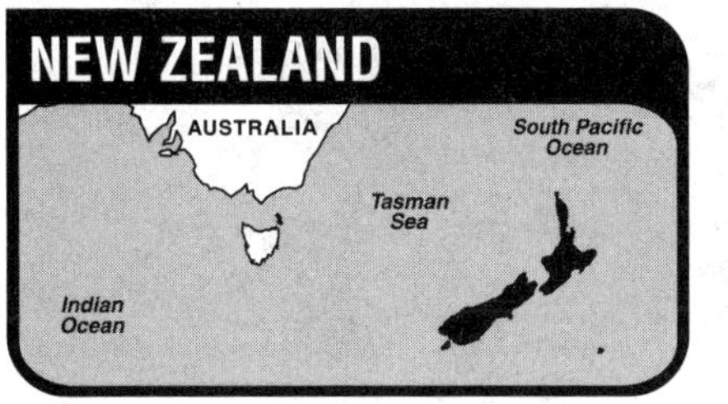

New Zealand, a parliamentary state located in the southwestern Pacific 1,250 miles (2,011 km.) east of Australia, has an area of 103,736 sq. mi. (269,056 sq. km.) and a population of 3.8 million. Capital: Wellington. Wool, meat, dairy products and some manufactured items are exported.

New Zealand was discovered and named by Dutch navigator Abel Tasman in 1642, and explored by British navigator Capt. James Cook who surveyed it in 1769 and annexed the land to Great Britain. The British government disavowed the annexation and for the next 70 years the only white settlers to arrive were adventurers attracted by the prospects of lumbering, sealing and whaling. Great Britain annexed the land in 1840 by treaty with the native chiefs and made it a dependency of New South Wales. The colony was granted self-government in 1852, a ministerial form of government in 1856, and full dominion status on Sept. 26, 1907. Full internal and external autonomy, which New Zealand had in effect possessed for many years, was formally extended in 1947. New Zealand is a member of the Commonwealth of Nations. Elizabeth II is Head of State as Queen of New Zealand.

RULERS:

British

MONETARY SYSTEM:

1 Shilling = 12 Pence
1 Pound = 20 Shillings to 1967
1 Pound = 20 Shillings (also 2 Dollars) to 1967
1 Dollar = 100 Cents, 1967-

RESERVE BANK OF NEW ZEALAND

1940 ND ISSUE

#158-162 portr. Capt. J. Cook at lower r. Sign. title: *CHIEF CASHIER*. Wmk: Maori chief. Printer: TDLR.

		VG	VF	UNC
158	**10 Shillings** ND (1940-67). Brown on multicolor underprint. Arms at upper center Kiwi at left, Waitangi Treaty signing scene at center on back.			
	a. Signature T. P. Hanna. (1940-55).	10.00	45.00	225.
	b. Signature G. Wilson. (1955-56).	12.50	55.00	325.
	c. Signature R. N. Fleming. without security thread. (1956-67).	10.00	50.00	300.
	d. As c. with security thread. (1967).	5.00	12.50	55.00

		VG	VF	UNC
159	**1 Pound** ND (1940-67). Purple on multicolor underprint. Arms at upper center Sailing ship on sea at left. on back.			
	a. Signature T. P. Hanna. (1940-55).	8.00	30.00	200.
	b. Signature G. Wilson. (1955-56).	10.00	40.00	275.
	c. Signature R. N. Fleming. without security thread. (1956-67).	8.00	30.00	215.
	d. As c. with security thread. (1967).	4.00	13.50	65.00

160 5 Pounds

ND (1940-67). Blue on multicolor underprint. Crowned arms at upper center Lake Pukaki and Mt. Cook on back.

	VG	VF	UNC
a. Signature T. P. Hanna. (1940-55).	12.50	60.00	225.
b. Signature G. Wilson. (1955-56).	12.50	65.00	275.
c. Signature R. N. Fleming. without security thread. (1956-67).	12.50	40.00	275.
d. As c. with security thread. (1967).	12.50	30.00	120.

161 10 Pounds

ND (1940-67). Green on multicolor underprint. Crowned arms, sailing ship at left. Flock of sheep at left. Center on back.

	VG	VF	UNC
a. Signature T. P. Hanna. (1940-55).	55.00	130.	875.
b. Signature G. Wilson. (1955-56).	70.00	225.	1000.
c. Signature R. N. Fleming. (1956-67).	50.00	100.	425.
d. As c. with security thread. (1967).	40.00	90.00	275.

162 50 Pounds

ND (1940-67). Red on multicolor underprint. Crowned arms, sailing ship at left. Dairy farm and Mt. Egmont on back.

	VG	VF	UNC
a. Signature T. P. Hanna. (1940-55).	450.	1100.	5000.
b. Signature G. Wilson. (1955-56).	500.	1150.	5500.
c. Signature R. N. Fleming. (1956-67).	225.	750.	2500.

1967 ND ISSUE

#163-168 Qn. Elizabeth II at r. on face. Birds and plants on back. Wmk: Capt. J. Cook. Printer: TDLR.

#163b-168b replacement notes: Special serial # prefix and * suffix.

163 1 Dollar

ND (1967-81). Brown on multicolor underprint. Pied fantail at center on back.

	VG	VF	UNC
a. Signature R. N. Fleming. (1967-68).	6.00	20.00	55.00
b. Signature D. L. Wilks. (1968-75).	3.50	10.00	30.00
c. Signature R. L. Knight. (1975-77).	2.00	7.50	18.00
d. Signature H. R. Hardie. (1977-81).	2.00	7.50	17.50
s. Specimen.	—	—	—

164 2 Dollars

ND (1967-81). Purple on multicolor underprint. Riffleman at center on back.

	VG	VF	UNC
a. Signature R. N. Fleming. (1967-68).	5.00	17.50	65.00
b. Signature D. L. Wilks. (1968-75).	5.00	15.00	45.00
c. Signature R. L. Knight. (1975-77).	4.00	12.50	30.00
d. Signature H. R. Hardie. (1977-81).	3.50	10.00	25.00
s. Specimen.	—	—	—

165 5 Dollars

ND (1967-81). Orange on multicolor underprint. Tui at center on back.

	VG	VF	UNC
a. Signature R. N. Fleming. (1967-68).	7.50	25.00	85.00
b. Signature D. L. Wilks. (1968-75).	12.50	50.00	250.
c. Signature R. L. Knight. (1975-77).	6.00	20.00	60.00
d. Signature H. R. Hardie. (1977-81).	5.00	15.00	55.00
s. Specimen.	—	—	—

166 10 Dollars

ND (1967-81). Blue on multicolor underprint. Kea at center on back.

	VG	VF	UNC
a. Signature R. N. Fleming. (1967-68).	15.00	35.00	140.
b. Signature D. L. Wilks. (1968-75.)	15.00	45.00	225.
c. Signature R. L. Knight. (1975-77).	15.00	35.00	200.
d. Signature H. R. Hardie. (1977-81).	12.00	25.00	130.
s. Specimen.	—	—	—

167 20 Dollars

ND (1967-81). Green on multicolor underprint. New Zealand pigeon at center on back.

	VG	VF	UNC
a. Signature R. N. Fleming. (1967-68).	25.00	50.00	180.
b. Signature D. L. Wilks. (1968-75).	35.00	75.00	400.
c. Signature R. L. Knight. (1975-77).	30.00	65.00	300.
d. Signature H. R. Hardie. (1977-81).	20.00	40.00	135.
s. Specimen.	—	—	—

168 100 Dollars

ND (1967-77). Red on multicolor underprint. Takahe at center on back.

	VG	VF	UNC
a. Signature R. N. Fleming. (1967-68).	120.	300.	1400.
b. Signature R. L. Knight. (1975-77).	100.	250.	900.
s. Specimen.	—	—	—

1981-83 ND Issue

#169-175 new portr. of Qn. Elizabeth II on face. Birds and plants on back. Wmk: Capt. J. Cook. Printer: BWC.

#169a, 170a, 171a, 171b, 172a, 172b and 173a replacement note: Special serial # prefix and * suffix.

169 1 Dollar

ND (1981-92). Dark brown on multicolor underprint. Back similar to #163.

	VG	VF	UNC
a. Signature H. R. Hardie with title: *CHIEF CASHIER.* (1981-85).	FV	3.50	6.50
b. Signature S. T. Russell with title: *GOVERNOR.* (1985-89).	FV	3.00	6.00
c. Signature D. T. Brash. (1989-92).	FV	2.50	5.00

170 2 Dollars

ND (1981-92). Purple on multicolor underprint. Back similar to #164.

	VG	VF	UNC
a. Signature H. R. Hardie with title: *CHIEF CASHIER.* (1981-85).	FV	4.50	9.00
b. Signature S.T. Russell with title: *GOVERNOR.* (1985-89).	FV	4.00	9.00
c. Signature D. T. Brash. (1989-92).	FV	3.50	7.00

171 5 Dollars

ND (1981-92). Orange on multicolor underprint. Back similar to #165.

	VG	VF	UNC
a. Signature H. R. Hardie with title: *CHIEF CASHIER.* (1981-85).	FV	12.00	25.00
b. Signature S.T. Russell with title: *GOVERNOR.* (1985-89).	FV	10.00	20.00
c. Signature D. T. Brash. (1989-92).	FV	10.00	20.00

172 10 Dollars

ND (1981-92). Blue on multicolor underprint. Back similar to #166.

	VG	VF	UNC
a. Signature H. R. Hardie with title: *CHIEF CASHIER.* (1981-85).	FV	22.50	47.50
b. Signature S.T. Russell with title: *GOVERNOR.* (1985-89).	FV	15.00	32.50
c. Signature D. T. Brash. (1989-92).	FV	9.00	35.00

173 20 Dollars

ND (1981-92). Green on multicolor underprint. Back similar to #167.

	VG	VF	UNC
a. Signature H. R. Hardie with title: *CHIEF CASHIER.* (1981-85).	FV	40.00	100.
b. Signature S.T. Russell with title: *GOVERNOR.* (1985-89).	FV	35.00	65.00
c. Signature D. T. Brash. (1989-92).	FV	30.00	55.00

174 50 Dollars

ND (1981-92). Yellow-orange on multicolor underprint. Morepork Owl at center on back.

	VG	VF	UNC
a. Signature H. R. Hardie, with title: Chief Cashier. (1981-85).	FV	70.00	200.
b. Signature D. T. Brash, with title: Governor. (1989-92).	FV	65.00	130.

175 100 Dollars

ND (1981-89). Red on multicolor underprint. Back similar to #168.

	VG	VF	UNC
a. Signature H. R. Hardie with title: *CHIEF CASHIER.* (1981-85).	FV	150.	350.
b. Signature S.T. Russell with title: *GOVERNOR.* (1985-89).	FV	135.	275.

1990 COMMEMORATIVE ISSUE

#176, 150th Anniversary - Treaty of Waitangi, 1840-1990

176 10 Dollars

	VG	VF	UNC
1990. Blue-violet and pale blue on multicolor underprint. Face design like #172, with addition of 1990 Commission logo, the White Heron (in red and white with date 1990) at right of Queen. Special inscription and scene of treaty signing on back. Watermark: Capt. J. Cook. Serial # prefix *BBB; CCC; DDD.* Printer: BWC.	FV	FV	25.00

Note: #176 w/prefix letters *AAA* was issued in 2, 4, 8, 16 and 32 subject panes. Market value is 10% over face value. Note: #176 w/serial # prefix *BBB* was also issued in a special folder.

1992 ND ISSUE

#177-181 wmk: Qn. Elizabeth II. Sign. D.T. Brash. Replacement notes: Serial # prefix *ZZ*. Printer: TDLR.

177 5 Dollars

ND (1992-). Brown and brown-orange on multicolor underprint. Mt. Everest at left, Sir Edmund Hillary at center. Back brown and blue; flora with Yellow-eyed penguin at center right.

	VG	VF	UNC
a. Issued note.	FV	4.00	15.00
b. Uncut block of 4 in special folder.	—	—	50.00
c. Uncut block of 8 in special folder.	—	—	140.

178 10 Dollars

ND (1992). Blue and purple on multicolor underprint. Camellia flowers at left, K. Sheppard at center right. Pair of blue ducks at center right on back.

	VG	VF	UNC
a. Issued note.	FV	8.00	35.00
b. Uncut pair in special folder.	—	—	35.00
c. Uncut block of 4 in special folder.	—	—	65.00

179	20 Dollars	VG	VF	UNC
	ND (1992). Green on multicolor underprint. Queen Elizabeth II at right, government building at left in underprint. Back pale green and blue; New Zealand falcons at center.			
	a. Issued note.	FV	17.00	50.00
	b. Uncut block of 4 in special folder.	—	—	125.
180	50 Dollars			
	ND (1992). Purple, violet and deep blue on multicolor underprint. Sir A. Ngata at right, Maori meeting house at left in underprint. Kokako at right on back.			
	a. Issued note.	FV	37.50	70.00
	b. Uncut block of 4 in special folder.	—	—	285.

181	100 Dollars	VG	VF	UNC
	ND (1992). Violet-brown and red on multicolor underprint. Lord Rutherford of Nelson at center, Nobel prize medal in underprint at left. Yellowhead on tree trunk at center right, moth at lower left on back.			
	a. Issued note.	FV	75.00	140.
	b. Uncut block of 4 in special folder.	—	—	550.
	s. Specimen.	—	—	—

1994 ND Issue

#182 and 183 replacement notes: Serial # prefix *ZZ*.

182	10 Dollars	VG	VF	UNC
	ND (1994). Like #178 but bright blue at center behind Whio ducks on back.	FV	FV	22.50
183	20 Dollars			
	ND (1994). Like #179 but bright green at center behind Karearea falcon on back.	FV	FV	40.00

1996 Commemorative Issue

#184, 70th Birthday - Qn. Elizabeth II

184	20 Dollars	VG	VF	UNC
	ND (1996). Green on multicolor underprint. Commemorative overprint on #183. Serial # prefix *ER*.	FV	75.00	200.

Note: Issued in a special folder w/a $5 Commemorative coin (3000).

1999 Issue

#185-189 printer: NPA (w/o imprint).

Note: See Collector Series for special sets.

185	5 Dollars	VG	VF	UNC
	(19)99. Similar to #177 but polymer plastic.			
	a. Signature D.T. Brash.	FV	FV	8.50
	b. Signature Alan Bollard.	FV	FV	8.50

186	10 Dollars	VG	VF	UNC
	(19)99; (20)03; (20)04. Blue and multicolor. Similar to #178 but polymer plastic.			
	a. Signature D.T. Brash.	FV	FV	14.00
	b. Signature Alan Bollard.	FV	FV	14.00

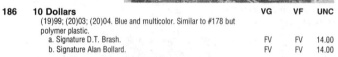

187	20 Dollars	VG	VF	UNC
	(19)99; (20)02. Gray and multicolor. Similar to #179 but polymer plastic.			
	a. Signature D.T. Brush.	FV	FV	27.50
	b. Signature Alan Bollard.	FV	FV	27.50

NOTICE

Readers with unlisted dates, signature varieties, etc. are invited to submit photocopies of their notes to: Standard Catalog of World Paper Money, 700 East State St. Iola, WI 54990-0001, E-Mail: george.cuhaj@fwpubs.com.

		VG	VF	UNC
188	**50 Dollars**			
	(19)99. Purple and multicolor. Similar to #180 but polymer plastic.			
	a. Signature D.T. Brash.	FV	FV	50.00
	b. Signatrue Alan Bollard.	FV	FV	50.00

		VG	VF	UNC
189	**100 Dollars**			
	(19)99. Brownish red and multicolor. Similar to #181 but polymer plastic.			
	a. Signature D.T. Brush.	FV	FV	95.00
	b. Signature Alan Bollard.	FV	FV	95.00

2000 COMMEMORATIVE ISSUE

#190, Millennium Commemorative

#190 printer: NPA (w/o imprint).

		VG	VF	UNC
190	**10 Dollars**			
	2000. Blue, orange and multicolor. Earth, map of New Zealand at left, ceremonial boat at center. Five sport activities on back. Polymer plastic.			
	a. Black serial #. Serial # prefix *AA; AB.*	FV	FV	17.50
	b. Red serial #. Serial # prefix *NZ.*	FV	FV	17.50

NOTICE

Readers with unlisted dates, signature varieties, etc. are invited to submit photocopies of their notes to: Standard Catalog of World Paper Money, 700 East State St. Iola, WI 54990-0001, E-Mail: george.cuhaj@fwpubs.com.

COLLECTOR SERIES

RESERVE BANK OF NEW ZEALAND

1990 ND COMMEMORATIVE ISSUE

		Issue Price	Mkt. Value
CS176	**10 Dollars**		
	1990. With special serial # prefix.		
	a. Serial # prefix *CWB* (for Country Wide Bank).	—	9.00
	b. Serial # prefix *FTC* (for Farmers Trading Co.).	—	9.00
	c. Serial # prefix *MBL* (for Mobil Oil Co.).	—	9.00
	d. Serial # prefix *RNZ* (for Radio New Zealand).	—	9.00
	e. Serial # prefix *RXX* (for Rank Xerox Co.).	—	9.00
	f. Serial # prefix *TNZ* (for Toyota New Zealand).	—	9.00

1992 ISSUE

		Issue Price	Mkt. Value
CS180	**50 Dollars**		
	ND (1993). Red serial #.	—	65.00

Note: Issued w/$50 phone card.

1993 ND ISSUE

		Issue Price	Mkt. Value
CS183	**20 Dollars**		
	As #183.		
	a. Uncut pair, with serial # prefix: *TRBNZA* on back in folder.	—	—
	b. In folder with $20 phone card. 2500 sets.	—	40.00

1999 ISSUE

		Issue Price	Mkt. Value
CS185	**5 Dollars**		
	As #185. Serial # prefix: *AA.*		
	a. Uncut pair.	—	20.00
	b. Uncut sheet of 40 notes. 150 sheets.	—	150.
CS186	**10 Dollars**		
	As #186. Serial # prefix: *AA.*		
	a. Uncut pair. 2,000 pairs.	—	25.00
	b. Uncut sheet of 40 notes. 150 sheets.	—	300.

	Issue Price	Mkt. Value
CS187 20 Dollars		
As #187. Serial # prefix: *AA.*		
a. Uncut pair. 4,000 pairs.	—	50.00
b. Uncut sheet of 40. 150 sheets.	—	600.
CS188 50 Dollars		
Expected new issue.	—	—
CS189 100 Dollars		
As #189. Serial # prefix: *AA.*		
a. Uncut pair. 1,000 pairs.	—	150.
b. Uncut sheet of 28. 100 sheets.	—	1800.

1999 COMMEMORATIVE ISSUE

#CS190, Millennium Commemorative

	Issue Price	Mkt. Value
CS190 10 Dollars		
As #190 but with bank overprint in red under 10 on face. Red serial #.		
a. Single note in folder with serial # prefix: *NZ.*	—	12.50
b. Uncut pair in folder with serial # prefix: *NZ.*	—	25.00
c. Uncut sheet of 20 with serial # prefix: *NZ.*	—	225.

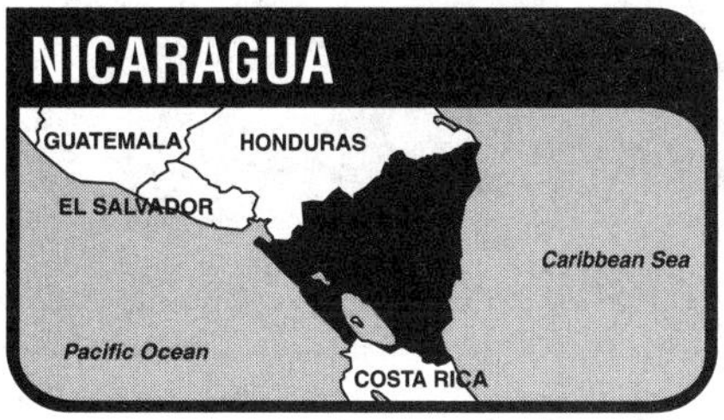

The Republic of Nicaragua, situated in Central America between Honduras and Costa Rica, has an area of 50,193 sq. mi (130,000 sq. km.) and a population of 4.69 million. Capital: Managua. Agriculture, mining (gold and silver) and hardwood logging are the principal industries. Cotton, meat, coffee, tobacco and sugar are exported.

Columbus sighted the coast of Nicaragua in 1502 during the course of his last voyage of discovery. It was first visited in 1522 by conquistadors from Panama, under command of Gonzalez Davila. After the first settlements were established in 1524 at Granada and Leon, Nicaragua was incorporated, for administrative purpose, in the Captaincy General of Guatemala, which included every Central American state but Panama. The Captaincy General declared its independence from Spain on Sept. 15, 1821. The next year Nicaragua united with the Mexican Empire of Agustin de Iturbide, then in 1823 with the Central American Republic. When the federation was dissolved, Nicaragua declared itself an independent republic in 1838.

MONETARY SYSTEM:

1 Peso = 100 Centavos to 1912
1 Córdoba = 100 Centavos, 1912-1987
1 New Córdoba = 1000 Old Córdobas, 1988-90
1 Córdoba Oro = 100 Centavos, 1990-

REPLACEMENT NOTES:

1985-dated issues printed by TDLR, ZA; ZB prefix.

REPUBLIC

BANCO CENTRAL DE NICARAGUA

DECRETO 26.4.1962

Series A

#107-114 portr. F. Hernandez Córdoba at ctr. on back. Printer: ABNC.

		VG	VF	UNC
107	**1 Córdoba** D.1962. Blue on multicolor underprint. Banco Central at upper center.	.15	1.00	7.50

		VG	VF	UNC
108	**5 Córdobas** D.1962. Green on multicolor underprint. C. Nicarao at upper center. Similar to #100.	.75	3.00	15.00

109	10 Córdobas	VG	VF	UNC
	D.1962. Red on multicolor underprint. Portrait M. de Larreynaga at upper center.			
	a. Issued note.	1.50	5.00	22.50
	s. Specimen.	—	—	—

110	20 Córdobas	VG	VF	UNC
	D.1962. Orange-brown on multicolor underprint. Portrait T. Martinez at upper center.	3.00	10.00	45.00

111	50 Córdobas	VG	VF	UNC
	D.1962. Purple on multicolor underprint. Portrait M. Jerez at upper center.	6.00	25.00	85.00

112	100 Córdobas	VG	VF	UNC
	D.1962. Red-brown on multicolor underprint. Portrait J. D. Estrada at upper center.	4.00	12.50	60.00
113	**500 Córdobas**			
	D.1962. Black on multicolor underprint. Portrait R. Dario at upper center.			
	a. Issued note.	50.00	175.	425.
	s. Specimen.	—	—	500.

114	1000 Córdobas	VG	VF	UNC
	D.1962. Brown on multicolor underprint. Portrait A. Somoza at upper center.			
	a. Issued note.	60.00	200.	550.
	s. Specimen.	—	—	500.

DECRETO 25.5.1968

Series B

#115-120 portr. F. Hernandez Córdoba on back. Printer: TDLR.

115	1 Córdoba	VG	VF	UNC
	D.1968. Blue on multicolor underprint. Like #107.			
	a. With 3 signature	.10	.50	2.00
	b. Pres. A. Somoza hand signature at left.	—	—	—

116	5 Córdobas	VG	VF	UNC
	D.1968. Green on multicolor underprint. Like #108.			
	a. Issued note.	.50	1.50	5.00
	s. Specimen.	—	—	—

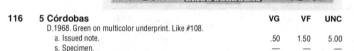

117	10 Córdobas	VG	VF	UNC
	D.1968. Red on multicolor underprint. Like #109.			
	a. Issued note.	.75	2.00	7.50
	s. Specimen.	—	—	—

Note: Some of #118-120 were apparently released w/o r.h. sign. after the Managua earthquake of 1972 damaged the Central Bank building.

118	20 Córdobas			
	D.1968. Orange-brown on multicolor underprint. Like #110.			
	a. With 3 signature	1.00	3.00	12.50
	b. Without right hand signature	—	—	—
119	**50 Córdobas**			
	D.1968. Purple on multicolor underprint. Like #111.			
	a. With 3 signature	4.00	8.00	30.00
	b. Without right hand signature	—	—	—
120	**100 Córdobas**			
	D.1968. Red-brown on multicolor underprint. Like #112.			
	a. With 3 signature	3.00	8.00	30.00
	b. Without right hand signature	—	—	—

DECRETO 27.4.1972

Series C

#121-128 printer: TDLR.

121	2 Córdobas	VG	VF	UNC
	D.1972. Olive-green on multicolor underprint. Banco Central at right. Furrows at left on back.			
	a. With 3 signature	.10	.25	3.00
	b. Without left hand signature	—	—	400.
	s. As a. Specimen.	—	—	35.00

122	5 Córdobas	VG	VF	UNC
	D.1972. Dark green on multicolor underprint. C. Nicarao standing at right with bow. Fruitseller at left on back.	.25	.75	4.00

123	10 Córdobas	VG	VF	UNC
	D.1972. Red on multicolor underprint. A. Castro standing at right atop rocks. Hacienda at left on back.	.25	1.00	6.00

124	20 Córdobas	VG	VF	UNC
	D.1972. Orange-brown on multicolor underprint. R. Herrera igniting cannon at right. Signing ceremony of abrogation of Chamorro-Bryan Treaty of 1912, Somoza at center on back.	.50	2.00	10.00

Note: #124 was issued on the 60th anniversary of the Chamorro-Bryan Treaty of 1912.

125	50 Córdobas	VG	VF	UNC
	D.1972. Purple on multicolor underprint. M. Jerez at right. Cows at left on back.	10.00	30.00	85.00

126	100 Córdobas	VG	VF	UNC
	D.1972. Violet on multicolor underprint. J. Dolores Estrada at right. National flower at left on back.	.50	2.50	10.00

127	500 Córdobas	VG	VF	UNC
	D.1972. Black on multicolor underprint. R. Darío at right. National Theater at left on back.	10.00	25.00	100.

128	1000 Córdobas	VG	VF	UNC
	D.1972. Brown on multicolor underprint. A. Somoza G. at right. View of Managua at left on back.			
	a. 3 signature	12.00	30.00	125.
	b. 2 signature (without right hand signature).	—	—	80.00

DECRETO 20.2.1978

Series D

#129-130 printer: TDLR.

129	20 Córdobas	VG	VF	UNC
	D.1978. Like #124.	.25	1.50	7.50

130	50 Córdobas	VG	VF	UNC
	D.1978. Like #125.	.25	2.50	9.00

DECRETO 16.8.1979

Series E, first issue

#131-133 w/square outer frame. Engraved. Printer: TDLR.

131	50 Córdobas	VG	VF	UNC
	D.1979. Purple on multicolor underprint. Comdt. C. F. Amador at right. Liberation of 19.7.1979 on back.	.50	1.50	5.00

132	100 Córdobas	VG	VF	UNC
	D.1979. Dark brown on multicolor underprint. Like #126.	.50	1.50	5.00

133	500 Córdobas	VG	VF	UNC
	D.1979. Deep blue on multicolor underprint. Like #127.	.50	2.50	7.00

1979 ND SECOND ISSUE

Series E, second issue

#134-139 underprint to edge. Wmk: Sandino. Printer: TDLR.

#134-137 lithographed.

134	10 Córdobas	VG	VF	UNC
	D.1979. Red on multicolor underprint. A. Castro standing atop rocks at right. Miners on back.	.25	.75	3.00

135	20 Córdobas	VG	VF	UNC
	D.1979. Orange-brown on multicolor underprint. Comdt. G. P. Ordoñez at right. Marching troops on back.	.25	.75	3.50

136	50 Córdobas	VG	VF	UNC
	D.1979. Purple on multicolor underprint. Comdt. C. F. Amador at right. Liberation of 19.7.1979 on back.	.25	1.00	4.00

		VG	VF	UNC
137	**100 Córdobas** D.1979. Brown on multicolor underprint. J. D. Estrada at right. Flower on back. Signature varieties.	.50	1.00	4.00

		VG	VF	UNC
138	**500 Córdobas** D.1979. Deep olive-green on multicolor underprint. Engraved. R. Darío at right. Teatro Popular at left on back. Signature varieties.	.50	1.75	6.00

		VG	VF	UNC
139	**1000 Córdobas** D.1979. Blue-gray on multicolor underprint. Engraved. Gen. A. C. Sandino at right. Hut (Sandino's birthplace) on back. Signature varieties.	2.50	15.00	45.00

RESOLUTION OF 6.8.1984

Series F

#140-143 wmk: Sandino. Printer: TDLR.

		VG	VF	UNC
140	**50 Córdobas** L.1984 (1985). Purple on multicolor underprint. Like #136.	.20	.50	2.00
141	**100 Córdobas** L.1984 (1985). Brown on multicolor underprint. Like #137.	.25	1.00	3.00

		VG	VF	UNC
142	**500 Córdobas** L.1984 (1985). Deep olive-green on multicolor underprint. Like #138.	.20	1.00	5.00
143	**1000 Córdobas** L.1984 (1985). Blue-gray on multicolor underprint. Like #139.	.50	2.00	9.00

RESOLUTION OF 11.6.1985

Series G

#144-146 wmk: Sandino. Replacement notes: Serial # prefix *ZA; ZB*. Printer: TDLR.

		VG	VF	UNC
144	**500 Córdobas** L.1985 (1987). Deep olive-green on multicolor underprint. Like #142. Lithographed.	.20	.75	4.00
145	**1000 Córdobas** L.1985 (1987). Dark gray on multicolor underprint. Like #143.			
	a. Engraved.	.25	1.00	3.00
	b. Lithographed.	.15	.50	2.00

		VG	VF	UNC
146	**5000 Córdobas** L.1985 (1987). Brown, orange and black on multicolor underprint. Map at upper center, Gen. D. Zeledon at right. National Assembly building on back.	.15	.50	2.50

A.P.E. DEL 26 OCT. 1987 ND PROVISIONAL ISSUE

#147-150 black ovpt. new denomination on face and back of old Series F and G notes printed by TDLR.

147	20,000 Córdobas on 20 Córdobas	VG	VF	UNC
	D.1987 (1987). Overprint on unissued 20 Cordobas Series F. Colors and design like #135.	.20	.75	2.50

148	50,000 Córdobas on 50 Córdobas	VG	VF	UNC
	D.1987 (1987). Overprint on #140.	.25	.75	3.00

149	100,000 Córdobas on 500 Córdobas	VG	VF	UNC
	D.1987 (1987). Overprint on #144.	.25	.75	4.00

150	500,000 Córdobas on 1000 Córdobas	VG	VF	UNC
	D.1987 (1987). Overprint on #145b. (Not issued).	.50	2.00	5.50

NOTICE

Readers with unlisted dates, signature varieties, etc. are invited to submit photocopies of their notes to: Standard Catalog of World Paper Money, 700 East State St. Iola, WI 54990-0001, E-Mail: george.cuhaj@fwpubs.com.

1985 (1988) Issue

#151-156 wmk: Sandino. Replacement notes: Serial # prefix *ZA; ZB*.

151	10 Córdobas	VG	VF	UNC
	1985 (1988). Green and olive on multicolor underprint. Comdt. C. F. Amador at right. Troop formation marching at left on back.	.10	.50	2.00

152	20 Córdobas	VG	VF	UNC
	1985 (1988). Blue-black and blue on multicolor underprint. Comdt. G. P. Ordoñez at right. Demonstration for agrarian reform at left on back.	.10	.50	2.50

153	50 Córdobas	VG	VF	UNC
	1985 (1988). Brown and dark red on multicolor underprint. Gen. J. D. Estrada at right. Medical clinic scene at left on back.	.10	.50	3.50

154	100 Córdobas	VG	VF	UNC
	1985 (1988). Deep blue, blue and gray on multicolor underprint. R. Lopez Perez at right. State council building at left on back.	.20	.50	4.00

		VG	VF	UNC
155	**500 Córdobas** 1985 (1988). Purple, blue and brown on multicolor underprint. R. Dario at right. Classroom with students at left on back.	.25	.75	4.00

		VG	VF	UNC
156	**1000 Córdobas** 1985 (1988). Brown on multicolor underprint. Gen. A. C. Sandino at right. Liberation of 19.7.1979 on back.			
	a. Engraved with watermark at left. Serial # prefix FA.	.25	.75	5.00
	b. Lithographed without watermark at left. Serial # prefix FC.	.25	.50	2.00

1988-89 ND Provisional Issue

		VG	VF	UNC
157	**5000 Córdobas** ND (1988). Overprint elements in black on face and back of #146. Face overprint: signature and title: *PRIMER VICE PRESIDENTE BANCO CENTRAL DE NICARAGUA* at left, two lines of text at lower center blocked out, guilloche added at right. Overprint: guilloche at left and right, same signature title as overprint on face at right on back.	.25	.50	2.50

#158 and 159 black ovpt. of new denominations on face and back of earlier notes. Ovpt. errors exist and are rather common.

		VG	VF	UNC
158	**10,000 Córdobas on 10 Córdobas** ND (1989). Overprint on #151.	.25	.75	3.00

		VG	VF	UNC
159	**100,000 Córdobas on 100 Córdobas** ND (1989). Overprint on #154.	.25	1.00	5.00

1989 ND Emergency Issue

#160 and 161 grid map of Nicaragua at ctr. on face and back. Wmk: Sandino.

		VG	VF	UNC
160	**20,000 Córdobas** ND (1989). Black on blue, yellow and multicolor underprint. Comdt. Cleto Ordoñez at right. Church of San Francisco Granada at left, map at center on back.	.25	1.00	4.50

		VG	VF	UNC
161	**50,000 Córdobas** ND (1989). Brown on purple, orange and multicolor underprint. Gen. J. D. Estrada at right. Hacienda San Jacinto at left, map at center on back.	.25	.75	3.50

1990 ND Provisional Issue

#162-164, black ovpt. new denomination on face and back of earlier notes.
Note: Ovpt. errors exist and are rather common.

		VG	VF	UNC
162	**200,000 Córdobas on 1000 Córdobas** ND (1990). Overprint on #156b.	.15	.40	1.75

163	**500,000 Córdobas on 20 Córdobas**	**VG**	**VF**	**UNC**
	ND (1990). Overprint on #152.	.25	1.00	3.50

164	**1 Million Córdobas on 1000 Córdobas**	**VG**	**VF**	**UNC**
	ND (1990). Overprint on #156b.	.25	1.00	3.50

1990 ND Emergency Issue

#165 and 166 wmk: Sandino head, repeated

165	**5 Million Córdobas**	**VG**	**VF**	**UNC**
	ND (1990). Purple and orange on red and multicolor underprint. Like #160.	.20	.50	2.00

166	**10 Million Córdobas**	**VG**	**VF**	**UNC**
	ND (1990). Purple and lilac on blue and multicolor underprint. Like #161.	.25	.75	2.50

1990; 1991-92 ND Issues

#173-177, 2 sign. varieties.

167	**1 Centavo**	**VG**	**VF**	**UNC**
	ND (1991). Purple on pale green and multicolor underprint.	FV	.05	.15

168	**5 Centavos**	**VG**	**VF**	**UNC**
	ND (1991). Red-violet on pale green and multicolor underprint. Two signature varieties.			
	a. Issued note.	FV	.05	.20
	s. Specimen.	—	—	100.

169	**10 Centavos**	**VG**	**VF**	**UNC**
	ND (1991). Olive-green on light green and multicolor underprint. Two signature varieties.			
	a. Issued note.	FV	.10	.25
	b. Specimen.	—	—	100.

170	**25 Centavos**	**VG**	**VF**	**UNC**
	ND (1991). Blue on pale green and multicolor underprint. Two signature varieties.			
	a. Issued note.	FV	—	.25
	s. Specimen.	—	—	100.

#171 and 172 printer: CBNC.

171	**1/2 Córdoba**	**VG**	**VF**	**UNC**
	ND (1991). Brown and green on multicolor underprint. F. H. de Córdoba at left, plant at right. Arms at center on green back.	FV	FV	.50

172 **1/2 Córdoba**

	VG	VF	UNC
ND (1992). Face like #171. Arms at left, national flower at right on green back.	FV	FV	.50

#173-177, 2 sign. varieties.

173 **1 Córdoba**

	VG	VF	UNC
1990. Blue on purple and multicolor underprint. Sunrise over field of maize at left, F. H. Córdoba at right. Back green and multicolor; arms at center. Printer: TDLR. Two signature varieties.	FV	FV	1.00

174 **5 Córdobas**

	VG	VF	UNC
ND (1991). Red-violet and deep olive-green on multicolor underprint. Indian Chief Diriangén at left, sorghum plants at right. R. Herrera firing cannon at British warship on green back. Printer: CBNC. Two signature varieties.	FV	FV	2.00

175 **10 Córdobas**

	VG	VF	UNC
1990. Green on blue and multicolor underprint. Sunrise over rice field at left, M. de Larreynaga at right. Back dark green and multicolor; arms at center. Printer: TDLR. Two signature varieties.	FV	FV	3.50

176 **20 Córdobas**

	VG	VF	UNC
ND (1990). Pale red-orange and dark brown on multicolor underprint. Sandino at left, coffee plant at right. E. Mongalo at left, fire in the Mesón de Rivas (1854) at center on green back. Two signature varieties. Printer: CBNC.	FV	FV	6.00

177 **50 Córdobas**

	VG	VF	UNC
ND (1991). Purple and violet on multicolor underprint. Dr. P. J. Chamorro at left, banana plants at right. Toppling of Somoza's statue and scene at polling place on green back. Series A: three signatures; Series B: two signatures. Printer: CBNC.	FV	FV	12.50

		VG	VF	UNC
178	**100 Córdobas**			
	1990. Blue and red on multicolor underprint. Sunrise over cotton field at left, R. Darío at right. Back green and multicolor; arms at center. Printer: TDLR. Three signatures. Series A.	FV	FV	26.00
178A	**500 Córdobas**			
	ND (1991). Brown and red on multicolor underprint. Estrada at right, cattle and sunrise at left. Arms at center on back. Printer: H&S.			
	a. Issued note.	FV	FV	50.00
	s. Specimen.	—	—	175.
178B	**1000 Córdobas**			
	ND (1991). Purple and brown on multicolor underprint. Coffee plants at left, peace demonstration at right. Printer: H&S.			
	a. Issued note.	FV	FV	90.00
	s. Specimen.	—	—	200.

1992-96 ISSUE

179 **1 Córdoba**

	VG	VF	UNC
1995. Blue on purple and multicolor underprint. Similar to #173. Printer: BABN. Series B.	FV	FV	1.00

		VG	VF	UNC
180	**5 Córdobas** 1995. Red, deep olive-green and brown on multicolor underprint. Similar to #174. Printer: F-CO.	FV	FV	1.75
181	**10 Córdobas** 1996. Green on blue and multicolor underprint. Similar to #175. Printer: G&D.	FV	FV	3.00

		VG	VF	UNC
182	**20 Córdobas** 1995. Pale red-orange and dark brown on multicolor underprint. Similar to #176. Printer: F-CO.	FV	FV	5.00

		VG	VF	UNC
183	**50 Córdobas** 1995. Purple and brown on multicolor underprint. Face similar to #177 but with two signatures. Arms at center on back. Printer: F-CO.	FV	FV	10.00

		VG	VF	UNC
184	**100 Córdobas** 1992. Blue and red on multicolor underprint. Like #178 but with two signatures. Series B.	FV	FV	22.50

NOTICE

Readers with unlisted dates, signature varieties, etc. are invited to submit photocopies of their notes to: Standard Catalog of World Paper Money, 700 East State St. Iola, WI 54990-0001, E-Mail: george.cuhaj@fwpubs.com.

1997 Issue

#185-187 printer: TDLR.

		VG	VF	UNC
185	**20 Córdobas** 1997. Orange-brown, green and multicolor. J. Santos Zelaya at right. Arms at center on back. Series C.	FV	FV	6.00

#186 Not assigned.

		VG	VF	UNC
187	**100 Córdobas** 1997. Blue and red on multicolor underprint. Like #184. Series C.	FV	FV	17.50

1999 Issue

		VG	VF	UNC
188	**10 Córdobas** 1999. Multicolor. Series D. Printer: F-CO.	FV	FV	2.50
189	**20 Córdobas** 1999. Similar to #182. Printer F-CO.	FV	FV	5.00

		VG	VF	UNC
189A	**50 Córdobas** 2001. Printer: G&D.	FV	FV	7.50
190	**100 Córdobas** 1999. Blue and red on multicolor underprint. Like #187 but with windowed security thread.	FV	FV	15.00

2002 Issue

		VG	VF	UNC
191	**10 Córdobas** 2002. Green on blue and multicolor underprint.	FV	FV	3.00

192 **20 Córdobas**

	VG	VF	UNC
2002. Pale red-orange and dark brown on multicolor underprint.	FV	FV	5.00

193 **50 Córdobas**

	VG	VF	UNC
2002. Purple and brown on multicolor underprint.	FV	FV	10.00

194 **100 Córdobas**

	VG	VF	UNC
2002. Blue and red on multicolor underprint.	FV	FV	15.00

195 **500 Córdobas**

	VG	VF	UNC
2002. Brown and red on multicolor underprint.	FV	FV	50.00

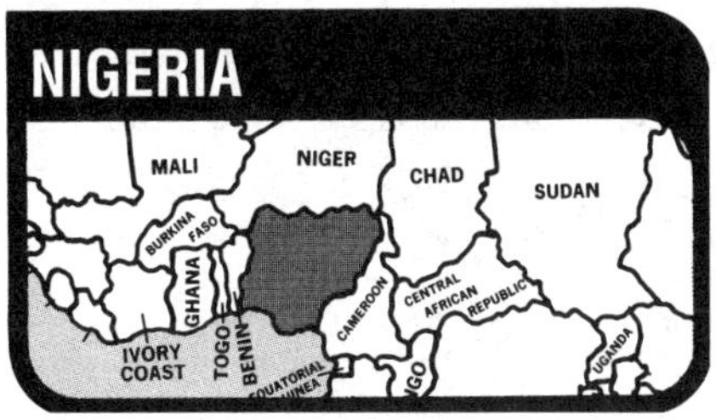

The Federal Republic of Nigeria, situated on the Atlantic coast of Africa between Benin and Cameroon, has an area of 356,667 sq. mi. (923,768 sq. km.) and a population of 128.79 million. Capital: Abuja. The economy is d on petroleum and agriculture. Crude oil, cocoa, tobacco and tin are exported.

Following the Napoleonic Wars, the British expanded their trade with the interior of Nigeria. British claims to a sphere of influence in that area were recognized by the Berlin Conference of 1885, and in the following year the Royal Niger Company was chartered. Direct British control of the territory was initiated in 1900, and in 1914 the amalgamation of northern and southern Nigeria into the Colony and Protectorate of Nigeria was effected. In 1960, following a number of territorial and constitutional changes, Nigeria was granted independence within the British Commonwealth as a federation of the northern, western and eastern regions. Nigeria altered its political relationship with Great Britain on Oct. 1, 1963, by proclaiming itself a republic. It did, however, elect to remain a member of the Commonwealth. The Supreme Commander of Armed Forces is the Head of the Federal Military Government.

On May 30, 1967, the Eastern Region of the republic - an area occupied principally by the proud and resourceful Ibo tribe - seceded from Nigeria and proclaimed itself the independent Republic of Biafra. Civil war erupted and raged for 31 months. Casualties, including civilian, were about two million, the majority succumbing to malnutrition and disease. Biafra surrendered to the federal government on January 15, 1970. After military coups in 1983 and 1985 the government was assumed by an Armed Forces Ruling Council. A transitional civilian council was formed in 1993. Nigeria was suspended from the Commonwealth in November 1995, but was re-admitted on May 29, 1999.

RULERS:

British to 1963

MONETARY SYSTEM:

1 Shilling = 12 Pence
1 Pound = 20 Shillings to 1973
1 Naira (10 Shillings) = 100 Kobo, 1973-

SIGNATURE VARIETIES

	GOVERNOR	CHIEF OF BANKING OPERATIONS		GOVERNOR	CHIEF OF BANKING OPERATIONS
1			2		
3			4		DIRECTOR OF DOMESTIC OPERATIONS
5			6		
	GOVERNOR	DIRECTOR OF CURRENCY OPERATIONS			DIRECTOR OF CURRENCY OPERATIONS
7			8		
9			10		
11			12		
13					

FEDERAL REPUBLIC OF NIGERIA

CENTRAL BANK OF NIGERIA

1967 ND ISSUE

Pound System

#6-13 bank bldg. at l. Wmk: Lion's head.

		VG	VF	UNC
6	**5 Shillings** ND (1967). Lilac and blue. Back lilac; log cutting.	2.00	20.00	140.
7	**10 Shillings** ND (1967). Green and brown. Back green; stacking grain sacks.	4.00	35.00	200.

		VG	VF	UNC
8	**1 Pound** ND (1967). Red and dark brown. Back red; man beating cluster from date palm at right.	.75	2.00	8.00
9	**5 Pounds** ND (1967). Blue-gray and blue-green on multicolor underprint. Back blue-gray; food preparation.	1.00	30.00	350.

1968 ND Issue

#10-13 designs similar to previous issue. Wmk: Lion's head.

		VG	VF	UNC
10	**5 Shillings** ND (1968). Green and orange on multicolor underprint. Back green. Similar to #6.			
	a. Right signature title: *GENERAL MANAGER.*	2.00	15.00	150.
	b. Right signature title: *CHIEF OF BANKING OPERATIONS.*	3.00	25.00	200.
	s. As a. Specimen.	—	—	25.00

		VG	VF	UNC
11	**10 Shillings** ND (1968). Blue and black on multicolor underprint. Back blue; similar to #7.			
	a. Right signature title: *GENERAL MANAGER.*	4.50	25.00	200.
	b. Right signature title: *CHIEF OF BANKING OPERATIONS.*	7.50	35.00	325.
	s. As a. Specimen.	—	—	25.00

		VG	VF	UNC
12	**1 Pound** ND (1968). Olive-brown and purple on multicolor underprint. Back olive-brown. Similar to #8.			
	a. Right signature title: *GENERAL MANAGER.*	4.50	25.00	200.
	b. Right signature title: *CHIEF OF BANKING OPERATIONS.*	7.50	35.00	325.
	s. As a. Specimen.	—	—	25.00

		VG	VF	UNC
13	**5 Pounds** ND (1968). Red-brown and blue on multicolor underprint. Back red-brown. Similar to #9.			
	a. Right signature title: *GENERAL MANAGER.*	20.00	75.00	500.
	b. Right signature title: *CHIEF OF BANKING OPERATIONS.*	25.00	100.	550.
	s. As a. Specimen.	—	—	60.00

1973; 1977 ND Issue

Naira System

#14-17 bank bldg. at l. ctr. Wmk: Heraldic eagle. Replacement notes: Serial # prefix *DZ/*.

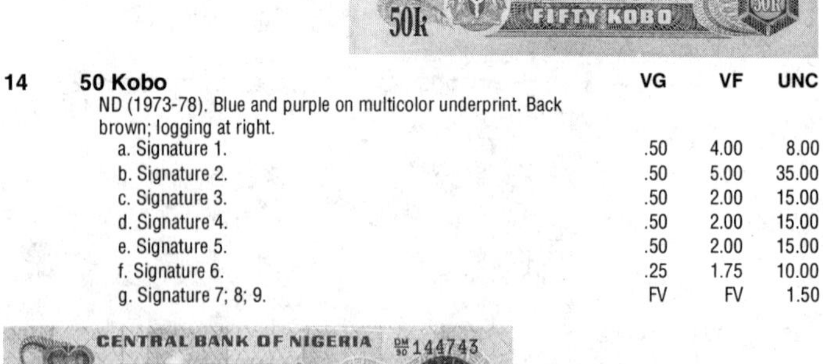

		VG	VF	UNC
14	**50 Kobo** ND (1973-78). Blue and purple on multicolor underprint. Back brown; logging at right.			
	a. Signature 1.	.50	4.00	8.00
	b. Signature 2.	.50	5.00	35.00
	c. Signature 3.	.50	2.00	15.00
	d. Signature 4.	.50	2.00	15.00
	e. Signature 5.	.50	2.00	15.00
	f. Signature 6.	.25	1.75	10.00
	g. Signature 7; 8; 9.	FV	FV	1.50

15	1 Naira	VG	VF	UNC
	ND (1973-78). Red and brown on multicolor underprint. Back red; stacking grain sacks.			
	a. Signature 1.	.75	5.00	12.50
	b. Signature 2.	.75	4.00	12.50
	c. Signature 3.	.75	4.00	12.50
	d. Signature 4.	2.00	17.50	50.00

16	5 Naira	VG	VF	UNC
	ND (1973-78). Blue-gray and olive-green on multicolor underprint. Back blue-gray; man beating cluster from date palm at right.			
	a. Signature 1.	5.00	15.00	70.00
	b. Signature 2.	3.00	10.00	50.00
	c. Signature 3.	15.00	60.00	275.
	d. Signature 4.	20.00	75.00	325.

17	10 Naira	VG	VF	UNC
	ND (1973-78). Carmine and dark blue on multicolor underprint. Back carmine; dam at center.			
	a. Signature 1.	15.00	35.00	110.
	b. Signature 2.	7.00	22.50	85.00
	c. Signature 3.	35.00	125.	400.
	d. Signature 4.	40.00	150.	475.
18	**20 Naira**			
	ND (1977-84). Yellow-green and black on red and multicolor underprint. Gen M. Muhammed at left. Arms at center right on back.			
	a. Signature 2.	30.00	100.	325.
	b. Signature 3.	20.00	60.00	200.
	c. Signature 4.	8.00	20.00	65.00
	d. Signature 5.	6.00	15.00	45.00
	e. Signature 6.	4.00	10.00	35.00

NOTICE

Readers with unlisted dates, signature varieties, etc. are invited to submit photocopies of their notes to: Standard Catalog of World Paper Money, 700 East State St. Iola, WI 54990-0001, E-Mail: george.cuhaj@fwpubs.com.

1979 ND Issue

#19-22 sign. titles: *GOVERNOR* and *DIRECTOR OF DOMESTIC OPERATIONS*. Wmk: Heraldic eagle.

19	1 Naira	VG	VF	UNC
	ND (1979-84). Red on orange and multicolor underprint. H. Macaulay at left. Mask at center right on back.			
	a. Signature 4.	.25	2.00	7.50
	b. Signature 5.	.25	1.00	5.00
	c. Signature 6.	.25	.75	3.00

20	5 Naira	VG	VF	UNC
	ND (1979-84). Green on multicolor underprint. Sir Abubakar Tafawa Balewa Alhaji at left. Dancers at center right on back.			
	a. Signature 4.	1.00	5.00	15.00
	b. Signature 5.	1.00	4.00	12.50
	c. Signature 6.	.50	3.00	10.00

21	10 Naira	VG	VF	UNC
	ND (1979-84). Brown, purple and violet on multicolor underprint. A. Ikoku at left. Two women with bowls on heads at center right on back.			
	a. Signature 4.	2.50	12.00	30.00
	b. Signature 5.	1.50	8.00	25.00
	c. Signature 6.	5.00	20.00	—

1984; 1991 ND Issue

#23-27 new colors and sign. Like #18-21 but reduced size. Wmk: Heraldic eagle.

23	1 Naira	VG	VF	UNC
	ND (1984-). Red, violet and green. Like #19. Back olive and light violet.			
	a. Signature title at right: *DIRECTOR OF DOMESTIC OPERATIONS*. Signature 6.	FV	1.00	3.00
	b. Signature title at right: *DIRECTOR OF CURRENCY OPERATIONS*. Signature 7.	FV	FV	2.50
	c. Titles as b. signature 8.	FV	FV	2.50
	d. Titles as b. signature 9.	FV	FV	2.50

24	5 Naira	VG	VF	UNC
	ND (1984-). Purple and brown-violet on multicolor underprint. Like #20.			
	a. Signature title at right: *DIRECTOR OF DOMESTIC OPERATIONS.* Signature 6.	FV	2.00	6.50
	b. Signature title at right: *DIRECTOR OF CURRENCY OPERATIONS.* Signature 7.	FV	1.00	4.00
	c. Titles as b. signature 8.	FV	FV	2.00
	d. Titles as b. signature 9.	FV	FV	2.00
	e. Titles as b. signature 10.	FV	FV	1.75
	f. ND. signature 11.	FV	FV	1.75
	g. 2001. signature 11.	FV	FV	1.75
	h. 2002. signature 11.	FV	FV	1.75
	i. 2004. signature 12.	FV	FV	1.75
	j. 2005. signature 12.	FV	FV	1.75
	k. 2005. signature 13.	FV	FV	1.75

25	10 Naira	VG	VF	UNC
	ND (1984-). Red-violet and orange on multicolor underprint. Back red. Like #21.			
	a. Signature title at right: *DIRECTOR OF DOMESTIC OPERATIONS.* Signature 6.	FV	2.50	9.00
	b. Signature title at right: *DIRECTOR OF CURRENCY OPERATIONS.* Signature 7.	FV	2.50	6.00
	c. Titles as b. Signature 8.	FV	FV	3.25
	d. Titles as b. Signature 9.	FV	FV	3.00
	e. Titles as b. Signature 10.	FV	FV	3.00
	f. 2001.Titles as b. Signature 11.	FV	FV	3.00
	g. 2003. Signature 12.	FV	FV	3.00
	h. 2004.	FV	FV	3.00
	i. 2005.	FV	FV	3.00

26	20 Naira	VG	VF	UNC
	ND (1984-). Dark blue-green, dark green and green on multicolor underprint. Like #18.			

26	20 Naira	VG	VF	UNC
	a. Signature title at right: *DIRECTOR OF DOMESTIC OPERATIONS.* Signature 6.	FV	5.00	20.00
	b. Signature title at right: *DIRECTOR OF CURRENCY OPERATIONS.* Signature 7.	FV	FV	6.00
	c. Titles as b. signature 8.	FV	FV	4.00
	d. Titles as b. signature 9.	FV	FV	4.00
	e. Titles as b. signature 10.	FV	FV	3.00
	f. 2001. signature 11.	FV	FV	3.00
	g. 2003. signature 11.	FV	FV	3.00
	h. 2003. signature 12.	FV	FV	3.00
	i. 2004. signature 12.	FV	FV	3.00
	j. 2005.	FV	FV	3.00

27	50 Naira	VG	VF	UNC
	ND (1991-). Dark blue, black and gray on multicolor underprint. Four busts reflecting varied citizenry at left center. Three farmers in field at center right, arms at lower right on back.			
	a. Signature 8.	FV	3.50	12.50
	b. Signature 9.	FV	FV	7.50
	c. Signature 10.	FV	FV	6.50
	d. 2001.Signature 11.	FV	FV	6.50
	e. 2005. signature 13.	FV	FV	6.50

1999-2001 ND ISSUE

#28-30 sign. 11.

28	100 Naira	VG	VF	UNC
	ND (1999-). Brown and red on multicolor underprint. Chief Obafemi Awolowo at left. Zuma rock on back.			
	a. Back with *Abuja Province* identification by rock. (1999).	FV	FV	10.00
	b. Back modified without identification. (2000).	FV	FV	8.00
	c. 2001. signature 11.	FV	FV	8.00
	d. 2003. signature 12.	FV	FV	8.00
	e. 2005. signature 13.	FV	FV	8.00

		VG	VF	UNC
29	**200 Naira** 2000; 2003; 2005. Brown, dark blue and green on multicolor underprint. Sir Ahmadu Bello at left and as watermark. Two cows and agricultural products on back.			
	a. 2000. signature 11.	FV	FV	10.00
	b. 2003. signature 12.	FV	FV	10.00
	c. 2005. signature 13.	FV	FV	10.00

		VG	VF	UNC
30	**500 Naira** 2001; 2002; 2005. Purple and olive-green on rose and multicolor underprint. Dr. Nnamdi Azikiwe at left and as watermark. Wide segmented security thread at left center. Oil platform at center right on back.			
	a. 2001. signature 11.	FV	FV	18.00
	b. 2002. signature 12.	FV	FV	18.00
	c. 2005. signature 13.	FV	FV	18.00

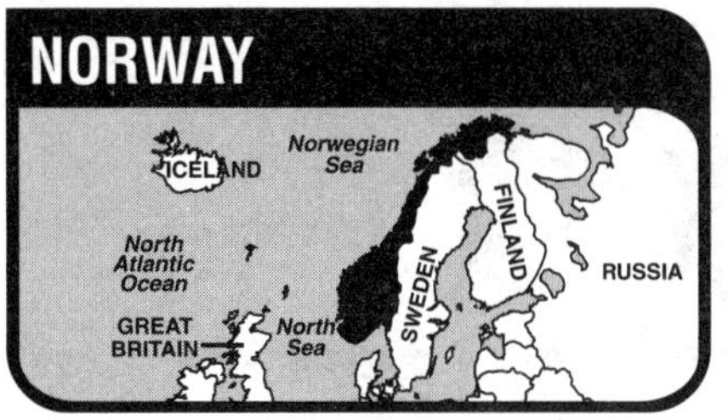

The Kingdom of Norway, a constitutional monarchy located in northwestern Europe, has an area of 150,000 sq. mi. (388,500 sq. km.) including the island territories of Spitzbergen (Svalbard) and Jan Mayen, and a population of 4.46 million. Capital: Oslo. The diversified economic of Norway includes shipping, fishing, forestry, agriculture and manufacturing. Nonferrous metals, paper and paperboard, paper pulp, iron, steel and oil are exported.

A United Norwegian kingdom was established in the 9th century, the era of the indomitable Norse Vikings who ranged far and wide, visiting the coasts of northwestern Europe, the Mediterranean, Greenland and North America. In the 13th century, the Norse kingdom was united briefly with Sweden, then passed, through the Union of Kalmar, 1397, to the rule of Denmark which was maintained until 1814. In 1814, Norway fell again under the rule of Sweden. The union lasted until 1905 when the Norwegian Parliament arranged a peaceful separation and invited a Danish prince (King Haakon VII) to occupy the throne of an independent Kingdom of Norway.

RULERS:

Olav V, 1957-1991
Harald V, 1991-

MONETARY SYSTEM:

1 Krone = 100 Øre, 1873-

KINGDOM

NORGES BANK

1948-55 ISSUE

#30-33 Replacement notes: Serial # prefix *Z*. Wmk: value repeated.

		VG	VF	UNC
30	**5 Kroner** 1955-63. Blue on gray and multicolor underprint. Portrait Fridtjof Nansen at left. Fishing scene on back.			
	a. Signature Brofoss - Thorp. 1955-57. Prefix A-F.	10.00	20.00	75.00
	b. Signature Brofoss - Ottesen. 1959-63. Prefix F-L.	7.50	17.50	65.00
	s. As a. Specimen.	—	150.	300.

		VG	VF	UNC
31	**10 Kroner** 1954-73. Yellow-brown on gray underprint. Portrait Christian Michelsen at left. Mercury with ships on back.			
	a. Signature Jahn - Thorp. 1954. Prefix A-D.	2.50	7.50	40.00
	b1. Signature Brofoss - Thorp. 1954-55. Prefix D-G.	2.00	7.00	35.00
	b2. Signature Brofoss - Thorp. 1955. Prefix H.	180.	350.	800.
	b3. Signature Brofoss - Thorp. 1956. Prefix H-I.	2.00	7.00	35.00
	b4. Signature Brofoss - Thorp. 1957. Prefix I.	12.50	40.00	100.
	b5. Signature Brofoss - Thorp. 1957-58. Prefix J-M.	2.00	7.00	35.00
	b6. Signature Brofoss - Thorp. 1958. Prefix N.	7.00	30.00	85.00
	c. Signature Brofoss - Ottesen. 1959-65. Prefix N-E.	2.00	4.00	20.00
	d. Signature Brofoss - Petersen. 1965-69. Prefix F-V.	FV	3.00	12.50
	e. Signature Brofoss - Odegaard. 1970. Prefix W-Ø.	FV	2.00	10.00
	f. Signature Wold - Odegaard. 1971-73. Prefix Á-R.	FV	1.75	7.50
	s. As a, d, f. Specimen.	—	150.	300.

#31 replacement notes: Serial # prefix *X* (1966-72) *Z* (1954-73).

		VG	VF	UNC
32	**50 Kroner**			
	1950-65. Dark green. Portrait Bjørnstjerne Björnson at upper left and as wmk., crowned arms at upper center Harvesting on back.			
	a1. Signature Jahn - Thorp. 1950-52. Prefix A.	15.00	55.00	200.
	a2. Signature Jahn - Thorp. 1952. Prefix B.	60.00	120.	550.
	a3. Signature Jan - Thorp. 1953-54. Prefix B.	15.00	55.00	200.
	b1. Signature Brofoss - Thorp. 1954. Prefix B.	70.00	150.	650.
	b2. Signature Brofoss - Thorp. 1955-58. Prefix B; C.	17.50	50.00	170.
	b3. Signature Brofoss - Thorp. 1958. Prefix D.	24.00	95.00	350.
	c. Signature Brofoss - Ottesen. 1959-65. Prefix D-F.	12.50	35.00	130.
	s. As a. 1951. Specimen.	—	—	—
33	**100 Kroner**			
	1949-62. Red. Portrait Henrik Wergeland at upper left and as wmk., crowned arms at upper center Logging on back.			
	a1. Signature Jahn - Thorp. 1949-52. Prefix A.	22.50	50.00	175.
	a2. Signature Jahn - Thorp. 1952. Prefix C.	800.	1250.	—
	a3. Signature Jahn - Thorp. 1953-54. Prefix C.	22.50	50.00	175.
	b. Signature Brofoss - Thorp. 1954-58. Prefix D-G.	20.00	50.00	175.
	c. Signature Brofoss - Ottesen. 1959-62. Prefix G-I.	20.00	40.00	140.

		VG	VF	UNC
34	**500 Kroner**			
	1948-76. Dark green. Portrait Niels Henrik Abel at upper left and as wmk., crowned supported arms at upper center Factory workers on back. Prefix A.			
	a. Signature Jahn - Thorp. 1948; 1951.	175.	350.	1000.
	b1. Signature Brofoss - Thorp. 1954; 1956.	175.	350.	1000.
	b2. Signature Brofoss - Thorp. 1958.	100.	200.	675.
	c. Signature Brofoss - Ottesen. 1960-64.	90.00	160.	550.
	d. Signature Brofoss - Petersen. 1966-69.	85.00	140.	400.
	e. Signature Brofoss - Odegaard. 1970.	80.00	130.	325.
	f. Signature Wold - Odegaard. 1971-76.	75.00	120.	275.
	s. As a. Specimen.	—	600.	850.

		VG	VF	UNC
35	**1000 Kroner**			
	1949-74. Red-brown. Portrait H. Ibsen at left and as wmk., crowned supported arms at upper center Old man and child on back. Prefix A.			
	a. Signature Jahn - Thorp. 1949; 1951; 1953.	175.	425.	800.
	b. Signature Brofoss - Thorp. 1955; 1958.	160.	290.	600.
	c. Signature Brofoss - Ottesen. 1961; 1962.	150.	225.	500.
	d. Signature Brofoss - Petersen. 1965-70.	140.	210.	400.
	e. Signature Brofoss - Odegaard. 1971-74.	130.	200.	325.
	s. As a. Specimen.	—	600.	850.

#34 and 35 replacement notes: Serial # prefix *G*.

1962-78 ISSUE

#36-40 arms at ctr.

#36 and 41 replacement notes: Serial # prefix *H* or *Q*.

		VG	VF	UNC
36	**10 Kroner**			
	1972-84. Dark blue on multicolor underprint. Fridtjof Nansen at left. Fisherman and cargo ship at right on back. Watermark: Value *10* repeated.			
	a. 1972. Replacement Prefix *Q*.	30.00	50.00	100.
	b. Signature Wold and Odegaard. 1973-76.	FV	4.00	11.00
	c. Signature Wold and Sagård. 1977-79; 1981-84.	FV	2.00	6.50
	s. As a. Specimen.	—	500.	900.

#37-40 replacement notes: Serial # prefix *X* or *Z*.

37	50 Kroner	VG	VF	UNC
	1966-83. Green on multicolor underprint. Bjørnstjerne Björnson at left and as watermark. Old church at right on back.			
	a. Signature Brofoss and Petersen. 1966-67; 1969. Prefix A-C.	12.00	25.00	80.00
	b. Signature Wold and Odegaard. 1971-73. Prefix C-E.	12.00	17.50	60.00
	c. As b. with security thread. 1974-75. Prefix F-G.	12.00	15.00	40.00
	d. Signature Wold and Sagård. 1976-83. Prefix H-R.	FV	12.50	35.00
	s. As a. Specimen.	—	450.	750.

38	100 Kroner	VG	VF	UNC
	1962-77. Red-violet on multicolor underprint. H. Wergeland at left and as watermark. Establishment of Constitution in 1814 at right on back.			
	a. Signature Brofoss and Ottesen. 1962-65. Prefix A-D.	FV	20.00	80.00
	b. Signature Brofoss and Petersen. 1965-69. Prefix D-H.	FV	17.50	80.00
	c. Signature Brofoss and Odegaard. 1970. Prefix M-P.	FV	17.50	55.00
	d. Signature Wold and Odegaard. 1971-76. Prefix P-C.	FV	17.50	50.00
	e. Signature Wold and Sagård. 1977. Prefix D-K.	FV	FV	40.00
	s. As a. Specimen.	—	450.	800.

39	500 Kroner	VG	VF	UNC
	1978-85. Green on brown underprint. Niels Henrik Abel at left and as watermark. University of Oslo at right on back.			
	a. Signature Wold and Sagård. 1978; 1982.	FV	100.	200.
	b. Signature Skånland and Sagård. 1985.	FV	100.	200.
	s. As a. Specimen.	—	1000.	1900.

NOTICE

Readers with unlisted dates, signature varieties, etc. are invited to submit photocopies of their notes to: Standard Catalog of World Paper Money, 700 East State St. Iola, WI 54990-0001, E-Mail: george.cuhaj@fwpubs.com.

40	1000 Kroner	VG	VF	UNC
	1975-87. Brown and violet on multicolor underprint. Henrik Ibsen at left and as watermark. Scenery on back.			
	a. Signature Wold and Odegaard. 1975. Prefix A.	FV	200.	275.
	b. Signature Wold and Sagård. 1978; 1980; 1982-85. Prefix A-C.	FV	160.	250.
	c. Signature Skånland and Sagård. 1985-87. Prefix C-E.	FV	140.	225.
	s. As a. Specimen.	—	800.	1400.

1977 ISSUE

41	100 Kroner	VG	VF	UNC
	1977-82. Purple on pink and multicolor underprint. Cahilla Collett at left and as watermark. Date at top left center. Filigree design on back. Signature Wold and Sagård.			
	a. Brown serial #. 1977.	FV	17.50	55.00
	b. Black serial #. 1979; 1980.	FV	17.50	45.00
	c. 1981; 1982.	FV	17.50	45.00
	s. As a. Specimen.	—	800.	1400.

1983-91 ISSUE

42	50 Kroner	VG	VF	UNC
	1984-95. Green on multicolor underprint. Aasmund Olavsson Vinje at left. Stone carving with soldier slaying dragon on back. Watermark: 50 repeated within diagonal bars.			
	a. Signature Wold and Sagård. 1984.	FV	15.00	30.00
	b. Signature Skånland and Sagård. 1985-87.	FV	9.00	22.50
	c. Signature Skånland and Johansen. 1989-90; 1993.	FV	9.00	17.50
	d. Signature Moland and Johansen. 1995.	FV	FV	15.00
	s. As a. Specimen.	—	800.	1400.

Note: #42d was also issued in a special "Last Edition" folder w/50 Øre coin dated 1996. (8400 pieces), Value $50.00.

43 100 Kroner — VG | VF | UNC

1983-94. Red-violet on pink and multicolor underprint. Similar to #41 but smaller printing size, and date at lower right.

	VG	VF	UNC
a. Signature Wold and Sagård. 1983.	FV	17.50	40.00
b. As a. but large date. 1984.	FV	17.50	40.00
c. Signature Skånland and Sagård. 1985-87.	FV	17.50	35.00
d. Signature Skånland and Johansen. 1988-93.	FV	15.00	27.50
e. Signature Moland and Johansen. 1994.	FV	FV	27.50

Note: #43e was also issued in a special "Last Edition" folder w/1 Krone coin dated 1996. (6000 issued). Value $50.

44 500 Kroner — VG | VF | UNC

1991; 1994; 1996; 1997. Blue-violet on multicolor underprint. Edvard Grieg at left. Floral mosaic at center on back. Watermark: Multiple portrait of Grieg vertically.

	VG	VF	UNC
a. Signature Skånland and Johansen. 1991.	FV	FV	125.
b. Signature Moland and Johansen. 1994.	FV	FV	100.
c. Signature Storvik and Johansen. 1996; 1997.	FV	FV	100.

45 1000 Kroner — VG | VF | UNC

1989; 1990. Purple and dark blue on multicolor underprint. C. M. Falsen at left. 1668 royal seal on back. Signature: Skånland and Johansen.

	VG	VF	UNC
a. Signature Skånland and Johansen. 1989; 1990.	FV	FV	200.
b. Signature Storvik and Johansen. 1998.	FV	FV	190.

1994-96 ISSUE

#46 and 47 sign. K. Storvik and S. Johansen.

46 50 Kroner — VG | VF | UNC

1996; 1998. Dark green on pale green and multicolor underprint. P. C. Asbjörnsen at right and as repeated vertical watermark. Water lilies and dragonfly on back.

	VG	VF	UNC
a. Signature Storvik and Johansen. 1996; 1998.	FV	FV	12.50
b. Signature Gjedrem and Johansen. 1999; 2000.	FV	FV	10.00

47 100 Kroner — VG | VF | UNC

1995; 1997-99. Deep brown-violet and red-violet on multicolor underprint. Kirsten Flagstad at right and as repeated vertical watermark. Theatre layout on back.

	VG	VF	UNC
a. Signature Storvik and Johansen. 1995; 1997; 1998. 10-digit serial # upper left and lower right. on face. Date on back.	FV	FV	25.00
b. Signature Gjedrem and Johansen. 1999. 10-digit serial # upper left, 8-digit # lower right. on face, where last four digits are the date.	FV	FV	20.00

Note: #47 was issued on the 100th birthday of famed singer Kirsten Flagstad in 1895.

48 200 Kroner — VG | VF | UNC

1994; 1998; 1999. Blue-black and dark blue on multicolor underprint. Kristian Birkeland at right and as repeated vertical watermark. Map of the North Pole; North America and Northern Europe at left center on back.

	VG	VF	UNC
a. Signature Moland and Johansen. 1994.	FV	FV	40.00
b. Signature Storvik and Johansen. 1998.	FV	FV	37.50
c. Signature Gjedrem and Johansen. 1999; 2000.	FV	FV	35.00

1999-2002 ISSUE

49	100 Kroner	VG	VF	UNC
	2003. Similar to #49 but with wide holographic strip at right. Signature: Gjdren and Eklund.	FV	FV	20.00

50	200 Kroner	VG	VF	UNC
	2002-03. Similar to #48 but with wide holographic strip at right.			
	a. 2002. signature Gjedrem and Johansen.	FV	FV	40.00
	b. 2003. signature Gjdrem and Eklund.	FV	FV	35.00

51	500 Kroner	VG	VF	UNC
	1999; 2000; 2002. Brown on tan and multicolor underprint. Sigrid Undste and wide holographic strip at right. Wreath of wheat and roses on back. Signature: Gjedrem and Johansen.	FV	FV	90.00

52	1000 Kroner	VG	VF	UNC
	2001. Lilac, blue, yellow and multicolor. Edvard Munch at right, wide holographic strip at right edge, part of his painting *Melancholy* at left center. Munch's great work *The Sun* on back. Signature: Gjedrem and Johansen.	FV	FV	250.

Listings for Nouméa, see New Caledonia

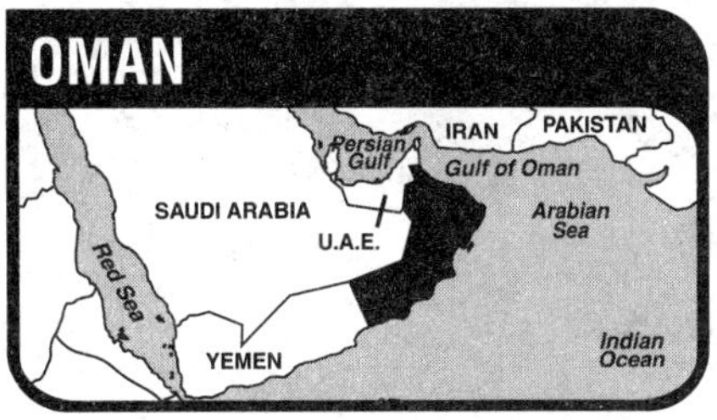

The Sultanate of Oman (formerly Muscat and Oman), an independent monarchy located in the southeastern part of the Arabian Peninsula, has an area of 82,030 sq. mi. (212,457 sq. km.) and a population of 2.72 million. Capital: Muscat. The economy is d on agriculture, herding and petroleum. Petroleum products, dates, fish and hides are exported.

The first European contact with Muscat and Oman was made by the Portuguese who captured Muscat, the capital and chief port, in 1508. They occupied the city, utilizing it as a naval and factory and holding it against land and sea attacks by Arabs and Persians until finally ejected by local Arabs in 1650. It was next occupied by the Persians who maintained control until 1741, when it was taken by Ahmed ibn Sa'id of the present ruling family. Muscat and Oman was the most powerful state in Arabia during the first half of the 19th century, until weakened by the persistent attack of interior nomadic tribes. British influence, initiated by the signing of a treaty of friendship with the Sultanate in 1798, remains a dominant fact of the civil and military phases of the government, although Britain recognizes the Sultanate as a sovereign state and there is no colonial relationship between them.

Sultan Sa'id bin Taimur was overthrown by his son, Qaboos bin Sa'id, on July 23, 1970. He changed the nation's name to the Sultanate of Oman.

RULERS:

Sa'id bin Taimur, AH1351-1390/1932-1970 AD
Qaboos bin Sa'id, AH1390-1419/1970-1999AD

MONETARY SYSTEM:

1 Rial Omani = 1000 Baiza (Baisa)
1 Rial Saidi = 1000 Baiza (Baisa)

MUSCAT AND OMAN

SULTANATE OF MUSCAT AND OMAN

1970 ND ISSUE

#1-6 arms at r. and as wmk.

1	100 Baiza	VG	VF	UNC
	ND (1970). Brown on blue-green and multicolor underprint.			
	a. Issued note.	1.00	2.00	5.00
	s. Specimen.	—	—	40.00
	ct. Color trial in violet.	—	—	150.

2	1/4 Rial Saidi	VG	VF	UNC
	ND (1970). Blue and brown on multicolor underprint. Jalali Fortress on back.			
	a. Issued note.	1.25	3.00	6.00
	s. Specimen.	—	—	45.00
	ct. Color trial in green.	—	—	150.

3	1/2 Rial Saidi	VG	VF	UNC
	ND (1970). Green and purple on multicolor underprint. Sumail Fortress on back.			
	a. Issued note.	2.00	4.00	10.00
	s. Specimen.	—	—	60.00
	ct. Color trial in purple.	—	—	150.

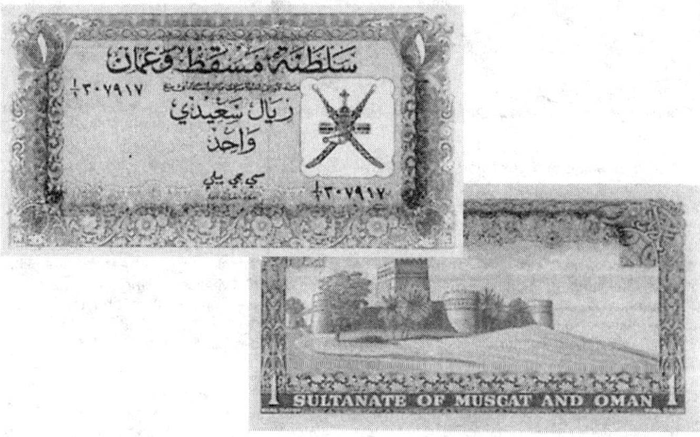

4	1 Rial Saidi	VG	VF	UNC
	ND (1970). Red and olive-green on multicolor underprint. Sohar Fort on back.			
	a. Issued note.	4.00	9.00	22.50
	s. Specimen.	—	—	90.00
	ct. Color trial in blue.	—	—	250.

5	5 Rials Saidi	VG	VF	UNC
	ND (1970). Purple and blue on multicolor underprint. Nizwa Fort on back.			
	a. Issued note.	20.00	40.00	80.00
	s. Specimen.	—	—	120.
	ct. Color trial in red.	—	—	300.

6	10 Rials Saidi	VG	VF	UNC
	ND (1970). Dark brown and blue on multicolor underprint. Mirani Fort on back.			
	a. Issued note.	30.00	70.00	160.
	s. Specimen.	—	—	175.
	ct. Color trial in blue-green.	—	—	400.

OMAN

OMAN CURRENCY BOARD

1973 ND ISSUE

#7-12 arms at r. and as wmk. Like #1-6.

#8-12 different fortresses on back.

7	100 Baiza	VG	VF	UNC
	ND (1973). Brown on blue-green and multicolor underprint. Like #1.			
	a. Issued note.	1.00	2.25	4.25
	s. Specimen.	—	—	35.00
	ct. Color trial. Violet-brown on multicolor underprint.	—	—	100.

8	1/4 Rial Omani	VG	VF	UNC
	ND (1973). Blue and brown on multicolor underprint. Like #2.			
	a. Issued note.	1.25	2.50	6.00
	s. Specimen.	—	—	35.00
	ct. Color trial. Green on multicolor underprint.	—	—	100.

9	1/2 Rial Omani	VG	VF	UNC
	ND (1973). Green and purple on multicolor underprint. Like #3.			
	a. Issued note.	2.00	3.00	9.00
	s. Specimen.	—	—	35.00
	ct. Color trial. Black and purple on multicolor underprint.	—	—	100.

10 1 Rial Omani
ND (1973). Red and olive-green on multicolor underprint. Like #4.

	VG	VF	UNC
a. Issued note.	3.00	9.00	17.50
s. Specimen.	—	—	50.00
ct. Color trial. Blue on multicolor underprint.	—	—	125.

11 5 Rials Omani
ND (1973). Purple and blue on multicolor underprint. Like #5.

	VG	VF	UNC
a. Issued note.	17.50	30.00	70.00
s. Specimen.	—	—	100.
ct. Color trial. Red and blue on multicolor underprint.	—	—	240.

12 10 Rials Omani
ND (1973). Dark brown and blue on multicolor underprint. Like #6.

	VG	VF	UNC
a. Issued note.	32.50	60.00	125.
s. Specimen.	—	—	140.
ct. Color trial in blue-green.	—	—	225.

CENTRAL BANK OF OMAN

1977; 1985 ND ISSUE

#13-19 arms at r. and as wmk.

13 100 Baisa
ND (1977). Light brown on multicolor underprint. Port of Qaboos on back.

	VG	VF	UNC
a. Issued note.	FV	2.00	3.00
s. Specimen.	—	—	100.

14 200 Baisa
ND (1985). Purple on multicolor underprint. Rustaq Fortress on back.

VG	VF	UNC
FV	2.00	3.50

15 1/4 Rial
ND (1977). Blue and brown on multicolor underprint. Back similar to #2.

	VG	VF	UNC
a. Issued note.	FV	2.50	5.00
s. Specimen.	—	—	100.

16 1/2 Rial
ND (1977). Green and purple on multicolor underprint. Back similar to #3.

	VG	VF	UNC
a. Issued note.	FV	4.00	8.00
s. Specimen.	—	—	100.

17 1 Rial
ND (1977). Red and brown on multicolor underprint. Back similar to #14.

	VG	VF	UNC
a. Issued note.	FV	8.00	16.00
s. Specimen.	—	—	100.

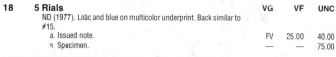

18	5 Rials	VG	VF	UNC
	ND (1977). Lilac and blue on multicolor underprint. Back similar to #15.			
	a. Issued note.	FV	25.00	40.00
	s. Specimen.	—	—	75.00

19	10 Rials	VG	VF	UNC
	ND (1977). Brown and blue on multicolor underprint. Back similar to #16.			
	a. Issued note.	FV	42.50	100.
	s. Specimen.	—	—	100.

20	20 Rials	VG	VF	UNC
	ND (1977). Gray-blue and orange on multicolor underprint. Sultan Qaboos bin Sa'id at right. Central Bank at left center on back. Watermark: Arms.			
	a. Issued note.	FV	75.00	150.
	s. Specimen.	—	—	150.

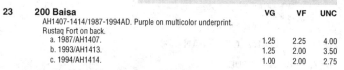

21	50 Rials	VG	VF	UNC
	ND. Olive-brown, blue and dark brown on multicolor underprint. Sultan at right. Jabreen Fort at left center on back.			
	a. Issued note.	150.	250.	375.
	s. Specimen.	—	—	350.

1985-90 Issue

#22-30 Sultan Qaboos bin Sa'id at r. and as wmk.

22	100 Baisa	VG	VF	UNC
	AH1408-1414/1987-1994AD. Light brown on multicolor underprint. Port of Qaboos on back.			
	a. 1987/AH1408.	1.25	2.00	3.50
	b. 1989/AH1409.	1.00	1.50	2.25
	c. 1992/AH1413.	4.00	8.00	24.00
	d. 1994/AH1414.	.75	1.50	2.00

23	200 Baisa	VG	VF	UNC
	AH1407-1414/1987-1994AD. Purple on multicolor underprint. Rustaq Fort on back.			
	a. 1987/AH1407.	1.25	2.25	4.00
	b. 1993/AH1413.	1.25	2.00	3.50
	c. 1994/AH1414.	1.00	2.00	2.75

		VG	VF	UNC
24	**1/4 Rial** 1989/AH1409. Blue, brown and red on multicolor underprint. Modern fishing industry on back.	1.40	3.25	4.75
25	**1/2 Rial** 1987/AH1408. Green on multicolor underprint. Aerial view of Sultan Qaboos University on back.	2.25	5.25	7.00

26	1 Rial	VG	VF	UNC
	AH1407-1414/1987-1994AD. Red, black and olive-brown on multicolor underprint. Sohar Fort at left on back.			
	a. 1987/AH1407.	5.00	10.00	15.00
	b. 1989/AH1409.	5.00	10.00	12.50
	c. 1994/AH1414.	FV	FV	8.00

27	5 Rials	VG	VF	UNC
	1990/AH1411. Dark rose, brown-violet and multicolor underprint. Fort Nizwa on back.	FV	27.50	45.00

28	10 Rials	VG	VF	UNC
	AH1408/1987AD; AH1413/1993AD. Dark brown, red-brown and blue on multicolor underprint. Fort Mirani at left center on back.			
	a. 1987/AH1408.	FV	55.00	80.00
	b. 1993/AH1413.	FV	50.00	70.00

29	20 Rials	VG	VF	UNC
	AH1407/1987AD; AH1414/1994AD. Brown, dark olive-brown and blue-gray on multicolor underprint. Similar to #20.			
	a. 1987/AH1408.	FV	110.	140.
	b. 1994/AH1414.	FV	100.	130.

30	50 Rials	VG	VF	UNC
	AH1405/1985AD; AH1413/1992AD. Olive-brown, blue and dark brown on multicolor underprint. Like #21 but with *Jabreen Fort* added at lower right on back.			
	a. 1985/AH1405.	FV	220.	325.
	b. 1992/AH1413.	FV	210.	300.
	s. As a. Specimen.	—	—	375.

Note: For note with similar design but w/o date, see #21.

1995 Issue

#31-38 Sultan Qaboos at r. and as wmk.

#31-36, 38 arms at upper l.

31	100 Baisa	VG	VF	UNC
	1995/AH1416. Deep olive-green, dark green-blue and purple on multicolor underprint. Faslajs irrigation system at center Verreaux's eagle and white oryx at center on back.	FV	1.00	1.75

32	200 Baisa	VG	VF	UNC
	1995/AH1416. Black, deep blue and green on multicolor underprint. Seeb & Salalah Airports at left center. Raysut Port and Marine Science & Fisheries Center at lower left, aerial view of Sultan Qaboos port center on back.	FV	1.50	3.00

		VG	VF	UNC
33	**1/2 Rial** 1995/AH1416. Dark brown and gray on multicolor underprint. Bahla Castle at center Nakhl Fort and Al-Hazm castle at lower left, Nakhl Fort at center on back.	FV	4.50	7.00
34	**1 Rial** 1995/AH1416. Deep purple, purple and blue-green on multicolor underprint. Sultan Qaboos Sports Complex, Burj al-Sahwa, road overpass at center Omani Khanjar, traditional silver bracelets and ornaments with shipbuilding in background underprint. on back.	FV	4.50	7.00

		VG	VF	UNC
35	**5 Rials** 1995/AH1416. Red on pale blue and multicolor underprint. Sultan Qaboos University building with clock tower at center Nizwa city view at left center on back.			
	a. Without reflective pattern of Khanjars (State Emblem) on back.	FV	22.50	40.00
	b. With reflective pattern of Khanjars on back.	FV	FV	32.50

		VG	VF	UNC
36	**10 Rials** 1995/AH1416. Dark brown on pale blue and multicolor underprint. al-Nahdha in Salalah Tower, Jabreen coconut palm and frankincense tree at center Mutrah Fort and Corniche at left center on back.	FV	FV	60.00

		VG	VF	UNC
37	**20 Rials** 1995/AH1416. Dark blue-green and olive-green on multicolor underprint. Central Bank of Oman building at center, minaret at right. Muscat Security Market at left, aerial view of Rysayl Industrial Area at center, Oman Chamber of Commerce building at upper right on back.	FV	FV	110.

		VG	VF	UNC
38	**50 Rials** 1995/AH1416. Purple and violet on multicolor underprint. Ministry of Finance and Economy building at center, Mirani Fort at right. Cabinet building at left, Ministry of Commerce and Industry building at center right on back.	FV	FV	250.

2000 Issue

#39-42 like #35-38 but w/holographic strip added at r.

		VG	VF	UNC
39	**5 Rials** 2000/AH1420. Red on multicolor underprint. Like #5.	FV	FV	27.50

		VG	VF	UNC
40	**10 Rials** 2000/1420AH. Brown on multicolor underprint. Like #36.	FV	FV	45.00

		VG	VF	UNC
41	**20 Rials** 2000/1420AH. Green on multicolor underprint. Like #37.	FV	FV	95.00

		VG	VF	UNC
42	**50 Rials** 2000/1420AH. Purple on multicolor underprint. Like #38.	FV	FV	225.

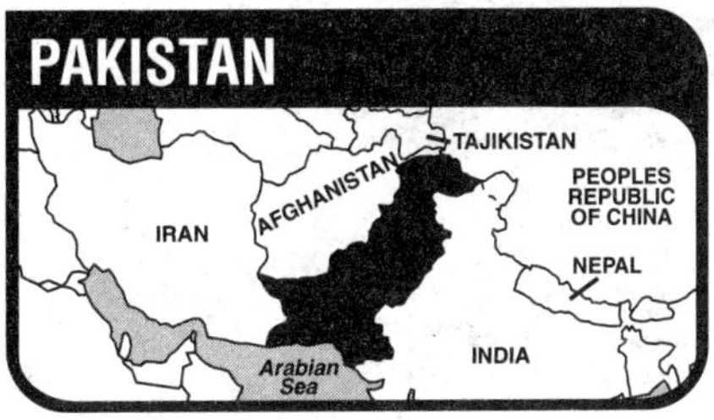

The Islamic Republic of Pakistan, located on the Indian subcontinent between India and Afghanistan, has an area of 310,404 sq. mi. (803,943 sq. m.) and a population of 156 million. Capital: Islamabad. Pakistan is mainly an agricultural land. Yarn, cotton, rice and leather are exported.

Afghan and Turkish intrusions into northern India between the 11th and 18th centuries resulted in large numbers of Indians being converted to Islam. The idea of a separate Moslem state independent of Hindu India developed in the 1930's and was agreed to by Britain in 1946. The Islamic majority areas of India, consisting of the separate geographic entities known as East and West Pakistan, achieved self-government as Pakistan, with dominion status in the British Commonwealth, when the British withdrew from India on Aug. 14, 1947. Pakistan became a republic in 1956. When a basic constitutional crisis initiated by the election of Dec. 1, 1970 - the first direct general election in Pakistani history - could not be resolved by the leaders of East and West Pakistan, the East Pakistanis seceded from the Islamic Republic of Pakistan (March 26, 1971) and formed the independent People's Republic of Bangladesh.

Pakistan was expelled from the Commonwealth on January 20, 1972 and re-admitted again on October 1, 1989.

MONETARY SYSTEM:

1 Rupee = 16 Annas to 1961
1 Rupee = 100 Paisa (Pice), 1961-

REPLACEMENT NOTES:

#24, 24A, 24B, 1/X or 2/X prefix. #25-33, X as first of double prefix letters.

REPUBLIC

GOVERNMENT OF PAKISTAN

1951-73 ND ISSUES

		VG	VF	UNC
8	**1 Rupee** ND (1951). Blue on multicolor underprint. Back violet. Archway at left. Center Like #4. 2 signature varieties.	15.00	60.00	100.
9	**1 Rupee** ND (1953-63). Blue on multicolor underprint. Like #8 but larger size serial #. Back blue. 6 signature varieties.	3.00	5.00	10.00

Note: The scarce sign. is Abdul Qadir, valued at $50. in Unc.

		VG	VF	UNC
9A	**1 Rupee** ND (1964). Blue on multicolor underprint. Back violet. Like #8 but differnt font for serial #. 3 signature varieties.	1.00	2.50	4.50

		VG	VF	UNC
10	**1 Rupee** ND (1973). Brown on multicolor underprint. Like #9.			
	a. Signature 1. *Attab Qazi.*	.50	1.50	3.50
	b. Signature 2. *Abdul Rauf.*	.50	1.50	3.00

STATE BANK OF PAKISTAN

CITY OVERPRINT VARIETIES

ঢাকা ڈھاکہ করাচী کراچی লাহোর لاہور

Dacca Karachi Lahore

Some notes exist w/Urdu and some w/Bengali ovpt. denoting city of issue, Dacca, Karachi or Lahore. These are much scarcer than the regular issues. Sign. varieties.

1957-66 ND ISSUE

#15-19 Portr. Mohammed Ali Jinnah and as wmk.

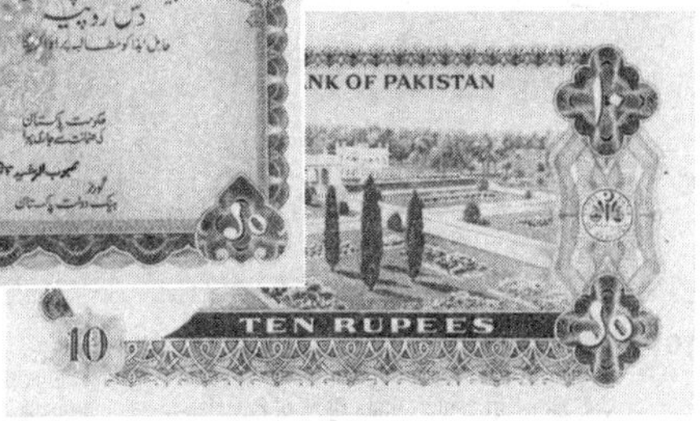

		VG	VF	UNC
15	**5 Rupees** ND (1966). Purple on light blue and maroon underprint. Mohammed Ali Jinnah at center. Terraces on back. Three signature varieties	2.00	3.50	6.00

16 **10 Rupees**
ND (1970). Brown on multicolor underprint. Portrait Mohammed Ali Jinnah at left. Shalimar Gardens on back. Two signature varieties.

	VG	VF	UNC
a. Latin signature	2.50	7.50	15.00
b. Urdu & Bengali signature	2.00	6.00	12.50

17 **50 Rupees**
ND (1964). Blue-green on peach underprint. Portrait Mohammed Ali Jinnah at center. Back green; sailing ships. Three signature varieties.

	VG	VF	UNC
a. Latin signature 2 signature varieties.	2.50	6.00	10.00
b. 1 Urdu and 1 Bengali signature of the same signatory.	2.50	6.00	10.00

18 **100 Rupees**
ND (1957). Green on violet and peach underprint. Mohammed Ali Jinnah at center. Badshahi Mosque in Lahore on back.

	VG	VF	UNC
a. Without overprint. 2 signature varieties.	3.00	6.00	10.00
b. Ovpt: *Dhaka.* 2 signature varieties.	3.00	6.00	10.00
c. Ovpt: *Karachi.* 2 signature varieties.	3.00	6.00	10.00
d. Ovpt: *Lahore.* 2 signature varieties.	3.00	6.00	10.00

19 **500 Rupees**
ND (1964). Red on gold and light green underprint. Mohammed Ali Jinnah at center. State Bank of Pakistan building on back.

	VG	VF	UNC
a. Ovpt: *Dhaka.*	15.00	25.00	50.00
b. Ovpt: *Karachi.* 2 signature varieties.	10.00	20.00	35.00
c. Ovpt: *Lahore.*	10.00	20.00	35.00

1973 ND Issue

#20-23 Mohammed Ali Jinnah at ctr. or l. and as wmk.

20 **5 Rupees**
ND (1972-78). Orange-brown on pale blue and dull green underprint. Mohammed Ali Jinnah at center. Terraces on back. Three signature varieties.

	VG	VF	UNC
a. Serial # prefix of single or double letters.	2.00	5.00	8.00
b. Serial # prefix fractional with double letters over numerals.	2.00	5.00	8.00

21 **10 Rupees**
ND (1972-75). Green on multicolor underprint. Mohammed Ali Jinnah at left. Shalimar Gardens, Lahore on back. Two signature varieties.

	VG	VF	UNC
a. Sans-serif font for serial #.	2.50	5.00	10.00
b. Serif font for serial #. Printer :TDLR without imprint.	5.00	10.00	20.00
c. Serial # prefix with two **.	15.00	40.00	100.

22 **50 Rupees**
ND (1972-78). Blue on multicolor underprint. Mohammed Ali Jinnah at center. Sailing ships on back. Three signature varieties.

VG	VF	UNC
5.00	12.50	25.00

			VG	VF	UNC
23	100 Rupees	ND (1973-78). Dark blue on multicolor underprint. Mohammed Ali Jinnah at left. Badshahi Mosque, Lahore, on back. Two signature varieties.	7.50	20.00	55.00

Note: The signature variety of Osman Ali is valued at $150. in Unc.

GOVERNMENT OF PAKISTAN

SIGNATURE VARIETIES

1	Abdur Rauf Shaikh	2	Aftab Ahmad Khan
3	Habibullah Baig	4	Izharul-Haq
5	Saeed Ahmad Qureshi	6	R. A. Akhund
7	Qazi Alimullah	8	Khalid Javed
9	Javed Talat	10	Mian Tayeb Hasan
11	Moeen Afzal	12	Mohammad Younus Khan

1975 ND ISSUE

			VG	VF	UNC
24	1 Rupee	ND (1974). Blue on light green and lilac underprint. Arms at right and as watermark. Minar-i-Pakistan monument at left on back. Lower border on face is 14mm high and includes text in four languages. Signature 1.	5.00	10.00	35.00

			VG	VF	UNC
24A	1 Rupee	ND (1975-81). Blue on light green and lilac underprint. Like #24, but new broader panel is 22mm high and without four-language text along bottom face. Arms at right and as watermark. Minar-i-Pakistan monument at left on back. Signature 1-3.	1.00	2.00	3.50

NOTICE

Readers with unlisted dates, signature varieties, etc. are invited to submit photocopies of their notes to: Standard Catalog of World Paper Money, 700 East State St. Iola, WI 54990-0001, E-Mail: george.cuhaj@fwpubs.com.

1981-83 ND ISSUE

رزقِ حلال عین عبادت ہے

URDU TEXT LINE A

حصولِ رزقِ حلال عبادت ہے

URDU TEXT LINE B

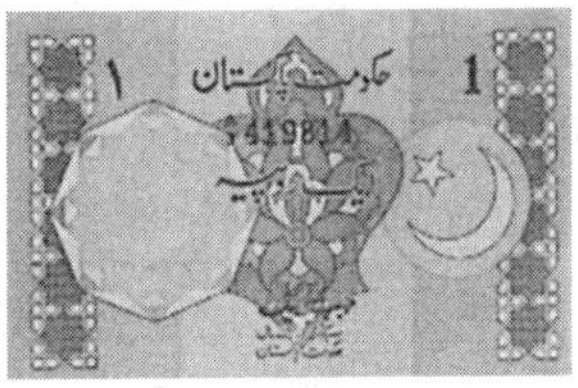

			VG	VF	UNC
25	1 Rupee	ND (1981-82). Dull brown on multicolor underprint. Arms at right and as watermark. Tomb of Allama Mohammed Iqbal on back. No Urdu text line at bottom on back. Serial # at upper center. Signature 3.	1.00	2.00	3.50

			VG	VF	UNC
26	1 Rupee	ND (1982). Dull brown on multicolor underprint. Like #25 but with Urdu text line A at bottom on back.			
		a. Serial # at upper center. Signature 3.	1.00	2.00	3.00
		b. Serial # at lower right. Signature 3.	1.00	2.00	3.00

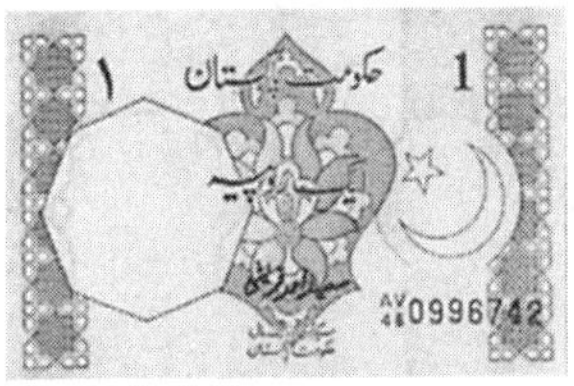

			VG	VF	UNC
27	1 Rupee	ND (1983-). Like #26 but with Urdu text line B at bottom on back.			
		a. Serial # at upper center. Signature 3.	.50	1.00	2.00
		b. Serial # at lower right. Signature 3.	.25	.50	1.00
		c. As a. Signature 4.	.50	1.00	2.00
		d. As b. Signature 4.	.25	.50	1.00
		e. As a. Signature 5.	.50	1.00	2.00
		f. As b. Signature 5.	.25	.50	1.00
		g. As a. Signature 6.	.50	1.00	2.00
		h. As b. Signature 6.	.25	.50	1.00
		i. As a. Signature 7.	.50	1.00	2.00
		j. As b. Signature 7.	.25	.50	1.00
		k. As b. Signature 8.	.25	.50	1.00
		l. As b. Signature 9.	.25	.50	1.00
		m. As b. Signature 10.	.25	.50	1.00
		n. As b. Signature 11.	.25	.50	1.00
		o. As b. Signature 13.	.25	.50	1.00

STATE BANK OF PAKISTAN

1976-77 ND ISSUE

#28-31 Mohammed Ali Jinnah at r. and as wmk. Serial # and sign. varieties.

			VG	VF	UNC
28	5 Rupees	ND (1976-84). Dark brown on tan and pink underprint. Khajak railroad tunnel on back. No Urdu text line beneath upper title on back. Two signature varieties.	1.00	2.50	4.00

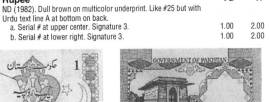

		VG	VF	UNC
29	**10 Rupees** ND (1976-84). Pale olive-green on multicolor underprint. View of Moenjodaro on back. No Urdu text line beneath upper title on back. Two signature varieties.	1.00	2.50	4.00
30	**50 Rupees** ND (1977-84). Purple on multicolor underprint. Main gate of Lahore fort on back. No Urdu text line beneath upper title on back. Two signature varieties.	2.50	5.00	12.50

		VG	VF	UNC
31	**100 Rupees** ND (1976-84). Red and orange on multicolor underprint. Islamic College, Peshawar, on back. No Urdu text line beneath upper title on back. Two signature varieties.	5.00	12.50	25.00

1981-82 ND Issue

#33-36 Mohammed Ali Jinnah at r. and as wmk.

#32 Deleted.

		VG	VF	UNC
33	**5 Rupees** ND (1981-82). Dark brown on tan and pink underprint. Like #28 but with Urdu text line A beneath upper title on back.	1.00	2.50	5.00
34	**10 Rupees** ND (1981-82). Pale olive-green on multicolor underprint. Like #29 but with Urdu text line A beneath upper title on back.	1.00	2.50	5.00

		VG	VF	UNC
35	**50 Rupees** ND (1981-82). Purple on multicolor underprint. Like #30 but with Urdu text line A beneath upper title on back.	3.00	7.50	12.50

		VG	VF	UNC
36	**100 Rupees** ND (1981-82). Red and orange on multicolor underprint. Like #31 but with Urdu text line A beneath upper title on back.	5.00	12.50	25.00

1983-88 ND Issue

		VG	VF	UNC
37	**2 Rupees** ND (1985-99). Pale purple on multicolor underprint. Arms at right and as watermark. Badshahi mosque on back. Urdu text line B beneath upper title on back. Five signature varieties.	1.00	2.00	4.00

Note: #37 shade varieties exist. #38-43 Mohammed Ali Jinnah at r. and as wmk.

		VG	VF	UNC
38	**5 Rupees** ND (1983-84). Dark brown on tan and pink underprint. Like #28 but with Urdu text line B beneath upper title on back. Six signature varieties.	FV	FV	1.00

		VG	VF	UNC
39	**10 Rupees** ND (1983-84). Pale olive-green on multicolor underprint. Like #29 but with Urdu text line B beneath upper title on back. Six signature varieties.	FV	FV	1.50

		VG	VF	UNC
40	**50 Rupees** ND (1986-). Purple on multicolor underprint. Like #30 but with Urdu text line B beneath upper title on back. Six signature varieties.	FV	FV	6.00
41	**100 Rupees** ND (1986-). Red and orange on multicolor underprint. Like #31 but with Urdu text line B beneath upper title on back. Six signature varieties.	FV	FV	7.50

		VG	VF	UNC
42	**500 Rupees** ND (1986-). Deep blue-green and olive-green on multicolor underprint. State Bank of Pakistan building at center on back. Six signature varieties.	FV	FV	30.00

		VG	VF	UNC
43	**1000 Rupees** ND (1988-). Deep purple and blue-black on multicolor underprint. Tomb of Jahangir on back. Four signature varieties.	FV	FV	50.00

1997 Commemorative Issue

#44, Golden Jubilee of Independence, 1947-1997

		VG	VF	UNC
44	**5 Rupees** 1997. Dull violet on light green and pale orange-brown underprint. Star-burst with text and dates at left, Mohammed Ali Jinnah at right and as watermark. Tomb of Shah Ruke-e-Alam at left center, bank seal at upper right on back.	2.00	3.50	5.00

Regional

State Bank of Pakistan

1950 ND Haj Pilgrim Issue

		VG	VF	UNC
R3	**10 Rupees** ND. Green on multicolor underprint. Like #16 but with overprint. Two signature varieties.	15.00	40.00	75.00

		VG	VF	UNC
R4	**10 Rupees** ND. Purple on multicolor underprint. Like #16 and #21 but with overprint.	5.00	7.00	10.00

		VG	VF	UNC
R5	**100 Rupees** ND. Brown on multicolor underprint. Like #23; black overprint.	50.00	100.	225.

1970 ND Haj Pilgrim Issue

Haj Pilgrim notes were discontinued in 1994 and notes on hand were destroyed.

		VG	VF	UNC
R6	**10 Rupees** ND (1978). Blue-black on multicolor underprint. Like #34; black overprint.	4.00	7.00	10.00

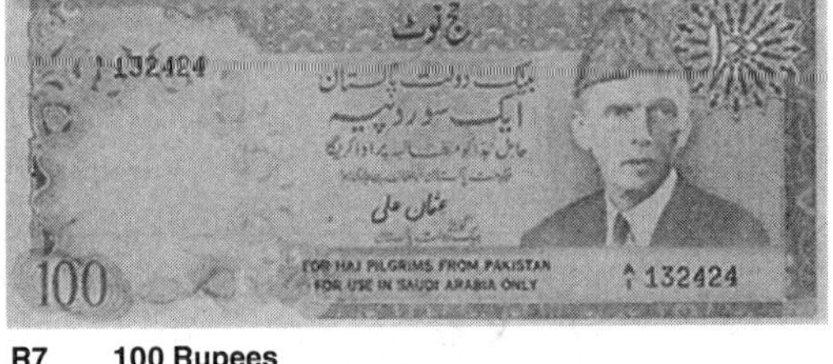

		VG	VF	UNC
R7	**100 Rupees** ND (1975-78). Gold on multicolor underprint. Like #31; dark brown overprint. Two signature varieties.	5.00	10.00	20.00

PAPUA NEW GUINEA

Papua New Guinea, an independent member of the British Commonwealth, occupies the eastern half of the island of New Guinea. It lies north of Australia near the equator and borders on West Irian. The country, which includes nearby Bismarck Archipelago, Buka and Bougainville, has an area of 176,280 sq. mi. (461,691 sq. km.) and a population of 4.81 million who are divided into more than 1,000 separate tribes speaking more than 700 mutually unintelligible languages. Capital: Port Moresby. The economy is agricultural, and exports include copra, rubber, cocoa, coffee, tea, gold and copper.

New Guinea, the world's largest island after Greenland, was discovered by Spanish navigator Jorge de Menezes, who landed on the northwest shore in 1527. European interests, attracted by exaggerated estimates of the resources of the area, resulted in the island being claimed in whole or part by Spain, the Netherlands, Great Britain and Germany.

Papua (formerly British New Guinea), situated in the southeastern part of the island of New Guinea, has an area of 90,540 sq. mi. (234,499 sq. km.) and a population of 740,000. It was temporarily annexed by Queensland in 1883 and by the British Crown in 1888. Papua came under control of the Australian Commonwealth in 1901 and became the Territory of Papua in 1900. Japan invaded New Guinea and Papua early in 1942, but Australian control was restored before the end of the year in Papua and in 1945 in New Guinea.

In 1884 Germany annexed the area known as German New Guinea (also Neu-Guinea or Kaiser Wilhelmsland) comprising the northern section of eastern New Guinea, and granted its administration and development to the New-Guinea Compagnie. Administration reverted to Germany in 1889 following the failure of the company to exercise adequate administration. While a German protectorate, German New Guinea had an area of 92,159 sq. mi. (238,692 sq. km.) and a population of about 250,000. Capital: Herbertshohe, later named Rabaul. Copra was the chief crop. Australian troops occupied German New Guinea in Aug. 1914, shortly after Great Britain declared war on Germany. It was mandated to Australia by the League of Nations in 1920 and known as the Territory of New Guinea. The territory was invaded and occupied by Japan in 1942. Following the Japanese surrender, it came under U.N. trusteeship, Dec. 13, 1946, with Australia as the administering power.

The Papua and New Guinea Act, 1949, provided for the government of Papua and New Guinea as one administrative unit. On Dec. 1, 1973, Papua New Guinea became self-governing with Australia retaining responsibility for defense and foreign affairs. Full independence was achieved on Sept. 16, 1975 and Papua New Guinea is now a member of the Commonwealth of Nations. The Queen of England is Chief of State.

RULERS:
British

MONETARY SYSTEM:
1 Kina = 100 Toea, 1975-

BRITISH ADMINISTRATION

BANK OF PAPUA NEW GUINEA

SIGNATURE VARIETIES	
1	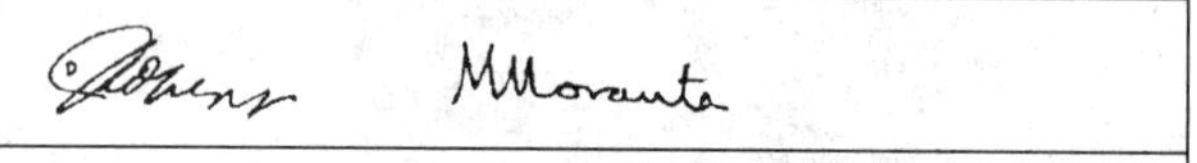
2	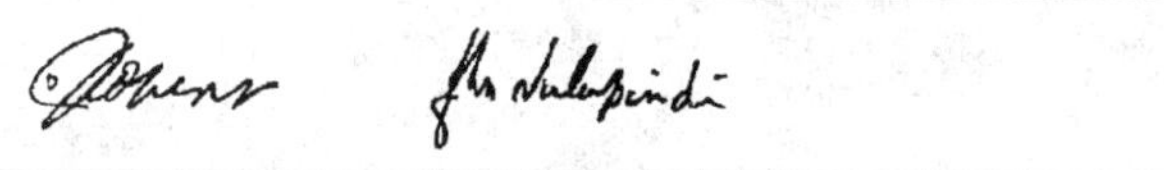
3	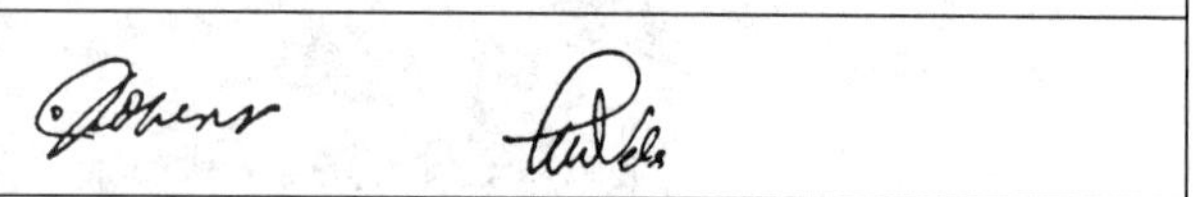
4	
5	
6	
7	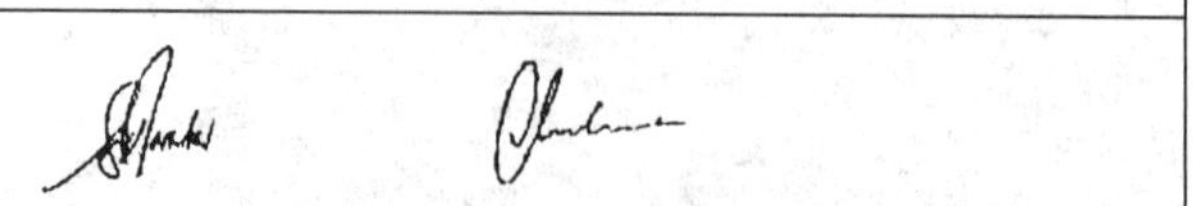
8	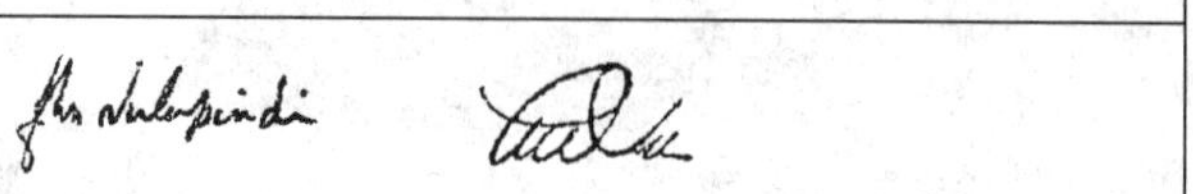
9	
10	

1975 ISSUE

#1-4 stylized Bird of Paradise at l. ctr. and as wmk.

			VG	VF	UNC
1	**2 Kina**	ND (1975). Black on light green and multicolor underprint. Artifacts on back. Signature 1.			
		a. Issued note.	1.50	6.00	17.50
		s. Specimen.	—	—	35.00

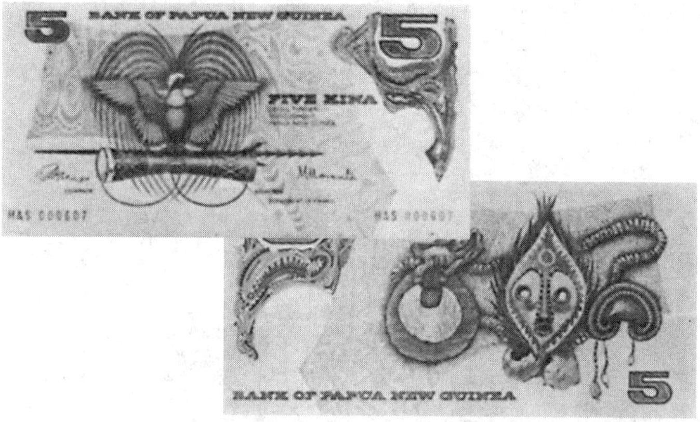

			VG	VF	UNC
2	**5 Kina**	ND (1975). Violet and purple on multicolor underprint. Mask at center right on back. Signature 1.	3.00	8.50	27.50

			VG	VF	UNC
3	**10 Kina**	ND (1975). Dark blue-green and purple on multicolor underprint. Bowl, ring and other artifacts on back. Signature 1.	7.50	20.00	60.00

			VG	VF	UNC
4	**20 Kina**	ND (1977). Dark brown and deep red on multicolor underprint. Boar's head at right on back. Signature 1.	10.00	25.00	80.00

1981-85 Issues

		VG	VF	UNC
5	**2 Kina**			
	ND (1981). Black and dark green on light green and multicolor underprint. Like #1. White strip 16mm wide at right.			
	a. Signature 1.	FV	FV	10.00
	b. Signature 2.	FV	7.50	30.00
	c. Signature 3.	FV	FV	7.50
6	**5 Kina**			
	ND (1981). Violet and purple on multicolor underprint. Like #2. White strip 22mm wide at right.			
	a. Signature 1.	FV	6.50	30.00
	b. Signature 2.	FV	7.00	32.50
7	**10 Kina**			
	ND (1985). Dark blue, purple and green on multicolor underprint. Like #3. White strip 18mm wide at right. Signature 1.	FV	10.00	50.00

#8 Held in Reserve.

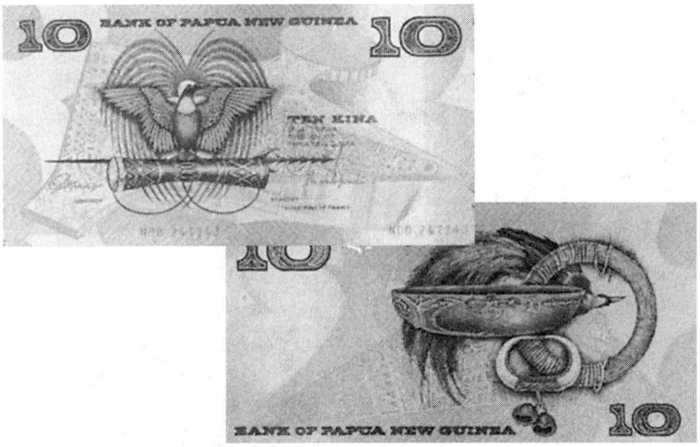

		VG	VF	UNC
9	**10 Kina**			
	ND (1988). Dark blue, dark green and brown-violet on multicolor underprint. Similar to #7 but different design elements in underprint representing a modern building. Ornate corner designs omitted on face and back.			
	a. Signature 2.	FV	15.00	85.00
	b. Signature 3.	FV	FV	25.00
	c. Signature 5.	FV	FV	22.50
	d. Signature 7.	FV	FV	22.50
	e. Signature 8.	FV	FV	22.50

		VG	VF	UNC
10	**20 Kina**			
	ND. Dark brown and deep red on multicolor underprint. Similar to #4 but different design elements in underprint.			
	a. Signature 3.	FV	FV	50.00
	b. Signature 6.	FV	FV	40.00
	c. Signature 8.	FV	FV	30.00
	d. Signature 10.	FV	FV	35.00

		VG	VF	UNC
11	**50 Kina**			
	ND (1989). Brown, red, blue and multicolor underprint. National Parliament building at center. Foreign Affairs Minister M. Somare at left center, ceremonial masks at right on back. Watermark: Central Bank logo. Signature 3. Paper.	FV	FV	75.00

1991 Commemorative Issue

#12, 9th South Pacific Games 1991

		VG	VF	UNC
12	**2 Kina**			
	1991. Black and dark green on light green and multicolor underprint. Similar to #5 but with stylized Bird of Paradise in clear circle at lower right. Polymer plastic. Signature 3. Printer: NPA (without imprint).	FV	FV	6.50

1992; 1993 ND Regular Issues

#12A, 13 and 14: stylized Bird of Paradise at l. ctr. and as wmk.

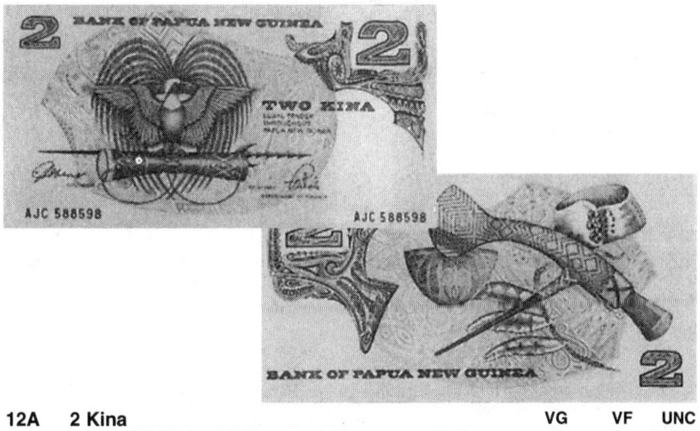

		VG	VF	UNC
12A	**2 Kina**			
	ND (1992). Black and dark green on light green and multicolor underprint. Like #5 but most design elements much lighter. Serial # darker and heavier type face. Signature 3. Paper.	FV	FV	6.00

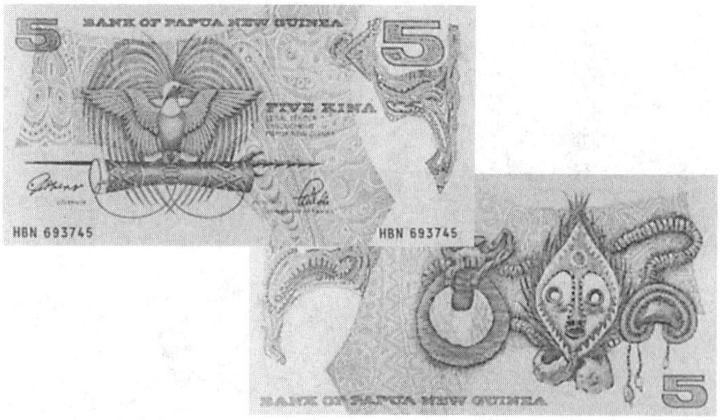

13 5 Kina

ND (1992). Violet and purple on multicolor underprint. Like #6 but most design elements much lighter. Serial # darker, heavier type face. Paper.

	VG	VF	UNC
a. Signature 3.	FV	FV	15.00
b. Signature 7.	FV	FV	15.00
c. Signature 9.	FV	FV	7.50
d. Signature 10.	FV	FV	5.00

14 5 Kina

ND (1993). Violet and purple on multicolor underprint. Like #13 but with segmented security thread and new signature title: *Secretary for Finance and Planning*. Paper.

	VG	VF	UNC
a. Signature 4.	FV	FV	12.50
b. Signature 5.	FV	FV	12.50

1995 ND Commemorative Issue

#15, 20th Anniversary of Independence

15 2 Kina

ND (1995). Black and dark green on light green and multicolor underprint. Similar to #12 but with ornate *20 ANNIVERSARY* logo at left, *PNG 20* at lower left. Signature 5. Polymer plastic. Printer: NPA (without imprint).

VG	VF	UNC
FV	FV	7.50

1996 ND Regular Issue

16 2 Kina

ND (1996). Black and dark green on light green and multicolor underprint. Similar to #12A and 15. Polymer plastic.

	VG	VF	UNC
a. Signature 6.	FV	FV	5.50
b. Signature 7.	FV	FV	5.50
c. Signature 10.	FV	FV	5.00

1998 Commemorative Issue

#17, Bank's 25th Anniversary

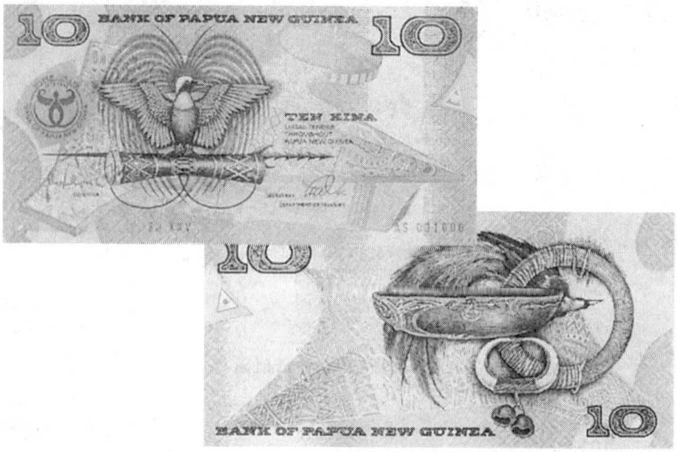

17 10 Kina

1998. Dark blue, dark green and brown-violet on multicolor underprint. Like #9, but signature 8. Silver Jubilee foil with arms and commemorative dates *1973-1998* at left, and *SJ XXV* at lower left center. Paper.

VG	VF	UNC
FV	FV	20.00

1999 Issue

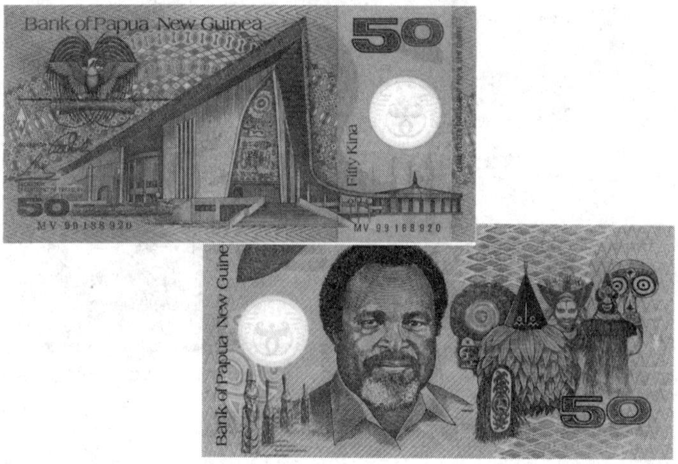

18 50 Kina

1999. Black and red on orange, yellow and multicolor underprint. Similar to #11 but with ornate window design. Polymer plastic. Printer: NPA (without imprint).

	VG	VF	UNC
a. Signature 9.	FV	FV	70.00
b. Signature 10.	FV	FV	65.00

2000 Commemorative Issue

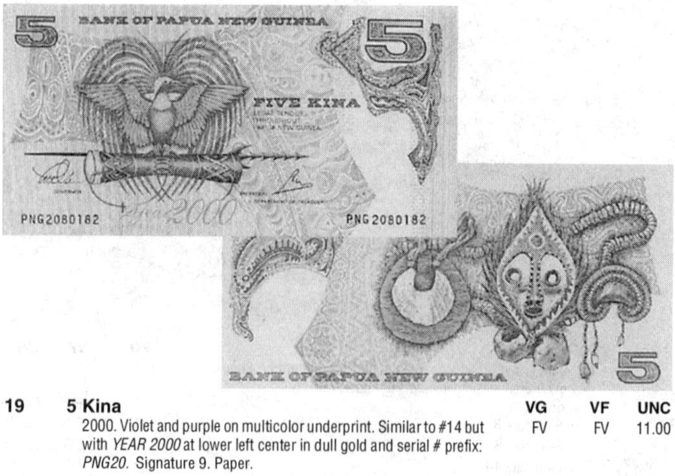

19 5 Kina

2000. Violet and purple on multicolor underprint. Similar to #14 but with *YEAR 2000* at lower left center in dull gold and serial # prefix: *PNG20*. Signature 9. Paper.

VG	VF	UNC
FV	FV	11.00

2000 SECOND COMMEMORATIVE ISSUE

#20 Currency Silver Jubilee

		VG	VF	UNC
20	**5 Kina** 2000. Similar to #19 but with silver imprint at lower center right and red inscription overprint at lower center: *PNG1942000 (19 4 2000 date)*. Paper. Signature 10.	FV	FV	10.00

2000 THIRD COMMEMORATIVE ISSUE

#21-25, Silver Jubilee of PNG. Sign. 10.

		VG	VF	UNC
21	**2 Kina** (20)00. Black and dark green on light green and multicolor underprint. Similar to #16 but with 25th Anniversary logo at left. Polymer plastic.	FV	FV	5.00

		VG	VF	UNC
22	**5 Kina** ND (2000). Similar to # 13 but with 25th Anniversary logo at lower right. Paper. Signature 10.	FV	FV	10.00

		VG	VF	UNC
23	**10 Kina** (20)00. Similar to #17 but with 25th Anniversary logo at left. Polymer plastic.	FV	FV	18.50

		VG	VF	UNC
24	**20 Kina** (20)00. Similat to #10 but with 25th Anniversary logo at left. Paper.	FV	FV	35.00

		VG	VF	UNC
25	**50 Kina** (20)00. Similar to #11 but with 25th Anniversary logo at upper left center. Polymer plasic. Signature 10.	FV	FV	65.00

2000 ISSUE

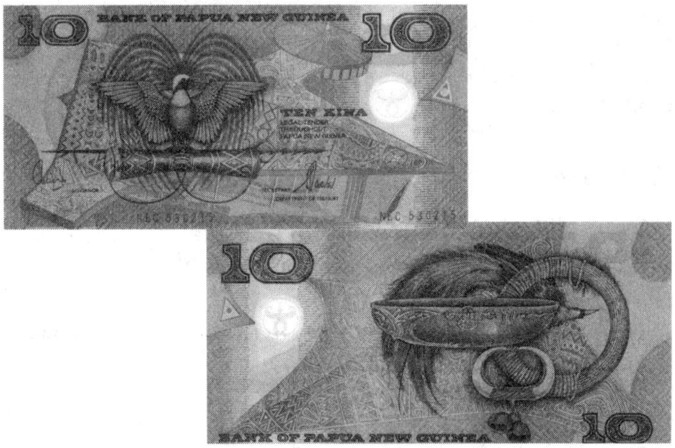

		VG	VF	UNC
26	**10 Kina** July, 2000. Similar to #9. Polymer plastic. Signature 10.	FV	FV	20.00

2004 ISSUE

#27, 30th Anniversary of the Bank.

		VG	VF	UNC
27	**20 Kina** 2004. Polymer plastic.	FV	FV	35.00

The Republic of Paraguay, a landlocked country in the heart of South America surrounded by Argentina, Bolivia and Brazil, has an area of 157,042 sq. mi. (406,752 sq. km.) and a population of 5.5 million, 95 percent of whom are of mixed Spanish and Indian descent. Capital: Asunción. The country is predominantly agrarian, with no important mineral deposits or oil reserves. Meat, timber, oilseeds, tobacco and cotton account for 70 percent of Paraguay's export revenue.

Paraguay was first visited by Alejo Garcia, a shipwrecked Spaniard, in 1520. The interior was explored by Sebastian Cabot in 1526 and 1529, when he sailed up the Paraná and Paraguay Rivers. Asunción, which would become the center of a province embracing much of southern South America, was established by the Spanish explorer Juan de Salazar on Aug. 15, 1537. For a century and a half the history of Paraguay was largely the history of the agricultural colonies established by the Jesuits in the south and east to Christianize the Indians. In 1811, following the outbreak of the South American wars of independence, Paraguayan patriots overthrew the local Spanish authorities and proclaimed their country's independence.

MONETARY SYSTEM:

1 Guaraní = 100 Céntimos, 1944-

REPUBLIC

BANCO CENTRAL DEL PARAGUAY

DECRETO LEY DE NO. 18 DEL 25 DE MARZO DE 1952

(FROM AUG.1963)

#192-201 arms at l. Sign. size and name varieties. Replacement notes: Serial # prefix *Z*. Printer: TDLR.

192	1 Guaraní	VG	VF	UNC
	L.1952. Green on multicolor underprint. Soldier at right. Black serial # at lower left and lower right. Banco Central on back. One signature variety.	.25	1.00	4.00

193	1 Guaraní	VG	VF	UNC
	L.1952. Green on multicolor underprint. Soldier at right. Palacio Legislativo on back. Two signature varieties.			
	a. Black serial # at lower left and lower right.	.10	.25	1.75
	b. Black serial # at upper left and lower right.	.10	.25	1.25
	s. As a. Specimen.	—	—	25.00

194	5 Guaraníes	VG	VF	UNC
	L.1952. Blue on multicolor underprint. Girl holding jug at right, black serial # at lower left and lower right. Hotel Guarani on back. One signature variety.	.25	1.50	6.00

195	5 Guaraníes	VG	VF	UNC
	L.1952. Black on multicolor underprint. Like #194. Two signature varieties.			
	a. Red serial # at lower left and lower right.	.10	.25	1.50
	b. Red serial # at upper left and lower right.	.10	.25	1.25
	s. As a. Specimen.	—	—	25.00

196	10 Guaraníes	VG	VF	UNC
	L.1952. Deep red on multicolor underprint. General Eugenio A. Garay at right. International bridge on back. Two signature varieties.			
	a. Black serial # at lower left and lower right.	.15	.40	2.25
	b. Black serial # at upper left and lower right.	.15	.40	2.00
	s. As a. Specimen.	—	—	25.00

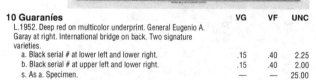

197	50 Guaraníes	VG	VF	UNC
	L.1952. Brown on multicolor underprint. Mariscal José F. Estigarribia at right. Country road on back. Two signature varieties.			
	a. Black serial # at lower left and lower right.	.50	1.75	7.00
	b. Black serial # at upper left and lower right.	.20	.75	4.00
	s. As a. Specimen.	—	—	25.00

198 100 Guaraníes

L.1952. Green on multicolor underprint. General José E. Diaz at right. Black serial # at lower left and lower right. Ruins of Humaita on back. One signature variety (large size signature.)

	VG	VF	UNC
a. Issued note.	.50	3.00	15.00
s. Specimen.	—	—	25.00

Note: Do not confuse green #198 w/later issue #205 also in green. #198 w/value: *CIEN GUARANIES* at bottom on back.

199 100 Guaraníes

L.1952. Orange on multicolor underprint. Like #198. Two signature varieties (small size signature.).

	VG	VF	UNC
a. Black serial # at lower left and lower right.	.50	2.50	7.00
b. Black serial # at upper left and lower right.	.50	1.00	3.00

200 500 Guaraníes

L.1952. Blue-gray on multicolor underprint. General Bernardino Caballero at right. Federal merchant ship on back. Two signature varieties.

	VG	VF	UNC
a. Black serial # at lower left and lower right.	.75	4.00	10.00
b. Black serial # at upper left and lower right.	.50	2.00	6.00
s. As a. Specimen.	—	—	25.00

201 1000 Guaraníes

L.1952. Purple on multicolor underprint. Mariscal Francisco Solano Lopez right. National shrine on back. Two signature varieties.

	VG	VF	UNC
a. Black serial # at lower left and lower right.	2.00	7.50	20.00
b. Black serial # at upper left and lower right.	1.00	6.00	15.00
s. As a. Specimen.	—	—	25.00

#202-204 printer: TDLR.

202 5000 Guaraníes

L.1952. Red-orange on multicolor underprint. Arms at center, Don Carlos Antonio López at right. López Palace on back. Two signature varieties.

	VG	VF	UNC
a. Black serial # at lower left and lower right.	7.50	25.00	60.00
b. Black serial # at upper left and lower right.	5.00	75.00	45.00
s. As a. Specimen.	—	—	25.00

203 10,000 Guaraníes

L.1952. Dark brown on multicolor underprint. Arms at center, Dr. José Caspar Rodriguez De Francia at right, black serial # at lower left and lower right. Historical scene from 14.5.1811 on back. One signature variety.

	VG	VF	UNC
a. Issued note.	10.00	40.00	100.
s. Specimen.	—	—	25.00

204 10,000 Guaraníes

L.1952. Dark brown on multicolor underprint. Like #203 but CASPAR changed to GASPAR below Francia. Two signature varieties.

	VG	VF	UNC
a. Black serial # at lower left and lower right.	10.00	40.00	100.
b. Black serial # at upper left and lower right.		30.00	75.00

1982; 1990 ND Issue

#205-210 replacement notes: Serial # prefix *Z*.

#205-209 like #199-203 except expression of values changed on back from Spanish to native Guaraní. Printer: TDLR.

205 100 Guaraníes — VG .10 | VF .25 | UNC 1.25

L.1952 (1982). Green on multicolor underprint. Like #199 but value on back stated as: SA GUARANI. Four signature varieties.

206 500 Guaraníes — VG FV | VF FV | UNC 1.75

L.1952 (1982). Blue-gray on multicolor underprint. Like #200 but value on back stated as: PO SA GUARANI. Six signature varieties.

207 1000 Guaraníes — VG FV | VF FV | UNC 2.00

L.1952 (1982). Purple on multicolor underprint. Like #201 but value on back stated as: SU GUARANI. Six signature varieties.

208 5000 Guaraníes — VG FV | VF FV | UNC 7.50

L.1952 (1982). Red-orange on multicolor underprint. Like #202 but value on back stated as: PO SU GUARANI. Six signature varieties.

209 10,000 Guaraníes — VG FV | VF FV | UNC 10.00

L.1952 (1982). Dark brown on multicolor underprint. Like #203 but value on back stated as: PA SU GUARANI. Five signature varieties.

210 50,000 Guaraníes — VG FV | VF FV | UNC 45.00

L.1952 (1990). Deep purple and light blue on multicolor underprint. Soldier at right, outline map of Paraguay at center. Back purple and olive-green on multicolor underprint. House of Independence at center. Watermark: Bust of soldier. Plain security thread. Three signature varieties. Printer: TDLR.

1994 ND Issue

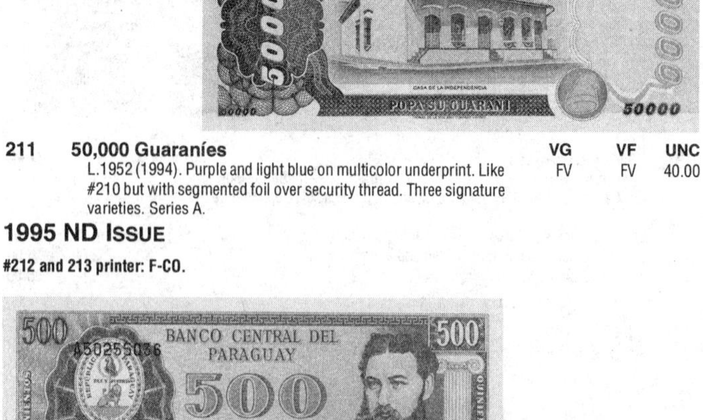

211 50,000 Guaraníes — VG FV | VF FV | UNC 40.00

L.1952 (1994). Purple and light blue on multicolor underprint. Like #210 but with segmented foil over security thread. Three signature varieties. Series A.

1995 ND Issue

#212 and 213 printer: F-CO.

212 **500 Guaraníes** | VG FV | VF FV | UNC 1.25
L.1952 (1995). Blue-gray on multicolor underprint. Like #206. Two signature varieties.

213 **1000 Guaraníes** | VG FV | VF FV | UNC 2.00
L.1952 (1995). Purple on multicolor underprint. Like #207.

LEY 489 DEL 29 DE JUNIO DE 1995; 1997-98 ISSUE

214 **1000 Guaraníes** | VG FV | VF FV | UNC 1.75
1998; 2001; 2003. Purple on multicolor underprint. Like #213. Series B. Printer: Ciccone Calcogra, S.A.

215 **5000 Guaraníes** | VG FV | VF FV | UNC 5.00
1997; 1998. Red-orange on multicolor underprint. Like #208. Silver foil over security thread. Printer: TDLR. Two signature varieties. Series B.

> **NOTICE**
> Readers with unlisted dates, signature varieties, etc. are invited to submit photocopies of their notes to: Standard Catalog of World Paper Money, 700 East State St. Iola, WI 54990-0001, E-Mail: george.cuhaj@fwpubs.com.

216 **10,000 Guaraníes** | VG FV | VF FV | UNC 7.50
1998; 2003. Brown. Like #209. Series B. Printer: Ciccone Calcogra, S.A.

217 **50,000 Guaraníes** | VG FV | VF FV | UNC 27.50
1997. Purple and light blue on multicolor underprint. Like #211. Printer: TDLR. Series B.

218 **50,000 Guaraníes** | VG FV | VF FV | UNC 27.50
1998. Like #217 but with staircase metallic impression at lower left corner on face. Series B. Printer: *(T)DLR.*

219 **100,000 Guaraníes** | VG FV | VF FV | UNC 50.00
1998. Green, yellow-brown and multicolor. San Rogue González de Santa Cruz at right. *Represa de Itaipu,* Itaipu Hydroelectric Dam on back. Printer: TDLR.

2000 Issue

		VG	VF	UNC
220	**5000 Guaraníes** 2000; 2003. Similar to #215. Series C. Printer: CC.	FV	FV	5.00

2002 Commemorative Issue

50th Anniversary of the Banco Cenral del Paraguay

		VG	VF	UNC
221	**1000 Guaraníes** 2002. Purple on multicolor underprint. Like #214 but with anniversary text below date. Printer: F-CO.	FV	FV	1.75

2004 Issue

		VG	VF	UNC
222	**1000 Guaraníes** 2004. Like #221 but without anniversary text. Printer: F-CO.	FV	FV	1.75

		VG	VF	UNC
223	**5000 Guaraníes** 2004. Brown.	FV	FV	5.00

		VG	VF	UNC
224	**10,000 Guaraníes** 2004. Green. Printer: (T)DLR.	FV	FV	10.00
225	**20,000 Guaraníes** 2004.	FV	FV	20.00

2005 Issue

		VG	VF	UNC
226	**1000 Guaraníes** 2005. Purple on multicolor underprint.. Francisco Solano Lopez at right. Church of the Assuncion at center on back. Printer: DLR.	FV	FV	2.00
227	**5000 Guaraníes** 2005. Orange on multicolor underprint. Don Carlos Antonio Lopez at right. Lopez Palace at center on back. Printer: DLR.	FV	FV	5.00
228	**20,000 Guaraníes** 2005. Multicolor.	FV	FV	—
229	**100,000 Guaraníes** 2004. Multicolor. Printer: DLR.	FV	FV	10.00
230	**100,000 Guaraníes** 2005. Multicolor. Printer: F-CO.	FV	FV	10.00

Collector Series

Banco Central del Paraguay

1979 Issue

		Issue Price	Mkt. Value
CS1	**100-10,000 Guaraníes** L.1972 (1979). 199b-202b, 204b overprint: SPECIMEN and with serial # prefix Maltese cross.	—	25.00

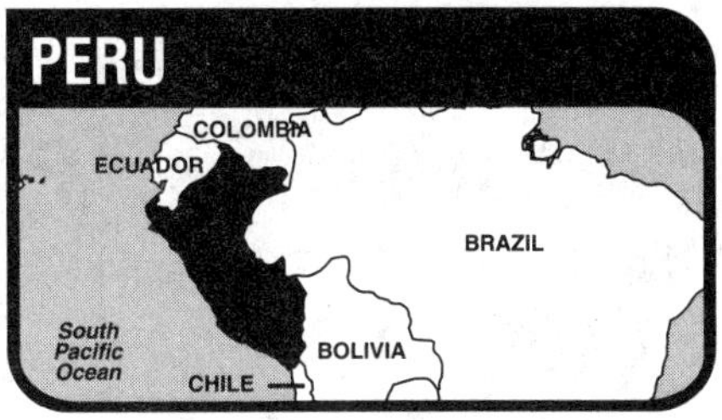

The Republic of Perú, located on the Pacific coast of South America, has an area of 496,222 sq. mi. (1,285,216 sq. km.) and a population of 25.66 million. Capital: Lima. The diversified economy includes mining, fishing and agriculture. Fish meal, copper, sugar, zinc and iron ore are exported.

Once part of a great Inca Empire that reached from northern Ecuador to central Chile, Perú was conquered in 1531-33 by Francisco Pizarro. Desirable as the richest of the Spanish viceroyalties, it was torn by warfare between avaricious Spaniards until the arrival in 1569 of Francisco de Toledo, who initiated 2 1/2 centuries of efficient colonial rule which made Lima the most aristocratic colonial capital and the stronghold of Spain's South American possessions. José de San Martín of Argentina proclaimed Perú's independence on July 28, 1821; Simón Bolívar of Venezuela secured it in Dec. of 1824 when he defeated the last Spanish army in South America. After several futile attempts to re-establish its South American empire, Spain recognized Perú's independence in 1879.

MONETARY SYSTEM:

1 Sol = 1 Sol de Oro = 100 Centavos, 1879-1985
1 Libra = 10 Soles
1 Inti = 1000 Soles de Oro, 1986-1991
1 Nuevo Sol = 100 Centimes = 1 Million Intis, 1991-

REPÚBLICA DEL PERÚ

BANCO CENTRAL DE RESERVA DEL PERU

LEY 10535, 1956 ISSUE

#76-80 seated Liberty holding shield and staff at ctr. Arms at ctr. on back. Sign. varieties.

		VG	VF	UNC
76	**5 Soles** 22.3.1956; 18.3.1960. Green on patterned light blue underprint. Seated Liberty holding shield and staff at center. Like #70. Arms at center. Printer: TDLR.	.50	1.50	5.00
77	**10 Soles** 9.7.1956. Orange on multicolor underprint. Seated Liberty holding shield and staff at center. Similar to #71. Arms at center. Printer: G&D.	2.00	6.00	20.00

#78-80 printer: TDLR.

		VG	VF	UNC
78	**50 Soles** 22.3.1956; 24.10.1957; 13.5.1959. Dark blue on lilac underprint. Seated Liberty holding shield and staff at center. Serial # at upper left and right. Like #72. Arms at center. Printer: TDLR.			
	a. Issued note.	1.50	4.50	17.50
	s. Specimen.	—	—	—
79	**100 Soles** 1956-61. Black on light blue underprint. Seated Liberty holding shield and staff at center. Like #73 but different guilloche. Black. Arms at center. Printer: TDLR.			
	a. *LIMA* at lower left 22.3.1956; 24.10.1957.	4.00	12.00	30.00
	b. *LIMA* at lower right. With date. 13.5.1959.	4.00	12.00	30.00
	c. As b. Series and serial # at lower left and upper right. 1.2.1961.	4.00	12.00	30.00
	s. As a. Specimen.	—	—	—

		VG	VF	UNC
80	**500 Soles** 1956-61. Brown on light brown and lilac underprint. Seated Liberty holding shield and staff at center. Similar to #74. Brown. Arms at center. Printer: TDLR.			
	a. Series and serial # at upper corners. 22.3.1956; 24.10.1957.	8.00	25.00	75.00
	b. Series and serial # at lower left and upper right. 10.12.1959; 16.6.1961.	8.00	25.00	75.00
	s. As b. Specimen.	—	—	—

1958 ISSUE

#81-82 printer: W&S.

		VG	VF	UNC
81	**5 Soles** 21.8.1958. Green. Seated Liberty holding shield and staff at center. Arms at center. Like #70 but different guilloche. Printer: W&S.	1.00	4.00	7.50

		VG	VF	UNC
82	**10 Soles** 21.8.1958. Orange on multicolor underprint. Seated Liberty holding shield and staff at center. Similar to #71. Orange. Arms at center. Printer: W&S.	1.00	4.00	15.00

1960 ISSUE

		VG	VF	UNC
82A	**10 Soles** 8.7.1960; 1.2.1961. Orange on multicolor underprint. Liberty seated holding shield and staff at center. Serial # and series at lower left and upper right. Printer: TDLR.	.75	1.50	6.00

REPUBLIC

BANCO CENTRAL DE RESERVA DEL PERÚ

LEY 13958, 1962; 1964 ISSUE

#83-87 Liberty seated holding shield and staff at ctr. Arms at ctr. on back. Printer: TDLR.

		VG	VF	UNC
83	**5 Soles de Oro** 9.2.1962; 20.9.1963; 18.6.1965; 18.11.1966; 23.2.1968. Green on multicolor underprint. Serial # at lower left and upper right. Series J.			
	a. Issued note.	.25	1.00	4.00
	s. Specimen.	—	—	25.00

		VG	VF	UNC
84	**10 Soles de Oro** 8.6.1962; 20.9.1963; 20.5.1966; 25.5.1967; 23.2.1968. Orange on multicolor underprint. Series I.			
	a. Issued note.	.25	1.50	4.00
	s. Specimen.	—	—	25.00

85 **50 Soles de Oro**

9.2.1962; 20.9.1963; 23.2.1968. Blue on multicolor underprint. Serial # at lower left and upper right. Series H.

	VG	VF	UNC
a. Issued note.	.75	3.50	12.50
s. Specimen.	—	—	25.00

86 **100 Soles de Oro**

13.3.1964; 23.2.1968. Black on light blue and multicolor underprint. Series G.

	VG	VF	UNC
a. Issued note.	2.00	6.00	20.00
s. Specimen.	—	—	25.00

87 **500 Soles de Oro**

9.2.1962; 20.9.1963; 20.5.1966; 23.2.1968. Brown on light brown and multicolor underprint. Series L.

	VG	VF	UNC
a. Issued note.	3.00	10.00	40.00
s. Specimen.	—	—	25.00

1962; 1965 Issue

#88-91 like #84-87. *Pagará al Portador* added under bank name at top ctr. Printer: ABNC.

88 **10 Soles de Oro**

	VG	VF	UNC
26.2.1965. Red-orange on light green and multicolor underprint. Series C.	.50	2.00	7.50

89 **50 Soles de Oro**

20.8.1965. Blue on multicolor underprint. Series B.

	VG	VF	UNC
a. Issued note.	1.00	5.00	20.00
s. Specimen.	—	—	100.

90 **100 Soles de Oro**

12.9.1962; 20.8.1965. Black on light blue and multicolor underprint. Series A.

	VG	VF	UNC
a. Issued note.	2.00	6.50	22.50
s. Specimen.	—	—	100.

91 **500 Soles de Oro**

		VG	VF	UNC
91	26.2.1965. Brown on multicolor underprint. Series P.	7.50	25.00	70.00

LEY 13 958 1968 ISSUE

#92-98 arms at ctr. 3 sign. Printer: TDLR.

Replacement notes: Serial # *Z999* . . .

92 **5 Soles de Oro**

	VG	VF	UNC
23.2.1968. Green on multicolor underprint. Artifacts at left, Inca Pachacútec at right. Fortaleza de Sacsahuaman on back. Series J.			
a. Issued note.	.25	.75	3.00
s. Specimen.	—	—	25.00

93 **10 Soles de Oro**

	VG	VF	UNC
23.2.1968. Red-orange on multicolor underprint. Building at left, Garcilaso Inca de la Vega at right. Lake Titicaca, boats on back. Series I.			
a. Issued note.	.20	.50	2.00
s. Specimen.	—	—	25.00

94 **50 Soles de Oro**

	VG	VF	UNC
23.2.1968. Blue-gray on multicolor underprint. Workers at left, Tupac Amaru II at right. Scene of historic town of Tinta on back. Series H.			
a. Issued note.	.25	1.00	5.00
s. Specimen.	—	—	25.00

95 **100 Soles de Oro**

	VG	VF	UNC
23.2.1968. Black on multicolor underprint. Dock workers at left, Hipolito Unanue at right. Church, site of first National Congress on back. Series G.			
a. Issued note.	.50	1.50	6.50
s. Specimen.	—	—	25.00

96 **200 Soles de Oro**

	VG	VF	UNC
23.2.1968. Purple on multicolor underprint. Fishermen at left, Ramon Castilla at right. Frigate *Amazonas* at center on back. Series Q.			
a. Issued note.	1.00	3.50	12.50
s. Specimen.	—	—	25.00

97 **500 Soles de Oro**

	VG	VF	UNC
23.2.1968. Brown on multicolor underprint., tan near center. Builders at left, Nicolas de Pierola at right. National mint on back. Series L.			
a. Issued note.	2.00	3.00	20.00
s. Specimen.	—	—	25.00

98 **1000 Soles de Oro**

23.2.1968. Violet on multicolor underprint. Miguel Grau at left, Francisco Bolognesi (misspelled BOLOGÑESI) at right. Scene of Machu Picchu on back. Series R.

	VG	VF	UNC
a. Issued note.	4.00	12.50	30.00
s. Specimen.	—	—	25.00

1969 ISSUE

#99-105 like #92-98 but text changed to: *De Acuerdo Con Su Ley Organica*. 2 sign. Printer: TDLR.

Replacement notes: Serial # *Z999 . . .*

		VG	VF	UNC
99	**5 Soles de Oro**			
	1969-74. Like #92. Series J.			
	a. 20.6.1969.	.10	.25	2.50
	b. 16.10.1970; 9.9.1971; 4.5.1972.	.10	.25	2.00
	c. 24.5.1973; 16.5.1974; 15.8.1974.	.10	.25	1.25
100	**10 Soles de Oro**			
	1969-74. Like #93. Series I.			
	a. 20.6.1969.	.10	.25	2.00
	b. 16.10.1970; 9.9.1971.	.10	.25	1.50
	c. 4.5.1972; 24.5.1973; 16.5.1974.	.10	.25	1.50
101	**50 Soles de Oro**			
	1969-74. Like #94. Series H.			
	a. 20.6.1969.	.20	.50	5.00
	b. 16.10.1970; 9.9.1971; 4.5.1972.	.20	.50	4.00
	c. 24.5.1973; 16.5.1974; 15.8.1974.	.20	.50	2.50
102	**100 Soles de Oro**			
	1969-74. Like #95. Series G.			
	a. 20.6.1969.	.25	1.00	5.00
	b. 16.10.1970; 9.9.1971; 4.5.1972.	.20	.50	3.50
	c. 24.5.1973; 16.5.1974; 15.8.1974.	.20	.50	3.00
103	**200 Soles de Oro**			
	1969-74. Like #96. Series Q.			
	a. 20.6.1969.	.50	3.00	10.00
	b. 24.5.1973; 16.5.1974; 15.8.1974.	.50	2.00	9.00

		VG	VF	UNC
104	**500 Soles de Oro**			
	1969-74. Like #97. Series L.			
	a. 20.6.1969.	1.00	5.00	20.00
	b. 16.10.1970; 9.9.1971; 4.5.1972; 24.5.1973.	1.00	4.00	15.00
	c. 16.5.1974; 15.8.1974.	.50	2.50	10.00

		VG	VF	UNC
105	**1000 Soles de Oro**			
	1969-73. Like #98 but *BOLOGNESI* correctly spelled at right. Series R.			
	a. 20.6.1969; 16.10.1970.	1.50	7.50	30.00
	b. 9.9.1971; 4.5.1972; 24.5.1973.	1.50	5.00	25.00

1975 ISSUE

#106-111 3 sign. Printer: TDLR.

Replacement notes: Serial # *Z999 . . .*

		VG	VF	UNC
106	**10 Soles de Oro**			
	2.10.1975. Like #93. Series I.	.10	.25	1.50

		VG	VF	UNC
107	**50 Soles de Oro**			
	2.10.1975. Like #94. Series H.	.10	.25	1.50
108	**100 Soles de Oro**			
	2.10.1975. Like #95. Series G.	.20	.50	2.50

#109 Not assigned.

		VG	VF	UNC
110	**500 Soles de Oro**			
	2.10.1975. Like #97. Pale green underprint near center. Series L.	1.00	3.00	15.00

		VG	VF	UNC
111	**1000 Soles de Oro**			
	2.10.1975. Like #98. Name correctly spelled. Series R.	2.00	5.00	27.50

1976-77 ISSUES

#112 and 113 w/o *Pagará al Portador* at top. W/o security thread. 3 sign. Printer: TDLR. Replacement notes: Serial # *Z999....*

		VG	VF	UNC
112	**10 Soles de Oro** 17.11.1976. Like #106. Series I. Printer: TDLR.	.10	.25	1.50
113	**50 Soles de Oro** 15.12.1977. Like #107. Series H. Printer: TDLR.	.10	.25	1.25

#114-115 printer: IPS-Roma.

114	**100 Soles de Oro** 22.7.1976. Green, brown and multicolor. Arms at left, Tupac Amaru II at right. Machu Picchu on back.	.10	.25	1.25

		VG	VF	UNC
115	**500 Soles de Oro** 22.7.1976. Green, blue and yellow. Arms at center, Jose Quiñones at right. Logging scene on back.	.05	.25	1.50

#116 and 117 printer: BDDK. Replacement notes: Serial # prefix *Y*, and suffix letter *A*.

		VG	VF	UNC
116	**1000 Soles de Oro** 22.7.1976. Black, green, brown and multicolor. Arms at center, Miguel Grau at right. Fishermen on back.	.50	2.00	7.50

		VG	VF	UNC
117	**5000 Soles de Oro** 1976-85. Brown and maroon on multicolor underprint. Arms at center, Col. Bolognesi at right and as watermark. Two miners in mine at left on back.			
	a. 22.7.1976.	1.00	2.50	10.00
	b. 5.11.1981.	.15	.50	2.50
	c. 21.6.1985.	.05	.25	1.50

1979 ISSUE

#117A *Deleted*. See #125A.

#118-120 denominations below coat-of-arms. Printer: TDLR. Replacement notes: Serial # prefix *Y* and suffix letter *A*.

		VG	VF	UNC
118	**1000 Soles de Oro** 1.2.1979; 3.5.1979. Black, green and multicolor. Adm. Grau at right and as watermark, arms at center. Fishermen and boats at left on back.	.50	1.00	3.00

		VG	VF	UNC
119	**5000 Soles de Oro** 1.2.1979. Brown-violet and multicolor. Similar to #117 but *CINCO MIL* added at bottom on face. Miners on back.	.50	1.50	7.50

		VG	VF	UNC
120	**10,000 Soles de Oro** 1.2.1979; 5.11.1981. Black, blue-violet and purple on multicolor underprint. Inca Garcilaso Inca de la Vega at right and as watermark. Indian digging at left, woman with flowers at center on back.	.50	3.00	15.00

NOTICE

Readers with unlisted dates, signature varieties, etc. are invited to submit photocopies of their notes to: Standard Catalog of World Paper Money, 700 East State St. Iola, WI 54990-0001, E-Mail: george.cuhaj@fwpubs.com.

1981 Issue

#121 *Deleted*. See #125B.

#122-125 portr. as wmk. Printer: ABNC. Replacement notes: Serial # prefix *Y*, suffix *A*.

		VG	VF	UNC
122	**1000 Soles de Oro**			
	5.11.1981. Black, green and multicolor. Similar to #118 but slightly modified guilloche in underprint at center.			
	a. Issued note.	.10	.30	1.50
	s. Specimen.	—	—	100.

		VG	VF	UNC
123	**5000 Soles de Oro**			
	5.11.1981. Black and red-brown on multicolor underprint. Similar to #119 but denomination is above signatures at center.	.25	1.00	5.00

		VG	VF	UNC
124	**10,000 Soles de Oro**			
	5.11.1981. Black, blue-violet and purple on multicolor underprint. Similar to #120 but slight variations on borders.	.50	2.00	7.00

		VG	VF	UNC
125	**50,000 Soles de Oro**			
	5.11.1981; 2.11.1984. Black and orange on multicolor underprint. Arms at center, Nicolas de Pierola at right. Drilling rig at left on back, helicopter approaching.			
	a. Issued note.	1.00	3.00	12.50
	s. Specimen.	—	—	150.

1982; 1985 Issue

Replacement notes: Serial # prefix *Y*, suffix *A* and *ZZ* respectively.

		VG	VF	UNC
125A	**500 Soles de Oro**			
	18.3.1982. Like #115 but printer: (T)DLR.	.25	.50	3.00
125B	**50,000 Soles de Oro**			
	23.8.1985. Black, orange and multicolor. Like #125. Printer: TDLR.	.75	2.25	6.50

1985 Provisional Issue

		VG	VF	UNC
126	**100,000 Soles de Oro**			
	23.8.1985. Overprint bank name and new denomination in red on face and back of #122.	50.00	150.	375.
127	**500,000 Soles de Oro**			
	23.8.1985. Overprint bank name and new denomination in red on face and back of #123.	—	—	—

1985-91 Issues

During the period from around 1984 and extending beyond 1990, Perú suffered from a hyperinflation that saw the Sol depreciate in value dramatically and drastically. A sudden need for new Inti banknotes caused the government to approach a number of different security printers in order to satisfy the demand for new notes.

#128-150 involve 7 different printers: BdM, BDDK, CdM-B, FNMT, G&D, IPS-Roma and TDLR. Listings proceed by denomination and in chronological order. All portr. appear also as wmk., and all notes have arms at ctr. on face.

Replacement notes:
BdM - Serial # prefix *Y*; *Z*. BDDK - Serial # prefix *Y*. FNMT - Serial # prefix *Y*. IPS-Roma - Serial # prefix Y; Z. TDLR - Serial # prefix Y;

		VG	VF	UNC
128	**10 Intis**			
	3.4.1985; 17.1.1986. Black, dark blue and purple on multicolor underprint. Ricardo Palma at right. Back aqua and purple; Indian farmer digging at left and another picking cotton at center. Printer: TDLR.	.05	.20	.50

NOTICE

Readers with unlisted dates, signature varieties, etc. are invited to submit photocopies of their notes to: Standard Catalog of World Paper Money, 700 East State St. Iola, WI 54990-0001, E-Mail: george.cuhaj@fwpubs.com.

		VG	VF	UNC
129	**10 Intis** 26.6.1987. Black, dark blue and purple on multicolor underprint. Like #128. Printer: IPS-Roma.	.05	.10	.35

		VG	VF	UNC
130	**50 Intis** 3.4.1985. Black, orange and green on multicolor underprint. Nicolas de Pierola at right. Drilling rig at left on back, helicopter approaching. Printer: TDLR.	.15	.50	2.00
131	**50 Intis** 1986; 1987. Black, orange and green on multicolor underprint. Like #130. Printer: CdM-Brazil.			
	a. 6.3.1986.	.05	.20	.75
	b. 26.6.1987.	.05	.20	.50

		VG	VF	UNC
132	**100 Intis** 1985-86. Black and dark brown on multicolor underprint. Ramon Castilla at right. Women workers by cotton spinning frame at left center on back. Printer: CdM-Brazil.			
	a. 1.2.1985; 1.3.1985.	.50	2.00	12.00
	b. 6.3.1986. With additional pink and light green vertical underprint at right.	.15	.50	2.00

		VG	VF	UNC
133	**100 Intis** 26.6.1987. Black and dark brown on multicolor underprint. Like #132b. Printer: BDDK.	.05	.10	.35

		VG	VF	UNC
134	**500 Intis** 1985; 1987. Deep brown-violet and olive-brown on multicolor underprint. Jose Cabriel Condorcanqui Tupac Amaru II at right. Mountains and climber at center on back. Printer: BDDK.			
	a. 1.3.1985.	.15	.30	3.00
	b. 26.6.1987. Ornate red-orange vertical strip at left end of design with added security thread underneath.	.05	.20	.50

		VG	VF	UNC
135	**500 Intis** 6.3.1986. Deep brown-violet and olive-brown on multicolor underprint. Similar to #134b. Printer: FNMT.	1.00	3.50	12.50

		VG	VF	UNC
136	**1000 Intis** 1986-88. Deep green, olive-brown and red on multicolor underprint. Mariscal Andres Avelino Caceres at right. Ruins off Chan Chan on back. Printer: TDLR.			
	a. 6.3.1986.	.10	.50	2.00
	b. 26.6.1987; 28.6.1988.	.05	.25	1.50

		VG	VF	UNC
137	**5000 Intis** 28.6.1988. Purple, deep brown and red-orange on multicolor underprint. Admiral Miguel Grau at right. Fishermen repairing nets on back. Printer: G&D.	.05	.15	.50
138	**5000 Intis** 28.6.1988. Purple, deep brown and red-orange on multicolor underprint. Like #137. Printer: IPS-Roma.	.25	1.00	3.50
139	**5000 Intis** 9.9.1988. Purple, deep brown and red-orange on multicolor underprint. Like #137. Without watermark. Printer: TDLR.	.25	1.00	4.50

		VG	VF	UNC
140	**10,000 Intis** 28.6.1988. Aqua, blue and orange on light green and multicolor underprint. Cesar Vallejo at right. Black and red increasing size serial # (anti-counterfeiting device). Santiago de Chuco street scene on back. Printer IPS-Roma.	.05	.25	.75

		VG	VF	UNC
141	**10,000 Intis** 28.6.1988. Dark blue and orange on light green and multicolor underprint. Like #140 but with broken silver security thread. Printer: TDLR.	.25	.75	3.00

		VG	VF	UNC
142	**50,000 Intis** 28.6.1988. Red, violet and dark blue on multicolor underprint. Victor Raul Haya de la Torre at right. Chamber of National Congress on back. Printer: IPS-Roma.	.25	.75	3.50
143	**50,000 Intis** 28.6.1988. Red, violet and dark blue on multicolor underprint. Like #142 but with segmented foil security thread. Printer: TDLR.	.50	1.50	5.00

#144-150 arms at ctr. Various printers.

		VG	VF	UNC
144	**100,000 Intis** 21.11.1988. Brown and black on multicolor underprint. Francisco Bolognesi at right. Local boats in Lake Titicaca on back. Bolognesi's printed image on watermark area at left. Printer: TDLR.	.25	.75	2.25

		VG	VF	UNC
144A	**100,000 Intis** 21.12.1988. Brown and black on multicolor underprint. Like #144 but with watermark: *F. Bolognesi.* Segmented foil over security thread.	.25	.75	2.50
145	**100,000 Intis** 21.12.1989. Like #144b, but with black security thread at right of arms. Printer: BdeM.	.25	.75	3.00
146	**500,000 Intis** 21.11.1988. Blue and blue-violet on multicolor underprint. Face like #128. Church of *La Caridád* (charity), site of first National Congress, on back. Ricardo Palma's printed image in watermark area at left. Printer: TDLR.	.25	1.00	6.50

		VG	VF	UNC
146A	**500,000 Intis** 21.12.1988. Blue and blue-violet on multicolor underprint. Like #146 but with watermark: *R. Palma.* Segmented foil over security thread.	.25	1.75	7.50

147 500,000 Intis
21.12.1989. Blue and blue-violet on multicolor underprint. Like #146A, but with black security thread at right. Printer: BdeM.

VG	VF	UNC
.25	1.25	5.50

148 1,000,000 Intis
5.1.1990. Red-brown, green and multicolor. Hipolito Unanue at right and as watermark. Medical college at San Fernando at left center on back. Printer: TDLR.

VG	VF	UNC
.25	1.00	5.00

149 5,000,000 Intis
5.1.1990. Brown, red and multicolor. Antonio Raimondi at right and as watermark. Indian comforting Raimundi on back. Printer: BdeM.

VG	VF	UNC
2.25	7.50	20.00

150 5,000,000 Intis
16.1.1991. Similar to #149 but plants printed on watermark area at left on face. Old building at right on back. Printer: IPS-Roma.

VG	VF	UNC
.50	2.00	7.50

1991; 1992 ISSUES

MONETARY REFORM:

1 Nuevo Sol = 1 Million Intis
#151-155 arms at upper r.

151 10 Nuevos Soles
1.2.1991. Dark green and blue-green on multicolor underprint. WW II era fighter plane as monument at upper center, José Abelardo Quiñones at right and as watermark. Biplane inverted (signifying pilot's death) at left center on back. Printer: TDLR.

VG	VF	UNC
FV	FV	9.50

151A 10 Nuevos Soles
10.9.1992. Dark green and blue-green on multicolor underprint. Like #151 but printer: IPS-Roma.

VG	VF	UNC
FV	FV	9.50

152 20 Nuevos Soles
1.2.1991. Black, brown and orange on multicolor underprint. Patio of San Marcos University at center, Raul Porras B. at right and as watermark. Palace of Torre Tagle at left center on back. Printer: TDLR.

VG	VF	UNC
FV	FV	22.50

#153-155 printer: IPS-Roma.

153 20 Nuevos Soles
25.6.1992. Black, brown and orange on multicolor underprint. Like #152.

VG	VF	UNC
FV	FV	17.50

154 50 Nuevos Soles
1.2.1991; 25.6.1992. Red-brown, blue-violet and black on multicolor underprint. Building at center, Abraham Valdelomar at right and as watermark. Laguna de Huacachina at left center on back.

VG	VF	UNC
FV	FV	40.00

155 100 Nuevos Soles
1.2.1991; 25.6.1992; 10.9.1992. Black, blue-black, red-violet and deep green on multicolor underprint. Arch monument at center, Jorge Basadre (Grohmann) at right and as watermark. National Library at left center on back.

	VG	VF	UNC
a. With Jorge Basadre. 1.2.1991.	FV	FV	75.00
b. With Jorge Basadre Grohmann. 10.9.1992.	FV	FV	70.00

1994; 1995 ISSUE

#156-161 similar to #151-155 but w/clear wmk. area.

		VG	VF	UNC
156	**10 Nuevos Soles** 16.6.1994. Dark green and blue-green on multicolor underprint. Like #151. Printer: TDLR.	FV	FV	7.50

		VG	VF	UNC
157	**10 Nuevos Soles** 20.4.1995. Dark green and blue-green on multicolor underprint. Like #156. Printer: G&D.	FV	FV	7.00

		VG	VF	UNC
158	**20 Nuevos Soles** 16.6.1994. Black, brown and orange on multicolor underprint. Like #152. Printer: TDLR.	FV	FV	15.00
159	**20 Nuevos Soles** 20.4.1995. Similar to #158.	FV	FV	14.00

#160-162 printer: IPS-Roma.

		VG	VF	UNC
160	**50 Nuevos Soles** 16.6.1994; 20.4.1995. Brown, deep blue and black on multicolor underprint. Like #154.	FV	FV	37.50

		VG	VF	UNC
161	**100 Nuevos Soles** 20.4.1995. Black, blue-black, red-violet and deep green on multicolor underprint. Like #155b.	FV	FV	65.00

		VG	VF	UNC
162	**200 Nuevos Soles** 20.4.1995. Red, brown-violet and dark blue on multicolor underprint. Isabel Flores de Oliva, St. Rose of Lima at right and as watermark. Well in underprint at center. Convent of Santo Domingo at left on back.	FV	FV	120.

1996 ISSUE

#163-165 printer: IPS-Roma.

		VG	VF	UNC
163	**10 Nuevos Soles** 25.4.1996. Like #156.	FV	FV	10.00

		VG	VF	UNC
164	**20 Nuevos Soles** 25.4.1996; 11.6.1997. Like #158.	FV	FV	15.00
165	**100 Nuevos Soles** 25.4.1996. Like #161.	FV	FV	65.00

1997 ISSUE

#166-167 printer: BABN.

		VG	VF	UNC
166	**10 Nuevos Soles** 11.6.1997; 6.8.1998; 20.5.1999; 1.3.2001. Dark green and blue-green on multicolor underprint. Like #157.	FV	FV	9.00
167	**20 Nuevos Soles** 11.6.1997. Like #158.	FV	FV	15.00

		VG	VF	UNC
168	**50 Nuevos Soles** 11.6.1997; 6.8.1998. Like #154. Printer: IPS-Roma.	FV	FV	37.50

1999 Issue

		VG	VF	UNC
169	**20 Nuevos Soles** 20.5.1999. Like #167. Printer: FNMT.	FV	FV	15.00

		VG	VF	UNC
169A	**50 Nuevos Soles** 20.5.1999. Like #168. Printer: (T)DLR.	FV	FV	37.50
170	**100 Nuevos Soles** 20.5.1999. Like #161. Printer: BABN.	FV	FV	65.00

Banco de Credito del Perú
Banco Central de Reserva del Perú

1985 Emergency Check Issue

		VG	VF	UNC
R2	**100,000 Soles** 2.9.1985. Black text on light blue text underprint. Two signature varieties.	35.00	150.	—

Banco de la Nación
Banco Central de Reserva del Perú

1985 Cheques Circulares de Gerencia Issue

#R6-R8 bank monogram at upper l.

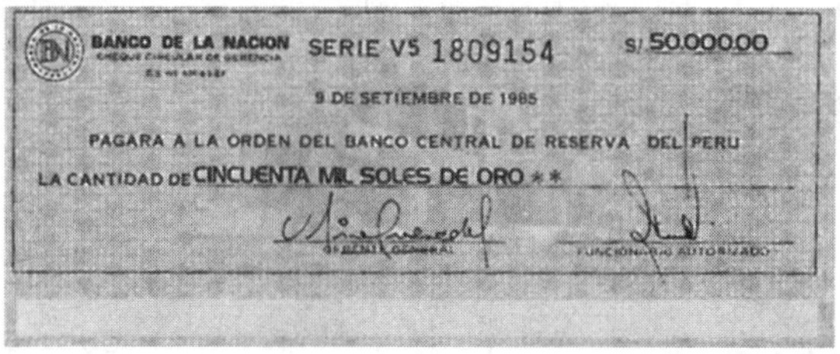

		VG	VF	UNC
R6	**50,000 Soles** 9.9.1985; 16.9.1985. Black text on tan underprint. Bank at center.	35.00	125.	—
R7	**100,000 Soles** 2.9.1985. Black text on light blue underprint. Like #R6.	35.00	125.	—
R8	**200,000 Soles** 2.9.1985. Black text on pink underprint. Like #R6.	35.00	125.	—

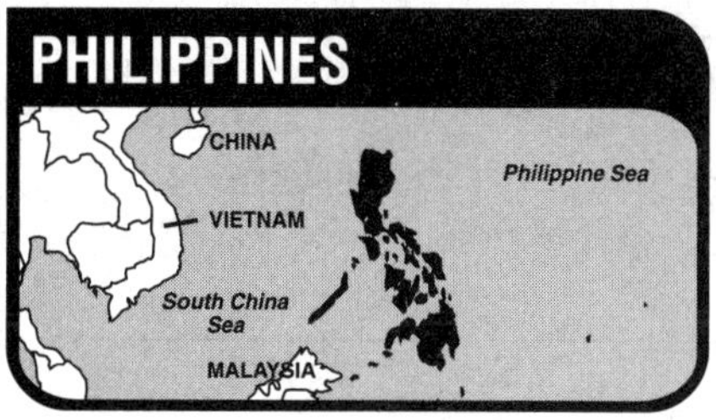

The Republic of the Philippines, an archipelago in the western Pacific 500 miles (805 km.) from the southeast coast of Asia, has an area of 115,830 sq. mi. (300,000 sq. km.) and a population of 75.04 million. Capital: Manila. The economy of the 7,000-island group is d on agriculture, forestry and fishing. Timber, coconut products, sugar and hemp are exported.

Migration to the Philippines began about 30,000 years ago when land bridges connected the islands with Borneo and Sumatra. Ferdinand Magellan claimed the islands for Spain in 1521. The first permanent settlement was established by Miguel de Legazpi at Cebu in April of 1565; Manila was established in 1572. A British expedition captured Manila and occupied the Spanish colony in Oct. of 1762, but it was returned to Spain by the treaty of Paris, 1763. Spain held the Philippines amid a growing movement of Filipino nationalism until 1898 when they were ceded to the United States at the end of the Spanish-American War. The Filipinos then fought unsuccessfully against the United States to maintain their independent Republic proclaimed by Emilio Aguinaldo. The country became a self-governing Commonwealth of the United States in 1935, and attained independence as the Republic of the Philippines on July 4, 1946. During World War II the Japanese had set up a puppet republic, but this quasi-government failed to achieve worldwide recognition. The occupation lasted from late 1941 to 1945. Ferdinand Marcos lost to Corazón Aquino in elections of 1986. Marcos then fled the country. In 1992 Fidel Ramos was elected president. He was succeeded in 1998 by Joseph E. Estrada, who was deposed in January 2001 and replaced by his vice-president Gloria Macapagal Arroyo.

RULERS:

Spanish to 1898
United States, 1898-1946

MONETARY SYSTEM:

1 Peso = 100 Centavos to 1967
1 Piso = 100 Sentimos, 1967-

Type1 Type 2 Type3 Type 4 Type 5

SIGNATURE VARIETIES

1	E. Quirino	
2	R. Magsaysay	M. Cuaderno
3	C. Garcia	M. Cuaderno
4	C. Garcia	A. Castillo
5	D. Macapagal	A. Castillo
6	F. Marcos	A. Castillo
7	F. Marcos	A. Calalang
8	F, Marcos	G. Licaros

SIGNATURE VARIETIES		
9	 F. Marcos	 J. Laya
10	 F. Marcos	 J. Fernandez
11	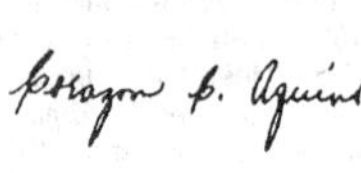 C. Aquino	 J. Fernandez
12	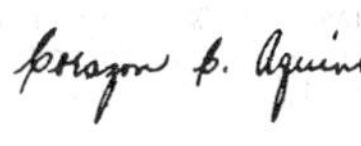 C. Aquino	 J. Cuisia
13	 M. Ramos	 J. Cuisia
14	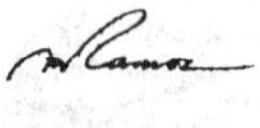 M. Ramos	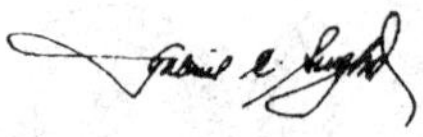 G.C. Singson
15	 J. E. Estrada	 G. C. Singson
16	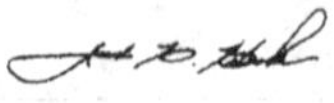 J.E. Estrada	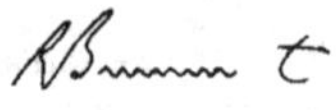 R. B. Buenaventura
17	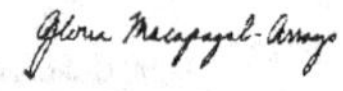 G. Macapagal-Arroyo	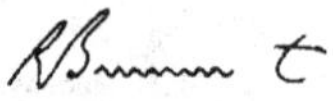 R. B. Buenaventura

Republic

Central Bank of the Philippines

1949 ND "English" Issues

#125, 127, and 129 sign. 1. Central Bank Seal at l., Type 1. Printer: SBNC.

		VG	VF	UNC
125	**5 Centavos** ND (1949). Red on tan underprint. Central Bank Seal Type 1 at left. Signature 1. Red. Printer: SBNC.	.15	.50	1.75

		VG	VF	UNC
126	**5 Centavos** ND. Red on tan underprint. Central Bank Seal Type 1 at left. Signature 2. Like #125. Red. Printer: W&S.			
	a. Issued note.	.10	.25	1.50
	p. Proof.	—	—	250.

		VG	VF	UNC
127	**10 Centavos** ND. Brownish purple on tan underprint. Central Bank Seal Type 1 at left. Signature 1. Brownish purple. Printer: SBNC.			
	a. Issued note.	.25	.50	2.50
	r. Remainder without serial #.	—	100.	250.

		VG	VF	UNC
128	**10 Centavos** ND. Like #127. Signature 2. Printer: W&S.	.25	.50	1.25
129	**20 Centavos** Central Bank Seal Type 1at left. Signature 1. ND. Green on light green underprint. Back green.			
	a. Issued note.	.25	.75	2.50
	r. Remainder without serial #.	—	100.	250.

#130-141 printer: TDLR.

		VG	VF	UNC
130	**20 Centavos** ND. Green on light green underprint. Back green.			
	a. Signature 2.	.20	.50	2.00
	b. Signature 3.	.20	.50	2.00
131	**50 Centavos** ND. Blue on light blue underprint. Back blue. Signature 2.			
	a. Issued note.	.20	.50	2.00
	p. Proof.	—	—	250.

#132-141 large Central Bank Seal Type 1 bank seal at lower r.

		VG	VF	UNC
132	**1/2 Peso** ND. Green on yellow and blue underprint. Ox-cart with Mt. Mayon in background at center. Back green. Signature 2.	.25	1.00	3.50

		VG	VF	UNC
133	**1 Peso** ND. Black on light gold and blue underprint. Portrait A. Mabini at left. Back black; Barasoain Church at center.			
	a. Signature 1. *GENUINE* in very light tan letters just beneath top heading on face.	7.50	25.00	110.
	b. Signature 1. without *GENUINE* on face.	.50	2.00	10.00
	c. Signature 2.	.75	2.50	15.00
	d. Signature 3.	.25	2.00	12.50
	e. Signature 4.	.50	1.25	8.00
	f. Signature 5.	.25	1.00	5.00
	g. Signature 6.	.10	.50	2.50
	h. Signature 7.	.10	1.00	3.00
	s1. Signature as a. Specimen.	—	—	200.
	s2. Signature as b. Specimen. (De La Rue).	—	—	200.
	s3. Signature as c. Specimen. (De La Rue).	—	—	200.
	s4. Signature as d. Specimen. (De La Rue).	—	—	200.
	s5. Signature as e. Specimen. (De La Rue).	—	—	200.

133	1 Peso	VG	VF	UNC
	s6. Signature as f. Specimen.	—	—	45.00
	s7. Signature as f. Specimen. (De La Rue).	—	—	250.
	s8. Signature as g. Specimen.	—	—	50.00
	s9. Signature as g. Specimen. (De La Rue).	—	—	250.
	10. Signature as h. Specimen.	—	—	30.00
	11. Signature as h. Specimen. (De La Rue).	—	—	250.

134	2 Pesos	VG	VF	UNC
	ND. Black on blue and gold underprint. Portrait J. Rizal at left. Back blue; landing of Magellan in the Philippines.			
	a. Signature 1.	1.50	7.50	15.00
	b. Signature 2.	.75	2.00	5.00
	c. Signature 4.	1.00	2.50	10.00
	d. Signature 5.	.15	.50	2.00
	p. Signature as b. Proof.	—	—	125.
	s1. Signature as a. Specimen. (De La Rue) Cancelled.	—	—	250.
	s2. Signature as b. Specimen.	—	—	60.00
	s3. Signature as b. Specimen. (De La Rue).	—	—	250.
	s4. Signature as c. Specimen. (De La Rue).		—	250.
	s5. Signature as d. Specimen.	—	—	60.00

135	5 Pesos	VG	VF	UNC
	ND. Black on yellow and gold underprint. Portrait M. H. del Pilar at left, Lopez Jaena at right. Back gold; newspaper "La Solidaridad".			
	a. Signature 1.	1.50	7.50	40.00
	b. Signature 2.	.75	3.50	12.50
	c. Signature 3.	.75	5.00	17.50
	d. Signature 4.	.75	3.00	10.00
	e. Signature 5.	.20	.50	3.00
	f. Signature 8.	.20	.50	2.00
	p. Proof.	—	—	150.
	s1. Signature as a. Specimen. (De La Rue).	—	—	250.
	s2. Signature as b. Specimen. (De La Rue).	—	—	250.
	s3. Signature as d. Specimen. (De La Rue).	—	—	250.
	s4. Signature as e. Specimen.	—	—	65.00
	s5. Signature as e. Specimen. (De La Rue).	—	—	200.
	s6. Signature as f. Specimen.	—	—	65.00

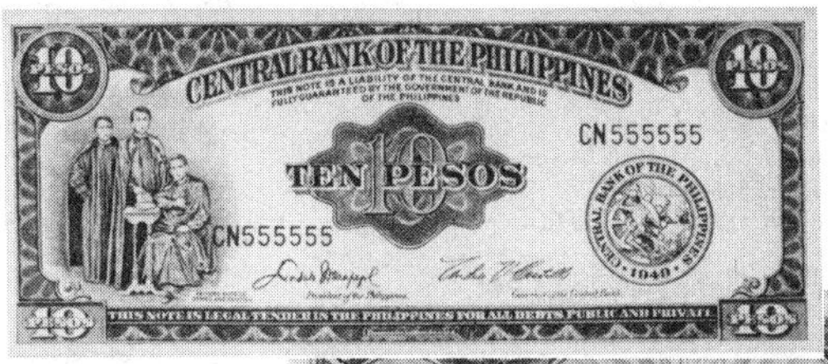

136	10 Pesos	VG	VF	UNC
	ND. Black on tan and light red underprint. Fathers Burgos, Gomez and Zamora at left. Back brown; monument.			
	a. Signature 1.	75.00	200.	500.
	b. Signature 2.	2.50	5.00	25.00
	c. Signature 3.	2.50	5.00	25.00
	d. Signature 4.	2.50	5.00	30.00
	e. Signature 5.	.25	.50	2.00
	f. Signature 8.	1.00	2.00	5.00
	s1. Signature as b. Specimen.	—	—	70.00
	s2. Signature as c. Specimen.	—	—	70.00
	s3. Signature as c. Specimen. (De La Rue).	—	—	250.
	s4. Signature as d. Specimen	—	—	75.00
	s5. Signature as d. Specimen. (De La Rue).	—	—	250.
	s6. Signature as e. Specimen. (De La Rue).	—	—	200.
	s7. Signature as f. Specimen.	—	—	70.00

137	20 Pesos	VG	VF	UNC
	ND. Black on yellow underprint. Portrait A. Bonifacio at left, E. Jacinto at right. Back brownish orange; flag and monument.			
	a. Signature 1.	10.00	75.00	200.
	b. Signature 2.	3.00	20.00	50.00
	c. Signature 4.	3.00	10.00	20.00
	d. Signature 5.	.50	1.50	2.25
	e. Signature 8.	.25	1.00	2.50
	p. Signature as d. Proof.	—	—	150.
	s1. Signature as a. Specimen.	—	—	175.
	s2. Signature as c. Specimen. (De La Rue).	—	—	200.
	s3. Signature as d. Specimen.	—	—	125.
	s4. Signature as d. Specimen (De La Rue).	—	—	175.
	s5. Signature as e. Specimen.	—	—	70.00

138	50 Pesos	VG	VF	UNC
	ND. Black on pink and light tan underprint. Portrait A. Luna at left. Back red; scene of blood compact of Sikatuna and Legaspi.			
	a. Signature 1.	125.	500.	—
	b. Signature 2.	15.00	50.00	125.
	c. Signature 3.	5.00	15.00	40.00
	d. Signature 5.	.25	1.00	2.50
	p. Signature as d. Proof.	—	—	175.
	s1. Signature as a. Specimen. (De La Rue).	—	—	500.
	s2. Signature as b. Specimen. (De La Rue).	—	—	300.
	s3. Signature as d. Specimen.	—	—	75.00
	s4. Signature as d. Specimen. (De La Rue).	—	—	500.

139	100 Pesos	VG	VF	UNC
	ND. Black on gold underprint. Portrait T. Sora at left. Back yellow; regimental flags. Signature 1.			
	a. Issued note.	2.00	6.00	15.00
	s. Specimen.	—	—	85.00

140	200 Pesos	VG	VF	UNC
	ND. Green on pink and light blue underprint. Portrait Pres. Manuel Quezon at left. Back green; Legislative building signature 1.			
	a. Issued note.	3.00	7.50	20.00
	s. Specimen (De La Rue).	—	—	350.

141	500 Pesos	VG	VF	UNC
	ND. Black on purple and light tan underprint. Portrait Pres. Manuel Roxas at left. Back purple; Central Bank. Signature 1.			
	a. Issued note.	10.00	25.00	70.00
	s. Specimen. (De La Rue).	—	—	300.

Bangko Sentral ng Pilipinas

1969 ND "Pilipino" Issue

#142-147 heading at top in double outline. Replacement notes: Serial # prefix "+".

142	1 Piso	VG	VF	UNC
	ND (1969). Blue and black on multicolor underprint. J. Rizal at left and as watermark. Central Bank Seal Type 2. Scene of Aguinaldo's Independence Declaration of June 12, 1898 on back.			
	a. Signature 7.	.20	.50	1.50
	b. Signature 8.	.15	.50	1.00
	s1. Signature as a. Specimen. (De La Rue).	—	—	100.
	s2. Signature as b. Specimen.	—	—	40.00

#143-145 printer: G&D (w/o imprint). Central Bank Seal Type 3.

143	5 Piso	VG	VF	UNC
	ND (1969). Green and brown on multicolor underprint. A. Bonifacio at left in brown and as watermark. Scene of the Katipunan organization on back.			
	a. Signature 7.	.25	1.50	2.25
	b. Signature 8.	.25	1.00	2.00
	s1. Signature as a. Specimen.	—	—	125.
	s2. Signature as b. Specimen.	—	—	25.00

144	10 Piso	VG	VF	UNC
	ND (1969). Brown on multicolor underprint. A. Mabini at left and as watermark. Barasoain Church on back.			
	a. Signature 7.	.25	1.50	5.00
	b. Signature 8.	.25	1.50	3.00
	s1. Signature as a. Specimen.	—	—	100.
	s2. Signature as b. Specimen.	—	—	25.00

145	20 Piso	VG	VF	UNC
	ND (1969). Orange and brown on multicolor underprint. M. L. Quezon at left in brown and as watermark. Malakanyang Palace on back.			
	a. Signature 7.	.50	2.00	8.00
	b. Signature 8.	.50	2.00	6.00
	s1. Signature as a. Specimen.	—	—	100.
	s2. Signature as b. Specimen.	—	—	50.00

146	50 Piso	VG	VF	UNC
	ND (1969). Red on multicolor underprint. S. Osmeña at left and as watermark. Central Bank Seal Type 2. Legislative building on back.			
	a. Signature 7.	2.00	5.00	15.00
	b. Signature 8.	1.75	3.00	10.00
	s1. Signature as a. Specimen. (De La Rue).	—	—	225.
	s2. Signature as b. Specimen.	—	—	30.00
	s3. Signature as b. Specimen. (De La Rue).	—	—	225.

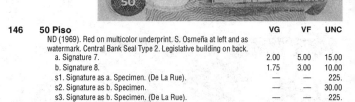

147	100 Piso	VG	VF	UNC
	ND (1969). Purple on multicolor underprint. M. Roxas at left and as watermark. Central Bank Seal Type 2. Old Central Bank on back.			
	a. Signature 7.	4.00	10.00	25.00
	b. Signature 8.	3.00	7.50	22.00
	p. Signature as a. Proof.	—	—	475.
	s1. Signature as a. Specimen.	—	—	50.00
	s2. Signature as a. Specimen. (De La Rue).	—	—	175.
	s3. Signature as b. Specimen.	—	—	50.00
	s4. Signature as b. Specimen. (De La Rue).	—	—	200.

1970's ND First Issue

#148-151 Central Bank Seal Type 2. Heading at top in single outline, l. and r. ends completely filled in. Sign. 8. Replacement notes: Serial # prefix "+".

		VG	VF	UNC
148	**5 Piso**			
	ND. Green on multicolor underprint. Like #143 but A. Bonifacio in green.			
	a. Issued note.	.25	.75	4.00
	s. Specimen.	—	—	20.00
149	**10 Piso**			
	ND. Brown on multicolor underprint. Like #144 but without white paper showing at sides on face or back.			
	a. Issued note.	.25	3.00	10.00
	s. Specimen.	—	—	40.00

		VG	VF	UNC
150	**20 Piso**			
	ND. Orange and blue on multicolor underprint. Like #145 but M. L. Quezon in orange.			
	a. Issued note.	.25	1.00	4.00
	s. Specimen.	—	—	75.00

		VG	VF	UNC
151	**50 Piso**			
	ND. Red on multicolor underprint. Similar to #146. Seal under denomination instead of over, signature closer, *LIMAMPUNG PISO* in one line, and other modifications.			
	a. Issued note.	1.00	5.00	15.00
	s. Specimen.	—	—	70.00

1970's ND Second Issue

#152-158 Central Bank Seal Type 2. Ovpt: *ANG BAGONG LIPUNAN* (New Society) on wmk. area, 1974-85.

Replacement notes: Serial # prefix "+".

#152-156, 158 sign. 8.

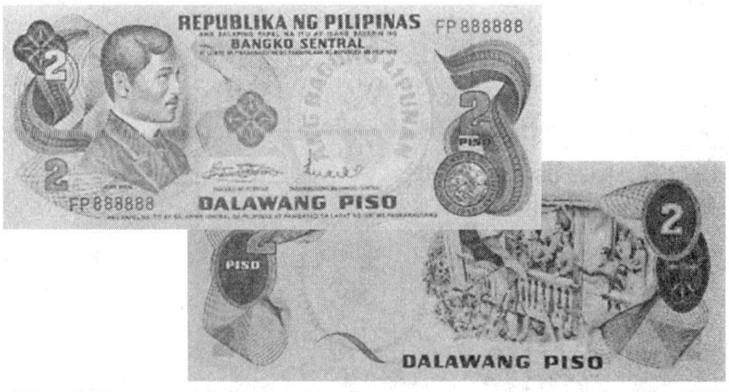

		VG	VF	UNC
152	**2 Piso**			
	ND. Blue on multicolor underprint. J. Rizal at left and as watermark. Scene of Aguinaldo's Independence Declaration of June 12, 1898 on back.			
	a. Issued note.	.20	.50	1.50
	s1. Specimen.	—	—	12.00
	s2. Specimen. (De La Rue).	—	—	225.

		VG	VF	UNC
153	**5 Piso**			
	ND. Green on multicolor underprint. Like #148.			
	a. Dark overprint.	.25	1.00	5.00
	b. Light overprint.	.25	1.00	4.00
	s1. Specimen.	—	—	20.00
	s2. Specimen. (De La Rue).	—	—	225.
154	**10 Piso**			
	ND. Brown on multicolor underprint. Like #149.			
	a. Issued note.	.25	.50	2.00
	s1. Specimen.	—	—	25.00
	s2. Specimen. (De La Rue).	—	—	225.

Note: Varieties of light or dark overprints.

		VG	VF	UNC
155	**20 Piso**			
	ND. Orange on multicolor underprint. Like #150.			
	a. Issued note.	.25	1.50	4.00
	s1. Specimen.	—	—	35.00
	s2. Specimen. (De La Rue).	—	—	250.
156	**50 Piso**			
	ND. Red on multicolor underprint. Like #151.			
	a. Brown signature title.	1.00	4.00	7.50
	b. Red signature title.	1.00	7.50	20.00
	s1. Signature as b. Specimen.	—	—	40.00
	s2. Signature as. b. Specimen. (De La Rue).	—	—	250.

		VG	VF	UNC
157	**100 Piso**			
	ND. Purple on multicolor underprint. Like #147. Bank seal in purple at left.			
	a. Signature 7.	2.50	15.00	40.00
	b. Signature 8.	2.00	7.50	20.00
	s1. Signature as a. Specimen.	—	—	200.
	s2. Signature as b. Specimen.	—	—	65.00

		VG	VF	UNC
158	**100 Piso**			
	ND. Purple on multicolor underprint. Face resembling #157 but heading at top solid letters, green bank seal at lower right, and denomination near upper right. Back similar to #157 but denomination at bottom.			
	a. Issued note.	10.00	25.00	60.00
	s. Specimen.	—	—	175.

1978 ND Issue

#159-167 Central Bank Seal Type 4. Replacement notes: Serial # prefix "+".

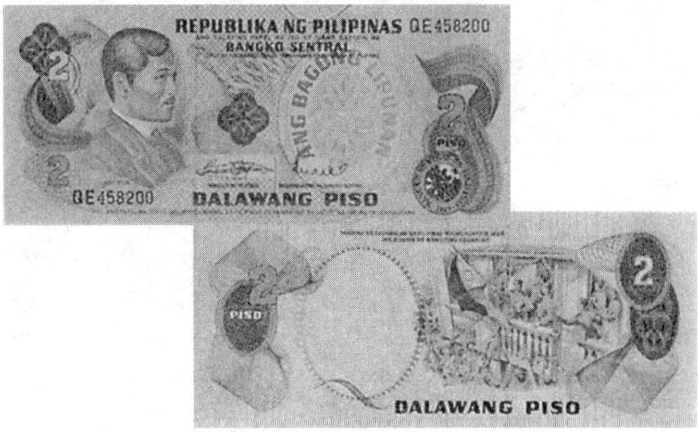

159	2 Piso	VG	VF	UNC
	ND. Blue on multicolor underprint. Like #152.			
	a. Signature 8.	.10	.30	1.50
	b. Signature 9. Black serial #.	.10	.50	1.50
	c. Signature 9. Red serial #.	.10	.30	1.00
	d. Signature as b. Uncut sheet of 4.	—	—	15.00
	s1. Signature as a. Specimen.	—	—	15.00
	s2. Signature as b. Specimen.	—	—	15.00

160	5 Piso	VG	VF	UNC
	ND. Green on multicolor underprint. Like #153.			
	a. Signature 8.	.15	.50	2.50
	b. Signature 9. Black serial #.	.15	1.00	3.00
	c. Signature 9. Red serial #.	.15	.40	1.50
	d. Signature 10.	.15	.40	2.00
	e. Signature as b. Uncut sheet of 4.	—	—	30.00
	f. Signature as d. Uncut sheet of 4.	—	—	30.00
	s1. Signature as a. Specimen.	—	—	15.00
	s2. Signature as b. Specimen.	—	—	20.00

161	10 Piso	VG	VF	UNC
	ND. Brown on multicolor underprint. Like #154.			
	a. Signature 8.	.10	.75	2.50
	b. Signature 9.	.10	1.00	5.00
	c. Signature 10. Black serial #.	.10	.50	2.00
	d. Signature 10. Red serial #.	.10	1.00	8.00
	e. Signature as b. Uncut sheet of 4.	—	—	35.00
	f. Signature as c. Uncut sheet of 4.	—	—	35.00
	s1. Signature as a. Specimen.	—	—	15.00
	s2. Signature as b. Specimen.	—	—	15.00

162	20 Piso	VG	VF	UNC
	ND. Orange and blue on multicolor underprint. Like #155.			
	a. Signature 8.	.25	1.00	4.00
	b. Signature 9.	.25	1.00	5.00
	c. Signature 10.	.25	1.00	3.00
	d. Signature as b. Uncut sheet of 4.	—	—	40.00
	e. Signature as d. Uncut sheet of 4.	—	—	40.00
	s1. Signature as a. Specimen.	—	—	20.00
	s2. Signature as b. Specimen.	—	—	30.00

163	50 Piso	VG	VF	UNC
	ND. Red on multicolor underprint. Like #156.			
	a. Signature 8.	.50	2.00	7.50
	b. Signature 9.	.50	1.50	4.00
	c. Signature 10.	.50	1.50	5.00
	s1. Signature as a. Specimen.	—	—	35.00
	s2. Signature as b. Specimen.	—	—	35.00

164	100 Piso	VG	VF	UNC
	ND. Purple and deep olive-green on multicolor underprint. Face like #158. New Central Bank complex with ships behind on back.			
	a. Signature 8.	2.00	10.00	27.50
	b. Signature 9.	1.00	4.00	8.00
	c. Signature 10. Black serial #.	.75	3.00	8.00
	s1. Signature as a. Specimen.	—	—	35.00
	s2. Signature as b. Specimen.	—	—	40.00

1978 Commemorative Issue

#165, Centennial - Birth of Pres. Osmeña, 1978

165	50 Piso	VG	VF	UNC
	1978. Black circular commemorative overprint at left on #163a.	1.00	4.00	15.00

1981 COMMEMORATIVE ISSUES

#166, Papal Visit of John Paul II, 1981

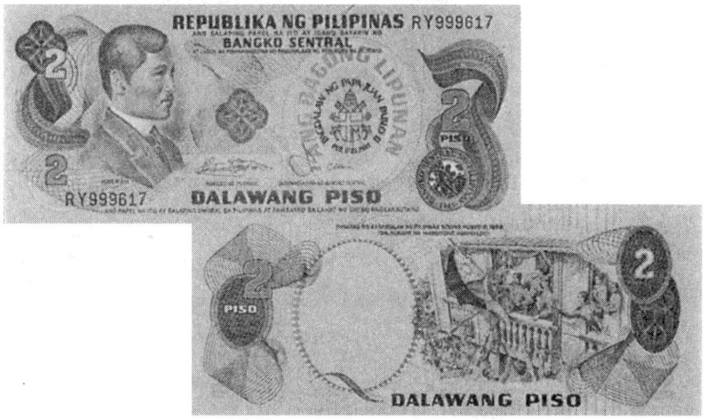

166	2 Piso	VG	VF	UNC
	1981. Black commemorative overprint at center right on #159b.			
	a. Regular prefix letters before serial #.	.10	.25	2.50
	b. Special prefix letters *JP* and all zero numbers (presentation).	—	—	100.

#167, Inauguration of Pres. Marcos, 1981

167	10 Piso	VG	VF	UNC
	1981. Black commemorative overprint at center right on #161b.			
	a. Regular prefix letters before serial #. Wide and narrow collar varieties.	.25	.50	2.00
	b. Special prefix letters *FM* and all zero numbers (presentation).	—	—	35.00
	s. As a. Specimen. Wide or narrow collar.	—	—	50.00

1985-91 ND ISSUE

#168-173 replacement notes: Serial # prefix "+".

168	5 Piso	VG	VF	UNC
	ND (1985-94). Deep green and brown on multicolor underprint. Aguinaldo at left center and as watermark, plaque with cannon at right. Aguinaldo's Independence Declaration of June 12, 1898 on back.			
	a. Signature 10. Black serial #.	FV	FV	2.00
	b. Signature 11. Black serial #.	FV	FV	1.00
	c. Signature as b. Red serial # (1990).	FV	FV	1.25
	d. Signature 12. Red serial #.	FV	FV	1.00
	e. Signature 13. Red serial #.	FV	FV	1.00
	f. Signature as b. Uncut sheet of 4.	—	—	30.00
	g. Signature as d. Uncut sheet of 4.	—	—	30.00
	h. Signature as e. Uncut sheet of 4.	—	—	15.00
	s1. Signature as b. Specimen.	—	—	15.00
	s2. Signature as c. Specimen.	—	—	15.00
	s3. Signature as d. Specimen.	—	—	20.00

169	10 Piso	VG	VF	UNC
	ND (1985-94). Dark brown, brown and blue-gray on multicolor underprint. Mabini at left center and as watermark, handwritten scroll at right. Barasoain church on back.			
	a. Signature 10.	FV	.50	3.00
	b. Signature 11.	FV	FV	1.50
	c. Signature 12. Black serial #.	FV	FV	2.00
	d. Signature as c. Red serial #.	FV	.50	5.00
	e. Signature 13.	—	—	2.00
	f. Signature as b. Uncut sheet of 4.	—	—	25.00
	g. Signature as b. Uncut sheet of 32.	—	—	100.
	s. Signature as b. Specimen.	—	—	25.00

170	20 Piso	VG	VF	UNC
	ND (1986-94). Orange and blue on multicolor underprint. Pres. M. Quezon at left center and as watermark, arms at right. Malakanyang Palace on back.			
	a. Signature 10. Black serial #.	FV	1.00	7.50
	b. Signature 11. Black serial #.	FV	FV	3.00
	c. Signature 12. Black serial #.	FV	FV	4.00
	d. Signature as c. Red serial #. Not confirmed.	—	—	—
	e. Signature 13. Red serial #.	FV	1.00	5.00
	f. Signature as e. Black serial #.	FV	FV	4.00
	g. Signature as b. Uncut sheet of 4.	—	—	45.00
	s. Signature as b. Specimen.	—	—	35.00

171	50 Piso	VG	VF	UNC
	ND (1987-94). Red and purple on multicolor underprint. Pres. Sergio Osmeña at left center and as watermark, gavel at right. Legislative building on back.			
	a. Signature 11. Black serial #.	FV	1.00	6.00
	b. Signature 12. Black serial #.	FV	FV	5.00
	c. Signature 13. Black serial #.	FV	FV	4.00
	s1. Signature as a. Specimen.	—	—	75.00
	s2. Signature as b. Specimen.	—	—	60.00
	s3. Signature as b. Uncut sheet of 4. Specimen.	—	—	30.00
	s4. Signature as c. Specimen.	—	—	35.00

172 100 Piso	VG	VF	UNC
ND (1987-94). Purple on multicolor underprint. Pres. M. Roxas at left center and as watermark, USA and Philippine flags at right. New Central Bank complex at left center with old building facade above on back.			
a. Signature 11. Black serial #.	FV	FV	7.50
b. Signature 11. Red serial #.	FV	FV	35.00
c. Signature 12. Black serial #.	FV	FV	12.50
d. Signature as b. Red serial #.	FV	FV	12.50
e. Signature 13. Red serial #.	FV	FV	10.00
f. Signature as d. Blue serial #.	FV	FV	7.50
s1. Signature as a. Specimen.	—	—	120.
s2. Signature as b. Specimen.	—	—	100.
s3. Signature as c. Specimen.	—	—	50.00
s4. Signature as d. Specimen.	—	—	50.00
s5. Signature as d. Specimen. Uncut sheet of 4.	—	—	25.00
s6. Signature as b. Specimen. Uncut sheet of 4.	—	—	75.00
s7. Signature as b. Specimen. Uncut sheet of 32.	—	—	200.
s8. Signature as e. Specimen. Blue serial #.	—	—	75.00
cr. Replacement note. Sign. as a. Red serial #. Rare.	—	—	—

173 500 Piso	VG	VF	UNC
ND (1987-94). Black and brown on multicolor underprint. Aquino at left center and as watermark, flag in underprint at center, typewriter at lower right. Various scenes and gatherings of Aquino's career on back.			
a. Signature 11.	FV	FV	40.00
b. Signature 12.	FV	FV	50.00
c. Signature 13.	FV	FV	30.00
s1. Signature as a. Specimen.	—	—	80.00
s2. Signature as b. Specimen.	—	—	55.00
s3. Signature as b. Specimen. Uncut sheet of 4.	—	—	75.00
174 1000 Piso			
ND (1991-94). Dark blue and blue-black on multicolor underprint. J. A. Santos, J. L. Escoda and V. Lim at left center and as watermark, flaming torch at right. Banawe rice terraces at left, to center, local carving and hut at center right on back.			
a. Signature 12.	FV	FV	85.00
b. Signature 13.	FV	FV	60.00

1986-91 Commemorative Issues

Commemorative ovpt. not listed were produced privately in the Philippines.

#175, Visit of Pres. Aquino to the United States

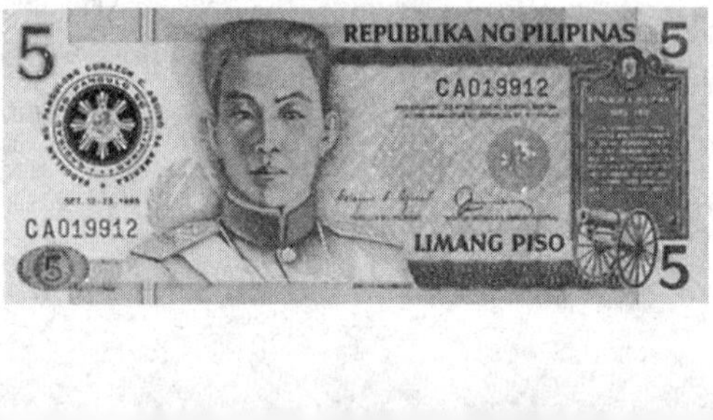

175 5 Piso	VG	VF	UNC
1986. Deep green and brown on multicolor underprint. Like #168 but with commemorative text, seal and visit dates in watermark area. Prefix letters CA. Signature 11.			
a. Serial #1-20,000 in special folder.	FV	FV	12.50
b. Serial # above 20,000.	FV	FV	1.50
c. Uncut sheet of 4.	—	—	30.00

#176, Canonization of San Lorenzo Ruiz

176 5 Piso	VG	VF	UNC
18.10.1987. Deep green and brown on multicolor underprint. Like #168 but with commemorative design, text and date in watermark area. Signature 11.			
a. Issued note.	FV	FV	1.50
b. Uncut sheet of 8 in special folder.	—	—	20.00

#177, 40th Anniversary of Central Bank

177 5 Piso	VG	VF	UNC
1989. Deep green and brown on multicolor underprint. Like #168 but with red commemorative design, text and date in watermark area. Signature 11.			
a. Issued note.	FV	FV	1.50
b. Uncut sheet of 8 in special folder.	—	—	20.00

#178, Women's Rights, 1990

178 5 Piso	VG	VF	UNC
1990. Deep green and brown on multicolor underprint. Like #168 but with black commemorative design in watermark area. Signature 11.			
a. Black serial #.	FV	FV	1.00
b. Red serial #.	FV	FV	4.00

#179, II Plenary Council, 1991

179 5 Piso	VG	VF	UNC
1991. Deep green and brown on multicolor underprint. Like #168 but with black commemorative design and date in watermark area. Red serial #. Signature 12.	FV	FV	1.00

1995 ND; 1998-99 ISSUE

#180-186 like #168-174 but w/Central Bank Seal Type 5 w/date 1993 at r.

#180 and 181 sign. 14.

		VG	VF	UNC
180	**5 Piso** ND (1995). Deep green and brown on multicolor underprint. Like #168.	FV	FV	1.00
181	**10 Piso** ND (1995-97). Dark brown and blue-gray on multicolor underprint. Like #169.			
	a. Red serial #.	FV	FV	1.50
	b. Signature as a. Black serial #.	FV	FV	3.00

		VG	VF	UNC
182	**20 Piso** ND (1997); 1998-. Orange and blue on multicolor underprint. Like #170.			
	a. Signature 14. Red serial #. ND.	FV	FV	2.50
	b. Signature 14. Black serial #.	FV	FV	3.00
	c. Signature 15. Black serial #. 1998; 1999.	FV	FV	2.50
	d. Signature 15. Blue serial #. 1999.	FV	FV	6.50
	e. Signature 16. Blue serial #. 2000.	FV	FV	5.00
	f. Signature 16. Blue serial #. 2001.	FV	FV	6.00
	g. Signature 17. Blue serial #. 2001.	FV	FV	3.50
	h. Signature 17. Black serial #. 2001; 2002; 2003; 2004, 2005.	FV	FV	3.00
	i. Signature 18. Black serial #. 2005.	FV	FV	3.50
	s1. As a. Specimen.	—	—	50.00
	s2. Uncut sheet of 4. Specimen.	—	—	100.

		VG	VF	UNC
183	**50 Piso** ND; 1998-2001. Red and purple on multicolor underprint. Like #171.			
	a. Signature 14. ND (1995).	FV	FV	4.00
	b. Signature as a. Red serial #. 1998.	FV	FV	6.00
	c. Signature 16. Red serial #. 1999; 2000; 2001.	FV	FV	4.00
	d. Signature 16. Black serial #. 2001.	FV	FV	8.00

		VG	VF	UNC
184	**100 Piso** ND; 1998-. Purple on multicolor underprint. Like #172.			
	a. Signature 14. ND.	FV	FV	10.00
	b. Signature as a. 1998.	FV	FV	8.00
	c. Signature 15. Red serial #. 1998.	FV	FV	5.00
	d. Signature as c. Black serial #. 1998; 1999.	FV	FV	6.00
	e. Signature 16. 1999; 2000.	FV	FV	7.00
	f. Signature 16. 2001.	FV	FV	12.50
	s. Signature as a. Specimen.	—	—	30.00

		VG	VF	UNC
185	**500 Piso** ND; 1998-2000. Black on multicolor underprint. Like #173.			
	a. Signature 14. ND; 1998.	FV	FV	30.00
	b. Signature 15. 1998; 1999.	FV	FV	25.00
	c. Signature 16; 1999; 2000.	FV	FV	35.00
	s. As a. Specimen.	—	—	50.00

		VG	VF	UNC
186	**1000 Piso** ND; 1998-2001. Dark blue on multicolor underprint. Like #174.			
	a. Signature 14. ND; 1998.	FV	FV	45.00
	b. Signature 15. 1998; 1999.	FV	FV	45.00
	c. Signature 16. 1999; 2000.	FV	FV	45.00
	d. Signature 17. 2001. Red serial #.	FV	FV	85.00
	s1. Signature as a. Specimen.	—	—	85.00
	s2. Signature as c. Specimen. 1999.	—	—	50.00

1997 ISSUE

187	10 Piso	VG	VF	UNC
	1997-. Dark brown and blue-gray on multicolor underprint. A. Mabini and A. Bonifacio at left center; flag, book, declaration and quill pen at right. Barasoain church at left, blood *Pacto de Sangre* meeting at lower right on back.			
	a. Signature 14. Single figure watermark. 1997.	FV	FV	2.00
	b. Signature 14. Single figure watermark. 1998.	FV	FV	2.00
	c. Signature 14. Double figures as watermark. Black serial #. 1998.	FV	FV	4.00
	d. Signature 14. Double figures as watermark. Red serial #.	FV	FV	20.00
	e. Signature 15. Red serial #. 1999.	FV	FV	2.50
	f. Signature 16. Red serial #. 1999; 2000; 2001.	FV	FV	3.00
	g. Signature 16. Red serial #.	FV	FV	7.00
	h. Signature 17. Red serial #. 2001.	FV	FV	2.00
	i. Signature 17. Black serial #. 2001.	FV	FV	3.00

1998 COMMEMORATIVE ISSUE

#188-190, Centennial of First Republic, 1898-1998

188	100 Piso	VG	VF	UNC
	ND (1997); 1998. Purple on multicolor underprint. Like #184 but with centennial design and inscription in rectangular frame at left in watermark area. Signature 14.			
	a. Without date at upper left. (1997).	FV	FV	6.00
	b. 1998 under value at left.	FV	FV	12.00
189	**2000 Piso**			
	1998. Multicolor. Pres. J. E. Estrada taking his oath of office on June 30, 1998 in the Barasoain Church at center. Re-enactment of the declaration of Philippine Independence at the Aguinaldo Shrine in Kawit, Cavite on June 12, 1998 by Pres. F. V. Ramos at center on back. Signature 15. Watermark: Estrada and Ramos. 216 x 133mm, issued in folder.	—	—	125.
190	**100,000 Piso**			
	1998. Green, yellow and brown. Pres. F. V. Ramos being greated by crowd, Bank seal at right. Pres. Ramos greeting crowd from inside enclosed porch. Signature 14.	—	—	3500.

Note: #190 only 1,000 pieces issued.

1999 COMMEMORATIVE ISSUE

#191, 50th Anniversary Bangko Sentral

191	50 Piso	VG	VF	UNC
	ND; 1999. Red and purple on multicolor underprint. Overprint on #183.			
	a. Without date at upper left. Signature 14.	FV	FV	3.50
	b. 1999 at upper left. Signature 15.	FV	FV	7.50

#192-194 held in reserve.

NOTICE

Readers with unlisted dates, signature varieties, etc. are invited to submit photocopies of their notes to: Standard Catalog of World Paper Money, 700 East State St. Iola, WI 54990-0001, E-Mail: george.cuhaj@fwpubs.com.

2001-02 ISSUE

#195-196 like #185-186 but w/iridescent denomination strip at l. ctr. and metallic segmented security strip at ctr. r.

193	50 Piso	VG	VF	UNC
	2001-2005. Red and purple on multicolor underprint. Like #183 but National Museum on back. Signature 17.			
	a. 2001; 2002; 2003; 2004. Signature 17.	FV	FV	4.00
	b. 2005. Signature 18. Black serial #.	FV	FV	5.00

194	100 Piso	VG	VF	UNC
	2001-2006. Purple on multicolor underprint. Like #188. Black serial #.			
	a. 2001; 2002; 2003; 2004. Signature 16, 17.	FV	FV	7.00
	b. 2005; 2006. Signature 18.	FV	FV	9.00
	c. 2005. Signature 18. Signature spelled Arrovo.	FV	FV	12.00

195	200 Piso	VG	VF	UNC
	2002; 2003; 2004. Green and purple on multicolor underprint. Diosdado Macapagal at left, Aguinaldo shrine at lower right. Scene of swearing in of Gloria Macapagal-Arroyo on back. Signature 17.	FV	FV	12.50

		VG	VF	UNC
196	**500 Piso** 2001; 2002; 2003; 2004; 2005. Black on multicolor underprint. Like #185. Signature 17.	FV	FV	20.00

		VG	VF	UNC
197	**1000 Piso** 2001-2005. Dark blue on multicolor underprint. Like #186.			
	a. 2001; 2002; 2003; 2004. Signature 17.	FV	FV	40.00
	b. 2005. Signatrue 18.	FV	FV	40.00

Collector Series

Bangko Sentral ng Pilipinas

1978 ND Issue

		VG	VF	UNC
CS1	**1978 ND 2-100 Piso** #159a-164a overprint: *SPECIMEN* and with serial # prefix Maltese cross.		—	50.00

The Republic of Poland, formerly the Polish Peoples Republic, located in central Europe, has an area of 120,725 sq. mi. (312,677 sq. km.) and a population of 38.73 million. Capital: Warsaw. The economy is essentially agricultural, but industrial activity provides the products for foreign trade. Machinery, coal, coke, iron, steel and transport equipment are exported.

Poland, which began as a Slavic duchy in the 10th century and reached its peak of power between the 14th and 16th centuries, has had a turbulent history of invasion, occupation or partition by Mongols, Turkey, Hungary, Sweden, Austria, Prussia and Russia.

The first partition took place in 1772. Prussia took Polish Pomerania. Russia took part of the eastern provinces. Austria took Galicia, in which lay the fortress city of Krakow (Cracow). The second partition occurred in 1793 when Russia took another slice of the eastern provinces and Prussia took what remained of western Poland. The third partition, 1795, literally removed Poland from the map. Russia took what was left of the eastern provinces. Prussia seized most of central Poland, including Warsaw. Austria took what was left of the south. Napoleon restored to Poland much of the territory lost to Prussia and Austria, but after his defeat another partition returned the Duchy of Warsaw to Prussia, made Kracow into a tiny republic, and declared what remained to be the Kingdom of Poland under the czar and in permanent union with Russia.

Poland re-emerged as an independent state recognized by the Treaty of Versailles on June 28, 1919, and maintained its independence until 1939 when it was invaded by Germany, then partitioned between Germany and Russia. Poland's present boundaries were determined by the U.S.-British-Russian agreement of Aug. 16, 1945. The Government of National Unity was replaced when the Polish Communist-Socialist faction won a decisive victory at the polls in 1947 and established a "People's Democratic Republic" of the Soviet type. In Dec. 1989, Poland became a republic once again.

MONETARY SYSTEM:

1 Marka = 100 Fenigow to 1919
1 Zloty = 100 Groszy, 1919-

Peoples Republic

Narodowy Bank Polski

Polish National Bank

1962; 1965 Issue

		VG	VF	UNC
140A	**20 Zlotych** 2.1.1965. Multicolor. Man at right, arms at upper left center. (Not issued).	—	—	—

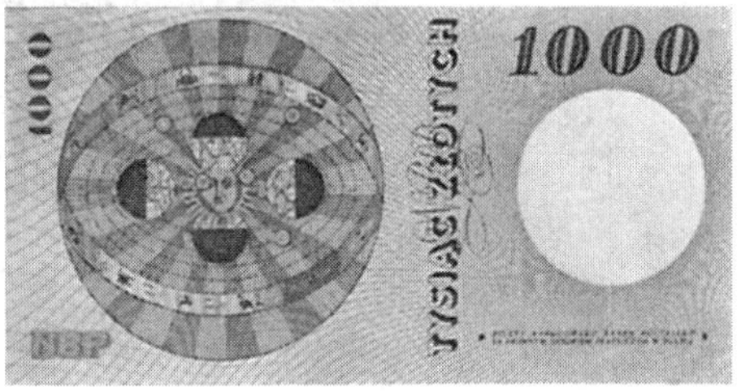

		VG	VF	UNC
141	**1000 Zlotych** 1962; 1965. Orange, red and green on multicolor underprint. Copernicus at center right and as watermark, arms at upper right. Zodiac signs in ornate sphere at left on back.			
	a. 29.10.1965. Series S.	1.50	5.00	20.00
	b. 29.10.1965. Series X.	10.00	25.00	120.
	s1. Specimen overprint: *WZOR*. 24.5.1962. (Not issued).	—	—	200.
	s2. Specimen overprint: *WZOR* with regular serial #. 29.10.1965.	—	—	30.00

1974-76 Issue

#142-146 eagle arms at lower ctr. or lower r. and as wmk. Sign. varieties.

142 50 Zlotych
1975-88. Olive-green on multicolor underprint. K. Swierczewski at center. Order of Grunwald at left on back.

	VG	VF	UNC
a. 9.5.1975.	.50	1.50	10.00
b. 1.6.1979; 1.6.1982.	.10	.30	2.75
c. 1.6.1986; 1.12.1988.	.10	.20	.75
s1. Specimen overprint: *WZOR*. 1975; 1986; 1988.	—	—	8.00
s2. Specimen overprint: *WZOR*. 1979.	—	—	7.00
s3. Specimen overprint: *WZOR*. 1982.	—	—	10.00

143 100 Zlotych
1975-88. Brown on lilac and multicolor underprint. L. Warynski at right. Old paper at left on back.

	VG	VF	UNC
a. 15.1.1975.	2.00	4.00	25.00
b. 17.5.1976.	1.00	2.00	8.00
c. 1.6.1979.	.25	.75	3.00
d. 1.6.1982.	.10	.20	2.00
e. 1.6.1986; 1.5.1988.	—	—	.50
s1. Specimen overprint: *WZOR*. 1975; 1982.	—	—	8.00
s2. Specimen overprint: *WZOR*. 1976.	—	—	7.00
s3. Specimen overprint: *WZOR*. 1979.	—	—	10.00

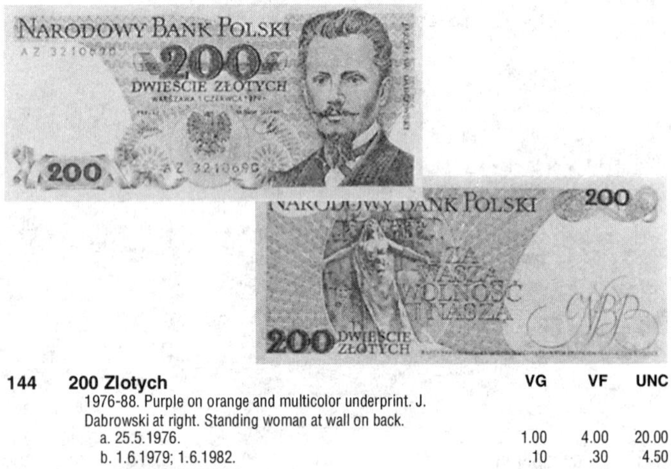

144 200 Zlotych
1976-88. Purple on orange and multicolor underprint. J. Dabrowski at right. Standing woman at wall on back.

	VG	VF	UNC
a. 25.5.1976.	1.00	4.00	20.00
b. 1.6.1979; 1.6.1982.	.10	.30	4.50
c. 1.6.1986; 1.12.1988.	.10	.25	1.00
s1. Specimen overprint: *WZOR*. 1976; 1986.	—	—	8.00
s2. Specimen overprint: *WZOR*. 1979.	—	—	7.00
s3. Specimen overprint: *WZOR*. 1982.	—	—	10.00

145 500 Zlotych
1974-82. Brown on tan and multicolor underprint. T. Kosciuszko at center. Arms and flag at left center on back.

	VG	VF	UNC
a. 16.12.1974.	2.00	7.00	30.00
b. 15.6.1976.	1.00	3.00	10.00
c. 1.6.1979.	.20	.75	7.00
d. 1.6.1982.	.10	.25	1.00
s1. Specimen overprint: *WZOR*. 1974; 1976.	—	—	8.00
s2. Specimen overprint: *WZOR*. 1979.	—	—	7.00
s3. Specimen overprint: *WZOR*. 1982.	—	—	10.00

146 1000 Zlotych
1975-82. Blue on olive-green and multicolor underprint. Copernicus at right. Atomic symbols on back.

	VG	VF	UNC
a. 2.7.1975.	2.00	4.00	35.00
b. 1.6.1979.	.25	1.25	10.00
c. 1.6.1982.	.15	.50	1.50
s1. Specimen overprint: *WZOR*. 1975; 1982.	—	—	10.00
s2. Specimen overprint: *WZOR*. 1979.	—	—	7.00

POLSKA RZECZPOSPOLITA LUDOWA

POLISH PEOPLES REPUBLIC

NARODOWY BANK POLSKI

POLISH NATIONAL BANK

1977 ISSUE

147 2000 Zlotych
1977-82. Dark brown on multicolor underprint. Mieszko I at right, arms at lower center and as watermark. B. Chrobry on back.

	VG	VF	UNC
a. 1.5.1977.	.25	1.00	5.00
b. 1.6.1979.	.50	1.75	13.50
c. 1.6.1982.	.20	.50	1.00
s1. Specimen overprint: *WZOR*. 1977.	—	—	10.00
s2. Specimen overprint: *WZOR*. 1979.	—	—	7.00
s3. Specimen overprint: *WZOR*. 1982.	—	—	15.00

1982 ISSUE

#148-150 wmk: Arms.

148 10 Zlotych

1.6.1982. Blue and green on multicolor underprint. J. Bem at left center, arms at lower right. Large value on back.

	VG	VF	UNC
a. Issued note.	.10	.25	1.50
s. Specimen overprint: *WZOR.*	—	—	10.00

149 20 Zlotych

1.6.1982. Brown and purple on multicolor underprint. R. Traugutt at left center, arms at lower right. Large value on back.

	VG	VF	UNC
a. Issued note.	.10	.25	.75
s. Specimen overprint: *WZOR.*	—	—	10.00

150 5000 Zlotych

1982-88. Dark green, purple and black on multicolor underprint. F. Chopin at right, arms at lower center. *Polonaise* music score at center on back.

	VG	VF	UNC
a. 1.6.1982.	.25	1.00	4.00
b. 1.6.1986.	FV	2.00	7.00
c. 1.12.1988.	FV	FV	2.50
s. Specimen overprint: *WZOR.*	—	—	12.50

1987-90 Issue

#151-158 arms at lower ctr. or lower r. and as wmk.

151 10,000 Zlotych

1.2.1987; 1.12.1988. Dark blue and red on green and multicolor underprint. S. Wyspianski at left center. Trees and city scene on back.

	VG	VF	UNC
a. 1.2.1987.	.50	2.25	10.00
b. 1.12.1988.	FV	.50	3.00
s. Specimen overprint: *WZOR.*	—	—	10.00

152 20,000 Zlotych

1.2.1989. Dark brown on tan and gold underprint. M. Curie at right. Scientific instrument on back.

	VG	VF	UNC
a. Issued note.	FV	1.25	4.00
s. Specimen overprint: *WZOR.*	—	—	10.00

153 50,000 Zlotych

1.12.1989. Dark brown and greenish black on multicolor underprint. S. Staszic at left center. Staszic Palace in Warsaw on back.

	VG	VF	UNC
a. Issued note.	FV	5.00	10.00
s. Specimen overprint: *WZOR.*	—	—	10.00

154 100,000 Zlotych

1.2.1990. Black and grayish blue on multicolor underprint. S. Moniuszko at right. Warsaw Theatre at left on back.

	VG	VF	UNC
a. Issued note.	FV	5.00	12.50
s. Specimen overprint: *WZOR.*	—	—	10.00

155 200,000 Zlotych

1.12.1989. Dark purple on red, tan and multicolor underprint. Coin of Sigismund III at lower center, arms at right. Back purple on brown underprint; Warsaw shield at left, view of Warsaw. Watermark: Geometric design repeated.

	VG	VF	UNC
a. Issued note.	FV	10.00	30.00
s. Specimen overprint: *WZOR.*	—	—	15.00

NOTICE

Readers with unlisted dates, signature varieties, etc. are invited to submit photocopies of their notes to: Standard Catalog of World Paper Money, 700 East State St. Iola, WI 54990-0001, E-Mail: george.cuhaj@fwpubs.com.

RZECZPOSPOLITA POLSKA

REPUBLIC OF POLAND

NARODOWY BANK POLSKI

POLISH NATIONAL BANK

1990-92 ISSUE

156	500,000 Zlotych	VG	VF	UNC
	20.4.1990. Dark blue-green and black on multicolor underprint. H. Sienkiewicz at left center. Shield with three books, also four flags on back.			
	a. Issued note.	FV	25.00	65.00
	s. Specimen overprint: *WZOR.*	—	—	37.50
157	**1,000,000 Zlotych**			
	15.2.1991. Brown-violet, purple and red on multicolor underprint. W. Reymont at right. Tree with rural landscape in background on back.			
	a. Issued note.	FV	50.00	150.
	s. Specimen overprint: *WZOR.*	—	—	70.00

158	2,000,000 Zlotych	VG	VF	UNC
	14.8.1992. Black and deep brown-violet on multicolor underprint. I. Paderewski at left center. Imperial eagle at left on back.			
	a. Issued note, misspelling *KONSTYTUCYJY* on back. Series A.	—	—	250.
	b. As a, but corrected spelling *KONSTYTUCYJNY* on back. Series B.	FV	90.00	200.
	s. Specimen overprint: *WZOR.*	—	—	100.

1993 ISSUE

#159-163 similar to #153, 154, 156-158 but modified w/color in wmk. area, eagle w/crown at lower ctr. or ctr. r. Wmk: Eagle's head.

159	50,000 Zlotych	VG	VF	UNC
	16.11.1993. Dark blue-green and brown on multicolor underprint. Similar to #153.			
	a. Issued note.	FV	3.00	7.00
	s. Specimen overprint: *WZOR.*	—	—	8.50

160	100,000 Zlotych	VG	VF	UNC
	16.11.1993. Black and grayish blue on multicolor underprint. Similar to #154.			
	a. Issued note.	FV	5.00	10.00
	s. Specimen overprint: *WZOR.*	—	—	10.00
161	**500,000 Zlotych**			
	16.11.1993. Dark blue-green and black on multicolor underprint. Similar to #156.			
	a. Issued note.	FV	20.00	30.00
	s. Specimen overprint: *WZOR.*	—	—	37.50

162	1,000,000 Zlotych	VG	VF	UNC
	16.11.1993. Brown-violet, purple and red on multicolor underprint. Similar to #157.			
	a. Issued note.	FV	45.00	100.
	s. Specimen overprint: *WZOR.*	—	—	70.00
163	**2,000,000 Zlotych**			
	16.11.1993. Black and deep brown on multicolor underprint. Similar to #158.			
	a. Issued note.	FV	95.00	200.
	s. Specimen overprint: *WZOR.*	—	—	100.

1990 (1996) "CANCELLED" ISSUE

Currency Reform

1 "new" Zloty = 10,000 "old" Zlotych

#164-172 arms at l. and as wmk. These notes were printed in Germany (w/o imprint). Before their release, it was decided a more sophisticated issue of notes should be prepared and these notes were later ovpt: *NIEOBIEGOWY* (non-negotiable) in red and released to the collecting community. Specimens are also known.

164	1 Zloty	VG	VF	UNC
	1.3.1990. Blue-gray and brown on multicolor underprint. Building in Gdynia at right. Sailing ship at left on back.			
	a. Cancelled note.	—	—	3.00
	s. Specimen overprint: *WZOR.*	—	—	25.00

165 2 Zlote

1.3.1990. Dark brown and brown on multicolor underprint. Mining conveyor tower at Katowice at right. Battle of Upper Silesia (1921) monument at left on back.

	VG	VF	UNC
a. Cancelled note.	—	—	3.00
s. Specimen overprint: *WZOR*.	—	—	25.00

166 5 Zlotych

1.3.1990. Deep green on multicolor underprint. Building in Zamosc at right. Order of Grunwald at left on back.

	VG	VF	UNC
a. Cancelled note.	—	—	3.00
s. Specimen overprint: *WZOR*.	—	—	25.00

167 10 Zlotych

1.3.1990. Red and purple on multicolor underprint. Building in Warsaw at right. Statue of Warszawa at left on back.

	VG	VF	UNC
a. Cancelled note.	—	—	3.00
s. Specimen overprint: *WZOR*.	—	—	25.00

168 20 Zlotych

1.3.1990. Brownish black and deep violet on multicolor underprint. Grain storage facility in Gdansk at right. Male statue at left on back.

	VG	VF	UNC
a. Cancelled note.	—	—	3.00
s. Specimen overprint: *WZOR*.	—	—	25.00

169 50 Zlotych

1.3.1990. Purple on lilac and multicolor underprint. Church in Wroclaw at right. Medallion at left on back.

	VG	VF	UNC
a. Cancelled note.	—	—	3.00
s. Specimen overprint: *WZOR*.	—	—	35.00

170 100 Zlotych

1.3.1990. Dark brown and black on orange and multicolor underprint. Building in Poznan at right. Medieval seal at left on back.

	VG	VF	UNC
a. Cancelled note.	—	—	3.00
s. Specimen overprint: *WZOR*.	—	—	35.00

171 200 Zlotych

1.3.1990. Black and deep purple on multicolor underprint. Buildings in Krakow at right. Medieval coin at left on back.

	VG	VF	UNC
a. Cancelled note.	—	—	3.00
s. Specimen overprint: *WZOR*.	—	—	25.00

172 500 Zlotych

1.3.1990. Black on green and multicolor underprint. Church in Gniezno at right. Medieval seal at left on back.

	VG	VF	UNC
a. Cancelled note.	—	—	3.00
s. Specimen overprint: *WZOR.*	—	—	25.00

1994 (1995) Regular Issue

#173-177 replacement notes: Serial # prefix *ZA*.

#173-175 arms at upper l. ctr.

173 10 Zlotych

25.3.1994 (1995). Dark brown, brown and olive-green on multicolor underprint. Prince Mieszko I at center right. Medieval denar of Mieszko I at left center on back.

	VG	VF	UNC
a. Issued note.	FV	FV	6.50
r. Replacement.	FV	FV	17.00
s. Specimen overprint: *WZOR.*	—	—	7.50

174 20 Zlotych

25.3.1994 (1995). Purple and deep blue on multicolor underprint. King Boleslaw I Chrobry at center right. Medieval denar of Boleslaw II at left center on back.

	VG	VF	UNC
a. Issued note.	FV	FV	10.00
r. Replacement.	FV	FV	27.00
s. Specimen overprint: *WZOR.*	—	—	12.50

175 50 Zlotych

25.3.1994 (1995). Blue-violet and deep blue and green on multicolor underprint. King Kazimierz III Wielki at center right. Eagle from seal, orb and sceptre at left center, town views of Cracow and Kazimierz on back.

	VG	VF	UNC
a. Issued note.	FV	FV	22.50
r. Replacement.	FV	FV	50.00
s. Specimen overprint.: *WZOR.*	—	—	35.00

176 100 Zlotych

25.3.1994 (1995). Olive-green on multicolor underprint. Wladyslaw II Jagiello at center right. Arms and Teutonic Knights' castle in Malbork on back.

	VG	VF	UNC
a. Issued note.	FV	FV	45.00
r. Replacement.	FV	FV	100.
s. Specimen overprint: *WZOR.*	—	—	65.00

177 200 Zlotych

25.3.1994. Brown on multicolor underprint. King Zygmunt I the old at center right. Arms and eagle in hexagon from the Zygmunt's chapel in the Wawel Cathedral and Wawel's court on back.

	VG	VF	UNC
a. Issued note.	FV	FV	85.00
r. Replacement.	FV	FV	170.
s. Specimen overprint: *WZOR.*	—	—	100.

2006 Commemorative Issue

178 50 Zlotych

16.10.2006. Light blue and yellow. Pope John Paul II at right center, hand raised in blessing. World map as background. Pope John Paul II seated at left, kissing hand of kneeling Cardinal Stefan Wyszynski at right. Text from letter to Poles, and rendering of Jasna Góra Monastery on back. — — 65.00

Foreign Exchange Certificates

Pekao Trading Co. (P.K.O.) / Bank Polska

Bon Towarowy (Trade Voucher)

1969 Series

#FX21-FX33 serial # prefix *E; F; G*.

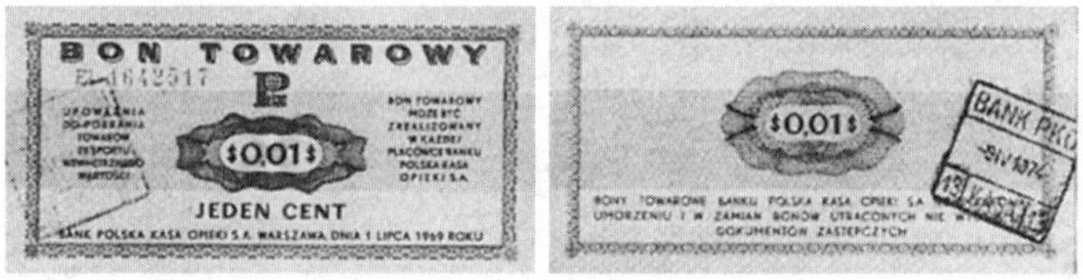

FX21 1 Cent

	VG	VF	UNC
1969. Black and blue on pale blue underprint. Back brown on pale blue underprint.	1.25	3.00	5.00

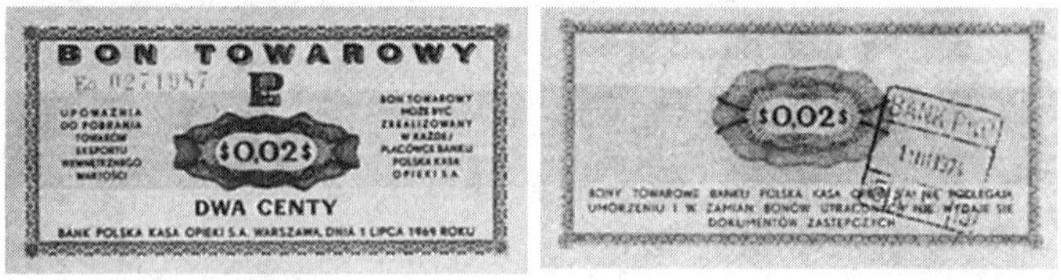

FX22 2 Cents

	VG	VF	UNC
1969. Black and green on orange and pink underprint. Back red on pink underprint.	1.25	3.00	5.00

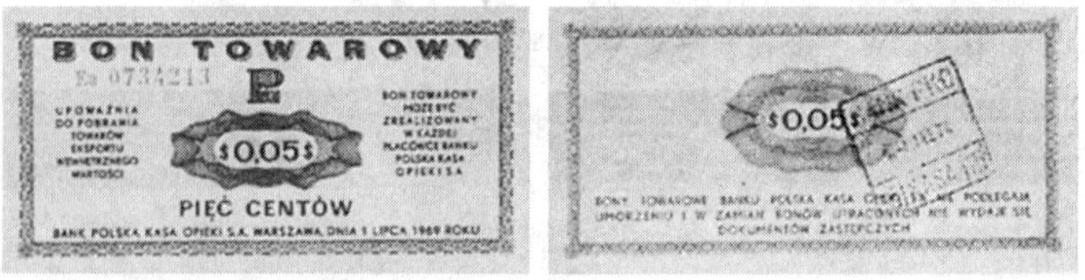

FX23 5 Cents

	VG	VF	UNC
1969. Black on orange underprint. Back brown on orange underprint.	1.50	4.50	7.50

		VG	VF	UNC
FX24	**10 Cents** 1969. Blue and black on orange and yellow underprint. Back olive on yellow underprint.	2.50	6.00	10.00
FX25	**20 Cents** 1969.	3.50	10.00	15.00
FX26	**50 Cents** 1969.	3.50	10.00	17.50
FX27	**1 Dollar** 1969. Brown and green on lilac and violet underprint.	5.00	12.50	20.00
FX28	**2 Dollars** 1969.	10.00	15.00	25.00
FX29	**5 Dollars** 1969.	10.00	25.00	—
FX30	**10 Dollars** 1969.	12.50	35.00	—
FX31	**20 Dollars** 1969.	17.50	45.00	—
FX32	**50 Dollars** 1969.	35.00	85.00	—
FX33	**100 Dollars** 1969.	100.	175.	—

1979 Series

#FX34-FX46 serial # prefix *H; I*.

		VG	VF	UNC
FX34	**1 Cent** 1979.	.50	1.50	2.50

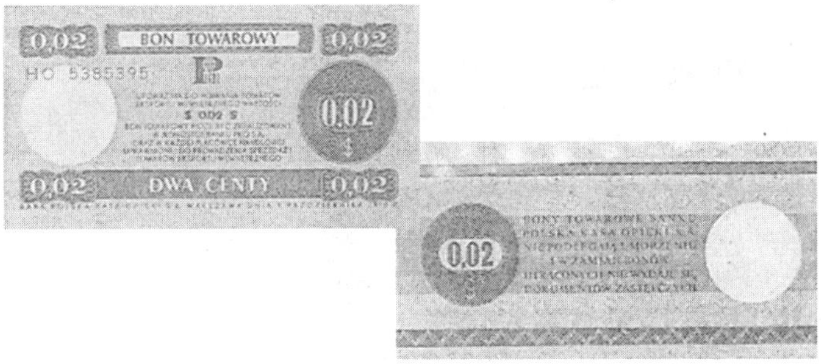

		VG	VF	UNC
FX35	**2 Cents** 1979. Brown on pink and tan underprint.	.75	1.75	3.00

		VG	VF	UNC
FX36	**5 Cents** 1979. Brown-violet on pale green and yellow underprint. Back lilac on light green underprint.	1.00	2.50	4.00

		VG	VF	UNC
FX37	**10 Cents** 1979. Deep green on pink and lilac underprint.	1.00	2.75	4.50

		VG	VF	UNC
FX38	**20 Cents** 1979.	1.25	3.00	5.00

		VG	VF	UNC
FX39	**50 Cents** 1979. Brown on orange and yellow underprint. Back red-brown on yellow underprint.	1.75	4.50	7.50
FX40	**1 Dollar** 1979. Olive-green on light blue and lilac underprint.	3.00	7.50	12.50
FX41	**2 Dollars** 1979.	5.00	12.00	20.00
FX42	**5 Dollars** 1979.	5.00	15.00	35.00
FX43	**10 Dollars** 1979.	12.00	30.00	50.00
FX44	**20 Dollars** 1979.	17.50	45.00	80.00
FX45	**50 Dollars** 1979.	30.00	75.00	125.
FX46	**100 Dollars** 1979.	50.00	125.	200.

Marynarski Bon Towarowy

Seamen's Trade Vouchers

1973 Series

#FX47-FX52 winged anchor w/knot at l.

		VG	VF	UNC
FX47	**1 Cent** 1.7.1973.	4.00	10.00	—
FX48	**2 Cents** 1.7.1973.	5.00	12.50	—
FX49	**5 Cents** 1.7.1973.	6.00	15.00	—
FX50	**10 Cents** 1.7.1973.	7.00	17.50	—
FX51	**20 Cents** 1.7.1973.	8.00	17.50	—
FX52	**50 Cents** 1.7.1973. Blue and green on green underprint. Anchor at left. Back black on green underprint.	10.00	20.00	—
FX53	**1 Dollar** 1.7.1973.	15.00	25.00	—
FX54	**2 Dollars** 1.7.1973.	20.00	30.00	—
FX55	**5 Dollars** 1.7.1973.	25.00	40.00	—
FX56	**10 Dollars** 1.7.1973.	35.00	50.00	—

Note: Higher denominations may have been issued.

Collector Series

Narodowy Bank Polski

ND (1948; 1965) Issue

		Issue Price	Mkt. Value
CS1	**Collector Set** Deep red ovpt: *WZOR* on 1948-dated 20, 50, 100, 500 Zlotych #137, 138, 139 and on 1965-dated 1000 Zlotych #141a. All with normal serial #.	—	75.00

1967 Issue

		Issue Price	Mkt. Value
CS2	**Collector Set** Red overprint: *WYSTAWA PIENIEDZY RADZIECKICH - LISTOPAD 1967* and *50 LAT WIELKIEGO PAZDZIERNIKA.* with *NBP* monogram at corners on faces of 1937 Russian 1, 3, 5, 10 Chervonetz #202-205. Made for the 50th anniversary of the Socialist revolution of 1917. Released by the National Bank of Poland in a special booklet.	—	50.00

1974 Issue

		Issue Price	Mkt. Value
CS3	**Collector Set** Reprints of 1944 Russian issue from 50 Groszy-500 Zlotych #104b-119b. Indicated as reprints of 1974 but without other overprint Made for the 30th anniversary of the Polish Peoples Republic.	—	20.00

1978 Issue

		Issue Price	Mkt. Value
CS4	**Collector Set** Dark blue-black overprint: *150 LAT BANKU POLSKIEGO 1828-1978* on faces of 1948-dated 20, 100 Zlotych #137, 139a. Made for 150th anniversary of Polish banknotes. Issued in a folder.	—	25.00

1979 Issues

		Issue Price	Mkt. Value
CS5	**Collector Set** Reprints of 1944 Soviet issue as #C3, but dated 1979 and with red overprint on face: *XXXV - LECIE PRL 1944-1979.* Made for the 35th anniversary of the Polish Peoples Republic.	—	25.00
CS6	**Collector Set** Reprint of 1919-dated 100 Marek with red overprint on face: *60-LECIE POLSKIEGO BANKNOTU PO ODZY SANIU NIEPODLEGLOSCI 1919-1979.* Made for 60th anniversary of modern Polish bank notes. Released by National Bank of Poland in a folder.	—	15.00
CS7	**Collector Set** Red overprint: *WYSTAWA WSPOLCZESNE MONETY I BANKNOTY POLSKIE I OBCE NBP 1979* on 1948 dated 2 Zlote #134. Issued in a small leatherette folder by the National Bank of Poland for a numismatic exposition.	—	10.00

1979-92 Issue

		Issue Price	Mkt. Value
CS8	**Collector Set** #142-157a, 148a with red overprint: *WZOR* on face; all zero serial # and additional black specimen # with star suffix. Red overprint: *SPECIMEN* on back.	—	300.

Note: Originally #CS8 was sold in a special booklet by Pekao Trading Company at its New York City, NY, and Warsaw offices. Currently available only from the Polish Numismatic Society.

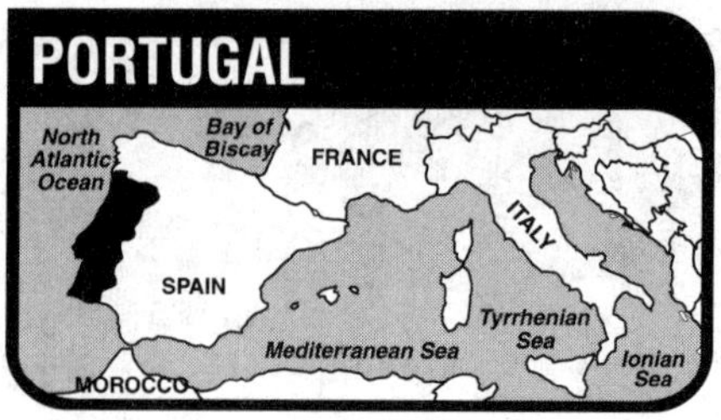

The Portuguese Republic, located in the western part of the Iberian Peninsula in southwestern Europe, has an area of 35,553 sq. mi. (91,905 sq. km.) and a population of 9.79 million. Capital: Lisbon. Portugal's economy is d on agriculture and a small but expanding industrial sector. Textiles, machinery, chemicals, wine and cork are exported.

After centuries of domination by Romans, Visigoths and Moors, Portugal emerged in the 12th century as an independent kingdom financially and philosophically prepared for the great period of exploration that would follow. Attuned to the inspiration of Prince Henry the Navigator (1394-1460), Portugal's daring explorers of the 14th and 15th centuries roamed the world's oceans from Brazil to Japan in an unprecedented burst of energy and endeavor that culminated in 1494 with Portugal laying claim to half the transoceanic world. Unfortunately for the fortunes of the tiny kingdom, the Portuguese proved to be inept colonizers. Less than a century after Portugal laid claim to half the world, English, French and Dutch trading companies had seized the lion's share of the world's colonies and commerce, and Portugal's place as an imperial power was lost forever. The monarchy was overthrown in 1910 and a republic established.

On April 25, 1974, the government of Portugal was seized by a military junta which reached agreements providing for independence for the Portuguese overseas provinces of Portuguese Guinea (Guinea-Bissau), Mozambique, Cape Verde Islands, Angola, and St. Thomas and Prince Islands (São Tomé e Príncipe).

MONETARY SYSTEM:

1 Escudo = 100 Centavos, 1910-2001
1 Euro = 100 Cents, 2002- Note: Prata = Silver, Ouro = Gold.

Republic

Banco de Portugal

1960; 1961 Issue

		VG	VF	UNC
163	**20 Escudos** 26.7.1960. Ch. 6A. Dark green and purple on multicolor underprint. Portrait Dom Antonio Luiz de Menezes at right and as watermark Back purple and m/c; bank seal at left. 8 signature varieties. Printer: BWC (without imprint).	10.00	35.00	90.00

		VG	VF	UNC
164	**50 Escudos** 24.6.1960. Ch. 7A. Blue on multicolor underprint. Arms at upper center, Fontes Pereira de Mello at right and as watermark Back dark green and m/c; bank seal at upper left, statue *The Thinker* at left. 8 signature varieties. Printer: TDLR (without imprint).	17.50	50.00	160.

NOTICE

Readers with unlisted dates, signature varieties, etc. are invited to submit photocopies of their notes to: Standard Catalog of World Paper Money, 700 East State St. Iola, WI 54990-0001, E-Mail: george.cuhaj@fwpubs.com.

165	100 Escudos	VG	VF	UNC
	19.12.1961. Ch. 6A. Deep violet and purple on orange, green and multicolor underprint. Pedro Nunes at right and as watermark, arms at upper center. Fountain and arches at left, bank seal at center on back. Seven signature varieties. Printer: BWC (without imprint).	17.50	50.00	140.

166	1000 Escudos	VG	VF	UNC
	30.5.1961. Ch. 8A. Purple on multicolor underprint. Queen Filipa de Lancastre at right and as watermark. Back blue. Printer: BWC (without imprint). Eight signature varieties.	40.00	180.	500.

1964-66 ISSUE

167	20 Escudos	VG	VF	UNC
	26.5.1964. Ch. 7. Olive-green and purple on multicolor underprint. Santo Antonio of Padua at right and as watermark. Church of Santo Antonio de Lisboa at left on back. Seven signature varieties.			
	a. Olive-brown underprint at left and right.	1.25	3.00	12.00
	b. Green underprint at left and right.	.75	1.75	7.00
	ct. Color trial. Blue and purple on multicolor underprint.	—	—	200.

168	50 Escudos	VG	VF	UNC
	28.2.1964. Ch. 8. Dark brown on multicolor underprint. Queen Isabella at right and as watermark. Old city Conimbria on back. Fifteen signature varieties.	1.00	2.25	9.00

169	100 Escudos	VG	VF	UNC
	1965; 1978. Ch. 7. Blue on light tan and multicolor underprint. Camilo Castello Branco at right and as watermark. City of Porto in 19th century at left on back.			
	a. 22 signature varieties. 30.11.1965.	1.25	3.00	12.00
	b. 6 signature varieties. 20.9.1978.	1.25	3.00	12.00

170	500 Escudos	VG	VF	UNC
	1966; 1979. Ch. 10. Brown on multicolor underprint. Old map at center, João II at right and as watermark. Compass-card or Rhumb-card and double statue on back. Printer: JEZ (without imprint).			
	a. 7 signature varieties. 25.1.1966.	6.00	20.00	65.00
	b. 9 signature varieties. 6.9.1979.	6.00	17.50	50.00

171	1000 Escudos	VG	VF	UNC
	2.4.1965. Ch. 9. Gray-blue on red-brown and multicolor underprint. Pillar at left, arms at upper center, Dom Diniz at right and as watermark. Scene of founding of University of Lisbon in 1290 on back. Printer: JEZ (without imprint). Seven signature varieties.	225.	750.	2400.

1967 ISSUE

			VG	VF	UNC
172	**1000 Escudos**	19.5.1967. Ch. 10. Blue, dark brown and violet on multicolor underprint. Flowers at left, Queen Maria II at right and as watermark. Her medallion portrait at left, Banco de Portugal in 1846 building at lower right on back. Printer: JEZ (without imprint). Twenty-four signature varieties.			
		a. Signature titles: *O GOVERNADOR* and *O ADMINISTRADOR.*	8.50	20.00	65.00
		b. Signature titles: *O VICE-GOVERNADOR* and *O ADMINISTRADOR.*	8.50	20.00	65.00

1968; 1971 ISSUE

			VG	VF	UNC
173	**20 Escudos**	27.7.1971. Ch. 8. Green (shades) on multicolor underprint. Garcia de Orta at right and as watermark. 16th century market in Goa on back. Fifteen signature varieties.	.50	1.25	5.00

			VG	VF	UNC
174	**50 Escudos**	1968; 1980. Ch. 9. Dark brown on multicolor underprint. Arms at left, Infante Dona Maria at right and as watermark. Sintra in 1507 on back.			
		a. 7 signature varieties. 28.5.1968.	1.00	2.50	10.00
		b. 9 signature varieties. 1.2.1980.	1.00	2.25	9.00

			VG	VF	UNC
175	**1000 Escudos**	1968-82. Ch. 11. Blue and black on multicolor underprint. Dom Pedro V at center and as watermark. Conjoined busts at left, ceremonial opening of the first railway at bottom center and right on back. Printer: BWC (without imprint).			
		a. 24 signature varieties. 28.5.1968.	6.00	17.50	50.00
		b. 8 signature varieties. 16.9.1980.	7.50	12.50	35.00
		c. 9 signature varieties. 3.12.1981.	7.50	12.50	35.00
		d. 9 signature varieties. 21.9.1982.	25.00	65.00	140.
		e. 11 signature varieties. 26.10.1982.	7.50	12.50	35.00
		ct. Color trial. Purple and green.	—	—	350.

1978; 1979 ISSUE

			VG	VF	UNC
176	**20 Escudos**	1978. Ch. 9. Green (shades) on multicolor underprint. Admiral Gago Coutinho at right and as watermark. Airplane on back. Large or small size numerals in serial #.			
		a. 6 signature varieties. 13.9.1978.	.40	1.50	6.00
		b. 6 signature varieties. 4.10.1978.	.40	1.25	5.00

			VG	VF	UNC
177	**500 Escudos**	4.10.1979 (1982). Ch. 11. Brown on multicolor underprint. Old street layout of part of Braga at center, Francisco Sanches at right and as watermark. 17th century street scene in Braga on back. Printer: JEZ (without imprint). Nine signature varieties.	3.75	8.50	27.50

1980-89 ISSUES

			VG	VF	UNC
178	**100 Escudos**	1980-85. Ch. 8. Dark blue on multicolor underprint. Manuel M. B. du Bocage seated at right and as watermark. Early 19th century scene of Rossio Square in Lisbon on back.			
		a. 8 signature varieties. Darker underprint through center 2.9.1980.	2.00	5.00	20.00
		b. 8 signature varieties. Light underprint through center 24.2.1981.	1.25	3.00	12.00

		VG	VF	UNC
178	**100 Escudos**			
	c. 7 signature varieties. 31.1.1984.	1.00	2.50	10.00
	d. 6 signature varieties. 12.3.1985.	1.00	2.50	10.00
	e. 6 signature varieties. 4.6.1985.	1.00	2.50	10.00
	s. Specimen.	—	—	135.
	ct. Color trial. Blue and green on multicolor underprint.	—	—	200.

		VG	VF	UNC
179	**100 Escudos**			
	1986-88. Ch. 9. Blue (shades) on multicolor underprint. Fernando Antonio Nogueira Pessoa at center right and as watermark. Rosebud on back.			
	a. 5 signature varieties. 16.10.1986.	1.00	2.50	10.00
	b. 8 signature varieties. 12.2.1987.	1.25	3.00	12.00
	c. Prefix letters *FIL*. 12.2.1987.	—	—	120.
	d. 8 signature varieties. 3.12.1987.	.85	2.00	8.00
	e. 6 signature varieties. 26.5.1988.	.85	2.00	8.00
	f. 6 signature varieties. 24.11.1988.	.85	2.00	8.00

Note: #179c was issued in a special folder w/an adhesive postage stamp affixed on the upper r. corner of the folder commemorating the 300th Anniversary of Portuguese Paper Money.

		VG	VF	UNC
180	**500 Escudos**			
	1987-94. Ch. 12. Brown and multicolor. José Xavier Mouzinho da Silveira at center right and as watermark, arms at upper left. Sheaf on back.			
	a. 8 signature varieties. 20.11.1987.	5.00	12.50	30.00
	b. 6 signature varieties. 4.8.1988.	4.50	10.00	27.50
	c. 6 signature varieties. 4.10.1989.	3.75	8.50	25.00
	d. 5 signature varieties. 13.2.1992.	3.75	8.50	25.00
	e. 7 signature varieties. 18.3.1993.	3.75	8.50	25.00
	f. 6 signature varieties. 4.11.1993.	3.75	8.50	25.00
	g. 5 signature varieties. 29.9.1994.	5.00	12.50	30.00

		VG	VF	UNC
181	**1000 Escudos**			
	1983-94. Ch. 12. Purple and dark brown on multicolor underprint. Teofilo Braga at center right and as watermark. Museum artifacts on back.			
	a. 9 signature varieties. 2.8.1983.	7.50	16.00	45.00
	b. 5 signature varieties. 12.6.1986.	7.50	17.50	47.50
	c. 8 signature varieties. 26.2.1987.	7.50	17.50	47.50
	d. 8 signature varieties. 3.9.1987.	7.50	17.50	47.50
	e. 6 signature varieties. 22.12.1988.	7.50	17.50	47.50
	f. 6 signature varieties. 9.11.1989.	7.50	17.50	47.50
	g. 5 signature varieties. 26.7.1990.	7.50	15.00	40.00
	h. 5 signature varieties. 20.12.1990.	7.50	15.00	40.00
	i. 5 signature varieties. 6.2.1992.	7.50	15.00	40.00
	j. 6 signature varieties. 17.6.1993.	7.50	12.50	32.50
	k. 6 signature varieties. 3.3.1994.	7.50	12.50	32.50

		VG	VF	UNC
182	**5000 Escudos**			
	1980-86. Ch. 1. Brown and multicolor. Antonio Sergio de Sousa at left center and as watermark. de Sousa walking at center on back. Printer: TDLR (without imprint).			
	a. 8 signature varieties. 10.9.1980.	35.00	75.00	170.
	b. 8 signature varieties. 27.1.1981.	35.00	70.00	160.
	c. 10 signature varieties. 24.5.1983.	35.00	70.00	150.
	d. 6 signature varieties. 4.6.1985.	35.00	70.00	150.
	e. 6 signature varieties. 7.1.1986.	35.00	70.00	150.
183	**5000 Escudos**			
	1987. Ch. 2. Olive-green and brown on multicolor underprint. Antero de Quental at center right and as watermark. Six hands with rope and chain at center on back.			
	a. 8 signature varieties. 12.2.1987.	30.00	45.00	120.
	b. 8 signature varieties. 3.12.1987.	30.00	45.00	120.

		VG	VF	UNC
184	**5000 Escudos**			
	1988-93. Ch. 2A. Olive-green and brown on multicolor underprint. Like #183.			
	a. 6 signature varieties. 28.10.1988.	30.00	45.00	120.
	b. 6 signature varieties. 6.7.1989.	30.00	50.00	125.
	c. 6 signature varieties. 19.10.1989.	30.00	45.00	120.
	d. 5 signature varieties. 31.10.1991.	30.00	45.00	120.
	e. 7 signature varieties. 18.3.1993.	30.00	45.00	120.
	f. 7 signature varieties. 2.9.1993.	30.00	45.00	120.

NOTICE

Readers with unlisted dates, signature varieties, etc. are invited to submit photocopies of their notes to: Standard Catalog of World Paper Money, 700 East State St. Iola, WI 54990-0001, E-Mail: george.cuhaj@fwpubs.com.

185	10,000 Escudos	VG	VF	UNC
	1989-91. Ch. 1. Orange, light brown and yellow. Dr. Antonio Gaetano de Abreu Preire Egas Moniz by human brain at center and as watermark. Nobel Prize medal, snakes, tree at center on back.			
	a. 6 signature varieties. 12.1.1989.	70.00	110.	250.
	b. 6 signature varieties. 14.12.1989.	70.00	100.	225.
	c. 5 signature varieties. 16.5.1991.	70.00	100.	220.

1991 ISSUE

186	2000 Escudos	VG	VF	UNC
	1991-93. Ch. 1. Dark brown and blue on multicolor underprint. Bartholomeu Dias at left and as watermark, astrolabe at center. Sailing ship at center, arms at right on back.			
	a. 5 signature varieties. 23.5.1991.	15.00	25.00	55.00
	b. 5 signature varieties. 29.8.1991.	15.00	35.00	80.00
	c. 6 signature varieties. 16.7.1992.	15.00	20.00	45.00
	d. 6 signature varieties. 21.10.1993.	15.00	30.00	70.00

1995-97 ISSUE

Note: #187-191, Quincentenary of Portuguese Discoveries Series

187	500 Escudos	VG	VF	UNC
	1997; 2000. Ch. 13. Violet and brown on multicolor underprint. João de Barros at right and as watermark, crowned shields on global view at upper center, angels below at left and right in underprint. Allegory of the Portuguese Discoveries at left center, illustrations from the *Grammer* at left in underprint on back.			
	a. 6 signature varieties. 17.4.1997.	FV	FV	12.50
	b. 6 signature varieties. 11.9.1997.	FV	FV	10.00
	c. 7.11.2000.	FV	FV	9.00

188	1000 Escudos	VG	VF	UNC
	1996; 1998; 2000. Ch. 13. Purple and brown on multicolor underprint. Pedro Alvares Cabral wearing helmet at right and as watermark, Brazilian arms at center. Old sailing ship at center, birds and animals of Brazilian jungle in underprint on back. Signature varieties.			
	a. 6 signature varieties. 18.4.1996.	FV	FV	25.00
	b. 6 signature varieties. 31.10.1996.	FV	FV	22.50
	c. 6 signature varieties. 12.3.1998; 21.5.1998.	FV	FV	22.50
	d. 7.11.2000.	FV	FV	20.00

189	2000 Escudos	VG	VF	UNC
	1995-97. Ch. 2. Blue-violet and deep blue-green on multicolor underprint. Bartholomeu Dias at right and as watermark, cruzado coin of Dom João II at upper center, sailing instrument below. Old sailing ship at center right, compass, map at left center on back.			
	a. 5 signature varieties. 21.9.1995.	FV	FV	40.00
	b. 6 signature varieties. 1.2.1996.	FV	FV	37.50
	c. 31.7.1997; 11.9.1997.	FV	FV	32.50
	d. 7.11.2000.	FV	FV	37.50

190	5000 Escudos	VG	VF	UNC
	1995-98. Ch. 3. Deep olive-green and brown-violet on underprint. Vasco da Gama at right and as watermark, medallion at upper center. Old sailing ship at center right, da Gama with authorities in Calcutta at left on back.			
	a. 5 signature varieties. 5.1.1995.	FV	FV	95.00
	b. 6 signature varieties. 12.9.1996.	FV	FV	90.00
	c. 6 signature varieties. 20.2.1997.	FV	FV	90.00
	d. 6 signature varieties. 11.9.1997.	FV	FV	85.00
	e. 2.7.1998.	FV	FV	85.00

191	10,000 Escudos	VG	VF	UNC
	1996-98. Ch. 2. Violet and dark brown on multicolor underprint. Infante Dom Henrique at right and as watermark, arms at center. Old sailing ship at center on back. Six signature varieties.			
	a. 2.5.1996.	FV	FV	150.
	b. 10.7.1997.	FV	FV	140.
	c. 12.2.1998; 12.7.1998.	FV	FV	140.

Note: For later issues used in Portugal see European Union listings.

PORTUGUESE GUINEA

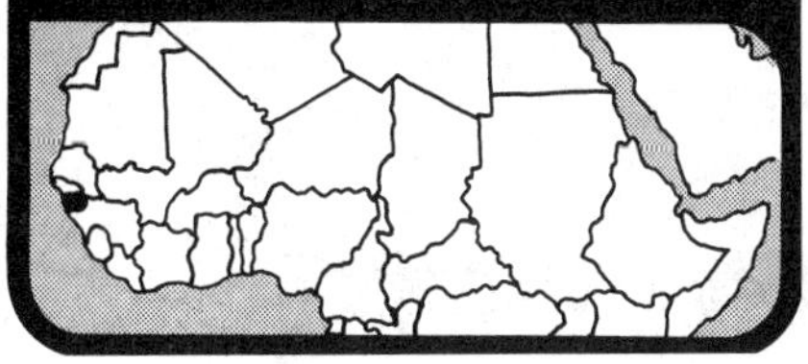

Portuguese Guinea (now Guinea-Bissau), a former Portuguese province off the west coast of Africa bounded on the north by Senegal and on the east and southeast by Guinea, had an area of 13,948 sq. mi. (36,125 sq. km.). Capital: Bissau. The province exported peanuts, timber and beeswax.

Portuguese Guinea was discovered by Portuguese navigator Nuno Tristao in 1446. Trading rights in the area were granted to Cape Verde islanders but few prominent posts were established before 1851, and they were principally coastal installations. The chief export of this colony's early period was slaves for South America, a practice that adversely affected trade with the native people and retarded subjection of the interior. Territorial disputes with France delayed final demarcation of the colony's frontiers until 1905.

The African Party for the Independence of Guinea-Bissau was founded in 1956, and several years later began a guerrilla warfare that grew in effectiveness until 1974, when the rebels controlled most of the colony. Portugal's costly overseas wars in her African territories resulted in a military coup in Portugal in April 1974, that appreciably brightened the prospects for freedom for Guinea-Bissau. In August, 1974, the Lisbon government signed an agreement granting independence to Portuguese Guinea effective Sept. 10, 1974. The new republic took the name of Guinea-Bissau.

RULERS:

Portuguese to 1974

MONETARY SYSTEM:

1 Mil Reis = 1000 Reis to 1910
1 Escudo = 100 Centavos, 1910-1975

Note: For later issues see Guinea-Bissau.

PORTUGUESE ADMINISTRATION

BANCO NACIONAL ULTRAMARINO, GUINÉ

DECRETOS - LEIS 39221 E 44891; 1964 ISSUE

#40-42 J. Teixeira Pinto at l., bank ship seal at r. Woman sitting, ships through the ages in background at ctr. on back.

40	50 Escudos	VG	VF	UNC
	30.6.1964. Dark green on lilac and multicolor underprint.			
	a. Issued note.	20.00	60.00	150.
	s. Specimen, punch hole cancelled.	—	—	120.

		VG	VF	UNC
41	**100 Escudos**			
	30.6.1964. Blue-green on multicolor underprint.			
	a. Issued note.	27.50	80.00	220.
	s. Specimen, punch hole cancelled.	—	—	150.
42	**500 Escudos**			
	30.6.1964. Brown on multicolor underprint.			
	a. Issued note.	50.00	150.	450.
	s. Specimen, punch hole cancelled.	—	—	200.

		VG	VF	UNC
43	**1000 Escudos**			
	30.4.1964. Red-orange on multicolor underprint. Portrait H. Barreto at right, bank ship seal at upper center. Woman standing, ships through the ages in background at left center on back. Printer: BWC.			
	a. Issued note.	35.00	100.	300.
	s. Specimen.	—	—	350.
	ct. Color trial. Brown on multicolor underprint.	—	—	200.

DECRETOS - LEIS 39221 E 44891; 1971 ISSUE

#44-46 Portuguese arms at upper ctr. Woman standing, ships through the ages in background at l. ctr., bank ship seal at lower l. on back.

		VG	VF	UNC
44	**50 Escudos**			
	17.12.1971. Olive-green on multicolor underprint. N. Tristao at right and as watermark.			
	a. Issued note.	6.00	20.00	50.00
	ct. Color trial. Green on multicolor underprint.	—	—	135.

		VG	VF	UNC
45	**100 Escudos**			
	17.12.1971. Blue on multicolor underprint. Portrait N. Tristao at right and as watermark.			
	a. Issued note.	6.00	20.00	55.00
	ct. Color trial. Olive on multicolor underprint.	—	—	135.

		VG	VF	UNC
46	**500 Escudos**			
	27.7.1971. Purple on multicolor underprint. Portrait H. Barreto at right.			
	a. Issued note.	30.00	90.00	275.
	ct. Color trial. Brown on multicolor underprint.	—	—	325.

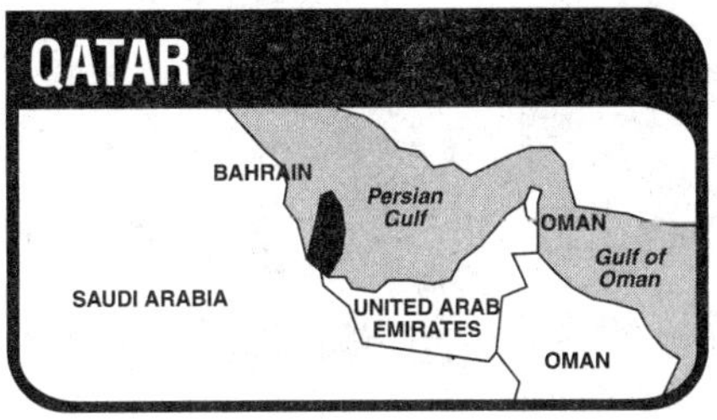

The State of Qatar, an emirate in the Persian Gulf between Bahrain and the United Arab Emirates, has an an area 4,247 sq. mi. (11,437 sq. km.) and a population of 700,000. Capital: Doha. Oil is the chief industry and export.

Qatar was under Turkish control from 1872 until the beginning of World War I when the Ottoman Turks evacuated the Qatar Peninsula. In 1916 Sheikh Abdullah placed Qatar under the protection of Great Britain and gave Britain responsibility for its defense and foreign relations. Qatar joined with Dubai in a monetary union and issued coins and paper money in 1966 and 1969. When Britain announced in 1968 that it would end treaty relationships with the Persian Gulf sheikhdoms in 1971, this union was dissolved. Qatar joined Bahrain and the seven trucial sheikhdoms (the latter now called the United Arab Emirates) in an effort to form a union of Arab emirates. However, the nine sheikhdoms were unable to agree on terms of union, and Qatar declared its independence as the State of Qatar on Sept. 3, 1971.

Also see Qatar and Dubai.

MONETARY SYSTEM:

1 Riyal = 100 Dirhem

EMIRATE

QATAR MONETARY AGENCY

1973 ND ISSUE

#1-6 arms in circle at r. Wmk: Falcon's head.

1	**1 Riyal**	VG	VF	UNC
	ND (1973). Red on lilac and multicolor underprint. Port of Doha at left on back.			
	a. Issued note.	.75	3.00	15.00
	s. Specimen.	—	—	35.00

2	**5 Riyals**	VG	VF	UNC
	ND (1973). Dark brown on lilac and multicolor underprint. National Museum at left on back.			
	a. Issued note.	2.00	8.00	35.00
	s. Specimen.	—	—	40.00

3	**10 Riyals**	VG	VF	UNC
	ND (1973). Green on multicolor underprint. Qatar Monetary Agency building at left on back.			
	a. Issued note.	3.50	10.00	40.00
	s. Specimen.	—	—	50.00

4	**50 Riyals**	VG	VF	UNC
	ND (1976). Blue on multicolor underprint. Offshore oil drilling platform at left on back.			
	a. Issued note.	70.00	275.	1100.
	s. Specimen.	—	—	500.

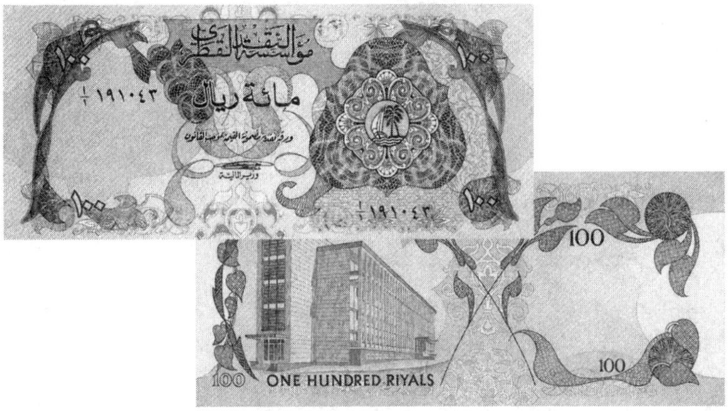

5	**100 Riyals**	VG	VF	UNC
	ND (1973). Olive-green and orange-brown on multicolor underprint. Ministry of Finance building at left on back.			
	a. Issued note.	FV	200.	700.
	s. Specimen.	—	—	225.

6	**500 Riyals**	VG	VF	UNC
	ND (1973). Blue-green on multicolor underprint. Mosque of the Sheikhs and minaret at left on back.			
	a. Issued note.	FV	600.	1600.
	s. Specimen.	—	—	700.

1980'S ND ISSUE

#7-13 arms at r. Wmk: Falcon's head.

		VG	VF	UNC
7	**1 Riyal** ND. Brown on multicolor underprint. City street scene in Doha at left center on back.	FV	1.50	5.00

		VG	VF	UNC
8	**5 Riyals** ND. Dark red and purple on multicolor underprint. Back red-brown, green and brown; sheep and plants at left center.			
	a. Watermark: Hawk, nostril visible, and top bill overlaps bottom.	FV	4.00	10.00
	b. Watermark: Hawk, without nostril, beak even.	FV	FV	8.00

		VG	VF	UNC
9	**10 Riyals** ND. Green on blue and multicolor underprint. National Museum at left center on back.	FV	5.00	15.00

		VG	VF	UNC
10	**50 Riyals** ND (1989). Blue on multicolor underprint. Furnace at a steel factory on back.	FV	20.00	50.00

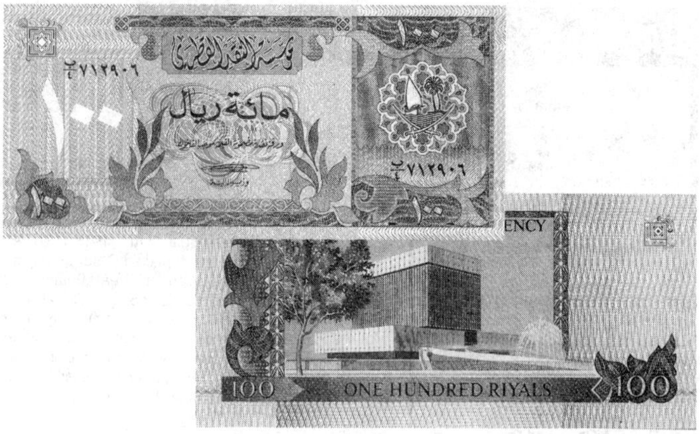

		VG	VF	UNC
11	**100 Riyals** ND. Green on multicolor underprint. Qatar Monetary Agency building at left center on back.	FV	30.00	65.00

		VG	VF	UNC
12	**500 Riyals** ND. Blue and green on multicolor underprint. Offshore oil drilling platform on vertical back.			
	a. Issued note.	FV	150.	275.
	s. Specimen.	—	—	200.

1985 ND ISSUE

		VG	VF	UNC
13	**1 Riyal** ND (1985). Brown on multicolor underprint. Face like #7. Back purple; boat beached at left, Ministry of Finance, Emir's Palace in background at center.			
	a. Watermark: Hawk, nostril visible, and top bill overlaps bottom.	FV	FV	2.25
	b. Watermark: Hawk, without nostril, beak even.	FV	FV	2.00

NOTICE

Readers with unlisted dates, signature varieties, etc. are invited to submit photocopies of their notes to: Standard Catalog of World Paper Money, 700 East State St. Iola, WI 54990-0001, E-Mail: george.cuhaj@fwpubs.com.

QATAR CENTRAL BANK

1996 ND ISSUE

#14-19 similar to #8-13 but w/two sign. Wmk: Falcon's head.

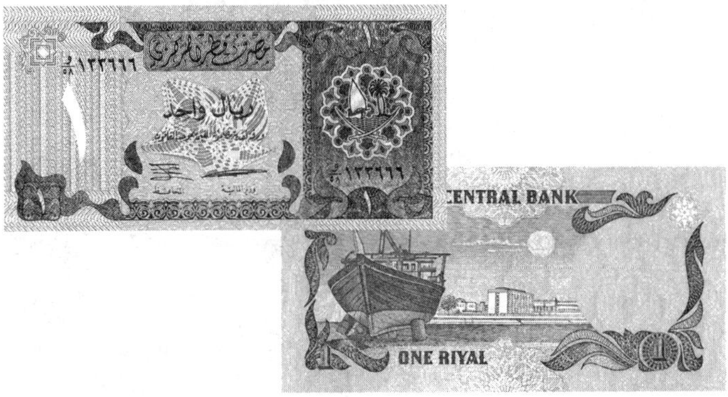

		VG	VF	UNC
14	**1 Riyal** ND (1996). Brown on multicolor underprint. Similar to #13.			
	a. Security thread reads: *QATAR MONETARY AGENCY.*	FV	FV	2.50
	b. Security thread reads: *QATAR CENTRAL BANK.*	FV	FV	2.00

		VG	VF	UNC
15	**5 Riyals** ND (1996). Red and purple on multicolor underprint. Similar to #8.			
	a. Security thread reads: *QATAR MONETARY AGENCY.*	FV	FV	9.00
	b. Security thread reads: *QATAR CENTRAL BANK.*	FV	FV	6.00

		VG	VF	UNC
16	**10 Riyals** ND (1996). Green and blue on multicolor underprint. Similar to #9.			
	a. Security thread reads: *QATAR MONETARY AGENCY.*	FV	FV	12.00
	b. Security thread reads: *QATAR CENTRAL BANK.*	FV	FV	8.00

		VG	VF	UNC
17	**50 Riyals** ND (1996). Blue on multicolor underprint. Similar to #10.	FV	FV	35.00

		VG	VF	UNC
18	**100 Riyals** ND (1996). Green on multicolor underprint. Similar to #11.	FV	FV	55.00

		VG	VF	UNC
19	**500 Riyals** ND (1996). Blue on multicolor underprint. Silver foil emblem at upper left. Similar to #12.	FV	FV	250.

2003 ND ISSUE

#20-25 wmk: Falcon's head at l.

		VG	VF	UNC
20	**1 Riyal** ND (2003). Purple and blue on multicolor underprint. Three native birds - Crested Lark, Eurasian Bee Eater and Lesser Sand Plover at left on back.	FV	FV	1.25

21 **5 Riyals**
ND (2003). Light and dark green on multicolor underprint. National Museum and native animals at left on back.

VG	VF	UNC
FV	FV	4.00

22 **10 Riyals**
ND (2003). Oranbe-brown and tan on multicolor underprint. Traditional Dhow and sand dunes Khor Al-Udeid at left on back.

VG	VF	UNC
FV	FV	7.00

23 **50 Riyals**
ND (2003). Rose on multicolor underprint. Qatar Central Bank building and Oyster and Pearl Monument at left on back.

VG	VF	UNC
FV	FV	35.00

24 **100 Riyals**
ND (2003). Green on multicolor underprint. Mosque of the Sheikhs and Al-Shaqab Institute at left on back.

VG	VF	UNC
FV	FV	50.00

25 **500 Riyals**
ND (2003). Light and dark blue on multicolor underprint. Royal Palace, Al-Wajbah Fort and Falcon's head at left on back.

VG	VF	UNC
FV	FV	225.

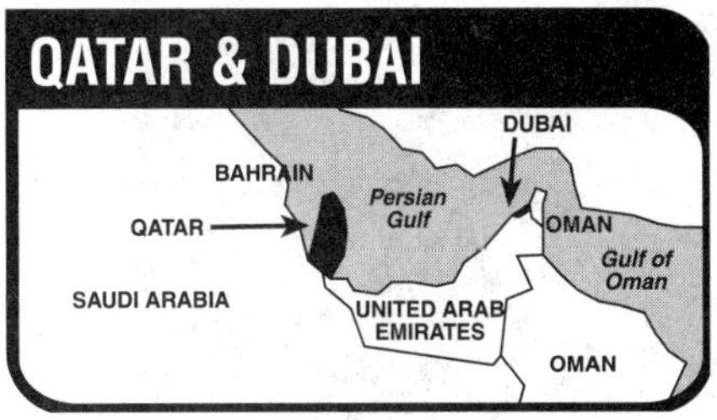

The State of Qatar, which occupies the Qatar Peninsula jutting into the Persian Gulf from eastern Saudi Arabia, has an area of 4,247 sq. mi. (11,000 sq. km.) and a population of 382,000. Capital: Doha. The traditional occupations of pearling, fishing and herding have been replaced in economics by petroleum-related industries. Crude oil, petroleum products, and tomatoes are exported.

Dubai is one of the seven sheikhdoms comprising the United Arab Emirates (formerly Trucial States) located along the southern shore of the Persian Gulf. It has a population of about 60,000. Qatar, which initiated protective treaty relations with Great Britain in 1820, achieved independence on Sept. 3, 1971, upon withdrawal of the British military presence from the Persian Gulf, and replaced its special treaty arrangement with Britain with a treaty of general friendship. Dubai attended independence on Dec. 1, 1971, upon termination of Britain's protective treaty with the trucial sheikhdoms, and on Dec. 2, 1971, entered into the union of the United Arab Emirates.

Despite the fact that the sultanate of Qatar and the sheikhdom of Dubai were merged under a monetary union, the two territories were governed independently from each other. Qatar now uses its own currency while Dubai uses the United Arab Emirates currency and coins.

MONETARY SYSTEM:

1 Riyal = 100 Dirhem

QATAR AND DUBAI CURRENCY BOARD

1960s ND ISSUE

#1-6 dhow, derrick and palm tree at l. Wmk: Falcon's head.

#		VG	VF	UNC
1	**1 Riyal** ND. Dark green on multicolor underprint.			
	a. Issued note.	5.00	50.00	165.
	s. Specimen, punch hole cancelled.	—	—	125.
2	**5 Riyals** ND. Purple on multicolor underprint.			
	a. Issued note.	20.00	100.	800.
	s. Specimen, punch hole cancelled.	—	—	200.

#		VG	VF	UNC
3	**10 Riyals** ND. Gray-blue on multicolor underprint.			
	a. Issued note.	40.00	175.	1100.
	s. Specimen, punch hole cancelled.	—	—	300.

#		VG	VF	UNC
4	**25 Riyals** ND. Blue on multicolor underprint.			
	a. Issued note.	500.	2000.	5000.
	s. Specimen, punch hole cancelled.	—	—	1500.
5	**50 Riyals** ND. Red on multicolor underprint.			
	a. Issued note.	350.	1500.	4000.
	s. Specimen, punch hole cancelled.	—	—	1300.

#		VG	VF	UNC
6	**100 Riyals** ND. Olive on multicolor underprint.			
	a. Issued note.	250.	1250.	3000.
	s. Specimen, punch hole cancelled.	—	—	1250.

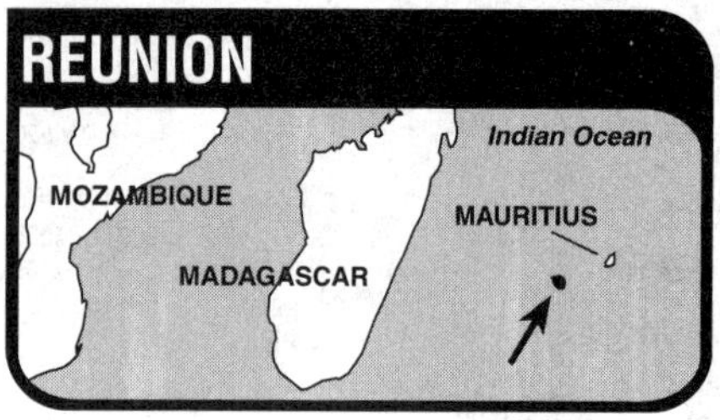

The Department of Reunion, an overseas department of France located in the Indian Ocean 400 miles (640 km.) east of Madagascar, has an area of 969 sq. mi. (2,510 sq. km.) and a population of 556,000. Capital: Saint-Denis. The island's volcanic soil is extremely fertile. Sugar, vanilla, coffee and rum are exported.

Although first visited by Portuguese navigators in the 16th century, Reunion was uninhabited when claimed for France by Capt. Goubert in 1638. It was first colonized as Isle de Bourbon by the French in 1662 as a layover station for ships rounding the Cape of Good Hope to India. It was renamed Reunion in 1793. The island remained in French possession except for the period of 1810-15, when it was occupied by the British. Reunion became an overseas department of France in 1946, and in 1958 voted to continue that status within the new French Union. Banque de France notes were introduced 1.1.1973.

MONETARY SYSTEM:

1 Franc = 100 Centimes
1 Nouveau Franc = 50 Old Francs, 1960

INSTITUT D'EMISSION DES DÉPARTEMENTS D'OUTRE-MER, RÉPUBLIQUE FRANÇAISE

DEPARTMENT DE LA RÉUNION

1964; 1965 ND ISSUE

		VG	VF	UNC
51	**500 Francs** ND (1964). Multicolor. Two girls at right, sailboat at left. Farmers with ox-carts on back.			
	a. Signature A. Postel-Vinay and P. Calvet.	25.00	150.	500.
	b. Signature A. Postel-Vinay and B. Clappier.	15.00	100.	400.
	s. Specimen.	—	—	175.

		VG	VF	UNC
52	**1000 Francs** ND (1964). Multicolor. Two women (symbol of the "Union Française") at right. Signature A. Postel-Vinay and P. Calvet.			
	a. Issued note.	20.00	125.	600.
	s. Specimen.	—	—	250.

		VG	VF	UNC
53	**5000 Francs** ND (1965). Brown on multicolor underprint. Gen. Schoelcher at center right. Signature A. Postel-Vinay and P. Calvet.			
	a. Issued note.	50.00	250.	1100.
	s. Specimen.	—	—	450.

1967 ND PROVISIONAL ISSUE

		VG	VF	UNC
54	**10 Nouveaux Francs on 500 Francs** ND (1967-71). Multicolor. Overprint on #51.			
	a. Signature A. Postel-Vinay and P. Calvet. (1967).	12.50	75.00	350.
	b. Signature A. Postel-Vinay and B. Clappier. (1971).	10.00	60.00	300.
55	**20 Nouveaux Francs on 1000 Francs** ND (1967-71). Multicolor. Overprint on #52.			
	a. Signature A. Postel-Vinay and P. Calvet. (1967).	12.50	100.	425.
	b. Signature A. Postel-Vinay and B. Clappier. (1971).	10.00	90.00	400.

		VG	VF	UNC
56	**100 Nouveaux Francs on 5000 Francs** ND (1967-71). Multicolor. Overprint on #53.			
	a. Signature A. Postel-Vinay and P. Calvet. (1967).	25.00	300.	900.
	b. Signature A. Postel-Vinay and B. Clappier. (1971).	22.50	225.	750.

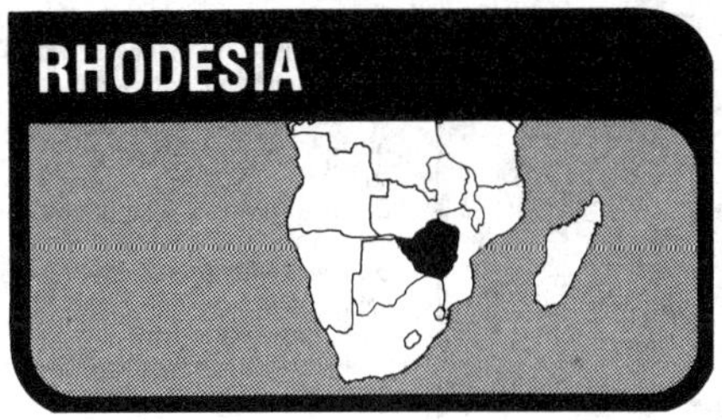

The "Republic of" Rhodesia (never recognized by the British government and was referred to as Southern Rhodesia, now Zimbabwe) located in the east-central part of southern Africa, has an area of 150,804 sq. mi. (390,580 sq. km.) and a population of 9.9 million. Capital: Harare. The economy is d on agriculture and mining. Tobacco, sugar, asbestos, copper and chrome ore and coal are exported.

The Rhodesian area, the habitat of paleolithic man, contains extensive evidence of earlier civilizations, notably the world-famous ruins of Zimbabwe, a gold-trading center that flourished about the 14th or 15th century AD. The Portuguese of the 16th century were the first Europeans to attempt to develop south-central Africa, but it remained for Cecil Rhodes and the British South Africa Co. to open the hinterlands. Rhodes obtained a concession for mineral rights from local chiefs in 1888 and administered his African empire (named Southern Rhodesia in 1895) through the British South Africa Co. until 1923, when the British government annexed the area after the white settlers voted for existence as a separate entity, rather than for incorporation into the Union of South Africa.

From Sept. of 1953 through 1963 Southern Rhodesia was joined with the British protectorates of Northern Rhodesia and Nyasaland into a multiracial federation. When the federation was dissolved at the end of 1963, Northern Rhodesia and Nyasaland became the independent states of Zambia and Malawi.

Britain was prepared to grant independence to Southern Rhodesia but declined to do so when the politically dominant white Rhodesians refused to give assurances of representative government. In November 1965, the white minority government of Southern Rhodesia unilaterally declared Southern Rhodesia an independent dominion. The United Nations and the British Parliament both proclaimed this unilateral declaration of independence null and void. Following a conference in London in December 1979, the opposition government conceded and it was agreed that the British government should resume control. In 1970, the government proclaimed a republic, but this too received no recognition. In 1979, the government purported to change the name of the Colony to Zimbabwe Rhodesia, but again this was never recognized. A British governor soon returned to Southern Rhodesia. One of his first acts was to affirm the nullification of the purported declaration of independence. On April 18, 1980, pursuant to an act of the British Parliament, the colony of Southern Rhodesia became independent within the commonwealth as the Republic of Zimbabwe.

RULERS:

British to 1970 (1980)

MONETARY SYSTEM:

1 Shilling = 12 Pence
1 Pound = 20 Shillings to 1970
1 Dollar = 100 Cents, 1970-80

BRITISH ADMINISTRATION

RESERVE BANK OF RHODESIA

1964 ISSUE

Pound System

#24-26 arms at upper ctr., Qn. Elizabeth II at r. Various date and sign. varieties. Wmk: C. Rhodes. Printer: BWC. Printed in England from engraved plates.

		VG	VF	UNC
24	**10 Shillings** 30.9.1964-16.11.1964. Blue on multicolor underprint. Blue portrait, black serial #. Tobacco field at left center on back.			
	a. Issued note.	20.00	80.00	425.
	ct. Color trial. Brown on multicolor underprint.	—	—	700.
25	**1 Pound** 3.9.1964-16.11.1964. Red on multicolor underprint. Red portrait, black serial #. Victoria Falls at left center on back.			
	a. Issued note.	10.00	60.00	300.
	ct. Color trial. Green on multicolor underprint.	—	—	600.

		VG	VF	UNC
26	**5 Pounds** 10.11.1964; 12.11.1964; 16.11.1964. Blue-green on multicolor underprint. Blue portrait, black serial #. Sable antelope at lower left. Zimbabwe ruins at left center on back.			
	a. Issued note.	15.00	65.00	275.
	ct. Color trial. Light blue on multicolor underprint.	—	—	850.

1966 ISSUE

#27-29 arms at upper ctr., Qn. Elizabeth II at r. Various date and sign. varieties. Wmk: C. Rhodes. Printed in Rhodesia (w/o imprint). Lithographed.

		VG	VF	UNC
27	**10 Shillings** 1.6.1966; 10.9.1968. Blue on multicolor underprint. Similar to #24 but with black portrait. Red serial #.			
	a. Issued note.	5.00	35.00	165.
	s. Specimen.	—	—	—
28	**1 Pound** 15.6.1966-14.10.1968. Pale red on multicolor underprint. Similar to #25 but brown portrait. Red serial #.			
	a. Issued note.	10.00	75.00	250.
	s. Specimen.	—	—	—
29	**5 Pounds** 1.7.1966. Blue-green on multicolor underprint. Similar to #26 but purple portrait. Red serial #.			
	a. Issued note.	30.00	225.	750.
	s. Specimen.	—	—	—

Note: Before the issue of #26, 28 and 29, a series of Rhodesian banknotes was printed in Germany by Giesecke and Devrient, Munich. An injunction prevented delivery of this issue and it was never released. Subsequently it was destroyed.

REPUBLIC

RESERVE BANK OF RHODESIA

1970-72 ISSUE

Dollar System

#30-33 bank logo at upper ctr., arms at r. Replacement notes: Serial # prefixes *W/1, X/1, Y/1, Z/1* respectively.

		VG	VF	UNC
30	**1 Dollar** 1970-79. Blue on multicolor underprint. Back like #27. Two signature varieties.			
	a. Watermark: C. Rhodes. 17.2.1970-18.8.1971.	2.00	7.50	30.00
	b. Watermark. as a. 14.2.1973-18.4.1978.	1.00	3.50	15.00
	c. Watermark: Zimbabwe bird. 2.8.1979.	1.00	2.50	12.50
	s. As b. Specimen.	—	—	—

		VG	VF	UNC
31	**2 Dollars** 1970-79. Red on multicolor underprint. Back like #28. Two signature varieties.			
	a. Watermark: C. Rhodes. 17.2.1970-4.1.1972.	2.00	10.00	40.00
	b. Watermark. as a. 29.6.1973-5.8.1977.	1.50	5.00	25.00
	c. Watermark. as a. 10.4.1979.	20.00	85.00	200.
	d. Watermark: Zimbabwe bird. 10.4.1979; 24.5.1979.	1.00	3.50	17.50
	s. As b, d. Specimen.	—	—	—

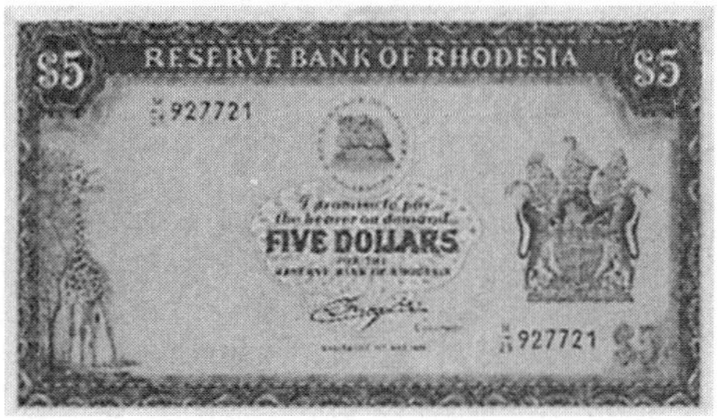

32	5 Dollars	VG	VF	UNC
	1972-79. Brown on multicolor underprint. Giraffe at lower left. Two lions on back. Two signature varieties.			
	a. Watermark: C. Rhodes. 16.10.1972.	3.00	10.00	35.00
	b. Watermark. as a. 1.3.1976; 20.10.1978.	2.50	10.00	35.00
	c. Watermark: Zimbabwe bird. 15.5.1979.	2.50	7.50	25.00
	s. Specimen.	—	—	—

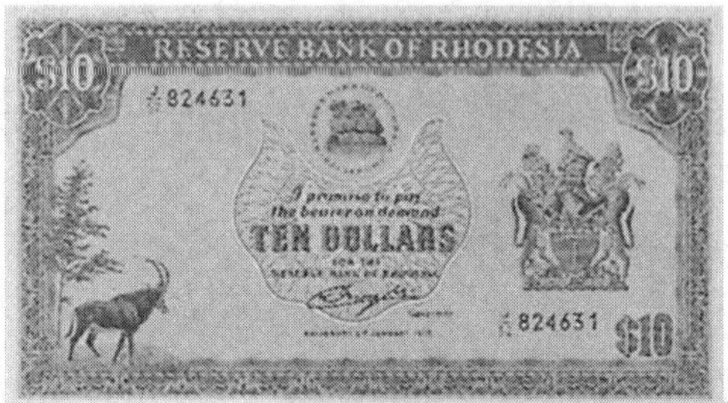

33	10 Dollars	VG	VF	UNC
	1970-79. Black on blue-green and multicolor underprint. Sable antelope at lower left. Back like #29. Two signature varieties.			
	a. Watermark: C. Rhodes. 17.2.1970-8.5.1972.	20.00	65.00	185.
	b. Watermark. as a. 20.11.1973-1.3.1976.	4.00	12.50	40.00
	c. Watermark: Zimbabwe bird. 2.1.1979.	3.50	12.50	35.00
	s. Specimen.	—	—	—

Note: For later issues see Zimbabwe.

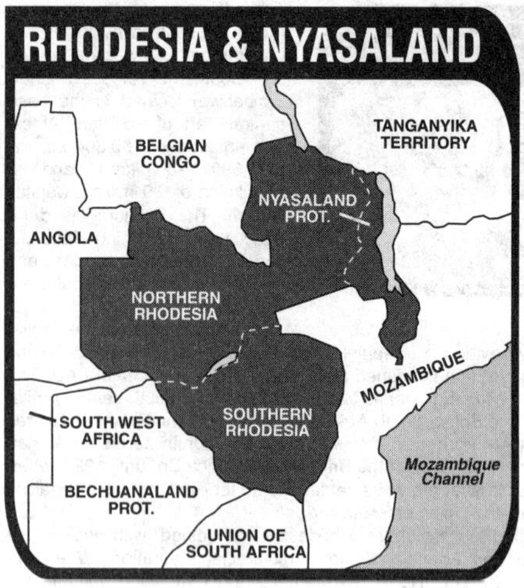

Rhodesia and Nyasaland (now the Republics of Malawi, Zambia and Zimbabwe) was located in the east-central part of southern Africa, had an area of 487,133 sq. mi. (1,261,678 sq. km.). Capital: Salisbury. The area was the habitat of paleolithic man, contains extensive evidence of earlier civilizations, notably the world-famous ruins of Zimbabwe, a gold-trading center that flourished about the 14th or 15th century AD. The Portuguese of the 16th century were the first Europeans to attempt to develop south-central Africa, but it remained for Cecil Rhodes and the British South Africa Co. to open the hinterlands. Rhodes obtained a concession for mineral rights from local chiefs in 1888 and administered his African empire (named Southern Rhodesia in 1895) through the British South Africa Co. until 1923, when the British government annexed the area after the white settlers voted for existence as a separate entity, rather than for incorporation into the Union of South Africa. From Sept. of 1953 through 1963 Southern Rhodesia was joined with the British protectorates of Northern Rhodesia and Nyasaland into a multiracial federation. When the federation was dissolved at the end of 1963, Northern Rhodesia and Nyasaland became the independent states of Zambia and Malawi.

Britain was prepared to grant independence to Southern Rhodesia but declined to do so when the politically dominant white Rhodesians refused to give assurances of representative government. On May 11, 1965, following two years of unsuccessful negotiation with the British government, Prime Minister Ian Smith issued a unilateral declaration of independence. Britain responded with economic sanctions supported by the United Nations. After further futile attempts to effect an accommodation, the Rhodesian Parliament severed all ties with Britain, and on March 2, 1970, established the Republic of Rhodesia.

On March 3, 1978, Prime Minister Ian Smith and three moderate black nationalist leaders signed an agreement providing for black majority rule. The name of the country was changed to Zimbabwe Rhodesia.

After the election of March 3, 1980, the country again changed its name to the Republic of Zimbabwe. The Federation of Rhodesia and Nyasaland (or the Central African Federation), comprising the British protectorates of Northern Rhodesia and Nyasaland and the self-governing colony of Southern Rhodesia, was located in the east-central part of southern Africa. The multiracial federation had an area of about 487,000 sq. mi. (1,261,330 sq. km.) and a population of 6.8 million. Capital: Salisbury, in Southern Rhodesia. The geographical unity of the three British possessions suggested the desirability of political and economic union as early as 1924. Despite objections by the African constituency of Northern Rhodesia and Nyasaland, who feared the dominant influence of prosperious and self governing Southern Rhodesia, the Central African Federation was established in Sept. of 1953. As feared, the Federation was effectively and profitably dominated by the European consituency of Southern Rhodesia despite the fact that the three component countries retained their basic prefederation political structure. It was dissolved at the end of 1963, largely because of the effective opposition of the Nyasaland African Congress. Northern Rhodesia and Nyasaland became independent states of Zambia and Malawi in 1964. Southern Rhodesia unilaterally declared its independence as Rhodesia the following year; this act was not recognized by the British Government.

RULERS:

British to 1963

MONETARY SYSTEM:

1 Shilling = 12 Pence
1 Pound = 20 Shillings to 1963

BRITISH ADMINISTRATION

BANK OF RHODESIA AND NYASALAND

1956 ISSUE

#20-23 portr. Qn. Elizabeth II at r. Various date and sign. varieties. Wmk: C. Rhodes. Printer: BWC.

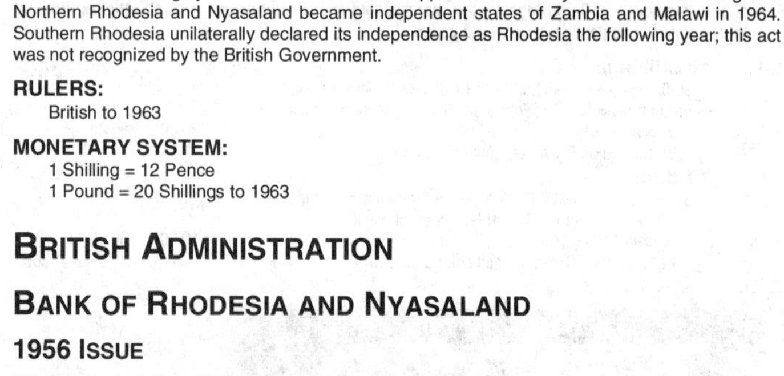

20	10 Shillings	VG	VF	UNC
	1956-61. Reddish brown on multicolor underprint. Fish eagle at lower left. River scene on back.			
	a. Signature A. P. Grafftey-Smith. 3.4.1956-17.6.1960.	45.00	250.	1000.
	b. Signature B. C. J. Richards. 30.12.1960-1.2.1961.	50.00	285.	1100.
	s. As a. Specimen punched hole cancelled. 3.4.1956.	—	—	450.
	ct. Color trial. Green on pink underprint.	—	—	850.

		VG	VF	UNC
21	**1 Pound**			
	1956-61. Green on multicolor underprint. Leopard at lower left. Zimbabwe ruins at center on back.			
	a. Signature A. P. Grafftey-Smith. 3.4.1956-17.6.1960.	35.00	225.	1100.
	b. Signature B. C. J. Richards. 23.12.1960-1.2.1961.	40.00	235.	1200.
	s. As a. Specimen punched hole cancelled. 2.5.1956.	—	—	550.
	ct. Color trial. Blue on orange underprint	—	—	850.
22	**5 Pounds**			
	1956-61. Blue on multicolor underprint. Sable antelope at lower left. Victoria Falls on back.			
	a. Signature A. P. Grafftey-Smith. 3.4.1956-17.6.1960.	85.00	375.	1400.
	b. Signature B. C. J. Richards. 23.1.1961-3.2.1961.	95.00	425.	1750.
	s. As a. Specimen punched hole cancelled. 3.4.1956.	—	—	900.
	ct. Color trial. Red-brown on blue underprint.	—	—	1350.

		VG	VF	UNC
23	**10 Pounds**			
	1956-61. Brown on multicolor underprint. Back gray-green; elephants at center.			
	a. Signature A. P. Grafftey-Smith. 3.4.1956-17.6.1960.	350.	1000.	—
	b. Signature B. C. J. Richards. 1.2.1961; 3.1.1961.	400.	1200.	—
	s. As a. Specimen punched hole cancelled. 3.4.1956.	—	—	1800.
	ct. Color trial. Green on multicolor underprint.	—	—	2250.

Note: For earlier issues refer to Southern Rhodesia in Volume 2. For later issues refer to Malawi, Zambia, Rhodesia and Zimbabwe in Volume 3.

Romania, located in southeast Europe, has an area of 91,699 sq. mi. (237,500 sq. km.) and a population of 22.5 million. Capital: Bucharest. Machinery, foodstuffs, raw minerals and petroleum products are exported. The area of Romania, generally referred to as Dacia, was inhabited by Dacians or Getae, a people of Thracian stock. The kingdom of Dacia existed as early as 200 BC. After military campaigns in 105-106 AD the Roman Emperor Trajan conquered Dacia and converted it into a Roman province. During the third century AD, raids by the Goths became such a menace that the Roman legions were withdrawn across the Danube in 271AD. Successive waves of invaders, including Goths, Huns, Gepidae, Avars and Slavs, made the country a battleground although the Romanized population preserved a Latin speech and identity. Through gradual assimilation of the Slavonic tribes, these people developed into a distinct ethnic group called Wallachians (Valachs or Vlachs).

With defeat in 1526, Hungary came under Turkish rule. Transylvania became a separate principality under the protection of the Sultan (1541).

At the close of the sixteenth century, the three principalities were united (Transylvania in 1599 and Moldavia in 1600) by Prince Mihai Viteazul of Wallachia, who made continual war on the Turks in an attempt to gain and maintain independence. The Ottomans restored their control of the principalities after Michael's death. The last Turkish vassal was eliminated in 1699 and Austria obtained the possession of Transylvania by the Treaty of Karlowitz. Under Hapsburg's administration, the region was made into a grand principality in 1765.

Because of the decline of Turkish power during the eighteenth century, the Austrian and later Russian influence became preeminent in the area.

After 1821 Romanian rulers were reestablished. The principalities, although remaining under Sultan control, were more autonomous. In 1829, the Turkish monopoly of commerce was abolished. Important institutional reforms were adopted.

The results of the European insurrectionist movements of 1848 saw the Moldovaian and Wallachian provisional revolutionary governments put down by Russo-Turkish military intervention. In 1867, Transylvania was incorporated under Hungarian administration. The question of the union of Wallachia and Moldavia was resolved in 1859. The two assemblies elected a single prince, Alexandru Ioan Cuza, establishing the fruition of Romania. Prince Cuza was deposed in 1866. A provisional government then elected Prince Karl of Hohenzollern-Sigmaringen, who as Carol I was vested as hereditary prince. A rapid modernization of the country was perceived. Romania was successful in a war against Turkey (1877-78) and proclaimed itself to be independent. The Congress of Berlin (1878) recognized this fact. In 1881, Carol I became king. In 1888, Romania became a constitutional monarchy with a bicameral legislature.

A new constitution was adopted in 1923. During this time the government struggled with domestic problems, agrarian reform and economic reconstruction.

The government was reorganized along Fascist lines between September 14, 1940 - January 23, 1941. A military dictatorship followed. Marshal Ion Antonescu installed himself as chief of state. When the Germans invaded the Soviet Union, Romania also became involved in recovering the regions of Bessarabia and northern Bukovina annexed by Stalin in 1940.

On August 23, 1944, King Mihai I proclaimed an armistice with the Allied Forces. The Romanian army drove out the Germans and Hungarians in northern Transylvania, but the country was subsequently occupied by the Soviet army. That monarchy was abolished on December 30, 1947, and Romania became a "People's Republic" d on the Soviet regime. With the accession of N. Ceausescu to power, Romania began to exercise a considerable degree of independence, refusing to participate in the 1968 invasion of Czechoslovakia. In 1965, it was proclaimed a "Socialist Republic". After 1977, an oppressed and impoverished domestic scene worsened.

On December 17, 1989, an anti-Communist revolt began in Timisoara. On December 22, 1989 the Communist government was overthrown by organized freedom fighters in Bucharest. Ceausescu and his wife were arrested and later executed. The new government has established a republic.

MONETARY SYSTEM:

10,000 "old" Lei = 1 "new" Leu, 1.7.2005
1 Leu = 100 Bani

Socialist Republic

Banca Nationala a Republicii Socialiste România

1966 Issue

#91-94 arms at ctr. Wmk: Rhombuses.

		VG	VF	UNC
91	**1 Leu**			
	1966. Olive-brown and tan.			
	a. Issued note.	.10	.40	2.50
	s. Specimen.	—	—	10.00
92	**3 Lei**			
	1966. Blue on orange and multicolor underprint.			
	a. Issued note.	.25	.75	3.50
	s. Specimen.	—	—	10.00

		VG	VF	UNC
93	**5 Lei**			
	1966. Brown and dark blue on multicolor underprint. Cargo ships at dockside on back.			
	a. Issued note.	.20	.60	3.50
	s. Specimen.	—	—	10.00

94	10 Lei	VG	VF	UNC
	.1966. Purple on multicolor underprint. Harvest scene on back.			
	a. Issued note.	.20	.75	4.50
	s. Specimen.	—	—	10.00

#95-97 arms at ctr. r. Wmk: Rhombuses.

95	25 Lei	VG	VF	UNC
	1966. Dark green on multicolor underprint. Portrait Tudor Vladimirescu at left. Large refinery on back.			
	a. Issued note.	.25	.75	5.50
	s. Specimen.	—	—	15.00

96	50 Lei	VG	VF	UNC
	1966. Dark green on multicolor underprint. Alexandru Ioan Cuza at left. Culture Palace in Iasi at center right on back.			
	a. Issued note.	.25	2.00	7.00
	s. Specimen.	—	—	15.00

97	100 Lei	VG	VF	UNC
	1966. Dark blue and purple on multicolor underprint. Portrait Nicolae Balcescu at left. The Athenaeum in Bucharest at center right on back.			
	a. Issued note.	.50	2.25	8.50
	s. Specimen.	—	—	20.00

REPUBLIC

BANCA NATIONALA A ROMÂNIEI

1991 ISSUE

98	500 Lei	VG	VF	UNC
	1991. Dark brown on multicolor underprint. Constantin Brâncusi at right and as watermark Brâncusi seated with statue at left. Center on back. Signature Isarescu.			
	a. Jan. 1991.	.75	5.00	16.00
	b. April 1991.	.25	1.50	6.00
	x. As b, with *APRILIED* (error). Reported not confirmed.	—	—	—

#99 renumbered to #101A.

1991-94 ISSUE

100	200 Lei	VG	VF	UNC
	Dec. 1992. Dull deep brown and brown-violet on multicolor underprint. Square-topped shield at left center, steamboat *Tudor Vladimirescu* above grey heron and Sulina Lighthouse in underprint. at center, Grigore Antipa at at right. Herons, fish, and net on outline of Danube Delta at left center on back. Watermark: Bank monogram repeated.	.10	.60	3.00

101 500 Lei

Dec. 1992. Dull deep green, reddish brown and violet on multicolor underprint. Square topped shield at left center, sculptures at center, Constantin Brâncusi at right. Sculptures at left center on back. Watermark: Bust right.

	VG	VF	UNC
a. Watermark: Bust facing as #98.	.20	3.00	9.00
b. Watermark: Bust to r.	.10	.60	2.50

		VG	VF	UNC
101A	**1000 Lei** Sept. 1991. Red-brown, blue-green and brown-orange on multicolor underprint. Circular shield at left center, sails of sailing ships at lower center, Mihai Eminescu at right and as watermark Putna monastery at left center on back. Signature Isarescu and Florescu.	1.00	3.00	12.00
102	**1000 Lei** May 1993. Similar to #101A but square-topped shield of arms at left center.	.20	1.00	3.50

		VG	VF	UNC
103	**5000 Lei** March 1992. Pale purple on multicolor underprint. Round seal at left center, church at center, Avram Iancu at right and as watermark. Church at left, the gate of Alba Iulia stronghold at left center, seal at center right on back.	1.00	4.00	18.00

		VG	VF	UNC
104	**5000 Lei** May 1993. Similar to #103 but square-topped shield at left center.	.50	1.50	5.00

		VG	VF	UNC
105	**10,000 Lei** Feb. 1994. Dull violet and reddish brown on multicolor underprint. Nicolae Iorga at right and as watermark, snake god Glycon at center. Statue of Fortuna at left, historical Museum in Bucharest at center, The Thinking Man of Hamangia at lower center right on back.	.50	2.00	7.00

1996-2000 Paper Issue

#106-110 arms at top l., bank monogram at upper ctr. r. Bank monogram at top r. on back.

		VG	VF	UNC
106	**1000 Lei** 1998. Blue-violet, dark green and olive-brown on multicolor underprint. Mihai Eminescu at right and as watermark, lily flower and quill pen at center. Lime and blue flowers at left center, ruins of ancient fort of Histria at center on back.	.10	.50	2.00

		VG	VF	UNC
107	**5000 Lei** 1998. Violet, dark brown and brown-orange on multicolor underprint. Lucian Blaga at right and as watermark, daffodil at center. Vine leaf at left center, roadside crucifix at center on back.	.25	1.00	3.50

108	10,000 Lei	VG	VF	UNC
	1999. Green-yellow and blue on multicolor underprint. Nicolae Iorga at right and as watermark, gentian flower at center. The church of Curtea de Arges monastery at center, Wallachian arms of Prince Constantin Brancoveanu (1686-1714) at left on back.	.50	1.25	5.00

109	50,000 Lei	VG	VF	UNC
	1996. Purple and red-violet on lilac and multicolor underprint. George Enescu at right and as watermark, floral ornament, musical notes at center, arms at upper left. Sphinx of Carpathian mountains at left center, musical chord from *Oedip King* above on back.	.50	3.00	18.00

109A	50,000 Lei	VG	VF	UNC
	2000. Purple and red-violet on lilac and multicolor underprint. Like #109 but violin shaped bronze area near portrait, and changed underprint design.	.50	1.00	8.50

110	100,000 Lei	VG	VF	UNC
	1998. Dull red on olive-green and multicolor underprint. Nicolae Grigorescu at right and as watermark, mallow flowers and artist's brush at center. Peasant girl with ewe at left, cottage at center on back.	1.00	2.50	14.00

1999 Commemorative Issue

#111, Total Solar Eclipse, August 11, 1999

111	2000 Lei	VG	VF	UNC
	1999. Blue on multicolor underprint. Imaginative reproduction of the Solar System at right, with the mention of the event. The map of Romania having the colors of the national flag, (blue, yellow, red) marking the area where the phenomenon of the solar eclipse was total at center on back. Polymer plastic.			
	a. Issued note.	.25	.50	2.00
	b. Serial # prefix 001A in folder. (One million pcs.)		—	8.00

2000-01 Polymer Issue

112	10,000 Lei	VG	VF	UNC
	2000. Green and blue on multicolor underprint. Similar to # 109. Signature Ghizari; Nitu. Polymer plastic.			
	a. Issued note.	.25	.50	3.00
	b. Uncut sheet of 4 (5000 sheets) .	—	—	12.50

113	50,000 Lei	VG	VF	UNC
	2000. Purple and red-violet on lilac and multicolor underprint. Like #109. Polymer plastic.			
	a. Issued note.	.25	1.00	4.50
	b. Uncut sheet of 4 (500 sheets).	—	—	40.00

114 100,000 Lei

	VG	VF	UNC
2001. Dull red on olive-green and multicolor underprint. Similar to #110. Signature Isarescu; Nitu. Polymer plastic.	.50	1.00	7.50

115 500,000 Lei

	VG	VF	UNC
2000. Brown on yellow and multicolor underprint. Aurel Vlaicu at right, edelweiss flower at center. Imperial Eagle head at center, *Vlaicu II* plane and *Gnome* engine sketch at left center on back. Polymer plastic.			
a. Issued note.	.50	2.50	25.00
b. Uncut sheet of 4 (2000 sheets) .	—	—	140.

116 1,000,000 Lei

	VG	VF	UNC
2003. Blue, green, violet and yellow. Luca Caragiale at right. Statue and building on back.	3.50	10.00	45.00

2005 Revaluation Issue

117 1 Leu

	VG	VF	UNC
2005.	FV	FV	1.25

118 5 Lei

	VG	VF	UNC
2005.	FV	FV	2.00

119 10 Lei

	VG	VF	UNC
2005.	FV	FV	4.00

120 50 Lei

	VG	VF	UNC
2005.	FV	FV	19.00

121 100 Lei

	VG	VF	UNC
2005.	FV	FV	38.00

122 500 Lei

	VG	VF	UNC
2005.	FV	FV	185.

Russia, (formerly the central power of the Union of Soviet Socialist Republics and now of the Commonwealth of Independent States) occupying the northern part of Asia and the far eastern part of Europe, has an area of 8,649,538 sq. mi. (17,075,450 sq. km.) and a population of 146.2 million. Capital: Moscow. Exports include machinery, iron and steel, oil, timber and nonferrous metals.

The first Russian dynasty was founded in Novgorod by the Viking, Rurik in 862 AD. Under Yaroslav the Wise (1019-54) the subsequent Kievan state (Kyiv's Rus') became one of the great commercial and cultural centers of Europe before falling to the Mongols in the 13th century, who ruled Russia until late in the 15th century when Ivan III threw off the Mongol yoke. The Russian Empire was enlarged and solidified during the reigns of Ivan the Terrible, Peter the Great and Catherine the Great, and by 1881 extended to the Pacific and into Central Asia.

Assignats, the first government paper money of the Russian Empire, were introduced in 1769, and gave way to State Credit Notes in 1843. Russia was put on the gold standard in 1897 and reformed its currency at that time.

All pre-1898 notes were destroyed as they were turned in to the Treasury, accounting for their uniform scarcity today.

The last Russian Czar, Nicholas II (1894-1917), was deposed by the provisional government under Prince Lvov and later Alexander Kerensky during the military defeat in World War I. This government rapidly lost ground to the Bolshevik wing of the Socialist Democratic Labor Party. During the Russian Civil War (1917-1922) many regional governments, national states and armies in the field were formed which issued their own paper money (see Vol. I).

After the victory of the Red armies, many of these areas became federal republics of the Russian Socialist Federal Soviet Republic (RSfSR), or autonomous soviet republics which united on Dec. 30, 1922, to form the Union of Soviet Socialist Republics (SSSR). Beginning with the downfall of the communist government in Poland (1989), other European countries occupied since WW II began democratic elections that spread into Russia itself, leaving the remaining states united in a newly founded Commonwealth of Independent States (C.I.S.). The USSR Supreme Soviet voted a formal end to the treaty of union signed in 1922 and dissolved itself.

MONETARY SYSTEM:

1 Ruble = 100 Kopeks, until 1997
1 Ruble = 1000 "old" Rubles, 1998-

А	а	А	а	A	С	с	С	с	S
Б	б	Б	б	B	Т	т	Т	т	T
В	в	В	в	V	У	у	У	у	U
Г	г	Г	г	G	Ф	ф	Ф	ф	F
Д	д	Д	д	D	Х	х	Х	х	Kh
Е	е	Е	е	ye	Ц	ц	Ц	ц	C
Ё	ё	Ё	ё	yo	Ч	ч	Ч	ч	ch
Ж	ж	Ж	ж	zh	Ш	ш	Ш	ш	sh
З	з	З	з	Z	Щ	щ	Щ	щ	shch
И	и	И	и	I	Ъ*)	ъ*)	—	ъ	'
Й	й	Й	й	J	Ы	ы	—	ы	
К	к	К	к	K	Ь**)	ь**)	—	ь	'
Л	л	Л	л	L	Э	э	Э	э	E
М	м	М	м	M	Ю	ю	Ю	ю	yu
Н	н	Н	н	N	Я	я	Я	я	ya
О	о	О	о	O	І	і	І	і	I
П	п	П	п	P	Ѣ	ѣ	Ѣ	ѣ	ye
Р	р	Р	р	R					

*) "hard", and **) "soft" signs; both soundless. I and Ѣ were dropped in 1918.

С.С.С.Р. - СОЮЗ СОВЕТСКИХ СОЦИАЛИСТИЧЕСКИХ

U.S.S.R. - UNION OF SOVIET SOCIALIST REPUBLICS

ГОСУДАРСТВЕННЫЙ КАЗНАЧЕЙСКИЙ БИЛЕТ

STATE TREASURY NOTE

1961 ISSUE

#222-224 arms at upper l. Wmk: Stars.

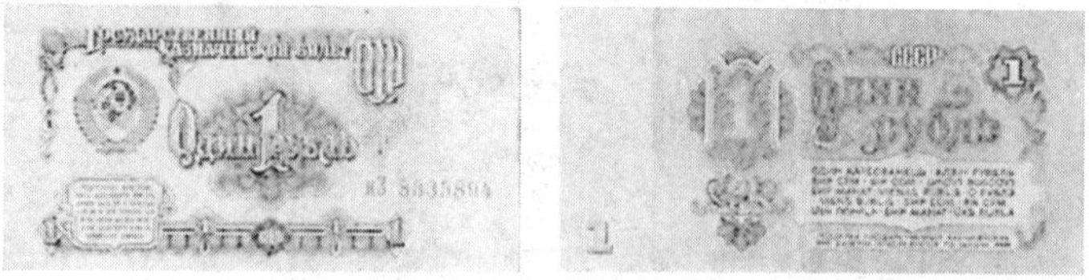

		VG	VF	UNC
222	**1 Ruble** 1961. Brown on pale green underprint. Back red on multicolor underprint.			
	a. Issued note.	.05	.10	.50
	s. Specimen.	—	—	15.00

		VG	VF	UNC
223	**3 Rubles** 1961. Dark green on multicolor underprint. View of Kremlin at center. Back light blue on green and multicolor underprint.			
	a. Issued note.	.05	.10	1.00
	s. Specimen.	—	—	15.00

		VG	VF	UNC
224	**5 Rubles** 1961. Blue on peach underprint. Kremlin Spasski tower at left. Back blue on multicolor underprint.			
	a. Issued note.	.05	.15	1.50
	s. Specimen.	—	—	15.00

БИЛЕТ ГОСУДАРСТВЕННОГО БАНКА С.С.С.Р.

STATE BANK NOTE U.S.S.R.

1961 ISSUE

		VG	VF	UNC
233	**10 Rubles** 1961. Red-brown on pale gold underprint. Arms at upper left, portrait V. I. Lenin at right. Watermark: Stars.			
	a. Issued note.	.10	.25	1.00
	s. Specimen.	—	—	15.00

#234-236 portr. V. I. Lenin at upper l., arms at upper ctr.

		VG	VF	UNC
234	**25 Rubles** 1961. Purple on pale light green underprint. Watermark: Stars.			

		VG	VF	UNC
234	**25 Rubles**			
	a. Lilac tinted paper. 124 x 61mm.	.25	1.00	5.00
	b. White paper. 121 x 62mm.	.10	.25	1.00
	s. Specimen.	—	—	15.00

		VG	VF	UNC
235	**50 Rubles** 1961. Dark green and green on green and pink underprint. Kremlin at upper center on back.			
	a. Issued note.	.25	1.00	8.00
	s. Specimen.	—	—	15.00

		VG	VF	UNC
236	**100 Rubles** 1961. Brown on light blue underprint. Kremlin tower at center with date on back. Watermark: Lenin.			
	a. Issued note.	.25	1.00	5.00
	s. Specimen.	—	—	15.00

1991 ISSUE

#237-243 similar to #222-236.
#237-239 wmk: Star in circle repeated.

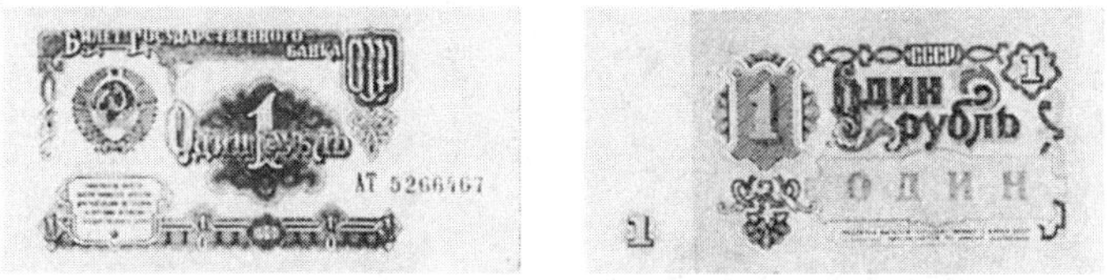

		VG	VF	UNC
237	**1 Ruble** 1991. Dark green and red-brown on tan underprint. Similar to #222.			
	a. Issued note.	.05	.10	.50
	s. Specimen.	—	—	15.00

		VG	VF	UNC
238	**3 Rubles** 1991. Green on blue and multicolor underprint. Similar to #223.			
	a. Issued note.	.10	.25	1.00
	s. Specimen.	—	—	15.00

		VG	VF	UNC
239	**5 Rubles** 1991. Blue-gray on light blue, pale green and pink underprint. Similar to #224.			
	a. Issued note.	.05	.25	1.00
	s. Specimen.	—	—	15.00

		VG	VF	UNC
240	**10 Rubles** 1991. Red-brown and green on multicolor underprint. Similar to #233.			
	a. Issued note.	.15	.25	1.25
	s. Specimen.	—	—	15.00

		VG	VF	UNC
241	**50 Rubles** 1991. Dark brown, green and red on multicolor underprint. Similar to #235.			
	a. Issued note.	.20	1.00	6.00
	s. Specimen.	—	—	15.00

		VG	VF	UNC
242	**100 Rubles** 1991. Deep red-brown and blue on multicolor underprint. Similar to #236 with date on face at right. Watermark: Lenin.			
	a. Issued note.	.25	.75	4.00
	s. Specimen.	—	—	15.00

243	100 Rubles	VG	VF	UNC
	1991. Like #242 but with added pink and green guilloche at right in watermark area, blue guilloche added at upper left on back. Watermark: Stars.			
	a. Issued note.	.25	.75	3.00
	ɔ. Ɛpɔoimɔn.	—	—	15.00

#244-246 portr. V. I. Lenin at upper l. and as wmk., arms at upper ctr. Different views of the Kremlin on back.

244	200 Rubles	VG	VF	UNC
	1991. Green and brown on multicolor underprint.	.50	3.00	10.00

245	500 Rubles	VG	VF	UNC
	1991. Red and green on multicolor underprint.	1.00	5.00	17.50

246	1000 Rubles	VG	VF	UNC
	1991. Brown and blue on green and multicolor underprint.	1.50	5.50	20.00

Russian Federation

РОССИЙСКАЯ ФЕДЕРАЦИЯ

Russian Federation

1992 Issue

247	50 Rubles	VG	VF	UNC
	1992. Brown and gray on green and multicolor underprint. Similar to #241. Watermark: Star in circle repeated.			
	a. Issued note.	.15	.50	1.50
	s. Specimen.	—	—	15.00

248	200 Rubles	VG	VF	UNC
	1992. Green and brown on multicolor underprint. Similar to #244, but guilloche added in watermark area on back. Watermark as #247.			
	a. Issued note.	.15	.75	2.50
	s. Specimen.	—	—	15.00

249	500 Rubles	VG	VF	UNC
	1992. Red, violet and dark green on multicolor underprint. Similar to #245, but guilloche added in watermark area on back. Watermark: Stars.			
	a. Issued note.	.15	.75	4.00
	s. Specimen.	—	—	15.00

		VG	VF	UNC
250	**1000 Rubles**			
	1992. Dark brown and deep green on multicolor underprint. Similar to #246, but guilloche added in watermark area on back. Watermark: Stars.			
	a. Issued note.	.15	.50	1.50
	s. Specimen.	—	—	15.00

1992 Government Privatization Check Issue

		VG	VF	UNC
251	**10,000 Rubles**			
	1992. Dark brown on multicolor underprint. Parliament White House in Moscow. Text indicating method of redemption into shares of government-owned property on back. Handstamp from bank added at bottom. Valid until Dec. 31, 1993.	7.50	15.00	35.00

Note: While not a regular banknote, #251 was easily negotiable and was widely distributed by the govt. It was to provide funds to allow citizens to "buy into" a business. Worth about $35. at time of issue (early 1992), inflation since then has cut its real value dramatically.

БАНК РОССИЙ

Bank of Russia

1992 Issue

		VG	VF	UNC
252	**5000 Rubles**			
	1992. Blue and maroon on multicolor underprint. St. Basil's Cathedral at left. Kremlin on back. Watermark: Stars. Signature Georgui Matiukhin.			
	a. Issued note.	.25	.50	1.50
	s. Specimen.	—	—	15.00

		VG	VF	UNC
253	**10,000 Rubles**			
	1992. Brown, black and red on multicolor underprint. Kremlin with new tricolor flag at left center and as watermark. Kremlin towers at center right on back.			
	a. Issued note.	.25	.75	2.00
	s. Specimen.	—	—	15.00

1993 Issue

#254-260 new tricolor flag over stylized Kremlin at l., monogram at upper r. or near ctr. on back.

#254-256 wmk: Stars within wavy lines repeated.

		VG	VF	UNC
254	**100 Rubles**			
	1993. Blue-black on pink and light blue underprint. Kremlin, Spasski Tower at center right on back.	.10	.25	1.00

		VG	VF	UNC
255	**200 Rubles**			
	1993. Brown on pink and multicolor underprint. Kremlin gate at center on back.	.10	.25	1.00

		VG	VF	UNC
256	**500 Rubles**			
	1993. Green, blue and purple on multicolor underprint. Kremlin at left center on back.	.05	.15	1.25

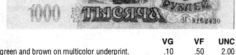

		VG	VF	UNC
257	**1000 Rubles** 1993. Green, olive-green and brown on multicolor underprint. Kremlin at center on back. Watermark: Stars.	.10	.50	2.00

#258-260 new flag over Kremlin at l. and as wmk. Kremlin at or near ctr. on back.

		VG	VF	UNC
258	**5000 Rubles** 1993; 1993/94. Blue, brown and violet on multicolor underprint.			
	a. 1993.	.50	2.50	10.00
	b. 1993//94.	.50	2.50	10.00

		VG	VF	UNC
259	**10,000 Rubles** 1993; 1993//94. Violet, greenish blue, brownish purple and multicolor.			
	a. 1993.	.50	4.00	15.00
	b. 1993//94.	.50	2.50	10.00

		VG	VF	UNC
260	**50,000 Rubles** 1993; 1993//94. Olive-green, black and reddish brown on multicolor underprint.			
	a. 1993.	1.00	5.00	30.00
	b. 1993//94.	1.00	5.00	30.00

1995 ISSUE

		VG	VF	UNC
261	**1000 Rubles** 1995. Dark brown and brown on multicolor underprint. Seaport of Vladivostok at left center, memorial column at center right and as watermark. Entrance to Vladivostok Bay at center on back. Watermark: *1000* and memorial column.	.25	.75	4.00

		VG	VF	UNC
262	**5000 Rubles** 1995. Deep blue-green and dark olive-green on multicolor underprint. Monument of the Russian Millennium in Novgorod at left center. Cathedral of St. Sophia at center and as watermark Old towered city wall at upper left center on back.	.25	1.00	4.00

		VG	VF	UNC
263	**10,000 Rubles** 1995. Dark brown and dark gray on multicolor underprint. Arch bridge over Yenisei River in Krasnoyarsk at left center, steeple at center right and as watermark. Hydroelectric dam at center on back.	.25	2.00	6.00

		VG	VF	UNC
264	**50,000 Rubles** 1995. Dark brown, grayish purple and black on multicolor underprint. Personification of river Neva on foot of Rostral Column, Peter and Paul Fortress in St. Petersburg. Rostral Column and Naval Museum at upper left center on back. Watermark: building with steeple.	.50	7.50	20.00

265 **100,000 Rubles**

	VG	VF	UNC
1995. Purple and brown on multicolor underprint. Apollo and chariot freize on Bolshoi (Great) Theatre in Moscow at center. Bolshoi Theatre on back. Watermark: building over value.	2.50	15.00	35.00

266 **500,000 Rubles**

	VG	VF	UNC
1995 (1997). Brown-violet on multicolor underprint. Statue of Peter the Great, sailing ship dockside in port of Arkhangelsk at center Monastery in Solovetsky Island on back.	10.00	40.00	125.

1997 (1998) "New Ruble" Issue

1 Ruble = 1000 "old" Rubles

#267-271 like #262-266.

267 **5 Rubles**

	VG	VF	UNC
1997 (1998). Deep blue-green and dark olive-green on multicolor underprint. Like #262.	.10	.25	2.00

268 **10 Rubles**

	VG	VF	UNC
1997 (1998); 2001. Dark brown and dark gray on multicolor underprint. Like #263.			
a. 1997.	.25	.35	2.50
b. 2001. Date in very small vertical text to l. of bridge.	.25	.35	2.50

269 **50 Rubles**

	VG	VF	UNC
1997 (1998). Dark brown, grayish purple and black on multicolor underprint. Like #264.	.50	1.75	4.00

270 **100 Rubles**

	VG	VF	UNC
1997 (1998). Violet and brown on multicolor underprint. Like #265.	1.00	4.00	7.50

271 **500 Rubles**

	VG	VF	UNC
1997 (1998). Brown-violet on multicolor underprint. Like #266.	5.00	16.00	35.00

272 **1000 Rubles**

	VG	VF	UNC
1997 (2000). St. Basil Cathedral on back.	5.00	32.00	65.00

2004 and 1997 Dated Issue

273 **10 Rubles**

	VG	VF	UNC
2004. Dark Brown and dark gray on multicolor underprint.	FV	FV	1.25

		VG	VF	UNC
274	**50 Rubles** 2004. Dark brown, grayish purple and black on multicolor underprint.	FV	FV	4.00
275	**100 Rubles** 2004. Violet and brown on multicolor underprint.	FV	FV	7.50

		VG	VF	UNC
276	**500 Rubles** 2004. Brown-violet on multicolor underprint.	15.00	20.00	35.00

		VG	VF	UNC
277	**1000 Rubles** 2004. Multicolor.	25.00	35.00	70.00

FOREIGN EXCHANGE CERTIFICATES

HARD CURRENCY NOTES

1965-68 BLUE BAND ISSUE

		VF	XF	UNC
FX10	**1 Kopek** 1965; 1966. Black on light orange underprint in dark green frame. Back dark green.			
	a. 1965.	.50	1.00	4.00
	b. 1966.	.50	1.00	3.50
FX11	**2 Kopek** 1965; 1966. Black on light orange underprint in dark green frame. Back dark green.			
	a. 1965.	.50	1.00	4.00
	b. 1966.	.50	1.00	3.50

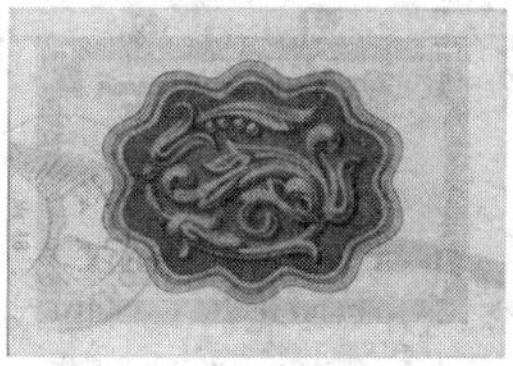

		VF	XF	UNC
FX12	**5 Kopek** 1965; 1966. Black on light orange underprint in dark green frame. Back dark green.			
	a. 1965.	.75	2.00	5.00
	b. 1966.	.75	2.00	5.00
	c. 1972.	.75	3.00	7.00
FX13	**10 Kopek** 1965; 1966. Black on light orange underprint in dark green frame. Back dark green.			
	a. 1965.	1.00	2.50	8.00
	b. 1966.	1.00	2.50	8.00
FX14	**25 Kopek** 1965; 1966. Black on light orange underprint in dark green frame. Back dark green.			
	a. 1965.	2.00	5.00	12.00
	b. 1966.	2.00	5.00	12.00
FX15	**50 Kopek** 1965. Black on light orange underprint in dark green frame. back dark green.	4.00	8.00	18.00

		VF	XF	UNC
FX16	**1 Ruble** 1965; 1966. Black on gray-green underprint in red-brown frame. Back red-brown.			
	a. 1965.	6.00	10.00	25.00
	b. 1966.	6.00	10.00	25.00
FX17	**3 Ruble** 1966; 1968. Black on gray-green underprint in red-brown frame. Back red-brown.			
	a. 1966.	8.00	15.00	35.00
	b. 1968.	12.00	25.00	45.00
FX18	**5 Ruble** 1965; 1968. Black on gray-green underprint in red-brown frame. Back red-brown.			
	a. 1965.	10.00	20.00	40.00
	b. 1968.	15.00	28.00	50.00

		VF	XF	UNC
FX19	**10 Rubles** 1967. Black on gray-green underprint in red-brown frame. Back red-brown.	16.00	30.00	60.00
FX20	**20 Rubles** 1965. Black on gray-green underprint in red-brown frame. Back red-brown.	20.00	40.00	75.00

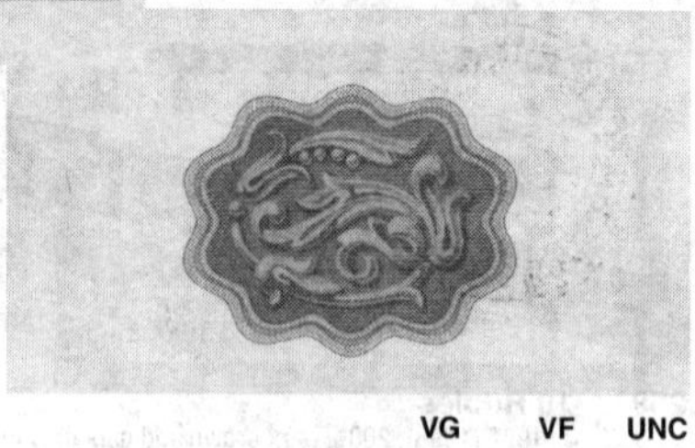

		VG	VF	UNC
FX21	**50 Rubles** 1972.	—	—	—
FX22	**100 Rubles** Reported not confirmed.	—	—	—

1972 Blue Band Issue

FX25-FX28 like previous issue but for text added to back.

		VF	XF	UNC
FX25	**2 Kopek** 1972. Black on light orange underprint in dark green frame. Back dark green.	1.50	3.00	6.00
FX26	**5 Kopek** 1972. Black on light orange underprint in dark green frame. Back dark green.	1.50	3.00	7.00
FX27	**10 Kopek** 1972. Black on light orange underprint in dark green frame. Back dark green.	1.50	3.00	10.00
FX28	**3 Ruble** 1972. Black on gray-green underprint in red-brown frame. Back red-brown.	12.50	25.00	45.00

1965-67 Yellow Band Issue

		VF	XF	UNC
FX30	**1 Kopek** 1965; 1966. Black on light orange underprint in dark green frame. Back dark green.			
	a. 1965.	1.00	2.00	6.00
	b. 1966.	.50	1.00	4.00
FX31	**2 Kopek** 1965; 1966. Black on light orange underprint in dark green frame. Back dark green.			
	a. 1965.	1.00	2.00	6.00
	b. 1966.	.75	1.50	5.00
FX32	**5 Kopek** 1965; 1966. Black on light orange underprint in dark green frame. Back dark green.			
	a. 1965.	1.50	3.00	7.00
	b. 1966.	1.00	2.00	6.00
FX33	**10 Kopek** 1965; 1966. Black on light orange underprint in dark green frame. Back dark green.			
	a. 1965.	2.00	4.00	8.00
	b. 1966.	1.75	3.50	7.50
FX34	**25 Kopeks** 1965; 1966. Black on light orange underprint in dark green frame. Back dark green.			
	a. 1965.	3.00	7.00	12.00
	b. 1966.	3.00	7.00	12.00
FX35	**50 Kopeks** Reported not confirmed.	—	—	—
FX36	**1 Ruble** 1965; 1967. Black on gray-green underprint in red-brown frame. Back red-brown.			
	a. 1965.	8.00	16.00	30.00
	b. 1967.	8.00	16.00	30.00
FX37	**3 Rubles** Reported not confirmed.	—	—	—
FX38	**5 Rubles** 1965. Black on gray-green underprint in red-brown frame. Back red-brown.	12.00	22.00	45.00
FX39	**10 Rubles** Reported not confirmed.	—	—	—
FX40	**20 Rubles** Reported not confirmed.	—	—	—
FX41	**50 Rubles** Reported not confirmed.	—	—	—
FX42	**100 Rubles** Reported not confirmed.	—	—	—

1965-66; 1972 No Band Issue

		VF	XF	UNC
FX45	**1 Kopek** 1965; 1966. Black on light orange underprint in dark green frame. Back dark green.			
	a. 1965.	.75	1.50	4.50
	b. 1966.	.50	1.00	4.00
FX46	**2 Kopek** 1965; 1966. Black on light orange underprint in dark green frame. Back dark green.			
	a. 1965.	.75	1.50	4.50
	b. 1966.	.50	1.00	4.00

		VG	VF	UNC
FX47	**5 Kopek** 1965; 1966; 1972. Black on light orange underprint in dark green frame. Back dark green.			
	a. 1965.	1.00	2.00	5.00
	b. 1966.	.75	1.50	4.50
	c. 1972.	1.25	2.50	6.50
FX48	**10 Kopek** 1966; 1972. Black on light orange underprint in dark green frame. Back dark green.			
	a. 1966.	2.00	4.00	8.00
	b. 1972.	2.50	5.00	10.00
FX49	**25 Kopek** 1966.Black on light orange underprint in dark green frame. Back dark green.	4.00	8.00	15.00
FX50	**50 Kopek** 1965. Black on light orange underprint in dark green frame. Back dark green.	5.00	10.00	20.00
FX51	**1 Ruble** 1966.Black on gray-green underprint in red-brown frame. Back red-brown.	8.00	16.00	28.00

		VG	VF	UNC
FX52	**3 Ruble** 1966.Black on gray-green underprint in red-brown frame. Back red-brown.	15.00	24.00	35.00
FX53	**5 Ruble** 1968.Black on gray-green underprint in red-brown frame. Back red-brown.	20.00	32.00	45.00
FX54	**10 Rubles** Reported not confirmed.	—	—	—
FX55	**20 Rubles** Reported not confirmed.	—	—	—
FX56	**50 Rubles** Reported not confirmed.	—	—	—
FX57	**100 Rubles** Reported not confirmed.	—	—	—

1976 Civilian Issue

		VG	VF	UNC
FX60	**1 Kopek** 1976. Light orange, brown, blue. Back light brown, purple.	.25	.50	1.50
FX61	**2 Kopek** 1976. Light orange, red-brown and blue. Back pink, dark green.	.35	.75	1.75
FX62	**5 Kopek** 1976. Light orange, dark and light blue. Back light blue and dark red.	.50	1.00	2.00
FX63	**10 Kopek** 1976. Light orange, dark and light blue. Back blue and dark green.	.75	1.50	3.00

		VG	VF	UNC
FX64	**25 Kopek** 1976. Light orange, blue and purple. Back lilac and dark turquoise.	1.00	2.00	4.50
FX65	**50 Kopek** 1976. Light orange, blue and green. Back green and brown.	2.00	4.00	8.00

		VG	VF	UNC
FX66	**1 Ruble** 1976. Red-brown, green and multicolor. Back brown and gray.	1.00	2.50	5.00

		VG	VF	UNC
FX67	**3 Ruble** 1976. Green, orange and multicolor. Back blue and green.	2.50	5.00	10.00

		VG	VF	UNC
FX68	**5 Ruble** 1976. Green, dark blue and multicolor. Back turquoise and blue-gray.	3.50	7.00	15.00
FX69	**10 Rubles** 1976. Light blue, red-brown and multicolor. Back light brown, light red.	5.00	12.00	25.00
FX70	**20 Rubles** 1976. Blue-green, dark red and multicolor. Back dark green and gray-red.	10.00	18.00	35.00

		VG	VF	UNC
FX71	**50 Rubles** 1976. Blue-green, green and red. Back brown-red and gray-green.	10.00	30.00	80.00
FX72	**100 Rubles** 1976. Turquoise and brown. Back dark blue-green and brown.	25.00	50.00	160.
FX73	**250 Rubles** 1976. Pink, brown and multicolor. Back olive and pink.	40.00	100.	200.

		VG	VF	UNC
FX74	**500 Rubles** 1977.	75.00	150.	300.

1976 MILITARY ISSUE

		VG	VF	UNC
M10	**1 Kopek** 1976. Light orange, brown, blue. Back light brown, purple.	7.50	16.00	35.00

		VG	VF	UNC
M11	**2 Kopek** 1976. Light orange, red-brown and blue. Back pink, dark green.	8.00	17.50	40.00
M12	**5 Kopek** 1976. Light orange, dark and light blue. Back light blue and dark red.	8.00	18.00	40.00
M13	**10 Kopek** 1976. Light orange, dark and light blue. Back blue and dark green.	10.00	20.00	45.00
M14	**25 Kopek** 1976. Light orange, blue and purple. Back lilac and dark turquoise. Reported not confirmed.	—	—	—
M15	**50 Kopek** 1976. Light orange, blue and green. Back green and brown.	15.00	30.00	60.00
M16	**1 Ruble** 1976. Red-brown, green and multicolor. Back brown and gray.	3.00	8.00	25.00
M17	**3 Ruble** 1976. Green, orange and multicolor. Back blue and green.	5.00	10.00	30.00
M18	**5 Ruble** 1976. Green, dark blue and multicolor. Black turquoise and blue-gray.	5.00	10.00	30.00
M19	**10 Rubles** 1976. Light blue, red-brown and multicolor. Back light brown, light red.	7.50	15.00	40.00
M20	**20 Rubles** 1976. Blue-green, dark red and multicolor. Back dark green and gray-red.	15.00	50.00	150.

		VG	VF	UNC
M21	**50 Rubles** 1976. Blue-green, green and red. Back brown-red and gray-green.	—	—	—
M22	**100 Rubles** 1976. Turquoise and brown. Back dark blue-green and brown.	15.00	50.00	325.
M23	**250 Rubles** 1976. Pink, brown and multicolor. Back olive and pink. Reported not confirmed.	—	—	—
M24	**500 Rubles** 1976. Reported not confirmed.	—	—	—

GOSBANK (ГОСУДАРСТВЕННЫЙ БАНК СССР)

1961 ISSUE

#FX80-FX85 issued in booklets. Used on ships to buy food.

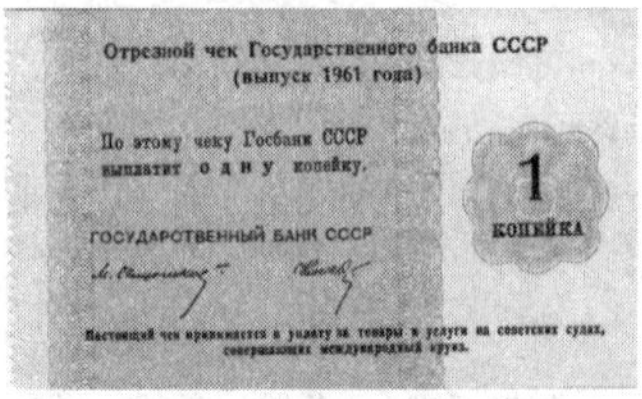

		VG	VF	UNC
FX80	**1 Kopek** 1961. 2 signature varieties.	1.00	2.00	4.00

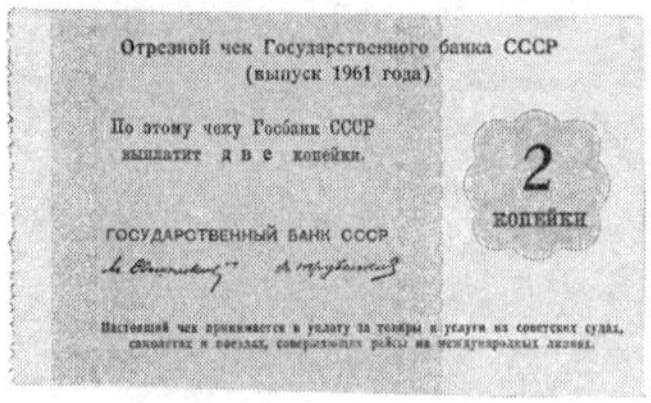

		VG	VF	UNC
FX81	**2 Kopek** 1961. Two signature varieties.	1.00	2.00	4.00
FX82	**5 Kopek** 1961.	2.00	5.00	10.00
FX83	**10 Kopek** 1961. Reported not confirmed.	—	—	—
FX84	**50 Kopek** 1961.	7.50	15.00	30.00
FX85	**1 Ruble** 1961. Reported not confirmed.	—	—	—

1967-74 SERIES

		VG	VF	UNC
FX90	**1 Kopek** 1970; 1972; 1974.	1.00	2.00	4.00
FX91	**2 Kopek** 1967; 1970.	1.00	2.00	4.00

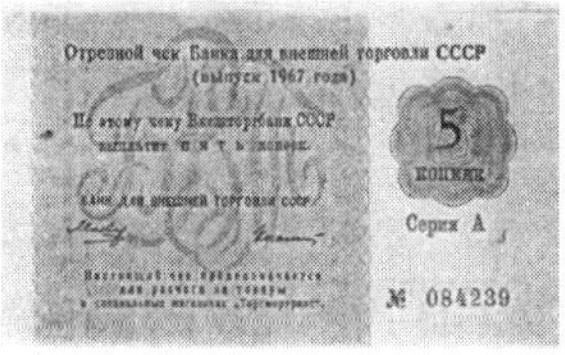

		VG	VF	UNC
FX92	**5 Kopek** 1967; 1970.	1.25	2.50	5.00
FX93	**10 Kopek** 1970.	1.50	3.00	6.00

1970-76 Issue

		VG	VF	UNC
FX95	**1 Kopek** 1970; 1974; 1976.	1.25	2.50	5.00
FX96	**2 Kopek** 1970; 1976.	1.50	2.50	5.00
FX97	**5 Kopek** 1976. Reported not confirmed.	—	—	—
FX98	**10 Kopek** 1976.	1.50	3.00	6.00

Vneshtorgbank (ВАНКА ДАЯВНЕШНЕЙ ТОРГОВАЙ ТОРГОВАЙ СССР)

1973 Issue

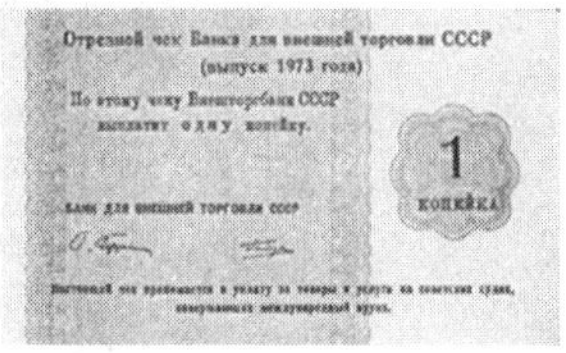

		VG	VF	UNC
FX100	**1 Kopek** 1973.	1.00	3.00	6.00
FX101	**2 Kopek** 1973.	—	—	—
FX102	**5 Kopek** 1973.	—	—	—
FX103	**10 Kopek** 1973.	—	—	—
FX104	**50 Kopek** 1973.	—	—	—
FX105	**1 Ruble** 1973.	—	—	—

1975 Issue

		VG	VF	UNC
FX110	**1 Kopek** 1975.	1.00	3.00	6.00
FX111	**2 Kopek** 1975.	1.50	3.50	7.00
FX112	**5 Kopek** 1975.	2.00	4.00	8.00
FX113	**10 Kopek** 1975.	2.50	4.50	9.00
FX114	**50 Kopek** 1975.	—	—	—
FX115	**1 Ruble** 1975.	—	—	—

1978 Issue

FX120-124 similar to FX95-98 but for new script on note.

		VG	VF	UNC
FX120	**5 Kopek** 1978.	1.00	2.50	5.00
FX121	**10 Kopek** 1978; 1980.	1.50	3.00	7.50

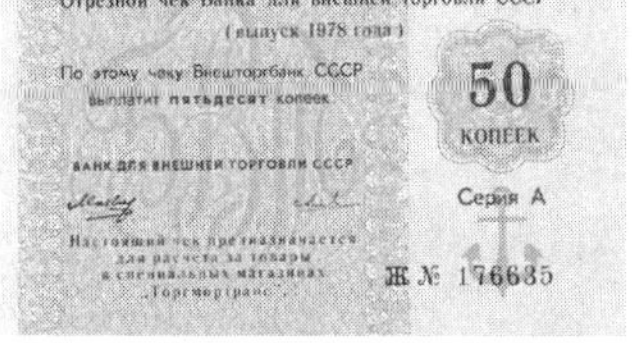

		VG	VF	UNC
FX122	**50 Kopek** 1978.	2.00	5.00	9.00
FX123	**1 Ruble** 1978.	3.00	8.00	14.00
FX124	**5 Ruble** 1978.	5.00	10.00	20.00

Bank of Foreign Trade

1977; 1980 Cruise Ship Series

		VG	VF	UNC
FX135	**1 Kopek** 1977; 1980.			
	a. 1977; 1980. Without serial #.	.15	.50	1.00
	b. 1977. With serial #.	.25	.75	1.50

		VG	VF	UNC
FX136	**2 Kopek** 1977; 1980.			
	a. 1977; 1980. Without serial #.	.15	.50	1.00
	b. 1977. With serial #.	.25	.75	1.50

		VG	VF	UNC
FX137	**5 Kopek** 1977; 1980.			
	a. 1977; 1980. Without serial #.	.25	.50	1.25
	b. 1977. With serial #. Reported not confirmed.	—	—	—

		VG	VF	UNC
FX138	**10 Kopek** 1977; 1980.			
	a. 1977; 1980. Without serial #. Reported not confirmed.	—	—	—
	b. 1977. With serial #.	.50	1.00	2.00
FX139	**50 Kopek** 1977; 1980.			
	a. Without serial #.	1.00	2.00	4.00
	b. With serial #.	1.00	2.00	4.00
FX140	**1 Ruble** 1977; 1980.			
	a. Without serial #.	2.00	4.00	8.00
	b. With serial #.	2.00	4.00	8.00

1985 Cruise Ship Series

This series has a white border around the printed area, the notes are larger than series 1977 and 1980.

		VG	VF	UNC
FX141	**5 Kopek** 1985.	.25	.75	1.50

		VG	VF	UNC
FX142	**10 Kopek** 1985.	.50	1.00	1.75

		VG	VF	UNC
FX143	**50 Kopek** 1985.	.75	1.50	2.50
FX144	**1 Ruble** 1985.	1.00	2.00	4.00

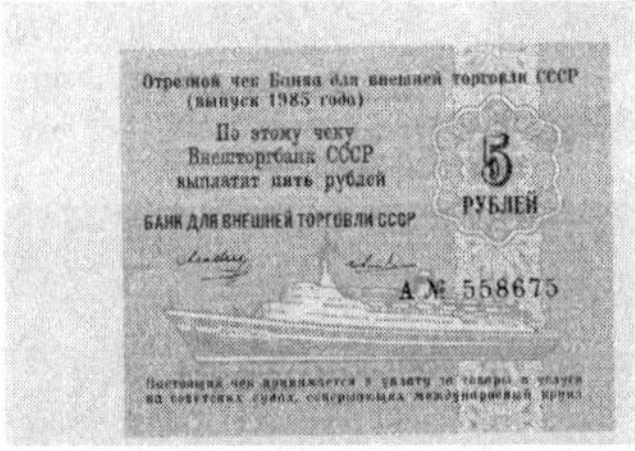

		VG	VF	UNC
FX145	**5 Ruble** 1985.	1.25	2.50	5.00

1979; 1980 Diplomatic Series

		VG	VF	UNC
FX146	**1 Kopek** 1979; 1980.	.10	.35	.75
FX147	**2 Kopek** 1979; 1980.	.15	.40	.85

		VG	VF	UNC
FX148	**5 Kopek** 1979; 1980.	.20	.50	1.00

		VG	VF	UNC
FX149	**10 Kopek** 1979; 1980.	.20	.50	1.00
FX150	**20 Kopek** 1979; 1980.	.20	1.00	2.00
FX151	**50 Kopek** 1979; 1980.	.50	1.00	2.00
FX152	**1 Ruble** 1979; 1980.	1.00	2.00	4.00
FX153	**2 Ruble** 1979; 1980.	1.00	2.50	5.00
FX154	**5 Ruble** 1979; 1980.	1.50	3.00	6.00
FX155	**10 Rubles** 1979; 1980. Rare.	—	—	—
FX156	**25 Rubles** 1979; 1980. Rare.	—	—	—

Bank for Foreign Economic Activity

1989 Series

		VG	VF	UNC
FX157	**5 Kopek** 1989.	.25	.75	1.50
FX158	**10 Kopek** 1989.	.50	1.00	1.75
FX159	**50 Kopek** 1989.	.75	1.50	2.50

		VG	VF	UNC
FX160	**1 Ruble** 1989.	1.00	2.00	4.00
FX161	**5 Ruble** 1989.	1.25	2.50	5.00
FX162	**10 Rubles** 1989. Rare.	—	—	—
FX163	**25 Rubles** 1989. Rare.	—	—	—

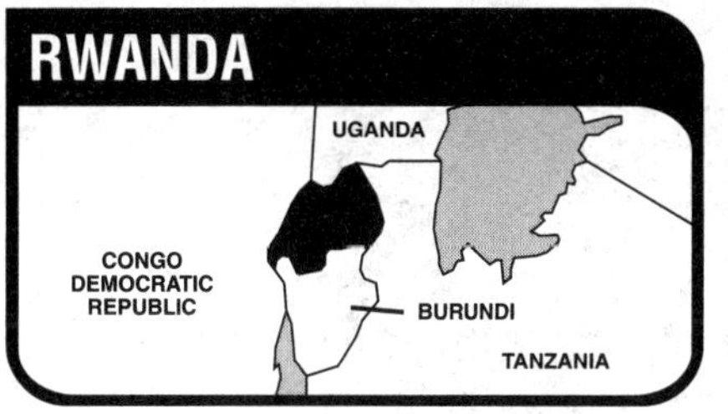

The Republic of Rwanda, located in central Africa between the Republic of the Congo and Tanzania, has an area of 10,169 sq. mi. (26,340 sq. km.) and a population of 7.67 million. Capital: Kigali. The economy is d on agriculture and mining. Coffee and tin are exported.

German lieutenant Count von Goetzen was the first European to visit Rwanda, 1894. Four years later the court of the Mwami (the Tutsi king of Rwanda) willingly permitted the kingdom to become a protectorate of Germany. In 1916, during the African campaigns of World War I, Belgian troops from the Congo occupied Rwanda. After the war it, together with Burundi, became a Belgian League of Nations mandate under the name of the Territory of Ruanda-Urundi. Following World War II, Ruanda-Urundi became a Belgian administered U.N. trust territory. The Tutsi monarchy was deposed by the U.N. supervised election of 1961, after which Belgium granted Rwanda internal autonomy. On July 1, 1962, the U.N. terminated the Belgian trusteeship and granted full independence to both Rwanda and Burundi. Banknotes were used in common with the Belgian Congo, and later with Burundi.

A coup in 1973 established a military government in the 1980's. There was increasing tension with refugees from neighboring Uganda, culminating in a 1990 Tutsi invasion. U.N. forces were posted in 1994-96 but civil strife continues.

Also see Belgian Congo, Rwanda-Burundi.

MONETARY SYSTEM:

1 Franc (Amafranga, Amafaranga) = 100 Centimes

REPLACEMENT NOTES:

#6e, 17:ZZ prefix. #12, VV prefix. Others probably exist.

REPUBLIC

BANQUE NATIONALE DU RWANDA

BANKI NASIYONALI Y'U RWANDA

1962 PROVISIONAL ISSUE

#1-5 ovpt: *BANQUE NATIONALE DU RWANDA* and sign. title: *LE GOUVERNEUR* on Banque d'Emission du Rwanda et du Burundi notes.

#1-3 stamped ovpt.

		Good	Fine	XF
1	**20 Francs** ND (1962 -old date 5.10.1960). Green on tan and pink underprint. Maroon or black overprint on Rwanda-Burundi #3.	70.00	190.	475.

		Good	Fine	XF
2	**50 Francs** ND (1962 -old dates 15.9.1960; 1.10.1960). Red on multicolor underprint. Maroon overprint on Rwanda-Burundi #4.	75.00	250.	600.

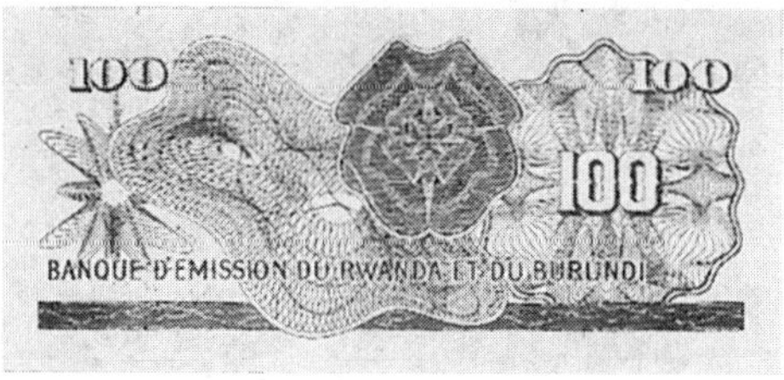

		Good	Fine	XF
3	**100 Francs** ND (1962 -old dates 15.9.1960; 1.10.1960; 31.7.1962). Blue on light green and tan underprint. Overprint on Rwanda-Burundi #5.			
	a. Black overprint.	75.00	150.	375.
	b. Purple overprint.	75.00	150.	375.
4	**500 Francs** ND (1962 -old dates 15.9.1960; 15.9.1961). Lilac-brown on multicolor underprint. Embossed overprint and blind embossed facsimile signature on Rwanda-Burundi #6.	300.	850.	1300.
5	**1000 Francs** ND (1962 -old dates 15.5.1961; 1.7.1962). Green on multicolor underprint. Embossed overprint and blind facsimile signature on Rwanda-Burundi #7.	250.	800.	1250.

1964 ISSUE

#6-10 various date and sign. title varieties. Replacement notes: Serial # prefix *ZZ*.

		VG	VF	UNC
6	**20 Francs** 1964-76. Brown on multicolor underprint. Flag of Rwanda at left. Four young boys at left center with pipeline in background at center on back.			
	a. Signature titles: *VICE-GOUVERNEUR* and *GOUVERNEUR*, with security thread. 1.7.1964; 31.3.1966; 15.3.1969; 1.9.1969.	1.00	7.50	15.00
	b. Signature titles: *VICE GOUVERNEUR* and *ADMINISTRATEUR*, with security thread. 1.7.1965.	1.25	10.00	20.00
	c. Signature titles: *GOUVERNEUR* and *ADMINISTRATEUR*, with security thread. 1.7.1971.	1.00	3.00	7.50
	d. Signature titles: *ADMINISTRATEUR* and *ADMINISTRATEUR*, with security thread. 30.10.1974.	.25	1.50	6.00
	e. Signature titles: *ADMINISTRATEUR* and *GOUVERNEUR*, without security thread. 1.1.1976.	.25	.75	1.00
	s1. As a. Specimen. 1.7.1964; 31.3.1966; 15.3.1969.	—	Unc	5.00
	s2. As b. Specimen. 1.7.1965.	—	Unc	3.50
	s3. As c. Specimen. 1.7.1971.	—	Unc	3.50
	s4. As d. Specimen. 30.10.1974.	—	Unc	6.00

		VG	VF	UNC
7	**50 Francs** 1964-76. Blue on green underprint. Map of Rwanda at left center. Miner at left with miners digging at center.			
	a. Signature titles: *VICE-GOUVERNEUR* and *GOUVERNEUR*, with security thread. 1.7.1964; 31.1.1966; 1.9.1969.	1.00	10.00	20.00
	b. Signature titles: *ADMINISTRATEUR* and *GOUVERNEUR*, with security thread. 1.7.1971; 30.10.1974.	.50	2.00	7.00
	c. Signature titles: *ADMINISTRATEUR* and *GOUVERNEUR*, without security thread. 1.1.1976.	.25	1.00	2.50
	s1. As a. Specimen. 1.7.1964; 31.1.1966; 1.9.1969.	—	—	4.00
	s2. As b. Specimen. 1.7.1971; 30.10.1974.	—	—	4.00

8	100 Francs	VG	VF	UNC
	1964-76. Purple on multicolor underprint. Map of Rwanda at left. Woman with basket on head at left, banana trees at center on back.			
	a. Signature titles: *VICE-GOUVERNEUR* and *GOUVERNEUR*, with security thread. 1.7.1964; 31.3.1966; 31.10.1969.	1.00	3.50	10.00
	b. Signature titles: *VICE-GOUVERNEUR* and *ADMINISTRATEUR*, with security thread. 1.7.1965.	2.50	8.00	20.00
	c. Signature titles: *ADMINISTRATEUR* and *GOUVERNEUR*, with security thread. 1.7.1971; 30.10.1974.	1.00	3.50	8.50
	d. Signature titles: *ADMINISTRATEUR* and *GOUVERNEUR*, without security thread. 1.1.1976.	.25	1.50	4.00
	s1. As a. Specimen. 1.7.1964; 31.10.1969.	—	—	6.00
	s2. As c. Specimen. 1.7.1971; 30.10.1974.	—	—	6.00

9	500 Francs	VG	VF	UNC
	1964-76. Dark green and multicolor. Arms of Rwanda at left. Man with basket on head at left, rows of plants in background on back.			
	a. Signature titles: *VICE-GOUVERNEUR* and *GOUVERNEUR*. 1.7.1964; 31.3.1966; 31.10.1969.	3.50	10.00	42.50
	b. Signature titles: *ADMINISTRATEUR* and *GOUVERNEUR*. 1.7.1971; 30.10.1974; 1.1.1976.	2.50	7.50	25.00
	s1. As a. Specimen. 1.7.1964; 31.3.1966.	—	—	12.50
	s2. As b. Specimen. 1.7.1971; 30.10.1974	—	—	12.50

10	1000 Francs	VG	VF	UNC
	1964-76. Red and multicolor. Arms of Rwanda at left. Man and terraced hills at center on back.			
	a. Signature titles: *VICE-GOUVERNEUR* and *GOUVERNEUR*. 1.7.1964; 31.3.1966; 15.3.1969.	7.50	25.00	80.00
	b. Signature titles: *ADMINISTRATEUR* and *GOUVERNEUR*. 1.7.1971; 30.10.1974.	7.50	20.00	45.00
	c. Printed signature titles like b. 1.1.1976.	5.00	15.00	30.00
	s1. As a. Specimen. 31.3.1966; 15.3.1969.	—	—	17.50
	s2. As b. Specimen. 1.7.1971.	—	—	17.50

1974 ISSUE

11	500 Francs	VG	VF	UNC
	19.4.1974. Green and multicolor. Gen. Habyarimana at left. Back like #9.			
	a. Issued note.	2.00	10.00	25.00
	s. Specimen.	—	—	10.00

1978 ISSUE

12	100 Francs	VG	VF	UNC
	1.1.1978. Gray on light blue and multicolor underprint. Zebras. Woman carrying child at left, mountains in background at center right on back.			
	a. Issued note.	.50	2.50	7.00
	s. Specimen.	—	—	12.50

13	500 Francs	VG	VF	UNC
	1.1.1978. Brown, orange and multicolor. Impalas. Eight drummers at left, strip mining at right on back.			
	a. Watermark: Impala's head.	1.00	7.50	15.00
	b. Without watermark.	20.00	60.00	150.
	s. As a. Specimen.	—	—	20.00

NOTICE

Readers with unlisted dates, signature varieties, etc. are invited to submit photocopies of their notes to: Standard Catalog of World Paper Money, 700 East State St. Iola, WI 54990-0001, E-Mail: george.cuhaj@fwpubs.com.

14	1000 Francs	VG	VF	UNC
	1.1.1978. Green and multicolor. Boys picking tea leaves at left. Tribal dancer at right on back. Watermark: Impala's head.			
	a. Issued note.	4.00	15.00	35.00
	s. Specimen.	—	—	25.00

15	5000 Francs	VG	VF	UNC
	1.1.1978. Green, blue and multicolor. Female with basket on her head at left, field workers at center. Lake and mountains on back. Watermark: Impala's head.			
	a. Issued note.	40.00	65.00	150.
	s. Specimen.	—	—	100.

1981 Issue

16	500 Francs	VG	VF	UNC
	1.7.1981. Brown and multicolor. Arms at left, three Impala at right. Men working in field at left on back. Watermark: Crowned crane's head.			
	a. Issued note.	2.00	7.50	22.50
	s. Specimen.	—	—	20.00

17	1000 Francs	VG	VF	UNC
	1.7.1981. Green, brown and multicolor. Two Watusi warriors at right. Two Eastern Gorillas at left, canoe in lake at right on back. Watermark: Crowned crane's head.			
	a. Issued note.	4.00	12.00	30.00
	s. Specimen.	—	—	32.50

1982 Issue

18	100 Francs	VG	VF	UNC
	1.8.1982. Black on lilac and multicolor underprint. Zebras at center and right. Back purple and multicolor; woman carrying baby at left, view of mountains at center. Watermark: Impala's head.	.25	1.50	4.00

1988-89 Issue

#19, 21 and 22 similar to #18, #17 and #15, but new spelling *AMAFARANGA* on back. Slight color differences and new sign. titles: *2E VICE-GOUVERNEUR and GOUVERNEUR*.

19	100 Francs	VG	VF	UNC
	24.4.1989. Similar to #18.	.25	1.25	3.00

#20 Not assigned.

21	1000 Francs	VG	VF	UNC
	1.1.1988; 24.4.1989. Similar to #17.	2.50	7.50	20.00

22 **5000 Francs**

	VG	VF	UNC
1.1.1988; 24.4.1989. Similar to #15.	7.50	30.00	60.00

1994 Issue

#23-25 mountainous landscape at ctr. r. Wmk: Impala's head. Printer: G&D (w/o imprint).

23 **500 Francs**

	VG	VF	UNC
1.12.1994. Blue-black, black and dark blue-green on multicolor underprint. Female Waterbuck at left center on back.	FV	FV	7.50

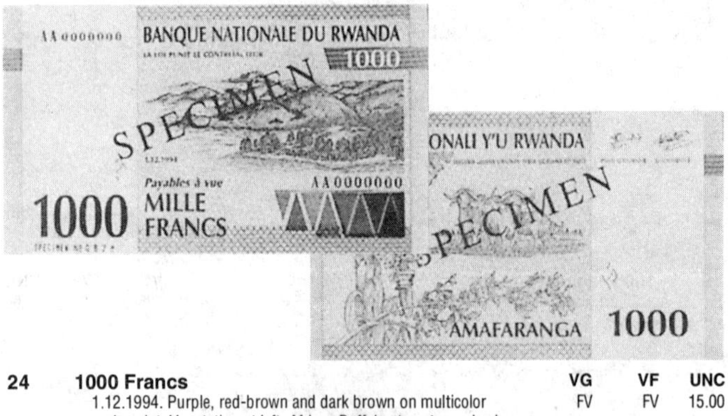

24 **1000 Francs**

	VG	VF	UNC
1.12.1994. Purple, red-brown and dark brown on multicolor underprint. Vegetation at left, African Buffalo at center on back.	FV	FV	15.00

25 **5000 Francs**

	VG	VF	UNC
1.12.1994. Dark brown, violet and purple on multicolor underprint. Reclining lion at left center on back.	FV	FV	50.00

1998 Issue

26 **500 Francs**

	VG	VF	UNC
1.12.1998. Blue and green on multicolor underprint. Mountain gorillas at right. National Museum of Butare and schoolchildren on back.	FV	FV	7.00

27 **1000 Francs**

	VG	VF	UNC
1.12.1998. Blue and brown on multicolor underprint. Volcano range at right. Tea plantation and cattle on back.	FV	FV	15.00

28 **5000 Francs**

	VG	VF	UNC
1.12.1998. Black, red and green on multicolor underprint. *Intore* dancers at right. National Bank building on back.	FV	FV	50.00

2003 Issue

		VG	VF	UNC
29	**100 Francs** 1.5.2003. Green, brown and blue on yellow underprint. Oxen and farmer plowing at center. Mountain and lake on back.	FV	FV	2.00

		VG	VF	UNC
30	**500 Francs** 1.7.2004. Green on tan and blue underprint.	FV	FV	6.00

		VG	VF	UNC
31	**1000 Francs** 1.7.2004. Blue on tan underprint. Doggett's Guenon.	FV	FV	12.50

Rwanda-Burundi, a Belgian League of Nations mandate and United Nations trust territory comprising the provinces of Rwanda and Burundi of the former colony of German East Africa, was located in central Africa between the present Republic of the Congo, Uganda and mainland Tanzania. The mandate-trust territory had an area of 20,916 sq. mi. (54,272 sq. km.).

For specific statistics and history of Rwanda and Burundi see individual entries.

When Rwanda and Burundi were formed into a mandate for administration by Belgium, their names were changed to Ruanda and Urundi and they were organized as an integral part of the Belgian Congo, during which time they used a common banknote issue with the Belgian Congo. After the Belgian Congo acquired independence as the Republic of the Congo, the provinces of Ruanda and Urundi reverted to their former names of Rwanda and Burundi and issued notes with both names on them. In 1962, both Rwanda and Burundi became separate independent states.

Also see Belgian Congo, Burundi and Rwanda.

MONETARY SYSTEM:

1 Franc = 100 Centimes

MANDATE - TRUST TERRITORY

BANQUE D'EMISSION DU RWANDA ET DU BURUNDI

1960 ISSUE

#1-7 various date and sign. varieties.

		VG	VF	UNC
1	**5 Francs** 1960-63. Light brown on green underprint. Impala at left.			
	a. 15.9.1960; 15.5.1961.	15.00	55.00	225.
	b. 15.4.1963.	17.50	65.00	275.

		Good	Fine	XF
2	**10 Francs** 15.9.1960; 5.10.1960. Dull gray on pale blue and pale orange underprint. Hippopotamus at left. Printer: TDLR.	15.00	65.00	240.

		Good	Fine	XF
3	**20 Francs** 15.9.1960; 5.10.1960. Green on tan and pink underprint. Crocodile at right. Printer: TDLR.	25.00	90.00	350.
4	**50 Francs** 15.9.1960; 1.10.1960. Red on multicolor underprint. Lioness at center right.	22.50	85.00	325.

		Good	Fine	XF
5	**100 Francs** 15.9.1960; 1.10.1960; 31.7.1962. Blue on light green and tan underprint. Zebu at left.	15.00	60.00	225.
6	**500 Francs** 15.9.1960; 15.5.1961; 15.9.1961. Lilac-brown on multicolor underprint. Black Rhinoceros at center right.	225.	850.	2000.

		Good	Fine	XF
7	**1000 Francs** 15.9.1960; 15.5.1961; 31.7.1962. Green on multicolor underprint. Zebra at right.			
	a. Issued note.	180.	750.	1750.
	ct. Color trial in purple on multicolor underprint.	—	Unc	1500.

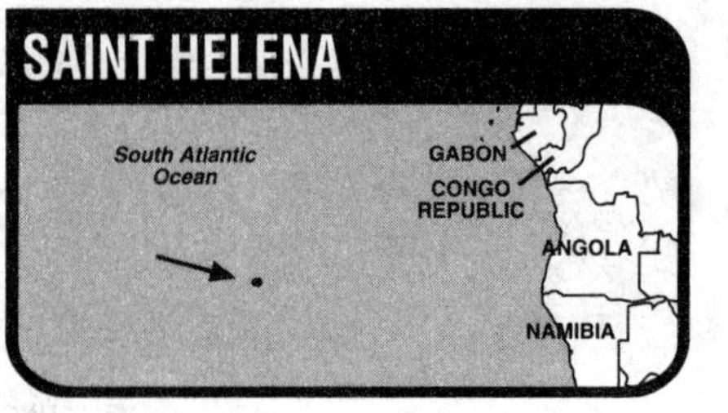

The Colony of St. Helena, a British colony located about 1,150 miles (1,850 km.) from the west coast of Africa, has an area of 47 sq. mi. (122 sq. km.) and a population of 5,700. Capital: Jamestown. Flax, lace and rope are produced for export. Ascension and Tristan da Cunha are dependencies of St. Helena.

The island was discovered and named by the Portuguese navigator João da Nova Castella in 1502. The Portuguese imported livestock, fruit trees and vegetables but established no permanent settlement. The Dutch occupied the island temporarily, 1645-1651. The original European settlement was founded by representatives of the British East India Company sent to annex the island after the departure of the Dutch. The Dutch returned and captured St. Helena from the British on New Year's Day, 1673, but were in turn ejected by a British force under Sir Richard Munden. Thereafter St. Helena was the undisputed possession of Great Britain. The island served as the place of exile for Napoleon, several Zulu chiefs, and and an ex-Sultan of Zanzibar.

St. Helena banknotes are also used on the islands of Assencion and Tristan de Cunia.

RULERS:

British

MONETARY SYSTEM:

1 Pound = 20 Shillings to 1971

1 Pound = 100 New Pence, 1971-

SIGNATURE VARIETIES	
1	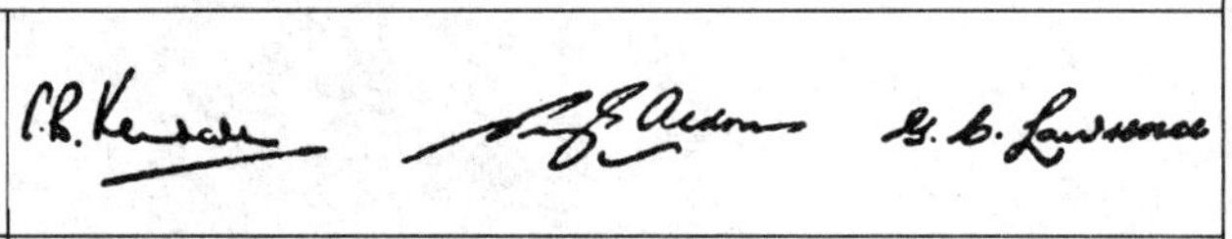
2	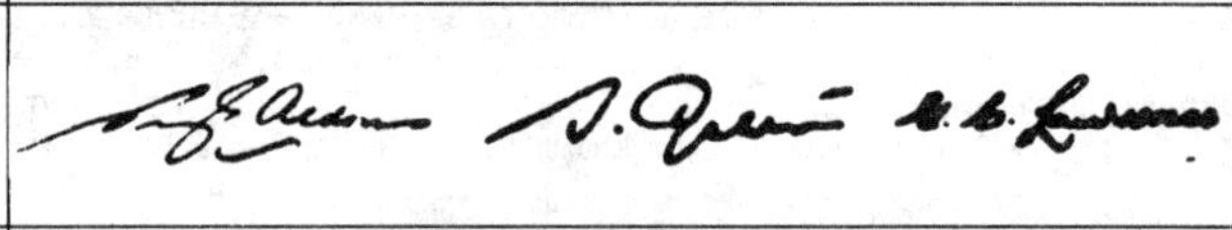
3	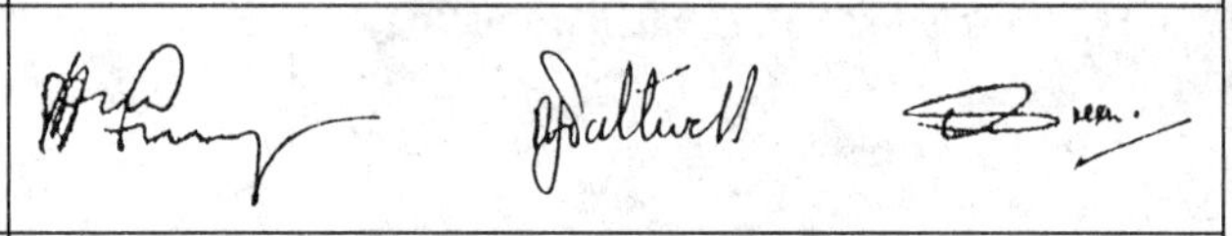
4	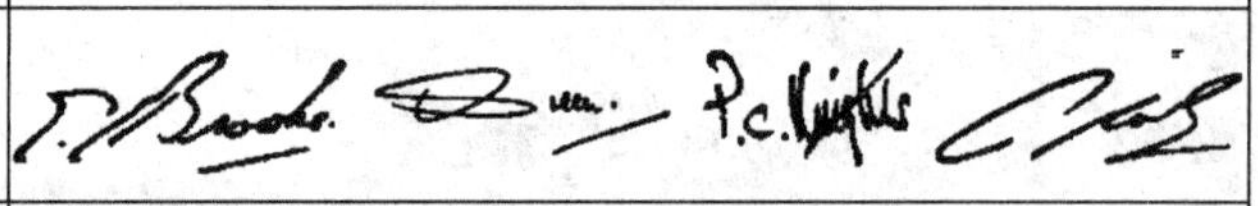
5	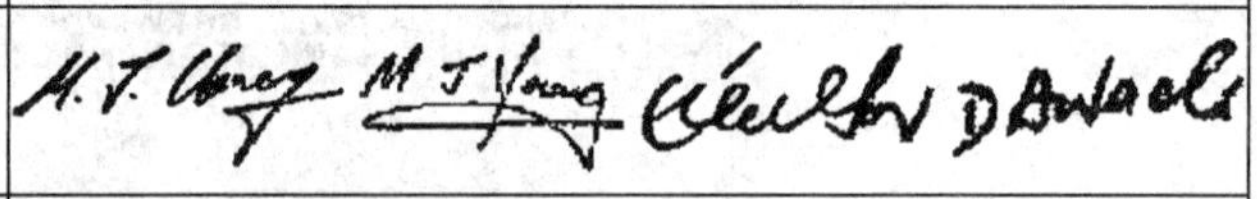
6	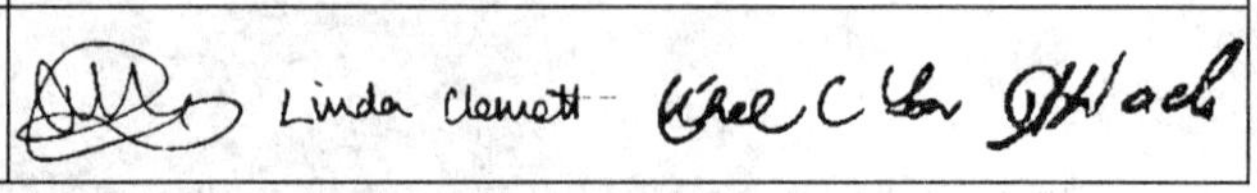

BRITISH ADMINISTRATION

GOVERNMENT OF ST. HELENA

1976; 1979 ND ISSUE

#5-8 views of the island at l., Qn. Elizabeth II at r.

#5-7 Royal arms w/motto at l., shield w/ship at ctr. r. on back.

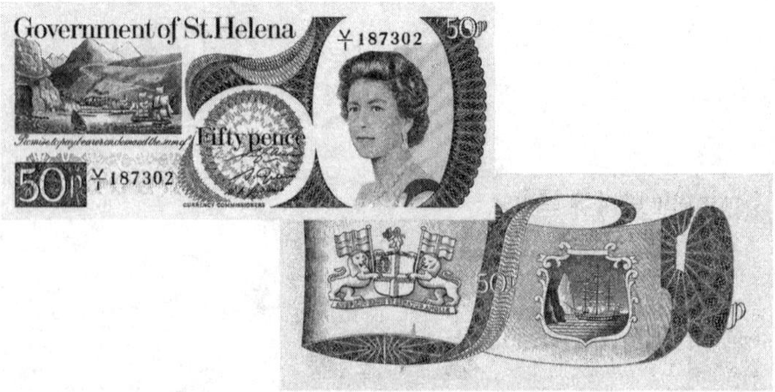

		VG	VF	UNC
5	**50 Pence** ND (1979). Purple on pink and pale yellow-green underprint. Correctly spelled *ANGLIAE* in motto. Signature 2.			
	a. Issued note.	FV	3.00	30.00
	s. Specimen.	—	—	—

Note: #5 w/serial #170,001-200,000 are non-redeemable.

6 **1 Pound**
ND (1976). Deep olive-green on pale orange and ochre underprint. Incorrect spelling *ANGLAE* in motto. 153 x 67mm.

	VG	VF	UNC
a. Issued note.	FV	10.00	65.00
s. Specimen.	—	—	—

7 **5 Pounds**
ND (1976). Blue on light brown underprint. 152x74mm.

	VG	VF	UNC
a. Incorrect spelling *ANGLAE* in motto. signature 1. (1976).	FV	10.00	80.00
b. Corrected spelling *ANGLIAE* in motto. signature 2. (1981).	FV	FV	40.00
s. As a. Specimen.	—	—	175.

8 **10 Pounds**
ND (1979). Pale red on multicolor underprint. Arms on back, correctly spelled *ANGLIAE* in motto. 159x80mm.

	VG	VF	UNC
a. Signature 2. (1979).	FV	FV	130.
b. Signature 3. (1985).	FV	FV	65.00
c. As a. Uncut sheet of 3.	—	—	400.
r. Remainder without signature or serial #.	—	—	220.
s. As a. Specimen.	—	—	—

NOTICE

Readers with unlisted dates, signature varieties, etc. are invited to submit photocopies of their notes to: Standard Catalog of World Paper Money, 700 East State St. Iola, WI 54990-0001, E-Mail: george.cuhaj@fwpubs.com.

1981; 1986 ND Issue

#9 and 10 Qn. Elizabeth II at r.

9 **1 Pound**
ND (1981). Deep olive-green on pale orange and ochre underprint. Like #6 but corrected spelling *ANGLIAE* in motto. Reduced size, 147 x 66mm. Signature 2.

	VG	VF	UNC
a. Issued note.	FV	FV	12.50
s. Specimen.	—	—	—

Note: #9 w/serial *#A/1* 350,000 - *A/1* 400,000 are non-redeemable.

10 **20 Pounds**
ND (1986). Dark brown on multicolor underprint. Harbor view at left center. Back light green; arms at center. Four signatures in block form. Signature 4. 164 x 85mm.

	VG	VF	UNC
a. Issued note.	FV	FV	110.
s. Specimen.	—	—	—

1998 ND Issue

11 **5 Pounds**
ND (1998). Similar to #7, but reduced size. Four signatures in block form. Signature 5. 135 x 71mm.

	VG	VF	UNC
a. Issued note.	FV	FV	35.00
s. Specimen.	—	—	100.

2004 Issues

#12-13, Qn. Elizabeth II at r. Year on back. 135x71mm. Four sign. in block form.

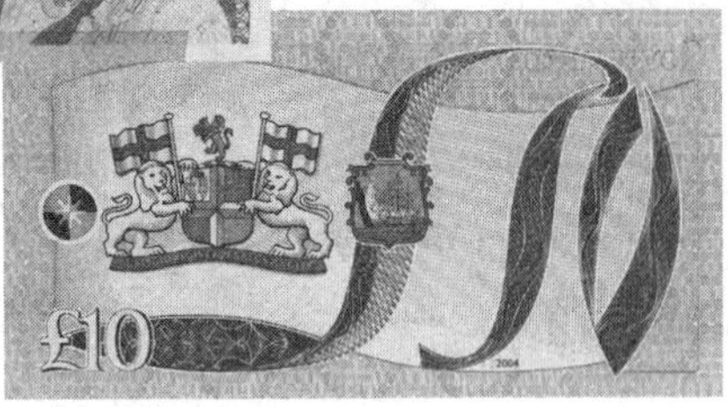

		VG	VF	UNC
12	**10 Pounds** 2004. Rose on multicolor underprint. Historic harbor view at left. Arms at left, large 10 at right on back.			
	a. Issued note.	FV	FV	60.00
	s. Specimen (300 issued).	—	—	115.

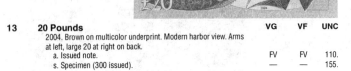

		VG	VF	UNC
13	**20 Pounds** 2004. Brown on multicolor underprint. Modern harbor view. Arms at left, large 20 at right on back.			
	a. Issued note.	FV	FV	110.
	s. Specimen (300 issued).	—	—	155.

SAINT PIERRE & MIQUELON

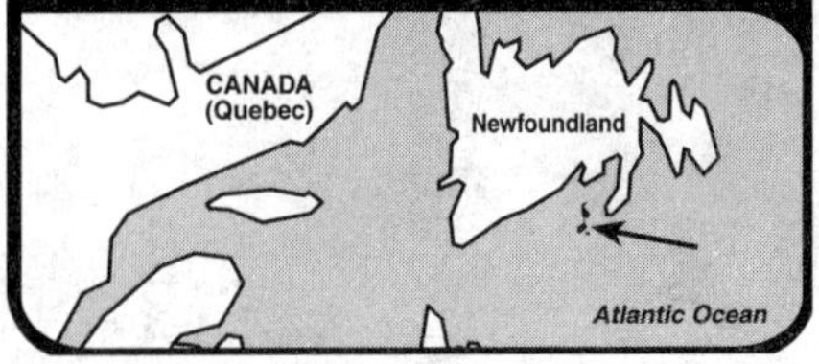

The Territorial Collectivity of St. Pierre and Miquelon, a French overseas territory located 10 miles (16 km.) off the south coast of Newfoundland, has an area of 93 sq. mi. (242 sq. km.) and a population of about 6,000. Capital: St. Pierre. The economy of the barren archipelago is d on cod fishing and fur farming Fish and fish products, and mink and silver fox pelts are exported.

The islands, occupied by the French in 1604, were captured by the British in 1702 and held until 1763 when they were returned to the possession of France and employed as a fishing station. They passed between France and England on six more occasions between 1778 and 1814 when they were awarded permanently to France by the Treaty of Paris. The rugged, soil-poor granite islands, which will support only evergreen shrubs, are all that remain to France of her extensive colonies in North America. In 1958 St. Pierre and Miquelon voted in favor of the new constitution of the Fifth Republic of France, thereby choosing to remain within the French Community.

Notes of the Banque de France circulated 1937-1942; afterwards notes of the Caisse Centrale de la France Libre and the Caisse Centrale de la France d'Outre-Mer were in use.

RULERS:

French

MONETARY SYSTEM:

1 Franc = 100 Centimes
5 Francs 40 Centimes = 1 Canada Dollar
1 Nouveau Franc = 100 "old" Francs, 1960-

French Administration

Caisse Centrale de la France d'Outre-Mer

Saint-Pierre-et-Miquelon

1960 ND Provisional Issue

#30-35 ovpt: *SAINT-PIERRE-ET-MIQUELON* and new denomination.

		VG	VF	UNC
30	**1 Nouveau Franc on 50 Francs** ND (1960). Multicolor. Overprint on Reunion #25.			
	a. Special series *A.1-Y.1* with 3 digit serial # and 5 digit control #.	10.00	40.00	200.
	b. Normal series with 5 digit serial # and 9 digit control #.	6.00	20.00	75.00
	s. As a, b. Specimen.	—	—	—

1961; 1963 ND Provisional Issue

		VG	VF	UNC
31	**1 Nouveau Franc on 50 Francs** ND (1961). Multicolor. B. d'Esnambuc at left, ship at right. Woman on back.	35.00	200.	650.

NOTICE

Readers with unlisted dates, signature varieties, etc. are invited to submit photocopies of their notes to: Standard Catalog of World Paper Money, 700 East State St. Iola, WI 54990-0001, E-Mail: george.cuhaj@fwpubs.com.

33 2 Nouveaux Francs on 100 Francs

		VG	VF	UNC
33	2 Nouveaux Francs on 100 Francs ND (1963). Multicolor. La Bourdonnais at left, two women at right. Woman looking at mountains on back.	10.00	45.00	100.

		VG	VF	UNC
33	10 Nouveaux Francs on 500 Francs ND (1964). Multicolor. Bldgs. and sailboat at left, 2 women at right. Ox-carts with wood and plants on back.	40.00	175.	425.

		VG	VF	UNC
34	20 Nouveaux Francs on 1000 Francs ND (1964). Multicolor. Two women at right. Women at right, two men in small boat on back.	70.00	225.	700.
35	100 Nouveaux Francs on 5000 Francs ND (1961). Multicolor. Gen. Schoelcher at center right. Family on back.	85.00	450.	2000.

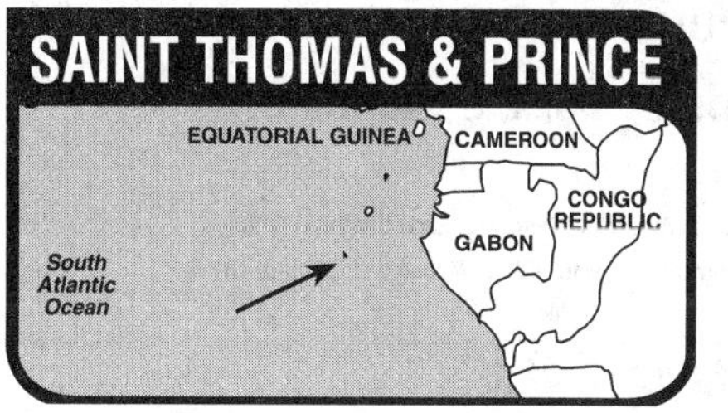

The Democratic Republic of Sao Tomé and Príncipe (formerly the Portuguese overseas province of St. Thomas and Prince Islands) is located in the Gulf of Guinea 150 miles (241 km.) off the West African coast. It has an area of 372 sq. ml. (960 sq. km.) and a population of 149,000. Capital: São Tomé. The economy of the islands is d on cocoa, copra and coffee.

St. Thomas and St. Prince were uninhabited when discovered by Portuguese navigators Joao de Santarem and Pedro de Escobar in 1470. After the failure of their initial settlement, 1485, the Portuguese successfully colonized St. Thomas with a colony of prisoners and exiled Jews, 1493. An initial prosperity d on the sugar trade gave way to a time of misfortune, 1567-1709, that saw the colony attacked and occupied or plundered by the French and Dutch; ravaged by the slave revolt of 1595; and finally rendered destitute by the transfer of the world sugar trade to Brazil. In the late 1800s, the colony turned from the production of sugar to cocoa, the basis of its present prosperity.

The islands were designated a Portuguese overseas province in 1951. On April 25, 1974, the government of Portugal was seized by a military junta which reached agreements providing for independence for the Portuguese overseas provinces of Portuguese Guinea (Guinea-Bissau), Mozambique, Cape Verde Islands, Angola, and St. Thomas and Prince Islands. The Democratic Republic of São Tomé and Príncipe was declared on July 12, 1975.

RULERS:

Portuguese to 1975

MONETARY SYSTEM:

1 Escudo = 100 Centavos, 1911-1976
1 Dobra = 100 Centimos, 1977-

PORTUGUESE ADMINISTRATION

BANCO NACIONAL ULTRAMARINO

S. TOMÉ E PRÍNCIPE

1956-64 ISSUE

#36-39 bank seal at l., Portuguese arms at lower ctr., D. Afonso V at lower r. Printer: BWC.

		VG	VF	UNC
40	1000 Escudos 11.5.1964. Green on multicolor underprint. J. de Santarem at right, bank arms at upper center. Woman, sailing ships at left center, arms at upper right on back.			
	a. Issued note.	25.00	95.00	250.
	s. Specimen, punch hole cancelled.	—	—	150.
	ct. Color trial. Purple on multicolor underprint.	—	—	300.

1974 CIRCULATING BEARER CHECK ISSUE

		VG	VF	UNC
41	100 Escudos 31.3.1974.	—	—	—
42	500 Escudos 28.4.1974.	—	—	—
43	500 Escudos 31.12.1974.	45.00	85.00	160.
43A	1000 Escudos 23.12.1974; 31.12.1974. Red.	45.00	85.00	160.

NOTICE

Readers with unlisted dates, signature varieties, etc. are invited to submit photocopies of their notes to: Standard Catalog of World Paper Money, 700 East State St. Iola, WI 54990-0001, E-Mail: george.cuhaj@fwpubs.com.

DEMOCRATIC REPUBLIC

BANCO NACIONAL DE S. TOMÉ E PRÍNCIPE

1976 PROVISIONAL ISSUE

#44-48 new bank name ovpt. in red on both sides of Banco Nacional Ultramarino notes.

#44-46 bank seal at l., Portuguese arms at lower ctr., Kg. D. Afonso V at r. Printer: BWC.

		VG	VF	UNC
44	**20 Escudos** 1.6.1976 (- old date 20.11.1958). Brown on multicolor underprint. Overprint on #36.	3.00	10.00	25.00

		VG	VF	UNC
45	**50 Escudos** 1.6.1976 (- old date 20.11.1958). Brown-violet on multicolor underprint. Overprint on #37.	3.00	10.00	30.00

		VG	VF	UNC
46	**100 Escudos** 1.6.1976 (- old date 20.11.1958). Purple on multicolor underprint. Overprint on #38.	5.00	15.00	45.00

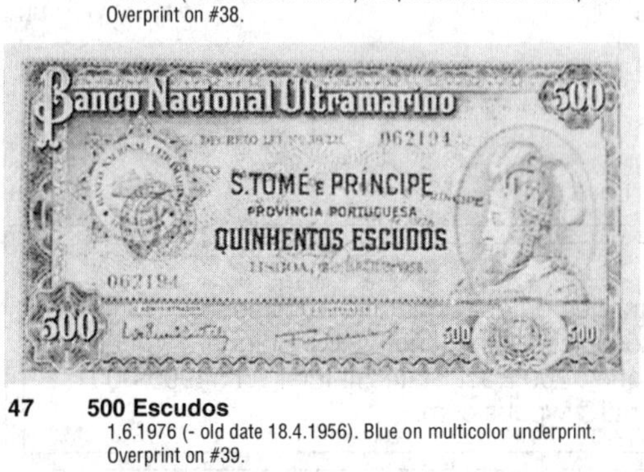

		VG	VF	UNC
47	**500 Escudos** 1.6.1976 (- old date 18.4.1956). Blue on multicolor underprint. Overprint on #39.	15.00	40.00	150.
48	**1000 Escudos** 1.6.1976 (- old date 11.5.1964). Green on multicolor underprint. Overprint on #40.	15.00	40.00	120.

#49 Deleted. See #43A.

1976 CIRCULATING BEARER CHECK ISSUE

		VG	VF	UNC
50	**500 Escudos** 21.6.1976. Black on pink and light aqua underprint. 167 x 75mm.	10.00	27.50	85.00
51	**1000 Escudos** 21.6.1976. 167 x 75mm.	12.50	35.00	100.

DECRETO-LEI NO. 50/76; 1977 ISSUE

#52-55 Rei Amador at r. and as wmk., arms at lower l. Sign. titles: *O MINISTRO DA COORDENACÃO ECONOMICA* and *O GOVERNADOR*. Printer: BWC.

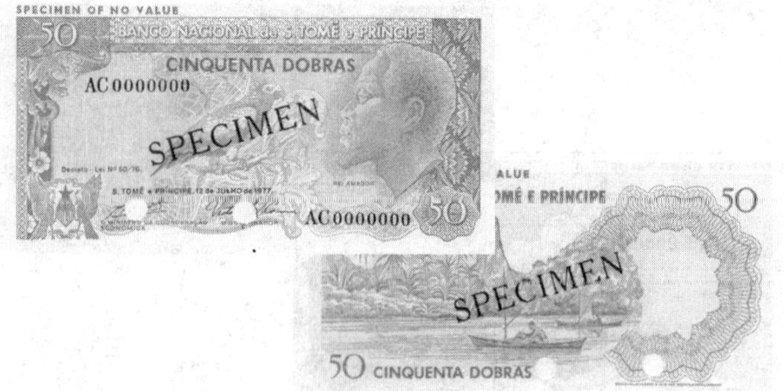

		VG	VF	UNC
52	**50 Dobras** 12.7.1977. Red and multicolor. African grey parrot at center in underprint. Scene with two fishermen in boats on back.			
	a. Issued note.	1.00	3.00	8.00
	s. Specimen.	—	—	125.

		VG	VF	UNC
53	**100 Dobras** 12.7.1977. Green and multicolor. Flower at center in underprint. Group of people preparing food on back.			
	a. Issued note.	1.50	4.00	10.00
	s. Specimen.	—	—	125.

		VG	VF	UNC
54	**500 Dobras** 12.7.1977. Purple and multicolor. Sea Turtle at center in underprint. Waterfall on back.			
	a. Issued note.	3.00	10.00	25.00
	s. Specimen.	—	—	150.

55	1000 Dobras	VG	VF	UNC
	12.7.1977. Blue and multicolor. Bananas at center in underprint. Fruit gatherer on back.			
	a. Issued note.	9.00	35.00	90.00
	s. Specimen.	—	—	200.

DECRETO-LEI NO. 6/82; 1982 ISSUE

#56-59 like #52-55 but w/sign. titles: *O MINISTRO DO PLANO* and *O GOVERNADOR*. Printer: BWC.

		VG	VF	UNC
56	**50 Dobras** 30.9.1982. Like #52.	.75	2.50	6.50
57	**100 Dobras** 30.9.1982. Like #53.	1.00	3.50	9.00
58	**500 Dobras** 30.9.1982. Like #54.	2.50	9.00	22.50

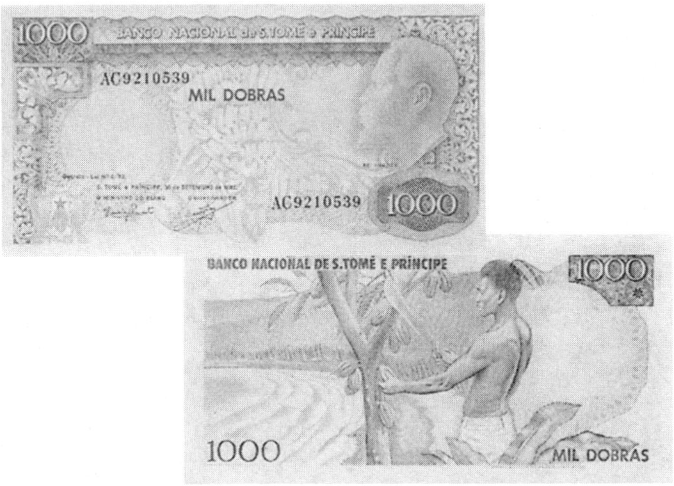

59	1000 Dobras	VG	VF	UNC
	30.9.1982. Like #55.	3.50	12.00	32.50

DECRETO-LEI NO. 1/88; 1989 ISSUE

#60-62 designs like #57-59 except sign. title at l.: *O MINISTRO DA ECONOMIA E FINANÇAS*. Printer: TDLR.

60	100 Dobras	VG	VF	UNC
	4.1.1989. Green and multicolor. Like #57.	.75	2.50	6.00

		VG	VF	UNC
61	**500 Dobras** 4.1.1989. Violet, red, orange and tan on multicolor underprint. Like #58.	1.00	4.00	9.00
62	**1000 Dobras** 4.1.1989. Blue, green and multicolor underprint. Like #59.	2.00	7.00	17.50

BANCO CENTRAL DE S.TOMÉ E PRÍNCIPE

DECRETO LEI NO. 29/93; 1993 ISSUE

#63 and 64 like #61 and 62. Ascending size serial #. Printer: TDLR.

63	500 Dobras	VG	VF	UNC
	26.8.1993. Violet, red, orange and tan on blue and multicolor underprint. Like #61 but arms at lower left is blue. Green serial # at right.	FV	FV	4.00

64	1000 Dobras	VG	VF	UNC
	26.8.1993. Purple and deep blue and blue-green on multicolor underprint. Similar to #62. Red serial # at right.	FV	FV	10.00

NOTICE

Readers with unlisted dates, signature varieties, etc. are invited to submit photocopies of their notes to: Standard Catalog of World Paper Money, 700 East State St. Iola, WI 54990-0001, E-Mail: george.cuhaj@fwpubs.com.

DECRETO LEI NO. 42/96; 1996 ISSUE

#65-68 Rei Amador at r. and as wmk., arms at upper ctr. r. Printer: TDLR. Replacement notes: Serial # prefix ZZ.

65	5000 Dobras	VG	VF	UNC
	22.10.1996. Purple, lilac and olive-green on multicolor underprint. Papa Figo bird (Principe Glossy Starling) at left center. Esplanade, modern building at left center on back.			
	a. One security thread.	FV	FV	10.00
	b. Two security threads.	FV	FV	8.00
	s. Specimen.	FV	FV	75.00

66	10,000 Dobras	VG	VF	UNC
	22.10.1996; 26.8.2004. Dark green, blue-violet and tan on multicolor underprint. Emerald Cuckoo at left center. Bridge over river at left center on back.			
	a. One security thread.	FV	FV	17.50
	b. Two security threads.	FV	FV	15.00
	s. Specimen.	—	—	75.00

67	20,000 Dobras	VG	VF	UNC
	22.10.1996; 26.8.2004. Red, olive-brown and blue-black on multicolor underprint. Sao Tome Oriole at left center. Beach scene at left center on back.			
	a. One security thread.	FV	FV	25.00
	b. Two security threads.	FV	FV	22.50
	s. Specimen.	—	—	75.00

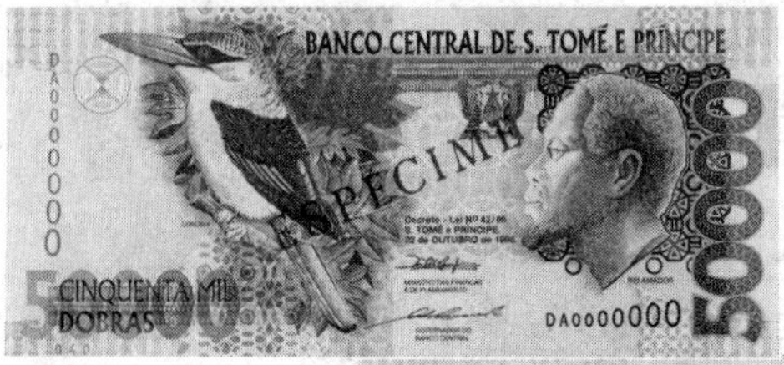

68	50,000 Dobras			
	22.10.1996; 26.8.2004. Brown, purple and red on multicolor underprint. Black-winged Kingfisher at left center. Central Bank building at left center on back.			
	a. One security thread.	—	Unc	50.00
	b. Two security threads.	—	Unc	50.00
	s. Specimen overprint: *ESPÉCIME*, 0's in serial #.	—	Unc	75.00

Listings for Samoa, see Western Samoa

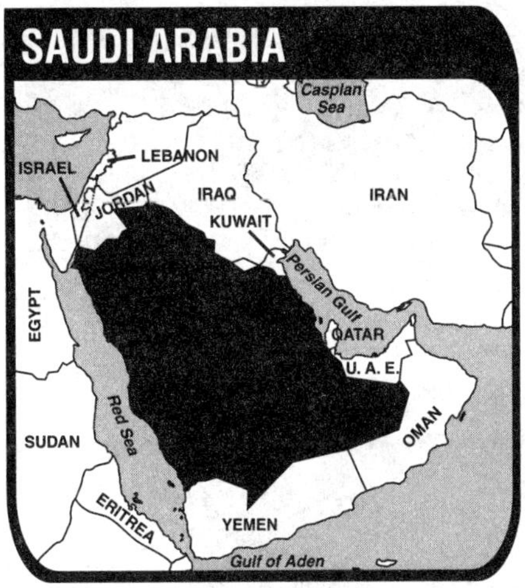

The Kingdom of Saudi Arabia, an independent and absolute hereditary monarchy comprising the former sultanate of Nejd, the old kingdom of Hejaz, Asir and El Hasa, occupies four-fifths of the Arabian peninsula. The kingdom has an area of 830,000 sq. mi. (2,149,690 sq. km.) and a population of 21.66 million. Capital: Riyadh. The economy is d on oil, which provides 85 percent of Saudi Arabia's revenue.

Mohammed united the Arabs in the 7th century and his followers founded a great empire with its capital at Medina. The Turks established nominal rule over much of Arabia in the 16th and 17th centuries, and in the 18th century divided it into principalities.

The Kingdom of Saudi Arabia was created by King Ibn-Saud (1882-1953), a descendant of earlier Wahabi rulers of the Arabian peninsula. In 1901 he seized Riyadh, capital of the Sultanate of Nejd, and in 1905 established himself as Sultan. In 1913 he captured the Turkish province of Hasa; took the Hejaz in 1925 and by 1926 most of Asir. In 1932 he combined Nejd and Hejaz into the single kingdom of Saudi Arabia. Asir was incorporated into the kingdom a year later.

One of the principal cities, Mecca, is the Holy center of Islam and is the scene of an annual Pilgrimage from the entire Moslem world.

RULERS:

Sa'ud Ibn Abdul Aziz, AH1373-1383/1953-1964AD
Faisal, AH1383-1395/1964-1975AD
Khaled, AH1395-1402/1975-1982AD
Fahd, AH1402-/1982AD-

MONETARY SYSTEM:

1 Riyal = 20 Ghirsh

REPLACEMENT NOTES:

#1-4, serial number starting w/Arabic "O".

KINGDOM

SAUDI ARABIAN MONETARY AGENCY

SIGNATURE VARIETIES

	GOVERNOR OF SAMA	MINISTER OF FINANCE
1	 Anwar Ali	 Tallal bin Abdul Aziz
2	 Anwar Ali	 Musa'id bin Abdul Rahman
3	 Abdul Aziz al-Qurashi	 Musa'id bin Abdul Rahman
4	 Abdul Aziz al-Qurashi	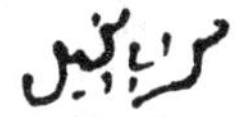 Muhammad Ali Aba Al-Khail
5	 Hamad Saud al-Sayyari	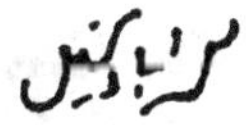 Muhammad Ali Aba Al-Khail
6	 Hamad Saud al-Sayyari	 Ibrahim bin Abdulaziz bin Abdullah al-Assaf

LAW OF 1.7. AH1379; 1961 ND ISSUE

#6-10 arms (palm tree and crossed swords) on back and as wmk. Embedded security thread.

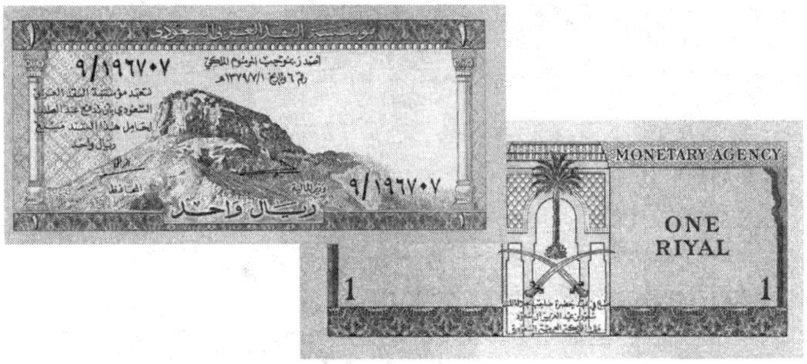

		VG	VF	UNC
6	**1 Riyal** L. AH1379 (1961). Brown on light blue and green underprint. Hill of Light at center. Back violet-brown and green. Signature #1.	2.00	10.00	45.00

		VG	VF	UNC
7	**5 Riyals** L. AH1379 (1961). Blue and green on multicolor underprint. Fortress at center.			
	a. Signature #1.	12.00	75.00	325.
	b. Signature #2.	20.00	100.	400.

		VG	VF	UNC
8	**10 Riyals** L. AH1379 (1961). Green on pink and multicolor underprint. Dhows in Jedda harbor.			
	a. Signature #1.	15.00	75.00	325.
	b. Signature #2.	20.00	100.	400.

		VG	VF	UNC
9	**50 Riyals** L. AH1379 (1961). Violet and olive-green on multicolor underprint. Derrick at center right.			
	a. Signature #1.	60.00	200.	800.
	b. Signature #2.	60.00	175.	800.

10	100 Riyals	VG	VF	UNC
	L. AH1379 (1961). Red on multicolor underprint. Building at left, archway in background at center, building at right.			
	a. Signature #1.	150.	650.	2000.
	b. Signature #2.	125.	550.	1750.

LAW OF 1.7. AH1379; 1968 ND ISSUE

#11-15 wmk: Arms. Embedded security thread.

11	1 Riyal	VG	VF	UNC
	L. AH1379 (1968). Purple on multicolor underprint. Goverment building at center right. Saudi arms on back.			
	a. Signature #2.	.50	3.00	15.00
	b. Signature #3.	.50	4.00	20.00
	s. As a. Specimen.	—	—	—

12	5 Riyals	VG	VF	UNC
	L. AH1379 (1968). Green on multicolor underprint. Airport. Oil loading on ships at dockside on back.			
	a. Signature #2.	3.00	15.00	60.00
	b. Signature #3.	5.00	25.00	100.

13	10 Riyals	VG	VF	UNC
	L. AH1379 (1968). Gray-blue on multicolor underprint. Mosque. Al-Masa Wall with arches on back. Signature #2.	2.50	15.00	60.00

14	50 Riyals	VG	VF	UNC
	L. AH1379 (1968). Brown on multicolor underprint. Courtyard of mosque at right. Saudi arms at left, row of palms at center on back.			
	a. Signature #2.	20.00	90.00	325.
	b. Signature #3.	17.50	80.00	300.

15	100 Riyals	VG	VF	UNC
	L. AH1379 (1966). Red on multicolor underprint. Government Building at center right. Derricks at left center on back.			
	a. Signature #2.	30.00	100.	400.
	b. Signature #3.	25.00	90.00	350.

LAW OF 1.7. AH1379; 1976; 1977 ND ISSUE

#16-19 portr. Kg. Faisal at r. and as wmk. Sign. 4.

16	1 Riyal	VG	VF	UNC
	L. AH1379 (1977). Red-brown on multicolor underprint. Hill of Light at center. Airport at left center on back.	.25	1.00	5.00

Incorrect Correct

17	5 Riyals	VG	VF	UNC
	L. AH1379 (1977). Green and brown on multicolor underprint. Irrigation canal at center. Dam at left center on back.			
	a. Incorrect Khamsa (five) in lower center panel of text.	1.50	6.00	25.00
	b. Correct Khamsa (five) in lower center panel of text.	1.00	2.50	15.00

18	10 Riyals	VG	VF	UNC
	L. AH1379 (1977). Lilac and brown on multicolor underprint. Oil drilling platform at center. Oil refinery on back.	FV	5.00	25.00

19	50 Riyals	VG	VF	UNC
	L. AH1379 (1976). Green, purple and brown on multicolor underprint. Arches of mosque at center. Courtyard of mosque at left center on back.	FV	20.00	75.00

NOTICE

Readers with unlisted dates, signature varieties, etc. are invited to submit photocopies of their notes to: Standard Catalog of World Paper Money, 700 East State St. Iola, WI 54990-0001, E-Mail: george.cuhaj@fwpubs.com.

20	100 Riyals	VG	VF	UNC
	L. AH1379 (1976). Blue and turquoise on multicolor underprint. Mosque at center, King 'Abd al-'Aziz Ibn Saud at right. Long building with arches on back.	FV	35.00	115.

LAW OF 1.7. AH1379; 1983; 1984 ND ISSUE

#21-26 wmk: Kg. Fahd.

Lower l. serial # fluoresces gold under UV light. Non-visible portr. of King fluoresces yellow under UV light.

#21-24 upper l. panel also exists w/unnecessary upper accent mark in "Monetary." at ctr. r. in text.

Incorrect Correct

21	1 Riyal	VG	VF	UNC
	L. AH1379 (1984). Dark brown on multicolor underprint. 7th century gold dinar at left, portrait King Fahd at center right. Flowers and landscape on back. Two signature varieties.			
	a. Incorrect text. signature 5.	FV	1.00	2.00
	b. Correct "Monetary." signature 5; 6.	FV	FV	1.25

22	5 Riyals	VG	VF	UNC
	L. AH1379 (1983). Purple, brown, and blue-green on multicolor underprint. Dhows at left, portrait King Fahd at center right. Oil refinery at center right on back.			
	a. Incorrect text. signature 5.	FV	1.50	5.00
	b. Correct "Monetary." signature 5.	FV	FV	4.00

23 **10 Riyals**

L. AH1379 (1983). Black, brown and purple on multicolor underprint. Fortress at left, portrait King Fahd at center right. Palm trees at center right on back.

	VG	VF	UNC
a. Incorrect text. signature 5.	FV	4.00	10.00
b. Correct "Monetary." signature 5.	FV	FV	7.00

24 **50 Riyals**

L. AH1379 (1983). Dark green and dark brown on multicolor underprint. Mosque of Omar (Dome of the Rock) in Jerusalem at left, portrait King Fahd at center right. Mosque at center on back.

	VG	VF	UNC
a. Incorrect text. signature 5.	FV	FV	40.00
b. Correct "Monetary." signature 5.	FV	FV	30.00

#25-26 Saudi arms in blind embossed latent image area at l. ctr.

25 **100 Riyals**

L. AH1379 (1984). Brown-violet and olive-green on multicolor underprint. Mosque at left, portrait King Fahd at center right. Mosque at center on back. Signature 5; 6.

	VG	VF	UNC
	FV	FV	55.00

NOTICE

Readers with unlisted dates, signature varieties, etc. are invited to submit photocopies of their notes to: Standard Catalog of World Paper Money, 700 East State St. Iola, WI 54990-0001, E-Mail: george.cuhaj@fwpubs.com.

Incorrect Correct

26 **500 Riyals**

L. AH1379 (1983). Purple and green on multicolor underprint. Courtyard at left, portrait King 'Abd al-'Aziz Ibn Saud at center right. Courtyard of Great Mosque at center on back.

	VG	VF	UNC
a. Incorrect "Five Hundred Riyals" in lower center panel of text. signature 5.	FV	150.	300.
b. Correct "Five Hundred Riyals" in lower center panel of text. signature 5.	FV	FV	225.

2000 COMMEMORATIVE ISSUE

#27 and 28, Centennial of Kingdom

27 **20 Riyals**

AH1419, 1999. Brown, red, gray and blue on multicolor underprint. Abdul Aziz at left center and as watermark. Annur Mouuntain at center, commemorative logo and text at left. Signature 6.

	VG	VF	UNC
	FV	FV	10.00

28 **200 Riyals**

2000. Red, brown, gray and green on multicolor underprint. Abdul Aziz at left center and as watermark. Al Mussmack Palace at lower right and its gate on back. Commemorative logo and text at right. Signature 6.

	VG	VF	UNC
	FV	FV	85.00

2003 ISSUE

		VG	VF	UNC
29	**100 Riyals** 2003. Brown, violet and multicolor. Hologram added at upper center.	FV	FV	50.00

		VG	VF	UNC
30	**500 Riyals** 2003. Purple, green and peach on multicolor underprint.	FV	FV	200.

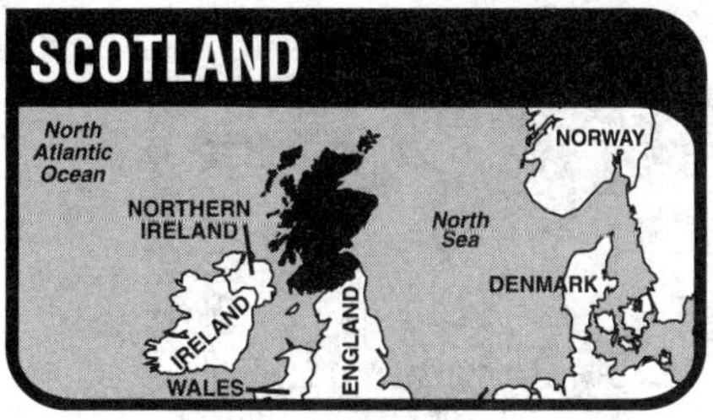

Scotland, a part of the United Kingdom of Great Britain and Northern Ireland, consists of the northern part of the island of Great Britain. It has an area of 30,414 sq. mi. (78,772 sq. km.). Capital: Edinburgh. Principal industries are agriculture, fishing, manufacturing and ship-building.

In the 5th century, Scotland consisted of four kingdoms; that of the Picts, the Scots, Strathclyde, and Northumbria. The Scottish kingdom was united by Malcolm II (1005-34), but its ruler was forced to payo homage to the English crown in 1174. Scotland won independence under Robert Bruce at Bannockburn in 1314 and was ruled by the house of Stuart from 1371 to 1688. The personal union of the kingdoms of England and Scotland was achieved in 1603 by the accession of King James VI of Scotland as James I of England. Scotland was united with England by Parliamentary act in 1707.

RULERS:

British

MONETARY SYSTEM:

1 Shilling = 12 Pence
1 Guinea = 21 Shillings
1 Pound Sterling = 12 Pounds Scots
1 Pound = 20 Shillings to 1971
1 Pound = 100 New Pence, 1971-1981
1 Pound = 100 Pence, 1982-

REPLACEMENT NOTES:

#111, Z/1, Z/2 or Z/3 prefix; #112 ZA or ZB prefix; #113 ZB prefix.

BRITISH ADMINISTRATION

BANK OF SCOTLAND

1935; 1938 ISSUE

		VG	VF	UNC
91	**1 Pound** 1937-43. Yellow-brown, dark brown and gray-blue. Like #86 but arms of the bank at left.			
	a. Signature Lord Elphinstone and A. W. M. Beveridge. 15.1.1935-15.9.1937.	15.00	80.00	225.
	b. Signature Lord Elphinstone and J. Macfarlane. 5.1.1939-7.5.1941.	15.00	75.00	200.
	c. Signature Lord Elphinstone and J. B. Crawford. 2.6.1942; 16.10.1943.	15.00	75.00	225.
	s. As c. Specimen.	—	—	175.
92	**5 Pounds** 1935-44. Like #86 but thistle motif at left.			
	a. Signature Lord Elphinstone and A. W. M. Beveridge. 17.1.1935-17.3.1938.	60.00	225.	600.
	b. Signature Lord Elphinstone and J. Macfarlane. Black value panels. 24.4.1939-16.10.1941.	60.00	225.	600.
	c. Signature Lord Elphinstone and J. B. Crawford. 5.6.1942-26.9.1944.	50.00	210.	550.
	s. As c. Specimen.	—	—	175.
93	**10 Pounds** 1938-63. Scottish arms in panel at left, medallion of Goddess of fortune below arms at right. Bank building on back.			
	a. Signature Lord Elphinstone and A. W. M. Beveridge. 24.1.1935; 28.6.1938.	250.	900.	2000.
	b. Signature Lord Elphinstone and J. B. Crawford. 16.7.1942; 15.10.1942.	225.	800.	1800.
	c. Signature Lord Bilsland and Sir Wm. Watson. 26.9.1963; 27.9.1963.	175.	500.	1350.
94	**20 Pounds** 1935-65. Like #93.			
	a. Signature Lord Elphinstone and A. W. M. Beveridge. 11.1.1935-22.7.1938.	100.	350.	1000.
	b. Signature Lord Elphinstone and J. Macfarlane. 16.5.1939; 12.7.1939.	100.	400.	1100.
	c. Signature Lord Elphinstone and J. B. Crawford. 5.6.1942-11.8.1952.	75.00	300.	800.
	d. Signature Lord Elphinstone and Sir Wm. Watson. 5.12.1952; 14.4.1953.	100.	375.	1000.
	e. Signature Sir J. Craig and Sir Wm. Watson. 6.4.1955-12.6.1956	60.00	250.	750.
	f. Signature Lord Bilsland and Sir Wm. Watson. 21.3.1958-3.10.1963.	60.00	250.	700.

NOTICE

Readers with unlisted dates, signature varieties, etc. are invited to submit photocopies of their notes to: Standard Catalog of World Paper Money, 700 East State St. Iola, WI 54990-0001, E-Mail: george.cuhaj@fwpubs.com.

95	**100 Pounds**	**VG**	**VF**	**UNC**
	1935-62. Like #93.			
	a. Signature Lord Elphinstone and A. W. M. Beveridge. 8.1.1935-12.8.1937.	450.	1450.	3200.
	b. Signature Lord Elphinstone and J. Macfarlane. 2.4.1940; 15.7.1940.	400.	1200.	2650.
	c. Signature Lord Elphinestone and J. B. Crawford. 10.6.1942; 14.12.1951.	350.	1000.	2400.
	d. Signature John Craig and Sir Wm. Watson. 14.9.1956-3.12.1956.	350.	950.	2200.
	e. Signature Lord Bilsland and Sir Wm. Watson. 24.3.1959-30.11.1962.	350.	900.	2100.

1961 Issue

102	**1 Pound**	**VG**	**VF**	**UNC**
	1961-65. Light brown and pale blue. Medallion at center, date below. Ship at center on back.			
	a. Imprint ends: *LD.* Signature Lord Bilsland and Sir Wm. Watson. 10.5.1961-13.2.1964.	4.00	20.00	70.00
	b. Imprint ends: *LTD.* Signature Lord Bilsland and Sir Wm. Watson. 4.5.1965; 11.5.1965.	4.00	20.00	70.00
	c. Magnetic ink encoded experimental note. Four short parallel lines overprinted at right and left borders. (1963-64).	—	—	400.
103	**5 Pounds**			
	14.9.1961-22.9.1961. Light brown and pale blue. Medallion at center, date below. Arms at left, ship at right on back. Reduced size. Signature Lord Bilsland and Sir Wm. Watson.	20.00	40.00	125.

#104 deleted, see #102.

1961; 1966 Issue

105	**1 Pound**	**VG**	**VF**	**UNC**
	1966; 1967. Light brown and pale blue. Similar to #102 but *EDINBURGH* and date at right. Signature Lord Polwarth and J. Letham with titles: *GOVERNOR* and *TREASURER & GENERAL MANAGER.* two watermark varieties.			
	a. Without electronic sorting marks on back. 1.6.1966.	4.00	17.50	60.00
	b. With electronic sorting marks on back. 3.3.1967.	4.00	17.50	60.00
	s. As b. Specimen.	—	—	—

106	**5 Pounds**	**VG**	**VF**	**UNC**
	1961-67. Blue and light brown. Medallion of fortune at center, numerals of value filled in at base. Arms at left, ship at right on back. Like #103.			
	a. Signature Lord Bilsland and Sir Wm. Watson with titles: *GOVERNOR* and *TREASURER.* 25.9.1961-12.1.1965.	15.00	35.00	120.
	b. Signature Lord Polwarth and Sir Wm. Watson. 7.3.1966-8.3.1966.	20.00	40.00	150.
	c. Lighter shades of printing. Signature Lord Polwarth and J. Letham with titles: *GOVERNOR* and *TREASURER & GENERAL MANAGER.* 1.2.1967; 2.2.1967.	15.00	35.00	120.
	d. Signature titles as b. with electronic sorting marks on back. 1.11.1967.	20.00	40.00	125.

1968; 1969 Issue

109	**1 Pound**	**VG**	**VF**	**UNC**
	1968; 1969. Ochre on blue and multicolor underprint. Arms at center flanked by two women. Arms at upper left, shield at upper center, sailing ship at upper right on back.			
	a. *EDINBURGH* 19mm in length. 17.7.1968.	5.00	20.00	65.00
	b. *EDINBURGH* 24mm in length. 18.8.1969.	5.00	20.00	65.00
	s. As b. Specimen.	—	—	—

110	**5 Pounds**	**VG**	**VF**	**UNC**
	1968-69. Green on multicolor underprint. Similar to #109.			
	a. *EDINBURGH* 19mm in length. 1.11.1968; 4.11.1968.	25.00	80.00	250.
	b. *EDINBURGH* 24mm in length. 8.12.1969; 9.12.1969.	25.00	80.00	250.

110A	**20 Pounds**	**VG**	**VF**	**UNC**
	5.5.1969. Scottish arms in panel at left, medallion of Goddess of Fortune below arms at center right. Signature: Lord Polwarth and J. Letham. with security thread. Watermark: Thistle.	60.00	150.	375.

Note: #110A was an emergency printing of 25,000 examples.

1970-74 ISSUE

#111-115 arms at ctr. flanked by 2 women. Sir W. Scott at r.

#111-113 replacement notes: #111 - Serial # prefix *Z/1, Z/2* or *Z/3;* #112 - Serial # prefix *ZA* or *ZB;* #113 - Serial # prefix *ZB*.

111	1 Pound	VG	VF	UNC
	1970-88. Green on multicolor underprint. Sailing ship at left, arms at upper center, medallion of Pallas seated at right on back.			
	a. Signature Lord Polwarth and T. W. Walker. 10.8.1970; 31.8.1971.	5.00	15.00	50.00
	b. Signature Lord Clydesmuir and T. W. Walker. 1.11.1972; 30.8.1973.	5.00	15.00	50.00
	c. Signature Lord Clydesmuir and A. M. Russell. 28.10.1974-3.10.1978.	3.00	5.00	22.50
	d. Signature Lord Clydesmuir and D. B. Pattullo. 15.10.1979; 4.11.1980.	3.00	5.00	15.00
	e. Signature T. N. Risk and D. B. Pattullo. 30.7.1981.	4.00	7.00	18.00
	f. Without sorting marks on back. Signature like e. 7.10.1983; 9.11.1984; 12.12.1985; 18.11.1986.	2.00	4.00	16.00
	g. Signature T. N. Risk and L. P. Burt. 19.8.1988.	2.00	3.00	10.00
	s. As a (1970); c (1974). Specimen.	—	Unc	125.

112	5 Pounds	VG	VF	UNC
	1970-88. Blue on multicolor underprint. Back similar to #111.			
	a. Signature Lord Polwarth and T. W. Walker. 10.8.1970; 2.9.1971.	20.00	50.00	150.
	b. Signature Lord Clydesmuir and T. W. Walker. 4.12.1972; 5.9.1973.	17.50	35.00	110.
	c. Signature Lord Clydesmuir and A. M. Russell. 4.11.1974; 1.12.1975; 21.11.1977; 19.10.1978.	15.00	30.00	90.00
	d. Signature Lord Clydesmuir and D. B. Pattullo. 28.9.1979; 28.11.1980.	15.00	25.00	75.00
	e. Signature T. N. Risk and D. B. Pattullo. 27.7.1981; 25.6.1982.	12.00	25.00	70.00
	f. Without encoding marks. 13.10.1983; 3.12.1985; 29.2.1988.	12.00	20.00	55.00
	s. As a (1970); c (1974). Specimen.	—	—	150.

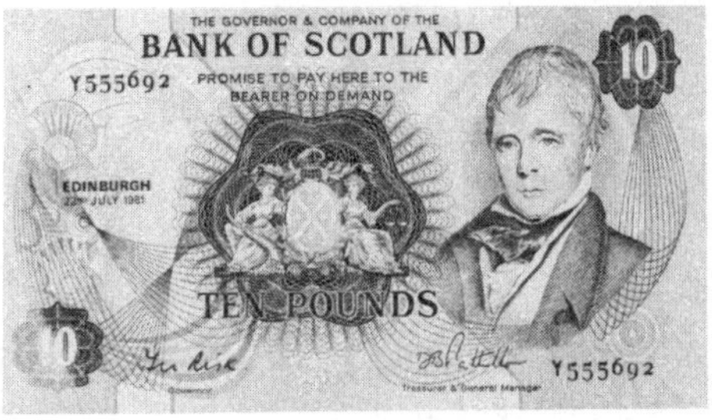

113	10 Pounds	VG	VF	UNC
	1974-90. Brown on multicolor underprint. Medallions of sailing ship at lower left, Pallas seated at upper left center, arms at right on back.			
	a. Signature Lord Clydesmuir and A. M. Russell. 1.5.1974-10.10.1979.	30.00	50.00	175.
	b. Signature Lord Clydesmuir and D. B. Pattullo. 5.2.1981.	30.00	50.00	160.
	c. Signature T. N. Risk and D. B. Pattullo. 22.7.1981; 16.6.1982; 14.10.1983; 17.9.1984; 8.1.1986; 20.10.1986; 6.8.1987.	20.00	30.00	35.00
	d. Signature T. N. Risk and P. Burt. 1.9.1989; 31.10.1990.	20.00	30.00	65.00

114	20 Pounds	VG	VF	UNC
	1970-87. Purple on multicolor underprint. Arms at upper left, above sailing ship with medallion of Pallas seated below, head office building at center on back.			
	a. Signature Lord Polwarth and T. W. Walker. 1.10.1970.	55.00	120.	350.
	b. Signature Lord Clydesmuir and T. W. Walker. 3.1.1973.	55.00	110.	300.
	c. Signature Lord Clydesmuir and A. M. Russell. 8.11.1974; 14.1.1977.	50.00	90.00	265.
	d. Signature Lord Clydesmuir and D. B. Pattullo. 16.7.1979; 2.2.1981.	45.00	80.00	225.
	e. Signature T. N. Risk and D. B. Pattullo. 4.8.1981-15.12.1987.	40.00	55.00	175.
	s. As a. Specimen. 1.10.1970.	—	—	250.
115	**100 Pounds**			
	1971-86. Red on multicolor underprint. Arms at upper left, medallions of sailing ship at lower left, Pallas seated at lower right, head office building at center on back.			
	a. Signature Lord Polwarth and T. W. Walker. 6.12.1971.	300.	525.	1250.
	b. Signature Lord Clydesmuir and T. W. Walker. 6.9.1973.	275.	500.	1200.
	c. Signature Lord Clydesmuir and A. M. Russell. 11.10.1978.	275.	450.	1000.
	d. Signature Lord Clydesmuir and D. B. Pattullo. 26.1.1981.	275.	425.	900.
	e. Signature T. N. Risk and D. B. Pattullo. 11.6.1982; 26.11.1986.	250.	350.	750.
	s. As a. Specimen.	—	—	300.

1990-92 STERLING ISSUE

#116-118 similar to previous issue but w/*STERLING* added below value. Smaller size notes.

116 5 Pounds VG VF UNC

1990-94. Blue on multicolor underprint. Similar to #112, but 135 x 70mm.

	VG	VF	UNC
a. Signature T. N. Risk and P. Burt. 20.6.1990.	FV	17.50	40.00
b. Signature D. B. Pattullo and P. Burt. 6.11.1991; 18.1.1993; 7.1.1994.	FV	15.00	35.00

117 10 Pounds

	VG	VF	UNC
7.5.1992; 9.3.1993; 13.4.1994. Deep brown on multicolor underprint. Similar to #113, but 142 x 75mm. Signature D. B. Pattullo and P. Burt.	FV	25.00	60.00

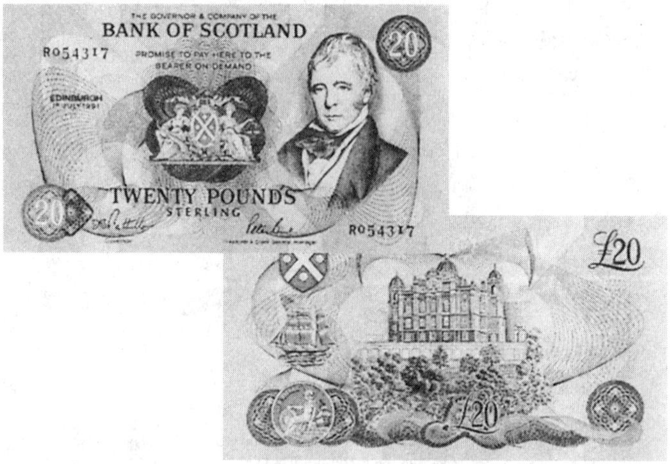

118 20 Pounds

	VG	VF	UNC
1.7.1991; 3.2.1992; 12.1.1993. Purple on multicolor underprint. Similar to #114 but reduced size, 148 x 81mm. Signature D. B. Pattullo and P. Burt.	FV	50.00	85.00

118A 100 Pounds

14.2.1990; 2.12.1992; 9.2.1994. Red on multicolor underprint. Similar to #115 but in Sterling added to denomination.

	VG	VF	UNC
a. 14.2.1990. Signature T.N. Risk and Peter Burt.	200.	285.	550.
b. 22.1.1992; 2.12.1992; 9.2.1994. Signature D.B. Pattullo and Peter Burt.	200.	275.	500.

1995 COMMEMORATIVE ISSUE

#119-122, Tercentenary - Bank of Scotland

#119-123 Sir W. Scott at l. and as wmk., bank arms at ctr. Bank head office bldg. at lower l., medallion of Pallas seated, arms and medallion of sailing ships at r. on back. Printer: TDLR (W/o imprint).

119 5 Pounds

1995-. Dark blue and purple on multicolor underprint. Oil well riggers working with drill at center on back.

	VG	VF	UNC
a. Signature D. Bruce Pattullo and Peter A. Burt. 4.1.1995. Signature titles as: *GOVERNOR* and *TREASURER & CHIEF GENERAL MANAGER*.	FV	FV	25.00
b. Signature D. Bruce Pattullo and Gavin Masterton. 13.9.1996.	FV	FV	20.00
c. Signature Alistair Grant and Gavin Masterton. 5.8.1998.	FV	FV	18.50
d. Signature Peter Burt and George Mitchell. 25.6.2002. Signature titles as: *GOVERNOR* and *TREASURER & MANAGING DIRECTOR*.	FV	FV	17.50
e. Signature Dennis Stevenson and Colin Matthew.	FV	FV	17.50

120 10 Pounds

1995-. Dark brown and deep olive-green on multicolor underprint. Workers by distilling equipment at center on back.

	VG	VF	UNC
a. Signature D. Bruce Pattullo and Peter A. Burt. 1.2.1995. Signature titles as: *GOVERNOR and TREASURER & CHIEF GENERAL MANAGER*.	FV	FV	42.50
b. Signature Bruce Pattullo and Gavin Masterton. 5.8.1997.	FV	FV	37.50
c. Signature Alistair Grant and Gavin Masterton. 18.8.1998.	FV	FV	35.00
d. Signature John Shaw and George Mitchell. 18.6.2001. Signature titles as: *GOVERNOR and TREASURER & MANAGING DIRECTOR*.	FV	FV	32.50
e. Signature George Mitchell. 26.11.2003; 24.9.2004. Signature title as: *GOVERNOR*.	FV	FV	30.00

#	Denomination	VG	VF	UNC
121	**20 Pounds**	VG	VF	UNC
	1995-. Violet and brown on multicolor underprint. Woman researcher at laboratory station at center on back.			
	a. Signature D. Bruce Pattullo and Peter A. Burt. 1.5.1995. Signature titles as: *GOVERNOR* and *TREASURER & CHIEF GENERAL MANAGER.*	FV	FV	80.00
	b. Signature Bruce Pattullo and Gavin Masterton. 25.10.1996; 1.4.1998.	FV	FV	70.00
	c. Signature Alistair Grant and Gavin Masterton. 22.3.1999. Signature titles as: *GOVERNOR* and *TREASURER & MANAGING DIRECTOR.*	FV	FV	67.50
	d. Signature John Shaw and George Mitchell. 18.6.2001.	FV	FV	65.00
	e. Signature George Mitchell. 26.11.2003; 24.9.2004. Signature title as: *GOVERNOR.*	FV	FV	65.00

#	Denomination	VG	VF	UNC
122	**50 Pounds**	VG	VF	UNC
	1995; 1999. Dark green and olive-brown on multicolor underprint. Music director and violinists at center on back.			
	a. Signature D. Bruce Pattullo and Peter A. Burt. 1.5.1995. Signature titles as: *GOVERNOR* and *TREASURER & MANAGING DIRECTOR.*	FV	110.	225.
	b. Signature Alistair Grant and Gavin Masterton. 15.4.1999. Signature titles as: *GOVERNOR* and *TREASURER & MANAGING DIRECTOR.*	FV	FV	175.
	c. Signature George Mitchell. 29.1.2003. Signature title as *GOVERNOR.*	FV	FV	160.
	d. Signature Dennis Stevenson and Colin Matthew.	FV	FV	150.

#	Denomination	VG	VF	UNC
123	**100 Pounds**	VG	VF	UNC
	1995-. Red-violet and red-orange on multicolor underprint. Golf outing at center on back.			
	a. Signature D. Bruce Pattullo and Peter A. Burt. 17.7.1995. Signature titles as: *GOVERNOR* and *TREASURER & CHIEF GENERAL MANAGER.*	FV	225.	450.
	b. Signature D. Bruce Pattullo and Gavin Masterton. 18.8.1997.	FV	FV	400.
	c. Signature Alistair Grant and Gavin Masterton. 19.5.1999. Signature titles as: *GOVERNOR and TREASURER & MANAGING DIRECTOR.*	FV	FV	350.
	d. Signature George Mitchell. 26.11.2003. Signature title as: *GOVERNOR.*	FV	FV	325.
	e. Signature Dennis Stevenson and Colin Matthew.	FV	FV	300.

BRITISH LINEN BANK

1961; 1962 ISSUE

#162-170 sideview of seated Britannia in emblem at l., arms at upper r. Back blue. Printer: TDLR.

#	Denomination	VG	VF	UNC
162	**1 Pound**	VG	VF	UNC
	30.9.1961. Blue and red.	7.50	22.50	75.00
163	**5 Pounds**			
	2.1.1961; 3.2.1961. Blue and red.	25.00	100.	300.
164	**20 Pounds**			
	14.2.1962; 5.3.1962; 4.4.1962. Blue and red.	75.00	275.	600.
165	**100 Pounds**			
	9.5.1962; 1.6.1962. Blue and red.	275.	450.	1250.

1962 ISSUE

#	Denomination	VG	VF	UNC
166	**1 Pound**	VG	VF	UNC
	1962-67. Blue and red. Similar to #162 but reduced size. 150 x 70mm.			
	a. Signature A. P. Anderson. 31.3.1962.	7.00	22.50	60.00
	b. Test note with lines for electronic sorting on back. 31.3.1962.	—	Unc	350.
	c. Signature T. W. Walker. 1.7.1963-13.6.1967.	5.00	17.50	50.00
	s. As a, c. Specimen.	—	Unc	150.
167	**5 Pounds**			
	21.9.1962-18.8.1964. Blue and red. Sir Walter Scott at right. 140 x 85mm.			
	a. Signature A. P. Anderson. 21.9.1962; 20.10.1962; 16.6.1962.	12.00	25.00	75.00
	b. Signature T. W. Walker. 16.6.1964; 17.7.1964; 18.8.1964.	12.00	25.00	75.00
	c. As b. Test note with lines for electronic sorting. 17.7.1964.	60.00	150.	400.

1967 ISSUE

#	Denomination	VG	VF	UNC
168	**1 Pound**	VG	VF	UNC
	13.6.1967. Blue on multicolor underprint. Similar to #166 but modified design and with lines for electronic sorting on back.	4.00	20.00	55.00

1968 ISSUE

#	Denomination	VG	VF	UNC
169	**1 Pound**	VG	VF	UNC
	1968-70. Blue on multicolor underprint. Sir W. Scott at right, supported arms at top center.			
	a. 29.2.1968; 5.11.1969.	4.00	20.00	55.00
	b. 20.7.1970.	10.00	40.00	100.
170	**5 Pounds**			
	22.3.1968; 23.4.1968; 24.5.1968. Blue and red. Similar to #167, but reduced size and many plate changes. 146 x 78 mm.	17.50	40.00	100.

CLYDESDALE AND NORTH OF SCOTLAND BANK LTD.

1950-51 ISSUE

191	1 Pound	VG	VF	UNC
	1950-60. Blue, red and orange. Ships at dockside at left, landscape (sheaves) at right. River scene with trees on back.			
	a. 1.11.1950-1.11.1956.	10.00	45.00	150.
	b. 1.5.1958-1.11.1960.	10.00	40.00	125.
	s. As a. Specimen.	—	—	200.

192	5 Pounds	VG	VF	UNC
	2.5.1951-1.3.1960. Purple. King's College at Aberdeen at lower left, Glasgow Cathedral at lower right.			
	a. Signature J. J. Campbell.	25.00	80.00	250.
	b. Signature R. D. Fairbairn.	25.00	85.00	250.

193	20 Pounds	VG	VF	UNC
	2.5.1951-1.8.1962. Green on multicolor underprint. Like #192. 180 x 97mm.			
	a. Signature J. J. Campbell.	45.00	90.00	350.
	b. Signature R. D. Fairbairn.	45.00	90.00	350.
194	**100 Pounds**	**VG**	**VF**	**UNC**
	2.5.1951. Blue. Like #192. 180 x 97mm. Signature J. J. Campbell.	400.	850.	1750.

1961 ISSUE

#195 and 196 arms at r.

195	1 Pound	VG	VF	UNC
	1.3.1961; 2.5.1962; 1.2.1963. Green on multicolor underprint. Ship and tug at center on back.			
	a. Issued note.	6.50	35.00	100.
	s. Specimen.	—	—	160.

196	5 Pounds	VG	VF	UNC
	20.9.1961; 1.6.1962; 1.2.1963. Dark blue on multicolor underprint. King's College at Aberdeen on back.	17.50	60.00	175.

CLYDESDALE BANK LIMITED

1963-64 ISSUE

197	1 Pound	VG	VF	UNC
	2.9.1963-3.4.1967. Green on multicolor underprint. Like #195.	6.00	20.00	70.00
198	**5 Pounds**			
	2.9.1963-1.9.1969. Blue and violet. Like #196.	15.00	55.00	175.

199	10 Pounds	VG	VF	UNC
	20.4.1964; 1.12.1967. Brown on multicolor underprint. Arms at right, University of Glasgow on back.	50.00	200.	650.

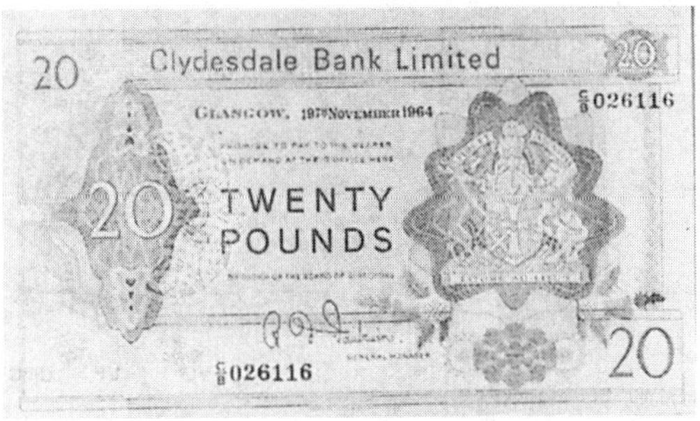

		VG	VF	UNC
200	**20 Pounds** 19.11.1964; 1.12.1967. Carmine on multicolor underprint. Arms at right. George Square in Glasgow on back.	60.00	175.	600.

		VG	VF	UNC
201	**100 Pounds** 1.2.1965; 29.4.1965; 1.2.1968. Violet on multicolor underprint. Multiple arch bridge across river at center on back.	250.	500.	1500.

1967 ISSUE

		VG	VF	UNC
202	**1 Pound** 3.4.1967; 1.10.1968; 1.9.1969. Green on multicolor underprint. Like #197 but lines for electronic sorting on back.	4.00	17.50	65.00

		VG	VF	UNC
203	**5 Pounds** 1.5.1967; 1.11.1968; 1.9.1969. Blue and violet on multicolor underprint. Like #198 but lines for electronic sorting on back.	15.00	55.00	175.

1971-81 ISSUE

#204-210 wmk: Old sailing ships.

		VG	VF	UNC
204	**1 Pound** 1971-81. Dark olive-green on multicolor underprint. Robert the Bruce at left. Scene of Battle of Bannockburn, 1314 on back.			
	a. Signature R. D. Fairbairn, with title: *GENERAL MANAGER.* 1.3.1971.	4.00	10.00	40.00
	b. Signature A. R. Macmillan, with title: *GENERAL MANAGER.* 1.5.1972; 1.8.1973.	4.00	10.00	45.00
	c. Signature A. R. Macmillan, with title: *CHIEF GENERAL MANAGER.* 1.3.1974-27.2.1981.	3.00	8.00	30.00
	s. As c. Specimen.	—	—	—

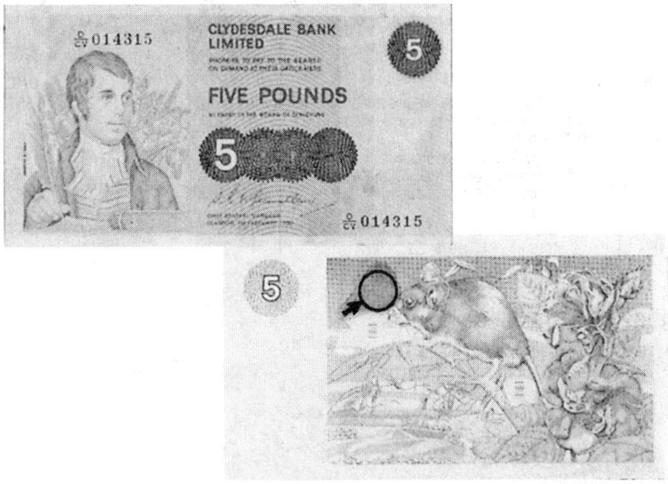

		VG	VF	UNC
205	**5 Pounds** 1971-80. Grayish lilac on multicolor underprint. Robert Burns at left. Harvest Mouse and rose from Burns' pomes on back.			
	a. Signature R. D. Fairbairn, with title: *GENERAL MANAGER.* 1.3.1971.	15.00	55.00	175.
	b. Signature A. R. Macmillan, with title: *GENERAL MANAGER.* 1.5.1972; 1.8.1973.	15.00	55.00	175.
	c. Signature A. R. Macmillan, with title: *CHIEF GENERAL MANAGER.* 1.3.1974; 6.1.1975; 2.2.1976; 31.1.1979; 1.2.1980.	12.50	30.00	80.00
	s. As c. Specimen.	—	—	—

#206 *Deleted.* See #205.

		VG	VF	UNC
207	**10 Pounds**			
	1972-81. Brown and pale purple on multicolor underprint. David Livingstone at left. Dromedary Camel and African scene on back.			
	a. Signature A. R. MacMillan, with title: *GENERAL MANAGER.* 1.3.1972; 1.8.1973.	30.00	100.	400.
	b. Signature A. R. MacMillan, with title: *CHIEF GENERAL MANAGER.* 1.3.1974-27.2.1981.	27.50	75.00	350.
208	**20 Pounds**			
	1972-81. Lilac on multicolor underprint. Lord Kelvin at left. Kelvin's lecture room at Glasgow University on back.			
	a. Signature A. R. MacMillan, with title: *GENERAL MANAGER.* 1.3.1972.	60.00	125.	450.
	b. Signature A. R. MacMillan, with title: *CHIEF GENERAL MANAGER.* 2.2.1976; 27.2.1981.	60.00	125.	400.

		VG	VF	UNC
209	**50 Pounds**			
	1.9.1981. Olive on multicolor underprint. A. Smith at left. Sailing ships, blacksmith implements and farm on back.	125.	210.	550.
210	**100 Pounds**			
	1972; 1975; 1976. Red on multicolor underprint. Lord Kelvin at left. Kelvin's lecture room at Glasgow University on back.			
	a. Signature A. R. MacMillan, with title: *GENERAL MANAGER.* 1.3.1972.	235.	450.	1150.
	b. Signature A. R. MacMillan, with title: *CHIEF GENERAL MANAGER.* 6.1.1975; 2.2.1976.	225.	425.	1050.

CLYDESDALE BANK PLC

1982-89 "STERLING" ISSUES

#211-217 wmk: Old sailing ship repeated vertically.

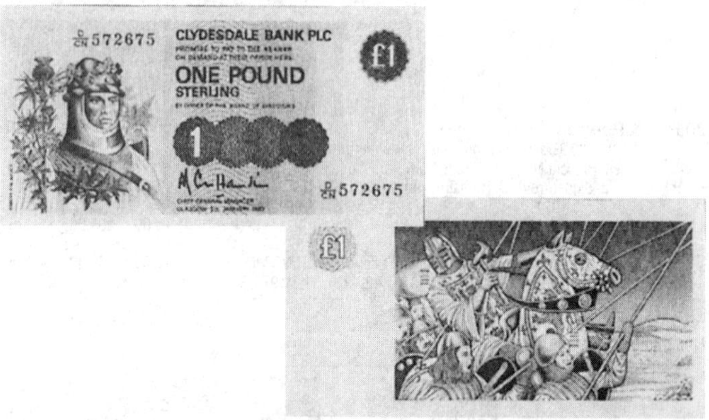

		VG	VF	UNC
211	**1 Pound**			
	1982-88. Dark olive-green on multicolor underprint. Like #204.			
	a. With sorting marks. Signature A. R. Macmillan. 29.3.1982.	3.50	8.00	22.50
	b. Like a. signature A. R. Cole Hamilton. 5.1.1983.	3.50	8.00	22.50
	c. Without sorting marks. Signature A. R. Cole Hamilton. 8.4.1985; 25.11.1985.	3.00	6.00	20.00
	d. Signature title: *CHIEF EXECUTIVE.* 18.9.1987; 9.11.1988.	3.00	5.00	15.00

		VG	VF	UNC
212	**5 Pounds**			
	1982-89. Blue on multicolor underprint. Like #205.			
	a. Signature A. R. Macmillan. 29.3.1982.	15.00	35.00	110.
	b. Signature A. R. Cole Hamilton. 5.1.1983.	12.50	30.00	95.00
	c. Without sorting marks. Signature A. R. Cole Hamilton. 18.9.1986.	12.50	30.00	90.00
	d. Signature title: *CHIEF EXECUTIVE.* 18.9.1987; 2.8.1988; 28.6.1989.	10.00	20.00	60.00
	s. As d. Specimen.	—	—	200.

		VG	VF	UNC
213	**10 Pounds**			
	1982-87. Brown and pale purple on multicolor underprint. Like #207.			
	a. Signature A. R. Macmillan. 29.3.1982; 5.1.1983.	25.00	60.00	275.
	b. Signature A. R. Cole Hamilton. 8.4.1985; 18.9.1986.	25.00	60.00	250.
	c. Signature title: *CHIEF EXECUTIVE.* 18.9.1987.	22.50	55.00	225.
	s. As d. Specimen.	—	—	—
214	**10 Pounds**			
	7.5.1988; 3.9.1989; 1.3.1990; 9.11.1990. Dark brown on multicolor underprint. D. Livingstone in front of map at left. Blantyre (Livingstone's birthplace) on back. Watermark: Sailing ships.	20.00	40.00	120.

		VG	VF	UNC
215	**20 Pounds**			
	1982-90. Lilac on multicolor underprint. Lord Kelvin at left. Lord Kelvin's lecture room at Glasgow University on back. Like #208.			
	a. Signature A. R. Macmillan. 29.3.1982.	50.00	125.	425.
	b. Signature A. R. Cole Hamilton. 5.1.1983; 8.4.1985.	50.00	110.	400.
	c. Signature title: *CHIEF EXECUTIVE.* 18.9.1987; 2.8.1990.	50.00	125.	425.

#216 *Deleted*. See #222.

		VG	VF	UNC
217	**100 Pounds** 1985; 1991. Red on multicolor underprint. Like #215. 163 x 90mm.			
	a. Signature title: *CHIEF GENERAL MANAGER*. 8.4.1985.	275.	500.	1000.
	b. Signature title: *CHIEF EXECUTIVE*. 9.11.1991.	260.	400.	800.

1989-96 "STERLING" ISSUE

#218-221 like #212-217 but reduced size notes. Wmk: Old sailing ship repeated vertically.

		VG	VF	UNC
218	**5 Pounds** 1990-. Black and gray on multicolor underprint. Similar to #212, but 135 x 70mm.			
	a. Signature A. R. Cole Hamilton. 2.4.1990.	—	Unc	30.00
	b. Signature F. Cicutto. 1.9.1994.	—	Unc	25.00
	c. Signature F. Goodwin. 21.7.1996; 1.12.1997.	—	Unc	20.00
	d. Signature G. Savage. 19.6.2002.	—	Unc	20.00

		VG	VF	UNC
219	**10 Pounds** 1992-97. Deep brown and green on multicolor underprint. Similar to #214 but with modified sailing ship outlines at right. 142 x 75mm.			
	a. Signature A. R. Cole Hamilton. 3.9.1992.	FV	32.50	70.00
	b. Signature Charles Love. 5.1.1993.	FV	30.00	65.00
	c. Signature F. Goodwin. 22.3.1996; 27.2.1997.	FV	30.00	60.00

NOTICE

Readers with unlisted dates, signature varieties, etc. are invited to submit photocopies of their notes to: Standard Catalog of World Paper Money, 700 East State St. Iola, WI 54990-0001, E-Mail: george.cuhaj@fwpubs.com.

		VG	VF	UNC
220	**20 Pounds** 1990-93. Violet, purple, brown and brown-orange on multicolor underprint. Robert the Bruce at left. His equestrian statue, Monymusk reliquary, Stirling Castle and Wallace Monument on back. 148 x 80mm.			
	a. Signature A. R. Cole Hamilton. 30.11.1990; 2.8.1991; 3.9.1992.	42.50	70.00	175.
	b. Signature Charles Love. 5.1.1993.	42.50	70.00	150.

		VG	VF	UNC
221	**20 Pounds** 1994-. Purple, dark brown and deep orange on multicolor underprint. Like #220. Ascending size serial # at upper left.			
	a. Signature F. Cicutto. 1.9.1994.	FV	50.00	95.00
	b. Signature F. Goodwin. 2.12.1996.	FV	40.00	80.00

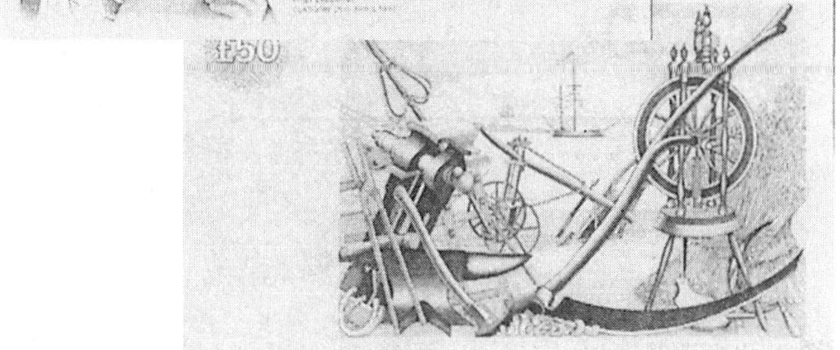

		VG	VF	UNC
222	**50 Pounds** 3.9.1989; 20.4.1992. Olive-green on multicolor underprint. Similar to #209. Signature A. R. Cole Hamilton.	FV	175.	450.
223	**100 Pounds** 2.10.1996. Purple, red and violet on multicolor underprint. Face similar to #217. Glasgow University on back. Signature F. Goodwin. Vertical serial # at right.	FV	240.	350.

1996 Commemorative Issue

#224, Poetry of Robert Burns

224	5 Pounds	VG	VF	UNC
	21.7.1996. Black and gray on multicolor underprint. Like #218 but with lines of poetry. Watermark: Sailing ship			
	a. "A man's a man for a'that - Then let us..."	FV	12.50	25.00
	b. "Tam O'Shanter - Now, wha this..."	FV	12.50	25.00
	c. "Ae Fond Kiss - But to see..."	FV	12.50	25.00
	d. "Scots wha hae - By oppressions woes..."	FV	12.50	25.00

Note: For sets w/matching serial # see Collector Series - CS1.

1996 Regular Issue

225	50 Pounds	VG	VF	UNC
	1996; 2003. Olive-green on multicolor underprint. Like #222 but reduced size. 157 x 85mm. Signature F. Goodwin.			
	a. 22.3.1996. Signature F. Goodwin.	FV	125.	225.
	b. 25.4.2003. Signature Ross Pinney as *Chief Operating Officer.*	FV	FV	175.

1997 Commemorative Issues

#226, Work of Mary Slessor

226	10 Pounds	VG	VF	UNC
	1997-. Dark brown and brown on multicolor underprint. M. Slessor at left and as watermark. Map of Calabar in Nigeria in wreath at center, sailing ship at upper left, Slessor seated below and with children at right.			
	a. Signature F. Goodwin. 1.5.1997.	—	Unc	40.00
	b. Signature J. Wright. 5.11.1998; 20.10.1999.	—	Unc	40.00
	c. Signature S. Targett. 26.1.2003.	—	Unc	40.00

226	10 Pounds	VG	VF	UNC
	d. Signature Ross Pimney. 25.4.2003.	—	Unc	32.50
	e. Signature David Thorburn as *Chief Operating Officer.* 21.11.2004.	—	Unc	32.50
	f. Signature David Thorburn, larger CB bank emblem. 14.3.2006.	FV	FV	32.50

Note: #226 exists w/serial # prefix *NAB* encapsulated in acrylic plastic w/text: *1987-1997 THE FIRST DECADE.* Market value $150. Non-encapsulated *NAB* market value in Unc. $70. #227, Commonwealth heads of government meeting in Edinburgh, Oct. 1997

227	20 Pounds	VG	VF	UNC
	30.9.1997. Purple, dark brown and deep orange on multicolor underprint. Face like #221. Edinburgh International Conference Centre at lower right, Clydesdale Bank plaza and Edinburgh Castle in background at center on back. Signature F. Goodwin.	FV	45.00	80.00

Note: #227 was issued w/serial # prefix: *CHG* (Special Commemorative prefix). Market value $70.

1997 Regular Issue

228	20 Pounds	VG	VF	UNC
	1.11.1997-. Purple, dark brown and deep orange on multicolor underprint. Like #221 but square design replaces *£20* at lower left, segmented foil over security thread, bank logo added to value panel at lower center right.			
	a. Signature Fred Goodwin. 1.11.1997.	FV	FV	90.00
	b. Signature John Wright. 12.10.1999.	FV	FV	70.00
	c. Signature Grahm Savage. 19.6.2002.	FV	FV	85.00
	d. Signature Steve Targett. 26.1.2003; 26.4.2003.	FV	FV	80.00
	e. Signature Ross Pinney. 25.4.2003.	FV	FV	62.50
	f. Signature David Thorburn as *Chief Operating Officer.* 21.11.2004.	FV	FV	62.50

1999 Commemorative Issue

#229, Glasgow as UK City of Architecture and Design

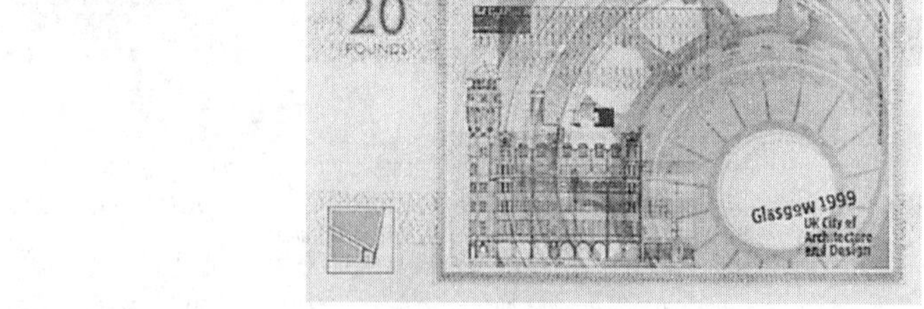

229	20 Pounds	VG	VF	UNC
	9.4.1999. Purple, brown and multicolor. Alex "Greek" Thompson at left. Holmwood House on back. Special text at lower right. on both sides.	FV	FV	80.00

2000 Commemorative Issues

#229A and 229B, special text: *COMMEMORATING THE YEAR 2000.*

229A	10 Pounds	VG	VF	UNC
	1.1.2000. Brown and green on multicolor underprint. Similar to #226 but commemorative text added at right.	FV	FV	40.00

229B	20 Pounds	VG	VF	UNC
	1.1.2000. Purple, dark brown and deep orange on multicolor underprint. Similar to #228 but commemorative text added at right.	FV	FV	70.00

#229C and 229D, Commemorating the 550th Anniversary of the University of Glasgow

2001 Commemorative Issues

			VG	VF	UNC
229C	50 Pounds	6.1.2001. Olive-green on multicolor underprint. Like #225 but with commemorative emblem and text at right.	FV	FV	175.

			VG	VF	UNC
229D	100 Pounds	6.1.2001. Purple, red and violet on multicolor underprint. Like #223 but with commemorative emblem and text at right.	FV	FV	350.

2005 Commemorative Issues

			VG	VF	UNC
229E	20 Pounds	2005. Similar to #228 but Clysesdale Bank Exchange in Glasgow on back. Signature David Thorburn.	FV	FV	70.00
229F	10 Pounds	2005. Similar to #226. Commonwealth Games on back. Serial # prefix *CG*.	FV	FV	32.50

National Commercial Bank of Scotland Limited

1961 Issue

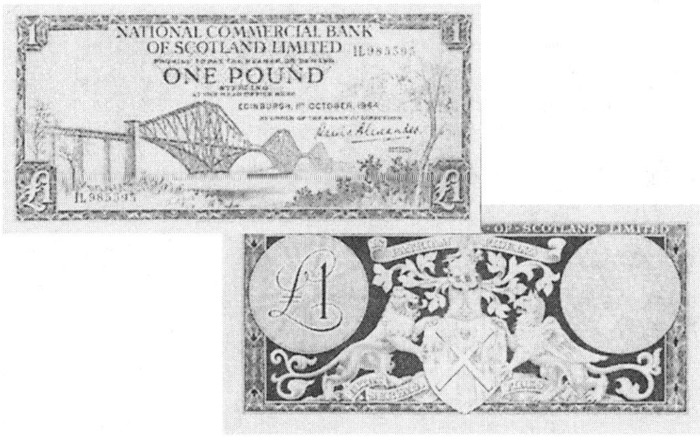

			VG	VF	UNC
269	1 Pound	1.11.1961-4.1.1966. Green on multicolor underprint. Forth Railway bridge. Arms at center on back. Reduced size, 151 x 72mm. Printer: BWC.			
		a. Issued note.	4.00	17.50	60.00
		s. Specimen.	—	—	160.

			VG	VF	UNC
270	5 Pounds	3.1.1961. Green on multicolor underprint. Arms at bottom center right. Forth Railway bridge on back. Reduced size: 159 x 90mm. Printer: W&S.	25.00	70.00	250.

1963-67 Issue

#271-273 printer: BWC.

			VG	VF	UNC
271	1 Pound	4.1.1967. Green on multicolor underprint. Like #269, but lines for electronic sorting on back. 152 x 72mm.			
		a. Issue note.	7.00	22.50	75.00
		s. Specimen.	—	—	—

			VG	VF	UNC
272	5 Pounds	2.1.1963; 1.8.1963; 1.10.1964; 4.1.1966; 1.8.1966. Blue on multicolor underprint. Arms at lower center Landscape with Edinburgh Castle, National Gallery on back. 142 x 85mm.			
		a. Issued note.	15.00	32.50	100.
		s. Specimen.	—	—	200.
273	10 Pounds	18.8.1966. Brown on multicolor underprint. Arms at lower center Forth Railway bridge on back. 151 x 94mm.	175.	300.	900.

1967; 1968 Issue

#274 and 275 printer: BWC.

		VG	VF	UNC
274	**1 Pound** 4.1.1968. Green on multicolor underprint. Similar to #271, but with Forth Railway Bridge and road bridge on face. Reduced size. 136 x 67mm.			
	a. Issued note.	6.00	17.50	60.00
	s. Specimen.	—	—	160.

		VG	VF	UNC
275	**5 Pounds** 4.1.1968. Blue, red and green on multicolor underprint. Like #272 but electronic sorting marks on back.			
	a. Issued note.	15.00	40.00	140.
	s. Specimen.	—	—	225.
275A	**20 Pounds** 1.6.1967. Red on multicolor underprint. Arms at lower right. Bridge on back. Printer: TDLR.			
	a. Issued note.	1500.	4000.	6000.
	s. Specimen.	—	—	600.
275B	**100 Pounds** 1.6.1967. Purple on multicolor underprint. Arms at lower right. Bridge on back. Printer: TDLR. Specimen.	—	—	1500.

ROYAL BANK OF SCOTLAND

1875; 1887 ISSUE

		Good	Fine	XF
319	**20 Pounds** 1877-1969. Blue and brown. Uniface.			
	a. Plate C. 1877-1911.	350.	850.	2500.
	b. Plate D. Yellow underprint. Imprint: W. & A. K. Johnston 1931-47.	100.	400.	1000.
	c. Plates E; F; G; H. underprint. without red. Imprint: W. & A. K. Johnston & G. W. Bacon Ltd. Both signature printed 1947-66.	90.00	275.	600.
320	**100 Pounds** 1877-1969. Blue and red. Uniface.			
	a. Plate C. 1877-1918.	1000.	2750.	—
	b. Plates D; E. Yellow underprint. 1918-60.	350.	750.	2200.
	c. Plates F; G. Imprint: W. & A. K. Johnston & G. W. Bacon Ltd. Both signature printed. 1960-66.	300.	700.	2000.

1952 ISSUE

		VG	VF	UNC
323	**5 Pounds** 1952-63. Blue and red on yellow underprint. Uniface. Like #317 but reduced size.			
	a. 2 signature Imprint: W. & A.K. Johnston Ltd. 2.1.1952-1.7.1953.	30.00	85.00	250.
	b. 3 signature Imprint: W. & A. K. Johnston & G. W. Bacon Ltd. 1.7.1953-1.2.1954.	35.00	150.	325.
	c. 2 signature Imprint: W. & A. K. Johnston & G. W. Bacon. 1.4.1955-3.1.1963.	25.00	60.00	175.

1955 ISSUE

		VG	VF	UNC
324	**1 Pound** 1955-64. Dark blue on yellow and brown underprint. Signature W. R. Ballantyne with title: *General Manager.* 152 x 85mm.			
	a. Without engraver's name on back. 1.4.1955-1.11.1955.	7.00	18.00	75.00
	b. With engraver's name W. H. Egan upside down and in very small letters below the r. hand bank building on back. 1.2.1956-1.7.1964.	6.00	15.00	60.00
	s. As a. Specimen.	—	—	—

1964 ISSUE

		VG	VF	UNC
325	**1 Pound** 1964-67. Black and brown on yellow underprint. Like #324, but 150 x 71mm.			
	a. Signature W. R. Ballantyne. 1.8.1964-1.6.1965.	7.00	22.50	75.00
	b. Signature G. P. Robertson. 2.8.1965-1.11.1967.	6.00	20.00	65.00
	s. As a. Specimen.	—	—	150.

		VG	VF	UNC
326	**5 Pounds** 1964-65. Dark blue, orange-brown and yellow. Uniface. Like #323, but 140 x 85mm.			
	a. 2.11.1964. Signature W. R. Ballantyne & A. G. Campbell.	25.00	70.00	200.
	b. 2.8.1965. Signature G. P. Robertson & A. G. Campbell.	25.00	70.00	200.
	s. As b. Specimen.	—	—	275.

1966; 1967 ISSUE

#327 and 328 portr. D. Dale at l. and as wmk., bank arms at lower r. Bank head office bldg. at ctr. and upper r. on back.

		VG	VF	UNC
327	**1 Pound**			
	1.9.1967. Green on multicolor underprint.			
	a. Issued note.	6.00	20.00	50.00
	s. Specimen.	—	—	125.

		VG	VF	UNC
328	**5 Pounds**			
	1.11.1966; 1.3.1967. Blue on multicolor underprint.	25.00	55.00	160.

ROYAL BANK OF SCOTLAND LIMITED

1969 ISSUE

#329-333 wmk: D. Dale. Sign. G. P. Robertson and J. B. Burke. Printer: BWC.

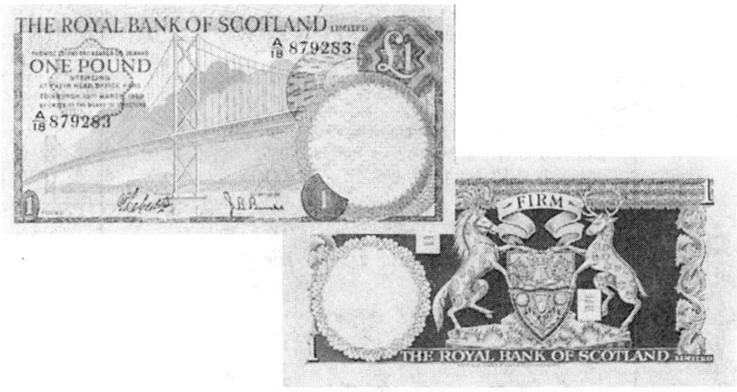

		VG	VF	UNC
329	**1 Pound**			
	19.3.1969. Green on multicolor underprint. Forth Road Bridge at left center, old Forth Railway bridge in background. Arms at center right on back.			
	a. Issued note.	4.00	10.00	50.00
	s. Specimen.	—	—	125.

		VG	VF	UNC
330	**5 Pounds**			
	19.3.1969. Blue on multicolor underprint. Arms at left. Edinburgh Castle on back.	20.00	45.00	140.

		VG	VF	UNC
331	**10 Pounds**			
	19.3.1969. Brown on multicolor underprint. Arms at center. Tay road bridge on back.	35.00	125.	400.

		VG	VF	UNC
332	**20 Pounds**			
	19.3.1969. Purple on multicolor underprint. Forth Road Bridge on back.	60.00	125.	475.

		VG	VF	UNC
333	**100 Pounds**			
	19.3.1969. Red on multicolor underprint. Similar to #332.			
	a. Issued note.	300.	600.	1250.
	s. Specimen.	—	—	—

1970 ISSUE

#334 and 335 like #329 and 330 but w/only 1 sign, J. B. Burke.

		VG	VF	UNC
334	**1 Pound**			
	15.7.1970. Green on multicolor underprint. Like #329.			
	a. Issued note.	4.00	12.50	50.00
	s. Specimen.	—	—	—

		VG	VF	UNC
335	**5 Pounds**			
	15.7.1970. Blue on multicolor underprint. Like #330.	20.00	50.00	150.

1972 ISSUE

#336-340 arms at r. Wmk: A. Smith. Printer: BWC.

		VG	VF	UNC
336	**1 Pound** 5.1.1972-1.5.1981. Dark green on multicolor underprint. Edinburgh Castle at left center on back.			
	a. Issued note.	4.00	9.00	32.50
	s. Specimen.	—	—	100.

		VG	VF	UNC
337	**5 Pounds** 5.1.1972; 2.4.1973; 1.5.1975; 3.5.1976; 1.5.1979; 1.5.1980; 1.5.1981. Blue on multicolor underprint. Culzean Castle at left center on back.			
	a. Issued note.	15.00	30.00	100.
	s. Specimen.	—	—	175.

		VG	VF	UNC
338	**10 Pounds** 5.1.1972; 15.12.1975; 2.5.1978; 10.1.1981. Brown on multicolor underprint. Glamis Castle at left center on back.			
	a. Issued note.	25.00	65.00	200.
	s. Specimen.	—	—	225.
339	**20 Pounds** 5.1.1972; 1.5.1981. Purple on multicolor underprint. Brodick Castle on back.	55.00	120.	300.

		VG	VF	UNC
340	**100 Pounds** 5.1.1972; 1.5.1981. Red on multicolor underprint. Balmoral Castle on back.	250.	500.	1000.

ROYAL BANK OF SCOTLAND PLC

1982-86 ISSUES

#341-345 arms at r. Sign. title varieties.

#341, replacement note: Serial # prefix *Y/1*.

		VG	VF	UNC
341	**1 Pound** 1982-85. Dark green on multicolor underprint. Like #336. Signature C. Winter. Printer: BWC.			
	a. With sorting marks. 3.5.1982.	5.00	15.00	50.00
	b. Without sorting marks. 1.10.1983; 4.1.1984; 3.1.1985.	3.00	6.00	20.00

		VG	VF	UNC
341A	**1 Pound** 1986. Dark green on multicolor underprint. Like #341. Printer: TDLR.			
	a. Signature C. Winter. 1.5.1986.	2.00	4.50	15.00
	b. Signature R. M. Maiden. 17.12.1986.	2.50	5.00	17.50

		VG	VF	UNC
342	**5 Pounds** 1982-86. Blue on multicolor underprint. Like #337. Printer: BWC.			
	a. Signature C. M. Winter. With electronic sorting marks. 3.5.1982; 5.1.1983.	12.00	40.00	130.
	b. Without sorting marks. 4.1.1984.	12.00	40.00	125.
	c. Signature C. M. Winter title larger size. 3.1.1985.	12.00	40.00	130.
	d. Signature R. M. Maiden. 17.12.1986.	12.00	40.00	120.

#342A *Deleted*. See #342d.

		VG	VF	UNC
343	**10 Pounds** 1982-86. Brown on multicolor underprint. Like #338. Printer: BWC.			
	a. Signature C. M. Winter. 3.5.1982; 4.1.1984; 3.1.1985.	25.00	65.00	200.
	b. Signature R. M. Maiden. 17.12.1986.	25.00	65.00	190.

		VG	VF	UNC
344	**20 Pounds** 3.5.1982; 3.1.1985. Purple on multicolor underprint. Like #339. Printer: BWC.	55.00	100.	300.
345	**100 Pounds** 3.5.1982. Red on multicolor underprint. Like #340. Printer: BWC.	225.	375.	850.

NOTICE

Readers with unlisted dates, signature varieties, etc. are invited to submit photocopies of their notes to: Standard Catalog of World Paper Money, 700 East State St. Iola, WI 54990-0001, E-Mail: george.cuhaj@fwpubs.com.

1987 ISSUE

#346-350 Lord Ilay at r. and as wmk. Printer: TDLR. Replacement notes: Serial # prefix: *Z/1*.

346	1 Pound	VG	VF	UNC
	25.3.1987. Dark green and green on multicolor underprint. Edinburgh Castle at left center on back.	FV	4.00	12.00

347	5 Pounds	VG	VF	UNC
	25.3.1987; 22.6.1988. Black and blue-black on multicolor underprint. Culzean Castle at left center on back.	10.00	20.00	47.50

348	10 Pounds	VG	VF	UNC
	25.3.1987; 24.2.1988; 22.2.1989; 24.1.1990. Deep brown and brown on multicolor underprint. Glamis Castle at left center on back. Signature right. M. Maiden.	FV	25.00	65.00

349	20 Pounds	VG	VF	UNC
	25.3.1987; 24.1.1990. Black and purple on multicolor underprint. Brodick Castle at left center on back. Signature right. M. Maiden.	40.00	55.00	130.

350	100 Pounds	VG	VF	UNC
	1987-. Red on multicolor underprint. Balmoral Castle at left. Center on back.			
	a. Signature R. M. Maiden, with title: *MANAGING DIRECTOR*. 25.3.1987; 24.1.1990.	FV	250.	600.
	b. Signature G. R. Mathewson, with title: *CHIEF EXECUTIVE*. 28.1.1992; 23.3.1994; 24.1.1996; 26.3.1997; 30.9.1998.	FV	FV	400.
	c. Signature G. R. Matthewson, with title: *GROUP CHIEF EXECUTIVE*. 30.3.1999.	FV	FV	375.
	d. Signature Fred Goodwin. 27.6.2000.	FV	FV	350.

1988-92 ISSUE

#351-355 similar to #346-350, but reduced size. Replacement notes: Serial # prefix: *Z/1*.

#351-354 Lord Ilay at r. and as wmk.

351	1 Pound	VG	VF	UNC
	1988-. Dark green and green on multicolor underprint. Similar to #346, but 127 x 65mm. Printer: TDLR.			
	a. Signature R. M. Maiden with title: *MANAGING DIRECTOR*. 13.12.1988; 26.7.1989; 19.12.1990.	FV	3.00	9.00
	b. Signature C. Winter with title: *CHIEF EXECUTIVE*. 24.7.1991.	FV	FV	7.00
	c. Signature G. R. Mathewson with title: *CHIEF EXECUTIVE*. 24.3.1992; 24.2.1993; 24.2.1994; 24.1.1996; 1.10.1997.	FV	FV	5.00
	d. Signature G. R. Mathewson, with title: *GROUP CHIEF EXECUTIVE*. 30.3.1999.	FV	FV	4.50
	e. Signature Fred Goodwin. 27.6.2000; 1.10.2001.	FV	FV	4.00

352	5 Pounds	VG	VF	UNC
	1988-. Black and blue-black on multicolor underprint. Similar to #347, but 135 x 70mm.			
	a. Signature R. M. Maiden, with title: *MANAGING DIRECTOR*. 13.12.1988; 24.1.1990.	FV	12.50	35.00

352	5 Pounds	VG	VF	UNC
	b. Signature G. R. Mathewson. with title: *CHIEF EXECUTITIVE.* 23.3.1994; 24.1.1996; 26.3.1997; 29.4.1998.	FV	10.00	25.00
	c. Signature G. R. Matthewson, with title: *GROUP CHIEF EXECUTIVE.* 30.3.1999.	FV	FV	35.00
	d. Signature Fred Goodwin. 27.6.2000; 20.1.2005.	FV	FV	17.50

353	10 Pounds	VG	VF	UNC
	1992- Deep brown and brown on multicolor underprint. Similar to #348, but 142 x 75mm.			
	a. Signature G. R. Mathewson, with title: *CHIEF EXECUTIVE.* 28.1.1992; 7.5.1992; 24.2.1993; 23.3.1994.	FV	FV	40.00
	b. Signature Fred Goodwin, with title. *GROUP CHIEF EXECUTIVE.* 27.6.2000; 1.10.2001.	FV	FV	35.00

354	20 Pounds	VG	VF	UNC
	1991-. Black and purple on multicolor underprint. Similiar to #349 but 150 x 81mm.			
	a. Signature C. Winter with title: *CHIEF EXECUTIVE.* 27.3.1991.	—	Unc	100.
	b. Signature G. R. Mathewson. 28.1.1992; 24.2.1993; 26.3.1997; 29.4.1998.	—	Unc	95.00
	c. Signature G. R. Mathewson, with title: *GROUP CHIEF EXECUTIVE.* 30.3.1999.	—	Unc	100.
	d. Signature Fred Goodwin. 27.6.2000.	—	Unc	65.00

#355 not assigned.

1992 COMMEMORATIVE ISSUE

#356, European Summit at Edinburgh, Dec. 1992

356	1 Pound	VG	VF	UNC
	8.12.1992. Dark green and green on multicolor underprint. Like #351c but with additional blue-violet overprint containing commemorative inscription at left. Serial # prefix: EC.			
	a. Issued note.	FV	FV	7.00
	s. Specimen.	—	—	100.

1994 REGULAR ISSUE

Lord Ilay at r. Replacement note: Serial # prefix *Y/1*.

357	1 Pound	VG	VF	UNC
	23.3.1994. Dark green and green on multicolor underprint. Like #351 but without watermark. Printer: BABN.	4.00	15.00	45.00

1994 COMMEMORATIVE ISSUE

#358, Centennial - Death of Robert Louis Stevenson

358	1 Pound	VG	VF	UNC
	3.12.1994. Dark green and green on multicolor underprint. Commemorative overprint in watermark area on #351c. Portrait right. L. Stevenson and images of his life and works on back. Serial # prefix: RLS.			
	a. Issued note.	FV	3.00	7.50
	s. Specimen.	—	—	100.

1997 COMMEMORATIVE ISSUE

#359, 150th Anniversary - Birth of Alexander Graham Bell, 1847-1997

359	1 Pound	VG	VF	UNC
	3.3.1997. Dark green and green on multicolor underprint. Overprint telephone, text and OVD on watermark area of face like #351c. Portrait Alexander Grahm Bell and images of his life and work on back. Serial # prefix: AGB.	FV	FV	5.00

1999 COMMEMORATIVE ISSUE

#360, Opening of the Scottish Parliament

360	1 Pound	VG	VF	UNC
	12.5.1999. Dark green on multicolor underprint. Overprint Scottish Parliament text at left on watermark area of face like #351c. Scottish Parliament building on back. Serial # prefix: SP.	FV	FV	5.00

NOTICE

Readers with unlisted dates, signature varieties, etc. are invited to submit photocopies of their notes to: Standard Catalog of World Paper Money, 700 East State St. Iola, WI 54990-0001, E-Mail: george.cuhaj@fwpubs.com.

2000 Commemorative Issue

#361, Birth centennial of the Queen Mother

		VG	VF	UNC
361	**20 Pounds** 4.8.2000. Black and purple on multicolor underprint. Gold crown with inscription beneath at left. Queen Mother on back. Serial # prefix: QETQM.	FV	FV	65.00
361A	**100 Pounds** 4.8.2000. Black and purple on multicolor underprint. Special presentation item for the Queen Mother. Unique	—	—	—

2002 Commemorative Issue

#362, Queen's Golden Jubilee. Printer: TDLR.

		VG	VF	UNC
362	**5 Pounds** 6.2.2002. Black and dark blue on multicolor underprint. Gold crown overprint at left. Back dark and light blue; 1952 and 2002 portraits of Queen Elizabeth II.	FV	FV	15.00

2004 Commemorative Issue

#363 250th Anniversary of St. Andrews Royal & Ancient Golf Club.

		VG	VF	UNC
363	**5 Pounds** 14.5.2004. Black and blue-black on multicolor underprint. Similar to #352 but shield and 1754 at left. Tom Morris and images of St. Andrews on back. Serial # prefix: *R&A*.	FV	FV	15.00

Note: Also available in a presentation folder.

2005 Commemorative Issues

500th Anniversary, College of Surgeons.

		VG	VF	UNC
364	**5 Pounds** 1.7.2005. Commemorative overprint at left. Serial # prefix RCS.	FV	FV	17.50

#365 Jack Nicholas retirement from Golf commemorative. RBS's sponsorship of the British Open at St. Andrew's.

		VG	VF	UNC
365	**5 Pounds** 14.7.2005. Commemorative overprint at left. Jack Nicolas on back. Serial # prefix JWN.	FV	FV	17.50

#366 New Bank Neadquarters at Gogarburn.

366	**50 Pounds** 14.9.2005. New Bank headquarters at Gogarburn on back. Serial # prefix RBS.	FV	FV	175.

2005 Regular Issue

367	**50 Pounds** 14.9.2005. Inverness Castle on back.	FV	FV	150.

Collector Series

Clydesdale Bank Plc

1996 Issue

		Issue Price	Mkt. Value
CS1	**1996 5 Pounds** Matched serial # (prefix R/B 0 - R/B 3) set #224a-224d.	—	90.00—

Serbia, a former inland Balkan kingdom (now a federated republic with Montenegro) has an area of 34,116 sq. mi. (88,361 sq. km.) Capital: Belgrade.

Serbia emerged as a separate kingdom in the 12th century and attained its greatest expansion and political influence in the mid-14th century. After the Battle of Kosovo, 1389, Serbia became a vassal principality of Turkey and remained under Turkish suzerainty until it was re-established as an independent kingdom by the 1887 Treaty of Berlin. Following World War I, which was in part caused by the assassination of Austrian Archduke Francis Ferdinand by a Serbian nationalist, Serbia joined with the Croats and Slovenes to form the new kingdom of the South Slavs with Petar I of Serbia as king. The name of the kingdom was later changed to Yugoslavia. Invaded by Germany during World War II, Serbia emerged as a constituent republic of the Socialist Federal Republic of Yugoslavia.

With the breakup of Yugoslavia, a Federation of Serbia and Montenegro was formed, with each state using independent currencies.

MONETARY SYSTEM:

1 Dinara ДИНАРА = 100 Para ПАРА

Note: For additional issues refer to Bosnia-Herzegovina and Croatia-Knin in Volume 3, Modern Issues.

Federation of Serbia and Montenegro

Narodna Banka Srbija

National Bank of Serbia

2003 Issue

			VG	VF	UNC
40	50 Dinara	2005. Purple and tan on multicolor underprint. Stevan Stojanovic Mokranjac at left center, violin, keyboard and music score at center. Mokranjac standing, scores and linear art from Gospel of Miroslav illuminated manuscript.			
		a. Issued note.	FV	FV	2.00
		s. Specimen.	—	—	—

			VG	VF	UNC
41	100 Dinara	2003. Light and dark blue on multicolor underprint. Nikola Tesla at left. Detail from the Tesla electromagnetic induction engine at center, Tesla at left on vertical format back.			
		a. Issued note.	—	—	4.00
		s. Specimen.	—	—	—

			VG	VF	UNC
42	200 Dinara	2005. Black and blue on tan underprint. Nadezda Petrovic at left center, Petrovic sculpture and Gracanica monastery at center. Petrovic photo as WWI nurse, Gracanica monastery and painting detail on vertical format back.			
		a. Issued note.	FV	FV	8.50
		s. Specimen.	—	—	—

			VG	VF	UNC
43	500 Dinara	2004. Green.			
		a. Issued note.	FV	FV	17.50
		s. Specimen.	—	—	—

			VG	VF	UNC
44	1000 Dinara	2003. Red on multicolor underprint. Dorde Vajfert at left. Vajfert seated, details of National Bank's interior on vertical format back.			
		a. Signature Mladjan Dinkic.	FV	FV	35.00
		b. Signature Kori Udovicki.	FV	FV	30.00
		s. Specimen.	—	—	—

45	5000 Dinara	VG	VF	UNC
	2003. Green on multicolor underprint. Slibodan Jovanovic at left. Jovanovic and Parliament building views on vertical format back.			
	a. Signature Mladjan Dinkic	FV	FV	150.
	b. Signature Kori Udovicki. Expected new issue.	—	—	—
	s. Specimen.	—	—	—

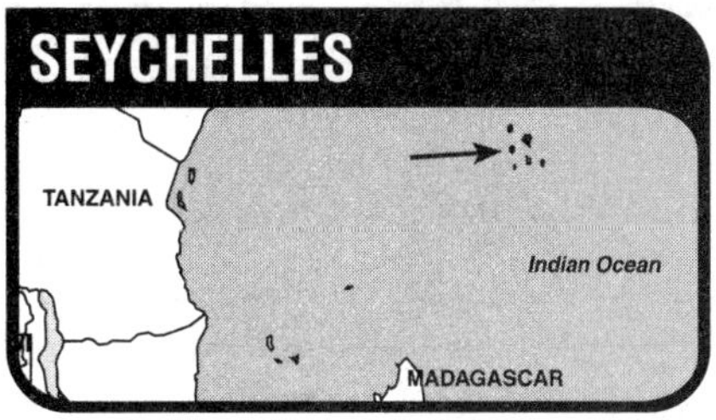

The Republic of Seychelles, an archipelago of 85 granite and coral islands situated in the Indian Ocean 600 miles (965 km.) northeast of Madagascar, has an area of 156 sq. mi. (455 sq. km.) and a population of 82,400. Among these islands are the Aldabra Islands, the Farquhar Group, and Ile Desroches, which the United Kingdom ceded to the Seychelles upon its independence. Capital: Victoria, on Mahe. The economy is d on fishing, a plantation system of agriculture and tourism. Copra, cinnamon and vanilla are exported.

Although the Seychelles are marked on Portuguese charts of the early 16th century, the first recorded visit to the islands, by an English ship, occurred in 1609. The Seychelles were annexed to France by Captain Lazare Picault in 1743 and permanently settled in 1768, with the intention of establishing spice plantations to compete with the Dutch monopoly of the spice trade. British troops seized the islands in 1810, during the Napoleonic Wars; they were formally ceded to Britain by the Treaty of Paris, 1814. The Seychelles were a dependency of Mauritius until Aug. 31, 1903, when they became a separate British Crown Colony. The colony was granted limited internal self-government in 1970, and attained independence on June 28, 1976, becoming Britain's last African possession to do so. Seychelles is a member of the Commonwealth of Nations. The president is the Head of State and of Government.

RULERS:

British to 1976

MONETARY SYSTEM:

1 Rupee = 100 Cents

BRITISH ADMINISTRATION

GOVERNMENT OF SEYCHELLES

1954 ISSUE

#11-13 portr. Qn. Elizabeth II in profile at r. #12 and 13 portr. Qn. Elizabeth II in profile at r. Denominations on back. Various date and sign. varieties. Printer: TDLR.

11	5 Rupees	VG	VF	UNC
	1954; 1960. Lilac and green.			
	a. 1.8.1954.	12.50	60.00	275.
	b. 1.8.1960.	7.50	50.00	265.

12	10 Rupees	VG	VF	UNC
	1954-67. Green and red. Like #11.			
	a. 1.8.1954.	12.50	85.00	850.
	b. 1.8.1960.	10.00	80.00	800.
	c. 1.5.1963.	10.00	75.00	750.
	d. 1.1.1967.	7.50	70.00	675.

13	50 Rupees	VG	VF	UNC
	1954-67. Black. Like #11.			
	a. 1.8.1954.	30.00	200.	2000.
	b. 1.8.1960.	27.50	175.	1750.
	c. 1.5.1963.	25.00	150.	1700.
	d. 1.1.1967.	25.00	150.	1600.

1968 ISSUE

#14-18 Qn. Elizabeth II at r. Wmk: Black parrot's head. Various date and sign. varieties.

14	5 Rupees	VG	VF	UNC
	1.1.1968. Dark brown on multicolor underprint. Seychelles black parrot at left.			
	a. Issued note.	3.00	20.00	65.00
	s. Specimen.	—	—	—
	ct. Color trial. Blue-green on multicolor underprint.	—	—	350.

15	10 Rupees	VG	VF	UNC
	1968; 1974. Light blue on multicolor underprint. Sea tortoise at left center. Letters *SCUM* discernible beneath tortoise's rear flipper at left.			
	a. 1.1.1968.	10.00	75.00	350.
	b. 1.1.1974.	7.50	60.00	275.
	s. As a. Specimen.	—	—	—

16	20 Rupees	VG	VF	UNC
	1968-74. Purple on multicolor underprint. Bridled tern at left center.			
	a. 1.1.1968.	15.00	125.	550.
	b. 1.1.1971.	12.50	60.00	300.
	c. 1.1.1974.	10.00	60.00	300.
	s. As c. Specimen.	—	—	—

17	50 Rupees	VG	VF	UNC
	1968-73. Olive on multicolor underprint. Sailing ship at left. Word *SEX* discernible in trees at right.			
	a. 1.1.1968.	40.00	200.	1250.
	b. 1.1.1969.	40.00	275.	1600.
	c. 1.10.1970.	25.00	175.	1200.
	d. 1.1.1972.	20.00	125.	600.
	e. 1.8.1973.	25.00	150.	700.
	s. As d. Specimen.	—	—	—
	ct. Color trial. Green on multicolor underprint.	—	—	1600.

18	100 Rupees	VG	VF	UNC
	1968-75. Red on multicolor underprint. Land turtles at left center.			
	a. 1.1.1968.	100.	650.	3000.
	b. 1.1.1969.	175.	1000.	3750.
	c. 1.1.1972.	80.00	600.	2200.
	d. 1.8.1973.	75.00	500.	2100.
	e. 1.6.1975.	75.00	500.	2000.
	s. Specimen.	—	—	—
	ct. Color trial. Blue on multicolor underprint.	—	—	2750.

REPUBLIC

REPUBLIC OF SEYCHELLES

1976; 1977 ND ISSUE

#19-22 Pres. J. R. Mancham at r. Wmk: Black parrot's head.

19	10 Rupees	VG	VF	UNC
	ND (1976). Dark blue and blue on multicolor underprint. Seashell at lower left. Hut with boats and cliffs on back.			
	a. Issued note.	1.50	5.00	17.50
	s. Specimen.	—	—	175.

20	20 Rupees	VG	VF	UNC
	ND (1977). Purple on multicolor underprint. Sea tortoise at lower left. Sailboat at left center on back.			
	a. Issued note.	3.00	10.00	30.00
	s. Specimen.	—	—	125.

21	50 Rupees	VG	VF	UNC
	ND (1977). Olive on multicolor underprint. Fish at lower left. Fishermen at left center on back.			
	a. Issued note.	6.00	25.00	80.00
	s. Specimen.	—	—	165.

22	100 Rupees	VG	VF	UNC
	ND (1977). Red and multicolor. Fairy terns at lower left. Dock area and islands on back.			
	a. Issued note.	10.00	40.00	135.
	s. Specimen.	—	—	235.

SEYCHELLES MONETARY AUTHORITY

1979 ND ISSUE

#23-27 vertical format on back. Wmk: Black parrot's head.

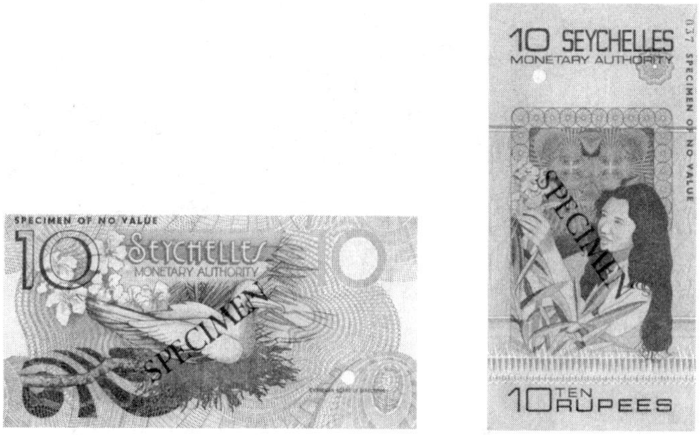

23	10 Rupees	VG	VF	UNC
	ND (1979). Blue, green and light red on multicolor underprint. Red-footed booby at center Girl picking flowers on back.			
	a. Issued note.	FV	2.50	6.50
	s. Specimen.	—	—	125.

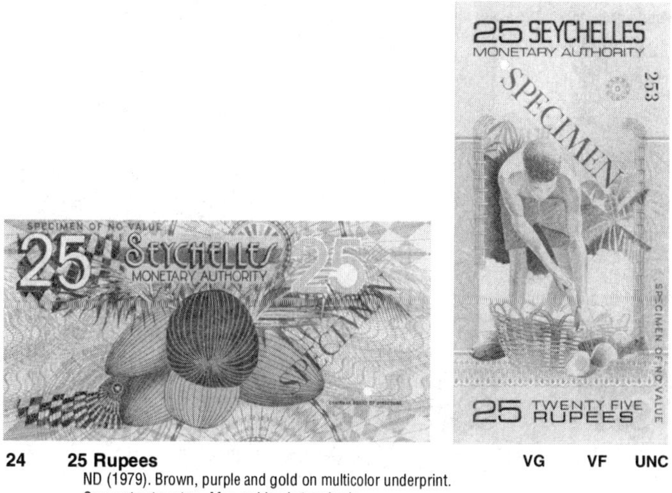

24	25 Rupees	VG	VF	UNC
	ND (1979). Brown, purple and gold on multicolor underprint. Coconuts at center. Man and basket on back.			
	a. Issued note.	FV	7.50	20.00
	s. Specimen.	—	—	125.

25	50 Rupees	VG	VF	UNC
	ND (1979). Olive-green, brown and lilac on multicolor underprint. Turtle at center. Buildings and palm trees on back.			
	a. Issued note.	FV	15.00	45.00
	s. Specimen.	—	—	150.

26	100 Rupees	VG	VF	UNC
	ND (1979). Red and light blue on multicolor underprint. Tropical fish at center. Man with tools, swordfish on back.			
	a. Issued note.	15.00	30.00	100.
	s. Specimen.	—	—	250.

Note: A shipment of #26 was lost at sea; only serial # A000,001 - A300,000 are valid numbers for exchange.

1980 ND Issue

27	100 Rupees	VG	VF	UNC
	ND (1980). Brown and light blue on multicolor underprint. Like #26.			
	a. Issued note.	FV	25.00	75.00
	s. Specimen, punch hole cancelled.	—	—	175.

Central Bank of Seychelles

1983 ND Issue

#28-31 like previous issue except for new bank name and sign. title. Wmk: Black parrot's head.

28	10 Rupees	VG	VF	UNC
	ND (1983). Blue, green and light red on multicolor underprint. Like #23.			
	a. Issued note.	FV	FV	6.00
	s. Specimen.	—	—	125.

29	25 Rupees	VG	VF	UNC
	ND (1983). Brown, purple and gold on multicolor underprint. Like #24.			
	a. Issued note.	FV	FV	15.00
	s. Specimen.	—	—	125.

30	50 Rupees	VG	VF	UNC
	ND (1983). Olive-green, brown and lilac on multicolor underprint. Like #25.			
	a. Issued note.	FV	FV	30.00
	s. Specimen.	—	—	150.

31	100 Rupees	VG	VF	UNC
	ND (1983). Brown and light blue on multicolor underprint. Like #27.			
	a. Issued note.	FV	FV	55.00
	s. Specimen.	—	—	175.

LABANK SANTRAL SESEL

CENTRAL BANK OF SEYCHELLES

1989 ND ISSUE

#32-35 bank at ctr., flying fish at l. and ctr. r. Wmk: Black parrot's head.

32	10 Rupees	VG	VF	UNC
	ND (1989). Blue-black and deep blue-green on multicolor underprint. Boy Scouts at lower left, image of man with flags and broken chain at right. Local people dancing to drummer at center on back.	FV	FV	6.00

33	25 Rupees	VG	VF	UNC
	ND (1989). Purple on multicolor underprint. Two men with coconuts at lower left, boy near palms at upper right. Primitive ox-drawn farm equipment on back.	FV	FV	15.00

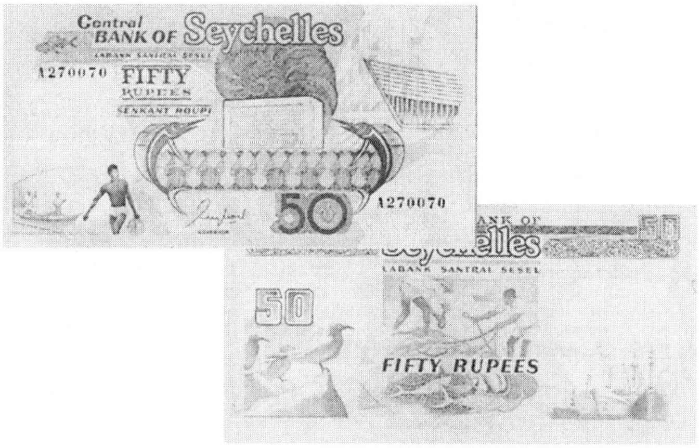

34	50 Rupees	VG	VF	UNC
	ND (1989). Dark green and brown on multicolor underprint. Two men in boat, Seychelles man at lower left, prow of boat in geometric outline at upper right. Lesser noddy at lower left, fishermen with nets at center, modern cargo ships at right on back.	FV	FV	27.50

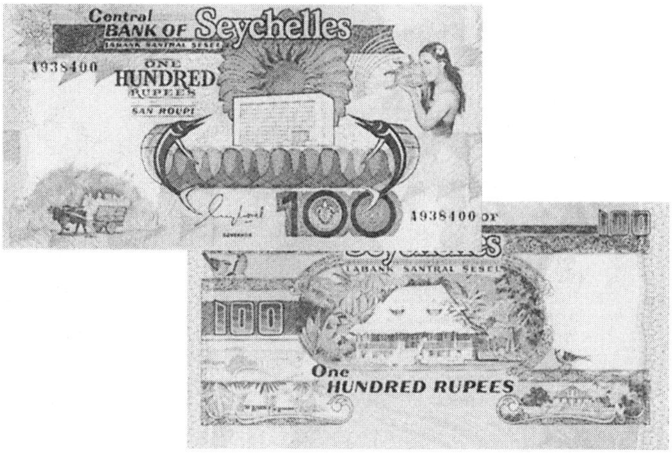

35	100 Rupees	VG	VF	UNC
	ND (1989). Red and brown on multicolor underprint. Men in ox-cart at lower left, girl with shell at upper right. Building at center on back.	FV	FV	50.00

1998 ND ISSUE

#36-39 arms at upper l. Cowry shells at upper l. on back. Wmk: Sea tortoise. Ascending size serial #.

36	10 Rupees	VG	VF	UNC
	ND (1998). Deep blue, dark green and green on multicolor underprint. Coco-de-Mer palm at center, black-spotted trigger fish at lower left. Coco-de-Mer palm fruit at lower left, FairyTerns at center, Hawksbill turtle at lower right on back.	FV	FV	5.00

		VG	VF	UNC
37	**25 Rupees**			
	ND (1998). Purple, violet and blue-violet on multicolor underprint. "Wrights gardenia" flower at center, Lion fish at lower left. "Bi-Centennary" monument at lower left, coconut crab at center, Seychelles blue pigeon at right on back.	FV	FV	14.00

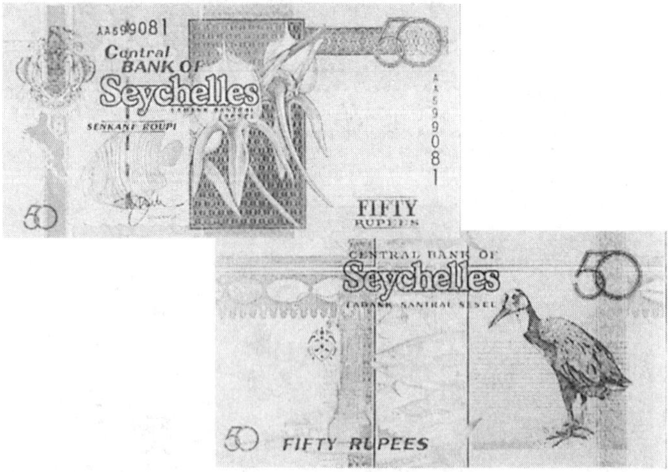

		VG	VF	UNC
38	**50 Rupees**			
	ND (1998). Dark green, deep olive-green and brown on multicolor underprint. *Paille en Que* orchids at center, Angel fish at lower left. Clock tower, autos at lower left, Yellow fin tuna at center, Flightless white throated rail or *Tiomitio* at right on back.	FV	FV	25.00

		VG	VF	UNC
39	**100 Rupees**			
	ND (1998). Red, brown-orange and violet on multicolor underprint. Pitcher plant at center, Vielle Babone Cecile fish at lower left. Shoreline at lower left, Bridled terns at center, giant land tortoise at lower right on back.	FV	FV	47.50

		VG	VF	UNC
40	**100 Rupees**			
	ND (2001). Red, brown-orange and violet on multicolor underprint. Similar to # 39, but with gold foil impression of sailfish on face.	FV	FV	45.00
41	**500 Rupees**			
	ND (2005). Brown and red orange on tan and multicolor underprint. Fish. Owl at right on back.	FV	FV	150.

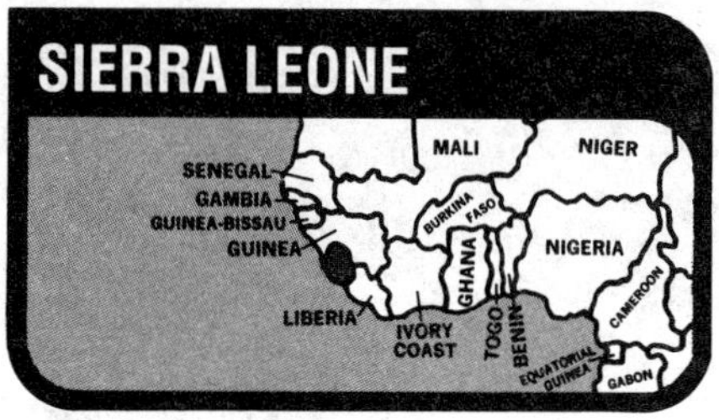

The Republic of Sierra Leone, a British Commonwealth nation located in western Africa between Guinea and Liberia, has an area of 27,699 sq. mi. (71,740 sq. km.) and a population of 4.87 million. Capital: Freetown. The economy is predominantly agricultural but mining contributes significantly to export revenues. Diamonds, iron ore, palm kernels, cocoa and coffee are exported.

The coast of Sierra Leone was first visited by Portuguese and British slavers in the 15th and 16th centuries. The first settlement at Freetown was established in 1787 as a refuge for freed slaves within the British Empire, runaway slaves from the United States and blacks discharged from the British armed forces. The first settlers were virtually wiped out by tribal attacks and disease. The colony was re-established under the auspices of the Sierra Leone Company and transferred to the British Crown in 1907. The interior region was secured and established as a protectorate in 1896. Sierra Leone became independent within the Commonwealth on April 27, 1961, and adopted a republican constitution ten years later. It is a member of the Commonwealth of Nations. The president is Chief of State and Head of Government.

RULERS:

British to 1971

MONETARY SYSTEM:

1 Leone = 100 Cents

REPUBLIC

BANK OF SIERRA LEONE

1964 ND ISSUE

#1-3 300-year-old cottonwood tree and court bldg. at l. on face. Sign. varieties. Wmk: Lion's head. Printer: TDLR.

		VG	VF	UNC
1	**1 Leone**			
	ND (1964-70). Green on multicolor underprint. Diamond mining on back.			
	a. ND (1964). Prefix A/1-A/6.	4.50	12.50	65.00
	b. ND (1969). Prefix A/7-A/8.	6.00	18.50	85.00
	c. ND (1970). Prefix A/9-A/12.	2.50	7.50	45.00
	s. As a. Specimen.	—	—	—

#2d replacement notes: Serial # prefix *Z1*.

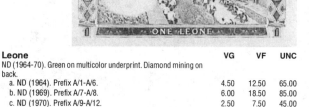

		VG	VF	UNC
2	**2 Leones**			
	ND (1964-70). Red on multicolor underprint. Village scene on back.			
	a. ND (1964). Prefix B/1-B/21.	5.00	15.00	60.00
	b. ND (1967). Prefix B/22-B/25.	6.00	17.50	85.00
	c. ND (1969). Prefix B/26-B/30.	6.00	17.50	85.00
	d. ND (1970). Prefix B/31-B/41.	5.00	15.00	70.00
	s. As a. Specimen.	—	—	—

3	5 Leones	VG	VF	UNC
	ND (1964). Purple on multicolor underprint. Dockside at Freetown at center right with boats in harbor on back. Prefix C/1.			
	a. Issued note.	20.00	75.00	450.
	s. Specimen.	—	—	—

1974-80 Issue

#4-8 Pres. S. Stevens at l. Printer: TDLR. Replacement notes: Serial # prefix *Z/1*.

4	50 Cents	VG	VF	UNC
	ND; 1979-84. Dark brown on multicolor underprint. Arms at upper left, flowers in underprint at right. Central Bank building at center on back.			
	a. ND (1972). Prefix D/1-D/2.	.75	2.00	6.00
	b. ND (1974). Prefix D/3-D/5.	.60	1.50	4.00
	c. Prefix D/6-D/8. 1.7.1979.	.50	1.00	3.00
	d. Prefix D/9; D/10. 1.7.1981.	.15	.50	1.50
	e. 4.8.1984.	.10	.25	.75
	s. As a. Specimen, without prefix.	—	—	—

#5-8 arms at upper r. on back. Wmk: Lion's head.

5	1 Leone	VG	VF	UNC
	1974-84. Olive-green and dark green on multicolor underprint. Central Bank building at center right on back.			
	a. Prefix A/1-A/7. 19.4.1974.	.75	2.25	7.50
	b. Prefix A/8-A/12. 1.1.1978.	1.00	4.00	10.00
	c. Prefix A/13-A/17. 1.3.1980.	.25	1.00	4.00
	d. Prefix A/18-A/26. 1.7.1981.	.25	.50	2.00
	e. 4.8.1984.	.25	.50	1.00

6	2 Leones	VG	VF	UNC
	1974-85. Red, deep red-orange and dark brown on multicolor underprint. Central Bank building at center right on back.			
	a. Prefix B/1-B/20. 19.4.1974.	1.25	3.50	10.00
	b. Prefix B/21-B/22. 1.1.1978.	6.00	15.00	65.00
	c. Prefix B/23-B/27. 1.7.1978.	1.00	4.00	12.50
	d. Prefix B/28-B/31. 1.7.1979.	.75	2.00	7.50

6	2 Leones	VG	VF	UNC
	e. Prefix B/32-B/37. 1.5.1980.	.75	2.00	7.00
	f. 1.7.1983.	.25	.75	3.00
	g. 4.8.1984.	.20	.45	1.25
	h. 4.8.1985.	.20	.45	1.25

7	5 Leones	VG	VF	UNC
	1975-85. Purple and blue-black on multicolor underprint. Plant leaves at center. Parliament building at center right on back.			
	a. Prefix C/1. 4.8.1975.	3.00	10.00	35.00
	b. Prefix C/2. 1.7.1978.	2.00	7.00	25.00
	c. Prefix C/3. 1.3.1980.	1.00	4.00	12.50
	d. Prefix C/4-C/6. 1.7.1981.	.75	3.00	7.50
	e. 19.4.1984.	.50	1.00	3.50
	f. 4.8.1984.	.50	1.00	3.50
	g. 4.8.1985.	.50	1.00	3.25
8	10 Leones			
	1981; 1984. Blue-gray, black and blue-green on multicolor underprint. Dredging operation at center right on back.			
	a. Prefix E/1-E/4. 1.7.1981.	1.00	4.00	12.50
	b. 19.4.1984.	.40	1.00	3.00
	c. 4.8.1984.	.40	1.00	3.00

1980 Commemorative Issue

#9-13, Commemorating The Organisation of African Unity Conference in Freetown

Note: #9-13 were prepared in special booklets (1800 sets).

9	50 Cents	VG	VF	UNC
	1.7.1980. Dark brown on multicolor underprint. Red overprint in four lines at upper left center on #4.	1.00	4.00	15.00

#10-13 red ovpt. in circle around wmk. area at r., date below.

10	1 Leone	VG	VF	UNC
	1.7.1980. Olive-green and dark green on multicolor underprint. Overprint on #5.	1.25	5.00	15.00

11	2 Leones	VG	VF	UNC
	1.7.1980. Red, deep red-orange and dark brown on multicolor underprint. Overprint on #6.	1.50	7.50	20.00

12	5 Leones	VG	VF	UNC
	1.7.1980. Purple and blue-black on multicolor underprint. Overprint on #7.	2.25	7.50	22.50

13	10 Leones	VG	VF	UNC
	1.7.1980. Blue-gray, black and blue-green on multicolor underprint. Overprint on #8.	2.50	10.00	30.00

1982 ISSUE

14	20 Leones	VG	VF	UNC
	1982; 1984. Brown, red and green on multicolor underprint. Tree at center, Pres. S. Stevens at right. Two youths pan mining (gold or diamonds) on back. Printer: BWC. Watermark: Lion's head.			
	a. 24.8.1982.	1.00	2.50	10.00
	b. 24.8.1984.	.25	1.00	4.00
	s. As a, b. Specimen.	—	—	100.

1988-93 ISSUE

#15-21 arms at upper ctr. Wmk: Lion's head. Replacement notes: Serial # prefix *Z/1*.

#15-19 Pres. Dr. Joseph Saidu Momoh at r.

15	10 Leones	VG	VF	UNC
	27.4.1988. Dark green and purple on multicolor underprint. Steer at left, farmer harvesting at center on back.	FV	.50	2.00

16	20 Leones	VG	VF	UNC
	27.4.1988. Brown, red and green on multicolor underprint. Like #14, but new president at right.	FV	.75	2.50

17	50 Leones	VG	VF	UNC
	1988-89. Purple, blue and black on multicolor underprint. Sports stadium at center. Dancers at left center on back.			
	a. Without imprint. 27.4.1988.	FV	1.50	3.00
	b. Printer: TDLR. 27.4.1989.	FV	.75	2.00

NOTICE

Readers with unlisted dates, signature varieties, etc. are invited to submit photocopies of their notes to: Standard Catalog of World Paper Money, 700 East State St. Iola, WI 54990-0001, E-Mail: george.cuhaj@fwpubs.com.

		VG	VF	UNC
18	**100 Leones** 1988-90. Blue and black on multicolor underprint. Building and ship at left center. Local designs at left and right, Central Bank building at left center on back.			
	a. Without imprint. 27.4.1988.	FV	1.00	5.00
	b. Printer: TDLR. 27.4.1989.	FV	.75	2.00
	c. 26.9.1990.	FV	FV	2.00

		VG	VF	UNC
19	**500 Leones** 27.4.1991. Red-brown and dark green on multicolor underprint. Modern building below arms at left center. Two fishing boats at left center, artistic carp at right on back.	FV	1.00	3.75

		VG	VF	UNC
20	**1000 Leones** 4.8.1993; 27.4.1996. Black, red and yellow on multicolor underprint. Bai Bureh at right, carving at lower center. Dish antenna at left center on back. Printer: TDLR.	FV	1.50	5.00

		VG	VF	UNC
21	**5000 Leones** 4.8.1993. Blue and violet on multicolor underprint. Sengbe Pieh at right, building at lower center. Dam at left center on back. Printer: TDLR.	FV	6.00	22.50

1995-2000 ISSUES

#22 Not assigned.

		VG	VF	UNC
23	**500 Leones** 27.4.1995 (1996); 15.7.1998; 2003. Blue-green, brown and green on multicolor underprint. K. Londo at right, arms at upper center, spearhead at left, building at lower center. Fishing boats at left center, artistic carp at right on back. Similar to #19. Watermark: Lion's head. Printer: TDLR.	FV	FV	3.00

		VG	VF	UNC
24	**1000 Leones** 15.7.1998; 2003. Multicolor.	FV	FV	5.00

		VG	VF	UNC
25	**2000 Leones** 1.1.2000. Brown and blue on multicolor underprint. I. T. A. Wallace-Johnson at right, cargo ship and storage shed at center. Modern building at left center on back. Printer: TDLR.	FV	FV	9.00

2002-2004 Issue

		VG	VF	UNC
27	**2000 Leones** 1.2.2002; 1.3.2003. Brown and blue on multicolor underprint. Like #25 but with metallic printing. Printer: TDLR.	FV	FV	9.00

		VG	VF	UNC
28	**5000 Leones** 1.2.2002. Multicolor.	FV	FV	22.50

		VG	VF	UNC
29	**10,000 Leones** 4.8.2004. Blue, green and Multicolor.	FV	FV	40.00

> ### NOTICE
> Readers with unlisted dates, signature varieties, etc. are invited to submit photocopies of their notes to: Standard Catalog of World Paper Money, 700 East State St. Iola, WI 54990-0001, E-Mail: george.cuhaj@fwpubs.com.

Collector Series

Bank of Sierra Leone

1972 ND Issue

#CS1, First Anniversary of Republic, 1972

		Issue Price	Mkt. Value
CS1	**ND (19.4.1972) - 50 Cents** #4 laminated in plastic with two 50 cent coins in special maroon case.	—	10.00

Note: #CS1 note has serial # all zeros but w/o specimen ovpt.

1979 ND Issue

		Issue Price	Mkt. Value
CS2	**ND (1979) 50 Cents - 5 Leones** #4, 5b-7b with overprint: *SPECIMEN* and serial # prefix Maltese cross.	—	20.00

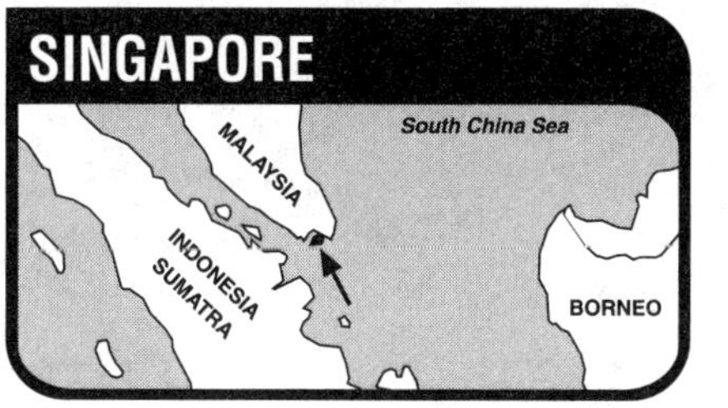

The Republic of Singapore, a British Commonwealth nation situated at the southern tip of the Malayan peninsula, has an area of 263 sq. mi. (682 sq. km.) and a population of 4.1 million. Capital: Singapore. The economy is d on electronics production, petrochemicals, pharmaceuticals and shipbuilding/repairs. It is a world financial, business E-commerce, oil refining and air services center, besides having the busiest port in terms of shipping tonnage and containers handled.

Singapore's modern. history - it was an important shipping center in the 14th century before the rise of Malacca and Penang - began in 1819 when Sir Thomas Stamford Raffles, an agent for the British East India Company, founded the town of Singapore. By 1825 its trade exceeded that of Malacca and Penang combined. The opening of the Suez Canal (1869) and the demand for rubber and tin created by the automobile and packaging industries combined to make Singapore one of the major ports of the world. In 1826 Singapore, Penang and Malacca were combined to form the Straits Settlements, which was made a Crown Colony in 1867. Singapore became a separate Crown Colony in 1946 when the Straits Settlements was dissolved. It joined in the formation of Malaysia in 1963, but broke away on Aug. 9, 1965, to become an independent republic. Continued economic prosperity has made Singapore an influential member of the Asian economic community. Singapore is a member of the Commonwealth of Nations. The president is Chief of State. The prime minister is Head of Government.

MONETARY SYSTEM:

1 Dollar = 100 Cents

REPUBLIC

BOARD OF COMMISSIONERS OF CURRENCY

SIGNATURE SEAL VARIETIES

Type I: Dragon, seal script, lion	**Type II: Seal script w/symbol**

1967-73 ND ISSUE

#1 and 2 wmk: Lion's head. Arms at r. Sign. varieties. Printer: BWC.

		VG	VF	UNC
1	**1 Dollar**			
	ND (1967-72) Blue on multicolor underprint. Light red flowers (Janet Kaneali Orchid) at center, arms at right. Apartment buildings on back.			
	a. Without red seal. Signature Lim Kim San (1967).	4.00	7.50	17.50
	b. Red signature seal Type I at center. Signature Dr. Goh Keng Swee (1970).	8.00	17.50	35.00
	c. Without red seal. Signature Hon Sui Sen (1971).	4.00	8.00	19.00
	d. Red signature seal Type II at center. Signature Hon Sui Sen (1972).	2.00	5.00	12.50

		VG	VF	UNC
2	**5 Dollars**			
	ND (1967-73). Green on multicolor underprint. Light orange flowers (T. M. A. Orchid) at center, arms at upper right. Busy scene on the Singapore River on back.			
	a. Without red seal. Signature Lim Kim San (1967).	15.00	35.00	90.00
	b. Red signature seal Type I at center. Signature Dr. Goh Keng Swee (1970).	80.00	200.	450.
	c. Without red seal. Signature Hon Sui Sen (1972).	30.00	60.00	150.
	d. Red signature seal Type II at center. Signature Hon Sui Sen (1973).	10.00	22.50	80.00

#3-5 wmk: Lion's head. Printer: TDLR.

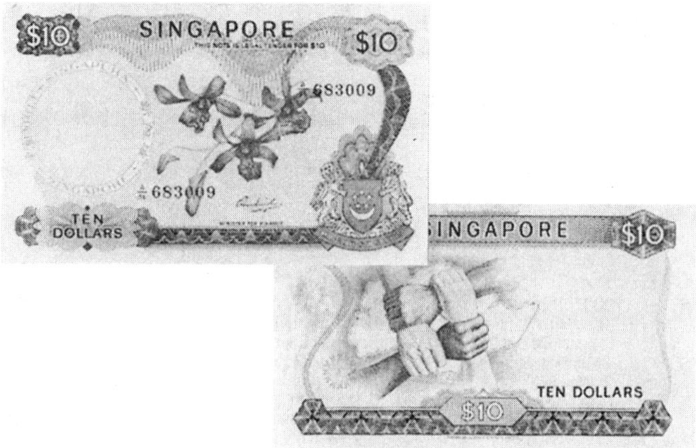

		VG	VF	UNC
3	**10 Dollars**			
	ND (1967-73). Red on multicolor underprint. Lilac flowers (Dendrobium Marjorie Orchid) at center, arms at lower right. Four hands clasping wrists over map of Singapore at left center on back.			
	a. Without red seal. Signature Lim Kim San (1967).	17.50	40.00	100.
	b. Red signature seal Type I at center. Signature Dr. Goh Keng Swee (1970).	25.00	50.00	100.
	c. Without red seal. Signature Hon Sui Sen (1972).	20.00	40.00	90.00
	d. Red signature seal Type II at center. Signature Hon Sui Sen (1973).	15.00	25.00	50.00
	s. As d. Specimen.	—	—	250.

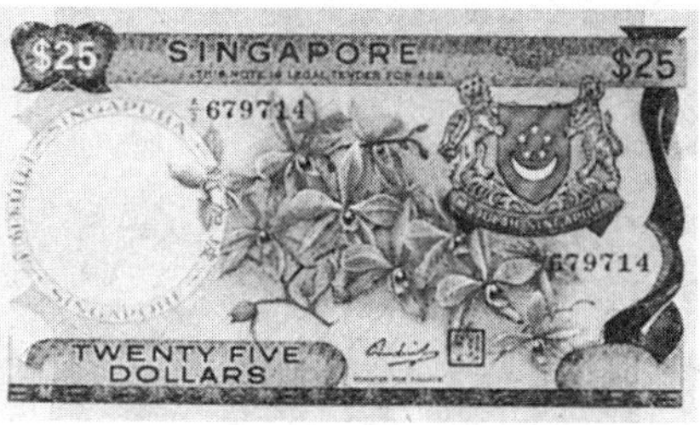

		VG	VF	UNC
4	**25 Dollars**			
	ND (1972). Dark brown on multicolor underprint. Yellow flowers (Renanthopsis Aurora Orchid) at center, arms at upper right. Supreme Court building on back.	60.00	80.00	130.

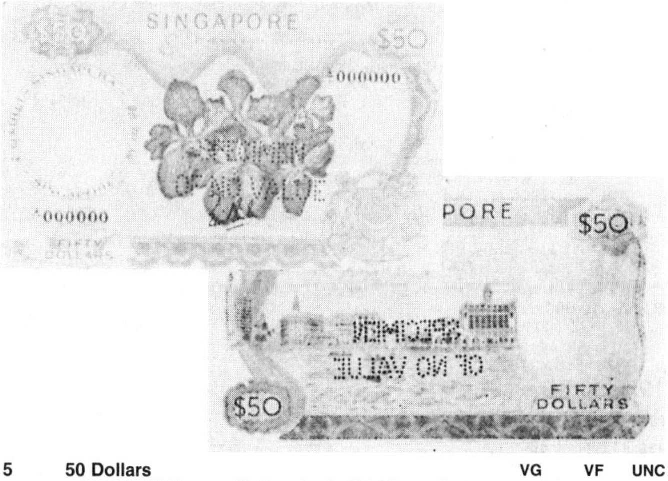

		VG	VF	UNC
5	**50 Dollars**			
	ND (1967-73). Blue on multicolor underprint. Violet flowers (Vanda Rothschildiana Orchid) at center, arms at lower right. Singapore seafront and Clifford Pier on back.			
	a. Without red seal. Signature Lim Kim San (1967).	70.00	125.	250.
	b. Red signature seal Type I at center. Signature Dr. Goh Keng Swee (1970).	90.00	225.	350.
	c. Without red seal. Signature Hon Sui Se Sen (1972).	45.00	85.00	200.
	d. Red signature seal Type II at center. Signature Hon Sui Sen (1973).	35.00	75.00	175.
	s. As d. Specimen.	—	—	400.

6	100 Dollars	VG	VF	UNC
	ND (1967-73). Blue and violet on multicolor underprint. Red flowers (Cattleya Orchid) at center, arms at right. Sailing vessels along Singapore waterfront on back. Watermark: Lion's head. Printer: BWC.			
	a. Without red seal. Signature Lim Kim San (1967).	90.00	150.	350.
	b. Red signature seal Type I at center. Signature Dr. Goh Keng Swee (1970).	125.	500.	825.
	c. Without red seal. Signature Hon Sui Sen (1972).	90.00	175.	375.
	d. Red signature seal Type II at center. Signature Hon Sui Sen (1973).	80.00	150.	325.
	s. Specimen.	—	—	525.

#7-8A wmk: Lion's head. Printer: TDLR.

7	500 Dollars	VG	VF	UNC
	ND (1972). Dark green, lilac on multicolor underprint. Pink flowers (Dendrobium Shangri-la) at center. Government offices at St. Andrew's road on back.	500.	700.	1100.
8	1000 Dollars			
	ND (1967-75). Purple on multicolor underprint. Lilac-brown colored flowers (Dendrobium Kimiyo Kondo) at center, arms at right. Victoria Theatre and Empress Palace on back.			
	a. Without red seal. Signature Lim Kim San (1967).	750.	1200.	1800.
	b. Red signature seal Type I at center. Signature Dr. Goh Keng Swee (1970).	800.	1500.	2200.
	c. Without red seal. Signature Hon Sui Sen (1973).	700.	1300.	2000.
	d. Red signature seal Type II at center. Signature Hon Sui Sen (1975).	650.	900.	1600.
8A	10,000 Dollars			
	ND (1973). Green on multicolor underprint. Orchids (Aranda Majulah) at center, arms at at right. The Istana (Presidential residence) at left. Center on back. Signature Hon Sui Sen.	FV	8000.	13,000.

1976-80 ND Issue

#9-17 city skyline along bottom, arms at upper r. Wmk: Lion's head.

#9 and 10 printer: BWC.

9	1 Dollar	VG	VF	UNC
	ND (1976). Blue-black on multicolor underprint. Black-naped tern at left. National Day parade passing large building at center right on back.	FV	FV	4.00

10	5 Dollars	VG	VF	UNC
	ND (1976). Green and brown on multicolor underprint. Red-whiskered bulbul at left. Ariel tram cars and view of harbor on back.	FV	FV	12.50

11	10 Dollars	VG	VF	UNC
	ND (1976). Red and dark blue on multicolor underprint. White collared kingfisher at left. Garden City with high rise public housing in background on back. Printer: TDLR.			
	a. With security thread (1979).	FV	20.00	60.00
	b. With segmented foil over security thread (1980).	FV	15.00	30.00

12	20 Dollars	VG	VF	UNC
	ND (1979). Brown, yellow and blue on multicolor underprint. Yellow-breasted Sunbird at left. Back brown; dancer at left, Concorde over Changi International airport center right. Printer: BWC.	20.00	40.00	55.00

NOTICE

Readers with unlisted dates, signature varieties, etc. are invited to submit photocopies of their notes to: Standard Catalog of World Paper Money, 700 East State St. Iola, WI 54990-0001, E-Mail: george.cuhaj@fwpubs.com.

		VG	VF	UNC
13	**50 Dollars**			
	ND (1976). Dark blue on multicolor underprint. White-rumped shama at left. School band on parade on back. Printer: TDLR.			
	a. With security thread.	FV	40.00	100.
	b. With segmented foil over security thread.	FV	35.00	85.00

		VG	VF	UNC
14	**100 Dollars**			
	ND (1977). Blue on multicolor underprint. Blue-throated Bee eater at left. Various ethnic dancers on back. Printer: BWC.	FV	100.	200.

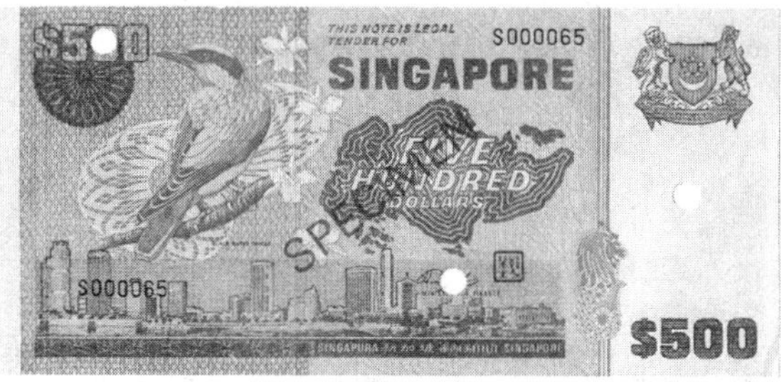

		VG	VF	UNC
15	**500 Dollars**			
	ND (1977). Green and multicolor. Black-naped oriole at left. Back green; view of island and oil refinery at center. Printer: TDLR.			
	a. Issued note.	FV	450.	750.
	s. Specimen.	—	—	—

		VG	VF	UNC
16	**1000 Dollars**			
	ND (1978). Violet and brown on multicolor underprint. Brahminy Kite bird at left. Container ship terminal on back. Printer: TDLR.	FV	750.	1250.

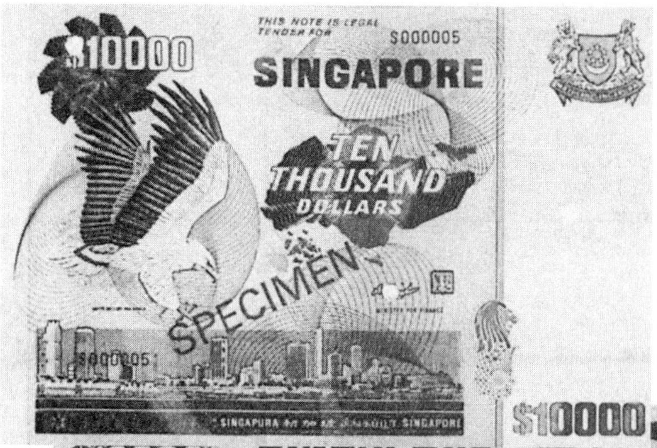

		VG	VF	UNC
17	**10,000 Dollars**			
	ND (1980). Green on multicolor underprint. White-bellied Sea Eagle at left. 19th century Singapore River scene above, modern view below on back. Printer: TDLR.			
	a. Issued note.	FV	8000.	10,000.
	s. Specimen, punched hole cancelled.	—	—	1500.

1984-89 ND Issue

#18-25 arms at upper l. Wmk: Lion's head. Printer: TDLR. Replacement notes: Serial # prefix *Z/1, Z/2,* etc.

		VG	VF	UNC
18	**1 Dollar**			
	ND (1987). Deep blue and green. Sailing ship *Sha Chuan* at left. Chinese Crasse and carp at lower right. Orchids and satellite tracking station at center, on back.			
	a. Signature Goh Keng Swee.	—	Unc	3.00
	b. Signature Hu Tsu Tau.	—	Unc	2.75
19	**5 Dollars**			
	ND (1989). Green and red-violet on multicolor underprint. Chinese lion with ball and Commerson's Anchovy at right. *Twkow* boats at left, View of the PSA container terminal at right on back.	FV	FV	7.50

		VG	VF	UNC
20	**10 Dollars**			
	ND (1988). Red-orange and violet on multicolor underprint. Trader vessel *Palari* at left, Phoenix and round scad at lower right. Stylized map at center, public housing at right on back.	FV	FV	10.00

#21 Not assigned.

NOTICE

Readers with unlisted dates, signature varieties, etc. are invited to submit photocopies of their notes to: Standard Catalog of World Paper Money, 700 East State St. Iola, WI 54990-0001, E-Mail: george.cuhaj@fwpubs.com.

		VG	VF	UNC
22	**50 Dollars**			
	ND (1987). Blue on multicolor underprint. Coastal vessel *Perak* at left. Mountain ducks and six-banded grouper at lower right. Two raised areas in circles at lower right. Benjamin Sheares Bridge and city view on back.			
	a. With security thread.	FV	FV	65.00
	b. With segmented foil over security thread.	FV	FV	60.00

		VG	VF	UNC
23	**100 Dollars**			
	ND (1985; 1995). Dark brown, violet and orange-brown on multicolor underprint. Passenger liner *Chusan* at left center. Slender shad and three raised areas in circles at lower right. Airplane above with Changi air terminal at center right on back.			
	a. With security thread. Signature Dr. Goh Keng Swee. (1985).	FV	FV	125.
	b. With segmented foil over "clear text" security thread With $100 *SINGAPORE* in four languages. (1995).	FV	FV	110.
	c. As b. signature Hu Tsu Tau.	FV	FV	125.

		VG	VF	UNC
24	**500 Dollars**			
	ND (1988). Green on multicolor underprint. Cargo vessel *Neptune Sardonyx* at left. Members of the three Armed Forces and the Civil Defence Force with outline map of Singapore on back.	FV	FV	450.

		VG	VF	UNC
25	**1000 Dollars**			
	ND (1984). Purple and red on multicolor underprint. Container ship *Neptune Garnet* at left center, Phoenix and Polka-dot grouper at lower right. Shipyard on back.			
	a. Signature Dr. Goh Keng Swee.	FV	FV	900.
	b. Signature Dr. Hu Tsu Tau.	FV	FV	850.
	s. As a. Specimen.	—	—	—
26	**10,000 Dollars**			
	ND (1987). Red and purple on multicolor underprint. General bulk carrier *Neptune Canopus* at left. Chinese dragon at center right. 1987 National Day parade on back.	FV	7000.	8000.

1990 ND Issue

#27 and 28 printer: TDLR. Replacement notes: Serial prefix *ZZ*.

		VG	VF	UNC
27	**2 Dollars**			
	ND (ca.1990). Orange and red on yellow-green underprint. Arms at upper left, *Tongkang* boat and two smaller boats at center. Chingay procession on back. Watermark: Lion's head. Printer: TDLR.	FV	FV	3.50

		VG	VF	UNC
28	**2 Dollars**			
	ND (1992). Deep purple and brown-violet on multicolor underprint. Like #27, but with ascending size serial #.	FV	FV	3.00

Note: #28 also issued in various uncut sheets from 2 to 40 subjects.

1992 Commemorative Issues

#29, 25th Anniversary - Board of Commissioners of Currency

		VG	VF	UNC
29	**2 Dollars**			
	ND(1992). Deep purple and brown-violet on multicolor underprint. Overprint: *25 YEARS OF CURRENCY 1967-1992...* on #28. (5000).			
	a. Issued note.	—	—	350.
	x. Without overprint text: *COMMISSONERS* (error).	—	—	380.

#30 and 31, 25th Anniversary of Independence

		VG	VF	UNC
30	**50 Dollars** 9.8.1990. Red and purple on multicolor underprint. Silver hologram of Yusof bin Ishak at center. Old harbor scene at left, modern buildings at right. First parliament at left, group of people below flag and arms at right on back. Plastic.	FV	FV	60.00

Note: #30 was issued in a special commemorative folder.

		VG	VF	UNC
31	**50 Dollars** ND (1990). Red and purple on multicolor underprint. Like #30 but without date.	FV	FV	75.00

1994 ND Commemorative Issue

#31A, 25th Anniversary - Board of Commissioners of Currency

		VG	VF	UNC
31A	**2 Dollars** ND (1994). Red overprint logo of the Board at left beneath arms on #28.	—	—	100.

Note: #31A was issued in the book *Prudence at the Helm, 1967-1992.*

1994 Regular Issue

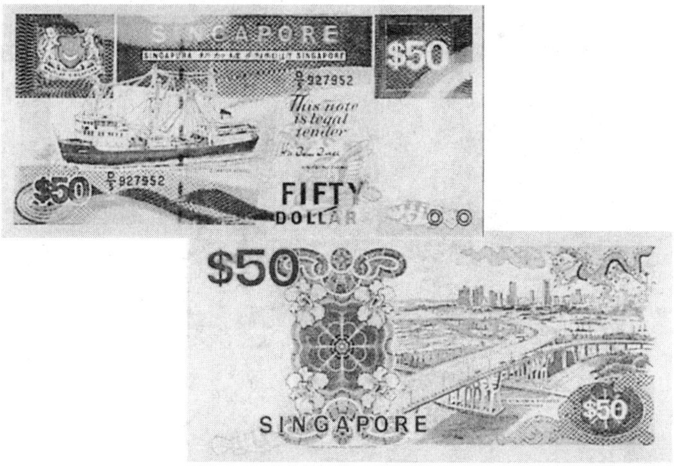

		VG	VF	UNC
32	**50 Dollars** ND (1994). Deep blue-black and red on multicolor underprint. Like #22. with segmented foil over security thread. Printer: TDLR.	FV	FV	55.00

1996 Commemorative Issue

#33, 25th Anniversary of Monetary Authority, 1971-1996

		VG	VF	UNC
33	**25 Dollars** 1.1.1996. Red-brown and green on multicolor underprint. Arms at upper left, Monetary Authority building at center. Optical variable device at left center in addition to many other security features. Financial sector skyline on back. Watermark: Lion's head. Signature Hu Tsu Tau.	FV	FV	60.00

Note: #33 was offered in 2 varieties of special booklets, wide, narrow and uncut sheets of 20 subjects.

1997 ND Regular Issue

#34 and 35 wmk: Lion's head. Printer: H&S.

		VG	VF	UNC
34	**2 Dollars** ND (1997). Deep purple and brown-violet on multicolor underprint. Like #28.	FV	FV	2.50

		VG	VF	UNC
35	**5 Dollars** ND (1997). Green and red-violet on multicolor underprint. Like #19.	FV	FV	6.00
36	**50 Dollars** ND (1997). Slate gray and red on multicolor underprint. Like #32. with segmented foil over "Cleartext" security thread. with $50 *SINGAPORE* in four languages. Watermark: Lion's head.	FV	FV	45.00

1998 ND Issue

		VG	VF	UNC
37	**2 Dollars** ND(1998). Deep purple and brown-violet on multicolor underprint. Like #34. Watermark: Lion's head. Printer: BABN.	FV	FV	2.50

1999 ND Issue

#38-45 Pres. Encik Yusof bin Ishak at r. and as wmk. Each back w/different theme.

		VG	VF	UNC
38	**2 Dollars** ND (1999). Purple, brown and underprint. Education - Victoria Bridge School, Raffles Institue, College of Medicine views with children on back.	FV	FV	2.50

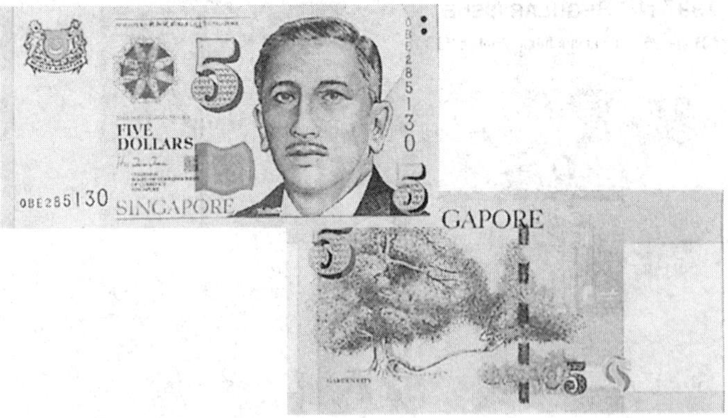

39	5 Dollars	VG	VF	UNC
	ND (1999). Green, red and multicolor. Garden City - trees and flowers, skyline in background on back.	FV	FV	6.00

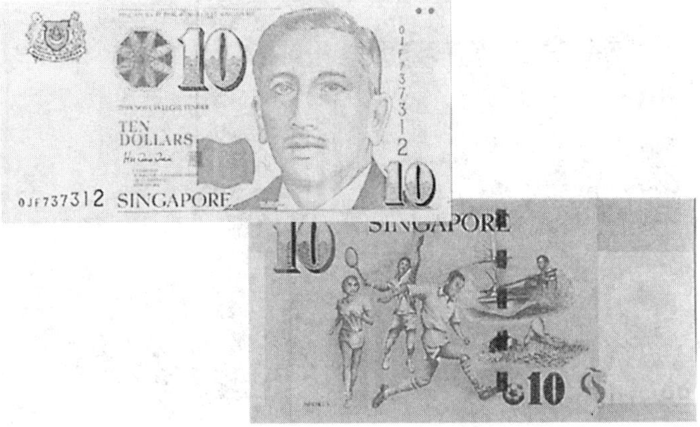

40	10 Dollars	VG	VF	UNC
	ND (1999). Red, brown and multicolor. Sports - swimming, tennis, soccer, sailing, running on back.	FV	FV	12.00

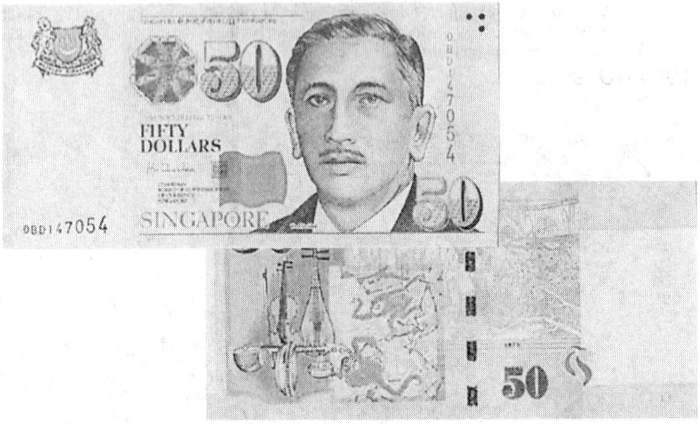

41	50 Dollars	VG	VF	UNC
	ND (1999). Slate blue and multicolor. Arts - music, graphics on back.	FV	55.00	65.00

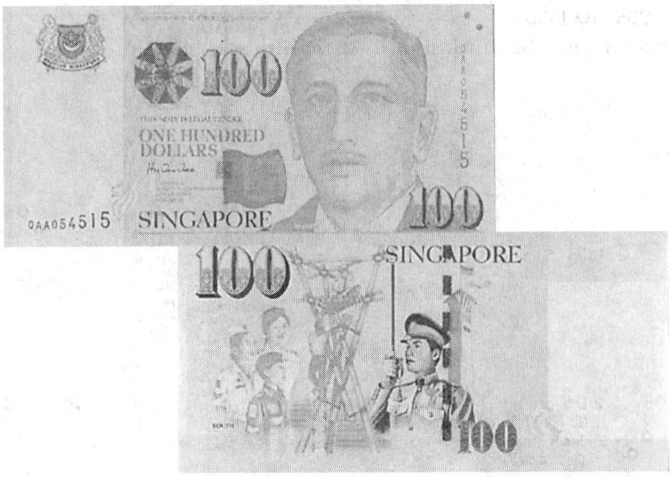

42	100 Dollars	VG	VF	UNC
	ND (1999). Orange, brown and multicolor. Youth - Members of the Singapore Red Cross, St. John's Ambulance Brigade, National Police Cadet Corps, Scouts with pioneering project, National Service officer with cereminial sword, Safti Military Institute tower on back.	FV	FV	100.

43	1000 Dollars	VG	VF	UNC
	ND (1999). Purple, lilac and multicolor. Parlament House at left, Istana (Presidential residence) at center, Supreme Court at right on back.	FV	FV	800.

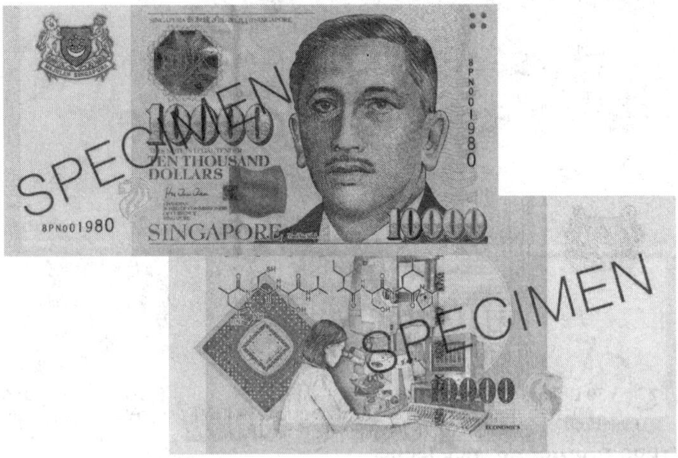

44	10,000 Dollars	VG	VF	UNC
	ND (1999). Light brown and multicolor. Technology - computer chip research lab on back.			
	a. Issued note.	FV	FV	7500.
	s. Specimen.	—	—	300.

2000 Issue

#45, Red ovpt. added to #38.

45	2 Dollars	VG	VF	UNC
	2000. Purple, brown and multicolor. #38 with 2000 overprint in red at upper right and lower left.	2.00	3.00	4.00

Monetary Authority of Sinapore

2005 Issue

		VG	VF	UNC
46	**2 Dollars** ND (2005). Like #38.	FV	FV	2.50
47	**5 Dollars** ND (2005). Like #39.	FV	FV	5.00

		VG	VF	UNC
48	**10 Dollars** ND (2005). Like #40 but polymer plastic.	FV	FV	10.00

		VG	VF	UNC
49	**50 Dollars** ND (2006)	FV	FV	50.00
50	**100 Dollars** Expected new issue.	—	—	—
51	**1000 Dollars** Expected new issue.	—	—	—
52	**10,000 Dollars** Expected new issue.	—	—	—

COLLECTOR SERIES

SINGAPORE

1989 ND ISSUES

		Issue Price	Mkt. Value
CS1	**ND (1989). 1 Dollar - 100 Dollars** #1a-3a, 5a and 6a overprint: *SPECIMEN.* (77 sets).	—	1850.
CS2	**ND (1989). 1 Dollar - 100 Dollars** #1c-3c, 5c and 6c overprint: *SPECIMEN.* (89 sets).	—	2250.
CS3	**ND (1989). 1 Dollar - 100 Dollars** #1d-3d, 4, 5d and 6d overprint: *SPECIMEN.* (82 sets).	—	2400.
CS4	**ND (1989). 1-100 Dollars** #9-11, 13 and 14 overprint: *SPECIMEN.* (311 sets).	—	1250.

2000 ISSUE

		Issue Price	Mkt. Value
CS5	**2 Dollars** Twin sets of albums, each with 3 Two Dollar notes that bear identical serial #s for the last 6 digits. Albums titled: *The Twin Collection of the Millennium Dragon Circa 2000 Singapore.*	—	15.00

SLOVAKIA

Slovakia as a republic has an area of 18,923 sq. mi. (49,011 sq. km.) and a population of 5.37 million. Capital: Bratislava. Textiles, steel, and wood products are exported.

Slovakia was settled by Slavic Slovaks in the 6th or 7th century and was incorporated into Greater Moravia in the 9th century. After the Moravian state was destroyed early in the 10th century, Slovakia was conquered by the Magyars and remained a land of the Hungarian crown until 1918, when it joined the Czechs in forming Czechoslovakia. In 1938, the Slovaks declared themselves an autonomous state within a federal Czecho-Slovak state. After the German occupation, Slovakia became nominally independent under the protection of Germany, March 16, 1939. Father Jozef Tiso was appointed President. Slovakia was liberated from German control in Oct. 1944, but in May 1945 ceased to be an independent Slovak state. In 1968 it became a constituent state of Czechoslovakia as Slovak Socialist Republic. In January 1991 the Czech and Slovak Federal Republic was formed, and after June 1992 elections, it was decided to split the federation into the Czech Republic and Slovakia on 1 January, 1993.

MONETARY SYSTEM:

1 Korun = 100 Halierov

REPUBLIC

SLOVENSKA REPUBLIKA

REPUBLIC OF SLOVAKIA

1993 ND PROVISIONAL ISSUE

#15-19 Czechoslovakian issue w/affixed adhesive stamps w/*SLOVENSKA / arms / REPUBLIKA*.

		VG	VF	UNC
15	**20 Korun** ND (1993- old date 1988). Black and light blue adhesive stamp on Czechoslovakia #95.	1.00	2.50	4.00

		VG	VF	UNC
16	**50 Korun** ND (1993- old date 1987). Black and yellow adhesive stamp on Czechoslovakia #96. Serial # prefixes: *F* and *I*.	2.25	3.50	8.00

		VG	VF	UNC
17	**100 Korun** ND (1993- old date 1961). Black and orange adhesive stamp on Czechoslovakia #91b. Series G37-.	4.00	5.00	9.00
18	**500 Korun** ND (1993- old date 1973). Adhesive stamp on Czechoslovakia #93. Serial # prefixes: *Z, V* and *W*.	17.50	25.00	50.00
19	**1000 Korun** ND (1993- old date 1985). Adhesive stamp on Czechoslovakia #98.	35.00	45.00	90.00

NÁRODNÁ BANKA SLOVENSKA

SLOVAK NATIONAL BANK

1993 ISSUE

#20-24 shield of arms at lower ctr. r. on back. Sign. varieties.

		VG	VF	UNC
20	**20 Korun**			
	1993; 1995; 1997; 1999; 2001. Black and green on multicolor underprint. Prince Pribina at right and as watermark. Nitra Castle at left on back. Printer: BABN.			
	a. Pale green underprint. 1.9.1993.	FV	FV	3.00
	b. As a. but with green underprint. at right. Security thread closer at center 1.6.1995.	FV	FV	2.50
	c. As b. 31.10.1997; 1.7.1999; 31.8.2001; 6.9.2004.	FV	FV	2.00
	d. As a. Serial # prefix A. Uncut sheet of 60 (6000 sheets).	—	—	60.00

		VG	VF	UNC
21	**50 Korun**			
	1993; 1995; 1999; 2002. Black, blue and aqua on multicolor underprint. St. Cyril and St. Method at right and as watermark. Medieval church at Drazovce and first 7 letters of Slavic alphabet on back. Printer: BABN.			
	a. 1.8.1993.	FV	FV	5.00
	b. Security thread closer to center 1.6.1995; 1.7.1999; 2.5.2002.	FV	FV	5.00
	c. As a. Serial # prefix A. Uncut sheet of 45 (4000 sheets).	—	—	100.

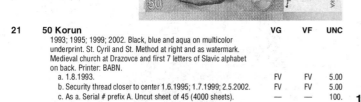

		VG	VF	UNC
22	**100 Korun**			
	1.9.1993. Red and black on orange and multicolor underprint. Madonna (by master woodcarver Pavol) from the altar of the Birth in St. Jacob's Church in Levoca at right. Levoca town view on back. Printer: TDLR.			
	a. 1.9.1993. Serial # prefix D.	FV	FV	9.00
	b. Serial # prefix A. Uncut sheet of 35 (4000 sheets).	—	—	165.

		VG	VF	UNC
23	**500 Korun**			
	1.10.1993. Dark gray and brown on multicolor underprint. Ludovit Stúr at right and as watermark. Bratislava Castle and St. Michael's Church at left on back. Printer: TDLR.			
	a. Serial # prefix E; F.	FV	FV	30.00
	b. Serial # prefix A. Uncut sheet of 28 (2500 sheets).	—	—	525.
	s. Specimen. Perforated: *SPECIMEN.*	—	—	—

		VG	VF	UNC
24	**1000 Korun**			
	1993; 1995; 1997. Dark gray and purple on red-violet and multicolor underprint. Andrej Hlinka at right and as watermark. Madonna of the Church of Liptovké Sliace near Ruzomberok and Church of St. Andrew in Ruzomberok at left center on back. Printer: TDLR.			
	a. 1.10.1993.	FV	FV	55.00
	b. Security thread closer to center 1.6.1995.	FV	FV	52.50
	c. Prefix B; G. 1.7.1997; 1.8.1997.	FV	FV	52.50
	d. As a. Serial # prefix A. Uncut sheet of 28 (1500 sheets).	—	—	1050.
	s. Specimen. Perforated: *SPECIMEN.*	—	—	—

1995; 1996 ISSUE

#25-29 shield of arms at lower ctr. r. on back.

		VG	VF	UNC
25	**100 Korun**			
	1996-97; 1999; 2001. Like #22 but red-orange replaces dull orange in corners on back.			
	a. Printer as: *TDLR.* 31.10.1996.	FV	FV	7.00
	b. Serial # prefix: *D, L.* 1.10.1997.	FV	FV	7.00
	c. Printer as: *DLR.* 1.7.1999; 10.10.2001.	FV	FV	6.00
	s. Specimen. Perforated: *SPECIMEN.*	—	—	—

26	200 Korun	VG	VF	UNC
	1.8.1995. Dark gray and blue-green on multicolor underprint. Anton Bernolák at right and as watermark. Trnava town view at left center on back. Printer: G&D.			
	a. Issued note.	FV	FV	10.00
	s. Specimen. Perforated: *SPECIMEN.*	—	—	—

27	500 Korun	VG	VF	UNC
	31.10.1996. Like #23 but blue underprint at left center and in corners on face, also in upper left center and in corners on back. Dark brown at center on back.			
	a. Issued note.	FV	FV	25.00
	s. Specimen. Perforated: *SPECIMEN.*	—	—	—

#28 not assigned.

29	5000 Korun	VG	VF	UNC
	3.4.1995. Brown-violet and pale yellow-brown on multicolor underprint. Milan Rastislav Štefánik at right, sun and moon at center. Štefánik's grave at Bradlo Hill, part of *Ursa Major* constellation, and a pasque flower at left center on back. Printer: G&D.			
	a. Issued note.	FV	FV	175.
	s. Specimen. Perforated: *SPECIMEN.*	—	—	—

1999-2000 ISSUE

Optical variable ink and dots added in wmk. areas. Printer: G&D.

30	200 Korun	VG	VF	UNC
	31.5.1999. Dark gray and blue-green on multicolor underprint. Like #26 but with optical variable ink in watermark area.	FV	FV	7.50
31	**500 Korun**	**VG**	**VF**	**UNC**
	30.10.2000. Dark gray and brown on multicolor underprint. Like #27 but with optical variable device in watermark area.	FV	FV	17.50

32	1000 Korun	VG	VF	UNC
	1.10.1999. Dark gray and purple on red-violet and multicolor underprint. Like #24 but with optical variable device in watermark area.	FV	FV	30.00

33 **5000 Korun** — VG FV — VF FV — UNC 150.
11.5.1999. Orange-brown and olive on multicolor underprint. Like #29 but with optical variable device in watermark area and addition of a Kinegram left center.

2000 Commemorative Issue

Previously Series *A* notes were available only as uncut sheets. These overprints caused problems with bank counting machines and were not in circulation for an extended period of time.

34 **20 Korun** — VG FV — VF FV — UNC 1.75
1.9.1993. Silver overprint on #20. 330,000 pcs.

35 **50 Korun** — VG FV — VF FV — UNC 2.50
1.8.1993. Silver overprint on #21. 168,750 pcs.

36 **100 Korun** — VG FV — VF FV — UNC 4.50
1.9.1993. Silver overprint on #22. 133,000 pcs.

37 **200 Korun** — VG FV — VF FV — UNC 7.50
1.8.1995. Silver overprint on #26. 108,000 pcs.

38 **500 Korun** — VG FV — VF FV — UNC 20.00
1.10.1993. Silver overprint on #23. 67,200 pcs.

39 **1000 Korun** — VG FV — VF FV — UNC 35.00
1.10.1993. Silver overprint on #24a. 40,600 pcs.

40 **5000 Korun** — VG FV — VF FV — UNC 175.
3.4.1995. Gold overprint on #29. 10,800 pcs.

2002 Issue

41 **200 Korun** — VG FV — VF FV — UNC 7.50
30.8.2002. Dark gray and blue-green on multicolor underprint. Like #30 but with additional security features. Printer: FCO.

42 **1000 Korun** — VG FV — VF FV — UNC 30.00
10.6.2002. Dark gray and purple on red-violet and multicolor underprint. Similar to #32 but with additional security features. Printer: (T)DLR.

43 **5000 Korun** — VG FV — VF FV — UNC 150.
17.11.2003. Orange-brown and olive on multicolor underprint. Like #33 but with additional security features.

The Republic of Slovenia is bounded in the north by Austria, northeast by Hungary, southeast by Croatia and to the west by Italy. It has an area of 5,246 sq. mi. (20,251 sq. km.) and a population of 1.99 million. Capital: Ljubljana. The economy is d on electricity, minerals, forestry, agriculture and fishing. Small industries are being developed during privatization.

The Roman Province of Pannonia (Croatia-Slavonia) was conquered by the Ostrogoths and later recovered by Justinian in 535. In 568 it was conquered by the Avars who were overthrown by the Croats around 640. After changing relations with the Franks, Byzantium, Venice, Moravia and a short-lived Bulgar State, it eventually came under Magyar conquerors led by King Koloman in 1102 who was crowned King of Croatia and Dalmatia at Belgrad. Croatia was an autonomous kingdom under the Holy Crown of St. Stephen for the next eight centuries, becoming a fortress against any further invasion by the Turks. By 1699 all Croatia-Slavonia was recovered from the Turks and was settled by many Serbian refugees from Turkey. Napoleon's rise to power created an "Illyrian" state of east Adriatic territories which Austria had acquired from Venice. All were restored by 1822. The Hungarian Revolution in 1848 developed a federalist policy dissolving any legal bond with Hungary but the Austrians remained in control. From 1868 to 1914 increased political activity developed which broke out in riots in 1883. The Croatian constitution was temporarily suspended by Hungary and a royal commissioner, Count Khuen-Hédervàry, was appointed. His 20 years of rule were very humiliating for Croatia. From 1903 onwards a national feeling developed leading to quarrels with Hungary in 1907 which resulted in Cuvaj being appointed as a dictator by Hungary in 1912. The church lost its autonomy and revolutionary movements followed. The dictatorship was abolished in 1913 with somewhat of a truce with Budapest when WW I broke out. This resulted in the union of the Yugoslav Provinces on Dec. 1, 1918. The lands originally settled by Slovenes in the 6th century were steadily encroached upon by Germans. Slovenia developed as part of Austro-Hungarian Empire after the defeat of the latter in World War I it became part of the Kingdom of the Serbs, Croats and Slovenes (Yugoslavia) established on December 1, 1918. A legal opposition group, the Slovene League of Social Democrats, was formed in Jan. 1989. In Oct. 1989 the Slovene Assembly voted a constitutional amendment giving it the right to secede from Yugoslavia. On July 2, 1990 the Assembly adopted a 'declaration of sovereignty' and in Sept. proclaimed its control over the territorial defense force on its soil. A referendum on Dec. 23 resulted in a majority vote for independence, which was formally declared on Dec. 26. In Feb. 1991 parliament ruled that henceforth Slovenian law took precedence over federal. On June 25, Slovenia declared independence, but agreed to suspend this for 3 months at peace talks sponsored by the EC. The moratorium having expired, Slovenia (and Croatia) declared their complete independence of the Yugoslav federation on Oct. 8, 1991.

MONETARY SYSTEM:

1 (Tolar) = 1 Yugoslavian Dinar
1 Tolar = 100 Stotinas

REPLACEMENT NOTES:

#11-19, ZA prefix.

REPUBLIC

BANKA SLOVENIJE (FIRST)

1989 ISSUE

		VG	VF	UNC
A1	**1 Lipa** 29.11.1989 (1990). Green. Plants at left, Dr. France Preseren at right. Slovenian Parliament on back.			
	a. Issued note.	3.00	8.00	20.00
	s. Specimen.	—	—	20.00

Note: reportedly 25,000 notes issued, of which more than 10,000 were distributed.

REPUBLIKA SLOVENIJA

1990-92 ISSUE

#1-10 pedimented behive at lower l., denomination numeral in guilloche over a representation of the dance of the Catrniolan bee on an underprint of honeycomb at ctr. r. Date given as first 2 numerals of serial #. Mountain ridge of Triglav at l. ctr. on back. Wmk: Symmetrical designs repeated.

Note: About 500 sets of Specimens #1s-10s were released to the general collecting public. Specimens exist with normal serial #'s and with 0's as serial #'s. Zero serial #'s are valued up to $20.00 each.

		VG	VF	UNC
1	**1 (Tolar)** (19)90. Dark olive-green on light gray and light olive-green underprint.			
	a. Issued note.	.05	.10	.30
	s1. Specimen overprint: *VZOREC.*	—	—	4.00
	s2. Specimen overprint *SPECIMEN.*	—	—	4.00

		VG	VF	UNC
B1	**50 (Tolarjev)** (19)90. Not issued.	—	—	50.00

Note: #B1 was not released in 1990, but sold to collectors with #9A about twelve years later.

		VG	VF	UNC
2	**2 (Tolarjev)** (19)90. Brown on tan and ochre underprint.			
	a. Issued note.	.05	.10	.40
	s1. Specimen overprint: *VZOREC.*	—	—	4.00
	s2. Specimen overprint: *SPECIMEN.*	—	—	4.00
3	**5 (Tolarjev)** (19)90. Maroon on pale maroon and pink underprint.			
	a. Issued note.	.05	.15	.50
	s1. Specimen overprint: *VZOREC.*	—	—	4.00
	s2. Specimen overprint: *SPECIMEN.*	—	—	4.00

		VG	VF	UNC
4	**10 (Tolarjev)** (19)90. Dark blue-green and grayish purple on light blue-green underprint.			
	a. Issued note.	FV	FV	3.00
	s1. Specimen overprint: *VZOREC.*	—	—	4.00
	s2. Specimen overprint: *SPECIMEN.*	—	—	4.00
5	**50 (Tolarjev)** (19)90. Dark gray on tan and light gray underprint.			
	a. Issued note.	FV	FV	5.00
	s1. Specimen overprint: *VZOREC.*		—	3.50
	s2. Specimen overprint: *SPECIMEN.*	—	—	4.00

		VG	VF	UNC
6	**100 (Tolarjev)** (19)90. Reddish brown and violet on orange and light violet underprint.			
	a. Issued note.	FV	FV	8.00
	s1. Specimen overprint:*VZOREC.*	—	—	3.50
	s2. Specimen overprint: *SPECIMEN.*	—	—	4.00

7	200 (Tolarjev)	VG	VF	UNC
	(19)90. Greenish black and dark brown on light gray and light green underprint.			
	a. Issued note.	FV	FV	25.00
	s. Specimen overprint: *SPECIMEN.*	—	—	4.00

8	500 (Tolarjev)	VG	VF	UNC
	(19)90; (19)92. Deep lilac and red on pink and pale blue underprint.			
	a. 1990.	FV	FV	25.00
	b. 1992.	FV	FV	40.00
	s1. Specimen overprint: *VZOREC.*	—	—	3.50
	s2. Specimen overprint: *SPECIMEN.*	—	—	4.00

9	1000 (Tolarjev)	VG	VF	UNC
	(19)91; (19)92. Dark blue-gray and gray on light gray and pale blue underprint.			
	a. 1991.	FV	FV	35.00
	b. 1992.	FV	FV	45.00
	s1. Specimen overprint: *VZOREC.* watermark: Column pedestal.	—	—	7.50
	s2. Specimen overprint: *SPECIMEN.* watermark: Column pedestal.	—	—	7.50
	s3. Specimen overprint: *SPECIMEN.* watermark: Snowflake (error).	—	—	150.

9A	2000 (Tolarjev)	VG	VF	UNC
	(19)91. Multicolor. (Not issued).	—	—	60.00

Note: #9A was not released into circulation, but sold along with #B1 to collectors about twelve years later.

10	5000 (Tolarjev)	VG	VF	UNC
	(19)92. Purple and lilac on pink underprint.			
	a. Issued note.	FV	FV	130.
	s1. Specimen overprint: *VZOREC.*	—	—	20.00
	s2. Specimen overprint: *SPECIMEN.*	—	—	10.00

BANKA SLOVENIJE

1992-93 ISSUE

#11-20 replacement notes: Serial # prefix *AZ* and possibly others.

11	10 Tolarjev	VG	VF	UNC
	15.1.1992. Black, brown-violet and brown-orange on multicolor underprint. P. Trubar at right and as watermark, Quill pen at left center. Ursuline church in Ljubljana at center on back.			
	a. Issued note.	FV	FV	.50
	s. Specimen overprint: *VZOREC.*	—	—	8.50

12	20 Tolarjev	VG	VF	UNC
	15.1.1992. Brownish black, deep brown and brown-orange on multicolor underprint. J. Vajkard Valvasor at right and as watermark, compass at left. Topographical outlines at left center, cherub arms at right on back.			
	a. Issued note.	FV	FV	.75
	s. Specimen overprint: *VZOREC.*	—	—	10.00

13	50 Tolarjev	VG	VF	UNC
	15.1.1992. Black, purple and brown-orange on multicolor underprint. J. Vega at right and as watermark, geometric design and calculations at left center. Academy at upper left, planets and geometric design at center on back.			
	a. Issued note.	FV	FV	1.50
	s. Specimen overprint: *VZOREC.*	—	—	12.50

14	100 Tolarjev	VG	VF	UNC
	15.1.1992. Black, blue-black and brown-orange on multicolor underprint. R. Jakopic at right and as watermark. Outline of the Jakopicev Pavilion at center right on back.			
	a. Issued note.	FV	FV	2.75
	s. Specimen overprint: *SPECIMEN* and *VZOREC.*	—	—	15.00

15	200 Tolarjev	VG	VF	UNC
	1992; 1997; 2001. Black, violet-brown and brown-orange on multicolor underprint. I. Gallus at right and as watermark, musical façade at left. Drawing of Slovenia's Philharmonic building at upper left, five lines of medieval music at upper center on back.			
	a. 15.1.1992.	FV	FV	20.00
	b. 8.10.1997.	FV	FV	3.25
	c. 15.1.2001.	FV	FV	3.00
	s. Specimen overprint: *SPECIMEN* and *VZOREC.*	—	—	17.50

16	500 Tolarjev	VG	VF	UNC
	1992; 2001. Black, red and brown-orange on multicolor underprint. J. Plecnik at right and as watermark. Drawing of the National and University Library of Ljubljana at left center on back.			
	a. 15.1.1992.	FV	FV	9.00
	b. 15.1.2001.	FV	FV	8.00
	s. Specimen overprint: *SPECIMEN* and *VZOREC.*	—	—	20.00

17	1000 Tolarjev	VG	VF	UNC
	15.1.1992. Brownish black, deep green and brown-orange on multicolor underprint. F. Preseren at right and as watermark The poem "Drinking Toast" at center on back.			
	a. Issued note.	FV	FV	22.50
	s. Specimen overprint: *SPECIMEN* and *VZOREC.*	—	—	25.00

18	1000 Tolarjev	VG	VF	UNC
	1.6.1993. Black, deep blue-green and brown-orange on multicolor underprint. Like #17 but modified portrait and other incidental changes including color.			
	a. Without *1000* in UV ink on back.	FV	FV	15.00
	b. With *1000* in UV ink on back.	FV	FV	15.00
	s. Specimen overprint: *SPECIMEN* and *VZOREC.*	—	—	25.00

19	5000 Tolarjev	VG	VF	UNC
	1.6.1993. Brownish black, dark brown and brown-orange on multicolor underprint. I. Kobilika at right and as watermark. National Gallery in Ljubljana at upper left on back.			
	a. Issued note.	FV	FV	80.00
	s. Specimen overprint: *SPECIMEN* and *VZOREC.*	—	—	30.00

20	10,000 Tolarjev	VG	VF	UNC
	28.6.1994. Black, purple and brown-orange on multicolor underprint. I. Cankar at right and as watermark. Chrysanthemum blossom at left on back.			
	a. Issued note.	FV	FV	110.
	s. Specimen overprint: *SPECIMEN* and *VZOREC*.	—	—	35.00

1997 Issue

21	5000 Tolarjev	VG	VF	UNC
	8.10.1997. Brownish black, dark brown and brown-orange on multicolor underprint. Like #19 but with scalloped kinegram with cameo portrait and value.			
	a. Kinegram 5000 vertical.	FV	FV	50.00
	b. Kinegram 5000 horizontal.	FV	FV	50.00
	s. Specimen overprint: *SPECIMEN* and *VZOREC*.	—	—	25.00

2000 Issue

22	1000 Tolarjev	VG	VF	UNC
	15.1.2000. Black, green and yellow. Similar to #18.			
	a. Issued note.	FV	FV	10.00
	s. Specimen overprint: *SPECIMEN* and *VZOREC*.	—	—	—

23	5000 Tolarjev	VG	VF	UNC
	15.1.2000. Black, green, red and orange. Similar to # 21a.			
	a. Issued note.	FV	FV	45.00
	s. Specimen overprint: *SPECIMEN* and *VZOREC*.	—	—	—

24	10,000 Tolarjev	VG	VF	UNC
	15.1.2000. Brown-black, purple and red. Similar to #20 but with holographic band at right. edge.			
	a. Issued note.	FV	FV	80.00
	s. Specimen overprint: *SPECIMEN* and *VZOREC*.	—	—	—

2000 Commemorative Issue

#25-27, 10th Anniversary of Bank Slovenije

		VG	VF	UNC
25	**100 Tolarjev** 2001. Like #14 but with special text overprint (10,000 pieces).	FV	FV	3.00
26	**1000 Tolarjev** 2001. Like #22 but with special text overprint (5,000 pieces)	FV	FV	10.00

27	10,000 Tolarjev	VG	VF	UNC
	2001. Like #24 but with special text overprint (1,000 pieces).	FV	FV	80.00

2004 Commemorative Issue

#28-30 EU entry on May 1, 2004.

		VG	VF	UNC
28	**100 Tolarjev** 2003. Multicolor. Like #14 but with special overprint (10,000 pieces).	FV	FV	7.50

		VG	VF	UNC
29	**1000 Tolarjev** 2003. Multicolor. Like #22 but with special overprint (5,000 pieces).	FV	FV	25.00

		VG	VF	UNC
30	**10,000 Tolarjev** 2003. Multicolor. Like #24 but with special overprint (1,000 pieces).	FV	FV	125.

2003 Issue

		VG	VF	UNC
31	**100 Tolarjev** 15.1.2003. Black and blue on multicolor underprint.			
	a. Issued note.	FV	FV	2.75
	s. Specimen overprint: *SPECIMEN* and *VZOREC.*	—	—	—

NOTICE

Readers with unlisted dates, signature varieties, etc. are invited to submit photocopies of their notes to: Standard Catalog of World Paper Money, 700 East State St. Iola, WI 54990-0001, E-Mail: george.cuhaj@fwpubs.com.

		VG	VF	UNC
32	**1000 Tolarjev** 15.1.2003; 15.1.2004; 15.1.2005. Black and green on multicolor underprint.			
	a. Issued note.	FV	FV	10.00
	s. Specimen overprint: *SPECIMEN* and *VZOREC.*	—	—	—

		VG	VF	UNC
33	**5000 Tolarjev** 15.1.2002. Black, green, red and orange. Similar to #23.			
	a. Issued note.	FV	FV	45.00
	s. Specimen.	—	—	—

		VG	VF	UNC
34	**10,000 Tolarjev** 15.1.2003; 15.1.2004. Black and purple on multicolor underprint. Iridescent ink added onto chrysanthemum on back.			
	a. Issued note.	FV	FV	80.00
	s. Specimen overprint: *SPECIMEN* and *VZOREC.*	—	—	—

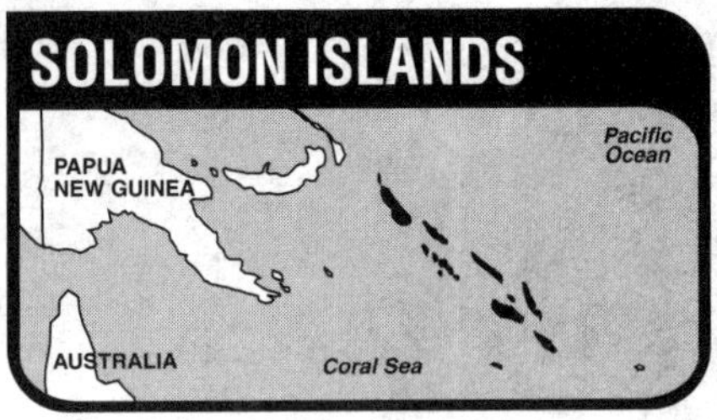

The Solomon Islands, located in the Southwest Pacific east of Papua New Guinea, has an area of 10,983 sq. mi. (28,450 sq. km.) and an estimated population of 444,000. Capital: Honiara. The most important islands of the Solomon chain are Guadalcanal (scene of some of the fiercest fighting of World War II), Malaitia, New Georgia, Florida, Vella Lavella, Choiseul, Rendova, San Cristobal, the Lord Howe group, the Santa Cruz islands, and the Duff group. Copra is the only important cash crop but it is hoped that timber will become an economic factor.

The Solomon Islands were discovered by Spanish navigator Alvaro de Mendana in 1567, and in 1569 he made an unsuccessful attempt to colonize them. European knowledge of the group would not be completed until the end of the 18th century. Germany declared a protectorate over the northern Solomons in 1885. The British protectorate over the southern Solomons was established in 1893. In 1899 Germany transferred its claim to all Solomon Islands except Buka and Bougainville to Great Britain in exchange for recognition of German claims in western Samoa. Australia occupied the two German held islands in 1914, and administered them after 1920.

The Japanese invaded the Solomons during 1942-43, but were driven out by an American counteroffensive after a series of bloody clashes.

Following World War II the Islands returned to the status of a British protectorate. In 1976 the protectorate was abolished and the Solomons became a self-governing dependency. Full independence was achieved on July 7, 1978. Solomon Islands is a member of the Commonwealth of Nations. Elizabeth II is Head of State as Queen of the Solomon Islands.

RULERS:

British

MONETARY SYSTEM:

1 Shilling = 12 Pence
1 Pound = 20 Shillings to 1966
1 Dollar = 100 Cents, 1966-

SIGNATURE VARIETIES

	CHAIRMAN	MEMBER		GOVERNOR	DIRECTOR
1			4		
2			5		
3			6		
	GOVERNOR	SEC. OF FINANCE		GOVERNOR	SEC. OF FINANCE
7		George Kiriau	8	Rick N. Houenipwela	

BRITISH ADMINISTRATION

SOLOMON ISLANDS MONETARY AUTHORITY

1977; 1981 ND ISSUE

Dollar System

#5-8 Qn. Elizabeth II at r. Wmk: Falcon. Printer: TDLR (w/o imprint). Replacement notes: Serial # prefix: *Z/1*.

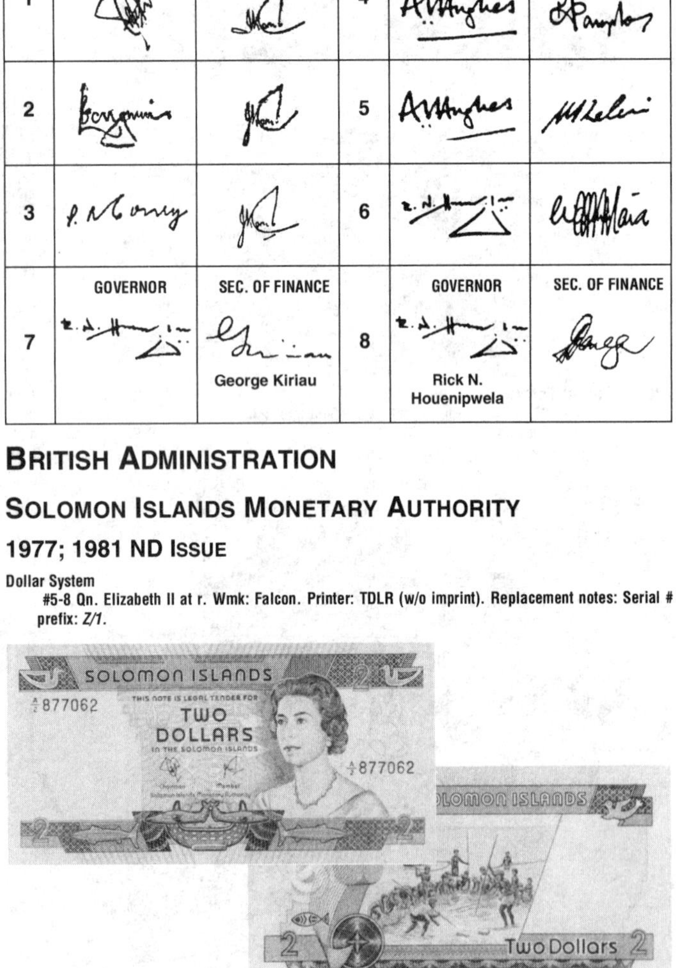

		VG	VF	UNC
5	**2 Dollars** ND (1977). Dark green on pink and pale green underprint. Fishermen on back. Signature 1.			
	a. Issued note.	1.00	2.00	10.00
	s. Specimen.	—	—	30.00

		VG	VF	UNC
6	**5 Dollars** ND (1977). Dark blue on multicolor underprint. Long boats and hut on back.			
	a. Signature 1.	2.25	5.00	25.00
	b. Signature 2.	2.25	6.00	30.00
	s. As a. Specimen.	—	—	30.00

		VG	VF	UNC
7	**10 Dollars** ND (1977). Purple and violet on multicolor underprint. Weaver on back.			
	a. Signature 1.	4.00	7.50	32.50
	b. Signature 2.	4.00	8.00	37.50
	s. As a. Specimen.	—	—	30.00

		VG	VF	UNC
8	**20 Dollars** ND (1981). Brown and deep orange on multicolor underprint. Line of people on back. Signature 3.	7.00	20.00	60.00

CENTRAL BANK OF SOLOMON ISLANDS

1984 ND ISSUE

#11 and 12 like #7 and 8 except for new bank name. Wmk: Falcon. Sign. 4. Replacement notes: Serial # prefix *Z/1*.

		VG	VF	UNC
11	**10 Dollars** ND (1984). Purple and violet on multicolor underprint.	FV	7.50	25.00

		VG	VF	UNC
12	**20 Dollars** ND (1984). Brown and dark orange on multicolor underprint.	FV	15.00	50.00

1986 ND Issue

#13-17 arms at r. Wmk: Falcon. Sign. 5. Replacement notes: Replacement notes: Serial # prefix *Y/1*.

#13-16 backs like #5-8.

		VG	VF	UNC
13	**2 Dollars** ND (1986). Green on multicolor underprint.			
	a. Issued note.	FV	FV	2.25
	s. Specimen.	—	—	25.00

		VG	VF	UNC
14	**5 Dollars** ND (1986). Dark blue, deep purple and violet on multicolor underprint.			
	a. Issued note.			
	s. Specimen.			

		VG	VF	UNC
15	**10 Dollars** ND (1986). Purple and violet on multicolor underprint.			
	a. Issued note.	FV	FV	10.00
	s. Specimen.	—	—	10.00

		VG	VF	UNC
16	**20 Dollars** ND (1986). Brown and deep orange on multicolor underprint.			
	a. Issued note.	FV	FV	20.00
	s. Specimen.	—	—	25.00

		VG	VF	UNC
17	**50 Dollars** ND (1986). Blue-green and purple on multicolor underprint. Butterflies and reptiles on back.			
	a. Issued note.	FV	FV	45.00
	s. Specimen.	—	—	30.00

1996; 1997 ND Issue

#18-22 similar to #13-17 but w/added security devices. Printing in wmk. area on back. Ascending size serial #. W/security thread. Wmk: Falcon. Replacement notes: Serial # prefix *X/1*.

		VG	VF	UNC
18	**2 Dollars** ND (1997). Greenish black and olive-green on multicolor underprint.	FV	FV	2.00

NOTICE

Readers with unlisted dates, signature varieties, etc. are invited to submit photocopies of their notes to: Standard Catalog of World Paper Money, 700 East State St. Iola, WI 54990-0001, E-Mail: george.cuhaj@fwpubs.com.

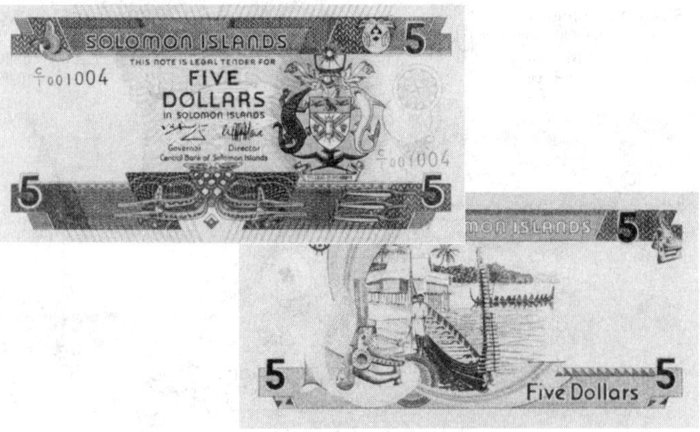

		VG	VF	UNC
19	**5 Dollars** ND (1997). Dark blue, deep purple and violet on multicolor underprint.	FV	FV	4.00

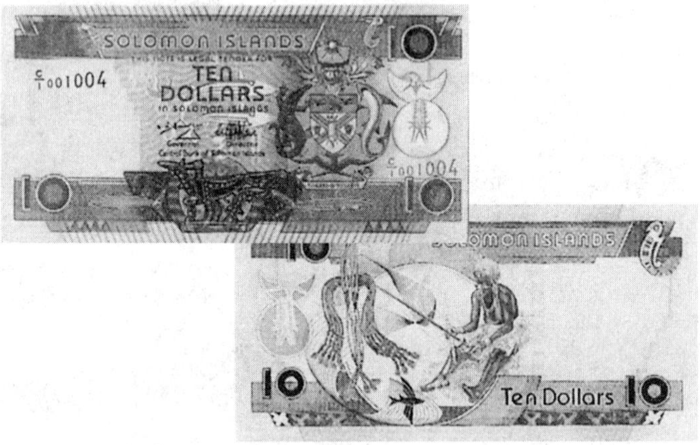

		VG	VF	UNC
20	**10 Dollars** ND (1996). Purple and red-violet on multicolor underprint.	FV	FV	7.00

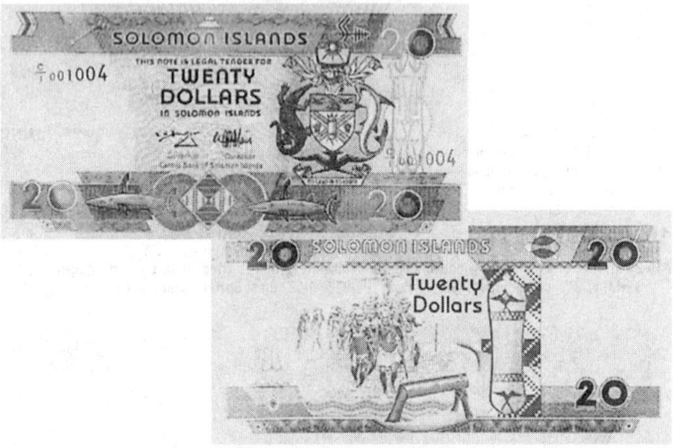

		VG	VF	UNC
21	**20 Dollars** ND (1996). Brown and brown-orange on multicolor underprint.	FV	FV	12.50

		VG	VF	UNC
22	**50 Dollars** ND (1996). Green, Blue-gray and purple on multicolor underprint.	FV	FV	30.00

2001 Commemorative Issue

#23, 25th Anniversary Central Bank of Solomon Islands

		VG	VF	UNC
23	**2 Dollars** (20)01. Dark and light green on multicolor underprint. Similar to #18 but with ornate window design. Silver imprint *CBSI Silver Jubilee* on face, and *COMMEMORATING CBSI SILVER JUBILEE* on back. Polymer plastic.	FV	FV	2.50

2001 ND Issue

		VG	VF	UNC
24	**50 Dollars** ND (2001). Green, blue-gray and purple on multicolor underprint. Similar to #22 but flag added at left center, segmented silver security strip at center right, and vertical serial # at right. Smaller size in width.	FV	FV	30.00

Collector Series

Solomon Islands Monetary Authority

1979 ND Issue

		Issue Price	Mkt. Value
CS1	**ND (1979) 2-10 Dollars** #5, 6b, 7b with overprint: *SPECIMEN* and serial # prefix Maltese cross.	—	25.00

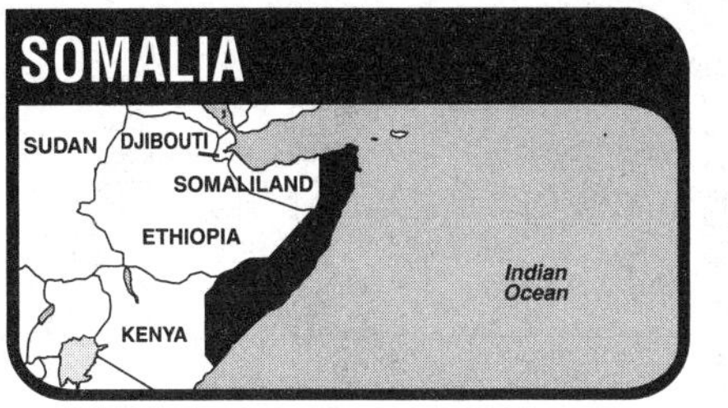

Somalia, the Somali Democratic Republic, comprising the former Italian Somaliland, is located on the coast of the eastern projection of the African continent commonly referred to as the *Horn*. It has an area of 178,201 sq. ml. (461,657 sq. km.) and a population of 11.53 million. Capitol Mogadishu. The economy is pastoral and agricultural. Livestock, bananas and hides are exported. The area of the British Somaliland Protectorate was known to the Egyptians at least 1,500 years B.C., and was occupied by the Arabs and Portuguese before British sea captains obtained trading and anchorage rights in 1827. The land of sandy clay and sporadic rainfall acquired a strategic importance with the opening of the Suez Canal in 1869. After negotiating treaties with the tribes, Britain declared the area a protectorate in 1888. Italy acquired Italian Somaliland in 1895 by purchase from the sultan of Zanzibar. Britain occupied Italian Somaliland in 1941 and administered it until April 1, 1950, when it was returned to Italy as a U.N. trusteeship. The British Somaliland protectorate became independent on June 26, 1960. Five days later it joined with Italian Somaliland to form the Somali Republic. The country was under a revolutionary military regime installed Oct. 21, 1969. After 11 years of civil war rebel forces fought their way into the capital. A. M. Muhammad became president in Aug. 1991 but interfactional fighting continued. A UN-sponsored truce was signed in March 1992 and a peace plan and pact was signed Jan. 15, 1993. The northern Somali National Movements (SNM) declared a secession of the northwestern Somaliland Republic on May 17, 1991 which is not recognized by the Somali Democratic Republic.

MONETARY SYSTEM:

1 Scellino = 1 Shilling = 100 Centesimi
1 Shilin = 1 Shilling = 100 Centi

REPUBLIC

BANCA NAZIONALE SOMALA

1962 ISSUE

#1-4 sign. title: *IL PRESIDENTE* at l. Wmk: Leopard's head. Printer OCV.

		VG	VF	UNC
1	**5 Scellini = 5 Shillings** 1962. Red on green and orange underprint. Antelope at left. Back orange-brown; dhow at center.			
	a. Issued note.	15.00	35.00	200.
	s. Specimen.	—	—	110.

		VG	VF	UNC
2	**10 Scellini = 10 Shillings** 1962. Green on red-brown and green underprint. Flower at left. Back brown and green; river scene at center right.			
	a. Issued note.	20.00	55.00	325.
	s. Specimen.	—	—	185.

		VG	VF	UNC
3	**20 Scellini = 20 Shillings** 1962. Brown on blue and gold underprint. Banana plant at left. Back brown and blue; bank building at center right.			
	a. Issued note.	25.00	75.00	600.
	s. Specimen.	—	—	750.

		VG	VF	UNC
4	**100 Scellini = 100 Shillings** 1962. Blue on green and orange underprint. Artcraft at left. Back blue and red; building.			
	a. Issued note.	35.00	125.	750.
	s. Specimen.	—	—	400.

1966 ISSUE

#5-8 slight changes in colors and design elements (w/o imprint). Wmk: Leopard's head.

		VG	VF	UNC
5	**5 Scellini = 5 Shillings** 1966. Similar to #1 but different guilloche in underprint. Back with blue underprint.			
	a. Issued note.	10.00	30.00	175.
	s. Specimen perforated: *ANNULLATO.*	—	—	100.
6	**10 Scellini = 10 Shillings** 1966. Similar to #2 but different guilloche in underprint. Back green with light tan underprint.			
	a. Issued note.	15.00	50.00	325.
	s. Specimen perforated: *ANNULLATO.*	—	—	225.
7	**20 Scellini = 20 Shillings** 1966. Similar to #3 but underprint is pink, blue and green. Brown bank building on back.			
	a. Issued note.	26.00	66.00	160.
	s. Specimen perforated: *ANNULLATO.*	—	—	325.
8	**100 Scellini = 100 Shillings** 1966. Similar to #4 but underprint is green, purple and tan.			
	a. Issued note.	35.00	120.	600.
	s. Specimen perforated: *ANNULLATO.*	—	—	435.

1968 ISSUE

#9-12 Wmk: Leopard's head. Sign. title *IL GOVERNATORE* at l.

		VG	VF	UNC
9	**5 Scellini = 5 Shillings** 1968. Red on green and orange underprint. Like #5.	15.00	40.00	250.
10	**10 Scellini = 10 Shillings** 1968. Green on red-brown and green underprint. Like #6.	20.00	55.00	450.
11	**20 Scellini = 20 Shillings** 1968. Brown on blue and gold underprint. Like #7.	25.00	85.00	575.
12	**100 Scellini = 100 Shillings** 1968. Blue on green and orange underprint. Like #8.	37.50	125.	850.

DEMOCRATIC REPUBLIC

BANCA NAZIONALE SOMALA

1971 ISSUE

#13-16 like #9-12. Wmk: Leopard's head. Sign. title: *IL GOVERNATORE* and *IL CASSIERE* at r.

		VG	VF	UNC
13	**5 Scellini = 5 Shillings** 1971. Purple-brown on blue, green and gold underprint. Like #9.			
	a. Issued note.	8.00	25.00	200.
	s. Specimen.	—	—	110.

		VG	VF	UNC
14	**10 Scellini = 10 Shillings** 1971. Green on red-brown and green underprint. Like #10.			
	a. Issued note.	10.00	30.00	325.
	s. Specimen.	—	—	175.

		VG	VF	UNC
15	**20 Scellini = 20 Shillings** 1971. Brown on blue and gold underprint. Like #11.			
	a. Issued note.	15.00	70.00	500.
	s. Specimen.	—	—	275.

		VG	VF	UNC
16	**100 Scellini = 100 Shillings** 1971. Blue on green and orange underprint. Like #12.			
	a. Issued note.	20.00	85.00	650.
	s. Specimen.	—	—	375.

BANKIGA QARANKA SOOMAALIYEED

SOMALI NATIONAL BANK

LAW OF 11.12.1974

#17-20 arms at l. Wmk: Sayyid Mohammed Aabdullah Hassan.

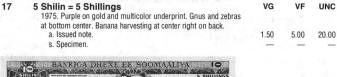

		VG	VF	UNC
17	**5 Shilin = 5 Shillings** 1975. Purple on gold and multicolor underprint. Gnus and zebras at bottom center. Banana harvesting at center right on back.			
	a. Issued note.	1.50	5.00	20.00
	s. Specimen.	—	—	—

		VG	VF	UNC
18	**10 Shilin = 10 Shillings** 1975. Dark green on pink and multicolor underprint. Minaret at left center. Shipbuilders at work at center right on back.	2.00	7.50	37.50

19	20 Shilin = 20 Shillings	VG	VF	UNC
	1975. Brown on multicolor underprint. Bank building at center. Cattle on back.	3.00	10.00	100.

20	100 Shilin = 100 Shillings	VG	VF	UNC
	1975. Blue on gold and multicolor underprint. Woman with baby, rifle and farm tools at left center. Dagathur Monument at center right. Workers in factory on back.	7.00	20.00	125.

BANKIGA DHEXE EE SOOMAALIYA

CENTRAL BANK OF SOMALIA

LAW OF 6.12.1977

#20A-24 arms at l. Black series and serial #. Wmk: Sayyid Mohammed Abdullah Hassan.

20A	5 Shilin = 5 Shillings	VG	VF	UNC
	1978. Purple on gold and multicolor underprint. Like #17.			
	a. Issued note.	4.00	12.50	45.00
	s. Specimen.	—	—	25.00

21	5 Shilin = 5 Shillings	VG	VF	UNC
	1978. Purple on gold and multicolor underprint. Similar to #20A but Cape Buffalo herd at bottom left center.	.50	2.00	12.50
22	**10 Shilin = 10 Shillings**			
	1978. Dark green on pink and multicolor underprint. Like #18.			
	a. Issued note.	1.00	4.00	25.00
	s. Specimen.	—	—	25.00

23	20 Shilin = 20 Shillings	VG	VF	UNC
	1978. Brown on multicolor underprint. Like #19.			
	a. Issued note.	2.00	7.50	40.00
	s. Specimen.	—	—	40.00

24	100 Shilin = 100 Shillings	VG	VF	UNC
	1978. Blue on gold and multicolor underprint. Like #20.			
	a. Issued note.	3.00	10.00	70.00
	s. Specimen.	—	—	25.00

LAW OF 5.4.1980

#26-28 arms at l. Red series and serial #. Different sign. title at l. Wmk: Sayyid Mohammed Abdullah Hassan. Replacement ntoes: Serial # prefix *Z001*.

#25 *Deleted*.

		VG	VF	UNC
26	**10 Shilin = 10 Shillings** 1980. Dark green on pink and multicolor underprint. Like #22.	.50	2.50	10.00

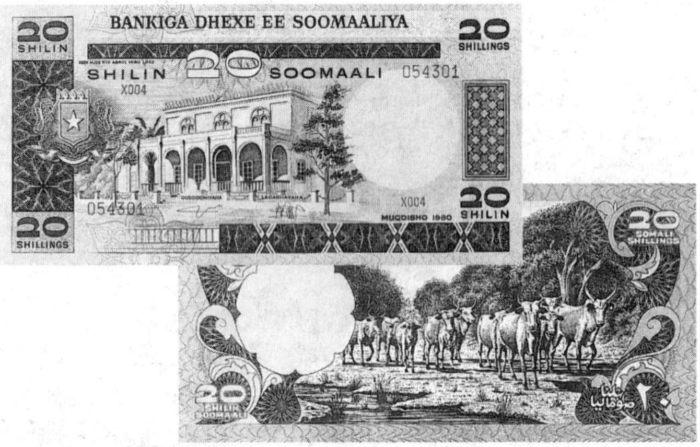

		VG	VF	UNC
27	**20 Shilin = 20 Shillings** 1980. Brown on multicolor underprint. Like #23.	1.00	5.00	27.50

		VG	VF	UNC
28	**100 Shilin = 100 Shillings** 1980. Blue on gold and multicolor underprint. Like #24.	2.00	7.50	30.00

LAW OF 9.12.1981

#29-30 wmk: Sayyid Mohammed Abdullah Hassan. Replacement notes: Serial # prefix *ZZ001*.

		VG	VF	UNC
29	**20 Shilin = 20 Shillings** 1981. Brown on multicolor underprint. Like #27.	2.00	10.00	37.50

		VG	VF	UNC
30	**100 Shilin = 100 Shillings** 1981. Blue on gold and multicolor underprint. Like #28.	2.00	7.50	30.00

LAW OF 30.12.1982; 1983 ISSUE

#31-35 arms at top l. ctr., star at or near lower ctr. Reduced size notes. Replacement notes: Serial # prefix *Z001*.

		VG	VF	UNC
31	**5 Shilin = 5 Shillings** 1983-87. Brown-violet. Cape Buffalo herd at left center. Harvesting bananas on back.			
	a. 1983.	.10	.50	2.50
	b. 1986..	.10	.40	2.00
	c. 1987.	.10	.25	1.00

#32-35 wmk: S. M. A. Hassan.

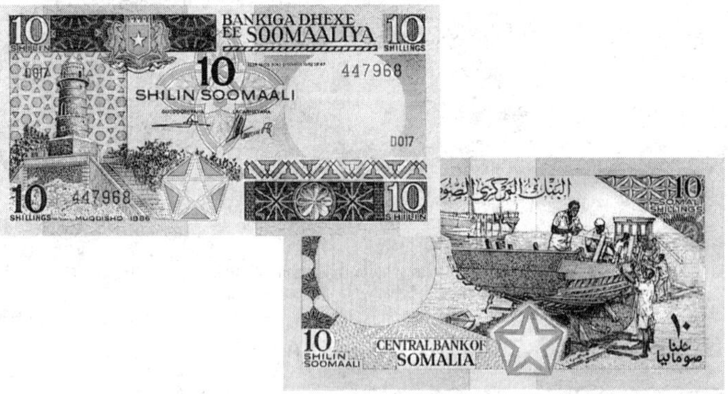

		VG	VF	UNC
32	**10 Shilin = 10 Shillings** 1983-87. Green and multicolor. Lighthouse at left. Shipbuilders at center right on back.			
	a. 1983.	.25	.75	3.00
	b. 1986.	.20	.50	2.00
	c. 1987.	.15	.50	1.75
33	**20 Shilin = 20 Shillings** 1983-89. Brown and multicolor. Bank at left. Back similar to #19.			
	a. 1983.	.25	1.50	5.00
	b. 1986.	.25	1.00	4.00
	c. 1987.	.20	.75	3.00
	d. 1989.	.15	.50	2.00

34 **50 Shilin = 50 Shillings**
1983-89. Red-brown and multicolor underprint. Walled city at left and center. Watering animals at center right on back.

34	50 Shilin = 50 Shillings	VG	VF	UNC
	a. 1983.	.50	1.50	6.00
	b. 1986; 1987. 2 signature varieties for 1987.	.15	.40	4.00
	c. 1988.	.15	.50	2.50
	d. 1989.	.10	.40	2.00

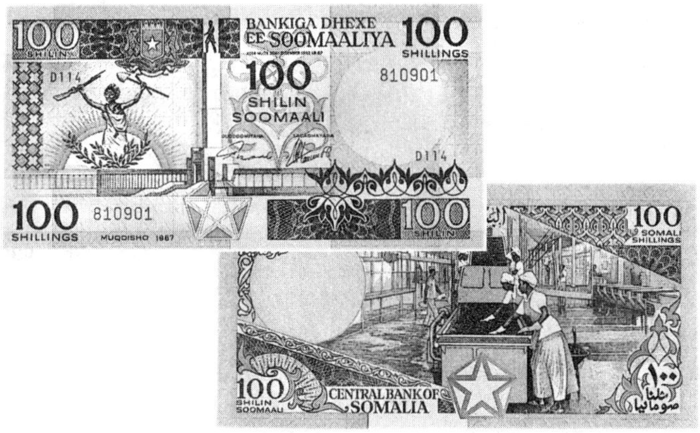

35	100 Shilin = 100 Shillings	VG	VF	UNC
	1983-89. Blue-black, dark blue and dark green on multicolor underprint. Similar to #20.			
	a. 1983.	.50	2.50	7.50
	b. 1986; 1987. Two signature varieties for 1987.	.30	1.00	4.00
	c. 1988.	.15	.50	2.50
	d. 1989.	.15	.40	2.00

LAW OF 1.1.1989

#36 and 37 arms at top l. ctr. Wmk: Sayyid Mohammed Abdullah Hassan.

36	500 Shilin = 500 Shillings	VG	VF	UNC
	1989; 1990; 1996. Green and aqua on multicolor underprint. Fishermen mending net at left center. Mosque at left center on back. Two signature varieties.			
	a. 1989.	FV	FV	6.00
	b. 1990.	FV	FV	5.50
	c. 1996.	FV	FV	5.00

LAW OF 1.1.1990; 1990 ISSUE

37	1000 Shilin = 1000 Shillings	VG	VF	UNC
	1990; 1996. Violet and orange on multicolor underprint. Women seated weaving baskets at left center; arms above. City view at bottom, Port of Mogadishu at upper center right on back.			
	a. 1990.	FV	FV	2.50
	b. 1996.	FV	FV	3.50

REGIONAL

MOGADISHU NORTH FORCES

1991 ISSUE

#R1 and R2 arms at top l. ctr. Wmk: Sayyid Mohammed Abdullah Hassan.

R1	20 N Shilin = 20 N Shillings	VG	VF	UNC
	1991. Purple, red-brown, brown-orange and olive-green on multicolor underprint. Trader leading camel in underprint at left center. Picking cotton at center right on back.	.50	1.50	7.00

R2	50 N Shilin = 50 N Shillings	VG	VF	UNC
	1991. Brown, green and black on multicolor underprint. Man working loom. Young person leading a donkey with three children on back.	1.75	5.00	15.00

PUNTLAND REGION

2000 (1999) ISSUE

R10	1000 Shilin = 1000 Shillings	VG	VF	UNC
	1990 (2000). Purple and orange on multicolor underprint. Lithographed copy of #37a.	.50	1.00	5.00

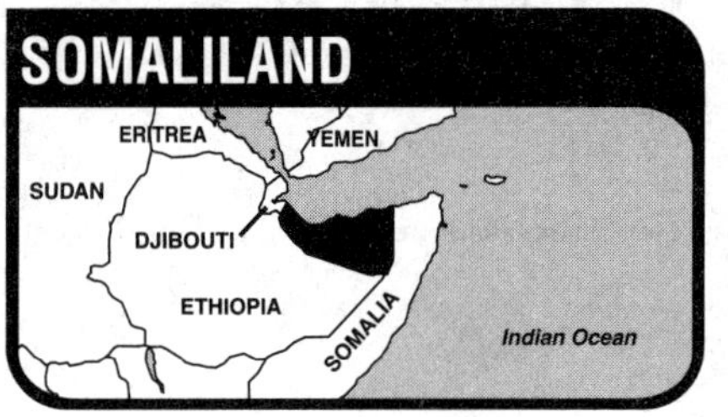

The Somaliland Republic, comprising the former British Somaliland Protectorate, is located on the coast of the northeastern projection of the African continent commonly referred to as the "Horn" on the southwestern end of the Gulf of Aden.

Bordered by Eritrea to the west, Ethiopia to west and south and Somalia to the east, it has an area of 68,000* sq. mi. (176,000* sq. km). Capital: Hargeysa. It is mostly arid and mounainous except for the gulf shoreline.

The Protectorate of British Somaliland was established in 1888 and from 1905 the territory was administered by a commissioner under the British Colonial Office. Italian Somaliland was administered as a colony from 1893 to 1941, when the territory was occupied by British forces. In 1950 the United Nations allowed Italy to resume control of Italian Somaliland under a trusteeship. In 1960 British and Italian Somaliland were united as Somalia, an independent republic outside the Commonwealth.

Civil War erupted in the late 1970's and continued until the capital of Somalia was taken in 1990. The United Nations provided aid and peacekeepers. A UN sponsored truce was signed in March 1992 and a peace plan and pact was signed Jan. 15, 1993. The northern Somali National Movement (SMN) declared a secession of the Somaliland Republic on May 17, 1991 which is not recognized by the Somali Democratic Republic.

The currency issued by the East African Currency Board was used in British Somaliland from 1945 to 1961. Somali currency was then used until 1995.

MONETARY SYSTEM:

1 Somaliland Shilling = 1 Shilin

SIGNATURE VARIETIES					
	Guddoomiyaha	Lacaghayaha		Lacaghayaha	Guddoomiyaha
1			4		

REPUBLIC

BAANKA SOMALILAND

1994 ISSUE

#1-4 bldg. at ctr. Greater Kudu at r. Traders w/camels on back.

1	5 Shillings = 5 Shilin	VG	VF	UNC
	1994. Bright green, olive-green and red-brown on multicolor underprint.			
	a. Issued note.	FV	FV	1.00
	s. Specimen.	—	—	100.

2	10 Shillings = 10 Shilin	VG	VF	UNC
	1994-96. Violet, purple and red-brown on multicolor underprint.			
	a. 1994.	FV	FV	1.25
	b. 1996.	FV	FV	1.00
	s. Specimen.	—	—	100.

3	20 Shillings = 20 Shilin	VG	VF	UNC
	1994-96. Brown and red-brown on multicolor underprint.			
	a. 1994.	FV	FV	2.25
	b. 1996.	FV	FV	2.00
	s. Specimen.	—	—	110.

4	50 Shillings = 50 Shilin	VG	VF	UNC
	1994-96. Blue-violet, blue-gray and red-brown on multicolor underprint.			
	a. 1994.	FV	FV	4.00
	b. 1996.	FV	FV	3.50
	s. Specimen.	—	—	110.

#5 and 6 bldg. at ctr. Ship dockside in background, herdsmen w/sheep at front ctr. on back.

5	100 Shillings = 100 Shilin	VG	VF	UNC
	1994-99. Brownish black and red-violet on multicolor underprint.			
	a. 1994.	FV	FV	6.50
	b. 1996.	FV	FV	5.00
	c. Signature 3. 1999.	FV	FV	5.00
	s. Specimen.	—	—	110.

6	500 Shillings = 500 Shilin	VG	VF	UNC
	1994-96. Purple, blue-black and blue-green on multicolor underprint.			
	a. 1994.	FV	FV	15.00
	b. 1996.	FV	FV	10.00
	s. Specimen.	—	—	125.

1996 ISSUE

7	50 Shillings = 50 Shilin	VG	VF	UNC
	1996, 1999. Blue-violet, blue-gray and violet on multicolor underprint. Like #4 but increased size. 130 x 58mm.			
	a. Signature 1.	FV	FV	2.50
	b. Signature 2.	FV	FV	2.25
	c. Signature 3. 1999.	FV	FV	2.25
	s. Specimen.	—	—	125.

1996 "BRONZE" COMMEMORATIVE ISSUE

#8-13, 5th Anniversary of Independence

#8-13 bronze ovpt. on face: ***5th Anniversary of Independence 18 May 1996 - Sanad Gurada 5ee Gobanimadda 18 May 1996***

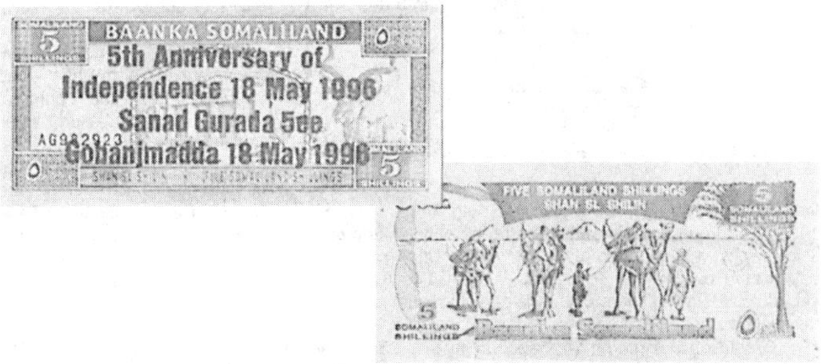

8	**5 Shillings = 5 Shilin** 18.5.1996 (- old date 1994). Overprint on #1.	VG FV	VF FV	UNC 1.75

9	**10 Shillings = 10 Shilin** 18.5.1996 (- old date 1994). Overprint on #2a.	VG FV	VF FV	UNC 2.00

10	**20 Shillings = 20 Shilin** 18.5.1996 (- old date 1994). Overprint on #3a.	VG FV	VF FV	UNC 3.00

11	**50 Shillings = 50 Shilin** 18.5.1996.	VG	VF	UNC
	a. overprint on #4a. (- old date 1994)	FV	FV	4.25
	b. overprint on #4b. 1996.	FV	FV	0.00

11A	**50 Shillings = 50 Shilin** 18.5.1996. Blue-violet, blue-gray and violet on multicolor underprint. Bronze overprint on #7a.	VG FV	VF FV	UNC 3.50

12	**100 Shillings = 100 Shilin** 18.5.1996 (- old date 1994). Overprint on #5a.	VG FV	VF FV	UNC 7.50

13	**500 Shillings = 500 Shilin** 18.5.1996 (- old date 1994). Overprint on #6a.	VG FV	VF FV	UNC 25.00

1996 "SILVER" COMMEMORATIVE ISSUE

#14-19, 5th Anniversary of Independence

#14-19 silver ovpt. on face: ***Sanad Gurada 5ee Gobanimadda 18 May 1996***

14	**5 Shillings = 5 Shilin** 18.5.1996 (- old date 1994). Overprint on #1.	VG FV	VF FV	UNC 1.75

15	**10 Shillings = 10 Shilin** 18.5.1996 (- old date 1994). Overprint on #2a.	VG FV	VF FV	UNC 2.00

16	**20 Shillings = 20 Shilin** 18.5.1996 (- old date 1994). Overprint on #3a.	VG FV	VF FV	UNC 3.00

		VG	VF	UNC
17	**50 Shillings = 50 Shilin** 18.5.1996.			
	a. overprint on #4a. (- old date 1994).	FV	FV	4.25
	b. overprint on #4b. 1996.	FV	FV	3.00

		VG	VF	UNC
17A	**50 Shillings = 50 Shilin** 1996. Blue-violet, blue-gray and violet on multicolor underprint. Overprint on #7b.	FV	FV	3.50

		VG	VF	UNC
18	**100 Shillings = 100 Shilin** 18.5.1996 (- old date 1994). Overprint on #5a.	FV	FV	7.50

		VG	VF	UNC
19	**500 Shillings = 500 Shilin** 18.5.1996 (- old date 1994). Overprint on #6a.	FV	FV	25.00

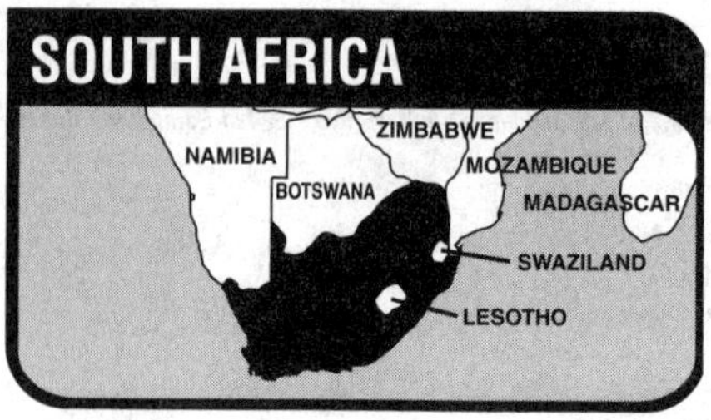

The Republic of South Africa, located at the southern tip of Africa, has an area, including the enclave of Walvis Bay, of 472,359 sq. mi. (1,221,040 sq. km.) and a population of 46.26 million. Capital: Administrative, Pretoria; Legislative, Cape Town; Judicial, Bloemfontein. Manufacturing, mining and agriculture are the principal industries. Exports include wool, diamonds, gold and metallic ores.

Portuguese navigator Bartholomeu Diaz became the first European to sight the region of South Africa when he rounded the Cape of Good Hope in 1488, but throughout the 16th century the only white men to come ashore were the survivors of ships wrecked while attempting the stormy Cape passage. The first permanent settlement was established by Jan van Riebeeck of the Dutch East India Company in 1652. In subsequent decades additional Dutch, Germans and Huguenot refugees from France settled in the Cape area to form the Afrikaner segment of today's population.

Great Britain captured the Cape colony in 1795, and again in 1806, receiving permanent title in 1814. To escape British political rule and cultural dominance, many Afrikaner farmers (Boers) migrated northward (the Great Trek) beginning in 1836, and established the independent Boer republics of the Transvaal (the South African Republic, Zuid-Afrikaansche Republiek) in 1852, and the Orange Free State in 1854. British political intrigues against the two republics, coupled with the discovery of diamonds and gold in the Boer-settled regions, led to the bitter Boer Wars (1880-1881, 1899-1902) and the incorporation of the Boer republics into the British Empire.

On May 31, 1910, the two former Boer republics (Transvaal and Orange Free State) were joined with the British colonies of Cape of Good Hope and Natal to form the Union of South Africa, a dominion of the British Empire. In 1934 the Union achieved status as a sovereign state within the British Empire. Political integration of the various colonies did not still the conflict between the Afrikaners and the English-speaking groups, which continued to have a significant impact on political developments. A resurgence of Afrikaner nationalism in the 1940s and 1950s led to a referendum in the white community authorizing the relinquishment of dominion status and the establishment of a republic. The decision took effect on May 31, 1961. The Republic of South Africa withdrew from the British Commonwealth in Oct., 1961. The apartheid era ended on April 27, 1994 with the first democratic election for all people of South Africa. Nelson Mandela was inaugurated as president on May 10, 1994. South Africa was readmitted to the Commonwealth of Nations.

South African currency carries inscriptions in both Afrikaans and English.

RULERS:

British to 1961

MONETARY SYSTEM:

1 Rand = 100 Cents (= 10 Shillings), 1961-

SIGNATURE VARIETIES

3	 M. H. de Kock, 1.7.1945-30.6.1962	4	 G. Rissik, 1.7.1962-30.6.1967
5	 T. W. de Jongh, 1.7.196731.12.1980	6	 G. P. C. de Kock, 1.1.1981-7.8.1989
7	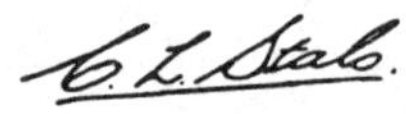 C. L. Stals, 8.8.1989-7.8.1999	8	 T. T. Mboweni, 8.8.1999-

REPUBLIC OF SOUTH AFRICA

SOUTH AFRICAN RESERVE BANK

1961 ND ISSUE

#102-108A portr. Jan van Riebeeck at l. and as wmk.

#102-105 replacement notes: Serial # prefix *Z/1; Y/1; X/1; W/1* respectively.

		VG	VF	UNC
102	**1 Rand** ND (1961-65). Rust brown on multicolor underprint. First line of bank name and value in English. 135 x 77mm.			
	a. Signature 3. (1961).	6.50	22.50	65.00
	b. Signature 4. (1962-65).	3.25	11.00	28.00
	s. As a. Specimen.	—	—	550.
103	**1 Rand** ND (1961-65). Rust brown on multicolor underprint. Like #102 but first line of bank name and value in Afrikaans. 137 x 78mm.			
	a. Signature 3. (1961).	6.50	22.50	65.00
	b. Signature 4. (1962-65).	3.25	11.00	27.50
104	**2 Rand** ND (1961-65). Blue on multicolor underprint. First line of bank name and value in English. 150 x 85mm.			
	a. Signature 3. (1961).	3.75	12.50	36.00
	b. Signature 4. (1962-65).	2.50	6.50	20.00

105	2 Rand	VG	VF	UNC
	ND (1961-65). Like #104 but first line of bank name and value in Afrikaans. 150 x 85mm.			
	a. Signature 3. (1961).	3.75	12.50	36.00
	b. Signature 4. (1962-65).	2.50	6.50	20.00
	s. As a. Specimen.	—	—	550.
106	**10 Rand**			
	ND (1961-65). Green and brown on multicolor underprint. First line of bank name and value in English. Sailing ship on back. 170 x 97mm.			
	a. Signature 3. (1961).	9.00	25.00	65.00
	b. Signature 4. (1962-65).	5.00	17.50	37.50

107	10 Rand	VG	VF	UNC
	ND (1961-65). Green and brown on multicolor underprint. Like #106 but first line of bank name and value in Afrikaans. 170 x 97mm.			
	a. Signature 3. (1961).	9.00	25.00	65.00
	b. Signature 4. (1962-65).	5.00	17.50	37.50
	s. Specimen.	—	—	550.

108	20 Rand	VG	VF	UNC
	ND (1961). Brown-violet. First line of bank name and value in English. Machinery on back. Signature 3.			
	a. Issued note.	16.00	50.00	160.
	s. Specimen.	—	—	550.

108A	20 Rand	VG	VF	UNC
	ND (1962-65). Like #108 but first line of bank name in Afrikaans. Signature 4.	15.00	50.00	160.

1966 ND Issue

#109-114 J. van Riebeeck at l. Replacement notes: Serial # prefix *Z/1; Y/1; X/1; W/1* respectively.

109	1 Rand	VG	VF	UNC
	ND (1066-72). Dark reddish brown on multicolor underprint. First lines of bank name and value in English. Rams in field on back. 126 x 64mm. Watermark: Springbok.			
	a. Signature 4. (1966).	1.00	2.50	13.50
	b. Signature 5. (1967).	.60	1.50	8.00
	s1. As a. Specimen.	—	—	35.00
	s2. As b. Specimen.	—	—	35.00

110	1 Rand	VG	VF	UNC
	ND (1966-72). Dark reddish brown on multicolor underprint. Like #109 but first lines of bank name and value in Afrikaans. 126 x 64mm. Watermark: Springbok.			
	a. Signature 4. (1966).	1.00	2.50	13.50
	b. Signature 5. (1967).	.60	1.50	8.00
	s1. As a. Specimen.	—	—	35.00
	s2. As b. Specimen.	—	—	35.00

111	5 Rand	VG	VF	UNC
	ND (1966-76). Purple on multicolor underprint. Covered wagons on trail at right corner. First lines of bank name and value in English. Factory with train on back. 133 x 70mm.			
	a. Signature 4. watermark: Springbok (1966).	4.00	15.00	90.00
	b. Signature 5. watermark: Springbok (1967-74).	2.00	6.00	17.50
	c. Signature 5. watermark: J. van Riebeeck (1975).	2.25	6.50	20.00
	s1. As a. Specimen.	—	—	35.00
	s2. As b. Specimen.	—	—	35.00

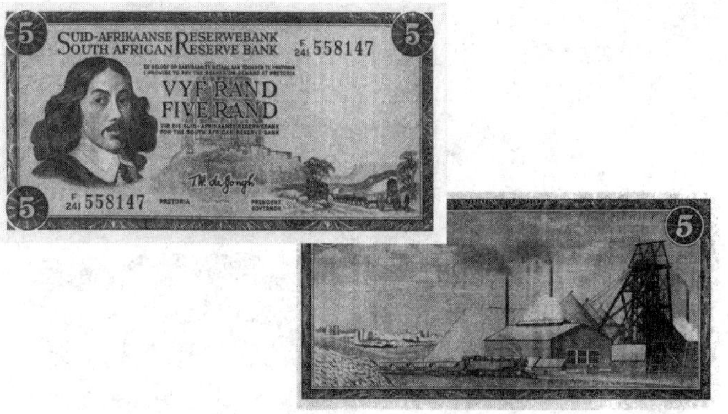

112	5 Rand	VG	VF	UNC
	ND (1966-76). Purple on multicolor underprint. Like #111 but first lines of bank name and value in Afrikaans.			
	a. Signature 4. watermark: Springbok (1966).	4.00	15.00	90.00
	b. Signature 5. watermark: Springbok (1967-74).	2.00	6.00	17.50
	c. Signature 5. watermark: J. van Riebeeck (1975).	2.25	6.50	20.00
	s1. As a. Specimen.	—	—	35.00
	s2. As b. Specimen.	—	—	

113	10 Rand	VG	VF	UNC
	ND (1966-76). Dark green and brown on multicolor underprint. Capital building at center. First lines of bank name and value in English. Old sailing ships on back. 140 x 76mm.			
	a. Signature 4. watermark: Springbok (1966).	2.50	10.00	35.00
	b. Signature 5. watermark: Springbok (1967-74).	2.00	5.00	16.50
	c. Signature 5. watermark: J. van Riebeeck (1975).	2.00	5.00	16.50
	s1. As a. Specimen.	—	—	50.00
	s2. As b. Specimen.	—	—	50.00

114	10 Rand	VG	VF	UNC
	ND (1966-76). Dark green and brown on multicolor underprint. Like #113 but first lines of bank name and value in Afrikaans. 140 x 76mm.			
	a. Signature 4. watermark: Springbok (1966).	2.50	10.00	35.00
	b. Signature 5. watermark: Springbok (1967-74).	2.00	5.00	16.50
	c. Signature 5. watermark: J. van Riebeeck (1975).	2.00	5.00	16.50
	s1. As a. Specimen.	—	—	50.00
	s2. As b. Specimen.	—	—	50.00

1973-84 ND ISSUE

#115-122 J. van Riebeeck at l.

115	1 Rand	VG	VF	UNC
	ND (1973-75). Dark reddish brown on multicolor underprint. Like #109 but 120 x 57mm. Signature 5.			
	a. Watermark: Springbok (1973).	.50	1.75	5.00
	b. Watermark: J. van Riebeeck (1975).	.75	2.00	6.00

116	1 Rand	VG	VF	UNC
	ND (1973-75). Dark reddish brown on multicolor underprint. Like #110 but 120 x 57mm. Signature 5.			
	a. Watermark: Springbok (1973).	.50	1.75	5.00
	b. Watermark: J. van Riebeeck (1975).	.65	2.00	6.00

117	2 Rand	VG	VF	UNC
	ND (1974-76). Blue on multicolor underprint. First lines of bank name and value in Afrikaans. Hydroelectric dam on back. 127 x 62mm. Signature 5.			
	a. Watermark: Springbok (1974).	.50	3.00	15.00
	b. Watermark: J. van Riebeeck (1976).	.50	4.50	16.00

#118-122 wmk: J. van Riebeek.

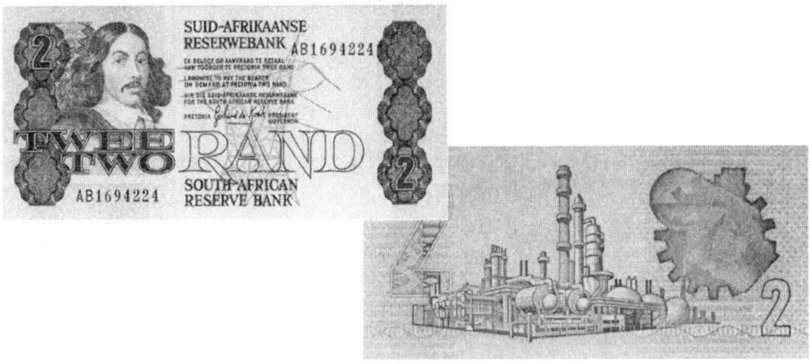

118	2 Rand	VG	VF	UNC
	ND (1978-90). Blue on multicolor underprint. Electrical tower at center. Refinery at left center on back. 120 x 57mm.			
	a. Signature 5. (1978-81).	.25	1.00	6.50
	b. Signature 6. Fractional numbering system. Without security thread (1981).	.50	3.00	20.00
	c. As b. With security thread. (1981-83).	.25	1.00	4.50
	d. As c. Alpha-numeric system. (1983-90).	.25	.50	3.50
	e. Signature 7. (1990).	.50	2.00	6.50

Note: #118b exists w/serial # w/sm. fractional letters and lg. numerals or larger letters w/sm. numerals.

119	5 Rand	VG	VF	UNC
	ND (1978-94). Purple on multicolor underprint. First lines of bank name and value in English. Diamond at center. Grain storage at left center on back. 127 x 63mm.			
	a. Signature 5. (1978-81).	1.00	2.50	13.50
	b. Signature 6. Fractional numbering system. Without security thread (1981).	12.50	40.00	165.
	c. As b. With security thread. (1981-89).	FV	1.50	14.00
	d. As c. Alpha-numeric system. (1989-90).	FV	2.50	12.00
	e. Signature 7. (1990-94).	FV	2.50	12.50

120	10 Rand	VG	VF	UNC
	ND (1978-93). Green on multicolor underprint. Flower at center. Bull and ram at left center on back. 134 x 70mm.			
	a. Signature 5. (1978-81).	1.50	4.50	17.00
	b. Signature 6. Fractional numbering system. Without security thread (1981).	2.50	12.50	55.00
	c. As b. With security thread. (1982-85).	FV	3.25	16.50
	d. As c. Alpha-numeric system. (1985-90).	FV	3.00	20.00
	e. Signature 7. (1990-93).	FV	2.00	12.50

121	20 Rand	VG	VF	UNC
	ND (1984-93). Brown on multicolor underprint. Building in underprint at center. Three sailing ships at left center with arms at right on back. 144 x 77mm.			
	a. Signature 5. (1978-81).	3.00	7.00	27.50
	b. Signature 6. Fractional numbering system. Without security thread (1981).	5.00	22.50	80.00
	c. As b. With security thread. (1982-85).	FV	5.00	25.00
	d. As c. Alpha-numeric system. (1985-90).	FV	10.00	50.00
	e. Signature 7. (1990-93).	FV	6.00	16.50

122	50 Rand	VG	VF	UNC
	ND (1984-90). Red on multicolor underprint. Lion in underprint at center. Local animals at lower left, mountains at center, plants at right on back. 147 x 83mm.			
	a. Signature 6. (1984).	7.50	15.00	40.00
	b. Signature 7. (1990).	10.00	22.50	50.00

1992-94 ISSUE

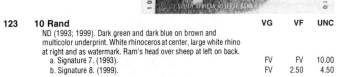

123	10 Rand	VG	VF	UNC
	ND (1993; 1999). Dark green and dark blue on brown and multicolor underprint. White rhinoceros at center, large white rhino at right and as watermark. Ram's head over sheep at left on back.			
	a. Signature 7. (1993).	FV	FV	10.00
	b. Signature 8. (1999).	FV	2.50	4.50

		VG	VF	UNC
124	**20 Rand** ND (1993; 1999). Deep brown and red-brown on multicolor underprint. Elephants at center, large elephant head at right and as watermark. Open pit mining at left center on back.			
	a. Signature 7 (1993).	FV	FV	10.00
	b. Signature 8 (1999).	FV	FV	7.50

		VG	VF	UNC
125	**50 Rand** ND (1992; 1999). Maroon, brown and deep blue-green on multicolor underprint. Lions with cub drinking water at center, male lion head at right and as watermark. Sasol oil refinery at lower left center on back.			
	a. Signature 7 (1992). Reddish lion drinking water (serial # prefix lower than AL).	FV	25.00	85.00
	b. Signature 7. (1992). Brownish blue lion drinking water. (serial # prefix greater than AL).	FV	FV	25.00
	c. Signature 8 (1999).	FV	FV	17.50
	x. Like a. Watermark on wrong side. Serial # prefix: *BP*.	FV	22.50	50.00

		VG	VF	UNC
126	**100 Rand** ND (1994; 1999). Blue-violet and dark gray on multicolor underprint. Cape buffalo at center and large water buffalo head at right and as watermark. Zebras along bottom from left to center on back.			
	a. Signature 7 (1994).	FV	FV	72.50
	b. Signature 8 (1999).	FV	FV	30.00

		VG	VF	UNC
127	**200 Rand** ND (1994; 1999). Orange on multicolor underprint. Leopard at center, large leopard's head at right. Dish antenna at upper left, modern bridge at lower left on back.			
	a. Signature 7 (1994).	FV	FV	85.00
	b. Signature 8 (1999).	FV	FV	60.00

2005 Issue

#128-132 silimar to #123-127 but with increased security features. Coat of arms at top left, various geometric shapes at lower portion of notes.

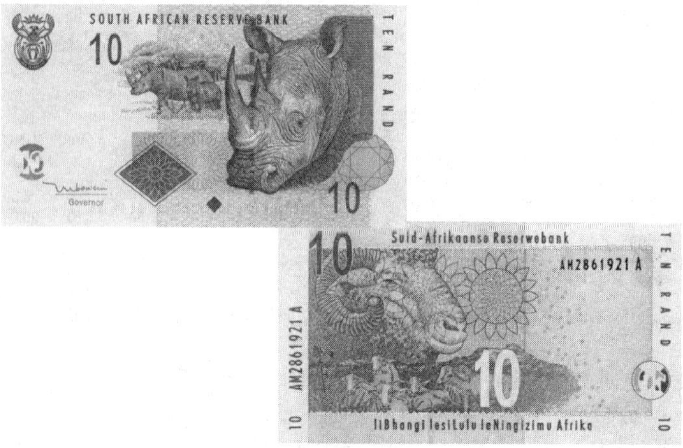

		VG	VF	UNC
128	**10 Rand** 2005. Green on multicolor underprint. Rhino head at right.	FV	FV	4.00

		VG	VF	UNC
129	**20 Rand** 2005. Brown on tan underprint. Elephant head at right.	FV	FV	7.00

		VG	VF	UNC
130	**50 Rand** 2005. Red on multicolor underprint. Lion head at right.	FV	FV	13.00

NOTICE

Readers with unlisted dates, signature varieties, etc. are invited to submit photocopies of their notes to: Standard Catalog of World Paper Money, 700 East State St. Iola, WI 54990-0001, E-Mail: george.cuhaj@fwpubs.com.

131	100 Rand	VG	VF	UNC
	2005. Blue on multicolor underprint. Buffalo head at right.	FV	FV	30.00

132	200 Rand	VG	VF	UNC
	2005. Brown on green and multicolor underprint. Leopard head at right.	FV	FV	60.00

The Spanish State, forming the greater part of the Iberian Peninsula of southwest Europe, has an area of 194,884 sq. mi. (504,750 sq. km.) and a population of 40.5 million including the Balearic and the Canary Islands. Capital: Madrid. The economy is d on agriculture, industry and tourism. Machinery, fruit, vegetables and chemicals are exported.

It is not known when man first came to the Iberian Peninsula - the Altamira caves off the Cantabrian coast approximately 50 miles west of Santander were fashioned in Paleolithic times. Spain was a battleground for centuries before it became a united nation, fought for by Phoenicians, Carthaginians, Greeks, Celts, Romans, Vandals, Visigoths and Moors. Ferdinand and Isabella destroyed the last Moorish stronghold in 1492, freeing the national energy and resources for the era of discovery and colonization that would make Spain the most powerful country in Europe during the 16th century. After the destruction of the Spanish Armada, 1588, Spain never again played a major role in European politics. Napoleonic France ruled Spain between 1808 and 1814. The monarchy was restored in 1814 and continued, interrupted by the short-lived republic of 1873-74, until the exile of Alfonso XIII in 1931, when the Second Republic was established. A bloody civil war ensued in 1936, and Francisco Franco established himself as ruler of fascist Spain after his forces, aided by the Italians and especially the Germans, defeated the Republican forces.

The monarchy was reconstituted in 1947 under the regency of General Francisco Franco, the king designate to be crowned after Franco's death. Franco died on Nov. 30, 1975. Two days after his passing, Juan Carlos de Borbón, the grandson of Alfonso XIII, was proclaimed King of Spain.

RULERS:

Francisco Franco, regent, 1937-1975
Juan Carlos I, 1975-

MONETARY SYSTEM:

1 Peseta = 100 Centimos 1874-2001
1 Euro = 100 Cents, 2002-

REPLACEMENT NOTES:

#150 and later, *9A, 9B, 9C* type prefix.

REPUBLIC

BANCO DE ESPAÑA

1965 (1970; 1971) ISSUE

#150-151 printer: FNMT.

150	100 Pesetas	VG	VF	UNC
	19.11.1965 (1970). Brown on multicolor underprint. Gustavo Adolfo Bécquer at center right, couple near fountain at lower left. Woman with parasol at center, Cathedral of Sevilla at left on back. Watermark: Woman's head.	1.50	6.00	15.00

		VG	VF	UNC
151	**1000 Pesetas** 19.11.1965 (1971). Green on multicolor underprint. San Isidoro at left and as watermark. Imaginary figure with basilica behind on back.	12.00	45.00	110.

1970-71 Issue

152 and 153 printer: FNMT.

		VG	VF	UNC
152	**100 Pesetas** 17.11.1970 (1974). Brown on pale orange and multicolor underprint. Manuel de Falla at right and as watermark. The summer residence of the Moorish kings in Granada at left center on back.			
	a. Issued note.	1.00	3.00	7.50
	s. Specimen.	—	—	—

		VG	VF	UNC
153	**500 Pesetas** 23.7.1971 (1973). Blue-gray and black on multicolor underprint. Jacinto Verdaguer at right and as watermark. View of Mt. Canigó with village of Vignolas d'Oris on back.			
	a. Issued note.	5.00	20.00	50.00
	s. Specimen.	—	—	—

> **NOTICE**
>
> Readers with unlisted dates, signature varieties, etc. are invited to submit photocopies of their notes to: Standard Catalog of World Paper Money, 700 East State St. Iola, WI 54990-0001, E-Mail: george.cuhaj@fwpubs.com.

1974 Commemorative Issue

#154, Centennial of the Banco de España's becoming the sole issuing bank, 1874-1974

		VG	VF	UNC
154	**1000 Pesetas** 17.9.1971 (1974). Green and black on multicolor underprint. José Echegaray at right and as watermark. Bank of Spain in Madrid and commemorative legend on back. Printer: FNMT.	FV	20.00	50.00

1976 Issue

		VG	VF	UNC
155	**5000 Pesetas** 6.2.1976 (1978). Purple and brown on multicolor underprint. King Carlos III at right and as watermark. Museum of Prado in Madrid at left center on back.	FV	85.00	200.

1982-87 Issue

#156-161 printer: FNMT.

		VG	VF	UNC
156	**200 Pesetas** 16.9.1980 (1984). Brown and orange on multicolor underprint. Leopoldo Garcí de las Alas, known as *Clarín* at right and as watermark, cross at lower center. Tree at left, cross at center on back.	2.00	7.00	20.00

		VG	VF	UNC
157	**500 Pesetas** 23.10.1979 (1983). Dark blue and black on multicolor underprint. Rosalia de Castro at right and as watermark. Villa at left center on back.	FV	8.00	25.00

		VG	VF	UNC
158	**1000 Pesetas** 23.10.1979 (1982). Gray-blue and green on multicolor underprint. Tree at center, Benito Pérez Galdos at right and as watermark. Rock formations, mountains and map of Canary Islands on back.	FV	12.50	35.00
159	**2000 Pesetas** 22.7.1980 (1983). Deep red and orange on multicolor underprint. Rose at center, Juan Ramón Jiménez at right and as watermark. Villa de la Rosa at left center on back.	FV	20.00	55.00

		VG	VF	UNC
160	**5000 Pesetas** 23.10.1979 (1982). Brown and purple on multicolor underprint. Fleur-de-lis at center, King Juan Carlos I at right and as watermark. Royal Palace in Madrid at left center on back.	FV	47.50	110.

		VG	VF	UNC
161	**10,000 Pesetas** 24.9.1985 (1987). Gray-black on multicolor underprint. Arms at center, King Juan Carlos I at right and as watermark. Back blue-gray on multicolor underprint. Felipe, Prince of Asturias at left, view of the Escorial at center.	FV	95.00	175.

1992 ISSUE

		VG	VF	UNC
162	**2000 Pesetas** 24.4.1992. Red-violet and orange on multicolor underprint. José Celistino Mutis observing flower at right and as watermark. Royal Botanical Garden and title page of Mutis' work on vertical format back. Two serial #.	FV	16.00	45.00

1992 (1996) ISSUE

#163-166 w/blurred *BANCO DE ESPAÑA* at r. margin.

Note: Issued for the 5th Centennial of the Discovery of America by Spain.

		VG	VF	UNC
163	**1000 Pesetas** 12.10.1992 (1996). Dark green, purple and red-brown on multicolor underprint. Hernán Cortes at right. Francisco Pizarro on vertical format back and as watermark.	FV	9.00	25.00

		VG	VF	UNC
164	**2000 Pesetas** 24.4.1992 (1996). Red-violet and orange on multicolor underprint. Like #162 but with modified portrait. One serial #.	FV	8.00	30.00

NOTICE

Readers with unlisted dates, signature varieties, etc. are invited to submit photocopies of their notes to: Standard Catalog of World Paper Money, 700 East State St. Iola, WI 54990-0001, E-Mail: george.cuhaj@fwpubs.com.

		VG	VF	UNC
165	**5000 Pesetas** 12.10.1992 (1996). Violet-brown, brown and red-brown on multicolor underprint. Christopher Columbus at right and as watermark. Astrolabe at lower center on vertical format back.	FV	40.00	90.00

		VG	VF	UNC
166	**10,000 Pesetas** 12.10.1992 (1996). Slate blue on multicolor underprint. King Juan Carlos I at right and as watermark, *Casa de América* in Madrid at lower center. de Ulloa y de Jorge Juan above astronomical navigation diagram on vertical format back.	FV	85.00	160.

Note: For later issues used in Spain, see European Union listings.

SRI (SHRI) LANKA

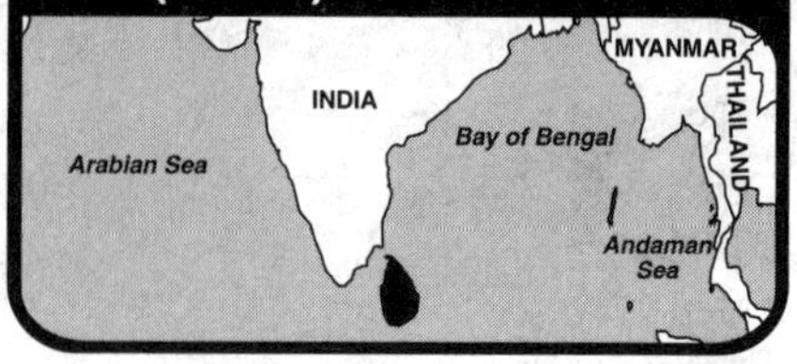

The Democratic Socialist Republic of Sri (Shri) Lanka (formerly Ceylon), situated in the Indian Ocean 18 miles (29 km.) southeast of India, has an area of 25,332 sq. mi. (65,610 sq. km.) and a population of 18.7 million. Capital: Colombo. The economy is chiefly agricultural. Tea, coconut products and rubber are exported.

The earliest known inhabitants of Ceylon, the Veddahs, were subjugated by the Sinhalese from northern India in the 6th century BC. Sinhalese rule was maintained until 1505 when the costal areas came under Portuguese control which was maintained for 150 years. The Portuguese were supplanted by the Dutch in 1658, who were in turn supplanted by the British who seized the Dutch colonies in 1796, and made them into Crown Colony in 1802. In 1815, the British conquered the independent Kingdom of Kandy in the central part of the island. Constitutional changes in 1931 and 1946 granted the Ceylonese a measure of autonomy and a parliamentary form of government. Ceylon became a self-governing dominion of the British Commonwealth on February 4, 1948. On May 22, 1972, the Ceylonese adopted a new constitution which declared Ceylon to be the Republic of Sri Lanka - 'Resplendent Island'. Sri Lanka is a member of the Commonwealth of Nations. The president is Chief of State. The prime minister is Head of Government.

See also Ceylon for earlier listings.

RULERS:

British, 1796-1972

MONETARY SYSTEM:

1 Rupee = 100 Cents, ca. 1830-

REPUBLIC

CENTRAL BANK OF CEYLON

1977 ISSUE

#81 and 82 Sri Lanka arms at r. Wmk: Chinze. Printer: BWC.

		VG	VF	UNC
81	**50 Rupees** 26.8.1977. Purple and green on multicolor underprint. Terraced hillside on back.	4.00	10.00	35.00

		VG	VF	UNC
82	**100 Rupees** 26.8.1977. Purple and brown on multicolor underprint. Shrine at left center on back.			
	a. Issued note.	5.00	12.50	65.00
	s. Specimen.	—	—	150.

1979 ISSUE

#83-88 backs vertical format. Wmk: Chinze. Replacement notes: Serial # prefix *Z/1*.

83	**2 Rupees**	VG	VF	UNC
	26.3.1979. Red on multicolor underprint. Fish at right. Butterfly and lizard on back.			
	a. Issued note.	.50	1.00	3.50
	s. Specimen.	—	—	100.

84	**5 Rupees**	VG	VF	UNC
	26.3.1979. Gray on multicolor underprint. Butterfly and lizard at right. Flying squirrel and White-faced Starling on back.			
	a. Issued note.	.75	1.75	6.50
	s. Specimen.	—	—	100.

85	**10 Rupees**	VG	VF	UNC
	26.3.1979. Green, brown and black on multicolor underprint. Sri Lanka Grey Hornbill in tree at center. Flowers and Yellow-eared Bulbul on back.			
	a. Issued note.	1.25	2.00	12.50
	s. Specimen.	—	—	125.

86	**20 Rupees**	VG	VF	UNC
	26.3.1979. Brown and green on multicolor underprint. Ceylon Wood Pigeon at center, monkey at right. Bird, tree and animals on back.			
	a. Issued note.	1.50	5.00	25.00
	s. Specimen.	—		150.

87	**50 Rupees**	VG	VF	UNC
	26.3.1979. Blue and brown on multicolor underprint. Butterfly at center, Red-faced Malcoha at right. Lizard and Ceylon Spurfowl on back.			
	a. Issued note.	3.00	12.50	90.00
	s. Specimen.	—	—	220.

88	**100 Rupees**	VG	VF	UNC
	26.3.1979. Gold, green and black on multicolor underprint. Snakes and tree at center, Sri Lanka Myna at right. Yellow-fronted Barbet in tree, butterfly below on back.			
	a. Issued note.	5.00	20.00	150.
	s. Specimen.	—	—	325.

NOTICE

Readers with unlisted dates, signature varieties, etc. are invited to submit photocopies of their notes to: Standard Catalog of World Paper Money, 700 East State St. Iola, WI 54990-0001, E-Mail: george.cuhaj@fwpubs.com.

1981 Issue

#89 and 90 backs vertical format. Wmk: Chinze.

89	500 Rupees	VG	VF	UNC
	1.1.1981; 1.1.1985. Brown and purple on multicolor underprint. Elephant with rider at right. Abhayagiri Stupa, Anuradhapura temple on hill on back.	20.00	50.00	125.

90	1000 Rupees	VG	VF	UNC
	1.1.1981. Green on multicolor underprint. Dam at right. Peacock and mountains on back.			
	a. Issued note.	30.00	75.00	250.
	s. Specimen.	—	—	—

1982 Issue

#91-95 backs vertical format. Wmk: Chinze. Printer: BWC.

91	5 Rupees	VG	VF	UNC
	1.1.1982. Light red on multicolor underprint. Ruins at right. Stone carving of deity and child on back.			
	a. Issued note.	FV	.25	2.75
	s. Specimen.	—	—	100.

92	10 Rupees	VG	VF	UNC
	1.1.1982; 1.1.1985. Olive-green on multicolor underprint. Temple of the Tooth in Kandy at right. Shrine on back.			
	a. Issued note.	.25	.50	4.50
	s. Specimen.	—	—	100.

93	20 Rupees	VG	VF	UNC
	1.1.1982; 1.1.1985. Purple and red on multicolor underprint. Moonstone at right. Dagoba Shrine on back.			
	a. Issued note.	.50	1.00	6.00
	s. Specimen.	—	—	110.

94	50 Rupees	VG	VF	UNC
	1.1.1982. Dark blue and dark brown on multicolor underprint. Building in Kelaniya at right. Ruins of temple at Polonnaruwa at center on back.			
	a. Issued note.	1.00	3.00	12.50
	s. Specimen.	—	—	125.

NOTICE

Readers with unlisted dates, signature varieties, etc. are invited to submit photocopies of their notes to: Standard Catalog of World Paper Money, 700 East State St. Iola, WI 54990-0001, E-Mail: george.cuhaj@fwpubs.com.

95 **100 Rupees** — VG VF UNC
1.1.1982. Orange and brown on multicolor underprint. Stone carving of lion at lower right. Parliament building on back.

	VG	VF	UNC
a. Issued note.	2.00	4.00	25.00
s. Specimen.	—	—	160.

SRÍ LANKÁ MAHA BÄNKUVA

CENTRAL BANK OF SRI LANKA

1987-89 ISSUE

#96-101 wmk: Chinze.

#96-100 similar to #89 and 92-95 but w/bank name changed in English from *CEYLON* to *Sri Lanka*. Printer: BWC.

		VG	VF	UNC
96	**10 Rupees** 1.1.1987; 21.11.1988; 21.2.1989; 5.4.1990. Green on multicolor underprint. Similar to #92.	FV	.40	2.50

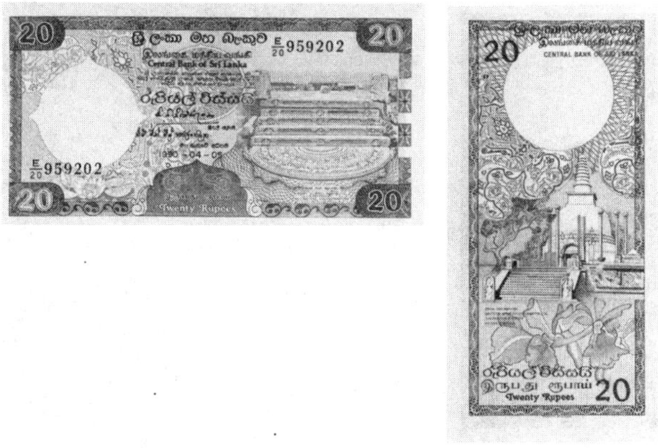

97 **20 Rupees** — VG VF UNC
1988-90. Purple and red on multicolor underprint. Similar to #93.

	VG	VF	UNC
a. 21.11.1988.	1.00	3.00	17.50
b. 21.2.1989; 5.4.1990.	FV	.75	3.75

		VG	VF	UNC
98	**50 Rupees** 21.2.1989; 5.4.1990. Blue and brown on multicolor underprint. Similar to #94.	FV	1.50	7.00
99	**100 Rupees** 1.1.1987; 1.2.1988; 21.2.1989; 5.4.1990. Orange and brown on multicolor underprint. Similar to #95.	FV	3.00	15.00
100	**500 Rupees** 1.1.1987; 21.11.1988; 21.2.1989; 5.4.1990. Brown and purple on multicolor underprint. Similar to #89 but with larger watermark area, vertical silver segmented security strip, bird and borders deeper red brown. Hill and temple in purple on back.	7.50	12.50	60.00

		VG	VF	UNC
101	**1000 Rupees** 1.1.1987; 21.2.1989; 5.4.1990. Deep green and purple on multicolor underprint. Victoria Dam at right. Peacock and University of Ruhuna on back. Printer: BWC.	FV	25.00	90.00

1991 ISSUE

#102-107 backs vertical format. Wmk: Chinze. Printer: TDLR. Replacement notes: Serial # prefix *Z/1*.

		VG	VF	UNC
102	**10 Rupees** 1.1.1991; 1.7.1992; 19.8.1994. Deep brown and green on multicolor underprint. Sinhalese Chinze at right. Painted stork at top left, Presidential Secretariat building in Colombo, flowers in lower foreground on back.	FV	.25	1.25

		VG	VF	UNC
103	**20 Rupees** 1.1.1991; 1.7.1992; 19.8.1994. Purple and red on multicolor underprint. Native bird mask at right. Two youths fishing, sea shells on back.	FV	.50	2.50

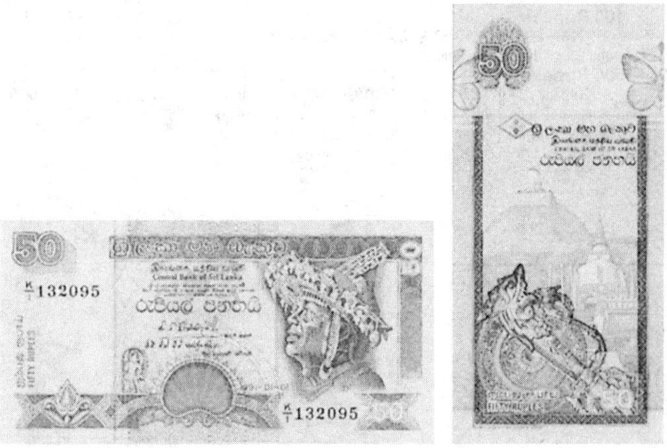

		VG	VF	UNC
104	**50 Rupees** 1.1.1991; 1.7.1992; 19.8.1994. Brown-violet, deep blue and blue-green on multicolor underprint. Male dancer with local headdress at right. Butterflies above temple ruins, with shield and ornamental sword hilt in lower foreground on back.	FV	.50	4.00

		VG	VF	UNC
105	**100 Rupees** 1991. Orange and dark brown on multicolor underprint. Decorative urn at right. Tea leaf pickers, two Rose-ringed Parakeets at bottom on back.			
	a. Without dot on value in Tamil at left. 1.1.1991.	FV	FV	35.00
	b. With dot on value in Tamil at left. 1.1.1991.	FV	FV	8.00
105A	**100 Rupees** 1.7.1992. Like #105a but back orange on multicolor underprint.	FV	FV	6.00

		VG	VF	UNC
106	**500 Rupees** 1991-92. Dark brown, purple and brown-orange on multicolor underprint. Musicians at right, dancer at left center. Stork-billed Kingfisher above temple and orchids on back.			
	a. 1.1.1991.	FV	FV	35.00
	b. 1.7.1992.	FV	10.00	50.00

		VG	VF	UNC
107	**1000 Rupees** 1.1.1991; 1.7.1992. Brown, dark green and purple on multicolor underprint. Chinze at lower left, two-headed bird at bottom center, elephant with trainer at right. Peacocks on palace lawn; lotus flowers above and Octagon Temple of the Tooth in Kandy on back.	FV	FV	65.00

1995 Issue

#108-113 backs have a vertical format. Enhanced latent image security feature at lower ctr. on face. Printer: TDLR.

		VG	VF	UNC
108	**10 Rupees** 15.11.1995. Like #102 but with additional security feature.	FV	FV	1.00
109	**20 Rupees** 15.11.1995. Like #103 but with additional security feature.	FV	FV	2.00
110	**50 Rupees** 15.11.1995. Like #104 but with additional security feature.	FV	FV	4.00

		VG	VF	UNC
111	**100 Rupees** 15.11.1995. Dark brown and orange on multicolor underprint. Like #105A but with additional security feature.	FV	FV	5.00
112	**500 Rupees** 15.11.1995. Like #106 but with additional security feature.	FV	FV	32.50
113	**1000 Rupees** 15.11.1995. Like #107 but with additional security feature.	FV	FV	50.00

1998 Commemorative Issue

#114, 50th Anniversary of Independence, 1948-1998

		VG	VF	UNC
114	**200 Rupees** 4.2.1998. Greenish black on blue, orange and multicolor underprint. Temple at upper center right above a collage of modern scenes across lower left to right. Palace at upper left center above collage of medieval scenes of British landing across lower left to right on back. Polymer plastic.			
	a. Red serial # in folder.	FV	FV	15.00
	b. Black serial #.	FV	FV	10.00

2001 Issue

		VG	VF	UNC
115	**10 Rupees** 2001; 2004. Like #108.			
	a. 12.12.2001.	FV	FV	.75
	b. 10.4.2004.	FV	FV	.50
116	**20 Rupees** 2001; 2004. Like #109.			
	a. 12.12.2001.	FV	FV	1.50
	b. 10.4.2004.	FV	FV	.75
117	**50 Rupees** 2001; 2004 Like #110.			
	a. 12.12.2001.	FV	FV	2.50
	b. 10.4.2004.	FV	FV	1.50
118	**100 Rupees** 2001; 2004. Like #111.			
	a. 12.12.2001.	FV	FV	4.00
	b. 10.4.2004.	FV	FV	
119	**500 Rupees** 2001; 2004. Like #112.			
	a. 12.12.2001.	FV	FV	17.50
	b. 10.4.2004.	FV	FV	15.00

		VG	VF	UNC
120	**1000 Rupees** 2001; 2004. Like #113.			
	a. 12.12.2001.	FV	FV	35.00
	b. 10.4.2004.	FV	FV	30.00

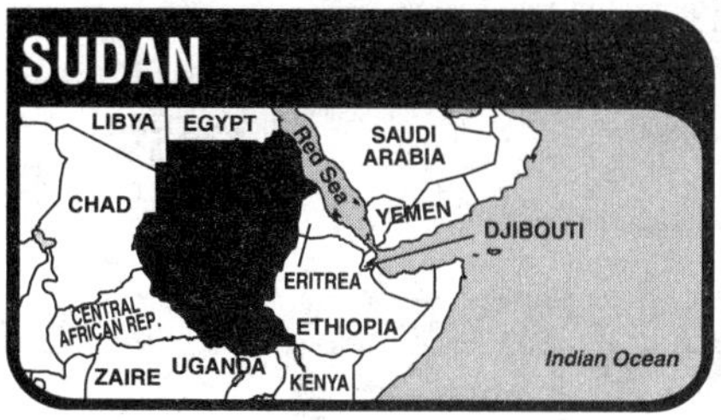

The Democratic Republic of the Sudan, located in northeast Africa on the Red Sea between Egypt and Ethiopia, has an area of 967,500 sq. mi. (2,505,810 sq. km.) and a population of 29.82 million. Capital: Khartoum. Agriculture and livestock raising are the chief occupations. Cotton, gum arabic and peanuts are exported.

The Sudan, site of the powerful Nubian kingdom of Roman times, was a collection of small independent states from the 14th century until 1820-22 when it was conquered and united by Mohammed Ali, Pasha of Egypt. Egyptian forces were driven from the area during the Mahdist revolt, 1881-98, but the Sudan was retaken by Anglo-Egyptian expeditions, 1896-98, and established as an Anglo-Egyptian condominium in 1899. Britain supplied the administrative apparatus and personnel, but the appearance of joint Anglo-Egyptian administration was continued until Jan. 9, 1954, when the first Sudanese self-government parliament was inaugurated.

The Sudan achieved independence on Jan. 1, 1956 with the consent of the British and Egyptian governments. On June 30, 1989 Gen. Omar Hassan Ahmad al-Bashir overthrew the civilian government in a military coup. The rebel guerrilla PLA forces are active in the south. Notes of Egypt were in use before 1956.

RULERS:

British, 1899-1954

MONETARY SYSTEM:

1 Ghirsh (Piastre) = 10 Millim (Milliemes)
1 Sudanese Pound = 100 Piastres to 1992
1 Dinar = 10 Old Sudanese Pounds, 1992

Republic

Bank of Sudan

1961-64 Issue

#6-10 various date and sign. varieties. Arms (desert camel rider) on back.

		VG	VF	UNC
6	**25 Piastres** 1964-68. Red on multicolor underprint. Soldiers in formation at left.			
	a. 6.3.1964; 20.1.1966.	6.00	25.00	200.
	b. 25.1.1967.	5.00	15.00	180.
	c. Without Arabic text *al-Khartoum.* 7.2.1968.	4.00	15.00	185.

		VG	VF	UNC
7	**50 Piastres** 1964-68. Green on multicolor underprint. Elephants at left.			
	a. 6.3.1964.	17.50	95.00	700.
	b. 25.1.1967.	20.00	100.	750.
	c. Without Arabic text *al-Khartoum.* 7.2.1968.	20.00	100.	750.

		VG	VF	UNC
8	**1 Pound** 1961-68. Blue on yellow and multicolor underprint. Dam at left.			
	a. 8.4.1961.	7.50	35.00	300.
	b. 2.3.1965.	7.50	35.00	300.
	c. 20.1.1966.	6.00	20.00	275.
	d. 25.1.1967.	6.00	20.00	275.
	e. Without Arabic text *al-Khartoum.* 7.2.1968.	5.00	20.00	250.

9	5 Pounds	VG	VF	UNC
	1962-68. Lilac-brown on multicolor underprint. Dhow at left.			
	a. 1.7.1962.	20.00	100.	950.
	b. 2.3.1965.	12.50	75.00	850.
	c. 20.1.1966.	10.00	70.00	725.
	d. 25.1.1967.	10.00	70.00	725.
	e. Without Arabic text *al-Khartoum*. 7.2.1968.	8.00	70.00	800.

10	10 Pounds	VG	VF	UNC
	1964-68. Gray-black on multicolor underprint. Bank of Sudan building at left.			
	a. 6.3.1964.	10.00	75.00	900.
	b. 20.1.1966.	12.50	85.00	950.
	c. 25.1.1967.	12.50	85.00	900.
	d. Without Arabic text *al-Khartoum*. 7.2.1968.	12.50	85.00	900.

1970 Issue

#11-15 Bank of Sudan at l. on face. Various date and sign. varieties. Printer: TDLR.

11	25 Piastres	VG	VF	UNC
	1970-80. Red on multicolor underprint. Textile industry on back.			
	a. Jan. 1970; Jan. 1971; Jan. 1972.	2.00	10.00	55.00
	b. 1.4.1973-28.5.1978.	.75	2.50	10.00
	c. 2.1.1980.	.50	1.00	7.50

12	50 Piastres	VG	VF	UNC
	1970-80. Green on multicolor underprint. University of Khartoum on back.			
	a. Jan. 1970; Jan. 1971; Jan. 1972.	1.50	15.00	75.00
	b. 1.4.1973-28.5.1978.	1.00	2.50	12.50
	c. 2.1.1980.	1.00	5.00	17.50

13	1 Pound	VG	VF	UNC
	1970-80. Blue on multicolor underprint. Ancient temple on back.			
	a. Watermark: Rhinoceros head. Jan. 1970; Jan. 1971.	5.00	20.00	75.00
	b. Watermark: Arms (secretary bird). Jan. 1972-28.5.1978.	1.00	3.00	30.00
	c. 2.1.1980.	1.00	4.00	35.00

14	5 Pounds	VG	VF	UNC
	1970-80. Brown and lilac on multicolor underprint. Domestic and wild animals on back.			
	a. Watermark: Rhinoceros head. Jan. 1970.	10.00	40.00	175.
	b. Watermark: Arms. Jan. 1971-28.5.1978.	5.00	25.00	175.
	c. 2.1.1980.	5.00	27.50	185.

15	10 Pounds	VG	VF	UNC
	1970-80. Purple and green on multicolor underprint. Transportation elements (ship, plane, etc.) on back.			
	a. Watermark: Rhinoceros head. Jan. 1970.	10.00	30.00	120.
	b. Watermark: Arms. Jan. 1971-28.5.1978.	7.50	20.00	90.00
	c. 2.1.1980.	5.00	15.00	35.00

Note: A large horad of #15 has recently come onto the market, resulting in a collapse in the value.

1981 Issue

#16-21 Pres. J. Nimeiri wearing national headdress at l., arms at ctr.

#18-21 wmk: Arms.

16	25 Piastres	VG	VF	UNC
	1.1.1981. Brown on multicolor underprint. Kosti bridge on back.	.25	1.00	2.50

		VG	VF	UNC
17	**50 Piastres** 1.1.1981. Purple on brown underprint. Bank of Sudan on back.	.50	1.25	4.50

		VG	VF	UNC
18	**1 Pound** 1.1.1981. Blue on multicolor underprint. People's Assembly on back.	1.00	4.00	17.50

		VG	VF	UNC
19	**5 Pounds** 1.1.1981. Green and brown on multicolor underprint. Back green; Islamic Centre Mosque in Khartoum at right.	2.00	6.00	30.00

		VG	VF	UNC
20	**10 Pounds** 1.1.1981. Blue and brown on multicolor underprint. Kenana sugar factory on back.	5.00	15.00	85.00
21	**20 Pounds** 1.1.1981. Green on multicolor underprint. Like #22 but without commemorative text.	7.50	30.00	135.

1981 Commemorative Issue

#22, 25th Anniversary of Independence

		VG	VF	UNC
22	**20 Pounds** 1.1.1981. Green on multicolor underprint. Pres. J. Nimeiri with native headdress at left, map at center, commemorative legend in circle at right around watermark, monument at right. Unity Monument at left, People's Palace at center right on back.	7.50	22.50	90.00

1983-84 Issue

#23-29 like previous issue but some in different colors.

		VG	VF	UNC
23	**25 Piastres** 1.1.1983. Red-orange on pale yellow underprint. Like #16.	.25	.50	1.50
24	**50 Piastres** 1.1.1983. Purple on brown underprint. Like #17.	.50	1.25	2.00
25	**1 Pound** 1.1.1983. Blue on multicolor underprint. Like #18 but building on back is blue only.	.50	1.25	2.50

		VG	VF	UNC
26	**5 Pounds** 1.1.1983. Green. Like #19.	1.00	4.00	17.50
27	**10 Pounds** 1.1.1983. Purple and red-brown on multicolor underprint. Like #20.	2.50	7.50	40.00
28	**20 Pounds** 1.1.1983. Green on multicolor underprint. Like #21.	5.00	12.50	65.00

		VG	VF	UNC
29	**50 Pounds** 25.5.1984. Brown-orange, blue and olive-brown on multicolor underprint. Pres. Nimeiri at left. Back blue on multicolor underprint; sailing ship at center, modern oil tanker at right. Watermark: Arms.	5.00	20.00	90.00

Law of 30.6.1985/AH1405

#30-36 outline map of Sudan at ctr. Bank of Sudan at ctr. r. on back. Wmk: Arms. Sign. title w/2 lines of Arabic text (Acting Governor).

Replacement notes: Serial # prefix *Z/1; Z/11; Z/21; Z/31; Z/41; Z/51; Z/61; Z/71.*

		VG	VF	UNC
30	**25 Piastres** L.1985. Purple on multicolor underprint. Camels at left.	.10	.40	1.50

		VG	VF	UNC
31	**50 Piastres** L.1985. Red on lilac and peach underprint. Lyre and drum at left, peanut plant at right.	.15	.50	2.50

#32-36 wmk: Arms.

		VG	VF	UNC
32	**1 Pound** L.1985. Green and blue on multicolor underprint. Cotton boll at left. Back blue on multicolor underprint.	.20	.75	3.00

		VG	VF	UNC
33	**5 Pounds** L.1985. Olive and brown on multicolor underprint. Cattle at left.	.50	5.00	30.00

		VG	VF	UNC
34	**10 Pounds** L.1985. Brown on multicolor underprint. City gateway at left.	2.00	7.50	45.00

		VG	VF	UNC
35	**20 Pounds** L.1985. Green and purple on multicolor underprint. Feluka at left.	5.00	30.00	250.

		VG	VF	UNC
36	**50 Pounds** L.1985. Brown, purple and red-orange on multicolor underprint. Columns along pool below National Museum at left, spear at right. Back red.	5.00	25.00	225.

1987-90 ISSUE

#37-43 sign. title in 1 line of Arabic text (Governor).

		VG	VF	UNC
37	**25 Piastres** 1987. Purple on multicolor underprint. Like #30.	.05	.15	.50

		VG	VF	UNC
38	**50 Piastres** 1987. Red on lilac and peach underprint. Like #31.	.05	.25	.75

		VG	VF	UNC
39	**1 Pound** 1987. Green and blue on multicolor underprint. Like #32.	.10	.25	1.00

#40-44 wmk: Arms.

40 5 Pounds

1987-90. Olive and brown on multicolor underprint. Like #33.

	VG	VF	UNC
a. 1987.	.25	.75	7.50
b. 1989.	.50	2.50	10.00
c. 1990.	.50	2.00	17.50

41 10 Pounds

1987-90. Brown on multicolor underprint. Like #34.

	VG	VF	UNC
a. 1987.	.50	1.50	22.50
b. 1989.	.75	3.00	25.00
c. 1990.	.75	3.00	25.00

42 20 Pounds

1987-90. Green and purple on multicolor underprint. Like #35.

	VG	VF	UNC
a. 1987.	.50	3.00	20.00
b. 1989.	.50	2.50	15.00
c. 1990.	.50	5.00	25.00

43 50 Pounds

1987; 1989; 1990. Brown, purple and red-orange on multicolor underprint. Like #36.

	VG	VF	UNC
a. 1987.	1.00	4.00	15.00
b. 1989.	1.00	3.50	10.00
c. 1990.	2.00	3.50	10.00

44 100 Pounds

1988-90. Brown, purple and deep green on multicolor underprint. Shield, University of Khartoum building at left, open book at lower right. Bank of Sudan and shiny coin design on back.

	VG	VF	UNC
a. 1988.	1.50	3.00	20.00
b. 1989; 1990.	.50	1.00	3.50

1991 Issue

#45-50 like #40-44. Wmk: Arms.

45 5 Pounds

	VG	VF	UNC
1991/AH1411. Red, orange and violet on multicolor underprint. Like #40. Back red-orange on multicolor underprint.	.20	.50	1.75

46 10 Pounds

	VG	VF	UNC
1991/AH1411. Black and deep green on multicolor underprint. Like #41. Back black on multicolor underprint.	.20	.75	2.00

47 20 Pounds

	VG	VF	UNC
1991/AH1411. Purple and violet on multicolor underprint. Like #42. Back violet on multicolor underprint.	.25	.75	2.50

48 50 Pounds

	VG	VF	UNC
1991/AH1411. Yellow-orange, brownish black and dark brown on multicolor underprint. Like #43. Back dark brown on multicolor underprint.	.50	1.00	3.50

49 100 Pounds

	VG	VF	UNC
1991/AH1411. Ultramarine and blue-green on multicolor underprint. Like #44. Ultramarine shield at left, light blue-green map image at center. Shiny light green coin design at right on back (partially engraved).	1.00	3.00	20.00

50 100 Pounds

	VG	VF	UNC
1991/AH1411; 1992/AH1412. Similar to #49 but colors rearranged. Blue-green shield at left, darker details on building and ultramarine map image at center. Pink coin design at right on back. (litho).	.50	1.00	3.00

1992-98 Issue

#51-55 People's Palace at ctr. or lower r. Wmk: Domed bldg. w/tower.

Note: First issues w/fractional serial # prefix (Type I) replaced w/local printings w/double letter serial # prefix (Type II).

51 5 Dinars

	VG	VF	UNC
1993/AH1413. Dark brown and red-orange on multicolor underprint. Plants including sunflowers at center on back. Serial # Type II. Replacement note: *GZ*.			
a. Issued note.	FV	FV	3.00
s. Specimen.	—	—	85.00

52 10 Dinars

	VG	VF	UNC
1993/AH1413. Deep red and dark brown on multicolor underprint. Domed building with tower at left center on back. Serial # Type II. Replacement note: *HZ*.			
a. Issued note.	FV	FV	3.50
s. Specimen.	—	—	85.00

53 25 Dinars

	VG	VF	UNC
1992/AH1412. Brownish black and green on multicolor underprint. Circular design at left on back.			
a. With artist's name *DOSOUGI* at lower right. Serial # Type I.	FV	FV	10.00
b. Without artist's name. Serial # Type I. Replacement note: *IZ*.	FV	FV	5.00
c. As b. Serial # Type II.	FV	FV	2.00

54	50 Dinars	VG	VF	UNC
	1992/AH1412. Dark blue-green, black and purple on multicolor underprint.			
	a. With artist's name *DOSOUGI* at lower right below palace. Serial # Type I.	FV	FV	20.00
	b. Without artist's name. 2 signature varieties. Serial # Type I.	FV	FV	4.50
	c. As b. Serial # Type II. Replacement note: *JZ*.	FV	FV	5.50
	d. As c. Segmented security thread. 7 or 8 digit serial #.	FV	FV	3.50

55	100 Dinars	VG	VF	UNC
	1994/AH1414. Black and deep brown-violet on multicolor underprint. Double doorway at center. Building at left center on back. Serial # Type I. Replacement note: *KZ*.	FV	FV	7.50

56	100 Dinars	VG	VF	UNC
	1994/AH1414. Black and deep brown-violet on multicolor underprint. Like #55 but with segmented foil over security thread. 7 or 8 digit serial #. Serial # Type II. Replacement note: *LZ*.	FV	FV	5.00

57	200 Dinars	VG	VF	UNC
	1998/AH1419. Green and black on multicolor underprint. Peoples Palace at right, crop line art at center. Building at upper center, line art at lower center on back.			
	a. 7 digit serial #. Embedded security thread.	FV	FV	8.00
	b. 8 digit serial #. Segmented security thread.	FV	FV	8.00

58	500 Dinars	VG	VF	UNC
	1998/AH1419. Red, black and green on multicolor underprint. Oil well and building on back. Serial # Type II.	FV	FV	10.00

59	1000 Dinars	VG	VF	UNC
	1996/AH1416. Green, yellow-brown and purple. Seal at left center, building in background at center. Building on back. Serial # Type II. Replacement note: *MZ*.	FV	FV	17.50

2002-03 Issue

60	200 Dinars	VG	VF	UNC
	2002/AH1424.	FV	FV	12.50

61	500 Dinars	VG	VF	UNC
	2003/AH1425.	FV	FV	7.50

		VG	VF	UNC
62	**1000 Dinars** Expected new issue.	—	—	—

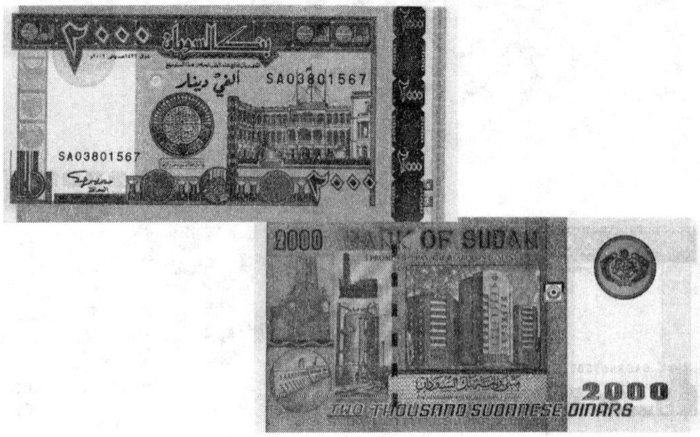

		VG	VF	UNC
63	**2000 Dinars** 2002/AH1421. Tan, blue, maroon and black on multicolor underprint. Dam, oil rig and Bank of Sudan building on back.	FV	FV	25.00

SURINAME

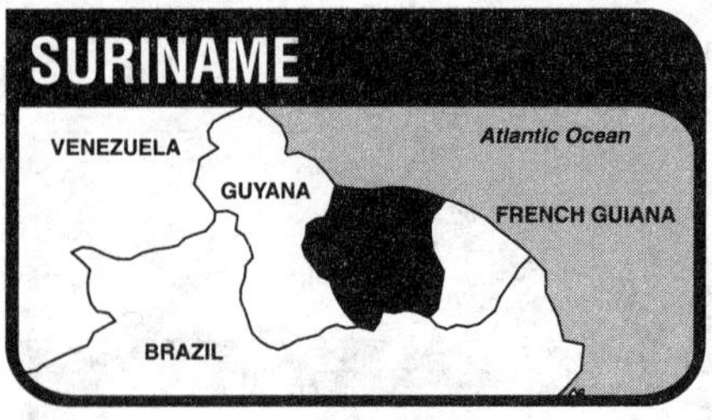

The Republic of Surinam, formerly known as Dutch Guiana, located on the north central coast of South America between Guyana and French Guiana, has an area of 63,037 sq. mi. (163,270 sq. km.) and a population of 452,000. Capital: Paramaribo. The country is rich in minerals and forests, and self-sufficient in rice, the staple food crop. The mining, processing and exporting of bauxite is the principal economic activity.

Lieutenants of Amerigo Vespucci sighted the Guiana coast in 1499. Spanish explorers of the 16th century, disappointed at finding no gold, departed leaving the area to be settled by the British in 1652. The colony prospered and the Netherlands acquired it in 1667 in exchange for the Dutch rights in Nieuw Nederland (state of New York). During the European wars of the 18th and 19th centuries, which were fought in part in the New World, Surinam was occupied by the British from 1799-1814. Surinam became an autonomous part of the Kingdom of the Netherlands on Dec. 15, 1954. Full independence was achieved on Nov. 25, 1975.

RULERS:

Dutch to 1975

MONETARY SYSTEM:

1 Gulden = 1 Florin = 100 Cents, to 2004
1 Dollar = 1000 "old" Gulden, 2004-

DUTCH ADMINISTRATION

MUNTBILJET

LAW 8.4.1960

#23-24 various date and sign. varieties. Printer: JEZ. Replacement notes: 6-digit serial number beginning with "1".

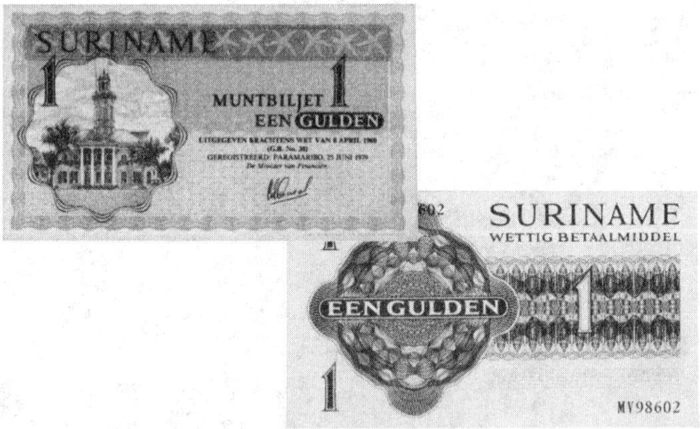

		VG	VF	UNC
116	**1 Gulden** 1961-86. Dark green with black text on pale olive-green and brown underprint. Building with tower and flag at left. Back brown and green.			
	a. Signature title: *De Minister van Financien* with printed Signature but without name. 1.8.1961-1.4.1969.	.75	2.00	10.00
	b. Signature in facsimile with printed name below. 1.4.1971.	.50	2.00	7.00
	c. Similar to b., but printed name of signer at right. 1.11.1974.	.50	2.00	5.50
	d. Like c. without printed name at right. 1.11.1974.	.50	2.00	5.50
	e. Similar to a., but shorter text, and signature title centered. 1.11.1974; 25.6.1979.	.40	1.50	7.00
	f. Similar to d., but signature title: *De Minister van Financien en Planning.* 1.9.1982.	.15	.50	2.50
	g. 2.1.1984.	.15	.50	2.25
	h. 1.12.1984.	.15	.50	2.25
	i. 1.10.1986.	.15	.50	2.00

		VG	VF	UNC
117	**2 1/2 Gulden** 1961; 1967. Red-brown. Girl wearing hat at left. Back red-brown and brown.			
	a. 2.1.1961.	.75	3.00	12.50
	b. 2.7.1967.	.75	2.25	7.50

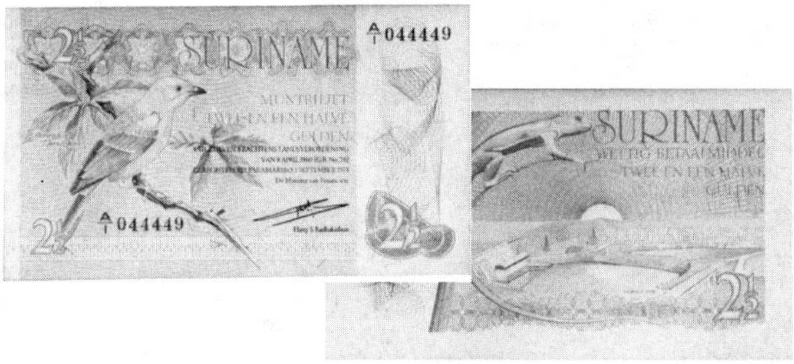

118	2 1/2 Gulden	VG	VF	UNC
	1973; 1978. Red-brown, light blue and multicolor. Blue-gray Tanager on branch at left. Three lines of text above signature title at center. Lizard and Afobaka Dam on back. Printer: BWC.			
	a. Signature title: *De Minister van Financien.* Printed name below Signature 1.9.1973.	.50	2.25	9.00
	b. Without printed name below signature 1.8.1978.	.20	.75	4.50
	s. Speciman.		—	
	s1. As a.		—	
	s2. As b.		—	

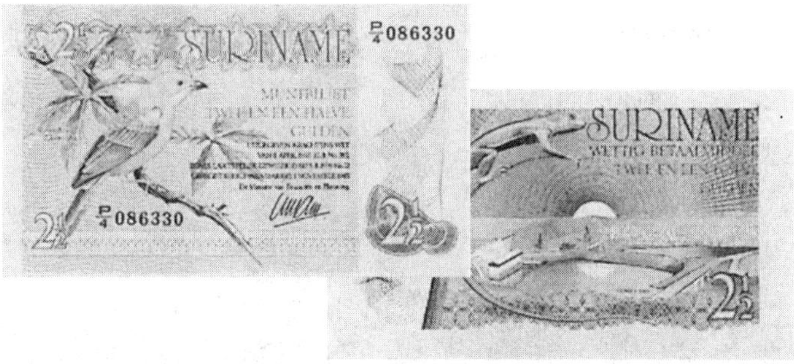

119	2 1/2 Gulden	VG	VF	UNC
	1.11.1985. Like #24A but four lines of text above signature with signature title: *De Minister van Financien en Planning*.			
	a. Issued note.	.20	.75	3.50
	s. Specimen.		—	

Centrale Bank van Suriname

1963 Issue

#30-34 different arms than 1957 issue on back. Wmk: Toucan's head. Printer: JEZ. Replacement notes: Serial # prefix *ZZ*.

120	5 Gulden	VG	VF	UNC
	1.9.1963. Blue on multicolor underprint. Two serial # varieties.			
	a. Small size serial #.	.10	.25	.75
	b. Large size serial #.	.10	.25	.75

121	10 Gulden	VG	VF	UNC
	1.9.1963. Orange on multicolor underprint.	.10	.25	1.00

122	25 Gulden	VG	VF	UNC
	1.9.1963. Green on multicolor underprint.	.50	3.00	10.00

123	100 Gulden	VG	VF	UNC
	1.9.1963. Purple on multicolor underprint.	1.00	5.00	12.50

124	1000 Gulden	VG	VF	UNC
	1.9.1963. Brown on multicolor underprint.	1.00	5.00	12.50

Note: #34 was sold in quantity by the Central Bank to the numismatic community.

Republic

Centrale Bank van Suriname

1982 Issue

#35-39 soldiers and woman at r. Bldg. w/flag on back. Wmk: Toucan's head. Printer: JEZ.

125	5 Gulden	VG	VF	UNC
	1.4.1982. Blue on multicolor underprint.	.15	.50	1.00

126	10 Gulden	VG	VF	UNC
	1.4.1982. Red on multicolor underprint.	.15	.40	1.25

127	25 Gulden	VG	VF	UNC
	1982; 1985. Green on multicolor underprint.			
	a. 1.4.1982.	1.00	2.50	5.00
	b. 1.11.1985.	.10	.25	.75

128	100 Gulden	VG	VF	UNC
	1982; 1985. Purple on multicolor underprint.			
	a. 1.4.1982.	5.00	10.00	20.00
	b. 1.11.1985.	.25	1.25	3.50

129	500 Gulden	VG	VF	UNC
	1.4.1982. Brown on multicolor underprint.	.25	1.00	7.50

Note: 1000 new notes of #39 were sold by the Central Bank to the numismatic community for USA $2.00 each.

1986-88 Issue

#40-44 Anton DeKom at l., militia at r., row of bldgs. across bottom. Toucan at l., speaker w/people at r. on back. Wmk: Toucan. Printer: TDLR.

130	5 Gulden	VG	VF	UNC
	1986; 1988. Blue on multicolor underprint.			
	a. 1.7.1986.	FV	.75	3.00
	b. 9.1.1988.	FV	FV	2.00

131	10 Gulden	VG	VF	UNC
	1986; 1988. Orange and red on multicolor underprint.			
	a. 1.7.1986.	FV	1.25	4.00
	b. 9.1.1988.	FV	FV	2.00

132	25 Gulden	VG	VF	UNC
	1986; 1988. Green on multicolor underprint.			
	a. 1.7.1986.	FV	2.00	8.00
	b. 9.1.1988.	FV	FV	3.50

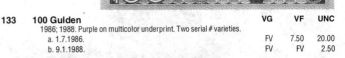

133	100 Gulden	VG	VF	UNC
	1986; 1988. Purple on multicolor underprint. Two serial # varieties.			
	a. 1.7.1986.	FV	7.50	20.00
	b. 9.1.1988.	FV	FV	2.50

134 250 Gulden

	VG	VF	UNC
9.1.1988. Blue-gray on multicolor underprint.	FV	2.00	8.00

135 500 Gulden

1.7.1986; 9.1.1988. Brown and orange on multicolor underprint.

	VG	VF	UNC
a. 1.7.1986.	FV	15.00	50.00
b. 9.1.1988.	FV	3.50	12.50

1991-97 ISSUE

#46-54 Central Bank bldg., Paramaribo at ctr. Toucan at l. ctr. and as wmk., arms at upper r. on back. Printer: TDLR.

136 5 Gulden

1991; 1995-96; 1998. Deep blue and green on multicolor underprint. Log trucks at upper left. Logging at center right on back.

	VG	VF	UNC
a. 9.7.1991.	FV	FV	1.50
b. 1.6.1995; 1.12.1996; 12.2.1998.	FV	FV	.25

137 10 Gulden

1991; 1995; 1998. Red and dark green on multicolor underprint. Bananas at upper left. Banana harvesting at center right on back.

	VG	VF	UNC
a. 9.7.1991.	FV	FV	3.00
b. 1.6.1995; 1.12.1996; 10.2.1998.	FV	FV	.25

138 25 Gulden

1991; 1995; 1996; 1998. Green and brown-orange on multicolor underprint. Track participants at upper left. Competition swimmer (Olympian Anthony Neste) in butterfly stroke at center right on back.

	VG	VF	UNC
a. 9.7.1991.	FV	FV	4.00
b. 1.6.1995.	FV	FV	3.50
c. 1.12.1996.	FV	FV	2.50
d. 10.2.1998.	FV	FV	2.50

139 100 Gulden

	VG	VF	UNC
9.7.1991. Violet and purple on multicolor underprint. Factory at upper left. Strip mining at center right on back.	FV	FV	6.50

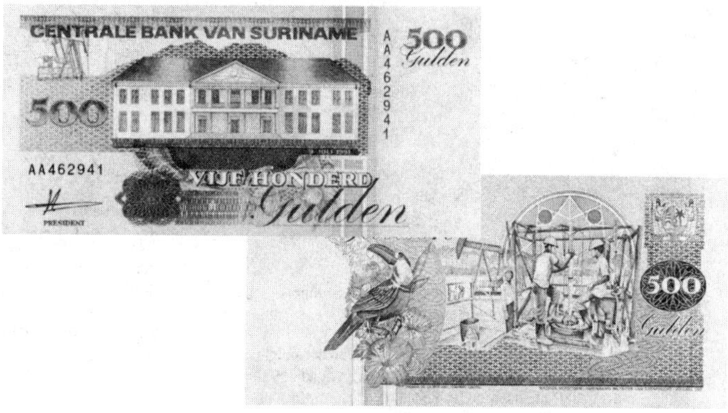

140 500 Gulden

	VG	VF	UNC
9.7.1991. Brown and red-orange on multicolor underprint. Crude oil pump at upper left. Drilling for crude oil at center right on back.	FV	FV	10.00

141 1000 Gulden

1993; 1995. Black and red on multicolor underprint. Combine at upper left. Combining grain at center right on back.

	VG	VF	UNC
a. 1.7.1993.	FV	FV	10.00
b. 1.3.1995.	FV	FV	5.00

		VG	VF	UNC
142	**2000 Gulden** 1.6.1995. Purple and green on multicolor underprint. Back like #46.	FV	FV	10.00

		VG	VF	UNC
143	**5000 Gulden** 5.10.1997; 1.2.1999. Purple on multicolor underprint. Long Billed Gnatwren, banana bunches on back.	FV	FV	20.00

		VG	VF	UNC
144	**10,000 Gulden** 5.10.1997. Green, red and multicolor. Silver segmented security thread. Bird, industrial complex on back.	FV	FV	37.50
145	**10,000 Gulden** 5.10.1997. Green, red and multicolor. Like #54 but purple segmented security thread. More red used on buildings at center and arms at left center on back than with #54.	FV	FV	37.50

2000 Issue

#56-64 arms at upper ctr. r. Ascending size serial #. Printer: TDLR.

		VG	VF	UNC
146	**5 Gulden** 1.1.2000. Blue and multicolor. Red-necked Woodpecker at left center. Flower on back.	FV	FV	1.00

		VG	VF	UNC
147	**10 Gulden** 1.1.2000. Green, purple, brown on multicolor underprint. Black-throated Mango at left center. Flower on back	FV	FV	1.25

		VG	VF	UNC
148	**25 Gulden** 1.1.2000. Blue and black on multicolor underprint. Red-billed Toucan at left center. Flower on back.	FV	FV	1.50

		VG	VF	UNC
149	**100 Gulden** 1.1.2000. Rose on multicolor underprint. Long-tailed Hermit at left center. Flower on back.	FV	FV	2.00

		VG	VF	UNC
150	**500 Gulden** 1.1.2000. Orange and green on multicolor underprint. Guianan Cock-of-the-Rock at left center. Flower on back.	FV	FV	2.50

151 **1000 Gulden**

	VG	VF	UNC
1.1.2000. Green and red on multicolor underprint. Royal Flycatcher at left center. Flower on back.	FV	FV	4.00

152 **5000 Gulden**

	VG	VF	UNC
1.1.2000. Green, yellow, blue and orange on multicolor underprint. Sun Parakeet at left center. Flowers on back.	FV	FV	12.50

153 **10,000 Gulden**

	VG	VF	UNC
1.1.2000. Brown, black and red on multicolor underprint. Ornate Hawk-eagle at left center. Flower on back.	FV	FV	20.00

154 **25,000 Gulden**

	VG	VF	UNC
1.1.2000. Brown and green on multicolor underprint. Specktacled Owl at left center. Flower and long leaves on back.	FV	FV	40.00

SURINAME WETTIG BETAALMIDDEL

2004 ISSUE

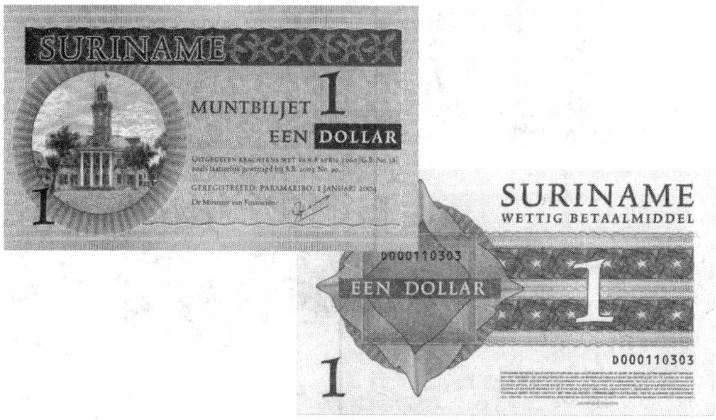

155 **1 Dollar**

	VG	VF	UNC
2004.	FV	FV	1.00

156 **2 1/2 Dollars**

	VG	VF	UNC
2004.	FV	FV	2.00

2004 ISSUE

157 **5 Dollars**

	VG	VF	UNC
2004.	FV	FV	2.00

158 **10 Dollars**

	VG	VF	UNC
2004.	FV	FV	2.50

159	20 Dollars	VG	VF	UNC
	2004.	FV	FV	10.00

160	50 Dollars	VG	VF	UNC
	2004.	FV	FV	20.00

161	100 Dollars	VG	VF	UNC
	2004.	FV	FV	40.00

SWAZILAND

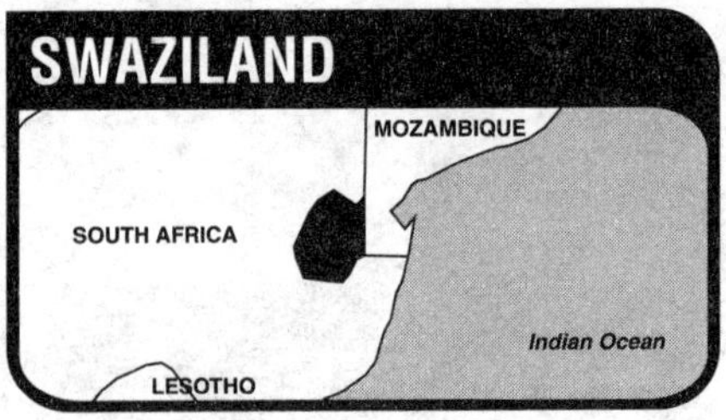

The Kingdom of Swaziland, located in southeastern Africa, has an area of 6,704 sq. mi. (17,360 sq. km.) and a population of 984,000. Capital: Mbabane (administrative); Lobamba (legislative). The diversified economy includes mining, agriculture and light industry. Asbestos, iron ore, wood pulp and sugar are exported.

The people of the present Swazi nation established themselves in an area including what is now Swaziland in the early 1800s. The first Swazi contact with the British came early in the reign of the extremely able Swazi leader King Mswati II when he asked the British for aid against Zulu raids into Swaziland. The British and Transvaal responded by guaranteeing the independence of Swaziland, 1881. South Africa assumed the power of protection and administration in 1894 and Swaziland continued under this administration until the conquest of the Transvaal during the Anglo-Boer War, when administration was transferred to the British government. After World War II, Britain began to prepare Swaziland for independence, which was achieved on Sept. 6, 1968 under the leadership of King Sobhuza II whose reign was of 61 years. His son, Prince Makhosetive was crowned King Mswati III on Apr. 25, 1986 at the age of 18 years. The kingdom is a member of the Commonwealth of Nations. The king of Swaziland is Chief of State. The prime minister is Head of Government.

RULERS:

British to 1968
Sobhuza II, 1968-82
Queen Ntombi, as regent, 1982-86
King Mswati III, 1986-

MONETARY SYSTEM:

1 Lilangeni = 100 Cents
(plural: Emalangeni)

SIGNATURE VARIETIES

	MINISTER FOR FINANCE	GOVERNOR
1	R. P. Stephens 1.6.1972 - 11.1.1979	E. A. Z. Mayisela 1.4.1974 - 31.10.1976
	J. L. F. Simelane 12.1.1979 - 20.11.1983	Deputy Governor H. B. B. Oliver 1.11.1976 - 30.6.1978 Acting Governor: A. D. Ockenden 1.6.1978 - 30.6.1981
2	J. L. F. Simelane 12.1.1979 - 20.11.1983	H. B. B. Oliver 1.7.1981 - 30.6.1992
3	Dr. S. S. Nxumalo 21.11.1983 - 8.6.1984	H. B. B. Oliver 1.7.1981 - 30.6.1992
4	B. S. Dlamini 27.8.1984 - 5.11.1993	H. B. B. Oliver 1.7.1981 - 30.6.1992
5	B. S. Dlamini 27.8.1984 - 5.11.1993	J. Nxumalo 1.7.1992 - 30.6.1997
6	I. S. Shabangu 10.11.1993 - 3.3.1995	J. Nxumalo 1.7.1992 - 30.6.1997
7A	Dr. D. von Wissell 3.3.1995 - 12.11.1996	J. Nxumalo 1.7.1992 - 30.6.1997
	minister for finance	governor
7B	Dr. D. von Wissell 3.3.1995 - 12.11.1996	J. Nxumalo 1.7.1992 - 30.6.1997

SIGNATURE VARIETIES		
8	T. Masuku 12.11.1996 - 19.11.1998	J. Nxumalo 1.7.1992 - 30.6.1997
9A	T. Masuku 12.11.1996 - 19.11.1998	M. G. Dlamini 1.7.1997 →
9B	T. Masuku 12.11.1996 - 19.11.1998	M. G. Dlamini 1.7.1997 →
	J. Charmichael 20.11.1998 - 14.2.2001	M. G. Dlamini 21.7.1997 →
10A	Majozi V. Sithole 15.2.2001 →	M. G. Dlamini 1.7.1997 →
10B	Majozi V. Sithole 15.2.2001 →	M. G. Dlamini 1.7.1997 →
11	Majozi V. Sithole	M. G. Dlamini

KINGDOM

MONETARY AUTHORITY OF SWAZILAND

1974-78 ND ISSUE

#1-5 Kg. Sobhuza II at l., Parliament House at bottom ctr. r. Sign. 1. Wmk: Shield and spears. Printer: TDLR. Replacement notes: Serial # prefix *Z*.

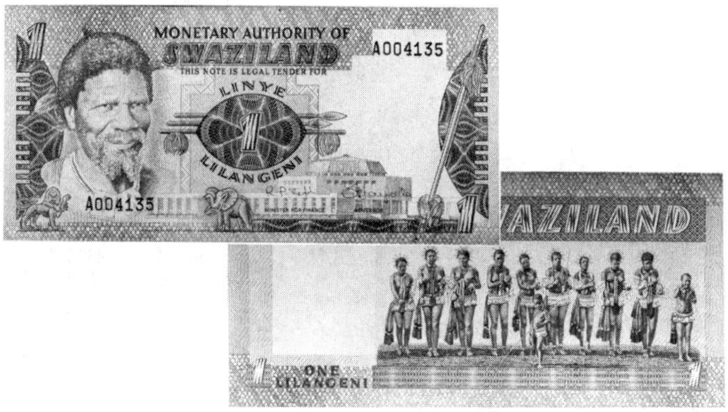

1	1 Lilangeni	VG	VF	UNC
	ND (1974). Red-brown on multicolor underprint. Princesses taking part in the *Ncwala* (kingship ceremony).			
	a. Issued note.	.50	.75	6.00
	s. Specimen. Serial # prefix *A; G*.	—	—	65.00

2	2 Emalangeni	VG	VF	UNC
	ND (1974). Dark brown on pink and multicolor underprint. Sugar mill on back.			
	a. Issued note.	.60	1.75	12.00
	s. Specimen. Serial # prefix *A; C*.	—	—	65.00

3	5 Emalangeni	VG	VF	UNC
	ND (1974). Dark green on yellow-green and multicolor underprint. Mantenga Falls and landscape on back.			
	a. Issued note.	1.50	5.00	37.50
	s. Specimen. Serial # prefix *A; B*.	—	—	65.00

4	10 Emalangeni	VG	VF	UNC
	ND (1974). Blue-black on blue and multicolor underprint. Asbestos mine on back.			
	a. Issued note.	4.00	10.00	80.00
	s. Specimen. Serial # prefix *A; B*.	—	—	65.00

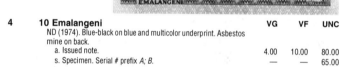

5	20 Emalangeni	VG	VF	UNC
	ND (1978). Purple and green on multicolor underprint. Agricultural products and cows on back.			
	a. Issued note.	12.50	35.00	185.
	s. Specimen. Serial # prefix *A*		—	65.00

CENTRAL BANK OF SWAZILAND

1981 COMMEMORATIVE ISSUE

#6 and 7, Diamond Jubilee of Kg. Sobhuza II

#6 and 7 printer: TDLR.

6 10 Emalangeni

1981. Blue-black on blue and multicolor underprint. Black commemorative text on watermark area. Back like #4. Watermark: Shield and spears. Signature 2.

	VG	VF	UNC
a. Issued note.	25.00	85.00	300.
s. Specimen. Serial # prefix *K*.	—	—	185.

7 20 Emalangeni

1981. Purple and green on multicolor underprint. Like #8. Back like #5. Watermark: Shield and spears. Signature 2.

	VG	VF	UNC
a. Issued note.	25.00	100.	335.
s. Specimen. Serial # prefix *C*.	—	—	185.

1982; 1983 ND Issue

#8-11 wmk: Shield and spears. Printer: TDLR. Replacement notes: Serial # prefix *Z*.

8 2 Emalangeni

ND (1983-86). Dark brown on pink and multicolor underprint. Like #2 but new issuer's name at top.

	VG	VF	UNC
a. Signature 2. (1983).	1.25	3.75	22.50
b. Signature 4. (1984).	.50	1.50	6.00
s1. As a. Specimen. Serial # prefix *F*.	—	—	65.00
s2. As b. Specimen. Serial # prefix *G, J*.	—	—	65.00

9 5 Emalangeni

ND (1982-86). Dark green on yellow-green and multicolor underprint. Like #3 but new issuer's name at top.

	VG	VF	UNC
a. Signature 2. (1982).	1.50	5.00	37.50
b. Signature 4. (1984).	1.00	2.00	11.00
s1. As a. Specimen. Serial # prefix *D; E*.	—	—	65.00
s2. As b. Specimen. Serial # prefix *F*.	—	—	65.00

10 10 Emalangeni

ND (1982-86). Blue-black on blue and multicolor underprint. Like #6 but without commemorative inscription on face.

	VG	VF	UNC
a. Signature 2. (1982).	7.50	25.00	135.
b. Signature 3. (1984).	6.50	22.50	120.
c. Signature 4. (1985).	1.25	4.00	16.50
s1. As a. Specimen. Serial # prefix *Q*.	—	—	65.00
s2. As b. Specimen. Serial # prefix *U*.	—	—	65.00
s3. As c. Specimen. Serial # prefix *W*.	—	—	65.00

11 20 Emalangeni

ND (1984-86). Purple and green on multicolor underprint. Like #7 but without commemorative inscription on face.

	VG	VF	UNC
a. Signature 3. (1984).	12.00	45.00	200.
b. Signature 4. (1985).	FV	8.00	38.50
s1. As a. Specimen. Serial # prefix *E*.	—	—	65.00
s2. As b. Specimen. Serial # prefix *F*.	—	—	65.00

1986 ND Issue

12 20 Emalangeni

ND (1986). Purple and green on multicolor underprint. King Mswati III at left, otherwise like #11. Printer: TDLR. Signature 4.

	VG	VF	UNC
a. Issued note.	3.00	6.50	30.00
s. Specimen. Serial # prefix *A*.	—	—	110.

1986; 1987 ND ISSUES

#13-16 Facing portr. of young Kg. Mswati III at l., arms at lower ctr. Wmk: Shield and spears. Sign. 4. Printer: TDLR. Replacement notes: Serial # prefix *Z*.

13	2 Emalangeni	VG	VF	UNC
	ND (1987). Dark brown and orange on multicolor underprint. Grey lourie, blue crane, hippos and other wildlife on back.			
	a. Issued note.	.50	1.50	7.00
	s. Specimen. Serial # prefix *A*.	—	—	110.

14	5 Emalangeni	VG	VF	UNC
	ND (1987). Dark green, dark brown and bright green on multicolor underprint. Warriors on back.			
	a. Issued note.	1.00	2.50	12.50
	s. Specimen. Serial # prefix *A*.	—	—	110.

15	10 Emalangeni	VG	VF	UNC
	ND (1986). Dark blue and black on multicolor underprint. Hydroelectric plant at Luphohlo and bird on back.			
	a. Issued note.	FV	3.50	20.00
	s. Specimen. Serial # prefix *A*; *F*.	—	—	110.

16	20 Emalangeni	VG	VF	UNC
	ND (1986). Violet, brown and purple on multicolor underprint. Cattle and truck on back.			
	a. Issued note.	6.00	32.50	160.
	s. Specimen. Serial # prefix *A*.	—	—	110.

1989 COMMEMORATIVE ISSUE

#17, 21st Birthday of Kg. Mswati III

17	20 Emalangeni	VG	VF	UNC
	19.4.1989. Like #16, with silver commemorative text and dates overprint on watermark area. Signature 4.			
	a. Issued note.	2.50	7.50	27.50
	s. Specimen. Serial # prefix *A*.	—	—	100.

1990; 1992 ND ISSUE

#18-22 printer: TDLR.

#18-21 similar to #13-16 but w/older portr. of Kg. Mswati III at l. facing half r. Backs like #13-16. Wmk: Shield and spears. Replacement notes: Serial # prefix *Z*.

18	2 Emalangeni	VG	VF	UNC
	ND (1992-95). Dark brown on multicolor underprint. Like #13.			
	a. Signature 4. (1992).	FV	1.50	5.00
	b. Signature 6. (1994).	1.00	4.00	15.00
	s1. As a. Specimen. Serial # prefix *M*.	—	—	100.
	s2. As b. Specimen. Serial # prefix *S*.	—	—	100.

19	5 Emalangeni	VG	VF	UNC
	ND (1990-95). Dark green, dark brown and bright green on multicolor underprint. Like #14.			
	a. Signature 4. (1990).	.75	2.50	8.50
	b. Signature 6. (1994).	2.00	7.50	37.50
	s1. As a. Specimen. Serial # prefix *D*.	—	—	100.
	s2. As b. Specimen. Serial # prefix *J*.	—	—	90.00

20	10 Emalangeni	VG	VF	UNC
	ND (1990-95). Dark blue and black on multicolor underprint. Like #15.			
	a. Signature 4. (1990).	1.25	4.50	22.50
	b. Signature 5. (1992).	1.50	5.00	25.00
	s1. As a. Specimen. Serial # prefix *J*.	—	—	100.
	s2. As b. Specimen. Serial # prefix *N*.	—	—	100.

		VG	VF	UNC
21	**20 Emalangeni**			
	ND (1990-95). Violet, brown and purple on multicolor underprint. Like #16.			
	a. Signature 4. (1990).	FV	9.00	37.50
	b. Signature 5. (1992).	FV	8.00	35.00
	s1. As a. Specimen. Serial # prefix *D.*	—	—	100.
	s2. As b. Specimen. Serial # prefix *G.*	—	—	100.

		VG	VF	UNC
22	**50 Emalangeni**			
	ND (1990-95). Dull red-brown, orange and dark green on multicolor underprint. King Mswati III at left. Central Bank seal at left center, head office building at right on back.			
	a. Signature 4. (1990).	FV	20.00	80.00
	b. Signature 6. (1995).	20.00	60.00	240.
	s1. As a. Specimen. Serial # prefix *A.*	—	—	90.00
	s2. As b. Specimen. Serial # prefix *C.*	—	—	85.00

1995 ND; 1995-98 Issue

#23-25 w/segmented foil over security thread.

		VG	VF	UNC
23	**5 Emalangeni**			
	ND (1995). Dark green, dark brown and bright green on multicolor underprint. Like #19 but warriors on back in dark brown. Ascending size serial #. Signature 7a. Printer: H&S.			
	a. Issued note.	FV	2.00	7.00
	s. Specimen. Serial # prefix *AA.*	—	—	85.00

#24 and 25 printer: F-CO.

		VG	VF	UNC
24	**10 Emalangeni**			
	ND (1995); 1997; 1998. Dark blue and black on multicolor underprint. Like #20.			
	a. Signature 7a. ND.	FV	13.00	32.50
	b. Signature 8. 8.4.1997.	FV	4.50	18.50
	c. Signature 9a. 1.4.1998.	FV	1.75	5.00
	s1. As a. Specimen. Serial # prefix *AA.*	—	—	85.00
	s2. As b. Specimen. Serial # prefix *AG.*	—	—	85.00
	s3. As c. Specimen. Serial # prefix *AK, AL, AN.*	—	—	85.00

		VG	VF	UNC
25	**20 Emalangeni**			
	ND (1995); 1997; 1998. Violet, brown and purple on multicolor underprint. Like #21.			
	a. Signature 7a. ND.	FV	5.00	22.50
	b. Signature 8. 8.4.1997.	FV	8.25	32.50
	c. Signature 9a. 1.4.1998.	FV	FV	8.50
	s1. As a. Specimen. Serial # prefix *AA.*	—	—	85.00
	s2. As b. Specimen. Serial # prefix *AF; AG.*	—	—	85.00
	s3. As c. Specimen. Serial # prefix *AK, AL.*	—	—	85.00

#26 and 27 OVD strip at r. w/C B of S repeated. Printer: G&D.

		VG	VF	UNC
26	**50 Emalangeni**			
	1995; 1998. Dull red-brown and dark green on multicolor underprint. Like #22.			
	a. Signature 7b. 1.4.1995.	FV	12.00	50.00
	b. Signature 9b. 1.4.1998.	FV	FV	24.00
	s1. As a. Specimen. Serial # prefix *AA.*	—	—	85.00
	s2. As b. Specimen. Serial # prefix *AA.*	—	—	85.00

		VG	VF	UNC
27	**100 Emalangeni**			
	6.9.1996. Dark brown on multicolor underprint. Central Bank seal at upper left center, rock formation at center on back. Signature 7b.			
	a. Issued note.	FV	FV	40.00
	s. Specimen. Serial # prefix *AA.*	—	—	85.00

1998 Commemorative Issue

#28, 30th Anniversary of Independence

28	200 Emalangeni	VG	VF	UNC
	6.9.1998. Dark green and green on multicolor underprint. Face like #27. Commemorative text vertically at left and right. Swazi villagers by thatched circular domed and fenced huts at center on back. Printer: G&D. Signature 9b.			
	a. Issued note.	FV	FV	65.00
	s. Specimen. Serial # prefix *AA*.	—	—	85.00

2001 ISSUE

#29-32 like #24-27 but with motto *GOD IS OUR SOURCE* added to back. Sign. 10.

#29-30 printer: F-CO.

29	10 Emalangeni	VG	VF	UNC
	1.4.2001. Dark Blue and black on multicolor underprint. Like #24.			
	a. Signature 10a.	FV	FV	3.75
	b. Signature 11.	FV	FV	3.75
	s. Specimen.	—	—	80.00

30	20 Emalangeni	VG	VF	UNC
	1.4.2001. Violet, brown and purple on multicolor underprint. Like #25.			
	a. Signature 10a.	FV	FV	6.50
	b. Signature 11.	FV	FV	6.50
	s. Specimen.	—	—	80.00

#31-32 printer: G&D.

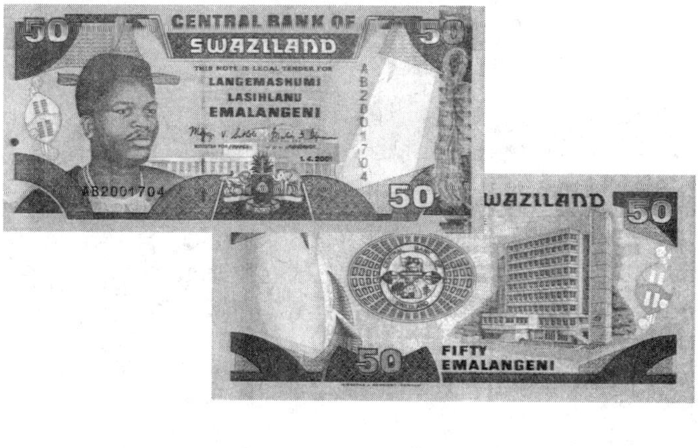

31	50 Emalangeni	VG	VF	UNC
	1.4.2001. Dull red-brown and dark green on multicolor underprint. Like #26.			
	a. Signature 10b.	FV	FV	17.00
	b. Signature 11.		FV	17.00
	s. Specimen.	—	—	80.00

32	100 Emalangeni	VG	VF	UNC
	1.4.2001. Dark brown on multicolor underprint. Like #27.			
	a. Signature 10b.	FV	FV	45.00
	b. Signature 11.	FV	FV	45.00
	s. Specimen.	—	—	80.00

2004 COMMEMORATIVE ISSUE

33	100 Emalangeni	VG	VF	UNC
	2004. Like #32 but with commemorative overprint in center. Signature 11.	FV	FV	35.00

COLLECTOR SERIES

MONETARY AUTHORITY OF SWAZILAND

1974 ISSUE

CS1	ND (1974). 1-20 Emalangeni	Issue Price	Mkt. Value
	#1-5 with overprint: *SPECIMEN* and serial # prefix Maltese cross.	—	80.00

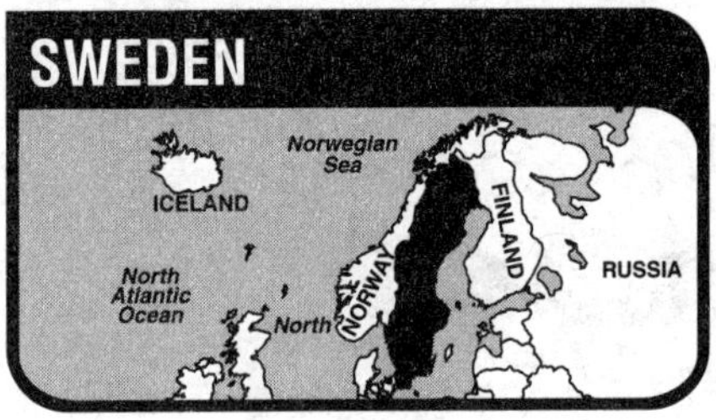

The Kingdom of Sweden, a limited constitutional monarchy located in northern Europe between Norway and Finland, has an area of 173,732 sq. mi. (449,964 sq. km.) and a population of 8.9 million. Capital: Stockholm. Mining, lumbering and a specialized machine industry dominate the economy. Machinery, paper, iron and steel, motor vehicles and wood pulp are exported.

Sweden was founded as a Christian stronghold by Olaf Skottkonung late in the 10th century. After conquering Finland late in the 13th century, Sweden, together with Norway, came under the rule of Denmark, 1397-1523, in an association known as the Union of Kalmar. Modern Sweden had its beginning in 1523 when Gustavus Vasa drove the Danes out of Sweden and was himself chosen king. Under Gustavus Adolphus II and Carl XII, Sweden was one of the great powers of 17th century Europe - until Carl invaded Russia, 1708, and was defeated at the Battle of Pultowa in June 1709. Early in the 18th century, a coalition of Russia, Poland and Denmark took away Sweden's Baltic empire and in 1809 Sweden was forced to cede Finland to Russia. Norway was ceded to Sweden by the Treaty of Kiel in January 1814. The Norwegians resisted for a time but later signed the Act of Union at the Convention of Moss in August 1814. The Union was dissolved in 1905 and Norway became independent.

A new constitution which took effect on Jan. 1, 1975, restricts the function of the king to a ceremonial role.

RULERS:

Gustaf VI Adolf, 1950-1973
Carl XVI Gustaf, 1973-

MONETARY SYSTEM:

1 Krona = 100 Öre

REPLACEMENT NOTES:

Issues since 1956 with asterisk following serial number. Asterisk following the serial number for note issued since 1956.

KINGDOM

SVERIGES RIKSBANK

1952-55 ISSUE

#42-43 replacement notes: Serial # suffix star.

42	5 Kronor	VG	VF	UNC
	1954-61. Dark brown on red and blue underprint. Beige paper with red safety fibers. Portrait King Gustaf VI Adolf at right center and as watermark Svea standing with shield at left. Center on back.			
	a. 1954.	.75	2.00	5.00
	b. 1955.	.75	2.00	5.00
	c. 1956.	.75	2.00	5.00
	d. 1959.	.75	2.00	7.50
	e. 1960.	.75	2.00	5.50
	f. 1961.	.75	2.00	4.00
	r1. Replacement, with star. 1956.	2.00	20.00	100.
	r2. Replacement, with star. 1959.	2.00	15.00	75.00
	r3. Replacement, with star. 1960. Rare.	—	—	—
	r4. Replacement, with star. 1961	2.00	15.00	75.00

43	10 Kronor	VG	VF	UNC
	1953-62. Gray-blue on multicolor underprint. Like #40. Portrait King Gustav Vasa at left and as watermark Arms at center on back. Blue date and serial #.			
	a. 1953.	FV	1.50	5.50
	b. 1954.	FV	1.50	5.50
	c. 1955.	FV	1.50	5.50
	d. 1956.	FV	1.50	5.00
	e. 1957.	FV	1.50	5.00
	f. 1958.	FV	1.50	5.00
	g. 1959.	FV	1.50	5.00
	h. 1960.	FV	2.00	10.00
	i. 1962.	FV	2.00	6.00
	r1. Replacement, with star. 1956.	2.00	30.00	120.
	r2. Replacement, with star. 1957.	2.00	20.00	70.00
	r3. Replacement, with star. 1958.	2.00	15.00	70.00
	r4. Replacement, with star. 1959.	2.00	15.00	75.00
	r5. Replacement, with star. 1960.	2.00	25.00	100.
	r6. Replacement, with star. 1962.	2.00	20.00	70.00

46	1000 Kronor	VG	VF	UNC
	1952-73. Brown and multicolor. Svea standing. King Gustaf V on back and as watermark.			
	a. Blue and red safety fibers. 1952.	FV	110.	500.
	b. 1957.	FV	110.	500.
	c. 1962.	FV	100.	450.
	d. 1965.	FV	100.	450.
	e. With security thread. 1971.	FV	90.00	400.
	f. 1973.	FV	90.00	350.

1958; 1959 ISSUE

#47 and 48 seated Svea at lower r. Kg. Gustaf Vasa at ctr. on back. Replacement notes: Serial # star suffix.

		VG	VF	UNC
47	**50 Kronor**			
	1959-62. Second signature at left. Sm. date and serial #.			
	a. 1959.	FV	12.50	35.00
	b. 1960.	FV	12.50	35.00
	c. 1961.	FV	25.00	75.00
	d. 1962.	FV	12.50	30.00
	r1. Replacement, with star. 1959.	12.50	20.00	120.
	r2. Replacement, with star. 1960.	12.50	20.00	100.
	r3. Replacement, with star. 1961.	12.50	20.00	100.
	r4. Replacement, with star. 1962.	FV	15.00	70.00
48	**100 Kronor**			
	1959-63. Second signature at left. Sm. date and serial #.			
	a. 1959.	FV	15.00	45.00
	b. 1960.	FV	15.00	45.00
	c. 1961.	FV	15.00	40.00
	d. 1962.	FV	15.00	35.00
	e. 1963.	FV	15.00	35.00
	r1. Remainder, with star. 1959.	15.00	25.00	120.
	r2. Remainder, with star. 1960.	15.00	20.00	100.
	r3. Remainder, with star. 1961.	15.00	20.00	90.00
	r4. Remainder, with star. 1962.	15.00	20.00	90.00
	r5. Remainder, with star. 1963.	10.00	15.00	100.

		VG	VF	UNC
49	**10,000 Kronor**			
	1958. Green and multicolor. King Gustaf VI Adolf at right and as watermark Svea standing with shield at crt. on back.	1200.	1750.	3000.

1962 ISSUE

#50 replacement notes: Star as serial # suffix.

		VG	VF	UNC
50	**5 Kronor**			
	1962-63. Dark brown on red and blue underprint. Like #42. Portrait King Gustaf VI Adolf at center. Svea standing with shield on back. Watermark: Esaias Tegnér (repeated). With security thread.			
	a. 1962.	.50	2.00	6.00
	b. 1963.	.50	1.50	3.00
	r1. Replacement, with star. 1962.	1.50	10.00	40.00
	r2. Replacement, with star. 1963.	—	—	15.00

1963-76 ISSUE

#51-55 replacement notes: Serial # suffix star.

		VG	VF	UNC
51	**5 Kronor**			
	1965-81. Purple, green and orange. King Gustav Vasa at right. Back blue and reddish brown; abstract design of rooster crowing at left. Beige paper. Watermark: Square with *5* repeated.			
	a. With year in dark red letter press. 1965-69.	.75	1.50	3.50
	b. With year in deep red offset. 1970.	.50	1.00	2.50
	c. As a. 1972-74; 1976-77.	.50	1.00	2.00
	d. With year in pale red offset. 1977-79; 1981.	.50	1.00	2.00

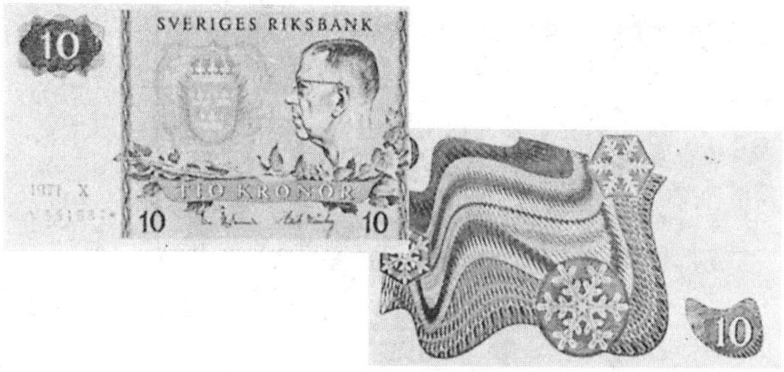

		VG	VF	UNC
52	**10 Kronor**			
	1963-90. Dark green, with red and blue guilloche at center. King Gustaf VI Adolf at right, arms at center. Northern lights and snowflakes at left center on back. Pale blue paper. Watermark: August Strindberg (repeated).			
	a. With year in dark red letter press. 1963.	1.00	2.50	4.50
	b. As a. 1966; 1968.	1.00	1.50	3.50
	c. As a. 1971; 1972; 1975.	1.00	1.50	3.00
	d. With year in pale red offset. Engraved signature 1976-77; 1979; 1983; 1985.	1.00	1.00	3.00
	e. As d. but withoutffset signature 1980-81; 1983-84; 1987-90.	.50	1.00	2.50

		VG	VF	UNC
53	**50 Kronor**			
	1965-90. Blue on green and brown underprint. King Gustaf III at right. Carl von Linné (Linnaeus) at center on back. Beige paper. Watermark: Anna Maria Lenngren (repeated).			
	a. Small watermark. 1965; 1967; 1970.	5.00	7.50	20.00
	b. Large watermark with year in dark red letter press. 1974; 1976.	5.00	7.50	17.50
	c. Large watermark as b. with year in red-brown offset. 1978; 1979; 1981.	5.00	7.50	15.00
	d. As c. Black serial #. 1982; 1984; 1986; 1989; 1990.	5.00	7.50	15.00

		VG	VF	UNC
54	**100 Kronor**			
	1965-85. Red-brown, blue and gray. King Gustav II Adolf at right. Figure head at left, Admiral ship *Vasa* of 1628 in center on back. Light blue paper. Watermark: Axel Oxenstierna (repeated).			
	a. Small watermark. 22mm. 1965; 1968; 1970.	10.00	15.00	30.00
	b. Large watermark. 27mm. with year in dark blue letter press. 1971; 1972; 1974; 1976.	10.00	15.00	25.00
	c. Large watermark. as b. with year in blue-green offset. 1978; 1980-83; 1985.	10.00	15.00	20.00

55	1000 Kronor	VG	VF	UNC
	1976-88. Red-brown on green and violet underprint. King Carl XIV Johan at right. Bessemer steel process on back. Watermark: Jacob Berzelius.			
	a. 1976-78.	100.	150.	300.
	b. 1980; 1981; 1983-86; 1988.	100.	125.	235.

1968 Commemorative Issue

#56, 300th Anniversary Sveriges Riksbank, 1668-1968

56	10 Kronor	VG	VF	UNC
	1968. Deep blue on multicolor underprint. Svea standing with ornaments at right. Back violet-brown; old Riksbank building at left center. Watermark: Crowned monogram King Charles XI.			
	a. Issued note.	1.00	2.00	6.00
	b. In printed banquet program folder with bank name, date and seal.	—	—	50.00

1985-89 Regular Issues

#57-65 the last digit of the year is first digit of the serial #. All notes have 2 sign. but only the right one is mentioned. Replacement notes: Serial # suffix star.

57	100 Kronor	VG	VF	UNC
	(198)6-(200)0. Blue-green and brown-violet on multicolor underprint. Carl von Linné (Linnaeus) at right and as watermark, building in background. Plants at left center. Bee pollinating flowers at center on back.			
	a. Watermark: Large portrait. Signature Bengt Dennis. (198)6; 7; 8; (199)2.	FV	FV	22.50
	b. Watermark: Small portrait repeated vertically. Signature Urban Bäckström. (199)6; 8; 9; (200)0.	FV	FV	20.00

58	500 Kronor	VG	VF	UNC
	(198)5-(198)6. Gray-blue and red-brown. King Carl XI at right and as watermark. Christopher Polhem seated at left center on back.			
	a. (198)5.	60.00	85.00	150.
	b. (198)6.	60.00	85.00	150.

59	500 Kronor	VG	VF	UNC
	(198)9-(200)0. Red and multicolor underprint. Similar to #58 but without white margin on face, also other slight changes.			
	a. Signature Bengt Dennis. (198)9; (199)1; 2.	FV	FV	120.
	b. Signature Urban Bäckström. (199)4; 5; 7; 8; 9; (200)0.	FV	FV	120.

60	1000 Kronor	VG	VF	UNC
	(198)9-(199)2. Brownish black on multicolor underprint. King Gustav Vasa at right and as watermark. Medieval harvest and threshing scene at left center on back.	FV	FV	175.

1991; 1996 ISSUE

		VG	VF	UNC
61	**20 Kronor** (199)1-(199)5. Dark blue on multicolor underprint. Horse-drawn carriage at lower center, Selma Lagerlöf at right and as watermark. Story scene with boy riding a snow goose in flight at left center on back. 130 x 72mm.			
	a. Signature Bengt Dennis. (199)1; 2.	FV	FV	7.50
	b. Signature Urban Bäckström. (199)4; 5.	FV	FV	5.00

		VG	VF	UNC
62	**50 Kronor** (199)6-(200)3. Deep olive-brown on multicolor underprint. Jenny Lind at center and as watermark (repeated), music lines at left, stage at right. Violin, treble clef with line of notes, abstract musical design on back.			
	a. Signature Urban Bäckström. (199)6; 7; 9; (200)0; 2.	FV	FV	10.00
	b. Signature Lars Heikensten. (200)3.	FV	FV	8.50

1997 ISSUE

		VG	VF	UNC
63	**20 Kronor** (199)7-(200)5. Purple on multicolor underprint. Like #61 but reduced size, 120 x 67mm.			
	a. Signature Urban Bäckström. (199)7; 8; 9; (200)1; 2.	FV	FV	4.00
	b. Signature Lars Heikensten. (200)3; 5.	FV	FV	3.50

2001 ISSUE

#64-65 w/enhanced security features.

		VG	VF	UNC
64	**100 Kronor** (200)1-(200)3. Blue-green and brown-violet on multicolor underprint. Like #57 but with foil hologram.			
	a. Signature Urban Bäckström. (200)1; 2.	FV	FV	20.00
	b. Signature Lars Heikensten. (200)3.	FV	FV	17.50

		VG	VF	UNC
65	**500 Kronor** (200)1-(200)3. Red on multicolor underprint. Like #59 but with foil hologram.			
	a. Signature Urban Bäckström. (200)1; 2.	FV	FV	80.00
	b. Signature Lars Heikensten. (200)3.	FV	FV	80.00

2005 COMMEMORATIVE ISSUE

#66 250th anniversary of the Tumba Paper Mill.

		VG	VF	UNC
66	**100 Kronor** 2005. Green on multicolor underprint. Seated Svea. Paper production and old map on back. Issued in a folder.	—	—	45.00

The Swiss Confederation, located in central Europe north of Italy and south of Germany, has an area of 15,941 sq. mi. (41,290 sq. km.) and a population of 7.41 million. Capital: Berne. The economy centers about a well developed manufacturing industry, however the most important economic factor is services (banks and insurance).

Switzerland, the habitat of lake dwellers in prehistoric times, was peopled by the Celtic Helvetians when Julius Caesar made it a part of the Roman Empire in 58 BC. After the decline of Rome, Switzerland was invaded by Teutonic tribes who established small temporal holdings which, in the Middle Ages, became a federation of fiefs of the Holy Roman Empire. As a nation, Switzerland originated in 1291 when the districts of Nidwalden, Schwyz and Uri united to defeat Austria and attain independence as the Swiss Confederation. After acquiring new cantons in the 14th century, Switzerland was made independent from the Holy Roman Empire by the 1648 Treaty of Westphalia. The revolutionary armies of Napoleonic France occupied Switzerland and set up the Helvetian Republic, 1798-1803. After the fall of Napoleon, the Congress of Vienna, 1815, recognized the independence of Switzerland and guaranteed its neutrality. The Swiss Constitutions of 1848, 1874, and 1999 established a union modeled upon that of the United States.

MONETARY SYSTEM:

1 Franc (Franken) = 10 Batzen = 100 Centimes (Rappen)
Plural: Francs, Franchi or Franken.

SIGNATURE VARIETIES

	PRESIDENT, BANK COUNCIL	DIRECTOR	CASHIER
39	Dr. Brenno Galli 1959-78	Dr. Walter Schwegler	Otto Kunz 1954-66
40	Dr. Brenno Galli	Dr. Riccardo Motta 1955-66	Otto Kunz
41	Dr. Brenno Galli	Dr. Max Iklé 1956-68	Otto Kunz
42	Dr. Brenno Galli 1959-78	Dr. Edwin Stopper 1966-74	Rudolf Aebersold 1954-66
43	Dr. Brenno Galli	Alexandre Hay 1966-75	Rudolf Aebersold
44	Dr. Brenno Galli	Max Iklé	Rudolf Aebersold
45	Dr. Brenno Galli	Dr. Fritz Leutwiler 1968-84	Rudolf Aebersold
46	Dr. Brenno Galli	Dr. Leo Schürmann 1974-80	Rudolf Aebersold
47	Dr. Brenno Galli	Dr. Pierre Languetin 1976-88	Rudolf Aebersold

NOTE: From #180 onward w/o the Chief Cashier's signature.

SIGNATURE VARIETIES

	PRESIDENT, BANK COUNCIL	DIRECTOR
48	Dr. Brenno Galli	Dr. Leo Schürmann
49	Dr. Brenno Galli	Alexandre Hay
50	Dr. Brenno Galli	Dr. Fritz Leutwiler
51	Dr. Brenno Galli	Dr. Pierre Languetin
52	Dr. Edmund Wyss 1978-86	Dr. Leo Schürmann
53	Dr. Edmund Wyss	Dr. Pierre Languetin
54	Dr. Edmund Wyss	Dr. Fritz Leutwiler
55	Dr. Edmund Wyss	Dr. Markus Lusser 1981-96
56	Dr. Edmund Wyss	Dr. Hans Meyer, 1985-2000
57	Dr. Francois Schaller 1986-89	Dr. Markus Lusser
58	Dr. Francois Schaller	Dr. Pierre Languetin
59	Dr. Francois Schaller	Dr. Hans Meyer
60	Dr. Francois Schaller	Jean Zwahlen (18mm)
61	Peter Gerber 1989-93	Dr. Markus Lusser

SIGNATURE VARIETIES		
	PRESIDENT, BANK COUNCIL	DIRECTOR
62	Peter Gerber	Jean Zwahlen (18mm)
63	Peter Gerber	Jean Zwahlen (15mm)
64	Peter Gerber	Dr. Hans Meyer
65	Dr. Jakob Schönenberger 1993-99	Dr. Markus Lusser
66	Dr. Jakob Schönenberger	Dr. Hans Meyer
67	Dr. Jakob Schönenberger	Jean Zwahlen (12mm)
68	Dr. Jakob Schönenberger	Dr. Jean-Pierre Roth 1996-
69	Dr. Jakob Schönenberger	Dr. Bruno Gehrig, 1996-2003
70	Eduard Belser, 1999-2002	Dr. Hans Meyer
71	Eduard Belser	Dr. Jean-Pierre Roth
72	Eduard Belser	Dr. Bruno Gehrig
73		
74		
75		
76		
77		

CONFEDERATION

SCHWEIZERISCHE NATIONALBANK

SWISS NATIONAL BANK

1954-61 ISSUE

#45-46 printer: OFZ.
Note: Sign. varieties listed after date.

45	10 Franken	VG	VF	UNC
	1955-77. Purple on red-brown underprint. Gottfried Keller at right. Carnation flower at left. Center on back. Printer: OFZ.			
	a. 25.8.1955. (34, 36, 37).	6.50	15.00	50.00
	b. 20.10.1955. (34, 36, 37).	6.50	15.00	50.00
	b2. 29.11.1956 (34, 37, 38).	6.50	15.00	50.00
	b2. 29.11.1956 (34, 37, 38).	6.50	15.00	50.00
	c. 29.11.1956. (34, 37, 38).	6.50	15.00	45.00

46	20 Franken	VG	VF	UNC
	1954-76. Blue on multicolor underprint. Gen. Guillaume-Henri Dufour at right. Silver thistle at left. Center on back. Printer: OFZ.			
	a. 1.7.1954 (34, 35, 36).	14.00	25.00	90.00
	b. 7.7.1955 (34, 36, 37).	14.00	25.00	90.00
	c. 20.10.1955 (34, 36, 37).	14.00	25.00	90.00
	d. 5.7.1956 (34, 37, 38).	14.00	25.00	90.00
	e. 4.10.1957 (34, 37, 38).	15.00	30.00	110.
	f. 18.12.1958 (34, 37, 38).	25.00	45.00	145.
	g. 23.12.1959 (39, 40, 41).	3.00	8.00	35.00
	h. 22.12.1960 (39, 40, 41).	3.00	8.00	37.50
	i. 26.10.1961 (39, 40, 41).	3.00	8.00	27.50
	j. 28.3.1963 (39, 40, 41).	3.00	8.00	26.00
	k. 2.4.1964 (39, 40, 41).	3.00	8.00	26.00
	l. 21.1.1965 (39, 40, 41).	3.00	8.00	26.00
	m. 23.12.1965 (39, 40, 41).	3.00	8.00	26.00
	n. 1.1.1967 (42, 43, 44).	3.00	10.00	32.50
	o. 30.6.1967 (42, 43, 44).	2.75	8.00	28.00
	p. 15.5.1968 (42, 43, 45).	2.75	8.00	28.00
	q. 15.1.1969 (42, 43, 45).	2.75	8.00	28.00
	r. 5.1.1970 (42, 43, 45).	2.75	8.00	28.00
	s. 10.2.1971 (42, 43, 45).	2.75	8.00	28.00
	s1. As a. Specimen.	—	—	50.00
	t. 24.1.1972 (42, 43, 45).	2.75	8.00	28.00
	u. 7.3.1973 (42, 43, 45).	2.75	8.00	28.00
	v. 7.2.1974 (42, 43, 45).	2.75	8.00	28.00
	w. 9.4.1976 (45, 46, 47).	2.50	7.50	25.00

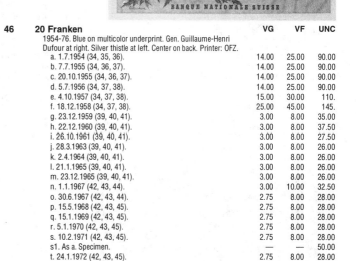

47	50 Franken	VG	VF	UNC
	1955-58. Green and red-brown on yellow-green underprint. Girl at upper right. Apple harvesting scene on back (symbolizing fertility). Printer: W&S.			
	a. 7.7.1955 (34, 36, 37).	25.00	42.50	200.
	b. 4.10.1957 (34, 37, 38).	20.00	37.50	125.
	c. 18.12.1958 (34, 37, 38).	150.	300.	750.

48	50 Franken	VG	VF	UNC
	1961-74. Green and red on multicolor underprint. Like #47.			
	a. 4.5.1961 (39, 40, 41).	25.00	60.00	200.
	b. 21.12.1961 (39, 40,41).	12.50	30.00	75.00
	c. 28.3.1963 (39, 40, 41).	30.00	85.00	220.
	d. 2.4.1964 (39, 40, 41).	35.00	90.00	225.
	e. 21.1.1965 (39, 40, 41).	12.50	30.00	80.00
	f. 23.12.1965 (39, 40, 41).	12.50	30.00	80.00
	g. 30.6.1967 (42, 43, 44).	12.50	30.00	80.00
	h. 15.5.1968 (42, 43, 45).	12.50	30.00	80.00
	i. 15.1.1969 (42, 43, 45).	12.50	30.00	75.00
	j. 5.1.1970 (42, 43, 45).	12.50	30.00	75.00
	k. 10.2.1971 (42, 43, 45).	12.50	30.00	75.00
	l. 24.1.1972 (42, 43, 45).	12.50	30.00	75.00
	m. 7.3.1973 (42, 43, 45).	12.50	30.00	75.00
	n. 7.2.1974 (42, 43, 45).	12.50	30.00	75.00
	s. As a. Specimen.	—	—	50.00

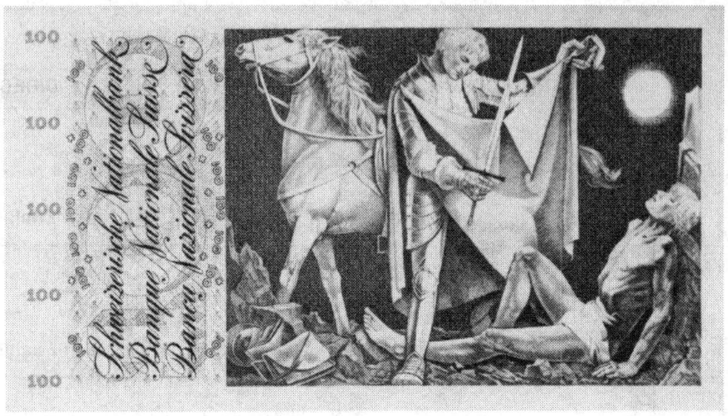

49	100 Franken	VG	VF	UNC
	1956-73. Dark blue and brown-olive on multicolor underprint. Boy's head at upper r with lamb. St. Martin cutting his cape (to share) at center right on back. Printer: TDLR.			
	a. 25.10.1956 (34, 37, 38).	30.00	57.50	200.
	b. 4.10.1957 (34, 37, 38).	30.00	55.00	170.
	c. 18.12.1958 (34, 37, 38).	32.50	60.00	320.
	d. 21.12.1961 (39, 40, 41);	15.00	30.00	135.
	e. 28.3.1963 (39, 40, 41).	15.00	30.00	135.
	f. 2.4.1964 (39, 40, 41).	15.00	30.00	135.
	g. 21.1.1965 (39, 40, 41).	15.00	32.50	135.
	h. 23.12.1965 (39, 40, 41).	16.00	35.00	180.
	i. 1.1.1967 (42, 43, 44).	16.00	35.00	170.
	j. 30.6.1967 (42, 43, 44).	14.00	27.50	125.
	k. 15.1.1969 (42, 43, 45).	14.00	25.00	125.
	l. 5.1.1970 (42, 43, 45).	16.00	35.00	130.
	m. 10.2.1971 (42, 43, 45).	12.00	25.00	120.
	n. 24.1.1972 (42, 43, 45).	12.00	25.00	120.
	o. 7.3.1973 (42, 43, 45).	12.00	25.00	120.
	s. As a. Specimen.	—	—	100.
50	500 Franken			
	1957-58. Red-brown and olive on multicolor underprint. Woman looking in mirror at right. Elders with 4 girls bathing at center right on back (Fountain of Youth). Printer: W&S.			
	a. 31.1.1957 (34, 37, 38).	250.	400.	900.
	b. 4.10.1957 (34, 37, 38).	200.	350.	800.
	c. 18.12.1958 (34, 37, 38).	300.	500.	1000.

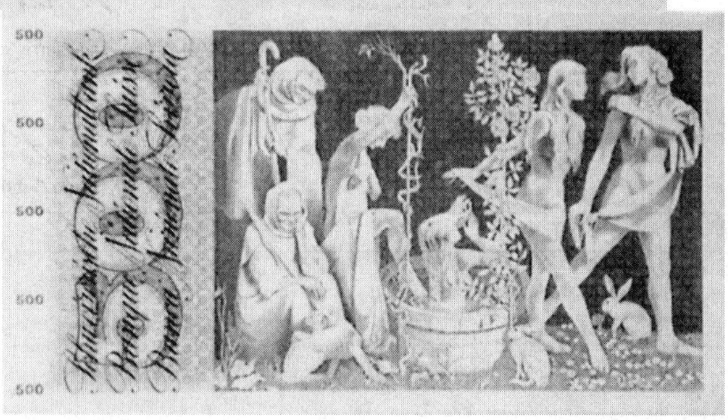

51	500 Franken	VG	VF	UNC
	1961-74. Brown-orange and olive on multicolor underprint. Like #50.			
	a. 21.12.1961 (39, 40, 41).	150.	275.	750.
	b. 28.3.1963 (39, 40, 41).	130.	240.	740.
	c. 2.4.1964 (39, 40, 41).	140.	250.	740.
	d. 21.1.1965 (39, 40, 41).	140.	250.	740.
	e. 1.1.1967 (42, 43, 44).	140.	250.	700.
	f. 15.5.1968 (42, 43, 45).	140.	250.	700.
	g. 15.1.1969 (42, 43, 45).	140.	250.	700.
	h. 5.1.1970 (42, 43, 45).	110.	235.	680.
	i. 10.2.1971 (42, 43, 45).	110.	235.	680.
	j. 24.1.1972 (42, 43, 45).	110.	235.	680.
	k. 7.3.1973 (42, 43, 45).	100.	230.	670.
	l. 7.2.1974 (42, 43, 45).	90.00	200.	650.
	s. As a. Specimen.	—	—	500.

52 1000 Franken
1954-74. Red-violet and turquoise on green and light violet underprint. Female head at upper right. allegorical scene *Dance Macabre* on back. Printer: TDLR.

	VG	VF	UNC
a. 30.9.1954 (34, 35, 36).	250.	500.	1900.
b. 4.10.1957 (34, 37, 38).	225.	425.	1650.
c. 18.12.1958 (34, 37, 38).	325.	650.	2000.
d. 22.12.1960 (39, 40, 41).	175.	350.	1550.
e. 21.12.1961 (39, 40, 41).	175.	350.	1550.
f. 28.3.1963 (39, 40, 41).	175.	350.	1400.
g. 21.1.1965 (39, 40, 41).	175.	350.	1300.
h. 1.1.1967 (42, 43, 44).	175.	350.	1300.
i. 5.1.1970 (42, 43, 45).	175.	350.	1300.
j. 10.2.1971 (42, 43, 45).	175.	350.	1175.
k. 24.1.1972 (42, 43, 45).	150.	300.	1175.
l. 1.10.1973 (42, 43, 45).	140.	280.	1175.
m. 7.2.1974 (42, 43, 45).	125.	260.	1150.
s. As a. Specimen.	—	—	1200.

1976-79 Issue; 6th Series

#53-59 series of notes printed in 4 languages - the traditional German, French and Italian plus Romansch; (Rhaeto - Romanic), the language of the mountainous areas of Graubünden Canton. Wmk. as portr. The first 2 numerals before the serial # prefix letter are date (year) indicators. Printer: OFZ.
Note: Sign. varieties listed after date.

53 10 Franken
(19)79-92. Orange-brown and multicolor. Leonhard Euler at right. Water turbine, light rays through lenses and Solar System in vertical format on back.

	VG	VF	UNC
a. 1979 (52, 53, 54).	FV	FV	15.00
b. 1980 (52, 53, 54).	FV	FV	13.00
c. 1981 (53, 54, 55).	FV	FV	12.00
d. 1982 (53, 54, 55).	FV	FV	12.00

53 10 Franken

	VG	VF	UNC
e. 1983 (53, 54, 55).	FV	FV	12.00
f. 1986 (53, 55, 56).	FV	FV	11.00
g. 1987 (57, 58, 59).	FV	FV	11.00
h. 1990 (61, 62, 63, 64). #62 is valued at $150 in Unc.	50.00	75.00	150.
i. 1991 (61, 63, 64).	FV	FV	10.00
j. 1992 (61, 62, 64).	FV	FV	10.00

54 20 Franken

	VG	VF	UNC
1978 (52, 53, 54). Light blue on multicolor underprint. Horace-Bénédict de Saussure at right, hygrometer at left. Fossel and early mountain expedition team hiking in the Alps on back. Underprint on face ends 2mm before the margin, only plain blue underprint visible within the 2mm.	FV	FV	35.00

55 20 Franken
(19)78-92. Blue and multicolor. Similar to #54, but underprint. at upper margin on face goes to the margin.

	VG	VF	UNC
a. 1978 (52, 53, 54).	FV	FV	42.50
b. 1980 (52, 53, 54).	FV	FV	30.00
c. 1981 (53, 54, 55).	FV	FV	27.50
d. 1982 (53, 54, 55).	FV	FV	27.50
e. 1983 (53, 54, 55).	FV	FV	32.50
f. 1986 (57, 58, 59).	FV	FV	32.50
g. 1987 (57, 58, 59).	FV	FV	25.00
h. 1989 (61, 62, 64).	FV	FV	25.00
i. 1990 (61, 63, 64).	FV	FV	22.50
j. 1992 (61, 63, 64).	FV	FV	20.00
s. Perforated: *SPECIMEN.*	—	—	250.

56 50 Franken
(19)78-88. Green and multicolor. Konrad Gessner at right. Eagle owl, *Primula auricu-la* plant and stars on vertical format back.

	VG	VF	UNC
a. 1978 (48, 50, 51).	FV	FV	62.50
b. 1979 (52, 53, 54).	FV	FV	57.50
c. 1980 (52, 53, 54).	FV	FV	57.50
d. 1981 (53, 54, 55).	FV	FV	55.00
e. 1983 (53, 54, 55).	FV	FV	52.50
f. 1985 (53, 55, 56).	FV	FV	52.50
g. 1986 (57, 58, 59).	FV	FV	50.00
h. 1988 (57, 59, 60).	FV	FV	50.00
s. Perforated: *SPECIMEN.*	—	—	350.

57 100 Franken
(19)75-93. Blue and multicolor. Francesco Borromini at right. Baroque architectural drawing and view of S. Ivo alla Sapienza on vertical format back.

	VG	VF	UNC
a. 1975 (48, 49, 50).	FV	FV	140.
b. 1977 (48, 50, 51).	FV	FV	140.

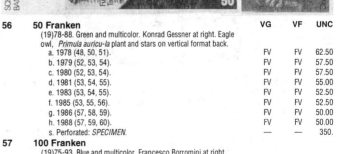

		VG	VF	UNC
57	**100 Franken**			
	c. 1980 (52, 53, 54).	FV	FV	140.
	d. 1981 (53, 54, 55).	FV	FV	120.
	e. 1982 (53, 54, 55).	FV	FV	120.
	f. 1983 (53, 54, 55).	FV	FV	120.
	g. 1984 (53, 54, 55).	FV	FV	130.
	h. 1986 (57, 58, 59).	FV	FV	120.
	i. 1988 (57, 59, 60).	FV	FV	135.
	j. 1989 (57, 59, 60).	FV	FV	120.
	k. 1991 (61, 63, 64).	FV	FV	105.
	l. 1992 (61, 63, 64).	FV	FV	105.
	m. 1993 (61, 63, 64).	FV	FV	100.
	s. Perforated: *SPECIMEN.*	—	—	400.

		VG	VF	UNC
58	**500 Franken**			
	(19)76-92. Brown and multicolor. Albrecht von Haller at right. Mountains (Gemmi Pass) at left. Anatomical muscles of the back, schematic blood circulation and a purple orchid flower on vertical format back.			
	a. 1976 (48, 50, 51).	FV	FV	625.
	b. 1986 (57, 58, 59).	FV	FV	600.
	c. 1992 (61, 63, 64).	FV	FV	550.
	s. Perforated: *SPECIMEN.*	—	—	500.

		VG	VF	UNC
59	**1000 Franken**			
	(19)77-93. Purple on multicolor underprint. Auguste Forel at right, diagrams through a brain and a nerve cell at left. Ants and ant-hill schematic on vertical format back.			
	a. 1977 (48, 50, 51).	FV	FV	1150.
	b. 1980 (52, 53, 54).	FV	FV	1100.
	c. 1984 (53, 54, 55).	FV	FV	1075.
	d. 1987 (57, 58, 59).	FV	FV	1050.
	e. 1988 (57, 59, 60).	FV	FV	1050.
	f. 1993 (61, 63, 64).	FV	FV	1000.
	s. Perforated: *SPECIMEN.*	—	—	1000.

1983-85 Reserve Issue

		VG	VF	UNC
60	**10 Franken** 1983. Orange-brown and multicolor. Leonhard Euler at right. Polyhedron in center, calculations, table for calculation of numbers and solar system diagram on back.	—	—	—
61	**20 Franken** 1985. Blue on multicolor underprint. Horace-Bénédict de Saussure at right, crystal in center. Hair hygrometer, mountains and mountain team hiking on back.	—	—	—
62	**50 Franken** 1985. Olive-green and multicolor. Konrad Gessner at right. Cherry tree branch, eagle, animals on back.	—	—	—
63	**100 Franken** 1985. Violet-blue and multicolor. Francesco Borromini at right, architectural motif at center. Drawing and tower of S. Ivo on back.	—	—	—
64	**500 Franken** 1985. Brown and multicolor. Albrecht von Haller at right, hexagonal structure of a cell in center. Anatomy plate and X-ray of a human thorax on back.	—	—	—
65	**1000 Franken** 1985. Violet and multicolor. Louis Agassiz at right, structure of the surface of a shellfish. Perch in three parts: head, skeleton and fossil, fishscales and ammonite on back.	—	—	—

1994-98 Issue; 8th Series

#66 71 vertical format, reduced size. First two numerals before serial # prefix letter indicates the year of printing. Many sophisticated security features added.

		VG	VF	UNC
66	**10 Franken**			
	(19)95; (19)96 (1997). Brown-orange, dark brown and blue on multicolor underprint. Architect Le Corbusier (Charles Édouard Jeanneret-Gris) at upper left and bottom center and as watermark. "Modular" measuring system and buildings in Chandigarh designed by Le Corbusier on back.			
	a. 1995. (65, 66, 67).	FV	FV	10.00
	b. 1996. (65, 66, 67).	FV	FV	9.50
67	**10 Franken**			
	Brown-orange, dark brown and blue on multicolor underprint. Like #66 but with microperforation '10' added.			
	a. 2000. (71, 72, 73).	FV	FV	9.50

68	**20 Franken**	VG	VF	UNC
	(19)94; (19)95. Red-violet and green on multicolor underprint. Composer Arthur Honegger at upper left and bottom center and as watermark. Trumpet valves at top, steam locomotive wheel at center, musical score and piano keys at bottom on back.			
	a. 1994. (65, 66, 67).	FV	FV	21.00
	b. 1995. (65, 66, 67).	FV	FV	20.00
69	**20 Franken**			
	(20)00; (20)03; (20)24. Red-violet and green on multicolor underprint. Like #67 but with microperforation '20' added.			
	a. 2000. (71, 72, 73).	FV	FV	19.00
	b. 2003. (74, 75, 76).	FV	FV	18.50
	c. 2004. (74, 76, 77).	FV	FV	18.50

70	**50 Franken**	VG	VF	UNC
	(19)94 (1995). Deep olive-green and purple on multicolor underprint. Artist Sophie Taeuber-Arp at upper left, bottom and as watermark. Examples of her abstract art works on back. (65, 66, 67).	FV	FV	50.00
71	**50 Franken**			
	2002 (2003)-. Deep olive-green and purple on multicolor underprint. Like #68 but with microperforation '50' added.			
	a. 2002 (71, 72, 73).	FV	FV	47.50
	b. 2004.	—	—	—

72	**100 Franken**	VG	VF	UNC
	(19)96-99. Dark blue, purple and brown-orange on multicolor underprint. Alberto Giacometti (artist) at upper left, bottom and as watermark. Bronze bust *Lotar II* at top, sculpture *Homme Qui Marche I* repeated at center, time-space relationship scheme at lower center on back.			
	a. 1996. (66, 68, 69).	FV	FV	100.
	b. 1997. (66, 68, 69).	FV	FV	95.00
	c. 1998. (66, 68, 69).	FV	FV	90.00
	d. 1999. (66, 68, 69).	FV	FV	90.00
	e. 2000. (71, 72, 73).	FV	FV	90.00

73	**200 Franken**	VG	VF	UNC
	(19)96; (20)00. Brown and purple on multicolor underprint. Author Charles-Ferdinand Ramuz at upper left and at bottom center and as watermark. Diablerets massif at top, Lavaux area by Lake Geneva repeated at center to bottom with partial manuscript overlay on back.			
	a. 1996 (66, 68, 69).	FV	FV	190.
	b. 2002 (71, 72, 73).	FV	FV	180.

74	**1000 Franken**	VG	VF	UNC
	(19)96 (1998); (19)99. Purple and violet on multicolor underprint. Jacob Burckhardt (art historian) at upper left, bottom and as watermark. Window and the Pergamon Altar at top, the Rotunda of the Pantheon in Rome and a section of the Façade of Palazzo Strozzi in Florence at center, overlapped by Burckhardt's view of history scheme on back.			
	a. 1996 (1998). (66; 67, 68).	FV	FV	950.
	b. 1999. (66, 68, 69).	FV	FV	925.

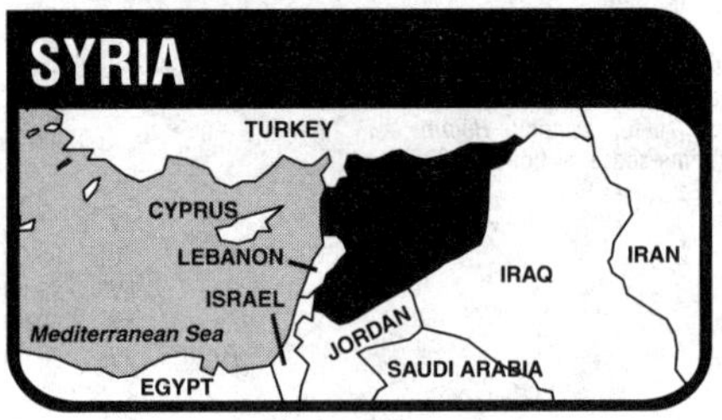

The Syrian Arab Republic, located in the Near East at the eastern end of the Mediterranean Sea, has an area of 71,498 sq. mi. (185,180 sq. km.) and a population of 16.13 million. Capital: Damascus. Agriculture and animal breeding are the chief industries. Cotton, crude oil and livestock are exported.

Ancient Syria, a land bridge connecting Europe, Africa and Asia, has spent much of its history in thrall to the conqueror's whim. Its subjection by Egypt about 1500 BC was followed by successive conquests by the Hebrews, Phoenicians, Babylonians, Assyrians, Persians, Macedonians, Romans, Byzantines and finally, in 636 AD, by the Moslems. The Arabs made Damascus, one of the oldest continuously inhabited cities of the world, the trade center and capital of an empire stretching from India to Spain. In 1517, following the total destruction of Damascus by the Mongols of Tamerlane, Syria fell to the Ottoman Turks and remained a Turkish province until World War I. The League of Nations gave France a mandate to the Levant states of Syria and Lebanon in 1920. In 1930, following a series of uprisings, France recognized Syria as an independent republic, but still subject to the mandate. Lebanon became fully independent on Nov. 22, 1943, and Syria on Jan. 1, 1944.

On Feb. 1, 1958, Egypt and Syria formed the United Arab Republic. Yemen joined on March 8 in an association known as the United Arab States. Syria withdrew from the United Arab Republic on Sept. 29, 1961, and on Dec. 26 Egypt dissolved its ties with Yemen in the United Arab States. Between 1961 and 1970 five coups brought in Lieut. Gen. Hafez el Assad as Prime Minister and in 1973 a new constitution was approved.

MONETARY SYSTEM:

1 Pound (Livre) = 100 Piastres

REPUBLIC

BANQUE CENTRALE DE SYRIE
CENTRAL BANK OF SYRIA

1958 ISSUE

#86-92 bank name in English on back. Wmk: Arabian horse's head.

#86-88 printer: The Pakistan Security Printing Corporation Ltd., Karachi (w/o imprint).

		VG	VF	UNC
86	**1 Pound** 1958/AH1377. Brown on multicolor underprint. Worker at right. Water wheel of Hama on back.			
	a. Issued note.	1.50	3.00	25.00
	s. Specimen.	—	—	25.00
87	**5 Pounds** 1958/AH1377. Green on multicolor underprint. Face similar to #86. Citadel of Aleppo on back.			
	a. Issued note.	5.00	15.00	85.00
	s. Specimen.	—	—	45.00

		VG	VF	UNC
88	**10 Pounds** 1958/AH1377. Purple on multicolor underprint. Face similar to #86. Courtyard of Omayad Mosque on back.			
	a. Issued note.	7.50	22.50	125.
	s. Specimen.	—	—	90.00

#89-92 printer: JEZ.

		VG	VF	UNC
89	**25 Pounds** 1958/AH1377. Blue on multicolor underprint. Girl with basket at right. Interior view of Azem Palace in Damascus on back.			
	a. Issued note.	8.00	30.00	120.
	s. Specimen.	—	—	150.
90	**50 Pounds** 1958/AH1377. Red and brown on multicolor underprint. Face similar to #89. Mosque of Sultan Selim on back.			
	a. Issued note.	8.00	30.00	120.
	s. Specimen.	—	—	175.
91	**100 Pounds** 1958;1962. Olive-green on multicolor underprint. Face similar to #89. Old ruins of Palmyra on back.			
	a. 1958.	15.00	65.00	225.
	b. 1962.	12.50	50.00	200.
	s. Specimen.	—	—	200.

		VG	VF	UNC
92	**500 Pounds** 1958/AH1377. Brown and purple on multicolor underprint. Motifs from ruins of Kingdom of Ugarit, head at right. Ancient religious wheel and cuneiform clay tablet on back.			
	a. Issued note.	35.00	150.	400.
	s. Specimen.	—	—	400.

1963-66 ISSUE

#93-98 wmk: Arabian horse's head. W/o imprint.

#93-95 worker at r.

		VG	VF	UNC
93	**1 Pound** 1963-82/AH1383-1402. Brown on multicolor underprint. Water wheel of Hama on back. Like #86.			
	a. Without security thread. 1963/AH1383.	1.00	3.00	10.00
	b. 1967/AH1387.	.75	2.50	8.00
	c. 1973/AH1393.	.50	1.50	5.00
	d. Security thread with *Central Bank of Syria* in small letters. 1978/AH1398.	.30	1.00	4.00
	e. 1982/AH1402.	.25	.75	3.00
	s. As a. Specimen.	—	—	85.00

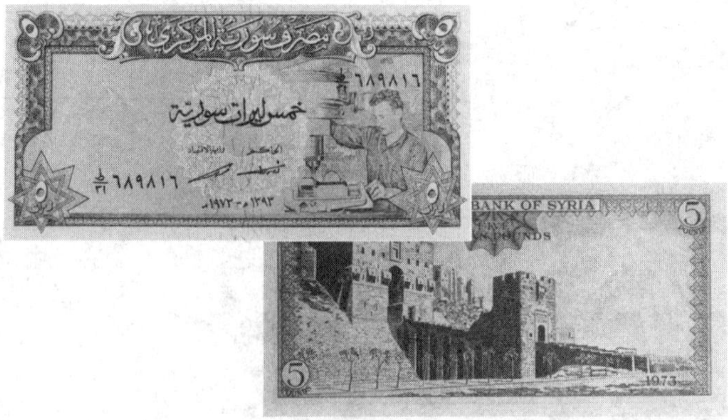

		VG	VF	UNC
94	**5 Pounds** 1963-73/AH1383-93. Green on multicolor underprint. Citadel of Aleppo on back. Like #87.			
	a. 1963/AH1383.	2.50	10.00	40.00
	b. 1967/AH1387.	1.75	6.00	35.00
	c. 1970.	1.00	4.00	25.00
	d. 1973/AH1393.	1.00	4.00	20.00

95	10 Pounds	VG	VF	UNC
	1965-73/AH138x-93. Purple on multicolor underprint. Courtyard of Omayad Mosque on back. Like #88.			
	a. 1965.	3.00	8.50	50.00
	b. 1968.	2.00	6.00	40.00
	c. 1973/AH1393.	1.50	5.00	25.00

96	25 Pounds	VG	VF	UNC
	1966-73/AH1386-93. Blue and brown on multicolor underprint. Worker at the loom at left. Bosra theater at center right on back.			
	a. 1966/AH1386.	4.00	25.00	150.
	b. 1970.	4.00	20.00	130.
	c. 1973/AH1393.	3.00	15.00	90.00
97	50 Pounds			
	1966-73/AH1386-93. Brown and olive-green on multicolor underprint. Arab driving combine at left. Fortress on back.			
	a. 1966/AH1386; 1970.	10.00	45.00	200.
	b. 1973/AH1393.	5.00	30.00	90.00

98	100 Pounds	VG	VF	UNC
	1966-74/AH1386-139x. Green and blue on multicolor underprint. Port installation at left. Back purple; dam at center.			
	a. 1966/AH1386.	12.50	40.00	110.
	b. 1968.	15.00	50.00	130.
	c. 1971/AH1391.	12.50	40.00	110.
	d. 1974.	10.00	30.00	90.00

1976-77 ISSUE

#99-105 wmk: Arabian horse's head. Shades vary between early and late printings.

99	1 Pound	VG	VF	UNC
	1977/AH1397. Orange and brown on multicolor underprint. Omayyad Mosque at center, craftsman at right. Back red-brown; combine at center.			
	a. Issued note.	1.00	3.00	12.50
	s. Specimen.	—	—	—

100	5 Pounds	VG	VF	UNC
	1977-91/AH1397-1412. Dark green on multicolor underprint. Bosra theater and statue of female warrior at right. Cotton picking and spinning frame on back.			
	a. Security thread. 1977/AH1397.	.75	2.50	7.50
	b. Security thread. With *Central Bank of Syria* in small letters. 1978/AH1398.	FV	FV	4.00
	c. 1982/AH1402.	FV	FV	3.00
	d. 1988/AH1408.	FV	FV	2.00
	e. 1991/AH1412.	FV	FV	1.50
	s. As a. Specimen.	—	—	—

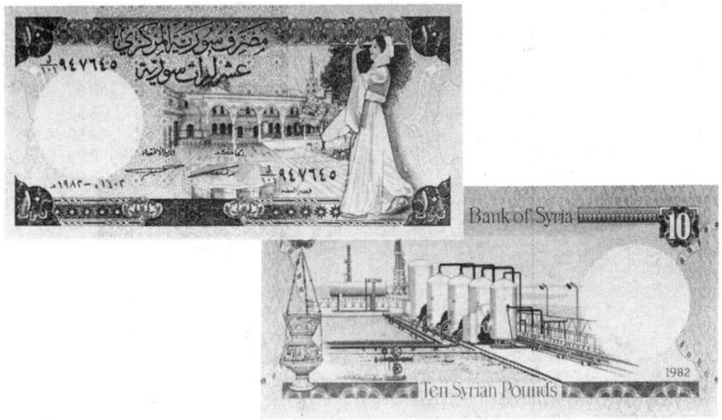

101	10 Pounds	VG	VF	UNC
	1977-91/AH1397-1412. Purple and violet on multicolor underprint. Al-Azem Palace in Damascus at center, dancing woman at right. Water treatment plant on back.			
	a. Like #100a. 1977/AH1397.	1.50	4.00	10.00
	b. Like #100b. 1978/AH1398.	FV	FV	3.50
	c. 1982/AH1402.	FV	FV	3.00
	d. 1988/AH1408.	FV	FV	1.50
	e. 1991/AH1412.	FV	FV	1.50

102	25 Pounds	VG	VF	UNC
	1977-91/AH1397-1412. Dark blue and dark green on multicolor underprint. Krak des Chevaliers castle at center, Saladdin at right. Central Bank building on back.			
	a. Like #100a. 1977/AH1397.	3.00	8.00	20.00
	b. Like #100b. 1978/AH1398.	FV	2.00	10.00
	c. 1982/AH1402.	FV	FV	7.00
	d. 1988/AH1408.	FV	FV	5.00
	e. 1991/AH1412.	FV	FV	4.00

103	50 Pounds	VG	VF	UNC
	1977-91/AH1397-1412. Brown, black and green on multicolor underprint. Dam at center, ancient statue at right. Citadel of Aleppo on back.			
	a. Like #100a. 1977/AH1397.	4.50	10.00	30.00
	b. Like #100b. 1978/AH1398.	FV	3.00	14.00
	c. 1982/AH1402.	FV	3.00	12.00
	d. 1988/AH1408.	FV	3.00	7.00
	e. 1991/AH1412.	FV	FV	6.00

104	100 Pounds	VG	VF	UNC
	1977-90/AH1397-1411. Dark blue, dark green and dark brown on multicolor underprint. Ancient Palmyra ruins at center, Queen Zenobia bust at right. Grain silos at Lattakia on back.			
	a. Like #100a. 1977/AH1397.	5.00	15.00	50.00
	b. Like #100b. 1978/AH1398.	FV	8.00	30.00
	c. 1982/AH1402.	FV	FV	17.50
	d. 1990/AH1411.	FV	FV	9.00

105	500 Pounds	VG	VF	UNC
	1976-90/AH1396-1411. Dark violet-brown and brown on multicolor underprint. Like #92.			
	a. 1976/AH1396.	FV	15.00	60.00
	b. 1979.	15.00	40.00	180.
	c. 1982/AH1402.	FV	20.00	80.00
	d. 1986.	FV	20.00	70.00
	e. 1990/AH1411.	FV	FV	45.00
	f. 1992/AH1413.	FV	FV	35.00

#106 not assigned.

1997-98 ISSUE

#107-109 wmk: Arabian horse's head.

107	50 Pounds	VG	VF	UNC
	1998/AH1419. Dark and light brown, green and lilac on multicolor underprint. Aleppo Citadel at center, water wheel of Hama at right. Al-Assad library, Abbyssian stadium and students on back.	FV	FV	3.00

108	100 Pounds	VG	VF	UNC
	1998/AH1419. Light blue, red-brown and purple on multicolor underprint. Bosra theater at center, ancient bust of Philip at right. Hajaz railway locomotive; Damascus station and road on back.	FV	FV	5.00

		VG	VF	UNC
109	**200 Pounds** 1997/AH1418. Red-orange, purple and light brown on multicolor underprint. Monument to the Unknown soldier at center, Islamic coin at lower center right, Statue of Saladdln at right. Cotton weaving and energy plant on back.	FV	FV	8.00

		VG	VF	UNC
110	**500 Pounds** 1998/AH1419 (2000). Gray and bluish-green on multicolor underprint. Queen Zenobia at right, Palmyra theater at center. Eufrate dam, irrigation and agricultural products on back.	FV	FV	24.00

		VG	VF	UNC
111	**1000 Pounds** 1997/AH1418. Green, blue and light brown on multicolor underprint. Omayyad Mosque main entrance at center, Islamic dinar coin and clay tablet at lower center, H. Assad at right and as watermark. Oil industry workers at left, harvesting machinery and fishing boat on back. Two slight varieties.	FV	FV	40.00

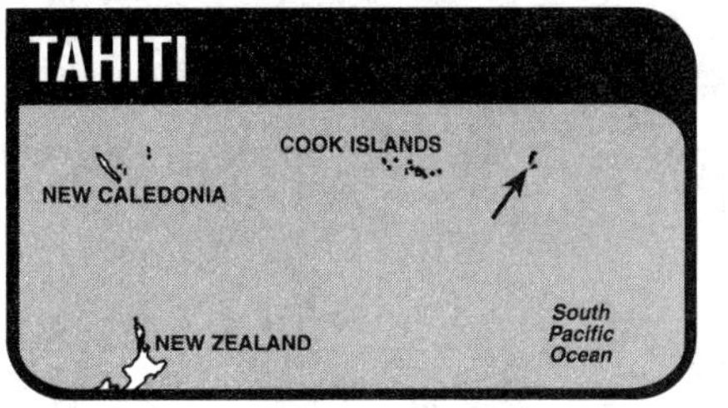

Tahiti, the largest island of the central South Pacific French overseas territory of French Polynesia, has an area of 402 sq. mi. (1,042 sq. km.) and a population of 79,024. Papeete on the northwest coast is the capital and administrative center of French Polynesia. Copra, sugar cane, vanilla and coffee are exported. Tourism is an important industry.

Capt. Samuel Wallis of the British Navy discovered Tahiti in 1768 and named it King George III Island. Louis-Antoine de Bougainville arrived the following year and claimed it for France. Subsequent English visits were by James Cook in 1769 and William Bligh in the HMS "Bounty" in 1788.

Members of the Protestant London Missionary Society established the first European settlement in 1797, and with the aid of the local Pomare family gained control of the entire island and established a "missionary kingdom" with a scriptural code of law. Nevertheless, Tahiti was subsequently declared a French protectorate (1842) and a colony (1880), and since 1958 is part of the overseas territory of French Polynesia.

RULERS:

French

MONETARY SYSTEM:

1 Franc = 100 Centimes

SIGNATURE VARIETIES

	DIRECTEUR GÉNÉRAL	PREÉSIDENT DU CONSEIL DE SURVEILLANCE
1	André Postel-Vinay, 1967-1972	Bernard Clappier, 1966-1972
2	Claude Panouillot, 1972-1973	André de Lattre, 1973
3	Claude Panouillot, 1974-1978	Marcel Theron, 1974-1979
4	Yves Roland-Billecart, 1979-1984	Gabriel Lefort, 1980-1984
5	Yves Roland-Billecart, 1985-	Jacques Waitzenegger, 1985-

FRENCH ADMINISTRATION

BANQUE DE L'INDOCHINE

PAPEETE

1939-40 ND ISSUE

14 **100 Francs**

ND (1939-65). Brown and multicolor. Woman wearing wreath and holding sm. figure of Athena at center Angkor statue on back.

	Good	Fine	XF
a. Signature M. Borduge and P. Baudouin with titles: *LE PRÉSIDENT* and *LE ADMINISTRATEUR DIRECTEUR GÉNÉRAL.*	20.00	85.00	300.
b. Signature titles: *LE PRÉSIDENT* and *LE ADMINISTRATEUR DIRECTEUR GÉNÉRAL.*	15.00	75.00	250.
c. Signature titles: *LE PRÉSIDENT* and *LE VICE-PRÉSIDENT DIRECTEUR GÉNÉRAL.*	12.00	60.00	225.
d. Signature titles: *LE PRÉSIDENT* and *LE DIRECTEUR GÉNÉRAL.*	10.00	50.00	200.

1951 ND Issue

21 **20 Francs**

ND (1951-63). Multicolor. Youth at left, flute player at right. Fruit at left, woman at right on back. Watermark: Man with hat.

	VG	VF	UNC
a. Signature titles: *LE PRÉSIDENT* and *LE DIRECTEUR GAL.* (1951).	12.50	50.00	125.
b. Signature titles: *LE PRÉSIDENT* and *LE VICE-PRÉSIDENT DIRECTEUR GÉNÉRAL* (1954-1958).	7.00	30.00	75.00
c. Signature titles: *LE PRÉSIDENT* and *LE DIRECTEUR GÉNÉRAL.* (1963).	5.00	20.00	50.00

Institut d'Emission d'Outre-Mer

1969-71 ND Issues

23 **100 Francs**

ND (1969). Brown and multicolor. Girl wearing wreath holding guitar at right, without *REPUBLIQUE FRANCAISE* near bottom center. Girl at left, town scene at center on back. Signature 1. Printed from engraved copper plates.

VG	VF	UNC
3.00	10.00	75.00

24 **100 Francs**

ND. (1971; 1973). Multicolor. Like #23 but with overprint: *REPUBLIQUE FRANCAISE* at bottom center. Signature 1.

	VG	VF	UNC
a. Printed from engraved copper plates. (1971).	6.00	25.00	60.00
b. Offset printing. (1973).	5.00	20.00	50.00

25 **500 Francs**

ND (1970-85). Blue and multicolor. Harbor view with boat in background at center, fisherman at lower right. Man at left, objects at right on back.

	VG	VF	UNC
a. Signature 1. (1970).	FV	30.00	75.00
b1. Signature 3. (1977).	FV	22.50	60.00
b2. Signature 3A.	FV	25.00	65.00
c. Signature 4. (1983).	FV	20.00	50.00
d. Signature 5. (1985).	FV	8.00	35.00

26 **1000 Francs**

ND (1969). Dark brown on red and multicolor underprint. Hut under palms at left, girl at right. Without *REPUBLIQUE FRANCAISE* overprint at bottom center. Kagu, deer, buildings, native carvings on back. Watermark: Marianne. Signature 1.

VG	VF	UNC
12.00	75.00	200.

27	1000 Francs	VG	VF	UNC
	ND (1971-85). Dark brown on multicolor underprint. Like #26 but with overprint: *REPUBLIQUE FRANCAISE* at lower left.			
	a. Signature 1. (1971).	FV	25.00	75.00
	b. Signature 3. (1977).	FV	22.50	65.00
	c. Signature 4. (1983).	FV	22.50	65.00
	d. Signature 5. (1985).	FV	20.00	50.00

28	5000 Francs	VG	VF	UNC
	ND (1971-85). Brown with black text on olive-green and multicolor underprint. Bougainville at left, sailing ships at center. Admiral Febvrier-Despointes at right, sailboat at center right on back.			
	a. Signature 1. (1971).	FV	70.00	210.
	b. Signature 2. (1975).	FV	65.00	175.
	c. Signature 4. (1982; 1984).	FV	60.00	160.
	d. Signature 5. (1985).	FV	60.00	135.

The Republic of Tajikistan, was formed from those regions of Bukhara and Turkestan where the population consisted mainly of Tajiks. It is bordered in the north and west by Uzbekistan and Kyrgyzstan, in the east by China and in the south by Afghanistan. It has an area of 55,240 sq. miles (143,100 sq. km.) and a population of 6.4 million. It includes 2 provinces of Khudzand and Khatlon together with the Gorno-Badakhshan Autonomous Region with a population of 5,092,603. Capital: Dushanbe. Tajikistan was admitted as a constituent republic of the Soviet Union on December 5, 1929. In Aug. 1990 the Tajik Supreme Soviet adopted a declaration of republican sovereignty, and in December 1991 the republic became a member of the Commonwealth of Independent States.

MONETARY SYSTEM:

1 Ruble = 100 Tanga, to 2000
1 Somoni = 1,000 Rubles
1 Somoni = 100 Diram

REPUBLIC

БОНКИ МИЛЛИИ ЧУМХУРИИ

NATIONAL BANK OF THE REPUBLIC OF TAJIKISTAN

1994 ISSUE

#1-8 arms at upper l. or l. *Majlisi Olii* (Parliament) on back. Wmk: Multiple stars. Printer: Goznak, Moscow, w/o imprint.

1	1 Ruble	VG	VF	UNC
	1994. Brown on multicolor underprint.			
	a. Issued note.	.05	.15	1.00
	s. Specimen.	—	—	—

2	5 Rubles	VG	VF	UNC
	1994. Deep blue on multicolor underprint.			
	a. Issued note.	.05	.15	1.00
	s. Specimen.	—	—	—

3	10 Rubles	VG	VF	UNC
	1994. Deep red on multicolor underprint.			
	a. Issued note.	.05	.15	1.00
	s. Specimen.	—	—	—

4	20 Rubles	VG	VF	UNC
	1994. Purple on multicolor underprint.			
	a. Issued note.	.05	.15	1.00
	s. Specimen.	—	—	—

5	50 Rubles	VG	VF	UNC
	1994. Dark olive-green on multicolor underprint.			
	a. Issued note. .	.05	.15	1.50
	s. Specimen.	—	—	—

6	100 Rubles	VG	VF	UNC
	1994. Blue-black and brown on multicolor underprint.			
	a. Issued note.	.10	.20	2.00
	s. Specimen.	—	—	—

7	200 Rubles	VG	VF	UNC
	1994. Deep olive-green and pale violet on multicolor underprint.			
	a. Issued note.	.15	.30	3.00
	s. Specimen.	—	—	—

8	500 Rubles	VG	VF	UNC
	1994. Brown-violet on multicolor underprint.			
	a. Issued note.	.25	.50	4.00
	s. Specimen.	—	—	—

9	1000 Rubles	VG	VF	UNC
	1994 (1999). Brown and purple on multicolor underprint.			
	a. Issued note.	.25	.50	5.00
	s. Specimen.	—	—	—

9A	5000 Rubles	VG	VF	UNC
	1994. Dark green and blue on multicolor underprint. Coat of Arms at left. Parliament building with flag on back. (Not issued).	—	—	35.00

9B	10,000 Rubles	VG	VF	UNC
	1994. Pink and brown on multicolor underprint. Coat of Arms at center. Parliament building with flag on back.			
	a. Unissued note.	—	—	35.00
	s. Specimen.	—	—	—

БОНКИ МИЛЛИИ ТОЧИКИСТОН

NATIONAL BANK OF TAJIKISTAN

1999 ISSUE

#10-19 Printed in Germany.

#10-13 wmk: two mountains over rectangle.

10	1 Diram	VG	VF	UNC
	1999 (2000). Brown on tan and red underprint. Sadriddin Ayni Theatre and Opera house at center. Pamir mountains on back.			
	a. Issued note.	.05	.15	1.00
	s. Specimen.	—	—	1.00
11	5 Diram			
	1999 (2000). Blue on tan underprint. Arbob Culture Palace at center. Shrine of Mirzo Tursunzoda on back.			
	a. Issued note.	.05	.15	1.00
	s. Specimen.	—	—	1.00
12	20 Diram			
	1999 (2000). Green on tan underprint. *Majlisi Olii* (Tajik Parliament) interior. Road pass in the mountains on back.			
	a. Issued note.	.05	.25	2.00
	s. Specimen.	—	—	1.50

13	50 Diram	VG	VF	UNC
	1999 (2000). Purple on tan underprint. Statue of Ismoili Somoni at center. Road in a valley on back.			
	a. Issued note.	.05	.35	1.50
	s. Specimen.	—	—	2.50

#14-19 wmk: as portrait.

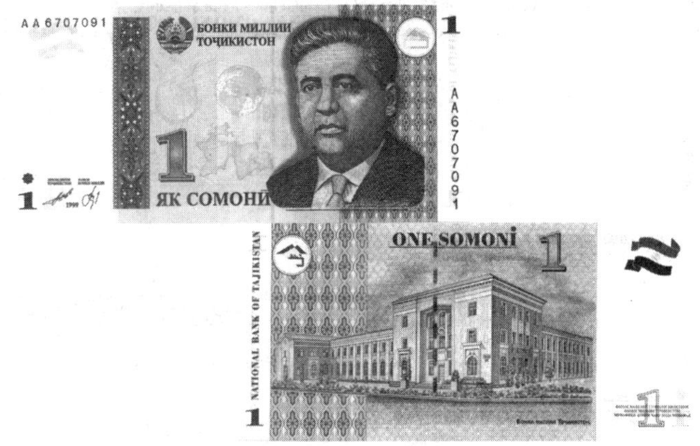

14	1 Somoni	VG	VF	UNC
	1999 (2000). Green and blue on multicolor underprint. Mirzo Tursunzoda (poet) at right. National Bank of Tajikistan building on back.			
	a. Issued note.	.05	.50	2.50
	s. Specimen.	—	—	5.00

15	5 Somoni	VG	VF	UNC
	1999 (2000). Blue and green on multicolor underprint. Sadriddin Ayni at right. Shrine of Abuabdullo Rudaki on back.			
	a. Issued note.	FV	1.50	6.00
	s. Specimen.	—	—	10.00

16	10 Somoni	VG	VF	UNC
	1999 (2000). Purple and orange-red. Mir Saiid Alii Hamadoni at right. Historical medieval monument on back.			
	a. Issued note.	.10	2.00	10.00
	s. Specimen.	—	—	17.50

NOTICE

Readers with unlisted dates, signature varieties, etc. are invited to submit photocopies of their notes to: Standard Catalog of World Paper Money, 700 East State St. Iola, WI 54990-0001, E-Mail: george.cuhaj@fwpubs.com.

#17-19 w/holographic strip at r.

17	20 Somoni	VG	VF	UNC
	1999 (2000). Brown and blue on multicolor underprint. Abuali Ibn Sino at right. Hissor fortress near Dushanbe on back.			
	a. Issued note.	.50	3.00	15.00
	s. Specimen.	—	—	22.50

18	50 Somoni	VG	VF	UNC
	1999 (2000). Dark blue and black on multicolor underprint. Bobojon Gafurov at right. *Choikhanai Sina,* a tea house in Dushanbe, on back.			
	a. Issued note.	1.00	3.00	15.00
	s. Specimen.	—	—	25.00

19	100 Somoni	VG	VF	UNC
	1999 (2000). Brown and blue on multicolor underprint. Ismoılı Somoni at right. Presidential Palace in Dushanbe on back.			
	a. Issued note.	1.00	3.00	25.00
	s. Specimen.	—	—	35.00

TANZANIA

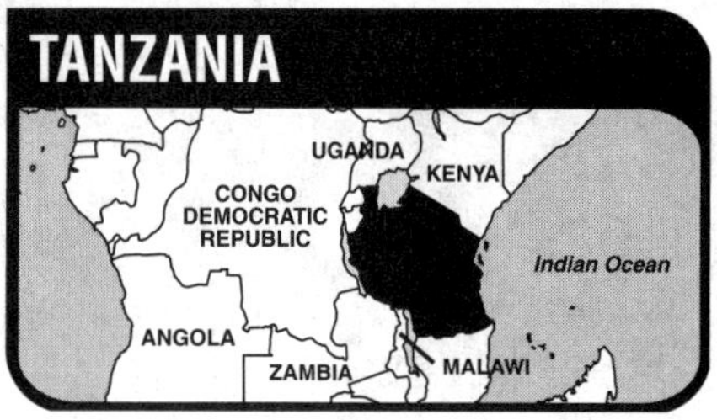

The United Republic of Tanzania, located on the east coast of Africa between Kenya and Mozambique, consists of Tanganyika and the islands of Zanzibar and Pemba. It has an area of 364,900 sq. mi. (945,090 sq. km.) and a population of 33.69 million. Capital: Dodoma. The chief exports are cotton, coffee, diamonds, sisal, cloves, petroleum products and cashew nuts.

German East Africa (Tanganyika), located on the coast of east-central Africa between British East Africa (now Kenya) and Portuguese East Africa (now Mozambique), had an area of 362,284 sq. mi. (938,216 sq. km.) and a population of about 6 million. Capital: Dar es Salaam. Chief products prior to German control were ivory and slaves; after German control, sisal, coffee and rubber. Germany acquired control of the area by treaties with coastal chiefs in 1884, established it as a protectorate in 1891, and proclaimed it the Colony of German East Africa in 1897. After World War I, Tanganyika was entrusted to Great Britain as a League of Nations mandate, and after World War II as a United Nations trust territory. Tanganyika became an independent nation within the British Commonwealth on Dec. 9, 1961.

The British Protectorate of Zanzibar and Pemba, and adjacent small islands, located in the Indian Ocean 22 miles (35 km.) off the coast of Tanganyika, comprised a portion of British East Africa. Zanzibar was also the name of a sultanate which included the Zanzibar and Kenya protectorates. Zanzibar has an area of 637 sq. mi. (1,651 sq. km.). Chief city: Zanzibar. Pemba has an area of 380 sq. mi. (984 sq. km.). Chief city: Chake Chake. The islands are noted for their cloves, of which Zanzibar is the world's foremost producer.

Zanzibar and Pemba share a common history. Zanzibar came under Portuguese control in 1503, was conquered by the Omani Arabs in 1698, became independent of Oman in 1860, and (with Pemba) came under British control in 1890. Britain granted the protectorate self-government in 1961, and independence within the British Commonwealth on Dec. 19, 1963. On April 26, 1964, Tanganyika and Zanzibar (with Pemba) united to form the United Republic of Tanganyika and Zanzibar. The name of the country was changed to Tanzania on Oct. 29, 1964. The president is Chief of State.

Also see East Africa and Zanzibar, (Vol. 2).

MONETARY SYSTEM:

1 Shilingi (Shilling) = 100 Senti

BANK OF TANZANIA

SIGNATURE VARIETIES

	MINISTER FOR FINANCE	GOVERNOR		MINISTER FOR FINANCE	GOVERNOR
1			2		
3			4		
5			6	WAZIRI WA FEDHA	GAVANA
7	WAZIRI WA FEDHA	GAVANA	7A		
8			9		
10			11		
12			13		
14					

1966 ND ISSUE

Note: Sign. 3-5 w/English titles on #2 and 3, changed to Swahili titles for later issues.

#1-5 arms at ctr., Pres. J. Nyerere at r. Wmk: Giraffe's head. Replacement notes: Serial # prefix *ZZ; ZY*.

		VG	VF	UNC
1	**5 Shillings**			
	ND (1966). Brown on multicolor underprint. Mountain view on back. Signature 1.			
	a. Issued note.	1.00	3.00	12.50
	s. Specimen.	—	—	25.00

		VG	VF	UNC
2	**10 Shillings**			
	ND (1966). Green on multicolor underprint. Sisal drying on back.			
	a. Signature 1.	1.50	3.00	9.00
	b. Signature 2.	2.00	4.00	10.00
	c. Signature 3.	7.50	30.00	225.
	d. Signature 4.	1.00	2.00	7.50
	e. Signature 5.	1.00	2.00	6.00
	s. As a. Specimen.	—	—	25.00

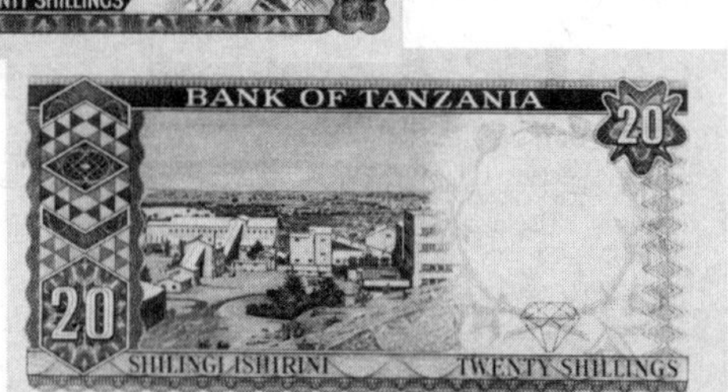

		VG	VF	UNC
3	**20 Shillings**			
	ND (1966). Blue on multicolor underprint. Work buildings on back.			
	a. Signature 1.	2.00	5.00	12.50
	b. Signature 2.	2.00	5.00	12.50
	c. Signature 3.	3.00	7.00	20.00
	d. Signature 4.	2.00	5.00	15.00
	e. Signature 5.	1.50	3.00	9.00
	s. As a. Specimen.	—	—	25.00

4 100 Shillings

ND (1966). Red on multicolor underprint. Masai herdsman with animals on back. Signature 1.

	VG	VF	UNC
a. Issued note.	17.50	60.00	375.
s. Specimen.	—	—	85.00

5 100 Shillings

ND (1966). Red on multicolor underprint. Various animals on back.

	VG	VF	UNC
a. Signature 1.	15.00	50.00	350.
b. Signature 3.	12.50	40.00	275.

BENKI KUU YA TANZANIA

1977-78 ND ISSUE

#6-8 arms at top ctr., Pres. J. Nyerere at r. Wmk: Giraffe's head. Replacement notes: Serial # prefix *ZZ; ZY*.

Note: For #6-8, sign. are shown in chronological order of appearance. It seems sign. 3 was used again following several later combinations.

6 10 Shilingi

ND (1978). Green on multicolor underprint. Monument and mountain at center on back.

	VG	VF	UNC
a. Signature 5.	.25	1.50	5.50
b. Signature 6.	.25	1.00	3.00
c. Signature 3. Signature titles: *WAZIRI WA FEDHA* and *GAVANA.*	.25	.75	2.50

7 20 Shilingi

ND (1978). Blue on multicolor underprint. Cotton knitting machine on back.

	VG	VF	UNC
a. Signature 5.	.50	2.25	7.50
b. Signature 6.	.50	2.25	4.50
c. Signature 3. Signature titles: *WAZIRI WA FEDHA* and *GAVANA.*	.50	2.25	5.00

8 100 Shilingi

ND (1977). Purple on multicolor underprint. Teacher and students at left, farmers at center on back.

	VG	VF	UNC
a. Signature 4.	2.00	6.00	27.50
b. Signature 5.	1.50	5.00	25.00
c. Signature 6.	1.00	4.00	17.50
d. Signature 3. Signature titles: *WAZIRI WA FEDHA* and *GAVANA.*	1.00	4.50	20.00

1985 ND ISSUE

#9-11 portr. of an older Pres. J. Nyerere at r., torch at l., arms at ctr. Islands of Mafia, Pemba and Zanzibar are omitted from map on back. Sign. 3. Wmk: Giraffe's head. Replacement notes: Serial # prefix *ZZ; ZY*.

9 20 Shilingi

ND (1985). Purple, brown on multicolor underprint. Tire factory scene on back.

	VG	VF	UNC
	.15	.50	2.50

10 50 Shilingi

ND (1985). Red-orange, light brown on multicolor underprint. Brick making on back.

	VG	VF	UNC
	.25	1.50	5.00

11 100 Shilingi

ND (1985). Blue, purple on multicolor underprint. Graduation procession on back.

	VG	VF	UNC
	.50	3.00	8.50

1986 ND ISSUE

#12-14 like #9-11 but w/islands of Mafia, Pemba and Zanzibar now included in map on back. Replacement notes: Serial # prefix *ZZ; ZY*.

12	20 Shilingi	VG	VF	UNC
	ND (1986). Like #9 but with islands in map on back. Signature 3. Signature titles: WAZIRI WA FEDHA and *GAVANA*.	.15	.50	2.00

13	50 Shilingi	VG	VF	UNC
	ND (1986). Like #10 but with islands in map on back. Signature 3. Signature titles: *WAZIRI WA FEDHA* and *GAVANA*.	.25	1.00	3.50

14	100 Shilingi	VG	VF	UNC
	ND (1986). Like #11 but with islands in map on back.			
	a. Signature 3 with titles: *WAZIRI WA FEDHA* and *GAVANA*.	.50	1.50	5.00
	b. Signature 8.	.25	1.00	4.00

1986-90 ND ISSUE

#15-18 arms at ctr., Pres. Mwinyi at r. Wmk: Giraffe's head. Replacement notes: Serial # prefix *ZZ; ZY*.

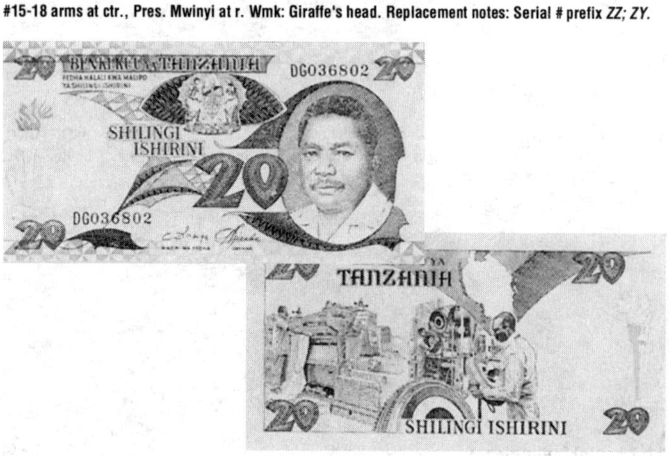

15	20 Shilingi	VG	VF	UNC
	ND (1987). Purple, red-brown on multicolor underprint. Back like #12. Signature 3 but with titles: *WAZIRI WA FEDHA* and *GAVANA*.	.10	.25	2.00

16	50 Shilingi	VG	VF	UNC
	ND (1986). Red-orange, light brown on multicolor underprint. Back like #13.			
	a. Signature 3 but with titles: *WAZIRI WA FEDHA* and *GAVANA*.	.25	1.00	4.00
	b. Signature 7.	.20	.75	3.00

18	200 Shilingi	VG	VF	UNC
	ND (1986). Black, orange and ochre on multicolor underprint. Two fishermen on back.			
	a. Signature 3 but with titles: *WAZIRI WA FEDHA* and *GAVANA*.	.50	2.00	7.50
	b. Signature 7.	1.00	4.00	15.00

1989-92 ND ISSUE

#19-22 similar to #16 and #18 but w/modified portr. Wmk: Giraffe's head. Replacement notes: Serial # prefix *ZZ; ZY*.

19	50 Shilingi	VG	VF	UNC
	ND (1992). Red-orange and light brown on multicolor underprint. Signature 8.	.10	.50	1.75

		VG	VF	UNC
20	**200 Shilingi** ND (1992). Black, orange and ochre on multicolor underprint. Signature 7, 8.	.50	1.50	6.00

		VG	VF	UNC
21	**500 Shilingi** ND (1989). Dark blue on multicolor underprint. Zebra at lower left. Harvesting on back.			
	a. Signature 3 but with titles: *WAZIRI WA FEDHA* and *GAVANA*.	2.50	10.00	35.00
	b. Signature 7.	1.50	5.00	22.50
	c. Signature 8.	1.00	3.00	17.50

		VG	VF	UNC
22	**1000 Shilingi** ND (1990). Green and brown on multicolor underprint. Elephants at lower left. Kiwira Coal Mine at left center, door to the Peoples Bank of Zanzibar at lower right on back. Signature 8.	1.50	5.00	22.50

1993; 1995 ND Issue

#23, 25-27 arms at ctr., Pres. Mwinyi at r. Wmk: Giraffe's head. Reduced size. Replacement notes: Serial # prefix *ZZ; ZY*.

		VG	VF	UNC
23	**50 Shilingi** ND (1993). Red-orange and brown on multicolor underprint. Wildebeest grazing at left. Men making bricks on back. Signature 9.	FV	FV	1.00

		VG	VF	UNC
24	**100 Shilingi** ND (1993). Blue and aqua on multicolor underprint. Kudu at left, arms at center, J. Nyerere at right. Graduation procession on back. Signature 9.	FV	FV	2.00

Note: #24 honors the 70th birthday of Julius Nyerere.

		VG	VF	UNC
25	**200 Shilingi** ND (1993). Black and orange on multicolor underprint. Leopards at left. Back similar to #18.			
	a. Signature 9.	FV	FV	3.50
	b. Signature 11.	FV	FV	3.00

		VG	VF	UNC
26	**500 Shilingi** ND (1993). Purple, blue-green and violet on multicolor underprint. Zebra at lower left. Back similar to #21 with arms at lower right.			
	a. Signature 9.	FV	FV	8.00
	b. Signature 10.	FV	FV	5.00
	c. Signature 11.	FV	FV	4.50

		VG	VF	UNC
27	**1000 Shilingi** ND (1993). Dark green, brown and orange-brown on multicolor underprint. Similar to #22.			
	a. Signature 9.	FV	FV	12.50
	b. Signature 10.	FV	FV	10.00
	c. Signature 11.	FV	FV	7.50

		VG	VF	UNC
28	**5000 Shilingi** ND (1995). Brown on multicolor underprint. Giraffes with Mt. Kilimanjaro in background on back. Signature 10.	FV	FV	27.50

		VG	VF	UNC
29	**10,000 Shilingi** ND (1995). Multicolor. Lion at lower left. Signature 10.	FV	FV	50.00

1997 ND ISSUE

#30-33 arms at upper ctr., giraffe's head at r. and as wmk. Sign. 12.

		VG	VF	UNC
30	**500 Shilingi** ND (1997). Blue-black and dark green on multicolor underprint. Zebra at lower left. Woman harvesting cloves at left center on back.	FV	FV	2.50

		VG	VF	UNC
31	**1000 Shilingi** ND (1997). Deep olive-green, red-orange and dark brown on multicolor underprint. Elephants at lower left. Industrial buildings at left center, door to the Peoples Bank of Zanzibar at lower right on back.	FV	FV	5.00

		VG	VF	UNC
32	**5000 Shilingi** ND (1997). Dark brown and purple on multicolor underprint. Rhinoceros at lower left. Giraffes with Mt. Kilimanjaro in background on back. Segmented foil over security thread.	FV	FV	16.00

		VG	VF	UNC
33	**10,000 Shilingi** ND (1997). Blue-black and dark gray on multicolor underprint. Lion at lower left. Vertical foil strip at right. Bank of Tanzania Head Office building at left center, Zanzibar House of Wonder at lower right on back.	FV	FV	32.00

2000 ND ISSUE

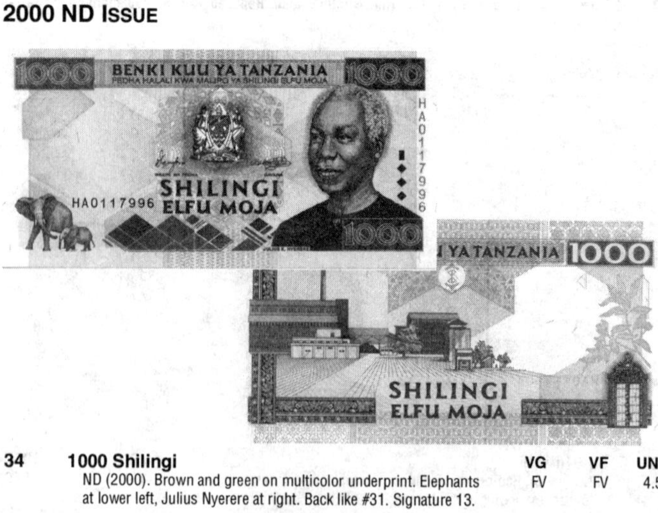

		VG	VF	UNC
34	**1000 Shilingi** ND (2000). Brown and green on multicolor underprint. Elephants at lower left, Julius Nyerere at right. Back like #31. Signature 13.	FV	FV	4.50

2003 ND Issue

#35-39 sign. 14. Printer: G&D.

		VG	VF	UNC
35	**500 Shilingi** ND (2003). Green and blue on multicolor underprint. Cape Buffalo at center right. Hospital at center, boats in background on back.	FV	FV	2.50

		VG	VF	UNC
36	**1000 Shilingi** ND (2003). Blue and slate blue on multicolor underprint. Julius Nyerere at center right. Palace on back.	FV	FV	5.00

		VG	VF	UNC
37	**2000 Shilingi** ND (2003). Brown, tan and green on multicolor underprint. Lion and Mt. Kilimanjaro at center. Fort on back.	FV	FV	7.50

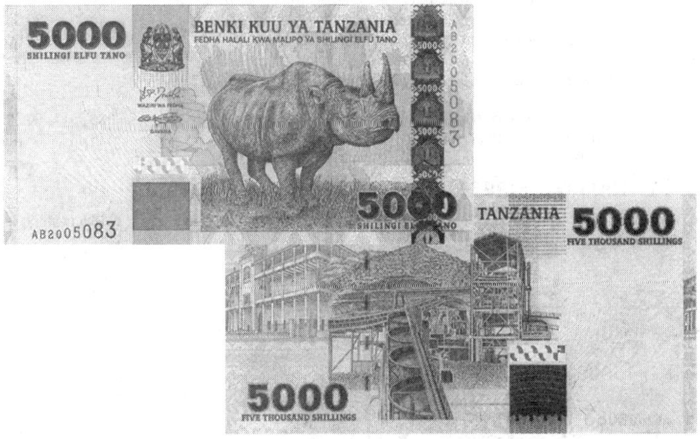

		VG	VF	UNC
38	**5000 Shilingi** ND (2003). Purple on multicolor underprint. Black Rhinoceros at center left. Mining and House of Wonder on back.	FV	FV	15.00

		VG	VF	UNC
39	**10,000 Shilingi** ND (2003). Rose and green on multicolor underprint. Elephant at center left. Central Bank building on back.	FV	FV	30.00

Sending Scanned Images by e-mail

Over the past two years or so, we have been receiving an ever-increasing flow of scanned images from sources world wide. Unfortunately, many of these scans could not be used due to the type of scan, or simple incompatibility with our systems. We appreciate the effort it takes to produce these images and accuracy they add to the catalog listings.

Here are a few simple instructions to follow when producing these scans. We encourage you to continue sending new images or upgrades to those currently illustrated and please do not hesitate to ask questions about this process.

- Scan all images within a resolution of 300 dpi.
- Size setting should be at 100%
- Please include in the e-mail the actual size of the image in millimeters height x width
- Scan in true 4-color
- Save images as 'tiff' and name in such a way which clearly indentifies the country of the note and catalog number
- Do not compress files
- Please e-mail with a request to confirm receipt of the attachment
- If you wish to send an image for "view only" and is not intended for print, a lower resolution (dpi) is fine
- Please send multiple images on a disc if available
- Please send images to george.cuhaj@fwpubs.com

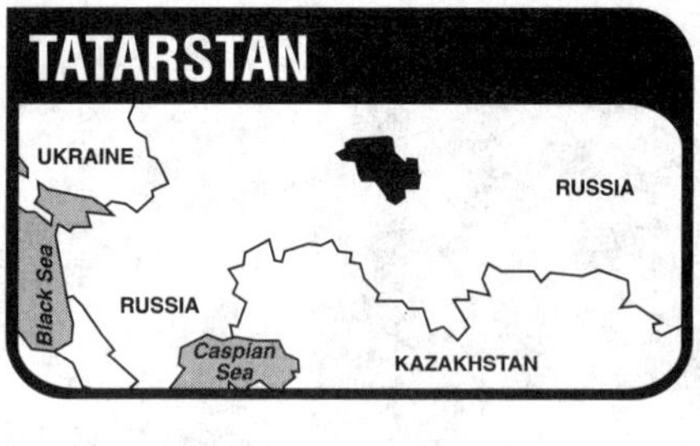

Tatarstan, an autonomous republic in the Russian Federation, is situated between the middle of the Volga River and its tributary Kama, extends east to the Ural mountains, covering 26,500 sq. mi. (68,000 sq. km.) and as of the 1970 census has a population of 3,743,600. Captial: Kazan. Tatarstan's economy combines its ancient traditions in the craftsmanship of wood, leather, cloth and ceramics with modern engineering, chemical, and food industries.

Colonized by the Bulgars in the 5th century, the territory of the Volga-Kama Bulgar State was inhabited by Turks. In the 13th century, Ghengis Khan conquered the area and established control until the 15th century when residual Mongol influence left Tatarstan as the Tatar Khanate, seat of the Kazar (Tatar) Khans. In 1552, under Ivan IV (the Terrible), Russia conquered, absorbed and controlled Tatarstan until the dissolution of the U.S.S.R.

Constituted as an autonomous republic on May 27, 1990, and as a sovereign state equal with Russia in April, 1992, Tatarstan, signed a treaty in February, 1994, defining it as a state united with the Commonwealth of Independent States.

MONETARY SYSTEM:

1 Ruble = 100 Kopeks

ТАТАРСКАЯ С.С.Р.

REPUBLIC OF TATARSTAN

TREASURY

1992 ND КУРОН - RUBLE CONTROL COUPON ISSUES

#1-3 red and green stripes w/black ТАТАРСКАЯ repeated on back.

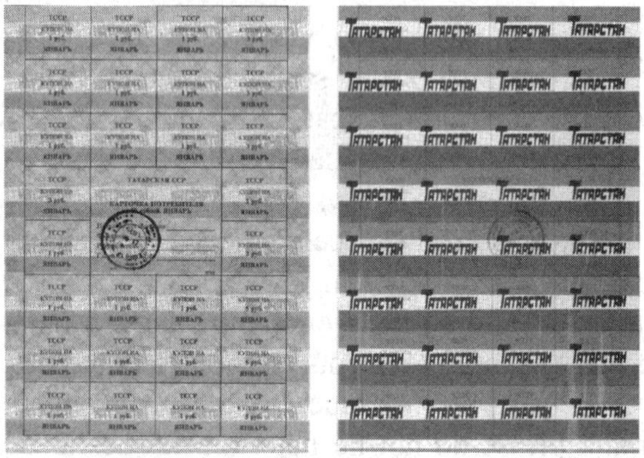

		VG	VF	UNC
1	**50 Rubles**			
	ND (1992). Black text on green underprint. With month: ЯНВАРЬ **(January).**			
	a. Issued full sheet.	4.50	10.00	15.00
	b. Remainder full sheet.	2.50	6.00	10.00
	c. Coupon.	.05	.20	.50

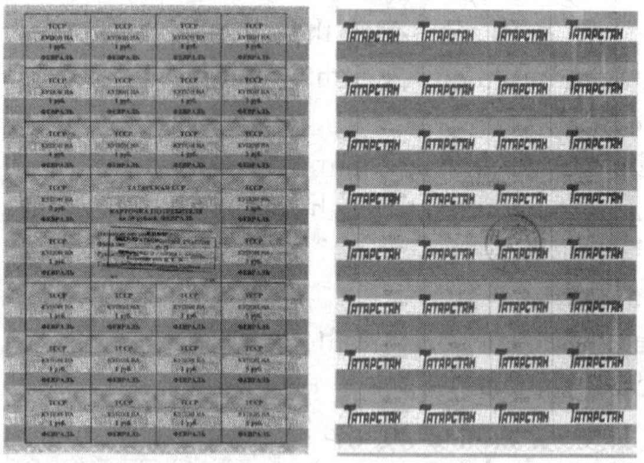

		VG	VF	UNC
2	**50 Rubles**			
	ND (1992). Black text on pink underprint. With month: ФЕВЯАЛЬ **(February).**			
	a. Issued full sheet.	3.00	7.50	15.00
	b. Remainder full sheet.	2.00	5.00	9.00
	c. Coupon.	.05	.20	.50

NOTICE

Readers with unlisted dates, signature varieties, etc. are invited to submit photocopies of their notes to: Standard Catalog of World Paper Money, 700 East State St. Iola, WI 54990-0001, E-Mail: george.cuhaj@fwpubs.com.

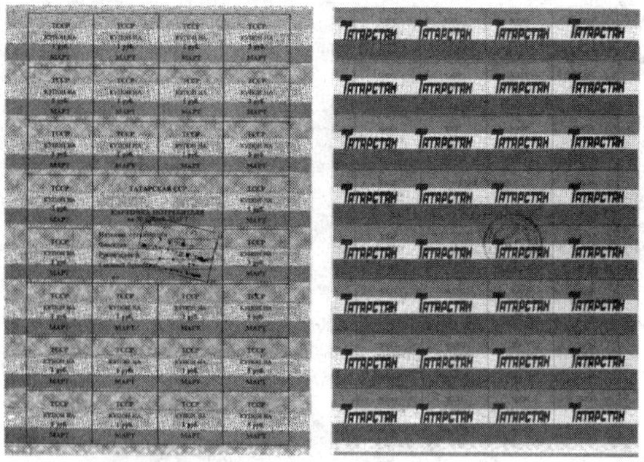

		VG	VF	UNC
3	**50 Rubles**			
	ND (1992). Black text on blue underprint. With month: МАРТ **(March).**			
	a. Issued full sheet.	3.00	7.50	15.00
	b. Remainder full sheet.	1.50	4.00	8.00
	c. Coupon.	.05	.20	.50

GOVERNMENT

1993 PRIVATIZATION CHECK ISSUE

		VG	VF	UNC
4A	**30,000 Rubles**			
	1993. Black text on green underprint. Arms with number. Back black text on white. Printer: USBN.			
	a. Issued note. With registration and without privatization book.	—	25.00	40.00
	b. Issued note. With registration and with privatization book.	—	40.00	80.00
	c. Not issued. All with coupons and without registration.	—	—	50.00
4B	**40,000 Rubles**			
	1993. Black text on green. Arms with number. Back black text on white. Printer: USBN.			
	a. Issued note. With registration and without privatization book.	—	17.50	30.00
	b. Issued note. With registration and with privatization book.	—	30.00	50.00
	c. Not issued. All with coupons and without registration.	—	—	50.00
4C	**60,000 Rubles**			
	1993. Black text on green underprint. Arms with number. Back black text on white. Printer: USBN (without imprint).			
	a. Issued note. With registration and without privatization book.	—	20.00	35.00
	b. Issued note. With registration and with privatization book.	—	35.00	60.00
	c. Not issued. All with coupons and without registration.	—	—	50.00
4D	**80,000 Rubles**			
	1993. Black text on green. Arms with number. Back black text on white. Printer: USBN.			
	a. Issued note. With registration and without privatization book.	—	25.00	40.00
	b. Issued note. With registration and with privatization book.	—	40.00	75.00
	c. Not issued. All with coupons and without registration.	—	—	50.00
4E	**90,000 Rubles**			
	1993. Black text on green. Arms with number. Black text on white. Printer: USBN.			
	a. Issued note. With registration and without privatization book.	—	30.00	50.00
	b. Issued note. With registration and with privatization book.	—	40.00	80.00
	c. Not issued. All with coupons and without registration.	—	—	50.00
4F	**100,000 Rubles**			
	1993. Black text on green. Arms with number. Black text on white. Printer: USBN.			
	a. Issued note. With registration and without privatization book.	—	35.00	60.00
	b. Issued note. With registration and with privatization book.	—	45.00	85.00
	c. Not issued. All with coupons and without registration.	—	—	—

1991; 1993 ND FIRST CURRENCY CHECK ISSUE

#5 and 6 state flag inside circle at l., stylized image of old castle Suumbeky in Kazan (ca. 16th century) in ornate frame at r. Uniface.

		VG	VF	UNC
5	**(100 Rubles)**			
	ND (1991-92). Blue-gray. 138 x 66mm. Watermark: Lozenges.			
	a. Gray underprint.	—	3.00	15.00
	b. Red underprint.	—	10.00	25.00
	c. Yellow underprint.	—	12.50	25.00
	d. Orange underprint.	—	12.50	25.00

Note: Issued statewide. Checks probably printed in 1991, as coat of arms was accepted later than flag, but issued to circulation in 1992.

		VG	VF	UNC
6	**(100 Rubles)**			
	ND (1993). Red and pink. Red and green arms at left, stylized image of old castle Suumbeky in ornate frame at right. Watermark: Lozenges. Uniface.			
	a. Gray underprint.	—	8.00	15.00
	b. Violet on pink underprint.	—	8.00	15.00
	c. dark blue on pale blue underprint.	—	8.00	15.00
	d. Brown underprint.	—	6.00	12.50
	e. Olive-green underprint.	—	8.00	15.00

Note: Issued for circulation in Kazan.

1994 ND Second Currency Check Issue

		VG	VF	UNC
7	**(200 Rubles)**			
	ND (1994). Medical emblem inside oval at right, stylized image of old castle Suumbeky in Kazan (ca. 16th century) at left. 105 x 53mm. Watermark: Lozenges. Uniface.			
	a. Blue-black and pale blue on multicolor underprint.	1.50	7.50	10.00
	b. Deep olive-green and green on tan and pale green underprint.	1.50	7.50	10.00

Note: Circulated in the republic from 3.10.1994 to 1.7.1995.

1993-95 ND Third Currency Check Issue

#8-12 arms at top ctr., Kazan Kremlin (ca. 16th century) at lower l., Arabic *Tatar* at r.
#8-11 wmk.: Mosaic.

		VG	VF	UNC
8	**(500 Rubles)**			
	ND (1993). Red-brown on multicolor underprint. Woman feeding geese on olive-green back. 105 x 53mm.	1.00	5.00	9.00

		VG	VF	UNC
9	**(500 Rubles)**			
	ND (1993). Green on multicolor underprint. Horses galloping at center on olive green back. 105 x 53mm.	1.00	5.00	9.00

		VG	VF	UNC
10	**(1000 Rubles)**			
	ND (1994). Pink on multicolor underprint. Gulls flying over raging waves on back. 105 x 53mm.	1.00	5.00	9.00
11	**(1000 Rubles)**			
	ND (1995). Blue on multicolor underprint. Deer at watering hole on back. 105 x 53mm.	1.00	5.00	9.00

Note: Checks #8-11 found in circulation before Aug. 1996.

1996 ND Fourth Currency Check Issue

		VG	VF	UNC
12	**(50 Shamil = 5000 Rubles)**			
	ND (1996). Kazan Kremlin (ca. 16th century) with English and Russian text "Tatarstan" in frame below. Women from national epic on back. 135 x 65mm. Watermark: light lines.			
	a. dark blue on pale blue-gray underprint.	1.00	4.00	12.50
	b. Deep green on pale green underprint.	1.00	4.00	12.50

Note: Check #12 found in circulation from Aug. 1996 to date.

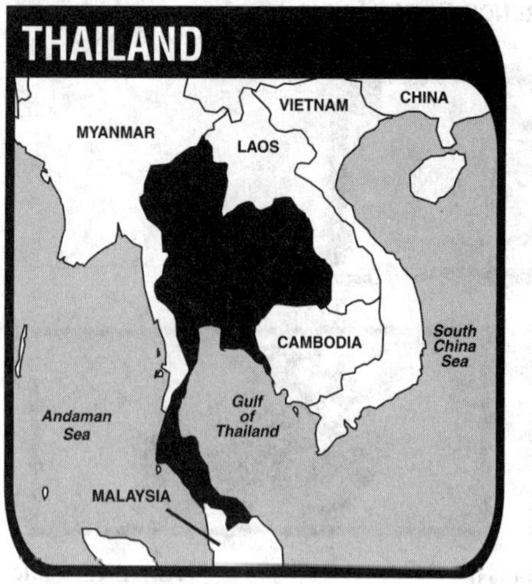

The Kingdom of Thailand, a constitutional monarchy located in the center of mainland southeast Asia between Burma and Lao, has an area of 198,457 sq. mi. (514,000 sq. km.) and a population of 60.49 million. Capital: Bangkok. The economy is d on agriculture and mining. Rubber, rice, teakwood, tin and tungsten are exported.

The history of Thailand, the only country in south and southeast Asia that was never colonized by an European power, dates from the 6th century AD when tribes of the Thai stock migrated into the area from the Asiatic continent, a process that accelerated with the Mongol invasion of China in the 13th century. After 400 years of sporadic warfare with the neighboring Burmese, King Taksin won the last battle in 1767. He founded a new capital, Dhonburi, on the west bank of Chao Praya River. King Rama I moved the capital to Bangkok in 1782.

The Thai were introduced to the Western world by the Portuguese, who were followed by the Dutch, British and French. Rama III of the present ruling dynasty negotiated a treaty of friendship and commerce with Britain in 1826, and in 1896 the independence of the kingdom was guaranteed by an Anglo-French accord. The absolute monarchy was changed into a constitutional monarchy in 1932. This was maintained when the name of the country was changed to Thailand in 1939.

In 1909 Siam ceded to Great Britain its suzerain rights over the dependencies of Kedah, Kelantan, Trengganu and Perlis, Malay states situated in southern Siam just north of British Malaya. This eliminated any British jurisdiction in Siam proper.

On December 8, 1941, after five hours of fighting, Thailand agreed to permit Japanese troops passage through the country to invade northern British Malaya. This eventually led to increased Japanese intervention and finally occupation of the country. On January 25, 1942, Thailand declared war on Great Britain and the United States. A free Thai guerrilla movement was soon organized to counteract the Japanese. In July 1943, Japan transferred the four northern Malay States back to Thailand. These were returned to Great Britain after peace treaties were signed in 1946.

RULERS:

Rama IX (Bhumiphol Adulyadej), 1946-

MONETARY SYSTEM:

1 Baht (Tical) = 100 Satang

SIGNATURE VARIETIES

	MINISTER OF FINANCE	GOVERNOR OF THE BANK OF THAILAND
34		
35		
36		
37		
38		
39	Chote Kvnakasem - no error -	Chote Kvnakasem
40		
41	S. Vinichchaikul	Puey Ungpakorn
42	S. Vinichchaikul	Bisudhi Nimmanhaemin
43	Boonma Wongesesawan	Bisudhi Nimmanhaemin

SIGNATURE VARIETIES

44	Sommai Hoontrakul	Bisudhi Nimmanhaemin
45	Sawet Piempongsarn	Bisudhi Nimmanhaemin
46	Boonchu Rojanasathien	Bisudhi Nimmanhaemin
47	Boonchu Rojanasathien	Sanoh Unakul
48	Sawet Piempongsarn	Sanoh Unakul
	MINISTER OF FINANCE	GOVERNOR OF THE BANK OF THAILAND
49	Suphat Suthatham	Sanoh Unakul
50	Gen. K. Chomanan	Sanoh Unakul
51	Gen. K. Chomanan	Nukul Prachuabmoh
52	Amnuey Virawan	Nukul Prachuabmoh
53	Sommai Hoontrakul	Nukul Prachuabmoh
54	Sommai Hoontrakul	Kamchorn Sathirakul
55	Suthee Singsaneh	Kamchorn Sathirakul
56	Pramual Sabhavasu	Kamchorn Sathirakul
57	Pramual Sabhavasu	Chavalit Thanachanan
57a	Virabongsa Ramangkul	Chavalit Thanachanan
58	Virabongsa Ramangkul	Vigit Supinit

SIGNATURE VARIETIES

59	Baham Silpa-acha	Vigit Supinit
60	Suthee Singsaneh	Vigit Supinit
61		Vigit Supinit
62	Pedro Malan, 1999-	Vigit Supinit
63	Tharin Nimanhaemin	Vigit Supinit
64	Sukariart Satirathai	Vigit Supinit
65	Bhodi Joonanord	Vigit Supinit
66	Bhodi Joonanord	Rerngchai Marakanond
67	Amnuey Virawan	Rerngchai Marakanond
68	Thanon Pithaya	Rerngchai Marakanond
69	Thanon Pithaya	Chaiwat Viboon
70	Kasit Pampiern	Chaiwat Viboon
71	Tharin Nimahaemin	Chaiwat Viboon
72	Tharin Nimahaemin	Jatumongkul Sonakul
73	Somkid Chatusripitak	Jatumongkul Sonakul
74	Somkid Chatusripitak	Pridi Teewakul

GOVERNMENT OF THAILAND

1953-56 ND ISSUE

#74-78 slightly modified portr. Kg. in Field Marshal's uniform w/collar insignia and 3 decorations. Black serial #. Printer: TDLR.

Small letters in 2-line text on back

Large letters in 2-line text on back.

		VG	VF	UNC
74	**1 Baht**			
	ND (1955). Blue on multicolor underprint. Like #69.			
	a. Watermark: Constitution. Red and blue security threads. signature 34.	.20	1.00	4.00
	b. Watermark: Constitution. Metal security strip. signature 34; 35 (Large size).	.20	1.00	3.50
	c. Watermark: King profile. Sm. letters in 2-line text on back. signature 35.	.10	.75	3.00
	d. Watermark: King profile. Larger letters in 2-line text on back. signature 36; 37; 38; 39; 40; 4l.	.10	.75	2.50
	s. As a; d. Specimen.	—	—	250.

		VG	VF	UNC
75	**5 Baht**			
	ND (1956). Purple on multicolor underprint. Like #70.			
	a. Watermark: Constitution. Red and blue security threads. signature 34.	5.00	15.00	50.00
	b. Watermark: Constitution. Metal security strip. signature 34; 35 (Large size).	.50	2.50	10.00
	c. Watermark: King profile. Sm. letters in 2-line text on back. signature 35; 36.	.50	2.00	5.00
	d. Watermark: King profile. Larger letters in 2-line text on back. signature 38; 39; 40; 41.	.50	1.50	4.50
	s. As a. Specimen.	—	—	250.

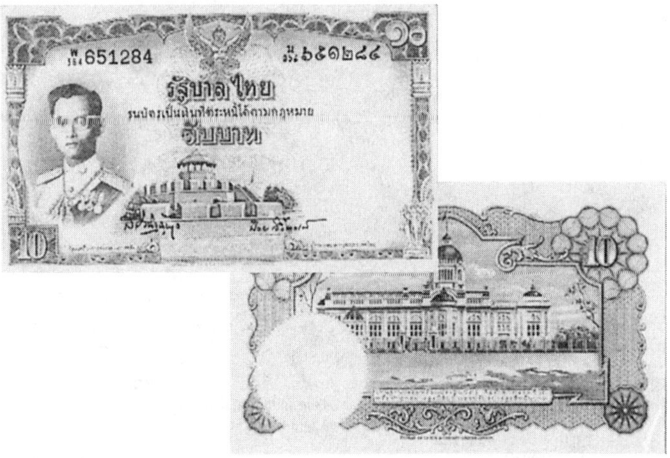

		VG	VF	UNC
76	**10 Baht**			
	ND (1953). Brown on multicolor underprint. Like #71.			

		VG	VF	UNC
76	**10 Baht**			
	a. Watermark: Constitution. Red and blue security threads. signature 34.	.50	2.50	8.00
	b. Watermark: Constitution. Metal security strip. signature 34; 35 (Large size).	.50	2.50	8.00
	c. Watermark: King profile. Sm. letters in 2-line text on back. signature 35; 36; 37; 38; 39.	.50	4.00	12.00
	d. Watermark: King profile. Larger letters in 2-line text on back. signature 39; 40; 41; 44.	.50	1.00	4.00
	s. As a. Specimen.	—	—	250.

		VG	VF	UNC
77	**20 Baht** ND (1953). Olive-green on multicolor underprint. Like #72.			
	a. Watermark: Constitution. Red and blue security threads. signature 34.	2.50	4.00	12.00
	b. Watermark: Constitution. Metal security strip. signature 34; 35 (Large size).	2.50	4.00	12.50
	c. Watermark: King profile. Sm. letters in 2-line text on back. signature 35; 37; 38.	6.00	10.00	30.00
	d. Watermark: King profile. Larger letters in 2-line text on back. signature 38; 39; 40; 41; 44.	.50	2.00	6.00
	s. As a. Specimen.	—	—	250.
78	**100 Baht** ND (1955). Red on multicolor underprint. Like #73.			
	a. Watermark: Constitution. Red and blue security threads. signature 34.	8.00	20.00	60.00
	b. Watermark: Constitution. Metal security strip. signature 34; 35; 37; 38.	4.00	12.50	25.00
	c. Watermark: King profile. Sm. letters in 2-line text on back. signature 38.	2.00	10.00	35.00
	d. Watermark: King profile. Larger letters in 2-line text on back. signature 38-41.	2.00	6.00	10.00
	s. As a; c. Specimen.	—	—	250.

BANK OF THAILAND

1968 ISSUE; SERIES 10

		VG	VF	UNC
79	**100 Baht** ND (1968). Red, blue and multicolor. Rama IX in uniform at right and as watermark. Royal barge on back. Signature 41; 42. Printer: TDLR.			
	a. Issued note.	3.50	7.50	15.00
	s. Specimen.	—	—	—

1969 COMMEMORATIVE ISSUE

SERIES 11

Printed in Thailand by the Thai Banknote Printing Works. Officially described as "Series Eleven". Kg. Rama IX wearing traditional robes at r., sign. of Finance Minister (above) and Governor of the Bank of Thailand (below) at ctr. Wmk: Rama IX. Reportedly 6,000 or 7,000 sets issued.

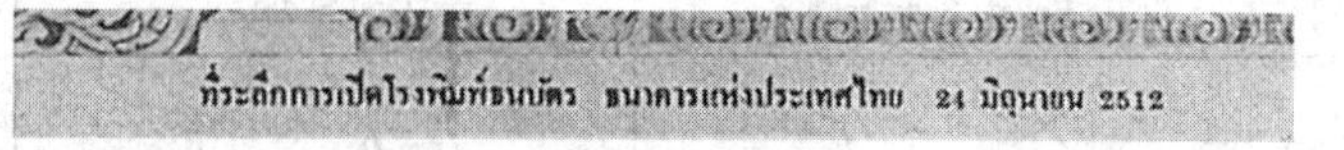

#80 and 81 text at bottom: *opening of the Thai Banknote Printing Works 24 June 2512* (1969).

		VG	VF	UNC
80	**5 Baht** 24.6.1969. Purple and multicolor. Aphonphimok Prasat Pavilion on back. Serial # prefix 00A. Signature 41.	—	—	150.

		VG	VF	UNC
81	**10 Baht** 24.6.1969. Brown on multicolor underprint. Wat Benchamabophitr temple on back. Serial # and signature like #80.	—	—	175.

1969-75 ND ISSUE; SERIES 11

#82-86 replacement notes: Serial # prefix *S-(W)*.

		VG	VF	UNC
82	**5 Baht** ND (1969). Purple and multicolor underprint. Like #80 but without commemorative line at bottom. Signature 41; 42.			
	a. Issued note.	.25	.50	2.00
	s. Specimen.	—	—	—

NOTICE

Readers with unlisted dates, signature varieties, etc. are invited to submit photocopies of their notes to: Standard Catalog of World Paper Money, 700 East State St. Iola, WI 54990-0001, E-Mail: george.cuhaj@fwpubs.com.

83	10 Baht	VG	VF	UNC
	ND (1969-78). Brown and multicolor. Like #81 but without commemorative line at bottom. Signature 41; 42; 43; 44; 45; 46; 47; 48; 49; 50; 51; 52; 53.			
	a. Issued note.	.25	.50	2.50
	s. Specimen.	—	—	—

84	20 Baht	VG	VF	UNC
	ND (1971-81). Dark green, olive-green and multicolor. Royal barge at left center on back. Signature 41; 42; 43; 44; 45; 46; 47; 48; 49; 50; 51; 52; 53.			
	a. Issued note.	.50	1.00	4.00
	s. Specimen.	—	—	—

85	100 Baht	VG	VF	UNC
	ND (1969-78). Red-brown and multicolor. Emerald Buddha section of Grand Palace on back.			
	a. Without black Thai overprint on face. Signature 42; 43; 44; 45; 46; 47; 48; 49.	2.00	4.50	10.00
	b. Black Thai overprint line just below upper signature for change of title. Signature 43.	5.00	12.50	25.00
	s. As a. Specimen.	—	—	40.00

86	500 Baht	VG	VF	UNC
	ND (1975-88). Purple and multicolor. Pra Prang Sam Yod Lopburi (three towers) on back. Signature 47; 49; 50; 51; 52; 53; 54; 55.			
	a. Issued note.	5.00	10.00	20.00
	s. Specimen.	—	—	—

1978-81 ND Issue; Series 12

#87-89 Kg. Rama IX wearing dk. Field Marshal's uniform at r. and as wmk. Sign. of Finance Minister (upper) and Governor of the Bank of Thailand (lower) at ctr. Replacement notes: Serial # prefix *S-(W)*.

87	10 Baht	VG	VF	UNC
	BE2523 (1980). Dark brown on multicolor underprint. Mounted statue of King Chulalongkorn on back. Signature 52; 53; 54; 55; 56; 57; 58; 59; 60; 61; 63; 66.	FV	.50	1.25

88	20 Baht	VG	VF	UNC
	BE2524 (1981). Dark green on multicolor underprint. King Taksin's statue at Chantaburi with three armed men on back. Signature 53-61; 63; 64; 66; 67; 72-74.	FV	.75	2.00

89	100 Baht	VG	VF	UNC
	ND (1978). Violet, red and orange on multicolor underprint. King Narasuan the Great atop elephant on back. Signature 49-63.	FV	2.00	6.00

1985-92 ND Issue; Series 13

#90-92 replacement notes: Serial # prefix *S-(W)*.

		VG	VF	UNC
90	**50 Baht**			

ND (1985-96). Dark blue and purple on multicolor underprint. King Rama IX facing at right, wearing traditional robe and as watermark. Palace at left, statue of King Rama VII at center, his arms and signature at upper left on back.

	VG	VF	UNC
a. King with pointed eartips. Signature 54.	FV	2.00	6.00
b. Darker blue color obscuring pointed eartips. Signature 54-60; 63.	FV	1.50	3.00

		VG	VF	UNC
91	**500 Baht**	FV	8.50	20.00

ND (1988-96). Purple and violet on multicolor underprint. King Rama IX at right in Field Marshal's uniform and as watermark. Statue at center right, palace in background in underprint at left center on back. Signature 55-61; 63.

		VG	VF	UNC
92	**1000 Baht**	FV	17.50	35.00

BE2535 (1992). Gray, brown, orange and multicolor. King at center right and as watermark. King Rama IX and Queen Sirikit greeting children at left center in underprint, viewing map at center right on back. Signature 62-64; 66-67; 69; 71-72.

1987 COMMEMORATIVE ISSUE

#93, King's 60th Birthday

		VG	VF	UNC
93	**60 Baht**			

BE2530 (5.12.1987). Dark brown on multicolor underprint. King Rama IX seated on throne at center, Victory crown at left, Royal regalia at right. Royal family seated with subjects on back. Signature 55.

	VG	VF	UNC
a. Issued note.	—	—	4.00
s. Specimen in blue folder.	—	—	100.

Note: A 40 Baht surcharge was added to issue price of #93, for charity work and the expense of the special envelope which came with each issued note.

1992 COMMEMORATIVE ISSUE

#94 and 95, 90th Birthday of Princess Mother

		VG	VF	UNC
94	**50 Baht**	FV	FV	3.00

ND (1992). Blue on multicolor underprint. Similar to #90. Two lines of text added under Princess Mother's watermark on face. Signature 57.

		VG	VF	UNC
95	**500 Baht**	FV	FV	20.00

ND (1992). Purple and multicolor. Similar to #91. Two lines of text added under Princess Mother's watermark on face. Signature 57.

#96, Qn. Sirikit's 60th Birthday

			VG	VF	UNC
96	**1000 Baht**	ND (1992). Black, deep olive-green and yellow-brown on multicolor underprint. Like #92 but with commemorative text in three lines under Queen Sirikit's watermark on face and back. Signature 61.	FV	FV	40.00

1994 ND Issue

			VG	VF	UNC
97	**100 Baht**	BE2537 (1994). Violet, red and brown-orange on multicolor underprint. King Rama IX at right. Statue of King Rama V and Rama VI with children; Royal initial emblem in center on back. Signature 63-65; 67-75.	FV	FV	4.00

1995 Commemorative Issue

Text at lower margin:

๑๒๐ ปี กระทรวงการคลัง วันที่ ๑๔ เมษายน พุทธศักราช ๒๕๓๘

#98, 120th Anniversary Ministry of Finance

			VG	VF	UNC
98	**10 Baht**	ND (1995). Dark brown on multicolor underprint. Like #87 but with commemorative text in lower margin. Signature 63.	—	—	2.00

1996 Commemorative Issue

#99 and 101, 50th Anniversary of Reign

			VG	VF	UNC
99	**50 Baht**	ND (1996). Purple on light blue and multicolor underprint. King Rama IX wearing Field Marshal's uniform at right and as a shadow design in clear area at left, royal seal of kingdom at upper right. Back like #90. Polymer plastic. Signature 66, 67. Printer: NPA (without imprint).	FV	FV	4.50

			VG	VF	UNC
100	**500 Baht**	ND (1996). Purple and red-violet on multicolor underprint. Similar to #103 but with Crowned Royal seal with *50* at center right, arms above dancers at right replacing crowned radiant Chakra at left center. Temple of the Emerald Buddha at left, King Rama I and Rama II at left center on back. Signature 64.	FV	FV	30.00

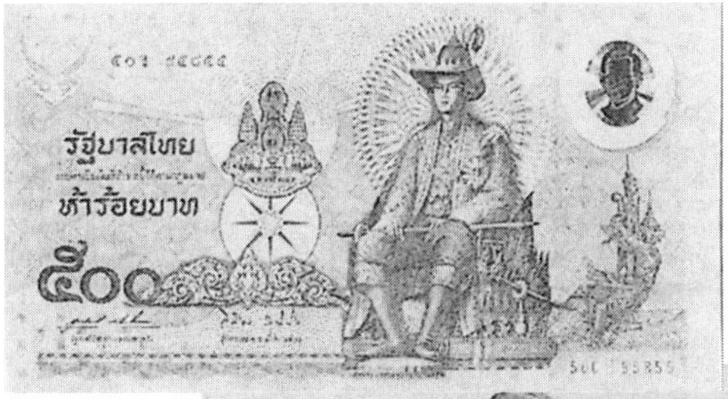

			VG	VF	UNC
101	**500 Baht**	ND (1996). Multicolor. King Rama IX seated in royal attire at center right, hologram of King at upper right. King holding map at center, waterfalls at left, farmers in terraced landscape at right on back. Polymer plastic. Signature 64; 66. Printer: NPA (without imprint).	—	—	40.00

Note: #101 was also issued in a box with booklet about the king. Issue price was $60.00.

1996-97 ND Regular Issue

		VG	VF	UNC
102	**50 Baht** BE2540. (1997). Black on light blue and multicolor underprint. King Rama IX in Field Marshal's uniform at center right, arms at upper left. King Rama VI seated at table at center right, royal arms at upper left center, medieval ship's prow at lower right on back. Signature 67, 71; 72; 74. Polymer plastic. Printer: NPA (without imprint).	FV	FV	3.00

		VG	VF	UNC
103	**500 Baht** BE2539 (1996). Purple and red-violet on multicolor underprint. King Rama IX at right and as watermark. Arms at upper left, radiant crowned Chakra seal on platform at left center. Back similar to #100. Signature 64; 66; 67; 69; 72.	FV	FV	20.00

1999 Commemorative Issue

#104, 72nd Birthday of King

		VG	VF	UNC
104	**1000 Baht** BE2542. 1999. Brown, orange and yellow on multicolor underprint. King Bhumibol at right center, green seal has scroll below. King with camera at right, Pa Sak Jolasid Dam at left on back. Signature 72.	FV	FV	35.00

2000 Commemorative Issue

#105, 106 Golden Wedding Anniversary

		VG	VF	UNC
105	**50 Baht** ND (2000). Brown and tan on multicolor underprint. Portrait of King and Queen. Views of their family life on back. 126 x 205mm. Issued in special folder. Signature 72.	—	—	25.00
106	**500,000 Baht** ND (2000). As #105 but for value. (1998 pieces printed).	—	—	25,000.

2000-01 ND Issue

		VG	VF	UNC
107	**500 Baht** ND (2001). Blue and rose on multicolor underprint. Portrait King Bhumibol at right. Statue and palace on back. Signature 74; 75.	FV	FV	16.00

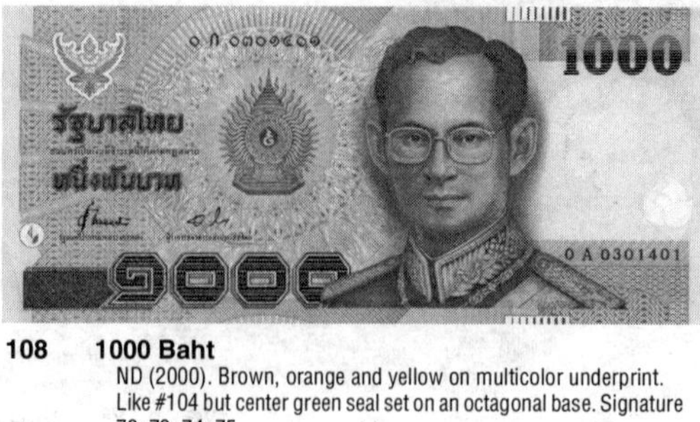

		VG	VF	UNC
108	**1000 Baht** ND (2000). Brown, orange and yellow on multicolor underprint. Like #104 but center green seal set on an octagonal base. Signature 72; 73; 74; 75.	FV	FV	32.50

2002 Commemorative Issue

		VG	VF	UNC
109	**20 Baht** ND (2003). Green on green and tan multicolor underprint. King Rama IX wearing Field Marshal's uniform at center right. Procession with King in military uniform and new bridge on back. Signature 74; 75.	FV	FV	1.50

		VG	VF	UNC
110	**100 Baht** ND (2002). Brown and slate blue on green and multicolor underprint. King Rama V and King Rama IX at right. Back slate blue on green underprint. Facsimile print of #12a. Signature 74; 75.	—	—	4.50

2004 Commemorative Issue

#111, Queen's 72nd Birthday. Issued in a folder.

		VG	VF	UNC
111	**100 Baht** 2004. Multicolor. King and Queen. Queen standing on back. Signature 74.	—	—	6.50

2004 Issue

		VG	VF	UNC
112	**50 Baht** ND (2004). Slate black on light blue and multicolor. Like #102 but paper.	FV	FV	2.00

Collector Series

1991 Commemorative Issue

#CS1, World Bank Group/IMF Annual Meetings

		Issue Price	Mkt. value
CS1	**1991 10, 20, 50, 100, 500 Baht** #87-91 with overprint: 1991 World Bank Group/IMF Annual Meetings in English and Thai. Specimen. (Issued in blue hanging folder).	—	600.

Military - Vietnam War

Auxiliary Military Payment Certificate Coupons

First Series

#M1-M8 issued probably from January to April or May, 1970. Larger shield at ctr. on face and back. Words *Coupon* below shield or at r., *Non Negotiable* at r. Small Thai symbol only at upper l. corner; denomination at 3 corners. Black print on check-type security paper.

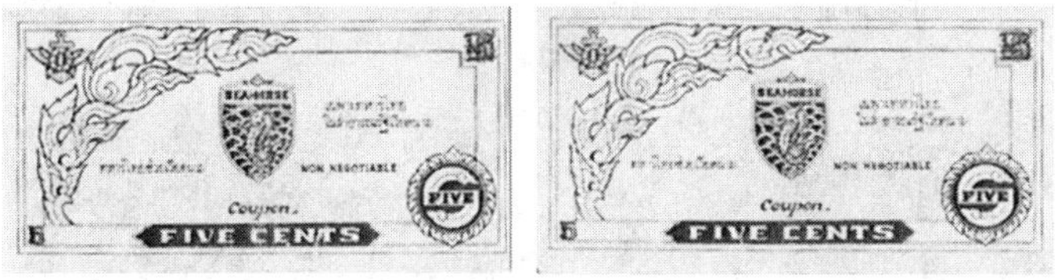

		Good	Fine	XF
M1	**5 Cents** ND (1970). Yellow paper. Seahorse shield design.	100.	250.	—
M2	**10 Cents** ND (1970). Light gray paper. Shield with leaping panther and *RTAVF. Non Negotiable* under shield; *Coupon* deleted.	100.	250.	—
M3	**25 Cents** ND (1970). Pink paper. Shield with *Victory Vietnam. Coupon* at right.	160.	400.	—
M4	**50 Cents** ND (1970). Light blue paper. Circle with shaking hands and *Royal Thai Forces Vietnam.*	160.	400.	—
M5	**1 Dollar** ND (1970). Yellow paper. Inscription *Victory Vietnam. Coupon* at right.	160.	400.	—
M6	**5 Dollars** ND (1970). Light gray paper. Seahorse in shield.	200.	500.	—
M7	**10 Dollars** ND (1970). Yellow paper. Shield with leaping panther.	225.	550.	—
M8	**20 Dollars** ND (1970). Light green paper. Circle with hands shaking.	225.	550.	—

Second Series

#M9-M16 issued April or May, 1970 to possibly Oct. 7, 1970. Shield designs similar to previous issue, but paper colors are different. Larger shield outline around each shield at l. ctr. *Coupon* in margin at lower ctr., denomination at all 4 corners.

		Good	Fine	XF
M9	**5 Cents** ND (1970). Yellow paper. Shield similar to #M1.	40.00	100.	—
M10	**10 Cents** ND (1970). Light green paper. Shield similar to #M2.	50.00	125.	—
M11	**25 Cents** ND (1970). Yellow paper. Shield similar to #M3.	60.00	150.	—
M12	**50 Cents** ND (1970). Light gray paper. Shield similar to #M4.	60.00	150.	—
M13	**1 Dollar** ND (1970). Pink paper. Shield similar to #M5.	60.00	150.	—
M14	**5 Dollars** ND (1970). Light green paper. Shield similar to #M6.	160.	400.	—

		Good	Fine	XF
M15	**10 Dollars** ND (1970). Pale yellow paper. Shield similar to #M7.	160.	400.	—
M16	**20 Dollars** ND (1970). Light green paper. Shield similar to #M8.	180.	450.	—

Third Series

#M17-M23 date of issue not known (Oct., 1970?). All notes w/hands shaking in shield at lower r. on face. Different shield designs at upper l. on back. More elaborate design across face and back.

		VG	VF	UNC
M17	**5 Cents** ND. Light gray, maroon and green.	22.50	75.00	300.

		VG	VF	UNC
M18	**10 Cents** ND. Light yellow and green.	22.50	75.00	300.

		VG	VF	UNC
M19	**25 Cents** ND. Green, pink and maroon.	40.00	125.	350.

		VG	VF	UNC
M20	**50 Cents** ND. Yellow, green, blue and red.	40.00	125.	350.

		VG	VF	UNC
M21	**1 Dollar** ND. Pink, blue and green.			
	a. Issued note.	125.	225.	—
	r. Remainder without serial #.	—	—	300.

		VG	VF	UNC
M22	**5 Dollars** ND. Yellow, green, blue and red.			
	a. Issued note.	600.	950.	—
	r. Remainder without serial #.			375.

		VG	VF	UNC
M23	**10 Dollars** ND. Green, maroon and dark red.			
	a. Issued note.	125.	225.	—
	r. Remainder without serial #.	—	—	350.

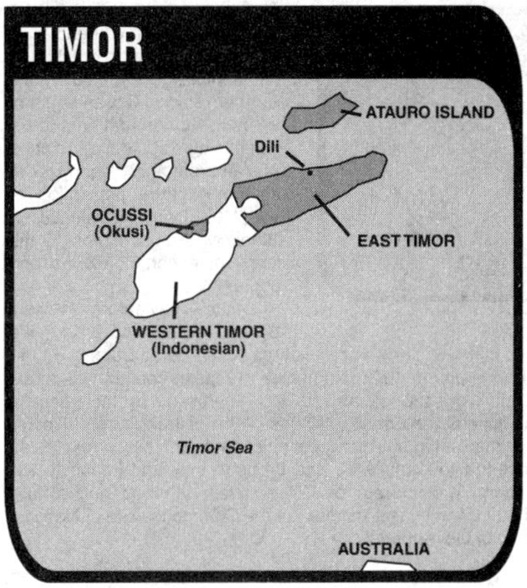

Timor, is an island between the Savu and Timor Seas, has an area, including the former colony of Portuguese Timor, of 11,883 sq. mi. (30,775 sq. km.) and a population of 1.5 million. Western Timor is administered as part of Nusa Tenggara Timur (East Nusa Tenggara) province. Capital: Kupang. The eastern half of the island, the former Portuguese colony, forms a single province, Timor Timur (East Timor). Originally the Portuguese colony also included the area around Ocussi-Ambeno and the small island of Atauro (Pulau Kambing) located north of Dili. Capital: Dili. Timor exports sandalwood, coffee, tea, hides, rubber and copra.

Portuguese traders reached Timor about 1520, and moved to the north and east when the Dutch established themselves in Kupang, a sheltered bay at the southwestern tip, in 1613. Treaties effective in 1860 and 1914 established the boundaries between the two colonies. Japan occupied the entire island during World War II. The former Dutch colony in the western part of the island became part of Indonesia in 1950.

At the end of Nov., 1975, the Portuguese Province of Timor attained independence as the People's Democratic Republic of East Timur. In Dec., 1975 or early in 1976 the government of the People's Democratic Republic was seized by a guerilla faction sympathetic to the Indonesian territorial claim to East Timur which ousted the constitutional government and replaced it with the Provisional Government of East Timur. On July 17, 1976, the Provisional Government enacted a law which dissolved the free republic and made East Timur the 24th province of Indonesia.

In 1999 a revolution suceeded, and it is once again an independent country. Note: For later issues see Indonesia.

MONETARY SYSTEM:

1 Escudo = 100 Centavos, 1958-1975

SIGNATURE VARIETIES

1		
2		
3		
4		
5		
6		
7		
8		

PORTUGUESE ADMINISTRATION

BANCO NACIONAL ULTRAMARINO

DECRETOS - LEI 39221E 44891; 1963-68 ISSUE

#26-30 portr. R. D. Aleixo at r. Bank ship seal at l., crowned arms at ctr. on back. Printer: BWC.

		VG	VF	UNC
26	**20 Escudos**			
	24.10.1967. Olive-brown on multicolor underprint. Signature 3-8.			
	a. Issued note.	.25	1.50	4.50
	s. Specimen.	—	—	—

		VG	VF	UNC
27	**50 Escudos**			
	24.10.1967. Blue on multicolor underprint. Signature 2; 4; 5; 6; 8.			
	a. Issued note.	.25	3.00	8.50
	s. Specimen.	—	—	160.

		VG	VF	UNC
28	**100 Escudos**			
	25.4.1963. Brown on multicolor underprint. Signature 1-3; 8.			
	a. Issued note.	.50	3.50	7.50
	s. Specimen. Punched hole cancelled.	—	—	160.

29	500 Escudos	VG	VF	UNC
	25.4.1963. Dark brown on multicolor underprint. Signature 1-3; 8; 9.			
	a. Issued note.	3.00	10.00	20.00
	s. Specimen.	—	—	175.

30	1000 Escudos	VG	VF	UNC
	21.3.1968. Green on multicolor underprint. Signature 2-8.			
	a. Issued note.	4.00	17.50	40.00
	s. Specimen.	—	—	185.

1969 ND Provisional Issue

		VG	VF	UNC
31	**20 Escudos**	—	—	—
	ND. Green on multicolor underprint. Régulo Jose Nunes at left. Bank seal at center, local huts on pilings at right on back. Specimen.			
32	**500 Escudos**			
	ND (1969 - old date 22.3.1967). Brown and violet on multicolor underprint. Overprint: *PAGAVEL EM TIMOR* on Mozambique #110, face and back.	150.	350.	750.

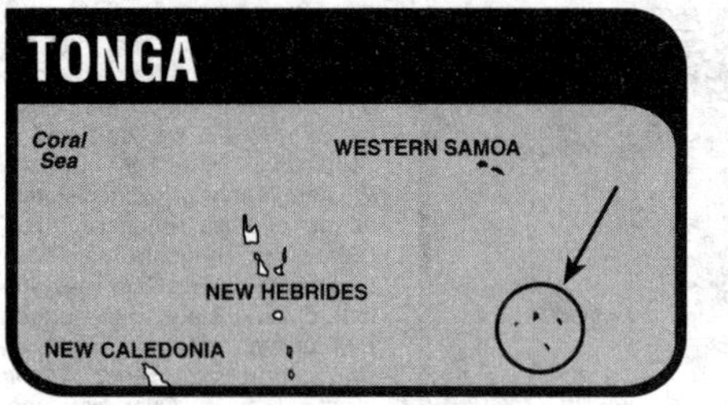

The Kingdom of Tonga (or Friendly Islands), a member of the British Commonwealth, is an archipelago situated in the southern Pacific Ocean south of Western Samoa and east of Fiji comprising 150 islands. Tonga has an area of 270 sq. mi. (748 sq. km.) and a population of 110,000. Capital: Nuku'alofa. Primarily agricultural, the kingdom exports bananas and copra.

Dutch navigators Willem Schouten and Jacob Lemaire were the first Europeans to visit Tonga in 1616. They were followed by the noted Dutch explorer Abel Tasman who visited the Tongatapu group in 1643. No further European contact was made until 1773 when British navigator Capt. James Cook arrived and, impressed by the peaceful deportment of the natives, named the islands the Friendly Islands. Within a few years of Cook's visit, Tonga was embroiled in a civil war that lasted until the great chief Taufa'ahau, who reigned as George Tupou I (1845-93), was converted to Christianity and brought unity and peace to the islands. Tonga became a self-governing protectorate of Great Britain in 1900 and a fully independent state on June 4, 1970. The monarchy is a member of the Commonwealth of Nations. The monarch is Chief of State and Head of Government.

RULERS:

Queen Salote III, 1918-1965
King Taufa'ahau IV, 1967-

MONETARY SYSTEM:

1 Shilling = 12 Pence
1 Pound = 20 Shillings to 1967
1 Pa'anga = 100 Seniti, 1967-

REPLACEMENT NOTES:

#18-24, Z/1 prefix.

Kingdom

Government of Tonga

1939-42 Issue

#9-12 w/denomination spelled out on both sides of arms at ctr. Printer: TDLR.

9	4 Shillings	VG	VF	UNC
	1941-66. Brown on multicolor underprint. *FOUR SHILLINGS* at left and right.			
	a. 1.12.1941-8.9.1947. 3 signature	20.00	100.	400.
	b. 7.2.1949; 15.2.1951; 20.7.1951; 6.9.1954.	20.00	100.	350.
	c. 19.9.1955-30.11.1959.	7.50	25.00	100.
	d. 24.10.1960-27.9.1966.	7.00	25.00	75.00
	e. 3.11.1966. 2 signature	5.00	20.00	50.00

10	10 Shillings	VG	VF	UNC
	1939-66. Green on multicolor underprint. *TEN SHILLINGS* at left and right.			
	a. 3.5.1940; 17.10.1941-28.11.1944. 3 signature	35.00	225.	—
	b. 9.7.1949-1955.	30.00	150.	400.
	c. 2.5.1956; 22.7.1957; 10.12.1958; 13.10.1959.	7.50	35.00	250.
	d. 24.10.1960; 28.11.1962; 29.7.1964; 22.6.1965.	7.00	30.00	100.
	e. 3.11.1966. 2 signature	5.00	22.50	65.00
11	**1 Pound**			
	1940-66. Red on multicolor underprint. *ONE POUND* at left and right.			
	a. 3.5.1940-7.11.1944. 3 signature	40.00	250.	—
	b. 15.6.1951; 11.9.1951; 19.9.1955.	30.00	175.	450.
	c. 2.5.1956; 10.12.1958; 30.11.1959; 12.12.1961.	20.00	70.00	300.
	d. 28.11.1962; 30.10.1964; 2.11.1965; 3.11.1966.	8.00	40.00	110.
	e. 2.12.1966. 2 signature	4.00	15.00	70.00

12	5 Pounds	VG	VF	UNC
	1942-66. Dark blue on multicolor underprint. *FIVE POUNDS* at left and right.			
	a. 11.3.1942-1945. 3 signature	550.	1750.	—
	b. 15.6.1951; 5.7.1955; 11.9.1956; 26.6.1958.	300.	1250.	—
	c. 30.11.1959; 2.11.1965.	175.	500.	1000.
	d. 2.12.1966. 2 signature	15.00	60.00	110.

PULE' ANGA 'O TONGA

GOVERNMENT OF TONGA

1967 ISSUE

#13-17 arms at lower l., Qn. Salote III at r. Various date and sign. varieties.

13	1/2 Pa'anga	VG	VF	UNC
	1967-73. Dark brown on pink underprint. Back brown and blue; coconut workers at left.			
	a. 3.4.1967.	5.00	20.00	75.00
	b. 19.5.1969.	5.00	35.00	100.
	c. 10.3.1970; 16.6.1970.	5.00	32.50	90.00
	d. 4.2.1971; 14.4.1971; 24.7.1972.	5.00	30.00	85.00
	e. 13.6.1973; 12.8.1973. 2 signatures.	6.00	30.00	125.
	s. ND. Specimen.	—	—	70.00

14	1 Pa'anga	VG	VF	UNC
	1967; 1970-71. Olive-green on multicolor underprint. Back olive and blue; river scene, palm trees.			
	a. 3.4.1967.	6.00	17.50	90.00
	b. 12.4.1967; 2.10.1967; 8.12.1967.	6.50	40.00	120.
	c. 10.3.1970; 16.6.1970.	7.00	45.00	130.
	d. 4.2.1971; 19.10.1971.	9.00	60.00	150.
	s. ND. Specimen.	—	—	70.00

15	2 Pa'anga	VG	VF	UNC
	1967-73. Red on multicolor underprint. Back red and brown; women making Tapa cloth.			
	a. 3.4.1967.	7.00	35.00	140.
	b. 2.10.1967; 8.12.1967.	7.00	50.00	170.
	c. 19.5.1969; 10.3.1970; 19.10.1971.	8.00	60.00	160.
	d. 24.7.1972; 10.11.1972; 2.8.1973.	7.50	60.00	175.
	e. 12.11.1973. 2 signatures.	10.00	80.00	275.
	s. ND. Specimen.	—	—	70.00

16	5 Pa'anga	VG	VF	UNC
	1967; 1973. Purple on multicolor underprint. Back purple and olive-green; Ha'amonga stone gateway.			
	a. 3.4.1967.	12.00	80.00	250.
	b. 13.6.1973.	15.00	90.00	325.
	c. 4.9.1973; 6.12.1973. 2 signatures.	17.50	110.	375.
	s. ND. Specimen.	—	—	100.

17	10 Pa'anga	VG	VF	UNC
	1967; 1973. Dark blue on multicolor underprint. Back blue and purple; Royal Palace.			
	a. 3.4.1967.	25.00	125.	550.
	b. 2.10.1967; 8.12.1967.	25.00	175.	600.
	c. 16.7.1973.	30.00	150.	750.
	s. ND. Specimen.	—	—	150.

1974; 1985 ISSUE

#18-22 arms at lower l., Portr. Kg. Taufa'ahau at r. Various date and sign. varieties. Replacement notes: Serial # prefix *Z/1*.

18	1/2 Pa'anga	VG	VF	UNC
	1974-83. Dark brown on pink underprint. Back like #13.			
	a. 2 signatures. 2.10.1974; 19.6.1975.	3.00	6.00	12.50
	b. 3 signatures. 12.1.1977; 17.5.1977; 10.9.1979.	1.00	3.00	12.50
	c. As b. 28.11.1979; 27.8.1980; 31.7.1981; 17.8.1982; 20.7.1083.	.75	2.00	8.00
	s. As a. Specimen.	—	—	—

		VG	VF	UNC
19	**1 Pa'anga** 1974-89. Olive-green on multicolor underprint. Back like #14.			
	a. 6.12.1973.	7.50	25.00	75.00
	b. 2 signatures. 31.7.1974; 19.6.1975; 21.8.1975; 5.8.1976; 21.1.1981; 18.5.1983.	1.25	3.50	12.50
	c. 3 signatures. 5.8.1976-11.6.1980; 31.7.1981-28.10.1982; 27.7.1983-30.6.1989.	FV	2.00	6.00
	s. As a. Specimen.	—	—	—

		VG	VF	UNC
20	**2 Pa'anga** 1974-89. Red on multicolor underprint. Back like #15.			
	a. 2 signatures. 2.10.1974; 19.6.1975; 21.8.1975; 21.1.1981.	1.50	3.50	12.50
	b. 3 signatures. 12.1.1977-27.8.1980;	2.50	4.00	15.00
	c. 3 signatures. 31.7.1981-30.6.1989.	1.50	2.75	9.00
	s. As a. Specimen.	—	—	—

		VG	VF	UNC
21	**5 Pa'anga** 1974-89. Purple on multicolor underprint. Back like #16.			
	a. 2 signatures. 2.10.1974; 19.6.1975; 21.1.1981.	FV	6.00	30.00
	b. 3 signatures. 21.12.1976-28.11.1980.	FV	5.00	20.00
	c. 3 signatures. 27.5.1981-30.6.1989.	FV	3.00	15.00
	s. As a. Specimen.	—	—	—
22	**10 Pa'anga** 1974-89. Dark blue on multicolor underprint. Back like #17.			
	a. 2 signatures. 31.7.1974; 3.9.1974; 19.6.1975; 21.1.1981.	FV	8.00	45.00
	b. 3 signatures. 12.12.1976-28.11.1980.	FV	6.50	32.50
	c. 3 signatures. 27.5.1981-30.6.1989.	FV	6.00	25.00
	s. As a. Specimen.	—	—	—
23	**20 Pa'anga** 1985-89. Orange on green and multicolor underprint. King in new design at center right and as watermark, arms at right. Tonga Development Bank on back.			
	a. 4.7.1985.	FV	35.00	130.
	b. 18.7.1985; 3.10.1985; 8.1.1986; 27.2.1987; 28.9.1987.	FV	27.50	45.00
	c. 20.5.1988; 14.12.1988; 23.1.1989; 30.6.1989.	FV	25.00	40.00

Note: #23a was made in limited quantities in celebration of the king's birthday.

KINGDOM OF TONGA

1988 ISSUE

		VG	VF	UNC
24	**50 Pa'anga** 1988-89. Brown and green on multicolor underprint. King in new design at center right and as watermark, arms at right. Vava'u Harbour on back.			
	a. 4.7.1988.	FV	60.00	175.
	b. 14.12.1988; 30.6.1989.	FV	55.00	100.

Note: #24a was made in limited quantities in celebration of the king's birthday. (5,000 pcs.).

NATIONAL RESERVE BANK OF TONGA

1992 ND ISSUE

#25-29 designs like #19-23. 2 sign. w/Tongan titles beneath.

		VG	VF	UNC
25	**1 Pa'anga** ND (1992-95). Olive-green on multicolor underprint. Like #19.	FV	FV	3.50

		VG	VF	UNC
26	**2 Pa'anga** ND (1992-95). Red on multicolor underprint. Like #20.	FV	FV	6.00

		VG	VF	UNC
27	**5 Pa'anga** ND (1992-95). Purple on multicolor underprint. Like #21.	FV	FV	15.00
28	**10 Pa'anga** ND (1992-95). Dark blue on multicolor underprint. Like #22.	FV	FV	25.00
29	**20 Pa'anga** ND (1992-95). Orange and green on multicolor underprint. Like #23.	FV	FV	45.00

1989 COMMEMORATIVE ISSUE

#30, Inauguration of National Reserve Bank of Tonga

		VG	VF	UNC
30	**20 Pa'anga** 1.7.1989. Orange on green and multicolor underprint. Similar to #24, but with commemorative text in circle on watermark area on face and back.	FV	20.00	60.00

1995 ND Issue

#31-34 Kg. Taufa'ahau at upper ctr. r. and as wmk., sign. varieties, arms at r. Printer: TDLR.

31	1 Pa'anga	VG	VF	UNC
	ND (1995). Olive-green and green on multicolor underprint. River scene, palm trees on back.			
	a. Signature N-D.	FV	2.00	6.00
	b. Signature U-F.	FV	FV	3.00

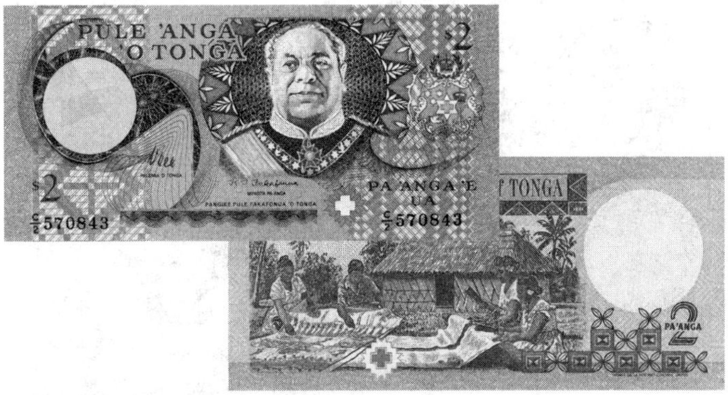

32	2 Pa'anga	VG	VF	UNC
	ND (1995). Red and reddish-brown on multicolor underprint. Women making Tapa cloth on back.			
	a. Signature N-D.	FV	3.00	7.50
	b. Signature U-F.	FV	FV	4.50

33	5 Pa'anga	VG	VF	UNC
	ND (1995). Purple and violet on multicolor underprint. Ha'amonga stone gateway on back.			
	a. Signature N-F.	FV	FV	10.00
	b. Signature U-U.	FV	FV	8.00

34	10 Pa'anga	VG	VF	UNC
	ND (1995). Dark blue on multicolor underprint. Royal Palace on back.			
	a. Signature N-D.	FV	20.00	35.00
	b. Signature U-F.	FV	FV	22.50
	c. Signature U-U.	FV	FV	17.50

35	20 Pa'anga	VG	VF	UNC
	ND. Orange and multicolor. Similar to #29.			
	a. Signature N-D.	FV	40.00	35.00
	b. Signature N-F.	FV	FV	40.00
	c. Signature U-U.	FV	FV	30.00

36	50 Pa'anga	VG	VF	UNC
	ND. Brown and green on multicolor underprint. Signature U-U.	FV	FV	85.00

Collector Series

Government of Tonga

1978 Issue

CS1	1978 1-10 Pa'anga	Issue Price	Mkt. Value
	#19b-22b overprint: *SPECIMEN* and prefix serial # Maltese cross.	—	70.00

TRANSNISTRIA

The Transnistria Moldavian Republic was formed in 1990, even before the separation of Moldavia from Russia. It has an area of 11,544 sq. mi. (29,900 sq. km). and a population of 700,000. Capital: Tiraspol.

The area was conquered from the Turks in the last half of the 18th Century, and in 1792 the capital city of Tiraspol was founded. After 1812, the area called Bessarabia (present Moldova and part of the Ukraine) became part of the Russian Empire. During the Russian Revolution, in 1918, the area was taken by Romanian troops, and in 1924 the Moldavian Autonomous SSR was formed on the left bank of the Dniester River. A Romanian occupation area between the Dniester and Bug Rivers called *Transnistria* was established in October 1941. Its center was the port of Odessa. A special issue of notes for use in Transnistria was made by the Romanian government. In 1944 the Russians recaptured Transnistria.

Once the Moldavian SSR declared independence in August 1991. Transnistria did not want to be a part of Moldavia. In 1992, Moldova tried to solve the issue militarily.

Transnistria has a president, parliament, army and police forces, but as yet is lacking international recognition.

MONETARY SYSTEM:

1 Ruble = 1,000 old Rubles (August 1994)
1 Ruble = 1,000,000 old Rubles (January 2001)

REPUBLIC

GOVERNMENT

1994 ND PROVISIONAL ISSUES

#1-15 issued 24.1.1994, invalidated on 1.12.1994.

The Bank purchased used Russian notes and placed stickers on them. Most collectors feel that "uncirculated" notes currently available were made after 1994.

		VG	VF	UNC
1	**10 Rublei** ND (1994- old date 1961). Green on pink tint adhesive stamp on Russia #233.	.10	.50	2.00

		VG	VF	UNC
2	**10 Rublei** ND (1994- old date 1991). Green on pink tint adhesive stamp on Russia #240.	.10	.50	2.00

		VG	VF	UNC
3	**25 Rublei** ND (1994- old date 1961). Red-violet on buff tint adhesive stamp on Russia #234.	.10	.50	2.50

		VG	VF	UNC
4	**50 Rublei** ND (1994- old date 1991). Red on pale green tint adhesive stamp on Russia #241.	.20	1.00	7.00
5	**50 Rublei** ND (1994- old date 1992). Red on pale green tint adhesive stamp on Russia #247.	.15	.75	4.00

		VG	VF	UNC
6	**100 Rublei** ND (1994- old date 1991). Black on pale blue tint adhesive stamp on Russia #242.	.25	2.00	7.50
7	**100 Rublei** ND (1994- old date 1991). Black on pale blue tint adhesive stamp on Russia #243.	.15	.75	4.50

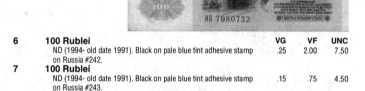

		VG	VF	UNC
8	**200 Rublei** ND (1994- old date 1991). Green on yellow tint adhesive stamp on Russia #244.	.50	4.00	17.50

		VG	VF	UNC
9	**200 Rublei** ND (1994- old date 1992). Green on yellow tint adhesive stamp on Russia #248.	.10	.50	3.50

		VG	VF	UNC
10	**500 Rublei** ND (1994- old date 1991). Blue adhesive stamp on Russia #245.	.50	4.00	22.50
11	**500 Rublei** ND (1994- old date 1992). Blue adhesive stamp on Russia #249.	.05	.25	3.50

		VG	VF	UNC
12	**1000 Rublei** ND (1994- old date 1991). Violet on yellow tint adhesive stamp on Russia #246.	.50	4.00	20.00
13	**1000 Rublei** ND (1994- old date 1992). Violet on yellow tint adhesive stamp on Russia #250.	.05	.25	3.00
14	**5000 Rublei** ND (1994- old date 1992). Dark brown on pale blue-gray tint adhesive stamp on Russia #252.	.15	.75	3.50

		VG	VF	UNC
14A	**5000 Rublei** ND (1994 -old date 1961). Adhesive stamp on Russia 5 Rubles #224.	.10	.50	2.00

		VG	VF	UNC
14B	**5000 Rublei** ND (1994 -old date 1991). Adhesive stamp on Russia 5 Rubles #239.	.10	.50	3.50
15	**10,000 Rublei** ND (1994- old date 1992). Purple on yellow tint adhesive stamp on Russia #253.	.20	.75	4.00

БАНКА НИСТРЯНЭ

BANKA NISTRIANA

1993; 1994 КУПОН KUPON ISSUE

#16-18 Alexander Vassilievitch Suvurov at r. Parliament bldg. at ctr. on back. Wmk: Block design.

Note: Postal adhesive stamps have been seen affixed to #16-18 to imitate revalidated notes.

		VG	VF	UNC
16	**1 Ruble** 1994. Dark green on multicolor underprint.	FV	.10	.30
17	**5 Rublei** 1994. Blue on multicolor underprint.	FV	.10	.40
18	**10 Rublei** 1994. Red-violet on multicolor underprint.	FV	.10	.50

#19-24 equestrian statue of A. V. Suvorov at r. Parliament bldg. on back. Wmk: Block design.

		VG	VF	UNC
19	**50 Rublei** 1993 (1994). Green on multicolor underprint.	FV	.15	1.00
20	**100 Rublei** 1993 (1994). Dark brown on multicolor underprint.	FV	.20	1.00
21	**200 Rublei** 1993 (1994). Red-violet on multicolor underprint.	FV	.25	2.00
22	**500 Rublei** 1993 (1994). Blue on multicolor underprint.	FV	.25	2.50
23	**1000 Rublei** 1993 (1994). Purple and red-violet on multicolor underprint.	FV	.50	2.00
24	**5000 Rublei** 1993 (1995). Black on deep olive-green and multicolor underprint.	FV	.75	3.50

#25 Not assigned.

1994 (1995) ISSUE

Currency Reform

1 Ruble = 1000 "Old" Rublei

		VG	VF	UNC
26	**1000 Rublei = 100,000 Rublei** 1994 (1995). Blue-violet and purple. V. Suvorov at right. Parliament building on back. Printed in Germany.	FV	.75	3.50

1995; ND (1996) PROVISIONAL ISSUE

27 **50,000 Rublei on 5 Rublei**

ND (1996 - old date 1994). Blue on multicolor underprint. Hologram with *50,000* at upper left on #17.

VG	VF	UNC
FV	.75	2.00

28 **50,000 Rublei = 500,000 Rublei**

1995 (1996). Brown-violet and brown on multicolor underprint. Bogdan Khmelnitsky at right. Drama and comedy theatre on back. Signature Vyacheslav Zagryatsky. Printed in Germany.

VG	VF	UNC
FV	.75	5.00

1996 ND Provisional Issue

#29-31, Gen. Alexander Vassilievitch Suvurov at l.

29 **10,000 Rublei on 1 Ruble**

ND (1996 - old date 1994). Dark green on multicolor underprint. Overprint on face and back of #16.

VG	VF	UNC
FV	.50	1.25

29A **10,000 Rublei on 1 Ruble**

1998. Green and tan on multicolor underprint. Overprint only on face of #16.

VG	VF	UNC
FV	FV	1.00

30 **50,000 Rublei on 5 Rublei**

ND (1996 - old date 1994). Blue on multicolor underprint. Overprint on face and back of #17.

VG	VF	UNC
FV	.25	1.50

31 **100,000 Rublei on 10 Rublei**

ND (1996 - old date 1994). Red-violet on multicolor underprint. Overprint on face and back of #18.

VG	VF	UNC
FV	.25	2.00

1997; 1999 Issue

32 **10,000 Rubles**

1999. Multicolor.

VG	VF	UNC
FV	1.00	3.00

33 **500,000 Rublei**

1997. Purple and violet on multicolor underprint. Like #24.

VG	VF	UNC
FV	1.00	3.00

2000 Issue

#34-37, Gen. Alexander Vassilievitch Suvurov at l.

34 **1 Ruble**

2000. Orange-brown on multicolor underprint. Gen. Alexander V. Suvorov at left. Kitskansky Bridgehead Memorial complex on back.

	VG	VF	UNC
a. Issued note.	FV	.50	1.00
s. Specimen.	—	—	—

35 **5 Rublei**

2000. Blue on multicolor underprint. Gen. Alexander V. Suvorov at left. *Kvint* destillery administrative building on back.

	VG	VF	UNC
a. Issued note.	FV	1.00	2.50
s. Specimen. ОБРАЗЕЦ.	—	—	—

36 **10 Rublei**

2000. Brown on multicolor underprint. Novo Nyametsky Monastery in Kitzkansk on back.

	VG	VF	UNC
a. Issued note.	FV	FV	4.50
s. Specimen.	—	—	—

37 **25 Rublei**

2000. Rose on multicolor underprint. Bendery fortress and a Russian soldiers' Memorial on back.

	VG	VF	UNC
a. Issued note.	FV	FV	9.00
s. Specimen.	—	—	—

38	50 Rublei	VG	VF	UNC
	2000. Deep green on multicolor underprint. Taras Shevchenko (poet) at left. Transnistria Parliament building on back.			
	a. Issued note.	FV	FV	15.00
	s. Specimen.	—	—	—

39	100 Rublei	VG	VF	UNC
	2000. Purple on multicolor underprint. Prince Dimitrie Cantemir at left. The Christmas Church on back.			
	a. Issued note.	FV	FV	30.00
	s. Specimen.	—	—	—

40	200 Rublei	VG	VF	UNC
	2004. Brown. Bust at left. 1757 Battle scene on back.	FV	FV	45.00

41	500 Rublei	VG	VF	UNC
	2004. Green. Catherine II at left. Fort on back.	FV	FV	100.

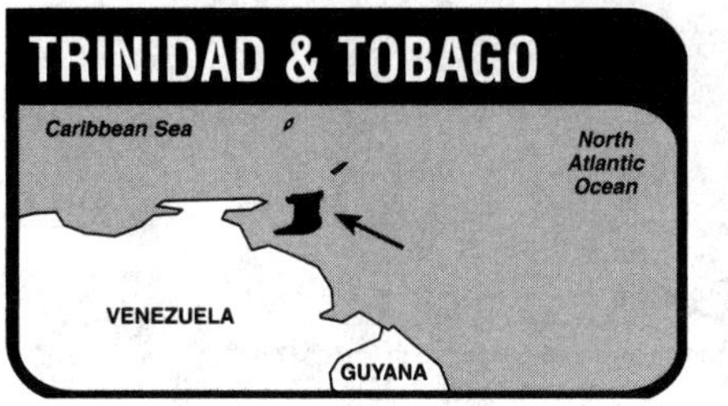

The Republic of Trinidad and Tobago, a member of the British Commonwealth situated 7 miles (11 km.) off the coast of Venezuela, has an area of 1,981 sq. mi. (5,130 sq. km.) and a population of 1.34 million. Capital: Port-of-Spain. The Island of Trinidad contains the world's largest natural asphalt bog. Birds of Paradise live on little Tobago, the only place outside of their native New Guinea where they can be found in a wild state. Petroleum and petroleum products are the mainstay of the economy. Petroleum products, crude oil and sugar are exported.

Trinidad and Tobago were discovered by Columbus in 1498. Trinidad remained under Spanish rule from the time of its settlement in 1592 until its capture by the British in 1797. It was ceded to the British in 1802. Tobago was occupied at various times by the French, Dutch and British before being ceded to Britain in 1814. Trinidad and Tobago were merged into a single colony in 1888. The colony was part of the Federation of the West Indies until Aug. 31, 1962, when it became an independent member of the Commonwealth of Nations. A new constitution establishing a republican form of government was adopted on Aug. 1, 1976. The president is Chief of State. The prime minister is Head of Government.

Notes of the British Caribbean Territories circulated between 1950-1964.

RULERS:

British to 1976

MONETARY SYSTEM:

1 Dollar = 100 Cents
5 Dollars = 1 Pound 10 Pence

SIGNATURE VARIETIES

1	J.F. Pierce	2	A.N. McLeod
3	J.E.Bruce	4	Linn OHB
5	W. Demas	6	N. Hareward
7	M. Duberan	8	

REPUBLIC

CENTRAL BANK OF TRINIDAD AND TOBAGO

1964 CENTRAL BANK ACT

#26-29 arms at l., portr. Qn. Elizabeth II at ctr. Central Bank bldg. at ctr. r. on back. Wmk: Bird of Paradise.

26	1 Dollar	VG	VF	UNC
	L.1964. Red on multicolor underprint. Oil rig in water at upper right on back.			
	a. Signature 1.	1.50	5.00	35.00
	b. Signature 2. Serial # single letter or fractional letters prefix.	2.00	5.50	45.00
	c. Signature 3.	1.00	4.00	30.00
	s. As a, c. Specimen.	—	—	125.

		VG	VF	UNC
27	**5 Dollars**			
	L.1964. Green on multicolor underprint. Crane loading sugar cane at upper right on back.			
	a. Signature 1.	7.50	30.00	250.
	b. Signature 2.	5.00	20.00	200.
	c. Signature 3.	2.00	15.00	85.00
	s. As a, c. Specimen.	—	—	200.

		VG	VF	UNC
28	**10 Dollars**			
	L.1964. Dark brown on multicolor underprint. Factory at upper right on back.			
	a. Signature 1.	20.00	85.00	1250.
	b. Signature 2.	15.00	75.00	1000.
	c. Signature 3.	10.00	35.00	350.
	s. As a, c. Specimen.	—	—	350.

		VG	VF	UNC
29	**20 Dollars**			
	L.1964. Purple on multicolor underprint. Cocoa pods at upper right on back.			
	a. Signature 1.	20.00	75.00	1000.
	b. Signature 2.	15.00	60.00	850.
	c. Signature 3.	10.00	37.50	325.
	s. As a, c. Specimen.	—	—	400.

1977 ND ISSUE

#30-35 authorization date 1964. Arms at ctr. Back like #26-29. Wmk: Bird of Paradise. Replacement notes: Serial # prefix *XX*.

		VG	VF	UNC
30	**1 Dollar**			
	L.1964 (1977). Red on multicolor underprint. Two scarlet Ibis at left. Back like #26.			
	a. Signature 3.	FV	.50	2.50
	b. Signature 4.	FV	1.00	4.00
	s. As a. Specimen.	—	—	150.

		VG	VF	UNC
31	**5 Dollars**			
	L.1964 (1977). Dark green on multicolor underprint. Branches and leaves at left. Back like #27.			
	a. Signature 3.	FV	1.00	6.00
	b. Signature 4.	FV	4.00	20.00
	s. As a. Specimen.	—	—	—

		VG	VF	UNC
32	**10 Dollars**			
	L.1964 (1977). Dark brown on multicolor underprint. Piping guan on branch at left. Signature 3. Back like #28.			
	a. Issued note.	FV	2.50	12.50
	s. Specimen.	—	—	—

		VG	VF	UNC
33	**20 Dollars**			
	L.1964 (1977). Purple on multicolor underprint. Flowers at left. Signature 3. Back like #29.			
	a. Issued note.	FV	5.00	25.00
	s. Specimen, punch hole cancelled.	—	—	—

34	50 Dollars	VG	VF	UNC
	L.1964 (1977). Dark brown on multicolor underprint. Long-billed starthroat at left. Net fishing at upper right on back. Signature 3.			
	a. 1963 (error date in authorization).	20.00	60.00	300.
	b. 1964 (corrected authorization date).	35.00	100.	650.
	s. As b. Specimen.	—	—	—

35	100 Dollars	VG	VF	UNC
	L.1964 (1977). Deep blue on multicolor underprint. Branch with leaves and berries at left. Huts and palm trees at upper right on back.			
	a. Signature 3.	FV	30.00	125.
	b. Signature 4.	FV	35.00	150.
	s. As a. Specimen.	—	—	—

CENTRAL BANK ACT CHAP. 79.02; 1985 ND ISSUE

#36-40 arms at ctr. Twin towered modern bank bldg. at ctr. on back. Wmk: Bird of Paradise. Replacement notes: Serial # prefix *XX*.

36	1 Dollar	VG	VF	UNC
	ND (1985). Red-orange and purple on multicolor underprint. Scarlet Ibis at left. Oil refinery at right on back.			
	a. Signature 4.	FV	FV	1.50
	b. Signature 5.	FV	FV	1.50
	c. Signature 6.	FV	FV	1.00
	d. Signature 7.	FV	FV	1.00
	s. Specimen.	—	—	150.

37	5 Dollars	VG	VF	UNC
	ND (1985). Dark green and blue on multicolor underprint. Blue crowned motmot at left. Woman at roadside produce stand at right on back.			
	a. Signature 4.	FV	FV	5.00
	b. Signature 5.	FV	FV	3.00
	c. Signature 6.	FV	FV	2.00
	d. Signature 7.	FV	FV	2.00
	s. Specimen.	—	—	150.

38	10 Dollars	VG	VF	UNC
	ND (1985). Dark green and brown on multicolor underprint. Piping guan on branch at left. Cargo ship dockside at right on back.			
	a. Signature 4.	FV	FV	7.50
	b. Signature 5.	FV	FV	6.00
	c. Signature 6.	FV	FV	4.00
	d. Signature 7.	FV	FV	4.00
	s. Specimen.	—	—	175.

39	20 Dollars	VG	VF	UNC
	ND (1985). Purple and green on multicolor underprint. White-tailed Saberwing in flowers at left. Steel drums at right on back.			
	a. Signature 4.	FV	FV	12.50
	b. Signature 5.	FV	FV	7.50
	c. Signature 6.	FV	FV	6.00
	d. Signature 7.	FV	FV	6.00
	s. Specimen.	—	—	175.

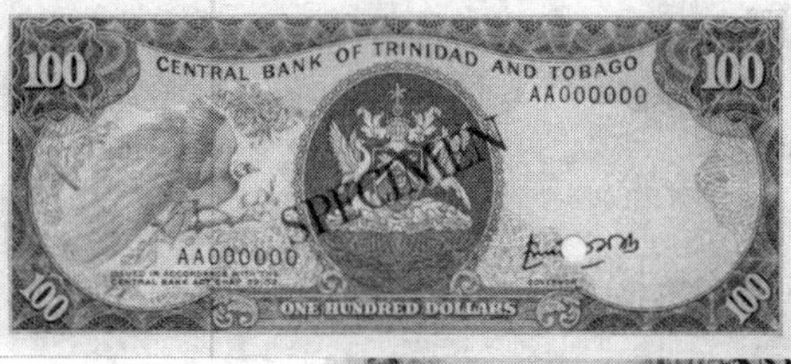

40	100 Dollars	VG	VF	UNC
	ND (1985). Deep blue on multicolor underprint. Greater Bird of Paradise at left. Oil rig at right on back.			
	a. Signature 4.	FV	FV	50.00
	b. Signature 5.	FV	FV	37.50
	c. Signature 6.	FV	FV	30.00
	d. Signature 7.	FV	FV	30.00
	s. Specimen.	—	—	225.

2002 ISSUE

#41-45 arms at ctr. Twin towered modern bank bldg. at ctr. on back. Wmk: Bird of Paradise. Segmented security thread.

41	1 Dollar	VG	VF	UNC
	2002. Red on multicolor underprint. Scarlet Ibis at left. Oil refinery at right on back.	FV	FV	1.00

42	5 Dollars	VG	VF	UNC
	2002. Green and blue on multicolor underprint. Blue crowned motmot at left. Woman at roadside produce stand at right on back.	FV	FV	2.00

43	10 Dollars	VG	VF	UNC
	2002. Dark green on multicolor underprint. Piping guan on branch at left. Cargo ship dockside at right on back.	FV	FV	4.00

44	20 Dollars	VG	VF	UNC
	2002. Purple on multicolor underprint. White-tailed Saberwing in flowers at left. Steel drums at right on back.	FV	FV	6.00

45	100 Dollars	VG	VF	UNC
	2002. Deep blue on multicolor underprint. Greater Bird of Paradise at left. Oil rig at right on back.	FV	FV	30.00

Sending Scanned Images by e-mail

Over the past two years or so, we have been receiving an ever-increasing flow of scanned images from sources world wide. Unfortunately, many of these scans could not be used due to the type of scan, or simple incompatibility with our systems. We appreciate the effort it takes to produce these images and accuracy they add to the catalog listings.

Here are a few simple instructions to follow when producing these scans. We encourage you to continue sending new images or upgrades to those currently illustrated and please do not hesitate to ask questions about this process.

- Scan all images within a resolution of 300 dpi.
- Size setting should be at 100%
- Please include in the e-mail the actual size of the image in millimeters height x width
- Scan in true 4-color
- Save images as 'tiff' and name in such a way which clearly indentifies the country of the note and catalog number
- Do not compress files
- Please e-mail with a request to confirm receipt of the attachment
- If you wish to send an image for "view only" and is not intended for print, a lower resolution (dpi) is fine
- Please send multiple images on a disc if available
- Please send images to george.cuhaj@fwpubs.com

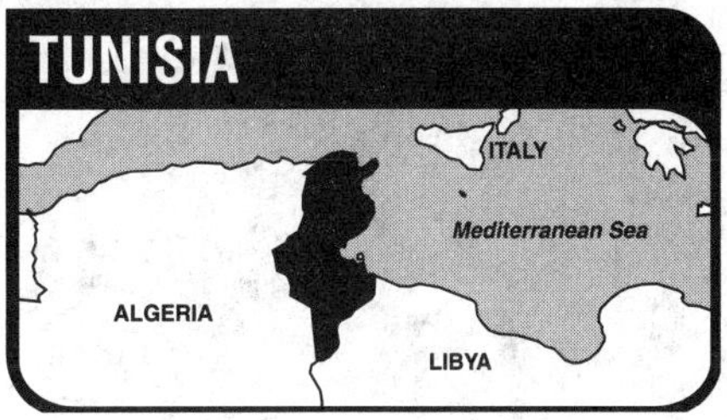

The Republic of Tunisia, located on the northern coast of Africa between Algeria and Libya, has an area of 63,170 sq. mi. (163,610 sq. km.) and a population of 9.84 million. Capital: Tunis. Agriculture is the backbone of the economy. Crude oil, phosphates, olive oil, and wine are exported.

Tunisia, settled by the Phoenicians in the 12th century BC, was the center of the seafaring Carthaginian empire. After the total destruction of Carthage, Tunisia became part of Rome's African province. It remained a part of of the Roman Empire (except for the 439-533 interval Vandal conquest) until taken by the Arabs, 648, who administered it until the Turkish invasion of 1570. Under Turkish control, the public revenue was heavily dependent upon the piracy of Mediterranean shipping, an endeavor that wasn't abandoned until 1819 when a coalition of powers threatened appropriate reprisal. Deprived of its major source of income, Tunisia underwent a financial regression that ended in bankruptcy, enabling France to establish a protectorate over the country in 1881. National agitation and guerrilla fighting forced France to grant Tunisia internal autonomy in 1955 and to recognize Tunisian independence on March 20, 1956. Tunisia abolished the monarchy and established a republic on July 25, 1957.

In 1975 the constitution was changed to make Bourguiba president for life. A two party system was started in 1981, but in the 1986 elections, all but the *Frout Nationals* boycotted. Bourguiba was ousted in 1987. His successor, Zine el Abidine Ben Ali introduced some democratic reforms, but a struggle with Islamic Fundamentalists lead to sporadic violence for some time.

RULERS:

French, 1881-1956

MONETARY SYSTEM:

1 Franc = 100 Centimes to 1960
1 Dinar = 1000 Millimes, 1960-

REPLACEMENT NOTES:

#61-89 with second prefix letter *R* added after regular letter.

REPUBLIC

BANQUE CENTRALE DE TUNISIE

1962 ISSUE

		VG	VF	UNC
61	**5 Dinars** 20.3.1962. Blue on multicolor underprint. Habib Bourguiba at right, bridge at left. Archways on back. Watermark: Arms.	6.00	50.00	300.

1965-69 ISSUE

		VG	VF	UNC
62	**1/2 Dinar** 1.6.1965. Blue on multicolor underprint. Habib Bourguiba at left and as watermark, mosque at right. Mosaic from Monastir on back.			
	a. Issued note.	3.00	25.00	135.
	s. Specimen.	—	—	100.

#63-65 Habib Bourguiba at r. and as wmk.

		VG	VF	UNC
63	**1 Dinar** 1.6.1965. Blue on purple and multicolor underprint. Factory at left. Mosaic on back.			
	a. Issued note.	3.00	25.00	100.
	s. Specimen.	—	—	100.

		VG	VF	UNC
64	**5 Dinars** 1.6.1965. Lilac-brown and green on multicolor underprint. Sadiki College at left. Mosaic with woman in sprays at left, arch at center, Sunface at lower right on back.			
	a. Issued note.	7.50	35.00	150.
	s. Specimen.	—	—	100.

		VG	VF	UNC
65	**10 Dinars** 1.6.1969. Multicolor. Refinery at left. Palm trees in field on back.			
	a. Issued note.	7.50	25.00	100.
	s. Specimen.	—	—	100.

1972 ISSUE

#66-68 Habib Bourguiba at r. and as wmk. Printer: (T)DLR.

		VG	VF	UNC
66	**1/2 Dinar** 3.8.1972. Brown on multicolor underprint. City with river at left. View of Tunis on back.			
	a. Issued note.	1.00	2.50	12.50
	s. Specimen.	—	—	40.00

NOTICE

Readers with unlisted dates, signature varieties, etc. are invited to submit photocopies of their notes to: Standard Catalog of World Paper Money, 700 East State St. Iola, WI 54990-0001, E-Mail: george.cuhaj@fwpubs.com.

67 **1 Dinar**

	VG	VF	UNC
3.8.1972. Purple on multicolor underprint. Old fort at left. Minaret at left, girl at center on back.			
a. Issued note.	1.50	5.00	22.50
s. Specimen.	—	—	40.00

68 **5 Dinars**

	VG	VF	UNC
3.8.1972. Green on multicolor underprint. Modern building at left. Amphitheater at El-Djem on back.			
a. Issued note.	5.00	15.00	50.00
s. Specimen.	—	—	40.00

1973 Issue

#69-72 H. Bourguiba at l. ctr. and as wmk.

69 **1/2 Dinar**

	VG	VF	UNC
15.10.1973. Green on multicolor underprint. Man with camel and trees at left. Landscape with sheep and assorted produce on back.	1.00	2.50	7.50

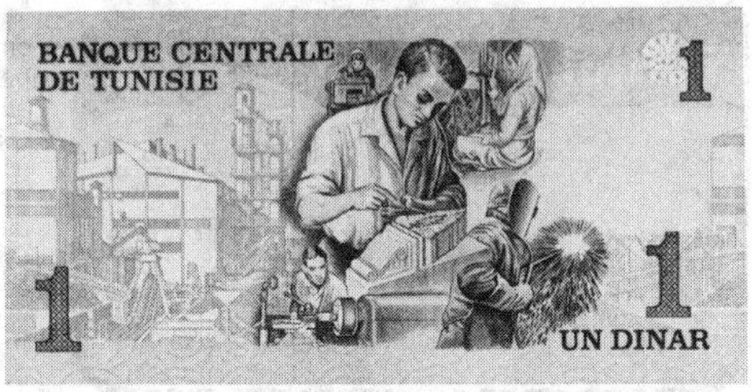

70 **1 Dinar**

	VG	VF	UNC
15.10.1973. Blue and green on multicolor underprint. Building at right. Industrial scenes on back.	1.00	3.00	10.00

71 **5 Dinars**

	VG	VF	UNC
15.10.1973. Dark brown on multicolor underprint. City view at left. Montage of old and new on back.	2.00	7.50	35.00

72 **10 Dinars**

	VG	VF	UNC
15.10.1973. Purple and brown on multicolor underprint. Refinery in background at center. Montage with students, column, train and drummers on back.	3.50	15.00	60.00

#73 not assigned.

1980 Issue

#74, 75 and 77 Habib Bourguiba at r. and as wmk.

74 **1 Dinar**

	VG	VF	UNC
15.10.1980. Red-brown and brown on red and multicolor underprint. Amphitheater at center. Village of Korbous in the "Cap Bon" on back.	.50	2.00	7.50

75 **5 Dinars**
15.10.1980. Brown, red-brown and olive-green on multicolor underprint. Buildings at center. Ruins and hills at left on back.

	VG	VF	UNC
75	1.50	5.00	30.00

76 **10 Dinars**
15.10.1980. Blue-green on bistre and multicolor underprint. Habib Bourguiba at left, building at center. Reservoir at center on back.

	VG	VF	UNC
76	3.00	15.00	85.00

77 **20 Dinars**
15.10.1980. Dark blue-green and brown on multicolor underprint. Amphitheater at center. Harbor of Sousse on back.

	VG	VF	UNC
77	FV	20.00	75.00

1983 Issue

#79-81 Habib Bourguiba on face and as wmk.

79 **5 Dinars**
3.11.1983. Red-brown and purple on lilac underprint. Habib Bourguiba at left, desert scene at bottom center. Hydroelectric dam at center right on back.

	VG	VF	UNC
79	FV	5.00	15.00

80 **10 Dinars**
3.11.1983. Blue and lilac on multicolor underprint. Workers at lower left center, Habib Bourguiba at center, offshore oil rig at right. Modern building at center, old city gateways at right on back.

	VG	VF	UNC
80	FV	10.00	35.00

81 **20 Dinars**
3.11.1983. Light blue and dark blue on green and multicolor underprint. Habib Bourguiba at left, building at bottom center. Building at lower left, aerial view of harbor at right on back.

	VG	VF	UNC
81	FV	20.00	60.00

1986 ISSUE

#82 and 83 Held in reserve.

84 **10 Dinars** | VG FV | VF 10.00 | UNC 30.00

20.3.1986. Yellow-brown on green underprint. Habib Bourguiba at left center and as watermark, agricultural scene at bottom center. Offshore oil rig at left center on back.

#85 Held in reserve.

1992-97 ISSUE

#86-89 replacement notes: *R* in denomination of lower r. serial #.

86 **5 Dinars** | VG FV | VF FV | UNC 12.50

7.11.1993. Green, olive-brown and black. Head of Hannibal at left center and as watermark, Carthage harbor fortress at right. "Nov. 7, 1987" collage at left center on back.

Note: #86 issued on the 6th anniversary of the overthrow of the Bourguiba Government.

87 **10 Dinars** | VG FV | VF FV | UNC 20.00

7.11.1994. Purple, blue-green and red-brown on multicolor underprint. Ibn Khaldoun at center and as watermark. Open book of "7 Novembre 1987" at left center on back. .

Note: #87 issued on the 7th anniversary of the overthrow of the Bourguiba Government.

87A **10 Dinars** | VG FV | VF FV | UNC 15.00

7.11.1994 (2005). Brown on multicolor underprint. Ibn Khaldoun at center and as watermark. Open book of '7 Novembre 1987' at left center on back.

88 **20 Dinars** | VG FV | VF FV | UNC 30.00

7.11.1992. Deep purple, blue-black and red-brown on multicolor underprint. K. Et-tounsi on horseback at left center, his head as watermark, buildings in background. Montage of city view; a "7" with 1987 date over flag on stylized dove at center on back.

Note: #88 issued on the 5th anniversary of the overthrow of the Bourguiba Government.

89 **30 Dinars** | VG FV | VF FV | UNC 45.00

7.11.1997. Green and yellow on multicolor underprint. Aboul El Kacem Chebbi at right and as watermark. Schoolgirls, sheep and weaver on back.

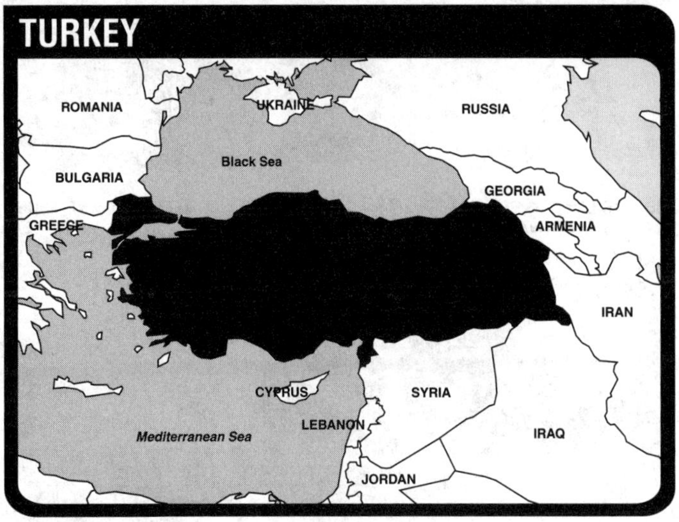

The Republic of Turkey, a parliamentary democracy of the Near East located partially in Europe and partially in Asia between the Black and the Mediterranean seas, has an area of 301,382 sq. mi. (780,580 sq. km.) and a population of 65.73 million. Capital: Ankara. Turkey exports cotton, hazelnuts and tobacco, and enjoys a virtual monopoly in meerschaum.

The Ottoman Turks, a tribe from Central Asia, first appeared in the early 13th century, and by the 17th century had established the Ottoman Empire which stretched from the Persian Gulf to the southern frontier of Poland, and from the Caspian Sea to the Algerian plateau. The defeat of the Turkish navy by the Holy League in 1571, and of the Turkish forces besieging Vienna in 1683, began the steady decline of the Ottoman Empire which, accelerated by the rise of nationalism, contracted its European border, and by the end of World War I deprived it of its Arab lands. The present Turkish boundaries were largely fixed by the Treaty of Lausanne in 1923. The sultanate and caliphate, the political and spiritual ruling institutions of the old empire, were separated and the sultanate abolished in 1922 by Mustafa Kemal Atatürk. On Oct. 29, 1923, Turkey formally became a republic and Atatürk was selected as the first president.

MONETARY SYSTEM:

1 Lira (Livre, Pound) = 100 Piastres

REPUBLIC

TÜRKIYE CÜMHURIYET MERKEZ BANKASI

CENTRAL BANK OF TURKEY

LAW 11 HAZIRAN 1930; 1961-65 ND ISSUE

#173-178 portr. Pres. K. Atatürk at r. and as wmk. Printer: DBM-A (w/o imprint).

173	5 Lira	VG	VF	UNC
	L.1930 (25.10.1961). Blue with orange, blue and multicolor guilloche. Back blue; Three women with baskets of hazelnuts at center.			
	a. Issue note.	3.00	10.00	60.00
	s. Specimen.	—	—	200.

174	5 Lira	VG	VF	UNC
	L.1930 (4.1.1965). Blue-green. Back blue-gray, like #173.			
	a. Issued note.	2.00	6.00	45.00
	s. Specimen.	—	—	200.

175	50 Lira	VG	VF	UNC
	L.1930 (1.6.1964). Brown on multicolor underprint. 3 signature Soldier holding rifle figure from the Victory statue at Ulus Square in Ankara at center on back.			
	a. Issued note.	5.00	20.00	75.00
	s. Specimen.	—	—	250.

176	100 Lira	VG	VF	UNC
	L.1930 (15.3.1962). Olive on orange and multicolor guilloche. Youth Park with bridge in Ankara on back.			
	a. Issued note.	12.50	50.00	125.
	s. Specimen.	—	—	350.

177	100 Lira	VG	VF	UNC
	L.1930 (1.10.1964). Like #176, but guilloche blue, lilac and multicolor. Different sign.			
	a. Issued note.	8.50	35.00	100.
	s. Specimen.	—	—	350.

178 500 Lira | VG | VF | UNC

L.1930 (1.12.1962). Purple and brown on multicolor underprint. Sultan Ahmet Mosque, the Obelisc and the Hippodrome in Istanbul on back.

	VG	VF	UNC
a. Issued note.	50.00	150.	400.
s. Specimen.	—	—	500.

LAW 11 HAZIRAN 1930; 1966-69 ND ISSUE

#179-183 Pres. Atatürk at r. and as wmk. 3 sign. Printer: DBM-A (w/o imprint).

		VG	VF	UNC
179	**5 Lira** L.1930 (8.1.1968). Grayish purple on multicolor underprint. Manavgat waterfall in Antalya at left center on back.	.25	1.00	4.00

		VG	VF	UNC
180	**10 Lira** L.1930 (4.7.1966). Green on multicolor underprint. Maiden's Tower on the Bosphorus in Istanbul at center on back.	1.00	3.00	9.00

		VG	VF	UNC
181	**20 Lira** L.1930 (15.6.1966). Orange-brown on multicolor underprint. Back dull brown on pale green underprint, mausoleum of of Atatürk in Ankara at center on back.			
	a. 7-digit serial #.	15.00	50.00	350.
	b. 8-digit serial #.	1.50	2.50	15.00
182	**100 Lira** L.1930 (17.3.1969). Like #176 but modified guilloche in pinkish red, blue and multicolor underprint. Different signature.	12.00	40.00	100.
183	**500 Lira** L.1930 (3.6.1968). Purple, brown and multicolor. Like #178.	30.00	90.00	300.

#184 Not assigned.

LAW OCAK 14 (JAN. 26), 1970; 1971-82 ND ISSUES

#185-191 Pres. Atatürk at r. and as wmk. 2 sign.

#185, 188, 190 and 191 replacement notes: Serial # prefix *Z91-Z95*.

		VG	VF	UNC
185	**5 Lira** L.1970 (1976). Like #179.	.15	.50	2.00

		VG	VF	UNC
186	**10 Lira** L.1970 (1975). Like #180.	.50	1.50	5.00

		VG	VF	UNC
187	**20 Lira** L.1970 (1974). Like #181.			
	a. Black signature. 2 varieties.	.25	1.00	5.00
	b. Brown signature.	.25	.50	1.00

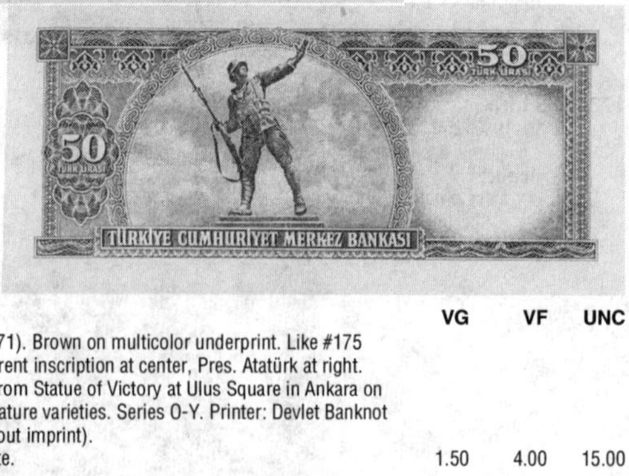

		VG	VF	UNC
187A	**50 Lira** L.1970 (2.8.1971). Brown on multicolor underprint. Like #175 except for different inscription at center, Pres. Atatürk at right. Soldier figure from Statue of Victory at Ulus Square in Ankara on back. Two signature varieties. Series O-Y. Printer: Devlet Banknot Matbaasi (without imprint).			
	a. Issued note.	1.50	4.00	15.00
	s. Specimen.	—	—	—

188 50 Lira

	VG	VF	UNC
L.1970 (1976). Dark brown on multicolor underprint. New portrait at right. Marble Fountain in Topkapi Palace in Istanbul on back. Two signature varieties.	.25	.50	2.00

189 100 Lira

	VG	VF	UNC
L.1970 (15.5.1972). Blue-green on multicolor underprint. Face similar to #188. Back brown; Mt. Ararat at center. Three signature varieties.			
a. Issued note.	.25	1.00	3.00
s. Specimen.	—	—	—

190 500 Lira

	VG	VF	UNC
L.1970 (1.9.1971). Dark blue and dark green on multicolor underprint. Main Gate of Istanbul University on back. Two signature varieties.	3.00	10.00	25.00

191 1000 Lira

	VG	VF	UNC
L.1970. Deep purple and brown-violet on multicolor underprint. Bosphorus River with boat and suspension bridge on back. Three signature varieties.	2.00	6.00	20.00

LAW OCAK 14 (JAN. 26), 1970; 1984-97 ND ISSUES

#192-204 Pres. Atatürk at r. and as wmk.

Some sign. varieties.

192 10 Lira

	VG	VF	UNC
L.1970 (1979). Dull gray-green on multicolor underprint. Young boy and girl in medallion in underprint at center. Children presenting flowers to Atatürk on back.	.10	.20	.50

193 10 Lira

	VG	VF	UNC
L.1970 (1982). Black on multicolor underprint. Like #192.	.10	.20	.50

194 100 Lira

	VG	VF	UNC
L.1970 (1984). Violet and brown on multicolor underprint. Fort of Ankara, Mehmet Akif Ersoy, his home and document on back.			
a. Watermark: Head small, bust facing right, dotted security thread.	.15	.30	1.25
b. Watermark: Head large, bust facing 3/4 right.	.10	.25	1.00

195 500 Lira

	VG	VF	UNC
L.1970 (1983). Blue on multicolor underprint. Clock Tower in Izmir at left center on back. Watermark varieties. Two signature varieties.	.25	.50	1.50

196 1000 Lira

	VG	VF	UNC
L.1970 (1986). Purple and blue on multicolor underprint. One dot for visually impaired at lower left. Istanbul coastline at left, Fathi Sultan Mehmet at center right on back. Two signature varieties.	.25	.75	1.75

196A 5000 Lira

	VG	VF	UNC
L.1970 (1981). Dark brown and olive-green on multicolor underprint. Mevlana Museum in Konya and figure of Mevlana at right on back.	4.00	12.00	35.00

197 5000 Lira

	VG	VF	UNC
L.1970 (1985). Dark brown, red-brown and blue on multicolor underprint. Seated Mevlana at left center, Mevlana Museum at center on back. Two signature varieties.	1.00	3.00	10.00

198 5000 Lira

	VG	VF	UNC
L.1970 (1990). Deep brown and deep green on multicolor underprint. Afsin-Elbistan thermal power plant at left center on back.	.25	1.25	4.00

199 10,000 Lira

	VG	VF	UNC
L.1970 (1982). Purple and deep green on multicolor underprint. Three dots for visally impaired at lower left. Back darker green and multicolor; Selimiye Mosque in Edirne, Mimar Sinan (architect) at center.	FV	1.75	10.00

200 10,000 Lira

	VG	VF	UNC
L.1970 (1989). Like #199 but back pale green.	FV	1.00	5.00

201 20,000 Lira

	VG	VF	UNC
L.1970 (1988). Red-brown and purple on multicolor underprint. New Central Bank building in Ankara at left center on back.	FV	FV	9.00

202 20,000 Lira

	VG	VF	UNC
L.1970 (1995). Like #201 but with lighter underprint at center. Red signature. Lithographed back in lighter shade. Series G-.	FV	FV	2.75

203 50,000 Lira

	VG	VF	UNC
L.1970 (1989). Blue-green and dark green on multicolor underprint. National Parliament House in Ankara at left center on back.			
a. Issued note.	FV	FV	7.50
b. Issued note. Serial # prefix *H01-H03.*	50.00	200.	650.

204 50,000 Lira

	VG	VF	UNC
L.1970 (1995). Like #203 but with value in gray on back. Series K-.	FV	FV	2.50

#205-211 Pres. Atatürk facing at ctr. r. and as wmk. Sign. varieties.

205 100,000 Lira

	VG	VF	UNC
L.1970 (1991). Reddish brown, dark brown and dark green on multicolor underprint. Equestrian statue of Atatürk at lower left center. Children presenting flowers to Atatürk at left center on back.	FV	FV	10.00

		VG	VF	UNC
206	**100,000 Lira** L.1970 (1997). Multicolor. Like #205 but without security device at upper right. Back lithographed; lighter brown color.	FV	FV	4.00

		VG	VF	UNC
207	**250,000 Lira** L.1970 (1992). Blue-gray, dark green and violet on multicolor underprint. Triangular security device at upper right. Kizilkale Fortress at Alunya at center on back.	FV	FV	10.00

		VG	VF	UNC
208	**500,000 Lira** L.1970 (1993). Purple, blue-black and violet on multicolor underprint. Square security device at upper right. Aerial view of Canakkale Martyrs Monument on back.	FV	FV	15.00

		VG	VF	UNC
209	**1,000,000 Lira** L.1970 (1995). Claret red and blue-gray on multicolor underprint. Atatürk dam in Sanliurfa on back.	FV	FV	20.00

		VG	VF	UNC
210	**5,000,000 Lira** L.1970 Ocak (January) 1997 (at bottom left). Dark brown and red-brown on multicolor underprint. Gold oval seal with AH1329 date at right. Anitkabir complex (mausoleum of Ataturk) in Ankara at left center on back.	FV	FV	25.00

LAW OCAK 14 (JAN. 26), 1970; 1998-2002 ND ISSUE

		VG	VF	UNC
211	**250,000 Lira** L.1970 (1998). Blue-gray and violet on multicolor underprint. Like #207 but triangular security device at upper right printed in solid ink. Back blue lithograph.	FV	FV	3.00

		VG	VF	UNC
212	**500,000 Lira** L.1970 (1998). Purple, blue-black and violet on multicolor underprint. Like #208 but without square security device at upper right. Black pale purple. Lithograph.	FV	FV	4.50

		VG	VF	UNC
213	**1,000,000 Lira** L.1970 (2002). Face same as #209. Back pale color, Lithograph. Name of dam changed to Sanliurfa-Adiyaman.	FV	FV	8.00

214 10,000,000 Lira | VG FV | VF FV | UNC 35.00

L.1970 (1999). Red and purple on multicolor underprint. Ataturk at left center. Square security device in gold at right. World map of 1513 by Piri Reis on back.

215 20,000,000 Lira | VG FV | VF FV | UNC 45.00

L.1970 (2000). Green and red. Atatük at center globe and olive branch behind. Efes ancient city on back.

2005 New Lira Issue

#216-221 Atatürk at ctr. or r. and as wmk.

Monetary reform: 100,000 "old" lira = 1 "new" lira

216 1 New Lira | VG FV | VF FV | UNC 3.00

2005. Claret red and blue. Atatürk Dam in Sanliurfa-Adiyaman on back.

NOTICE

Readers with unlisted dates, signature varieties, etc. are invited to submit photocopies of their notes to: Standard Catalog of World Paper Money, 700 East State St. Iola, WI 54990-0001, E-Mail: george.cuhaj@fwpubs.com.

217 5 New Lira | VG FV | VF FV | UNC 11.00

2005. Greenish brown. Mausolem of Atatürk on back.

218 10 New Lira | VG FV | VF FV | UNC 20.00

2005. Greenish brown. World map of 1513 by Piri Reis on back.

219 20 New Lira | VG FV | VF FV | UNC 40.00

2005. Green. Ancient city of Ephesus on back.

220	50 New Lira	VG	VF	UNC
	2005. Orange. Goreme National Park, Capadoccia, on back.	FV	FV	75.00

221	100 New Lira	VG	VF	UNC
	2005. Blue. Ishak Pasha Palace, Dogu Bayazit, on back.	FV	FV	135.

The Turkmenistan Republic covers the territory of the Trans-Caspian Region of Turkestan, the Charjiui Vilayet of Bukhara and the part of Khiva located on the right bank of the Oxus. Bordered on the north by the Autonomous Kara-Kalpak Republic (a constituent of Uzbekistan), by Iran and Afghanistan on the south, by the Uzbek Republic on the east and the Caspian Sea on the west. It has an area of 186,400 sq. mi. (488,100 sq. km.) and a population of 4.48 million. Capital: Ashgabat (formerly Poltoratsk). Main occupation is agricultural products including cotton and maize. It is rich in minerals, oil, coal, sulphur and salt,and is also famous for it's carpets, Turkoman horses and Karakul sheep.

The Turkomans arrived in Transcaspia as nomadic Seluk Turks in the 11th century. They often became subjected to one of the neighboring states. Late in the 19th century the Russians invaded with their first victory in 1877, arriving in Ashkhabad in 1882 resulting in submission of the Turkmen tribes. By 1884, the Transcaspian province of Russian Turkestan was formed. During WW I the Russian government tried to conscript the Turkmen; this led to a revolt in Oct. 1916 under the leadership of Aziz Chapykov. In 1918 the Turks captured Baku from the Red army and the British sent a contingent to Merv to prevent a German-Turkish offensive toward Afghanistan and India. In mid-1919 the Bureau of Turkistan Moslem Communist Organizations was formed in Moscow hoping to develop one large republic including all surrounding Turkic areas within a Soviet federation. A Turkistan Autonomous Soviet Socialist Republic was formed and was partitioned into five republics according to the principle of nationalities. On Oct. 27, 1924, Turkmenistan became a Soviet Socialist Republic and was accepted as a member of the U.S.S.R. on Jan. 29, 1925. In Aug. 1990 the Turkmen Supreme Soviet adopted a declaration of sovereignty followed by a declaration of independence in Oct. 1991. It joined the Commonwealth of Independent States in December. A new constitution was adopted in 1992 providing for an executive presidency.

REPUBLIC

TÜRKMENISTANYÑ MERKEZI DÖWLET BANKY

CENTRAL BANK OF TURKMENISTAN

1993 ND; 1995-98 ISSUE

#1-9 arms at l. on back. Wmk: Rearing Arabian horse. Sign. Khudaiberdy Orazov. Replacement notes: Serial # prefix *ZZ*.

1	1 Manat	VG	VF	UNC
	ND (1993). Brown and tan on orange and multicolor underprint. Ylymlar Academy at center, native craft at right. Shield at left, Temple at center on back.	FV	.15	.75

2	5 Manat	VG	VF	UNC
	ND (1993). Blue and green on multicolor underprint. Building at center. Building at center on back.	—	.25	1.00

#3-10 Pres. S. Niazov at r.

		VG	VF	UNC
3	**10 Manat** ND (1993). Brown and pale orange on multicolor underprint. Government Building at center. Back red-violet; Government Building at center on back.	—	.25	1.50

		VG	VF	UNC
4	**20 Manat** ND (1993); 1995. Blue-gray and blue on multicolor underprint. National library at center. Large Building at center on back.			
	a. ND (1993).	.15	.25	3.00
	b. 1995.	—	.15	1.50

		VG	VF	UNC
5	**50 Manat** ND (1993); 1995. Brown and green on multicolor underprint. Monument at center. Mosque ruins on back.			
	a. ND (1993).	.15	.25	3.00
	b. 1995.	.15	.25	1.75

		VG	VF	UNC
6	**100 Manat** ND (1993); 1995. Dark blue and dark gray on multicolor underprint. Presidential Palace at center. Sultan Sanjaryn mausoleum on back.			
	a. ND (1993).	.50	1.00	5.00
	b. 1995.	—	.25	1.75

		VG	VF	UNC
7	**500 Manat** ND (1993); 1995. Violet, dark brown and orange on multicolor underprint. National theatre at center. Hanymyn mausoleum on back.			
	a. ND (1993).	.25	1.25	7.50
	b. 1995.	.15	1.00	5.00
8	**1000 Manat** 1995. Green on multicolor underprint. Building at center. Arms at center on back.	FV	1.00	7.50
9	**5000 Manat** 1996. Violet, purple and red on multicolor underprint. Building at center. Arms on back.	FV	1.00	8.50
10	**10,000 Manat** 1996. Dark brown on multicolor underprint. Presidential palace at center. Arms on back.	FV	2.00	10.00

		VG	VF	UNC
11	**10,000 Manat** 1998. Light blue, light brown, and red on multicolor underprint. Palace of Turkmenbashy. Back light blue, violet, and purple on multicolor underprint, Mosque of Saparmurat at center.	FV	2.00	10.00

1999-2003 ISSUE

		VG	VF	UNC
12	**5000 Manat** 1999; 2000. Violet, purple and red on multicolor underprint. Like #9.			
	a. 1999. Signature Khudaiberdy Orazov.	FV	1.00	7.50
	b. 2000. Signature S. Kandymov.	FV	1.00	7.50

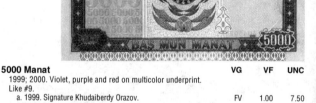

		VG	VF	UNC
13	**10,000 Manat** 1999. Light blue and light brown on multicolor underprint. Pres. Niyazov with medals at right. Palace of Turkmenbashy at center. Mosque of Saparmurat on back. Like #11. Signature Khudaiberdy Orazov.	FV	1.50	10.00

		VG	VF	UNC
14	**10,000 Manat** 2000. Face like #13 but stars and crescent at upper left. Circular design at upper right on back. Signature S. Kandymov.	FV	FV	10.00

		VG	VF	UNC
15	**10,000 Manat** 2003. Like #14 but arms at upper left.	FV	FV	10.00

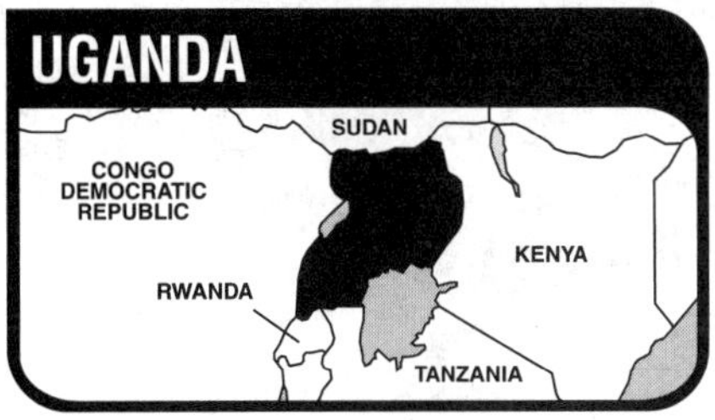

The Republic of Uganda, a former British protectorate located astride the equator in east-central Africa, has an area of 91,134 sq. mi. (236,036 sq. km.) and a population of 15.25 million. Capital: Kampala. Agriculture, including livestock, is the basis of the economy; there is some mining of copper, tin, gold and lead. Coffee, cotton, copper and tea are exported.

Uganda was first visited by Arab slavers in the 1830s. They were followed in the 1860s by British explorers searching for the headwaters of the Nile. The explorers, and the missionaries who followed them into the Lake Victoria region of south-central Africa in 1877-1879, found well developed African kingdoms dating back several centuries. In 1894 the local native Kingdom of Buganda was established as a British protectorate that was extended in 1896 to encompass an area substantially the same as the present Republic of Uganda. The protectorate was given a ministerial form of government in 1955, full internal self-government on March 1, 1962, and complete independence on Oct. 9, 1962. Uganda is a member of the Commonwealth of Nations. The president is Chief of State and Head of Government.

Notes of East African Currency Board circulated before Bank of Uganda notes were available. Also see East Africa.

MONETARY SYSTEM:

1 Shilling = 100 Cents

Caution: Several years ago the Bank of Uganda sold quantities of demonetized notes, most of which were made available for only $1.00 per note. Condition of notes thus sold is not reported. A listing of some pieces NOT available from the bank includes #4, 6a, 7a, 8a and b, 9a and b, 13a, 14a, 21, 23, and 24a and b.

REPUBLIC

BANK OF UGANDA

1966 ND ISSUE

#1-5 sign. titles: *GOVERNOR* and *SECRETARY*. Wmk: Hand. Replacement notes: Serial # prefix *Z/1* (5/ and 10/); *Y/1; X/1; W/1* respectively.

		VG	VF	UNC
1	**5 Shillings** ND (1966). Dark blue on multicolor underprint. Arms at right. River and waterfall on back.			
	a. Issued note.	.25	1.50	5.00
	s. Specimen.	—	—	25.00
	ct. Color trial.	—	—	75.00
2	**10 Shillings** ND (1966). Brown on multicolor underprint. Arms at center. Workers picking cotton on back.			
	a. Issued note.	.50	2.50	5.00
	s. Specimen.	—	—	25.00
	ct. Color trial.	—	—	125.

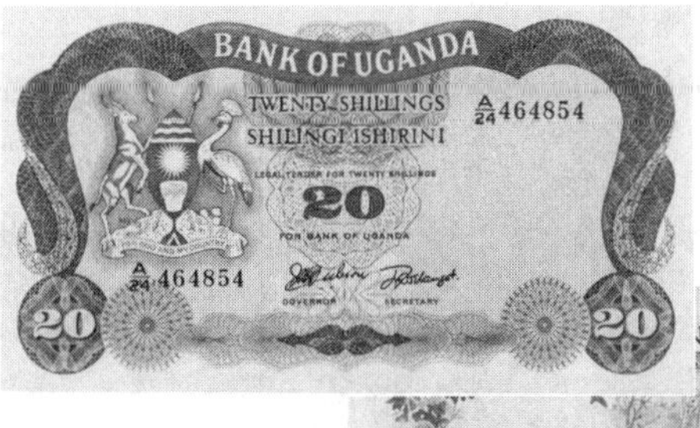

3 **20 Shillings** | VG | VF | UNC

ND (1966). Purple on multicolor underprint. Marabou stork, Green Monkey, Lion, Elephants, Zebra and Impala on back.

	VG	VF	UNC
a. Issued note.	.50	2.00	6.00
s. Specimen.	—	—	25.00
ct. Color trial.	—	—	250.

4 **100 Shillings**

ND (1966). Green on multicolor underprint. Crowned crane at left, without *FOR BANK OF UGANDA* just below value at center. Building at right on back.

	VG	VF	UNC
a. Issued note.	15.00	75.00	750.
s. Specimen.	—	—	125.
ct. Color trial.	—	—	500.

5 **100 Shillings**

ND (1966). Green on multicolor underprint. Like #4 but with text: *FOR BANK OF UGANDA* under value at face center.

	VG	VF	UNC
a. Issued note.	.25	1.50	6.00
s. Specimen.	—	—	25.00

1973-77 ND Issue

SIGNATURE VARIETIES					
1	GOVERNOR	SECRETARY	2	GOVERNOR	SECRETARY

#5A-9 Pres. Idi Amin at l., arms at lower r. Wmk: Crested crane. Replacement notes: Serial # prefix *Z/1* (5/ and 10/); *Y/1; X/1; W/1* respectively.

5A **5 Shillings**

	VG	VF	UNC
ND (1977). Blue on multicolor underprint. Woman picking coffee beans on back.	.25	.50	2.50

6 **10 Shillings**

ND (1973). Brown on multicolor underprint. Elephants, antelope and hippopotamus on back.

	VG	VF	UNC
a. Signature titles: *GOVERNOR* and *DIRECTOR*.	7.50	40.00	285.
b. Signature titles: *GOVERNOR* and *SECRETARY*. Signature 1.	1.00	2.50	12.50
c. Signature titles as b. Signature 2.	.25	1.00	5.00
s. As a. Specimen.	—	—	80.00

7 **20 Shillings**

ND (1973). Purple and brown on multicolor underprint. Large building on back.

	VG	VF	UNC
a. Signature titles: *GOVERNOR* and *DIRECTOR*.	7.50	50.00	300.
b. Signature titles: *GOVERNOR* and *SECRETARY*. Signature 1.	2.00	10.00	75.00
c. Signature titles as b. Signature 2.	.50	2.00	6.50
s. As a. Specimen.	—	—	90.00

8 **50 Shillings**

ND (1973). Blue (shade) on multicolor underprint. Hydroelectric dam on back.

	VG	VF	UNC
a. Signature titles: *GOVERNOR* and *DIRECTOR*.	7.50	40.00	275.
b. Signature titles: *GOVERNOR* and *SECRETARY*. Signature 1.	2.50	8.00	85.00
c. Signature titles as b. Signature 2.	.50	2.00	6.00
s. As a. Specimen.	—	—	135.

9	100 Shillings	VG	VF	UNC
	ND (1973). Green (shades) on multicolor underprint. Scene of lake and hills on back.			
	a. Signature titles: *GOVERNOR* and *DIRECTOR.*	7.50	30.00	150.
	b. Signature titles: *GOVERNOR* and *SECRETARY.* Signature 1.	3.00	12.50	85.00
	c. Signature titles as b. Signature 2.	.75	2.00	8.50
	s. As a. Specimen.	—	—	110.

1979 Issue

#10-14 Bank of Uganda at l. Sign. titles: *GOVERNOR* and *DIRECTOR*. Wmk: Crested crane's head. Replacement notes: Serial # prefix *Z/1* (5/ and 10/); *Y/1; X/1; W/1* respectively.

10	5 Shillings	VG	VF	UNC
	ND (1979). Blue on multicolor underprint. Back like #5A.	.05	.20	1.00

11	10 Shillings	VG	VF	UNC
	ND (1979). Brown on multicolor underprint. Back like #6.			
	a. Light printing on bank.	.25	1.50	5.00
	b. Dark printing on bank.	.25	.50	2.00

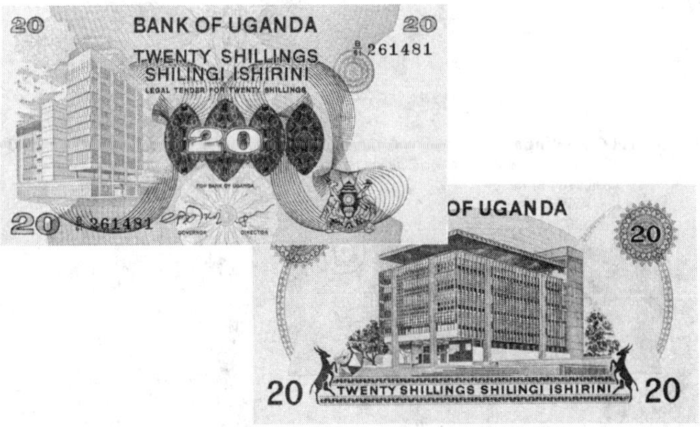

12	20 Shillings	VG	VF	UNC
	ND (1979). Purple and brown on multicolor underprint. Back like #7.			
	a. Light printing on bank.	.50	2.00	7.50
	b. Dark printing on bank.	.25	.50	2.50

13	50 Shillings	VG	VF	UNC
	ND (1979). Dark blue and purple on multicolor underprint. Back like #8.			
	a. Light printing on bank.	5.00	17.50	100.
	b. Dark printing on bank.	.25	1.00	4.50

14	100 Shillings	VG	VF	UNC
	ND (1979). Green (shades) on multicolor underprint. Back like #9.			
	a. Light printing on bank.	1.50	3.00	12.00
	b. Dark printing on bank.	1.00	2.50	8.50

1982 Issue

#15-19 arms at l. Sign. titles: *GOVERNOR* and *SECRETARY*. Wmk: Crested crane's head. Replacement notes: Serial # prefix *Z/1* (5/ and 10/); *Y/1; X/1; W/1* respectively.

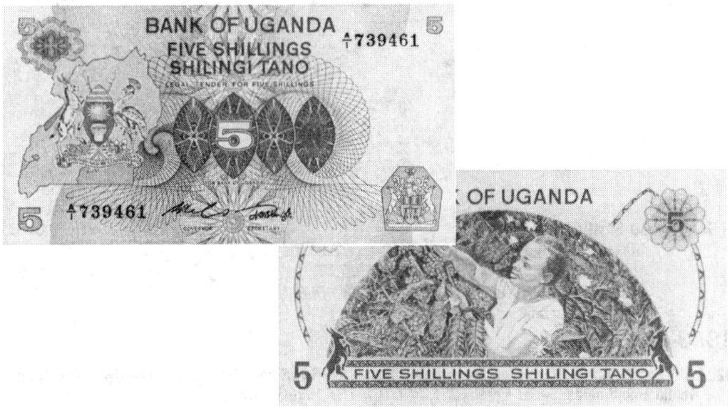

15	5 Shillings	VG	VF	UNC
	ND (1982). Olive-green on multicolor underprint. Back like #5A.	.10	.25	1.00

16	10 Shillings	VG	VF	UNC
	ND (1982). Purple on multicolor underprint. Back like #6.	.10	.50	2.50

17 **20 Shillings**

	VG	VF	UNC
ND (1982). Green, dark red and multicolor. Back like #7.	.25	2.00	7.00

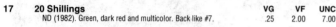

18 **50 Shillings**

	VG	VF	UNC
ND (1982). Brown, orange and multicolor. Back like #8.			
a. Signature titles: *GOVERNOR* and *SECRETARY.*	.25	.75	3.00
b. Signature titles: *GOVERNOR* and *DEPUTY GOVERNOR.*	.25	1.00	10.00

19 **100 Shillings**

	VG	VF	UNC
ND (1982). Red-violet, orange and multicolor. Back like #9.			
a. Signature titles: *GOVERNOR* and *SECRETARY.*	.25	1.00	3.50
b. Signature titles: *GOVERNOR* and *DEPUTY GOVERNOR.* Small or large prefix letter and # before serial #.	.25	1.50	5.00

1983-85 Issue

#20-23 Pres. Milton Obote at l. on face. Sign. titles: *GOVERNOR* and *DEPUTY GOVERNOR.* Wmk: Hand. Replacement notes: Serial # prefix *X/1; W/1; U/1; T/1; S/1* respectively.

20 **50 Shillings**

	VG	VF	UNC
ND (1985). Brown and orange on multicolor underprint. Back like #8.	.25	1.00	3.00

21 **100 Shillings**

	VG	VF	UNC
ND (1985). Red-violet and orange on multicolor underprint. Back like #9.	.50	4.00	20.00

22 **500 Shillings**

	VG	VF	UNC
ND (1983). Blue, purple and multicolor. Cattle and harvesting on back. Serial # prefix varieties as #19b.			
a. Issued note.	.25	1.00	5.00
s. Specimen.	—	—	10.00

23 **1000 Shillings**

	VG	VF	UNC
ND (1983). Red and multicolor. Building on back. Serial # prefix varieties as #19b.			
a. Issued note.	.50	4.00	22.50
s. Specimen.	—	—	12.50

24 5000 Shillings VG VF UNC

1985-86. Purple and multicolor. Arms at left. Building with clock tower at center right on back.

	VG	VF	UNC
a. Watermark: Hand. 1985.	2.50	6.00	30.00
b. Watermark: Crested crane. 1986.	.50	1.50	5.00

1985-86 Issue

#25 and 26 face similar to #24. Wmk: Crested crane's head. Replacement notes: Serial # prefix *U/1; T/1* respectively.

	VG	VF	UNC
25 500 Shillings 1986. Blue, purple and multicolor. Back like #22.	.25	.75	2.00

	VG	VF	UNC
26 1000 Shillings 1986. Red and multicolor. Back like #23.	.25	1.00	3.00

1987 Issue

#27-34 replacement notes: Serial # prefix *ZZ*.

#27-32 arms at upper l., map at ctr. Printer: TDLR.

	VG	VF	UNC
27 5 Shillings 1987. Brown on multicolor underprint. Arms at right also. Crowned crane, hippo, elephant and waterbuck on back.	.10	.30	1.50

	VG	VF	UNC
28 10 Shillings 1987. Green on multicolor underprint. Arms at right also. Two antelope grazing, two men fishing in canoe at center on back.	.10	.30	1.50

#29-34 wmk: Crested crane's head.

29 20 Shillings VG VF UNC

1987-88. Purple, blue-black and violet on multicolor underprint. Modern buildings at center right on back.

	VG	VF	UNC
a. Imprint on back. 1987.	.10	.50	2.50
b. Without imprint. 1988.	.10	.25	1.50

30 50 Shillings VG VF UNC

1987-98. Red, orange and dark brown on multicolor underprint. Parliament building at center right on back.

	VG	VF	UNC
a. Imprint on back. 1987.	.15	.50	2.50
b. Without imprint. 1988; 1989.	.15	.50	2.00
c. 1994; 1996; 1997; 1998.	.10	.25	1.00

31 100 Shillings VG VF UNC

1987-98. Deep blue-violet, black and aqua on multicolor underprint. High Court building with clock tower at center right on back.

	VG	VF	UNC
a. Signature titles: *GOVERNOR* and *SECRETARY, TREASURY.* Imprint on back. 1987.	.25	1.00	3.00
b. As a. but without imprint on back. 1988.	.15	.75	1.50
c. As b. but with signature titles: *GOVERNOR* and *SECRETARY.* 1994; 1996; 1997; 1998.	.10	.25	1.00

NOTICE

Readers with unlisted dates, signature varieties, etc. are invited to submit photocopies of their notes to: Standard Catalog of World Paper Money, 700 East State St. Iola, WI 54990-0001, E-Mail: george.cuhaj@fwpubs.com.

32	200 Shillings	VG	VF	UNC
	1987-98. Brown, orange and olive-brown on multicolor underprint. Worker in textile factory at center right on back.			
	a. 1987.	.15	.50	3.00
	b. 1991; 1994; 1996; 1998.	.15	.50	1.50

1991 Issue

33	500 Shillings	VG	VF	UNC
	1991. Dark brown and deep purple on multicolor underprint. Elephant at left, arms at upper center and lower right. Uganda Independence Monument at left, municipal building with clock tower at center on back.			
	a. Signature titles: *GOVERNOR* and *SECRETARY, TREASURY.*	FV	.75	4.00
	b. Signature titles: *GOVERNOR* and *SECRETARY.*	FV	1.00	4.50
	s. As a. Specimen.	—	—	25.00

34	1000 Shillings	VG	VF	UNC
	1991. Black, deep brown-violet and dark green on multicolor underprint. Farmers at left, arms at upper center and lower right. Grain storage facility at center on back.			
	a. Signature titles: *GOVERNOR* and *SECRETARY, TREASURY.*	FV	2.50	5.00
	b. Signature titles: *GOVERNOR* and *SECRETARY.*	FV	1.25	4.00

1993-95 Issue

#35-38 arms at upper ctr. Ascending size serial # vertically at l. Wmk: Crested crane's head. Replacement notes: Serial # prefix *ZZ*.

35	500 Shillings	VG	VF	UNC
	1994; 1996-98. Like #33. Segmented foil over security thread. Ascending size serial # at left.			
	a. 1994; 1996.	FV	FV	4.00
	b. 1997; 1998.	FV	2.50	5.00

36	1000 Shillings	VG	VF	UNC
	1994; 1996; 1998; 1999. Like #34. Segmented foil over security thread. Ascending size serial # at left.	FV	1.25	3.50

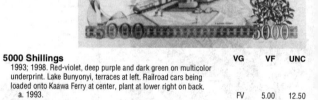

37	5000 Shillings	VG	VF	UNC
	1993; 1998. Red-violet, deep purple and dark green on multicolor underprint. Lake Bunyonyi, terraces at left. Railroad cars being loaded onto Kaawa Ferry at center, plant at lower right on back.			
	a. 1993.	FV	5.00	12.50
	b. 1998.	FV	FV	12.00

38	10,000 Shillings	VG	VF	UNC
	1995; 1998. Green and red on multicolor underprint. Musical instruments at left. Owen Falls dam, kudu on back.			
	a. 1995.	FV	10.00	25.00
	b. 1998.	FV	FV	22.50

1999-2002 Issue

#39-41 like #36-38 but color variances and w/added security devices.

39 1000 Shillings VG FV · VF FV · UNC 3.00
2000; 2003. Like #36 but arms at upper center in brown and green. Numerals of value at lower right all in dark brown.

39A 1000 Shillings VG FV · VF FV · UNC 3.00
2001. Like #39 but different security devices.

40 5000 Shillings VG FV · VF FV · UNC 10.00
2000; 2002. Like #37 but with silver leaf overlay at upper left center and security V symbol at lower right.

41 10,000 Shillings VG FV · VF FV · UNC 17.50
2001; 2003. Red, green, brown and multicolor. Like #38 but with changes in security devices.

41A 5000 Shillings VG FV · VF FV · UNC 10.00
2002. Like #40 but different devices added.

42 20,000 Shillings VG FV · VF FV · UNC 30.00
1999; 2002. Green on multicolor underprint. Crested crane at left, arms at upper center. Silver vertical OVD strip with repeated value at right. Modern building on back. Watermark: Arms. Two signature varieties.

2003-04 Issue

43 1000 Shillings VG FV · VF FV · UNC 3.00
2005. Multicolor. Silver OVD strip at right.

		VG	VF	UNC
44	**5000 Shillings** 2004; 2005. Multicolor.	FV	FV	7.50

		VG	VF	UNC
45	**10,000 Shillings** 2004. Multicolor.	FV	FV	12.50

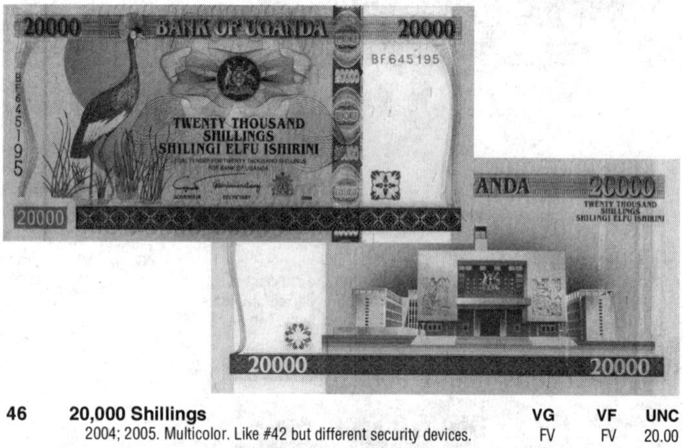

		VG	VF	UNC
46	**20,000 Shillings** 2004; 2005. Multicolor. Like #42 but different security devices.	FV	FV	20.00

		VG	VF	UNC
47	**50,000 Shillings** 2003. Brown. Monument at left. Cotton harvest on back.	FV	FV	45.00

Ukraine is bordered by Russia to the east, Russia and Belarus to the north, Poland, Slovakia and Hungary to the west, Romania and Moldova to the southwest and in the south by the Black Sea and the Sea of Azov. It has an area of 233,088 sq. mi. (603,700 sq. km.) and a population of 50.8 million. Capital: Kyiv (Kiev). Coal, grain, vegetables and heavy industrial machinery are major exports.

The territory of Ukraine has been inhabited for over 30,000 years. As the result of its location, Ukraine has served as the gateway to Europe for millennia and its early history has been recorded by Arabic, Greek, Roman, as well as Ukrainian historians.

Ukraine, which was known as Rus' until the sixteenth century (and from which the name Russia was derived in the 17th century), became the major political and cultural center of Eastern Europe in the 9th century. The Rus' Kingdom, under a dynasty of Varangian origin, because of its position on the intersection of the north-south Scandinavia to Byzantium and the east-west Orient to Europe trade routes, became a focal point of world trade. At its apex Rus' stretched from the Baltic to the Black Sea and from the upper Volga River in the east, almost to the Vistula River in the west. In 988 the Rus' adopted Christianity from Byzantium. The Mongol invasion in 1240 brought an end to the might of the Rus' Kingdom.

In the seventeenth century, after almost four hundred years of Mongol, Lithuanian, Polish, and Turkish domination, the Cossack State regained Ukrainian independence. The Hetman State lasted until the mid-eighteenth century and was followed by a period of foreign rule: Eastern Ukraine was controlled by Russia; Western Ukraine came under relatively benign Austro-Hungarian rule.

With the disintegration of the Russian and Austro-Hungarian Empires in 1917 and 1918, Eastern Ukraine declared its full independence on January 22, 1918 and Western Ukraine followed suit on November 1 of that year. On January 22, 1919 both parts united into one state that had to defend itself on three fronts: from the "Red" Bolsheviks and their puppet Ukrainian Soviet Republic formed in Kharkiv, from the "White" czarist Russian forces, and from Poland. Ukraine lost the war. In 1920, Eastern Ukraine was occupied by the Bolsheviks and in 1922 was incorporated into the Soviet Union. There followed a brief resurgence of Ukrainian language and culture until it was suppressed in 1928. Western Ukraine was partitioned between Poland, Romania, Hungary and Czechoslovakia.

During the period of independence 1917-1920, Ukraine issued its own currency in Karbovanets denominations under the Central Rada of social-democrats (#1-11) and in Hryvnia denominations during the monarchy of Hetman Pavlo Skoropadsky (#12-19 and #29-34). During WW II German occupation forces issued Karbowanez currency.

On August 24, 1991 Ukraine once again declared its independence. On December 5, 1991 the Ukrainian Parliament abrogated the 1922 treaty which incorporated Ukraine into the Soviet Union.

During the changeover from the Ruble currency of the Soviet Union to the Karbovanets of Ukraine, as a transition measure and to restrict unlicensed export of scarce goods, coupon cards (202 x 82mm), similar to ration cards, were issued in various denominations. They were valid for one month and were given to employees in amounts equal to their pay. Each card contained multiples of 1, 3, 5, 10, 25 and sometimes 50 Karbovanets valued coupons, to be cut apart. They were supposed to be used for purchases together with ruble notes. In January 1992 Ukraine began issuing individual coupons in Karbovanets denominations from 1 krb to 100 krb (printed in France and dated 1991). They were replaced by the Hryvnia.

Ukraine is a charter member of the United Nations.

MONETARY SYSTEM:

1 Karvovanets (Karbovantsiv) КАРБОВАНЕЦЬ, КАРБОВАНЦІВ = 1 Russian Ruble, 1991-96
1 Hryvnia (Hryvni, Hryven) ГРИВНЯ (ГРИВНІ, ГРИВЕНЬ) = 100,000 Karbovantsiv, 1996-

УКРАЇНСЬКА Р.С.Р.

TREASURY

1990 ND КУПОН RUBLE CONTROL COUPON ISSUE

#68 various authorization handstamps in registry. Uniface.

		VG	VF	UNC
68	**Karbovantsiv - Various amounts** ND (1990). Sheet of 28 coupons and registry. Жовтень.	—	—	4.00

#69-74 not assigned.

1991 КУПОН RUBLE CONTROL COUPON ISSUE

Consumer cards (coupons) were not legal tender but without them the U.S.S.R. rubles could not perform functions of money within Ukraine's territory.

#75 various authorization handstamps in registry. Uniface.

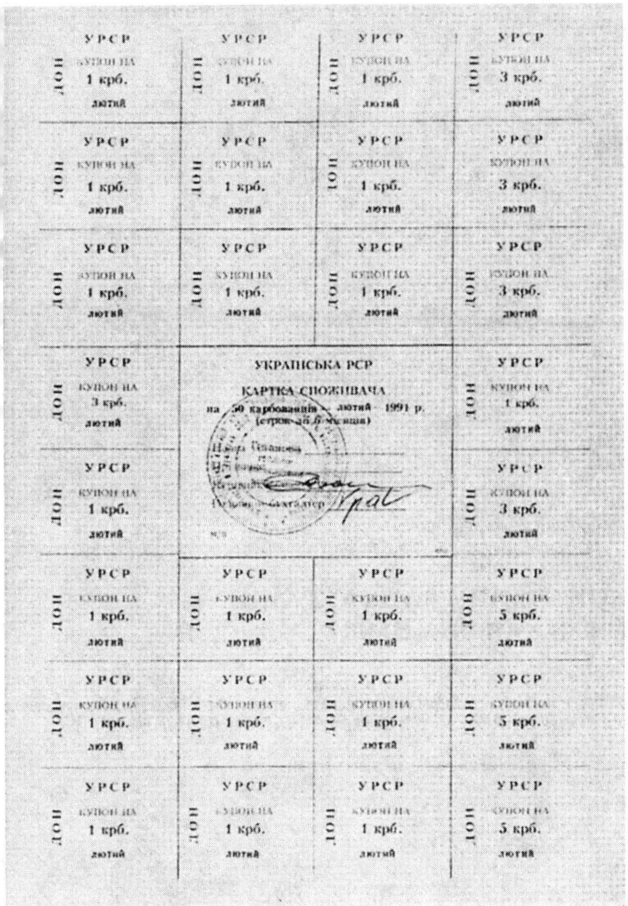

		VG	VF	UNC
75	**Karbovantsiv - Various amounts**	VG	VF	UNC
	1991. Sheet of 28 coupons and registry.	—	—	4.00

#76-80 not assigned.

НАЦІОНАЛЬНИЙ БАНК УКРАЇНИ

UKRAINIAN NATIONAL BANK

1991 КУПОН CONTROL COUPON ISSUE

Karbovanets System

Originally issued at par and temporarily to be used jointly with Russian rubles in commodity purchases as a means of currency control (similar to Ruble Control Coupons above). They soon became more popular while the ruble slowly depreciated in exchange value. This did not last very long and the karbovanets has since suffered a higher inflation rate than the Russian ruble.

#81-87 Lybid, Viking sister of the founding brothers, at l. Cathedral of St. Sophia in Kiev at l. ctr. on back. All notes w/o serial #. Wmk. paper. All denominations had the value, i.e. *3 KRB*, printed sideways with fluorescent ink at l. Printer: ISPB (France) (Imprimerie Spéciale de Banque (France))

		VG	VF	UNC
81	**1 Karbovanets**	VG	VF	UNC
	1991. Dull brown and pale orange on yellow underprint.			
	a. Issued note.	.05	.10	.25
	s. Specimen.	—	—	45.00

		VG	VF	UNC
82	**3 Karbovantsi**	VG	VF	UNC
	1991. Greenish gray and pale orange on yellow underprint.			
	a. Issued note.	.05	.10	.25
	b. Issued note with imprint *3 Kpe* at left.	.05	.10	.50
	s. As a. Specimen.	—	—	45.00

		VG	VF	UNC
83	**5 Karbovantsiv**	VG	VF	UNC
	1991. Dull blue-violet and pale orange on yellow underprint.			
	a. Issued note.	.05	.20	.50
	s. Specimen.	—	—	45.00

		VG	VF	UNC
84	**10 Karbovantsiv**	VG	VF	UNC
	1991. Pink and pale orange on yellow underprint.			
	a. Issued note.	.05	.20	1.00
	s. Specimen.	—	—	45.00

		VG	VF	UNC
85	**25 Karbovantsiv**	VG	VF	UNC
	1991. Purple and pale orange on yellow underprint.			
	a. Issued note.	.15	.50	4.00
	s. Specimen.	—	—	45.00

		VG	VF	UNC
86	**50 Karbovantsiv**	VG	VF	UNC
	1991. Blue-green and pale orange on yellow underprint.			
	a. Issued note.	.10	.35	1.50
	b. Issued note with *50 Kps* at left.	.20	.70	.30
	s. As a. Specimen.	—	—	45.00

		VG	VF	UNC
87	**100 Karbovantsiv**	VG	VF	UNC
	1991. Brown-violet and pale orange on yellow underprint.			
	a. Issued note.	.50	1.50	4.50
	s. Specimen.	—	—	45.00
87A	**250 Karbovantsiv**			
	1991. Blue and red. (Not Issued). Specimen.	—	—	—
87B	**500 Karbovantsiv**			
	Reported, not confirmed.	—	—	—

1992 ISSUE

#88-91 founding Viking brothers Kyi, Shchek and Khoryv w/sister Libyd in bow of boat at l. Backs like #81-87. All notes w/serial #. Wmk. paper. Replacement notes: Serial # prefix .../99 in denominator. Printer: TDLR (w/o imprint).

		VG	VF	UNC
88	**100 Karbovantsiv**	VG	VF	UNC
	1992. Orange on lilac and ochre underprint.			
	a. Issued note.	.10	.50	1.75
	r. Replacement note.	.50	2.50	6.00
	s. Specimen.	—	—	10.00

89	200 Karbovantsiv	VG	VF	UNC
	1992. Dull brown and silver on lilac and ochre underprint.			
	a. Issued note.	.25	1.25	5.00
	r. Replacement note.	.50	2.50	7.00
	s. Specimen.	—	—	10.00

90	500 Karbovantsiv	VG	VF	UNC
	1992. Blue-green and silver on lilac and ochre underprint.			
	a. Issued note.	.25	1.00	4.00
	r. Replacement note.	.50	2.50	6.00
	s. Specimen.	—	—	25.00

91	1000 Karbovantsiv	VG	VF	UNC
	1992. Red-violet and light green on lilac and ochre underprint.			
	a. Issued note.	.25	.75	2.00
	r. Replacement note.	.50	2.50	6.00
	s. Specimen.	—	—	25.00

GOVERNMENT

TREASURY

1992 СЕРТИФІКАТ - COMPENSATION CERTIFICATE ISSUE

#91A and 91B church at l., small arms at upper r. Text on back. The exact use of these notes has come into question.

91A	1,000,000 Karbovantsiv	VG	VF	UNC
	1992. Dull blue-green, orange and gray on pale orange and pale green underprint.	.75	2.00	5.00

NOTICE

Readers with unlisted dates, signature varieties, etc. are invited to submit photocopies of their notes to: Standard Catalog of World Paper Money, 700 East State St. Iola, WI 54990-0001, E-Mail: george.cuhaj@fwpubs.com.

91B	2,000,000 Karbovantsiv	VG	VF	UNC
	1992. Green, orange and pink with black text on light blue, pink and multicolor underprint.	1.00	3.00	8.00

НАЦІОНАЛЬНИЙ БАНК УКРАЇНИ
UKRAINIAN NATIONAL BANK

1993 ISSUE

#92 and 93 similar to #88-91, but trident symbol added at l. on face; at r. on back. Replacement notes: Serial # prefix *001/92-001/99; 001/99* for notes dated 1993. Printer: TDLR (w/o imprint).

92	2000 Karbovantsiv	VG	VF	UNC
	1993. Blue and olive-green on aqua and gold underprint.			
	a. Issued note.	.25	.75	2.50
	s. Specimen.	—	—	10.00

93	5000 Karbovantsiv	VG	VF	UNC
	1993; 1995. Red-orange and olive-brown on pale blue and ochre underprint.			
	a. 1993.	.10	.25	1.25
	b. 1995.	.50	2.50	5.00
	r. Replacement note. 1993.	1.00	3.00	6.00
	s1. Specimen. 1993; 1995.	—	—	25.00
	s2. As b. Specimen.	—	—	15.00

#94-97 statue of St. Volodymyr standing w/long cross at l. Bldg. facade at l. on back. Trident at l. on face, at r. on back. Wmk: Ornamental shield repeated vertically. Replacement notes: Serial # prefix *001/92-001/99; 001/99* for notes dated 1993. Printer: TDLR (Serial # as a fraction) or Banknote Printing and Minting works of the National Bank of Ukraine, Kyiv (BPMW) (serial # prefix is 2 letters) (Both w/o imprint).

94	10,000 Karbovantsiv	VG	VF	UNC
	1993-96. Apple green and tan on pale blue and ochre underprint.			
	a. 1993.	.10	.25	2.00
	b. 1995.	.05	.20	.50
	c. 1996. Watermark: Zig-zag of 4 bars. (parquet-paper).	.10	.25	1.50
	s1. Specimen. 1993.	—	—	25.00
	s2. Specimen. 1995; 1996.	—	—	15.00

		VG	VF	UNC
95	**20,000 Karbovantsiv**			
	1993-96. Lilac and tan on blue and yellow underprint.			
	a. 1993.	.10	.50	2.00
	b. 1994; 1995.	.10	.25	1.00
	c. 1996. Watermark: Zig-zag of 4 bars. (parquet-paper).	.10	.50	2.00
	s1. Specimen. 1993.	—	—	25.00
	s2. Specimen. 1994; 1996.	—	—	15.00

		VG	VF	UNC
96	**50,000 Karbovantsiv**			
	1993-95. Dull orange and blue on multicolor underprint.			
	a. 1993.	.15	.50	4.00
	b. 1994; 1995.	.20	.75	2.50
	s1. Specimen. 1993.	—	—	25.00
	s2. Specimen. 1994.	—	—	15.00

		VG	VF	UNC
97	**100,000 Karbovantsiv**			
	1993; 1994. Gray-green and ochre on multicolor underprint. Watermark: Trident shield repeated.			
	a. Prefix fraction before serial #. 1993.	.50	1.25	6.00
	b. Prefix letters with serial #. 1994.	.25	.75	3.00
	s1. Specimen. 1993.	—	—	30.00
	s2. Specimen. 1994.	—	—	17.50

#98 and 99 statue of St. Volodymyr standing w/long cross at r. Opera house at l. ctr. on back. Wmk: Trident shield repeated. Replacement notes: Serial # prefix *001/92-001/99; 001-99* for notes dated 1994.

		VG	VF	UNC
98	**200,000 Karbovantsiv**			
	1994. Dull red-brown and light blue on aqua and gray underprint. Back multicolor.			
	a. Prefix fraction before serial #. 1994.	.75	2.50	10.00
	b. Prefix letters with serial #. 1994.	.50	1.50	5.00
	s1. Specimen. 1994. Serial # prefix as a fraction.	—	—	30.00
	s2. Specimen. 1994.	—	—	17.50

		VG	VF	UNC
99	**500,000 Karbovantsiv**			
	1994. Light blue and lilac on yellow and gray underprint.			
	a. Issued note.	1.00	3.00	12.50
	s. Specimen.	—	—	30.00

1995 Issue

		VG	VF	UNC
100	**1,000,000 Karbovantsiv**			
	1995. Dark brown on pale orange, light blue and multicolor underprint. Statue of T. G. Shevchenko at right, arms at lower left. Kiev State University at left center, arms at lower right on back.			
	a. Issued note.	1.50	4.50	17.50
	s. Specimen.	—	—	30.00

1995 Privatization Certificate Issue

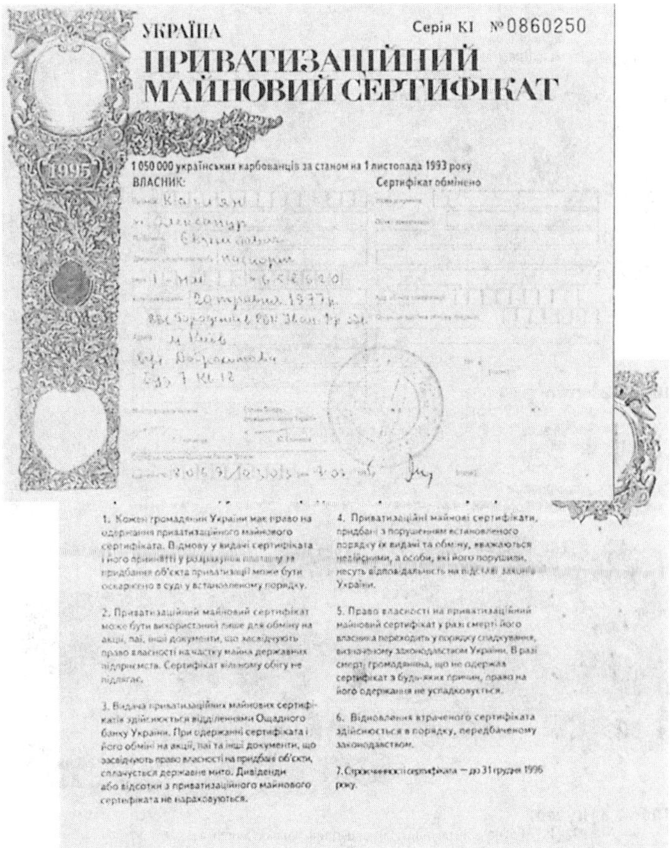

		VG	VF	UNC
101	**1,050,000 Karbovantsiv**			
	1995. Dark gray on light gray and ochre underprint. Arms at upper left. Text on back.	2.00	7.50	25.00

#102 not assigned.

1992 (1996) Regular Issue

SIGNATURE VARIETIES			
1	В.Гетьмаан Getman	2	В.Матвієнко Matvienko
3	Yuschenko	3A	Yuschenko
4	Stelmah	5	Tigipko

#103-107 wmk: Trident repeated. Printer: CBNC (w/o imprint). Replacement notes: First digit of serial # is *9*.

103	**1 Hryvnia**	VG	VF	UNC
	1992 (1996). Olive-brown on multicolor underprint. Ruins of Kherson at center. St. Volodymr at center on back.			
	a. Signature 1.	—	.25	1.00
	b. Signature 2.	—	.25	1.00
	c. Signature 3.	—	.25	1.00
	s. As a. Specimen.	—	—	25.00

104	**2 Hryvni**	VG	VF	UNC
	1992 (1996). Brown on multicolor underprint. Cathedral of St. Sophia at center. Prince Yaroslav at center on back.			
	a. Signature 1.	—	FV	1.50
	b. Signature 2.	—	FV	3.00
	c. Signature 3.	—	FV	1.50
	s. As a. Specimen.	—	—	25.00

105	**5 Hryven**	VG	VF	UNC
	1992 (1996). Blue-gray on multicolor underprint. Illinska Church in Subotiv at center. B. Khmelnytsky at center on back.			
	a. Signature 1.	—	FV	3.00
	b. Signature 2.	—	FV	4.00
	c. Signature 3.	—	FV	2.50
	s. As a. Specimen.	—	—	25.00

106	**10 Hryven**	VG	VF	UNC
	1992 (1996). Purple on multicolor underprint. Kyiv-Pecherska Monastery at center. I. Mazepa at center on back.			
	a. Signature 1.	FV	FV	5.00
	b. Signature 3.	FV	FV	4.50

107	**20 Hryven**	VG	VF	UNC
	1992 (1996). Brown on multicolor underprint. Lviv Opera House at center. Ivan Franko at center on back.			
	a. Signature 1.	FV	5.00	8.50
	b. Signature 3.	FV	5.00	8.50
107A	**50 Hryven**	VG	VF	UNC
	1992. Man at center (Not issued). Printer: CBNC.	—	—	—
107B	**100 Hryven**	VG	VF	UNC
	1992. Man at center (Not issued). Printer: CBNC.	—	—	—

1994-98 ND and Dated Issue

108	**1 Hryvnia**	VG	VF	UNC
	1994; 1995. Grayish brown and green on multicolor underprint. St. Volodymyr at center right and as watermark. City of Khersonnes at center on back. Signature 3.			
	a. 1994 (1996).	FV	FV	1.00
	b. 1995 (1997).	FV	FV	1.00
	s. Specimen. 1994.	—	—	35.00

109	**2 Hryvni**	VG	VF	UNC
	1995; 2001. Multicolor. Prince Yaroslav at center right and as watermark. Cathedral of St. Sophia in Kyiv on back.			
	a. 1995 (1997).	FV	FV	1.75
	b. 2001.	FV	FV	2.00
	s. As a. Specimen.	—	—	30.00

110	5 Hryven	VG	VF	UNC
	1994; 1997; 2001. Multicolor. Bohdan Khmelnytsky at center right. Illinska Church in Subotiv at center on back. Printer: TDLR (without imprint).			
	a. 1994 (1997).	FV	FV	2.50
	b. 1997 (1998).	FV	FV	2.50
	c. 2001.	FV	FV	2.50
	s. As a. Specimen.	—	—	30.00

111	10 Hryven	VG	VF	UNC
	1994; 2000. Multicolor. L. Mazepa at center right and as watermark. Kyiv-Pecherska Monastery at center on back.			
	a. 1994 (1997). Printer: TDLR.	FV	FV	4.50
	b. 2000. Ukranian printer.	FV	FV	4.50
	s. As a. Specimen.	—	—	30.00

112	20 Hryven	VG	VF	UNC
	1995; 2000. Multicolor. Ivan Franko at right and as watermark. Opera House in Lviv on back.			
	a. 1995. with segmented security thread.	FV	FV	7.50
	b. 2000.	FV	FV	7.50
	s. As a. Specimen.	—	—	30.00

113	50 Hryven	VG	VF	UNC
	ND (1996). Purple and dark blue-gray on multicolor underprint. M. Hrushevsky at right and as watermark. Parliament building at center on back.			
	a. Signature 1.	FV	FV	20.00
	b. Signature 3.	FV	FV	20.00
	s. Specimen.	—	—	150.
	x. Watermark. T. Shevchenko (error). Rare.	—	—	—

114	100 Hryven	VG	VF	UNC
	ND (1996). Brown and dark green on multicolor underprint. T. Shevchenko at right and as watermark. Cathedral of St. Sophia in Kyiv at center, statue of St. Volodymyr standing at left on back.			
	a. Signature 1.	FV	FV	35.00
	b. Signature 3.	FV	FV	35.00
	s. Specimen.	—	—	175.

115	200 Hryven	VG	VF	UNC
	ND (2001).Black and blue on multicolor underprint. Lesia Ukrainka (L. P. Kosach) at right and as watermark. Castle gate on back. Signature 1.	FV	FV	65.00

#116 formerly listed has been changed to 110b.

2003 Issue

		VG	VF	UNC
116	**1 Hryvnia** 2004; 2005. Multicolor.	FV	FV	1.00
117	**2 Hryven** 2004; 2005. Multicolor.	FV	FV	2.00
118	**5 Hryven** 2004; 2005 Multicolor.	FV	FV	2.50

119	10 Hryven	VG	VF	UNC
	2003; 2004, 2005. Multicolor.	FV	FV	4.50

120	20 Hryven	VG	VF	UNC
	2003; 2004, 2005. Multicolor.	FV	FV	7.50

		VG	VF	UNC
121	**50 Hryven** 2004; 2005. Multicolor.	FV	FV	20.00

COLLECTOR SERIES

НАЦІОНАЛЬНИЙ БАНК УКРАЇНИ

UKRAINIAN NATIONAL BANK

1996 ISSUE

		Issue Price	Mkt. Value
CS1	**1 Hryvnia** #103 and 2 Karbovantsiv 1996 Independence coins in a folder.	—	—

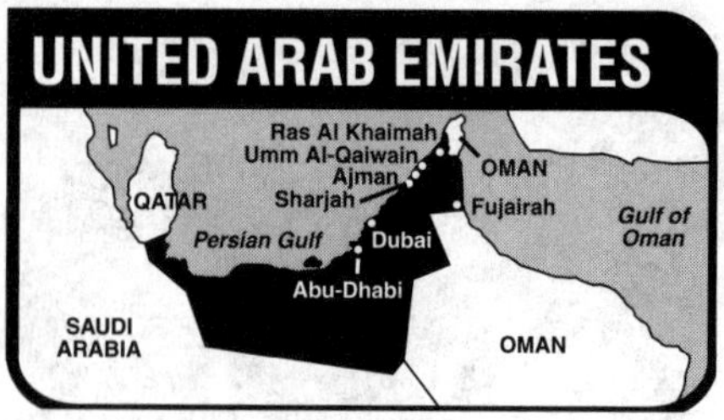

The seven United Arab Emirates (formerly known as the Trucial Sheikhdoms or States), located along the southern shore of the Persian Gulf, are comprised of the Sheikhdoms of Abu Dhabi, Dubai, Sharjah, Ajman, Umm al Qaiwain, Ras al-Khaimah and Fujairah. They have a combined area of about 32,000 sq. mi. (83,600 sq. km.) and a population of 2.44 million. Capital: Abu Dhabi. Since the oil strikes of 1958-60, the economy has centered on petroleum.

The Trucial States came under direct British influence in 1892 when the maritime truce treaty, enacted after the suppression of pirate activity along the Trucial Coast, was enlarged to enjoin the states from disposing of any territory, or entering into any foreign agreements, without British consent in return for British protection from external aggression. In March of 1971 Britain reaffirmed its decision to terminate its treaty relationships with the Trucial Sheikhdoms, whereupon the seven states joined with Bahrain and Qatar in an effort to form a union of Arab emirates under British protection. When the prospective members failed to agree on terms of union, Bahrain and Qatar declared their respective independence in Aug. and Sept. 1971. Six of the Sheikhdoms united to form the United Arab Emirates on Dec. 2, 1971. Ras al-Khaimah joined a few weeks later.

MONETARY SYSTEM:

1 Dirham = 1000 Fils

SHEIKHDOMS

UNITED ARAB EMIRATES CURRENCY BOARD

1973; 1976 ND ISSUE

#1-6 dhow, camel caravan, palm tree and oil derrick at l. Wmk: Arabian horse's head. Printer: (T)DLR.

		VG	VF	UNC
1	**1 Dirham** ND (1973). Green on multicolor underprint. Police station at center right on back.			
	a. Issued note.	1.00	5.00	25.00
	s. Specimen.	—	—	75.00

		VG	VF	UNC
2	**5 Dirhams** ND (1973). Purple on multicolor underprint. Fortress Fujairah at center right on back.			
	a. Issued note.	3.50	12.50	50.00
	s. Specimen.	—	—	75.00

3	10 Dirhams	VG	VF	UNC
	ND (1973). Gray-blue on multicolor underprint. Aerial view of Umm al-Qaiwan at center right on back.			
	a. Issued note.	3.00	10.00	50.00
	s. Specimen.	—	—	100.

4	50 Dirhams	VG	VF	UNC
	ND (1973). Red on multicolor underprint. Sheikh's Palace of Ajman at center right on back.			
	a. Issued note.	10.00	45.00	250.
	s. Specimen.	—	—	225.

5	100 Dirhams	VG	VF	UNC
	ND (1973). Olive-green on multicolor underprint. Ras al-Khaimah city at center right on back.			
	a. Issued note.	15.00	65.00	325.
	s. Specimen.	—	—	325.

6	1000 Dirhams	VG	VF	UNC
	ND (1976). Blue on multicolor underprint. Fortress at center right on back.			
	a. Issued note.	125.	750.	2500.
	s. Specimen.	—	—	750.

UNITED ARAB EMIRATES CENTRAL BANK

1982; 1983 ND ISSUE

#7-11 arms at upper ctr., sparrowhawk at l. on back. Wmk: Sparrowhawk's head.

7	5 Dirhams	VG	VF	UNC
	ND (1982). Brown on multicolor underprint. Sharjah Market at right. Seacoast cove with tower on back.			
	a. Issued note.	FV	4.00	12.00
	s. Specimen.	—	—	50.00

8	10 Dirhams	VG	VF	UNC
	ND (1982). Green on multicolor underprint. Arab dagger at right. Ideal farm with trees at left center on back.			
	a. Issued note.	FV	6.00	25.00
	s. Specimen.	—	—	50.00

9	50 Dirhams	VG	VF	UNC
	ND (1982). Purple, dark brown and olive on multicolor underprint. Oryx at right. Al Jahilie Fort at left center on back.			
	a. Issued note.	25.00	45.00	100.
	s. Specimen.	—	—	95.00

		VG	VF	UNC
10	**100 Dirhams** ND (1982). Red, violet and black on multicolor underprint. Al Fahidie Fort at right. Dubai Trade center at left center on back.			
	a. Issued note.	FV	50.00	100.
	s. Specimen.	—	—	100.

		VG	VF	UNC
11	**500 Dirhams** ND (1983). Dark blue, purple and brown on multicolor underprint. Sparrowhawk at right. Mosque in Dubai at left center on back.			
	a. Issued note.	FV	175.	375.
	s. Specimen.	—	—	350.

1989-96 ISSUES

#12-15 and 17 similar to #7-11 w/condensed Arabic text in titles, modified designs and slight color variations. Large value outline type in wmk. area. Silver arms at upper ctr. Arabic serial # in red at l., electronic sorting style in black at r. Wmk: Sparrowhawk's head.

		VG	VF	UNC
12	**5 Dirhams** 1993-/AH1414-1995-/AH1416. Dark brown, red-orange and violet on multicolor underprint. Similar to #7.			
	a. 1993/AH1414.	FV	5.00	10.00
	b. 1995/AH1416.	FV	FV	7.50

		VG	VF	UNC
13	**10 Dirhams** 1993-/AH1414-199/AH1416. Green and pale olive-green on multicolor underprint. Similar to #8.			
	a. 1993/AH1414.	FV	7.50	16.00
	b. 1995/AH1416.	FV	5.00	10.00

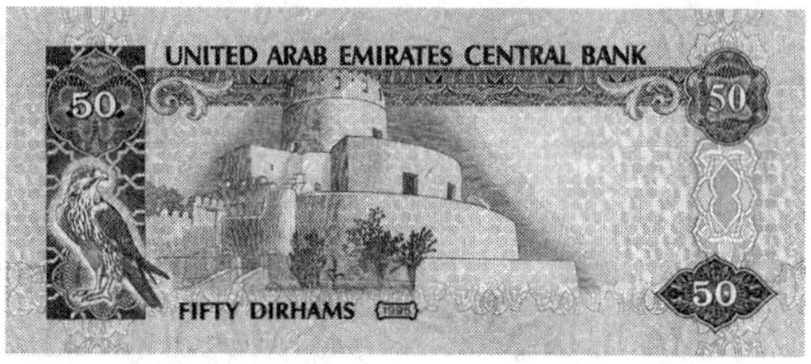

		VG	VF	UNC
14	**50 Dirhams** 1995-/AH1415-1996/AH1417. Purple, black and violet on multicolor underprint. With segmented foil over security thread. Similar to #9.			
	a. 1995/AH1415.	FV	FV	50.00
	b. 1996/AH1417.	FV	FV	45.00

		VG	VF	UNC
15	**100 Dirhams** 1993-/AH1414-1995/AH1416. Red, red-violet and black on multicolor underprint. Fortress at left center on back. With segmented foil over security thread. Similar to #10.			
	a. 1993/AH1414.	—	Unc	80.00
	b. 1995/AH1416.	—	Unc	70.00

		VG	VF	UNC
16	**200 Dirhams** 1989/AH 1410. Brown, green and multicolor. Sharia Court building and Zayed Sports City on face. Central Bank building at left center on back. With segmented foil over security thread.	FV	FV	110.
17	**500 Dirhams** 1993/AH1414. Dark blue, black, purple and silver on multicolor underprint. With segmented foil over security thread. Similar to #11.	FV	FV	350.
18	**500 Dirhams** 1996/AH1416. Dark blue, black, purple and silver on multicolor underprint. Like #17 but with kinegram added at lower left.	FV	FV	325.

1997-2000 ISSUE

#19-25 similar to #12-19 but wmk. area shaded.

		VG	VF	UNC
19	**5 Dirhams** 2000-04. Brown and orange. Similar to #12 but with color and minor design variations.			
	a. 2000/AH1420.	FV	FV	6.00
	b. 2001/AH1422.	FV	FV	5.00
	c. 2004/AH1425.	FV	FV	5.00

		VG	VF	UNC
20	**10 Dirhams** 1998-2004. Similar to #13.			
	a. 1998/AH1419.	FV	FV	9.00
	b. 2001/AH1422.	FV	FV	8.00
	c. 2004/AH1425.	FV	FV	8.00

		VG	VF	UNC
21	**20 Dirhams** 1997/AH1418; 2000/AH1421. Green, blue and multicolor. Dubai Creek Golf and Yacht Club at right. Dhow on back.			
	a. 1997/AH1419.	FV	FV	18.00
	b. 2000/AH/1420.	FV	FV	16.00

		VG	VF	UNC
22	**50 Dirhams** 1998/AH1419. Similar to #14.	FV	FV	35.00

		VG	VF	UNC
23	**100 Dirhams** 1998/AH1419. Similar to #15 but without value over watermark area on face.	FV	FV	60.00

		VG	VF	UNC
24	**500 Dirhams** 1998/AH1419; 2000/AH1420. Similar to #18 but with wide silver foil at right, silver seal at left.			
	a. 1998/AH1419.	FV	FV	260.
	b. 2000/AH1420.	FV	FV	250.

		VG	VF	UNC
25	**1000 Dirhams** 1998/AH1419; 2000/AH1421. Brown, green and multicolor. Palace corner tower at right. Holographic strip vertically at right. City view on back.			
	a. 1998/AH1419.	FV	FV	425.
	b. 2000/AH1420.	FV	FV	375.

2003-04 ISSUE

#26-28 Dallah (coffee pot) added to wmk. area.

		VG	VF	UNC
27	**50 Dirhams** 2004/AH1425. Similar to #22.	FV	FV	27.50

		VG	VF	UNC
28	**100 Dirhams** 2003/AH1423; 2004/AH1425. Similar to #23 but with silver overprint of tower at upper right.	FV	FV	45.00

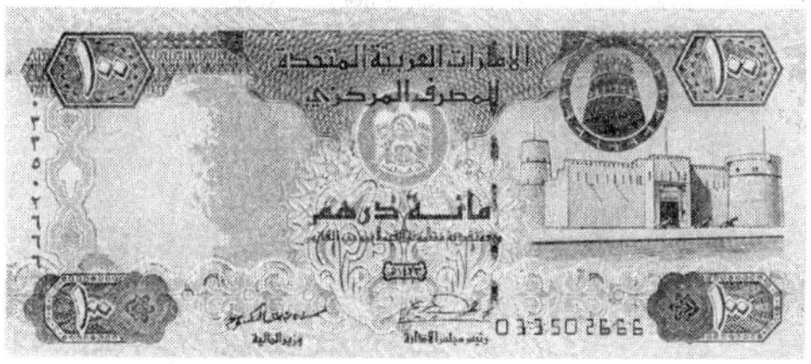

		VG	VF	UNC
29	**500 Dirhams** 2004/AH1424. Blue on multicolor underprint.	FV	FV	200.

UNITED STATES OF AMERICA

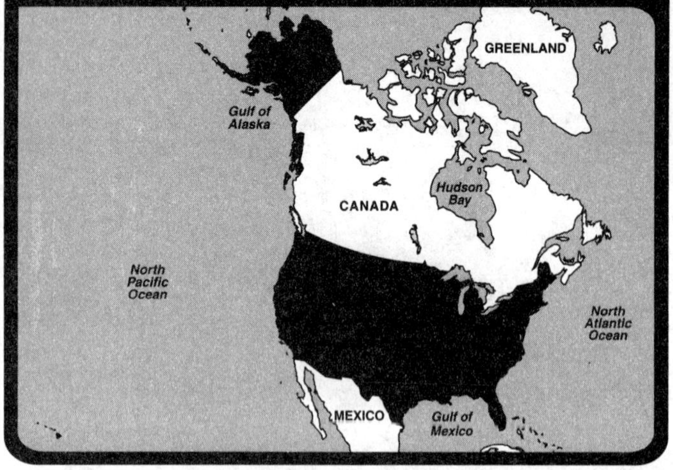

The area of the North American continent currently controlled by the United States of America was originally inhabited by numerous groups of Indian tribes. Some of these groups settled in particular areas, creating permanent settlements, while others were nomadic, traveling great distances and living off the land.

English explorers John and Sebastian Cabot reached Nova Scotia in what is today Canada in 1497; in 1534 the French gained a foothold with the explorations of Jacques Cartier. In 1541 the Spanish explorer Coronado traversed the south central portion of the country in what was to become the states of New Mexico, Texas, Nebraska and Oklahoma. In 1542 another Spaniard, Juan Cabrillo navigated north from Mexico along the Pacific coastline to California. The Spanish set up the first permanent settlement of Europeans in North America at St. Augustine, Florida in 1565. In 1607 the English settled in Jamestown, Virginia, and in 1620 at Plymouth, Massachusetts. This was followed closely by Dutch settlements in Albany and New York in 1624, and in 1638 the Swedes arrived in Delaware. From their foothold in Canada, French explorers pushed inland through the Great Lakes. Jean Nicolet explored what was to become Wisconsin in 1634, and in 1673 explorers Marquette and Joliet reached Iowa. In the 1650s the Dutch won the Swedish lands, and in 1664 the English gained control of the Dutch lands, thus giving the English control all along the Atlantic Coast. The resulting thirteen British colonies; New Hampshire, Vermont, Massachusetts, Rhode Island, Connecticut, New York, Pennsylvania, Delaware, Maryland, Virginia, North Carolina, South Carolina and Georgia formed the nucleus of what would become the United States of America.

From this point on tensions grew between the English, who could not expand westward from their settlements along the Atlantic Coast, and the French who had settled inland into the Ohio river valley. This dispute ended in 1763 after a war with the French loosing control of lands east of the Mississippi river. Manufacturing, textiles and other industry was developing at this time, and by 1775 about one-seventh of the world's production of raw iron came from the colonies. From 1771-1783 the war for American Independence was fought by the colonists against the English, and settled by the Peace of Paris in 1783. Americans gained control of lands south of the St. Lawrence and Great Lakes, and east of the Mississippi, with the exception of Florida which would remain under Spanish control until 1821. At the close of the war, the population was about 3 million, many of whom lived on self-sufficient family farms. Fishing, lumbering and the production of grains for export were becoming major economic endeavors. The newly independent states formed a loose confederation, but in 1787 approved the Constitution of the United States which is the framework for the goverment today. In 1789 it's first president, George Washington was elected, and the capitol was set up in New York City. In 1800 the capitol was moved to a planned city, Washington, D.C. where it remains.

Westward expansion was an inevitability as population grew. French territory west of the Mississippi, stretching to the northern Pacific was purchased in 1804 under the presidency of Thomas Jefferson, who then sent out Lewis and Clark on expedition of discovery. Spain granted independence to Mexico in 1821, which included lands which would become the states of California, New Mexico, Arizona and Texas. From 1836-1845 Texas was an independent republic, not joining the United States until 1845. Upon losing a war with the United States, Mexico ceded California (including most of Arizona and New Mexico) to the United States in 1848. Gold was discovered in California that year, and western migration took off on overland wagon trains or around-the-horn sail and steam ships. Hawaii came under U.S. protection in 1851. As the country developed in the 19th century, the northern states increased in commerce and industry while the southern states developed a vast agricultural through the use of slave labor. Northern political and social threats to slavery lead twelve southern states to secede from the Union in 1860 forming the Confederate States of America. The ensuing Civil War lasted until 1865, at which time slavery was abolished and the States reunited.

In 1867 Alaska was purchased from Russia. The transcontinental railroad was completed in 1869. The central region of the country west of the Mississippi River and east of the Rocky Mountains was the last to be developed, beginning after the Civil War, with the establishment of cattle ranches and farms. Between 1870 and 1891 the nomadic Native American population clashed with settlers and federal troops. By 1891 the Native Americans were confined to reservations.

At the close of the 19th century the United States embarked on a colonial mission of its own, with advances into Cuba, Puerto Rico, Panama, Nicaragua and the Philippines. This resulted in the Spanish-American War which was quickly decided, ending Spanish colonial dominance, and signaling the rise of the United States as a world power. Slow to enter both World Wars of the 20th century, it was a major contributor to the conclusion of both, making it one of the major nations of the 20th century.

MONETARY SYSTEM:

1 Dollar = 100 Cents

SIGNATURE VARIETIES

SERIES	TREASURER	SECRETARY
1963	Kathryn O'Hay Granahan	C. Douglas Dillon
1963A	Kathryn O'Hay Granahan	Henry H. Fowler
1963B	Kathryn O'Hay Granahan	Joseph W. Barr
1969	Dorothy Andrews Elston	David M. Kennedy
1969A	Dorothy Andrews Kabis	David M. Kennedy
1969B	Dorothy Andrews Kabis	John B. Connally
1969C	Romana Acosta Banuelos	John B. Connally
1969D	Romana Acosta Banuelos	George P. Schultz
1974	Francine I. Neff	William E. Simon
1977	Azie Taylor Morton	W. Michael Blumenthal
1977A	Azie Taylor Morton	J. William Miller
1981	Angela M. Buchanan	Donald T. Regan
1981A	Katherine Davalos Ortega	Donald T. Regan
1985	Katherine Davalos Ortega	John A. Baker III
1988	Katherine Davalos Ortega	Nicholas F. Brady
1988A-1990	Catalina Vasquez Villalpando	Nicholas F. Brady
1993	Mary Ellen Withrow	Lloyd Bentson
1995, 1996	Mary Ellen Withrow	Robert E. Rubin
1999	Mary Ellen Withrow	Lawrence Summers
2001	Rosario Marin	Paul H. O'Neill
2003, 2004	Rosario Marin	John Snow
2003A, 2004A	Anna Escobedo Cabral	John Snow
2006	Anna Escobedo Cabral	Henry M. Paulson Jr.

BANKNOTE DESIGNS

1 DOLLAR	Portr. George Washington. Great Seal flanking ONE on back.
2 DOLLAR	Portr. Thomas Jefferson. Monticello on back to 1963, signing of the Declaration of Independence, 1976; 1995 series.
5 DOLLAR	Portr. Abraham Lincoln. Lincoln Memorial on back.
10 DOLLAR	Portr. Alexander Hamilton. U. S. Treasury bldg. on back.
20 DOLLAR	Portr. Andrew Jackson. White House on back.
50 DOLLAR	Portr. Ulysses S. Grant. U. S. Capitol bldg. on back.
100 DOLLAR	Portr. Benjamin Franklin. Independence Hall on back.

REPLACEMENT NOTES:

All issues since about 1916 have a star either before or after the serial number, depending on type of note.

All government notes of the United States, since issue of the Demand Notes in 1861, are still valid as legal tender.

The different types of currency are treated in a number of specialized catalogs such as the following:

Friedberg, Robert; *Paper Money of the United States.*

Hickman, John and Oakes, Dean; *Standard Catalog of National Bank Notes.*

Krause, Chester L. and Lemke, Robert F.; *Standard Catalog of United States Paper Money.*

Detailed information, as given in these catalogs, is not repeated here. The following listing is limited to the individual types and their principal varieties. Sign. varieties in earlier issues are not detailed.

REPUBLIC

UNITED STATES NOTES

SERIES OF 1963

Replacement Notes: Serial # suffix is an *.

#		VG	VF	UNC
382	**2 Dollars**			
	a. 1963.	FV	FV	10.00
	b. 1963A.	FV	FV	13.00
383	**5 Dollars**			
	1963.	FV	9.00	20.00

SERIES OF 1966

#		VG	VF	UNC
384	**100 Dollars**			
	1966.	FV	125.	550.

FEDERAL RESERVE NOTES - SMALL SIZE

Green Treasury seal. Replacement notes: Serial # suffix is an *. Imprinted #, letter and name (in seal at l.) of 1 of the 12 Federal Reserve Banks:

A-1: (Boston)	E-5: (Richmond)	I-9: (Minneapolis)
B-2: (New York)	F-6: (Atlanta)	J-10: (Kansas City)
C-3: (Philadelphia)	G-7: (Chicago)	K-11: (Dallas)
D-4: (Cleveland)	H-8: (St. Louis)	L-12: (San Francisco)

1963 SERIES

#		VG	VF	UNC
443	**1 Dollar**			
	a. 1963. (A-L).	FV	FV	4.00
	b. 1963A. (A-L).	FV	FV	4.00
	c. 1963B. (B; E; G; J; L).	FV	FV	5.00
444	**5 Dollars**			
	a. 1963. (A-D; F-H: J-L).	FV	FV	20.00
	b. 1963A. (A-L).	FV	FV	15.00
445	**10 Dollars**			
	a. 1963. (A-H; J-L).	FV	FV	50.00
	b. 1963A. (A-L).	FV	FV	37.50
446	**20 Dollars**			
	a. 1963. (A-B; D-H; J-L).	FV	FV	75.00
	b. 1963A. (A-L).	FV	FV	60.00
447	**50 Dollars**			
	1963A. (A-L).	FV	FV	150.
448	**100 Dollars**			
	1963A. (A-L).	FV	FV	275.

1969 SERIES

#		VG	VF	UNC
449	**1 Dollar**			
	a. 1969. (A-L).	FV	FV	4.00
	b. 1969A. (A-L).	FV	FV	4.00
	c. 1969B. (A-L).	FV	FV	4.00
	d. 1969C. (B; D-L).	FV	FV	5.00
	e. 1969D. (A-L).	FV	FV	5.00
450	**5 Dollars**			
	a. 1969. (A-L).	FV	FV	15.00
	b. 1969A. (A-L).	FV	FV	20.00
	c. 1969B. (A-L).	FV	FV	50.00
	d. 1969C. (A-L).	FV	FV	20.00
451	**10 Dollars**			
	a. 1969. (A-L).	FV	FV	35.00
	b. 1969A. (A-L).	FV	FV	35.00
	c. 1969B. (A-L).	FV	FV	100.
	d. 1969C. (A-L).	FV	FV	40.00
452	**20 Dollars**			
	a. 1969. (A-L).	FV	FV	60.00
	b. 1969A. (A-L).	FV	FV	75.00
	c. 1969B. (B; D-L).	FV	FV	150.
	d. 1969C. (A-L).	FV	FV	50.00
453	**50 Dollars**			
	a. 1969. (A-L).	FV	FV	200.
	b. 1969A. (A-L).	FV	FV	200.
	c. 1969B. (A-B; E-G; K).	FV	FV	120.
	d. 1969C. (A-L).	FV	FV	150.
454	**100 Dollars**			
	a. 1969. (A-L).	FV	FV	225.
	b. 1969A. (A-L).	FV	FV	225.
	c. 1969C. (A-L).	FV	FV	225.

1974 SERIES

#		VG	VF	UNC
455	**1 Dollar**			
	1974. (A-L).	FV	FV	4.00
456	**5 Dollars**			
	1974. (A-L).	FV	FV	15.00
457	**10 Dollars**			
	1974. (A-L).	FV	FV	35.00
458	**20 Dollars**			
	1974. (A-L).	FV	FV	60.00
459	**50 Dollars**			
	1974. (A-L).	FV	FV	200.
460	**100 Dollars**			
	1974. (A-L).	FV	FV	200.

1976 SERIES

#461, U.S. Bicentennial - Trumbull's painting *Signing of the Declaration of Independence*

#		VG	VF	UNC
461	**2 Dollars**			
	1976. (A-L).	FV	FV	6.00

Note: #461 is also available in uncut sheets of 4, 16 and 32 notes.

1977 SERIES

#		VG	VF	UNC
462	**1 Dollar**			
	a. 1977. (A-L).	FV	FV	4.00
	b. 1977A. (A-L).	FV	FV	4.00
463	**5 Dollars**			
	a. 1977. (A-L).	FV	FV	10.00
	b. 1977A. (A-I)	FV	FV	18.00
464	**10 Dollars**			
	a. 1977. (A-L).	FV	FV	40.00
	b. 1977A. (A-L).	FV	FV	35.00
465	**20 Dollars**			
	1977. (A-L).	FV	FV	60.00
466	**50 Dollars**			
	1977. (A-L).	FV	FV	175.
467	**100 Dollars**			
	1977. (A-L).	FV	FV	225.

1981 SERIES

Note: Since Oct. 1981 the Bureau of Engraving and Printing has made available to collectors uncut sheets of 4, 16, and 32 notes of the $1.00 and $2.00 denominations.

#		VG	VF	UNC
468	**1 Dollar**			
	a. 1981. (A-L).	FV	FV	4.00
	b. 1981A. (A-L).	FV	FV	4.00
469	**5 Dollars**			
	a. 1981. (A-L).	FV	FV	20.00
	b. 1981A. (A-L).	FV	FV	20.00
470	**10 Dollars**			
	a. 1981. (A-L).	FV	FV	40.00
	b. 1981A. (A-L).	FV	FV	40.00
471	**20 Dollars**			
	a. 1981. (A-L).	FV	FV	75.00
	b. 1981A. (A-L).	FV	FV	60.00
472	**50 Dollars**			
	a. 1981. (A-L).	FV	FV	200.
	b. 1981A. (A-L).	FV	FV	225.
473	**100 Dollars**			
	a. 1981. (A-L).	FV	FV	275.
	b. 1981A. (A-L).	FV	FV	275.

1985 SERIES

#		VG	VF	UNC
474	**1 Dollar**			
	1985. (A-L).	FV	FV	4.00
475	**5 Dollars**			
	1985. (A-L).	FV	FV	15.00
476	**10 Dollars**			
	1985. (A-L).	FV	FV	35.00
477	**20 Dollars**			
	1985. (A-L).	FV	FV	50.00
478	**50 Dollars**			
	1985. (A-L).	FV	FV	120.
479	**100 Dollars**			
	1985. (A-L).	FV	FV	175.

1988 SERIES

#		VG	VF	UNC
480	**1 Dollar**			
	a. 1988. (A-L).	FV	FV	4.00
	b. 1988A. (A-L).	FV	FV	4.00
	c. 1988A Web Press. (A-C; E-G).	FV	8.00	40.00
481	**5 Dollars**			
	a. 1988. (A-L).	FV	FV	15.00
	b. 1988A. (A-L).	FV	FV	15.00
482	**10 Dollars**			
	1988A (A-L).	FV	FV	35.00
483	**20 Dollars**			
	1988A (A-L).	FV	FV	50.00
484	**50 Dollars**			
	1988 (A-L).	FV	FV	150.
485	**100 Dollars**			
	1988 (A-L).	FV	FV	200.

1990 Series

#486-489 w/additional row of micro-printing: *THE UNITED STATES OF AMERICA* repeated around portr. Filament w/value and *U.S.A.* repeated inversely at l.

		VG	VF	UNC
486	**10 Dollars** 1990. (A-L).	FV	FV	20.00
487	**20 Dollars** 1990. (A-L).	FV	FV	30.00
488	**50 Dollars** 1990. (A-L).	FV	FV	100.
489	**100 Dollars** 1990. (A-L).	FV	FV	150.

1993 Series

		VG	VF	UNC
490	**1 Dollar**			
	a. 1993. (A-G; L).	FV	FV	2.00
	b. 1993. Web Press. (G-I; K; L).	FV	4.00	15.00
491	**5 Dollars** 1993 (A-C; E-L).	FV	FV	15.00
492	**10 Dollars** 1993 (A-D, F-H, J, L).	FV	FV	20.00
493	**20 Dollars** 1993. (A-L).	FV	FV	40.00
494	**50 Dollars** 1993 (A, B, D, E, G, H, J, K).	FV	FV	135.
495	**100 Dollars** 1993. (A-L).	FV	FV	150.

1995 Series

		VG	VF	UNC
496	**1 Dollar**			
	a. 1995. (A-L).	FV	FV	2.00
	b. 1995. Web Press. (A; B; D; F).	FV	4.00	17.50
497	**2 Dollars** 1995. (F).	FV	FV	4.00
498	**5 Dollars** 1995 (A-L).	FV	FV	10.00
499	**10 Dollars** 1995 (A-L).	FV	FV	25.00
500	**20 Dollars** 1995 (B-L).	FV	FV	40.00

Federal Reserve Notes

Green Treasury seal. Replacement notes: Serial # suffix is an *. Imprinted #, letter and name (in seal at l.) of 1 of the 12 Federal Reserve Banks:

A-1: (Boston)	E-5: (Richmond)	I-9: (Minneapolis)
B-2: (New York)	F-6: (Atlanta)	J-10: (Kansas City)
C-3: (Philadelphia)	G-7: (Chicago)	K-11: (Dallas)
D-4: (Cleveland)	H-8: (St. Louis)	L-12: (San Francisco)

1996 Series

#501-503 redesigned and enlarged portr. on face at l. ctr. and as wmk. Green value at lower r. Security thread at l. Backs similar to #493-495.

		VG	VF	UNC
501	**20 Dollars** 1996. (A1-L12).	FV	FV	30.00
502	**50 Dollars** 1996 (A1-L12).	FV	FV	60.00
503	**100 Dollars** 1996 (A1-L12).	FV	FV	115.

1999 Series

#505-507 redesigned and enlarged portr. on face at l. ctr. and as wmk.

		VG	VF	UNC
504	**1 Dollar** 1999 (A-L).	FV	FV	2.00

NOTICE

Readers with unlisted dates, signature varieties, etc. are invited to submit photocopies of their notes to: Standard Catalog of World Paper Money, 700 East State St. Iola, WI 54990-0001, E-Mail: george.cuhaj@fwpubs.com.

		VG	VF	UNC
505	**5 Dollars** 1999 (A1-L12).	FV	FV	10.00
506	**10 Dollars** 1999 (A1 L12).	FV	FV	15.00
507	**20 Dollars** 1999 (A1-L12).	FV	FV	30.00
508	**100 Dollars** 1999(A1-L12).	FV	FV	115.

2001 Series

		VG	VF	UNC
509	**1 Dollar** 2001 (A-L).	FV	FV	2.00
510	**5 Dollars** 2001 (A1-L12).	FV	FV	10.00
511	**10 Dollars** 2001 (A1-L12).	FV	FV	20.00
512	**20 Dollars** 2001 (A1-L12).	FV	FV	30.00
513	**50 Dollars** 2001 (A1-L12).	FV	FV	60.00

		VG	VF	UNC
514	**100 Dollars** 2001 (A1-L12).	FV	FV	115.

2003 Series

		VG	VF	UNC
515	**1 Dollar**			
	a. 2003 (A-L).	FV	FV	2.00
	b. 2003A (A-L).	FV	FV	2.00
516	**2 Dollars**			
	a. 2003 (A1-L12)	FV	FV	7.50
	b. 2003A (A1-L12)	FV	FV	7.50
517	**5 Dollars**			
	2003 (A1-L12).	FV	FV	10.00
	b. 2003A (A1-L12)	FV	FV	10.00
518	**10 Dollars** 2003 (A1-L12).	FV	FV	17.50
519	**100 Dollars**			
	a. 2003 (A1-L12)	FV	FV	120.
	b. 2003 A (A1-L12)	FV	FV	120.

2004 Series

#520-522 redesigned face and back, color underprint.

		VG	VF	UNC
520	**10 Dollars** 2004A.	FV	FV	15.00
521	**20 Dollars** 2004. Black on light green, blue and tan underprint. Jackson at left center. Back green. White House at center on back.			
	a. 2004 (A1-L12).	FV	FV	27.50
	b. 2004A (A1-A12).	FV	FV	27.50
522	**50 Dollars**			
	a. 2004 (A1-L12).	FV	FV	60.00
	b. 2004A (A1-A12).	FV	FV	60.00

2006 SERIES

		VG	VF	UNC
523	**20 Dollars** 2006.	FV	FV	30.00
524	**50 Dollars** 2006.	FV	FV	60.00
525	**100 Dollars** 2006.	FV	FV	120.

MILITARY PAYMENT CERTIFICATES

SERIES 591

26.5.1961 to 6.1.1964.

#M43-M46 Head of Statue of Liberty at r.

		VF	UNC
M43	**5 Cents** ND (1961). Lilac on green and yellow underprint.	3.50	55.00

		VF	UNC
M44	**10 Cents** ND (1961). Blue on lilac underprint.	4.00	65.00
M45	**25 Cents** ND (1961). Green on purple underprint.	17.50	140.

		VF	UNC
M46	**50 Cents** ND (1961). Brown on aqua underprint.	35.00	240.

		VF	UNC
M47	**1 Dollar** ND (1961). Red on purple and multicolor underprint. Portrait woman facing left at right.	25.00	275.

		VF	UNC
M48	**5 Dollars** ND (1961). Blue on multicolor underprint. Woman at left.	550.	4500.
M49	**10 Dollars** ND (1961). Green on multicolor underprint. Portrait woman 3/4 facing left at right.	200.	2000.

SERIES 611

6.1.1964 to 28.4.1969.

#M50-M53 Liberty head profile facing r. at l.

		VF	UNC
M50	**5 Cents** ND (1964). Blue on multicolor underprint.	5.00	40.00

		VF	UNC
M51	**10 Cents** ND (1964). Green on multicolor underprint.	5.00	45.00
M52	**25 Cents** ND (1964). Brown on multicolor underprint.	30.00	275.
M53	**50 Cents** ND (1964). Lilac on multicolor underprint.	30.00	275.

		VF	UNC
M54	**1 Dollar** ND (1964). Green on multicolor underprint. Portrait woman with tiara facing at left.	5.00	100.
M55	**5 Dollars** ND (1964). Red on multicolor underprint. Woman facing at center.	125.	2000.

		VF	UNC
M56	**10 Dollars** ND (1964). Blue on violet and multicolor underprint. Portrait woman facing left at center.	130.	1400.

SERIES 641

31.8.1965 to 21.10.1968.

#M57-M60 woman at l. Eagle with outstretched wings clasping fasces at ctr. on back.

		VG	VF	UNC
M57	**5 Cents** ND (1965). Purple on blue underprint.		1.00	13.50

		VF	UNC
M58	**10 Cents** ND (1965). Green on dark red underprint.	1.00	18.50
M59	**25 Cents** ND (1965). Red on blue-green underprint.	2.50	24.00
M60	**50 Cents** ND (1965). Orange on multicolor underprint.	3.50	35.00

		VF	UNC
M61	**1 Dollar** ND (1965). Light red on multicolor underprint. Woman at right.	4.00	45.00

		VF	UNC
M62	**5 Dollars** ND (1965). Green on multicolor underprint. Woman with wreath of flowers at center. Woman facing right at center on back.	17.50	250.

		VF	UNC
M63	**10 Dollars** ND (1965). Brown on orange and multicolor underprint. Portrait woman facing right at center. Liberty head facing at center on back.	10.00	250.

SERIES 661

21.10.1968 to 11.8.1969.

#M64-M67 woman wearing scarf at l.

		VF	UNC
M64	**5 Cents** ND (1968). Light green and lilac on multicolor underprint.	.50	10.00
M65	**10 Cents** ND (1968). Blue and violet on multicolor underprint.	.50	10.00
M66	**25 Cents** ND (1968). Brown and orange on multicolor underprint.	2.00	27.50
M67	**50 Cents** ND (1968). Red and green on multicolor underprint.	2.00	22.50

		VF	UNC
M68	**1 Dollar** ND (1968). Blue on multicolor underprint. Portrait woman 3/4 facing left at right. Mountain scene on back.	5.00	24.00
M69	**5 Dollars** ND (1968). Dark brown on red and multicolor underprint. Woman holding flowers at center. Girl's head at center on back.	5.00	30.00

		VF	UNC
M70	**10 Dollars** ND (1968). Red and orange on multicolor underprint. Woman holding fasces at left. Woman facing left at center right on back.	200.	1850.
M71	**20 Dollars** ND (1968). Black, brown and blue on multicolor underprint. Woman at center. Standing woman at left on back.	125.	1450.

SERIES 651

28.4.1969 to 19.11.1973.

#M72A-M74 similar to Series 641 except for colors and the addition of a "Minuteman statue" at l.

		VF	UNC
M72A	**5 Cents** ND (1969). Dark blue on multicolor underprint.	—	700.
M72B	**10 Cents** ND (1969). Red-violet on multicolor underprint.	—	700.
M72C	**25 Cents** ND (1969). Aqua blue on multicolor underprint.	—	700.

		VF	UNC
M72D	**50 Cents** ND (1969). Dark brown on multicolor underprint.	—	275.

		VF	UNC
M72E	**1 Dollar** ND (1969). Green on violet and multicolor underprint. Portrait woman facing left at right.	6.00	45.00

NOTICE

Readers with unlisted dates, signature varieties, etc. are invited to submit photocopies of their notes to: Standard Catalog of World Paper Money, 700 East State St. Iola, WI 54990-0001, E-Mail: george.cuhaj@fwpubs.com.

		VF	UNC
M73	**5 Dollars** ND (1969). Brown on green and multicolor underprint. Portrait woman facing with wreath of flowers at center.	50.00	275.
M74	**10 Dollars** ND (1969). Violet on multicolor underprint. Woman at center.	50.00	275.

SERIES 681

11.8.1969 to 7.10.1970.

#M75-M78 submarine at r. Astronaut in spacewalk at ctr. on back.

		VF	UNC
M75	**5 Cents** ND (1969). Green and blue.	1.00	12.50
M76	**10 Cents** ND (1969). Violet and blue.	1.00	16.00
M77	**25 Cents** ND (1969). Red and blue.	2.00	27.50

		VF	UNC
M78	**50 Cents** ND (1969). Brown and blue.	3.00	25.00
M79	**1 Dollar** ND (1969). Violet on multicolor underprint. Air Force pilot at right. Four Thunderbirds in formation at center on back.	3.00	25.00

		VF	UNC
M80	**5 Dollars** ND (1969). Purple and green. Sailor at center. Eagle at center on back.	10.00	125.

		VF	UNC
M81	**10 Dollars** ND (1969). Blue-green and black. Infantryman (Green Beret) at center. Tank at center on back.	30.00	300.
M82	**20 Dollars** ND (1969). Brown, pink and blue. Portrait soldier facing wearing helmet at center. B-52 bomber at center on back.	30.00	1100.

SERIES 691

#M83-M85 not assigned.

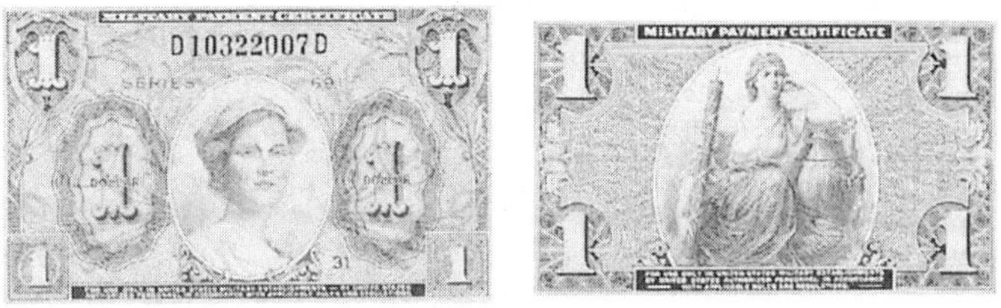

		VF	UNC
M87	**1 Dollar** ND (1969). Slate gray on light blue underprint. Woman's portrait at center. Allegorical female seated at center on back.	—	250.

		VF	UNC
M88	**5 Dollars** ND (1969). Brown on light blue underprint. Woman's head at left looking right. Woman's head at center.	—	1000.

		VF	UNC
M89	**10 Dollars** ND (1969). Turquoise on light blue and red underprint. Bust of woman at center. Young girl's head at center on back.	—	1000.

		VF	UNC
M90	**20 Dollars** ND (1969). Purple on blue and light blue underprint. Veiled woman's head at center. Eagle perched on rock at center on back.	—	300.

SERIES 692

7.10.1970 to 15.3.1973.

#M83-M86 sculpture of seated Roman warrior at l. (National Archives, Washington DC façade). Eagle at ctr. on back.

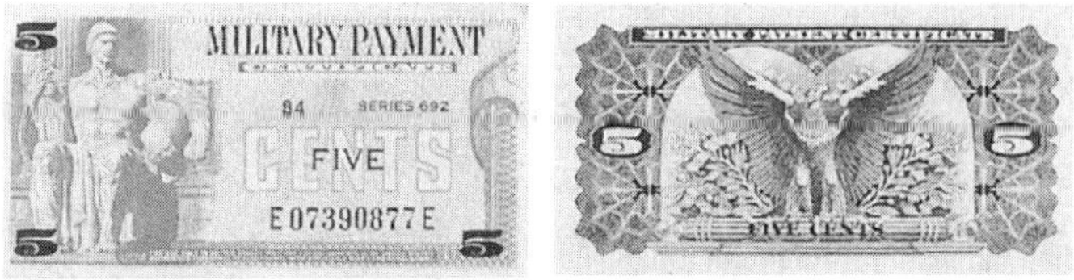

		VF	UNC
M91	**5 Cents** ND (1970). Red-brown and lilac on multicolor underprint.	1.00	16.50
M92	**10 Cents** ND (1970). Green and blue on multicolor underprint.	1.00	17.50
M93	**25 Cents** ND (1970). Dark blue on yellow and multicolor underprint.	3.00	30.00
M94	**50 Cents** ND (1970). Purple on yellow and multicolor underprint.	4.00	40.00

		VF	UNC
M95	**1 Dollar** ND (1970). Blue-green on multicolor underprint. Portrait woman facing right at left, flowers at bottom center. Buffalo at center on back.	8.00	95.00
M96	**5 Dollars** ND (1970). Brown on orange and multicolor underprint. Girl and flowers at center. Elk family at left center on back.	50.00	1000.
M97	**10 Dollars** ND (1970). Blue on pink and multicolor underprint. Indian Chief Hollow Horn Bear at center. Eagle at left center on back.	75.00	1150.
M98	**20 Dollars** ND (1970). Violet on orange and multicolor underprint. Indian Chief Ouray at center. Dam on back.	30.00	1200.

SERIES 701

#M99-M102 not assigned.

		VF	UNC
M103	**1 Dollar** ND (1970). Light green on brown and orange underprint. Washington Irving and open books. Hay harvesting on back.	—	750.

		VF	UNC
M104	**5 Dollars** ND (1970). Purple on green underprint. Thomas Edison at right, light bulb at center, Benjamin Franklin and kite/key at left. Rocky Mountain vista on back at left center.	—	750.

		VF	UNC
M105	**10 Dollars** ND (1970). Red-brown on tan underprint. Mt. Vernon at center, George Washington at right. Mountain vista at left on back.	—	750.

		VF	UNC
M106	**20 Dollars** ND (1970). Brown on light blue-green underprint. Steamboat *Clermont* at left, Robert Fulton at right. Coastline vista at center right on back.	—	750.

AAFES (ARMY AND AIR FORCE EXCHANGE SERVICE)

FIRST ISSUE

		VG	VF	UNC
M121	**5 Cents** Large value in red on both sides. (1A51).	FV	FV	.25
M122	**10 Cents** Large vlaue in blue on both sides. (1A101).	FV	FV	.50
M123	**25 Cents** Large value in white on both sides. (1A251).	FV	FV	.75

SECOND ISSUE

		VG	VF	UNC
M124	**5 Cents** A-10 Thunderbolt II. (2A51).	FV	FV	.25
M125	**5 Cents** B-2 Spirit. (2B51).	FV	FV	.25
M126	**5 Cents** Patriot missile truck. (2C51).	FV	FV	.25
M127	**5 Cents** Paratroopers skyjumping. (2D51).	FV	FV	.25
M128	**5 Cents** B-52 Stratofortress. (2E51).	FV	FV	.25
M129	**5 Cents** A-7 Corsair II. (2F51).	FV	FV	.25
M130	**5 Cents** AH-64 Apache helicopter. (2G51).	FV	FV	.25
M131	**5 Cents** Operation Iraqi Freedom legend in clouds from a Patriot missle launching. (2H51).	FV	FV	.25
M132	**5 Cents** Two F-15 Eagles, sun in background. (2J51).	FV	FV	.25
M133	**5 Cents** Two F-15 Eagles, one banking. (2K51).	FV	FV	.25
M134	**5 Cents** K-Dog, Navy's bottle-nose dolphin jumping upwards. (2L51).	FV	FV	.25
M135	**5 Cents** CH-47 Chinook helicopter transporting tank. (2M51).	FV	FV	.25
M136	**10 Cents** AC-130 Spectre front view. (2A101).	FV	FV	.50
M137	**10 Cents** Two F-16 Fighting Falcons. (2B101).	FV	FV	.50
M138	**10 Cents** Two H-60 Black Hawk helicopters and a CH-47 Chinook helicopter. (2C101).	FV	FV	.50
M139	**10 Cents** Operation Iraqi Freedom legend, surface-to-air missile launcher. (2D101).	FV	FV	.50
M140	**10 Cents** F-15 Eagle in banking turn. (2E101).	FV	FV	.50
M141	**10 Cents** Warheads on bombs. (2F101).	FV	FV	.50
M142	**10 Cents** Two soldiers in protective masks and MOPP gear. (2G101).	FV	FV	.50
M143	**10 Cents** Troops around an artillery piece. (2H101).	FV	FV	.50
M144	**10 Cents** Battleship firing. (2J101).	FV	FV	.50
M145	**10 Cents** Four pilots being assisted into four F-15 Eagles. (2K101).	FV	FV	.50
M146	**10 Cents** Soldier aiming a machine gun. (2L101).	FV	FV	.50
M147	**10 Cents** M1A1Tank advancing right. (2M101).	FV	FV	.50
M148	**25 Cents** CH-46 Sea Knight helicopter. (2A251).	FV	FV	.75
M149	**25 Cents** F-16 Fighting Falcon diving. (2B251).	FV	FV	.75
M150	**25 Cents** Close-up of soldier wearing protective mask. (2C251).	FV	FV	.75
M151	**25 Cents** Two UH-1Iroquois helicopters advancing forward. (2D251).	FV	FV	.75
M152	**25 Cents** E-3 Sentry AWACS. (2E251).	FV	FV	.75
M153	**25 Cents** Pilot in cockpit of F-16 Fighting Falcon as seen from above. (2F251).	FV	FV	.75
M154	**25 Cents** Operation Iraqi Freedom legend, top of tank. (2G251).	FV	FV	.75

		VG	VF	UNC
M155	**25 Cents** Hovercraft. (2H251).	FV	FV	.75
M156	**25 Cents** F/A-18 Hornet in a banking turn. (2J251).	FV	FV	.75
M157	**25 Cents** Mother of all Bombs MOAB, in flight. (2K251).	FV	FV	.75
M158	**25 Cents** H-60 helicopter with soldier on ladder. (2L251).	FV	FV	.75
M159	**25 Cents** Humvee. (2M251).	FV	FV	.75

THIRD ISSUE

		VG	VF	UNC
M160	**5 Cents** 2003. Soldier inspecting mouth of child. (3A51).	FV	FV	.25
M161	**5 Cents** 2003. Soldier seated in vehicle, flag in background. (3B51).	FV	FV	.25
M162	**5 Cents** 2003. Soldier standing by flag. (3C51).	FV	FV	.25
M163	**5 Cents** 2003. Child on shoulders of soldier. (3D51).	FV	FV	.25
M164	**5 Cents** 2003. Soldier wearing protective MOPP gear. (3E51).	FV	FV	.25
M165	**5 Cents** 2003. *Operation Iraqi Freedom* legend. H-3 Sea King helicopter and soldier. (3F51).	FV	FV	.25
M166	**5 Cents** 2003. SWIFT hight speed vessel, HSV 2. Wave piercing catamaran. (3G51).	FV	FV	.25
M167	**5 Cents** 2003. Statue of Liberty and HH-65 Dolphin helicopter. (3H51).	FV	FV	.25
M168	**5 Cents** 2003. *We go where you go* legend. Soldier at BX/PX store. (3J51).	FV	FV	.25
M169	**5 Cents** 2003. *Proudly serving those who serve* legend, flag background. (3K51).	FV	FV	.25
M170	**5 Cents** 2003. KC-Extender refueling F/A-22 Raptor. (3L51).	FV	FV	.25
M171	**5 Cents** 2003. F/A-18 Hornet. (3M51).	FV	FV	.25
M172	**10 Cents** 2003. AH-640 Apache-Longbow helicopter. (3A101).	FV	FV	.50
M173	**10 Cents** 2003. Child's face and flag. (3B101).	FV	FV	.50
M174	**10 Cents** 2003. Soldier and flag. (3C101).	FV	FV	.50
M175	**10 Cents** 2003. *Operation Iraqi Freedom* legend. Flight deck crewmember in red/white helmet. (3D101).	FV	FV	.50
M176	**10 Cents** F-16 Fighting Falcon, view over pilot's shoulder. (3E101).	FV	FV	.50
M177	**10 Cents** 2003. Soldier left, rock pile in background. (3F101).	FV	FV	.50
M178	**10 Cents** 2003. Flair of a rocket. (3G101).	FV	FV	.50
M179	**10 Cents** 2003. Seated soldier with shoulder missile launcher. (3H101).	FV	FV	.50
M180	**10 Cents** 2003. Soldier looking over barrel of weapon. (3J101).	FV	FV	.50
M181	**10 Cents** 2003. Soldier with machine gun on H-60 Black Hawk helicopter. (3K101).	FV	FV	.50
M182	**10 Cents** 2003. Amphibious tank. (3L101).	FV	FV	.50
M183	**10 Cents** 2003. C-130 Hercules dumping red liquid during flight. (3M101).	FV	FV	.50
M184	**25 Cents** 2003. Silhouette of soldier with machine gun facing right. (3A251).	FV	FV	.75
M185	**25 Cents** 2003. Silhouette of soldier with mounted machine gun facing left. (3B251).	FV	FV	.75
M186	**25 Cents** 2003. *Operation Iraqi Freedom* legend. Soldier saluting flag. (3C251).	FV	FV	.75
M187	**25 Cents** 2003. Two AV-8B Harrier jets on approach. (3D251).	FV	FV	.75
M188	**25 Cents** 2003. Silhouette of soldier on vehicle. (3E251).	FV	FV	.75
M189	**25 Cents** 2003. V-22 Osprey lifting off from carrier deck. (3F251).	FV	FV	.75
M190	**25 Cents** 2003. Soldier inspecting child's ear. (3G251).	FV	FV	.75
M191	**25 Cents** 2003. Lineup of C-130 Hercules cargo planes on runway. (3H251).	FV	FV	.75
M192	**25 Cents** 2003. U.S. Coast Guard Barque *Eagle*, the Academy's training vessel based in New London, Connecticut. (3J251).	FV	FV	.75
M193	**25 Cents** 2003. *Operation Enduring Freedom* legend. Soldier at console. (3K251).	FV	FV	.75
M194	**25 Cents** 2003. American flag on deck of an Aircraft carrier. (3L251).	FV	FV	.75
M195	**25 Cents** 2003. Three Marines in dress uniform. (3M251).	FV	FV	.75

FOURTH ISSUE

		VG	VF	UNC
M196	**5 Cents** 2004. F-35 flying right. (4A51).	FV	FV	.25
M197	**5 Cents** 2004. Sailor holding child. (4B51).	FV	FV	.25
M198	**5 Cents** 2004. Soldier and child. (4C51).	FV	FV	.25
M199	**5 Cents** 2004. CH-47 Chinook helicopter transporting cargo in net. (4D51).	FV	FV	.25
M200	**5 Cents** 2004. Patrial view, B-17 Flying Fortress. (4E51).	FV	FV	.25
M201	**5 Cents** 2004. *Operation Iraqi Freedom* legend. Soldier with machine gun. (4F51).	FV	FV	.25
M202	**5 Cents** 2004. Sailor walking away, toward row of flags. (4G51).	FV	FV	.25
M203	**5 Cents** 2004. Female soldier facing, looking thru gun. (4H51).	FV	FV	.25
M204	**5 Cents** 2004. *We go where you go!* legend. Female soldier. (4J51).	FV	FV	.25
M205	**5 Cents** 2004. *Proudly serving those who serve* legend. Three female soldiers. (4K51).	FV	FV	.25
M206	**5 Cents** 2004. WWII era troops landing off on an amphibious craft. (4L51).	FV	FV	.25
M207	**5 Cents** 2004. Lookout tower silhouette. (4M51).	FV	FV	.25
M208	**10 Cents** 2004. Soldier standing left, holding rifle. (4A101).	FV	FV	.50
M209	**10 Cents** 2004. WWII era female assembling an aircraft. (4B101).	FV	FV	.50
M210	**10 Cents** 2004. Soldier holding an object. (4B101).	FV	FV	.50
M211	**10 Cents** 2004. *Operation Iraqi Freedom* legend. Two soldiers in desert. (4D101).	FV	FV	.50
M212	**10 Cents** 2004. Navy ship #3 superstructure and flag. (4E101).	FV	FV	.50
M213	**10 Cents** 2004. H-60 Black Hawk helicopter approaching. (4F101).	FV	FV	.50
M214	**10 Cents** 2004. *Operation Enduring Freedom* legend. Oil well smoke. (4G101).	FV	FV	.50
M215	**10 Cents** 2004. Bradley fighting vehicle profile left. (4H101).	FV	FV	.50
M216	**10 Cents** 2004. Eight WWII crewmembers by plane. (4J101).	FV	FV	.50
M217	**10 Cents** 2004. Two soldiers near burning item. (4K101).	FV	FV	.50
M218	**10 Cents** 2004. B-1B Lancer cockpit. (4L101).	FV	FV	.50
M219	**10 Cents** 2004. H-60 Black Hawk helicopter on aircraft carrier. (4M101).	FV	FV	.50
M220	**25 Cents** 2004. Two soldiers helping another get into a deep-sea diving suit. (4A251).	FV	FV	.75
M221	**25 Cents** 2004. U.S. Coast Guard craft with men standing under deck canopy. (4B251).	FV	FV	.75
M222	**25 Cents** 2004. Vietnam era soldier with purchase from PX. (4C251).	FV	FV	.75
M223	**25 Cents** 2004. Child with small flag. (4D251).	FV	FV	.75
M224	**25 Cents** 2004. Five WWII era pilots. (4E251).	FV	FV	.75
M225	**25 Cents** 2004. WWII era submarine officer looking thru periscope. (4F251).	FV	FV	.75
M226	**25 Cents** 2004. AV-BB Harrier lifting off from carrier deck. (4G251).	FV	FV	.75
M227	**25 Cents** 2004. WWII era aircraft #63 approaching aircraft carrier. (4H251).	FV	FV	.75
M228	**25 Cents** 2004. Machine gunner atop Humvee. (4J251).	FV	FV	.75
M229	**25 Cents** 2004. *Operation Enduring Freedom* legend. C-130 Hercules cargo plane. (4K251).	FV	FV	.75
M230	**25 Cents** 2004. *Operation Iraqi Freedom* legend. Soldier with machine gun. (4L251).	FV	FV	.75
M231	**25 Cents** 2004. H-60 Black Hawk helicopter above soldier in the desert. (4M251).	FV	FV	.75

FIFTH ISSUE

		VG	VF	UNC
M232	**5 Cents** 2004. *Proudly serving those who serve* legend. Burger King ad on deplaning truck. (5A51).	FV	FV	.25
M233	**5 Cents** 2004. Soldiers lined up at a BX/PX grand opening. (5B51).	FV	FV	.25
M234	**5 Cents** 2004. BX/PX sign, soldiers around. (5C51).	FV	FV	.25

		VG	VF	UNC
M235	**5 Cents** 2004. Flight deck officer sending off P-51 Mustang. (5D51).	FV	FV	.25
M236	**5 Cents** 2004. HH-53 Jolly Green Giant helicopter in flight. (5E51).	FV	FV	.25
M237	**5 Cents** 2004. F-86 Sabre accending skyward. (5F51).	FV	FV	.25
M238	**5 Cents** 2004. Soldier with Iraqi blue topped building in background. (5G51).	FV	FV	.25
M239	**5 Cents** 2004. H-60 Black Hawk helicopter and sunset. (5H51). *Operation Iraqi Freedom,* legend.	FV	FV	.40
M240	**5 Cents** 2004. Six TBM Avenger bombers in formation. (5J51).	FV	FV	.25
M241	**5 Cents** 2004. Five jets comprised of: F-15E Strike Eagles, F-15 Eagle and F-16 Fighting Falcon in formation. Burning oil wells in distance. (5K51).	FV	FV	.25
M242	**5 Cents** 2004. Coast Guard vessel. (5L51).	FV	FV	.25
M243	**5 Cents** 2004. Capt. Charles "Chuck" Yeager with Bell XS-1. (5M51).	FV	FV	.25
M244	**10 Cents** 2004. Six crewmembers of the B-29 Super Fortress *Enola Gay.* (5A101).	FV	FV	.50
M245	**10 Cents** 2004. Soldier with infant, wife, flag behind. (5B101).	FV	FV	.50
M246	**10 Cents** 2004. *Operation Enduring Freedom* legend. F-14 Tomcat and crew member on flight deck. (5C101).	FV	FV	.50
M247	**10 Cents** 2004. Guard tower and razor wire. (5D101).	FV	FV	.50
M248	**10 Cents** 2004. Humvee in flood waters in Djibouti. (5E101).	FV	FV	.50
M249	**10 Cents** 2004. Soldier silhouette with night vision scope. (5F101).	FV	FV	.50
M250	**10 Cents** 2004. 4B-24 Liberator in flight. (5G101).	FV	FV	.50
M251	**10 Cents** 2004. Soldiers boarding rear of C-130 Hercules cargo transport. (5H101).	FV	FV	.50
M252	**10 Cents** 2004. Pilot standing before F-4 Phantom II. (5J101).	FV	FV	.50
M253	**10 Cents** 2004. Soldier with goggles and chains. (5K101).	FV	FV	.50
M254	**10 Cents** 2004. Sailor greeting young daughter. *Bassett* on denomination side. (5K101).	FV	FV	.50
M255	**10 Cents** 2004. Soldier seated with rifle in field. (5M101).	FV	FV	.50
M256	**25 Cents** 2004. KC-B5 Stratotanker refueling F-16 Fighting Falcon. (5A251).	FV	FV	.75
M257	**25 Cents** 2004. B-1B Lancer flying away. (5B251).	FV	FV	.75
M258	**25 Cents** 2004. Soldier standing next to flag reading letter. (5C251).	FV	FV	.75
M259	**25 Cents** 2004. Six F-16 Falcons, USAF *Thunderbirds* in formation. (5D251).	FV	FV	.75
M260	**25 Cents** 2004. Four airmen under wing. WWII Tuskeegee airmen. (5E251).	FV	FV	.75
M261	**25 Cents** 2004. F/A Hornet crossing the sound barrier. (5F251).	FV	FV	.75
M262	**25 Cents** 2004. Humvee in rearview mirror. (5G251). *Operation Enduring Freedom,* legend.	FV	FV	1.00
M263	**25 Cents** 2004. WACS in front of B-17 Flying Fortress. (5H251).	FV	FV	.75
M264	**25 Cents** 2004. Flag raising on Iwo Jima. (5J251).	FV	FV	.75
M265	**25 Cents** 2004. *Operation Iraqi Freedom* legend. Man and german shepard. (5K251).	FV	FV	.75
M266	**25 Cents** 2004. B-17 Flying fortress and crew. (5L251).	FV	FV	.75
M267	**25 Cents** 2004. *Operation Iraqi Freedom* legend. Crew member performing maintenance on plane nose. (5M251).	FV	FV	.75

SIXTH ISSUE

Due to the use of selected Elvis Presley images, this issue was limited to 50,000 pieces of each design.

		VG	VF	UNC
M268	**5 Cents** 2005. P-51 Mustang. (6A51).	FV	FV	.75
M269	**5 Cents** 2005. Two soldiers; one seated and one standing. (6B51).	FV	FV	.75
M270	**5 Cents** 2005. B-17 Flying Fortress *Our Mom* and crew. (6C51).	FV	FV	.75

		VG	VF	UNC
M271	**5 Cents** 2005. A-10 Thunderbolt II in the sky, seen from below. (6D51).	FV	FV	.75
M272	**5 Cents** 2005. Soldier looking in hillside cave. (6E51).	FV	FV	.75
M273	**5 Cents** 2005. Air Force One, VC-25 in flight. (6F51).	FV	FV	.75
M274	**5 Cents** 2005. OH-58 Kiowa Warrior helicopter, sun behind. (6G51).	FV	FV	.75
M275	**5 Cents** 2005. *Operation Iraqi Freedom* legend. Soldier kneeling with gun. (6H51).	FV	FV	.75
M276	**5 Cents** 2005. *Operation Enduring Freedom* legend. Two soldiers walking, white domed building in background. (6J51).	FV	FV	.75
M277	**5 Cents** 2005. CH-46 Sea Knight helicopter, soldiers jumping out back. (6K51).	FV	FV	.75
M278	**5 Cents** 2005. Two soldiers launching mortar. (6L51).	FV	FV	.75
M279	**5 Cents** 2005. Elvis Presley in fatigues leaning against barrack wall. (6M51).	FV	FV	3.00
M280	**10 Cents** 2005. CH-47 Chinook helicopter in desert, soldier with gun. (6A101).	FV	FV	1.00
M281	**10 Cents** 2005. Six soldiers outside large tent, rainbow in background. (6B101).	FV	FV	1.00
M282	**10 Cents** 2005. HH-60 Dolphin helicopter in flight. (6C101).	FV	FV	1.00
M283	**10 Cents** 2005. Elvis Presley in dress uniform standing on river bridge. (6D101).	FV	FV	3.00
M284	**10 Cents** 2005. Elvis Presley advancing between vertical opening. (6E101).	FV	FV	3.00
M285	**10 Cents** 2005. Elvis Presley leaning against building wall. (6F101).	FV	FV	3.00
M286	**10 Cents** 2005. Navy football player - Midshipman. (6G101).	FV	FV	1.00
M287	**10 Cents** 2005. Air Force football player - Falcons. (6H101).	FV	FV	1.00
M288	**10 Cents** 2005. Army football player - Black Knights. (6J101).	FV	FV	1.00
M289	**10 Cents** 2005. Soldier sitting with child. (6K101).	FV	FV	1.00
M290	**10 Cents** 2005. Soldier walking amongst confiscated weapons. (6L101).	FV	FV	1.00
M291	**10 Cents** 2005. Three sholdiers advancing with weapons pointed. (6M101). *Operation Enduring Freedom,* legend.	FV	FV	1.50
M292	**25 Cents** 2005. Female sailor and young child. (6A251).	FV	FV	1.50
M293	**25 Cents** 2005. Soldier profile clutching rifle. Image from #M81. (6B251).	FV	FV	1.50
M294	**25 Cents** 2005. Submarine conning tower. (6C251).	FV	FV	1.50
M295	**25 Cents** 2005. Tank with explosions in background. (6D251).	FV	FV	1.50
M296	**25 Cents** 2005. B-1B Lancer flying before pyramids. (6E251).	FV	FV	1.50

		VG	VF	UNC
M297	**25 Cents** 2005. *Operation Iraqi Freedom* legend. Red Cross H-60 Black Hawk helicopter. (6F251).	FV	FV	1.50
M298	**25 Cents** 2005. Soldier standing before Humvee. (6G251). *Operation Enduring Freedom,* legend.	FV	FV	2.00
M299	**25 Cents** 2005. SR-71 Black Bird as seen from above. (6H251).	FV	FV	1.50
M300	**25 Cents** 2005. Army NASCAR. (6J251).	FV	FV	1.50
M301	**25 Cents** 2005. F/A-18 Hornet takeoff from aircraft carrier. (6K251).	FV	FV	1.50
M302	**25 Cents** 2005. Flag montage of the Allies: United States, Australia and Great Britain. (6L251).	FV	FV	1.50
M303	**25 Cents** 2005. *Proudly serving those who serve* legend. Soldiers with banner. (6M251).	FV	FV	1.50

SEVENTH ISSUE

		VG	VF	UNC
M304	**5 Cents** 2005. General Eisenhower talking to 101st Airborne troops before the Normandy invasion. (7A51).	FV	FV	.25
M305	**5 Cents** 2005. Five soldiers before AAFES store. (7B51).	FV	FV	.25
M306	**5 Cents** 2005. Soldier and Medal of Honor. (7C51).	FV	FV	.25

		VG	VF	UNC
M307	**5 Cents** 2005. Pilot close-up. Vignette from MPC #M79. (7D51).	FV	FV	.25
M308	**5 Cents** 2005. Ronald Reagan in tie close-up. (7E51).	FV	FV	.25
M309	**5 Cents** 2005. Two soldiers with guns beside Humvee. (7F51).	FV	FV	.25
M310	**5 Cents** 2005. Soldier giving kid candy in street. (7G51).	FV	FV	.25
M311	**5 Cents** 2005. *Operation Iraqi Freedom* legend. Plane in flight right. (7H51).	FV	FV	.25
M312	**5 Cents** 2005. Four WWII planes above aircraft carrier. (7J51).	FV	FV	.25
M313	**5 Cents** 2005. Soldier holding Purple Heart. (7K51).	FV	FV	.25
M314	**5 Cents** 2005. *Operation Enduring Freedom* legend. Tank. (7L51).	FV	FV	.25
M315	**5 Cents** 2005. Four soldiers around artillery piece. (7M51).	FV	FV	.25
M316	**10 Cents** 2005. Mom holding child, soldier inspecting child's mouth. (7A101). *Operation Enduring Freedom,* legend.	FV	FV	.75
M317	**10 Cents** 2005. John F. Kennedy, shirtless in PT boat. (7B101).	FV	FV	.50
M318	**10 Cents** 2005. George H. W. Bush close-up portrait as WWII pilot. (7C101).	FV	FV	.50
M319	**10 Cents** 2005. Gerald Ford in uniform wearing necktie. (7D101).	FV	FV	.50
M320	**10 Cents** 2005. Soldier holding silver star. (7D101).	FV	FV	.50
M321	**10 Cents** 2005. Two soldiers with guns behind sandbag line. (7E101).	FV	FV	.50
M322	**10 Cents** 2005. *Operation Iraqi Freedom* legend. Amphibious tank. (7G101).	FV	FV	.50
M323	**10 Cents** 2005. Air Force NASCAR #21. (7H101).	FV	FV	.50
M324	**10 Cents** 2005. Coast Guard NASCAR #44. (7J101).	FV	FV	.50
M325	**10 Cents** 2005. Marines NASCAR. (7K101).	FV	FV	.50
M326	**10 Cents** 2005. Navy NASCAR #14. (7L101).	FV	FV	.50
M327	**10 Cents** 2005. National Guard NASCAR #16. (7M101).	FV	FV	.50
M328	**25 Cents** 2005. Jet from the front and above. (7A251).	FV	FV	.75
M329	**25 Cents** 2005. George H. W. Bush standing before WWII era plane. (7B251).	FV	FV	.75
M330	**25 Cents** 2005. Soldier standing with rifle. (7C251).	FV	FV	.75
M331	**25 Cents** 2005. *Operation Iraqi Freedom* legend. Three soldiers standing in line advancing forward. (7D251).	FV	FV	.75
M332	**25 Cents** 2005. Two soldiers atop tank. (7E251).	FV	FV	.75
M333	**25 Cents** 2005. Two soldiers by BX/PX sign superimposed on Iraq Campaign Medal. (7F251).	FV	FV	.75
M334	**25 Cents** 2005. Soldier directing excavator. (7G251).	FV	FV	.75
M335	**25 Cents** 2005. Soldier standing with British and American Flags atop vehicle. (7H251).	FV	FV	.75
M336	**25 Cents** 2005. Soldier playing bagpipes, flanked by flags. (7J251).	FV	FV	.75
M337	**25 Cents** 2005. Helicopter superimpsed on Afghanistan Campaign medal design. (7K251).	FV	FV	.75
M338	**25 Cents** 2005. Two soldiers walking in street with machine guns. (7L251). *Operation Enduring Freedom,* legend.	FV	FV	1.00
M339	**25 Cents** 2005. Army NHRA dragster. (7M251).	FV	FV	.75

Sending Scanned Images by e-mail

Over the past two years or so, we have been receiving an ever-increasing flow of scanned images from sources world wide. Unfortunately, many of these scans could not be used due to the type of scan, or simple incompatibility with our systems. We appreciate the effort it takes to produce these images and accuracy they add to the catalog listings.

Here are a few simple instructions to follow when producing these scans. We encourage you to continue sending new images or upgrades to those currently illustrated and please do not hesitate to ask questions about this process.

- Scan all images within a resolution of 300 dpi.
- Size setting should be at 100%
- Please include in the e-mail the actual size of the image in millimeters height x width
- Scan in true 4-color
- Save images as 'tiff' and name in such a way which clearly indentifies the country of the note and catalog number
- Do not compress files
- Please e-mail with a request to confirm receipt of the attachment
- If you wish to send an image for "view only" and is not intended for print, a lower resolution (dpi) is fine
- Please send multiple images on a disc if available
- Please send images to george.cuhaj@fwpubs.com

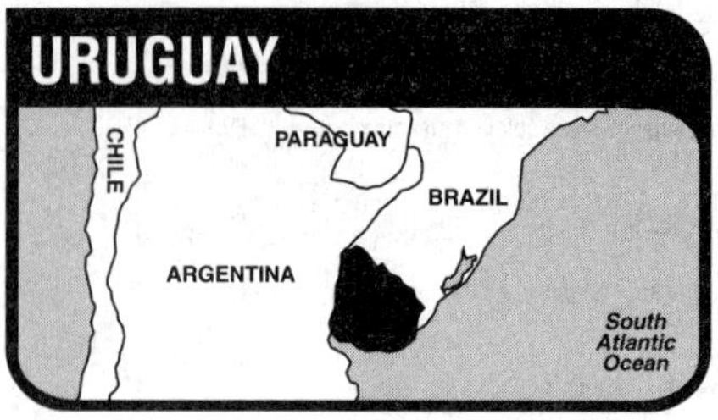

The Oriental Republic of Uruguay (so called because of its location on the east bank of the Uruguay River) is situated on the Atlantic coast of South America between Argentina and Brazil. This most advanced of South American countries has an area of 68,536 sq. mi. (176,220 sq. km.) and a population of 3.27 million. Capital: Montevideo. Uruguay's chief economic asset is its rich, rolling grassy plains. Meat, wool, hides and skins are exported.

Uruguay was discovered in 1516 by Juan Diaz de Solis, a Spaniard, but settled by the Portuguese who founded Colonia in 1680. Spain contested Portuguese possession and, after a long struggle, gained control of the country in 1778. During the general South American struggle for independence, Uruguay's first attempt was led by gaucho soldier José Gervasio Artigas leading the Banda Oriental which was quelled by Spanish and Portuguese forces in 1811. The armistice was soon broken and Argentine forces from Buenos Aires cast off the Spanish bond in the Plata region in 1814, only to be reconquered by the Portuguese from Brazil in the struggle of 1816-20. Revolt flared anew in 1825 and independence was reasserted in 1828 with the help of Argentina. The Uruguayan Republic was established in 1830.

In 1919, a new constitution established a plural executive, but this was abolished in 1933. A presidential government existed from 1933 to 1951 at which time a collective form of leadership was formed through 1966. Strikes and riots in the 1960's brought the military to power until 1985 when Julio Maria Sanguinetti established a government of national unity.

MONETARY SYSTEM:

1 Peso = 100 Centésimos, 1860-1975
1 Doblon = 10 Pesos, 1860-1875
1 Nuevo Peso = 1000 Old Pesos, 1975-1993
1 Peso Uruguayo = 1000 Nuevos Pesos, 1993-

BANCO CENTRAL DEL URUGUAY

Office Titles:

1-Gerente General, Secretario General, Presidente
2-Co-Gerente General, Secretario General, Presidente
3-p.Gerente General, Secretario General, Presidente
4-Gerente General, Secretario General, Vicepresidente
5-Gerente General, Secretario General, 2o Vicepresidente
6-p.Gerente General, Secretario General, Vicepresidente
7-Secretario General, Presidente

1967 ND PROVISIONAL ISSUE

#42-45 Banco Central was organized in 1967 and used notes of previous issuing authority w/Banco Central sign. title ovpt. Series D. Printer: TDLR.

42	10 Pesos	VG	VF	UNC
	L.1939 (1967). Purple on multicolor underprint. J. G. Artigas at lower center, arms at upper left. Farmer with 3-team ox-cart on back. Like #37. Signature title: 1.			
	a. Bank name below title: *Banco Central de la República.*	1.00	3.00	10.00
	b. Bank name below title: *Banco Central del Uruguay.*	.50	2.50	7.50

42A	50 Pesos	VG	VF	UNC
	L.1939 (1967). Blue and brown on multicolor underprint. Warrior wearing helmet at right, arms at upper left. Group of people with flag on back. Like #38.			
	a. Bank name below all 3 signature signature title: 1.	1.00	3.00	7.50
	b. Bank name below 2 signature at right. signature title: 3.	1.00	3.00	10.00

43	100 Pesos	VG	VF	UNC
	L.1939 (1967). Red and brown. "Constitution" at right, arms at center. People in town square on back. Like #39.			
	a. Bank name below 3 signature *Banco Central del Uruguay.* signature title: 1, 3; *PRESIDENTE* at right.	1.50	3.50	12.00
	b. Bank name below 2 signature at l.: *Banco Central del Uruguay.* signature title: 4; 6 *VICE PRESIDENTE* at right.	1.00	3.50	12.00
	c. Bank name below 2 signature at right. signature title: 3.	1.50	3.50	12.00

44	500 Pesos	VG	VF	UNC
	L.1939. Green and blue. "Industry" at right, arms at upper left. People with symbols of agriculture on back. Like #40.			
	a. Signature Like #42a.	1.50	6.00	17.50
	b. Signature like #42b.	1.50	6.00	17.50

45	1000 Pesos	VG	VF	UNC
	L.1939. Purple and black on pale yellow underprint. Jose Gervasio Artigas at right, arms at upper left. Man on horseback at center on back. Like #41. Signature like #42a.	4.00	8.00	25.00

1967 ND Issue

#46-51 Jose Gervasio Artigas at ctr. Sign. and sign. title varieties. Printer: TDLR.

46	50 Pesos	VG	VF	UNC
	ND (1967). Deep blue on light green and lilac underprint. Arms at left. Group of 33 men with flag on back. Series A. Signature titles: 1, 2, 4.			
	a. Issued note.	.10	.25	1.75
	s. Specimen.	—	—	55.00

47	100 Pesos	VG	VF	UNC
	ND (1967). Red on lilac and light gold underprint. Arms at left. Man presiding at independence meeting on back. Signature titles: 1, 2, 3.			
	a. Issued note.	.10	.25	1.75
	s. Specimen.	—	—	55.00

#48-51 wmk: Arms.

48	500 Pesos	VG	VF	UNC
	ND (1967). Green and blue on orange and light green underprint. Dam on back. Signature titles 1, 2.			
	a. Issued note.	.50	1.25	7.00
	s. Specimen.	—	—	55.00

49	1000 Pesos	VG	VF	UNC
	ND (1967). Purple and black on blue and yellow underprint. Large building on back. Signature titles: 1, 2, 3, 4.			
	a. Issued note.	.50	1.25	6.00
	s. Specimen.	—	—	60.00

50	5000 Pesos	VG	VF	UNC
	ND (1967). Brown and blue-green on lilac and light blue underprint. Bank on back.			
	a. Series A; B. Signature titles: 1, 4, 5, 6.	2.00	5.00	25.00
	b. Series C. Signature title: 2.	.25	1.00	4.50
	s. Specimen.	—	—	60.00

51	10,000 Pesos	VG	VF	UNC
	ND (1967). Dark green and black on yellow and light orange underprint. Building on back.			
	a. Series A. Signature title: 1.	5.00	12.50	35.00
	b. Series A. Signature title: 6.	6.00	15.00	40.00
	c. Series B. Signature titles: 2, 3, 4.	5.00	12.50	30.00
	s. Specimen.	—	—	65.00

1974 ND Issue

#52 and 53 sign. varieties. Wmk: Artigas.

#52 replacement notes: Serial # prefix *R*.

		VG	VF	UNC
52	**1000 Pesos** ND (1974). Violet and dark green on multicolor underprint. Arms at upper left center, Artigas at right. Building on back. Printer: CdeM-A. Signature title: 2.	.25	1.00	3.00

#53 replacement notes: First digit of 8 digit serial # is *9*.

		VG	VF	UNC
53	**10,000 Pesos** ND (1974). Orange on multicolor underprint, arms at upper left center, J. G. Artigas at right. Palace Esteze at left center on back. Printer: TDLR.			
	a. Series A. signature titles: 2.	1.00	3.00	10.00
	b. Series B. signature titles: 2.	.75	2.50	7.00
	c. Series C. signature titles: 1.	.50	2.00	6.00

1975 ND Provisional Issue

#54-58 new value ovpt. in black on wmk. area on face only.

		VG	VF	UNC
54	**0.50 Nuevo Peso on 500 Pesos** ND (1975). Overprint on #48. Signature titles: 1.	.10	.25	1.50

		VG	VF	UNC
55	**1 Nuevo Peso on 1000 Pesos** ND (1975). Overprint on #49. Signature titles: 1.	.25	1.00	3.50

#56 and 57 replacement notes: 8 digit serial # prefix *R*.

		VG	VF	UNC
56	**1 Nuevo Peso on 1000 Pesos** ND (1975). Overprint on #52. Signature titles: 2.	.25	1.00	4.00

		VG	VF	UNC
57	**5 Nuevos Pesos on 5000 Pesos** ND (1975). Brown on multicolor underprint. J. G. Artigas at right, arms at left center, overprint new value at left. Old Banco de la República on back. Printer: CdM-A. Signature titles: 2.	.25	1.25	5.00

		VG	VF	UNC
58	**10 Nuevos Pesos on 10,000 Pesos** ND (1975). Overprint on #53c. Signature titles: 1.	1.00	4.00	15.00

Ley No. 14.316; 1975 ND Issue

#59-60 arms near ctr., J. G. Artigas at r. and as wmk. Old govt. palace on back. Printer: TDLR.

		VG	VF	UNC
59	**50 Nuevos Pesos** ND (1975). Deep blue on multicolor underprint. Series A. 3 signatures. Sign. titles: 1.	2.00	5.00	9.00

60	100 Nuevos Pesos	VG	VF	UNC
	ND (1975). Olive-green on multicolor underprint. Series A. 3 signatures. Sign. titles: 1.	2.50	6.00	15.00

LEY NO. 14.316; 1978-88 ND ISSUES

#61-64A similar to previous issue but w/o text: *PAGARA .... A LA VISTA* at ctr. Printer: TDLR.
Replacement notes: 8 digit serial # starting w/*9*.

61	50 Nuevos Pesos	VG	VF	UNC
	ND (1978-87). Similar to #59.			
	a. 2 Signature. Series B (1978). Signature titles: 7.	.25	1.50	6.00
	b. 3 Signature. Series C (1980). Signature titles: 1.	.25	1.00	5.00
	c. 2 Signature. Series D (1981). Signature titles: 7.	.10	.75	3.00
	d. 3 Signature. Series E (1987). Signature titles: 1.	.10	.50	2.00

61A	50 Nuevos Pesos	VG	VF	UNC
	ND (1988-89). Like #61 but J. G. Artigas portrait printed in watermark area. Series F (1988); Series G (1989). Signature titles: 1.	.05	.20	.75

62	100 Nuevos Pesos	VG	VF	UNC
	ND (1978-86). Similar to #60.			
	a. 2 Signature. Series B (1978). Signature titles: 7.	.50	2.50	7.50
	b. 3 Signature. Series C (1980); Series D (1981).	.15	.50	3.00
	c. Series E (1985); Series F (1986). Signature titles: 1.	.05	.25	1.00

62A	100 Nuevos Pesos	VG	VF	UNC
	ND (1987). Olive-green on multicolor underprint. Like #62 but J. G. Artigas portrait printed in watermark area. Series G (1987). Signature titles: 1.	.05	.50	2.00

63	500 Nuevos Pesos	VG	VF	UNC
	ND (1978-85). Red on multicolor underprint.			
	a. 2 Signature. Series A (1978). Signature titles: 7.	1.00	4.00	12.50
	b. 3 Signature. Series B (1978); Series C (1985). Signature titles: 1.	.25	.75	3.50

63A	500 Nuevos Pesos	VG	VF	UNC
	ND (1991). Red on multicolor underprint. Like #63 but J. G. Artigas portrait printed in watermark area. Series D (1991). Signature titles: 1.	.20	.50	1.50

64	1000 Nuevos Pesos	VG	VF	UNC
	ND(1978-81). Purple on multicolor underprint.			
	a. 2 Signature. Series A (1978). signature titles: 7.	2.00	4.50	12.50
	b. 3 Signature. Series B (1981). Signature titles: 1.	.50	1.50	5.00

		VG	VF	UNC
64A	**1000 Nuevos Pesos** ND (1991-92). Purple on multicolor underprint. Like #64 but Jose Gervasio Artigas portrait printed in watermark area.			
	a. Series C (1991). Signature titles: 1.	.25	1.00	3.50
	b. Series D (1992). Signature titles: 1.	.20	.50	2.50

		VG	VF	UNC
65	**5000 Nuevos Pesos** ND (1983). Deep brown, orange-brown and blue on multicolor underprint. Arms at top left center, Brig. Gen. Juan Antonio Lavalleja at right. Back multicolor; 1830 scene of pledging allegiance at center. Series A; B; C. Printer: TDLR. Signature titles: 1.	.50	1.50	5.00

Ley No. 14.316; 1986; 1987 ND Issue

#66 replacement notes: Series A-R. Wmk: J. G. Artigas.

		VG	VF	UNC
66	**200 Nuevos Pesos** 1986. Dark and light green on brown and multicolor underprint. Quill and scroll at left, arms at center, J. E. Rodo at right. Rodo Monument at center, statuary at left and center on back. Series A. Printer: C. Ciccone S.A. Signature titles: 1.	.10	.25	1.50

		VG	VF	UNC
67	**10,000 Nuevos Pesos** ND (1987). Purple, dark blue, dark olive-green and violet on multicolor underprint. Plaza of Democracy with flag at left center. 19 departmental arms on back. Printer: ABNC. Signature titles: 1.			
	a. Overprint gold gilt bars on description and law designation. Series A.	7.50	25.00	75.00
	b. No overprint bars on new inscription at left, *DECRETO-LEY NO. 14.316* at upper right. Series B; C.	.75	2.00	7.50
	s. Entire note as printed and without overprint. Series A. Specimen.	—	—	—

Note: On #67 the description *Plaza de la Nacionalidad Oriental/Monumento a la bandera* and *LEY 14.316* ovpt. was being blocked out because of a change of government from military to elected civil administration before the notes were released. The new government took the prepared notes, ovpt. the legend relating to the old government and issued them (Series A). Only Specimen notes are known w/o the ovpt.

1989-92 Issue

#68-73 arms at upper l., latent image (silver oval #69-73) at upper r. w/letters B/CU. Wmk: J. G. Artigas. Sign. titles: 1. Printer: TDLR.

		VG	VF	UNC
67A	**1000 Nuevos Pesos** 1989. Brown and orange on multicolor underprint. Pedro Figari at right. Allegory of Music on back. Overprint: *NO EMITIDO.* Specimen. (Not issued.)	—	—	35.00

		VG	VF	UNC
68	**2000 Nuevos Pesos** 1989. Dark brown and orange on multicolor underprint. J. M. Blanes at center right. Altar of the Homeland (allegory of the Republic) on back. Series A.	.25	.50	2.00

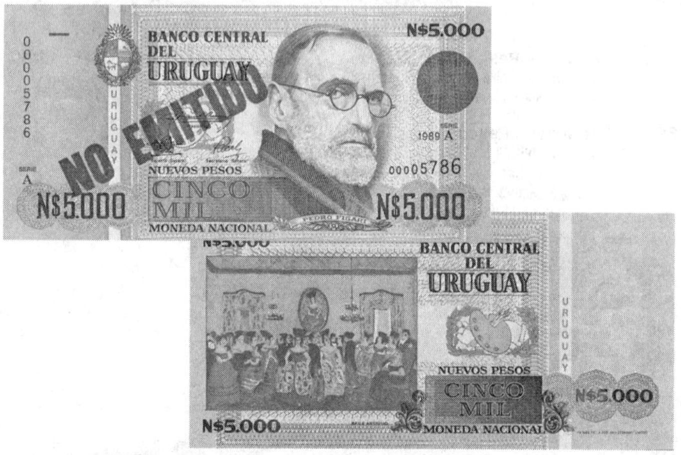

		VG	VF	UNC
68A	**5000 Nuevos Pesos** 1989. Brown and orange on multicolor underprint. Pedro Figari at right. *Baile Antiguo* (old dance) on back. Overprint: *NO EMITIDO.* Specimen. (Not issued.)	—	—	35.00

68B	10,000 Nuevos Pesos	VG	VF	UNC
	1989. Brown and orange on multicolor underprint. Alfredo Vasquez Acevedo at right. University of the Republic. Overprint: *NO EMITIDO*. Specimen. (Not issued.)	—	—	35.00

69	20,000 Nuevos Pesos	VG	VF	UNC
	1989; 1991. Dark green and violet on multicolor underprint. Dr. J. Zorrilla de San Martin at center right. Manuscript and allegory of the legend of the homeland (Victory with wings) on back. Series A.	.50	3.50	8.00

70	50,000 Nuevos Pesos	VG	VF	UNC
	1989; 1991. Black, violet and red on multicolor underprint. José Pedro Varela at center right. Varela Monument at left on back. Series A.	1.50	7.50	17.50

71	100,000 Nuevos Pesos	VG	VF	UNC
	1991. Purple and dark brown on multicolor underprint. Eduardo Fabini at right center. Musical allegory on back. Series A.	3.00	15.00	32.50

72	200,000 Nuevos Pesos	VG	VF	UNC
	1992. Dark brown and violet and orange on multicolor underprint. Pedro Figari at center right. Old dance at left on back. Series A.	5.00	27.50	65.00
73	**500,000 Nuevos Pesos**			
	1992. Blue-gray, violet and pale red on multicolor underprint. Alfredo Vaquez Acevedo at center right. University of Montevideo at left on back. Series A.	10.00	65.00	125.

1994-97 ISSUE

Currency Reform

1 Peso Uruguayo = 1000 Nuevos Pesos, 1993-

73A	5 Pesos Uruguayos	VG	VF	UNC
	ND (1997). Dark brown, red-brown and blue on multicolor underprint. Like 5000 Nuevos Pesos #65. Series A.	FV	FV	2.00

73B	10 Pesos Uruguayos	VG	VF	UNC
	ND (1995). Purple, dark blue, dark olive-green and violet on multicolor underprint. Like 10,000 Nuevos Pesos #67. Printer: G&D.			
	a. With Decreto-Ley No.14.316 (error). Series A.	FV	FV	4.00
	b. Without Ley. Series B.	FV	FV	3.50

NOTICE

Readers with unlisted dates, signature varieties, etc. are invited to submit photocopies of their notes to: Standard Catalog of World Paper Money, 700 East State St. Iola, WI 54990-0001, E-Mail: george.cuhaj@fwpubs.com.

#74-77 like #69-73 but w/new denominations. Arms at upper l. Series A. Wmk: J. G. Artigas. Printer: TDLR.

74	20 Pesos Uruguayos	VG	VF	UNC
	1994. Dark green and violet on multicolor underprint. Like #69.	FV	FV	4.50

75	50 Pesos Uruguayos	VG	VF	UNC
	1994. Black, red and violet on multicolor underprint. Like #70. Series A, B.	FV	FV	10.00

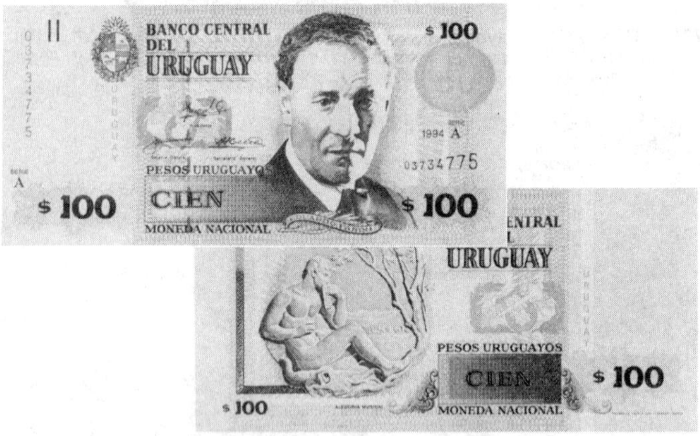

76	100 Pesos Uruguayos	VG	VF	UNC
	1994; 1997. Purple and dark brown on multicolor underprint. Like #71. Series A; B; C.	FV	FV	17.50

77	200 Pesos Uruguayos	VG	VF	UNC
	1995; 2000. Dark brown-violet on multicolor underprint. Like #72. Series A, B.	FV	FV	35.00

78	500 Pesos Uruguayos	VG	VF	UNC
	1994, 1999. Blue-gray, violet and pale red on multicolor underprint. Like #73.	FV	FV	75.00

79	1000 Pesos Uruguayos	VG	VF	UNC
	1995. Brown and olive-green on multicolor underprint. Juana de Ibarbourou at right. Palm tree in Ibarbourou Square at left, books on back.	FV	FV	140.

Note: #79 issued in celebration of the 100th birthday of Juana de Ibarbourou.

1998 Issue

#80-81 printer: (T)DLR.

80	5 Pesos Uruguayos	VG	VF	UNC
	1998. Brown and orange-brown on blue and multicolor underprint. Joaquín Torres Garcia at right center. Garcia's painting at left on back. Series A.	FV	FV	2.00

81 **10 Pesos Uruguayos**

1998. Slate black and light rose on multicolor underprint. Eduardo Acevedo Vásquez at right. Agronomy building at left on back. Series A.

VG	VF	UNC
FV	FV	3.00

1999 ISSUE

82 **500 Pesos Uruguayos**

1999. Blue on multicolor underprint. Like #78, but printer: FC-O. Series B.

VG	VF	UNC
FV	FV	75.00

2000 ISSUE

83 **20 Pesos Uruguayos**

2000; 2003. Like # 74 but Series C; D.

VG	VF	UNC
FV	FV	4.50

84 **50 Pesos Uruguayos**

2000; 2003. Like # 75 but Series B, C.

VG	VF	UNC
FV	FV	10.00

85 **100 Pesos Uruguayos**

2000; 2003. Like #76 but Series C, D.

VG	VF	UNC
FV	FV	35.00

2003 ISSUE

86 **2000 Pesos Uruguayos**

2003. Gray and light olive-green. Dámaso Antonio Larrañaga at right. National Library on back. Series A.

VG	VF	UNC
FV	FV	250.

The Republic of Uzbekistan (formerly the Uzbek S.S.R.), is bordered on the north by Kazakhstan, to the east by Kirghizia and Tajikistan, on the south by Afghanistan and on the west by Turkmenistan. It has an area of 172,741 sq. mi. (447,400 sq. km.) and a population of 23.5 million. Capital: Tashkent. Crude oil, natural gas, coal, copper and gold deposits make up the chief resources, while intensive farming, based on artificial irrigation, provides an abundance of cotton.

The original population was believed to be Iranian towards the north while the southern part hosted the satrapies of Sogdiana and Bactria, members of the Persian empire and once part of the empire of Alexander of Macedon. The Mongol invasion of Jenghiz Khan in 1219-20 brought destruction and great ethnic changes among the population. The khanate of Khiva, in 1688, became a vassal of Persia, but recovered its independence in 1747. While the Uzbek emirs and khans ruled central Turkestan, in the north were the Kazakhs, in the west lived the nomadic Turkmens, in the east dwelled the Kirghiz, and in the southeast was the homeland of the Persian-speaking Tajiks. In 1714-17 Peter the Great sent a military expedition against Khiva which ended in a disaster. In 1853 Ak-Mechet ("White Mosque," renamed Perovsk, later Kzyl Orda), was conquered by the Russians, and the following year the fortress of Vernoye (later Alma Ata) was established. On July 29, 1867, Gen. C. P. Kaufmann was appointed governor general of Turkestan with headquarters in Tashkent. On July 5 Mozaffar ed-Din, emir of Bukhara, signed a treaty making his country a Russian vassal state with much-reduced territory. Khiva was conquered by Gen. N. N. Golovachev, and on Aug. The czarist government did not attempt to Russify the indigenous Turkic or Tajik populations, preferring to keep them backward and illiterate. The revolution of March 1917 created a confused situation in the area. On Sept. 18, 1924, the Uzbek and Turkmen peoples were authorized to form S.S.R.'s of their own, and the Kazakhs, Kirghiz and Tajiks to form autonomous S.S.R.'s. On Oct. 27, 1924, the Uzbek and Turkmen S.S.R. were officially constituted and the former was formally accepted on Jan. 15, 1925, as a member of the U.S.S.R. Tajikistan was an autonomous soviet republic within Uzbekistan until Dec. 5, 1929, when it became a S.S.R. On Dec. 5, 1936, Uzbekistan was territorially increased by incorporating into it the Kara-Kalpak A.S.S.R., which had belonged to Kazakhstan until 1930 and afterward had come under direct control of the R.S.F.S.R.

On June 20, 1990 the Uzbek Supreme Soviet adopted a declaration of sovereignty, and in Aug. 1991, following an unsuccessful coup, it declared itself independent as the 'Republic of Uzbekistan', which was confirmed by referendum in December. That same month Uzbekistan became a member of the CIS.

Monetary System:

1 Sum (Ruble) = 100 Kopeks, 1991
1 Sum = 1,000 Sum Coupon, 1994
1 CўМ (Sum) = 100 ТИЙИН (Tiyin)

REPUBLIC

GOVERNMENT

КУПОНГА КАРТОЧКА - 1993 RUBLE CONTROL COUPONS

#43-52 and 58 uniface.

		VG	VF	UNC
43	**10 and 25 Coupons**			
	ND (1993). Black on pale blue underprint.			
	a. Full sheet of 35 coupons with 2 registries.	—	—	3.00
	b. Top half sheet of 10 coupons with registry.	—	—	2.00
	c. Bottom half sheet of 25 coupons with registry.	—	—	2.00
	d. Coupon.	—	—	.10
44	**10 and 25 Coupons**			
	ND (1993). Black on orange underprint.			
	a. Full sheet of 35 coupons with 2 registries.	—	—	3.00
	b. Top half sheet of 10 coupons with registry.	—	—	2.00
	c. Bottom half sheet of 25 coupons with registry.	—	—	2.00
	d. Coupon.	—	—	.10
45	**10 and 25 Coupons**			
	ND (1993). Black on pink underprint.			
	a. Full sheet of 35 coupons with 2 registries.	—	—	5.00
	b. Top half sheet of 10 coupons with registry.	—	—	2.00
	c. Bottom half sheet of 25 coupons with registry.	—	—	2.00
	d. Coupon.	—	—	.10
46	**50 Coupons**			
	ND (1993). Black on pale ochre underprint.			
	a. Full sheet of 28 coupons with registry.	—	—	3.00
	b. Coupon.	—	—	.10
47	**100 Coupons**			
	ND (1993). Black on violet underprint.			
	a. Full sheet of 100 coupons with registry.	—	—	3.00
	b. Coupon.	—	—	.10

NOTICE

Readers with unlisted dates, signature varieties, etc. are invited to submit photocopies of their notes to: Standard Catalog of World Paper Money, 700 East State St. Iola, WI 54990-0001, E-Mail: george.cuhaj@fwpubs.com.

		VG	VF	UNC
48	**100 Coupons**			
	ND (1993). Black on tan underprint.			
	a. Full sheet of 100 coupons with registry.	—	—	3.00
	b. Coupon.	—	—	.10
49	**100 Coupons**			
	ND (1993). Black on light blue underprint.			
	a. Full sheet of 100 coupons with registry.	—	—	3.00
	b. Coupon.	—	—	.10
50	**150 Coupons**			
	ND (1993). Red on pale gray underprint.			
	a. Full sheet of 150 coupons with registry.	—	—	3.00
	b. Coupon.	—	—	.10
51	**200 Coupons**			
	ND (1993). Black on pink underprint.			
	a. Full sheet of 200 coupons with registry.	—	—	3.00
	b. Coupon.	—	—	.10
52	**200 Coupons**			
	ND (1993). Black on tan underprint.			
	a. Full sheet of 200 coupons with registry.	—	—	.10
	b. Coupon.	—	—	.10

#53-57 not assigned.

		VG	VF	UNC
58	**2000 Coupons**			
	ND (1993). Blue on pink underprint. Uniface.			
	a. Full sheet of 28 coupons with registry.	—	—	4.00
	b. Coupon.	—	—	.10

#59 and 60 not assigned.

УЗБЕКИСТОН ДАВЛАТ БАНКИ

BANK OF UZBEKISTAN

1992 (1993) ISSUE

#61-72 arms at l. Mosque at ctr. on back. Printer: H&S (w/o imprint).

#61-65 wmk: Flower pattern repeated.

		VG	VF	UNC
61	**1 Sum**			
	1992 (1993). Blue-gray on light blue and gold underprint.			
	a. Issued note.	.05	.10	.25
	s. Specimen.	—	—	25.00

		VG	VF	UNC
62	**3 Sum**			
	1992 (1993). Green on light blue and gold underprint.			
	a. Issued note.	.05	.10	.50
	s. Specimen.	—	—	25.00
63	**5 Sum**			
	1992 (1993). Purple on light blue and gold underprint.			
	a. Issued note.	.05	.10	1.00
	s. Specimen.	—	—	25.00
64	**10 Sum**			
	1992 (1993). Red on light blue and gold underprint.			
	a. Issued note.	.05	.10	1.00
	s. Specimen.	—	—	25.00
65	**25 Sum**			
	1992 (1993). Blue-green on light blue and gold underprint. Back green.			
	a. Issued note.	—	.20	1.00
	s. Specimen.	—	—	25.00

#66-72 wmk: Lg. detailed cotton flower.

		VG	VF	UNC
66	**50 Sum**			
	1992 (1993). Rose on light blue and gold underprint.			
	a. Issued note.	.10	.25	3.00
	s. Specimen.	—	—	25.00

		VG	VF	UNC
67	**100 Sum**			
	1992 (1993). Dark brown on light blue and gold underprint. Back blue.			
	a. Issued note.	.10	.50	4.00
	s. Specimen.	—	—	25.00
68	**200 Sum**			
	1992 (1993). Violet on light blue and gold underprint.			
	a. Issued note.	.15	.75	4.50
	s. Specimen.	—	—	25.00
69	**500 Sum**			
	1992 (1993). Orange on light blue and gold underprint. Back light tan.			
	a. Larger and italicized serial #.	.10	.50	2.00
	b. Smaller and regular serial #.	.25	1.50	5.00
	s. Specimen.	—	—	25.00
70	**1000 Sum**			
	1992 (1993). Brown on lilac and pale green underprint.			
	a. Prefix letters same size as the numbers.	.15	.75	3.00
	b. Serial # prefix letters taller than the numbers.	.15	.75	4.00
	s. Specimen.	—	—	30.00

		VG	VF	UNC
71	**5000 Sum**			
	1992 (1993). Blue-gray on lilac and pale green underprint.			
	a. Issued note.	.50	2.50	12.50
	s. Specimen.	—	—	25.00
72	**10,000 Sum**			
	1992 (1993). Red-orange on lilac and pale green underprint.			
	a. Issued note. Serial # height of 3 or 3.5mm.	.25	2.00	10.00
	s. Specimen.	—	—	30.00

ЎЗБЕКИСТОН РЕСПУБЛИКАСИ МАРКАЗИЙ БАНКИ

CENTRAL BANK OF UZBEKISTAN REPUBLIC

1994; 1997 ISSUE

#73-80 wmk. paper. Replacement notes: serial # prefix *ZZ*.

		VG	VF	UNC
73	**1 Sum**			
	1994. Dark green on multicolor underprint. Arms at left. Building, fountain at center right on back.	FV	FV	1.50

		VG	VF	UNC
74	**3 Sum** 1994. Violet and red-violet on multicolor underprint. Arms at left. Mosque of Çaçma Ayub Mazar in Bukhara on back.	FV	FV	2.50

#75-79 arms at upper ctr. and as wmk.

		VG	VF	UNC
75	**5 Sum** 1994. Dark blue and red-violet on multicolor underprint. Ali Shir Nawai Monument in Tashkent at center right on back.	FV	FV	2.00

		VG	VF	UNC
76	**10 Sum** 1994. Purple and blue-gray on multicolor underprint. Tomb of Tamerlane in Samarakand at center right on back.	FV	FV	2.00

		VG	VF	UNC
77	**25 Sum** 1994. Dark blue and brown on multicolor underprint. Mausoleum Kazi Zadé Rumi in the necropolis Shakhi-Zinda in Samarkand at center right on back.	FV	FV	2.00

		VG	VF	UNC
78	**50 Sum** 1994. Dark brown, olive-brown and dull brown-orange on multicolor underprint. Esplanade in Reghistan and the two Medersas in Samarkand at center right on back.	FV	FV	2.50

		VG	VF	UNC
79	**100 Sum** 1994. Purple and blue on multicolor underprint. Stylized facing peacocks at left. *Drubja Narodov* palace in Tashkent at center right on back.	FV	FV	3.00

		VG	VF	UNC
80	**200 Sum** 1997. Dark blue, black, deep purple on green and multicolor underprint. Arms at left and as watermark. Sunface over mythological tiger at center on back.	FV	FV	4.00

		VG	VF	UNC
81	**500 Sum** 1999. Red, blue and green on multicolor underprint. Arms at left and as watermark. Equestrian statue at center right on back.	FV	FV	5.00

		VG	VF	UNC
82	**1000 Sum** 2001. Brown & purple. Arms at left and as watermark. Amir Temur Museum on back.	FV	FV	7.50

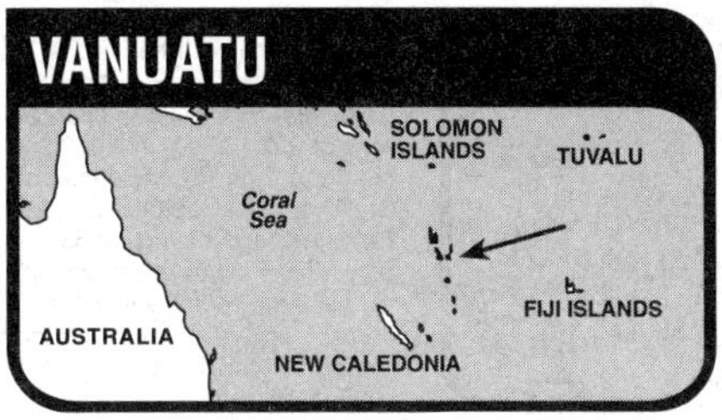

Vanuatu (formerly the New Hebrides Condominium), a group of islands located in the South Pacific 500 miles (800 km.) west of Fiji, were under the joint sovereignty of Great Britain and France. The islands have an area of 5,700 sq. mi. (14,763 sq. km.) and a population of *181,350, mainly Melanesians of mixed blood. Capital: Vila. The volcanic and coral islands, while malarial and subject to frequent earthquakes, are extremely fertile, and produce copra, coffee, tropical fruits and timber for export.

The New Hebrides were discovered by Portuguese navigator Pedro de Quiros in 1606, visited by French explorer Bougainville in 1768, and named by British navigator Capt. James Cook in 1774. Ships of all nations converged on the islands to trade for sandalwood prompting France and Britain to relinquish their individual claims and declare the islands a neutral zone in 1878. The New Hebrides were placed under the control of a mixed Anglo-French commission of naval officers during the native uprisings of 1887, and established as a condominium under the joint sovereignty of France and Great Britain in 1906. Independence for the area was attained in 1982 under the new name of Vanuatu.

RULERS:

British and French to 1982

MONETARY SYSTEM:

100 Vatu = 100 Francs

SIGNATURE VARIETIES

1	President	General Manager	2	Governor	Minister of Finance
3	President	General Manager	4	Governor	Minister of Finance

INDEPENDENT

BANQUE CENTRALE DE VANUATU

CENTRAL BANK OF VANUATU
CENTRAL BANK BLONG VANUATU

1982; 1989 ND ISSUE

#1-4 arms w/Melanesian chief standing w/spear at ctr. r. Wmk: Melanesian male head. Printer: BWC.

		VG	VF	UNC
1	**100 Vatu**			
	ND (1982). Dark green on multicolor underprint. Cattle among palm trees at left center on back. Signature 1.			
	a. Issued note.	1.00	2.50	15.00
	s. Specimen.	—	—	160.

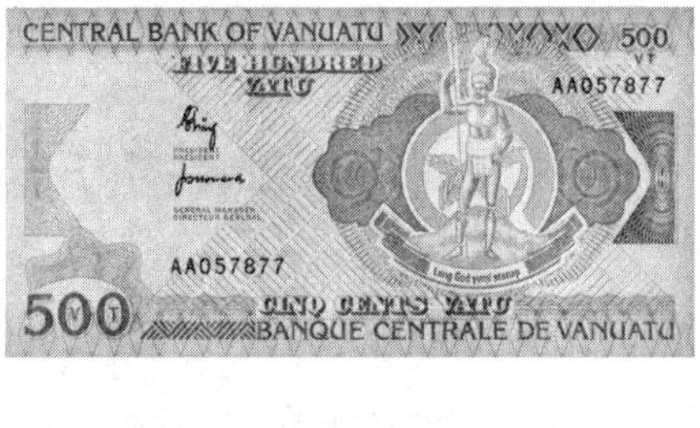

		VG	VF	UNC
2	**500 Vatu**			
	ND (1982). Light red on multicolor underprint. Three carvings at left, two men beating upright hollow log drums at left center on back. Signature 1.			
	a. Issued note.	FV	5.00	20.00
	s. Specimen.	—	—	180.

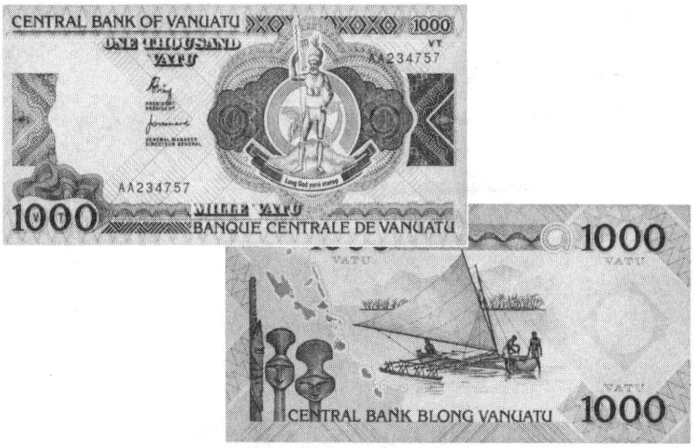

		VG	VF	UNC
3	**1000 Vatu**			
	ND (1982). Black on light orange, green and multicolor underprint. Three carvings at lower left, three men in outrigger sailboat at center on back. Signature 1.			
	a. Issued note.	FV	12.50	35.00
	s. Specimen.	—	—	225.
4	**5000 Vatu**			
	ND (1989). Brown and lilac on multicolor underprint. Man watching another *Gol* diving from log tower at center on back. Signature 2.	FV	50.00	95.00

BANQUE DE RESERVE DE VANUATU

RESERVE BANK OF VANUATU
RESERVE BANK BLONG VANUATU

1993 ND ISSUE

#5-7 like #2-4 but w/new bank name. Sign. 3. Wmk: Melanesian male head.

		VG	VF	UNC
5	**500 Vatu**			
	ND (1993). Light red on multicolor underprint. Like #2.	FV	FV	12.50

#		VG	VF	UNC
6	**1000 Vatu** ND (1993). Black on light orange, green and multicolor underprint. Like #3.	FV	FV	22.50
7	**5000 Vatu** ND. Expected new issue.	—	—	—

1995 ND Issue

#		VG	VF	UNC
8	**200 Vatu** ND (1995). Purple and violet on multicolor underprint. Arms with Melanesian chief standing with spear at center right. Statue of family life, "Traditional parliament in session" and flag on back. Watermark: Melanesian male head. Signature 4. Printer: TDLR.	FV	FV	7.50

1995 Commemorative Issue

#9, 15th Anniversary of Independence

#		VG	VF	UNC
9	**200 Vatu** ND (1995). Purple and violet on multicolor underprint. Commemorative text overprint in watermark area at left on #8.	FV	FV	7.50

2002 ND Issue

#		VG	VF	UNC
10	**1000 Vatu** ND (2002). Black and green on orange underprint. Printer: (T)DLR.	FV	FV	22.50

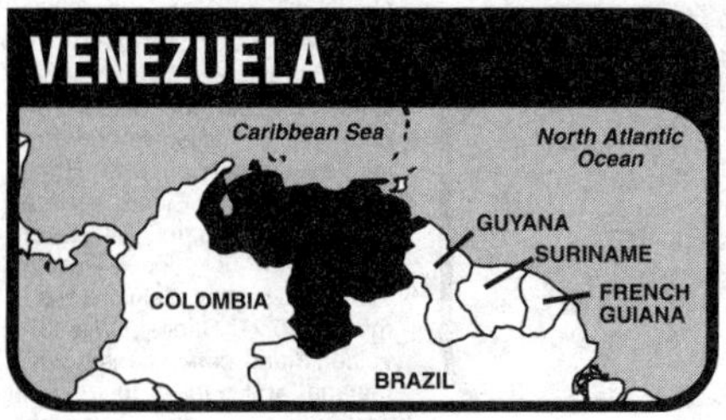

The Republic of Venezuela, located on the northern coast of South America between Colombia and Guyana, has an area of 352,145 sq. mi. (912,050 sq. km.) and a population of 24.17 million. Capital: Caracas. Petroleum and mining provide 90 percent of Venezuela's exports although they employ less than 2 percent of the work force. Coffee, grown on 60,000 plantations, is the chief crop.

Columbus discovered Venezuela on his third voyage in 1498. Initial exploration did not reveal Venezuela to be a land of great wealth. An active pearl trade operated on the off-shore islands and slavers raided the interior in search of Indians to be sold into slavery, but no significant mainland settlements were made before 1567 when Caracas was founded. Venezuela, the home of Bolívar, was among the first South American colonies to revolt against Spain in 1810. Independence was attained in 1821 but not recognized by Spain until 1845. Together with Ecuador, Panama and Colombia, Venezuela was part of "Gran Colombia" until 1830 when it became a sovereign and independent state.

MONETARY SYSTEM:

1 Bolívar = 100 Centimos, 1879-

Banco Central de Venezuela

1940-45 Issues

#31-37 Simon Bolivar on front. Arms on back. Printer: ABNC. (Series I, W not used).

#		VG	VF	UNC
31	**10 Bolívares** 19.7.1945-11.3.1960. Purple on multicolor underprint. Portrait Simon Bolívar at left, Antonio Jose de Sucre at right. Arms at right on back.			
	a. 19.7.1945-17.5.1951.	5.00	40.00	125.
	b. 31.7.1952. Serial # prefix F-G.	15.00	50.00	100.
	c. 23.7.1953-17.4.1958.	5.00	30.00	60.00
	d. 18.6.1959-11.3.1960.	5.00	20.00	45.00
	s. As a. Specimen. without signature Punched hole cancelled.	—	—	175.
32	**20 Bolívares** 15.2.1941-18.6.1959. Dark green on multicolor underprint. Portrait Simon Bolívar at right. Arms at left. on back.			
	a. 15.2.1941-17.1.1952.	15.00	60.00	125.
	b. 21.8.1952. Serial # prefix G-H.	20.00	50.00	100.
	c. 23.7.1953-18.6.1959.	5.00	30.00	75.00
	s. As a. Specimen. without signature Punched hole cancelled.	—	—	75.00
33	**50 Bolívares** 12.12.1940-11.3.1960. Black on multicolor underprint. Portrait Simon Bolívar at left. Back orange; arms at right.			
	a. 12.12.1940-17.1.1952.	25.00	100.	250.
	b. 23.7.1953. Serial # prefix C.	25.00	125.	225.
	c. 22.4.1954-11.3.1960.	15.00	65.00	125.
	s. As a. Specimen. without signature Punched hole cancelled.	—	—	125.
35	**500 Bolívares** 10.12.1940-21.12.1940. Blue on multicolor underprint. Portrait Simon Bolívar at right. Arms at left. on back.	250.	1000.	—
36	**500 Bolívares** 21.1.1943-29.11.1946. Red on multicolor underprint. Like #35.	250.	1000.	—

1947 Issue

#		VG	VF	UNC
37	**500 Bolívares** 1947-71. Orange on multicolor underprint. Like #35.			
	a. 14.8.1947-21.8.1952.	75.00	250.	—
	b. 23.7.1953-29.5.1958.	30.00	125.	300.
	c. 11.3.1960-17.8.1971.	17.50	80.00	200.
	s. As b. Specimen. without signature Punched hole cancelled.	—	—	135.

1952-53 Issue

#38-41 cruder and differently engraved portr. of Simon Bolívar and Antonio Jose de Sucre. Monument at ctr. on back. Printer: TDLR.

#		VG	VF	UNC
38	**10 Bolívares** 31.7.1952. Purple on multicolor underprint. Similar to #31. Arms at right on back. Series E, F. 7 digit serial #.	30.00	125.	350.
39	**20 Bolívares** 21.8.1952. Similar to #43. Arms at left. on back. Series G. 7 digit serial #.	35.00	175.	450.
40	**50 Bolívares** 26.2.1953; 23.7.1953. Simon Bolívar at left, *CINCUENTA BOLÍVARES* at right. Arms at right on back. Series C. 7 digit serial #.	50.00	135.	450.
41	**100 Bolívares** 23.7.1953. Portrait Simon Bolívar at right. Arms at left. on back. Series C, D. 7 digit serial #.	25.00	125.	425.

1960-61 ISSUE

#42-44 printer: TDLR.

		VG	VF	UNC
42	**10 Bolívares**			
	6.6.1961. Purple on multicolor underprint. Portrait Simon Bolívar at left. Antonio Jose de Sucre at right. Arms at right, monument to Battle of Carabobo at center on back. Face similar to #31, back like #38. Series E-J. 7 digit serial #.			
	a. Issued note.	2.50	15.00	35.00
	s. Specimen with black overprint: *SPECIMEN*. Serial # prefix *E*.	—	—	12.50

		VG	VF	UNC
43	**20 Bolívares**			
	1960-66. Dark green on multicolor underprint. Face similar to #32. Portrait Simon Bolívar at right, bank name in 1 line. Arms at left, monument at center on back. 7 digit serial #.			
	a. 11.3.1960. Serial # prefix *U-X*.	4.00	20.00	50.00
	b. 6.6.1961. Serial # prefix *X-Z*.	4.00	15.00	40.00
	c. 7.5.1963. Serial # prefix *A-B*.	4.00	—	40.00
	d. 2.6.1964. Serial # prefix *C-D*.	4.00	15.00	40.00
	e. 10.5.1966. Serial # prefix *E-G*.	4.00	15.00	40.00
	s1. Specimen with red ovpt: *SPECIMEN*. Paper with colored planchettes. Serial # prefix *X*.	—	—	15.00
	s2. Specimen with red ovpt: *ESPECIMEN SIN VALOR*. Paper with security thread. Punched hole cancelled.	—	—	15.00
	s3. Specimen with black ovpt: *SPECIMEN*. Serial # prefix *U*.	—	—	15.00

		VG	VF	UNC
44	**50 Bolívares**			
	6.6.1961; 7.5.1963. Black on multicolor underprint. Modified portrait of Simon Bolívar at left, value *CINCUENTA BOLIVARES* at right. Back orange; monument at center, arms at right on back. 7 digit serial #. Serial # prefix *H-J; J-K*.			
	a. Issued note.	8.00	50.00	125.
	s. Specimen with red ovpt: *SPECIMEN SIN VALOR*. Punched hole cancelled.	—	—	17.50

1963-67 ISSUE

#45-48 monument to Battle of Carabobo on back similar to #42-44. Printer: TDLR.

		VG	VF	UNC
45	**10 Bolívares**			
	1963-70. Purple on multicolor underprint. Similar to #42 but much different portrait of Antonio Jose de Sucre at right. 7-digit serial #.			
	a. 7.5.1963. Serial # prefix *K-N*.	1.00	2.50	15.00
	b. 2.6.1964. Serial # prefix *P-T*.	1.00	2.50	12.50
	c. 10.5.1966. Serial # prefix *T-V; X-Z*.	1.00	2.50	12.50
	d. 8.8.1967. Serial # prefix *A-D*.	1.00	2.50	10.00
	e. 5.3.1968. Serial # prefix *G-H; J-K*.	1.00	2.50	10.00
	f. 19.11.1968. Serial # prefix *E-F*.	1.00	2.50	7.50
	g. 27.1.1970. Serial # prefix *L-N; P-U*.	1.00	2.50	7.50
	s. Specimen with red overprint: *ESPECIMEN SIN VALOR*. ND. Punched hole cancelled.	—	—	30.00

		VG	VF	UNC
46	**20 Bolívares**			
	1967-74. Green on orange and blue underprint. Portrait Simon Bolívar at right and as watermark, bank name in three lines. Arms without circle at left on back.			
	a. 8.8.1967. Serial # prefix *H-J*.	1.00	4.00	20.00
	b. 5.3.1968. Serial # prefix *L-M*.	1.00	3.50	17.50
	c. 30.9.1969. Serial # prefix *K*.	1.00	3.50	17.50
	d. 27.1.1970. Serial # prefix *N; P-R*.	1.00	3.00	15.00
	e. 29.1.1974. Serial # prefix *Y-Z* (7 digits); *A-C* (7 or 8 digits).	1.00	3.00	15.00
	s1. Specimen with red overprint: *ESPECIMEN SIN VALOR*. ND. Punched hole cancelled.	—	—	15.00
	s2. Specimen with red overprint as S1. 27.1.1970.	—	—	15.00

		VG	VF	UNC
47	**50 Bolívares**			
	1964-72. Black on orange and green underprint. Portrait Simon Bolívar at left. *CINCUENTA BOLÍVARES* above *50* at center. Back orange; like #44.			
	a. 2.6.1964. Serial # prefix *K-L*.	2.00	6.00	40.00
	b. 27.7.1965. Serial # preifx *L-M*.	2.00	6.00	30.00
	c. 10.5.1966. Serial # prefix *M-N*.	2.00	6.00	30.00
	d. 8.8.1967. Serial # prefix *P*.	2.00	6.00	30.00
	e. 18.3.1969. Serial # prefix *P-Q*.	2.00	6.00	30.00
	f. 7.4.1970. Serial # prefix *Q-S*.	2.00	6.00	30.00
	g. 22.2.1972. Serial # prefix *T-U*.	2.00	6.00	30.00
	s. Specimen with red overprint: *ESPECIMEN SIN VALOR*. ND.	—	—	37.50

		VG	VF	UNC
48	**100 Bolívares**			
	1963-73. Brown on multicolor underprint. Portrait Simon Bolívar at right and as watermark. Arms at left on back.			
	a. 7.5.1963. Serial # prefix *M-N.*	2.00	5.00	40.00
	b. 2.6.1964. Serial # prefix *P-Q.*	2.00	5.00	40.00
	c. 27.7.1965. Serial # prefix *Q.*	2.00	5.00	40.00
	d. 10.5.1966. Serial # prefix Q-R.	2.00	5.00	40.00
	e. 8.8.1967. Serial # prefix *S-T.*	2.00	5.00	40.00
	f. 18.3.1969. Serial # prefix *U-V.*	2.00	5.00	40.00
	g. 26.5.1970. Serial # prefix *X-Y.*	2.00	5.00	40.00
	h. 17.8.1971. Serial # prefix *Z; A-B.*	2.00	5.00	40.00
	i. 24.10.1972. Serial # prefix *C-D.*	2.00	5.00	40.00
	j. 6.2.1973. Serial # prefix *E-F.*	2.00	5.00	40.00
	s1. Specimen with red overprint: *ESPECIMEN SIN VALOR.* ND.	—	—	20.00
	s2. Specimen with red overprint: *SPECIMEN* and TDLR oval stampings. ND. Punched hole cancelled.	—	—	95.00

1966 Commemorative Issue

#49, 400th Anniversary Founding of Caracas 1567-1967

		VG	VF	UNC
49	**5 Bolívares**			
	10.5.1966. Blue on green and yellow underprint. Scene of the founding and commemorative text at center and left, portrait Simon Bolívar at right. Back blue; city arms at left, early map (1578) of the city at center, national arms at right. Printer: ABNC. Serial # prefix *A-D.*	FV	3.00	22.50

1968-71 Issue

		VG	VF	UNC
50	**5 Bolívares**			
	1968-74. Red on multicolor underprint. Simon Bolívar at left, Francisco de Miranda at right. Arms at left, National Pantheon at center on back. Printer: TDLR.			
	a. 24.9.1968. Serial # prefix *E; F.*	.75	2.25	10.00
	b. 29.4.1969. Serial # prefix *H-J.*	.50	2.00	10.00
	c. 30.9.1969. Serial # prefix *G; H.*	.50	2.00	10.00
	d. 27.1.1970. Serial # prefix *J-M.*	.50	1.50	8.50
	e. 22.6.1971. Serial # prefix *M-P.*	.25	1.50	6.00
	f. 11.4.1972. Serial # prefix *P; R.*	.25	1.50	6.00
	g. 13.3.1973. Serial # prefix *S; T.*	.25	1.00	5.00
	h. 29.1.1974. Serial # prefix *U-Z* (7 digits); *A-E* (7 or 8 digits).	.25	1.00	5.00
	r. Remainder without date, signature or serial #.	—	—	8.00
	s. Specimen.	—	—	10.00

		VG	VF	UNC
51	**10 Bolívares**			
	1971-79. Purple on green and lilac underprint. Similar to #45. Printer: ABNC.			
	a. 22.6.1971. dark blue serial # with prefix *U-A.*	.75	2.50	12.50
	b. 11.4.1972. Serial # prefix *A-H.*	.75	2.00	10.00
	c. 13.3.1973. Serial # prefix *H-R.*	.50	1.50	9.00
	d. 29.1.1974. Serial # prefix *R-Z; A-H.*	.50	1.50	9.00
	e. 27.1.1976. Serial # prefix *J-Y.*	.50	1.50	8.00
	f. 7.6.1977. Serial # prefix *Y-C.*	.50	1.50	7.00
	g. 18.9.1979. Black serial # with prefix *C; D.*	.50	1.50	7.50
	s1. Specimen with red overprint: *MUESTRA.* Punched hole cancelled. 11.4.1972.	—	—	12.50
	s2. Specimen with red overprint: *MUESTRA.* Punched hole cancelled. 27.1.1976.	—	—	12.50
	s3. Specimen with red overprint: *MUESTRA.* Punched hole cancelled. 7.6.1977.	—	—	12.50
	s4. Specimen with red overprint: *MUESTRA.* Punched hole cancelled. 18.9.1979.	—	—	12.50

		VG	VF	UNC
52	**20 Bolívares**			
	1971; 1972. Dark green on multicolor underprint. Similar to #46. Printer: ABNC.			
	a. 22.6.1971. Serial # prefix *S-T.*	.75	2.00	12.50
	b. 11.4.1972. Serial # prefix *U-V; X-Y.*	.75	2.00	12.50
	s. Specimen with red overprint: *MUESTRA.* Punched hole cancelled. 11.4.1972.	—	—	12.50

1971-74 Issue

		VG	VF	UNC
53	**20 Bolívares**			
	1974-79. Dark green on multicolor underprint. Jose Antonio Paez at right and as watermark. Arms at left, monument to Battle of Carabobo at center on back. Printer: ABNC. 7 or 8 digit serial #.			
	a. 23.4.1974. Serial # prefix *A-H; J.*	.50	1.50	9.00
	b. 7.6.1977. Serial # prefix *J-N; P-T.*	.50	1.50	8.00
	c. 18.9.1979. Serial # prefix *T-V; X-Z; A-D.* 7 or 8-digit serial #.	.50	1.50	9.00
	s1. Specimen with red overprint: *ESPECIMEN SIN VALOR.* 23.4.1974.	—	—	10.00
	s2. Specimen with red overprint: *MUESTRA.* Punched hole cancelled. 7.6.1977.	—	—	10.00
	s3. Specimen with red overprint: *MUESTRA.* Punched hole cancelled. 18.9.1979.	—	—	10.00

54	50 Bolívares	VG	VF	UNC
	1972-77. Purple, orange and multicolor. Academic building at center, Andres Bello at right and as watermark. Back orange; arms at left, bank at center Printer: TDLR.			
	a. 21.11.1972. Serial # prefix *A-B.*	1.00	4.00	15.00
	b. 29.1.1974. Serial # prefix *B-D.*	1.00	4.00	14.50
	c. 27.1.1976. Serial # prefix *D-F.*	1.00	4.00	15.00
	d. 7.6.1977. Serial # prefix *F-H; J-N.*	.75	3.00	12.50
	s. Specimen with red overprint: *ESPECIMEN SIN VALOR.* 21.11.1972.	—	—	17.50

55	100 Bolívares	VG	VF	UNC
	1972-81. Dark brown and brown-violet on multicolor underprint. Simon Bolívar at right and as watermark. National Capitol at left, arms at right on back. Printer: BDDK.			
	a. Red serial #. 21.11.1972. Serial # prefix *A-D.*	4.00	12.50	65.00
	b. Watermark: Bolívar. 5.3.1974. Serial # prefix *D-H; J.*	3.00	10.00	45.00
	c. Blue serial #. *B-C* added to watermark. 27.1.1976.	1.50	5.00	27.50
	d. 23.11.1976. Serial # prefix *Q-V; X-Z; A* (8 digit serial #.)	1.50	5.00	27.50
	e. 12.12.1978. Serial # prefix *A-H; J-M.*	1.00	5.00	25.00
	f. 18.9.1979. Serial # prefix *N; P-V; X-Z; A-F.*	1.00	5.00	25.00
	g. 1.9.1981. Serial # prefix *F-H; J-N; P-R.*	1.00	4.50	20.00
	s1. Specimen with red overprint: *ESPECIMEN SIN VALOR.* 21.11.1972.	—	—	15.00
	s2. Specimen. 27.1.1976.	—	—	15.00

56	500 Bolívares	VG	VF	UNC
	1971-72. Brown and blue on multicolor underprint. Simon Bolívar at left and as watermark, horsemen with rifles riding at center. Back brown; dam at center, arms at right. Serial # prefix *A.* Printer: TDLR.			
	a. 9.11.1971.	4.00	15.00	50.00
	b. 11.1.1972.	2.00	8.50	45.00
	s. Specimen with red overprint: *ESPECIMEN SIN VALOR.* ND.	—	—	22.50

1980 Issue

57	10 Bolívares	VG	VF	UNC
	29.1.1980. Purple on multicolor underprint. Antonio Jose de Sucre at right. Arms at left, officers on horseback at center right on back. Serial # prefix *A.* 7 or 8 digit serial #. Printer: ABNC.			
	a. Issued note.	.25	1.00	3.00
	p. Uniface Proofs, face and back. 29.1.1980.	—	—	150.
	s. Specimen with red overprint: *MUESTRA.* Punched hole cancelled.	—	—	10.00

1980-81 Commemorative Issues

#58, Bicentennial Birth of Andres Bello, 1781-1981

58	50 Bolívares	VG	VF	UNC
	27.1.1981. Dark brown and green on multicolor underprint. Andres Bello at right and as watermark Arms at left, scene showing Bello teaching young Bolívar on back. Serial # prefix *A.* Printer: TDLR.			
	a. Issued note.	.50	3.00	12.50
	s. Specimen.	—	—	—

#59, 150th Anniversary Death of Simon Bolívar, 1830-1980

59	100 Bolívares	VG	VF	UNC
	29.1.1980. Red, purple and black on multicolor underprint. Simon Bolívar at right and as watermark, his tomb at center right. Arms at left, scene of hand to hand combat aboard ship on back. Serial # prefix *A.* Printer: TDLR.			
	a. Issued note.	2.00	5.00	27.50
	s. Specimen with red overprint: *ESPECIMEN SIN VALOR.*	—	—	15.00

1981-88 ISSUES

#60-67 w/o imprint.

60	10 Bolívares	VG	VF	UNC
	6.10.1981. Purple on light blue and multicolor underprint. Similar to #57 but underprint is different, and there are many significant plate changes. Printer: CdM-B (without imprint).			
	a. 7 or 8 digit serial #. Serial # prefix: *B-D.*	FV	.50	3.50
	s. Specimen with red overprint: *MUESTRA.*	—	—	12.50

61	10 Bolívares	VG	VF	UNC
	1986-95. Purple on light green and lilac underprint. Like #51, but *CARACAS* removed from upper center beneath bank title. Printer: ABNC (without imprint).			
	a. 18.3.1986. Serial # prefix: *D-F.*	FV	FV	2.00
	b. 31.5.1990. Serial # prefix: *G-H, J-L.*	FV	FV	1.00
	c. 8.12.1992. Serial # prefix: *L-N, P.*	FV	FV	1.00
	d. 5.6.1995. Serial # prefix: *P-U.*	FV	FV	1.00
	s. Specimen. Overprint: *MUESTRA SIN VALOR.*	—	—	—

62	10 Bolívares	VG	VF	UNC
	3.11.1988. Purple on ochre underprint. Like #45, but *CARACAS* removed from upper center beneath bank title. Serial # prefix *F-G.* Printer: TDLR (without imprint).	FV	FV	1.00

63	20 Bolívares	VG	VF	UNC
	1981-95. Dark green on multicolor underprint. Similar to #53 but *CARACAS* deleted under bank title. Title 82mm, horizontal central design in left center guilloche. Printer: TDLR (without imprint).			
	a. 6.10.1981. Serial # prefix: *D-H, J.*	FV	FV	3.00
	b. 7.9.1989. Serial # prefix: *X-Z, A-H, J.*	FV	FV	2.50
	c. 31.5.1990. Serial # prefix: *X.*	FV	FV	2.00
	d. 8.12.1992. Short design in guilloche. Serial # prefix: *D-H, J-N, P-Z, A.*	FV	FV	2.00
	e. 5.6.1995. Serial # prefix: *A-E.*	FV	FV	1.00
	f. 10.2.1998. Serial # prefix: *E-F.*	FV	FV	1.00
	s. Specimen.	—	—	10.00

Note: Central design in l.h. guilloche:

64	20 Bolívares	VG	VF	UNC
	25.9.1984. Dark green on multicolor underprint. Like #63, but title 84mm and without central design in left center guilloche, also other minor plate differences. Latent image *BCV* in guilloches easily seen. Serial # prefix *J* (8 digits);*K-N; P-S* (7 or 8 digit serial #.) Printer: CdM-B (without imprint).	FV	FV	3.00

64A	20 Bolívares	VG	VF	UNC
	7.7.1987. Dark green on multicolor underprint. Like #63 but printer: ABNC (without imprint). Serial # prefix *T-X.* 7 or 8 digit serial *#.*	FV	FV	2.50

65	50 Bolívares	VG	VF	UNC
	1985-98. Purple, black and orange on multicolor underprint. Like #54, but *CARACAS* removed under bank name. Printer: BDDK (without imprint).			
	a. 10.12.1985. Serial # prefix: *N, P-S.*	FV	FV	4.00
	b. 3.11.1988. Serial # prefix: *S-V, X-Z, A.*	FV	FV	4.00
	c. 31.5.1990. Serial # prefix: *A-H, J-K.*	FV	FV	3.00
	d. 8.12.1992. Serial # prefix: *K, L-N, P-V, X-Z.* 7 or 8 digit serial #.	FV	FV	2.50
	e. 5.6.1995. Serial # prefix: *Q-U.*	FV	FV	2.00
	f. 5.2.1998. Serial # prefix: *U-V.*	FV	FV	1.50
	g. 13.10.1998. Serial # prefix: *V-Z.*	FV	FV	1.50
	s. Specimen. 10.12.1985. Serial # prefix *N.*	—	—	20.00

66	100 Bolívares	VG	VF	UNC
	1987-98. Dark brown and brown-violet on multicolor underprint. Like #55. Printer: BDDK (without imprint).			
	a. 3.2.1987. Serial # prefix: *R-V, X-Z, A-H, J-K.*	FV	FV	5.00
	b. 16.3.1989. Serial # prefix: *K-N, P-V, X-Z, A-G.*	FV	FV	3.50
	c. 31.5.1990. Serial # prefix: *G-H, J-N, P-V, X-Y.*	FV	FV	3.50
	d. 12.5.1992. Serial # prefix: *Y-Z, A-E.*	FV	FV	2.00
	e. 8.12.1992. Serial # prefix: *E-H, K-N.*	FV	FV	2.00
	f. 5.2.1998. Serial # prefix: *E-G.*	FV	FV	2.00
	g. 13.10.1998.	FV	FV	2.00

67	500 Bolívares	VG	VF	UNC
	1981-98. Purple and black on multicolor underprint. Simon Bolívar at right and as watermark. Back green and multicolor; arms at left, orchids at center. Printer: BDDK (without imprint).			
	a. 25.9.1981. Serial # prefix: *A.*	FV	5.00	30.00
	b. 3.2.1987. Serial # prefix: *B-C.*	FV	FV	15.00
	c. 16.3.1989. Serial # prefix: *C-F.*	FV	FV	15.00
	d. 31.5.1990. Serial # prefix: *F-H, J-N, P-V, X-Z, A-C.*	FV	FV	5.00
	e. 5.6.1995. Serial # prefix: *C-H, J-N, P-Q.*	FV	FV	5.00
	f. 5.2.1998. Serial # prefix: *Q-Z.*	FV	FV	2.50

1989 Issue

#68 and 69 replacement notes: Serial # prefix *X XX* and *W*.

68	1 Bolívar	VG	VF	UNC
	5.10.1989. Purple on blue and green underprint. Large *1* at left, coin with Simon Bolívar at right. Arms at left, rosette at right on back. Watermark paper. Printer: BDDK (without imprint). Serial # prefix: *A-D; X.*	FV	FV	.25

69	2 Bolívares	VG	VF	UNC
	5.10.1989. Blue and brownish gray on light blue underprint. Coin head of Simon Bolívar at right. Large *2* at left, arms at right on back. Printer: USBNC (without imprint). Serial # prefix: *AA-AH, AJ-AM, AW-AZ, BA, BJ, BL, BN, BP, BU-BW, XX.*	FV	FV	.50

70	5 Bolívares	VG	VF	UNC
	21.9.1989. Red on multicolor underprint. Like #50, but *CARACAS* removed from upper center beneath bank title on face and back. Lithographed. Printer: TDLR (without imprint).			
	a. 7 digit serial #. Serial # prefix: *F-Z (no I or O.)*	FV	FV	1.00
	b. 8 digit serial #. Serial # prefix: *A-E, W.*	FV	FV	.50

1989 Commemorative Issue

#71, Bicentennial Birth of General Rafael Urdaneta, 1789-1989

71	20 Bolívares	VG	VF	UNC
	20.10.1987 (1989). Deep green and black on multicolor underprint. General Rafael Urdaneta at right and as watermark. Battle of Lake Maracaibo at left center on back. Serial # prefix *A-C.*	FV	FV	2.00

1990-94 Issue

#72 and 73 w/o imprint.

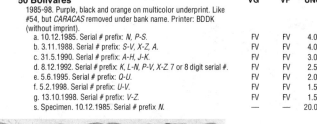

72	50 Bolívares	VG	VF	UNC
	31.5.1990. Purple, black and orange on multicolor underprint. Similar to #65 but modified plate design, ornaments in "50's". Back deeper orange. Serial # prefix *A-H; J-K.*	FV	FV	2.50

#73-75 arms at upper r. on back.

73	1000 Bolívares	VG	VF	UNC
	1991-92. Red-violet on multicolor underprint. Part of independence text at far left, Simon Bolívar at left and as watermark. Signing of the Declaration of Independence at center right on back.			
	a. Dot instead of accent above *i* (error) in *Bolívares* on face and back. 8.8.1991. Serial # prefix: *A.*	3.00	10.00	45.00
	b. Accent above *í* in *Bolívares* on face and back. 30.7.1992. Serial # prefix: *A.*	FV	FV	25.00
	c. As b. 8.12.1992. Serial # prefix: *A* (8-digits); *B* (8 or 9-digits).	FV	FV	4.00
	s1. As a. Specimen.	—	—	40.00
	s2. As b. Specimen.	—	—	40.00

74	2000 Bolívares	VG	VF	UNC
	1994; 1995. Dark green and black on multicolor underprint. Antonio Jose de Sucre at right and as watermark. Value at lower left in green. Scene of Battle of Ayacucho at left center on back.			
	a. 12.5.1994. Serial # prefix: *A.*	FV	FV	7.50
	b. Serial # prefix: *A-B.* 21.12.1995. Large serial #.	FV	FV	6.00

75	5000 Bolívares	VG	VF	UNC
	1994; 1996. Dark brown and brown-violet on multicolor underprint. Simon Bolívar at right and as watermark. Gathering at palace for Declaration of Independence at center on back.			
	a. 12.5.1994. Serial # prefix *A.*	FV	FV	15.00
	b. 14.3.1996. Serial # prefix *A-B.*	FV	FV	15.00

1994 ISSUE

76	1000 Bolívares	VG	VF	UNC
	1994-98. Red-violet on multicolor underprint. Like #73 but with green OVD *1000* at lower right.			
	a. 17.3.1994. Serial # prefix. *C-E.* (8 or 9-digits).	FV	FV	3.00
	b. 5.6.1995. Serial # prefix: *E-H, J, W.* (9 digits).	FV	FV	3.00
	c. 5.2.1998. Serial # prefix: *J-M, Z.* (8 or 9 digits).	FV	FV	2.50
	d. 6.8.1998. Serial # prefix: *M-Q, Z.* (8 or 9 digits)	FV	FV	2.50
	e. 10.9.1998.	FV	FV	2.50

1997 ISSUE

77	2000 Bolívares	VG	VF	UNC
	1997; 1998. Dark green, brown and black on multicolor underprint. Like #74 but with *2000* at lower left in black.			
	a. 16.6.1997. Serial # prefix *B-C.*	FV	FV	9.00
	b. 10.2.1998 Serial # prefix *C-D.*	FV	FV	9.00
	c. 6.8.1998. Serial # prefix: D-F.	FV	FV	9.00

78	5000 Bolívares	VG	VF	UNC
	1997-98 Brown and red-brown on multicolor underprint. Simon Bolivar at left center. Back like #75.			
	a. 16.6.1997. Serial # prefix: *B-C.*	FV	FV	17.50
	b. 10.2.1998. Serial # prefix: *C-D.*	FV	FV	15.00
	c. 6.8.1998. Serial # prefix: *D-F.*	FV	FV	15.00

1998 ISSUE

Replacement notes are indicated by a *Z* serial # prefix for all notes dated 1998 but for the 5.6.1998 1000 Bolívares which uses a *W*.

		VG	VF	UNC
79	**1000 Bolívares** 10.9.1998. Violet on multicolor underprint. Simon Bolívar at right. Panteon Nacional at right center on back. Serial # prefix: *A*.	FV	FV	2.50

		VG	VF	UNC
80	**2000 Bolívares** 29.10.1998. Olive green and gray. Andrea Bello at right. Pico Bolívar mountain range at right center. Serial # prefix: *A*.	FV	FV	5.00

		VG	VF	UNC
81	**10,000 Bolívares** 10.2.1998. Black, red and olive-brown on multicolor underprint. Simon Bolívar at right and as watermark. Teresa Carreño Theatre at left center, arms at top center right on back. Serial # prefix: *Z, A-B*.	FV	FV	27.50

NOTICE

Readers with unlisted dates, signature varieties, etc. are invited to submit photocopies of their notes to: Standard Catalog of World Paper Money, 700 East State St. Iola, WI 54990-0001, E-Mail: george.cuhaj@fwpubs.com.

		VG	VF	UNC
82	**20,000 Bolívares** 24.8.1998. Green on multicolor underprint. Simon Rodriguez at right. Arms at left, parrot at left. center, Angel Falls at center right on back. Serial # prefix: *Z, A-B*.	FV	FV	45.00

		VG	VF	UNC
83	**50,000 Bolívares** 24.8.1998. Orange and multicolor. Dr. Jose Maria Vargas at center. Central University at center, araguaney flower at left on back. Printer: CMV. Serial # prefix: *A*.	FV	FV	50.00

REPÚBLICA BOLIVARIANA DE VENEZUELA

2000-01 ISSUE

#91-93 printer: CMV.

		VG	VF	UNC
91	**5000 Bolívares** 25.5.2000; 13.8.2002. Blue and multicolor. Francisco de Miranda at right and as watermark. Electric power dam at Guri at center on back.	FV	FV	7.50

92	10,000 Bolívares	VG	VF	UNC
	25.5.2000; 15.8.2001; 13.8.2002; 25.4.2004. Black on brown and multicolor underprint. Antonio J. Sucre at center right. Supreme Court building at center on back. Serial # prefix: *A*.	FV	FV	20.00

93	20,000 Bolívares	VG	VF	UNC
	16.8.2001. Green on multicolor underprint. Simon Rodriguez at right. Like #82.	FV	FV	30.00

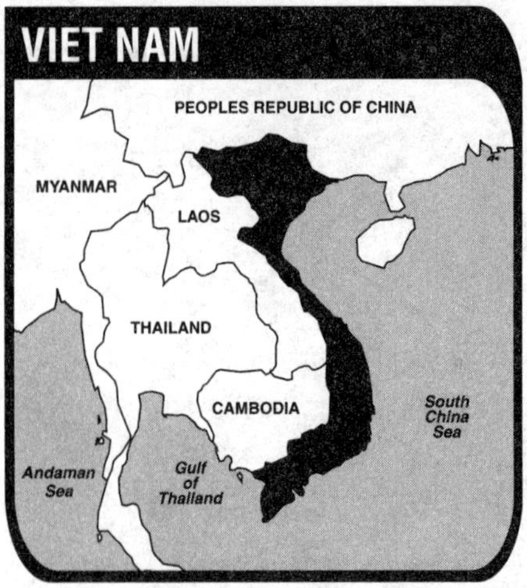

The Socialist Republic of Viet Nam, located in Southeast Asia west of the South China Sea, has an area of 127,300 sq. mi. (329,560 sq. km.) and a population of 80.55 million. Capital: Hanoi. Agricultural products, saltwater fish, shellfish, coal, mineral ores and electronic products are exported.

The Viet Namese originated in North China, from where they were driven southward by the Han Chinese. They settled in the Red River Delta in northern Viet Nam. By 208 BC, much of present-day southern China and northern Viet Nam was incorporated into the independent kingdom of Nam Viet. China annexed Nam Viet in 111 BC and ruled it until 939, when independence was reestablished. The new state then expanded until it included much of Cambodia and southern Viet Nam. Viet Nam was reconquered by the Chinese in 1407; and although they were driven out, the country was divided into two, not to be reunited until 1802.

During the latter half of the 19th century, the French gradually overran Viet Nam. Cochin-China, fell to the French in 1862-67. In 1884, France established protectorates over Annam, the central region of Viet Nam and Tonkin in the north. Cambodia, Cochin-China, Annam and Tonkin were incorporated into the Indo-Chinese Union in 1887.

At the start of World War II, many nationalists, communist and non-communist alike, fled to China and joined the League for the Independence of Viet Nam ("Viet Minh") to free Viet Nam from French rule. The Japanese occupied Viet Nam during World War II. As the end of the war drew near, the Vichy French administration and granted Viet Nam independence under a government headed by Bao Dai, emperor of Annam. The Bao Dai government collapsed at the end of the war, and on September 2, 1945, the Viet Minh proclaimed the existence of an independent Viet Nam consisting of Cochin-China, Annam and Tonkin, and set up a provisional Communist government of the Democratic Republic of Viet Nam. France recognized the new government as a free state, but later reneged and in 1949 reinstalled Bao Dai as ruler of Viet Nam and extended the regime within the French Union. The first Indochina War, against the state that raged on to the disastrous defeat of the French by the Viet Minh on May 7, 1954.

An agreement of July 21, 1954, provided for a temporary division of Viet Nam at the 17th parallel of latitude, with the Democratic Republic of Viet Nam (North Viet Nam) to the north, and the Republic of Viet Nam (South Viet Nam) to the south. In October 1955, South Viet Nam held a referendum and authorized the establishment of a republic. This Republic of Viet Nam was proclaimed on October 26, 1955, and was recognized immediately by the Western powers.

The Democratic Republic of Viet Nam, working through Viet Cong guerrillas, instigated subversion in South Viet Nam which led to the second Indochina War. This war, from the viewpoint of the North was merely a continuation of the first (anti-French) war, which came to a brief halt in 1973 but did not end until April 30, 1975 when South Viet Nam surrendered. The National Liberation Front for South Viet Nam, the political arm of the Viet Cong, assumed governmental power in the south. On July 2, 1976, North and South Viet Nam were united as the Socialist Republic of Viet Nam with Hanoi as the capital.

MONETARY SYSTEM:

1 Hao = 10 Xu
1 Dông = 100 Xu
1 Dông = 100 "Old" Dong, 1951

Note: HCM = Ho Chi Minh

DEMOCRATIC REPUBLIC

NGÂN HÀNG NHÀ NU'Ó'C VIÊT NAM

STATE BANK OF VIET NAM

1964 ND; 1972; 1975 ISSUE

74A	20 Dông	VG	VF	UNC
	1969. Olive on dark green underprint. HCM at left. Coat of arms at right. Tractor on back. (Not issued).	—	—	400.

75	2 Xu	VG	VF	UNC
	ND (1964). Purple on green underprint. Arms at center.			
	a. Issued note.	4.00	15.00	75.00
	s. Specimen.	—	—	200.

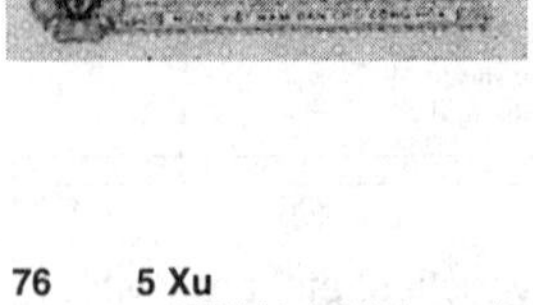

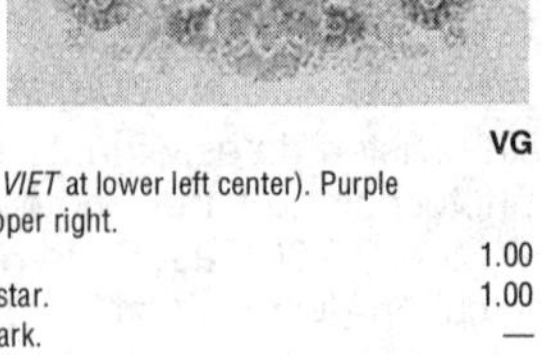

76	5 Xu	VG	VF	UNC
	1975 (date in light brown above *VIET* at lower left center). Purple on brown underprint. Arms at upper right.			
	a. Watermark: 15mm stars.	1.00	3.00	10.00
	b. Watermark: 30mm radiant star.	1.00	3.00	10.00
	s. Specimen. Without watermark.	—	—	15.00

		VG	VF	UNC
77	**1 Hao**			
	1972. Violet on multicolor underprint. Arms at center. Woman feeding pigs on back. 103 x 57mm.			
	a. Watermark: 15mm stars. Series KG-?.	1.00	3.00	10.00
	b. Watermark: 32mm encircled stars. Series MK-?.	1.00	3.00	10.00
	c. Without watermark. Series ML.	1.00	3.00	10.00
	s. Specimen. Without watermark.	—	—	15.00
77A	**1 Hao**			
	1972. Violet on multicolor underprint. Like #77 but reduced size, 96 x 48mm. Specimen.	—	Unc	20.00

		VG	VF	UNC
78	**2 Hao**			
	1975. Brownish gray on green and peach underprint. Arms at center, two men spraying rice field on back.			
	a. Issued note.	1.00	3.00	10.00
	s. Specimen.	—	—	15.00

SOCIALIST REPUBLIC

The country was united under the name of Socialist Republic of Viet Nam on July 2, 1976 after the Democratic Republic of (North) Viet Nam and the southern Peoples Revolutionary Government with assistance from China, Eastern Europe and the Soviet Union, won their long war against the Republic of (South) Viet Nam.

NGÂN HÀNG NHÀ NU'Ó'C VIÊT NAM

STATE BANK OF VIET NAM

1976 DATED ISSUE

Northern 1958 and Southern 1966-dated notes were exchanged in 1978 for 1976-dated notes to unify the currency of North and South Viet Nam. All of the old northern and southern Xu and Hao notes continued as legal tender, but the old Dong notes were overstamped with ***Da Thu*, marked with an *X*, and/or destroyed.**

		VG	VF	UNC
79	**5 Hao**			
	1976. Purple on multicolor underprint. Coconut palms amd river scene on back.			
	a. Issued note.	.25	1.00	3.00
	s. Specimen.	—	—	100.

		VG	VF	UNC
80	**1 Dông**			
	1976. Brown on multicolor underprint. Arms at center. Factory on back.			
	a. Issued note.	.25	1.00	3.00
	s. Specimen.	—	—	20.00

		VG	VF	UNC
81	**5 Dông**			
	1976. Blue-gray and green on pink underprint. Back green on yellow underprint; two women with fish in foreground, boats in harbor in background.			

		VG	VF	UNC
81	**5 Dông**			
	a. Issued note. Watermark: Flower. Block letter at left, serial # at right.	.25	1.00	4.00
	b. Block letter and serial # together. Without watermark.	.25	1.00	3.00
	s. Specimen.	—	—	20.00

		VG	VF	UNC
82	**10 Dông**			
	1976. Purple and brown on multicolor underprint. Elephants logging at center on back. (Counterfeits known.)			
	a. Issued note.	.25	1.00	5.00
	s. Specimen.	—	—	25.00

		VG	VF	UNC
83	**20 Dông**			
	1976. Blue on pink and green underprint. HCM at right, arms at left. Tractors and dam on back.			
	a. Issued note.	.25	2.00	10.00
	s. Specimen.	—	—	25.00
84	**50 Dông**			
	1976. Red-brown on pink and green underprint. HCM at right, arms at left. Hong Gay open pit mining scene on back. 2 serial # varieties.			
	a. Issued note.	.25	1.25	7.00
	s. Specimen.	—	—	25.00

SOCIALIST REPUBLIC OF VIET NAM

NGÂN HÀNG NHÀ NU'Ó'C VIÊT NAM

STATE BANK OF VIET NAM

1980; 1981 ISSUE

		VG	VF	UNC
85	**2 Dông**			
	1980 (1981). Brown on multicolor underprint. Arms at center. River scene on back.			
	a. Issued note.	.25	.75	2.00
	s. Specimen.	—	—	15.00

86	10 Dông	VG	VF	UNC
	1980 (1981). Brown on multicolor underprint. Arms at right. House and trees on back.			
	a. Issued note.	.25	.75	4.00
	s. Specimen.	—	—	15.00

87	30 Dông	VG	VF	UNC
	1981 (1982). Purple, brown and multicolor. Arms at left. center, HCM at right. Harbor scene on back. Large and small serial # varieties.			
	a. Issued note.	.50	1.50	8.00
	b. Large serial #.	5.00	15.00	35.00
	s1. Specimen overprint: *SPECIMEN*.	—	—	25.00
	s2. Specimen overprint: *GIAY MÂU*.	—	—	35.00

88	100 Dông	VG	VF	UNC
	1980 (1981). Brown, dark blue and multicolor. Portrait HCM at right and as watermark, arms at center. Back blue, purple and brown; boats and rock formations in sea cove. Large or small digits in serial #.			
	a. Issued note.	.25	1.00	8.00
	s. Specimen.	—	—	30.00

1985 Issue

#89-93 Tower of Ha Noi at l. ctr., arms at r. on face.

89	5 Hao	VG	VF	UNC
	1985. Red-violet on light blue underprint. Large 5 at center on back.			
	a. Issued note.	.25	2.00	4.00
	s. Specimen.	—	—	15.00

90	1 Dông	VG	VF	UNC
	1985. Blue-green on multicolor underprint. Sampans along rocky coastline on back.			
	a. Issued note.	.15	.50	2.00
	s. Specimen.	—	—	15.00

91	2 Dông	VG	VF	UNC
	1985. Purple on multicolor underprint. Sampans anchored along coastline on back.			
	a. Issued note.	.20	.75	2.00
	s. Specimen.	—	—	15.00

92	5 Dông	VG	VF	UNC
	1985. Green on multicolor underprint. Sampans anchored in river on back.			
	a. Issued note.	.15	.50	2.00
	s. Specimen.	—	—	15.00

93	10 Dông	VG	VF	UNC
	1985. Brown-violet on multicolor underprint. Village along stream at center on back.			
	a. Issued note.	.25	.75	3.00
	s. Specimen.	—	—	15.00

#94-99 HCM at r.

		VG	VF	UNC
94	**20 Dông** 1985 (1986). Brown, dark purple and multicolor. Arms at center right. One pillar pagoda in Hanoi on back.			
	a. Issued note.	.25	.75	2.00
	s. Specimen.	—	—	15.00

		VG	VF	UNC
95	**30 Dông** 1985 (1986). Blue and multicolor. Arms at left. Large building with clock tower at center on back.			
	a. Issued note.	.50	1.25	5.00
	s. Specimen.	—	—	15.00

		VG	VF	UNC
96	**50 Dông** 1985. Green, brown and multicolor. Arms at left center. Thac Ba hydro power plant and reservoir (Hoang Lien Son Province) on back.			
	a. Issued note.	.50	1.50	7.00
	s. Specimen.	—	—	15.00

		VG	VF	UNC
97	**50 Dông** 1985 (1987). Blue-gray on orange and multicolor underprint. Arms at center. Thang Loing bridge crossing the Red River (north of Ha Noi) at center on back.			
	a. Issued note.	.25	.75	3.00
	s. Specimen.	—	—	15.00

		VG	VF	UNC
98	**100 Dông** 1985. Brown, green, yellow and multicolor. Arms at left center. Planting rice on back. Watermark: HCM.			
	a. Issued note.	.25	2.50	15.00
	s. Specimen.	—	—	15.00

		VG	VF	UNC
99	**500 Dông** 1985. Red on blue and multicolor underprint. Arms at upper center. Bim Son Cement plant (Thanh Hoa Province) at left center on back. Watermark: HCM.			
	a. Issued note.	1.00	3.00	12.50
	s. Specimen.	—	—	20.00

1987; 1988 Issue

#100-104 HCM at r., arms at l. or l. ctr.

		VG	VF	UNC
100	**200 Dông** 1987. Red-brown and tan on multicolor underprint. Field workers at left and tractor at center right on back.			
	a. Small serial digits.	.10	.50	1.00
	b. Large serial digits.	1.00	3.00	5.00
	s. Specimen.	—	—	15.00

101 500 Dông

1988 (1989). Red-brown and red on multicolor underprint. Dockside view on back.

	VG	VF	UNC
a. Small serial digits.	.25	.50	2.00
b. Large serial digits.	1.00	3.00	5.00
s. Specimen.	—	—	15.00

#102-104 wmk: HCM.

102 1000 Dông

1987 (1988). Dark brown and deep olive-green on multicolor underprint. Open pit mining equipment at left center on back.

	VG	VF	UNC
a. Issued note.	1.00	3.00	15.00
s. Specimen.	—	—	15.00

103 2000 Dông

1987 (1988). Dark and light brown on green and multicolor underprint. Back dark purple; Pha Lai thermo power plant (Hai Hung Province) at left center.

	VG	VF	UNC
a. Issued note.	1.00	4.00	30.00
s. Specimen.	—	—	15.00

104 5000 Dông

1987 (1989). Deep blue, purple, brown and green on multicolor underprint. Offshore oil rigs at left center on back.

	VG	VF	UNC
a. Issued note.	1.00	2.00	8.00
s. Specimen.	—	—	15.00

1988-91 ISSUE

#106-111 HCM at r., arms at l. or l. ctr.

105 100 Dông

1991 (1992). Light brown on multicolor underprint. Temple and pagoda at left center on back.

	VG	VF	UNC
a. Small serial digits.	.25	.50	1.00
b. Large serial digits.	1.00	3.00	5.00
s1. Specimen withou overprintt: *TIEN MÂU.*	—	—	20.00
s2. Specimen without overprint: *SPECIMEN.*	—	—	40.00

106 1000 Dông

1988 (1989). Purple on gold and multicolor underprint. Elephant logging at center on back.

	VG	VF	UNC
a. Small serial digits.	.10	.25	1.50
b. Large serial digits.	1.00	3.00	5.00
s. Specimen.	—	—	15.00

107 2000 Dông

1988 (1989). Brownish purple on lilac and multicolor underprint. Women workers in textile factory on back.

	VG	VF	UNC
a. Small serial digits.	.15	.50	2.00
b. Large serial digits.	1.00	3.00	5.00
s. Specimen.	—	—	15.00

108 5000 Dông

1991 (1993). Dark blue on multicolor underprint. Electric lines on back.

	VG	VF	UNC
a. Issued note.	.25	.75	3.00
s. Specimen.	—	—	15.00

#109-111 wmk: HCM.

109	10,000 Đông	VG	VF	UNC
	1990 (1992). Red and red-violet on multicolor underprint. Junks along coastline at center on back.			
	a. Issued note.	1.25	1.50	10.00
	s. Specimen.	—	—	15.00

110	20,000 Đông	VG	VF	UNC
	1991 (1993). Blue-green on multicolor underprint. Arms at center. Packing factory on back.			
	a. Issued note.	1.00	1.25	8.00
	s. Specimen.	—	—	20.00

111	50,000 Đông	VG	VF	UNC
	1990 (1993). Dark olive-green and black on multicolor underprint. Arms at upper left center. Date at lower right. Dockside view on back.			
	a. Issued note.	1.75	3.50	20.00
	s. Specimen.	—	—	30.00

1992 Bank Cheque Issue

#112-114A Negotiable Bank Cheques/Certificates with expiration dates used for high value merchandise and large transactions. Specimens are valued a 2x the Unc. price.

112	100,000 Đông	VG	VF	UNC
	1992-94.	20.00	50.00	200.

> **NOTICE**
>
> Readers with unlisted dates, signature varieties, etc. are invited to submit photocopies of their notes to: Standard Catalog of World Paper Money, 700 East State St. Iola, WI 54990-0001, E-Mail: george.cuhaj@fwpubs.com.

113	500,000 Đông	VG	VF	UNC
	1992-2000.	25.00	75.00	150.

		VG	VF	UNC
114	1,000,000 Đông 1992-2001.	50.00	100.	250.
114A	5,000,000 Đông 1992-2001.	100.	300.	600.

1993; 1994 Regular Issue

115	10,000 Đông	VG	VF	UNC
	1993. Red and red-violet on multicolor underprint. Like #109 but with optical registry device at lower left, modified underprint color around arms. Back brown-violet on multicolor underprint.			
	a. Issued note.	FV	FV	4.00
	s. Specimen.	—	—	20.00

		VG	VF	UNC
116	**50,000 Dông** 1994. Dark olive-green and black on multicolor underprint. Like #111 but with date under HCM.			
	a. Issued note.	FV	FV	8.00
	s. Specimen.	—	—	20.00

		VG	VF	UNC
117	**100,000 Dông** 1994 (2000). Brown and light green on multicolor underprint. HCM at right. HCM's house on back.			
	a. Issued note.	FV	FV	20.00
	s. Specimen.	—	—	20.00

2001 Commemorative Issue

#118, 50th Anniversary National Bank of Viet Nam

Released in a special folder. Face value is minimal.

		VG	VF	UNC
118	**50 Dông** 2001. Rose on multicolor underprint. HCM at right center. Building on back. Commemorative text in clear area at upper left on face, and upper right on back. Polymer plastic.			
	a. Issued note.	—	—	30.00
	s. Specimen.	—	—	—

> **NOTICE**
>
> Readers with unlisted dates, signature varieties, etc. are invited to submit photocopies of their notes to: Standard Catalog of World Paper Money, 700 East State St. Iola, WI 54990-0001, E-Mail: george.cuhaj@fwpubs.com.

2003 Issue

#119-121 HCM at r. Polymer plastic. Printed originally at NPA, later printings done at the State Printing Works in Viet Nam.

		VG	VF	UNC
119	**50,000 Dông** (20)03; (20)04; (20)05; (20)06. Rose on multicolor underprint. Buildings in Hua on back. Polymer plastic. Issued in official folder.			
	a. Issued note.	FV	FV	8.00
	s. Specimen.	—	—	—

		VG	VF	UNC
120	**100,000 Dông** (20)04; (20)05; (20)06. Green on multicolor underprint. Van Mieu Quoc Tu Giam (National University) on back. Ploymer plastic.			
	a. Issued note.	FV	FV	15.00
	s. Specimen.	—	—	—

		VG	VF	UNC
121	**500,000 Dông** (20)03; (20)04; (20)05; (20)06. Blue and pink on multicolor underprint. HCM's birthplace in Kim Lien, Nghean Province on back. Polymer plastic.			
	a. Issued note.	FV	FV	70.00
	s. Specimen.	—	—	—

FOREIGN EXCHANGE CERTIFICATES

NGÂN HANG NGOAI THUONG VIET NAM

BANK FOR FOREIGN TRADE

1987 ND DÔNG B ISSUE

#FX1-FX5 green on pale blue and yellow unpt. Back pale blue.

FX1 10 Dông B
ND (1987).

	VG	VF	UNC
a. Series AA; AB (not issued).	—	—	5.00
s. Specimen. Series EE.	—	—	10.00

FX2 50 Dông B
ND (1987).

	VG	VF	UNC
a. Series AD (not issued).	—	—	5.00
s. Specimen. Series EE.	—	—	10.00

FX3 100 Dông B
ND (1987).

	VG	VF	UNC
a. Series AC (not issued).	—	—	5.00
s. Specimen. Series EE.	—	—	10.00

FX4 200 Dông B
ND (1987).

	VG	VF	UNC
a. Series AD (not issued).	—	—	5.00
s. Specimen. Series EE.	—	—	10.00

FX5 500 Dông B
ND (1987).

	VG	VF	UNC
a. Series AC (not issued).	—	—	5.00
s. Specimen. Series EE.	—	—	10.00

FX6 1000 Dông B
ND (1987). Red-violet on pink and pale orange underprint. Back pink.

	VG	VF	UNC
a. Issued note. Series AE.	—	—	5.00
s. Specimen. Series EE.	—	—	10.00

FX7 5000 Dông B
ND (1987). Brown on ochre underprint. Back ochre.

	VG	VF	UNC
a. Issued note. Series AA; AB; AE.	—	—	5.00
s. Specimen. Series EE.	—	—	10.00

PHIÊU' THAY NGOAI TÊ

1981 US DOLLAR A ISSUE

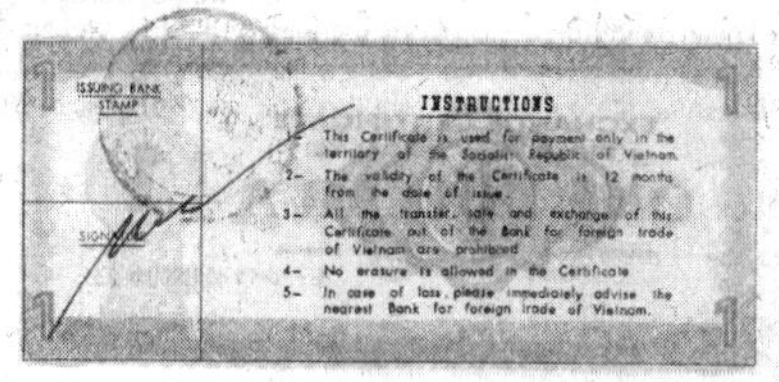

FX8 1 Dollar
1981-84. Green on peach and light blue underprint. Series AD.

	VG	VF	UNC
a. Issued note with validation overprint.	400.	900.	—
b. Unissued note without validation overprint.	—	—	800.

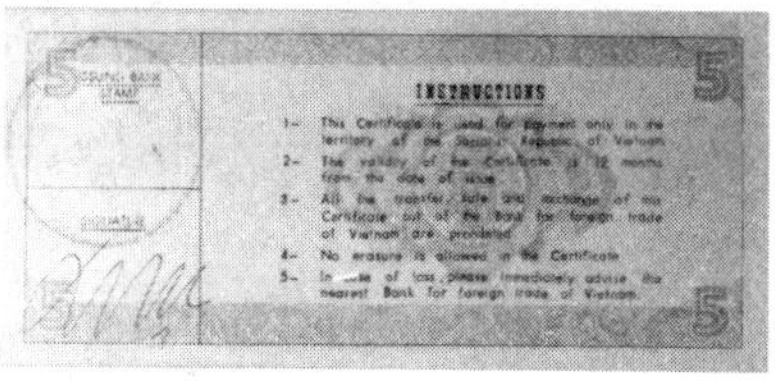

FX9 5 Dollars
1981-84. Purple on peach and light blue underprint. Series AF.

	VG	VF	UNC
a. Issued note with validation overprint.	400.	900.	—
b. Unissued note without validation overprint.	—	—	800.

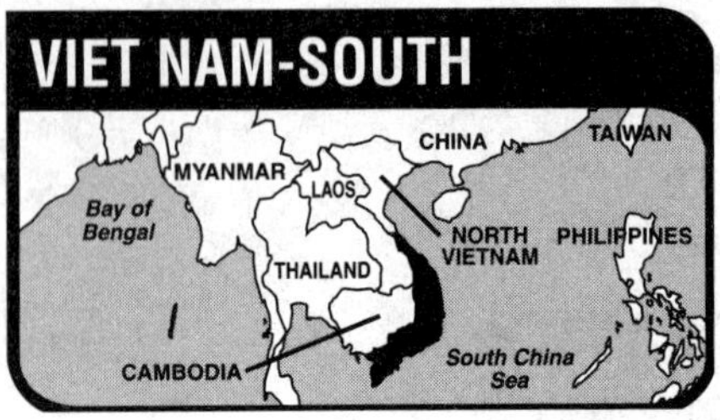

South Viet Nam (the former Republic of Viet Nam), located in Southeast Asia, bounded by North Viet Nam on the north, Laos and Cambodia on the west, and the South China Sea on the east and south, had an area of 66,280 sq. mi. (171,665 sq. km.) and a population of 20 million. Capital: Saigon. The economy of the area is predominantly agricultural.

South Viet Nam, the direct successor to the French-dominated regime (also known as the State of Viet Nam), was created after the first Indochina War (between the French and the Viet-Minh) by the Geneva agreement of 1954 which divided Viet Nam at the 17th parallel of latitude. Elections which would have reunified North and South Viet Nam in 1956 never took place, and the North continued the war for unification of Viet Nam under the the Democratic Republic of (North) Viet Nam. The Republic of Viet Nam surrendered unconditionally on April 30, 1975. There followed a short period of coexistence of the two Viet Namese states, but the South was governed by the North through the Peoples Revolutionary Government (PRG). On July 2, 1976, South and North Viet Nam joined to form the Socialist Republic of Viet Nam.

Also see Viet Nam.

MONETARY SYSTEM

1 Dông = 100 Xu

VIET NAM - SOUTH

NGÂN-HÀNG QUÔ'C-GIA VIÊT-NAM

NATIONAL BANK OF VIET NAM

1962 ND ISSUE

#5-6 printer: SBNC.

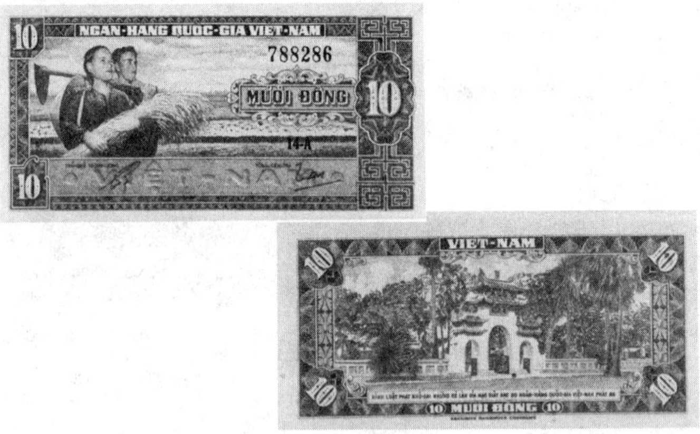

		VG	VF	UNC
5	**10 Dông** ND (1962). Red. Young farm couple at left. Ornate arch on back. Shade varieties.			
	a. Issued note.	.50	2.00	8.00
	p. Uniface face or back proof.	—	—	150.
	s. Specimen. *GIAY MAU.*	—	—	150.

		VG	VF	UNC
6	**20 Dông** ND (1962). Brown. Ox cart at left. Woman digging on back.			
	a. Issued note.	2.00	6.00	35.00
	p. Uniface face or back proof.	—	—	150.
	s. Specimen. *GIAY MAU.*	—	—	175.
	x. Counterfeit.	—	—	—

		VG	VF	UNC
6A	**500 Dông** ND (1962). Green-blue on gold and pinkish underprint. Dragon at left, palace-like building at left center. Farmer with two water buffalos at right on back. Watermark: Ngo Dinh Diem.			
	a. Issued note.	100.	200.	700
	s1. Specimen. *GIAY MAU.*	—	—	1000.
	s2. Specimen. TDLR oval.	—	—	1000.

1964; 1966 ND ISSUES

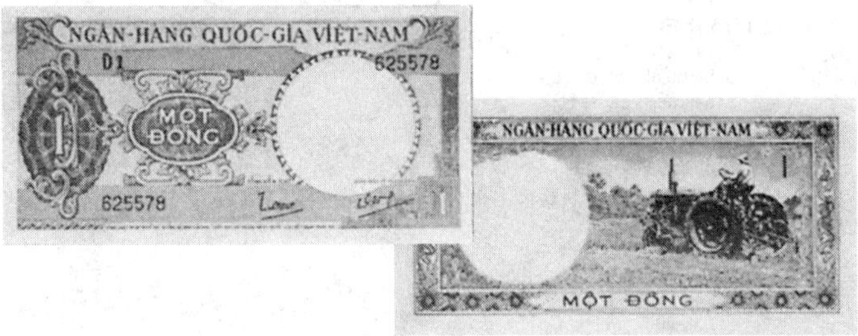

		VG	VF	UNC
15	**1 Dông** ND (1964). Light and dark brown on orange and light blue underprint. Back red-brown; farm tractor at right. Watermark: Plant.			
	a. Issued note.	1.00	3.00	5.00
	s1. Specimen. *GIAY MAU.*	—	—	1200.
	s2. Specimen. TDLR oval.	—	—	1200.

		VG	VF	UNC
16	**20 Dông** ND (1964). Green on multicolor underprint. Stylized fish at center on back. Watermark: Dragon's head.			
	a. Issued note.	.25	.75	9.00
	s. Specimen. *GIAY MAU.*	—	—	300.

Note: Three different #16 specimens have been reported This indicates that more varieties of issued notes may exist. Please report all new varieties to the editors.

		VG	VF	UNC
17	**50 Dông** ND (1966). Purple on multicolor underprint. Leaf tendrils at right.			
	a. Issued note.	1.00	5.00	25.00
	s. Specimen. *GIAY MAU.*	—	—	300.

18 **100 Dông**

ND (1966). Light and dark brown on light blue underprint. Building with domed roof at right. Power plant, water reservoir and dam on back. Watermark: Plant.

	VG	VF	UNC
a. Issued note.	1.00	5.00	35.00
s1. Specimen. Red overprint *GIAY MAU.*	—	—	300.
s2. Specimen. Black overprint	—	—	300.

19 **100 Dông**

ND (1966). Red on multicolor underprint. Le Van Duyet in national costume at left. Building and ornate gateway at center right on back.

	VG	VF	UNC
a. Watermark: Demon's head.	1.00	10.00	40.00
b. Watermark: Le Van Duyet's head.	.25	3.00	15.00
s1. As a. Specimen.	—	—	500.
s2. As b. Specimen.	—	—	500.

20 **200 Dông**

ND (1966). Dark brown on multicolor underprint. Nguyen-Hue, warrior, at left. Warrior on horseback leading soldiers on back.

	VG	VF	UNC
a. Watermark: Demon's head.	1.00	10.00	45.00
b. Watermark: Nguyen Hue's head.	.25	3.00	25.00
s1. As a. Specimen.	—	—	500.
s2. As b. Specimen.	—	—	500.

#21 *Deleted.* See #6A.

22 **500 Dông**

ND (1964). Brown on multicolor underprint. Museum in Saigon at center Stylized creatures at center on back. Watermark: Demon's head.

	VG	VF	UNC
a. Issued note.	3.00	12.50	50.00
s1. Specimen.	—	—	300.
s2. Specimen. TDLR oval.	—	—	600.

23 **500 Dông**

ND (1966). Blue on multicolor underprint. Trâ'n-Hu'ng-Dao, warrior, at left and as watermark Sailboat and rocks in water at center right on back.

	VG	VF	UNC
a. Issued note.	1.00	5.00	25.00
s. Specimen. TDLR oval.	—	—	500.
x. Counterfeit. Series S; U; X.	—	—	15.00

1969-71 ND Issue

#24-29 bank bldg. at r. Lathework on all backs. Wmk. as #23.

24 **20 Dông**

ND (1969). Red on multicolor underprint.

	VG	VF	UNC
a. Issued note.	.25	.50	5.00
s. Specimen. *GIAY MAU.*	—	—	175.

25 **50 Dông**

ND (1969). Blue-green on multicolor underprint.

	VG	VF	UNC
a. Issued note.	.25	.50	5.00
s. Specimen. *GIAY MAU.*	—	—	175.

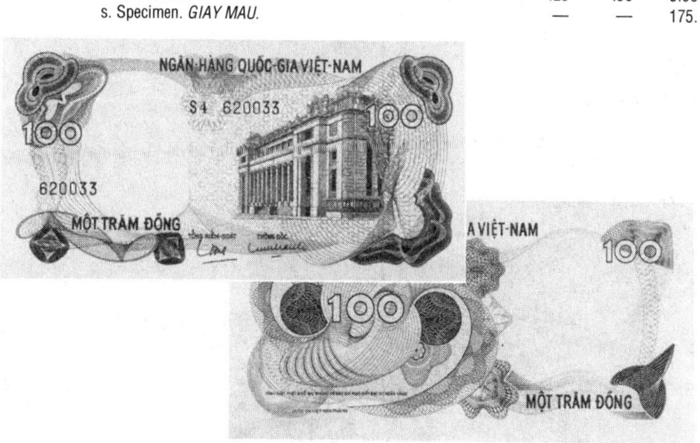

26 **100 Dông**

ND (1970). Dark green on multicolor underprint.

	VG	VF	UNC
a. Issued note.	.25	.75	5.00
s. Specimen. *GIAY MAU.*	—	Unc	175.

27 200 Dông

ND (1970). Purple on multicolor underprint.

	VG	VF	UNC
a. Issued note.	.50	1.25	25.00
s. Specimen.	—	—	300.

28 500 Dông

ND (1970). Orange and dark brown on multicolor underprint. Back orange and pale olive-green on multicolor underprint.

	VG	VF	UNC
a. Issued note.	.25	.75	5.00
s. Specimen.	—	—	200.

#28A *Deleted*. See #28. Note: The brown and black variety previously listed as #28A is believed to be the result of oxidation.

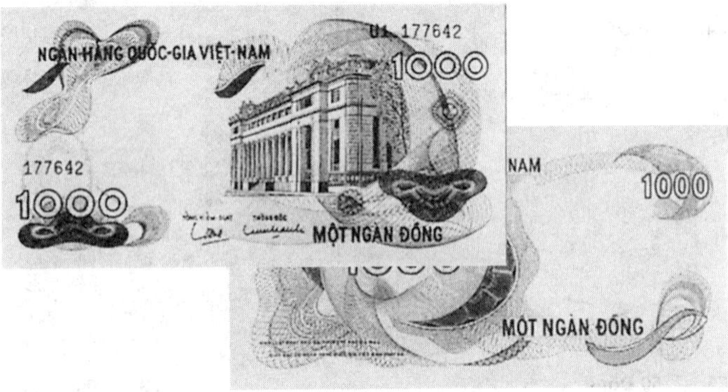

29 1000 Dông

ND (1971). Turquoise on multicolor underprint.

	VG	VF	UNC
a. Issued note.	1.00	5.00	15.00
s. Specimen. *GIAY MAU.*	—	—	250.

1972; 1975 ND Issue

#30-36 Palace of Independence at r. Wmk: Young woman's head in profile.

30 50 Dông

ND (1972). Blue-gray on multicolor underprint. Three horses at left center on back.

	VG	VF	UNC
a. Issued note.	.25	.50	4.00
s. Specimen.	—	—	400.

31 100 Dông

ND (1972). Green on multicolor underprint. Farmer with two water buffalos at left center on back.

	VG	VF	UNC
a. Issued note.	.25	.75	5.00
s. Specimen.	—	—	400.

32 200 Dông

ND (1972). Wine red on multicolor underprint. Three deer at left center on back.

	VG	VF	UNC
a. Issued note.	1.00	2.50	15.00
s. Specimen. TDLR oval.	—	—	500.

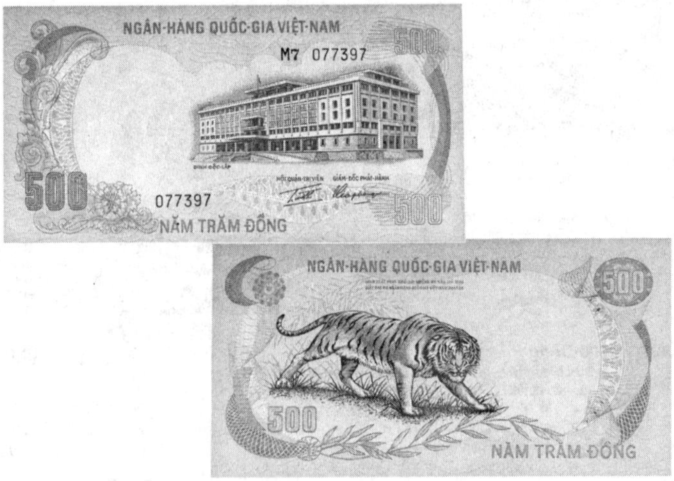

33 500 Dông

ND (1972). Orange and olive-brown on multicolor underprint. Tiger at left center on back.

	VG	VF	UNC
a. Issued note.	.50	1.25	6.00
s. Specimen.	—	—	500.

Note: The brown and olive-brown variety previously listed as #33A is believed to be the result of oxidation by leading authorities. #33A *Deleted*. See #33.

34	1000 Dông	VG	VF	UNC
	ND (1972). Blue on multicolor underprint. Three elephants carrying loads at left center on back.			
	a. Issued note.	.50	1.25	5.00
	s. Specimen.	—	—	500.

34A	1000 Dông	VG	VF	UNC
	ND (1975). Green and multicolor. Stylized fish at left, Truong Cong Dinh at right. Dinh's tomb at upper left, stylized fish at right on back. Specimen. (Not issued).	—	—	4500.

#35 and 36 printer: TDLR.

35	5000 Dông	VG	VF	UNC
	ND (1975). Brown, blue and multicolor. Leopard at left center on back. (Not issued).			
	a. Normal serial #.	30.00	80.00	500.
	s. Specimen.	—	—	600.

36	10,000 Dông	VG	VF	UNC
	ND (1975). Violet and multicolor. Water buffalo at left center on back. (Not issued).			
	a. Normal serial #.	50.00	80.00	500.
	s. Specimen. *GIAY MAU.*	—	—	600.

NGÂN HÀNG VIÊT NAM

1966 DATED (1975) TRANSITIONAL ISSUE

#37-44 constitute a transitional issue of the Peoples Revolutionary Government that took over on April 30, 1975. The notes are dated 1966 but were not issued until 1975. They were used until the South's economic system was merged with that of the Democratic Republic of Viet Nam in 1978.

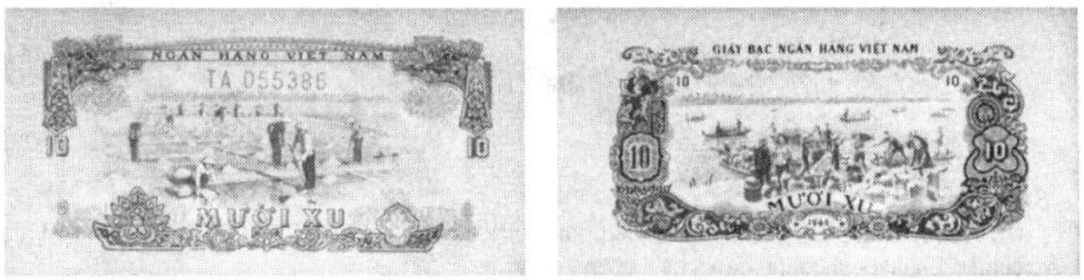

37	10 Xu	VG	VF	UNC
	1966 (1975). Brown on multicolor underprint. Drying salt at center Unloading boats on back.			
	a. Issued note.	.50	1.25	3.00
	s. Specimen.	—	—	15.00

38	20 Xu	VG	VF	UNC
	1966 (1975). Blue on multicolor underprint. Workers on rubber plantation at center. Soldiers greeting farmers with oxen on back.			
	a. Issued note.	.50	1.25	3.00
	s. Specimen.	—	—	15.00

39	50 Xu	VG	VF	UNC
	1966 (1975). Brownish purple on multicolor underprint. Harvesting cane at center. Women weaving rugs on back.			
	a. Issued note.	.50	2.50	8.00
	s. Specimen.	—	—	20.00

40	1 Dông	VG	VF	UNC
	1966 (1975). Red-orange on multicolor underprint. Boats on canal at center. Workers in field on back.			
	a. Issued note.	1.00	3.00	10.00
	s. Specimen.	—	—	20.00

41	2 Dông	VG	VF	UNC
	1966 (1975). Blue and green on multicolor underprint. Houseboats under a bridge at center. Soldiers and workers on back.			
	a. Issued note.	1.50	5.00	15.00
	s. Specimen.	—	—	20.00

		VG	VF	UNC
42	**5 Dông** 1966 (1975). Purple on multicolor underprint. Four women in textile factory at center. Armed soldiers with downed helicopters on back.			
	a. Issued note.	2.00	6.00	20.00
	s. Specimen.	—	—	25.00

		VG	VF	UNC
43	**10 Dông** 1966 (1975). Red on multicolor underprint. Three women and train at center. Soldiers and people with flag on back.			
	a. Issued note.	4.00	20.00	40.00
	s. Specimen.	—	—	25.00

		VG	VF	UNC
44	**50 Dông** 1966 (1975). Green and blue on multicolor underprint. Workers in factory at center. Combine harvester on back.			
	a. Issued note.	12.00	75.00	200.
	s. Specimen.	—	—	50.00

REGIONAL

ÚY BAN TRUNG U'O'NG

CENTRAL COMMITTEE OF THE NATIONAL FRONT FOR THE LIBERATION OF SOUTH VIETNAM

1963 ND ISSUE

#R1-R8 were printed in China for use in territories under control of the National Liberation Front. They were never issued, but many were captured during a joint US/South Viet Nam military operation into Cambodia. Except for #R2, relatively few survived in uncirculated condition.

		VG	VF	UNC
R1	**10 Xu** ND (1963). Purple and multicolor. Star at center.	.25	1.00	3.00
R2	**20 Xu** ND (1963). Red-brown on aqua and multicolor underprint. Star at center.	.25	1.00	5.00
R3	**50 Xu** ND (1963). Green and multicolor. Star at center.	.50	2.00	8.00

		VG	VF	UNC
R4	**1 Dông** ND (1963). Light brown on multicolor underprint. Harvesting at center. Schoolroom on back.	1.00	3.00	8.00

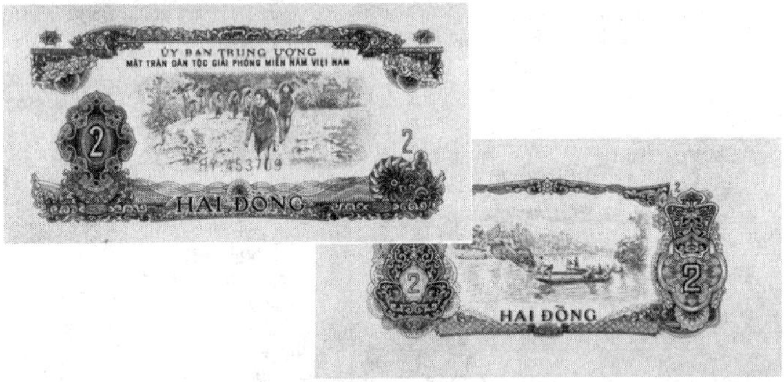

		VG	VF	UNC
R5	**2 Dông** ND (1963). Blue on multicolor underprint. Women in convoy at center. Fishermen with boats on back.	1.00	5.00	25.00
R6	**5 Dông** ND (1963). Lilac on multicolor underprint. Women harvesting at center. Women militia patrol on back.	1.50	6.00	50.00

		VG	VF	UNC
R7	**10 Dông** ND (1963). Green on multicolor underprint. Harvesting scene at center. War scene on back.	7.50	40.00	125.

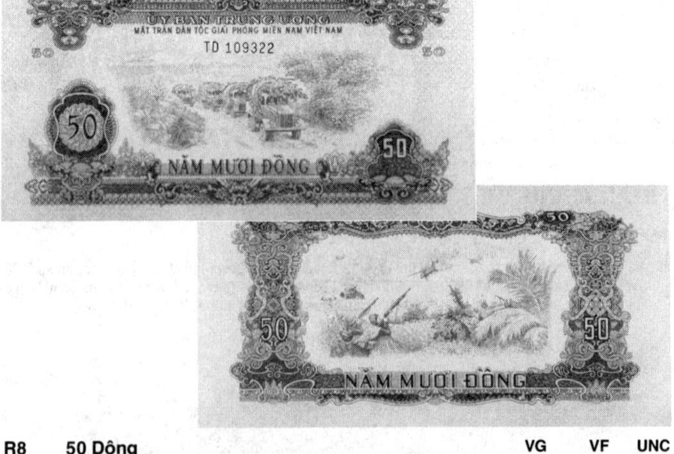

		VG	VF	UNC
R8	**50 Dông** ND (1963). Orange on multicolor underprint. Truck convoy at center. Soldiers shooting down helicopters on back.	12.50	75.00	175.

WEST AFRICAN STATES

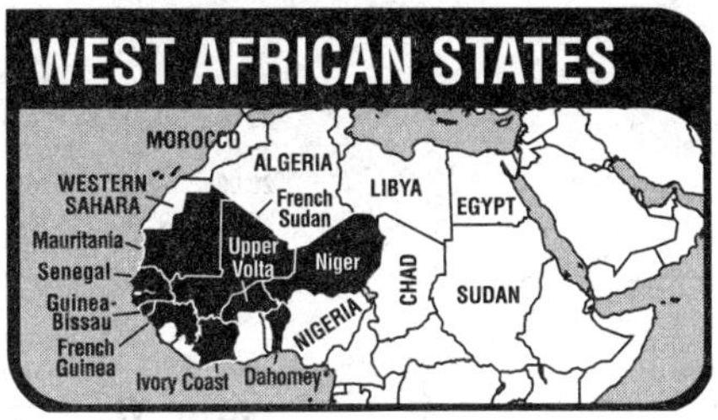

The West African States, a former federation of eight French colonial territories on the northwest coast of Africa, had an area of 1,813,079 sq. mi. (4,742,495 sq. km.) and a population of about 60 million. Capital: Dakar. The constituent territories were Mauritania, Senegal, Dahomey, French Sudan, Ivory Coast, Upper Volta, Niger and French Guinea.

The members of the federation were overseas territories within the French Union until Sept. of 1958 when all but French Guinea approved the constitution of the Fifth French Republic, thereby electing to become autonomous members of the new French Community. French Guinea voted to become the fully independent Republic of Guinea. The other seven attained independence in 1960. The French West Africa territories were provided with a common currency, a practice which was continued as the monetary union of the West African States which provides a common currency to the autonomous republics of Dahomey (now Benin), Mali, Senegal, Upper Volta (now Burkina Faso) Ivory Coast, Togo, Niger, and Guinea-Bissau.

MONETARY SYSTEM:

1 Franc = 100 Centimes

DATING:

The year of issue on the current notes appear in the first 2 digits of the serial number, i.e. (19)91, (19)92, etc.

SIGNATURE VARIETIES

	LE PRÉSIDENT	LE DIRECTEUR GÉNÉRAL	DATE
1			Various dates - 1959 20.3.1961
2			20.3.1961
3			20.12.1964
4			2.3.1965; ND
5			ND
6			ND
7			ND
8			ND
9			ND
	LE PRÉSIDENT DU CONSEIL DES MINISTRES	LE GOUVERNEUR	DATE
10			ND
11			ND (1977); 1977
12			ND (1978); 1978; 1979
13			ND (1980); 1980

SIGNATURE VARIETIES

14			ND (1977); 1977; 1988; 1989
15			ND (1981); 1981; 1982
16			ND (1983); 1983
17			1981; 1983; 1984
18			ND (1984); 1984
19			1984; 1985
20			1986; 1987
21			1989
22			1991
23			1992
24			1992
25			1993
26			1994
27			1994; 1995
28			1996; 1997
29			1999
30			2000; 2001
31			2002; 2003
32			2003

NOTICE

Readers with unlisted dates, signature varieties, etc. are invited to submit photocopies of their notes to: Standard Catalog of World Paper Money, 700 East State St. Iola, WI 54990-0001, E-Mail: george.cuhaj@fwpubs.com.

WEST AFRICAN STATES

Note: Beginning with signature #21 the signature positions have been reversed on the 500 Francs.

BANQUE CENTRALE DES ETATS DE L'AFRIQUE DE L'OUEST

A FOR COTE D'IVOIRE (IVORY COAST)

1959-65; ND ISSUE

101A 100 Francs

1961-65; ND. Dark brown, orange and multicolor. Design like #201B.

	VG	VF	UNC
a. Engraved. Signature 1. 20.3.1961.	8.00	20.00	65.00
b. Signature 2. 20.3.1961.	8.00	20.00	65.00
c. Litho. Signature 2. 20.3.1961.	10.00	25.00	70.00
d. Signature 3. 2.12.1964.	10.00	25.00	70.00
e. Signature 4. 2.3.1965.	8.00	20.00	65.00
f. Signature 4. ND.	5.00	15.00	45.00
g. Signature 5. ND.	5.00	15.00	45.00

102A 500 Francs

1959-64; ND. Brown, green and multicolor. Field workers at left, mask carving at right. Woman at left, farmer on tractor at right on back. Watermark: Woman's head.

	VG	VF	UNC
a. Engraved. signature 1. 15.4.1959.	25.00	55.00	150.
b. Signature 1. 20.3.1961.	12.00	35.00	90.00
c. Signature 2. 20.3.1961.	12.00	35.00	90.00
d. Signature 3. 2.12.1964.	25.00	55.00	150.
e. Signature 5. ND.	12.00	35.00	90.00
f. Signature 6. ND.	10.00	30.00	75.00
g. Litho. signature 6. ND.	13.00	40.00	100.
h. Signature 7. ND.	12.00	35.00	90.00
i. Signature 8. ND.	20.00	50.00	120.
j. Signature 9. ND.	8.00	25.00	60.00
k. Signature 10. ND.	5.00	15.00	45.00
l. Signature 11. ND.	5.00	15.00	40.00
m. Signature 12. ND.	7.50	25.00	90.00

103A 1000 Francs

1959-65; ND. Brown, blue and multicolor. Man and woman at center Man with rope suspension bridge in background and pineapples on back. Watermark: Man's head.

	VG	VF	UNC
a. Engraved. signature 1. 17.9.1959.	50.00	150.	—
b. Signature 1. 20.3.1961.	15.00	45.00	110.
c. Signature 2. 20.3.1961.	15.00	45.00	110.
d. Signature 4. 2.3.1965.	30.00	80.00	—
e. Signature 5. ND.	8.00	25.00	60.00
f. Signature 6. ND.	8.00	25.00	60.00
g. Litho. signature 6. ND.	8.00	25.00	60.00
h. Signature 7. ND.	10.00	30.00	70.00
i. Signature 8. ND.	12.00	40.00	90.00
j. Signature 9. ND.	8.00	25.00	60.00
k. Signature 10. ND.	5.00	15.00	40.00
l. Signature 11. ND.	5.00	15.00	35.00
m. Signature 12. ND.	5.00	15.00	35.00
n. Signature 13. ND.	5.00	15.00	35.00

104A 5000 Francs

1961-65; ND. Blue, brown and multicolor. Bearded man at left, building at center. Woman, corn grinders and huts on back.

	VG	VF	UNC
a. Signature 1. 20.3.1961.	35.00	100.	300.
b. Signature 2. 20.3.1961.	25.00	75.00	200.
c. Signature 3. 2.12.1964.	25.00	75.00	200.
d. Signature 4. 2.3.1965.	35.00	100.	—
e. Signature 6. ND.	25.00	50.00	175.
f. Signature 7. ND.	25.00	50.00	175.
g. Signature 8. ND.	35.00	100.	—
h. Signature 9. ND.	20.00	45.00	160.
i. Signature 10. ND.	20.00	40.00	150.
j. Signature 11. ND.	20.00	40.00	150.

1977-81; ND ISSUE

#105A-109A smaller size notes.

105A 500 Francs

1979-80. Lilac, light olive-green and multicolor. Artwork at left, long horn animals at center, man wearing hat at right. Cultivated palm at left, aerial view at center, mask at right on back. Watermark: Woman in profile.

	VG	VF	UNC
a. Signature 12. 1979.	3.00	10.00	25.00
b. Signature 13. 1980.	3.00	7.50	20.00

106A 500 Francs

1981-90. Pale olive-green and multicolor. Design like #105A.

	VG	VF	UNC
a. Signature 14. 1988.	.50	1.00	6.00
b. Signature 15. 1981. (BF).	5.00	15.00	35.00
c. Signature 15. 1981. (F-CO).	.50	3.00	7.00
d. Signature 15. 1982. (BF).	6.00	20.00	50.00
e. Signature 17. 1981. (F-CO).	6.00	20.00	50.00
f. Signature 17. 1983.	.50	3.00	7.00
g. Signature 18. 1984.	.50	3.00	7.00
h. Signature 19. 1984.	.50	3.00	7.00
i. Signature 19. 1985.	.50	3.00	7.00
j. Signature 20. 1986.	.50	1.00	6.00
k. Signature 20. 1987.	.50	3.00	10.00
l. Signature 21 (reversed order). 1989.	.50	1.00	5.00
m. Signature 22. 1990.	.50	1.00	5.00

Note: #106A w/10-digit small serial # were printed by Banque de France (BF) while those w/9-digit large serial # were printed by F-CO.

107A 1000 Francs

1981-90. Brown on multicolor underprint. Artwork at left, open pit mine at center, woman at right and as watermark. Wood carver with finished works on back.

	VG	VF	UNC
a. Signature 14. 1988.	1.00	2.00	10.00
b. Signature 15. 1981.	1.00	4.00	12.00
c. Signature 17. 1981.	1.00	4.00	12.00
d. Signature 18. 1984.	1.00	4.00	12.00
e. Signature 19. 1984.	1.00	12.00	30.00
f. Signature 19. 1985.	1.00	4.00	12.00
g. Signature 20. 1986.	1.00	2.00	10.00
h. Signature 20. 1987.	1.00	2.00	10.00
i. Signature 21. 1989.	1.00	2.00	9.00
j. Signature 22. 1990.	1.00	2.00	9.00

108A 5000 Francs

1977-91. Black and red on multicolor underprint. Woman at left, fish and boats on shore at center, carving at right. Carvings, fishing boats and mask on back.

	VG	VF	UNC
a. Signature 11. 1977.	15.00	25.00	60.00
b. Signature 12. 1978.	15.00	25.00	60.00
c. Signature 12. 1979.	25.00	45.00	100.
d. Signature 13. 1980.	25.00	50.00	110.
e. Signature 14. 1977.	20.00	35.00	80.00
f. Signature 14. 1988.	5.00	10.00	35.00
g. Signature 14. 1989.	5.00	10.00	35.00
h. Signature 15. 1981.	7.00	20.00	50.00
i. Signature 15. 1982.	7.00	20.00	50.00
j. Signature 16. 1983.	35.00	60.00	—
k. Signature 17. 1983.	20.00	35.00	80.00
l. Signature 18. 1984.	15.00	25.00	60.00
m. Signature 19. 1984.	7.00	20.00	50.00
n. Signature 19. 1985.	7.00	20.00	50.00
o. Signature 20. 1986.	20.00	35.00	80.00
p. Signature 20. 1987.	5.00	10.00	35.00
q. Signature 21. 1990.	5.00	10.00	35.00
r. Signature 22. 1991.	5.00	10.00	40.00

109A 10,000 Francs

ND (1977-92). Red-brown on multicolor underprint. Two men seated operating primitive spinning apparatus, woman with headwear at right and as watermark. Figurine and girl at left, modern textile spinning machine at center on back.

	VG	VF	UNC
a. Signature 11. ND.	20.00	35.00	85.00
b. Signature 12. ND.	20.00	35.00	95.00
c. Signature 13. ND.	20.00	35.00	95.00
d. Signature 14. ND.	10.00	20.00	60.00
e. Signature 15. ND.	10.00	20.00	65.00
f. Signature 18. ND.	20.00	35.00	85.00
g. Signature 19. ND.	25.00	40.00	100.
h. Signature 20. ND.	10.00	20.00	60.00
i. Signature 21. ND.	10.00	20.00	55.00
j. Signature 22. ND.	10.00	20.00	55.00
k. Signature 23. ND.	10.00	20.00	55.00

1991-92 ISSUE

#113A and 114A were first issued on 19.9.1994.

110A 500 Francs

(19)91-(20)02. Dark brown and dark green on multicolor underprint. Man at right and as watermark, flood control dam at center. Farmer riding spray rig behind garden tractor at center, native art at left on back.

	VG	VF	UNC
a. Signature 22. (19)91.	.25	1.00	4.00
b. Signature 23. (19)92.	1.00	4.00	10.00
c. Signature 25. (19)93.	.25	1.00	4.00
d. Signature 26. (19)94.	.25	1.00	4.00
e. Signature 27. (19)95.	.25	1.00	3.00
f. Signature 28. (19)96.	.25	1.00	3.00
g. Signature 28. (19)97.	.25	1.00	3.00
h. Signature 28. (19)98.	.25	1.00	3.00
i. Signature 28. (19)99.	.25	1.00	3.00
j. Signature 29. (19)99.	.25	1.00	3.00
k. Signature 30. (20)01.	.25	1.00	3.00
l. Signature 31. (20)02.	.25	1.00	3.00

111A 1000 Francs

(19)91-(20)03. Dark brown-violet on tan, yellow and multicolor underprint. Workmen hauling peanuts to storage at center, woman's head at right and as watermark. Twin statues and mask at left, two women with baskets, elevated riverside storage bins in background at center on back.

	VG	VF	UNC
a. Signature 22. (19)91.	.50	1.00	7.00
b. Signature 23. (19)92.	.50	1.00	7.00
c. Signature 25. (19)93.	.50	1.00	7.00
d. Signature 26. (19)94.	.50	1.00	7.00
e. Signature 27. (19)95.	.50	1.00	6.00
f. Signature 28. (19)96.	.50	1.00	6.00
g. Signature 28. (19)97.	.50	1.00	6.00
h. Signature 28. (19)98.	.50	1.00	6.00
i. Signature 29. (19)99.	.50	1.00	6.00
j. Signature 30. (20)01.	.50	1.00	5.00
k. Signature 31. (20)02.	.50	1.00	5.00
l. Signature 31. (20)03.	.50	1.00	5.00

112A 2500 Francs

(19)92-(19)94. Deep purple and dark brown on lilac and multicolor underprint. Dam at center, young woman's head at right and as watermark. Statue at left, harvesting and spraying of fruit at left center on back.

	VG	VF	UNC
a. Signature 23. (19)92.	1.00	4.00	20.00
b. Signature 25. (19)93.	1.00	4.00	20.00
c. Signature 27. (19)94.	1.00	4.00	20.00

113A 5000 Francs

(19)92-(20)03. Dark brown and deep blue on multicolor underprint. Woman wearing headdress adorned with cowrie shells at right and as watermark, smelting plant at center. Women with children and various pottery at left center on back.

	VG	VF	UNC
a. Signature 23. (19)92.	1.00	4.00	27.50
b. Signature 25. (19)93.	1.00	4.00	27.50
c. Signature 27. (19)94.	1.00	4.00	27.50
d. Signature 27. (19)95.	1.00	4.00	25.00
e. Signature 28. (19)96.	1.00	4.00	25.00
f. Signature 28. (19)97.	1.00	4.00	25.00
g. Signature 28. (19)98.	1.00	4.00	25.00
h. Signature 29. (19)98.	1.00	4.00	25.00
i. Signature 29. (19)99.	1.00	4.00	25.00
j. Signature 30. (20)00.	1.00	4.00	25.00
k. Signature 30. (20)01.	1.00	4.00	25.00
l. Signature 31. (20)02.	1.00	4.00	25.00
m. Signature 31. (20)03.	1.00	4.00	25.00

114A 10,000 Francs

(19)92-(20)01. Dark brown on multicolor underprint. Headman with scepter at right and as watermark, skyscraper at center. Native art at left, woman crossing vine bridge over river at center on back.

	VG	VF	UNC
a. Signature 25. (19)92.	1.00	7.00	50.00
b. Signature 27. (19)94.	1.00	7.00	50.00
c. Signature 27. (19)95.	1.00	7.00	45.00
d. Signature 28. (19)96.	1.00	7.00	45.00
e. Signature 28. (19)97.	1.00	7.00	40.00
f. Signature 28. (19)98.	1.00	7.00	40.00
g. Signature 29. (19)98.	1.00	7.00	35.00
h. Signature 29. (19)99.	1.00	7.00	35.00
i. Signature 30. (20)00.	1.00	7.00	35.00
j. Signature 30. (20)01.	1.00	7.00	35.00

2003 ISSUE

115A 1000 Francs

(20)03-. Red-brown on red and multicolor underprint.

	VG	VF	UNC
a. Signature 32. (20)03.	FV	FV	6.00
b. Signature 32. (20)04.	FV	FV	6.00

116A 2000 Francs

(20)03-. Blue on light blue and multicolor underprint.

	VG	VF	UNC
a. Signature 32. (20)03.	FV	FV	10.00
b. Signature 32. (20)04.	FV	FV	8.00

117A 5000 Francs

(20)03-. Multicolor.

	VG	VF	UNC
a. Signature 32. (20)03.	FV	FV	25.00
b. Signature 32. (20)04.	FV	FV	17.50

118A 10,000 Francs

(20)03-. Multicolor.

	VG	VF	UNC
a. Signature 32. (20)03.	FV	FV	40.00
b. Signature 32. (20)04.	FV	FV	30.00

1959-65; ND ISSUE

201B 100 Francs

1961-65; ND. Like #101A.

	VG	VF	UNC
a. Engraved. Signature 1. 20.3.1961.	12.00	40.00	120.
b. Signature 2. 20.3.1961.	10.00	35.00	100.
c. Litho. Signature 2. 20.3.1961.	10.00	35.00	100.
d. Signature 3. 2.12.1964.	12.00	40.00	120.
e. Signature 4. 2.3.1965.	7.50	20.00	65.00
f. Signature 4. ND.	5.00	15.00	45.00

202B 500 Francs

1961-64; ND. Like #102A.

	VG	VF	UNC
a. Signature 1. 20.3.1961.	50.00	—	—
b. Engraved signature 2. 20.3.1961.	25.00	65.00	150.
d. Signature 3. 2.12.1964.	—	—	—
e. Signature 4. 2.3.1965.	50.00	—	—
f. Signature 5. ND.	20.00	55.00	130.
g. Signature 6. ND.	10.00	30.00	80.00
h. Litho. Signature 7. ND.	12.00	35.00	90.00
i. Signature 8. ND.	50.00	125.	—
j. Signature 9. ND.	8.00	25.00	75.00
k. Signature 10. ND.	5.00	20.00	60.00
l. Signature 11. ND.	4.00	15.00	45.00

203B 1000 Francs

1961-65; ND. Like #103A.

	VG	VF	UNC
a. Engraved. Signature 1. 17.9.1959.	35.00	90.00	—
b. Signature 1. 20.3.1961.	35.00	90.00	—
c. Signature 2. 20.3.1961.	35.00	90.00	—
d. Signature 4. 2.3.1965.	25.00	60.00	140.
g. Signature 6. ND.	8.00	30.00	70.00
h. Litho. Signature 6. ND.	7.00	25.00	60.00
i. Signature 7. ND.	25.00	60.00	150.
j. Signature 8. ND.	10.00	35.00	100.
k. Signature 9. ND.	10.00	35.00	100.
l. Signature 10. ND.	5.00	15.00	50.00
m. Signature 11. ND.	5.00	15.00	45.00
n. Signature 12. ND.	5.00	15.00	50.00

204B 5000 Francs

1961; ND. Like #104A.

	VG	VF	UNC
a. Signature 1. 20.3.1961.	50.00	150.	—
b. Signature 2. 20.3.1961.	50.00	150.	—
h. Signature 6. ND.	25.00	75.00	200.
j. Signature 7. ND.	25.00	75.00	200.
k. Signature 9. ND.	20.00	50.00	175.
l. Signature 10. ND.	20.00	50.00	175.

1977-81; ND ISSUE

#205B-209B smaller size notes.

205B 500 Francs

1979-80. Like #105A.

	VG	VF	UNC
a. Signature 12. 1979.	6.00	20.00	50.00
b. Signature 13. 1980.	3.00	10.00	25.00

206B 500 Francs

1981-90. Like #106A.

	VG	VF	UNC
a. Signature 14. 1988.	4.00	12.00	—
b. Signature 15. 1981. (BF).	.50	3.00	10.00
c. Signature 15. 1981. (F-CO).	.50	3.00	10.00
d. Signature 15. 1982. (BF).	6.00	25.00	50.00
e. Signature 17. 1981. (F-CO).	6.00	25.00	—
f. Signature 17. 1983. (BF).	6.00	25.00	—
g. Signature 18. 1984.	.50	3.00	10.00
h. Signature 19. 1984.	.50	3.00	10.00
i. Signature 19. 1985.	2.00	8.00	20.00
j. Signature 20. 1986.	1.00	2.00	6.00
k. Signature 20. 1987.	2.00	8.00	20.00
l. Signature 21. 1989.	2.00	8.00	20.00
m. Signature 22. 1990.	1.00	2.00	6.00

Note: #206B w/10-digit small serial # were printed by Banque de France (BF) while those w/9-digit large serial # were printed by F-CO.

207B 1000 Francs

1981-90. Like #107A.

	VG	VF	UNC
a. Signature 14. 1988.	1.00	3.00	12.00
b. Signature 15. 1981.	1.00	5.00	20.00
c. Signature 18. 1984.	1.00	4.00	15.00
d. Signature 19. 1984.	10.00	40.00	—
e. Signature 19. 1985.	1.00	4.00	15.00
f. Signature 20. 1986.	1.00	3.00	12.00
g. Signature 20. 1987.	1.00	3.00	12.00
h. Signature 21. 1989.	5.00	25.00	—
i. Signature 22. 1990.	1.00	3.00	10.00

208B 5000 Francs	VG	VF	UNC
1977-92. Like #108A.			
a. Signature 12. 1979.	20.00	35.00	75.00
b. Signature 14. 1977.	20.00	35.00	80.00
c. Signature 14. 1988.	35.00	75.00	—
d. Signature 14. 1989.	5.00	10.00	35.00
e. Signature 15. 1981.	7.00	25.00	65.00
f. Signature 15. 1982.	7.00	20.00	55.00
g. Signature 17. 1983.	35.00	75.00	—
h. Signature 18. 1984.	35.00	75.00	—
i. Signature 19. 1985.	35.00	75.00	—
j. Signature 20. 1986.	35.00	75.00	—
k. Signature 20. 1987.	7.00	20.00	55.00
l. Signature 21. 1990.	5.00	10.00	35.00
m. Signature 22. 1991.	5.00	10.00	55.00
n. Signature 22. 1992.	5.00	10.00	30.00
o. Signature 23. 1992.	5.00	10.00	30.00
p. Signature 24. 1992.	20.00	40.00	—

209B 10,000 Francs	VG	VF	UNC
ND (1977-92). Like #109A.			
a. Signature 11. ND.	40.00	75.00	175.
b. Signature 12. ND.	40.00	75.00	—
c. Signature 14. ND.	15.00	40.00	100.
d. Signature 15. ND.	15.00	35.00	90.00
e. Signature 16. ND.	40.00	75.00	—
f. Signature 18. ND.	40.00	75.00	—
g. Signature 19. ND.	10.00	35.00	90.00
h. Signature 20. ND.	35.00	60.00	—
i. Signature 21. ND.	10.00	20.00	60.00
j. Signature 22. ND.	10.00	20.00	60.00
k. Signature 23. ND.	10.00	20.00	60.00

1991-92 ISSUE

210B 500 Francs	VG	VF	UNC
(19)91-(20)02. Like #110A.			
a. Signature 22. (19)91.	.25	1.00	5.00
b. Signature 22. (19)92.	1.00	5.00	15.00
c. Signature 23. (19)92.	1.00	5.00	15.00
d. Signature 25. (19)93.	.25	1.00	5.00
e. Signature 26. (19)94.	.25	1.00	5.00
f. Signature 27. (19)95.	.25	1.00	4.00
g. Signature 28. (19)96.	.25	1.00	4.00
h. Signature 28. (19)97.	.25	1.00	4.00
i. Signature 28. (19)98.	.25	1.00	4.00
j. Signature 29. (19)99.	.25	1.00	4.00
k. Signature 30. (20)00.	.25	1.00	4.00
l. Signature 30. (20)01.	.25	1.00	4.00
m. Signature 31. (20)02.	.25	1.00	4.00

211B 1000 Francs	VG	VF	UNC
(19)91-(20)02. Like #111A.			
a. Signature 22. (19)91.	.50	2.00	8.00
b. Signature 22. (19)92.	2.00	10.00	25.00
c. Signature 23. (19)92.	2.00	10.00	25.00
d. Signature 25. (19)93.	2.00	10.00	25.00
e. Signature 26. (19)94.	.50	1.50	8.00
f. Signature 27. (19)95.	.50	1.50	7.00
g. Signature 28. (19)96.	.50	1.50	7.00
h. Signature 28. (19)97.	.50	1.50	6.00
i. Signature 28. (19)98.	.50	1.50	6.00
j. Signature 29. (19)99.	.50	1.50	7.00
k. Signature 30. (20)00.	.50	1.50	6.00
l. Signature 30. (20)01.	.50	1.50	6.00
m. Signature 31. (20)02.	.50	1.50	6.00
n. Signature 31. (20)03.	.50	1.50	6.00

212B 2500 Francs	VG	VF	UNC
(19)92-(19)94. Like #112A.			
a. Signature 23. (19)92.	1.00	4.00	20.00
b. Signature 25. (19)93.	1.00	4.00	20.00
c. Signature 27. (19)94.	1.00	4.00	20.00

213B 5000 Francs	VG	VF	UNC
(19)92-(20)02. Like #113A.			
a. Signature 23. (19)92.	1.00	5.00	27.50
b. Signature 25. (19)93.	1.00	5.00	27.50
c. Signature 27. (19)94.	1.00	5.00	27.50
d. Signature 27. (19)95.	1.00	5.00	27.50
e. Signature 28. (19)96.	1.00	5.00	27.50
f. Signature 28. (19)97.	1.00	5.00	27.50
g. Signature 28 (19)98.	1.00	5.00	28.00
h. Signature 29. (19)98.	1.00	5.00	28.00
i. Signature 29. (19)99.	1.00	5.00	25.00
j. Signature 30. (20)00.	1.00	5.00	25.00
k. Signature 30. (20)01.	1.00	5.00	25.00
l. Signature 31. (20)02.	1.00	5.00	25.00
m. Signature 31. (20)03.	1.00	5.00	25.00

214B 10,000 Francs	VG	VF	UNC
(19)92-(20)01. Like #114A.			
a. Signature 25. (19)92.	2.00	8.00	50.00
b. Signature 27. (19)94.	2.00	8.00	50.00
c. Signature 27. (19)95.	2.00	8.00	45.00
d. Signature 28. (19)96.	2.00	8.00	45.00
e. Signature 28. (19)97.	2.00	8.00	45.00
f. Signature 28. (19)98.	2.00	8.00	45.00
g. Signature 29. (19)98.	2.00	8.00	45.00
h. Signature 29. (19)99.	2.00	8.00	45.00
i. Signature 30. (20)00.	2.00	8.00	45.00
j. Signature 30. (20)01.	2.00	8.00	45.00

2003 ISSUE

215B 1000 Francs	VG	VF	UNC
(20)03-. Red-brown on red and multicolor underprint.			
a. Signature 32. (20)03.	FV	FV	6.00
b. Signature 32. (20)04.	FV	FV	6.00

216B 2000 Francs	VG	VF	UNC
(20)03-. Blue on light blue and multicolor underprint.			
a. Signature 32. (20)03.	FV	FV	10.00
b. Signature 32. (20)04.	FV	FV	8.00

217B 5000 Francs	VG	VF	UNC
(20)03-. Multicolor.			
a. Signature 32. (20)03.	FV	FV	25.00
b. Signature 32. (20)04.	FV	FV	17.50

218B 10,000 Francs	VG	VF	UNC
(20)03-. Multicolor.			
a. Signature 32. (20)03.	FV	FV	40.00
b. Signature 32. (20)04.	FV	FV	30.00

1961; ND ISSUE

301C 100 Francs	VG	VF	UNC
1961-65; ND. Like #101A.			
a. Engraved. signature 1. 20.3.1961.	15.00	45.00	140.
b. Signature 2. 20.3.1961.	12.00	40.00	120.
c. Litho. Signature 2. 20.3.1961.	30.00	60.00	—
d. Signature 3. 2.12.1964.	—	—	—
e. Signature 4. 2.3.1965.	7.50	25.00	75.00
f. Signature 4. ND.	7.50	17.50	55.00

302C 500 Francs	VG	VF	UNC
1961-65; ND. Like #102A.			
a. Signature 1. 15.4.1959.	50.00	100.	—
b. Signature 1. 20.3.1961.	50.00	100.	—
c. Engraved. Signature 2. 20.3.1961.	25.00	75.00	160.
d. Signature 4. 20.3.1961.	20.00	65.00	—
e. Signature 4. 2.3.1965.	25.00	75.00	—
f. Signature 5. ND.	25.00	75.00	—
g. Signature 6. ND.	15.00	40.00	110.
h. Litho. Signature 6. ND.	10.00	30.00	100.
i. Signature 7. ND.	20.00	60.00	140.
k. Signature 8. ND.	15.00	40.00	90.00
l. Signature 9. ND.	7.50	25.00	75.00
m. Signature 11. ND.	5.00	15.00	45.00
n. Signature 12. ND.	5.00	15.00	50.00

303C 1000 Francs	VG	VF	UNC
1961; ND. Like #103A.			
a. Signature 1. 17.9.1959.	65.00	175.	—
b. Signature 1. 20.3.1961.	75.00	—	—
d. Signature 2. 20.3.1961.	30.00	90.00	—

303C 1000 Francs

	VG	VF	UNC
e. Signature 4. 2.3.1965.	65.00	175.	—
f. Signature 5. ND.	65.00	175.	—
g. Signature 6. ND.	25.00	60.00	140.
h. Signature 6. ND. Litho.	35.00	100.	—
i. Signature 7. ND.	20.00	45.00	120.
j. Signature 8. ND.	25.00	60.00	150.
k. Signature 9. ND.	10.00	30.00	80.00
l. Signature 10. ND.	5.00	15.00	50.00
m. Signature 11. ND	5.00	15.00	45.00
n. Signature 12. ND.	5.00	15.00	50.00
o. Signature 13. ND.	8.00	20.00	55.00

304C 5000 Francs
1961; ND. Like #104A.

	VG	VF	UNC
a. Signature 1. 20.3.1961.	35.00	90.00	300.
b. Signature 2. 20.3.1961.	100.	—	—
d. Signature 4. 2.3.1965.	100.	—	—
h. Signature 6. ND.	25.00	75.00	—
i. Signature 7. ND.	25.00	75.00	—
k. Signature 9. ND.	20.00	60.00	190.
l. Signature 11. ND.	20.00	50.00	175.

1977-81; ND Issues

#305C-309C smaller size notes.

305C 500 Francs
1979-80. Like #105A.

	VG	VF	UNC
a. Signature 12. 1979.	3.00	10.00	25.00
b. Signature 13. 1980.	2.50	8.00	20.00

306C 500 Francs
1981-90. Like #106A.

	VG	VF	UNC
a. Signature 14. 1988.	.60	3.00	7.00
b. Signature 15. 1981. (BF).	.50	3.00	10.00
c. Signature 15. 1981. (F-CO).	.50	3.00	8.00
d. Signature 15. 1982. (BF).	6.00	15.00	40.00
e. Signature 17. 1981. (F-CO).	6.00	15.00	—
f. Signature 17. 1983. (BF).	6.00	15.00	—
g. Signature 18. 1984.	.50	3.00	8.00
h. Signature 19. 1984.	.50	3.00	8.00
i. Signature 19. 1985.	.50	3.00	8.00
j. Signature 20. 1986.	.50	3.00	8.00
k. Signature 20. 1987.	3.00	10.00	25.00
l. Signature 21. 1989.	3.00	10.00	25.00
m. Signature 22. 1990.	.50	2.00	7.00

Note: #306C w/10-digit small serial # were printed by Banque de France (BF) while those w/9-digit large serial # were printed by F-CO.

307C 1000 Francs
1981-90. Like #107A.

	VG	VF	UNC
a. Signature 14. 1988.	1.00	3.00	10.00
b. Signature 15. 1981.	1.00	4.00	15.00
c. Signature 17. 1981.	5.00	25.00	—
d. Signature 18. 1984.	5.00	25.00	—
e. Signature 19. 1984.	5.00	25.00	—
f. Signature 19. 1985.	5.00	25.00	—
g. Signature 20. 1986.	1.00	4.00	15.00
h. Signature 20. 1987.	1.00	3.00	10.00
i. Signature 21. 1989.	1.00	4.00	15.00
j. Signature 22. 1990.	1.00	3.00	10.00

308C 5000 Francs
1977-92. Like #108A.

	VG	VF	UNC
a. Signature 12. 1978.	20.00	35.00	80.00
b. Signature 12. 1979.	20.00	35.00	80.00
c. Signature 14. 1977.	20.00	35.00	80.00
d. Signature 14. 1988.	5.00	10.00	35.00
e. Signature 14. 1989.	5.00	10.00	40.00
f. Signature 15. 1981.	5.00	20.00	60.00
g. Signature 15. 1982.	5.00	20.00	55.00
h. Signature 17. 1983.	5.00	20.00	55.00
i. Signature 18. 1984.	20.00	35.00	80.00
k. Signature 19. 1985.	5.00	20.00	60.00
l. Signature 20. 1986.	5.00	25.00	75.00
m. Signature 20. 1987.	5.00	25.00	70.00

308C 5000 Francs

	VG	VF	UNC
n. Signature 21. 1990.	5.00	10.00	35.00
o. Signature 22. 1991.	5.00	10.00	35.00
p. Signature 22. 1992.	5.00	10.00	35.00
q. Signature 23. 1992.	5.00	10.00	35.00
r. Signature 24. 1992.	20.00	40.00	—

309C 10,000 Francs
ND (1977-92). Like #109A.

	VG	VF	UNC
a. Signature 11. ND.	40.00	75.00	175.
b. Signature 12. ND.	25.00	50.00	100.
c. Signature 13. ND.	25.00	50.00	100.
d. Signature 14. ND.	30.00	65.00	150.
e. Signature 15. ND.	25.00	55.00	120.
f. Signature 20. ND.	10.00	30.00	80.00
g. Signature 21. ND.	8.00	15.00	55.00
h. Signature 22. ND.	8.00	15.00	55.00
i. Signature 23. ND.	8.00	15.00	55.00

1991 Issue

310C 500 Francs
(19)91-(20)02. Like #110A.

	VG	VF	UNC
a. Signature 22. (19)91.	.25	1.00	5.00
b. Signature 23. (19)92.	1.00	5.00	15.00
c. Signature 25. (19)93.	.25	1.00	7.00
d. Signature 26. (19)94.	.25	1.00	5.00
e. Signature 27. (19)95.	.25	1.00	4.00
f. Signature 28. (19)96.	.25	1.00	3.00
g. Signature 28. (19)97.	.25	1.00	3.00
h. Signature 28. (19)98.	.25	1.00	3.00
i. Signature 29. (19)99.	.25	1.00	3.00
j. Signature 30. (20)00.	.25	1.00	3.00
k. Signature 30. (20)01.	.25	1.00	3.00
l. Signature 31. (20)02.	.25	1.00	3.00

311C 1000 Francs
(19)91-(20)02. Like #111A.

	VG	VF	UNC
a. Signature 22. (19)91.	.50	1.50	8.00
b. Signature 22. (19)92.	3.00	8.00	25.00
c. Signature 23. (19)92.	3.00	8.00	25.00
d. Signature 25. (19)93.	.50	1.50	8.00
e. Signature 26. (19)94.	.50	1.50	7.00
f. Signature 27. (19)95.	.50	1.50	6.00
g. Signature 28. (19)96.	.50	1.50	6.00
h. Signature 28. (19)97.	.50	1.50	6.00
i. Signature 28. (19)98.	.50	1.50	6.00
j. Signature 29. (19)99.	.50	1.50	6.00
k. Signature 30. (20)00.	.50	1.50	6.00
l. Signature 30. (20)01.	.50	1.50	6.00
m. Signature 31. (20)02.	.50	1.50	6.00
n. Signature 31. (20)03.	.50	1.50	6.00

312C 2500 Francs
(19)92-(19)94. Like #112A.

	VG	VF	UNC
a. Signature 23. (19)92.	1.00	4.00	20.00
b. Signature 25. (19)93.	1.00	4.00	25.00
c. Signature 27. (19)94.	1.00	4.00	20.00

313C 5000 Francs
(19)92-(20)02. Like #113A.

	VG	VF	UNC
a. Signature 23. (19)92.	1.00	5.00	27.50
b. Signature 25. (19)93.	1.00	5.00	27.50
c. Signature 27. (19)94.	1.00	5.00	27.50
d. Signature 27. (19)95.	1.00	5.00	25.00
e. Signature 28. (19)96.	1.00	5.00	25.00
f. Signature 28. (19)97.	1.00	5.00	25.00
g. Signature 28. (19)98.	1.00	5.00	25.00
h. Signature 29. (19)98.	1.00	5.00	25.00
i. Signature 29. (19)99.	1.00	5.00	26.00
j. Signature 30. (20)00.	1.00	5.00	26.00
k. Signature 30. (20)01.	1.00	5.00	26.00
l. Signature 31. (20)02.	1.00	5.00	26.00
m. Signature 31. (20)03.	1.00	5.00	25.00

		VG	VF	UNC
314C	**10,000 Francs**			
	(19)92-(20)01. Like #114A.			
	a. Signature 25. (19)92.	2.00	8.00	50.00
	b. Signature 27. (19)94.	2.00	8.00	50.00
	c. Signature 27. (19)95.	2.00	8.00	45.00
	d. Signature 28. (19)96.	2.00	8.00	45.00
	e. Signature 28. (19)97.	2.00	8.00	45.00
	f. Signature 28. (19)98.	2.00	8.00	45.00
	g. Signature 29. (19)98.	2.00	8.00	45.00
	h. Signature 29. (19)99.	2.00	8.00	45.00
	i. Signature 30. (20)00.	2.00	8.00	45.00
	j. Signature 30. (20)01.	2.00	8.00	45.00

2003 ISSUE

		VG	VF	UNC
315C	**1000 Francs**			
	(20)03-. Red-brown on red and multicolor underprint.			
	a. Signature 32. (20)03.	FV	FV	6.00
	b. Signature 32. (20)04.	FV	FV	6.00

		VG	VF	UNC
316C	**2000 Francs**			
	(20)03-. Blue on light blue and multicolor underprint.			
	a. Signature 32. (20)03.	FV	FV	10.00
	b. Signature 32. (20)04.	FV	FV	8.00
317C	**5000 Francs**	VG	VF	UNC
	(20)03-. Multicolor.			
	a. Signature 32. (20)03.	FV	FV	25.00
	b. Signature 32. (20)04.	FV	FV	17.50

		VG	VF	UNC
318C	**10,000 Francs**			
	(20)03-. Multicolor.			
	a. Signature 32. (20)03.	FV	FV	40.00
	b. Signature 32. (20)04.	FV	FV	30.00

1959-61; ND ISSUE

		Good	Fine	XF
401D	**100 Francs**			
	20.3.1961. Like #101A. Signature left.	65.00	175.	—
402D	**500 Francs**			
	1959; 1961. Like #102A.			
	a. Signature I. 15.4.1959.	100.	300.	—
	b. Signature I. 20.3.1961.	—	—	—
403D	**1000 Francs**			
	1959; 1961. Like #103A.			
	a. Signature I. 17.9.1959.	85.00	250.	500.
	b. Signature I. 20.3.1961.	85.00	250.	500.
404D	**5000 Francs**			
	20.3.1961. Like #104A. Signature left.	150.	350.	650.

1981; ND ISSUE

#405D-408D smaller size notes.

		VG	VF	UNC
405D	**500 Francs**			
	1981-90. Like #106A.			
	a. Signature 14. 1988.	.50	2.00	7.00
	b. Signature 15. 1981. (BF).	.50	3.00	9.00
	c. Signature 17. 1981. (F-CO).	.50	3.00	9.00
	e. Signature 19. 1985.	.50	2.00	8.00
	f. Signature 20. 1986.	1.00	5.00	12.50
	g. Signature 20. 1987.	1.00	5.00	12.50
	h. Signature 21. 1989.	1.00	5.00	12.50
	i. Signature 22. 1990.	.50	2.00	5.00

Note: #405D w/10-digit small serial # were printed by Banque de France (BF) while those w/9-digit large serial # were printed by F-CO.

		VG	VF	UNC
406D	**1000 Francs**			
	1981-90. Like #107A.			
	a. Signature 14. 1988.	1.00	2.00	10.00
	b. Signature 15. 1981.	1.00	4.00	12.00
	c. Signature 17. 1981.	4.00	10.00	30.00
	f. Signature 19. 1985.	4.00	10.00	30.00
	g. Signature 20. 1986	4.00	10.00	30.00
	h. Signature 20. 1987.	4.00	10.00	30.00
	i. Signature 21. 1989.	1.00	2.00	9.00
	j. Signature 22. 1990.	1.00	2.00	10.00
407D	**5000 Francs**			
	1981-92. Like #108A.			
	a. Signature 14. 1988.	7.00	10.00	50.00
	b. Signature 14. 1989.	20.00	35.00	75.00
	c. Signature 15. 1981.	7.00	20.00	50.00
	d. Signature 17. 1984.	7.00	20.00	50.00
	e. Signature 18. 1984.	25.00	45.00	80.00
	f. Signature 19. 1985.	7.00	20.00	50.00
	g. Signature 20. 1986.	7.00	20.00	50.00
	h. Signature 20. 1987.	7.00	20.00	50.00
	i. Signature 21. 1990.	5.00	10.00	40.00
	j. Signature 22. 1991.	5.00	10.00	35.00
	k. Signature 23. 1992.	5.00	10.00	40.00
	l. Signature 24. 1992.	7.00	20.00	50.00
408D	**10,000 Francs**			
	ND (1981-92). Like #109A.			
	a. Signature 14. ND.	10.00	25.00	80.00
	b. Signature 15. ND.	10.00	25.00	80.00
	c. Signature 18. ND.	25.00	55.00	120.
	d. Signature 19. ND.	25.00	55.00	120.
	e. Signature 20. ND.	10.00	20.00	70.00
	f. Signature 21. ND.	10.00	20.00	55.00
	g. Signature 22. ND.	10.00	20.00	55.00

1991-92 ISSUE

		VG	VF	UNC
410D	**500 Francs**			
	(19)91-(20)02. Like #110A.			
	a. Signature 22. (19)91.	.25	1.00	4.00
	b. Signature 23. (19)92.	3.00	6.00	15.00
	c. Signature 25. (19)93.	.25	1.00	4.00
	d. Signature 26. (19)94.	.25	1.00	4.00
	e. Signature 27. (19)95.	.25	1.00	3.00

		VG	VF	UNC
410D	**500 Francs**			
	f. Signature 28. (19)96.	.25	1.00	3.00
	g. Signature 28. (19)97.	.25	1.00	3.00
	h. Signature 28. (19)98.	.25	1.00	3.00
	i. Signature 29. (19)99.	.25	1.00	3.00
	j. Signature 30. (20)00.	.25	1.00	3.00
	k. Signature 30. (20)01.	.25	1.00	3.00
	l. Signature 31. (20)02.	.25	1.00	3.00
	m. Signature 31. (20)03.	.25	1.00	4.00

		VG	VF	UNC
411D	**1000 Francs**			
	(19)91-(20)02. Like #111A.			
	a. Signature 22. (19)91.	.50	1.50	7.00
	b. Signature 23. (19)92.	1.50	10.00	25.00
	c. Signature 25. (19)93.	.50	1.50	7.00
	d. Signature 26. (19)94.	.50	1.50	7.00
	e. Signature 27. (19)95.	.50	1.50	6.00
	f. Signature 28. (19)96.	.50	1.50	6.00
	g. Signature 28. (19)97.	.50	1.50	6.00
	h. Signature 28. (19)98.	.50	1.50	6.00
	i. Signature 29. (19)99.	.50	1.50	6.00
	j. Signature 30. (20)00.	.50	1.50	6.00
	k. Signature 30. (20)01.	.50	1.50	6.00
	l. Signature 31. (20)02.	.50	1.50	6.00
	m. Signature 31. (20)03.	.50	1.50	6.00
412D	**2500 Francs**			
	(19)92-(19)94. Like #112A.			
	a. Signature 23. (19)92.	1.00	4.00	20.00
	b. Signature 25. (19)93.	1.00	4.00	30.00
	c. Signature 27. (19)94.	1.00	4.00	20.00
413D	**5000 Francs**			
	(19)92-(20)02. Like #113A.			
	a. Signature 23. (19)92.	1.00	5.00	27.50
	b. Signature 27. (19)94.	1.00	5.00	27.50
	c. Signature 27. (19)95.	1.00	5.00	27.50
	d. Signature 28. (19)96.	1.00	5.00	25.00
	e. Signature 28. (19)97.	1.00	5.00	25.00
	f. Signature 28. (19)98.	1.00	5.00	25.00
	g. Signature 29. (19)98.	1.00	5.00	25.00
	h. Signature 29. (19)99.	1.00	5.00	26.00
	i. Signature 30. (20)00.	1.00	5.00	25.00
	j. Signature 30. (20)01.	1.00	5.00	25.00
	k. Signature 31. (20)02.	1.00	5.00	25.00
	l. Signature 32. (20)03.	1.00	5.00	25.00
414D	**10,000 Francs**			
	(19)92-(20)02. Like #114A.			
	a. Signature 25. (19)92.	2.00	8.00	50.00
	b. Signature 27. (19)94.	2.00	8.00	50.00
	c. Signature 27. (19)95.	2.00	8.00	45.00
	d. Signature 28. (19)96.	2.00	8.00	45.00
	e. Signature 28. (19)97.	2.00	8.00	45.00
	f. Signature 28. (19)98.	2.00	8.00	45.00
	g. Signature 29. (19)98.	2.00	8.00	45.00
	h. Signature 29. (19)99.	2.00	8.00	45.00
	i. Signature 30. (20)00.	2.00	8.00	45.00
	j. Signature 30. (20)01.	2.00	—	45.00

2003 Issue

		VG	VF	UNC
415D	**1000 Francs**			
	(20)03-. Red on light red and multicolor underprint.			
	a. Signature 32. (20)03.	FV	FV	6.00
	b. Signature 32. (20)04.	FV	FV	6.00
416D	**2000 Francs**			
	(20)03-. Red-brown on red and multicolor underprint.			
	a. Signature 32. (20)03.	FV	FV	10.00
	b. Signature 32. (20)04.	FV	FV	8.00

		VG	VF	UNC
417D	**5000 Francs**			
	(20)03-. Multicolor.			
	a. Signature 32. (20)03.	FV	FV	25.00
	b. Signature 32. (20)04.	FV	FV	17.50
	c. Signature 33. (20)05.	FV	FV	17.50
418D	**10,000 Francs**	**VG**	**VF**	**UNC**
	(20)03-. Multicolor.			
	a. Signature 32. (20)03.	FV	FV	40.00
	b. Signature 32. (20)04.	FV	FV	30.00

1959-64; ND Issue

		Good	Fine	XF
501E	**100 Francs**			
	1961-65; ND. Like #101A.			
	b. Signature 1. 20.3.1961.	30.00	90.00	250.
	c. Signature 3. 2.12.1964.	30.00	90.00	250.
	e. Signature 4. 2.3.1965.	25.00	85.00	225.
	f. Signature 4. ND.	25.00	85.00	225.
502E	**500 Francs**			
	1959-64; ND. Like #102A.			
	a. Engraved. signature 1. 15.4.1959.	55.00	120.	400.
	b. Signature 1. 20.3.1961.	45.00	100.	350.
	c. Signature 2. 20.3.1961.	45.00	100.	350.
	e. Signature 4. 2.3.1965.	45.00	100.	350.
	f. Signature 5. ND.	45.00	100.	350.
	g. Signature 6. ND.	45.00	100.	350.
	h. Litho. signature 6. ND.	45.00	100.	350.
	i. Signature 7. ND.	45.00	100.	350.
503E	**1000 Francs**			
	1961-65; ND. Like #103A.			
	a. Signature 1. 17.9.1959.	100.	—	—
	b. Engraved. Signature 1. 20.3.1961.	55.00	130.	400.
	e. Signature 4. 2.3.1965.	45.00	130.	350.
	g. Signature 6. ND.	45.00	120.	350.
	h. Litho. Signature 6. ND.	45.00	120.	350.
504E	**5000 Francs**			
	1961-65; ND. Like #104A.			
	a. Signature 1. 20.3.1961.	65.00	150.	450.
	b. Signature 2. 20.3.1961.	65.00	150.	450.
	c. Signature 4. 2.3.1965.	65.00	150.	450.
	d. Signature 6. ND.	60.00	130.	400.
	e. Signature 7. ND.	60.00	130.	400.

1959-65; ND Issue

		VG	VF	UNC
601H	**100 Francs**			
	1961-65; ND. Like #101A.			
	a. Engraved. Signature 1. 20.3.1961.	15.00	45.00	140.
	b. Signature 2. 20.3.1961.	12.00	40.00	120.
	c. Litho. Signature 2. 20.3.1961.	12.00	40.00	120.
	d. Signature 3. 2.12.1964.	20.00	55.00	160.
	e. Signature 4. 2.3.1965.	8.00	25.00	75.00
	f. Signature 4. ND.	7.00	17.50	55.00
602H	**500 Francs**			
	1959-65; ND. Like #102A.			
	a. Engraved. signature 1. 15.4.1959.	50.00	125.	—
	c. Signature 2. 20.3.1961.	50.00	125.	—
	d. Signature 3. 2.12.1964.	25.00	75.00	175.
	e. Signature 4. 2.3.1965.	25.00	75.00	175.
	f. Signature 5. ND.	45.00	100.	—
	g. Signature 6. ND.	10.00	30.00	100.
	h. Litho. signature 6. ND.	10.00	30.00	100.
	i. Signature 7. ND.	20.00	65.00	150.
	j. Signature 8. ND.	10.00	30.00	100.
	k. Signature 9. ND.	8.00	25.00	80.00
	l. Signature 10. ND.	75.00	—	—
	m. Signature 11. ND.	5.00	15.00	55.00

603H 1000 Francs
1959-65; ND. Like #103A.

	VG	VF	UNC
a. Signature 1. 17.9.1959.	—	—	—
b. Signature 1. 20.3.1961.	30.00	65.00	175.
c. Signature 2. 20.3.1961.	75.00	—	—
e. Signature 4. 2.3.1965.	30.00	65.00	175.
f. Signature 5. ND.	30.00	65.00	175.
g. Signature 6. ND.	10.00	35.00	90.00
h. Litho. signature 6. ND.	20.00	45.00	125.
i. Signature 7. ND.	10.00	35.00	100.
j. Signature 8. ND.	30.00	65.00	—
k. Signature 9. ND	8.00	30.00	70.00
l. Signature 10. ND.	5.00	15.00	50.00
m. Signature 11. ND.	5.00	15.00	45.00
n. Signature 12. ND.	5.00	15.00	50.00
o. Signature 13. ND.	5.00	20.00	60.00

604H 5000 Francs
1961; 1965; ND. Like #104A.

	VG	VF	UNC
a. Signature 1. 20.3.1961.	100.	—	—
b. Signature 2. 20.3.1961.	40.00	150.	—
d. Signature 4. 2.3.1965.	40.00	150.	—
e. Signature 6. ND.	40.00	150.	—
i. Signature 7. ND.	40.00	150.	—
k. Signature 9. ND.	20.00	60.00	190.
l. Signature 10. ND.	20.00	60.00	190.
m. Signature 11. ND.	20.00	50.00	175.

1977-81; ND ISSUE

#605H-608H smaller size notes.

605H 500 Francs
1979-80. Like #105A.

	VG	VF	UNC
a. Signature 12. 1979.	6.00	17.50	40.00
b. Signature 13. 1980.	3.00	7.50	20.00

606H 500 Francs
1981-90. Like #106A.

	VG	VF	UNC
a. Signature 14. 1988.	.50	2.00	7.00
b. Signature 15. 1981. (BF).	6.00	15.00	35.00
c. Signature 15. 1981. (F-CO).	.50	3.00	8.00
d. Signature 15. 1982. (BF).	10.00	—	—
e. Signature 17. 1981. (F-CO).	.50	3.00	8.00
f. Signature 18. 1984.	10.00	45.00	—
g. Signature 19. 1984.	10.00	—	—
h. Signature 19. 1985.	8.00	—	—
i. Signature 20. 1986.	.50	2.00	7.00
j. Signature 20. 1987	.50	3.00	8.00
k. Signature 21. 1989.	.50	2.00	6.00
l. Signature 22. 1990.	.50	2.00	6.00

607H 1000 Francs
1981-90. Like #107A.

	VG	VF	UNC
a. Signature 14. 1988.	1.00	2.00	10.00
b. Signature 15. 1981.	1.00	4.00	15.00
c. Signature 17. 1981.	10.00	—	—
d. Signature 18. 1984.	5.00	15.00	40.00
e. Signature 19. 1984.	5.00	20.00	50.00
f. Signature 19. 1985.	1.00	4.00	15.00
g. Signature 20. 1986.	1.00	2.00	10.00
h. Signature 20. 1987.	1.00	2.00	10.00
i. Signature 21. 1989.	1.00	2.00	10.00
j. Signature 22. 1990.	1.00	2.00	10.00

608H 5000 Francs
1977-90. Like #108A.

	VG	VF	UNC
a. Signature 12. 1978.	20.00	35.00	80.00
b. Signature 12. 1979.	20.00	35.00	80.00
c. Signature 13. 1980.	30.00	50.00	110.
d. Signature 14. 1977.	20.00	35.00	80.00
e. Signature 14. 1989.	7.00	10.00	35.00
f. Signature 15. 1981.	7.00	20.00	60.00
g. Signature 15. 1982.	7.00	20.00	55.00
h. Signature 17. 1983.	7.00	20.00	55.00
i. Signature 18. 1984.	20.00	35.00	80.00
j. Signature 19. 1985.	7.00	20.00	55.00
k. Signature 20. 1986.	7.00	20.00	55.00
l. Signature 20. 1987.	5.00	10.00	35.00
m. Signature 21. 1990.	5.00	10.00	35.00
n. Signature 27. 1995.	5.00	10.00	35.00

609H 10,000 Francs
ND (1977). Like #109A.

	VG	VF	UNC
a. Signature 11. ND.	30.00	55.00	130.
b. Signature 12. ND.	50.00	—	—
c. Signature 13. ND.	50.00	—	—
d. Signature 14. ND.	10.00	20.00	65.00
e. Signature 15. ND.	15.00	35.00	90.00
f. Signature 18. ND.	30.00	55.00	130.
g. Signature 19. ND.	30.00	55.00	130.
h. Signature 20. ND.	10.00	20.00	65.00
i. Signature 21. ND.	10.00	20.00	60.00
j. Signature 22. ND.	10.00	20.00	50.00

1991-92 ISSUE

610H 500 Francs
(19)91-(20)02. Like #110A.

	VG	VF	UNC
a. Signature 22. (19)91.	.25	1.00	4.00
b. Signature 23. (19)92.	1.00	5.00	15.00
c. Signature 25. (19)93.	.25	1.00	5.00
d. Signature 26. (19)94.	.25	1.00	4.00
e. Signature 27. (19)95.	.25	1.00	3.00
f. Signature 28. (19)96.	.25	1.00	3.00
g. Signature 28. (19)97.	.25	1.00	3.00
h. Signature 28. (19)98.	.25	1.00	3.00
i. Signature 29. (19)99.	.25	1.00	3.00
j. Signature 30 (20)00.	.25	1.00	3.00
k. Signature 30. (20)01.	.25	1.00	3.00
l. Signature 31. (20)02.	.25	1.00	3.00

611H 1000 Francs
(19)91-(20)02. Like #111A.

	VG	VF	UNC
a. Signature 22. (19)91.	.50	1.50	8.00
b. Signature 23. (19)92.	.50	1.50	8.00
c. Signature 25. (19)93.	.50	1.50	8.00
d. Signature 26. (19)94.	.50	1.50	7.00
e. Signature 27. (19)95.	.50	1.50	6.00
f. Signature 28. (19)96.	.50	1.50	6.00
g. Signature 28. (19)97.	.50	1.50	6.00
h. Signature 28. (19)98.	.50	1.50	6.00
i. Signature 29. (19)99.	.50	1.50	6.00
j. Signature 30. (20)00.	.50	1.50	6.00
k. Signature 30. (20)02.	.50	1.50	6.00
l. Signature 31. (20)03.	.50	1.50	6.00

612H 2500 Francs
(19)92-(19)94. Like #112A.

	VG	VF	UNC
a. Signature 23. (19)92.	1.00	4.00	20.00
b. Signature 25. (19)93.	1.00	4.00	20.00
c. Signature 27. (19)94.	1.00	4.00	20.00

613H 5000 Francs
(19)92-(20)02. Like #113A.

	VG	VF	UNC
a. Signature 23. (19)92.	1.00	5.00	27.50
b. Signature 27. (19)94.	1.00	5.00	27.50
c. Signature 27. (19)95.	1.00	5.00	27.50
d. Signature 28. (19)96.	1.00	5.00	27.50
e. Signature 28. (19)97.	1.00	5.00	27.50
f. Signature 28. (19)98.	1.00	5.00	25.00
g. Signature 29. (19)98.	1.00	5.00	25.00
h. Signature 29. (19)99.	1.00	5.00	25.00
i. Signature 30. (20)00.	1.00	5.00	25.00
j. Signature 30. (20)01.	1.00	5.00	25.00
k. Signature 31. (20)02.	1.00	5.00	25.00
l. Signature 31. (20)03.	1.00	5.00	25.00

614H 10,000 Francs
(19)92-(20)01. Like #114A.

	VG	VF	UNC
a. Signature 25. (19)92.	2.00	8.00	50.00
b. Signature 27. (19)94.	2.00	8.00	50.00
c. Signature 27. (19)95.	2.00	8.00	45.00
d. Signature 28. (19)96.	2.00	8.00	45.00
e. Signature 28. (19)97.	2.00	8.00	45.00
f. Signature 28. (19)98.	2.00	8.00	45.00
g. Signature 29. (19)98.	2.00	8.00	45.00
h. Signature 29. (19)99.	2.00	8.00	45.00
i. Signature 30. (20)00.	2.00	8.00	45.00
j. Signature 30. (20)01.	2.00	8.00	45.00

2003 ISSUE

615H 1000 Francs
(20)03-. Red-brown on red and multicolor underprint.

	VG	VF	UNC
a. Signature 32. (20)03.	FV	FV	6.00
b. Signature 32. (20)04.	FV	FV	6.00

616H 2000 Francs
(20)03-. Blue on light blue and multicolor underprint.

	VG	VF	UNC
a. Signature 32. (20)03.	FV	FV	10.00
b. Signature 32. (20)04.	FV	FV	8.00

		VG	VF	UNC
617H	**5000 Francs**			
	(20)03-. Multicolor.			
	a. Signature 32. (20)03.	FV	FV	25.00
	b. Signature 32. (20)04.	FV	FV	17.50
618H	**10,000 Francs**			
	(20)03-. Multicolor.			
	a. Signature 32. (20)03.	FV	FV	40.00
	b. Signature 32. (20)04.	FV	FV	30.00

1959-65; ND Issue

		VG	VF	UNC
701K	**100 Francs**			
	1961-65; ND. Like #101A.			
	a. Engraved. Signature 1. 20.3.1961.	15.00	35.00	100.
	b. Signature 2. 20.3.1961.	10.00	25.00	70.00
	c. Litho. Signature 2. 20.3.1961.	10.00	25.00	70.00
	d. Signature 3. 2.12.1964.	10.00	25.00	80.00
	e. Signature 4. 2.3.1965.	8.00	20.00	65.00
	f. Signature 4. ND.	5.00	15.00	45.00
	g. Signature 5. ND.	15.00	35.00	100.
702K	**500 Francs**			
	1959-65; ND. Like #102A.			
	a. Engraved. signature 1. 15.4.1959.	25.00	55.00	150.
	b. Signature 1. 20.3.1961.	15.00	45.00	120.
	c. Signature 2. 20.3.1961.	15.00	45.00	120.
	d. Signature 3. 2.12.1964.	15.00	45.00	120.
	e. Signature 4. 2.3.1965.	12.00	40.00	100.
	f. Signature 5. ND.	18.00	50.00	130.
	g. Signature 6. ND.	8.00	25.00	75.00
	h. Litho. signature 6. ND.	8.00	25.00	75.00
	i. Signature 7. ND.	12.00	40.00	100.
	j. Signature 8. ND.	12.00	40.00	100.
	k. Signature 9. ND.	5.00	20.00	60.00
	l. Signature 10. ND.	4.00	15.00	50.00
	m. Signature 11. ND.	4.00	12.00	40.00
	n. Signature 12. ND.	4.00	15.00	45.00

		VG	VF	UNC
703K	**1000 Francs**			
	1959-65; ND. Like #103A.			
	a. Engraved. signature 1. 17.9.1959.	20.00	60.00	150.
	b. Signature 1. 20.3.1961.	20.00	60.00	150.
	c. Signature 2. 20.3.1961.	12.00	45.00	110.
	e. Signature 4. 2.3.1965.	12.00	45.00	110.
	f. Signature 5. ND.	35.00	90.00	—
	g. Signature 6. ND.	35.00	90.00	—
	h. Litho. signature 6. ND.	5.00	15.00	50.00
	i. Signature 7. ND.	8.00	20.00	60.00
	j. Signature 8. ND.	8.00	20.00	60.00
	k. Signature 9. ND.	5.00	15.00	50.00
	l. Signature 10. ND.	4.00	12.00	40.00
	m. Signature 11. ND.	4.00	10.00	35.00
	n. Signature 12. ND.	4.00	12.00	40.00
	o. Signature 13. ND.	4.00	12.00	40.00
704K	**5000 Francs**			
	1961-65; ND. Like #104A.			
	b. Signature 1. 20.3.1961.	30.00	80.00	225.
	c. Signature 2. 20.3.1961.	30.00	80.00	225.
	d. Signature 3. 2.12.1964.	30.00	80.00	225.
	e. Signature 4. 2.3.1965.	25.00	65.00	180.
	h. Signature 6. ND.	20.00	45.00	150.
	i. Signature 7. ND.	25.00	65.00	180.
	j. Signature 8. ND.	75.00	—	—
	k. Signature 9. ND.	20.00	65.00	180.
	l. Signature 10. ND.	20.00	45.00	160.
	m. Signature 11. ND.	20.00	40.00	140.

1977-81; ND Issue

#705K-709K smaller size notes.

		VG	VF	UNC
705K	**500 Francs**			
	1979-80. Like #105A.			
	a. Signature 12. 1979.	3.00	10.00	25.00
	b. Signature 13. 1980.	2.50	8.00	20.00
706K	**500 Francs**			
	1981-90. Like #106A.			
	a. Signature 14. 1988.	.50	1.00	6.00
	b. Signature 15. 1981 (BF).	5.00	15.00	35.00
	c. Signature 15. 1981. (F-CO).	.50	3.00	7.00
	d. Signature 15. 1982. (BF).	1.00	4.00	9.00
	e. Signature 17. 1981. (F-CO).	.50	3.00	7.00
	f. Signature 17. 1983. (BF).	1.00	4.00	9.00
	g. Signature 18. 1984.	.50	3.00	7.00
	h. Signature 19. 1985.	.50	3.00	7.00
	i. Signature 20. 1986.	.50	1.00	6.00
	j. Signature 20. 1987.	.50	1.00	6.00
	k. Signature 21. (reversed order). 1989.	.50	1.00	5.00
	l. Signature 22. 1990.	.50	1.00	5.00

Note: #706K w/10-digit small serial # were printed by Banque de France (BF) while those w/9-digit large serial # were printed by F-CO.

		VG	VF	UNC
707K	**1000 Francs**			
	1981-90. Like #107A.			
	a. Signature 14. 1988.	1.00	2.00	10.00
	b. Signature 15. 1981.	1.00	4.00	12.00
	c. Signature 17. 1981.	1.00	4.00	12.00
	d. Signature 18. 1984.	1.00	4.00	12.00
	e. Signature 19. 1984.	5.00	20.00	—
	f. Signature 19. 1985.	1.00	4.00	12.00
	g. Signature 20. 1986.	1.00	2.00	10.00
	h. Signature 20. 1987.	1.00	2.00	10.00
	i. Signature 21. 1989.	1.00	2.00	9.00
	j. Signature 22. 1990.	1.00	2.00	9.00
708K	**5000 Francs**			
	1977-92. Like #108A.			
	a. Signature 12. 1978.	15.00	25.00	60.00
	b. Signature 12. 1979.	20.00	35.00	90.00
	c. Signature 13. 1980.	25.00	45.00	110.
	d. Signature 14. 1977.	15.00	25.00	60.00
	e. Signature 14. 1989.	7.00	15.00	50.00
	f. Signature 15. 1982.	25.00	45.00	110.
	g. Signature 16. 1983.	30.00	50.00	130.
	h. Signature 17. 1983.	15.00	25.00	60.00
	i. Signature 18. 1984.	17.50	25.00	60.00
	j. Signature 19. 1985.	20.00	50.00	—
	k. Signature 20. 1986.	20.00	50.00	—
	l. Signature 20. 1987.	5.00	10.00	35.00
	m. Signature 21. 1990.	5.00	10.00	35.00
	n. Signature 22. 1991.	5.00	10.00	35.00
	o. Signature 22. 1992.	5.00	10.00	35.00
	p. Signature 23. 1992.	5.00	10.00	35.00
	q. Signature 24. 1992.	5.00	10.00	35.00
709K	**10,000 Francs**			
	ND. (1977-92). Like #109A.			
	a. Signature 11. ND.	20.00	35.00	95.00
	b. Signature 12. ND.	20.00	35.00	95.00
	c. Signature 13. ND.	20.00	40.00	100.
	d. Signature 14. ND.	10.00	20.00	60.00
	e. Signature 15. ND.	10.00	20.00	65.00
	f. Signature 16. ND.	20.00	45.00	110.
	h. Signature 18. ND.	10.00	25.00	75.00
	i. Signature 19. ND.	20.00	35.00	100.
	j. Signature 20. ND.	10.00	20.00	60.00
	k. Signature 21. ND.	10.00	20.00	55.00
	l. Signature 22. ND.	10.00	20.00	55.00
	m. Signature 23. ND.	10.00	20.00	55.00

1991-92 Issue

		VG	VF	UNC
710K	**500 Francs**			
	(19)91-(20)02. Like #110A.			

		VG	VF	UNC
710K	**500 Francs**			
	a. Signature 22. (19)91.	.25	1.00	4.00
	b. Signature 23. (19)92.	.25	1.00	4.00
	c. Signature 25. (19)93.	.25	1.00	4.00
	d. Signature 26. (19)94.	.25	1.00	4.00
	e. Signature 27. (19)95.	.25	1.00	3.00
	f. Signature 28. (19)96.	.25	1.00	3.00
	g. Signature 28. (19)97.	.25	1.00	3.00
	h. Signature 28. (19)98.	.25	1.00	3.00
	i. Signature 29. (19)99.	.25	1.00	3.00
	j. Signature 30. (20)00.	.25	1.00	3.00
	k. Signature 30. (20)01.	.25	1.00	3.00
	l. Signature 31. (20)02.	.25	1.00	3.00
711K	**1000 Francs**			
	(19)91-(20)02. Like #111A.			
	a. Signature 22. (19)91.	.50	1.00	7.00
	b. Signature 23. (19)92.	.50	1.00	7.00
	c. Signature 25. (19)93.	.50	1.00	7.00
	d. Signature 26. (19)94.	.50	1.00	10.00
	e. Signature 27. (19)95.	.50	1.00	6.00
	f. Signature 28. (19)96.	.50	1.00	6.00
	g. Signature 28. (19)97.	.50	1.00	6.00
	h. Signature 28. (19)98.	.50	1.00	6.00
	i. Signature 29. (19)99.	.50	1.00	6.00
	j. Signature 30. (20)00.	.50	1.00	6.00
	k. Signature 30. (20)01.	.50	1.00	6.00
	l. Signature 31. (20)02.	.50	1.00	6.00
	m. Signature 31. (20)03.	.50	1.00	6.00

		VG	VF	UNC
712K	**2500 Francs**			
	(19)92-(19)94. Like #112A.			
	a. Signature 23. (19)92.	1.00	4.00	20.00
	b. Signature 25. (19)93.	1.00	4.00	20.00
	c. Signature 27. (19)94.	1.00	4.00	20.00
713K	**5000 Francs**			
	(19)92-(20)02. Like #113A.			
	a. Signature 23. (19)92.	1.00	4.00	27.00
	b. Signature 25. (19)93.	1.00	4.00	27.00
	c. Signature 27. (19)94.	1.00	4.00	27.00
	d. Signature 27. (19)95.	1.00	4.00	27.00
	e. Signature 28. (19)96.	1.00	4.00	27.00
	f. Signature 28. (19)97.	1.00	4.00	25.00
	g. Signature 28. (19)98.	1.00	4.00	25.00
	h. Signature 29. (19)98.	1.00	4.00	25.00
	i. Signature 29. (19)99.	1.00	4.00	25.00
	j. Signature 30. (20)00.	1.00	4.00	25.00
	k. Signature 30. (20)01.	1.00	4.00	25.00
	l. Signature 31. (20)02.	1.00	4.00	25.00
	m. Signature 31. (20)03.	1.00	4.00	25.00
714K	**10,000 Francs**			
	(19)92-(20)01. Like #114A.			
	a. Signature 25. (19)92.	1.50	7.00	50.00
	b. Signature 27. (19)94.	1.50	7.00	50.00
	c. Signature 27. (19)95.	1.50	7.00	45.00
	d. Signature 28. (19)96.	1.50	7.00	45.00
	e. Signature 28. (19)97.	1.50	7.00	45.00
	f. Signature 28. (19)98.	1.50	7.00	45.00
	g. Signature 29. (19)98.	1.50	7.00	45.00
	h. Signature 29. (19)99.	1.50	7.00	45.00
	i. Signature 30. (20)00.	1.50	7.00	45.00
	j. Signature 30. (20)01.	1.50	7.00	45.00

2003 Issue

		VG	VF	UNC
715K	**1000 Francs**			
	(20)03-. Red-brown on red and multicolor underprint.			
	a. Signature 32. (20)03.	FV	FV	6.00
	b. Signature 32. (20)04.	FV	FV	6.00

		VG	VF	UNC
716K	**2000 Francs**			
	(20)03-. Blue on light blue and multicolor underprint.			
	a. Signature 32. (20)03.	FV	FV	10.00
	b. Signature 32. (20)04.	FV	FV	8.00
717K	**5000 Francs**			
	(20)03-. Multicolor.			
	a. Signature 32. (20)03.	FV	FV	25.00
	b. Signature 32. (20)04.	FV	FV	17.50
718K	**10,000 Francs**			
	(20)03-. Multicolor.			
	a. Signature 32. (20)03.	FV	FV	40.00
	b. Signature 32. (20)04.	FV	FV	30.00

1959-65; ND Issue

		VG	VF	UNC
801T	**100 Francs**			
	1961-65; ND. Like #101A.			
	a. Engraved. Signature 1. 20.3.1961.	15.00	35.00	100.
	b. Signature 2. 20.3.1961.	10.00	25.00	70.00
	c. Litho. Signature 2. 20.3.1961.	10.00	25.00	70.00
	d. Signature 3. 2.12.1964.	11.00	28.00	80.00
	e. Signature 4. 2.3.1965.	8.00	20.00	60.00
	f. Signature 4. ND.	5.00	15.00	45.00
	g. Signature 5. ND.	11.00	28.00	80.00
802T	**500 Francs**			
	1959-61; ND. Like #102A.			
	a. Engraved. signature 1. 15.4.1959.	25.00	55.00	150.
	b. Signature 1. 20.3.1961.	35.00	100.	—
	c. Signature 2. 20.3.1961.	35.00	100.	—
	f. Signature 5. ND.	25.00	55.00	150.
	g. Signature 6. ND.	8.00	25.00	75.00
	i. Litho. signature 7. ND.	20.00	50.00	130.
	j. Signature 8. ND.	20.00	50.00	130.
	k. Signature 9. ND.	5.00	20.00	60.00
	l. Signature 10. ND.	10.00	30.00	90.00
	m. Signature 11. ND.	1.00	5.00	30.00
803T	**1000 Francs**			
	1959-65; ND. Like #103A.			
	a. Engraved. signature 1. 17.9.1959.	75.00	—	—
	b. Signature 1. 20.3.1961.	20.00	60.00	150.
	c. Signature 2. 20.3.1961.	35.00	90.00	—
	e. Signature 4. 2.3.1965.	20.00	60.00	140.
	f. Signature 5. ND.	20.00	60.00	150.
	g. Signature 6. ND.	10.00	30.00	70.00
	h. Litho. signature 6. ND.	25.00	70.00	—
	i. Signature 7. ND.	10.00	30.00	70.00
	j. Signature 8. ND.	35.00	90.00	—
	k. Signature 9. ND.	5.00	20.00	50.00
	l. Signature 10. ND.	5.00	15.00	40.00
	m. Signature 11. ND.	4.00	10.00	35.00
	n. Signature 12. ND.	5.00	15.00	40.00
	o. Signature 13. ND.	5.00	15.00	40.00
804T	**5000 Francs**			
	1961; ND. Like #104A.			
	b. Signature 1. 20.3.1961.	35.00	90.00	250.
	h. Signature 6. ND.	25.00	75.00	200.
	i. Signature 7. ND.	50.00	150.	—
	j. Signature 8. ND.	50.00	150.	—
	k. Signature 9. ND.	25.00	65.00	175.
	m. Signature 11. ND.	20.00	40.00	140.

1977-81; ND Issue

#805T-809T smaller size notes.

		VG	VF	UNC
805T	**500 Francs**			
	1979. Like #105A. Signature 12.	3.00	8.00	20.00
806T	**500 Francs**			
	1981-90. Like #106A.			
	a. Signature 14. 1988.	6.00	15.00	—
	b. Signature 15. 1981. (BF).	1.00	3.00	7.00
	c. Signature 15. 1981. (F-CO).	1.00	3.00	7.00
	d. Signature 15. 1982. (BF).	1.50	5.00	20.00
	e. Signature 17. 1981. (F-CO).	1.50	5.00	20.00
	f. Signature 18. 1984.	6.00	15.00	40.0
	g. Signature 19. 1984.	1.00	5.00	10.

806T 500 Francs

	VG	VF	UNC
h. Signature 19. 1985.	.50	3.00	7.00
i. Signature 20. 1986.	.50	1.00	6.00
j. Signature 20. 1987.	.50	1.00	6.00
k. Signature 21. 1989.	.50	1.00	5.00
l. Signature 22. 1990.	.50	1.00	5.00

Note: #806T w/10-digit small serial # were printed by Banque de France (BF) while those w/9-digit large serial # were printed by F-CO.

807T 1000 Francs
1981-90. Like #107A.

	VG	VF	UNC
a. Signature 14. 1988.	1.00	2.00	10.00
b. Signature 15. 1981.	1.00	4.00	12.00
c. Signature 17. 1981.	2.00	6.00	25.00
d. Signature 18. 1984.	2.00	6.00	25.00
e. Signature 19. 1984.	5.00	15.00	—
f. Signature 19. 1985.	1.00	4.00	12.00
g. Signature 20. 1986.	5.00	15.00	—
h. Signature 20. 1987.	1.00	2.00	10.00
i. Signature 21. 1989.	1.00	2.00	9.00
j Signature 22. 1990.	1.00	2.00	9.00

808T 5000 Francs
1977-92. Like #108A.

	VG	VF	UNC
a. Signature 12. 1978.	20.00	35.00	90.00
b. Signature 12. 1979.	20.00	35.00	90.00
c. Signature 14. 1977.	15.00	25.00	60.00
d. Signature 14. 1989.	5.00	10.00	35.00
e. Signature 15. 1981.	25.00	45.00	—
f. Signature 15. 1982.	25.00	45.00	—
g. Signature 17. 1983.	40.00	—	—
h. Signature 18. 1984.	15.00	25.00	60.00
i. Signature 20. 1987.	5.00	10.00	35.00
j. Signature 21. 1990.	5.00	10.00	35.00
k. Signature 22. 1991.	5.00	10.00	35.00
l. Signature 22. 1992.	5.00	10.00	35.00
m. Signature 23. 1992.	5.00	10.00	35.00
n. Signature 24. 1992.	5.00	10.00	35.00

809T 10,000 Francs
ND. (1977-92). Like #109A.

	VG	VF	UNC
a. Signature 11. ND.	20.00	40.00	95.00
b. Signature 12. ND.	35.00	90.00	—
c. Signature 13. ND.	35.00	90.00	—
d. Signature 14. ND.	35.00	90.00	—
e. Signature 15. ND.	10.00	20.00	65.00
f. Signature 16. ND.	20.00	45.00	110.
h. Signature 18. ND.	10.00	20.00	65.00
k. Signature 22. ND.	10.00	20.00	55.00
l. Signature 23. ND.	10.00	20.00	55.00

1991-92 ISSUE

810T 500 Francs
(19)91-(20)02. Like #110A.

	VG	VF	UNC
a. Signature 22. (19)91.	.25	1.00	4.00
b. Signature 23. (19)92.	1.00	5.00	15.00
c. Signature 25. (19)93.	.25	1.00	4.00
d. Signature 26. (19)94.	.25	1.00	4.00
e. Signature 27. (19)95.	.25	1.00	3.00
f. Signature 28. (19)96.	.25	1.00	3.00
g. Signature 28. (19)97.	.25	1.00	3.00
h. Signature 28. (19)98.	.25	1.00	3.00
i. Signature 29. (19)99.	.25	1.00	3.00
j. Signature 30. (20)00.	.25	1.00	3.00
k. Signature 30. (20)01.	.25	1.00	3.00
l. Signature 31. (20)02.	.25	1.00	3.00

811T 1000 Francs
(19)91-(20)02. Like #111A.

	VG	VF	UNC
a. Signature 22. (19)91.	.50	1.50	7.00
b. Signature 23. (19)92.	.50	1.50	7.00
c. Signature 25. (19)93.	.50	1.50	7.00
d. Signature 26. (19)94.	.50	1.50	7.00
e. Signature 27. (19)95.	.50	1.50	6.00
f. Signature 28. (19)96.	.50	1.50	6.00
g. Signature 28. (19)97.	.50	1.50	6.00
h. Signature 28. (19)98.	.50	1.50	6.00
i. Signature 29. (19)99.	.50	1.50	6.00
j. Signature 30. (20)00.	.50	1.50	6.00
k. Signature 30. (20)01.	.50	1.50	6.00
l. Signature 31. (20)02.	.50	1.50	6.00
m. Signature 31. (20)03.	.50	1.50	6.00

812T 2500 Francs
(19)92-(19)94. Like #112A.

	VG	VF	UNC
a. Signature 23. (19)92.	1.00	4.00	20.00
b. Signature 25. (19)93.	1.00	4.00	20.00
c. Signature 27. (19)94.	1.00	4.00	20.00

813T 5000 Francs
(19)92-(20)02. Like #113A.

	VG	VF	UNC
a. Signature 23. (19)92.	1.00	5.00	27.50
b. Signature 25. (19)93.	1.00	5.00	27.50
c. Signature 27. (19)94.	1.00	5.00	27.50
d. Signature 27. (19)95.	1.00	5.00	25.00
e. Signature 28. (19)97.	1.00	5.00	25.00
f. Signature 28. (19)98.	1.00	5.00	25.00
g. Signature 29. (19)98.	1.00	5.00	25.00
h. Signature 29. (19)99.	1.00	5.00	25.00
i. Signature 30. (20)00.	1.00	5.00	25.00
j. Signature 30. (20)01.	1.00	5.00	25.00
k. Signature 31. (20)02.	1.00	5.00	25.00
l. Signature 31. (20)03.	1.00	5.00	25.00

814T 10,000 Francs
(19)92-(20)01. Like #114A.

	VG	VF	UNC
a. Signature 25. (19)92.	1.50	8.00	50.00
b. Signature 27. (19)94.	1.50	8.00	50.00
c. Signature 27. (19)95.	1.50	8.00	45.00
d. Signature 28. (19)96.	1.50	8.00	45.00
e. Signature 28. (19)97.	1.50	8.00	45.00
f. Signature 29. (19)99.	1.50	8.00	45.00
g. Signature 30. (20)00.	1.50	8.00	45.00
h. Signature 30. (20)01.	1.50	8.00	45.00

2003 ISSUE

815T 1000 Francs
(20)03-. Red-brown on red and multicolor underprint.

	VG	VF	UNC
a. Signature 32. (20)03.	FV	FV	6.00
b. Signature 32. (20)04.	FV	FV	6.00

816T 2000 Francs
(20)03-. Blue on light blue and multicolor underprint.

	VG	VF	UNC
a. Signature 32. (20)03.	FV	FV	10.00
b. Signature 32. (20)04.	FV	FV	8.00

817T 5000 Francs
(20)03-. Multicolor.

	VG	VF	UNC
a. Signature 32. (20)03.	FV	FV	25.00
b. Signature 32. (20)04.	FV	FV	17.50

818T 10,000 Francs
(20)03-. Multicolor.

	VG	VF	UNC
a. Signature 32. (20)03.	FV	FV	40.00
b. Signature 32. (20)04.	FV	FV	30.00

NOTICE

Readers with unlisted dates, signature varieties, etc. are invited to submit photocopies of their notes to: Standard Catalog of World Paper Money, 700 East State St. Iola, WI 54990-0001, E-Mail: george.cuhaj@fwpubs.com.

1997 ISSUE

		VG	VF	UNC
910S	**500 Francs** (19)97-(19)99. Like #110A.			
	a. Signature 28. (19)97.	.25	1.00	5.00
	b. Signature 28. (19)98.	.25	1.00	3.00
	c. Signature 29. (19)99.	.25	1.00	3.00
	d. Signature 30. (20)00.	.25	1.00	3.00
	f. Signature 31. (20)02.	.25	1.00	3.00
911S	**1000 Francs** (19)97-(19)99. Like #111A.			
	a. Signature 28. (19)97.	.50	2.00	8.00
	b. Signature 28. (19)98.	.50	2.00	6.00
	c. Signature 29. (19)99.	.50	2.00	6.00
	e. Signature 30. (20)01.	.50	2.00	6.00
	f. Signature 31. (20)02.	.50	2.00	6.00

		VG	VF	UNC
913S	**5000 Francs** (19)97-(20)00. Like #113A.			
	a. Signature 28. (19)97.	1.50	6.00	32.50
	b. Signature 28. (19)98.	1.50	6.00	25.00
	c. Signature 29. (19)98.	1.50	6.00	26.00
	d. Signature 29. (19)99.	1.50	6.00	26.00
	e. Signature 30. (20)00.	1.50	6.00	26.00
	g. Signature 31. (20)02.	1.50	6.00	25.00
	h. Signature 31. (20)03.	1.50	6.00	25.00
914S	**10,000 Francs** (19)97-(19)98. Like #114A.			
	a. Signature 28. (19)97.	2.50	15.00	55.00
	b. Signature 28. (19)98.	2.50	15.00	50.00
	d. Signature 29. (19)99.	2.50	15.00	45.00
	e. Signature 30. (20)00.	2.50	15.00	45.00

2003 ISSUE

		VG	VF	UNC
915S	**1000 Francs** (20)03-. Red-brown on red and multicolor underprint.			
	a. Signature 32. (20)03.	FV	FV	6.00
	b. Signature 32. (20)04.	FV	FV	6.00
916S	**2000 Francs** (20)03-. Blue on light blue and multicolor underprint.			
	a. Signature 32. (20)03.	FV	FV	10.00
	b. Signature 32. (20)04.	FV	FV	8.00
917S	**5000 Francs** (20)03-. Multicolor.			
	a. Signature 32. (20)03.	FV	FV	17.50
	b. Signature 32. (20)04.	FV	FV	17.50
918S	**10,000 Francs** (20)03-. Multicolor.			
	a. Signature 32. (20)03.	FV	FV	40.00
	b. Signature 32. (20)04.	FV	FV	30.00

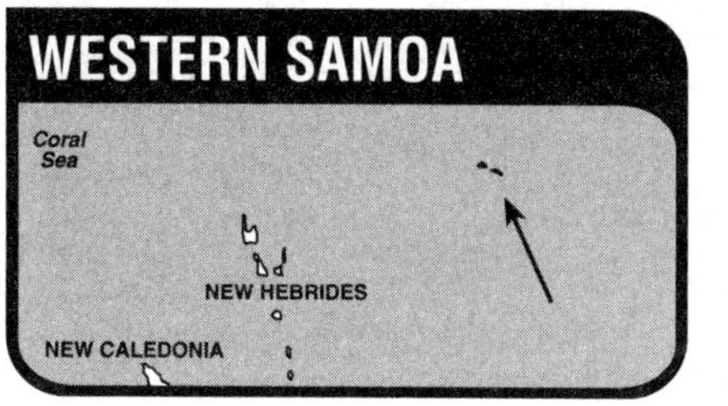

The Independent State of Western Samoa (formerly German Samoa), located in the Pacific Ocean 1,600 miles (2,574 km.) northeast of New Zealand, has an area of 1,097 sq. mi. (2,860 sq. km.) and a population of 157,000. Capital: Apia. The economy is d on agriculture, fishing and tourism. Copra, cocoa and bananas are exported.

The Samoan group of islands was discovered by Dutch navigator Jacob Roggeveen in 1772. Great Britain, the United States and Germany established consular representation at Apia in 1847, 1853 and 1861 respectively. The conflicting interests of the three powers produced the Berlin agreement of 1889 which declared Samoa neutral and had the effect of establishing a tripartite protectorate over the islands. A further agreement, 1899, recognized the rights of the United States in those islands east of 171 deg. west longitude (American Samoa) and of Germany in the other islands (Western Samoa). New Zealand occupied Western Samoa at the start of World War I and administered it as a League of Nations mandate and U.N. trusteeship until Jan. 1, 1962, when it became an independent state.

Western Samoa is a member of the Commonwealth of Nations. The Chief Executive is Chief of State. The prime minister is the Head of Government. The present Head of State, Malietoa Tanumafili II, holds his position for life. Future Heads of State will be elected by the Legislature Assembly for five-year terms.

RULERS:

British, 1914-1962
Malietoa Tanumafili II, 1962-

MONETARY SYSTEM:

1 Shilling = 12 Pence
1 Pound = 20 Shillings to 1967
1 Tala = 100 Sene, 1967-

NEW ZEALAND ADMINISTRATION

TERRITORY OF WESTERN SAMOA

1920-22 TREASURY NOTE ISSUE

By Authority of New Zealand Government

#7-9 various date and sign. varieties. Printer: BWC.

Note: Some of these notes may appear to be ND, probably through error or washed out, faded or worn off hand-stamped dates.

		Good	Fine	XF
7	**10 Shillings** 1922-59. Black on brown and green underprint. Palm trees along beach at center.			
	a. 3.3.1922.	—	—	—
	b. Signature title: *MINISTER OF EXTERNAL AFFAIRS FOR NEW ZEALAND* at left. 13.4.1938-21.11.1949.	50.00	175.	500.
	c. Signature title: *MINISTER OF ISLAND TERRITORIES FOR NEW ZEALAND* at left. 24.5.1951-27.5.1958; 29.10.1959.	75.00	250.	700.
	d. Signature title: *HIGH COMMISSIONER* at left. 20.3.1957-22.12.1959.	35.00	150.	500.
8A	**1 Pound** 1948-61. Purple on multicolor underprint. Like #8 but *STERLING* omitted from center.			
	a. Signature title: *MINISTER OF ISLAND TERRITORIES FOR NEW ZEALAND* at left. 6.8.1948-7.8.1958.	100.	400.	1250.
	b. Signature title: *HIGH COMMISSIONER* at left. 20.4.1959; 10.12.1959; 1.5.1961.	65.00	225.	1000.

BANK OF WESTERN SAMOA

1960-61 PROVISIONAL ISSUE

#10-12 red ovpt: *Bank of Western Samoa, Legal Tender in Western Samoa by virtue of the Bank of Western Samoa Ordinance 1959* on older notes. Various date and sign. varieties.

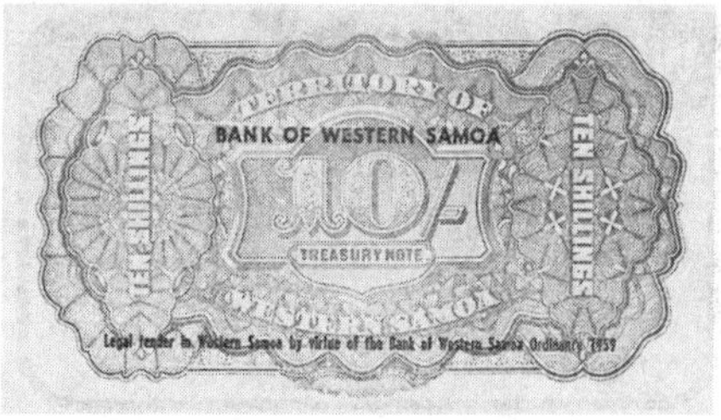

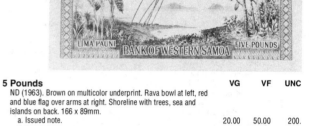

		VG	VF	UNC
10	**10 Shillings** 1960-61; ND. Overprint on #7.			
	a. Signature title: *HIGH COMMISSIONER* blocked out at lower left, with *MINISTER OF FINANCE* below. 8.12.1960; 1.5.1961.	35.00	150.	550.
	b. ND. signature title: *MINISTER OF FINANCE* in plate without ovpt., at lower left	35.00	150.	550.
11	**1 Pound** 1960-61. Overprint on #8.			
	a. Signature title: *HIGH COMMISSIONER* blocked out at lower left, with *MINISTER OF FINANCE* below. 8.11.1960; 1.5.1961.	65.00	300.	1150.
	b. Signature title: *MINISTER OF FINANCE* in plate without ovpt., at lower left 1.5.1961.	65.00	275.	1100.
12	**5 Pounds** 1.5.1961. Overprint on #9A.	500.	1750.	4500.

STATE

FALE TUPE O SAMOA I SISIFO

BANK OF WESTERN SAMOA

1963 ND ISSUE

		VG	VF	UNC
13	**10 Shillings** ND (1963). Dark green on multicolor underprint. Arms at left, boat at right. Hut and two palms at center on back.			
	a. Issued note.	2.50	10.00	65.00
	s. Specimen.	—	—	50.00

		VG	VF	UNC
14	**1 Pound** ND (1963). Blue on multicolor underprint. Palms and rising sun at left and right, arms at center. Small Building and lagoon at center on back. 159 x 83mm.			
	a. Issued note.	5.00	20.00	100.
	s. Specimen.	—	—	50.00

		VG	VF	UNC
15	**5 Pounds** ND (1963). Brown on multicolor underprint. Rava bowl at left, red and blue flag over arms at right. Shoreline with trees, sea and islands on back. 166 x 89mm.			
	a. Issued note.	20.00	50.00	200.
	s. Specimen.	—	—	200.

1967 ND ISSUE

Tala System

SIGNATURE VARIETIES			
1	MANAGER	2	MANAGER
3	MANAGER	4	SENIOR MANAGER

		VG	VF	UNC
16	**1 Tala** ND (1967). Dark green on multicolor underprint. Like #13.			
	a. Signature 1.	1.50	8.00	55.00
	b. Signature 2.	1.00	7.00	45.00
	c. Signature 3.	1.00	7.00	35.00
	d. Signature 4.	1.50	8.00	40.00
	s. Signature as a, b, d. Specimen.	—	—	40.00

		VG	VF	UNC
17	**2 Tala** ND (1967). Blue on multicolor underprint. Like #14, but 144 x 77mm.			
	a. Signature 1.	3.00	7.50	45.00
	b. Signature 3.	2.50	5.00	40.00
	c. Signature 4.	4.00	8.00	50.00
	s. Signature as a, c. Specimen.	—	—	50.00

#	Denomination	VG	VF	UNC
18	**10 Tala** ND (1967). Brown on multicolor underprint. Like #15, but 150 x 76mm.			
	a. Signature 1.	15.00	75.00	300.
	b. Signature 2.	15.00	90.00	350.
	c. Signature 3.	12.00	30.00	150.
	d. Signature 4.	12.00	35.00	165.
	s. Signature as a, b, d. Specimen.	—	—	60.00

KOMITI FAATINO O TUPE A SAMOA I SISIFO

MONETARY BOARD OF WESTERN SAMOA

1980-84 ND ISSUE

#19-23 national flag at l. ctr. on face and ctr. r. on back. Arms at lower ctr. r. on back. Wmk: M. Tanumafili II.

#	Denomination	VG	VF	UNC
19	**1 Tala** ND (1980). Dark green on multicolor underprint. Two weavers at right. Two fishermen in canoe at left center on back.	.75	2.00	10.00

#	Denomination	VG	VF	UNC
20	**2 Tala** ND (1980). Deep blue-violet on multicolor underprint. Woodcarver at right. Hut with palms on small island at left center on back.	1.50	3.00	15.00

#	Denomination	VG	VF	UNC
21	**5 Tala** ND (1980). Red on multicolor underprint. Child writing at right. Small port city at left center on back.	3.50	7.00	27.50

#	Denomination	VG	VF	UNC
22	**10 Tala** ND (1980). Dark brown and purple on multicolor underprint. Man picking bananas at right. Shoreline landscape on back.	7.50	30.00	135.
23	**20 Tala** ND (1984). Brown and orange-brown on multicolor underprint. Fisherman with net at right. Round building at left on back.	30.00	90.00	350.

#24 not assigned.

FALETUPE TUTOTONU O SAMOA

CENTRAL BANK OF SAMOA

1985 ND ISSUE

#25-30 like #20-23 but w/new issuer's name. Wmk: M. Tanumafili II.

#	Denomination	VG	VF	UNC
25	**2 Tala** ND (1985). Deep blue-violet on multicolor underprint. Like #20.	FV	FV	4.00
26	**5 Tala** ND (1985). Red on multicolor underprint. Like #21.	FV	FV	6.50
27	**10 Tala** ND (1985). Dark brown and purple on multicolor underprint. Like #22.	FV	FV	10.00
28	**20 Tala** ND (1985). Brown and orange-brown on multicolor underprint. Like #23.	FV	FV	20.00

#29-30 M. Tanumafili II at r.

#	Denomination	VG	VF	UNC
29	**50 Tala** ND (ca.1990). Green on multicolor underprint. Former home of Robert Louis Stevenson, current residence of Head of State at center. Man performing traditional knife dance on back.	FV	FV	40.00
30	**100 Tala** ND (ca.1990). Violet and light brown on multicolor underprint. Flag and Parliament building at center. Harvest scene on back.	FV	FV	65.00

1990 COMMEMORATIVE ISSUE

#31, Golden Jubilee of Service of the Head of State, Susuga Malietoa Tanumafili II, 1990

#	Denomination	VG	VF	UNC
31	**2 Tala** ND (1990). Brown, blue and purple on multicolor underprint. Samoan village at center, M. Tanumafili II at right. Clear area at lower right containing a Rava bowl visible from both sides. Family scene at center, arms at upper right on back. Polymer plastic. Printer: NPA (without imprint).			
	a. Text on face partly engraved. Serial # prefix *AAA.*	FV	FV	6.50
	b. Printing as a. Uncut sheet of 4 subjects. Serial # prefix *AAB.*	—	—	25.00
	c. Face completely lithographed, deeper blue, purple and dull brown. Serial # prefix *AAC.*	FV	FV	3.50
	d. Serial # prefix: *AAD.*	FV	FV	3.50
	e. Serial # prefix: *AAE.*	FV	FV	3.50

Note: #31a was also issued in a special folder.

2002 ND ISSUE

#	Denomination	VG	VF	UNC
32	**2 Tala** ND (2003). Brown, blue and purple on multicolor underprint. Expected new issue.	—	—	—

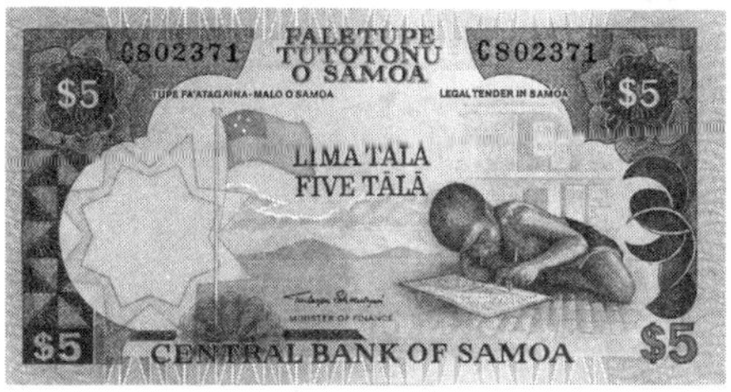

#	Denomination	VG	VF	UNC
33	**5 Tala** ND (2002). Red on multicolor underprint. Like #26.	FV	FV	6.50

NOTICE

Readers with unlisted dates, signature varieties, etc. are invited to submit photocopies of their notes to: Standard Catalog of World Paper Money, 700 East State St. Iola, WI 54990-0001, E-Mail: george.cuhaj@fwpubs.com.

		VG	VF	UNC
34	**10 Tala** ND (2002). Dark brown and purple on multicolor underprint. Like #27.	FV	FV	10.00

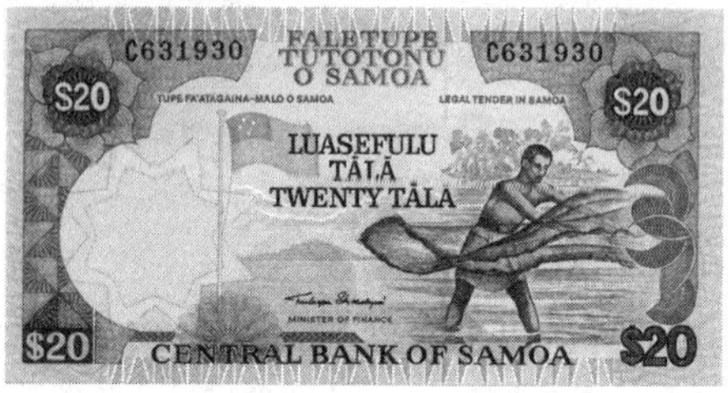

		VG	VF	UNC
35	**20 Tala** ND (2002). Brown and orange-brown on multicolor underprint. Like #28	FV	FV	20.00

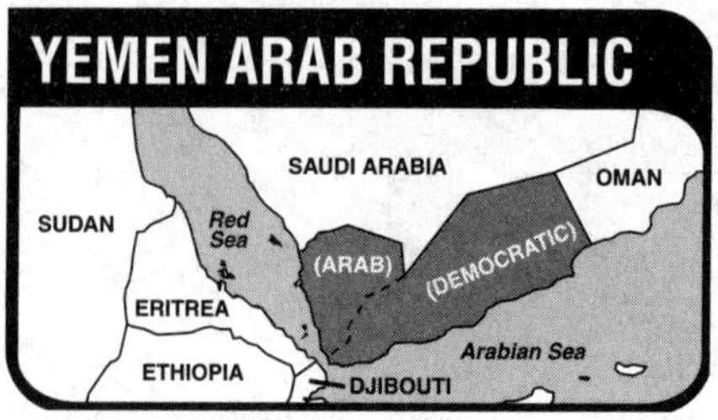

The Yemen Arab Republic, located in the southwestern corner of the Arabian Peninsula, has an area of 75,290 sq. mi. (195,000 sq. km.) and a population of 18.12 million. Capital: San'a. The industries of Yemen, one of the world's poorest countries, are agriculture and local handicrafts. Qat (a mildly narcotic leaf), coffee, cotton and rock salt are exported.

One of the oldest centers of civilization in the Near East, Yemen was once part of the Minaean Kingdom and of the ancient Kingdom of Sheba, after which it was captured successively by Egyptians, Ethiopians and Romans. It was converted to the Moslem religion in 628 AD and administered as a caliphate until 1538, when it came under Turkish occupation which was maintained until 1918 when autonomy was achieved through revolution.

On Feb. 1, 1958, Egypt and Syria formed the United Arab Republic. Yemen joined on March 8 in an association known as the United Arab States. Syria withdrew from the United Arab Republic on Sept. 29, 1961, and on Dec. 26 Egypt dissolved its ties with Yemen in the United Arab States.

Provoked by the harsh rule of Imam Mohammed al-Badr, last ruler of the Kingdom of Mutawwakkilite, the National Liberation Front seized control of the government on Sept. 27, 1962. Badr fled to Saudi Arabia.

An agreement for a constitution for a unified state was reached in Dec. 1989 uniting the Yemen Arab Republic with the People's Democratic Republic of Yemen into the Republic of Yemen on May 22, 1990. Both currencies circulated for a number of years, but the PDR dinar lost legal tender status on June 11, 1996.

RULERS:

Imam Ahmad, AH1367-1382/1948-1962AD
Imam al-Badr, AH1382-1388/1962-1968AD

MONETARY SYSTEM:

1 Rial = 40 Buqshas
1 Rial = 100 Fils (from April 1, 1995).

SIGNATURE VARIETIES

1	**Minister of the Treasury** **Abdul Ghani Ali, 1964**	2	**Minister of the Treasury and Economy** **Abdul Ghani Ali, 1967**
3	**Minister of the Treasury** **Ahmad al-Ruhumi, 1966 (actually inverted)**	4	**Minister of the Treasury** **Ahmad Abdu Said, 1968**
5	**Governor & Chairman, CBY** **Abdul Aziz Abdul Ghani, 1971-85**	6	**Governor & Chairman, CBY** **Abdulla Mohamed al-Sanabani, 1978-85**
7	**Governor & Chairman, CBY** **Abdulla Mohamed al-Sanabani, 1978-85**	8	**Governor, CBY** **Muhammad Ahmad Gunaid, 1985-94**
9	**Governor, CBY** **Aluwi Salih al-Salami, 1994**	10	**Governor, CBY** **Ahmed Abdul Rahman al-Samani, 1997-**

ARAB REPUBLIC

YEMEN CURRENCY BOARD

1964 ND ISSUE

#1-3 wmk: Arms.

		VG	VF	UNC
1	**1 Rial**			
	ND (1964; 1967). Green on multicolor underprint. Arms at left. Houses in Sana'a with minaret at center on back.			
	a. Signature 1. (1964).	2.50	15.00	100.
	b. Signature 2. (1967).	3.50	20.00	125.
	s. As a. Specimen.	—	—	225.

		VG	VF	UNC
2	**5 Rials**			
	ND (1964; 1967). Red on multicolor underprint. Arms at left. Lion of Timna sculpture at right on back.			
	a. Signature 1. (1964).	7.00	65.00	275.
	b. Signature 2. (1967).	8.00	75.00	300.
	s. As a. Specimen.	—	—	300.

		VG	VF	UNC
3	**10 Rials**			
	ND (1964; 1967). Blue-green on multicolor underprint. Arms at left. Dam at right on back.			
	a. Signature 1. (1964).	15.00	75.00	350.
	b. Signature 2. (1967).	15.00	75.00	350.
	s. As a. Specimen.	—	—	300.

1966-71 ND ISSUE

#4-10 wmk: Arms.

		VG	VF	UNC
4	**10 Buqshas**	1.25	4.00	17.50
	ND (1966). Brown on multicolor underprint. Lion of Timna sculpture at left. Ancient dedication stone from a temple at Ma'rib at right on back. Signature 3.			

		VG	VF	UNC
5	**20 Buqshas**	1.00	6.00	35.00
	ND (1966). Green on multicolor underprint. Tall alabaster head at left. Back olive-green; ruins of the Bara'an temple at right. Signature 3.			

#6-8 backs like #1-3.

		VG	VF	UNC
6	**1 Rial**			
	ND (1969). Green on multicolor underprint. Alabaster head at left. House in Sana'a with minaret on back. Signature 4.			
	a. Issued note.	2.00	15.00	75.00
	s. Specimen.	—	—	175.

		VG	VF	UNC
7	**5 Rials**			
	ND (1969). Red on multicolor underprint. Bronze lion's head sculpture at left. Lion of Timna sculpture at right on back. Signature 4.			
	a. Issued note.	7.50	45.00	200.
	s. Specimen.	—	—	250.

		VG	VF	UNC
8	**10 Rials**			
	ND (1969). Blue-green on multicolor underprint. Shadhili Mosque at left. Dam at right on back. Signature 4.			
	a. Issued note.	6.00	35.00	175.
	s. Specimen.	—	—	250.

		VG	VF	UNC
9	**20 Rials**			
	ND (1971). Purple and blue-green on multicolor underprint. Palace on the rock at Wadi Dahr. Back purple and gold; city view of Sana'a. Signature 4.			
	a. Issued note.	8.00	30.00	150.
	s. Specimen.	—	—	—

		VG	VF	UNC
10	**50 Rials**			
	ND (1971). Dark olive-green on multicolor underprint. Crossed *jambiyas* (daggers) at left. Coffee branch and tree, mountains in background at center right on back. Signature 4.	7.50	35.00	175.

CENTRAL BANK OF YEMEN

1973-77 ND ISSUES

#11-16 wmk: Arms.

		VG	VF	UNC
11	**1 Rial**			
	ND (1973). Green on multicolor underprint. Al Baqiliyah Mosque at left. Coffee plants with mountains in background at center on back.			
	a. Signature 5.	.10	.50	2.50
	b. Signature 7.	.50	2.50	7.50
	s. Specimen.	—	—	—
	ct. Color trial.	—	—	—

		VG	VF	UNC
12	**5 Rials**			
	ND (1973). Red on multicolor underprint. Buildings in Wadi Du'an at left. Beit al Midie on high rock hill at center on back. Signature 5.			
	a. Issued note.	.50	2.50	10.00
	s. Specimen.	—	—	—

		VG	VF	UNC
13	**10 Rials**			
	ND (1973). Blue-green on multicolor underprint. Bronze head of King Dhamer Ali at left. Republican Palace in Sana'a at center on back.			

		VG	VF	UNC
13	**10 Rials**			
	a. Signature 5.	1.00	3.50	15.00
	b. Signature 7.	.50	2.50	12.50
	s. Specimen.	—	—	—
	ct. Color trial.	—	—	—

		VG	VF	UNC
14	**20 Rials**			
	ND (1973). Purple on multicolor underprint. Marble sculpture of seated figure with grapes at left. Back purple and brown; terraced slopes along mountain at center right. Signature 5.			
	a. Issued note.	1.00	3.00	15.00
	ct. Color trial.	—	—	—

		VG	VF	UNC
15	**50 Rials**			
	ND (1973). Dark olive-green on multicolor underprint. Bronze statue of Ma'adkarib at left. Bab al Yemen (main gate of Sana'a) on back.			
	a. Signature 5.	1.00	5.00	35.00
	b. Signature 7.	.50	2.00	10.00
	s. Specimen.	—	—	—

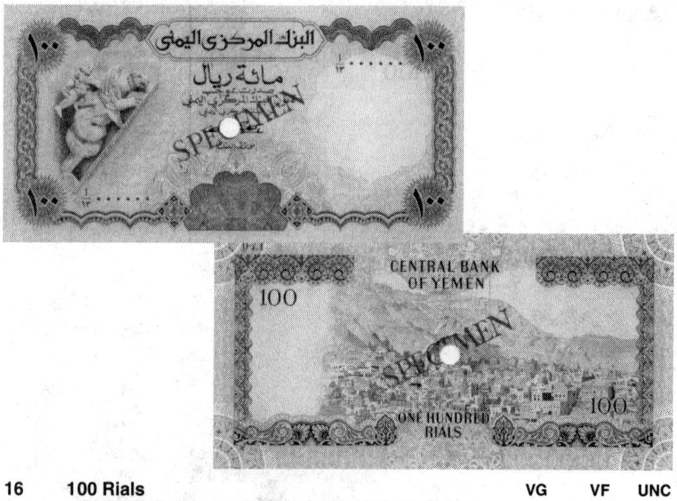

		VG	VF	UNC
16	**100 Rials**			
	ND (1976). Red-violet on multicolor underprint. Marble sculpture of cherub and griffin at left. View of Ta'izz on back. Signature 5.			
	a. Issued note.	10.00	40.00	200.
	s. Specimen.	—	—	—

1979-85 ND Issues

#16B-21A wmk: Arms.

		VG	VF	UNC
16B	**1 Rial** ND (1983). Like #11, but darker green and smaller serial #. Clearer underprint design over watermark area at right. Signature 7.	.10	.25	1.00

		VG	VF	UNC
17	**5 Rials** ND (1981). Red on orange and multicolor underprint. Dhahr al Dahab at left. Fortress Qal'at al Qahira overlooking Ta'izz at center right on back.			
	a. Signature 5. (1981).	.25	1.00	5.00
	b. Signature 7. (1983).	.15	.75	5.00
	c. Signature 8. (1991).	.10	.40	2.00

		VG	VF	UNC
18	**10 Rials** ND (1981). Blue on green and multicolor underprint. Village of Thulla at left. Al Baqiliyah Mosque on back.			
	a. Signature 5. (1981).	.50	2.00	12.50
	b. Signature 7. (1983).	.25	2.00	7.50

		VG	VF	UNC
19	**20 Rials** ND (1985). Purple on multicolor underprint. Face like #14. View of San'a on back.			

		VG	VF	UNC
19	**20 Rials**			
	a. Bank title on tan underprint. on back. Signature 7. (1983). 4mm serial #.	1.00	7.50	35.00
	b. As a. Signature 8. 3mm serial #.	.50	3.00	15.00
	c. Bank title on light brown underprint of vertical lines on back. Signature 8.	.50	2.00	10.00
	s. Specimen.	—	—	—

#20 *Deleted.* See #26.

		VG	VF	UNC
21	**100 Rials** ND (1979). Red-violet on multicolor underprint. Al Ashrafiya Mosque and Ta'izz city view at left. View of San'a with mountains on back. Signature 6.	1.00	5.00	25.00

		VG	VF	UNC
21A	**100 Rials** ND (1984). Red-violet on multicolor underprint. Face like #16 but different signature. Central Bank of Yemen building at center right on back. Signature 7.			
	a. Issued note.	.75	2.50	10.00
	s. Specimen.	—	—	—

1990-97 ND Issues

#23-31 wmk: Arms.

		VG	VF	UNC
23	**10 Rials** ND (1990-). Blue and black on multicolor underprint. Al Baqilyah Mosque at left. Back blue and brown; Ma'rib Dam at center right, *10* at upper corners. Two watermark varieties. Signature 8.	FV	FV	3.00

		VG	VF	UNC
24	**10 Rials**			
	ND (ca.1992). Face like #23. Back like #23, but with *10* at upper left and lower right. *10* with Arabic text: *Sadd Marib* near lower right. Signature 8.	FV	FV	3.00

		VG	VF	UNC
25	**20 Rials**			
	ND (1995). Dark brown on multicolor underprint. Arch ends straight border across upper center Marble sculpture of cupid with grapes at left. Coastal view of Aden, dhow on back. Signature 8.	FV	FV	5.00

		VG	VF	UNC
26	**20 Rials**			
	ND (1990). Dark brown on multicolor underprint. Face like #25. Different city view of San'a without minarets or dhow at center right on back. Signature 8.			
	a. Without shading around title of the bank.	FV	3.00	10.00
	b. With shading around title of the bank.	FV	2.00	5.00

		VG	VF	UNC
27	**50 Rials**			
	ND (1993). Black and deep olive-brown on multicolor underprint. Face like #15. Shibam city view at center right. Without Arabic title at lower left on back. Signature 8.	FV	FV	4.50
27A	**50 Rials**			
	ND (199?). Black and deep olive-brown on multicolor underprint. Like #27 but with Arabic title *Shibam Hadramaut* at lower left. on back. Signature 8, 9.	FV	FV	4.50

		VG	VF	UNC
28	**100 Rials**			
	ND (1993). Violet, purple and black on multicolor underprint. Ancient culvert in Aden at left. City view of Sana'a on back. Signature 8, 9.	FV	FV	3.00

		VG	VF	UNC
29	**200 Rials**			
	ND (1996). Deep blue-green on multicolor underprint. Alabaster sculpture of a man at left. Harbor view of Mukalla at center right on back. Signature 9.	FV	FV	7.50

		VG	VF	UNC
30	**500 Rials**			
	ND (1997). Blue-violet and red-brown on multicolor underprint. Central Bank of Yemen building at left. Bara'an temple ruins in brown at right on back. Signature 9.	FV	FV	12.00

1998-2001 ND Issues

#31-32 holographic strip w/arms repeated at l. Sign. 10.

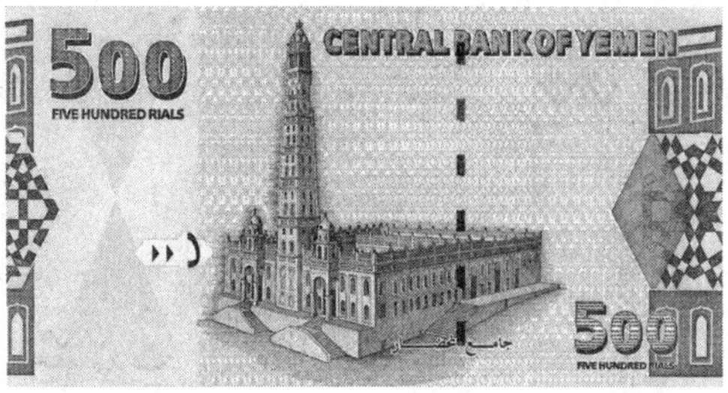

		VG	VF	UNC
31	**500 Rials** AH1422/2001. Light blue and gray on beige and multicolor underprint. Palace on the Rock at left. Al Muhdar mosque in Tarim, Hadramaut at center on back.	FV	FV	12.00

		VG	VF	UNC
32	**1000 Rials** ND (1998). Dark brown and dark green on multicolor underprint. Sultan's palace in Seiyun, Hadramaut at center. Bab al-Yemen and old city of Sana'a on back.	FV	FV	20.00

		VG	VF	UNC
33	**1000 Rials** 2004/AH1424. Dark brown and dark green on multicolor underprint. Similar to #15 but with color changes and date on front at lower right.	FV	FV	20.00

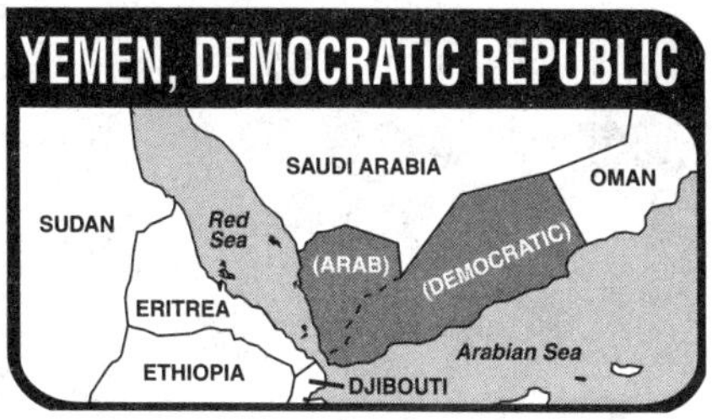

The People's Democratic Republic of Yemen, (formerly the Peoples Republic of Southern Yemen) was located on the southern coast of the Arabian Peninsula. It had an area of 128,560 sq. mi. (332,968 sq. km.). Capital: Aden. It consisted of the port city of Aden, 17 states of the former South Arabian Federation, 3 small sheikhdoms, 3 large sultanates, Quaiti, Kathiri and Mahri, which made up the Eastern Aden Protectorate, and Socotra, the largest island in the Arabian Sea. The port of Aden is the area's most valuable natural resource. Cotton, fish, coffee and hides are exported.

Between 1200 BC and the 6th century AD, what is now the People's Democratic Republic of Yemen was part of the Minaean kingdom. In subsequent years it was controlled by Persians, Egyptians and Turks. Aden, one of the cities mentioned in the Bible, had been a port for trade between the East and West for 2,000 years. British rule began in 1839 when the British East India Co. seized control to put an end to the piracy threatening trade with India. To protect their foothold in Aden, the British found it necessary to extend their control into the area known historically as the Hadramaut, and to sign protection treaties with the sheikhs of the hinterland. Eventually, 15 of the 16 Western Protectorate states, the Wahidi state of the Eastern Protectorate, and Aden Colony joined to form the Federation of South Arabia. In 1959, Britain agreed to prepare South Arabia for full independence, which was achieved on Nov. 30, 1967, at which time South Arabia, including Aden, changed its name to the People's Republic of Southern Yemen. On Dec. 1, 1970, following the overthrowing of the new government by the National Liberation Front, Southern Yemen changed its name to the People's Democratic Republic of Yemen. On May 22, 1990 the People's Democratic Republic merged with the Yemen Arab Republic into a unified Republic of Yemen. The YDR currency ceased to circulate on June 11, 1996.

MONETARY SYSTEM:

1 Dinar = 1000 Fils

FEDERATED STATE

SIGNATURE VARIETIES			
1		2	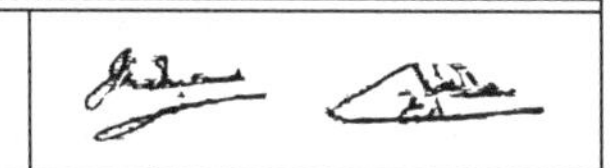
3	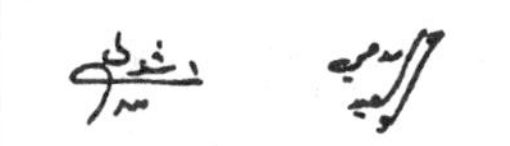	4	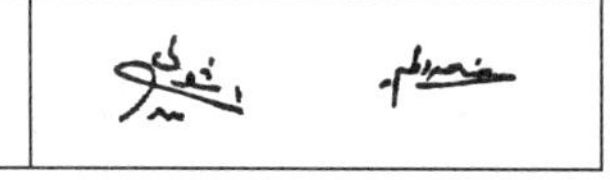

SOUTH ARABIAN CURRENCY AUTHORITY

1965 ND ISSUE

#1-5 Aden harbor, dhow at ctr. Wmk: Camel's head. Printer: TDLR.

		VG	VF	UNC
1	**250 Fils** ND (1965). Brown on multicolor underprint. Date palm at center on back.			
	a. Signature 1.	2.50	7.50	35.00
	b. Signature 2.	.50	3.00	12.50
	s. As a. Specimen.	—	—	35.00

2 500 Fils

		VG	VF	UNC
2	**500 Fils** ND (1965). Green on multicolor underprint. Date palm at center, heads of wheat at lower left. on back.			
	a. Signature 1.	3.50	20.00	85.00
	b. Signature 2.	2.00	6.00	30.00
	s. As a. Specimen.	—	—	50.00

		VG	VF	UNC
3	**1 Dinar** ND (1965). Dark blue on multicolor underprint. Date palm at center, branch of a cotton plant at left on back.			
	a. Signature 1.	7.50	25.00	150.
	b. Signature 2.	3.50	15.00	45.00
	s. As a. Specimen.	—	—	75.00

		VG	VF	UNC
4	**5 Dinars** ND (1965). Red on multicolor underprint. Date palm at center, cotton plant branch and millet flanking on back.			
	a. Signature 1.	17.50	75.00	350.
	b. Signature 2.	7.50	15.00	75.00
	s. As a. Specimen.	—	—	100.

		VG	VF	UNC
5	**10 Dinars** ND (1967). Deep olive-green on multicolor underprint. Date palm at center, cotton branch, corn cobs and heads of wheat around on back. Signature 2.	22.50	90.00	350.

PEOPLES DEMOCRATIC REPUBLIC

BANK OF YEMEN

1984 ND ISSUE

#6-9 similar to #1-5 but w/o English on face and w/new bank name on back. Capital: *ADEN* added to bottom r. on back. Wmk: Camel's head.

		VG	VF	UNC
6	**500 Fils** ND (1984). Green on multicolor underprint. Similar to #2.	.50	2.00	12.50

		VG	VF	UNC
7	**1 Dinar** ND (1984). Dark blue on multicolor underprint. Similar to #3.	1.00	5.00	20.00

8	5 Dinars	VG	VF	UNC
	ND (1984). Red on multicolor underprint. Similar to #4.			
	a. Signature 3.	5.00	20.00	100.
	b. Signature 4.	3.00	10.00	32.50

9	10 Dinars	VG	VF	UNC
	ND (1984). Deep olive-green on multicolor underprint. Similar to #5.			
	a. Signature 3.	7.50	22.50	110.
	b. Signature 4.	5.00	20.00	55.00

The Federal Republic of Yugoslavia is a Balkan country located on the east shore of the Adriatic Sea bordering Bosnia-Herzegovina and Croatia to the west, Hungary and Romania to the north, Bulgaria to the east, and Albania and Macedonia to the south. It has an area of 39,449 sq. mi. (102,173 sq. km.) and a population of 10.5 million. Capital: Belgrade. The chief industries are agriculture, mining, manufacturing and tourism. Machinery, nonferrous metals, meat and fabrics are exported.

The first South-Slavian State - Yugoslavia - was proclaimed on Dec. 1, 1918, after the union of the Kingdom of Serbia, Montenegro and the South Slav territories of Austria-Hungary; it then changed its official name from the Kingdom of the Serbs, Croats, and Slovenes to the Kingdom of Yugoslavia on Oct. 3, 1929. The Royal government of Yugoslavia attempted to remain neutral in World War II but, yielding to German pressure, aligned itself with the Axis powers in March of 1941; a few days later it was overthrown by a military-led coup and its neutrality reasserted. The Nazis occupied the country on April 17, and throughout the remaining years were resisted by a number of guerrilla armies, notably that of Marshal Josip Broz known as Tito. After the defeat of the Axis powers, a leftist coalition headed by Tito abolished the monarchy and, on Jan. 31, 1946, established a "People's Republic". Tito's rival General Draza Mihajlovic, who led the Chetniks against the Germans and Tito's forces, was arrested on March 13, 1946 and executed the following day after having been convicted by a partisan court.

The Federal Republic of Yugoslavia was composed of six autonomous republics: Serbia, Croatia, Slovenia, Bosnia-Herzegovina, Macedonia and Montenegro with two autonomous provinces within Serbia: Kosovo-Metohija and Vojvodina. The collapse of the Socialist Federal Republic of Yugoslavia during 1991-92 has resulted in the autonomous republics of Croatia, Slovenia, Bosnia-Herzegovina and Macedonia declaring their respective independence.

The Federal Republic of Yugoslavia was proclaimed in 1992; it consists of the former Republics of Serbia and Montenegro.

MONETARY SYSTEM:

1 Dinar = 100 Para
1 Dinar = 100 *Old* Dinara, 1965
1 Dinar = 10,000 *Old* Dinara, 1990-91
1 Dinar = 10 *Old* Dinara, 1992
1 Dinar = 1 Million *Old* Dinara, 1.10.1993
1 Dinar = 1 Milliard *Old* Dinara, 1.1.1994
1 Novi Dinar = 1 German Mark = 12,000,000 Dinara, 1.24.94

SIGNATURE VARIETIES

	VICE GOVERNOR	GOVERNOR
5	Isak Sion	Nikola Maljanich
6	Borivoje Jelich	Nikola Maljanich
7	Branislav Colanovich	Nikola Maljanich
8	Branislav Colanovich	Ivo Perishin
9	Joshko Shtrukelj	Branislav Colanovich
10	Ilija Marjanovich	Ksente Bogoev
11	Miodrag Veljkovich	Radovan Makich

SIGNATURE VARIETIES

12	Dr. Slobodan Stanojevich	Radovan Makich
13	Dr. Slobodan Stanojevich	Dushan Vlatkovitch
14	Mitja Gaspari	Dushan Vlatkovitch
15		Dushan Vlatkovitch
16		Vuk Ognjanovich
17		Borivoje Atanockovich
18		
19	Bozidar Gazivoda	
20	Bozidar Gazivoda	Dragoslav Avramovich

SOCIALIST FEDERAL REPUBLIC

НАРОДНА БАНКА ЈУГОСЛАВИЈЕ

NARODNA BANKA JUGOSLAVIJE

NATIONAL BANK OF YUGOSLAVIA

1963 ISSUE

#73-76 sign. 5. Replacement notes: Serial # prefix *ZA*.

		VG	VF	UNC
73	**100 Dinara** 1.5.1963. Dark red on multicolor underprint. Woman wearing national costume at left. View of Dubrovnik at center on back.			
	a. Issued note.	.10	.25	2.00
	s. Specimen.	—	—	40.00

		VG	VF	UNC
74	**500 Dinara** 1.5.1963. Dark green on multicolor underprint. Farm woman with sickle at left. Two combine harvesters at center on back.			
	a. Issued note.	.50	1.00	4.00
	s. Specimen.	—	—	50.00

		VG	VF	UNC
75	**1000 Dinara** 1.5.1963. Dark brown on multicolor underprint. Male steelworker at left. Factory complex at center on back.			
	a. Issued note.	.50	1.00	4.00
	s. Specimen.	—	—	30.00
76	**5000 Dinara** 1.5.1963. Dark blue on multicolor underprint. Relief of Mestrovic at left. Parliament building in Belgrade at center on back.			
	a. Issued note.	10.00	30.00	150.
	s. Specimen.	—	—	30.00
	x. Error. without serial #.	60.00	125.	225.

1965 ISSUE

#77-80 sign. 6. Replacement notes: Serial # prefix *ZA*.

		VG	VF	UNC
77	**5 Dinara** 1.8.1965. Dark green on multicolor underprint. Like #74. 134 x 64mm.			
	a. Small numerals in serial #.	.50	3.00	25.00
	b. Large numerals in serial #.	.50	1.50	15.00
	s. Specimen.	—	—	40.00
78	**10 Dinara** 1.8.1965. Dark brown on multicolor underprint. Like #75. 143 x 66mm.			
	a. Serial # like #77a.	.50	1.50	15.00
	b. Serial # like #77b.	1.00	5.00	25.00
	s. Specimen.	—	—	40.00
79	**50 Dinara** 1.8.1965. Dark blue on multicolor underprint. Like #76. 151 x 72mm.			
	a. Serial # like #77a.	1.00	5.00	40.00
	b. Serial # like #77b.	1.00	5.00	50.00
	s. Specimen.	—	—	40.00

		VG	VF	UNC
80	**100 Dinara** 1.8.1965. Red on multicolor underprint. Equestrian statue "Peace" of Augustincic in garden of United Nations, New York at left.			
	a. Serial # like #77a.	.75	4.00	20.00
	b. Serial # like #77b, but without security thread.	.50	2.00	10.00
	c. Serial # like #77b, but with security thread. 7 digit serial #.	.25	.75	5.00
	s. Specimen.	—	—	40.00

1968-70 Issue

#81-84 lg. numerals of value at l. ctr. on back. Sign. 7 or 8. Replacement notes: Serial # prefix *ZA*.

		VG	VF	UNC
81	**5 Dinara**			
	1.5.1968. Dark green on multicolor underprint. Face like #77. 123 x 59mm.			
	a. Serial # like #77a.	.05	.20	1.00
	b. Serial # like #77b.	.05	.20	1.00
	s. Specimen.	—	—	30.00

		VG	VF	UNC
82	**10 Dinara**			
	1.5.1968. Dark brown on multicolor underprint. Face like #78. 131 x 63mm.			
	a. Serial # like #77a.	.25	1.00	20.00
	b. Serial # like #80b.	.50	3.00	25.00
	c. Serial # like #80c.	.05	.15	.50
	s. Specimen.	—	—	30.00

		VG	VF	UNC
83	**50 Dinara**			
	1.5.1968. Dark blue on multicolor underprint. Face like #79. 139 x 66mm.			
	a. Serial # like #77a.	.50	1.50	20.00
	b. Serial # like #80b.	.20	.50	4.00
	c. Serial # like #80c.	.10	.25	1.00
	s. Specimen.	—	—	45.00
84	**500 Dinara**			
	1.8.1970. Dark olive-green on multicolor underprint. Statue of N. Tesla seated with open book at left.			
	a. Without security thread. signature 8.	.15	.50	2.50
	b. With security thread.	.50	1.50	6.00

1974 Issue

#85 and 86 sign. 9. Replacement notes: Serial # prefix *ZA*.

		VG	VF	UNC
85	**20 Dinara**			
	19.12.1974. Purple on multicolor underprint. Ship dockside at left. Two prefix letters plus 6 or 7-digit serial #.	.10	.25	1.50
86	**1000 Dinara**			
	19.12.1974. Blue-black on multicolor underprint. Woman with fruit at left.	.25	1.00	4.50

1978 Issue

#87-92 long, 2-line sign. title at l. and different sign. Replacement notes: Serial # prefix *ZA; ZB; ZC*.

		VG	VF	UNC
87	**10 Dinara**			
	1978; 1981. Dark brown on multicolor underprint. Like #82.			
	a. Signature 10. 12.8.1978.	.10	.20	.75
	b. Signature 11. 4.11.1981.	.10	.20	.75
88	**20 Dinara**			
	1978; 1981. Purple on multicolor underprint. Like #85.			
	a. Signature 10. 12.8.1978.	.05	.15	.75
	b. Signature 11. 4.11.1981.	.10	.25	2.00
89	**50 Dinara**			
	1978; 1981. Dark blue on multicolor underprint. Like #83.			
	a. Signature 10. 12.8.1978.	.05	.20	1.00
	b. Signature 11. 4.11.1981.	.05	.20	1.00

		VG	VF	UNC
90	**100 Dinara**			
	1978. Red on multicolor underprint. Like #80.			
	a. Signature 10. 12.8.1978.	.10	.25	1.25
	b. Signature 11. 4.11.1981.	.10	.25	1.25
	c. Signature 13. 16.5.1986.	.10	.20	1.00

		VG	VF	UNC
91	**500 Dinara**			
	1978; 1981; 1986. Dark olive-green on multicolor underprint. Like #84.			
	a. Signature 10. 12.8.1978.	.15	.50	2.00
	b. Signature 11. 4.11.1981.	.10	.50	1.00
	c. Signature 13. 16.5.1986.	.15	.50	2.00

92	1000 Dinara	VG	VF	UNC
	1978; 1981. Blue-black on multicolor underprint. Like #86.			
	a. Signature 10 with title at right: *GUVERNE* in Latin without final letter *R* (engraving error). Series AF. 12.8.1978.	.25	1.00	7.50
	b. As a. Series AR.	1.00	3.00	15.00
	c. Corrected signature title.	.15	.50	3.00
	d. Signature 11. 4.11.1981.	.05	.25	1.00

1985-89 ISSUE

93	5000 Dinara	VG	VF	UNC
	1.5.1985. Deep blue on multicolor underprint. Josip Broz Tito at left and as watermark, arms at center. Jajce in Bosnia at center on back. Signature 12.			
	a. Corrected year of Tito's death - *1980.*	.10	.50	3.50
	x. Error: Tito's death date as *1930* instead of *1980.*	2.00	10.00	65.00

#94 not assigned.

95	20,000 Dinara	VG	VF	UNC
	1.5.1987. Brown on multicolor underprint. Miner at left and as watermark, arms at center. Mining equipment at center on back. Signature 13.	.05	.25	1.50

96	50,000 Dinara	VG	VF	UNC
	1.5.1988. Green and blue on multicolor underprint. Girl at left and as watermark, arms at center. City of Dubrovnik at center on back. Signature 13.	.50	1.00	3.50

#97-100 sign. 14.

97	100,000 Dinara	VG	VF	UNC
	1.5.1989. Violet and red on multicolor underprint. Young girl at left and as watermark, arms at center. Abstract design with letters and numbers at center right on back.	.20	.75	3.50

98	500,000 Dinara	VG	VF	UNC
	Aug. 1989. Deep purple and blue on lilac underprint. Arms at left, Partisan monument "Kozara" at right. Partisan monument "Sutjeska" at center on back.			
	a. Issued note.	.25	1.50	7.00
	s. Specimen.	—	—	50.00

99	1,000,000 Dinara	VG	VF	UNC
	1.11.1989. Light olive-green on orange and gold underprint. Young woman at left and as watermark, arms at center. Stylized stalk of wheat on back.	.25	1.50	10.00

100	2,000,000 Dinara	VG	VF	UNC
	Aug. 1989. Pale olive-green and brown on light orange underprint. Face like #98. Partisan "V3" monument at Kragujevac at center on back.			
	a. Issued note.	2.00	12.50	65.00
	s. Specimen.	—	—	50.00

1990 First Issue

#101 and 102 sign. 14. Replacement notes: Serial # prefix *ZA*.

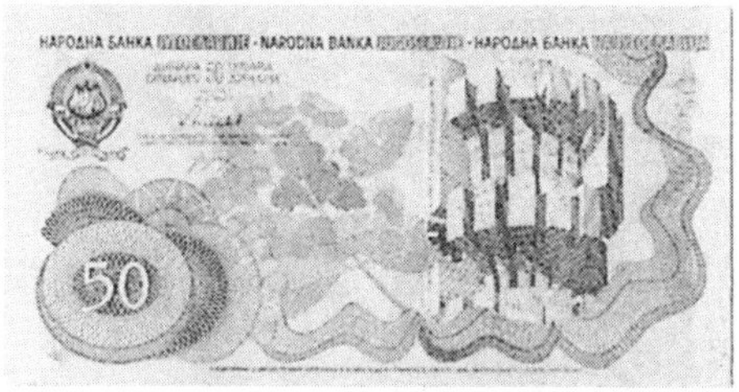

101	50 Dinara	VG	VF	UNC
	1.1.1990. Deep purple and blue on lilac underprint. Similar to #98.			
	a. Issued note.	.50	3.00	25.00
	s. Specimen.	—	—	50.00

101A	100 Dinara	VG	VF	UNC
	ND (1990). Black and dark olive-green on pink and yellow-green underprint. Marshal Tito at right, flags in underprint at center, arms at upper left. Partisan monument "Sutjeska" at center on back. (Not issued).	—	—	1000.

102	200 Dinara	VG	VF	UNC
	1.1.1990. Pale olive-green and brown on light orange underprint. Similar to #100.			
	a. Issued note.	1.00	4.00	25.00
	s. Specimen.	—	—	50.00

1990 Second Issue

#103-107 arms at ctr. Sign. 14. Replacement notes: Serial # prefix *ZA*.

103	10 Dinara	VG	VF	UNC
	1.9.1990. Violet and red on multicolor underprint. Similar to #97.	.05	.20	1.50

104	50 Dinara	VG	VF	UNC
	1.6.1990. Purple. Young boy at left and as watermark. Roses at center right on back.	.05	.25	1.50
105	100 Dinara			
	1.3.1990. Light olive-green on orange and gold underprint. Similar to #99.	.20	.50	7.00
106	500 Dinara			
	1.3.1990. Blue and purple. Young man at left and as watermark Mountain scene on back.	.20	.50	7.00

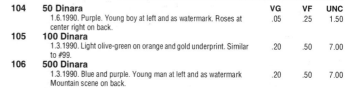

106A	500 Dinara	VG	VF	UNC
	Brown and orange. Like #106. (Not issued).	—	—	225.

107	1000 Dinara	VG	VF	UNC
	26.11.1990. Brown and orange. N. Tesla at left and as watermark. High frequency transformer on back.	.25	1.00	12.50

1991 Issue

#107A-111 year date only. Sign. 15. Replacement notes: Serial # prefix *ZA*.

		VG	VF	UNC
107A	**10 Dinara** 1991. Purple, black and lilac. Like #103. (Not issued).	—	—	175.

		VG	VF	UNC
107B	**50 Dinara** 1991. Orange and red. Like #104. (Not issued).	—	—	175.
108	**100 Dinara** 1991. Black and olive-brown on yellow underprint. Similar to #105.	.10	.50	1.50
109	**500 Dinara** 1991. Brown, dark brown and orange on tan underprint. Similar to #106.	.25	.50	2.50
110	**1000 Dinara** 1991. Blue and purple. Similar to #107.	.20	.50	7.00
111	**5000 Dinara** 1991. Purple, red-orange and blue-gray on gray underprint. Ivo Andric at left and as watermark. Multiple arch stone bridge on the Drina River at Visegrad at center on back.	.50	1.50	7.50

1992 Issue

#112-117 National Bank monogram arms at ctr. Similar to previous issues. Replacement notes: Serial # prefix *ZA*.

#112-115 sign. 15.

		VG	VF	UNC
112	**100 Dinara** 1992. Pale blue and purple. Similar to #105.	.20	.40	1.00
113	**500 Dinara** 1992. Pale purple and lilac. Similar to #106.	.15	.50	4.00
114	**1000 Dinara** 1992. Red, orange and purple on lilac underprint. Similar to #107.	.25	.50	7.50
115	**5000 Dinara** 1992. Deep blue-green, purple and deep olive-brown on gray underprint. Similar to #111.	.25	1.50	6.00
116	**10,000 Dinara** 1992. Varied shades of brown and salmon on tan underprint. Similar to #103. Signature 16.			
	a. With dot after date.	.10	.20	2.00
	b. Without dot after date.	.10	.20	2.00
117	**50,000 Dinara** 1992. Purple, olive-green and deep blue-green. Similar to #104. Signature 16.	.25	.75	4.50

1993 Issue

#118-127 replacement notes: Serial # prefix *ZA*.

#118-123 sign. 16.

		VG	VF	UNC
118	**100,000 Dinara** 1993. Olive-green on orange and gold underprint. Face like #112. Sunflowers at center right on back.	.15	.50	3.50

		VG	VF	UNC
119	**500,000 Dinara** 1993. Blue-violet and orange on multicolor underprint. Face like #113. Koponik Sky Center on back.	.50	2.50	20.00
120	**1,000,000 Dinara** 1993. Purple on blue, orange and multicolor underprint. Face like #117. Iris flowers at center right on back.	.50	4.00	20.00

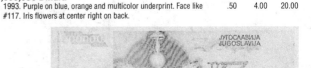

		VG	VF	UNC
121	**5,000,000 Dinara** 1993. Violet, lilac, turquoise and multicolor. Face like #114. Vertical rendition of high frequency transformer at center, hydroelectric dam at right on back.	.15	.50	3.00

		VG	VF	UNC
122	**10,000,000 Dinara** 1993. Slate blue, light and dark brown. Face like #115. National library at center right on back.	.20	.50	3.00
123	**50,000,000 Dinara** 1993. Black and orange. Face like #116. Belgrade University on back.	.25	.75	5.00

#124-127 sign. 17.

		VG	VF	UNC
124	**100,000,000 Dinara** 1993. Grayish purple and blue. Face like #113. Academy of Science at center right on back.	.20	.50	3.00
125	**500,000,000 Dinara** 1993. Black and lilac. Face like #118. Department of Agriculture building on back.	.25	1.00	6.00

		VG	VF	UNC
126	**1,000,000,000 Dinara** 1993. Red and purple on orange and blue-gray underprint. Face like #123. Parliament building (National Assembly) at center on back.	.25	2.50	12.50

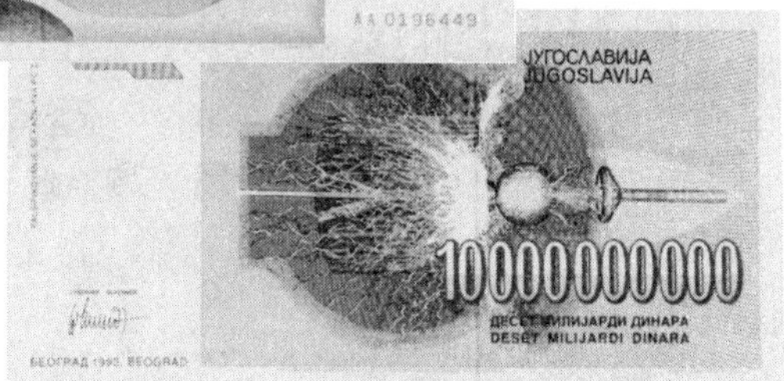

		VG	VF	UNC
127	**10,000,000,000 Dinara** 1993. Black, purple and red. Like #114.	.25	1.50	10.00

1993 Reform Issue

#128-137 replacement notes: Serial # prefix *ZA*.

#128-130 sign. 17.

		VG	VF	UNC
128	**5000 Dinara** 1993. Pale reddish brown, pale olive-green and orange. Face like #114. Tesla Museum at center right on back.	.25	1.00	6.00

		VG	VF	UNC
129	**10,000 Dinara** 1993. Gray and green on orange and olive-green underprint. Vuk. Stefanovic Karadzic at left. Orthodox church, house on back.	.25	.75	5.00

		VG	VF	UNC
130	**50,000 Dinara** 1993. Dark blue on pink and aqua underprint. Petar II Petrovic Niegos Prince-Bishop of Montenegro, at left. Monastery in Cetinje at right on back.	.10	.50	2.00

#131-137 sign. 18.

		VG	VF	UNC
131	**500,000 Dinara** 1993. Dark green on blue-green and yellow-orange underprint. Dositej Obradovic at left. Monastery Hopovo at center right on back.	.25	.50	2.00

		VG	VF	UNC
132	**5,000,000 Dinara** 1993. Dark brown on orange, blue-green and pale olive-brown underprint. Karadjordj Petrovich, Prince of Serbia, at left. Orthodox church at center right on back.	.20	.50	2.00

		VG	VF	UNC
133	**50,000,000 Dinara** 1993. Red and purple on orange and lilac underprint. Michajlo Pupin at left. Telephone Exchange building at center right on back.	.10	.25	2.00

		VG	VF	UNC
134	**500,000,000 Dinara** 1993. Purple on aqua, brown-orange and dull pink underprint. Jovan Cvijich at left. University at center right on back.	.20	.50	3.00

		VG	VF	UNC
135	**5,000,000,000 Dinara** 1993. Olive-brown on light green, ochre and orange underprint. D. Jaksich at left. Monastery in Vrazcevsnitza at center right on back.			
	a. Issued note.	.20	.50	3.00
	s. Specimen with red overprint.	—	—	60.00

		VG	VF	UNC
136	**50,000,000,000 Dinara** 1993. Dark brown on blue-violet, orange, red-violet and gray underprint. Serbian Prince Milan Obrenovich at left. Villa of Obrenovich at center right on back.	.25	.75	5.00

		VG	VF	UNC
137	**500,000,000,000 Dinara** 1993. Red-violet on orange, pale blue-gray and olive-brown underprint. Poet J. Zmaj at left. National Library at center right on back.			
	a. Issued note.	.50	1.50	10.00
	s. Specimen with red overprint.	—	—	70.00

1994 Issue

#138-143 wmk. paper. Sign. 18.

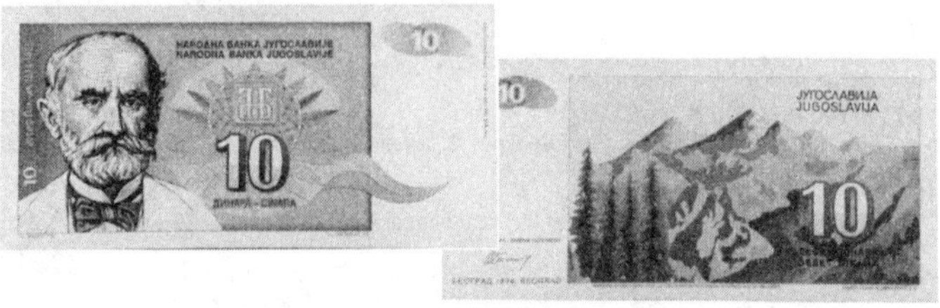

		VG	VF	UNC
138	**10 Dinara** 1994. Chocolate brown on brown and gray-green underprint. Joseph Panchic at left. Back aqua; mountain view, pine trees at center right. Without serial #.			
	a. Issued note without serial #.	.10	.50	1.00
	b. With serial #, serial # prefix *AR*.	—	—	—
	s. Specimen with red overprint.	—	—	40.00

Note: Violet or orange specimen ovpts. are forgeries. Notes w/serial #s were privately added.

		VG	VF	UNC
139	**100 Dinara** 1994. Grayish purple on pink and pale blue underprint. Similar to #128.			
	a. Issued note without serial #.	.10	.25	1.00
	s. Specimen with red overprint.	—	—	40.00

Note: examples are know with serial #s privately added.

		VG	VF	UNC
140	**1000 Dinara** 1994. Dark olive-gray on red-orange, olive-brown and lilac underprint. Similar to #130.			
	a. Issued note.	.20	.50	2.00
	s. Specimen with red overprint.	—	—	40.00

141	5000 Dinara	VG	VF	UNC
	1994. Dark blue on lilac, orange and aqua underprint. Similar to #131.			
	a. Issued note.	.20	.50	2.00
	s. Specimen with red overprint.	—	—	40.00

142	50,000 Dinara	VG	VF	UNC
	1994. Dull red and lilac on orange underprint. Similar to #132.			
	a. Issued note.	.20	.75	3.00
	s. Specimen with red overprint	—	Unc	40.00

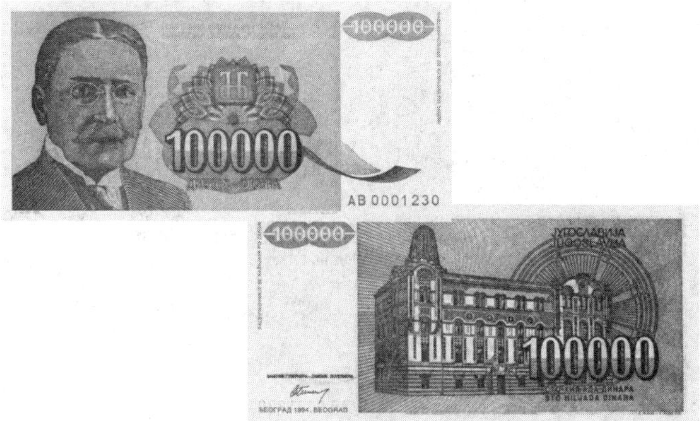

142A	100,000 Dinara	VG	VF	UNC
	1994. Red-brown on ochre and pale olive-green underprint. Like #133. Michajlo Pupin at left. Telephone Exchange building on back. Without serial #. (Not issued).	—	—	350.

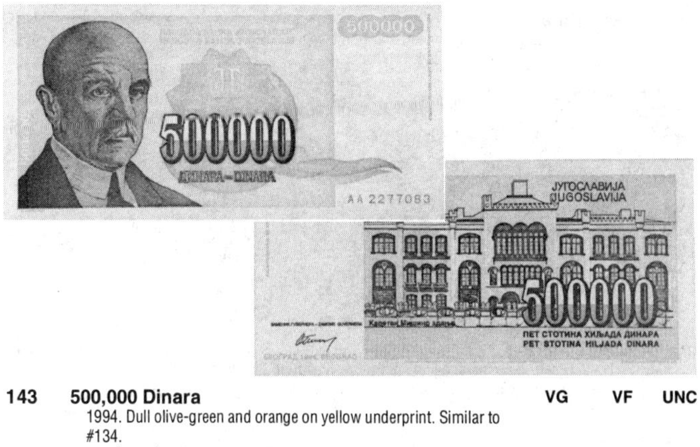

143	500,000 Dinara	VG	VF	UNC
	1994. Dull olive-green and orange on yellow underprint. Similar to #134.			
	a. Issued note.	.10	.40	1.50
	s. Specimen with red overprint.	—	—	40.00

1994 Provisional Issue

144	10,000,000 Dinara	VG	VF	UNC
	1994 (-old date 1993). Red overprint: *1994* on face and back with new silver overprint. Signature 18 and signature title on back on #122.			
	a. Issued note.	.20	1.00	5.00
	s. Specimen with red overprint.	—	—	50.00

1994 Reform Issues

#145-147 wmk: Diamond grid. Sign. 19.

Note: #145-147 withdrawn from circulation on 1.1.1995.

145	1 Novi Dinar	VG	VF	UNC
	1.1.1994. Blue-gray and brown on pale olive-green and tan underprint. Similar to #138.	.25	1.00	4.00

146	5 Novih Dinara	VG	VF	UNC
	1.1.1994. Red-brown and pink on ochre and pale orange underprint. Similar to #139.	.50	2.50	15.00

147	10 Novih Dinara	VG	VF	UNC
	1.1.1994. Purple and pink on aqua and olive-green underprint. Similar to #140.	.50	2.50	15.00

1994; 1996 ISSUE

#148-152 arms w/double-headed eagle at upper ctr. Wmk: Symmetrical design repeated.

#148-150 sign. 20. Replacement notes: Serial # prefix *3A*.

		VG	VF	UNC
148	**5 Novih Dinara** 3.3.1994. Black, deep purple and violet. NicolaTesla at left. Back like #146.	FV	.25	2.00

		VG	VF	UNC
149	**10 Novih Dinara** 3.3.1994. Purple, violet and brown. Like #147.	FV	.50	3.75

		VG	VF	UNC
150	**20 Novih Dinara** 3.3.1994. Dark green, brown-orange and brown. Similar to #135.	FV	.75	6.00

#151 and 152 sign. 19. Replacement notes: Serial # prefix *ZA*.

		VG	VF	UNC
151	**50 Novih Dinara** June 1996. Black and blue. Similar to #136.	FV	1.50	12.50

		VG	VF	UNC
152	**100 Novih Dinara** Oct. 1996. Black on olive-brown and grayish green underprint. Similar to #141.	FV	2.50	25.00

2000-01 ISSUE

#153-157 Portr. as wmk. Arms at upper l. on vertical backs.

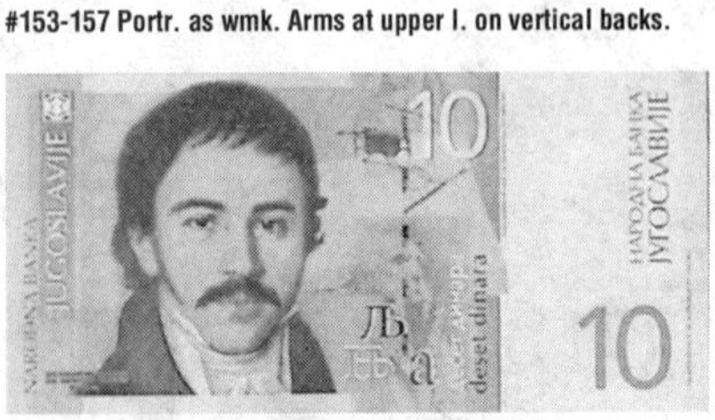

		VG	VF	UNC
153	**10 Dinara** 2000. Brown on ochre-yellow and green underprint. Stefanovich Karadzic at left. Karadzic and alphabet on back.			
	a. Signature Dusan Vlatkovic (not issued).	—	—	150.
	b. Signature Mladjan Dinkich.	FV	FV	1.25

		VG	VF	UNC
154	**20 Dinara** 2000 (2001). Green and black on tan underprint. Petar II Petrovic Njegos, Prince-Bishop of Montenegro at left. Statue from Njegos' mausoleum, mosaic and mountains on back.	FV	FV	1.75

		VG	VF	UNC
155	**50 Dinara** 2000. Light and dark violet on tan underprint. Stevan Stojanovic Mokranjac at left, piano keyboard at lower center. Full-length photo and musical bars on back.	FV	FV	3.50

		VG	VF	UNC
156	**100 Dinara** 2000. Blue on green and tan underprint. Nikola Tesla at left, motor at lower center. Tesla photo, schematic of electro-magnetic induction engine, dove on back.	FV	FV	5.50

		VG	VF	UNC
157	**200 Dinara** 2001. Black and blue on tan underprint. Nadezda Petrovic at left. Figure of the artist and Gracanica monastery on back.	FV	FV	12.50

		VG	VF	UNC
158	**1000 Dinara** 2001. Red on blue and tan underprint. Dorde Vajfert at left. Vajfert portrait and Central Bank interior on back.	FV	FV	40.00

		VG	VF	UNC
159	**5000 Dinara** 2002. Green, violet and gray on multicolor underprint. Slobodan Jovanovic at left. Details of the federal parliament.	FV	—	175.

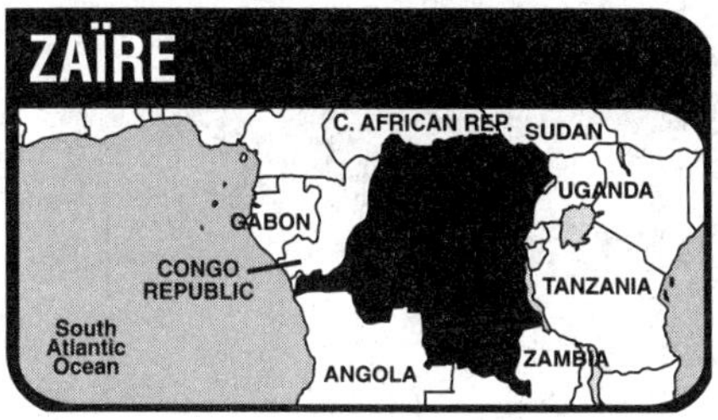

The Republic of Zaïre (formerly the Congo Democratic Republic) located in the south-central part of Africa, has an area of 905,568 sq. mi. (2,345,409 sq. km.) and a population of 43.81 million. Capital: Kinshasa. The mineral-rich country produces copper, tin, diamonds, gold, zinc, cobalt and uranium.

In ancient times the territory comprising Zaïre was occupied by Negrito peoples (Pygmies) pushed into the mountains by Bantu and Nilotic invaders. The interior was first explored by the American correspondent Henry Stanley, who was subsequently commissioned by King Leopold II of Belgium to conclude development treaties with the local chiefs. The Berlin conference of 1885 awarded the area to Leopold, who administered and exploited it as his private property until it was annexed to Belgium in 1908. Following the eruption of bloody independence riots in 1959, Belgium granted the Belgian Congo independence as the Republic of the Congo on June 30, 1960. The Belgian Congo attained independence with the distinction of being the most ill-prepared country to ever undertake self-government. Without a single doctor, lawyer or engineer, with no organized unit capable of maintaining law and order, independence disintegrated into an orgy of anarchy. Provinces seceded. Intertribal warfare erupted. Belgian troops intervened to protect Belgian citizens from retributive massacre. By 1961, four groups were fighting for political dominance. The most serious threat to the viability of the country was posed by the secession of mineral-rich Katanga province on July 11, 1960.

After two and one-half years of sporadic warfare with a U.N. military force, Katanga's leaders capitulated, Jan. 14, 1963 and the rebellious province was partioned into three provinces. The nation officially changed its name to Zaïre on Oct. 27, 1971. In May 1997, the dictator was overthrown after a three-year rebellion. The country changed its name to the Democratic Republic of the Congo.

See also Rwanda, Rwanda-Burundi or Congo Democratic Republic.

MONETARY SYSTEM:

1 Franc = 100 Centimes to 1967
1 Zaïre = 100 Makuta, 1967-1993
1 Nouveau Zaïre = 100 N Makuta = 3 million "old" Zaïres, 1993-1998

Banque du Zaïre

	GOVERNOR		GOVERNOR
3	 J. Sambwa Mbagui	4	 Bofossa W. Amba
5	 EmonyJ	6	 Sambwa Mbagui
7	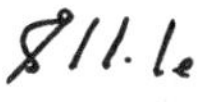 Pay Pay wa Syakassighe	8	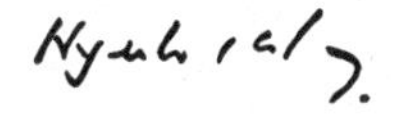 Nyembo Shabanga
9	 B. Mushaba	10	 Ndiang Kabul
11	 L. O. Djamboleka		

Republic

Banque du Zaïre

1971-80 Issues

#16-25 Mobutu at l. and as wmk., leopard at lower r. facing r. Various date and sign. varieties. Printer: G&D. Replacement notes: Serial # suffix *Z*.

		VG	VF	UNC
16	**50 Makuta** 1973-78. Red, dark brown and multicolor. Man and structure in water on back. Intaglio.			
	a. Red guilloche at left center on back. Signature 3. 30.6.1973; 4.10.1974; 4.10.1975.	1.00	6.00	30.00
	b. Red and purple guilloche at left center on back. Signature 3. 24.6.1976; 24.6.1977.	1.50	7.00	35.00
	c. Guilloche as b. Sign 4. 20.5.1978.	1.00	5.00	24.00

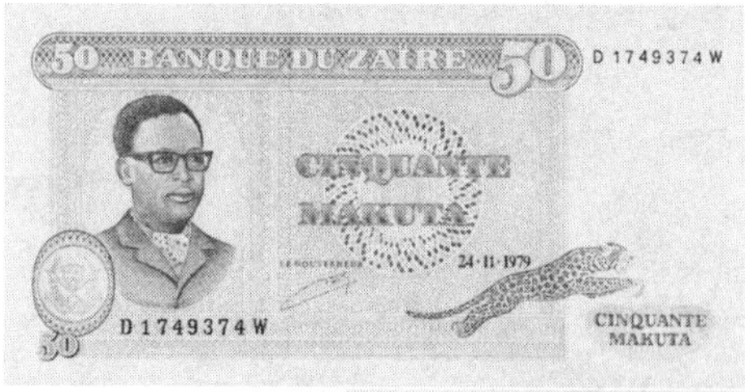

		VG	VF	UNC
17	**50 Makuta** 1979; 1980. Like #16 but slight color differences. Lithographed.			
	a. Signature 5. 24.11.1979.	.40	1.25	7.00
	b. Signature 3. 14.10.1980.	.40	1.25	6.00

		VG	VF	UNC
18	**1 Zaïre** 1972-77. Brown and multicolor. Factory, pyramid, flora and elephant tusks at center right on back. Intaglio.			
	a. Signature 3 with title: *LE GOUVERNEUR* placed below line. 15.3.1972; 27.10.1974; 20.5.1975; 27.10.1975; 27.10.1976.	1.00	2.25	14.00
	b. Signature 4 with title: *LE GOUVERNEUR* placed above line. 27.10.1977.	.75	2.00	10.00

		VG	VF	UNC
19	**1 Zaïre**			
	1979-81. Like #18 but slight color differences. Lithographed.			
	a. Signature 5. 22.10.1979.	.40	1.25	5.25
	b. Signature 3. 27.10.1980; 20.5.1981.	.25	1.00	4.50

		VG	VF	UNC
20	**5 Zaïres**			
	24.11.1972. Green, black, brown and multicolor. Carving at left, hydroelectric dam at center right on back. Like Congo #14. Signature 3.	15.00	50.00	200.

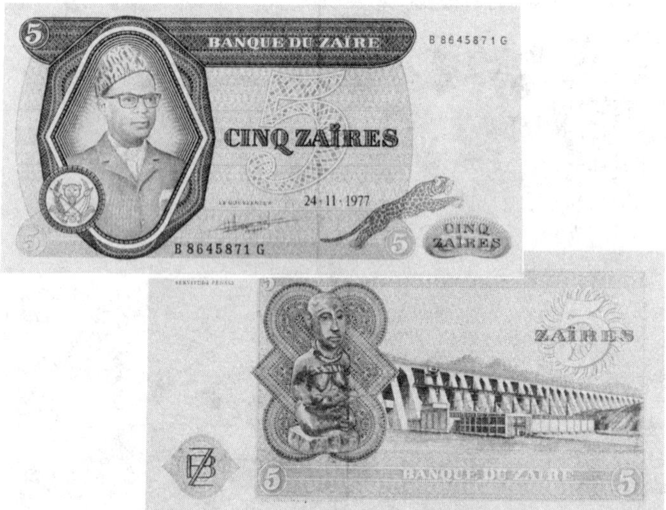

		VG	VF	UNC
21	**5 Zaïres**			
	1974-77. Green, black, brown and multicolor. Similar to #20 but Mobutu with cap.			
	a. Signature 3. 30.11.1974; 30.6.1975; 24.11.1975; 24.11.1976.	2.50	7.50	30.00
	b. Signature 4. 24.11.1977.	1.00	3.00	14.00
	s. As a. Specimen.	—	—	75.00
22	**5 Zaïres**			
	1979; 1980. Blue, brown, violet and multicolor. Like #21.			
	a. Signature 5. 20.5.1979.	.50	2.00	9.50
	b. Signature 3. 27.10.1980.	.75	3.00	17.50
	s. Specimen. 20.5.1979.	—	—	65.00

NOTICE

Readers with unlisted dates, signature varieties, etc. are invited to submit photocopies of their notes to: Standard Catalog of World Paper Money, 700 East State St. Iola, WI 54990-0001, E-Mail: george.cuhaj@fwpubs.com.

		VG	VF	UNC
23	**10 Zaïres**			
	1972-77. Dark brown and blue on multicolor underprint. Similar to Congo #15 but arms with hand holding torch at left center on back.			
	a. Signature 3. 30.6.1972; 22.6.1974; 30.6.1975; 30.6.1976; 27.10.1976.	4.00	12.00	65.00
	b. Signature 4. 27.10.1977.	1.00	3.00	15.00
	s. As a. Specimen without serial #.	—	—	85.00

		VG	VF	UNC
24	**10 Zaïres**			
	1979; 1981. Green, brown and multicolor. Like #23.			
	a. Signature 5. 24.6.1979.	1.00	4.00	17.50
	b. Signature 3. 4.1.1981.	1.00	3.00	15.00
	s. Specimen. 24.6.1979.	—	—	85.00

		VG	VF	UNC
25	**50 Zaïres**			
	1980. Red, violet, brown and multicolor. Face similar to #21. Arms at left center on back.			
	a. Signature 5. 4.2.1980.	5.00	12.50	47.50
	b. Signature 3. 24.11.1980.	5.00	20.00	70.00
	s. Specimen. 4.2.1980.	—	—	100.

1982-85 Issues

#26-31 replacement notes: Serial # suffix *Z*. #26-29 leopard at lower l. facing l. Mobutu in civilian dress at ctr. r. and as wmk. Sign. varieties.

		VG	VF	UNC
26	**5 Zaïres** 17.11.1982. Blue, black and multicolor. Hydroelectric dam at center right on back. Printer: G&D. Signature 6.			
	a. Issued note.	.25	1.00	5.00
	s. Specimen.	—	—	85.00
26A	**5 Zaïres** 24.11.1985. Like #26, but printer: HdMZ. Signature 7.	.20	.50	1.75

		VG	VF	UNC
27	**10 Zaïres** 27.10.1982. Green, black and multicolor. Arms with hand holding torch on back. Printer: G&D. Signature 6.			
	a. Issued note.	.50	1.00	5.50
	s. Specimen.	—	—	50.00
27A	**10 Zaïres** 27.10.1985. Like #27, but printer: HdMZ. Signature 7.	.20	.50	1.75

#28 and 29 printer: G&D.

		VG	VF	UNC
28	**50 Zaïres** 1982; 1985. Purple, blue and multicolor. Back blue and multicolor; men fishing with stick nets at center.			
	a. Signature 6. 24.11.1982.	.75	2.50	15.00
	b. Signature 7. 24.6.1985.	.50	1.50	9.00
	s. Specimen.	—	—	50.00

		VG	VF	UNC
29	**100 Zaïres** 1983; 1985. Dark brown, orange and multicolor. Bank of Zaïre at center right on back.			
	a. Signature 6. 30.6.1983.	.75	3.00	16.50
	b. Signature 7. 30.6.1985.	.25	1.00	7.50
	s. Specimen.	—	—	50.00

#30 and 31 leopard at lower l. facing l., Mobutu in military dress at ctr. r. and as wmk., arms at lower r. Printer: G&D.

		VG	VF	UNC
30	**500 Zaïres** 1984; 1985. Gray, purple and multicolor. Suspension bridge over river at center right on back.			
	a. Signature 6. 14.10.1984.	3.00	15.00	70.00
	b. Signature 7. 14.10.1985.	1.25	6.00	30.00
	s. Specimen.	—	75.00	100.

		VG	VF	UNC
31	**1000 Zaïres** 24.11.1985. Blue-black and green on multicolor underprint. Civic building, water fountain at center right on back. Signature 7.			
	a. Issued note.	2.00	6.00	15.00
	s. Specimen.	—	85.00	125.

1988-92 Issues

#32-46 Mobutu in military dress at r. and as wmk., leopard at lower l. ctr. facing l., arms at lower r. Reduced size notes. Replacement notes: serial # suffix *Z*.

#32-36 printer: HdMZ.

		VG	VF	UNC
32	**50 Zaïres** 30.6.1988. Green and multicolor. Men fishing with stick nets at left on back. Similar to #28. Signature 7.			
	a. Issued note.	.10	.50	1.50
	s. Specimen.	—	45.00	55.00

		VG	VF	UNC
33	**100 Zaïres** 14.10.1988. Blue and multicolor. Bank of Zaïre at left center on back. Similar to #29. Signature 7.			
	a. Issued note.	.15	.75	3.00
	s. Specimen.	—	45.00	55.00

		VG	VF	UNC
34	**500 Zaïres** 24.6.1989. Brown, orange and multicolor. Suspension bridge over river at left center on back. Similar to #30. Signature 7.			
	a. Issued note.	.25	1.25	6.00
	s. Specimen.	—	50.00	65.00

35	1000 Zaïres	VG	VF	UNC
	24.11.1989. Purple, brown and multicolor. Civic building, fountain at left center on back. Similar to #31. Signature 7.			
	a. Issued note.	.50	4.00	21.00
	s. Specimen.	—	60.00	75.00

36	2000 Zaïres	VG	VF	UNC
	1.10.1991. Purple and peach on multicolor underprint. Men fishing with stick nets at left, carved figure at center right on back. (Smaller size than #35.) signature 8.			
	a. Issued note.	.25	.75	2.50
	s. Specimen.	—	55.00	65.00

#37 and 38 printer: G&D. Replacement notes: Serial # suffix *Z*.

37	5000 Zaïres	VG	VF	UNC
	20.5.1988. Blue, green and multicolor. Factory at left, elephant tusks and plants at center on back. Signature 7.			
	a. Brown triangle at lower right.	6.00	30.00	150.
	b. Green triangle at lower right.	.25	1.25	6.00

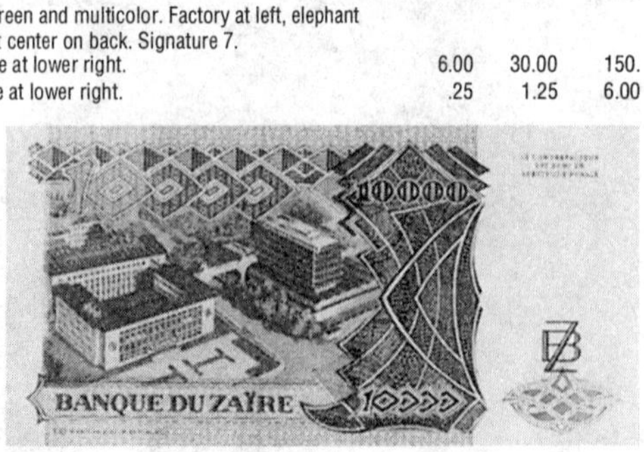

38	10,000 Zaïres	VG	VF	UNC
	24.11.1989. Purple, brown-orange and red on multicolor underprint. Government Building complex at left center on back. Signature 7.			
	a. Issued note.	.25	1.25	5.50
	s. Specimen.	—	50.00	65.00

39	20,000 Zaïres	VG	VF	UNC
	1.7.1991. Black on multicolor underprint. Bank of Zaïre at left, other buildings across center on back. Similar to #29. Printer: HdMZ. Signature 8.			
	a. Issued note.	.25	.50	3.50
	s. Specimen.	—	60.00	70.00

#40 and 41 printer: G&D. Replacement notes: Serial # suffix *Z*.

40	50,000 Zaïres	VG	VF	UNC
	24.4.1991. Wine and blue-black on multicolor underprint. Family of Western Gorillas on back. Signature 7.			
	a. Issued note.	.75	2.50	8.00
	s. Specimen.	—	60.00	70.00

41	100,000 Zaïres	VG	VF	UNC
	4.1.1992. Black and deep olive-green on multicolor underprint. Domed building at left center on back. Signature 8.			
	a. Issued note.	.50	1.25	6.00
	s. Specimen.	—	50.00	65.00

42 200,000 Zaïres | VG | VF | UNC

1.3.1992. Deep purple and deep blue on multicolor underprint. Back similar to #31; civic building and fountain at left center Printer: HdMZ. Signature 8.

	VG	VF	UNC
a. Issued note.	.25	1.00	5.50
s. Specimen.	—	50.00	65.00

#43 and 44 printer: G&D.

43 500,000 Zaïres | VG | VF | UNC

15.3.1992. Brown and orange on multicolor underprint. Hydroelectric dam at left center on back. Signature 8.

	VG	VF	UNC
a. Issued note.	.50	1.50	7.75
s. Specimen.	—	50.00	65.00

44 1,000,000 Zaïres | VG | VF | UNC

31.7.1992. Red-violet and deep red on multicolor underprint. Suspension bridge at left center on back. Signature 8. | .50 | 3.00 | 12.00

45 1,000,000 Zaïres

1993. Like #44. Printer: HdMZ.

	VG	VF	UNC
a. Signature 8. 15.3.1993.	.75	2.50	13.00
b. Signature 9. 17.5.1993; 30.6.1993.	.50	1.25	7.00
s. Specimen.	—	60.00	85.00

46 5,000,000 Zaïres | VG | VF | UNC

1.10.1992. Deep brown and brown on multicolor underprint. Factory, pyramids at center, flora and elephant tusks at left on back. Printer: H&S. Signature 8.

	VG	VF	UNC
a. Issued note.	.50	2.00	8.25
s. Specimen.	—	60.00	75.00

1993 Issue

#47-58 leopard at lower l., Mobutu in military dress at r., arms at lower r. Replacement notes: serial # suffix *Z*.

#47 and 48 Independence Monument at l. on back. W/o wmk. Printer: G&D.

#49-58 wmk: Mobutu.

47 1 Nouveau Mikuta | VG | VF | UNC

24.6.1993. Light brown on pink and multicolor underprint. Signature 9. | .05 | .20 | .75

48 5 Nouveaux Makuta | VG | VF | UNC

24.6.1993. Black on pale violet and blue-green underprint. Signature 9. | .05 | .20 | 1.00

#49 and 51 printer: HdMZ (CdM-A).

49 10 Nouveaux Makuta | VG | VF | UNC

24.6.1993. Green on multicolor underprint. Factory, pyramids at center, flora and elephant tusks at left on back. Signature 9. | .10 | .50 | 1.75

#50 *Not assigned.*

51 50 Nouveaux Makuta | VG | VF | UNC

24.6.1993. Brown-orange on light green and multicolor underprint. Chieftain at left, men fishing with stick nets at center on back. Signature 9. | .10 | .30 | 1.25

#52-54 printer: G&D.

52 **1 Nouveau Zaïre** — VG / VF / UNC
24.6.1993. Violet and purple on multicolor underprint. Banque du Zaïre at left center on back. Signature 9. — .10 / .30 / 1.75

53 **5 Nouveaux Zaïres** — VG / VF / UNC
24.6.1993. Brown on multicolor underprint. Back like #41.
a. Signature 9. — .20 / .50 / 1.75
b. Signature 10. — .50 / 1.50 / 4.00

54 **10 Nouveaux Zaïres** — VG / VF / UNC
24.6.1993. Dark gray and dark blue-green on multicolor underprint. Back like #31. Signature 9. — .25 / .75 / 3.00

55 **10 Nouveaux Zaïres**
24.6.1993. Dark gray and dark blue-green on multicolor underprint. Back like #31. Printer: HdMZ (CdM-A). Signature 9. — .15 / .50 / 1.75

#56 and 57 printer: HdMZ (CdM-A).

56 **20 Nouveaux Zaïres** — VG / VF / UNC
24.6.1993. Brown and blue on pale green and lilac underprint. Back similar to #42. Signature 9. — .20 / .75 / 3.50

57 **50 Nouveaux Zaïres** — VG / VF / UNC
24.6.1993. Brown and deep red on multicolor underprint. Back like #43. Signature 9. — .20 / .75 / 4.00

58 **100 Nouveaux Zaïres** — VG / VF / UNC
1993-94. Grayish purple and blue-violet on aqua and ochre underprint. Back like #44. Printer: G&D.
a. Signature 9. 24.6.1993. — .50 / 1.00 / 4.75
b. Signature 10. 15.2.1994. — .50 / 1.25 / 5.50

58A **100 Nouveaux Zaïres**
1993. Grayish purple and blue-violet on aqua and ochre underprint. Like #58a. Printer: HdMZ. — .50 / 1.00 / 4.75

1994-96 Issues

#59-77 a leopard at lower l. ctr., Mobutu in military dress at r. and as wmk., arms at lower r.

Replacement notes: serial # suffix *Z*.

#59-61 printer: HdMZ.

59 **50 Nouveaux Zaïres** — VG / VF / UNC
15.2.1994. Dull red-violet and red on multicolor underprint. Like #57. Signature 10. — .50 / 2.00 / 8.25

60 **100 Nouveaux Zaïres** — VG / VF / UNC
15.2.1994. Grayish purple and blue-violet on aqua and ochre underprint. Like #58. Signature 10. — .25 / 1.00 / 4.75

61 **200 Nouveaux Zaïres**
15.2.1994. Deep olive-brown on orange and multicolor underprint. Men fishing with stick nets at left center on back. Signature 10. — .05 / .25 / 3.00

62 **200 Nouveaux Zaïres**
15.2.1994. Deep olive-brown on orange and multicolor underprint. Like #61. Printer: G&D. — .10 / .50 / 3.00

63 **500 Nouveaux Zaïres**
15.2.1994. Gray and deep olive-green on multicolor underprint. Banque du Zaïre at left center on back. Printer: HdMZ. — .10 / .50 / 1.75

64 **500 Nouveaux Zaïres**

	VG	VF	UNC
15.2.1994. Gray and deep olive-green on multicolor underprint. Like #63. Printer: G&D.	.10	.50	4.00

64A **500 Nouveaux Zaïres**

	VG	VF	UNC
15.2.1994. Like #63. Serial # prefix *X*. Printed in Argentina.	.20	1.00	4.75

65 **500 Nouveaux Zaïres**

	VG	VF	UNC
30.1.1995. Blue on multicolor underprint. Large value on back. Signature 11.	.10	.50	1.75

66 **1000 Nouveaux Zaïres**

	VG	VF	UNC
30.1.1995. Olive-green and olive-gray on multicolor underprint. Printer: G&D. Signature 11.	.20	1.00	4.75

67 **1000 Nouveaux Zaïres**

	VG	VF	UNC
30.1.1995. Like #66. Printer: HdMZ. Signature 11.	.10	.75	4.00

68 **5000 Nouveaux Zaïres**

	VG	VF	UNC
30.1.1995. Brown-violet and red-violet on multicolor underprint. Printer: G&D. Signature 11.	.50	2.00	9.50

69 **5000 Nouveaux Zaïres**

	VG	VF	UNC
31.1.1995. Brown-violet and red-violet on multicolor underprint. Like #68. Printer: HdMZ. Signature 11.	.25	1.25	7.00

#70-77 w/OVD vertical band at l.

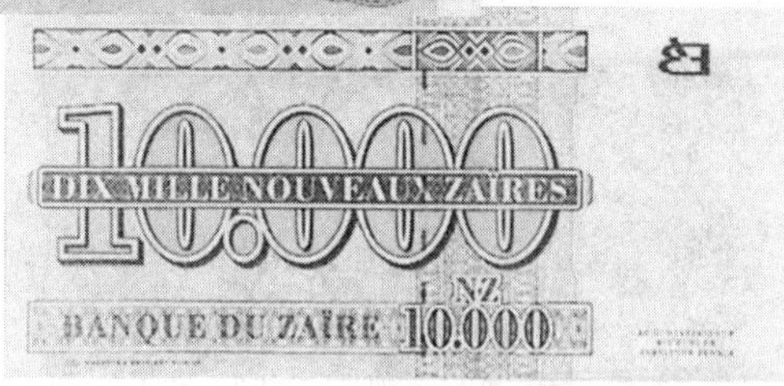

70 **10,000 Nouveaux Zaïres**

	VG	VF	UNC
30.1.1995. Blue-violet on multicolor underprint. Printer: G&D. Signature 11.	.30	1.50	7.50

71 **10,000 Nouveaux Zaïres**

	VG	VF	UNC
30.1.1995. Blue-violet on multicolor underprint. Like #70. Printer: HdMZ. Signature 11.	.25	1.25	6.00

72 **20,000 Nouveaux Zaïres**

	VG	VF	UNC
30.1.1996. Brown on multicolor underprint. Printer: G&D. Signature 11.	.40	1.50	7.00

73 **20,000 Nouveaux Zaïres**

	VG	VF	UNC
30.1.1996. Brown on multicolor underprint. Like #72. Printer: HdMZ. Signature 11.	.40	1.50	7.00

74 **50,000 Nouveaux Zaïres**

	VG	VF	UNC
30.1.1996. Violet and pale blue on multicolor underprint. Printer: G&D. Signature 11.	.75	3.00	12.00

75 **50,000 Nouveaux Zaïres**

	VG	VF	UNC
30.1.1996. Violet and pale blue on multicolor underprint. Like #74. Printer: HdMZ. Signature 11.	.75	3.00	12.00

76 **100,000 Nouveaux Zaïres**

	VG	VF	UNC
30.6.1996. Dull orange on green and multicolor underprint. Printer: G&D. Signature 11.	.50	2.00	9.50

77 **100,000 Nouveaux Zaïres**

	VG	VF	UNC
30.6.1996. Dull orange on green and multicolor underprint. Like #76. Printer: HdMZ. Signature 11.	.50	2.00	9.50

77A **100,000 Nouveaux Zaïres**

	VG	VF	UNC
30.6.1996. Gray and blue-green on multicolor underprint. Like #76 and 77. Printer: HdMZ.	1.00	4.50	20.00

#78 and 79 Mobutu at r. and as wmk. Printer: G&D. Sign. 11.

78 **500,000 Nouveaux Zaïres**

	VG	VF	UNC
25.10.1996. Green and yellow-green on multicolor underprint. Map of Zaïre, family in canoe on back.			
a. Issued note.	.75	3.00	12.00
s. Specimen.	—	—	40.00

79 **1,000,000 Nouveaux Zaïres**

	VG	VF	UNC
25.10.1996. Light violet and red on multicolor underprint. Diamonds at lower left center. Map of Zaïre, mining facility on back.			
a. Issued note.	1.00	4.00	17.50
s. Specimen.	—	—	75.00

REGIONAL

Validation Ovpt:

Type I: Circular handstamp: *REPUBLIQUE DU ZAÏRE-REGION DU BAS-ZAÏRE; GARAGE - STA/BANANA* around arms.

BANQUE DU ZAÏRE BRANCHES

Note: #R3 and R4 are just 2 examples of handstamps applied to notes being turned in for exchange for a new issue. It appears that is some locations (i.e. Bas Fleuve, Bas Zaïre and Shaba Sons) there were not enough of the new notes to trade for the older ones. In such cases, an ovpt. was applied to the older piece indicating its validity and acceptability for future redemption into new currency. A number of different ovpt. are known, and more information is needed.

1980's ND PROVISIONAL ISSUE

			Good	Fine	XF
R3	**5 Zaïres**				
	1980's ND (- old date 1972-77). Handstamp on #21b.				
		a. 1972.	5.00	15.00	60.00
		b. 1974-76.	3.00	7.00	30.00
		c. 1977.	1.00	3.00	7.50
R4	**10 Zaïres**				
	1980's ND (-old date various). Handstamp on #23b.				
		a. 1975-76.	4.00	7.00	30.00
		b. 1977.	1.00	3.00	10.00

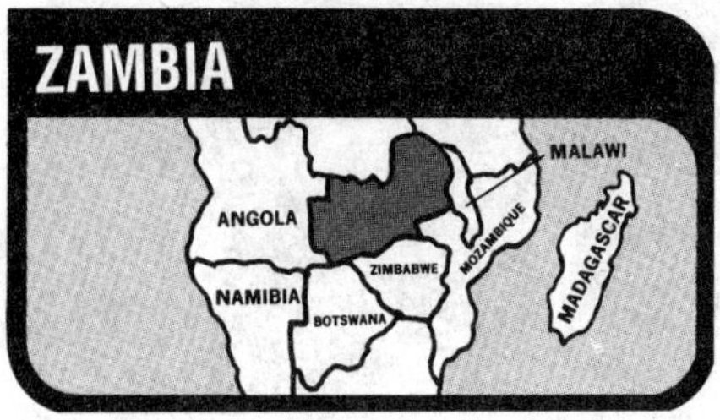

The Republic of Zambia (formerly Northern Rhodesia), a landlocked country in south-central Africa, has an area of 290,586 sq. mi. (752,614 sq. km.) and a population of nearly 9.87 million. Capital: Lusaka. The economy is d principally on copper, of which Zambia is the world's third largest producer. Copper, zinc, lead, cobalt and tobacco are exported.

The area that is now Zambia was brought within the British sphere of influence in 1888 by empire builder Cecil Rhodes, who obtained mining concessions in south-central Africa from indigenous chiefs. The territory was ruled by the British South Africa Company, which Rhodes established, until 1924 when its administration was transferred to the British government as a protectorate. In 1953, Northern Rhodesia was joined with Nyasaland and the colony of Southern Rhodesia to form the Federation of Rhodesia and Nyasaland. Northern Rhodesia seceded from the Federation on Oct. 24, 1964, and became the independent Republic of Zambia. It is a member of the Commonwealth of Nations. The president is Chief of State.

Zambia adopted a decimal currency system on Jan. 16, 1969.

Also see Rhodesia and Malawi.

RULERS:

British to 1964

MONETARY SYSTEM:

1 Shilling = 12 Pence
1 Pound = 20 Shillings to 1968
1 Kwacha = 100 Ngwee, 1968-

SIGNATURE VARIETIES

1	R. C. Hallet, 1964-67	2	Dr. J. B. Zulu, 1967-70
3	V. S. Musakanya, 1970-72	4	B. R. Kuwani, 1972-76, 1982-84
5	L. J. Mwananshiku, 1976-81	6	D. A. R. Phiri, 1984-8
7	Dr. L. S. Chivuno, 1986-88	8	F. Nkhoma, 1988-9
9	J. A. Bussiere, 1991- (ca.1993)	10	D. Mulaisho, 1993-95
11	Dr. J. Mwanza, 1995-2002	12	K. Fundanga 2002 -

REPUBLIC

BANK OF ZAMBIA

1963 ND ISSUE

		VG	VF	UNC
A1	**1 Pound** 1963. Blue on lilac underprint. Fisherman with net and boat at center, portrait Queen Elizabeth II at right. Back purple; Ross's Turaco at left center Imprint: H&S (Not issued).	—	—	2750.

Note: #A1 exists in a number of different color varieties.

1964 ND ISSUE

#1-3 sign. 1. Arms at upper ctr. Wmk: Wildebeest's head. Printer: TDLR .

			VG	VF	UNC
1	**10 Shillings**				
	ND (1964). Brown on multicolor underprint. Chaplins Barbet bird at right. Farmers plowing with tractor and oxen on back.				
		a. Issued note.	70.00	150.	400.
		s. Specimen.	—	—	300.

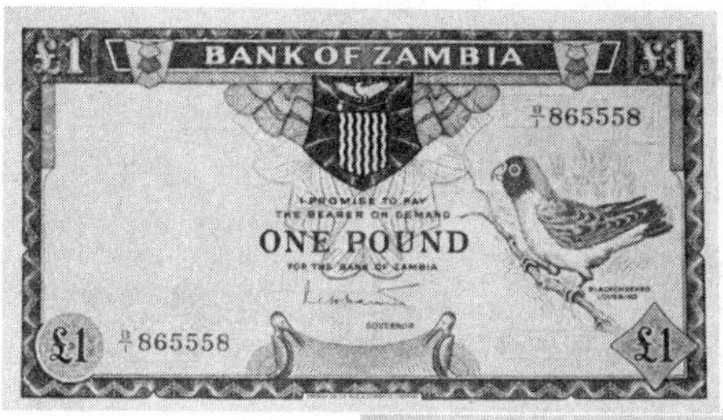

2	1 Pound	VG	VF	UNC
	ND (1964). Green on multicolor underprint. Black-cheeked Lovebird at right. Mining tower and conveyors at left center on back.			
	a. Issued note.	100.	200.	900.
	s. Specimen.	—	—	300.

3	5 Pounds	VG	VF	UNC
	ND (1964). Blue on multicolor underprint. Wildebeest at right. Victoria Falls of Zambezi at left center on back.			
	a. Issued note.	175.	450.	2500.
	s. Specimen.	—	—	400.

1968 ND Issue

#4-8 Pres. K. Kaunda at r. Dot between letter and value. Sign. 2. Printer: TDLR. Replacement notes: Serial # prefix *1/Z; 1/Y; 1/X; 1/W; 1/V* respectively.

4	50 Ngwee	VG	VF	UNC
	ND (1968). Red-violet on multicolor underprint. Arms at left. Two antelope on back. Without watermark.			
	a. Issued note.	10.00	27.50	80.00
	s. Specimen.	—	—	75.00

#5-8 arms at upper ctr. Wmk: Kaunda.

5	1 Kwacha	VG	VF	UNC
	ND (1968). Dark brown on multicolor underprint. Farmers plowing with tractor and oxen on back.			
	a. Issued note.	11.50	40.00	95.00
	s. Specimen.	—	—	80.00
6	2 Kwacha			
	ND (1968). Green on multicolor underprint. Back like #2; mining tower and conveyors at left center.			
	a. Issued note.	12.50	50.00	140.
	s. Specimen.	—	—	120.
7	10 Kwacha			
	ND (1968). Blue on multicolor underprint. Back like #3; waterfall at center.			
	a. Issued note.	35.00	100.	700.
	s. Specimen.	—	—	170.
8	20 Kwacha			
	ND (1968). Purple on multicolor underprint. National Assembly on back.			
	a. Issued note.	50.00	200.	900.
	s. Specimen.	—	—	220.

1969 ND Issue

#9-13 Pres. K. Kaunda at r., w/o dot between letter and value. Backs and wmks. like #4-8. Replacement notes: Serial # prefix *1/Z; 1/Y; 1/X; 1/W; 1/V* respectively.

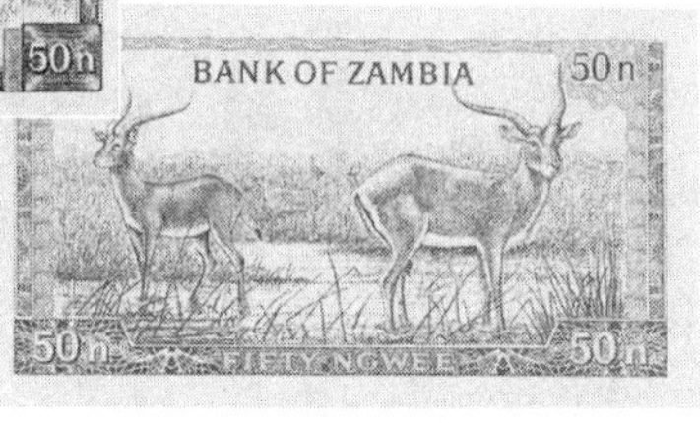

9	50 Ngwee	VG	VF	UNC
	ND (1969). Red-violet on multicolor underprint. Like #4.			
	a. Signature 3.	4.00	20.00	75.00
	b. Signature 4.	2.50	9.00	40.00
	s. As c. Specimen.	—	—	50.00

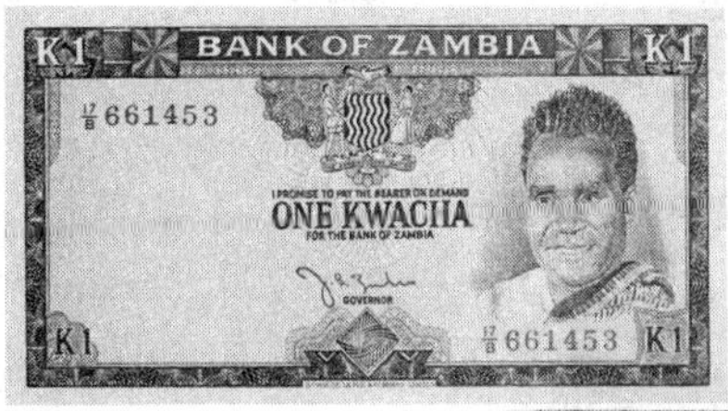

10	1 Kwacha	VG	VF	UNC
	ND (1969). Dark brown on multicolor underprint. Like #5.			
	a. Signature 2.	4.00	20.00	75.00
	b. Signature 3.	2.50	9.00	40.00
	s. Specimen.	—	—	50.00

11	2 Kwacha	VG	VF	UNC
	ND (1969). Green on multicolor underprint. Like #6.			
	a. Signature 2.	7.00	40.00	200.
	b. Signature 3.	6.00	30.00	200.
	c. Signature 4.	5.00	22.50	160.
	s. As s. Specimen.	—	—	90.00

12	10 Kwacha	VG	VF	UNC
	ND (1969). Blue on multicolor underprint. Like #7.			
	a. Signature 2.	20.00	75.00	350.
	b. Signature 3.	25.00	100.	600.
	c. Signature 4.	18.00	60.00	300.
	s. Specimen.	—	—	90.00

13	20 Kwacha	VG	VF	UNC
	ND (1969). Purple on multicolor underprint. Like #8.			
	a. Signature 2.	25.00	75.00	500.
	b. Signature 3.	50.00	150.	650.
	c. Signature 4.	7.50	25.00	75.00
	s. Specimen.	—	—	120.

1973 ND Issue

#14 and 15 Pres. K. Kaunda at r. and as wmk., arms at upper ctr. Replacement notes: Serial # prefix *1/Z; 1/U* respectively.

14	50 Ngwee	VG	VF	UNC
	ND (1973). Black on lilac and multicolor underprint. Miners on back. Without watermark. Printer: TDLR. Signature 4.			
	a. Issued note.	1.00	5.00	12.50
	s. Specimen.	—	—	40.00

15	5 Kwacha	VG	VF	UNC
	ND (1973). Red-violet on multicolor underprint. Children by school on back. Signature 4.			
	a. Issued note.	25.00	150.	450.
	s. Specimen.	—	—	200.

1973 ND Commemorative Issue

#16, Birth of the Second Republic, December 13, 1972

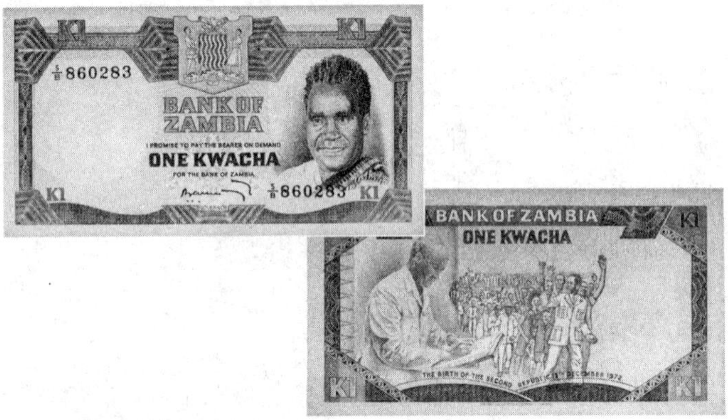

16	1 Kwacha	VG	VF	UNC
	ND (1973). Red-orange and brown on multicolor underprint. Pres. K. Kaunda at right and as watermark. Document signing, commemorative text and crowd on back. Printer: TDLR. Signature 4.			
	a. Issued note.	4.00	12.50	40.00
	s. Specimen.	—	—	40.00

1974 ND Issue

#17 and 18 Pres. K. Kaunda at r. and as wmk., arms at upper ctr. Sign. 4. Printer: BWC. Replacement notes: Serial # prefix *1/W; 1/V* respectively.

17	10 Kwacha	VG	VF	UNC
	ND (1974). Blue on multicolor underprint. Waterfalls at left center on back.			
	a. Issued note.	20.00	100.	350.
	s. Specimen.	—	—	175.
18	20 Kwacha			
	ND (1974). Purple and red on multicolor underprint. National Assembly on back.			
	a. Issued note.	17.50	65.00	260.
	s. Specimen.	—	—	220.

1974-76 ND ISSUE

#19-22A earlier frame design, arms at upper ctr. Older Pres. K. Kaunda at r. but same wmk. as previous issues. Printer: TDLR. Replacement notes: Serial # prefix *1/Y; 1/X; 1/U; 1/W* respectively.

		VG	VF	UNC
19	**1 Kwacha**			
	ND (1976). Brown on multicolor underprint. Back like #5. Signature 5.			
	a. Issued note.	1.50	6.00	12.50
	s. Specimen.	—	—	30.00
20	**2 Kwacha**			
	ND (1974). Green on multicolor underprint. Back like #6. Signature 4.			
	a. Issued note.	1.50	7.00	22.50
	s. Specimen.	—	—	30.00
21	**5 Kwacha**			
	ND (1976). Brown and violet on multicolor underprint. Back like #16. Signature 5.			
	a. Issued note.	3.00	10.00	35.00
	s. Specimen.	—	—	55.00
22	**10 Kwacha**			
	ND (1976). Blue on multicolor underprint. Back like #17. Signature 5.			
	a. Issued note.	3.50	20.00	50.00
	s. Specimen.	—	—	75.00

		VG	VF	UNC
22A	**20 Kwacha**			
	ND. Purple, red and multicolor. Back like #13. (Not issued.)	—	—	—

1980; 1986 ND ISSUE

#23-28 Pres. K. Kaunda at r. and as wmk., African fish eagle at l. ctr. Printer: TDLR. Replacement notes: Serial # prefix *Z/1*.

		VG	VF	UNC
23	**1 Kwacha**			
	ND (1980-88). Dark brown on multicolor underprint. Workers picking cotton at left. Center on back.			
	a. Signature 5.	.40	1.00	4.00
	b. Signature 7.	.25	.50	1.50
	s. Specimen.	—	—	40.00

		VG	VF	UNC
24	**2 Kwacha**			
	ND (1980-88). Olive-green on multicolor underprint. Teacher with student at left, school building at center on back.			
	a. Signature 5.	.50	1.25	6.50
	b. Signature 6.	.50	1.00	4.00
	c. Signature 7.	.25	.75	2.25
	s. Specimen.	—	—	40.00

		VG	VF	UNC
25	**5 Kwacha**			
	ND (1980-88). Brown on multicolor underprint. Hydroelectric dam at left. Center on back.			
	a. Signature 5.	.50	1.75	7.50
	b. Signature 4.	1.00	7.50	35.00
	c. Signature 6.	.25	.50	3.50
	d. Signature 7.	.25	.50	3.00
	s. Specimen.	—	—	40.00

		VG	VF	UNC
26	**10 Kwacha**			
	ND (1980-88). Blue, green and black on multicolor underprint. Bank at left. Center on back.			
	a. Signature 5.	2.00	8.00	42.50
	b. Signature 4 in black.	3.00	15.00	85.00
	c. Signature 4 in blue.	2.50	10.00	70.00
	d. Signature 6.	2.00	5.00	12.50
	e. Signature 7.	1.00	2.50	5.00
	s. Specimen.	—	—	40.00

		VG	VF	UNC
27	**20 Kwacha**			
	ND (1980-88). Green and olive-brown on multicolor underprint. Woman with basket on head at center right on back.			
	a. Signature 5.	3.00	12.00	50.00
	b. Signature 4 in black.	4.00	15.00	120.
	c. Signature 4 in dark green.	2.50	8.00	65.00
	d. Signature 6.	2.00	7.00	15.00
	e. Signature 7.	1.00	2.50	7.50
	s. Specimen.	—	—	60.00

28	50 Kwacha	VG	VF	UNC
	ND (1986-88). Purple, violet and multicolor. "Chainbreaker" statue at left, modern building at left center on back. Signature 7.			
	a. Issued note.	1.00	3.00	10.00
	s. Specimen.	—	—	60.00

1989 ND Issue

#29-33 Pres. K. Kaunda at r. and as wmk., fish eagle at lower l., butterfly over arms at ctr. "Chainbreaker" statue at l. on back.

29	2 Kwacha	VG	VF	UNC
	ND (1989). Olive-brown on multicolor underprint. Rhinoceros head at lower left facing left, cornfield at center, tool at right on back. Signature 8.			
	a. Issued note.	.25	.50	1.75
	s. Specimen.	—	—	40.00

30	5 Kwacha	VG	VF	UNC
	ND (1989). Brown and red-orange on multicolor underprint. Back brown; lion cub head facing at lower left, building at center, jar at right. Signature 8.			
	a. Issued note.	.30	.70	2.50
	s. Specimen.	—	—	40.00
31	10 Kwacha			
	ND (1989-91). Black, dark blue and red-violet on multicolor underprint. Back dark blue; giraffe head at lower left, facing left, building at center, carving of man's head at right.			
	a. Signature 8.	.40	1.00	5.00
	b. Signature 9.	.30	.90	3.00
	s. Specimen.	—	—	40.00
32	20 Kwacha			
	ND (1989-91). Dark olive-green, brown and blue on multicolor underprint. Back dark green; Dama gazelle head at lower left, facing 3/4 left, building at center, carving of man's head at right.			
	a. Signature 8.	.50	1.00	5.00
	b. Signature 9.	.30	1.00	5.00
	s. Specimen.	—	—	60.00

33	50 Kwacha	VG	VF	UNC
	ND (1989-91). Red-violet and purple on multicolor underprint. Zebra head at lower left, facing left, manufacturing at center, carving of woman's bust at right on back.			
	a. Signature 8.	.75	5.50	30.00
	b. Signature 9.	.50	3.50	10.00
	s. Specimen.	—	—	60.00

1991 ND Issue

#34-35 older Pres. K. Kaunda at r. and as wmk., fish eagle at l., tree over arms at ctr. "Chainbreaker" statue at l. on back. Sign. 9.

34	100 Kwacha	VG	VF	UNC
	ND (1991). Purple, red and blue on multicolor underprint. Water buffalo head at left, facing Victoria Falls of Zambezi with rainbow through center on back.			
	a. Issued note.	.50	1.50	7.50
	s. Specimen.	—	—	50.00

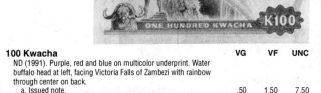

35	500 Kwacha	VG	VF	UNC
	ND (1991). Brown on multicolor underprint. Elephant at left, workers picking cotton at center on back.			
	a. Issued note.	1.00	2.50	10.00
	s. Specimen.	—	Unc	60.00

1992; 1996 ND Issue

#36-42 seal of arms w/date at lower l., fish eagle at r. Wmk: Fish eagle's head. "Chainbreaker" statue at lower ctr. r. on back. Printer: TDLR. Replacement notes: Serial # prefix *1/X*.

36	20 Kwacha	VG	VF	UNC
	1992. Green on multicolor underprint. Fig tree at center, Kudu at left, 3/4 facing left, State House at Lusaka at center on back.			
	a. Signature 10.	.10	.50	3.00
	b. Signature 11.	.10	.50	2.50
	s. Specimen.	—	—	40.00

37	50 Kwacha	VG	VF	UNC
	1992; 2001; 2003; 2006. Red on multicolor underprint. Sausage tree at center, Zebra at left. Copper refining at Nkana Mine at center on back.			
	a. 1992. Signature 10.	.20	.60	3.25
	b. 1992. Signature 11.	.20	.60	3.00
	c. 2001. Signature 11.	FV	.50	2.75
	d. 2003. Signature 12.	FV	.50	2.50
	e. 2006. Signature 12.	FV	FV	1.25
	s. Specimen.	—	—	40.00

38	100 Kwacha	VG	VF	UNC
	1992; 2001; 2003; 2005; 2006. Deep purple on multicolor underprint. Palm tree at center. Water buffalo head facing at left, Victoria falls at center on back. Serial # varieties.			
	a. 1992. Signature 10.	FV	.60	3.00
	b. 1992. Signature 11.	FV	.60	3.00
	c. 2001. Signature 11.	FV	—	2.50
	d. 2003. Signature 12.	FV	FV	2.00
	e. 2005. Signature 12.	FV	FV	2.00
	f. 2006. Signatrue 12.	FV	FV	2.25
	s. Specimen.	—	—	40.00

39	500 Kwacha	VG	VF	UNC
	1992; 2001; 2003. Brown on multicolor underprint. Baobab tree. Elephant head at left, workers picking cotton at center on back.			
	a. 1992. signature 10.	FV	1.75	6.00
	b. 1992. signature 11.	FV	1.00	5.00
	c. 2001. signature 11.	FV	FV	3.00
	d. 2003. signature 12.		FV	3.00
	s. Specimen.	—	—	40.00

40	1000 Kwacha	VG	VF	UNC
	1992 (1996); 2001; 2003. Red-violet, deep orange and dark olive-green on multicolor underprint. Jacaranda tree. Aardvark at left, Sorghum farmer on tractor at center on back.			
	a. 1992 (1996). Signature 11.	FV	1.25	5.50
	b. 2001. Signature 11.	FV	.75	4.50
	c. 2003. Signature 12.	FV	FV	3.00
	s. Specimen.	—	—	40.00

41	5000 Kwacha	VG	VF	UNC
	1992 (1996); 2001; 2003, 2005; 2006. Purple, dark brown and deep red on multicolor underprint. Murera / Acacia / Mopani tree at center. Lion facing at left, root cassava plant at center on back.			
	a. 1992 (1996). Signature 11.	FV	2.50	10.00
	b. 2001. Signature 11.	FV	1.75	5.50
	c. 2003. Signature 12.	FV	1.00	4.50
	d. 2005. Signature 12.	FV	FV	3.00
	e. 2006. Signature 12.	FV	FV	2.00
	s. Specimen.	—	—	40.00

42	10,000 Kwacha	VG	VF	UNC
	1992 (1996). Aqua, brown-violet and yellow-brown on multicolor underprint. Musuku tree at center. Porcupine at left, harvesting rice paddy at center on back. Signature 11.			
	a. Issued note.	FV	5.00	17.50
	s. Specimen.	—	—	50.00

2001 Issue

43	10,000 Kwacha	VG	VF	UNC
	2001-6. Aqua, brown-violet and yellow-brown on multicolor underprint. Like #42 but with foil fish eagle head at lower left.			
	a. 2001. Signature 11. Foil fish eagle faces left.	FV	FV	7.00
	b. 2003. Signature 12.	FV	FV	6.00
	c. 2003. Date as denominator. Foil fish eagle head points right.	FV	FV	6.00
	d. 2005. Signature 12.	FV	FV	6.00
	e. 2006. Signature 12.	FV	FV	6.00

2003 Issue

44	500 Kwacha	VG	VF	UNC
	2003-6. Multicolor. Polymer plastic.			
	a. 2003. Serial # wears off.	—	—	15.00
	b. 2003. Second printing.	FV	FV	1.00
	c. 2004. Signature 12.	FV	FV	1.00
	d. 2005. Signature 12.	FV	FV	1.00
	e. 2006. Signature 12.	FV	FV	1.00

45	1000 Kwacha	VG	VF	UNC
	2003-6. Multicolor. Polymer plastic.			
	a. 2003. Serial # wears off.	—	—	20.00
	b. 2003. Second Printing.	FV	FV	3.00
	c. 2004. Signature 12.	FV	FV	3.00
	d. 2005. Signature 12.	FV	FV	3.00
	e. 2006. Signature 12.	FV	FV	3.00

46	20,000 Kwacha	VG	VF	UNC
	2003-6. Multicolor.			
	a. 2003. Signature 12.	FV	FV	10.00
	b. 2005. Signature 12.	FV	FV	10.00
	c. 2006. Signature 12.	FV	FV	10.00

47	50,000 Kwacha	VG	VF	UNC
	2003, 2006. Multicolor.			
	a. 2003. Signature 12.	FV	FV	25.00
	b. 2006. Signature 12.	FV	FV	25.00

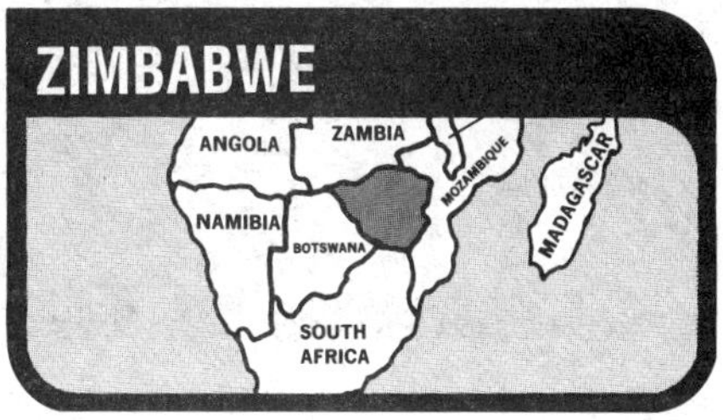

The Republic of Zimbabwe (formerly Rhodesia or Southern Rhodesia), located in the east-central part of southern Africa, has an area of 150,820 sq. mi. (390,580 sq. km.) and a population of 12.39 million. Capital: Harare (formerly Salisbury). The economy is d on agriculture and mining. Tobacco, sugar, asbestos, copper and chrome ore and coal are exported.

The Rhodesian area, the habitat of paleolithic man, contains extensive evidence of earlier civilizations, notably the world-famous ruins of Zimbabwe, a gold-trading center that flourished about the 14th or 15th century AD. The Portuguese of the 16th century were the first Europeans to attempt to develop south-central Africa, but it remained for Cecil Rhodes and the British South Africa Co. to open the hinterlands. Rhodes obtained a concession for mineral rights from local chiefs in 1888 and administered his African empire (named Southern Rhodesia in 1895) through the British South Africa Co. until 1923, when the British government annexed the area after the white settlers voted for existence as a separate entity, rather than for incorporation into the Union of South Africa. From Sept. of 1953 through 1963 Southern Rhodesia was joined with the British protectorates of Northern Rhodesia and Nyasaland into a multiracial federation. When the federation was dissolved at the end of 1963, Northern Rhodesia and Nyasaland became the independent states of Zambia and Malawi.

Britain was prepared to grant independence to Southern Rhodesia but declined to do so when the politically dominant white Rhodesians refused to give assurances of representative government. In November 1965, the white minority government of Southern Rhodesia unilaterally declared Southern Rhodesia an independent dominion. The United Nations and the British Parliament both proclaimed this unilateral declaration of independence null and void. In 1970, the government proclaimed a republic, but this too received no recognition. In 1979, the government purported to change the name of the colony to Zimbabwe Rhodesia, but again this was never recognized. Following a conference in London in December 1979, the opposition government conceded and it was agreed that the British government should resume control. A British governor soon returned to Southern Rhodesia. One of his first acts was to affirm the nullification of the purported declaration of independence. On April 18, 1980, pursuant to an act of the British Parliament, the Colony of Southern Rhodesia became independent within the Commonwealth as the Republic of Zimbabwe.

For earlier issues see Rhodesia.

MONETARY SYSTEM:

1 Dollar = 100 Cents

SIGNATURE/TITLE VARIETIES

	GOVERNOR		GOVERNOR
1	Dr. D. C. Krogh	2	K. Moyana
3	L. Tsumba	4	Dr. D. C. Krogh
5	Dr. K. J. Moyana	6	Dr. L. L. Tsumba
7	C. Chikaura	8	Dr. G. Gono
	FINANCE DIRECTOR		OPERATIONS DIRECTOR
A	Priscilla P. Mutembwa		Stephen J. Newton-Howes

ZIMBABWEAN BIRD WATERMARK VARIETIES

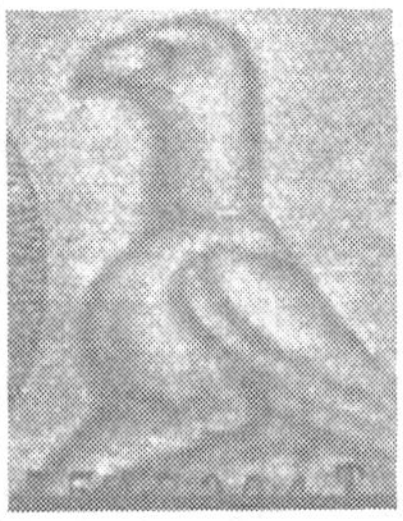	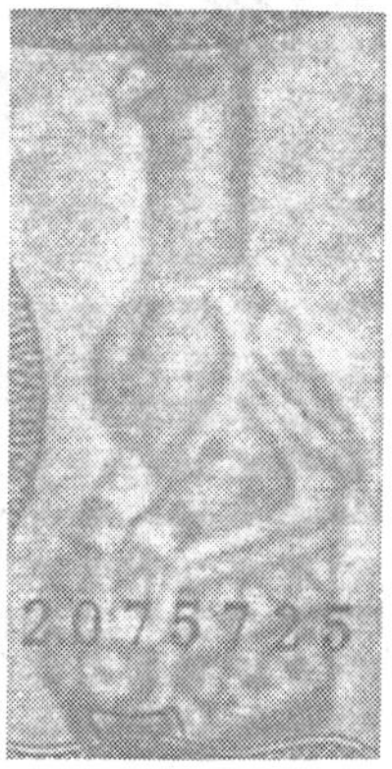	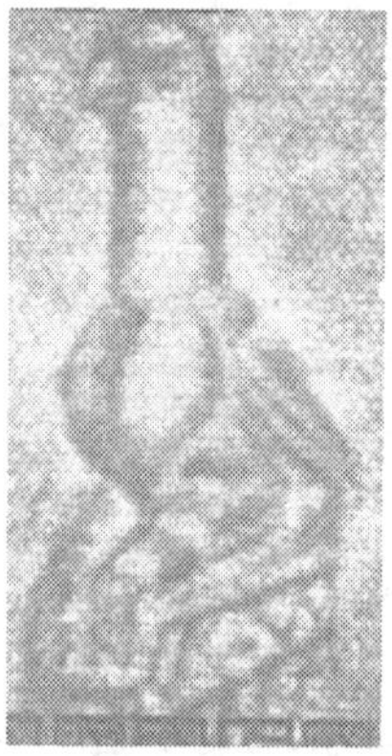
Type A Profile short neck	Type B 3/4 view medium neck	Type C 3/4 view long neck

RESERVE BANK OF ZIMBABWE

1980 ISSUE

#1-4 Chiremba balancing rock formation, Epworth (Harare) at ctr. r. Sign. varieties. Wmk: Zimbabwe bird. Replacement notes: Serial # prefix: *AW; BW; CW; DW* respectively.

1	2 Dollars	VG	VF	UNC
	1980 (1981); 1983; 1994. Blue and multicolor. Water buffalo at left. Tigerfish at center, Kariba Dam and reservoir at right on back.			
	a. Signature 1. Salisbury. 1980.	.50	2.25	10.00
	b. Signature 2. Harare. 1983.	.25	1.25	5.00
	c. Signature 3. Watermark: Type A. 1994.	.20	.75	3.75
	d. Signature 3. Watermark: Type B. 1994.	4.75	22.50	95.00

2	5 Dollars	VG	VF	UNC
	1980 (1981); 1982-83; 1994. Green and multicolor. Zebra at left. Village scene with two workers on back.			
	a. Signature 1. Salisbury. 1980.	1.75	5.50	24.00
	b. Signature 1. Harare. 1982.	1.25	5.00	22.50
	c. Signature 2. 1983.	.25	1.50	6.50
	d. Signature 3. 1994. Watermark: Type A.	.75	2.75	11.00
	e. Signature 3. 1994. Watermark: Type B.	3.00	12.50	50.00

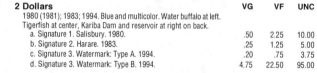

		VG	VF	UNC
3	**10 Dollars** 1980 (1981); 1982-83; 1994. Red and multicolor. Sable antelope at left. View of Harare and Freedom Flame monument on back.			
	a. Signature 1. Salisbury. 1980.	2.25	10.00	50.00
	b. Signature 1. Salisbury. 1982 (error).	5.00	20.00	100.
	c. Signature 1. Harare. 1982.	4.50	20.00	85.00
	d. Signature 2. 1983.	.75	2.75	11.00
	e. Signature 3. 1994.	.25	1.50	6.50

		VG	VF	UNC
4	**20 Dollars** 1980 (1982); 1982-83; 1994. Blue, black and dark green on multicolor underprint. Giraffe at left. Elephant and Victoria Falls on back.			
	a. Signature 1. Salisbury. 1980.	4.25	17.50	70.00
	b. Signature 1. Harare. 1982.	15.00	75.00	300.
	c. Signature 2. 1983.	1.25	5.00	15.00
	d. Signature 3. 1994.	.75	3.50	14.00

1994; 1997; 2001 Issues

#5-6 Chiremba balancing rock formation, Epworth (Harare) at ctr. r. Wmk: Zimbabwe bird, Type C. Sign. 3.

Replacement notes: Serial # prefix *AA; AB; AC; AD; AE;* and *AF* respectively.

		VG	VF	UNC
5	**5 Dollars** 1997. Brown, red-orange and purple on multicolor underprint. Terraced hills at center right on back.			
	a. Light brown back (litho).	.15	.75	3.00
	b. Darker brown back (intaglio).	.05	.20	1.00

		VG	VF	UNC
6	**10 Dollars** 1997. Red-brown, deep green and blue-black on multicolor underprint. Chilolo Cliffs at center right on back.	FV	FV	.35

		VG	VF	UNC
7	**20 Dollars** 1997. Deep blue, purple and gray-green on multicolor underprint. Victoria Falls at center right.	FV	FV	.40
8	**50 Dollars** 1994. Dark brown, olive-brown and red-orange on multicolor underprint. Great Zimbabwe ruins on back.	FV	FV	.50

		VG	VF	UNC
9	**100 Dollars** 1995. Brownish black and purple on multicolor underprint. Aerial view of Kariba Dam and reservoir at center right on back.	FV	FV	.60

		VG	VF	UNC
10	**500 Dollars** 2001. Dark brown and red on multicolor underprint. Hwange power station on back. Hologram silver foil at left, *500* added to bird watermark.	FV	FV	4.00

NOTICE

Readers with unlisted dates, signature varieties, etc. are invited to submit photocopies of their notes to: Standard Catalog of World Paper Money, 700 East State St. Iola, WI 54990-0001, E-Mail: george.cuhaj@fwpubs.com.

11 500 Dollars

	VG	VF	UNC
2001. Dark brown on tan and multicolor underprint. Like #10, without foil at left.	FV	FV	1.00

12 1000 Dollars

	VG	VF	UNC
2003. Brown, purple and green on multicolor underprint. Elephants on back.	FV	FV	1.00

2003 EMERGENCY CARGILL BEARERCHECKS

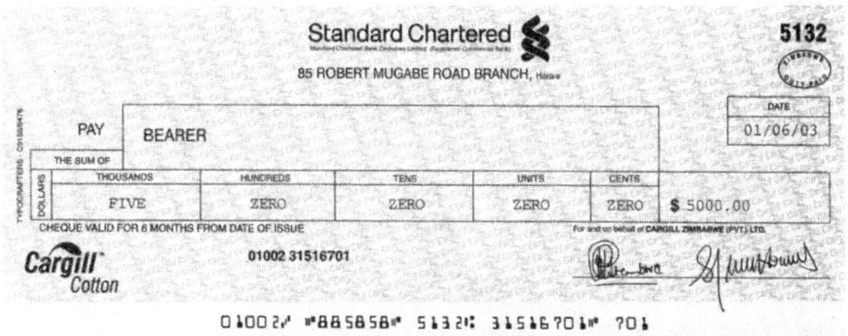

13 5000 Dollars

	VG	VF	UNC
2003. Watermark: Cotton plant. Printer: Typocrafters.			
a. 1.6.2003. Green.	5.00	20.00	85.00
b. 1.9.2003. Blue.	7.50	25.00	100.

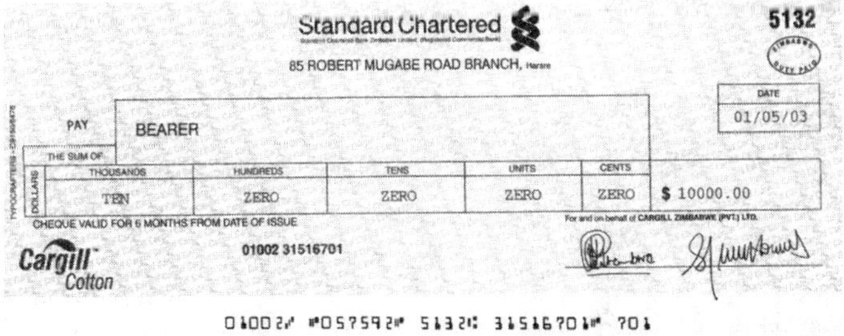

14 10,000 Dollars

	VG	VF	UNC
2003. Blue. Watermark: Cotton plant. Printer: Typocrafters.			
a. 1.5.2003.	10.00	45.00	175.
b. 1.9.2003.	12.00	55.00	200.

2003 EMERGENCY TRAVELLERS' CHECKS

#13-18 Reserve bank of Zimbabwe logo. Wave pattern on back. Pink and green unpt. Wmk: Zimbabwe bird, Type 1. Sign. 4.

		VG	VF	UNC
15	**1000 Dollars** 2003. Gray.	FV	5.00	20.00
16	**5000 Dollars** 2003. Red.	FV	3.00	15.00

17 10,000 Dollars

	VG	VF	UNC
2003. Light blue.	FV	7.50	25.00

18 20,000 Dollars

	VG	VF	UNC
2003. Olive green.	FV	10.00	35.00

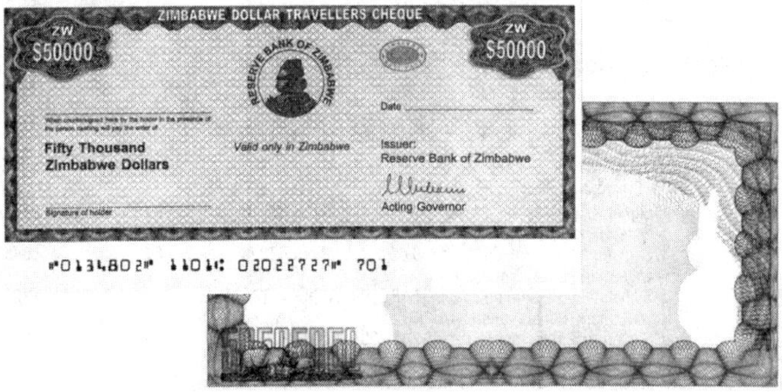

19 50,000 Dollars

	VG	VF	UNC
2003. Dark blue.	FV	20.00	75.00

20 100,000 Dollars

	VG	VF	UNC
2003. Brown.	FV	35.00	175.

2003 EMERGENCY BEARER CHECKS

#19-21 Rezerve Bank of Zimbabwe logo. Printed on paper stock from #8, $50.00. Wmk: Zimbabwe bird, Type 3.

21	5000 Dollars	VG	VF	UNC
	2003. Blue.			
	a. Signature 4. Redemption date: 31.1.2004. No RZB in watermark. Serial # prefix: A.	FV	5.00	20.00
	b. Signature 4. Redemption date: 30.6.2004. No RBZ in watermark. Serial # prefix: B-C.	FV	2.00	12.50
	c. Signature 5. Redemption date: 31.12.2004. With RZB in watermark. Serial # prefix: AA.	FV	2.50	10.00
	d. Signature 5. Redemption date: 31.12.2004. *GOVERNOR / DR. G. GONO.*	FV	1.25	5.00

22	10,000 Dollars	VG	VF	UNC
	2003. Red.			
	a. Signature 4. Redemption date: 31.1.2004. Without RZB in watermark. Serial # prefix: E.	FV	10.00	45.00
	b. Signature 4. Redemption date: 30.6.2004. Without RZB in watermark. Serial # prefix: F-G.	FV	3.75	30.00
	c. Signature 5. Redemption date: 31.12.2004. With RZB in watermark. Serial # prefix: BA.	FV	4.50	32.50
	d. Signature 5. Redemption date: 31.12.2004. With RZB in watermark. *GOVERNOR / DR. G. GONO.*	FV	FV	10.00

23	20,000 Dollars	VG	VF	UNC
	2003. Brown.			
	a. Signature 4. Redemption date: 31.1.2004. Without RZB in watermark. Serial # prefix: J.	FV	12.50	85.00
	b. Signature 4. Redemption date: 30.6.2004. Without RZB in watermark. Serial # prefix: K-L.	FV	6.25	50.00
	c. Signature 5. Redemption date: 31.12.2004. Without RZB in watermark. Serial # prefix: AA.	FV	55.00	225.
	d. Signature 5. Redemption date: 31.12.2004. *GOVERNOR* with RZB in watermark. Serial # prefix AA.	FV	7.50	50.00
	e. Signature 5. Redemption date: 31.12.2004. *GOVERNOR / DR. G. GONO.* with RZB in watermark.	FV	FV	35.00

2004 Emergency Cargill BearerChecks

24	10,000 Dollars	VG	VF	UNC
	1.4.2004. Blue.	3.00	12.50	45.00

25	20,000 Dollars	VG	VF	UNC
	1.4.2004. Green.	5.00	20.00	75.00

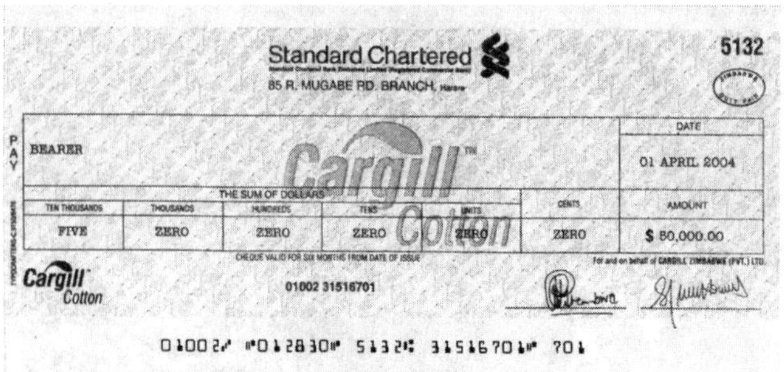

26	50,000 Dollars	VG	VF	UNC
	1.4.2004. Orange.	10.00	35.00	125.

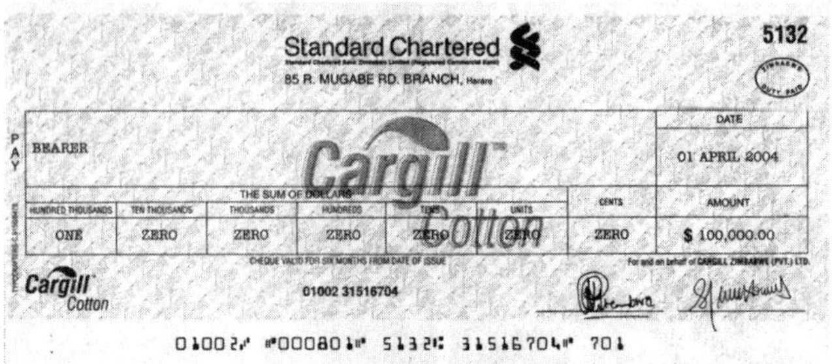

27	100,000 Dollars	VG	VF	UNC
	1.4.2004. Red.	12.00	40.00	150.

Collecting Paper Money

by Albert Pick
Translated by E. Sheridan

"To kill a person needs no knife . . .
a piece of paper that is written
. . . or printed on suffices."

With this observation the Chinese, as the inventors of paper, wished to emphasize the great need for responsibility in dealing with this material.

There is hardly any application of paper qualified to such a degree as paper money in providing that it is within man's power to have it be a benefit or a curse to mankind. On the one hand, lack of credit and a shortage of legal tender have been overcome by issues of paper money to serve trade and industry commensurate with economic development; yet on the other hand, the immense increase in the volume of paper money in inflationary periods has been the cause of economic and personal catastrophes. The many issues of paper money retaining their full value were mostly destroyed after redemption and have largely faded from the memory of man. The paper money originating during times of inflation and then becoming worthless has outlived the period, since it was no longer redeemable, and it acts as a constant reminder of the period of monetary devaluation.

Thus, paper money is considered by many people around the world as legal tender with an inglorious tradition. As negatively as periods of inflation influence the opinion of a superficial observer of the history of paper money, these relics of a monetary devaluation have positively influenced the collecting of paper money.

Frequently, the hope of a later redemption may have contributed toward placing the old notes in safekeeping. Later on, attempts were made to complete the series of notes and in this manner the first collections may have originated; perhaps even as early as the time of the French Revolution, when in addition to the French assignats and the "mandats Territoriaux," the regional issues of "Billets de confiance" were in circulation. In the United States, too, there was a very early opportunity to collect paper money as the Colonial and Continental bills, notes of the Confederate States and the numerous notes, rich in design, of the many 19th century banks became worthless as a circulating medium.

In our own time, an ever increasing number of persons come into contact with foreign currencies through international travel – and even war. A particularly pleasing note is retained as a souvenir and not infrequently becomes the cornerstone of a bank note collection. Here, it is a feature of the bank note that because of its relatively large surface (compared with a coin or postage stamp) it offers space for many motifs and frequently impresses the viewer with the quality of its printing on high-grade paper. The catalogs published in recent years provide the necessary reference tools for building a collection, and thus it is small wonder that the number of paper money collectors is steadily on the increase.

Particularly for the novice collectors not yet fully acquainted with the collecting sphere, hints are given regarding the different types of paper money, various avenues of collecting, historical backgrounds and the possibilities for building a specialized collection.

Government Paper Money

—Bank Notes—

Emergency Money

For some would-be collectors, the lack of knowledge and the means for easy orientation in a hobby causes a decline in interest and often ends in a short-lived participation. Conversely, an interested person can become a real collector if he is aided in acquainting himself with his new hobby and in finding the right way to develop a meaningful collection.

The collector of paper money should know from the start which items belong to his collecting sphere and what paper money represents.

In contrast to coins, which in the past represented money of intrinsic value guaranteed by virtue of the material in which they were struck, paper money is money of no intrinsic value; it is printed paper without material value.

Today, in common hobby parlance, we categorize as paper money all forms of money made of paper or printed on a paper-like material. Only a few decades ago, the term paper money, as applied to government issues, stood in contrast to other monetary forms of paper such as bank notes. Whereas the government paper money had to be considered general legal tender because the government was obliged to accept the notes at face value

France, 3 Livres, siege note, Mainz 1793

Germany, 2 Groschen, siege note of Kolberg, 1807

Italy, 500 Lire

Italy 1000 Lire, Banca d'Italia

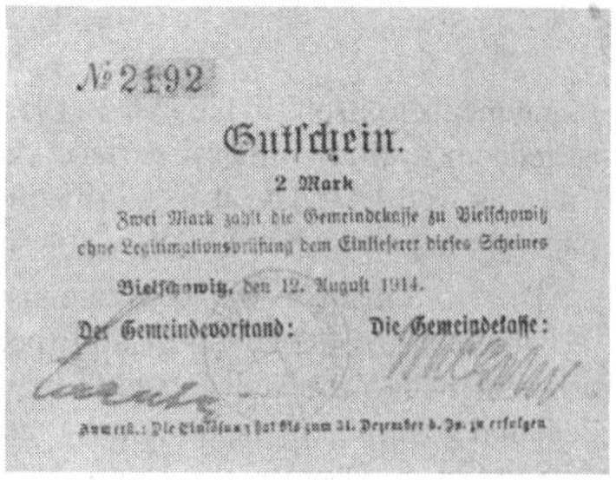

Germany, 2 Mark, Emergency money note of Bielschowitz, 1914

Germany, Emergency money note of Bremen, 1922

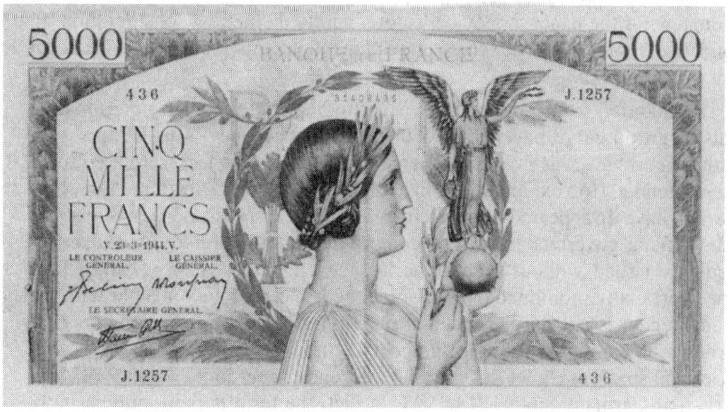

France, 5000 Francs, Banque de France, 1944

New Zealand, 2 Dollars with bird

Indonesia, 100 Rupiah with flowers, 1959

Seychelles, 10 Rupees with sea turtles

in payments to itself, in the case of the bank note, the issuing bank promises to redeem it at any time at its face value for legal tender. Still, in former times as well as today, it was difficult to recognize what was government paper money and what was bank notes.

There are many examples in the history of paper money of the adoption of bank notes by the government. Especially in times of distress, if the government had overtaxed a bank for its purposes, the bank's notes were declared government paper money (e.g. Spain, 1794, the notes of the Banco de San Carlos, and Austria, 1866). The opposite situation was less frequent; i.e., a bank adopting government paper money and making it into bank notes, yet there are also examples of this (Oldenburg, 1869). In our time, however, the difference between government paper money and the bank note is generally no longer discernible. This often involves differences contingent only on tradition or the organization of the government or banking authority which are of no consideration when using the notes as legal tender.

Differentiating between government paper money and the bank note remains for the paper money collector a purely theoretical consideration. In practice, few collectors exclude one or the other from their collecting except in rare instances.

In addition to the government paper money and the bank note, there is also a third kind of paper money, the emergency money. This form of substitute currency was issued to overcome a shortage or lack of government legal tender (for example, in times of distress, as a substitute for coins which have disappeared from circulation). Sometimes issued by authority of the official government or other competent authorizing body, but also frequently issued without such authority, these emergency issues may have been officially prohibited or tacitly tolerated, and accepted on a par with the legal tender issues they replaced, if only in a small district. Among the best known of such issues are the "notgeld," a familiar expression even to non-German speaking collectors for the emergency paper money issues of Austria and Germany circa 1914-1923. In fact, the term is being increasingly applied to many other emergency issues as well.

General Collection - Specialized Collection

A bank note collection does not always develop in a straight line direction. The interest in paper money is in many cases of a general nature and thus the individual collects everything he encounters. The general collection thus formed often does not please the collector as his interest matures. He may then select those collecting spheres that interest him most and will either dispose of all other notes not fitting those spheres or add to his collection only those notes which fit into his newly specialized collection. The sooner he can decide the limits of his collecting interests, the sooner he can concentrate on building his collection.

Thematic Collection

The creation of general paper money collections will increasingly become a matter only for the museums. The majority of private collectors can occupy themselves only with specialized spheres for financial reasons or lack of time, and even within these spheres the rare pieces may remain generally unobtainable for them. Thus, collectors are increasingly turning their attention to the aesthetic qualities of paper money. The idea of thematic collecting is becoming quite strong. The underlying causes for this are not only the financial considerations and the inability to acquire the rarest pieces, but also in the pleasure obtained from the beauty of individual notes.

Over the last decade a number of countries have stimulated interest in collecting bank notes by designs with definite motifs. Thus, indigenous birds are depicted on the different values of the Reserve Bank of New Zealand. In the Seychelles and a number of African states, notes show illustrations of animals. Representations of flowers are present on the Israeli notes of 1955 and the 1959 Indonesian currency. According to his choice of subject, the taste of the collector is not always adequate for building a collection which will find general recognition. With more ambitious themes, he is obliged to acquire some basic knowledge about the topic he has chosen. The wealth of motifs is inexhaustible, so that possibilities offer themselves even for very special themes.

Varieties

Even in the consideration of varieties, opinions of collectors differ. One collector is content to acquire one note of each basic type, and will ignore minor differences; another is interested in watermark varieties, various dates of issue, serial numbers, sheet marks, signatures, printers, color varieties and other differences within a type. It is by no means easy for a collector to determine what he will include along these lines and what he will leave out. The differences of material value in the one collecting sphere, and which frequently occur in varying combinations, can be of no consequence for another collecting sphere. A few examples will show that general guidelines, applying to all areas of paper money collecting, are impossible.

In the case of German Reichsbank notes from 1883-1914, the few dates varieties which delimit the different issues are included by almost all collectors. On the other hand, all date varieties are not even considered by the most specialized collectors of Belgian notes since the notes bear the date of the day of printing. In this instance collectors are usually satisfied with one note of each year. In areas such as Scottish, Italian and Romanian notes, there are also numerous date varieties and collectors who specialize in them. On United States paper money there are only year dates, sometimes followed by a letter suffix. This year date, as a rule, changes only when the type of note changes; while the letter following the year date moves forward by one if the signature change.

Example: $1 Silver Certificate
1928-D, signature Julian/Woodin
1928-E, Julian/Morgenthau
1934, Julian/Morgenthau

The notes dated 1928 have the Treasury seal on the left, those with 1934, on the right. On U.S. notes the year date hardly permits the date of issue to be determined, a better clue being taken from the suffix letter, or better still, the signatures.

Signature varieties are practically unknown for some countries, such as with German Reichsbank notes. Other countries, however, change note signatures with any change in officials (France, Belgium, Great Britain, several South American countries and others). Since these changes in signature are also important in determining the date of issue (such as with modern British notes which carry no date), these different signatures are of interest to all collectors. A change of signature in notes issued at the same time was already known on assignats of the 18th century. It is still found today with notes of the Scandinavian countries and Switzerland, where a signature

China 1 Kuan, Ming Dynasty, 14th century

Netherlands, 20 Stuiver cardboard coin of the City of Leyden, 1574

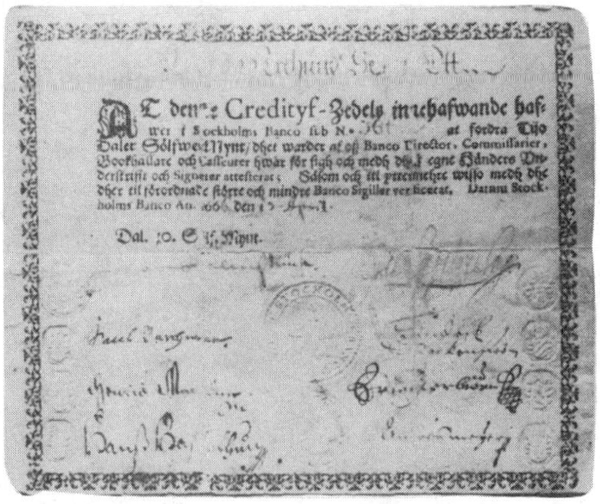

Sweeden, 10 Daler silver, Stockholms Banco, 1666, one of the oldest European banknotes

often does not change over lengthy periods (such as that of the bank president). Only the specialized collectors will deal with these changing signatures and they, too, must content themselves with the lower values.

Since variations in serial numbers, printers and colors do not occur too often in paper money, they are often included in a collection. Such things as prefix and suffix letters with serial numbers and sheet marks or plate numbers, on the other hand, may interest only specialized collectors, and then only when the bank note material is correspondingly plentiful.

History of Paper Money

In the 13th century, the famous Venetian, Marco Polo, undertook a journey to China. His records of this journey contain the first Western reports regarding the production and the use of paper money, a currency still incomprehensible for European conditions of that time, due to its lack of intrinsic worth. His contemporaries did not give credence to Marco Polo's report. Only much later were his accounts actually verified in the form of Chinese notes of the 14th century (Ming Dynasty) produced in the same manner. Today, such bluish-tinted notes are found in many of the larger collections, and it is now known that they were not the oldest notes, but stood at the end of a development which began already in the 7th century A.D. The Chinese, who called paper money "flying money" because of its light weight and ability to circulate over a wide area, had a well organized bank note clearing system as early as the 10th century.

Along with the first bank notes, the first counterfeiters also made their appearance. Numerous files still in existence provide information regarding the fight waged by the Chinese against these forgers.

The first European paper money is of much more recent origin. It was emergency money issued in 1483 by the Spaniards during the siege by the Moors. Since up to the present day not a single one of these notes has been discovered, it may be assumed that they were all destroyed after their redemption. In contrast to this, the cardboard coins produced in 1574 by the beleaguered citizens of Leyden are preserved in various denominations. The cities of Leyden and Middelburg were lacking silver for the striking of coins during the siege by the Spaniards, so they took as a material the covers of Catholic parish registers. The cardboard coins may indeed be described as the oldest preserved European money consisting of paper, but on the other hand, they are not true paper money.

Only 300 years after Marco Polo's account of Chinese paper money, the Stockholms Banco in Sweden issued the first European bank notes for circulation. The cause for the issuing of these notes was the devaluation of the copper plate money introduced in 1644. In the search for a legal tender for a transition period, Johann Palmstruch suggested the issue of so-called "Kreditivsedlar." In 1661 the first notes were issued made out in Riksdaler specie and Daler silver. It is assumed that this involved forms where the denomination and currency were inserted in handwriting. More is known about the second issue which occurred in 1662-1664. In this instance the denomination was imprinted. In 1666 the third, considerably augmented, issue was ordered. Of these notes for 10, 25, 50 and 100 Daler silver, approximately 60 specimens have been preserved.

At this time, the so-called Goldsmith Notes were already known in England. The transactions of the English goldsmiths also included brokerage and money changing. When King Charles I demanded a part of the ready money for himself, deposited by merchants in the Tower or in the office of the Chief Cashier of the government, the merchants went in search of new depositories and discovered these in the vaults of the goldsmiths. With this deposited money, the goldsmiths began speculating and were thus also able to pay interest. Withdrawal periods were laid down for deposits yielding interest, those not yielding interest being repaid on demand. The goldsmiths thus became bankers, issuing notes in respect to the deposits which, as required, were made out to the bearer without an indication of name. For the purpose of facilitating the redemption of parts of the deposited money, possibly for third parties, the notes were even issued in smaller denominations in round sums, and these notes can be considered forerunners of bank notes.

The desire for an independent credit institution was strengthened when some goldsmiths went bankrupt on the king's refusal to discharge some debts which fell due. In 1694 the Bank of England was founded, and its first notes were similar to the notes of the goldsmiths. Acts of Parliament strengthened the special position of the Bank, and merchants increasingly came to realize that support of the Bank provided them backing in time of crisis; thus the Bank of England succeeded in obtaining a firm foundation.

In Scotland, one year later than in England, a central bank, the Bank of Scotland, was also founded. In Norway, then a Danish province, the issue of

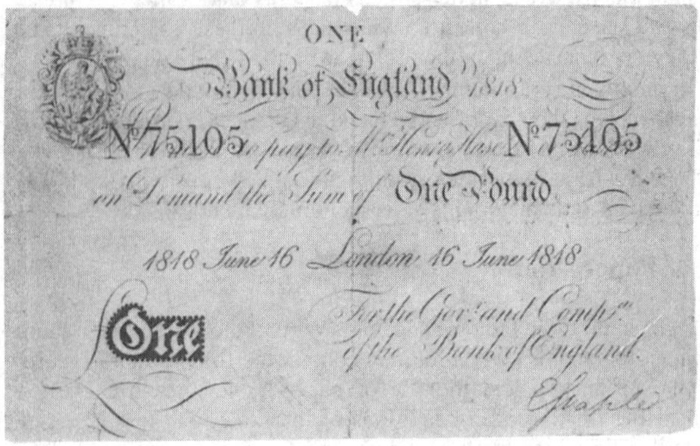

Great Britain, 1 Pound, Bank of England, 1818

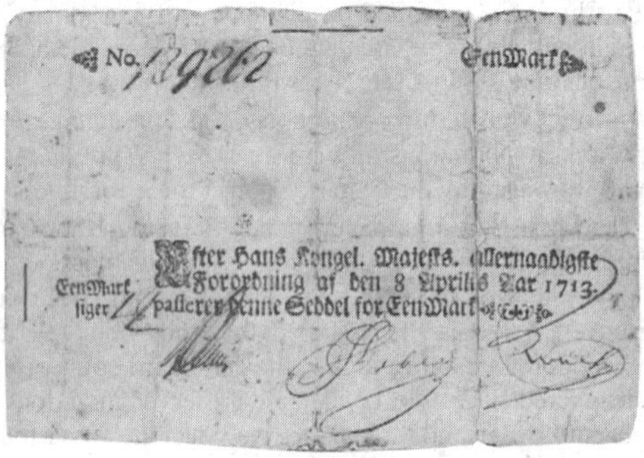

Denmark, 1 Mark, 1713

non-interest bearing notes occurred in the same year on the initiative of the merchant Thor Mohlen. In Denmark itself, King Frederick IV had paper money produced 18 years later, in 1713, during the Nordic Wars.

The poor financial position of France forced King Louis XIV to carry out a "reformation" of the coins in circulation. In 1703 he ordered coins to be withdrawn, overstamped, and then reissued at a higher rate. Receipts were issued for the withdrawn coins and this so-called coin scrip was declared legal tender.

The continued indebtedness of the government persisted even after the king's death, and it was therefore not astonishing that the Scotsman John Law's ideas for the restoration of the government finances were gladly seized upon. Law wished to increase circulation of money by issuing bank notes and promoting credit. In 1716 he received permission for founding the Banque Generale which issued "Ecus" (Taler) in the form of notes. In 1718 the bank was taken over by the government. With the notes later made out to "Livres Tournois" and the shares of the two colonial companies "Compagnie des Indes" and "Compagnie D'Occident," Law indulged in a dangerous financial and stock exchange scheme which resulted in 1720 in a tremendous catastrophe. The bank was closed and Law had to leave France, abandoning his assets.

This was not to remain the only French experiment with paper money in the 18th century. France's ever-unfavorable financial position deteriorated still further through the revolution. The receding revenues of the government faced increased demands in the face of burgeoning expenditures. In accordance with a plan worked out by Tallyrand, the first assignats were issued in 1790, for which confiscated Church property was to serve as security. Notes of the first issue bore interest, while the later issues did not.

For relieving the shortage of small change, many towns and municipalities issued so-called "Billets de confiance," of which a few thousand types were in circulation. The government, too, was not printing assignats in small denominations. Simultaneously the issues of higher value were continually being increased.

The Royal Assignats were substituted at the inception of the Republic by new issues which were themselves superceded in 1795, upon the introduction of the metric system, by assignats of Franc currency. On January 1, 1796, over 27 million Livres in assignats were in circulation, the value of which merely amounted to one-half of one percent of the face value.

For the purpose of restoring confidence in the currency, it was decided to abolish the assignats and to issue a new type of paper money, the "Mandats Territoriaux." At a conversion ratio of 30 to 1, "Promesses des Mandats Territoriaux" were initially issued for the assignats to be converted. The actual mandats were later issued only in small quantities. Even this new kind of paper money was unable to put a brake on inflation, though. Within a few weeks the value of the mandats dropped by 95 percent. By November, 1796, all notes were declared worthless.

After the disappearance of the assignats and mandats, a number of note-issuing banks originated. Their notes, however, circulated only in small quantities. Out of one of these banks, the "Caisse des Comptes Courants," the Bank of France was founded in 1800, due mainly to the influence of Napoleon.

In other European countries, too, attempts were made in the 18th century to eliminate the financial difficulties of the government by issuing paper money. In Russia, the Assignation Bank was established in 1768. Its paper money was widely accepted. However, when the government began circulating ever increasing quantities of notes during the second war against the Turks (1787-1792), confidence waned and the notes lost value. Since that time Russia has continued to issue government paper money in an uninterrupted sequence.

The Austrian Wars of Succession and the battles under Maria Theresia with Frederick the Great had encumbered the Austrian government heavily with debts. At that time, attention was turned to the issue of paper money. The "Banco del Giro," founded in 1703, was originally supposed to issue obligations for circulation, but confidence in this bank was found wanting, so the plan was quickly abandoned. Only when administration of the bank was transferred to the city of Vienna and the name changed to "Wiener Stadt-Banco" did the mistrust disappear.

In 1759 the first provisional paper money issue came about. It was superceded by the true government paper money in 1762. Initially these notes, termed "Bancozettel" (Bank Scrip), were popular, but when government indebtedness continually rose because of wars, and various new issues in ever-greater quantities became necessary, the notes lost value. The war with

Poland, 10 Groszy, 1974

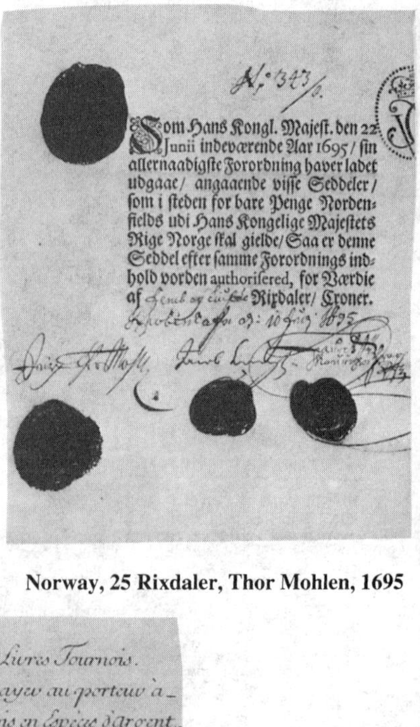

Norway, 25 Rixdaler, Thor Mohlen, 1695

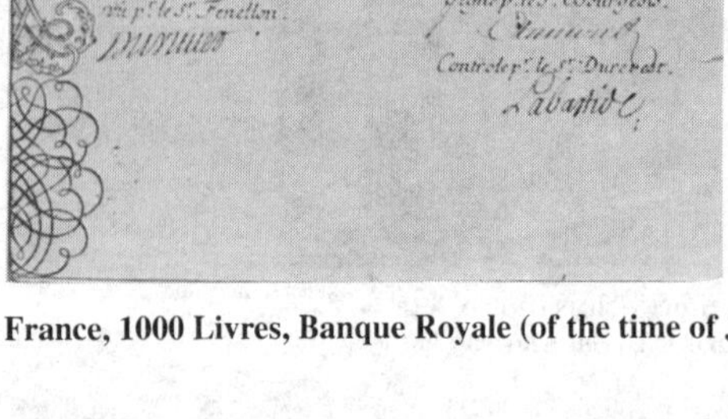

France, 1000 Livres, Banque Royale (of the time of John Law), 1719

France produced the peak of indebtedness and the government found itself incapable of continuing to redeem the notes. Only a monetary reform could prevent national bankruptcy. Thus, it was decided in 1811 to issue "Redemption Notes," which could be converted at the ratio of 1:5 for the old Banco scrip.

Soon the value of these new notes also dropped and they were followed in 1813 by another kind of paper money, the "Anticipation Notes" (anticipatory of future taxes). The end of the Napoleonic Wars gave rise to a new hope for a peaceful economic development and a stable currency. In 1816 the "Austrian National Scrip Bank" was established to create legal tender of stable value with its notes.

The first German money of paper material was the issue of the previously mentioned cardboard coins in the Dutch towns of Leyden and Middelburg in 1574. Whereas these were emergency money, the "Banco Scrip" issued in 1705 by the Elector Johann Wilhelm can be considered the first real paper money in Germany. The Elector had founded the "Banco di gyro d'affrancatione," whose notes were in fact made out to individual names, but were transferable.

In Ansbach-Bayreuth the "Hochfurstlich Brandenburgische Muntz-Banco" made out so-called "Banco-Billets" (Bank Scrip) by the middle of the 18th century. However, in exactly the same manner as the interest-bearing bank notes of the "Hochfurstlich Brandenburg-Anspach-Bayreuthische Hof-Banco," founded in 1780, they remained of little importance in the way of a legal tender.

The fear of monetary devaluation by the introduction of paper money was too deeply rooted in Germany. Until the end of the 18th century and partly until the middle of the 19th century such issues were planned but decisions postponed.

USA, 20 Dollars, Georgia, Bank of Commerce, 1857

Germany, 1 Taler, Saxony, 1855

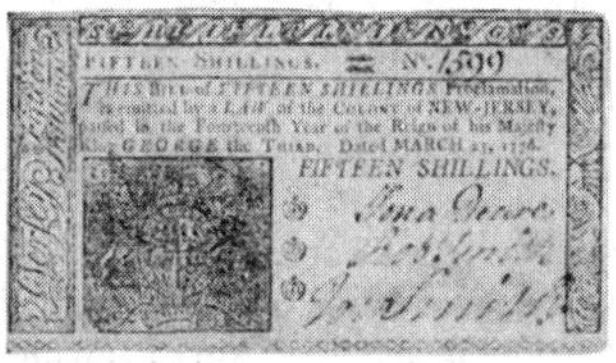

USA, 15 Shillings, New Jersey, 1776

Germany, 5 Thaler, Prussia, 1806

In Prussia the first notes were issued by the "Konigliche Giro-und Lehnbank" founded in 1765. The notes, in denominations of Pound-Banco, however, remained of little importance in circulation. Only those notes issued from 1820 onwards gained any importance. The bank name was changed to "Preussische Bank" in 1847, from which the Reichsbank originated in 1876.

Of greater importance at the beginning of the 19th century was the Prussian government paper money, the "Tresorscheine" (bank-safe notes).

In Bavaria, attempts were made at the end of the 18th and the beginning of the 19th century to create an issue of government paper money by issuing diverse monetary substitutes. Government indebtedness was therefore not less than in countries with paper money issues.

It was the time of peace following the Napoleonic Wars that brought a slow financial recovery. But the lack of credit and shortage of legal tender, due to the favorable development of trade, was not eliminated until 1835, when the Bayerische Hypotheken-und Wechselbank was founded. This institution in subsequent years issued notes of 10 and 100 Gulden and remained the only Bavarian central bank until the foundation of the German Reich.

At the beginning of the 19th century, paper money remained unpopular in Germany. A change occurred after 1848, when some German states felt the need to produce their own paper money to protect themselves against notes of smaller states whose issue quantities far exceeded the circulation requirements of their own areas. The larger states could then prohibit the circulation of these notes within their boundaries. The decisive step on the way toward centralization of banks in Germany occurred in 1875 with the new Bank Act and the foundation of the Reichsbank. The last four banks retained their issuing rights up to 1935.

In Italy the banking system developed earlier than in all other European countries. Deposit receipts and promissory notes made out by the banks existing as early as the Middle Ages, such as the "Casa di St. Giorgio," in Genoa, the "Banco di Sant' Ambrogio" in Milan and the "Banco di Rialto" in Venice, were transferable with an endorsement. These notes can be considered forerunners of modern bank notes. Real bank notes, however, were first issued in the middle of the 18th century in the Kingdom of Sardinia. Subsequently came the notes of the "Sacro Monte della Pieta di Roma" and those of the "Banco di Santo Spirito di Roma."

In Poland, issues of paper money first appeared during the 18th century. Rebels under the leadership of Kosciuszko issued various kinds of notes in 1794. With the crushing of the rebellion, paper money issues also ceased. Only in the Duchy of Warsaw, created by Napoleon (personal union with the Kingdom of Saxony), did paper money circulate again, so-called currency notes resembling Saxon currency tickets in their design.

It might be expected that paper money became known in America much later than in Europe. But exactly like in Europe, North America became acquainted with money of no intrinsic value in the 1600s.

The inadequate supply of coins in Canada under French colonial administration led to a chronic lack of legal tender. In order to at least ensure the soldiers' pay, the Canadians resorted to self-help and utilized quartered playing cards, to which the treasurer's seal and signatures of the Governor and Administrator were added, as paper currency. In 1685 the first money of this nature was circulated. It was the intention to withdraw these emer-

Italy, 7 Scudi, Banco di Santo Spirito di Roma, 1786

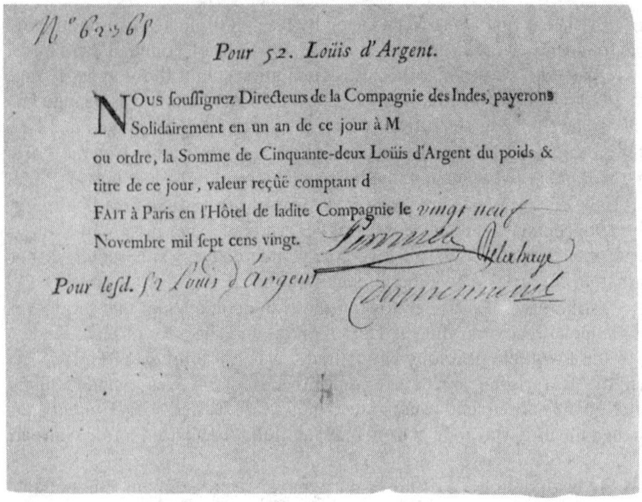

France, 52 Louis d' Argent, Compagnie des Indies, Banque Royale (of the time of John Law), 1720

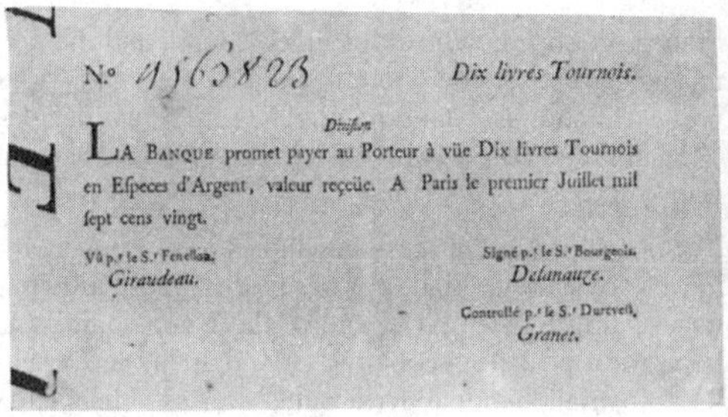

France, 10 Livres (of the time of John Law), 1720

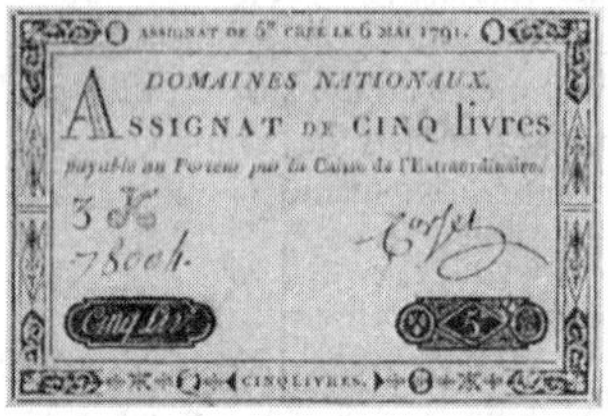

France, 5 Livres, Royal Assignat, 1791

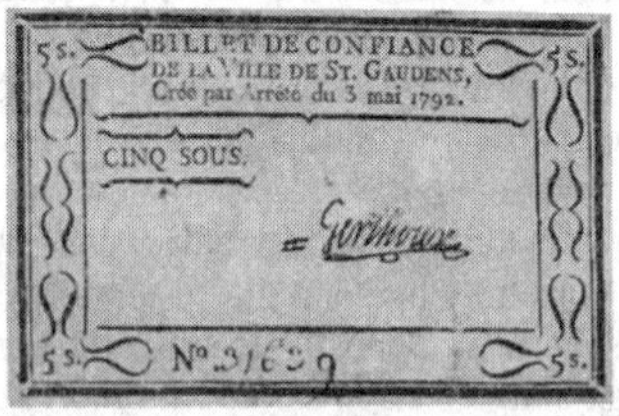

France, 5 Sous, Billet de confiance, St. Gaudens, 1972

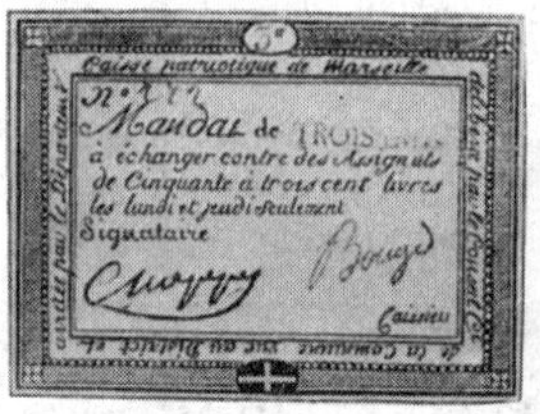

France, 3 Livres, Billet de Confiance, Marseille, 1792

France, 4000 Livres, Assignat, 1792

France, 2000 Francs, Assignat, 1794

gency items of legal tender immediately after adequate coin supplies arrived, but this did not happen. Further issues which included half or whole cards followed, gaining circulation throughout the whole of the colony. The money remained valid until 1718/19 when the governor had it withdrawn from circulation and prohibited further issues.

In 1729, new issues of this strange money were recorded and from then on circulated in ever increasing quantities. When the British took over the Canadian territories in 1759, more than 14 million Livres of such notes were in circulation. Because the French government refused to redeem the notes, the value of playing card money dropped considerably until an agreement was finally reached for its redemption.

In 1690, the Colony of Massachusetts lacked the necessary metallic currency to pay its soldiers returning from Canada and this led to the production of the Colonial Bills of Credit. A few years later other colonies, such as Connecticut, New Hampshire, New Jersey, New York, Pennsylvania, Rhode Island and South Carolina followed with similar issues. It was believed that an increase in the paper money would foster general prosperity, thus great quantities of new notes were constantly being created. Benjamin Franklin was also of this opinion, as may be seen from his treatise "A Modeste Inquiry Into the Nature and Necessity of a Paper Money." All attempts by the British government to bring the devaluation of paper money to an end at the beginning of the 18th century failed, and thus, America with its Colonial bills encountered the same experience France had with its John Law notes: they became completely worthless.

After the battle of Lexington in 1775, a new attempt was made to issue paper money in the form of Continental bills issued by order of the Continental Congress. After being in circulation for just a year, the notes had already lost some of their value. By 1777, ten dollars in Continental bills was worth only one silver dollar. In 1780, one silver dollar fetched 75 of the Continental currency. By 1781, the ratio was 1000 to 1. George Washington at the time observed in a letter that a wagon full of notes was just sufficient for purchasing a wagon full of provisions.

Liberal laws in the 19th century allowed an almost incalculable number of private note-issuing banks to form, many of which circulated worthless, sometimes fraudulent note issues. So-called "wildcat banks" established their offices in such remote areas - where there were more wildcats than people - as to make redemption of their notes virtually impossible. In the New England states, by contrast, the introduction of severe penalties against swindlers and the rise of an effective clearing house system allowed a solid banking system to develop.

Due to the Civil War, the currency confusion which existed in time of peace was further compounded, particularly as the Confederate States of America and its constituent states began issuing notes which quickly became worthless. However, it was also during the Civil War that the first United States government paper money originated, the beginning of an unbroken string of notes which remain legal tender to this day.

The American bills of the last century, rich in design and well printed, are popular with collectors today, abroad as well as in the U.S.

In most of the civilized world the development towards centralizing the bank note system took place during the second half of the 19th century or in the first decades of the 20th century. Central banks were established which ousted the private or local banks issuing notes, or at least considerably limited their influence on circulating paper money issues.

Until a few years ago, paper money could be described as the most modern form of currency, but we are today on the threshold of a new development. The system of payment by check, some two decades ago common only in business, is increasingly gaining in importance. The use of checks in the private sector has today become a matter of course. Just beyond is the use of the credit card and other electronic fund transfers which may someday create a moneyless society. The development of money from the precoin era to the days of coin as the dominant legal tender to the paper money which ousted the coin is again about to begin a new era.

Collecting Early Note Issues

Within the scope of a general collection, a collector attempting to acquire notes from the beginnings of the history of paper money will soon discover that he will hardly be in a position, due to the lack of available and affordable material, to form a review of the early history of paper money with the individual specimens he has purchased.

The oldest bank note obtainable is the Chinese Ming note. This note is indeed rare, but it is still feasible today to acquire it. The Leyden cardboard coins, too, considered to be the earliest European form of money made of paper, are still obtainable. Considerably more difficult, if not impossible, is the situation regarding the Swedish notes of the 17th century, the early Bank of England notes, the Norwegian Thor Mohlen notes and the French coin scrip. These notes are all firmly entrenched in museums and other major collections. The few specimens occasionally placed on the market fetch very high prices. Only a modicum of good fortune, along with strong financial standing, can assist in building a collection of these early notes.

It looks a little more favorable for the collector with regard to John Law notes. Of the 1720 issues (January and July), the 10 Livres note is still procurable. More difficult, though, is the 100 Livres note. The 50 and 1000 Livres of 1720 and the notes of 1719 are offered only rarely and at high prices.

French assignats and mandats of 1792-1794 are still relatively easy to obtain today, and with a great deal of endurance and collector's skill, it is possible to assemble a specialized collection.

Of the "Billets de Confiance" orginating from the same period, notes of the different local authorities and towns, there are several thousands. These notes may indeed represent the oldest group of emergency money notes. With a lot of patience a collector may gather a small collection of some 100 notes of this description during the course of several years, if he is able to build on a collection bought from French collectors.

Austria, 10 gulden (form), 1762

1 Fun

2 Fun

Japan, Hansatsu (clan or local notes)

Apart from those already mentioned, not many European notes remain from the 18th century which are within the reach of the collector.

In Poland the treasury notes in denominations of 5 and 10 Groszy, 4, 5, 10 and 25 Zloty, issued in 1794 during the Kosciuszko uprising, are obtainable. The other denominations, 1, 50 and 100 Zloty, are rare, with the 500 and 1000 Zloty practically unobtainable. The Taler notes of the Duchy of Warsaw, reminiscent of Saxony currency tickets, are also still procurable. Danish notes of 1792 until the beginning of the 19th century belong to the already expensive class of old notes from that country still on the market. Equally, Swedish and Norwegian notes of the 18th century are still obtainable. The same applies to the latter as to the Danish notes, being highly popular in Scandinavia and therefore achieving correspondingly high prices.

The old Russian notes appearing in private collections generally originate from the beginning of the 19th century. Older notes are very rare and are found only as singles in key collections.

American Colonial and Continental bills issued at the end of the 18th century can be purchased without difficulty, even though prices for such notes rose considerably in the U.S. during the 1976 Bicentennial celebration.

Among older non-European notes, mention should be made of the Japanese "Hansatsu" or "Shisatsu." These narrow, bookmark-like and thematically rich notes were issued by the many different Daimios (territorial

Austria, 10 Kreuzer,
Emergency money note,
Marienthal (Bohemia), 1848

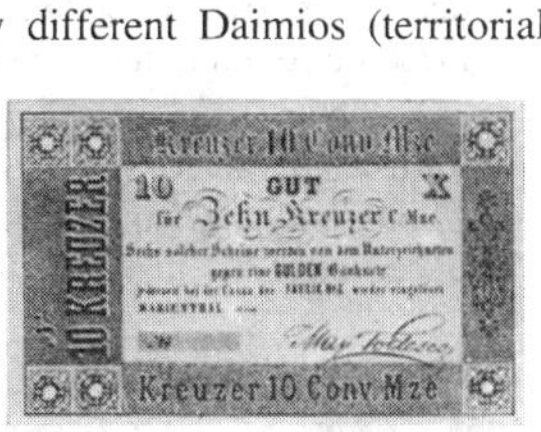

Italy, 50 Lire, Torino, 1765

Portugal, 10 Milreis, 1799

rulers) and impress the Western collector as exotic. There are many thousands of these notes available relatively cheaply. They are hard to attribute, but perhaps a Japanese collector or dealer can help.

Of the first Austrian issues through 1796, none of the original notes are offered. The low denominations of the 1800 and 1806 issues, on the other hand, are still plentiful and inexpensive today. Among the numerous other Austrian issues of the 19th century there are partly decorative notes available at a favorable price.

Among collectors of national German notes, the number of whom is rising steadily, many are now attempting to obtain German notes issued before 1871. Such old German notes, including issues of private banks in Mark currency up to 1914, can be acquired in only a few pieces. The systematic building of this type of collection is no longer feasible today.

The difficulty in procuring bank notes from the beginnings of paper money history may stimulate collectors to acquire at least some singles which are then given prominent display as very noteworthy showpieces, independently of the building of the rest of the collection.

Counterfeiters

The battle against counterfeiters pervades the entire history of paper money. The Chinese occupied themselves with protection against counterfeits by enforcing strict regulations. Forgers were given the death penalty, and the informer received a reward along with the property of the criminal. The essential aids in the battle against counterfeiting were, and remain, the finesse in printing techniques and paper manufacture, in connection with which the watermark and, during the last century, the printing of the guilloches, play a special part.

The recognition of old notes as counterfeits generally requires great experience on the part of the collector. The lack of means of comparison renders recognition difficult and frequently such notes are in a collection for many years before they are recognized. This discovery is not as painful for a paper money collector as it would be for collectors of other objects, since the value of a contemporary counterfeit bank note is little less than the original in many cases. With common notes, the counterfeit may well be worth more than the original.

Collectors of paper money differentiate between counterfeiting and alteration. A counterfeit note is false in all its parts; whereas an altered note originated from a genuine note. If, for example, an overprint has been added later, or the denomination was raised on a genuine note, then it is termed an alteration.

Most counterfeiters fail because of special types of processing machines which are not available for their use in imitating genuine production methods. Even professional qualifications and artistic abilities will not suffice for coping with the sophisticated security techniques employed by prominent bank note printers, especially with modern paper money.

If, however, such counterfeits were carried out at the instigation of the government or official authorities, then the possibility existed for achieving so-called "perfect" counterfeits. The two best-known examples in this respect are found in the last century and during World War II.

After Napoleon's entry into Vienna, he ordered the printing blocks for the Austrian Banco Scrip to be imitated, and notes, distinguishable from originals only by paper tint, to be printed in Paris. Despite the ban pronounced after his marriage to Princess Marie Louise on issuing the notes, such counterfeits did enter circulation. Russian ruble notes, too, were forged on Napoleon's instructions.

With the greatest bank note forgery of all time, known under the code of "Operation Bernhard," the press, radio and television have repeatedly occupied themselves with the postwar period, particularly since such counterfeit notes were subsequently discovered in Lake Toplitz, Austria. Books have also been written on this subject. The German Security Service prepared counterfeit Bank of England notes during World War II after careful preparatory work in laboratories hidden in concentration camps. The finest machinery and specifically produced watermarked paper were used by experts and inmates of the camps. These notes, circulated via neutral foreign countries (the payment to the spy "Cicero" became known especially), were so identical to the genuine notes that the Bank of England was compelled to withdraw the subject issue from circulation.

There are also notes which were imitated to the detriment of collectors. After the issuing of the first notgeld notes in 1914, the number of notgeld collectors began increasingly steadily during subsequent years. The high demand for these first issues prompted some local authorities and other issuing offices to produce reprints of these sometimes primitively printed notes. In contrast to the rare originals, these reprints are generally considerably cheaper.

The numerous fancy issues of notgeld, intended for the collector in the period 1920-1922, also belong here.

Particularly easy is the counterfeiting of overprinting on notes. The stamp "Fezzan," on the 5-Franc note of the Banque de l'Afrique Occidentale, is an example of such a forgery and can be differentiated only with difficulty from the original stamp.

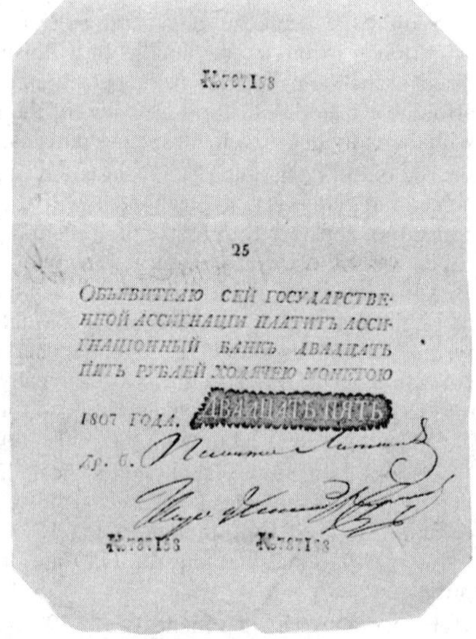

Falsification of a Russian 25 Rubles note of 1807 (by Napoleon's Army

Germany, Alteration to 100 Mark of a genuine 20 Mark note, issued by Allied Military administration authority

Germany, Falsification of an English 50 Pound note (World War II)

Brazil, Alteration of a genuine 10 Milreis note to 100 Milreis

COUNTRY / BANK IDENTIFICATION GUIDE

Afghanistan / Bank of Afghanistan

Algeria / Banque Centrale D' Algerie

Armenia / Armenia Republic Bank

Armenia / Armenia Republic Bank

Belarus / Belarus National Bank

Belarus / Belarus National Bank

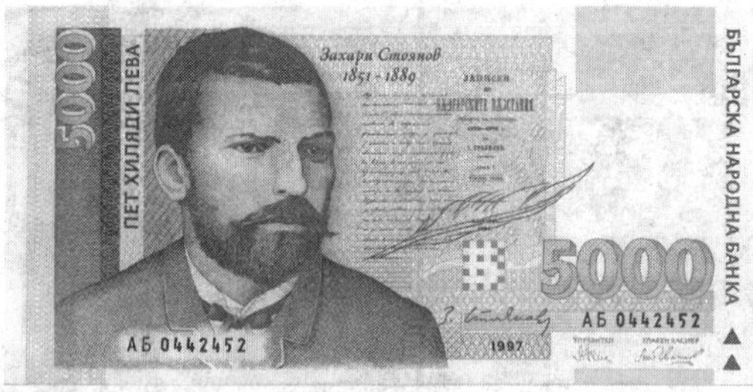

Bulgaria / Bulgarian National Bank

Cambodia / National Bank of Cambodia

COUNTRY / BANK IDENTIFICATION GUIDE

Georgia / Georgian National Bank

Kyrgystan / Kyrgyz Bank

Greece / Bank of Greece

Lao / Bank of the Lao PDR

Kazakhstan / Kazakhsta National Bank

Libya / Bank of Libya

North Korea / Korean Central Bank

Macedonia / National Bank of the Republic of Macedonia

Mongolia / Mongol Bank

Transnistria / Banka Nistriana

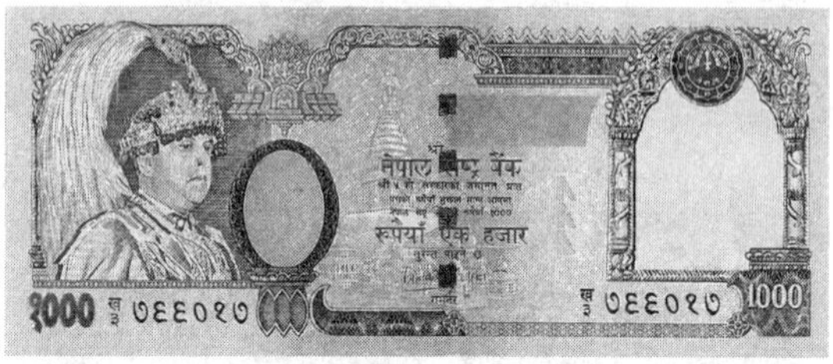

Nepal / State Bank

Uzbekistan / Central Bank of Uzbekistan Republic

Thailand / Bank of Thailand

Ukraine / Ukrainian National Bank

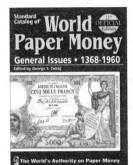

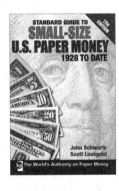

BANK NOTE PRINTERS

Printers' names, abbreviations or monograms will usually appear as part of the frame design or below it on face and/or back. In some instances the engraver's name may also appear in a similar location on a note. The following abbreviations identify printers for many of the notes listed in this volume:

ABNC .... American Bank Note Company (USA)
BABN(C) .... British American Bank Note Co., Ltd. (Canada)
B&S .... Bouligny & Schmidt (Mexico)
BDDK .... Bunddesdruckerei (Germany)
BEPP .... Bureau of Engraving & Printing, Peking (China)
BF .... Banque de France (France)
BFL .... Barclay & Fry Ltd. (England)
BWC .... Bradbury, Wilkinson & Co. (England)
CABB .... Compania Americana de Billetes de Banco (ABNC)
CBC .... Columbian Banknote Co. (US)
CBNC .... Canadian Bank Note Company (Canada)
CC .... Ciccone Calcografica S.A. (Italy)
CCBB .... Compania Columbiana de Billetes de Banco (CBC)
CdM- .... Casa da Moeda (Brazil)
CdM- .... Casa de Moneda (Argentina, Chile, etc.)
CHB .... Chung Hua Book Co. (China)
CMN .... Casa de Moneda de la Nacion (Argentina)
CMPA .... Commercial Press (China)
CNBB .... Compania Nacional de Billetes de Banco (NBNC)
CONB .... Continental Bank Note Company (US)
CPF .... Central Printing Factory (China)
CSABB .... Compania Sud/Americana de Billetes de Banco .... (Argentina)
CS&E .... Charles Skipper & East (England)
DLR .... De La Rue (England)
DTB .... Dah Tung Book Co., and Ta Tung Printing (China)
E&C .... Evans & Cogswell (CSA)
EAW .... E.A. Wright (US)
FLBN .... Franklin-Lee Bank Note Company (US)
FNMT .... Fabrica Nacional de Moneda y Timbre (Spain)
G&D .... Giesecke & Devrient (Germany)
HBNC .... Hamilton Bank Note Compay (USA)
HKB .... Hong Kong Banknote (Hong Kong)
HKP .... Hong Kong Printing Press (Hong Kong)
H&L .... Hoyer & Ludwig, Richmond, Virginia (CSA)
HLBNC .... Homer Lee Bank Note Co. (US)
H&S .... Harrison & Sons Ltd. (England)
IBB .... Imprenta de Billetes-Bogota (Colombia)
IBSFB .... Imprenta de Billetes-Santa Fe de Bogota (Colombia)
IBNC .... International Bank Note Company (US)
JBNC .... Jeffries Bank Note Company (US)
JEZ .... Joh. Enschede en Zonen (Netherlands)
K&B .... Keatinge & Ball (CSA)
KBNC .... Kendall Bank Note Company, New York (USA)
LN .... Litografia Nacional (Colombia)
NAL .... Nissen & Arnold (England)
NBNC .... National Bank Note Company (US)
OCV .... Officina Carte-Valori (Italy)
ODBI .... Officina Della Banca D'Italia (Italy)
OFZ .... Orell Füssli, Zurich (Switzerland)
P&B .... Perkins & Bacon (England)
PBC .... Perkins, Bacon & Co. (England)
PB&P .... Perkins, Bacon & Petch (England)
SBNC .... Security Banknote Company (US)
TDLR .... Thomas De La Rue (England)
UPC .... Union Printing Co. (China)
UPP .... Union Publishers & Printers Fed. Inc. (China)
USBNC .... United States Banknote Corp. (US)
WDBN .... Western District Banknote Fed. Inc.
W&S .... Waterlow & Sons Ltd. (England)
WPCo .... Watson Printing Co. (China)
WWS .... W.W. Sprague & Co. Ltd. (England)

SPECIMEN NOTES

To familiarize private banks, central banks, law enforcement agencies and treasuries around the world with newly issued currency, many nations provide them with special "Specimen" examples of their notes. Specimens are actual bank notes, complete with dummy or all zero serial numbers and signatures and bearing the overprinted and/or perforated word "SPECIMEN" in the language of the country of origin itself or where the notes were printed.

Some countries have made specimen notes available for sale to collectors. These include Cuba, Czechoslovakia, Poland and Slovakia after World War II and a special set of four denominations of Jamaica notes bearing red matched star serial numbers. Also, in 1978, the Franklin Mint made available to collectors specimen notes from 15 nations, bearing matching serial numbers and a Maltese cross device used as a prefix. Several other countries have also participated in making specimen notes available to collectors at times.

Aside from these collectors issues, specimen notes may sometimes command higher prices than regular issue notes of the same type, even though there are far fewer collectors of specimens. In some cases, notably older issues in high denominations, specimens may be the only form of such notes available to collectors today. Specimen notes are not legal tender or redeemable, thus have no real "face value" which also is indicated on some examples.

The most unusual forms of specimens were produced by Waterlow and Sons. They printed special off colored notes for salesman's sample books adding the word SPECIMEN and their seal. These salesman's samples are not included in catalog listings. In most cases they are less valuable than true color specimens but may command a premium in more popularly collected countries.

Some examples of how the word "SPECIMEN" is represented in other languages or on notes of other countries follow:

AMOSTRA: Brazil
CAMPIONE: Italy
CONTOH: Malaysia
EKSEMPLAAR: South Africa
ESPÉCIME: Portugal and Colonies
ESPECIMEN: Various Spanish-speaking nations
GIAY MAU: Vietnam
MINTA: Hungary
MODELO: Brazil
MODEL: Albania
MUSTER: Austria, Germany
MUESTRA: Various Spanish-speaking nations
NUMUNEDIR GECMEZ: Turkey
ORNEKTIR GECMEZ: Turkey
ОБРАЗЕЦ or **ОБРАЗЕЦЪ:** Bulgaria, Russia, U.S.S.R.
PARAUGS: Latvia
PROFTRYK: Sweden
UZORAK: Croatia
WZOR: Poland
ЗАГВАР: Mongolia

نموذج or نموذج : Arabic
نمونه :Persian
نمونه :Pakistan
דוגמא : Israel
ແບບປາງ : Laos
見本 : Japan
見樣券 : Korea (old)
樣本 : China (printed or perforated)
見樣 : Korea (old)
គំរូ : Kampuchea
견양 : Korea (new)

SECURITY DEVICES

ASCENDING SIZE SERIAL NUMBER - A serial number with each digit slightly increasing in height and width. Both horizontal and vertical formats have been used. Czech Republic and Slovakia are among the countries where this may be found.

BAR CODE AND NUMERALS - Used mainly by banks for checks. Some countries have used these on banknotes. Scotland has a bar code, and Canada has used it with serial numbers. Sometimes magnetic.

COLORED FIBERS - Fibers usually red, blue or green, that are added either into the pulp mix to be randomly flowed onto the paper as it is made, or distributed onto the drying paper in particular areas of the page forming 'bars' of colored fibers, quite visible to the naked eye.

EMBEDDED SECURITY THREAD - A high strength thread, sometimes magnetic, embedded into the paper at the beginning of the drying stage. Looks to the eye as a solid dark strip within the paper.

FACE-BACK OPTICAL REGISTRATION DESIGN (TRANSPARENT REGISTER) - A design technique where half of an image in a framed area is printed on the face, and the other half is printed on the back, in exact register, so when held to a light, the two half images form one full image.

FOIL IMPRINTS - Shaped metal foil applied to the printed note, usually with an adhesive. Sometimes the foil is embossed with an image.

HOLOGRAM - Shiny application to the note containing an image that changes in design and color depending upon the viewing angle.

INVISIBLE PRINTING - Designs printed with inks detectable only when viewed under bright sunlight or ultraviolet light. Sometimes used to replace the more expensive watermark on low value notes.

LATENT IMPRESSIONS -Portions of the note containing sculptured engraving, making some legends or designs visible only when held to the light at certain angles.

KINEGRAM(r) - Similar to a foil imprint, the design and color changes at different viewing angles.

METALLIC INK - An ink with very fine granules of metal, thus giving the ink a metallic sheen.

MICRO PRINTING - Very small letters added to an intaglio printing plate, sometimes as single lines, or in multiple repeating lines forming a larger block in the underprint design. Intaglio printing keeps the design sharp and clear, but if the note is counterfeit the microprinted area usually becomes muddy and unclear.

OPTICAL VARIABLE DEVICE (OVD) - A foil that displays a three-dimensional image when viewed under proper lighting conditions. Similar to foil imprints.

OPTICALLY VARIABLE INK - An ink when printed in a special pattern changes shades when viewed and then tilted slightly.

PLANCHETTES - Tiny multicolored discs of paper embedded into the pulp mix or randomly sprinkled throughout the paper as it is drying.

RAISED MARKS - A type of braille design in notes, enabling blind people to identify note values.

SEGMENTED SECURITY THREAD -A continuous security thread, usually wide and with lettering, that is added into the paper during the drying process. Once added, a special tool is used to scrape the wet paper off only above the thread, and usually in a particular pattern, thus exposing alternate areas of the embedded thread.

UV-ULTRAVIOLET (FLOURESCENT) - When viewed in a darkened area, and exposed to a special low or high frequency UV light, a design, value, or paper fibers will glow.

WATERMARK - Extensively used as a security measure, the watermark is created by a raised design on a drying cylinder applied towards the end of the paper manufacturing process. The raised design causes a thin area in the paper which when held to the light reveals an image. This image can be words, design, or a portrait. Recent developments have made graduations available. Thus, rather than a light/dark watermark, a gradual light to dark fade can be achieved.